W9-AFU-724

2017 U.S. MASTER TAX GUIDE®

100TH EDITION

Wolters Kluwer Editorial Staff Publications

Access the Latest Tax Developments and Your Free CPE Course

A special webpage created by Wolters Kluwer for the U.S. Master Tax Guide® will keep you up-to-date with late-breaking tax guidance and legislative developments occurring after publication of the 2017 edition. Visit ***CCHGroup.com/TaxUpdates*** to find the information you'll need to keep U.S. Master Tax Guide your first source for practical tax guidance. You will also find a link to your free Top Federal Tax Issues for 2017 course – a great and easy way to earn valuable CPE credit!

Wolters Kluwer

This publication is designed to provide accurate and authoritative information in regard to the subject matter covered. It is sold with the understanding that the publisher is not engaged in rendering legal, accounting, or other professional service. If legal advice or other expert assistance is required, the services of a competent professional person should be sought.

ISBN: 978-0-8080-4364-5 (paperback edition)

ISBN: 978-0-8080-4474-1 (hardbound edition)

© 2016 CCH Incorporated and its affiliates. All rights reserved.

2700 Lake Cook Road
Riverwoods, IL 60015
800 248 3248
CCHGroup.com

No claim is made to original government works; however, within this Product or Publication, the following are subject to CCH Incorporated's copyright: (1) the gathering, compilation, and arrangement of such government materials; (2) the magnetic translation and digital conversion of data, if applicable; (3) the historical, statutory and other notes and references; and (4) the commentary and other materials.

Printed in the United States of America

Preface

Income taxation in the United States has been around for over 100 years. From the very beginning, Wolters Kluwer was there and is still setting the standard as the number one quick reference resource for tax professionals. Wolters Kluwer is proud to serve the tax professional community with this new edition of the *U.S. Master Tax Guide* ®. The 100th Edition of this industry standard explains the complex set of tax rules and is designed to provide fast and reliable answers to tax questions affecting individuals and businesses. In all, 29 chapters contain comprehensive, timely, and precise explanations of the ever-changing federal income tax rules for individuals, businesses, estates, and trusts.

The 2017 Edition reflects all significant IRS guidance, including but not limited to, amendments to partnership regulations, penalty guidance on compliance with the health care reform, accounting method changes, and important regulations that affect the preparation of 2016 tax returns. In addition, coverage includes changes to the Code from enactment of several minor legislative actions, including but not limited to, the Trade Facilitation and Trade Enforcement Act of 2015 (P.L. 114-125), which increases penalties for failure to file tax returns, the Recovering Missing Children Act (P.L. 114-184), which allows for disclosure of tax information related to missing and abused children, the FAA Extension, Safety, and Security Act of 2016 (P.L. 114-190) and the Airport and Airway Extension Act of 2016 (P.L. 114-141), which extends expenditure authority and excise taxes for the FAA until September 30, 2017, and the United States Appreciation for Olympians and Paralympians Act of 2016 (P.L. 114-239), which allows exclusion from gross income of monetary award received from the U.S. Olympic Committee.

In an effort to keep users of the *Guide* current on events taking place after the date of publication, Wolters Kluwer has established a website at *CCHGroup.com/TaxUpdates* for any late-breaking 2016 year-end tax legislation or for other significant tax developments that might affect the *Guide's* coverage.

As in previous editions, major legislative provisions are highlighted at ¶ 2 and reflected throughout the *Guide*, while important non-legislative tax developments are conveniently highlighted at ¶ 3. In addition, the *Guide* comes complete with many timesaving features that help practitioners quickly and easily determine how particular tax items and situations should be treated (see the following page for a listing and description of these "Key Features"). The *Guide* also contains a handy Quick Tax Facts card that can be detached for an at-a-glance reference to key tax figures and other often-referenced amounts for the 2016 tax year.

Not only does the *U.S. Master Tax Guide* ® assist in the preparation of 2016 tax returns, it also serves as a reference tool for more comprehensive tax research and tax planning via extensive footnotes and other references to the Internal Revenue Code, Income Tax Regulations, and Wolters Kluwer's STANDARD FEDERAL TAX REPORTS ®, FEDERAL ESTATE AND GIFT TAX REPORTER, TAX RESEARCH CONSULTANT, and Practical Tax Explanations series.

For additional analysis of new and complex tax issues, and as a way to earn valuable continuing education credits, *Top Federal Tax Issues for 2017* is provided along with the *Guide*. This course provides helpful insights for the practitioner to keep abreast of the most significant new rules and changes by explaining the most important new provisions and developments in 2016 specifically applicable to 2017 and the IRS rules and regulations that go into effect in 2017. It also examines current audit and litigation issues that have developed over the past year that create a new environment for tax strategies initiated in 2016.

Finally, for treatment of state tax topics, please refer to Wolters Kluwer's *State Tax Guidebooks* (12 states available–CA, CT, FL, IL, MA, MI, NJ, NY, NC, OH, PA and TX) and Wolters Kluwer's *State Tax Handbook* covering all 50 states and the District of Columbia.

November 2016

Key Features

In addition to 29 chapters of tax law explanations, the *U.S. Master Tax Guide*® provides a wealth of information in the pages that lead up to Chapter 1. Some of these timesaving tools and features are described below, listed by paragraph location.

OVERVIEW (¶ 1-6): The Overview division contains informative features available to facilitate research and dealing with clients, including the following.

- "Tax Legislation," a highlight of provisions from this year's enacted tax legislation.
- "What's New on 2016 Returns," a highlight of changes affecting preparation of 2016 tax returns.
- "AGI Phaseout Thresholds," includes a number of tax items subject to phaseout restrictions.
- "Where to File Returns," a listing of income tax return mailing addresses.
- "2017 Tax Calendar," shows the filing dates for 2016 tax returns and tax payments throughout 2017.

TAX RATES (¶ 11-53): This section contains the 2016 and 2017 tax rate schedules for individuals and estates and trusts, the corporate tax rate schedule and related rates, and the estate and gift tax rate schedule, as well as a listing of key excise tax rates.

CHECKLISTS (¶ 55-65): A collection of checklists designed to provide tax return preparers with quick references to assist in answering common questions regarding the inclusion of items in income, the deductibility of certain expenses, the treatment of various medical expenses, the availability of tax credits, and a list of IRS forms to use.

SPECIAL TAX TABLES (¶ 83-88): This is a collection of often-used interest rates and percentages including:

- Applicable Federal Rates (AFRs)
- Adjusted Applicable Federal Rates
- Federal Long-Term Tax-Exempt Rates
- Low-Income Housing Credit percentages

ADDITIONAL FORMATS: To provide flexibility for users, the *Guide* is available in either a softbound or hardbound print edition and an e-Book version. The *Guide* is also available on *IntelliConnect*, Wolters Kluwer's industry-leading research platform that combines the quick-reference ease and reliability of the *Guide* with current primary sources including the Internal Revenue Code, Income Tax Regulations, cases, IRS rulings, and more.

TAX UPDATE RESOURCE: As a courtesy to our customers, Wolters Kluwer has established a website at *CCHGroup.com/TaxUpdates* for users of the *Guide* to visit periodically in order to stay current with post-publication tax legislation and key tax developments.

Wolters Kluwer, CCH Tax and Accounting

EDITORIAL STAFF

Joshua Braunstein, *Vice President, Research and Learning*

Mark L. Friedlich, J.D., *Senior Director, Global Content Assets*

Kristine Kelley, *Senior Director, Editorial*

Elizabeth Albers, M.B.A., *Director, Content Solutions and Optimization*

Jennifer M. Lowe, J.D., *Editorial Director, Tax*

Sarah Stevens, J.D., LL.M., M.B.A., *Director, News, Thought Leadership, and Specialty Publications*

Explanation and Analysis

David Becker, J.D.

Dan Billings, J.D.

Glenn L. Borst, J.D., LL.M.

Anne E. Bowker, J.D., LL.M.

John Buchanan, J.D., LL.M.

Mildred Carter, J.D.

Casie Cooper

Kurt Diefenbach, J.D., *Managing Editor*

Liliana Dimitrova, LL.B., LL.M.

Karen Elsner, C.P.A.

Alicia C. Ernst, J.D.

Elena Eyber, J.D.

Shannon Jett Fischer, J.D.

Donna M. Flanagan, J.D.

Mary Jo Gagnon, C.P.A.

Bruno L. Graziano, J.D., M.S.A.

Joy A. Hail, J.D., LL.M., *Managing Editor*

Michael Henaghan, J.D., LL.M., *Managing Editor*

Kathleen M. Higgins

Caroline L. Hosman, J.D., LL.M.

David M. Jaffe, J.D.

Daniel C. Johnson, J.D., LL.M.

Nitasha A. Kadam, J.D.

Thomas K. Lauletta, J.D.

Adam R. Levine, J.D., LL.M.

Laura M. Lowe, J.D., *Managing Editor*

Mark A. Luscombe, J.D., LL.M, C.P.A., *Principal Analyst*

Chantal M. Mahler

Sheri Wattles Miller, J.D.

Robert A. Morse, J.D., LL.M.

Jonathan Mosier, J.D., LL.M.

John J. Mueller, J.D., LL.M., *Managing Editor*

Jean T. Nakamoto, J.D.

Jerome Nestor, J.D., M.B.A., C.P.A., *Managing Editor*

Karen A. Notaro, J.D., LL.M., *Managing Editor*

Lawrence A. Perlman, J.D., LL.M., C.P.A.

Deborah M. Petro, J.D., LL.M.

Robert Recchia, J.D., M.B.A., C.P.A.

Betty Ross, J.D.

John W. Roth, J.D., LL.M.

Carolyn M. Schiess, J.D.

Michael G. Sem, J.D.

James Solheim, J.D., LL.M.

Raymond G. Suelzer, J.D., LL.M.

Kenneth L. Swanson, J.D., LL.M.

Laura A. Tierney, J.D.

Kelley Wolf, J.D., LL.M.

Susan M. Zengerle, J.D., LL.M., *Managing Editor*

Washington News Staff

Jessica Jeane, J.D.

George G. Jones, J.D., LL.M., *Managing Editor*

Jalisa D. Mathis, J.D., LL.M.

George L. Yaksick, Jr., J.D.

Electronic and Print Production

David Allan,
Senior Digital/Print Coordinator

John Barrett,
Senior Production/Design Manager

Angela D. Bretschneider

Douglas Bretschneider

Josalyn Coleman,
Associate Marketing Manager

Jim Donnelly

Amelia Eslava

Debra Fogg

Laila Gaidulis

Patrick Gallagher

Mary Ellen Guth

Christine Hansen

Meghan Klick

Andrejs Makwitz

Redgie Martinez,
Design Manager

Tina Medina

Helen Miller

Jennifer Nelson

Elaine Ogawa,
Managing Editor

Jose Robles,
Product Line and Channel Manager

Jennifer K. Schencker

David Schuster

Monika Stefan

Tuan Tran

Christopher Zwirek

DETAILED TABLE OF CONTENTS

Paragraph

Overview

Looking Back 1
Tax Legislation 2
What's New on 2016 Returns 3
AGI Phaseout Thresholds 4
Where to File Returns 5
2017 Tax Calendar 6

Tax Rates

Tax Rate Schedules for 2016 and 2017 11
2016 Tax Table—Individuals 25
Corporation Income Tax Rates 33
Estate and Gift Taxes 40
Other Taxes 47

Checklists

Checklist for Items of Income 55
Checklist for Deductions 57
Checklist for Medical Expenses 59
Checklist for Credits 61
Checklist for Forms 63
Guide to Information Returns 64
Checklist for Types of Payments 65

Special Tax Tables

Applicable Federal Rates 83
Adjusted Applicable Federal Rates 84
Federal Long-Term Tax-Exempt Rates 85
Applicable Credit Percentages for Low-Income Housing 86
Earned Income Credit 87
Average Itemized Deductions 88

Chapter 1: Individuals

Filing of Tax Returns 101
Computation of Tax Liability 123
Personal and Dependency Exemptions 133
Filing Status 152
Tax Treatment of Decedent's Final Return 178

Chapter 2: Corporations

Corporate Formation 201
Return and Payment of Tax 211
Computation of Tax Liability 219
Estimated Tax 241
Accumulated Earnings Tax 251
Personal Service Corporations 273
Personal Holding Companies 275
Controlled Corporate Groups 289
Consolidated Returns 295

Paragraph

Chapter 3: S Corporations
S Corporation Status . . . 301
Taxation of Shareholders . . . 309
Tax Treatment of Distributions . . . 323
Taxation of Corporation . . . 335
Returns and Tax Year . . . 351

Chapter 4: Partnerships
Choice of Entity . . . 401
Publicly Traded Partnerships . . . 403
Partnership-Level Issues . . . 404
Partnership Loss Deductions . . . 425
Partner's Distributive Share of Partnership Items . . . 428
Sale and Liquidation of Partner's Interest . . . 434
Partnership Contributions, Distributions, and Basis . . . 443
Family Partnerships . . . 474
Organization, Syndication, Start-Up Costs . . . 477
Electing Large Partnerships . . . 482

Chapter 5: Trusts—Estates
Estates and Trusts as Taxable Entities . . . 501
Fiduciary Return and Payment of Tax . . . 510
Taxation of Estates and Trusts . . . 514
Income Distribution Deduction . . . 542
Taxation of Beneficiaries . . . 554
Grantor Trusts . . . 571
Other Special Trusts . . . 590

Chapter 6: Exempt Organizations
Overview . . . 601
Code Sec. 501(c)(3) Organizations . . . 602
Private Foundations . . . 631
Unrelated Business Taxable Income . . . 655
Taxable Income from Debt-Financed Property . . . 687
Other Tax-Exempt Organizations . . . 692

Chapter 7: Income
What Is "Income" . . . 701
Ownership of Income . . . 704
Salaries, Wages, and Benefits . . . 713
Interest . . . 724
Dividends . . . 733
Dividends: Distribution in Redemption of Stock . . . 742
Dividends: Earnings and Profits . . . 747
Business Income . . . 759
Rents and Royalties . . . 762
Farming Income . . . 767
Alimony Payments . . . 771
Other Income . . . 785
Shareholder's or Employee's Bargain Purchase . . . 789
Creditor's Financial Income . . . 793

Paragraph

Below-Market Interest Loans 795
Recoveries 799

Chapter 8: Exclusions from Gross Income

Exclusions from Gross Income 801
Life Insurance and Death Benefits 803
Annuities 817
Bequests and Gifts 847
Personal Injuries and Disability Proceeds 851
Cancellation of Debt 855
Education Benefits 863
Tax-Favored Savings Accounts 870
Other Exclusions from Gross Income 871
Excludable Military Benefits 891

Chapter 9: Business Expenses

Trade or Business Expenses 901
Compensation Paid 906
Entertainment, Meal, and Gift Expenses 910
Taxes 920
Charitable Contributions 927
Interest 937
Employee's Expenses 941
Transportation and Car Expenses 945
Traveling Expenses Away from Home 949
Home Office and Vacation Home Expenses 961
Other Business Expenses 968
Domestic Production Activities 980A
Expenses of Professional Persons 981
Farmer's Expenses 982
Landlord or Tenant Expenses 986
Mining Company's Expenses 987
Uniform Capitalization Rules 990
Incentives for Economically Distressed Communities 999A

Chapter 10: Nonbusiness Expenses

Deductions, Generally 1001
Adjusted Gross Income (AGI) 1005
Phaseout of Itemized Deductions 1014
Medical Expenses 1015
Taxes, Generally 1021
Real Property Taxes 1028
Interest 1043
Prepaid Interest 1055
Charitable Contributions 1058
Moving Expenses 1073
Miscellaneous Itemized Deductions 1079
Production of Income Expenses 1085

Paragraph

Chapter 11: Losses—Passive Activity Losses
Deduction of Losses 1101
Casualty and Theft Losses 1121
Bad Debts 1135
Net Operating Losses (NOLs) 1145
At-Risk Limitations 1155
Passive Activity Limits on Losses and Credits 1165
Rental Activities Subject to Passive Activity Rules 1181
Tax-Exempt Use Property 1191
Hobby Losses 1195

Chapter 12: Depreciation, Amortization and Depletion
DEPRECIATION
Allowance for Depreciation 1201
Basis for Depreciation 1203
Section 179 Expense Election 1208
Limitations on Automobiles and Other Listed Property 1211
Depreciation Methods 1216
Leased Property 1234
Modified Accelerated Cost Recovery System (MACRS) 1236
Accelerated Cost Recovery System (ACRS) 1252
Class Life ADR System 1282
Deductions for Refiners 1285
Deduction for Energy Efficiency Improvements 1286
AMORTIZATION
Allowance for Amortization 1287
DEPLETION
What is Depletion? 1289
Mineral Production Payments 1291
Percentage Depletion 1294

Chapter 13: Tax Credits
Nonrefundable Credits 1301
Limitation on Nonrefundable Credits 1315
Refundable Credits 1321
Health Care Credits 1331
Nonbusiness Energy Credits 1341
Alternative Motor Vehicle Credit 1345
Foreign Tax Credit 1361
General Business Credits 1365
Tax Credit Bonds 1371

Chapter 14: Alternative Minimum Tax
AMT Liability 1401
AMT Preferences and Adjustments 1425
Credits Against Minimum Tax 1470

Chapter 15: Tax Accounting
Accounting Period 1501
Accounting Method 1515
Timing of Income and Expenses 1533

Paragraph

Long-Term Contracts 1551
Inventories 1553
Allocation and Reconstruction of Income 1573

Chapter 16: Basis for Gain or Loss

Computing Gain or Loss 1601
Property Acquired by Purchase 1611
Property Acquired by Gift or Bequest 1630
Property Acquired by Exchange 1648
Other Acquired Property 1678
Valuation Rules 1695

Chapter 17: Sales and Exchanges—Capital Gains

SALES AND EXCHANGES

Sales and Exchanges of Property 1701
Gain or Loss from Sale of Residence 1705
Involuntary Conversion 1713
Transactions Between Related Persons 1717
Tax-Free Exchanges 1719

CAPITAL GAINS

Treatment of Capital Gain or Loss 1735
Section 1231 1747
Capital Loss Limitation, Carryover, Carryback 1752
Subdivision of Real Estate 1762
Patents, Royalties, and Franchises 1767
Disposition of Depreciable Property 1779
Farmers' Recapture 1797

Chapter 18: Installment Sales—Deferred Payments

INSTALLMENT SALES

Installment Method 1801
Computation of Income 1813
Related-Party Sales 1833
Repossessions of Property 1838
Dispositions of Installment Obligations 1846
Corporate Liquidations 1856

DEFERRED PAYMENTS

Imputed Interest 1859
Treatment of Interest 1883

Chapter 19: Securities Transactions

Taxation of Securities Transactions 1901
Gains and Losses on Small Business Stock 1905
Worthless Securities 1916
Options 1919
Wash Sales 1935
Short Sales 1944
Commodities and Related Instruments 1947
Corporate Bonds and Other Debt Instruments 1950
Accounting Issues 1973

Paragraph

Chapter 20: Health and Employee Benefits
Employer Health Insurance Mandate 2001
Health and Welfare Benefits 2011
HSAs, HRAs, and FSAs 2035
Cafeteria Plans 2045
Other Employee Benefits 2055
Fringe Benefits Under Code Sec. 132 2085

Chapter 21: Retirement Plans
Types of Retirement Plans 2101
Qualified Plan Requirements 2111
Taxation of Distributions and Rollovers 2141
Traditional IRAs 2155
Roth IRAs 2171
SIMPLE Plans and SEPs 2181
Sec. 403(b), Sec. 457, and Nonqualified Plans 2191

Chapter 22: Corporate Acquisitions—Reorganizations—Liquidations
Corporate Division 2201
Corporate Reorganization 2205
Corporate Liquidation 2253
Carryforwards 2277

Chapter 23: Special Corporate Status
Mutual Funds 2301
Real Estate Investment Trusts 2326
Real Estate Mortgage Investment Conduits 2343
Insurance Companies 2370
Other Special Entities 2383

Chapter 24: Foreign Income and Transactions
Overview 2401
U.S. Citizens and Residents Living Abroad 2402
Nonresident Aliens and Foreign Corporations 2425
Reporting Foreign Assets of U.S. Taxpayers 2465
Foreign Tax Credit or Deduction 2475
U.S. Shareholders of Foreign Corporations 2487
Other Foreign Tax Rules 2495

Chapter 25: Returns—Payment of Tax
Filing Returns 2501
Payment of Tax 2525
Deadlines 2549
Information Returns and Payment at Source 2565
Reportable Transactions and Tax Shelters 2591

Chapter 26: Withholding—Estimated Tax
WITHHOLDING
Withholding on Wages 2601
Computation of Withholding on Wages 2612
Withholding on Non-Wage Payments 2642
FICA and FUTA Taxes 2648

Paragraph

Return and Payment by Employer 2650
Self-Employment Tax 2664
ESTIMATED TAX
Payment of Estimated Taxes 2682

Chapter 27: Examination of Returns—Collection of Tax
Organization of IRS 2701
Examination 2708
Assessment and Collection of Tax 2711
Liens and Levies 2751
Mitigation of Effect of Statute of Limitations 2756
Refunds and Credits 2759
The Courts 2776

Chapter 28: Penalties—Interest
Failure to File Returns or Pay Tax 2801
Document and Information Return Penalties 2814
Underpayments of Tax—Interest 2838
Underpayments of Tax—Penalties 2854
Underpayments of Estimated Tax 2875
Erroneous Tax Refund Claims 2891
Unauthorized Return Disclosures or Inspections 2892
Criminal Penalties 2898

Chapter 29: Estate, Gift and Generation-Skipping Transfer Tax
Transfer Tax System 2901
Gift Tax 2903
Estate Tax 2912
Generation-Skipping Transfer Tax 2942
Transfer Tax on Gifts and Bequests from Expatriates 2948

Topical Index . . . . . page 939

Filing 2016 Returns

OVERVIEW

	Par.
Looking Back	1
Tax Legislation	2
What's New on 2016 Returns	3
AGI Phaseout Thresholds	4
Where to File Returns	5
2017 Tax Calendar	6

¶ 1 Looking Back — 100 Years of the *U.S. Master Tax Guide®*

Before the 20th Century, the United States had made several attempts at imposing a federal income tax. An act imposing an income tax in 1861 in order to fund the U.S. Civil War was allowed to lapse in 1872. The Wilson-Gorman Tariff Act of 1894 included a relatively modest income tax provision, but the U.S. Supreme Court in 1895 found that it was a "direct tax" and violated Article I, Section 2 of the U.S. Constitution, requiring that any direct tax be apportioned among the states according to population. Even in 1787, this would have been difficult, but by the end of the 19th Century, with massive population surges in the United States coupled with an increasingly mobile citizenry, it was effectively impossible. There could not be an income tax in the United States without a constitutional amendment. That would come less than 20 years later with the 16th Amendment in 1913.

Around the time the Supreme Court was striking down the second federal income tax, a Chicago businessman named William Kix Miller formed a company to assist lawyers with the more mundane tasks of legal work (e.g. legal filing, court document work, etc.). This business would form the basis for what would become Commerce Clearing House. A few years later, a Chicago banker named Oakleigh Thorne purchased an interest in the company with an eye towards expanding into the burgeoning field of legislative coverage and regulatory guidance. By the time of the 16th Amendment, Commerce Clearing House had established the infrastructure to step in and provide the legal market, as well as a newly-established tax accounting market, with coverage needed to comply and plan for the requirements of the first federal income tax act.

After immediate success in 1913 with what would become the Standard Federal Tax Reporter, Commerce Clearing House saw the need to provide a smaller and more manageable product for the more casual professional. The Standard Federal Tax Reporter was (and is today) a comprehensive product covering the entirety of the federal income tax. Many tax professionals, however do not need comprehensive guidance, they only need high level tax explanations because tax compliance and planning is not their primary professional focus. So, in 1917, Kix Miller worked with his partner, Arnold Baar, and created the *U.S. Income and War Tax Guide*, the forerunner of the *U.S. Master Tax Guide®*.

Unlike our modern Internal Revenue Code, the first revenue acts in the United States were not codified, which meant that a fresh revenue act had to be passed every year to keep the government funded. The first Internal Revenue Act of 1913 was small, only about 20 pages, and even by 1917, it was only about 25 pages. Accordingly, the first *U.S. Income and War Tax Guide* was also small, only 124 pages (including the entire 1917 Revenue Act). As the original name was no longer applicable, the *U.S. Income and War Tax Guide* became the *U.S. Income Tax Guide* in 1932, and the now-familiar *U.S. Master Tax Guide®* in 1934.

As the United States grew and expanded, the revenue acts grew and expanded. As they expanded, so did the coverage provided by Commerce Clearing House. By 1934, the year's revenue act had grown to 93 pages. By 1935, a very small percentage of Americans were even required to file a return and pay income taxes (only about one out of 32), but the Supreme Court's holding in *Gregory v. Helvering*, making a distinction between tax planning and tax evasion, led to an explosion in the tax planning field. By that time, the 1935 *U.S. Master Tax Guide®* had grown to 230 pages to meet the needs of tax professionals to plan for and comply with increasingly complex tax laws.

The following decades would bring codification of the revenue laws (first in 1939, with significant revisions in 1954 and 1986) as well as dozens of significant revenue acts with hundreds of smaller acts. By the time of printing the 100th Edition of the *U.S. Master Tax Guide®*, the Internal Revenue Code has swelled to over 2,000 pages and the *U.S. Master Tax Guide®* to more than 1,000 pages. As the laws changed and grew more complex, the need for regulations and non-regulatory IRS guidance has grown as well. All this time, the *U.S. Master Tax Guide®* has continued to adapt, grow, and reorganize while maintaining the early commitment to provide tax, accounting, and legal professionals with the legislative and regulatory guidance, as well analysis they need to provide their clients and customers with exceptional service. By the mid-1990's, the *U.S. Master Tax Guide®* made its first appearance electronically; first on CD-ROM, then on the Internet, and finally as an e-Book. Also around this time, Commerce Clearing House become CCH, and then Wolters Kluwer, and it continues to be an industry leader in providing guidance and analysis to tax professionals around the world.

As the *U.S. Master Tax Guide®* begins its second century, Wolters Kluwer continues to build on the foundation laid by the thousands of editors, analysts, production editors, printers, proofreaders, researchers, reporters, marketers, and salespersons who worked to make the *U.S. Master Tax Guide®* an essential part of tax professionals' day-to-day lives.

¶ 2 Tax Legislation

After years of routine temporary extensions of some popular tax breaks, the Protecting Americans from Tax Hikes (PATH) Act of 2015 (P.L. 114-113) enacted on December 18, 2015, made permanent many of these items. Individual tax provisions made permanent include, but are not limited to, the deduction for state and local taxes, the Hope Scholarship/American Opportunity tax credit (AOTC), the teacher expense deduction, and qualified charitable distributions from IRAs. Business tax provisions made permanent include, but are not limited to, the increased Code Sec. 179 expensing limit, the research credit, and 15-year straight-line recovery period for qualified leasehold improvements, restaurant buildings, and retail improvements.

The PATH Act also extends or modifies many other tax provisions through the 2016 tax year and beyond. For individuals these include the tuition and fees deduction, the deduction of mortgage insurance premiums, and the exclusion of mortgage debt on a principal residence. For businesses, the PATH Act extends bonus depreciation under a phase-down schedule through 2019, as well as extends the work opportunity credit and various energy credits. It also included a delay on the excise tax on so-called Cadillac medical plans and the medical device excise tax.

In addition to the PATH Act, following legislation has been enacted during the past year:

- The United States Appreciation for Olympians and Paralympians Act of 2016 (P.L. 114-239) excludes from gross income of any individual with adjusted gross income of $1 million or less the value of medals and any prize money received from the U.S. Olympic Committee (USOC) on account of competition in the Olympic or Paralympic Games.

- The FAA Extension, Safety, and Security Act of 2016 (P.L. 114-190) and the Airport and Airway Extension Act of 2016 (P.L. 114-141) extended through September 30, 2017, the expenditure authority for the Airport and Airway Trust Fund of the United States, excise taxes on aviation fuel, airline passenger tickets, and air cargo, and special rules applicable to fractional ownership aircraft flights as noncommercial aviation.

- The Recovering Missing Children Act (P.L. 114-184) permits Federal law enforcement officials to seek an ex parte court order for the disclosure of return and return information under Code Sec. 6103 in cases of missing or exploited children, and to disclose the information to certain officers and employees of State or local law enforcement agencies.

- The Trade Facilitation and Trade Enforcement Act of 2015 (P.L. 114-125) increases the penalty under Code Sec. 6651 for failure to file a return effective for returns required to be filed in calendar years after 2015. For taxpayers who fail to file their returns more than 60 days after the due date or extended due date, the minimum penalty tax is the lesser of $205 or 100 percent of the unpaid tax.

For information on further legislative and other key tax-related developments following publication of the *U.S. Master Tax Guide*®, visit the *U.S. Master Tax Guide*® website at *CCHGroup.com/TaxUpdates*.

¶ 3 What's New on 2016 Returns

The *U.S. Master Tax Guide* ® reflects all of the important administrative and judicial developments of 2016, including final regulations, major court decisions, and important rulings of the Internal Revenue Service. Legislative highlights are at ¶ 2. Following are additional highlights of the changes in 2016 with the greatest impact on individuals and businesses.

Individuals

Income levels at which individuals must file income tax returns have increased for 2016 . . . . . ¶ 101
Basic standard deduction amounts have increased for 2016 . . . . . ¶ 126
The deduction for each personal exemption is $4,050 for 2016 . . . . . ¶ 133
The applicable threshold amount for phaseout of itemized deductions and personal exemptions for high-income taxpayers has increased for 2016 . . . . . ¶ 133, ¶ 1014
"Kiddie" tax amount is $2,100 for 2016 . . . . . ¶ 706
Updated discussion of the extended health coverage tax credit . . . . . ¶ 1333

Business Expenses

The standard mileage rate for all business use of a car is 54 cents per mile for 2016 . . . . . ¶ 947
Per diem rates under the high-low method of substantiating travel expenses are $282 for high-cost localities and $189 for low-cost localities for travel after September 30, 2016 . . . . . ¶ 954A

Depreciation, Amortization and Depletion

The maximum Code Sec. 179 deduction for 2016 is $500,000 . . . . . ¶ 1208
The Code Sec. 179 investment limitation for 2016 is $2,010,000 . . . . . ¶ 1208
Updated discussion of the capitalization regulations (the "repair regs") which a taxpayer generally has the option of applying for tax years beginning on or after January 1, 2012 . . . . . ¶ 903, ¶ 1238, ¶ 1240

Tax Credits

For 2016, the maximum earned income credit for eligible taxpayers with no qualifying children is $506, with one qualifying child is $3,373, with two qualifying children is $5,572, and with three or more qualifying children is $6,269 . . . . . ¶ 87, ¶ 1322
The child tax credit is $1,000 . . . . . ¶ 1305
The education tax credits (Hope Scholarship/American Opportunity and lifetime learning) are $2,500 and $2,000, respectively, ... ¶ 1303

Retirement and Benefits

The transportation fringe benefit exclusion amount for employer-provided parking, transit passes, and commuter highway vehicles is $255 per month for 2016. . . . . ¶ 2091
Updated discussion of the requirement for applicable large employers to provide minimum essential health coverage to employees . . . . . ¶ 2001
Updated discussion of the requirement to reconcile advanced payments of the premium tax credit . . . . . ¶ 1331

Withholding

The 2016 OASDI wage base for FICA and self-employment tax purposes is $118,500 . . . . . ¶ 47, ¶ 49, ¶ 2648, ¶ 2670
The 2016 wage threshold for "Nanny Tax" reporting is $2,000 . . . . . ¶ 2652

Estate, Gifts and Generation-Skipping Transfer Tax

Updated discussion of basis reporting requirements . . . . . ¶ 1633, ¶ 2938

¶ 4 AGI Phaseout Thresholds

Adjusted gross income (AGI) levels in excess of certain phaseout thresholds limit the following deductions, credits, and other tax benefits. This chart provides the beginning point for the 2016 thresholds and the ending point of the phaseout, where applicable.

Tax Item	*Taxpayers Affected*	*Phaseout—Begin*	*Phaseout—End*
Itemized Deductions (Overall Limit)	joint and surviving spouse filers	$311,300	N/A
	head-of-household filers	$285,350	N/A
	single filers	$259,400	N/A
	married individuals filing separately	$155,650	N/A
Floor on Itemized Medical Expenses Deduction	taxpayers under 65	10% of AGI	N/A
	taxpayers 65 or older (before January 1, 2017)	7.5% of AGI	N/A
Floor on Miscellaneous Itemized Deductions	all taxpayers	2% of AGI	N/A
Itemized Deduction of Casualty Loss	all taxpayers	10% of AGI	N/A
Personal Exemption	joint or surviving spouse filers	$311,300	$433,800
	head of household filers	$285,350	$407,850
	single filers	$259,400	$381,900
	married individuals filing separately	$155,650	$216,900
Child Tax Credit*	single, head of household	$75,000	phaseout varies by taxpayer
	married filing separately	$55,000	phaseout varies by taxpayer
	joint filers	$110,000	phaseout varies by taxpayer
Dependent Care Credit	single, head of household, joint filers	35% credit if AGI not over $15,000	20% credit if AGI over $43,000
Elderly and Disabled Credit	single, head of household	$7,500	$17,500
	joint filers	$10,000	$20,000 if one qualifying spouse; $25,000 if two qualifying spouses
	married filing separately	$5,000	$12,500
Adoption Credit*	all filers	$201,920	$241,920
Adoption Assistance Programs*	all filers	$201,920	$241,920
Earned Income Credit	single, head of household, surviving spouse, no child	$8,270	$14,880
	single, head of household, surviving spouse, one child	$18,190	$39,296
	single, head of household, surviving spouse, two children	$18,190	$44,648
	single, head of household, surviving spouse, three or more children	$18,190	$47,955
	joint filers, no child	$13,820	$20,430

Tax Item	*Taxpayers Affected*	*Phaseout—Begin*	*Phaseout—End*
	joint filers, one child	$23,740	$44,846
	joint filers, two children	$23,740	$50,198
	joint filers, three or more children	$23,740	$53,505
American Opportunity Credit*	single, head of household	$80,000	$90,000
	joint filers	$160,000	$180,000
Lifetime Learning Credit*	single, head of household	$55,000	$65,000
	joint filers	$111,000	$131,000
Student Loan Interest Deduction*	single, head of household	$65,000	$80,000
	joint filers	$130,000	$160,000
Savings Bonds Interest Exclusion*	single, head of household	$77,550	$92,550
	joint filers	$116,300	$146,300
Coverdell Education Savings Accounts*	single, head of household, married filing separately	$95,000	$110,000
	joint filers	$190,000	$220,000
IRA Deduction* (for taxpayers covered by retirement plan at work)	single, head of household	$61,000	$71,000
	joint filers (contributing spouse covered by retirement plan at work)	$98,000	$118,000
	joint filers (contributing spouse not covered by retirement plan at work; other spouse is covered by retirement plan at work)	$184,000	$194,000
	married filing separately	$0	$10,000
Roth IRA Contribution*	single, head of household	$117,000	$132,000
	joint filers	$184,000	$194,000
	married filing separately	$0	$10,000
Rental Real Estate Passive Losses	single, head of household, joint filers	$100,000	$150,000
	married filing separately	$50,000	$75,000

* Modified AGI, as defined by the relevant Code sections, is used instead of AGI.

¶ 5 Where to File Returns

Individuals. Listed below are the mailing addresses to use for filing self-prepared individual income tax return and by individuals filing returns prepared by a tax professionals (¶ 111). Individual taxpayers and tax professionals may also consult the IRS website https://www.irs.gov/uac/where-to-file-paper-tax-returns-with-or-without-a-payment or the Where to File Interactive Chart on CCH® IntelliConnect® for the most current mailing addresses.

The first two lines of the address should be Department of the Treasury, Internal Revenue Service, but no street address is needed. To facilitate processing for all taxpayers of the 50 states and the District of Columbia who do not need to enclose a payment with the return, each form (1040, 1040A, 1040EZ) uses a different ZIP+4 ZIP Code extension. If you are filing a client's Form 1040A and are not enclosing a payment, use the address in the middle column with the ZIP Code extension, -0015. If you are filing a client's Form 1040EZ and are not enclosing a payment, use the address in the middle column with the ZIP Code extension, -0014. If a payment is enclosed with the form, each form (1040, 1040A, 1040EZ) uses the same mailing address shown in the last column below.

If you are filing **Form 1040** *and are located in:*	*And are not enclosing a payment, mail your return to:*	*And are enclosing a payment, mail your return to:*
Alabama, Georgia, Kentucky, New Jersey, North Carolina, South Carolina, Tennessee, Virginia	Kansas City, MO 64999-0002	P.O. Box 931000 Louisville, KY 40293-1000
Florida, Louisiana, Mississippi, Texas	Austin, TX 73301-0002	P.O. Box 1214 Charlotte, NC 28201-1214
Alaska, Arizona, California, Colorado, Hawaii, Idaho, Nevada, New Mexico, Oregon, Utah, Washington, Wyoming	Fresno, CA 93888-0002	P.O. Box 7704 San Francisco, CA 94120-7704
Arkansas, Illinois, Indiana, Iowa, Kansas, Michigan, Minnesota, Montana, Nebraska, North Dakota, Ohio, Oklahoma, South Dakota, Wisconsin	Fresno, CA 93888-0002	P.O. Box 802501 Cincinnati, OH 45280-2501
Connecticut, Delaware, District of Columbia, Maine, Maryland, Massachusetts, Missouri, New Hampshire, New York, Pennsylvania, Rhode Island, Vermont, West Virginia	Kansas City, MO 64999-0002	P.O. Box 37008 Hartford, CT 06176-7008

If you are filing **Form 1040** *and are located in:*	*And are not enclosing a payment, mail your return to:*	*And are enclosing a payment, mail your return to:*
A foreign country, U.S. possession or territory*, or use an APO or FPO address, or file Form 2555, 2555-EZ or 4563, or are a dual-status alien	Austin, TX 73301-0215 USA	P.O. Box 1303 Charlotte, NC 28201-1303 USA

* For residents of American Samoa, Puerto Rico, Guam, the U.S. Virgin Islands, or the Northern Mariana Islands, see IRS Pub. 570 for the filing requirements for both U.S. possessions and Federal income tax returns along with a list of address of where to file each type of return.

Corporations and Partnerships. A corporation or partnership should file Form 1120 or Form 1065 in accordance with the "Where to File" addresses listed in the instructions to the forms. A corporation or partnership is "located in" the place where it has its principal place of business or principal office or agency. If a corporation or partnership is without a principal office or agency or principal place of business in the United States, returns are to be filed with the Internal Revenue Service Center in Ogden, Utah.

Estates and Trusts. A fiduciary of an estate or trust, including the fiduciary of a charitable or split interest trust (described in Code Sec. 4947(a)) or of a pooled income fund (described in Code Sec. 642(c)(5)), should generally file Form 1041 in accordance with the instructions to the form. A fiduciary is "located in" the place where he or she resides or has his or her principal place of business.

Private Delivery Services (PDSs). Certain private delivery services designated by the IRS are available to meet the "timely mailed as timely filing/paying" rule for tax returns and payments (Notice 2016-30, modifying and superseding Notice 2015-38, modifying Rev. Proc. 97-19). The designated private delivery services can be found at the IRS website https://www.irs.gov/uac/private-delivery-services-pds. The PDSs have special rules for determining the postmark date under Code Sec. 7502(f).

¶ 6 2017 Tax Calendar

Each date shown below is the last day for filing the return or making the payment of tax indicated. For income tax returns, the due dates apply to calendar-year taxpayers only. Employment tax due dates are determined on a calendar-year basis for all taxpayers. **If any statutory due date falls on a Saturday, Sunday, or legal holiday, the due date is the next succeeding day that is not a Saturday, Sunday, or legal holiday (national, District of Columbia, or statewide in the state where the return is to be filed).**

This day 2017	Tax Return Due Dates
Jan. 17th—	**Estimated Taxes.** Final installment of 2016 estimated tax (Form 1040-ES) by individuals unless income tax return is filed with final payment by January 31, 2017. Payment in full of estimated tax by farmers and fishermen unless income tax returns are filed by March 1, 2017.
	Final installment of 2016 estimated tax (Form 1041-ES) by trusts, calendar-year estates, and certain residuary trusts in existence more than two years, unless Form 1041 is filed and taxes are paid in full by January 31, 2017.
Jan. 31st—	**Employers' Taxes.** Employers of nonagricultural and nonhousehold employees file return on Form 941 for withheld income and FICA taxes in last quarter of 2016.[1]
	Employers of agricultural workers must file the annual Form 943 to report income and FICA taxes withheld on 2016 wages.[1]
	Employers must file Form 940, annual return of federal unemployment (FUTA) taxes for 2016.[1]
	Withholding. Employees' statements (Form W-2 and Form 1099-R) for amounts withheld in 2016 to be furnished by employer to employees. Copy A of Form W-2 (together with transmittal Form W-3) must be filed with the Social Security Administration, whether filed electronically or on paper.
	Individuals. Individuals, other than farmers and fishermen, who owed, but did not pay, estimated tax on January 17th must file final 2016 income tax return and pay tax in full to avoid late payment penalty.
	Trusts and Estates. Trusts, as well as estates and certain residuary trusts in existence more than two years, that owed but did not pay estimated tax on January 17th must file final 2016 income tax return and pay tax in full to avoid late payment penalty.
	Information Returns. Annual statements must be furnished to recipients of: gambling winnings (Form W-2G); dividends and liquidating distributions (Form 1099-DIV); interest, including interest on bearer certificates of deposit (Form 1099-INT); patronage dividends (Form 1099-PATR); original issue discount (Form 1099-OID); certain government payments, including unemployment compensation and state and local tax refunds of $10 or more (Form 1099-G); royalty payments of $10 or more, rent or other business payments of $600 or more, prizes and awards of $600 or more, crop insurance proceeds of $600 or more, fishing boat proceeds, medical and health care payments of $600 or more, nonemployee compensation payments in box 7 (Form 1099-MISC); debt canceled by certain financial entities including financial institutions, credit unions, and Federal Government agencies of $600 or more (Form 1099-C); distributions from retirement or profit-sharing plans, IRAs, SEPs, or insurance contracts (Form 1099-R); payments received from a third party settlement entity (Form 1099-K). See ¶ 64 for a chart of information returns and due dates.

This day 2017	Tax Return Due Dates
	Businesses, tax-exempt organizations, and educational institutions that receive certain payments must furnish annual statements to payors of: $600 or more of mortgage interest (Form 1098); $600 or more of student loan interest (Form 1098-E); qualified tuition and expenses (Form 1098-T). See ¶ 64 for a chart of information returns and due dates.
	Information called for on Form 8300 must be provided to each payer in a transaction of more than $10,000 in cash at any time during 2016. Form 8300 must be filed with the IRS by the 15th day after the date of the transaction.
	Partnerships must provide a copy of Form 8308 to the transferor and transferee in any exchange of a partnership interest that involved unrealized receivables or substantially appreciated inventory items. Form 8308 must be filed with the IRS with a partnership's income tax return for the year in which the exchange took place.
	Trustees or issuers of IRAs or SEPs must provide participants with a statement of the account's value and required minimum distribution (RMD), if applicable, on Form 5498. Participants and IRS must be provided with IRA plan contribution information by May 31st.
Feb. 15th—	**Individuals.** Last day for filing Form W-4 by employees who wish to claim exemption from withholding of income tax for 2017.
	Information Returns. Annual statements must be furnished to recipients of proceeds from broker and barter exchange transactions (Form 1099-B); proceeds from real estate transactions of $600 or more (Form 1099-S); broker payments of $10 or more in lieu of dividends or tax-exempt interest, and gross proceeds of $600 or more paid to an attorney (Form 1099-MISC).
Feb. 28th—	**Information Returns.** Annual 1099 series returns (together with transmittal Form 1096) for paper filings or, if filing electronically, by March 31, must be filed with the IRS to report payments to recipients who received Form 1099 on January 31st, as indicated above.
	Businesses, tax-exempt organizations, and educational institutions that receive certain payments must file with the IRS (together with transmittal Form 1096) for paper filings, or if filing electronically, by March 31; Form 1098 for $600 or more of mortgage interest received; Form 1098-E for $600 or more student loan interest received; and Form 1098-T for payments of qualified tuition and expenses. See ¶ 64 for a chart of information returns and due dates.
	Withholding. Form W-2G and Form 1099-R for 2016 "A" copies (together with transmittal Form 1096) for paper filings or, if filing electronically, by March 31st, must be filed with the IRS.
Mar. 1st—	**Individuals.** Last day for farmers and fishermen who owed, but did not pay, estimated tax on January 17th to file 2016 calendar-year income tax return and pay tax in full to avoid late payment penalty.
	Partnerships. Last day for filing income tax return for calendar-year partnership (Form 1065) and to provide each partner with a copy of Schedule K-1. Returns for fiscal-year partnerships are due on the 15th
Mar. 15th—	day of the 3rd month after the close of the tax year.
	Last day for calendar-year U.S. partnerships to file application (Form 7004) for automatic six-month extension to file 2016 income tax return.
	Last day for calendar-year partnerships to file an amended return (Form 1065X) for 2013.

This day 2017 — **Tax Return Due Dates**

S Corporations. Last day for filing income tax return for calendar-year S corporation (Form 1120S) and to provide each shareholder with a copy of Schedule K-1. Returns for fiscal-year S corporations are due on the 15th day of the 3rd month after the close of the tax year.

Last date for filing application (Form 7004) by S corporations for automatic six-month extension to file 2016 income tax return.

Last date for filing Form 2553 to elect to be treated as an S corporation beginning with calendar year 2017. The penalty for filing the election late is to postpone treatment as an S corporation until calendar year 2018.

Withholding. File returns on Form 1042 and Form 1042-S to report tax withheld at the source from nonresident aliens, foreign corporations, foreign partnerships and foreign fiduciaries of a trust or estate.

ABLE Accounts. Trustees of ABLE accounts must furnish copy of 5498-QA to participants. ABLE account information must be report to the IRS by May 31.

Mar. 31st— **Information Returns—Electronic Filing.** Due date for filing Form 1099 series (for reporting certain payments made) and Form 1098 series (for reporting receipt of certain payments) with the IRS electronically. See ¶ 64 for a chart of information returns and due dates.

Withholding—Electronic Filing. Last day for filing Form W-2G with the IRS if filing electronically.

Apr. 18th—* **Individuals.** Income tax and self-employment tax returns of individuals for calendar year 2016 and income tax returns of calendar-year decedents who died in 2016 (Form 1040, Form 1040A, or Form 1040EZ). Fiscal-year individuals must file returns or requests for extension by the 15th day of the 4th month after the close of the tax year.

Last day for calendar-year individuals to file application (Form 4868) for automatic six-month extension to file 2016 income tax return.

Individuals' information returns (Form 5471) with respect to foreign corporations to be filed with Form 1040.

Last day for individuals to file amended income tax returns (Form 1040X) for the calendar year 2013.

Estimated Tax. Calendar-year corporations pay first installment of 2017 estimated income taxes (Form 1120-W). Fiscal-year corporations are to make payments on the 15th day of the 4th, 6th, 9th, and 12th months of the tax year.

Payment of first installment of 2017 estimated income taxes (Form 1040-ES) by calendar-year individuals, other than farmers and fishermen. Estimated tax payments for fiscal-year individuals are due on the 15th day of the 4th, 6th, and 9th months of the tax year and the 1st month of the following tax year.

Trusts and calendar-year estates and certain residuary trusts in existence more than two years must make first payment of estimated taxes for 2017 (Form 1041-ES). Fiscal-year estates must make payments on the 15th day of the 4th, 6th, and 9th months of the fiscal year and the 1st month of the following fiscal year.

This day 2017 **Tax Return Due Dates**

Corporations. Due date of 2016 income tax returns (Form 1120) for calendar-year C corporations, including domestic corporations and foreign corporations with offices in the United States. Fiscal-year C corporations with a U.S. office generally must file by the 15th day of the 4th month following the close of the tax year. C corporations with a fiscal tax year ending on June 30, however, must file their returns by the 15th day of the 3rd month following the close of the tax year.

Last date for filing application (Form 7004) by calendar-year C corporations for automatic five-month extension to file 2016 income tax return.

Form 5452 for reporting nontaxable corporate distributions made to shareholders during calendar year 2016 should be filed by calendar-year corporations with income tax return. Fiscal-year corporations file Form 5452 with income tax return for first fiscal year ending after calendar year in which distributions were made.

Calendar-year corporations must file 2016 information return (Form 5471) with respect to foreign corporations. Fiscal-year corporations file form with income tax return.

Last date for a calendar-year corporation to file an amended income tax return (Form 1120X) for the calendar year 2013.[2]

Trusts and Estates. Fiduciary income tax return (Form 1041) for calendar year 2016. Fiscal-year estates must file by the 15th day of the 4th month following close of the tax year.

Last day for calendar year estates and trusts to file application (Form 7004) for automatic five-month extension of time to file 2016 income tax return.

Last day for estates and trusts to file amended tax returns (Form 1041) for calendar year 2013.

Information Returns. Annual information return (Form 1041-A) for split-interest trusts and complex trusts claiming charitable deductions under Code Sec. 642(c) and annual information return (Form 5227) for charitable remainder trusts, pooled income funds, and Code Sec. 4947(a)(2) trusts must be filed.

Apr. 30— **Coverdell ESAs.** Trustees of Coverdell education savings accounts (ESA) must furnish copy of Form 5498-ESA to participants. Coverdell ESA information must be report to the IRS by May 31.

May 1st— **Employers' Taxes.** Employers of nonagricultural and nonhousehold employees must file return on Form 941 to report income tax withholding and FICA taxes for the first quarter of 2017.[3]

May 15th— **Exempt Organizations.** Annual information return (Form 990) for 2016 by calendar-year organizations exempt or claiming exemption from tax under Code Sec. 501 or Code Sec. 4947(a)(1). Fiscal-year organizations must file by 15th day of 5th month after close of the tax year.

Calendar-year private foundations and Code Sec. 4947(a) trusts treated as private foundations must file Form 990-PF, and private foundations must pay the first quarter installment of estimated excise tax on net investment or tax on unrelated business income. Fiscal-year organizations must file by 15th day of 5th month after close of tax year, for both Form 990-PF and estimated taxes referred to above.

Calendar-year Code Sec. 501(a) organizations with unrelated business income must file income tax return on Form 990-T. Fiscal-year organizations must file by 15th day of 5th month following close of tax year.

This day 2017 **Tax Return Due Dates**

Last day for calendar year exempt organizations to file application (Form 8868) for automatic six-month extension of time to file Form 990 for the 2016 tax year. Form 8868 is also used for an automatic six-month extension of an exempt organization to file Form 990-T.

May 31st— **Information Returns.** Trustees must report on Form 5498 contributions, including rollover contributions, to any IRA, SEP, SIMPLE, and Roth IRA, as well as Roth conversions, IRA recharacterizations, and the fair market value (FMV) of the account. Participants of IRAs and SEPs must be provided statement of account's value and required minimum distribution by January 31.

Trustees must report contributions, including rollover contributions, to Coverdell ESAs (5498-ESA) and ABLE accounts 5498-QA. Coverdell ESA contributions must be reported to the beneficiary by April 30. ABLE account contributions must be reported to the beneficiary by March 15.

Trustees must report to the IRS and participants (5498-SA) contributions to a health savings account (HSA), including transfers and rollovers, or Archer medical savings account (MSA) and the fair market value of an HSA, Archer MSA, or Medicare Advantage MSA.

June 15th— **Individuals.** Last day for nonresident alien individuals not subject to withholding to file income tax return for calendar year 2016.

Estimated Tax. Calendar-year corporations must pay second installment of 2017 estimated tax (Form 1120-W).

Payment of second installment of 2017 estimated tax by individuals (Form 1040-ES), other than farmers and fishermen, by trusts and by estates (Form 1041-ES), and certain residuary trusts in existence more than two years. Nonresident aliens who have no wages subject to U.S. withholding must make first payment (Form 1040-ES (NR)).

Corporations. Last day for calendar-year foreign corporation that does not maintain an office or place of business in United States to file income tax return (Form 1120F) for calendar year 2016. Fiscal-year foreign corporations without offices in the United States must filed by the 15th day of the 6th month following the close of the tax year.

Last day for calendar year foreign corporation without offices in the United States to file application (Form 7004) for automatic six-month extension of time to file 2016 income tax return.

July 31st— **Employers' Taxes.** Employers of nonagricultural and nonhousehold employees must file return on Form 941 to report income tax withholding and FICA taxes for the second quarter of 2016.[4]

Sept. 15th— **Estimated Tax.** Payment of third installment of 2017 estimated tax by calendar-year corporations (Form 1120-W).

Payment of third installment of 2017 estimated tax by individuals (Form 1040-ES), other than farmers and fishermen, by trusts and by estates (Form 1041-ES), and certain residuary trusts in existence more than two years.

C Corporations. Last day for filing 2016 income tax return by calendar-year C corporations (Form 1120) that obtained automatic five-month filing extension.

Exempt Organizations. Last day for exempt calendar-year farmers' cooperatives to file 2016 income tax returns (Form 1120-C). Fiscal-year cooperatives must file by the 15th day of the 9th month following the close of the tax year. An automatic six-month extension of the filing date may be obtained by filing Form 7004.

This day 2017	Tax Return Due Dates
	Estates and Trusts. Last day for filing 2016 Form 1041 for calendar-year estates and trusts that obtained an automatic five-month filing extension.
	Partnerships. Last day for filing 2016 Form 1065 for calendar-year partnerships that obtained an automatic six-month filing extension.Form 1120S
	S Corporations. Last day for filing 2016 Form 1120S for calendar-year S corporation that obtained an automatic six-month filing extension.
October 16th—	**Individuals.** Last day for filing 2016 income tax return (Form 1040) by calendar-year individuals who obtained automatic six-month filing extension.
Oct. 31st—	**Employers' Taxes.** Employers of nonagricultural and nonhousehold employees must file return on Form 941 to report income tax withholding and FICA taxes for the third quarter of 2016.[5]
Dec. 15th—	**Estimated Tax.** Payment of last installment of 2017 estimated tax by calendar-year corporations (Form 1120-W).
This day 2018	
Jan. 16th—	**Estimated Taxes.** Final installment of 2016 estimated tax (Form 1040-ES) by individuals unless income tax return is filed with final payment by January 31, 2018. Payment in full of estimated tax by farmers and fishermen unless income tax returns are filed by March 1, 2018.
	Final installment of 2016 estimated tax (Form 1041-ES) by trusts, calendar-year estates, and certain residuary trusts in existence more than two years, unless Form 1041 is filed and taxes are paid in full by January 31, 2018.
Jan. 31st—	**Individuals.** Final income tax return for 2017 by calendar-year individuals (Form 1040) and by trusts and estates (Form 1041) in existence more than two years who owed but did not pay 2017 estimated tax otherwise due January 16th.

* The due date is due to the observance of Emancipation Day Holiday in the District of Columbia closing all Federal offices on Monday, April 17th. Maine or Massachusetts will also observe Patriot's Day on Monday, April 17th.

[1] If timely deposits in full payment of tax due were made, the due date for Form 940, Form 941, and Form 943 is February 10, 2017.

[2] Fiscal-year corporations generally must file within three years of the date the original return was due.

[3] If timely deposits in full payment of taxes due were made, the due date for Form 941 is May 10, 2017.

[4] If timely deposits in full payment of taxes due were made, the due date for Form 941 is August 10, 2017.

[5] If timely deposits in full payment of taxes due were made, the due date for Form 941 is November 10, 2017.

EMPLOYMENT TAX DEPOSITS

Income Tax Withholding, FICA Taxes, Backup Withholding. Employment taxes are withheld income tax, FICA contributions, and backup withholding on reportable payments. Generally, an employer must make either MONTHLY or SEMIWEEKLY deposits during a calendar year based upon the aggregate amount of employment taxes paid during the "lookback" period. The lookback period for each calendar year is the 12-month period that ended the preceding June 30. Thus, an employer's obligation to make deposits in 2017 will be based upon the aggregate employment taxes paid during the period July 1, 2015, through June 30, 2016 (¶ 2651). New employers are considered to have an aggregate tax liability of zero for any calendar quarter in which the employer did not exist.

Monthly Deposits. Monthly deposits are required if the aggregate amount of employment taxes reported by the employer for the lookback period is $50,000 or less. Monthly deposits are due on the 15th day of the following month in which the payments were made.

Semiweekly Deposits. An employer is a semiweekly depositor for the entire calendar year if the aggregate amount of employment taxes during the lookback period exceeds $50,000. Further, a monthly depositor will become a semiweekly depositor on the first day after the employer becomes subject to the One-Day Rule, discussed later. Semiweekly deposits are generally due on either Wednesday or Friday—depending upon the timing of the employer's pay period. Employers with payment dates, i.e., paydays, that fall on Wednesday, Thursday, or Friday must deposit the employment taxes on or before the following Wednesday. Employers with payment dates that fall on Saturday, Sunday, Monday, or Tuesday must make their deposit on or before the following Friday. An employer will always have three business days in which to make the deposit. Thus, if any of the three weekdays following the close of a semiweekly period is a holiday, then the employer will have an additional business day in which to make the deposit.

One-Day Rule. If an employer has accumulated $100,000 or more of undeposited employment taxes, then the taxes must be deposited by the close of the next banking day.

Federal Unemployment (FUTA) Taxes. The calendar year is divided into four quarters for purposes of determining when deposits of federal unemployment tax (FUTA) are necessary. The periods end on March 31, June 30, September 30, and December 31. If the employer's FUTA tax liability is $500 or less, then the employer does not have to deposit the tax, instead the amount may be carried forward and added to the liability for the next quarter to determine if a deposit is required. If the employer owes more than $500 in undeposited FUTA tax at the end of a quarter, including any FUTA tax carried forward from an earlier quarter, then the tax owed must be deposited by the end of the next month by either a electronic funds transfer (EFTPS) direct or a EFTPS financial institution.

Schedules and Tables

TAX RATES

	Par.
Tax Rate Schedules for 2016 and 2017	11
2016 Tax Table—Individuals	25
Corporation Income Tax Rates	33
Estate and Gift Taxes	40
Other Taxes	47

TAX RATE SCHEDULES FOR 2016 AND 2017

NOTE. The 2016 Tax Rate Schedules reproduced below are based on the rate changes and inflation adjustments to the tax brackets released by the IRS in Rev. Proc. 2015-53. The 2017 Tax Rate Schedules reproduced below are based on the rate changes and inflation adjustments to the tax brackets released by the IRS in Rev. Proc. 2016-55.

The 2016 and 2017 tax rate schedules for single individuals are at ¶ 11; for married individuals filing jointly and surviving spouses, see ¶ 13; for married individuals filing separately, see ¶ 15; for heads of households, see ¶ 17; and for estates and nongrantor trusts, see ¶ 19.

¶ 11 SCHEDULE X: Single Individuals

2016

Taxable Income Over	But Not Over	Pay	+	% on Excess	of the amount over—
$0—	$9,275	$0		10%	$0
9,275—	37,650	927.50		15	9,275
37,650—	91,150	5,183.75		25	37,650
91,150—	190,150	18,558.75		28	91,150
190,150—	413,350	46,278.75		33	190,150
413,350—	415,050	119,934.75		35	413,350
415,050—	. . . . .	120,529.75		39.6	415,050

2017

Taxable Income Over	But Not Over	Pay	+	% on Excess	of the amount over—
$0—	$9,325	$0		10%	$0
9,325—	37,950	932.50		15	9,325
37,950—	91,900	5,226.25		25	37,950
91,900—	191,650	18,713.75		28	91,900
191,650—	416,700	46,643.75		33	191,650
416,700—	418,400	120,910.25		35	416,700
418,400—	. . . . .	121,505.25		39.6	418,400

¶ 13 SCHEDULE Y-1: Married Filing Jointly and Surviving Spouses

2016

Taxable Income Over	But Not Over	Pay	+	% on Excess	of the amount over—
$0—	$18,550	$0		10%	$0
18,550—	75,300	1,855.00		15	18,550
75,300—	151,900	10,367.50		25	75,300
151,900—	231,450	29,517.50		28	151,900
231,450—	413,350	51,791.50		33	231,450
413,350—	466,950	111,818.50		35	413,350
466,950—	. . . . .	130,578.50		39.6	466,950

2017

Taxable Income Over	But Not Over	Pay	+	% on Excess	of the amount over—
$0—	$18,650	$0		10%	$0
18,650—	75,900	1,865.00		15	18,650
75,900—	153,100	10,452.50		25	75,900
153,100—	233,350	29,752.50		28	153,100
233,350—	416,700	52,222.50		33	233,350
416,700—	470,700	112,728.00		35	416,700
470,700—	. . . . .	131,628.00		39.6	470,700

¶ 15 SCHEDULE Y-2: Married Individuals Filing Separately

2016

Taxable Income Over	But Not Over	Pay	+	% on Excess	of the amount over—
$0—	$9,275	$0		10%	$0
9,275—	37,650	927.50		15	9,275
37,650—	75,950	5,183.75		25	37,650
75,950—	115,725	14,758.75		28	75,950
115,725—	206,675	25,895.75		33	115,725
206,675—	233,475	55,909.25		35	206,675
233,475—	. . . . .	65,289.25		39.6	233,475

2017

Taxable Income Over	But Not Over	Pay	+	% on Excess	of the amount over—
$0—	$9,325	$0		10%	$0
9,325—	37,950	932.50		15	9,325
37,950—	76,550	5,226.25		25	37,950
76,550—	116,675	14,876.25		28	76,550
116,675—	208,350	26,111.25		33	116,675
208,350—	235,350	56,364.00		35	208,350
235,350—	. . . . .	65,814.00		39.6	235,350

¶ 17 SCHEDULE Z: Heads of Households

2016

Taxable Income Over	But Not Over	Pay	+	% on Excess	of the amount over—
$0—	$13,250	$0		10%	$0
13,250—	50,400	1,325.00		15	13,250
50,400—	130,150	6,897.50		25	50,400
130,150—	210,800	26,835.00		28	130,150
210,800—	413,350	49,417.00		33	210,800
413,350—	441,000	116,258.50		35	413,350
441,000—	. . . . .	125,936.00		39.6	441,000

2017

Taxable Income Over	But Not Over	Pay	+	% on Excess	of the amount over—
$0—	$13,350	$0		10%	$0
13,350—	50,800	1,335.00		15	13,350
50,800—	131,200	6,952.50		25	50,800
131,200—	212,500	27,052.50		28	131,200
212,500—	416,700	49,816.50		33	212,500
416,700—	444,550	117,202.50		35	416,700
444,550—	. . . . .	126,950.00		39.6	444,550

¶ 19 INCOME TAX RATE SCHEDULES FOR USE BY ESTATES AND NONGRANTOR TRUSTS

2016

Taxable Income Over	But Not Over	Pay	+	% on Excess	of the amount over—
$0—	$2,550	$0		15%	$0
2,550—	5,950	382.50		25	2,550
5,950—	9,050	1,232.50		28	5,950
9,050—	12,400	2,100.50		33	9,050
12,400—	. . . . .	3,206.00		39.6	12,400

2017

Taxable Income Over	But Not Over	Pay	+	% on Excess	of the amount over—
$0—	$2,550	$0		15%	$0
2,550—	6,000	382.50		25	2,550
6,000—	9,150	1,245.00		28	6,000
9,150—	12,500	2,127.00		33	9,150
12,500—	. . . . .	3,232.50		39.6	12,500

Caution: This is a draft 2016 Tax Computation Worksheet. At the time of publication, the IRS had not yet released the 2016 Tax Computation Worksheet. For the latest information, see CCHGroup.com/TaxUpdates.

¶ 20 2016 Tax Computation Worksheet

2016 Tax Computation Worksheet—Line 44

See the instructions for line 44 to see if you must use the worksheet below to figure your tax.

Note. If you are required to use this worksheet to figure the tax on an amount from another form or worksheet, such as the Qualified Dividends and Capital Gain Tax Worksheet, the Schedule D Tax Worksheet, Schedule J, Form 8615, or the Foreign Earned Income Tax Worksheet, enter the amount from that form or worksheet in column (a) of the row that applies to the amount you are looking up. Enter the result on the appropriate line of the form or worksheet that you are completing.

DRAFT AS OF October 7, 2016

Section A—Use if your filing status is **Single.** Complete the row below that applies to you.

Taxable income. If line 43 is—	**(a)** Enter the amount from line 43	**(b)** Multiplication amount	**(c)** Multiply (a) by (b)	**(d)** Subtraction amount	**Tax.** Subtract (d) from (c). Enter the result here and on Form 1040, line 44
At least $100,000 but not over $190,150	$	× 28% (0.28)	$	$ 6,963.25	$
Over $190,150 but not over $413,350	$	× 33% (0.33)	$	$ 16,470.75	$
Over $413,350 but not over $415,050	$	× 35% (0.35)	$	$ 24,737.75	$
Over $415,050	$	× 39.6% (0.396)	$	$ 43,830.05	$

Section B—Use if your filing status is **Married filing jointly** or **Qualifying widow(er).** Complete the row below that applies to you.

Taxable income. If line 43 is—	**(a)** Enter the amount from line 43	**(b)** Multiplication amount	**(c)** Multiply (a) by (b)	**(d)** Subtraction amount	**Tax.** Subtract (d) from (c). Enter the result here and on Form 1040, line 44
At least $100,000 but not over $151,900	$	× 25% (0.25)	$	$ 8,457.50	$
Over $151,900 but not over $231,450	$	× 28% (0.28)	$	$ 13,014.50	$
Over $231,450 but not over $413,350	$	× 33% (0.33)	$	$ 24,587.00	$
Over $413,350 but not over $466,950	$	× 35% (0.35)	$	$ 32,854.00	$
Over $466,950	$	× 39.6% (0.396)	$	$ 54,333.70	$

Section C—Use if your filing status is **Married filing separately.** Complete the row below that applies to you.

Taxable income. If line 43 is—	**(a)** Enter the amount from line 43	**(b)** Multiplication amount	**(c)** Multiply (a) by (b)	**(d)** Subtraction amount	**Tax.** Subtract (d) from (c). Enter the result here and on Form 1040, line 44
At least $100,000 but not over $115,725	$	× 28% (0.28)	$	$ 6,507.25	$
Over $115,725 but not over $206,675	$	× 33% (0.33)	$	$ 12,293.50	$
Over $206,675 but not over $233,475	$	× 35% (0.35)	$	$ 16,427.00	$
Over $233,475	$	× 39.6% (0.396)	$	$ 27,166.85	$

Section D—Use if your filing status is **Head of household.** Complete the row below that applies to you.

Taxable income. If line 43 is—	**(a)** Enter the amount from line 43	**(b)** Multiplication amount	**(c)** Multiply (a) by (b)	**(d)** Subtraction amount	**Tax.** Subtract (d) from (c). Enter the result here and on Form 1040, line 44
At least $100,000 but not over $130,150	$	× 25% (0.25)	$	$ 5,702.50	$
Over $130,150 but not over $210,800	$	× 28% (0.28)	$	$ 9,607.00	$
Over $210,800 but not over $413,350	$	× 33% (0.33)	$	$ 20,147.00	$
Over $413,350 but not over $441,000	$	× 35% (0.35)	$	$ 28,414.00	$
Over $441,000	$	× 39.6% (0.396)	$	$ 48,700.00	$

2016 TAX TABLE—INDIVIDUALS

Caution: This is a draft 2016 Tax Table. At the time of publication, the IRS had not yet released the 2016 Tax Table. For the latest information, see CCHGroup.com/TaxUpdates.

¶ 25 2016 Tax Table for Use with Form 1040

□ The Tax Table that follows is for use with Form 1040. A similar Tax Table applies to Forms 1040A and 1040EZ.

2016 TAX TABLE Based on Taxable Income. For persons with taxable incomes of less than $100,000.

Read down the income columns of the tax table until you find the line covering the taxable income shown on line 43 of Form 1040 (line 27 of Form 1040A or line 6 of Form 1040EZ). Then read across that income line until you find the column heading that describes your filing status. Enter the tax found there on line 44 of Form 1040 (line 28 of Form 1040A or line 10 of Form 1040EZ).

Caution: This is a draft 2016 Tax Table. At the time of publication, the IRS had not yet released the 2016 Tax Table. For the latest information, see CCHGroup.com/TaxUpdates.

2016 Tax Table

See the instructions for line 44 to see if you must use the Tax Table below to figure your tax.

Example. Mr. and Mrs. Brown are filing a joint return. Their taxable income on Form 1040, line 43, is $25,300. First, they find the $25,300-25,350 taxable income line. Next, they find the column for married filing jointly and read down the column. The amount shown where the taxable income line and filing status column meet is $2,871. This is the tax amount they should enter on Form 1040, line 44.

Sample Table

At Least	But Less Than	Single	Married filing jointly*	Married filing separately	Head of a household
		Your tax is—			
25,200	25,250	3,320	2,856	3,320	3,121
25,250	25,300	3,328	2,864	3,328	3,129
25,300	25,350	3,335	2,871	3,335	3,136
25,350	25,400	3,343	2,879	3,343	3,144

DRAFT AS OF October 7, 2016

If line 43 (taxable income) is— At least	But less than	And you are— Single	Married filing jointly *	Married filing separately	Head of a household
		Your tax is—			
0	5	0	0	0	0
5	15	1	1	1	1
15	25	2	2	2	2
25	50	4	4	4	4
50	75	6	6	6	6
75	100	9	9	9	9
100	125	11	11	11	11
125	150	14	14	14	14
150	175	16	16	16	16
175	200	19	19	19	19
200	225	21	21	21	21
225	250	24	24	24	24
250	275	26	26	26	26
275	300	29	29	29	29
300	325	31	31	31	31
325	350	34	34	34	34
350	375	36	36	36	36
375	400	39	39	39	39
400	425	41	41	41	41
425	450	44	44	44	44
450	475	46	46	46	46
475	500	49	49	49	49
500	525	51	51	51	51
525	550	54	54	54	54
550	575	56	56	56	56
575	600	59	59	59	59
600	625	61	61	61	61
625	650	64	64	64	64
650	675	66	66	66	66
675	700	69	69	69	69
700	725	71	71	71	71
725	750	74	74	74	74
750	775	76	76	76	76
775	800	79	79	79	79
800	825	81	81	81	81
825	850	84	84	84	84
850	875	86	86	86	86
875	900	89	89	89	89
900	925	91	91	91	91
925	950	94	94	94	94
950	975	96	96	96	96
975	1,000	99	99	99	99

If line 43 (taxable income) is— At least	But less than	And you are— Single	Married filing jointly *	Married filing separately	Head of a household
		Your tax is—			
1,000					
1,000	1,025	101	101	101	101
1,025	1,050	104	104	104	104
1,050	1,075	106	106	106	106
1,075	1,100	109	109	109	109
1,100	1,125	111	111	111	111
1,125	1,150	114	114	114	114
1,150	1,175	116	116	116	116
1,175	1,200	119	119	119	119
1,200	1,225	121	121	121	121
1,225	1,250	124	124	124	124
1,250	1,275	126	126	126	126
1,275	1,300	129	129	129	129
1,300	1,325	131	131	131	131
1,325	1,350	134	134	134	134
1,350	1,375	136	136	136	136
1,375	1,400	139	139	139	139
1,400	1,425	141	141	141	141
1,425	1,450	144	144	144	144
1,450	1,475	146	146	146	146
1,475	1,500	149	149	149	149
1,500	1,525	151	151	151	151
1,525	1,550	154	154	154	154
1,550	1,575	156	156	156	156
1,575	1,600	159	159	159	159
1,600	1,625	161	161	161	161
1,625	1,650	164	164	164	164
1,650	1,675	166	166	166	166
1,675	1,700	169	169	169	169
1,700	1,725	171	171	171	171
1,725	1,750	174	174	174	174
1,750	1,775	176	176	176	176
1,775	1,800	179	179	179	179
1,800	1,825	181	181	181	181
1,825	1,850	184	184	184	184
1,850	1,875	186	186	186	186
1,875	1,900	189	189	189	189
1,900	1,925	191	191	191	191
1,925	1,950	194	194	194	194
1,950	1,975	196	196	196	196
1,975	2,000	199	199	199	199

If line 43 (taxable income) is— At least	But less than	And you are— Single	Married filing jointly *	Married filing separately	Head of a household
		Your tax is—			
2,000					
2,000	2,025	201	201	201	201
2,025	2,050	204	204	204	204
2,050	2,075	206	206	206	206
2,075	2,100	209	209	209	209
2,100	2,125	211	211	211	211
2,125	2,150	214	214	214	214
2,150	2,175	216	216	216	216
2,175	2,200	219	219	219	219
2,200	2,225	221	221	221	221
2,225	2,250	224	224	224	224
2,250	2,275	226	226	226	226
2,275	2,300	229	229	229	229
2,300	2,325	231	231	231	231
2,325	2,350	234	234	234	234
2,350	2,375	236	236	236	236
2,375	2,400	239	239	239	239
2,400	2,425	241	241	241	241
2,425	2,450	244	244	244	244
2,450	2,475	246	246	246	246
2,475	2,500	249	249	249	249
2,500	2,525	251	251	251	251
2,525	2,550	254	254	254	254
2,550	2,575	256	256	256	256
2,575	2,600	259	259	259	259
2,600	2,625	261	261	261	261
2,625	2,650	264	264	264	264
2,650	2,675	266	266	266	266
2,675	2,700	269	269	269	269
2,700	2,725	271	271	271	271
2,725	2,750	274	274	274	274
2,750	2,775	276	276	276	276
2,775	2,800	279	279	279	279
2,800	2,825	281	281	281	281
2,825	2,850	284	284	284	284
2,850	2,875	286	286	286	286
2,875	2,900	289	289	289	289
2,900	2,925	291	291	291	291
2,925	2,950	294	294	294	294
2,950	2,975	296	296	296	296
2,975	3,000	299	299	299	299

(Continued)

* This column must also be used by a qualifying widow(er).

Caution: This is a draft 2016 Tax Table. At the time of publication, the IRS had not yet released the 2016 Tax Table. For the latest information, see CCHGroup.com/TaxUpdates.

2016 Tax Table — *Continued*

DRAFT AS OF October 7, 2016

If line 43 (taxable income) is—		And you are—			
At least	But less than	Single	Married filing jointly *	Married filing separately	Head of a household
		Your tax is—			
3,000					
3,000	3,050	303	303	303	303
3,050	3,100	308	308	308	308
3,100	3,150	313	313	313	313
3,150	3,200	318	318	318	318
3,200	3,250	323	323	323	323
3,250	3,300	328	328	328	328
3,300	3,350	333	333	333	333
3,350	3,400	338	338	338	338
3,400	3,450	343	343	343	343
3,450	3,500	348	348	348	348
3,500	3,550	353	353	353	353
3,550	3,600	358	358	358	358
3,600	3,650	363	363	363	363
3,650	3,700	368	368	368	368
3,700	3,750	373	373	373	373
3,750	3,800	378	378	378	378
3,800	3,850	383	383	383	383
3,850	3,900	388	388	388	388
3,900	3,950	393	393	393	393
3,950	4,000	398	398	398	398
4,000					
4,000	4,050	403	403	403	403
4,050	4,100	408	408	408	408
4,100	4,150	413	413	413	413
4,150	4,200	418	418	418	418
4,200	4,250	423	423	423	423
4,250	4,300	428	428	428	428
4,300	4,350	433	433	433	433
4,350	4,400	438	438	438	438
4,400	4,450	443	443	443	443
4,450	4,500	448	448	448	448
4,500	4,550	453	453	453	453
4,550	4,600	458	458	458	458
4,600	4,650	463	463	463	463
4,650	4,700	468	468	468	468
4,700	4,750	473	473	473	473
4,750	4,800	478	478	478	478
4,800	4,850	483	483	483	483
4,850	4,900	488	488	488	488
4,900	4,950	493	493	493	493
4,950	5,000	498	498	498	498
5,000					
5,000	5,050	503	503	503	503
5,050	5,100	508	508	508	508
5,100	5,150	513	513	513	513
5,150	5,200	518	518	518	518
5,200	5,250	523	523	523	523
5,250	5,300	528	528	528	528
5,300	5,350	533	533	533	533
5,350	5,400	538	538	538	538
5,400	5,450	543	543	543	543
5,450	5,500	548	548	548	548
5,500	5,550	553	553	553	553
5,550	5,600	558	558	558	558
5,600	5,650	563	563	563	563
5,650	5,700	568	568	568	568
5,700	5,750	573	573	573	573
5,750	5,800	578	578	578	578
5,800	5,850	583	583	583	583
5,850	5,900	588	588	588	588
5,900	5,950	593	593	593	593
5,950	6,000	598	598	598	598

If line 43 (taxable income) is—		And you are—			
At least	But less than	Single	Married filing jointly *	Married filing separately	Head of a household
		Your tax is—			
6,000					
6,000	6,050	603	603	603	603
6,050	6,100	608	608	608	608
6,100	6,150	613	613	613	613
6,150	6,200	618	618	618	618
6,200	6,250	623	623	623	623
6,250	6,300	628	628	628	628
6,300	6,350	633	633	633	633
6,350	6,400	638	638	638	638
6,400	6,450	643	643	643	643
6,450	6,500	648	648	648	648
6,500	6,550	653	653	653	653
6,550	6,600	658	658	658	658
6,600	6,650	663	663	663	663
6,650	6,700	668	668	668	668
6,700	6,750	673	673	673	673
6,750	6,800	678	678	678	678
6,800	6,850	683	683	683	683
6,850	6,900	688	688	688	688
6,900	6,950	693	693	693	693
6,950	7,000	698	698	698	698
7,000					
7,000	7,050	703	703	703	703
7,050	7,100	708	708	708	708
7,100	7,150	713	713	713	713
7,150	7,200	718	718	718	718
7,200	7,250	723	723	723	723
7,250	7,300	728	728	728	728
7,300	7,350	733	733	733	733
7,350	7,400	738	738	738	738
7,400	7,450	743	743	743	743
7,450	7,500	748	748	748	748
7,500	7,550	753	753	753	753
7,550	7,600	758	758	758	758
7,600	7,650	763	763	763	763
7,650	7,700	768	768	768	768
7,700	7,750	773	773	773	773
7,750	7,800	778	778	778	778
7,800	7,850	783	783	783	783
7,850	7,900	788	788	788	788
7,900	7,950	793	793	793	793
7,950	8,000	798	798	798	798
8,000					
8,000	8,050	803	803	803	803
8,050	8,100	808	808	808	808
8,100	8,150	813	813	813	813
8,150	8,200	818	818	818	818
8,200	8,250	823	823	823	823
8,250	8,300	828	828	828	828
8,300	8,350	833	833	833	833
8,350	8,400	838	838	838	838
8,400	8,450	843	843	843	843
8,450	8,500	848	848	848	848
8,500	8,550	853	853	853	853
8,550	8,600	858	858	858	858
8,600	8,650	863	863	863	863
8,650	8,700	868	868	868	868
8,700	8,750	873	873	873	873
8,750	8,800	878	878	878	878
8,800	8,850	883	883	883	883
8,850	8,900	888	888	888	888
8,900	8,950	893	893	893	893
8,950	9,000	898	898	898	898

If line 43 (taxable income) is—		And you are—			
At least	But less than	Single	Married filing jointly *	Married filing separately	Head of a household
		Your tax is—			
9,000					
9,000	9,050	903	903	903	903
9,050	9,100	908	908	908	908
9,100	9,150	913	913	913	913
9,150	9,200	918	918	918	918
9,200	9,250	923	923	923	923
9,250	9,300	928	928	928	928
9,300	9,350	935	933	935	933
9,350	9,400	943	938	943	938
9,400	9,450	950	943	950	943
9,450	9,500	958	948	958	948
9,500	9,550	965	953	965	953
9,550	9,600	973	958	973	958
9,600	9,650	980	963	980	963
9,650	9,700	988	968	988	968
9,700	9,750	995	973	995	973
9,750	9,800	1,003	978	1,003	978
9,800	9,850	1,010	983	1,010	983
9,850	9,900	1,018	988	1,018	988
9,900	9,950	1,025	993	1,025	993
9,950	10,000	1,033	998	1,033	998
10,000					
10,000	10,050	1,040	1,003	1,040	1,003
10,050	10,100	1,048	1,008	1,048	1,008
10,100	10,150	1,055	1,013	1,055	1,013
10,150	10,200	1,063	1,018	1,063	1,018
10,200	10,250	1,070	1,023	1,070	1,023
10,250	10,300	1,078	1,028	1,078	1,028
10,300	10,350	1,085	1,033	1,085	1,033
10,350	10,400	1,093	1,038	1,093	1,038
10,400	10,450	1,100	1,043	1,100	1,043
10,450	10,500	1,108	1,048	1,108	1,048
10,500	10,550	1,115	1,053	1,115	1,053
10,550	10,600	1,123	1,058	1,123	1,058
10,600	10,650	1,130	1,063	1,130	1,063
10,650	10,700	1,138	1,068	1,138	1,068
10,700	10,750	1,145	1,073	1,145	1,073
10,750	10,800	1,153	1,078	1,153	1,078
10,800	10,850	1,160	1,083	1,160	1,083
10,850	10,900	1,168	1,088	1,168	1,088
10,900	10,950	1,175	1,093	1,175	1,093
10,950	11,000	1,183	1,098	1,183	1,098
11,000					
11,000	11,050	1,190	1,103	1,190	1,103
11,050	11,100	1,198	1,108	1,198	1,108
11,100	11,150	1,205	1,113	1,205	1,113
11,150	11,200	1,213	1,118	1,213	1,118
11,200	11,250	1,220	1,123	1,220	1,123
11,250	11,300	1,228	1,128	1,228	1,128
11,300	11,350	1,235	1,133	1,235	1,133
11,350	11,400	1,243	1,138	1,243	1,138
11,400	11,450	1,250	1,143	1,250	1,143
11,450	11,500	1,258	1,148	1,258	1,148
11,500	11,550	1,265	1,153	1,265	1,153
11,550	11,600	1,273	1,158	1,273	1,158
11,600	11,650	1,280	1,163	1,280	1,163
11,650	11,700	1,288	1,168	1,288	1,168
11,700	11,750	1,295	1,173	1,295	1,173
11,750	11,800	1,303	1,178	1,303	1,178
11,800	11,850	1,310	1,183	1,310	1,183
11,850	11,900	1,318	1,188	1,318	1,188
11,900	11,950	1,325	1,193	1,325	1,193
11,950	12,000	1,333	1,198	1,333	1,198

(Continued)

* This column must also be used by a qualifying widow(er).

Need more information or forms? Visit IRS.gov.

Caution: This is a draft 2016 Tax Table. At the time of publication, the IRS had not yet released the 2016 Tax Table. For the latest information, see CCHGroup.com/TaxUpdates.

2016 Tax Table — *Continued*

DRAFT AS OF October 7, 2016

If line 43 (taxable income) is—		And you are—			
At least	But less than	Single	Married filing jointly *	Married filing separately	Head of a household
		Your tax is—			
12,000					
12,000	12,050	1,340	1,203	1,340	1,203
12,050	12,100	1,348	1,208	1,348	1,208
12,100	12,150	1,355	1,213	1,355	1,213
12,150	12,200	1,363	1,218	1,363	1,218
12,200	12,250	1,370	1,223	1,370	1,223
12,250	12,300	1,378	1,228	1,378	1,228
12,300	12,350	1,385	1,233	1,385	1,233
12,350	12,400	1,393	1,238	1,393	1,238
12,400	12,450	1,400	1,243	1,400	1,243
12,450	12,500	1,408	1,248	1,408	1,248
12,500	12,550	1,415	1,253	1,415	1,253
12,550	12,600	1,423	1,258	1,423	1,258
12,600	12,650	1,430	1,263	1,430	1,263
12,650	12,700	1,438	1,268	1,438	1,268
12,700	12,750	1,445	1,273	1,445	1,273
12,750	12,800	1,453	1,278	1,453	1,278
12,800	12,850	1,460	1,283	1,460	1,283
12,850	12,900	1,468	1,288	1,468	1,288
12,900	12,950	1,475	1,293	1,475	1,293
12,950	13,000	1,483	1,298	1,483	1,298
13,000					
13,000	13,050	1,490	1,303	1,490	1,303
13,050	13,100	1,498	1,308	1,498	1,308
13,100	13,150	1,505	1,313	1,505	1,313
13,150	13,200	1,513	1,318	1,513	1,318
13,200	13,250	1,520	1,323	1,520	1,323
13,250	13,300	1,528	1,328	1,528	1,329
13,300	13,350	1,535	1,333	1,535	1,336
13,350	13,400	1,543	1,338	1,543	1,344
13,400	13,450	1,550	1,343	1,550	1,351
13,450	13,500	1,558	1,348	1,558	1,359
13,500	13,550	1,565	1,353	1,565	1,366
13,550	13,600	1,573	1,358	1,573	1,374
13,600	13,650	1,580	1,363	1,580	1,381
13,650	13,700	1,588	1,368	1,588	1,389
13,700	13,750	1,595	1,373	1,595	1,396
13,750	13,800	1,603	1,378	1,603	1,404
13,800	13,850	1,610	1,383	1,610	1,411
13,850	13,900	1,618	1,388	1,618	1,419
13,900	13,950	1,625	1,393	1,625	1,426
13,950	14,000	1,633	1,398	1,633	1,434
14,000					
14,000	14,050	1,640	1,403	1,640	1,441
14,050	14,100	1,648	1,408	1,648	1,449
14,100	14,150	1,655	1,413	1,655	1,456
14,150	14,200	1,663	1,418	1,663	1,464
14,200	14,250	1,670	1,423	1,670	1,471
14,250	14,300	1,678	1,428	1,678	1,479
14,300	14,350	1,685	1,433	1,685	1,486
14,350	14,400	1,693	1,438	1,693	1,494
14,400	14,450	1,700	1,443	1,700	1,501
14,450	14,500	1,708	1,448	1,708	1,509
14,500	14,550	1,715	1,453	1,715	1,516
14,550	14,600	1,723	1,458	1,723	1,524
14,600	14,650	1,730	1,463	1,730	1,531
14,650	14,700	1,738	1,468	1,738	1,539
14,700	14,750	1,745	1,473	1,745	1,546
14,750	14,800	1,753	1,478	1,753	1,554
14,800	14,850	1,760	1,483	1,760	1,561
14,850	14,900	1,768	1,488	1,768	1,569
14,900	14,950	1,775	1,493	1,775	1,576
14,950	15,000	1,783	1,498	1,783	1,584

If line 43 (taxable income) is—		And you are—			
At least	But less than	Single	Married filing jointly *	Married filing separately	Head of a household
		Your tax is—			
15,000					
15,000	15,050	1,790	1,503	1,790	1,591
15,050	15,100	1,798	1,508	1,798	1,598
15,100	15,150	1,805	1,513	1,805	1,606
15,150	15,200	1,813	1,518	1,813	1,614
15,200	15,250	1,820	1,523	1,820	1,621
15,250	15,300	1,828	1,528	1,828	1,629
15,300	15,350	1,835	1,533	1,835	1,636
15,350	15,400	1,843	1,538	1,843	1,644
15,400	15,450	1,850	1,543	1,850	1,651
15,450	15,500	1,858	1,548	1,858	1,659
15,500	15,550	1,865	1,553	1,865	1,666
15,550	15,600	1,873	1,558	1,873	1,674
15,600	15,650	1,880	1,563	1,880	1,681
15,650	15,700	1,888	1,568	1,888	1,689
15,700	15,750	1,895	1,573	1,895	1,696
15,750	15,800	1,903	1,578	1,903	1,704
15,800	15,850	1,910	1,583	1,910	1,711
15,850	15,900	1,918	1,588	1,918	1,719
15,900	15,950	1,925	1,593	1,925	1,726
15,950	16,000	1,933	1,598	1,933	1,734
16,000					
16,000	16,050	1,940	1,603	1,940	1,741
16,050	16,100	1,948	1,608	1,948	1,749
16,100	16,150	1,955	1,613	1,955	1,756
16,150	16,200	1,963	1,618	1,963	1,764
16,200	16,250	1,970	1,623	1,970	1,771
16,250	16,300	1,978	1,628	1,978	1,779
16,300	16,350	1,985	1,633	1,985	1,786
16,350	16,400	1,993	1,638	1,993	1,794
16,400	16,450	2,000	1,643	2,000	1,801
16,450	16,500	2,008	1,648	2,008	1,809
16,500	16,550	2,015	1,653	2,015	1,816
16,550	16,600	2,023	1,658	2,023	1,824
16,600	16,650	2,030	1,663	2,030	1,831
16,650	16,700	2,038	1,668	2,038	1,839
16,700	16,750	2,045	1,673	2,045	1,846
16,750	16,800	2,053	1,678	2,053	1,854
16,800	16,850	2,060	1,683	2,060	1,861
16,850	16,900	2,068	1,688	2,068	1,869
16,900	16,950	2,075	1,693	2,075	1,876
16,950	17,000	2,083	1,698	2,083	1,884
17,000					
17,000	17,050	2,090	1,703	2,090	1,891
17,050	17,100	2,098	1,708	2,098	1,899
17,100	17,150	2,105	1,713	2,105	1,906
17,150	17,200	2,113	1,718	2,113	1,914
17,200	17,250	2,120	1,723	2,120	1,921
17,250	17,300	2,128	1,728	2,128	1,929
17,300	17,350	2,135	1,733	2,135	1,936
17,350	17,400	2,143	1,738	2,143	1,944
17,400	17,450	2,150	1,743	2,150	1,951
17,450	17,500	2,158	1,748	2,158	1,959
17,500	17,550	2,165	1,753	2,165	1,966
17,550	17,600	2,173	1,758	2,173	1,974
17,600	17,650	2,180	1,763	2,180	1,981
17,650	17,700	2,188	1,768	2,188	1,989
17,700	17,750	2,195	1,773	2,195	1,996
17,750	17,800	2,203	1,778	2,203	2,004
17,800	17,850	2,210	1,783	2,210	2,011
17,850	17,900	2,218	1,788	2,218	2,019
17,900	17,950	2,225	1,793	2,225	2,026
17,950	18,000	2,233	1,798	2,233	2,034

If line 43 (taxable income) is—		And you are—			
At least	But less than	Single	Married filing jointly *	Married filing separately	Head of a household
		Your tax is—			
18,000					
18,000	18,050	2,240	1,803	2,240	2,041
18,050	18,100	2,248	1,808	2,248	2,049
18,100	18,150	2,255	1,813	2,255	2,056
18,150	18,200	2,263	1,818	2,263	2,064
18,200	18,250	2,270	1,823	2,270	2,071
18,250	18,300	2,278	1,828	2,278	2,079
18,300	18,350	2,285	1,833	2,285	2,086
18,350	18,400	2,293	1,838	2,293	2,094
18,400	18,450	2,300	1,843	2,300	2,101
18,450	18,500	2,308	1,848	2,308	2,109
18,500	18,550	2,315	1,853	2,315	2,116
18,550	18,600	2,323	1,859	2,323	2,124
18,600	18,650	2,330	1,866	2,330	2,131
18,650	18,700	2,338	1,874	2,338	2,139
18,700	18,750	2,345	1,881	2,345	2,146
18,750	18,800	2,353	1,889	2,353	2,154
18,800	18,850	2,360	1,896	2,360	2,161
18,850	18,900	2,368	1,904	2,368	2,169
18,900	18,950	2,375	1,911	2,375	2,176
18,950	19,000	2,383	1,919	2,383	2,184
19,000					
19,000	19,050	2,390	1,926	2,390	2,191
19,050	19,100	2,398	1,934	2,398	2,199
19,100	19,150	2,405	1,941	2,405	2,206
19,150	19,200	2,413	1,949	2,413	2,214
19,200	19,250	2,420	1,956	2,420	2,221
19,250	19,300	2,428	1,964	2,428	2,229
19,300	19,350	2,435	1,971	2,435	2,236
19,350	19,400	2,443	1,979	2,443	2,244
19,400	19,450	2,450	1,986	2,450	2,251
19,450	19,500	2,458	1,994	2,458	2,259
19,500	19,550	2,465	2,001	2,465	2,266
19,550	19,600	2,473	2,009	2,473	2,274
19,600	19,650	2,480	2,016	2,480	2,281
19,650	19,700	2,488	2,024	2,488	2,289
19,700	19,750	2,495	2,031	2,495	2,296
19,750	19,800	2,503	2,039	2,503	2,304
19,800	19,850	2,510	2,046	2,510	2,311
19,850	19,900	2,518	2,054	2,518	2,319
19,900	19,950	2,525	2,061	2,525	2,326
19,950	20,000	2,533	2,069	2,533	2,334
20,000					
20,000	20,050	2,540	2,076	2,540	2,341
20,050	20,100	2,548	2,084	2,548	2,349
20,100	20,150	2,555	2,091	2,555	2,356
20,150	20,200	2,563	2,099	2,563	2,364
20,200	20,250	2,570	2,106	2,570	2,371
20,250	20,300	2,578	2,114	2,578	2,379
20,300	20,350	2,585	2,121	2,585	2,386
20,350	20,400	2,593	2,129	2,593	2,394
20,400	20,450	2,600	2,136	2,600	2,401
20,450	20,500	2,608	2,144	2,608	2,409
20,500	20,550	2,615	2,151	2,615	2,416
20,550	20,600	2,623	2,159	2,623	2,424
20,600	20,650	2,630	2,166	2,630	2,431
20,650	20,700	2,638	2,174	2,638	2,439
20,700	20,750	2,645	2,181	2,645	2,446
20,750	20,800	2,653	2,189	2,653	2,454
20,800	20,850	2,660	2,196	2,660	2,461
20,850	20,900	2,668	2,204	2,668	2,469
20,900	20,950	2,675	2,211	2,675	2,476
20,950	21,000	2,683	2,219	2,683	2,484

(Continued)

* This column must also be used by a qualifying widow(er).

Caution: This is a draft 2016 Tax Table. At the time of publication, the IRS had not yet released the 2016 Tax Table. For the latest information, see CCHGroup.com/TaxUpdates.

2016 Tax Table — *Continued*

DRAFT AS OF October 7, 2016

If line 43 (taxable income) is—		And you are—			
At least	But less than	Single	Married filing jointly *	Married filing separately	Head of a household
		Your tax is—			
21,000					
21,000	21,050	2,690	2,226	2,690	2,491
21,050	21,100	2,698	2,234	2,698	2,499
21,100	21,150	2,705	2,241	2,705	2,506
21,150	21,200	2,713	2,249	2,713	2,514
21,200	21,250	2,720	2,256	2,720	2,521
21,250	21,3	2,728	2,264	2,728	2,529
21,300	21,350	2,735	2,271	2,735	2,536
21,350	21,400	2,743	2,279	2,743	2,544
21,400	21,450	2,750	2,286	2,750	2,551
21,450	21,500	2,758	2,294	2,758	2,559
21,500	21,550	2,765	2,301	2,765	2,566
21,550	21,600	2,773	2,309	2,773	2,574
21,600	21,650	2,780	2,316	2,780	2,581
21,650	21,700	2,788	2,324	2,788	2,589
21,700	21,750	2,795	2,331	2,795	2,596
21,750	21,800	2,803	2,339	2,803	2,604
21,800	21,850	2,810	2,346	2,810	2,611
21,850	21,900	2,818	2,354	2,818	2,619
21,900	21,950	2,825	2,361	2,825	2,626
21,950	22,000	2,833	2,369	2,833	2,634
22,000					
22,000	22,050	2,840	2,376	2,840	2,641
22,050	22,100	2,848	2,384	2,848	2,649
22,100	22,150	2,855	2,391	2,855	2,656
22,150	22,200	2,863	2,399	2,863	2,664
22,200	22,250	2,870	2,406	2,870	2,671
22,250	22,300	2,878	2,414	2,878	2,679
22,300	22,350	2,885	2,421	2,885	2,686
22,350	22,400	2,893	2,429	2,893	2,694
22,400	22,450	2,900	2,436	2,900	2,701
22,450	22,500	2,908	2,444	2,908	2,709
22,500	22,550	2,915	2,451	2,915	2,716
22,550	22,600	2,923	2,459	2,923	2,724
22,600	22,650	2,930	2,466	2,930	2,731
22,650	22,700	2,938	2,474	2,938	2,739
22,700	22,750	2,945	2,481	2,945	2,746
22,750	22,800	2,953	2,489	2,953	2,754
22,800	22,850	2,960	2,496	2,960	2,761
22,850	22,900	2,968	2,504	2,968	2,769
22,900	22,950	2,975	2,511	2,975	2,776
22,950	23,000	2,983	2,519	2,983	2,784
23,000					
23,000	23,050	2,990	2,526	2,990	2,791
23,050	23,100	2,998	2,534	2,998	2,799
23,100	23,150	3,005	2,541	3,005	2,806
23,150	23,200	3,013	2,549	3,013	2,814
23,200	23,250	3,020	2,556	3,020	2,821
23,250	23,300	3,028	2,564	3,028	2,829
23,300	23,350	3,035	2,571	3,035	2,836
23,350	23,400	3,043	2,579	3,043	2,844
23,400	23,450	3,050	2,586	3,050	2,851
23,450	23,500	3,058	2,594	3,058	2,859
23,500	23,550	3,065	2,601	3,065	2,866
23,550	23,600	3,073	2,609	3,073	2,874
23,600	23,650	3,080	2,616	3,080	2,881
23,650	23,700	3,088	2,624	3,088	2,889
23,700	23,750	3,095	2,631	3,095	2,896
23,750	23,800	3,103	2,639	3,103	2,904
23,800	23,850	3,110	2,646	3,110	2,911
23,850	23,900	3,118	2,654	3,118	2,919
23,900	23,950	3,125	2,661	3,125	2,926
23,950	24,000	3,133	2,669	3,133	2,934

If line 43 (taxable income) is—		And you are—			
At least	But less than	Single	Married filing jointly *	Married filing separately	Head of a household
		Your tax is—			
24,000					
24,000	24,050	3,140	2,676	3,140	2,941
24,050	24,100	3,148	2,684	3,148	2,949
24,100	24,150	3,155	2,691	3,155	2,956
24,150	24,200	3,163	2,699	3,163	2,964
24,200	24,250	3,170	2,706	3,170	2,971
24,250	24,300	3,178	2,714	3,178	2,979
24,300	24,350	3,185	2,721	3,185	2,986
24,350	24,400	3,193	2,729	3,193	2,994
24,400	24,450	3,200	2,736	3,200	3,001
24,450	24,500	3,208	2,744	3,208	3,009
24,500	24,550	3,215	2,751	3,215	3,016
24,550	24,600	3,223	2,759	3,223	3,024
24,600	24,650	3,230	2,766	3,230	3,031
24,650	24,700	3,238	2,774	3,238	3,039
24,700	24,750	3,245	2,781	3,245	3,046
24,750	24,800	3,253	2,789	3,253	3,054
24,800	24,850	3,260	2,796	3,260	3,061
24,850	24,900	3,268	2,804	3,268	3,069
24,900	24,950	3,275	2,811	3,275	3,076
24,950	25,000	3,283	2,819	3,283	3,084
25,000					
25,000	25,050	3,290	2,826	3,290	3,091
25,050	25,100	3,298	2,834	3,298	3,099
25,100	25,150	3,305	2,841	3,305	3,106
25,150	25,200	3,313	2,849	3,313	3,114
25,200	25,250	3,320	2,856	3,320	3,121
25,250	25,300	3,328	2,864	3,328	3,129
25,300	25,350	3,335	2,871	3,335	3,136
25,350	25,400	3,343	2,879	3,343	3,144
25,400	25,450	3,350	2,886	3,350	3,151
25,450	25,500	3,358	2,894	3,358	3,159
25,500	25,550	3,365	2,901	3,365	3,166
25,550	25,600	3,373	2,909	3,373	3,174
25,600	25,650	3,380	2,916	3,380	3,181
25,650	25,700	3,388	2,924	3,388	3,189
25,700	25,750	3,395	2,931	3,395	3,196
25,750	25,800	3,403	2,939	3,403	3,204
25,800	25,850	3,410	2,946	3,410	3,211
25,850	25,900	3,418	2,954	3,418	3,219
25,900	25,950	3,425	2,961	3,425	3,226
25,950	26,000	3,433	2,969	3,433	3,234
26,000					
26,000	26,050	3,440	2,976	3,440	3,241
26,050	26,100	3,448	2,984	3,448	3,249
26,100	26,150	3,455	2,991	3,455	3,256
26,150	26,200	3,463	2,999	3,463	3,264
26,200	26,250	3,470	3,006	3,470	3,271
26,250	26,300	3,478	3,014	3,478	3,279
26,300	26,350	3,485	3,021	3,485	3,286
26,350	26,400	3,493	3,029	3,493	3,294
26,400	26,450	3,500	3,036	3,500	3,301
26,450	26,500	3,508	3,044	3,508	3,309
26,500	26,550	3,515	3,051	3,515	3,316
26,550	26,600	3,523	3,059	3,523	3,324
26,600	26,650	3,530	3,066	3,530	3,331
26,650	26,700	3,538	3,074	3,538	3,339
26,700	26,750	3,545	3,081	3,545	3,346
26,750	26,800	3,553	3,089	3,553	3,354
26,800	26,850	3,560	3,096	3,560	3,361
26,850	26,900	3,568	3,104	3,568	3,369
26,900	26,950	3,575	3,111	3,575	3,376
26,950	27,000	3,583	3,119	3,583	3,384

If line 43 (taxable income) is—		And you are—			
At least	But less than	Single	Married filing jointly *	Married filing separately	Head of a household
		Your tax is—			
27,000					
27,000	27,050	3,590	3,126	3,590	3,391
27,050	27,100	3,598	3,134	3,598	3,399
27,100	27,150	3,605	3,141	3,605	3,406
27,150	27,200	3,613	3,149	3,613	3,414
27,200	27,250	3,620	3,156	3,620	3,421
27,250	27,300	3,628	3,164	3,628	3,429
27,300	27,350	3,635	3,171	3,635	3,436
27,350	27,400	3,643	3,179	3,643	3,444
27,400	27,450	3,650	3,186	3,650	3,451
27,450	27,500	3,658	3,194	3,658	3,459
27,500	27,550	3,665	3,201	3,665	3,466
27,550	27,600	3,673	3,209	3,673	3,474
27,600	27,650	3,680	3,216	3,680	3,481
27,650	27,700	3,688	3,224	3,688	3,489
27,700	27,750	3,695	3,231	3,695	3,496
27,750	27,800	3,703	3,239	3,703	3,504
27,800	27,850	3,710	3,246	3,710	3,511
27,850	27,900	3,718	3,254	3,718	3,519
27,900	27,950	3,725	3,261	3,725	3,526
27,950	28,000	3,733	3,269	3,733	3,534
28,000					
28,000	28,050	3,740	3,276	3,740	3,541
28,050	28,100	3,748	3,284	3,748	3,549
28,100	28,150	3,755	3,291	3,755	3,556
28,150	28,200	3,763	3,299	3,763	3,564
28,200	28,250	3,770	3,306	3,770	3,571
28,250	28,300	3,778	3,314	3,778	3,579
28,300	28,350	3,785	3,321	3,785	3,586
28,350	28,400	3,793	3,329	3,793	3,594
28,400	28,450	3,800	3,336	3,800	3,601
28,450	28,500	3,808	3,344	3,808	3,609
28,500	28,550	3,815	3,351	3,815	3,616
28,550	28,600	3,823	3,359	3,823	3,624
28,600	28,650	3,830	3,366	3,830	3,631
28,650	28,700	3,838	3,374	3,838	3,639
28,700	28,750	3,845	3,381	3,845	3,646
28,750	28,800	3,853	3,389	3,853	3,654
28,800	28,850	3,860	3,396	3,860	3,661
28,850	28,900	3,868	3,404	3,868	3,669
28,900	28,950	3,875	3,411	3,875	3,676
28,950	29,000	3,883	3,419	3,883	3,684
29,000					
29,000	29,050	3,890	3,426	3,890	3,691
29,050	29,100	3,898	3,434	3,898	3,699
29,100	29,150	3,905	3,441	3,905	3,706
29,150	29,200	3,913	3,449	3,913	3,714
29,200	29,250	3,920	3,456	3,920	3,721
29,250	29,300	3,928	3,464	3,928	3,729
29,300	29,350	3,935	3,471	3,935	3,736
29,350	29,400	3,943	3,479	3,943	3,744
29,400	29,450	3,950	3,486	3,950	3,751
29,450	29,500	3,958	3,494	3,958	3,759
29,500	29,550	3,965	3,501	3,965	3,766
29,550	29,600	3,973	3,509	3,973	3,774
29,600	29,650	3,980	3,516	3,980	3,781
29,650	29,700	3,988	3,524	3,988	3,789
29,700	29,750	3,995	3,531	3,995	3,796
29,750	29,800	4,003	3,539	4,003	3,804
29,800	29,850	4,010	3,546	4,010	3,811
29,850	29,900	4,018	3,554	4,018	3,819
29,900	29,950	4,025	3,561	4,025	3,826
29,950	30,000	4,033	3,569	4,033	3,834

(Continued)

* This column must also be used by a qualifying widow(er).

Caution: This is a draft 2016 Tax Table. At the time of publication, the IRS had not yet released the 2016 Tax Table. For the latest information, see CCHGroup.com/TaxUpdates.

2016 Tax Table — *Continued*

DRAFT AS OF October 7, 2015

If line 43 (taxable income) is—		And you are—			
At least	But less than	Single	Married filing jointly *	Married filing separately	Head of a household
		Your tax is—			
30,000					
30,000	30,050	4,040	3,576	4,040	3,841
30,050	30,100	4,048	3,584	4,048	3,849
30,100	30,150	4,055	3,591	4,055	3,856
30,150	30,200	4,063	3,599	4,063	3,864
30,200	30,250	4,070	3,606	4,070	3,871
30,250	30,300	4,078	3,614	4,078	3,879
30,300	30,350	4,085	3,621	4,085	3,886
30,350	30,400	4,093	3,629	4,093	3,894
30,400	30,450	4,100	3,636	4,100	3,901
30,450	30,500	4,108	3,644	4,108	3,909
30,500	30,550	4,115	3,651	4,115	3,916
30,550	30,600	4,123	3,659	4,123	3,924
30,600	30,650	4,130	3,666	4,130	3,931
30,650	30,700	4,138	3,674	4,138	3,939
30,700	30,750	4,145	3,681	4,145	3,946
30,750	30,800	4,153	3,689	4,153	3,954
30,800	30,850	4,160	3,696	4,160	3,961
30,850	30,900	4,168	3,704	4,168	3,969
30,900	30,950	4,175	3,711	4,175	3,976
30,950	31,000	4,183	3,719	4,183	3,984
31,000					
31,000	31,050	4,190	3,726	4,190	3,991
31,050	31,100	4,198	3,734	4,198	3,999
31,100	31,150	4,205	3,741	4,205	4,006
31,150	31,200	4,213	3,749	4,213	4,014
31,200	31,250	4,220	3,756	4,220	4,021
31,250	31,300	4,228	3,764	4,228	4,029
31,300	31,350	4,235	3,771	4,235	4,036
31,350	31,400	4,243	3,779	4,243	4,044
31,400	31,450	4,250	3,786	4,250	4,051
31,450	31,500	4,258	3,794	4,258	4,059
31,500	31,550	4,265	3,801	4,265	4,066
31,550	31,600	4,273	3,809	4,273	4,074
31,600	31,650	4,280	3,816	4,280	4,081
31,650	31,700	4,288	3,824	4,288	4,089
31,700	31,750	4,295	3,831	4,295	4,096
31,750	31,800	4,303	3,839	4,303	4,104
31,800	31,850	4,310	3,846	4,310	4,111
31,850	31,900	4,318	3,854	4,318	4,119
31,900	31,950	4,325	3,861	4,325	4,126
31,950	32,000	4,333	3,869	4,333	4,134
32,000					
32,000	32,050	4,340	3,876	4,340	4,141
32,050	32,100	4,348	3,884	4,348	4,149
32,100	32,150	4,355	3,891	4,355	4,156
32,150	32,200	4,363	3,899	4,363	4,164
32,200	32,250	4,370	3,906	4,370	4,171
32,250	32,300	4,378	3,914	4,378	4,179
32,300	32,350	4,385	3,921	4,385	4,186
32,350	32,400	4,393	3,929	4,393	4,194
32,400	32,450	4,400	3,936	4,400	4,201
32,450	32,500	4,408	3,944	4,408	4,209
32,500	32,550	4,415	3,951	4,415	4,216
32,550	32,600	4,423	3,959	4,423	4,224
32,600	32,650	4,430	3,966	4,430	4,231
32,650	32,700	4,438	3,974	4,438	4,239
32,700	32,750	4,445	3,981	4,445	4,246
32,750	32,800	4,453	3,989	4,453	4,254
32,800	32,850	4,460	3,996	4,460	4,261
32,850	32,900	4,468	4,004	4,468	4,269
32,900	32,950	4,475	4,011	4,475	4,276
32,950	33,000	4,483	4,019	4,483	4,284

If line 43 (taxable income) is—		And you are—			
At least	But less than	Single	Married filing jointly *	Married filing separately	Head of a household
		Your tax is—			
33,000					
33,000	33,050	4,490	4,026	4,490	4,291
33,050	33,100	4,498	4,034	4,498	4,299
33,100	33,150	4,505	4,041	4,505	4,306
33,150	33,200	4,513	4,049	4,513	4,314
33,200	33,250	4,520	4,056	4,520	4,321
33,250	33,300	4,528	4,064	4,528	4,329
33,300	33,350	4,535	4,071	4,535	4,336
33,350	33,400	4,543	4,079	4,543	4,344
33,400	33,450	4,550	4,086	4,550	4,351
33,450	33,500	4,558	4,094	4,558	4,359
33,500	33,550	4,565	4,101	4,565	4,366
33,550	33,600	4,573	4,109	4,573	4,374
33,600	33,650	4,580	4,116	4,580	4,381
33,650	33,700	4,588	4,124	4,588	4,389
33,700	33,750	4,595	4,131	4,595	4,396
33,750	33,800	4,603	4,139	4,603	4,404
33,800	33,850	4,610	4,146	4,610	4,411
33,850	33,900	4,618	4,154	4,618	4,419
33,900	33,950	4,625	4,161	4,625	4,426
33,950	34,000	4,633	4,169	4,633	4,434
34,000					
34,000	34,050	4,640	4,176	4,640	4,441
34,050	34,100	4,648	4,184	4,648	4,449
34,100	34,150	4,655	4,191	4,655	4,456
34,150	34,200	4,663	4,199	4,663	4,464
34,200	34,250	4,670	4,206	4,670	4,471
34,250	34,300	4,678	4,214	4,678	4,479
34,300	34,350	4,685	4,221	4,685	4,486
34,350	34,400	4,693	4,229	4,693	4,494
34,400	34,450	4,700	4,236	4,700	4,501
34,450	34,500	4,708	4,244	4,708	4,509
34,500	34,550	4,715	4,251	4,715	4,516
34,550	34,600	4,723	4,259	4,723	4,524
34,600	34,650	4,730	4,266	4,730	4,531
34,650	34,700	4,738	4,274	4,738	4,539
34,700	34,750	4,745	4,281	4,745	4,546
34,750	34,800	4,753	4,289	4,753	4,554
34,800	34,850	4,760	4,296	4,760	4,561
34,850	34,900	4,768	4,304	4,768	4,569
34,900	34,950	4,775	4,311	4,775	4,576
34,950	35,000	4,783	4,319	4,783	4,584
35,000					
35,000	35,050	4,790	4,326	4,790	4,591
35,050	35,100	4,798	4,334	4,798	4,599
35,100	35,150	4,805	4,341	4,805	4,606
35,150	35,200	4,813	4,349	4,813	4,614
35,200	35,250	4,820	4,356	4,820	4,621
35,250	35,300	4,828	4,364	4,828	4,629
35,300	35,350	4,835	4,371	4,835	4,636
35,350	35,400	4,843	4,379	4,843	4,644
35,400	35,450	4,850	4,386	4,850	4,651
35,450	35,500	4,858	4,394	4,858	4,659
35,500	35,550	4,865	4,401	4,865	4,666
35,550	35,600	4,873	4,409	4,873	4,674
35,600	35,650	4,880	4,416	4,880	4,681
35,650	35,700	4,888	4,424	4,888	4,689
35,700	35,750	4,895	4,431	4,895	4,696
35,750	35,800	4,903	4,439	4,903	4,704
35,800	35,850	4,910	4,446	4,910	4,711
35,850	35,900	4,918	4,454	4,918	4,719
35,900	35,950	4,925	4,461	4,925	4,726
35,950	36,000	4,933	4,469	4,933	4,734

If line 43 (taxable income) is—		And you are—			
At least	But less than	Single	Married filing jointly *	Married filing separately	Head of a household
		Your tax is—			
36,000					
36,000	36,050	4,940	4,476	4,940	4,741
36,050	36,100	4,948	4,484	4,948	4,749
36,100	36,150	4,955	4,491	4,955	4,756
36,150	36,200	4,963	4,499	4,963	4,764
36,200	36,250	4,970	4,506	4,970	4,771
36,250	36,300	4,978	4,514	4,978	4,779
36,300	36,350	4,985	4,521	4,985	4,786
36,350	36,400	4,993	4,529	4,993	4,794
36,400	36,450	5,000	4,536	5,000	4,801
36,450	36,500	5,008	4,544	5,008	4,809
36,500	36,550	5,015	4,551	5,015	4,816
36,550	36,600	5,023	4,559	5,023	4,824
36,600	36,650	5,030	4,566	5,030	4,831
36,650	36,700	5,038	4,574	5,038	4,839
36,700	36,750	5,045	4,581	5,045	4,846
36,750	36,800	5,053	4,589	5,053	4,854
36,800	36,850	5,060	4,596	5,060	4,861
36,850	36,900	5,068	4,604	5,068	4,869
36,900	36,950	5,075	4,611	5,075	4,876
36,950	37,000	5,083	4,619	5,083	4,884
37,000					
37,000	37,050	5,090	4,626	5,090	4,891
37,050	37,100	5,098	4,634	5,098	4,899
37,100	37,150	5,105	4,641	5,105	4,906
37,150	37,200	5,113	4,649	5,113	4,914
37,200	37,250	5,120	4,656	5,120	4,921
37,250	37,300	5,128	4,664	5,128	4,929
37,300	37,350	5,135	4,671	5,135	4,936
37,350	37,400	5,143	4,679	5,143	4,944
37,400	37,450	5,150	4,686	5,150	4,951
37,450	37,500	5,158	4,694	5,158	4,959
37,500	37,550	5,165	4,701	5,165	4,966
37,550	37,600	5,173	4,709	5,173	4,974
37,600	37,650	5,180	4,716	5,180	4,981
37,650	37,700	5,190	4,724	5,190	4,989
37,700	37,750	5,203	4,731	5,203	4,996
37,750	37,800	5,215	4,739	5,215	5,004
37,800	37,850	5,228	4,746	5,228	5,011
37,850	37,900	5,240	4,754	5,240	5,019
37,900	37,950	5,253	4,761	5,253	5,026
37,950	38,000	5,265	4,769	5,265	5,034
38,000					
38,000	38,050	5,278	4,776	5,278	5,041
38,050	38,100	5,290	4,784	5,290	5,049
38,100	38,150	5,303	4,791	5,303	5,056
38,150	38,200	5,315	4,799	5,315	5,064
38,200	38,250	5,328	4,806	5,328	5,071
38,250	38,300	5,340	4,814	5,340	5,079
38,300	38,350	5,353	4,821	5,353	5,086
38,350	38,400	5,365	4,829	5,365	5,094
38,400	38,450	5,378	4,836	5,378	5,101
38,450	38,500	5,390	4,844	5,390	5,109
38,500	38,550	5,403	4,851	5,403	5,116
38,550	38,600	5,415	4,859	5,415	5,124
38,600	38,650	5,428	4,866	5,428	5,131
38,650	38,700	5,440	4,874	5,440	5,139
38,700	38,750	5,453	4,881	5,453	5,146
38,750	38,800	5,465	4,889	5,465	5,154
38,800	38,850	5,478	4,896	5,478	5,161
38,850	38,900	5,490	4,904	5,490	5,169
38,900	38,950	5,503	4,911	5,503	5,176
38,950	39,000	5,515	4,919	5,515	5,184

(Continued)

* This column must also be used by a qualifying widow(er).

Caution: This is a draft 2016 Tax Table. At the time of publication, the IRS had not yet released the 2016 Tax Table. For the latest information, see CCHGroup.com/TaxUpdates.

2016 Tax Table — *Continued*

DRAFT AS OF October 17, 2016

If line 43 (taxable income) is—		And you are—			
At least	But less than	Single	Married filing jointly *	Married filing separately	Head of a household
		Your tax is—			
39,000					
39,000	39,050	5,528	4,926	5,528	5,191
39,050	39,100	5,540	4,934	5,540	5,199
39,100	39,150	5,553	4,941	5,553	5,206
39,150	39,200	5,565	4,949	5,565	5,214
39,200	39,250	5,578	4,956	5,578	5,221
39,250	39,300	5,590	4,964	5,590	5,229
39,300	39,350	5,603	4,971	5,603	5,236
39,350	39,400	5,615	4,979	5,615	5,244
39,400	39,450	5,628	4,986	5,628	5,251
39,450	39,500	5,640	4,994	5,640	5,259
39,500	39,550	5,653	5,001	5,653	5,266
39,550	39,600	5,665	5,009	5,665	5,274
39,600	39,650	5,678	5,016	5,678	5,281
39,650	39,700	5,690	5,024	5,690	5,289
39,700	39,750	5,703	5,031	5,703	5,296
39,750	39,800	5,715	5,039	5,715	5,304
39,800	39,850	5,728	5,046	5,728	5,311
39,850	39,900	5,740	5,054	5,740	5,319
39,900	39,950	5,753	5,061	5,753	5,326
39,950	40,000	5,765	5,069	5,765	5,334
40,000					
40,000	40,050	5,778	5,076	5,778	5,341
40,050	40,100	5,790	5,084	5,790	5,349
40,100	40,150	5,803	5,091	5,803	5,356
40,150	40,200	5,815	5,099	5,815	5,364
40,200	40,250	5,828	5,106	5,828	5,371
40,250	40,300	5,840	5,114	5,840	5,379
40,300	40,350	5,853	5,121	5,853	5,386
40,350	40,400	5,865	5,129	5,865	5,394
40,400	40,450	5,878	5,136	5,878	5,401
40,450	40,500	5,890	5,144	5,890	5,409
40,500	40,550	5,903	5,151	5,903	5,416
40,550	40,600	5,915	5,159	5,915	5,424
40,600	40,650	5,928	5,166	5,928	5,431
40,650	40,700	5,940	5,174	5,940	5,439
40,700	40,750	5,953	5,181	5,953	5,446
40,750	40,800	5,965	5,189	5,965	5,454
40,800	40,850	5,978	5,196	5,978	5,461
40,850	40,900	5,990	5,204	5,990	5,469
40,900	40,950	6,003	5,211	6,003	5,476
40,950	41,000	6,015	5,219	6,015	5,484
41,000					
41,000	41,050	6,028	5,226	6,028	5,491
41,050	41,100	6,040	5,234	6,040	5,499
41,100	41,150	6,053	5,241	6,053	5,506
41,150	41,200	6,065	5,249	6,065	5,514
41,200	41,250	6,078	5,256	6,078	5,521
41,250	41,300	6,090	5,264	6,090	5,529
41,300	41,350	6,103	5,271	6,103	5,536
41,350	41,400	6,115	5,279	6,115	5,544
41,400	41,450	6,128	5,286	6,128	5,551
41,450	41,500	6,140	5,294	6,140	5,559
41,500	41,550	6,153	5,301	6,153	5,566
41,550	41,600	6,165	5,309	6,165	5,574
41,600	41,650	6,178	5,316	6,178	5,581
41,650	41,700	6,190	5,324	6,190	5,589
41,700	41,750	6,203	5,331	6,203	5,596
41,750	41,800	6,215	5,339	6,215	5,604
41,800	41,850	6,228	5,346	6,228	5,611
41,850	41,900	6,240	5,354	6,240	5,619
41,900	41,950	6,253	5,361	6,253	5,626
41,950	42,000	6,265	5,369	6,265	5,634

If line 43 (taxable income) is—		And you are—			
At least	But less than	Single	Married filing jointly *	Married filing separately	Head of a household
		Your tax is—			
42,000					
42,000	42,050	6,278	5,376	6,278	5,641
42,050	42,100	6,290	5,384	6,290	5,649
42,100	42,150	6,303	5,391	6,303	5,656
42,150	42,200	6,315	5,399	6,315	5,664
42,200	42,250	6,328	5,406	6,328	5,671
42,250	42,300	6,340	5,414	6,340	5,679
42,300	42,350	6,353	5,421	6,353	5,686
42,350	42,400	6,365	5,429	6,365	5,694
42,400	42,450	6,378	5,436	6,378	5,701
42,450	42,500	6,390	5,444	6,390	5,709
42,500	42,550	6,403	5,451	6,403	5,716
42,550	42,600	6,415	5,459	6,415	5,724
42,600	42,650	6,428	5,466	6,428	5,731
42,650	42,700	6,440	5,474	6,440	5,739
42,700	42,750	6,453	5,481	6,453	5,746
42,750	42,800	6,465	5,489	6,465	5,754
42,800	42,850	6,478	5,496	6,478	5,761
42,850	42,900	6,490	5,504	6,490	5,769
42,900	42,950	6,503	5,511	6,503	5,776
42,950	43,000	6,515	5,519	6,515	5,784
43,000					
43,000	43,050	6,528	5,526	6,528	5,791
43,050	43,100	6,540	5,534	6,540	5,799
43,100	43,150	6,553	5,541	6,553	5,806
43,150	43,200	6,565	5,549	6,565	5,814
43,200	43,250	6,578	5,556	6,578	5,821
43,250	43,300	6,590	5,564	6,590	5,829
43,300	43,350	6,603	5,571	6,603	5,836
43,350	43,400	6,615	5,579	6,615	5,844
43,400	43,450	6,628	5,586	6,628	5,851
43,450	43,500	6,640	5,594	6,640	5,859
43,500	43,550	6,653	5,601	6,653	5,866
43,550	43,600	6,665	5,609	6,665	5,874
43,600	43,650	6,678	5,616	6,678	5,881
43,650	43,700	6,690	5,624	6,690	5,889
43,700	43,750	6,703	5,631	6,703	5,896
43,750	43,800	6,715	5,639	6,715	5,904
43,800	43,850	6,728	5,646	6,728	5,911
43,850	43,900	6,740	5,654	6,740	5,919
43,900	43,950	6,753	5,661	6,753	5,926
43,950	44,000	6,765	5,669	6,765	5,934
44,000					
44,000	44,050	6,778	5,676	6,778	5,941
44,050	44,100	6,790	5,684	6,790	5,949
44,100	44,150	6,803	5,691	6,803	5,956
44,150	44,200	6,815	5,699	6,815	5,964
44,200	44,250	6,828	5,706	6,828	5,971
44,250	44,300	6,840	5,714	6,840	5,979
44,300	44,350	6,853	5,721	6,853	5,986
44,350	44,400	6,865	5,729	6,865	5,994
44,400	44,450	6,878	5,736	6,878	6,001
44,450	44,500	6,890	5,744	6,890	6,009
44,500	44,550	6,903	5,751	6,903	6,016
44,550	44,600	6,915	5,759	6,915	6,024
44,600	44,650	6,928	5,766	6,928	6,031
44,650	44,700	6,940	5,774	6,940	6,039
44,700	44,750	6,953	5,781	6,953	6,046
44,750	44,800	6,965	5,789	6,965	6,054
44,800	44,850	6,978	5,796	6,978	6,061
44,850	44,900	6,990	5,804	6,990	6,069
44,900	44,950	7,003	5,811	7,003	6,076
44,950	45,000	7,015	5,819	7,015	6,084

If line 43 (taxable income) is—		And you are—			
At least	But less than	Single	Married filing jointly *	Married filing separately	Head of a household
		Your tax is—			
45,000					
45,000	45,050	7,028	5,826	7,028	6,091
45,050	45,100	7,040	5,834	7,040	6,099
45,100	45,150	7,053	5,841	7,053	6,106
45,150	45,200	7,065	5,849	7,065	6,114
45,200	45,250	7,078	5,856	7,078	6,121
45,250	45,300	7,090	5,864	7,090	6,129
45,300	45,350	7,103	5,871	7,103	6,136
45,350	45,400	7,115	5,879	7,115	6,144
45,400	45,450	7,128	5,886	7,128	6,151
45,450	45,500	7,140	5,894	7,140	6,159
45,500	45,550	7,153	5,901	7,153	6,166
45,550	45,600	7,165	5,909	7,165	6,174
45,600	45,650	7,178	5,916	7,178	6,181
45,650	45,700	7,190	5,924	7,190	6,189
45,700	45,750	7,203	5,931	7,203	6,196
45,750	45,800	7,215	5,939	7,215	6,204
45,800	45,850	7,228	5,946	7,228	6,211
45,850	45,900	7,240	5,954	7,240	6,219
45,900	45,950	7,253	5,961	7,253	6,226
45,950	46,000	7,265	5,969	7,265	6,234
46,000					
46,000	46,050	7,278	5,976	7,278	6,241
46,050	46,100	7,290	5,984	7,290	6,249
46,100	46,150	7,303	5,991	7,303	6,256
46,150	46,200	7,315	5,999	7,315	6,264
46,200	46,250	7,328	6,006	7,328	6,271
46,250	46,300	7,340	6,014	7,340	6,279
46,300	46,350	7,353	6,021	7,353	6,286
46,350	46,400	7,365	6,029	7,365	6,294
46,400	46,450	7,378	6,036	7,378	6,301
46,450	46,500	7,390	6,044	7,390	6,309
46,500	46,550	7,403	6,051	7,403	6,316
46,550	46,600	7,415	6,059	7,415	6,324
46,600	46,650	7,428	6,066	7,428	6,331
46,650	46,700	7,440	6,074	7,440	6,339
46,700	46,750	7,453	6,081	7,453	6,346
46,750	46,800	7,465	6,089	7,465	6,354
46,800	46,850	7,478	6,096	7,478	6,361
46,850	46,900	7,490	6,104	7,490	6,369
46,900	46,950	7,503	6,111	7,503	6,376
46,950	47,000	7,515	6,119	7,515	6,384
47,000					
47,000	47,050	7,528	6,126	7,528	6,391
47,050	47,100	7,540	6,134	7,540	6,399
47,100	47,150	7,553	6,141	7,553	6,406
47,150	47,200	7,565	6,149	7,565	6,414
47,200	47,250	7,578	6,156	7,578	6,421
47,250	47,300	7,590	6,164	7,590	6,429
47,300	47,350	7,603	6,171	7,603	6,436
47,350	47,400	7,615	6,179	7,615	6,444
47,400	47,450	7,628	6,186	7,628	6,451
47,450	47,500	7,640	6,194	7,640	6,459
47,500	47,550	7,653	6,201	7,653	6,466
47,550	47,600	7,665	6,209	7,665	6,474
47,600	47,650	7,678	6,216	7,678	6,481
47,650	47,700	7,690	6,224	7,690	6,489
47,700	47,750	7,703	6,231	7,703	6,496
47,750	47,800	7,715	6,239	7,715	6,504
47,800	47,850	7,728	6,246	7,728	6,511
47,850	47,900	7,740	6,254	7,740	6,519
47,900	47,950	7,753	6,261	7,753	6,526
47,950	48,000	7,765	6,269	7,765	6,534

(Continued)

* This column must also be used by a qualifying widow(er).

Caution: This is a draft 2016 Tax Table. At the time of publication, the IRS had not yet released the 2016 Tax Table. For the latest information, see CCHGroup.com/TaxUpdates.

2016 Tax Table — *Continued*

DRAFT AS OF OCTOBER 7, 2016

If line 43 (taxable income) is—		And you are—			
At least	But less than	Single	Married filing jointly *	Married filing separately	Head of a household
		Your tax is—			
48,000					
48,000	48,050	7,778	6,276	7,778	6,541
48,050	48,100	7,790	6,284	7,790	6,549
48,100	48,150	7,803	6,291	7,803	6,556
48,150	48,200	7,815	6,299	7,815	6,564
48,200	48,250	7,828	6,306	7,828	6,571
48,250	48,300	7,840	6,314	7,840	6,579
48,300	48,350	7,853	6,321	7,853	6,586
48,350	48,400	7,865	6,329	7,865	6,594
48,400	48,450	7,878	6,336	7,878	6,601
48,450	48,500	7,890	6,344	7,890	6,609
48,500	48,550	7,903	6,351	7,903	6,616
48,550	48,600	7,915	6,359	7,915	6,624
48,600	48,650	7,928	6,366	7,928	6,631
48,650	48,700	7,940	6,374	7,940	6,639
48,700	48,750	7,953	6,381	7,953	6,646
48,750	48,800	7,965	6,389	7,965	6,654
48,800	48,850	7,978	6,396	7,978	6,661
48,850	48,900	7,990	6,404	7,990	6,669
48,900	48,950	8,003	6,411	8,003	6,676
48,950	49,000	8,015	6,419	8,015	6,684
49,000					
49,000	49,050	8,028	6,426	8,028	6,691
49,050	49,100	8,040	6,434	8,040	6,699
49,100	49,150	8,053	6,441	8,053	6,706
49,150	49,200	8,065	6,449	8,065	6,714
49,200	49,250	8,078	6,456	8,078	6,721
49,250	49,300	8,090	6,464	8,090	6,729
49,300	49,350	8,103	6,471	8,103	6,736
49,350	49,400	8,115	6,479	8,115	6,744
49,400	49,450	8,128	6,486	8,128	6,751
49,450	49,500	8,140	6,494	8,140	6,759
49,500	49,550	8,153	6,501	8,153	6,766
49,550	49,600	8,165	6,509	8,165	6,774
49,600	49,650	8,178	6,516	8,178	6,781
49,650	49,700	8,190	6,524	8,190	6,789
49,700	49,750	8,203	6,531	8,203	6,796
49,750	49,800	8,215	6,539	8,215	6,804
49,800	49,850	8,228	6,546	8,228	6,811
49,850	49,900	8,240	6,554	8,240	6,819
49,900	49,950	8,253	6,561	8,253	6,826
49,950	50,000	8,265	6,569	8,265	6,834
50,000					
50,000	50,050	8,278	6,576	8,278	6,841
50,050	50,100	8,290	6,584	8,290	6,849
50,100	50,150	8,303	6,591	8,303	6,856
50,150	50,200	8,315	6,599	8,315	6,864
50,200	50,250	8,328	6,606	8,328	6,871
50,250	50,300	8,340	6,614	8,340	6,879
50,300	50,350	8,353	6,621	8,353	6,886
50,350	50,400	8,365	6,629	8,365	6,894
50,400	50,450	8,378	6,636	8,378	6,904
50,450	50,500	8,390	6,644	8,390	6,916
50,500	50,550	8,403	6,651	8,403	6,929
50,550	50,600	8,415	6,659	8,415	6,941
50,600	50,650	8,428	6,666	8,428	6,954
50,650	50,700	8,440	6,674	8,440	6,966
50,700	50,750	8,453	6,681	8,453	6,979
50,750	50,800	8,465	6,689	8,465	6,991
50,800	50,850	8,478	6,696	8,478	7,004
50,850	50,900	8,490	6,704	8,490	7,016
50,900	50,950	8,503	6,711	8,503	7,029
50,950	51,000	8,515	6,719	8,515	7,041

If line 43 (taxable income) is—		And you are—			
At least	But less than	Single	Married filing jointly *	Married filing separately	Head of a household
		Your tax is—			
51,000					
51,000	51,050	8,528	6,726	8,528	7,054
51,050	51,100	8,540	6,734	8,540	7,066
51,100	51,150	8,553	6,741	8,553	7,079
51,150	51,200	8,565	6,749	8,565	7,091
51,200	51,250	8,578	6,756	8,578	7,104
51,250	51,300	8,590	6,764	8,590	7,116
51,300	51,350	8,603	6,771	8,603	7,129
51,350	51,400	8,615	6,779	8,615	7,141
51,400	51,450	8,628	6,786	8,628	7,154
51,450	51,500	8,640	6,794	8,640	7,166
51,500	51,550	8,653	6,801	8,653	7,179
51,550	51,600	8,665	6,809	8,665	7,191
51,600	51,650	8,678	6,816	8,678	7,204
51,650	51,700	8,690	6,824	8,690	7,216
51,700	51,750	8,703	6,831	8,703	7,229
51,750	51,800	8,715	6,839	8,715	7,241
51,800	51,850	8,728	6,846	8,728	7,254
51,850	51,900	8,740	6,854	8,740	7,266
51,900	51,950	8,753	6,861	8,753	7,279
51,950	52,000	8,765	6,869	8,765	7,291
52,000					
52,000	52,050	8,778	6,876	8,778	7,304
52,050	52,100	8,790	6,884	8,790	7,316
52,100	52,150	8,803	6,891	8,803	7,329
52,150	52,200	8,815	6,899	8,815	7,341
52,200	52,250	8,828	6,906	8,828	7,354
52,250	52,300	8,840	6,914	8,840	7,366
52,300	52,350	8,853	6,921	8,853	7,379
52,350	52,400	8,865	6,929	8,865	7,391
52,400	52,450	8,878	6,936	8,878	7,404
52,450	52,500	8,890	6,944	8,890	7,416
52,500	52,550	8,903	6,951	8,903	7,429
52,550	52,600	8,915	6,959	8,915	7,441
52,600	52,650	8,928	6,966	8,928	7,454
52,650	52,700	8,940	6,974	8,940	7,466
52,700	52,750	8,953	6,981	8,953	7,479
52,750	52,800	8,965	6,989	8,965	7,491
52,800	52,850	8,978	6,996	8,978	7,504
52,850	52,900	8,990	7,004	8,990	7,516
52,900	52,950	9,003	7,011	9,003	7,529
52,950	53,000	9,015	7,019	9,015	7,541
53,000					
53,000	53,050	9,028	7,026	9,028	7,554
53,050	53,100	9,040	7,034	9,040	7,566
53,100	53,150	9,053	7,041	9,053	7,579
53,150	53,200	9,065	7,049	9,065	7,591
53,200	53,250	9,078	7,056	9,078	7,604
53,250	53,300	9,090	7,064	9,090	7,616
53,300	53,350	9,103	7,071	9,103	7,629
53,350	53,400	9,115	7,079	9,115	7,641
53,400	53,450	9,128	7,086	9,128	7,654
53,450	53,500	9,140	7,094	9,140	7,666
53,500	53,550	9,153	7,101	9,153	7,679
53,550	53,600	9,165	7,109	9,165	7,691
53,600	53,650	9,178	7,116	9,178	7,704
53,650	53,700	9,190	7,124	9,190	7,716
53,700	53,750	9,203	7,131	9,203	7,729
53,750	53,800	9,215	7,139	9,215	7,741
53,800	53,850	9,228	7,146	9,228	7,754
53,850	53,900	9,240	7,154	9,240	7,766
53,900	53,950	9,253	7,161	9,253	7,779
53,950	54,000	9,265	7,169	9,265	7,791

If line 43 (taxable income) is—		And you are—			
At least	But less than	Single	Married filing jointly *	Married filing separately	Head of a household
		Your tax is—			
54,000					
54,000	54,050	9,278	7,176	9,278	7,804
54,050	54,100	9,290	7,184	9,290	7,816
54,100	54,150	9,303	7,191	9,303	7,829
54,150	54,200	9,315	7,199	9,315	7,841
54,200	54,250	9,328	7,206	9,328	7,854
54,250	54,300	9,340	7,214	9,340	7,866
54,300	54,350	9,353	7,221	9,353	7,879
54,350	54,400	9,365	7,229	9,365	7,891
54,400	54,450	9,378	7,236	9,378	7,904
54,450	54,500	9,390	7,244	9,390	7,916
54,500	54,550	9,403	7,251	9,403	7,929
54,550	54,600	9,415	7,259	9,415	7,941
54,600	54,650	9,428	7,266	9,428	7,954
54,650	54,700	9,440	7,274	9,440	7,966
54,700	54,750	9,453	7,281	9,453	7,979
54,750	54,800	9,465	7,289	9,465	7,991
54,800	54,850	9,478	7,296	9,478	8,004
54,850	54,900	9,490	7,304	9,490	8,016
54,900	54,950	9,503	7,311	9,503	8,029
54,950	55,000	9,515	7,319	9,515	8,041
55,000					
55,000	55,050	9,528	7,326	9,528	8,054
55,050	55,100	9,540	7,334	9,540	8,066
55,100	55,150	9,553	7,341	9,553	8,079
55,150	55,200	9,565	7,349	9,565	8,091
55,200	55,250	9,578	7,356	9,578	8,104
55,250	55,300	9,590	7,364	9,590	8,116
55,300	55,350	9,603	7,371	9,603	8,129
55,350	55,400	9,615	7,379	9,615	8,141
55,400	55,450	9,628	7,386	9,628	8,154
55,450	55,500	9,640	7,394	9,640	8,166
55,500	55,550	9,653	7,401	9,653	8,179
55,550	55,600	9,665	7,409	9,665	8,191
55,600	55,650	9,678	7,416	9,678	8,204
55,650	55,700	9,690	7,424	9,690	8,216
55,700	55,750	9,703	7,431	9,703	8,229
55,750	55,800	9,715	7,439	9,715	8,241
55,800	55,850	9,728	7,446	9,728	8,254
55,850	55,900	9,740	7,454	9,740	8,266
55,900	55,950	9,753	7,461	9,753	8,279
55,950	56,000	9,765	7,469	9,765	8,291
56,000					
56,000	56,050	9,778	7,476	9,778	8,304
56,050	56,100	9,790	7,484	9,790	8,316
56,100	56,150	9,803	7,491	9,803	8,329
56,150	56,200	9,815	7,499	9,815	8,341
56,200	56,250	9,828	7,506	9,828	8,354
56,250	56,300	9,840	7,514	9,840	8,366
56,300	56,350	9,853	7,521	9,853	8,379
56,350	56,400	9,865	7,529	9,865	8,391
56,400	56,450	9,878	7,536	9,878	8,404
56,450	56,500	9,890	7,544	9,890	8,416
56,500	56,550	9,903	7,551	9,903	8,429
56,550	56,600	9,915	7,559	9,915	8,441
56,600	56,650	9,928	7,566	9,928	8,454
56,650	56,700	9,940	7,574	9,940	8,466
56,700	56,750	9,953	7,581	9,953	8,479
56,750	56,800	9,965	7,589	9,965	8,491
56,800	56,850	9,978	7,596	9,978	8,504
56,850	56,900	9,990	7,604	9,990	8,516
56,900	56,950	10,003	7,611	10,003	8,529
56,950	57,000	10,015	7,619	10,015	8,541

(Continued)

* This column must also be used by a qualifying widow(er).

Caution: This is a draft 2016 Tax Table. At the time of publication, the IRS had not yet released the 2016 Tax Table. For the latest information, see CCHGroup.com/TaxUpdates.

2016 Tax Table — *Continued*

DRAFT AS OF October 7, 2016

If line 43 (taxable income) is—		And you are—			
At least	But less than	Single	Married filing jointly *	Married filing separately	Head of a household
		Your tax is—			
57,000					
57,000	57,050	10,028	7,626	10,028	8,554
57,050	57,100	10,040	7,634	10,040	8,566
57,100	57,150	10,053	7,641	10,053	8,579
57,150	57,200	10,065	7,649	10,065	8,591
57,200	57,250	10,078	7,656	10,078	8,604
57,250	57,300	10,090	7,664	10,090	8,616
57,300	57,350	10,103	7,671	10,103	8,629
57,350	57,400	10,115	7,679	10,115	8,641
57,400	57,450	10,128	7,686	10,128	8,654
57,450	57,500	10,140	7,694	10,140	8,666
57,500	57,550	10,153	7,701	10,153	8,679
57,550	57,600	10,165	7,709	10,165	8,691
57,600	57,650	10,178	7,716	10,178	8,704
57,650	57,700	10,190	7,724	10,190	8,716
57,700	57,750	10,203	7,731	10,203	8,729
57,750	57,800	10,215	7,739	10,215	8,741
57,800	57,850	10,228	7,746	10,228	8,754
57,850	57,900	10,240	7,754	10,240	8,766
57,900	57,950	10,253	7,761	10,253	8,779
57,950	58,000	10,265	7,769	10,265	8,791
58,000					
58,000	58,050	10,278	7,776	10,278	8,804
58,050	58,100	10,290	7,784	10,290	8,816
58,100	58,150	10,303	7,791	10,303	8,829
58,150	58,200	10,315	7,799	10,315	8,841
58,200	58,250	10,328	7,806	10,328	8,854
58,250	58,300	10,340	7,814	10,340	8,866
58,300	58,350	10,353	7,821	10,353	8,879
58,350	58,400	10,365	7,829	10,365	8,891
58,400	58,450	10,378	7,836	10,378	8,904
58,450	58,500	10,390	7,844	10,390	8,916
58,500	58,550	10,403	7,851	10,403	8,929
58,550	58,600	10,415	7,859	10,415	8,941
58,600	58,650	10,428	7,866	10,428	8,954
58,650	58,700	10,440	7,874	10,440	8,966
58,700	58,750	10,453	7,881	10,453	8,979
58,750	58,800	10,465	7,889	10,465	8,991
58,800	58,850	10,478	7,896	10,478	9,004
58,850	58,900	10,490	7,904	10,490	9,016
58,900	58,950	10,503	7,911	10,503	9,029
58,950	59,000	10,515	7,919	10,515	9,041
59,000					
59,000	59,050	10,528	7,926	10,528	9,054
59,050	59,100	10,540	7,934	10,540	9,066
59,100	59,150	10,553	7,941	10,553	9,079
59,150	59,200	10,565	7,949	10,565	9,091
59,200	59,250	10,578	7,956	10,578	9,104
59,250	59,300	10,590	7,964	10,590	9,116
59,300	59,350	10,603	7,971	10,603	9,129
59,350	59,400	10,615	7,979	10,615	9,141
59,400	59,450	10,628	7,986	10,628	9,154
59,450	59,500	10,640	7,994	10,640	9,166
59,500	59,550	10,653	8,001	10,653	9,179
59,550	59,600	10,665	8,009	10,665	9,191
59,600	59,650	10,678	8,016	10,678	9,204
59,650	59,700	10,690	8,024	10,690	9,216
59,700	59,750	10,703	8,031	10,703	9,229
59,750	59,800	10,715	8,039	10,715	9,241
59,800	59,850	10,728	8,046	10,728	9,254
59,850	59,900	10,740	8,054	10,740	9,266
59,900	59,950	10,753	8,061	10,753	9,279
59,950	60,000	10,765	8,069	10,765	9,291

If line 43 (taxable income) is—		And you are—			
At least	But less than	Single	Married filing jointly *	Married filing separately	Head of a household
		Your tax is—			
60,000					
60,000	60,050	10,778	8,076	10,778	9,304
60,050	60,100	10,790	8,084	10,790	9,316
60,100	60,150	10,803	8,091	10,803	9,329
60,150	60,200	10,815	8,099	10,815	9,341
60,200	60,250	10,828	8,106	10,828	9,354
60,250	60,300	10,840	8,114	10,840	9,366
60,300	60,350	10,853	8,121	10,853	9,379
60,350	60,400	10,865	8,129	10,865	9,391
60,400	60,450	10,878	8,136	10,878	9,404
60,450	60,500	10,890	8,144	10,890	9,416
60,500	60,550	10,903	8,151	10,903	9,429
60,550	60,600	10,915	8,159	10,915	9,441
60,600	60,650	10,928	8,166	10,928	9,454
60,650	60,700	10,940	8,174	10,940	9,466
60,700	60,750	10,953	8,181	10,953	9,479
60,750	60,800	10,965	8,189	10,965	9,491
60,800	60,850	10,978	8,196	10,978	9,504
60,850	60,900	10,990	8,204	10,990	9,516
60,900	60,950	11,003	8,211	11,003	9,529
60,950	61,000	11,015	8,219	11,015	9,541
61,000					
61,000	61,050	11,028	8,226	11,028	9,554
61,050	61,100	11,040	8,234	11,040	9,566
61,100	61,150	11,053	8,241	11,053	9,579
61,150	61,200	11,065	8,249	11,065	9,591
61,200	61,250	11,078	8,256	11,078	9,604
61,250	61,300	11,090	8,264	11,090	9,616
61,300	61,350	11,103	8,271	11,103	9,629
61,350	61,400	11,115	8,279	11,115	9,641
61,400	61,450	11,128	8,286	11,128	9,654
61,450	61,500	11,140	8,294	11,140	9,666
61,500	61,550	11,153	8,301	11,153	9,679
61,550	61,600	11,165	8,309	11,165	9,691
61,600	61,650	11,178	8,316	11,178	9,704
61,650	61,700	11,190	8,324	11,190	9,716
61,700	61,750	11,203	8,331	11,203	9,729
61,750	61,800	11,215	8,339	11,215	9,741
61,800	61,850	11,228	8,346	11,228	9,754
61,850	61,900	11,240	8,354	11,240	9,766
61,900	61,950	11,253	8,361	11,253	9,779
61,950	62,000	11,265	8,369	11,265	9,791
62,000					
62,000	62,050	11,278	8,376	11,278	9,804
62,050	62,100	11,290	8,384	11,290	9,816
62,100	62,150	11,303	8,391	11,303	9,829
62,150	62,200	11,315	8,399	11,315	9,841
62,200	62,250	11,328	8,406	11,328	9,854
62,250	62,300	11,340	8,414	11,340	9,866
62,300	62,350	11,353	8,421	11,353	9,879
62,350	62,400	11,365	8,429	11,365	9,891
62,400	62,450	11,378	8,436	11,378	9,904
62,450	62,500	11,390	8,444	11,390	9,916
62,500	62,550	11,403	8,451	11,403	9,929
62,550	62,600	11,415	8,459	11,415	9,941
62,600	62,650	11,428	8,466	11,428	9,954
62,650	62,700	11,440	8,474	11,440	9,966
62,700	62,750	11,453	8,481	11,453	9,979
62,750	62,800	11,465	8,489	11,465	9,991
62,800	62,850	11,478	8,496	11,478	10,004
62,850	62,900	11,490	8,504	11,490	10,016
62,900	62,950	11,503	8,511	11,503	10,029
62,950	63,000	11,515	8,519	11,515	10,041

If line 43 (taxable income) is—		And you are—			
At least	But less than	Single	Married filing jointly *	Married filing separately	Head of a household
		Your tax is—			
63,000					
63,000	63,050	11,528	8,526	11,528	10,054
63,050	63,100	11,540	8,534	11,540	10,066
63,100	63,150	11,553	8,541	11,553	10,079
63,150	63,200	11,565	8,549	11,565	10,091
63,200	63,250	11,578	8,556	11,578	10,104
63,250	63,300	11,590	8,564	11,590	10,116
63,300	63,350	11,603	8,571	11,603	10,129
63,350	63,400	11,615	8,579	11,615	10,141
63,400	63,450	11,628	8,586	11,628	10,154
63,450	63,500	11,640	8,594	11,640	10,166
63,500	63,550	11,653	8,601	11,653	10,179
63,550	63,600	11,665	8,609	11,665	10,191
63,600	63,650	11,678	8,616	11,678	10,204
63,650	63,700	11,690	8,624	11,690	10,216
63,700	63,750	11,703	8,631	11,703	10,229
63,750	63,800	11,715	8,639	11,715	10,241
63,800	63,850	11,728	8,646	11,728	10,254
63,850	63,900	11,740	8,654	11,740	10,266
63,900	63,950	11,753	8,661	11,753	10,279
63,950	64,000	11,765	8,669	11,765	10,291
64,000					
64,000	64,050	11,778	8,676	11,778	10,304
64,050	64,100	11,790	8,684	11,790	10,316
64,100	64,150	11,803	8,691	11,803	10,329
64,150	64,200	11,815	8,699	11,815	10,341
64,200	64,250	11,828	8,706	11,828	10,354
64,250	64,300	11,840	8,714	11,840	10,366
64,300	64,350	11,853	8,721	11,853	10,379
64,350	64,400	11,865	8,729	11,865	10,391
64,400	64,450	11,878	8,736	11,878	10,404
64,450	64,500	11,890	8,744	11,890	10,416
64,500	64,550	11,903	8,751	11,903	10,429
64,550	64,600	11,915	8,759	11,915	10,441
64,600	64,650	11,928	8,766	11,928	10,454
64,650	64,700	11,940	8,774	11,940	10,466
64,700	64,750	11,953	8,781	11,953	10,479
64,750	64,800	11,965	8,789	11,965	10,491
64,800	64,850	11,978	8,796	11,978	10,504
64,850	64,900	11,990	8,804	11,990	10,516
64,900	64,950	12,003	8,811	12,003	10,529
64,950	65,000	12,015	8,819	12,015	10,541
65,000					
65,000	65,050	12,028	8,826	12,028	10,554
65,050	65,100	12,040	8,834	12,040	10,566
65,100	65,150	12,053	8,841	12,053	10,579
65,150	65,200	12,065	8,849	12,065	10,591
65,200	65,250	12,078	8,856	12,078	10,604
65,250	65,300	12,090	8,864	12,090	10,616
65,300	65,350	12,103	8,871	12,103	10,629
65,350	65,400	12,115	8,879	12,115	10,641
65,400	65,450	12,128	8,886	12,128	10,654
65,450	65,500	12,140	8,894	12,140	10,666
65,500	65,550	12,153	8,901	12,153	10,679
65,550	65,600	12,165	8,909	12,165	10,691
65,600	65,650	12,178	8,916	12,178	10,704
65,650	65,700	12,190	8,924	12,190	10,716
65,700	65,750	12,203	8,931	12,203	10,729
65,750	65,800	12,215	8,939	12,215	10,741
65,800	65,850	12,228	8,946	12,228	10,754
65,850	65,900	12,240	8,954	12,240	10,766
65,900	65,950	12,253	8,961	12,253	10,779
65,950	66,000	12,265	8,969	12,265	10,791

(Continued)

* This column must also be used by a qualifying widow(er).

Caution: This is a draft 2016 Tax Table. At the time of publication, the IRS had not yet released the 2016 Tax Table. For the latest information, see CCHGroup.com/TaxUpdates.

2016 Tax Table — *Continued*

DRAFT AS OF October 17, 2016

If line 43 (taxable income) is—		And you are—			
At least	But less than	Single	Married filing jointly *	Married filing separately	Head of a household
		Your tax is—			
66,000					
66,000	66,050	12,278	8,976	12,278	10,804
66,050	66,100	12,290	8,984	12,290	10,816
66,100	66,150	12,303	8,991	12,303	10,829
66,150	66,200	12,315	8,999	12,315	10,841
66,200	66,250	12,328	9,006	12,328	10,854
66,250	66,300	12,340	9,014	12,340	10,866
66,300	66,350	12,353	9,021	12,353	10,879
66,350	66,400	12,365	9,029	12,365	10,891
66,400	66,450	12,378	9,036	12,378	10,904
66,450	66,500	12,390	9,044	12,390	10,916
66,500	66,550	12,403	9,051	12,403	10,929
66,550	66,600	12,415	9,059	12,415	10,941
66,600	66,650	12,428	9,066	12,428	10,954
66,650	66,700	12,440	9,074	12,440	10,966
66,700	66,750	12,453	9,081	12,453	10,979
66,750	66,800	12,465	9,089	12,465	10,991
66,800	66,850	12,478	9,096	12,478	11,004
66,850	66,900	12,490	9,104	12,490	11,016
66,900	66,950	12,503	9,111	12,503	11,029
66,950	67,000	12,515	9,119	12,515	11,041
67,000					
67,000	67,050	12,528	9,126	12,528	11,054
67,050	67,100	12,540	9,134	12,540	11,066
67,100	67,150	12,553	9,141	12,553	11,079
67,150	67,200	12,565	9,149	12,565	11,091
67,200	67,250	12,578	9,156	12,578	11,104
67,250	67,300	12,590	9,164	12,590	11,116
67,300	67,350	12,603	9,171	12,603	11,129
67,350	67,400	12,615	9,179	12,615	11,141
67,400	67,450	12,628	9,186	12,628	11,154
67,450	67,500	12,640	9,194	12,640	11,166
67,500	67,550	12,653	9,201	12,653	11,179
67,550	67,600	12,665	9,209	12,665	11,191
67,600	67,650	12,678	9,216	12,678	11,204
67,650	67,700	12,690	9,224	12,690	11,216
67,700	67,750	12,703	9,231	12,703	11,229
67,750	67,800	12,715	9,239	12,715	11,241
67,800	67,850	12,728	9,246	12,728	11,254
67,850	67,900	12,740	9,254	12,740	11,266
67,900	67,950	12,753	9,261	12,753	11,279
67,950	68,000	12,765	9,269	12,765	11,291
68,000					
68,000	68,050	12,778	9,276	12,778	11,304
68,050	68,100	12,790	9,284	12,790	11,316
68,100	68,150	12,803	9,291	12,803	11,329
68,150	68,200	12,815	9,299	12,815	11,341
68,200	68,250	12,828	9,306	12,828	11,354
68,250	68,300	12,840	9,314	12,840	11,366
68,300	68,350	12,853	9,321	12,853	11,379
68,350	68,400	12,865	9,329	12,865	11,391
68,400	68,450	12,878	9,336	12,878	11,404
68,450	68,500	12,890	9,344	12,890	11,416
68,500	68,550	12,903	9,351	12,903	11,429
68,550	68,600	12,915	9,359	12,915	11,441
68,600	68,650	12,928	9,366	12,928	11,454
68,650	68,700	12,940	9,374	12,940	11,466
68,700	68,750	12,953	9,381	12,953	11,479
68,750	68,800	12,965	9,389	12,965	11,491
68,800	68,850	12,978	9,396	12,978	11,504
68,850	68,900	12,990	9,404	12,990	11,516
68,900	68,950	13,003	9,411	13,003	11,529
68,950	69,000	13,015	9,419	13,015	11,541

If line 43 (taxable income) is—		And you are—			
At least	But less than	Single	Married filing jointly *	Married filing separately	Head of a household
		Your tax is—			
69,000					
69,000	69,050	13,028	9,426	13,028	11,554
69,050	69,100	13,040	9,434	13,040	11,566
69,100	69,150	13,053	9,441	13,053	11,579
69,150	69,200	13,065	9,449	13,065	11,591
69,200	69,250	13,078	9,456	13,078	11,604
69,250	69,300	13,090	9,464	13,090	11,616
69,300	69,350	13,103	9,471	13,103	11,629
69,350	69,400	13,115	9,479	13,115	11,641
69,400	69,450	13,128	9,486	13,128	11,654
69,450	69,500	13,140	9,494	13,140	11,666
69,500	69,550	13,153	9,501	13,153	11,679
69,550	69,600	13,165	9,509	13,165	11,691
69,600	69,650	13,178	9,516	13,178	11,704
69,650	69,700	13,190	9,524	13,190	11,716
69,700	69,750	13,203	9,531	13,203	11,729
69,750	69,800	13,215	9,539	13,215	11,741
69,800	69,850	13,228	9,546	13,228	11,754
69,850	69,900	13,240	9,554	13,240	11,766
69,900	69,950	13,253	9,561	13,253	11,779
69,950	70,000	13,265	9,569	13,265	11,791
70,000					
70,000	70,050	13,278	9,576	13,278	11,804
70,050	70,100	13,290	9,584	13,290	11,816
70,100	70,150	13,303	9,591	13,303	11,829
70,150	70,200	13,315	9,599	13,315	11,841
70,200	70,250	13,328	9,606	13,328	11,854
70,250	70,300	13,340	9,614	13,340	11,866
70,300	70,350	13,353	9,621	13,353	11,879
70,350	70,400	13,365	9,629	13,365	11,891
70,400	70,450	13,378	9,636	13,378	11,904
70,450	70,500	13,390	9,644	13,390	11,916
70,500	70,550	13,403	9,651	13,403	11,929
70,550	70,600	13,415	9,659	13,415	11,941
70,600	70,650	13,428	9,666	13,428	11,954
70,650	70,700	13,440	9,674	13,440	11,966
70,700	70,750	13,453	9,681	13,453	11,979
70,750	70,800	13,465	9,689	13,465	11,991
70,800	70,850	13,478	9,696	13,478	12,004
70,850	70,900	13,490	9,704	13,490	12,016
70,900	70,950	13,503	9,711	13,503	12,029
70,950	71,000	13,515	9,719	13,515	12,041
71,000					
71,000	71,050	13,528	9,726	13,528	12,054
71,050	71,100	13,540	9,734	13,540	12,066
71,100	71,150	13,553	9,741	13,553	12,079
71,150	71,200	13,565	9,749	13,565	12,091
71,200	71,250	13,578	9,756	13,578	12,104
71,250	71,300	13,590	9,764	13,590	12,116
71,300	71,350	13,603	9,771	13,603	12,129
71,350	71,400	13,615	9,779	13,615	12,141
71,400	71,450	13,628	9,786	13,628	12,154
71,450	71,500	13,640	9,794	13,640	12,166
71,500	71,550	13,653	9,801	13,653	12,179
71,550	71,600	13,665	9,809	13,665	12,191
71,600	71,650	13,678	9,816	13,678	12,204
71,650	71,700	13,690	9,824	13,690	12,216
71,700	71,750	13,703	9,831	13,703	12,229
71,750	71,800	13,715	9,839	13,715	12,241
71,800	71,850	13,728	9,846	13,728	12,254
71,850	71,900	13,740	9,854	13,740	12,266
71,900	71,950	13,753	9,861	13,753	12,279
71,950	72,000	13,765	9,869	13,765	12,291

If line 43 (taxable income) is—		And you are—			
At least	But less than	Single	Married filing jointly *	Married filing separately	Head of a household
		Your tax is—			
72,000					
72,000	72,050	13,778	9,876	13,778	12,304
72,050	72,100	13,790	9,884	13,790	12,316
72,100	72,150	13,803	9,891	13,803	12,329
72,150	72,200	13,815	9,899	13,815	12,341
72,200	72,250	13,828	9,906	13,828	12,354
72,250	72,300	13,840	9,914	13,840	12,366
72,300	72,350	13,853	9,921	13,853	12,379
72,350	72,400	13,865	9,929	13,865	12,391
72,400	72,450	13,878	9,936	13,878	12,404
72,450	72,500	13,890	9,944	13,890	12,416
72,500	72,550	13,903	9,951	13,903	12,429
72,550	72,600	13,915	9,959	13,915	12,441
72,600	72,650	13,928	9,966	13,928	12,454
72,650	72,700	13,940	9,974	13,940	12,466
72,700	72,750	13,953	9,981	13,953	12,479
72,750	72,800	13,965	9,989	13,965	12,491
72,800	72,850	13,978	9,996	13,978	12,504
72,850	72,900	13,990	10,004	13,990	12,516
72,900	72,950	14,003	10,011	14,003	12,529
72,950	73,000	14,015	10,019	14,015	12,541
73,000					
73,000	73,050	14,028	10,026	14,028	12,554
73,050	73,100	14,040	10,034	14,040	12,566
73,100	73,150	14,053	10,041	14,053	12,579
73,150	73,200	14,065	10,049	14,065	12,591
73,200	73,250	14,078	10,056	14,078	12,604
73,250	73,300	14,090	10,064	14,090	12,616
73,300	73,350	14,103	10,071	14,103	12,629
73,350	73,400	14,115	10,079	14,115	12,641
73,400	73,450	14,128	10,086	14,128	12,654
73,450	73,500	14,140	10,094	14,140	12,666
73,500	73,550	14,153	10,101	14,153	12,679
73,550	73,600	14,165	10,109	14,165	12,691
73,600	73,650	14,178	10,116	14,178	12,704
73,650	73,700	14,190	10,124	14,190	12,716
73,700	73,750	14,203	10,131	14,203	12,729
73,750	73,800	14,215	10,139	14,215	12,741
73,800	73,850	14,228	10,146	14,228	12,754
73,850	73,900	14,240	10,154	14,240	12,766
73,900	73,950	14,253	10,161	14,253	12,779
73,950	74,000	14,265	10,169	14,265	12,791
74,000					
74,000	74,050	14,278	10,176	14,278	12,804
74,050	74,100	14,290	10,184	14,290	12,816
74,100	74,150	14,303	10,191	14,303	12,829
74,150	74,200	14,315	10,199	14,315	12,841
74,200	74,250	14,328	10,206	14,328	12,854
74,250	74,300	14,340	10,214	14,340	12,866
74,300	74,350	14,353	10,221	14,353	12,879
74,350	74,400	14,365	10,229	14,365	12,891
74,400	74,450	14,378	10,236	14,378	12,904
74,450	74,500	14,390	10,244	14,390	12,916
74,500	74,550	14,403	10,251	14,403	12,929
74,550	74,600	14,415	10,259	14,415	12,941
74,600	74,650	14,428	10,266	14,428	12,954
74,650	74,700	14,440	10,274	14,440	12,966
74,700	74,750	14,453	10,281	14,453	12,979
74,750	74,800	14,465	10,289	14,465	12,991
74,800	74,850	14,478	10,296	14,478	13,004
74,850	74,900	14,490	10,304	14,490	13,016
74,900	74,950	14,503	10,311	14,503	13,029
74,950	75,000	14,515	10,319	14,515	13,041

(Continued)

* This column must also be used by a qualifying widow(er).

Caution: This is a draft 2016 Tax Table. At the time of publication, the IRS had not yet released the 2016 Tax Table. For the latest information, see CCHGroup.com/TaxUpdates.

2016 Tax Table — *Continued*

DRAFT AS OF OCTOBER 17, 2016

If line 43 (taxable income) is— At least	But less than	And you are— Single	Married filing jointly *	Married filing separately	Head of a household
		Your tax is—			
75,000					
75,000	75,050	14,528	10,326	14,528	13,054
75,050	75,100	14,540	10,334	14,540	13,066
75,100	75,150	14,553	10,341	14,553	13,079
75,150	75,200	14,565	10,349	14,565	13,091
75,200	75,250	14,578	10,356	14,578	13,104
75,250	75,300	14,590	10,364	14,590	13,116
75,300	75,350	14,603	10,371	14,603	13,129
75,350	75,400	14,615	10,386	14,615	13,141
75,400	75,450	14,628	10,399	14,628	13,154
75,450	75,500	14,640	10,411	14,640	13,166
75,500	75,550	14,653	10,424	14,653	13,179
75,550	75,600	14,665	10,436	14,665	13,191
75,600	75,650	14,678	10,449	14,678	13,204
75,650	75,700	14,690	10,461	14,690	13,216
75,700	75,750	14,703	10,474	14,703	13,229
75,750	75,800	14,715	10,486	14,715	13,241
75,800	75,850	14,728	10,499	14,728	13,254
75,850	75,900	14,740	10,511	14,740	13,266
75,900	75,950	14,753	10,524	14,753	13,279
75,950	76,000	14,765	10,536	14,766	13,291
76,000					
76,000	76,050	14,778	10,549	14,780	13,304
76,050	76,100	14,790	10,561	14,794	13,316
76,100	76,150	14,803	10,574	14,808	13,329
76,150	76,200	14,815	10,586	14,822	13,341
76,200	76,250	14,828	10,599	14,836	13,354
76,250	76,300	14,840	10,611	14,850	13,366
76,300	76,350	14,853	10,624	14,864	13,379
76,350	76,400	14,865	10,636	14,878	13,391
76,400	76,450	14,878	10,649	14,892	13,404
76,450	76,500	14,890	10,661	14,906	13,416
76,500	76,550	14,903	10,674	14,920	13,429
76,550	76,600	14,915	10,686	14,934	13,441
76,600	76,650	14,928	10,699	14,948	13,454
76,650	76,700	14,940	10,711	14,962	13,466
76,700	76,750	14,953	10,724	14,976	13,479
76,750	76,800	14,965	10,736	14,990	13,491
76,800	76,850	14,978	10,749	15,004	13,504
76,850	76,900	14,990	10,761	15,018	13,516
76,900	76,950	15,003	10,774	15,032	13,529
76,950	77,000	15,015	10,786	15,046	13,541
77,000					
77,000	77,050	15,028	10,799	15,060	13,554
77,050	77,100	15,040	10,811	15,074	13,566
77,100	77,150	15,053	10,824	15,088	13,579
77,150	77,200	15,065	10,836	15,102	13,591
77,200	77,250	15,078	10,849	15,116	13,604
77,250	77,300	15,090	10,861	15,130	13,616
77,300	77,350	15,103	10,874	15,144	13,629
77,350	77,400	15,115	10,886	15,158	13,641
77,400	77,450	15,128	10,899	15,172	13,654
77,450	77,500	15,140	10,911	15,186	13,666
77,500	77,550	15,153	10,924	15,200	13,679
77,550	77,600	15,165	10,936	15,214	13,691
77,600	77,650	15,178	10,949	15,228	13,704
77,650	77,700	15,190	10,961	15,242	13,716
77,700	77,750	15,203	10,974	15,256	13,729
77,750	77,800	15,215	10,986	15,270	13,741
77,800	77,850	15,228	10,999	15,284	13,754
77,850	77,900	15,240	11,011	15,298	13,766
77,900	77,950	15,253	11,024	15,312	13,779
77,950	78,000	15,265	11,036	15,326	13,791

If line 43 (taxable income) is— At least	But less than	And you are— Single	Married filing jointly *	Married filing separately	Head of a household
		Your tax is—			
78,000					
78,000	78,050	15,278	11,049	15,340	13,804
78,050	78,100	15,290	11,061	15,354	13,816
78,100	78,150	15,303	11,074	15,368	13,829
78,150	78,200	15,315	11,086	15,382	13,841
78,200	78,250	15,328	11,099	15,396	13,854
78,250	78,300	15,340	11,111	15,410	13,866
78,300	78,350	15,353	11,124	15,424	13,879
78,350	78,400	15,365	11,136	15,438	13,891
78,400	78,450	15,378	11,149	15,452	13,904
78,450	78,500	15,390	11,161	15,466	13,916
78,500	78,550	15,403	11,174	15,480	13,929
78,550	78,600	15,415	11,186	15,494	13,941
78,600	78,650	15,428	11,199	15,508	13,954
78,650	78,700	15,440	11,211	15,522	13,966
78,700	78,750	15,453	11,224	15,536	13,979
78,750	78,800	15,465	11,236	15,550	13,991
78,800	78,850	15,478	11,249	15,564	14,004
78,850	78,900	15,490	11,261	15,578	14,016
78,900	78,950	15,503	11,274	15,592	14,029
78,950	79,000	15,515	11,286	15,606	14,041
79,000					
79,000	79,050	15,528	11,299	15,620	14,054
79,050	79,100	15,540	11,311	15,634	14,066
79,100	79,150	15,553	11,324	15,648	14,079
79,150	79,200	15,565	11,336	15,662	14,091
79,200	79,250	15,578	11,349	15,676	14,104
79,250	79,300	15,590	11,361	15,690	14,116
79,300	79,350	15,603	11,374	15,704	14,129
79,350	79,400	15,615	11,386	15,718	14,141
79,400	79,450	15,628	11,399	15,732	14,154
79,450	79,500	15,640	11,411	15,746	14,166
79,500	79,550	15,653	11,424	15,760	14,179
79,550	79,600	15,665	11,436	15,774	14,191
79,600	79,650	15,678	11,449	15,788	14,204
79,650	79,700	15,690	11,461	15,802	14,216
79,700	79,750	15,703	11,474	15,816	14,229
79,750	79,800	15,715	11,486	15,830	14,241
79,800	79,850	15,728	11,499	15,844	14,254
79,850	79,900	15,740	11,511	15,858	14,266
79,900	79,950	15,753	11,524	15,872	14,279
79,950	80,000	15,765	11,536	15,886	14,291
80,000					
80,000	80,050	15,778	11,549	15,900	14,304
80,050	80,100	15,790	11,561	15,914	14,316
80,100	80,150	15,803	11,574	15,928	14,329
80,150	80,200	15,815	11,586	15,942	14,341
80,200	80,250	15,828	11,599	15,956	14,354
80,250	80,300	15,840	11,611	15,970	14,366
80,300	80,350	15,853	11,624	15,984	14,379
80,350	80,400	15,865	11,636	15,998	14,391
80,400	80,450	15,878	11,649	16,012	14,404
80,450	80,500	15,890	11,661	16,026	14,416
80,500	80,550	15,903	11,674	16,040	14,429
80,550	80,600	15,915	11,686	16,054	14,441
80,600	80,650	15,928	11,699	16,068	14,454
80,650	80,700	15,940	11,711	16,082	14,466
80,700	80,750	15,953	11,724	16,096	14,479
80,750	80,800	15,965	11,736	16,110	14,491
80,800	80,850	15,978	11,749	16,124	14,504
80,850	80,900	15,990	11,761	16,138	14,516
80,900	80,950	16,003	11,774	16,152	14,529
80,950	81,000	16,015	11,786	16,166	14,541

If line 43 (taxable income) is— At least	But less than	And you are— Single	Married filing jointly *	Married filing separately	Head of a household
		Your tax is—			
81,000					
81,000	81,050	16,028	11,799	16,180	14,554
81,050	81,100	16,040	11,811	16,194	14,566
81,100	81,150	16,053	11,824	16,208	14,579
81,150	81,200	16,065	11,836	16,222	14,591
81,200	81,250	16,078	11,849	16,236	14,604
81,250	81,300	16,090	11,861	16,250	14,616
81,300	81,350	16,103	11,874	16,264	14,629
81,350	81,400	16,115	11,886	16,278	14,641
81,400	81,450	16,128	11,899	16,292	14,654
81,450	81,500	16,140	11,911	16,306	14,666
81,500	81,550	16,153	11,924	16,320	14,679
81,550	81,600	16,165	11,936	16,334	14,691
81,600	81,650	16,178	11,949	16,348	14,704
81,650	81,700	16,190	11,961	16,362	14,716
81,700	81,750	16,203	11,974	16,376	14,729
81,750	81,800	16,215	11,986	16,390	14,741
81,800	81,850	16,228	11,999	16,404	14,754
81,850	81,900	16,240	12,011	16,418	14,766
81,900	81,950	16,253	12,024	16,432	14,779
81,950	82,000	16,265	12,036	16,446	14,791
82,000					
82,000	82,050	16,278	12,049	16,460	14,804
82,050	82,100	16,290	12,061	16,474	14,816
82,100	82,150	16,303	12,074	16,488	14,829
82,150	82,200	16,315	12,086	16,502	14,841
82,200	82,250	16,328	12,099	16,516	14,854
82,250	82,300	16,340	12,111	16,530	14,866
82,300	82,350	16,353	12,124	16,544	14,879
82,350	82,400	16,365	12,136	16,558	14,891
82,400	82,450	16,378	12,149	16,572	14,904
82,450	82,500	16,390	12,161	16,586	14,916
82,500	82,550	16,403	12,174	16,600	14,929
82,550	82,600	16,415	12,186	16,614	14,941
82,600	82,650	16,428	12,199	16,628	14,954
82,650	82,700	16,440	12,211	16,642	14,966
82,700	82,750	16,453	12,224	16,656	14,979
82,750	82,800	16,465	12,236	16,670	14,991
82,800	82,850	16,478	12,249	16,684	15,004
82,850	82,900	16,490	12,261	16,698	15,016
82,900	82,950	16,503	12,274	16,712	15,029
82,950	83,000	16,515	12,286	16,726	15,041
83,000					
83,000	83,050	16,528	12,299	16,740	15,054
83,050	83,100	16,540	12,311	16,754	15,066
83,100	83,150	16,553	12,324	16,768	15,079
83,150	83,200	16,565	12,336	16,782	15,091
83,200	83,250	16,578	12,349	16,796	15,104
83,250	83,300	16,590	12,361	16,810	15,116
83,300	83,350	16,603	12,374	16,824	15,129
83,350	83,400	16,615	12,386	16,838	15,141
83,400	83,450	16,628	12,399	16,852	15,154
83,450	83,500	16,640	12,411	16,866	15,166
83,500	83,550	16,653	12,424	16,880	15,179
83,550	83,600	16,665	12,436	16,894	15,191
83,600	83,650	16,678	12,449	16,908	15,204
83,650	83,700	16,690	12,461	16,922	15,216
83,700	83,750	16,703	12,474	16,936	15,229
83,750	83,800	16,715	12,486	16,950	15,241
83,800	83,850	16,728	12,499	16,964	15,254
83,850	83,900	16,740	12,511	16,978	15,266
83,900	83,950	16,753	12,524	16,992	15,279
83,950	84,000	16,765	12,536	17,006	15,291

(Continued)

* This column must also be used by a qualifying widow(er).

Need more information or forms? Visit IRS.gov.

Caution: This is a draft 2016 Tax Table. At the time of publication, the IRS had not yet released the 2016 Tax Table. For the latest information, see CCHGroup.com/TaxUpdates.

2016 Tax Table — *Continued*

DRAFT AS OF OCT 17, 2016

If line 43 (taxable income) is—		And you are—			
At least	But less than	Single	Married filing jointly *	Married filing separately	Head of a household
		Your tax is—			
84,000					
84,000	84,050	16,778	12,549	17,020	15,304
84,050	84,100	16,790	12,561	17,034	15,316
84,100	84,150	16,803	12,574	17,048	15,329
84,150	84,200	16,815	12,586	17,062	15,341
84,200	84,250	16,828	12,599	17,076	15,354
84,250	84,3	16,840	12,611	17,090	15,366
84,300	84,350	16,853	12,624	17,104	15,379
84,350	84,400	16,865	12,636	17,118	15,391
84,400	84,450	16,878	12,649	17,132	15,404
84,450	84,500	16,890	12,661	17,146	15,416
84,500	84,550	16,903	12,674	17,160	15,429
84,550	84,600	16,915	12,686	17,174	15,441
84,600	84,650	16,928	12,699	17,188	15,454
84,650	84,700	16,940	12,711	17,202	15,466
84,700	84,750	16,953	12,724	17,216	15,479
84,750	84,800	16,965	12,736	17,230	15,491
84,800	84,850	16,978	12,749	17,244	15,504
84,850	84,900	16,990	12,761	17,258	15,516
84,900	84,950	17,003	12,774	17,272	15,529
84,950	85,000	17,015	12,786	17,286	15,541
85,000					
85,000	85,050	17,028	12,799	17,300	15,554
85,050	85,100	17,040	12,811	17,314	15,566
85,100	85,150	17,053	12,824	17,328	15,579
85,150	85,200	17,065	12,836	17,342	15,591
85,200	85,250	17,078	12,849	17,356	15,604
85,250	85,300	17,090	12,861	17,370	15,616
85,300	85,350	17,103	12,874	17,384	15,629
85,350	85,400	17,115	12,886	17,398	15,641
85,400	85,450	17,128	12,899	17,412	15,654
85,450	85,500	17,140	12,911	17,426	15,666
85,500	85,550	17,153	12,924	17,440	15,679
85,550	85,600	17,165	12,936	17,454	15,691
85,600	85,650	17,178	12,949	17,468	15,704
85,650	85,700	17,190	12,961	17,482	15,716
85,700	85,750	17,203	12,974	17,496	15,729
85,750	85,800	17,215	12,986	17,510	15,741
85,800	85,850	17,228	12,999	17,524	15,754
85,850	85,900	17,240	13,011	17,538	15,766
85,900	85,950	17,253	13,024	17,552	15,779
85,950	86,000	17,265	13,036	17,566	15,791
86,000					
86,000	86,050	17,278	13,049	17,580	15,804
86,050	86,100	17,290	13,061	17,594	15,816
86,100	86,150	17,303	13,074	17,608	15,829
86,150	86,200	17,315	13,086	17,622	15,841
86,200	86,250	17,328	13,099	17,636	15,854
86,250	86,300	17,340	13,111	17,650	15,866
86,300	86,350	17,353	13,124	17,664	15,879
86,350	86,400	17,365	13,136	17,678	15,891
86,400	86,450	17,378	13,149	17,692	15,904
86,450	86,500	17,390	13,161	17,706	15,916
86,500	86,550	17,403	13,174	17,720	15,929
86,550	86,600	17,415	13,186	17,734	15,941
86,600	86,650	17,428	13,199	17,748	15,954
86,650	86,700	17,440	13,211	17,762	15,966
86,700	86,750	17,453	13,224	17,776	15,979
86,750	86,800	17,465	13,236	17,790	15,991
86,800	86,850	17,478	13,249	17,804	16,004
86,850	86,900	17,490	13,261	17,818	16,016
86,900	86,950	17,503	13,274	17,832	16,029
86,950	87,000	17,515	13,286	17,846	16,041

If line 43 (taxable income) is—		And you are—			
At least	But less than	Single	Married filing jointly *	Married filing separately	Head of a household
		Your tax is—			
87,000					
87,000	87,050	17,528	13,299	17,860	16,054
87,050	87,100	17,540	13,311	17,874	16,066
87,100	87,150	17,553	13,324	17,888	16,079
87,150	87,200	17,565	13,336	17,902	16,091
87,200	87,250	17,578	13,349	17,916	16,104
87,250	87,300	17,590	13,361	17,930	16,116
87,300	87,350	17,603	13,374	17,944	16,129
87,350	87,400	17,615	13,386	17,958	16,141
87,400	87,450	17,628	13,399	17,972	16,154
87,450	87,500	17,640	13,411	17,986	16,166
87,500	87,550	17,653	13,424	18,000	16,179
87,550	87,600	17,665	13,436	18,014	16,191
87,600	87,650	17,678	13,449	18,028	16,204
87,650	87,700	17,690	13,461	18,042	16,216
87,700	87,750	17,703	13,474	18,056	16,229
87,750	87,800	17,715	13,486	18,070	16,241
87,800	87,850	17,728	13,499	18,084	16,254
87,850	87,900	17,740	13,511	18,098	16,266
87,900	87,950	17,753	13,524	18,112	16,279
87,950	88,000	17,765	13,536	18,126	16,291
88,000					
88,000	88,050	17,778	13,549	18,140	16,304
88,050	88,100	17,790	13,561	18,154	16,316
88,100	88,150	17,803	13,574	18,168	16,329
88,150	88,200	17,815	13,586	18,182	16,341
88,200	88,250	17,828	13,599	18,196	16,354
88,250	88,300	17,840	13,611	18,210	16,366
88,300	88,350	17,853	13,624	18,224	16,379
88,350	88,400	17,865	13,636	18,238	16,391
88,400	88,450	17,878	13,649	18,252	16,404
88,450	88,500	17,890	13,661	18,266	16,416
88,500	88,550	17,903	13,674	18,280	16,429
88,550	88,600	17,915	13,686	18,294	16,441
88,600	88,650	17,928	13,699	18,308	16,454
88,650	88,700	17,940	13,711	18,322	16,466
88,700	88,750	17,953	13,724	18,336	16,479
88,750	88,800	17,965	13,736	18,350	16,491
88,800	88,850	17,978	13,749	18,364	16,504
88,850	88,900	17,990	13,761	18,378	16,516
88,900	88,950	18,003	13,774	18,392	16,529
88,950	89,000	18,015	13,786	18,406	16,541
89,000					
89,000	89,050	18,028	13,799	18,420	16,554
89,050	89,100	18,040	13,811	18,434	16,566
89,100	89,150	18,053	13,824	18,448	16,579
89,150	89,200	18,065	13,836	18,462	16,591
89,200	89,250	18,078	13,849	18,476	16,604
89,250	89,300	18,090	13,861	18,490	16,616
89,300	89,350	18,103	13,874	18,504	16,629
89,350	89,400	18,115	13,886	18,518	16,641
89,400	89,450	18,128	13,899	18,532	16,654
89,450	89,500	18,140	13,911	18,546	16,666
89,500	89,550	18,153	13,924	18,560	16,679
89,550	89,600	18,165	13,936	18,574	16,691
89,600	89,650	18,178	13,949	18,588	16,704
89,650	89,700	18,190	13,961	18,602	16,716
89,700	89,750	18,203	13,974	18,616	16,729
89,750	89,800	18,215	13,986	18,630	16,741
89,800	89,850	18,228	13,999	18,644	16,754
89,850	89,900	18,240	14,011	18,658	16,766
89,900	89,950	18,253	14,024	18,672	16,779
89,950	90,000	18,265	14,036	18,686	16,791

If line 43 (taxable income) is—		And you are—			
At least	But less than	Single	Married filing jointly *	Married filing separately	Head of a household
		Your tax is—			
90,000					
90,000	90,050	18,278	14,049	18,700	16,804
90,050	90,100	18,290	14,061	18,714	16,816
90,100	90,150	18,303	14,074	18,728	16,829
90,150	90,200	18,315	14,086	18,742	16,841
90,200	90,250	18,328	14,099	18,756	16,854
90,250	90,300	18,340	14,111	18,770	16,866
90,300	90,350	18,353	14,124	18,784	16,879
90,350	90,400	18,365	14,136	18,798	16,891
90,400	90,450	18,378	14,149	18,812	16,904
90,450	90,500	18,390	14,161	18,826	16,916
90,500	90,550	18,403	14,174	18,840	16,929
90,550	90,600	18,415	14,186	18,854	16,941
90,600	90,650	18,428	14,199	18,868	16,954
90,650	90,700	18,440	14,211	18,882	16,966
90,700	90,750	18,453	14,224	18,896	16,979
90,750	90,800	18,465	14,236	18,910	16,991
90,800	90,850	18,478	14,249	18,924	17,004
90,850	90,900	18,490	14,261	18,938	17,016
90,900	90,950	18,503	14,274	18,952	17,029
90,950	91,000	18,515	14,286	18,966	17,041
91,000					
91,000	91,050	18,528	14,299	18,980	17,054
91,050	91,100	18,540	14,311	18,994	17,066
91,100	91,150	18,553	14,324	19,008	17,079
91,150	91,200	18,566	14,336	19,022	17,091
91,200	91,250	18,580	14,349	19,036	17,104
91,250	91,300	18,594	14,361	19,050	17,116
91,300	91,350	18,608	14,374	19,064	17,129
91,350	91,400	18,622	14,386	19,078	17,141
91,400	91,450	18,636	14,399	19,092	17,154
91,450	91,500	18,650	14,411	19,106	17,166
91,500	91,550	18,664	14,424	19,120	17,179
91,550	91,600	18,678	14,436	19,134	17,191
91,600	91,650	18,692	14,449	19,148	17,204
91,650	91,700	18,706	14,461	19,162	17,216
91,700	91,750	18,720	14,474	19,176	17,229
91,750	91,800	18,734	14,486	19,190	17,241
91,800	91,850	18,748	14,499	19,204	17,254
91,850	91,900	18,762	14,511	19,218	17,266
91,900	91,950	18,776	14,524	19,232	17,279
91,950	92,000	18,790	14,536	19,246	17,291
92,000					
92,000	92,050	18,804	14,549	19,260	17,304
92,050	92,100	18,818	14,561	19,274	17,316
92,100	92,150	18,832	14,574	19,288	17,329
92,150	92,200	18,846	14,586	19,302	17,341
92,200	92,250	18,860	14,599	19,316	17,354
92,250	92,300	18,874	14,611	19,330	17,366
92,300	92,350	18,888	14,624	19,344	17,379
92,350	92,400	18,902	14,636	19,358	17,391
92,400	92,450	18,916	14,649	19,372	17,404
92,450	92,500	18,930	14,661	19,386	17,416
92,500	92,550	18,944	14,674	19,400	17,429
92,550	92,600	18,958	14,686	19,414	17,441
92,600	92,650	18,972	14,699	19,428	17,454
92,650	92,700	18,986	14,711	19,442	17,466
92,700	92,750	19,000	14,724	19,456	17,479
92,750	92,800	19,014	14,736	19,470	17,491
92,800	92,850	19,028	14,749	19,484	17,504
92,850	92,900	19,042	14,761	19,498	17,516
92,900	92,950	19,056	14,774	19,512	17,529
92,950	93,000	19,070	14,786	19,526	17,541

(Continued)

* This column must also be used by a qualifying widow(er).

Caution: This is a draft 2016 Tax Table. At the time of publication, the IRS had not yet released the 2016 Tax Table. For the latest information, see CCHGroup.com/TaxUpdates.

2016 Tax Table — *Continued*

DRAFT AS OF DECEMBER 15, 2016

If line 43 (taxable income) is—		And you are—			
At least	But less than	Single	Married filing jointly *	Married filing separately	Head of a household
		Your tax is—			
93,000					
93,000	93,050	19,084	14,799	19,540	17,554
93,050	93,100	19,098	14,811	19,554	17,566
93,100	93,150	19,112	14,824	19,568	17,579
93,150	93,200	19,126	14,836	19,582	17,591
93,200	93,250	19,140	14,849	19,596	17,604
93,250	93,300	19,154	14,861	19,610	17,616
93,300	93,350	19,168	14,874	19,624	17,629
93,350	93,400	19,182	14,886	19,638	17,641
93,400	93,450	19,196	14,899	19,652	17,654
93,450	93,500	19,210	14,911	19,666	17,666
93,500	93,550	19,224	14,924	19,680	17,679
93,550	93,600	19,238	14,936	19,694	17,691
93,600	93,650	19,252	14,949	19,708	17,704
93,650	93,700	19,266	14,961	19,722	17,716
93,700	93,750	19,280	14,974	19,736	17,729
93,750	93,800	19,294	14,986	19,750	17,741
93,800	93,850	19,308	14,999	19,764	17,754
93,850	93,900	19,322	15,011	19,778	17,766
93,900	93,950	19,336	15,024	19,792	17,779
93,950	94,000	19,350	15,036	19,806	17,791
94,000					
94,000	94,050	19,364	15,049	19,820	17,804
94,050	94,100	19,378	15,061	19,834	17,816
94,100	94,150	19,392	15,074	19,848	17,829
94,150	94,200	19,406	15,086	19,862	17,841
94,200	94,250	19,420	15,099	19,876	17,854
94,250	94,300	19,434	15,111	19,890	17,866
94,300	94,350	19,448	15,124	19,904	17,879
94,350	94,400	19,462	15,136	19,918	17,891
94,400	94,450	19,476	15,149	19,932	17,904
94,450	94,500	19,490	15,161	19,946	17,916
94,500	94,550	19,504	15,174	19,960	17,929
94,550	94,600	19,518	15,186	19,974	17,941
94,600	94,650	19,532	15,199	19,988	17,954
94,650	94,700	19,546	15,211	20,002	17,966
94,700	94,750	19,560	15,224	20,016	17,979
94,750	94,800	19,574	15,236	20,030	17,991
94,800	94,850	19,588	15,249	20,044	18,004
94,850	94,900	19,602	15,261	20,058	18,016
94,900	94,950	19,616	15,274	20,072	18,029
94,950	95,000	19,630	15,286	20,086	18,041
95,000					
95,000	95,050	19,644	15,299	20,100	18,054
95,050	95,100	19,658	15,311	20,114	18,066
95,100	95,150	19,672	15,324	20,128	18,079
95,150	95,200	19,686	15,336	20,142	18,091
95,200	95,250	19,700	15,349	20,156	18,104
95,250	95,300	19,714	15,361	20,170	18,116
95,300	95,350	19,728	15,374	20,184	18,129
95,350	95,400	19,742	15,386	20,198	18,141
95,400	95,450	19,756	15,399	20,212	18,154
95,450	95,500	19,770	15,411	20,226	18,166
95,500	95,550	19,784	15,424	20,240	18,179
95,550	95,600	19,798	15,436	20,254	18,191
95,600	95,650	19,812	15,449	20,268	18,204
95,650	95,700	19,826	15,461	20,282	18,216
95,700	95,750	19,840	15,474	20,296	18,229
95,750	95,800	19,854	15,486	20,310	18,241
95,800	95,850	19,868	15,499	20,324	18,254
95,850	95,900	19,882	15,511	20,338	18,266
95,900	95,950	19,896	15,524	20,352	18,279
95,950	96,000	19,910	15,536	20,366	18,291
96,000					
96,000	96,050	19,924	15,549	20,380	18,304
96,050	96,100	19,938	15,561	20,394	18,316
96,100	96,150	19,952	15,574	20,408	18,329
96,150	96,200	19,966	15,586	20,422	18,341
96,200	96,250	19,980	15,599	20,436	18,354
96,250	96,300	19,994	15,611	20,450	18,366
96,300	96,350	20,008	15,624	20,464	18,379
96,350	96,400	20,022	15,636	20,478	18,391
96,400	96,450	20,036	15,649	20,492	18,404
96,450	96,500	20,050	15,661	20,506	18,416
96,500	96,550	20,064	15,674	20,520	18,429
96,550	96,600	20,078	15,686	20,534	18,441
96,600	96,650	20,092	15,699	20,548	18,454
96,650	96,700	20,106	15,711	20,562	18,466
96,700	96,750	20,120	15,724	20,576	18,479
96,750	96,800	20,134	15,736	20,590	18,491
96,800	96,850	20,148	15,749	20,604	18,504
96,850	96,900	20,162	15,761	20,618	18,516
96,900	96,950	20,176	15,774	20,632	18,529
96,950	97,000	20,190	15,786	20,646	18,541
97,000					
97,000	97,050	20,204	15,799	20,660	18,554
97,050	97,100	20,218	15,811	20,674	18,566
97,100	97,150	20,232	15,824	20,688	18,579
97,150	97,200	20,246	15,836	20,702	18,591
97,200	97,250	20,260	15,849	20,716	18,604
97,250	97,300	20,274	15,861	20,730	18,616
97,300	97,350	20,288	15,874	20,744	18,629
97,350	97,400	20,302	15,886	20,758	18,641
97,400	97,450	20,316	15,899	20,772	18,654
97,450	97,500	20,330	15,911	20,786	18,666
97,500	97,550	20,344	15,924	20,800	18,679
97,550	97,600	20,358	15,936	20,814	18,691
97,600	97,650	20,372	15,949	20,828	18,704
97,650	97,700	20,386	15,961	20,842	18,716
97,700	97,750	20,400	15,974	20,856	18,729
97,750	97,800	20,414	15,986	20,870	18,741
97,800	97,850	20,428	15,999	20,884	18,754
97,850	97,900	20,442	16,011	20,898	18,766
97,900	97,950	20,456	16,024	20,912	18,779
97,950	98,000	20,470	16,036	20,926	18,791
98,000					
98,000	98,050	20,484	16,049	20,940	18,804
98,050	98,100	20,498	16,061	20,954	18,816
98,100	98,150	20,512	16,074	20,968	18,829
98,150	98,200	20,526	16,086	20,982	18,841
98,200	98,250	20,540	16,099	20,996	18,854
98,250	98,300	20,554	16,111	21,010	18,866
98,300	98,350	20,568	16,124	21,024	18,879
98,350	98,400	20,582	16,136	21,038	18,891
98,400	98,450	20,596	16,149	21,052	18,904
98,450	98,500	20,610	16,161	21,066	18,916
98,500	98,550	20,624	16,174	21,080	18,929
98,550	98,600	20,638	16,186	21,094	18,941
98,600	98,650	20,652	16,199	21,108	18,954
98,650	98,700	20,666	16,211	21,122	18,966
98,700	98,750	20,680	16,224	21,136	18,979
98,750	98,800	20,694	16,236	21,150	18,991
98,800	98,850	20,708	16,249	21,164	19,004
98,850	98,900	20,722	16,261	21,178	19,016
98,900	98,950	20,736	16,274	21,192	19,029
98,950	99,000	20,750	16,286	21,206	19,041
99,000					
99,000	99,050	20,764	16,299	21,220	19,054
99,050	99,100	20,778	16,311	21,234	19,066
99,100	99,150	20,792	16,324	21,248	19,079
99,150	99,200	20,806	16,336	21,262	19,091
99,200	99,250	20,820	16,349	21,276	19,104
99,250	99,300	20,834	16,361	21,290	19,116
99,300	99,350	20,848	16,374	21,304	19,129
99,350	99,400	20,862	16,386	21,318	19,141
99,400	99,450	20,876	16,399	21,332	19,154
99,450	99,500	20,890	16,411	21,346	19,166
99,500	99,550	20,904	16,424	21,360	19,179
99,550	99,600	20,918	16,436	21,374	19,191
99,600	99,650	20,932	16,449	21,388	19,204
99,650	99,700	20,946	16,461	21,402	19,216
99,700	99,750	20,960	16,474	21,416	19,229
99,750	99,800	20,974	16,486	21,430	19,241
99,800	99,850	20,988	16,499	21,444	19,254
99,850	99,900	21,002	16,511	21,458	19,266
99,900	99,950	21,016	16,524	21,472	19,279
99,950	100,000	21,030	16,536	21,486	19,291

$100,000 or over use the Tax Computation Worksheet

* This column must also be used by a qualifying widow(er).

Need more information or forms? Visit IRS.gov.

CORPORATION INCOME TAX RATES

¶ 33 Corporations

The corporate tax rates are as follows:

Taxable Income Over	But Not Over	Pay	+	% on Excess	of the amount over—
$0—	$50,000	$0		15%	$0
50,000—	75,000	7,500		25	50,000
75,000—	100,000	13,750		34	75,000
100,000—	335,000	22,250		39	100,000
335,000—	10,000,000	113,900		34	335,000
10,000,000—	15,000,000	3,400,000		35	10,000,000
15,000,000—	18,333,333	5,150,000		38	15,000,000
18,333,333—	. . . . .			35	0

Taxable income of certain personal service corporations is taxed at a flat rate of 35 percent (¶ 219).

¶ 34 Controlled Group of Corporations

A controlled group of corporations is subject to the regular corporate income tax rates (¶ 33) as though the group is one corporation (¶ 289).

¶ 35 Personal Holding Companies

In addition to regular corporate income taxes (¶ 33), a special tax is imposed on any corporation which is a personal holding company. For tax years beginning after December 31, 2012, the additional tax is 20 percent of the corporation's undistributed personal holding company income (¶ 275).

¶ 36 Insurance Companies and Regulated Investment Companies

The regular corporate tax rates (¶ 33) apply to an insurance company's taxable income (¶ 2370 and ¶ 2378). In the case of regulated investment companies (RIC or mutual fund), the corporate tax rates apply to investment company taxable income (¶ 2303).

¶ 37 Accumulated Earnings Tax

In addition to regular corporate income taxes (¶ 33), a corporation may be subject to a special tax on its accumulated taxable income. For tax years beginning after December 31, 2012, the tax is 20 percent of the corporation's accumulated taxable income. A corporation is entitled to a $250,000 accumulated earnings credit ($150,000 for personal service corporations) against the tax (¶ 251).

¶ 38 Foreign Corporations

The income of a foreign corporation that is not effectively connected with a U.S. trade or business is taxed at a rate of 30 percent unless a lower tax rate is provided under a income tax treaty (¶ 2431). Domestic corporate rates (¶ 33) apply to the income of a foreign corporation that is effectively connected with a U.S. trade or business (¶ 2425).

¶ 39 Real Estate Investment Trusts

A real estate investment trust (REIT) will be subject to regular corporate income tax rates (¶ 33) on its real estate investment trust taxable income (¶ 2329).

ESTATE AND GIFT TAXES

¶ 40 Unified Transfer Tax Rate Schedules

The basic estate and gift tax rate structure that applied to decedents dying and gifts made during 2010 through 2012 continues to apply for estates of decedents dying and gifts made after December 31, 2012, with the exception of the rates that apply to taxable transfers in excess of $500,000. Accordingly, the maximum tax rate is 40 percent for transfers made after December 31, 2012 (Code Sec. 2001). The unified tax rate schedules for years after 2012 and for 2010—2012 are as follows:

Unified Transfer Tax Rate Schedule After 2012

Column A	Column B	Column C	Column D
Taxable amount over	*Taxable amount not over*	*Tax on amount in column A*	*Rate of tax on excess over amount in column A*
$0	$10,000	$0	18 %
10,000	20,000	1,800	20
20,000	40,000	3,800	22
40,000	60,000	8,200	24
60,000	80,000	13,000	26
80,000	100,000	18,200	28
100,000	150,000	23,800	30
150,000	250,000	38,800	32
250,000	500,000	70,800	34
500,000	750,000	155,800	37
750,000	1,000,000	248,300	39
1,000,000	. . . . .	345,800	40

Unified Transfer Tax Rate Schedule, 2010*—2012

Column A	Column B	Column C	Column D
Taxable amount over	*Taxable amount not over*	*Tax on amount in column A*	*Rate of tax on excess over amount in column A*
$0	$10,000	$0	18 %
10,000	20,000	1,800	20
20,000	40,000	3,800	22
40,000	60,000	8,200	24
60,000	80,000	13,000	26
80,000	100,000	18,200	28
100,000	150,000	23,800	30
150,000	250,000	38,800	32
250,000	500,000	70,800	34
500,000	. . . . .	155,800	35

*The estates of decedents dying in 2010 were allowed to elect out of the estate tax regime, effectively reducing their estate tax rate to zero (Act Sec. 301(c) of the Tax Relief, Unemployment Insurance Reauthorization, and Job Creation Act of 2010 (P.L. 111-312)).

Generation-Skipping Transfer (GST) Tax. All GSTs are subject to tax at a flat rate equal to the product of the maximum federal estate tax rate under the unified rate schedule (40 percent for 2013 and thereafter) and the "inclusion ratio" (¶ 2943).

Nonresident Aliens. The transfer tax rates that apply to U.S. citizens and resident aliens also apply to nonresident aliens, for certain property situated within the United States (¶ 2903 and ¶ 2940).

¶ 41 Transfer Tax Credits, Exclusions, and Exemptions

Estate Tax Applicable Credit and Basic Exclusion Amounts, 2011—2017

Year	*Applicable Credit Amount*	*Applicable Exclusion Amount*
2011	1,730,800	5,000,000
2012	1,772,800	5,120,000
2013	2,045,800	5,250,000
2014	2,081,800	5,340,000
2015	2,117,800	5,430,000
2016	2,125,800	5,450,000
2017	2,141,800	5,490,000

Gift Tax Applicable Credit and Basic Exclusion Amounts, 2011—2017

Year	*Applicable Credit Amount*	*Applicable (Lifetime) Exclusion Amount*
2011	1,730,800	5,000,000
2012	1,772,800	5,120,000
2013	2,045,800	5,250,000
2014	2,081,800	5,340,000
2015	2,117,800	5,430,000
2016	2,125,800	5,450,000
2017	2,141,800	5,490,000

Gift Tax Annual Exclusion. There is an annual exclusion of $14,000 per donee for gifts made in 2016 ($14,000 per donee for 2017), with an annual maximum of $28,000 per donee for spouses who use gift-splitting in 2016 ($28,000 per donee in 2017) (¶ 2905).

Generation Skipping Transfer (GST) Tax Exemption Amounts, 2011—2017

Year	*Exemption Amount*
2011	5,000,000
2012	5,120,000
2013	5,250,000
2014	5,340,000
2015	5,430,000
2016	5,450,000
2017	5,490,000

Nonresident Aliens. The annual gift tax exclusion is available to nonresident alien donors (¶ 2905). Where permitted by treaty, the estate of a nonresident alien is allowed a credit equal to the unified credit available to a U.S. citizen multiplied by the proportion of the decedent's entire gross estate situated in the United States (¶ 2940). In computing the credit, property is not treated as situated in the United States if such property is exempt from tax under any treaty. In other cases, a unified credit of $13,000 is allowed. The estate of a resident of a U.S. possession is entitled to a unified credit equal to the greater of (1) $13,000; or (2) $46,800 multiplied by the percentage of the decedent's gross estate situated in the United States (Code Sec. 2102).

With respect to the gift tax, no portion of the unified credit may be used as a credit against gift taxes payable on a lifetime transfers by a nonresident alien.

¶ 43 State Death Taxes

Estates of decedents may claim a deduction in determining the value of the gross estate for estate, inheritance, legacy, or succession taxes paid to any state or the District of Columbia (¶ 2933).

OTHER TAXES

¶ 47 Self-Employment Taxes

For calendar year 2016, a tax rate of 15.3 percent is imposed on net earnings from self-employment. The rate consists of a 12.4 percent component for Social Security (old-age, survivors, and disability insurance (OASDI)) and a 2.9 percent component for Medicare hospital insurance (HI). The OASDI rate applies only to net earnings from self-employment up to the OASDI wage base of $118,500 in 2016. The Medicare rate applies to all net earnings in 2016 (¶ 2664). The Medicare rate is increased by 0.9 percent to 3.8 percent for net earnings from self-employment in excess of $200,000 ($250,000 in the case of a joint return; $125,000 in the case of a married individual filing separately). In the case of a joint return, the additional 0.9 percent tax for Medicare is imposed on the combined income of both spouses. For 2017, the OASDI rate applies to net earnings from self-employment up to the OASDI wage base of $127,200. The Medicare rate applies to all net earnings in 2017.

¶ 49 Employment Taxes

FICA Taxes. Under the Federal Insurance Contributions Act (FICA), taxes are imposed on both employers and employees on wages paid to the employee for Social Security (old-age, survivors, and disability insurance (OASDI)), and Medicare hospital insurance (HI) (¶ 2648). For calendar year 2016, the tax rate on both the employer's and the employee's portion of wages is 7.65 percent (15.3 percent total), consisting of a 6.2 percent rate for OASDI and a 1.45 percent rate for Medicare. The OASDI rate for employers and employees applies only to wages up to the OASDI wage base of $118,500 in 2016. The Medicare rate applies to all wages in 2016. The Medicare rate on the employee's portion of wages is increased 0.9 percent to 2.35 percent for wages in excess of $200,000 ($250,000 in the case of a joint return; $125,000 in the case of a married individual filing separately). In the case of a joint return, the additional 0.9 percent tax for Medicare is imposed on the combined income of both spouses. For 2017, the OASDI rate applies to wages up to the OASDI wage base of $127,200. The Medicare rate applies to all wages in 2017.

Medicare Payments. Medicare Part B premiums qualify as deductible medical expenses (¶ 1019).

Unemployment Compensation. Under the Federal Unemployment Tax Act (FUTA), a tax is imposed on the first $7,000 of wages paid to a covered employee by an employer who employs one or more persons in covered employment in each of 20 days in a year, each day being in a different week, or who has a payroll for covered employment of at least $1,500 in a calendar quarter in the current or preceding calendar year (¶ 2649). The FUTA tax rate is 6.0 percent for wages paid in 2016. Since employers are allowed credits against the FUTA rate through participation in state unemployment insurance laws, the net FUTA rate actually paid by most employers is 0.6 percent in 2016, except when credit reductions are in effect in a state. The unemployment tax also applies to any person who paid total cash wages of $1,000 or more to a household employee during any calendar quarter in the current or preceding calendar year.

Railroad Retirement Tax. The Railroad Retirement and Survivors' Improvement Act provides benefits similar to those as under Social Security and Medicare. Tier I benefits are financed by taxes on employers and employees equal to those under FICA. The tax rate on the employer's and the employee's portion of wages for calendar year 2016 is 7.65 percent (15.3 percent total), consisting of a 6.2 percent rate for OASDI and a 1.45 percent rate for Medicare. The OASDI rate for employers and employees applies only to wages up to the OASDI wage base of $118,500 in 2016. The Medicare rate applies to all wages in 2016. The Medicare rate on the employee's portion of wages is increased 0.9 percent to 2.35 percent for wages in excess of $200,000 ($250,000 in the case of a joint return; $125,000 in the case of a married individual filing separately). In the case of a joint return, the additional 0.9 percent tax for Medicare is imposed on the combined income of both spouses. For 2017, the OASDI rate applies to wages up to the OASDI wage base of $127,200. The Medicare rate applies to all wages in 2017.

Tier II benefits are also available equivalent to a private pension plan and financed with employers and employees contributing a certain percentage of pay toward the system to finance benefits. For calendar year 2016, a tier II tax rate of 13.1 percent for employers and 4.9 percent for employees is imposed on annual compensation within a compensation base of $88,200. For calendar year 2017, the tier II tax rate will be imposed on annual compensation within a compensation base of $94,500.

¶ 53 Excise Taxes

Identified below are various excise taxes.

FUELS

Gasoline

Gasoline (per gallon) . . . . . 18.4¢

Diesel fuel, biodiesel, and kerosene

Diesel fuel (except if used on a farm for farming purposes) (per gallon) . . . . . 24.4¢

Diesel fuel for use in trains (per gallon) . . . . . 0.1¢

Diesel-water fuel emulsions (per gallon) . . . . . 19.8¢

Kerosene (except if used in a farm for farming purposes) (per gallon) . . . . . 24.4¢

B-100 (100 percent biodiesel) (per gallon) . . . . . 24.4¢

Special fuels

Special motor fuel (per gallon) . . . . . 18.4¢

Liquefied petroleum gas (LPG) . . . . . 18.3¢

"P Series" fuels . . . . . 18.4¢

Compressed natural gas (CNG) (per energy equivalent of a gallon of gasoline) . . . . . 18.3¢

Liquefied hydrogen . . . . . 18.4¢

Any liquid fuel derived from coal (including peat) through the Fischer-Tropsch process (per gallon) . . . . . 24.4¢

Liquid fuel derived from biomass (per gallon) . . . . . 24.4¢

Liquefied natural gas (LNG) (per gallon) . . . . . 24.3¢

Liquefied gas derived from biomass (per gallon) . . . . . 18.4¢

Qualified ethanol produced from coal (per gallon) . . . . . 18.4¢

Qualified methanol produced from coal (per gallon) . . . . . 18.4¢

Partially exempt ethanol produced from natural gas (per gallon) . . . . . 11.4¢

Partially exempt methanol produced from natural gas (per gallon) . . . . . 9.25¢

Fuel used on inland waterways

Inland waterways fuel use tax (per gallon) . . . . . 29.1¢

Aviation fuels

Kerosene used in commercial aviation (when removed from a refinery or terminal directly into the fuel tank of an aircraft) (per gallon) . . . . . 4.4¢

Kerosene used in noncommercial aviation (when removed from a refinery or terminal directly into the fuel tank of an aircraft) (per gallon) . . . . . 21.9¢

Noncommercial aviation gasoline (per gallon) . . . . . 19.4¢

Fuel used in fractional aircraft ownership program flights (per gallon) . . . . . 14.1¢ surtax

Fuel credits

Second generation biofuel (per gallon) . . . . . $1.01 credit until 2017

Biodiesel and biodiesel mixtures (per gallon) . . . . . $1.00 credit until 2017

Agri-biodiesel (per gallon) . . . . . $1.00 credit until 2017

Agri-biodiesel if benefited from the small agri-biodiesel producer credit (per gallon) . . . . . $1.10 credit until 2017

Renewable diesel and renewable diesel mixtures (per gallon) . . . . . $1.00 credit until 2017

Alternative fuel (as defined in Code Sec. 6426(d)(2)) (per gallon) . . . . . 50¢ credit until 2017 (including for liquefied hydrogen)

Crude oil

Crude oil (per barrel) . . . . . 8¢; 9¢ as of 1/1/17

HEAVY TRUCKS, TRAILERS

Truck chassis or body (that is suitable for use with a vehicle in excess of 33,000 lbs. gross vehicle weight)	12% of retail price
Trailer and semitrailer chassis or body (that is suitable for use with a trailer or semitrailer in excess of 26,000 lbs. gross vehicle weight)	12% of retail price
Parts and accessories installed on taxable vehicles within 6 months after being placed in service (when cost of parts or accessories exceeds $1,000)	12% of retail price

HIGHWAY-TYPE TIRES

Tires with load capacity of 3,500 lbs. or less	No tax
Tires with load capacity over 3,500 lbs.	9.45¢ for each 10 lbs. of tire load capacity over 3,500 lbs.
Super single tires designed for steering	9.45¢ for each 10 lbs. of tire load capacity over 3,500 lbs.
Super single tires not designed for steering	4.725¢ for each 10 lbs. of tire load capacity over 3,500 lbs.
Biasply tires	4.725¢ for each 10 lbs. of tire load capacity over 3,500 lbs.

GAS GUZZLER TAX

Mileage ratings per gallon of at least 22.5	$ 0
Mileage ratings per gallon of at least 21.5 but less than 22.5	1,000
Mileage ratings per gallon of at least 20.5 but less than 21.5	1,300
Mileage ratings per gallon of at least 19.5 but less than 20.5	1,700
Mileage ratings per gallon of at least 18.5 but less than 19.5	2,100
Mileage ratings per gallon of at least 17.5 but less than 18.5	2,600
Mileage ratings per gallon of at least 16.5 but less than 17.5	3,000
Mileage ratings per gallon of at least 15.5 but less than 16.5	3,700
Mileage ratings per gallon of at least 14.5 but less than 15.5	4,500
Mileage ratings per gallon of at least 13.5 but less than 14.5	5,400
Mileage ratings per gallon of at least 12.5 but less than 13.5	6,400
Mileage ratings per gallon of less than 12.5	7,700

FACILITIES AND SERVICES

Communications

Local telephone service and teletypewriter service	3%

Transportation by air

Domestic passenger tickets	7.5% plus $4 (from 1/1/16-12/31/16) for each flight segment (excepting segments to or from rural airports)
Alaska and Hawaii passenger tickets (amount per person per departure) (from 1/1/16-12/31/16)	$8.90
International passenger tickets (amount per person for each arrival and for each departure) (from 1/1/16-12/31/16)	$17.80
Air freight waybill	6.25%

Transportation by water

Persons	$3.00
Port use tax on imports (harbor maintenance tax)	0.125% of cargo value

ALCOHOL TAXES

Distilled spirits (per gallon) $13.50
Beer (per barrel—31 gallons or less) . . . . . $18.00, generally
First 60,000 barrels removed during calendar year by U.S. brewer producing not more than 2 million barrels during year (per barrel) $7.00

Wines

Not more than 14% alcohol (per gallon) $1.07
More than 14 to 21% alcohol (per gallon) $1.57
More than 21 to 24% alcohol (per gallon) $3.15
More than 24% alcohol (per gallon) $13.50
Artificially carbonated wines (per gallon) $3.30
Champagne and other sparkling wines (per gallon) $3.40
Hard cider derived from apples containing at least ½ of 1% and less than 7% alcohol (per gallon) $0.226

TOBACCO TAXES

Cigars weighing not more than 3 lbs. (per 1,000) $50.33
Cigars weighing more than 3 lbs. . . . . 52.75% of sales price, not to exceed 40.26 cents per cigar
Cigarettes weighing not more than 3 lbs. (per 1,000) $50.33
Cigarettes weighing more than 3 lbs. (per 1,000) $105.69
Cigarette papers (per 50 papers) . . . . . 3.15¢
Cigarette tubes (per 50 tubes) . . . . . 6.30¢
Snuff (per pound) $1.51
Chewing tobacco (per pound) . . . . . 50.33¢
Pipe tobacco (per pound) $2.8311
Roll-your-own tobacco (per pound) $24.78

WAGERING TAXES

State authorized wagers placed with bookmakers and lottery operators . . . . . 0.25% of wager amt.
Unauthorized wagers placed with bookmakers and lottery operators . . . . . 2% of wager amt.
License fee on state authorized persons accepting wagers (per year, per person) $50
License fee on unauthorized persons accepting wagers (per year, per person) $500

HIGHWAY MOTOR VEHICLE USE TAX

Vehicles of less than 55,000 lbs. . . . . No tax
Vehicles of 55,000 lbs.—75,000 lbs. (per year) . . . . . $100 per year + $22 for each 1,000 lbs. (or fraction thereof) over 55,000 lbs.
Vehicles over 75,000 lbs. (per year) $550

FIREARMS

Transfer taxes (per firearm) . . . . . $5 (concealable weapons) or $200
Occupational taxes (per year) . . . . . $1,000 (importers or manufacturers), or $500 (dealers, small importers and manufacturers)
Pistols and revolvers . . . . . 10% of sales price
Firearms other than pistols and revolvers . . . . . 11% of sales price
Ammunition (shells and cartridges) . . . . . 11% of sales price

OTHER TAXES

Electric outboard motors	3% of sales price
Fishing tackle boxes	3% of sales price
Sport fishing equipment	10% of sales price
Bows with a peak draw weight of at least 30 pounds	11% of sales price
Quivers, broadheads, points	11% of sales price
Arrow shafts	49¢ per shaft (from 1/1/2016 through 12/31/2016) 50¢ per shaft (from 1/1/2017 through 12/31/2017)
Coal—underground mines	$1.10 per ton, not to exceed 4.4% of sales price
Coal—surface mines	55¢ per ton, not to exceed 4.4% of sales price
Vaccines	75¢ per dose on taxable vaccines
Indoor tanning services	10% of amount paid
Casualty insurance and indemnity, fidelity and surety bonds (per dollar of premium paid)	4¢
Life insurance, sickness and accident policies, and annuity contracts (per dollar of premium paid)	1¢
Reinsurance of taxable contracts above (per dollar of premium paid)	1¢

Preparing Income Tax Returns

CHECKLISTS

	Par.
Checklist for Items of Income	55
Checklist for Deductions	57
Checklist for Medical Expenses	59
Checklist for Credits	61
Checklist for Forms	63
Guide to Information Returns	64
Checklist for Types of Payments	65

¶ 55 Checklist for Items of Income

The determination of whether an item of income is includible in income and, thus, taxable, or whether it is excludable from income is crucial to the determination of tax liability. An item that is includible increases tax liability, depending on the amount, whereas an excludable item decreases tax liability. The following chart, which is arranged alphabetically by income item, indicates whether the item is includible or excludable from income. A reference to further details in the 2017 *U.S. Master Tax Guide*® is also provided.

Income Item	*Includible in Income*	*Paragraph Reference*
Accident and health insurance premiums, employer-paid (except for long-term care benefits provided through flexible spending accounts and subject to limitation as to medical savings accounts and health savings accounts)	No	¶ 2013
Accident and health plans proceeds (under insurance purchased by taxpayer or under employee supported plans) where premiums did not give taxpayer a previous medical expense deduction	No	¶ 2015
		¶ 1288;
Agreement not to compete, payments received for	Yes	¶ 1743
Alaska Permanent Fund dividends	Yes	¶ 105
Alimony, support and separate maintenance payments, receipt of	Yes	¶ 773
Allowances received by dependents of members of the Armed Forces	No	¶ 896
Annuities (amounts in excess of cost)	Yes	¶ 819
Annuities, interest on advance premiums	Yes	¶ 724
Annuity contract, death benefit (amount in excess of cost)	Yes	¶ 817
Antitrust action, punitive damages recovered	Yes	¶ 852
Armed Forces pay (except "combat zone" or "missing" status pay)	Yes	¶ 891
Athletic facilities on employer's premises, value of use	No	¶ 2094
Attorney's contingent fee, includible in plaintiff's gross income	Yes	¶ 852
Awards and prizes, generally	Yes	¶ 785
Back pay	Yes	¶ 852
Bad debts, prior taxes and interest on taxes, recovery of, provided no tax benefit in prior year	No	¶ 799
Bargain purchases from employer to extent discount exceeds gross profit percentage	Yes	¶ 789

Income Item	*Includible in Income*	*Paragraph Reference*
Barter income	Yes	¶ 785
Beauty contest winners, receipt of scholarships and amounts for personal appearances	Yes	¶ 785
Bequests and devises, generally	No	¶ 847
Bonds, state, city, etc., interest on, generally	No	¶ 724
Bonuses	Yes	¶ 713
Buried treasure	Yes	¶ 785
Business interruption insurance proceeds:		
. based on income experience	Yes	¶ 759
. based on per diem idleness	No	¶ 759
Business profits	Yes	¶ 759
Business relocation payments	Yes	¶ 759
Business subsidies for construction or contributions by customer or potential customer	Yes	¶ 759
Cancellation of debt	Yes	¶ 855
Capital contributions to corporation	No	¶ 1660
Car pool receipts by car owner for transportation of other employees	No	¶ 945
Car used for business purposes by full-time car salesperson, value of use	No	¶ 947
Checks, uncashed by payee, for previously deducted items	Yes	¶ 1543
Child or dependent care plan benefits, employer-subsidized, limited	No	¶ 2065
Child support payments	No	¶ 776
Christmas bonuses from employer, based on percentage of salary (aside from token gifts such as hams, turkeys, etc., given for goodwill)	Yes	¶ 713
Civil Rights Act violation, back pay recovery	Yes	¶ 852
Clergy fees and contributions received unless earned as agent of religious order	Yes	¶ 713
COBRA premium assistance	No	¶ 2013
"Combat zone" pay, military	No	¶ 895
Commissions	Yes	¶ 713
Commodity credit loans, receipt of (optional)	Yes	¶ 769
Compensated Work Therapy program payments for veterans and their families	No	¶ 891
Compensation, property received, value of	Yes	¶ 1681
Contract cancellation, payments received for	Yes	¶ 1563
Contribution in aid of construction	Yes	¶ 1660
Damages:		
. back pay	Yes	¶ 852
. personal physical injuries or sickness	No	¶ 852
. slander or libel of personal reputation	Yes	¶ 852
Death benefits:		
. employer paid, in general	Yes	¶ 2011
. government plan, public safety officer	No	¶ 813
Debts:		
. cancellation of, related to principal residence, from 2007 through 2016, up to $2,000,000	No	¶ 855
. gratuitous cancellation of	No	¶ 855; ¶ 2903
. nongratuitous cancellation of	Yes	¶ 855
Defamation damage award, compensating injury to business and professional reputation	Yes	¶ 852
Deferred income under certain nonqualified deferred compensation plans	Yes	¶ 2199

Income Item	*Includible in Income*	*Paragraph Reference*
Dependent care assistance program payments, limited	No	¶ 2065
Disability payments, other than for loss of wages, all taxpayers, including veterans	No	¶ 891; ¶ 2025
Disability pensions, Veterans' Administration	No	¶ 891
Disaster unemployment payments	Yes	¶ 722
Discharge of indebtedness:		
. debt on a principal residence, from 2007 through 2016, up to $2,000,000	No	¶ 855
. gratuitous	No	¶ 855; ¶ 2903
. nongratuitous	Yes	¶ 855
Dividends, stock distributed in lieu of money	Yes	¶ 733
Drawing account, excess cancelled by employer	Yes	¶ 713
Educational assistance, employer-provided under a nondiscriminatory plan, up to $5,250 per year	No	¶ 2067
Embezzlement proceeds	Yes	¶ 785
Employee achievement awards, qualified	No	¶ 2069
Employee discount, qualified	No	¶ 2088
Employment contract, amounts received by employee for cancellation	Yes	¶ 713
Endowment policies, generally as to non-annuity payments until cost is recovered	No	¶ 841
Farm income	Yes	¶ 767
Farmers, government payments to offset operating losses or lack of profits	Yes	¶ 767
Fellowships and scholarships, degree programs	No	¶ 865
Financial counseling:		
. fees, employer-paid	Yes	¶ 713
. services, employer-provided, related to a qualified retirement plan	No	¶ 2093
Foreign earned income (limited exclusion)	Yes	¶ 2402
Foster parents, reimbursements for care of a qualified foster child	No	¶ 883
Fringe benefits:		
. athletic facilities	No	¶ 2094
. *de minimis* fringe benefit	No	¶ 2089
. employee discounts	No	¶ 2088
. in general	No	¶ 2085
. military base realignment and closure benefits	No	¶ 2095
. moving expenses reimbursements	No	¶ 2092
. no-additional-cost-services	No	¶ 2087
. retirement planning services	No	¶ 2093
. transportation fringe benefit	No	¶ 2091
. working condition fringe benefits	No	¶ 2090
Future services, prepayment for	Yes	¶ 1537
Gain on sale of personal residence:		
. up to $250,000 ($500,000 for joint filers)	No	¶ 1705
Gains:		
. condemnation of nonresidential property unless award is used for replacement	Yes	¶ 1716
. discount on later sale or redemption of bonds purchased with excess number of interest coupons detached (stripped bonds)	Yes	¶ 1952
. obligations purchased or satisfied for less than face value	Yes	¶ 1958
. partner's sale of asset to partnership	Yes	¶ 432
. sales of depreciable property	Yes	¶ 1780

Income Item	*Includible in Income*	*Paragraph Reference*
. sales of goodwill	Yes	¶ 1743
. sales of patents	Yes	¶ 1767
. sales of property, generally	Yes	¶ 1701
. sales of stock in foreign corporations	Yes	¶ 2487
Gambling winnings:		
. illegal	Yes	¶ 785
. legal	Yes	¶ 785
Gifts	No	¶ 849
Government employees, additional compensation as inducement to accept foreign service employment ("post differentials")	Yes	¶ 714
Health insurance proceeds, not paid by the insured's employer or financed by the insured's employer through contributions that were not included in the employee's gross income	No	¶ 851
Health Savings Accounts partner's/shareholder's contributions made by partnership/S corporation	Yes	¶ 2035
Hedging transactions, commodity futures transactions	Yes	¶ 1949
Hobby income (nonprofit activities, deductions limited)	Yes	¶ 1195
Illegal transactions, gains from: gambling, betting, lotteries, illegal businesses, embezzlement, protection money, etc.	Yes	¶ 785
Illness, employee's compensation during, except to extent qualifying as insurance benefits	Yes	¶ 851
Incentive stock options	No	¶ 1925
Income tax refunds:		
. state, to extent of tax benefit from prior deduction	Yes	¶ 799
Inheritances	No	¶ 847
Insider's profits	Yes	¶ 1760
Insurance policy dividends:		
. distributed, up to total of all net premiums paid	No	¶ 809
. retained by insurer and applied against premium	No	¶ 809
Insurance proceeds:		
. business interruption insurance, based on lost income	Yes	¶ 759
. use or occupancy, actual loss of net profits	Yes	¶ 759
Interest-free loans:		
. loans in excess of *de minimis* amount, deemed interest	Yes	¶ 795
. loans within *de minimis* amount	No	¶ 795
Interest on:		
. bank deposits or accounts	Yes	¶ 724
. bonds, debentures, or notes	Yes	¶ 724
. claim awarded by judgment	Yes	¶ 852
. condemnation awards	Yes	¶ 1716
. deferred legacies	Yes	¶ 847
. federal obligations	Yes	¶ 724
. insurance contracts	Yes	¶ 724
. refund of federal taxes	Yes	¶ 2765
Involuntary conversions, gain from, if reinvested	No	¶ 1713
Juror's mileage allowance	No	¶ 713
Jury fees	Yes	¶ 1010
Layoff pay benefits:		
. supplemental unemployment benefit plan, company-financed	Yes	¶ 722
Lease cancellation, payments received for	Yes	¶ 762

Income Item	*Includible in Income*	*Paragraph Reference*
Leased retail space, cash or rent reductions received for construction or improvements	No	¶ 764
Lessee's improvements, value of to lessor upon termination of lease	No	¶ 764
Libel or slander of personal reputation, exemplary damages	Yes	¶ 852
Life insurance contract, distributed from qualified plan	Yes	¶ 2055
Life insurance dividends:		
. distributed, up to total of all net premiums paid	No	¶ 809
. retained by insurer and applied against premium	No	¶ 809
Life insurance dividends, veterans	No	¶ 891
Life insurance, group-term premiums paid by employer, to extent of employer's cost of $50,000 or less of insurance	No	¶ 2055
Life insurance proceeds, paid on death of the insured	No	¶ 803
Living expenses paid by insurance while damaged home being repaired	No	¶ 877
Lodging, furnished on employer's premises, for employer's convenience, and as a condition of employment	No	¶ 2089
Losses, previously deducted, reimbursement for or expense items	Yes	¶ 799
Meals, cost of, furnished on employer's premises for employer's convenience	No	¶ 2089
Medical care reimbursements, employer-financed accident and health plan	No	¶ 2015
Medical loss ratio (MLR) rebates:		
. insurance premiums previously deducted	Yes	¶ 2031
. insurance premiums not previously deducted	No	¶ 2031
Military personnel, basic pay	Yes	¶ 895
Military service, employer-payments to employees	Yes	¶ 896
Mortgage indebtedness, prepayment at a discount to the extent of the discount	Yes	¶ 855
Moving expenses, qualified, employer-reimbursement	No	¶ 2092
National Labor Relations Board, back-pay award	Yes	¶ 2604
National Service Life Insurance dividends	No	¶ 891
Nobel prize and similar awards if donated by recipient to qualified entity	No	¶ 785
Nonqualified deferred compensation plan, assets set aside to fund	Yes	¶ 2199
Obligations, federal interest on	Yes	¶ 724
Old age, disability, survivors' benefit payments, Social Security or Railroad Retirement Acts, below base amount	No	¶ 716
Parsonage, rental value of, furnished to a minister or rabbi as part of compensation; rental allowances if used to rent or provide a home	No	¶ 875
Partnership, distributive share of taxable income	Yes	¶ 431
Patents, sale to controlled foreign corporation	Yes	¶ 2491
Pensions:		
. annuities, etc., for personal injuries or sickness resulting from active service in armed forces of any country, National Oceanic and Atmospheric Administration, or U.S. Public Health Service	No	¶ 851
. distributions attributable to employer contributions	Yes	¶ 2141
Personal physical injuries, damages	No	¶ 852
Political campaign contributions, with exceptions	No	¶ 696

Income Item	*Includible in Income*	*Paragraph Reference*
Prizes	Yes	¶ 785
Professional fees	Yes	¶ 713
Pulitzer prize and similar awards if donated by recipient to qualified entity	No	¶ 785
Punitive damages	Yes	¶ 852
Purchases, nondiscriminatory employee-discounts	No	¶ 2088
Railroad Retirement Act benefits, below base amount	No	¶ 716
Rebates, credits, price reductions received by customers	No	¶ 759
Rent reductions received by retail tenants for construction or improvements	No	¶ 764
Rents	Yes	¶ 762
Retirement pay attributable to employer contributions other than veterans' disability retirement pay	Yes	¶ 2141
Reward, informer's	Yes	¶ 713
Royalties	Yes	¶ 763
Salaries, including those of state and federal employees and amounts employer withholds for income, Social Security, and Railroad Retirement taxes	Yes	¶ 701; ¶ 714
Scholarships and fellowships, degree programs, qualified	No	¶ 865
Security deposits, when retained by lessor (advance rent)	Yes	¶ 1537
Sickness and injury benefits:		
. employer's plan, subject to limitations	No	¶ 851
. workers' compensation equivalent	No	¶ 851
Social Security old age, disability and survivor's benefits, below base amount	No	¶ 716
State contracts, profits on	Yes	¶ 759
Stock distributions in general	No	¶ 733A
. convertible preferred stock or debentures	Yes	¶ 733A
. disproportionate distributions	Yes	¶ 733A
. distributions of common and preferred stock	Yes	¶ 733A
. dividends on preferred stock	Yes	¶ 733A
. increasing shareholder's proportionate interest	Yes	¶ 733A
. in lieu of money	Yes	¶ 733A
Stock options, incentive	No	¶ 1925
Strike benefits, generally	Yes	¶ 702
Strike benefits, union and non-union employees in need, paid in form of food, clothes, etc.	No	¶ 702
Supper money, employer-paid, occasional due to overtime work	No	¶ 2089
Supplemental security income (SSI) payments	No	¶ 716
Support payment, received from former spouse as alimony	Yes	¶ 772
Surviving spouse, decedent's salary continued, depending on intent as a gift	No	¶ 719
Survivor annuities, paid to family of public safety officer	No	¶ 813
Taxes:		
. employees', employer-paid	Yes	¶ 713
. refunds of, not previously deducted or deducted without tax benefit	No	¶ 799
Tenancy, payments for surrender of	Yes	¶ 676
Tips	Yes	¶ 717
Treasure trove	Yes	¶ 785
Treaty-exempt income	No	¶ 2450
Tuition, employer-paid under qualified plans	No	¶ 2067
Unemployment benefit plans, supplemental payments	Yes	¶ 722

Income Item	*Includible in Income*	*Paragraph Reference*
Unemployment benefits	Yes	¶ 722
U.S. Savings Bonds, earned increase during year, if cash-method taxpayer elects	Yes	¶ 730
Use and occupancy insurance proceeds, income experience	Yes	¶ 877
Vacation fund allowance, union agreement	Yes	¶ 713
Veterans Administration payments	No	¶ 893
Veterans' benefits, generally	No	¶ 891
Veterans' bonuses, state	No	¶ 896
Virtual currency, received for goods or services	Yes	¶ 785
Wages	Yes	¶ 713
Workers' Compensation Acts, payments related to occupational injuries	No	¶ 851
"Wrap-around" annuity contracts sold by life insurance companies, interest on	Yes	¶ 817

¶ 57 Checklist for Deductions

The Internal Revenue Code permits a number of wide-ranging deductions that may be taken into account in arriving at taxable income. The Code contains a number of rules and restrictions concerning the expenses that qualify as deductions and the taxpayers who may claim them. Although deductions generally reduce taxable income, deductions from gross income, available to all qualifying taxpayers, must be distinguished from deductions from adjusted gross income (AGI), available only to those taxpayers who itemize. Certain miscellaneous itemized deductions, including unreimbursed employee business expenses and investment expenses, are deductible by an individual only if the aggregate amount of such deductions exceeds two percent of AGI (¶ 1079). In addition, deductions that can be taken currently must be distinguished from those that can be taken over a number of tax years through depreciation or amortization.

The chart below lists a number of expenses that a taxpayer might incur. The chart indicates for each expense a symbol(s) representing the possible availability of a deduction, its timing, and whether it is deductible from gross income or AGI. Many deductions have special rules. The chart also provides the 2017 *U.S. Master Tax Guide*® paragraph number where further information on the deduction may be found.

The following symbols are used:

D/GI = Deductible from gross income

D/AGI = Deductible from AGI

D/Am = Deductible over a period of time

ND = Nondeductible

Abandonment of business real property	D/GI, ¶ 1109
Accident and health plans	
. employer contributions	D/GI, ¶ 908
Accounting fees	
. business	D/GI, ¶ 901
. capital transactions	D/Am, ¶ 903
. connected with trade or business	D/GI, ¶ 901
. investors	D/AGI, ¶ 1086
. organization of business ($5,000 deduction and excess amortizable over 15 years)	D/GI, D/Am, ¶ 904
. reorganization of business	ND, ¶ 904
Accounting system, installation	D/GI, ¶ 991
Administrative expenses of estate	D/AGI, ¶ 2925
Admissions to political dinners, programs, inaugural balls, etc.	ND, ¶ 976
Advertising expenses	
. business cards	D/GI, ¶ 969
. catalogs	D/Am, ¶ 969
. generally	D/GI, ¶ 969
. home demonstrations	D/GI, ¶ 969
. package design costs	D/GI, ¶ 969
. political programs and publications	ND, ¶ 969
. prizes and contests	D/GI, ¶ 969
. product launch costs	D/GI, ¶ 969
. promotional activities	D/GI, ¶ 918
Airline pilot, special clothing	D/AGI, ¶ 1083
Airplane, heavy maintenance expenses	D/GI, ¶ 901
Alcohol fuels credit, unused	D/Am, ¶ 1365I
Alimony payments	D/GI, ¶ 1008
Amortization of premium on taxable bonds (optional)	D/AGI, ¶ 1079
Appraisal fees	
. acquisition of capital asset	ND, ¶ 990
. connection with trade or business	D/AGI, ¶ 1092
Architect's fees (capital expenditure)	D/Am, ¶ 903
Architectural services	
. domestic production activities	D/GI, ¶ 980F
Attorney's and accountant's fees in contesting tax claims (nonbusiness)	D/AGI, ¶ 1092
Attorney's fees	
. accounting suit by former partner, defense of	D/GI, ¶ 1093
. acquisition of corporate control	ND, ¶ 237
. business debts, collection of	D/GI, ¶ 1093
. civil rights suits	D/GI, ¶ 1093
. condemnation proceeding, defense of	ND, ¶ 1093
. disbarment proceedings	D/GI, ¶ 981

. divorce
. . obtaining alimony . . D/GI, ¶ 1093
. . proceedings . . . . . ND, ¶ 1093
. . property settlement . ND, ¶ 1093
. personal affairs . . . . . ND, ¶ 1093
. slander prosecution (personal) . . . . . ND, ¶ 1093
. tax advice on investments . . . . . D/AGI, ¶ 1086; ¶ 1983
. title clearance
. . land . . . . . ND, ¶ 1093
. . stock . . . . . ND, ¶ 1093
. will preparation . . . . . ND, ¶ 973
Automobile expenses
. business use by employee
. . unreimbursed . . . . . D/AGI, ¶ 947
. business use by self-employed person
. . chauffeur's salary . . . D/GI, ¶ 906
. . cost of car . . . . . D/GI, D/Am, ¶ 1214
. . garage rentals . . . . . D/GI, ¶ 946
. . gas . . . . . D/GI, ¶ 946
. . insurance . . . . . D/GI, ¶ 946
. . license fees . . . . . D/GI, ¶ 946
. . loss on sale . . . . . D/GI, ¶ 946
. . oil and lubrication . . D/GI, ¶ 946
. . parking . . . . . D/GI, ¶ 946
. . repairs . . . . . D/GI, ¶ 946
. . tires . . . . . D/GI, ¶ 946
. . washing . . . . . D/GI, ¶ 946
. nonbusiness casualty loss (limited) . . . . . D/AGI, ¶ 1121
. pleasure use . . . . . ND, ¶ 1211
. rural mail carriers (limited) . . . . . D/AGI, ¶ 947
Bad debts
. business . . . . . D/GI, ¶ 1135
. nonbusiness . . . . . D/GI, ¶ 1143
Bar admission and examination fees . . . . . ND, ¶ 981
Baseball player's uniforms . D/AGI, ¶ 1083
Black lung benefits trust, employer contributions . D/GI, ¶ 692
Bookmakers, business expenses . . . . . D/GI, ¶ 785
Building property, energy efficient property for commercial buildings (through 2016) . . . . . D/GI, ¶ 977D
Building replacements (capital expenditure) . . . D/Am, ¶ 991
Burglar alarm system, cost of installing (business capital expenditure) . . . . . D/Am, ¶ 991
Burial expenses . . . . . ND, ¶ 2925
Business bad debts . . . . . D/GI, ¶ 1135
Business conventions
. cruise ship (limited) . . D/GI, ¶ 959
. foreign conventions (limited) . . . . . D/GI, ¶ 960
. political conventions (must be related to trade or business) . . . D/GI, ¶ 959; ¶ 976
. travel expenses . . . . . D/GI, ¶ 949
Business expenses . . . . . D/GI, ¶ 901
Business meals . . . . . 50% D/GI, ¶ 914
Business start-up expenses ($5,000 deduction and excess amortizable over 15 years) . . . . . D/GI, D/Am, ¶ 904
Campaign contributions . . ND, ¶ 976
Capital expenditures . . . . . ND, D/Am, ¶ 991
Capital loss individual (limited) . . . . . D/GI, ¶ 1754
Car expenses (see "Automobile expenses")
Career counseling costs . . D/AGI, ¶ 1081
Carrying charges (charged seperately) . . . . . D/AGI, ¶ 1614
Casualty losses (nonbusiness casualty losses limited) . D/AGI, ¶ 1121
Charitable contributions
. corporations (limited) . D/GI, ¶ 927
. . inventory-type property . . . . . D/GI, ¶ 930
. . scientific research property . . . . . D/GI, ¶ 930
. individuals (limited) . . D/AGI, ¶ 1058; ¶ 1059
. . appreciated property . D/AGI, ¶ 1062
. where organization carries on lobbying activities . . . . . ND, ¶ 974
Child support payments . . . ND, ¶ 776
Circulation expenditures, newspapers, magazine periodicals . . . . . D/GI, ¶ 971
Classroom expenses, teachers . . . . . D/GI, ¶ 1011B
Clinical testing deduction if credit is elected . . . . . ND, ¶ 1365S
Club dues (limited) . . . . . D/AGI, ¶ 913A
Coal royalty contracts
. expenses related to . . . ND, ¶ 1289
. if there is no production, or no income, under contracts . . . . . D/AGI, ¶ 1289
Commissions
. paid as compensation . D/GI, ¶ 906
. sale of real estate or securities
. . dealers . . . . . D/GI, ¶ 1983
. . other taxpayers . . . . ND, ¶ 906

Commissions on sale of real estate and securities, dealer only (other than taxpayers deduct from selling price) D/GI, ¶ 1983
Commuting expenses . . . . ND, ¶ 945
Compensation, reasonable . D/GI, ¶ 906
Computer software (business use)
. development costs . . . D/GI, D/Am, ¶ 980
. leased software . . . . . D/GI, ¶ 980
. purchased software . . D/Am, ¶ 980
Construction
. domestic production activities . . . . . D/GI, ¶ 980F
Contributions by employer to employer-financed accident and health plans for benefit of employees . . . . . D/GI, ¶ 908
Contributions by employer to state unemployment insurance and state disability funds . . . . . D/GI, ¶ 922
Contributions by members to a labor union (voluntary) ND, ¶ 1080
Contributions paid (within certain limits) during year to charitable, etc., organizations . . . . . D/AGI, ¶ 1058
Convention (political) programs, cost of advertising in . . . . . ND, ¶ 976
Conventions (see "Business conventions")
Cooperative housing corporation, share of taxes or interest paid by . . . . . D/AGI, ¶ 1040
Copyright costs . . . . . D/Am, ¶ 1006A
Cost recovery, business property or property held for the production of income . . . . . D/Am, ¶ 1201
Credit and debit card convenience fees for paying taxes . . . . . D/AGI, ¶ 1092
Cruise ship business conventions (limited) . . . D/GI, ¶ 959
Custodian fees . . . . . D/AGI, ¶ 1086
Day care providers
. standard meal deduction . . . . . D/GI, ¶ 964
Defending title to property (capital expenditure) . . . ND, ¶ 1611
Demolition of structure . . . ND, ¶ 1105
Dependents . . . . . D/AGI, ¶ 137
Depletion . . . . . D/Am, ¶ 1289
Depreciation, business property or property held for production of income . D/Am, ¶ 1201
. election to expense (limited) . . . . . D/GI, ¶ 1208
Diaper service . . . . . ND, ¶ 1015
Disbarment proceedings, attorneys' fees and expenses in defending . . D/GI, ¶ 981
Doctor's staff privilege fees at hospital (capital expenditures) . . . . . D/Am, ¶ 981
Domestic production activities . . . . . D/GI, ¶ 980A
Dues
. chamber of commerce . D/GI, ¶ 913A
. charitable, religious, educational organizations . . . . . D/AGI, ¶ 1059
. clubs organized for business, pleasure, recreation, or any other social purpose . . . . . ND, ¶ 913
. professional associations . . . . . D/GI, ¶ 981
. union dues . . . . . D/AGI, ¶ 1080
Education expenses
. higher education expenses (through 2016) . . . . . D/GI, ¶ 1011A
Education expenses (employee)
. maintaining or improving required skills . . . . . D/AGI, ¶ 1082
. minimum requirements for job . . . . . ND, ¶ 1082
. new trade or business . ND, ¶ 1082
Educational assistance plan payments . . . . . D/GI, ¶ 2067
Efficiency engineers' fees . . D/GI, ¶ 901
Electricity
. domestic production activities . . . . . D/GI, ¶ 980
Embezzlement loss . . . . . D/GI, ¶ 1123
Employee's expenses
. entertaining customers
. . reimbursed expenses D/GI, ¶ 915
. . unreimbursed expenses . . . . . 50% D/AGI, ¶ 910
. meals and lodging away from home
. . reimbursed . . . . . D/GI, ¶ 954
. . unreimbursed lodging . . . . . D/AGI, ¶ 949
. . unreimbursed meals . 50% D/AGI, ¶ 910
. move to a new work location . . . . . D/GI, ¶ 1073
. transportation expenses
. . unreimbursed (limited) . . . . . D/AGI, ¶ 916
Employees' life insurance, paid by employer
. employee beneficiary . D/GI, ¶ 909
. employer beneficiary . ND, ¶ 909

Employees, payments for injuries to, not compensated by insurance; disability benefits . . . . . D/GI, ¶ 2015
Employees, severance payments to . . . . . D/GI, ¶ 2075
Employees, training expenses for . . . . . D/GI, ¶ 1082
Employment, fees for obtaining . . . . . D/AGI, ¶ 1081
Employment taxes
. employer's payment under Federal Unemployment Tax Act
. . employer (but not deductible if paid on wages of domestics) . D/GI, ¶ 2650
. employer's taxes under Federal Insurance Contributions Act
. . employer (deductible only as business expense) . . . . . D/GI, ¶ 923
. employer's taxes under Railroad Retirement Act
. . employer (deductible only as business expense) . . . . . D/GI, ¶ 716
. Federal Unemployment Tax Act . . . . . D/GI, ¶ 2649
. Railroad Retirement Act . . . . . D/GI, ¶ 716
. Social Security Act . . . D/GI, ¶ 923
Energy efficient property, commercial building property (through 2016) . D/GI, ¶ 977D
Engineering services
. domestic production activities . . . . . D/GI, ¶ 980F
Entertainment expenses (business, nonemployee)
. athletic club dues . . . . ND, ¶ 913A
. facilities owned and used by the taxpayer . . . . ND, ¶ 913
. food
. . furnished to employees on premises . . . . . D/GI, ¶ 915
. . meals directly related to business . . . . . 50% D/GI, ¶ 911
. . provided for customers . . . . . 50% D/GI, ¶ 914
Environmental protection agency, sulfur regulation compliance (limited) . . . D/GI, ¶ 1285
Estate tax . . . . . ND, ¶ 2912
Excess deductions on termination of estate or trust . . . . . D/AGI, ¶ 507
Excise taxes on personal goods . . . . . ND, ¶ 1611
Expenditures violating public policy . . . . . ND, ¶ 973
Farmers
. domestic production activities. . . . . D/GI, ¶ 980G
. fertilizers, lime, etc. . . D/GI, ¶ 985
. soil and water conservation . . . . . D/GI, ¶ 982
Federal income tax . . . . . ND, ¶ 924
Federal National Mortgage Association
. first buyers, excess of issue price over market value on date of issuance . . . . . D/GI, ¶ 975
Fiduciaries' fees . . . . . D/AGI, ¶ 528
Film and television
. domestic production activities . . . . . D/GI, ¶ 980D
. small film and television production (limited) . D/GI, ¶ 901
Finance charges other than carrying charges or loan fees (limited) . . . . . D/AGI, ¶ 1043
Fines and penalties
. child labor violations . . ND, ¶ 972
. Fair Labor Standards Act awards . . . . . D/GI, ¶ 972
. federal income tax penalties . . . . . ND, ¶ 972
. generally . . . . . ND, ¶ 972
. NLRB awards . . . . . D/GI, ¶ 972
. overweight or over-length trucks . . . . . ND, ¶ 972
. violations of federal law ND, ¶ 972
. Walsh-Healey Act awards . . . . . ND, ¶ 972
Firefighter
. meals and lodging on overnight duty at station . . . . . ND, D/AGI, ¶ 954A
. rubber coat, helmet, boots, etc. . . . . D/AGI, ¶ 1083
Fishing boat crews (commercial), members' protective clothing . . . . D/AGI, ¶ 1083
Foreign conventions (with limitations) . . . . . D/GI, ¶ 960
Foreign taxes (unless taken as credit)
. by payor . . . . . D/AGI, ¶ 2485
Forfeitures
. business transactions
. . advance payments . . D/GI, ¶ 1006
. . lease deposits . . . . . D/GI, ¶ 1006
. . purchase price . . . . D/GI, ¶ 1006
. interest
. . premature withdrawal from time savings account . . . . . D/GI, ¶ 1111

Fringe benefits
. cost of providing noncash benefits . . . . . D/GI, ¶ 2085
Funeral expenses . . . . . ND, ¶ 2925
Furnishings and fixtures, business cost . . . . . D/Am ¶ 1021
Gambling losses (limited) . D/AGI, ¶ 1113
Gas
. domestic production activities . . . . . D/GI, ¶ 980D
Gift tax . . . . . ND, ¶ 2905
Gifts (business), but limited to $25 per donee per year D/GI, ¶ 918
Gifts to charity
. corporations (limited) . D/GI, ¶ 927
. . computer equipment (through 2011) . . . . D/GI, ¶ 930
. . inventory-type property . . . . . D/GI, ¶ 930
. . scientific research property . . . . . D/GI, ¶ 930
. individuals (limited) . . D/AGI, ¶ 1059
. . appreciated property . D/AGI, ¶ 1062
. where organization carries on lobbying activities . . . . . ND, ¶ 974
Gifts to employees
. awards for length of service (limited) . . . . D/GI, ¶ 919
. gifts valued above $25 . ND, ¶ 918
. gifts valued at $25 or less . . . . . D/GI, ¶ 919
Gifts to individuals . . . . . ND, ¶ 2903
Golden parachutes
. excess parachute payments . . . . . ND, ¶ 907
. parachute payments . . D/GI, ¶ 907
Golf course
. land preparation costs, modern greens . . . . D/Am, ¶ 991
. maintenance and operating costs . . . . D/GI, ¶ 991
. original construction . . ND, ¶ 991
Hobby losses . . . . . ND, ¶ 1195
Home office (limited) . . . . D/GI, ¶ 961
. employee . . . . . D/AGI, ¶ 961
. principal place of business . . . . . D/GI, ¶ 961
. storage of product samples . . . . . D/GI, ¶ 961
House rent . . . . . ND, ¶ 986
Illegal business, legitimate expenses . . . . . D/GI, ND, ¶ 972
Illegal drugs . . . . . ND, ¶ 972
Impairment-related work expenses
. attendant care services at work . . . . . D/AGI, ¶ 901
. necessary expenses at work . . . . . D/AGI, ¶ 901
Import duties (unless as a business expense) . . . . ND, ¶ 1003
Improvements made by lessee, depreciation and amortization . . . . . D/Am, ¶ 1234
Income tax (state) . . . . . D/AGI, ¶ 924
Income tax liability, cost of determining . . . . . D/AGI, ¶ 973
Income tax returns, cost of preparing (nonbusiness) . D/AGI, ¶ 973
Individual retirement account, contributions (limited) . . D/GI, ¶ 2157
Infringement litigation in course of business . . . . D/GI, ¶ 973
Inheritance tax . . . . . ND, ¶ 2912
Injuries to employees, payments for, not compensated by insurance . . . . . D/GI, ¶ 2015
Insurance expenses
. business
. . casualty . . . . . D/GI, ¶ 968
. . malpractice . . . . . D/GI, ¶ 981
. individuals (medical) . D/AGI, ¶ 1019
. . self-employed individuals (health insurance) . . . . . D/GI, ¶ 908
. insured employees
. . employee or other beneficiary . . . . . D/GI, ¶ 908
. . employer beneficiary ND, ¶ 804
. . key employees . . . . D/GI, ¶ 804
. personal residence . . . ND, ¶ 1047
. required for credit
. . premiums paid by creditor . . . . . D/GI, ¶ 1048A
. . premiums paid by debtor . . . . . ND, ¶ 1048A
Intangible assets (as defined in Code Sec. 197) . . . . . D/Am, ¶ 1288
Interest and carrying charges related to a commodity straddle position in excess of income generated by straddle position . . . . . ND, ¶ 1949
Interest (with exceptions and limitations, see below) . . D/AGI, ¶ 937
. education loans (limited) . . . . . D/GI, ¶ 1011
. interest related to tax-exempt income . . . . ND, ¶ 970
. interest related to life insurance contracts (limited) . . . . . D/AGI, ¶ 2055; ¶ 2057
. personal obligations (limited) . . . . . ND, ¶ 1043
. points, purchase of residence . . . . . D/AGI, ¶ 1055
. prepaid . . . . . D/Am, D/GI, ¶ 1055

. property held for production of rent or royalties . . . . . D/GI, ¶ 1006A
. trade or business debts D/GI, ¶ 937
Interest forfeiture
. premature withdrawal from time savings account . . . . . D/GI, ¶ 1111
Interest on tax deficiencies
. corporation . . . . . D/GI, ¶ 937A
. individual, generally . . ND, ¶ 937A
. . related to trade or business . . . . . D/GI, ND, ¶ 937A
. underpayment attributable to nondisclosed reportable transaction . . . . . ND, ¶ 2838
Investigatory costs
. acquisition of specific business . . . . . ND, ¶ 904
. . business search . . . . D/GI, D/Am, ¶ 904
Investor's expenses (except incurred in earning tax-exempt interest) . . . . . D/AGI, ¶ 1086
ISO 9000 costs . . . . . D/GI, ¶ 901
Job hunting expenses
. new trade or business . ND, ¶ 1081
. resume preparation costs . . . . . D/AGI, ¶ 1081
. same trade or business D/AGI, ¶ 1081
. travel and transportation to new area . . . . . D/AGI, ¶ 1081
Jockey's riding apparel . . . D/AGI, ¶ 1083
Labor union dues . . . . . D/AGI, ¶ 1080
Laundry, dry cleaning, pressing charges (business travel) . . . . . D/AGI, ¶ 901
Legal expenses and fees
. business . . . . . D/GI, ¶ 973
. investors . . . . . D/AGI, ¶ 1086
. production of income . D/AGI, ¶ 1093
. tax determination . . . . D/AGI, ¶ 1092
Legislators
. congressional living expenses, away from home
. . expenses of moving to capital . . . . . D/AGI, ¶ 956
. state
. . local transportation . D/AGI, ¶ 956
. . meals and lodging . . D/AGI, ¶ 956
. . travel expenses . . . . D/AGI, ¶ 956
License fees
. treated as personal property tax . . . . . D/AGI, ¶ 1021
Life insurance premiums, debts incurred to purchase, paid by employer . . . . . D/GI, ¶ 909
. employee or other beneficiary . . . . . D/GI, ¶ 909
. employer beneficiary . ND, ¶ 804
Loan cost—stock reacquisition . . . . . ND, ¶ 1043
Lobbying expense
. appearances before legislative bodies . . . ND, ¶ 974
. expenditures to influence voters . . . . . ND, ¶ 974
. professional lobbyist's expenses . . . . . D/GI, ¶ 974
Losses
. gambling (trade or business) . . . . . D/AGI, ¶ 1113
. net operating loss . . . . D/GI, ¶ 1145
. sale or exchange of property
. . business property . . D/GI, ¶ 1007
. . related parties . . . . . ND, ¶ 905
. . capital assets (business motive) . . . . . D/GI, ¶ 1007
. theft or casualty
. . individual property . . D/AGI, ¶ 1121; ¶ 1123
. . rent-or royalty-generating property . D/GI, ¶ 1006A
. worthless stock and securities . . . . . D/GI, ¶ 1916
Lump sum distribution-ordinary income portion . D/GI, ¶ 2143
Machinery
. incidental repairs . . . . D/GI, ¶ 991
Materials and supplies, business (incidentals) . . D/GI, ¶ 901
Maternity clothes . . . . . ND, ¶ 1016
Meals provided for employees
. employer's cost of providing meals on premises . . . . . D/GI, ¶ 2089
. meals directly related to business . . . . . 50% D/GI, ¶ 911
Medical, dental and hospital expenses (to the extent exceeding 10% of adjusted gross income; 7.5% of AGI for taxpayers age 65 or older) . . . . . D/AGI, ¶ 59; ¶ 1015
Medical savings account . . D/GI, ¶ 2035; ¶ 2037
Mine development expenditures . . . . . D/GI, ¶ 988
Mine exploration expenditures . . . . . D/GI, ¶ 987
Mortgages
. insurance premiums (through 2016) . . . . D/AGI, ¶ 1048A
. interest . . . . . D/AGI, ¶ 1047
Moving expenses
. meals . . . . . ND, ¶ 1073

. other expenses
. . employee, reimbursed . . . . . D/GI, ¶ 1073
. . employee, unreimbursed . . . . . D/GI ¶ 1073
. . self employed . . . . . D/GI, ¶ 1073
Moving machinery . . . . . D/GI, ¶ 901
Musician's clothing, used exclusively in business . . D/AGI, ¶ 1083
National Labor Relations Board award to employees, payment by employer . . . D/GI, ¶ 2604
Net operating loss deduction . . . . . D/GI, ¶ 1430
New business, cost of starting up ($5,000 deduction and excess amortizable over 15 years) . . . . . D/GI, D/Am, ¶ 904
Nonbusiness bad debts (limited) . . . . . D/GI, ¶ 1007
Nontrade or nonbusiness expenses incurred in preserving income-producing property . . . . D/AGI, ¶ 1085
Nurse's uniform . . . . . D/AGI, ¶ 1083
Office in home (limited)
. employee . . . . . D/AGI, ¶ 965
. principal place of business . . . . . D/GI, ¶ 945
Office supplies . . . . . D/GI, ¶ 963
Operating loss in prior or subsequent year . . . . . D/GI, ¶ 1145
Organization expenses of corporation ($5,000 deduction and excess amortizable over 15 years) . . . . . D/GI, D/Am, ¶ 904
Original construction of greens on a golf course . ND, ¶ 991
Outside salesperson
. meals—see Meals, employees' business
. moving expenses—see Moving expenses
. travel expenses . . . . . D/AGI, ¶ 941B; ¶ 1073
Package design costs . . . . D/GI, ¶ 969
Partners' fixed or guaranteed payments for services or for use of capital (allowed as business deduction to partnership) . . . . . D/GI, ¶ 421
Partnership organization expenses, unless election to amortize . . . . . ND, ¶ 477
Passport fee, business trip . D/GI, ¶ 955
Passport fee (except for business purposes) . . . . ND, ¶ 955
Penalties . . . . . generally ND, ¶ 972
. Environmental Protection Agency:
. . Clean Air Act violation . . . . . ND, ¶ 972
. . nonconformance penalty . . . . . D/GI, ¶ 972
. penalty on early withdrawal of time deposit . . . . . D/GI, ¶ 1111
Performing artists (limitation on gross income)
. employee business expenses . . . . . D/GI, ¶ 941A
Permanent improvements
. business property . . . D/Am, ¶ 1201
. tenants . . . . . D/Am, ¶ 764
"Points" on home mortgage (if customarily required in geographic area in which indebtedness was incurred) . . . . . D/AGI, ¶ 1055
Police officer's uniform and cost of cleaning . . . . . D/AGI, ¶ 1083
Political contributions
. corporations, businesses, etc. . . . . ND, ¶ 976
. individuals . . . . . ND, ¶ 976
Political publications, cost of advertising in . . . . . ND (generally), ¶ 976
Postage costs, business . . . D/GI, ¶ 901
Premiums paid on a business insurance "professional overhead expense disability policy" . . . . . D/GI, ¶ 908A
Prepaid interest or finance charges . . . . . D/Am, ¶ 1055
Prizes and contests—see "Promotional activities"
Professional associations, dues
. unreimbursed employee expense . . . . . D/AGI, ¶ 981
Professional books and journals and information services
. unreimbursed employee expense . . . . . D/AGI, ¶ 981
Promotional activities
. coupons . . . . . D/GI, ¶ 918
. prizes and contests . . . D/GI, ¶ 969
Protective clothing . . . . . D/AGI, ¶ 1083
Raffle tickets, cost of . . . . . ND, ¶ 1061
Railroad retirement tax paid by employers . . . . . D/GI, ¶ 716
Railway trainman's uniform D/AGI, ¶ 1083
Real estate impact fees . . . ND, ¶ 1288A

Reconditioning and health-restoring expenses of employees paid by employers . . . . . D/GI, ¶ 1016
Refinery property (limited) . D/GI, ¶ 977C
Reforestation costs . . . . . D/GI, D/Am, ¶ 530
Reimbursed expenses (otherwise deductible) . . D/GI, ¶ 942
Removal of architectural and transportation barriers to the handicapped and elderly (limited) . . . . . D/AGI, ¶ 1365M
Rent, business property . . . D/GI, ¶ 986
Reorganization expenditures . . . . . ND, ¶ 904
Repairs to business property . . . . . D/GI, D/Am, ¶ 903
Repairs to personal residence . . . . . ND, ¶ 966
Research and experimental expenditures connected with a trade or business . D/GI, D/Am, ¶ 979
Restaurant smallwares (limited) . . . . . D/GI, ¶ 1825
Retirement plans, contributions to
. employer . . . . . D/GI, ¶ 2115
. individuals (limited) . . D/GI, ¶ 2121; ¶ 2157; ¶ 2171; ¶ 2183; ¶ 2189
. savings incentive match plan for employees (SIMPLE) . . . . . D/GI, ¶ 2183; ¶ 2185
. self-employed individuals . . . . . D/GI, ¶ 2107
. simplified employee pension contributions D/GI, ¶ 2189
Return, federal or state income tax, gift tax, etc., cost of having prepared (including investor) . . . . D/AGI, ¶ 973
Safe deposit boxes, rental for protection of income producing property
. investor . . . . . D/AGI, ¶ 1085
Salaries
. bonuses . . . . . D/GI, ¶ 906
. commissions . . . . . D/GI, ¶ 906
. related parties . . . . . D/GI, ¶ 915
Salespersons' expenses
. reimbursed . . . . . D/GI, ¶ 942
. unreimbursed . . . . . D/AGI ¶ 942
. . automobile expenses D/AGI, ¶ 946
. . entertaining customers, reimbursed . . . . . D/GI, ¶ 915
. . entertaining customers, unreimbursed . . . . . 50% D/AGI, ¶ 910
. . gifts to customers (up to $25) . . . . . D/AGI, ¶ 918
. . membership dues in business or social clubs . . . . . ND, ¶ 981
. . subscriptions to business, professional or trade publications, if for business reasons . D/AGI, ¶ 981
. . transportation expenses, unreimbursed . . . . . D/AGI, ¶ 916
. . travel expenses . . . . D/AGI, ¶ 949
Sales tax (state) . . . . . D/AGI, ¶ 1021
Self-employment tax (limited to 50%) . . . . . D/GI, ¶ 2664
Servants, social security taxes paid for . . . . . ND, ¶ 923
Severance payments . . . . . D/GI, ¶ 2075
Shareholder's proxy fight expenses . . . . . D/AGI, ¶ 309
Smallwares, restaurant (limited) . . . . . D/GI, ¶ 1825
Social Security taxes
. employees . . . . . ND, ¶ 923
. employers . . . . . D/GI (only as business expense), ¶ 923
Soil and water conservation expenditures, farmers . . D/GI, D/Am, ¶ 982
Stamp taxes
. dealers/investors . . . . D/GI, ¶ 1611
. trade or business . . . . D/GI, ¶ 1611
. transfer of personal residence . . . . . ND, ¶ 1611
Start-up expenditures, business ($5,000 deduction and excess amortizable over 15 years) . . . . . D/GI, D/Am, ¶ 904
Stock redemption costs . . . ND, ¶ 742
Subscriptions, professional journals (self-employed) . D/GI, ¶ 981
Supplemental unemployment compensation benefits, repayments by recipients D/GI, ¶ 1009
Surgeon's uniform (employee) . . . . . D/AGI, ¶ 1083
Tax penalty payments . . . . ND, ¶ 972
Tax refresher course, lawyer's . . . . . D/GI, ¶ 981
Tax returns, cost of preparation
. business . . . . . D/GI, ¶ 1092
. individual . . . . . D/AGI, ¶ 1092

Taxes . . . . . ¶ 1021
. automobile excise taxes . . . . . D/Am, ¶ 126
Teachers, classroom expenses . . . . . D/GI, ¶ 1011B
Telephone service (as a business expense) . . . . D/GI, ¶ 961
Theft loss
. business . . . . . D/GI, ¶ 1123
. nonbusiness . . . . . D/AGI, ¶ 1123
Timber
. reforestation expenses ($10,000 deduction and excess amortizable over 7 years) . . . . . D/GI, D/Am, ¶ 1287
. post-establishment fertilization . . . . . D/GI, ¶ 901
Tires (see "Automobile expenses" and "Truck tires")
Title costs (perfecting or defending title to property, including costs of defending condemnation proceedings) (capital expenditure) . . . . . D/Am, ¶ 1611
Tools, unreimbursed cost, useful life of one year or less . . . . . D/AGI, ¶ 901
Trade association dues, unreimbursed employee expenses . . . . . D/AGI, ¶ 981
Trade or business expenses (securities dealers and traders) . . . . . D/GI, ¶ 1086
Trademark and trade name expenditures . . . . . D/Am, ¶ 1288
Transfer taxes . . . . . ND, ¶ 41
Travel expenses (employees)
. commuting expenses . ND, ¶ 945
. reimbursed . . . . . D/GI, ¶ 954
. unreimbursed . . . . . D/AGI, ¶ 952
. . baseball players (including meals and lodging) . . . . . D/AGI, ¶ 954
. . business and pleasure trips . . . . . D/AGI, ¶ 952
. . commercial fishing boat crew members, for travel, meals, and lodging away from home port . . . . . D/AGI, ¶ 952
. . congressmen, up to $3,000 of living expenses . . . . . D/AGI, ¶ 950
. . expenses of traveling from principal place to minor place of business . . . . . D/AGI, ¶ 952
. . government employees, expenses in excess of per diem allowances . . . . . D/AGI, ¶ 953
. . lawyers . . . . . D/AGI, ¶ 981
. . meals, reimbursed . . D/GI, ¶ 954
. . meals, unreimbursed 50% D/AGI, ¶ 952
. . members of Congress, up to $3,000 of living expenses . . . . . D/AGI, ¶ 950
. . National Guard and Military Reserve members (limited) . . D/GI, ¶ 950
. . physician, medical conventions . . . . . D/AGI, ¶ 959
. . railroad employees' meals and lodging while away from "home terminal" . . . . . D/AGI, ¶ 916
. . salespersons . . . . . D/AGI, ¶ 1079
. . teachers, scientific meetings and conventions . . . . . D/AGI, ¶ 959
. . truck drivers' (long line) meals and lodging while away from "home terminal" . . . . . D/AGI, ¶ 949
Truck tires
. replacement tires (limited) . . . . . D/GI, ¶ 946
. with life less than a year . . . . . D/GI, ¶ 946
Truck use tax (unless as business expense) . . . . ND, ¶ 1021
Uncollectible notes (see "Bad debts")
Uniform and special clothing costs
. baseball uniforms . . . . D/AGI, ¶ 1083
. clothing required for business . . . . . D/AGI, ¶ 1083
. employer-reimbursed costs . . . . . D/GI, ¶ 1083
. jockey's riding apparel . D/AGI, ¶ 1083
. nurses' uniforms . . . . D/AGI, ¶ 1083
. protective clothing . . . D/AGI, ¶ 1083
. work shoes, metal tipped . . . . . D/AGI, ¶ 1083
Union payments
. dues . . . . . D/AGI, ¶ 1080
. fines . . . . . D/AGI, ¶ 972
Utilities, personal . . . . . ND, ¶ 963
Wages and salaries . . . . . D/GI, ¶ 906
Waiters, waitresses
. special uniforms . . . . D/AGI, ¶ 1083
Water, potable
. domestic production activities . . . . . D/GI, ¶ 980D
Work shoes, metal tipped for protection of worker . . . D/AGI, ¶ 1083

¶ 59 Checklist for Medical Expenses

Generally, a medical expense deduction is allowed for expenses incurred in the diagnosis, cure, mitigation, treatment or prevention of disease, or for the purpose of affecting any structure or function of the body for the individual or for the individual's spouse or dependents (¶ 1016). The deduction covers expenses that have not been reimbursed by medical insurance or other sources.

Despite the broad scope of medical expenses, not every expense incurred for medical care is deductible. Also, there is a 10-percent-of-adjusted-gross-income floor on the medical expense deduction for most taxpayers (for tax years ending before January 1, 2017, the floor is 7.5 percent if a taxpayer or spouse is age 65 or older before the close of the tax year). The chart, below, lists specific types of expenses and whether or not a deduction for the expense is permitted. The user can easily check whether an official determination has been made as to the deductibility of a particular type of expense.

Medical Expense	*Deductible*	*Authority*
Abortion		
. legal	Yes	Rev. Rul. 73-201, 1973-1 CB 140, as clarified by Rev. Rul. 73-603, 1973-2 CB 76, and Rev. Rul. 97-9, 1997-1 CB 77
Accident and health insurance		
. medical care portion separately stated and reasonable in amount	Yes	Code Sec. 213(d)(1)(D) and (d)(6); Reg. § 1.213-1(e)(4)
. medical care portion not separately stated or, if separately stated, not reasonable in amount	No	Code Sec. 213(d)(6)(A); Reg. § 1.213-1(e)(4)
Acupuncture	Yes	Rev. Rul. 72-593, 1972-2 CB 180
Adoption		
. medical costs of adopted child	Yes	Rev. Rul. 60-255, 1960-2 CB 105
. medical costs of natural mother	No	*B.L. Kilpatrick*, 68 TC 469, Dec. 34,493
Air conditioner		
. allergy relief	Yes	Rev. Rul. 55-261, 1955-1 CB 307
. cystic fibrosis relief	Yes	*R. Gerard*, 37 TC 826, Dec. 25,331 (Acq.)
. detachable, for sick person's use only	Yes	Reg. § 1.213-1(e)(1)(iii)
. permanent improvement to property (if not directly related to medical care)	No	Reg. § 1.213-1(e)(1)(iii); *G.W. Wade*, 61-2 USTC ¶ 9709
Alcoholism, treatment of	Yes	Rev. Rul. 73-325, 1973-2 CB 75
Ambulance hire	Yes	Reg. § 1.213-1(e)(1)(ii)
Anticipated medical expenses	No	*W.B. Andrews*, 37 TCM 744, Dec. 35,144(M), TC Memo. 1978-174
Attendant to accompany blind or deaf student	Yes	Rev. Rul. 64-173, 1964-1 CB (Part 1) 121; *R.A. Baer Est.*, 26 TCM 170, Dec. 28,352(M), TC Memo. 1967-34
Automobile (see Car)		
Baby sitting expenses to enable parent to see doctor	No	Rev. Rul. 78-266, 1978-2 CB 123
Birth control pills	Yes	Rev. Rul. 73-200, 1973-1 CB 140
Blind persons		
. attendant to accompany student	Yes	Rev. Rul. 64-173, 1964-1 (Part I) CB 121
. braille books and magazines, excess cost over cost of regular editions	Yes	Rev. Rul. 75-318, 1975-2 CB 88
. seeing-eye dog	Yes	Rev. Rul. 55-261, 1955-1 CB 307
. special education (see Schools, special)		

Medical Expense	*Deductible*	*Authority*
. special educational aids to mitigate condition	Yes	Rev. Rul. 58-223, 1958-1 CB 156
Breast pumps and supplies	Yes	Announcement 2011-14, 2011-9 IRB 532
Capital expenditures		
. home modifications for handicapped individual	Yes	Rev. Rul. 87-106, 1987-2 CB 67
. permanent improvement to property, if not directly related to medical care	No	Reg. § 1.213-1(e)(1)(iii)
. primary purpose medical care	Yes	Reg. § 1.213-1(e)(1)(iii)
Car		
. depreciation on	No	*M.S. Gordon,* 37 TC 986, Dec. 25,364; *R.K. Weary,* CA-10, 75-1 USTC ¶ 9173, *cert. denied,* 423 US 838
. equipping to accommodate wheelchair passengers, excess cost of	Yes	Rev. Rul. 70-606, 1970-2 CB 66
. insurance, medical coverage for persons other than taxpayer, spouse and children	No	Rev. Rul. 73-483, 1973-2 CB 75
. special controls for a person with a disability	Yes	Rev. Rul. 66-80, 1966-1 CB 57
Chauffeur, salary of	No	*W.E. Buck,* 47 TC 113, Dec. 28,175
Chemical dependency treatment (see Alcoholism, treatment of, and Drug addiction, recovery from)		
Childbirth preparation classes		
. "coach"	No	IRS Letter Ruling 8919009
. mother, for obstetrical care	Yes	IRS Letter Ruling 8919009
Chiropractors	Yes	Rev. Rul. 55-261, 1955-1 CB 307, as modified by Rev. Rul. 63-91, 1963-1 CB 54
Christian Science practitioners	Yes	Rev. Rul. 55-261, 1955-1 CB 307, as modified by Rev. Rul. 63-91, 1963-1 CB 54
Clarinet and lessons, alleviation of severe teeth malocclusion	Yes	Rev. Rul. 62-210, 1962-2 CB 89
Clothing, suitable for use other than therapy	No	*M.C. Montgomery,* 51 TC 410, Dec. 29,270, aff'd on other issues, CA-6, 70-2 USTC ¶ 9466
Computer data bank, storage and retrieval of medical records	Yes	Rev. Rul. 71-282, 1971-2 CB 166
Contact lenses	Yes	Reg. § 1.213-1(e)(1)(iii); Rev. Rul. 74-429, 1974-2 CB 83
. replacement insurance	Yes	Rev. Rul. 74-429, 1974-2 CB 83
Contraceptives, prescription	Yes	Rev. Rul. 73-200, 1973-1 CB 140
Cosmetic surgery		
. necessary to ameliorate a deformity arising from a congenital abnormality, personal injury, or disfiguring disease	Yes	Code Sec. 213(d)(9); Senate Finance Committee Report to P.L. 101-508
. unnecessary	No	Code Sec. 213(d)(9); Senate Finance Committee Report to P.L. 101-508
Crime victims, compensated medical expenses of	No	Rev. Rul. 74-74, 1974-1 CB 18
Crutches	Yes	Reg. § 1.213-1(e)(1)(iii)

Medical Expense	*Deductible*	*Authority*
Dancing lessons	No	*R.C. France,* CA-6, 82-1 USTC ¶ 9225, aff'g 40 TCM 508, Dec. 37,023(M), TC Memo. 1980-215
Deaf persons		
. hearing aid	Yes	Rev. Rul. 55-261, 1955-1 CB 307
. hearing-aid animal	Yes	Rev. Rul. 68-295, 1968-1 CB 92
. lip reading expenses for the deaf	Yes	Rev. Rul. 55-261, 1955-1 CB 307
. notetaker, deaf student	Yes	*R.A. Baer Est.,* 26 TCM 170, Dec. 28,352(M), TC Memo. 1967-34
. special education (see Schools, special)		
. telephone, specially equipped, including repairs	Yes	Rev. Rul. 71-48, 1971-1 CB 99, as amplified by Rev. Rul. 73-53, 1973-1 CB 139
. television, closed-caption decoder	Yes	Rev. Rul. 80-340, 1980-2 CB 81
. visual alert system	Yes	IRS Letter Ruling 8250040
Dental fees	Yes	Reg. § 1.213-1(e)(1)(ii)
Dentures (artificial teeth)	Yes	Reg. § 1.213-1(e)(1)(ii)
Deprogramming services	No	IRS Letter Ruling 8021004
Diagnostic fees	Yes	Reg. § 1.213-1(e)(1)(ii)
Diapers		
. diaper service	No	Rev. Rul. 55-261, 1955-1 CB 307
. disposable, to alleviate severe neurological disease	Yes	IRS Letter Ruling 8137085
Doctors' fees	Yes	Reg. § 1.213-1(e)(1)(i); Rev. Rul. 55-261, 1955-1 CB 307
Domestic aid, for nursing-type service	Yes	Rev. Rul. 58-339, 1958-2 CB 106
Drug addiction, recovery from	Yes	Rev. Rul. 72-226, 1972-1 CB 96
Drugs and medicines		
. illegal/controlled substances, even when prescribed	No	Rev. Rul. 97-9, 1997-1 CB 77
. over-the-counter (non-prescription)	No	Code Sec. 213(b); Rev. Rul. 2003-58, 2003-1 CB 959
. prescription, legal	Yes	Code Sec. 213(b)
Dust elimination system	No	*F.S. Delp,* 30 TC 1230, Dec. 23,167
Dyslexia, language training	Yes	Rev. Rul. 69-607, 1969-2 CB 40
Ear piercing	No	Rev. Rul. 82-111, 1982-1 CB 48
Electrolysis	No	Code Sec. 213(d)(9); Senate Finance Committee Report to P.L. 101-508
Elevator, alleviation of cardiac condition	Yes	Reg. § 1.213-1(e)(1)(iii); *J.E. Berry,* DC Okla., 58-2 USTC ¶ 9870, 174 FSupp 748; Rev. Rul. 59-411, 1959-2 CB 100, as modified by Rev. Rul. 83-33, 1983-1 CB 70
Equipment, supplies, or diagnostic devices for medical care, non-prescription	Yes	Rev. Rul. 2003-58, 2003-1 CB 959
Eye examinations and glasses	Yes	Reg. § 1.213-1(e)(1)(ii) and (iii)
Fallout shelter, prevention of disease	No	*F.H. Daniels,* 41 TC 324, Dec. 26,414
Fertility enhancement	Yes	IRS Letter Ruling 200318017; IRS Pub. 502
Fluoride device; on advice of dentist	Yes	Rev. Rul. 64-267, 1964-2 CB 69
Founder's fee, prepaid, to retirement home; portion attributable to medical care	Yes	Rev. Rul. 76-481, 1976-2 CB 82, as clarified by Rev. Rul. 93-72, 1993-2 CB 77
Funeral expenses	No	*K.P. Carr,* 39 TCM 253, Dec. 36,352(M), TC Memo. 1979-400

Medical Expense	*Deductible*	*Authority*
Furnace	No	*J.L. Seymour,* 14 TC 1111, Dec. 17,675
Glasses	Yes	Reg. § 1.213-1(e)(1)(ii)
Gravestone	No	*C.W. Libby Est.,* 14 TCM 699, Dec. 21,110(M), TC Memo. 1955-180
Guide animals (see Service animals)		
Hair transplants, surgical	No	Code Sec. 213(d)(9); Senate Finance Committee Report to P.L. 101-508
Halfway house or specially selected home, for adjustment from mental hospital	Yes	Rev. Rul. 69-499, 1969-2 CB 39; IRS Letter Ruling 7714016
Handicapped persons (see, also, specific handicap or equipment)		
. home modification (see Capital expenditures)		
. special training or education (see Schools, special)		
Health club dues		
. not related to a particular medical condition	No	Rev. Rul. 55-261, 1955-1 CB 307
. prescribed by physician for medical condition	Yes	Rev. Rul. 55-261, 1955-1 CB 307
Health Maintenance Organization (HMO)	Yes	Reg. § 1.213-1(e)(4); IRS Pub. 502
Hearing aids (see Deaf persons)		
Hospital care, in-patient	Yes	Reg. § 1.213-1(e)(1)(v)
Hospital services	Yes	Reg. § 1.213-1(e)(1)(ii)
Hygienic supplies	No	Reg. § 1.213-1(e)(2); *O.G. Russell,* 12 TCM 1276, Dec. 19,973(M)
Indian medicine man	Yes	*R.H. Tso,* 40 TCM 1277, Dec. 37,260(M), TC Memo. 1980-339
Insulin	Yes	Code Sec. 213(b)
Insurance		
. accident and health insurance (see Accident and health insurance)		
. hospital insurance (HI) payroll tax paid	No	Rev. Rul. 66-216, 1966-2 CB 100
. long term care insurance (within limits)	Yes	Code Secs. 213(d)(1)(D) and 7702B
. Medicare A premiums (voluntarily enrolled taxpayer)	Yes	Rev. Rul. 79-175, 1979-1 CB 117
. Medicare B premiums	Yes	Reg. § 1.213-1(e)(4)
. premiums for loss of income	No	Reg. § 1.213-1(e)(4)
. premiums for loss of life, limb or sight	No	Reg. § 1.213-1(e)(4)
. premiums for medical care	Yes	Reg. § 1.213-1(e)(4)
. self-employed	Yes	Code Sec. 162(l)
Iron lung	Yes	Rev. Rul. 55-261, 1955-1 CB 307
Laboratory fees	Yes	Reg. § 1.213-1(e)(1)(ii)
Lactation expenses	Yes	Announcement 2011-14, 2011-9 IRB 532
Laetrile, prescribed	No	Rev. Rul. 97-9, 1997-1 CB 77
Lamaze classes (see Childbirth preparation classes)		
Laser eye surgery	Yes	Rev. Rul. 2003-57, 2003-1 CB 959
Lead paint, removal	Yes	Rev. Rul. 79-66, 1979-1 CB 114
Legal expenses		
. authorization of treatment for mental illness	Yes	Rev. Rul. 71-281, 1971-2 CB 165
. divorce upon medical advice	No	*J.H. Jacobs,* 62 TC 813, Dec. 32,773

Medical Expense	*Deductible*	*Authority*
Lifetime medical care fee, prepaid, to retirement home; portion attributable to medical care	Yes	Rev. Rul. 75-302, 1975-2 CB 86, Rev. Rul. 75-303, 1975-2 CB 87, as clarified by Rev. Rul. 93-72, 1993-2 CB 77
Limbs, artificial	Yes	Reg. § 1.213-1(e)(1)(ii)
Lodging		
. care not provided in hospital or equivalent outpatient facility	No	*A.L. Polyak,* 94 TC 337, Dec. 46,443
. limited to $50 per night per person	Yes	Code Sec. 213(d)(2)
Long term care expenses	Yes	Code Secs. 213(d)(1)(C) and 7702B
Marriage counseling	No	Rev. Rul. 75-319, 1975-2 CB 88
Maternity clothes	No	Rev. Rul. 55-261, 1955-1 CB 307
Mattress, prescribed for alleviation of arthritis	Yes	Rev. Rul. 55-261, 1955-1 CB 307
Nursing home, medical reasons	Yes	*W.B. Counts,* 42 TC 755, Dec. 26,893 (Acq.)
Nursing services (including board and employer's portion of social security tax if paid by taxpayer)	Yes	Reg. § 1.213-1(e)(1)(ii); Rev. Rul. 57-489, 1957-2 CB 207
Obstetrical expenses	Yes	Reg. § 1.213-1(e)(1)(ii)
Operations		
. illegal	No	Reg. § 1.213-1(e)(1)(ii)
. legal	Yes	Reg. § 1.213-1(e)(1)(ii)
Optometrists	Yes	Rev. Rul. 55-261, 1955-1 CB 307
Orthodontia	Yes	Reg. § 1.213-1(e)(1)(ii)
Orthopedic shoes, excess cost	Yes	IRS Letter Ruling 8221118
Osteopaths	Yes	Rev. Rul. 55-261, 1955-1 CB 307, as modified by Rev. Rul. 63-91, 1963-1 CB 54
Oxygen equipment, breathing difficulty	Yes	Rev. Rul. 55-261, 1955-1 CB 307
Patterning exercises, handicapped child	Yes	Rev. Rul. 70-170, 1970-1 CB 51
Plumbing, special fixtures for handicapped	Yes	Rev. Rul. 70-395, 1970-2 CB 65
Pregnancy test kit	Yes	IRS Pub. 502
Prosthesis	Yes	Reg. § 1.213-1(e)(1)(ii)
Psychiatric care	Yes	Rev. Rul. 55-261, 1955-1 CB 307
Psychologists	Yes	Rev. Rul. 63-91, 1963-1 CB 54
Psychotherapists	Yes	Rev. Rul. 63-91, 1963-1 CB 54
Reclining chair for cardiac patient	Yes	Rev. Rul. 58-155, 1958-1 CB 156
Reconstructive surgery, after mastectomy for breast cancer	Yes	Rev. Rul. 2003-57, 2003-1 CB 959
Remedial reading for dyslexic child	Yes	Rev. Rul. 69-607, 1969-2 CB 40
Residence, loss on sale, move medically recommended	No	Rev. Rul. 68-319, 1968-1 CB 92
Retirement home, cost of medical care	Yes	Reg. § 1.213-1(e)(1)(v); *H.W. Smith Est.,* 79 TC 313, Dec. 39,273 (Acq.)
Sanitarium rest home, cost of medical care (and meals and lodging, if warranted by individual's condition)	Yes	Reg. § 1.213-1(e)(1)(v)
Schools, special, relief of handicap	Yes	Reg. § 1.213-1(e)(1)(v); Rev. Rul. 58-533, 1958-2 CB 108; Rev. Rul. 70-285, 1970-1 CB 52; Rev. Rul. 78-340, 1978-2 CB 124
Scientology "audits" and "processing"	No	*D.H. Brown,* CA-8, 75-2 USTC ¶ 9718, aff'g 62 TC 551, Dec. 32,701; Rev. Rul. 78-190, 1978-1 CB 74
Self-help, medical	No	*B. Doody,* 32 TCM 547, Dec. 32,006(M), TC Memo. 1973-126

Medical Expense	*Deductible*	*Authority*
Service animals		
. hearing-aid animal	Yes	Rev. Rul. 68-295, 1968-1 CB 92
. other	Yes	Senate Finance Committee Report to P.L. 100-647
. seeing-eye dog	Yes	Reg. § 1.213-1(e)(1)(iii); Rev. Rul. 55-261, 1955-1 CB 307
Sexual dysfunction, therapy for	Yes	Rev. Rul. 75-187, 1975-1 CB 92
Smoking, program to stop	Yes	Rev. Rul. 99-28, 1999-1 CB 1269
Spiritual guidance	No	*M. Miller,* 40 TCM 243, Dec. 36,911(M), TC Memo. 1980-136
Sterilization operation, legal	Yes	Rev. Rul. 73-603, 1973-2 CB 76, clarifying Rev. Rul. 73-201, 1973-1 CB 140
Swimming pool, treatment of polio or arthritis	Yes	*C.B. Mason,* DC Hawaii, 57-2 USTC ¶ 10,012; Rev. Rul. 83-33, 1983-1 CB 70
Tattoos	No	Rev. Rul. 82-111, 1982-1 CB 48
Taxicab to doctor's office	Yes	Rev. Rul. 55-261, 1955-1 CB 307
Teeth		
. artificial	Yes	Reg. § 1.213-1(e)(1)(ii)
. whitening procedure	No	Rev. Rul. 2003-57, 2003-1 CB 959
Telephone, specially equipped		
. deaf persons	Yes	Rev. Rul. 71-48, 1971-1 CB 99, amplified by Rev. Rul. 73-53, 1973-1 CB 139
. modified for person in an iron lung	Yes	Rev. Rul. 55-261, 1955-1 CB 307
Television, closed caption decoder	Yes	Rev. Rul. 80-340, 1980-2 CB 81
Therapy, received as medical treatment	Yes	Reg. § 1.213-1(e)(1)(ii)
Toilet articles	No	Reg. § 1.213-1(e)(2); *O.G. Russell,* 12 TCM 1276, Dec. 19,973(M)
Transplant, donor's costs of	Yes	Rev. Rul. 68-452, 1968-2 CB 111; Rev. Rul. 73-189, 1973-1 CB 139
Transportation, cost incurred essentially and primarily for medical care	Yes	Code Sec. 213(d)(1)(B); Reg. § 1.213-1(e)(1)(iv)
Trips, general health improvement	No	Reg. § 1.213-1(e)(1)(ii) and (iv)
Vacations, health restorative	No	Reg. § 1.213-1(e)(1)(ii) and (iv); Rev. Rul. 57-130, 1957-1 CB 108
Vacuum cleaner, alleviation of dust allergy	No	Rev. Rul. 76-80, 1976-1 CB 71
Vasectomy, legal	Yes	Rev. Rul. 73-201, 1973-1 CB 140, clarified by Rev. Rul. 73-603, 1973-2 CB 76, and Rev. Rul. 97-9, 1997-1 CB 77
Visual alert system for hearing impaired	Yes	IRS Letter Ruling 8250040
Weight loss program		
. for treatment of specific disease	Yes	Rev. Rul. 2002-19, 2002-1 CB 778
. to improve appearance, prescribed	No	Rev. Rul. 79-151, 1979-1 CB 116; IRS Pub. 502
Wheelchair	Yes	Reg. § 1.213-1(e)(1)(iii)
Wig, prescribed to alleviate mental discomfort resulting from disease	Yes	Rev. Rul. 62-189, 1962-2 CB 88
X-rays	Yes	Reg. § 1.213-1(e)(1)(ii)

¶ 61 Checklist for Credits

The Internal Revenue Code provides for a number of credits that may be taken into account when arriving at a tax liability. A tax credit directly reduces a taxpayer's tax liability dollar for dollar, rather than reducing the taxpayer's taxable income as a deduction does. Both individual and business taxpayers are eligible for tax credits, and certain credits are available to both types of taxpayers.

The two charts below show the availability of the nonbusiness and business credits. All paragraph references are to the 2017 *U.S. Master Tax Guide*®. The date ranges are time periods for which the credits are available for calendar-year taxpayers. Fiscal-year taxpayers should consult the referenced paragraph to determine if any special requirements are applicable.

Nonbusiness Credits

Nonbusiness Credits	*Years Available*	*Paragraph Reference*
Adoption credit:		
. nonrefundable	After 12/31/2011	¶ 1307
Alternative fuel vehicle refueling property credit:		
. non-hydrogen property	1/1/2006—12/31/2016	¶ 1355
. hydrogen property	Until 12/31/2014	¶ 1355
Alternative motor vehicle credit:		
. fuel cell motor vehicle credit	Until 12/31/2016	¶ 1346
Child and dependent care credit	Permanent	¶ 1301
Child tax credit	Permanent	¶ 1305
Earned income credit	Permanent	¶ 1322
Educational credits:		
. Hope Scholarship/American Opportunity tax credit (AOTC)	Permanent	¶ 1303
. Lifetime learning credit (LLC)	Permanent	¶ 1303
Elderly and permanently and totally disabled credit	Permanent	¶ 1302
Foreign tax credit	Permanent	¶ 2475
Health insurance costs credit:		
. for TAA and/or alternative TAA eligible individuals	Until 12/31/2020	¶ 1332
. for PBGC eligible individuals	Until 12/31/2020	¶ 1332
Health insurance premium assistance credit	After 12/31/2013	¶ 1331
Minimum tax credit:		
. nonrefundable	Permanent	¶ 1309
Mortgage interest credit	Permanent	¶ 1306
Mutual fund capital gains credit	Permanent	¶ 1330
Nonbusiness energy property credit:		
. lifetime limit of $500	1/1/2011—12/31/2016	¶ 1341
Plug-in electric drive motor vehicle credit:		
. generally	1/1/2010 until phased out	¶ 1351
. 2-wheeled vehicles	1/1/2012—12/31/2013, 1/1/2015—12/31/2016	¶ 1351
. 3-wheeled vehicles	1/1/2012—12/31/2014	¶ 1351
Residential energy efficient property credit		
. generally	Until 12/31/2016	¶ 1342
. qualified solar electric and water heating property	Until 12/31/2021	¶ 1342
Retirement savings contributions credit	Permanent	¶ 1304
Tax credit bonds:		
. build America bond credit	Bonds issued between 2/18/2009—12/31/2010	¶ 1378

Nonbusiness Credits	*Years Available*	*Paragraph Reference*
. new clean renewable energy bond credit	Bonds issued after 10/3/2008	¶ 1374
. qualified energy conservation bond credit	Bonds issued after 10/3/2008	¶ 1375
. qualified forestry conservation bond credit	Bonds issued between 5/23/2008—5/22/2010	¶ 1373
. school construction bond credit	Bonds issued between 2/18/2009—12/31/2010	¶ 1377
. zone academy bond credit	Bonds issued between 10/4/2008—12/31/2016	¶ 1376
Withheld tax on wages credit	Permanent	¶ 1321

Business Credits

Business Credits	*Years Available*	*Paragraph Reference*
Alcohol fuels credit:		
. second generation biofuel	1/1/2009—12/31/2016	¶ 1365I
Alternative fuel vehicle refueling property credit:		
. non-hydrogen property	Until 12/31/2016	¶ 1355
. hydrogen property	Until 12/31/2014	¶ 1355
Alternative motor vehicle credit:		
. fuel cell motor vehicle credit	Until 12/31/2016	¶ 1346
Biodiesel and renewable diesel fuels credit:		
. small agri-biodiesel producer credit	Until 12/31/2016	¶ 1365X
. renewable biodiesel	Until 12/31/2016	¶ 1365X
. other biodiesel	Until 12/31/2016	¶ 1365X
Carbon dioxide sequestration credit	10/3/2008—until phased out	¶ 1365JJ
Coal production credit	Permanent	¶ 1365D
Disabled access credit	Permanent	¶ 1365M
Distilled spirits excise tax carrying credit	Permanent	¶ 1365Z
Electricity produced from renewable resources credit (available 5 to 10 years after facilities are placed in service):		
. electricity from wind facilities	Construction beginning before 1/1/2020	¶ 1365N
. Indian coal production facilities	Placed in service before 1/1/2016	¶ 1365N
. refined coal facilities	Placed in service before 12/31/2011	¶ 1365N
. small irrigation power facilities	Placed in service before 10/3/2008	¶ 1365N
. all other facilities	Construction beginning before 1/1/2017	¶ 1365N
Employer credit for differential wage payments to military personnel	Permanent	¶ 1365II
Employer credit for providing child care	Permanent	¶ 1365V
Empowerment zone credit	Until 12/31/2016	¶ 1365O
Energy credit	Permanent[1]	¶ 1365C
Energy efficient appliance credit	Until 12/31/2013	¶ 1365DD
Energy efficient home credit	Until 12/31/2016	¶ 1365CC
Energy project credit	After 2/17/2009	¶ 1365F

Business Credits	*Years Available*	*Paragraph Reference*
Enhanced oil recovery credit	Permanent	¶ 1329
Federal excise fuel tax credit	Permanent	¶ 1329
FICA tip credit	Permanent	¶ 1365R
Foreign tax credit	Permanent	¶ 2475
Gasification project credit	Permanent	¶ 1365E
General business credit	See specific credit component	¶ 1365
Health insurance credit for small employers	After 12/31/2009	¶ 1333
Indian employment credit	Until 12/31/2016	¶ 1365Q
Investment credit	See specific credit component	¶ 1365A
Low-income housing credit	Permanent	¶ 1365K
Low sulfur diesel fuel production credit	Permanent	¶ 1365Y
Mine rescue team training credit	Until 12/31/2016	¶ 1365GG
Minimum tax credit	Permanent	¶ 1309
New markets tax credit	Until 12/31/2019; carryforward amounts until 12/31/2024	¶ 1365T
Nonconventional source fuel production credit	For coke or coke gas produced before 1/1/2010 that is sold no later than four years after the coke or coke gas is first sold	¶ 1365BB
Nuclear power facilities production credit	Until 12/31/2020	¶ 1365AA
Oil and gas from marginal wells producers credit	Permanent	¶ 1365KK
Orphan drug credit	Permanent	¶ 1365S
Pension plan startup costs credit for small employers	Permanent	¶ 1365U
Plug-in electric drive motor vehicle credit:		
. generally	1/1/2010 until phased out	¶ 1351
. 2-wheeled vehicles	1/1/2012—12/31/2013, 1/1/2015—12/31/2016	¶ 1351
. 3-wheeled vehicles	1/1/2012—12/31/2014	¶ 1351
Puerto Rico and U.S. possessions credit (available only to existent claimants from American Samoan companies)	Until 12/31/2016	¶ 1362
Railroad track maintenance credit	Until 12/31/2016	¶ 1365W
Rehabilitation credit	Permanent	¶ 1365B
Research credit	Permanent	¶ 1365J
Work opportunity credit:		
. generally	Until 12/31/2019	¶ 1365G
. qualified veteran	11/22/2011—12/31/2019	¶ 1365G

[1] Exceptions apply.

¶ 63 Checklist for Forms

The following chart lists key forms in use by the IRS and provides paragraph references to the main discussions of those forms in the 2017 *U.S. Master Tax Guide*®.

Form	*Paragraph reference*
56	¶ 2747
433-A	¶ 2723
433-B	¶ 2723
656	¶ 2723
706	¶ 2938; ¶ 2944
706, Schedule A	¶ 2912
706, Schedule A-1	¶ 2922
706, Schedule B	¶ 2912
706, Schedule C	¶ 2912
706, Schedule D	¶ 2915
706, Schedule E	¶ 2919
706, Schedule F	¶ 2912
706, Schedule G	¶ 2913; ¶ 2914
706, Schedule H	¶ 2918
706, Schedule I	¶ 2917
706, Schedule J	¶ 2925
706, Schedule K	¶ 2925
706, Schedule L	¶ 2925
706, Schedule M	¶ 2926
706, Schedule O	¶ 2932
706, Schedule Q	¶ 2934
706, Schedule R	¶ 2944
706, Schedule R-1	¶ 2944
706-A	¶ 2922
706-CE	¶ 2934
706-D	¶ 2937
706-GS(D)	¶ 2944
706-GS(T)	¶ 2944
706-NA	¶ 2940
709	¶ 2910
712	¶ 2915
843	¶ 2813
851	¶ 295
866	¶ 2721
870	¶ 2712
906	¶ 2721
911	¶ 2707
940	¶ 2650
941	¶ 2650
943	¶ 2650
944	¶ 2650
945	¶ 2650
966	¶ 211
970	¶ 1565
972	¶ 259
973	¶ 259
976	¶ 2317
982	¶ 855
990	¶ 625
990, Schedule C	¶ 613
990-BL	¶ 625
990-EZ	¶ 625
990-PF	¶ 625
990-T	¶ 658
990-W	¶ 633
1023	¶ 623
1024	¶ 692
1028	¶ 698
1040	¶ 105
1040, Schedule A	¶ 1014
1040, Schedule B	¶ 105
1040, Schedule C	¶ 105
1040, Schedule D	¶ 128
1040, Schedule E	¶ 105
1040, Schedule EIC	¶ 1322
1040, Schedule F	¶ 767
1040, Schedule H	¶ 2652
1040, Schedule J	¶ 767
1040, Schedule R	¶ 1302
1040, Schedule SE	¶ 2664
1040A	¶ 105
1040A, Schedule EIC	¶ 1322
1040-C	¶ 2411
1040-ES	¶ 2685
1040-EZ	¶ 105
1040NR	¶ 2425
1040NR-EZ	¶ 2425
1040-PR	¶ 2501
1040-SS	¶ 2501
1040-V	¶ 2525
1040X	¶ 2505
1041	¶ 510
1041, Schedule I	¶ 1401
1041, Schedule J	¶ 567
1041, Schedule K-1	¶ 510
1041-A	¶ 537
1041-ES	¶ 511
1041-QFT	¶ 575
1041-T	¶ 511
1042	¶ 2455
1042-S	¶ 2455
1042-T	¶ 2455
1045	¶ 1145
1065	¶ 406
1065, Schedule D	¶ 1758
1065, Schedule K-1	¶ 406
1066	¶ 2343
1066, Schedule Q	¶ 2344
1098	¶ 2565
1098-C	¶ 1070A
1098-E	¶ 2565
1098-T	¶ 2565
1099-A	¶ 2565
1099-B	¶ 2565
1099-C	¶ 2565
1099-DIV	¶ 2565
1099-G	¶ 2565
1099-H	¶ 2565
1099-INT	¶ 2565
1099-K	¶ 2565
1099-MISC	¶ 2565
1099-OID	¶ 1952
1099-PATR	¶ 2565
1099-R	¶ 2565
1099-S	¶ 2565
1116	¶ 2476
1118	¶ 2476
1120	¶ 211
1120, Schedule PH	¶ 275
1120, Schedule UTP	¶ 2501

Form	*Paragraph reference*
1120-C	¶ 698
1120-F	¶ 2425
1120-FSC	¶ 2501
1120-H	¶ 699
1120-IC-DISC	¶ 2501
1120-L	¶ 2370
1120-ND	¶ 2501
1120-PC	¶ 2501
1120-POL	¶ 696
1120-REIT	¶ 2326
1120-RIC	¶ 2301
1120S	¶ 351
1120-SF	¶ 2501
1120X	¶ 2759
1122	¶ 295
1127	¶ 2537
1128	¶ 1513
1138	¶ 1145
1139	¶ 2773
1310	¶ 178
2063	¶ 2411
2106	¶ 942; ¶ 1215
2120	¶ 147
2210	¶ 2875
2210-F	¶ 2875
2220	¶ 241
2350	¶ 2509
2438	¶ 2305; ¶ 2329
2439	¶ 1330; ¶ 2305; ¶ 2329
2441	¶ 1301
2553	¶ 306
2555	¶ 2408
2555-EZ	¶ 2408
2848	¶ 2708A
3115	¶ 1529
3468	¶ 1365A
3520	¶ 588
3520-A	¶ 588
3800	¶ 1365
3903	¶ 1073
3921	¶ 2565
3922	¶ 2565
4070	¶ 2605
4070A	¶ 717
4136	¶ 1329
4137	¶ 717
4255	¶ 1365A
4361	¶ 2667
4466	¶ 247
4562	¶ 1201; ¶ 1208; ¶ 1214
4563	¶ 2414
4626	¶ 1401
4684	¶ 1121; ¶ 1123
4720	¶ 590A; ¶ 610; ¶ 614; ¶ 617; ¶ 635; ¶ 637
4768	¶ 2938
4797	¶ 1208; ¶ 1211; ¶ 1713; ¶ 1747; ¶ 1779
4868	¶ 2509
4876-A	¶ 2498
4952	¶ 1094
4970	¶ 567
4972	¶ 2143
5213	¶ 1195
5227	¶ 537
5304-SIMPLE	¶ 2181
5305-SEP	¶ 2189
5305-SIMPLE	¶ 2181
5329	¶ 2127; ¶ 2151; ¶ 2161; ¶ 2169; ¶ 2173
5405	¶ 1324
5471	¶ 2487
5498	¶ 2565
5500	¶ 2137
5500-SF	¶ 2137
5558	¶ 2137
5695	¶ 1341; ¶ 1342
5713	¶ 2496
5735	¶ 1362
5768	¶ 613
5884	¶ 1365G
6198	¶ 1155
6251	¶ 1401
6252	¶ 1801
6478	¶ 1365I
6765	¶ 1365J
6781	¶ 1948
7004	¶ 2509
8027	¶ 2605
8082	¶ 415
8275	¶ 2856; ¶ 2858; ¶ 2863
8275-R	¶ 2856; ¶ 2858; ¶ 2863
8282	¶ 627
8283	¶ 1070A
8288	¶ 2442
8288-A	¶ 2442
8288-B	¶ 2442
8300	¶ 2565
8332	¶ 139A
8379	¶ 163
8396	¶ 1306
8582	¶ 1169
8582-CR	¶ 1169
8586	¶ 1365K
8594	¶ 1620
8596	¶ 2565
8596-A	¶ 2565
8606	¶ 2160; ¶ 2165; ¶ 2173¶ 2173; ¶ 2177
8611	¶ 1365K
8615	¶ 103
8621	¶ 2490
8689	¶ 2416
8716	¶ 1501
8801	¶ 1309; ¶ 1327
8802	¶ 2450
8804	¶ 2503
8809	¶ 2455
8810	¶ 1169
8811	¶ 2343
8812	¶ 1305
8814	¶ 103
8815	¶ 863
8818	¶ 863
8820	¶ 1365S
8822	¶ 2711
8822-B	¶ 2711
8824	¶ 1721; ¶ 1732

Form	*Paragraph reference*
8825	¶ 1169
8826	¶ 1365M
8827	¶ 1309
8828	¶ 105
8829	¶ 961
8832	¶ 201
8833	¶ 2450
8834	¶ 1354
8835	¶ 1365N
8839	¶ 1307
8840	¶ 2409
8843	¶ 2409
8844	¶ 1365O
8845	¶ 1365Q
8846	¶ 1365R
8849	¶ 1329
8850	¶ 1365G
8854	¶ 2412
8855	¶ 516
8857	¶ 162
8859	¶ 1308
8863	¶ 1303
8864	¶ 1365X
8865	¶ 2487
8866	¶ 1229
8867	¶ 2518
8868	¶ 2509
8869	¶ 304
8871	¶ 696
8872	¶ 696
8874	¶ 1365T
8875	¶ 2340
8879	¶ 2517
8880	¶ 1304
8881	¶ 1365U
8882	¶ 1365V
8885	¶ 1332
8886	¶ 2592
8886-T	¶ 619
8888	¶ 2155
8889	¶ 2035
8898	¶ 2414
8899	¶ 627
8900	¶ 1365W
8903	¶ 980A
8906	¶ 1365Z
8907	¶ 1365BB
8908	¶ 1365CC
8909	¶ 1365DD
8910	¶ 1345
8911	¶ 1355
8912	¶ 1371
8918	¶ 2593
8919	¶ 105
8923	¶ 1365GG
8925	¶ 804
8927	¶ 2317
8928	¶ 2015
8930	¶ 2141
8931	¶ 1365HH
8932	¶ 1365II
8933	¶ 1365JJ
8936	¶ 1351
8938	¶ 2572
8940	¶ 623
8941	¶ 1333
8944	¶ 2503
8948	¶ 2503
8949	¶ 1735
8955-SSA	¶ 2137
8959	¶ 2648
8960	¶ 129
9465	¶ 2529
HUD-1	¶ 1055
SS-4	¶ 2652
SS-5	¶ 116
SS-8	¶ 2602
T	¶ 1772
W-2	¶ 2565
W-2G	¶ 2642
W-3	¶ 2650
W-4	¶ 2634
W-4P	¶ 2643
W-4S	¶ 2604
W-4V	¶ 2629
W-7	¶ 2579
W-7A	¶ 2579
W-8BEN	¶ 2455
W-8ECI	¶ 2455
W-8EXP	¶ 2455
W-8IMY	¶ 2455
W-9	¶ 2579

¶ 64 Guide to Information Returns

The following chart lists information returns in use by the IRS. It provides reportable payment types and amounts, as well as the due dates for filing the returns with the IRS and for providing statements to a payee or other person.

(If any date shown falls on a Saturday, Sunday, or legal holiday, the due date is the next business day.)

				Due Date	
Form	**Title**	**What To Report**	**Amounts To Report**	**To IRS**	**To Recipient (unless indicated otherwise)**
1042-S	Foreign Person's U.S. Source Income Subject to Withholding	Income such as interest, dividends, royalties, pensions and annuities, etc., and amounts withheld under Chapter 3 (nonresident aliens and foreign corporations). Also, distributions of effectively connected income by publicly traded partnerships or nominees.	See form instructions	March 15	March 15
1097-BTC	Bond Tax Credit	Tax credit bond credits to shareholders.	All amounts	February 28*	On or before the 15th day of the 2nd calendar month after the close of the calendar month in which the credit is allowed
1098	Mortgage Interest Statement	Mortgage interest (including points) and certain mortgage insurance premiums you received in the course of your trade or business from individuals and reimbursements of overpaid interest.	$600 or more	February 28*	(To Payer/ Borrower) January 31
1098-C	Contributions of Motor Vehicles, Boats, and Airplanes	Information regarding a donated motor vehicle, boat, or airplane.	Gross proceeds of more than $500	February 28*	(To Donor) 30 days from date of sale or contribution
1098-E	Student Loan Interest Statement	Student loan interest received in the course of your trade or business.	$600 or more	February 28*	January 31
1098-MA	Mortgage Assistance Payment	Assistance payments paid to homeowners from funds allocated from the Housing Finance Authority Innovation Fund for the Hardest Hit Housing Markets (HFA Hardest Hit Fund) or the Emergency Homeowner's Loan Program.	All amounts	February 28*	January 31
1098-Q	Qualified Longevity Annuity Contract Information	Status of a contract that is intended to be a qualifying longevity annuity contract (QLAC), defined in section A-17 of Reg. § 1.401(a)(9)-6, that is purchased or held under any plan, annuity, or account described in Code Secs. 401(a), 403(a), 403(b), or 408 (other than a Roth IRA) or eligible governmental plan under Code Sec. 457(b).	All amounts	February 28	January 31

Form	Title	What To Report	Amounts To Report	Due Date To IRS	Due Date To Recipient (unless indicated otherwise)
1098-T	Tuition Statement	Qualified tuition and related expenses, reimbursements or refunds, and scholarships or grants (optional).	See instructions	February 28*	January 31
1099-A	Acquisition or Abandonment of Secured Property	Information about the acquisition or abandonment of property that is security for a debt for which you are the lender.	All amounts	February 28*	(To Borrower) January 31
1099-B	Proceeds From Broker and Barter Exchange Transactions	Sales or redemptions of securities, futures transactions, commodities, and barter exchange transactions.	All amounts	February 28*	February 15**
1099-C	Cancellation of Debt	Cancellation of a debt owed to a financial institution, the Federal Government, a credit union, RTC, FDIC, NCUA, a military department, the U.S. Postal Service, the Postal Rate Commission, or any organization having a significant trade or business of lending money.	$600 or more	February 28*	January 31
1099-CAP	Changes in Corporate Control and Capital Structure	Information about cash, stock, or other property from an acquisition of control or the substantial change in capital structure of a corporation.	Over $1000	February 28*	(To Shareholders) January 31
1099-DIV	Dividends and Distributions	Distributions, such as dividends, capital gain distributions, or nontaxable distributions, that were paid on stock and liquidation distributions.	$10 or more, except $600 or more for liquidations	February 28*	January 31**
1099-G	Certain Government Payments	Unemployment compensation, state and local income tax refunds, agricultural payments, and taxable grants.	$10 or more for refunds and unemployment	February 28*	January 31
1099-INT	Interest Income	Interest income.	$10 or more ($600 or more in some cases)	February 28*	January 31**
1099-K	Payment Card and Third Party Network Transactions	Payment card transactions.	All amounts	February 28*	January 31
		Third party network transactions.	$20,000 or more **and** 200 or more transactions	February 28*	January 31
1099-LTC	Long-Term Care and Accelerated Death Benefits	Payments under a long-term care insurance contract and accelerated death benefits paid under a life insurance contract or by a viatical settlement provider.	All amounts	February 28*	January 31

Form	Title	What To Report	Amounts To Report	Due Date To IRS	Due Date To Recipient (unless indicated otherwise)
1099-MISC	Miscellaneous Income	Rent or royalty payments; prizes and awards that are not for services, such as winnings on TV or radio shows (including payments reported pursuant to an election described in Reg. § 1.1471-4(d)(5)(i)(A) or reported as described in Reg. § 1.1471-4(d)(2)(iii)(A)).	$600 or more, except $10 or more for royalties	February 28+**	January 31**
	(Also, use to report direct sales of $5,000 or more of consumer goods for resale.)	Payments to crew members by owners or operators of fishing boats including payments of proceeds from sale of catch.	All amounts	February 28*	January 31**
		Code Sec. 409A income from nonqualified deferred compensation plans (NQDCs).	All amounts	February 28*	January 31**
		Payments to a physician, physicians' corporation, or other supplier of health and medical services. Issued mainly by medical assistance programs or health and accident insurance plans.	$600 or more	February 28*	January 31**
		Payments for services performed for a trade or business by people not treated as its employees (including payments reported pursuant to an election described in Reg. § 1.1471-4(d)(5)(i)(A) or reported as described in Reg. § 1.1471-4(d)(2)(iii)(A)). Examples: fees to subcontractors or directors and golden parachute payments.	$600 or more	February 28*	January 31**
		Fish purchases paid in cash for resale.	$600 or more	February 28*	January 31**
		Crop insurance proceeds.	$600 or more	February 28*	January 31**
		Substitute dividends and tax-exempt interest payments reportable by brokers.	$10 or more	February 28*	February 15**
		Gross proceeds paid to attorneys.	$600 or more	February 28*	February 15**
		A U.S. account for Chapter 4 purposes (FATCA) to which you made no payments during the year that are reportable on any applicable Form 1099 (or a U.S. account to which you made payments during the year that do not reach the applicable reporting threshold for any applicable Form 1099) reported pursuant to an election described in Reg. § 1.1471-4(d)(5)(i)(A).	All amounts (including $0)	February 28*	January 31**

Form	Title	What To Report	Amounts To Report	Due Date To IRS	Due Date To Recipient (unless indicated otherwise)
1099-OID	Original Issue Discount	Original issue discount including amounts reported pursuant to an election described in Reg. § 1.1471-4(d)(5)(i)(A) or reported as described in Reg. § 1.1471-4(d)(2)(iii)(A)).	$10 or more	February 28*	January 31**
1099-PATR	Taxable Distributions Received From Cooperatives	Distributions from cooperatives passed through to their patrons including any domestic production activities deduction and certain pass-through credits.	$10 or more	February 28*	January 31
1099-Q	Payments From Qualified Education Programs (Under Sections 529 and 530)	Earnings from qualified tuition programs and Coverdell Educational Savings Accounts (ESAs).	All amounts	February 28*	January 31
1099-R	Distributions From Pensions, Annuities, Retirement or Profit-Sharing Plans, IRAs, Insurance Contracts, etc.	Distributions from retirement or profit-sharing plans, any IRA, insurance contracts, and IRA recharacterizations (including payments reported pursuant to an election described in Reg. § 1.1471-4(d)(5)(i)(B) or reported as described in Reg. § 1.1471-4(d)(2)(iii)(A)).	$10 or more	February 28*	January 31
1099-S	Proceeds From Real Estate Transactions	Gross proceeds from the sale or exchange of real estate and certain royalty payments.	Generally, $600 or more	February 28*	February 15
1099-SA	Distributions From an HSA, Archer MSA, or Medicare Advantage MSA	Distributions from an HSA, Archer MSA, or Medicare Advantage MSA.	All amounts	February 28*	January 31
3921	Exercise of an Incentive Stock Option Under Section 422(b)	Transfer of stock pursuant to the exercise of an incentive stock option under Code Sec. 422(b).	All amounts	February 28*	January 31
3922	Transfer of Stock Acquired Through an Employee Stock Purchase Plan Under Section 423(c)	Transfer of stock acquired through an employee stock purchase plan under Code Sec. 423(c).	All amounts	February 28*	January 31
5498	IRA Contribution Information	Contributions (including rollover contributions) to any individual retirement arrangement (IRA) including a SEP, SIMPLE, and Roth IRA; Roth conversions; IRA recharacterizations; and the fair market value (FMV) of the account.	All amounts	May 31	(To Participant) For FMV/RMD Jan 31; For contributions, May 31
5498-ESA	Coverdell ESA Contribution Information	Contributions (including rollover contributions) to a Coverdell ESA.	All amounts	May 31	April 30
5498-QA	ABLE Account Contributions Information	Contributions (including rollover contributions) to an ABLE account.	All amounts	May 31	March 15

Form	Title	What To Report	Amounts To Report	Due Date To IRS	Due Date To Recipient (unless indicated otherwise)
5498-SA	HSA, Archer MSA, or Medicare Advantage MSA Information	Contributions to an HSA (including transfers and rollovers) or Archer MSA and the FMV of an HSA, Archer MSA, or Medicare Advantage MSA.	All amounts	May 31	(To Participant) May 31
W-2G	Certain Gambling Winnings	Gambling winnings from horse racing, dog racing, jai alai, lotteries, keno, bingo, slot machines, sweepstakes, wagering pools, poker tournaments, etc.	Generally, $600 or more; $1,200 or more from bingo or slot machines; $1,500 or more from keno	February 28*	January 31
W-2	Wage and Tax Statement	Wages, tips, other compensation; Social Security, Medicare, and withheld income taxes. Include bonuses, vacation allowances, severance pay, certain moving expense payments, some kinds of travel allowances, and third-party payments of sick pay.	See separate instructions	**(TO SSA)** January 31	**(To Recipient)** January 31

+ **Note:** If any payments for nonemployee compensation are reported in box 7, the due date is January 31.
* The due date is March 31 if filed electronically.
** The due date is March 15 for reporting by trustees and middlemen of widely-held financial investment trusts (WHFITs).

¶ 65 Checklist for Types of Payments

The following chart lists common payments and the forms used to file and report them. It is not a complete list of all payments, and the absence of a payment from the list does not indicate that the payment is not reportable.

Type of Payment	Report on Form
ABLE (Achieve a Better Living Experience) accounts:	
Contributions	5498-QA
Distributions	1099-QA
Abandonment	1099-A
Accelerated death benefits	1099-LTC
Acquisition of control	1099-CAP
Agriculture payments	1099-G
Allocated tips	W-2
Alternate TAA payments	1099-G
Annuities	1099-R
Archer MSAs:	
Contributions	5498-SA
Distributions	1099-SA
Attorney, fees and gross proceeds	1099-MISC
Auto reimbursements:	
Employee	W-2
Nonemployee	1099-MISC
Awards:	
Employee	W-2
Nonemployee	1099-MISC
Barter exchange income	1099-B
Bond tax credit	1097-BTC
Bonuses:	
Employee	W-2
Nonemployee	1099-MISC
Broker transactions	1099-B
Cancellation of debt	1099-C
Capital gain distributions	1099-DIV
Car expenses:	
Employee	W-2
Nonemployee	1099-MISC
Changes in capital structure	1099-CAP
Charitable gift annuities	1099-R
Commissions:	
Employee	W-2
Nonemployee	1099-MISC
Commodities transactions	1099-B
Compensation:	
Employee	W-2
Nonemployee	1099-MISC
Contributions of motor vehicles, boats, and airplanes	1098-C
Cost of current life insurance protection	1099-R
Coverdell Educational Savings Accounts (ESAs):	
Contributions	5498-ESA
Distributions	1099-Q
Crop insurance proceeds	1099-MISC
Damages	1099-MISC
Death benefits	1099-R
Accelerated death benefits	1099-LTC
Debt cancellation	1099-C
Dependent care payments	W-2
Direct rollovers	1099-Q, 1099-R, 5498
Direct sales of consumer products for resale	1099-MISC
Directors' fees	1099-MISC
Discharge of indebtedness	1099-C
Dividends	1099-DIV
Donation of motor vehicle	1098-C
Education loan interest	1098-E
Employee business expense reimbursement	W-2
Employee compensation	W-2
Excess deferrals, excess contributions, distributions of	1099-R
Exercise of incentive stock option under Code Sec. 422(b)	3921
Fees, employee	W-2
Fees, nonemployee	1099-MISC
Fishing boat crew members proceeds	1099-MISC
Fish purchases for cash	1099-MISC
Foreclosures	1099-A
Foreign persons' income	1042-S
401(k) contributions	W-2
404(k) dividend	1099-DIV
Gambling winnings	W-2G
Golden parachute:	
Employee	W-2
Nonemployee	1099-MISC
Grants, taxable	1099-G
Health care services	1099-MISC
Health savings accounts (HSAs):	
Contributions	5498-SA
Distributions	1099-SA
Income attributable to domestic production activities, deduction for	1099-PATR
Income tax refunds, state and local	1099-G
Indian gaming profits paid to tribal members	1099-MISC
Interest income	1099-INT
Tax-exempt	1099-INT
Interest, mortgage	1098
Individual Retirement Account (IRA):	
Contributions	5498
Distributions	1099-R
Life insurance contract distributions	1099-R, 1099-LTC
Liquidation, distributions in	1099-DIV
Loans, distribution from pension plan	1099-R
Long-term care benefits	1099-LTC
Medicare Advantage MSAs:	
Contributions	5498-SA
Distributions	1099-SA
Medical services	1099-MISC
Mileage:	
Employee	W-2
Nonemployee	1099-MISC
Military retirement	1099-R
Mortgage assistance payments	1098-MA
Mortgage interest	1098
Moving expense	W-2
Nonemployee compensation	1099-MISC
Nonqualified deferred compensation:	
Beneficiary	1099-R
Employee	W-2
Nonemployee	1099-MISC
Original issue discount (OID)	1099-OID
Patronage dividends	1099-PATR
Payment card transactions	1099-K

Type of Payment	Report on Form
Pensions	1099-R
Points	1098
Prizes:	
Employee	W-2
Nonemployee	1099-MISC
Profit-sharing plan	1099-R
Punitive damages	1099-MISC
Qualified longevity annuity contract information	1098-Q
Qualified plan distributions	1099-R
Qualified tuition program (QTP) payments	1099-Q
Real estate transactions	1099-S
Recharacterized IRA contributions	1099-R, 5498
Refund, state and local tax	1099-G
Rents	1099-MISC
Retirement	1099-R
Roth conversion IRAs:	
Contributions	5498
Distributions	1099-R
Roth IRAs:	
Contributions	5498
Distributions	1099-R
Royalties	1099-MISC, 1099-S
Timber, pay-as-cut contract	1099-S
Sales:	
Real estate	1099-S
Securities	1099-B
Code Sec. 1035 exchange	1099-R
SEPs:	
Contributions	W-2, 5498
Distributions	1099-R
Severance pay	W-2
Sick pay	W-2
SIMPLEs:	
Contributions	W-2, 5498
Distributions	1099-R
Student loan interest	1098-E
Substitute payments in lieu of dividends or tax-exempt interest	1099-MISC
Supplemental unemployment	W-2
Tax refunds, state and local	1099-G
Third-party network payments	1099-K
Tips	W-2
Traditional individual retirement accounts (Traditional IRAs):	
Contirbutions	5498
Distributions	1099-R
Transfer of stock acquired through an employee stock purchase plan under Code Sec. 423(c)	3922
Tuition	1098-T
Unemployment benefits	1099-G
Vacation allowance:	
Employee	W-2
Nonemployee	1099-MISC
Wages	W-2

SPECIAL TAX TABLES

	Par.
Applicable Federal Rates	83
Adjusted Applicable Federal Rates	84
Federal Long-Term Tax-Exempt Rates	85
Applicable Credit Percentages for Low-Income Housing	86
Earned Income Credit	87
Average Itemized Deductions	88

¶ 83 Applicable Federal Rates

Following are the monthly applicable federal interest rates for January 2016 through November 2016 published by the IRS for purposes of testing imputed interest in below-market interest loans (¶ 795) and debt-for-property transactions (¶ 1954). The rates are also relevant under the golden parachute rules (¶ 907) and for testing interest in connection with deferred payments for the use of property (¶ 1859).

In the case of below-market interest loans that are demand or gift loans, an amount deemed the "foregone" interest is treated as transferred from the lender to the borrower and retransferred by the borrower to the lender as interest. In order to simplify the computation of such foregone interest, the IRS prescribes a "blended annual rate," which is 0.73% on loans for the calendar year 2016.

	Period for Compounding			
	Annual	*Semiannual*	*Quarterly*	*Monthly*
January 2016				
Short-Term				
AFR	.75	.75	.75	.75
110% AFR	.83	.83	.83	.83
120% AFR	.90	.90	.90	.90
130% AFR	.98	.98	.98	.98
Mid-Term				
AFR	1.81	1.80	1.80	1.79
110% AFR	1.99	1.98	1.98	1.97
120% AFR	2.17	2.16	2.15	2.15
130% AFR	2.35	2.34	2.33	2.33
150% AFR	2.72	2.70	2.69	2.68
175% AFR	3.17	3.15	3.14	3.13
Long-Term				
AFR	2.65	2.63	2.62	2.62
110% AFR	2.91	2.89	2.88	2.87
120% AFR	3.18	3.16	3.15	3.14
130% AFR	3.45	3.42	3.41	3.40

	Period for Compounding			
	Annual	*Semiannual*	*Quarterly*	*Monthly*
February 2016				
Short-Term				
AFR	.81	.81	.81	.81
110% AFR	.89	.89	.89	.89
120% AFR	.97	.97	.97	.97
130% AFR	1.05	1.05	1.05	1.05
Mid-Term				
AFR	1.82	1.81	1.81	1.80
110% AFR	2.00	1.99	1.99	1.98
120% AFR	2.18	2.17	2.16	2.16
130% AFR	2.36	2.35	2.34	2.34
150% AFR	2.74	2.72	2.71	2.70
175% AFR	3.20	3.17	3.16	3.15
Long-Term				
AFR	2.62	2.60	2.59	2.59
110% AFR	2.88	2.86	2.85	2.84
120% AFR	3.14	3.12	3.11	3.10
130% AFR	3.41	3.38	3.37	3.36
March 2016				
Short-Term				
AFR	.65	.65	.65	.65
110% AFR	.72	.72	.72	.72
120% AFR	.78	.78	.78	.78
130% AFR	.85	.85	.85	.85
Mid-Term				
AFR	1.48	1.47	1.47	1.47
110% AFR	1.63	1.62	1.62	1.61
120% AFR	1.77	1.76	1.76	1.75
130% AFR	1.92	1.91	1.91	1.90
150% AFR	2.22	2.21	2.20	2.20
175% AFR	2.59	2.57	2.56	2.56
Long-Term				
AFR	2.33	2.32	2.31	2.31
110% AFR	2.57	2.55	2.54	2.54
120% AFR	2.80	2.78	2.77	2.76
130% AFR	3.04	3.02	3.01	3.00
April 2016				
Short-Term				
AFR	.70	.70	.70	.70
110% AFR	.77	.77	.77	.77
120% AFR	.84	.84	.84	.84
130% AFR	.91	.91	.91	.91
Mid-Term				
AFR	1.45	1.44	1.44	1.44
110% AFR	1.59	1.58	1.58	1.57
120% AFR	1.74	1.73	1.73	1.72
130% AFR	1.88	1.87	1.87	1.86
150% AFR	2.17	2.16	2.15	2.15
175% AFR	2.54	2.52	2.51	2.51
Long-Term				
AFR	2.25	2.24	2.23	2.23
110% AFR	2.48	2.46	2.45	2.45
120% AFR	2.71	2.69	2.68	2.68
130% AFR	2.93	2.91	2.90	2.89

		Period for Compounding			
		Annual	*Semiannual*	*Quarterly*	*Monthly*
May 2016					
	Short-Term				
	AFR	.67	.67	.67	.67
110%	AFR	.74	.74	.74	.74
120%	AFR	.80	.80	.80	.80
130%	AFR	.87	.87	.87	.87
	Mid-Term				
	AFR	1.43	1.42	1.42	1.42
110%	AFR	1.57	1.56	1.56	1.55
120%	AFR	1.71	1.70	1.70	1.69
130%	AFR	1.86	1.85	1.85	1.84
150%	AFR	2.14	2.13	2.12	2.12
175%	AFR	2.51	2.49	2.48	2.48
	Long-Term				
	AFR	2.24	2.23	2.22	2.22
110%	AFR	2.47	2.45	2.44	2.44
120%	AFR	2.70	2.68	2.67	2.67
130%	AFR	2.92	2.90	2.89	2.88
June 2016					
	Short-Term				
	AFR	.64	.64	.64	.64
110%	AFR	.70	.70	.70	.70
120%	AFR	.77	.77	.77	.77
130%	AFR	.83	.83	.83	.83
	Mid-Term				
	AFR	1.41	1.41	1.41	1.41
110%	AFR	1.56	1.55	1.55	1.55
120%	AFR	1.70	1.69	1.69	1.68
130%	AFR	1.84	1.83	1.83	1.82
150%	AFR	2.13	2.12	2.11	2.11
175%	AFR	2.49	2.47	2.46	2.46
	Long-Term				
	AFR	2.24	2.23	2.22	2.22
110%	AFR	2.47	2.45	2.44	2.44
120%	AFR	2.70	2.68	2.67	2.67
130%	AFR	2.92	2.90	2.89	2.88
July 2016					
	Short-Term				
	AFR	.71	.71	.71	.71
110%	AFR	.78	.78	.78	.78
120%	AFR	.85	.85	.85	.85
130%	AFR	.92	.92	.92	.92
	Mid-Term				
	AFR	1.43	1.42	1.42	1.42
110%	AFR	1.57	1.56	1.56	1.55
120%	AFR	1.71	1.70	1.70	1.69
130%	AFR	1.86	1.85	1.85	1.84
150%	AFR	2.14	2.13	2.12	2.12
175%	AFR	2.51	2.49	2.48	2.48
	Long-Term				
	AFR	2.18	2.17	2.16	2.16
110%	AFR	2.40	2.39	2.38	2.38
120%	AFR	2.62	2.60	2.59	2.59
130%	AFR	2.84	2.82	2.81	2.80

		Period for Compounding			
		Annual	*Semiannual*	*Quarterly*	*Monthly*
August 2016					
	Short-Term				
	AFR	.56	.56	.56	.56
110%	AFR	.62	.62	.62	.62
120%	AFR	.67	.67	.67	.67
130%	AFR	.73	.73	.73	.73
	Mid-Term				
	AFR	1.18	1.18	1.18	1.18
110%	AFR	1.30	1.30	1.30	1.30
120%	AFR	1.43	1.42	1.42	1.42
130%	AFR	1.54	1.53	1.53	1.53
150%	AFR	1.78	1.77	1.77	1.76
175%	AFR	2.08	2.07	2.06	2.06
	Long-Term				
	AFR	1.90	1.89	1.89	1.88
110%	AFR	2.09	2.08	2.07	2.07
120%	AFR	2.28	2.27	2.26	2.26
130%	AFR	2.48	2.46	2.45	2.45
September 2016					
	Short-Term				
	AFR	.61	.61	.61	.61
110%	AFR	.67	.67	.67	.67
120%	AFR	.73	.73	.73	.73
130%	AFR	.79	.79	.79	.79
	Mid-Term				
	AFR	1.22	1.22	1.22	1.22
110%	AFR	1.34	1.34	1.34	1.34
120%	AFR	1.47	1.46	1.46	1.46
130%	AFR	1.60	1.59	1.59	1.58
150%	AFR	1.84	1.83	1.83	1.82
175%	AFR	2.15	2.14	2.13	2.13
	Long-Term				
	AFR	1.90	1.89	1.89	1.88
110%	AFR	2.09	2.08	2.07	2.07
120%	AFR	2.28	2.27	2.26	2.26
130%	AFR	2.48	2.46	2.45	2.45
October 2016					
	Short-Term				
	AFR	.66	.66	.66	.66
110%	AFR	.73	.73	.73	.73
120%	AFR	.79	.79	.79	.79
130%	AFR	.86	.86	.86	.86
	Mid-Term				
	AFR	1.29	1.29	1.29	1.29
110%	AFR	1.43	1.42	1.42	1.42
120%	AFR	1.56	1.55	1.55	1.55
130%	AFR	1.69	1.68	1.68	1.67
150%	AFR	1.95	1.94	1.94	1.93
175%	AFR	2.27	2.26	2.25	2.25
	Long-Term				
	AFR	1.95	1.94	1.94	1.93
110%	AFR	2.14	2.13	2.12	2.12
120%	AFR	2.34	2.33	2.32	2.32
130%	AFR	2.54	2.52	2.51	2.51

		Period for Compounding			
		Annual	*Semiannual*	*Quarterly*	*Monthly*
November 2016					
	Short-Term				
	AFR	.68	.68	.68	.68
110%	AFR	.75	.75	.75	.75
120%	AFR	.82	.82	.82	.82
130%	AFR	.88	.88	.88	.88
	Mid-Term				
	AFR	1.33	1.33	1.33	1.33
110%	AFR	1.47	1.46	1.46	1.46
120%	AFR	1.61	1.60	1.60	1.59
130%	AFR	1.74	1.73	1.73	1.72
150%	AFR	2.01	2.00	2.00	1.99
175%	AFR	2.34	2.33	2.32	2.32
	Long-Term				
	AFR	2.07	2.06	2.05	2.05
110%	AFR	2.28	2.27	2.26	2.26
120%	AFR	2.49	2.47	2.46	2.46
130%	AFR	2.70	2.68	2.67	2.67

¶ 84 Adjusted Applicable Federal Rates

Code Sec. 1288 provides that, in determining original issue discount on tax-exempt obligations, an adjustment must be made to the applicable federal rates (¶ 83) to take into account the tax exemption for interest on the obligations.

Adjusted Applicable Federal Rates

	Annual Compounding	SemiAnnual Compounding	Quarterly Compounding	Monthly Compounding
January 2016				
Short-term rate	.57%	.57%	.57%	.57%
Mid-term rate	1.46%	1.45%	1.45%	1.45%
Long-term rate	2.65%	2.63%	2.62%	2.62%
February 2016				
Short-term rate	.61%	.61%	.61%	.61%
Mid-term rate	1.39%	1.39%	1.39%	1.39%
Long-term rate	2.53%	2.51%	2.50%	2.50%
March 2016				
Short-term rate	.55%	.55%	.55%	.55%
Mid-term rate	1.12%	1.12%	1.12%	1.12%
Long-term rate	2.27%	2.26%	2.25%	2.25%
April 2016				
Short-term rate	.46%	.46%	.46%	.46%
Mid-term rate	1.12%	1.12%	1.12%	1.12%
Long-term rate	2.25%	2.24%	2.23%	2.23%
May 2016				
Short-term rate	.63%	.63%	.63%	.63%
Mid-term rate	1.26%	1.26%	1.26%	1.26%
Long-term rate	2.24%	2.23%	2.22%	2.22%
June 2016				
Short-term rate	.64%	.64%	.64%	.64%
Mid-term rate	1.16%	1.16%	1.16%	1.16%
Long-term rate	2.15%	2.14%	2.13%	2.13%
July 2016				
Short-term rate	.65%	.65%	.65%	.65%
Mid-term rate	1.16%	1.16%	1.16%	1.16%
Long-term rate	2.08%	2.07%	2.06%	2.06%
August 2016				
Short-term rate	.56%	.56%	.56%	.56%
Mid-term rate	1.03%	1.03%	1.03%	1.03%
Long-term rate	1.82%	1.81%	1.81%	1.80%
September 2016				
Short-term rate	.45%	.45%	.45%	.45%
Mid-term rate	.91%	.91%	.91%	.91%
Long-term rate	1.41%	1.41%	1.41%	1.41%

October 2016

	Annual Compounding	*SemiAnnual Compounding*	*Quarterly Compounding*	*Monthly Compounding*
Short-term rate	.49%	.49%	.49%	.49%
Mid-term rate	.96%	.96%	.96%	.96%
Long-term rate	1.45%	1.44%	1.44%	1.44%

November 2016

	Annual Compounding	*SemiAnnual Compounding*	*Quarterly Compounding*	*Monthly Compounding*
Short-term rate	.51%	.51%	.51%	.51%
Mid-term rate	.99%	.99%	.99%	.99%
Long-term rate	1.54%	1.53%	1.53%	1.53%

¶ 85 Federal Long-Term Tax-Exempt Rates

Code Sec. 382 provides that the long-term tax-exempt rate for purposes of net operating loss carryforwards shall be the highest of the adjusted federal long-term rates (¶ 84) for the three months ending with the month in which the particular ownership change occurs. Each rate below is the highest for the 3-month period.

Long-Term Tax-Exempt Rates

Month	*Rate*
January 2016	2.65%
February 2016	2.65%
March 2016	2.65%
April 2016	2.25%
May 2016	2.27%
June 2016	2.25%
July 2016	2.24%
August 2016	2.15%
September 2016	2.08%
October 2016	1.82%
November 2016	1.54%

¶ 86 Applicable Credit Percentages for Low-Income Housing

Code Sec. 42 provides that applicable credit percentages for low-income housing are to be computed so that the present value of the 10 annual credit amounts at the beginning of the 10-year credit period equals either 70% or 30% of the qualified basis of the low-income units in a project. The discount rate for determining the present value in these computations is a rate equal to 72% of the average of the month's AFR for mid-term and long-term obligations. The applicable credit percentage for new construction or rehabilitation expenditures not federally subsidized is indicated under the 70% rate column. The applicable credit percentage for subsidized construction or rehabilitation expenditures and the acquisition of existing housing is indicated under the 30% rate column. See ¶ 1365K.

Applicable Credit Percentages for Low-Income Housing

Month	*70% Rate*	*30% Rate*
January 2016	7.51%	3.22%
February 2016	7.51%	3.22%
March 2016	7.44%	3.19%
April 2016	7.42%	3.18%
May 2016	7.42%	3.18%
June 2016	7.42%	3.18%
July 2016	7.41%	3.18%
August 2016	7.35%	3.15%
September 2016	7.36%	3.15%
October 2016	7.37%	3.16%
November 2016	7.39%	3.17%

Caution: This is a draft 2016 Earned Income Credit (EIC) Table. At the time of publication, the IRS had not yet released the 2016 Earned Income Credit (EIC) Table. For the latest information, see CCHGroup.com/TaxUpdates.

¶ 87 Earned Income Credit

The earned income credit tables are used in conjunction with the Form 1040 or Form 1040A, and Schedule EIC. The Schedule EIC must be filed with the taxpayer's tax return in order to claim the earned income credit. The credit, as computed on the EIC Worksheet found in the Form 1040 instructions, is entered on the appropriate line of Form 1040 or Form 1040A. Form 1040EZ may be used to claim the earned income credit in limited circumstances.

Caution: This is a draft 2016 Earned Income Credit (EIC) Table. At the time of publication, the IRS had not yet released the 2016 Earned Income Credit (EIC) Table. For the latest information, see CCHGroup.com/TaxUpdates.

2016 Earned Income Credit (EIC) Table

Caution. This is **not** a tax table.

1. To find your credit, read down the "At least - But less than" columns and find the line that includes the amount you were told to look up from your EIC Worksheet.

2. Then, go to the column that includes your filing status and the number of qualifying children you have. Enter the credit from that column on your EIC Worksheet.

Example. If your filing status is single, you have one qualifying child, and the amount you are looking up from your EIC Worksheet is $2,455, you would enter $842.

If the amount you are looking up from the worksheet is–		And your filing status is– Single, head of household, or qualifying widow(er) and the number of children you have is–			
		0	1	2	3
At least	But less than	Your credit is–			
2,400	2,450	186	825	970	1,091
2,450	2,500	189	842	990	1,114

DRAFT AS OF October 7, 2016

If the amount you are looking up from the worksheet is–		And your filing status is– Single, head of household, or qualifying widow(er) and the number of children you have is–				Married filing jointly and the number of children you have is–			
		0	1	2	3	0	1	2	3
At least	But less than	Your credit is–				Your credit is–			
$1	$50	$2	$8	$10	$11	$2	$8	$10	$11
50	100	6	26	30	34	6	26	30	34
100	150	10	43	50	56	10	43	50	56
150	200	13	60	70	79	13	60	70	79
200	250	17	77	90	101	17	77	90	101
250	300	21	94	110	124	21	94	110	124
300	350	25	111	130	146	25	111	130	146
350	400	29	128	150	169	29	128	150	169
400	450	33	145	170	191	33	145	170	191
450	500	36	162	190	214	36	162	190	214
500	550	40	179	210	236	40	179	210	236
550	600	44	196	230	259	44	196	230	259
600	650	48	213	250	281	48	213	250	281
650	700	52	230	270	304	52	230	270	304
700	750	55	247	290	326	55	247	290	326
750	800	59	264	310	349	59	264	310	349
800	850	63	281	330	371	63	281	330	371
850	900	67	298	350	394	67	298	350	394
900	950	71	315	370	416	71	315	370	416
950	1,000	75	332	390	439	75	332	390	439
1,000	1,050	78	349	410	461	78	349	410	461
1,050	1,100	82	366	430	484	82	366	430	484
1,100	1,150	86	383	450	506	86	383	450	506
1,150	1,200	90	400	470	529	90	400	470	529
1,200	1,250	94	417	490	551	94	417	490	551
1,250	1,300	98	434	510	574	98	434	510	574
1,300	1,350	101	451	530	596	101	451	530	596
1,350	1,400	105	468	550	619	105	468	550	619
1,400	1,450	109	485	570	641	109	485	570	641
1,450	1,500	113	502	590	664	113	502	590	664
1,500	1,550	117	519	610	686	117	519	610	686
1,550	1,600	120	536	630	709	120	536	630	709
1,600	1,650	124	553	650	731	124	553	650	731
1,650	1,700	128	570	670	754	128	570	670	754
1,700	1,750	132	587	690	776	132	587	690	776
1,750	1,800	136	604	710	799	136	604	710	799
1,800	1,850	140	621	730	821	140	621	730	821
1,850	1,900	143	638	750	844	143	638	750	844
1,900	1,950	147	655	770	866	147	655	770	866
1,950	2,000	151	672	790	889	151	672	790	889
2,000	2,050	155	689	810	911	155	689	810	911
2,050	2,100	159	706	830	934	159	706	830	934
2,100	2,150	163	723	850	956	163	723	850	956
2,150	2,200	166	740	870	979	166	740	870	979
2,200	2,250	170	757	890	1,001	170	757	890	1,001
2,250	2,300	174	774	910	1,024	174	774	910	1,024
2,300	2,350	178	791	930	1,046	178	791	930	1,046
2,350	2,400	182	808	950	1,069	182	808	950	1,069
2,400	2,450	186	825	970	1,091	186	825	970	1,091
2,450	2,500	189	842	990	1,114	189	842	990	1,114
2,500	2,550	193	859	1,010	1,136	193	859	1,010	1,136
2,550	2,600	197	876	1,030	1,159	197	876	1,030	1,159
2,600	2,650	201	893	1,050	1,181	201	893	1,050	1,181
2,650	2,700	205	910	1,070	1,204	205	910	1,070	1,204
2,700	2,750	208	927	1,090	1,226	208	927	1,090	1,226
2,750	2,800	212	944	1,110	1,249	212	944	1,110	1,249

If the amount you are looking up from the worksheet is–		And your filing status is– Single, head of household, or qualifying widow(er) and the number of children you have is–				Married filing jointly and the number of children you have is–			
		0	1	2	3	0	1	2	3
At least	But less than	Your credit is–				Your credit is–			
2,800	2,850	216	961	1,130	1,271	216	961	1,130	1,271
2,850	2,900	220	978	1,150	1,294	220	978	1,150	1,294
2,900	2,950	224	995	1,170	1,316	224	995	1,170	1,316
2,950	3,000	228	1,012	1,190	1,339	228	1,012	1,190	1,339
3,000	3,050	231	1,029	1,210	1,361	231	1,029	1,210	1,361
3,050	3,100	235	1,046	1,230	1,384	235	1,046	1,230	1,384
3,100	3,150	239	1,063	1,250	1,406	239	1,063	1,250	1,406
3,150	3,200	243	1,080	1,270	1,429	243	1,080	1,270	1,429
3,200	3,250	247	1,097	1,290	1,451	247	1,097	1,290	1,451
3,250	3,300	251	1,114	1,310	1,474	251	1,114	1,310	1,474
3,300	3,350	254	1,131	1,330	1,496	254	1,131	1,330	1,496
3,350	3,400	258	1,148	1,350	1,519	258	1,148	1,350	1,519
3,400	3,450	262	1,165	1,370	1,541	262	1,165	1,370	1,541
3,450	3,500	266	1,182	1,390	1,564	266	1,182	1,390	1,564
3,500	3,550	270	1,199	1,410	1,586	270	1,199	1,410	1,586
3,550	3,600	273	1,216	1,430	1,609	273	1,216	1,430	1,609
3,600	3,650	277	1,233	1,450	1,631	277	1,233	1,450	1,631
3,650	3,700	281	1,250	1,470	1,654	281	1,250	1,470	1,654
3,700	3,750	285	1,267	1,490	1,676	285	1,267	1,490	1,676
3,750	3,800	289	1,284	1,510	1,699	289	1,284	1,510	1,699
3,800	3,850	293	1,301	1,530	1,721	293	1,301	1,530	1,721
3,850	3,900	296	1,318	1,550	1,744	296	1,318	1,550	1,744
3,900	3,950	300	1,335	1,570	1,766	300	1,335	1,570	1,766
3,950	4,000	304	1,352	1,590	1,789	304	1,352	1,590	1,789
4,000	4,050	308	1,369	1,610	1,811	308	1,369	1,610	1,811
4,050	4,100	312	1,386	1,630	1,834	312	1,386	1,630	1,834
4,100	4,150	316	1,403	1,650	1,856	316	1,403	1,650	1,856
4,150	4,200	319	1,420	1,670	1,879	319	1,420	1,670	1,879
4,200	4,250	323	1,437	1,690	1,901	323	1,437	1,690	1,901
4,250	4,300	327	1,454	1,710	1,924	327	1,454	1,710	1,924
4,300	4,350	331	1,471	1,730	1,946	331	1,471	1,730	1,946
4,350	4,400	335	1,488	1,750	1,969	335	1,488	1,750	1,969
4,400	4,450	339	1,505	1,770	1,991	339	1,505	1,770	1,991
4,450	4,500	342	1,522	1,790	2,014	342	1,522	1,790	2,014
4,500	4,550	346	1,539	1,810	2,036	346	1,539	1,810	2,036
4,550	4,600	350	1,556	1,830	2,059	350	1,556	1,830	2,059
4,600	4,650	354	1,573	1,850	2,081	354	1,573	1,850	2,081
4,650	4,700	358	1,590	1,870	2,104	358	1,590	1,870	2,104
4,700	4,750	361	1,607	1,890	2,126	361	1,607	1,890	2,126
4,750	4,800	365	1,624	1,910	2,149	365	1,624	1,910	2,149
4,800	4,850	369	1,641	1,930	2,171	369	1,641	1,930	2,171
4,850	4,900	373	1,658	1,950	2,194	373	1,658	1,950	2,194
4,900	4,950	377	1,675	1,970	2,216	377	1,675	1,970	2,216
4,950	5,000	381	1,692	1,990	2,239	381	1,692	1,990	2,239
5,000	5,050	384	1,709	2,010	2,261	384	1,709	2,010	2,261
5,050	5,100	388	1,726	2,030	2,284	388	1,726	2,030	2,284
5,100	5,150	392	1,743	2,050	2,306	392	1,743	2,050	2,306
5,150	5,200	396	1,760	2,070	2,329	396	1,760	2,070	2,329
5,200	5,250	400	1,777	2,090	2,351	400	1,777	2,090	2,351
5,250	5,300	404	1,794	2,110	2,374	404	1,794	2,110	2,374
5,300	5,350	407	1,811	2,130	2,396	407	1,811	2,130	2,396
5,350	5,400	411	1,828	2,150	2,419	411	1,828	2,150	2,419
5,400	5,450	415	1,845	2,170	2,441	415	1,845	2,170	2,441
5,450	5,500	419	1,862	2,190	2,464	419	1,862	2,190	2,464
5,500	5,550	423	1,879	2,210	2,486	423	1,879	2,210	2,486
5,550	5,600	426	1,896	2,230	2,509	426	1,896	2,230	2,509

(Continued)

Need more information or forms? Visit IRS.gov.

Caution: This is a draft 2016 Earned Income Credit (EIC) Table. At the time of publication, the IRS had not yet released the 2016 Earned Income Credit (EIC) Table. For the latest information, see CCHGroup.com/TaxUpdates.

Earned Income Credit (EIC) Table - *Continued*

(Caution. This is **not** a tax table.)

If the amount you are looking up from the worksheet is–		And your filing status is– Single, head of household, or qualifying widow(er) and the number of children you have is–				Married filing jointly and the number of children you have is–			
		0	1	2	3	0	1	2	3
At least	But less than	Your credit is–				Your credit is–			
5,600	5,650	430	1,913	2,250	2,531	430	1,913	2,250	2,531
5,650	5,700	434	1,930	2,270	2,554	434	1,930	2,270	2,554
5,700	5,750	438	1,947	2,290	2,576	438	1,947	2,290	2,576
5,750	5,800	442	1,964	2,310	2,599	442	1,964	2,310	2,599
5,800	5,850	446	1,981	2,330	2,621	446	1,981	2,330	2,621
5,850	5,900	449	1,998	2,350	2,644	449	1,998	2,350	2,644
5,900	5,950	453	2,015	2,370	2,666	453	2,015	2,370	2,666
5,950	6,000	457	2,032	2,390	2,689	457	2,032	2,390	2,689
6,000	6,050	461	2,049	2,410	2,711	461	2,049	2,410	2,711
6,050	6,100	465	2,066	2,430	2,734	465	2,066	2,430	2,734
6,100	6,150	469	2,083	2,450	2,756	469	2,083	2,450	2,756
6,150	6,200	472	2,100	2,470	2,779	472	2,100	2,470	2,779
6,200	6,250	476	2,117	2,490	2,801	476	2,117	2,490	2,801
6,250	6,300	480	2,134	2,510	2,824	480	2,134	2,510	2,824
6,300	6,350	484	2,151	2,530	2,846	484	2,151	2,530	2,846
6,350	6,400	488	2,168	2,550	2,869	488	2,168	2,550	2,869
6,400	6,450	492	2,185	2,570	2,891	492	2,185	2,570	2,891
6,450	6,500	495	2,202	2,590	2,914	495	2,202	2,590	2,914
6,500	6,550	499	2,219	2,610	2,936	499	2,219	2,610	2,936
6,550	6,600	503	2,236	2,630	2,959	503	2,236	2,630	2,959
6,600	6,650	506	2,253	2,650	2,981	506	2,253	2,650	2,981
6,650	6,700	506	2,270	2,670	3,004	506	2,270	2,670	3,004
6,700	6,750	506	2,287	2,690	3,026	506	2,287	2,690	3,026
6,750	6,800	506	2,304	2,710	3,049	506	2,304	2,710	3,049
6,800	6,850	506	2,321	2,730	3,071	506	2,321	2,730	3,071
6,850	6,900	506	2,338	2,750	3,094	506	2,338	2,750	3,094
6,900	6,950	506	2,355	2,770	3,116	506	2,355	2,770	3,116
6,950	7,000	506	2,372	2,790	3,139	506	2,372	2,790	3,139
7,000	7,050	506	2,389	2,810	3,161	506	2,389	2,810	3,161
7,050	7,100	506	2,406	2,830	3,184	506	2,406	2,830	3,184
7,100	7,150	506	2,423	2,850	3,206	506	2,423	2,850	3,206
7,150	7,200	506	2,440	2,870	3,229	506	2,440	2,870	3,229
7,200	7,250	506	2,457	2,890	3,251	506	2,457	2,890	3,251
7,250	7,300	506	2,474	2,910	3,274	506	2,474	2,910	3,274
7,300	7,350	506	2,491	2,930	3,296	506	2,491	2,930	3,296
7,350	7,400	506	2,508	2,950	3,319	506	2,508	2,950	3,319
7,400	7,450	506	2,525	2,970	3,341	506	2,525	2,970	3,341
7,450	7,500	506	2,542	2,990	3,364	506	2,542	2,990	3,364
7,500	7,550	506	2,559	3,010	3,386	506	2,559	3,010	3,386
7,550	7,600	506	2,576	3,030	3,409	506	2,576	3,030	3,409
7,600	7,650	506	2,593	3,050	3,431	506	2,593	3,050	3,431
7,650	7,700	506	2,610	3,070	3,454	506	2,610	3,070	3,454
7,700	7,750	506	2,627	3,090	3,476	506	2,627	3,090	3,476
7,750	7,800	506	2,644	3,110	3,499	506	2,644	3,110	3,499
7,800	7,850	506	2,661	3,130	3,521	506	2,661	3,130	3,521
7,850	7,900	506	2,678	3,150	3,544	506	2,678	3,150	3,544
7,900	7,950	506	2,695	3,170	3,566	506	2,695	3,170	3,566
7,950	8,000	506	2,712	3,190	3,589	506	2,712	3,190	3,589
8,000	8,050	506	2,729	3,210	3,611	506	2,729	3,210	3,611
8,050	8,100	506	2,746	3,230	3,634	506	2,746	3,230	3,634
8,100	8,150	506	2,763	3,250	3,656	506	2,763	3,250	3,656
8,150	8,200	506	2,780	3,270	3,679	506	2,780	3,270	3,679
8,200	8,250	506	2,797	3,290	3,701	506	2,797	3,290	3,701
8,250	8,300	506	2,814	3,310	3,724	506	2,814	3,310	3,724
8,300	8,350	501	2,831	3,330	3,746	506	2,831	3,330	3,746
8,350	8,400	498	2,848	3,350	3,769	506	2,848	3,350	3,769
8,400	8,450	494	2,865	3,370	3,791	506	2,865	3,370	3,791
8,450	8,500	490	2,882	3,390	3,814	506	2,882	3,390	3,814
8,500	8,550	486	2,899	3,410	3,836	506	2,899	3,410	3,836
8,550	8,600	482	2,916	3,430	3,859	506	2,916	3,430	3,859
8,600	8,650	479	2,933	3,450	3,881	506	2,933	3,450	3,881
8,650	8,700	475	2,950	3,470	3,904	506	2,950	3,470	3,904
8,700	8,750	471	2,967	3,490	3,926	506	2,967	3,490	3,926
8,750	8,800	467	2,984	3,510	3,949	506	2,984	3,510	3,949
8,800	8,850	463	3,001	3,530	3,971	506	3,001	3,530	3,971
8,850	8,900	459	3,018	3,550	3,994	506	3,018	3,550	3,994
8,900	8,950	456	3,035	3,570	4,016	506	3,035	3,570	4,016
8,950	9,000	452	3,052	3,590	4,039	506	3,052	3,590	4,039
9,000	9,050	448	3,069	3,610	4,061	506	3,069	3,610	4,061
9,050	9,100	444	3,086	3,630	4,084	506	3,086	3,630	4,084
9,100	9,150	440	3,103	3,650	4,106	506	3,103	3,650	4,106
9,150	9,200	436	3,120	3,670	4,129	506	3,120	3,670	4,129
9,200	9,250	433	3,137	3,690	4,151	506	3,137	3,690	4,151
9,250	9,300	429	3,154	3,710	4,174	506	3,154	3,710	4,174
9,300	9,350	425	3,171	3,730	4,196	506	3,171	3,730	4,196
9,350	9,400	421	3,188	3,750	4,219	506	3,188	3,750	4,219
9,400	9,450	417	3,205	3,770	4,241	506	3,205	3,770	4,241
9,450	9,500	413	3,222	3,790	4,264	506	3,222	3,790	4,264
9,500	9,550	410	3,239	3,810	4,286	506	3,239	3,810	4,286
9,550	9,600	406	3,256	3,830	4,309	506	3,256	3,830	4,309
9,600	9,650	402	3,273	3,850	4,331	506	3,273	3,850	4,331
9,650	9,700	398	3,290	3,870	4,354	506	3,290	3,870	4,354
9,700	9,750	394	3,307	3,890	4,376	506	3,307	3,890	4,376
9,750	9,800	391	3,324	3,910	4,399	506	3,324	3,910	4,399
9,800	9,850	387	3,341	3,930	4,421	506	3,341	3,930	4,421
9,850	9,900	383	3,358	3,950	4,444	506	3,358	3,950	4,444
9,900	9,950	379	3,373	3,970	4,466	506	3,373	3,970	4,466
9,950	10,000	375	3,373	3,990	4,489	506	3,373	3,990	4,489
10,000	10,050	371	3,373	4,010	4,511	506	3,373	4,010	4,511
10,050	10,100	368	3,373	4,030	4,534	506	3,373	4,030	4,534
10,100	10,150	364	3,373	4,050	4,556	506	3,373	4,050	4,556
10,150	10,200	360	3,373	4,070	4,579	506	3,373	4,070	4,579
10,200	10,250	356	3,373	4,090	4,601	506	3,373	4,090	4,601
10,250	10,300	352	3,373	4,110	4,624	506	3,373	4,110	4,624
10,300	10,350	348	3,373	4,130	4,646	506	3,373	4,130	4,646
10,350	10,400	345	3,373	4,150	4,669	506	3,373	4,150	4,669
10,400	10,450	341	3,373	4,170	4,691	506	3,373	4,170	4,691
10,450	10,500	337	3,373	4,190	4,714	506	3,373	4,190	4,714
10,500	10,550	333	3,373	4,210	4,736	506	3,373	4,210	4,736
10,550	10,600	329	3,373	4,230	4,759	506	3,373	4,230	4,759
10,600	10,650	326	3,373	4,250	4,781	506	3,373	4,250	4,781
10,650	10,700	322	3,373	4,270	4,804	506	3,373	4,270	4,804
10,700	10,750	318	3,373	4,290	4,826	506	3,373	4,290	4,826
10,750	10,800	314	3,373	4,310	4,849	506	3,373	4,310	4,849
10,800	10,850	310	3,373	4,330	4,871	506	3,373	4,330	4,871
10,850	10,900	306	3,373	4,350	4,894	506	3,373	4,350	4,894
10,900	10,950	303	3,373	4,370	4,916	506	3,373	4,370	4,916
10,950	11,000	299	3,373	4,390	4,939	506	3,373	4,390	4,939
11,000	11,050	295	3,373	4,410	4,961	506	3,373	4,410	4,961
11,050	11,100	291	3,373	4,430	4,984	506	3,373	4,430	4,984
11,100	11,150	287	3,373	4,450	5,006	506	3,373	4,450	5,006
11,150	11,200	283	3,373	4,470	5,029	506	3,373	4,470	5,029
11,200	11,250	280	3,373	4,490	5,051	506	3,373	4,490	5,051
11,250	11,300	276	3,373	4,510	5,074	506	3,373	4,510	5,074
11,300	11,350	272	3,373	4,530	5,096	506	3,373	4,530	5,096
11,350	11,400	268	3,373	4,550	5,119	506	3,373	4,550	5,119
11,400	11,450	264	3,373	4,570	5,141	506	3,373	4,570	5,141
11,450	11,500	260	3,373	4,590	5,164	506	3,373	4,590	5,164
11,500	11,550	257	3,373	4,610	5,186	506	3,373	4,610	5,186
11,550	11,600	253	3,373	4,630	5,209	506	3,373	4,630	5,209
11,600	11,650	249	3,373	4,650	5,231	506	3,373	4,650	5,231
11,650	11,700	245	3,373	4,670	5,254	506	3,373	4,670	5,254
11,700	11,750	241	3,373	4,690	5,276	506	3,373	4,690	5,276
11,750	11,800	238	3,373	4,710	5,299	506	3,373	4,710	5,299
11,800	11,850	234	3,373	4,730	5,321	506	3,373	4,730	5,321
11,850	11,900	230	3,373	4,750	5,344	506	3,373	4,750	5,344
11,900	11,950	226	3,373	4,770	5,366	506	3,373	4,770	5,366
11,950	12,000	222	3,373	4,790	5,389	506	3,373	4,790	5,389
12,000	12,050	218	3,373	4,810	5,411	506	3,373	4,810	5,411
12,050	12,100	215	3,373	4,830	5,434	506	3,373	4,830	5,434
12,100	12,150	211	3,373	4,850	5,456	506	3,373	4,850	5,456
12,150	12,200	207	3,373	4,870	5,479	506	3,373	4,870	5,479
12,200	12,250	203	3,373	4,890	5,501	506	3,373	4,890	5,501
12,250	12,300	199	3,373	4,910	5,524	506	3,373	4,910	5,524
12,300	12,350	195	3,373	4,930	5,546	506	3,373	4,930	5,546
12,350	12,400	192	3,373	4,950	5,569	506	3,373	4,950	5,569
12,400	12,450	188	3,373	4,970	5,591	506	3,373	4,970	5,591
12,450	12,500	184	3,373	4,990	5,614	506	3,373	4,990	5,614
12,500	12,550	180	3,373	5,010	5,636	506	3,373	5,010	5,636
12,550	12,600	176	3,373	5,030	5,659	506	3,373	5,030	5,659
12,600	12,650	173	3,373	5,050	5,681	506	3,373	5,050	5,681
12,650	12,700	169	3,373	5,070	5,704	506	3,373	5,070	5,704
12,700	12,750	165	3,373	5,090	5,726	506	3,373	5,090	5,726
12,750	12,800	161	3,373	5,110	5,749	506	3,373	5,110	5,749

(Continued)

Caution: This is a draft 2016 Earned Income Credit (EIC) Table. At the time of publication, the IRS had not yet released the 2016 Earned Income Credit (EIC) Table. For the latest information, see CCHGroup.com/TaxUpdates.

Earned Income Credit (EIC) Table - *Continued*

(**Caution.** This is **not** a tax table.)

If the amount you are looking up from the worksheet is–		And your filing status is– Single, head of household, or qualifying widow(er) and the number of children you have is–				Married filing jointly and the number of children you have is–			
		0	1	2	3	0	1	2	3
At least	But less than	Your credit is–				Your credit is–			
12,800	12,850	157	3,373	5,130	5,771	506	3,373	5,130	5,771
12,850	12,900	153	3,373	5,150	5,794	506	3,373	5,150	5,794
12,900	12,950	150	3,373	5,170	5,816	506	3,373	5,170	5,816
12,950	13,000	146	3,373	5,190	5,839	506	3,373	5,190	5,839
13,000	13,050	142	3,373	5,210	5,861	506	3,373	5,210	5,861
13,050	13,100	138	3,373	5,230	5,884	506	3,373	5,230	5,884
13,100	13,150	134	3,373	5,250	5,906	506	3,373	5,250	5,906
13,150	13,200	130	3,373	5,270	5,929	506	3,373	5,270	5,929
13,200	13,250	127	3,373	5,290	5,951	506	3,373	5,290	5,951
13,250	13,300	123	3,373	5,310	5,974	506	3,373	5,310	5,974
13,300	13,350	119	3,373	5,330	5,996	506	3,373	5,330	5,996
13,350	13,400	115	3,373	5,350	6,019	506	3,373	5,350	6,019
13,400	13,450	111	3,373	5,370	6,041	506	3,373	5,370	6,041
13,450	13,500	107	3,373	5,390	6,064	506	3,373	5,390	6,064
13,500	13,550	104	3,373	5,410	6,086	506	3,373	5,410	6,086
13,550	13,600	100	3,373	5,430	6,109	506	3,373	5,430	6,109
13,600	13,650	96	3,373	5,450	6,131	506	3,373	5,450	6,131
13,650	13,700	92	3,373	5,470	6,154	506	3,373	5,470	6,154
13,700	13,750	88	3,373	5,490	6,176	506	3,373	5,490	6,176
13,750	13,800	85	3,373	5,510	6,199	506	3,373	5,510	6,199
13,800	13,850	81	3,373	5,530	6,221	506	3,373	5,530	6,221
13,850	13,900	77	3,373	5,550	6,244	501	3,373	5,550	6,244
13,900	13,950	73	3,373	5,572	6,269	498	3,373	5,572	6,269
13,950	14,000	69	3,373	5,572	6,269	494	3,373	5,572	6,269
14,000	14,050	65	3,373	5,572	6,269	490	3,373	5,572	6,269
14,050	14,100	62	3,373	5,572	6,269	486	3,373	5,572	6,269
14,100	14,150	58	3,373	5,572	6,269	482	3,373	5,572	6,269
14,150	14,200	54	3,373	5,572	6,269	479	3,373	5,572	6,269
14,200	14,250	50	3,373	5,572	6,269	475	3,373	5,572	6,269
14,250	14,300	46	3,373	5,572	6,269	471	3,373	5,572	6,269
14,300	14,350	42	3,373	5,572	6,269	467	3,373	5,572	6,269
14,350	14,400	39	3,373	5,572	6,269	463	3,373	5,572	6,269
14,400	14,450	35	3,373	5,572	6,269	459	3,373	5,572	6,269
14,450	14,500	31	3,373	5,572	6,269	456	3,373	5,572	6,269
14,500	14,550	27	3,373	5,572	6,269	452	3,373	5,572	6,269
14,550	14,600	23	3,373	5,572	6,269	448	3,373	5,572	6,269
14,600	14,650	20	3,373	5,572	6,269	444	3,373	5,572	6,269
14,650	14,700	16	3,373	5,572	6,269	440	3,373	5,572	6,269
14,700	14,750	12	3,373	5,572	6,269	436	3,373	5,572	6,269
14,750	14,800	8	3,373	5,572	6,269	433	3,373	5,572	6,269
14,800	14,850	4	3,373	5,572	6,269	429	3,373	5,572	6,269
14,850	14,900	*	3,373	5,572	6,269	425	3,373	5,572	6,269
14,900	14,950	0	3,373	5,572	6,269	421	3,373	5,572	6,269
14,950	15,000	0	3,373	5,572	6,269	417	3,373	5,572	6,269
15,000	15,050	0	3,373	5,572	6,269	413	3,373	5,572	6,269
15,050	15,100	0	3,373	5,572	6,269	410	3,373	5,572	6,269
15,100	15,150	0	3,373	5,572	6,269	406	3,373	5,572	6,269
15,150	15,200	0	3,373	5,572	6,269	402	3,373	5,572	6,269
15,200	15,250	0	3,373	5,572	6,269	398	3,373	5,572	6,269
15,250	15,300	0	3,373	5,572	6,269	394	3,373	5,572	6,269
15,300	15,350	0	3,373	5,572	6,269	391	3,373	5,572	6,269
15,350	15,400	0	3,373	5,572	6,269	387	3,373	5,572	6,269
15,400	15,450	0	3,373	5,572	6,269	383	3,373	5,572	6,269
15,450	15,500	0	3,373	5,572	6,269	379	3,373	5,572	6,269
15,500	15,550	0	3,373	5,572	6,269	375	3,373	5,572	6,269
15,550	15,600	0	3,373	5,572	6,269	371	3,373	5,572	6,269
15,600	15,650	0	3,373	5,572	6,269	368	3,373	5,572	6,269
15,650	15,700	0	3,373	5,572	6,269	364	3,373	5,572	6,269
15,700	15,750	0	3,373	5,572	6,269	360	3,373	5,572	6,269
15,750	15,800	0	3,373	5,572	6,269	356	3,373	5,572	6,269
15,800	15,850	0	3,373	5,572	6,269	352	3,373	5,572	6,269
15,850	15,900	0	3,373	5,572	6,269	348	3,373	5,572	6,269
15,900	15,950	0	3,373	5,572	6,269	345	3,373	5,572	6,269
15,950	16,000	0	3,373	5,572	6,269	341	3,373	5,572	6,269
16,000	16,050	0	3,373	5,572	6,269	337	3,373	5,572	6,269
16,050	16,100	0	3,373	5,572	6,269	333	3,373	5,572	6,269
16,100	16,150	0	3,373	5,572	6,269	329	3,373	5,572	6,269
16,150	16,200	0	3,373	5,572	6,269	326	3,373	5,572	6,269
16,200	16,250	0	3,373	5,572	6,269	322	3,373	5,572	6,269
16,250	16,300	0	3,373	5,572	6,269	318	3,373	5,572	6,269
16,300	16,350	0	3,373	5,572	6,269	314	3,373	5,572	6,269
16,350	16,400	0	3,373	5,572	6,269	310	3,373	5,572	6,269
16,400	16,450	0	3,373	5,572	6,269	306	3,373	5,572	6,269
16,450	16,500	0	3,373	5,572	6,269	303	3,373	5,572	6,269
16,500	16,550	0	3,373	5,572	6,269	299	3,373	5,572	6,269
16,550	16,600	0	3,373	5,572	6,269	295	3,373	5,572	6,269
16,600	16,650	0	3,373	5,572	6,269	291	3,373	5,572	6,269
16,650	16,700	0	3,373	5,572	6,269	287	3,373	5,572	6,269
16,700	16,750	0	3,373	5,572	6,269	283	3,373	5,572	6,269
16,750	16,800	0	3,373	5,572	6,269	280	3,373	5,572	6,269
16,800	16,850	0	3,373	5,572	6,269	276	3,373	5,572	6,269
16,850	16,900	0	3,373	5,572	6,269	272	3,373	5,572	6,269
16,900	16,950	0	3,373	5,572	6,269	268	3,373	5,572	6,269
16,950	17,000	0	3,373	5,572	6,269	264	3,373	5,572	6,269
17,000	17,050	0	3,373	5,572	6,269	260	3,373	5,572	6,269
17,050	17,100	0	3,373	5,572	6,269	257	3,373	5,572	6,269
17,100	17,150	0	3,373	5,572	6,269	253	3,373	5,572	6,269
17,150	17,200	0	3,373	5,572	6,269	249	3,373	5,572	6,269
17,200	17,250	0	3,373	5,572	6,269	245	3,373	5,572	6,269
17,250	17,300	0	3,373	5,572	6,269	241	3,373	5,572	6,269
17,300	17,350	0	3,373	5,572	6,269	238	3,373	5,572	6,269
17,350	17,400	0	3,373	5,572	6,269	234	3,373	5,572	6,269
17,400	17,450	0	3,373	5,572	6,269	230	3,373	5,572	6,269
17,450	17,500	0	3,373	5,572	6,269	226	3,373	5,572	6,269
17,500	17,550	0	3,373	5,572	6,269	222	3,373	5,572	6,269
17,550	17,600	0	3,373	5,572	6,269	218	3,373	5,572	6,269
17,600	17,650	0	3,373	5,572	6,269	215	3,373	5,572	6,269
17,650	17,700	0	3,373	5,572	6,269	211	3,373	5,572	6,269
17,700	17,750	0	3,373	5,572	6,269	207	3,373	5,572	6,269
17,750	17,800	0	3,373	5,572	6,269	203	3,373	5,572	6,269
17,800	17,850	0	3,373	5,572	6,269	199	3,373	5,572	6,269
17,850	17,900	0	3,373	5,572	6,269	195	3,373	5,572	6,269
17,900	17,950	0	3,373	5,572	6,269	192	3,373	5,572	6,269
17,950	18,000	0	3,373	5,572	6,269	188	3,373	5,572	6,269
18,000	18,050	0	3,373	5,572	6,269	184	3,373	5,572	6,269
18,050	18,100	0	3,373	5,572	6,269	180	3,373	5,572	6,269
18,100	18,150	0	3,373	5,572	6,269	176	3,373	5,572	6,269
18,150	18,200	0	3,373	5,572	6,269	173	3,373	5,572	6,269
18,200	18,250	0	3,367	5,565	6,261	169	3,373	5,572	6,269
18,250	18,300	0	3,359	5,554	6,251	165	3,373	5,572	6,269
18,300	18,350	0	3,351	5,544	6,240	161	3,373	5,572	6,269
18,350	18,400	0	3,343	5,533	6,230	157	3,373	5,572	6,269
18,400	18,450	0	3,335	5,523	6,219	153	3,373	5,572	6,269
18,450	18,500	0	3,327	5,512	6,208	150	3,373	5,572	6,269
18,500	18,550	0	3,319	5,501	6,198	146	3,373	5,572	6,269
18,550	18,600	0	3,311	5,491	6,187	142	3,373	5,572	6,269
18,600	18,650	0	3,303	5,480	6,177	138	3,373	5,572	6,269
18,650	18,700	0	3,295	5,470	6,166	134	3,373	5,572	6,269
18,700	18,750	0	3,287	5,459	6,156	130	3,373	5,572	6,269
18,750	18,800	0	3,279	5,449	6,145	127	3,373	5,572	6,269
18,800	18,850	0	3,271	5,438	6,135	123	3,373	5,572	6,269
18,850	18,900	0	3,263	5,428	6,124	119	3,373	5,572	6,269
18,900	18,950	0	3,255	5,417	6,114	115	3,373	5,572	6,269
18,950	19,000	0	3,247	5,407	6,103	111	3,373	5,572	6,269
19,000	19,050	0	3,239	5,396	6,093	107	3,373	5,572	6,269
19,050	19,100	0	3,231	5,386	6,082	104	3,373	5,572	6,269
19,100	19,150	0	3,223	5,375	6,072	100	3,373	5,572	6,269
19,150	19,200	0	3,215	5,365	6,061	96	3,373	5,572	6,269

* If the amount you are looking up from the worksheet is at least $14,850 but less than $14,880, and you have no qualifying child, your credit is $1.
If the amount you are looking up from the worksheet is $14,880 or more, and you have no qualifying child, you can't take the credit.

(Continued)

Caution: This is a draft 2016 Earned Income Credit (EIC) Table. At the time of publication, the IRS had not yet released the 2016 Earned Income Credit (EIC) Table. For the latest information, see CCHGroup.com/TaxUpdates.

Earned Income Credit (EIC) Table - *Continued*

(**Caution.** This is **not** a tax table.)

If the amount you are looking up from the worksheet is–		And your filing status is– Single, head of household, or qualifying widow(er) and the number of children you have is–				Married filing jointly and the number of children you have is–			
		0	1	2	3	0	1	2	3
At least	But less than	Your credit is–				Your credit is–			
19,200	19,250	0	3,207	5,354	6,051	92	3,373	5,572	6,269
19,250	19,300	0	3,199	5,343	6,040	88	3,373	5,572	6,269
19,300	19,350	0	3,191	5,333	6,029	85	3,373	5,572	6,269
19,350	19,400	0	3,183	5,322	6,016	81	3,373	5,572	6,269
19,400	19,450	0	3,175	5,312	6,008	77	3,373	5,572	6,269
19,450	19,500	0	3,167	5,301	5,999	73	3,373	5,572	6,269
19,500	19,550	0	3,159	5,291	5,987	69	3,373	5,572	6,269
19,550	19,600	0	3,151	5,280	5,977	65	3,373	5,572	6,269
19,600	19,650	0	3,143	5,270	5,966	62	3,373	5,572	6,269
19,650	19,700	0	3,135	5,259	5,956	58	3,373	5,572	6,269
19,700	19,750	0	3,128	5,249	5,945	54	3,373	5,572	6,269
19,750	19,800	0	3,120	5,238	5,935	50	3,373	5,572	6,269
19,800	19,850	0	3,112	5,228	5,924	46	3,373	5,572	6,269
19,850	19,900	0	3,104	5,217	5,914	42	3,373	5,572	6,269
19,900	19,950	0	3,096	5,207	5,903	39	3,373	5,572	6,269
19,950	20,000	0	3,088	5,196	5,893	35	3,373	5,572	6,269
20,000	20,050	0	3,080	5,186	5,882	31	3,373	5,572	6,269
20,050	20,100	0	3,072	5,175	5,872	27	3,373	5,572	6,269
20,100	20,150	0	3,064	5,164	5,861	23	3,373	5,572	6,269
20,150	20,200	0	3,056	5,154	5,850	20	3,373	5,572	6,269
20,200	20,250	0	3,048	5,143	5,840	16	3,373	5,572	6,269
20,250	20,300	0	3,040	5,133	5,829	12	3,373	5,572	6,269
20,300	20,350	0	3,032	5,122	5,819	8	3,373	5,572	6,269
20,350	20,400	0	3,024	5,112	5,808	4	3,373	5,572	6,269
20,400	20,450	0	3,016	5,101	5,798	*	3,373	5,572	6,269
20,450	20,500	0	3,008	5,091	5,787	0	3,373	5,572	6,269
20,500	20,550	0	3,000	5,080	5,777	0	3,373	5,572	6,269
20,550	20,600	0	2,992	5,070	5,766	0	3,373	5,572	6,269
20,600	20,650	0	2,984	5,059	5,756	0	3,373	5,572	6,269
20,650	20,700	0	2,976	5,049	5,745	0	3,373	5,572	6,269
20,700	20,750	0	2,968	5,038	5,735	0	3,373	5,572	6,269
20,750	20,800	0	2,960	5,028	5,724	0	3,373	5,572	6,269
20,800	20,850	0	2,952	5,017	5,714	0	3,373	5,572	6,269
20,850	20,900	0	2,944	5,007	5,703	0	3,373	5,572	6,269
20,900	20,950	0	2,936	4,996	5,693	0	3,373	5,572	6,269
20,950	21,000	0	2,928	4,985	5,682	0	3,373	5,572	6,269
21,000	21,050	0	2,920	4,975	5,671	0	3,373	5,572	6,269
21,050	21,100	0	2,912	4,964	5,661	0	3,373	5,572	6,269
21,100	21,150	0	2,904	4,954	5,650	0	3,373	5,572	6,269
21,150	21,200	0	2,896	4,943	5,640	0	3,373	5,572	6,269
21,200	21,250	0	2,888	4,933	5,629	0	3,373	5,572	6,269
21,250	21,300	0	2,880	4,922	5,619	0	3,373	5,572	6,269
21,300	21,350	0	2,872	4,912	5,608	0	3,373	5,572	6,269
21,350	21,400	0	2,864	4,901	5,598	0	3,373	5,572	6,269
21,400	21,450	0	2,856	4,891	5,587	0	3,373	5,572	6,269
21,450	21,500	0	2,848	4,880	5,577	0	3,373	5,572	6,269
21,500	21,550	0	2,840	4,870	5,566	0	3,373	5,572	6,269
21,550	21,600	0	2,832	4,859	5,556	0	3,373	5,572	6,269
21,600	21,650	0	2,824	4,849	5,545	0	3,373	5,572	6,269
21,650	21,700	0	2,816	4,838	5,535	0	3,373	5,572	6,269
21,700	21,750	0	2,808	4,828	5,524	0	3,373	5,572	6,269
21,750	21,800	0	2,800	4,817	5,513	0	3,373	5,572	6,269
21,800	21,850	0	2,792	4,806	5,503	0	3,373	5,572	6,269
21,850	21,900	0	2,784	4,796	5,492	0	3,373	5,572	6,269
21,900	21,950	0	2,776	4,785	5,482	0	3,373	5,572	6,269
21,950	22,000	0	2,768	4,775	5,471	0	3,373	5,572	6,269
22,000	22,050	0	2,760	4,764	5,461	0	3,373	5,572	6,269
22,050	22,100	0	2,752	4,754	5,450	0	3,373	5,572	6,269
22,100	22,150	0	2,744	4,743	5,440	0	3,373	5,572	6,269
22,150	22,200	0	2,736	4,733	5,429	0	3,373	5,572	6,269
22,200	22,250	0	2,728	4,722	5,419	0	3,373	5,572	6,269
22,250	22,300	0	2,720	4,712	5,408	0	3,373	5,572	6,269
22,300	22,350	0	2,712	4,701	5,398	0	3,373	5,572	6,269
22,350	22,400	0	2,704	4,691	5,387	0	3,373	5,572	6,269
22,400	22,450	0	2,696	4,680	5,377	0	3,373	5,572	6,269
22,450	22,500	0	2,688	4,670	5,366	0	3,373	5,572	6,269
22,500	22,550	0	2,680	4,659	5,356	0	3,373	5,572	6,269
22,550	22,600	0	2,672	4,649	5,345	0	3,373	5,572	6,269
22,600	22,650	0	2,664	4,638	5,334	0	3,373	5,572	6,269
22,650	22,700	0	2,656	4,627	5,324	0	3,373	5,572	6,269
22,700	22,750	0	2,648	4,617	5,313	0	3,373	5,572	6,269
22,750	22,800	0	2,640	4,606	5,303	0	3,373	5,572	6,269
22,800	22,850	0	2,632	4,596	5,292	0	3,373	5,572	6,269
22,850	22,900	0	2,624	4,585	5,282	0	3,373	5,572	6,269
22,900	22,950	0	2,616	4,575	5,271	0	3,373	5,572	6,269
22,950	23,000	0	2,608	4,564	5,261	0	3,373	5,572	6,269
23,000	23,050	0	2,600	4,554	5,250	0	3,373	5,572	6,269
23,050	23,100	0	2,592	4,543	5,240	0	3,373	5,572	6,269
23,100	23,150	0	2,584	4,533	5,229	0	3,373	5,572	6,269
23,150	23,200	0	2,576	4,522	5,219	0	3,373	5,572	6,269
23,200	23,250	0	2,568	4,512	5,208	0	3,373	5,572	6,269
23,250	23,300	0	2,560	4,501	5,198	0	3,373	5,572	6,269
23,300	23,350	0	2,552	4,491	5,187	0	3,373	5,572	6,269
23,350	23,400	0	2,544	4,480	5,177	0	3,373	5,572	6,269
23,400	23,450	0	2,536	4,470	5,166	0	3,373	5,572	6,269
23,450	23,500	0	2,528	4,459	5,155	0	3,373	5,572	6,269
23,500	23,550	0	2,520	4,448	5,145	0	3,373	5,572	6,269
23,550	23,600	0	2,512	4,438	5,134	0	3,373	5,572	6,269
23,600	23,650	0	2,504	4,427	5,124	0	3,373	5,572	6,269
23,650	23,700	0	2,496	4,417	5,113	0	3,373	5,572	6,269
23,700	23,750	0	2,488	4,406	5,103	0	3,373	5,572	6,269
23,750	23,800	0	2,480	4,396	5,092	0	3,367	5,565	6,261
23,800	23,850	0	2,472	4,385	5,082	0	3,359	5,554	6,251
23,850	23,900	0	2,464	4,375	5,071	0	3,351	5,544	6,240
23,900	23,950	0	2,456	4,364	5,061	0	3,343	5,533	6,230
23,950	24,000	0	2,448	4,354	5,050	0	3,335	5,523	6,219
24,000	24,050	0	2,440	4,343	5,040	0	3,327	5,512	6,208
24,050	24,100	0	2,432	4,333	5,029	0	3,319	5,501	6,198
24,100	24,150	0	2,424	4,322	5,019	0	3,311	5,491	6,187
24,150	24,200	0	2,416	4,312	5,008	0	3,303	5,480	6,177
24,200	24,250	0	2,408	4,301	4,998	0	3,295	5,470	6,166
24,250	24,300	0	2,400	4,290	4,987	0	3,287	5,459	6,156
24,300	24,350	0	2,392	4,280	4,976	0	3,279	5,449	6,145
24,350	24,400	0	2,384	4,269	4,966	0	3,271	5,438	6,135
24,400	24,450	0	2,376	4,259	4,955	0	3,263	5,428	6,124
24,450	24,500	0	2,368	4,248	4,945	0	3,255	5,417	6,114
24,500	24,550	0	2,360	4,238	4,934	0	3,247	5,407	6,103
24,550	24,600	0	2,352	4,227	4,924	0	3,239	5,396	6,093
24,600	24,650	0	2,344	4,217	4,913	0	3,231	5,386	6,082
24,650	24,700	0	2,336	4,206	4,903	0	3,223	5,375	6,072
24,700	24,750	0	2,329	4,196	4,892	0	3,215	5,365	6,061
24,750	24,800	0	2,321	4,185	4,882	0	3,207	5,354	6,051
24,800	24,850	0	2,313	4,175	4,871	0	3,199	5,343	6,040
24,850	24,900	0	2,305	4,164	4,861	0	3,191	5,333	6,029
24,900	24,950	0	2,297	4,154	4,850	0	3,183	5,322	6,019
24,950	25,000	0	2,289	4,143	4,840	0	3,175	5,312	6,008
25,000	25,050	0	2,281	4,133	4,829	0	3,167	5,301	5,998
25,050	25,100	0	2,273	4,122	4,819	0	3,159	5,291	5,987
25,100	25,150	0	2,265	4,111	4,808	0	3,151	5,280	5,977
25,150	25,200	0	2,257	4,101	4,797	0	3,143	5,270	5,966
25,200	25,250	0	2,249	4,090	4,787	0	3,135	5,259	5,956
25,250	25,300	0	2,241	4,080	4,776	0	3,128	5,249	5,945
25,300	25,350	0	2,233	4,069	4,766	0	3,120	5,238	5,935
25,350	25,400	0	2,225	4,059	4,755	0	3,112	5,228	5,924
25,400	25,450	0	2,217	4,048	4,745	0	3,104	5,217	5,914
25,450	25,500	0	2,209	4,038	4,734	0	3,096	5,207	5,903
25,500	25,550	0	2,201	4,027	4,724	0	3,088	5,196	5,893
25,550	25,600	0	2,193	4,017	4,713	0	3,080	5,186	5,882

DRAFT AS OF 01-06-2016

* If the amount you are looking up from the worksheet is at least $20,400 but less than $20,430, and you have no qualifying children, your credit is $1.
If the amount you are looking up from the worksheet is $20,430 or more, and you have no qualifying children, you can't take the credit.

(Continued)

Caution: This is a draft 2016 Earned Income Credit (EIC) Table. At the time of publication, the IRS had not yet released the 2016 Earned Income Credit (EIC) Table. For the latest information, see CCHGroup.com/TaxUpdates.

Earned Income Credit (EIC) Table - *Continued*

(**Caution.** This is **not** a tax table.)

If the amount you are looking up from the worksheet is–		And your filing status is– Single, head of household, or qualifying widow(er) and the number of children you have is–				Married filing jointly and the number of children you have is–			
		0	1	2	3	0	1	2	3
At least	But less than	Your credit is–				Your credit is–			
25,600	25,650	0	2,185	4,006	4,703	0	3,072	5,175	5,872
25,650	25,700	0	2,177	3,995	4,692	0	3,064	5,164	5,861
25,700	25,750	0	2,169	3,985	4,682	0	3,056	5,154	5,850
25,750	25,800	0	2,161	3,975	4,671	0	3,048	5,143	5,840
25,800	25,850	0	2,153	3,964	4,661	0	3,040	5,133	5,829
25,850	25,900	0	2,145	3,954	4,650	0	3,032	5,122	5,819
25,900	25,950	0	2,137	3,943	4,640	0	3,024	5,112	5,808
25,950	26,000	0	2,129	3,932	4,629	0	3,016	5,101	5,798
26,000	26,050	0	2,121	3,922	4,618	0	3,008	5,091	5,787
26,050	26,100	0	2,113	3,911	4,608	0	3,000	5,080	5,777
26,100	26,150	0	2,105	3,901	4,597	0	2,992	5,070	5,766
26,150	26,200	0	2,097	3,890	4,587	0	2,984	5,059	5,756
26,200	26,250	0	2,089	3,880	4,576	0	2,976	5,049	5,745
26,250	26,300	0	2,081	3,869	4,566	0	2,968	5,038	5,735
26,300	26,350	0	2,073	3,859	4,555	0	2,960	5,028	5,724
26,350	26,400	0	2,065	3,848	4,545	0	2,952	5,017	5,714
26,400	26,450	0	2,057	3,838	4,534	0	2,944	5,007	5,703
26,450	26,500	0	2,049	3,827	4,524	0	2,936	4,996	5,693
26,500	26,550	0	2,041	3,817	4,513	0	2,928	4,985	5,682
26,550	26,600	0	2,033	3,806	4,503	0	2,920	4,975	5,671
26,600	26,650	0	2,025	3,796	4,492	0	2,912	4,964	5,661
26,650	26,700	0	2,017	3,785	4,482	0	2,904	4,954	5,650
26,700	26,750	0	2,009	3,775	4,471	0	2,896	4,943	5,640
26,750	26,800	0	2,001	3,764	4,460	0	2,888	4,933	5,629
26,800	26,850	0	1,993	3,753	4,450	0	2,880	4,922	5,619
26,850	26,900	0	1,985	3,743	4,439	0	2,872	4,912	5,608
26,900	26,950	0	1,977	3,732	4,429	0	2,864	4,901	5,598
26,950	27,000	0	1,969	3,722	4,418	0	2,856	4,891	5,587
27,000	27,050	0	1,961	3,711	4,408	0	2,848	4,880	5,577
27,050	27,100	0	1,953	3,701	4,397	0	2,840	4,870	5,566
27,100	27,150	0	1,945	3,690	4,387	0	2,832	4,859	5,556
27,150	27,200	0	1,937	3,680	4,376	0	2,824	4,849	5,545
27,200	27,250	0	1,929	3,669	4,366	0	2,816	4,838	5,535
27,250	27,300	0	1,921	3,659	4,355	0	2,808	4,828	5,524
27,300	27,350	0	1,913	3,648	4,345	0	2,800	4,817	5,513
27,350	27,400	0	1,905	3,638	4,334	0	2,792	4,806	5,503
27,400	27,450	0	1,897	3,627	4,324	0	2,784	4,796	5,492
27,450	27,500	0	1,889	3,617	4,313	0	2,776	4,785	5,482
27,500	27,550	0	1,881	3,606	4,303	0	2,768	4,775	5,471
27,550	27,600	0	1,873	3,596	4,292	0	2,760	4,764	5,461
27,600	27,650	0	1,865	3,585	4,281	0	2,752	4,754	5,450
27,650	27,700	0	1,857	3,574	4,271	0	2,744	4,743	5,440
27,700	27,750	0	1,849	3,564	4,260	0	2,736	4,733	5,429
27,750	27,800	0	1,841	3,553	4,250	0	2,728	4,722	5,419
27,800	27,850	0	1,833	3,543	4,239	0	2,720	4,712	5,408
27,850	27,900	0	1,825	3,532	4,229	0	2,712	4,701	5,398
27,900	27,950	0	1,817	3,522	4,218	0	2,704	4,691	5,387
27,950	28,000	0	1,809	3,511	4,208	0	2,696	4,680	5,377
28,000	28,050	0	1,801	3,501	4,197	0	2,688	4,670	5,366
28,050	28,100	0	1,793	3,490	4,187	0	2,680	4,659	5,356
28,100	28,150	0	1,785	3,480	4,176	0	2,672	4,649	5,345
28,150	28,200	0	1,777	3,469	4,166	0	2,664	4,638	5,334
28,200	28,250	0	1,769	3,459	4,155	0	2,656	4,627	5,324
28,250	28,300	0	1,761	3,448	4,145	0	2,648	4,617	5,313
28,300	28,350	0	1,753	3,438	4,134	0	2,640	4,606	5,303
28,350	28,400	0	1,745	3,427	4,124	0	2,632	4,596	5,292
28,400	28,450	0	1,737	3,417	4,113	0	2,624	4,585	5,282
28,450	28,500	0	1,729	3,406	4,102	0	2,616	4,575	5,271
28,500	28,550	0	1,721	3,395	4,092	0	2,608	4,564	5,261
28,550	28,600	0	1,713	3,385	4,081	0	2,600	4,554	5,250
28,600	28,650	0	1,705	3,374	4,071	0	2,592	4,543	5,240
28,650	28,700	0	1,697	3,364	4,060	0	2,584	4,533	5,229
28,700	28,750	0	1,689	3,353	4,050	0	2,576	4,522	5,219
28,750	28,800	0	1,681	3,343	4,039	0	2,568	4,512	5,208
28,800	28,850	0	1,673	3,332	4,029	0	2,560	4,501	5,198
28,850	28,900	0	1,665	3,322	4,018	0	2,552	4,491	5,187
28,900	28,950	0	1,657	3,311	4,008	0	2,544	4,480	5,177
28,950	29,000	0	1,649	3,301	3,997	0	2,536	4,470	5,166
29,000	29,050	0	1,641	3,290	3,987	0	2,528	4,459	5,155
29,050	29,100	0	1,633	3,280	3,976	0	2,520	4,448	5,145
29,100	29,150	0	1,625	3,269	3,966	0	2,512	4,438	5,134
29,150	29,200	0	1,617	3,259	3,955	0	2,504	4,427	5,124

If the amount you are looking up from the worksheet is–		And your filing status is– Single, head of household, or qualifying widow(er) and the number of children you have is–				Married filing jointly and the number of children you have is–			
		0	1	2	3	0	1	2	3
At least	But less than	Your credit is–				Your credit is–			
29,200	29,250	0	1,609	3,248	3,945	0	2,496	4,417	5,113
29,250	29,300	0	1,601	3,237	3,934	0	2,488	4,406	5,103
29,300	29,350	0	1,593	3,227	3,923	0	2,480	4,396	5,092
29,350	29,400	0	1,585	3,216	3,913	0	2,472	4,385	5,082
29,400	29,450	0	1,577	3,206	3,902	0	2,464	4,375	5,071
29,450	29,500	0	1,569	3,195	3,892	0	2,456	4,364	5,061
29,500	29,550	0	1,561	3,185	3,881	0	2,448	4,354	5,050
29,550	29,600	0	1,553	3,174	3,871	0	2,440	4,343	5,040
29,600	29,650	0	1,545	3,164	3,860	0	2,432	4,333	5,029
29,650	29,700	0	1,537	3,153	3,850	0	2,424	4,322	5,019
29,700	29,750	0	1,530	3,143	3,839	0	2,416	4,312	5,008
29,750	29,800	0	1,522	3,132	3,829	0	2,408	4,301	4,998
29,800	29,850	0	1,514	3,122	3,818	0	2,400	4,290	4,987
29,850	29,900	0	1,506	3,111	3,808	0	2,392	4,280	4,978
29,900	29,950	0	1,498	3,101	3,797	0	2,384	4,269	4,966
29,950	30,000	0	1,490	3,090	3,787	0	2,376	4,259	4,955
30,000	30,050	0	1,482	3,080	3,776	0	2,368	4,248	4,945
30,050	30,100	0	1,474	3,069	3,766	0	2,360	4,238	4,934
30,100	30,150	0	1,466	3,058	3,755	0	2,352	4,227	4,924
30,150	30,200	0	1,458	3,048	3,744	0	2,344	4,217	4,913
30,200	30,250	0	1,450	3,037	3,734	0	2,336	4,206	4,903
30,250	30,300	0	1,442	3,027	3,723	0	2,329	4,196	4,892
30,300	30,350	0	1,434	3,016	3,713	0	2,321	4,185	4,882
30,350	30,400	0	1,426	3,006	3,702	0	2,313	4,175	4,871
30,400	30,450	0	1,418	2,995	3,692	0	2,305	4,164	4,861
30,450	30,500	0	1,410	2,985	3,681	0	2,297	4,154	4,850
30,500	30,550	0	1,402	2,974	3,671	0	2,289	4,143	4,840
30,550	30,600	0	1,394	2,964	3,660	0	2,281	4,133	4,829
30,600	30,650	0	1,386	2,953	3,650	0	2,273	4,122	4,819
30,650	30,700	0	1,378	2,943	3,639	0	2,265	4,111	4,808
30,700	30,750	0	1,370	2,932	3,629	0	2,257	4,101	4,797
30,750	30,800	0	1,362	2,922	3,618	0	2,249	4,090	4,787
30,800	30,850	0	1,354	2,911	3,608	0	2,241	4,080	4,776
30,850	30,900	0	1,346	2,901	3,597	0	2,233	4,069	4,766
30,900	30,950	0	1,338	2,890	3,587	0	2,225	4,059	4,755
30,950	31,000	0	1,330	2,879	3,576	0	2,217	4,048	4,745
31,000	31,050	0	1,322	2,869	3,565	0	2,209	4,038	4,734
31,050	31,100	0	1,314	2,858	3,555	0	2,201	4,027	4,724
31,100	31,150	0	1,306	2,848	3,544	0	2,193	4,017	4,713
31,150	31,200	0	1,298	2,837	3,534	0	2,185	4,006	4,703
31,200	31,250	0	1,290	2,827	3,523	0	2,177	3,996	4,692
31,250	31,300	0	1,282	2,816	3,513	0	2,169	3,985	4,682
31,300	31,350	0	1,274	2,806	3,502	0	2,161	3,975	4,671
31,350	31,400	0	1,266	2,795	3,492	0	2,153	3,964	4,661
31,400	31,450	0	1,258	2,785	3,481	0	2,145	3,954	4,650
31,450	31,500	0	1,250	2,774	3,471	0	2,137	3,943	4,640
31,500	31,550	0	1,242	2,764	3,460	0	2,129	3,932	4,629
31,550	31,600	0	1,234	2,753	3,450	0	2,121	3,922	4,618
31,600	31,650	0	1,226	2,743	3,439	0	2,113	3,911	4,608
31,650	31,700	0	1,218	2,732	3,429	0	2,105	3,901	4,597
31,700	31,750	0	1,210	2,722	3,418	0	2,097	3,890	4,587
31,750	31,800	0	1,202	2,711	3,407	0	2,089	3,880	4,576
31,800	31,850	0	1,194	2,700	3,397	0	2,081	3,869	4,566
31,850	31,900	0	1,186	2,690	3,386	0	2,073	3,859	4,555
31,900	31,950	0	1,178	2,679	3,376	0	2,065	3,848	4,545
31,950	32,000	0	1,170	2,669	3,365	0	2,057	3,838	4,534
32,000	32,050	0	1,162	2,658	3,355	0	2,049	3,827	4,524
32,050	32,100	0	1,154	2,648	3,344	0	2,041	3,817	4,513
32,100	32,150	0	1,146	2,637	3,334	0	2,033	3,806	4,503
32,150	32,200	0	1,138	2,627	3,323	0	2,025	3,796	4,492
32,200	32,250	0	1,130	2,616	3,313	0	2,017	3,785	4,482
32,250	32,300	0	1,122	2,606	3,302	0	2,009	3,775	4,471
32,300	32,350	0	1,114	2,595	3,292	0	2,001	3,764	4,460
32,350	32,400	0	1,106	2,585	3,281	0	1,993	3,753	4,450
32,400	32,450	0	1,098	2,574	3,271	0	1,985	3,743	4,439
32,450	32,500	0	1,090	2,564	3,260	0	1,977	3,732	4,429
32,500	32,550	0	1,082	2,553	3,250	0	1,969	3,722	4,418
32,550	32,600	0	1,074	2,543	3,239	0	1,961	3,711	4,408
32,600	32,650	0	1,066	2,532	3,228	0	1,953	3,701	4,397
32,650	32,700	0	1,058	2,521	3,218	0	1,945	3,690	4,387
32,700	32,750	0	1,050	2,511	3,207	0	1,937	3,680	4,376
32,750	32,800	0	1,042	2,500	3,197	0	1,929	3,669	4,366

(Continued)

DRAFT AS OF 08-31-2016

Caution: This is a draft 2016 Earned Income Credit (EIC) Table. At the time of publication, the IRS had not yet released the 2016 Earned Income Credit (EIC) Table. For the latest information, see CCHGroup.com/TaxUpdates.

Earned Income Credit (EIC) Table - *Continued*

(**Caution.** This is **not** a tax table.)

If the amount you are looking up from the worksheet is–		And your filing status is– Single, head of household, or qualifying widow(er) and the number of children you have is–				Married filing jointly and the number of children you have is–			
		0	1	2	3	0	1	2	3
At least	But less than	Your credit is–				Your credit is–			
32,800	32,850	0	1,034	2,490	3,186	0	1,921	3,659	4,355
32,850	32,900	0	1,026	2,479	3,176	0	1,913	3,648	4,345
32,900	32,950	0	1,018	2,469	3,165	0	1,905	3,638	4,334
32,950	33,000	0	1,010	2,458	3,155	0	1,897	3,627	4,324
33,000	33,050	0	1,002	2,448	3,144	0	1,889	3,617	4,313
33,050	33,100	0	994	2,437	3,134	0	1,881	3,606	4,303
33,100	33,150	0	986	2,427	3,123	0	1,873	3,596	4,292
33,150	33,200	0	978	2,416	3,113	0	1,865	3,585	4,281
33,200	33,250	0	970	2,406	3,102	0	1,857	3,574	4,271
33,250	33,300	0	962	2,395	3,092	0	1,849	3,564	4,260
33,300	33,350	0	954	2,385	3,081	0	1,841	3,553	4,250
33,350	33,400	0	946	2,374	3,071	0	1,833	3,543	4,239
33,400	33,450	0	938	2,364	3,060	0	1,825	3,532	4,229
33,450	33,500	0	930	2,353	3,049	0	1,817	3,522	4,218
33,500	33,550	0	922	2,342	3,039	0	1,809	3,511	4,208
33,550	33,600	0	914	2,332	3,028	0	1,801	3,501	4,197
33,600	33,650	0	906	2,321	3,018	0	1,793	3,490	4,187
33,650	33,700	0	898	2,311	3,007	0	1,785	3,480	4,176
33,700	33,750	0	890	2,300	2,997	0	1,777	3,469	4,166
33,750	33,800	0	882	2,290	2,986	0	1,769	3,459	4,155
33,800	33,850	0	874	2,279	2,976	0	1,761	3,448	4,145
33,850	33,900	0	866	2,269	2,965	0	1,753	3,438	4,134
33,900	33,950	0	858	2,258	2,955	0	1,745	3,427	4,124
33,950	34,000	0	850	2,248	2,944	0	1,737	3,417	4,113
34,000	34,050	0	842	2,237	2,934	0	1,729	3,406	4,102
34,050	34,100	0	834	2,227	2,923	0	1,721	3,395	4,092
34,100	34,150	0	826	2,216	2,913	0	1,713	3,385	4,081
34,150	34,200	0	818	2,206	2,902	0	1,705	3,374	4,071
34,200	34,250	0	810	2,195	2,892	0	1,697	3,364	4,060
34,250	34,300	0	802	2,184	2,881	0	1,689	3,353	4,050
34,300	34,350	0	794	2,174	2,870	0	1,681	3,343	4,039
34,350	34,400	0	786	2,163	2,860	0	1,673	3,332	4,029
34,400	34,450	0	778	2,153	2,849	0	1,665	3,322	4,018
34,450	34,500	0	770	2,142	2,839	0	1,657	3,311	4,008
34,500	34,550	0	762	2,132	2,828	0	1,649	3,301	3,997
34,550	34,600	0	754	2,121	2,818	0	1,641	3,290	3,987
34,600	34,650	0	746	2,111	2,807	0	1,633	3,280	3,976
34,650	34,700	0	738	2,100	2,797	0	1,625	3,269	3,966
34,700	34,750	0	731	2,090	2,786	0	1,617	3,259	3,955
34,750	34,800	0	723	2,079	2,776	0	1,609	3,248	3,945
34,800	34,850	0	715	2,069	2,765	0	1,601	3,237	3,934
34,850	34,900	0	707	2,058	2,755	0	1,593	3,227	3,923
34,900	34,950	0	699	2,048	2,744	0	1,585	3,216	3,913
34,950	35,000	0	691	2,037	2,734	0	1,577	3,206	3,902
35,000	35,050	0	683	2,027	2,723	0	1,569	3,195	3,892
35,050	35,100	0	675	2,016	2,713	0	1,561	3,185	3,881
35,100	35,150	0	667	2,005	2,702	0	1,553	3,174	3,871
35,150	35,200	0	659	1,995	2,691	0	1,545	3,164	3,860
35,200	35,250	0	651	1,984	2,681	0	1,537	3,153	3,850
35,250	35,300	0	643	1,974	2,670	0	1,530	3,143	3,839
35,300	35,350	0	635	1,963	2,660	0	1,522	3,132	3,829
35,350	35,400	0	627	1,953	2,649	0	1,514	3,122	3,818
35,400	35,450	0	619	1,942	2,639	0	1,506	3,111	3,808
35,450	35,500	0	611	1,932	2,628	0	1,498	3,101	3,797
35,500	35,550	0	603	1,921	2,618	0	1,490	3,090	3,787
35,550	35,600	0	595	1,911	2,607	0	1,482	3,080	3,776
35,600	35,650	0	587	1,900	2,597	0	1,474	3,069	3,766
35,650	35,700	0	579	1,890	2,586	0	1,466	3,058	3,755
35,700	35,750	0	571	1,879	2,576	0	1,458	3,048	3,744
35,750	35,800	0	563	1,869	2,565	0	1,450	3,037	3,734
35,800	35,850	0	555	1,858	2,555	0	1,442	3,027	3,723
35,850	35,900	0	547	1,848	2,544	0	1,434	3,016	3,713
35,900	35,950	0	539	1,837	2,534	0	1,426	3,006	3,702
35,950	36,000	0	531	1,826	2,523	0	1,418	2,995	3,692
36,000	36,050	0	523	1,816	2,512	0	1,410	2,985	3,681
36,050	36,100	0	515	1,805	2,502	0	1,402	2,974	3,671
36,100	36,150	0	507	1,795	2,491	0	1,394	2,964	3,660
36,150	36,200	0	499	1,784	2,481	0	1,386	2,953	3,650
36,200	36,250	0	491	1,774	2,470	0	1,378	2,943	3,639
36,250	36,300	0	483	1,763	2,460	0	1,370	2,932	3,629
36,300	36,350	0	475	1,753	2,449	0	1,362	2,922	3,618
36,350	36,400	0	467	1,742	2,439	0	1,354	2,911	3,608
36,400	36,450	0	459	1,732	2,428	0	1,346	2,901	3,597
36,450	36,500	0	451	1,721	2,418	0	1,338	2,890	3,587
36,500	36,550	0	443	1,711	2,407	0	1,330	2,879	3,576
36,550	36,600	0	435	1,700	2,397	0	1,322	2,869	3,565
36,600	36,650	0	427	1,690	2,386	0	1,314	2,858	3,555
36,650	36,700	0	419	1,679	2,376	0	1,306	2,848	3,544
36,700	36,750	0	411	1,669	2,365	0	1,298	2,837	3,534
36,750	36,800	0	403	1,658	2,354	0	1,290	2,827	3,523
36,800	36,850	0	395	1,647	2,344	0	1,282	2,816	3,513
36,850	36,900	0	387	1,637	2,333	0	1,274	2,806	3,502
36,900	36,950	0	379	1,626	2,323	0	1,266	2,795	3,492
36,950	37,000	0	371	1,616	2,312	0	1,258	2,785	3,481
37,000	37,050	0	363	1,605	2,302	0	1,250	2,774	3,471
37,050	37,100	0	355	1,595	2,291	0	1,242	2,764	3,460
37,100	37,150	0	347	1,584	2,281	0	1,234	2,753	3,450
37,150	37,200	0	339	1,574	2,270	0	1,226	2,743	3,439
37,200	37,250	0	331	1,563	2,260	0	1,218	2,732	3,429
37,250	37,300	0	323	1,553	2,249	0	1,210	2,722	3,418
37,300	37,350	0	315	1,542	2,239	0	1,202	2,711	3,407
37,350	37,400	0	307	1,532	2,228	0	1,194	2,700	3,397
37,400	37,450	0	299	1,521	2,218	0	1,186	2,690	3,386
37,450	37,500	0	291	1,511	2,207	0	1,178	2,679	3,376
37,500	37,550	0	283	1,500	2,197	0	1,170	2,669	3,365
37,550	37,600	0	275	1,490	2,186	0	1,162	2,658	3,355
37,600	37,650	0	267	1,479	2,175	0	1,154	2,648	3,344
37,650	37,700	0	259	1,468	2,165	0	1,146	2,637	3,334
37,700	37,750	0	251	1,458	2,154	0	1,138	2,627	3,323
37,750	37,800	0	243	1,447	2,144	0	1,130	2,616	3,313
37,800	37,850	0	235	1,437	2,133	0	1,122	2,606	3,302
37,850	37,900	0	227	1,426	2,123	0	1,114	2,595	3,292
37,900	37,950	0	219	1,416	2,112	0	1,106	2,585	3,281
37,950	38,000	0	211	1,405	2,102	0	1,098	2,574	3,271
38,000	38,050	0	203	1,395	2,091	0	1,090	2,564	3,260
38,050	38,100	0	195	1,384	2,081	0	1,082	2,553	3,250
38,100	38,150	0	187	1,374	2,070	0	1,074	2,543	3,239
38,150	38,200	0	179	1,363	2,060	0	1,066	2,532	3,228
38,200	38,250	0	171	1,353	2,049	0	1,058	2,521	3,218
38,250	38,300	0	163	1,342	2,039	0	1,050	2,511	3,207
38,300	38,350	0	155	1,332	2,028	0	1,042	2,500	3,197
38,350	38,400	0	147	1,321	2,018	0	1,034	2,490	3,186
38,400	38,450	0	139	1,311	2,007	0	1,026	2,479	3,176
38,450	38,500	0	131	1,300	1,996	0	1,018	2,469	3,165
38,500	38,550	0	123	1,289	1,986	0	1,010	2,458	3,155
38,550	38,600	0	115	1,279	1,975	0	1,002	2,448	3,144
38,600	38,650	0	107	1,268	1,965	0	994	2,437	3,134
38,650	38,700	0	99	1,258	1,954	0	986	2,427	3,123
38,700	38,750	0	91	1,247	1,944	0	978	2,416	3,113
38,750	38,800	0	83	1,237	1,933	0	970	2,406	3,102
38,800	38,850	0	75	1,226	1,923	0	962	2,395	3,092
38,850	38,900	0	67	1,216	1,912	0	954	2,385	3,081
38,900	38,950	0	59	1,205	1,902	0	946	2,374	3,071
38,950	39,000	0	51	1,195	1,891	0	938	2,364	3,060
39,000	39,050	0	43	1,184	1,881	0	930	2,353	3,049
39,050	39,100	0	35	1,174	1,870	0	922	2,342	3,039
39,100	39,150	0	27	1,163	1,860	0	914	2,332	3,028
39,150	39,200	0	19	1,153	1,849	0	906	2,321	3,018

DRAFT October 2016

(Continued)

Caution: This is a draft 2016 Earned Income Credit (EIC) Table. At the time of publication, the IRS had not yet released the 2016 Earned Income Credit (EIC) Table. For the latest information, see CCHGroup.com/TaxUpdates.

Earned Income Credit (EIC) Table - *Continued*

(**Caution.** This is **not** a tax table.)

If the amount you are looking up from the worksheet is–		And your filing status is– Single, head of household, or qualifying widow(er) and the number of children you have is–				Married filing jointly and the number of children you have is–			
		0	1	2	3	0	1	2	3
At least	But less than	Your credit is–				Your credit is–			
39,200	39,250	0	11	1,142	1,839	0	898	2,311	3,007
39,250	39,300	0	*	1,131	1,828	0	890	2,300	2,997
39,300	39,350	0	0	1,121	1,817	0	882	2,290	2,986
39,350	39,400	0	0	1,110	1,807	0	874	2,279	2,976
39,400	39,450	0	0	1,100	1,796	0	866	2,269	2,965
39,450	39,500	0	0	1,089	1,786	0	858	2,258	2,955
39,500	39,550	0	0	1,079	1,775	0	850	2,248	2,944
39,550	39,600	0	0	1,068	1,765	0	842	2,237	2,934
39,600	39,650	0	0	1,058	1,754	0	834	2,227	2,923
39,650	39,700	0	0	1,047	1,744	0	826	2,216	2,913
39,700	39,750	0	0	1,037	1,733	0	818	2,206	2,902
39,750	39,800	0	0	1,026	1,723	0	810	2,195	2,892
39,800	39,850	0	0	1,016	1,712	0	802	2,184	2,881
39,850	39,900	0	0	1,005	1,702	0	794	2,174	2,870
39,900	39,950	0	0	995	1,691	0	786	2,163	2,860
39,950	40,000	0	0	984	1,681	0	778	2,153	2,849
40,000	40,050	0	0	974	1,670	0	770	2,142	2,839
40,050	40,100	0	0	963	1,660	0	762	2,132	2,828
40,100	40,150	0	0	952	1,649	0	754	2,121	2,818
40,150	40,200	0	0	942	1,638	0	746	2,111	2,807
40,200	40,250	0	0	931	1,628	0	738	2,100	2,797
40,250	40,300	0	0	921	1,617	0	731	2,090	2,786
40,300	40,350	0	0	910	1,607	0	723	2,079	2,776
40,350	40,400	0	0	900	1,596	0	715	2,069	2,765
40,400	40,450	0	0	889	1,586	0	707	2,058	2,755
40,450	40,500	0	0	879	1,575	0	699	2,048	2,744
40,500	40,550	0	0	868	1,565	0	691	2,037	2,734
40,550	40,600	0	0	858	1,554	0	683	2,027	2,723
40,600	40,650	0	0	847	1,544	0	675	2,016	2,713
40,650	40,700	0	0	837	1,533	0	667	2,005	2,702
40,700	40,750	0	0	826	1,523	0	659	1,995	2,691
40,750	40,800	0	0	816	1,512	0	651	1,984	2,681
40,800	40,850	0	0	805	1,502	0	643	1,974	2,670
40,850	40,900	0	0	795	1,491	0	635	1,963	2,660
40,900	40,950	0	0	784	1,481	0	627	1,953	2,649
40,950	41,000	0	0	773	1,470	0	619	1,942	2,639
41,000	41,050	0	0	763	1,459	0	611	1,932	2,628
41,050	41,100	0	0	752	1,449	0	603	1,921	2,618
41,100	41,150	0	0	742	1,438	0	595	1,911	2,607
41,150	41,200	0	0	731	1,428	0	587	1,900	2,597
41,200	41,250	0	0	721	1,417	0	579	1,890	2,586
41,250	41,300	0	0	710	1,407	0	571	1,879	2,576
41,300	41,350	0	0	700	1,396	0	563	1,869	2,565
41,350	41,400	0	0	689	1,386	0	555	1,858	2,555
41,400	41,450	0	0	679	1,375	0	547	1,848	2,544
41,450	41,500	0	0	668	1,365	0	539	1,837	2,534
41,500	41,550	0	0	658	1,354	0	531	1,826	2,523
41,550	41,600	0	0	647	1,344	0	523	1,816	2,512
41,600	41,650	0	0	637	1,333	0	515	1,805	2,502
41,650	41,700	0	0	626	1,323	0	507	1,795	2,491
41,700	41,750	0	0	616	1,312	0	499	1,784	2,481
41,750	41,800	0	0	605	1,301	0	491	1,774	2,470
41,800	41,850	0	0	594	1,291	0	483	1,763	2,460
41,850	41,900	0	0	584	1,280	0	475	1,753	2,449
41,900	41,950	0	0	573	1,270	0	467	1,742	2,439
41,950	42,000	0	0	563	1,259	0	459	1,732	2,428
42,000	42,050	0	0	552	1,249	0	451	1,721	2,418
42,050	42,100	0	0	542	1,238	0	443	1,711	2,407
42,100	42,150	0	0	531	1,228	0	435	1,700	2,397
42,150	42,200	0	0	521	1,217	0	427	1,690	2,386
42,200	42,250	0	0	510	1,207	0	419	1,679	2,376
42,250	42,300	0	0	500	1,196	0	411	1,669	2,365
42,300	42,350	0	0	489	1,186	0	403	1,658	2,354
42,350	42,400	0	0	479	1,175	0	395	1,647	2,344

If the amount you are looking up from the worksheet is–		And your filing status is– Single, head of household, or qualifying widow(er) and the number of children you have is–				Married filing jointly and the number of children you have is–			
		0	1	2	3	0	1	2	3
At least	But less than	Your credit is–				Your credit is–			
42,400	42,450	0	0	468	1,165	0	387	1,637	2,333
42,450	42,500	0	0	458	1,154	0	379	1,626	2,323
42,500	42,550	0	0	447	1,144	0	371	1,616	2,312
42,550	42,600	0	0	437	1,133	0	363	1,605	2,302
42,600	42,650	0	0	426	1,122	0	355	1,595	2,291
42,650	42,700	0	0	415	1,112	0	347	1,584	2,281
42,700	42,750	0	0	405	1,101	0	339	1,574	2,270
42,750	42,800	0	0	394	1,091	0	331	1,563	2,260
42,800	42,850	0	0	384	1,080	0	323	1,553	2,249
42,850	42,900	0	0	373	1,070	0	315	1,542	2,239
42,900	42,950	0	0	363	1,059	0	307	1,532	2,228
42,950	43,000	0	0	352	1,049	0	299	1,521	2,218
43,000	43,050	0	0	342	1,038	0	291	1,511	2,207
43,050	43,100	0	0	331	1,028	0	283	1,500	2,197
43,100	43,150	0	0	321	1,017	0	275	1,490	2,186
43,150	43,200	0	0	310	1,007	0	267	1,479	2,175
43,200	43,250	0	0	300	996	0	259	1,468	2,165
43,250	43,300	0	0	289	986	0	251	1,458	2,154
43,300	43,350	0	0	279	975	0	243	1,447	2,144
43,350	43,400	0	0	268	965	0	235	1,437	2,133
43,400	43,450	0	0	258	954	0	227	1,426	2,123
43,450	43,500	0	0	247	943	0	219	1,416	2,112
43,500	43,550	0	0	236	933	0	211	1,405	2,102
43,550	43,600	0	0	226	922	0	203	1,395	2,091
43,600	43,650	0	0	215	912	0	195	1,384	2,081
43,650	43,700	0	0	205	901	0	187	1,374	2,070
43,700	43,750	0	0	194	891	0	179	1,363	2,060
43,750	43,800	0	0	184	880	0	171	1,353	2,049
43,800	43,850	0	0	173	870	0	163	1,342	2,039
43,850	43,900	0	0	163	859	0	155	1,332	2,028
43,900	43,950	0	0	152	849	0	147	1,321	2,018
43,950	44,000	0	0	142	838	0	139	1,311	2,007
44,000	44,050	0	0	131	828	0	131	1,300	1,996
44,050	44,100	0	0	121	817	0	123	1,289	1,986
44,100	44,150	0	0	110	807	0	115	1,279	1,975
44,150	44,200	0	0	100	796	0	107	1,268	1,965
44,200	44,250	0	0	89	786	0	99	1,258	1,954
44,250	44,300	0	0	78	775	0	91	1,247	1,944
44,300	44,350	0	0	68	764	0	83	1,237	1,933
44,350	44,400	0	0	57	754	0	75	1,226	1,923
44,400	44,450	0	0	47	743	0	67	1,216	1,912
44,450	44,500	0	0	36	733	0	59	1,205	1,902
44,500	44,550	0	0	26	722	0	51	1,195	1,891
44,550	44,600	0	0	15	712	0	43	1,184	1,881
44,600	44,650	0	0	**	701	0	35	1,174	1,870
44,650	44,700	0	0	0	691	0	27	1,163	1,860
44,700	44,750	0	0	0	680	0	19	1,153	1,849
44,750	44,800	0	0	0	670	0	11	1,142	1,839
44,800	44,850	0	0	0	659	0	***	1,131	1,828
44,850	44,900	0	0	0	649	0	0	1,121	1,817
44,900	44,950	0	0	0	638	0	0	1,110	1,807
44,950	45,000	0	0	0	628	0	0	1,100	1,796
45,000	45,050	0	0	0	617	0	0	1,089	1,786
45,050	45,100	0	0	0	607	0	0	1,079	1,775
45,100	45,150	0	0	0	596	0	0	1,068	1,765
45,150	45,200	0	0	0	585	0	0	1,058	1,754
45,200	45,250	0	0	0	575	0	0	1,047	1,744
45,250	45,300	0	0	0	564	0	0	1,037	1,733
45,300	45,350	0	0	0	554	0	0	1,026	1,723
45,350	45,400	0	0	0	543	0	0	1,016	1,712
45,400	45,450	0	0	0	533	0	0	1,005	1,702
45,450	45,500	0	0	0	522	0	0	995	1,691
45,500	45,550	0	0	0	512	0	0	984	1,681
45,550	45,600	0	0	0	501	0	0	974	1,670

* If the amount you are looking up from the worksheet is at least $39,250 but less than $39,296, and you have one qualifying child, your credit is $4.
If the amount you are looking up from the worksheet is $39,296 or more, and you have one qualifying child, you can't take the credit.

** If the amount you are looking up from the worksheet is at least $44,600 but less than $44,648, and you have two qualifying children, your credit is $5.
If the amount you are looking up from the worksheet is $44,648 or more, and you have two qualifying children, you can't take the credit.

*** If the amount you are looking up from the worksheet is at least $44,800 but less than $44,846, and you have one qualifying child, your credit is $4.
If the amount you are looking up from the worksheet is $44,846 or more, and you have one qualifying child, you can't take the credit.

(Continued)

DRAFT AS OF October 7, 2016

Caution: This is a draft 2016 Earned Income Credit (EIC) Table. At the time of publication, the IRS had not yet released the 2016 Earned Income Credit (EIC) Table. For the latest information, see CCHGroup.com/TaxUpdates.

Earned Income Credit (EIC) Table - *Continued*

(**Caution.** This is **not** a tax table.)

If the amount you are looking up from the worksheet is–		And your filing status is– Single, head of household, or qualifying widow(er) and the number of children you have is–				Married filing jointly and the number of children you have is–			
		0	1	2	3	0	1	2	3
At least	But less than	Your credit is–				Your credit is–			
45,600	45,650	0	0	0	491	0	0	963	1,660
45,650	45,700	0	0	0	480	0	0	952	1,649
45,700	45,750	0	0	0	470	0	0	942	1,638
45,750	45,800	0	0	0	459	0	0	931	1,628
45,800	45,850	0	0	0	449	0	0	921	1,617
45,850	45,900	0	0	0	438	0	0	910	1,607
45,900	45,950	0	0	0	428	0	0	900	1,596
45,950	46,000	0	0	0	417	0	0	889	1,586
46,000	46,050	0	0	0	406	0	0	879	1,575
46,050	46,100	0	0	0	396	0	0	868	1,565
46,100	46,150	0	0	0	385	0	0	858	1,554
46,150	46,200	0	0	0	375	0	0	847	1,544
46,200	46,250	0	0	0	364	0	0	837	1,533
46,250	46,300	0	0	0	354	0	0	826	1,523
46,300	46,350	0	0	0	343	0	0	816	1,512
46,350	46,400	0	0	0	333	0	0	805	1,502
46,400	46,450	0	0	0	322	0	0	795	1,491
46,450	46,500	0	0	0	312	0	0	784	1,481
46,500	46,550	0	0	0	301	0	0	773	1,470
46,550	46,600	0	0	0	291	0	0	763	1,459
46,600	46,650	0	0	0	280	0	0	752	1,449
46,650	46,700	0	0	0	270	0	0	742	1,438
46,700	46,750	0	0	0	259	0	0	731	1,428
46,750	46,800	0	0	0	248	0	0	721	1,417
46,800	46,850	0	0	0	238	0	0	710	1,407
46,850	46,900	0	0	0	227	0	0	700	1,396
46,900	46,950	0	0	0	217	0	0	689	1,386
46,950	47,000	0	0	0	206	0	0	679	1,375
47,000	47,050	0	0	0	196	0	0	668	1,365
47,050	47,100	0	0	0	185	0	0	658	1,354
47,100	47,150	0	0	0	175	0	0	647	1,344
47,150	47,200	0	0	0	164	0	0	637	1,333
47,200	47,250	0	0	0	154	0	0	626	1,323
47,250	47,300	0	0	0	143	0	0	616	1,312
47,300	47,350	0	0	0	133	0	0	605	1,301
47,350	47,400	0	0	0	122	0	0	594	1,291
47,400	47,450	0	0	0	112	0	0	584	1,280
47,450	47,500	0	0	0	101	0	0	573	1,270
47,500	47,550	0	0	0	91	0	0	563	1,259
47,550	47,600	0	0	0	80	0	0	552	1,249
47,600	47,650	0	0	0	69	0	0	542	1,238
47,650	47,700	0	0	0	59	0	0	531	1,228
47,700	47,750	0	0	0	48	0	0	521	1,217
47,750	47,800	0	0	0	38	0	0	510	1,207
47,800	47,850	0	0	0	27	0	0	500	1,196
47,850	47,900	0	0	0	17	0	0	489	1,186
47,900	47,950	0	0	0	6	0	0	479	1,175
47,950	48,000	0	0	0	*	0	0	468	1,165
48,000	48,050	0	0	0	0	0	0	458	1,154
48,050	48,100	0	0	0	0	0	0	447	1,144
48,100	48,150	0	0	0	0	0	0	437	1,133
48,150	48,200	0	0	0	0	0	0	426	1,122
48,200	48,250	0	0	0	0	0	0	415	1,112
48,250	48,300	0	0	0	0	0	0	405	1,101
48,300	48,350	0	0	0	0	0	0	394	1,091
48,350	48,400	0	0	0	0	0	0	384	1,080
48,400	48,450	0	0	0	0	0	0	373	1,070
48,450	48,500	0	0	0	0	0	0	363	1,059
48,500	48,550	0	0	0	0	0	0	352	1,049
48,550	48,600	0	0	0	0	0	0	342	1,038
48,600	48,650	0	0	0	0	0	0	331	1,028
48,650	48,700	0	0	0	0	0	0	321	1,017
48,700	48,750	0	0	0	0	0	0	310	1,007
48,750	48,800	0	0	0	0	0	0	300	996

If the amount you are looking up from the worksheet is–		And your filing status is– Single, head of household, or qualifying widow(er) and the number of children you have is–				Married filing jointly and the number of children you have is–			
		0	1	2	3	0	1	2	3
At least	But less than	Your credit is–				Your credit is–			
48,800	48,850	0	0	0	0	0	0	289	986
48,850	48,900	0	0	0	0	0	0	279	975
48,900	48,950	0	0	0	0	0	0	268	965
48,950	49,000	0	0	0	0	0	0	258	954
49,000	49,050	0	0	0	0	0	0	247	943
49,050	49,100	0	0	0	0	0	0	236	933
49,100	49,150	0	0	0	0	0	0	226	922
49,150	49,200	0	0	0	0	0	0	215	912
49,200	49,250	0	0	0	0	0	0	205	901
49,250	49,300	0	0	0	0	0	0	194	891
49,300	49,350	0	0	0	0	0	0	184	880
49,350	49,400	0	0	0	0	0	0	173	870
49,400	49,450	0	0	0	0	0	0	163	859
49,450	49,500	0	0	0	0	0	0	152	849
49,500	49,550	0	0	0	0	0	0	142	838
49,550	49,600	0	0	0	0	0	0	131	828
49,600	49,650	0	0	0	0	0	0	121	817
49,650	49,700	0	0	0	0	0	0	110	807
49,700	49,750	0	0	0	0	0	0	100	796
49,750	49,800	0	0	0	0	0	0	89	786
49,800	49,850	0	0	0	0	0	0	78	775
49,850	49,900	0	0	0	0	0	0	68	764
49,900	49,950	0	0	0	0	0	0	57	754
49,950	50,000	0	0	0	0	0	0	47	743
50,000	50,050	0	0	0	0	0	0	36	733
50,050	50,100	0	0	0	0	0	0	26	722
50,100	50,150	0	0	0	0	0	0	15	712
50,150	50,200	0	0	0	0	0	0	**	701
50,200	50,250	0	0	0	0	0	0	0	691
50,250	50,300	0	0	0	0	0	0	0	680
50,300	50,350	0	0	0	0	0	0	0	670
50,350	50,400	0	0	0	0	0	0	0	659
50,400	50,450	0	0	0	0	0	0	0	649
50,450	50,500	0	0	0	0	0	0	0	638
50,500	50,550	0	0	0	0	0	0	0	628
50,550	50,600	0	0	0	0	0	0	0	617
50,600	50,650	0	0	0	0	0	0	0	607
50,650	50,700	0	0	0	0	0	0	0	596
50,700	50,750	0	0	0	0	0	0	0	585
50,750	50,800	0	0	0	0	0	0	0	575
50,800	50,850	0	0	0	0	0	0	0	564
50,850	50,900	0	0	0	0	0	0	0	554
50,900	50,950	0	0	0	0	0	0	0	543
50,950	51,000	0	0	0	0	0	0	0	533
51,000	51,050	0	0	0	0	0	0	0	522
51,050	51,100	0	0	0	0	0	0	0	512
51,100	51,150	0	0	0	0	0	0	0	501
51,150	51,200	0	0	0	0	0	0	0	491
51,200	51,250	0	0	0	0	0	0	0	480
51,250	51,300	0	0	0	0	0	0	0	470
51,300	51,350	0	0	0	0	0	0	0	459
51,350	51,400	0	0	0	0	0	0	0	449
51,400	51,450	0	0	0	0	0	0	0	438
51,450	51,500	0	0	0	0	0	0	0	428
51,500	51,550	0	0	0	0	0	0	0	417
51,550	51,600	0	0	0	0	0	0	0	406
51,600	51,650	0	0	0	0	0	0	0	396
51,650	51,700	0	0	0	0	0	0	0	385
51,700	51,750	0	0	0	0	0	0	0	375
51,750	51,800	0	0	0	0	0	0	0	364
51,800	51,850	0	0	0	0	0	0	0	354
51,850	51,900	0	0	0	0	0	0	0	343
51,900	51,950	0	0	0	0	0	0	0	333
51,950	52,000	0	0	0	0	0	0	0	322

DRAFT AS OF October 17, 2016

* If the amount you are looking up from the worksheet is at least $47,950 but less than $47,955, and you have three qualifying children, your credit is $1.
If the amount you are looking up from the worksheet is $47,955 or more, and you have three qualifying children, you can't take the credit.

** If the amount you are looking up from the worksheet is at least $50,150 but less than $50,198, and you have two qualifying children, your credit is $5.
If the amount you are looking up from the worksheet is $50,198 or more, and you have two qualifying children, you can't take the credit.

(Continued)

Caution: This is a draft 2016 Earned Income Credit (EIC) Table. At the time of publication, the IRS had not yet released the 2016 Earned Income Credit (EIC) Table. For the latest information, see CCHGroup.com/TaxUpdates.

Earned Income Credit (EIC) Table - *Continued*

(**Caution.** This is **not** a tax table.)

If the amount you are looking up from the worksheet is–		And your filing status is–							
		Single, head of household, or **qualifying widow(er)** and the number of children you have is–				**Married filing jointly** and the number of children you have is–			
		0	1	2	3	0	1	2	3
At least	But less than	Your credit is–				Your credit is–			
52,000	52,050	0	0	0	0	0	0	0	312
52,050	52,100	0	0	0	0	0	0	0	301
52,100	52,150	0	0	0	0	0	0	0	291
52,150	52,200	0	0	0	0	0	0	0	280
52,200	52,250	0	0	0	0	0	0	0	270
52,250	52,300	0	0	0	0	0	0	0	259
52,300	52,350	0	0	0	0	0	0	0	248
52,350	52,400	0	0	0	0	0	0	0	238
52,400	52,450	0	0	0	0	0	0	0	227
52,450	52,500	0	0	0	0	0	0	0	217
52,500	52,550	0	0	0	0	0	0	0	206
52,550	52,600	0	0	0	0	0	0	0	196
52,600	52,650	0	0	0	0	0	0	0	185
52,650	52,700	0	0	0	0	0	0	0	175
52,700	52,750	0	0	0	0	0	0	0	164
52,750	52,800	0	0	0	0	0	0	0	154

If the amount you are looking up from the worksheet is–		And your filing status is–							
		Single, head of household, or **qualifying widow(er)** and the number of children you have is–				**Married filing jointly** and the number of children you have is–			
		0	1	2	3	0	1	2	3
At least	But less than	Your credit is–				Your credit is–			
52,800	52,850	0	0	0	0	0	0	0	143
52,850	52,900	0	0	0	0	0	0	0	133
52,900	52,950	0	0	0	0	0	0	0	122
52,950	53,000	0	0	0	0	0	0	0	112
53,000	53,050	0	0	0	0	0	0	0	101
53,050	53,100	0	0	0	0	0	0	0	91
53,100	53,150	0	0	0	0	0	0	0	80
53,150	53,200	0	0	0	0	0	0	0	69
53,200	53,250	0	0	0	0	0	0	0	59
53,250	53,300	0	0	0	0	0	0	0	48
53,300	53,350	0	0	0	0	0	0	0	38
53,350	53,400	0	0	0	0	0	0	0	27
53,400	53,450	0	0	0	0	0	0	0	17
53,450	53,500	0	0	0	0	0	0	0	6
53,500	53,505	0	0	0	0	0	0	0	1

DRAFT AS OF October 7, 2016

¶ 88 Average Itemized Deductions

For those taxpayers who itemize their deductions on Schedule A of Form 1040, the following chart should be of special interest. Based on preliminary statistics for 2014 returns, the chart shows the average deductions of taxpayers for tax year 2014 for interest (¶ 1043), taxes (¶ 1021), medical and dental expenses (¶ 1015), and charitable contributions (¶ 1058). While it may be interesting for those who itemize their deductions to compare them with these average figures, the chart should *not* be considered as indicating amounts that would be allowed by the IRS. In any case, taxpayers must be able to substantiate claimed itemized deductions.

Individual Income Tax Returns, Preliminary Data, 2014, Table 1 (Source: *Spring 2016 Statistics of Income (SOI) Bulletin*).

PRELIMINARY AVERAGE ITEMIZED DEDUCTIONS FOR TAX YEAR 2014 BY ADJUSTED GROSS INCOME RANGES

Adjusted Gross Income Ranges	*Medical Expenses*	*Taxes*	*Interest*	*Charitable Contributions*
Under $ 15,000	$8,787	$3,566	$7,129	$1,427
$ 15,000 to $ 30,000	8,477	3,376	6,619	2,339
$ 30,000 to $ 50,000	8,209	4,098	6,511	2,594
$ 50,000 to $ 100,000	9,614	6,679	7,553	3,147
$ 100,000 to $ 200,000	11,122	10,983	9,147	4,130
$ 200,000 to $ 250,000	18,092	17,763	11,642	5,786
$ 250,000 or more	38,992	50,679	16,982	21,596

Chapter 1
INDIVIDUALS

	Par.
Filing of Tax Returns	101
Computation of Tax Liability	123
Personal and Dependency Exemptions	133
Filing Status	152
Tax Treatment of Decedent's Final Return	178

Filing of Tax Returns

101. Who Must File an Individual Tax Return. All U.S. citizens and resident aliens (¶ 2409) are liable for federal income tax on their worldwide income, without regard to whether the income arose from sources within or outside of the United States (Code Sec. 1; Reg. § 1.1-1(b)).[1] For each tax year, a return (¶ 105) must be filed by a U.S. citizen or a resident alien who has at least a specified minimum amount of gross income.

Filing Thresholds. The filing threshold for most individuals is the sum of the applicable exemption amount (¶ 133) and the applicable standard deduction amount (¶ 126) for the tax year (Code Sec. 6012).[2] The additional standard deduction for taxpayers age 65 or older at the end of the tax year is also taken into account for determining the filing threshold amount; the additional standard deduction for taxpayers who are blind at the end of the tax year is *not* considered. A taxpayer's gross income for this purpose is computed without regard to the exclusion of gain from the sale of a personal residence (¶ 1705) and the exclusion of foreign earned income and housing expenses for U.S. citizens and residents living abroad (¶ 2402).

Generally, the gross income levels at which individuals must file income tax returns for 2016 are:

Single individual (including individuals treated as unmarried for tax purposes; see ¶ 173)	$10,350
Single individual, 65 or older	11,900
Married individual, separate return	4,050
Married couple, joint return	20,700
Married couple, joint return, one spouse 65 or older	21,950
Married couple, joint return, both spouses 65 or older	23,200
Head of household	13,350
Head of household, 65 or older	14,900
Qualifying widow(er) (surviving spouse)	16,650
Qualifying widow(er) (surviving spouse), 65 or older	17,900

Generally, the gross income levels at which individuals must file income tax returns for 2017 are:

Single individual (including individuals treated as unmarried for tax purposes; see ¶ 173)	$10,400
Single individual, 65 or older	11,950
Married individual, separate return	4,050
Married couple, joint return	20,800
Married couple, joint return, one spouse 65 or older	22,050
Married couple, joint return, both spouses 65 or older	23,300
Head of household	13,400
Head of household, 65 or older	14,950
Qualifying widow(er) (surviving spouse)	16,750
Qualifying widow(er) (surviving spouse), 65 or older	18,000

References are to Standard Federal Tax Reports; Tax Research Consultant; and Practical Tax Explanations.

[1] ¶ 3260, ¶ 3265; INDIV: 100; § 1,001

[2] ¶ 35,142; FILEIND: 15,152; § 1,305.05

The income levels for a married couple filing a joint return are not applicable if, at the close of their tax year, the couple does not share the same household or if some other taxpayer is entitled to claim a dependency exemption for either spouse, e.g., a married student who is supported by a parent. In this case, a return for 2016 must be filed if gross income equals $4,050 or more ($4,050 or more for 2017).

Dependents. A child or other individual who can be claimed as a dependent on another person's tax return must file a return if that individual's income exceeds certain threshold amounts for earned or unearned income (Code Sec. 6012(a)(1)(C)).[3] Earned income includes salaries, wages, tips, professional fees, and taxable scholarship and fellowship grants. Unearned income includes investment-type income such as taxable interest, ordinary dividends, capital gain distributions, unemployment compensation, Social Security benefits, pensions, annuities, cancellation of debt income, and distributions of unearned income from a trust. The parent of a child who is subject to the kiddie tax and who has income only from interest or dividends may elect to report the child's income on the parent's return (¶ 103). The child will then *not* have to file a return.

With respect to a dependent child or other individual who is *neither* age 65 or older, or blind, at the end of 2016 and for whom a dependency exemption is allowable to another taxpayer (¶ 137), a return must be filed for the 2016 tax year if the individual has:

- over $1,050 of unearned income ($1,050 for 2017);
- over $6,300 of earned income ($6,350 for 2017); or
- a total of unearned and earned income which exceeds the larger of $1,050 or earned income up to $5,950 ($6,000 for 2017) plus $350.

All married dependents under age 65 with gross income of at least $5 whose spouse files a separate return on Form 1040 and itemizes deductions on Schedule A must file a return.

With respect to a dependent child or other individual who is *either* age 65 or older, or blind, at the end of 2016, and for whom a dependency exemption is allowed to another taxpayer (¶ 137), a return must be filed if the dependent's:

- earned income exceeds the basic standard deduction amount for an unmarried individual plus the additional standard deduction amounts to which he or she is entitled;
- unearned income exceeds the sum of $1,050 plus the additional standard deduction amounts to which he or she is entitled; or
- gross income exceeds the greater of (1) the total of earned income plus $350 (but not to exceed the basic standard deduction amount for an unmarried individual) plus the additional standard deduction amounts to which he or she is entitled; or (2) $1,050 plus the additional standard deduction amounts to which he or she is entitled (¶ 126).

If a guardian or other person is charged with the care of a minor individual or the minor individual's property, or a person under a disability, the return for the individual should be filed by the responsible person, unless already filed by the individual or some other person (¶ 504).

Return Requirement. If the applicable gross income test for the filing threshold is met, then a return must still be filed even though the individual's exemptions and deductions are such that no tax would be due. If the gross income test is *not* met, then a return should be filed whenever a refund of tax or any refundable credit, i.e., the earned income credit, is available. A return is also required if:

References are to Standard Federal Tax Reports; Tax Research Consultant; and Practical Tax Explanations.

[3] ¶ 35,142; FILEIND: 15,152; § 1,305.05

- net earnings from self-employment in 2016 are at least $400 (¶ 2664);
- Social Security and/or Medicare (commonly referred to as FICA) taxes are due on tip income not reported to an employer (¶ 717) or on wages received from an employer who did not withhold the taxes;
- uncollected Social Security, Medicare, or Railroad Retirement Tax Act (RRTA) taxes are due on tips reported to an employer or on group-term life insurance;
- liability for alternative minimum tax is incurred (¶ 1401);
- additional tax on a qualified retirement plan or individual retirement account (IRA) is due as calculated on Form 5329 (¶ 2169);
- additional tax on a health savings account (HSA) (¶ 2035) or Archer medical savings account (MSA) (¶ 2037) is due as calculated on Form 5329;
- household employment taxes are due (¶ 2652);
- tax is due from the recapture of any of the following: the first-time homebuyer credit (¶ 1324); the investment credit (¶ 1365A); the low-income housing credit (¶ 1365K); the new markets credit (¶ 1365T); the qualified plug-in electric drive motor vehicle credit (¶ 1351); the Indian employment credit (¶ 1365Q); the alternative motor vehicle credit (¶ 1345); the employer-provided child care credit (¶ 1365V); the alternative fuel vehicle refueling property credit (¶ 1355); the education credits (¶ 1303); or on the disposition of a home purchased with a federally subsidized mortgage; or
- wages of $108.28 or more were earned from a church or qualified church-controlled organization that is exempt from employer FICA taxes (¶ 2601).

Any person who is required to file an income tax return must report on that return the amount of tax-exempt interest received or accrued during the tax year (¶ 724) (Code Sec. 6012(d)).

103. Returns of Children or Dependents. A child or dependent is generally taxed in the same manner as any other taxpayer on income, including wages, income from property, and trust income (¶ 554). Special rules, however, apply for calculating a child's tax liability if he or she is required to file a return (¶ 101). First, no personal exemption is allowed to an individual eligible to be claimed as a dependent on another taxpayer's return (¶ 135) (Code Sec. 151(d)(2)).[4] Second, the basic standard deduction for dependents in 2016 is limited to the greater of $1,050 or the sum of $350 plus earned income, but not in excess of $6,300, the standard deduction amount for unmarried individuals ($1,050, $350, and $6,350, respectively, for 2017) (¶ 126) (Code Sec. 63(c)(5); Rev. Proc. 2015-53; Rev. Proc. 2016-55).[5] Finally, if a child's income tax is not paid, an assessment made against the child will be treated as if it were made against the child's parent to the extent that the tax is attributable to amounts received for the child's services (Code Sec. 6201(c)).[6]

Kiddie Tax. Ordinarily, a child's tax liability is computed in the same manner as any other taxpayer after taking into account the limits on the personal exemption and standard deduction, if applicable (¶ 123). Certain children with investment income may be subject to tax on that income at the parent's top marginal rate if this results in a higher tax than would apply at the child's rate (Code Sec. 1(g)).[7] This is commonly referred to as the "kiddie tax," and it applies if:

- the child is required to file a tax return;
- the child does not file a joint return for the tax year;
- the child's investment income is more than $2,100 for 2016 (more than $2,100 for 2017);

References are to Standard Federal Tax Reports; Tax Research Consultant; and Practical Tax Explanations.

[4] ¶ 8000; FILEIND: 15,152.25; § 1,505

[5] ¶ 6020; FILEIND: 15,152.25; § 1,505

[6] ¶ 37,502; INDIV: 18,156.10; § 3,005.30

[7] ¶ 3260; INDIV: 18,154; § 1,510.05

- either parent of the child is alive at the end of the year; and
- the child is:

  — under the age of 18 at the end of the tax year;

  — under the age of 19 at the end of the tax year and does not provide more than half of his or her own support with earned income; or

  — under the age of 24 at the end of the tax year, a full-time student, and does not provide more than half of his or her own support with earned income.

The kiddie tax applies to the child's net unearned income, which is the portion of the child's adjusted gross income (AGI) for the tax year that is not attributable to earned income. This amount is further reduced by the limitation on the dependent standard deduction amount ($1,050 for 2016; $1,050 for 2017) and by the greater of either $1,050 in 2016 ($1,050 for 2017) or the child's itemized deductions (¶ 1014) relating to the production of the unearned income (Code Sec. 1(g)(4)). Even though, under state law, compensation for a child's personal services may be treated as belonging to the parent, and even though the money is not retained by the child, it is considered gross income of the child for federal income tax purposes (Reg. § 1.73-1).[8]

The marginal tax rate of the parent with the greater amount of taxable income applies in the case of married individuals filing separately. If the child's parents are divorced or legally separated and the custodial parent has not remarried, the return of the custodial parent should be used. If the custodial parent has remarried, the stepparent is treated as the child's parent for purposes of determining the marginal tax rate. Form 8615 is used to figure the kiddie tax.

Parent's Election. The parents of a child may elect to include on their return the unearned income of a child to avoid the kiddie tax (Code Sec. 1(g)(7); Rev. Proc. 2015-53; Rev. Proc. 2016-55). The election can only be made if all of the following requirements are met:

- the child is required to file a tax return and would otherwise be subject to the kiddie tax;
- the child's only income for the tax year is from interest and dividends, including Alaska Permanent Fund dividends;
- the income was more than $1,050 but less than $10,500 for 2016 ($1,050 and $10,500 in 2017, respectively);
- no estimated tax payments were made for the year in the child's name and Social Security number, including any overpayment of tax from the previous tax year; and
- the child is not subject to backup withholding.

The election is made by filing Form 8814. Electing parents are then taxed on their child's income in excess of $2,100 for the 2016 tax year (in excess of $2,100 for 2017). They must also report an additional tax liability of either $105 ($105 for 2017) if the child's taxable income is more than $1,050 (more than $1,050 for 2017) or 10 percent of the child's income if it is less than $1,050 (less than $1,050 for 2017).

105. Forms in Use for 2016. Three principal forms are available for use by the majority of individuals for filing income tax returns. These forms include Form 1040, a shorter return form, Form 1040A, and for certain taxpayers with no dependents, Form 1040EZ. If the applicable filing conditions are met, any of the forms in the 1040 series may serve as a separate return or as a joint return. If a married person's filing status is married filing separately and the taxpayer uses Form 1040 and itemizes deductions, then his or her spouse can file Form 1040 and either itemize deductions or claim a standard deduction of zero. If the individual decides to claim a standard deduction of zero, he or

References are to Standard Federal Tax Reports; Tax Research Consultant; and Practical Tax Explanations.

[8] ¶ 6150; INDIV: 18,152; § 3,005.30

she may choose to file Form 1040A. These rules do not apply to a spouse who is eligible to file as unmarried or as head of household (¶ 173).

Form 1040EZ. For the 2016 tax year, the simplified income tax return, Form 1040EZ, may be used by a taxpayer who:

- is filing as single or married filing jointly (a taxpayer who was a nonresident alien at any time during the year may file Form 1040EZ *only* if his or her filing status is married filing jointly);
- does not claim any dependents (¶ 137);
- does not claim any adjustments to gross income (¶ 1005);
- does not claim any tax credits other than the earned income tax credit (¶ 1322);
- is under age 65 and not blind, including the spouse if filing a joint return, at the end of 2016;
- has taxable income of less than $100,000 (¶ 123);
- has income from *only* wages, salaries, tips, unemployment compensation, taxable scholarships and/or fellowship grants, Alaska Permanent Fund dividends, and taxable interest income not exceeding $1,500;
- has his or her earned tips included in boxes 5 and 7 of Form W-2;
- does not owe household employment taxes on wages paid to a household employee; and
- is not a debtor in a chapter 11 bankruptcy case filed after October 16, 2005.

If the taxpayer does *not* meet *all* the requirements, then he or she must use either Form 1040 or Form 1040A.

Form 1040A. For the 2016 tax year, Form 1040A may be used by an unmarried individual filing as single, a married couple filing jointly or separately, an individual filing as head of household (¶ 173), or a qualifying widow(er) with a dependent child (a surviving spouse) (¶ 175) if the taxpayer:

- has gross income only from: wages, salaries, tips; interest and ordinary dividends (including Alaska Permanent Fund dividends); capital gains distributions; taxable scholarship and fellowship grants; taxable distributions from IRAs, pensions and annuities; unemployment compensation; and taxable Social Security or railroad retirement benefits;
- has only adjustments to gross income for IRA contributions (¶ 2157), student loan interest paid (¶ 1011), tuition and fees paid (¶ 1011A), or teacher classroom expenses paid (¶ 1011B);
- does not itemize deductions (¶ 1014);
- has taxable income of less than $100,000;
- does not claim any tax credits other than the child tax credit (¶ 1305), the additional child tax credit, the educational credits (¶ 1303), the earned income credit (¶ 1322), the child and dependent care credit (¶ 1301), the elderly and disabled credit (¶ 1302), the retirement savings contributions credit (¶ 1304), or the premium assistance credit (¶ 1331); and
- does not have an alternative minimum tax (AMT) adjustment on stock acquired from the exercise of an incentive stock option (¶ 1435).

Form 1040A may also be used by taxpayers who received dependent care benefits (¶ 2065) or owe tax from the recapture of an education credit (¶ 1303) or the AMT (¶ 1401).

Form 1040. For the 2016 tax year, Form 1040 must be used by a taxpayer if he or she:

- has taxable income of $100,000 or more;
- itemizes deductions (¶ 1014);

- has income that cannot be reported on Form 1040EZ or 1040A, including tax-exempt interest from private activity bonds issued after August 7, 1986 (¶ 729), self-employment (net earnings of at least $400) (¶ 2667), rents and royalties (¶ 762 and ¶ 763), taxable state and local income tax refunds (¶ 799), alimony received (¶ 771), capital gains (¶ 1735), business income (¶ 759), or farm income (¶ 767);
- claims any credit against tax other than those credits which may be claimed on Form 1040A;
- claims any adjustments to income other than the adjustments listed for Form 1040A;
- receives in any month tips of $20 or more that are not reported fully to the employer, has a Form W-2 that shows allocated tips that must be reported in income, owes Social Security or Medicare tax on tips not reported to the employer, or has a Form W-2 that shows any uncollected Social Security, Medicare, or Railroad Retirement Tax Act (RRTA) taxes on tips or on group-term life insurance;
- owes or claims any of the items set out as *Other Taxes* in the discussion following, with the exception of the alternative minimum tax;
- is the grantor of, or transferor to, a foreign trust (¶ 588);
- can exclude foreign earned income received as a U.S. citizen (¶ 2402) or resident alien, certain income received from sources in Puerto Rico due to being a bona fide resident of Puerto Rico, or certain income received from sources in a U.S. possession while a resident of American Samoa (¶ 2414);
- receives or pays accrued interest on securities transferred between interest payment dates (¶ 728);
- earns wages of $108.28 or more from a church or church-controlled organization that is exempt from employer social security taxes;
- receives any nontaxable dividends or capital gain distributions;
- is reporting original issue discount in an amount more or less than that shown on Form 1099-OID;
- receives income as a partner (¶ 415 and ¶ 431), an S corporation shareholder (¶ 309), or a beneficiary of an estate or trust (¶ 554);
- has financial accounts in foreign countries (exceptions apply if the combined value of the accounts was $10,000 or less or if the accounts were with a U.S. military banking facility operated by a U.S. financial institution) (¶ 2570);
- is reporting household employment taxes (¶ 2652);
- receives a health savings account (HSA) funding distribution from his or her individual retirement account (IRA) (¶ 2035);
- is a debtor in a bankruptcy case filed after October 16, 2005; or
- must repay the first-time homebuyer credit (¶ 1324).

Calculating Taxable Income. The basic Form 1040 is a single-sheet, two-page form. To it are added any necessary supporting schedules or forms, depending upon the particular circumstances of the individual taxpayer. Adjustments to gross income on the bottom of page 1 of Form 1040 (commonly referred to as above-the-line deductions) are principally those deductions that may be taken whether or not the standard deduction is employed. They include the deductions for:

- teacher classroom expenses (¶ 1011B);
- employee business expenses of certain fee-basis state or local government officials (¶ 941), performing artists (¶ 941A), and reservist's business expenses (¶ 941E);
- health savings accounts (HSAs) and Archer medical savings accounts (MSAs) (¶ 2035 and ¶ 2037);
- moving expenses (¶ 1073);

- one-half of self-employment tax (¶ 2664);
- contributions to self-employed retirement plans (¶ 2107);
- health insurance premiums paid by self-employed individuals (¶ 908);
- the forfeited interest penalty for premature withdrawals from a time savings account (¶ 1111);
- alimony paid (¶ 771);
- contributions to individual retirement arrangements (IRAs) (¶ 2157);
- student loan interest (¶ 1011);
- qualified tuition and fees (¶ 1011A);
- the domestic production activities deduction (¶ 980A);
- jury duty pay given to an employer (¶ 941 and ¶ 1010);
- amortization of forestation or reforestation expenses (¶ 1287);
- repayment of supplemental unemployment benefits (¶ 1009);
- contributions to Code Sec. 501(c)(18) pension plans (¶ 602);
- contributions by certain chaplains to Code Sec. 403(b) plans (¶ 2191);
- expenses incurred with respect to the rental of personal property (¶ 1006A); and
- attorney's fees and court costs for certain federal claims (¶ 1093).

Once adjusted gross income (AGI) is determined, the appropriate personal exemption amount, and either itemized deductions or the standard deduction amount, are subtracted from AGI to calculate taxable income.

Credits. A number of credits whose excess over tax liability is not refundable in the current year are subtracted from the resulting tax in the following order:

- foreign tax credit (¶ 2475);
- credit for child and dependent care expenses (¶ 1301);
- education credits (¶ 1303);
- retirement savings contributions credit (¶ 1304);
- child tax credit (¶ 1305);
- residential energy credit (¶ 1341);
- credit for the elderly or for the permanently and totally disabled (¶ 1302);
- mortgage interest credit (¶ 1306);
- alternative fuel vehicle refueling property credit (personal use) (¶ 1355);
- general business credit (¶ 1365);
- credit for prior year alternative minimum tax (¶ 1309);
- the new clean renewable energy bond credit (¶ 1374); and
- the qualified plug-in electric drive motor vehicle credit (personal use) (¶ 1351).

Other Taxes. The following taxes are then added:

- alternative minimum tax (¶ 1401);
- self-employment tax (¶ 2664);
- Social Security, Medicare, and/or RRTA tax owing on tip income not reported to the employer, computed on Form 4137, and employee FICA, Medicare, and/or RRTA tax on tips where the employer did not withhold proper amounts, computed on Form 8919 (¶ 2606);
- excess contribution, excess distribution, and premature distribution taxes for IRAs and qualified pension or annuity plans, excess accumulations in qualified pension plans (including IRAs), Archer MSAs and HSAs, or early distribution tax

for a modified endowment contract entered into after June 20, 1988, computed on Form 5329 (¶ 2035, ¶ 2037, ¶ 2151, ¶ 2161, and ¶ 2197);

- household employment taxes (¶ 2652);
- recapture of any of the following: the first-time homebuyer credit (¶ 1324); the investment credit (¶ 1365A); the low-income housing credit (¶ 1365K); the new markets credit (¶ 1365T); the qualified plug-in electric drive motor vehicle credit (¶ 1351); the Indian employment credit (¶ 1365Q); the alternative motor vehicle credit (¶ 1345); the employer-provided child care credit (¶ 1365V); the alternative fuel vehicle refueling property credit (¶ 1355); education credits (¶ 1303); household employment taxes (¶ 2650); or on the disposition of a home purchased with a federally subsidized mortgage;
- the individual responsibility payment ("penalty") for failure to maintain minimal essential health care coverage (¶ 131);
- the "Section 72(m)(5) excess benefits tax" imposed on a five-percent owner of a business who receives a distribution of excess benefits from a qualified pension or annuity plan;
- uncollected Social Security, Medicare, and/or RRTA tax on tips with respect to employees who received wages that were insufficient to cover the Social Security, Medicare, and RRTA tax due on tips reported to their employers;
- uncollected Social Security, Medicare, and/or RRTA tax on group-term life insurance (¶ 2055);
- the additional 0.9-percent Medicare tax on high-income wage earners (¶ 2648);
- the 3.8-percent net investment income tax on high-income individuals (¶ 129);
- any excise tax due on "golden parachute" payments (¶ 907); and
- tax on accumulated distribution of trusts.

Payments. To arrive at final tax due or refund owed, the taxpayer subtracts from the above balance the following:

- federal income tax withheld (¶ 2601);
- 2016 estimated tax payments and amounts applied from 2015 return;
- earned income credit (¶ 1322);
- amounts paid with the application for automatic filing extension (¶ 2509);
- additional child tax credit (¶ 1305);
- refundable portion of the American Opportunity tax credit (AOTC) (¶ 1303);
- excess Social Security tax and/or Tier 1 railroad retirement (RRTA) tax withheld from individuals paid more than a total of $118,500 in wages in 2016 ($127,200 in 2017) by two or more employers (excess Tier 2 RRTA tax withheld from individuals paid more than a total of $88,200 ($94,500 in 2017) by two or more employers is claimed on Form 843, not Form 1040) (¶ 2648);
- health insurance costs credit (¶ 1332);
- credit for excise tax on gasoline and special fuels used in business and credit on certain diesel-powered vehicles (¶ 1329);
- a shareholder's share of capital gains tax paid by a regulated investment company (mutual fund) (¶ 2305); and
- the refundable portion of long-term unused prior year minimum tax credit (expired) (¶ 1327).

Schedules and Supporting Documents. The following schedules and forms are filed with the basic Form 1040 as needed:

- Schedule A for itemizing deductions;

• Schedule B for reporting (a) more than $1,500 of ordinary dividend income and/or other stock distributions, (b) more than $1,500 of taxable interest income or claiming the exclusion of interest from series EE U.S. savings bonds issued after 1989 used for higher educational expenses, and (c) any interests in foreign accounts and trusts;

• Schedule C or Schedule C-EZ for claiming profit or loss from a sole proprietorship;

• Schedule D for reporting a summary of capital gains and losses;

• Schedule E for reporting income or loss from (a) rents and royalties, (b) partnerships and S corporations, (c) estates and trusts, and (d) real estate mortgage investment conduits (REMICs);

• Schedule EIC for providing information regarding the earned income credit;

• Schedule F for computing income and expenses from farming;

• Schedule H for reporting employment taxes for domestic workers paid $2,000 or more during 2016;

• Schedule J for reporting farm income averaging;

• Schedule R for claiming the tax credit for the elderly or the disabled;

• Schedule SE for computing the tax due on income from self-employment;

• Form 2106 or 2106-EZ for computing employee business expenses;

• Form 3903 for calculating moving expenses;

• Form 4562 for reporting depreciation and amortization;

• Form 4684 for reporting personal casualty or theft losses;

• Form 4797 for reporting gains and losses from sales of business assets or from involuntary conversions other than casualty or theft losses (business casualty and theft losses are reported on Form 4684, Section B);

• Form 6251 for computing the alternative minimum tax;

• Form 8283 for claiming a deduction for a noncash charitable contribution where the total claimed value of the contributed property exceeds $500;

• Form 8582 for computing the amount of passive activity loss;

• Form 8606 for reporting nondeductible IRA contributions, for figuring the basis of an IRA, and for calculating nontaxable distributions;

• Form 8615 for computing the tax for certain children who have investment income in excess of $2,100 in 2016;

• Form 8814 for electing to report a child's unearned income on the parents' income tax return;

• Form 8829 for figuring allowable expenses for business use of a home;

• Form 8834 for figuring the personal credit amount for the purchase of a qualified plug-in electric or electric vehicle credit;

• Form 8853 for figuring the allowable deduction for contributions to an Archer Medical Savings Account (Archer MSA);

• Form 8888 for direct deposit of income tax refunds into more than one account including, but not limited to, individual retirement accounts;

• Form 8889 for figuring the allowable deduction for contributions to a Health Savings Account (HSA);

• Form 8919, for reporting uncollected Social Security and Medicare taxes on wages;

• Form 8949 for reporting sales and exchanges of capital assets;

• Form 8959, for reporting additional Medicare tax on high-income wage earners; and

- Form 8960, for reporting the net investment income tax by high-income individuals.

The following forms are for computing and claiming credits:

- Form 1116 to compute the foreign tax credit for individuals, estates or trusts;
- Form 2441 to figure the child and dependent care credit;
- Form 3800 if any of the components of the general business credit are claimed;
- Form 5405 for calculating the amount of the credit recapture for first-time homebuyer claims (¶ 1324);
- Form 5884 to calculate the work opportunity credit;
- Form 8396 to figure the mortgage interest credit and any carryforwards;
- Form 8801 to compute the credit for prior year alternative minimum tax including the refundable portion;
- Form 8812 to claim the additional child tax credit;
- Form 8828 to compute the recapture of a federal mortgage subsidy;
- Form 8834 to determine the amount of qualified electric vehicle passive activity credits from prior years;
- Form 8839 to claim the adoption credit;
- Form 8863 to claim the education credits;
- Form 8880 to claim the credit for qualified retirement savings contributions;
- Form 8882 to claim the credit for employer-provided child care facilities and services;
- Form 8885 to claim the health insurance costs credit;
- Form 8903 to claim the deduction for domestic production activity;
- Form 8910 to claim the alternative motor vehicle credit;
- Form 8911 to claim the alternative fuel vehicle refueling property credit; and
- Form 8912 to claim the credit for holders of tax credit bonds;

IRS Computation of Tax. Any taxpayer who files an individual tax return by the due date, April 18, 2017, can have the IRS compute the tax under certain conditions on Form 1040, Form 1040A, and Form 1040EZ. The IRS may also figure the credit for the elderly or the disabled and the earned income credit. See IRS Pub. 17 for the requirements to have the IRS compute a taxpayer's tax liability or these credits. These returns must have all applicable lines completed, be signed (by both spouses if filing jointly) and dated. If taxpayers want to designate a friend, family member or any other person to be allowed to discuss their 2016 tax return with the IRS, they must check the Yes box in the Third Party Designee area and provide the necessary information. Inclusion of a daytime telephone number of the taxpayer will speed the process should any questions arise. Form W-2 and any other required forms necessary to complete the return should be attached. If the taxpayer overpaid his or her taxes for the year, the IRS will refund that amount. If an amount is due, the taxpayer must pay the amount no later than 30 days from the billing date or due date of the return; failure to do so may result in penalties and interest.

Rounding Off Amounts. Dollar amounts on the return and accompanying schedules and forms may be rounded off to the nearest whole dollar.

107. Due Date for Individual Returns. Individual income tax returns are generally due on or before the 15th day of the 4th month following the close of the tax year (April

15 in the case of a calendar-year taxpayer) (¶ 2505) (Code Sec. 6072; Reg. § 1.6072-1).[9] U.S. citizens and resident aliens living outside the country have an additional two months to file their returns (June 15 in the case of a calendar-year taxpayer). Similarly, a nonresident alien who has wages *not* subject to withholding generally may also file a return as late as the 15th day of the 6th month after the close of the tax year. A nonresident alien who has wages subject to withholding, however, must file a return by the 15th day of the 4th month following the close of the tax year. If any due date falls on a Saturday, Sunday, or legal holiday, the return must be filed on the first following business day (¶ 2549) (Code Sec. 7503; Reg. § 301.7503-1).[10] An individual taxpayer can obtain—without seeking IRS approval—an automatic six-month extension of time to file his or her tax return (¶ 109).

An individual may correct an error in a return, without incurring interest or penalties, by filing an amended return (Form 1040X) and paying any additional tax due on or before the last day prescribed for filing the original return. For further information regarding amended returns, see ¶ 2505.

109. Extension for Filing. An individual may obtain an automatic six month extension for filing Forms 1040, 1040A or 1040EZ by filing Form 4868 before the due date of the return, accompanied by a reasonable estimate of tax due for the year (¶ 2509) (Reg. § 1.6081-4).[11] U.S. citizens or residents who live and have a main place of business or post of duty outside the U.S. and Puerto Rico, or who are in military or naval service on duty outside the U.S. and Puerto Rico, generally file their income tax return by the 15th of the sixth month after the close of the tax year (June 15 in the case of a calendar-year taxpayer). These individuals, upon filing of Form 4868, are given an automatic additional four-month extension for the filing of their return (Reg. § 1.6081-5).[12] An automatic extension of time for filing a return will not extend the time for payment of any tax due, and interest and penalties may apply. Finally, interest will be charged on any unpaid tax from the original due date of the return.

111. Where to File Returns. The IRS strongly encourages all taxpayers to file their returns electronically through the IRS's e-file system. For individuals who prefer to mail their income tax returns, the returns are filed with the Internal Revenue Service Center for the region in which the individual's residence or principal place of business is located (Code Sec. 6091; Reg. § 1.6091-2).[13] Taxpayers must be aware that income tax returns which include a tax payment are mailed to a different address than returns showing a refund or no tax liability. For example, U.S. citizens living abroad, nonresident aliens, and certain other taxpayers must file their income tax returns if no payment of tax is required at the IRS Service Center located in Austin, Texas. If a payment is required, the return should be filed at the IRS Service Center in Charlotte, North Carolina. For a list of addresses of filing locations, see ¶ 5.

116. Identifying Number. Every taxpayer must record his or her taxpayer identification number (TIN) on the income tax return (Code Sec. 6109(a); Reg. § 301.6109-1).[14] This is either the taxpayer's Social Security number (SSN), Individual Taxpayer Identification Number (ITIN) (for use by resident or nonresident aliens who do not qualify for a Social Security number), or Adoption Taxpayer Identification Number (ATIN) (a temporary taxpayer identification number for use by individuals in the process of adopting a child for whom they are unable to obtain a Social Security number until the adoption is final) (¶ 2579). If a taxpayer does not have a TIN, he or she should apply for either a Social Security number using Form SS-5, an ITIN using Form W-7, or an ATIN using Form W-7A. Taxpayers must provide TINs for dependents and qualifying children for the purpose of claiming a dependency exemption (¶ 133), the earned income tax credit (¶ 1322), the child care credit (¶ 1301), the adoption credit (¶ 1307), and the child tax

References are to Standard Federal Tax Reports; Tax Research Consultant; and Practical Tax Explanations.

[9] ¶ 36,720, ¶ 36,721; FILEIND: 18,052.20; § 1,325.05

[10] ¶ 42,630, ¶ 42,631; FILEBUS: 15,056; § 1,325.05

[11] ¶ 36,793; FILEBUS: 15,104; § 1,325.10

[12] ¶ 36,795; FILEBUS: 15,104.15; § 1,325.10

[13] ¶ 36,800, ¶ 36,808; FILEBUS: 12,150; § 1,325.20

[14] ¶ 36,960, ¶ 36,961; FILEBUS: 12,106; § 1,335

credit (¶ 1305). An ATIN, however, cannot be used for purposes of claiming the earned income tax credit. It should be noted that to in order to claim the refundable earned income tax or child tax credit, the TIN must be issued on or before the due date of the return. Individuals claiming the earned income tax credit must also include TINs for themselves and their spouses, if married. Failure to include a correct TIN will be treated as a mathematical or clerical error, as will instances when the information provided differs from the information on file with the IRS that is obtained from the Social Security Administration (Code Sec. 6213(g)(2)(F)).[15] The parent of any child to whom the rules governing taxation of unearned income of minor children apply must provide his or her TIN to the child for inclusion on the child's tax return (¶ 103).

117. Estimated Taxes. Individuals are required to make estimated tax payments if the amount of tax they pay through withholding on wages and other payments will not adequately cover their tax liability for the year (¶ 2875). As 2016 ends, the first responsibility of the calendar-year taxpayer is to review payments of estimated tax for 2016 to make sure that these tax payments and the income tax withheld from wages during the year are sufficient to avoid penalties on the last installment, which is due January 17, 2017. The 2016 estimated tax payments, plus income tax withheld from wages, are credited against tax due for 2016. Any underpayment of tax must be made up by a payment with the final return, and any overpayment is either refunded or credited against the estimated tax for the next year, whichever the taxpayer elects on the return (¶ 2682). For the special rules related to estimated tax payments for farmers and fishermen, see ¶ 2691.

Overpayment. An individual who has been making payments of estimated tax for 2016, and who finds that by paying the installment scheduled for January 17, 2017, he or she will overpay the 2016 tax, may:

- make the payment as scheduled on or before January 17, 2017, file the return on or before April 18, 2017, and direct whether the overpayment should be refunded or credited toward the 2017 estimated tax;
- reduce the payment due on or before January 17, 2017, so that the estimated tax payments plus withholding will meet the tax liability that will be shown on the return to be filed on or before April 18, 2017;
- pay enough estimated tax to cover the minimum requirement as described at ¶ 2875 in order to avoid a penalty on the January 17, 2017, payment and then pay any difference on the final return, filed on or before April 18, 2017; or
- file the final return on or before January 31, 2017, add up all payments of estimated tax plus any withholding, and use this return for a final accounting of 2016 tax liability.

Underpayment. The law provides a penalty for underpayment of estimated tax. A taxpayer can avoid this penalty by paying the minimum installment authorized under one of the exceptions described at ¶ 2682. The taxpayer may file the tax return for calendar year 2016 on or before January 31, 2017, and pay any balance of tax that may still be due for 2016. Under this method, no penalty will apply for failure to make the last quarterly installment, and any penalty for underpayment of any of the three earlier installments will not be increased (¶ 2688).

Computation of Tax Liability

123. Taxable Income of Individuals. An individual computes his or her tax liability for a tax year by multiplying taxable income by the applicable tax rate, subtracting allowable credits, and adding other taxes. The computation of taxable income starts with gross income (¶ 701), from which certain deductions (commonly referred to as either adjustments to gross income or above-the-line deductions) are subtracted to determine the taxpayer's adjusted gross income (AGI) (¶ 1005). After AGI is determined, certain

References are to Standard Federal Tax Reports; Tax Research Consultant; and Practical Tax Explanations.

[15] ¶ 37,545; FILEBUS: 12,106; § 1,335

other deductions are subtracted from a taxpayer's AGI to determine his or her taxable income. These include the deduction for personal and dependency exemptions (¶ 133), the standard deduction (¶ 126), or, in lieu of the standard deduction, the taxpayer's itemized deductions (¶ 1014). Once taxable income is determined, the taxpayer's tax liability is generally computed by applying the appropriate tax rates based on the taxpayer's filing status (single, married filing jointly, head of household, surviving spouse, or married filing separately). Subject to certain exceptions, taxpayers *must* use either the tax rate tables or tax schedules issued by the IRS to compute their income tax. See ¶ 128 for a discussion of the tax rate tables and tax schedules.

126. Standard Deduction. An individual taxpayer who does not elect to itemize deductions (¶ 1014) computes taxable income by subtracting from adjusted gross income (AGI) the standard deduction and the deduction for personal exemptions (¶ 133). Taxpayers have a choice of itemizing deductions or claiming the standard deduction, whichever will result in a higher deduction. The standard deduction amount is the sum of the basic standard deduction, plus the additional standard deduction amounts for aged and blind taxpayers.[16]

Basic Standard Deduction. The basic standard deduction amount varies according to the taxpayer's filing status and is adjusted annually for inflation. The basic standard deduction amounts available to individuals in 2016 are (Code Sec. 63(c)(2); Rev. Proc. 2015-53):

Filing status	*2016 standard deduction amount*
Married filing jointly and surviving spouses	$12,600
Married filing separately	6,300
Head of household filers	9,300
Single filers	6,300

The basic standard deduction amounts available to individuals in 2017 are (Rev. Proc. 2016-55):

Filing status	*2017 standard deduction amount*
Married filing jointly and surviving spouses	$12,700
Married filing separately	6,350
Head of household filers	9,350
Single filers	6,350

A taxpayer who can be claimed as a dependent on another taxpayer's return is limited to a smaller standard deduction regardless of whether the individual actually is claimed as a dependent. The dependent's basic standard deduction may not exceed the greater of $1,050 ($1,050 for 2017) or the sum of $350 and the individual's earned income, up to the applicable standard deduction amount (for single taxpayers: $6,300 for 2016; $6,350 for 2017) (Code Sec. 63(c)(5); Rev. Proc. 2015-53; Rev. Proc. 2016-55).[17] The limit applies to the basic standard deduction and not to any additional amount such as for elderly or blind taxpayers. A scholarship or fellowship grant that is *not* excludable from the dependent's gross income (¶ 865) is considered earned income for this purpose (IRS Pub. 501).

Elderly and/or Blind Taxpayers. Taxpayers who are age 65 or older, or blind, or both, at the end of the tax year receive an additional standard deduction amount that is added to the basic standard deduction shown in the table above. The additional amount is $1,250 for tax years beginning in 2016 for married individuals, whether filing jointly or separately, and surviving spouses ($1,250 for 2017). The additional amount is $1,550 for tax years beginning in 2016 for unmarried individuals, whether filing as single or as head of household ($1,550 for 2017) (Code Sec. 63(f), Reg. § 1.151-1; Rev. Proc. 2015-53; Rev. Proc. 2016-55).[18] Two additional standard deduction amounts are allowed to an individual who is both over 65 and blind at the end of the tax year. Thus, married

References are to Standard Federal Tax Reports; Tax Research Consultant; and Practical Tax Explanations.

[16] ¶ 6020, ¶ 6023.10; FILEIND: 12,100; § 1,010.15

[17] ¶ 6020; FILEIND: 12,106; § 1,010.15

[18] ¶ 6020, ¶ 8001; FILEIND: 12,104; § 1,010.15

taxpayers filing jointly, both of whom are over 65 and blind, would claim four of the additional standard deduction amounts.

A taxpayer claiming the additional standard deduction must be either age 65 or blind, or both, before the close of the tax year. An individual who reaches age 65 on January 1st of any year is deemed to have reached that age on the preceding December 31st. A taxpayer claiming the additional amount for blindness must obtain a certified statement from a doctor or registered optometrist. The statement, which should be kept with the taxpayer's records, must state either that: (1) the individual cannot see better than 20/200 in the better eye with glasses or contact lenses; or (2) the individual's field of vision is 20 degrees or less.

A married taxpayer filing separately may claim the additional amounts for a spouse who had no gross income for the year and was not claimed as a dependent by another taxpayer (Code Sec. 151(b)). A taxpayer who claims a dependency exemption for an individual who is either age 65 or older, blind, or both may *not* claim the additional standard deduction amounts for that individual.

Taxpayers Ineligible for Standard Deduction. When married taxpayers file separate returns, both spouses should either itemize their deductions or claim the standard deduction. This is because if one spouse itemizes and the other does not, the non-itemizing spouse's standard deduction amount will be zero, even if such spouse is age 65 or older, or blind, or both. This rule does not apply if one spouse qualifies to file as head-of-household. A zero standard deduction amount also applies to nonresident aliens, estates or trusts, common trust funds, or partnerships, and to individuals with short tax years due to a change in their annual accounting period (Code Sec. 63(c)(6)).[19] Taxpayers who itemize even though their itemized deductions are less than the standard deduction must check the box on the last line of Schedule A of Form 1040 to make this election.

128. Tax Rates and Tables for Individuals. Most individuals determine their income tax liability by applying the appropriate tax rate to their taxable income (¶ 123) based on their filing status (¶ 152 and ¶ 173). There are seven tax rates for individuals, which are 10, 15, 25, 28, 33, 35, and, for individuals with taxable income in excess of the applicable threshold amount, 39.6 percent (Code Sec. 1(i)).[20] All threshold amounts are subject to inflation adjustment. The applicable threshold amounts for 2016 are $466,950 for married taxpayers filing jointly or surviving spouse filers, $441,000 for head of household filers, $415,050 for unmarried individuals other than head of household and surviving spouse filers, and $233,475 for married taxpayers filing separately (Rev. Proc. 2015-53). The applicable threshold amounts for 2017 are $470,700 for married taxpayers filing jointly or surviving spouse filers, $444,550 for head of household filers, $418,400 for unmarried individuals other than head of household and surviving spouse filers, and $235,350 for married taxpayers filing separately (Rev. Proc. 2016-55).

For 2016, the 10-percent bracket applies to the first $9,275 of taxable income for single filers and married taxpayers filing separately ($9,325 for 2017), the first $13,250 of taxable income for head-of-household filers ($13,350 for 2017), and the first $18,550 of taxable income for married taxpayers filing jointly and surviving spouses ($18,650 for 2017) (Rev. Proc. 2015-53; Rev. Proc. 2016-55). The upper limit of the 15-percent tax bracket for joint filers is 200 percent of the upper limit of the 15-percent tax bracket for single filers (Code Sec. 1(f)(8)).

Subject to certain exceptions listed later, individuals *must* use either the tax rate tables or tax schedules issued by the IRS to compute their income tax (Code Sec. 3).[21] Taxpayers whose taxable income is less than $100,000 *must* use the tax tables reproduced at ¶ 25. Taxpayers whose taxable income is $100,000 or more *must* use the Tax Computation Worksheet in the Form 1040 Instructions (reproduced at ¶ 20), which is based on the tax rate schedules at ¶ 11 for single taxpayers, ¶ 13 for married individuals

References are to Standard Federal Tax Reports; Tax Research Consultant; and Practical Tax Explanations.

[19] ¶ 6020; FILEIND: 12,108; § 1,010.15

[20] ¶ 3260; FILEIND: 15,054; § 1,015

[21] ¶ 3345; FILEIND: 15,054.10; § 1,015

filing jointly and surviving spouses, ¶ 15 for married individuals filing separately, and ¶ 17 for heads of households, in order to compute their tax. Taxpayers may *not* use the table if they file short-period returns because of a change in their annual accounting periods (¶ 1507).

Tax Calculation on Form 8615. Form 8615 must be used to figure the tax of a child subject to the *kiddie tax* rules (¶ 103). Taxpayers required to calculate their tax on Form 8615 may compute taxable income using Form 1040 or Form 1040A. Form 8615 is not filed if the child's parent elects to include the child's unearned income on the parent's return.

Capital Gain Tax Calculation. Taxpayers who had a net capital gain from a sale or exchange (¶ 1736) use Form 1040, Schedule D, Part III, to determine which of the capital gains tax worksheets to use to calculate the amount of tax on the capital gains. Taxpayers with sales or exchanges of assets taxed at the 28-percent rate or with unrecaptured Code Sec. 1250 gains, or both, complete the "Schedule D Tax Worksheet" in the Instructions to Schedule D of Form 1040. All other taxpayers, including those with only qualified dividends and net capital gains from a distribution of a regulated investment company (RIC/mutual fund), complete the "Qualified Dividends and Capital Gains Tax Worksheet" in the Form 1040 or 1040A instructions.

129. Net Investment Income Tax. An individual is subject to an additional 3.8 percent tax for tax years beginning after December 31, 2012, on the lesser of net investment income for the tax year or the excess modified adjusted gross income (MAGI) for the tax year over a threshold amount (Code Sec. 1411; Reg. § 1.1411-2).[22] The net investment tax is determined using Form 8960. Although the tax is an addition to the regular income tax liability, it is taken into account for purposes of calculating estimated tax payments and underpayment penalties (Code Sec. 6654(a) and (f)). The tax also applies to the net investment income of estates and trusts (¶ 517).

For individuals, the net investment income tax is 3.8 percent of the lesser of (1) the taxpayer's net investment income for the tax year, or (2) the excess of MAGI for the tax year over the threshold amount of $200,000 ($250,000 for married taxpayers filing jointly and surviving spouses, and $125,000 for a married taxpayer filing separately). MAGI is the taxpayer's adjusted gross income (AGI) increased by any foreign income excluded from gross income for the year under Code Sec. 911 less any deductions, exclusions, or credits properly allocable to such foreign income.

The net investment income tax applies to all individuals subject to U.S. taxation other than nonresident aliens (Reg. § 1.1411-2). Special rules apply to U.S. citizens or residents married to a nonresident alien. The default position is that these couples are treated as married filing separately for purposes of the tax. If they elect to file jointly under Code Sec. 6013(g) (¶ 152), however, these couples may also make a separate election to apply the joint return election for net investment income tax purposes, so that the tax applies to their combined investment income.

Net investment income is the excess of the sum of the following items, less any otherwise allowable deductions properly allocable to such income or gain (Reg. § 1.1411-4):

(a) gross income from interest, dividends, annuities, royalties, rents, and substitute interest and dividend payments, but not to the extent this income is derived in the ordinary course of an active trade or business;

(b) other gross income (not described in (a)) from a passive activity under Code Sec. 469 (¶ 1169), or from a trade or business of a trader trading in financial instruments or commodities; and

References are to Standard Federal Tax Reports; Tax Research Consultant; and Practical Tax Explanations.

[22] ¶ 32,602, ¶ 32,603H; INDIV: 69,150; § 1,022.10

(c) net gain included in computing taxable income that is attributable to the disposition of property, but not to the extent the property was held in an active trade or business.

Any item that is excluded from gross income for regular income tax purposes is also excluded from net investment income and MAGI (Reg. § 1.1411-1(d)(4)). Some examples of such items are: excludable gain on the sale of a taxpayer's personal residence; veterans' benefits; and tax-exempt bond interest.

Net investment income generally does not include income and gain derived in the ordinary course of a trade or business, unless the trade or business is a passive activity or that of a trader trading in financial instruments or commodities. If an individual owns or engages in a trade or business directly (or indirectly through owning a disregarded entity), the determination of whether gross income is derived in a trade or business is made at the individual level. If an individual owns an interest in a trade or business through one or more passthrough entities, e.g., a partnership or S corporation, the determination of whether gross income is derived in a passive activity is made at the owner level, and the determination of whether gross income is derived in the trade or business of a trader trading in financial instruments or commodities is made at the entity level (Reg. § 1.1411-4(b)). Similar rules apply for determining whether net gain is attributable to property held in a trade or business. For purposes of determining net gain, a disposition is a sale, exchange, transfer, conversion, cash settlement, cancellation, termination, lapse, expiration, or other disposition. Net gain cannot be less than zero, and losses from dispositions of capital assets are allowed to offset gains, unless the asset's disposition is subject to the net investment income tax. The $3,000 deduction ($1,500 for married individuals filing separate returns) under Code Sec. 1211 (¶ 1752) may not be taken against losses on capital assets but may be taken against other net investment income (Reg. § 1.1411-4). Losses deductible under Code Sec. 165, including losses attributable to casualty, theft, and abandonment or other worthlessness (¶ 1101), are applied to calculate net gains, and then any excess losses are applied as properly allocable deductions against investment income (Reg. § 1.1411-4(d)).

Property held in a trade or business does not generally include an interest in a partnership or stock in an S corporation, so gain from the disposition of such an interest or stock is usually treated as net gain. However, special rules apply upon the disposition of an active interest in a partnership or S corporation (Prop. Reg. § 1.1411-7).

The net investment income tax rules might cause taxpayers to reconsider the way they have previously grouped activities for passive activity loss purposes under Code Sec. 469. In light of this concern, taxpayers subject to the net investment income tax are provided with a one-time election to regroup activities under Code Sec. 469 to allow for realignment of grouped activities to properly reflect the interaction of the Code Sec. 469 rules and income for net investment income tax purposes. Further, regrouping may be done on an amended return if the taxpayer was not subject to net investment income tax on the original return (Reg. § 1.469-11(b)(3)(iv)).[23]

Net investment income includes any income, gain, or loss that is attributable to an investment of working capital (Reg. § 1.1411-6). Net investment income does not include a distribution from qualified employee benefit plans or arrangements, including: a qualified pension, profit sharing, and stock-bonus plan; qualified annuity plan under Code Sec. 403(a) or (b); a traditional or Roth IRA; or a Code Sec. 457 plan of a government or tax-exempt organization (Reg. § 1.1411-8). However, a distribution from a qualified plan or arrangement that is includible in gross income is taken into account for determining the taxpayer's MAGI in the net investment income tax calculation.

Special rules are provided for self-employed individuals (Reg. § 1.1411-9) and controlled foreign corporations and passive foreign investment companies (Reg. § 1.1411-10).

References are to Standard Federal Tax Reports; Tax Research Consultant; and Practical Tax Explanations.

[23] ¶ 21,965F; INDIV: 69,160.20; § 17,415.05

131. Individual Health Care Coverage Mandate. Effective for tax years beginning after December 31, 2013, an individual is required to either maintain minimum essential health care coverage or make a shared responsibility payment, i.e., a penalty payment for failure to maintain minimum essential health care coverage (Code Sec. 5000A; Reg. §§ 1.5000A-1—1.5000A-5).[24] The shared responsibility payment (i.e., the penalty) is imposed on an applicable individual for each month he or she fails to maintain minimum essential health care coverage for him- or herself, or his or her dependents.

If the taxpayer qualifies to claim an individual as a dependent on his or her income tax return (¶ 137), then the taxpayer, rather than the dependent, is liable for the shared responsibility payment that would otherwise be imposed on the dependent during the taxpayer's tax year, regardless of whether the taxpayer actually claims the dependency exemption (Reg. § 1.5000A-1(c)). If an individual qualifies as a dependent of more than one taxpayer, the taxpayer who properly claims the dependency exemption is liable for the penalty. If no one claims the dependency exemption, the taxpayer with priority under the rules of Code Sec. 152 will be liable for the penalty. Special rules govern who is responsible for dependents that are placed for adoption, adopted, or placed in foster care. Married taxpayers who file a joint return are jointly liable for the penalty that is imposed on either one of them for any month during the tax year.

The penalty is included on the taxpayer's income tax return for the tax year that includes the month for which the penalty is imposed (Code Sec. 5000A(b)(2)). It must be paid upon notice and demand by the IRS, and is assessed and collected in the same manner as other tax imposed under the Code (Reg. § 1.5000A-5). A taxpayer, however, will not be subject to any criminal prosecution or criminal penalty for failing to timely pay the penalty. In addition, the IRS cannot file a notice of lien or levy on any property to collect any unpaid penalty but they may use any overpayment due the taxpayer to offset any liability for the penalty.

Applicable Individuals. Every individual is an applicable individual subject to the penalty for failure to maintain minimum health care coverage, unless he or she is a member of a specific group whose members are not considered applicable individuals (Code Sec. 5000A(d); Reg. § 1.5000A-3). Members of these groups include:

- individuals who have obtained a religious conscience exemption as a member of a recognized religious sect or division described in Code Sec. 1402(g)(1), i.e., groups objecting to private and public insurance, and who adhere to the established tenets or teachings of the sect or division;

- individuals who are members of a health care sharing ministry, which is an organization described under Code Sec. 501(c)(3), and tax exempt under Code Sec. 501(a), whose members share the same ethical and religious beliefs and share medical expenses among themselves, that retains members even after they develop a medical condition, that has been in existence since December 31, 1999, whose members have shared all medical expenses continuously since then, and that conducts an annual audit that is performed by an independent certified public accountant and made public upon request;

- individuals who are not U.S. citizens or nationals, or are not lawfully present in the United States; and

- individuals who are incarcerated, except for those incarcerated while waiting for disposition of their charges.

There are also a number of exemptions from maintaining minimal health care coverage (Code Sec. 5000A(e)). An individual who is otherwise an applicable individual may be exempt from the penalty if he or she:

References are to Standard Federal Tax Reports; Tax Research Consultant; and Practical Tax Explanations.

[24] ¶ 34,962, ¶ 34,962D—¶ 34,962L; HEALTH: 3,050; § 42,001

- cannot afford health care coverage, meaning that the individual's required contribution exceeds eight percent of his or her household income;
- has household income below his or her income thresholds for filing an income tax return for the tax year (¶ 101);
- lacked minimum essential coverage for a continuous period of less than three months;
- is a member of an Indian tribe as defined for purposes of the Indian employment credit under Code Sec. 45A; or
- experiences a hardship with respect to the capability to obtain coverage under a qualified health plan.

A taxpayer's minimum required contribution for purposes of the unaffordable coverage exemption is either (1) the annual premium for self-only minimum essential coverage of an employer-sponsored plan, or (2) the annual premium of the single lowest cost bronze plan available in the individual market through a Health Benefit Exchange, reduced by the health care credit under Code Sec. 36B (¶ 1331) (Code Sec. 5000A(e)(1)(B)). The required contribution percentage is indexed to premium costs. For plan years beginning in 2016, the required contribution percentage is 8.13 percent (Rev. Proc. 2014-62). For plan years beginning in 2017, the required contribution percentage is 8.16 percent (Rev. Proc. 2016-24).

The taxpayer's household income for this purpose is the sum of his or her modified adjusted gross income (MAGI), plus the MAGI of all other individuals in the taxpayer's family for whom the taxpayer is allowed a dependency exemption deduction and who were required to file an income tax return for the tax year (Code Sec. 5000A(c)(4)). MAGI is the taxpayer's adjusted gross income (AGI) increased by any exclusion from gross income under Code Sec. 911, foreign earned income and housing costs, plus any tax-exempt interest received during the tax year. Household income must be increased by any required contribution made through a salary reduction agreement and excluded from the individual's gross income, e.g., health insurance premiums paid through a cafeteria plan.

Example 1: Susanna is an unmarried individual with no dependents. In November 2016, Susanna is eligible to enroll in self-only coverage under a plan offered by her employer for calendar year 2017. If she enrolls in this plan, she is required to pay $5,000 of the total annual premium. In 2017, Susanna's annual income is $60,000. Her minimum required contribution is $5,000, the portion of the annual premium that she pays for self-only coverage. Susanna will be considered to lack affordable coverage for 2017 because her required contribution ($5,000) is greater than 8.16 percent of her household income ($60,000 x 8.16% = $4,896) (Reg. § 1.5000A-3(e)(3)(iii), Ex. 1).

Example 2: Bill and Kate are married and file a joint return for 2017. They have two children. In November 2016, Bill is eligible to enroll in self-only coverage in his employer's sponsored plan for calendar year 2017, with his total annual premium being $5,000. Kate and the children are eligible for family coverage under the same plan, at a total annual premium of $20,000. The family's total household income for 2017 is $90,000. Bill's minimum required contribution is equal to his premium for self-only coverage ($5,000). Bill has affordable coverage available for himself, because the annual premium for self-only coverage ($5,000) is less than 8.16 percent of his household income ($90,000 x 8.16% = $7,344). The required minimum contribution for Kate and the two children is Bill's share of the cost for family coverage ($20,000). Kate and the two children lack affordable health care coverage because their required minimum contribution ($20,000) exceeds 8.16 percent of their household income ($90,000 x 8.16% = $7,344) (Reg. § 1.5000A-3(e)(3)(iii), Ex. 2).

A short lapse of minimum essential coverage, i.e., short coverage gap, is defined as a continuous period of less than three months. The continuous period is determined without regard to the calendar year. If the taxpayer has more than one continuous lapse of coverage, only the first lapsed period will be counted for this exception (Code Sec. 5000A(e)(4); Reg. § 1.5000A-3(j)).

Example 3: Dave has minimum essential coverage in the current year from January 1 through March 2. After March 2, he does not have minimum essential coverage until he enrolls in an employer sponsored plan effective on June 15. Dave has minimum essential coverage for January, February and March, and June through December. Coverage on the first day of the month qualifies the entire month to be considered a coverage month. Dave is considered without minimum essential coverage for April and May, a continuous period of only two months. Dave will qualify for the short term coverage gap exemption (Reg. § 1.5000A-3(j)(4), Ex. 1).

Hardship exemption certificates are issued by an Exchange and certify that an individual has suffered a hardship as defined in 45 CFR 166.605(g) with respect to obtaining minimum essential coverage (Reg. § 1.5000A-3(h)(2)). The IRS has issued guidance on certain hardship exemptions which may be claimed on a Federal income tax return without obtaining hardship certificate (Notice 2014-76). These hardship exemptions are;

- when two or more members of a family whose combined cost of employer-sponsored coverage is considered unaffordable,
- when gross income is below the applicable return filing threshold,
- for individuals eligible through an Indian Health Care Provider, and
- for certain individuals residing in state that did not expand Medicaid eligibility under section 2001(a) of the Affordable Care Act.

Minimum Essential Coverage. Minimum essential coverage means health care coverage under a government-sponsored program (Medicare, Medicaid, CHIP, etc.), an eligible employer-sponsored plan, a health insurance plan offered in the individual market, a group health plan in which the individual was enrolled on March 23, 2010, an eligible expatriate health plan (for plans issued or modified on or after July 1, 2015), or any other coverage recognized by the IRS (Code Sec. 5000A(f); Reg. § 1.5000A-2; Notice 2015-43; Proposed Reg. § 1.5000A-2(c)(1)(i)(D)). Minimum essential coverage does not include health insurance coverage that consists of excepted benefits, such as accident or disability benefits, liability insurance, workers compensation, credit-only insurance, automobile medical payments, or coverage for on-site medical clinics. Applicable to tax years beginning after December 31, 2013, certain government-sponsored limited benefit coverage (e.g., line of duty coverage for inactive service members, Medicaid coverage for the medically needy, etc.) does not constitute minimum essential coverage (Reg. § 1.5000A-2).

If benefits are provided under a separate policy, certificate, or insurance contract, then excepted benefits also include: (1) limited scope dental or vision benefits, benefits for long-term care, nursing home care, home health care, community-based care, or any combination thereof, and other similar limited benefits; (2) coverage only for a specified disease or illness; (3) hospital indemnity or other fixed indemnity insurance; and (4) Medicare supplemental health insurance, coverage supplemental to the medical and dental coverage provided to military personnel, and similar supplemental coverage provided to coverage under a group health plan.

Amount of Penalty. The penalty for failing to maintain minimum essential health care coverage, i.e., the shared responsibility payment, for any month is the lesser of:

- the national average premium for a bronze-level coverage plan offered through an Exchange for the tax year for a family that is the size of the taxpayer's family; or
- the sum of a "monthly penalty" amounts for each individual in the taxpayer's family (Code Sec. 5000A(c)(1); Reg. § 1.5000A-4).

The monthly national average premium for qualified health plans that have a bronze level of coverage and are offered through Exchanges in 2016 is $223 per individual and $1,115 for a shared responsibility family with five or more members (Rev. Proc. 2016-43).

The monthly penalty amount is equal to 1/12 multiplied by the greater of:

- the flat dollar amount, or
- the excess income amount.

The flat dollar amount is the lesser of:

- the sum of the applicable dollar amounts for all applicable individuals in the taxpayer's family who lack minimum essential coverage and whom the taxpayer is required to insure, or
- 300 percent of the applicable dollar amount for the calendar year with or within which the tax year ends.

The applicable dollar amount is $695 for 2016 ($695 for 2017). The applicable dollar amount is adjusted for inflation after 2016. Special rules apply for individuals under the age of 18 (Reg. § 1.5000A-4(b)(2); Rev. Proc. 2016-55).

The excess income amount is the product of the income percentage times the excess of the taxpayer's household income over the taxpayer's applicable filing threshold (¶ 101). The income percentage is two and one-half percent for 2016 and thereafter.

Example 4: George is an unmarried individual with no dependents. He does not have minimum essential health care coverage for any month during 2016 and does not qualify for an exemption. For 2016, his household income is $40,000, and his applicable filing threshold is $10,350. George's flat dollar amount is $695. To determine his payment using the income formula, he must subtract $10,350 (filing threshold) from $40,000 (2016 household income). The result is $29,650. Two and one-half percent of $29,650 equals $741. The annual national average premium for bronze level coverage for 2016 is $2,676 ($223 x 12). Because $741 is greater than $695 and less than $2,676, George's shared responsibility payment for 2016 is $741, or $61.75 for each month he is uninsured and subject to penalty in 2016 (1/12 x $741).

Personal and Dependency Exemptions

133. Exemption Amount. An individual may claim a personal exemption deduction (¶ 135) and an exemption deduction for each person he or she claims as a dependent (¶ 137) on his or her tax return. The amount of a personal exemption (for the taxpayer and spouse) and of a dependency exemption (for each of the taxpayer's dependents) is adjusted annually for inflation. The exemption amount is $4,050 for 2016 ($4,050 for 2017) (Code Sec. 151(d); Rev. Proc. 2015-53; Rev. Proc. 2016-55).[25] The dependency exemption is denied to claimants who fail to provide the dependent's correct taxpayer identification number on the return claiming the dependency exemption (Code Sec. 151(e)).

Taxpayers whose adjusted gross income (AGI) exceeds an applicable threshold amount based on filing status must reduce the amount of their otherwise allowable exemption deduction (Code Sec. 151(d)(3)).[26] The applicable threshold amounts for 2016 are:

- $311,300 for married individuals filing a joint return and surviving spouses ($313,800 for 2017);
- $285,350 for heads of households ($287,650 for 2017);
- $259,400 for single individuals ($261,500 for 2017); and
- $155,650 for married individuals filing a separate return ($156,900 for 2017).

The threshold amounts are subject to inflation adjustment for tax years beginning after 2013. The taxpayer's deduction for personal and dependency exemptions is reduced by two percent for each $2,500 or fraction thereof by which the AGI exceeds the threshold amount. In the case of a married individual filing separately, the exemption reduction will be reduced by two percent for each $1,250 or fraction thereof by which AGI exceeds the threshold amount. In no case will the deduction for exemptions be reduced by more than 100 percent.

References are to Standard Federal Tax Reports; Tax Research Consultant; and Practical Tax Explanations.

[25] ¶ 8000, ¶ 8005.12; FILEIND: 6,050; § 1,205

[26] ¶ 8000; FILEIND: 6,052; § 1,205

135. Personal Exemptions. An individual may generally claim a personal exemption deduction for himself or herself equal to the exemption amount for the year ($4,050 for 2016; $4,050 for 2017) (¶ 133) on his or her tax return, plus any exemptions for dependents (¶ 137) (Code Sec. 151(b); Reg. § 1.151-1; Rev. Proc. 2015-53; Rev. Proc. 2016-55).[27] *No* exemption, however, is allowed to an individual who is eligible to be claimed as a dependent on another taxpayer's return. Thus, students who work part-time during the year or for the summer may *not* claim a personal exemption on their own return if their parents, or any other taxpayers, are *entitled* to claim them on their return. If dependents who are not allowed their own exemptions have gross income in an amount not exceeding $1,050 in 2016 ($1,050 for 2017), they will *not* be taxed on that amount and need *not* file income tax returns (¶ 101).

Spouses are allowed at least two personal exemptions when filing a joint return, even if one spouse has no income. If spouses file a joint return, neither can be claimed as a dependent on the return of any other taxpayer. If spouses file separate returns, each must take his or her own exemption on their respective return. If spouses file separate returns and one of the spouses has no gross income and is *not* the dependent of another taxpayer, then the spouse with gross income may claim the personal exemption for the other spouse on his or her separate return. A married taxpayer who files a separate return may *not* claim two exemptions for his or her spouse, one as a spouse and one as a dependent.

A resident alien may claim his or her own personal exemption and, if he or she files a joint return, may claim a similar exemption for his or her spouse. However, unless one of the elections noted at ¶ 2410 applies, the filing of a joint return is *not* permissible if either spouse was a nonresident alien at any time during the tax year (Code Sec. 6013(a)(1); Reg. § 1.6013-1(b)).[28]

137. Exemption for Dependent. A taxpayer may claim an exemption deduction ($4,050 for 2016; $4,050 for 2017) for each person he or she claims as a dependent that is a qualifying child (¶ 137A) or qualifying relative (¶ 137B), in addition to his or her personal exemption deduction (¶ 135) (Code Secs. 151(c) and 152; Rev. Proc. 2015-53; Rev. Proc. 2016-55).[29] Anyone claimed as a dependent, or the taxpayer's spouse if filing a joint return, by another taxpayer, however, is barred from claiming another individual as a dependent (Code Sec. 152(b)(1)). Thus, an individual cannot be claimed as a dependent if he or she files a joint return with his or her spouse for the same tax year, unless the return was filed as a claim for refund (¶ 138). The individual to be claimed as a dependent must also be a U.S. citizen, national, or resident of the United States or a contiguous country.

137A. Qualifying Child Definition. A individual taxpayer is allowed to claim a dependency exemption (¶ 137) for each person who is a qualifying child (Code Sec. 152(c)).[30] The following five requirements must all be met for an individual to be considered a qualifying child.

- *Relationship.* The individual must bear one of the following relationships to the taxpayer:

  — a son, daughter, stepson, stepdaughter, or a descendant of such child; or

  — a brother, sister, stepbrother, stepsister, or a descendant of such relative (Code Sec. 152(c)(2) and (f)(1)).

The relationship test includes foster and adopted children. An eligible foster child is a child who is placed with the taxpayer by an authorized placement agency or by

References are to Standard Federal Tax Reports; Tax Research Consultant; and Practical Tax Explanations.

[27] ¶ 8000, ¶ 8001; FILEIND: 6,104; § 1,210.05

[28] ¶ 35,160, ¶ 35,161; FILEIND: 3,250; § 37,125.15

[29] ¶ 8000, ¶ 8007; FILEIND: 6,150; § 1,201

[30] ¶ 8007; FILEIND: 6,154; § 1,215.05

a decree issued by the courts. An eligible adopted child includes both a legally adopted child and a child legally placed for adoption.

• *Age.* The individual must be younger than the taxpayer, and either under the age of 19 at the end of the calendar year, or under the age of 24 at the end of the calendar year and a full-time student. An individual who is totally and permanently disabled (¶ 1302) at any time during the year satisfies the age requirement regardless of his or her age (Code Sec. 152(c)(3)). An individual is a full-time student if enrolled or registered for at least part of five calendar months in a year at a qualified educational institution or a qualified on-farm training program (Code Sec. 152(f)(2); Reg. § 1.151-3(b)).

• *Principal Place of Abode.* The individual must have the same principal place of abode as the taxpayer for more than one-half of the year (Code Sec. 152(c)(1)(B)). Temporary absences for illness, school, vacation, or military service may count as time living with the taxpayer. Special rules apply in the case of children of divorced or separated parents (¶ 139A). A child who is born or dies during the tax year is considered as living with the taxpayer for the entire year if the taxpayer's home was the child's home for the entire time he or she was alive (Rev. Rul. 73-156).

• *Support.* The individual must *not* provide more than one-half of his or her own support for the year (Code Sec. 152(c)(1)(D) and (f)(5)). For this purpose, if the individual is the taxpayer's child and is a full-time student, amounts received as scholarships are not considered support.

• *Joint Return.* The individual cannot have filed a joint return with his or her spouse except as a claim for refund (¶ 138) (Code Sec. 152(c)(1)(E)).

In the event that an individual may be claimed as the qualifying child by two or more taxpayers, the taxpayers may decide between themselves who will claim the individual as a qualifying child. If the taxpayers cannot agree and more than one taxpayer is entitled to claim the individual as a qualifying child, regardless of whether they file a return and actually claim the qualifying child, the IRS will disallow all but one of the claims based on the tie-breaking rules discussed at ¶ 139.

If the child or individual fails to meet all the requirements to be considered a qualifying child, the individual may still be claimed as a dependent if he or she meets all the requirements for a qualifying relative (¶ 137B).

137B. Qualifying Relative Definition. An individual taxpayer is allowed to claim a dependency exemption (¶ 137) for each individual who is a qualifying relative and who fails to meet the requirements to be considered a qualifying child (¶ 137A). The following four requirements must all be met for an individual to be considered a qualifying relative (Code Sec. 152(d)).[31]

• *Relationship.* The individual must bear one of the following relationships to the taxpayer:

— a child, stepchild, adopted child, eligible foster child, or a descendant of such child (see ¶ 137A for the definition of adopted and foster child);

— a brother, sister, stepbrother, stepsister, half brother, or half sister;

— a parent, grandparent, or other direct ancestor (other than foster parent), as well as any stepparent;

— a brother or sister of the taxpayer's parent (aunt or uncle), and any son or daughter of the taxpayer's brother or sister (niece or nephew);

— a son-in-law, daughter-in-law, father-in-law, mother-in-law, brother-in-law or sister-in-law; or

References are to Standard Federal Tax Reports; Tax Research Consultant; and Practical Tax Explanations.

[31] ¶ 8007; FILEIND: 6,156; § 1,220.05

— an individual who, for the entire year, has the same principal place of abode as the taxpayer and is a member of the taxpayer's household (temporary absences for illness, school, vacation, or military service are permitted) (Code Sec. 152(d)(2)).

Once established, a relationship does not terminate due to divorce or death of a spouse.

• *Gross Income.* The individual's gross income for the calendar year (¶ 143) in which the taxpayer's tax year begins must be less than the exemption amount for the year (¶ 133) ($4,050 for 2016; $4,050 for 2017) (Code Sec. 152(d)(1)(B); Rev. Proc. 2015-53; Rev. Proc. 2016-55).

• *Support.* Over half of the individual's total support for that calendar year must have been furnished by the taxpayer (¶ 147) (Code Sec. 152(d)(1)(C)).

• *Not A Qualifying Child.* The individual must *not* be the qualifying child of the taxpayer or of any other taxpayer for the tax year (¶ 137A) (Code Sec. 152(d)(1)(D)).

For purposes of the requirement that an individual not be the qualifying child of another taxpayer, an unrelated child who lives with and is supported by a taxpayer may be claimed as a qualifying relative if the other individual for whom the child is a qualifying child does not file a return or files a return solely to claim a refund of withheld taxes (Notice 2008-5). For example, a boyfriend would be allowed to claim a dependency exemption for his girlfriend's unrelated child provided she is not required to file a return under Code Sec. 6012 or, if she files a return, it is only for the purpose of claiming a refund. If she files a return to claim the earned income credit, then she is considered to have filed a return and the boyfriend is denied the dependency exemption.

In the event that an individual can be claimed as the qualifying relative by two or more taxpayers, the taxpayers may decide between themselves who will claim the individual as a qualifying relative. If the taxpayers cannot agree and more than one taxpayer is entitled to claim the individual as a qualifying relative, regardless of whether they file a return and actually claim the qualifying relative, the IRS will disallow all but one of the claims based on the tie-breaking rules discussed at ¶ 139.

138. Married Dependents. A married individual cannot be claimed as a dependent (¶ 133) if he or she joins with his or her spouse to file a joint return (¶ 154) (Code Sec. 152(b)(2)).[32] Thus, a parent cannot claim a married child as a dependent if the child has filed a joint return with his or her spouse. The only exception to this rule is if the sole purpose for the married dependent filing the joint return was to obtain a refund and neither the dependent nor the spouse would have a tax liability if they had filed separately (Rev. Rul. 65-34). In this situation, the IRS views the return as simply a claim for refund.

139. Two or More Taxpayers Claiming the Same Qualifying Child. An individual may meet the requirements to be a qualifying child or qualifying relative of more than one taxpayer. Only one taxpayer, however, can claim the individual for purposes of claiming the dependency exemption (¶ 137). Generally, if an individual may be claimed as a qualifying child by two or more taxpayers, the taxpayers may decide between themselves who will treat the child as a qualifying child, subject to the tie-breaking rules. If the taxpayers cannot agree and more than one taxpayer is entitled to claim the individual as a qualifying child, regardless of whether a return is filed and the qualifying child is claimed, the IRS will disallow all but one of the claims based on the following tie-breaking rules (Code Sec. 152(c)(4); Notice 2006-86):[33]

References are to Standard Federal Tax Reports; Tax Research Consultant; and Practical Tax Explanations.

[32] ¶ 8005.56, ¶ 8007; FILEIND: 6,152; § 1,210.05

[33] ¶ 8007; FILEIND: 6,154.25; § 1,215.35

- If only one of the taxpayers is the child's parent, then the child is the qualifying child for the parent.
- If the child's parents do not file a joint return, then the child is the qualifying child of the parent with whom the child lived with the longest during the year.
- If the child resided with both parents equally during the year and the parents do not file a joint return, then the child is the qualifying child of the parent with the highest adjusted gross income (AGI).
- If none of the taxpayers claiming the child are the child's parent, then the child is the qualifying child of the person with the highest AGI.
- If the parents may claim the child as a qualifying child, but do not actually do so, then the child may be the qualifying child of any other taxpayer but only if the other taxpayer's AGI is higher than the AGI of either parent.

When applying the tie-breaking rules above, the taxpayer is allowed to claim the child as a qualifying child for purposes of the dependency exemption (¶ 137), head-of-household filing status (¶ 173), the child tax credit (¶ 1305), the dependent care credit (¶ 1301), the exclusion for dependent care benefits (¶ 2065), and the earned income credit (¶ 1322).

For a discussion of the separate tie-breaker rules for divorced and separated parents, see ¶ 139A.

139A. Exemptions for Children of Divorced Parents. The dependency exemption for a child who is a qualifying child or qualifying relative of divorced or separated parents usually will go to the parent who has primary custody of the child for the calendar year. The custodial parent is determined by the number of nights in which the child resided with the parent (Code Sec. 152(e); Reg. § 1.152-4).[34] When the child spends an equal amount of time with each parent, the parent with the higher adjusted gross income (AGI) is allowed to claim the dependency exemption.

The custodial parent, however, can waive the dependency exemption and the child may be treated as the qualifying child or qualifying relative of the noncustodial parent if all of the following requirements are met:

- the parents are divorced or legally separated under a decree of divorce or separate maintenance, separated under a written separation agreement, or lived apart at all times during the last six months of the calendar year, including parents who were never married and who do not live together;
- one or both parents provided more than half of the child's total support for the calendar year determined without regard to any multiple support agreement (¶ 147); however, when a parent has remarried, support received from the parent's spouse is treated as received from the parent (Code Sec. 152(d)(5)(B));
- one or both parents have legal custody of the child for more than half of the calendar year; and
- the custodial parent makes a written declaration on Form 8332 that he or she will not claim the exemption and the noncustodial parent attaches the declaration to his or her tax return for each year the exemption is claimed.

If all of the above requirements are met, the noncustodial parent may claim the child as a qualifying child for purposes of the dependency exemption (¶ 137), the child tax credit (¶ 1305), and any education credits attributable to educational expenses made for the child by the noncustodial parent (¶ 1303). Even if the dependency exemption is released, the custodial parent may still claim the child as a qualifying child for purposes of the head of household filing status (¶ 173), dependent care credit (¶ 1301), exclusion of dependent care benefits (¶ 2065), and earned income tax credit (¶ 1322) (Notice 2006-86).

References are to Standard Federal Tax Reports; Tax Research Consultant; and Practical Tax Explanations.

[34] ¶ 8007, ¶ 8150; FILEIND: 6,158.05; § 1,215.40

Moreover, so long as the first three requirements listed above are met, regardless of whether the custodial parent releases the claim to an exemption, if the child is the qualifying child or qualifying relative of one of the parents, he or she can be treated as a dependent of both parents for purposes of:

(1) the child's receipt of benefits under a parent's employer-provided health care plan (¶ 2015);

(2) contributions to an accident or health plan by a parent's employer on behalf of the child (¶ 2013);

(3) the child's use of a fringe benefit that qualifies as a no-additional-cost service or qualified employee discount (¶ 2087 and ¶ 2088, respectively);

(4) the child's deductible medical expense (¶ 1015); and

(5) the child's qualified medical expenses paid from distributions from a health savings account (HSA) or Archer medical savings account (MSA) that are excludable from gross income (¶ 2035 and ¶ 2037, respectively) (Rev. Proc. 2008-48).

141. Claiming the Dependency Exemption. Personal exemptions are claimed on Form 1040 or 1040A. The taxpayer, spouse, and dependents are listed in the "Exemptions" section on page 1 of either form. The total number of exemptions is then multiplied by the exemption amount ($4,050 for 2016; $4,050 for 2017) and used to figure taxable income (¶ 133). On a joint return, the dependency exemption is allowed if the dependent is the qualifying child or qualifying relative of one of the spouses (¶ 137) (Reg. § 1.152-2(d); Rev. Proc. 2015-53; Rev. Proc. 2016-55).[35]

If a parent is barred from claiming an exemption for a child because that child fails to meet either the qualifying child (¶ 137A) or qualifying relative (¶ 137B) requirements, the child may claim a personal exemption on his or her own return. Also a dependent, whether a qualifying child or a qualifying relative, who has earned income on which tax has been withheld should file a return even though he or she is claimed as a dependent by another. The return will serve as a claim for refund of the tax withheld if the dependent incurs no tax liability. If a dependent child of the taxpayer has only earned income in excess of the standard deduction amount for the year (¶ 126), unearned income in excess of, for 2016, $1,050, gross income exceeding the larger of, for 2016, $1,050 or the standard deduction amount for the year, or self-employment income of $400 or more, a return must be filed whether or not the child is claimed as a dependent (¶ 101 and ¶ 2670).

In a community property state (¶ 710), if a child's support is derived from community income, some or all of the exemptions may, by agreement, be taken by either spouse on a separate return. A single exemption amount, however, may *not* be divided between them.[36]

143. Gross Income of a Qualifying Relative Dependent. For an individual to be a qualifying relative for purposes of the dependency exemption (¶ 137B), his or her gross income for the calendar year in which the taxpayer's tax year begins must be less than the exemption amount for that year ($4,050 for 2016; $4,050 for 2017) (Rev. Proc. 2015-53; Rev. Proc. 2016-55) (¶ 133). In determining whether a dependent has gross income in excess of the exemption amount, it is statutory gross income, not gross sales, adjusted gross, net or any other amount of income, that is counted. Thus, gross income is taken into account without deductions. For example, gross rents are counted, without reduction for rental expenses or depreciation. A partner's share of partnership gross income, rather than net income, is counted. Any income excludable from the claimed dependent's gross income, i.e., exempt interest, disability, or Social Security, however, is disregarded, as well as income received by a permanently and totally disabled individual at a sheltered workshop school (Code Sec. 152(d)(4); IRS Pub. 17).[37] Excludable income is counted in determining whether the taxpayer has furnished over half of the dependent's support (¶ 147).

References are to Standard Federal Tax Reports; Tax Research Consultant; and Practical Tax Explanations.

[35] ¶ 8050; FILEIND: 6,152; § 1,201

[36] ¶ 8005.23; INDIV: 24,160; § 1,201

[37] ¶ 8007; FILEIND: 6,156.20; § 1,220.15

Example: Paul's mother, who lived in his home, earned $500 in 2016 from baby-sitting. She was injured in an accident and received $2,650 in compensatory damages. Paul contributed $2,000 for her support in 2016. The damage award is not taxable income and is not counted for purposes of the $4,050 gross income test, but if Paul's mother spent at least $1,500 of this amount (plus the $500 she received for baby-sitting) in 2016 for her own support, Paul could *not* claim her as a dependent because he would not have furnished *more* than one-half of her support. If less than $2,000 was spent by Paul's mother for her own support, Paul would be entitled to the dependency exemption.

147. Support of a Qualifying Relative Dependent. For an individual to be a qualifying relative for purposes of the dependency exemption (¶ 137B), a taxpayer must furnish more than one-half of the *total* support for the individual for the tax year. See, however, the special rule for children of divorced parents at ¶ 139A (Code Sec. 152(d)(1); Reg. § 1.152-1).[38] Thus, if an individual provides more than one-half of his or her own support for the tax year, then generally no other taxpayer can meet the support test and no one can claim that individual as a qualifying relative. If any other individual taxpayer provides more than one-half of a person's support, only that other taxpayer can meet the support test, except in the case of certain divorced parents (¶ 139A).

Multiple Support Agreement. If no one taxpayer provides more than one-half of the support for an individual, any taxpayer who actually provides more than 10 percent of the individual's support can be treated as having met the support test if a multiple support agreement is filed (Code Sec. 152(d)(3); Reg. § 1.152-3).[39] To be eligible to use a multiple support agreement, more than one-half of the individual's support must be received from a group of persons including the taxpayer, each of whom would otherwise have been entitled to claim the individual as a dependent if they each had furnished more than one-half of the individual's support, and no one taxpayer furnished more than one-half of that support. The person claiming the dependency exemption completes Form 2120 verifying that each person who contributed more than 10 percent of the support signed a written declaration stating that he or she will not claim the exemption. The statement must include the calendar year for which the waiver for claiming the dependency exemption applies, the name of the qualifying relative, and the name, address and Social Security number of the person waiving the exemption claim. These statements must be retained with the taxpayer's records in the event the taxpayer is called upon to justify claiming the dependency exemption.

Support Defined. The support test is applied by comparing the amount of support provided by the taxpayer with the total amount of support received by the dependent from all sources during the calendar year in which the taxpayer's tax year begins. "Total" support is the sum of:

- the fair rental value of lodging furnished to a qualifying relative dependent;
- the costs of all items of expense paid out directly by or for the benefit of the qualifying relative dependent, such as clothing, education, medical and dental care, gifts, transportation, church contributions, and entertainment and recreation; and
- a proportionate share of the expenses incurred in supporting the whole household that cannot be directly attributed to each individual, such as food.[40]

The proportionate share of household expenses does not include items that represent the cost of maintaining a house, such as heat, electricity, repairs, taxes, etc., because these costs are accounted for in the fair rental value of the lodging furnished to the dependent. Medical care includes the premiums paid on a medical care policy, but not the benefits provided by the policy. Medicare benefits, both basic and supplementary, as well as Medicaid, are also disregarded in determining support.

Certain capital expenditures qualify as items of support, such as the cost of an automobile purchased for a qualifying relative dependent and the cost of furniture and

References are to Standard Federal Tax Reports; Tax Research Consultant; and Practical Tax Explanations.

[38] ¶ 8007, ¶ 8008; FILEIND: 6,156.15; § 1,220.20

[39] ¶ 8007, ¶ 8100; FILEIND: 6,156.15; § 1,220.20

[40] ¶ 8005.54, ¶ 8005.80; FILEIND: 6,160; § 1,220.20

appliances. However, the following have been held not to be items of support: (1) income and Social Security taxes paid by a dependent child from his own income; (2) funeral expenses of a qualifying relative dependent; (3) costs incurred by a parent in exercising visitation rights, and (4) life insurance premium costs.[41]

In determining whether a taxpayer furnished more than one-half of a qualifying relative dependent's total support, the support provided by the taxpayer, by the dependent, and by third parties must be taken into account. In addition, only the amount of the cash actually expended for items of support is taken into account. The source and tax status of money used to provide support is, generally, not controlling. It may come from taxable income, tax-exempt receipts, and loans. Furthermore, the year in which the support is received, and not the year of payment of the indebtedness incurred, is controlling in determining whether over one-half of the support is furnished by the taxpayer, regardless of his or her method of tax accounting.[42]

In the case of the taxpayer's child (¶ 137), or stepchild who is a student, any amounts received as scholarships do not have to be taken into account (Reg. § 1.152-1(c)).[43] Educational benefits received under the U.S. Navy's educational assistance program are *not* considered to be scholarships.[44]

Survivor and old-age insurance benefits received under the Social Security Act and used for support are considered as having been contributed by the recipient to his or her own support.[45] Benefit payments made to an individual under state public assistance laws and measured solely by the needs of the recipient are considered as having been used entirely by that individual for his or her own support unless it is shown otherwise.[46] Amounts expended by a state for the training and education of handicapped children, including children with intellectual disabilities who qualify as "students" and are in a state institution that qualifies as an "educational institution," are not considered to constitute support, except where the state assumes custody of the child involved.[47] Aid to Families with Dependent Children (AFDC) payments are considered support by the state and not by the parent.[48]

149. Effect of Death on Exemption. The personal or dependency exemption amount claimed by a taxpayer (¶ 133) is not reduced because of the death of a taxpayer, his or her spouse, or a dependent during the tax year (Reg. § 1.152-1(b)).[49]

Example 1: A child is born on December 31, 2016, and dies in January 2017. A full exemption is allowed for the child in both years.

The death of one spouse will also *not* deprive the survivor of the right to claim the exemptions of the deceased. The crucial date for determining marital status is the last day of the tax year. If a spouse dies during the tax year, however, this determination is made as of the date of death (Code Sec. 7703(a)).[50]

On the final separate return of a decedent, in addition to the deceased's own personal exemption, the exemptions for the surviving spouse may be taken if the surviving spouse had no gross income and was not a dependent of anyone else (¶ 135). Further, since the dependency exemption is based upon furnishing over half the support during the calendar year in which the tax year of the taxpayer begins, a decedent who furnished over half the support to a person otherwise qualifying as a dependent would be entitled to the full exemption for such dependent, without proration.

References are to Standard Federal Tax Reports; Tax Research Consultant; and Practical Tax Explanations.

[41] ¶ 8005.38, ¶ 8005.80; FILEIND: 6,152.05; § 1,220.20

[42] ¶ 8005.81; FILEIND: 6,160.10; § 1,220.20

[43] ¶ 8008; FILEIND: 6,158.20; § 1,220.20

[44] ¶ 8005.62; FILEIND: 6,158.20; § 1,220.20

[45] ¶ 8005.71; FILEIND: 6,160.25; § 1,220.20

[46] ¶ 8005.60; FILEIND: 6,160.25; § 1,220.20

[47] ¶ 8005.72; FILEIND: 6,160.25; § 1,220.20

[48] ¶ 8005.60; FILEIND: 6,160.25; § 1,220.20

[49] ¶ 8008; FILEIND: 6,158.10; § 1,220.10

[50] ¶ 43,170; FILEIND: 3,202; § 1,210.10

Example 2: Allen furnishes the full support for his aged father up to the date of Allen's death on September 1, 2016, and over one-half of the total support for the year. A $4,050 exemption is allowed for the father on Allen's final return. But if Allen died on April 1 and his brother, Bob, supported their father for the balance of the year, incurring a larger expense than Allen did during the first part of the year, Bob would be entitled to the exemption. If the support in the latter case was furnished equally by Bob and another brother, Carl, from April 1 on, and if none of the three brothers furnished over half of the father's support for the calendar year, any one of them, including the executor of Allen's estate (on Allen's final return), could take the exemption if the other two brothers renounced their right to the exemption for that year (¶ 147). Regardless of the amount of support, no exemption is allowed to any of the three brothers for their father if the father had gross income of $4,050 or more during calendar year 2016 (¶ 137B).

150. Missing and/or Kidnapped Children. A dependency exemption may be claimed for any child of the taxpayer, regardless of whether the child qualifies as a qualifying child or qualifying relative, if the child is presumed by a law enforcement agency to have been kidnapped by someone other than a member of the family and had resided at the taxpayer's principal place of abode for more than one-half of the portion of the year before the kidnapping (Code Sec. 152(f)(6)).[51]

Filing Status

152. Joint Return—Who May File. Married taxpayers may elect to file a joint return or file as married persons filing separately. In most cases, it is more beneficial for married taxpayers to file a joint return (¶ 156). Spouses may file a joint return even though one spouse has no income or deductions (Code Sec. 6013; Reg. § 1.6013-1),[52] but only if:

- their tax years begin on the same date;
- they are not legally separated under a decree of divorce or separate maintenance on the last day of the tax year; and
- neither is a nonresident alien at any time during the year.

Marital status for federal tax purposes depends on state law. Taxpayers married in compliance with the laws of one state remain married regardless of where they reside. Recognition of this principle has been extended to common-law marriages (Rev. Rul. 58-66). Although, at one time, the principle had also been extended to same-sex couples (Rev. Rul. 2013-17, obsoleted by T.D. 9785), under the U.S. Supreme Court decision in *J. Obergefell v. R. Hodges* (SCt, 2015-1 USTC ¶ 50,357), all states must recognize and license same-sex marriages. In light of *Obergefell*, the IRS has issued final regulations, effective as of September 2, 2016, providing that a marriage of two individuals will be recognized for federal tax purposes if that marriage would be recognized by the state, possession, or territory of the United States in which the marriage was entered into; and that two individuals entering into a relationship denominated as marriage under the laws of a foreign jurisdiction are married for federal tax purposes if the relationship would be recognized as marriage under the laws of at least one state, possession, or territory of the United States (Reg. § 301.7701-18(b)).[53] On the other hand, a domestic partnership, civil union, or other similar formal relationship will not be treated as a marriage for federal tax purposes if the relationship is not called a "marriage" under state or foreign law (Reg. § 301.7701-18(c)).[54] Same-sex married couples may elect to amend any prior open tax years under these rules.

A U.S. citizen or resident and his or her nonresident alien spouse, however, can elect to file a joint return if they agree to be taxed on their worldwide income and supply all necessary books and records and other information pertinent to the determination of

References are to Standard Federal Tax Reports; Tax Research Consultant; and Practical Tax Explanations.

[51] ¶ 8007; FILEIND: 6,158.15; § 1,215.10

[52] ¶ 35,160, ¶ 35,161; FILEIND: 18,056; § 1,320.05

[53] ¶ 43,116; FILEIND: 3,202: FILEIND: 18,056.10; § 46,951

[54] ¶ 43,116; FILEIND: 3,202: FILEIND: 18,056.10; § 46,951

tax liability (¶ 2410) (Code Sec. 6013(g)). Further, a one-time election to file a joint return is available in the year in which a nonresident alien spouse becomes a resident (Code Sec. 6013(h)).

If married persons are on a calendar-year basis or have fiscal years that begin on the same date, then they can file a joint return. However, if they have different tax years for some reason other than the intervention of death (¶ 164), then they cannot file a joint return. If newly married spouses with different tax years want to change the year of one spouse to coincide with that of the other so as to be able to file jointly, then they may do so by following the rules described at ¶ 1513. Spouses may file a joint return even though they have different accounting methods, e.g., one is on the cash basis and the other is on the accrual basis, if such methods clearly reflect their income.

Even though married persons are not living together on the last day of the tax year, they may still file a joint return if they are *not* legally separated under a decree of divorce or separate maintenance on that date (Reg. § 1.6013-4).[55] Spouses who are separated under an interlocutory decree of divorce are considered married and are entitled to file a joint return until the decree becomes final. However, certain married individuals living apart may file separate returns as heads of households (¶ 173).

Spouses of military personnel serving in a combat zone and missing in action may file a joint return for any tax year until the tax year beginning two years after the termination of combat activities in that zone (Code Sec. 6013(f)).[56]

154. Joint Return—Election to File. When married individuals file separate returns for a tax year, they can elect to make a joint return for that year after the period for timely filing has expired. This change of filing status is usually achieved by the filing of an amended return on Form 1040X within three years of the last date prescribed by law for the filing of the separate return or returns, without taking into account any extension of time granted to either spouse (Code Sec. 6013(b)(2)).[57] However, the change to a joint return cannot be made:

- after either spouse timely files a petition with the Tax Court pursuant to a notice of deficiency which was mailed to either spouse for the tax year;
- after either spouse commences a suit in any court for the recovery of any part of the tax for such tax year;
- after either spouse enters into a closing agreement with respect to such tax year; or
- after either spouse has compromised any civil or criminal case arising with respect to such tax year.

Once a joint return has been filed for a tax year, the spouses may *not* thereafter file separate returns after the time for filing the return of either spouse has expired (Reg. § 1.6013-1(a)).[58] The exception being if either spouse dies during the tax year, then only the executor or administrator of the estate of the deceased spouse may elect to change from a joint to a separate return (¶ 168).

The Tax Court has ruled that a couple could elect to file a joint return even though the IRS had previously prepared and filed returns for the husband with a status of married filing separately (*J.V. Millsap*, Dec. 45,179, 91 TC 926). The IRS's filing of substitute returns did not bar the taxpayer from contesting either the deficiency or the IRS's choice of his filing status. The former standard that the IRS's choice precludes taxpayers from selecting a different filing status will be applied only when the issue is appealable to the U.S. Court of Appeals for the Tenth Circuit (*R.E. Smalldridge*, CA-10, 86-2 USTC ¶ 9764).

References are to Standard Federal Tax Reports; Tax Research Consultant; and Practical Tax Explanations.

[55] ¶ 35,165; FILEIND: 18,056.10; § 1,320.10

[56] ¶ 35,160; FILEIND: 18,056.30; § 1,320.10

[57] ¶ 35,160; FILEIND: 18,056.05; § 1,320.25

[58] ¶ 35,161; FILEIND: 18,056.05; § 1,320.25

156. Joint Return v. Separate Return. It is generally more beneficial for married taxpayers to file a joint return (¶ 152). The filing of a joint return will result in a savings of tax in those instances in which differences in the tax rate brackets for joint and separate returns result in higher tax rates for married individuals filing separately. Unlike with separate returns, taxable income (¶ 123) on a joint return is the entire taxable income amount of the couple. Although there are two taxpayers on the joint return, there is only one taxable income amount and only one adjusted gross income (AGI) amount (Reg. § 1.6013-4).[59] In addition, the total exemptions (¶ 135) of spouses are subtracted in determining taxable income.

> **Example:** For 2016, Joe has taxable income in the amount of $14,500, and his wife, Trisha, has taxable income in the amount of $37,750. If they elect to file a joint return, they will not be subject to the 25-percent tax rate because their combined taxable income of $52,250 does not exceed the $75,300 threshold amount for 2016 (¶ 13). If they elect to file separate returns, however, $100, which represents the portion of Trisha's income that exceeds the $37,650 threshold, falls within the 25-percent tax bracket for the year (¶ 15).

Also, if only one spouse has income, it would be impractical for the income earner to use married filing separately status. This filing status carries a basic standard deduction of $6,300 for 2016, whereas joint filers have a basic standard deduction of $12,600 for 2016 (¶ 126). It should be noted that a married individual generally may *not* claim the credit for the elderly or permanently disabled (¶ 1302), the child and dependent care credit (¶ 1301), the earned income credit (¶ 1322), or the educational credits (¶ 1303) unless he or she files a joint return with his or her spouse.

There are circumstances under which married taxpayers might reduce their tax liability by filing separate returns. For example, a spouse whose medical expenses are high, but not high enough to exceed 10 percent of the AGI reported on a joint return (7.5 percent of AGI for tax years ending before January 1, 2017, for individuals age 65 or older by the end of the tax year), may exceed the AGI threshold on a separate return (¶ 1015). In light of the two-percent-of-AGI floor on miscellaneous itemized deductions (¶ 1014), a spouse who incurs substantial unreimbursed employee business or investment expenses might be better off filing separately. The same rationale holds true for casualty and disaster loss deductions, which are subject to a 10-percent-of-AGI floor (¶ 1131).

Actual tax comparisons should be made using both joint and separate returns if there is doubt as to which method produces a more favorable result. Considerations other than tax savings might enter into the decision to file a separate, rather than a joint return. For example, one spouse may wish to avoid a tax deficiency liability assessed against the other spouse (¶ 162).

162. Joint Return—Liability for Taxes. Spouses are liable jointly and individually for the entire amount of tax, penalties, and interest arising out of a joint return (Code Sec. 6013(d)(3)).[60] Relief is available under certain circumstances, commonly referred to as "innocent spouse relief" (Code Sec. 6015).[61] Three types of innocent spouse relief are available to the electing spouse: liability relief (commonly referred to as innocent spouse relief) (Code Sec. 6015(b)), separation of liability relief (Code Sec. 6015(c)), or equitable relief (Code Sec. 6015(f)). A spouse must generally request one of these types of relief on Form 8857 within two years of the IRS beginning collection of a tax deficiency or assessment. Equitable relief requests, however, may be requested within the limitations period for filing any claim for refund (¶ 2763) or for the collection of tax (¶ 2735) (Notice 2011-70).

Any determination by the IRS regarding any type of innocent spouse relief is reviewable in the Tax Court.[62] Notice of the election for relief is required to be given to

References are to Standard Federal Tax Reports; Tax Research Consultant; and Practical Tax Explanations.

[59] ¶ 35,165; FILEIND: 18,056.35; § 1,320.05

[60] ¶ 35,160; FILEIND: 18,056.40; § 1,320.30

[61] ¶ 35,185; INDIV: 18,050; § 39,040.05

[62] ¶ 35,192.815; INDIV: 18,052.20; § 39,040.05

the non-electing spouse, who may participate in any hearings on the relief requested (Code Sec. 6015(h)(2); Reg. § 1.6015-6(a)(1)).[63] The Tax Court has held that the non-electing spouse has the right to a "stand-alone" hearing regarding the appropriateness of granting relief to the electing spouse (*T. Corson*, Dec. 53,882, 114 TC 354); *K.A. King*, Dec. 53,994, 115 TC 118). However, the appellate courts have limited the jurisdiction of the Tax Court with regard to spousal relief. The Tax Court has no jurisdiction to make any spousal relief determination unless the IRS has issued a deficiency notice to the taxpayer (*G.A. Ewing*, CA-9, 2006-1 USTC ¶ 50,191; *T.E. Bartman*, CA-8, 2006-1 USTC ¶ 50,298). There are additional requirements for jurisdictions located in community property states (IRS Pub. 555).

Liability Relief (Innocent Spouse Relief). To qualify for liability relief (commonly referred to as innocent spouse relief), the requesting taxpayer must meet *all* the following requirements:

- filed a joint return for the tax year which has an *understatement of tax* due to *erroneous items* of the other spouse;
- establish that at the time of signing the tax return the taxpayer did not know, or have reason to know, there was an understatement of tax; and
- show that it would be unfair to hold the innocent spouse liable for the understatement of tax, taking into account all the facts and circumstances (Code Sec. 6015(b)).[64]

A key element for the IRS will be whether the electing spouse received any substantial benefits, or later was divorced or separated from, or deserted by, the other spouse.

Separation of Liability Relief. Alternatively, the taxpayer may elect to obtain relief by separation of liabilities (Code Sec. 6015(c)).[65] To qualify, an individual must have filed a joint return, and either:

- be no longer married to, or be legally separated from, the spouse with whom the joint return was filed, or
- must *not* have been a member of the same household with the other spouse for a 12-month period ending on the date of the filing of Form 8857.

The burden of proof on income and deductions is on the taxpayer who elects relief under separation of liability.

Equitable Relief. Should an individual fail to qualify for either of the first two types of relief, he or she may still obtain relief from the tax liabilities, interest and penalties by electing equitable relief (Code Sec. 6015(f)).[66] The taxpayer must show that, under *all* facts and circumstances, it would be unfair to be held liable for the understatement or underpayment of taxes. The IRS has issued guidance for taxpayers seeking equitable relief (Rev. Proc. 2013-34).

Taxpayers filing bankruptcy petitions. The running of the statute of limitations on filing a Tax Court petition to determine the appropriate innocent spouse relief is suspended for a taxpayer who is prohibited from filing a petition due to the automatic stay provision under the bankruptcy law (Code Sec. 6015(e), as added by the Protecting Americans from Tax Hikes (PATH) Act of 2015 (P.L. 114-113)). The running of the statute of limitations is also suspended on filing a Tax Court petition to determine the appropriate relief available in collection cases (Code Sec. 6330(d)(1) and (d)(2), as amended and added byP.L. 114-113).

Proper venue. Tax Court decisions rendered in cases involving the determination of innocent spouse relief under Code Sec. 6015, collection by lien under Code Sec. 6320, or levy under Code Sec. 6330 follow the general rule for appellate review (Code Sec. 7482(b)(1), as amended by P.L. 114-113).

References are to Standard Federal Tax Reports; Tax Research Consultant; and Practical Tax Explanations.

[63] ¶ 35,185, ¶ 35,187E; INDIV: 18,052.15; § 39,040.25

[64] ¶ 35,185; INDIV: 18,054; § 39,040.10

[65] ¶ 35,185; INDIV: 18,056; § 39,040.15

[66] ¶ 35,185; INDIV: 18,058; § 39,040.20

163. Joint Return—Injured Spouse Claim. When married taxpayers file a joint return and one spouse has not paid child or spousal support, or certain federal debts, e.g., student loans, all or part of the tax overpayment shown on the joint return may be used to satisfy the past-due debt of the delinquent spouse. The nonobligated spouse may, however, be entitled to a refund of his or her part of the overpayment if that individual:

- is not required to pay the past-due amount;
- received and reported income, i.e., wages, taxable interest, etc., on the joint return; and
- made and reported payments, i.e., withheld federal income taxes or estimated taxes, on the joint return (Financial Management Service Reg. § 285.3).[67]

To make this type of claim, the nonobligated spouse can either write "Injured Spouse" in the upper left corner of the jointly-filed Form 1040 and attach Form 8379, or file Form 8379 by itself after filing the joint return.

164. Joint Return—Effect of Death. A joint return may be filed when one or both spouses died during the year, and the tax year of both began on the same day, whether this year is a fiscal or calendar year. When a joint return is filed, it is treated as if the tax years of both spouses ended on the closing date of the surviving spouse's tax year (Reg. § 1.6013-3).[68]

166. Joint Return—Surviving Spouse. A surviving spouse who is a widow(er) with dependent children may continue to use the tax rates for married taxpayers filing jointly for two tax years immediately following the year of death of his or her spouse (¶ 175). A surviving spouse may *not* file a joint return in the year the other spouse dies if the surviving spouse remarries before the close of the tax year. The surviving spouse may, however, file a joint return with his or her new spouse for that year if all other requirements are met. The surviving spouse may not file a joint return with the deceased spouse if the tax year of either spouse is a fractional part of a year resulting from a change of accounting period (Reg. § 1.6013-1(d)).[69]

Example: Stan and Tracy file joint returns on a calendar-year basis. Tracy dies on March 1, 2016. Thereafter, Stan receives permission to change his accounting period to a fiscal year beginning July 1, 2016. A joint return cannot be filed for the short tax year ending June 30, 2016.

168. Joint Return—Return with a Deceased Spouse. Generally, where one spouse dies, a joint return can be filed only by the executor or administrator and the survivor (¶ 178). The surviving spouse, alone, however, may file a joint return if:

- no return was filed by the decedent for the tax year at issue;
- no executor or administrator was appointed; and
- no executor or administrator was appointed before the last day for filing the return of the surviving spouse, including any extensions of time for filing.

Even if all of the above tests are met, an administrator or executor, subsequently appointed, may disaffirm a joint return made by the surviving spouse by filing a separate return for the decedent. This disaffirmance must be made within one year after the last day allowed for filing the return of the surviving spouse including extensions. If a disaffirmance is made, then the already filed joint return will be considered the survivor's separate return. The survivor's tax will be figured by excluding all of the items properly includible in the return of the deceased spouse (Reg. § 1.6013-1(d)).[70]

References are to Standard Federal Tax Reports; Tax Research Consultant; and Practical Tax Explanations.

[67] ¶ 38,527; INDIV: 18,062, IRS: 33,102; § 40,015.15

[68] ¶ 35,164; FILEIND: 18,056.25; § 1,320.05

[69] ¶ 35,161; FILEIND: 18,056.20, FILEIND: 18,056.25; § 38,145.05

[70] ¶ 35,161; FILEIND: 18,056.25; § 1,320.20

173. Head of Household Filing Status. Individuals who qualify to file as head of household are generally entitled to a higher standard deduction (¶ 126) and lower tax rates than single individuals. See Tax Rate Schedule Z (¶ 17) or the Tax Computation Worksheet (¶ 20) and the "Head of a Household" column in the Tax Table (¶ 25). In order to qualify for head of household status, an individual must be unmarried or considered unmarried, and not a surviving spouse (¶ 175) at the close of the tax year (Code Sec. 2(b)).[71] In addition, the taxpayer must maintain a household which, for more than one-half of the tax year, is the principal place of abode of a qualifying individual who is a member of the household.

A qualifying individual includes a qualifying child of the taxpayer for dependency exemption purposes (¶ 137A) determined without regard to the rules for divorced parents (¶ 139A). A child is not a qualifying individual for head-of-household status purposes, however, if the child is married at the close of the taxpayer's tax year and (i) files a joint return with his or her spouse (Code Sec. 152(b)(2)), or (ii) is not a U.S. citizen, a U.S. national, or a resident of the United States, Canada, or Mexico (Code Sec. 152(b)(3)). For purposes of this requirement, an adopted child or a foster child, as defined under the qualifying child rules, is treated as the taxpayer's child by blood.

A qualifying individual also includes any other person who is a dependent of the taxpayer if the taxpayer is entitled to claim a dependency deduction for that person (¶ 137). A taxpayer, however, cannot claim head-of-household status if the only reason for being able to claim an individual as a dependent is based on either the individual living as a member of the taxpayer's household for the full year as a qualifying relative (¶ 137B), or claiming the dependency exemption under a multiple support agreement (¶ 147).

An individual qualifies for head of household status if a *separate* household is maintained for a parent for the tax year. The separate household must be the parent's principal place of abode, and the parent must qualify as the child's dependent (¶ 137). A parent's principal place of abode can include residence in a rest home or home for the aged. An institutionalized or hospitalized dependent, other than a parent, may also qualify a taxpayer as head of a household if the taxpayer can prove that the taxpayer's home was the "principal" place of abode of the dependent, even though the dependent may never return home because of the nature of the infirmity (Code Sec. 2(b)(1)(B); Reg. § 1.2-2(b)(4)).[72]

Marital Status. The marital status of an individual for the purpose of applying the head of household rates is determined at the end of a tax year. A taxpayer is considered to be unmarried at the end of a tax year if his or her spouse was a nonresident alien at any time during the tax year, or if he or she is legally separated from his or her spouse under a decree of divorce or separate maintenance at the close of the tax year. A taxpayer under an interlocutory decree of divorce is not legally separated. A widow or widower may not use the head of household rates in those tax years in which he or she is eligible to use the joint tax rates under the surviving spouse rules discussed at ¶ 175.

A married taxpayer will be considered unmarried and eligible for head of household status if the taxpayer's spouse was not a member of the household for the last six months of the year and if the household is the principal place of abode of a child for whom the taxpayer is entitled to a dependency exemption (¶ 137) (Code Secs. 2(c) and 7703(b)).[73] The taxpayer, however, will still be eligible for head-of-household status even if no dependency exemption is available for a child because the taxpayer waived the exemption (¶ 139A). A nonresident alien who is considered unmarried may not use the head of household tax rate but must use the tax rate schedule for single individuals (Reg. § 1.2-2(b)(6)).[74]

References are to Standard Federal Tax Reports; Tax Research Consultant; and Practical Tax Explanations.

[71] ¶ 3310; FILEIND: 3,150; § 1,115.05

[72] ¶ 3310, ¶ 3325; FILEIND: 3,154; § 1,115.30

[73] ¶ 3310, ¶ 43,170; FILEIND: 3,204; § 1,115.10

[74] ¶ 3325; FILEIND: 3,250; § 1,115.10

Maintains Household. An individual taxpayer "maintains a household" if (1) the taxpayer furnishes, with funds attributable to him or her, more than one-half the cost of maintaining the home during the tax year and (2) at least one of the qualifying individuals described previously lives there for more than one-half of the year except for temporary absence. An exemption is made for institutionalized or hospitalized dependents. Birth or death of a qualifying individual during the year will not disqualify the taxpayer as the head of a household if the individual lived in the household during the part of the year when he or she was alive (Code Sec. 2(b)(1); Reg. § 1.2-2(c)).[75]

The cost of maintaining a household includes the expenses incurred for the mutual benefit of the occupants by reason of its use as the principal place of abode. These expenses include property taxes, mortgage interest, rent, utility charges, upkeep and repairs, property insurance, food consumed on the premises, and other household expenses. They do *not* include the cost of clothing, education, medical treatment, vacations, life insurance, transportation, food consumed off the premises, or the value of services rendered by the taxpayer or by any person who qualifies the taxpayer as head of a household (Reg. § 1.2-2(d)).[76]

175. Surviving Spouse Filing Status. A surviving spouse (qualifying widow(er)) may use the joint return tax rates for two tax years following the year of death of the husband or wife, but *only* if the survivor remains unmarried and maintains a household (¶ 173) that, for the entire tax year, is the principal place of abode of a child, adopted child, foster child, or stepchild for whom the taxpayer is entitled to the dependency exemption (¶ 137) (Code Sec. 2(a); Reg. § 1.2-2(a)).[77] See ¶ 164 for a discussion of filing a joint return for the year of death of one spouse.

A widow(er) who qualifies as a surviving spouse uses the joint return rate schedule (Schedule Y-1) at ¶ 13, the Tax Computation Worksheet at ¶ 20 or the Tax Table at ¶ 25 and must use either Form 1040 or Form 1040A. This benefit is afforded a surviving spouse only if he or she was entitled to file a joint return with the deceased spouse for the tax year in which the deceased spouse died.

It should be emphasized that the benefit entitles the survivor only to the joint return tax rates; it does not authorize him or her to file a joint return or claim any personal exemptions other than his or her own and those of the dependent or dependents for whom the household is maintained. For 2016, a qualifying widow(er) (surviving spouse) with dependent children is generally entitled to joint return rate benefits if the spouse died at any time during 2014 or 2015 (Code Sec. 2(a)(1)(A)).

In determining eligibility for filing as a surviving spouse, the date of death of a person serving in a combat zone who was missing in action is considered to be two years after the termination of combat activities in that zone, unless death has been established at an earlier time (Code Sec. 2(a)(3)).

176. Single Filing Status. Unmarried individuals who do not qualify to file their returns as a married individual (¶ 152), as a surviving spouse (¶ 175), or as a head of household (¶ 173) must file their returns as a single taxpayer (Code Sec. 1(c)).[78] See ¶ 103 for a discussion on the filing requirements for a child with earned and unearned income.

Tax Treatment of Decedent's Final Return

178. Who Must File for a Decedent. An income tax return must be filed for a deceased person who would have been required to file a return if he or she were still alive during the tax year (¶ 101) (Code Sec. 6012). This final return covers a short year, including the part of the year up to the date of death. A decedent's final return is due at the same time his or her return would have been due had he or she lived (¶ 107).[79] The

References are to Standard Federal Tax Reports; Tax Research Consultant; and Practical Tax Explanations.

[75] ¶ 3310, ¶ 3325; FILEIND: 3,154.05; § 1,115.15

[76] ¶ 3325; FILEIND: 3,154.10; § 1,115.15

[77] ¶ 3310, ¶ 3325; FILEIND: 3,100; § 1,120

[78] ¶ 3,260; FILEIND: 3,050; § 1,110

[79] ¶ 35,142; ACCTNG: 24,256; § 1,305.10

final return is filed on Form 1040, 1040A, or 1040EZ if the decedent met the gross income filing test for the short period, or otherwise would have been required to file a return, e.g., the decedent had more than $400 of self-employment earnings. The word "DECEASED," the decedent's name, and the date of death should be written across the top of page 1 of the return.

The return for the decedent must be filed by his or her administrator, executor, or any other person charged with responsibility for the decedent's affairs. The surviving spouse should, however, file the decedent's final return if there is no executor or administrator. A surviving spouse may also file a joint return for the decedent's final year (¶ 168). Whoever files the return for the decedent may file a separate return or a joint return (¶ 164). All personal exemptions to which the decedent was entitled while he or she was alive may be claimed. If a refund is due, the personal representative must attach to the return either Form 1310 or a copy of the court certificate showing his or her appointment. A surviving spouse filing a joint return with the decedent can claim the refund without attaching Form 1310.

180. Due Date of Final Return. The final return of a decedent is due by the date on which the return would have been due had death not occurred (¶ 107). Thus, for a calendar-year taxpayer who died in 2016, the final return is due by April 18, 2017 (Reg. § 1.6072-1(a)).[80]

182. How Decedent Income Is Treated. When a cash-basis taxpayer dies, only income actually or constructively received up to the date of death is included in the final return. If the decedent was on the accrual basis of accounting, income accrued up to the date of death is included in the final return. Income that accrues *only because of death*, however, is not included (Code Sec. 451; Reg. § 1.451-1(b)).[81] These rules also apply to successive decedents as rights to receive "income in respect of a prior decedent" (Reg. § 1.691(a)-1(c)).[82]

Any amount of gross income *not* reported on the return of the decedent is, when received, includible in the income of the person receiving such amounts by inheritance or survivorship as "income in respect of a decedent." The person receiving the income may be the decedent's estate or, if the estate does not collect an item of income but distributes the right to receive it to a testamentary trust or to the heir, next of kin, legatee, or devisee, it is included in the income of such trust, heir, next of kin, legatee, or devisee (Code Sec. 691(a); Reg. § 1.691(a)-2).[83]

The depreciation recapture rules under Code Secs. 1245 and 1250 apply to sales or other dispositions of property subject to those rules where the income therefrom is treated as income on the decedent's final return or as income in respect of a decedent under Code Sec. 691. See ¶ 1779 and following for a complete discussion. These rules, however, do not apply to transfers of depreciable property at death (Code Secs. 1245(b)(2) and 1250(d)(2)).[84]

184. Installment Obligations Paid to Decedent. Collections on an installment obligation acquired from a decedent are treated as items of income in respect of a decedent (¶ 182) if the decedent had been reporting the profit on the installment basis (Code Sec. 691(a)(4); Reg. § 1.691(a)-5).[85] If, however, the obligor of the installment obligation acquires the uncollected obligation, then the decedent's estate is considered to have made a taxable disposition of the installment obligation. Thus, any previously unreported gain will be recognized by the estate. This rule also applies if the obligation is canceled because of the death of the payee or if the estate allows the obligation to become unenforceable because it is canceled by the executor.

References are to Standard Federal Tax Reports; Tax Research Consultant; and Practical Tax Explanations.

[80] ¶ 36,721; ACCTNG: 24,256.05; § 1,305.10

[81] ¶ 21,002, ¶ 21,003; ACCTNG: 9,408; § 38,145.05

[82] ¶ 24,901; ESTTRST: 6,060; § 38,145.05

[83] ¶ 24,900, ¶ 24,902; ESTTRST: 6,054; § 38,145.05

[84] ¶ 30,902, ¶ 31,000; DEPR: 18,104; § 38,145.05

[85] ¶ 24,900, ¶ 24,905; ESTTRST: 6,056, ESTTRST: 6,116; § 18,370

187. Deductions for Decedents. Deductible expenses and other items are not accrued on the final return of a decedent unless his or her accounting method requires it, but are deductible instead by the estate or person who pays them or is liable for their payment (Code Sec. 461; Reg. § 1.461-1(b)).[86] Similar treatment is given to the foreign tax credit (Code Sec. 691(b); Reg. § 1.691(b)-1).[87]

Expenses for medical care of the decedent, paid out of his or her estate within one year from the date of death, are deductible on the decedent's final income tax return (Reg. § 1.213-1(d)).[88] However, the estate must attach a statement, in duplicate, to the decedent's return waiving the right to claim the deduction on the estate tax return.

Business expenses, income-producing expenses, interest, and taxes for which the decedent was liable but which were not properly allowable as a deduction on his or her last return will be allowed when paid as a deduction by the estate or, if the estate was not liable, then as a deduction by the person who by reason of the decedent's death acquires—subject to such obligation—an interest in property of the decedent (Reg. § 1.691(b)-1(a)).[89] The percentage depletion deduction is allowed only to the person who receives the income in respect of the decedent to which the deduction relates (Reg. § 1.691(b)-1(b)).

189. How Recipient Treats Decedent's Income. A decedent's income that is to be accounted for by the recipient retains the same character it would have had in the hands of the decedent (Code Sec. 691(a)(3); Reg. § 1.691(a)-3).[90] Thus, if the income would have been earned income, exempt income, or interest to the decedent, it is the same kind of income to the recipient.

191. Deduction of Estate Taxes. If a person includes in gross income an item of income that had accrued as of the date of death of a decedent or prior successive decedents, so that it was included in the valuation of the estate for estate tax purposes, that person may take a corresponding deduction based on the estate tax attributable to the net value of the income item (Code Sec. 691(c); Reg. § 1.691(c)-1).[91] This deduction is taken by individuals on Form 1040 and by estates and trusts on Form 1041. In the case of individuals, it may be taken only if deductions are itemized on Schedule A. For individuals, as well as for estates and trusts, the deduction is not subject to the two-percent-of-adjusted-gross-income (AGI) floor on miscellaneous deductions (Code Sec. 67(b)(7)).[92] In the case of any generation-skipping transfer tax imposed on a taxable termination or a direct skip as a result of the death of the transferor, a deduction is available for the portion of this tax attributable to items of gross income that were not properly includible in the gross income of the trust before the date of such termination (Code Sec. 691(c)(3)).[93]

References are to Standard Federal Tax Reports; Tax Research Consultant; and Practical Tax Explanations.

[86] ¶ 21,802, ¶ 21,805; ESTTRST: 6,206, ESTTRST: 6,208; § 38,145.05

[87] ¶ 24,900, ¶ 24,907; ESTTRST: 6,206.30; § 3,050

[88] ¶ 12,541; ESTTRST: 6,208.05; § 7,220

[89] ¶ 24,907; ESTTRST: 6,206.05; § 32,925.05

[90] ¶ 24,900, ¶ 24,901; ESTTRST: 6,056; § 32,910

[91] ¶ 24,900, ¶ 24,909; ESTTRST: 6,156; § 32,925.10

[92] ¶ 6060; FILEIND: 12,054; § 7,110.10

[93] ¶ 24,900; ESTTRST: 6,158; § 32,925.10

Chapter 2
CORPORATIONS

	Par.
Corporate Formation	201
Return and Payment of Tax	211
Computation of Tax Liability	219
Estimated Tax	241
Accumulated Earnings Tax	251
Personal Service Corporations	273
Personal Holding Companies	275
Controlled Corporate Groups	289
Consolidated Returns	295

Corporate Formation

201. How Organizations Are Taxed. A corporation, like any business entity, is formed by one or more persons to conduct a business venture and divide profits among investors (Reg. § § 301.7701-2 and 301.7701-3).[1] A corporation files a charter or articles of incorporation in a state, in a U.S. possession, with a foreign government (¶ 2425), or (in certain cases) with the U.S. government. It prepares bylaws, has its business affairs overseen by a board of directors, and issues stock. Under the check-the-box regulations (¶ 402A), entities formed under a corporation statute are automatically classified as corporations and may not elect to be treated as any other kind of entity; other entities are allowed to elect corporate status on Form 8832. Thus, an entity that is a partnership or limited liability company (¶ 402B) under the laws of the state in which it is formed may elect to be taxed as a C corporation or an S corporation under the Code. However, partnerships that are publicly traded are taxed as corporations unless 90 percent or more of the gross income consists of qualifying passive-type income (Code Sec. 7704; Reg. § § 1.7704-1 and 1.7704-3).[2]

For tax purposes, the predominant forms of business enterprises are C corporations, S corporations (¶ 301), partnerships (¶ 401), and sole proprietorships. These different forms are treated differently under federal tax law and care should be taken in choosing the appropriate entity for the business. Although many of the Code's provisions apply to all of these entities, some areas of the law are specially tailored for each type. The classification of an entity will have a lingering tax impact throughout the entity's existence.

Of the types of business organizations, income earned in a C corporation is generally subject to the toughest tax bite, as the earnings are taxed twice. First, a *corporate* income tax is imposed on the corporation's net earnings (¶ 219). Then, after the earnings are distributed to shareholders as dividends, each shareholder must pay taxes separately on its share of the dividends (¶ 733–¶ 740). A corporation can reduce, or even eliminate, its federal income tax liability by distributing its income as salary to shareholder-employees who actually perform valuable services for the corporation (¶ 713). Although this can reduce taxation at the corporate level, employees who receive payments from a corporation in exchange for services must still pay tax on the amount received as salary or wages.

References are to Standard Federal Tax Reports; Tax Research Consultant; and Practical Tax Explanations.

[1] ¶ 43,082, ¶ 43,083; CCORP: 100, PART: 3,102; § 30,015.05, § 30,015.10

[2] ¶ 43,180, ¶ 43,180B, ¶ 43,181D; PART: 3,250

This scheme of taxation differs radically from that applied to partnerships, limited liability companies, S corporations, and sole proprietorships. These entities generally do not pay an entity-level tax on their earnings. There is no income tax on partnerships (¶ 404) or on limited liability companies (¶ 402B) treated as partnerships for federal tax purposes. Nor (in most cases) is there an S corporation income tax (¶ 319) or sole proprietorship income tax. Rather, the owners or members of these entities are taxed on their share of the entity's earnings.

203. Tax-Free Contributions in Exchange for Stock. A corporation is formed by the transfer of money or property from shareholders to the corporate entity in return for corporate stock. If one or more shareholders transfer money or property to a corporation solely in exchange for stock of that corporation, and if the shareholders control the corporation immediately after the exchange, neither the shareholders nor the corporation recognize any gain or loss (Code Secs. 351(a) and 1032).[3] To be considered in "control," the transferring shareholders—as a group—must own, immediately after the exchange: (1) at least 80 percent of the total combined voting power of all classes of stock entitled to vote, and (2) at least 80 percent of the total number of shares of all other classes of stock (Code Sec. 368(c)).[4] The exchanges need not actually be simultaneous to avoid nonrecognition of gain (Reg. § 1.351-1(a)(1)).[5] Rather, all that is required is a situation where the rights of the parties have been previously defined and the execution of the agreement proceeds in an orderly manner.

Money or property transferred to a controlled corporation generally includes all property, tangible or intangible, with certain limitations (Code Sec. 351(d)).[6] Stock issued for services, indebtedness of the corporation that is not evidenced by a security, or interest on indebtedness of the corporation that accrued on or after the beginning of the transferor's holding period for the debt are not considered issued in return for property.

Shareholders can be individuals, estates, trusts, partnerships, or other corporations (Reg. § 1.351-1(a)(1)).[7] However, the rules permitting tax-free transfers to a corporation in exchange for corporate stock do not apply if the transferee corporation is an investment company (Code Sec. 351(e)(1)).[8]

If the transferor owners receive additional property along with the stock when they transfer property to the corporation, the transfer can still qualify as a contribution to a controlled corporation described in Code Sec. 351 (Code Sec. 351(b); Reg. § 1.351-2(a)).[9] The shareholders are taxed on any additional property received ("boot"). Thus, gain is recognized, but only to the extent of the cash received plus the fair market value of the additional property received. No loss is recognized on the transfer.

Assumption of Liabilities. If property transferred in what would otherwise be a Code Sec. 351 tax-free transaction is subject to liabilities, the acceptance of the transfer or the assumption of the liabilities does not prevent the transaction from being tax free (Code Sec. 357).[10] This rule does not apply if the principal purpose of the transfer is tax avoidance or if liabilities assumed by the transferee exceed the transferor's basis in the property.

Bankruptcy. A debtor must recognize gain or loss upon its transfer of assets to a controlled corporation pursuant to a plan approved by a bankruptcy court (other than a reorganization plan) in which the stock is exchanged (Code Sec. 351(e)(2)).[11] Essentially, the transaction is treated as if the property had first been transferred to the creditors and then transferred by them to the controlled corporation. If less than all the stock is transferred to creditors, only a proportionate share of the gain or loss must be

References are to Standard Federal Tax Reports; Tax Research Consultant; and Practical Tax Explanations.

[3] ¶ 16,402, ¶ 29,622; CCORP: 3,050; § 26,101

[4] ¶ 16,750; CCORP: 3,054; § 26,105.05

[5] ¶ 16,403; CCORP: 3,054.05; § 26,105.05

[6] ¶ 16,402; CCORP: 3,052; § 26,110.05

[7] ¶ 16,403; CCORP: 3,050; § 26,101

[8] ¶ 16,402; CCORP: 3,062

[9] ¶ 16,402, ¶ 16,404B; CCORP: 3,102.10; § 26,120

[10] ¶ 16,520; CCORP: 3,106; § 26,125.05

[11] ¶ 16,402; CCORP: 3,114

recognized. Both the basis of the stock and of the assets are adjusted for the gain or loss recognized on the transfer to the corporation. Note that this rule does not apply to a transfer by one corporation to another corporation in a bankruptcy case. Instead, the transfer is considered a Code Sec. 368(a)(1)(G) reorganization and its tax consequences are determined accordingly (¶ 2247).

Reporting Requirements. If a person is a significant transferor and receives stock of a corporation in exchange for property in a Code Sec. 351 transaction, then the person and the corporation must each attach to their tax return a complete statement of all the facts pertinent to the exchange, including:

(1) the name and employer identification number (if any) of the transferee corporation (for the significant transferor's statement), or the name and taxpayer identification number (if any) of every significant transferor (for the transferee corporation's statement);

(2) the date(s) of the transfer(s) of assets;

(3) effective generally for exchanges occurring before March 28, 2016, the aggregate fair market value and basis of the assets transferred by the significant transferor (for the significant transferor's statement) or received by the transferee corporation (for the transferee corporation's statement); effective generally for exchanges occurring on or after March 28, 2016, the fair market value and basis of the property transferred by the significant transferor (for the significant transferor's statement) or received by the transferee corporation (for the transferee corporation's statement) in the exchange, determined immediately before the transfer and aggregated as follows:

(a) importation property transferred in a loss importation transaction (a transaction subject to the anti-loss importation rule of Code Sec. 362(e)(1));

(b) loss duplication property transferred in a loss duplication transaction (a transaction subject to the anti-loss duplication rule of Code Sec. 362(e)(2));

(c) property with respect to which any gain or loss is recognized on the transfer (without regard to whether such property is also identified in (a) or (b), above); and

(d) property not described in (a), (b) or (c), above.

(4) the date and control number of any private letter ruling(s) issued by the IRS in connection with the Code Sec. 351 exchange (Reg. § 1.351-3).[12]

The transferee corporation does not have to file a statement, however, if a significant transferor's statement that includes the required information is attached to the same return for the same Code Sec. 351 exchange. For this purpose, a significant transferor is a person that owns immediately after the exchange, at least five percent of the corporation's outstanding stock if the stock owned is publicly traded, or at least one percent of the corporation's outstanding stock if the stock owned is not publicly traded.

Return and Payment of Tax

211. Annual and Short-Period Corporate Returns. A corporation must file an income tax return using Form 1120, even if it has no income or no tax is due (Code Sec. 6012(a)(2); Reg. § 1.6012-2).[13] For tax years beginning after December 31, 2015, Form 1120 generally must be filed on or before the 15th day of the fourth month following the close of the corporation's tax year (April 15 for calendar-year corporations) (Code Sec. 6072; Reg. § 1.6072-2).[14] However, in the case of a corporation with a fiscal tax year ending on June 30, Form 1120 must be filed on or before the 15th day of the third month following the close of its tax year for tax years beginning before December 31, 2025. For tax years beginning before January 1, 2016, a corporation must file Form 1120 on or before the 15th day of the third month following the close of its tax year (March 15 for a

References are to Standard Federal Tax Reports; Tax Research Consultant; and Practical Tax Explanations.

[12] ¶ 16,404C; CCORP: 3,404; § 26,165

[13] ¶ 35,142, ¶ 35,145; FILEBUS: 3,052.05; § 39,025

[14] ¶ 36,720, ¶ 36,724; FILEBUS: 3,052.05; § 26,030.05

calendar-year corporations). If the last day of a corporation's tax year does not end on the last day of a month (as in the case of a dissolved corporation whose tax year ends on the date of dissolution), the return is due on or before the 15th day of the third or fourth full month (depending on the tax year) following the date of dissolution. If the due date for filing a return falls on a Saturday, Sunday, or legal holiday, the return must be filed by the first following business day (¶ 2549). Timely mailing generally is regarded as timely filing (¶ 2553). A corporation is generally entitled to an automatic extension of six months for filing its returns (¶ 2509).

A corporation's tax year generally may be a calendar year or a fiscal year (¶ 1501). Restrictions apply, however, to the choice of tax years by S corporations, personal service corporations, REITs, or REMICs. A corporation's return generally may not cover a period of more than a year except that a corporation may elect to use an annual filing period that fluctuates between 52 and 53 weeks (¶ 1505). A return may cover less than a year if a corporation was formed during the year or dissolved during the year. For example, if a corporation elects the calendar year method but starts operations on August 1, it must report income from August 1 to December 31. If a calendar-year corporation dissolves on June 30, it must file a short-period return covering the period from January 1 to June 30. In addition to filing its regular income tax return, a corporation that has adopted a resolution to dissolve itself or liquidate all or part of its stock must file Form 966 (Code Sec. 6043; Reg. § 1.6043-1).[15]

215. Due Date for Payment of Corporate Taxes. The due date for the payment of a corporation's taxes is generally the same as the due date for the filing of a return, without regard to filing extensions—the 15th day of the fourth or third month (depending on the tax year) that follows the close of its tax year (¶ 211) (Code Sec. 6151).[16] A corporation that anticipates a tax liability of $500 or more must estimate its taxes and make quarterly estimated tax payments (including estimated payments of the alternative minimum tax) using electronic fund transfers. If the liability exceeds the total estimated payments, the corporation must pay the remaining amount by the due date of its return. Failure to pay estimated taxes may be penalized (¶ 241). Corporations may file for an extension of time to file returns or to pay taxes (¶ 2509 and ¶ 2537).

Computation of Tax Liability

219. Corporate Tax Rates. Corporations are subject to the following tax rates on their taxable income (Code Secs. 11 and 1201):[17]

If taxable income is:					
Over—	*But not over—*	*Tax is—*			*Of the amt. over—*
$0	$50,000			15%	$0
50,000	75,000	$7,500	+	25%	50,000
75,000	100,000	13,750	+	34%	75,000
100,000	335,000	22,250	+	39%	100,000
335,000	10,000,000	113,900	+	34%	335,000
10,000,000	15,000,000	3,400,000	+	35%	10,000,000
15,000,000	18,333,333	5,150,000	+	38%	15,000,000
18,333,333	—			35%	0

Qualified Personal Service Corporations. The corporate graduated rates do not apply to qualified personal service corporations. Such corporations are instead taxed at a flat rate of 35 percent of taxable income (¶ 273). Qualified personal service corporations perform services in the fields of health, law, engineering, architecture, accounting (including the preparation of tax returns), actuarial science, the performing arts, or

References are to Standard Federal Tax Reports; Tax Research Consultant; and Practical Tax Explanations.

[15] ¶ 35,880, ¶ 35,881; FILEBUS: 9,352, CCORP: 27,054; § 38,145.10

[16] ¶ 37,080; FILEBUS: 6,102.05; § 39,305.05

[17] ¶ 3365, ¶ 30,352; CCORP: 100, SALES: 15,210; § 16,527.10, § 26,010

consulting. Substantially all of the stock of a personal service corporation is held by employees, retired employees, or their estates (Code Secs. 11(b)(2) and 448(d)(2)).[18]

Foreign Corporations. Foreign corporations are taxed at regular U.S. corporate rates on most income that is effectively connected with a U.S. trade or business (¶ 2429) and subject to a flat 30-percent withholding tax on U.S.-source fixed or determinable income that is not effectively connected (¶ 2431). Tax treaties between the U.S. and foreign countries may provide for lower rates or exemptions from taxation.

Additional Taxes. In addition to the regular corporate income tax, the alternative minimum tax (AMT) may be imposed on a corporation having tax preference items (¶ 1401). A corporation is exempt from the AMT if it is the corporation's first year or it is a small corporation with average annual gross receipts for the three-tax-year period (or portion thereof) ending before the current tax year not in excess of $7.5 million (¶ 1415). The $7.5-million amount is reduced to $5 million for the corporation's first three-tax-year period. Certain corporations used by their shareholders for the purpose of avoiding taxes might also be subject to the accumulated earnings tax (¶ 251–¶ 269) or the personal holding company tax (¶ 275–¶ 287).

Certain Timber Gains. For a tax year beginning in 2016, a 23.8-percent alternative tax rate applies to corporations on the portion of a corporation's taxable income that consists of qualified timber gain (Code Sec. 1201(b), as amended by the Protecting Americans from Tax Hikes (PATH) Act of 2015 (P.L. 114-113)).[19] The tax is equal to the sum of (1) 23.8 percent of the least of qualified timber gain, net capital gain, or taxable income, plus (2) 35 percent of any excess of taxable income over the sum of the amounts for which a tax was determined under Code Sec. 1201(a)(1) and the 23.8-percent computation. Qualified timber gain is the net gain from the sale or exchange of timber described in Code Sec. 631(a) (cutting of standing timber) and Code Sec. 631(b) (disposal of timber with a retained economic interest or outright sale). The special rate applies only to timber that has been held for more than 15 years.

221. Corporate Taxable Income. The corporate tax rates (¶ 219) are applied to a corporation's taxable income, which is the corporation's gross income for the year minus allowable deductions (Code Sec. 11).[20] The principal items of corporation income include gross sales receipts, dividends and interest received, rent and royalty income, and capital gains. The common deductions for a corporation include compensation paid to officers and workers, expenses for repairs and maintenance of property, taxes, licenses, interest paid, depreciation and depletion, advertising, and deductible amounts paid to pension and profit-sharing plans and employee benefit programs. In addition, a corporation may be entitled to special deductions for dividends received from other corporations (¶ 223), affiliates (¶ 229), and foreign corporations (¶ 231), as well as deductions for organizational expenses (¶ 237) and domestic production activities (¶ 239 and ¶ 980A).

A corporation generally must use the accrual method of accounting to determine when income and expenses are reported (¶ 1515). The cash basis of accounting may be used, however, by a qualified personal service corporation (¶ 219), a corporation engaged in a farming business (¶ 1519), or a corporation whose average annual gross receipts do not exceed $5 million for the three tax years preceding the current tax year (Code Sec. 448).[21] Securities dealers must use the mark-to-market method of accounting (¶ 1903).

223. Dividends Received from Other Corporations. A corporation is entitled to a special deduction from gross income for dividends received from a domestic corporation that is subject to income tax (Code Sec. 243).[22] The deduction is: (1) 70 percent of dividends from a corporation if the recipient corporation owns less than 20 percent of

References are to Standard Federal Tax Reports; Tax Research Consultant; and Practical Tax Explanations.

[18] ¶ 3365, ¶ 20,800; CCORP: 100; § 27,110

[19] ¶ 30,352; SALES: 15,210; § 16,527.10

[20] ¶ 3365; CCORP: 100; § 26,001

[21] ¶ 20,800; ACCTNG: 6,050; § 38,215.05

[22] ¶ 13,051; CCORP: 9,050; § 26,501

the distributing corporation; (2) 80 percent of dividends received from a 20-percent-owned corporation—a corporation having at least 20 percent (but generally less than 80 percent) of its stock owned by the recipient corporation; (3) 100 percent of qualifying dividends received from members of the same affiliated group (generally, 80-percent-or-more common ownership) to which the recipient corporation belongs (¶ 229); and (4) 100 percent of dividends received by a small business investment company (¶ 2392). These rules also apply to dividends received from a foreign corporation that are paid out of the earnings and profits of a taxable domestic predecessor corporation (¶ 231).

The aggregate amount of dividends-received deductions that may be taken by a corporation is limited to 70 percent (80 percent in the case of 20-percent-owned corporations) of its taxable income, computed without regard to any net operating loss deduction, the domestic production activities deduction, dividends-received deduction, dividends-paid deduction in the case of public utilities prior to December 19, 2014, the deduction for the U.S.-source portion of dividends from 10-percent-owned foreign corporations, the deduction for certain dividends received from wholly owned foreign subsidiaries, capital loss carryback, or adjustment for nontaxed portions of extraordinary dividends received. This limitation is applied first with respect to any 80-percent-deductible dividends and then separately for 70-percent-deductible dividends (after reducing taxable income by the 80-percent-deductible dividends), but it does not apply for the year if the full deduction results in a net operating loss (Code Sec. 246(b)).[23] Further, it does not apply in the case of dividends received by a small business investment company.

The dividends-received deduction is not allowed in computing the accumulated earnings tax (¶ 251) or the tax on personal holding companies (¶ 275). The deduction is allowed to a resident foreign corporation, as well as to a domestic corporation. No deduction is allowed for dividends received from a corporation exempt from income tax (including an exempt farmers' cooperative) during the tax year or the preceding year (Code Sec. 246(a)).[24]

Holding Period. The dividends-received deduction is only allowed if the underlying stock is held for at least 46 days during the 91-day period beginning on the date 45 days before the ex-dividend date of the stock (Code Sec. 246(c)).[25] If the stock is cumulative preferred stock with an arrearage of dividends, it must be held at least 91 days during the 181-day period beginning on the date 90 days before the ex-dividend date. The ex-dividend date is the first day the stock trades without a buyer having a right to an announced dividend and, to account for the delay needed to accommodate settlement, is normally two business days before the record date (the day when the company determines who is the record owner of the stock). A person who buys stock on the trading day before the ex-dividend date will receive a dividend, while a person who buys the stock on the ex-dividend date will not.

The holding period is reduced for any period during which the taxpayer's risk of loss with respect to the stock is diminished because the taxpayer (1) has an option to sell, is under an obligation to sell, or has made (and not closed) a short sale of substantially identical stock or securities; (2) is the grantor of an option to purchase substantially identical stock or securities; or (3) has reduced the risk loss by virtue of holding one or more other positions with respect to substantially similar or related property.

Debt-Financed Portfolio Stock. The dividends-received deduction is reduced for dividends received from debt-financed portfolio stock by a percentage related to the amount of debt incurred to purchase such stock. The deduction is calculated by multiplying the difference between 100 percent and the average portfolio indebtedness by 70 percent (80 percent in the case of 20-percent-owned corporations) (Code Sec. 246A).[26] However, any required reduction is limited to the amount of the interest

References are to Standard Federal Tax Reports; Tax Research Consultant; and Practical Tax Explanations.

[23] ¶ 13,200; CCORP: 9,212; § 26,510.15

[24] ¶ 13,200; CCORP: 9,062; § 26,510.10

[25] ¶ 13,200; CCORP: 9,204; § 26,510.20

[26] ¶ 13,250; CCORP: 9,208

deduction allocable to the related dividend. In addition, the reduction does not apply to dividends that are eligible for 100-percent dividends-received deduction for (1) qualifying dividends received from a member of an affiliated group, and (2) dividends received from a small business investment company.

Other Limitations. Capital gain dividends from a regulated investment company (mutual fund) or a real estate investment trust, and distributions that are a return of capital, do not qualify for the dividends-received deduction (Code Sec. 243(d)).[27] Additionally, the deduction is not allowed to the extent that the taxpayer is under an obligation (pursuant to a short sale or otherwise) to make related payments with respect to positions in substantially similar or related property (Code Sec. 246(c)(1)(B)).[28]

Prior to December 19, 2014, the deduction for dividends received on certain preferred stock of a public utility was reduced to the extent the public utility was allowed a dividends-paid deduction (Code Secs. 244 and 247, prior to repeal by the Tax Technical Corrections Act of 2014 (P.L. 113-295)).[29]

227. Debt-Equity Rules. For instruments issued by corporations and advances made to corporations, a question can arise as to whether such instruments and advances are treated as bona fide debt of the corporation or as an equity interest in the corporation. If they are treated as a bona fide debt, the corporation can deduct interest payments as a business expense and the shareholders can receive principal payments as a tax-free return of capital. However, if they are treated as stock, the corporation cannot deduct payments made with respect to such instruments.

The Code lists five factors that may be considered in making the debt-equity determination (Code Sec. 385):[30]

(1) whether there is a written, unconditional promise to pay on demand or on a specified date a sum certain in money in return for an adequate consideration in money or money's worth, and to pay a fixed rate of interest;

(2) whether there is subordination to or preference over any indebtedness of the corporation;

(3) the ratio of debt to equity of the corporation;

(4) whether there is convertibility into the stock of the corporation; and

(5) the relationship between holdings of stock in the corporation and holdings of the interest in question.

The courts have developed other guidelines to be used in making a debt-equity determination.[31]

Code Sec. 385 Debt-Equity Regulations. Final and temporary regulations provide guidance on the classification of certain related-party instruments as debt or stock for federal tax purposes (Reg. §§ 1.385-1, 1.385-2, and 1.385-3; Temp. Reg. §§ 1.385-3T and 1.385-4T).[32] The regulations generally apply to debt instruments issued between related corporations that are members of an expanded group. An expanded group is defined by reference to the term affiliated group in Code Sec. 1504(a), subject to certain modifications, and generally includes all corporations connected to a common parent that owns, directly or indirectly, 80 percent of the vote or value of each such corporation.

Foreign issuers, S corporations, non-controlled regulated investment companies, and non-controlled real estate investment trusts are excluded from the application of the Code Sec. 385 regulations. In addition, the regulations generally do not apply to debt instruments issued by partnerships, but contain certain anti-abuse provisions intended to prevent the use of controlled partnerships to avoid these rules. Intercompany obligations issued between members of a consolidated group are also outside the scope of these regulations.

References are to Standard Federal Tax Reports; Tax Research Consultant; and Practical Tax Explanations.

[27] ¶ 13,051; CCORP: 9,062; § 26,510.10

[28] ¶ 13,200; CCORP: 9,206

[29] ¶ 13,100, ¶ 13,300; CCORP: 9,210, CCORP: 9,250

[30] ¶ 17,340; CCORP: 3,301

[31] ¶ 15,704.264; CCORP: 3,304

[32] ¶ 17,350B, ¶ 17,350D, ¶ 17,350F, ¶ 17,350G, ¶ 17,350J; CCORP: 3,302

The Code Sec. 385 regulations require preparation and maintenance of documentation necessary to substantiate the tax treatment of certain related-party instruments as debt (Reg. § 1.385-2).[33] This generally means that taxpayers must be able to provide evidence of (i) the issuer's unconditional and binding obligation to pay a sum certain; (ii) the holder's rights as a creditor; (iii) the issuer's ability to repay the loan; and (iv) the issuer's and holder's actions that are consistent with a debtor-creditor relationship, such as payment of interest and principal and actions taken on default. The documentation must be prepared by the time the issuer's federal income tax return is filed, taking into account any applicable extensions.

For instruments that fail to satisfy the documentation rules, a rebuttable presumption to stock treatment applies if the expanded group demonstrates a high degree of compliance with these rules. If the expanded group does not demonstrate a high degree of compliance with the documentation rules, the instrument for which the documentation requirements are not met would be treated as stock for tax purposes and any tax benefit claimed by the taxpayer with respect to the treatment of the instrument as debt will be disallowed.

The documentation requirements apply to expanded group instruments provided that (i) stock of any member of the expanded group is publicly traded; (ii) the expanded group's total assets reported on financial statements exceed $100 million; and (iii) the expanded group's annual total revenue reported on financial statements exceeds $50 million.

The Code Sec. 385 regulations also recharacterize a purported debt instrument as stock if the instrument is issued between expanded group members as part of a transaction that does not finance new investment in the operations of the issuer (Reg. § 1.385-3 and Temp. Reg. § 1.385-3T).[34] Subject to a variety of exceptions for more ordinary course transactions, the debt recharacterization rules apply to instruments distributed from a U.S. issuer to a parent corporation, or other highly-related entity. The debt recharacterization rules also apply to the use of instruments, other than certain qualified short-term debt instruments, to fund acquisitions of related-party stock and internal asset reorganizations, as well as multi-step transactions that have an economically similar result.

Taxpayers can exclude the first $50 million of debt that otherwise would be recharacterized as stock under these rules. The debt recharacterization rules generally do not apply to debt instruments issued by dealers in securities or by regulated financial or insurance companies. Other exceptions, such as a subsidiary stock exception, an earnings and profits exception, and a net equity contribution exception, also apply.

The Code Sec. 385 regulations apply generally to tax years ending on or after January 19, 2017, subject to a number of transition rules. Debt instruments issued before April 5, 2016, are not covered by the regulations, and for purposes of the debt recharacterization rules, distributions and acquisitions (and similar transactions) before that date are grandfathered. The documentation rules apply to debt instruments issued on or after January 1, 2018.

229. 100-Percent Dividends-Received Deduction for Affiliates. Affiliated corporations are allowed a 100-percent dividends-received deduction for qualifying dividends received from members of the affiliated group (Code Sec. 243).[35] A qualifying dividend is any dividend received by a corporation that is a member of the same affiliated group as the corporation distributing it.

If the affiliated group includes at least one life insurance company, no dividend by any member of the group will be treated as qualified unless a special election is in effect for the tax year in which the dividend is received. If any member of an affiliated group elects the foreign tax credit, then all members of the group that pay or accrue foreign

References are to Standard Federal Tax Reports; Tax Research Consultant; and Practical Tax Explanations.

[33] ¶ 17,350D; CCORP: 3,302.10

[34] ¶ 17,350F, ¶ 17,350G; CCORP: 3,302.15

[35] ¶ 13,051; CCORP: 9,100; § 26,505

taxes must elect the credit in order for any dividend paid by a member of the group to qualify for the 100-percent dividends-received deduction.

231. Dividends from Foreign Corporations. A domestic corporation is entitled to a 70-percent (80-percent in the case of 20-percent-owned corporations (¶ 223)) deduction of the U.S.-source portion of dividends received from a foreign corporation that is at least 10 percent owned, by vote and value, by the domestic corporation (Code Sec. 245(a)).[36]

The U.S.-source portion of a dividend is the amount that bears the same ratio to the dividend as undistributed U.S. earnings bear to total undistributed earnings. U.S. earnings include (i) income of the foreign corporation that is effectively connected with a U.S. trade or business and that is subject to U.S. income tax, or (ii) dividends received from 80-percent-or-more-owned (directly or indirectly) domestic corporations (Code Sec. 245(a)(5)).[37] For this purpose, dividends received from regulated investment companies (RICs) and real estate investment trusts (REITs) on or after December 18, 2015, are not treated as dividends received from domestic corporations (Code Sec. 245(a)(12), as added by the Protecting Americans from Tax Hikes (PATH) Act of 2015 (P.L. 114-113)).[38]

A 100-percent dividends-received deduction is allowed to a domestic corporation for dividends paid by a wholly owned foreign subsidiary out of its earnings and profits for the tax year (Code Sec. 245(b)).[39] All of the foreign subsidiary's gross income must be effectively connected with a U.S. trade or business.

Debt-Financed Portfolio Stock. Any reduction in the dividends-received deduction resulting from the rules concerning debt-financed portfolio stock (¶ 223) must be computed before applying the above ratios.

237. Organizational Expenditures. A corporation may elect to deduct up to $5,000 of any organizational expenses it incurs in the tax year in which it begins business (Code Sec. 248; Reg. § 1.248-1).[40] A taxpayer is deemed to have made an election to deduct and amortize organizational expenses in the tax year in which the active trade or business to which the expenditures relate begins. A taxpayer may choose to forego the deemed election by clearly electing to capitalize its organizational expenditures on a timely filed federal income tax return, including extensions, for the tax year in which the active trade or business to which the expenditures relate begins. The $5,000 deducted for organizational expenses must be reduced by the amount by which the expenses exceed $50,000. Any remaining balance of organizational expenditures that are not immediately deductible must be amortized over a 180-month period.

Organizational expenditures are those that are (1) connected directly with the creation of the corporation, (2) chargeable to capital account, and (3) of a character that would be amortizable over the life of the corporation if its life were limited by its charter. They include expenses of temporary directors and organizational meetings, state fees for incorporation privileges, accounting service costs incident to organization, and legal service expenditures, such as for drafting of documents, minutes of organizational meetings, and terms of the original stock certificates.

Expenditures connected with issuing or selling stock or with the transfer of assets to a corporation are not amortizable. Instead, such costs must be netted against the proceeds of the stock sale. Pre-opening or start-up expenses, such as employee training, advertising, and expenses of lining up suppliers or potential customers, are not organizational expenses, but may be amortizable as start-up expenditures (¶ 904). Likewise, corporate expenditures that are incurred in investigating the creation or acquisition of an active trade or business or in creating such a trade or business do not qualify for amortization as organizational expenses, but may qualify as start-up expenses (Rev. Rul. 99-23).[41]

References are to Standard Federal Tax Reports; Tax Research Consultant; and Practical Tax Explanations.

[36] ¶ 13,150; CCORP: 9,152; § 26,510.10

[37] ¶ 13,150; CCORP: 9,152.10; § 26,510.10

[38] ¶ 13,150; CCORP: 9,152.10; § 26,510.10

[39] ¶ 13,150; CCORP: 9,154; § 26,510.10

[40] ¶ 13,350, ¶ 13,351; BUSEXP: 9,452.05; § 9,210.05

[41] ¶ 12,371.25; DEPR: 21,404.10; § 9,205.10

239. Domestic Production Activities. A corporation may claim a deduction against gross income equal to the applicable percentage of its qualified production activities income (QPAI) or its taxable income, whichever is less (i.e., the manufacturer's deduction (¶ 980A)). The amount of the deduction for any tax year, however, may not exceed 50 percent of the W-2 wages the taxpayer deducts in calculating its QPAI.

Estimated Tax

241. Penalty for Underpayment of Corporate Estimated Tax. A corporation that anticipates a tax bill of $500 or more must estimate its income tax liability for the current tax year and pay four quarterly estimated tax installments using electronic funds transfers during that year (Code Sec. 6655).[42] Any underpayment of a required installment results in an addition to tax on the amount of the underpayment for the period of underpayment. The addition to tax is based on current interest rates (¶ 2838). The period of underpayment begins with the due date of the underpaid installment and ends with the earlier of (1) the date that the underpayment is satisfied, or (2) the 15th day of the fourth month after the close of the tax year for tax years beginning after 2015, except for certain fiscal year corporations (the 15th day of the third month after the close of the tax year for tax years beginning before 2016) (¶ 211). Each estimated tax payment is credited against unpaid installments in the order in which they are required to be paid.

No addition to tax applies if the tax shown on the return, or the actual tax if no return is filed, is less than $500. If there is an underpayment, the taxpayer may use Form 2220 to determine whether the addition to tax applies and, if so, the amount of the penalty. However, a corporation is not required to file the form, as the IRS will determine any penalty owed and notify the corporation of the amount due (Instructions to Form 2220).

What is the Tax? The tax liabilities to which corporate estimated tax applies are: (1) the corporate income tax (¶ 219), the alternative tax on corporate capital gains (¶ 1738), or the income tax imposed on insurance companies (¶ 2370), whichever applies; (2) the alternative minimum tax (¶ 1401); and (3) the tax on gross transportation income of foreign corporations (Code Sec. 887).[43] For this purpose, the 30-percent tax on fixed, determinable, annual or periodic income of a foreign corporation not effectively connected with a U.S. business is considered a corporate income tax (¶ 2431). The total expected tax liability is reduced by the sum of the credits against tax. Special rules apply for estimating the book income adjustment by corporations that use the annualization method to calculate estimated tax liability (¶ 245).

243. Time and Amount of Corporate Estimated Tax Payments. For calendar-year corporations, estimated tax installments are due on April 15, June 15, September 15, and December 15. Installments of fiscal-year corporations are due on the 15th day of the fourth, sixth, ninth, and twelfth months of the tax year (Code Sec. 6655).[44] If any due date falls on a Saturday, Sunday, or legal holiday (¶ 2549), the payment is due on the first following business day. Corporations required to deposit taxes must transfer their tax deposits electronically from their accounts to the IRS's general account (Reg. § 31.6302-1(h)).[45]

To avoid a penalty for underpayment of estimated taxes (¶ 241), each installment must equal at least 25 percent of the lesser of:

(1) 100 percent of the tax shown on the current year's tax return or of the actual tax if no return is filed, or

References are to Standard Federal Tax Reports; Tax Research Consultant; and Practical Tax Explanations.

[42] ¶ 39,565; FILEBUS: 6,050, FILEBUS: 6,056, FILEBUS: 6,058; § 26,015.05, § 26,015.10

[43] ¶ 27,580; INTL: 3,602

[44] ¶ 39,565; FILEBUS: 6,054.05; § 26,015.10

[45] ¶ 38,055B; FILEBUS: 6,106.10; § 39,320.20

(2) 100 percent of the tax shown on the corporation's return for the preceding tax year, provided a positive tax liability was shown and the preceding tax year consisted of 12 months (Code Sec. 6655(d))[46] (but see special limitation on "*Large Corporations,*" following).

A lower installment amount may be paid if it is shown that use of an annualized income method or, for corporations with seasonal incomes, an adjusted seasonal method would result in a lower required installment (¶ 245).

Example: The X Corporation, a calendar-year taxpayer, estimates at the end of March that its federal income tax for the current tax year would be $800,000. Accordingly, it pays $200,000 [25% of ($800,000 × 100%)]of estimated tax by April 15, and another $200,000 by June 15. At the end of August, a recalculation shows that its tax for the year is expected to be $1 million. Assuming that there is no later change in the estimated tax, the estimated tax installments for September and December are computed as follows:

Estimated tax required to be paid by 9/15 [75% of ($1 million × 100%)]	$750,000
Less payments made in April and June	$400,000
Payment due in September	$350,000
Payment due in December [25% of ($1 million × 100%)]	$250,000
Total estimated tax payments	$1,000,000

Large Corporations. A large corporation—one with taxable income of at least $1 million in any one of the three immediately preceding tax years—is prohibited from using its prior year's tax liability (method (2), above), *except* in determining the first installment of its tax year (Code Sec. 6655(d)(2) and (g)(2)).[47] Any reduction in a large corporation's first installment as a result of using the prior year's tax must be recaptured in the corporation's second installment. In applying the $1-million test, taxable income is computed without regard to net operating loss carryovers or capital loss carrybacks. Also, a controlled group of corporations (¶ 291) must divide a single $1-million amount among its members.

Corporations with $1 Billion in Assets. Corporations with $1 billion or more in assets are required to make larger and smaller estimated tax payments in certain months in 2017 (Act Sec. 4 of the Amendment to Africa Growth and Opportunity Act (P.L. 112-163)). Specifically, for a payment due in July, August, or September of 2017, the amount due is 100.25 percent of the estimated tax the taxpayer would otherwise be required to pay. For a payment in October, November, or December of 2017, the amount due is 99.75 percent of the amount that would otherwise be due.

In addition, the amount of any required installment of estimated tax due by such corporations in July, August, or September of 2020 is 108 percent of the estimated tax amount otherwise due. The estimated tax payment due in October, November, or December of 2020 is 92 percent of the estimated tax amount otherwise due (Act Sec. 803 of the Trade Preferences Extension Act of 2015 (P.L. 114-27)).

245. Annualization and Seasonal Income Methods. A corporation may make a lower required installment payment of estimated taxes (¶ 243) where its annualized income installment or adjusted seasonal installment is less than the regular amount of the required installment. The annualized income installment is the product of the tax on the corporation's taxable income (including alternative minimum taxable income) for the corresponding portion of the tax year on an annualized basis, and reduced by all prior required installments for the tax year (Code Sec. 6655(e); Reg. § 1.6655-2).[48] A corporation can choose between using the standard monthly periods or either of two optional monthly periods. An election to use either of the two optional monthly periods

References are to Standard Federal Tax Reports; Tax Research Consultant; and Practical Tax Explanations.

[46] ¶ 39,565; FILEBUS: 6,052.05; § 26,015.05, § 26,015.15

[47] ¶ 39,565; FILEBUS: 6,052.05; § 26,015.05

[48] ¶ 39,565, ¶ 39,568; FILEBUS: 6,052.10; § 26,015.10

is effective only for the year of election. The election must be made on or before the date required for the first installment payment.

Installment	*Standard Monthly Periods*	*Optional Monthly Periods #1*	*Optional Monthly Periods #2*
1st	first 3 months	first 2 months	first 3 months
2nd	first 3 months	first 4 months	first 5 months
3rd	first 6 months	first 7 months	first 8 months
4th	first 9 months	first 10 months	first 11 months

To annualize income, multiply the income for the applicable period by 12 and divide by the number of months in the period. A corporation that uses the annualization method and switches to another method during the same tax year must, in its first installment under the new method, recapture 100 percent of any reduction achieved in the earlier installments.

Adjusted Seasonal Installments. Adjusted seasonal installments may be used only if the average of the corporation's taxable income for the same six-month period in the three preceding years was 70 percent or more of annual taxable income. An adjusted seasonal installment is the excess (if any) of (a) 100 percent of the amount determined by following the four steps set forth below, over (b) the aggregate amount of all prior required installments for the tax year. The steps are as follows:

(1) take the taxable income for the portion of the tax year up to the month in which the installment is due (filing month);

(2) divide this amount by the base period percentage for such months;

(3) determine the tax on the result; and

(4) multiply the tax by the base period percentage for the filing month and all preceding months during the tax year.

For any period of months, the base period percentage is the average percentage that the taxable income for the corresponding months in each of the three preceding tax years bears to the taxable income for those years (Code Sec. 6655(e)(3); Reg. § 1.6655-3).[49]

247. Quick Refund for Estimated Tax Overpayment. A corporation may apply for a refund of an overpayment of estimated tax immediately after the close of its tax year if its overpayment is at least 10 percent of the expected tax liability and amounts to at least $500. Overpayment, for this purpose, is the excess of the estimated tax paid over what the corporation expects its final income tax liability to be at the time the application is filed. The application must be filed by the 15th day of the fourth month after the close of the tax year for tax years beginning after 2015, except for certain fiscal year corporations (the 15th day of the third month after the close of the tax year for tax years beginning before 2016) (¶ 211), and before the day on which the corporation files its income tax return for the tax year for which a quick refund is requested (Code Sec. 6425; Reg. § § 1.6425-1—1.6425-3).[50] The taxpayer should file Form 4466. An extension of time to file Form 1120 will not extend the time for filing Form 4466.

Accumulated Earnings Tax

251. Accumulated Earnings Tax. In addition to being liable for regular income taxes, every corporation (other than personal holding companies (¶ 277), tax-exempt organizations (¶ 601), and passive foreign investment companies (¶ 2490)) may be liable for the accumulated earnings tax. The tax is in the form of a penalty and applies if a corporation is formed or used for the purpose of avoiding the imposition of income tax upon its shareholders by permitting its earnings or profits to accumulate instead of being distributed (Code Secs. 531 and 532).[51] A corporation is presumed to be availed of for a tax avoidance purpose if its earnings are accumulated beyond the reasonable needs of its business (¶ 265). The tax may be imposed on a corporation without regard to the number of shareholders, so it applies to both closely held and publicly held corporations.

References are to Standard Federal Tax Reports; Tax Research Consultant; and Practical Tax Explanations.

[49] ¶ 39,565, ¶ 39,570; FILEBUS: 6,052.10; § 26,015.10

[50] ¶ 38,840—¶ 38,843; IRS: 33,358; § 26,015.20

[51] ¶ 23,001, ¶ 23,010; CCORP: 18,250; § 26,901

The accumulated earnings tax is 20 percent of the corporation's accumulated taxable income (¶ 253) (Code Sec. 531).[52] For tax years beginning before January 1, 2013, the rate is 15 percent. There is no particular form that a corporation files to compute the tax. Instead, the IRS enforces the tax by reaching a conclusion whether enough dividends were paid during the tax year based on the corporation's filed income tax return. Interest on any underpayment is computed from the date the corporation's tax return is due without regard to extensions (¶ 211) (Code Sec. 6601(b)(4)).[53]

253. Accumulated Taxable Income. The accumulated earnings tax (¶ 251) is imposed on a corporation's accumulated taxable income for the tax year. Accumulated taxable income is the corporation's taxable income with certain adjustments, and minus the sum of the dividends-paid deduction (¶ 259) and the accumulated earnings credit (¶ 261). The adjustments to taxable income include the following:

(1) A deduction is allowed for federal income taxes, as well as for income, war, and excess profits taxes of foreign countries and U.S. possessions (to the extent not allowed as deductions in computing taxable income) accrued during the tax year, regardless of the accounting method used. The deduction will not include any accumulated earnings tax or personal holding company tax paid.

(2) Charitable contributions for the tax year are deductible without regard to the 10-percent-of-taxable-income limitation (¶ 927).

(3) No deduction is allowed for dividends received from other corporations (¶ 223).

(4) The net operating loss deduction is not allowed.

(5) A corporation (other than a mere holding company or investment company) is allowed a deduction for net capital losses incurred for the tax year determined without regard to capital loss carryovers. However, the deduction is reduced by the lesser of (1) the capital gains deducted in earlier years that have not already been used in a previous year to reduce the capital loss reduction, or (2) the corporation's accumulated earnings and profits at the close of the preceding year.

(6) A deduction is allowed for net capital gains for the year taking into account capital loss carryovers, reduced by the taxes attributable to them. In the case of a foreign corporation, only net capital gains that are effectively connected with the conduct of a trade or business within the United States and that are not exempt under treaty are taken into account.

(7) No capital loss carryback or carryover is allowed.

(8) A controlled foreign corporation (CFC) is allowed to deduct the amount of its subpart F income that is required to be included in the income of its U.S. shareholders (¶ 2488). However, if the corporation would otherwise calculate its accumulated taxable income on a gross basis, then the corporation's deduction must be reduced by any deduction that may have reduced a U.S. shareholder's income inclusion (Code Sec. 535; Reg. § 1.535-2).[54]

Although exempt interest income is excludable from accumulated taxable income for purposes of determining the accumulated earnings tax base, it is considered for purposes of determining whether earnings and profits have been accumulated beyond the reasonable needs of the business (¶ 265) (Rev. Rul. 70-497).[55]

References are to Standard Federal Tax Reports; Tax Research Consultant; and Practical Tax Explanations.

[52] ¶ 23,001; CCORP: 18,250; § 26,901

[53] ¶ 39,410; PENALTY: 9,054.05; § 40,105.15

[54] ¶ 23,040, ¶ 23,042; CCORP: 18,252; § 26,905.10

[55] ¶ 23,018.897; CCORP: 18,150; § 26,910.10

Holding or Investment Companies. If a corporation is a mere holding or investment company, then in determining its accumulated taxable income: (1) net capital losses may not be deducted, (2) net short-term capital gains are deductible only to the extent of any capital loss carryovers, and (3) accumulated earnings and profits cannot be less than they would have been had the rules in (1) and (2) been applied in computing earnings and profits (Code Sec. 535(b)(8)).[56]

Foreign Corporations. A foreign corporation is subject to U.S. income tax on U.S. source income, including the accumulated earnings tax (¶ 2425). Thus, foreign source income is generally excluded from accumulated taxable income. However, if 10 percent or more of the earnings and profits of any foreign corporation is derived from U.S. sources, then any distribution out of such earnings and profits (and any interest payment) retains its character as U.S.-source income upon receipt by a U.S.-owned foreign corporation (Code Sec. 535(d)).[57] A U.S.-owned foreign corporation is any foreign corporation in which 50 percent or more of voting power or total value is held directly or indirectly by U.S. persons.

259. Dividends-Paid Deduction. Dividends paid by regulated investment companies (mutual funds), real estate investment trusts (REITs), personal holding companies, and corporations subject to the accumulated earnings tax are deductible in determining accumulated taxable income (¶ 253) (Code Sec. 561).[58] The deduction is the sum of dividends paid during the tax year, consent dividends, and, in the case of a personal holding company, dividends carried over from the two preceding tax years (¶ 275). The deduction is unaffected by the taxpayer's accounting method, but rather is based upon the amount of dividends actually paid by the corporation and received by the shareholder. A corporation subject to the accumulated earnings tax is required, and a personal holding company may elect, to deduct dividends paid within 3½ months of the end of the tax year (within 2½ months of the end of the tax year for tax years beginning before January 1, 2016, or for tax years beginning before December 31, 2025, in the case of a corporation with a fiscal tax year ending on June 30) (Code Sec. 563).[59]

The dividends-paid deduction may be claimed for any payment that is a distribution of property to shareholders with respect to their stock and paid out of earnings and profits (¶ 747) (Code Sec. 562).[60] For a personal holding company, however, the deduction is up to the amount of undistributed personal holding company income, regardless of its earnings and profits (Code Sec. 316(b)(2)(A)).[61] No deduction is allowed for preferential dividends. On the other hand, distributions in complete liquidation of a corporation other than a personal holding company are included as part of the deduction. Distributions in complete liquidation of a personal holding company can be included depending on whether the distributee is a noncorporate or corporate shareholder. For a regulated investment company, the deduction is computed without regard to capital gain dividends and exempt-interest dividends (¶ 2303). For a REIT, the deduction is computed without regard to excluded net income from foreclosure property (¶ 2329).

Consent Dividend. A consent dividend is any dividend that a shareholder agrees to include in taxable income, even though the corporation does not make an actual distribution (Code Sec. 565).[62] The consent dividend is treated as paid by the corporation on the last day of its tax year and immediately contributed as paid-in capital by the shareholder. A consent dividend may be paid only with respect to consent stock, which is either common stock or preferred stock with unlimited participation; thus, the consent dividend must not be a preferential dividend. Shareholders consent on Form 972 that the corporation includes with Form 973 when filing its return to claim the dividends-paid deduction for consent dividends.

References are to Standard Federal Tax Reports; Tax Research Consultant; and Practical Tax Explanations.

[56] ¶ 23,040; CCORP: 18,104

[57] ¶ 23,040; CCORP: 18,052

[58] ¶ 23,450; CCORP: 9,300; § 26,905.15

[59] ¶ 23,490; CCORP: 9,308; § 26,905.15

[60] ¶ 23,470; CCORP: 9,304; § 26,905.15

[61] ¶ 15,702; CCORP: 9,304.05

[62] ¶ 23,530; CCORP: 9,316; § 26,905.15

261. Accumulated Earnings Credit. For a corporation other than a holding or investment company, the accumulated earnings credit allowed in computing accumulated taxable income (¶ 253) is an amount equal to the part of the earnings and profits of the tax year retained for the reasonable needs of the business, reduced by the net capital gain (which is itself reduced by the amount of income tax attributable to it). A minimum amount of $250,000 ($150,000 for personal service corporations (¶ 219)) may be accumulated from past and present earnings combined by all corporations, including holding or investment companies. This minimum amount is the only credit allowable to a holding or investment company (Code Sec. 535(c)).[63] Only one $250,000 accumulated earnings credit is allowed to a controlled group of corporations (¶ 291) (Code Sec. 1561(a)(2)).[64] The single credit is to be divided equally among the corporations.

263. Basis of Liability for Accumulated Earnings Tax. Although the accumulated earnings tax is computed as a percentage of the corporation's accumulated taxable income (¶ 253), liability for the tax hinges on whether the corporation was formed or availed of to avoid the income tax on income otherwise receivable by its shareholders. A corporation can be subject to the accumulated earnings tax for a year in which it has accumulated taxable income on hand even though, because of a stock redemption, no earnings and profits were accumulated for the tax year (*GPD, Inc.*, CA-6, 75-1 USTC ¶ 9142).[65]

The courts have shifted the focus of attention from earnings and profits to liquidity.[66] The reason for this change in emphasis is that the earnings-and-profits figure often is no indication of the funds available to the corporation to meet its business needs and pay dividends to its shareholders. Whether a corporation can be subjected to the accumulated earnings tax is therefore determined by comparing the reasonable needs of its business (¶ 265) to its total liquid assets at the end of the year. Liquid assets include the corporation's cash and marketable securities.

265. Reasonable Needs of the Business. In order to justify an accumulation of income (¶ 251), there must be a reasonable business need for it and a definite plan for its use. Since a corporation is given a credit (¶ 261) for its reasonable business needs (including reasonably anticipated needs) in figuring the accumulated earnings tax, the resolution of most disputes hinges on this issue (¶ 267).

The Code does not contain a comprehensive definition of reasonable business needs. However, a number of acceptable and unacceptable grounds for accumulating income are listed in the regulations (Code Sec. 537(b); Reg. § 1.537-2).[67] Acceptable grounds include: (1) business expansion and plant replacement; (2) acquisition of a business through purchase of stock or assets; (3) debt retirement; (4) working capital; and (5) investments or loans to suppliers or customers necessary to the maintenance of the corporation's business. The self-insurance of product liability risks is also a business need for which earnings and profits may be accumulated to a reasonable extent.

Unacceptable grounds include: (1) loans to shareholders and expenditures for their personal benefit; (2) loans to relatives or friends of shareholders or to others who have no reasonable connection with the business; (3) loans to a commonly controlled corporation; (4) investments that are not related to the business; and (5) accumulations to provide against unrealistic hazards.

Courts have used an operating-cycle approach to determine the amount of working capital a corporation needs. An operating cycle consists of (1) an inventory cycle (conversion of cash and raw materials into inventory), (2) a receivables cycle (conversion of inventory into accounts receivable and cash), and, possibly, (3) a credit cycle (accounts payable turnover).[68]

References are to Standard Federal Tax Reports; Tax Research Consultant; and Practical Tax Explanations.

[63] ¶ 23,040; CCORP: 18,254; § 26,905.20

[64] ¶ 33,340; CCORP: 18,254, CCORP: 42,054

[65] ¶ 23,045.37; CCORP: 18,100

[66] ¶ 23,045.65, ¶ 23,074.36; CCORP: 18,170; § 26,910.10

[67] ¶ 23,070, ¶ 23,072; CCORP: 18,154; § 26,910.10

[68] ¶ 23,074.625; CCORP: 18,158

A stock redemption under Code Sec. 303 to pay death taxes and expenses (¶ 745) and a redemption of stock in order to bring a private foundation within the 20-percent excess business holdings limit (¶ 640) are good cause for an accumulation of income (Code Sec. 537(a)).[69] Although other types of stock redemptions are not accorded this certainty, accumulations to redeem a minority interest (or the interest of one of two 50-percent stockholders) have been approved where they would eliminate dissent, would prevent the minority interest from falling into hostile hands, or were an essential ingredient of an employee incentive plan. Court decisions in this area show that except in rare circumstances, the redemption of a majority interest is not good cause for accumulating income.[70]

267. Burden of Proof of Reasonable Business Needs. On the issue of whether a corporation has accumulated income in excess of the reasonable needs of its business (¶ 265), the burden of proof in the Tax Court is on the government in two instances (Code Sec. 534; Reg. § 1.534-2).[71] First, the burden is on the government if, in advance of a formal deficiency notice, it does not notify the corporation by certified or registered mail of its intention to assess a deficiency based in whole or in part on the accumulated earnings tax or fails to state the tax years at issue. Second, in the event of such notification, the burden falls on the government if the corporation responds within 60 days with a statement of the grounds on which it relies to establish the reasonableness of all or any part of its accumulation of income. In other courts, the burden of proof is wholly on the corporation.

269. Tax Avoidance Intent for Accumulated Earnings Tax. One of the conditions that must exist before a corporation can be subject to the accumulated earnings tax (¶ 251) is an intent to avoid the income tax on its shareholders (Code Sec. 533).[72] If the corporation accumulates income beyond the reasonable needs of its business (or if it is a mere holding or investment company), a presumption of tax avoidance intent arises. This presumption can be overcome by showing that tax avoidance was not one of the purposes of the accumulation of income (*Donruss Co.*, 69-1 USTC ¶ 9167; *Shaw-Walker*, 69-1 USTC ¶ 9198).[73]

Personal Service Corporations

273. Personal Service Corporations. A personal service corporation (PSC) is one that furnishes personal services performed by employee-owners (Code Secs. 269A and 280H; Proposed Reg. § 1.269A-1(a)).[74] An employee-owner is an employee who owns, directly or indirectly, more than 10 percent of the outstanding stock of the corporation on any day during the corporation's tax year. The IRS may allocate income, deductions, credits, exclusions, or other allowances between the PSC and its employee-owners in order to prevent tax evasion or avoidance or to clearly reflect the income of both if: (1) substantially all of the services of a PSC are performed for, or on behalf of, one other corporation, partnership, or other entity, and (2) the principal purpose for forming or using the PSC is the avoidance or evasion of income tax by reducing the income of any employee-owner or securing the benefit of any expense, deduction, credit, exclusion or other allowance for any employee-owner that would not otherwise be available. The purpose of evading or avoiding income tax can be shown by a reduction in the tax liability of, or the increase of tax benefits to, an employee-owner or by any other increase in tax benefits. Code Sec. 280H restricts the amount that can be deducted by a PSC for amounts paid to owners if the corporation has elected a noncalendar tax year.

References are to Standard Federal Tax Reports; Tax Research Consultant; and Practical Tax Explanations.

[69] ¶ 23,070; CCORP: 18,168; § 26,910.10

[70] ¶ 23,018.895; CCORP: 18,168.15

[71] ¶ 23,020, ¶ 23,022; CCORP: 18,200

[72] ¶ 23,015; CCORP: 18,100; § 26,910.05

[73] ¶ 23,018.26; CCORP: 18,102; § 26,910.05

[74] ¶ 14,300, ¶ 14,301, ¶ 15,160; ACCTNG: 24,550, ACCTNG: 30,150; § 27,101

Personal Holding Companies

275. Tax on Personal Holding Companies. In addition to being liable for regular income taxes, a corporation that is a personal holding company (¶ 277) will be liable for a separate tax on its undistributed personal holding company income (¶ 281). The personal holding company tax was enacted when the highest corporate income tax rate was well below the highest individual income tax rate. It was designed to prevent individuals from establishing a corporation to receive and hold investment income or compensation so that it would be taxed at a lower rate (i.e., "incorporated pocketbooks"). Even though the corporate and individual income tax rates have somewhat equalized, the personal holding company tax still applies.

The personal holding company tax is 20 percent of a corporation's undistributed personal holding company income (Code Sec. 541; Reg. § 1.541-1).[75] For tax years beginning before January 1, 2013, the tax rate is 15 percent. Undistributed personal holding company income is computed by making the following adjustments to the corporation's taxable income, not just its personal holding company income (Code Sec. 545):[76]

(1) A deduction is allowed for federal income taxes, as well as for income, war, and excess profits taxes of foreign countries and U.S. possessions (to the extent not allowed as deductions in computing taxable income) accrued during the tax year, regardless of the accounting method used. The deduction does not include any accumulated earnings tax or personal holding company tax paid.

(2) Charitable contributions for the tax year are deductible but the 20-to-50-percent contribution base for individuals (¶ 1059) must be used, rather than the 10-percent base normally allowed to corporations (¶ 927).

(3) No deduction is allowed for dividends received from other corporations (¶ 223).

(4) The net operating loss deduction is not allowed.

(5) A deduction is allowed for net capital gains for the year, reduced by the taxes attributable to them. In the case of a foreign corporation, only net capital gains that are effectively connected with the conduct of a trade or business within the United States and that are not exempt under treaty are taken into account.

(6) Any deduction for ordinary and necessary business expenses, as well as depreciation, attributable to the operation and maintenance of property owned or operated by the corporation is limited to the aggregate rental income or other compensation earned from the property, unless the corporation shows that the compensation received was the highest available, the property was held in a bona fide business operated for profit, and either there was a reasonable expectation of a profit or the property was necessary for carrying on the corporation's business.

After these adjustments are made, the dividends-paid deduction is deducted from the adjusted taxable income (¶ 259). The amount of deduction for a personal holding company includes a dividend carryover from the two preceding tax years (Code Sec. 564).[77] The carryover is the excess of the dividends paid in the two preceding years over the income for such years. Any remaining balance is the corporation's undistributed personal holding company income.

Personal holding company taxes are computed and reported on Schedule PH, which is attached to the corporation's Form 1120.

277. Personal Holding Company Defined. A personal holding company is any corporation in which at least 60 percent of adjusted ordinary gross income for the tax year is personal holding company income (¶ 281), and at any time during the last half of the tax year more than 50 percent in value of its outstanding stock is owned, directly or

References are to Standard Federal Tax Reports; Tax Research Consultant; and Practical Tax Explanations.

[75] ¶ 23,152, ¶ 23,153; CCORP: 36,250; § 27,001

[76] ¶ 23,250; CCORP: 36,250; § 27,010.20

[77] ¶ 23,510; CCORP: 9,314; § 27,010.20

indirectly, by or for not more than five individuals (¶ 285) (Code Sec. 542; Reg. § § 1.542-1—1.542-3).[78] For this purpose, individuals include: a qualified pension, profit-sharing, or stock bonus plan (¶ 2101); a supplemental unemployment benefit (SUB) trust (¶ 692); a private foundation (¶ 631); or part of a trust permanently set aside or used exclusively for charitable purposes (¶ 537).

Certain corporations are exempt from the personal holding company tax (¶ 275), even though they meet the income and stock ownership qualifications (Code Sec. 542(c)). These include tax-exempt corporations (¶ 601); banks or domestic building and loan associations (¶ 2383); certain lending and finance companies that meet gross income, deduction, and loan tests; life insurance companies (¶ 2370); surety companies; corporations in bankruptcy or similar proceedings (unless the purpose of the proceedings is to avoid the personal holding company tax); and foreign corporations. A small business investment company (¶ 2392) is exempt from personal holding company tax if it is licensed by the Small Business Administration, but not if any shareholder of the company owns directly or indirectly a five-percent-or-more proprietary interest in a small business concern to which the investment company provides funds, or five percent or more in value of outstanding stock of such a concern.

281. Personal Holding Company Income. Personal holding company income for purposes of the personal holding company tax (¶ 275) means the portion of the adjusted ordinary gross income that consists of (Code Sec. 543):[79]

(1) dividends (other than dividends received by a U.S. shareholder from a controlled foreign corporation, effective for tax years ending on or after December 19, 2014), interest, royalties (other than mineral, oil and gas, copyright, or computer software royalties), and annuities (such income does not, however, include interest received by a broker or dealer in connection with any securities or money market instruments held as inventory or primarily for sale to customers, margin accounts, or any financing for a customer secured by securities or money market instruments);

(2) rents, unless they constitute 50 percent or more of the adjusted ordinary gross income, and unless the sum of dividends paid during the tax year, dividends paid after the close of the tax year but considered paid on the last day of the year, and consent dividends (¶ 259), equals or exceeds the amount by which personal holding company income exceeds 10 percent of the ordinary gross income;

(3) mineral, oil, and gas royalties, unless (a) they constitute 50 percent or more of the adjusted ordinary gross income, (b) the other personal holding company income for the tax year is not more than 10 percent of the ordinary gross income, and (c) the ordinary and necessary business expense deductions, other than compensation for personal services rendered by shareholders, are 15 percent or more of adjusted ordinary gross income;

(4) copyright royalties, unless (a) apart from royalties derived from the works of shareholders, they make up 50 percent or more of the ordinary gross income, (b) personal holding company income for the tax year (not taking into account copyright royalties and dividends in any corporation in which the taxpayer owns at least 50 percent of all classes of voting stock and at least 50 percent of the value of all classes of stock) is 10 percent or less of the ordinary gross income, and (c) ordinary and necessary business expense deductions, other than compensation for personal services rendered by shareholders and deductions for royalties, equal or exceed 25 percent of the amount by which the ordinary gross income exceeds the sum of royalties paid or accrued and depreciation allowed;

(5) rents from the distribution and exhibition of produced films (i.e., rents from a film interest acquired before the film production was substantially complete) unless such rents are 50 percent or more of the ordinary gross income;

References are to Standard Federal Tax Reports; Tax Research Consultant; and Practical Tax Explanations.

[78] ¶ 23,190—¶ 23,193; CCORP: 36,000; § 27,001

[79] ¶ 23,210; CCORP: 36,150; § 27,010.15

(6) amounts received as compensation for the use of, or right to use, tangible property of the corporation where, at any time during the tax year, 25 percent or more in value of the outstanding stock of the corporation is owned, directly or indirectly, by or for an individual entitled to the use of the property, whether such right is obtained directly from the corporation or by means of a sublease or other arrangement (but this paragraph applies only if the corporation's other personal holding company income, computed with certain adjustments, for the tax year is more than 10 percent of its ordinary gross income);

(7) amounts received by a corporation from contracts for personal services, including gain from the sale or other disposition thereof, if (a) some person other than the corporation has the right to designate (by name or by description) the individual who is to perform the services or if the individual who is to perform the services is designated (by name or by description) in the contract and (b) at some time during the tax year 25 percent or more in value of the outstanding stock of the corporation is owned, directly or indirectly, by or for the individual who has performed, is to perform, or may be designated (by name or by description) as the one to perform such services; and

(8) income required to be reported by a corporate beneficiary under the income tax provisions relating to estates and trusts.

Active Business Computer Software Royalties. Active business computer software royalties received in connection with the licensing of computer software are excluded from personal holding company income (Code Sec. 543(d)).[80] To qualify for the exclusion: (1) the royalties must be derived by a corporation actively engaged in the trade or business of developing, manufacturing, or producing computer software; (2) the royalties must make up at least 50 percent of the corporation's gross income; (3) business and research expenses relating to the royalties must equal or exceed 25 percent of ordinary gross income; and (4) dividends must equal or exceed the excess of personal holding company income over 10 percent of ordinary gross income. If one member of an affiliated group receives software royalties, it will be treated as having met the above requirements if another member meets the requirements.

283. Adjusted Ordinary Gross Income. In determining whether 60 percent or more of a corporation's adjusted ordinary gross income is personal holding company income (¶ 281), the following adjustments must be made to ordinary gross income (Code Sec. 543(b)(2)):[81]

(1) Rental income must be reduced by deductions for depreciation and amortization, property taxes, interest, and rents paid that are attributable to such income.

(2) Income from mineral, oil, and gas royalties and from working interests in oil and gas wells must be reduced by deductions for depreciation, amortization and depletion, property and severance taxes, interest, and rents paid that are attributable to such income.

(3) Interest on U.S. bonds held for sale by a dealer who is making a primary market for these obligations, and interest on condemnation awards, judgments, and tax refunds, must be excluded.

(4) Rent received from the lease of tangible personal property manufactured by a taxpayer engaged in substantial manufacturing or production of property of the same type must be reduced by deductions for depreciation and amortization, taxes, rent, and interest paid that are attributable to such income.

All capital gains are excluded in determining whether the 60-percent test has been met because it is based on adjusted ordinary gross income.

References are to Standard Federal Tax Reports; Tax Research Consultant; and Practical Tax Explanations.

[80] ¶ 23,210; CCORP: 36,156.15

[81] ¶ 23,210; CCORP: 36,106; § 27,010.10

285. Constructive Ownership of Personal Holding Company. The following constructive ownership rules apply in determining whether (1) a corporation is a personal holding company (¶ 277), (2) amounts received under a personal service contract are personal holding company income (¶ 281), (3) copyright royalties are personal holding company income, or (4) compensation for the use of property is personal holding company income (Code Sec. 544; Reg. § 1.544-1):[82]

(1) Stock owned, directly or indirectly, by or for a corporation, partnership, estate, or trust is considered owned proportionately by its shareholders, partners, or beneficiaries.

(2) An individual is considered to own the stock owned, directly or indirectly, by or for his or her family (brothers and sisters (whole or half blood), spouse, ancestors, and lineal descendants), or by or for his or her partner.

(3) If any person has an option to acquire stock, such stock is considered owned by such person. An option to acquire an option, and each one of a series of such options, is regarded as an option to acquire stock. This rule is applied in preference to rule (2), above, when both rules apply.

(4) Stock constructively owned by a corporation, partnership, estate, or trust will be reattributed to its owners or beneficiaries so that they are treated as constructive owners of the stock. However, stock constructively and not actually owned by an individual will not be reattributed.

(5) Outstanding securities convertible into stock (whether or not during the tax year) are considered outstanding stock, but only if the effect of the inclusion of all such securities is to make the corporation a personal holding company.

287. Deficiency Dividend Deduction for Personal Holding Company Tax. If a deficiency is determined in the personal holding company tax (¶ 275), the corporation may then distribute dividends and, in redetermining the undistributed personal holding company income, reduce or eliminate the deficiency by means of a deduction for deficiency dividends in the amount of the dividends so paid (Code Sec. 547; Reg. § § 1.547-1—1.547-7).[83] The distribution must be made within 90 days after the deficiency determination. Claim for the deduction must be filed within 120 days of the determination.

Controlled Corporate Groups

289. Allocation of Tax Benefits of Certain Controlled Corporations. A controlled group of corporations (¶ 291) is allowed only one set of graduated income tax brackets for regular income tax purposes (¶ 219) and one $250,000 accumulated earnings credit for the accumulated earning tax (¶ 261). Controlled groups are also allowed one $40,000 exemption amount for alternative minimum tax purposes (¶ 1410). Each of these items is to be allocated equally among the members of the group unless they all consent to a different apportionment (Code Sec. 1561).[84]

Dividends-Received Deduction. If a parent-subsidiary controlled group is also an affiliated group, a 100-percent dividends-received deduction may be taken with respect to dividends paid from one member to another (¶ 223). A 70-percent deduction is allowed for distributions between members of a brother-sister controlled group.

291. Controlled Group of Corporations. There are three types of controlled corporate groups—parent-subsidiary, brother-sister, and combined groups (Code Sec. 1563(a)).[85] A parent-subsidiary controlled group exists if: (1) one or more chains of corporations are connected through stock ownership with a common parent corporation; (2) 80 percent or more of the voting power or value of the stock of each corporation in the group other than the parent is owned by one or more corporations in the group;

References are to Standard Federal Tax Reports; Tax Research Consultant; and Practical Tax Explanations.

[82] ¶ 23,230, ¶ 23,231; CCORP: 36,058

[83] ¶ 23,290—¶ 23,297; CCORP: 36,300; § 27,015

[84] ¶ 33,340; CCORP: 42,050

[85] ¶ 33,360; CCORP: 42,102, CCORP: 42,104, CCORP: 42,106

and (3) the common parent owns at least 80 percent of the voting power or value of the stock of one of the other corporations in the group (not counting stock owned directly by other members).

A brother-sister controlled group exists if five or fewer persons (individuals, estates, or trusts) own stock possessing more than 50 percent of the total combined voting power of all classes of stock entitled to vote, or more than 50 percent of the total value of all stock, taking into account the stock ownership of each person only to the extent the person owns stock in each corporation.

A combined group consists of three or more corporations, each of which is a member of either a parent-subsidiary controlled group or a brother-sister controlled group, and at least one of which is the common parent of a parent-subsidiary group and also is a member of a brother-sister group.

293. Controlled Group of Corporations—Expenses, Interest, and Losses. Controlled groups of corporations are subject to the related-party transaction rules of Code Sec. 267 (¶ 1717), under which controlled members must use a matching rule that defers the deductibility of an expense or interest by a payor until the payment is included in the payee's income (Code Sec. 267(a)(2)).[86] Also, losses on sales between members of a controlled group must be deferred until the property is sold to an unrelated person (Code Sec. 267(f)).[87] The loss-deferral rule does not apply, however, to sales to a domestic international sales corporation (DISC) (¶ 2498), to sales of inventory in the ordinary course of business if one of the parties is a foreign corporation, or to loan repayment losses attributable to foreign currency value reductions.

Consolidated Returns

295. Consolidated Returns. An affiliated group of corporations may file a consolidated income tax return for the tax year instead of filing separate returns (Code Sec. 1501).[88] An affiliated group is one or more chains of includible corporations connected through stock ownership with a common parent corporation that is an includible corporation if (1) the common parent directly owns stock possessing at least 80 percent of the total voting power of at least one of the other includible corporations and has a value equal to at least 80 percent of the total value of the stock of the corporation, and (2) stock meeting the 80-percent test in each includible corporation other than the common parent is owned directly by one or more of the other includible corporations (Code Sec. 1504(a)).[89]

A consolidated return may be filed only if all corporations that were members of the affiliated group *at any time* during the tax year consent prior to the last day for filing the return. The making of a consolidated return is such consent. The common parent corporation, when filing a consolidated return, must attach Form 851. In addition, for the first year a consolidated return is filed, each subsidiary must attach a Form 1122 (consent to be included in the consolidated return) (Code Sec. 1501; Reg. § 1.1502-75(b)).[90] A subsidiary may be treated as if it filed a Form 1122, even though it failed to do so, if the affiliated group meets certain requirements (Rev. Proc. 2014-24).[91]

The following corporations may not file consolidated returns (Code Sec. 1504(b)):[92]

(1) tax-exempt corporations (¶ 601), except that such organizations may be affiliated with other such organizations at least one of which is organized only to hold title for exempt organizations and from which the others derive income;

(2) life insurance companies (¶ 2370), except for those included in the group at the election of the common parent (Code Sec. 1504(c));[93]

References are to Standard Federal Tax Reports; Tax Research Consultant; and Practical Tax Explanations.

[86] ¶ 14,150; BUSEXP: 21,160; § 17,605

[87] ¶ 14,150; CCORP: 42,260, SALES: 39,112

[88] ¶ 33,121; CCORP: 45,050, CONSOL: 7,000

[89] ¶ 33,260; CCORP: 45,052, CONSOL: 7,050

[90] ¶ 33,121, ¶ 33,195; CCORP: 45,102, CONSOL: 9,100

[91] ¶ 33,168.564; CCORP: 45,102, CONSOL: 9,102

[92] ¶ 33,260; CCORP: 45,054, CONSOL: 7,100

[93] ¶ 33,260; CCORP: 45,054.10, CONSOL: 7,106

(3) foreign corporations, except for Canadian or Mexican subsidiaries for which the common parent makes an election to treat them as domestic corporations includible in the consolidated group (Code Sec. 1504(d));[94]

(4) corporations electing the Code Sec. 936 possessions tax credit (¶ 1362);

(5) regulated investment companies (mutual funds) and real estate investment trusts (but see ¶ 2340 for circumstances in which a REIT may treat income and deductions of a qualified subsidiary as its own);

(6) domestic international sales corporations (DISCs); and

(7) S corporations.

297. Advantages and Disadvantages of Consolidated Returns. The advantages of filing a consolidated income tax return (¶ 295) include: (1) offsetting operating losses of one company against the profits of another (see the rule for dual resident companies, following); (2) offsetting capital losses of one company against the capital gains of another (subject to a limitation on pre-acquisition losses of newly acquired corporations (¶ 2285)); (3) avoidance of tax on intercompany distributions; (4) deferral of income on intercompany transactions; (5) use by the corporate group of the excess of one member's foreign tax credit over its limitation; and (6) designation of the parent corporation (or another corporation in certain cases) as an agent of the group for all tax purposes.

The disadvantages include: (1) the effect on later years' returns; (2) deferral of losses on intercompany transactions; (3) additional bookkeeping required to keep track of deferred intercompany transactions; (4) intercompany profit in inventories still within the group must be reflected in annual inventory adjustments; (5) possible elimination of foreign tax credits when the limiting fraction is diminished because of lack of foreign income on the part of some members; and (6) possible accumulated earnings tax liability (¶ 251) when the consolidated accumulated earnings and profits of the group exceed the minimum credit amount.

Dual Resident Companies. If a U.S. corporation is subject to foreign tax on its worldwide income, or on a residence basis as opposed to a source basis, any net operating loss it incurs in a year cannot reduce the taxable income of any other member of a U.S. affiliated group for any tax year (Code Sec. 1503(d); Reg. §§ 1.1503(d)-1—1.1503(d)-8).[95]

Preferred Dividends. Income out of which a member of an affiliated group, other than a common parent, distributes preferred dividends to a nonmember may not be offset by the group's net operating losses or capital losses (Code Sec. 1503(f)).[96] Taxes on that income may not be offset by most group tax credits.

Golden Parachutes. All members of an affiliated group are treated as a single corporation when determining excessive payments that are contingent on a change in corporate control (¶ 907) (Code Sec. 280G(d)(5)).[97]

References are to Standard Federal Tax Reports; Tax Research Consultant; and Practical Tax Explanations.

[94] ¶ 33,260; CCORP: 45,054.05, CONSOL: 7,108.05

[95] ¶ 33,240, ¶ 33,245—¶ 33,252; CCORP: 45,264, CONSOL: 63,400—CONSOL: 64,100

[96] ¶ 33,240; CCORP: 45,318, CONSOL: 75,100

[97] ¶ 15,150; COMPEN: 30,050; § 45,020.05

Chapter 3

S CORPORATIONS

	Par.
S Corporation Status	301
Taxation of Shareholders	309
Tax Treatment of Distributions	323
Taxation of Corporation	335
Returns and Tax Year	351

S Corporation Status

301. S Corporations — Generally. An S corporation is a corporation that elects and is eligible to choose S corporation status (¶ 303–¶ 305) and whose shareholders consent to the corporation's election (¶ 306). In general, an S corporation does not pay any income tax (with exceptions discussed in ¶ 335 and following). Instead, the corporation's income and deductions are passed through to its shareholders. The shareholders must then report the income and deductions on their own income tax returns.

To the extent the S corporation rules (Code Sec. 1361 and following) do not apply, S corporations are governed by the regular (C corporation) corporate tax rules. Thus, while the taxation of income earned by, and the allocation of losses incurred by, S corporations closely parallel the taxation of partnerships with respect to items of income and loss, S corporations generally are treated as regular corporations for purposes of the rules relating to corporate distributions, redemptions, liquidations, and reorganizations, as well as contributions of capital by shareholders (Code Sec. 1371).[1]

303. Corporations Eligible to Elect S Corporation Status. To qualify as an S corporation, a corporation must be a "small business corporation" and meet all of the following requirements (Code Sec. 1361; Reg. § 1.1361-1(b)).[2]

- The entity must be a domestic corporation that is organized under the laws of any state or U.S. territory, or a domestic eligible entity (i.e., a partnership or limited liability company (LLC)) that elects to be taxed as a corporation under the check-the-box rules (Reg. § § 1.1361-1(c) and 301.7701-3).[3]
- The corporation may have as shareholders only individuals, estates, certain trusts, and certain tax-exempt organizations (¶ 304). Partnerships and corporations cannot be shareholders.
- Only U.S. citizens or residents can be shareholders.
- The corporation can have only one class of stock (¶ 305).

A few limited types of corporations are ineligible to be small business corporations including (Code Sec. 1361(b)(2)):[4]

- a financial institution that uses the reserve method of accounting;
- an insurance company taxed under subchapter L of the Code (¶ 2370);
- a corporation that has elected to take the Puerto Rico and possessions tax credit (¶ 1362); or
- a domestic international sales corporation (DISC) or former DISC.

References are to Standard Federal Tax Reports; Tax Research Consultant; and Practical Tax Explanations.

[1] ¶ 32,140; SCORP: 368; § 28,901

[2] ¶ 32,021, ¶ 32,024A; SCORP: 150; § 28,001

[3] ¶ 32,024A, ¶ 43,083; PART: 3,102, SCORP: 152; § 30,005.30

[4] ¶ 32,021; SCORP: 154; § 28,001

An existing domestic eligible entity that is treated as a partnership for tax purposes is allowed to change its tax status and elect to be taxed as an S corporation. In other words, provided requirements that apply to check-the-box elections and S corporations are met, the entity may elect to change its tax status from partnership to corporation and also file an S election. There will be no intervening C year between the partnership tax year and the S tax year, so long as the check-the-box and S elections are effective on the same date and both sets of deadlines are met (Rev. Rul. 2009-15).[5]

100-Shareholder Limitation. An S corporation can have no more than 100 shareholders (Code Sec. 1361(b)(1)(A) and (c)).[6] In certain cases, two or more shareholders can be counted as only one shareholder for this purpose if they are related in particular ways. For example, two spouses (and their estates) are counted as a single shareholder. In addition, all qualifying members of a family who hold stock in the corporation are treated as one shareholder of the S corporation. A family is defined as a common ancestor, the lineal descendants of the common ancestor, and the spouses (or former spouses) of the common ancestor and the descendants. The common ancestor can be no more than six generations removed from the youngest shareholder who is treated as a member of the family on the latest of: (1) the date the S corporation election is made (¶ 306); (2) the earliest date that a family member first holds stock in the corporation; or (3) October 22, 2004. Additionally, in determining whether certain children are lineal descendants and members of a family, any legally adopted child, any child lawfully placed with the individual for legal adoption, and any eligible foster child are treated as a child by blood. The estate of a family member is treated as a member of the family for purposes of determining the number of shareholders.

304. Eligible S Corporation Shareholders. All shareholders of an S corporation must be individuals, estates, certain specified trusts, or certain tax-exempt organizations (Code Sec. 1361(b)(1)(B)).[7] Partnerships and C corporations are not eligible to hold stock in an S corporation. The prohibition on a partnership holding S corporation stock does not extend to a limited liability company (LLC) with a single, individual member that is taxed as a disregarded entity under the check-the-box rules. The owner of the single-member LLC is treated as the owner of the S corporation stock. A single-member LLC that checks the box to be taxed as a C corporation may not hold stock in an S corporation. A taxpayer who holds only restricted bank director stock is not considered a shareholder for determining whether an S corporation has an ineligible shareholder (Code Sec. 1361(f)).

Trusts. Trusts eligible to hold S corporation shares include grantor trusts (where the grantor is regarded as the shareholder) and voting trusts (where each beneficiary is treated as a shareholder) (Code Sec. 1361(c)(2); Reg. § 1.1361-1(h)).[8]

A trust that qualifies as a traditional or Roth individual retirement arrangement (IRA) is generally not an eligible S corporation shareholder (*Taproot Administrative Services, Inc.*, Dec. 57,950, 133 TC 202 (2009), aff'd, CA-9, 2012-1 USTC ¶ 50,256; Rev. Rul. 92-73).[9] An IRA, however, may hold stock in a bank or depository holding company that is an S corporation if the IRA held the stock as of October 22, 2004 (Code Sec. 1361(c)(2)(A)(vi)).[10] If the IRA decides to sell the bank stock, it can sell the stock to the IRA beneficiary within 120 days after the corporation makes the S corporation election without violating the prohibited transaction rules.

Any testamentary trust that receives S corporation stock is an eligible S corporation shareholder unless the trust is treated as an eligible shareholder only for two years after the deemed owner's death. The IRS may extend the two-year limit under an extension for estate tax payments. A charitable remainder trust is not an eligible S corporation shareholder (Rev. Rul. 92-48).[11]

References are to Standard Federal Tax Reports; Tax Research Consultant; and Practical Tax Explanations.

[5] ¶ 32,053.36; LLC: 18,200; § 28,010.05

[6] ¶ 32,021; SCORP: 156; § 28,005.05

[7] ¶ 32,021; SCORP: 158; § 28,010.05

[8] ¶ 32,021, ¶ 32,024A; SCORP: 158.20; § 28,010.10, § 28,010.20

[9] ¶ 32,026.815; SCORP: 158.35; § 28,010.40

[10] ¶ 32,021; SCORP: 158.35; § 28,010.40

[11] ¶ 24,468.22; SCORP: 160.05; § 28,715.05

ESBTs. An electing small business trust (ESBT) can be an S corporation shareholder so long as the trust does not have as a beneficiary any person other than an individual, estate, or organization eligible to accept charitable contributions under Code Sec. 170 (other than a political entity) (Code Sec. 1361(c)(2)(A)(v), (c)(2)(B)(v), and (e)).[12] ESBTs also cannot have any interest acquired by purchase (i.e., acquired with a cost basis).

To qualify as an ESBT, the trustee must file an election by signing and filing a statement with the IRS service center where the S corporation files its income tax return (Reg. § 1.1361-1(m)). The election statement must identify the trust, its potential current beneficiaries, the S corporations in which the trust currently owns stock, and the first date on which the trust owned the stock. It must include words identifying it as an ESBT election statement under Code Sec. 1361(e)(3), the effective date of the election, and representations that the trust qualifies as an ESBT and that all potential current beneficiaries are eligible shareholders. A trust is treated as an ESBT as of the effective date of the election. Once effective, the election applies to the tax year in which it is made and all subsequent tax years unless it is revoked with IRS consent.

Some types of trusts are not permitted to be ESBTs. Ineligible trust types include qualified subchapter S trusts (see following), any trust that is exempt from income tax, and charitable remainder unitrusts (CRUTs) and charitable remainder annuity trusts (CRATs) (Reg. § 1.1361-1(m)(iv)).

Each potential current beneficiary of an ESBT is treated as a shareholder, except that for any period in which there is no potential current beneficiary of the trust, the trust itself is treated as the shareholder. A potential current beneficiary is a person who is entitled to a distribution from the trust or who may receive a distribution at the discretion of any person. Any person who may benefit from a power of appointment is not a potential current beneficiary if the power has not been exercised. If the potential current beneficiaries of an ESBT would disqualify an entity from S corporation status, the ESBT has a grace period of one year to dispose of its stock in the S corporation, thereby avoiding disqualification.

QSSTs. A qualified subchapter S trust (QSST) whose beneficiary chooses to be treated as owner of the S corporation stock held by the trust also may hold stock in an S corporation (Code Sec. 1361(d); Reg. § 1.1361-1(j)).[13] A QSST must own stock in at least one S corporation and must distribute all of its income to one individual who is a U.S. citizen or resident. The QSST beneficiary is taxed on all items of income, loss, deduction, and credit attributable to the S corporation stock held by the QSST. However, the QSST, not the beneficiary, is treated as the owner of the S corporation stock for purposes of determining the tax consequences of the trust's disposition of the S corporation stock. In addition, the terms of the QSST must provide:

- there may be only one income beneficiary at any time;
- trust corpus may be distributed only to the income beneficiary;
- each income interest must end no later than the death of the income beneficiary; and
- if the trust ends at any time during the life of the income beneficiary, it must distribute all of its assets to the beneficiary.

Successive income beneficiaries are permitted. The income beneficiary's election to treat the trust as a QSST may be revoked only with the consent of the IRS. The election is effective for up to two months and 15 days before the election date. A separate election must be made with respect to each corporation the stock of which is held by the trust and must be made by each successive income beneficiary.

References are to Standard Federal Tax Reports; Tax Research Consultant; and Practical Tax Explanations.

[12] ¶ 32,021; SCORP: 158.30; § 28,010.30

[13] ¶ 32,021, ¶ 32,024A; SCORP: 160; § 28,010.25

Exempt Organizations as Shareholders. Certain tax-exempt organizations can be S corporation shareholders: qualified pension, profit-sharing, and stock bonus plans; charitable organizations; and Code Sec. 501(c)(3) organizations.

QSSS. Even though a corporation generally cannot be an S corporation shareholder, an S corporation is permitted to own a qualified subchapter S subsidiary (QSSS or QSub) (Code Sec. 1361(b)(3)).[14] This includes any domestic corporation that qualifies as an S corporation and is 100 percent owned by an S corporation parent that elects to treat it as a QSSS. A QSSS is not taxed as a separate corporation, and all its tax items are treated as belonging to the parent. Form 8869 is used to elect QSub treatment for wholly-owned corporate subsidiaries.

305. Single Class of Stock Requirement. An S corporation may have only one class of stock outstanding. The shares must confer identical rights to distribution and liquidation proceeds (Code Sec. 1361(b)(1)(D) and (c)(5); Reg. § 1.1361-1(l)).[15] Differences in voting rights are permitted. In addition, a corporate obligation that qualifies as "straight debt" is not considered a second class of stock. Buy-sell and redemption agreements restricting transferability of the stock are generally disregarded in determining whether the corporation has a single class of stock.

Stock of an S corporation does not include stock received for the performance of services that is substantially nonvested, unless the holder has made a Code Sec. 83(b) election to include the value of the stock in income (Reg. § 1.1361-1(b)(3)).[16] However, stock warrants, call options, or other similar rights to purchase stock (collectively, "options") generally are treated as stock of the corporation if the options are substantially certain to be exercised at a strike price substantially below fair market value. This rule does not apply if the option was issued:

- to a commercial lender;
- in connection with the performance of services, provided the option is nontransferable and does not have a readily ascertainable fair market value when issued (¶ 713); or
- at a strike price that is at least 90 percent of the stock's fair market value (Reg. § 1.1361-1(l)(4)(iii)).[17]

In addition, restricted bank director stock is not taken into account as outstanding stock in applying the provisions of subchapter S (Code Sec. 1361(f)(1)).[18] Accordingly, it is not treated as a second class of stock in the S corporation.

306. How to Make an S Election. The election of S corporation status must be made by a qualified corporation (¶ 303–¶ 305), with the unanimous consent of the shareholders, on or before the 15th day of the 3rd month of its tax year in order for the election to be effective beginning with the year when made (Code Sec. 1362(a), (b), and (c); Reg. § 1.1362-6).[19] The election is made on Form 2553. The corporation must meet all of the eligibility requirements for the pre-election portion of the tax year, and all persons who were shareholders during the pre-election portion also must consent to the election. If these requirements are not met during the pre-election period, the election becomes effective the following year.

A domestic eligible entity (¶ 402A) may file both its check-the-box and S elections simply by filing Form 2553. It does not need to file Form 8832, Entity Classification Election. The two elections will apply as of the same effective date (Reg. § 301.7701-3(c)(1)(v)(C)).[20]

Late Elections. A simplified procedure is available for obtaining relief from a late or invalid S corporation election, electing small business trust (ESBT) election, qualified subchapter S trust (QSST) election, or qualified subchapter S subsidiary (QSub) election

References are to Standard Federal Tax Reports; Tax Research Consultant; and Practical Tax Explanations.

[14] ¶ 32,021; SCORP: 550; § 28,020.05

[15] ¶ 32,021, ¶ 32,024A; SCORP: 162; § 28,015.05

[16] ¶ 32,024A; SCORP: 162.05

[17] ¶ 32,024A; SCORP: 162.15; § 28,015.10

[18] ¶ 32,021; SCORP: 162.05

[19] ¶ 32,040, ¶ 32,047; SCORP: 200; § 28,105.05

[20] ¶ 43,083; STAGES: 6,154.10; § 28,125

(¶ 304). Relief is generally available if a request for relief is filed within three years and 75 days after the date on which the election is intended to be effective (Rev. Proc. 2013-30).[21] An entity may request relief for a late S corporation election by filing with the applicable IRS service center: (1) a properly completed Form 2553 with Form 1120S for the corporation's current tax year; (2) a properly completed Form 2553 with a Form 1120S for one of the corporation's late-filed prior-year Forms 1120S; or (3) a properly completed Form 2553 submitted independently of Form 1120S.

The simplified procedure for requesting late-election relief also applies where a domestic eligible entity has failed to timely file both its S corporation election and its election to be treated as a corporation under the check-the-box rules (¶ 402A). An entity that obtains relief under the simplified procedure is treated as having made both an election to be classified as an association taxable as a corporation and an S corporation election as of the same date.

Community Property. Shareholders in community property states are also eligible for automatic relief for late S elections if their spouses did not file timely shareholder consents (Rev. Proc. 2004-35).[22] To qualify for relief, the S corporation election must be invalid solely because the spouse's signature is missing from the election form. Shareholders must alert the IRS that they are seeking relief under Rev. Proc. 2004-35 and identify the number of shares they own as of the date of the election. Each spouse must sign a separate statement indicating his or her consent to the election.

307. Termination of S Election. S corporation status is automatically terminated if any event occurs that would prohibit the corporation from making the election in the first place (Code Sec. 1362(d)(2); Reg. § 1.1362-2(b)).[23] The election is ended as of the date on which the disqualifying event occurs. Also, if a corporation has accumulated earnings and profits as of the end of three consecutive years, and the corporation's passive investment income exceeds 25 percent of its gross receipts in each of those three years, its S election is terminated beginning with the following tax year (Code Sec. 1362(d)(3); Reg. § 1.1362-2(c)).[24] For this purpose, dividends received by an S corporation from a C corporation subsidiary of which the S corporation owns 80 percent or more of stock are not treated as passive investment income to the extent the dividends are attributable to the earnings and profits derived from the active conduct of a trade or business.

An S corporation election may be revoked with the consent of shareholders holding more than 50 percent of the outstanding shares of stock (voting and nonvoting) on the day the revocation is made. A revocation may designate a prospective effective date (Code Sec. 1362(d)(1); Reg. § 1.1362-2(a)).[25] If no date is specified, a revocation made on or before the 15th day of the 3rd month of a corporation's tax year is effective on the first day of the tax year. A revocation made after this date is effective on the first day of the following tax year.

If an election is terminated or revoked, the corporation may not reelect S corporation status without IRS consent until the 5th year after the year in which the termination or revocation became effective (Code Sec. 1362(g); Reg. § 1.1362-5).[26] An S corporation whose status as a qualified subchapter S subsidiary (QSSS or QSub) (¶ 304) has ended also cannot elect to be treated as a QSub until the 5th year after the year in which the termination was effective (Code Sec. 1361(b)(3)(D)).[27]

In addition to formally filing an election to terminate S corporation status, an S corporation can simply create a situation that bars it from being an S corporation. An election to revoke S corporation status relates back to the beginning of the tax year only

References are to Standard Federal Tax Reports; Tax Research Consultant; and Practical Tax Explanations.

[21] ¶ 32,053.41; SCORP: 206; § 28,140.05

[22] ¶ 32,053.41; SCORP: 206; § 28,115.10

[23] ¶ 32,040, ¶ 32,043; SCORP: 304; § 28,210

[24] ¶ 32,040, ¶ 32,043; SCORP: 306; § 28,215.05

[25] ¶ 32,040, ¶ 32,043; SCORP: 302; § 28,205.05

[26] ¶ 32,040, ¶ 32,046; SCORP: 312; § 28,130

[27] ¶ 32,021; SCORP: 558; § 28,020.10

if the election is made before the 16th day of the third month of the corporation's tax year; elections made after that date apply to the next tax year. One way to avoid this rule and terminate S corporation status immediately is to create another corporation and transfer one share of S corporation stock to the new corporation. Because corporations cannot be S corporation shareholders, the S corporation status ends on the date the share of stock is transferred to a disqualified shareholder, and it is not necessary to wait until the next tax year for the revocation of the S corporation election to become effective.

Reorganizations. A corporation's subchapter S election does not terminate merely because it is a party to a reorganization (¶ 2221) if it continues to meet the S corporation eligibility requirements.[28] Typically, this issue arises because the reorganization results in an ineligible shareholder owning stock of the S corporation. For example, the IRS ruled that the S election of a corporation that was acquired by another corporation in a stock-for-stock B reorganization terminated on the date of acquisition. On the other hand, the IRS has ruled that A, C, and F reorganizations did not cause the S elections of the respective corporations to terminate when all owners of the corporations after the transaction were eligible S corporation shareholders.

Frequently, reorganizations can involve transfers of the same corporate stock several times to different parties as part of the transaction. The intermediate parties may be deemed to hold the stock only for an instant before transferring it to its ultimate holder. The question arises whether a corporation's subchapter S election terminates where one or more of these intermediate parties is not an eligible S corporation shareholder. This issue is not addressed by the Code or regulations. However, the IRS has privately ruled that having shareholders who acquire a corporation's stock only to immediately transfer it to another party does not cause the corporation's S election to terminate (LTRs 200453007 and 9010042).

Correction of Inadvertent Terminations. If a corporation's subchapter S election is inadvertently terminated or invalid when made, and the corporation makes a timely correction, the IRS can waive the termination or can permit the election (Code Sec. 1362(f); Reg. § 1.1362-4).[29] The IRS is also authorized to provide a waiver where an election to treat family members as one shareholder or to treat a corporation as a QSub is invalid when made or inadvertently terminated. To obtain a waiver, the corporation must correct any condition that either barred it from qualifying as an subchapter S corporation, or otherwise made an election invalid, and must obtain any required shareholder consents. All shareholders must agree to make such adjustments as may be required by the IRS.

Election to End Tax Year. If a shareholder terminates his or her interest in an S corporation and all affected shareholders consent to the termination, the tax year can be treated as two tax years, the first of which ends on the date of termination (Code Sec. 1377(a)(2)).[30] Affected shareholders include the shareholder whose interest is terminated and all shareholders to whom that shareholder has transferred shares during the tax year.

Taxation of Shareholders

309. Taxation of S Corporation Shareholders. Each shareholder of an S corporation separately accounts for his or her pro rata share of corporate items of income, deduction, loss, and credit in his or her tax year in which the corporation's tax year ends (Code Sec. 1366(a); Reg. §§ 1.1366-1(a) and 1.1377-1).[31] Certain items must be separately stated if they could affect the shareholder's individual tax liability (¶ 320). A shareholder's share of each item generally is computed based on the number of shares held on each day of the corporation's tax year.

References are to Standard Federal Tax Reports; Tax Research Consultant; and Practical Tax Explanations.

[28] ¶ 32,053.69; SCORP: 304.10; § 28,920

[29] ¶ 32,040, ¶ 32,045; SCORP: 308; § 28,220

[30] ¶ 32,240; SCORP: 402.15; § 28,445.10, § 28,445.15

[31] ¶ 32,080, ¶ 32,081, ¶ 32,240C; SCORP: 402; § 28,405

The character of an item included in a shareholder's pro rata share of S corporation income is generally determined as if the item were realized directly from the source from which the corporation realized it, or incurred in the same manner in which the corporation incurred it, subject to exceptions (Code Sec. 1366(b); Reg. § 1.1366-1(b)).[32] Thus, when income passes through from the S corporation to the shareholder, the character of that income passes through as well. For example, if an S corporation makes a charitable contribution to a qualifying organization, a shareholder's pro rata share of the S corporation's charitable contribution is characterized as made to a qualifying organization.

Similarly, if an S corporation has capital gain on the sale or exchange of a capital asset, a shareholder's pro rata share of that gain is also characterized as a capital gain, regardless of whether the shareholder is otherwise a dealer in that type of property. However, this rule does not apply when the S corporation is formed or availed of for a principal purpose of selling or exchanging contributed property that, in the hands of the shareholder, would not have produced capital gain if sold or exchanged by the shareholder. The same exception applies when the S corporation is formed or availed of for a principal purpose of selling or exchanging contributed property that, in the hands of a shareholder, would have produced capital loss if sold or exchanged by the shareholder. Any loss recognized by the corporation is treated as a capital loss to the extent that, immediately before the contribution, the adjusted basis of the property in the hands of the shareholder exceeded the fair market value of the property.

Duty of Consistency. A shareholder of an S corporation must treat a subchapter S item in a manner consistent with the treatment of that item on the S corporation's return (Code Sec. 6037).[33] Any shareholder who does not treat the item consistently must file a statement identifying the inconsistency.

At-Risk and Passive Activity Rules. The at-risk rules disallow losses that exceed an investor's amount at risk (¶ 1155). Generally, the amount at risk is the amount of investment that an investor could lose. The at-risk rules apply to all individuals, including S corporation shareholders, and are applied at the shareholder level (Code Sec. 465).[34] The at-risk amount is determined at the close of the S corporation's tax year. Thus, an S corporation shareholder who realizes that his or her at-risk amount is low, and wishes to deduct an anticipated S corporation net loss, can make additional contributions to the corporation.

Likewise, passive activity loss (PAL) rules generally are applied at the shareholder level (¶ 1169) (Code Sec. 469).[35] However, several determinations that affect the application of the PAL rules must be made at the corporate level. For example, the determination of whether an activity constitutes a trade or business, as opposed to a rental activity, is made at the corporate level. The distinction between portfolio and nonportfolio income is also made at the corporate level. This information is conveyed via the Schedule K-1 (Form 1120S) that is provided to the shareholder by the corporation. The shareholder then uses the information to apply the PAL and at-risk limitations when preparing his or her individual tax return.

Since a qualified subchapter S trust (QSST) (¶ 304) is treated as the shareholder when it disposes of S corporation stock, the application of the at-risk and PAL rules would normally be determined at the trust level, not the beneficiary level. However, to ensure that the beneficiary can take disallowed losses on the QSST's disposition of the stock, the at-risk and passive activity loss rules apply as if the beneficiary disposed of the stock (Code Sec. 1361(d)(1)(C)).[36]

Small Business Stock. Since S corporations are not entitled to ordinary loss treatment from the sale of qualified small business stock under Code Sec. 1244 (¶ 1911), and

References are to Standard Federal Tax Reports; Tax Research Consultant; and Practical Tax Explanations.

[32] ¶ 32,080, ¶ 32,081; SCORP: 402.05; § 28,420

[33] ¶ 35,520; PART: 60,402, SCORP: 402.05; § 28,425

[34] ¶ 21,850; SCORP: 406; § 28,430.30

[35] ¶ 21,960; BUSEXP: 33,050; § 28,430.35

[36] ¶ 32,021; SCORP: 160; § 17,435.20

the character of loss items passes through to shareholders, S corporation shareholders cannot claim ordinary losses incurred by the S corporation from the sale of qualified small business stock (*V.D. Rath*, Dec. 49,266, 101 TC 196 (1993)).[37] However, when the S corporation stock itself is qualified small business stock, shareholders may claim ordinary loss deductions if all the requirements are met.

312. Domestic Production Activities of S Corporation Shareholders. An S corporation cannot claim the domestic production activities deduction (DPAD) (¶ 980A). Instead, the deduction is determined at the shareholder level (Code Sec. 199(d)(1); Reg. § 1.199-5(c)).[38] Generally, each shareholder computes the deduction separately on Form 8903 by aggregating his or her pro rata share of qualified production activity (QPA) items of the S corporation (i.e., income, expenses) with his or her share of QPA items from other sources. The shareholder does not have to be directly engaged in the S corporation's trade or business to claim the deduction on the basis of his or her share of QPA items.

For purposes of determining the deduction, the activities of an S corporation are not attributed to its shareholders (or vice-versa) (Reg. § 1.199-5(g)). For example, if the S corporation manufactures qualified domestic production activities property within the United States and then distributes the property to the shareholder who subsequently sells, licenses, leases, or otherwise disposes of the property, then the income derived by the shareholder will not qualify as domestic production gross receipts (DPGR). A limited exception is provided for expanded affiliated groups.

Allocation of Items. A shareholder's pro rata share of expenses allocable to the S corporation's QPA is taken into account even if the corporation has no taxable income (Reg. § 1.199-5-(c)(1)(i)). If the shareholder is unable to claim a loss or deduction of the corporation for regular tax purposes (i.e., at-risk, passive loss, or basis limitations), then the loss or deduction cannot be used when computing the DPAD. The amount of any loss or deduction is subject to proportionate reduction if it is only partially allowed for regular tax purposes. Also, a loss or deduction that is temporarily disallowed for regular tax purposes may be taken into account in computing the DPAD in the tax year that it is allowed for regular tax purposes.

Instead of taking into account his or her pro rata share of each QPA item of the S corporation, a shareholder may compute his or her deduction by combining his or her pro rata share of the S corporation's qualified production activities income (QPAI) and W-2 wages with his or her QPAI and W-2 wages from other sources. This option applies only if the S corporation has elected to use the small business overall method for allocating costs, expenses, and other deductions to its DPGR (¶ 980G). Special rules apply to 20-percent shareholders of S corporations engaged in film or television production.

Sale of Stock. Gain or loss recognized on the sale of S corporation stock is not taken into account by a shareholder in computing his or her QPAI (Reg. § 1.199-5(f)). This is because the sale of an interest in the corporation does not reflect the realization of DPGR by the entity.

W-2 Wage Limitation. A shareholder of an S corporation computes the W-2 wage limitation (¶ 980C) for the DPAD by aggregating his or her share of W-2 wages from the S corporation allocable to DPGR with W-2 wages allocable to DPGR from other sources.

314. S Corporations and the Net Investment Income Tax. Individuals, trusts, and estates are subject to a 3.8-percent tax on the lesser of their net investment income for the tax year or the excess of their modified adjusted gross income (MAGI) for the tax year over a threshold amount (¶ 129). S corporations are not subject to the net investment income (NII) tax, but S corporation shareholders may be subject to the tax on income items related to their investments in the corporation.

References are to Standard Federal Tax Reports; Tax Research Consultant; and Practical Tax Explanations.

[37] ¶ 30,800.59; SALES: 18,154; § 28,440.25

[38] ¶ 12,468, ¶ 12,472D; BUSEXP: 6,214; § 6,020.05

Allocations of Net Investment Income (NII). NII generally includes income and gain from passive activities. It does not include gross income derived in the ordinary course of a trade or business. Thus, income from a trade or business conducted by the S corporation in which the shareholder actively participates is not considered NII to the shareholder (Reg. § 1.1411-4(b)(2)).[39] Income from a trade or business that is a passive activity with respect to the shareholder is, however, included in the shareholder's NII. In other words, the shareholder's distributive share of income earned by the S corporation that would be NII had it been earned directly by the shareholder is considered NII to the shareholder. In addition, if the S corporation is engaged in the trade or business of trading in financial instruments or commodities, the income or loss from that trade or business is excluded from the shareholder's NII without regard to whether the shareholder is himself or herself engaged in the trade or business.

Dispositions of S Corporation Stock. Net gain or loss upon the disposition of S corporation stock is considered NII only to the extent it would be taken into account as such by the shareholder if all S corporation property were sold at fair market value immediately before the disposition (Code Sec. 1411(c)(4); Proposed Reg. § 1.1411-7).[40] Specifically, gain or loss from property used in the S corporation's trade or business is excluded from NII, unless the trade or business is a passive activity with respect to the shareholder or involves trading in financial instruments or commodities.

315. Basis in S Corporation Stock. An S corporation shareholder's basis in his or her stock is determined under the same rules that apply to C corporation shareholders. Thus, the original basis of the shareholder's stock is the purchase price for the stock (i.e, money or the fair market value of any property given in exchange for the stock) (Code Sec. 1012).[41] Stock acquired by gift normally carries over the donor's basis (¶ 1630). The basis of stock acquired from a decedent is its fair market value on the date of the decedent's death or on the alternate valuation date, if elected (¶ 1633). During the time the corporation is an S corporation, each shareholder must make adjustments to his or her stock (¶ 317).

Similarly, the rules providing for contributions to controlled corporations under Code Sec. 351 (¶ 203) and tax-free corporate reorganizations under Code Sec. 368 (¶ 2209) generally apply to S corporations (Code Sec. 1371).[42] Thus, the basis of stock received under a tax-free reorganization is equal to the transferor's basis in the property transferred plus any gain realized, and minus the fair market value of the boot received and any loss recognized in the transaction.

Stock for Services. An S corporation may grant stock to an employee or other service provider as part of a compensation package. Typically, in a stock-for-services arrangement, S corporation stock may be transferred to an employee at a particular price or for nothing, with the rights to the stock becoming vested only after a number of years of employment. The value of the S stock at that vesting point usually has appreciated from its value at the time of transfer. The difference between the amount that the employee pays for the S stock and the fair market value of the stock at the time the employee's rights to the stock are vested must be included in the employee's ordinary gross income (¶ 713). The S corporation gets a compensation deduction for the amount the employee includes in income in the year the employee includes it in income.

317. Adjustments to Basis in S Corporation Stock. The stock basis of each S corporation shareholder (¶ 315) is *increased* by the shareholder's portion of:

- income items of the corporation, including tax-exempt income, that are separately computed and passed through to the shareholder;
- the income of the corporation that is not separately computed; and

References are to Standard Federal Tax Reports; Tax Research Consultant; and Practical Tax Explanations.

[39] ¶ 32,604; INDIV: 69,160.15, ESTTRST: 12,256

[40] ¶ 32,602, ¶ 32,604N; INDIV: 69,160.40; § 1,022.15

[41] ¶ 29,330; SALES: 6,050; § 28,605.10

[42] ¶ 32,140; CCORP: 3,202, CCORP: 39,256; § 26,130

- the excess of the corporation's deductions for depletion (¶ 1289) over the basis of the property subject to depletion (Code Sec. 1367(a)(1); Reg. § 1.1367-1(b)).[43]

A shareholder's basis is *decreased* by the portion of:

- distributions that are not includible in the shareholder's income (¶ 309);
- all loss and deduction items of the corporation that are separately stated and passed through to the shareholder (but see the later discussion with respect to charitable contributions of appreciated property);
- the nonseparately computed loss of the corporation;
- any expense of the corporation not deductible in computing its taxable income and not properly chargeable to capital account; and
- the amount of the shareholder's deduction for depletion with respect to oil and gas wells to the extent that it does not exceed his or her proportionate share of the adjusted basis of such property (Code Sec. 1367(a)(2); Reg. § 1.1367-1(c)).[44]

If a shareholder's stock basis is reduced to zero, the remaining net decrease attributable to losses and deductions is applied to reduce any basis in debt owed to the shareholder by the corporation (¶ 318). Distributions may not be applied against basis in debt. Any net increase in basis in a subsequent year is applied to restore the basis of debt before it may be applied to increase the shareholder's stock basis.

Generally, stock basis adjustments are determined as of the close of the corporation's tax year, and the adjustments are effective as of that date. However, if a shareholder disposes of stock during the corporation's tax year, the adjustments with respect to that stock are effective immediately before the disposition (Reg. § 1.1367-1(d)).[45] An adjustment for a nontaxable item is determined for the tax year in which the item would have been includible or deductible under the corporation's method of accounting for federal income tax purposes if the item had been subject to federal income taxation.

Charitable Deductions. A shareholder's reduction of basis in S corporation stock by reason of a charitable contribution of property made by the corporation equals the shareholder's pro rata share of the adjusted basis of the contributed property (Code Sec. 1367(a)(2), as amended by the Protecting Americans from Tax Hikes (PATH) Act of 2015 (P.L. 114-113)). For charitable contributions of property in tax years beginning after December 31, 2014, a shareholder's basis in S corporation stock is reduced by the shareholder's pro rata share of the contribution. The amount of the contribution is generally the fair market value of the property, subject to the gain limitations of Code Secs. 170(e) and 1367(a)(2)(B).

Cancellation of Debt. Discharge of debt income of an S corporation that is excluded from the corporation's income (¶ 855) is not taken into account as an item of income that flows through to any shareholder (¶ 309); therefore, it does not increase a shareholder's basis in S corporation stock (Code Sec. 108(d)(7)(A); Reg. § 1.108-7(d)).[46]

318. Basis in S Corporation Debt. For purposes of deducting S corporation losses, a shareholder has basis in certain debts of the S corporation to the shareholder (Code Sec. 1366(d)(1)(B); Reg. § 1.1366-2(a)(2)).[47] For transactions occurring on or after July 23, 2014, the debt in question must run directly to the shareholder and represent a bona fide debt of the S corporation. Federal tax principles generally determine whether debt is bona fide, based on all relevant facts and circumstances. Unlike a partner in a partnership, an S corporation shareholder does not receive basis or an increase in basis for debt of the S corporation to an outside lender. A mere guaranty by the shareholder of the S corporation's debt to a third party also does not increase the shareholder's basis, including acting as a surety, accommodation party, or in any similar capacity relating to the loan.

References are to Standard Federal Tax Reports; Tax Research Consultant; and Practical Tax Explanations.

[43] ¶ 32,100, ¶ 32,100B; SCORP: 410.05; § 28,610.05

[44] ¶ 32,100, ¶ 32,100B; SCORP: 410.05; § 28,615

[45] ¶ 32,100B; SCORP: 410.05; § 28,620

[46] ¶ 7002, ¶ 7006; SALES: 12,212.10, SCORP: 404.10; § 28,610.10

[47] ¶ 32,080, ¶ 32,082; SCORP: 404.05; § 28,630.05, § 28,630.10

For transactions occurring before July 23, 2014, a shareholder has basis in debt owed to the shareholder by the S corporation only to the extent that the shareholder has made an "actual economic outlay" (*M.G. Underwood*, Dec. 33,016, 63 TC 468 (1975), aff'd, CA-5, 76-2 USTC ¶ 9557).[48] In other words, only the kind of debt that proves an actual investment by the shareholder, not merely a promise by the shareholder for some future outlay, increases the shareholder's basis. The S corporation's debt must run directly to the shareholder, not merely to an entity in which he or she is an owner. Thus, debt running from the S corporation to a pass-through entity in which the shareholder has an interest will not be attributed to the shareholder for this purpose.

The basis that a shareholder has in debt owed to that shareholder by the S corporation must be adjusted like the shareholder's basis in stock. Adjustments to stock are calculated before the basis in debt is affected (Code Sec. 1367(b)(2); Reg. § 1.1367-2).[49] When decreases relating to losses, deductions, noncapital, nondeductible expenses, and certain oil and gas depletion deductions have reduced stock basis to zero, any excess is applied to reduce debt basis. Any debt by the corporation to the shareholder that has been satisfied by the corporation, disposed of, or forgiven by the shareholder during the tax year, and is not held by the shareholder at the close of that year is not subject to basis reduction. Generally, the adjustments to debt basis are made as of the close of the tax year. If the shareholder terminates his or her interest in the corporation during the tax year, however, the adjustments in basis to debt are applied with respect to any S corporation debt held by the shareholder immediately before the termination of the shareholder's interest in the corporation. If there is a reduction in the shareholder's basis in S corporation debt, any net increase in any subsequent tax year is applied first to the restoration of that reduction before any increase is applied to stock basis.

319. S Corporation's Taxable Income. An S corporation must compute its taxable income for purposes of determining the amount of income, gain, loss, deduction and credit passed through to its shareholders (¶ 309). Computation of an S corporation's taxable income parallels the computation of the taxable income of an individual, except that organizational expenditures may be amortized (¶ 237) and the reduction in certain corporate tax benefits (¶ 1445) is applied if the S corporation was a C corporation for any of its three immediately preceding tax years. Moreover, certain deductions allowed to individuals, such as those for personal exemptions, charitable contributions, medical expenses, alimony, and net operating losses, are not allowed to the S corporation when calculating taxable income (Code Sec. 1363(b)).[50] Certain items must be separately stated when passed through to shareholders (¶ 320).

An S corporation cannot carry forward or carry back any item from a year that the corporation is not an S corporation to a year that the corporation is an S corporation (Code Sec. 1371(b)).[51] Thus, no carryforward or carryback, such as with a net operating loss, arising from a tax year for which a corporation is a C corporation may be carried to a tax year for which the corporation is an S corporation. Also, no carryforward or carryback arises at the corporate level in a tax year for which a corporation is an S corporation. However, a tax year for which a corporation is an S corporation is treated as a tax year for purposes of determining the number of tax years to which an item may be carried back or carried forward. Thus, while the item remains intact during the time the corporation is an S corporation, those years count for any carryforward period applicable to the item.

References are to Standard Federal Tax Reports; Tax Research Consultant; and Practical Tax Explanations.

[48] ¶ 32,084.325; SCORP: 404.05; § 28,630.10

[49] ¶ 32,100, ¶ 32,100C; SCORP: 410.10; § 28,630.15

[50] ¶ 32,060; SCORP: 352; § 28,401

[51] ¶ 32,140; SCORP: 354; § 28,415

320. Separately Stated Items of S Corporation Income. Certain items of the taxable income of an S corporation (¶ 319) must be separately stated (Code Sec. 1363(b)).[52] These items must be reported and computed separately from items that can be combined. Items that must be separately stated include, but are not limited to:

- net income or loss from rental activities, including rental real estate activities;
- portfolio income or loss and expenses related to portfolio income or loss;
- Code Sec. 1231 net gain or loss;
- charitable contributions, grouped by the percentage limitations of Code Sec. 170(b);
- Code Sec. 179 expense deductions;
- the low-income housing credit;
- investment interest expense;
- tax preference and adjustment items needed to compute shareholders' alternative minimum tax;
- gains and losses from wagering transactions;
- medical, dental, etc., expenses;
- itemized deductions;
- capital gain or loss grouped by applicable holding periods;
- foreign taxes paid or accrued;
- tax-exempt income; and
- passive activity items for each of the corporation's activities (Code Sec. 1366(a)(1)(A); Reg. § 1.1366-1(a)).[53]

Each shareholder must also take into account his or her pro rata share of the nonseparately computed income or loss of the S corporation. Nonseparately computed income or loss is the corporation's gross income less the deductions allowed to the corporation, determined by excluding any item requiring separate computation.

Nonbusiness Bad Debts. An S corporation may claim a nonbusiness bad debt deduction (¶ 1143) in the same manner as an individual when computing an S corporation's taxable income. Accordingly, an S corporation that incurs a nonbusiness bad debt must separately state the debt as a short-term capital loss (Rev. Rul. 93-36). On the other hand, partially or wholly worthless business debts are included in nonseparately stated S corporation income or loss (¶ 1135).

321. Limits on S Corporation Deductions. A shareholder's currently deductible share of an S corporation's losses and deductions for any tax year is limited to the total of his or her adjusted basis in the corporation's stock (¶ 315) and any bona fide debt of the S corporation owed to the shareholder (¶ 318) (Code Sec. 1366(d)).[54]

An S corporation's itemized deductions are separately stated items (¶ 320). Thus, the two-percent of adjusted gross income floor on miscellaneous itemized deductions (¶ 1079) is applied at the shareholder level rather than at the S corporation level (Temp. Reg. § 1.67-2T(b)(1)).[55] Shareholders of an S corporation take into account separately their pro rata share of the corporation's miscellaneous itemized deductions, add them to their other individual miscellaneous deductions, and deduct them to the extent they exceed two percent of their individual adjusted gross income.

References are to Standard Federal Tax Reports; Tax Research Consultant; and Practical Tax Explanations.

[52] ¶ 32,060; SCORP: 352; § 28,405

[53] ¶ 32,080, ¶ 32,081; SCORP: 352.05; § 28,405

[54] ¶ 32,080; SCORP: 404; § 28,430.15

[55] ¶ 6062; INDIV: 39,102.05; § 28,440.45

The election to expense the cost of Code Sec. 179 property (¶ 1208) is made at the S corporation level (Reg. § 1.179-1(h)).[56] The dollar, investment, and taxable income limitations apply at both the S corporation and shareholder levels (Code Sec. 179(d)(8); Reg. § 1.179-2).[57]

Charitable Deductions. When an S corporation makes a charitable contribution of property, each shareholder reduces the his or her stock basis by his or her pro rata share of the S corporation's adjusted basis in the contributed property (Code Sec. 1367(a)(2), as amended by the Protecting Americans from Tax Hikes (PATH) Act of 2015 (P.L. 114-113)). The stock basis limitation on deductions does not apply to a charitable contribution of appreciated property to the extent the shareholder's pro rata share of the contribution exceeds the shareholder's pro rata share of the adjusted basis of the property. (Code Secs. 1366(d)(4) and 1367(a)(2), as amended by P.L. 114-113; Rev. Rul. 2008-16).[58]

Suspended Losses and Deductions. If, for a tax year, the amount of the loss or deduction of a shareholder is limited, the excess is treated, for that individual shareholder, as incurred by the S corporation in the next tax year and may be carried forward until used by that shareholder (Code Sec. 1366(d)(2)).[59] Disallowed losses and deductions may be transferred only to a current or former spouse of the shareholder when the S corporation stock is transferred between spouses or incident to divorce in a nontaxable transaction (¶ 1734).

If the shareholder's losses or deductions are limited for the last tax year in which the corporation is an S corporation, the excess is treated as incurred by the shareholder on the last day of the corporation's post-termination transition period (¶ 329) (Code Sec. 1366(d)(3)). The excess amount cannot exceed the shareholder's adjusted basis of the stock in the corporation, determined at the close of the last day of the post-termination transition period. The losses or deductions taken into account during this period reduce the shareholder's basis of stock in the corporation. Losses of an S corporation that are suspended under the at-risk rules (¶ 1155) are carried forward to the post-termination period.

322. Employee Benefits Provided to S Corporation Shareholders. The tax treatment of fringe benefits (¶ 2085) paid to owner-employees of an S corporation is different from the tax treatment for other employees (Code Sec. 1372).[60] Fringe benefits paid to S corporation employees who are not shareholders, or who own two percent or less of the outstanding S corporation stock, are tax free. They can be excluded from the employees' taxable wages and are deductible as fringe benefits by the corporation. On the other hand, owner-employees owning more than two percent of the S corporation stock are not treated as employees for fringe benefit purposes, and their fringe benefits may not be tax free. Instead, more-than-two-percent owners are treated in the same manner as partners in a partnership (¶ 421).

Health Insurance Expenses. An owner-employee who owns more than two percent of the S corporation stock can deduct 100 percent of the amount paid for medical insurance for himself or herself, his or her spouse, and dependents under a plan established by the S corporation (Code Sec. 162(l)(1) and (5); Notice 2008-1).[61] The S corporation must either pay the plan's premium payments itself or must reimburse the shareholder for the payments.

For purposes of the deduction, a more-than-two-percent shareholder's wages from the S corporation are treated as the shareholder's earned income. No deduction is allowed in excess of an individual's earned income (within the meaning of Code Sec. 401(c)) derived from the trade or business with respect to which the plan providing the health insurance is established.

References are to Standard Federal Tax Reports; Tax Research Consultant; and Practical Tax Explanations.

[56] ¶ 12,121; DEPR: 12,156; § 28,440.15

[57] ¶ 12,120, ¶ 12,122; DEPR: 12,112; § 9,815.15, § 28,440.15

[58] ¶ 32,080, ¶ 32,101.27; SCORP: 402.10; § 28,440.10

[59] ¶ 32,080; SCORP: 404; § 28,430.25

[60] ¶ 32,160; SCORP: 352.20; § 28,801

[61] ¶ 8500, ¶ 32,161.50; SCORP: 352.20; § 28,815

Note that reimbursement plans are generally no longer in compliance with group health plan rules, and may incur an excise tax of $100 per day per affected employer (Code Sec. 4980D). However, under transition relief, two-percent shareholder-employee arrangements of S corporations are not subject to the excise tax and not required to file Form 8928 solely as a result of having such an arrangement (Notice 2015-17). Until the IRS issues further guidance, the deduction rules discussed previously will continue to apply.

Tax Treatment of Distributions

323. S Corporation Distributions. Distributions of cash or property received by a shareholder from an S corporation are taxable depending on whether the corporation has earnings and profits. An S corporation generally has no earnings and profits unless attributable to tax years when the corporation was not an S corporation. An S corporation may also succeed to the earnings and profits of an acquired or merged corporation.

For an S corporation without earnings and profits, distributions are treated first as a nontaxable return of capital to the extent of the shareholder's basis in stock, and then as gain from the sale or exchange of property (Code Sec. 1368(b); Reg. § 1.1368-1(c)).[62]

For an S corporation with earnings and profits, unless an election is made to distribute the earnings and profits as dividends (¶ 333), distributions are treated as:

- a nontaxable return of capital, to the extent of the corporation's accumulated adjustments account (AAA) (¶ 325);
- dividends, to the extent of the S corporation's accumulated earnings and profits;
- a nontaxable return of capital, to the extent of the shareholder's remaining stock basis; and
- gain from the sale or exchange of property (Code Sec. 1368(c); Reg. § 1.1368-1(d)).[63]

Before applying these rules, the shareholder's stock basis and the AAA are adjusted for the corporate items passed through from the corporate tax year during which the distribution is made.

If an employee stock ownership plan (ESOP) holds S corporation shares that are employer securities, and the ESOP takes out a loan to purchase the employer securities, the prohibited transaction rules will not apply to distributions by the S corporation that are used to repay the loan, and the plan's status as an ESOP will not be jeopardized (Code Sec. 4975(f)(7)).[64]

325. Accumulated Adjustments Account. The accumulated adjustments account (AAA) is used to compute the tax effect of distributions made by an S corporation with accumulated earnings and profits (¶ 323) (Code Sec. 1368(e); Reg. § 1.1368-2).[65] The AAA is generally a measure of the corporation's accumulated gross income, less expenses, that has not been distributed. The AAA is zero on the first day of a corporation's first S corporation tax year. It is *increased* by:

- all corporate income items (excluding tax-exempt income items) that are separately stated and passed through to shareholders (¶ 320);
- nonseparately computed corporate income; and
- the excess of deductions for depletion over the basis of the property subject to depletion.

References are to Standard Federal Tax Reports; Tax Research Consultant; and Practical Tax Explanations.

[62] ¶ 32,120, ¶ 32,120B; SCORP: 452; § 28,505

[63] ¶ 32,120, ¶ 32,120B; SCORP: 454; § 28,510.05, § 28,510.20

[64] ¶ 34,400; RETIRE: 75,302

[65] ¶ 32,120, ¶ 32,120C; SCORP: 458; § 28,510.10

The AAA is *decreased* by:

- certain nontaxable corporate distributions;
- all loss and deduction items of the corporation that are separately stated and passed through (other than items that are not deductible in computing taxable income and not properly chargeable to capital account);
- the nonseparately computed loss of the corporation;
- the nondeductible amounts that are unrelated to the production of tax-exempt income; and
- the amount of the shareholder's deduction for oil and gas depletion.

As indicated previously, an S corporation's AAA is not increased by tax-exempt income, and it is not decreased by an expense related to the tax-exempt income. For example, premiums paid by an S corporation on an employer-owned life insurance contract (COLI), of which the S corporation is a beneficiary, do not reduce the S corporation's AAA. Nor is the AAA increased by death benefits received by the corporation under the policy that meets one of the exceptions for COLI (¶ 804) (Rev. Rul. 2008-42).[66]

No adjustment is made for federal taxes that arose when the corporation was a C corporation. Because the AAA may become negative, the account becomes positive only after the negative balance is restored by later income (Code Sec. 1368(e)(1)(A); Reg. § 1.1368-2).[67] The amount in the AAA as of the close of a tax year is determined without regard to any net negative adjustment for the tax year. A negative adjustment occurs in any tax year in which negative adjustments to the account exceed increases to the account.

Distributions received by an S corporation shareholder in a stock redemption that is treated as a Code Sec. 301 distribution are treated as distributions that reduce the S corporation's AAA (Rev. Rul. 95-14).[68] For a distribution in redemption of an S corporation's stock, if the redemption is treated as an exchange under Code Sec. 302 or 303, the AAA is decreased by an amount determined by multiplying the account balance by the number of shares redeemed and dividing the product by the total number of shares outstanding. This adjustment is made before the distribution rules are applied (Code Sec. 1368(e)(1)(B)).

The AAA relates only to the most recent continuous period in which the corporation has been an S corporation. However, the period does not include tax years beginning before January 1, 1983 (Code Sec. 1368(e)(2); Reg. § 1.1368-2(a)).[69] If corporate distributions during a tax year exceed the amount in the AAA at the end of that year, the balance of the account is allocated among distributions in proportion to their respective sizes (¶ 329) (Code Sec. 1368(c)).[70]

329. Post-Termination Distributions by S Corporations. If a corporation terminates its election to be an S corporation, it has the opportunity for a limited period of time to unfreeze the income that was previously taxed to shareholders under the pass-through rules but that was not actually distributed. Specifically, any cash distribution by the corporation with respect to its stock during the post-termination transition period is applied against and reduces the adjusted basis of the stock to the extent that the amount of the distribution does not exceed the accumulated adjustments account (AAA) (¶ 325) (Code Secs. 1371(e) and 1377(b)).[71]

The post-termination transition period is:

- the period beginning on the day after the last day of the corporation's last tax year as an S corporation and ending on the later of: (i) the day which is one year after such last day, or (ii) the due date for filing the return for the last tax year as an S corporation including extensions;

References are to Standard Federal Tax Reports; Tax Research Consultant; and Practical Tax Explanations.

[66] ¶ 32,121.20; SCORP: 458.05; § 28,510.10

[67] ¶ 32,120, ¶ 32,120C; SCORP: 458.05, SCORP: 458.10; § 28,510.10

[68] ¶ 32,121.20; SCORP: 458.15; § 28,510.10

[69] ¶ 32,120, ¶ 32,120C; SCORP: 458.05; § 28,510.10

[70] ¶ 32,120; SCORP: 454; § 28,510.10

[71] ¶ 32,140, ¶ 32,240; SCORP: 462; § 28,515

- the 120-day period beginning on the date of any determination pursuant to an audit of the taxpayer which follows the termination of the corporation's S election and which adjusts a subchapter S item of income, loss, or deduction of the corporation arising during the S period (Code Sec. 1368(e)(2));[72] or

- the 120-day period beginning on the date of a determination that the corporation's S election had ended for a previous tax year.

If the AAA is not exhausted by the end of the post-termination transition period, it disappears. Any distributions made thereafter are taxed under the usual C corporation rules—first, as a distribution of current earnings and profits; next, as a distribution of accumulated earnings and profits; then, as a return of capital to the extent of the shareholder's basis; and, finally, as a capital gain. Because the AAA is always reflected in the basis of the shareholder's stock, failure to exhaust it during the transition period moves it, in effect, below current and accumulated earnings and profits in the priority system for distributions. The grace period for post-termination distributions applies only to cash distributions. It does not apply to noncash distributions. A noncash distribution is taxed under the usual C corporation rules.

333. S Corporation Election to Distribute Earnings. An S corporation can avoid the priority system (¶ 323) for treatment of distributions by electing to treat distributions as dividends (Code Sec. 1368(e)(3); Reg. § 1.1368-1(f)(2)).[73] An S corporation might elect to treat a distribution as a taxable dividend if it wants to avoid a termination of its S status on account of excess passive investment income. All shareholders who receive a distribution during the tax year must consent to this treatment. If the election is made, the corporation is not required to distribute its entire accumulated adjustments account (AAA) (¶ 325) at the end of its tax year before it can pay a dividend.

Taxation of Corporation

335. Taxation of S Corporation. Since an S corporation is a pass-through entity (¶ 301 and ¶ 309), it is generally not subject to federal income taxes. However, an S corporation may be liable for the following corporate-level tax liabilities and is required to make estimated tax payments attributable to them:

- the tax imposed on built-in gains or capital gains (¶ 337);

- the tax on excess net passive income (¶ 341);

- the recapture of the investment credit on the disposition of property placed in service before 1985; and

- the recapture of benefits from using the last-in, first-out (LIFO) inventory method of accounting upon conversion to an S corporation (¶ 339) (Code Sec. 6655(g)(4)).[74]

If the S corporation was incorporated after 1982, immediately became an S corporation, and has no earnings or profits, only the capital gains tax applies. If the S corporation was incorporated and elected S corporation status before 1987, the tax on built-in gains does not apply.

337. Tax on Built-In Gains of S Corporation. A corporate-level tax ("built-in gains tax") is imposed on S corporations that dispose of assets that appreciated in value during tax years when the corporation was a C corporation (Code Sec. 1374).[75] The built-in gains tax applies only to corporations that made S corporation elections after 1986. However, a tax imposed on certain capital gains of S corporations applies to corporations that made S elections before 1987.

References are to Standard Federal Tax Reports; Tax Research Consultant; and Practical Tax Explanations.

[72] ¶ 32,120; SCORP: 462; § 28,515

[73] ¶ 32,120, ¶ 32,120B; SCORP: 456; § 28,510.25

[74] ¶ 39,565; SCORP: 362, SCORP: 370; § 28,315.05, § 29,020.15

[75] ¶ 32,201; SCORP: 356; § 28,305.05

An S corporation may be liable for tax on its built-in gains if:

- it was a C corporation prior to making its S corporation election;
- it has a net recognized built-in gain within the recognition period; and
- the net recognized built-in gain for the tax year does not exceed the net unrealized built-in gain minus the net recognized built-in gain for prior years in the recognition period, to the extent that such gains were subject to tax.

Net recognized built-in gain is the lesser of: (1) the amount that would be the taxable income of the S corporation if only recognized built-in gains and recognized built-in losses were taken into account, or (2) the corporation's taxable income (Code Sec. 1374(d)(2); Reg. § 1.1374-2).[76] For a corporation that made its S corporation election on or after March 31, 1988, any net recognized built-in gain that is not subject to the built-in gains tax due to the net income limitation is carried forward. The amount of recognized built-in gain passed through and taxed to shareholders is reduced by the tax imposed on the built-in gain and paid by the S corporation (Code Sec. 1366(f)(2)).[77]

A recognized built-in loss is any loss recognized during the recognition period on the disposition of any asset to the extent that the S corporation establishes that: (1) the asset was held by the S corporation at the beginning of its first tax year as an S corporation; and (2) the loss is not greater than the excess of (a) the adjusted basis of the asset at the beginning of the corporation's first tax year as an S corporation, over (b) the fair market value of the asset at that time.

Recognition Period. The recognition period for net built-in gain is the five-year period beginning on the first day on which the corporation is an S corporation (Code Sec. 1374(d)(7), as amended by the Protecting Americans from Tax Hikes (PATH) Act of 2015 (P.L. 114-113); Reg. § 1.1374-1(d)).[78] For example, if the first day of the recognition period is July 12, 2012, the last day of the recognition period is July 11, 2017. If the S corporation sells an asset within the recognition period under the installment method (¶ 1801), all the payments received (whether within the recognition period or not) are treated as received in the tax year of the sale. The recognition period applies separately with respect to any asset acquired in a carryover basis transaction (Code Sec. 1374(d)(8)).

Amount of Tax. The tax is computed by applying the highest corporate income tax rate to the S corporation's net recognized built-in gain for the tax year. The amount of the net recognized built-in gain is taxable income. However, any net operating loss carryforward arising in a tax year in which the corporation was a C corporation is allowed as a deduction against the net recognized built-in gain of the S corporation. Capital loss carryforwards may also be used to offset recognized built-in gains (Code Sec. 1374(b) and (d); Reg. § 1.1374-5).[79] Furthermore, business tax credit carryovers of an S corporation arising in a tax year in which the corporation was a C corporation can offset the built-in gains tax of the S corporation (Code Sec. 1374(b)(3)(B); Reg. § 1.1374-6).[80]

339. LIFO Recapture by S Corporation. A C corporation that maintains its inventory using the last-in, first-out (LIFO) method (¶ 1565) for its last tax year before an S corporation election becomes effective must include in gross income a LIFO recapture amount when it converts to S corporation status. LIFO recapture is also required for transfers of inventory from a C corporation to an S corporation in a tax-free reorganization (Code Sec. 1363(d); Reg. § 1.1363-2).[81] The LIFO recapture amount is the amount, if any, by which the amount of the inventory assets using the first-in, first-out (FIFO) method (¶ 1564) exceeds the inventory amount of such assets under the LIFO method.

References are to Standard Federal Tax Reports; Tax Research Consultant; and Practical Tax Explanations.

[76] ¶ 32,201, ¶ 32,202B; SCORP: 356.05; § 28,305.20

[77] ¶ 32,080; SCORP: 402.05; § 28,305.65

[78] ¶ 32,201, ¶ 32,201C; SCORP: 356.05; § 28,305.15

[79] ¶ 32,201, ¶ 32,202H; SCORP: 356.10, SCORP: 356.25; § 28,305.40

[80] ¶ 32,201, ¶ 32,202J; SCORP: 356.30; § 28,305.45

[81] ¶ 32,060, ¶ 32,061B; SCORP: 352.35; § 28,315.05

The tax attributable to the inclusion in income of any LIFO recapture amount is payable by the corporation in four equal installments. The first payment is due on or before the due date of the corporate tax return for the electing corporation's last tax year as a C corporation. The three subsequent installments are due on or before the respective due dates of the S corporation's returns for the three succeeding tax years. No interest is payable on these installments if they are paid by the respective due dates.

341. Passive Investment Income of S Corporation. An S corporation with accumulated earnings and profits and total passive investment income totaling more than 25 percent of gross receipts is subject to an income tax computed by multiplying the corporation's excess net passive income by the highest corporate income tax rate (Code Sec. 1375; Reg. § 1.1375-1).[82] Passive investment income is gross receipts derived from royalties, rents, dividends, interest (excluding interest on installment sales of inventory to customers and gross receipts from certain lending and financing businesses), and annuities (Code Sec. 1362(d)(3)(C); Reg. § 1.1362-2(c)(5)).[83] Income derived by an S corporation in the ordinary course of its trade or business is generally excluded from the definition of passive investment income. For an S corporation bank (including a bank holding company and a depository institution holding company), passive investment income does not include interest earned by the bank or any dividends received on assets that the bank is required to hold. The exception for assets applies to stock in the Federal Reserve Bank, the Federal Home Loan Bank, or the Federal Agriculture Mortgage Bank, and participation certificates issued by a Federal Intermediate Credit Bank.

Excess net passive income is the amount that bears the same ratio to net passive income as the amount of passive investment income that exceeds 25 percent of gross receipts bears to passive investment income (Code Sec. 1375(b); Reg. § 1.1375-1(b)).[84] Net passive income is passive investment income reduced by any allowable deduction directly connected with the production of such income except for the net operating loss (NOL) deduction (¶ 1145) and the special deductions allowed to corporations in computing taxable income (¶ 221—¶ 237). Excess net passive income cannot exceed the corporation's taxable income for the tax year computed without regard to any NOL deduction and without regard to the special deductions allowed to corporations, other than the deduction for organizational expenditures (¶ 237). Passive investment income is determined without taking into account any recognized built-in gain or loss during the recognition period (¶ 337). This means that S corporations without earnings and profits cannot be taxed on excess net passive income if they have no taxable income. This can happen if the corporation has NOLs and income from passive investments. The tax is not merely carried over; there is no tax due if during the year the corporation did not have taxable income.

The tax on excess net passive income reduces each item of passive income by the amount of tax attributable to it, and thereby reduces the amount of passive investment income that each shareholder must take into account in computing gross income (Code Sec. 1366(f)(3)).[85]

The only credits allowable against the passive investment income tax are those for certain uses of gasoline and special fuels (¶ 1329) (Code Sec. 1375(c); Reg. § 1.1375-1(c)).[86]

The IRS may waive the tax on excess net passive income if the S corporation establishes: (1) that it made a good-faith determination that it had no C corporation earnings and profits at the close of the tax year, and (2) within a reasonable time after determining that it did have C corporation earnings and profits at the close of the tax year, those earning and profits were distributed (Code Sec. 1375(d); Reg. § 1.1375-1(d)).[87]

References are to Standard Federal Tax Reports; Tax Research Consultant; and Practical Tax Explanations.

[82] ¶ 32,220, ¶ 32,221; SCORP: 360; § 28,310.05

[83] ¶ 32,040, ¶ 32,043; SCORP: 360; § 28,310.20

[84] ¶ 32,220, ¶ 32,221; SCORP: 358; § 28,310.10

[85] ¶ 32,080; SCORP: 356, SCORP: 402.05; § 28,310.05, § 28,310.30

[86] ¶ 32,220, ¶ 32,221; SCORP: 360; § 28,310.05

[87] ¶ 32,220, ¶ 32,221; SCORP: 360; § 28,310.25

349. Foreign Income of S Corporation. Foreign taxes paid by an S corporation pass through to shareholders who can elect to treat them as deductions or credits on their individual returns (Code Sec. 1373).[88] Since an S corporation is treated as a partnership rather than a corporation, for purposes of the foreign tax credit provisions of the Code, neither it nor its shareholders may claim the indirect foreign tax credit (¶ 2475) for taxes paid by a foreign corporation in which the S corporation is a shareholder. The foreign loss recapture rules apply to an S corporation that previously passed foreign losses through to the shareholders and subsequently terminates its S corporation status. For the purpose of computing the amount of foreign losses that must be recaptured, the making or termination of an S corporation election is treated as a disposition of a trade or business.

Returns and Tax Year

351. S Corporation Returns. An S corporation is required to file Form 1120S for each tax year that the election to be treated as an S corporation is in effect (¶ 303), regardless of whether the corporation has taxable income for that year (Reg. § 1.6012-2(h)).[89] Form 1120S is due on or before the 15th day of the third month following the close of the tax year (March 15th for a calendar-year S corporation) (Code Sec. 6072(b); Reg. § 1.6037-1(b)).[90] An S corporation may obtain an automatic six-month extension of time to file its return by filing Form 7004 on or before the due date of its Form 1120S (Reg. § 1.6081-3(a)).[91]

An S corporation must provide to each shareholder a copy of the information shown on Schedule K-1 that is attached to Form 1120S. The information must be provided on or before the day the corporation files Form 1120S (Code Sec. 6037(b)).[92]

An S corporation that fails to timely file any required return may be subject to penalties (¶ 353).

353. Failure to File Penalties for S Corporations. An S corporation that fails to timely file Form 1120S (¶ 351) (or files an incomplete return) is liable for a penalty of $195 per shareholder, per month for a maximum of twelve months, unless reasonable cause is shown (Code Sec. 6699).[93] For returns required to be filed after December 31, 2014, the $195 amount is adjusted annually for inflation and remains $195 for tax years beginning in 2016 ($200 for 2017) (Rev. Proc. 2015-53; Rev. Proc. 2016-55). An S corporation may not contest the penalty assessment in the Tax Court but can pay the entire penalty and then sue for a refund.

An S corporation may also be subject to penalties for failure to furnish Schedules K-1 to its shareholders (Code Sec. 6722).[94] See ¶ 2823 for more details.

355. Tax Year of S Corporation. The tax year of an S corporation must be a permitted year. Permitted years include the calendar year, a tax year elected under Code Sec. 444 (¶ 1501), a 52-53 week tax year ending with reference to the calendar year or a tax year elected under Code Sec. 444, or any other tax year for which the corporation establishes a business purpose to the satisfaction of the IRS (Reg. § 1.1378-1(a)).[95] The procedures for an S corporation to establish a business purpose are contained in Rev. Proc. 2006-46.[96]

An S corporation may elect to have a tax year other than its required tax year. Generally, this election may be made only if the deferral period of the tax year elected is not longer than three months. The S corporation makes this election by filing Form 8716 (¶ 1501). If such an election is made, the S corporation may be required to make certain tax payments.

References are to Standard Federal Tax Reports; Tax Research Consultant; and Practical Tax Explanations.

[88] ¶ 32,180; SCORP: 364; § 13,405.20, § 28,410.05

[89] ¶ 35,145; SCORP: 500; § 29,010.10

[90] ¶ 35,521; SCORP: 500; § 29,010.10

[91] ¶ 36,790; FILEBUS: 15,104.10; § 29,010.10

[92] ¶ 35,520; SCORP: 500; § 29,010.10

[93] ¶ 40,023; PENALTY: 3,208.45; § 29,010.20

[94] ¶ 40,230; PENALTY: 3,204; § 29,010.20

[95] ¶ 32,261; SCORP: 252, SCORP: 258; § 28,410.15

[96] ¶ 32,262.10; SCORP: 256; § 28,410.15

Chapter 4
PARTNERSHIPS

	Par.
Choice of Entity	401
Publicly Traded Partnerships	403
Partnership-Level Issues	404
Partner Loss Deductions	425
Partner's Distributive Share of Partnership Items	428
Sale and Liquidation of Partner's Interest	434
Partnership Contributions, Distributions, and Basis	443
Family Partnerships	474
Organization, Syndication, Start-Up Costs	477
Electing Large Partnerships	482

Choice of Entity

401. Partnership Defined. A partnership includes a syndicate, group, pool, joint venture, or other unincorporated organization that carries on any business, financial operation, or venture, and that is not a trust, estate, or corporation within the meaning of the Code (Code Sec. 761).[1] A noncorporate entity with at least two members can be classified under the check-the-box rules (¶ 402A) either as a partnership or as an association taxable as a corporation. A noncorporate entity with one member can be taxed either as a corporation or as a sole proprietorship (Reg. § 301.7701-3).[2]

401A. Limited Partnerships. A limited partnership is a partnership (¶ 401) that has one or more general partners and one or more limited partners. Limited partnerships are formed under the limited partnership laws of each state. Unlike general partnerships in which all the partners are responsible for partnership liabilities, limited partners are not responsible for partnership liabilities beyond the amount of their investments. In addition, under state law, limited partners cannot participate in partnership management.

401B. Limited Liability Partnerships. Limited liability partnerships (LLPs) are partnerships (¶ 401) that are generally used by professionals such as accountants, attorneys, and doctors. An LLP is a general partnership in which each individual partner remains liable for his or her own liabilities as well as the liabilities arising out of the wrongful acts or omissions of those over whom the partner has supervisory duties. For this reason, they are sometimes used for large professional partnerships with hundreds of partners scattered over the country or even on different continents.

Each state and the District of Columbia have LLP-enabling legislation. Some states offer members of LLPs limited protection from partnership liabilities, such as limiting the protection to malpractice claims against other partners. Other states offer full protection from liabilities, including the partnership's contractual liabilities. These are called "full shield" states.

As a practical matter, LLPs are most often used to give liability protection to partners in an existing partnership. The conversion of an existing partnership to an LLP does not create a new partnership, as the IRS has ruled that the registration of a general partnership as a registered LLP does not cause a termination of the partnership (¶ 410) (Rev. Rul. 95-55).[3] In such a case, the partnership must continue to use the same method

References are to Standard Federal Tax Reports; Tax Research Consultant; and Practical Tax Explanations.

[1] ¶ 25,600; PART: 3,100; § 30,015.05

[2] ¶ 43,083; PART: 3,102; § 30,015.10

[3] ¶ 25,202.27; PART: 3,108; § 30,005.15

of accounting used before its registration as an LLP. Each partner's total percentage interest in the partnership's profits, losses, and capital remains the same after the registration.

Limited Liability Limited Partnerships. Some states have passed legislation allowing limited liability limited partnerships (LLLPs). These entities operate like a traditional limited partnership, but the general partner also has the limited personal liability of a partner in a limited liability partnership.

402. Exclusion from Partnership Provisions. An entity that would otherwise be considered a partnership (¶ 401) may elect to not be treated as partnership or not have all or part of the partnership rules under Subchapter K of the Code in two situations. Application of the partnership tax rules can be avoided where the income of the partners can be adequately determined without partnership-level computation and in the case of certain partnerships consisting solely of a married couple.

Unincorporated organizations may elect not to be taxed as partnerships if they are used either for investment purposes only or for the joint production, extraction, or use—but not the sale—of property under an operating agreement (Code Sec. 761(a)).[4] The exclusion also can be used by securities dealers for a short period for the purpose of underwriting, selling, or distributing a particular issue of securities. The exclusion can be elected only if the partners' incomes can be determined without computing the entity's income first.

An unincorporated organization may choose to be completely or only partially excluded from the partnership provisions. However, the IRS does not allow an organization making the partial election to be excluded from the tax-year conformity rules (¶ 416) or from the limitations on the allowance of losses (¶ 425) (Rev. Rul. 57-215).[5] The election removes the entity from all or a portion of the subchapter K partnership provisions.

Qualified Joint Ventures. A trade or business co-owned by a married couple who file a joint return may elect to be taxed as a qualified joint venture instead of a partnership for federal tax purposes (Code Sec. 761(f)).[6] A qualified joint venture is a joint venture involving the conduct of a trade or business if: (1) the only members of the joint venture are a married couple, (2) both spouses materially participate in the trade or business, and (3) both spouses elect to have the provision apply. The IRS takes the position that qualified joint ventures include only businesses that are owned and operated by spouses as co-owners, and do not include businesses that are run as a state-law entity, such as a limited liability company (IRS Pub. 1635).

All items of income, gain, loss, deduction, and credit from a qualified joint venture are divided between the spouses in accordance with their respective interests in the venture. Each spouse takes into account his or her respective share of these items as a sole proprietor. Each spouse should account for his or her respective share on a separate Schedule C or Schedule F of Form 1040. Each spouse may also need to file Schedule SE for self-employment tax purposes.

402A. Check-the-Box Regulations. Any business entity not required to be treated as a corporation for federal tax purposes may choose its own classification (Reg. § 301.7701-3).[7] An entity with two or more members can be classified either as a partnership or as an association taxed as a corporation. An entity with only one member can choose to be taxed as a corporation or it can be disregarded as an entity separate from its owner. Form 8832 is used by an entity to elect how it will be classified for federal tax purposes.

References are to Standard Federal Tax Reports; Tax Research Consultant; and Practical Tax Explanations.

[4] ¶ 25,600; PART: 3,350; § 30,015.20

[5] ¶ 25,602.11; PART: 3,356.15; § 30,015.20

[6] ¶ 25,600; PART: 3,358; § 30,015.20

[7] ¶ 43,083; PART: 3,102; § 30,015.10

Domestic entities with two or more members that do not file an election have a default classification of partnership. A single-member limited liability company (SMLLC) cannot elect partnership status because a partnership, by definition, has two or more partners (¶ 401). A domestic entity with one member that does not elect to be taxed as a corporation is considered a disregarded entity—i.e., it is ignored and the taxpayer is treated as a sole proprietorship. Thus, a domestic LLC will be taxed as a partnership or disregarded entity unless it files an election to be taxed as a corporation. An election not to be taxed as a partnership on Form 8832 applies to all Code provisions, and this election is different than the election under Code Sec. 761 which removes an entity from some or all parts of Subchapter K of the Code (¶ 402).

Foreign Business Entities. The check-the-box rules apply somewhat differently to foreign business organizations. Entities listed in Reg. § 301.7701-2(b)(8) are considered corporations and are not eligible to be partnerships under the check-the-box rules. Any other foreign entity may be taxed as either a corporation or partnership (or a disregarded entity if it has one owner). A foreign business entity where all owners have limited liability will generally be treated as a corporation unless it elects to be taxed as a partnership. A foreign business entity where one or more owners has unlimited liability will generally be taxed as a partnership unless it elects to be taxed as a corporation. Thus, the foreign equivalent of an LLC (such as a German *GmbH*), where all members have limited liability, will be taxed as a corporation unless it elects to be taxed as a partnership. The default classification for foreign and domestic entities existing before January 1, 1997, is the classification the entity claimed immediately prior to that date.

Note that the term "limited liability" is not precisely defined by the regulations, and it may be uncertain whether the IRS would consider a given foreign law to provide for limited liability for all members of an entity. It will usually be easier and safer for practitioners to file an election under the check-the-box rules for a foreign entity rather than to determine what its default classification would be.

402B. Limited Liability Companies. A state-registered limited liability company (LLC) can be taxed as a partnership for federal income tax purposes. However, its members, like corporate shareholders, are not personally liable for the entity's debts or liabilities. Under the check-the-box rules (¶ 402A), an LLC can choose partnership status to avoid taxation at the entity level as an association taxed as a corporation.

Unlike limited partners, LLC members may participate in management without risking personal liability for company debts. In addition, no limitations are placed on the number of owners of LLCs taxed as partnerships. Contrast this to S corporations, which have a maximum number of shareholders. There is also no limitation on the different types of owners of an LLC. S corporations may generally only have U.S. resident individuals or certain types of trusts as shareholders. Additional advantages over S corporations include the ability to make disproportionate allocations and distributions (Code Sec. 704)[8] and to distribute appreciated property to members without the recognition of gain (Code Sec. 731(b)).[9] Members may also exchange appreciated property for membership interests without the recognition of gain or loss (Code Sec. 721).[10]

Conversion from Partnership to LLC. A conversion of a partnership into an LLC that is taxed as a partnership for federal income tax purposes is treated as a nontaxable partnership-to-partnership conversion (Rev. Rul. 95-37).[11] The conversion is treated as a contribution of assets to the new partnership under Code Sec. 721 and does not result in gain or loss to the partners. The tax results are the same whether the LLC is formed in the same state as the former partnership or a different state. Upon a conversion, the tax year of the converting partnership does not close with respect to any of the partners, and the resulting LLC does not need to obtain a new taxpayer identification number.

References are to Standard Federal Tax Reports; Tax Research Consultant; and Practical Tax Explanations.

[8] ¶ 25,120; PART: 30,000; § 30,501

[9] ¶ 25,320; PART: 33,152; § 30,530.05

[10] ¶ 25,240; PART: 9,050; § 30,105.10

[11] ¶ 25,243.13; PART: 3,106.10; § 30,930.20

Conversion from C Corporation to LLC. The conversion of an existing C corporation into an LLC taxed as a partnership is generally treated as a liquidation of the corporation and thus a taxable event for both the corporation and the shareholders (Code Sec. 7701; LTR 9701029).[12] The possible tax hit diminishes the attractiveness of existing corporate entities converting to LLCs. This is especially true if the corporation holds appreciated property. Only a corporation with little or no net worth and shareholders with bases exceeding the amount of any distribution can escape this tax result. The conversion can be accomplished in one of two ways: (1) the assets of the corporation can be contributed to the LLC in return for membership interests, which are then distributed to the shareholders in liquidation of the corporation; or (2) the corporation can distribute its assets in complete liquidation, and the shareholders can then contribute their undivided interests in the assets to the LLC in exchange for membership interests.

Conversion from S Corporation to LLC. For an S corporation to convert to an LLC taxed as a partnership, it must undergo the same process as a C corporation discussed above. However, unlike a C corporation, when an S corporation distributes appreciated assets to its shareholders in exchange for their stock, there is no double tax. Because the S corporation is a flowthrough entity, the gain incurred at the corporate level passes through to the shareholders and is generally included in income on the shareholder's tax return.

Any gain recognized by the shareholder as a result of the gain attributable to the liquidating distribution increases the shareholder's stock basis. The shareholder's increased basis then reduces the amount of gain recognized or increases the amount of loss recognized. Thus, with one exception relating to the built-in gains tax (¶ 337) there is a single level of taxation. Although, with an S corporation, there is usually only this one level of taxation, rather than the two levels of taxation inherent with the C corporation, this single level of taxation may still be enough to dissuade an S corporation from converting to an LLC.

Series LLCs. Several states permit the creation of separate series within an LLC. The debts and other liabilities of each series are enforceable only against that series. Each series is recognized as a distinct entity for state law purposes and each series can have its own separate business purposes. A series can be terminated without affecting the other series of the LLC. Under proposed regulations, effective when they are finalized, each series of a series organization (such as a series LLC) would be treated for federal tax purposes as an entity formed under local law, regardless of whether local law actually treats the series as a separate entity (Prop. Reg. § 301.7701-1(a)(5)).[13]

Publicly Traded Partnerships

403. Publicly Traded Partnerships. A publicly traded partnership (PTP) is taxed as a corporation unless 90 percent or more of its gross income is derived from qualifying passive income sources—interest, dividends, rents from real property, gain from the disposition of real property, mining and natural resource income, and gain from the disposition of capital assets or section 1231 property held for the production of such income (Code Sec. 7704).[14] A PTP is a partnership with interests traded on an established securities market or readily tradable on a secondary market (or its substantial equivalent), including master limited partnerships.

A partnership that was publicly traded on December 17, 1987, continues to be treated as a partnership rather than a corporation if it meets certain conditions (Code Sec. 7704(g); Reg. § 1.7704-2(a)(1)).[15] A grandfather rule exempts electing 1987 partnerships from corporate treatment if the partnership existed as a PTP or was treated as having existed as a PTP on December 17, 1987, elected to continue its partnership status, and does not add a substantial new line of business. A grandfathered electing 1987 partnership must pay an annual 3.5-percent tax on any income from the conduct of an active business.

References are to Standard Federal Tax Reports; Tax Research Consultant; and Practical Tax Explanations.

[12] ¶ 43,080; LLC: 18,150

[13] ¶ 43,081A; STAGES: 24,200

[14] ¶ 43,180; PART: 3,250

[15] ¶ 43,180, ¶ 43,181; PART: 3,256

Partnership-Level Issues

404. Partners, Not Partnership, Subject to Tax. A partnership does not pay federal income tax; rather, items of partnership income, gain, loss, deduction, and credit flow through to the partners who are taxed on their distributive shares of partnership taxable income. However, a partnership is a tax-reporting entity that must file an annual partnership return (¶ 406). In determining federal income tax, a partner must take into account his or her distributive share of partnership income or loss for the year, as well as his or her distributive share of certain separately stated items (¶ 431) of partnership income, gain, loss, deduction, or credit. A partner's distributive share of partnership items is includible on his or her individual income tax return (or corporate income tax return for corporate partners) for his or her tax year in which the partnership tax year ends (Code Sec. 706(a)).[16]

A partner is generally not taxed on distributions of cash, marketable securities, and property received from the partnership, except to the extent that any money and marketable securities distributed exceeds the partner's adjusted basis in his or her partnership interest immediately before the distribution (¶ 453). Taxable gain can also result from distributions of property that were contributed to a partnership with a built-in gain (if property has a fair market value in excess of its adjusted basis) and from property distributions that are characterized as sales and exchanges (¶ 432).

A 3.8-percent net investment income (NII) tax applies to individuals, estates, and trusts, but not to partnerships (¶ 129) (Code Sec. 1411).[17] Income from trades or businesses conducted by partnerships is not considered net investment income. However, income from a trade or business that is a passive activity with respect to the partner is included in the partner's net investment income. Thus, the partner's distributive share of income earned by a partnership that would otherwise be net investment income in the hands of the partner is considered net investment income to the partner.

406. Partnership Return (Form 1065). A partnership is generally required to file Form 1065 for each partnership tax year to report the income, gains, losses, deductions, credits, etc., from the operation of the partnership (Code Sec. 6031(a); Reg. § 1.6031(a)-1).[18] This includes a foreign partnership unless it has no income effectively connected with a U.S. trade or business and no U.S. partners at any time during the partnership's tax year.

For tax years beginning after December 31, 2015, Form 1065 is due on or before the 15th day of the *third* month (the *fourth* month for prior tax years) following the close of the tax year (March 15 for a calendar-year partnership) (Code Sec. 6072(b)).[19] Although Code Sec. 6063[20] states that the return may be signed by any one of the partners, the instructions to Form 1065 indicate that the form must be signed by one of the partnership's general partners or, in the case of a limited liability company (LLC), by one of the member-managers (¶ 415). Form 7004 is used to apply for an automatic five-month filing extension (Reg. § 1.6081-2).[21] For partnership returns for tax years beginning after December 31, 2015, the maximum extension period will increase to six months (Act Sec. 2006(b)(1) of the Surface Transportation and Veterans Health Care Choice Improvement Act of 2015 (P.L. 114-41)).

A partnership that fails to timely file Form 1065 or files an incomplete return is liable for a penalty of $195 per partner for 2016 ($200 for 2017), per month or fraction of a month up to a maximum of twelve months, unless reasonable cause is shown (Code Sec. 6698; Rev. Proc. 2015-53; Rev. Proc. 2016-55).[22]

References are to Standard Federal Tax Reports; Tax Research Consultant; and Practical Tax Explanations.

[16] ¶ 25,160; PART: 6,052; § 30,125

[17] ¶ 32,602; INDIV: 69,160.60; § 1,022.15

[18] ¶ 35,381, ¶ 35,383; PART: 18,160.05; § 30,435

[19] ¶ 36,720; PART: 18,160.05; § 30,435

[20] ¶ 36,640; PART: 18,160.05; § 30,435

[21] ¶ 36,788; PART: 18,160.05; § 30,435

[22] ¶ 39,995; PART: 18,162.10; § 30,435

Reasonable cause exists only if significant mitigating factors are present, or the failure to file arose from factors beyond the filer's control, and the filer establishes that it acted in a responsible manner both before and after the failure. A partnership may not contest the penalty assessment in the Tax Court but must pay the entire penalty and then sue for a refund. Certain domestic partnerships with 10 or fewer partners do not have to pay the penalty if all partners have fully reported their distributive shares on timely filed income tax returns (Rev. Proc. 84-35).[23]

Schedule K-1s. A partnership required to file Form 1065 for the tax year generally must furnish each partner with a Schedule K-1 on or before the due date for Form 1065 (Code Sec. 6031(b); Temp. Reg. § 1.6031(b)-1T(a); Rev. Proc. 2012-17).[24] Schedule K-1 can be provided in an electronic format to partners, but the partnership must first obtain their consent. The partnership may be subject to penalties for failure to furnish Schedule K-1 to its partners (¶ 2823).

The Schedule K-1 should provide the partner's distributive share of partnership income, gain, loss, deduction, or credit, and any additional information that is necessary to enable the partner to determine the correct income tax treatment of a partnership item. Generally effective for returns filed for partnership tax years beginning after December 31, 2017, Schedule K-1s may not be amended by the partnership after the due date of Form 1065 unless the partnership elects to apply the post-2017 audit adjustment rules at the partner level (see ¶ 413).

410. Changes in Ownership Interests of Partnerships. The tax year of a partnership closes with respect to a partner whose entire interest in the partnership ends, whether by a sale of the entire interest or otherwise (Code Sec. 706(c)(2)(A)).[25] The sale of a portion of a partnership interest does not result in the closing of the partnership's tax year with respect to the selling partner.

In the case of a sale, exchange, gift, or liquidation of a partner's entire interest in a partnership, the partnership "closes the books" as to that partner (Code Sec. 706(c)(2)(A); Reg. § 1.706-1(c)(2)).[26] In this case, the date of the disposition of the partnership interest is treated *as to the withdrawing partner* as if it is the close of the tax year. That partner's share of the partnership tax items is then determined as of that date, and the partner must include his or her share of partnership tax items in income for the tax year in which his or her partnership interest ends. However, a partnership does not have to make an interim closing of the books. Instead, a retiring partner's share of income may, by agreement among the partners, be estimated by taking a pro rata portion of the amount of such items the partner would have included in income had he or she remained a partner until the end of the partnership tax year. The prorated amount may be based on the portion of the tax year that has elapsed prior to the sale, exchange, or liquidation, or may be determined under any other method that is reasonable.

Technical Terminations. A partnership is considered to terminate if, within a 12-month period, there is a sale or exchange of 50 percent or more of the total interests in partnership capital and profits (Code Sec. 708(b)(1)(B)).[27]

Changes in Partnership Interests During Tax Year. If there is a change in any partner's interest in the partnership (for instance, because of the retirement of a partner, entry of a new partner, or simply a change in the allocations of partnership items), each remaining partner's distributive share must take into account the varying interests during the partnership tax year (Code Sec. 706(d); Reg. §§ 1.706-1 and 1.706-4; Prop. Reg. § 1.706-4).[28] The varying interests rule generally may be satisfied either by using an interim closing of the books or by prorating income, losses, etc., for the entire year. Special rules apply with respect to cash-basis items and tiered partnerships.

References are to Standard Federal Tax Reports; Tax Research Consultant; and Practical Tax Explanations.

[23] ¶ 40,000.10; PART: 18,162.10; § 30,435

[24] ¶ 35,385, ¶ 35,389.16; PART: 18,162.15; § 30,435

[25] ¶ 25,160; PART: 6,154; § 38,145.15

[26] ¶ 25,160, ¶ 25,161; PART: 24,112; § 30,910.05

[27] ¶ 25,200; PART: 51,100; § 31,010.05

[28] ¶ 25,160, ¶ 25,161, ¶ 25,163J, ¶ 25,163M; PART: 24,114, PART: 24,116; § 30,425.10, § 30,910.05

If there is a change in any partner's interest in the partnership, the distributive shares of certain cash-method items are determined by assigning the appropriate portion of each item to each day to which it is attributable and then by allocating the daily portions among the partners in proportion to their interests in the partnership at the close of each day. For this purpose, cash-method items are interest, taxes, payments for services or for the use of property, and any other item specified in the regulations. Cash-method items deductible or includible within the tax year but attributable to a time period before the beginning of the tax year (for example, payment during the tax year for services performed in the prior tax year) are assigned to the first day of the tax year. If persons to whom such items are allocable are no longer partners on the first day of the tax year, then their portion of the items must be capitalized by the partnership and allocated to the basis of partnership assets (¶ 459). Cash-method items attributable to periods following the close of the tax year (for example, properly deductible prepaid expenses) are assigned to the last day of the tax year.

In the case of changes in a partner's interest in an upper-tier partnership that has an ownership interest in a lower-tier partnership, each partner's distributive share of any items of the upper-tier partnership attributable to the lower-tier partnership is determined by: (1) assigning the appropriate portion of each such item to the appropriate days of the upper-tier partnership's tax year on which the upper-tier partnership is a partner in the lower-tier partnership; and (2) allocating the assigned portion among the partners in proportion to their interests in the upper-tier partnership as of the close of each day (Code Sec. 706(d)(3)).[29]

413. Partnership Audits and Adjustments (Post-2017). Effective for returns filed for partnership tax years beginning after December 31, 2017, a single set of rules for auditing partnerships and their partners at the partnership level applies, replacing the TEFRA audit rules (¶ 415) as well as the rules for electing large partnerships (¶ 482). A partnership can elect to apply the new rules to returns filed for partnership tax years beginning after November 2, 2015, and before January 1, 2018 (Act Sec. 1101 of the Bipartisan Budget Act of 2015 (P.L. 114-74).

Generally, an election to have the new partnership rules apply must be made within 30 days of the date of the IRS notice of selection for examination, and must be made as prescribed by the rules (Temp. Reg. § 301.9100-22T).[30] A partnership that has not been issued a notice of selection may also make the election in order to file an administrative adjustment request (AAR). During the period of at least 30 days after the IRS receives a valid election and before it mails any notice of an administrative proceeding, the partnership may file an AAR (Code Sec. 6227, as added by the Bipartisan Budget Act of 2015 (P.L. 114-74)).[31]

Under the post-2017 audit rules, the IRS will examine a partnership's items of income, gain, loss, deduction, or credit, and any partners' distributive shares of the items, for a particular year of the partnership (reviewed year). Any adjustments (including penalties) are taken into account by the partnership and not the individual partners in the year the audit or any judicial review is completed (adjustment year) (Code Sec. 6221, as added by P.L. 114-74).[32] Partnerships with 100 or fewer qualifying partners for whom a Schedule K-1 of Form 1065 is required to be provided may opt out of these rules and be audited under the rules applicable to individuals.

A partner must generally treat on its income tax return a partnership item in a manner consistent with the treatment of that item on the partnership return (Code Sec. 6222, as added by P.L. 114-74)).[33] Any underpayment of tax attributable to failure to meet the consistency requirement is treated as if the underpayment were due to a mathematical or clerical error. An additional tax will not be assessed for a failure to meet the consistency requirement if certain notification requirements are met. However, accuracy-related and fraud penalties may apply if the partner disregards the requirement.

References are to Standard Federal Tax Reports; Tax Research Consultant; and Practical Tax Explanations.

[29] ¶ 25,160; PART: 24,114; § 30,910.05

[30] ¶ 47,037; PART: 60,700; § 31,270

[31] ¶ 37,983; PART: 60,702

[32] ¶ 37,950; PART: 60,700

[33] ¶ 37,956; PART: 60,700

A partnership must designate a person with substantial presence in the United States as the partnership representative (replacing the concept of tax-matter partner under the TEFRA rules) (Code Sec. 6223, as added by P.L. 114-74).[34] The representative has the sole authority to act on behalf of the partnership for purposes of the partnership audit rules and all partners are bound by the representative's actions. The IRS may select a representative if none is selected by the partnership.

Partnership Adjustments. In the event that the IRS adjusts any item of a partnership's income, gain, loss, deduction, or credit, or partners' distributive shares of such items, the partnership must pay an imputed underpayment in the adjustment year based on the highest rate of tax in effect for the reviewed year (Code Secs. 6225 and 6241(2), as added by P.L. 114-74 and amended by the Protecting Americans from Tax Hikes (PATH) Act of 2015 (P.L. 114-113)).[35] The IRS may modify the imputed underpayment in certain situations (for example, where a partner files an amended return or is a tax-exempt entity). No deduction is permitted for the imputed underpayment (Code Sec. 6241(4), as added by P.L. 114-74). In addition, if a partnership ceases to exist before a partnership adjustment takes effect, the adjustment is taken into account by the former partners under IRS regulations (Code Sec. 6241(7), as added by P.L. 114-74).

As an alternative to paying an imputed underpayment, a partnership may elect within 45 days of the date of the notice of final partnership adjustment to apply the adjustment at the partner level rather than at the partnership level (Code Sec. 6226, as added by P.L. 114-74 and amended by P.L. 114-113).[36] If the election is made, the partnership must furnish to each partner for the reviewed year an adjusted Schedule K-1 indicating their share of any adjustment to be used in filing an amended return. Penalties and additions to tax arising due to the adjustment continue to be determined at the partnership level. However, interest on an imputed underpayment passed through to a partner is computed at the partner level (Code Sec. 6233, as added by P.L. 114-74).[37]

As under the pre-2018 audit rules, a partnership may file an AAR for one or more partnership items for the tax year (Code Sec. 6227, as added by P.L. 114-74).[38] Any administrative adjustment is taken into account in the year the request is made by the partnership, or in the year the request is made by the partnership and partners if the election not to apply the adjustment at the partnership level is made.

Administrative Procedures. The IRS is required to provide notice of proceedings and adjustments to the partnership and partnership representative (Code Sec. 6231, as added by P.L. 114-74).[39] Any imputed underpayment with respect to any partnership adjustment is treated as if it were a tax imposed for assessment and collection purposes, subject to certain restrictions (Code Sec. 6232, as added by P.L. 114-74).[40] Within 90 days after the date on which a notice of final partnership adjustment is mailed, the partnership may petition for readjustment with the proper court (Code Secs. 6234 and 6241(5), as added by P.L. 114-74 and amended by P.L. 114-113).[41] The statute of limitations for making adjustments for any partnership tax year is generally three years, but may be extended if there is a modification of an imputed underpayment or a notice of proposed partnership adjustment issued by the IRS (Code Sec. 6235, as added by P.L. 114-74 and amended by P.L. 114-113).[42]

415. Partnership Audits and Adjustments (Pre-2018). Effective for returns filed for partnership tax years beginning before January 1, 2018, the determination of the tax treatment of partnership items is generally made at the partnership level in a single administrative partnership proceeding. The Tax Equity and Fiscal Responsibility Act of 1982 (P.L. 97-248) provides rules (TEFRA audit rules) governing proceedings that must

References are to Standard Federal Tax Reports; Tax Research Consultant; and Practical Tax Explanations.

[34] ¶ 37,962; PART: 60,700

[35] ¶ 37,971, ¶ 38,032; PART: 60,702

[36] ¶ 37,977; PART: 60,702

[37] ¶ 38,004; PART: 60,702, PART: 60,704

[38] ¶ 37,983; PART: 60,702

[39] ¶ 37,992; PART: 60,704

[40] ¶ 37,998; PART: 60,704

[41] ¶ 38,010, ¶ 38,032; PART: 60,704

[42] ¶ 38,021; PART: 60,704

be conducted at the partnership level for the assessment and collection of tax deficiencies or for tax refunds arising out of the partners' distributive shares of partnership items (Code Secs. 6221—6233).[43] See also ¶ 482 for special rules applicable to electing large partnerships with 100 or more partners.

The TEFRA audit rules, as well as the electing large partnership rules, are repealed for returns filed for partnership tax years beginning after December 31, 2017 (Act Sec. 1101 of the Bipartisan Budget Act of 2015 (P.L. 114-74)). In their place, a single set of rules for partnership audits and adjustments at the partnership level will apply. A partnership may elect to apply the new audit rules to returns filed for partnership tax years beginning after November 2, 2015. See ¶ 413 for a discussion of the post-2017 partnership audit rules.

Under the pre-2018 TEFRA audit rules, notice of the beginning of administrative proceedings and the resulting final partnership administrative adjustment (FPAA) must be given to all partners whose names and addresses are furnished to the IRS, except those with less than a one-percent interest in partnerships that have more than 100 partners (Code Sec. 6223).[44] A group of partners having an aggregate profits interest of five percent or more may request notice to be mailed to a designated partner.

Each partnership should have a tax matters partner (TMP) who is to receive notice on behalf of small partners not entitled to notice and who keeps all of the partners informed of all administrative and judicial proceedings at the partnership level (Code Sec. 6231).[45] The TMP is either the general partner designated as such by the partnership or, in the absence of a designation, the general partner with the largest interest in partnership profits for the relevant tax year. Settlement agreements may be entered into between the TMP and the IRS that bind the parties to the agreement, and may extend to other partners who request to enter into consistent settlement agreements (Code Sec. 6224).[46]

Consistency Requirement. Each partner is required to treat partnership items on his or her return in a manner consistent with the treatment of such items on the partnership return (Code Sec. 6222).[47] A partner may be penalized for intentionally disregarding this requirement. The consistency requirement may be waived if the partner files Form 8082 identifying the inconsistency or shows that it resulted from an incorrect schedule furnished by the partnership.

The IRS may apply entity-level audit procedures when it appears from the return that such procedures should apply. The IRS's determination will stand even if it later proves to be erroneous (Code Sec. 6231(g)).[48]

Innocent Spouse Relief. Innocent spouse relief is available with respect to partnership-level proceedings (Code Sec. 6230).[49] If the spouse of a partner in a partnership subject to the TEFRA audit rules asserts that the innocent spouse rules apply with respect to a liability attributable to any adjustment to a partnership item, the spouse may file a request for an abatement of the assessment with the IRS. The spouse must file the request within 60 days after the notice of a computational adjustment has been mailed by the IRS. Upon receipt of the request, the IRS must abate the assessment. If the IRS chooses to reassess the abated tax, it then has 60 days after the date of the abatement in which to make any reassessment. In such a scenario, the regular deficiency procedures apply.

If the taxpayer claiming innocent spouse relief files a Tax Court petition under Code Sec. 6213 with respect to the request for abatement, the Tax Court can determine only whether the innocent spouse requirements have in fact been satisfied. For purposes of

References are to Standard Federal Tax Reports; Tax Research Consultant; and Practical Tax Explanations.

[43] ¶ 37,565—¶ 37,900; PART: 60,050; § 31,105

[44] ¶ 37,590; PART: 60,150; § 31,110.15

[45] ¶ 37,770; PART: 60,100; § 31,110.10

[46] ¶ 37,640; PART: 60,200; § 31,110.10

[47] ¶ 37,570; PART: 60,058; § 31,115

[48] ¶ 37,770; PART: 60,054; § 31,105

[49] ¶ 37,750; PART: 60,312

this determination, the treatment of the TEFRA partnership items under the settlement, the FPAA, or the court decision (whichever is appropriate) that gave rise to the liability in question is conclusive.

Small Partnership Exception. The TEFRA audit rules do not apply to partnerships with 10 or fewer partners if each partner is an individual U.S. resident, C corporation, or estate, and each partner's share of any partnership item is the same as his or her distributive share of every other partnership item. However, these small partnerships may elect to have the TEFRA audit rules apply using Form 8893 (Code Sec. 6231(a)(1)(B)).[50] The partnership also can allocate items without jeopardizing its exception from the TEFRA audit rules. Once a small partnership elects to have the TEFRA rules apply, the election cannot be revoked without IRS consent.

416. Partnership's Required Tax Year. A partnership generally cannot have a tax year other than its majority-interest tax year (Code Sec. 706(b)).[51] This is the tax year that, on each testing day, constitutes the tax year of one or more partners having an aggregate interest in partnership profits and capital of more than 50 percent. The testing day is the first day of the partnership's tax year (determined without regard to the majority-interest rule). A partnership that changes to a majority-interest tax year is generally not required to change to another tax year for the two tax years following the year of change.

If the partnership has no majority-interest tax year, then its tax year must be the same as the tax year of all of the partnership's principal partners (partners who individually own five percent or more of the partnership's profits or capital) (Code Sec. 706(b)(1)(B)(ii)).[52] Partnerships that are unable to determine a tax year under either of the foregoing methods must adopt a tax year that results in the least aggregate deferral of income to the partners (Reg. § 1.706-1).[53] A partnership may avoid the tax year rules if it can establish a business purpose for selecting a different tax year (Code Sec. 706(b)(1)(C); Reg. § 1.706-1(b)(2)).[54]

Code Sec. 444 Election. Certain partnerships are permitted to make an election to have a tax year other than the normally required tax year (Code Sec. 444).[55] For any tax year for which an election is made, a partnership generally must make a required payment that is intended to represent the tax on the income deferred through the use of a tax year other than a required year. The payment is due on May 15 of the calendar year following the calendar year in which the Code Sec. 444 election year begins (¶ 1501) (Code Sec. 7519; Temp. Reg. § 1.7519-2T(a)(4)(ii)).[56]

417. Partnership Taxable Income. While a partnership is not subject to tax (¶ 404), its taxable income is the key feature by which the partnership passes through its income or loss to its partners (Code Sec. 701).[57] Each partner generally must account for his or her distributive share of partnership taxable income in computing income tax. The partner's share of partnership tax items is reported to him or her by the partnership on Schedule K-1 of Form 1065. A partner's basis in his or her partnership interest is increased by his or her distributive share of partnership taxable income, while the partner's basis generally decreases by the amount distributed to the partner by the partnership. Thus, if a partnership distributes all of its taxable income by the end of the partnership tax year, the basis of each partner's interest in the partnership does not change (Code Secs. 705 and 731(a)).[58]

The taxable income of a partnership is computed in the same manner as that of an individual except that the following deductions and carryovers are not allowed to a partnership:

References are to Standard Federal Tax Reports; Tax Research Consultant; and Practical Tax Explanations.

[50] ¶ 37,770; PART: 60,054; § 31,105

[51] ¶ 25,160; PART: 6,102; § 30,120.10

[52] ¶ 25,160; PART: 6,104; § 30,120.15

[53] ¶ 25,161; PART: 6,106; § 30,120.20

[54] ¶ 25,160, ¶ 25,161; PART: 6,108

[55] ¶ 20,600; PART: 6,110; § 30,120.30

[56] ¶ 42,770, ¶ 42,773; PART: 6,110; § 30,120.05

[57] ¶ 25,060; PART: 18,050; § 30,401

[58] ¶ 25,140, ¶ 25,320; PART: 15,056, PART: 15,058; § 30,210.15

- the deduction for personal exemptions (¶ 133);
- the deduction for foreign taxes (note that the taxes are allocated to the partners as separately stated items);
- the net operating loss deduction (which is determined at the partner level, not the partnership level) (¶ 1145);
- the deduction for charitable contributions (which is allocated to the partners as a separately stated item) (¶ 1058);
- individuals' itemized deductions (medical expenses, etc. (¶ 1014));
- the capital loss carryover (which is determined at the partner level, not the partnership level) (¶ 1754);
- the domestic production activities deduction (which is determined at the partner level, not the partnership level) (¶ 980A); and
- depletion deductions with respect to oil and gas wells (which are allocated to the partners as separately stated items) (¶ 1289) (Code Sec. 703(a); Reg. § 1.703-1).[59]

In addition, certain items of gain, loss, etc. must be separately stated (¶ 431).

418. Partnership Anti-Abuse Regulations. Regulations give the IRS the power to recast transactions that attempt to use the partnership provisions for tax-avoidance purposes (Reg. § 1.701-2).[60] Under the rules, a partnership must be *bona fide* and each partnership transaction must be entered into for a substantial business purpose. The form of each transaction must be respected under substance-over-form rules. In addition, the tax consequences to each partner of partnership operations and transactions must accurately reflect the partners' economic agreement and clearly reflect each partner's income. Whether there is a principal purpose of substantially reducing the present value of the partners' aggregate tax liability is determined at the partnership level.

In abusive situations, the IRS can treat a partnership as the aggregate of its partners, in whole or in part, as appropriate to carry out the purpose of any Code provision or regulation. However, to the extent that a Code provision or regulation prescribes treatment of the partnership as an entity and the treatment and ultimate tax results are clearly contemplated by the provision, the IRS will not recast a transaction.

419. Elections by Partnerships. Most elections affecting the computation of income derived from a partnership must be made by the partnership. Thus, elections as to methods of accounting, methods of computing depreciation, the Code Sec. 179 expensing election, the election not to use the installment sales provision, the option to expense intangible drilling and development costs, and similar elections must be made by the partnership and must apply to all partners, insofar as the partnership transactions are concerned (Reg. § 1.703-1(b)).[61] In the case of an involuntary conversion of partnership property, the partnership also must purchase replacement property and elect nonrecognition of gain treatment (Rev. Rul. 66-191).[62]

Individual partners may make elections to: (1) use as a credit or as a deduction their distributive shares of foreign taxes of the partnership, (2) deduct or capitalize their shares of the partnership's mining exploration expenditures, or (3) reduce basis in connection with discharge of indebtedness under Code Sec. 108 (Code Sec. 703(b)).[63]

Regulations provide for an automatic six-month extension for making elections if the time for making the election also is the due date of the return for which the election is made (Reg. § § 301.9100-1, 301.9100-2, and 301.9100-3).[64]

References are to Standard Federal Tax Reports; Tax Research Consultant; and Practical Tax Explanations.

[59] ¶ 25,100, ¶ 25,101; PART: 18,052; § 30,405

[60] ¶ 25,061B; PART: 3,110; § 30,130

[61] ¶ 25,101; PART: 18,152; § 30,301

[62] ¶ 29,650.704; SALES: 27,166.10; § 30,301

[63] ¶ 25,100; PART: 18,154; § 30,301

[64] ¶ 44,014, ¶ 44,014AE, ¶ 44,014AG; FILEBUS: 15,150; § 39,220

421. Guaranteed Payments to Partners. Any fixed or guaranteed payments to partners for services or the use of capital made without regard to partnership income are treated as paid to a nonpartner for purposes of computing partnership gross income and business expense deductions (¶ 432). Thus, guaranteed payments are regarded as ordinary income to the recipient and deductible by the partnership if they are ordinary and necessary business expenses (¶ 901) (Code Sec. 707(c); Reg. §§ 1.707-1(c) and 1.707-4).[65] This rule applies only to the extent that the amounts paid are in fact guaranteed payments determined without regard to the income of the partnership. The partner must report the payments on his or her return for the tax year within or with which ends the partnership year in which the partnership deducted the payments as paid or accrued under its method of accounting.

Example 1: In the AB partnership, Ann is the managing partner and is entitled to receive a fixed annual payment of $100,000 for her services, without regard to the income of the partnership. Her distributive share of partnership profit and loss is 10 percent. After deducting her guaranteed payment, the partnership has $300,000 ordinary income. Ann must include $130,000 ($100,000 guaranteed payment plus $30,000 distributive share) as ordinary income for her tax year within or with which the partnership tax year ends. If the partnership had shown a $100,000 loss after deduction of Ann's guaranteed payment, her guaranteed payment ($100,000) would be reported as income, and her $10,000 distributive share of the loss, subject to the limitations on partnership losses (¶ 425), would be taken into account on her individual tax return.

If a partner is entitled to a minimum payment and the percentage of profits is less than the minimum payment, the guaranteed payment is the difference between the minimum payment and the distributive share of the profits determined before the deduction of the minimum payment (Reg. § 1.707-1(c)).[66] Only the amount of the guaranteed payment may qualify as a deductible business expense of the partnership.

Example 2: The AB partnership agreement provides that Ann is to receive 30% of partnership income before taking into account any guaranteed payments, but not less than $100,000. The income of the partnership is $600,000, and Ann is entitled to $180,000 (30% of $600,000) as her distributive share. Because her distributive share exceeds the minimum amount that was guaranteed, no part of the $180,000 is a guaranteed payment. If the partnership had income of only $200,000, Ann's distributive share would have been $60,000 (30% of $200,000), and the remaining $40,000 payable to Ann would have been a guaranteed payment.

A partner who receives a guaranteed salary payment is not regarded as an employee of the partnership for the purpose of withholding of income or Social Security taxes, or for pension plans. The guaranteed salary is includible in self-employment income for the purpose of the self-employment tax along with the partner's share of ordinary income or loss of the partnership (Reg. § 1.707-1(c); Rev. Rul. 56-675).[67]

Fringe Benefits. The value of fringe benefits (¶ 2085) provided to a partner for services rendered in the capacity as a partner is generally treated as a guaranteed payment (Code Sec. 162(l); Rev. Rul. 91-26).[68] As such, the value of the benefit is generally deductible by the partnership as an ordinary and necessary business expense; and the value of the benefit is included in the partner's gross income unless specifically excluded from a partner's income under another Code provision. Thus, a payment of premiums by a partnership for a partner's health or accident insurance is generally deductible by the partnership and included in the partner's gross income. As an alternative, a partnership may choose to account for premiums paid for a partner's insurance by reducing that partner's distributions. In this case, the premiums are not deductible by the partnership and all partners' distributive shares are unaffected by payment of the premiums. A partner can deduct 100 percent of the cost of the health insurance premiums paid on his or her behalf.

References are to Standard Federal Tax Reports; Tax Research Consultant; and Practical Tax Explanations.

[65] ¶ 25,180, ¶ 25,181, ¶ 25,181C; PART: 27,100; § 30,735.05

[66] ¶ 25,181; PART: 27,110; § 30,735.15

[67] ¶ 25,181, ¶ 25,183.30; PART: 27,112; § 30,735.20

[68] ¶ 8500, ¶ 25,183.16; PART: 27,104; § 21,225, § 30,735.10

Partner Loss Deductions

425. Partnership Loss Limited to Partner's Basis. The amount of partnership loss (including capital loss) that may be recognized by a partner is limited to the amount of the adjusted basis (before reduction by the current year's loss) of the partner's interest in the partnership at the end of the partnership tax year in which the loss occurred. Any disallowed loss is carried forward to, and may be deducted by the partner in, subsequent partnership tax years to the extent that his or her basis exceeds zero before deducting the loss (Reg. § 1.704-1(d)).[69] Techniques that have been used to increase a partner's basis so that he or she can deduct losses that otherwise would be unavailable include making additional contributions to the capital of the partnership (¶ 443) and increasing the partner's share of partnership liabilities (¶ 447). However, a partner's recognition of losses may be further limited to amount the partner has at-risk in partnership activities (¶ 426), and the amount of passive-activity income (¶ 427).

426. Partners and the At-Risk Rules. A partners' deduction for partnership losses for any tax year is generally limited to the amount the partner has at risk in the partnership for the year (¶ 1155). Thus, the at-risk limits apply at the partner level, and not the partnership level (Code Sec. 465; Temp. Reg. § 1.469-2T(d)(6)).[70] A partner is not at risk for any portion of a partnership liability for which he or she has no personal liability. The at-risk loss limitation rules are applied after taking into account the basis limitation for partners' losses (¶ 425), but before taking into account the limitations that apply to computing any passive activity loss for the year (¶ 427).

Real Estate Exception. The at-risk rules generally apply to the holding of property in the same manner as they apply to other activities (Code Sec. 465(b)(6)).[71] However, an exception applies to the holding of real estate. A taxpayer is at risk with respect to qualified nonrecourse financing that is secured by the real property used in the activity of holding real estate. Thus, lending provided by any person actively and regularly engaged in the business of lending money is qualified nonrecourse financing. Such lenders generally include banks, savings and loan associations, credit unions, insurance companies regulated under federal, state, or local law, or pension trusts. Further, qualified nonrecourse financing includes a loan made by any federal, state, or local government or a governmental entity, or a loan that is guaranteed by any federal, state, or local government. Convertible debt cannot be treated as qualified nonrecourse financing.

Qualified nonrecourse financing can be provided by a related persons (generally, family members, fiduciaries, and corporations, or partnerships in which a person has at least a 10-percent interest) if the financing from the related person is commercially reasonable and on substantially the same terms as loans involving unrelated persons.

427. Partnerships and the Passive Activity Loss Rules. A partner's deduction for partnership losses for any tax year is generally limited by the passive activity rules (¶ 1169) which apply at the partner level to his or her share of any loss or credit attributable to a passive activity of the partnership (Code Sec. 469).[72] The passive activity limits are applied only after taking into account the basis limitation for the partners' losses (¶ 425) and the at-risk limits (¶ 426).

A partnership may engage in both passive and nonpassive activities. For example, a partnership may engage in business that is a passive activity of its limited partners (who normally do not participate in the management of a limited partnership), and it may also have investment assets that produce portfolio income (not a passive activity). Thus, a partner who disposes of his or her interest in a partnership must allocate any gain or

References are to Standard Federal Tax Reports; Tax Research Consultant; and Practical Tax Explanations.

[69] ¶ 25,121; PART: 15,202; § 30,430.10

[70] ¶ 21,850, ¶ 21,963; PART: 15,204; § 17,301

[71] ¶ 21,850; BUSEXP: 42,160; § 17,305.10

[72] ¶ 21,960; PART: 15,206; § 30,430.05, § 30,430.20

loss among the various activities of the partnership in order to determine the amount that is passive gain or loss and the amount that is nonpassive gain or loss. In general, the allocation is made in accordance with the relative value of the partnership's assets.

To allow a partner to make these calculations, a partnership must report separately a partner's share of income, losses, and credits from each of its trade or business activities, rental real estate activities, and rental activities other than rental real estate. The separate activities must be reported on a statement attached to the Schedule K-1 of Form 1065 provided to the partner (Instructions to Form 1065). A partnership's portfolio income, which is excluded from passive income, must also be separately reported.

A passive activity of a partner generally is: (1) a trade or business activity in which the partner does not materially participate, or (2) any rental activity. Except as otherwise provided, an interest in an activity as a limited partner in a limited partnership is not one in which the partner materially participates (Temp. Reg. § 1.469-5T(e)(2)).[73] If a partnership reports amounts from more than one activity on a partner's Schedule K-1 and one or more of the activities is passive to the partner, the partnership must attach a statement detailing the income, losses, deductions, and credits from each passive activity, and identifying the line of Schedule K-1 on which that amount is included.

427A. Net Operating Loss Deduction of Partners. The benefit of the net operating loss deduction (¶ 1145) is not allowed to the partnership but instead to its partners (Reg. § 1.702-2).[74] For purposes of determining net operating loss, each partner takes into account his or her distributive share of income, gain, loss, deduction, and credit of the partnership as if each item were realized directly from the source from which it was realized by the partnership or incurred in the same manner as it was incurred by the partnership.

Partner's Distributive Share of Partnership Items

428. Allocations of Partnership Items Under Partnership Agreement. A partner's distributive share of income, gain, loss, deduction, or credit is generally determined by the partnership agreement. Allocations of any partnership item must have substantial economic effect (Code Sec. 704(b); Reg. § 1.704-1(b)).[75] If a partnership agreement does not provide for the allocation of partnership items or if partnership allocations lack substantial economic effect, the partner's distributive share is determined according to his or her interest in the partnership.

Economic Effect. Allocations have economic effect if they are consistent with the underlying economic arrangement of the partners (Reg. § 1.704-1(b)(2)(ii)).[76] For instance, a limited partner who has no risk under the partnership agreement other than his or her initial capital contribution ordinarily may not be allocated losses attributable to a partnership recourse liability to the extent such losses exceed the capital contribution. Recourse losses ordinarily must be allocated to the partners (usually the general partners) who bear the ultimate burden of discharging the partnership's liability. A partnership's nonrecourse deductions—those attributable to those liabilities of the partnership for which no partner bears personal liability such as a mortgage secured only by a building and the land on which it is located)—are deemed to lack economic effect and must be allocated according to the partners' interests in the partnership (¶ 448).

Partnership allocations may be deemed to have substantial economic effect if the requirements of *optional* safe harbor provisions are met (Reg. § 1.704-1(b)(2)).[77] Generally, to satisfy the safe harbor, a partnership must maintain its "book" capital accounts as set out by Reg. § 1.704-1 and make tax allocations consistent with the capital accounts. A second safe harbor in Reg. § 1.704-2 applies to the allocation of nonrecourse deductions.

References are to Standard Federal Tax Reports; Tax Research Consultant; and Practical Tax Explanations.

[73] ¶ 21,965; PART: 15,206; § 17,435.20

[74] ¶ 25,084; PART: 18,306; § 30,405

[75] ¶ 25,120, ¶ 25,121; PART: 21,100; § 30,610.05

[76] ¶ 25,121; PART: 21,150; § 30,610.05

[77] ¶ 25,121; PART: 21,150, PART: 21,358; § 30,610.10

Substantiality. The economic effect of an allocation is generally considered substantial if there is a reasonable possibility that the allocation will substantially affect the dollar amounts to be received by the partners from the partnership, independent of tax consequences (Reg. § 1.704-1(b)(2)(iii)).[78]

Contributed Property. Income, gain, loss, and deductions attributable to property contributed to a partnership by a partner must be allocated among the partners to take into account the variation between the property's fair market value and its basis to the partnership at the time of contribution (Code Sec. 704(c)).[79] The partnership's basis in the contributed property at the time of contribution in exchange for a partnership interest is the basis of the property in the hands of the contributing partner. Any built-in gain or loss with respect to the contributed property must be allocated to the contributing partner. A similar rule applies to contributions by cash-method partners of accounts payable and other accrued but unpaid items.

When allocating tax items to property contributed to a property, three reasonable allocation methods are permitted—the traditional method, the traditional method with curative allocations, and the remedial allocation method (Reg. § 1.704-3).[80] The IRS has announced that it will issue regulations denying the nonrecognition of gain (¶ 721) with respect to contribution of property to a partnership that has a foreign partner related to the U.S. transferor, unless the partnership adopts the gain deferral method (GDM) as its remedial allocation method. The regulations will retroactively apply to transfers occurring on or after August 6, 2015, and to transfers occurring before that date resulting from entity classification elections filed on or after August 6, 2015 (Notice 2015-54).[81]

Special rules also prevent use of allocations to improperly shift the tax consequences associated with contributed property among partners in a partnership (Reg. § 1.704-3(a)(10)).[82] Under the anti-abuse rule, an allocation method is not reasonable if the property contribution and the corresponding allocation of tax items regarding the property are made with a view to shifting the tax consequences of built-in gain or loss among the partners in a manner that substantially reduces the present value of the partners' aggregate tax liability (¶ 418). Also, the distribution of built-in gain or loss property to partners other than the contributing partner within seven years of its contribution to the partnership may result in the recognition of gain or loss to the contributing partner (¶ 453).

430. Disproportionate Partnership Distributions. Disproportionate distribution rules apply if an actual or constructive distribution to a partner changes his or her proportionate interest in a partnership's unrealized receivables or inventory. The purpose of these rules is to prevent conversion of ordinary income to capital gain on the distribution or a change in share of unrealized receivables or substantially appreciated inventory.

A disproportionate distribution is treated as a sale or exchange of the receivables or inventory items from the partnership to the partner (Code Sec. 751(b)).[83] This results in ordinary income rather than capital gain. These rules cannot be avoided through the use of tiered partnerships (Code Sec. 751(f)). Sale or exchange treatment does not apply to a distribution of property that the distributee contributed to the partnership or to payments to a retiring partner or a successor in interest of a deceased partner.

Although the substantially appreciated inventory test was dropped for most appreciated inventory in the case of a sale or exchange of a partnership interest (¶ 434), it remains in effect for disproportionate distributions from a partnership to its partners. Inventory is considered to be substantially appreciated if its fair market value exceeds the partnership's basis in the property by 120 percent or more. The inventory need not appreciate in value after the partnership acquired it to satisfy the 120-percent test.

References are to Standard Federal Tax Reports; Tax Research Consultant; and Practical Tax Explanations.

[78] ¶ 25,121; PART: 21,200; § 30,615.05

[79] ¶ 25,120; PART: 9,150; § 30,625.05

[80] ¶ 25,134; PART: 9,059

[81] ¶ 25,243.145; PART: 9,059

[82] ¶ 25,134; PART: 9,152.05; § 30,625.05

[83] ¶ 25,500; PART: 30,100; § 30,540.10

431. Separate Reporting of Partnership Items. Each partner of a partnership must account separately for his or her distributive share of the following partnership items on his or her tax return (Code Sec. 702):[84]

- short-term capital gains and losses,
- long-term capital gains and losses,
- gains and losses from sales or exchanges of property used in a trade or business or subject to involuntary conversion (¶ 1747),
- charitable contributions (¶ 1061),
- dividends for which there is a dividends-received deduction (¶ 223),
- taxes paid or accrued to foreign countries and to U.S. possessions (¶ 2475),
- taxable income or loss, exclusive of items requiring separate computation, and
- other items required to be stated separately either by Reg. § 1.702-1[85] or because separate statement could affect the income tax liability of any partner, including:
  - — recovery of bad debts, prior taxes, and delinquency amounts,
  - — gains and losses from wagering transactions (¶ 785),
  - — soil and water conservation expenditures (¶ 982),
  - — deductible investment expenses (¶ 1085),
  - — medical and dental expenses (¶ 1015),
  - — alimony payments (¶ 771),
  - — amounts paid to cooperative housing corporations (¶ 1040),
  - — intangible drilling and development costs (¶ 989),
  - — alternative minimum tax adjustments and tax preference items (¶ 1425 and ¶ 1430),
  - — investment tax credit recapture (¶ 1365A),
  - — recapture of mining exploration expenditures (¶ 987),
  - — information necessary for partners to compute oil and gas depletion allowances (¶ 1289),
  - — cost of recovery property being currently expensed (¶ 1208),
  - — work opportunity tax credit (¶ 1365G),
  - — alcohol fuels credit (¶ 1365I),
  - — net earnings from self-employment (¶ 2670),
  - — investment interest (¶ 1094),
  - — income or loss to the partnership on certain distributions of unrealized receivables and inventory items to a partner (¶ 453),
  - — any items subject to a special allocation under the partnership agreement (¶ 428),
  - — contributions (and the deductions for contributions) made on a partner's behalf to qualified retirement plans (¶ 2115 and ¶ 2117), and
  - — income and expenses from domestic production activities (¶ 431A).

The need for a separate statement of various partnership items gives rise to the separate reporting of these items on Form 1065 and Schedule K K-1.

Partnerships that regularly carry on a trade or business are required to furnish to tax-exempt partners a separate statement of items of unrelated business taxable income (Code Sec. 6031(d)).[86]

References are to Standard Federal Tax Reports; Tax Research Consultant; and Practical Tax Explanations.

[84] ¶ 25,080; PART: 18,054; § 30,410

[85] ¶ 25,081; PART: 18,054; § 30,410

[86] ¶ 35,381; PART: 18,162.15; § 30,410

431A. Domestic Production Activities by Partnerships. A partnership cannot claim the deduction for qualified domestic production activities (¶ 980A and following). Instead, the deduction is determined at the partner level (Code Sec. 199(d)(1); Reg. § 1.199-5(b)(1)).[87] Each partner generally computes its deduction separately on Form 8903 by aggregating its proportionate share of qualified production activity (QPA) items of the partnership (i.e., income, expenses) with its share of QPA items from other sources. The partner does not have to be directly engaged in the partnership's trade or business to claim the deduction on the basis of its share of QPA items.

A partner will not be treated as directly conducting the QPA of the partnership (and vice versa) with respect to property transferred between the parties (Reg. § 1.199-5(g)).[88] For example, if a partner manufactures qualified production property within the United States and then contributes the property to the partnership, which subsequently sells, licenses, leases, or otherwise disposes of the property, then the income derived by the partnership will not qualify as domestic production gross receipts (DPGR). A limited exception is provided for certain qualifying oil and gas partnerships and expanded affiliated groups.

Allocation of Items. QPA items of a partnership are allocated to each partner as any other tax item (¶ 428). This includes special allocations of QPA items, subject to the rules of Reg. § 1.704-1(b), including the rules for determining substantial economic effect (¶ 428). A partner's distributive share of expenses allocable to the partnership's QPA must be taken into account even if the partnership has no taxable income. If a partner is unable to claim a loss or deduction for regular tax purposes (i.e., at-risk, passive loss, or basis limitations), then the loss or deduction cannot be taken into account in computing the Code Sec. 199 deduction. The amount of any loss or deduction is subject to proportionate reduction if it is only partially allowed for regular tax purposes. Also, a loss or deduction that is temporarily disallowed for regular tax purposes may be used in computing the Code Sec. 199 deduction in the tax year in which the loss or deduction is allowed for regular tax purposes.

Instead of taking into account its distributive share of each QPA item of the partnership, a partner may compute its deduction by combining its distributive share of the partnership's qualified production activities income (QPAI) and W-2 wages with its QPAI and W-2 wages from other sources. This option applies only if the partnership has elected to use the small business overall method for allocating costs, expenses, and other deductions to its DPGR (¶ 980A and following). A partner's share of QPAI from a partnership may be less than zero under this method.

Special rules apply to 20-percent partners of partnerships engaged in film or television production (Code Sec. 199(d)(1)(A)(iv)).[89]

Sale of Partnership Interest. Gain or loss recognized on the sale of a partnership interest will not be taken into account by a partner in computing its QPAI (Reg. § 1.199-5(f)).[90] This is because the sale of the partnership interest does not reflect the realization of DPGR by the entity. However, if the taxpayer receives a distribution of unrealized receivables or partnership inventory for its entire partnership interest (Code Sec. 751 property (¶ 434 and ¶ 436)), then any gain or loss that would be attributable to the sale or other disposition of such assets which would give rise to QPAI may be taken into account by the partner.

W-2 Wage Limitation. A partner computes the W-2 wage limitation for the Code Sec. 199 deduction by aggregating its share of W-2 wages from the partnership allocable to DPGR with its W-2 wages allocable to DPGR from other sources.

References are to Standard Federal Tax Reports; Tax Research Consultant; and Practical Tax Explanations.

[87] ¶ 12,468, ¶ 12,472D; BUSEXP: 6,212.05, BUSEXP: 6,212.10; § 30,415.05

[88] ¶ 12,472D; BUSEXP: 6,212.10; § 30,415.05

[89] ¶ 12,468; BUSEXP: 6,152

[90] ¶ 12,472D; BUSEXP: 6,212.05, BUSEXP: 6,212.10

432. Members' Dealings with Own Partnership. Transactions between a partnership and partner may be deemed to be between a partnership and a nonpartner under certain circumstances (Code Sec. 707(a)).[91] This rule prevents the use of disguised payments to circumvent the requirement that a partnership capitalize certain expenses (such as syndication and organization expenses).

Disguised Sales or Payments for Services. In order to prevent such manipulation, a transaction is treated as if it occurred between a partnership and a nonpartner for income tax purposes if:

- a partner performs services for a partnership or transfers property to a partnership,
- there is a related direct or indirect allocation and distribution to the partner, and
- the performance of the partner's service (or the partner's transfer of property) and the allocation and distribution, when viewed together, are properly characterized as a transaction that occurred between the partnership and the partner acting as a nonpartner (Code Sec. 707).[92]

If this rule applies to a transaction, then the allocation and distribution made by the partnership to the partner is recharacterized as a payment for services or property. In this case, the payment must be capitalized where required or otherwise treated in a manner consistent with its recharacterization. The partners' shares of taxable income or loss must then be redetermined.

Whether a transfer constitutes a disguised sale is based on facts and circumstances. However, contributions and distributions made within a two-year period are presumed to be a sale, while such transactions occurring more than two years apart are presumed not to be a sale (Reg. § 1.707-3(c) and (d)).[93] Under proposed regulations, effective when finalized, the primary factor in determining whether a payment is a disguised payment for services is whether the payment is subject to significant entrepreneurial risk (Prop. Reg. § 1.707-2).[94] Exceptions to the disguised sale rules are provided for guaranteed payments for capital, reasonable preferred returns, operating cash flow distributions, and reimbursements of preformation capital expenditures, subject to certain limitations (Reg. § 1.707-4). A partner is permitted on or after October 5, 2016, limited aggregation of property for purposes of the applying the limitations for reimbursements of capital expenditures (Reg. § 1.707-4(d)).[95]

A transfer of a nonqualified liability from a partner to a partnership is treated as a transfer of consideration to the partner to the extent of the excess of the amount of the liability over the partner's share of that liability immediately after the transfer (Reg. § 1.707-5(a)(1)).[96] Temporary regulations effective October 5, 2016 provide that, for disguised sale purposes only, a partner's share of any partnership liability, whether recourse or nonrecourse, is generally the same percentage used to determine the partner's share of the partnership's excess nonrecourse liabilities, which are generally determined in accordance with the partner's share of partnership profits (¶ 448) (Temp. Reg. § 1.707-5T(a)(2)).[97]

References are to Standard Federal Tax Reports; Tax Research Consultant; and Practical Tax Explanations.

[91] ¶ 25,180; PART: 27,050; § 30,701

[92] ¶ 25,180; PART: 27,058; § 30,715.05

[93] ¶ 25,181B; PART: 27,058.05; § 30,715.15, § 30,715.20

[94] ¶ 25,181AD; PART: 27,050; § 30,710.05

[95] ¶ 25,181C; PART: 27,058.10; § 30,715.25

[96] ¶ 25,181D; PART: 27,058.15; § 30,715.65

[97] ¶ 25,181DK; PART: 27,058.15; § 30,715.65.

Transactions Between Controlled Partnerships. Special rules also apply to controlled partnerships. No loss deduction is allowed from a sale or exchange of property (other than an interest in the partnership) between a partnership and a person whose interest in the partnership's capital *or* profits is more than 50 percent. A loss deduction is also not allowed if the sale or exchange is between two partnerships in which the same persons own more than 50 percent of the capital or profits interests (Code Sec. 707(b)(1)).[98] In either case, if one of the purchasers or transferees realizes gain on a later sale, the gain is taxable only to the extent it exceeds the amount of the disallowed loss attributable to the property sold. Gain recognized on transactions involving controlled partnerships is treated as ordinary income if the property sold or exchanged is not a capital asset in the hands of the transferee (Code Sec. 707(b)(2)).[99]

Code Sec. 267 disallows deductions for losses from the sale or exchange of property between related persons, including a partnership and a corporation controlled by the same persons (¶ 1717). This loss-denial rule does not apply to a transaction between a partnership and a partner. The rule does apply, however, to a transaction between a partnership and a person who, with respect to a partner, is a related person under Code Sec. 267(b) (Reg. § 1.267(b)-1(b)).[100] In addition to the disallowance of losses, accrued interest and expense deductions are not deductible until paid if the amount giving rise to the deduction is owed to a related cash-method taxpayer. For purposes of this rule, a partnership and persons holding interests in the partnership (actually or constructively) or persons related (under Code Sec. 267(b) or 707(b)(1)) to actual or constructive partners are treated as related persons (¶ 905 and ¶ 1540B) (Code Sec. 267(e)(1)).[101]

Sale and Liquidation of Partner's Interest

434. Purchase or Sale of a Partnership Interest. The sale or exchange of a partnership interest generally is treated as the sale of a single capital asset rather than a sale of each of the underlying partnership properties (Code Sec. 741).[102] The amount of gain or loss is based on the partner's basis in his or her partnership interest and the amount realized on the sale (Code Sec. 721).[103] A partner may recognize ordinary income or loss under the constructive sale rules if he or she receives a disproportionate distribution of partnership unrealized receivables or inventory (¶ 430). In addition, the sale or exchange of a partnership interest is distinguishable from the liquidation or redemption of a partner's entire interest in a partnership (¶ 435).

If a partner abandons or forfeits his or her partnership interest, the partner recognizes a loss equal to his or her basis in the partnership interest. Thus, a partner with a zero basis in its partnership interest is not allowed an abandonment loss (*E.J. LeBlanc*, FedCl, 2010-1 USTC ¶ 50,104). If the partnership has liabilities, the abandoning partner is deemed to have received a distribution from the partnership when he or she is relieved of the liabilities. In such a case, the partner's loss is the basis in his or her interest less any liabilities of which the partner is relieved. If there are no partnership liabilities of which the partner is relieved, the abandoning partner has an ordinary loss because no sale or exchange has taken place (*B.P. Citron*, Dec. 47,513, 97 TC 200 (1991); *G.G. Gannon*, Dec. 18,304, 16 TC 1134 (1951)).[104] If there are partnership liabilities of which the abandoning partner is relieved, the resulting gain or loss is a capital gain or loss (*A.O. Stilwell*, Dec. 27,950, 46 TC 247 (1966)).[105] Even a *de minimis* actual or deemed distribution generally results in capital loss treatment to the partner. Capital loss also occurs if the transaction is, in substance, a sale or exchange (Rev. Rul. 93-80).[106]

References are to Standard Federal Tax Reports; Tax Research Consultant; and Practical Tax Explanations.

[98] ¶ 25,180; PART: 27,152; § 30,720.10

[99] ¶ 25,180; PART: 27,154; § 30,720.15

[100] ¶ 14,153; PART: 27,152; § 30,720.10

[101] ¶ 14,150; PART: 27,160; § 30,730.05

[102] ¶ 25,440; PART: 39,050; § 30,905.05

[103] ¶ 25,240; PART: 39,052, PART: 39,054; § 30,905.05

[104] ¶ 25,442.12, ¶ 25,422.545; PART: 39,058.05; § 30,905.45, § 30,905.50

[105] ¶ 25,422.545; PART: 39,058.10; § 30,905.10

[106] ¶ 25,442.12; PART: 36,104.15; § 30,905.45

Net Investment Income. For purposes of the 3.8-percent net investment income (NII) tax, net gain or loss upon the disposition of a partnership interest is considered net investment income only to the extent it would be taken into account by the partner if all partnership property were sold at fair market value immediately before the disposition (¶ 129) (Code Sec. 1411).[107]

Unrealized Receivables and Inventory. A partner recognizes ordinary income or loss on any portion of a sale of a partnership interest that is attributable to his or her share of the partnership's unrealized receivables and inventory (¶ 436) (Code Sec. 751(a)).[108] The gain is measured by the portion of the selling price attributable to unrealized receivables and inventory, and the partner's basis in the assets. The partner's basis is the basis the partner's share of partnership unrealized receivables and inventory would have if these assets were distributed to the partner in a current distribution (Reg. § 1.751-1(a)(2)).[109] Capital gain or loss is determined by subtracting the partner's remaining basis from the rest of the amount realized (Reg. § 1.741-1(a)).[110]

435. Liquidation or Redemption of Partnership Interest. If a partner's entire interest in a partnership is liquidated or redeemed, he or she recognizes gain to the extent any money or marketable securities received exceeds his or her basis in the partnership interest immediately before the distribution (Code Sec. 731(a)(1) and (c)).[111] If only partnership property is received as part of the liquidating distribution, then no gain is recognized except to the extent provided for payments to retiring partners (¶ 438) and unrealized receivables and inventory (¶ 436). The partner's basis in any distributed partnership property received is equal to his or her partnership interest, less the amount of money and marketable securities received (¶ 456).

A partner recognizes loss from a distribution in liquidation of his or her entire partnership interest if no property other than money, unrealized receivables, and inventory are distributed to the partner. The loss is equal to the excess of the partner's basis in the partnership interest exceeds the amount of money received, plus the basis of the distributed receivables and inventory (Code Sec. 731(a)(2)).[112]

> **Example:** Martin has an adjusted basis in his partnership interest of $100,000. He retires from the partnership and receives as a distribution in liquidation of his share of partnership property. This includes $50,000 cash and inventory with a basis to him of $30,000. Martin can recognize a loss of $20,000, his basis minus the money received and his basis in the inventory distributed to him ($100,000 – ($50,000 + $30,000) = $20,000).

If a partner receives money or property in exchange for any part of his or her partnership interest, the amount attributable to the partner's share of the partnership's unrealized receivables or inventory items results in ordinary income or loss. This treatment applies to the unrealized receivables portion of the payments to a retiring partner or successor in interest of a deceased partner only if that part is not treated as paid in exchange for partnership property. The rationale behind this rule is that the inventory or the accounts receivable would give rise to ordinary income had the partnership interest not been sold. However, if the partner does not sell the distributed inventory items within five years from the date of distribution, the gain can be recognized as a capital gain (Code Sec. 735(a)(2)).[113] For this purpose, inventory does not include real estate or depreciable trade or business property (¶ 436) (Code Sec. 735(c)(1)).[114]

For exchanges of partnership interests involving unrealized receivables or inventory, the partnership must file an information return describing the exchange, and must furnish statements to each party (Reg. § 1.6050K-1).[115]

References are to Standard Federal Tax Reports; Tax Research Consultant; and Practical Tax Explanations.

[107] ¶ 32,602; INDIV: 69,156; § 1,022.10

[108] ¶ 25,500; PART: 42,050; § 30,905.25

[109] ¶ 25,501; PART: 42,054; § 30,905.25

[110] ¶ 25,441; PART: 42,052; § 30,905.25

[111] ¶ 25,320; PART: 36,102; § 30,515.10

[112] ¶ 25,320; PART: 36,104.05; § 30,515.15

[113] ¶ 25,400; PART: 36,202; § 30,915.10

[114] ¶ 25,400; PART: 36,202; § 30,915.05

[115] ¶ 36,241; PART: 42,058; § 30,915.20

436. Unrealized Receivables and Inventory Items of Partnerships. Unrealized receivables of a partnership include any rights to income for services or goods that are not capital assets that have not been included in gross income under the method of accounting employed by the partnership (Code Sec. 751(c); Reg. § 1.751-1(c)).[116] This classification generally relates to cash-method partnerships that have acquired a contractual or legal right to income for goods or services. It usually does not apply to an accrual-method partnership because it has already included unrealized receivables in gross income.

Unrealized receivables also includes certain property to the extent of the amount of gain that would have been realized and recharacterized or recaptured as ordinary income by the partnership if it had sold the property at its fair market value at the time of the sale or exchange of the partnership interest being considered. The types of property covered, which include depreciable personal property and real property, are listed in the flush language of Code Sec. 751(c). This property is not treated as an unrealized receivable (¶ 438), relating to payments in liquidation of a retiring or deceased partner's interest.

"Inventory items" of a partnership is defined more broadly than the term itself might suggest (Code Sec. 751(d); Reg. § 1.751-1(d)(2)).[117] It includes not only inventory, but also any other assets that would not be treated either as capital assets or section 1231 assets (generally, depreciable property and land used in a trade or business) if they were sold by the partnership (or by the partner, if he or she had held them). Thus, the term might include a copyright or artistic work, accounts receivable for services and inventory, or any unrealized receivables.

Distributions of inventory made in exchange for all or a part of a partner's interest in other partnership property, including money, are governed by the "substantially appreciated" rule (¶ 430) (Code Sec. 751(b); Reg. § 1.751-1(d)).[118] Thus, gain from such distributions is taxed as ordinary income if the fair market value of the partnership's inventory exceeds 120 percent of its adjusted basis.

438. Payments to Retired Partner or Deceased Partner's Successor. Payments made by a partnership in liquidation of the interest of a retiring or deceased partner are considered distributions by the partnership to the extent that the payments are in exchange for the partner's interest in partnership property. Otherwise, they are considered a distributive share of partnership income or a guaranteed payment (Code Secs. 736 and 761(d)).[119] This provision does not apply if the estate or other successor in interest of a deceased partner continues as a partner in its own right under local law (Reg. § 1.736-1(a)(1)).[120] In addition, it applies only to payments made by the partnership and not to transactions such as the sale of a partnership interest between the partners.

Under Code Sec. 731, distributions are generally nontaxable except to the extent that money distributed exceeds the partner's adjusted basis in his or her partnership interest (¶ 453); that excess is treated as capital gain. However, all gain relating to inventory is treated as being from the sale of a noncapital asset (¶ 436).[121] The partners' valuation in an arm's-length agreement of a retiring or deceased partner's interest in partnership property is presumptively correct, but that presumption may be rebutted (Reg. § 1.736-1(b)(1)).[122]

Payments for unrealized receivables and goodwill are treated as distributive shares of partnership income or as guaranteed payments if: (1) capital is not a material income-producing factor, and (2) the retiring or deceased partner was a general partner (Code Sec. 736(b)(2) and (3)).[123] Such payments are deductible by the partnership. If these two

References are to Standard Federal Tax Reports; Tax Research Consultant; and Practical Tax Explanations.

[116] ¶ 25,500, ¶ 25,501; PART: 42,100; § 30,540.15

[117] ¶ 25,500, ¶ 25,501; PART: 42,152; § 30,540.20

[118] ¶ 25,500, ¶ 25,501; PART: 30,050; § 30,915.05

[119] ¶ 25,420, ¶ 25,600; PART: 48,050; § 30,560.05

[120] ¶ 25,421; PART: 48,050; § 30,560.05

[121] ¶ 25,500; PART: 48,050; § 30,575

[122] ¶ 25,421; PART: 48,050; § 30,565.10

[123] ¶ 25,420; PART: 48,150; § 30,565.05, § 30,575

requirements are not met, payments for goodwill are treated as payments for partnership property and do not create a deduction for the partnership. However, payments for goodwill can be treated as payments for property if: (1) the goodwill was originally purchased by the partnership or otherwise acquired in a transaction resulting in a cash basis to the partnership, *or* (2) the partnership agreement calls for a reasonable payment for goodwill.

Such payments result in capital gain or loss to the extent of the partnership's basis in the goodwill. In fixing the amount attributable to goodwill, an amount arrived at under an arm's-length agreement generally is accepted by the IRS. A formula approach involving the capitalization of earnings in excess of a fair market rate of return on the partnership's net tangible assets may be used, but only where there is no better basis for making such a determination (Rev. Rul. 68-609).[124]

Amounts not considered as distributions by the partnership made for an interest in the partnership property are treated as either distributive shares of partnership income or guaranteed payments (Code Sec. 736(a)).[125] If the payments are determined by reference to partnership income, they are taxed as a distributive share to the recipient; if not, they are treated as guaranteed payments (¶ 421). Accordingly, if the payments consist of a percentage of partnership profits, they reduce the distributive shares of income of the remaining partners. If they are guaranteed payments, the effect is the same because they are deductible as business expenses in determining partnership taxable income. In either event, the payments are treated as ordinary income in the hands of the recipient partner.

Example 1: Partnership ABC is a personal service partnership and its balance sheet is as follows:

Assets			Liabilities and Capital		
	Adjusted basis	Market value		Adjusted basis	Market value
Cash	$130,000	$130,000	Liabilities .	$30,000	$30,000
Accounts receivable . .	0	300,000	Capital:		
			A	100,000	210,000
Capital and Sec. 1231 assets .	200,000	230,000	B	100,000	210,000
			C	100,000	210,000
Total	$330,000	$660,000	Total .	$330,000	$660,000

General Partner A retires from the partnership in accordance with an agreement under which his share of liabilities (⅓ of $30,000) is assumed. In addition, he is to receive $90,000 in the year of retirement, plus $100,000 in each of the two succeeding years, for a total of $300,000 (including his $10,000 share of liabilities) for his partnership interest. The value of A's interest in the partnership's section 736(b) property is $120,000 (⅓ of $360,000, which is the sum of $130,000 cash and $230,000, the fair market value of section 1231 assets). The accounts receivable are not included in A's interest in partnership property because A is a general partner in a partnership in which capital is not a material income-producing factor. Assuming that the basis of A's interest is $110,000 ($100,000, the basis of his capital investment, plus $10,000, his share of partnership liabilities), he realizes a capital gain of $10,000 on the sale of his interest in partnership property. The $180,000 balance to be received by him is treated as guaranteed payments taxable as ordinary income.

The $100,000 that A receives in each of the three years would ordinarily be allocated as follows: $40,000 as payment for A's interest in section 736(b) property ($120,000/$300,000 × $100,000) and the balance of $60,000 as guaranteed payments. While the $10,000 capital gain is normally recognized in the first year, A may elect to prorate the gain over the three-year period.

References are to Standard Federal Tax Reports; Tax Research Consultant; and Practical Tax Explanations.

[124] ¶ 25,422.51; PART: 48,308, VALUE: 12,050; § 30,565.05, § 30,575

[125] ¶ 25,420; PART: 48,150; § 30,910.10

Example 2: Assume the same facts as in Example 1 above, except that the agreement provides for payments to A for three years of a percentage of annual income instead of a fixed amount. As a result, all payments received by A are treated as payments for A's interest in partnership property until he has received $120,000. After that, the payments are treated as a distributive share of partnership income to A (Reg. § 1.736-1(b)(7)).

For income tax purposes, a retired partner or a deceased partner's successor is treated as a partner until his or her interest has been completely liquidated (Reg. § 1.736-1(a)(6)).[126]

440. Partner Receiving Income In Respect of a Decedent. All payments to the successor of a deceased partner under Code Sec. 736(a)—which relates to payments made in liquidation of a deceased partner's interest and considered as a distributive share or a guaranteed payment (¶ 438)—are income in respect of a decedent (Code Sec. 753; Reg. § 1.753-1).[127] The payments are taxed to the recipient when received to the extent that they are not properly includible in the short tax year ending with the decedent's death (¶ 182). The estate or heir of a deceased partner is also treated as receiving income in respect of a decedent to the extent that amounts are received from an outsider in exchange for rights to future payments by the partnership representing distributive shares or guaranteed payments.

Partnership Contributions, Distributions, and Basis

443. Contribution to Partnership. No gain or loss is recognized by either a partnership or any of its partners upon a contribution of property to the partnership in exchange for a partnership interest (Code Sec. 721(a); Reg. § 1.721-1).[128] This is true whether the contribution is made to an existing partnership or to a newly formed partnership. However, a partner must recognize any gain realized on the transfer of appreciated property to a partnership that would be treated as an investment company if the partnership were incorporated (Code Secs. 707(c) and 721(b)).[129] Further, the value of a capital interest in a partnership that is transferred to a partner in exchange for his or her services is taxable to the partner as ordinary income provided that the interest is not subject to a substantial risk of forfeiture (¶ 713) (Reg. § 1.721-1(b)).[130] The receipt of a profits interest in exchange for services rendered is not taxable as ordinary income (Rev. Proc. 93-27, clarified by Rev. Proc. 2001-43; Notice of Proposed Rulemaking (NPRM) REG-115452-14).[131]

The IRS has announced that it will issue regulations to ensure that when a U.S. person contributes property with built-in gain to a partnership that has foreign partners related to the transferor, income or gain attributable to the property will be taken into account by the transferor. The regulations will retroactively apply to transfers occurring on or after August 6, 2015, and to transfers occurring before that date resulting from entity classification elections filed on or after August 6, 2015 (Notice 2015-54).

Basis of Partner's Interest. The basis of a partner's interest acquired by a contribution of property is the amount of the money contributed, plus the adjusted basis to the contributing partner of any property contributed (Code Sec. 722).[132] If a partner receives a partnership interest as compensation for services rendered or to be rendered, and this results in taxable income to the incoming partner, that income is added to the basis of the partnership interest (Reg. § 1.722-1).[133] If the contributed property is subject to debt, or if liabilities of the partner are assumed by the partnership, the basis of the contributing partner's interest is reduced by the portion of the debt assumed by the other partners (¶ 447) (Code Sec. 752).[134] The assumption of the partner's debt by others is treated as a distribution of money to the partner and as a contribution of money by those assuming the debt.

References are to Standard Federal Tax Reports; Tax Research Consultant; and Practical Tax Explanations.

[126] ¶ 25,421; PART: 48,050; § 31,005.10, § 31,005.15

[127] ¶ 25,540, ¶ 25,541; PART: 48,304; § 32,901

[128] ¶ 25,240, ¶ 25,241; PART: 9,050; § 30,105.05

[129] ¶ 25,180, ¶ 25,240; PART: 9,058; § 30,105.10

[130] ¶ 25,241; PART: 12,050; § 30,115.15

[131] ¶ 25,243.12, ¶ 49,657; PART: 12,100; § 30,115.15

[132] ¶ 25,260; PART: 15,050; § 30,205.05

[133] ¶ 25,261; PART: 12,152; § 30,205.15

[134] ¶ 25,520; PART: 9,100; § 30,220.10

Basis of Property to Partnership. The basis to the partnership of property contributed by a partner is the adjusted basis of such property in the hands of the contributing partner at the time of the contribution and any gain the partner recognized on the transfer (Code Sec. 723).[135] However, a federal court of appeals held that the basis of a nonbusiness asset (for example, a personal automobile) converted to a business asset upon contribution to a partnership was its fair market value at the time of contribution (*L.Y.S. Au*, CA-9, 64-1 USTC ¶ 9447).[136] The holding period of a contributed asset includes the period during which it was held by the contributing partner (Reg. § 1.723-1).[137]

Only the contributing partner may take into account any built-in loss. In determining items allocated to the noncontributing partners, the basis of the contributed property is the property's fair market value at the time of contribution (Code Sec. 704(c)(1)(C)).[138] Proposed regulations effective for partnership contributions occurring on or after the regulations are finalized would clarify that the basis adjustment is initially equal to the built-in loss associated with the property and then is adjusted in a manner generally similar to basis adjustments on transfers of partnership interests (¶ 467) (Prop. Reg. § 1.704-3(f)).[139]

Contributions of Unrealized Receivables, Inventory, and Capital Loss Property. Unrealized receivables and inventory items contributed by the partner to the partnership retain their ordinary income character in the hands of the partnership (Code Sec. 724).[140] That is, unrealized receivables remain ordinary income property up to the time of disposal by the partnership, and inventory items remain ordinary income property for the five-year period beginning on the date of contribution. In addition, a partner's contribution of property with a built-in capital loss results in retention of the property's capital loss status in the hands of the partnership to the extent of built-in loss for the five-year period beginning on the date of contribution.

To prevent avoidance of these rules through the partnership's exchange of contributed unrealized receivables, inventory items, or capital loss property in a nonrecognition transaction (or series of transactions), the rule applies to any substituted basis property resulting from the exchange. It does not apply, however, to any stock in a C corporation received in an exchange of property for stock if the contributor is in control following the exchange (Code Secs. 351 and 735(c)(2)).[141] For this purpose, control is at least 80 percent of the total combined voting power of all classes of stock entitled to vote and at least 80 percent of the total number of shares of all other classes of stock of the corporation (Code Sec. 368(c)).[142]

445. Increases and Decreases in Basis of Partner's Interest. The basis of a partner's interest in a partnership (¶ 443) is *increased* by his or her distributive share of partnership taxable income, the partnership's tax-exempt income, and the excess of partnership deductions for depletion over the basis to the partnership of the depletable property (Code Sec. 705).[143] The basis of the partner's interest in a partnership is *decreased* (but not below zero) by distributions to the partner from the partnership (¶ 453). In addition, the partner's basis is also *decreased* by the sum of the partner's share of partnership losses and partnership expenditures not deductible in computing its taxable income and not chargeable to capital account, and the partner's depletion deduction for oil and gas wells. Distributions are taken into account before losses in adjusting the partner's interest basis (Rev. Rul. 66-94).[144]

References are to Standard Federal Tax Reports; Tax Research Consultant; and Practical Tax Explanations.

[135] ¶ 25,280; PART: 9,056; § 30,105.10

[136] ¶ 25,282.02; PART: 9,056

[137] ¶ 25,281; PART: 9,056; § 30,105.20

[138] ¶ 25,120; PART: 45,112; § 30,625.05

[139] ¶ 25,134BB; PART: 45,112

[140] ¶ 25,300; PART: 9,250; § 30,105.20

[141] ¶ 16,402, ¶ 25,400; PART: 36,202; § 30,105.20

[142] ¶ 16,750; CCORP: 3,054; § 26,105.10

[143] ¶ 25,140; PART: 15,056, PART: 15,058; § 30,210.10, § 30,210.15

[144] ¶ 25,144.12; PART: 15,060; § 30,210.20

Example: Partner A of ABC partnership has an $80,000 basis for her partnership interest. During the tax year, she receives cash distributions of $50,000, and her share of the partnership's losses is $40,000. Her interest is adjusted as follows:

Basis at beginning of year	$80,000	
Less cash distributions	50,000	$30,000
Less share of losses ($40,000) but only to the extent that the basis is not reduced below zero		30,000
Adjusted basis for interest		0

Because basis is decreased by distributions received before reduction by A's share of partnership losses, no gain is recognized on the cash distribution. However, $10,000 of A's share of partnership loss is disallowed and carried forward to subsequent tax years (¶ 425).

The basis of partnership interests may also be determined by reference to proportionate shares of the adjusted basis of partnership property that would be distributable if the partnership were to be terminated. This alternative rule is available only in limited circumstances—if a partner cannot practicably apply the general rule or when the IRS approves (Code Sec. 705(b); Reg. § 1.705-1(b)).[145]

For determining a partner's basis in his or her partnership interest, or for figuring gain or loss on a distribution, advances or drawings of money or property against a partner's distributive share of income are treated as current distributions made on the last day of the partnership's tax year (Reg. § 1.731-1(a)(1)(ii)).[146] Money received by a partner under an obligation to repay the partnership is not a distribution but is a loan that is treated as a transaction between the partnership and a nonpartner (Reg. §§ 1.707-1(a) and 1.731-1(c)(2)).[147]

447. Partnership Liabilities Treated as Distributions or Contributions. Any increase in a partner's share of partnership liabilities, including a partner's assumption of partnership liabilities or receipt of partnership property subject to a liability (limited to the fair market value of the encumbered property), is treated as a contribution of money that increases a partner's basis in his or her interest (¶ 445) (Code Secs. 722 and 752(a)).[148] A decrease in a partner's share of partnership liabilities is treated as a distribution of money by the partnership, which decreases the distributee partner's basis in his or her partnership interest (but not below zero) (Code Secs. 733 and 752(b)).[149] When a partner's basis has been reduced to zero, such deemed distributions can result in taxable gain (¶ 453).

448. Allocation of Partnership Liabilities. Partners' shares of partnership liabilities (and corresponding allocations of basis) depend upon whether the liability is "recourse" or "nonrecourse." In addition, separate rules apply in the case of nonrecourse debts of the partnership if a partner is the lender or has guaranteed repayment of the debt.

Recourse Liabilities. Liabilities are recourse to the extent that a partner bears the economic risk of loss if the liability is not satisfied by the partnership. Recourse liabilities are allocated in accordance with the partners' economic risk of loss (Reg. § 1.752-2(a)).[150] Economic risk of loss is generally borne by a partner to the extent that he or she must make a contribution to the partnership (including the obligation to restore a deficit capital account) or pay a creditor if all partnership assets, including money, were deemed worthless and all partnership liabilities were due and payable (Reg. § 1.752-2(b)(1)).[151] Thus, a limited partner cannot be allocated recourse liabilities in excess of his or her capital contribution and future contribution obligations unless he

References are to Standard Federal Tax Reports; Tax Research Consultant; and Practical Tax Explanations.

[145] ¶ 25,140, ¶ 25,141; PART: 15,100; § 30,210.25

[146] ¶ 25,321; PART: 33,052.10; § 30,210.20

[147] ¶ 25,181, ¶ 25,321; PART: 33,052.05; § 30,210.20

[148] ¶ 25,260, ¶ 25,520; PART: 9,100; § 30,215.05

[149] ¶ 25,360, ¶ 25,520; PART: 9,100; § 30,215.05

[150] ¶ 25,523; PART: 15,254; § 30,215.15

[151] ¶ 25,523; PART: 15,254.10; § 30,215.15

or she has agreed to restore any deficit in his or her capital account or to indemnify other partners for their debts with respect to a liability.

Recourse liabilities must be allocated to a partner if a related person bears the risk of loss for the liability (Reg. § 1.752-4(b)).[152] A partner does not bear the economic risk of loss if he or she is entitled to reimbursement from other partners or the partnership—for example, through an indemnification agreement or a state law right to subrogation (Reg. § 1.752-2(b)(5)).[153] Under temporary regulations effective October 5, 2016, a partner or related person generally does not bear the economic risk of loss with respect to a bottom-dollar payment obligation, generally defined as an obligation other than one in which the partner or related person is liable for the full amount of a payment obligation to the extent that any amount of a partnership liability is not otherwise satisfied (Temp. Reg. § 1.752-2T(b)(3)(ii)).[154]

Nonrecourse Liabilities. Nonrecourse liabilities are liabilities for which no partner bears the economic risk of loss—for example, a mortgage on an office building that is secured only by a lien on the building and on the rents, but with no personal obligation to repay the loan on the part of any of the owners. Such liabilities are generally shared by the partners in a manner that correlates with their allocations of deductions attributable to the liabilities (¶ 428).[155] A partner's share of nonrecourse liabilities of a partnership equals the sum of: (1) the partner's share of partnership minimum gain, (2) the amount of any taxable gain that would be allocated to the partner if the partnership disposed of all partnership property subject to one or more nonrecourse liabilities of the partnership in full satisfaction of the liabilities and no other consideration, and (3) the partner's share of the excess nonrecourse liabilities as determined in accordance with the partner's share of partnership profits (Reg. § 1.752-3(a)).[156]

Although excess nonrecourse liabilities are allocated in accordance with the partners' respective profits interests, the partnership agreement may state the partners' interests for purposes of sharing nonrecourse liabilities, provided that the stated sharing ratios are reasonably consistent with the allocation of significant item of partnership income or gain among the partners. Because no partner bears the economic risk of loss for nonrecourse liabilities, limited partners may be allocated shares of such liabilities (and the basis in such liabilities) in amounts exceeding their total capital contribution obligations.

Partner Nonrecourse Loans and Guarantees. A partner who lends money to the partnership on a nonrecourse basis bears the economic risk of loss for the liability. Likewise, a partner who guarantees an otherwise nonrecourse liability bears the risk of loss to the extent of his or her guarantee (Reg. § 1.752-2(d)(2)).[157]

A loss incurred on the abandonment or worthlessness of a partnership interest is an ordinary loss if sale or exchange treatment does not apply. If there is an actual or deemed distribution to the partner, or if the transaction is otherwise in substance a sale or exchange, the partner's loss is a capital loss except as provided if the partner receives a disproportionate distribution of partnership unrealized realized receivables or inventory (¶ 430). A deemed distribution includes the relief from partnership debts in which the abandoning partner shares. As with other losses, the partners must establish the finality and uncollectibility of the loss (Reg. § 1.165-1(d)).[158]

453. Gain or Loss on Distribution to Partners. The income of a partnership is taxable to the partners in accordance with their distributive shares of partnership taxable income (¶ 428). It does not matter when or if the income is actually distributed to the partners. However, distributions to partners decrease the partners' bases for their partnership interests (¶ 445).

References are to Standard Federal Tax Reports; Tax Research Consultant; and Practical Tax Explanations.

[152] ¶ 25,525; PART: 15,254.20; § 30,215.35

[153] ¶ 25,523; PART: 15,254.25; § 30,215.15

[154] ¶ 25,523DB; PART: 15,254.15; § 30,215.15.

[155] ¶ 25,120; PART: 15,254.10; § 30,215.20

[156] ¶ 25,524; PART: 21,358; § 30,215.20

[157] ¶ 25,523; PART: 15,254.20; § 30,215.25

[158] ¶ 9803; INDIV: 54,256; § 16,905.20

Example 1: A partner contributes $100,000 to the capital of a partnership. During the first year, his share of the partnership taxable income is $25,000, but only $10,000 of this amount is actually distributed to him. The $25,000 taxable income increases his basis to $125,000, and the $10,000 distribution decreases it to $115,000.

No gain or loss is recognized by a partnership on a distribution of property to a partner, including money (Code Sec. 731(b); Reg. § 1.731-1(b)).[159] However, a partnership may have to recognize gain or loss on the distribution of unrealized receivables or substantially appreciated inventory items that are treated as a sale or exchange of property between the partnership and the distributee partner (¶ 436).

A partner recognizes gain on the distribution of property from the partnership, but only to the extent any money or marketable securities received exceeds his or her basis in the partnership immediately before the distribution (Code Sec. 731(a)(1) and (c)).[160] This rule applies both to current distributions and distributions in liquidation of a partner's entire interest in the partnership. If only partnership property is received by the partner, then no gain is recognized except to the extent provided for payments to retiring partners (¶ 438) and unrealized receivables and inventory (¶ 436). The partner's basis in any property received is equal to his or her partnership interest, less the amount of money and marketable securities received (¶ 456).

Example 2: Partner A purchases a partnership interest for $100,000. During the first year, A receives a cash distribution of $100,000 and a distribution of property with a fair market value of $30,000. He recognizes no gain on the distributions since the amount of money distributed does not exceed A's basis for his partnership interest ($100,000). If he had received a cash distribution of $130,000, a $30,000 gain would have been recognized.

No loss is recognized by a partner on the distribution of property from the partnership, except in liquidation of the partner's entire interest in the partnership, and then only if the distribution is limited to money, unrealized receivables, and inventory (¶ 435). The loss is equal to the excess of the partner's basis in the partnership interest over the amount of money received, plus the basis of the distributed receivables and inventory (Code Sec. 731(a)(2)).[161]

Example 3: A partner whose basis for his partnership interest is $100,000 retires from the partnership, receiving $50,000 in cash, and inventory items having a basis to the partnership of $30,000. The taxpayer has a capital loss of $20,000.

A distribution of property encumbered by a liability may cause a partner's share of partnership liabilities to decrease, resulting in a deemed distribution of money to that partner (¶ 447). For instance, if a partner receives a distribution of property subject to a secured liability, the liability becomes a personal liability of the distributee partner, and there is a decrease in the liabilities of all other partners who had been allocated a share of the liability. These partners must decrease the bases in their partnership interests in the amount of their deemed distributions (but not below zero), and any amounts deemed distributed in excess of their respective bases are taxable as capital gain.

The nonrecognition rules of Code Sec. 731 may not apply if, within a short period before or after property is contributed to a partnership, there is a distribution of either: (1) other partnership property to the contributing partner, or (2) the contributed property to another partner (Code Sec. 707(a)(2)(B); Reg. § 1.731-1(c)(3)).[162] If the distribution is made in order to effect an exchange of property between the partnership and a partner, or between two or more partners, then the transaction is treated as an

References are to Standard Federal Tax Reports; Tax Research Consultant; and Practical Tax Explanations.

[159] ¶ 25,320, ¶ 25,321; PART: 33,000; PART: 36,000; § 30,530.05

[160] ¶ 25,320; PART: 36,102; § 30,515.10

[161] ¶ 25,320; PART: 36,104.05; § 30,515.15

[162] ¶ 25,180, ¶ 25,321; PART: 27,058; § 30,595.05

exchange and the disguised sale rules (¶ 432) may apply. There is a presumption that distributions made within two years of a contribution are made as part of a sale arrangement (Reg. § 1.707-3(c)).[163] The presumption can be rebutted if the facts and circumstances clearly establish that there is no sale (Reg. § 1.707-4).[164]

A partner who contributes property to a partnership may have to recognize gain or loss if the contributed property is distributed by the partnership to another partner within seven years (¶ 454).

454. Partnership Distribution of Contributed Property. A partner who contributes property to a partnership may have to recognize gain or loss if the contributed property is distributed by the partnership to another partner within seven years (Code Sec. 704(c)).[165] The gain or loss recognized under this rule is limited to the difference between the property's tax basis and its fair market value at the time of contribution. Upon distribution of the property within the seven-year period, the precontributed gain or loss recognized is equal to the amount that would have been allocated to the contributing partner had the partnership sold the property rather than distributed it to a partner. Appropriate adjustments must be made to the basis of the contributing partner's partnership interest and to the basis of the distributed property to reflect any gain or loss recognized (¶ 445 and ¶ 456).

The recognition rule does not apply if the property is distributed to the contributing partner (or its successor). Also, the rule does not apply with respect to certain distributions made as part of an exchange of like-kind property.

A similar rule may cause a partner contributing appreciated property to recognize precontribution gain if the partner receives a distribution of other partnership property (except money or marketable securities) within a seven-year period (Code Sec. 737(b)).[166] Precontribution gain must be recognized to the extent that it exceeds the partner's basis for his or her partnership interest at the time the distribution is received.

456. Basis of Property Distributed to Partner. The basis of property received in a distribution from a partnership other than in liquidation of a partner's interest is ordinarily the same as the basis in the hands of the partnership immediately prior to distribution (Code Sec. 732(a)).[167] In no case may the basis of property in the hands of the partner exceed the basis of his or her partnership interest reduced by the amount of money distributed to the partner in the same transaction.

> **Example 1:** A partner has a basis of $100,000 for his partnership interest. He receives a nonliquidating distribution of $40,000 in cash and property with a basis to the partnership of $80,000. The basis to the partner of the distributed property is $60,000 ($100,000 minus $40,000). The partnership can recover the $20,000 difference by making the election to adjust the basis of its remaining assets to take up the unused basis (¶ 459).

The basis of property distributed *in liquidation* of a partner's interest is the basis of the distributee's partnership interest less any money received in the same transaction (Code Sec. 732(b)).[168]

A distributee partner's basis adjustment is allocated among distributed assets, first to unrealized receivables and inventory items in an amount equal to the partnership's basis in each property (Code Sec. 732(c)).[169] For this purpose, unrealized receivables includes any property the sale of which would create ordinary income (Code Sec. 751(c)).[170] For example, this would include depreciation-recapture property. However, the amount of unrealized receivables is limited to that amount that would be treated as ordinary income if the property were sold at fair market value.

References are to Standard Federal Tax Reports; Tax Research Consultant; and Practical Tax Explanations.

[163] ¶ 25,181B; PART: 27,058.05; § 30,715.15

[164] ¶ 25,181C; PART: 27,058.05; § 30,715.05

[165] ¶ 25,120; PART: 33,156; § 30,590.05

[166] ¶ 25,425; PART: 33,154; § 30,595.05

[167] ¶ 25,340; PART: 33,162; § 30,510.30

[168] ¶ 25,340; PART: 36,150; § 30,510.30

[169] ¶ 25,340; PART: 33,162.15; § 30,510.35

[170] ¶ 25,500; PART: 42,106; § 30,540.15

Basis is allocated first to the extent of each distributed property's adjusted basis to the partnership. Any remaining basis adjustment that is an increase is allocated among properties with unrealized appreciation in proportion to their respective amounts of unrealized appreciation (to the extent of each property's appreciation) and then in proportion to their respective fair market values.

Example 2: A partnership has two assets, a tractor and a steam shovel. Both assets are distributed to a partner whose adjusted basis in his partnership interest is $550,000. The tractor has a basis to the partnership of $50,000 and a fair market value of $400,000. The steam shovel has a basis to the partnership of $100,000 and a fair market value of $100,000. Basis is first allocated to the tractor in the amount of $50,000 and to the steam shovel in the amount of $100,000 (their adjusted bases to the partnership). The remaining basis adjustment is an increase of $400,000 (the partner's $550,000 basis minus the partnership's total basis of $150,000 in the distributed assets). Basis is then allocated to the tractor in the amount of $350,000, its unrealized appreciation, with no allocation to the steam shovel attributable to unrealized appreciation because its fair market value equals the partnership's adjusted basis. The remaining basis adjustment of $50,000 is allocated in the ratio of the assets' fair market values, which are $40,000 to the tractor (for a total basis of $440,000) and $10,000 to the steam shovel (for a total basis of $110,000).

If the remaining basis adjustment is a decrease, it is allocated among properties with unrealized depreciation in proportion to their respective amounts of unrealized depreciation (to the extent of each property's depreciation), and then in proportion to their respective adjusted bases, taking into account the adjustments already made. Accordingly, a partner's substituted basis in distributed partnership property is allocated among multiple properties based on the fair market value of the distributed properties.

Optional Basis Adjustments. If a partner has acquired his or her partnership interest (1) by purchase from a former partner or another partner, or (2) from a deceased partner, then the partner can elect to have a special basis adjustment for property (other than money) received in a distribution from the partnership within two years after the partnership interest was acquired (Code Sec. 732(d)).[171] This can be done if the partnership has not made an election to have the special basis adjustment apply to its assets. The partner's election accomplishes substantially the same result as if the partnership had made the election. The special basis adjustment is the difference between the amount paid for the partnership interest and the partner's share of the adjusted basis of partnership assets.

The special basis adjustment applies to property received in current distributions as well as to distributions in complete liquidation of the partner's interest. If the partner makes the election when a distribution of depreciable or depletable property is received, the special basis adjustment is not diminished by any depletion or depreciation on that portion of the basis of partnership property that arises from the special basis adjustment (Reg. § 1.732-1(d)(1)(iv)). Depletion or depreciation on that portion for the period before distribution is allowed or allowable only if the partnership made the election.

If a transferee-partner wishes to make the election, it must be made on his or her tax return for the year of the distribution if the distribution includes any property subject to depreciation, depletion, or amortization. If the distribution does not include any such property, the election may be made with the return for any tax year not later than the first tax year in which the basis of the distributed property is pertinent in determining income tax.

459. Optional Adjustment to Basis of Partnership Assets. If the basis of distributed assets in the hands of the distributee partner is less than the basis of the assets in the hands of the partnership (¶ 458), there may be an "unused" basis. The partnership may elect to adjust the basis of its remaining assets to take up this unused basis (¶ 470) (Code Secs. 734, 754, and 755).[172]

References are to Standard Federal Tax Reports; Tax Research Consultant; and Practical Tax Explanations.

[171] ¶ 25,340; PART: 45,100; § 30,520.05

[172] ¶ 25,380, ¶ 25,560, ¶ 25,580; PART: 45,050; § 30,805.05

If gain is recognized by a partner because of a distribution of money (¶ 453), a similar increase in the partnership's basis of its remaining assets may be made. If the election is made, the partnership may have to decrease the basis of its remaining assets. The decrease would be required for the excess of the basis of distributed assets to the partner over the basis that the partnership had for those assets, in the event of a distribution in liquidation of a partner's interest. Decrease would also be required to the extent that any distribution to a partner resulted in loss to the partner. Loss results to the partner only if the distribution terminates the partner's interest and generally consists only of money, unrealized receivables, and inventories.

Example: An equal three-person partnership has the following assets:

	Partnership's Basis	*Fair Market Value*
Cash	$120,000	$120,000
Land	60,000	120,000
Securities	90,000	120,000
Total	$270,000	$360,000

If a partner retires and the partnership pays him $120,000 for the fair market value of his partnership interest, the partnership is really distributing $40,000 as his pro rata share of the partnership's cash and paying him $80,000 for his ⅓ interest in the land and securities. However, the retiring partner's share of the partnership's basis for these properties totals only $50,000. Therefore, the partnership, if it wishes to reflect the $30,000 excess cost, may elect to adjust the basis of the land and securities.

A partnership is barred from increasing the adjusted basis of remaining property following a distribution of an interest in another partnership if the other partnership has not made a consistent Code Sec. 754 election. In other words, tiered partnerships must make consistent elections.

The allocation of any increase or decrease in basis is made among the various partnership assets or categories of assets (Code Sec. 755).[173] These rules contemplate generally that the allocation will be made first to like-kind assets and will reduce the difference between fair market value and basis of each asset adjusted.

No allocation of basis decrease may be made to stock of a corporate partner. The basis decrease must be allocated to other partnership property. The partnership recognizes gain to the extent the decrease in basis exceeds the basis of the other partnership assets.

462. Character of Gain or Loss on Disposition of Distributed Property. A partner recognizes ordinary gain or loss on the disposition of unrealized receivables or inventory items distributed by the partnership (¶ 436), regardless of whether the property has substantially appreciated in value (Code Sec. 735; Reg. § 1.735-1).[174] In the case of inventory items, this rule applies only if the sale takes place within five years of the date of distribution. If the sale takes place after the five-year period, gain may be treated as capital gain if the assets are capital assets in the hands of the partner at that time.

If a partner disposes of distributed unrealized receivables or inventory items in a nonrecognition transaction (or series of transactions), these rules apply to treat gain or loss on the substituted basis property as ordinary income or loss, except in the case of stock in a C corporation received in a Code Sec. 351 exchange. The House Committee Report to the Deficit Reduction Act of 1984 (P.L. 98-369) states that it is intended that the basis-tainting rules regarding distributed property apply only for the period during which the underlying rules as to character of gain or loss under Code Sec. 735 would apply if the property were not disposed of in a nonrecognition transaction. For example, if an inventory item was distributed by the partnership, and the partner subsequently disposed of it in a nonrecognition transaction, ordinary income treatment would apply to

References are to Standard Federal Tax Reports; Tax Research Consultant; and Practical Tax Explanations.

[173] ¶ 25,580; PART: 45,150; § 30,520.05

[174] ¶ 25,400, ¶ 25,401; PART: 33,166.05, PART: 36,202; § 30,535.05

any substitute basis property only for the duration of the five-year period beginning on the date of the original distribution.

467. Adjustment of Basis on Sale of Partnership Interest. The transfer of a partnership interest by a partner generally does not affect the basis of partnership assets. However, the partnership may elect to adjust the basis of partnership assets to reflect the difference between the partner's basis for his or her partnership interest (generally, the purchase price) and his or her proportionate share of the adjusted basis of all partnership property (his or her share of the partnership's adjusted basis in the partnership property). The election applies only to the transferee partner and applies where there is a transfer of an interest in a partnership by sale or exchange or upon the death of a partner, but not upon the contribution of property (including money) to the partnership (Code Sec. 743; Reg. § 1.743-1(a)).[175]

Basis adjustments must be made to undistributed partnership property any time there is a transfer of a partnership interest and immediately after the transfer the partnership has a substantial built-in loss (more than $250,000), whether or not the partnership has a Code Sec. 754 election in effect (Code Sec. 743(a) and (d)).[176]

The amount of the increase or decrease is an adjustment affecting the transferee partner only (Code Sec. 743(b)).[177] In addition, a partner's proportionate share of the adjusted basis of partnership property is determined in accordance with his or her interest in partnership capital. Where, however, an agreement on contributed property is in effect, the agreement must be taken into account in determining a partner's proportionate share.

A Code Sec. 743 basis adjustment is mandatory in the case of a transferred partnership interest with a substantial built-in loss. A substantial built-in loss exists if the partnership's adjusted basis in the property is more than $250,000 over the fair market value. An electing investment partnership is excepted from this rule. It will not be treated as having a substantial built-in loss; therefore, it is not required to make basis adjustments to partnership property (Code Sec. 743(e)(1)).[178]

The basis adjustment must be allocated among the partnership assets or categories of assets (¶ 459).

470. Election for Partnership Basis Adjustment. A partnership makes a basis adjustment election (¶ 459 and ¶ 467) by filing a statement, signed by a partner, with its partnership return for the first year to be covered by the election (Reg. § 1.754-1).[179] The election applies to all property distributions and transfers of partnership interests taking place in the year of the election and in all later partnership tax years until revoked. An automatic extension of 12 months from the original deadline for making the basis adjustment election is generally available, provided the taxpayer takes corrective action within that 12-month extension period (Reg. § 301.9100-2).[180]

Family Partnerships

474. Family Partnerships. The family partnership is a common device for splitting income among family members and having more income taxed in the lower tax brackets. A person is recognized as a partner for income tax purposes if he or she owns a capital interest in a partnership in which capital is a material income-producing factor, whether or not the partnership interest was acquired by gift from another person (Code Sec. 761(b), as amended by the Bipartisan Budget Act of 2015 (P.L. 114-74); Reg. § 1.704-1(e)).[181] If capital is *not* a material income-producing factor, a partnership resulting from a gift of an interest might be disregarded as an invalid attempt to assign income.

References are to Standard Federal Tax Reports; Tax Research Consultant; and Practical Tax Explanations.

[175] ¶ 25,480, ¶ 25,481; PART: 45,100; § 30,810

[176] ¶ 25,480; PART: 45,112; § 30,810

[177] ¶ 25,480; PART: 45,100; § 30,810

[178] ¶ 25,480; PART: 45,112; § 30,810

[179] ¶ 25,561; PART: 45,250; § 30,825

[180] ¶ 44,014AE; PART: 45,256; § 30,825

[181] ¶ 25,600, ¶ 25,121; PART: 54,100; § 31,301

In any event, if all the income is attributable to the personal efforts of the donor, the donor is taxed on the entire income. In addition, the donee's distributive share of income must be proportionate to his or her capital interest, and his or her control over the partnership must be consistent with his or her status as partner. Family limited partnerships are also used for estate planning purposes (¶ 2903).

Organization, Syndication, Start-Up Costs

477. Partnership Syndication and Organization Fees. No deduction is generally allowed a partnership or a partner for the costs of organizing a partnership (organization fees) or of selling partnership interests (syndication fees) (with certain exceptions) (¶ 481) (Code Sec. 709; Reg. § 1.709-1).[182] Guaranteed payments (¶ 421) made to partners for their services in organizing a partnership are capital expenditures and are not deductible by the partnership.

A partnership may elect to deduct up to $5,000 in organizational expenses, generally in the same manner as start-up expenditures (¶ 481) (Code Sec. 709(b)).[183] The $5,000 amount is reduced (but not below zero) by the amount by which the organizational expenditures exceed $50,000. The remainder of the organizational expenditures may be amortized ratably over a 180-month period, beginning with the month the active trade or business begins. The partnership is deemed to have made an election to deduct and amortize such expenses for the tax year in which the active trade or business to which the expenditures relate begins. A partnership may choose to forgo the deemed election by affirmatively electing to capitalize its organizational expenditures on a timely filed federal income tax return, including extensions, for the tax year in which begins the active trade or business to which the expenditures relate (Reg. § 1.709-1(b)(2)).[184]

A new partnership formed after a technical termination (¶ 410) must continue amortizing organizational expenses over the remainder of the amortization period originally established by the terminating partnership (Reg. § 1.708-1(b)(6)).[185]

481. Partnership Start-Up Expenditures. Taxpayers that pay or incur start-up costs for a trade or business and who subsequently enter the trade or business can elect to expense up to $5,000 of the costs (¶ 904). The $5,000 deduction amount is reduced dollar for dollar when the start-up expenses exceed $50,000. The balance of start-up expenses (if any) are amortized over a period of not less than 180 months, starting with the month in which the business begins (Code Sec. 195).[186] The election must be made on Form 4562 no later than the date (including extensions) for filing the return for the tax year in which the business begins or is acquired (Reg. § 1.195-1(b)).[187] Taxpayers that do not make the election must capitalize the expenses.

In the case of start-up expenses incurred by the partnership itself and for which an election is made, the amortization deduction is taken into account in computing partnership income. In the case of qualifying investigatory expenses incurred in connection with acquiring a partnership interest, the deduction is taken by the partner who has incurred the expenses. A new partnership formed after a technical termination (¶ 410) must continue amortizing start-up expenses over the remainder of the amortization period originally established by the terminating partnership (Reg. § 1.708-1(b)(6)).[188]

Electing Large Partnerships

482. Simplified Reporting for Electing Large Partnerships. A partnership with 100 or more members in the preceding tax year may elect large partnership status for returns filed for tax years beginning before January 1, 2018. Partnerships making this election combine most items of partnership income, deduction, credit, and loss at the

References are to Standard Federal Tax Reports; Tax Research Consultant; and Practical Tax Explanations.

[182] ¶ 25,220, ¶ 25,221C; PART: 18,200; § 9,210.15

[183] ¶ 25,220; PART: 18,200; § 9,210.15

[184] ¶ 25,221C; PART: 18,206.05; § 9,215

[185] ¶ 25,201; PART: 51,256.45; § 31,020.05

[186] ¶ 12,370; PART: 18,104.10; § 9,205.05

[187] ¶ 12,370F; DEPR: 21,406

[188] ¶ 25,201; PART: 51,256.45; § 31,020.05

partnership level, and pass through net amounts to the partners (Code Secs. 771—777).[189] Special modifications apply to partnerships engaged in oil and gas activities, and to partnerships with residual interests in real estate mortgage investment conduits (REMICs). Service partnerships and commodity pools generally are unable to elect large partnership treatment. Electing large partnerships are subject to audit and procedural rules separate from the general TEFRA audit rules.

The taxable income of an electing large partnership for returns filed for tax years beginning before January 1, 2018, is computed in the same manner as for an individual, except that certain items are separately stated, and specified modifications apply (Code Sec. 773).[190] For example, miscellaneous itemized deductions are not separately reported to the partners, and in place of the two-percent floor, 70 percent of the itemized deductions are disallowed at the partnership level. The remaining 30 percent is allowed at the partnership level in determining the large partnership's taxable income and is not subject to the two-percent floor at the partner level. Tax credits other than the low-income housing credit, the rehabilitation credit, and the credit for producing fuel from nonconventional sources are reported as a single item. Credit recapture also is recognized at the partnership level.

For electing large partnerships, the netting of capital gains and losses for returns filed for tax years beginning before January 1, 2018, occurs at the partnership level (Code Sec. 773).[191] Passive activity items are separated from capital gains stemming from partnership portfolio income. Each partner separately takes into account the partner's distributive shares of net capital gain or net capital loss for passive activity and portfolio items. Any partnership gains and losses under Code Sec. 1231 (¶ 1747) are netted at the partnership level. Net gain is treated as long-term capital gain, and any net loss is treated as ordinary loss and consolidated with the partnership's other taxable income.

The TEFRA audit rules that normally apply to partnerships for returns filed for partnership tax years beginning before January 1, 2018, do not apply to electing large partnerships (¶ 415). An electing large partnership, like other partnerships, appoints a representative to handle IRS matters (Code Sec. 6255(b)).[192] Unlike under the TEFRA rules, however, the representative does not have to be a partner. In addition, only the partnership, and not the individual partners, receives notice of partnership adjustments (Code Sec. 6245(b)).[193] Only the partnership has the right to appeal the adjustment (Code Sec. 6247(a)).[194] After a partnership-level adjustment, prior-year partners and prior tax years generally are not affected. Instead, the adjustments generally are passed through to current partners. However, prior years can be affected if there has been a partnership dissolution or a finding that the shares of a distribution to partners were erroneous.

The electing large partnerships rules, as well as the TEFRA audit rules, are repealed for returns filed for partnership tax years beginning after December 31, 2017, and a single set of rules will apply for partnership audits and adjustments (Act Sec. 1101 of the Bipartisan Budget Act of 2015 (P.L. 114-74)). A partnership may elect to apply the new rules for returns filed for partnership tax years beginning after November 2, 2015. See ¶ 413 for a discussion of the post-2017 partnership audit rules as well as the election to apply those rules earlier.

References are to Standard Federal Tax Reports; Tax Research Consultant; and Practical Tax Explanations.

[189] ¶ 25,604—¶ 25,628; PART: 3,450

[190] ¶ 25,612; PART: 18,452, PART: 18,454

[191] ¶ 25,612; PART: 18,452, PART: 18,454

[192] ¶ 37,949Q; PART: 60,652

[193] ¶ 37,937; PART: 60,660

[194] ¶ 37,949D; PART: 60,662

Chapter 5

TRUSTS □ ESTATES

	Par.
Estates and Trusts as Taxable Entities	501
Fiduciary Return and Payment of Tax	510
Taxation of Estates and Trusts	514
Income Distribution Deduction	542
Taxation of Beneficiaries	554
Grantor Trusts	571
Other Special Trusts	590

Estates and Trusts as Taxable Entities

501. Trust, Estate, and Fiduciary Defined. A trust is a separate taxable entity for federal income tax purposes. A trust usually involves an arrangement created either by a will upon the creator's death or by a trust instrument that may take effect during the creator's life (Reg. § 301.7701-4(a)).[1] Under either arrangement, a trustee takes title to the property in order to protect or conserve it for beneficiaries. Usually, the beneficiaries merely accept the trust's benefits. However, even if the beneficiaries are the persons who planned or created it, the trust will still be recognized as a separate taxable entity if its purpose is to vest the trustee with the responsibility to protect and preserve property on behalf of beneficiaries who cannot share in the discharge of this responsibility. Federal tax law provides specific guidelines for what constitutes a business trust or investment trust (¶ 502) and a liquidating trust (¶ 503). Some types of trusts are governed by special tax rules, such as grantor trusts (¶ 571), charitable trusts (¶ 590), and common trust funds (¶ 595).

Decedents' estates are also considered separate taxable entities for income tax purposes during the period of administration (¶ 507). Other types of estates are discussed at ¶ 504—¶ 506.

Trustees, executors, and certain receivers are considered fiduciaries. A fiduciary is a person who occupies a position of special confidence toward another, who holds in trust property in which another person has the beneficial title or interest, or who receives and controls income of another (Reg. § 301.7701-6).[2] However, a person who is an agent of another person is not necessarily a fiduciary for federal income tax purposes, even though a fiduciary relationship may be said to exist for state law purposes. For example, when a person receives income as an agent, intermediary debtor, or conduit, and the income is paid over to another, the agent is not considered a fiduciary for tax purposes. The fiduciary is responsible for computing the entity's income tax liability and paying the resulting tax (¶ 510), and may be personally liable for any tax delinquencies if others are paid in preference to the IRS (¶ 512).

Small Business Trusts. An electing small business trust (ESBT) is a special kind of trust permitted to be a shareholder in an S corporation. An ESBT has no beneficiaries other than individuals or estates eligible to be S corporation shareholders, except that charitable organizations may hold contingent remainder interests. The portion of any ESBT that consists of stock in one or more S corporations is treated as a separate trust (¶ 304 and ¶ 516).

Qualified Domestic Trusts. A qualified domestic trust (QDOT) is a trust that meets certain requirements and is subject to a special estate tax. Property that is transferred

References are to Standard Federal Tax Reports; Tax Research Consultant; and Practical Tax Explanations.

[1] ¶ 43,090; ESTTRST: 3,050; § 32,005.05

[2] ¶ 43,094; ESTTRST: 100; § 32,030.05

from a citizen decedent to a nonresident alien spouse will not qualify for the usual estate tax marital deduction unless it is transferred from the decedent to a QDOT (¶ 2926).

Foreign Trusts and Estates. A foreign trust is a trust in which (1) no court within the United States can exercise primary supervision over the trust's administration (court test), and (2) no U.S. person has the authority to control all of the trust's substantial decisions (control test). A foreign estate is an estate whose income, from non-U.S. sources which is not effectively connected with the conduct of a trade or business in the United States (¶ 2431), is not includible in gross income for federal income tax purposes (Code Sec. 7701(a)(30) and (31); Reg. § 301.7701-7).[3]

502. Business and Investment Trusts. A business or commercial trust is a trust created as a means of carrying on a profit-making business, usually using capital or property supplied by the beneficiaries (Reg. § 301.7701-4(b)).[4] The trustees or other designated persons are, in effect, managers of the undertaking, whether appointed or controlled by the beneficiaries. This arrangement is treated for federal tax purposes as an association which may be taxed as a corporation or partnership, and is distinguishable from the type of trust discussed at ¶ 501. The fact that the trust property is not supplied by beneficiaries is not sufficient in itself to avoid the trust being classified and taxed as a business entity.

An investment trust may also be taxed as an association, rather than a trust, if there is a power under the trust agreement to vary the investment of the certificate holders (Reg. § 301.7701-4(c)).[5] However, if this power is lacking, the arrangement is taxed as a trust. Unit investment trusts, as defined in the Investment Company Act of 1940, that are set up to hold mutual fund shares for investors are also not taxed as trusts. Instead, their income is taxed directly to the investors (Reg. § 1.851-7).[6]

503. Liquidating Trusts. A liquidating trust formed for the primary purpose of liquidating and distributing the assets transferred to it is taxed as a trust, and not as an association, despite the possibility of profit (Reg. § 301.7701-4(d)).[7] All activities of the trust must be reasonably necessary for, and consistent with, accomplishing the primary purpose of liquidation and distribution. If the liquidation is unreasonably prolonged, or if the liquidation purpose becomes so obscured by business activities that the declared purpose of liquidation can be said to have been lost or abandoned, the arrangement is no longer a liquidating trust.

504. Estate of Minor, Incompetent, or Person Under a Disability. The estate of an infant, incompetent person, or other person under a disability is not a taxable entity separate from the person for whom the fiduciary (¶ 501) is acting (Reg. § 1.641(b)-2(b)).[8] Therefore, the estate of such a person is not required to file a fiduciary return on Form 1041.

A guardian is generally required to file a tax return as an agent for a minor or legally disabled person if the individual would otherwise be required to file a return (Code Sec. 6012(b)(2); Reg. § 1.6012-3(b)(3)).[9] However, a minor can file a return for himself or herself or have someone else file it, relieving the guardian of this obligation. For the tax year during which an incompetent person is declared competent and the fiduciary is discharged, the former incompetent person must file the tax return. An agent filing a return for another person should file Form 2848, granting power of attorney, with the taxpayer's return (Reg. § 1.6012-1(a)(5)).[10] If an agent is used, both the agent and the taxpayer for whom the return is made may be liable for penalties for erroneous, false, or fraudulent returns. One spouse may execute a valid return on behalf

References are to Standard Federal Tax Reports; Tax Research Consultant; and Practical Tax Explanations.

[3] ¶ 43,080, ¶ 43,097; INTL: 3,552.15; § 32,190, § 32,610.30

[4] ¶ 43,090; ESTTRST: 3,102; § 30,005.35

[5] ¶ 43,090; ESTTRST: 3,154; § 30,005.35

[6] ¶ 26,407; RIC: 3,150; § 45,430.05

[7] ¶ 43,090; ESTTRST: 3,158; § 32,125

[8] ¶ 24,265; FILEIND: 18,064; § 39,030.25

[9] ¶ 35,142, ¶ 35,146; FILEIND: 18,064; § 1,305.25, § 39,020.05

[10] ¶ 35,143; FILEBUS: 12,102; § 41,205.05

of his or her mentally incompetent or disabled spouse prior to appointment of a legal guardian without a formal power of attorney (Rev. Rul. 56-22).[11]

505. Bankruptcy Estate of Individual Debtor. Property held by a trustee in bankruptcy for an individual under Chapter 7 (liquidation) or Chapter 11 (business reorganization) of the Bankruptcy Code is considered the estate of the debtor (Code Sec. 1398).[12] The estate is treated as a separate taxable entity unless the bankruptcy case is dismissed. The fiduciary of a Chapter 7 or Chapter 11 bankruptcy estate is obligated to file the estate's return. If the bankruptcy plan creates a liquidating trust, the fiduciary must file the trust's return (Code Sec. 6012(b)(4)).[13] The bankruptcy trustee must file a Form 1041 for the bankruptcy estate for any tax year in which the estate in bankruptcy has gross income that equals or exceeds the sum of the personal exemption amount (¶ 133), plus the basic standard deduction for married persons filing separately (¶ 126) for the year ($10,350 for 2016; $10,400 for 2017) (Code Sec. 6012(a)(8)). The tax year for which the fiduciary files a return begins on the date of the bankruptcy petition filing. The return may be for a calendar year or a fiscal year. A trustee in bankruptcy has no authority to file a return on Form 1040 for a bankrupt individual; the individual must file an individual return.

Taxable income for bankruptcy estates is computed in the same manner as for individuals, including the right to a personal exemption, but the tax rates for married persons filing separately apply (¶ 15) (Code Sec. 1398(c); Instructions to Form 1041). If a bankruptcy estate does not itemize deductions, it can claim the standard deduction available for a married person filing separately (¶ 126).

A separate taxable entity is not created when a case is brought under Chapter 13 of the Bankruptcy Code, which involves adjustment of debts of an individual with regular income. A separate taxable entity also is not created when an individual is in receivership (Reg. § 1.641(b)-2(b)).[14]

506. Bankruptcy Estate of Partnership or Corporate Debtor. The commencement of bankruptcy proceedings for a partnership or corporation does not create a separate taxable entity (Code Sec. 1399).[15] Thus, there is no obligation imposed upon the bankruptcy trustee to file a Form 1041 on behalf of the estate. However, a receiver, trustee in dissolution, trustee in bankruptcy, or assignee who, by order of a court, has possession of or holds title to all or substantially all the property or business of a corporation must file the income tax return for the corporation on Form 1120 (Reg. § 1.6012-3(b)(4)).[16] The receiver, trustee, or assignee must file the return whether or not it is operating the property or business of the corporation. A receiver in charge of only *a small part* of the property of a corporation, such as a receiver in mortgage foreclosure proceedings, need not file the return. Bankrupt partnerships must file their returns on Form 1065.

507. Termination of Estates and Trusts. An estate is recognized as a taxable entity only during the period of administration or settlement (i.e., the period actually required by the executor or administrator to perform the ordinary duties of administration, such as collection of assets, payment of debts and legacies, etc.) (Reg. § 1.641(b)-3(a)).[17] This is true whether the period is longer or shorter than that specified under local law for estate settlement. However, estate administration may not be unduly prolonged. For federal tax purposes, the estate is considered terminated after the expiration of a reasonable period for the performance of administration duties, or when all estate assets have been distributed except for a reasonable amount set aside in good faith for the payment of contingent liabilities and expenses. If the estate has joined in making a valid election to treat a qualified revocable trust as part of the estate (¶ 516), then it does not terminate prior to the end of the election period.

References are to Standard Federal Tax Reports; Tax Research Consultant; and Practical Tax Explanations.

[11] ¶ 35,150.734; FILEIND: 18,064; § 39,020.05

[12] ¶ 32,410; INDIV: 66,050, INDIV: 66,066

[13] ¶ 35,142; INDIV: 66,066.05; § 32,030.05

[14] ¶ 24,265; INDIV: 66,052.10

[15] ¶ 32,420; INDIV: 66,150

[16] ¶ 35,146; FILEBUS: 3,068

[17] ¶ 24,266; ESTTRST: 9,054, ACCTNG: 24,256.10; § 32,005.10, § 38,145.20

A trust is recognized as a taxable entity until the trust property has been distributed to successors, plus a reasonable time after this event as is necessary for the trustee to complete trust administration (Reg. § 1.641(b)-3(b)).[18] A trust is also considered terminated when all the assets have been distributed except for a reasonable amount set aside in good faith to pay contingent liabilities and expenses (other than a claim by a beneficiary in that capacity).

Once an estate or trust is considered terminated for tax purposes, its gross income, deductions, and credits subsequent to termination are considered to be the gross income, deductions, and credits of the persons who succeed to the property (Reg. § 1.641(b)-3(d)).

Fiduciary Return and Payment of Tax

510. Return of Estate or Trust by Fiduciary. A fiduciary must file a return on Form 1041 for an estate or trust if: (1) the estate has gross income of $600 or more for the tax year; (2) the trust (other than a trust exempt under Code Sec. 501(a)) has for the tax year any taxable income, or gross income of $600 or more regardless of the amount of taxable income; (3) any beneficiary of the estate or trust is a nonresident alien (unless the trust is exempt under Code Sec. 501(a)); or (4) an individual's bankruptcy estate under Chapter 7 or Chapter 11 of the Bankruptcy Code has gross income equal to or greater than the sum of the personal exemption amount, plus the basic standard deduction amount for married individuals filing separately (¶ 505) (Code Sec. 6012(a); Reg. § 1.6012-3).[19] A foreign estate or foreign trust (¶ 501) generally must file Form 1040NR (Instructions to Form 1041).

When there is more than one fiduciary, the return can be filed by any one of them. However, when an estate has both domiciliary and ancillary representatives, each representative must file a return (Reg. § 1.6012-3(a)(1) and (3)). A trustee of two or more trusts must file a separate return for each trust, even though the trusts were created by the same grantor for the same beneficiaries (Reg. § 1.6012-3(a)(4)). Two or more trusts may be treated as one trust under certain circumstances (¶ 515).

The return must be filed on or before the 15th day of the fourth month following the close of the tax year (Code Sec. 6072(a)).[20] For returns filed by estates, and returns filed by trusts for tax years beginning before January 1, 2016, an automatic five-month extension of time for filing the fiduciary return is available by filing Form 7004 on or before the due date for filing Form 1041, and making a proper estimate of the amount of tax due for the tax year (Reg. § 1.6081-6; Instructions to Form 7004). An automatic 5½-month extension is available for returns filed by trusts for tax years beginning after December 31, 2015 (Act Sec. 2006(b) of the Surface Transportation and Veterans Health Care Choice Improvement Act of 2015 (P.L. 114-41)).[21] The automatic extension period is six months for an individual's Chapter 7 or 11 bankruptcy estate (¶ 505) or for a qualified funeral trust (¶ 575). The automatic extension does not extend the time for payment of any tax due on the return. In addition, the extension to file does not extend the time for a beneficiary of the estate or trust to file its income tax return or to pay any tax on the beneficiary's return.

The fiduciary of an estate or trust need not file a copy of the will or trust instrument with the estate or trust income tax return unless requested by the IRS (Reg. § 1.6012-3(a)(2)).[22] If requested, the fiduciary should file a copy (including any amendments), accompanied by a written declaration of truth and completeness and a statement indicating the provisions of the will or trust instrument that determine the extent to which estate or trust income is taxable to the estate or trust, the beneficiaries, or the grantor.

References are to Standard Federal Tax Reports; Tax Research Consultant; and Practical Tax Explanations.

[18] ¶ 24,266; ESTTRST: 9,054, ACCTNG: 24,256.10; § 32,005.15, § 38,145.20

[19] ¶ 35,142, ¶ 35,146; IRS: 30,256.10, IRS: 66,152.05; § 32,610.05, § 39,030.10

[20] ¶ 36,720; FILEIND: 18,052.20; § 32,610.15, § 39,205.25

[21] ¶ 36,797; FILEBUS: 15,104.20; § 32,610.15, § 39,215.20

[22] ¶ 35,146; IRS: 30,256.10, IRS: 66,152.05; § 32,610.15

An estate or trust that is obligated to file an income tax return must furnish a copy of Schedule K-1 of Form 1041 to each beneficiary (1) who receives a distribution from the estate or trust for the year, or (2) to whom any item with respect to the tax year is allocated (Code Sec. 6034A).[23] This statement must contain the information required to be shown on the return and be furnished on or before the date on which the return is to be filed. In addition, a copy must be attached to Form 1041 (Instructions to Form 1041). A penalty may be assessed for each failure to file or furnish a correct information return (¶ 2816) or payee statement (¶ 2823).

Accounting Period. When filing its first return, an estate may choose the same accounting period as the decedent, or it may choose a calendar tax year or any fiscal tax year. If it chooses the decedent's accounting period, its first return will be for a short period to cover the unexpired term of the decedent's regular tax year (Code Secs. 441 and 443).[24] An exemption of $600 is allowed on a short-period return, without proration (¶ 534) (Reg. § 1.443-1(a)(2)).[25] However, if the estate gets approval from the IRS to change the accounting period, the exemption on the short-period return must be prorated (Reg. § 1.443-1(b)(1)(v)).

Trusts (other than trusts exempt from tax under Code Sec. 501 and wholly charitable trusts under Code Sec. 4947(a)) must adopt a calendar tax year (Code Sec. 644).[26] Thus, a trust must generally file Form 1041 on or before April 15 following the close of the tax year. If April 15 falls on a weekend or holiday, the due date is the next day that is not a Saturday, Sunday, or legal holiday (¶ 2549). An existing trust that is required to change its tax year must annualize any income earned in the short year. A trust must obtain IRS approval to change its annual accounting period to its required (calendar) tax year (¶ 1513).

Payment of Tax. The entire income tax liability of an estate or trust must be paid on or before the due date for its return (Code Sec. 6151).[27] In addition, estates that have been in existence for more than two years and both new and existing trusts must pay estimated tax in the same manner as individuals (¶ 511).

511. Payment of Estimated Tax by Estate or Trust. Estates and trusts are generally required to make quarterly estimated tax payments in the same manner as individuals (¶ 2682). However, estates and grantor trusts that receive the residue of a probate estate under the grantor's will are only required to make estimated tax payments for tax years that end two or more years after the decedent's death (Code Sec. 6654(l)).[28]

Estates or trusts with a short tax year must pay installments of tax on or before the 15th day of the fourth, sixth and ninth months of the tax year, and the 15th day of the first month of the following tax year (¶ 2685). The amount of each installment in a short tax year is determined by dividing the required annual payment by the number of payments required for that year (Notice 87-32).[29]

Estates and trusts generally have 45 days (rather than the 15 days allowed individuals) to compute the payments under the estimated tax annualization rules. The payment due dates are unchanged (Code Sec. 6654(l)).[30] First-time filers must file Form 1041-ES, which includes vouchers to be included with quarterly payments. After the first payment, the IRS should provide pre-printed vouchers. A fiduciary paying estimated tax for more than one trust should submit a separate Form 1041-ES and a separate check for each trust. However, a fiduciary may submit a single check for multiple trusts if a separate estimated tax voucher is submitted for each trust (Announcement 87-32).[31]

References are to Standard Federal Tax Reports; Tax Research Consultant; and Practical Tax Explanations.

[23] ¶ 35,460; ESTTRST: 100; § 32,610.20, § 39,155.35

[24] ¶ 20,302, ¶ 20,500; ACCTNG: 24,252; § 32,025, § 38,140.05, § 38,145.20

[25] ¶ 20,501; ESTTRST: 12,052; § 32,350, § 38,140.05

[26] ¶ 24,350; ACCTNG: 24,104, ACCTNG: 24,252.25; § 32,025, § 32,610.15

[27] ¶ 37,080; ESTTRST: 100, FILEBUS: 6,102; § 39,305.05

[28] ¶ 39,550; FILEIND: 21,058; § 32,615.05

[29] ¶ 39,560.82; FILEIND: 21,058; § 32,615.05

[30] ¶ 39,550; FILEIND: 21,050; § 1,410, § 32,615.05, § 40,225.10

[31] ¶ 39,560.82; FILEIND: 21,058; § 32,615.05

The trustee of a trust, or the fiduciary of an estate whose tax year is reasonably expected to be its last tax year, may elect to treat any or all of an estimated tax payment as a payment made by the beneficiary and credited toward the beneficiary's tax liability (Code Sec. 643(g)).[32] If elected, the payment is not treated as an estimated tax payment made by the estate or trust. The election is made on Form 1041-T and must be filed on or before the 65th day after the close of the tax year (March 6, 2017, for calendar year 2016).

512. Personal Liability of Fiduciary. Any fiduciary (other than a trustee acting under the Bankruptcy Code) who pays any debt due by the decedent or the estate, in whole or in part, before federal tax obligations are satisfied becomes personally liable for the tax of the estate to the extent of such payments (Reg. § 1.641(b)-2; 31 U.S.C. § 3713).[33] However, the fiduciary is not liable for amounts paid out for debts that have priority over the federal taxes due and owing on the estate, such as a decedent's funeral expenses or probate administration costs. Further, an executor or administrator who pays other debts is not personally liable unless the executor or administrator has either personal knowledge of a tax due the United States or knowledge that would put a reasonably prudent person on notice that such tax debts exist.[34] Discharge of the fiduciary does not terminate the fiduciary's personal liability for the payment of other debts of the estate without satisfying prior tax claims.

Taxation of Estates and Trusts

514. Taxation of Estates and Trusts—Introduction. An estate or trust is a separate taxable entity (¶ 501). Its entire income for its tax year generally must be reported on Form 1041, which must be filed by the fiduciary (¶ 510). If income is required to be distributed currently or is properly distributed to a beneficiary, the estate or trust is regarded as a conduit with respect to that income. It is allowed a deduction for the portion of gross income that is currently distributable to the beneficiaries or is properly paid or credited to them (¶ 542—¶ 545). The beneficiaries are generally taxed on the part of the income currently distributed, and the estate or trust is taxed on the portion that it has accumulated. The income allocated to a beneficiary retains the same character in the beneficiary's hands that it had in the hands of the estate or trust (Reg. § § 1.652(b)-1 and 1.662(b)-1).[35]

For purposes of the income taxation of estates and nongrantor trusts, the term income (without specifying gross income, taxable income, undistributed net income, or distributable net income) refers to income of the estate or trust for the tax year determined under the terms of its governing instrument and applicable local law—that is, income as it would be computed in an accounting to the court having jurisdiction over the estate or trust (Code Sec. 643(b); Reg. § 1.643(b)-1).[36] Trust provisions that depart fundamentally from concepts of income and principal are not recognized for tax purposes. However, an allocation of amounts between income and principal pursuant to applicable local law will be respected if local law provides for a reasonable apportionment between the income and remainder beneficiaries of the trust's total return for the year, including ordinary income, tax-exempt income, capital gains, and appreciation.

Income items of an estate or trust are discussed at ¶ 520—¶ 527. Ordinary deductions of an estate or trust are discussed at ¶ 528—¶ 536. The charitable contribution deduction is discussed at ¶ 537—¶ 538. The deduction for distributions to beneficiaries and the concept of distributable net income (DNI) are discussed at ¶ 542—¶ 549. The treatment of tax credits of an estate or trust is discussed at ¶ 540.

References are to Standard Federal Tax Reports; Tax Research Consultant; and Practical Tax Explanations.

[32] ¶ 24,320; ESTTRST: 27,054, FILEIND: 21,054.10; § 1,410, § 32,615.10

[33] ¶ 24,265, ¶ 40,730; IRS: 60,202; § 32,030.10, § 34,410.07, § 39,545

[34] ¶ 40,735.25; IRS: 60,206; § 32,030.10, § 34,410.07, § 39,545

[35] ¶ 24,383, ¶ 24,425; ESTTRST: 24,154, ESTTRST: 30,106; § 32,005.05, § 32,501, § 32,701

[36] ¶ 24,320, ¶ 24,329; ESTTRST: 18,050; § 32,010.10

515. Multiple Trusts. One grantor may create several trusts, and the income may be taxed separately for each trust. When there is intent to create separate trusts for multiple beneficiaries, the fact that the corpus of each trust is kept in one fund will not necessarily defeat the grantor's intent. Although it is not necessary to divide the corpus physically in order to carry out the intent of the parties, it is necessary to comply literally with the terms of the trust instrument in other respects.[37]

Two or more trusts, however, will be treated as one trust if (1) the trusts have substantially the same grantor or grantors and substantially the same primary beneficiary or beneficiaries, and (2) a principal purpose of the trusts is the avoidance of income tax (Code Sec. 643(f)).[38] A special safe-harbor provision applies to any trust that was irrevocable on March 1, 1984, except to the extent that corpus is contributed to the trust after that date.

516. Computation of Tax for Estates and Trusts. An estate or trust computes its tax liability by using the separate estate and trust income tax rate schedule at ¶ 19. The taxable income of an estate or trust for purposes of regular income tax is determined by subtracting from its gross income (¶ 520) allowable deductions (¶ 528), amounts distributable to beneficiaries (to the extent of distributable net income (DNI)) (¶ 543), and the proper exemption (¶ 534) (Code Sec. 641; Reg. § § 1.641(a)-1 and 1.641(b)-1).[39]

The alternative minimum tax (AMT) of an estate or trust is computed by determining DNI under the general rules (¶ 543), subject to further adjustments under the minimum tax rules. The AMT is computed on Part III of Schedule I, Form 1041 (¶ 1401).

Grantor trusts and employees' trusts are subject to special tax treatment (¶ 571 and ¶ 2101).

Qualified Revocable Trusts. A trustee of a qualified revocable trust (QRT) and the executor, if any, of a decedent's estate may join in an election to treat the revocable trust as part of the estate (Code Sec. 645; Reg. § 1.645-1).[40] The election allows the revocable trust to enjoy certain income tax treatment that would otherwise be accorded only to the decedent's estate, such as claiming the unlimited deduction for amounts permanently set aside for charity without first actually paying the amount (¶ 537), waiving the active participation requirement under the passive loss rules for two years after the decedent's death (¶ 1165), and qualifying for amortization of reforestation expenditures (¶ 530). A QRT is any trust or portion of a trust that, on the date of the decedent's death, is treated as owned by the decedent as grantor by reason of a power to revoke the trust (¶ 582), but without regard to powers held by the decedent's spouse (¶ 578). The election is made on Form 8855 which must be filed by the due date (including extensions) of the Form 1041 for the first tax year of the related estate or filing trust. The election period begins on the date of the decedent's death, and ends on the earlier of the day on which both the trust and related estate have distributed all of their assets, or the day before the applicable date, which is either (1) two years after the date of death, if no federal estate tax return is required, or (2) six months after the final determination of estate tax liability, if a federal estate tax return must be filed.

Electing Small Business Trust. An electing small business trust (ESBT) (¶ 501) is taxed in a different manner than other trusts (Code Sec. 641(c); Reg. § 1.641(c)-1).[41] First, the portion of the ESBT that consists of stock in one or more S corporations is treated as a separate trust for purposes of computing the income tax attributable to the S corporation stock held by the trust. This portion of the trust's income is taxed at the highest rate imposed on estates and trusts, and includes:

References are to Standard Federal Tax Reports; Tax Research Consultant; and Practical Tax Explanations.

[37] ¶ 24,267.67; ESTTRST: 3,202; § 32,185

[38] ¶ 24,320; ESTTRST: 3,204; § 32,185

[39] ¶ 24,260, ¶ 24,262, ¶ 24,264; ESTTRST: 100; § 32,005.05, § 32,010, § 32,015, § 32,020

[40] ¶ 24,355, ¶ 24,356; ESTTRST: 39,300; § 32,105.10

[41] ¶ 24,260, ¶ 24,266F; SCORP: 166.35; § 32,165

(1) the items of income, loss, deduction, or credit allocated to the trust as an S corporation shareholder;

(2) gain or loss from the sale of the S corporation stock;

(3) any state or local income taxes and administrative expenses of the trust properly allocable to the S corporation stock; and

(4) any interest expense paid or accrued on debt incurred to acquire S corporation stock.

Capital losses are allowed in computing an ESBT's income only to the extent of capital gains. Moreover, no deduction is allowed for amounts distributed to beneficiaries and, except as described above, no additional deductions or credits are allowed. Also, the ESBT's income is not included in the DNI of the trust and, therefore, is not included in the beneficiaries' income. Furthermore, no item relating to the S corporation stock is apportioned to any beneficiary. The trust's AMT exemption amount is zero. Special rules apply upon termination of all or a part of the ESBT (¶ 304).

Special rules apply for calculating the 3.8-percent net investment income tax (¶ 517) of an ESBT (Reg. § 1.1411-3(c)).[42]

Gifts from Expatriates. A domestic trust that receives property, directly or indirectly, by gift, devise, bequest, or inheritance from a covered expatriate (¶ 2412) after the date of expatriation must pay a tax equal to the value of such covered gift or bequest multiplied by the greater of the highest federal estate tax rate or the highest federal gift tax rate in effect. Similarly, a covered gift or bequest made to a foreign trust (¶ 501) is subject to the tax, but only at the time a distribution of income or principal is made to a U.S. citizen or resident from the trust that is attributable to the covered gift or bequest. A foreign trust can elect to be treated as a domestic trust for these purposes; the election can be revoked with IRS consent (¶ 2948).

517. Net Investment Income Tax of Estates and Trusts. Effective for tax years beginning after December 31, 2012, an estate or trust is liable for a 3.8-percent net investment income tax on the lesser of: (1) its undistributed net investment income for the tax year, or (2) any excess of its adjusted gross income determined under Code Sec. 67(e) (¶ 528) over the dollar amount at which the highest tax bracket for estates and trusts begins for the tax year ($12,400 for 2016; $12,500 for 2017; ¶ 19) (Code Sec. 1411(a)(2); Reg. § 1.1411-3).[43] An estate or trust's undistributed net investment income is its net investment income (¶ 129) reduced by distributions of net investment income to beneficiaries, and by deductions for amounts of net investment income paid or permanently set aside for a charitable purpose (¶ 537) (Reg. § 1.1411-3(e)).

The tax does not apply to several types of trusts, including (1) trusts that are exempt from federal income taxes; (2) trusts whose unexpired interests are devoted to one or more charitable purposes described in Code Sec. 170(c)(2)(B); (3) grantor trusts (¶ 571); (4) Electing Alaska Native Settlement Trusts; (5) cemetery perpetual care funds under Code Sec. 642(i); and (6) any other trust, fund, or account that is statutorily exempt from federal income tax (Code Sec. 1411(e)(2); Reg. § 1.1411-3(b)). The tax applies to individual debtors' Chapter 7 and Chapter 11 bankruptcy estates (¶ 505). The tax does not apply to foreign trusts or foreign estates (¶ 501), but does apply to distributions of current year income by foreign trusts or foreign estates to their U.S. beneficiaries (Reg. § 1.1411-3(e)(3)).

520. Gross Income of Estates and Trusts. The gross income of an estate or trust is generally determined in the same manner as that of an individual (Code Sec. 641(b); Reg. § 1.641(a)-2).[44] It includes all items of income received during the tax year, including:

References are to Standard Federal Tax Reports; Tax Research Consultant; and Practical Tax Explanations.

[42] ¶ 32,603L; ESTTRST: 12,256.20

[43] ¶ 32,602, ¶ 32,603L; ESTTRST: 12,256; § 32,022

[44] ¶ 24,260, ¶ 24,263; ESTTRST: 9,052, ESTTRST: 24,100; § 32,201

(1) income accumulated in trust for the benefit of unborn or unascertained persons or persons with contingent interests;

(2) income accumulated or held for future distribution under the terms of the will or trust;

(3) income that is to be distributed currently by the fiduciary to the beneficiaries, and income collected by the guardian of an infant that is to be held or distributed as the court may direct;

(4) income received by the estate of a deceased person during the period of administration or settlement of the estate; and

(5) income that, at the discretion of the fiduciary, may be either distributed to the beneficiaries or accumulated.

Although all the items above are includible in gross income, the tax liability may rest on either the estate or trust as a separate entity or on the beneficiary (¶ 542).

The allocation of income and deductions between a decedent's estate and the surviving spouse in community property states depends on state community property laws. In most states, the surviving spouse is taxed on one-half of the income flowing from the community property of the estate.[45]

522. Real Estate Income of Estates. State law determines whether income from real estate during the period of administration is taxable to the decedent's estate or to the heirs or devisees (¶ 520). The IRS has ruled that if state law provides that real property is subject to administration, income derived from the property is taxable to the estate even though legal title may pass directly to the heirs or devisees. However, if the administrator is not entitled to possession or control of real property, income from the property is taxable to the heirs or devisees and not to the estate. Even if the property is not subject to the administrator's control, all or a part of the gain from a sale of property is taxable to the estate to the extent that the property was sold, under state law, to raise funds for its administration (Rev. Rul. 57-133; Rev. Rul. 59-375).[46]

523. Personal Property Income of Estates. Income from personal property, including a gain from the sale or exchange of such property, is taxable to the estate (¶ 520). This is because title to personal property vests in the administrator or executor immediately upon appointment and does not pass to the heirs or legatees until the estate is fully administered and distribution is ordered or approved by the courts, and notwithstanding the fact that the basis of the property distributed relates back to the date of the decedent's death.[47]

524. Sale of Property by Estates and Trusts. The gain or loss realized on the sale of property acquired by an estate, trust, or beneficiary is determined under special basis rules, the applicability of which depends on how the property was acquired and the nature of the property sold (¶ 1601 and ¶ 1701).

For estates of decedents dying in 2010, if the executor elected *not* to have the federal estate tax apply to the estate, then the decedent's estate, a qualified revocable trust (¶ 516), or an heir may be able to exclude from gross income the gain on the sale of the decedent's personal residence (Code Sec. 121(d)(11), prior to repeal by the Tax Relief, Unemployment Insurance Reauthorization, and Job Creation Act of 2010 (P.L. 111-312); Act Sec. 301 of P.L. 111-312).[48] The general rules for the personal residence gain exclusion are discussed at ¶ 1705. This exclusion is not available for estates of 2010 decedents whose executors did not make the special election, or for estates of decedents dying after 2010.

References are to Standard Federal Tax Reports; Tax Research Consultant; and Practical Tax Explanations.

[45] ¶ 2350.2473; INDIV: 24,200, ESTTRST: 9,108; § 32,205.25

[46] ¶ 24,267.5204; ESTTRST: 9,102; § 32,205.30

[47] ¶ 24,267.515; ESTTRST: 9,052; § 32,210.05

[48] ¶ 7260; REAL: 15,150; § 1,610.30, § 34,901

526. Gain on Transfer of Property to Beneficiary. Gain or loss is generally realized by an estate or trust, or by the other beneficiaries, on the distribution of property in kind that satisfies a beneficiary's right to receive a specific dollar amount, specific property other than the property distributed, or other income if income is required to be distributed currently (Reg. § 1.661(a)-2(f)).[49] A special rule generally limits gain recognized on transfers to qualified heirs of property for which a special use valuation election under Code Sec. 2032A was made (¶ 2922) (Code Sec. 1040).[50] However, for estates of decedents dying in 2010 for which the executor elected *not* to have the federal estate tax apply, this rule limits gain on exchanges that satisfy pecuniary bequests with appreciated property (former Code Sec. 1040, prior to repeal by the Tax Relief, Unemployment Insurance Reauthorization, and Job Creation Act of 2010 (P.L. 111-312); Act Sec. 301 of P.L. 111-312).

For purposes of the rule limiting gain on transfers to qualified heirs of special use valuation property, a marital deduction trust (¶ 2926) comprising a portion of the residuary estate and measured by a percentage of the value of the adjusted gross estate is considered as being provided for in a fixed dollar amount (Rev. Rul. 60-87).[51] Upon a distribution of property to such a trust, the estate realizes gain or loss equal to the difference between the property's fair market value at the distribution date and its federal estate tax value.

Distribution of a stated percentage of trust corpus to the beneficiary before termination of the trust is not considered a satisfaction of a trust obligation for a definite amount of cash or equivalent value in property. Instead, it is treated as a partial distribution of a share of the trust principal. Thus, there is no sale or exchange, and neither the trustee nor the beneficiary realizes taxable income (Rev. Rul. 55-117).[52] However, a trustee or executor may elect to recognize gain or loss on the distribution of noncash property to a beneficiary as if the property had been sold to the beneficiary at its fair market value (Code Sec. 643(e)(3)).[53] The election is made on the return for the year of distribution and applies to all distributions made by the estate or trust during its entire tax year. Thus, an election to recognize gain or loss cannot be made separately for each distribution.

In the event the election is made, the beneficiary's basis in the distributed property is the estate's or trust's adjusted basis just prior to the distribution, adjusted by the gain or loss recognized by the estate or trust. If the election is not made, the beneficiary's basis is the same as the trust's or estate's, and any gain or loss is recognized by the beneficiary when the beneficiary disposes of the property.

Gain recognition on certain property distributions to expatriates is discussed at ¶ 566.

527. Income of Foreign Estates and Trusts. For purposes of computing the taxable income of a foreign estate or foreign trust (¶ 501), the estate or trust is treated as a nonresident alien individual who is not present in the United States at any time (¶ 2409 and ¶ 2425) (Code Sec. 641(b)).[54]

The estate of a nonresident alien is taxed on its income received from U.S. sources, including capital gains and dividends (Rev. Rul. 68-621).[55] The estate is allowed a deduction for distributions to both nonresident aliens and U.S. beneficiaries to the extent that these distributions are not in excess of its distributable net income (¶ 545). The portion of the distribution allocated to capital gains is not includible in the gross income of nonresident alien beneficiaries if they have not resided in the United States for a period of at least 183 days (¶ 2435). However, the portion of a distribution that represents dividends is includible in the gross income of nonresident alien beneficiaries. The fiduciary must withhold U.S. taxes from these dividend distributions at the statutory rate or the applicable treaty rate.

References are to Standard Federal Tax Reports; Tax Research Consultant; and Practical Tax Explanations.

[49] ¶ 24,402; ESTTRST: 21,150; § 32,215, § 32,520

[50] ¶ 29,779, ¶ 29,780; ESTTRST: 21,252; § 18,225

[51] ¶ 24,267.5281; ESTTRST: 21,158; § 32,520

[52] ¶ 24,267.5281; ESTTRST: 21,158; § 32,505.15, § 32,520

[53] ¶ 24,320; ESTTRST: 21,102; § 32,505.15, § 32,520

[54] ¶ 24,260; ESTTRST:100; § 32,005.05

[55] ¶ 24,267.4985; ESTTRST: 30,106; § 32,005.05, § 37,005

528. Deductions of Estates and Trusts—Generally. Estates and trusts are generally allowed the same deductions as individuals in computing taxable income (Code Sec. 641(b); Reg. § 1.641(b)-1).[56] However, the standard deduction available to estates and trusts is zero (Code Sec. 63(c)(6)(D)).[57] In addition, special rules govern the computation of certain deductions and the allocation of deductions between the beneficiaries and the estate or trust (¶ 529—¶ 538). Further, the estate or trust is permitted to claim a deduction for certain distributions to beneficiaries (¶ 544 and ¶ 545). The limitation on the amount of allowable itemized deductions for higher-income individuals (¶ 1014) does not apply to estates and trusts (Code Sec. 68(e)).[58]

Two-Percent Floor on Itemized Deductions. An estate or trust is generally subject to the two-percent-of-adjusted-gross-income (AGI) floor on miscellaneous itemized deductions (¶ 1079) (Code Sec. 67(e)).[59] The AGI of an estate or trust is computed in the same manner as it is for an individual (¶ 1005), except that the following deductions are allowed from gross income: (1) deductions for expenses paid or incurred in connection with the administration of the estate or trust that would not have been incurred had the property not been so held; (2) the personal exemption deduction allowed to estates and trusts (¶ 534); and (3) the deduction for distribution to beneficiaries (¶ 544 and ¶ 545). The IRS has regulatory authority to apply the two-percent floor at the beneficiary level, rather than the entity level, with respect to simple trusts.

The U.S. Supreme Court has ruled that only estate or trust expenses that would be uncommon, unusual, or unlikely for a hypothetical individual to incur are not subject to the two-percent floor (*M.J. Knight, Trustee,* SCt, 2008-1 USTC ¶ 50,132).[60] These types of costs would not "commonly" or "customarily" be incurred by individuals. Hence, investment advisory fees incurred by an estate or trust are generally subject to the two-percent floor. Expenses incurred in administering a bankruptcy estate are fully deductible from gross income (CCA 200630016).

Regulations consistent with *Knight* provide that a cost is subject to the two-percent floor to the extent that it commonly or customarily would be incurred by a hypothetical individual holding the same property (Reg. § 1.67-4(a)).[61] Rules are provided for four specific categories of costs: ownership costs, tax preparation fees, investment advisory fees, and appraisal fees. Fees for investment advice are generally subject to the two-percent floor, but certain incremental costs of investment advice beyond the amount normally charged to an individual investor are not. A single fee or commission (a "bundled fee") paid by an estate or nongrantor trust must be allocated between the costs that are subject to the two-percent floor and those that are not (Reg. § 1.67-4(c)). The allocation can be made using any reasonable method. Note that, for tax years beginning before January 1, 2015, taxpayers are not required to determine the portion of a bundled fiduciary fee that is subject to the two-percent floor. Instead, taxpayers may deduct 100 percent of the bundled fiduciary fee without regard to the two-percent floor (Reg. § 1.67-4(d); Notice 2011-37).[62]

529. Deductible Expenses of Estates and Trusts. An estate or trust is generally allowed deductions for any ordinary and necessary expenses incurred in carrying on a trade or business (¶ 901), in the production of income or the management or conservation of income-producing property (¶ 1085), or in connection with the determination, collection, or refund of any tax (¶ 1092). Reasonable amounts paid or incurred by a fiduciary on account of administration, including fiduciary fees and litigation expenses, are deductible as well. Such expenses are deductible even if the estate or trust is not engaged in a trade or business, unless the expenses were for the production or collection of tax-exempt income (Reg. § 1.212-1(i)).[63]

References are to Standard Federal Tax Reports; Tax Research Consultant; and Practical Tax Explanations.

[56] ¶ 24,260, ¶ 24,264; ESTTRST: 12,000; § 32,301

[57] ¶ 6020; ESTTRST: 12,050; § 32,301

[58] ¶ 6080; ESTTRST: 12,054; § 32,301

[59] ¶ 6060; ESTTRST: 12,054; § 32,345

[60] ¶ 6064.75; ESTTRST: 12,054; § 32,345

[61] ¶ 6063C; ESTTRST: 12,054; § 32,345

[62] ¶ 6063C, ¶ 6064.75; ESTTRST: 12,054; § 32,345

[63] ¶ 12,521; ESTTRST: 12,054, ESTTRST: 12,056; § 32,315.05

Deductions are not allowed for: (1) expenses that are allocable to one or more classes of income exempt from tax (other than interest income); or (2) any amount relating to expenses for the production of income that is allocable to tax-exempt interest income (¶ 970). The IRS allows a deduction for an executor's or administrator's commissions, as paid or accrued, except the portion allocable to tax-exempt income.[64]

Alimony Payments. An estate can deduct the value of periodic alimony payments it makes under the rules regarding deductions for distributions to beneficiaries.[65]

Double Deductions Prohibited. Amounts deductible as administration expenses or losses for estate tax (¶ 2925) or generation-skipping transfer tax (¶ 2942) purposes may not also be deducted, or offset against the sales price of property in determining gain or loss (i.e., selling expenses) for income tax purposes by the estate or any other person (Code Sec. 642(g); Reg. § 1.642(g)-1).[66] However, the estate can deduct such items for income tax purposes if it files a statement (in duplicate) that the items have not been claimed as deductions for estate tax purposes and that all rights to deduct them for such purposes are waived.

Note that one deduction or portion of a deduction may be allowed for income tax purposes if the appropriate statement is filed, while another deduction or portion is allowed for estate tax purposes (Reg. § 1.642(g)-2).[67] Deductions for taxes, interest, business expenses, and other items accrued *at the decedent's date of death* are allowed as a deduction for estate tax purposes as claims against the estate, and are also allowed as a deduction in respect of a decedent for income tax purposes. However, the estate cannot take an income tax deduction for the decedent's medical and dental expenses that it has paid. These expenses can only be claimed on the estate tax return or the decedent's final income tax return (¶ 1018).

530. Depreciation and Depletion Deductions of Estates and Trusts. Depreciation and depletion deductions must be apportioned between an estate or trust and its beneficiaries (Code Secs. 167(d), 611(b), and 642(e); Reg. § § 1.167(h)-1, 1.611-1(c), and 1.642(e)-1).[68] Different rules govern estates and trusts.

For a trust, the allowable deduction for depreciation or depletion is apportioned between the income beneficiaries and the trustee on the basis of the trust income allocable to each. However, if the trust instrument or local law requires or permits the trustee to maintain a reserve for depreciation or depletion, the deduction is first allocated to the trustee to the extent that income is set aside for the reserve. Any part of the deduction in excess of the income set aside for the reserve is then apportioned between the income beneficiaries and the trust on the basis of the trust income allocable to each. No effect is given to any allocation that gives any beneficiary or trustee a share of the deduction greater than a pro rata share of the trust income. The allocation is disregarded despite any provisions in the trust instrument, unless the trust instrument or local law requires or permits the trustee to maintain a reserve for depreciation or depletion.

For an estate, the depreciation or depletion allowance is apportioned between the estate and the heirs, legatees, and devisees on the basis of the income from the property allocable to each.

Section 179 Election. Although an estate or trust is entitled to take MACRS depreciation on qualified assets, neither can make a Code Sec. 179 election to expense depreciable business assets (¶ 1208) (Code Sec. 179(d)(4)).[69]

References are to Standard Federal Tax Reports; Tax Research Consultant; and Practical Tax Explanations.

[64] ¶ 12,523.51, ¶ 24,686.80; ESTTRST: 12,058; § 32,315.15

[65] ¶ 6094.31, ¶ 24,267.403, ¶ 24,407.56; ESTTRST: 27,052.10; § 1,905.20, § 32,310

[66] ¶ 24,280, ¶ 24,299; ESTTRST: 9,200, ESTTRST: 9,202; § 32,310

[67] ¶ 24,300; ESTTRST: 9,202; § 32,310

[68] ¶ 11,002, ¶ 11,048, ¶ 23,920, ¶ 23,922, ¶ 24,280, ¶ 24,297; ESTTRST: 12,102; § 32,335.05

[69] ¶ 12,120; DEPR: 12,050; § 32,335.05

Reforestation Expenditures. Estates can elect to expense reforestation expenditures and amortize any excess expenditures (¶ 1287) (Code Sec. 194).[70] Trusts cannot elect the expense deduction but can elect to amortize such expenditures. Total reforestation expenditures incurred must be apportioned between the income beneficiaries and the fiduciary. Amounts apportioned to a beneficiary must be taken into account in determining the dollar limit on the reforestation expenditures that the beneficiary can expense.

531. Losses and Bad Debt Deductions of Estates and Trusts. An estate or trust can deduct losses from a trade or business or from transactions entered into for profit (¶ 1101). Similarly, the rules governing nonbusiness casualty and theft losses (¶ 1121) apply to an estate or trust. Thus, after the $100-per-occurrence floor has been satisfied, losses in excess of nonbusiness casualty and theft gains are deductible to the extent that they exceed 10 percent of the adjusted gross income (AGI) of the estate or trust. For this purpose, an estate's or trust's administration expenses are allowable as a deduction in computing its AGI (Code Sec. 165(h)(4)(C)).[71]

A nonbusiness casualty or theft loss sustained or discovered during the settlement of an estate is deductible on the estate's income tax return only if it has not been allowed for estate tax purposes (Code Sec. 165(h)(4)(D); Reg. §§ 1.165-7(c) and 1.165-8(b)).[72] A statement to this effect should be filed with the return for the year for which the deduction is claimed.

Net Operating Losses. An estate or trust is allowed a deduction for net operating losses (NOLs) (¶ 1145) (Reg. § 1.642(d)-1).[73] However, an estate cannot deduct an NOL (or a capital loss (¶ 1752)) sustained by a decedent during the decedent's last tax year. These losses must be deducted on the decedent's final return.[74] In addition, in computing gross income and deductions for the NOL calculation, a trust must not take into account income and deductions attributable to the grantor or any substantial owner under the grantor trust rules (¶ 571). Also, an estate or trust cannot claim the deductions for charitable contributions (¶ 537) and distributions to beneficiaries (¶ 544 and ¶ 545) in calculating NOLs.

Bad Debts. An estate or trust is entitled to claim bad debt deductions under the rules governing individuals (¶ 1135).

Passive Losses. The passive activity loss rules (¶ 1165) apply to estates and trusts, but not grantor trusts (¶ 1173).

532. Deduction of Taxes by Estates and Trusts. An estate or trust is entitled to the same deductions for taxes as individuals (¶ 1021). In addition, an estate or trust is permitted an offset of the allocable federal estate tax against income in respect of a decedent (¶ 191). The portion of state income taxes allocable to exempt income, other than exempt interest income, is not deductible (¶ 970). The portion of state income taxes attributable to exempt interest income and to income subject to federal income tax is deductible (Rev. Rul. 61-86).[75]

533. Deduction of Interest by Estates and Trusts. Interest paid or accrued during the tax year is deductible by an estate or trust under the same rules that apply to individuals (¶ 1043) (Code Sec. 163).[76] However, there are a number of important differences. For example, interest owed and accrued at the death of the decedent can be deducted on the estate's income tax return as a deduction in respect of the decedent for the tax year in which the interest is paid. If the interest accrues after the decedent's death, it may be claimed as either an estate tax deduction or an income tax deduction (¶ 529). In addition, interest is not deductible by an estate or trust on a debt incurred, or

References are to Standard Federal Tax Reports; Tax Research Consultant; and Practical Tax Explanations.

[70] ¶ 12,330; FARM: 24,112; § 32,335.15

[71] ¶ 9802; ESTTRST: 12,060.10; § 7,705.10, § 32,401

[72] ¶ 9802, ¶ 10,004, ¶ 10,100; ESTTRST: 12,060.10; § 7,705.15, § 32,401

[73] ¶ 24,296; ESTTRST: 12,062; § 32,401, § 32,410

[74] ¶ 24,267.451; ESTTRST: 6,208.15, ESTTRST: 12,062; § 32,401

[75] ¶ 9502.453; ESTTRST: 12,064; § 32,325

[76] ¶ 9102; ESTTRST: 12,064; § 32,320

continued, to purchase or carry obligations the interest on which is wholly exempt from federal income taxes (¶ 970). Personal interest of an estate or trust is also nondeductible (¶ 1043). Further, the deduction for investment interest may not exceed net investment income for the tax year (Code Sec. 163(d)).[77] Net capital gain attributable to the disposition of property held for investment is generally excluded from investment income for purposes of computing this limitation. However, a special election is available to increase net capital gain includible in investment income by reducing the amount eligible for capital gain treatment (¶ 1094).

534. Personal Exemption Amount of Estates and Trusts. An estate can claim a personal exemption of $600 in determining its taxable income (Code Sec. 642(b); Reg. § 1.642(b)-1).[78] A simple trust (¶ 542)—one that is required to distribute all of its income currently—is allowed an exemption of $300. A complex trust is entitled to a $100 exemption. If a final distribution of assets has been made during the year, all income of the estate or trust must be reported as distributed to the beneficiaries, without reduction for the amount claimed for the exemption (¶ 535).

A qualified disability trust, whether taxed as a simple or complex trust, can claim an exemption in the amount available to an unmarried individual who is not a surviving spouse or head of a household (¶ 133) (Code Sec. 642(b)(2)(C)). For tax years beginning after December 31, 2012, the exemption for a qualified disability trust is subject to phase-out.

535. Loss Carryovers and Excess Deductions of Estates and Trusts. A beneficiary succeeding to the property of an estate or trust can deduct a net operating loss (NOL) carryover (¶ 1149 and ¶ 1153), a capital loss carryover (¶ 562 and ¶ 1754), and deductions in excess of gross income for the year in which the estate or trust terminates (Code Sec. 642(h); Reg. § § 1.642(h)-1—1.642(h)-5).[79] Excess deductions on termination of an estate or trust are allowed only in computing taxable income and must be taken into account in computing the beneficiary's tax preference items. Such deductions may not be used in computing adjusted gross income. In computing excess deductions, the deductions for personal exemptions and amounts set aside for charitable purposes are disregarded. The deduction is claimed as an itemized deduction or capital loss (depending on its nature) on the beneficiary's tax return filed for the year in which the estate or trust terminates.

An individual debtor's bankruptcy estate (¶ 505) succeeds to certain tax attributes of the debtor, including any NOL carryover (Code Sec. 1398(g)).[80] The tax attributes that become part of the estate are determined as of the first day of the debtor's tax year in which the bankruptcy case commences. If any carryback year of the estate is a tax year before the estate's first tax year, the carryback is taken into account in the tax year of the debtor that corresponds to such carryback year and may offset the pre-bankruptcy income of the debtor (Code Sec. 1398(j)(2)(A)). When the estate closes upon the issuance of a final decree, the debtor succeeds to the same attributes as the estate, including any unused NOL carryover (Code Sec. 1398(i)). The debtor, however, cannot carry an unused NOL carryback from a tax year that ended after commencement of the bankruptcy case to a tax year that precedes the tax year in which the bankruptcy case was commenced (Code Sec. 1398(j)(2)(B)).

536. Domestic Production Activities Deduction of Estates and Trusts. An estate or a nongrantor trust, and the beneficiaries of the estate or trust, may claim the deduction for domestic production activities (¶ 980A) (Code Sec. 199(d)(1)(B); Reg. § 1.199-5(e)).[81] In computing the deduction, an estate or trust apportions W-2 wages, domestic production gross receipts (DPGR), cost of goods sold allocable to DPGR, and

References are to Standard Federal Tax Reports; Tax Research Consultant; and Practical Tax Explanations.

[77] ¶ 9102; ESTTRST: 12,064; § 7,414, § 7,420.05, § 32,320

[78] ¶ 24,280, ¶ 24,286; ESTTRST: 12,052; § 32,350

[79] ¶ 24,280, ¶ 24,301—¶ 24,305; ESTTRST: 12,150; § 32,415

[80] ¶ 32,410; INDIV: 66,106, INDIV: 66,108; § 3,420.10, § 17,010.05

[81] ¶ 12,468, ¶ 12,472D; BUSEXP: 6,216; § 6,020.20, § 32,355

expenses, losses and deductions properly allocable to DPGR between the beneficiaries and the fiduciary, and among the beneficiaries. The nine-percent applicable percentage limitation on the deduction is applied to the lesser of the estate's or trust's qualified production activities income (QPAI) or its adjusted gross income (AGI), as determined under the AGI computation rules for estates and trusts (¶ 528).

The estate or trust calculates each beneficiary's share (as well as the estate's or trust's own share, if any) of the estate's or trust's QPAI and W-2 wages at the estate or trust level. The QPAI and W-2 wages are allocated to each beneficiary and to the estate or trust based on the relative proportion of the estate's or trust's distributable net income (DNI) for the tax year that is distributed or required to be distributed to the beneficiary or is retained by the estate or trust (¶ 542 and ¶ 543). If the estate or trust has no DNI for the tax year, QPAI and W-2 wages are allocated entirely to the estate or trust.

Each beneficiary computes his or her Code Sec. 199 deduction by combining their share of QPAI and W-2 wages from the estate or trust with their share of QPAI and W-2 wages from other sources. When determining its total QPAI and W-2 wages from such other sources, the beneficiary does not take into account the items allocated from the estate or trust. The beneficiary's share of W-2 wages from the estate or trust is determined under the law applicable to pass-through entities based on the beginning date of the estate's or trust's tax year, not the beneficiary's tax year (Reg. § 1.199-5(e)(3)).

Grantor Trust. For a grantor trust (¶ 571), the owner computes its QPAI with respect to the owned portion of the trust as if that QPAI had been generated by activities performed directly by the owner (Reg. § 1.199-5(d)). Similarly, for purposes of the wage limitation (¶ 980C), the owner takes into account its share of the trust's W-2 wages that are attributable to the owned portion of the trust. The nongrantor trust provisions (discussed above) do not apply to the owned portion of the trust.

537. Charitable Deductions of Estates and Trusts—Generally. Estates and complex trusts are allowed an unlimited charitable deduction for amounts paid to recognized charities (¶ 1061) out of gross income (other than unrelated business income of a trust (¶ 538)) under the terms of the governing instrument during the tax year (Code Sec. 642(c)).[82] For example, amounts bequeathed to charity that are paid out of corpus under state law are not deductible from income as charitable contributions or as distributions to beneficiaries.[83] However, payments in compromise of bequests to charity are deductible.[84] Limitations on the charitable deduction for estates and trusts are discussed at ¶ 538.

The trustee or administrator may elect to treat charitable payments made during the year following the close of a tax year as having been paid in the earlier year for deduction purposes (Code Sec. 642(c)(1); Reg. § 1.642(c)-1(b)).[85] The election must be made no later than the time, including extensions, prescribed by law for filing the income tax return for the tax year in which payment is made. The election is binding for the tax year for which it is made and may not be revoked after the time for making the election has expired.

Estates may also claim an unlimited deduction for amounts of gross income permanently set aside for charitable purposes (Reg. § 1.642(c)-2).[86] The income must be permanently set aside for a purpose specified in Code Sec. 170(c) or it must be used exclusively for: (1) religious, charitable, scientific, literary, or educational purposes; (2) the prevention of cruelty to children or animals; or (3) the establishment, acquisition, maintenance, or operation of a nonprofit public cemetery. For most complex trusts, the unlimited deduction for gross income that is permanently set aside for charitable purposes does not apply.

References are to Standard Federal Tax Reports; Tax Research Consultant; and Practical Tax Explanations.

[82] ¶ 24,280, ¶ 24,308.1135; ESTTRST: 15,050; § 32,340.05

[83] ¶ 24,308.115; ESTTRST: 15,050; § 32,340.05, § 32,340.20

[84] ¶ 24,308.105; ESTTRST: 15,260; § 32,340.20

[85] ¶ 24,280, ¶ 24,288; ESTTRST: 15,200; § 32,340.05

[86] ¶ 24,290; ESTTRST: 15,250, ESTTRST: 15,252; § 32,340.15

A provision in a governing instrument or local law that specifically identifies the source out of which amounts are to be paid, permanently set aside, or used for charitable purposes must have economic effect independent of income tax consequences in order to be respected for federal tax purposes (Reg. § 1.642(c)-3(b)(2)).[87]

Pooled income funds (¶ 593) may claim a set-aside deduction only for gross income attributable to gain from the sale of a long-term capital asset that is permanently set aside for the benefit of the charity (Reg. § 1.642(c)-2(c)).[88] No deduction is allowed with respect to gross income of the fund that is (1) attributable to income other than net long-term capital gains or (2) earned with respect to amounts transferred to the fund before August 1, 1969. The investment and accounting requirements applicable to trusts also apply to pooled income funds.

The charitable deduction is normally computed on Schedule A of Form 1041. However, pooled income funds claiming the set-aside deduction for long-term capital gain and nonexempt charitable trusts under Code Sec. 4947(a)(1) treated as private foundations (¶ 631) must compute their deduction on a separate schedule, rather than Schedule A. Also, a nonexempt charitable trust not treated as a private foundation must file Form 990 or Form 990-EZ in addition to Form 1041 if its gross receipts are normally more than $50,000. However, the trust may file Form 990 or Form 990-EZ to satisfy its Form 1041 filing requirement if it has zero taxable income (¶ 625).

Every trust claiming a charitable deduction for amounts permanently set aside (other than nonexempt charitable trusts under Code Sec. 4947(a)(1), and split-interest trusts under Code Sec. 4947(a)(2)) is required to file an information return on Form 1041-A generally by April 15 following the close of the trust's calendar year (Code Sec. 6034).[89] Form 1041-A does not have to be filed if the trust must distribute all of its income for the tax year (a simple trust). Split-interest trusts (pooled income funds (¶ 593), charitable remainder trusts (¶ 590), and charitable lead trusts (¶ 2932)) file their information return on Form 5227.

Both the trust and the trustee can be liable for a penalty of $10 per day for 2016, up to a maximum of $5,000, for failure to timely file Form 1041-A ($10 per day for 2017, up to a $5,000 maximum) (Code Sec. 6652(c)(2) and (7); Rev. Proc. 2015-53; Rev. Proc. 2016-55).[90] A split-interest trust that fails to file or to provide the required information on Form 5227 can be liable for a penalty of $20 per day for 2016, up to a maximum of $10,000 ($20 per day for 2017, up to a $10,000 maximum). If the split-interest trust's gross income exceeds $255,000 for 2016, the penalty is $100 per day, up to a maximum of $51,000 ($100 per day for 2017, up to a $51,000 maximum, if gross income exceeds $257,000). An additional penalty may be assessed against the person required to file the return if he or she knowingly fails to file it. Criminal penalties also apply for willful failure to file a return and filing a false or fraudulent return (Reg. § 1.6034-1(d)).[91]

538. Limitations on Charitable Deductions of Trusts. A trust is not entitled to an unlimited charitable deduction (¶ 537) for income that is allocable to its unrelated business income for the tax year (Code Secs. 642(c)(4) and 681(a); Reg. §§ 1.642(c)-3(d), 1.681(a)-1, and 1.681(a)-2).[92] The unrelated business income of a trust is computed in much the same manner as the unrelated business taxable income (UBTI) of a tax-exempt organization (¶ 655 and ¶ 687). However, in computing unrelated business income, a trust can claim deductions for payments to charities, subject to the percentage limitations applicable to individuals' charitable deductions (¶ 1058).

References are to Standard Federal Tax Reports; Tax Research Consultant; and Practical Tax Explanations.

[87] ¶ 24,291; ESTTRST: 15,064; § 32,340.20

[88] ¶ 24,290; ESTGIFT: 45,252.45; § 32,340.30

[89] ¶ 35,440; ESTTRST: 15,360; § 39,155.30

[90] ¶ 39,480; PENALTY: 3,208; § 33,605.05, § 39,155.30

[91] ¶ 35,441; IRS: 66,150, IRS: 66,200; § 40,245.05, § 41,625.25

[92] ¶ 24,280, ¶ 24,291, ¶ 24,840, ¶ 24,841, ¶ 24,842; ESTTRST: 15,352; § 32,340.05, § 33,901

Charitable deductions are not allowed for otherwise deductible gifts to an organization upon which a tax has been imposed for termination of private foundation status, unless the IRS has abated the tax (¶ 649) (Code Sec. 508(d)(1) and (3)).[93] General contributors will be denied deductions after the organization is notified of the loss of its private foundation status. Substantial contributors (¶ 635) will be denied deductions in the year in which action is taken to terminate the organization's private foundation status.

If a charitable contribution consists of gain from the sale of qualified small business stock (section 1202 stock) held for more than five years (¶ 1905), the charitable deduction amount must be adjusted for any gain excluded from gross income (Code Sec. 642(c)(4)).[94]

Deductions are also denied for contributions to any private foundation, nonexempt charitable trust, or split-interest trust, as defined in Code Sec. 4947, that fails to meet the governing instrument requirements for private foundations (Code Sec. 508(d)(2)).[95] Deductions for gifts and bequests to any organization are disallowed during the period that the organization fails to notify the IRS that it is claiming exempt status as a charitable organization (¶ 623). Churches, organizations with gross receipts of $5,000 or less, and certain other organizations designated by the IRS are exempt from the notification requirements. Charitable deductions are also disallowed for bequests and gifts to a foreign private foundation after the IRS notifies it that it has engaged in a prohibited transaction, or for a year in which such an organization loses its exempt status for engaging in such a transaction (Code Sec. 4948(c)(4)).[96]

540. Estate and Trust Income Tax Credits. The tax credits allowed to individuals (¶ 1301—¶ 1391) are generally allowed to estates and trusts in computing income tax liability (Reg. § 1.641(b)-1).[97] The credits typically must be apportioned between the estate or trust and the beneficiaries on the basis of the income allocable to each. However, the foreign tax credit (¶ 1361) is allocated according to the proportionate share of the foreign taxes (Code Sec. 642(a); Reg. § 1.642(a)(2)-1).[98]

The general business tax credit is a limited nonrefundable credit against income tax that is claimed after all other nonrefundable credits are claimed (¶ 1365). The amount of the general business tax credit may not exceed the net income tax minus the greater of the tentative minimum tax or 25 percent of the net regular tax liability over $25,000. For estates and trusts, the $25,000 amount must be reduced to an amount that bears the same ratio to $25,000 as the portion of the income of the estate or trust that is not allocated to the beneficiaries bears to the total income of the estate or trust (Code Sec. 38(c)(6)(D)).[99] Any unused credit can be carried back one year and forward 20 years (Code Sec. 39).[100]

Estates and trusts are also entitled to claim various refundable tax credits, including the credit for federal income tax withheld on wages and backup withholding (¶ 1321 and ¶ 2645), the credit for taxes paid on undistributed capital gain of a regulated investment company (¶ 1330), and the credit for federal excise taxes paid on fuels (¶ 1329).

Income Distribution Deduction

542. Simple v. Complex Trust. The deduction allowed to simple trusts (¶ 544) and to estates and complex trusts (¶ 545) for distributions to beneficiaries is determined by reference to distributable net income (DNI) (¶ 543).

References are to Standard Federal Tax Reports; Tax Research Consultant; and Practical Tax Explanations.

[93] ¶ 22,790; EXEMPT: 21,502; § 33,240.05

[94] ¶ 24,280; ESTTRST: 15,304; § 16,605.05

[95] ¶ 22,790; EXEMPT: 21,504; § 33,205.20

[96] ¶ 34,160; EXEMPT: 21,352; § 33,205.10, § 33,240.15

[97] ¶ 24,264; ESTTRST: 12,200, ESTTRST: 12,204; § 32,305

[98] ¶ 24,280, ¶ 24,282; ESTTRST: 12,202; § 13,405.20, § 32,305

[99] ¶ 4250; ESTTRST: 12,204, BUSEXP: 54,056; § 13,605.10

[100] ¶ 4300; BUSEXP: 54,056, BUSEXP: 54,058; § 13,605.15

A simple trust is a trust that: (1) is required to distribute all of its income currently whether or not distributions of current income are in fact made; and (2) does not allow any amount to be paid or set aside for charitable contributions (Code Sec. 651; Reg. § 1.651(a)-1).[101] A trust may be a simple trust even though, under local law or the governing trust instrument, capital gains must be allocated to corpus. The income required to be distributed in order for the trust to qualify as a simple trust is the income determined under local law and the governing instrument (Code Sec. 643(b); Reg. § 1.643(b)-1).[102] This will generally include only ordinary income because capital gains under most trust instruments and state laws are considered corpus. A trust will lose its classification as a simple trust (but not its $300 exemption) for any year during which it distributes corpus (¶ 544). Thus, a trust can never be a simple trust during the year of termination or in a year of partial liquidation (Reg. § 1.651(a)-3).[103]

A complex trust is any trust other than a simple trust described above (Reg. § 1.661(a)-1).[104] The same rules that apply to complex trusts generally also apply to estates.

Loans by Foreign Trusts. A foreign trust (¶ 501) will not be treated as a simple trust if it makes a loan of cash, cash equivalents, or marketable securities to, or permits the uncompensated use of any other trust property by, a grantor or beneficiary who is a U.S. person or a party related to such a grantor or beneficiary (Code Sec. 643(i)).[105] The amount of the loan or the fair market value of the property's use is treated as a distribution by the trust for purposes of the distribution deduction (¶ 545), the gross income of trust beneficiaries (¶ 556), and the treatment of excess trust distributions (¶ 567). For trust property other than a loan of cash or marketable securities, distribution treatment does not apply if the trust is paid the fair market value for the property's use within a reasonable time period. Any subsequent transaction between the trust and the original borrower regarding the loan principal—such as the complete or partial repayment, satisfaction, cancellation, or discharge of the loan—or the return of the property used is disregarded.

543. Distributable Net Income (DNI). The deductions allowable to an estate or trust for amounts paid or credited to beneficiaries (¶ 544 and ¶ 545) are limited to the entity's distributable net income (DNI). The entity's DNI may also limit the amount of the distribution taxable to the beneficiary (¶ 554) and it is a factor in applying the conduit rule (¶ 559).

The DNI of an estate or trust generally consists of the same items of gross income and deductions that make up the taxable income of the estate or trust. However, there are important modifications: (1) no deduction is allowed for distributions to beneficiaries; (2) the deduction for the personal exemption is disallowed (¶ 534); (3) tax-exempt interest on state and local bonds is included, reduced by amounts which would be deductible but for the disallowance of deductions on expenses and interest related to tax-exempt income; (4) for a foreign trust (¶ 501), gross income from outside the United States (reduced by amounts which would be deductible but for the disallowance of deductions on expenses related to tax-exempt income) and within the United States is included; (5) capital gains are excluded if they are allocable to corpus and are not (a) paid, credited, or required to be distributed to any beneficiary during the tax year, or (b) paid, permanently set aside, or to be used for a charitable purpose (¶ 537); (6) capital losses are excluded except to the extent of their use in determining the amount of capital gains paid, credited, or required to be distributed to any beneficiary during the tax year; and (7) in the case of a simple trust, extraordinary dividends or taxable stock dividends that the fiduciary, acting in good faith, allocates to corpus are excluded (Code Sec. 643(a); Reg. §§ 1.643(a)-0—1.643(a)-7).[106] The DNI of the estate or trust is deter-

References are to Standard Federal Tax Reports; Tax Research Consultant; and Practical Tax Explanations.

[101] ¶ 24,360, ¶ 24,361; ESTTRST: 24,050; § 32,501, § 32,510

[102] ¶ 24,320, ¶ 24,329; ESTTRST: 24,052; § 32,010.10

[103] ¶ 24,363; ESTTRST: 24,056; § 32,501

[104] ¶ 24,401; ESTTRST: 24,050; § 32,501, § 32,515.05

[105] ¶ 24,320; ESTTRST: 18,200; § 32,501

[106] ¶ 24,320, ¶ 24,321—¶ 24,328; ESTTRST: 18,050; § 32,505.05

mined by taking into account a net operating loss (NOL) deduction (¶ 531 and ¶ 556).[107] However, the exclusion of gain from the sale or exchange of qualified small business stock (section 1202 stock) held for more than five years (¶ 1905) is not taken into account in determining DNI (Code Sec. 643(a)(3)).[108]

544. Deduction for Distributions to Beneficiaries of a Simple Trust. A simple trust (¶ 542) may deduct the amount of income that the trustee is under a duty to distribute currently to beneficiaries, even if the trustee makes the actual distribution after the close of the tax year (Code Sec. 651; Reg. §§ 1.651(a)-2 and 1.651(b)-1).[109] If other amounts are distributed—such as a payment from corpus to meet the terms of an annuity payable from income or corpus—the complex trust rules apply for that year, except that the $300 personal exemption (¶ 534) is still allowed (Reg. § 1.642(b)-1).[110] If the income required to be distributed exceeds distributable net income (DNI), the distribution deduction is limited to DNI (¶ 543), computed without including tax-exempt income and related deductions.

545. Deduction for Distributions to Beneficiaries of Complex Trust or Estate. An estate or complex trust (¶ 542) may deduct any amount of income for the tax year that is required to be distributed currently to beneficiaries (Code Sec. 661(a); Reg. § 1.661(a)-2).[111] This includes any amount required to be distributed that may be paid out of income or corpus, to the extent that it is in fact paid out of income. An estate or complex trust may also deduct any other amounts properly paid or credited or required to be distributed in the tax year, including amounts distributable at the discretion of the fiduciary and a distribution in kind. The amount to be taken into account in determining the deduction depends on whether the estate or trust elected to recognize gain on a noncash distribution of property in kind (¶ 526). In no case may the deduction exceed the distributable net income (DNI) of the estate or trust (¶ 543).

Special provisions exclude from the estate or trust's distribution deduction any unlimited charitable contribution (¶ 537), and certain gifts or bequests of a specific sum of money or specific property if paid or distributed all at once or in not more than three installments (¶ 556 and ¶ 564) (Code Sec. 663(a); Reg. §§ 1.663(a)-1 and 1.663(a)-2).[112] Also, an estate or trust cannot include in the distribution deduction for the current tax year an amount deemed distributed to a beneficiary in a prior tax year (Reg. § 1.663(a)-3).[113]

Where a will is silent, state law determines whether income or gain during the period of estate administration is properly paid or credited to a legatee (Rev. Rul. 71-335).[114] Also, a testamentary trustee can be a legatee or beneficiary for the purpose of a taxable distribution.[115]

When estate or trust income is of varying types, the distribution deduction is treated as consisting of the same proportion of each class of items entering into the DNI calculation as the total of each class bears to total DNI (Code Sec. 661(b); Reg. § 1.661(b)-1).[116] However, items will be allocated in accordance with a trust instrument or local law providing for a different method of allocation. No deduction is allowed to the estate or trust for the part of a beneficiary's distribution that consists of DNI that is not included in the gross income of the estate or trust, such as tax-exempt interest income (Code Sec. 661(c); Reg. § 1.661(c)-1).[117]

References are to Standard Federal Tax Reports; Tax Research Consultant; and Practical Tax Explanations.

[107] ¶ 24,296, ¶ 24,431.493; ESTTRST: 12,062; § 32,410, § 32,505.05

[108] ¶ 24,320; ESTTRST: 18,056; § 16,605, § 32,505.05

[109] ¶ 24,360, ¶ 24,362, ¶ 24,366; ESTTRST: 24,102; § 32,510

[110] ¶ 24,286; ESTTRST: 24,100; § 32,510

[111] ¶ 24,400, ¶ 24,402; ESTTRST: 27,056; § 32,515.05

[112] ¶ 24,440, ¶ 24,441, ¶ 24,442; ESTTRST: 27,102, ESTTRST: 27,104; § 32,515.05

[113] ¶ 24,443; ESTTRST: 27,106; § 32,515.05

[114] ¶ 24,407.78; ESTTRST: 27,054; § 32,515.05

[115] ¶ 24,407.7951; ESTTRST: 30,050

[116] ¶ 24,400, ¶ 24,403; ESTTRST: 27,056; § 32,515.05, § 32,515.10

[117] ¶ 24,400, ¶ 24,405; ESTTRST: 27,056; § 32,515.05

In applying the above rule, all deductions entering into the computation of DNI (including charitable contributions) are allocated among the different types of income that make up the DNI in the following manner (Reg. § § 1.652(b)-3 and 1.661(b)-2):[118]

(1) The deductions *directly* attributable to an income class are allocated to that income. For example, real estate taxes, repairs, the trustee's share of depreciation, fire insurance premiums, etc., would be allocated to rental income.

(2) The deductions *not directly* attributable to a specific income class (such as trustee's commissions, safe deposit box rental, and state income and personal property taxes) may be allocated to any income item (including capital gains) included in computing DNI. However, a trust with nontaxable income must allocate a portion of these deductions to nontaxable income.

(3) Any excess deductions from step (1) may be assigned to any other class of income (including capital gains) in the manner described in step (2). However, excess deductions attributable to tax-exempt income may not be offset against any other class of income. Also, excess deductions from a passive activity (¶ 1169) cannot be allocated to income from a nonpassive activity, or to portfolio income earned by the estate or trust (Instructions to Form 1041).

For purposes of the computation, the unlimited charitable deduction (¶ 537) is first allocated ratably among all classes of income entering into DNI before any other expenses, unless a different allocation is specified by the governing instrument or local law (Reg. § § 1.643(a)-5 and 1.661(b)-2).[119] The charitable deduction is allocated by multiplying it by a ratio: the numerator is the amount of each single class of income, and the denominator is the total of all income classes.

Examples illustrating the allocations are provided at ¶ 559.

546. Estate or Complex Trust's 65-Day Election. The fiduciary of an estate or complex trust can elect annually to treat any distribution or any portion of a distribution to a beneficiary made within the first 65 days following the end of a tax year as having been distributed in the prior year (Code Sec. 663(b); Reg. § § 1.663(b)-1 and 1.663(b)-2).[120] The election is made on Form 1041, is irrevocable for the year involved, and is binding for that year only. The amount to which the election can apply is the greater of: (1) the estate or trust's income (¶ 514); or (2) distributable net income (DNI) (¶ 543) for the tax year, reduced by any amounts paid, credited, or required to be distributed during the tax year other than those amounts that are subject to the 65-day election. There is no 65-day election for distributions of accumulated income (¶ 567).

548. Annuities Distributable from Income or Corpus. In the case of recurring distributions, payments by an estate or trust (where the amounts to be distributed, paid, or credited are a charge upon the corpus *or* the income) are usually taxable to the beneficiary and deductible by the estate or trust, to the extent that they are made from income (Code Sec. 661(a)(1); Reg. § 1.661(a)-2(b)).[121]

549. Widow(er)'s Allowance. A widow(er)'s or dependent's statutory allowance or award for support during administration of the estate is deductible by an estate if it is paid pursuant to a court order or decree or under local law (Reg. § 1.661(a)-2(e)).[122] The allowance can be paid from either income or principal, but the deduction is limited to the estate's distributable net income (DNI) for the year (¶ 543). Such payments are includible in the recipient's income to the extent of his or her share of the estate's DNI (Reg. § § 1.662(a)-2(c) and 1.662(a)-3(b)).[123] The allowance is treated as a distribution to a

References are to Standard Federal Tax Reports; Tax Research Consultant; and Practical Tax Explanations.

[118] ¶ 24,386, ¶ 24,404; ESTTRST: 27,056, ESTTRST: 30,250; § 32,515.10

[119] ¶ 24,326, ¶ 24,404; ESTTRST: 27,056, ESTTRST: 30,256; § 32,515.05, § 32,515.10

[120] ¶ 24,440, ¶ 24,444, ¶ 24,445; ESTTRST: 30,304; § 32,515.30

[121] ¶ 24,400, ¶ 24,402; ESTTRST: 27,052; § 32,515.05

[122] ¶ 24,402; ESTTRST: 27,052.10; § 32,525.10

[123] ¶ 24,422, ¶ 24,423; ESTTRST: 27,052.10; § 32,710.05

beneficiary, even if it is considered to be a debt of the estate rather than a payment to a beneficiary under local law (Rev. Rul. 75-124).[124]

Taxation of Beneficiaries

554. Taxation of Simple Trust Beneficiary. A beneficiary of a simple trust (¶ 542) must include in gross income the income that is required to be distributed currently to the beneficiary (¶ 514), whether or not it is actually distributed during the tax year, up to the amount of distributable net income (DNI) (¶ 543) (Code Sec. 652; Reg. §§ 1.652(a)-1—1.652(b)-3).[125] If the income required to be distributed exceeds DNI, only a proportionate share of each item is includible in the beneficiary's income. Each income item retains the same character (such as rent, dividends, etc.) that it had in the hands of the trust, and is treated as consisting of the same proportion of each class of items entering into the DNI calculation as the total of each class bears to total DNI, unless the trust instrument specifically allocates a particular type of income to a particular beneficiary. Deductions reflected in the computation of DNI are allocated among the various types of income (¶ 545). On termination of a trust, unused loss carryovers and excess deductions of the trust are allowed to certain beneficiaries (¶ 535). The amounts reported on the beneficiary's return must be consistent with the amounts reported on the trust return (¶ 2823) (Code Sec. 6034A(c)).[126]

Net Investment Income Tax. For purposes of determining the 3.8-percent net investment income tax (¶ 129), net investment income includes a beneficiary's share of DNI to the extent that the character of such income constitutes gross income from certain income items (e.g., interest, dividends, annuities, royalties, rents, gross income from a passive trade or business or from a trader's financial instrument trading business, etc.) or net gain attributable to the disposition of certain property, with further computations for the trust's undistributed net investment income (¶ 517) (Reg. § 1.1411-4(e)(1)).[127]

556. Taxation of Beneficiary of Estate or Complex Trust. A beneficiary of a complex trust (¶ 542) or a decedent's estate must include in gross income the income that is required to be distributed currently to the beneficiary (¶ 514), whether or not it is actually distributed during the tax year, plus any other amounts that are properly paid, credited, or required to be distributed to the beneficiary for the year (Code Sec. 662; Reg. § 1.662(a)-1).[128] For example, income of a trust is taxable to the beneficiaries even where there is no direction as to distribution or accumulation and state law requires distribution.[129] If a fiduciary elects to treat a distribution to a beneficiary made in the year as an amount paid in a prior year (¶ 546), the amount covered by the election is included in the beneficiary's income for the year for which the trust takes the deduction. Special rules also apply to distributions by certain trusts out of accumulated income (¶ 567).

If the amount of income required to be distributed currently to all beneficiaries exceeds distributable net income (DNI) (¶ 543) (computed without the charitable deduction (¶ 537)), then each beneficiary includes in income an amount that bears the same ratio to DNI as the amount of income required to be distributed currently to the beneficiary bears to the amount required to be distributed currently to all beneficiaries (Reg. § 1.662(a)-2(b)).[130]

If the sum of income required to be distributed currently, plus other amounts properly paid, credited, or required to be distributed, exceeds DNI, then the beneficiary includes such other amounts in gross income only to the extent that DNI exceeds income required to be distributed currently (Reg. § 1.662(a)-3(c)).[131] If the other amounts are paid, credited, or required to be distributed to more than one beneficiary,

References are to Standard Federal Tax Reports; Tax Research Consultant; and Practical Tax Explanations.

[124] ¶ 24,431.84; ESTTRST: 27,052.10; § 32,525.10

[125] ¶ 24,380—¶ 24,386; ESTTRST: 24,150; § 32,705.05

[126] ¶ 35,460; ESTTRST: 100; § 32,701

[127] ¶ 32,604; ESTTRST: 12,256.10; § 32,705.05

[128] ¶ 24,420, ¶ 24,421; ESTTRST: 30,000; § 32,710.05

[129] ¶ 24,431.65; ESTTRST: 24,052.05; § 32,710.05

[130] ¶ 24,422; ESTTRST: 30,108; § 32,710.05

[131] ¶ 24,423; ESTTRST: 30,154; § 32,710.05

each beneficiary includes in gross income his or her proportionate share of such other amounts includible in gross income. The beneficiary's proportionate share is the amount which bears the same ratio to DNI (after subtracting income required to be distributed currently) as the other amounts distributed to the beneficiary bear to the other amounts distributed to all beneficiaries. The amount to be used in determining the beneficiary's share of estate or trust income depends on whether the estate or trust elected to recognize gain on the distribution (¶ 526).

Any amount which, under a will or trust instrument, is used in full or partial discharge or satisfaction of a legal obligation of any person is included in that person's gross income as though the amount was directly distributed to him or her as a beneficiary (Reg. § 1.662(a)-4).[132] A legal obligation includes an obligation to support another person only if it is not affected by the adequacy of the dependent's own resources. The amount of trust income included in the gross income of a person obligated to support a dependent is limited by the extent of the person's legal obligation under local law. For example, in the case of a parent's obligation to support his or her child, to the extent that the support obligation (including education) is determined under local law by the family's station in life and the means of the parent, it is determined without consideration of the trust income in question. This rule does not pertain to alimony payments or income of an alimony trust (¶ 771).

If a net operating loss carryback of the estate or trust (¶ 531) reduces the DNI of the estate or trust for the prior tax year to which the NOL is carried, the beneficiary's tax liability for the prior year may be recomputed based upon the revised DNI of the estate or trust (Rev. Rul. 61-20).[133]

In allocating the various types of income to the beneficiaries so as to give effect to these tax rules, the amount reflected in the trust's or estate's DNI is determined first. It is charged with directly related expenses and a proportionate part of other expenses, including the unlimited charitable deduction (¶ 537) to the extent it is chargeable to income of the current year (Reg. §§ 1.662(b)-1 and 1.662(b)-2).[134] Each beneficiary's share of income paid, credited, or required to be distributed to the beneficiary is then multiplied by fractions, for each class of income, in which the numerator is the amount of such income included in DNI (whether the aggregate is more or less than the DNI), and the denominator is the total DNI (¶ 545). However, if the governing instrument specifies or local law requires a different allocation, such allocation is to be followed. These computations are illustrated at ¶ 559.

Special provisions exclude certain amounts from the beneficiary's gross income (and from the estate or trust's distribution deduction) (Code Sec. 663(a); Reg. §§ 1.663(a)-1, 1.663(a)-2, and 1.663(a)-3).[135] Any amount paid, permanently set aside, or to be used for charitable purposes and allowable for the unlimited charitable deduction (¶ 537) cannot be part of the distribution deduction or treated as an amount distributed for purposes of determining the beneficiary's gross income. Additionally, amounts deemed to be distributed to a beneficiary in a *prior* tax year cannot be deducted by the estate or trust, and are not included in the beneficiary's gross income for the current tax year. Certain gifts or bequests of a specific sum of money or specific property if paid or distributed all at once or in not more than three installments are also excluded (¶ 564).

On termination of an estate or trust, unused loss carryovers and excess deductions of the estate or trust are allowed to certain beneficiaries (¶ 535).

The amounts reported on the beneficiary's return must be consistent with the amounts reported on the estate or trust return (¶ 2823) (Code Sec. 6034A(c)).[136]

References are to Standard Federal Tax Reports; Tax Research Consultant; and Practical Tax Explanations.

[132] ¶ 24,424; ESTTRST: 30,052; § 32,710.05

[133] ¶ 24,431.493; ESTTRST: 12,062; § 32,410

[134] ¶ 24,425, ¶ 24,426; ESTTRST: 30,106; § 32,710.05

[135] ¶ 24,440—¶ 24,443; ESTTRST: 27,100; § 32,710.05, § 32,710.15

[136] ¶ 35,460; ESTTRST: 100; § 32,701

Net Investment Income Tax. For purposes of determining the 3.8-percent net investment income tax (¶ 129), net investment income includes a beneficiary's share of DNI to the extent that the character of such income constitutes gross income from certain income items (e.g., interest, dividends, annuities, royalties, rents, gross income from a passive trade or business or from a trader's financial instrument trading business, etc.) or net gain attributable to the disposition of certain property, with further computations for the estate's or trust's undistributed net investment income (¶ 517) (Reg. § 1.1411-4(e)(1)).[137]

557. Separate Shares as Separate Estates or Trusts. Where an estate or trust has two or more beneficiaries and is to be administered in well-defined and separate shares, the shares must be treated as separate estates or trusts in determining the amount of distributable net income (DNI) allocable to the beneficiaries (¶ 554 and ¶ 556) (Code Sec. 663(c); Reg. §§ 1.663(c)-1—1.663(c)-5).[138] This rule limits the tax liability of a beneficiary on a distribution of income and corpus where the income is being accumulated for the benefit of another beneficiary. The separate-share treatment is mandatory, not elective. A trustee or an executor must apply it even if separate and independent accounts are not maintained for each share, or if assets are not physically segregated.

The separate-share rule does not affect situations in which a single trust instrument creates not one, but several separate trusts, as opposed to separate shares in the same trust. It also does not apply to trusts that provide for successive interests (e.g., a trust that provides a life estate to A and remainder to B).

The treatment of separate shares as separate estates or trusts applies *only* for determining DNI in computing the distribution deduction allowable to the estate or trust and the amount includible in the income of the beneficiary. It cannot be applied to obtain more than one deduction for the personal exemption or to split the income of the estate or trust into several shares so as to be taxed at a lower-bracket rate.

559. How the Complex Trust Rules Operate. The examples below illustrate computations of distributable net income (DNI) (¶ 543), the distributive share of a beneficiary (¶ 544 and ¶ 545), and the taxable income of a complex trust. No "throwback" distributions (¶ 567) are involved.

Example 1: Trust income: A complex trust has the following items of income in 2016:

Dividends	$16,000
Taxable interest	10,000
Exempt interest	10,000
Rent	4,000
Long-term capital gain allocable to corpus	6,000
The trust has expenses as follows:	
Expenses directly allocable to rent	$2,000
Commissions allocable to income	3,000
Commissions allocable to corpus	1,500

On these facts, the trust would have income of $40,000 (¶ 514). The income items consist of dividends, taxable interest, exempt interest and rent. No expenses or charges against income or corpus are subtracted; only receipts treated as income under local law and the governing instrument are counted (e.g., rent). Also, the long-term capital gain is excluded from this income in order to apply the conduit rule (as illustrated in Example 3) because it is not income under local law. It is, however, included in the taxable income computation.

References are to Standard Federal Tax Reports; Tax Research Consultant; and Practical Tax Explanations.

[137] ¶ 32,604; ESTTRST: 12,256.10; § 32,710.05

[138] ¶ 24,440, ¶ 24,446—¶ 24,449; ESTTRST: 27,200; § 32,515.20

Example 2: Distributable net income: In computing the trust's DNI, the net amount of tax-exempt interest is added to the net income of the trust (after subtracting any charitable contribution). The net amount of tax-exempt interest is the full amount of such interest minus any expenses directly allocable to it and a proportionate part of all general expenses such as commissions. As indicated in Example 1, there are $4,500 in general expenses (i.e., expenses not directly allocable to rental income), so 25 percent ($10,000/$40,000) of $4,500, or $1,125, is allocated to the exempt interest ($10,000), leaving a net of $8,875. This $1,125 must also be excluded from the deductions claimed by the trust as an expense indirectly related to the production of exempt interest income and therefore disallowed by Code Sec. 265 (¶ 970). Accordingly, DNI is $33,500, computed as follows:

Dividends		$16,000
Taxable interest		10,000
Exempt interest ($10,000 less $1,125 allocable to exempt interest)		8,875
Rent		4,000
Total		$38,875
Deductions:		
Rent expense	$2,000	
Commissions ($4,500 less $1,125 allocable to exempt interest)	3,375	5,375
Distributable net income		$33,500

Example 3: Taxable income of beneficiary: There is one beneficiary to whom the trustee must distribute $20,000 under the terms of the trust instrument. The first step in computing the amount taxable to the beneficiary is to determine the extent to which each income item is reflected in DNI, allocating expenses to the various items. Those allocable to exempt interest have already been reflected in the $8,875 figure carried into DNI in Example 2, so no further allocation of that item is needed. Allocation is needed for dividends, rent, and taxable interest income, but this allocation does not have to be proportionate. Expenses directly related to any source or type of income must be allocated directly to that income, but general expenses can be allocated to any taxable income the taxpayer wishes when computing DNI as long as no deficit is created for any item. In this example, it is assumed the trustee allocates all general expenses to taxable interest. Accordingly, the trustee charges the entire $3,375 of general expenses to the taxable interest ($10,000) so that the $33,500 DNI, for the purpose of applying the conduit rule, is deemed to have been derived from:

Rent	$2,000
Taxable interest	6,625
Dividends	16,000
Tax-exempt interest	8,875
	$33,500

The total corresponds to the DNI and is only an intermediate or identification step. Because the amounts actually distributable are less than the amount of DNI, the next step is to multiply each of the above amounts by $20,000/$33,500 to determine what part of each is taxable to the beneficiary and deductible by the trust. Using these figures (the same result could be obtained by determining $2,000/$33,500 of $20,000, $6,625/$33,500 of $20,000, and so on), the apportionment is as follows:

Rent	$1,194.03
Taxable interest	3,955.22
Dividends	9,552.24
Tax-exempt interest	5,298.51
	$20,000.00

The beneficiary's share of income and deductions is reported on Schedule K-1 of Form 1041. The beneficiary will omit the $5,298.51 tax-exempt interest in reporting income from the trust. The $1,194.03 rent, $9,552.24 dividend, and $3,955.22 taxable interest income should be reported on the beneficiary's Form 1040.

Example 4: Taxable income of the trust: The trust is allowed a deduction for the amount required to be distributed currently up to the amount of its DNI, but not for any portion that consists of tax-exempt income. The deduction for distributions, therefore, is $14,701.49 ($20,000 minus $5,298.51). Taxable income of the trust is then computed as follows:

Dividends	$16,000.00	
Taxable Interest	10,000.00	
Rent	4,000.00	
Long-term capital gain	6,000.00	$36,000.00
Less:		
Expenses allocable to rent	$2,000.00	
Commissions allocable to income ($3,000 minus the 25% [$750] allocable to exempt interest)	2,250.00	
Commissions allocable to corpus ($1,500 minus the 25% [$375] allocable to exempt interest)	1,125.00	
Distribution to beneficiary	14,701.49	
Exemption	100.00	20,176.49
Taxable income		$15,823.51

562. Capital Gain or Loss of Estate or Trust. Capital gains, whether long or short term, are generally excluded from distributable net income (DNI) (i.e., are taxed to an estate or trust) to the extent allocated to corpus and not (1) paid, credited, or required to be distributed to any beneficiary during the tax year, or (2) paid, permanently set aside, or to be used for a charitable purpose (Code Sec. 643(a)(3); Reg. § 1.643(a)-3).[139] Capital gains are included in DNI, however, to the extent they are: (1) allocated to income; (2) allocated to corpus but consistently treated by the fiduciary as part of a distribution to a beneficiary; or (3) allocated to corpus but actually distributed to a beneficiary or used by the fiduciary in determining the amount that is distributed or required to be distributed to a beneficiary (¶ 543).

A net capital loss of an estate or trust will reduce the taxable income of the estate or trust, but no part of the loss is deductible by the beneficiaries. If the estate or trust distributes all of its income, the capital loss will not result in a tax benefit for the year of the loss. Losses from the sale or exchange of capital assets are first netted at the trust level against any capital gains, except for capital gains utilized by the fiduciary in determining the amount to be distributed to a particular beneficiary (Reg. § 1.643(a)-3(d)).[140] On termination of an estate or trust, any unused capital loss carryover of the estate or trust is available to the beneficiaries (¶ 535).

564. Gift or Bequest by Estates and Trusts. An estate or trust may not deduct as a distribution to a beneficiary, and a beneficiary does not include in income, a gift or bequest of a specific sum of money or specific property that is paid or credited in three installments or less (Code Sec. 663(a)(1); Reg. § 1.663(a)-1).[141] However, an amount will *not* be treated as an excluded gift or bequest if the governing instrument provides that the specific sum is payable only from the income of the estate or trust. The following are also *not* treated as an excluded gift or bequest of a sum of money or specific property: (1) an annuity, or periodic gifts of specific property in lieu of or having the effect of an annuity; (2) a residuary estate or the corpus of a trust; or (3) a gift or bequest paid in a lump sum or in three installments or less, if required by the governing instrument to be paid in more than three installments. In determining the number of installments, gifts or bequests of articles of personal use (e.g., personal and household effects, cars, etc.) are disregarded. Also disregarded are transfers of specific real estate, title to which passes directly from the decedent to the devisee under local law.

565. Beneficiary's Tax Year Different From Estate's or Trust's. If a beneficiary has a different tax year from that of an estate or complex trust (¶ 542), the amount to be

References are to Standard Federal Tax Reports; Tax Research Consultant; and Practical Tax Explanations.

[139] ¶ 24,320, ¶ 24,324; ESTTRST: 18,056; § 32,505.10

[140] ¶ 24,324; ESTTRST: 18,058; § 32,505.10

[141] ¶ 24,440, ¶ 24,441; ESTTRST: 27,102; § 32,710.15

included in the beneficiary's gross income must be based on the distributable net income (DNI) of the estate or trust (¶ 543) and the amounts paid, credited, or required to be distributed to the beneficiary for any tax year or years of the estate or trust ending with or within his or her tax year (Code Sec. 662(c); Reg. § 1.662(c)-1).[142] Similarly, if a beneficiary of a simple trust has a tax year different from that of the trust, the amount that the beneficiary includes in gross income must be based on the amount of the trust's income for any tax year or years ending with or within his or her tax year (Code Sec. 652(c); Reg. § 1.652(c)-1).[143]

566. Distributions to Expatriates by Nongrantor Trusts. If a covered expatriate (¶ 2412) is a beneficiary of a nongrantor trust on the day before the individual's expatriation date, and receives a direct or indirect distribution of any property from the trust, the trustee must deduct and withhold 30 percent of the taxable portion of the distribution (Code Sec. 877A(f)).[144] Additionally, if the fair market value of the property distributed exceeds the adjusted basis in the hands of the trust, the trust must recognize gain as if the property were sold to the expatriate at its fair market value.

The taxable portion of the distribution is that portion which would be includible in the covered expatriate's gross income had the expatriate continued to be subject to tax as a U.S. citizen or resident. A nongrantor trust is the portion of any trust of which the individual is not considered the owner under the grantor trust rules (¶ 571) as determined immediately before the beneficiary's expatriation date.

The withholding rules apply in a manner similar to those that apply to nonresident aliens (¶ 2455), but the distribution item is not subject to the nonresident alien withholding tax itself or the withholding tax on wages (¶ 2601). Further, the covered expatriate is treated as having waived any claim to a withholding reduction under any treaty with the United States, unless the expatriate agrees to other treatment that the IRS deems appropriate. Items subject to withholding are taxed according to the rules that apply to nonresident aliens (¶ 2429 and ¶ 2431).

567. "Throwback" of Accumulated Income. Special "throwback rules" generally apply to trust distributions made in tax years beginning before August 6, 1997 (Code Secs. 665—668).[145] Although the throwback rules have been repealed for most trusts, they continue to apply to trusts created before March 1, 1984, that would be treated as multiple trusts under Code Sec. 643(f), and to foreign trusts (¶ 501) and domestic trusts that were once treated as foreign trusts.

The throwback rules are designed to prevent the accumulation of trust income by a complex or accumulation trust over a period of years with a distribution to a beneficiary only in low-income years. The rules have the effect of carrying back to preceding years any distributions in excess of distributable net income (DNI) (¶ 543) for the distribution year and taxing them to the beneficiaries as if they were distributed in the year the income was accumulated by the trust. This additional income is taxed to the beneficiary in the year that the beneficiary receives the accumulation distribution, but the beneficiary's tax liability is computed on Form 4970 under special rules. Beneficiaries who receive the accumulation distribution from a foreign trust report it and the partial tax on Form 3520. Schedule J of Form 1041 is used to determine the amount, the year, and the character of the additional distributions taxable to beneficiaries under the throwback rules; the trustee must give a copy of Part IV of Schedule J to each beneficiary. The beneficiary is allowed an offset or credit against the partial tax for the proportionate part of the trust's tax for the prior year, thus eliminating any double tax on the income. Beneficiaries of estates are not subject to the throwback rules.

References are to Standard Federal Tax Reports; Tax Research Consultant; and Practical Tax Explanations.

[142] ¶ 24,420, ¶ 24,427; ESTTRST: 30,306; § 32,710.10

[143] ¶ 24,380, ¶ 24,387; ESTTRST: 24,158; § 32,705.15

[144] ¶ 27,430; EXPAT: 3,320; § 37,135

[145] ¶ 24,480, ¶ 24,500, ¶ 24,520, ¶ 24,540; ESTTRST: 33,000; § 32,715.05

Grantor Trusts

571. Overview of Grantor Trust Rules. Under the grantor trust rules, a person (i.e., the grantor) who transfers property to a trust and retains certain powers or interests (¶ 576—¶ 584) is treated as the owner of the trust property for income tax purposes (Code Sec. 671).[146] As a result, the income, deductions, and credits attributable to the trust are included in determining the grantor's taxable income to the extent of the owned portion of the trust. For income tax purposes, conversion of a nongrantor trust to a grantor trust is not a transfer of the property held by the nongrantor trust to the owner of the grantor trust, so the owner is not required to recognize gain (CCA 200923024).

Family Trusts. Income-producing property is often conveyed in trust for the benefit of a family member in an effort to split any income generated by the property or to otherwise lessen the original owner's tax liability. However, there must be an actual transfer of property to accomplish the desired tax savings; it is not enough to transfer income generated by the property.

In addition, the limitations of the grantor trust rules prevent a taxpayer from escaping tax on the income from property where the taxpayer in effect remains the property owner by retaining control over the trust. For example, a "family estate" trust (i.e., a trust to which an individual transfers personal assets and the right to income in exchange for the beneficial enjoyment of such assets and compensation) is taxed as a grantor trust (Rev. Rul. 75-257).[147] The grantor's assignment of lifetime services or salary to the trust is not recognized for income tax purposes. Such trusts are deemed a "nullity" for income tax purposes and their income is taxable to the persons who created them. Acceptance of this broad economic principle deprives a grantor of any possible refuge in the technicalities of the grantor trust provisions. Expenses incurred in setting up family estate trusts are not deductible under Code Sec. 212.[148] Intra-family transfers of income-producing property cannot also be used to reduce income tax liability by shifting income from the parents' higher tax bracket to their child's generally lower tax bracket. Under the kiddie tax rules, if the net unearned income of the child exceeds an annual inflation-adjusted amount, it is taxed at the parents' top marginal rate (¶ 143).

Net Investment Income Tax. A grantor trust is not subject to the 3.8-percent net investment income tax (¶ 129 and ¶ 517) (Reg. § 1.1411-3(b)(1)).[149] Instead, for purposes of calculating the net investment income of the grantor or other person who is taxable on trust income (¶ 585), each item of income or deduction included in computing his or her taxable income under the grantor trust rules must be treated as if it had been received by, or paid to, the grantor or other person.

575. Funeral Trusts. A qualified funeral trust (QFT) is a nonforeign funeral trust that elects not to be treated as a grantor trust (¶ 571), so that the income tax on the annual earnings of the trust is payable by the trustee (Code Sec. 685).[150] A QFT is generally an arrangement that would otherwise be treated as a grantor trust, under which an individual purchases funeral services or necessary property for himself or herself, or for another individual, from a funeral home prior to death and funds the purchase via contributions. There are no dollar limitations on contributions to a QFT, but the contributions must be held, invested, and reinvested by the trust solely to make payments for funeral services or property upon the individual's or the other trust beneficiaries' death.

If the election is made, the income tax rate schedule generally applicable to estates and trusts (¶ 19) is applied to the trust by treating each beneficiary's interest as a separate trust. However, the trust is not entitled to a personal exemption (¶ 534). The trustee's election must be made separately for each such separate trust. No gain or loss is recognized to a purchaser of a funeral trust contract as a result of any payment from the trust to the purchaser due to the cancellation of the contract.

References are to Standard Federal Tax Reports; Tax Research Consultant; and Practical Tax Explanations.

[146] ¶ 24,680; ESTTRST: 36,000; § 32,801

[147] ¶ 24,783.1973; ESTTRST: 3,116; § 46,530.10

[148] ¶ 12,523.50; BUSEXP: 12,064.40; § 46,530.10

[149] ¶ 32,603L; ESTTRST: 12,256.05; § 32,801

[150] ¶ 24,895; ESTTRST: 39,350; § 32,175

The trustee elects QFT status by filing Form 1041-QFT. The election must be filed no later than the due date (with extensions) for filing the trust income tax return for the year of election. The election applies to each trust reported in the QFT return. The trustee can use the form to file for a single QFT or multiple QFTs having the same trustee. The election may be made for the trust's first eligible year or for any subsequent year. Once made, the election cannot be revoked without IRS consent.

576. Trusts With Reversionary Interest in Grantor. A grantor is considered to be the owner of any portion of a trust (¶ 571) in which the grantor or the grantor's spouse (¶ 578) has a reversionary interest in either the trust corpus or income if the value of the interest exceeds five percent of the value of that portion of the trust (Code Sec. 673).[151] The value of the interest is measured as of the inception of the portion of the trust in which the grantor holds an interest. In determining whether the grantor's reversionary interest exceeds the five-percent threshold, the maximum exercise of discretion in the grantor's favor is assumed. Any postponement of the reacquisition or enjoyment of the interest is considered to be a new transfer in trust. However, no trust income is included in the grantor's income that would not have been included absent postponement. In addition, a grantor is exempt from the reversionary interest rule if the interest takes effect only upon the death of a beneficiary who is a minor lineal descendant of the grantor (under age 21) and if the beneficiary has the entire present interest in all or part of the trust.

578. Powers Held by Grantor's Spouse. A grantor is treated as holding any power or interest in a trust (¶ 571) that is held by a person who was the grantor's spouse at the time the power or interest was created, or who became the grantor's spouse after creation of the power or interest (but only with respect to periods that the individual was the grantor's spouse) (Code Sec. 672(e)).[152] Thus, the grantor trust provisions cannot be avoided by having the spouse of the grantor possess prohibited powers or interests (e.g., spousal remainder trusts). Individuals who are legally separated under a decree of divorce or separate maintenance are not considered to be married for this purpose.

579. Power to Control Beneficial Enjoyment. A grantor of a trust (¶ 571) is taxed on trust income if the grantor or the grantor's spouse (¶ 578) retains the power to control the beneficial enjoyment of trust property or income without the consent of an adverse party (e.g., power to change beneficiaries or to change remainder interests) (Code Sec. 674; Reg. § 1.674(a)-1).[153] There are a number of exceptions to this rule including, but not limited to: (1) an unexercised power to apply income to support a dependent (¶ 137); (2) power to allocate income among charitable beneficiaries; (3) power to distribute corpus limited by a reasonably definite standard; and (4) power to withhold income temporarily (Reg. § § 1.674(b)-1—1.674(d)-2).[154]

581. Retention of Administrative Powers. The grantor of a trust (¶ 571) is taxed on trust income if the grantor or the grantor's spouse (¶ 578) retains administrative powers enabling the grantor to obtain, by dealings with the trust, financial benefits that would not be available in an arm's-length transaction (Code Sec. 675; Reg. § 1.675-1).[155] For example, if the grantor or his or her spouse borrows trust corpus or income at any time during a tax year, the grantor is taxed on the trust income for that entire year, even if the grantor repays the loan with interest during the same year (Rev. Rul. 86-82).[156]

582. Power to Revoke Trust. If a grantor creates a trust (¶ 571) and reserves a right to revoke it, the income of the trust is treated as the grantor's income (Code Sec. 676; Reg. § § 1.676(a)-1 and 1.676(b)-1).[157] The trust income is not taxed to the grantor if the power can only affect the beneficial enjoyment of the income after the occurrence of

References are to Standard Federal Tax Reports; Tax Research Consultant; and Practical Tax Explanations.

[151] ¶ 24,710; ESTTRST: 39,050; § 32,810

[152] ¶ 24,700; ESTTRST: 36,054; § 32,805.20

[153] ¶ 24,720, ¶ 24,721; ESTTRST: 45,050; § 32,815.05

[154] ¶ 24,722—¶ 24,725; ESTTRST: 45,050, ESTTRST: 45,052; § 32,815.10

[155] ¶ 24,740, ¶ 24,741; ESTTRST: 45,100; § 32,820.05

[156] ¶ 24,742.10; ESTTRST: 45,106; § 32,820.10

[157] ¶ 24,760, ¶ 24,761, ¶ 24,762; ESTTRST: 39,250; § 32,825

an event such that the grantor would not be treated as the owner if the power were a reversionary interest (¶ 576). However, the grantor may be treated as the owner after the event occurs unless the power to revoke is then relinquished.

584. Income for Grantor's Benefit. The grantor of a trust (¶ 571) is taxed on trust income that is or may be accumulated for or distributed to the grantor or the grantor's spouse, or used to pay life insurance premiums on either the grantor's or the spouse's life (except for policies irrevocably payable to charities) (Code Sec. 677; Reg. §§ 1.677(a)-1 and 1.677(b)-1).[158] To the extent that trust income may be used in satisfaction of the grantor's legal obligation to support a beneficiary (such as a child, but not a spouse), it is regarded as distributable to the grantor. If the discretion to so use the income is not in the grantor acting as such, but in another person (for example, the trustee or the grantor acting as trustee or co-trustee), then that income is includible in the grantor's gross income only to the extent that it is actually used for the beneficiary's support or maintenance. In addition, any capital gain under state law that is added to trust corpus is taxable to the grantor if the corpus reverts to the grantor upon termination of the trust (Reg. §§ 1.671-3(b)(2) and 1.677(a)-1(f); Rev. Rul. 58-242; Rev. Rul. 75-267).[159]

585. Income Taxable to Person Other Than Grantor. A person other than the grantor of a trust (¶ 571), including a beneficiary, may be taxed on the trust's income if that person has a power, exercisable alone, to vest trust corpus or income in himself or herself (Code Sec. 678; Reg. §§ 1.678(a)-1—1.678(d)-1).[160] For example, if a father establishes a trust for the benefit of his children, but the trust provides that the grantor's brother may take trust property at any time, the brother is treated as the owner and trust income is taxed to him. This rule does not apply if the power is renounced or disclaimed within a reasonable period. This rule also does not apply to a power over income as originally granted or later modified, if the grantor of the trust or a transferor to a foreign trust (¶ 588) is treated as the trust owner under the other grantor trust rules.

A U.S. person who is a beneficiary of a trust is treated as the grantor to the extent that the beneficiary transferred property, directly or indirectly and for less than adequate consideration, to a foreign person who otherwise would have been treated as the owner under the grantor trust rules (Code Sec. 672(f)(5)).[161]

586. Return for Grantor Trust. Items of income, deduction, or credit that are treated as belonging to a trust grantor or another person (¶ 571) are generally not reported by the trust on Form 1041 (Reg. § 1.671-4).[162] Instead, these items are reflected on the income tax return of the grantor (or other person who is taxable on the trust income). A separate statement should be attached to Form 1041 stating the name, taxpayer identification number, and address of the person to whom the income is taxable, and setting forth the income, deductions, and credits; however, there are other optional reporting methods available to certain types of grantor trusts. Widely held fixed investment trusts have specific information reporting requirements (Reg. § 1.671-5).[163]

588. Foreign Grantor Trust Rules. Any U.S. person transferring property to a foreign trust (¶ 501) (other than certain employee benefit plans and charitable trusts) that has a U.S. beneficiary will be treated as the owner of that portion of the trust attributable to the property transferred (Code Sec. 679).[164] The IRS can presume that the trust has a U.S. beneficiary unless the transferor submits to the IRS any information that the IRS requires regarding the transfer, and demonstrates to the IRS's satisfaction that: (1) under the terms of the trust, no part of the trust's income or corpus may be paid or accumulated during the tax year to or for the benefit of a U.S. person, even if that

References are to Standard Federal Tax Reports; Tax Research Consultant; and Practical Tax Explanations.

[158] ¶ 24,780—¶ 24,782; ESTTRST: 42,000; § 32,830.05, § 32,830.10, § 32,830.15

[159] ¶ 24,684, ¶ 24,781, ¶ 24,783.101, ¶ 24,783.34; ESTTRST: 39,150, ESTTRST: 42,054; § 32,830.40

[160] ¶ 24,800—¶ 24,804; ESTTRST: 36,200; § 32,805.10

[161] ¶ 24,700; ESTTRST: 36,056.05; § 32,801

[162] ¶ 24,685; ESTTRST: 36,104; § 32,610.25

[163] ¶ 24,685K; ESTTRST: 36,300

[164] ¶ 24,820; ESTTRST: 36,250; § 32,801, § 32,805.10

person's interest is contingent on a future event; and (2) no part of the trust's income or corpus could be paid to or for the benefit of a U.S. person if the trust were terminated at any time during the tax year. The transferor must ensure that the trust satisfies certain reporting requirements, and submit any information the IRS may require regarding the foreign trust (Code Secs. 6048(b) and 6677(a)).[165] A foreign trust with at least one U.S. owner must file Form 3520-A in order for the U.S. owner to satisfy its annual information reporting requirements. The U.S. grantor trust rules (¶ 571) generally do not apply to any portion of a trust that would otherwise be deemed to be owned by a foreign person (Code Sec. 672(f)).[166]

U.S. persons who are treated as owners of foreign trusts under the grantor trust rules (¶ 571) must file Form 3520.

Other Special Trusts

590. Charitable Remainder Trusts. Whenever there is a noncharitable income beneficiary of a trust, gifts of remainder interests qualify for a charitable contribution deduction only if the trust is a charitable remainder annuity trust (CRAT) or a charitable remainder unitrust (CRUT) (Code Sec. 664; Reg. §§ 1.664-1, 1.664-2 and 1.664-3).[167] Charitable contribution deductions are denied for gifts of remainder interests in all other types of trusts. However, if the donor gives *all* the interests in a trust to charity, the above rules do not apply, and a deduction is allowable (¶ 1070).

Qualification. An *annuity trust* is a trust from which a sum certain or a specified amount is to be paid to the income beneficiary (Code Sec. 664(d)(1); Reg. §§ 1.664-1 and 1.664-2). The specified amount cannot be less than five percent or more than 50 percent of the initial net fair market value of all property placed in trust, and it must be paid at least annually to the income beneficiary. Furthermore, the value of the charitable remainder interest must be at least 10 percent of the initial net fair market value of all of the property placed in trust. There are several provisions designed to provide relief to trusts that do not meet the 10-percent test. In addition, under the "probability of exhaustion" test, no charitable deduction is allowed if there is a greater than five percent probability that the life beneficiary or beneficiaries will survive exhaustion of the CRAT assets. The IRS has provided a sample provision that can be used as an alternative to satisfying the probability of exhaustion test, applicable to trusts created on or after August 8, 2016 (Rev. Proc. 2016-42).[168] No contributions can be made to a CRAT after the initial contribution, and the governing instrument must contain a prohibition against future contributions.

A *unitrust* is a trust that specifies that the income beneficiary is to receive annual payments based on a fixed percentage of the net fair market value of the trust's assets as determined each year (Code Sec. 664(d)(2); Reg. §§ 1.664-1 and 1.664-3). The fixed percentage cannot be less than five percent or more than 50 percent of the net fair market value of the trust's assets for the year. However, a qualified CRUT may provide for the distribution each year of five percent of the net fair market value of its assets or the amount of the trust income, whichever is lower. For this purpose, trust income excludes capital gains, and trust assets must be valued annually. The payment requirement may not be discretionary with the trustee. Additional contributions can be made to a unitrust. For most transfers in trust, the value of the charitable remainder interest with respect to each contribution to the unitrust must be at least 10 percent of the net fair market value of such contributed property as of the date the property is contributed to the trust. If an additional contribution would cause the trust to fail the 10-percent remainder test, then the contribution will be treated as a transfer to a separate trust under regulations. Other provisions may provide relief to trusts that fail to meet the 10-percent test.

References are to Standard Federal Tax Reports; Tax Research Consultant; and Practical Tax Explanations.

[165] ¶ 36,000, ¶ 39,815; ESTTRST: 36,258; § 39,135.15

[166] ¶ 24,700; ESTTRST: 36,056.05; § 32,801

[167] ¶ 24,460, ¶ 24,461, ¶ 24,464, ¶ 24,465; ESTGIFT: 45,200; § 32,150

[168] ¶ 24,468.28; ESTGIFT: 45,202.48; § 32,150.15

In the case of the early termination of a net income only charitable remainder unitrust (NICRUT) or a net income with make-up CRUT (NIMCRUT), the remainder interest is computed on the basis that an amount equal to five percent of the net fair market value of the trust assets (or a greater amount, if required by the trust instrument) is to be distributed each year, with any net income limit to be disregarded (Code Sec. 664(e), as amended by the Protecting Americans from Tax Hikes Act of 2015 (P.L. 114-113)).[169] This provision applies to terminations of trusts occurring after December 18, 2015.

CRATs and CRUTs cannot have noncharitable remainder interests. The remainder interests generally must pass to a charity upon the termination of the last income interest, and the trust instrument must contain a provision that determines how the final payment of a specified distribution is to be made. However, a charitable trust may make certain limited qualified gratuitous transfers of qualified employer securities to an employee stock ownership plan (ESOP) without adversely affecting the status of the charitable remainder trust.

To avoid the possible disqualification of a charitable remainder trust due to a surviving spouse's right of election against the grantor spouse's estate under state law, the IRS created a safe harbor requiring the surviving spouse to irrevocably waive the right (Rev. Proc. 2005-24). Until further guidance is published, the IRS will disregard the existence of a right of election *without* requiring a waiver, but only if the surviving spouse does not exercise the right (Notice 2006-15).[170]

There may be more than one noncharitable income beneficiary, either concurrently or successively, and the income interest may be a life estate or for a term of years not in excess of 20 years. However, a contingency clause may be placed in the trust instrument providing that the noncharitable interest is to terminate and the charitable remainder interest is to be accelerated upon the happening of an event, such as the remarriage of the noncharitable beneficiary (Code Sec. 664(f)).[171] The income beneficiary can receive only a specified or fixed amount from the trust, and the trustee cannot have additional power to invade corpus or to alter, amend, or revoke the trust for the benefit of the noncharitable income beneficiary. The trustee cannot be restricted from investing in income-producing assets (Reg. § 1.664-1(a)(3)).[172]

Division of Trust. The IRS has provided guidelines for dividing a CRAT or a CRUT into two or more separate and equal trusts without violating the charitable remainder trust requirements (Rev. Rul. 2008-41).[173]

Reporting. A CRAT or CRUT does not file Form 1041, but instead is required to file Form 5227. In addition, the fiduciary of a CRAT or CRUT may be required to file other returns regarding the excise tax on unrelated business taxable income (¶ 590A), and the excise taxes on private foundations that apply to charitable remainder trusts (¶ 591). Form 5227 must generally be filed on or before the 15th day of the fourth month following the close of the tax year of the trust (Rev. Proc. 83-32).[174]

590A. Taxation of Charitable Remainder Trust. A charitable remainder annuity trust (CRAT) or a charitable remainder unitrust (CRUT) (¶ 590) is generally exempt from income tax (Code Sec. 664(c); Reg. § 1.664-1).[175] However, if a CRAT or CRUT has unrelated business taxable income (UBTI) (¶ 670), it is subject to a 100-percent excise tax on its UBTI, but will retain its tax-exempt status. The excise tax is treated as paid from corpus, and trust income that is UBTI is income of the trust for purposes of determining the character of distributions made to beneficiaries (¶ 590B). The tax is reported on Form 4720, which must be filed by the due date for Form 5227 (¶ 590). The

References are to Standard Federal Tax Reports; Tax Research Consultant; and Practical Tax Explanations.

[169] ¶ 24,460; ESTGIFT: 45,204; § 34,315.20

[170] ¶ 24,468.18; ESTGIFT: 45,202.15, ESTGIFT: 45,204.05; § 32,150.25

[171] ¶ 24,460; ESTGIFT: 45,202.20, ESTGIFT: 45,204.20; § 32,150.25

[172] ¶ 24,461; ESTGIFT: 45,200; § 32,150.25

[173] ¶ 24,468.12; ESTTRST: 15,354; § 32,150.25

[174] ¶ 24,468.20; ESTTRST: 15,360; § 32,150.25

[175] ¶ 24,460, ¶ 24,461; ESTTRST: 15,354, ESTGIFT: 45,200; § 32,150, § 32,601, § 33,901

rule preventing the IRS from filing an additional deficiency notice once a taxpayer files a Tax Court petition challenging the deficiency also applies to this tax. In addition to the tax on UBTI, a charitable remainder trust may be subject to the income and excise taxes imposed on private foundations (¶ 591).

590B. Treatment of Charitable Remainder Trust Beneficiaries. Under either a charitable remainder annuity trust (CRAT) or a charitable remainder unitrust (CRUT) (¶ 590), the amount paid to a beneficiary is considered as having the following characteristics in the beneficiary's hands: (1) ordinary income to the extent of the trust's ordinary income for the tax year and its undistributed ordinary income from prior years; (2) capital gains to the extent of the trust's capital gains for the tax year and its undistributed capital gains, determined on a cumulative net basis, for prior years; (3) other income (including tax-exempt interest) to the extent of the trust's other income for the tax year and its undistributed other income from prior years; and (4) a distribution of trust corpus (Code Sec. 664(b); Reg. § § 1.664-1—1.664-4).[176] Items within the ordinary income and capital gains categories are assigned to different subcategories based on the federal income tax rate applicable to each type of income within the category. Categories of income that are taxed at the same rate can be combined into a single class if the tax rate will not change in the future. If the tax rate is temporary, then the categories must be maintained as separate groups (Reg. § 1.664-1(d)(1)(i)).[177]

The characterizations of income items distributed or deemed distributed at any time during the tax year of the charitable remainder trust are determined as of the end of the tax year. Distributions are subject to the tax rate applicable to the income class from which the distribution is derived, not the tax rate applicable when the income was received by the trust (Reg. § 1.664-1(d)(1)(ii)(a)). Gains and losses of long-term capital gain classes are netted prior to netting short-term capital loss against any class of long-term capital gain (Reg. § 1.664-1(d)(1)(iv)).

Net Investment Income Tax. While CRATs and CRUTs are not subject to the 3.8-percent net investment income tax (¶ 129 and ¶ 517), special rules apply for calculating the tax applicable to CRAT and CRUT distributions to beneficiaries (Reg. § 1.1411-3(d)).[178]

591. Private Foundation Rules Applicable to Charitable Trusts. The income and excise taxes imposed on private foundations extend to all nonexempt charitable trusts with certain modifications (Code Sec. 4947).[179] First, a nonexempt trust that devotes all of its unexpired interests to charitable, religious, educational, and other purposes that enable contributors to obtain a charitable deduction is treated as a private foundation (¶ 631). Thus, it may be subject to the excise taxes on: investment income (¶ 633), self-dealing (¶ 635), failure to distribute income (¶ 637), excess business holdings (¶ 640), investments that jeopardize charitable purposes (¶ 642), and certain taxable expenditures (lobbying, electioneering, etc.) (¶ 644). For this purpose, unexpired interests include life or term income interests, interests in trust corpus, and remainder interests.

Second, a nonexempt trust that does not devote all of its unexpired interests to charitable purposes (split-interest trust) is subject to the excise taxes on self-dealing, excess business holdings, investments that jeopardize charitable purposes, and certain taxable expenditures (lobbying, electioneering, etc.) as if it were a private foundation. However, the taxes apply to income to be paid to trust beneficiaries under the terms of the trust instrument only if the trust was a charitable remainder annuity trust (CRAT) or charitable remainder unitrust (CRUT) (¶ 590). The taxes do not, in any event, apply to amounts in trust for which a deduction is not allowable if segregated from deductible amounts.

References are to Standard Federal Tax Reports; Tax Research Consultant; and Practical Tax Explanations.

[176] ¶ 24,460—¶ 24,466; ESTGIFT: 45,210; § 32,150

[177] ¶ 24,461; ESTGIFT: 45,210; § 32,150

[178] ¶ 32,603L; ESTTRST: 12,256.25

[179] ¶ 34,140; EXEMPT: 21,300; § 33,201

In addition, the taxes on excess business holdings and investments that jeopardize charitable purposes do not apply to a split-interest trust if: (1) the charity is only an income beneficiary and its beneficial interest is no more than 60 percent of the value of the trust property; or (2) the charity's only interest in the trust is as a remainderman. Split-interest trusts are treated like private foundations with regard to the rules on governing instruments and the tax on involuntary termination of status for repeated or willful violations (¶ 631 and ¶ 649).

The excise tax on investment income and failure to distribute income do not apply to split-interest trusts under any circumstances.

593. Pooled Fund Arrangements. A pooled income fund is generally a trust to which a person transfers an irrevocable remainder interest in property for the benefit of a public charity while retaining an income interest in the property for the life of one or more beneficiaries living at the time of the transfer (Code Sec. 642(c)(5); Reg. § 1.642(c)-5).[180] Income, estate, and gift tax charitable contribution deductions are allowed for the value of remainder interests in property transferred to a pooled income fund (Code Sec. 642(c)(3)). To protect the value of depreciable property that will pass to the charitable remainderman, the governing instrument of the pooled income fund must provide for the creation of a depreciation reserve.[181] In addition, the fund: (1) must commingle all property contributed to it; (2) cannot invest in tax-exempt securities; and (3) must be maintained by the recipient charity with no donor or income beneficiary acting as a trustee. The charity does not have to act as trustee of the fund.

Each person who has an income interest resulting from a transfer of property to the fund must be paid an annual income based on the fund's yearly rate of return (i.e., the trust cannot accumulate income for any beneficiary). A pooled income fund's method of calculating its yearly rate of return must be supported by a full statement attached to the fund's annual income tax return. The fund and its beneficiaries are taxable under the rules applicable to trusts, except that the grantor trust rules (¶ 571) do not apply. In addition to its income tax return, a pooled income fund must file an annual information return on Form 5227 regarding its charitable deductions (¶ 537).

595. Common Trust Fund. Each participant in a common trust fund (¶ 2389) must report its share of the taxable income of the fund, whether or not distributed or distributable. The taxable income of a common trust fund is computed in much the same manner as an individual's taxable income, except that: (1) the charitable contribution deduction is not allowed; (2) gains and losses from the sale or exchange of capital assets must be segregated, and the fund cannot benefit from capital loss carryovers; (3) ordinary taxable income or net loss is computed without regard to capital gains or losses; and (4) the net operating loss deduction is not allowed (Code Sec. 584).[182]

References are to Standard Federal Tax Reports; Tax Research Consultant; and Practical Tax Explanations.

[180] ¶ 24,280, ¶ 24,293; ESTGIFT: 45,252; § 32,340.30

[181] ¶ 24,308.1877, ¶ 24,308.1880; ESTGIFT: 45,252; § 32,340.30

[182] ¶ 23,630; RIC: 12,300

Chapter 6

EXEMPT ORGANIZATIONS

	Par.
Overview	601
Code Sec. 501(c)(3) Organizations	602
Private Foundations	631
Unrelated Business Taxable Income	655
Taxable Income from Debt-Financed Property	687
Other Tax-Exempt Organizations	692

Overview

601. Overview of Tax-Exempt Organizations. A variety of organizations may qualify for exemption from federal income taxation. The most common basis for exempt status is as a charitable organization under Code Sec. 501(c)(3) (¶ 602). Charitable organizations can be either publicly supported or private foundations. While all charitable organizations are subject to limitations on how they operate, private foundations may be subject to excise taxes for engaging in prohibited activities (¶ 631). In addition to charitable organizations under Code Sec. 501(c)(3), there are a number of organizations that qualify for exempt status if they have a socially beneficial purpose (¶ 692). Regardless of how an entity qualifies as a tax-exempt organization, it may still be subject to federal income tax on any business income not related to its exempt purpose (¶ 655) and any income arising from debt-financed property (¶ 687). All tax-exempt organizations are also subject to various reporting requirements, such as annual information reporting (¶ 625), involvement in tax shelter transactions (¶ 619), and other disclosure requirements (¶ 627).

Code Sec. 501(c)(3) Organizations

602. Charitable Organizations Under Code Sec. 501(c)(3). Code Sec. 501 provides that various classes of nonprofit organizations may be exempt from federal income tax unless they are feeder organizations (¶ 694)[1] or they engage in certain prohibited transactions.[2] The most common basis for invoking tax-exempt status falls under Code Sec. 501(c)(3)'s broad exemption for religious, charitable, scientific, literary, and educational organizations (collectively referred to as charitable organizations).[3] Charitable organizations are generally either public charities or private foundations (¶ 631). Among other benefits, exempt status conferred by Code Sec. 501(c)(3) allows a public charity to receive tax-deductible contributions from its donors (¶ 627 and ¶ 1061). Any corporation, community chest, fund, trust, or foundation may qualify for the exemption. Application for recognition of Code Sec. 501(c)(3) federal tax-exempt status is made on Form 1023 or Form 1023-EZ (¶ 623).

To qualify for tax-exempt status under Code Sec. 501(c)(3), the entity must be organized and operated exclusively for religious (¶ 604), charitable, scientific, educational, or literary purposes; prevention of cruelty to children or animals; promotion of amateur sports competition; or testing for public safety. What constitutes a charitable purpose is interpreted broadly and may include purposes beyond those explicitly stated in Code Sec. 501(c)(3). For example, a charitable purpose can include: providing relief to the poor or disadvantaged; the advancement of education, religion, or science; or lessening the burdens of government through the promotion of social welfare or other

References are to Standard Federal Tax Reports; Tax Research Consultant; and Practical Tax Explanations.

[1] ¶ 22,670; EXEMPT: 15,350; § 33,001

[2] ¶ 22,680; EXEMPT: 12,208; § 33,825.15

[3] ¶ 22,602; EXEMPT: 3,000, EXEMPT: 9,000; § 33,005.05

community development (Reg. § 1.501(c)(3)-1(d)).[4] An educational organization can include a childcare center whose services are available to the general Code Sec. 501(k)).[5] Regardless of an entity's charitable purpose, it must meet certain organizational, operational, and private benefit tests to qualify as a tax-exempt charitable organization.

Organizational Test. The organizational test requires that the entity's articles of organization specifically limit its purpose to one or more exempt purposes, including that its assets are dedicated to an exempt purpose (Reg. § 1.501(c)(3)-1(b)).[6] The articles of organization also must not expressly permit the organization to carry on activities that do not further the organization's exempt purpose, except where the nonexempt activities are an insubstantial part of the organization's activities. For example, the articles of organization must not allow more than an insubstantial part of the organization's activities to consist of carrying on propaganda or attempting to influence legislation (¶ 613); or authorize the organization to directly or indirectly participate or intervene in any political campaign on behalf of or in opposition to any candidate for public office (¶ 614). Whether an organization meets the organizational requirement is determined exclusively from the language of the articles of organization and not from the activities conducted by the organization. For this purpose, "articles of organization" include trust instruments, corporate charters, articles of association, or any other written instrument that created an organization.

Operational Test. The operational test requires an entity to be operated exclusively for one or more exempt purposes. This means the organization engages primarily in activities that accomplish one or more of its exempt purposes (Reg. § 1.501(c)(3)-1(c)).[7] Only an insubstantial part of the entity's activities may be in the furtherance of nonexempt purposes. Whether an organization has a substantial nonexempt purpose is determined by taking into account all facts and circumstances, including the size and extent of all of the organization's activities. If the entity is an "action organization," then it will *not* be considered as operated exclusively for an exempt purpose. An entity is an action organization if it devotes a substantial part of its activities to attempting to influence legislation or if it participates in political campaigns. However, if an organization fails the operational test because it is an action organization, it may still qualify for tax-exempt status as a social welfare organization under Code Sec. 501(c)(4) (¶ 692). If a charitable organization provides commercial-type insurance as an insubstantial part of its activities, then the insurance activity will be treated as an unrelated trade or business (¶ 655) (Code Sec. 501(m) and (n)).[8]

An entity will not be considered as operating exclusively for exempt purposes if any of its net earnings inure in whole or in part to the benefit of private shareholders or individuals. A private shareholder or individual is any person having a personal and private interest in the activities of the organization, such as founders of the organization, employees, board members, or family members of officers, employees, etc. The inurement prohibition does not prohibit all payments to a private shareholder or individual but instead is directed at payments that are made for purposes other than as reasonable compensation for goods or services (¶ 617).

Private Benefit Test. An organization is not organized or operated exclusively for charitable purposes unless it serves a public rather than a outside private interest (as opposed to inside interests addressed by the inurement prohibition under the operation test). The question of private benefit often arises in situations in which a charitable organization enters into partnerships and other joint ventures with for-profit entities. The charitable organization can form such ventures and still satisfy the operational test only if it is permitted to act exclusively in furtherance of its exempt purpose and only incidentally for the benefit of the for-profit partners (Rev. Rul. 98-15).[9] In addition, the

References are to Standard Federal Tax Reports; Tax Research Consultant; and Practical Tax Explanations.

[4] ¶ 22,608; EXEMPT: 3,150; § 33,105

[5] ¶ 22,602; EXEMPT: 3,300; § 33,105

[6] ¶ 22,608; EXEMPT: 3,050; § 33,115

[7] ¶ 22,608; EXEMPT: 3,100; § 33,120

[8] ¶ 22,602; EXEMPT: 15,160

[9] ¶ 22,609.411; EXEMPT: 15,452, EXEMPT: 15,458; § 33,125

for-profit party cannot be allowed to control or use the charitable organization's activities or assets for its own benefit unless the control or use is incidental.

Charitable Hospitals. In addition to the requirements that apply to all Code Sec. 501(c)(3) organizations, each hospital organization operated by a charitable organization is subject to four requirements, on a facility-by-facility basis: (1) each facility must conduct and implement a community health needs assessment; (2) each facility must adopt, implement, and widely publicize a written financial assistance policy; (3) each facility may not bill patients who qualify for financial assistance more than the amount generally billed to insured patients; and (4) the facility (or affiliates) may not undertake extraordinary collection actions against patients (Code Sec. 501(r); Reg. §§1.501(r)-0—1.501(r)-7).[10] If a hospital organization fails to meet the community health needs assessment requirement, an excise tax of $50,000 for any applicable year is imposed on the hospital (Code Sec. 4959).[11] The IRS has provided procedures that a charitable hospital organization may use to correct and disclose certain failures to meet the requirements (Rev. Proc. 2015-21).[12]

604. Churches and Religious Organizations. A church or religious organization is exempt from federal income tax and eligible to receive tax-deductible contributions if it meets the Code Sec. 501(c)(3) requirements (¶ 602). The term "church" is not specifically defined in the Code but is used in its generic sense as a place of worship including, for example, mosques and synagogues. It also includes conventions or associations of churches, as well as integrated auxiliaries of a church. For this purpose, a convention or association of churches is a cooperative undertaking by churches of the same or differing denominations (Rev. Rul. 74-224).[13] The fact that the convention or association may extend membership to individuals and those individuals have voting rights will not cause it to lose exempt status (Code Sec. 7701(n)).[14]

It is important to distinguish churches from other religious organizations. To balance the need for the IRS to combat efforts on the part of some individuals and organizations to use churches to avoid taxes, and the equally important need to protect legitimate churches from undue IRS interference in their activities, the Code and regulations contain detailed rules governing when the IRS may inquire into or examine the activities of a "church" (Code Sec. 7611; Reg. §301.7611-1; Prop. Reg. §301.7611-1; NPRM REG-112756-09).[15] Religious organizations that are not churches may still be eligible for tax-exempt status, including nondenominational ministries, interdenominational and ecumenical organizations, and other entities whose principal purpose is the study or advancement of religion (IRS Pub. 1828). Unlike churches, however, religious organizations that want to be tax exempt must apply to the IRS for tax-exempt status by filing Form 1023 or Form 1023-EZ (¶ 623).

A religious or apostolic association that does not meet the requirements to be a Code Sec. 501(c)(3) organization may nonetheless qualify as exempt from federal income taxation if it has a common or community treasury. The exemption applies even if the association engages in business for the common good of its members, provided that the members include in their gross income their pro rata share of the association's taxable income as dividends received, whether distributed or not (Code Sec. 501(d); Reg. §1.501(d)-1).[16] There is no official exemption application form for this purpose but the association must file Form 1065 each tax year for information purposes (Reg. §1.6033-2(e)).[17]

607. Supporting Organizations. A charitable organization under Code Sec. 501(c)(3) that carries out its exempt purpose by providing support to other tax-exempt organizations (usually public charities) (¶ 602) is considered a public charity rather than

References are to Standard Federal Tax Reports; Tax Research Consultant; and Practical Tax Explanations.

[10] ¶ 22,602, ¶ 22,608C—¶ 22,608W; EXEMPT: 3,154

[11] ¶ 34,256; EXEMPT: 3,154

[12] ¶ 22,609.30; EXEMPT: 3,154

[13] ¶ 11,620.205; EXEMPT: 21,052

[14] ¶ 43,080; EXEMPT: 21,052

[15] ¶ 42,910, ¶ 42,912, ¶ 42,912C; IRS: 18,406

[16] ¶ 22,602, ¶ 22,659; EXEMPT: 3,202

[17] ¶ 35,422; EXEMPT: 12,054.20

a private foundation (¶ 631). To qualify as a supporting organization, an organization must not only meet the requirements to be a charitable organization under Code Sec. 501(c)(3) but must also be:

- organized and operated exclusively for the benefit of, to perform the functions of, or to carry out the purposes of a public charity (organizational and operational tests);
- operated or controlled by a public charity (relationship test); and
- not controlled either directly or indirectly by a disqualified person (¶ 635), other than a foundation manager or publicly supported charity (lack of control test) (Code Sec. 509(a)(3)).[18]

To satisfy the relationship test, a supporting organization must hold one of three close relationships with the supported organization (Reg. § 1.509(a)-4; Prop. Reg. § 1.509(a)-4).[19] In a Type I relationship, the supported organization must exercise a substantial degree of control over the programs, activities, and policies of the supporting organization (comparable to a parent-subsidiary relationship). In a Type II relationship, there must be common control or supervision by persons controlling or supervising both the supporting organization and the supported organization (comparable to brother-sister corporations). In a Type III relationship, the supporting organization must be operated in connection with the supported organization by being responsive to its needs and demands, and by being significantly involved in its operations to the point that the supported organization is dependent upon the supporting organization for the type of support it provides. Regardless of whether these relationship requirements are met, if a Type I or Type III organization supports an organization that is controlled by a donor, then the supporting organization will be treated as a private foundation rather than as a public charity (Code Sec. 509(f)(2)).

A number of special rules also apply to Type III supporting organizations. Each tax year, a Type III organization must provide each supported organization with any information that may be required by the IRS to ensure that the relationship requirements of being a Type III organization are met (Code Sec. 509(f)(1)). This may include the Type III organization's annual information return (Form 990), any tax return filed (Form 990-T), and any annual report. In addition, a Type III organization may not be operated in connection with any public charity that is organized outside the United States. Similarly, a trust will not be considered to be a Type III organization *solely* based on the facts that it is a charitable trust under state law, the public charity is a beneficiary of the trust, and the public charity has the power to enforce the trust terms (Act Sec. 1241(c) of P.L. 109-280).

Tax-exempt organizations use Form 8940 to request determinations about a change in type of supporting organization.

610. Donor Advised Funds. A Code Sec. 501(c)(3) charitable organization (other than a private foundation) may establish a donor advised fund that is a separate account where contributions made by a donor to the organization under which the donor (or person appointed by the donor) reasonably expects to provide nonbinding advice regarding distributions or investments (Code Sec. 4966(d)(2)).[20] The donor may be entitled to a charitable deduction for contributions to a donor advised fund (¶ 1061), but only if the sponsoring organization legally owns and controls the contributions. For this purpose, a donor advised fund does not include any fund that only makes distributions to a single identified organization or governmental entity. It also does not include a fund that allows the donor to provide advice as to which individuals receive grants for travel, study, or similar purposes through a committee that is appointed by the sponsoring organization that is not controlled by a donor or group of donors with advisory privileges and under which all grants are made on an objective and nondiscriminatory basis. The IRS has discretionary authority to exempt a fund or account from treatment as a donor

References are to Standard Federal Tax Reports; Tax Research Consultant; and Practical Tax Explanations.

[18] ¶ 22,800; EXEMPT: 21,200; § 33,020.05

[19] ¶ 22,804, ¶ 22,804B; EXEMPT: 21,200; § 33,020.10

[20] ¶ 34,317; EXEMPT: 33,000; § 33,720.05

advised fund. The charitable organization must provide information to the IRS when it applies for tax-exempt status (¶ 623) whether it maintains or intends to maintain the donor advised fund, and the manner in which it plans to operate those funds (Code Sec. 508(f)).[21]

An excise tax is imposed on any "taxable distribution" from a donor advised fund that is any distribution to a natural person or other person for a purpose other than an exempt purpose under Code Sec. 501(c)(3) (¶ 602) (Code Sec. 4966).[22] It also includes any distribution to a disqualified supporting organization (¶ 607), unless the sponsoring organization exercises responsibility for the distribution (Notice 2006-109, modified by Notice 2014-4).[23] A taxable distribution does not include any distribution to a 50-percent organization (¶ 1059), to the sponsoring organization, or to another donor advised fund. The excise tax is 20 percent of the distribution and is imposed on the sponsoring organization. A separate five-percent excise tax is imposed on any fund manager who knowingly agrees to the distribution (up to $10,000 per distribution). A fund manager includes any officer, director, or trustee of the sponsoring organization, as well as an employee having authority with respect to the distribution. Fund managers who knowingly participate in the transaction are jointly and severally liable for the five-percent tax. The taxes on both the sponsoring organization and the fund manager are reported on Form 4720. The IRS has discretionary authority to abate both taxes (¶ 647).

An excise tax is also imposed if a donor advised fund makes a distribution to any person that results in (directly or indirectly) a more-than-incidental benefit to the donor, donor advisor, member of the donor's family, or any entity in which the donor holds more than a 35-percent ownership interest (Code Sec. 4967).[24] The tax is 125 percent of the benefit received and is imposed on the donor, donor advisor, and related persons who recommended the distribution or received the prohibited benefit. A tax of 10 percent of the benefit (up to $10,000) is also imposed on fund managers who agreed to make a distribution knowing it would confer a more-than-incidental benefit. All persons liable for the taxes are jointly and severally liable. If the taxes are imposed, the IRS has discretionary authority to abate them (¶ 647). However, neither tax will be imposed if the distribution is subject to tax as an excess benefit transaction (¶ 617). Also, a donor advised fund is treated as a private foundation for purposes of the excise tax on excess business holdings (¶ 640).

613. Limitations on Lobbying Activities. An organization that otherwise qualifies as a Code Sec. 501(c)(3) charitable organization is denied tax-exempt status if: (1) a *substantial* part of its activities consists of carrying on propaganda or attempting to influence legislation, or (2) it participates or intervenes in any political campaign on behalf of, or in opposition to, any candidate for public office (Code Sec. 501(h); Reg. § 1.501(h)-1).[25] If a charitable organization engages in substantial legislative activity or participates in any political campaign, then it is an action organization (¶ 602) and not operated exclusively for one or more exempt purposes (Reg. § 1.501(c)(3)-1(c)(3)).[26] There are no specific guidelines as to what constitutes *substantial* legislative activities for this purpose; instead it is determined on the facts and circumstances of each case. However, the IRS has issued guidance for the facts and circumstances to be evaluated in determining whether or not a Code Sec. 501(c)(3) organization has participated or intervened in a political campaign for public office (Rev. Rul. 2007-41).[27] If the organization has made a political expenditure, it will be subject to an excise tax (¶ 614).

As an alternative to the substantial part test, many charitable organizations may elect on Form 5768 a sliding scale limitation on expenditures to objectively determine their permissible level of lobbying activities (Code Sec. 501(h); Reg. § 1.501(h)-2).[28] The

References are to Standard Federal Tax Reports; Tax Research Consultant; and Practical Tax Explanations.

[21] ¶ 22,790; EXEMPT: 33,056; § 33,720.05

[22] ¶ 34,317; EXEMPT: 33,150; § 33,720.10

[23] ¶ 34,317C.20; EXEMPT: 33,150; § 33,720.10

[24] ¶ 34,319; EXEMPT: 33,200; § 33,720.15

[25] ¶ 22,602, ¶ 22,663; EXEMPT: 6,100; § 33,710.05

[26] ¶ 22,608; EXEMPT: 6,102; § 33,710.05

[27] ¶ 22,609.103; EXEMPT: 6,104; § 33,710.05

[28] ¶ 22,602, ¶ 22,664; EXEMPT: 6,150; § 33,710.05

election can be made at any time during the organization's tax year. It is effective for the entire tax year and all succeeding years until revoked. Organizations that may not make this election include: churches or a convention or association of churches (¶ 604), private foundations (¶ 631), and supporting organizations (¶ 607) for social welfare organizations, labor unions, trade associations, and organizations that test for public safety (¶ 692).

The basic permitted level for lobbying expenditures (but not grassroots lobbying) is 20 percent of the first $500,000 of the electing organization's exempt-purpose expenditures for the year, 15 percent of the second $500,000, 10 percent of the third $500,000, and five percent of any additional expenditures with a maximum annual limitation of $1 million (Code Sec. 4911).[29] In the case of so-called grassroots lobbying—attempts to influence the public on legislative matters—the basic permitted level is limited to 25 percent of the general lobbying level described above. An excise tax of 25 percent is imposed on any excess lobbying expenditures above these limits. In addition, if an organization's lobbying expenditures normally—on an average over a four-year period—exceed 150 percent of these limits (computed on Schedule C of Form 990), the organization will lose its tax-exempt status (Reg. § 1.501(h)-3).[30]

614. Excise Tax on Political Expenditures. A 10-percent excise tax is imposed on a Code Sec. 501(c)(3) organization for each political expenditure made during the tax year (Code Sec. 4955).[31] For this purpose, a political expenditure is generally defined as any amount paid or incurred by the organization in connection with any participation or intervention in any political campaign on behalf of (or in opposition to) any candidate for public office (¶ 613). A separate 2.5-percent excise tax (up to $5,000) is imposed on any organization manager who agrees to the making of the expenditure if the manager knows that it is a political expenditure, unless the agreement is not willful and due to reasonable cause. An organization manager includes a director, officer, trustee, or any individual with comparable responsibilities.

If the political expenditure is not corrected within a "taxable period," then a second-tier excise tax is imposed on the organization equal to 100 percent of the amount of the expenditure. Organization managers who refuse to agree to all or part of the correction are also subject to a second-tier tax of 50 percent of the amount of the expenditure (up to $10,000). If more than one manager is liable for either the first- or second-tier taxes, then each manager is jointly and severally liable for them. The taxable period is the period beginning on the date on which the taxable expenditure is made and ending on the earlier of the date on which a deficiency notice for the first-tier tax is mailed or it is assessed. A correction of a political expenditure means the foundation takes all reasonable means to recover the expenditure to the extent possible and establishes safeguards to prevent future political expenditures. If full recovery is not possible, then the foundation must take whatever corrective action is prescribed by the IRS. Both the first and second levels of taxes may be abated under certain circumstances (¶ 647). The organization's taxes are reported on Form 4720.

617. Excess Benefit Transactions. An excise tax is imposed on any "excess benefit transaction" involving a charitable organization under Code Sec. 501(c)(3) other than a private foundation (¶ 631), a social welfare organization under Code Sec. 501(c)(4) (¶ 692), or a qualified nonprofit health insurance issuer under Code Sec. 501(c)(29) (Code Sec. 4958).[32] The tax may be applied instead of, or in addition to, the organization being disqualified as an exempt organization due to the prohibition on private inurement (¶ 602). An excess benefit transaction is any transaction in which an economic benefit is provided to a "disqualified person" by the organization that exceeds any consideration given. It also includes any grant, loan, or other payment from a donor advised fund (¶ 610) or a qualified supporting organization (¶ 607) to a disqualified person.

References are to Standard Federal Tax Reports; Tax Research Consultant; and Practical Tax Explanations.

[29] ¶ 33,960; EXEMPT: 6,156.05; § 33,710.05

[30] ¶ 22,665; EXEMPT: 6,160; § 33,710.05

[31] ¶ 34,240; EXEMPT: 6,106; § 33,710.10

[32] ¶ 34,250; EXEMPT: 6,056; § 33,705.30

The tax is imposed on the disqualified person and is 25 percent of the amount of the excess benefit or the amount of the grant, loan, or other compensation received from a donor advised fund or qualified supporting organization. A manager of the exempt organization who knowingly participates in the transaction is subject to a separate excise tax of 10 percent, up to $20,000 per act. Managers who knowingly participate in the transaction are jointly and severally liable for the 10-percent tax. A manager will not be liable if participation is not willful and due to reasonable cause. For this purpose, a manager includes a director, officer, trustee, and any other individual of the exempt organization with comparable responsibilities.

If the excess benefit is not corrected within the "taxable period" (¶ 614), then a second-tier excise tax is imposed on the disqualified person equal to 200 percent of the amount of the excess benefit, grant, loan, or other payment. If more than one person is liable for either the first- or second-tier taxes on disqualified persons, then these persons are jointly and severally liable for them. The taxes on disqualified persons and organization managers are reported on Form 4720. However, both levels of taxes may be abated under certain circumstances (¶ 647). In addition, private foundations are subject to different sanctions (¶ 635).

Disqualified Persons. For this purpose, a disqualified person is a person who is in a position to exercise substantial influence over the affairs of the exempt organization (including a qualified supporting organization), regardless of the individual's title. Certain family members and entities in which a disqualified person holds at least a 35-percent ownership interest are also treated as disqualified persons. In the case of any donor advised fund, a disqualified person includes any donor, donor advisor, and investment advisor to the fund, as well as any family member or any entity controlled by such persons. A disqualified person with respect to a qualified supporting organization includes any substantial contributor (¶ 635), family member of a substantial contributor, or a 35-percent controlled entity.

619. Involvement in Tax Shelter Transactions. Generally, a tax-exempt entity that is a party to a prohibited tax shelter transaction (¶ 2591), or that becomes a party to a subsequently listed transaction at any time during the tax year, is subject to an excise tax on a percentage of the entity's net income or proceeds attributable to the prohibited transaction (Code Sec. 4965).[33] The rate of tax depends on whether the exempt entity *knew or had reason to know* that the transaction was a prohibited tax shelter transaction at the time it became a party to the transaction. In addition, any manager of a tax-exempt entity who approves or otherwise causes the exempt entity to be a party to a prohibited tax shelter transaction at any time during the tax year, and knew or had reason to know that the transaction was a prohibited tax shelter transaction, must pay a separate excise tax for each approval. For this purpose, a tax-exempt entity includes any tax-exempt organization under Code Sec. 501(c) or religious organization under Code Sec. 501(d), including any charitable organization and any qualified retirement plan, as well as individual retirement account (IRA), health savings account (HSA), Archer medical savings account (MSA), qualified tuition plan, and qualified ABLE account. The tax-exempt entity must disclose that it is a party to a prohibited tax shelter transaction on Form 8886-T, as well as the identity of any other party (including both taxable and tax-exempt parties) to the transaction which is known by the entity (Code Sec. 6033(a)(2); Reg. § 1.6033-5).[34] The entity or certain entity managers may be liable for a penalty if the disclosure requirement is not met (Code Sec. 6652(c)(3)).[35]

623. Application and Modification of Tax-Exempt Status. Charitable organizations seeking exempt status under Code Sec. 501(c)(3) must file an application for exemption on Form 1023 or Form 1023-EZ within 15 months (or 27 months with an automatic 12-month extension) from the end of the month in which they are organized (Code Sec.

References are to Standard Federal Tax Reports; Tax Research Consultant; and Practical Tax Explanations.

[33] ¶ 34,305; EXEMPT: 6,252; § 33,715

[34] ¶ 35,420, ¶ 35,424E; EXEMPT: 6,254; § 33,715

[35] ¶ 39,480; EXEMPT: 6,254; § 33,715

508; Reg. § 1.508-1; Temp. Reg. § 1.508-1T).[36] Form 1023-EZ, which can only be filed electronically, is meant for organizations with gross receipts of $50,000 or less and assets of $250,000 or less (Rev. Proc. 2016-5). An organization that fails to file a timely notice will not qualify for exempt status for any period prior to the date actual notice is given. A second notification is required to be included on the application if the organization wants to claim public charity status. An organization that fails to notify the IRS of public charity status will be presumed to be a private foundation (¶ 631). An organization will be a publicly supported organization qualifying for public charity status in its first five years if it can reasonably be expected to receive the requisite public support during the period (Reg. § 1.170A-9(f)(4)(v)).[37]

Organizations that are not required to file an application for exempt status or notification of public charity status include: (1) any organization (other than a private foundation) whose annual gross receipts normally do not exceed $5,000; (2) churches and their affiliates; (3) any subordinate organization (other than a private foundation) covered by a group exemption of a parent; and (4) certain nonexempt charitable trusts (¶ 591) (Reg. § 1.508-1(a)(3)). However, for such an organization to establish its exemption with the IRS and receive a determination letter, it should file the appropriate information return as proof of its exemption (¶ 625) (Reg. § 1.508-1(a)(4)).

The IRS will issue a favorable determination letter or exemption ruling if the organization's application and supporting documents establish that it meets the particular requirements under which it is claiming tax-exempt status (Rev. Proc. 2016-5).[38] A ruling may also be modified or revoked by the IRS at any time (Reg. § 601.201(n)(6)).[39] Revocations generally occur prospectively but a retroactive revocation may occur where: (1) the IRS was not fully or correctly informed as to the material facts on which the exemption ruling was based, or (2) there have been material changes in law or fact after the original ruling was issued.

If an organization receives an unfavorable exemption ruling, or its exempt status is revoked, it may seek judicial review only after it has exhausted all administrative remedies with the IRS. If an adverse ruling is issued (or if the IRS fails to issue a ruling), the organization can seek a declaratory judgment that it qualifies for exempt status (Code Sec. 7428).[40] If the organization has actually begun operations before it receives an adverse ruling (or its exempt status is revoked retroactively), it may either pay the taxes on its activities it thought were exempt and file for a refund or it can protest the assessment of any taxes in the Tax Court. An organization whose tax-exempt status has been revoked because it did not file annual information returns for three consecutive years (¶ 625) can apply for reinstatement of its status (Rev. Proc. 2016-5).[41]

Tax-exempt organizations use Form 8940 to request determinations (other than initial exemption applications) about their tax-exempt status. These determinations include advance approval for foundation set-asides and scholarship approvals, change in type of supporting organization, and termination of foundation status.

625. Annual Information Return for Tax-Exempt Organizations. All tax-exempt organizations are generally required to file an annual information return with the IRS, including organizations whose application for exemption is pending, as well as nonexempt charitable trusts (¶ 591) (Code Sec. 6033; Reg. § 1.6033-2).[42] For most organizations, the return is filed on or before the 15th day of the fifth month following the close of the organization's tax year on Form 990, Form 990-EZ, or Form 990-N, depending on its gross receipts and total assets. For returns filed for tax years beginning before January 1, 2016, an automatic three-month extension is available; an automatic six-month

References are to Standard Federal Tax Reports; Tax Research Consultant; and Practical Tax Explanations.

[36] ¶ 22,790, ¶ 22,791, ¶ 22,791F; EXEMPT: 12,054; § 33,505

[37] ¶ 11,662; EXEMPT: 21,102; § 7,565.10

[38] ¶ 22,604.10; EXEMPT: 12,054; § 33,535

[39] ¶ 43,356; EXEMPT: 12,104; § 33,801

[40] ¶ 41,720; EXEMPT: 12,150; § 33,801

[41] ¶ 43,360.173; EXEMPT: 12,054; § 33,605.20

[42] ¶ 35,420, ¶ 35,422; EXEMPT: 12,252; § 33,605.05

extension is available for returns filed for tax years beginning after December 31, 2015 (Reg. § 1.6081-9(a); Act Sec 2006(b) of the Surface Transportation and Veterans Health Care Choice Improvement Act of 2015 (P.L. 114-41)).[43]

Other forms may be required for certain organizations. For example, private foundations file Form 990-PF (¶ 631), farmers' cooperatives file Form 1120-C (¶ 698), religious and apostolic organizations file Form 1065 (¶ 604), and black lung benefits trusts file Form 990-BL. Organizations that exclude exempt function income from their gross income may be required to file a variation of Form 1120 in lieu of, or in addition to, Form 990 or Form 990-EZ, such as political organizations, which file Form 1120-POL (¶ 696), and certain homeowner associations, which file Form 1120-H (¶ 699).

Exempt organizations that are not required to file Form 990 or Form 990-EZ, regardless of gross receipts and total assets, include: any organization (other than a private foundation or supporting organization (¶ 607)) that has annual gross receipts of $50,000 or less; any church (including its integrated auxiliary) and convention or association of churches (¶ 604); an exclusively religious activity of a religious order; church-sponsored mission societies; governmental units exempt from taxation; corporations organized under an act of Congress; certain schools affiliated with a church or religious order; and certain foreign or U.S. possession organizations (Code Sec. 6033(a)(3); Reg. § 1.6033-2(g)(1); Rev. Proc. 2011-15).[44] An exempt organization that is not required to file Form 990 or Form 990-EZ because its annual gross receipts normally do not exceed $50,000 is still required to file an annual information return electronically on Form 990-N (Code Sec. 6033(i); Reg. § 1.6033-6; Rev. Proc. 2011-15).[45]

Information Required. Form 990 and Form 990-EZ require an exempt organization to provide information on its finances, governance, compliance with certain federal tax filings and requirements, compensation paid to certain persons, exempt and nonexempt activities, and, in the case of a charitable hospital, the needs identified in its community health needs assessments and a copy of its audited financial statements (Code Sec. 6033(b)). Additional schedules and information are required to be completed depending upon the activities and type of the organization. For example, a charitable organization under Code Sec. 501(c)(3) must include information on its lobbying activities (¶ 613) and any donor advised funds (¶ 610) it sponsors (Code Sec. 6033(e) and (k)). A qualified nonprofit health insurance issuer under Code Sec. 501(c)(29) must include information on the amount of reserves on hand, and the amount of reserves required by each state in which the issuer is licensed to issue qualified health plans (Code Sec. 6033(m)). If an organization was tax-exempt for any of its last five tax years preceding its dissolution, liquidation, termination, or substantial contraction, then it must also include on Form 990 or Form 990-EZ information relating to that event (Code Sec. 6043(b); Reg. § 1.6043-3(b)).[46] Organizations exempt from reporting information on their dissolution or termination include churches, organizations other than private foundations with $5,000 or less in annual gross receipts, and other organizations specified in the regulations.

Disclosure. Tax-exempt organizations, including private foundations, must make available for public inspection, at the organization's principal, regional, and district offices (having three or more employees) during regular business hours, its three most recent annual information returns, as well as a copy of its application for exemption. Charitable organizations must also make available for public inspection any returns related to the organization's unrelated business taxable income (¶ 670) filed in the previous three tax years (Code Sec. 6104; Reg. § 301.6104(d)-3).[47] Organizations do not have to honor requests if they reasonably believe that the request is part of a harass-

References are to Standard Federal Tax Reports; Tax Research Consultant; and Practical Tax Explanations.

[43] ¶ 36,798K; FILEBUS: 15,104.35, EXEMPT: 12,252; § 33,605.05

[44] ¶ 35,420, ¶ 35,422, ¶ 35,425.24; EXEMPT: 12,252.05; § 33,605.05

[45] ¶ 35,420, ¶ 35,424J, ¶ 35,425.33; EXEMPT: 12,252.05; § 33,605.15

[46] ¶ 35,880, ¶ 35,885; EXEMPT: 12,252.30; § 33,605.05

[47] ¶ 36,900, ¶ 36,910E; EXEMPT: 12,258; § 33,615

ment campaign. Requests may be made either in person or in writing. Copies of an organization's Form 990 must be furnished immediately for requests made in person and within 30 days for written requests. Organizations are permitted to charge a reasonable fee for reproduction and mailing costs. An exempt organization can comply with these disclosure requirements by posting information on its website.

Penalties. A penalty is imposed on each tax-exempt organization that fails to file an annual information return, files a late return without reasonable cause, or fails to file the information return on dissolution or substantial contraction (Code Sec. 6652(c)(1) and (7); Rev. Proc. 2015-53; Rev. Proc. 2016-55).[48] The penalty is adjusted annually for inflation and is $20 per day for 2016 ($20 per day for 2017), up to a maximum for one return of $10,000 for 2016 ($10,000 for 2017) or five percent of the organization's gross receipts for the years, whichever is less.

For organizations with gross receipts in excess of $1,020,000 for 2016 ($1,028,500 for 2017), the penalty increases to $100 per day for 2016 ($100 per day for 2017), up to a maximum for any return of $51,000 for 2016 ($51,000 for 2017). An additional penalty of $10 a day for 2016 ($10 for 2017), up to a maximum $5,000 on any return for 2016 ($5,000 for 2017) is imposed on any officer, trustee, employee, etc., who fails to file the return without reasonable cause after requested by the IRS. There is no monetary penalty on an organization that is required to file Form 990-N but fails to do so.

If an organization fails to file an annual return for three consecutive years, its exempt status is automatically revoked (Code Sec. 6033(j)).[49] An organization whose tax-exempt status has been revoked because it did not file annual information returns for three consecutive years can apply for reinstatement of its status (Rev. Proc. 2016-5).[50]

Failure to comply with the public disclosure requirements results in a penalty of $20 per day for 2016 ($20 per day for 2017), with a maximum of $10,000 for any annual return for 2016 ($10,000 for any annual return for 2017) (Code Sec. 6652(c)(1)(C) and (D)). There is no maximum penalty for failure to disclose the organization's exemption application. The penalty for a willful failure to comply with the public disclosure requirements is $5,000 for each return or application (Code Sec. 6685).[51]

627. Other Reporting and Disclosure Requirements of Tax-Exempt Organizations. In addition to filing an application for tax-exempt status (¶ 623) and annual information returns (¶ 625), tax-exempt organizations (other than private foundations (¶ 631)) have a number of other filing requirements.

Nondeductible Contributions. All tax-exempt organizations that are not eligible to receive deductible charitable contributions (such as lobbying groups, political action committees, labor unions, trade associations, social clubs, and political organizations (¶ 692 and ¶ 1061)) must disclose this fact in a conspicuous and easily recognizable format in their fundraising solicitations (Code Sec. 6113).[52] Violation of this requirement without reasonable cause will subject an organization to a penalty of $1,000 per day of solicitation (up to $10,000 for any calendar year); a higher penalty will apply if the failure was intentional (Code Sec. 6710).[53]

Quid Pro Quo Contributions. Charitable organizations are required to inform donors in a written statement that quid pro quo contributions in excess of $75 are deductible only to the extent that the contributions exceed the value of goods or services provided by the organization (Code Sec. 6115).[54] Failure to make the required disclosure subjects the organization to a penalty of $10 per contribution unless due to reasonable cause (Code Sec. 6714).[55] A quid pro quo contribution is any payment made partly as a contribution to the organization and partly in consideration for goods or services provided by the organization (e.g., fundraising dinners and auctions).

References are to Standard Federal Tax Reports; Tax Research Consultant; and Practical Tax Explanations.

[48] ¶ 39,480; PENALTY: 3,208.15; § 33,615

[49] ¶ 35,420; EXEMPT: 12,252.15; § 33,605.05

[50] ¶ 43,360.173; EXEMPT: 12,054; § 33,605.20

[51] ¶ 39,871; EXEMPT: 12,258; § 33,615

[52] ¶ 37,040; EXEMPT: 12,302; § 33,620.15

[53] ¶ 40,115; EXEMPT: 12,302.25; § 33,620.15

[54] ¶ 37,065; EXEMPT: 12,306; § 33,620.05

[55] ¶ 40,180; EXEMPT: 12,306.20; § 33,620.05

Donated Vehicles. A charitable organization is required to provide a donor of a motor vehicle, boat, or airplane with a contemporaneous written acknowledgment of the donation using Form 1098-C, including a certification of the organization's use or sale of the vehicle (¶ 1070A). A donee organization that fails to provide the acknowledgment or that provides a fraudulent acknowledgment will be subject to a penalty (Code Sec. 6720).[56]

Donated Intellectual Property. A charitable organization that receives or accrues net income during a tax year from a qualified intellectual property contribution must file an information return on Form 8899 and provide a copy to the donor (¶ 1062A). The return is required for any tax year that occurs during the 10-year period beginning on the date of the contribution and if the legal life of the donated property has not expired. The organization will be subject to a penalty for failure to file the return (¶ 2816).

Dispositions of Donated Property. A charitable organization is required to file a donee information return on Form 8282 if it sells or otherwise disposes of any charitable deduction property within three years after donated to the organization (Code Sec. 6050L(a)).[57] Charitable donation property is any property (other than cash or public securities) for which the donor claims a charitable contribution deduction of more than $5,000 and for which the organization signed an acknowledgment on Form 8283. The organization will be subject to a penalty for failure to file the return (¶ 2816).

Private Foundations

631. Private Foundations. Charitable organizations under Code Sec. 501(c)(3) are either public charities or private foundations (¶ 602). A public charity is an organization that has broad public support or that actively functions in a supporting relationship to such an organization. A private foundation typically is funded by one individual, family, or corporation. Thus, a private foundation is any Code Sec. 501(c)(3) organization *other than*:

- a charitable deduction donee listed in Code Sec. 170(b)(1)(A) (¶ 1059);
- a publicly supported organization receiving more than ⅓ of its annual support from members and the public, and not more than ⅓ of its support from investment income and unrelated business income (¶ 655);
- a qualified supporting organization (¶ 607); or
- an organization operated for public safety testing (Code Sec. 509; Reg. § 1.509(a)-3).[58]

An organization that fails the public support test for two consecutive years will be treated as a private foundation as of the beginning of the second year of failure for certain purposes. The organization will be treated as a private foundation for all purposes beginning the first day of the third consecutive year.

Like all Code Sec. 501(c)(3) organizations, a private foundation must provide notice to the IRS for it to be exempt from taxation (¶ 623). However, even if notice is provided, a private foundation will be denied tax-exempt status unless its governing instrument specifically prohibits it from accumulating income (¶ 637), engaging in certain prohibited activities including acts of self-dealing (¶ 635), retaining excess business holdings (¶ 640), making investments that jeopardize its charitable purpose (¶ 642), or making certain taxable expenditures (¶ 644) (Code Sec. 508(e)).[59] All private foundations must also file an annual information return on Form 990-PF reporting gross income, receipts, disbursements, etc. (¶ 625). If at any time during the tax year the foundation has at least $5,000 of assets, it must also include information on its assets, managers, and grants or contributions made during the year (Code Sec. 6033(c); Reg. § 1.6033-3).[60]

References are to Standard Federal Tax Reports; Tax Research Consultant; and Practical Tax Explanations.

[56] ¶ 40,207; INDIV: 51,456.25; § 33,610.35

[57] ¶ 36,260; EXEMPT: 12,262; § 33,610.10

[58] ¶ 22,800, ¶ 22,803; EXEMPT: 21,000; § 33,205.05

[59] ¶ 22,790; EXEMPT: 21,450; § 33,205.20

[60] ¶ 35,420, ¶ 35,423; EXEMPT: 21,552; § 33,205.15

633. Investment Income of Private Foundations. A two-percent excise tax is imposed on the "net investment income" of a private foundation (¶ 631) for each tax year (Code Sec. 4940).[61] The tax is reduced to one percent if the foundation satisfies certain requirements as to the amount of charitable distributions it made during the year and if it was not liable for the excise tax on undistributed income (¶ 637) in any of the preceding five tax years. The excise tax is reported on the foundation's annual return, Form 990-PF. Estimated payments of the foundation's liability for the tax (as well as its unrelated business taxable income (UBTI) (¶ 670)) are computed on Form 990-W. The first-quarter installment is due by the 15th day of the fifth month following the foundation's tax year (May 15 for calendar year foundations) (Code Sec. 6655(g)(3)).[62] The net investment income of a private foundation generally includes the foundation's gross investment income and net capital gain, less the ordinary and necessary business expenses incurred for the production or collection of gross investment income. Gross investment income includes interest, dividends, rents, royalties, and payments with respect to securities loans, as well as any similar source of income such as income from annuities and notional principal contracts. It does not include income to the extent it is taken into account as UBTI, including any gain or loss from the sale or disposition of property (no capital loss carryovers or carrybacks are allowed).

The tax on investment income will not apply to an exempt "operating foundation," which is any operating foundation that has been publicly supported for at least 10 years, at all times during the tax year it is governed by representatives at least 75 percent of whom represent the public, and at no time during the tax year does it have an officer who is a disqualified individual. For this purpose, a disqualified individual is a substantial contributor to the foundation, an owner of more than 20 percent of a business or trust that is a substantial contributor, or a member of the family of any of the preceding. An operating foundation is a foundation that spends at least 85 percent of the lesser of its adjusted net income or its minimum investment return in carrying on its exempt activities (Code Sec. 4942(j)(3); Reg. § 53.4942(b)-1).[63] A nonoperating private foundation is generally a grantmaking organization that does not operate its own charitable program.

635. Prohibitions on Self-Dealing by Private Foundations. Certain acts of self-dealing are prohibited between a disqualified person and a private foundation (¶ 631) (Code Sec. 4941).[64] This includes the sale or exchange of property, loans or other extensions of credit, the furnishing of goods or services, payments of compensation, or the transfer of income or assets to the disqualified person. It does not include the pro rata division of a trust that qualifies as a charitable remainder trust (¶ 590) into two separate trusts (Rev. Rul. 2008-41).[65] For this purpose, a disqualified person includes:

- a substantial contributor (any person who contributes more than $5,000 if that amount is more than two percent of the total contributions received by the foundation before the end of its tax year);
- a foundation manager, including an officer, director, or trustee;
- the owner of more than 20 percent of a corporation, partnership, trust, or other enterprise that is a substantial contributor;
- a member of the family of any of the preceding (including spouse, ancestor, child, grandchild, great grandchild, or spouse of any of these descendants);
- a corporation, trust, estate, or partnership more than 35 percent of which is owned or held by any of the preceding; and
- a government official (Code Sec. 4946).[66]

References are to Standard Federal Tax Reports; Tax Research Consultant; and Practical Tax Explanations.

[61] ¶ 34,000; EXEMPT: 24,050; § 33,210.05

[62] ¶ 39,565; EXEMPT: 15,204; § 33,245

[63] ¶ 34,040, ¶ 34,044; EXEMPT: 24,450; § 33,210.10

[64] ¶ 34,020; EXEMPT: 24,150; § 33,215.05

[65] ¶ 34,031.65; EXEMPT: 24,200

[66] ¶ 34,120; EXEMPT: 24,700; § 33,205.25

The disqualified person is subject to a 10-percent excise tax on the amount involved in any act of self-dealing for each year in the taxable period. Any foundation manager who knowingly participates in the self-dealing act is subject to a five-percent excise tax on the amount involved but only if participation was willful and not due to reasonable cause. A second-level tax of 200 percent (50 percent on the manager) applies if the prohibited act is not corrected within the taxable period. For this purpose, the taxable period begins on the date the self-dealing act occurs and ends on the earliest of: (1) the date the deficiency notice for the first-level tax is mailed; (2) the date the first-level tax is assessed; or (3) the date the act of self-dealing is completely corrected (Code Sec. 4941(e)).[67] The maximum tax imposed on a foundation manager is $20,000 per act for each level of tax. The IRS has discretionary authority to abate both levels of tax for the manager and the disqualified person (¶ 647). However, a third-level tax may be imposed or the foundation's status may be terminated (¶ 649) if there are repeated or flagrant acts of self-dealing (Code Sec. 6684).[68] The initial excise tax on an act of self-dealing is reported on Form 4720.

637. Undistributed Income of Private Foundations. A private foundation (¶ 631) other than an operating foundation (¶ 633) is required to annually distribute its minimum investment return for the tax year, which equals five percent of the foundation's net investment assets (adjusted for certain taxes and loan repayments). Failure to do so will cause the foundation to be subject to an excise tax of 30 percent of any undistributed income (Code Sec. 4942).[69] Undistributed income is the amount the minimum investment return of the foundation exceeds the amount of qualifying distributions made during the tax year. Qualifying distributions include distributions to public charities and private operating foundations, and payments for expenses and assets used for charitable purposes. It does not generally include payments made by the nonoperating private foundation to a supporting organization (¶ 607).

If the foundation fails to make the necessary distributions within the taxable period, then a second-level tax will be imposed equal to 100 percent of the undistributed income. The taxable period is the period that begins on the first day of the tax year, and ends on the earlier of the date the deficiency notice for the initial tax is mailed or it is assessed. The IRS has discretionary authority to abate both levels of tax (¶ 647). However, a third-level tax may be imposed or the foundation's status may be terminated (¶ 649) if there are repeated or flagrant acts of failure to distribute income (Code Sec. 6684).[70] The initial excise tax on undistributed income is reported on Form 4720.

640. Excess Business Holdings of Private Foundations. A private foundation (¶ 631) is allowed to own a certain amount of business enterprises jointly with disqualified persons (¶ 635). However, to curb any abuses, the foundation is subject to a 10-percent excise tax on any excess business holdings during the tax year (Code Sec. 4943).[71] If the excess business holdings are not divested within the taxable period (¶ 637), then a second-level tax of 200 percent is imposed. The permitted amount of business ownership that a private foundation and disqualified person may have in any enterprise that is not substantially related to the exempt purposes of the foundation is generally 20 percent. If third parties have effective control of the business enterprise, then the limit is 35 percent. Special rules apply to certain grandfathered holdings. The IRS has discretionary authority to abate both levels of tax (¶ 647). However, a third-level tax may be imposed or the foundation's status may be terminated (¶ 649) if there are repeated or flagrant acts of excess business holdings (Code Sec. 6684).[72]

The excise tax on excess business holdings will apply to donor advised funds (¶ 610) and certain qualified supporting organizations (¶ 607). In applying the tax to donor advised funds, a disqualified person is defined as any donor, a member of the donor's family, or a 35-percent controlled entity (Code Sec. 4943(e)). A qualified

References are to Standard Federal Tax Reports; Tax Research Consultant; and Practical Tax Explanations.

[67] ¶ 34,020; EXEMPT: 24,150; § 33,215.05

[68] ¶ 39,865; EXEMPT: 24,162; § 33,215.05

[69] ¶ 34,040; EXEMPT: 24,300; § 33,220.05

[70] ¶ 39,865; EXEMPT: 24,162; § 33,220.05

[71] ¶ 34,060; EXEMPT: 24,500; § 33,225.05

[72] ¶ 39,865; EXEMPT: 24,162; § 33,225.05

supporting organization will be subject to the excess business holdings tax only if it is a Type III supporting organization, or a Code Sec. 501(c)(3) organization that meets the organizational and operational test of a qualified supporting organization and it is not controlled by a disqualified person (Code Sec. 4943(f)). For this purpose, a disqualified person with respect to the supporting organization is any person with substantial influence over the organization (or any family member of such a person), as well as any substantial contributor, family member of a substantial contributor, or 35-percent controlled entity.

642. Investments Jeopardizing Exempt Purpose of Private Foundations. A 10-percent excise tax is imposed on any investment of a private foundation (¶ 631) that jeopardizes the foundation's exempt status (Code Sec. 4944; Reg. § 53.4944-1).[73] A jeopardizing investment is generally one that shows a lack of reasonable business care and prudence in providing for the foundation's short-and long-term financial needs. Examples of investments that will be closely scrutinized include trading in securities on margin, trading in commodity futures, investing in working interests in oil and gas wells, and selling short. Investments made by a private foundation that are not program-related investments (PRIs) but are made at least partially for charitable purposes are not jeopardizing investments (Reg. § 53.4944-3; Notice 2015-62).[74] A 10-percent excise tax is also imposed on any foundation manager who knowingly participates in such an investment (up to $10,000 per investment), unless the participation is not willful but due to a reasonable cause. A second-level tax of 25 percent is imposed on the foundation if the jeopardy situation is not corrected within the taxable period (¶ 637). Any foundation manager who refuses to agree to part or all of the correction will be subject to a second-level tax of five percent of the investment (up to $20,000). If more than one foundation manager is liable for either level of tax, then all such managers are jointly and severally liable for them. The IRS has discretionary authority to abate both levels of tax (¶ 647). However, a third-level tax may be imposed on either the foundation or a manager, or the foundation's status may be terminated (¶ 649), if there are repeated or flagrant acts of jeopardizing investments (Code Sec. 6684).[75]

644. Lobbying and Other Prohibited Expenditures of Private Foundations. A private foundation (¶ 631) is subject to a 20-percent excise tax on the amount of any taxable expenditure made during the tax year. Any foundation manager who, without reasonable cause, willfully agrees to the expenditure knowing it is improper is subject to a five-percent excise tax on the expenditure (up to $10,000) (Code Sec. 4945).[76] A taxable expenditure generally includes any amount paid by the foundation for legislative or political purposes, or any grant to an individual for travel, study, or other similar purpose (unless made under objective standards). It also includes any grant to any organization unless the grantee organization is a public charity, qualified supporting organization (¶ 607), exempt operating foundation (¶ 633), or the nonoperating private foundation exercises responsibility for the expenditure of the grant. A taxable expenditure does not include the pro rata division of a trust that qualifies as a charitable remainder trust (¶ 590) into two separate trusts (Rev. Rul. 2008-41).[77] A second-level tax of 100 percent is imposed on the foundation if the taxable expenditure is not corrected within the taxable period (¶ 637). Any foundation manager who refuses to agree to part or all of the correction will be subject to a second-level tax of 50 percent of the investment (up to $20,000). If more than one foundation manager is liable for either level of tax, then all such managers are jointly and severally liable for them. The IRS has discretionary authority to abate both levels of tax for the foundation or the manager (¶ 647). However, a third-level tax may be imposed or the foundation's status may be terminated (¶ 649) if there are repeated or flagrant acts of taxable expenditures (Code Sec. 6684).[78]

References are to Standard Federal Tax Reports; Tax Research Consultant; and Practical Tax Explanations.

[73] ¶ 34,080, ¶ 34,081; EXEMPT: 24,600; § 33,230.05

[74] ¶ 34,083, ¶ 34,087.60; EXEMPT: 24,608, EXEMPT: 24,610.10; § 33,230.10

[75] ¶ 39,865; EXEMPT: 24,162; § 33,230.05

[76] ¶ 34,100; EXEMPT: 24,650; § 33,235.05

[77] ¶ 34,031.65; EXEMPT: 24,650

[78] ¶ 39,865; EXEMPT: 24,162; § 33,235.05

647. Abatement of Certain Taxes on Tax-Exempt Organizations. The IRS has discretionary authority not to assess certain first-tier excise taxes imposed on tax-exempt organizations, or to abate such taxes if already assessed, or to provide a credit or refund if the tax is already collected. The IRS will exercise this authority only if the violation giving rise to the imposition of the excise tax in question was due to reasonable cause and not willful neglect, and is corrected within the correction period (Code Sec. 4962).[79] First-tier excise taxes to which this relief may apply include: all of the excise taxes imposed on private foundations and disqualified persons (¶ 631), except for the tax on acts of self-dealing (¶ 635); the excise tax on the lobbying and political activities of public charities (¶ 614); the excise tax on excess benefit transactions (¶ 617); and the excise taxes on taxable distributions and prohibited benefits from donor advised funds (¶ 610). The IRS may withhold or abate an assessment of any second-tier excise taxes if the taxable event in question is corrected voluntarily during the correction period (Code Sec. 4961).[80] The correction period begins on the date of the taxable event and ends 90 days after the deficiency notice for the second-tier tax is mailed (Code Sec. 4963).[81]

649. Termination of Private Foundation Status. The status of any organization as a private foundation (¶ 631) may be terminated voluntarily or involuntarily (Code Sec. 507).[82] A voluntary termination requires the foundation to notify the IRS of its plan to terminate. An involuntary termination occurs when the IRS notifies the foundation of the intent to terminate its status because of willful repeated violations or a willful and flagrant violation giving rise to excise taxes on the foundation. In either case, the private foundation must pay a termination tax equal to the lesser of: (1) the aggregate amount of tax benefits received by the foundation and any of its substantial contributors (¶ 635) since its inception resulting from its exempt status under Code Sec. 501(c)(3); or (2) the value of its net assets. The pro rata division of a trust that qualifies as a charitable remainder trust (¶ 590) into two separate trusts does not terminate private foundation status or cause the termination tax to apply (Rev. Rul. 2008-41).[83]

The IRS may abate a portion or all of the termination tax if, prior to providing notice to the IRS of its voluntary termination, the foundation distributes all of its net assets to another private foundation or public charity described in Code Sec. 170(b)(1)(A) (¶ 1059) that has been in existence for at least five years immediately before the distribution. Under these circumstances, the transfer of assets is not a termination of the foundation's status. Instead, the foundation retains its status until it gives actual notice of its termination to the IRS. When notice is provided after all net assets are transferred, then the termination tax will be zero (but the distributions may give rise to excise taxes). The termination tax may also be abated if the foundation becomes a public charity within 12 months or it actually operates as a public charity for at least five years. However, notice of termination must be provided to the IRS prior to the beginning of the 12-month or five-year termination period.

Tax-exempt organizations use Form 8940 to request determinations about termination of foundation status.

Unrelated Business Taxable Income

655. Tax-Exempt Organizations Subject to Unrelated Business Income Tax. Although a variety of nonprofit organizations with charitable or socially beneficial purposes may be granted tax-exempt status under Code Sec. 501, they are still subject to a tax on unrelated business income (¶ 658) (Code Sec. 511).[84] Unrelated business income is income from a trade or business regularly carried on by the exempt organization (¶ 664) that is not substantially related (¶ 667) to the organization's exempt purposes (Code Sec. 512).[85] All types of exempt organizations, except government instrumentali-

References are to Standard Federal Tax Reports; Tax Research Consultant; and Practical Tax Explanations.

[79] ¶ 34,280; EXEMPT: 24,750; § 33,220.10

[80] ¶ 34,260; EXEMPT: 24,750; § 33,220.10

[81] ¶ 34,300; EXEMPT: 24,756; § 33,220.10

[82] ¶ 22,771; EXEMPT: 27,000; § 33,240.05

[83] ¶ 34,031.65; EXEMPT: 27,000

[84] ¶ 22,820; EXEMPT: 15,000; § 33,905

[85] ¶ 22,830; EXEMPT: 15,050; § 33,910

ties (other than colleges or universities) and federally licensed businesses or educational institutions sponsored by a religious order, are subject to the tax (Reg. § 1.511-2).[86] Additionally, title-holding companies may be exempt from tax on unrelated business income if the holding corporation and the payee organization file a consolidated return.

658. Unrelated Business Income Tax Rate and Payment. Tax-exempt organizations subject to the unrelated business income tax (¶ 655) are taxed on their unrelated business taxable income (UBTI) (¶ 670) at ordinary corporate income tax rates (¶ 219) or, if the organization is not incorporated, at trust income tax rates (¶ 19) (Code Sec. 511(a)).[87] Organizations taxed on UBTI are also subject to the alternative minimum tax (AMT) for items of tax preference that enter into the computation of UBTI (¶ 1401). Returns are made on Form 990-T for each tax year that the organization has gross income of $1,000 or more from an unrelated trade or business. The form is filed at the same time as the organization's annual information return (¶ 625) (Reg. § 1.6012-2(e)).[88] Estimated payments of the exempt organization's liability for UBTI are computed on Form 990-W. The first-quarter installment is due by the 15th day of the fifth month following the organization's tax year (May 15 for calendar year organizations) (Code Sec. 6655(g)(3)).[89]

664. Business Regularly Carried on by Tax-Exempt Organizations. The unrelated business taxable income (UBTI) of a tax-exempt organization (¶ 670) is its gross income from any unrelated trade or business *regularly* carried on by the organization, minus any deductions for expenses related to the trade or business (¶ 682) (Code Sec. 512(a); Reg. §§ 1.512(a)-1 and 1.513-1(c)).[90] A trade or business generally includes any activity carried on for the production of income from selling goods or performing services. In determining whether a trade or business is regularly carried on, the frequency and continuity with which an activity is pursued is judged with comparable commercial activities of nonexempt organizations. In the case of a social club, voluntary employees' beneficiary association (VEBA), or an organization for the payment of supplemental unemployment benefits (SUB) (¶ 692), UBTI is subject to tax only to the extent that it is not set aside for the purposes that constitute the basis for the organization's exemption (Code Sec. 512(a)(3); Temp. Reg. § 1.512(a)-5T).[91]

667. Business Unrelated to Exempt Function of Tax-Exempt Organizations. The unrelated business taxable income (UBTI) of a tax-exempt organization (¶ 670) includes any income from a business *not substantially related* to the organization's exempt purpose (Code Sec. 513; Reg. § 1.513-1).[92] A business activity is not substantially related to an organization's exempt purpose if it does not contribute importantly to accomplishing that purpose (other than through the production of funds). Whether an activity contributes importantly depends on the facts, including the size and extent of the activities involved in relation to the exempt function they serve. A number of activities will *not* be considered an unrelated trade or business, including any trade or business that:

- has substantially all the work in carrying on the business performed for the organization without compensation;
- is carried on by a Code Sec. 501(c)(3) organization or governmental college or university primarily for the convenience of its members, students, etc.;
- consists of selling merchandise, substantially all of which has been received by the organization as gifts or contributions;

References are to Standard Federal Tax Reports; Tax Research Consultant; and Practical Tax Explanations.

[86] ¶ 22,822; EXEMPT: 15,058; § 33,905

[87] ¶ 22,820; EXEMPT: 15,202; § 33,901

[88] ¶ 35,145; EXEMPT: 15,204; § 33,901

[89] ¶ 39,565; EXEMPT: 15,204; § 33,901

[90] ¶ 22,830, ¶ 22,831, ¶ 22,841; EXEMPT: 15,054, EXEMPT: 15,252; § 33,910, § 33,915

[91] ¶ 22,830, ¶ 22,834; EXEMPT: 15,206, EXEMPT: 15,208; § 33,910, § 33,915

[92] ¶ 22,840, ¶ 22,841; EXEMPT: 15,056; § 33,920

- is a qualified entertainment activity or a qualified convention and trade show activity (¶ 685) (Code Sec. 513(d));

- in the case of a public charity hospital, performs services that a tax-exempt cooperative hospital organization may perform (¶ 699) (Code Sec. 513(e));

- consists of conducting any bingo games if the games are conducted in accordance with local law and do not compete with profit-making businesses (Code Sec. 513(f));

- in the case of a mutual or cooperative telephone or electric company, engages in qualified pole rentals (Code Sec. 513(g));

- includes exchanging or renting member donor lists between exempt organizations or distributing low-cost articles ($10.60 for 2016; $10.70 for 2017) incidental to the solicitation of charitable contributions (Code Sec. 513(h); Rev. Proc. 2015-53; Rev. Proc. 2016-55); or

- involves soliciting and receiving qualified sponsorship payment (Code Sec. 513(i)) (¶ 685).

670. Unrelated Business Taxable Income Defined. The unrelated business taxable income (UBTI) of a tax-exempt organization is its gross income from any unrelated trade or business regularly carried on (¶ 664 and ¶ 667), less the deductions directly connected with the trade or business (¶ 682) (Code Sec. 512).[93] The following income items (and any related deductions) are generally excluded from the calculation of UBTI: dividends, interest, annuities and royalties (¶ 673); rents from real property or incidental rents from personal property leased with real property (¶ 676); gains or losses from the disposition of property other than stock in trade (¶ 679); certain research income; certain amounts received from controlled entities and foreign corporations; income of a mutual or cooperative electric company derived from the sale of electricity from its members; and gains or losses on the disposition of qualified brownfield sites. Annual dues not exceeding $161 for 2016 ($162 for 2017) that are paid to an exempt agricultural or horticultural organization will also be excluded from UBTI (Code Sec. 512(d); Rev. Proc. 2015-53; Rev. Proc. 2016-55).

An exempt organization's UBTI calculation must include its share of income and deductions from an unrelated trade or business conducted by a partnership (including a publicly traded partnership) or S corporation in which it is a partner or shareholder (Code Sec. 512(c) and (e)). However, if the tax year of the organization differs from the partnership's, then the amounts used to calculate UBTI will be based on the income and deductions of the partnership in the tax year that ends within the tax year of the exempt organization. In addition, the organization's share of S corporation income and deductions must be included regardless of whether they would normally be excluded from UBTI (dividends, interest, royalties, etc.).

673. Unrelated Business Taxable Income—Investment Income. The unrelated business taxable income (UBTI) of a tax-exempt organization (¶ 670) generally will *not* include investment income such as dividends, interest, annuities, royalties, payments with respect to securities loans, amounts received or accrued as consideration for entering into agreements to make loans, and income derived from notional principal contracts (as well as income from ordinary investments that are substantially similar) (Code Sec. 512(b); Reg. § 1.512(b)-1(a)).[94] Royalties for this purpose include amounts paid to an exempt organization for use of its name, trademarks, and other intellectual property rights in connection with the sale of merchandise or services.[95] However,

References are to Standard Federal Tax Reports; Tax Research Consultant; and Practical Tax Explanations.

[93] ¶ 22,830; EXEMPT: 15,200, EXEMPT: 15,300; § 33,935.05

[94] ¶ 22,830, ¶ 22,835; EXEMPT: 15,302; § 33,935.05

[95] ¶ 22,837.83; EXEMPT: 15,310; § 33,935.05

where an exempt organization provides active services in relation to marketing products or services associated with its name or other rights, the income may not be excluded as royalty income. The exclusion for investment income also does not apply to income from debt-financed property (¶ 687).

Membership Organizations. Special rules apply to certain membership organizations including a social and recreational club, voluntary employees' beneficiary association (VEBA), or a supplemental unemployment compensation benefit trust (SUB) (¶ 692). Unlike other exempt organizations, these organizations cannot exclude investment income from UBTI and losses from nonexempt activities cannot generally be used to offset investment income. However, gross income does not include exempt function income, which is income from dues, fees, and charges for providing facilities and services for members, dependents, and guests, as well as income set aside for charitable purposes or by a VEBA to provide insurance benefits (Code Sec. 512(a)(3)).[96] An exclusion also applies for gain such organizations realize on the sale of assets used in pursuing their exempt function to the extent the proceeds are reinvested (within a four-year period) in other assets for such purposes. A title-holding corporation whose income is payable to a membership organization will be treated as the exempt organization for this purpose. To prevent bypassing these limitations through termination of tax-exempt status, a *nonexempt* social club or other membership organization operated primarily to furnish goods or services to members may deduct the cost of furnishing these goods, services, insurance, etc., only to the extent of membership-related income (Code Sec. 277).[97] A nonexempt social club or VEBA is also not allowed to claim the corporate dividends-received deduction (¶ 223).

Look-Through Rules. If an exempt organization receives or accrues a payment of interest, annuity, royalty or rent (but not a dividend) from an entity that it controls, then the payment is includible in the organization's UBTI to the extent it either reduces the net unrelated business income of the controlled entity or increases its net unrelated losses (Code Sec. 512(b)(13), as amended by the Protecting Americans from Tax Hikes (PATH) Act of 2015 (P.L. 114-113)).[98] However, any payment made pursuant to a binding written contract in effect on August 17, 2006, (or renewal of such a contract) is included in UBTI only to the extent it exceeds the amount of the payment if it were made as if the parties were not related (i.e., arms-length transaction).

A valuation misstatement penalty applies to excess payments that are included in UBTI. In addition, the exempt organization must report the payments from a controlled entity on its annual return (Code Sec. 6033(h)).[99] The threshold of control of a subsidiary which triggers UBTI is having more than 50-percent ownership (more than 50 percent of stock by vote or value in a corporation, or more than 50 percent of a profits, capital, or beneficial interest of a partnership or other entity). The constructive ownership rules of Code Sec. 318 apply for this purpose (¶ 743).

676. Unrelated Business Taxable Income—Rents. Excluded from the unrelated business taxable income (UBTI) of a tax-exempt organization (¶ 670) are amounts received from the rental of real property, including those rents from personal property leased with real property so long as they are incidental in relation to the total amount of rents under the lease (10 percent or less of total rents from all leased property) (Code Sec. 512(b)(3); Reg. § 1.512(b)-1(c)).[100] However, payments for the use or occupancy of rooms and other space (for example, in a hotel, boarding house, storage facility) where services are also provided primarily for the occupant's convenience and are not those customarily rendered in rental for occupancy only (such as maid service) are not rents from real property. Rents are taxable if they are: (1) rents from real property leased with personal property where more than 50 percent of the rent is attributable to the personal property; (2) rents from both real and personal property if the amount of the rents

References are to Standard Federal Tax Reports; Tax Research Consultant; and Practical Tax Explanations.

[96] ¶ 22,830; COMPEN: 54,350, EXEMPT: 15,206, EXEMPT: 15,208; § 33,935.05

[97] ¶ 14,600; ACCTNG: 12,216; § 33,420.25

[98] ¶ 22,830; EXEMPT: 15,304; § 33,935.05

[99] ¶ 35,420; EXEMPT: 15,304; § 33,935.05

[100] ¶ 22,830, ¶ 22,835; EXEMPT: 15,306; § 33,935.05

depends on the income or profits derived by any person from the leased property (other than an amount based on a fixed percentage of gross receipts or sales); and (3) unrelated income from debt-financed property (¶ 687).

679. Unrelated Business Taxable Income—Gains and Losses. Excluded from the unrelated business taxable income (UBTI) of a tax-exempt organization (¶ 670) are all gains or losses from the sale, exchange or other disposition (including involuntary conversions and casualties) of property *other than*: (1) stock in trade or other property of a kind properly includible in inventory; (2) property held primarily for sale to customers in the ordinary course of a trade or business; or (3) timber cutting that the organization has elected to consider as a sale or exchange (Code Sec. 512(b)(5); Reg. § 1.512(b)-1(d)).[101] The exclusion also applies to all gains or losses recognized in connection with the organization's investment activities from the lapse or termination of options to buy and sell securities (whether or not written by the organization), as well as options to buy or sell real property. The exclusion does not apply to gains from the sale or other disposition of debt-financed property (¶ 687). Gains from certain pension plan investments in property of troubled financial institutions are also excluded (Code Sec. 512(b)(16)).

682. Unrelated Business Taxable Income—Deductions. In computing unrelated business taxable income (UBTI) (¶ 670), a tax-exempt organization is entitled to deduct all ordinary and necessary business expenses *directly connected* with carrying on the unrelated trade or business (¶ 667). To be directly connected with the conduct of an unrelated business, deductions must have a proximate and primary relationship to carrying on the business. Expenses attributable to an exempt activity generally are not deductible unless: (1) the unrelated business exploits the exempt activity; (2) the business is of a type normally carried on for profit by a taxable organization; and (3) the exempt activity is of a type normally carried on by a taxable organization in carrying on its business. If facilities or personnel are used for both exempt functions and the conduct of an unrelated business, expenses must be allocated on a reasonable basis (Code Sec. 512(a) and (b)(12); Reg. § 1.512(a)-1).[102]

In addition to deduction of ordinary and necessary business expenses, an exempt organization is allowed a specific deduction of $1,000, as well as the deduction for charitable contributions allowed to corporations (¶ 927), net operating losses (NOLs) (¶ 1145), and domestic production activities (equal to the appropriate percentage of the lesser of qualified production activities income or unrelated business taxable income, rather than taxable income (¶ 980A)). The charitable contribution deduction is allowed whether or not directly connected with the carrying on of the trade or business but is limited to 10 percent of the organization's UBTI, computed without regard to the contributions deduction (Code Sec. 512(b)(10)). An exempt trust that is subject to the unrelated business income tax at trust rates generally is allowed a deduction for charitable contributions in the same amounts as allowed for individuals (¶ 1058). With respect to the NOL deduction, the deduction must only reflect taxable business income and carryovers and items attributable to exempt income and expenses are disregarded (Code Sec. 512(b)(6)).

685. Advertising, Sponsorships, and Trade Shows. The sale of advertising in a periodical, journal, or magazine of a tax-exempt organization is considered an unrelated business of the organization (¶ 667) that exploits an exempt activity when the advertising activity is regularly carried on (¶ 664) (Reg. § 1.512(a)-1(d) and (f)).[103] An activity such as advertising does not lose its identity as a trade or business merely because it is carried on within a larger complex of other activities which may or may not be related to the organization's exempt purpose (Reg. § 1.513-1(b)).[104] As a result, advertising reve-

References are to Standard Federal Tax Reports; Tax Research Consultant; and Practical Tax Explanations.

[101] ¶ 22,830, ¶ 22,835; EXEMPT: 15,302; § 33,935.05

[102] ¶ 22,830, ¶ 22,831; EXEMPT: 15,250; § 33,930

[103] ¶ 22,831; EXEMPT: 15,158; § 33,925.05

[104] ¶ 22,841; EXEMPT: 15,158; § 33,925.05

nue is used in computing the organization's unrelated business taxable income (UBTI) (¶ 670) but may be offset by the expenses directly related to the advertising business activity. If facilities and personnel are both used to carry on exempt activities and unrelated advertising, the expenses must be allocated on a reasonable basis.

For this purpose, income realized by an exempt organization from the sponsorship of a public event will generally constitute advertising services. However, the solicitation and receipt of qualified sponsorship payments by an exempt organization is not an unrelated business, and the payments are excluded from computing UBTI (Code Sec. 513(i); Reg. § 1.513-4).[105] A qualified sponsorship payment is any payment by a payor engaged in a trade or business that does not expect any substantial return from the exempt organization other than the use or acknowledgment of the payor's name, logo, or product lines in connection with the activities of the tax-exempt organization. A qualified sponsorship payment does *not* include any payment:

- for advertising the payor's product or services, including messages that contain qualitative or comparative language, price information, an endorsement, or an inducement to purchase, sell or use the payor's products and services;
- contingent upon factors indicating the degree of public exposure at one or more events (attendance, broadcast ratings);
- that entitles the payor to the use or acknowledgment of the business name, logo, or product lines in the exempt organization's publication; or
- made in connection with a qualified convention or trade show activity (a convention or trade show conducted by a charitable organization (¶ 602), social welfare program, labor organization, or business league (¶ 692) that has as one of its purposes the promotion of interest in the products and services of the industry in general, or the education of the attendees regarding new developments or products and services related to the exempt activities of the organizations (Reg. § 1.513-3)).[106]

Taxable Income from Debt-Financed Property

687. Unrelated Debt-Financed Income. A percentage of income from debt-financed property must be included in a tax-exempt organization's unrelated business taxable income (UBTI) (¶ 670) regardless of whether the organization is engaged in a trade or business (Code Sec. 514(a); Reg. § 1.514(a)-1).[107] The percentage included in UBTI is the same percentage (not to exceed 100 percent) as the average acquisition indebtedness on the property (¶ 689) for the tax year divided by the average amount of the adjusted basis of the property. Deductions with respect to each debt-financed property are allowed by applying the same percentage to expenses related to the property, except for any deduction resulting from the carryback or carryover of net capital losses (¶ 1752). For this purpose, debt-financed property generally means any property held to produce income, including gain from its disposition (for example, rental real estate, corporate stock, etc.) on which there is an acquisition indebtedness at any time during the tax year (or preceding 12 months if the property is disposed of during the tax year) (Code Sec. 514(b); Reg. § 1.514(b)-1(a)).[108] Certain property, however, is not debt-financed property even if it is held to produce income (¶ 691).

689. Acquisition Indebtedness on Debt-Financed Property. For any debt-financed property of a tax-exempt organization (¶ 687), acquisition indebtedness is the outstanding amount of principal debt: (1) incurred to acquire or improve property; (2) incurred before the acquisition or improvement if it would not have been incurred but for the acquisition or improvement; and (3) incurred after acquisition or improvement if it would not have been incurred but for the acquisition or improvement and was reasonably foreseeable at the time (Code Sec. 514(c); Reg. § 1.514(c)-1).[109]

References are to Standard Federal Tax Reports; Tax Research Consultant; and Practical Tax Explanations.

[105] ¶ 22,840, ¶ 22,843G; EXEMPT: 15,122; § 33,925.05

[106] ¶ 22,843; EXEMPT: 15,112; § 33,925.05

[107] ¶ 22,850, ¶ 22,851; EXEMPT: 18,050; § 33,940.05

[108] ¶ 22,850, ¶ 22,853; EXEMPT: 18,100; § 33,940.05

[109] ¶ 22,850, ¶ 22,854; EXEMPT: 18,200; § 33,940.15

If property is acquired subject to a mortgage, the amount of the mortgage (or similar lien) is considered acquisition indebtedness, even if the organization does not assume or agree to pay the debt. However, when mortgaged property is received by bequest or devise (or by gift under certain circumstances), the debt will not be treated as an acquisition indebtedness for 10 years from the date of acquisition. A lien for taxes or assessments under state law will be treated similar to a mortgage to the extent the amount becomes due and the organization has an opportunity to pay it.

Acquisition indebtedness does not include debt that was incurred by an exempt organization in the exercise of its exempt purpose. Generally, it also does not include debt incurred by certain qualified organizations (qualified employee benefits trust; an exempt school; exempt title-holding company; retirement income account of church plan) in acquiring or improving real property. Annuities may be excluded from the definition of acquisition indebtedness, as well as certain obligations insured by the Federal Housing Administration or incurred by a small business investment company (¶ 2392).

691. Exceptions to Debt-Financed Property. The following types of property are excluded from the definition of debt-financed property of a tax-exempt organization (¶ 687):

(1) property substantially all the use of which (85 percent or more) is related to the exercise or performance of the organization's tax-exempt function (special rules apply to real property used as a medical clinic);

(2) property to the extent that its income is subject to tax as income from carrying on an unrelated trade or business (however, if any gain on disposition of the property is not included in unrelated business taxable income (¶ 655), it may be income from debt-financed property (¶ 679));

(3) property to the extent that its income is from certain research activities and is excluded from gross income of an unrelated trade or business;

(4) property to the extent it is used in a business where substantially all of the work of carrying on the business is performed without compensation, the Code Sec. 501(c)(3) organization carrying on the business does so primarily for the convenience of members, students, patients, etc., or the business consists of selling merchandise substantially all of which has been received as contributions; and

(5) certain brownfield site property to the extent the gain or loss from its sale or exchange would be excluded from gross income of an unrelated trade or business (Code Sec. 514(b); Reg. § 1.514(b)-1).[110]

For (1), (3), and (4) above, property use by a related organization is taken into account in determining use of an tax-exempt organization. In addition, special rules apply to life income contracts and real property located in the neighborhood of other property owned and used for exempt purposes by the tax-exempt organization.

Other Tax-Exempt Organizations

692. Other Tax-Exempt Organizations under Code Sec. 501(c). In addition to charitable organizations (¶ 602), Code Sec. 501 exempts other types of nonprofit organizations from federal income tax unless they are feeder organizations (¶ 694). Among the most common are civic leagues and social welfare organizations, business leagues, social and recreation clubs, and fraternal beneficiary societies. Contributions to these organizations are generally *not* deductible as charitable contributions. An organization described in this section generally files an application for exemption on Form 1024 and an annual information return on Form 990 (¶ 625).

Social Welfare Organizations and Civic Leagues. A civic league or organization is exempt from federal income taxes if it is not organized for profit and is operated

References are to Standard Federal Tax Reports; Tax Research Consultant; and Practical Tax Explanations.

[110] ¶ 22,850, ¶ 22,853; EXEMPT: 18,100; § 33,940.10

exclusively for the promotion of social welfare (Code Sec. 501(c)(4)).[111] This includes a local association of employees if the membership is limited to the employees of a designated employer in a particular municipality and whose net earnings are devoted exclusively to charitable, educational, or recreational purposes. An exemption is not allowed if any part of the net earnings of the civic league or organization inures to the benefit of any private shareholder or individual (¶ 602). If the organization provides an excess benefit to certain persons, an excise tax may be imposed (¶ 617).

A civic league or organization will be considered to be operated exclusively for the promotion of social welfare if it *primarily* engages in promoting the common good and general welfare of the community (for example, volunteer fire departments or community association) (¶ 699). Promoting social welfare does not include participation or intervention in the political campaign of any candidate for office. In addition, the promotion of social welfare does not include the operation of a social club for the benefit of its members or carrying on a business similar to for-profit organizations (Reg. § 1.501(c)(4)-1).[112] This includes providing commercial-type insurance unless it is an insubstantial part of the organization's activities, in which case the activity will be treated as an unrelated trade or business (¶ 655) (Code Sec. 501(m) and (n)).[113]

Any Code Sec. 501(c)(4) organization organized after December 18, 2015, is required to notify the IRS that it exists and is operating as a 501(c)(4) organization within 60 days of being established (Code Sec. 506, as added by the Protecting Americans from Tax Hikes (PATH) Act of 2015 (P.L. 114-113); Temp. Reg. § 1.506-1T).[114] If the organization fails to file the required notification within the 60-day (or extended) deadline, a penalty of $20 per day will be imposed for as many days as the failure continues, up to a maximum penalty of $5,000. Alternatively, the IRS may provide a written demand to an organization that is already violating this notification requirement and specify some reasonable future date as a deadline for this organization to submit the notice. The same $20 per day up to a maximum $5,000 penalty applies to managers if the organization fails to comply by the date specified in the demand letter (Code Sec. 6652(c)(4), as added by P.L. 114-113). Notification is electronically submitted on Form 8976. The organization must include with its first annual information return filed after submitting the notification: (1) the name, address, and taxpayer identification number of the organization; (2) the date on which, and the state or other jurisdiction under the laws of which, the organization was organized; and (3) a statement of the purpose of the organization (Code Sec. 6033(f)(2), as added by P.L. 114-113).

Labor, Agricultural, and Horticultural Organizations. A qualifying labor, agricultural, or horticultural organization is tax-exempt if: (1) no net earnings of the organization inure to the benefit of any member; and (2) it has as its objective the betterment of the conditions of those engaged in such pursuits, the improvement of the grade of their products, and the development of a higher degree of efficiency in their respective occupations (Code Sec. 501(c)(5); Reg. § 1.501(c)(5)-1).[115] This does not include administration of any type of retirement plan. Generally, a qualifying labor organization is an association of workers such as a labor union. An agricultural and horticultural organization is involved with raising livestock, forestry, harvesting crops or aquatic resources, the cultivation of useful or ornamental plants, and similar pursuits (Code Sec. 501(g); IRS Pub. 557).

Business Leagues. A business league, chamber of commerce, real estate board, board of trade, or professional football league is tax-exempt if it is not organized for profit and no part of its net earnings inures to the benefit of any private shareholder or individual (Code Sec. 501(c)(6); Reg. § 1.501(c)(6)-1).[116] A business league is an association of persons having some common business interest, a purpose to promote the common interest and not engaging in a regular business of a kind ordinarily carried on

References are to Standard Federal Tax Reports; Tax Research Consultant; and Practical Tax Explanations.

[111] ¶ 22,602; EXEMPT: 9,300; § 33,405.05

[112] ¶ 22,610; EXEMPT: 9,300; § 33,405.05

[113] ¶ 22,602; EXEMPT: 15,160.10, EXEMPT: 15,160.15; § 33,405.05

[114] ¶ 22,740, ¶ 22,742; EXEMPT: 9,312; § 33,405.17

[115] ¶ 22,602, ¶ 22,612; EXEMPT: 9,050; § 33,410.05

[116] ¶ 22,602, ¶ 22,614; EXEMPT: 9,100; § 33,415.05

for profit. For example, an association engaged in furnishing information to prospective investors is not a business league because its activities do not further any common business interest.

Social Clubs. A social club or similar organization is exempt from federal income taxes if it is organized and operated exclusively for pleasure, recreation, and other nonprofitable purposes and no part of its net earnings inures to the benefit of any person having an interest in the activities of the organization (Code Sec. 501(c)(7); Reg. § 1.501(c)(7)-1; IRS Pub. 557).[117] Membership in the club must be limited, but personal contact, commingling, and fellowship must exist between the members. In addition, the club's charter, bylaws, other governing instrument, or any written policy statement must not provide for discrimination against any person on the basis of race, color, or religion (Code Sec. 501(i)). A club that in good faith limits its membership to the members of a particular religion to further the teachings or principles of that religion will not be considered as discriminating on the basis of religion. The restriction on religious discrimination, however, does not apply to an auxiliary club of a fraternal beneficiary society if that society limits its membership to the members of a particular religion.

A social club is generally only exempt if it is supported solely by membership fees, dues, and assessments. The club cannot be engaged in any business activities, such as making its facilities available to the public or by selling real estate, timber, or other products. However, a club may receive up to 35 percent of its gross income, including investment income, from sources outside of its membership. Up to 15 percent of the gross receipts may be derived from the use of the club's facilities or services by the public, or from other activities not furthering social or recreational purposes for members. If an organization has outside income that is more than these limits, all the facts and circumstances will be taken into account in determining whether the organization qualifies for exempt status (IRS Pub. 557).

Fraternal Beneficiary Societies. A fraternal beneficiary society, order, or association is exempt from federal income taxes if: (1) it operates under the lodge system for the exclusive benefit of the members of a fraternity itself operating under the lodge system; and (2) it provides for the payment of life, sickness, accident, or other benefits to the members of such society, order, or association or their dependents (Code Sec. 501(c)(8)).[118] Contributions by an individual to a fraternal beneficiary society are deductible as charitable contributions if the gift is used exclusively for religious, charitable, scientific, literary, or educational purposes, or for the prevention of cruelty to children or animals (¶ 1061). A domestic fraternal society, order, or association that operates under the lodge system but does not provide for the payment of life, sickness, accident, or other benefits may nonetheless qualify for exemption if its net earnings are devoted exclusively to religious, charitable, scientific, literary, educational, and fraternal purposes (Code Sec. 501(c)(10)).

Other Nonprofit Organizations. Other nonprofit organizations that may be exempt from federal income taxes under Code Sec. 501(c) include:

- corporations organized under an Act of Congress (Code Sec. 501(c)(1));
- title-holding corporations for exempt organizations (Code Sec. 501(c)(2) and (25));
- voluntary employees' beneficiary associations (VEBAs) providing life, sickness, accident, and other benefits to members or their dependents or beneficiaries (Code Secs. 501(c)(9) and 505);
- local teachers' retirement fund associations (Code Sec. 501(c)(11));
- local benevolent life insurance associations (Code Sec. 501(c)(12));
- cemetery companies (Code Sec. 501(c)(13));
- state-chartered credit unions and mutual reserve funds (Code Sec. 501(c)(14));

References are to Standard Federal Tax Reports; Tax Research Consultant; and Practical Tax Explanations.

[117] ¶ 22,602, ¶ 22,616; EXEMPT: 9,400; § 33,420.05

[118] ¶ 22,602; EXEMPT: 9,150; § 33,425.05

- mutual insurance companies or associations (other than life insurance) (Code Sec. 501(c)(15));
- corporations used to finance crop operations (¶ 698) (Code Sec. 501(c)(16));
- supplemental unemployment benefit (SUB) trusts (Code Sec. 501(c)(17));
- employee funded pension trusts created before June 25, 1959 (Code Sec. 501(c)(18));
- posts or organizations for veterans, members of the armed services, and their families (Code Sec. 501(c)(19));
- black lung benefit trusts (Code Sec. 501(c)(21));
- domestic trusts set up to pay for withdrawal liability from multi-employer pension plans under ERISA (Code Sec. 501(c)(22));
- veterans organizations created before 1880 (Code Sec. 501(c)(23));
- trusts set up by a corporation in connection with the termination of its pension, profit sharing, or stock bonus plan (Code Sec. 501(c)(24));
- state-sponsored high-risk health coverage organizations (Code Sec. 501(c)(26));
- state-sponsored workers' compensation reinsurance organizations (Code Sec. 501(c)(27));
- national railroad retirement investment trust (Code Sec. 501(c)(28));
- a qualified nonprofit health insurance issuer under the Consumer Operated and Oriented Plan (CO-OP) program established by the Secretary of Health and Human Services (Code Sec. 501(c)(29)); and
- a reinsurance entity established or entered into a contract with by a state government to collect payments and make payments to the health insurance issuers that cover high-risk individuals in the individual market during the three-year period beginning January 1, 2014 (Act Sec. 1341(a) of the Patient Protection and Affordable Care Act of 2010 (P.L. 111-148)).

694. Feeder Organizations. An organization whose primary purpose is to operate a trade or business, with all the profits paid to one or more tax-exempt entities, is known as a feeder organization (Code Sec. 502; Reg. § 1.502-1).[119] The fact that the income is turned over to a tax-exempt organization does not entitle the feeder organization to tax-exempt status. A feeder organization is subject to tax unless its activities are an integral part of the exempt activities of the parent organization. A trade or business of a feeder organization does *not* include: (1) rentals if the rents received would not be subject to the unrelated business income tax (¶ 655); (2) any trade or business if substantially all the work of carrying on the trade or business is performed by unpaid individuals or volunteers; or (3) any trade or business that sells merchandise, substantially all of which has been donated or contributed.

696. Political Organizations. A political organization is generally considered tax exempt to the extent that it is organized and operated to accept contributions and make expenditures for influencing the selection, nomination, election, or appointment of any individual to public office (Code Sec. 527).[120] Examples of political organizations include political parties; federal, state, or local candidate committees; political action committees (PACs); and certain newsletters and segregated funds. The exempt function income of a political organization consists solely of: (1) contributions of money or property; (2) membership dues or fees; or (3) proceeds from a political fundraising event or the sale of political campaign materials. Any other income received (less deductions not related to exempt functions) is taxed at the highest income tax rate for corporations and capital gains. In calculating its taxable income, a political organization is permitted a $100

References are to Standard Federal Tax Reports; Tax Research Consultant; and Practical Tax Explanations.

[119] ¶ 22,670, ¶ 22,671; EXEMPT: 15,350; § 33,301

[120] ¶ 22,900; EXEMPT: 9,850; § 33,428.05

deduction, but it will not be allowed a net operating loss deduction (¶ 1145), a dividends received deduction (¶ 223), or other special deductions allowed to corporations (¶ 221).

Political organizations with taxable income must determine and report their tax on Form 1120-POL. Political organizations with $25,000 or more of gross receipts ($100,000 for certain state or local organizations) must also file an annual information return on Form 990 or Form 990-EZ (Code Sec. 6033(g)).[121] All political organizations must notify the IRS electronically on Form 8871 of their existence within 24 hours of establishment (Code Sec. 527(i)). They must also provide periodic reports on Form 8872 of the contributions they receive and their expenditures (Code Sec. 527(j)). Organizations do not have to meet these two requirements if they have gross receipts of less than $25,000, are already required to file similar reports with the Federal Election Commission, or are certain state or local political organizations. Failure to provide notification will result in all income (including exempt function income) being taxed. In addition, failure to provide periodic reports will result in all undisclosed contributions and expenditures being taxed. A safe harbor is provided that waives the amounts due for failing to comply with the reporting requirements due to reasonable cause but not willful neglect (Rev. Proc. 2007-27).[122] The public disclosure of all returns and forms filed by a political organization is required (Code Sec. 6104).[123]

698. Farmers' Cooperatives. A cooperative (or federation of cooperatives) of farmers, fruit growers, and persons engaged in similar pursuits may qualify for tax-exempt status if the cooperative is organized and operated to market the members' products and return to them net proceeds, or purchase supplies and equipment for the use of members at cost plus expenses (Code Sec. 521; Reg. § 1.521-1).[124] The cooperative can deal with nonmembers, so long as the business does not account for more than 15 percent of all of its business. Application for exemption is filed on Form 1028. A farmers' association that has capital stock will not be denied exemption if: (1) the dividend rate is fixed at the legal rate of interest for the state of incorporation or eight percent (whichever is greater), and (2) substantially all of the stock is owned by producers who market their products or purchase their supplies through the association. A farmers' cooperative will also not be denied exemption if it computes its net earnings by offsetting certain earnings and losses in determining any amount available for distribution to patrons (Code Sec. 1388(j)(1)).[125]

Exempt farmers' cooperatives, and nonexempt corporations operating on a cooperative basis, are subject to regular corporate income and capital gain taxes and must file Form 1120-C to report taxable income (Code Secs. 1381 and 1382; Reg. § 1.1382-3).[126] In computing taxable income, all cooperatives are allowed certain deductions from gross income in addition to other deductions allowed to corporations (¶ 221). For example, an exempt farmers' cooperative is permitted a deduction for any dividends paid on capital stock, for amounts paid on a patronage basis arising from certain nonpatronage earnings, and for amounts paid in redemption of certain nonqualified written notices of allocation. In addition, all cooperatives are allowed a deduction for any patronage dividend paid or allocated to its members during the tax year. A patronage dividend is an amount paid to a member:

- on the basis of quantity or value of business done with the cooperative;
- under an obligation of the cooperative to pay such amount, where the obligation existed before the cooperative received the amount paid; and
- which is determined by reference to the net earnings of the cooperative from business done with or for its members. However, net earnings will not be reduced by amounts paid as dividends on capital stock to the extent that the dividends are in addition to amounts otherwise payable to patrons (Code Sec. 1388(a)).[127]

References are to Standard Federal Tax Reports; Tax Research Consultant; and Practical Tax Explanations.

[121] ¶ 35,420; EXEMPT: 9,864; § 33,428.30

[122] ¶ 22,911.70; EXEMPT: 9,864; § 33,428.30

[123] ¶ 36,900; EXEMPT: 9,864; § 33,428.30

[124] ¶ 22,880, ¶ 22,881; FARM: 12,200

[125] ¶ 32,380; FARM: 12,250

[126] ¶ 32,300, ¶ 32,320, ¶ 32,323; FARM: 12,100, FARM: 12,150, FARM: 12,200; § 36,040

[127] ¶ 32,380; FARM: 12,104; § 36,040

699. Additional Exempt Organizations. There are a number of organizations other than charitable (¶ 602) and social (¶ 692) that may be exempt from federal income taxes, including homeowners' associations, credit counseling organizations, and cooperative service organizations.

Homeowners' Association. A homeowners' association formed to own and maintain common areas and enforce covenants to preserve the appearance of a development may qualify as a tax-exempt social welfare organization under Code Sec. 501(c)(4) (¶ 692). A homeowners' association that is not exempt as a social welfare organization and that is either a condominium management, real estate management, or timeshare association, may nonetheless elect to exclude certain exempt function income from its gross income, including membership dues, fees, and assessments from member-owners (Code Sec. 528).[128] Electing associations are taxed at a flat rate of 30 percent (32 percent for timeshare associations) on both ordinary income and capital gains which are nonexempt. Form 1120-H is used by the association to make the election for each tax year and to report annual taxable income.

Credit Counseling Organizations. An organization that provides credit counseling services as a substantial purpose may not qualify as a tax-exempt organization unless it qualifies as a Code Sec. 501(c)(3) charitable or educational organization (¶ 602) or a Code Sec. 501(c)(4) social welfare organization (¶ 692) (Code Sec. 501(q)).[129] In addition, the organization: (1) must provide services tailored to customers' specific needs; (2) must not refuse to provide services to customers due to inability to pay or ineligibility for debt management plan enrollment; (3) make no loans to customers; (4) have a reasonable fee policy and must not pay or receive referral fees; (5) have limited ownership of related service providers; and (6) have independent board members with public interests.

Cooperative Service Organizations. A cooperative hospital service organization is exempt from federal income taxation if it performs specifically listed services for two or more patron hospitals that are tax exempt under Code Sec. 501(c)(3) or if it is owned and operated by the federal government or by a state or local government (Code Sec. 501(e)).[130] Services that may be performed include data processing, purchasing (including purchasing insurance on a group basis, such as malpractice and general liability insurance), laboratory, billing and collection (including the purchase of patron accounts receivable on a recourse basis), food, personnel, and clinical services. It does not include laundry services.[131] A cooperative arrangement formed and controlled by a group of exempt educational organizations for the collective investment of their funds may also qualify for tax-exempt status (Code Sec. 501(f)).[132] These organizations qualify for exemption only if all of the relevant requirements of Code Sec. 501(c)(3) are also satisfied.

References are to Standard Federal Tax Reports; Tax Research Consultant; and Practical Tax Explanations.

[128] ¶ 22,920; EXEMPT: 9,500; § 33,429.05

[129] ¶ 22,602; EXEMPT: 10,050; § 33,105

[130] ¶ 22,602; EXEMPT: 3,154

[131] ¶ 22,662.30; EXEMPT: 3,154

[132] ¶ 22,602; EXEMPT: 3,300

Chapter 7
INCOME

	Par.
What Is "Income"	701
Ownership of Income	704
Salaries, Wages, and Benefits	713
Interest	724
Dividends	733
Dividends: Distribution in Redemption of Stock	742
Dividends: Earnings and Profits	747
Business Income	759
Rents and Royalties	762
Farming Income	767
Alimony Payments	771
Other Income	785
Shareholder's or Employee's Bargain Purchase	789
Creditor's Financial Income	793
Below-Market Interest Loans	795
Recoveries	799

What Is "Income"

701. Gross Income Defined. Gross income for federal income tax purposes means all income from whatever source derived, except for those items specifically excluded by the Code (Code Sec. 61; Reg. § 1.61-1).[1] A nonexclusive list of specific items that are included in gross income is provided in Code Sec. 61 and includes:

- compensation for services, including fees, commissions, fringe benefits, and similar items (¶ 713);
- gross income from business (¶ 759 and ¶ 767);
- gains from dealings in property (¶ 1701);
- interest (¶ 724);
- rents (¶ 762);
- royalties (¶ 763);
- dividends (¶ 733);
- alimony and separate maintenance payments (¶ 771);
- annuities (¶ 817);
- income from life insurance and endowment contracts (Reg. § 1.61-10);[2]
- pensions (¶ 718);
- income from the discharge of indebtedness (¶ 855);
- a partner's share of partnership income (¶ 404);
- income in respect of a decedent (¶ 182); and
- income from an interest in an estate or trust (¶ 554 and ¶ 556).

Although nearly every type of accession to wealth appears to fall within this comprehensive definition, income items should be checked against the specific exclu-

References are to Standard Federal Tax Reports; Tax Research Consultant; and Practical Tax Explanations.

[1] ¶ 5502, ¶ 5503; INDIV: 6,050; § 3,001

[2] ¶ 5708; INDIV: 30,350; § 46,615.20

sions in Code Secs. 101—140 (¶ 801). For special rules relating to foreign income, see ¶ 2401. For a detailed list of income items and exclusions, see the Checklist for Items of Income at ¶ 55. For a discussion of the income tax treatment of gifts and inheritances of property, see ¶ 847 and ¶ 849.

702. Determining Income. Court decisions have developed a concept of "income" that is quite different from the layman's concept. The U.S. Supreme Court has defined income as an undeniable accession to wealth, clearly realized, and over which the taxpayer has complete dominion (*Glenshaw Glass Co.*, SCt, 55-1 USTC ¶ 9308).[3] Further, the Supreme Court pointed out that it has repeatedly given a liberal construction to this broad definition of what constitutes gross income in recognition of Congress's intent to tax all gain unless specifically exempted. In addition to those items specifically excludable from gross income by law (¶ 801), certain other items are not considered income.

Return of Capital. A return of capital, such as repayment of a loan, is not income unless the loan has been previously deducted as a bad debt, resulting in a tax benefit.[4] Similarly, car pool reimbursements are not income even if only one person provides the car and does the driving.[5]

Damages. Damages, other than punitive damages, that compensate an injured person for personal physical injuries or physical sickness are excludable from gross income (¶ 852). Damages received for personal nonphysical injuries, such as employment discrimination or injury to reputation, are generally taxable.[6] Interest on a judgment, including mandatory prejudgment interest, is generally includible in income.[7] See ¶ 759 for treatment of damages awarded for business claims.

Attorney Fees and Court Costs. Court costs and attorney fees paid in connection with an action based on unlawful discrimination under federal law, as well as certain other claims (i.e., whistleblower actions), are deductible from gross income in determining adjusted gross income (¶ 1093).

Governmental Assistance. Many types of government assistance payments are not included in income if they are for the promotion of general welfare. For example, rental assistance payments made by the Department of Housing and Urban Development under the National Housing Act and relocation payments made under the Housing and Community Development Act of 1974 are nontaxable.[8] However, payments made by individuals or other nongovernmental entities are not considered payments for the general welfare and are taxable.[9]

Gift v. Income. The characterization of a payment or transfer as either a gift or taxable income must be made on a case-by-case basis.[10] The U.S. Supreme Court, for example, has held that the value of a "gift" transferred to a business friend for furnishing the names of potential customers is taxable compensation (¶ 849).[11]

Strike and Lockout Benefits. Strike benefits received from a labor union may be treated as nontaxable gifts when the benefits paid in the form of food, clothing, and rent are: (1) given to both member and nonmember strikers, (2) dependent upon individual need, (3) dependent on the unavailability of unemployment compensation or local public assistance, and (4) given without conditions. The fact that benefits are paid only to union members is not, of itself, determinative as to taxability.[12]

Unrealized Appreciation. Unrealized appreciation in the value of property is not income.[13]

References are to Standard Federal Tax Reports; Tax Research Consultant; and Practical Tax Explanations.

[3] ¶ 5900.51; INDIV: 6,052; § 3,001

[4] ¶ 5504.103, ¶ 5504.6305; INDIV: 6,058; § 17,101

[5] ¶ 5504.144; INDIV: 33,554; § 4,015

[6] ¶ 5900.14, ¶ 5900.49, ¶ 5900.57; INDIV: 6,354; § 3,810.05

[7] ¶ 6662.513; INDIV: 12,112; § 3,805.35

[8] ¶ 5504.184; INDIV: 33,354; § 4,050

[9] ¶ 5504.193; INDIV: 6,368

[10] ¶ 6553.115; INDIV: 33,100; § 3,615

[11] ¶ 5507.294; INDIV: 33,102; § 3,605.05

[12] ¶ 6553.46; COMPEN: 6,068; § 22,110.40

[13] ¶ 5504.119; INDIV: 6,052; § 3,001

Ownership of Income

704. Tax Liability. In the vast majority of cases, the identity of the taxpayer is clear. The taxpayer is simply the person who is legally entitled to receive income. Thus, an individual who receives wages for services is obviously the person who must pay income tax on the wages. Under certain circumstances, however, a person may be taxed on income even though at the time of payment another receives it because of an anticipatory assignment of income (¶ 705). Special rules also affect the treatment of unearned income of a minor (¶ 706), income from property held in joint tenancy (¶ 709), and income of taxpayers living in community property states (¶ 710).

705. Assignment of Income. Generally, an individual can escape tax on income from property only if the individual makes a valid gift or assignment of the income-producing property itself, as distinguished from an assignment of the income. The U.S. Supreme Court has held that an individual who gave his spouse the legally enforceable right to receive the future income generated by his law practice was still taxable on that income (*G.C. Earl*, SCt, 2 USTC ¶ 496).[14] In another case, the Court ruled that an individual who gave his son interest coupons, which were detached from bonds that he owned, was liable for the tax on the interest accrued before the gift and later paid to his son (*P.R.G. Horst*, SCt, 40-2 USTC ¶ 9787).[15] See ¶ 706 for the taxation of the unearned income of minor and certain dependent children.

706. Unearned Income of Minor Child. The amount of net unearned income of a child meeting certain statutory requirements that exceeds an annual inflation-adjusted amount ($2,100 for 2016; $2,100 for 2017) generally is taxed at the parents' highest marginal federal income tax rate. This is referred to as the "kiddie tax." It is designed to lessen the effectiveness of intra-family transfers of income-producing property that would shift income from the parents' higher marginal tax rate to the child's generally lower tax rate, to reduce a family's overall income tax liability. The kiddie tax applies to a child's unearned income regardless of source, and requires a calculation of the parents' allocable tax, which is the increase in the parents' tax liability that results from adding the net unearned income of all of the parents' children meeting the kiddie tax requirements to the parents' taxable income (Code Sec. 1(g)).[16]

See ¶ 103 for more details on the kiddie tax, as well as the parents' election to include a child's unearned income on their return. See ¶ 143 for discussion of dependents with earned income.

709. Joint Tenancy and Tenancy in Common. When property is held in joint tenancy with a right of survivorship, income from the property, including gain or loss upon its sale, is divided between the owners to the extent that each is entitled under state law to share in the income. There must be evidence that the joint ownership was bona fide and not used merely as a tax-avoidance scheme. These rules also apply to tenants in common.[17]

710. Community Property Income. In community property states (Arizona, California, Idaho, Louisiana, Nevada, New Mexico, Texas, Washington, and Wisconsin), property acquired by a married couple during their marriage while they reside in the state is generally regarded as owned by the spouses together, each owning an undivided interest in the whole property. Similarly, income from the property is divided equally between the spouses. Although each state has exceptions in classifying income as separate income or community income, the general rule is that salaries, wages, and other compensation for the services of either or both of the spouses, as well as income from community real and personal property, are community income; but it does not follow in every state that income from separate property is separate income. The states also differ in their treatment of property acquired by inheritance or intestate succession. The IRS can disallow the benefits of any community property law to a spouse for any

References are to Standard Federal Tax Reports; Tax Research Consultant; and Practical Tax Explanations.

[14] ¶ 6553.74; INDIV: 27,052; § 4,110

[15] ¶ 2150.64; INDIV: 27,052; § 4,135.05

[16] ¶ 3260; INDIV: 18,154; § 1,510.05

[17] ¶ 2250.35; INDIV: 18,100

income that the spouse treats as his or hers alone if that spouse fails to notify the other spouse of the nature and amount of the income before the due date, including extensions, for filing the return for the tax year in which the income was derived (Code Sec. 66(b); Reg. § 1.66-3).[18]

Same-Sex Married Couples and Registered Domestic Partners. A marriage of two individuals is recognized for federal tax purposes if the marriage would be recognized by the state, possession, or territory of the United States in which the marriage was entered into, regardless of where the individuals are domiciled. A marriage conducted in a foreign jurisdiction will also be recognized for federal tax purposes if that marriage would be recognized in at least one state, possession, or territory of the United States, regardless of where the individuals are domiciled. Thus, legally-married same-sex couples are recognized as married for federal tax purposes, and the terms "spouse", "husband", and "wife" mean an individual lawfully married to another individual, regardless of sex (Reg. § 301.7701-18).[19] See ¶ 152.

A marriage for federal tax purposes does not include registered domestic partnerships, civil unions, or other similar relationships recognized under state law that are not denominated as a marriage under that state's law. Nonetheless, registered domestic partners in Nevada, Washington, or California generally must follow state community property laws (CCA 201021050; IRS Pub. 555).[20] Thus, each partner must report one-half of the combined community income on his or her federal income tax return.

711. Joint v. Separate Return in Community Property States. If separate returns are filed by a married couple residing in a community property state (¶ 710), each spouse must report one-half of the community income (Reg. § 1.66-1).[21] In Idaho, Louisiana, Texas, and Wisconsin, income from the separate property of a spouse is community income, with one-half being allocable to each spouse. In the other community property states, income from separate property is separate income.[22] Each spouse filing a separate return must use Form 8958 to allocate income, deductions, credits, and other return amounts between the spouses.

It is usually more beneficial to file a joint return. There are some situations, however, when filing separate returns may be beneficial for married spouses (¶ 156). See ¶ 152 for more details on filing joint returns.

Nonresident Alien Spouse. A U.S. citizen or resident alien who is married to a nonresident alien may elect to file a joint return if both agree to be taxed on their worldwide income (¶ 2410). If the couple does not make this election and has community income, any community income that is earned income, trade or business income, partnership income, or income from separate property is treated as the separate income of the spouse to whom the particular income item is associated (¶ 2438) (Code Sec. 879).[23]

Separated Spouses. The usual community property rules do not apply to spouses living apart from each other if: (1) they are separated for the entire calendar year; (2) they file separate returns; (3) either or both spouses have community earned income; and (4) they do not transfer between each other more than a *de minimis* amount of the earned income before the end of the calendar year (Code Sec. 66(a); Reg. § 1.66-2).[24] Instead, their community income is treated as if one of the spouses is a nonresident alien and they did not elect to file a joint return.

Innocent Spouse Relief. A requesting spouse may receive relief from federal income tax liability for an item of community income that would be properly treated as the income of the nonrequesting spouse under the Code Sec. 879 rules (¶ 2438) if: (1) the requesting spouse does not file a joint return for the tax year in question, and does not

References are to Standard Federal Tax Reports; Tax Research Consultant; and Practical Tax Explanations.

[18] ¶ 6050, ¶ 6050F; INDIV: 24,050, INDIV: 24,152; § 39,035.45

[19] ¶ 43,166; FILEIND: 3,202; § 45,901

[20] ¶ 6051.60; FILEIND: 3,202; § 45,922

[21] ¶ 6050B; FILEIND: 3,212.05; § 45,910.20

[22] ¶ 2350.2475; INDIV: 24,050; § 45,915.20

[23] ¶ 27,460; INDIV: 24,156; § 45,925

[24] ¶ 6050, ¶ 6050D; INDIV: 24,060.05; § 45,920.05

include the community income item in his or her gross income; (2) the requesting spouse establishes that he or she did not know and had no reason to know of the item; and (3) under the facts and circumstances, it would be inequitable to include the item in the requesting spouse's gross income. If these requirements are not met, the IRS may still provide relief from a tax liability or deficiency arising from the community income item if failure to do so would be inequitable (Code Sec. 66(c), Reg. § 1.66-4).[25] The IRS has issued guidance for taxpayers seeking equitable relief in Rev. Proc. 2013-34.[26]

Salaries, Wages, and Benefits

713. Compensation for Personal Services. All compensation for personal services, no matter what the form of payment, must be included in gross income (Reg. § 1.61-2).[27] Wages, salaries, commissions, bonuses, fringe benefits that do not qualify for statutory exclusions, tips, payments based on a percentage of profits, rewards, directors' fees, jury fees, election officials' fees, retirement pay and pensions, and other forms of compensation are income in the year received and not in the year earned, unless the taxpayer reports income on an accrual basis (¶ 1515).

Example: A cash-method salesperson who receives commissions in January 2017 for sales made in 2016 must include those amounts on the 2017 return.

Under the claim-of-right doctrine (¶ 1543), a taxpayer receiving income under a claim of right and without restrictions on its use or disposition is taxed on that income in the year received, even though the right to retain the income is not yet fixed or the taxpayer may later be required to return it.[28]

Compensation is income even though the amount is not fixed in advance, as in the case of marriage fees, baptismal offerings, and similar sums received by a member of the clergy.[29] A year-end bonus is usually taxable, particularly if based on salary or length of service. Severance pay and vacation pay are also taxable as compensation. The value of a turkey, ham, or other nominally valued item distributed to an employee on holidays is *not* reportable income even though the employer is entitled to deduct the cost as a business expense. However, a distribution of cash, a gift certificate or gift card, or a similar item of value readily convertible to cash, must be included in the employee's income.[30]

The amount of compensation reported on the taxpayer's return is the gross amount before any reductions for withheld income tax or social security taxes, union dues, insurance, or other deductions by the employer.

Child's Earned Income. Compensation for the services of a child are included in the child's gross income, even if the compensation is or must be received by the parent rather than the child (¶ 103).

Restricted Property Transfers. If stock or other property is given as compensation for services instead of cash, the fair market value (FMV) of the property is included in income unless the property is subject to a substantial risk of forfeiture (Code Sec. 83; Reg. § 1.83-1).[31] The FMV of the property included in income becomes its basis to the employee. If the property is sold to the employee for less than its market value, the difference between the amount paid and the value of the property is also income.

If the stock or other property is subject to a substantial risk of forfeiture, no amount is included in income until the year that the property becomes substantially vested as the result of the removal of the risk of forfeiture (Code Sec. 83(a); Reg. § 1.83-1(a)(1)).[32] However, any income (e.g., a dividend) from property that is subject to a substantial risk of forfeiture, or from the right to use such property, is included in income as compensation when received (Rev. Proc. 80-11; Rev. Proc. 83-38).[33] Property is considered

References are to Standard Federal Tax Reports; Tax Research Consultant; and Practical Tax Explanations.

[25] ¶ 6050, ¶ 6050H; INDIV: 24,154; § 45,920.10

[26] ¶ 6051.20; INDIV: 18,060; § 45,920.10

[27] ¶ 5506; COMPEN: 6,050; § 3,005.05

[28] ¶ 21,005.122; ACCTNG: 27,050; § 4,225.05

[29] ¶ 5507.141; COMPEN: 6,050; § 3,005.05

[30] ¶ 5507.2942; COMPEN: 6,350; § 21,120

[31] ¶ 6380, ¶ 6381; COMPEN: 18,050; § 21,401

[32] ¶ 6380, ¶ 6381; COMPEN: 6,104; § 21,430.05

[33] ¶ 6390.63; COMPEN: 18,550; § 21,435

substantially vested when it is either (1) transferable to another person who is not required to give up the property or its value if the substantial risk of forfeiture occurs, or (2) no longer subject to a substantial risk of forfeiture (Code Sec. 83(c)(1); Reg. § 1.83-3).[34]

A substantial risk of forfeiture exists if the right to the property is conditioned on (1) the future performance or refraining from performance of substantial services by any person, or (2) the occurrence of a condition related to a purpose of the transfer if the possibility of forfeiture is substantial (Code Sec. 83(c)(1); Reg. § 1.83-3(c)). For property transferred on or after January 1, 2013: (1) a substantial risk of forfeiture may be established *only* by the two conditions described above; (2) in determining whether a substantial risk of forfeiture exists due to a condition related to the purpose of the transfer, the likelihood that the forfeiture event will occur and that the forfeiture will be enforced must both be considered; and (3) except as provided in Reg. § 1.83-3(j) or (k), transfer restrictions do not create a substantial risk of forfeiture if the restriction is violated, even if the violation results in forfeiture of property or in liability for damages, penalties or fees.

A taxpayer who receives property subject to a substantial risk of forfeiture may elect to include in gross income in the year the property is received the FMV of the property less any amount paid for the property. This is known as a "section 83(b) election" (Code Sec. 83(b); Reg. § 1.83-2).[35] The election can only be revoked with the consent of the IRS. Once the value of the property is included in income, any subsequent appreciation is not taxed as compensation to the person who performed the services. If the property is forfeited after the election is made and before it is substantially vested, the forfeiture is treated as a sale or exchange on which a loss is realized, equal to any excess of the amount paid for the property minus any amount realized upon the forfeiture.

The taxpayer makes the election by filing a written statement with the IRS center where the tax return is filed no later than 30 days after the date the property was transferred. To facilitate e-filing, the IRS issued regulations for property transferred on or after January 1, 2016, that eliminates the need to attach the election statement to the taxpayer's return (Reg. § 1.83-2(c) and (g)).[36] The IRS has provided sample language that may be used for making the election, as well as examples of the tax consequences of the election (Rev. Proc. 2012-29).[37]

Stock Options. Nonstatutory stock options (NSOs) are discussed at ¶ 1923. Incentive stock options (ISOs) are discussed at ¶ 1925 and ¶ 1927. Employee stock purchase plans (ESPPs) are discussed at ¶ 1929 and ¶ 1931.

Employee Benefits. Compensation for personal services includes any benefits an employer provides to an employee which are not otherwise excludable from income (Reg. § 1.61-21).[38] Excludable employee benefits include:

- amounts received under employer-financed accident and health plans (¶ 2015);
- employer contributions to provide the accident and health benefits (¶ 2013);
- employer contributions to a health savings account (HSA) (¶ 2035), Archer medical savings account (MSA) (¶ 2037), health reimbursement arrangement (HRA) (¶ 2039), or flexible spending arrangement (FSA) (¶ 2041);
- premiums for group-term life insurance to the extent coverage does not exceed $50,000 (¶ 2055);
- qualified adoption expenses reimbursed under an employer adoption assistance program (¶ 2063);
- child and dependent care assistance benefits (¶ 2065);

References are to Standard Federal Tax Reports; Tax Research Consultant; and Practical Tax Explanations.

[34] ¶ 6380, ¶ 6383; COMPEN: 18,202, COMPEN: 18,210; § 21,415.05

[35] ¶ 6380, ¶ 6382; COMPEN: 18,300; § 21,475.05

[36] ¶ 6382; COMPEN: 18,304; § 21,475.20

[37] ¶ 6390.77; COMPEN: 18,304; § 21,475.20

[38] ¶ 5906; COMPEN: 33,000; § 3,005.05

- educational assistance benefits (¶ 2067);
- employee achievement awards to the extent deductible by the employer (¶ 2069);
- qualified moving expense reimbursements (¶ 2092); and
- certain other fringe benefits (¶ 2085).

Some excludable employee benefits may be provided to an employee through the employer's cafeteria plan (¶ 2045).

Employer-Provided Vehicle. An employee who uses an employer-provided vehicle for more than *de minimis* personal use receives a taxable fringe benefit from his or her employer. The amount includible in an employee's wages is determined by the fair market value of the vehicle's availability (¶ 2059).

Vacation and Club Expenses. The portion of an employee's vacation, athletic club, or health resort expenses that is paid by the employer is taxable to the employee.[39]

Occupational Disability or Insurance Benefit. Compensation received under a workers' compensation act for personal injuries or sickness and amounts received under a policy of accident and health insurance are excludable from gross income (¶ 851).

714. Compensation of Federal or State Employee. The salaries of all employees or officials of the United States government are taxed the same as those of other individuals (Code Sec. 3401(c)). This is also true for state and local government employees.[40]

715. Treatment of Excessive Salaries. Although an employer is denied a deduction for compensation paid to the extent that the payment is unreasonable (¶ 906), the full amount of the payment is includible in the recipient's income. In the case of an employee-shareholder, excessive compensation may be treated as dividend income. Excessive salaries are taxed only to the extent of the gain if the excess amounts are determined to be payments to the recipient for property rather than compensation (Reg. § 1.162-8).[41]

716. Social Security and Equivalent Railroad Retirement Benefits. A portion of a taxpayer's social security benefits or an equivalent portion of tier 1 railroad retirement benefits may be taxable (Code Sec. 86).[42] The amount includible in gross income is the lesser of one-half of the annual benefits received or one-half of the excess of the taxpayer's provisional income over a specified base amount. If the taxpayer's provisional income exceeds an adjusted base amount, up to 85 percent of the benefits may be included (see *85-Percent Inclusion*, following). The Form 1040 Instructions contain a worksheet for computing the taxable amount.

Provisional income is the taxpayer's modified adjusted gross income (MAGI) plus one-half of the social security or tier 1 railroad retirement benefits received. MAGI is the taxpayer's adjusted gross income (¶ 1005), plus any tax-exempt interest received. Adjusted gross income is determined without including any social security benefits or equivalent railroad retirement benefits, and without subtracting the following items from gross income: interest income from U.S. savings bonds used to finance higher education (¶ 863), amounts paid under an employer's adoption assistance program (¶ 2063), deductible domestic production activities income (¶ 980A), deductible student loan interest (¶ 1011), deductible tuition and related expenses (for tax years before 2017) (¶ 1011A), foreign earned income and foreign housing expenses attributable to living and working abroad (¶ 2402), and certain income of bona fide residents of U.S. possessions (¶ 2414) or Puerto Rico (¶ 2415). The base amount is: $32,000 for joint filers; $0 if married filing separately and the taxpayer lived with his or her spouse at any time during the tax year; and $25,000 for married individuals filing separately who live apart from their spouse for the entire year and for individuals filing as single or head-of-household.

References are to Standard Federal Tax Reports; Tax Research Consultant; and Practical Tax Explanations.

[39] ¶ 5507.47; COMPEN: 33,104; § 3,005.05

[40] ¶ 33,502; COMPEN: 6,650; § 22,005.15

[41] ¶ 8639; COMPEN: 6,074; § 9,301

[42] ¶ 6420; INDIV: 6,200; § 3,301

Example 1: John and Jane Mapes have an adjusted gross income of $24,000 for 2016. John, who is retired, receives social security benefits of $7,200 per year. The couple also receives $6,000 a year from a mutual fund that invests solely in tax-exempt municipal bonds. On their joint return for 2016, the couple would make the following computation to determine how much, if any, of John's social security benefits must be included in their gross income:

(1) Adjusted gross income	$24,000
(2) Plus: All tax-exempt interest	6,000
(3) Modified adjusted gross income	30,000
(4) Plus: One-half of social security benefits	3,600
(5) Provisional income	33,600
(6) Less: Base amount	32,000
(7) Excess above base amount	1,600
(8) One-half of excess above base amount	800
(9) One-half of social security benefits	3,600
(10) Amount includible in gross income (lesser of (8) or (9))	800

Social security benefits are the monthly benefits under Title II of the Social Security Act (Code Sec. 86(d)(1)).[43] Supplemental security income (SSI) payments are authorized by Title XVI of the Social Security Act, and thus are *not* included in gross income. Although tier 2 railroad retirement benefits are not taken into account under the above rules, these benefits are taxed in the same manner as benefits paid under qualified retirement plans (Code Sec. 72(r)).[44]

85-Percent Inclusion. Up to 85 percent of an individual's social security benefits or tier 1 railroad retirement benefits may be includible in gross income. This affects taxpayers whose provisional income exceeds the adjusted base amount, which is: $44,000 for married taxpayers filing jointly; $0 for married taxpayers filing separately and not living apart during the entire tax year; and $34,000 for all other taxpayers (Code Sec. 86(c)(2)).

Those who exceed the appropriate adjusted base amount must include in gross income the lesser of: (1) 85 percent of social security benefits, or (2) the sum of 85 percent of the excess of provisional income over the adjusted base amount, plus the smaller of: (a) the amount that would otherwise be includible if the second threshold did not apply (i.e., the amount calculated under the 50-percent rules discussed previously), or (b) one-half of the difference of the adjusted base amount over the base amount (i.e., $6,000 for joint filers; $0 for married filing separately and not living apart from their spouse; $4,500 for all other taxpayers).

Example 2: Assume the same facts as in Example 1 above, except that the Mapes' provisional income is increased from $33,600 to $53,600. The includible amount is determined as follows:

(1) Provisional income	$53,600
(2) Adjusted base amount	44,000
(3) Excess of (1) over (2)	9,600
(4) 85% of amount in (3)	8,160
(5) Amount otherwise includible: lesser of (a) ½ of benefits received ($3,600) or (b) ½ of the excess of provisional income minus base amount ($10,800)	3,600
(6) One-half of adjusted base amount minus base amount (for joint filers)	6,000
(7) Lesser of (5) or (6)	3,600
(8) Sum of amounts in (4) and (7)	11,760
(9) 85% of social security benefits	6,120
(10) Amount includible in gross income (lesser of (8) or (9))	6,120

References are to Standard Federal Tax Reports; Tax Research Consultant; and Practical Tax Explanations.

[43] ¶ 6420; INDIV: 6,204; § 3,305

[44] ¶ 6102; INDIV: 6,204; § 24,101

Individual Retirement Account (IRA) Contributions. Employed individuals who are covered by a retirement plan and receiving social security benefits must make a special computation to determine the allowable IRA deduction amount (¶ 2157).

717. Tip Income. Tips are amounts paid freely by a customer to a person providing a service and are generally taxable such as amounts received by cab drivers, waiters, barbers, hotel, railroad and cruise ship employees, etc. (Reg. § 1.61-2(a)(1)).[45] In the absence of proof of the actual amount of tips received, tip income may be reconstructed on the basis of average tips in a given locality for a given type of service.[46]

Tipped employees may use Form 4070A, which should be retained with the individual's tax records, to maintain a daily record of their tips. Cash, check, and credit card tips totalling $20 or more per month are reported to the employer on Form 4070 or a similar statement by the 10th day of the following month in which they are received (IRS Pub. 531). An employer may also allow tips to be reported electronically (Reg. § 31.6053-1).[47]

Form 4137 is used to compute an employee's liability for Social Security and Medicare taxes on monthly tips of $20 or more that were not reported to the employer or on tips allocated by a large food and beverage establishment. If an employer was unable to withhold Social Security and Medicare taxes on reported tip income, the uncollected taxes are shown on Form W-2 and reported as an additional tax on the tipped employee's income tax return. Noncash tips and tips of less than $20 per month are not subject to Social Security and Medicare tax. These amounts, however, are subject to income tax and must be reported on the employee's return.

See ¶ 2605 regarding the duty to report tips monthly to employer on Form 4070, ¶ 2606 regarding the employer's withholding requirements, and ¶ 1365R regarding an employer credit for its portion of Social Security taxes on employee cash tips.

718. Pension. A pension paid to a retired employee is usually taxable compensation (¶ 2101 and ¶ 2141) (Reg. § 1.61-11).[48]

719. Salary Payments to Employee's Survivor. The IRS and the Tax Court have generally taken the position that salary payments made to the surviving spouse of a deceased employee are taxable income, while several U.S. Courts of Appeal have viewed the payments as tax-free gifts.[49] Unpaid salary owed to a taxpayer at the time of his or her death is typically treated as income in respect of a decedent (¶ 182).

720. Compensation Other Than in Cash. When compensation for services is paid for in property, the fair market value (FMV) of the property at the time of receipt must be included in gross income (Reg. § 1.61-2(d)).[50] A note received in payment for services and not merely as security for the payment, comes within this rule and its FMV must be included in income. A portion of each payment received under the note is excludable from gross income as a recovery of capital (Reg. § 1.61-2(d)(4)).[51]

722. Unemployment Compensation. Recipients of unemployment compensation benefits must include in income the entire annual amount of benefits received (Code Sec. 85; Reg. § 1.85-1).[52] If an employee contributes to a governmental unemployment compensation program but is not allowed to deduct his or her contributions, amounts the employee receives under the program are not unemployment compensation until he or she has recovered the total amount of nondeductible contributions. Payments to laid-off employees from company-financed supplemental unemployment benefit plans (also referred to as "guaranteed annual wage" plans) constitute taxable income to the employees in the year received.[53] Payors report unemployment compensation on Form 1099-G.

References are to Standard Federal Tax Reports; Tax Research Consultant; and Practical Tax Explanations.

[45] ¶ 5506; COMPEN: 6,058; § 21,301

[46] ¶ 5507.4651, ¶ 35,111.58; ACCTNG: 3,168; § 21,325.05

[47] ¶ 36,461; PAYROLL: 3,406; § 21,305.10

[48] ¶ 5710; RETIRE: 42,300; § 3,040

[49] ¶ 5507.4741, ¶ 6507.83; COMPEN: 48,206; § 3,605.05

[50] ¶ 5506; SALES: 6,062, COMPEN: 6,104; § 3,005.10

[51] ¶ 5506, ¶ 5508.35; COMPEN: 6,106; § 3,005.10

[52] ¶ 6410, ¶ 6411; INDIV: 6,208; § 3,075

[53] ¶ 5507.60; INDIV: 6,208

723. Deferred Compensation. Not all compensation is paid in the year when services are rendered. Some may be deferred to a later year. There are two types of deferred compensation arrangements—funded and unfunded.

Funded Arrangements. If deferred compensation is contributed to a trust or is used to purchase an annuity or other insurance contract, the arrangement is funded and a participant may be subject to tax on his or her portion of trust's income (¶ 2199).

Unfunded Arrangements. If the deferral takes the form of an employer's unsecured promise (i.e., not represented by a note) to pay compensation for current services at some time in the future, and if the employee uses the cash method of accounting, the amount promised is not includible in the employee's gross income until it is received or made available (¶ 906) (Rev. Rul. 60-31, modified by Rev. Rul. 64-279 and Rev. Rul. 70-435).[54] This rule is not altered merely because the employee agrees with the employer in advance to receive compensation on a deferred basis, so long as the agreement is made before the taxpayer obtains an unqualified and unconditional right to the compensation (*J.F. Oates,* CA-7, 53-2 USTC ¶ 9596).[55]

Unfunded Plans of State and Local Governments and Other Tax-Exempt Organizations. The treatment of unfunded deferred compensation plans is modified for participants in plans maintained by state and local governments and other tax-exempt organizations other than churches and qualified church-controlled organizations (Code Sec. 457).[56] For distributions from an eligible nongovernment plan, the deferred compensation is includible in income only when received by, or unconditionally made available to, a participant. For distributions from an eligible government plan, the deferred compensation is included in gross income only when actually paid. If a plan is not an eligible plan, the present value of the deferred compensation is includible in gross income for the first tax year in which there is no substantial risk of forfeiture, and the tax treatment of any amount made available to a participant is determined under the annuity rules. See ¶ 2193 for further discussion of 457 plans.

Unfunded Plans of Taxable Employers. An unfunded plan of a taxable employer is not subject to the limitations that apply to a tax-exempt employer. As a practical matter, however, an unfunded plan of a taxable employer is limited to providing benefits in excess of those permitted under qualified plans or benefits for highly compensated and managerial employees. This is because any other unfunded deferred compensation plan of a taxable employer would be subject to participation, vesting, funding, and fiduciary standards of the Employee Retirement Income Security Act of 1974 (ERISA) (P.L. 93-406) (ERISA Secs. 4(b)(5), 201(2), 301(a)(3), and 401(a)(1)). See ¶ 2197 and ¶ 2199 for a discussion of nonqualified deferred compensation plans.

Interest

724. Interest Generally. All interest received or accrued by a taxpayer is generally included in gross income and fully taxable (Reg. § 1.61-7).[57] Exceptions exist for interest on tax-exempt state or municipal bonds, including qualified private activity bonds (¶ 729), and interest on U.S. savings bonds used to pay qualified educational expenses (¶ 863). A cash-basis taxpayer is taxed on interest when received. Interest on bank deposits, coupons payable on bonds, etc., is considered available to a cash-basis taxpayer under the doctrine of constructive receipt and is taxed when credited or due (¶ 1533).

Interest earned on corporate obligations is generally taxed when actually received by, or credited to, a cash-basis taxpayer (Reg. § 1.61-7(a)). The same rule applies to interest on certificates of deposit, time obligations, and similar deposit arrangements on which interest is credited periodically and can be withdrawn without penalty, even though the principal cannot be withdrawn without penalty prior to maturity. However, interest on a six-month certificate that is not credited or made available to the holder without penalty before maturity is not includible in the holder's income until the certificate is redeemed or matures (Rev. Rul. 80-157, amplified by Rev. Rul. 82-42).[58]

References are to Standard Federal Tax Reports; Tax Research Consultant; and Practical Tax Explanations.

[54] ¶ 21,009.1967; COMPEN: 15,202; § 25,610.15

[55] ¶ 21,009.135; COMPEN: 15,202; § 25,610.15

[56] ¶ 21,531; COMPEN: 15,150; § 25,310.10 , § 25,315.05

[57] ¶ 5702; INDIV: 12,052; § 3,101

[58] ¶ 21,009.3247; INDIV: 12,102, INDIV: 12,110.10; § 3,101

Increments in value of growth savings certificates are taxable in the year that the increase occurs because the certificate holder has a present right to redeem the certificate (Rev. Rul. 66-44).[59] Any increment in the value of life insurance or annuity due to prepaid premiums or premium deposits is income when made available to the policyholder for withdrawal or when credited against premiums payable.[60] Interest on a judgment is taxable even if the underlying award is nontaxable.[61]

When a bond with defaulted interest coupons is bought "flat" (i.e., the price covers both principal and unpaid interest), any interest received that was in default on the date of purchase is not taxable but is a return of capital. If the bond is sold, this amount must be applied to reduce the basis. If interest is received for a period which *follows* the date of purchase, it is taxable in full (Reg. § 1.61-7(c)).[62]

Under the accrual method, interest is taxable as it accrues even though it is payable later. An exception to this rule applies when it is discovered before the close of the tax year that the interest owed to the taxpayer will not be collected.[63]

State and Local Bonds—Tax Credit Bonds. The federal government provides financial assistance to state and local governmental agencies by excluding from the gross income of the recipient the interest on certain tax-exempt state and local bonds. Bond interest is not tax free, however, when it is derived from certain state or local bonds that are nonqualified private activity bonds (¶ 729), bonds that have not been issued in registered form, arbitrage bonds, hedge bonds, or federally guaranteed bonds (Code Secs. 103, 148, and 149).[64]

The federal government also authorizes the issuers of such bonds to issue tax credit bonds. A tax credit bond essentially provides the issuer with a tax-free loan. Instead of interest payments, the bond holders receive a tax credit on their federal income tax at the specified credit rate, and the issuer only has to repay the principal. The bond holders must include the credit amount in income, then claim the credit against tax on their return. In effect, the holders will usually receive the same net amount from the credit as they would receive in interest from a conventional state or local bond. See ¶ 1371 for discussion of tax credit bonds.

"Thank You" Points. A depositor who received airline tickets by redeeming "thank you" award points from a bank for making a deposit or maintaining a balance in his account received something "in the nature of interest" which constituted gross income (*P.H. Shankar*, Dec. 60,001, 143 TC 140 (2014)).[65]

726. Interest on Foreclosed Mortgaged Property. The U.S. Supreme Court has held that when a taxpayer forecloses on a mortgage and purchases the property at a foreclosure sale by bidding on the property for the full amount of the mortgage plus accrued unpaid interest, taxable income is realized in the amount of the accrued interest even if the fair market value (FMV) of the property is less than the principal due on the mortgage (*Midland Mutual Life Ins. Co.*, SCt, 37-1 USTC ¶ 9114). Other courts have applied this rule to *voluntary* conveyances by the mortgagor in consideration for the cancellation of the principal and interest of the mortgage. There is no interest income, however, in the case of a voluntary conveyance if the property is worth less than the principal of the loan.[66] Nor is any taxable income realized if only the principal of the mortgage is bid on. For repossessions of real property, see ¶ 1841.

References are to Standard Federal Tax Reports; Tax Research Consultant; and Practical Tax Explanations.

[59] ¶ 21,009.1142; INDIV: 12,102, INDIV: 12,110.10; § 38,315.15

[60] ¶ 5504.2665; INDIV: 12,118, INDIV: 30,352; § 3,101

[61] ¶ 30,575.166; INDIV: 12,112; § 3,805.35

[62] ¶ 5702, ¶ 5704.3062; INDIV: 12,252.25; § 45,415.15

[63] ¶ 5704.32; INDIV: 12,254; § 3,101

[64] ¶ 6600, ¶ 7870, ¶ 7900; SALES: 51,050; § 3,105

[65] ¶ 5704.302; INDIV: 12,052; § 3,101

[66] ¶ 5704.338; REAL: 6,154

If a creditor bids on a property for a debt, a loss may be deductible if the property is worth less than the debt.[67] Any such loss must take into account the basis and FMV of the property bid on, and therefore a loss may exist even though the creditor bid on the property for more than the debt (*Hadley Falls Trust Co.*, CA-1, 40-1 USTC ¶ 9352).[68] The FMV of the mortgaged property is presumed to be the amount bid on, in the absence of clear and convincing proof to the contrary (Reg. § 1.166-6). See ¶ 1135 for a discussion of the bad debt deduction, and ¶ 1139 for discussion of secured bad debt.

Seller-Provided Financing. A taxpayer who receives or accrues qualified residence interest (¶ 1047) from seller-provided financing must include on his or her income tax return the name, address and taxpayer identification number of the person from whom the interest was received or accrued (Code Sec. 6109(h)).[69] Failure to provide this information will expose the taxpayer to information reporting penalties (¶ 2833).

727. Imputed Interest. Holders of bonds or other obligations issued at a discount may be required to include in gross income a portion of the discount as imputed interest in each year the obligation is held, even though no interest corresponding to the amount is paid or accrued during the period (¶ 1952). Holders of notes or other debt instruments that were issued in exchange for property or services may be required to include in gross income imputed interest if no interest is provided in the debt instrument or the rate of interest is less than the applicable federal rate (AFR) (¶ 1954). Other loans bearing interest at less than the AFR may also result in imputed interest income to the lender (¶ 795).

728. Bond Transaction Between Interest Dates. When a bond is sold between interest dates, part of the sales price represents the interest earned up to the date of sale. The seller reports that portion as interest income in the year of the sale (Reg. § 1.61-7(d)).[70] Because the buyer has paid for the accrued interest as part of the sales price, the interest is a return of capital if it is later paid which reduces the buyer's basis in the bond, rather than taxable interest income, except to the extent it exceeds the amount paid the seller (Reg. § 1.61-7(c)). This interest adjustment has no effect on the cost of the bond and no connection with the adjustment for amortizable bond premium (¶ 1967).

729. Private Activity Bonds. Although interest on obligations of a state or local government is generally excludable from gross income (¶ 724), interest on a is generally not tax free when it is derived from a private activity bond that does not qualify for tax exemption (Code Sec. 103(b)).[71] A private activity bond is part of a state or local government bond issue in which: (1) more than 10 percent of the bond proceeds is to be used for a private business use; and (2) more than 10 percent of the payment of principal or interest is secured by an interest in property to be used for a private business use or payments for such property, or is to be derived from payments for property or borrowed money used for a private business use. Alternatively, part of an issue may instead qualify as a private activity bond if the amount of the bond proceeds to be used to make or finance loans to persons other than government units exceeds the lesser of five percent of the proceeds or $5 million (Code Sec. 141).[72] Certain bonds issued by a governmental unit to fund the acquisition of existing electric and gas generation and transmission systems are generally treated as private activity bonds (Code Sec. 141(d)).

Private activity bonds that *do* qualify for tax exemption include exempt facility bonds, qualified veterans' mortgage bonds, qualified student loan bonds, qualified redevelopment bonds, qualified Code Sec. 501(c)(3) bonds, qualified mortgage bonds, and qualified small-issue bonds (Code Secs. 141—145; IRS Pub. 550).[73] Qualified private activity bonds must meet the applicable volume cap requirements of Code Sec. 146 and the applicable requirements of Code Sec. 147 (Code Sec. 141(e)).

References are to Standard Federal Tax Reports; Tax Research Consultant; and Practical Tax Explanations.

[67] ¶ 10,750.10; BUSEXP: 48,204

[68] ¶ 10,670.123; BUSEXP: 48,204, REAL: 6,152.10

[69] ¶ 36,960; REAL: 6,056.15; § 18,515.05

[70] ¶ 5702; INDIV: 12,252.20; § 3,101

[71] ¶ 6600; SALES: 51,100; § 3,105.10

[72] ¶ 7702; SALES: 51,100; § 3,105.10

[73] ¶ 7702, ¶ 7740, ¶ 7780, ¶ 7810, ¶ 7821; SALES: 51,150; § 3,105.10

Exempt facility bonds may include certain enterprise zone facility bonds, New York Liberty bonds, Gulf Opportunity Zone (GO Zone) bonds, and recovery zone facility bonds, as well as Midwestern disaster area bonds and Hurricane Ike disaster area bonds (Code Secs. 1394, 1400L(d), 1400N(a)(1), and 1400U-3; Act Secs. 702 and 704, Emergency Economic Stabilization Act of 2008 (P.L. 110-343)).[74] Qualified mortgage bonds may include certain GO Zone bonds, Midwestern disaster area bonds, and Hurricane Ike disaster area bonds. Qualified small issue bonds include tribal manufacturing facility bonds (Code Sec. 7871(c)(3)).[75]

Tax Preference Items. Tax-exempt interest on private activity bonds is ordinarily considered a tax preference for purposes of the alternative minimum tax (AMT) (Code Sec. 57(a)(5)).[76] Thus, the amount of interest received is taken into account in computing alternative minimum taxable income (AMTI) for AMT purposes (¶ 1425). However, exempt interest is *not* a tax preference item on qualified 501(c)(3) bonds, New York Liberty bonds, GO Zone bonds, Midwestern disaster area bonds, or Hurricane Ike disaster area bonds, as well as the following bonds if issued after July 30, 2008: certain exempt facility bonds, qualified mortgage bonds, or qualified veterans' mortgage bonds. Additionally, exempt interest on private activity bonds issued in 2009 or 2010 is *not* treated as a tax preference item.

730. Interest on U.S. Savings Bonds. Interest on U.S. savings bonds is fully taxable (¶ 731). An accrual basis taxpayer reports interest on U.S. savings bonds each year as it accrues. A cash basis taxpayer generally reports U.S. savings bond interest in the year received (¶ 1515). Series HH and H bonds, which the U.S. Treasury no longer issues, were issued at face value, and interest was paid every six months. Paper Series EE and Series E bonds are issued at a discount, and interest is payable on redemption. Electronic Series EE bonds and inflation-indexed Series I bonds are issued at face value, and accrued interest is payable at maturity (IRS Pub. 550).

For a cash basis taxpayer, none of the interest on Series EE, E, or I bonds is taxable until the earlier of (1) the year the bonds are cashed in or disposed, or (2) the year in which they mature. The taxpayer *may*, however, elect to report the interest income on these bonds each year as it accrues (Code Sec. 454; Reg. § 1.454-1(a); IRS Pub. 550).[77]

Trades for Series H or HH bonds are no longer allowed. When such trades were available, taxable income was not recognized if Series EE or E bonds on which interest reporting was postponed were traded for Series HH or H bonds, unless cash was received in the trade. Any cash received was taxed to the extent of interest earned on the Series EE or E bonds. When the Series HH or H bonds mature, or, when they are disposed of prior to maturity, the difference between their redemption value and cost is reported as interest income. Cost is the amount paid for the Series EE or E bonds plus any additional amount paid for the Series HH or H bonds. A taxpayer could have elected to treat all previously unreported accrued interest on Series EE or E bonds traded for Series HH bonds as income in the year of the trade (IRS Pub. 550).

For individuals, Interest income from U.S. savings bonds is generally reported on Schedule B of the taxpayer's Form 1040 or Form 1040A. An individual who redeems a qualified U.S. savings bond and uses the interest to pay certain higher education expenses may be able to exclude from gross income some or all of the interest redeemed (¶ 863).

731. Issues of U.S. Obligations. Interest on all obligations of the United States and its agencies and instrumentalities (i.e., U.S. Treasury bills, notes, and bonds) issued after February 28, 1941, is subject to federal taxes to the same extent as private obligations (Reg. § § 1.61-7(b)(2) and (3), and 1.103-4).[78]

References are to Standard Federal Tax Reports; Tax Research Consultant; and Practical Tax Explanations.

[74] ¶ 32,391, ¶ 32,473, ¶ 32,483, ¶ 32,524; SALES: 51,200, SALES: 51,350; § 3,105.10

[75] ¶ 43,944; SALES: 51,056.15

[76] ¶ 5300; FILEIND: 30,252; § 15,315

[77] ¶ 21,500, ¶ 21,501; INDIV: 12,150; § 3,115.10

[78] ¶ 5702, ¶ 6606; SALES: 51,052; § 3,115.05

Dividends

733. Dividends. Dividends on stock that are paid out of the corporation's earnings profits (¶ 747) whether in the form or cash or other property are generally included in the shareholder's gross income (Code Secs. 61(a)(7), 301, and 316).[79] If a dividend is in cash, the amount of the dividend is the amount of the cash. If the dividend is in both cash and noncash property, the amount of the dividend is the amount of the cash plus the fair market value (FMV) of the property distributed (¶ 735). Special rules apply to distributions received by 20-percent corporate shareholders (Code Sec. 301(e)).[80]

Dividends are generally taxed as ordinary income. However, qualified dividend income received by an individual, estate, or trust is taxed at capital gains rates. Qualified dividend income is defined as dividends received during the tax year from a domestic corporation or a qualified foreign corporation (Code Sec. 1(h)(11)).[81] The capital gains rate for noncorporate taxpayers is 20 percent for individuals, estates, and trusts in the 39.6-percent income tax bracket; 15 percent for individuals, estates, and trusts in the 25-, 28-, or 33-percent income tax bracket; 0 percent for individuals in the 10- or 15-percent income tax brackets; and 0 percent for estates and trusts in the 15-percent income tax bracket. Individuals, estates, and trusts subject to the 20-percent capital gains rate may also be subject to the net investment income tax of 3.8 percent, which brings the capital gains rate for higher-income taxpayers to 23.8 percent. See ¶ 129 for discussion of the net investment income tax and ¶ 1736 for discussion of capital gains rates.

Corporate stock dividends passed through to investors by a mutual fund or other regulated investment company (RIC), partnership, real estate investment trust (REIT), or held by a common trust fund are also eligible for the reduced rate assuming the distribution would otherwise be classified as qualified dividend income.

Investments in tax-deferred retirement vehicles such as regular IRAs, 401(k)s, and deferred annuities receive no benefit from the rate reduction. Distributions from these accounts are taxed at ordinary income tax rates even if the funds represent dividends paid on the stocks held in the account.

The reduced tax rates also do not apply to dividends paid by corporations such as credit unions, mutual insurance companies, farmers' cooperatives, nonprofit voluntary employee benefit associations (VEBAs), mutual savings banks, building and loan associations, and certain stock owned for short terms (Code Sec. 1(h)(11)(B)(ii)).[82] Special rules apply to Code Sec. 306 stock (see ¶ 739). Special rules also apply to dividends received from foreign corporations (Code Sec. 1(h)(11)(C)).

Holding Period. To qualify for the lower rate on qualified dividend income, shareholders are required to hold the stock from which the dividend is paid for more than 60 days in the 121-day period beginning 60 days before the ex-dividend date. The ex-dividend date is the date following the record date on which the corporation finalizes the list of shareholders who will receive the dividend (Code Sec. 1(h)(11)(B)(iii)).[83]

733A. Stock Dividends and Stock Rights. Generally, a stockholder need not include in gross income the value of stock received as a stock dividend (Code Sec. 305(a); Reg. §§ 1.305-1—1.305-8).[84] However, the following distributions by a corporation of its stock or stock rights are taxed as a dividend (¶ 733):

- distributions in lieu of money (Reg. § 1.305-2);
- disproportionate distributions (Reg. § 1.305-3);
- convertible preferred stock and debentures (Reg. § 1.305-6);
- distributions of common and preferred stock (Reg. § 1.305-4);
- certain transactions increasing a shareholder's proportionate interest (Reg. § 1.305-7); and
- dividends on preferred stock, unless the limited exception applies (Reg. § 1.305-5).

References are to Standard Federal Tax Reports; Tax Research Consultant; and Practical Tax Explanations.

[79] ¶ 5502, ¶ 15,302, ¶ 15,702; CCORP: 6,050; § 3,030.05

[80] ¶ 15,302; CCORP: 12,160; § 26,601

[81] ¶ 3260; CCORP: 6,062, SALES: 15,202.55; § 3,030.05, § 26,230

[82] ¶ 3260; SALES: 15,202.55; § 3,030.05, § 26,230

[83] ¶ 3260; CCORP: 6,062; § 3,030.05, § 26,230

[84] ¶ 15,400, ¶ 15,401—¶ 15,401H, ¶ 15,402; CCORP: 6,252; § 3,030.15, § 26,235.05

An increase in the conversion ratio of convertible preferred stock made solely to account for stock dividends or stock splits on the stock into which the convertible stock can be converted is tax free.

The basis of the stock, stock rights, or fractional shares acquired in a nontaxable distribution is an allocable portion of the basis of the stock on which the distribution was made. To determine the basis of the stock received in a tax-free distribution, the shareholder allocates a part of the basis of the stock previously held to the new stock or stock rights. The basis is allocated between the old stock and the new stock or stock rights in proportion to the fair market values of each on the date of the distribution, not the record date (Code Sec. 307; Reg. § 1.307-1).[85] If the fair market value of rights received in the distribution is less than 15 percent of the fair market value of the old stock, the shareholder takes a basis of zero in the stock rights unless the shareholder elects to allocate a portion of the basis of the old stock in a statement attached to a timely filed return for the year in which the rights were received. An election, once made, is irrevocable (Reg. § 1.307-2).[86]

Any corporation that receives an extraordinary dividend with respect to any share of stock that the corporation has not held for more than two years before the dividend announcement date must reduce its basis in such stock, but not below zero, by the untaxed portion of the extraordinary dividend received. An extraordinary dividend is a dividend that equals or exceeds 10 percent (five percent in the case of stock preferred as to dividends) of the shareholder's adjusted basis in the stock (Code Sec. 1059).[87]

733B. Corporate Debt v. Equity. A number of factors are used to determine whether, for federal income tax purposes, a corporation has issued a debt or equity instrument. These factors include the source of the payments made to the holder and whether there is an unconditional promise to pay a sum certain together with a fixed rate of interest. For instruments issued after October 24, 1992, the corporate issuer's characterization of the nature of the instrument made at the time of issuance is binding upon the corporation and all the holders, but not the IRS. Interest holders are not bound, however, by the issuer's characterization if they disclose any inconsistent treatment on their tax returns (Code Sec. 385(c)).[88]

The IRS closely scrutinizes debt instruments that contain a combination of debt and equity characteristics (Notice 94-47). Of particular interest are instruments that contain equity features such as an unreasonably long maturity or an ability to repay principal with the issuer's stock. No deduction is allowed for any interest paid or accrued on a "disqualified debt instrument" issued after June 8, 1997 (Code Sec. 163(l)).[89] A disqualified debt instrument means any debt that is payable in equity of the issuer or a related party, or equity held by the issuer or any related party in any other person, but only if: (1) a substantial portion of the principal or interest is required to be paid or converted, or at the issuer's or related party's option is payable in, or convertible into, equity of the issuer or any other person; (2) a substantial portion of the principal or interest is required to be determined, or may be determined at the option of the issuer or a related party, by reference to the value of equity of the issuer or any other person; or (3) the debt is part of an arrangement reasonably expected to result in a transaction described in (1) or (2). An exception to the no deduction rule applies for certain instruments issued by dealers in securities.

In addition, the IRS examines corporate transactions designed to produce interest deductions with respect to a related issuance of stock and to provide companies with significant tax advantages in satisfying their equity capital requirements (Notice 94-48). The overall substance of an arrangement whereby a corporation creates a partnership that issues notes to investors and uses most of its capital to buy stock of the corporation is viewed by the IRS as merely an issuance of preferred stock by the corporation. Thus, such a corporation could not deduct an allocable portion of interest expense on the note without an offsetting inclusion of dividend income.

References are to Standard Federal Tax Reports; Tax Research Consultant; and Practical Tax Explanations.

[85] ¶ 15,500, ¶ 15,501; SALES: 6,302, CCORP: 6,250; § 26,235.10

[86] ¶ 15,501B; SALES: 6,302; § 26,235.10

[87] ¶ 30,020, ¶ 30,021; SALES: 6,358; § 26,201, § 26,245

[88] ¶ 17,340; CCORP: 3,300; § 26,201

[89] ¶ 9102; BUSEXP: 21,216

734. When Is a Dividend Received. A dividend (¶ 737) on corporate stock is taxable when it is unqualifiedly made subject to the demand of the shareholder (Code Sec. 301; Reg. § 1.301-1(b)).[90] For cash-method shareholders, this generally occurs when payment is actually received. For accrual-method shareholders, this occurs when the dividend is constructively received or at the time of declaration. As an exception to the constructive receipt rule, a dividend is taxable when the check is actually received, even though it may be dated and mailed in an earlier tax year, unless the recipient requested delivery by mail in order to delay recognition of income. Therefore, both accrual and cash basis taxpayers essentially may use the cash method for including dividends in income and must report the income as received.[91]

Voluntary repayment of a dividend legally declared and distributed does not negate the receipt of dividend income by a shareholder.[92] Also, dividends paid by regulated investment companies (i.e., RICs or mutual funds) are not always taxable when received (¶ 2323).

For individuals, dividends and interest in excess of $1,500 must be reported on Schedule B of the taxpayer's Form 1040 or Form 1040A.

735. Dividend Paid in Property. If any part of a dividend (¶ 737) is paid in a form other than cash, the property received must be included in gross income at its fair market value (FMV) at the date of distribution, regardless of whether it is the same date on which the distribution is includible in gross income (Code Sec. 301(b)(1) and (3)).[93] When property is distributed to a corporate shareholder, the adjusted basis of the property in the hands of the distributing corporation at the time of the distribution, plus any gain recognized by the distributing corporation, is substituted for the FMV of the property if the adjusted basis is less than the FMV.

The amount of income realized on a distribution is reduced, but not below zero, by the amount of any liability to which property is subject or which is assumed by the shareholder (Code Sec. 301(b)(2); Reg. § 1.301-1).[94] The basis of property received in a distribution is the fair market value of the property (Code Sec. 301(d)).

If a distribution is paid in property having an FMV in excess of the corporation's earnings and profits, the dividend is limited to accumulated and current earnings and profits. The portion of the distribution that is not a dividend is applied to reduce the basis of the stock. If the amount of the nondividend distribution exceeds the basis of the stock, the excess is treated as a gain from the sale or exchange of property (Code Sec. 301(c)).

736. Gain or Loss to Corporation on Nonliquidating Distributions. A corporation does not recognize a gain or loss on the distribution of its stock, or rights to its stock, to shareholders. Similarly, a corporation generally does not recognize gain or loss on the distribution to its shareholders of corporate property (Code Sec. 311(a)).[95] A corporation generally must recognize gain, however, when it distributes appreciated property to its shareholders in any ordinary, nonliquidating distribution to the extent that the fair market value (FMV) of the property exceeds its adjusted basis (Code Sec. 311(b)).[96] Gain or loss rules applicable to corporations on liquidating distributions are discussed at ¶ 2257.

739. Disposition of Section 306 Stock. Code Sec. 306 is designed to prevent shareholders from receiving nontaxable stock dividends or stock distribution in connection with a reorganization, and disposing of the stock to avoid dividend income (¶ 733).[97]

References are to Standard Federal Tax Reports; Tax Research Consultant; and Practical Tax Explanations.

[90] ¶ 15,302, ¶ 15,303; CCORP: 6,060; § 3,030.05

[91] ¶ 21,009.1235; CCORP: 6,060; § 3,030.05

[92] ¶ 15,704.46, ¶ 15,704.473; CCORP: 6,058; § 3,030.05

[93] ¶ 15,302; CCORP: 6,150; § 26,205

[94] ¶ 15,302, ¶ 15,303; CCORP: 6,154; § 26,205

[95] ¶ 15,550; CCORP: 6,100; § 26,235.10

[96] ¶ 15,550; CCORP: 6,152; § 26,210

[97] ¶ 15,450; CCORP: 24,050; § 26,235.25

This is accomplished by denying capital gain treatment when the stockholder disposes of certain stock referred to as section 306 stock. Section 306 stock includes: (1) stock other than common stock received as a tax-free stock dividend, (2) stock other than common stock received in certain tax-free divisions or reorganizations, and (3) stock, including common stock, with a substituted or carryover basis determined by reference to other section 306 stock (Code Sec. 306(a)(1)(D) and (c)).[98]

If section 306 stock is redeemed by a corporation (¶ 742), the amount realized by shareholder is considered a distribution of property and treated as ordinary income or a taxable distribution to the extent that it is made out of earnings and profits (¶ 733 and ¶ 747). If section 306 stock is sold or disposed of by a shareholder other than by a redemption, the amount realized by the shareholder is treated as ordinary income to the extent that the amount realized is not more than the amount that would have been realized as a dividend if, instead of the stock, the corporation had distributed cash in an amount equal to the fair market value of the stock. Thus, it would be ordinary income up to the stockholder's share of the amount of earnings and profits of the corporation available for distribution. Section 306 stock is not subject to these rules under certain circumstances (¶ 740).

A shareholder who received a preferred stock dividend on common stock and who donated the dividend to a tax-exempt charitable foundation realized no income on the stock transfer. In addition, the donor would not realize any income from the later sale of the section 306 stock by the foundation.[99]

740. Special Rules and Exceptions for Code Sec. 306 Stock. A holder of section 306 stock (¶ 739) is not subject to the ordinary income recognition rule for a transfer of the stock if the disposition occurs as part of a transaction that cannot be used to bail out earnings and profits. The rules governing gain realized on section 306 stock do not apply to a disposition (Code Sec. 306(b)):[100]

- if it is not a redemption,

  — is not made, directly or indirectly, to a related person under the constructive ownership rules, and

  — terminates the entire stock interest of the shareholder in the corporation, including stock constructively owned;

- if it is a complete redemption of all the stock held in the corporation by the shareholder or in redemption of stock held by a shareholder who is not a corporation and in partial liquidation of the distributing corporation;

- if it is redeemed in a complete liquidation of the corporation;

- to the extent that gain or loss to the shareholder is not recognized with respect to the disposition; or

- if the IRS is satisfied that the distribution of the stock and the disposition or redemption, simultaneously or previously, of the stock on which the distribution was made were not in pursuance of a plan having federal income tax avoidance as one of its principal purposes.

The sale of new preferred stock to an employees' trust, however, was held not to be within the scope of Code Sec. 306(a).[101]

References are to Standard Federal Tax Reports; Tax Research Consultant; and Practical Tax Explanations.

[98] ¶ 15,450; CCORP: 24,152; § 26,235.25

[99] ¶ 15,452.19; CCORP: 24,150; § 26,235.25

[100] ¶ 15,450; CCORP: 24,200; § 26,235.25

[101] ¶ 15,452.21; CCORP: 24,200; § 26,235.25

Dividends: Distribution in Redemption of Stock

742. Redemption of Stock as a Dividend. If a corporation cancels or redeems its stock in such a manner as to make the distribution equivalent to a dividend distribution (¶ 747), the amount received by the shareholder to the extent that it is paid out of earnings and profits is a taxable dividend (Reg. § 1.302-1).[102] Whether a distribution in connection with a cancellation or redemption of stock is equivalent to a taxable dividend depends on the facts in each case.

A cancellation or redemption of a part of the stock, pro rata among all the shareholders, will generally be considered as resulting in a dividend distribution (Reg. § 1.302-2).[103] A redemption can be treated as an exchange of stock, rather than as a dividend, if one of the following four tests is met (Code Sec. 302(b)):[104] (1) the redemption is substantially disproportionate with respect to the shareholder; (2) the redemption terminates the shareholder's entire interest in the corporation; (3) the redemption is not substantially equivalent to a dividend; (4) the redemption is of stock held by a noncorporate shareholder and is made in partial liquidation of the redeeming corporation; or (5) the redemption is of stock of a publicly offered regulated investment company (RIC or mutual fund) if the redemption is upon the stockholder's demand and the RIC issues only stock that is redeemable upon such demand. Amounts received by a shareholder in a distribution in complete liquidation of a corporation are not equivalent to the distribution of a taxable dividend (Code Sec. 331).[105]

A distribution is substantially disproportionate as to a shareholder if, after the redemption, the shareholder owns less than 50 percent of the combined voting power of all classes of voting stock and there is an exchange of stock but not a dividend. Further, the ratio of the shareholder's holdings of voting stock after the redemption to all the voting stock must be less than 80 percent of the ratio of the voting stock the shareholder owned immediately before the redemption to the entire voting stock in the corporation. In addition, a distribution is not substantially disproportionate unless the stockholder's ownership of common stock, whether voting or nonvoting, after and before redemption also meets the 80-percent test (Reg. § 1.302-3).[106]

If a shareholder is entirely bought out, the transaction is treated as an exchange of the stock, and no part of the distribution is taxed as a dividend (Reg. § 1.302-4).[107]

A distribution that is in redemption of stock held by a noncorporate shareholder in partial liquidation of the distributing corporation is a distribution in exchange for the stock and is not taxed as a dividend (Code Sec. 302(b)(4)).[108]

Stock Redemption Expenses. A corporation is not allowed a deduction for any amount paid or incurred in connection with any redemption of its stock or the stock of any related person (¶ 432 and ¶ 1717). This restriction does not apply to deductions for interest paid or accrued within the tax year on indebtedness, deductions for dividends paid in connection with the redemption of stock in a RIC or mutual fund, or deductions for amounts properly allocable to indebtedness and amortized over the term of the debt (Code Sec. 162(k)).[109]

743. Constructive Ownership of Stock. Certain provisions relating to corporate distributions and adjustments treat an individual as constructively owning stock held by a related person. Under these constructive ownership rules an individual is treated as owning stock owned, directly or indirectly, by a spouse if not legally separated under a decree of divorce or separate maintenance, children, including adopted children, grandchildren, and parents (Code Sec. 318(a)(1); Reg. §§ 1.318-1, 1.318-2).[110] Stock constructively owned by an individual under the family attribution rule is not treated as

References are to Standard Federal Tax Reports; Tax Research Consultant; and Practical Tax Explanations.

[102] ¶ 15,326 ; CCORP: 21,102; § 26,305.05

[103] ¶ 15,327; CCORP: 21,250; § 26,305.05

[104] ¶ 15,325; CCORP: 21,150; § 26,301

[105] ¶ 16,002; CCORP: 27,050; § 26,320.05

[106] ¶ 15,328; CCORP: 21,150; § 26,315.05

[107] ¶ 15,329; CCORP: 21,204; § 26,320.05

[108] ¶ 15,325; CCORP: 21,700; § 26,330

[109] ¶ 8500; BUSEXP: 9,412.05; § 26,365

[110] ¶ 15,900, ¶ 15,901, ¶ 15,902; CCORP: 21,500; § 26,310.05

owned by that individual for the purpose of applying the constructive stock ownership rule to make another the owner of such stock (Reg. § 1.318-4).[111]

Stock owned directly or indirectly by or for a partnership, S corporation, or estate is considered as being owned proportionately by the partners, S corporation shareholders, or beneficiaries. Stock owned directly or indirectly by or for a partner, S corporation shareholder, or beneficiary is treated as being owned by the partnership, S corporation, or estate (Code Sec. 318(a)(2) and (3)).[112]

Stock owned directly or indirectly by or for a trust is considered as being owned by its beneficiaries in proportion to their actuarial interests in the trust. Stock owned directly or indirectly by or for a beneficiary of a trust is considered as being owned by the trust. However, a contingent beneficial interest of not more than five percent of the value of the trust property is not to be taken into account (Code Sec. 318(a)(2) and (3); Reg. § 1.318-2).[113]

If 50 percent or more in value of the stock in a corporation is owned directly or indirectly by or for any person, that person is considered as owning the stock owned directly or indirectly by or for the corporation in the proportion that the value of the stock the person owns bears to the value of all the stock in the corporation. The corporation, on the other hand, is considered as owning the stock owned directly or indirectly by or for any person holding 50 percent or more in value of its stock directly or indirectly (Code Sec. 318(a)(2)(C) and (a)(3)(C)).[114]

744. Redemption of Stock Through Use of Related Corporations. If stock of an issuing corporation is acquired by a corporation that is controlled by the issuing corporation, the amount paid for the stock is a dividend by the issuing corporation provided that it is redemption that would be considered a taxable dividend (¶ 742). Also, when the stock of one corporation is sold to a related corporation (i.e., brother-sister corporations), the sale proceeds are considered as distributed in redemption of the stock of the corporation which bought it. If the sales are related, it is immaterial whether they are made simultaneously (Reg. § 1.304-2).[115] Whether the sales are related is determined upon the facts and circumstances surrounding all the sales. To the extent that a redemption involving related corporations is treated as a distribution under Code Sec. 301, the transferor and the acquiring corporation are treated as if the transferor had transferred the stock involved to the acquiring corporation in exchange for stock of the acquiring corporation, in a Code Sec. 351(a) nontaxable contribution of capital, and then the acquiring corporation had redeemed the stock it was deemed to have issued (Code Sec. 304(a)(1)).[116]

745. Redemption of Stock to Pay Estate Taxes and Expenses. A distribution of property by a corporation in redemption of its stock that has been included in the gross estate of a decedent for estate tax purposes can qualify as a sale or exchange of the stock to the extent that the amount of the distribution does not exceed the sum of the estate, generation-skipping transfer, inheritance, legacy, and succession taxes on the estate, including interest, plus the funeral and administration expenses allowable as deductions from the gross estate for federal estate tax purposes (Code Sec. 303(a) and (d)).[117] For discussion of the estate tax, see ¶ 2901 and following.

To qualify for this treatment, the redemption must have been made after the decedent's death and not later than 90 days after the period of limitations on assessment of the federal estate tax, which is three years after the return is filed (Code Sec. 303(b)(1)). When a petition for redetermination of an estate tax deficiency has been filed with the Tax Court, the redemption period is extended to any time before the expiration of 60 days after the decision of the Tax Court becomes final. A distribution made more

References are to Standard Federal Tax Reports; Tax Research Consultant; and Practical Tax Explanations.

[111] ¶ 15,905; CCORP: 21,502; § 26,310.30

[112] ¶ 15,900; CCORP: 21,504, CCORP: 21,506; § 26,310.15, § 26,310.20

[113] ¶ 15,900, ¶ 15,902; CCORP: 21,508; § 26,310.20

[114] ¶ 15,900; CCORP: 21,510; § 26,310.15

[115] ¶ 15,377; CCORP: 21,450

[116] ¶ 15,375; CCORP: 21,450

[117] ¶ 15,350; CCORP: 21,650; § 26,340.05

than 60 days after the decision of the Tax Court becomes final can be timely, provided it is made within 90 days after expiration of the three-year period.[118]

In order for the redemption not to be treated as a taxable dividend, the value of the decedent's stock in the redeeming corporation must exceed 35 percent of the gross estate, after the deductions for allowable funeral and administration expenses and losses (Code Sec. 303(b)(2)). The shares must be redeemed from a person whose interest in the estate is reduced by payment of estate, generation-skipping transfer, inheritance, and succession taxes or funeral and administration expenses (Code Sec. 303(b)(3)).

If stock in a corporation is the subject of a generation-skipping transfer occurring at the same time and as a result of the death of an individual, the tax imposed on the transfer is treated as an estate tax for purposes of the redemption rules. The period of distribution is measured from the date of the generation-skipping transfer, and the relationship of stock to the decedent's estate is measured with reference solely to the amount of the generation-skipping transfer (Code Sec. 303(d)).[119]

Dividends: Earnings and Profits

747. Source of Dividend Distributions. A distribution received by a shareholder from a corporation must be paid out of earnings and profits of the distributing corporation (¶ 748) to be subject to income tax as a dividend (¶ 733). A dividend is any distribution made by a corporation to its shareholders out of its earnings and profits accumulated after February 28, 1913, or out of the earnings and profits of the current tax year, computed as of the close of the tax year without diminution by reason of any distributions made during the tax year, and without regard to the amount of the earnings and profits at the time the distribution was made (Code Sec. 316; Reg. § 1.316-1).[120]

In order to determine the source of a distribution, consideration should be given to: (1) the earnings and profits of the tax year; (2) the earnings and profits accumulated since February 28, 1913, but only in the case when, and to the extent that, the distributions made during the tax year are not regarded as out of the earnings and profits of that year; (3) the earnings and profits accumulated before March 1, 1913, only after all of the earnings and profits of the tax year and all the earnings and profits accumulated since February 28, 1913, have been distributed; and (4) sources other than earnings and profits only after the earnings and profits have been distributed (Reg. § 1.316-2).[121]

If the current year's earnings and profits are sufficient to cover all distributions made during the year, each distribution is a taxable dividend. If the year's cash distributions exceed current earnings and profits, a part of the earnings and profits must be allocated proportionately to each distribution, on the basis of the following formula: distribution × (current earnings and profits ÷ total distributions). The remaining portion of each distribution not covered by current earnings and profits is then treated as a taxable dividend to the extent of accumulated earnings and profits. If these are not sufficient to cover the remaining portion of any distribution, they are to be applied against each distribution in chronological order until exhausted.

748. Computation of Earnings and Profits. In computing earnings and profits, all income that is exempt from tax must be included, as well as all items includible in gross income (Reg. § 1.312-6).[122] Thus, exempt income such as life insurance proceeds and fully tax-exempt interest on state or municipal obligations is included. Similarly, cancellation of indebtedness income and intercorporate dividends are included.

The starting point for the computation of earnings and profits is the corporation's taxable income, which is then adjusted to more accurately reflect true economic income available for distribution. This involves the different treatment of certain items from their treatment for tax purposes, including depreciation, depletion, certain reserves, and other

References are to Standard Federal Tax Reports; Tax Research Consultant; and Practical Tax Explanations.

[118] ¶ 15,353.80; CCORP: 21,650; § 26,340.25

[119] ¶ 15,350; CCORP: 21,662; § 26,340.05

[120] ¶ 15,702, ¶ 15,703; CCORP: 12,050; § 26,215

[121] ¶ 15,703B; CCORP: 12,050; § 26,215

[122] ¶ 15,611; CCORP: 12,102; § 26,601

items. In many cases, gain or loss from a sale or other disposition of property will be included in earnings and profits at the time and to the extent that it is recognized for tax purposes (Reg. § 1.312-7).[123] There are exceptions to this general rule and the corporation's earnings and profits are very unlikely to be the same as the corporation's taxable income. For example, income from installment sales is treated differently than earnings and profits (¶ 756). As another example, some items that are required to be capitalized for income tax purposes are deducted in the computation of earnings and profits (Rev. Rul. 60-123).[124]

The general rule on the distribution of property, including cash, by a corporation is that the earnings and profits for future distributions are reduced by the amount of money distributed, the principal amount of any obligations of the corporation distributed, and the adjusted basis of any other property distributed (Reg. § 1.312-1).[125] If appreciated property is distributed with respect to stock, earnings and profits must be increased by the amount of the gain realized upon the distribution even if the gain is not recognized for purposes of computing taxable income. There are special rules for distributions to 20-percent corporate shareholders (¶ 733).

749. Effect of Deficit on Earnings and Profits. Even if there is an operating deficit at the beginning of the year, total dividends paid are taxable to the extent of profits for the *entire* year (¶ 747) (Reg. § 1.316-1(e)).[126]

750. Effect of Loss on Earnings and Profits. A loss for a preceding year cannot be used to decrease the earnings and profits of the tax year (¶ 747) (Reg. § 1.312-6(d)).[127]

751. Redemptions and Earnings and Profits. A corporation that distributes amounts in redemption of its stock can reduce its post-February 28, 1913, accumulated earnings and profits only by the ratable share of those earnings and profits attributable to the redeemed stock (¶ 747) (Code Sec. 312(n)(7)).[128]

752. Effect of Reorganization on Earnings and Profits. When a corporate reorganization results in no recognized gain or loss, the company's life as a continuing venture does not stop, so that what were earnings and profits of the original company remain, for purposes of distribution of dividend, earnings and profits of the continuing corporation (¶ 747).[129]

753. Effect of Nontaxable Distribution on Earnings and Profits. Nontaxable stock dividends or stock rights (¶ 733A) do not reduce earnings and profits (¶ 747). The same rule applies to distributions of the stock or securities, or rights to acquire stock or securities, of other corporations and distributions of property or money when they were nontaxable to the recipient when made (Code Sec. 312(d)).[130]

754. Distribution Other Than a Dividend. Any distribution that is a dividend is included in gross income (¶ 733). The portion of a distribution that is not a dividend reduces the adjusted basis of the shareholder's stock. Any excess of distributions over the basis is treated as a gain from the sale or exchange of property (Code Sec. 301(c)).[131]

755. Effect of Depreciation on Earnings and Profits. Depreciation claimed on the corporation's income tax return that is in excess of the straight-line method increases the corporation's current earnings and profits (¶ 747) (Code Sec. 312(k)).[132] For tangible property placed in service in tax years beginning after 1986, the alternative MACRS method is used to compute depreciation in order to determine the corporation's earn-

References are to Standard Federal Tax Reports; Tax Research Consultant; and Practical Tax Explanations.

[123] ¶ 15,611B; CCORP: 12,100; § 26,610

[124] ¶ 15,612.4425; CCORP: 12,050

[125] ¶ 15,601; CCORP: 12,152; § 26,615.05

[126] ¶ 15,703; CCORP: 12,050; § 26,605.05

[127] ¶ 15,611, ¶ 15,612.45; CCORP: 12,050; § 26,605.10

[128] ¶ 15,600; CCORP: 12,210; § 26,305.05

[129] ¶ 15,612.68, ¶ 17,031.21; CCORP: 12,200; § 26,601

[130] ¶ 15,600; CCORP: 12,156; § 26,235.10

[131] ¶ 15,302; CCORP: 12,050; § 26,215

[132] ¶ 15,600; CCORP: 12,108; § 26,625.15

ings and profits (¶ 1247). For depreciable assets first placed in service after 1980, but before 1987, the adjustment to earnings and profits for depreciation is determined under the straight-line ACRS, using extended recovery periods (¶ 1252).[133] For assets placed in service before 1981, the amount of the depreciation deduction for the purpose of computing earnings and profits is generally the amount allowable under the traditional straight-line method, although a corporation that uses the permissible non-accelerated depreciation method (e.g., the machine-hour method) can use that method for earnings and profits purposes.

Also, in computing the earnings and profits of a corporation, any amount that can be deducted under certain provisions can be deducted ratably over a period of five years, beginning with the year the amount is otherwise deductible (Code Sec. 312(k)(3)(B)).[134] This includes property that can be expensed under Code Sec. 179 (¶ 1208), environmental expenses deducted under Code Sec. 179B (¶ 1285), the cost of refinery property deducted under Code Sec. 179C (¶ 1285A), the cost of energy-efficient property deducted under Code Sec. 179D (¶ 1286), and the cost of advanced mine safety equipment deducted under Code Sec. 179E (¶ 989A; ¶ 1237).[135]

756. Effect of Installment Sales on Earnings and Profits. A corporation that sells property on the installment method of accounting (¶ 1801) is treated for earnings and profits purposes as if it had not used the installment method (¶ 747) (Code Sec. 312(n)(5)).[136]

757. Effect of LIFO Reserve Changes on Earnings and Profits. A corporation's earnings and profits (¶ 747) generally must be increased or decreased by the amount of any change in the corporation's "LIFO recapture amount" at the end of each tax year (Code Sec. 312(n)(4)).[137] The LIFO recapture amount is the amount, if any, by which the inventory amount of the inventory assets under the first-in, first-out (FIFO) method (¶ 1564) exceeds the inventory amount of the inventory assets under the last-in, first-out (LIFO) method (¶ 1565).

Business Income

759. Business Income or Profit. Gross income of a taxpayer includes "gross income derived from business," which is usually the same as gross profit, *not* gross receipts (Code Sec. 61(a)(2); Reg. § 1.61-3(a)).[138] Gross profit is the total receipts from sales minus the cost of the goods sold, plus investment income and income from other sources. In the case of most mercantile businesses, cost of goods sold includes the purchase price of the article sold plus delivery costs, warehousing, etc. In a manufacturing firm it includes the entire factory cost—materials, direct labor, and factory overhead, including depreciation attributable to manufacturing processes—applicable to goods manufactured and sold. Gross income derived from business is determined without subtracting selling expenses, losses, or other items not ordinarily used in computing costs of goods sold, as well as amounts paid for bribes, kickbacks, fines or penalties for which a business deduction would not be allowed (¶ 972). Cost of goods sold should be determined according to the accounting method consistently used by the taxpayer (¶ 1515).

Damages for Lost Profit or Capital. Damage awards and amounts received in settlement of claims for business injuries that represent compensation for lost profits are included in gross income and taxable as ordinary income. This rule applies to proceeds from business interruption insurance, liquidated damages, and awards for breach of contract. Damages received for injury to goodwill are a nontaxable return of capital to the extent that the amounts received do not exceed the taxpayer's basis in goodwill. Similarly, compensation for injury to, or loss of, capital is treated as a nontaxable return of capital to the extent of basis. Any excess is treated as capital gain if received for

References are to Standard Federal Tax Reports; Tax Research Consultant; and Practical Tax Explanations.

[133] ¶ 15,612.31; CCORP: 12,108; § 11,001, § 26,625.15

[134] ¶ 15,600; DEPR: 3,452; § 26,625.10

[135] ¶ 12,120—¶ 12,139; DEPR: 12,050; § 26,625.10

[136] ¶ 15,600; CCORP: 12,106; § 26,625.25

[137] ¶ 15,600; CCORP: 12,106; § 26,625.45

[138] ¶ 5502, ¶ 5511; INDIV: 6,050; § 3,010

damage to a capital asset.[139] Punitive damages, such as treble damages under antitrust laws, constitute taxable ordinary income (Reg. § 1.61-14(a)).[140] See ¶ 852 for damages arising out of employment discrimination claims.

760. Tax Credits Included in Income. If the taxpayer claims a credit for gasoline and special fuels on Form 4136 (¶ 1329), the amount of the credit must be included in gross income to the extent that a business deduction for the products was taken.[141] A cash-basis taxpayer must claim the credit and include the amount in gross income in the same tax year. An accrual-basis taxpayer should include the credit in the gross income for the tax year in which the fuel was actually used (IRS Pub. 510).

A taxpayer must include the amounts of the alcohol fuels credit (¶ 1365I), which is the second generation biofuel producer credit only, and the biodiesel fuels credit (¶ 1365X) in gross income for the tax year in which they were earned (Code Sec. 87).[142] The total credit allowable must be included even if the taxpayer could not use the credit currently because of the credit limitation based on tax liability.

Rents and Royalties

762. Rents. Amounts received or accrued as rents in payment for the use of property must be included in gross income (Code Sec. 61(a)(5); Reg. § 1.61-8).[143] The payment by a lessee of any expenses of a lessor is generally considered additional rental income to the lessor (¶ 765). Consideration received by the lessor for cancellation of a lease is in substitution for rental payments and not a return of capital. Any reduction in the value of property due to cancellation of a lease is a deductible loss only when fixed by a closed transaction (*W.M. Hort*, SCt, 41-1 USTC ¶ 9354).[144] Rental activities are generally treated as passive activities (¶ 1181).

For individuals, expenses attributable to property held for the production of rents are deductible in computing adjusted gross income (AGI) (¶ 1006A). An individual lessor generally reports rental real estate income and expenses on Schedule E of Form 1040. However, Schedule C or Schedule C-EZ of Form 1040 is used instead if the taxpayer provided significant services to the real property lessee. In addition, Schedule C is used to report income and expenses from the rental of personal property if the taxpayer is in the business of renting personal property. If the taxpayer is not in the business of renting personal property, the income is reported as other income on Form 1040 and the expenses are reported as an adjustment to AGI (Instructions to Form 1040).

See ¶ 966 for special rules affecting a taxpayer's rental of his or her residence or vacation home.

763. Royalties. Royalties from copyrights on literary, musical, or artistic works and similar property or from a patent on an invention are includible in gross income (Code Sec. 61(a)(6); Reg. § 1.61-8(a)).[145] Royalties received from oil, gas, or other mineral properties are also includible in gross income. For the treatment of royalties on the disposition of an interest in timber, coal, and iron ore, see ¶ 1772. For the depletion allowance for royalties, see ¶ 1289.

For individuals, expenses attributable to property held for the production of royalties are deductible in computing adjusted gross income (AGI) (¶ 1006A). Royalty income and expenses are generally reported on Schedule E of Form 1040. However, Schedule C or Schedule C-EZ of Form 1040 is used to report royalties received by the holder of an operating oil, gas, or mineral interest, and by self-employed writers, inventors, artists, etc.

References are to Standard Federal Tax Reports; Tax Research Consultant; and Practical Tax Explanations.

[139] ¶ 5900.14, ¶ 5900.15, ¶ 5900.26; INDIV: 6,354; § 3,810.10, § 3,810.20

[140] ¶ 5815; INDIV: 6,356; § 3,810.25

[141] ¶ 4150, ¶ 5602.35; INDIV: 6,376; § 13,540

[142] ¶ 6430; INDIV: 6,376; § 3,085

[143] ¶ 5502, ¶ 5705; REAL: 12,050; § 3,020

[144] ¶ 5706.5162; REAL: 12,252; § 3,020, § 18,630

[145] ¶ 5502, ¶ 5705; SALES: 24,250, FARM: 18,150; § 3,025

764. Improvements by Lessee. Ordinarily, on the termination of a lease, a lessor of real property excludes any income derived from improvements made on the property by the lessee (Code Sec. 109; Reg. § 1.109-1).[146] This exclusion applies to improvements that revert to the lessor upon expiration of a lease as well as to those acquired by the lessor upon forfeiture of a lease prior to the end of the full term. If the improvements represent a liquidation-in-kind of lease rentals, the exclusion does not apply to the extent that the improvements represent such liquidation.

If the lessee makes improvements in lieu of paying rent during the lease term, the lessor has rental income to the extent of the fair market value of the improvements in the year they were made (Reg. § § 1.61-8(c) and 1.109-1).[147] This treatment of lessee improvements depends on the parties' intention, which may be indicated by the lease terms or the surrounding circumstances.

Construction Allowances. A retail tenant that receives cash or rent reductions from a lessor of retail space with respect to a lease of 15 years or less entered into after August 5, 1997, does not include that amount in gross income, if the tenant uses the amounts for construction or improvement of nonresidential real property that is part of the retail space and used in the tenant's trade or business (Code Sec. 110(a); Reg. § 1.110-1).[148] The lessor must depreciate the improvement as MACRS nonresidential real property (¶ 1234 and ¶ 1240). If the improvement is disposed or abandoned at the termination of the lease, the lessor must continue to depreciate after the improvement was disposed of or abandoned and may claim a gain or loss by reference to the remaining adjusted basis of the improvement (¶ 1109).

765. Lessor's Obligations Paid by Lessee. If a lessee pays any of the lessor's expenses, such as property taxes, the payment is additional rental income to the lessor (Reg. § 1.61-8(c)).[149] When the taxes paid are income to the lessor, they may be treated as if paid by the lessor in determining their deductibility (¶ 986). If a lessee agrees to pay, in lieu of rent, a dividend on the lessor's stock or interest on its mortgages, the payments will result in rental income to the lessor.[150]

Farming Income

767. Farming As a Business. Income from farming is treated in the same way as income from any other business (¶ 759). Every individual, partnership, or corporation that cultivates, operates, or manages a farm for gain or profit, either as owner or tenant, is designated as a farmer (Reg. § 1.61-4(d)).[151] A person who cultivates or operates a farm for recreation or pleasure, and who experiences a continual net loss from year to year, generally lacks a profit motive and may not deduct the losses (¶ 1195).

An individual engaged in farming for profit must file a Schedule F of Form 1040 to report income and expenses from the farming activity. Partnerships engaged in farming must file Schedule F along with Form 1065, and estates and trusts engaged in farming must file Schedule F along with Form 1041. Corporations engaged in farming must file the appropriate Form 1120. An individual farmer must also file Schedule SE of Form 1040 for computing earnings from self-employment (¶ 2676).

Cash Basis. The general rules for all cash-basis taxpayers also apply to a farmer on the cash basis (¶ 1515). A cash-basis farmer does not use inventories, and includes in gross income all cash and the value of merchandise or other property received from the sale of livestock and produce that have been raised, profits from the sale of livestock or other items that have been purchased, amounts received from breeding fees, rental fees, and other incidental farm income, all subsidy or conservation payments treated as income, and income received from all other sources (Reg. § 1.61-4).[152] A cash-basis

References are to Standard Federal Tax Reports; Tax Research Consultant; and Practical Tax Explanations.

[146] ¶ 7020, ¶ 7021; SALES: 42,252, REAL: 12,304; § 18,625

[147] ¶ 5705, ¶ 7021; SALES: 42,252; § 18,625

[148] ¶ 7030, ¶ 7032; REAL: 12,312; § 4,035

[149] ¶ 5705; REAL: 12,066, REAL: 12,070; § 18,610.20

[150] ¶ 5706.564; REAL: 12,070; § 18,610.20

[151] ¶ 5601; FARM: 3,052; § 36,305

[152] ¶ 5601; FARM: 3,056; § 36,310.05

farmer may defer recognition of gain from the sale of a crop delivered in one year until the following year if a valid contract with the purchaser or the purchaser's agent prohibits payment until the following year, but not if the payment is deferred merely at the seller's request. If the sales contract states that the farmer has the right to the proceeds of the sale from the purchaser at any time after delivery of the item, the farmer must include the sales price in his or her gross income in the year of the sale, regardless of when payment is received.[153]

Profit from the sale of livestock or other items purchased by a farmer is computed by deducting the cost from the sales price. For the sale of animals that originally were purchased as draft or work animals, or for breeding or dairy purposes and not for resale, the profit is the difference between the sale price and the depreciated basis of the animal sold (Reg. § 1.61-4(a)).

A cash-basis farmer who receives insurance proceeds as a result of destruction or damage to crops may elect to include the proceeds in income in the year after the year of damage if the farmer can show that the income from the crops would normally have been reported in the following year. This includes payments received under the Agricultural Act of 1949, Title II of the Disaster Assistance Act of 1988, or Title I of the Disaster Assistance Act of 1989 as a result of damage to crops caused by drought, flood, or other natural disaster, or the inability to plant crops because of such a natural disaster (Code Sec. 451(d); Reg. § 1.451-6; Rev. Rul. 91-55).[154]

A cash-method farmer who is forced to sell more livestock than usual in the current year due to drought, flood, or other weather-related conditions, in an area designated as eligible for assistance by the federal government, may elect to be taxed on the forced sale income (gain that normally would not have been realized in the year of the forced sale) in the following year if the farmer can show that, under usual business practices, the additional animals would not have been sold in the current year except for the weather-related condition (Code Sec. 451(e); Reg. § 1.451-7).[155]

Accrual Method. A farmer on the accrual method (¶ 1515) must use inventories taken at the start and the end of the tax year (Reg. § 1.61-4(b)).[156] Although many farmers may use the cash method, the accrual method of accounting is required for certain farming corporations and partnerships (¶ 1519), and for all farming tax shelters including farming syndicates (¶ 1521).

Gross profit of a farmer on the accrual basis is calculated by: (1) adding the inventory value of livestock and other products on hand at the end of the year, plus the amount received from the sale of livestock and other products during the year, miscellaneous income items (i.e., breeding fees, rental fees, other incidental farm income), all subsidy or conservation payments treated as income, and gross income from all other sources, and then (2) subtracting from that total the sum of the inventory value of livestock and products on hand at the beginning of the year and the cost of livestock and products purchased during the year, but not livestock held for draft, dairy, or breeding purposes, unless they are included in inventory (Reg. § 1.61-4(b)).

Livestock raised or purchased for sale must be inventoried (¶ 1569). Livestock purchased for draft, breeding, or dairy purposes and not for sale may be inventoried, or instead may be treated as capital assets subject to depreciation if the method used is consistently followed from year to year. If inventoried livestock is sold, its cost must not be taken as an additional deduction in computing taxable income, because the cost is reflected in the inventory (Reg. § 1.61-4(b)). Sales of livestock held for draft, breeding, or dairy purposes are generally reported on Form 4797.

Other Methods. Two other inventory methods are available to farmers—the farm-price method and the unit-livestock-price method (¶ 1569).

References are to Standard Federal Tax Reports; Tax Research Consultant; and Practical Tax Explanations.

[153] ¶ 21,009.453; FARM: 3,056; § 36,035

[154] ¶ 21,002, ¶ 21,018, ¶ 21,021.28; FARM: 3,202; § 36,020

[155] ¶ 21,002, ¶ 21,020; FARM: 3,204; § 36,035

[156] ¶ 5601; FARM: 3,058, FARM: 3,100; § 36,315

Income Averaging. An individual engaged in a farming business or fishing business may elect to average farm income over three years (Code Sec. 1301; Reg. § 1.1301-1).[157] The tax imposed in any tax year equals the sum of the tax computed on taxable income reduced by the amount of farm income elected for averaging plus the increase in tax that would result if taxable income for each of the three prior tax years were increased by an amount equal to one-third of the elected farm income. Schedule J of Form 1040 is used to report the income averaging.

Other Matters. For income from the sale of farm property other than inventory, see the discussion beginning at ¶ 1701. For tax shelter farming operations, see ¶ 1521. For expenses of a farmer, see ¶ 982—¶ 985. For the application of the uniform capitalization rules to a farming business, see ¶ 999.

768. Patronage Dividend. A cooperative and its patrons are taxed in a way that the business earnings of the cooperative are taxable currently either to the cooperative or, through patronage dividends, to the patrons (¶ 698) (Code Secs. 1382 and 1385).[158]

769. Commodity Credit Corporation Loan. Income from the sale of a crop is normally reported in the year of the sale. If, however, the farmer has pledged all or part of the crop production to secure a Commodity Credit Corporation (CCC) loan, the farmer may elect to report the loan proceeds as income in the year received rather than reporting the income in the year of the sale. IRS permission is not required to begin reporting CCC loans in this manner, but once a loan has been reported in income in the year received, all succeeding loans must be reported in the same way unless the IRS grants permission to change the reporting method. The election is made on Schedule F of Form 1040. The amount reported as income becomes the farmer's basis in the commodity and is used to determine gain or loss upon the ultimate disposition of the commodity (Code Sec. 77; Reg. §§ 1.77-1 and 1.77-2).[159] The IRS has adopted procedures for automatic approval of an accounting method change to report CCC loans as loans rather than as income (Rev. Proc. 2016-29).[160]

The repayment amount for a loan secured by an eligible commodity is generally based on the lower of the original loan rate or the alternative repayment rate for the commodity as of the repayment date. Thus, on repayment a market gain may be realized if the loan is repaid when the alternative rate is lower than the original loan rate (Notice 2007-63).[161] When a CCC loan is repaid, regardless of the manner of repayment, the CCC is required to file an information return reporting market gain associated with the repayment (Code Sec. 6039J(a)).[162] The CCC is to report market gain from the repayment of a CCC loan on Form 1099-G.

Alimony Payments

771. Tax Treatment of Alimony Payments. Alimony and separate maintenance payments are income to the recipient/payee and are deductible by the payor if certain requirements are met (¶ 772 and ¶ 773) (Code Secs. 61(a)(8), 62(a)(10), 71 and 215).[163] Alimony payments are taken as a deduction from gross income in arriving at the payor's adjusted gross income (AGI) (¶ 1005) and therefore may be claimed by taxpayers regardless of whether they itemize.

772. Requirements for Alimony and Separate Maintenance Payments. Payments made under a divorce or separation instrument are includible in the gross income of the recipient/payee and deductible by the payor as alimony or separate maintenance payments (¶ 771 and ¶ 773) if the following requirements are met:

References are to Standard Federal Tax Reports; Tax Research Consultant; and Practical Tax Explanations.

[157] ¶ 31,787, ¶ 31,789; FARM: 3,300; § 36,401

[158] ¶ 32,320, ¶ 32,360; FARM: 12,102; § 36,040

[159] ¶ 6300, ¶ 6301, ¶ 6302; FARM: 3,170; § 36,005.15

[160] ¶ 6304.20; ACCTNG: 21,302.10; § 36,005.15

[161] ¶ 6304.50; FARM: 3,170.20; § 36,005.15

[162] ¶ 35,699G; FILEBUS: 9,378; § 36,005.15

[163] ¶ 5502, ¶ 6002, ¶ 6090, ¶ 12,570; INDIV: 21,150; § 1,901

- the payment is in cash, including checks and money orders payable on demand;
- the payment is received by or on behalf of a spouse under a divorce or separation instrument;
- the instrument does not designate the payment as being not includible in the recipient/payee's gross income and not deductible by the payor;
- spouses who are legally separated under a decree of divorce or separate maintenance cannot be members of the same household at the time the payment is made;
- there is no liability to make any payment for any period after the death of the payee spouse, or to make any payment, either in cash or property, as a substitute for such payments after the death of the payee spouse;
- the spouses must not file joint returns with each other; and
- the payment is not fixed by the instrument as child support (¶ 776) (Code Sec. 71(b), (c), and (e); Temp. Reg. § 1.71-1T).[164]

A divorce or separation instrument is defined as: (1) a divorce or separate maintenance decree or a written instrument incident to such a decree, (2) a written separation agreement, or (3) a decree that is not a divorce or separate maintenance decree but requires a spouse to make payments for the support or maintenance of the other spouse (Code Sec. 71(b)(2)).[165]

773. Year of Taxability or Deductibility of Alimony Payments. Alimony and separate maintenance payments are generally included in the recipient's income and deductible from the payor's gross income (¶ 771 and ¶ 772). Both spouses are treated as if they are on the cash method of accounting for purposes of including and deducting alimony payments, even if either or both use the accrual method. Thus, alimony and separate maintenance payments are included in the payee-spouse's gross income when received (Code Sec. 71(a); Reg. § 1.71-1)[166] Also, alimony and separate maintenance payments are deductible by the payer-spouse in the year paid (Code Sec. 215; Reg. § 1.215-1).[167] A recapture rule prevents the front-loading of alimony payments (¶ 774).

774. Three-Year Recapture of Excess Alimony Payments. A special recapture rule may apply to *excess* alimony and separate maintenance payments (¶ 771 and ¶ 772) if payments decrease or end during the first three calendar years (Code Sec. 71(f)).[168] Its purpose is to prevent property settlement payments from qualifying for alimony treatment.

The rule requires the recapture of excess amounts that have been treated as alimony or separate maintenance either during the calendar year in which payments began (the first post-separation year) or in the next succeeding calendar year (the second post-separation year). The payor-spouse must include excess alimony payments in gross income in his or her tax year beginning in the third post-separation year. The payee, who previously included the payments in gross income, is entitled to deduct the amount recaptured from gross income in his or her tax year beginning in the third post-separation year.

Excess alimony payments are equal to the sum of the excess payments made in the first post-separation year, plus the excess payments made in the second post-separation year. For the first post-separation year, the excess payment amount is the excess, if any, of the total alimony paid in the first post-separation year minus the sum of $15,000, plus the average of the amount of alimony paid in the second post-separation year less excess payments for that year, plus the amount of alimony paid in the third post-separation year. Thus, for the first post-separation year, the following formula is used:

References are to Standard Federal Tax Reports; Tax Research Consultant; and Practical Tax Explanations.

[164] ¶ 6090, ¶ 6092; INDIV: 21,200; § 1,905.05

[165] ¶ 6090; INDIV: 21,204, INDIV: 21,300; § 1,905.15

[166] ¶ 6090, ¶ 6091; INDIV: 21,156; § 1,901

[167] ¶ 12,570, ¶ 12,571; INDIV: 21,156; § 1,901

[168] ¶ 6090; INDIV: 21,350; § 1,910.05

$$\text{1st year excess payments} = \text{alimony paid in 1st year} - \left(\$15{,}000 + \frac{\left[\left(\text{alimony paid in 2nd year} - \text{excess payments in 2nd year} \right) + \text{alimony paid in 3rd year} \right]}{2} \right)$$

To calculate the excess payments for the first year, it is necessary to determine the excess payments for the second post-separation year. The amount of excess payments for the second year is the excess, if any, of the amount of alimony paid during the second year minus the sum of $15,000, plus the amount of alimony paid in the third year. Thus, for the second post-separation year, the following formula is used:

$$\text{2nd year excess payments} = \text{alimony paid in 2nd year} - \left(\text{alimony paid in 3rd year} + \$15{,}000 \right)$$

Example 1: In 2014, Mr. Black makes payments totalling $50,000 to his ex-wife. He makes no payments in either 2015 or 2016. Assuming none of the exceptions set forth below apply, $35,000 will be recaptured in 2016. Mr. Black will have to report an additional $35,000 in income, while his ex-wife will be entitled to a $35,000 reduction in income.

Example 2: In 2014, Ms. Gold makes payments totalling $50,000 to her ex-husband. In 2015, she makes $20,000 in payments, but in 2016 she makes no payments. Assuming that none of the exceptions set forth below apply, the total amount that must be recaptured in 2016 (year three) is $32,500. This represents $5,000 from 2015 (year two) ($20,000 minus $15,000) and $27,500 from 2014 (year one). The amount recaptured from year one equals the excess of $50,000 over the sum of $15,000 plus $7,500. The $7,500 is the average of the payments for years two and three after reducing the payments by the $5,000 recaptured for year two ($20,000 payment in year two plus $0 payment in year three minus the $5,000 that was required to be recaptured equals $15,000; divided by two equals $7,500).

IRS Pub. 504 contains a worksheet for computing alimony recapture.

Exceptions to Recapture Rule. There are several exceptions to the recapture rule (Code Sec. 71(f)(5)).[169] Recapture is not required if, before the end of the third post-separation year, the alimony or separate maintenance payments terminate because either party dies or the payee-spouse remarries. The recapture rule also does not payments made under temporary support orders, such as payments made under an interlocutory decree of divorce or payments being made pendente lite (Code Sec. 71(b)(2)(C)). Recapture is not required if the alimony or separate maintenance payments fluctuate because of a continuing liability—over at least a three-year period—to pay a fixed portion of income from the earnings of a business or property or from compensation from employment or self-employment. Additionally, the recapture rule does not apply if alimony or separate maintenance payments decline by $15,000 or less over the three-year period.

775. Indirect Alimony Payments. When a beneficial interest in a trust is transferred or created incident to a divorce or separation, the beneficiary-spouse is entitled to the same treatment as the beneficiary of a regular trust, notwithstanding that the payments by the trust qualify as alimony or otherwise discharge a support obligation (¶ 771 and ¶ 772) (Code Sec. 682; Reg. §§ 1.682(a)-1, 1.682(b)-1).[170] The payor spouse cannot claim a deduction for a trust distribution to the payee spouse if the distribution is not includible in the payor's gross income (Code Sec. 215(d)).[171]

776. Child Support. Payments that a divorce or separation instrument fixes as payable to support the payor's child are not considered alimony or separate maintenance

References are to Standard Federal Tax Reports; Tax Research Consultant; and Practical Tax Explanations.

[169] ¶ 6090; INDIV: 21,356; § 1,910.10

[170] ¶ 24,860, ¶ 24,861, ¶ 24,862; INDIV: 21,214; § 2,210.10

[171] ¶ 12,570; INDIV: 21,214; § 2,210.10

payments (¶ 772), and thus are not deductible by the payor or taxable to the payee (Code Sec. 71(c); Reg. § 1.71-1(e); Temp. Reg. § 1.71-1T(c)).[172] If any amount specified in the instrument is to be reduced based on a contingency set out in the instrument relating to a child—such as attaining a specified age, dying, leaving school, or marrying—the amount of the specified reduction is treated as child support from the outset. The same rule applies if the reduction called for by the instrument is to occur at a time that can clearly be associated with such contingency. Thus, payments that vary with the status of a child are not deductible.

> **Example:** A divorce instrument provides that alimony payments will be reduced by $500 per month when a child reaches age 18. Under these circumstances, $500 of each payment is treated as child support.

778. Property Transfers Between Spouses Incident to Divorce. No gain or loss is recognized to the transferor on a transfer of property, either outright or in trust, between spouses or between former spouses incident to divorce (Code Sec. 1041; Temp. Reg. § 1.1041-1T).[173] The transfer is treated as a gift to the transferee, and thus the property's value is not includible in the transferee's gross income. The transferee's basis in the property is equal to the transferor's adjusted basis. A transfer between former spouses is incident to divorce if it occurs within one year after the marriage ceases or is related to the cessation of the marriage.

Nonrecognition of gain or loss is not available to the transferor if the transferee is a nonresident alien, or if there is a transfer in trust to the extent that liabilities assumed by the transferee, including liabilities to which the property is subject, exceed the transferor's adjusted basis in the property. The transferee's basis is increased for any such gain recognized by the transferor.

Other Income

785. Taxation of Miscellaneous or Other Income. Several income items are considered miscellaneous or other income (IRS Pub. 525; Instructions for Form 1040).

Prizes and Awards. Amounts received as prizes and awards are generally includible in the recipient's gross income, subject to several exceptions (Code Sec. 74, as amended by United States Appreciation for Olympians and Paralympians Act of 2016 (P.L. 114-239)).[174] An individual may exclude qualified scholarships and fellowships from gross income (¶ 865), as well employee achievement awards to the extent that the cost of the award is deductible by the employer (¶ 919).

Awards received by an individual for religious, charitable, scientific, educational, artistic, literary, or civic achievement are excludable from gross income, but only if: (1) the taxpayer is selected without any action on his or her part to enter the contest or proceeding; (2) the taxpayer is not required to render substantial future services as a condition to receiving the award; and (3) the award is transferred unused by the payor to a charitable organization or governmental unit designated by the recipient. For example, Nobel and Pulitzer Prize recipients may not exclude from income the value of their awards unless these conditions are met. Prize money awarded to a U.S. athlete by the United States Olympic Committee (USOC) after December 31, 2015, as well as the fair market value of any medal received on account of competition in the Olympic or Paralympic Games, are excluded from the athlete's gross income if the individual's adjusted gross income (AGI) does not otherwise exceed $1 million ($500,000 if married filing separately).

Gambling Income and Illegal Gains. Gain arising from gambling, betting and lotteries is includible in gross income. A gain from an illegal transaction, such as bootlegging, extortion, embezzlement or fraud, is also includible.[175] Gambling losses are discussed at ¶ 1113.

References are to Standard Federal Tax Reports; Tax Research Consultant; and Practical Tax Explanations.

[172] ¶ 6090, ¶ 6091, ¶ 6092; INDIV: 21,450; § 2,001

[173] ¶ 29,800, ¶ 29,801; INDIV: 21,050; § 2,101, § 18,230

[174] ¶ 6200; INDIV: 33,150; § 3,060

[175] ¶ 5504.22, ¶ 5901.25, ¶ 5901.30, ¶ 5901.35, ¶ 5901.40; INDIV: 6,250; § 3,085

Bartering. The value of bartered services is includible in gross income, usually on Schedule C or Schedule C-EZ of Form 1040. If the barter involves an exchange of property, a different form may be required for reporting purposes. For example, if the owner of an apartment building permits an artist to use an apartment in exchange for works of art created by the artist, the building owner reports the fair market value of the art as rental income on Schedule E of Form 1040, and the artist reports the fair rental value of the apartment as income on Schedule C or C-EZ (IRS Pub. 525).[176]

If two individuals are members of a barter club and each agrees to exchange services, the value of the services received by each is includible in gross income. Barter clubs must report exchanges on Form 1099-B (¶ 2565).[177] Trade or credit units used by a barter club to account for transactions are also includible in gross income when credited to the taxpayer's account.[178]

Cancelled Debt. If a debt is cancelled or forgiven, other than as a gift or bequest, the cancelled amount generally must be included in gross income (Code Sec. 61(a)(12); Reg. § 1.61-12).[179] Cancelled nonbusiness debt income is reported as other income on Form 1040. Whether or not the interest portion of the cancelled debt must be included in income depends on whether the interest would be deductible if paid. Exclusions of discharged debt are discussed in ¶ 855.

Insurance. Life insurance proceeds are generally excludable (¶ 803—¶ 809). However, if dividends received exceed the total net premiums paid for the contract, this is reportable income.

Recoveries. The recovery of an amount for which the taxpayer claimed a deduction or credit in an earlier tax year is generally reported as other income on Form 1040 in the tax year of the recovery (¶ 799).

Jury Duty Pay. Jury pay is reportable as other income on Form 1040 (Reg. § 1.61-2(a)(1)).[180] It may be deductible, however, by an employee required to surrender it to his or her employer (¶ 1010).

Certain Taxable Distributions. Distributions from a Coverdell education savings account (Coverdell ESA or ESA) (¶ 867) or a qualified tuition program (QTP or 529 plan) (¶ 869) that exceed the amount used to pay for qualified education expenses and are not part of a qualified rollover are includible in income. A similar rule applies to distributions from health savings accounts (HSAs) (¶ 2035), Archer medical savings accounts (Archer MSAs) (¶ 2037), and qualified ABLE accounts (¶ 870). If an individual fails to remain eligible for an HSA, he or she may have to include a portion of amounts contributed to the account in gross income (¶ 2035).

Below-Market Loans. If a below-market gift or demand loan is made, the forgone interest (at the federal rate) is interest income (¶ 795).

Income From the Rental of Personal Property. If an individual rents personal property, any rental income is includible in gross income. An individual lessor generally reports income and expenses from the rental of personal property on Schedule C or Schedule C-EZ of Form 1040 if the taxpayer is in the business of renting personal property. If the taxpayer is not in the business of renting personal property, the income is reported as other income on Form 1040 and any expenses are reported as an adjustment to AGI (¶ 1006A), but only up to the amount of income (¶ 1195).

Hobbies. Income from an activity not engaged for profit is considered other income. Deductions for expenses related to the activity may be limited (¶ 1195).

Recapture of Charitable Tax Benefits. The recapture of a charitable contribution deduction for property disposed of within three years of contribution (¶ 1062) or the recapture of a charitable contribution deduction relating to the contribution of a partial interest (¶ 1063) is considered other income.

References are to Standard Federal Tax Reports; Tax Research Consultant; and Practical Tax Explanations.

[176] ¶ 5508.15; INDIV: 6,378, COMPEN: 6,110; § 3,085

[177] ¶ 35,920; FILEBUS: 9,260; § 3,085

[178] ¶ 5508.15; INDIV: 6,378; § 3,085

[179] ¶ 5502, ¶ 5801; SALES: 12,150; § 3,401

[180] ¶ 5506; COMPEN: 6,102; § 3,005.05

Treasure Trove. Treasure trove or other found property is gross income for the tax year in which it is reduced to undisputed possession, to the extent of its value in U.S. currency (Reg. § 1.61-14).[181]

Virtual Currency. Virtual currency is a digital representation of value that functions as a medium of exchange, a unit of account, or a store of value. Convertible virtual currency (e.g., Bitcoin), which has an equivalent value in or acts as a substitute for real currency, is treated as property for federal tax purposes. Transactions using convertible virtual currency are subject to the general tax principles that apply to property transactions. A taxpayer who receives convertible virtual currency as payment for goods or services must include in gross income the currency's fair market value, measured in U.S. dollars, as of the date it was received. If a taxpayer successfully "mines" convertible virtual currency (e.g., uses computer resources to validate Bitcoin transactions and maintain the public Bitcoin transaction ledger), the currency's fair market value is includible in gross income as of the date of receipt (Notice 2014-21).[182]

Sharing Economy. The sharing economy allows individuals and groups to use technology advancements to arrange transactions that generate revenue from their assets, such as cars and homes, or from services they provide, such as household chores or technology services. The internet is generally used to connect suppliers to consumers. The sharing economy is also used to connect workers and businesses for short-term work. Income received is generally taxable, even if the recipient does not receive a Form 1099, Form W-2, or some other income statement. Depending upon the circumstances, some or all business expenses may be deductible. Participants in the sharing economy who are employees at another job can often avoid the need to make estimated tax payments by having more tax withheld from their paychecks. The IRS has a website at https://www.irs.gov/businesses/small-businesses-self-employed/sharing-economy-tax-center to help taxpayers involved in the sharing economy quickly locate the resources they need to help them meet their tax obligations (IRS News Release IR-2016-110).

Shareholder's or Employee's Bargain Purchase

789. Shareholder's or Employee's Bargain Purchase. If an employer transfers property to an employee or an independent contractor at less than its fair market value (FMV), whether or not the transfer is in the form of a sale or exchange, the difference between the amount paid for the property and its FMV at the time of the transfer is income to the purchaser as compensation for personal services (Reg. § 1.61-2(d)(2)).[183] Note, however, that qualified employee discounts are excludable from income (¶ 2088). See ¶ 713 for discussion of restricted property transferred in connection with the performance of services.

If a corporation transfers property to a shareholder at less than the property's FMV, the shareholder is treated as having received a distribution from the transferor-corporation and is subject to the general tax rules for including it in income (¶ 733, ¶ 735) (Reg. § 1.301-1(j)).[184] For treatment of securities transactions as potential income, see ¶ 1901.

In computing the gain or loss on a later sale of the property, its basis is the amount paid for the property, increased by the amount previously included in income in the case of the employee or independent contractor, or by the amount of the distribution in the case of the shareholder.

Creditor's Financial Income

793. Creditor's Financial Income. A cash-basis creditor reports interest on loans or obligations as it is received. An accrual-basis creditor reports this type of interest as it is earned (i.e., over the term of the loan, as installment payments are due, etc.), or when it is received if payment is received earlier than when due (¶ 724).

References are to Standard Federal Tax Reports; Tax Research Consultant; and Practical Tax Explanations.

[181] ¶ 5815; INDIV: 6,360; § 3,085

[182] ¶ 5508.20; INDIV: 6,054; § 19,601

[183] ¶ 5506; COMPEN: 6,150; § 3,005.05

[184] ¶ 15,303; CCORP: 6,060, CCORP: 6,312.05; § 3,030.05, § 26,225.05

Rule of 78s. The IRS will *not* give any tax effect to a provision in a loan agreement that provides interest must be allocated in accordance with the Rule of 78s, because that method of allocating interest does not accurately reflect the true cost of borrowing. Under the Rule of 78s, the interest payable for a payment period is determined by multiplying the total interest for the loan by the following fraction: number of payment periods remaining (including the period for which the interest is being determined)/the sum of the digits of the payment periods.[185]

Loan Commission. A loan commission is taxed to an accrual-basis lender in the year the loan is made. A commission deducted from the face amount of the loan is taxed to a cash-basis lender only when received upon payment of the loan or sale of the obligation.[186]

Below-Market Interest Loans

795. Imputed Interest on Below-Market Interest Loans. Loans that carry little or no interest are generally recharacterized as arm's-length transactions in which the lender is treated as having made to the borrower a demand loan bearing an interest rate that is less than the statutory federal rate of interest, or a term loan in which the loan amount is more than the present value of all payments due under the loan (Code Sec. 7872).[187] Concurrently, there is deemed to be a transfer in the form of gift, dividend, contribution to capital, compensation, or other manner of payment, depending upon the nature of the loan, from the lender to the borrower which, in turn, is retransferred by the borrower to the lender to satisfy the accruing interest. These rules apply to: (1) gift loans, (2) corporation-shareholder loans, (3) compensation loans between employer and employee or between independent contractor and client, (4) tax-avoidance loans, (5) any below-market interest loans in which the interest arrangement has a significant effect on either the lender's or borrower's tax liability, and (6) loans to certain continuing care facilities that are not exempt from the rules.

In the case of a demand loan or a gift loan, the imputed interest amount is deemed to be transferred from the lender to the borrower on the last day of the calendar year of the loan. As for a term loan, other than a gift loan, the imputed amount is deemed to have been transferred on the date the loan was made.

Exceptions. A *de minimis* exception applies to gift loans totalling $10,000 or less between individuals if the loan is not directly attributable to the purchase or carrying of income-producing assets (Code Sec. 7872(c)(2)). There is also a $10,000 *de minimis* exception for compensation-related or corporation-shareholder loans that do not have tax avoidance as a principal purpose (Code Sec. 7872(c)(3)). Further, in the case of gift loans between individuals where the total amount outstanding does not exceed $100,000, the amount deemed transferred from the borrower to the lender at the end of the year will be imputed to the lender only to the extent of the borrower's annual net investment income (Code Sec. 7872(d)). For this purpose, net investment income is the excess of investment income minus investment expenses, as under the noncorporate deduction for interest paid on investment debt (¶ 1094). If such income does not exceed $1,000, no imputed interest is deemed transferred to the lender.

The below-market interest rate rules also do not apply to below-market loans owed by a facility which, on the last day of the year in which the loan is made, is a qualified continuing care facility, if the loan was made pursuant to a continuing care contract, and if the lender or his or her spouse reaches age 62 before the close of the tax year (Code Sec. 7872(h)).[188]

Employee Relocation Loans. In the case of an employer loan to an employee made in connection with the purchase of a principal residence at a new place of work, the applicable federal rate (AFR) for testing the loan is the rate as of the date the written

References are to Standard Federal Tax Reports; Tax Research Consultant; and Practical Tax Explanations.

[185] ¶ 9104.62; INDIV: 48,264; § 7,405.20

[186] ¶ 20,620.214; COMPEN: 6,302; § 18,510

[187] ¶ 43,956; INDIV: 12,200; § 19,401

[188] ¶ 43,956; INDIV: 12,208.20; § 19,430.15

contract to purchase the residence was entered into (Code Sec. 7872(f)(11); Temp. Reg. §1.7872-5T(c)(1)).[189] Additionally, employee relocation loans meeting certain requirements are exempt from the below-market interest loan rules. The special treatment for employee relocation loans applies only under circumstances in which the moving expense deduction would be allowed (¶ 1073 and ¶ 1075).

Recoveries

799. Tax Treatment of Recoveries. The receipt of an amount that was part of a deduction or credit taken in an earlier tax year is considered a recovery and generally must be included, partially or totally, in income in the year of receipt (Code Sec. 111; Reg. §1.111-1).[190] Common types of recoveries are refunds, reimbursements, and rebates. Refunds of federal income taxes are not included in income because the taxes are not allowed as a deduction from income. Interest on amounts recovered is income in the year of the recovery.

When the refund or other recovery is for amounts that were paid in separate years, the recovery must be allocated between these years.

> **Example 1:** Marcia VanNauker paid her 2016 estimated state income tax liability of $4,000 in four equal installments in April, June, and September of 2016 and in January of 2017. In May of 2017, she received a $400 refund based on her 2016 state income tax return. Because the tax liability was paid in two years, the amount recovered must be allocated pro rata between the years in which the liability was paid. Since 75 percent of the liability was paid in 2016, 75 percent of the $400 refund ($300) is for amounts paid in 2016 and is a recovery item in 2017 when received. The remaining $100 is offset against the otherwise deductible state tax payments made in 2017.

Itemized Deduction Recoveries. Recoveries of amounts that may be claimed only as itemized deductions (¶ 1014) are not includible if the taxpayer did not itemize in the prior tax year for which the recovery was received. If a deduction was taken, the includible amount is limited to the amount of the deduction. Thus, the amount of the recovery included in income is the lesser of the amount deducted or the amount recovered.

> **Example 2:** Brent Martin receives a $1,500 medical expense reimbursement in 2016 for expenses incurred in 2015. However, due to the threshold on medical expenses, he was able to claim only a $450 deduction in 2015. The amount that he must include in income in 2016 is $450.

For situations in which an individual's itemized deductions for the prior tax year were reduced or phased-out because his or her adjusted gross income (AGI) exceeded a threshold amount, and the taxpayer recovers all or a portion of the previously deducted amount in a later tax year, the amount includible in income in the year of receipt is the difference between (1) the amount of the prior year's itemized deductions (after the overall limitation has been applied) minus (2) the deductions that would have been claimed (i.e., the greater of (a) itemized deductions after the overall limitation, or (b) the standard deduction) had the individual paid the proper amount in the prior year and not received a recovery or refund in the later year (Rev. Rul. 93-75).[191]

A taxpayer who recovers any itemized deduction claimed in a prior tax year must generally include in gross income the entire recovered amount in the tax year it is received if, in the prior tax year: (1) itemized deductions exceeded the standard deduction by at least the recovered amount, and were not subject to the phaseout; (2) the deduction for the recovered item equals or exceeds the recovered amount; and (3) the taxpayer had taxable income, had no unused tax credits, and was not subject to the alternative minimum tax. If a taxpayer receives a refund of state or local income tax or state or local general sales tax, the entire refund amount must be recovered if, in addition to the three requirements listed above, the excess of the state or local tax that

References are to Standard Federal Tax Reports; Tax Research Consultant; and Practical Tax Explanations.

[189] ¶ 43,956, ¶ 43,957D; INDIV: 12,210.05; § 19,430.10

[190] ¶ 7060, ¶ 7061; INDIV: 6,300; § 4,210

[191] ¶ 7062.63; INDIV: 6,302.15; § 4,215

the taxpayer elected to deduct minus the state or local tax that the taxpayer elected not to deduct is more than the refund amount of the tax deducted.

IRS Pub. 525 contains a worksheet for computing the amount of a taxable itemized deduction recovery.

Special Rules for Recovery of State Tax Refunds. Taxpayers may elect to deduct state and local sales taxes instead of state and local income taxes (¶ 1021). If a taxpayer makes this choice, the maximum state and local tax refund amount that he or she may have to include in income in the year the refund is received is limited to the excess of the tax that the taxpayer chose to deduct for the prior tax year minus the tax he or she did not choose to deduct for the prior year (IRS Pub. 525).

If the taxpayer pays state income taxes in Year 1, and then in Year 2 receives a refund of the state income taxes that were paid in Year 1, the refund is not taxable if, in Year 1, the taxpayer (a) did not itemize his or her deductions, or (b) elected to deduct state and local general sales taxes instead of state and local income taxes (Instructions to Form 1040).

Nonitemized Deduction Recoveries. A taxpayer that receives a recovery of a prior year deduction amount which was not required to be itemized must include the recovery amount in income in the year of receipt, but only up to the amount of the deduction that reduced the taxpayer's income tax in the prior year. If the taxpayer has both itemized and nonitemized recoveries, the amount includible in income is determined by first figuring the amount of the nonitemized recovery to include in income, adding that amount to AGI, then determining the amount of the itemized recovery to include in income (IRS Pub. 525).

Amounts Recovered for Credits. If a taxpayer claims a tax credit in a prior tax year, other than the foreign tax credit (¶ 2475) or investment tax credit (¶ 1365A), and during the current tax year there is a downward price adjustment or a similar adjustment on the item for which the credit was claimed, the taxpayer's income tax for the current year is increased by the amount of the credit that is attributable to the adjustment (Code Sec. 111(b)). There is no tax increase, however, if the credit did not reduce income tax in the prior year.

Chapter 8
EXCLUSIONS FROM GROSS INCOME

	Par.
Exclusions from Gross Income	801
Life Insurance and Death Benefits	803
Annuities	817
Bequests and Gifts	847
Personal Injury and Disability Proceeds	851
Cancellation of Debt	855
Education Benefits	863
Tax-Favored Savings Accounts	870
Other Exclusions from Gross Income	871
Excludable Military Benefits	891

Exclusions from Gross Income

801. Exclusions from Gross Income. Gross income includes all income that is not specifically excludable by statute or administrative and judicial decisions. In addition to the items listed in Code Secs. 101—140, the following are excludable from gross income:

- items of income that, under the U.S. Constitution, are not taxable by the federal government;
- items of income that are exempt from tax under the provisions of any act of Congress not inconsistent with, or repealed by, the revenue acts; and
- items that are nontaxable under the provisions of foreign tax treaties designed to prevent double taxation.

These exclusions and exemptions should not be confused with deductions from gross income (i.e., losses, expenses, bad debts, etc.) which must be shown on a tax return. An exclusion generally does *not* have to be shown on a return.

Life Insurance and Death Benefits

803. Life Insurance Proceeds. Life insurance contract proceeds paid by reason of the death of the insured are generally excluded from gross income regardless of whether they represent the return of premiums paid, the increased value of the policy due to investment, or the death benefit feature—the policy proceeds exceeding the value of the contract immediately prior to the death of the insured (Code Sec. 101; Reg. §§ 1.101-1(a) and 1.101-3).[1] It is immaterial whether the proceeds are received in a single sum or otherwise (¶ 805). However, if the proceeds are left with the insurer under an agreement to pay interest, any interest earned and paid is income to the recipient. In addition, there is a limit on the amount of proceeds of a company-owned life insurance (COLI) contract that may be excluded from gross income (¶ 804).

A contract must qualify as a life insurance contract under applicable state or foreign law and meet either a cash value accumulation test or a guideline premium/cash value corridor test (Code Sec. 7702).[2] If a contract does not satisfy at least one of these tests, it will be treated as a combination of term insurance and a currently taxable deposit fund, and the policyholder must treat income on the contract as ordinary income in any year paid or accrued.

References are to Standard Federal Tax Reports; Tax Research Consultant; and Practical Tax Explanations.

[1] ¶ 6502, ¶ 6503, ¶ 6508; INDIV: 30,302, INDIV: 30,306; § 3,515.05

[2] ¶ 43,150; INDIV: 30,400; § 3,505

Amounts received before the insured's death under a life insurance contract on the life of a terminally or chronically ill individual are also excludable from gross income (Code Sec. 101(g)).[3] For chronically, but not terminally, ill individuals, the exclusion is subject to a maximum amount per day, adjusted for inflation, under policies that pay a set amount each day known as per diem policies. If a portion of a life insurance contract benefit is assigned or sold to a viatical settlement provider, any amount received from the sale or assignment is generally excludable.

804. Company-Owned Life Insurance (COLI). In the case of a company-owned life insurance (COLI) contract issued after August 17, 2006, there is a limit on the amount of proceeds paid by reason of the death of the employee that may be excludable from gross income (¶ 803) (Code Sec. 101(j)).[4] The applicable policyholder, the employer, or a related person generally may only exclude an amount not exceeding the total of the premiums and other amounts paid by the policyholder, with any excess death benefits being includible in gross income.

Exceptions. The income inclusion rule does not apply to an amount received by reason of the death of certain insured individuals if notice and consent requirements are satisfied. This exception applies if the insured:

- was an employee of the applicable policyholder at any time during the 12-month period before the insured's death; or
- at the time the contract was issued with respect to the policyholder, was
  - — a director,
  - — a highly compensated employee under Code Sec. 414(q), determined without regard to the election regarding the top-paid 20 percent of the employees (¶ 2114), or
  - — a highly compensated individual under Code Sec. 105(h)(5), who is in the group of the highest paid 35 percent of employees (¶ 2017).

The inclusion rule also does not apply if certain notice and consent requirements are satisfied with respect to proceeds that are paid:

- to a member of the insured's family (¶ 1717);
- to any individual who is the designated beneficiary of the insured under the contract, other than the applicable policyholder;
- to a trust established for the benefit of the insured's family or a designated beneficiary; or
- to the estate of the insured.

In addition, the rule does not apply to proceeds that are used to buy an equity interest, or capital or profits interest, in the policyholder from the insured's heir.

An officer, director, or highly compensated employee within the meaning of Code Sec. 414(q) is an employee for these purposes. The exceptions to the inclusion rule apply only if the insured is a U.S. citizen or resident.

Notice and Consent. To keep excess benefits from being included in income, the policyholder must satisfy the following notice and consent requirements before the issuance of the insurance contract:

- the employee must be notified in writing that the policyholder intends to insure the life of the employee and of the maximum face amount for which the employee can be insured;
- the employee must provide written consent to being insured under the contract and acknowledge that such coverage may continue after the insured terminates employment; and
- the employee must be informed in writing that an applicable policyholder will be a beneficiary of any proceeds payable upon death of the employee.

References are to Standard Federal Tax Reports; Tax Research Consultant; and Practical Tax Explanations.

[3] ¶ 6502; INDIV: 30,350; § 3,515.10

[4] ¶ 6502; INDIV: 30,304; § 3,515.15

Annual Reporting. The policyholder of the contract must also satisfy annual reporting and record retention requirements (Code Sec. 6039I; Reg. § 1.6039I-1).[5] A policyholder satisfies the reporting requirements by attaching Form 8925 to the policyholder's tax return.

805. Installment Options for Life Insurance Proceeds. If the beneficiary of a life insurance policy receives the proceeds in installments (¶ 803), any interest element in the life insurance proceeds accruing after the date of the insured's death is included in the income of the beneficiary (Code Sec. 101(d); Reg. § 1.101-4).[6]

807. Transfer of Life Insurance Policy. If a life insurance policy is transferred for valuable consideration, payments on account of the death of the insured are income to the transferee to the extent that they exceed the premiums and other consideration given for the life insurance policy (¶ 845). If the policy is transferred as a tax-free exchange or gift, however, the donor's investment basis in the contract is carried over to the donee, and the death benefits are excludable from gross income. The benefits are also excludable if the contract is transferred to the insured, a partner of the insured, a partnership including the insured, or a corporation in which the insured is a shareholder or officer (Code Sec. 101(a)(2); Reg. § 1.101-1(b)).[7]

809. Life Insurance Dividends. Amounts received from an annuity policy prior to the annuity starting date in the nature of dividends, or return of premiums or other consideration, are not taxable until the amounts received exceed the aggregate of premiums or other consideration paid or deemed to have been paid for the annuity. Amounts received in the nature of dividends after the start date of the annuity may be fully taxable (¶ 823) (Code Sec. 72(e); Reg. § 1.72-11(b)).[8]

813. Death Benefits of Public Safety Officers. The amount paid as a survivor annuity to the spouse, former spouse, or child of a public safety officer killed in the line of duty is excludable from the recipient's gross income if the annuity is provided under a governmental plan (Code Sec. 101(h)).[9] For death benefits of public safety officers not paid as an annuity, see ¶ 851.

Gross income also does not include amounts paid by an employer by reason of the death of an employee who is a specified terrorist victim or an astronaut killed in the line of duty. The exclusion applies to death benefits from a qualified plan that satisfy the incidental death benefit rule (Code Sec. 101(i)).[10]

Annuities

817. Exclusion Ratio for Annuities. Amounts received as an annuity under any annuity, endowment, or life insurance contract, and paid out for reasons other than death of the insured, are excludable from gross income to the extent of the taxpayer's basis in the contract (Code Sec. 72; Reg. §§ 1.72-1—1.72-11).[11] The tax-free portion of the income is spread evenly over the annuitant's life expectancy. For contracts with an annuity starting date before 1987, however, the exclusion remains the same no matter how long the annuitant lives. The annuity rules also apply to contracts whose payments are made over a prescribed number of years. For Armed Forces personnel annuities, see ¶ 891.

A contract, with certain exceptions, will not be treated as an annuity contract unless it provides that: (1) if the contract holder dies on or after the annuity starting date, but before the entire interest in the contract is distributed, the remainder must be distributed at least as rapidly as under the method used as of the day the holder died, and (2) the entire interest in the contract must be distributed within five years of the holder's death (Code Sec. 72(s)).[12]

References are to Standard Federal Tax Reports; Tax Research Consultant; and Practical Tax Explanations.

[5] ¶ 35,699C, ¶ 35,699D; FILEBUS: 9,376; § 3,515.15

[6] ¶ 6502, ¶ 6510; INDIV: 30,308; § 3,515.05

[7] ¶ 6502, ¶ 6503; INDIV: 30,310; § 3,515.05

[8] ¶ 6102, ¶ 6113; COMPEN: 48,058; § 3,510

[9] ¶ 6502; INDIV: 33,560; § 3,530.05

[10] ¶ 6502; INDIV: 33,562; § 3,530.10

[11] ¶ 6102; ¶ 6102B—¶ 6113; INDIV: 30,056; § 3,210

[12] ¶ 6102; INDIV: 30,206; § 3,260.05

To determine the portion of the annuity that is excludable from the recipient's gross income, an exclusion ratio is to be determined for each contract (¶ 819). This ratio is usually determined by dividing the investment in the contract by the expected return (Code Sec. 72(b); Reg. § 1.72-2).[13] The exclusion ratio is then applied to the total amount received as an annuity during the tax year. Any excess amount over the portion determined by the application of the exclusion ratio is includible in the recipient's gross income (Reg. § 1.72-4). In the case of distributions from an individual retirement arrangement (IRA), the exclusion ratio is determined by dividing the employee's total nondeductible contributions by the balance of the account. For this purpose, all of an individual's IRAs and distributions during a year are aggregated (¶ 2165). A nontaxable distribution of IRA assets is reported on Form 8606 (Instructions to Form 8606; IRS Pub. 590).

For annuities with a starting date *after* 1986, the exclusion of a portion of each annuity payment cannot be continued indefinitely. Once the total of all exclusions taken for payments under the annuity contract equals the investment in the contract, all subsequent payments are included in gross income in full (Code Sec. 72(b)(2)). On the other hand, if the annuitant dies before the investment in the contract is fully recovered tax free through the annuity exclusion, a deduction is provided for the annuitant's last year in an amount equal to the unrecovered portion of the investment (Code Sec. 72(b)(3)).

Partial Annuitization of Annuity Contracts. For amounts received in tax years beginning after December 31, 2010, if any amount is received as an annuity for a period of 10 years or more, or for the lives of one or more individuals, under any portion of an annuity, endowment, or life insurance contract, then that portion of the contract is treated as a separate contract (Code Sec. 72(a)(2)). Thus, a portion of the contract may be annuitized, while the balance is not annuitized. In these cases, the investment in the contract is allocated on a pro rata basis between each portion of the contract from which amounts are received as an annuity and the portion of the contract from which amounts are not received as an annuity. The allocation is made for purposes of applying:

- the rules relating to the exclusion ratio (¶ 819);
- the definitions of the investment in the contract (¶ 821), the expected return (¶ 825), and the annuity starting date (¶ 823); and
- the rules for amounts not received as an annuity.

In addition, a separate annuity starting date is determined with respect to each portion of the contract from which amounts are received as an annuity.

819. The Exclusion Ratio Formula. The excludable portion of an annuity payment is the annuity payment multiplied by the exclusion ratio (¶ 817). The remainder is taxable to the recipient, whether they are the primary annuitant or a secondary annuitant under a joint annuity or joint and survivor annuity. The exclusion ratio is the investment in the contract (¶ 821) divided by the expected return (¶ 825) under the contract as of the annuity starting date (¶ 823). For example, if as of the annuity starting date a taxpayer's investment in an annuity contract is $6,000 and the expected return is $10,000, then the exclusion ratio is $6,000/$10,000 or 60 percent. If the taxpayer receives a monthly annuity payment of $200, then the monthly exclusion is $120 ($200 × 60 percent).

821. Investment in the Contract Defined. In determining the exclusion ratio for an annuity (¶ 819), the investment in the contract generally is the total amount of premiums or other consideration paid for the contract, less amounts, if any, received before the annuity starting date and not included in gross income (Code Sec. 72(c)(1); Reg. § 1.72-6).[14] However, owner-employees may not include the deductible costs of purchasing insurance as part of their investment in the contract (Code Sec. 72(m)(2); Reg. § 1.72-17A(c)). A special adjustment is provided for a refund annuity (¶ 837). For

References are to Standard Federal Tax Reports; Tax Research Consultant; and Practical Tax Explanations.

[13] ¶ 6102, ¶ 6102D; INDIV: 30,050; § 3,210

[14] ¶ 6102, ¶ 6107; INDIV: 30,060; § 3,220.05

special rules for computing an employee's investment in an annuity received through an employer, see ¶ 2143.

Nonresident Aliens. Certain employer or employee contributions made by or on behalf of a nonresident alien are not considered part of the individual's investment in the contract. The excluded contributions are those:

- made with respect to compensation for labor or services by an employee who was a nonresident alien at the time the labor or services were performed and treated as from sources outside the United States; and

- that were not subject to tax by the United States or a foreign country but would have been subject to tax if paid in cash.

Thus, contributions to a foreign pension plan are included in the calculation of the participant's basis only if the participant has been subject to tax on the contribution by the United States or a foreign country (Code Sec. 72(w)).[15]

823. Annuity Starting Date Defined. In determining the exclusion ratio for an annuity (¶ 819), the annuity starting date is the first day of the first period for which an amount is received as an annuity under the contract. This is the later of:

- the date upon which the obligations of the contract become fixed; or

- the first day of the period (year, half-year, quarter, or month, depending on whether the payments are made annually, semi-annually, quarterly, or monthly) that ends on the date of the first annuity payment (Code Sec. 72(c)(4); Reg. § 1.72-4(b)).[16]

825. Expected Return Computation. In determining the exclusion ratio for an annuity (¶ 819), the expected return under the contract is limited to amounts receivable as an annuity or as annuities. If no life expectancy is involved, as in the case of installment payments for a fixed number of years, the expected return is found by totaling the amounts to be received (Code Sec. 72(c)(3); Reg. § 1.72-5(a) and (c)).[17] To determine the expected return under contracts involving life expectancy, actuarial tables prescribed by the IRS must be used. The tables provide a multiplier, based on life expectancy, that is applied to the annual payment to obtain the expected return under the contract (Reg. § 1.72-9).

The expected return will vary, depending on when contributions were made and when amounts were received as an annuity. Gender-neutral tables must be used if the total investment in the contract is made after June 30, 1986. If there was an investment in the contract as of June 30, 1986, and there has been a further investment in the contract after that date, an individual may elect to calculate the exclusion under a special rule. Under this rule, an exclusion amount is calculated using the gender-based tables—as if the investment in the contract as of June 30, 1986, were the only investment in the contract. Then a second exclusion is calculated, using the gender-neutral tables, as if the post-June 30, 1986, investment were the only investment. The two exclusion amounts are then added together to produce the final exclusion. Although the gender-based annuity tables formerly in effect must generally still be used if all contributions were made prior to June 30, 1986, an election may be made to use the updated tables if the annuity payments are received after June 30, 1986 (Reg. § § 1.72-5 and 1.72-6).[18]

For use in the following examples, a portion of Table V (gender-neutral for post-June 30, 1986, investment in the contract (Reg. § 1.72-9))[19] for ordinary life annuities for one life is reproduced below:

References are to Standard Federal Tax Reports; Tax Research Consultant; and Practical Tax Explanations.

[15] ¶ 6102; RETIRE: 42,304.05; § 3,220.05

[16] ¶ 6102, ¶ 6104; INDIV: 30,054.15; § 3,205

[17] ¶ 6102, ¶ 6106; INDIV: 30,058; § 3,215.05

[18] ¶ 6106, ¶ 6107; INDIV: 30,058; § 3,215.05

[19] ¶ 165; INDIV: 30,058.05; § 910

TABLE V.—ORDINARY LIFE ANNUITIES—ONE LIFE—EXPECTED RETURN MULTIPLES

Age	*Multiple*	*Age*	*Multiple*
55	28.6	64	20.8
56	27.7	65	20.0
57	26.8	66	19.2
58	25.9	67	18.4
59	25.0	68	17.6
60	24.2	69	16.8
61	23.3	70	16.0
62	22.5	71	15.3
63	21.6	72	14.6

Example 1: In 2016, X purchases for $8,000 an annuity that provides for payments to him of $50 per month for life. At the annuity starting date, his age at his nearest birthday is 64 years. Table V (gender-neutral) must be used since all investment in the contract is post-June 1986. The table shows that for an individual of X's age, the multiple to be used in computing the expected return is 20.8. X's expected return and annual exclusion, therefore, are computed as follows:

Annual payment ($50 per month × 12 months)		$600
Table V multiple		20.8
Expected return ($600 × 20.8)		$12,480
Exclusion ratio	$\frac{8,000}{12,480}$, or 64.10%	
Annual exclusion (64.10% of $600)		$384.60

If payments under the contract are made quarterly, semiannually, or annually, or if the interval between the annuity starting date and the date of the first payment is less than the interval between future payments, an adjustment of the multiple found in the actuarial tables may be required (Reg. § 1.72-5).[20] The amount of the adjustment is found in the following table:

If the number of whole months from the annuity starting date to the first payment date is	0-1	2	3	4	5	6	7	8	9	10	11	12
And payments under the contract are to be made:												
Annually	+.5	+.4	+.3	+.2	+.1	0	0	–.1	–.2	–.3	–.4	–.5
Semiannually	+.2	+.1	0	0	–.1	–.2	..	..	..	..	..	..
Quarterly	+.1	0	–.1	..	..	..	..	..	..	..	..	..

Example 2: Assume the same facts as in Example 1 above, except that the payments under the contract are to be made semiannually in the amount of $300, the first payment being made six full months from the annuity starting date. The table shows the adjustment to be "–.2". Therefore, X's multiple from Table V, 20.8, is adjusted by subtracting 0.2. His adjusted multiple then is 20.6, and his expected return and semiannual exclusion are computed as follows:

Annual payment ($300 × 2)		$600
Table V adjusted multiple		20.6
Expected return ($600 × 20.6)		$12,360
Exclusion ratio	$\frac{8,000}{12,360}$, or 64.72%	
Semiannual exclusion (64.72% of $300)		$194.16

References are to Standard Federal Tax Reports; Tax Research Consultant; and Practical Tax Explanations.

[20] ¶ 6106; INDIV: 30,058.10; § 3,215.10

There is a simpler computation that may be used, but only if the annuity amount does not vary from year to year. This computation determines the annual exclusion by dividing the taxpayer's investment in the contract by the appropriate multiple from the actuarial tables.

Example 3: Assume the same facts as in Example 1 above. X's annual exclusion is computed as follows:

Cost of annuity	$8,000
Annual payment ($50 per month × 12 months)	$600
Table V multiple	20.8
Annual exclusion $\frac{8,000}{20.8}$	$385
Annual taxable income ($600 less $385)	$215

827. Joint and Survivor Annuities and Joint Annuities. In the case of a joint and survivor annuity contract that provides the first annuitant with a fixed monthly income for life and, after his or her death, provides an identical monthly income for life to the second annuitant, the multiple used in computing expected return is found in Table II (gender-based) or Table VI (gender-neutral) under the ages of the living annuitants as of the annuity starting date (Reg. § 1.72-5(b)).[21] For use in the following example, a portion of Table VI (gender-neutral for post-June 30, 1986, investment in the contract) providing expected return multiples for ordinary joint life and last survivor annuities for two lives is reproduced below.

TABLE VI.—ORDINARY JOINT LIFE AND LAST SURVIVOR ANNUITIES—TWO LIVES— EXPECTED RETURN MULTIPLES

Ages	65	66	67	68	69	70	71	72
65	25.0	24.6	24.2	23.8	23.4	23.1	22.8	22.5
66	24.6	24.1	23.7	23.3	22.9	22.5	22.2	21.9
67	24.2	23.7	23.2	22.8	22.4	22.0	21.7	21.3
68	23.8	23.3	22.8	22.3	21.9	21.5	21.2	20.8
69	23.4	22.9	22.4	21.9	21.5	21.1	20.7	20.3
70	23.1	22.5	22.0	21.5	21.1	20.6	20.2	19.8
71	22.8	22.2	21.7	21.2	20.7	20.2	19.8	19.4
72	22.5	21.9	21.3	20.8	20.3	19.8	19.4	18.9

Example: In 2016, Y purchased a joint and survivor annuity providing for payments of $200 a month to be made to Y for life and upon his death, to his wife Z during her lifetime. At the annuity starting date Y's age at his nearest birthday is 68 and Z's is 66. The annuity cost is $44,710. The expected return is as follows:

Annual payment ($200 × 12)	$2,400
Table VI multiple (age 68; age 66)	23.3
Expected return ($2,400 × 23.3)	$55,920

The annual exclusion for both Y and Z is computed as follows:

Exclusion ratio $\frac{44,710}{55,920}$, or 79.95%	
Annual exclusion (79.95% of $2,400)	$1,918.80

If a joint and survivor annuity provides for a different monthly income, rather than an identical monthly income, payable to the second annuitant, there is a special computation of expected return that involves the use of both Table I and Table II or Table V and Table VI, whichever are applicable. If a contract involving two annuitants provides for fixed monthly payments to be made as a joint life annuity until the death of the first annuitant—, in other words, only as long as both remain alive—the expected return for the contract is determined under either Table IIA or Table VIA, whichever is applicable. Adjustment of the multiple obtained from the annuity tables, as explained at

References are to Standard Federal Tax Reports; Tax Research Consultant; and Practical Tax Explanations.

[21] ¶ 6106; INDIV: 30,066; § 3,215.15

¶ 825 for single life annuities, may also be necessary for joint and survivor annuities and joint annuities if payments are made less often than monthly or if the first payment is accelerated.

829. Special Types of Annuities. To compute the exclusion ratio (¶ 819) for a contract that is acquired for a single consideration and that provides for the payment of two or more annuity obligations or elements, the investment in the contract is divided by the aggregate of the expected returns under all the annuity elements (Reg. § § 1.72-4(e), 1.72-5(e), and 1.72-6(b)).[22] In the case of variable annuities, a special rule is provided for determining the portion of each payment to be an amount received as an annuity and excludable from gross income each year (Reg. § 1.72-2(b)(3)).[23] The computation of the expected return for temporary life annuities is determined by multiplying the total of the annuity payments to be received annually by the multiple shown in Table IV or Table VIII of Reg. § 1.72-9, whichever is applicable. The computation uses the annuitant's age as of the annuity starting date, and if applicable, the annuitant's gender and the nearest whole number of years in the specified period (Reg. § 1.72-5(a)(3)—(5)).[24]

835. Exclusion for Year Annuity Begins. If the first payment an annuitant receives from an annuity is for a fractional part of a year, the annuitant need only determine the exclusion ratio (¶ 819) as a percentage and apply it to the payment received for the fractional part of the payment period, resulting in the amount of the annuitant's exclusion for the tax year (Reg. § 1.72-4(a)).[25]

> **Example:** John purchased an annuity that provides for semiannual payments of $3,000. The annuity starting date is November 1, and on December 31, John received $1,000 as his first payment under the contract. John's exclusion percentage is 70 percent. He may exclude 70 percent of $1,000, or $700, from his calendar-year income.

837. Refund Annuity. If an annuity contract has a refund feature, including a contract for a life annuity with a minimum period of payments, an adjustment must be made to the original investment in the contract when determining the exclusion ratio (¶ 819). The original investment in the contract must be reduced by the value of the refund payment or minimum payments as of the annuity starting date (Code Sec. 72(b)(4) and (c); Reg. § 1.72-7).[26] The computation of the adjustment is detailed and involves the use of Table III (gender-based) or Table VII (gender-neutral) of Reg. § 1.72-9.[27]

Generally, an annuity contract contains a refund feature if:

- the annuity payments depend, in whole or in part, upon the continuing life of one or more persons;
- there are payments on or after the death of the annuitant if a specified amount or a stated number of payments has not been made prior to death; and
- the payments are in the nature of a refund of the consideration paid (Code Sec. 72(c)(2); Reg. § 1.72-7).[28]

839. Employee's Annuity. Amounts received as an annuity from qualified employee plans under Code Sec. 401(a), employee annuities under Code Sec. 403(a), and annuity contracts under Code Sec. 403(b) are subject to a simplified method for computing the taxable and tax-free portion of the distributions (Code Sec. 72(d); Notice 98-2).[29]

Post-November 18, 1996, Annuities. Under the simplified method for annuity starting dates beginning after November 18, 1996, but before January 1, 1998, the total number of monthly annuity payments expected to be received is based on the primary

References are to Standard Federal Tax Reports; Tax Research Consultant; and Practical Tax Explanations.

[22] ¶ 6104, ¶ 6106, ¶ 6107; INDIV: 30,070; § 3,205

[23] ¶ 6102D; INDIV: 30,068; § 3,235

[24] ¶ 6106; INDIV: 30,058.15; § 3,215.05

[25] ¶ 6104; INDIV: 30,056; § 3,210

[26] ¶ 6102, ¶ 6108; INDIV: 30,068; § 3,220.05

[27] ¶ 165; INDIV: 30,062; § 3,220.10

[28] ¶ 6102, ¶ 6108; INDIV: 30,062, RETIRE: 42,304; § 3,220.10

[29] ¶ 17,502, ¶ 18,270, ¶ 6102, ¶ 6140.82; RETIRE: 42,304.10; § 24,405.10

annuitant's age at the annuity starting date. The same expected number of payments applies to a single life annuity or a joint and survivor annuity. The expected number of payments is set forth in the following table:

Age of Primary Annuitant on the Annuity Starting Date	*Number of Anticipated Payments*
55 and under	360
56-60	310
61-65	260
66-70	210
71 and over	160

For annuity starting dates after December 31, 1997, annuities paid over the life of a single individual have anticipated payments as listed in the table above. If, however, the annuity is payable over the lives of more than one individual, the number of anticipated payments is listed in the table below:

Combined Age of Annuitants	*Number of Anticipated Payments*
110 and under	410
More than 110 but not more than 120	360
More than 120 but not more than 130	310
More than 130 but not more than 140	260
More than 140	210

The number of anticipated payments listed in the table above is based on the employee's age on the annuity starting date. If the number of payments is fixed under the terms of the annuity, that number is to be used rather than the number of anticipated payments listed in the table.

Example 1: At retirement, Jeff Anderson, age 65, begins receiving retirement benefits in the form of a joint and 50-percent survivor annuity to be paid for the joint lives of Jeff and his wife, Jan, age 59. Jeff's annuity starting date is January 1, 2016. Jeff contributed $24,000 to the plan and has received no distributions prior to the annuity starting date. He will receive a monthly retirement benefit of $1,000, and his wife Jan will receive a monthly survivor benefit of $500 upon his death. Jeff's investment in the contract is $24,000 (the after-tax contributions to the plan). The set number of monthly payments will be 310 (Jeff's age plus Jan's age at the starting date of the annuity equals 124). The tax-free portion of each $1,000 monthly annuity payment to Jeff is $77.42, determined by dividing Jeff's investment ($24,000) by the number of monthly payments (310). If Jeff has not recovered the full $24,000 investment at his death, Jan will exclude $77.42 from each $500 monthly annuity payment. Any annuity payments received after 310 payments have been made will be includible in gross income. If Jeff and his wife die before 310 payments have been made, a deduction is allowed on the survivor's last income tax return in the amount of the unrecovered investment.

The simplified method does not apply if the primary annuitant has attained age 75 on the annuity starting date unless there are fewer than five years of guaranteed payments under the annuity (Code Sec. 72(d)(1)(E)). Also, if in connection with commencement of annuity payments, the recipient receives a lump-sum payment that is not part of the annuity stream, then the payment is taxed under the annuity rules of Code Sec. 72(e) as if received before the annuity starting date and the investment in the contract used to calculate the simplified exclusion ratio for the annuity payments is reduced by the amount of the payment (Code Sec. 72(d)(1)(D)).

Pre-November 19, 1996, Annuities. The IRS provided an elective alternative to application of the usual annuity rules for distributions from qualified plans when the annuity starting date was before November 19, 1996. This is a simplified safe-harbor method for determining the tax-free and taxable portions of certain annuity payments made from qualified employee plans, employee annuities, and annuity contracts (Notice

88-118).[30] Distributees who elected to use this method are considered to have complied with Code Sec. 72(b). Payors may also use this method to report the taxable portion of the annuity payments on Form 1099-R. The safe-harbor method may be used *only* if the following three conditions are met:

- the annuity payments depend upon the life of the distributee or the joint lives of the distributee and beneficiary;
- the annuity payments are made from an employee plan qualified under Code Sec. 401(a), an employee annuity under Code Sec. 403(a), or an annuity contract under Code Sec. 403(b); and
- the distributee is less than age 75 when annuity payments commence or, if the distributee is age 75 or older, there are fewer than five years of guaranteed payments.

Under the safe-harbor method, the total number of monthly annuity payments expected to be received is based on the distributee's age at the annuity starting date rather than on the life expectancy tables in Reg. § 1.72-9. The same expected number of payments applies to a distributee whether the individual is receiving a single life annuity or a joint and survivor annuity. These payments are set forth in the following table:

Age of Distributee	*Number of Payments*
55 and under	300
56-60	260
61-65	240
66-70	170
71 and over	120

Under the safe-harbor method, the distributee recovers the investment in the contract in level amounts over the number of monthly payments determined from the above table. The portion of each monthly annuity payment that is excluded from gross income by a distributee who uses the safe-harbor method for income tax purposes is a level dollar amount determined by dividing the investment in the contract, including any applicable death benefit exclusion, by the set number of annuity payments from the above table as follows:

$$\frac{\text{Investment}}{\text{Number of monthly payments}} = \text{Tax-free portion of monthly annuity}$$

For distributees with annuity starting dates after 1986, annuity payments received after the investment is recovered, usually after the set number of payments has been received, are fully includible in gross income.

Example 2: Assume the same facts as in Example 1 above, except Jeff's annuity start date was January 1, 1996. Under the safe-harbor method, Jeff's investment in the contract is $24,000 (the after-tax contributions to the plan). The set number of monthly payments for a distributee who is age 65 is 240. The tax-free portion of each $1,000 monthly annuity payment to Jeff is $100, determined by dividing Jeff's investment ($24,000) by the number of monthly payments (240). If Jeff has not recovered the full $24,000 investment at his death, Jan will also exclude $100 from each $500 monthly annuity payment. Any annuity payments received after 240 payments have been made will be fully includible in gross income. If Jeff and his wife die before 240 payments have been made, a deduction is allowed on the survivor's last income tax return in the amount of the unrecovered investment.

The dollar amount is excluded from each monthly payment even if the annuity payment amount changes. If the amount excluded is greater than the amount of the monthly annuity, because of decreased survivor payments, each monthly annuity payment is excluded completely until the entire investment is recovered. If annuity payments cease before the set number of payments has been made, a deduction for the unrecovered investment is allowed on the distributee's last tax return. If payments are

References are to Standard Federal Tax Reports; Tax Research Consultant; and Practical Tax Explanations.

[30] ¶ 6140.82; RETIRE: 42,304.15; § 24,405.10

made to multiple beneficiaries, the excludable amount is based on the oldest beneficiary's age. A pro rata portion is excluded by each beneficiary.

General Rules. For purposes of these rules, the investment in the contract (¶ 821) is determined without regard to the adjustment made for a refund feature (Code Sec. 72(d)(1)(C)). In any case where the annuity payments are not made on a monthly basis, appropriate adjustments must be made to take into account the basis on which the payments are actually made (Code Sec. 72(d)(1)(F)). Employee contributions under a defined contribution plan may be treated as a separate contract (Code Sec. 72(d)(2)). Railroad Retirement Act Tier 2 benefits received by retired railroad workers and their survivors are subject to federal income tax in the same manner as pension plan benefits paid by private employers (Code Sec. 72(r)).[31]

841. Discharge of Annuity Obligation. Any amount received, whether in a single sum or otherwise, under an annuity, endowment, or life insurance contract in full discharge of the obligation under the contract as a refund of the consideration paid for the contract or any amount received under such contract on its complete surrender, redemption, or maturity is includible in gross income to the extent the amounts exceed the investment in the contract (Code Sec. 72(e); Reg. § 1.72-11).[32] The remainder is taxable to the recipient, whether the recipient is the primary annuitant or a secondary annuitant under a joint annuity or joint and survivor annuity. A penalty is imposed on a policyholder who receives a premature distribution (for example, before age 59½ unless one of a number of exceptions such as death or disability applies) (Code Sec. 72(q)).[33]

843. Installment Options for Annuities. If an insured elects under an option in an insurance contract to receive the proceeds as an annuity instead of a lump sum, and the election is made within 60 days after the day on which the lump sum first became payable, no part of it is includible in gross income under the doctrine of constructive receipt (Code Sec. 72(h); Reg. § 1.72-12).[34] The installment payments are taxed in accordance with the annuity rules.

845. Transfer of Annuities. If a life insurance, endowment, or annuity contract is transferred for a valuable consideration, and the proceeds of the contract are paid to the transferee for reasons other than the death of the insured (for example, on surrender, redemption, or maturity of the contract), the transferee, including a beneficiary of, or the estate of, a transferee, is treated as follows:

- if the proceeds are received as an annuity or in installments for a fixed period, the transferee computes the amount excludable from gross income under the exclusion ratio formula (¶ 819); or
- if the proceeds are received in a lump sum, the transferee includes in gross income only that portion of the proceeds in excess of the consideration paid.

Regardless of how the proceeds are received and included in gross income, the transferee's consideration paid consists of the actual value of the consideration paid for the transfer, plus the amount of premiums or other consideration paid after the transfer. This transferee rule, however, does not apply if the transferred contract has a basis for gain or loss in the hands of the transferee determined by reference to the transferor's basis, as in the case of a gift or tax-free exchange (Code Sec. 72(g); Reg. § 1.72-10).[35]

A loss realized upon the surrender or forfeiture of an annuity contract by the original purchaser is deductible as an ordinary loss under Code Sec. 165, the basis of the contract being its cost less the amounts previously excluded from gross income (Rev. Rul. 61-201).[36] The loss is deducted as a miscellaneous itemized deduction subject to the two-percent-of-adjusted-gross-income limitation (¶ 1079) (IRS Pub. 575).

References are to Standard Federal Tax Reports; Tax Research Consultant; and Practical Tax Explanations.

[31] ¶ 6102; INDIV: 33,358

[32] ¶ 6102, ¶ 6113; INDIV: 30,102.10; § 3,230.10

[33] ¶ 6102; INDIV: 30,204; § 3,255

[34] ¶ 6102, ¶ 6117; INDIV: 30,208; § 3,265.35

[35] ¶ 6102, ¶ 6112; INDIV: 30,064; § 3,220.05

[36] ¶ 9900.111; INDIV: 30,216; § 3,245.10

Bequests and Gifts

847. Bequests Excluded from Gross Income. The value of property acquired by bequest, devise, or inheritance is excludable from gross income (Code Sec. 102; Reg. § 1.102-1).[37] The *income* flowing from the property, however, is *not* excludable from gross income under this rule. For example, amounts received as investment income from the property or as profit from the sale of the property are not excludable. The exclusion also does not apply if the bequest consists of income from property. Thus, a bequest of annual rent from the testator's property for 10 years is taxable income to the beneficiary. The beneficiary is required to include in gross income each year the amount of the annual rent. For the basis of inherited property, see ¶ 1633—¶ 1639.

A bequest of a specific sum of money or specific property from an estate or trust may be excluded from gross income if it is paid or credited all at once or in not more than three installments (Code Sec. 663(a)(1); Reg. § 1.663(a)-1).[38] An amount which is paid from the estate or trust income may qualify as a bequest for this purpose if the amount could have been paid from either income or principal. An amount that can only be paid from the estate or trust income, however, will not be treated as a bequest and thus *not* excludable from gross income even when paid in less than four installments.

849. Gifts Excluded from Gross Income. The value of a gift is excludable from gross income, but *any income* from the gift, including profit upon sale, is taxable (Code Sec. 102).[39] A gift of income from the property of an estate or trust is not excluded from gross income except in the case of a gift of a specific sum or specific property paid or credited all at once or in not more than three installments (¶ 847). For a donee's basis for gift property, see ¶ 1630.

Tips are not gifts and are therefore taxable (¶ 717). Food, clothing, and rent payments furnished as strike benefits by a labor union to a needy worker participating in a strike may be considered gifts. In determining whether a gift was made, the fact that benefits were paid only to union members is not controlling.[40]

The exclusion from gross income applicable to the value of property acquired by gift does not apply to any amount transferred by or for an employer to, or for the benefit of, an employee (Code Sec. 102(c)).[41] However, certain employee achievement awards (¶ 2069) and certain fringe benefits provided by employers are excludable (¶ 2085).

Personal Injury and Disability Proceeds

851. Occupational Disability or Insurance Benefit. Compensation received under a workers' compensation act for personal injuries or sickness, and amounts received by a taxpayer under a policy of accident and health insurance, are excludable from gross income (Code Sec. 104(a)(1); Reg. § 1.104-1).[42] The exclusion also applies to benefits having the characteristics of life insurance proceeds paid under a workers' compensation act to the survivors of a deceased employee (Reg. § 1.101-1(a)).[43] For a discussion of disability income plans, see ¶ 2025.

Amounts received as a pension, annuity, or similar allowance for personal injuries or sickness resulting from active service in the armed forces of any country or in the National Oceanic and Atmospheric Administration (formerly the Coast and Geodetic Survey) or the Public Health Service, or as a disability annuity payable under section 808 of the Foreign Service Act of 1980, are also excludable from gross income (Code Sec. 104(a)(4); Reg. § 1.104-1).[44] The exclusion generally is limited to amounts received for combat-related injury or illness. However, it will not be less than the maximum amount of disability compensation from the Veterans Administration to which the individual is, or would be, entitled upon application (Code Sec. 104(b)).

References are to Standard Federal Tax Reports; Tax Research Consultant; and Practical Tax Explanations.

[37] ¶ 6550, ¶ 6551; INDIV: 33,102, INDIV: 33,104; § 3,601

[38] ¶ 24,440, ¶ 24,441; INDIV: 33,104; § 32,710.05g

[39] ¶ 6550; INDIV: 33,102, INDIV: 33,104; § 3,601, § 3,615

[40] ¶ 6553.46; COMPEN: 6,068; § 22,110.40

[41] ¶ 6550; INDIV: 33,102.05; § 3,605.10

[42] ¶ 6660, ¶ 6661; INDIV: 33,406, HEALTH: 12,200; § 3,705.10

[43] ¶ 6503; INDIV: 30,302.05

[44] ¶ 6660, ¶ 6661; INDIV: 33,410; § 42,210

Benefits that are payable under state law for occupational injury or illness arising out of employment are nontaxable if the benefits are in the nature of workers' compensation payments (Reg. § 1.104-1(b)).[45] No fault insurance disability benefits received by a passenger injured in an automobile accident under the automobile owner's policy as compensation for loss of income or earning capacity are also excludable from gross income.[46]

If an otherwise excludable amount is for reimbursement of medical expenses previously deducted for tax purposes, the amount must be included in gross income to the extent of the prior deduction. If a portion of an award is specifically allocated to future injury-related medical expenses, the future expenses must be offset by the awarded portion and are not deductible to that extent.[47]

Terrorist Attacks. Disability income received by an individual for injuries received in a terrorist attack while the individual was performing services as a U.S. employee outside the United States is also excludable from gross income (Code Sec. 104(a)(5)).[48]

Death Benefits Received by Beneficiaries of Public Safety Officers. Effective for payments made on or after May 22, 2015, death benefits or other amounts received by qualified beneficiaries or surviving dependents of a public safety officer who has died as the direct and proximate result of a personal injury sustained in the line of duty are excludable from gross income (Code Sec. 104(a)(6)).[49] The requirement that the exclusion applies only if the amounts are received under a statute in the nature of a workers' compensation act no longer applies to the payment of these types of benefits. For death benefits received as an annuity by beneficiaries of public safety officers, see ¶ 813.

852. Damages for Personal Injuries or Sickness. Amounts received as damages, other than punitive damages, on account of *personal physical injuries or sickness* are excludable from gross income (Code Sec. 104(a)(2)).[50] Damages for emotional distress, including the physical symptoms of emotional distress, may not be treated as damages on account of a personal physical injury or sickness, except to the extent of amounts paid for medical care attributable to emotional distress. Accordingly, back pay received in satisfaction of a claim for denial of a promotion due to employment discrimination is not excludable because it is completely independent of, and *not* damages received on account of, personal physical injuries or sickness (Rev. Rul. 96-65).

Interest and Punitive Damage Awards. Interest included in an award of damages for personal injury is includible in gross income.[51] Also, punitive damages arising out of personal physical injury action are includible in gross income (Code Sec. 104(a)(2)).[52] Punitive damages may be excludable from income, however, if received in a civil action for wrongful death and the applicable state law provides that *only* punitive damages may be awarded (Code Sec. 104(c)).

Attorney's Fees. The full amount of a litigant's award, including the attorney's contingent fee, regardless of whether paid directly to the attorney or to the individual, is includible in the litigant's gross income under the anticipatory assignment of income theory (*J.W. Banks II*, SCt, 2005-1 USTC ¶ 50,155).[53] See ¶ 973 for a discussion of business legal expenses and ¶ 1093 for a discussion of nonbusiness legal expenses.

Cancellation of Debt

855. Cancellation or Discharge of Debt. A taxpayer generally realizes income equal to the portion of a debt that is cancelled or discharged other than as a gift or bequest (¶ 785). However, income from the discharge of a debt may be excluded from gross income for:

References are to Standard Federal Tax Reports; Tax Research Consultant; and Practical Tax Explanations.

[45] ¶ 6661; INDIV: 33,406; § 3,705.05

[46] ¶ 6662.24; INDIV: 33,408; § 42,205

[47] ¶ 6662.41; INDIV: 33,402.10; § 7,210.05

[48] ¶ 6660; HEALTH: 12,256; § 3,710

[49] ¶ 6660; INDIV: 33,560; § 3,705.10

[50] ¶ 6660; INDIV: 33,402; § 3,805.05

[51] ¶ 6662.513; INDIV: 12,112; § 3,805.35

[52] ¶ 6660; INDIV: 33,402.05; § 3,805.30

[53] ¶ 6662.515; INDIV: 6,358.05; § 3,805.40

- a debt discharge in a bankruptcy action under Title 11 of the U.S. Code in which the taxpayer is under the jurisdiction of the court and the discharge is either granted by, or is under a plan approved by, the court;
- a discharge when the taxpayer is insolvent outside bankruptcy;
- a discharge of qualified farm indebtedness;
- a discharge of qualified real property business indebtedness;
- a discharge of qualified principal residence indebtedness occurring before January 1, 2017; and
- a discharge of a student loan provided the student works for a certain period of time in certain professions for any of a broad class of employers (Code Sec. 108).[54]

Form 982 is filed with a debtor's income tax return to report excludable income from the discharge of a debt.

A corporation that satisfies a debt by transferring corporate stock to its creditor, or a partnership that transfers a capital or profits interest in the partnership to a creditor, is treated as if it has paid the creditor with money equal to the fair market value of the stock or interest. The corporation or partnership will thus have income from discharge of debt to the extent that the principal of the debt exceeds the value of the stock or partnership interest and any other property transferred (Code Sec. 108(e)(8)).[55] A similar rule applies to debtors, corporate or noncorporate, issuing debt instruments in satisfaction of debt (Code Sec. 108(e)(10)).

Discharge of debt income can result even if the cancelled debt is nonrecourse, i.e., no individual is personally liable for repayment of the debt. Thus, where property securing a nonrecourse debt is transferred in exchange for cancellation of the debt, such as a foreclosure sale, the amount realized from the sale or exchange includes the principal amount of the debt discharged. The IRS has ruled that the writedown of the principal amount of a nonrecourse note by a holder who was not the seller of the property results in the realization of discharge of debt income, even if there is no disposition of the property (Rev. Rul. 91-31).[56]

Effect of Exclusion on Tax Attributes. When an amount is excluded from gross income as the result of a discharge of debt in a Title 11 bankruptcy case, insolvency, or qualified farm indebtedness, a taxpayer is required to reduce its tax attributes. The reduction in the foreign tax credit, minimum tax credit, passive activity credit, and general business credit carryovers is to be made at a rate of 33⅓ cents per dollar of excluded income (Code Sec. 108(b)(3)(B)).[57]

Insolvency. For this purpose, insolvency refers to an excess of liabilities over the fair market value of assets immediately prior to discharge. This exclusion is limited to the amount by which the taxpayer is insolvent. The taxpayer's insolvent amount includes the amount by which a nonrecourse debt exceeds the fair market value of the property securing the debt, but only to the extent that the excess nonrecourse debt is discharged.[58]

Nonrecourse debt in excess of the property's fair market value is separated into two components for purposes of the insolvency exception. First, the excess nonrecourse debt that is forgiven is treated as a liability for purposes of the insolvency exception. Otherwise, the debt discharge could result in a tax when the debtor lacks the ability to pay it. Second, the excess of nonrecourse debt that is not forgiven is not treated as a liability for purposes of the insolvency exception. The IRS's reasoning is that nondischarged debt does not directly impede the taxpayer's ability to pay tax on discharge of recourse or nonrecourse debt, and thus, is not relevant in determining the extent of his insolvency (Rev. Rul. 92-53). The IRS has extended these principles to determine the

References are to Standard Federal Tax Reports; Tax Research Consultant; and Practical Tax Explanations.

[54] ¶ 7002; SALES: 12,152, SALES: 12,202; § 3,420.05

[55] ¶ 7002; SALES: 12,254; § 3,401

[56] ¶ 5802.34; SALES: 12,154; § 3,415

[57] ¶ 7002; SALES: 12,206; § 3,420.05

[58] ¶ 7010.38; SALES: 12,200; § 3,420.15

extent a partner may be insolvent due to the partnership's discharged nonrecourse debt, as determined for each partner under the rules of Code Sec. 704(b) (Rev. Rul. 2012-14, amplifying Rev. Rul. 92-53).

Qualified Farm Debt. Income arising from the discharge of qualified farm indebtedness owed to an unrelated lender, including a federal, state, or local government or agency, or instrumentality of such an agency, may be excluded from a taxpayer's gross income if certain requirements are met. The debt must be incurred directly in connection with the operation by the taxpayer of the trade or business of farming. Also, at least 50 percent of the taxpayer's aggregate gross receipts for the three tax years preceding the tax year in which the discharge occurs must be attributable to the trade or business of farming. The discharge of debt income is excludable only to the extent absorbed by tax attributes (credits are reduced at a rate of 33⅓ cents per dollar of excluded income) and the adjusted bases of qualified property (i.e., any property held or used in a trade or business or for the production of income) (Code Sec. 108(g)). Basis reduction occurs first with respect to depreciable property, then with respect to land used in the business of farming, and finally with respect to other qualified property (Code Sec. 1017(b)(4)).[59]

Qualified Real Property Business Debt. A taxpayer other than a C corporation may elect to exclude from gross income amounts realized from the discharge of debt incurred or assumed in connection with real property used in a trade or business and secured by that property (Code Sec. 108(a)(1)(D) and (c)).[60] If the debt is incurred or assumed after 1992, it must be incurred or assumed to acquire, construct, reconstruct, or substantially improve the real property. The excludable amount is limited to the excess of the outstanding principal amount of the debt over the fair market value of the business real property reduced by the outstanding principal amount of any other qualified business indebtedness secured by the property. Also, the exclusion may not exceed the aggregate adjusted bases of depreciable real property held by the taxpayer immediately before discharge. The excluded amount reduces the basis of depreciable real property.

The election to exclude income from the discharge of qualified real property business debt must be filed with the taxpayer's timely income tax return, including extensions, for the tax year in which the discharge occurs (Reg. § 1.108-5(b)). The election is only revocable with the consent of the IRS and is made on Form 982. A taxpayer who fails to make a timely election must request consent to file a late election under Reg. § 301.9100-3.

Qualified Principal Residence Debt. An individual may exclude from gross income a limited amount of qualified principal residence indebtedness discharged on or after January 1, 2007, but before January 1, 2017, or subject to an arrangement that is entered into and evidenced in writing before January 1, 2017 (Code Sec. 108(a)(1)(E), as amended by the Protecting Americans from Tax Hikes (PATH) Act of 2015 (P.L. 114-113)).[61]

An individual's acquisition indebtedness is indebtedness with respect to his or her principal residence if it is incurred in the acquisition, construction, or substantial improvement of that residence, and the debt is secured by the residence (¶ 1048). The amount of excludable is limited to $2 million ($1 million for married taxpayers filing separately) (Code Sec. 108(h)(2)). Qualified principal residence interest also includes refinancing of the debt, but only to the extent of the amount of the refinanced debt. Principal residence has the same meaning for purposes of the exclusion as it does for purposes of exclusion of gain from the sale of a principal residence (¶ 1705) (Code Sec. 108(h)(5)).

Several rules are included to prevent the abuse of the exclusion of income from the discharge of qualified principal residence indebtedness. The discharge of a loan will not be excludable from gross income if it is as a result of (1) services performed for the lender, or (2) other factors unrelated to either the financial condition of the taxpayer or a decline in value of the residence. In addition, if only a portion of discharged debt is

References are to Standard Federal Tax Reports; Tax Research Consultant; and Practical Tax Explanations.

[59] ¶ 7002; SALES: 12,152.15; § 3,420.20

[60] ¶ 7002; SALES: 12,152.20; § 3,420.30

[61] ¶ 7002; SALES: 12,152.25; § 3,420.35

qualified principal residence indebtedness, the exclusion applies only to the amount of discharged debt that exceeds the portion of the debt that is not qualified principal residence indebtedness. The basis of the taxpayer's principal residence is reduced, but not below zero, by the amount of qualified principal residence interest that is excluded from income (Code Sec. 108(h)).

Student Loans. A special income exclusion applies to the discharge of all or part of a student loan if, pursuant to the loan agreement, the discharge is made because the individual works for a specified period of time in certain professions for any of a broad class of employers (for example, as a doctor or nurse in an underserved rural area) (Code Sec. 108(f)).[62] The loan must be made by: (1) a federal, state, or local government or instrumentality, agency, or subdivision of that government; (2) a tax-exempt public benefit corporation that has assumed control of a public hospital with public employees; or (3) an educational institution if (a) it received funds to loan from an entity described in (1) or (2), above, or (b) the student serves, pursuant to a program of the institution, in an occupation or area with unmet needs under the direction of a governmental unit or a tax-exempt Code Sec. 501(c)(3) organization. Loans refinanced through such a program by the institution or certain tax-exempt organizations also qualify for the exclusion.

Effective for tax years beginning after January 1, 2015, Federal student loans discharged under either the Department of Education's Closed School or Defense of Repayment discharge processes do not have to include the discharged debt in gross income (Rev. Proc. 2015-57). Nor will the IRS pursue these individuals for increases in tax resulting from the discharge of debts if in a prior year the individual received the benefit of claiming either an educational credit or deduction. This guidance is in response to the large number of federal loans being discharge by students or former students of for-profit educational institutions.

Deferral of Discharge of Debt Income Resulting from Reacquisition of Debt. A limited deferral is allowed for the discharge or debt income in connection with the reacquisition in 2009 or 2010 of an applicable business debt (Code Sec. 108(i)).[63] At the election of the taxpayer, income from the discharge of the applicable business debt is includible in gross income ratably over a five-year period beginning in 2014 in the case of a reacquisition occurring in 2009 or 2010.

If the taxpayer issued a new debt instrument for the debt instrument being reacquired, and there is original issue discount (OID) with respect to the original instrument, the taxpayer can deduct the OID ratably over the same period as that for which the discharge of indebtedness income is deferred. If a debt instrument was issued by the taxpayer and the proceeds were used to reacquire a debt instrument also issued by the taxpayer, the new instrument is treated as being issued for the instrument being reacquired. The election to defer OID income is made on an instrument-by-instrument basis, and is irrevocable once made.

Special rules address the application of Code Sec. 108(i) to C corporations, S corporations, and partnerships, including, under certain circumstances, a required acceleration of any remaining items of a C corporation's deferred cancellation of indebtedness income (Reg. §§ 1.108(i)-0—1.108(i)-3).[64]

Education Benefits

863. U.S. Savings Bond Income Used for Higher Education Expenses. An individual who redeems any qualified U.S. savings bond during the year in order to pay qualified higher education expenses may exclude from gross income amounts received, provided certain requirements are met (Code Sec. 135).[65] A qualified U.S. savings bond is any such bond issued after 1989 to an individual who has reached age 24 before the date of issuance and which was issued at a discount under 31 U.S.C. § 3105 (Series I or EE bonds). Qualified higher education expenses include tuition and fees required for

References are to Standard Federal Tax Reports; Tax Research Consultant; and Practical Tax Explanations.

[62] ¶ 7002; SALES: 12,152.10; § 3,420.25

[63] ¶ 7002; SALES: 12,252; § 3,420.40

[64] ¶ 7009C—¶ 7009N; SALES: 12,252; § 3,420.40

[65] ¶ 7550; INDIV: 12,162; § 3,120.05

enrollment or attendance at an eligible educational institution of either a taxpayer, the taxpayer's spouse, or any dependent of the taxpayer for whom the taxpayer is allowed a deduction exemption (¶ 137). Also, taxpayers are entitled to the exclusion if the redemption proceeds are contributed to a qualified tuition program (QTP or 529 plan) (¶ 869).

A taxpayer must be able to verify the amount of interest excluded. Therefore, the following records should be kept:

- A written record of each post-1989 Series EE U.S. savings bond that is cashed in. It must include the serial number, issue date, face value, and total redemption proceeds (principal and interest) of each bond. Form 8818 may be used for this purpose.
- Some form of documentation to show that qualified higher education expenses were paid during the year. This could include canceled checks, credit card receipts, or bills from the educational institution.

The amount that may be excludable is limited when the aggregate proceeds of qualified U.S. savings bonds redeemed by a taxpayer during a tax year exceed the qualified higher education expenses paid during that year (Code Sec. 135(b)(1)). Qualified higher education expenses must be reduced by the sum of: any qualified scholarship that is not includible in gross income (¶ 865); any educational assistance allowance under certain chapters of title 38 of the United States Code; any payment other than a gift or inheritance that is exempt from tax including employer-provided educational assistance (¶ 2067), or any payment, waiver, or reimbursement under a qualified tuition program (¶ 869) (Code Sec. 135(d)(1)). The amount must be further reduced by expenses taken into account for the American opportunity credit or lifetime learning credit (¶ 1303), as well as amounts taken into account in determining the exclusion for distributions from a qualified tuition program or the exclusion for distributions from an Coverdell education savings account (¶ 867) (Code Sec. 135(d)(2)).

The exclusion is subject to a phaseout in the years in which the bonds are cashed and the tuition is paid (Code Sec. 135(b)(2)(B)).[66] For 2016, the phaseout range is $116,300—$146,300 for joint filers and $77,550—$92,550 for all other filers (Rev. Proc. 2015-53). For 2017, the phaseout range is $117,250—$147,250 for joint filers and $78,150—$93,150 for all other filers (Rev. Proc. 2016-55).

Below the phaseout threshold, taxpayers may exclude bond interest up to the amount of qualified higher education expenses. Above the upper phaseout limit, no exclusion is allowed. For those falling within the ranges, the amount of interest excludable from income is reduced, depending on the taxpayer's modified adjusted gross income (AGI). Modified AGI (MAGI) is adjusted gross income *after* applying the partial exclusion for Social Security and tier 1 railroad retirement benefits (¶ 716), the deduction for contributions to a traditional IRA (¶ 2157), and adjustments for limitations on passive activity losses and credits (¶ 1169). In addition, MAGI is calculated *before* the exclusion of interest from U.S. Savings bonds, the exclusion for qualified adoption expenses (¶ 2063), the domestic production activities deduction (¶ 980A), the deduction for interest paid on qualified student loans (¶ 1011), the deduction for qualified tuition and related expenses (¶ 1011A), the foreign income exclusion (¶ 2402), and the exclusions for income from sources within Puerto Rico and the U.S. possessions (¶ 2414 and ¶ 2415) (Code Sec. 135(c)(4)). This exclusion is not available to married individuals who file separate returns. The amount of excludable savings bond interest is determined using Form 8815, which is then filed with the taxpayer's Form 1040 or Form 1040A.

865. Scholarships and Fellowship Grants. Any amount received as a qualified scholarship by an individual is excluded from gross income if the individual is a candidate for a degree at a qualified educational organization, which normally maintains a regular faculty and curriculum and normally has a regularly enrolled body of students in attendance where its educational activities are regularly carried on (Code Sec. 117; Reg. § 1.117-1).[67] A qualified scholarship includes any amount received by an individual

References are to Standard Federal Tax Reports; Tax Research Consultant; and Practical Tax Explanations.

[66] ¶ 7550; INDIV: 12,162; § 3,120.15

[67] ¶ 7170, ¶ 7172; INDIV: 60,060; § 3,905.05

as a scholarship or fellowship grant so long as the amount was used for qualified tuition and related expenses, which are (1) tuition and fees required for enrollment or attendance at a qualified educational organization, and (2) fees, books, supplies, and equipment required for courses of instruction at the organization. A qualified scholarship does not include amounts used for incidental expenses such as room and board, travel, research, clerical help, equipment, and other expenses that are *not* required for either enrollment or attendance, or in a course of instruction at an educational organization (Prop. Reg. § 1.117-6(c)(2)).

Tuition Reduction. The amount of any qualified tuition reduction to employees of educational institutions is similarly excludable from gross income (Code Sec. 117(d)).[68] The tuition reduction must be provided to an employee of a qualified educational organization as defined under Code Sec. 170(b)(1)(A)(ii). The reduction can be for education provided by the employer or by another qualified educational organization. Moreover, it can be for education provided to the employee, the employee's spouse, dependent child, or other person treated as an employee (¶ 2085). However, it can only be used for education below the graduate level unless it is for the education of an employee who is a graduate student and who is engaged in teaching or research activities for the employer. Benefits under a qualified tuition reduction program may be excludable only if the program does not discriminate in favor of highly compensated employees.

Employer-Related Grants. Employer-related grants are *not* excludable from gross income if they are considered to be compensation or an incentive to employees (Rev. Proc. 76-47).[69] When educational scholarships are made available to or for the benefit of employees on a preferential basis, such preferential grants suggest an intent to provide additional compensation or an employment incentive and are included in gross income unless they are shown to fall outside the pattern of employment. This is true even if the grants are made by an independent third party, such as a private foundation or a voluntary employees' beneficiary association (VEBA). Educational grants are considered to fall outside the pattern of employment only if seven conditions and at least one of two percentage tests are satisfied. The seven conditions are:

- The programs must not be used by the employer, the private foundation, or the organizer to recruit or to induce employees to continue their employment or otherwise follow a course of action sought by the employer.
- Selection of grant recipients must be made by a committee consisting wholly of individuals totally independent, except for participation on this committee, and separate from the private foundation, its organizer, and the employer concerned.
- The program must impose identifiable minimum requirements for grant eligibility, and these requirements must be related to the purpose of the program.
- Selection of grant recipients must be based solely upon substantial objective standards that are completely unrelated to the employment of the recipients or their parents and to the employer's line of business.
- A grant may not be terminated because the recipient or the recipient's parent terminates employment with the employer subsequent to the awarding of the grant regardless of the reason for the termination of employment. If a grant is awarded for one academic year and the recipient must reapply for a grant for a subsequent year, the recipient may *not* be considered ineligible for a further grant simply because that individual or the individual's parent is no longer employed by the employer.
- The courses of study for which grants are available must not be limited to those that would be of particular benefit to the employer or to the foundation.
- The terms of the grant and the courses of study for which grants are available must meet all other requirements for the exclusion and must be consis-

References are to Standard Federal Tax Reports; Tax Research Consultant; and Practical Tax Explanations.

[68] ¶ 7170; INDIV: 60,060.10; § 3,910

[69] ¶ 7183.29; INDIV: 60,060.10; § 3,905.15

tent with a disinterested purpose of enabling the recipients to obtain an education in their individual capacities solely for their personal benefit. The terms of the grant must not include any conditional or unconditional commitments, understandings, or obligations suggesting that the studies are undertaken by the recipients for the benefit of the employer or the foundation, or have as their objective the accomplishment of any purpose of the employer or the foundation, even though consistent with its exempt status, other than enabling the recipients to obtain an education in their individual capacities and solely for their personal benefit.

Under the percentage tests, the number of grants awarded under the program to children of employees must not exceed either (1) 25 percent of the children who were eligible for such grants, were applicants for the grants, and were considered by the selection committee making such grants; or (2) 10 percent of the number of employees' children who can be shown to be eligible for grants in that year, whether or not they submitted an application.

Compensation for Teaching, Research, or Other Services Performed. The exclusions for qualified scholarships and qualified tuition reductions do not apply to amounts representing payments for teaching, research, or other services performed by the student that are required as a condition for receiving the qualified scholarship or qualified tuition reduction (Code Sec. 117(c)).[70] Athletic scholarships awarded to students who are expected, but not required, to participate in sports qualify for exclusion (Rev. Rul. 77-263). The IRS will follow Rev. Rul. 77-263 regardless of any decision of the National Labor Relation Board (NLRB) in respect to employment status of student athletes (INFO 2014-0016).

Under an exception, amounts received by degree candidates from the National Health Service Corps (NHSC) Scholarship Program, the Armed Forces Health Professions Scholarship and Financial Assistance Program or a comprehensive student work-learning-service program operated by a work college (both terms defined under section 448(e) of the Higher Education Act of 1965 (P.L. 89-329)) for tuition, fees, books, supplies, and required equipment are excluded from the recipient's gross income even though there is a future service obligation connected to these qualified scholarships (Code Sec. 117(c)(2), as amended by the Protecting Americans from Tax Hikes (PATH) Act of 2015 (P.L. 114-113)). Amounts received by health care professionals under the NHSC Loan Repayment Program are excludable from gross income and employment taxes (Code Sec. 108(f)(4)). This provision also extends to loan repayments received under similar state programs qualified for funding under the Public Health Service Act and repayments under other state loan repayment or forgiveness programs that are intended to provide for increased availability of health care services in underserved or health professional shortage areas.

867. Coverdell Education Savings Accounts. Individuals may open a Coverdell Education Savings Account (Coverdell ESA), formerly called an education IRA, which is created exclusively to help pay for the qualified education expenses of a designated beneficiary (Code Sec. 530).[71] A Coverdell ESA is a tax-exempt trust or custodial account organized in the United States. At the time it is organized the trust must be designated as a Coverdell ESA and the designated beneficiary must be under age 18 or a special needs individual. Contributions to a Coverdell ESA must be made in cash and are *not* deductible. In addition, the maximum annual contribution that can be made is limited to $2,000 a year excluding rollovers. The annual contribution is phased out for joint filers with modified adjusted gross income (MAGI) at or above $190,000 and less than $220,000 (at or above $95,000 and less than $110,000 for single filers). The reduction in permitted contributions based on MAGI applies only to individual contributors. Thus, contributions made by entities, such as a corporation or tax-exempt organization, are not subject to the phaseout rules. Amounts remaining in the account must be distributed within 30 days after the beneficiary reaches age 30, or 30 days after the death of the beneficiary (see *Rollovers*, following).

References are to Standard Federal Tax Reports; Tax Research Consultant; and Practical Tax Explanations.

[70] ¶ 7170; INDIV: 60,060.15; § 3,905.10

[71] ¶ 22,950; INDIV: 60,202; § 1,810.05

Coordination with Other Educational Benefits. Qualified expenses will first be reduced for tax-exempt scholarships or fellowship grants (¶ 865) and any other tax-free educational benefits. Expenses will then be reduced for amounts taken into account in determining the American Opportunity and lifetime learning credits (¶ 1303). Where a student receives distributions from both a Coverdell ESA and a qualified tuition plan (QTP or 529 plan) (¶ 869) that together exceed any remaining expenses, the expenses must be allocated between the distributions (Code Sec. 530(d)(2)(C) and (D)).

Distributions. Contributions to Coverdell ESAs are generally treated as gifts to the beneficiaries. Distributions from Coverdell ESAs are excludable from gross income to the extent that the distribution does not exceed the qualified higher education expenses incurred by the designated beneficiary during the year in which the distribution is made (Code Sec. 530(d)(2)(A)). Qualified distributions are excludable regardless of whether the designated beneficiary attends an eligible educational institution on a full-time, half-time, or less than half-time basis. However, room and board expenses constitute qualified higher education expenses only if the student is enrolled at an eligible institution on at least a half-time basis (see *Qualifying Education Expenses*, following).

Distributions are deemed paid from both contributions, which are always tax free, and earnings, which may be excludable. The amount of contributions distributed is determined by multiplying the distribution by the ratio that the aggregate amount of contributions bears to the total balance of the account at the time the distribution is made (Code Sec. 530(d)(1)).

If aggregate distributions exceed expenses during the tax year, qualified education expenses are deemed to be paid from a pro rata share of both principal and interest. Thus, the portion of earnings excludable from gross income is based on the ratio that the qualified higher education expenses bear to the total amount of the distribution. The remaining portion of earnings are included in the gross income of the distributee.

Distributions Not Used for Education. If a designated beneficiary receives a distribution from a Coverdell ESA that is includible in gross income, a 10-percent addition to tax or penalty will apply to the distribution (Code Sec. 530(d)(4)(A)). The 10-percent addition to tax does not apply to distributions: (1) made to a designated beneficiary or the estate of a designated beneficiary after the designated beneficiary's death; (2) attributable to the designated beneficiary being disabled as defined under Code Sec. 72(m)(7); (3) made on account of a scholarship or allowance (¶ 1303), received by the account holder to the extent the amount of the distribution does not exceed the amount of the scholarship or allowance; or (4) that constitute the return of excess contributions and earnings thereon, although earnings are includible in income (Code Sec. 530(d)(2)(A)).

Military Academy Attendance. Since recipients of appointments to military academies are required to fulfill service obligations, the appointments are generally not considered scholarships and the 10-percent penalty applies. Withdrawals from Coverdell ESAs made on account of the beneficiary's attendance at a service academy are not subject to the penalty to the extent the distribution is used for the costs of advanced education (Code Sec. 530(d)(4)). The penalty waiver covers appointments to the United States Military, Navy, Air Force, Coast Guard, and Merchant Marine Academies.

Rollovers. Amounts held in a Coverdell ESA may be distributed and put into a Coverdell ESA for a member of the designated beneficiary's family. These distributions will not be included in the distributee's gross income provided the rollover occurs within 60 days of the distribution. Similarly, any change in the beneficiary of a Coverdell ESA does not constitute a distribution for gross income purposes if the new beneficiary is a member of the family of the original beneficiary and of the same or higher generation. A person's family members are determined under the qualified tuition program rules of Code Sec. 529(e)(2) (Code Sec. 530(d)(5)). Amounts held in a Coverdell ESA may also be rolled over into another Coverdell ESA for the benefit of the same beneficiary.

Qualified Education Expenses. Qualified education expenses include expenses for elementary, secondary, undergraduate, and graduate level education. Tuition, fees, books, supplies, equipment, and special needs services if required are qualified education expenses for the designated beneficiary to attend undergraduate or graduate level courses at an eligible education institution. The term also includes room and board provided that the student incurring the expense is enrolled at an eligible education institution on at least a half-time basis.

Qualified elementary and secondary expenses also include expenses for academic tutoring, the purchase of computer technology or equipment, Internet access or related services, room and board, uniforms, transportation, and supplementary items and services such as extended day programs as required or provided by the school (Code Secs. 529(e)(3)(A) and 530(b)(3)).[72] Computer expenses do *not* include software designed for sports, games, or hobbies unless the nature of the software is predominately educational.

Eligible Educational Institution. An eligible educational institution is generally an accredited post-secondary educational institution offering credit toward a bachelor's degree, an associate's degree, a graduate-level or professional degree, or other recognized post-secondary credential. Generally, proprietary and post-secondary vocational institutions are eligible educational institutions (Code Sec. 529(e)(3)). Elementary and secondary schools (i.e., kindergarten through grade 12) are also eligible institutions. Schools may be public, private, or religious (Code Sec. 530(b)(3)).

Prohibited Uses of Accounts. A Coverdell ESA will lose its tax-exempt status if it engages in a prohibited transaction or is pledged as security for a loan. Prohibited transactions include loans and use of account assets by the beneficiary or a fiduciary (Code Sec. 4975(c)).[73]

Transfers Upon Death or Divorce. Death or divorce of the designated beneficiary need not cause a taxable distribution to the spouse or ex-spouse. The transfer of a beneficiary's interest in a Coverdell ESA to a spouse or ex-spouse under a divorce or separation agreement is not a taxable transfer, and after the transfer the interest in the account is treated as belonging to the spouse or ex-spouse (Code Sec. 530(d)(7)).[74]

Estate and Gift Tax Treatment. Any contribution to a Coverdell ESA is treated as a completed gift of a present interest from the contributor to the beneficiary at the time of the contribution. Contributions are eligible for the annual gift tax exclusion (¶ 2905) and are excludable for purposes of the generation-skipping transfer tax (Code Sec. 530(d)(3)).[75]

Military Death Benefits as Contributions. An individual who receives a military death gratuity or Servicemembers' Group Life Insurance payment may contribute up to the full amount into a Coverdell ESA without regard to the annual contribution limit and the income phase-out of the limit that would otherwise apply. A military death benefit contribution to a Coverdell ESA will be considered a tax-free rollover contribution if it is made within one year of the date on which the amount is received, and does not exceed the total amount of gratuity and life insurance payments received, less the amount of such payments contributed to a Roth IRA or to another Coverdell ESA. Such rollovers will be disregarded for purposes of the limit on the number of tax-free rollovers per year (Code Sec. 530(d)(9)).

869. Qualified Tuition Programs (QTPs or 529 Plans). Distributions from a qualified tuition program (QTP, also known as a qualified tuition plan, Code Sec. 529 plan, or 529 plan) are generally not excluded from the gross income of the donor or the designated beneficiary, as long as the distributions do not exceed the beneficiary's qualified higher education expenses (Code Sec. 529(c)(3)(B)). A QTP is a program under which an individual may prepay tuition credits or make cash contributions to an account on behalf of a beneficiary for payment of qualified higher education expenses. The program must be established and maintained by a state, state agency, or by an eligible educational institution (i.e., virtually any accredited public, nonprofit, or private college or university). Eligible schools generally include any accredited post-secondary educational institution, so long as contributions made to the program are held in a qualified trust (i.e., one which meets the requirements under Code Sec. 408(a)(2) and (5)).[76] A QTP is exempt from all federal income taxation, except for the tax imposed on unrelated business income (¶ 655 and following) (Code Sec. 529).[77]

References are to Standard Federal Tax Reports; Tax Research Consultant; and Practical Tax Explanations.

[72] ¶ 22,950; INDIV: 60,206; § 1,810.25

[73] ¶ 34,400; INDIV: 60,202.35; § 24,020.10

[74] ¶ 22,950; INDIV: 60,202.30; § 1,810.40

[75] ¶ 22,950; INDIV: 60,202.10; § 1,810.15

[76] ¶ 18,902; INDIV: 60,204, RETIRE: 66,100; § 1,805.10

[77] ¶ 22,940; INDIV: 60,204, EXEMPT: 9,950; § 1,805.05

Form 990-T. While a QTP is generally exempt from income taxation, colleges and universities of states and other governmental units, as well as subsidiary corporations wholly owned by such colleges and universities, may be required to file Form 990-T to report any the tax on unrelated business taxable income (UBTI).

Contributions. Contributions to a QTP on behalf of any beneficiary cannot exceed the necessary amount of qualified higher education expenses (QHEEs) for the beneficiary as determined under the program. There are no adjusted gross income phaseout limits. In addition, a taxpayer can contribute to both a QTP and a Coverdell account (¶ 867) in the same year for the same beneficiary.

Qualified Higher Education Expenses (QHEEs). For this purpose, QHEEs include tuition, fees, books, supplies, and equipment required by an educational institution for enrollment or attendance. For tax years beginning after December 31, 2014, QHEEs also include amounts paid for computers and peripheral equipment, software, and internet access and related services if the items are to be used primarily by the beneficiary during any of the years the beneficiary is enrolled at an eligible educational institution. QHEEs also include the reasonable cost of room and board if the beneficiary is enrolled at least half-time (Code Sec. 529(e)(3), as amended by the Protecting Americans from Tax Hikes (PATH) Act of 2015 (P.L. 114-113)).[78] Certain expenses of special needs beneficiaries may also be considered QHEEs. The amount of QHEEs must be reduced by the amount of any other tax free benefits received, such scholarship or fellowship grants excluded from gross income (¶ 865) or the education credits (¶ 1303).

Distributions. Any part of a distribution from a QTP representing the amount paid or contributed to the QTP is excludable from gross income to the extent that the distribution is used to pay for QHEEs. The designated beneficiary generally does not have to include in gross income any earnings distributed from a QTP, if the total distribution is less than or equal to adjusted qualified education expenses (Code Sec. 529(c)(3)). Distributions that exceed the beneficiary's QHEEs are generally taxed under the Code Sec. 72 annuity rules (¶ 817). The part of any distribution from a QTP that represents amounts paid or contributed to the account represent a return of the investment in the account. Any distribution from a QTP used to pay QHEEs that are later refunded to the designated beneficiary after December 31, 2014, is not taxed if the beneficiary recontributes the refunded amount to a QTP, generally within 60 days (Code Sec. 529(c)(3)(D), as added by P.L. 114-113)). Distributions of program earnings in excess of the beneficiary's QHEEs are includable in income and subject to an additional 10-percent tax (Code Sec. 529(c)(6)).[79]

Rollovers and Transfers. Generally, amounts can be rolled over from one QTP to another for the benefit of the same designated beneficiary, or another beneficiary who is a member of the same family, without tax consequences. In order to qualify for rollover treatment, a distribution from the first QTP must be paid into the second QTP no later than the 60th day after the payment or distribution is made. If the rollover is made to another QTP of the same beneficiary, then only one such transfer is permitted within 12 months of the previous transfer to any QTP for that designated beneficiary (Code Sec. 529(c)(3)).[80]

Estate and Gift Tax Treatment. A contribution to a QTP is treated as a completed gift of a present interest for gift tax purposes (Code Sec. 529(c)(2)). Thus, the contribution qualifies for the annual gift tax exclusion (¶ 2905). If a donor's contribution exceeds the annual exclusion amount, then he or she may elect to take the excess into account ratably over five years. A QTP contribution does not qualify for the unlimited gift tax exclusion for money used to pay educational expenses (¶ 2907). No portion of a contribution is generally includible in the estate of a donor unless the donor dies during the five-year period in which excess contributions to a QTP are being ratably taken into account.

References are to Standard Federal Tax Reports; Tax Research Consultant; and Practical Tax Explanations.

[78] ¶ 22,940; INDIV: 60,206; § 1,805.20

[79] ¶ 22,940; INDIV: 60,204.15; § 1,805.35

[80] ¶ 22,940; INDIV: 60,204.20; § 1,805.45

Tax-Favored Savings Accounts

870. Qualified ABLE Accounts. In tax years beginning after December 31, 2014, tax-favored savings accounts can be established under the Achieve a Better Living Experience (ABLE) program to encourage individuals and families to provide private funding to assist disabled individuals in maintaining a healthy, independent, and quality life style (Code Sec. 529A).[81] ABLE programs are modeled along the lines of qualified tuition programs under Code Sec. 529 (¶ 869). A qualified ABLE program is established by a state, or agency or instrumentality of a state, under which a person may make contributions for the benefit of an eligible individual to an ABLE account established for the purpose of meeting the qualified disability expenses of the account's designated beneficiary. The program must limit a designated beneficiary to *one* ABLE account. However, an ABLE account can be established for a beneficiary who is not a resident of the state maintaining the ABLE program (Code Sec. 529A(b)(1), as amended by the Protecting Americans from Tax Hikes (PATH) Act of 2015 P.L. 114-113).

A qualified ABLE program must also provide:

- all contributions must be in cash and that the aggregate of all annual contributions cannot exceed the annual gift tax exclusion amount for the year (¶ 2905);
- separate accounting for each designated beneficiary;
- no designated beneficiary may, directly or indirectly, direct the investment of any contribution or earnings more than twice a year; and
- no interest in, or portion of, an ABLE account can be pledged as security for a loan.

An ABLE account is an account established by an eligible individual, owned by the eligible individual, and maintained under a qualified ABLE program (Code Sec. 529A(e)). A designated beneficiary of an ABLE account is the eligible individual who established the account and is the owner of the account. An eligible individual is an individual who is disabled or blind, with the onset of the disability or blindness occurring before the individual attains age 26. The person must either be entitled to benefits based on blindness or disability under title II of the Social Security Act, or must have a disability certificate on file with the IRS for the tax year. In order to ensure that a designated beneficiary is limited to one ABLE account, proposed regulations provide that a qualified ABLE program must obtain a verification, signed under penalties of perjury, that the eligible individual has no other ABLE accounts, other than one that will terminate and roll over into the new account (Prop. Reg. § 1.529A-2(c)(2)).

Means Tested Federal Benefit Programs. For purposes of determining eligibility of a designated beneficiary for, or the amount to be received from, any other federal welfare assistance program the following items are disregarded: (1) the amount held in any ABLE account of the designated beneficiary (except amounts in excess of $100,000 are considered a resource of the designated beneficiary); (2) any contributions to the ABLE account, and (3) any distributions (except those for housing expenses) for qualified disability expenses (Act Sec. 103, Division B, of P.L. 113-295). Additionally, any supplemental security income program benefits under title IX of the Social Security Act are not terminated with respect to an individual due to excess resources of the individual, but are suspended instead.

Contributions. A person may make nondeductible contributions to an ABLE account for the benefit of an eligible individual (Code Sec. 529A(b)(1)). Contributions must be in cash and the aggregate annual contribution amount cannot exceed the annual gift tax exclusion amount for the year (¶ 2905). The limit does not apply to rollover contributions. Aggregate total contributions, including contributions from any prior ABLE program on behalf of a designated beneficiary, may not exceed the limits established by the state for its qualified tuition program with respect to the amount necessary to provide for a beneficiary's qualified higher education expenses (¶ 869).

References are to Standard Federal Tax Reports; Tax Research Consultant; and Practical Tax Explanations.

[81] ¶ 22,949.01; INDIV: 30,550; § 1,851.

A six-percent excise tax applies to excess contributions to ABLE accounts (Code Sec. 4973(a)(6) and (h)). Any contribution which is distributed out of the ABLE account in a timely-made corrective distribution is not an excess contribution subject to the excise tax. A corrective distribution must be made on or before the day prescribed by law, including extensions of time, for filing the individual's return for that tax year. The corrective distribution must include any net income attributable to the contribution, which is deemed to have been earned and received in the tax year in which the contribution is made (Code Sec. 529A(b)(2)).

For gift and generation-skipping transfer taxes, any contribution to an ABLE account in a qualified ABLE program on behalf of a designated beneficiary is treated as a completed gift and not as a future interest in property (Code Sec. 529A(c)(2)). A contribution does not qualify for the unlimited gift tax exclusion for money used to pay educational expenses (¶ 2907). Distributions from an ABLE account to the designated beneficiary are not treated as a taxable gift. Transfers made by reason of change of beneficiary or the ABLE program are not subject to gift or generation-skipping transfer taxes.

Distributions. Distributions from an ABLE account for a tax year are not includible in gross income unless they exceed the amount of qualified disability expenses incurred during the tax year (Code Sec. 529A(c)(1)). If the distribution is in excess of qualified disability expenses, the amount includible in gross income is the excess amount reduced by an amount in the same ratio as the expenses bear to the distributions.

Qualified disability expenses include any expense related to the eligible individual's blindness or disability that is expended for the benefit of an eligible individual who is the designated beneficiary of an ABLE account (Code Sec. 529A(e)(5)). These include expenses for: education, housing, transportation, employment training and support, assistive technology and personal support services, health, prevention and wellness, financial management and administrative services, legal fees, oversight and monitoring, and funeral and burial expenses. Under proposed regulations, qualified expenses include basic living expenses and are not limited to items for which there is a medical necessity or that solely benefit a disabled individual (Prop. Reg. § 1.529A-2(h)).

Distribution amounts that are not excludable from gross income are taxed similarly to annuity payments under Code Sec. 72 (¶ 817), unless excludable under another provision of the Internal Revenue Code. For this purpose, all distributions during a tax year are treated as one distribution and the value of the contract, income on the contract, and investment on the contract are computed as the close of the calendar year in which the tax year begins. In addition, any designated beneficiary who receives a distribution from an ABLE account that is includible in gross income incurs an additional 10-percent tax on the includible income (Code Sec. 529A(c)(3)). The 10-percent addition to tax does not apply if the payment or distribution is made to a beneficiary (or to the estate of the designated beneficiary) on or after the death of the designated beneficiary.

Rollovers and Changes in Beneficiaries. A rollover from one ABLE account to another (whether in the same ABLE program or a different ABLE program) that meets certain conditions is not includible in the distributee's gross income. To escape income inclusion, the rollover amount must be paid into another ABLE account not later than the 60th day after the date of payment or distribution. The ABLE account accepting the payment must be established for the designated beneficiary or an eligible individual who is a family member of the designated beneficiary (Code Sec. 529A(c)(1)(C)). This nonrecognition provision does not apply to rollovers that occur within 12 months from the date of a previous transfer to any qualified ABLE program for the benefit of the designated beneficiary.

In the event of a change of designated beneficiary during the tax year, the change is not considered a distribution required to be included in gross income if the new beneficiary is an eligible individual for the tax year and a member of the family of the former designated beneficiary. Family members include any eligible individual who is a brother, sister, stepbrother, or stepsister, including legal adopted siblings (Code Sec. 529A(e)(4)).

Once an ABLE account in a qualified ABLE program is established, no account subsequently established for a designated beneficiary can be treated as an ABLE account. There is an exception, however, for an ABLE account opened to facilitate the rollover from an ABLE account for the same beneficiary or to change a beneficiary as long as the first ABLE account is terminated no later than the end of the 60th day after the date of the distribution (Code Sec. 529A(c)(4)).

Transfer to State. Upon the death of a designated beneficiary, all amounts remaining in the qualified ABLE account, subject to any outstanding payments due for qualified disability expenses, not in excess of the amount equal to the total medical assistance paid for the beneficiary after the establishment of the account, net of any premiums paid from the account or paid by or an on behalf of the beneficiary to a Medicaid Buy-In program under any state Medicaid plan established under title IX of the Social Security Act is distributed to the state when the state files a claim for payment (Code Sec. 529A(f)). The state is to be treated as a creditor, rather than a beneficiary, and distribution of any excess funds is not subject to taxation.

Bankruptcy Treatment. A debtor must declare any interest he or she holds in an ABLE account upon filing of a bankruptcy petition (11 U.S.C. § 521(c)). In addition, any amounts in an ABLE account are excludable from the property of a bankruptcy estate with respect to a debtor under 11 U.S.C. § 541(b) if the debtor's contributions were made not later than 365 days prior to the date of filing of the bankruptcy petition.

Other Exclusions from Gross Income

871. Exclusion or Rollover of Certain Stock Gains. Noncorporate taxpayers may exclude from gross income a certain percentage of capital gain from the sale or exchange of qualified small business stock held for more than five years and issued after August 10, 1993 (¶ 1905). Noncorporate taxpayers may also elect to roll over capital gain from the sale of qualified business stock held for more than six months if other qualified small business stock is purchased during the 60-day period beginning on the date of sale (¶ 1907). Individuals and C corporations may elect to defer recognition of capital gain realized upon the sale of publicly traded securities if the sale proceeds are used within 60 days to purchase common stock or a partnership interest in a specialized small business investment company (SSBIC) (¶ 1909).

873. Exclusion of Certain Employee Benefits. Compensation for personal services includes any benefits an employer provides to an employee which are not otherwise excludable from income (Reg. § 1.61-2(a)).[82] Excludable employee benefits include:

- amounts received under employer-financed accident and health plans (¶ 2015);
- employer contributions to provide the accident and health benefits (¶ 2013);
- employer contributions to a health savings account (HSA) (¶ 2035), Archer medical savings account (MSA) (¶ 2037), health reimbursement arrangement (HRA) (¶ 2039), or flexible spending arrangement (FSA) (¶ 2041);
- premiums for group-term life insurance to the extent coverage does not exceed $50,000 (¶ 2055);
- qualified adoption expenses reimbursed under an employer adoption assistance program (¶ 2063);
- child and dependent care assistance benefits (¶ 2065);
- educational assistance benefits (¶ 2067);
- employee achievement awards to the extent deductible by the employer (¶ 2069); and
- certain other fringe benefits (¶ 2085).

Some excludable employee benefits may be provided to an employee through the employer's cafeteria plan (¶ 2045).

References are to Standard Federal Tax Reports; Tax Research Consultant; and Practical Tax Explanations.

[82] ¶ 5506; COMPEN: 6,050; § 3,005.05

875. Minister's Home or Rental Allowance. Ministers of the gospel may exclude from gross income the rental value of homes furnished by churches as part of their compensation (Code Sec. 107; Reg. § 1.107-1).[83] This includes the portion of a retired minister's pension designated as a rental allowance by the national governing body of a religious denomination having complete control over the retirement fund.[84] The exclusion also applies to the rental value of a residence furnished to a retired minister but not a widow.[85]

A minister is entitled to deduct mortgage interest and real property taxes paid on a personal residence even if the amounts expended are derived from a rental allowance that is excludable from the minister's gross income (Code Sec. 265(a)(6)).[86]

877. Reimbursed Living Expenses. A taxpayer whose principal residence is damaged or destroyed by fire, storm, or other casualty and who must temporarily occupy another residence during the repair can exclude from gross income any insurance payments received as reimbursement for *increased* living expenses during such period (Code Sec. 123; Reg. § 1.123-1).[87] The exclusion also applies to a person who is denied access to his principal residence by governmental authorities because of the occurrence or threat of occurrence of a casualty.

The exclusion is limited to the excess of actual living expenses incurred by the taxpayer and members of the household over the normal living expenses they would have incurred during the period. The exclusion covers additional costs incurred in renting suitable housing and any extraordinary expenses for transportation, food, utilities, and miscellaneous items.

The IRS has specifically provided that taxpayers who received relocation payments during the period beginning November 19, 2015, through May 31, 2016, due to the gas leak at the Southern California Gas Company Aliso Canyon storage field would not be required to include the relocation payments in income (Announcement 2016-25).

881. Government Cost-Sharing Payments. Agricultural and forestry cost-sharing payments made by state or federal governments may be excluded from gross income if:

- the Secretary of Agriculture determines that the payments were made primarily for soil and water conservation, environmental protection or restoration, wildlife habitat development, or forest improvement, and
- the Treasury Department determines that the payments do not result in a substantial increase in the annual income derived from the property with respect to which the payments were made (Code Sec. 126).[88]

No adjustment to the basis of the property involved is made for the payments and no income tax deduction or credit may be taken with respect to them. Further, if the property or improvement purchased with the payments is disposed of within 20 years, the payment amounts are recaptured as ordinary income. A 100-percent recapture rate applies if disposition occurs within the first 10 years, with an annual decrease of 10 percent thereafter (Code Sec. 1255; Temp. Reg. § § 16A.1255-1 and 16A.1255-2).[89]

883. Foster Care Payments. Amounts received by a foster care provider from a state or qualified foster care placement agency are excludable from gross income if received for providing care for a qualified foster individual placed in the taxpayer's home or received as a difficulty of care payment (Code Sec. 131).[90] A qualified foster care placement agency is an placement agency that is licensed or certified by a state or local government, or an entity designated by such a government, to make foster care payments to foster care providers.

References are to Standard Federal Tax Reports; Tax Research Consultant; and Practical Tax Explanations.

[83] ¶ 6850, ¶ 6851; COMPEN: 6,554; § 3,005.20

[84] ¶ 6852.12; COMPEN: 6,556; § 3,005.20

[85] ¶ 6852.31; COMPEN: 6,556; § 3,005.20

[86] ¶ 14,050; INDIV: 48,554.05; § 46,110.10

[87] ¶ 7300, ¶ 7301; INDIV: 33,450; § 4,005

[88] ¶ 7330; FARM: 3,168; § 36,005.10

[89] ¶ 31,080, ¶ 31,081, ¶ 31,082; FARM: 3,168.15; § 16,715.05

[90] ¶ 7400; INDIV: 33,250, INDIV: 33,252; § 4,010.05

A difficulty of care payment is a payment for the additional care required because the qualified foster individual placed in the taxpayer's home has a physical, mental, or emotional handicap. Effective for payments received on or after January 3, 2014, qualified Medicaid waiver payments will be treated as difficulty of care payments excludable from gross income, regardless of whether the care provider is related or unrelated to the eligible individual (Notice 2014-7).

Regular foster care payments are *not* excludable to the extent they are made for more than five individuals in the home who have attained age 19. In the case of difficulty of care payments, payments are *not* excludable to the extent they are made for more than 10 individuals under age 19 and more than five individuals who have attained 19 years of age.

887. Disaster Relief Payments. Individuals who are the victims of a disaster may exclude from gross income qualified disaster relief payments received (Code Sec. 139).[91] This exclusion also applies for self-employment and employment tax purposes. Thus, no withholding is required for qualified disaster relief payments. However, the exclusion does not apply to any individual, or a representative, identified by the Attorney General to have been a participant or conspirator in a terrorist action.

Disaster Relief Payments Defined. Qualified disaster relief payments include payments, from any source, made to or for the benefit of an individual:

- to reimburse or pay reasonable and necessary personal, family, living, or funeral expenses incurred as a result of a qualified disaster;
- to reimburse or pay reasonable and necessary expenses incurred for the repair or rehabilitation of a personal residence or for the repair, rehabilitation, or replacement of its contents to the extent attributable to a qualified disaster;
- by a common carrier that sells or furnishes transportation (e.g., commercial airlines) for death or personal physical injuries as a result of a qualified disaster; or
- if such amount is paid by a federal, state, or local government in connection with a qualified disaster to promote the general welfare.

Taxpayers in a federally declared disaster (formerly known as a presidentially declared disaster) area who receive grants from state programs, charitable organizations, or employers to cover medical, transportation, or temporary housing expenses may exclude these grants from gross income (Rev. Rul. 2003-12). However, qualified disaster relief payments do not include payments for any expense compensated for by insurance or otherwise, or payments in the nature of income replacement, such as payments to individuals of lost wages, unemployment compensation, or payments in the nature of business income replacement.

A qualified disaster is:

- a disaster that results from a terroristic or military action as defined under Code Sec. 692(c)(2);
- a federally declared disaster as defined under Code Sec. 165(i)(5)(A);
- a disaster that results from an accident involving a common carrier, or from any other event, which is determined by the IRS to be of a catastrophic nature; or
- a disaster determined by an applicable federal, state or local authority, as determined by the IRS, to warrant assistance.

Air Transportation Safety Act. Taxpayers who are eligible to receive payments under Section 406 of the Air Transportation Safety and System Stabilization Act as a result of physical harm or death incurred from the terrorist-related aircraft crashes can exclude the payments from gross income (Code Sec. 139(f)).

References are to Standard Federal Tax Reports; Tax Research Consultant; and Practical Tax Explanations.

[91] ¶ 7646; INDIV: 33,310.05; § 4,055.10

889. Other Excluded Income. Several other items of income are excluded from gross income.

Holocaust Reparation Payments. Restitution or reparation payments received by persons who suffered Nazi persecution and survived the Holocaust are excludable from gross income (Act Sec. 2 of the Holocaust Restitution Tax Fairness Act of 2002 (P.L. 107-358)).[92] The exclusion extends to any interest earned on the payments. The excludable payments are also *not* included when applying any tax provision that takes into account excluded income in computing modified adjusted gross income, such as the taxation of Social Security benefits.

Native American Health Care Benefits. The amount of qualified health care benefits provided by Indian tribal governments to a member of an Indian tribe or a member's spouse or dependents are excludable from the beneficiary's gross income (Code Sec. 139D).[93] See ¶ 2027 for further discussion of Indian health care benefits.

Energy Conservation Subsidies. The value of any subsidy provided, directly or indirectly, by a public utility to a customer for the purchase or installation of energy conservation measures for a dwelling unit is excludable from the customer's gross income (Code Sec. 136).[94] Energy conservation measures are any installations or modifications designed to reduce the consumption of electricity or natural gas or to improve management of energy demand.

Wrongfully Incarcerated Individuals. Amounts paid to a wrongfully incarcerated individual for civil damages, restitution, or other monetary awards—including compensatory or statutory damages and restitution imposed in a criminal matter—that relate to the individual's incarceration for the federal or state criminal offense for which he or she was convicted are excluded from gross income (Code Sec. 139F, as added by the Protecting Americans from Tax Hikes (PATH) Act of 2015 (P.L. 114-113)).[95] A credit or refund claim based on this exclusion for any period before December 18, 2015, may be allowed or made even if it would otherwise be disallowed by operation of any law or rule of law, if the individual filed the claim by December 19, 2016 (Act Sec. 304(d) of P.L. 114-113; IRS News Release IR-2016-88).

Clean Coal Power Grants. An eligible noncorporate recipient can exclude from gross income certain grants, awards, or allowances received under the Clean Coal Power Initiative (Act Sec. 402 of the Energy Policy Act of 2005 (P.L. 109-58)) in tax years beginning after December 31, 2011 (Act Sec. 343 of P.L. 114-113).

Other Exclusions. Exclusions are also available to human trafficking victims (Notice 2012-12) and certain settlements received by Native Americans (Notice 2013-1, appendix modified by Notice 2014-38). The IRS has provided guidance on whether a medical loss ratio (MLR) rebate paid to a health insurance policyholder is excludable from the policyholder's gross income as a returned premium (¶ 2031).

Excludable Military Benefits

891. Armed Forces Benefits. Amounts received from a pension, annuity, or similar payment for *personal injuries* or *sickness* that resulted from combat-related service in the armed forces of *any* country, the National Oceanic and Atmospheric Administration, or the Public Health Service, or from a disability annuity under the provisions of section 808 of the Foreign Service Act of 1980, are excludable from gross income (¶ 851) (Code Sec. 104(a)(4); Reg. § 1.104-1(e)).[96]

Retirement pay received from the government by Armed Service members is *not* excludable from gross income (Code Sec. 61(a)(11)).[97] Disability retirement pay that is computed on the basis of the percentage of disability is fully excludable from gross income, but disability retirement pay that is computed by reference to years of service is

References are to Standard Federal Tax Reports; Tax Research Consultant; and Practical Tax Explanations.

[92] ¶ 5504.0285; INDIV: 33,308; § 3,835

[93] ¶ 7649N; INDIV: 33,512; § 3,715

[94] ¶ 7560; INDIV: 33,552; § 4,001

[95] ¶ 7649ZA; INDIV: 33,550

[96] ¶ 6660, ¶ 6661; INDIV: 33,410; § 42,210

[97] ¶ 5502, ¶ 5507.121; HEALTH: 12,254; § 45,805.40

excludable only to the extent allowed under the percentage-of-disability method (Reg. § 1.104-1(e)).[98]

Dividends and proceeds from maturing government endowment insurance contracts under the National Service Life Insurance Act of 1940 and all other acts relating to veterans are excludable from gross income.[99] Interest on dividends left on deposit with the Department of Veterans Affairs is also excludable. If an individual uses accumulated dividends to buy additional paid-up National Service Life Insurance, neither the dividends nor the paid-up insurance is taxable (Rev. Rul. 91-14).

Veterans' benefits under any law administered by the Department of Veterans Affairs are excludable from gross income.[100] This includes: educational, training, or subsistence allowances; disability compensation and pension payments for disabilities; compensation for participation in a work therapy program; and grants for homes designed for wheelchair living; grants for motor vehicles for veterans who lost their sight or the use of their limbs; and veterans' pensions (38 USC § 5301 and following).

893. Armed Forces Allowances. Allowances for subsistence, uniforms, quarters, travel, and moving furnished to a commissioned officer, chief warrant officer, warrant officer, or enlisted personnel of the Armed Forces, National Oceanic and Atmospheric Administration, or Public Health Service are excludable from gross income (Reg. § 1.61-2(b)).[101]

Housing and cost-of-living allowances received by Armed Forces members to cover the excess cost of quarters and subsistence while on permanent duty at a post outside the United States are also excludable from gross income (Rev. Rul. 61-5).[102] The same rule applies to family separation allowances received on account of overseas assignment.[103] The fact that a member of the military service, National Oceanic and Atmospheric Administration, or Public Health Service receives a tax-free housing allowance will not bar a deduction for mortgage interest or real property taxes on the member's home (Code Sec. 265(a)(6)).[104]

895. Combat Zone Compensation. Enlisted members of the Armed Forces and warrant officers, both commissioned and noncommissioned, may exclude from gross income all pay received for any month during any part of which they served in a combat zone or were hospitalized as a result of wounds, disease, or injury incurred while serving in a combat zone. The exclusion for months of hospitalization does not apply for any month beginning more than two years after the termination of combatant activities in the zone. The same exclusion applies to commissioned officers, but it is limited to the maximum enlisted amount. This amount is the highest rate of basic pay at the highest pay grade that enlisted personnel may receive, plus the amount of hostile fire/imminent danger pay that the officer receives (Code Sec. 112; Reg. § 1.112-1).[105]

The following areas, among others, have been designated combat zones qualifying American military personnel serving in these areas for special tax benefits:

- by Executive Order No. 13239 Afghanistan and its airspace, including Jordan, Kyrgyzstan, Pakistan, Tajikistan, and Uzbekistan effective on September 19, 2001; the Philippines from January 9, 2002, through September 30, 2015; Djibouti effective on July 1, 2002; Yeman effective April 10, 2002, and Somalia and Syria effective on January 1, 2004,

- by Executive Order No. 13119 the Federal Republic of Yugoslavia (Serbia/Montenegro), Albania, Kosovo, the Adriatic Sea, and the Ionian Sea above the 39th parallel effective on March 24, 1999, and

References are to Standard Federal Tax Reports; Tax Research Consultant; and Practical Tax Explanations.

[98] ¶ 6661, ¶ 6662.79; HEALTH: 12,252; § 45,805.35

[99] ¶ 5504.74; ESTGIFT: 21,164

[100] ¶ 5504.785; HEALTH: 12,254; § 4,065.30

[101] ¶ 5506, ¶ 7222.79; COMPEN: 6,606; § 45,805.25

[102] ¶ 5507.111; COMPEN: 33,110

[103] ¶ 5507.110; COMPEN: 33,110

[104] ¶ 14,050; INDIV: 48,554; § 7,420.05

[105] ¶ 7080, ¶ 7081; COMPEN: 6,604; § 3,005.15a

- by Executive Order No. 12744 the Persian Gulf, the Red Sea, the Gulf of Oman, part of the Arabian Sea that is north of 10 degrees north latitude and west of 68 degrees east longitude, the Gulf of Aden and the total land areas of Iraq, Kuwait, Saudi Arabia, Oman, Bahrain, Qatar, and the United Arab Emirates, including Jordan effective on March 19, 2003, and Lebanon effective on February 12, 2015, due to their direct air support of military operations.

For a complete list of designated combat zones, see IRS Pub. 3.

Combat pay excludable from gross income may nevertheless be included in earned income for purposes of the earned income tax credit (¶ 1322) and calculating the refundable portion of the child tax credit (¶ 1305). Similarly, combat pay may be treated as compensation in determining the amount military personnel can contribute to their individual retirement accounts (IRAs) (¶ 2155).

896. Qualified Military Benefits. A variety of benefits for military personnel were excludable from gross income under a variety of statutes, regulations, and long-standing administrative practices prior to enactment of the Tax Reform Act of 1986 (P.L. 99-514). In the 1986 Act, it was determined that, in the future, no such exclusions would be permitted except under some provision of the Internal Revenue Code. However, the Act added to the Code a provision that, in effect, grandfathered all of the previous non-Code exclusions (Code Sec. 134).[106] Under this provision, all such exclusions that were in effect on September 9, 1986, continue to be in effect. If a benefit in effect on September 9, 1986, is thereafter modified or adjusted for increases in the cost of living under authority existing on that date, the adjustments are also excludable. Benefits not otherwise categorized as qualified military benefits but provided in connection with an individual's status or service as a member of the uniformed services may be excluded from gross income under other Code sections if their requirements for exclusion are met.

Death Gratuity Payments. Section 1478, Title 10, of the U.S. Code provides that upon notification of the death of military personnel on active duty or combat-related activities (i.e., duty training) a death gratuity will be paid to or for the survivor of the service member. The death gratuity payment amount is $100,000 (National Defense Authorization Act for Fiscal Year 2006, (P.L. 109-163)). The exclusion from gross income is also allowed for any adjustment in the amount of the death gratuity payments. The limitation on post-September 9, 1986, modifications does not apply to this benefit. Thus, cost-of-living adjustments or other increases in the gratuity amount will not be subject to tax.

Dependent Care Assistance Program. Qualified military benefits include dependent care assistance provided under a dependent care assistance program (¶ 2065) for a current or former uniformed forces service member or for a dependent (Code Sec. 134(b)(4)).

Veterans' Bonuses and Payments. The definition of qualified military benefit includes bonus payments by a state or local government entity to a member or former member of the military, or to any dependents of such a member. The payment must be made only by reason of the member's service in a combat zone. Thus, the state or local program under which the bonus is paid must specify that the bonus is *only* available with respect to members who served in a combat zone (Code Sec. 134(b)(6)).

References are to Standard Federal Tax Reports; Tax Research Consultant; and Practical Tax Explanations.

[106] ¶ 7500; COMPEN: 6,606, COMPEN: 6,608; § 4,065.20

Chapter 9
BUSINESS EXPENSES

	Par.
Trade or Business Expenses	901
Compensation Paid	906
Entertainment, Meal, and Gift Expenses	910
Taxes	920
Charitable Contributions	927
Interest	937
Employee's Expenses	941
Transportation and Car Expenses	945
Traveling Expenses Away from Home	949
Home Office and Vacation Home Expenses	961
Other Business Expenses	968
Domestic Production Activities	980A
Expenses of Professional Persons	981
Farmer's Expenses	982
Landlord or Tenant Expenses	986
Mining Company's Expenses	987
Uniform Capitalization Rules	990
Incentives for Economically Distressed Communities	999A

Trade or Business Expenses

901. Deductibility of Business Expenses—Generally. A taxpayer, whether a corporation, an individual, a partnership, a trust, or an estate, generally may deduct from gross income the ordinary and necessary expenses of carrying on a trade or business that are paid or incurred during the tax year (Code Sec. 162; Reg. § 1.162-1).[1] Business expenses incurred by a cash-basis taxpayer while conducting a business but paid in a year after terminating the business are deductible as business expenses in the year paid (Rev. Rul. 67-12).[2] However, a deduction is not permitted for any expenditure that is a capital expense (¶ 903). Expenses for property used for both business and personal activities must be allocated between the different activities. The origin and character of a claim control whether an expense is a deductible business expense or a nondeductible personal expense.

Ordinary and Necessary. Whether a business expense is ordinary and necessary is based on the facts surrounding the expense. An expense is necessary if it is appropriate and helpful to the taxpayer's business (*S.B. Heininger*, SCt, 44-1 USTC ¶ 9109).[3] An expense is ordinary if it is one that is common and accepted in the particular business activity.

Trade or Business. A "trade or business," although not defined in the tax law, has been characterized as an activity carried on for a livelihood or for profit. A profit motive must be present and some type of economic activity must be conducted. In determining whether an activity is engaged in for profit, all facts and circumstances with respect to the activity are taken into account (Reg. § 1.183-2(b)).[4] No one factor is conclusive in making this determination. In addition, it is not intended that only the factors described below are to be taken into account in making the determination, or that a determination

References are to Standard Federal Tax Reports; Tax Research Consultant; and Practical Tax Explanations.

[1] ¶ 8500, ¶ 8501; BUSEXP: 3,100; § 9,001

[2] ¶ 8520.1546; BUSEXP: 3,058.20; § 9,001

[3] ¶ 8520.517; BUSEXP: 3,100; § 9,010.05

[4] ¶ 12,173; BUSEXP: 15,150; § 17,210.05

is to be made on the basis that the number of factors, whether or not listed in the regulations, indicating a lack of profit objective exceeds the number of factors indicating a profit objective, or vice versa. Among the factors that should normally be taken into account are the following: the manner in which the taxpayer carries on the activity; the expertise of the taxpayer or his or her advisors; the time and effort expended by the taxpayer in carrying on the activity; the expectation that assets used in the activity may appreciate in value; the success of the taxpayer in carrying on other similar or dissimilar activities; the taxpayer's history of income or losses with respect to the activity; the amount of occasional profits, if any, that are earned; the financial status of the taxpayer; and elements of personal pleasure or recreation.

903. Capital Expenditures. A taxpayer may not currently deduct a capital expenditure. Broadly defined, a capital expenditure is (1) any amount paid out for new buildings or permanent improvements or betterments made to increase the value of any property or estate, or (2) any amount expended in restoring property or in making good the exhaustion thereof for which an allowance has been made (Code Sec. 263; Reg. § 1.263(a)-1).[5] Capital expenditures are included in basis (¶ 1611) and are generally recovered through depreciation, amortization or depletion (¶ 1201). Amounts paid or incurred for incidental repairs and maintenance of property are not capital expenditures.

Capital expenses include amounts paid to produce or acquire tangible or intangible property, to improve tangible property, to facilitate the acquisition of a trade or business or a change in a business entity's capital structure, or to acquire or create an interest in land. They also include amounts paid in corporate financings and restructurings, such as amounts paid by bondholders and shareholders to be used in corporate reorganizations, voluntary contributions by shareholders to a corporation, and amounts paid by a holding company to carry out a guaranty of dividends on the stock of a subsidiary corporation in certain circumstances (Reg. § 1.263(a)-1(d)).[6]

Taxpayers may elect to treat certain capital expenditures as deductible or deferred expenses, or treat certain deductible expenses as capital expenditures (Reg. § 1.263(a)-6).[7] These include expenses related to newspaper or magazine circulation (¶ 971); research and experiments (¶ 979); soil and water conservation (¶ 982); Code Sec. 179 property (¶ 1208); sulfur regulation compliance (¶ 1285); refineries (¶ 1285A); energy efficient commercial buildings (¶ 1286); advanced mine safety equipment (¶ 989A); fertilizer (¶ 985); film, television production, and live theatrical production (¶ 977B); removal of barriers to the handicapped and elderly (¶ 1287); tertiary injectants; reforestation (¶ 1287); business start-up (¶ 904); corporate organization (¶ 237); carrying charges (¶ 1614); mine development (¶ 988); and partnership organization and syndication (¶ 477).

Repair Regulations—Effective Date and Accounting Method Changes. Final "repair" regulations relating to amounts paid to acquire, produce, or improve tangible property apply to tax years beginning on or after January 1, 2014 (T.D. 9636). For tax years beginning during 2012 and 2013, a taxpayer could, but was not required to, apply either the final regulations or the prior temporary regulations (T.D. 9564). Taxpayers who apply the final regulations may rely on Sec. 11.08 of Rev. Proc. 2016-29 for automatic change of accounting method procedures to comply with the repair regulations, generally effective for changes filed on or after May 5, 2016, for a year of change ending on or after September 30, 2015. Sec. 10.11 of Rev. Proc. 2015-14 contains the relevant automatic change procedures for complying with the repair regulations for changes filed on or after January 16, 2015 and before May 5, 2016. For earlier filed changes, see Appendix Sec. 10.11 of Rev. Proc. 2011-14, as modified by Rev. Proc. 2014-16 and Rev. Proc. 2012-19.[8]

References are to Standard Federal Tax Reports; Tax Research Consultant; and Practical Tax Explanations.

[5] ¶ 13,700, ¶ 13,701; BUSEXP: 9,000; § 10,201

[6] ¶ 13,701; BUSEXP: 9,000; § 10,201

[7] ¶ 13,704J; BUSEXP: 9,102; § 10,201

[8] ¶ 13,709.105; BUSEXP: 9,099; § 9,930.05, § 10,215.05

A small business taxpayer does not have to file Form 3115 to comply with the final repair regulations for its first tax year beginning in 2014 (Rev. Proc. 2015-20). The regulations are applied on a cut-off basis to amounts paid or incurred in tax years beginning on or after January 1, 2014. Therefore, no Code Sec. 481(a) adjustment (¶ 1531) is required. A small business taxpayer is a taxpayer with one or more separate and distinct trades or businesses that has either:

(1) total assets of less than $10 million as of the first day of the tax year for which the change in method of accounting is effective, or

(2) average annual gross receipts of $10 million or less for the prior three tax years.

A qualifying taxpayer chooses this relief if it does not file Form 3115 for its 2014 tax year. The relief applies to all accounting method changes required by Sec. 10.11 of Rev. Proc. 2015-14, as clarified and modified, and as modified and superseded by Sec. 11.08 of Rev. Proc. 2016-29, to comply with the final repair regulations. A taxpayer choosing this relief, however, may not file an accounting method change for the 2014 tax year to make the late partial disposition election described in Sec. 6.33 of Rev. Proc. 2015-14, as clarified and modified, and as modified and superseded by Sec. 6.10 of Rev. Proc. 2016-29, to claim losses on previously retired structural components (¶ 1239). An electing taxpayer may also not file an accounting method change described in Sec. 6.37 (Sec. 6.14 of Rev. Proc. 2016-29) relating to permissible changes in identifying assets or portions of assets disposed of from multiple asset accounts and mass asset accounts, and Sec. 6.38 and Sec. 6.39 (Sec. 6.15 and Sec. 6.16 of Rev. Proc. 2016-29) relating to recognition of gain and loss on dispositions of buildings and structural components or section 1245 property that are considered disposed of without making a partial disposition election. An electing taxpayer also does not receive audit protection for expenditures paid or incurred prior to the first tax year beginning on or after January 1, 2014.

Acquired or Produced Tangible Property. Taxpayers are required to capitalize amounts paid or incurred to produce or acquire a unit of tangible real or personal property, including leasehold improvement property, land and land improvements, buildings, machinery, equipment, furniture, and fixtures unless a current deduction is allowed under the *de minimis* safe harbor (see *De Minimis Expensing Safe Harbor,* following) or the rules that apply to materials and supplies (see *Materials and Supplies,* following). Capitalized amounts include the invoice price, amounts that facilitate the acquisition of the property (i.e., transactions costs), and costs for work performed before the taxpayer places the property in service (e.g., repairs). Amounts paid to acquire real or personal property for resale are also capitalized (Reg. § 1.263(a)-2).[9]

An amount facilitates the acquisition of property if the amount is paid in the process of investigating or otherwise pursuing the acquisition or production of the property. Inherently facilitative costs of acquiring or producing property that must be capitalized are amounts paid for: (a) transporting the property, e.g., shipping fees and moving costs; (b) appraisals and valuations; (c) negotiating the terms or structure of the acquisition; (d) tax advice on the acquisition; (e) application fees, bidding costs, or similar expenses; (f) preparing and reviewing the documents that effectuate the acquisition of the property, e.g., preparing the bid, offer, sales contract, or purchase agreement; (g) title examination and evaluation; (h) obtaining regulatory approval of the acquisition; (i) securing permits related to the acquisition, including application fees; (j) conveying property between the parties, including sales and transfer taxes, and title registration costs; (k) finders' fees or brokers' commissions, including contingency fees; (l) architectural, geological, survey, engineering, environmental, or inspection services pertaining to particular properties; and (m) services provided by a qualified intermediary or other facilitator of a like-kind exchange (Reg. § 1.263(a)-2(f)).

Activities performed in the process of determining whether to acquire real property and which real property to acquire are currently deductible. However, inherently facilitative amounts are capitalized even if paid or incurred during the "whether and which" process (Reg. § 1.263(a)-2(f)(2)(iii)).

References are to Standard Federal Tax Reports; Tax Research Consultant; and Practical Tax Explanations.

[9] ¶ 13,703; BUSEXP: 9,080; § 10,215.05

Employee compensation and overhead do not facilitate the acquisition of real or personal property but may need to be capitalized under the Code Sec. 263A uniform capitalization rules to property produced by the taxpayer or to property acquired for resale (¶ 990). However, a taxpayer may elect to capitalize employee compensation and overhead on a timely filed original federal tax return (including extensions) for the tax year during which the amounts are paid or incurred (Reg. § 1.263(a)-2(f)(2)(iv)).

De Minimis Expensing Safe Harbor. A taxpayer who meets certain requirements may make an annual *de minimis* safe harbor expensing election on a timely filed income tax return (including extensions) (Reg. § 1.263(a)-1(f)).[10] A taxpayer electing the safe harbor may not capitalize any amount paid in the tax year for the acquisition or production of a unit of tangible property nor treat as a material or supply an amount paid for tangible property that costs no more than a specified amount: up to $5,000 for a taxpayer with an applicable financial statement (AFS), and up to $2,500 ($500 for tax years beginning before 2016) for a taxpayer without an AFS (Notice 2015-82). However, the uniform capitalization rules (¶ 990) may require a taxpayer to capitalize amounts that are deductible under the safe harbor as a direct and allocable indirect cost of property produced by the taxpayer or property acquired for resale.

A taxpayer with an AFS may elect the *de minimis* expensing safe harbor for a tax year if (1) at the beginning of the tax year, it has written accounting procedures treating as an expense for non-tax purposes amounts paid or incurred for property that cost less than a certain dollar amount or that has an economic useful life of 12 months or less and (2) it treats such amounts paid or incurred during the tax year as an expense on the AFS. If the taxpayer does not have an AFS, the accounting procedures in effect at the beginning of the tax year do not need to be written. However, the taxpayer must expense the amount paid for the property on its books and records according to its accounting procedures.

Repairs. Expenses that keep tangible property in an ordinarily efficient operating condition and do not add to its value or appreciably prolong its useful life are generally deductible as repair and maintenance costs (Reg. § 1.162-4).[11] Taxpayers may elect to capitalize certain repair expenses (see *Election to Capitalize Repair and Maintenance Costs,* following).

Improvements. Expenses that improve a unit of property are capitalized (Reg. § 1.263(a)-3).[12] A unit of property is improved if the amounts paid for activities performed after the property is placed in service by the taxpayer either result in a betterment to the unit of property, restore the unit of property, or adapt the unit of property to a new or different use. A taxpayer generally must capitalize all the direct costs of an improvement, as well as all the indirect costs, such as otherwise deductible repair costs, that directly benefit or are incurred by reason of an improvement. Indirect costs that do not directly benefit and are not incurred by reason of an improvement generally are not capital improvements, regardless of whether they are paid or incurred at the same time as a capital improvement.

A betterment is an expenditure that:

- ameliorates a material condition or defect that existed prior to the taxpayer's acquisition of the unit of property or arose during the production of the property, whether or not the taxpayer was aware of the condition or defect at the time of acquisition;
- is for a material addition to the unit of property, such as a physical enlargement, expansion, extension, or addition of a new major component;
- is for a material increase in the capacity of the unit of property, such as additional cubic or linear space; or
- is reasonably expected to materially increase the productivity, efficiency, strength, quality, or output of the unit of property (Reg. § 1.263(a)-3(j)(1)).

References are to Standard Federal Tax Reports; Tax Research Consultant; and Practical Tax Explanations.

[10] ¶ 13,701; BUSEXP: 9,080; § 10,215.15

[11] ¶ 8620; BUSEXP: 9,150; § 9,930.05

[12] ¶ 13,704; BUSEXP: 9,090; § 10,215.12

An amount is paid to restore a unit of property if:

- the taxpayer replaces a component of a unit of property and deducts a loss for that component, other than a casualty loss, for example, by making a partial disposition election under Reg. § 1.168(i)-8(d);

- the taxpayer replaces a component of a unit of property and realizes gain or loss by selling or exchanging the component;

- the expenditure is for the restoration of damage to a unit of property caused by a casualty and the taxpayer is required to make a basis adjustment to the unit of property on account of a casualty loss or the receipt of insurance;

- the expenditures return a unit of property to its ordinary efficient operating condition after the property has deteriorated to a state of disrepair and is no longer functional for its intended use;

- the expenditures rebuild a unit of property to a like-new condition after the end of its class life (i.e., its MACRS alternative depreciation system recovery period); or

- the expenditures are for the replacement of a part or a combination of parts that comprise a major component or a substantial structural part of a unit of property (Reg. § 1.263(a)-3(k)(1)).

Repair expenditures paid in connection with a casualty are currently deductible if the capitalized restoration expenditures exceed the adjusted basis of the property prior to reduction by the casualty loss deduction or insurance reimbursement. If the capitalized restoration expenditures do not exceed the adjusted basis, but the sum of the capitalized restoration expenditures and repair expenditures exceed the adjusted basis, then the repair expenditures not used to offset the adjusted basis may be deducted (Reg. § 1.263(a)-3(k)(4)(i) and (k)(7), Example 5). Repair expenditures are not deductible if a basis adjustment is made to a property on account of a casualty loss or event, such as the receipt of insurance (Reg. § 1.263(a)-3(k)(1)(iii)).

An adaptation to a new or different use is a type of improvement that is capitalized. In general, an amount is paid to adapt a unit of property to a new or different use if the adaptation is not consistent with the taxpayer's ordinary use of the unit of property at the time it was originally placed in service by the taxpayer (Reg. § 1.263(a)-3(l)).

Removal Costs. If a taxpayer disposes of a depreciable asset, including a partial disposition under Reg. § § 1.168(i)-1(e)(1)(ii) or 1.168(i)-8(d), and has taken into account the adjusted basis of the asset or component of the asset in realizing gain or loss, then the costs of removing the asset or component are deductible. If a taxpayer disposes of a component of a unit of property, but the disposal is not a disposition, then the taxpayer must capitalize the removal cost if it directly benefits or is incurred by reason of an improvement to the unit of property (Reg. § 1.263(a)-3(g)(2)). For example, the cost of removing shingles on a roof is deductible if the replacement costs are a deductible repair. However, if the entire roof is replaced and the replacement costs are capitalized, then the removal costs are capitalized provided the taxpayer does not make a partial disposition election (¶ 1239) and claim a loss deduction on the replaced roof. Special rules apply to demolitions (¶ 1105).

Remodel-Refresh Safe Harbor. A qualified taxpayer engaged in the trade or business of operating a retail establishment or a restaurant may adopt a safe harbor method of accounting under which 25 percent of qualified remodel/refresh costs are capital expenditures under Code Sec. 263(a) and the uniform capitalization rules of Code Sec. 263A, and 75 percent of such costs are currently deductible (Rev. Proc. 2015-56; Sec. 11.10 of Rev. Proc. 2016-29). A qualified taxpayer must have an applicable financial statement (AFS) as defined in Reg.§ 1.263(a)-1(f). The building and improvements capitalized under the safe harbor must be placed in separate MACRS general asset accounts (GAAs). A late election to place the building in a GAA may be made in the tax year that the safe harbor is first used as part of the safe harbor accounting method change. Improvements that are depreciable under MACRS and made prior to the year that the safe harbor is first used generally must also be placed in a GAA by making a late election. A taxpayer may not make a partial disposition election (¶ 1239) to claim retirement losses on building components once this safe harbor is used. The safe harbor accounting method change is applied on a cut-off basis unless the taxpayer revokes any prior year partial disposition elections on an amended return filed within the limitations period for the tax year for which the election was made or files an accounting method change to revoke any partial disposition elections that were made in prior tax years. The method change to revoke prior partial disposition elections is only allowed for a tax year beginning after December 31, 2013, and ending before December 31, 2016 (Sec. 6.20(3) of Rev. Proc. 2016-29). Taxpayers who applied Temp. Reg.§ 1.168(i)-8T or the general asset account rules under Temp. Reg.§ 1.168(i)-1T in a tax year beginning before January 1, 2014 to claim losses on building components may not use the safe harbor until an accounting method change is filed to comply with the final regulations (Reg.§ 1.168(i)-8 or Reg.§ 1.168(i)-1) (¶ 1239). The positive Code Sec. 481(a) adjustment related to the losses previously claimed under the temporary regulations or partial disposition losses under the final regulations is included in income in a single tax year (i.e., the year of change).[13]

Routine Maintenance Safe Harbor. Under a safe harbor, routine maintenance activities on a unit of property do not improve that unit (Reg. § 1.263(a)-3(i)).[14] Routine maintenance activities are the recurring activities expected to be performed to keep a unit of property in ordinarily efficient operating order. The activities are routine only if at the time the unit of property is placed in service the taxpayer reasonably expects to perform the activities more than once during the class life (i.e., MACRS alternative depreciation system recovery period) of the unit of property or, in the case of a building, more than once during a ten-year period beginning on the date the taxpayer places the building in service.

Routine maintenance *does not* include amounts paid or incurred for a betterment or adaptation. The following types of restorations also do not qualify: the cost of replacing components if a retirement loss is claimed or gain or loss is realized upon a sale of the replaced component; amounts paid for the restoration of damage to a unit of property for which a basis adjustment as a result of a casualty loss or casualty event is required; and the cost of restoring deteriorated and nonfunctional property to its ordinarily efficient operating condition. In addition, routine maintenance does not include amounts paid for repairs, maintenance, or improvement of rotable and temporary spare parts if the taxpayer applies the optional method of accounting for such spare parts. Routine maintenance may include the replacement of a major component or substantial structural part of a unit of property.

Routine maintenance performed on a building structure or any of its building systems qualifies for the routine maintenance safe harbor. However, repairs, maintenance, or improvement of network assets (e.g., railroad track, oil and gas pipelines, water and sewage pipelines, power transmission and distribution lines, and telephone and cable lines) does not qualify for the safe harbor.

The routine maintenance safe harbor is an accounting method and not an election.

Building Improvements Safe Harbor for Small Taxpayers. A taxpayer with $10 million or less of average annual gross receipts in the three preceding tax years may elect not to capitalize improvements on a building, condominium, or cooperative that has an unadjusted basis (generally cost) of $1 million or less if the total amount paid or incurred for repairs, maintenance, and improvements for the tax year of the election does not exceed the lesser of (1) $10,000 or (2) two percent of the unadjusted basis of the building. Amounts deducted under the *de minimis* safe harbor or the safe harbor for routine maintenance are counted toward the $10,000 limit. This election must be made by the due date of the return (including extensions) for the year of the election. The improvements safe harbor for small taxpayers is applied separately to each eligible building

References are to Standard Federal Tax Reports; Tax Research Consultant; and Practical Tax Explanations.

[13] ¶ 11,275B, ¶ 11,276Q; BUSEXP: 9,096.30; § 10,215.12

[14] ¶ 13,704; BUSEXP: 9,096.10; § 10,215.40

owned or leased by the taxpayer. A lessee's unadjusted basis of a leased building or leased building space is equal to the total amount of undiscounted rent paid or expected to be paid over the entire lease term, including expected renewal periods (Reg. § 1.263(a)-3(h)).[15]

Election to Capitalize Repair and Maintenance Costs. A taxpayer may elect on a timely filed original return (including extensions) to capitalize as improvements all amounts paid during the tax year for repair and maintenance of tangible property, if the taxpayer incurs these amounts in carrying on its trade or business and treats them as capital expenditures on its books and records for the tax year covered by the election. An electing taxpayer cannot currently deduct the repair and maintenance amounts affected by the election. The election does not apply to amounts paid for repairs or maintenance of rotable or temporary spare parts to which the optional method of accounting under Reg. § 1.162-3(e) is applied (Reg. § 1.263(a)-3(n)).[16]

Unit of Property. All components that are functionally interdependent comprise a single unit of property. Components are functionally interdependent if the placing in service of one component is dependent on the placing in service of the other components (Reg. § 1.263(a)-3(e)).[17] Although a building, including its structural components, is a unit of property, the improvement rules are applied separately to each building system and the building structure. A building structure consists of a building as defined in Reg. § 1.48-1(e)(1) and its structural components as defined in Reg. § 1.48-1(e)(2), *other than* those designated as building systems. Designated building systems, including their components, that are separate from the building structure are:

(1) heating, ventilation, and air conditioning (HVAC) systems, including motors, compressors, boilers, furnace, chillers, pipes, ducts, and radiators;

(2) plumbing systems, including pipes, drains, valves, sinks, bathtubs, toilets, water and sanitary sewer collection equipment, and site utility equipment;

(3) electrical systems, including wiring, outlets, junction boxes, lighting fixtures and associated connectors, and site utility equipment;

(4) all escalators;

(5) all elevators;

(6) fire-protection and alarm systems, including sensing devices, computer controls, sprinkler heads, sprinkler mains, associated pipes or plumbing, pumps, visual and audible alarms, alarms control panels, heat and smoke detection devices, fire escapes, fire doors, emergency exit lighting and signage, and fire fighting equipment;

(7) security systems for the protection of the building and its occupants, including windows and door locks, security cameras, recorders, monitors, motion detectors, security lighting, alarm systems, entry and access systems, and related junction boxes, wiring and conduits;

(8) gas distribution systems, including associated pipes and equipment used to distribute gas to and from the property line and between buildings; and

(9) any other structural components designated as a building system by the IRS in published guidance (Reg. § 1.263(a)-3(e)(2)(ii)(B)).

Example: A taxpayer replaces the steps on the sole escalator in a building. The improvement rules are applied separately to the escalator because it is a building system. Since the steps are a major component of the escalator, the cost of replacing the steps is for a restoration and must be capitalized. If the improvement rules applied to the entire building, including its building systems, then the steps might not be considered a major component of the building and a repair deduction could be claimed. Generally, the larger the unit of property the more likely an expenditure is for a repair.

References are to Standard Federal Tax Reports; Tax Research Consultant; and Practical Tax Explanations.

[15] ¶ 13,704; BUSEXP: 9,096.20; § 10,215.12b

[16] ¶ 13,704; BUSEXP: 9,096.25; § 9,930.05.

[17] ¶ 13,704; BUSEXP: 9,094; § 10,215.12.

Materials and Supplies. The cost of nonincidental materials and supplies are deducted in the tax year they are first used or consumed, while the cost of incidental materials and supplies for which no inventories or records of consumption are kept is deductible in the tax year when paid or incurred if taxable income is clearly reflected (Reg. § 1.162-3(a)).[18] However, materials and supplies that improve tangible property are capitalized (Reg. § 1.263(a)-3(c)). In addition, the uniform capitalization rules (¶ 990) require taxpayers to capitalize the direct and allocable indirect costs, including the cost of materials and supplies, of property produced by the taxpayer and property acquired for resale. Taxpayers may also be required to include in inventory certain materials and supplies (¶ 1553) (Reg. § 1.162-3(b)). Finally, the cost of materials and supplies that meet the requirements of the *de minimis* safe harbor are deductible in the year paid or incurred if a taxpayer makes the *de minimis* safe harbor election.

"Materials and supplies" mean tangible property that is used or consumed in the taxpayer's business operations, is not inventory, and is:

- a component that is acquired to maintain, repair, or improve a unit of tangible property owned, leased, or serviced by the taxpayer, but is not acquired as part of any single unit of tangible property;
- fuel, lubricants, water, and similar items that are reasonably expected to be consumed in 12 months or less, beginning when used in a taxpayer's operations;
- a unit of property that has an economic useful life of 12 months or less, beginning when the property is used or consumed in the taxpayer's operations;
- a unit of property with an acquisition or production cost of $200 or less; or
- identified as a material or supply by the IRS in published guidance (Reg. § 1.162-3(c)(1)).

Rotable, Temporary, and Standby Emergency Parts. Rotable and temporary spare parts are materials and supplies and their cost is deducted in the year used or consumed unless the taxpayer uses the optional method of accounting to deduct their cost in the year of installation (Reg. § 1.162-3(c)(2)).[19] If the election is not made, rotable and temporary spare parts are treated as used or consumed in the year they are discarded (Reg. § 1.162-3(a)(3)).

Rotable spare parts are parts that are acquired for installation on a unit of property, removable from that unit of property, generally repaired or improved, and either reinstalled on the same or other property or stored for later installation. Temporary spare parts are parts that are used temporarily until a new or repaired part can be installed and then are removed and stored for later installation (Reg. § 1.162-3(c)(2)).

A taxpayer may elect to capitalize and depreciate the cost of rotable, temporary, and standby emergency spare parts. The election does not apply to rotable and temporary spare parts for which the optional method of accounting is used (Reg. § 1.162-3(d)).

The *de minimis* safe harbor election does not apply to rotable, temporary, or standby emergency spare parts that a taxpayer elects to capitalize and depreciate, or to rotable and temporary spare parts that are accounted for under the optional method (Reg. § 1.162-3(f)).

Intangible Property. Amounts must be capitalized if they are paid or incurred for: (1) specific categories of expenditures that are incurred in acquiring, creating, or enhancing, or that facilitate the acquisition or creation of, an intangible that is acquired from another person in a purchase or similar transaction; (2) certain rights, privileges, or benefits that are created or originated by the taxpayer; (3) a separate and distinct intangible asset; or (4) a future benefit that the IRS identifies in published guidance (Reg. § 1.263(a)-4).[20]

904. Business Start-Up Costs. Taxpayers who enter into a trade or business can elect to expense up to $5,000 of their start-up costs. The maximum $5,000 deduction is reduced dollar for dollar when the start-up expenses exceed $50,000. The balance of

References are to Standard Federal Tax Reports; Tax Research Consultant; and Practical Tax Explanations.

[18] ¶ 8600; BUSEXP: 18,558; § 9,935.05

[19] ¶ 8600; BUSEXP: 18,558; § 9,935.05

[20] ¶ 13,704C; BUSEXP: 9,104.20; § 10,210.05

start-up expenses, if any, are amortized over the 180-month period starting with the month in which the business begins (Code Sec. 195).[21] The taxpayer must make the election no later than the date for filing the return (including extensions) for the tax year in which the business begins or is acquired. The election is made by completing Part VI of Form 4562. A taxpayer who does not make the election must capitalize the expenses.

A taxpayer is deemed to elect to deduct and amortize start-up expenses for the tax year in which the active trade or business begins. A taxpayer may forego the deemed election by affirmatively electing to capitalize its start-up costs on a timely filed federal income tax return (including extensions) for the tax year in which the active trade or business begins. The election either to deduct and amortize start-up costs, or capitalize them, applies to all start-up expenses that are related to the active trade or business (Reg. § 1.195-1).[22]

Start-up expenses are those paid or incurred in connection with:

- investigating the creation or acquisition of an active trade or business;
- creating an active trade or business; or
- any activity engaged in for profit or for the production of income before the day the active trade or business begins, in anticipation of that activity becoming an active trade or business.

The start-up expense must also be a cost that would be allowable as a deduction if it were paid or incurred in connection with an existing active business in the same field (Code Sec. 195(c)).[23]

Start-up costs do not include any amount with respect to which a deduction is allowed for interest on indebtedness (¶ 1043), taxes (¶ 1021), or research and experimental expenses (¶ 979). If the trade or business is disposed of completely by the taxpayer before the end of the 180-month period, any remaining deferred expenses may be deductible as a loss (¶ 1101) (Code Sec. 195(b)(2)).[24]

The organizational costs of business entities are a separate class of expense from start-up expenses, though subject to similar rules. Corporate organization fees are discussed at ¶ 237. Costs of organizing a partnership are discussed at ¶ 477 and ¶ 481.

905. Expenses, Interest Deductions, and Losses—Related Taxpayers. When the payor and payee are related taxpayers (¶ 1717), and the payor is on the accrual method of accounting and the payee is on the cash method, no deduction is allowed for any trade or business expense or interest payable to the payee until the payee includes the payment in income (Code Sec. 267(a)(2)).[25] A similar rule denies a deduction for a loss (except for a loss from a distribution in corporate liquidation) for property sold or exchanged between related taxpayers (Code Sec. 267(a) and (d)).[26] However, the transferee's gain on a later sale or exchange of the property is recognized only to the extent that it exceeds the previously disallowed loss.

Compensation Paid

906. Compensation for Personal Service. A taxpayer carrying on a trade or business is entitled to deduct reasonable salaries or other compensation for personal services. The deduction is allowable for the year in which the salary is paid or incurred (Code Sec. 162(a)(1); Reg. § 1.162-7).[27]

Publicly held corporations generally cannot deduct compensation paid to certain covered employees that exceeds $1 million per tax year (Code Sec. 162(m); Reg. § 1.162-27).[28] A "covered employee" is any employee of the taxpayer who, as of the close of the tax year, is:

References are to Standard Federal Tax Reports; Tax Research Consultant; and Practical Tax Explanations.

[21] ¶ 12,370; DEPR: 21,400; § 9,201

[22] ¶ 12,370F; BUSEXP: 12,252; § 9,215

[23] ¶ 12,370; DEPR: 21,400; § 9,205.10

[24] ¶ 12,370; DEPR: 21,450; § 9,205.05

[25] ¶ 14,150; ACCTNG: 12,150; § 17,601

[26] ¶ 14,150; SALES: 39,100; § 17,605

[27] ¶ 8500, ¶ 8635; COMPEN: 9,050; § 9,305.05

[28] ¶ 8500, ¶ 9051B; COMPEN: 12,350; § 9,310

- the principal executive officer of the taxpayer, including an individual acting in that capacity; or

- one of the three highest compensated officers for the tax year and, therefore, must have his or her compensation reported to shareholders under SEC rules (Notice 2007-49).[29]

The $1 million limit does not apply to certain "performance-based compensation" payable solely on account of attaining one or more performance goals (Code Sec. 162(m)(4)(C); Reg. § 1.162-27(e)).[30] Performance-based compensation can include compensation issued in the form of stock rights and options exercised when the plan specifies the maximum number of shares that may be granted to all employees in the aggregate. Performance-based compensation attributable to stock rights or stock options must include a specific per-employee limitation on the amount granted (Reg. § 1.162-27(e)(2)(vi)(A)).

Awards paid under a corporate bonus plan are not qualified performance-based compensation if the plan allows payments to be made, even if the specified performance goals have not been met, upon the employee's retirement, termination without cause, or voluntary termination of employment for good reason (Rev. Rul. 2008-13).[31] If the bonus was paid solely for attaining a performance goal, the goal must be determined by a compensation committee consisting solely of two or more outside directors. An outside director cannot be a current employee, a former employee who receives compensation during the year, or a current or former officer (Rev. Rul. 2008-32).[32]

Reasonable compensation is the amount that would ordinarily be paid for like services by like enterprises in like circumstances (Reg. § 1.162-7(b)(3)).[33] Thus, whether compensation is reasonable in a given situation depends on the relevant facts and circumstances, including personal ability, responsibility of the position, and local economic conditions. The U.S. Court of Appeals for the Seventh Circuit has used an independent-investor test that presumes that compensation is reasonable if the company's investors earn their expected rate of return (*Exacto Spring Corporation*, CA-7, 99-2 USTC ¶ 50,964).[34] A bonus is deductible if it is paid for services performed, and, when added to other salaries, it does not exceed reasonable compensation (Reg. § 1.162-9).[35] Compensation paid to a relative is deductible if the relative performs needed services that would otherwise be performed by an unrelated party. The deduction is limited to the amount that would have been paid to a third party (*Transport Mfg. & Equip. Co.*, CA-8, 70-2 USTC ¶ 9627).[36] The IRS does not rule in advance on whether compensation is reasonable in amount (Rev. Proc. 2016-3).[37]

Officer-Stockholders of Closely Held Corporations. Officer-stockholders of closely held corporations may deduct repayments of salary to their corporation that are made under an agreement requiring such repayments if the IRS determines the salaries are excessive (Rev. Rul. 69-115).[38] The agreement must be legally enforceable and in existence *before* the excess salary is paid.

Deferred Compensation Plans. For unfunded deferred compensation plans, the employer deducts compensation when the compensation, or amount attributable to it, is included in the gross income of the recipient (¶ 723) (Code Sec. 404(a)(5) and (b)(1)).[39] Other benefits that are excluded from the recipient's gross income are deductible when they otherwise would have been includible but for the exclusion (Code Sec.

References are to Standard Federal Tax Reports; Tax Research Consultant; and Practical Tax Explanations.

[29] ¶ 8636.2763; COMPEN: 12,354

[30] ¶ 8500, ¶ 9051B; COMPEN: 12,356; § 9,310

[31] ¶ 8636.2768; COMPEN: 12,356.10

[32] ¶ 8636.2764; COMPEN: 12,356.10; § 9,310.15

[33] ¶ 8635; COMPEN: 9,100; § 9,305.10

[34] ¶ 8637.227, ¶ 8637.57; COMPEN: 9,114; § 9,305.10

[35] ¶ 8641; COMPEN: 9,054; § 9,335

[36] ¶ 8637.752; COMPEN: 9,202; § 9,305.20

[37] ¶ 8637.692; COMPEN: 9,054

[38] ¶ 8640.165; COMPEN: 9,456; § 7,101

[39] ¶ 18,330; COMPEN: 15,250; § 25,605

404(b)(2)).[40] This rule also applies to compensation paid to independent contractors (Code Sec. 404(d)).[41]

A plan is unfunded if it consists of an unsecured promise to pay compensation at some time in the future. If the employer sets aside a reserve for the future obligation, the plan is unfunded if the employee has no rights in the reserve or its earnings and if the reserve remains solely the property of the employer or other payor, subject to the claims of creditors (Rev. Rul. 55-525).[42]

A plan is presumed to defer compensation if the compensation is received after the 15th day of the third calendar month after the end of the employer's tax year in which the related services are rendered. This presumption may be overcome if the employer establishes that it was administratively or economically impractical to avoid the deferral of compensation beyond the 2½-month period. Payments within the 2½-month period are not deferred compensation and may be accrued by an accrual-method employer in the year earned by the employee (Temp. Reg. § 1.404(b)-1T, Q&A-2).[43]

For a discussion of rules governing the employer's deduction for compensation for deferred compensation plans, see ¶ 2117 and ¶ 2199.

Health Insurance Providers. The deduction for compensation or remuneration paid to officers, directors, or employees of covered health insurance providers, including those that provide services for or on behalf of covered health insurance providers, is limited to $500,000 for disqualified tax years beginning after December 31, 2012 (Code Sec. 162(m)(6); Reg. § 1.162-31).[44] A disqualified tax year is any tax year in which the employer is a covered health insurance provider. For tax years beginning after December 31, 2012, a covered health insurance provider is a health insurance issuer, as defined under Code Sec. 9832(b)(2), for any tax year during which at least 25 percent of the gross premiums it receives from providing health insurance coverage is from providing minimum essential coverage (¶ 131). A *de minimis* exception applies if health insurance premiums are less than two percent of gross revenues. For tax years beginning after 2009 and before 2013, a covered health insurance provider is a health insurance issuer that receives premiums from providing health insurance coverage.

Deduction Limit for TARP Recipients. Under the Troubled Asset Relief Program (TARP) established by the Emergency Economic Stabilization Act of 2008 (P.L. 110-343), the federal government may purchase troubled assets from financial institutions. A TARP participant's deduction for compensation paid to a covered executive is limited to $500,000 in each year that TARP financial assistance remains outstanding (Code Sec. 162(m)(5)).[45] According to the Treasury Department web site, the Treasury is winding down its remaining TARP investments.

907. Golden Parachutes. A corporation that enters into a contract agreeing to pay an employee additional compensation if control or ownership of the corporation changes cannot take a deduction for an "excess parachute payment" made to a "disqualified individual" (Code Sec. 280G).[46] A disqualified individual is an officer, shareholder, or highly compensated person who performs personal services for the corporation as an employee or independent contractor. A personal service corporation is treated as an individual. The disqualified individual is subject to an excise tax of 20 percent of the excess parachute payment in addition to the income tax due (Code Sec. 4999(a)).[47]

Parachute Payment Defined. A parachute payment is any payment in the nature of compensation to a disqualified individual if:

References are to Standard Federal Tax Reports; Tax Research Consultant; and Practical Tax Explanations.

[40] ¶ 18,330; COMPEN: 12,108.10; § 25,605

[41] ¶ 18,330; COMPEN: 15,252; § 25,605

[42] ¶ 18,352.48; COMPEN: 15,050; § 25,610.15

[43] ¶ 18,354; COMPEN: 15,254; § 24,005

[44] ¶ 8500, ¶ 9051I; COMPEN: 12,360; § 9,310.05

[45] ¶ 8500; COMPEN: 12,358; § 9,310.05

[46] ¶ 15,150; COMPEN: 30,050; § 21,805.15

[47] ¶ 34,940; COMPEN: 30,250; § 21,820

- the payment is contingent on a change in the ownership or effective control of the corporation or a substantial portion of the assets of the corporation; and
- the aggregate present value of the contingent payments equals or exceeds three times the individual's base amount.

A payment in the nature of compensation to a disqualified individual made under an agreement that violates any securities law or regulations is also a parachute payment. Parachute payments do not include reasonable compensation for personal services to be rendered on or after the date of change or for personal services actually rendered before the date of change, or payments to or from certain qualified plans (Code Sec. 280G(b)).[48]

Base Amount. The base amount is the individual's annualized includible compensation for the base period (the most recent five tax years ending before the date on which the ownership or control changed, or the portion of that period during which the disqualified individual performed personal services for the corporation) (Code Sec. 280G(b)(3)(A) and (d)(2)).[49]

Exceptions. A parachute payment generally does not include any payment made to a disqualified individual by a small business corporation. It also does not include a payment from a corporation if, immediately before the change in ownership or control, none of the corporation's stock was readily tradable on an established securities market and the payment met shareholder approval requirements (Code Sec. 280G(b)(5)).[50]

Excess Parachute Payment. An excess parachute payment is the portion of any parachute payment that exceeds the base amount, reduced, in the case of a change-in-control parachute payment, by the excess of the amount of the payment determined to be reasonable compensation for services performed before the date of the change, over average compensation. (Code Sec. 280G(b)).[51]

908. Contributions for Employee Benefits and Health Insurance. An employer's deduction for contributions to a funded welfare benefit plan for sickness, accident, hospitalization, or medical benefits is governed by Code Sec. 419 (¶ 2011) (Temp. Reg. § 1.162-10T).[52] Although amounts that are added to a self-insurance reserve account are not currently deductible, actual claims charged to the account are deductible (*General Dynamics Corp.*, SCt, 87-1 USTC ¶ 9280).[53] Group health plans that fail to provide COBRA continuing coverage to qualified beneficiaries may subject employers to an excise tax (Code Sec. 4980B).[54]

Self-Employed Persons. Self-employed persons may deduct 100 percent of amounts paid during the year for health insurance for themselves and their spouses and dependents (Code Sec. 162(l)).[55] The deduction cannot exceed the taxpayer's net earned income derived from the trade or business for which the insurance plan was established, minus the deduction for 50 percent of the self-employment tax and/or the deduction for contributions to qualified retirement plans, self-employed pensions (SEPs), or SIMPLE plans. The deduction is not available for amounts paid during any month, or part of a month, that the self-employed individual was able to participate in a subsidized health plan maintained by his or her employer or spouses' employer. The IRS has issued guidance providing optional calculation methods to resolve the circular relationship between the health insurance premium assistance credit (¶ 1331) and the self-employed health insurance deduction (Rev. Proc. 2014-41).[56]

Children Under the Age of 27. Children under the age of 27 are considered dependents of a taxpayer for purposes of the deduction for the health insurance costs of a self-employed person, spouse, and dependents. A child includes: a son, daughter, stepson, or

References are to Standard Federal Tax Reports; Tax Research Consultant; and Practical Tax Explanations.

[48] ¶ 15,150; COMPEN: 30,100; § 21,815.05

[49] ¶ 15,150; COMPEN: 30,150; § 21,805.25

[50] ¶ 15,150; COMPEN: 30,110; § 21,815.15

[51] ¶ 15,150; COMPEN: 30,150; § 21,805.25

[52] ¶ 8751; COMPEN: 42,100; § 9,345

[53] ¶ 8522.3947; BUSEXP: 18,210; § 9405.30, § 9,345

[54] ¶ 34,600; HEALTH: 24,100; § 42,850.05

[55] ¶ 8500; HEALTH: 15,100; § 5,401

[56] ¶ 8522.405; HEALTH: 3,322; § 42,015.20

stepdaughter of the taxpayer; a foster child placed with the taxpayer by an authorized placement agency or by judgment, decree, or other order of any court of competent jurisdiction; and a legally adopted child of the taxpayer or a child who has been lawfully placed with the taxpayer for legal adoption (Code Sec. 152(f)(1)).[57]

Excise Tax on High-Cost Employer-Provided Insurance. A 40-percent excise tax will be imposed on health coverage providers starting in 2020 to the extent that the aggregate value of employer-sponsored health coverage for an employee exceeds a threshold amount (Code Sec. 4980I as amended by the Protecting Americans from Tax Hikes (PATH) Act of 2015 (P.L. 114-113).[58]

908A. Disability Payments. A business or professional person may deduct premiums on a policy that pays overhead expenses during a period of disability, but the proceeds under such a policy are includible in gross income (Rev. Rul. 55-264).[59] When an insurance premium is paid in advance for more than one year, only a pro rata portion of the premium is deductible for each year, regardless of the taxpayer's method of accounting (Reg. § 1.461-1; Rev. Rul. 70-413).[60]

908B. Employer-Provided Day Care. An employer's payments to a day care center are a deductible business expense where the purpose of providing the day care is:

- to provide employees with a place to send their children while at work, so that the employees can be reassured that the children are receiving proper care;
- to reduce absenteeism, increase productivity, and reduce company training costs; and
- to reduce employee turnover (Rev. Rul. 73-348).[61]

An S corporation, however, could not deduct amounts it paid for day care for its sole shareholder's preschool children where there was no direct relationship to the corporation's business, and it did not pay day care expenses for any of its other employees (*F.M. Settimo,* Dec. 56,694(M), 92 TCM 473 (2006)).[62]

Up to $5,000 of employer-provided child or dependent care assistance services is excludable from the employee's gross income (¶ 2065).

909. Life Insurance Premiums. Premiums paid by an employer for insurance on the life of an officer or employee are deductible only if it can be shown that:

- premium payments are in the nature of additional compensation;
- total compensation, including premiums, is not unreasonable; and
- the employer is not directly or indirectly a beneficiary under the policy (*L. Hyman & Co.*, Dec. 6447, 21 BTA 159; *Brown Agency, Inc.*, Dec. 6615, 21 BTA 1111).[63]

However, an employer cannot deduct premiums paid under a split dollar arrangement (¶ 2057).

An employer can deduct premiums on group-term life insurance covering the lives of employees only if the employer is not a direct or indirect beneficiary (Code Sec. 264(a)(1); Reg. § 1.264-1).[64] The premiums generally represent income to the employee to the extent that the coverage exceeds $50,000 (¶ 2055).

Generally, no deduction is allowed for interest paid or accrued on a debt incurred or continued to purchase or carry any single premium life insurance, endowment or annuity contract. If substantially all the premiums on a life insurance or endowment contract are paid within four years from the date of purchase, or if an amount is deposited with the insurer for payment of a substantial number of future premiums, it is regarded as a single premium contract (Code Sec. 264(a)(2) and (c)).[65]

References are to Standard Federal Tax Reports; Tax Research Consultant; and Practical Tax Explanations.

[57] ¶ 8007; FILEIND: 6,154.05; § 1,215.10

[58] ¶ 34,619ZE; HEALTH: 9,302

[59] ¶ 8522.385; BUSEXP: 18,220; § 9,415.05

[60] ¶ 21,805, ¶ 21,817.21; BUSEXP: 18,216; § 9,420.05

[61] ¶ 8752.21; BUSEXP: 3,104; § 9,010.15

[62] ¶ 8520.517; BUSEXP: 3,104; § 9,010.15

[63] ¶ 8522.386, ¶ 8636.27; BUSEXP: 18,154.05; § 9405.05

[64] ¶ 14,002, ¶ 14,003; COMPEN: 48,100; § 21,005.05

[65] ¶ 14,002; INDIV: 48,556; § 9405.05

Interest on a debt incurred to purchase or continue a life insurance, endowment, or annuity contract under a purchase plan that contemplates the systematic borrowing of part or all of the increases in cash value is not deductible (Code Sec. 264(a)(3)).[66] However, an interest deduction is allowed in limited situations (Code Sec. 264(d)). Special rules may permit the deduction of interest incurred for key person policies owned by corporations (Code Sec. 264(e)).[67]

Entertainment, Meal, and Gift Expenses

910. Entertainment Expenses. Special limits are imposed by Code Sec. 274 on the deduction of business-related entertainment, meals, and gift expenses in addition to those imposed by other Code sections. Specifically, entertainment, amusement, or recreation costs are not deductible unless they are (1) *directly related* to the active conduct of a trade or business (¶ 911), or (2) for entertainment directly before or after a substantial and bona fide business discussion *associated with* the conduct of that trade or business (¶ 912) (Code Sec. 274(a)(1)). Specific exceptions to these general requirements are discussed at ¶ 915.

Entertainment includes entertaining guests at nightclubs, sporting events, theaters, etc. A taxpayer's trade or business is considered in applying an objective test as to what constitutes entertainment. For example, a ticket to a play is generally an entertainment expense, but it might be a business expense if the taxpayer is a professional theater critic (Code Sec. 274(a)(1)(A); Reg. § 1.274-2(b)(1)(ii)).[68] Only 50 percent of meal and entertainment expenses is deductible (¶ 916), but there are numerous exceptions to this limit (¶ 917).

Two-Percent-of-AGI Floor. An employee claims most unreimbursed business expenses as a miscellaneous itemized deduction subject to the two-percent-of-adjusted-gross-income (AGI) limitation on Schedule A of Form 1040 (¶ 1079). Any percentage limit, e.g., 50 percent on meal and entertainment expenses, must be taken into account before applying the two-percent-of-AGI floor (¶ 942) (Code Sec. 67; Temp. Reg. § 1.67-1T(a)).[69] Certain employees may deduct their unreimbursed expenses directly from gross income (¶ 941B).

911. Directly Related Test. For an entertainment expense to meet the directly related test for a deductible business expense (¶ 910), the taxpayer must have had more than a general expectation of deriving income, or some other specific business benefit, from the entertainment at some indefinite future time. The taxpayer must engage in the active conduct of business with the person being entertained, and the active conduct of business must be the principal aspect of the combined business and entertainment (Reg. § 1.274-2(c)).[70]

912. Associated Entertainment. Entertainment expenses associated with the active conduct of the taxpayer's business are deductible if they directly precede or follow a bona fide and substantial business discussion (¶ 910). This includes goodwill expenditures to obtain new business or encourage continuation of existing business relationships. The business discussion must be the principal aspect of the combined entertainment and business discussion and must represent an active effort by the taxpayer to obtain income or other specific business benefit (Reg. § 1.274-2(d)).[71]

References are to Standard Federal Tax Reports; Tax Research Consultant; and Practical Tax Explanations.

[66] ¶ 14,002; INDIV: 48,556; § 9,405.15

[67] ¶ 14,002; COMPEN: 48,062; § 9,405.15

[68] ¶ 14,402, ¶ 14,405; BUSEXP: 24,550; § 9,610.05, § 9,635.05

[69] ¶ 6060, ¶ 6061; BUSEXP: 12,102, FILEIND: 12,054; § 9,635.05

[70] ¶ 14,405; BUSEXP: 24,558; § 9,615

[71] ¶ 14,405; BUSEXP: 24,560; § 9,615

913. Entertainment Facility. No business deduction is allowed for any expense for entertainment facilities, such as yachts, hunting lodges, swimming pools, tennis courts, or bowling alleys (¶ 910) (Code Sec. 274(a)(1)(B)).[72] However, expenses for recreational facilities primarily for the benefit of employees generally are deductible (Reg. § 1.274-2(f)(2)(v)).[73]

913A. Club Dues. Club dues generally are not a business expense deduction. This rule extends to business, social, athletic, luncheon, sporting, airline, and hotel clubs (Code Sec. 274(a)(3); Reg. § 1.274-2(a)(2)(iii)).[74] However, dues paid to professional or public service organizations (e.g., accounting associations, or Kiwanis and Rotary clubs) are deductible if they are paid for business reasons and the organization's principal purpose is *not* to conduct entertainment activities for members or their guests or to provide those parties with access to entertainment facilities.

914. Entertainment-Related Meals. Generally, an entertainment-related meal expense is *not* deductible unless the taxpayer establishes that the expense is directly related to the active conduct of a trade or business. However, if a meal expense directly precedes or follows a substantial and bona fide business discussion, including a business meeting at a convention, then it is deductible if it is established that the expense was associated with the active conduct of a trade or business. The taxpayer must be able to substantiate the expense (¶ 953) (Code Sec. 274(d); Temp. Reg. § 1.274-5T(c) and (f)).[75]

There are two additional restrictions placed on the deduction of meal expenses: (1) meal expenses generally are not deductible if neither the taxpayer nor the taxpayer's employee is present at the meal, and (2) a deduction will not be allowed for food and beverages to the extent that such expense is lavish or extravagant under the circumstances. These restrictions do not apply to the expenses described in exceptions (2), (3), (4), (7), (8), and (9) at ¶ 915 (Code Sec. 274(k)).[76]

915. Exceptions to Entertainment Rules. The following entertainment expenses are not subject to the special rules for the deduction of entertainment expenses (¶ 912, ¶ 913, and ¶ 914). They are deductible as long as they meet the ordinary and necessary requirements and are properly substantiated (Code Sec. 274(e); Reg. § 1.274-2(f)(2)).[77] However, they may be subject to the 50-percent limit on meals and entertainment expenses (¶ 916 and ¶ 917). The exceptions are:

(1) food and beverages for employees furnished on the business premises;

(2) expenses for services, goods, and facilities that are treated as compensation and as wages for withholding tax purposes (however, if the recipient is a specified individual such as an officer, director, or 10-percent shareholder or related person, the employer's deduction is limited to the compensation reported);

(3) reimbursed expenses, but only:

(a) if the services relating to the expenses are performed for an employer that has not treated the expenses as wages subject to withholding; or

(b) if the services are performed for a person other than an employer and the taxpayer incurring the reimbursed expenses accounts to that person;

(4) recreational expenses primarily for employees who are not highly compensated (¶ 2114) (e.g., a company picnic);

(5) expenses of employees', stockholders', agents', or directors' business meetings;

(6) expenses directly related and necessary to attendance at a business meeting of a tax-exempt business league, including a real estate board, chamber of commerce or board of trade;

(7) expenses for goods, services, and facilities made available to the public;

References are to Standard Federal Tax Reports; Tax Research Consultant; and Practical Tax Explanations.

[72] ¶ 14,402; BUSEXP: 24,650; § 9,625.10

[73] ¶ 14,405; BUSEXP: 24,562.20; § 9,630.25

[74] ¶ 14,402, ¶ 14,405; BUSEXP: 24,658; § 9,625.15

[75] ¶ 14,402, ¶ 14,410; BUSEXP: 24,810; § 10,105

[76] ¶ 14,402; BUSEXP: 24,562; § 9,601

[77] ¶ 14,402, ¶ 14,405; BUSEXP: 24,562; § 9,630.10

(8) expenses for entertainment sold to customers in a bona fide transaction for adequate consideration; and

(9) expenses for goods, services, and facilities that are furnished to a nonemployee as entertainment, amusement or recreation and are includible in the recipient's income as compensation for services (¶ 713) or as a taxable prize or award (¶ 785).

916. 50-Percent Limit for Meal and Entertainment Expenses. The business deduction for meal and entertainment expenses is generally limited to 50 percent of such expenses. Food and beverage costs incurred in the course of travel away from home fall within the scope of this rule (Code Sec. 274(n)).[78] The 50-percent limit is applied only after determining the amount of the otherwise allowable deductions. For instance, the portion of a travel meal that is lavish and extravagant must first be subtracted from the meal cost before the 50-percent limit is applied. Related expenses, such as taxes, tips, room rental and parking fees, must be included in the total expense before applying the 50-percent limit. Allowable deductions for transportation costs to and from a business meal are not reduced.

Transportation Workers. The deductible percentage of the cost of meals consumed while away from home by individuals subject to Department of Transportation hours of service rules (e.g., interstate truck and bus drivers and certain railroad, airline, and merchant marine employees) is 80 percent (Code Sec. 274(n)(3)).[79]

Leased Employees. If an employee or independent contractor incurs unreimbursed meal and incidental expenses (M&IE) in connection with the performance of services for a third party, the 50-percent limit applies to any deduction claimed by the employee or independent contractor (Reg. § 1.274-2(f)(2)(iv)).[80] However, if an employee or independent contractor accounts for the expenses to a leasing company and is reimbursed under an allowance arrangement with a payment that is treated as compensation, the leasing company, rather than the employee or independent contractor, bears the expense and is subject to the 50-percent limit. Similarly, if the leased company accounts for the expenses to the third party and is reimbursed under an allowance arrangement, the third party bears the expenses and is subject to the 50-percent limit on its deduction.

917. Exceptions to 50-Percent Limit for Meal and Entertainment Expenses. The following expenses are *not* subject to the 50-percent limit on meal and entertainment expense deductions (80-percent limit for certain transportations workers) (¶ 916):

(1) expenses described in categories (2), (3), (4), (7), (8), and (9) at ¶ 915;

(2) food and beverage expenses associated with benefits that are excludable from the recipient's gross income as a *de minimis* fringe benefit (¶ 2089);

(3) the cost of a ticket package to a sporting event and related expenses if the event is organized to benefit a tax-exempt organization, all net proceeds are contributed to the organization, and volunteers perform substantially all of the work in carrying out the event; in other situations, a deduction for a ticket is limited to the ticket's face value;

(4) an employee's meal expenses incurred while moving that are reimbursed by the employer and includible in the employee's gross income; these expenses are not deductible (¶ 1073); and

(5) expenses for food and beverages provided to employees on certain (a) vessels and (b) oil or gas platforms and drilling rigs and their support camps (Code Sec. 274(l)(1) and (n)).[81]

Skyboxes. When a skybox is rented for more than one event, the deduction may not exceed the price of non-luxury box seats (subject to the usual 50-percent limit) (Code Sec. 274(l)(2)).[82]

References are to Standard Federal Tax Reports; Tax Research Consultant; and Practical Tax Explanations.

[78] ¶ 14,402; BUSEXP: 24,600; § 9,635

[79] ¶ 14,402; BUSEXP: 24,606; § 9,640.60

[80] ¶ 49,544; BUSEXP: 24,604; § 9,635.05

[81] ¶ 14,402; BUSEXP: 24,604; § 9,640.05

[82] ¶ 14,402; BUSEXP: 24,662; § 9,650

Tickets to College Sporting Events. For any payment to or for an institution of higher education that would be allowable as a charitable deduction but for the fact that the taxpayer thereby receives (directly or indirectly) the right to purchase tickets for seating at an athletic event in an athletic stadium of the institution, 80 percent of that payment is treated as a charitable contribution (Code Sec. 170(l)).[83]

918. Business Gifts. Deductions for business gifts, whether made directly or indirectly, are limited to $25 per recipient per year (Code Sec. 274(b)(1); Reg. § 1.274-3).[84] Items clearly of an advertising nature that cost $4 or less and signs, display racks, or other promotional materials given for use on business premises are not gifts.

919. Employee Achievement Awards. An employer may deduct up to $400 of the cost of an employee achievement award for all nonqualified plan awards to each employee (Code Sec. 274(j)).[85] The deduction for the cost of a qualified plan award made to a particular employee is limited to $1,600 per year, taking into account all other qualified and nonqualified awards made to that employee during the tax year.

An employee achievement award is an item of tangible personal property awarded to an employee as part of a meaningful presentation for length-of-service or safety achievements and under circumstances that do not create a significant likelihood of disguised compensation (¶ 2069). Tangible personal property does not include cash, gift certificates, or other intangible property such as vacations, meals, lodging, tickets to events, stocks, bond, and other securities.

A qualified plan award is an employee achievement award provided under an established written plan or program that does not discriminate in favor of highly compensated employees (¶ 2114) as to eligibility or benefits. An employee achievement award is not a qualified plan award if the average cost of all employee achievement awards under the plan exceeds $400. This average cost calculation includes the entire cost of all qualified plan awards other than awards of nominal value.

A length of service award does not qualify if it is received during the employee's first five years of service or if the employee has received another length of service award (other than an award excludable as a *de minimis* fringe benefit (¶ 2089)) during the year or within the last four years. An award is not a safety achievement award if it is made to a manager, administrator, clerical employee, or other professional employee, or if, during the tax year, awards for safety achievement previously have been made to more than 10 percent of the employees, excluding managers, administrators, clerical employees, or other professional employees.

Taxes

920. Taxes Directly Attributable to Business. Business taxpayers can deduct the taxes listed at ¶ 1021 and any other state, local, and foreign taxes paid or accrued within the tax year to the extent that they are directly attributable to a trade or business or to property held for the production of rents or royalties (Code Sec. 164(a)).[86] Any tax not listed at ¶ 1021 that is paid or accrued by the taxpayer in connection with the acquisition of property is treated as part of the cost of the acquired property or, if in connection with the disposition of property, as a reduction in the amount realized.

The uniform capitalization rules require some taxpayers to capitalize certain taxes that would otherwise be deductible (¶ 990–¶ 999).

921. Business Deduction for Federal Unemployment Insurance Tax. The Federal Unemployment Tax Act (FUTA) tax (¶ 2649) is an *excise* tax, so the employer may deduct it as a business expense if it represents an ordinary and necessary expense paid or incurred during the tax year in the conduct of a trade or business (Reg. § 1.164-2(f)).[87] The FUTA tax is deductible as a business expense after application of credits for the

References are to Standard Federal Tax Reports; Tax Research Consultant; and Practical Tax Explanations.

[83] ¶ 11,600; INDIV: 51,052.40; § 7,510.75

[84] ¶ 14,402, ¶ 14,406; BUSEXP: 24,706; § 9,945.05

[85] ¶ 14,402; BUSEXP: 24,714, BUSEXP: 24,716; § 9,340.10

[86] ¶ 9500; BUSEXP: 21,454; § 9,940.10

[87] ¶ 9503; INDIV: 45,112.35; § 9,365

employer's contributions to the state unemployment fund (Code Sec. 3302(a)(1)). On the cash basis (¶ 1515), the tax is deductible when paid. On the accrual basis (¶ 1540), the deduction may be accrued for the calendar year in which the wages were paid even though the tax is not due until the following year.

922. Business Deduction for State Unemployment Insurance and Disability Fund Contributions. An employer's contributions to a state unemployment insurance fund are deductible as taxes only if they are classified as taxes under state law and are incurred in carrying on a trade or business or for the production of income.[88] If the state does not classify the contributions as taxes, the employer may be able to deduct them as business expenses. Similar treatment applies to employer contributions to state disability funds.[89] An employee who is required to contribute to a state unemployment compensation fund may claim an itemized deduction for the contribution as a state income tax.[90] Also, compulsory employee contributions to state disability funds are deductible as itemized deductions for state income taxes. However, employees cannot deduct their contributions to private disability benefit plans. See also the checklist at ¶ 57.

923. Business Deduction for FICA Taxes. An employer's share of the Federal Insurance Contributions Act (FICA) tax for Social Security and Medicare (¶ 2648) is an *excise* tax, so the employer may deduct it as a business expense if it represents an ordinary and necessary expense paid or incurred during the tax year in the conduct of a trade or business or for the production of income (Reg. § 1.164-2(f)).[91] The employer contribution on wages paid to a domestic worker is not deductible unless it qualifies as a business expense (*R.A. Biggs*, CA-6, 71-1 USTC ¶ 9306).[92]

An employee's portion of FICA taxes is not deductible (¶ 1025). However, if the employer pays the employee's portion of the tax without deduction from the employee's wages under an agreement with the employee, the amount is deductible by the employer as a business expense, and is also wage income to the employee (Rev. Rul. 86-14).[93]

A self-employed individual may deduct from gross income 50 percent of the self-employment tax imposed for the tax year, other than the additional 0.9-percent Medicare tax on incomes over a certain threshold (¶ 2664) (Code Sec. 164(f)).[94]

924. Deduction for Federal and State Income Tax. Federal income taxes are not deductible in determining taxable income (Code Sec. 275).[95] However, they are deductible in determining the amount of a corporation's income subject to the accumulated earnings tax (¶ 251) and the personal holding company tax (¶ 275) (Reg. § § 1.535-2 and 1.545-2).[96] Corporations and partnerships may deduct their state income taxes as business expenses. State income taxes that are based on net business income may be deducted only by self-employed individuals as an itemized deduction on Schedule A of Form 1040. However, if the state income tax is based on gross business income, the tax may be deducted as a business expense (Temp. Reg. § 1.62-1T(d)).[97]

Charitable Contributions

927. Charitable Deduction Limits for Corporations. A corporation's deduction for charitable contributions is limited to 10 percent of its taxable income for the year, computed without regard to:

References are to Standard Federal Tax Reports; Tax Research Consultant; and Practical Tax Explanations.

[88] ¶ 8752.692—¶ 8752.694, ¶ 9502.31; BUSEXP: 21,506.05; § 9,415.05

[89] ¶ 8752.2959; BUSEXP: 21,506.05

[90] ¶ 9502.31; INDIV: 45,112.20, BUSEXP: 21,506.10; § 22,301

[91] ¶ 9503; INDIV: 45,112.35; § 9,365

[92] ¶ 9502.30; INDIV: 45,152.10, PAYROLL: 9,050; § 22,210.60

[93] ¶ 8636.49; INDIV: 45,112.35; § 9,005.20, § 22,210.45

[94] ¶ 9500; BUSEXP: 21,504; § 7,340

[95] ¶ 14,500; BUSEXP: 21,350; § 7,345

[96] ¶ 23,042, ¶ 23,252; CCORP: 18,252, CCORP: 36,254; § 26,905.05, § 27,001

[97] ¶ 6003; INDIV: 45,100; § 9,940.10

- the deduction for charitable contributions;
- the corporate deductions for dividends received and for dividends paid on certain preferred stock of public utilities;
- the limitation on the deduction for bond premium;
- any net operating loss or capital loss carryback to the tax year; and
- the deduction for domestic production activities. (Code Sec. 170(b)(2); Reg. § 1.170A-11).[98]

Corporate donors that qualify as farmers or ranchers may deduct certain qualified conservation contributions of real property interests (¶ 1063), up to the excess of the donor's taxable income (computed as described above) over all other allowable charitable contributions (which cannot exceed 10 percent of the donor's taxable income computed as described above) (Code Sec. 170(b)(2)(B), as amended by the Protecting Americans from Tax Hikes (PATH) Act of 2015 (P.L. 114-113)). For contributions made in tax years beginning after December 31, 2015, similar enhanced treatment also applies to Native Corporation donors for qualified conservation contributions of land that was conveyed under the Alaska Native Claims Settlement Act (Code Sec. 170(b)(2)(C), as added by P.L. 114-113).

Charitable contributions that exceed the 10-percent limit may be carried over to the corporation's five succeeding tax years, but deductions in those years are also subject to the maximum limitation (Code Sec. 170(d)(2)). Excess qualified conservation contributions by qualified corporate farmers and ranchers (and by Native Corporations in tax years beginning after 2015) are carried over to the 15 succeeding tax years (Code Sec. 170(b)(2)(B), as amended by P.L. 114-113).

Except for the carryover rule, a deduction is allowed only for a charitable contribution paid during the tax year. An accrual-basis corporation, however, may elect to treat as paid during the tax year all or a portion of a contribution that is actually paid within three-and-one-half months after the close of the tax year if it was authorized by the board of directors during the year (Code Sec. 170(a)(2)). For tax years beginning before January 1, 2016 (or before January 1, 2026 for C corporations whose tax year ends on June 30), the contribution must be made within two-and-one-half months after the close of the tax year.[99]

930. Charitable Contributions of Inventory or Scientific Property. Generally, the deduction for a charitable contribution of ordinary income property is the fair market value of that property less the amount that would have been ordinary income if the property had been sold at its fair market value on the date of the contribution (¶ 1062). There are exceptions to this rule in the case of certain contributions by corporations.

Inventory-Type Property. If a corporation, other than an S corporation, makes a gift of inventory, property held for sale to customers in the ordinary course of business, or depreciable or real property used in the trade or business, it may deduct its basis for the property, plus one-half of the property's unrealized appreciation. The claimed deduction, however, may not exceed twice the basis of the property (Code Sec. 170(e)(3)(B)).[100] Moreover, no deduction is allowed for any part of the appreciation that would be ordinary income resulting from recapture. To qualify, the gift must be made to a qualified public charity or a private operating foundation, and the donee's use of the property must be for the care of infants or the ill or needy.

Scientific Research Property. A corporation, other than an S corporation, a personal holding company, or a service organization, is entitled to the same deduction for a contribution of certain ordinary income property to an institution of higher education or to an exempt scientific research organization for research purposes as that for inventory-type property (Code Sec. 170(e)(4)).[101] To qualify as a research contribution:

References are to Standard Federal Tax Reports; Tax Research Consultant; and Practical Tax Explanations.

[98] ¶ 11,600, ¶ 11,672; CCORP: 9,350; § 7,575.05

[99] ¶ 11,600; CCORP: 9,352; § 7,575.10

[100] ¶ 11,600; CCORP: 9,354; § 7,575.25

[101] ¶ 11,600; CCORP: 9,354; § 7,575.25

- the contributed property must be tangible personal property that is inventory or held for the sale to customers;
- the contributed property must be scientific equipment or apparatus that was constructed or assembled by the donor;
- the contribution must be made within two years of construction or assembly;
- the original use of the property must be by the donee;
- substantially all of the donee's use of the property must be in the United States, for research or experimentation, or for research training, in physical or biological sciences;
- the donee may not transfer the property for money, other property, or services; and
- the donor must receive a written statement from the donee that the organization will comply with the use and transfer requirements.

930A. Charitable Contributions of Food. Corporate and noncorporate taxpayers are entitled to an enhanced deduction for charitable donations of food inventory from any trade or business (Code Sec. 170(e)(3)(C), as amended by the Protecting Americans from Tax Hikes (PATH) Act of 2015 (P.L. 114-113)).[102] Thus, the deduction rules for inventory-type property apply to such donations (¶ 930). The food inventory must consist of items fit for human consumption and be contributed to a qualified charity or private operating foundation for use in the care of the ill, the needy, or infants.

A noncorporate taxpayer's total deduction for food inventory donations during the tax year is limited to a maximum of 15 percent of the taxpayer's net income from all trades and businesses from which the donations are made during the tax year (10 percent for tax years beginning before January 1, 2016). Further, a C corporation's deduction for tax years beginning after December 31, 2015, is limited to 15 percent of the corporation's taxable income (¶ 927). Excess contributions are carried forward to the five succeeding tax years.

For tax years beginning after December 31, 2015, other special rules (1) coordinate the overall corporate deduction limitation with the food inventory contribution rules; (2) include a presumption concerning the basis of food inventory donated by certain businesses; and (3) include presumptions that may be used when valuing certain donated food inventory (Code Sec. 170(e)(3)(C)(iii), (iv), and (v), as added by P.L. 114-113).

931. Contribution Rules for Corporations. The rules concerning a deduction for the following charitable contributions are the same regardless of whether the contribution is made by a corporate or a noncorporate taxpayer:

- gifts of appreciated property (¶ 1062),
- use of property—partial interests (¶ 1063),
- reduction for interest (¶ 1065),
- gift of future interest in tangible personal property (¶ 1069),
- transfers in trust (¶ 1070),
- appraisals (¶ 1071), and
- denial of deduction (¶ 1068).

See ¶ 1070A for discussion of the reporting, recordkeeping, and substantiation rules for charitable contributions.

References are to Standard Federal Tax Reports; Tax Research Consultant; and Practical Tax Explanations.

[102] ¶ 11,600; INDIV: 51,152.15; § 7,525.20

Interest

937. Business Deduction for Interest. Interest expense or other borrowing costs incurred in a trade or business or in the production of rental or royalty income is generally deductible from gross income (Code Sec. 163).[103] However, interest paid on debt that is allocable to the production of certain property must be capitalized (¶ 993). Special rules also apply for prepaid interest (¶ 1055), investment interest paid by noncorporate taxpayers (¶ 1094), a debt instrument with original issue discount (¶ 1952), and a debt obligation that must be in registered form (¶ 1963).

Interest on debt incurred to purchase or carry commodity investments that are part of a straddle is not currently deductible. The interest must be added to the basis of the commodity. Hedging transactions, however, are exempted from this capitalization rule (¶ 1948 and ¶ 1949).

Earnings Stripping. A corporation cannot deduct excessive interest paid if the interest will not be taxed as income to the recipient (Code Sec. 163(j)).[104] A corporate partner's share of interest paid or accrued to or by the partnership is treated as paid or accrued by or to the corporation directly.

Corporate Indebtedness Incurred to Acquire Another Corporation's Stock. A corporation's annual deduction for interest on a debt incurred to acquire stock or two-thirds of the operating assets of another corporation is generally limited to $5 million (Code Sec. 279).[105]

937A. Interest on Income Tax Liability. Interest paid or accrued on income tax assessed on an individual's federal, state, or local income tax liability is *not* a business deduction even though the tax due is related to income from a trade or business (Temp. Reg. § 1.163-9T(b)(2)(i)(A)).[106] This rule also applies to an individual's partnership and S corporation activities. See ¶ 2723 and ¶ 2724 for interest allocations pursuant to compromise and partial payments. Penalties on deficiencies and underestimated tax cannot be deducted.

Employee's Expenses

941. Employee Business Expenses. The performance of services as an employee is considered to be a trade or business. Thus, employee business expenses are generally deductible. *Reimbursed* employee business expenses are deductible from gross income (Code Sec. 62(a)(2)(A)).[107] However, reimbursements that are paid under an accountable plan are excluded from the employee's gross income, and the employee may not deduct reimbursed costs as a business expense (¶ 942). *Unreimbursed* employee business expenses are deductible as miscellaneous itemized deductions, subject to the two-percent-of-adjusted-gross-income (AGI) limitation (¶ 1079) and the 50-percent limit for meal and entertainment expenses (80 percent for employees subject to the Department of Transportation's hours of service limitations) (¶ 916), if applicable. Special rules apply to qualified performing artists (¶ 941A), statutory employees (¶ 941B), impairment-related work expenses (¶ 1084), fee-based government employees (¶ 941D), schoolteachers (¶ 941C), and members of the National Guard or Armed Forces Reserves (¶ 941E). Jury duty pay surrendered to an employer in exchange for regular salary is deductible from the employee's gross income (¶ 1010).

941A. Performing Artist. A qualified performing artist may deduct business expenses in arriving at adjusted gross income on Form 2106 or Form 2106-EZ. Generally, to qualify for this deduction an individual must:

References are to Standard Federal Tax Reports; Tax Research Consultant; and Practical Tax Explanations.

[103] ¶ 9102; BUSEXP: 21,000; § 9,915

[104] ¶ 9102; BUSEXP: 21,210; § 26,201

[105] ¶ 14,700; CCORP: 9,400

[106] ¶ 9400; INDIV: 48,350; § 7,345

[107] ¶ 6002; INDIV: 36,050; § 5,310

- render services in the performing arts during the tax year for at least two employers;
- have total business deductions attributable to the performance of such services that exceed 10 percent of the income received from such services; and
- have adjusted gross income of $16,000 or less (Code Sec. 62(b)).[108]

941B. Statutory Employees. Statutory employees may deduct their allowable business expenses from gross income (Code Sec. 3121(d); Rev. Rul. 90-93).[109] A statutory employee includes:

- a full-time traveling or city salesperson who solicits orders from wholesalers, restaurants, or similar establishments on behalf of a principal where the merchandise sold is for resale (e.g., food sold to a restaurant) or for supplies used in the buyer's business;
- a full-time life insurance agent whose principal business activity is selling life insurance and/or annuity contracts for one life insurance company;
- an agent-driver or commission-driver engaged in distributing meat, vegetables, bakery goods, beverages (other than milk), or laundry or dry cleaning services; and
- a home worker performing work on material or goods furnished by the employer.

An employer should indicate on the worker's Form W-2 whether the worker is classified as a statutory employee. Statutory employees report their wages, income, and allowable expenses on Schedule C or C-EZ of Form 1040. Statutory employees are not liable for self-employment tax because their employers must treat them as employees for FICA and FUTA purposes (except for full-time life insurance agents and home workers, who are not considered employees for FUTA purposes).

941C. School Teachers. An inflation-adjusted amount of classroom expenses paid or incurred by an eligible educator is deductible as an above-the-line adjustment to gross income (¶ 1011B) (Code Sec. 62(a)(2)(D), as amended by the Protecting Americans from Tax Hikes (PATH) Act of 2015 (P.L. 114-113)). The maximum deduction for expenses incurred in 2016 is $250 ($250 for 2017) (Rev. Proc. 2016-14; Rev. Proc. 2016-55).[110]

941D. Fee-Based Government Officials. Expenses paid or incurred with respect to services performed by an official as an employee of a state or local government are deductible in computing adjusted gross income (Code Sec. 62(a)(2)(C)).[111] The employee must be compensated in whole or in part on a fee basis.

941E. National Guard and Reserve Members. Members of the National Guard and the U.S. Armed Forces Reserves may claim an above-the-line deduction for travel expenses paid or incurred in connection with service more than 100 miles away from home (Code Secs. 62(a)(2)(E) and 162(p)).[112] This type of travel is travel away from home in the pursuit of a trade or business, so it is subject to the normal business deduction rules (such as the 50-percent reduction in deductible meal costs), but it is available even if the taxpayer is not considered to be acting as an employee. The amount of deductible expenses is limited to the federal per diem rate for the locality of the meeting or training session.

942. Reimbursed and Unreimbursed Employee Business Expenses. The tax treatment of an employee's reimbursed business expenses depends on whether the employer's reimbursement or expense allowance arrangement is an accountable or nonaccountable plan (¶ 952A) (Code Sec. 62; Reg. § 1.62-2).[113] A reimbursement under an *accountable* plan is not reported as income on the employee's Form W-2, the employee cannot deduct the reimbursed expense, and the 50-percent limit on deduc-

References are to Standard Federal Tax Reports; Tax Research Consultant; and Practical Tax Explanations.

[108] ¶ 6002; INDIV: 36,058; § 5,315

[109] ¶ 8524.2547; INDIV: 63,154; § 5,305

[110] ¶ 6002; INDIV: 36,364; § 5,325

[111] ¶ 6002; INDIV: 36,050; § 5,320

[112] ¶ 6002, ¶ 8500; FILEIND: 9,054.25; § 5,330

[113] ¶ 6002, ¶ 6004; INDIV: 36,054; § 10,120.05

tions for meals and entertainment applies to the employer (¶ 916). If the employee's deductible business expenses exceed the amounts paid by the accountable plan, and these expenses are adequately substantiated (¶ 943), then the excess expenses are deductible as miscellaneous itemized deductions, subject to the two-percent-of-adjusted-gross-income (AGI) limitation (¶ 1079) and the 50-percent limit for meals and entertainment. A reimbursement under a *nonaccountable* plan is included in the employee's income and, along with unreimbursed expenses, can be deducted by the employee as miscellaneous itemized deductions. The deductible expenses must be adequately substantiated, and the deduction is subject to the two-percent-of-AGI floor, and the 50-percent limit for meals and entertainment. The employee reports the expenses on Form 2106 or Form 2106-EZ.

943. Substantiation for Employees' Returns. Business expenses that exceed the reimbursements received under an accountable plan (¶ 952A), that are reimbursed under a nonaccountable plan, or that are not reimbursed at all may be deducted by an employee (¶ 942). As with any other deductible expense, the employee must adequately substantiate business expenses in order to deduct them.

More specific substantiation requirements apply with respect to the following expenses: expenses with respect to travel away from home (including meals and lodging), entertainment expenses, business gifts, and expenses in connection with the use of "listed property" (¶ 1211). These expenses must generally be substantiated by adequate records or other sufficient evidence corroborating the taxpayer's own statement (Code Sec. 274(d); Temp. Reg. § 1.274-5T).[114] The expenses must be substantiated as to amount, time, place, and business purpose. For entertainment and gift expenses, the business relationship of the person being entertained or receiving the gift must also be substantiated.

Substantiation by Adequate Records. A contemporaneous log is not required, but a record of the elements of the expense or the business use of the listed property made at or near the time of the expenditure or use, supported by sufficient documentary evidence, has a high degree of credibility. Adequate accounting generally requires the submission of an account book, expense diary or log, or similar record maintained by the employee that records expenses at or near the time they are incurred. Documentary evidence, such as receipts or paid bills, is not generally required for expenses that are less than $75. Documentary evidence is required, however, for all lodging expenses (Reg. § 1.274-5(c)(2)(iii)).[115] The employee should also maintain a record of any amounts charged to the employer.

Substantiation of Meal and Incidental Expenses. An employee may substantiate deductible meal and/or incidental expenses (M&IE) either by retaining evidence of the actual expenses or by use of the standard meal allowance (¶ 954B). The amount of the standard meal allowance varies by location, and for some locations, by the time of year. An individual using the standard meal allowance must still keep records, such as a daily planner or log, to prove the time, place, and business purpose of the expenses. There is no standard lodging amount similar to the standard meal allowance. Employees must be able to substantiate the actual cost of their lodging in order to deduct it.

Transportation and Car Expenses

945. Local Transportation Expenses. A taxpayer's local transportation costs (including self-employed persons and statutory employees) for travel between two specific business locations, whether in the same or different businesses, are deductible from gross income as an ordinary and necessary business expense (Reg. § 1.162-1(a)).[116] The manner of the deduction generally depends on whether the employee is reimbursed under an accountable plan (¶ 942). Local transportation expenses are generally those incurred for the business use of a car. However, they also include the cost of travel by rail, bus, or taxi.

References are to Standard Federal Tax Reports; Tax Research Consultant; and Practical Tax Explanations.

[114] ¶ 14,402, ¶ 14,410; BUSEXP: 24,800; § 10,105.05, § 10,110.05

[115] ¶ 14,408F; BUSEXP: 24,806.15; § 10,105.15

[116] ¶ 8501; BUSEXP: 24,450; § 8,005

Commuting Expenses. Commuting expenses between a taxpayer's residence and a business location within the area of the taxpayer's tax home generally are not deductible (Reg. § § 1.162-2(e) and 1.262-1(b)(5)).[117] However, a deduction is allowed for expenses incurred in excess of ordinary commuting expenses for transporting job-related tools and materials (*D. Fausner*, SCt, 73-2 USTC ¶ 9515).[118] An individual who works at two or more different places in a day may deduct the costs of getting from one place to the other (Rev. Rul. 55-109, modified by Rev. Rul. 90-23).[119]

There is an exception to the general rule that commuting expenses are not deductible. If a taxpayer has at least one regular place of business away from home, then daily transportation expenses for commuting between the taxpayer's residence and a temporary work location in the same trade or business can be deducted (¶ 951) (Rev. Rul. 99-7).[120] For this purpose, a temporary work location is defined using a one-year standard. If employment at a work location is realistically expected to last (and does in fact last) for one year or less, the employment is temporary, absent facts and circumstances to the contrary. Employment at a work location is not temporary if it is realistically expected to last for more than one year, or if there is no realistic expectation that it will last for one year or less, regardless of whether it in fact lasts for more than one year. A taxpayer may at first realistically expect that employment at a work location will last one year or less, but, at a later date, realistically expect that the work will last for more than one year. In this situation, the employment is treated as temporary, unless facts and circumstances indicate otherwise, until the date that the taxpayer's realistic expectation changes. After that date, the employment is treated as not temporary.

Travel from a Home Office. An individual who uses his or her home as a principal place of business (¶ 961) may deduct transportation expenses between the home and another work location in the same trade or business (Rev. Rul. 99-7).[121] This rule applies regardless of whether the work location is temporary or regular and regardless of the distance.

946. Car Expense. Expenses for gasoline, oil, tires, repairs, insurance, depreciation, parking fees and tolls, licenses, and garage rent incurred for cars used in a trade or business are deductible (¶ 947) to the extent the expenses are attributable to business (Code Sec. 162; Reg. § 1.162-1).[122] Generally, an employee's unreimbursed expenses can be deducted only as a miscellaneous itemized deduction subject to the two-percent-of-adjusted-gross-income (AGI) floor (¶ 941). See ¶ 1208—¶ 1215 concerning the expensing election and depreciation of a car.

947. Substantiation of Car Expenses. A taxpayer can substantiate car expenses by keeping an exact record of the amount paid for gasoline, insurance, and other costs. In lieu of calculating the operating and fixed costs allocable to business purposes, however, taxpayers may use the standard mileage rate method as a simplified way to compute deductions for car expenses (Code Sec. 274(d); Temp. Reg. § 1.274-5T).[123]

Standard Mileage Rate. Under the standard mileage method, the taxpayer determines the allowable deduction by multiplying all the business miles driven during the year by the standard mileage rate. The business portion of parking fees and tolls may be deducted in addition to the standard mileage rate. The standard mileage rate is 54 cents per mile in 2016 (Rev. Proc. 2010-51; Notice 2016-1).[124]

The standard mileage rate method may be used by businesses, self-employed individuals, or employees in computing the deductible costs of operating automobiles they own or lease for business purposes. The business standard mileage rate may not be used to compute the deductible expenses of five or more automobiles owned or leased by a taxpayer and used simultaneously (i.e., a fleet operation). Using the standard

References are to Standard Federal Tax Reports; Tax Research Consultant; and Practical Tax Explanations.

[117] ¶ 8527, ¶ 13,601; BUSEXP: 24,458; § 8,010.05

[118] ¶ 8590.25; BUSEXP: 24,460; § 8,010.05

[119] ¶ 8570.175; BUSEXP: 24,454; § 8,010.05

[120] ¶ 8570.143; BUSEXP: 24,458; § 8,010.15

[121] ¶ 8570.143; BUSEXP: 24,456; § 8,010.20

[122] ¶ 8500, ¶ 8501; BUSEXP: 24,500; § 9,910

[123] ¶ 14,402, ¶ 14,410; BUSEXP: 24,502; § 8,065

[124] ¶ 8590.55; BUSEXP: 24,502; § 8,065

mileage rate in the first year of business use is considered an election to exclude the car from MACRS depreciation (¶ 1236). In determining the owner's adjusted basis in the vehicle, depreciation is considered to have been allowed at the rate of 24 cents per mile for 2016 (Rev. Proc. 2010-51; Notice 2016-1).[125]

Fixed and Variable Rate (FAVR) Method. The fixed and variable rate allowance (FAVR) also can be used to substantiate automobile expenses. An employer's FAVR allowance includes a combination of payments such as a cents-per-mile rate to cover the employee's variable operating costs (gas, oil, tires, etc.) plus a flat amount to cover the employee's fixed costs (depreciation or lease payments, insurance, etc.). The maximum standard automobile cost for purposes of the FAVR allowance for 2016 is $28,000 ($31,000 for trucks and vans) (Rev. Proc. 2010-51; Notice 2016-1).[126] At least five employees must be covered by a FAVR arrangement at all times during the calendar year, and at no time can the majority of covered employees be management employees. Additional requirements must also be met.

Postal workers. Rural mail carriers receive a qualified reimbursement for expenses incurred for the use of their vehicles for collecting and delivering mail in a rural route. They are allowed a miscellaneous itemized deduction, subject to the two-percent-of-adjusted-gross-income limitation, for their automobile expenses that exceed their qualified reimbursement (Code Sec. 162(o)).[127] Qualified reimbursements in excess of actual automobile expenses continue to be excluded from gross income (H.R. Conf. Rep. No. 108-755).

948. Interest on Car Loans. Interest paid by an employee on a car loan is nondeductible personal interest (¶ 1043). A self-employed taxpayer may claim the interest paid on the business portion of a car as a business expense. The nonbusiness portion is nondeductible personal interest (Code Sec. 163(a)).[128]

Traveling Expenses Away from Home

949. Traveling Expenses Generally. A taxpayer may deduct ordinary and necessary traveling expenses incurred while away from home in the conduct of a trade or business (Code Sec. 162(a)(2); Reg. § 1.162-2).[129] Individuals are away from home if it is reasonable for them to need to sleep or rest while their duties require them to be away from the general area of their tax homes for a period substantially longer than an ordinary workday. In some cases, travel expenses may be deductible even though the taxpayer is away from home for less than 24 hours.

Local Lodging. Expenses paid or incurred for lodging when not traveling away from home (i.e. local lodging) are generally nondeductible personal expenses (¶ 1003). However, local lodging expenses may be deductible as ordinary and necessary expenses of a taxpayer's trade or business, including the trade or business of being an employee, depending on the facts and circumstances (Reg. § 1.162-32).[130] Under a safe harbor for certain local lodging at business meetings and conferences, an individual's local lodging expenses are ordinary and necessary business expenses if:

(1) the lodging is necessary for the individual to participate fully in or be available for a bona fide business meeting, conference, training activity, or other business function;

(2) the lodging is for a period that does not exceed five calendar days and does not recur more than once per calendar quarter;

(3) if the individual is an employee, the employer requires the employee to remain at the meeting or function overnight; and

References are to Standard Federal Tax Reports; Tax Research Consultant; and Practical Tax Explanations.

[125] ¶ 14,417.50; BUSEXP: 24,506.05; § 10,125.15

[126] ¶ 8590.55; BUSEXP: 24,912.106; § 10,125.20

[127] ¶ 8500; BUSEXP: 24,506.15; § 8,050

[128] ¶ 9102; INDIV: 48,350; § 8,205

[129] ¶ 8500, ¶ 8527; BUSEXP: 24,050; § 9,510.05

[130] ¶ 9051K; BUSEXP: 24,052; § 9,505

(4) the lodging is not lavish or extravagant under the circumstances and does not provide any significant element of personal pleasure, recreation, or benefit.

950. Tax Home Defined. A individual's tax home for purposes of deducting travel expenses (¶ 949) is : (1) the taxpayer's regular or principal (if there is more than one regular) place of business, or (2) if there is no regular or principal place of business because of the nature of the work, the taxpayer's regular place of abode in a real and substantial sense (Rev. Rul. 75-432).[131] A taxpayer who does not fall within either category is an itinerant or someone who has a home wherever he or she happens to be working. Thus, the taxpayer is never away from home for purposes of deducting traveling expenses.

For a taxpayer with multiple areas of business activity or places of regular employment, the principal place of business is the tax home. In determining the principal place of an individual's business, the following factors are considered:

(1) the time spent on business activity in each area;

(2) the amount of business activity in each area; and

(3) the amount of the resulting financial return in each area (Rev. Rul. 54-147; *F. Markey*, CA-6, 74-1 USTC ¶ 9192).

Business travel expenses incurred while away from the principal place of business are deductible.[132]

The tax home of a member of the U.S. Congress is the member's residence in the state or district that the member represents. However, deduction for meals and lodging while in Washington, D.C., are limited to $3,000 per year, after applying the two-percent-of-adjusted-gross-income (AGI) floor for miscellaneous itemized deductions (Code Sec. 162(a)).[133]

A member of the U.S. Armed Forces is not away from home while at the individual's permanent duty station (*H.A. Stidger*, SCt, 67-1 USTC ¶ 9309).[134] However, members of the National Guard and Reserves can deduct qualifying travel expenses as an above-the-line deduction when attending meetings or training sessions (¶ 941E).

951. Temporary v. Indefinite Test. In determining when an individual is away from home for purposes of deducting travel expenses (¶ 949), the nature of the stay and the length of time away from the individual's principal place of business are of prime importance. If the assignment is temporary in nature, the taxpayer is considered away from home and a travel expense deduction is allowed. If the assignment is for an indefinite period of time, the location of the assignment becomes the individual's new tax home, and the individual may not deduct traveling expenses while there. When an individual works away from home at a single location for more than one year, the employment is indefinite, and related travel expenses are not deductible (Code Sec. 162(a); Rev. Rul. 93-86; Rev. Rul. 99-7).[135] Employment expected to last more than one year is classified as indefinite, regardless of whether the work actually exceeds a year. Employment that is expected to, and does in fact, last for one year or less is temporary.

The one-year rule does not apply to federal employees certified by the Attorney General as traveling on behalf of the United States in temporary duty status to investigate or prosecute, or to provide support services for the investigation or prosecution of, a federal crime. Such employees may deduct their travel expenses even if their assignment is expected to last for more than one year (Code Sec. 162(a)).

952. Deductible Travel Expenses. The costs of the following items are ordinarily deductible, if paid or incurred while a business owner or employee is traveling away from home on business (¶ 949): meals and lodging; transportation, including a reasona-

References are to Standard Federal Tax Reports; Tax Research Consultant; and Practical Tax Explanations.

[131] ¶ 8550.269; BUSEXP: 24,100; § 9,510.05

[132] ¶ 8570.175; BUSEXP: 24,104; § 9,510.15

[133] ¶ 8500; BUSEXP: 24,120

[134] ¶ 8570.1236; BUSEXP: 24,120.20; § 9,505

[135] ¶ 8500, ¶ 8570.1327, ¶ 8570.143; BUSEXP: 24,110; § 9,510.25

ble amount for baggage; necessary samples and display materials; hotel rooms, sample rooms, telephone and fax services, and public stenographers; and the costs, including depreciation (¶ 1211), of maintaining and operating a car for business purposes (Reg. § 1.162-2).[136]

No deduction is allowed for the travel expenses of a spouse, dependent, or other individual who accompanies the taxpayer or employee on a business trip unless the companion is an employee of the person who is paying or reimbursing the expenses, the companion's travel serves a bona fide business purpose, and the companion's expenses are otherwise deductible (Code Sec. 274(m)(3)).[137]

A taxpayer may deduct traveling expenses between the principal place of business and place of business at a temporary or minor post of duty. When the taxpayer's family lives at the temporary or minor post, however, the taxpayer's deduction for meals and lodging is limited to the portion of those expenses that is allocable to the taxpayer's presence there in the actual performance of the taxpayer's duties (Rev. Rul. 55-604).[138]

The deduction for the cost of meals and lodging while away from home on business is limited to amounts that are not lavish or extravagant under the circumstances (Code Sec. 162(a)(2)).[139] The deduction for meals is limited to 50 percent of the total expenses (¶ 916).

952A. Accountable v. Nonaccountable Plans. The arrangement under which an employer reimburses business expenses incurred by employees or provides advances to cover such expenses is either an accountable plan or a nonaccountable plan. Amounts paid under an accountable plan are deductible by the employer and not reported as income to the employee. Amounts paid under a nonaccountable plan are deductible by the employer as compensation reportable on the employee's Form W-2 and subject to withholding requirements. Withholding rules relating to employee expense reimbursements are explained at ¶ 2607 and ¶ 2608. The tax treatment of an employee's business expenses and reimbursements under each type of plan is explained at ¶ 942.

An accountable plan must satisfy the following three conditions:

(1) the expenses covered under the plan must have a business connection;

(2) the plan must require employees to substantiate the covered expenses; and

(3) the plan must require employees who receive advances to return any amounts in excess of their substantiated expenses (Reg. § 1.62-2(c)).[140]

If a plan satisfies these requirements, but an employee fails to return an excess advance to the employer within a reasonable period, only the amount of the substantiated expenses is treated as paid under an accountable plan. The retained excess is treated as paid under a nonaccountable plan. If a plan does not satisfy these requirements, an employee cannot force the employer to treat it as an accountable plan by substantiating the expenses and returning the excess.

Business Connection. The business connection requirement is satisfied if the expenses are deductible business expenses of the employer, paid or incurred in connection with the performance of services as an employee. If a plan also covers bona fide expenses that are related to the employer's business but not deductible, such as travel that is not away from home, the plan is treated as two separate arrangements, one accountable, the other nonaccountable (Reg. § 1.62-2(d)).[141]

Substantiation. The substantiation required by an accountable plan must be sufficient to substantiate the expense under the general rules for substantiating business expense deductions, which vary depending on the type of expense (Reg. § 1.62-2(e)).[142]

References are to Standard Federal Tax Reports; Tax Research Consultant; and Practical Tax Explanations.

[136] ¶ 8527; BUSEXP: 24,052; § 9,501

[137] ¶ 14,402; BUSEXP: 24,200; § 9,530

[138] ¶ 8570.175; BUSEXP: 24,104; § 9,505

[139] ¶ 8500; BUSEXP: 24,556; § 9,635

[140] ¶ 6004; INDIV: 36,056; § 10,120.10

[141] ¶ 6004; INDIV: 36,056.05; § 10,120.10

[142] ¶ 6004; INDIV: 36,056.10; § 10,120.10

If the expense is for travel, meals, lodging, entertainment, gifts, or attributable to the use of listed property (¶ 1211), the substantiation requirement is satisfied if enough information is submitted to the employer to satisfy substantiation requirements (¶ 953), including travel and car expenses deemed substantiated.

Other expenses, such as expenses for printing a report, are substantiated if enough information is submitted to the employer to enable the employer to identify the specific nature of each expense and to conclude that the expense was attributable to the employer's business activities. The elements of each expense should be substantiated, including the amount, place, time or date, and business purpose.

Deemed Substantiation of Employee's Reimbursed Expenses. An employee's expenses are deemed to be substantiated, for purposes of the accountable plan requirements, if the employee provides an adequate accounting of the expenses to the employer in the form of adequate records (Reg. § 1.274-5(f)(4)).[143] The adequate accounting requirement can be satisfied as to the amount of car expenses and lodging and/or meals and incidental expenses by using the per diem allowances discussed at ¶ 947 and ¶ 954–¶ 954B. An employee or self-employed worker who deducts unreimbursed lodging expenses on his or her own return must have evidence of the actual costs.

Return of Excess Advances. The return-of-excess-advances requirement is satisfied if employees are required to return amounts received in excess of the expenses that are substantiated or deemed substantiated within a reasonable period of time (Reg. § 1.62-2(f)).[144] Advances must be provided within a reasonable period before the covered expenses are expected to be paid or incurred and must be reasonably calculated not to exceed the anticipated expenses. If an employee fails to return the excess within a reasonable period of time, only amounts paid that are not in excess of the amounts substantiated are treated as paid under an accountable plan. Excess amounts retained are treated as paid under a nonaccountable plan and must be included in the employee's income. An accountable plan that reimburses expenses under an IRS-approved mileage (¶ 947) or per diem allowance (¶ 954–¶ 954B) must require the return of the portion that relates to days or miles of travel not substantiated.

Reasonable Period of Time. The provision of advances, the substantiation of expenses, and the return of excess advances must each take place within a reasonable period of time. A reasonable period depends on facts and circumstances, but there are two safe harbor methods: the fixed date method and the periodic statement method (Reg. § 1.62-2(g)).[145] Under the fixed date method, the following are treated as occurring within a reasonable period of time:

(1) advance payments made within 30 days of when an expense is paid or incurred;

(2) substantiation provided within 60 days after expenses are paid or incurred; or

(3) return of excess amounts within 120 days after expenses are paid or incurred.

The periodic statement method is a safe harbor for determining reasonable time substantiation and the return of excess advances. Under this method, the employer must:

(1) give each employee periodic statements (no less than quarterly) that set forth the amounts paid under the reimbursement arrangement in excess of the substantiated amount, and

(2) request that the employee either substantiate or return the excess amounts within 120 days of the statement date. An expense substantiated or amount returned within that period satisfies the reasonable period requirement.

References are to Standard Federal Tax Reports; Tax Research Consultant; and Practical Tax Explanations.

[143] ¶ 14,408F; BUSEXP: 24,800; § 10,115.10

[144] ¶ 6004; INDIV: 36,056.15; § 10,120.10

[145] ¶ 6004; INDIV: 36,056.10; § 10,120.15

953. Substantiation Requirements for Business Expenses. If a return is audited, the taxpayer must be able to prove that any deducted business expense was actually paid or incurred. Small expenses and those that are clearly related to the business may be substantiated by the taxpayer's statement or by keeping receipts, sales slips, invoices, cancelled checks, or other evidence of payments. The following expenses, which are particularly susceptible to abuse, must generally be substantiated by adequate records or sufficient evidence corroborating the taxpayer's own statement: expenses with respect to travel away from home (including meals and lodging), entertainment expenses, business gifts, and expenses in connection with the use of listed property such as cars and computers (¶ 1211) (Code Sec. 274(d); Temp. Reg. § 1.274-5T).[146] The expenses must be substantiated as to amount, time, place, and business purpose. For entertainment and gift expenses, the business relationship of the person being entertained or receiving the gift must also be substantiated. An employer's reimbursement arrangement must require employees to satisfy these substantiation requirements in order to be an accountable plan (¶ 952A).

Substantiation by Adequate Records. A contemporaneous log is not required, but a record of the elements of the expense or the business use of the listed property made at or near the time of the expenditure or use, supported by sufficient documentary evidence, has a high degree of credibility. Adequate accounting generally requires the submission of an account book, expense diary or log, or similar record maintained by the employee and recorded at or near the time the expense is incurred. Documentary evidence, such as receipts or paid bills, is not generally required for expenses that are less than $75. However, documentary evidence is required for all lodging expenses (Reg. § 1.274-5(c)(2)(iii)).[147] The employee should also maintain a record of any amounts charged to the employer.

The *Cohan* rule, which allows the courts to estimate the amount of a taxpayer's business expenses when adequate records do not exist, does not apply to expenses covered by the substantiation rules of Code Sec. 274(d) (Temp. Reg. § 1.274-5T(a)(1)).[148] However, if a taxpayer establishes that the records were lost due to circumstances beyond the taxpayer's control, such as destruction by fire or flood, then the taxpayer has a right to substantiate claimed deductions by a reasonable construction of the expenditures or use (Temp. Reg. § 1.274-5T(c)(5)).[149]

Employees of the executive and judicial branches and certain employees of the legislative branch of the federal government may substantiate their requests for reimbursement of ordinary and necessary business expenses with an account book or expense log instead of submitting documentary evidence (e.g., receipts or bills) (Rev. Proc. 97-45).[150]

954. Per Diem Methods for Substantiating Employers' Meals and Lodging Expenses. A taxpayer must substantiate the amount, time, place, and business purpose of expenses paid or incurred in traveling away from home (¶ 953). Although the taxpayer has the option of keeping the actual records of travel expenses, the IRS has provided per diem allowances under which the amount of away-from-home meals and incidental expenses (M&IE) may be deemed to be substantiated. These per diem allowances eliminate the need for substantiating actual costs (Rev. Proc. 2011-47).[151] A taxpayer who uses per diem allowances to calculate the deductible amount must still substantiate the time, place, and business purpose of the travel by adequate records or other evidence.

Although most frequently used in the employer-employee relationship, per diem allowances may be used in arrangements between any payor and payee, such as between independent contractors and those contracting with them. However, employees related to the payor under the related party rules of Code Sec. 267(b) (using a 10-percent common ownership standard (¶ 1717)) cannot use per diem substantiation methods.

References are to Standard Federal Tax Reports; Tax Research Consultant; and Practical Tax Explanations.

[146] ¶ 14,402, ¶ 14,410; BUSEXP: 24,800; § 10,105

[147] ¶ 14,408F; BUSEXP: 24,806.15; § 10,105.15

[148] ¶ 14,410; BUSEXP: 24,802; § 10,105.05

[149] ¶ 14,410; BUSEXP: 24,806; § 10,105.25

[150] ¶ 14,417.38; BUSEXP: 24,906.106; § 10,105.05

[151] ¶ 14,417.421; BUSEXP: 24,808; § 10,125.10

Employees. The per diem method can be used to substantiate an employee's reimbursed expenses (for purposes of the employer's return) only if the reimbursement arrangement is an accountable plan (¶ 952A) and the allowance:

(1) is paid with respect to ordinary and necessary expenses incurred or that the employer reasonably expects to be incurred by an employee for lodging and/or M&IE while traveling away from home in connection with the performance of services as an employee;

(2) is reasonably calculated not to exceed the amount of the expense or the anticipated expenses; and

(3) is paid at the applicable federal per diem rate, a flat rate, or stated schedule.

Types of Per Diem Allowances. There are three types of per diem allowances:

(1) lodging plus M&IE, which provides a per diem allowance to cover lodging as well as meals and incidental expenses (¶ 954A);

(2) M&IE only, which provides a per diem allowance for meals and incidental expenses only (¶ 954B); and

(3) incidental expenses only, to be used when no meal or lodging expenses are incurred (¶ 954B) (Rev. Proc. 2011-47).[152]

"Incidental expenses" has the same meaning as in the Federal Travel Regulations (41 C.F.R. 300-3.1). Under those regulations, incidental expenses include *only* fees and tips given to porters, baggage carriers, hotel staff, and staff on ships. Transportation between places of lodging or business and places where meals are taken, and the mailing cost of filing travel vouchers and paying employer-sponsored charge card billings, are not incidental expenses. Taxpayers using per diem rates may separately deduct or be reimbursed for such transportation and mailing expenses (Notice 2015-63).[153]

Expenses of laundry, lodging taxes, and telephone calls are not incidental expenses (IRS Pub. 463). Lodging taxes for travel within the continental United States and for nonforeign travel outside the continental United States are reimbursable miscellaneous expenses. However, lodging taxes have not been removed from the foreign per diem rates set by the U.S. State Department (41 C.F.R. 301-11.27).

Allowances Exceeding Federal Rates. If expenses are substantiated using a per diem amount, regardless of whether it covers lodging plus M&IE or only M&IE, any reimbursement that exceeds the relevant federal per diem rates for that type of allowance must be included in the employee's (or independent contractor's) gross income. The excess portion is treated as paid under a nonaccountable plan; thus, it must be reported on the employee's Form W-2 and is subject to withholding (Reg. § 1.62-2(h)(2)(i)(B)(1)).[154]

954A. Lodging Plus Meals and Incidental Expenses Per Diem. Under the lodging plus meals and incidental expenses (M&IE) per diem method (¶ 954), the amount of an employee's (or other payee's) reimbursed expenses that is deemed substantiated (for purposes of the employer's return) is equal to the lesser of the employer's per diem allowance or the federal per diem amount for the locality of travel for the period in which the employee is away from home (Rev. Proc. 2011-47).[155] The employer is not required to produce lodging receipts if per diem allowances are used to substantiate such expenses. The locality of travel is the place where the employee stops for sleep or rest. Employees and self-employed individuals may determine their allowable deductions for

References are to Standard Federal Tax Reports; Tax Research Consultant; and Practical Tax Explanations.

[152] ¶ 14,417.421; BUSEXP: 24,912.05; § 10,125.10

[153] ¶ 14,417.421; BUSEXP: 24,912.05; § 10,125.10

[154] ¶ 6004; BUSEXP: 24,904; § 10,125.10

[155] ¶ 14,417.421; BUSEXP: 24,912.05; § 10,125.10

unreimbursed M&IE while away from home by using the applicable federal M&IE rate (¶ 954B). However, unreimbursed lodging costs must be substantiated by required records, e.g., hotel receipts.

Per Diem Rates. The federal per diem rate for lodging plus M&IE depends upon the locality of travel. For various geographic areas within the continental United States (the 48 contiguous states plus the District of Columbia) (CONUS), the federal per diem rate for a given locality is equal to the sum of a maximum lodging amount and the M&IE rate for that locality. There are also federal per diem rates for nonforeign localities outside of the continental United States (OCONUS), such as Alaska, Hawaii, Puerto Rico, and U.S. possessions. Rates are also established for foreign travel (foreign OCONUS).

Rates for CONUS, OCONUS, and foreign travel are published under the Federal Travel Regulations for government travel and are updated periodically (Rev. Proc. 2011-47).[156] The travel rates are issued to coincide with the government's fiscal year of October to September.

High-Low Method. Instead of using the maximum per diem rates from the CONUS table, taxpayers can compute per diem allowances for travel within the continental United States under the high-low method, which is a simplified method for determining a lodging plus M&IE per diem. This method divides all CONUS localities into two categories: low-cost or high-cost localities (Rev. Proc. 2011-47).[157]

For travel on or after October 1, 2016, through September 30, 2017, the following per diem rates for lodging expenses and M&IE were set by the IRS for high-cost and low-cost localities (Notice 2016-58):

	Lodging expense rate	*M&IE rate*	*Maximum per diem rate*
High-cost locality	$214	$68	$282
Low-cost locality	132	57	189

For travel on or after October 1, 2015, through September 30, 2016, the following per diem rates for lodging expenses and M&IE were set by the IRS for high-cost and low-cost localities (Notice 2015-63):

	Lodging expense rate	*M&IE rate*	*Maximum per diem rate*
High-cost locality	$207	$68	$275
Low-cost locality	128	57	185

Some areas are treated as high-cost during certain periods of the year (e.g., peak tourist season) and as low-cost during other periods. Thus, employers who use the high-low method must determine whether the employee traveled in a high-cost area and if the area was classified as high-cost during the actual period of travel.

If the high-low method is used for an employee, then the payor may not use the actual federal maximum per diem rates for that employee during the calendar year for travel within the continental United States. However, for travel outside the continental United States (OCONUS), the employer may use the applicable federal OCONUS rates, the M&IE-only rate, or reimbursement of actual expenses.

Proration of M&IE Allowance. If an individual is traveling away from home for only a portion of the day, there are two alternative methods that may be used to prorate the per diem rate or the M&IE rate. Under the first method, 75 percent of the M&IE rate (or the M&IE portion of the per diem rate) is allowed for each partial day during which an employee or self-employed individual is traveling on business. Under the second method, referred to as the reasonable business practice method, the M&IE rate may be prorated using any method that is consistently applied and in accordance with reasonable business practice. For example, if an employee travels from 9 a.m. one day until 5 p.m. the next day, a proration method that gives an amount equal to two times the M&IE rate is treated as in accordance with reasonable business practice (Rev. Proc. 2011-47).[158]

References are to Standard Federal Tax Reports; Tax Research Consultant; and Practical Tax Explanations.

[156] ¶ 14,417.421; BUSEXP: 24,912; § 660, § 670, § 680, § 690

[157] ¶ 14,417.421; BUSEXP: 24,912.05; § 10,125.10

[158] ¶ 14,417.421; BUSEXP: 24,808; § 10,125.10

Transition Rules. Taxpayers may continue to use the per diem rates effective prior to October 1, 2016, for the remainder of 2016, or they may begin to use the new per diem rates for reimbursement for travel, as long as they use either the pre-October 1 rates or the updated rates for the October 1 through December 31 period consistently. Taxpayers who used the per diem method or the high-low substantiation method to reimburse travel expenses during the first nine months of calendar-year 2016 must continue to use that method for the remainder of calendar-year 2016. However, taxpayers who use the high-low method during the first nine months of calendar-year 2016 may either continue to use the rates and localities in effect before October 1, 2016, or use the updated rates and localities in effect for travel on and after October 1, 2016, as long as they use the same rates and localities consistently for all employees reimbursed under the high-low method.

954B. Meals-and-Incidental-Expense-Only Per Diem Allowances. A meals-and-incidental-expenses-only per diem allowance may be used to substantiate an employee's or other payee's meal and incidental expenses (M&IEs) for purposes of the employer's return (Rev. Proc. 2011-47).[159] The amount that is deemed substantiated is equal to the lesser of the per diem allowance or the amount computed at the federal M&IE rate for the locality of travel for the period that the employee is away from home. If M&IEs are substantiated using a per diem allowance, the entire amount is treated as a food and beverage expense subject to the 50-percent limitation on meal and entertainment expenses (¶ 916).

The M&IE rate must be prorated for partial days of travel away from home (¶ 954A). If an employee's meals are provided by the employer, even though the employee may be working from home, the employee is entitled to deduct only the incidental expense portion of the applicable federal per diem M&IE rates (*R.J. Zbylut*, Dec. 57,348(M), 95 TCM 1172 (2008)).[160]

Self-Employed Persons and Employees. Self-employed individuals and employees whose expenses are not reimbursed may also use the M&IE-only rate to substantiate M&IEs while traveling away from home. The taxpayer must actually prove through adequate records or sufficient corroborative evidence (¶ 953) the time, place, and business purpose of the travel, and lodging costs must be proven by documentary evidence (e.g., a receipt).

Optional Method for Incidental-Expenses-Only Deduction. Taxpayers may use an optional method to deduct only incidental expenses in lieu of using actual expenses. Taxpayers who do not incur any meal expenses may deduct $5 per calendar day (or partial day) as ordinary and necessary incidental expenses, paid or incurred, while traveling to any CONUS or OCONUS localities (Notice 2016-58; Notice 2015-63).[161] The optional method is subject to the proration rules for partial days and substantiation requirements for taxpayers who use the per diem method for substantiation (Rev. Proc. 2011-47).[162] The optional method for incidental expenses only cannot also be used by taxpayers who use the following per diem methods:

(1) the lodging plus M&IE per diem method;

(2) the M&IE-only method; or

(3) the high-low method and the optional M&IE-only method (¶ 954A).

Transportation Workers. The M&IE rates for travel away from home for both self-employed persons and employees in the transportation industry are $63 on or after October 1, 2015, for CONUS localities, and $68 on or after October 1, 2015, for OCONUS localities (Notice 2016-58; Notice 2015-63).[163] An individual is in the transportation

References are to Standard Federal Tax Reports; Tax Research Consultant; and Practical Tax Explanations.

[159] ¶ 14,417.421; BUSEXP: 24,808; § 10,125.10

[160] ¶ 14,417.421; BUSEXP: 24,808; § 10,125.10

[161] ¶ 14,417.421; BUSEXP: 24,912; § 10,125.10

[162] ¶ 14,417.421; BUSEXP: 24,808; § 10,125.10

[163] ¶ 14,417.421; BUSEXP: 24,912; § 10,125.10

industry only if the individual's work: (1) directly involves moving people or goods by airplane, barge, bus, ship, train, or truck, and (2) regularly requires travel away from home that involves travel to localities with differing federal M&IE rates during a single trip.

Under a calendar-year convention for the transportation industry, taxpayers who used the federal M&IE rates during the first nine months of calendar year 2016 to substantiate an individual's travel expenses may not use the special transportation industry rates for that individual until January 1, 2017 (Rev. Proc. 2011-47).[164] Likewise, taxpayers who used the special transportation industry rates for the first nine months of calendar year 2016 to substantiate an individual's travel expenses may not use the federal M&IE rates for that individual until January 1, 2017.

955. Foreign Travel. Traveling expenses (including meals and lodging) for travel outside of the United States generally must be allocated between time spent on the trip for business and time spent for pleasure (¶ 949) (Code Sec. 274(c); Reg. § 1.274-4).[165] Travel is outside the United States if it is not from one point in the United States to another point in the United States. Travel outside the United States does not include any travel within the United States.

When the trip is for one week or less, or when the time spent on personal activities is less than 25 percent of the total time away from home, no allocation is required and all expenses are deductible. When the foreign trip is longer than a week (seven consecutive days counting the day of return but not the day of departure) or 25 percent or more of the time away from home is spent for personal reasons, deductible travel expenses are limited to those that are allocable to the taxpayer's business or management of income-producing property (Reg. § 1.274-4(d)).[166]

No allocation is required on a foreign trip when (1) the individual traveling had no substantial control over the arranging of the business trip, or (2) a personal vacation was not a major consideration in making the trip. An employee traveling under a reimbursement or expense account allowance arrangement does not have substantial control over the arranging of a business trip unless the employee owns at least 10 percent of the employer, or the employee is a managing executive of the employer who can, without being vetoed, decide on whether and when to make the trip (Reg. § 1.274-4(f)(5).[167]

For special rules governing expenses of attending foreign conventions, seminars, and other similar meetings, see ¶ 959 and ¶ 960.

956. Travel Expenses of State Legislators. A state legislator whose residence is further than 50 miles from the state capitol building may elect to be deemed to be away from home in the pursuit of a trade or business on any day that the legislature is in session (including periods of up to four consecutive days when the legislature is not in session) or on any day when the legislature is not in session but the legislator's presence is formally recorded at a committee meeting (Code Sec. 162(h)).[168]

957. Luxury Water Travel. A deduction for transportation by ocean liner, cruise ship, or other form of water transportation is limited to a daily amount equal to twice the highest per diem travel amount allowable to employees of the federal government while on official business away from home within the United States. The limitation does not apply to any expense allocable to a convention, seminar, or other meeting that is held on a cruise ship (¶ 959). Separately stated meal and entertainment expenses are subject to the 50-percent limitation rule (¶ 916), prior to the application of the per diem limitation. Statutory exceptions to the 50-percent limit apply (¶ 917) (Code Sec. 274(m)(1)).[169]

References are to Standard Federal Tax Reports; Tax Research Consultant; and Practical Tax Explanations.

[164] ¶ 14,417.28; BUSEXP: 24,808; § 10,125.10

[165] ¶ 14,402, ¶ 14,408; BUSEXP: 24,300; § 9,535.05

[166] ¶ 14,408; BUSEXP: 24,304.10; § 9,535.15

[167] ¶ 14,408; BUSEXP: 24,304.15; § 9,535.20

[168] ¶ 8500; BUSEXP: 24,120; § 9,510

[169] ¶ 14,402; BUSEXP: 24,400; § 9,545.10

958. Travel as a Form of Education. Travel expenses are not deductible if the expense would be deductible only on the basis that the travel itself constitutes a form of education (Code Sec. 274(m)(2)).[170] See also ¶ 1082.

959. Convention Expenses. Deductible travel expenses include those incurred in attending a convention related to the taxpayer's business, even though the taxpayer is an employee (Code Sec. 274(h); Reg. § 1.162-2(d)).[171] The fact that an employee uses vacation or leave time or that attendance at the convention is voluntary does not necessarily negate the deduction. For the rules applicable to foreign conventions, see ¶ 960. Expenses for a convention or meeting in connection with investments, financial planning, or other income-producing property are not deductible.

Cruise Ships. A maximum $2,000 annual deduction is available for expenses incurred for conventions on U.S. cruise ships (Code Sec. 274(h)(2)).[172] This deduction applies only if:

(1) all ports of such cruise ship are located in the United States or in U.S. possessions;

(2) the taxpayer establishes that the convention is directly related to the active conduct of his or her trade or business; and

(3) the taxpayer includes certain specified information in the return on which the deduction is claimed.

960. Foreign Conventions. No deduction is allowed for expenses allocable to a convention, seminar, or meeting held outside the North American area unless the taxpayer establishes that the meeting is directly related to the active conduct of his or her trade or business and that it is reasonable for the meeting to be held outside the North American area (Code Sec. 274(h)).[173] The factors taken into account are:

(1) the purpose of the meeting and the activities taking place there;

(2) the purposes and activities of the sponsoring organization or group;

(3) the places where the sponsoring organization's or group's active members reside and where its other meetings have been or will be held; and

(4) other relevant factors that the taxpayer may present.

Expenses for foreign conventions on cruise ships are never deductible.

The North American area is the 50 states of the United States and the District of Columbia, U.S. possessions, Canada, Mexico, the Republic of the Marshall Islands, the Federated States of Micronesia, and the Republic of Palau. Costs incurred in attending conventions held in the Caribbean or on certain Pacific Islands may also be deductible if the host country is a designated beneficiary country, there is a bilateral or multilateral agreement in effect providing for the exchange of tax information with the United States, and the country has not been found to discriminate in its tax laws against conventions held in the United States. A list of qualifying countries is provided in Rev. Rul. 2016-16, effective June 27, 2016. For conventions prior to that date, use the list provided in Rev. Rul. 2011-26.[174]

Home Office and Vacation Home Expenses

961. Home Office Deduction. Expenses for the business use of the taxpayer's home are deductible only if they are attributable to a portion of the home used exclusively on a regular basis:

(1) as the principal place of any business carried on by the taxpayer;

(2) as a place of business that is used by patients, clients, or customers in meeting or dealing with the taxpayer in the normal course of business; or

References are to Standard Federal Tax Reports; Tax Research Consultant; and Practical Tax Explanations.

[170] ¶ 14,402; INDIV: 60,122.20; § 9,501

[171] ¶ 8527, ¶ 14,402; BUSEXP: 24,160; § 9,515

[172] ¶ 14,402; BUSEXP: 24,162; § 9,545.05

[173] ¶ 14,402; BUSEXP: 24,350; § 9,540

[174] ¶ 14,408A.62; BUSEXP: 24,350; § 9,540

(3) in connection with the taxpayer's business, if the taxpayer is using a separate structure that is appurtenant to, but not attached to, the home (Code Sec. 280A(c)).[175]

If the taxpayer is an employee, the business use of the home must be for the convenience of the employer (¶ 965). The allowable deduction is computed on Form 8829. The amount deductible is limited to either the taxpayer's actual expenses related to the office or an amount determined under a safe harbor method (¶ 963).

To satisfy the exclusive use test, a specific portion of the taxpayer's home generally must be used solely for the purpose of carrying on a trade or business. This requirement is not met if the portion is used for both business and personal purposes. However, a wholesale or retail seller or an auction or consignment seller whose dwelling unit is the sole fixed location of the trade or business may deduct the ordinary and necessary expenses allocable to space within the dwelling unit that is used to store inventory or product samples, provided that the space is used on a regular basis and is a separately identifiable space suitable for storage (Code Sec. 280A(c)(2); IRS Fact Sheet FS-2007-23).[176] Another special exception applies to licensed day care operators (¶ 964).

A home office is the taxpayer's principal place of business if the taxpayer uses it exclusively and regularly to administer or manage the trade or business and does not conduct substantial administrative or management activities at any other fixed location. This test can be satisfied by taxpayers who:

(1) have others conduct administrative or management activities at locations other than the taxpayer's home office (e.g., billing activities);

(2) carry out administrative and management activities at sites that are not fixed locations of the business (e.g., cars or hotel rooms) in addition to performing the activities at the home office;

(3) conduct an insubstantial amount of administrative and management activities at a fixed location other than the home office (e.g., occasionally doing minimal paperwork at another fixed location); and

(4) conduct substantial nonadministrative and nonmanagement business activities at a fixed location other than the home office (e.g., meeting with or providing services to customers, clients, or patients at another fixed location) (Instructions to Form 8829; IRS Pub. 587).[177]

Residential Telephone. Basic local telephone service charges on the first line in a residence are not deductible as business expenses. Additional charges for long-distance calls, equipment, optional services (e.g., call waiting), or additional telephone lines may be deductible (Code Sec. 262(b)).[178]

963. Limitation on Home Office Deductions. The home office deduction (¶ 961) cannot exceed the gross income from the activity, reduced by the home expenses that would be deductible in the absence of any business use (e.g., mortgage interest, property taxes, etc.) and the business expenses not related to the use of the home (Code Sec. 280A(c)(5)).[179] Business expenses related to the home office expenses are deducted in the following specific order:

(1) business expenses that are not allocable to the use of the home (such as office supplies);

(2) home expenses that would be deductible even if the home was not used as a place of business (such as mortgage interest and real estate taxes);

(3) household expenses that are allocable to the business use (such as utilities and insurance); and

(4) allocable depreciation.

References are to Standard Federal Tax Reports; Tax Research Consultant; and Practical Tax Explanations.

[175] ¶ 14,850; BUSEXP: 27,150; § 8,101

[176] ¶ 8521.112; BUSEXP: 27,158; § 8,125

[177] ¶ 14,850.017; BUSEXP: 27,152.05; § 8,120.10

[178] ¶ 13,600; BUSEXP: 27,056.15; § 8,205

[179] ¶ 14,850; BUSEXP: 27,300; § 8,140

The deduction of the expenses under items (3) and (4) above cannot create a loss. Unused expenses under items (3) and (4) are carried over to the next year but are still subject to the same limitation rules.

Optional Safe Harbor. A taxpayer may elect a simplified safe harbor method to compute the home office deduction for tax years beginning on or after January 1, 2013, without having to substantiate, calculate, and allocate deductible home office expenses (Rev. Proc. 2013-13).[180] Under the safe harbor, the deduction is equal to $5 times the number of square feet of the home office, up to a maximum of 300 square feet (so the safe-harbor deduction is limited to $1,500). The deduction also cannot exceed the taxpayer's gross income from the business. If the safe harbor deduction exceeds the income limit, the excess cannot be carried forward to the next year. A taxpayer whose home office expenses are reimbursed by an employer cannot use the safe harbor. A taxpayer who uses the safe harbor cannot deduct actual home office expenses, though business expenses unrelated to the business use of the home may still be deducted.

964. Home Office Deduction for Day Care Services. Taxpayers who use their personal residences on a regular basis in the trade or business of providing qualifying day care services (for the care of children, handicapped persons, or the elderly) do not have to meet the exclusive use test under the home office deduction rules (¶ 961) in order to deduct business-related expenses (Code Sec. 280A(c)(4)).[181] However, the deduction is available only if the taxpayer has applied for, has been granted, or is exempt from having a license, certification, or approval as a day care center or as a family or group day care home under applicable state law. The deduction of expenses allocable to day care use is limited as described at ¶ 963. Additionally, if the portion of the home used for day care purposes is not used exclusively for those purposes, the taxpayer must also allocate expenses based on the number of hours the space is used for day care, compared to the total hours it is available for any use. The taxpayer must file Form 8829.

965. Home Office Deduction by Employees. In order for employees to qualify for the home office deduction (¶ 961), they must not only meet the exclusive use requirement, but the exclusive use of the home office must be for the convenience of their employers (Code Sec. 280A(c)(1) and (6)).[182] However, an employee cannot claim a home office deduction for any portion of the home rented to the employer, except for expenses such as home mortgage interest and real property taxes that are deductible absent business use. Generally, an employee's home office expenses must be taken as a miscellaneous itemized deduction, subject to the two-percent-of-adjusted-gross-income floor on Schedule A of Form 1040 (¶ 1079). Statutory employees (¶ 941B) claim home office deductions on Schedule C of Form 1040.

966. Deductions on Rental Residence or Vacation Home. Special rules limit the deductions that may be taken by an individual or an S corporation in connection with the rental of a residence or vacation home, or a portion thereof, that is also used as the taxpayer's residence (Code Sec. 280A).[183] A vacation home is a dwelling unit, including a house, apartment, condominium, house trailer, boat, or similar property. Deductions that may be claimed without regard to whether or not the home is used for trade or business or for the production of income (e.g., mortgage interest, property taxes, or a casualty loss) are not limited.

Personal Usage Defined. A vacation home is used by the taxpayer for personal purposes for a day if it is used for any part of the day:

(1) for personal purposes by the taxpayer, any other person who owns an interest in the home, or the relatives (spouses, brothers, sisters, ancestors, and lineal descendants) of either;

References are to Standard Federal Tax Reports; Tax Research Consultant; and Practical Tax Explanations.

[180] ¶ 14,854.62; BUSEXP: 27,172; § 8,140

[181] ¶ 14,850; BUSEXP: 27,160; § 46,710.15

[182] ¶ 14,850; BUSEXP: 27,166; § 8,130.05, § 8,130.10

[183] ¶ 14,850; BUSEXP: 27,100, BUSEXP: 27,200; § 1,701, § 1,720.05

(2) by any individual who uses the home under a reciprocal arrangement, whether or not rent is charged; and

(3) by any other individual who uses the home unless a fair rental is charged.

If the taxpayer rents the home at a fair rental value to any person, including a relative, for the renter to use as a principal residence, the renter's use is not personal use by the taxpayer. This exception applies to a renter who owns an interest in the home only if the rental is under a shared equity financing agreement.

Rental Use of Fewer Than 15 Days. If the property is rented for fewer than 15 days during the year, rental expenses are not deductible and the rental income is excluded from the taxpayer's gross income (Code Sec. 280A(g)).[184]

Rental Use Exceeding 14 Days. If the property is rented for more than 14 days during the year, rental expenses are deductible. If the home is used as a personal residence for more than the greater of 14 days or 10 percent of the number of days the home is rented at a fair market rental during the year, rental deductions are limited to the gross rental income. If the taxpayer does not use the home as a personal residence, the rental deductions are not limited to the rental income. The deduction may also be reduced or eliminated under the passive activity loss rules (¶ 1169) or the hobby loss rules if the rental activity is not engaged in for profit (¶ 1195).

Ordering of Deduction. Rental expenses are deducted in a specific order from gross rental income. Mortgage interest, real property taxes, and casualty losses attributable to the rental use are deducted first. Next, operating expenses other than depreciation attributable to the rental use are deducted. Last, depreciation and other basis adjustments attributable to rental income are deducted. These expenses are allocated to rental use based on the ratio that the total number of rental days bears to the total days used for all purposes during the year. When the taxpayer's personal use exceeds the greater of either 14 days or 10 percent of the rental days, the IRS limits the deductible rental expenses in the same manner as that prescribed under the hobby loss rules at ¶ 1195 (i.e., the total deductions may not exceed the gross rental income, and expenses are allocated to rental use based on the total days rented divided by the total days used). However, the Tax Court has held that mortgage interest and real estate taxes should be allocated based on the ratio of the total days rented to the total days in the year, because those expenses are assessed on an annual basis regardless of the days the property is used (*D.D. Bolton*, Dec. 38,075, 77 TC 104 (1981); *E.G. McKinney*, Dec. 38,077(M), 42 TCM 467 (1981)).[185] This approach can effectively reduce the amount of mortgage interest and real estate taxes that is allocated to the rental use and, thus, leave more gross rental income available to offset allocated rental expenses.

Example: Sam rents out his vacation home for 91 days and uses the home for personal purposes for 30 days during the year. He has $2,700 in gross rental income, and he pays $621 of real property taxes and $2,854 of mortgage interest. He has $2,693 in additional expenses for maintenance, repair, and utilities.

The IRS allocation of all expenses would be based on 75 percent (91 days rented ÷ 121 days used). In contrast, the Tax Court would allocate taxes and interest based on 25 percent (91 days rented ÷ 365 days) and use the 75-percent limitation for the additional expenses for maintenance, repair, etc.

	IRS	*Tax Court*
1. Gross rental income	$2,700	$2,700
2. Less: Interest ($2,854)	- 2,141	- 714
Property tax ($621)	- 466	- 155
3. Remaining available income	$93	$1,831
4. Utilities, maintenance, etc.	- 93	- 1,831
5. Net income	$0	$0

References are to Standard Federal Tax Reports; Tax Research Consultant; and Practical Tax Explanations.

[184] ¶ 14,850; BUSEXP: 27,204; § 1,735

[185] ¶ 14,858.15; BUSEXP: 27,304; § 1,720.10

	IRS	Tax Court
6. Unused expense allowable as itemized deductions:		
Interest	$713	$2,140
Property tax	155	466
7. Total allowable deductions	$3,568	$5,306

Bed and Breakfast Inns. The special restrictions on deductions related to a residence used for business and personal purposes do not apply to the portion of the residence used exclusively as a bed and breakfast inn. Expenses related to that portion of a residence may be limited under the hobby loss rules (¶ 1195) (Code Sec. 280A(f)).[186]

967. Conversion of Property. Individuals who convert their principal residences into rental units (or vice versa) are not considered to have used the unit for personal purposes for any day during the tax year that occurs before (or after) a qualified rental period for purposes of applying the deduction limitation (¶ 966) allocable to the qualified rental period (Code Sec. 280A(d)(4)).[187] The expenses, however, must be allocated between the periods of rental and personal use. A qualified rental period is a consecutive period of 12 or more months, beginning (or ending) during the tax year, during which the unit is rented or held for rental at its fair market value. The 12-month rental requirement does not apply if the residence is sold or exchanged before it has been rented or held for rental for the full 12 months.

Example: Sue moved out of her principal residence on February 28, 2015, to accept employment in another town. The house was rented at its fair market value from March 15, 2015, through May 14, 2016. The use of the house as a principal residence from January 1 through February 28, 2015, is not counted as personal use. If Sue moved back and reoccupied the home on June 1, 2016, the use of the house as a principal residence from June 1 through December 31, 2016, is not counted as personal use.

Other Business Expenses

968. Fire and Casualty Insurance Premiums. A premium paid for insurance against losses from fire, accident, storm, theft, or other casualty is deductible if it is an ordinary and necessary expense of a business (Reg. § 1.162-1).[188] However, the uniform capitalization rules may require that insurance costs on real or tangible personal property produced or acquired for resale be included in inventory or capitalized, rather than being deducted (¶ 990–¶ 999).

An insurance company's agreement to reimburse future remediation costs that a business is certain to incur is not an insurance contract because it does not involve the requisite risk shifting. Therefore, the business's payments to the insurer are not deductible insurance premiums (Rev. Rul. 2007-47, amplifying Rev. Rul. 89-96).[189]

969. Advertising Expenses. Advertising expenses are deductible if they are reasonable in amount and bear a reasonable relation to the business. Deductible expenses may be intended to develop goodwill as well as gain immediate sales. The cost of advertising is deductible when paid or incurred, even though the advertising program extends over several years or is expected to result in benefits extending over a period of years (Rev. Rul. 92-80).[190] When a catalog is not replaced annually, the Tax Court and the IRS require the printing costs to be amortized over the expected life of the catalog. However, some courts have held to the contrary, treating catalog costs as regular advertising expenses (*Sheldon & Co.*, CA-6, 54-2 USTC ¶ 9526).[191] The costs of public service or other impartial advertising, such as advertising designed to encourage the public to register and to vote, are deductible (Rev. Rul. 62-156).[192]

References are to Standard Federal Tax Reports; Tax Research Consultant; and Practical Tax Explanations.

[186] ¶ 14,850; BUSEXP: 27,054.15; § 1,705

[187] ¶ 14,850; BUSEXP: 27,208; § 1,715.20

[188] ¶ 8501; BUSEXP: 18,202; § 9,415.05

[189] ¶ 8522.3915; BUSEXP: 18,200; § 9,415.05

[190] ¶ 8851.152; BUSEXP: 18,252; § 9,901

[191] ¶ 21,817.2075; BUSEXP: 18,260; § 9,901

[192] ¶ 8952.40; BUSEXP: 18,252; § 9,901

Expenses for advertising in political programs or for admission to political fund-raising or inaugural functions and similar events are not deductible (Code Sec. 276).[193] This rule also applies to admission to any dinner or program if any part of the proceeds of the event directly or indirectly inures to or for the use of a political party or a political candidate.

Package Design Costs. Package design costs include the graphic arrangement or design of shapes, colors, words, pictures, lettering, and other elements on a given product package, or the design of a container with respect to its shape or function (Reg. § 1.263(a)-4(b)(3)(v)).[194] The Tax Court has held that packaging design costs are a deductible advertising expense even though the design provided the company with significant future benefits (*RJR Nabisco*, Dec. 52,786(M), 76 TCM 71 (1998) (Nonacq.)).[195]

970. Expenses of Earning Tax-Exempt Income. No deduction is allowed for any expense allocable to the earning of tax-exempt income (Code Sec. 265; Reg. § 1.265-1).[196] No deduction is allowed for interest paid on a debt incurred or continued in order to purchase or carry tax-exempt bonds or other obligations, regardless of whether the interest expense was incurred in business, in a profit-inspired transaction, or in any other connection.

Banks, thrift institutions, and other financial institutions generally may not deduct any portion of their interest expenses allocable to tax-exempt interest on obligations acquired after August 7, 1986. This includes amounts paid in respect of deposits, investment certificates, or withdrawable or repurchasable shares. There is a *de minimis* safe harbor exception to the 100-percent disallowance rule, however, for bonds issued in 2009 and 2010 (Code Sec. 265(b)(7)).[197]

Qualified tax-exempt obligations that are issued by a qualified small issuer are not taken into account as investments in tax-exempt bonds and, therefore, are not subject to the 100-percent disallowance rule. Instead, only 20 percent of the interest expense allocable to qualified tax-exempt obligations is disallowed. A qualified small issuer is an issuer that reasonably anticipates that the amount of its tax-exempt obligations, other than certain private activity bonds, will not exceed $10 million during the calendar year. A qualified tax-exempt obligation is a tax-exempt obligation that (1) is issued after August 7, 1986, by a qualified small issuer; (2) is not a private activity bond; and (3) is designated by the issuer as qualifying for the exception from the general rule (Code Sec. 265(b)(3)).[198]

971. Circulation Expenses. Any expenditure to establish, maintain, or increase the circulation of a newspaper, magazine, or other periodical may be deducted in the year paid or incurred even though the taxpayer reports only an allocable portion of the subscription income for each year of the subscription period (¶ 1537) (Code Sec. 173; Reg. § 1.173-1).[199] Taxpayers may also elect to capitalize circulation expenses and amortize them over a three-year period (¶ 1450).

972. Fines, Penalties, Kickbacks, Drug Trafficking. A fine or a penalty paid to a government for the violation of any law is not a deductible business expense (Code Sec. 162(f)).[200] Any illegal bribe or kickback paid directly or indirectly to a domestic government official or employee is not deductible. Bribes and kickbacks paid directly or indirectly to an employee or official of a foreign government are not deductible if they are unlawful under the federal Foreign Corrupt Practices Act of 1977. No deduction is allowed for any payment made directly or indirectly to any person if the payment is a bribe, kickback, or other illegal payment under any U.S. law or under any generally enforced state law that subjects the payor to a criminal penalty or to the loss of license or

References are to Standard Federal Tax Reports; Tax Research Consultant; and Practical Tax Explanations.

[193] ¶ 14,550; BUSEXP: 18,310; § 9,120.05

[194] ¶ 13,704C; BUSEXP: 9,104.10; § 9,970

[195] ¶ 8851.1338; BUSEXP: 18,252.10; § 9,970

[196] ¶ 14,050, ¶ 14,051; BUSEXP: 18,600, RIC: 12,204.20; § 7,420.05, § 9,001

[197] ¶ 14,050; RIC: 12,204.20

[198] ¶ 14,050; SALES: 51,054.80

[199] ¶ 12,030, ¶ 12,031; DEPR: 21,252; § 11,520

[200] ¶ 8500; BUSEXP: 18,800; § 9,105, § 9,115

privilege to engage in a trade or business (Code Sec. 162(c)(2) and (3); Reg. § 1.162-18).[201] A deduction is also denied for any kickback, rebate, or bribe made by any provider of services, supplier, physician, or other person in connection with furnishing items or services or making or receiving payments under Medicare, Medicaid, or a federally funded state plan approved under Medicare or Medicaid. For all the above purposes, a kickback includes a payment in consideration of the referral of a client, patient, or customer.

If a taxpayer is convicted of or pleads guilty or no contest to a criminal violation of an antitrust law that contains a treble damage provision, no deduction is allowed for two-thirds of the amount paid to satisfy the judgment or in settlement of a suit brought under section 4 of the Clayton Act (Code Sec. 162(g); Reg. § 1.162-22).[202]

No deduction is allowed for a federal tax penalty (Reg. § 1.162-21(b)(1)(ii)).[203] No deduction or credit is allowed for amounts paid or incurred in the illegal trafficking in drugs listed in the federal Controlled Substances Act, even if the substance is legal under applicable state law. However, an adjustment to gross receipts for the cost of goods sold is permitted (Code Sec. 280E; *Olive*, CA-9, 2015-2 USTC ¶ 50,377).[204] Damage awards paid in connection with the violation of a federal civil statute and similar penalties may be deductible if they are compensatory, rather than punitive, in nature (Reg. § 1.162-21(b)(2)).[205]

973. Business Legal Expenses. Legal expenses paid or incurred in connection with a business transaction or primarily for the purpose of preserving existing business reputation and goodwill are ordinarily deductible (*F.W. Staudt*, Dec. 20,040(M), 12 TCM 1417 (1953)).[206] Legal fees may be deductible even if no litigation is involved. Legal expenses include attorneys' fees, fees or expenses of accountants and expert witnesses, and court stenographic and printing charges.

The deductibility tests are substantially the same as those for other business expenses and preclude a current deduction for a legal expense incurred in the acquisition of capital assets (Reg. § 1.263(a)-2).[207] Litigation costs must also be capitalized when, under the origin of the claim test (or the nature of the claim leading to the payments), they are incurred to acquire a capital asset.

Deductible business expenses include the cost of tax return preparation that is properly allocable to the business, as well as expenses incurred in resolving asserted tax deficiencies relating to the business (*D. Pistoresi*, Dec. 53,243(M), 77 TCM 1368 (1999); *C. Wood*, Dec. 25,086, 37 TC 70 (1961) (Acq.).[208]

For the deductibility of legal expenses arising from the determination of nonbusiness taxes or income-producing property, see ¶ 1092 and ¶ 1093.

974. Lobbying Expenses. Lobbying expenses directed towards influencing federal or state legislation are generally not deductible (Code Sec. 162(e); Reg. § 1.162-20(c)).[209] Under a *de minimis* exception, the prohibition does not apply to any in-house expenditures if the expenditures do not exceed $2,000 during the tax year. Lobbying expenses pertaining to local legislation are deductible.

975. Federal National Mortgage Association Stock. Initial holders of stock issued by the Federal National Mortgage Association may deduct, as a business expense, the excess of the price paid over the market price of the stock on the date of issuance (Code Sec. 162(d); Reg. § 1.162-19(a)).[210] The basis in the stock is reduced to reflect the deduction.

References are to Standard Federal Tax Reports; Tax Research Consultant; and Practical Tax Explanations.

[201] ¶ 8500, ¶ 8857; BUSEXP: 18,800; § 9,105

[202] ¶ 8500, ¶ 8955; BUSEXP: 18,800; § 9,125

[203] ¶ 8953; INDIV: 45,060; § 9,115

[204] ¶ 15,050, ¶ 15,050.25; BUSEXP: 18,808; § 9,110

[205] ¶ 8953; BUSEXP: 18,650; § 9,115

[206] ¶ 8526.4503; BUSEXP: 18,052.05; § 9,920.05

[207] ¶ 8526.4162, ¶ 13,703; BUSEXP: 18,054.05; § 9,920.05

[208] ¶ 8520.73; BUSEXP: 18,050; § 9,920.05

[209] ¶ 8500, ¶ 8951; BUSEXP: 18,302; § 9,120.05

[210] ¶ 8500, ¶ 8859; SALES: 6,372.35

976. Political Contributions. Contributions made to a political candidate or party are not deductible as a business expense (Code Sec. 162(e)(1)(B)).[211]

977A. Small Refiners' Deduction for Upgrades to Produce Low Sulfur Fuels. Small refiners may elect to deduct a portion of the cost to upgrade their facilities to produce low-sulfur fuels (Code Sec. 179B).[212] Qualified small refiners may deduct up to 75 percent of the capital costs paid or incurred for the purposes of complying with the Highway Diesel Fuel Sulfur Control Requirements of the Environmental Protection Agency (¶ 1285).

977B. Domestic Film and Television Productions Deduction. A taxpayer may elect to deduct the cost of any qualified film or television production commenced before January 1, 2017, as well as the cost of any live theatrical production commenced after December 31, 2015, and before January 1, 2017 (Code Sec. 181, as amended by the Protecting Americans from Tax Hikes (PATH) Act of 2015 (P.L. 114-113)).[213] The maximum deduction is $15 million ($20 million for films produced in certain low-income or distressed communities). See ¶ 1229 for general discussion of the amortization of film and television production costs.

977C. New Refinery Property Deduction (Expired). The builders of new liquid fuel refineries could elect to deduct up to 50 percent of the cost of building a qualified refinery property that was placed in service after August 8, 2005, and before January 1, 2014 (Code Sec. 179C).[214] The expensing deduction was also available with respect to refineries processing liquid fuel directly from shale or tar sands (¶ 1285A).

977D. Energy-Efficient Commercial Buildings Deduction. Taxpayers may deduct a portion of the costs of installing energy-efficient systems into commercial buildings (Code Sec. 179D, as amended by the Protecting Americans from Tax Hikes (PATH) Act of 2015 (P.L. 114-113)).[215] The maximum deduction is generally $1.80 per square foot of a qualified commercial property, reduced by the deductions taken in prior tax years. Qualified systems include interior lighting, heating, cooling, ventilation, hot water systems, and the building envelope. The deduction is available for qualified commercial property placed in service after December 31, 2005, but before January 1, 2017 (¶ 1286).

978. Expenses of Mercantile and Manufacturing Businesses. Merchants and manufacturers generally are subject to the uniform capitalization rules. See the discussion at ¶ 990–¶ 999. However, ordinary and necessary business expenses not covered by such rules may be currently deducted (Reg. § 1.162-1).[216]

979. Research and Experimental Expenses. A taxpayer may elect to deduct certain research and experimental expenses by claiming the deduction on the income tax return for the first tax year in which the costs are paid or incurred in connection with its business (Code Sec. 174; Reg. § 1.174-2).[217] Only costs of research in the laboratory or for experimental purposes, whether carried on by the taxpayer or on behalf of the taxpayer by a third party, are deductible. Market research and normal product testing costs are not research expenditures. Once made, the election is applicable to all research costs incurred in the project for the current and all subsequent years. A credit is also allowed for increased research and experimental expenses (¶ 1365J).

The costs of obtaining a patent, including attorneys' fees paid or incurred in making and perfecting a patent application, qualify as research or experimental expenditures, but the costs of acquiring another's patent, model, production, or process do not qualify (Reg. § 1.174-2(a)(1)).[218] If the taxpayer elects to defer the expenses, the right to amortize ceases when the patent issues. Unrecovered expenditures are recovered

References are to Standard Federal Tax Reports; Tax Research Consultant; and Practical Tax Explanations.

[211] ¶ 8500; BUSEXP: 18,310; § 9,120.05

[212] ¶ 12,134; BUSEXP: 18,908

[213] ¶ 12,144; DEPR: 12,300; § 10,235

[214] ¶ 12,137; BUSEXP: 18,900; § 10,245

[215] ¶ 12,138; BUSEXP: 18,950; § 10,250

[216] ¶ 8501; BUSEXP: 3,050; § 10,310.05

[217] ¶ 12,040, ¶ 12,043; BUSEXP: 9,102.10; § 9,705.05

[218] ¶ 12,043; DEPR: 21,300; § 9,705.10

through depreciation over the life of the patent (Reg. § 1.174-4(a)(4)).[219] A purchased patent may qualify as a section 197 intangible to be amortized over 15 years (¶ 1288).

980. Computer Software Costs. The tax treatment of computer software used in a trade or business depends on whether the taxpayer has leased the software, developed it internally, or purchased it (Code Sec. 162; Reg. § 1.162-11; Rev. Proc. 2000-50).[220]

Generally, rental payments for leased software are deductible as business expenses over the term of the lease in the same manner as any other rental payments (Rev. Proc. 2000-50).[221] However, acquired computer software is amortizable over 15 years if it is a section 197 intangible (¶ 1288). Software that is not a section 197 intangible is amortized using the straight-line method over a period of 36 months beginning on the first day of the month that the software is placed in service.

Costs incurred by a taxpayer to develop software for sale to others or for internal use may be treated like research and experimental expenses (¶ 979) and may be deducted currently, amortized as research expenses over a 60-month period (or shorter if established as appropriate), or amortized as software expenses over a 36-month period, so long as the costs are treated consistently (Rev. Proc. 2000-50).[222]

Computer software is any program designed to cause a computer to perform a desired function (Code Secs. 167(f)(1)(B) and 197(e)(3)(B); Rev. Proc. 2000-50).[223] It does not include any database or similar item unless the database or item is in the public domain and is incidental to the operation of otherwise qualifying computer software.

Software Bundled with Hardware. Software costs that are included, but not separately stated, in the cost of computer hardware are capitalized and depreciated as part of the hardware (Reg. § 1.167(a)-14(b)(2)).[224] In other words, the entire amount is treated as the cost of hardware (tangible property) and is depreciable under MACRS over a five-year recovery period.

Web Site Development Costs. The IRS has yet to issue formal guidance on the treatment of web site development costs.

Domestic Production Activities

980A. Domestic Production Activities Deduction. A taxpayer may claim a deduction against gross income equal to nine percent of (i) its qualified production activities income (QPAI) (¶ 980B) or (ii) adjusted gross income for individuals, estates and trusts, determined without regard to the domestic production activities. In the case of C corporations, the deduction for AMT purposes is equal to the relevant percentage of the lesser of QPAI, or AMT income, determined with regard to the deduction. (Code Sec. 199).[225] Form 8903 is used to calculate the deduction.

The amount of the domestic production activities deduction for any tax year, however, may not exceed 50 percent of the W-2 wages paid by the taxpayer (¶ 980C) that are allocable to the taxpayer's domestic production gross receipts (¶ 980D).

980B. Qualified Production Activities Income. A taxpayer's qualified production activities income (QPAI) is its domestic production gross receipts (DPGR) attributable to the actual conduct of a trade or business during the tax year (¶ 980D), reduced by: (1) the cost of goods sold allocable to DPGR; and (2) other deductions, expenses, and losses that are properly allocable to DPGR (Code Sec. 199(c)(1); Reg. §§ 1.199-1(c) and 1.199-4).[226]

Oil-Related QPAI. Taxpayers with QPAI that is attributable to the production, refining, processing, transportation or distribution of oil, gas or any of their primary

References are to Standard Federal Tax Reports; Tax Research Consultant; and Practical Tax Explanations.

[219] ¶ 12,046; DEPR: 21,300; § 9,710

[220] ¶ 8500, ¶ 8753, ¶ 8754.1695; DEPR: 15,162.85; § 11,535.05

[221] ¶ 8754.1695; BUSEXP: 18,856.106; § 11,535.15

[222] ¶ 8754.1695; DEPR: 21,308.20; § 11,535.25

[223] ¶ 8500, ¶ 11,030D, ¶ 8754.1695; DEPR: 21,054.15; § 11,410.25

[224] ¶ 11,030D; DEPR: 15,162.85; § 11,535.20

[225] ¶ 12,468; BUSEXP: 6,000; § 6,001

[226] ¶ 12,468, ¶ 12,472, ¶ 12,472C; BUSEXP: 6,000; § 6,015.05

products (oil-related QPAI) must reduce the domestic production activities deduction by three percent of the least of:

(1) the taxpayer's oil-related qualified production activities income for the tax year;

(2) the taxpayer's qualified production activities income for the tax year; or

(3) an individual's modified adjusted gross income, or any other taxpayer's taxable income (determined without regard to the domestic production activities deduction) (Code Sec. 199(d)(9)).

In computing oil-related QPAI for tax years beginning after 2015 and before 2022, an independent oil refiner allocates only 25 percent of its oil-related transportation costs to domestic production gross receipts. An independent oil refiner must be in the trade or business of refining oil, must have less than 500,000 barrels in average daily worldwide crude oil production for the tax year; and must not have had more than $1 billion in gross receipts for its last tax year ending in 2005 (Code Sec. 199(c)(3)(C), as added by the Consolidated Appropriations Act, 2016 (P.L. 114-113).[227] This reduction in allocated costs effectively increases the refiner's deduction.

980C. W-2 Wage Limitation for Code Sec. 199 Deduction. The deduction for domestic production activities (¶ 980A) may not exceed 50 percent of the W-2 wages paid by the taxpayer to its employees for the calendar year ending during the tax year that are properly allocable to the taxpayer's domestic gross production receipts (the wages that the taxpayer deducts in calculating its qualified production activities income (¶ 980B)) (Code Sec. 199(b)(2); Reg. § 1.199-2(a)).[228]

W-2 wages are amounts required to be reported for wages and compensation on Form W-2, plus compensation deferred under Code Sec. 457 plans and elective deferrals under other employer plans (i.e., 401(k)s, 403(b)s, SIMPLEs, and SEPs, as well as designated Roth contributions) (Reg. § 1.199-2(e)).[229] While all of these payments are reported on Form W-2, no single box includes all types of payments. Thus, taxpayers may use one of three methods for computing W-2 wages (Rev. Proc. 2006-47):[230]

(1) *Unmodified box method:* Under the unmodified box method, W-2 wages are the lesser of: (a) the total amount entered for all employees in Box 1 (wages, tips, other compensation) or (b) the total amount entered for all employees in Box 5 (Medicare wages and tips).

(2) *Modified Box 1 method:* Under the modified Box 1 method, the total amount reported in Box 1 for all employees is reduced by (a) amounts included in Box 1 that are not wages subject to federal income tax withholding and (b) amounts included in Box 1 that are not wages but the taxpayer has elected to withhold income on (e.g., supplemental unemployment compensation benefits and certain sick pay). The result is then increased by the total amount reported in Box 12 for all employees that are coded D, E, F, G, or S to arrive at the taxpayer's W-2 wages.

(3) *Tracking wages method:* Under the tracking wages method, the taxpayer actually tracks total wages paid to its employees that are subject to federal income tax withholding and that are reported on Form W-2 (not including supplemental unemployment benefits). The result is then increased by the amount reported in Box 12 and coded D, E, F, G, or S to arrive at the taxpayer's W-2 wages.

[231]

Amounts that a taxpayer treats as W-2 wages in one tax year (e.g., nonqualified deferred compensation) may not be treated as W-2 wages in another tax year or as W-2 wages of another taxpayer. In addition, an employer with a short tax year must use a modified version of the tracking wages method (Reg. § 1.199-2(b); Rev. Proc. 2006-47). A

References are to Standard Federal Tax Reports; Tax Research Consultant; and Practical Tax Explanations.

[227] ¶ 12,468; BUSEXP: 6,052.10; § 6,010

[228] ¶ 12,468, ¶ 12,472A; BUSEXP: 6,054; § 6,010

[229] ¶ 12,472A; BUSEXP: 6,054; § 6,010

[230] ¶ 12,476.75; BUSEXP: 6,054; § 6,010

[231] ¶ 12,472AC, ¶ 12,472GC; BUSEXP: 6,054; § 6,010

taxpayer that acquires a major portion of a trade or business may not take into account wages paid to common law employees of the predecessor employer for services rendered to the predecessor employer, even if those wages are reported on Forms W-2 furnished by the taxpayer (Rev. Proc. 2006-47). For tax years beginning on or after August 27, 2015, if an acquisition or disposition of a trade or business causes more than one taxpayer to be an employer of the acquired or disposed of business's employees during the calendar year, the taxpayer's W-2 wages for that year are allocated between each taxpayer, based on the period when the business's employees were employed by the taxpayer, regardless of which permissible method is used for reporting W-2 wages on Form W-2 (Temp. Reg. §§ 1.199-2T(c)(1), 1.199-8T(i)(10)).

980D. Domestic Production Gross Receipts (DPGR). Domestic production gross receipts (DPGR) are the gross receipts of the taxpayer that are derived from:

(1) the lease, rental, license, sale, exchange, or other disposition of:

(a) qualifying production property (generally, tangible personal property, computer software, and sound recordings) manufactured, produced, grown, or extracted by the taxpayer in whole or in significant part within the United States;

(b) any qualified film produced by the taxpayer in the United States; or

(c) electricity, natural gas, or potable water produced by the taxpayer in the United States;

(2) construction performed within the United States; and

(3) engineering or architectural services performed in the United States for construction projects located in the United States (Code Sec. 199(c)(4)).[232]

DPGR does not include gross receipts from:

(1) the sale of food and beverages prepared by the taxpayer at a retail establishment;

(2) transmission or distribution of electricity, natural gas, or potable water; or

(3) the lease, rental, license, sale, exchange, or other disposition of land.

The United States includes all 50 states and the District of Columbia, as well as the territorial waters of the United States, and the seabed and subsoil of submarine areas that are adjacent to the territorial waters of the United States and over which it has exclusive rights, in accordance with international law, with respect to the exploration and exploitation of natural resources (Reg. § 1.199-3(h)).[233] The United States generally does not include possessions and territories of the United States or the airspace or space over the United States. However, for its first eleven tax years beginning after December 31, 2005, and before January 1, 2017, a taxpayer can take into account its Puerto Rico business activity in calculating its DPGR and qualified production activities income (QPAI), if all of the taxpayer's gross receipts from Puerto Rican sources are subject to U.S. income taxation (Code Sec. 199(d)(8), as amended by the Protecting Americans from Tax Hikes (PATH) Act of 2015 (P.L. 114-113)).[234] For purposes of the 50-percent-of-W-2-wages limitation (¶ 980C), those taxpayers can take into account wages paid to bona fide residents of Puerto Rico for services performed in Puerto Rico.

A taxpayer generally may use any reasonable method to allocate its gross receipts between DPGR and non-DPGR. However, the taxpayer must use a specific identification method if the information is readily available and can be used without undue burden or expense (Reg. § 1.199-1(d)).[235] Under several *de minimis* safe harbors, allocation is not required when less than five percent of gross receipts are DPGR (or non-DPGR).

References are to Standard Federal Tax Reports; Tax Research Consultant; and Practical Tax Explanations.

[232] ¶ 12,468; BUSEXP: 6,100; § 6,015.10

[233] ¶ 12,472B; BUSEXP: 6,150; § 6,015.10

[234] ¶ 12,468; BUSEXP: 6,104.05; § 6,015.10

[235] ¶ 12,472; BUSEXP: 6,102.05; § 6,015.20

DPGR must be determined on an item-by-item basis (Reg. § 1.199-3(d)).[236] Thus, a taxpayer cannot determine DPGR on a division-by-division, product-line-by-product-line, or transaction-by-transaction basis. This prevents a taxpayer from isolating loss activities from other activities in order to maximize its deduction. An "item" is defined as property, or any portion of property, that is offered to sale to customers and that meets all of the requirements of the manufacturer's deduction.

Generally, gross receipts derived from the performance of a service other than construction, engineering, and architectural activities do not qualify as DPGR (Reg. § 1.199-3(i)).[237] There are several exceptions to this rule. A taxpayer may include in DPGR the gross receipts derived from a qualified warranty, a qualified delivery, distribution, or installation, and provision of a qualified operating manual, as well as a *de minimis* amount (less than five percent of the gross receipts) for embedded services with respect to an underlying item of qualifying property, and services provided under a qualified computer software maintenance agreement. A service is embedded if its price is not separately stated from the amount charged for the qualified property.

If a taxpayer exchanges qualified production property it manufactured, produced, etc., for other property in a taxable or nontaxable exchange, the value of the property received may be treated as DPGR. However, unless the taxpayer further manufactures, produces, etc., the property received, any gross receipts from the subsequent sale are not DPGR even if the property was qualified property in the hands of the transferor. Generally, DPGR also does not include any gross receipts derived by the taxpayer from the lease, rental, or license of qualified production property for use by any related person (Code Sec. 199(c)(7)).[238]

980E. Qualified Production Property (QPP). Only one taxpayer may claim the domestic production activities deduction with respect to the manufacture, production, growth, or extraction (MPGE) of qualifying production property (QPP) (tangible personal property, computer software, and sound recordings), as well as the disposition of electricity, natural gas, potable water, or a qualified film (Reg. § 1.199-3(f)(1)).[239] The deduction is claimed by the taxpayer who has the benefits and burdens of ownership of the property under federal income tax principles during the period that the qualifying activity occurs.

The QPP must be MPGE by the taxpayer in whole or in significant part within the United States. QPP is MPGE in significant part in the United States if the MPGE activity performed within the United States is substantial in nature. This is determined on a facts-and-circumstances basis taking into account the nature and relative value added by the taxpayer's U.S. activity (Reg. § 1.199-3(e) and (g)).[240] Under a safe harbor, the significant-part requirement is satisfied if the taxpayer's conversion costs, i.e., direct labor and related factory expenses, to MPGE the property within the United States account for 20 percent or more of the total cost of goods sold of the property (Reg. § 1.199-3(g)(3)). Packaging, repackaging, labeling, and minor assembly operations are not so substantial in nature as to qualify as the MPGE of QPP. In addition, research and experimental activities and the creation of intangibles (other than computer software and sound recordings) do not qualify as substantial activities and may be excluded in calculating the safe harbor.

980F. Construction, Engineering, or Architectural Activities. For taxpayers actively engaged in construction, engineering and architectural businesses, domestic production gross receipts (DPGR) includes the proceeds from the sale, exchange, or other disposition of real property constructed by the taxpayer in the United States (whether or not sold or completed), including compensation for the performance of construction services by the taxpayer and any qualified construction warranty (Reg. § 1.199-3(m)).[241] It also includes proceeds derived from engineering or architectural

References are to Standard Federal Tax Reports; Tax Research Consultant; and Practical Tax Explanations.

[236] ¶ 12,472B; BUSEXP: 6,100; § 6,015.05

[237] ¶ 12,472B; BUSEXP: 6,160; § 6,015.10

[238] ¶ 12,468; BUSEXP: 6,104; § 6,015.15

[239] ¶ 12,472B; BUSEXP: 6,160.25; § 6,015.10

[240] ¶ 12,472B; BUSEXP: 6,160.25; § 6,015.10

[241] ¶ 12,472B; BUSEXP: 6,156; § 6,015.10

services performed in the United States for real property construction projects. DPGR does not include proceeds from the lease or rental of real property constructed by the taxpayer. Nor does it include gross receipts attributable to the sale or other disposition of land (though the taxpayer may reduce its cost related to DPGR by the cost of the land).

980G. Allocation of Costs and Deductions for Code Sec. 199. To allocate cost of goods sold (CGS) between domestic production gross receipts (DPGR) and non-DPGR, a taxpayer must use a reasonable method that is satisfactory to the IRS based on all facts and circumstances (Reg. § 1.199-4(b)).[242] Reasonable methods may be based on gross receipts, number of units sold, number of units produced, or total production costs. Ordinarily, it is not reasonable for a taxpayer to use one method to allocate gross receipts between DPGR and non-DPGR and a different method to allocate CGS that is not demonstrably more accurate, unless the taxpayer can specifically identify CGS allocable to DPGR without undue burden or expense.

Three methods are provided for apportioning deductions properly allocable to DPGR. For purposes of all three methods, net operating losses (NOLs) and deductions not attributable to the actual conduct of a trade or business (i.e., the standard deduction or personal exemptions) may not be allocated or apportioned to DPGR (Reg. § § 1.199-4(c) and 1.199-8(c)):[243]

(1) The *Section 861 method* must be used by a taxpayer unless it is eligible and chooses to use one of the other methods. Under the Section 861 method, a taxpayer must allocate a deduction to the relevant class of gross income and then apportion the deduction within each class between DPGR and non-DPGR (Reg. § 1.199-4(d)).[244] If non-DPGR is treated as DPGR under a safe harbor or *de minimis* rule, deductions related to the non-DPGR must be apportioned to DPGR.

(2) Under the *simplified deduction method*, deductions other than CGS may be ratably apportioned between DPGR and non-DPGR based on relative gross receipts (Reg. § 1.199-4(e)).[245] A taxpayer is eligible to use this method if: (a) its average annual gross receipts during the three previous tax years is $100 million or less or (b) its total assets at the end of the tax year attributable to its trade or business are $10 million or less. A pass-through entity's eligibility is determined at the owner level and, except for trusts and estates, the method is also applied at the owner level.

(3) Under the *small business simplified overall method*, a qualifying small taxpayer may ratably apportion its total costs for the tax year (including CGS and other deductions) between DPGR and non-DPGR based on relative gross receipts (Reg. § 1.199-4(f)).[246] A taxpayer is eligible to use this method if: (a) its average annual gross receipts during the three previous years is $5 million or less; (b) it is engaged in the business of farming and is not required to use the accrual method of accounting; or (c) it is eligible to use the cash method of accounting under Rev. Proc. 2002-28 (¶ 1515). Estates and nongrantor trusts cannot use this method.

Wage Expense Safe Harbor. A taxpayer using either the Section 861 method of cost allocation or the simplified deduction method may allocate W-2 wages to DPGR by multiplying W-2 wages by the ratio of the wage expense included in calculating qualified production activities income (QPAI) to the total wage expense used in calculating taxable income (or adjusted gross income, if applicable), without regard to any wage expense disallowed by Code Secs. 465, 469, 704(d), or 1366(d) (Reg. § 1.199-2(e)(2)).[247] The taxpayer must use the same expense allocation and apportionment methods that it uses to determine QPAI to allocate and apportion wage expense for purposes of this safe harbor. A taxpayer that uses the small business simplified overall method may use a safe harbor to allocate W-2 wages to DPGR according to the ratio of DPGR to total gross receipts.

References are to Standard Federal Tax Reports; Tax Research Consultant; and Practical Tax Explanations.

[242] ¶ 12,472C; BUSEXP: 6,108.05; § 6,015.20

[243] ¶ 12,472C, ¶ 12,472G; BUSEXP: 6,108.05; § 6,015.20

[244] ¶ 12,472C; BUSEXP: 6,108.10; § 6,015.20

[245] ¶ 12,472C; BUSEXP: 6,108.15; § 6,015.20

[246] ¶ 12,472C; BUSEXP: 6,108.20; § 6,015.20

[247] ¶ 12,472A; BUSEXP: 6,054.20; § 6,010

980H. Application of Code Sec. 199 to Pass-Through Entities. The deduction for domestic production activities (¶ 980A) is generally applied at the shareholder, partner, or similar level of a pass-through entity (Code Sec. 199(d)(1); Reg. § 1.199-5).[248] The entity allocates to each partner or shareholder its share of the entity's qualified production activities income (QPAI) and W-2 wages. Only an eligible entity may calculate QPAI and W-2 wages at the entity level. An eligible entity is:

(1) an eligible Code Sec. 861 partnership,

(2) an eligible widely-held pass-through entity, or

(3) an eligible small pass-through entity (Rev. Proc. 2007-34).[249]

Entities that are ineligible to calculate QPAI and W-2 wages at the entity level include qualifying in-kind partnerships (under Reg. § 1.199-3(i)(7)) and EAG partnerships (as described in Reg. § 1.199-3(i)(8)).

The owner of a pass-through entity generally is not treated as directly conducting the qualified production activities of the entity, and vice versa, with respect to property transferred between the entity and the owner. Domestic production gross receipts (DPGR) generally do not include gain or loss recognized on the sale, exchange, or other disposition of an interest in a pass-through entity (Reg. § 1.199-5).[250]

Special rules permit patrons of agricultural or horticultural cooperatives to claim the deduction for their portion of any patronage dividend or per-unit allocation received that is allocable to the QPAI of the cooperative (Code Sec. 199(d)(3); Reg. § 1.199-6).[251] For a discussion of the application of the deduction to S corporations, see ¶ 312; for partnerships, see ¶ 431A; and for nongrantor trusts and estates, see ¶ 536.

Expenses of Professional Persons

981. Professional Persons. A professional person may deduct expenses incurred for using a car to make professional calls, dues to professional organizations, rent paid for office space, and other ordinary and necessary business expenses. Amounts for books and equipment may be deducted if the useful life of the item is not more than one year (Reg. § 1.162-6).[252]

No deduction is allowed for dues paid to any club organized for business, pleasure, recreation, or other social purposes (Code Sec. 274(a)(3); Reg. § 1.274-2(a)(2)(iii)).[253] However, this disallowance does not extend to dues paid to professional organizations (e.g., bar and accounting associations) or public service organizations (e.g., Kiwanis and Rotary clubs) (¶ 913A).

A professional who incurs unreimbursed expenses in performing services as an employee may deduct them only as itemized deductions subject to the two-percent-of-adjusted-gross-income floor (¶ 941 and ¶ 1079).

Information Services. Amounts paid for subscriptions to professional journals and information services that have a useful life of one year or less, are deductible by a lawyer, accountant or other taxpayer who buys a service in connection with the performance of his or her duties (*J.I. Peyser*, Dec. 13,076(M), 1 TCM 807 (1943); *G. Nehus*, Dec. 50,308(M), 68 TCM 1503 (1994)).[254] The cost of a professional library having a more permanent value should be capitalized.

Other Expenses. A deduction is allowed to members of the clergy, lawyers, merchants, professors, and physicians for expenses incurred in attending business conventions (¶ 959) (Reg. § 1.162-2).[255] For foreign conventions, see ¶ 960. A member of the medical profession is allowed a deduction for business entertainment, subject to the rules discussed at ¶ 910, so long as there is a direct relationship between the expense

References are to Standard Federal Tax Reports; Tax Research Consultant; and Practical Tax Explanations.

[248] ¶ 12,468, ¶ 12,472D; BUSEXP: 6,212; § 6,020.10

[249] ¶ 12,476.55; BUSEXP: 6,212.10, BUSEXP: 6,214; § 6,020.05

[250] ¶ 12,472D; BUSEXP: 6,212; § 6,020.05

[251] ¶ 12,468, ¶ 12,472E; BUSEXP: 6,204; § 6,020.05

[252] ¶ 8633; BUSEXP: 3,050; § 9,005.25

[253] ¶ 14,402, ¶ 14,405; BUSEXP: 24,658; § 9,625

[254] ¶ 8634.1206, ¶ 8634.1208; BUSEXP: 3,050; § 45,120.05

[255] ¶ 8527; BUSEXP: 24,160; § 9,515

and the development or expansion of a medical practice (*R.A. Sutter*, Dec. 19,966, 21 TC 170 (1953) (Acq.)).[256] A doctor's staff privilege fee paid to a hospital is a capital expenditure (*G.L. Heigerick*, Dec. 27,846, 45 TC 475 (1966)).[257] For other deductions, see the checklist at ¶ 57.

Farmer's Expenses

982. Farming Expenses. Deductions are permitted for expenses incurred in carrying on the business of farming, including a horticultural nursery business (Reg. § 1.162-12).[258] Allowable deductions include costs for small tools expected to last one year or less; for feeding and raising livestock (excluding produce grown on the farm and labor of the taxpayer); and for gasoline, repairs, and upkeep of a car or truck used wholly in the business of farming, or a portion of the cost if the vehicle is used for both farming and personal use. Special rules apply to certain property produced in a farming business (¶ 999) and to farm tax shelters (¶ 1519). See ¶ 767 for income averaging rules. Expenses for the purchase of farm machinery or equipment, breeding, dairy or work animals, a car, and drilling water wells for irrigation are capital items usually subject to depreciation.

Conservation Expenses. A farmer may generally elect to deduct soil and water conservation expenditures that are not depreciable or otherwise deductible if they would increase the basis of the property absent the election to deduct them (Code Sec. 175; Reg. § § 1.175-1—1.175-6).[259] However, current deductions for soil and water conservation expenses are limited to those that are consistent with a conservation plan approved by the Soil Conservation Service of the U.S.D.A. or, in the absence of a federally approved plan, a soil conservation plan of a comparable state agency. The election does not apply to expenses related to the draining or filling of wetlands or to land preparation for the installation or operation of center pivot irrigation systems. The deduction is limited annually to 25 percent of the taxpayer's gross income from farming. Excess expenses can be carried over to succeeding tax years, but in each year the total deduction is limited to 25 percent of that year's gross income from farming.

Deductible soil and water conservation expenses include such costs as: leveling; grading; construction, control, and protection of diversion channels, drainage ditches, outlets, and ponds; planting of windbreaks; and other treatment or moving of earth. Also deductible are endangered species recovery expenditures paid or incurred by a taxpayer engaged in the business of farming for the purpose of achieving site-specific management actions recommended in recovery plans approved pursuant to the Endangered Species Act of 1973 (P.L. 93-205). No current deduction is allowed for the purchase, construction, installation, or improvement of depreciable masonry, tile, metal, or wood structures, appliances, and facilities, such as tanks, reservoirs, pipes, canals, and pumps. Assessments levied by a soil or water conservation or drainage district to defray district expenses may also be deductible.

Schedule F Loss Limitation. The amount of net farm losses that can be claimed for any tax year in which a taxpayer, other than a C corporation, has received applicable subsidies is limited to the greater of $300,000 ($150,000 for a married taxpayer filing separately) or the taxpayer's aggregate net farm income for the five preceding tax years (Code Sec. 461(j)).[260] Any farm loss that exceeds this limitation is excess farm loss, which is carried forward to the next tax year as a farming deduction.

983. Land Clearing Expenses. Land clearing expenditures must be capitalized and added to the farmer's basis in the land (*AMFAC, Inc.*, CA-9, 80-2 USTC ¶ 9630).[261] However, business expenses for ordinary maintenance activities related to property already used in farming (e.g., brush clearing) are currently deductible (*E.G. Barham*, DC Ga., 69-1 USTC ¶ 9356).[262]

References are to Standard Federal Tax Reports; Tax Research Consultant; and Practical Tax Explanations.

[256] ¶ 8523.2717; BUSEXP: 24,160; § 9,610.05

[257] ¶ 8634.1154; BUSEXP: 9,100; § 10,201

[258] ¶ 8755; FARM: 9,050; § 36,101

[259] ¶ 12,060—¶ 12,066; FARM: 9,150; § 36,110.05

[260] ¶ 21,802; FARM: 9,208; § 36,215

[261] ¶ 12,068.27; FARM: 9,102; § 36,101

[262] ¶ 8520.7455; FARM: 9,168; § 36,320.10

984. Development Costs. Farmers generally have the option of deducting or capitalizing certain developmental expenses that are ordinary and necessary business expenses (¶ 999). However, plants produced by farms that have a preproductive period of more than two years must be capitalized. For certain farms (corporations, partnerships, and tax shelters) that are required to use the accrual method, the expenses must be capitalized regardless of the length of the preproductive period. Special rules apply to farming syndicates (¶ 1521).

985. Expensing Fertilizer Costs. A farmer, other than a farm syndicate, may elect to deduct current expenses otherwise chargeable to capital accounts for fertilizer, lime, ground limestone, marl, or other materials for enriching, neutralizing, or conditioning land used in farming. If no election is made, expenditures producing benefits extending over more than one year are capitalized and recovered by amortization (Code Sec. 180; Reg. § 1.180-1 and 1.180-2).[263] The election, which is effective only for the tax year claimed, is made by claiming the deduction on the return. For farm syndicates and prepayments by cash-basis farmers, see ¶ 1519, ¶ 1521, and ¶ 1539.

Landlord or Tenant Expenses

986. Landlord or Tenant. A tenant may deduct rent paid for business property, as well as any amounts such as property taxes and interest that the lease requires the tenant to pay on behalf of the landlord (Code Sec. 162(a)(3); Reg. § 1.162-11).[264] An amount paid by a *lessee* for cancellation of a lease on business property is generally deductible (*A.J. Cassatt*, CA-3, 43-2 USTC ¶ 9579).[265] However, payments by the *lessor* for the cancellation of a lease are generally capital expenditures, amortizable over the unexpired term of the canceled lease (*Peerless Weighing & Vending Machine Corp*, Dec. 29,713, 52 TC 850 (1969)).[266]

Under the one-year rule, a cash-basis taxpayer can deduct otherwise allowable rent attributable to the current or a previous year in the year in which the taxpayer actually pays the rent (Reg. § 1.461-1(a)).[267] This is true even though most of the lease term is in the following year if the lease expires within a year of payment. Prepaid rent for a lease extending more than one year from the date of payment must be capitalized and amortized over the term of the lease. Some rental payments are subject to the uniform capitalization rules (¶ 990). For an improvement made by the lessee on leased premises, see ¶ 1234.

If an owner of property occupies part of the property as a personal residence and rents part of it, expenses and depreciation allocable to the rented space may be deductible (¶ 966).

Payments made under a conditional sales contract are not deductible as rent. A conditional sales contract generally exists when at least a portion of the rental payments is applied to the purchase of the property under advantageous terms (IRS Fact Sheet FS-2007-14).[268]

Under certain conditions, taxpayers who are in the business of producing real property or tangible personal property for resale, or who purchase property for resale, may not claim rental or lease expenses as a current deduction. Instead, they must include some or all of these costs in the basis of the property they produce or acquire for resale under the uniform capitalization rules. These costs are recovered when the property is sold (IRS Fact Sheet FS-2007-14).

References are to Standard Federal Tax Reports; Tax Research Consultant; and Practical Tax Explanations.

[263] ¶ 12,140; ¶ 12,141, ¶ 12,142; FARM: 9,064; § 36,115, § 36,320.20

[264] ¶ 8500; ¶ 8753; REAL: 12,050; § 18,605

[265] ¶ 8754.16; REAL: 12,252.10; § 18,605.15

[266] ¶ 13,709.417; REAL: 12,252.20; § 18,605.15

[267] ¶ 21,805; ACCTNG: 6,316; § 38,405

[268] ¶ 8754.5497; SALES: 42,056.15

Mining Company's Expenses

987. Mine Exploration. Mining companies may elect to deduct domestic exploration expenses (except for oil or gas), but the amount deducted must be recaptured once the mine reaches production stage or is sold (Code Sec. 617).[269] The company recaptures the deduction by electing either to (1) include in income for that year the previously deducted exploration expenditures chargeable to the mine, increase the basis of the property by the amount included in income, and subsequently recover this amount through depletion, or (2) forgo depletion from the property that includes or comprises the mine until the forgone deductions equal the exploration expenditures previously deducted.

Expenses not recaptured by one of these methods are recaptured on the sale or other disposition of the mining property, with the amount recaptured treated as ordinary income. Certain transfers are not subject to these recapture rules (Code Sec. 617(b) and (d)(3)).[270]

Deductions allowed a corporation, other than an S corporation, for mineral exploration and development costs (¶ 988) must be reduced by 30 percent (Code Sec. 291(b)).[271] The 30 percent of expenses that cannot be deducted must be capitalized and amortized over a 60-month period on Form 4562. Taxpayers may also elect to capitalize mine exploration expenses and amortize them over a 10-year period (¶ 1450).

Geological and geophysical (G&G) expenditures paid or incurred in connection with oil and gas exploration or development in the United States must be amortized ratably over a 24-month period beginning on the mid-point of the tax year that the expenses were paid or incurred. If a property or project is abandoned or retired during the 24-month amortization period, any remaining basis must continue to be amortized (Code Sec. 167(h)).[272] Major integrated oil companies must ratably amortize any G&G costs over seven years.

988. Mine Development. Expenses paid or incurred with respect to a domestic mine or other natural deposit, other than oil or gas, after the existence of ores or minerals in commercially marketable quantities has been discovered can be deducted currently, unless the taxpayer elects to treat them as deferred expenses and deduct them ratably as the ore or mineral is sold (Code Sec. 616; Reg. § 1.616-1).[273] These expenses do not include those made for the acquisition or improvement of depreciable property. However, depreciation allowances are considered development costs.

The 30-percent reduction in the allowable deduction and the election to amortize over a 10-year period (discussed at ¶ 987 in the case of exploration expenses) applies also to mine development expenses (Code Sec. 291(b)).[274]

988A. Foreign Mine Exploration and Development. Foreign mining exploration and development expenses (other than oil, gas, or geothermal wells) are recovered over a 10-year, straight-line amortization schedule beginning with the tax year in which they were paid or incurred (Code Secs. 616(d) and 617(h)).[275] However, the taxpayer may elect to add such expenses to the adjusted basis of the property for purposes of computing cost depletion.

989. Oil, Gas, or Geothermal Well Drilling Expense. Operators of a domestic oil, gas, or geothermal well may elect to currently deduct intangible drilling and development costs (IDCs) rather than charging them to capital and recovering them through depletion or depreciation (Code Sec. 263(c); Reg. § 1.612-4).[276] The election is binding upon future years. IDCs generally include all expenses made by the operator incident to and necessary for the drilling of wells and the preparation of wells for the production of

References are to Standard Federal Tax Reports; Tax Research Consultant; and Practical Tax Explanations.

[269] ¶ 24,110; FARM: 21,052; § 11,630

[270] ¶ 24,110; FARM: 21,058.20; § 11,630

[271] ¶ 15,190; FARM: 21,102; § 11,630

[272] ¶ 11,002; FARM: 21,176; § 11,501

[273] ¶ 24,090, ¶ 24,091; FARM: 21,110; § 11,630

[274] ¶ 15,190; FARM: 21,118; § 11,630

[275] ¶ 24,090, ¶ 24,110; FARM: 21,052; § 11,630

[276] ¶ 13,700, ¶ 23,949; FARM: 21,150; § 45,525.15

oil, gas, or geothermal energy that are neither for the purchase of tangible property nor part of the acquisition price of an interest in the property. IDCs include labor, fuel, materials and supplies, truck rent, repairs to drilling equipment, and depreciation for drilling equipment.

An integrated oil company (generally, a producer that is not an independent producer) must reduce the deduction for IDCs otherwise allowable by 30 percent (Code Sec. 291(b)).[277] The amount disallowed as a current expense deduction must be amortized over a 60-month period. Taxpayers may elect to capitalize, rather than currently deduct, IDCs and amortize these expenditures over a 60-month period (¶ 1450).

If the operator elects to capitalize IDCs, and the well proves to be nonproductive, i.e., a dry hole, the operator may elect to deduct those costs as an ordinary loss (Reg. § 1.612-4(b)(4)).[278] The election, once made, is binding for all years.

Foreign Wells. Operators may not opt to currently deduct IDCs for wells located outside the U.S. (Code Sec. 263(i)).[279] Such costs must be recovered over a 10-year straight-line amortization schedule or, at the operator's election, added to the adjusted basis of the property for cost depletion. Dry hole expenses incurred outside the U.S. are currently deductible.

989A. Advanced Mine Safety Equipment Expensing. A taxpayer may elect to expense 50 percent of the cost of advanced mine safety equipment placed in service before January 1, 2017 (Code Sec. 179E, as amended by the Protecting Americans from Tax Hikes (PATH) Act of 2015 (P.L. 114-113)).[280] The cost of any eligible equipment that is expensed under Code Sec. 179 cannot be taken into account in calculating this special deduction for mine safety equipment. The deduction is subject to recapture as ordinary income under the Code Sec. 1245 depreciation recapture rules.

Uniform Capitalization Rules

990. Uniform Capitalization Rules. Taxpayers subject to the uniform capitalization rules must capitalize all direct costs and an allocable portion of most indirect costs that are associated with production or resale activities. The uniform capitalization rules apply to the following:

(1) real or tangible personal property produced by the taxpayer for use in a trade or business or in an activity engaged in for profit;

(2) real or tangible personal property produced by the taxpayer for sale to customers; and

(3) real or personal property, both tangible and intangible, acquired by the taxpayer for resale. However, the uniform capitalization rules do not apply to personal property acquired for resale if the taxpayer's average annual gross receipts for the preceding three tax years do not exceed $10 million (Code Sec. 263A).[281]

Costs attributable to producing or acquiring property generally are capitalized by charging them to capital accounts or basis, and costs attributable to property that is inventory in the hands of the taxpayer generally are capitalized by including them in inventory.

Property Excepted from Rules. Among the classes of property excepted from the rules are:

(1) property produced by the taxpayer for its own use other than in a trade or business or in an activity conducted for profit;

(2) research and experimental expenditures (¶ 979);

References are to Standard Federal Tax Reports; Tax Research Consultant; and Practical Tax Explanations.

[277] ¶ 15,190; FARM: 21,154.10; § 45,525.15

[278] ¶ 23,949; FARM: 21,152.10; § 45,525.15

[279] ¶ 13,700; FARM: 21,152.20; § 45,525.15

[280] ¶ 12,139; BUSEXP: 19,000; § 10,255

[281] ¶ 13,800; BUSEXP: 9,050; § 10,301

(3) capital costs incurred in complying with EPA sulfur regulations (¶ 977A), intangible drilling and development costs (¶ 989), and mine development and exploration (¶ 987 and ¶ 988);

(4) any property produced by the taxpayer under a long-term contract;

(5) any costs incurred in raising, growing or harvesting trees (including the costs associated with the underlying real property) other than trees bearing fruit, nuts, or other crops and ornamental trees (those that are six years old or less when severed from the roots); and

(6) amounts allowable as a deduction under Code Sec. 59(e), relating to the optional ten-year write-off of certain tax preferences under the alternative minimum tax rules, with respect to mining exploration and development costs, research and experimental expenditures, and intangible drilling costs (60-month write-off for IDCs), but not circulation expenditures (¶ 1450).

990A. Writers, Photographers, and Artists. The uniform capitalization rules do not apply to expenses paid or incurred by a self-employed individual, including expenses of a corporation owned by a free-lancer and directly related to the activities of a qualified employee-owner, in the business of being a writer, photographer, or artist whose personal efforts create or may reasonably be expected to create the product (Code Sec. 263A(h)).[282] Generally, expenses for producing jewelry, silverware, pottery, furniture, and similar household items are not exempt.

991. Costs Required To Be Capitalized. Generally, direct material and labor costs and indirect costs must be capitalized with respect to property that is produced or acquired for resale (Code Sec. 263A(a)(2); Reg. § 1.263A-1(e)).[283] Direct material costs include the costs of materials that become an integral part of the subject matter and materials that are consumed in the ordinary course of the activity. Direct labor costs include the cost of labor that can be identified or associated with a particular activity such as basic compensation, overtime pay, vacation pay, and payroll taxes.

Indirect costs include all costs other than direct material and labor costs. Indirect costs require a reasonable allocation to determine the portion of such costs that are attributable to each activity of the taxpayer. Indirect costs include: repair and maintenance of equipment or facilities; utilities; rental of equipment, facilities, or land; indirect labor and contract supervisory wages; indirect materials and supplies; depreciation, amortization and cost recovery allowance on equipment and facilities (to the extent allowable as deductions); certain administrative costs; insurance; contributions paid to or under a stock bonus, pension, profit-sharing, annuity, or other deferred compensation plan; rework labor, scrap and spoilage; and certain engineering and design expenses.

992. Costs Not Required To Be Capitalized. Costs that are not required to be capitalized with respect to property produced or acquired for resale include marketing, selling, advertising and distribution expenses (Reg. § 1.263A-1(e)(4)(iv)).[284] The IRS procedures allow for the capitalization or amortization of package design costs (Rev. Proc. 98-39).[285] Other costs that need not be capitalized include bidding expenses incurred in the solicitation of contracts not awarded the taxpayer; certain general and administrative expenses; and compensation paid to officers attributable to the performance of services that do not directly benefit or are not incurred by reason of a particular production activity.

993. Interest Capitalization Rules. Interest costs paid or incurred during the production period to finance the construction, building, installation, manufacture, development, or improvement of real or tangible personal property that is produced by the taxpayer must be capitalized in certain cases (Code Sec. 263A(f); Reg. § 1.263A-8).[286] This rule applies to property that is produced by the taxpayer for use in its trade or business or in an activity for profit with: (1) a long useful life (real property or any other

References are to Standard Federal Tax Reports; Tax Research Consultant; and Practical Tax Explanations.

[282] ¶ 13,800; BUSEXP: 9,062; § 10,305.10

[283] ¶ 13,800, ¶ 13,811; BUSEXP: 9,056; § 10,310.15

[284] ¶ 13,811; BUSEXP: 9,052; § 10,310.30

[285] ¶ 13,709.469; BUSEXP: 9,350; § 9,970

[286] ¶ 13,800, ¶ 13,852; BUSEXP: 9,060; § 10,330.05

property with a class life of 20 years or more), (2) an estimated production period exceeding two years, or (3) an estimated production period exceeding one year and a cost exceeding $1 million. The production period begins on the date production of the property starts and ends on the date the property is ready to be placed in service or is ready to be held for sale. Interest capitalization is not required for property acquired for resale (e.g., inventory held by a dealer), and interest that constitutes qualified residence interest (¶ 1047).

The taxpayer is treated as producing any property that is produced for the taxpayer under a contract (Code Sec. 263A(g)(2)).[287] Thus, the taxpayer-customer must capitalize its share of this interest expense allocable to capital costs, including progress payments, advances to the contractor, and an allocable portion of the taxpayers general and administrative expenses.

In determining whether interest expense is allocable to the production of property, interest on a debt that financed production or construction costs of a particular asset is first allocated and capitalized as part of the cost of the item (Reg. §§ 1.263A-9 and 1.263A-11).[288] Interest on other loans is also subject to capitalization under an avoided-cost rule to the extent of the production or construction costs that exceed the amount of this direct debt. An assumed interest rate based on the average interest rates on the taxpayer's outstanding debt, excluding debt specifically traceable to production or construction, may be used for this purpose. Production or construction expenditures include cumulative production costs (including previously capitalized interest) required to be capitalized.

Interest relating to property used to produce property subject to the interest capitalization rules is also subject to capitalization to the extent that interest is allocable to the produced property as determined under the above rules (Code Sec. 263A(f)(3)).[289]

For flow-through entities (i.e., partnerships, S corporations, estates, and trusts), the interest capitalization rules are applied first at the entity level and then at the beneficiary level (Code Sec. 263A(f)(2)(C)).

994. Property Acquired for Resale. Unless the taxpayer elects to use the simplified resale method at ¶ 995, the rules applicable to the production of property apply to costs incurred with respect to property acquired for resale in a trade or business or in an activity conducted for profit (Code Sec. 263A(b)).[290] Property held for resale may include literary, musical, or artistic compositions; stocks; certificates, notes, bonds, debentures, or other evidence of indebtedness; or an interest in or right to subscribe to or purchase of any of the foregoing, and other intangible properties. However, personal property acquired for resale is not subject to the uniform capitalization rules if the taxpayer's average annual gross receipts for the three preceding tax years (or if less, the number of preceding tax years the taxpayer and any predecessor has been in existence) do not exceed $10 million. The uniform capitalization rules apply to real property acquired for resale, regardless of the taxpayer's gross receipts.

995. Simplified Methods of Accounting for Resale Costs. Most taxpayers may elect to use one of the simplified resale methods for allocating costs to property acquired for resale (Reg. § 1.263A-3(d)).[291] However, a single trade or business that consists of both production and resale activities must use the simplified production method (¶ 996). Under the simplified resale methods, preliminary inventory balances are calculated without including the additional costs (¶ 996) required to be capitalized. The amount of additional costs attributable to prior periods and the amount of additional costs determined to be capitalized for the current period are then taken into account with the inventory balances as initially calculated in order to arrive at an ending inventory balance.

References are to Standard Federal Tax Reports; Tax Research Consultant; and Practical Tax Explanations.

[287] ¶ 13,800; BUSEXP: 9,060; § 10,330.10

[288] ¶ 13,856, ¶ 13,864; ACCTNG: 15,208.30; § 10,330.15

[289] ¶ 13,800; BUSEXP: 9,060; § 10,330.15

[290] ¶ 13,800; BUSEXP: 9,052.25; § 10,305.15

[291] ¶ 13,824; BUSEXP: 9,056.35; § 10,325.05

The following categories of costs are required to be capitalized with respect to property acquired for resale, regardless of whether a taxpayer elects one of the simplified resale methods: (1) off-site storage or warehousing; (2) purchasing; (3) handling, processing, assembly, and repackaging; and (4) certain general and administrative expenses (Reg. § 1.263A-3(c)).

996. Simplified Method of Accounting for Production Costs. Most taxpayers may elect to use the simplified production method to account for the additional costs required to be capitalized with respect to property produced by the taxpayer that is: (1) stock in trade or other property properly includible in inventory, or (2) noninventory property held primarily for sale to customers in the ordinary course of business (Reg. § 1.263A-2(b)(2)(i)).[292] Proposed regulations would provide a modified simplified production method that will be effective when the final regulations are published in the Federal Register (Prop. Reg. § 1.263A-2(c)).[293]

Categories of property eligible for the simplified production method also include properties constructed by a taxpayer for use in its trade or business if the taxpayer: (1) is also producing inventory property that is substantially identical in nature and is produced in the same manner, or (2) produces such property on a routine and repetitive basis.

997. Simplified Service Cost Method. A simplified method is available for determining capitalizable mixed service costs for eligible property (Reg. § 1.263A-1).[294] The election to use the simplified method must be made independently from other allowable simplified methods.

999. Capitalization of Farming Business Expenses. The uniform capitalization rules apply to plants and animals produced by certain farming businesses (corporations, partnerships, and tax shelters) that are required to use the accrual method. For other farming businesses, the uniform capitalization rules apply only to plants produced in the farming business that have a preproductive period of more than two years (Code Sec. 263A(d)(1)).[295]

Generally, the rules do not apply to costs that are attributable to the replanting, cultivation, maintenance, and development of any plants (of the same type of crop) bearing an edible crop for human consumption (normally eaten or drunk by humans) that were lost or damaged as the result of freezing temperatures, disease, drought, pests, or casualty (Code Sec. 263A(d)(2)).[296] Replanting or maintenance costs may be incurred on property other than the damaged property if the acreage does not exceed the acreage of the damaged property.

A farming business is a trade or business involving the cultivation of land or the raising or harvesting of any agricultural or horticultural commodity (Code Sec. 263A(e)(4)).[297] Examples include a nursery or sod farm; the raising of ornamental trees (including evergreen trees six years old or less when severed from their roots); the raising or harvesting of trees bearing fruit, nuts, or other crops; and the raising, shearing, feeding, caring for, training, and managing of animals.

Any farmer, other than a corporation, partnership, or tax shelter required to use the accrual method, may elect not to apply the uniform capitalization rules to any plant produced in the farming business (Code Sec. 263A(d)(3) and (e); Reg. § 1.263A-1(b)(3)).[298] However, the election may not be made for any costs incurred within the first four years in which any almond or citrus trees were planted.

References are to Standard Federal Tax Reports; Tax Research Consultant; and Practical Tax Explanations.

[292] ¶ 13,817; ACCTNG: 15,210.05; § 10,320.20

[293] ¶ 13,817C; ACCTNG: 15,210.05; § 10,320.20

[294] ¶ 13,811; ACCTNG: 15,212; § 10,315.15

[295] ¶ 13,800; FARM: 9,104; § 10,305.20

[296] ¶ 13,800; FARM: 9,104; § 36,320.15

[297] ¶ 13,800; FARM: 9,104; § 36,320.25

[298] ¶ 13,800, ¶ 13,811; FARM: 9,104; § 36,320.20

Unless IRS consent is obtained, farmers may elect out of the uniform capitalization rules only for the first tax year during which the farmer produces property that would normally be subject to rules (Code Sec. 263A(d)(3)).[299] Once the election is made, it is revocable only with the consent of the IRS.

Incentives for Economically Distressed Communities

999A. Tax Incentives for Distressed Communities. Special tax incentives are intended to encourage the development of economically distressed areas by businesses located in empowerment zones (¶ 999B), renewal communities (¶ 999C), and the District of Columbia Enterprise Community Zone (¶ 999D). The locations of qualifying empowerment zones and renewal communities are listed in the instructions to Form 8844.

999B. Empowerment Zones. Geographic areas may be designated as empowerment zones for purposes of enhanced tax benefits through December 31, 2016 (Code Sec. 1391(d)(1)(A)(i), as amended by the Protecting Americans from Tax Hikes (PATH) Act of 2015 (P.L. 114-113)).[300] The IRS issued guidance on the process for extending any empowerment zone designation until December 31, 2016 (Notice 2016-28.

Work Opportunity Credit. Employers may claim the work opportunity credit for certain first-year wages paid or incurred to "designated community residents" and "qualified summer youth employees" hired before January 1, 2020, and living within certain economically distressed areas (¶ 1365G) (Code Sec. 51(c)(4), as amended by P.L. 114-113, and (d)).[301]

Increased section 179 allowance for property placed in service in an empowerment zone. See ¶ 1208.

60-Percent Gain Exclusion for Small Business Stock. Taxpayers other than corporations may exclude 60 percent of the gain on the sale or exchange of qualified small business stock that is attributable to periods before January 1, 2019, if the small business corporation qualifies as an empowerment zone business, and the taxpayer acquired the stock after December 21, 2001, and held it for more than five years (¶ 1905) (Code Sec. 1202(a)(2)(C)).[302]) The exclusion is reduced to 50 percent for gain attributable to periods after 2018 (Code Sec. 1202(a)(1)). In general, the corporation must qualify as an enterprise zone during substantially all of the time the stock is held. The end of the empowerment zone designation on December 31, 2016, is ignored in determining whether the corporation qualified as an enterprise zone during substantially all of the time the stock was held. Gain from the sale of small business stock of a qualified business entity in the District of Columbia enterprise zone is not eligible for the increased exclusion.

999C. Renewal Communities (Expired). Even though renewal community status terminated after December 31, 2009, the capital gain exclusion continued to be available prior to 2015.

Renewal Community Capital Gain Exclusion. Gross income does not include capital gain (or section 1231 gain) from the sale or exchange of a qualified community asset held for more than five years and acquired after December 31, 2001, and before January 1, 2010 (Code Sec. 1400F).[303] Gain attributable to periods before 2002 and after 2014 does not qualify for the exclusion.

A qualified community asset that is sold or otherwise transferred to a subsequent purchaser qualifies for the capital gain exclusion for the purchaser provided that the stock or partnership interest continues to represent an interest in a renewal community business or the tangible property continues to be used in a renewal community business (Code Secs. 1400B(b)(4)(B)(ii) and 1400F(b)(4)(B)).

References are to Standard Federal Tax Reports; Tax Research Consultant; and Practical Tax Explanations.

[299] ¶ 13,800; FARM: 9,104; § 36,320.20

[300] ¶ 32,385; BUSEXP: 57,000; § 10,001

[301] ¶ 4800; BUSEXP: 54,250; § 13,805.05

[302] ¶ 30,372; BUSEXP: 57,056.10; § 9,001

[303] ¶ 32,437; BUSEXP: 57,204.05; § 9,001

Gain on tangible property that is substantially improved by a taxpayer before January 1, 2010, and any land on which such property is located qualifies for the exclusion if during any 24-month period beginning after December 31, 2001, additions to the basis of the property exceed the greater of the adjusted basis of the property at the start of the 24-month period or $5,000.

Special rules apply that limit the exclusion in the same way as with DC Zone assets (¶ 999D) (Code Secs. 1400B(e) and 1400F(c)(3)).[304]

999D. District of Columbia. Gross income does not include qualified capital gain from the sale or exchange of any DC Zone asset held for more than five years (Code Sec. 1400B).[305] Although the DC Zone designation terminated on January 1, 2012, capital gain exclusion for a D.C. Zone asset is available until December 31, 2016, for assets acquired prior to 2012.

In general, a DC Zone asset includes only:

(1) DC Zone business stock—stock originally issued after December 31, 1997, and acquired before January 1, 2012, for cash from a domestic corporation that is a DC Zone business;

(2) a DC Zone partnership interest—a capital or profits interest in a domestic partnership interest originally issued after December 31, 1997, and acquired before January 1, 2012, for cash from a partnership that is a DC Zone business; and

(3) DC Zone business property—tangible property acquired by purchase (as defined in Code Sec. 179(d)(2)) after December 31, 1997, and before January 1, 2012, the original use of which commences with the taxpayer in the taxpayer's DC Zone business. The property may not be acquired from a related person or another member of a controlled group (Code Sec. 1400B(b).

A taxpayer who acquires stock, a partnership interest, or tangible property from another person in whose hands the asset was a DC Zone asset may also qualify for the exclusion.

Qualified capital gain is gain recognized on the sale or exchange of a DC Zone asset that is a capital asset or a Section 1231 asset (i.e., depreciable personal property and real property). It does not include gain attributable to periods before January 1, 1998, or after December 31, 2016, gain that would be recaptured as ordinary income under the Code Sec. 1245 depreciation recapture rules, gain that would be recaptured as ordinary income under the Code Sec. 1250 recapture rules if all depreciation on real property (rather than depreciation in excess of straight-line) was subject to recapture, and gain attributable to a transaction with a related person within the meaning of Code Sec. 267(b) or Code Sec. 707(b)(1).

District of Columbia Enterprise Zone. Before January 1, 2012, the District of Columbia Enterprise Zone (DC Zone) was treated as an empowerment zone, and qualifying taxpayers were generally entitled to the same special tax incentives (¶ 999B) applicable to other empowerment zones (Code Sec. 1400).[306] The $5,000 credit that was available to certain first-time homebuyers within the District of Columbia expired on December 31, 2011 (¶ 1308). However, the termination of the DC Zone designation is disregarded for purposes of determining whether any property is a DC Zone asset eligible for the capital gain exclusion described above (Code Sec. 1400B(b)(5)).

References are to Standard Federal Tax Reports; Tax Research Consultant; and Practical Tax Explanations.

[304] ¶ 32,426, ¶ 32,437; SALES: 15,354.15

[305] ¶ 32,426; SALES: 15,352.15; § 16,525.05

[306] ¶ 32,422; BUSEXP: 57,056.30; § 10,001

Chapter 10
NONBUSINESS EXPENSES

	Par.
Deductions, Generally	1001
Adjusted Gross Income (AGI)	1005
Phaseout of Itemized Deductions	1014
Medical Expenses	1015
Taxes, Generally	1021
Real Property Taxes	1028
Interest	1043
Prepaid Interest	1055
Charitable Contributions	1058
Moving Expenses	1073
Miscellaneous Itemized Deductions	1079
Production of Income Expenses	1085

Deductions, Generally

1001. Categories of Deductions for Individuals. Tax deductions for individuals fall into two basic categories: (1) those deductible from gross income to arrive at adjusted gross income (AGI), usually referred to as adjustments to gross income or above-the-line deductions (¶ 1005); and (2) those deductible from AGI, either in the form of itemized deductions (¶ 1014) or the standard deduction based on the individual's filing status (¶ 126). All the deductions claimed, along with the taxpayer's personal and dependency exemptions (¶ 133), reduces an individual's gross income to determine taxable income (Code Sec. 63).[1]

1003. Personal Expenses. A personal, living, or family expense is *not* deductible unless the Code specifically provides otherwise (Reg. § 1.262-1).[2] Nondeductible expenses include, but are not limited to, rent and insurance premiums paid for the taxpayer's own dwelling, life insurance premiums paid by the insured, and payments for food, clothing, domestic help, and upkeep of an automobile.

Adjusted Gross Income (AGI)

1005. Adjustments to Gross Income (Above-the-Line Deductions). Adjusted gross income (AGI) of an individual is an intermediate figure between gross income and taxable income. It is the starting point for computing certain deductions, credits, and other tax benefits that are based on, or limited by, income (Code Sec. 62; Temp. Reg. § 1.62-1T).[3] See the chart at ¶ 4 for a listing of the 2016 AGI phaseout thresholds.

AGI is gross income minus the following deductions:

- expenses of a trade or business carried on by the taxpayer, except for services as an employee (¶ 1006);
- certain expenses of qualified performing artists (¶ 941A), fee-based government employees (¶ 941D), and members of the National Guard or Armed Forces Reserves (¶ 941E);
- expenses attributable to rental or royalty property (¶ 1006A);
- losses from the sale or exchange of property (¶ 1007);
- alimony payments (¶ 1008);

References are to Standard Federal Tax Reports; Tax Research Consultant; and Practical Tax Explanations.

[1] ¶ 6020; FILEIND: 9,000, FILEIND: 12,000; § 1,010.05

[2] ¶ 13,601; INDIV: 39,052; § 8,201, § 8,205

[3] ¶ 6002, ¶ 6003; FILEIND: 9,000; § 5,001

- certain repayments of supplemental unemployment compensation benefits (¶ 1009);
- jury duty pay remitted to employer (¶ 1010);
- interest on education loans (¶ 1011);
- unreimbursed classroom expenses incurred by eligible educators (¶ 1011B);
- post-secondary tuition and related expenses (¶ 1011A);
- 50 percent of the self-employment taxes imposed on the taxpayer for the year (¶ 1027 and ¶ 2664);
- contributions to traditional individual retirement accounts (IRAs) (¶ 2157);
- contributions by a self-employed person to pension, profit-sharing, and annuity plans (¶ 2107);
- contributions to health savings account (HSA) (¶ 2035) and Archer medical savings account (MSA) (¶ 2037);
- depreciation or depletion allowed to a life tenant of property, or to an income beneficiary of property held in trust, or to an heir, legatee, or devisee of an estate (¶ 1090);
- interest forfeited to a bank, savings association, etc., on premature withdrawals from time savings accounts or deposits (¶ 1111);
- amortization of reforestation expenses (¶ 1287);
- moving expenses (¶ 1073);
- attorney fees and court costs paid in connection with an unlawful federal discrimination claim, or a whistleblower award for providing information on tax law violations (¶ 1093); and
- domestic production activities (also referred to as the manufacturer's deduction or DPAD) (¶ 980A).

The Code specifically allows a deduction from gross income for expenses paid or incurred in connection with the performance of services as an employee under a reimbursement or expense allowance arrangement with the employer or third party (Code Sec. 62(a)(2)(A)). In practice, employee expenses that are reimbursed under an accountable plan are *not* reported on the taxpayer's return. Generally, employee expenses that are not reimbursed or reimbursed under a nonaccountable plan are deductible, if adequately substantiated, only as miscellaneous itemized deductions subject to the two-percent-of-adjusted-gross-income limitation (¶ 1079) and the 50-percent limit for meals and entertainment (¶ 916).

1006. Trade or Business Deductions of Individuals. Expenses directly attributable to a trade or business carried on by an individual are deductible in computing adjusted gross income (AGI). All deductible business expenses are subtracted from the gross receipts from the trade or business to arrive at the net profit or loss calculated on Schedule C, Schedule C-EZ, or Schedule F of Form 1040. For this purpose, the performance of services as an employee is *not* considered to be a trade or business. However, the practice of a profession, not as an employee, is considered the conduct of a trade or business (Code Sec. 62(a)(1); Temp. Reg. § 1.62-1T(d)).[4] See ¶ 941 and following for business deductions that are available to employees.

1006A. Expenses of Individuals Attributable to Rental or Royalty Property. Ordinary and necessary expenses of an individual attributable to property held for the production of rents or royalties may be deducted in calculating adjusted gross income (AGI), even if the property is not actually producing income (Code Sec. 62(a)(4); Temp. Reg. § 1.62-1T(c))[5] These deductions include interest, taxes, depreciation, depletion, losses, etc. (Reg. § 1.212-1).[6]

References are to Standard Federal Tax Reports; Tax Research Consultant; and Practical Tax Explanations.

[4] ¶ 6002, ¶ 6003; FILEIND: 9,052; § 5,005, § 9,101

[5] ¶ 6002, ¶ 6003; FILEIND: 9,058; § 7,801, § 7,875.05

[6] ¶ 12,521; BUSEXP: 12,158.05; § 7,875.10

Rental real estate and royalty expenses are subtracted from gross income of the activity to arrive at net income or loss calculated on Schedule E of Form 1040. Income and expenses from the rental of personal property, however, is reported on Schedule C or Schedule C-EZ of Form 1040 if the taxpayer is in the business of renting personal property. If the taxpayer is not in the business of renting personal property, the income is reported on line 21 of Form 1040. The expenses are reported as an adjustment to AGI (an above-the-line deduction) by entering the amount and "PPR" on the dotted line next to line 36 of Form 1040 and including the amount in the total for that line (Instructions to Form 1040).

Property held for the production of royalties includes intangible as well as tangible property. Therefore, depreciation on a patent or copyright may be deducted. Similarly, operating owners, lessees, sublessors or sublessees, or purchasers of royalty interests can deduct their shares of a depletion allowance on natural resources (¶ 1201 and ¶ 1289).

Expenses must be pro rated if a property is devoted to rental purposes for part of a year and to personal use for the other part. See ¶ 966 for special rules governing the deduction of expenses of rental vacation homes. For the applicability of the at-risk and passive activity rules, see ¶ 1155 and ¶ 1165.

1007. Losses of Individuals from Sales or Exchanges. Any allowable loss from the sale or exchange of business or investment property may be claimed as a deduction by an individual in calculating adjusted gross income (AGI) (Code Sec. 62(a)(3); Temp. Reg. § 1.62-1T(c)(4)).[7] This includes losses from sales or exchanges of capital assets (¶ 1735), losses that are treated as losses from sales or exchanges of capital assets such as worthless securities or nonbusiness bad debts, and any allowable losses from sales or exchanges of noncapital assets (¶ 1701). A loss on an involuntary conversion is deductible in computing AGI only if it is attributable to property used in a trade or business or property held for the production of rents or royalties (¶ 1101 and ¶ 1713). A taxpayer may be entitled, however, to an itemized deduction for the involuntary conversion of property used for personal purposes if the loss arises from a casualty (¶ 1121 and ¶ 1123).

Capital losses of an individual are deductible only to the extent of capital gains, plus $3,000 of ordinary income (¶ 1752). Form 8949 and Schedule D of Form 1040 are used to calculate capital gains and losses, and the result is reported on line 13 of Form 1040 (Instructions to Form 1040). Losses of a taxpayer from the sale or exchange of noncapital assets used in a trade or business or for the production of income are calculated on Form 4797 and reported on line 14 of Form 1040 (Instructions for 4797 and Form 1040).

1008. Deduction for Alimony Paid. Alimony or separate maintenance payments made by an individual are deductible from gross income in the year paid as an adjustment to gross income (an above-the-line deduction) in calculating adjusted gross income (AGI), regardless of whether the taxpayer uses the cash or accrual method of accounting (Code Secs. 62(a)(10) and 215).[8] Back alimony is deductible in the year paid if it would have been deductible if paid on time.[9] See ¶ 771 and following for more details.

1009. Repayment of Unemployment Compensation Benefits. Repayments of supplemental unemployment compensation benefits to trusts or voluntary employees' beneficiary associations (VEBAs) required because of subsequent receipt of trade readjustment allowances under the Trade Act of 1974 are deductible from gross income as an adjustment to gross income (an above-the-line deduction) in calculating adjusted gross income (AGI) (Code Sec. 62(a)(12)).[10] The deduction is claimed by entering the amount and "Sub-Pay TRA" on the dotted line next to line 36 of Form 1040 and including

References are to Standard Federal Tax Reports; Tax Research Consultant; and Practical Tax Explanations.

[7] ¶ 6002, ¶ 6003; FILEIND: 9,056; § 5,010

[8] ¶ 6002, ¶ 12,570; INDIV: 21,150; § 1,945

[9] ¶ 6094.80; INDIV: 21,154; § 1,945

[10] ¶ 6002; FILEIND: 9,074; § 5,035

the amount in the total for that line (Instructions to Form 1040). Repayment of most other unemployment compensation benefits in a year following the year of receipt are deductible as an itemized deduction on Schedule A of Form 1040 (IRS Pub. 525). If the repayment of either type of unemployment compensation exceeds $3,000, the taxpayer may compute the tax for the tax year of the repayment under the claim-of-right doctrine (¶ 1543).

1010. Jury Duty Pay. An employee can deduct jury duty pay surrendered to an employer who continued to pay the employee's normal salary while the employee was on jury duty (Code Sec. 62(a)(13)).[11] The deduction is claimed as an adjustment to gross income (an above-the-line deduction) in calculating adjusted gross income (AGI) by entering the amount and "Jury Pay" on the dotted line next to line 36 of Form 1040 and including the amount in the total for that line (Instructions to Form 1040).

1011. Student Loan Interest Deduction. Interest paid by an individual during the tax year on any qualified education loan is deductible from gross income as an adjustment to gross income (an above-the-line deduction) in calculating adjusted gross income (AGI) on Form 1040 or Form 1040A (Code Secs. 62(a)(17) and 221).[12] The debt must be incurred by the taxpayer solely to pay qualified higher education expenses. The maximum deductible amount of interest is $2,500, but the amount of any deduction is reduced or phased out based on the taxpayer's modified adjusted gross income (MAGI). For 2016, the maximum deduction is reduced when MAGI exceeds $65,000 ($130,000 for joint returns) and is completely eliminated when MAGI is $80,000 ($160,000 for joint returns) (Rev. Proc. 2015-53). For 2017, the maximum deduction is reduced when MAGI exceeds $65,000 ($135,000 for joint filers) and is completely eliminated when MAGI is $80,000 ($165,000 for joint filers) (Rev. Proc. 2016-55).

1011A. Tuition and Fees Deduction. For tax years beginning before January 1, 2017, an individual may claim an adjustment to gross income (an above-the-line deduction) in calculating adjusted gross income (AGI) for qualifying tuition and related expenses paid for enrollment or attendance by the taxpayer, the taxpayer's spouse or dependent at any accredited post-secondary institution. The deductible amount is based on the taxpayer's AGI. The maximum deduction is $4,000 for taxpayers with AGI of $65,000 or less ($130,000 for joint filers), and $2,000 for taxpayers with AGI above $65,000 but less than or equal to $80,000 ($130,000 and $160,000, respectively, for joint filers). No deduction is available to taxpayers with AGI above $80,000 ($160,000 for joint filers) (Code Secs. 62(a)(18) and 222, as amended by the Protecting Americans from Tax Hikes (PATH) Act of 2015 (P.L. 114-113)).[13] The deduction is claimed on Form 8917 and then reported on the appropriate line of Form 1040 or Form 1040A. For tax years beginning after June 29, 2015, taxpayers are required to attached Copy B of Form 1098-T to their return in order to claim the deduction.

1011B. Teachers' Classroom Expense Deduction. Eligible educators are allowed an above-the-line deduction in calculating adjusted gross income (AGI) of up to $250 for 2016 (up to $250 for 2017) for unreimbursed expenses incurred in connection with books, supplies (other than nonathletic supplies for courses in health or physical education), computer equipment, and supplementary materials used in the classroom (Code Sec. 62(a)(2)(D), as amended by the Protecting Americans from Tax Hikes (PATH) Act of 2015 (P.L. 114-113); Rev. Proc. 2016-14; Rev. Proc. 2016-55).[14] An eligible educator is an individual who, for at least 900 hours during a school year, is a kindergarten through grade 12 teacher, instructor, counselor, principal, or aide in a school that provides elementary or secondary education as determined under state law (Code Sec. 62(d)(1)).

References are to Standard Federal Tax Reports; Tax Research Consultant; and Practical Tax Explanations.

[11] ¶ 6002; FILEIND: 9,076; § 5,040

[12] ¶ 6002, ¶ 12,692; INDIV: 60,054; § 5,901

[13] ¶ 6002, ¶ 12,770; INDIV: 60,064; § 5,201, § 5,210

[14] ¶ 6002; INDIV: 36,364; § 5,325

Phaseout of Itemized Deductions

1014. Phaseout of Itemized Deductions. Once an individual determines adjusted gross income (AGI) (¶ 1005), he or she may claim certain itemized deductions of personal expenses specifically authorized by the Code in determining taxable income. Alternatively, he or she can simplify their deductions by claiming a standard deduction based on their filing status rather than itemizing deductions (¶ 126). An amended return may be filed to change the election to claim itemized deductions or standard deduction. In the case of married individuals filing separate returns, however, the amended return may only be filed if both spouses consent (Code Sec. 63(e)).[15]

Itemized deductions are reported on Schedule A of Form 1040 and include deductions for medical and dental expenses (¶ 1015), certain taxes (¶ 1021 and ¶ 1028), interest (¶ 1043), charitable contributions (¶ 1058), casualty and theft losses (¶ 1121 and ¶ 1123), and certain miscellaneous expenses (¶ 1079). An individual whose AGI exceeds an applicable threshold amount based on filing status must reduce the total amount of otherwise allowable itemized deductions. The threshold amounts are adjusted annually for inflation (Code Sec. 68; Rev. Proc. 2015-53; Rev. Proc. 2016-55):[16]

Filing status	*2016*	*2017*
Married filing jointly and surviving spouses	$311,300	$313,800
Head of household	$285,350	$287,650
Single individual	$259,400	$261,500
Married filing separately	$155,650	$156,900

If a taxpayer's AGI exceeds the applicable threshold amount, he or she must reduce the amount of allowable itemized deductions by the lesser of: (1) three percent of the excess of the taxpayer's AGI over the applicable threshold amount, or (2) 80 percent of allowable itemized deductions reduced by the deductions for medical expenses, investment interest, casualty and theft losses, and wagering losses. The reduction is applied after all other limitations on itemized deductions are applied, including the charitable contribution limit (¶ 1059), the limit on certain meal and entertainment expenses (¶ 916), and the two-percent-of-AGI limitation on miscellaneous itemized deductions (¶ 1079). No reduction of itemized deductions is required for tax years beginning before January 1, 2013, since the reduction of itemized deduction was phased out for these years.

Medical Expenses

1015. Medical and Dental Expenses. An itemized deduction (¶ 1014) is allowed to an individual for expenses paid during the tax year for the medical care of the taxpayer or the taxpayer's spouse or dependent to the extent that the expenses exceed 10 percent of the taxpayer's adjusted gross income (AGI) (Code Sec. 213).[17] For individuals who attain age 65 before the close of the year, the threshold to claim an itemized deduction for unreimbursed medical expenses is 7.5 percent of AGI for tax years beginning before January 1, 2017. On a joint return, the percentage limitation is based on the total AGI of both spouses. The expenses are reported on Schedule A of Form 1040.

The deduction may be taken for any person who was the taxpayer's dependent or spouse when the services were rendered or the expenses were paid (Reg. § 1.213-1(e)(3)).[18] For this purpose, a dependent is the same as for claiming a dependency exemption (¶ 137) except that dependent status is determined without regard to whether the dependent claims any dependency exemptions, files a joint return, or has gross income in excess of the exemption amount for the tax year (Code Sec. 213(a); Reg. § 1.213-1(a)(3)). In addition, a child of divorced parents is treated as the dependent of both parents, even without a declaration by the custodial parent releasing the claim to the dependency exemption (¶ 139A) (Code Sec. 213(d)(5); Rev. Proc. 2008-48).

References are to Standard Federal Tax Reports; Tax Research Consultant; and Practical Tax Explanations.

[15] ¶ 6020; FILEIND: 12,052; § 7,010

[16] ¶ 6080; FILEIND: 12,056; § 7,015

[17] ¶ 12,540; INDIV: 42,000, INDIV: 42,300; § 7,201

[18] ¶ 12,541; INDIV: 42,356; § 7,205

The itemized deduction for medical expenses is limited to unreimbursed medical expenses (Code Sec. 213(a); Reg. § 1.213-1(g)). Reimbursement received for expenses deducted in a previous tax year is includible in gross income in the year received to the extent the expenses were previously deducted. Reimbursement for an earlier tax year in which no deduction was claimed is excludable from gross income.

Although medical expenses are generally deductible in the year paid, advance payments generally are *not* deductible until services are rendered (Reg. § 1.213-1(a)).[19] However, prepayments for lifetime care in a retirement home, nursing center, or similar institution are deductible in the year paid if the obligation to pay was incurred at the time the payment was made and the promise to provide lifetime care was conditioned on the payment (Rev. Rul. 93-72). Charges to credit cards qualify as payment of medical expenses in the year the expenses are charged, regardless of when the credit card company is paid (Rev. Rul. 78-39).

See ¶ 1016 for the definition of medical expenses, ¶ 1017 for the treatment of drugs and supplies, ¶ 1018 for the treatment of medical expenses paid after death, ¶ 1019 for health insurance premiums, ¶ 2035 for deductible contributions to health savings accounts (HSAs), and ¶ 2037 for deductible contributions to Archer medical savings accounts (MSAs).

1016. Medical Expenses Defined. Medical expenses eligible to be deducted as itemized deductions (¶ 1015) include amounts paid for the diagnosis, cure, mitigation, treatment, or prevention of disease, or for the purpose of affecting any structure or function of the body (Code Sec. 213; IRS Pub. 502).[20] This includes the costs of equipment, supplies, and diagnostic devices needed for these purposes. Medical care expenses must be primarily to alleviate or prevent a physical or mental defect or illness to be deductible, and not merely beneficial to general health, such as vitamins or a vacation.

Deductible medical expenses include premiums paid for medical insurance that covers medical care expenses (¶ 1019). This includes supplemental insurance such as Medicare Part B and Part D, and premiums for qualified long-term care insurance contracts that do not exceed certain limits. Medical expenses that are deductible also include qualified long-term care services, as well as transportation and lodging costs incurred on trips primarily for and essential to medical care. The lodging deduction is limited to amounts that are not lavish or extravagant and cannot exceed $50 per night for each individual (Code Sec. 213(d)(2)). The lodging deduction may also be claimed for a person who must accompany the individual seeking medical care. Meals, however, are not deductible. When transportation expenses are deductible as a medical expense, the cost of operating a car may be calculated at a standard rate of 19 cents per mile for 2016, plus parking fees and tolls (Rev. Proc. 2010-51; Notice 2016-1). Medical expenses do not include any amount allowable as a child or dependent care credit (¶ 1301) (Code Sec. 213(e)) or funeral expenses.[21]

The medical expenses deduction is not limited to amounts paid for the least expensive form of medical care applicable. A physician's recommendation is also not necessary when the expenditures are for items that are wholly medical in nature and serve no other function. Thus, amounts paid by a healthy individual for self-initiated diagnostic tests and similar procedures, such as an annual physical, a full body scan, or a self-administered pregnancy test kit, are deductible (Rev. Rul. 2007-72).

Most expenses to prevent conception and birth are deductible, as well as fertility enhancement expenses (IRS Pub. 502). Expenses for elective cosmetic surgery are *not* deductible unless the surgery or procedure is necessary to ameliorate a deformity arising from, or directly related to, a congenital abnormality, a personal injury resulting from accident or trauma, or a disfiguring disease. Cosmetic surgery includes any procedure directed at improving the patient's appearance that does not meaningfully promote the proper function of the body or prevent or treat illness or disease (Code Sec. 213(d)(9)). Thus, costs to whiten teeth discolored by age are not deductible, but costs for breast reconstruction after a mastectomy and for vision correction by laser surgery

References are to Standard Federal Tax Reports; Tax Research Consultant; and Practical Tax Explanations.

[19] ¶ 12,541; INDIV: 42,250; § 7,215.05

[20] ¶ 12,540; INDIV: 42,052; § 7,225

[21] ¶ 12,543.452; INDIV: 42,082.10; § 7,230

are deductible (Rev. Rul. 2003-57). A weight-loss program is a medical expense if undertaken to relieve a disease or defect, such as obesity or hypertension (Rev. Rul. 2002-19). Smoking-cessation programs, whether or not prescribed, and prescription drugs to alleviate symptoms of nicotine withdrawal are also medical expenses, but over-the-counter gums or patches are not (Rev. Rul. 99-28).

Special schooling for a physically or mentally handicapped child or one needing psychiatric treatment is deductible (Rev. Rul. 78-340). Amounts paid for inpatient treatment of alcoholism or drug addiction at a therapeutic center and for meals and lodging furnished as a necessary incident to the treatment are deductible (Rev. Rul. 73-325). Amounts paid to acquire, train, and maintain a dog or other service animal for assisting a blind, deaf, or physically disabled individual are deductible (Rev. Rul. 55-261; Rev. Rul. 57-461; Rev. Rul. 68-295).

The entire cost of maintenance in a nursing home or home for the aged, including meals and lodging, is a medical expense if an individual is there because of a physical condition and the availability of medical care is a principal reason for the individual's residence. If an individual is in such an institution primarily for personal or family reasons, then only that portion of the cost attributable to medical or nursing care, excluding meals and lodging, is deductible. Payments to perform both nursing care and housework may be deducted only to the extent of the nursing cost.[22]

Expenditures for home improvements and additions that are primarily for medical care qualify as a deductible medical expense only to the extent that the cost of the improvement exceeds any increase in the value of the affected property (Reg. § 1.213-1(e)(1)).[23] The entire cost of any improvement that does not increase the value of the property is deductible. Deductions have been allowed for the installation of an elevator, a swimming pool, and a central air-conditioning system. Expenditures incurred to remove structural barriers to accommodate the condition of a physically handicapped person generally do not improve the value of the residence and, therefore, are fully deductible (Rev. Rul. 87-106). The entire cost of special equipment used to mitigate the effects of a physical impairment is also deductible.

See ¶ 59 for a checklist of medical expenses.

1017. Medical Expense Deduction for Medicines and Drugs. In computing the deduction for medicine and drugs, only amounts paid for insulin and prescription medications may be taken into account (Code Sec. 213(b)).[24] Although amounts paid for over-the-counter (OTC) medicines or drugs are not taken into account in calculating the deduction, amounts paid for OTC equipment, supplies, or diagnostic devices may be deductible medical expenses (Rev. Rul. 2003-58).

Example: In 2016, a taxpayer (who has not attained age 65 during the year) with an adjusted gross income of $48,000 paid $2,750 to a doctor for medical services, $3,325 to a hospital, $340 for prescription drugs, and $250 for OTC cold remedies and vitamins. His medical expense deduction is computed as follows:

Doctor	$2,750
Hospital	3,325
Medicine and drugs	340
OTC remedies and vitamins	0
Total medical expenses	$6,415
Less: 10% of $48,000 (adjusted gross income)	4,800
Allowable deduction	$1,615

1018. Medical Expenses Paid After Death. A decedent's medical expenses that are paid by his or her estate within one year of the day after the decedent's death are treated as paid when incurred and may be deducted on his or her income tax return for the year incurred if the estate waives an estate tax deduction for the expenses (Reg. § 1.213-1(d)).[25] Alternatively, the estate may deduct the medical expenses as a claim against the estate for federal estate tax purposes (¶ 2925). Medical expenses disallowed

References are to Standard Federal Tax Reports; Tax Research Consultant; and Practical Tax Explanations.

[22] ¶ 12,543.726, ¶ 12,543.727; INDIV: 42,066; § 7,245, § 7,250

[23] ¶ 12,541; INDIV: 42,064; § 7,285.05

[24] ¶ 12,540; INDIV: 42,056; § 7,235

[25] ¶ 12,541; INDIV: 42,256; § 7,220

for income tax purposes because of the 10-percent-of-adjusted gross income limitation (7.5 percent for taxpayers age 65 or older for tax years beginning before January 1, 2017) (¶ 1015) may *not* be claimed on the estate tax return when the estate allocates medical expenses between a decedent's final income tax and estate tax returns (Rev. Rul. 77-357).

1019. Health and Accident Insurance Premiums. A medical expense deduction is allowed for premiums paid for medical care insurance, including contact lens insurance, subject to the 10-percent-of-adjusted gross income limitation (7.5 percent for taxpayers age 65 or older for tax years beginning before January 1, 2017) (¶ 1015) (Code Sec. 213(d)(1)(D); Reg. § 1.213-1(e)(4)).[26] If the insurance contract provides payments for more than medical care, such as an indemnity for loss of income or life, limb or sight, premiums are deductible only to the extent a reasonable charge for the medical care is stated separately in the contract or in a separate statement from the insurer. Premiums paid by a taxpayer under age 65 for insurance covering medical care expenses of the taxpayer, the taxpayer's spouse, or a dependent after the taxpayer turns 65 are considered to be medical expenses in the year paid if the premiums are payable on a level payment basis under the contract: (1) for a period of 10 years or more or (2) until the year the taxpayer reaches age 65, but in no case for a period of less than five years.

Amounts paid as employment taxes (¶ 2648) for hospital insurance under the Medicare program are *not* medical expenses. Thus, the basic cost of Medicare insurance (Medicare Part A) is not deductible unless the individual is not covered by Social Security and voluntarily paid premiums to be covered. In addition, premiums voluntarily paid for supplemental Medicare insurance (Medicare Part B) and Medicare prescription drug insurance (Medicare Part D) are deductible (IRS Pub. 502). Self-employed individuals can deduct from gross income 100 percent of amounts paid for health insurance coverage (¶ 908), including premiums for all Medicare parts (CCA 201228037).

Long-Term Care Insurance. Premiums paid for a qualified long-term care insurance contract are a medical expense, but the deductible amount of the premium is adjusted annually for inflation and limited by the age of the individual at the close of the tax year (Code Sec. 213(d); Rev. Proc. 2015-53; Rev. Proc. 2016-55).[27] The maximum deductible amount is adjusted annually for inflation and is:

Age at close of tax year	*2016*	*2017*
40 or less	$390	$410
Over 40 but not over 50	$730	$770
Over 50 but not over 60	$1,460	$1,530
Over 60 but not over 70	$3,900	$4,090
Over	$4,870	$5,110

1020. Archer Medical Savings Accounts. Eligible individuals may claim an adjustment to gross income (an above-the-line deduction) in calculating adjusted gross income (AGI) for contributions they make during the tax year to their Archer medical savings account (Archer MSA). Individuals who are self-employed or work for small employers may be able to maintain Archer MSAs to pay medical expenses, provided that the accounts are used in conjunction with a high deductible health insurance plan (HDHP) (Code Sec. 220; Notice 96-53).[28] For a complete discussion of eligible individuals, contributions, and distributions from Archer MSAs, see ¶ 2037.

1020A. Health Savings Accounts. Eligible individuals with high-deductible health insurance plans (HDHP) may claim an adjustment to gross income (an above-the-line deduction) in calculating adjusted gross income (AGI) for contributions they make during the tax year to their health savings account (HSA). Individuals—and employees, through an employer's cafeteria plan—can establish HSAs to reimburse them for qualified medical expenses paid during the year (Code Sec. 223).[29] For a complete discussion on contributions, eligible individuals, the definition of high-deductible health plans, and taxation of distributions, see ¶ 2035.

References are to Standard Federal Tax Reports; Tax Research Consultant; and Practical Tax Explanations.

[26] ¶ 12,540, ¶ 12,541; INDIV: 42,100; § 7,240.05

[27] ¶ 12,540; INDIV: 42,114.05; § 7,240.15

[28] ¶ 12,670; INDIV: 42,500; § 42,601

[29] ¶ 12,776; INDIV: 42,450; § 42,501

Taxes, Generally

1021. Taxes Deductible as Itemized Deductions. Taxes paid or accrued by an individual not directly connected with a trade or business or with property held for production of rents or royalties may be deducted only as an itemized deduction on Schedule A of Form 1040. These include (Code Sec. 164):[30]

- state, local, or foreign real property tax (¶ 1026 and ¶ 1028);
- state or local personal property tax;
- state, local, or foreign income, war profits, or excess profits tax (¶ 1023 and ¶ 2475);
- generation-skipping transfer tax imposed on income distributions (¶ 2942); and
- state and local general sales tax (at the taxpayer's election and in lieu of state and local income taxes).

State and local taxes imposed on personal property are deductible if three conditions are met: the tax must be (1) *ad valorem*, i.e., substantially in proportion to the value of the property, (2) imposed on an annual basis, and (3) imposed with respect to personal property (Reg. § 1.164-3(c)).[31] Payment for car registration and licensing or a motor vehicle tax may be deductible as a personal property tax if it is imposed annually and assessed in proportion to the value of the car.

A taxpayer can elect to deduct *either* state and local income taxes or general state and local sales taxes (Code Sec. 164(b)(5), as amended by the Protecting Americans from Tax Hikes (PATH) Act of 2015 (P.L. 114-113)). If the taxpayer elects to deduct the general state and local sales taxes paid, he or she can claim either the total amount paid by substantiation with receipts, or the amount from IRS tables in the instructions to Schedule A, plus the amounts of general state and local sales taxes paid on the purchase a motor vehicle, boat, or other items determined by the IRS (Notice 2005-31).

If a foreign trust receives a gift or bequest from a covered expatriate (¶ 2412), a tax is imposed on the gift or bequest, and is payable by a U.S. citizen or resident beneficiary who receives from the trust a distribution attributable to the gift or bequest (¶ 516). The distribution recipient is allowed an income tax deduction on Schedule A for the amount of the tax paid or accrued, but only to the extent the tax is imposed on the portion of the distribution included in the recipient's gross income (¶ 2948).

See ¶ 1022 for when a tax is deductible, ¶ 1025 for nondeductible taxes, and ¶ 1027 for the deductibility of self-employment taxes.

1022. Taxes Deductible When Paid or Accrued. A deduction for taxes is allowed only for the year in which the taxes are paid or accrued (Code Sec. 164).[32] The failure to deduct taxes in the proper year does not allow the taxpayer to deduct the taxes in a later year. Instead, the taxpayer must file an amended return for the year the taxes were paid or accrued.

Cash-basis taxpayers deduct taxes in the year paid, including amounts withheld from wages, payments of estimated tax, and payments applicable to other tax years (¶ 1515). However, advance payments of estimated taxes made by a cash-basis taxpayer may not be deducted when paid if the taxpayer cannot reasonably determine that there is an additional amount owed (Rev. Rul. 82-208).

Accrual-basis taxpayers may generally deduct taxes in the year they accrue (¶ 1515). The date when a tax becomes due and payable is not necessarily its accrual date. State income taxes accrue during the year in which the income is earned.[33] Uncontested additional assessments accrue at the same time they would have accrued upon a correct original assessment.[34] See ¶ 1031 and ¶ 1034 for the accrual of real estate taxes.

References are to Standard Federal Tax Reports; Tax Research Consultant; and Practical Tax Explanations.

[30] ¶ 9500; INDIV: 45,000; § 7,301

[31] ¶ 9506; INDIV: 45,104; § 7,320

[32] ¶ 9500; INDIV: 45,200; § 7,310

[33] ¶ 9502.445, ¶ 21,817.115; INDIV: 45,202; § 7,310, § 7,325

[34] ¶ 9502.10; INDIV: 45,200; § 7,310

A contested tax accrues when the taxpayer transfers cash or property to satisfy the tax, if the contest exists after the transfer and a deduction would have otherwise been allowed for the year of transfer. This rule does not apply to taxes imposed by a foreign country or U.S. possession (Code Sec. 461(f)).[35]

1023. Deduction of Foreign Income and Profits Taxes. Foreign income and profits taxes are deductible only if no foreign tax credit under Code Sec. 901 is claimed for them on the taxpayer's U.S. income tax return (Code Sec. 275(a)(4)). The taxpayer must choose either the credit or the deduction; the taxes cannot be divided to support both a credit and a deduction. Foreign taxes accrue in the period for which they are imposed (¶ 2475 through ¶ 2485).

1025. Nondeductible Taxes. Taxes that cannot be deducted either as an itemized deduction by an individual, or as incurred in a trade or business or activity engaged in for profit, include (Code Sec. 275):[36]

- federal income taxes, including Social Security and railroad retirement taxes paid by employees and one-half of the self-employment taxes (¶ 2664);
- federal war profits and excess profits taxes;
- estate, inheritance, legacy, succession, and gift taxes (¶ 2901);
- income, war profits, and excess profits taxes imposed by a foreign country or a U.S. possession, if the taxpayer chooses to take a foreign tax credit for these taxes (¶ 2475);
- taxes on real property that must be treated as imposed on another taxpayer because of apportionment between buyer and seller (¶ 1032);
- certain additions to taxes imposed on public charities, private foundations, qualified pension plans, real estate investment trusts, stock compensation of insiders in expatriated corporations, golden parachute payments, and greenmail; and
- the annual fee imposed on drug manufacturers and importers for U.S. branded prescription drug sales after December 31, 2010, and the annual fee imposed on certain health insurance providers after December 31, 2013 (Act Secs. 9008(f) and 9010(f) of the Patient Protection and Affordable Care Act (P.L. 111-148)).

1026. Deduction of Assessments and Taxes for Local Benefits. Any tax that is in reality an assessment for local benefits such as streets, sidewalks, and similar improvements is *not* deductible by a property owner, except where it is levied for the purpose of maintenance and repair or of meeting interest charges on local benefits. It is the taxpayer's burden to show the allocation of amounts assessed to the different purposes (Code Sec. 164(c)(1); Reg. § 1.164-4).[37]

1027. Deduction of Self-Employment Tax. A self-employed individual can deduct one-half (50 percent) of the self-employment tax imposed for the tax year as an adjustment to gross income (an above-the-line-deduction) in calculating adjusted gross income (AGI) for that year (Code Sec. 164(f)).[38] The deduction, however, does not include the additional 0.9 Medicare tax imposed on self-employment income of certain high-income taxpayers (¶ 2664). The 50-percent deduction is attributable to a trade or business carried on by the taxpayer that does not consist of the performance of services by the taxpayer as an employee.

References are to Standard Federal Tax Reports; Tax Research Consultant; and Practical Tax Explanations.

[35] ¶ 21,802; INDIV: 45,208; § 38,430.15

[36] ¶ 14,500; INDIV: 45,150; § 7,345

[37] ¶ 9500, ¶ 9508; INDIV: 45,156; § 7,315.05

[38] ¶ 9500; INDIV: 45,114; § 5,050

Real Property Taxes

1028. Deductible Real Property Taxes. Local, state, and foreign real property taxes are generally deductible only by the person upon whom they are imposed in the year in which they were paid or accrued (Code Sec. 164(a)(1); Reg. § 1.164-1(a)).[39] Real property taxes are taxes imposed on interests in real property and levied for the general public welfare. These taxes do not include taxes assessed for local benefits (¶ 1026) (Reg. § 1.164-3).[40] State or local tax includes only taxes imposed by a state, the District of Columbia, U.S. possession, or a political subdivision thereof. Foreign tax includes taxes imposed by the authority of a foreign country or its political subdivisions. If real property is sold, any real property taxes must be apportioned between the buyer and seller (¶ 1032). A buyer or seller of real property using the accrual method of accounting may elect to accrual real estate taxes ratably (¶ 1031).

Stockholder-owners in a cooperative housing corporation may deduct their proportionate shares of the taxes paid by the corporation (¶ 1040). Condominium unit owners may also deduct real property taxes paid on their personal interests in the property (Rev. Rul. 64-31). Homeowner association assessments, however, are not deductible as real property taxes because the assessments are not paid to the state or a political subdivision (Rev. Rul. 76-495).[41]

Ministers and military personnel are allowed to deduct taxes paid on their homes, even if they receive a parsonage or military allowance excludable from gross income (¶ 1050). Cash-basis mortgagors that pay taxes directly to the mortgagee are entitled to deduct the taxes in the year when the mortgagee pays the taxing authority.

Real Property Construction Period Interest and Taxes. Interest and taxes on real property paid or incurred during the construction period generally must be capitalized (¶ 991 and ¶ 993) (Code Sec. 263A).[42]

Carrying Charges on Real Property. If a taxpayer elects to capitalize taxes on unimproved and unproductive real property, no deduction is allowed for those taxes (¶ 1614) (Code Sec. 266).[43]

1031. Real Property Taxes for Accrual Method Taxpayers. The economic performance rule generally delays an accrual-method taxpayer's deduction for real property taxes until they are paid (¶ 1540). An accrual basis seller or buyer, however, may elect to accrue real property taxes that are related to a definite period of time ratably over that period (Code Sec. 461(c); Reg. § 1.461-1(c)).[44] Alternatively, if the real estate taxes are a "recurring item," a taxpayer may elect to accrue the taxes and claim the deduction on the date the tax is assessed or becomes a lien against the property (Code Sec. 461(h)(3); Reg. § 1.461-5).[45] Either election may be made without IRS consent for the first tax year in which a taxpayer accrues real property taxes. For later years, the IRS has provided automatic consent procedures for taxpayers to make the elections (¶ 1529).

Making the Election. Whether a taxpayer should make the election to ratably accrue property taxes or adopt the recurring item exception to the economic performance rule depends on the taxpayer's tax year and lien date of the jurisdiction in which the real property is located. Except where taxes are prepaid, either option is more favorable than the payment rule.

> **Example 1:** X is a calendar-year, accrual-method taxpayer who owns Blackacre in Cook County. The real property tax year for the county is the calendar year and 2016 real property taxes were assessed and became a lien on the property on January 1, 2016. One-half of the taxes are due on March 1, 2017, and the other half on August 1, 2017. Under its three options for accruing real property taxes, X would allocate his deduction between 2016 and 2017 as follows:

References are to Standard Federal Tax Reports; Tax Research Consultant; and Practical Tax Explanations.

[39] ¶ 9500, ¶ 9501; INDIV: 45,102; § 7,315.05

[40] ¶ 9506; INDIV: 45,100, INDIV: 45,156; § 7,315.05

[41] ¶ 9502.422, ¶ 9502.515; INDIV: 45,052; § 7,315.05

[42] ¶ 13,800; REAL: 3,054; § 10,320.05, § 10,330.05

[43] ¶ 14,100; REAL: 3,112; § 10,220

[44] ¶ 21,802, ¶ 21,805; INDIV: 45,206.10; § 7,315.15, § 38,440

[45] ¶ 21,802, ¶ 21,811; ACCTNG: 12,104.10; § 38,435.10

- *Payment rule.* 2016: none. 2017: 12/12.
- *Ratable accrual.* 2016: 12/12. 2017: none.
- *Recurring item exception.* 2016: 12/12 (provided that X adopted the recurring item exception on either a timely filed original return or on an amended return filed after paying the second installment but before September 15, 2017). 2017: none.

Example 2: Assume X owns Greenacre in DeKalb County, where taxes for the fiscal year ending September 30, 2017, were assessed and became a lien on the property on October 1, 2016. Taxes are due on October 1, 2017. Under the three options for accruing real property taxes, X would allocate his deduction between 2016 and 2017 as follows:

- *Payment rule.* 2016: none. 2017: 12/12.
- *Ratable accrual.* 2016: 3/12. 2017: 9/12.
- *Recurring item exception.* 2016: none (because taxes are not due until more than 8½ months after end of 2016). 2017: 12/12. X could, however, advance his entire deduction into 2016 by prepaying his real property taxes on or before September 15, 2017.

1032. Apportionment of Real Property Tax Upon Sale. If real property is sold, then any real property taxes imposed on the property must be apportioned between the buyer and the seller for purposes of deducting the taxes (¶ 1028). The taxes are allocated based on the number of days each party held the property during the real property tax year. Taxes imposed on the property up to, but not including the date of sale, are allocated to the seller. Taxes imposed on the property beginning with the date of sale are allocated to the buyer. Proration is required whether or not the buyer and seller actually agree to apportion the tax and regardless of the lien dates under local law (Code Sec. 164(d); Reg. § 1.164-6).[46]

Example: A sells his farm to B on August 1, 2016. Both use the cash- and calendar-year basis of accounting. Taxes for the real property tax year, April 1, 2016, to March 31, 2017, become due and payable on May 15, 2017. B pays the real estate taxes when they fall due. Regardless of any agreement between the parties, 122/365 of the real estate taxes are allocated to and may be deducted by A and 243/365 of the taxes are allocated to and may be deducted by B.

For a discussion of the impact of the buyer's and seller's method of accounting on the timing of the deduction for allocated real estate taxes, see ¶ 1034.

Real Property Tax Year. The real property tax year is the period to which the tax relates under state law or local law. If a state and one or more local governmental units each imposes a tax, the real property tax year for each tax must be determined (Reg. § 1.164-6(c)).[47]

If property is sold after the real property tax becomes a personal liability or a lien but before the beginning of the related real property tax year, the seller may not deduct any amount for real property taxes for the related real property tax year. To the extent that the buyer holds the property for that real property tax year, the buyer may deduct the amount of the taxes for the tax year in which they are paid or accrued. Conversely, where the property is sold before the tax becomes a personal liability or a lien but after the end of the related real property tax year, the buyer cannot deduct any amount for taxes for the related real property tax year. To the extent that the seller holds the property for that real property tax year, the seller may deduct the amount of the taxes for the tax year they are paid or accrued (Reg. § 1.164-6(b)(1)(ii) and (iii)).[48]

Only real estate taxes arising during the real property tax year in which the sale takes place are allocated between the buyer and seller. Delinquent taxes from any prior year cannot be allocated to the buyer (Reg. § 1.164-6(b)(2)). Also, if a taxpayer pays and deducts real estate taxes in a year prior to the sale in excess of the portion allocated to him or her for the real property tax year, then the excess is required to be included in

References are to Standard Federal Tax Reports; Tax Research Consultant; and Practical Tax Explanations.

[46] ¶ 9500, ¶ 9603; INDIV: 45,300; § 7,315.10

[47] ¶ 9603; INDIV: 45,312; § 7,315.10b

[48] ¶ 9603; INDIV: 45,308, INDIV: 45,310; § 7,315.10c

his or her gross income in the year of sale, subject to the tax benefit rule (¶ 799) (Reg. § 1.164-6(d)(5)).[49]

Example: C is a cash-basis taxpayer whose real property tax is due and payable on November 30 for the next calendar year, which is also the real property tax year. He paid the 2016 real property taxes on November 30, 2015, and deducted them on his 2015 income tax return. On June 30, 2016, C sold the real property. Only the taxes from January 1 through June 29, 2016, or 180/366 of those paid, are treated as imposed on C. The excess amount deducted on his 2015 income tax return is includible in his gross income in 2016.

1034. Accounting for Allocated Real Estate Taxes. The tax year in which a taxpayer deducts real estate taxes allocated to him or her (¶ 1032) is affected by the taxpayer's method of accounting and by the date of the tax lien or liability. If the *seller* uses the cash method of accounting, the portion of taxes apportioned to him or her may be deducted in the tax year of the sale, whether or not actually paid in that tax year, if: (1) the buyer is liable for the real estate tax for the real property tax year; or (2) the seller is liable for the real estate tax for the real property tax year and the tax is not payable until after the date of sale. When the tax is not a liability of any person, the person who holds the property at the time the tax becomes a lien on the property is considered liable for the tax (Reg. § 1.164-6(d)(1) and (3)).[50]

If the *buyer* uses the cash method of accounting, the portion of real estate taxes apportioned to him or her may be deducted in the tax year of the sale, whether or not the tax is actually paid by the buyer in the tax year of the sale, if the seller is liable for the real estate tax. When the tax is not a liability of any person, the person who holds the property at the time the tax becomes a lien on the property is considered liable for the tax (Reg. § 1.164-6(d)(2) and (3)).[51]

If either the buyer or seller uses the accrual method of accounting and has not elected to accrue real estate taxes ratably (¶ 1031), the portion of their tax liability that may not be deducted for any tax year is treated as if accrued on the date of sale (Reg. § 1.164-6(d)(6)).[52]

Example: In County X the real property tax year is the calendar year and the real property tax becomes a lien on November 30 of the year. There is no personal liability for the tax. A is an accrual-method seller who sells real property to B on June 30, 2016. Neither party has elected to accrue real property taxes. A's share is 181/366 (January 1—June 29) of the tax and accrues on June 30, the date of the sale. She may deduct her share for her tax year within which June 30 falls. B's share of the tax is 185/366 (June 30—December 31) and accrues on November 30, the lien date. He may deduct his share for his tax year within which November 30 falls.

1040. Cooperative Housing Corporation. A tenant-stockholder may deduct amounts paid or accrued to the cooperative housing corporation (CHC) to the extent that they represent the tenant's proportionate share of: (1) real estate taxes on the apartment building or houses and the land on which they are situated; or (2) interest on debt contracted in the acquisition, construction, alteration, rehabilitation, or maintenance of such building, houses, or land (Code Sec. 216; Reg. § 1.216-1).[53] The limitations on deductible residential interest apply (¶ 1047).

For purposes of the deduction, a corporation is a CHC if:

- the corporation has only one class of outstanding stock;
- solely by reason of owning the stock, each stockholder is entitled to occupy a house or apartment in a building owned or leased by the corporation;
- no stockholder is entitled to receive any distribution which is not out of the corporation's earnings and profits, except on a partial or complete liquidation; and

References are to Standard Federal Tax Reports; Tax Research Consultant; and Practical Tax Explanations.

[49] ¶ 9603; INDIV: 45,318; § 4,210, § 7,315.10c

[50] ¶ 9603; INDIV: 45,316; § 7,315.10

[51] ¶ 9603; INDIV: 45,316; § 7,315.10

[52] ¶ 9603; INDIV: 45,318; § 7,315.10

[53] ¶ 12,600, ¶ 12,601; REAL: 9,200; § 7,445

- 80 percent or more of the corporation's gross income is derived from tenant-stockholders, 80 percent or more of the total square footage of its property is at all times used or available for use by the tenant-stockholders for residential purposes or purposes ancillary to residential use, or 90 percent or more of the corporation's expenses paid or incurred are for the acquisition, construction, management, maintenance, or care of the property for the tenant-stockholders' benefit.

Under the 80-percent-of-gross-income test, amounts received from tenant-stockholders to defray expenses for items like secretarial services, parking, utilities, recreation facilities, cleaning and related services are included in gross income derived from tenants, while amounts received from commercial leases and the operation of a business other than housing are excluded (Rev. Rul. 55-556). Income attributable to a unit that a governmental entity is entitled to occupy under a lease or stock ownership is also excluded (Code Sec. 216(b)(4); Reg. § 1.216-1(e)(4)).[54]

Interest

1043. Deduction of Interest by Individuals. An individual may generally deduct interest paid or accrued during the tax year, subject to certain exceptions and limitations (Code Sec. 163).[55] Deductible interest must pertain to a debt of the taxpayer and result from a debtor-creditor relationship based upon a valid and enforceable obligation to pay a fixed or determinable sum of money.[56]

Personal Interest. An individual is not allowed to claim any deduction for personal interest paid or accrued during the tax year (Code Sec. 163(h); Temp. Reg. § 1.163-9T).[57] Personal interest is any interest incurred by an individual *other than*:

- interest paid or accrued on indebtedness properly allocable to a trade or business, other than services as an employee (¶ 937);
- investment interest, but limited to net investment income (¶ 1094);
- home mortgage interest (qualified residence interest) paid or accrued on acquisition indebtedness or home equity indebtedness secured by any qualified residence of the taxpayer (¶ 1047);
- student loan interest (¶ 1011);
- interest taken into account in computing income or loss from a passive activity of the taxpayer (¶ 1165); and
- underpayment interest on estate tax payments that are deferred because of a reversionary or remainder interest in property (¶ 2939).

Any interest paid or accrued by an individual that does not fall into one of these categories is not deductible. This includes: interest on a car loan if the car is used for personal use; interest on credit cards, retail installment contracts, and revolving charge accounts incurred for personal expenses; and late payment charges by a public utility (IRS Pub. 17). In addition, expenses that are similar to interest are not deductible, including interest incurred to purchase or carry tax-exempt bonds (¶ 970), and interest incurred on loans incurred or continued to pay premiums on certain insurance contracts (¶ 909).

Nondeductible personal interest also includes interest paid on underpayments of individual federal, state, or local income taxes and on indebtedness used to pay the taxes, regardless of whether any portion of the additional tax due is attributable to trade or business income. This includes interest paid by trusts, S corporations and other pass-through entities on underpayments of state or local income taxes. Nondeductible personal interest also includes most interest on deferred taxes, other than underpayment interest on deferred estate tax payments because of a reversionary or remainder interest in property (Temp. Reg. § 1.163-9T).[58]

References are to Standard Federal Tax Reports; Tax Research Consultant; and Practical Tax Explanations.

[54] ¶ 12,600, ¶ 12,601; REAL: 9,108

[55] ¶ 9102; INDIV: 48,000; § 7,401

[56] ¶ 9104.264, ¶ 9104.344, ¶ 9104.728; INDIV: 48,200; § 7,405.10, § 7,405.15

[57] ¶ 9102, ¶ 9400; INDIV: 48,350; § 7,410

[58] ¶ 9400; INDIV: 48,350; § 7,410

Time for Deducting Interest. If a taxpayer is allowed an interest deduction, his or her method of accounting determines when it may be claimed (¶ 1515). A cash-basis taxpayer deducts interest in the year paid. In the case of prepaid interest, however, interest must be capitalized and deducted as if on the accrual basis unless it meets the exception for home mortgage interest (¶ 1055). An accrual-basis taxpayer deducts interest in the year in which it accrues, but the taxpayer must use the cash-basis for interest owed to a related taxpayer (¶ 1540B).

1047. Home Mortgage Interest Deduction. Although personal interest generally is not deductible (¶ 1043), interest payments attributable to purchase of a qualified residence are deductible by an individual in the year paid or accrued as a itemized deduction on Schedule A of Form 1040. Qualified residence interest or home mortgage interest is interest that is paid or accrued during the tax year on acquisition indebtedness and/or home equity indebtedness with respect to any qualified residence (¶ 1048) (Code Sec. 163(h)(3)).[59] It also can include interest on a loan secured by a qualified residence in a state where the security instrument is otherwise restricted by a debtor protection law. Interest paid or accrued by a trust or estate is deductible if the debt is secured by a beneficiary's qualified residence. If a taxpayer holds a mortgage credit certificate (¶ 1306), any home mortgage interest deduction must be reduced by the amount of any credit allowed (Code Sec. 163(g)).[60] See ¶ 1048A for treatment of certain mortgage insurance premiums as qualified residence interest.

Points and Prepaid Interest. Points paid by a borrower to obtain a home mortgage in exchange for a lower interest rate are prepaid interest and generally cannot be deducted as home mortgage interest in the year paid. Instead, they must be capitalized and deducted ratably over the life of the loan. See ¶ 1055, however, for circumstances under which points may be deducted in the year paid.

Qualified Residence. A qualified residence for this purpose includes the taxpayer's principal residence, and one other residence such as a vacation home that is not rented out at any time during the tax year or that is used by the taxpayer for a number of days exceeding the greater of 14 days or 10 percent of the number of days that it is rented out at a fair rental value (Code Sec. 163(h)(4)).[61] Married taxpayers who file separate returns are treated as one taxpayer, with each entitled to take into account one residence unless both consent in writing to having only one taxpayer take into account both residences.

Seller-Provided Financing. For seller-provided financing, taxpayers deducting qualified residence interest must include on Schedule A the name, address and taxpayer identification number (TIN) of the person to whom interest is paid or accrued (Code Sec. 6109(h); Instructions to Schedule A).[62]

1048. Acquisition and Home Equity Indebtedness Defined. Acquisition indebtedness is debt incurred in acquiring, constructing, or substantially improving a qualified residence and is secured by the residence for purposes of the home mortgage interest deduction (¶ 1047). Refinanced debt remains acquisition debt to the extent that it does not exceed the principal amount of acquisition debt immediately before refinancing (Code Sec. 163(h)(3)(B) and (C); IRS Pub. 936).[63] Home equity indebtedness is any nonacquisition debt that is secured by a qualified residence to the extent it does not exceed the fair market value of the residence reduced by any acquisition indebtedness. Interest on such debt is deductible even if the proceeds are used for personal expenditures.

Limitations. The aggregate amount of acquisition indebtedness may not exceed $1 million ($500,000 if married filing separately) (Code Sec. 163(h)(3)(B) and (C); Notice 88-74).[64] In addition, the total amount of debt that is treated as debt incurred in acquiring, constructing, or substantially improving a residence may not exceed the cost

References are to Standard Federal Tax Reports; Tax Research Consultant; and Practical Tax Explanations.

[59] ¶ 9102; INDIV: 48,400; § 18,515.05

[60] ¶ 9102; INDIV: 48,050; § 18,515.05

[61] ¶ 9102; INDIV: 48,400; § 18,515.10

[62] ¶ 36,960; REAL: 6,050; § 18,515.05

[63] ¶ 9102; INDIV: 48,400; § 18,515.15, § 18,515.20

[64] ¶ 9102, ¶ 9402.15; REAL: 6,056.15; § 18,515.15, § 18,515.20

of the residence, including the cost of any improvements. The aggregate amount of home equity indebtedness may not exceed $100,000 ($50,000 if married filing separately). Home equity debt is also limited to the fair market value of the residence less the total amount of the acquisition debt.

The dollar limits on acquisition debt and home equity debt apply to unmarried co-owners on a per-taxpayer basis, and not a per-residence basis (*B.H. Voss*, CA-9, 2015-2 USTC ¶ 50,427 (Acq)).[65] The IRS has also ruled that home acquisition debt may also constitute home equity debt to the extent the debt exceeds the $1 million/$500,000 limit for acquisition debt, but subject to the $100,000/$50,000 and fair market value limits for home equity debt (Rev. Rul. 2010-25). Thus, an individual can deduct interest paid on up to $1.1 million of such debt ($550,000 if married filing separately) as qualified residence interest. Interest attributable to debt over these limits is nondeductible personal interest (¶ 1043).

Example 1: A buys a home to be used as a principal residence for $375,000 that is secured by a mortgage in the amount of $350,000. The mortgage qualifies as home acquisition debt because the loan amount does not exceed the home's cost. Thus, since the acquisition indebtedness is less than $1 million, the entire amount of the interest payments is deductible.

Example 2: The fair market value of B's home is $310,000, and the balance of the mortgage (home acquisition debt) is $295,000. B takes out a home equity loan in the amount of $42,500. B's home equity debt, on which interest payments will be deductible as qualified home equity indebtedness, is limited to $15,000: the smaller of (1) the $100,000 maximum limit or (2) the excess of the home's fair market value ($310,000) over the home acquisition debt ($295,000).

Pre-October 13, 1987, Indebtedness. Interest on acquisition indebtedness incurred on or before October 13, 1987, is fully deductible, and is not subject to the $1 million limitation ($500,000 if married filing separately). The amount of this grandfathered debt reduces the amount of the limitation available for new acquisition debt, e.g., for improvements. Grandfathered debt is any debt incurred on or before October 13, 1987, that is secured by a qualified residence on that date and at all times thereafter before the interest is paid or accrued. It also includes debt secured by a qualified residence to refinance existing pre-October 13, 1987 debt, to the extent that the refinancing does not increase the principal amount or extend the term of the debt beyond the existing term of the acquisition debt immediately before the refinancing. If acquisition debt is not amortized over its term, as in the case of a balloon note, interest on any otherwise qualified refinancing is deductible for the term of the first refinancing for up to 30 years (Code Sec. 163(h)(3)(D)).[66]

1048A. Deduction of Mortgage Insurance Premiums. Premiums paid or accrued before January 1, 2017, for qualified mortgage insurance in connection with acquisition indebtedness (¶ 1048) are deductible as home mortgage interest by an individual as an itemized deduction on Schedule A of Form 1040 (¶ 1047) (Code Sec. 163(h)(3)(E), as amended by the Protecting Americans from Tax Hikes (PATH) Act of 2015 (P.L. 114-113), and 163(h)(4)(E)).[67] For every $1,000 by which the taxpayer's adjusted gross income (AGI) exceeds $100,000, however, the amount of premiums treated as interest is reduced by 10 percent. For married taxpayers filing separately, the amount of premiums treated as interest is reduced by 10 percent for every $500 that AGI exceeds $50,000. The deduction does not apply with respect to mortgage insurance contracts issued before January 1, 2007, or to premiums paid, accrued, or properly allocable to any period after December 31, 2016. Qualified mortgage insurance for this purpose is mortgage insurance provided by the Department of Veterans Affairs (VA), the Federal Housing Administration (FHA), or the Rural Housing Service, as well as private mortgage insurance.

For prepaid mortgage insurance, except VA or Rural Housing Service contracts, amounts paid that are allocable to periods after the payment year are capitalized and treated as paid in the allocable periods. Prepaid premiums must be allocated ratably over

References are to Standard Federal Tax Reports; Tax Research Consultant; and Practical Tax Explanations.

[65] ¶ 9402.12; REAL: 6,056.15; § 18,515.15, § 18,515.20

[66] ¶ 9102; REAL: 6,056

[67] ¶ 9102; REAL: 6,060; § 18,520

the shorter of the stated term of the mortgage or 84 months, beginning with the month in which the insurance was obtained. If the mortgage is satisfied before the end of its term, no deduction is allowed for any premium allocable to periods after the mortgage is satisfied (Code Sec. 163(h)(4)(F); Reg. § 1.163-11).[68]

1049. Deduction of Redeemable Ground Rents. Annual or periodic payments of redeemable ground rent, except amounts paid in redemption of this rent, are treated as interest paid on mortgage indebtedness (Code Sec. 163(c)).[69] Therefore, such ground rents are subject to the rules pertaining to qualified residences (¶ 1047). A redeemable ground rent is a ground rent payable under a freely assignable lease that, including possible renewal periods, is for a term in excess of 15 years, where the lessee has a right to terminate the lease and buy the lessor's interest in the land by paying a set amount, and the lessor's interest is primarily a security interest to protect the rental payments (Code Sec. 1055(c)(1); Reg. § 1.1055-1).[70]

1050. Deduction of Mortgage Interest of Ministers and Military Personnel. Ministers and military personnel are allowed to deduct mortgage interest on their qualified residences (¶ 1047) even though they receive a parsonage or military housing allowance that is excludable from gross income (Code Sec. 265(a)(6)).[71] Military personnel includes members of the Army, Navy, Air Force, Marine Corps, Coast Guard, National Oceanic and Atmospheric Administration, and Public Health Service (Rev. Rul. 87-32).

Prepaid Interest

1055. Deductibility of Prepaid Interest by Cash-Basis Taxpayers. A cash-basis taxpayer generally cannot take a current deduction for prepaid interest, other than for points on certain home mortgage loans described below. Instead, the taxpayer must deduct prepaid interest over the period of the loan to the extent that the interest represents the cost of using the borrowed funds during each tax year in the period (Code Sec. 461(g)).[72] This rule does not contemplate that interest will be treated as paid in equal payments over the term of the loan. Thus, interest paid on an amortizing loan as part of an equal constant payment, including principal and interest, is not subject to the prepaid interest rule merely because the payments consist of a larger interest portion in the earlier years of the loan than in later years.

Points on a home mortgage loan are deductible in the year paid if: (1) the loan is used to purchase or improve the taxpayer's principal residence and the loan is secured by the home; (2) the payment of points is an established practice in the area where the loan is made; and (3) the amount paid does not exceed the points generally charged in the area for a home loan (Code Sec. 461(g)(2)).[73] Taxpayers may also choose to amortize points over the life of their loan in certain circumstances (Rev. Proc. 87-15; IRS Pub. 936).[74]

Under a safe harbor, the IRS treats as deductible in the year paid any points paid by a cash-basis taxpayer that:

- are designated as points on the settlement statement (Form HUD-1) as points, loan discount, discount points, or loan origination fees, including amounts so designated on VA and FHA loans;
- are calculated as a percentage of the principal loan amount;
- are paid to acquire the taxpayer's principal residence in connection with a loan secured by that residence;
- are paid directly by the taxpayer, which may include earnest money, an escrow deposit, or down payment applied at closing, and not derived from loan proceeds; points paid by a seller, including points charged to the seller, are

References are to Standard Federal Tax Reports; Tax Research Consultant; and Practical Tax Explanations.

[68] ¶ 9102, ¶ 9401D; REAL: 6,060; § 18,520

[69] ¶ 9102; REAL: 6,052.45; § 18,515.05

[70] ¶ 29,940, ¶ 29,941; REAL: 6,052.45; § 18,515.05

[71] ¶ 14,050; INDIV: 48,554; § 18,515.05

[72] ¶ 21,802; ACCTNG: 6,312.05; § 38,410.45

[73] ¶ 21,802; INDIV: 48,256; § 18,515.35

[74] ¶ 9402.58; REAL: 6,054.05; § 18,515.35

considered directly paid by the taxpayer from funds not derived from loan proceeds if they are subtracted by the taxpayer from the purchase price of the residence in computing its basis; and

- conform to an established business practice of charging points for loans for the acquisition of personal residences in the area.

No part of the points may be in lieu of appraisal, inspection, title, and attorney fees, property taxes, or other amounts that are ordinarily stated separately on the settlement statement (Rev. Proc. 94-27).

The safe harbor does not apply to points paid for a loan to acquire a principal residence to the extent the principal amount exceeds the limit on acquisition indebtedness (¶ 1048). Nor does it apply to points paid on home improvement loans, second or vacation home loans, refinancing or home equity loans, or lines of credit. The fact that a taxpayer cannot satisfy the requirements of the safe harbor does not necessarily mean that points are not currently deductible. It does mean that the IRS will not automatically consider them to be currently deductible.

Refinancing. Points paid to refinance a home mortgage are not deductible in full in the year paid, but must be deducted ratably over the period of the loan because they are incurred for the repayment of the taxpayer's existing indebtedness and are not paid in connection with the purchase or improvement of the home. The U.S. Court of Appeals for the Eighth Circuit, however, allowed a full deduction in the year paid for points on a long-term home mortgage loan refinancing a short-term balloon loan used to acquire the home (*J.R. Huntsman*, CA-8, 90-2 USTC ¶ 50,340, nonacq. except in the Eighth Circuit).[75] Also, the portion of the points allocable to the proceeds of a refinancing that are used for improvements may be deducted in the year paid. The portion allocable to the repayment of existing indebtedness or other purposes is deducted ratably over the period of the loan (Rev. Rul. 87-22).[76]

Charitable Contributions

1058. Charitable Contributions by Individuals. An individual may claim an itemized deduction (¶ 1014) for contributions to a qualified charitable organization on Schedule A of Form 1040 (Code Sec. 170).[77] The charitable deduction for any one tax year is limited to a percentage of the taxpayer's contribution base determined by the type of organization receiving the donation and the type of property donated (¶ 1059). Any amount in excess of the percentage limitation for the tax year may be carried forward for five years (¶ 1060). When married individuals file a joint return, the percentage limitation depends on their aggregate contribution base. A limit also applies to the amount of a charitable deduction allowed for gifts of appreciated property, and is imposed before applying the percentage limitation (¶ 1062).

A charitable contribution is a contribution or gift to a qualifying organization (¶ 1061). Except in the case of a carryover of a deduction, a taxpayer may deduct the fair market value of property contributed to charity subject to the percentage limitation, only in the year of payment, regardless of when the contribution was pledged (Reg. § 1.170A-1(a)).[78] Contributions charged to a bank credit card, however, are deductible in the year charged even though paid in a later year. A contribution made by text message is deductible in the year the donor sends the text message if the contribution is charged to the donor's telephone or wireless account (IRS Pub. 526). Special rules apply to taxpayers recognized by the Alaska Eskimo Whaling Commission as whaling captains (Code Sec. 170(n)).[79]

IRA Distributions. Individuals age 70½ or older may distribute up to $100,000 tax-free from their individual retirement accounts (IRAs) to certain charitable organizations without including the distribution in gross income (¶ 2165). A qualified charitable distribution must be made directly by the trustee to a 50-percent organization (¶ 1059),

References are to Standard Federal Tax Reports; Tax Research Consultant; and Practical Tax Explanations.

[75] ¶ 9402.62; ACCTNG: 6,312.05; § 18,515.35

[76] ¶ 9402.60; ACCTNG: 6,312.05; § 18,515.35

[77] ¶ 11,600; INDIV: 51,000; § 7,501

[78] ¶ 11,600, ¶ 11,615; INDIV: 51,402; § 7,505.10

[79] ¶ 11,600; INDIV: 51,052.55

but *not* to a supporting organization or a donor advised fund (¶ 1061), and the entire distribution must otherwise be deductible as a charitable donation, disregarding the percentage limitations, even though the individual cannot claim a charitable deduction for the donation.

Partnerships and S Corporations. A partnership cannot claim a charitable contribution deduction in determining its taxable income. Each partner, however, is allowed a deduction for the partner's distributive share of the partnership's charitable contribution (¶ 417). See also ¶ 1061 for special rules regarding partnership donations of clothing and household items. An S corporation also cannot claim a charitable contribution deduction in determining its taxable income. A shareholder, however, reduces his or her basis in S corporation stock for his or her pro rata share of the corporation's charitable contribution (¶ 317).

1059. Percentage Limits on Individuals' Charitable Contributions. An individual's charitable contribution deduction for any tax year (¶ 1058) is limited to a percentage of the individual's contribution base determined by the type of organization receiving the donation and the type of property donated (Code Sec. 170(b)(1); Reg. § 1.170A-8(a)).[80] The deduction limit also depends on whether the donation of property is made to the charitable organization or for its use (¶ 1063). A donation of an income interest in property is made for the use of the charity, whether or not it is transferred in trust. A donation of a remainder interest in property is made for the use of the organization if it is transferred in trust to be held and administered for the organization. Charitable contributions that exceed the deduction limit may be carried forward to subsequent tax year (¶ 1060).

Contribution Base. An individual's contribution base is the taxpayer's adjusted gross income (AGI) (¶ 1005), computed without regard to the charitable deduction and any net operating loss carryback (¶ 1149) (Code Sec. 170(b)(1)(G); Reg. § 1.170A-8(a)).[81] When a married couple files a joint return, the percentage limitations are applied against the couple's aggregate income.

Percentage Limits. Contributions of ordinary income property (¶ 1062) to tax-exempt organizations (public charities) are limited to a maximum deduction of 50 percent of a taxpayer's contribution base for the tax year (Code Sec. 170(b)(1)(A), as amended by the Protecting Americans from Tax Hikes (PATH) Act of 2015 (P.L. 114-113); Reg. § 1.170A-9).[82] Contributions of capital gain property to public charities are limited to a maximum deduction of 30 percent of the taxpayer's contribution base for the tax year (Code Sec. 170(b)(1)(C)).[83] Public charities for this purpose include:

(1) churches or conventions or associations of churches (¶ 604);

(2) educational institutions;

(3) hospitals or medical research organizations, not including home health care organizations, convalescent homes, homes for children or the aged, or vocational institutions that train handicapped individuals;

(4) endowment foundations in connection with a state college or university;

(5) state, federal or local government units, if the contribution is made for exclusively public purposes;

(6) organizations referred to in Code Sec. 170(c)(2) (¶ 1061) normally receiving a substantial part of their support from the public or a governmental unit;

(7) private operating foundations (¶ 633);

(8) private nonoperating foundations (¶ 631 and ¶ 633) that distribute all contributions received to public charities and private operating foundations, or make certain other qualifying distributions, within 2½ months after the end of the tax year;

References are to Standard Federal Tax Reports; Tax Research Consultant; and Practical Tax Explanations.

[80] ¶ 11,600, ¶ 11,661; INDIV: 51,250; § 7,565.05

[81] ¶ 11,600, ¶ 11,661; INDIV: 51,252; § 7,565.05

[82] ¶ 11,600, ¶ 11,662; INDIV: 51,254, INDIV: 51,256; § 7,565.05, § 7,565.10

[83] ¶ 11,600; INDIV: 51,256; § 7,565.20

(9) private foundations (¶ 631) that pool all contributions into a common fund and allow a substantial contributor to designate a recipient charity, where income from the pool is distributed within 2½ months after the tax year in which it was realized and corpus attributable to any donor's contribution is distributed to a charity not later than one year after the death of the donor or surviving spouse with the right to designate the recipients of the corpus;

(10) publicly supported organizations normally receiving

(a) more than ⅓ of their support in each tax year from the public and organizations listed at (1)—(6), above, in the form of grants, gifts, contributions, or membership fees, and gross receipts from an activity that is not an unrelated trade or business (less certain receipts), and

(b) not more than ⅓ of their support from gross investment income and unrelated business taxable income (less taxes);

(11) certain supporting organizations (¶ 607); and

(12) for contributions made on and after December 18, 2015, certain agricultural research organizations.

The deduction limitation on contributions of ordinary income property to qualified charitable organizations other than public charities described above, and on gifts *for the use of* public charities, is the lesser of: (1) 30 percent of the taxpayer's contribution base, or (2) the excess of 50 percent of the taxpayer's contribution base for the tax year over the amount of charitable contributions qualifying for the 50-percent deduction ceiling, including carryovers (Code Sec. 170(b)(1)(B)).[84] Contributions of capital gain property to qualified charitable organizations other than public charities described above are subject to a 20-percent contribution base limitation (Code Sec. 170(b)(1)(D)).[85] Qualified public charities which are not public charities include veterans' organizations, fraternal societies, nonprofit cemeteries, and certain private nonoperating foundations.

Charitable contributions made by bona fide residents of U.S. possessions (¶ 2414) or Puerto Rico (¶ 2415) are deductible only to the extent allocable to income that is *not* excluded possession-source or Puerto Rico-source income (Reg. § 1.170A-1(j)(9)).[86] For deduction limitations on charitable contributions by corporations, see ¶ 927.

Qualified Conservation Contributions. Individual donors who make a qualified conservation contribution (QCC) of real property (¶ 1063) are allowed to claim their QCC deduction against the 50-percent contribution base minus their deduction for all other charitable contributions, and any excess over this amount can be carried forward for 15 years. These rules are applied separately from the rules that apply to other donations (Code Sec. 170(b)(1)(E), as amended P.L. 114-113).[87]

Qualified Farmers and Ranchers. Individual taxpayers with more than 50 percent of gross income from farming or ranching making a QCC of real property have their QCC deduction limited to 100 percent of the contribution base minus their deduction for all other charitable contributions. The 100-percent limit only applies if the contribution includes a restriction that the property must remain generally available for agriculture or livestock production (Code Sec. 170(b)(1)(E), as amended by P.L. 114-113). An enhanced charitable deduction for a QCC of real property by certain corporate farmers and ranchers is limited to the excess of the corporation's taxable income over the amount of other allowable charitable contributions, which is limited to 10 percent of taxable income (¶ 927).

References are to Standard Federal Tax Reports; Tax Research Consultant; and Practical Tax Explanations.

[84] ¶ 11,600; INDIV: 51,258, INDIV: 51,260; § 7,565.15

[85] ¶ 11,600; INDIV: 51,260; § 7,565.25

[86] ¶ 11,615; INDIV: 51,150; § 7,501

[87] ¶ 11,600; INDIV: 51,256.20; § 7,565.30

1060. Carryover of Excess Charitable Contributions of Individuals. Individual taxpayers may carry forward for five years their charitable contributions that exceed the deductible ceiling for the year of the contribution (¶ 1059) (Code Sec. 170(b)(1)(D)(ii) and (d); Reg. § 1.170A-10).[88] The amount of the excess that may be deducted in any carryover year is limited to the lesser of:

- the remaining portion of any excess contribution not already deducted; or
- an amount equal to 50 percent (or 30 percent for capital gain carryover) of the taxpayer's contribution base after first deducting the sum of the charitable contributions (to which the 50-percent or 30-percent limitation applies) paid in the carryover year and any excess contributions that have precedence in order of time over the present carryover.

The excess must be reduced to the extent that it reduces taxable income as computed for net operating loss (NOL) carrybacks and carryovers (¶ 1149) and increases the NOL deduction for a tax year succeeding the contribution year.

Qualified Conservation Contribution Carryover. If the value of a taxpayer's qualified conservation contribution (QCC) (¶ 1059) exceeds the special higher limit for such a donation, the excess can be carried forward for 15 years (Code Sec. 170(b)(1)(E)(ii)).[89]

1061. Charitable Contributions That Are Deductible. A charitable contribution is deductible only if it is a contribution or gift to, or for the use of, the following qualified organizations:

- the United States, a state, a local government, the District of Columbia, or a U.S. possession, for exclusively public purposes;
- a corporation, trust or community chest, fund, or foundation, created or organized in the United States or a possession or under the law of the United States, a possession, a state, or the District of Columbia, organized and operated exclusively for religious, charitable, scientific, literary, or educational purposes, or to foster national or international amateur sports competition, or for the prevention of cruelty to children or animals; no part of the charity's net earnings may inure to the benefit of any private shareholder or individual. Also, the organization must not be disqualified for tax exemption under Code Sec. 501(c)(3) by attempting to influence legislation;
- a cemetery company owned and operated exclusively for the benefit of its members or any corporation chartered solely for burial purposes as a cemetery corporation and not operated for profit or for the benefit of any private shareholder or individual;
- a post or organization of war veterans, or its auxiliary society or unit, organized in the United States or its possessions, if no part of the net earnings inures to the benefit of any private shareholder or individual; or
- a domestic fraternal society, order, or association, operating under the lodge system, by only individual donors if the contributions are used exclusively for religious, charitable, scientific, literary or educational purposes, or for the prevention of cruelty to children or animals (Code Sec. 170(c)).[90]

A contribution is not deductible unless it is made to, or for the use of, qualified organizations listed above. The donee organization must be qualified at the time of the contribution. It is the organization's responsibility to ensure that its character, purposes, activities, and method of operation satisfy the qualification requirements, so that donors have assurance that their contributions are deductible at the time made (Rev. Proc. 2011-33). The IRS maintains an electronic database that may be used to determine whether a tax-exempt organization qualifies to receive tax-deductible charitable contributions. The database can be found on the IRS's website at https://www.irs.gov/charities-non-profits/exempt-organizations-select-check.

References are to Standard Federal Tax Reports; Tax Research Consultant; and Practical Tax Explanations.

[88] ¶ 11,600, ¶ 11,663; INDIV: 51,262; § 7,570.05

[89] ¶ 11,600; INDIV: 51,256.20; § 7,565.30

[90] ¶ 11,600; INDIV: 51,100; § 7,505.05, § 7,520.05

Contributions made to individuals or nonqualified organizations are not deductible.[91] If specific requirements are met, however, a charitable deduction is allowed for the cost of maintaining a student in the taxpayer's home (¶ 1064). The fact that an organization is tax-exempt under Code Sec. 501 does not guarantee that contributions to the organization will be deductible. Moreover, organizations that otherwise qualify to receive deductible donations can be disqualified for activities that violate public policy or for influencing or participating in legislation or political campaigns.[92] Special rules apply for contributions to private foundations and certain trusts (¶ 538) (Code Sec. 170(f)(1)).

Clothing and Household Items. A deduction for a donation of clothing and household items is allowed only if the donated property is in good used condition or better. Household items do not include food, paintings, antiques, other objects of art, jewelry, gems, or collections. The IRS can deny a deduction for such donated property that is of minimal value. These restrictions do not apply if: (1) a deduction of more than $500 is claimed for the single clothing or household item, and (2) a qualified appraisal for that item is attached to the return (¶ 1071). For partnerships and S corporations, the restrictions are applied at the entity level, and denial of the deduction is at the partner or shareholder level (Code Sec. 170(f)(16)).[93]

Contributions of Services. The value of service rendered to a charitable organization is *not* deductible as a charitable contribution (Reg. § 1.170A-1(g); Rev. Rul. 162).[94] An out-of-pocket unreimbursed expense, such as for uniforms, telephone, or equipment, incurred in rendering such service, however, is a deductible contribution (Rev. Rul. 84-61). No deduction is allowed for an out-of-pocket expenditure made by any person on behalf of a charitable organization other than an organization described in Code Sec. 501(h)(5) relating to churches if the expenditure is made for the purpose of influencing legislation (Code Sec. 170(f)(6)). No charitable or business deduction is allowed for contributions made to organizations that conduct lobbying activities relating to matters of direct financial interest to the donor, unless the donor's direct conduct of the activities would have given rise to a business expense deduction (¶ 974) (Code Sec. 170(f)(9)).[95] See ¶ 2073 for a discussion of payments under leave-based donation programs in which an employer makes charitable donations in exchange for an employee's election to forgo paid leave.

Travel Expenses. Charitable deductions are allowed for transportation or other travel expenses, including meals and lodging, incurred in the performance of services away from home on behalf of a charitable organization if there is no significant element of personal pleasure, recreation or vacation. If there is such an element, deductions are denied even though the expenses are paid directly by the individual, indirectly through a contribution to the organization, or by reimbursement by the organization. This rule does not apply to the extent that an individual pays for travel for third parties who are participants in the charitable activity. However, deductions are disallowed where two unrelated taxpayers pay each other's travel expenses or members of a group contribute to a fund that pays for all travel expenses (Code Sec. 170(j)).[96] Individuals who qualify for a deduction for the use of an automobile during the year may use the statutory standard mileage rate of 14 cents per mile, plus parking fees and tolls, in lieu of a deduction based on the actual expenses incurred. Depreciation and insurance are not includible in the deductible contribution (Code Sec. 170(i)).[97]

Fund-Raising Activities. An amount paid for a ticket to a charity event such as a ball, bazaar, show, or athletic event is presumed to represent the purchase price for an item of value. The burden is on the taxpayer to show either that the payment is not a purchase or that the payment exceeds the fair market value of the admission or other privileges associated with the event. The purchase price of a raffle ticket is not deductible (Rev. Rul. 83-130; Rev. Proc. 90-12).[98]

References are to Standard Federal Tax Reports; Tax Research Consultant; and Practical Tax Explanations.

[91] ¶ 11,620.111; INDIV: 51,120

[92] ¶ 11,620.32; INDIV: 51,118

[93] ¶ 11,600; INDIV: 51,152; § 7,595

[94] ¶ 11,615, ¶ 11,620.65; INDIV: 51,056; § 7,540

[95] ¶ 11,600; INDIV: 51,118.15; § 7,540

[96] ¶ 11,600; INDIV: 51,056.15; § 7,545

[97] ¶ 11,600; INDIV: 51,056.15; § 7,545

[98] ¶ 11,620.511, ¶ 11,620.512, ¶ 11,620.513; INDIV: 51,052.40; § 7,510.05

Example: A pays $20 to see a special showing of a motion picture, the net proceeds of which go to a qualified charitable organization. Printed on the ticket is "Contribution—$20." If the regular price for the movie is $9, A made a contribution of $11 to a qualified charitable organization.

A fund-raising organization that provides token benefits to contributors can advise them that their donations are fully deductible only if the token benefits have an insubstantial value. If items are mailed to potential donors, the organization can advise that a contribution is fully deductible only if the items are low cost, provided for free, and not distributed at the donor's request or consent. A charity that receives a *quid pro quo contribution* in excess of $75 must provide a statement to the donor describing what portion of the donation represents consideration for goods or services (¶ 627).

Eighty percent of an otherwise deductible payment made to a college or university for the right to purchase tickets to an athletic event, including tickets to skyboxes, is treated as a charitable contribution regardless of whether the tickets would have been available if the payment had not been made (Code Sec. 170(l); IRS Letter Ruling 200004001).[99]

Transfers of property to a charitable organization that are directly related to the donor's business and made with a reasonable expectation of financial return equivalent to the value of the transfers do not qualify for a charitable deduction but may qualify as a trade or business expense (Reg. § 1.170A-1(c)(5)).[100]

Donor Advised Funds. The deduction for a contribution made to a donor advised fund (¶ 610) is allowed only if: (1) the fund's sponsoring organization is not a cemetery, a war veterans' organization, a lodge, or a Type III supporting organization that is not a "functionally integrated Type III supporting organization" (¶ 607), and (2) the donor obtains a contemporaneous written acknowledgment from the sponsoring organization that the organization has exclusive legal control over the assets contributed (Code Sec. 170(f)(18)).[101] Distributions from donor advised funds that are for noncharitable purposes are taxable, as are certain transactions between a donor advised fund and its donors, donor advisors, or related persons (¶ 610).

1062. Charitable Contributions of Appreciated Property. The amount of a noncash charitable contribution is generally the property's fair market value at the time of the contribution, reduced by limitations that apply to certain appreciated property (Code Sec. 170(e); Reg. §§ 1.170A-1(c) and 1.170A-4).[102] The deductible amount for appreciated property depends on whether it is ordinary income property, capital gain property, or a combination of both. The reduction rules described below do not apply if, due to the transfer of the contributed property, the donor recognizes income or gain in the same tax year in which the contribution is made.

Ordinary Income Property. Ordinary income property is property that, if sold at its fair market value on the date of contribution, would give rise to ordinary income or short-term capital gain. A charitable contribution deduction for such property is limited to the fair market value of the property less the amount that would be ordinary income. Ordinary income property includes inventory and stock in trade, artworks and manuscripts created by the donor, letters and memoranda, capital assets held one year or less, and section 306 stock (¶ 739 and ¶ 740) (Code Sec. 170(e)(1)(A); Reg. § 1.170A-4(b)(1)).[103]

Capital Gain Property. Capital gain property includes any asset on which long-term capital gain would be realized if the taxpayer sold the asset for fair market value on the date of contribution. A charitable contribution of capital gain property is generally deductible at their fair market value on the date of contribution. An individual's contribution must be reduced, however, by the potential long-term gain (appreciation) if:

References are to Standard Federal Tax Reports; Tax Research Consultant; and Practical Tax Explanations.

[99] ¶ 11,600, ¶ 11,680.10; INDIV: 51,052.40; § 7,510.75

[100] ¶ 11,615; INDIV: 51,154; § 7,505.05

[101] ¶ 11,600; EXEMPT: 33,100; § 7,520.40

[102] ¶ 11,600, ¶ 11,615, ¶ 11,632; INDIV: 51,200; § 7,525.05

[103] ¶ 11,600, ¶ 11,632; INDIV: 51,204; § 7,525.10

- the property is contributed to certain private nonoperating foundations (¶ 633) (a deduction is, however, allowed for the fair market value of qualified appreciated stock, which is publicly traded stock that would produce long-term capital gain if sold (Code Sec. 170(e)(5)));
- the gift is tangible personal property put to a use that is unrelated to the purpose or function upon which the organization's exemption is based;
- the gift is tangible personal property but without regard to whether a deduction greater than the donor's basis has been allowed, that the organization sells, exchanges, or disposes of in the tax year when the contribution was made, and the organization has not made a certification regarding the property (see "*Recapture of Charitable Tax Benefits*," following);
- the donation consists of patents, certain copyrights, trademarks, trade names, trade secrets, know-how, certain software, or similar intellectual property or applications or registrations of such property;
- the donation consists of taxidermy property contributed by the person who prepared, stuffed or mounted the property, or who paid or incurred the cost of preparation, stuffing or mounting; or
- the taxpayer elects to disregard the special 30-percent capital gains limitation in favor of the 50-percent limitation (Code Sec. 170(e)(1)(B); Reg. § 1.170A-4(b)(2)).[104]

Combination Property. The charitable contribution deduction is specially computed if the donor's sale of the property at fair market value would have produced both ordinary income and capital gain (Code Sec. 170(e)(1)). The fair market value is reduced by the ordinary income that would have resulted from the sale, and the remainder of the fair market value is treated as capital gain property, subject to the above rules. The types of property to which this special computation applies include property subject to depreciation recapture (¶ 1779 and ¶ 1788) and to recapture of farmland expenditures (¶ 1797), as well as interests in oil, gas, or geothermal property.

Recapture of Charitable Tax Benefits. If a donee organization disposes of "applicable property" within three years of the contribution and does not provide certification regarding the property, the donor taxpayer will be required to include as ordinary income for the year of the disposition the difference between the amount of the charitable deduction allowed for the donated capital gains property and the donor's basis. Applicable property is appreciated tangible personal property with a claimed value over $5,000, the use of which the donee certifies as related to its exempt function or purpose, and for which a deduction greater than the donor's basis is allowed. The certification is a written statement, signed under penalty of perjury by an officer of the donee, which either: (1) certifies that the property's use was *substantial and related* to the donee's exempt purpose, and describes how the property was used and how such use furthered the exempt purpose, or (2) states the donee's intended use of the property at the time of the contribution and certifies that such use became impossible or infeasible to implement (Code Sec. 170(e)(7)).[105]

Food Inventories. Noncorporate and corporate taxpayers are allowed to claim an enhanced deduction for certain donations of food inventories from a trade or business subject to certain limits (¶ 930A).

1062A. Additional Charitable Deduction for Income from Intellectual Property. A taxpayer who contributes qualified intellectual property to a charitable organization is allowed an additional charitable deduction based on a sliding-scale percentage of net income received by, or accrued to, the donee that is allocable to donated qualified intellectual property over a 10-year period. Qualified intellectual property includes patents and other intellectual property (¶ 1062), but does not include property donated to certain private nonoperating foundations (¶ 633). The additional deduction is allowed only to the extent that the total amount calculated using the sliding scale exceeds the

References are to Standard Federal Tax Reports; Tax Research Consultant; and Practical Tax Explanations.

[104] ¶ 11,600, ¶ 11,632; INDIV: 51,206, INDIV: 51,208, INDIV: 51,210; § 7,525.15

[105] ¶ 11,600; INDIV: 51,206.20; § 7,525.15c

deduction amount claimed on the property contribution without regard to the additional amount. The donor must inform the donee at the time of the contribution of its intent to treat the donation as a qualified intellectual property contribution. A donee, other than certain private foundations, that receives or accrues net income during a tax year from any qualified intellectual property contribution must make an information return and provide a copy to the donor (Code Secs. 170(m) and 6050L(b); Notice 2005-41).[106]

1063. Charitable Contributions of Partial Interests. No charitable deduction is generally allowed for contributions to charitable organizations of less than the taxpayer's entire interest in the property, except in the following cases: (1) a contribution of an undivided portion of a taxpayer's entire interest in property, e.g., a one-fourth interest in property; (2) a contribution of a remainder interest in a personal residence or farm; (3) a qualified conservation contribution; or (4) where a charitable deduction would have been allowed had the interest been transferred in trust (¶ 538 and ¶ 1070) (Code Sec. 170(f)(3); Reg. § 1.170A-7).[107]

Fractional Interest in Tangible Personal Property. No deduction is allowed for a contribution of an undivided portion of a taxpayer's entire interest in tangible personal property unless all interest in the property is held immediately before the contribution by the taxpayer, or the taxpayer and the donee. If the taxpayer makes an additional contribution later, then the charitable deduction is equal to the lesser of the fair market value of the property used to determine the deduction for the initial fractional contribution or the property at the time of the additional contribution. The deduction will be recaptured if, on or before the earlier of the 10th anniversary of the initial fractional contribution or the donor's date of death, either: (1) the donor fails to contribute the remaining interests to the donee, or (2) the donee fails to take substantial physical possession of the property and use it in a manner related to its exempt purpose. The recaptured amount will be subject to interest and a 10-percent additional tax, i.e, a penalty (Code Sec. 170(o)).[108] See ¶ 1069 for a discussion of charitable contributions of future interests in tangible personal property.

Qualified Conservation Contributions (QCC). A QCC is a contribution of a qualified real property interest to a qualified organization exclusively for conservation purposes that are protected in perpetuity. Qualified real property includes a donor's entire interest in real property other than an interest in subsurface oil, gas, or other minerals, and the right to access to such minerals, a remainder interest, and a restriction granted in perpetuity on the property's use (i.e., an easement). A qualified organization includes certain governmental units, public charities that meet certain public support tests, and certain supporting organizations. A qualified conservation purpose includes: (1) preserving land for public outdoor recreation or education; (2) protecting a relatively natural habitat of fish, wildlife, or plants; (3) preserving open space for the public's scenic enjoyment or under a governmental conservation policy that will yield significant public benefit; and (4) preserving an historically important land area or certified historic structure (Code Sec. 170(h); Reg. § 1.170A-14).[109] For any QCC, the deduction is reduced by an amount equal to the contribution's fair market value multiplied by a fraction: the sum of the rehabilitation credits (¶ 1365B) allowed to the taxpayer for the five preceding tax years on any building that is part of the donation, over the building's fair market value on the contribution date (Code Sec. 170(f)(14)).

Facade Easements. A facade easement may qualify as a QCC. There are several requirements for contributions of facade easements regarding buildings located in registered historic districts and certified as being of historic significance. The easement must preserve the building's entire exterior and prohibit any change that is inconsistent with the exterior's historical character. Both the donor and donee must certify in writing that the donee: (1) is a qualified organization whose purpose is environmental protection, land conservation, or open space or historic preservation and (2) has the resources and a commitment to manage and enforce the restriction. The donor's return must

References are to Standard Federal Tax Reports; Tax Research Consultant; and Practical Tax Explanations.

[106] ¶ 11,600, ¶ 36,260, ¶ 11,660.32; INDIV: 51,168; § 7,585

[107] ¶ 11,600, ¶ 11,651; INDIV: 51,350; § 7,550.05

[108] ¶ 11,600; INDIV: 51,354; § 7,550.15b

[109] ¶ 11,600, ¶ 11,701; INDIV: 51,364; § 7,550.20

include a qualified appraisal of the property interest (¶ 1071), photographs of the building's entire exterior, and a description of all restrictions on the building's development (Code Sec. 170(h)(4)(B)). Taxpayers who seek deductions over $10,000 for such contributions must submit a statutory $500 filing fee with their return (Code Sec. 170(f)(13)).

1064. Charitable Contribution for Care of Unrelated Student in the Home. A charitable contribution deduction may be claimed for unreimbursed amounts spent to maintain a full-time elementary or high school student, who is *not* a dependent or relative, in the taxpayer's home under a written agreement with a program sponsored by a charitable organization providing educational opportunities for students. The deduction is limited to actual expenditures, up to $50 per month, while the student is a member of the taxpayer's household. A dependent for this purpose is defined as the same as for claiming a dependency exemption (¶ 137), but without regard to whether the dependent claims dependency exemptions, files a joint return or has gross income in excess of the exemption amount (Code Sec. 170(g); Reg. § 1.170A-2).[110]

1065. Reduction of Charitable Contribution for Interest. The amount of a taxpayer's charitable contribution (¶ 1058) must be reduced by the amount of interest the taxpayer has paid or will pay attributable to a donated liability-encumbering property that the donee or any other person assumes and that is attributable to a period after the contribution is made. If the gift is a bond, note, or other evidence of debt, the amount of the contribution is further reduced by the interest that is paid or to be paid by the taxpayer-donor on debt incurred or continued to purchase or carry such bond that is attributable to any period prior to the contribution (Code Sec. 170(f)(5); Reg. § 1.170A-3).[111]

1069. Charitable Contribution of Future Interest in Tangible Personal Property. When a taxpayer transfers to a charitable organization a future interest in tangible personal property, such as a painting, manuscript, sculpture, or other art object, a charitable contribution deduction is *not* allowed until all intervening interests in, and rights to, the actual possession or enjoyment of the property have expired or are held by persons other than the taxpayer, related taxpayers, and controlled partnerships (Code Sec. 170(a)(3); Reg. § 1.170A-5).[112] This rule applies whether the property is contributed in trust or outright. The amount deductible is the value of the property at the time the contribution is considered made, but reduced by limitations that apply to appreciated property (¶ 1062). See ¶ 1063 for a discussion of charitable contributions of fractional interests in tangible personal property.

1070. Charitable Contributions in Trust. No charitable deduction is allowed for the value of a contribution in trust of any interest in property that is less than the taxpayer's entire interest in the property (¶ 1063) unless the trust is a pooled income fund (¶ 593), a charitable remainder annuity trust, or a charitable remainder unitrust (¶ 590). If the donor gives *all* the interests in a trust to charity, a deduction is allowable (Code Sec. 170(f)(2); Reg. § 1.170A-6).[113]

1070A. Recordkeeping Requirements for Charitable Contributions. Any taxpayer who claims a charitable contribution deduction (¶ 938 and ¶ 1058) must maintain records to substantiate that the contributions were actually made, in the amounts claimed on the tax return.

Cash Donations. No deduction will be allowed for contributions of cash, checks, or other monetary gifts, *regardless of the amount*, unless the donor maintains either: (1) a bank record, including a cancelled check, a bank or credit union statement, or a credit card statement; or (2) a receipt, letter, or other written communication from the donee, indicating the donee's name and the contribution date and amount (Code Sec. 170(f)(17); IRS Pub. 526).[114]

References are to Standard Federal Tax Reports; Tax Research Consultant; and Practical Tax Explanations.

[110] ¶ 11,600, ¶ 11,621; INDIV: 51,120; § 7,535

[111] ¶ 11,600, ¶ 11,631; INDIV: 51,160

[112] ¶ 11,600, ¶ 11,634; INDIV: 51,360; § 7,560

[113] ¶ 11,600, ¶ 11,635; INDIV: 51,366; § 7,555.05

[114] ¶ 11,600; INDIV: 51,454; § 7,600.10

Payroll Deductions. For charitable contributions made by payroll deduction, the taxpayer must retain: (1) a pay stub, Form W-2, or other employer-furnished document indicating the amount withheld for payment to the donee organization; and (2) a pledge card or other document prepared by the donee organization, or at its direction, showing the donee's name. For contributions of $250 or more from a single paycheck, the pledge card or other document must also include a statement that the donee does not provide goods or services in whole or partial consideration for any contributions made to it by payroll deduction (Notice 2006-110; IRS Pub. 526). The deduction from each paycheck is a separate charitable contribution.

Lump-Sum Donations Through CFC. To substantiate a lump-sum charitable contribution made through the Combined Federal Campaign (CFC) or similar programs, such as the United Way which distribute the amounts received to one or more qualified organizations (¶ 1061), the CFC organization must provide the donor with a written communication that includes the name of the donee organization that is the ultimate recipient of the contribution. This requirement is in addition to those for contributions of $250 or more (see *Contributions of $250 or More,* following) (Notice 2008-16).

Noncash Donations of Less than $250. For each noncash donation for which a charitable deduction of less than $250 is claimed, the taxpayer generally must maintain a receipt from the donee indicating the donee's name, the date and location of the donation, and a detailed description, but not the value, of the donated property. If it would be impracticable to obtain a receipt, the donor must maintain reliable written records regarding each item contributed (Reg. § 1.170A-13(b)).[115]

Contributions of $250 or More. Charitable contributions of $250 or more must be substantiated by a contemporaneous written acknowledgment from the donee organization unless the donee files a return with the IRS reporting the information that would be included in the written acknowledgment. Generally, the acknowledgment must include: (1) the amount of cash contributed and a description of any property contributed; (2) a description and good-faith estimate of the value of any goods or services with more than insubstantial value received in exchange for the contributions; and (3) if the donee provides any intangible religious benefits, a statement to that effect (Code Sec. 170(f)(8); Reg. § 1.170A-13(f)).[116]

Noncash Donations of More than $500. For noncash contributions for which a deduction of more than $500 is claimed, the taxpayer must satisfy the general contemporaneous written acknowledgment requirement for contributions of $250 or more described above. In addition, the taxpayer must include with its return for the tax year of the contribution a written description of the donated property in Section A of Form 8283. This requirement, however, does not apply to a C corporation that is not a personal service corporation or closely-held C corporation (Code Sec. 170(f)(11); Reg. § 1.170A-13(b)).[117] A noncash contribution that exceeds $5,000 must also be appraised and described in Section B of Form 8283 (¶ 1071) (Code Sec. 170(f)(11); Reg. § 1.170A-13(c)).[118]

If either of these additional documentation requirements are not met, the charitable contribution deduction will be denied unless the failure is due to reasonable cause and not willful neglect. The taxpayer must also maintain written records that include: (1) the manner and approximate date of acquisition of the property by the taxpayer, or if the property was created, produced, or manufactured by or for the taxpayer, the approximate date the property was substantially completed; and (2) the adjusted basis of the donated property (Reg. § 1.170A-13(b)(3); IRS Pub. 526).

Donations of Clothing or Household Items. Donations of clothing or household items that are *not* in good used condition or better are allowed only if a deduction of more than $500 is claimed for a single item and a qualified appraisal (¶ 1071) for that item is attached to the return (IRS Pub. 526).

References are to Standard Federal Tax Reports; Tax Research Consultant; and Practical Tax Explanations.

[115] ¶ 11,685; INDIV: 51,456; § 7,600.10

[116] ¶ 11,600, ¶ 11,685; INDIV: 51,454; § 7,600.15

[117] ¶ 11,600, ¶ 11,685; INDIV: 51,456.15; § 7,600.10b

[118] ¶ 11,600, ¶ 11,685; INDIV: 51,456.20; § 7,600.25

Vehicle Donations. Taxpayers donating to a charity a car, truck, boat, or aircraft valued at over $500 must obtain from the charity and attach to his or her return either a Form 1098-C or a similar contemporaneous written acknowledgment of the contribution. The acknowledgment must identify the donor taxpayer, list the taxpayer's and the qualified vehicle's identification number, and include a description and good faith estimate of the value of any goods or services provided by the charity in exchange for the vehicle. If the goods or services consist solely of intangible religious benefits, the acknowledgment must say so.

If the charity sells the vehicle without significant intervening use or material improvement, the acknowledgment must also certify that the vehicle was sold in an arm's-length transaction between unrelated parties, list the gross proceeds, and state that the deduction may not exceed the gross proceeds. If the charity retains the vehicle for its significant use or makes a material improvement, the acknowledgment must certify the use or improvement, the time frame the charity will use the vehicle, and that the vehicle will not be transferred before the use or improvement is completed. The taxpayer is then allowed to claim the fair market value of the vehicle as a charitable donation (Code Sec. 170(f)(12); Notice 2005-44; Notice 2006-1).[119]

If the charity sells the vehicle to a needy individual at a price significantly below fair market value, or gratuitously transfers the vehicle, the taxpayer can claim the donated vehicle's fair market value only if the sale or transfer directly furthers the charity's purpose. However, if a charity sells the vehicle at auction, the IRS will not accept as substantiation an acknowledgment stating that the vehicle is to be transferred to a needy individual for significantly below fair market value. In that case, the donor taxpayer may claim a deduction greater than $500, but only to the extent that the gross sale proceeds exceed that amount and the donor substantiates the contribution with an acknowledgment listing the gross proceeds (Notice 2007-70).

Qualified Conservation Contributions (QCCs). Documentation and certification requirements must be met for certain QCCs of facade easements (¶ 1063).

1071. Appraisals for Charitable Contributions. A charitable deduction will be denied to a taxpayer for a noncash contribution of over $5,000 unless the taxpayer obtains a qualified written appraisal of the donated property. An exception exists if the failure is due to reasonable cause and not to willful neglect. (Code Sec. 170(f)(11); Reg. § 1.170A-13(c); Notice 2006-96).[120] A summary of the appraisal must be made on Section B of Form 8283 and attached the taxpayer's return for the tax year the donation is made. The qualified appraisal itself, however, must be attached to the taxpayer's return for any charitable contributions valued in excess of $500,000. See ¶ 1070A for other substantiation requirements.

For purposes of determining the threshold dollar amounts for the reporting requirements for appraisals, all similar items of noncash property, whether donated to a single donee or multiple donees, are aggregated and treated as a single property donation. For partnerships and S corporations, the requirements are applied at the entity level, but if the entities fail to meet the requirements, denial of the deduction will be made at the partner or shareholder level. The appraisal requirement is waived for closely held corporations and personal service corporations.

No qualified appraisal is required for cash, publicly traded securities, patents and other intellectual property (¶ 1062), inventory or stock in trade (¶ 1741), or a qualified vehicle sold by the donee organization without any significant intervening use or material improvement and for which an acknowledgment is provided (¶ 1070A). In the case of nonpublicly traded stock with a claimed value between $5,000 and $10,000, only the appraisal summary on Form 8283 is required.

Qualified Appraisal. A qualified appraisal is an appraisal conducted by a qualified appraiser under generally-accepted appraisal standards and other IRS guidance. It must relate to an appraisal made no earlier than 60 days before the contribution of the

References are to Standard Federal Tax Reports; Tax Research Consultant; and Practical Tax Explanations.

[119] 11,600; INDIV: 51,456.25; § 7,590.05

[120] ¶ 11,600, ¶ 11,685; INDIV: 51,458; § 7,600.25

appraised property by the taxpayer to the charitable organization. The qualified appraisal must be signed and dated by the qualified appraiser, and it may not involve fees based on the assessed value of the property. The appraisal fees incurred by an individual in determining the fair market value of donated property are not treated as part of the charitable contribution, but they may be claimed by an individual as a miscellaneous itemized deduction subject to the two-percent-of-adjusted-gross-income (AGI) limitation (¶ 1079).

A qualified appraiser is an individual who has either earned an appraisal designation from a recognized professional organization or otherwise meet minimum requirements, must regularly perform appraisals for pay, and must meet any other requirements prescribed by the IRS. A qualified appraiser must also demonstrate verifiable education and experience in valuing the type of property being appraised, and must not have been prohibited from practicing before the IRS during the three-year period ending on the appraisal date (Code Sec. 170(f)(11)(E); Reg. § 1.170A-13(c); Notice 2006-96).[121]

Accuracy-Related Penalties. Appraisers are subject to civil penalties for certain appraisals that result in substantial or gross valuation misstatements (Code Sec. 6695A).[122]

Moving Expenses

1073. Moving Expense Deduction. Employees and self-employed individuals may claim an adjustment to gross income (an above-the-line deduction) in calculating adjusted gross income (AGI) for the reasonable expenses of moving themselves and their families if the move is related to starting work in a new location (Code Sec. 217).[123] The deduction is computed on Form 3903 and reported on Form 1040. A taxpayer must satisfy both the minimum distance condition and the minimum period of employment condition to deduct moving expenses (¶ 1075).

Deductible moving expenses are limited to the cost of (1) transportation of household goods and personal effects and (2) travel to the new residence, including lodging but not meals (Code Sec. 217(b)).[124] Where an automobile is used in making the move, a taxpayer may deduct either: (1) the actual out-of-pocket expenses incurred, such as gasoline and oil, but not repairs, depreciation, etc., or (2) a standard mileage allowance of 19 cents per mile for 2016, plus parking fees and tolls (Rev. Proc. 2010-51; Notice 2016-1).[125] In the case of foreign moves, a deduction is also allowed for reasonable expenses of moving household goods and personal effects to and from storage, and of storing them while the new place of work abroad is the taxpayer's principal place of work (Code Sec. 217(h)).[126] A foreign move for this purpose is the commencement of work by the taxpayer at a new principal place of work located outside the United States and its possessions.

Employer Reimbursements. An employee may exclude any qualified moving expenses reimbursement from gross income and wages as a fringe benefit (¶ 2092). A qualified moving expenses reimbursement includes any amount received directly or indirectly by the employee from an employer as payment or reimbursement of expenses that would be deductible as moving expenses if directly paid or incurred by the employee (Code Sec. 132(a)(6) and (g)).[127] Any amount, other than a qualified reimbursement received or accrued from an employer as a payment for or reimbursement of moving expenses must be included in the employee's gross income as compensation for services (Code Sec. 82).[128] Any nonqualified reimbursement is also considered wages subject to income tax withholding (Code Sec. 3401(a)(15); Reg. § 31.3401(a)(15)-1).[129]

References are to Standard Federal Tax Reports; Tax Research Consultant; and Practical Tax Explanations.

[121] ¶ 11,600, ¶ 11,685; INDIV: 51,458.05, INDIV: 51,458.15; § 7,600.25

[122] ¶ 39,971; PENALTY: 3,334; § 7,600.25

[123] ¶ 12,620; INDIV: 39,104; § 5,101

[124] ¶ 12,620; INDIV: 39,106.05; § 5,105.05

[125] ¶ 12,623.11; INDIV: 39,106.10; § 5,105.15

[126] ¶ 12,620; INDIV: 39,126; § 5,101

[127] ¶ 7420; INDIV: 39,130; § 5,130

[128] ¶ 6374; INDIV: 39,130; § 5,130

[129] ¶ 33,502, ¶ 33,528; COMPEN: 33,116; § 22,110.10p

Members of the Armed Forces. An individual who is a member of the Armed Forces on active duty may exclude from gross income the value of moving and storage expenses that are furnished in kind by the military or cash reimbursements or allowances to the extent of expenses actually paid or incurred incident to a permanent change of station. These expenses need not be reported and such moves are exempt from the time and mileage requirements. An income exclusion is also provided for moving and storage expenses incurred by the spouse or dependents of an Armed Forces member, even if they do not reside with the member either before or after the move. Reimbursements in excess of actual expenses are includible in the member's income as wages, while expenses in excess of reimbursements are deductible (Code Sec. 217(g); Reg. § 1.217-2(g)(2)(ii)).[130]

1075. Eligibility for Moving Expense Deduction. An individual must meet a distance test, a length-of-employment test, and a commencement-of-work test in order to deduct moving expenses (¶ 1073). A taxpayer who is a member of the Armed Forces on active duty does not have to meet the distance and time tests if his or her move is because of a permanent change of station (Code Sec. 217(g)(1)).[131]

The new principal place of work must be at least 50 miles farther from the taxpayer's old residence than the old residence was from the taxpayer's old place of work. If there was no old place of work, the new place of work must be at least 50 miles from the old residence (Code Sec. 217(c)(1)).[132]

During the 12-month period immediately following the move, the taxpayer must be employed full time for at least 39 weeks. A self-employed taxpayer must be employed or performing services full time for at least 78 weeks of the 24-month period immediately following the move and at least 39 weeks during the first 12 months. The full-time work requirement is waived due to death, disability, involuntary separation from work other than for willful misconduct, or transfer to another location for the benefit of the employer (Code Sec. 217(c)(2) and (d)).[133]

Generally, the move must be in connection with the commencement of work at the new location and the moving expenses must be incurred within one year from the time the taxpayer first reports to the new job or business. If the move is not made within one year, the expenses will not be deductible unless it can be shown that circumstances prevented the taxpayer from incurring the expenses within that period (Reg. § 1.217-2(a)(3)).[134]

An eligible taxpayer is permitted to deduct moving expenses even though the 39- or 78-week employment requirement has not been satisfied by the due date for the return including extensions for the tax year in which the moving expenses were incurred and paid. A taxpayer who fails to meet the requirements, however, must either file an amended return or include as gross income on the next year's return the amount previously claimed as expenses (Code Sec. 217(d); Reg. § 1.217-2(d)(3)).[135]

An individual who retires from an overseas job may deduct moving expenses incurred in returning to the United States. A surviving spouse or dependent who shared the residence of a decedent who worked outside the United States at the time of death may also deduct moving expenses incurred in returning to the United States within six months after the death (Code Sec. 217(i)).[136]

Miscellaneous Itemized Deductions

1079. Miscellaneous Itemized Deductions. Certain itemized deductions of an individual (¶ 1014) are treated as miscellaneous itemized deductions, and are only allowed to the extent that their total exceeds two percent of the individual's adjusted gross income (AGI) (Code Sec. 67(a); Reg. § 1.67-1T).[137] The deductions are reported on

References are to Standard Federal Tax Reports; Tax Research Consultant; and Practical Tax Explanations.

[130] ¶ 12,620, ¶ 12,622; INDIV: 39,122; § 5,135

[131] ¶ 12,620; INDIV: 39,122; § 5,135

[132] ¶ 12,620; INDIV: 39,118; § 5,120.10

[133] ¶ 12,620; INDIV: 39,120; § 5,120.15

[134] ¶ 12,622; INDIV: 39,114; § 5,115

[135] ¶ 12,620, ¶ 12,622; INDIV: 39,120.20; § 5,120.15, § 5,125

[136] ¶ 12,620; INDIV: 39,124;

[137] ¶ 6060, ¶ 6061; INDIV: 39,100; § 7,105.05

lines 21 through 23 on Schedule A of Form 1040. The two-percent-of-AGI limit is applied after other deduction limits, such as the 50-percent limit on meals and entertainment (¶ 916).

Indirect deductions from pass-through entities are subject to the two-percent-of-AGI limitation because they are treated as if they were incurred by the individual taxpayer. This rule applies to partnerships, S corporations, grantor trusts, common trust funds, real estate mortgage investment conduits (REMICs), nonpublicly offered regulated investment companies (RICs), and any other pass-through entity not specifically exempted by the IRS (Code Sec. 67(c); Temp. Reg. § 1.67-2T).[138] The pass-through rule does not apply to estates and trusts (other than grantor trusts) because they are generally treated as individuals (¶ 528).

Miscellaneous itemized deductions subject to the two-percent-of-AGI limitation may be divided into two broad categories: (1) unreimbursed employee business expenses, and (2) other expenses incurred for the production or collection of income, or the preparation of taxes. Unreimubrsed employee expenses that a taxpayer pays during the year are reported on Form 2106. Statutory employees, such as full-time life insurance salespersons, however, are not treated as employees for purposes of deducting expenses incurred in their business. Thus, their expenses may be claimed as trade or business expenses on Schedule C of Form 1040 (¶ 941B).

Itemized deductions *not* subject to the two-percent-of-AGI limitation and reported on Schedule A include those which are permitted by other Code provisions, including the deductions medical and dental expenses (¶ 1015), certain taxes (¶ 1021 and ¶ 1028), interest (¶ 1043), charitable contributions (¶ 1058), and casualty and theft losses (¶ 1121 and ¶ 1123). Other miscellaneous itemized deductions *not* subject to the two-percent-of-AGI limit are reported on line 28 of Schedule A and include:

- estate tax in the case of income in respect of a decedent (¶ 191);
- deductions allowable in connection with personal property used in a short sale (¶ 1944);
- deductions relating to computation of tax when the taxpayer restores an amount in excess of $3,000 held under claim of right (¶ 1543);
- deductions where annuity payments cease before an investment is recovered pursuant to Code Sec. 72(b)(3) (¶ 817);
- amortizable bond premiums (¶ 1967);
- deductions of taxes, interest, and business depreciation by a cooperative housing corporation tenant-stockholder (¶ 1040);
- gambling losses (¶ 785 and ¶ 1113); and
- impairment-related work expenses (¶ 1084) (Code Sec. 67(b)).[139]

1080. Union Dues. Union dues, initiation fees, and out-of-work-benefit assessments are deductible as a miscellaneous itemized deduction on Schedule A of Form 1040, subject to the two-percent-of-adjusted-gross-income (AGI) limitation (¶ 1079) (Reg. § 1.162-15(c)).[140] A union member cannot, however, deduct the part of a dues payment, assessment, or contribution that provides funds for payment of sickness, accident, or death benefits or the funds for contributions to a pension plan, even if the union requires the taxpayer to contribute. A self-employed individual may deduct union dues as a business expense (¶ 1006).

1081. Job-Hunting Expenses. Individuals may deduct all expenses incurred in seeking employment in the *same* trade or business regardless of whether or not the search is successful. The expenses are deductible only as a miscellaneous itemized deduction on Schedule A of Form 1040, subject to the two-percent-of-adjusted-gross-income (AGI) limitation (¶ 1079).

References are to Standard Federal Tax Reports; Tax Research Consultant; and Practical Tax Explanations.

[138] ¶ 6060, ¶ 6062; INDIV: 39,102; § 7,105.40

[139] ¶ 6060; INDIV: 39,100; § 7,110.05

[140] ¶ 8852, ¶ 8853.20; INDIV: 36,302; § 7,105.35

Job-hunting expenses include the typing, printing, and mailing of resumes, and travel and transportation expenses. Travel and transportation expenses to and from an area are deductible only if the trip relates primarily to seeking new employment. If the travel is primarily personal in nature, only the actual expenses of the search at the destination are deductible.[141] Job-hunting expenses are not deductible if an individual is seeking employment in a *new* trade or business even if employment is secured. Individuals cannot deduct job-hunting expenses if they are seeking their first job, entering a new trade or business, or if there is a substantial lack of continuity between the time of their past employment and the seeking of new employment.

1082. Work-Related Education Expenses. An individual who is an employee or self-employed may deduct his or her education expenses as a business expense, even if the education leads to a degree, if the education either:

- maintains or improves skills *required* in the taxpayer's employment or other trade or business, including refresher courses, current developments courses, or academic or vocational courses; or
- meets the express *requirements* of the taxpayer's employer, or of laws or regulations, *imposed* for a bona fide business purpose of the employer and as a condition to the taxpayer's retention of an established employment relationship, status, or rate of compensation (Reg. § 1.162-5(a); IRS Pub. 970).[142]

Education in excess of the minimum requirement may qualify as education undertaken to maintain or improve the required skills.

Educational expenses that are personal or constitute an inseparable aggregate of personal and capital expenditures are not deductible, even though they may maintain or improve a skill or meet the express requirements of the employer or under law (Reg. § 1.162-5(b)(1)). Nondeductible capital or personal education expenses are those that: (1) are required of the taxpayer in order to meet the minimum educational requirements for qualification in the taxpayer's present employment, trade, or business, or (2) qualify the taxpayer for a new trade or business.

The minimum education necessary to qualify for a position or other trade or business is determined from a consideration of such factors as requirements of the employer, laws or regulations, and the standards of the profession, trade, or business involved. The fact that an individual is already performing service in an employment status does not mean he or she has met the minimum educational requirements. However, once an individual has met the minimum requirements in effect when he or she enters the employment, profession, or trade or business, the individual is treated as continuing to meet those requirements even though they have changed. For these individuals, expenses for meeting the new requirements would be deductible (Reg. § 1.162-5(b)(2)).[143]

A change of duties is not a new trade or business if the new duties and the taxpayer's present employment involve the same general work. Thus, there is no new trade or business when a teacher moves from an elementary to a secondary school, from one subject to another, or from a teaching position to a principal's position (Reg. § 1.162-5(b)(3)).[144]

Reporting Deductible Education Expenses. An employee generally figures his or her deduction for work-related education expenses, as well as other employee business expenses on Form 2106. The deduction is claimed as a miscellaneous itemized deduction on Schedule A of Form 1040, subject to the two-percent of adjusted gross income (AGI) limitation (¶ 1079). The amount reported on Schedule A must be reduced by the amount of any tuition or fees deduction claimed (¶ 1011A). A self-employed individual deducts work-related education expenses from total business income on his or her Schedule C of Form 1040.

References are to Standard Federal Tax Reports; Tax Research Consultant; and Practical Tax Explanations.

[141] ¶ 8524.25; INDIV: 36,250; § 7,105.15

[142] ¶ 8631; INDIV: 60,102; § 7,901

[143] ¶ 8631; INDIV: 60,114, INDIV: 60,116; § 7,915.10

[144] ¶ 8631; INDIV: 60,118; § 7,915.05

Professional Expenses. A taxpayer may deduct unreimbursed expenditures for such items as dues paid to professional societies and subscription fees paid for professional journals, books, etc., as a miscellaneous itemized deduction, subject to the two-percent of AGI limitation (IRS Pub. 529).[145] The cost of technical books of relatively permanent value used in connection with professional work is a capital expenditure and must be depreciated (IRS Pub. 946) (¶ 1240).[146]

Travel as a Form of Education. No deduction is allowed for travel as a form of education, such as when a French teacher spends summers in Paris to maintain familiarity with the language (Code Sec. 274(m)(2)).[147] Travel in pursuit of an education, however, may be deductible if the educational expense itself is deductible as a business expense; for example, a French teacher travels to Paris to take otherwise deductible classes that are offered only at the Sorbonne.[148]

1083. Uniforms and Special Clothing. An individual may deduct the unreimbursed cost and upkeep of a uniform used in a trade or business, including laundering and cleaning, if the uniform is required as a condition of employment and is not adaptable to general wear, such as protective clothing, special work shoes and gloves, and shop caps. Both conditions must be present for the cost of the clothing to be deductible.[149] Individuals in the Armed Forces on full-time active duty may not deduct the cost of uniforms, but Armed Forces reservists may deduct the unreimbursed cost, less nontaxable uniform allowance, of a uniform required at drills or other functions if they are prohibited from wearing it for regular use (Reg. § 1.262-1(b)(8)).[150]

The deduction of unreimbursed cost and maintenance of uniforms is claimed as a miscellaneous itemized deduction on Schedule A of Form 1040, subject to the two-percent-of-adjusted-gross-income (AGI) limitation (¶ 1079). Uniform expense reimbursements paid under an accountable plan are not reported on the employee's Form W-2 or included in the employee's income (¶ 943). Costs that exceed the reimbursement are deductible as a miscellaneous itemized deduction. Reimbursement made under a nonaccountable plan must be included in income but may be deducted as miscellaneous itemized deduction.

1084. Impairment-Related Work Expenses. Ordinary and necessary business expenses incurred by a handicapped worker for attendant care services at the worker's place of employment, or for other expenses in connection with the worker's place of employment that are necessary for the individual to be able to work, are claimed as a miscellaneous itemized deduction but *not* subject to the two-percent-of-adjusted-gross-income limitation (¶ 1079). Handicapped persons include individuals who have a physical or mental disability, including blindness or deafness that limits employment, or a physical or mental impairment, including sight or hearing impairment, that substantially limits one or more major life activities (Code Sec. 67(b)(6) and (d); IRS Pub. 529).[151] A taxpayer who claims the deduction for impairment-related work expenses must file Form 2106 with his or her tax return. A self-employed individual claims the deduction on Schedule C of Form 1040, etc.

Production of Income Expenses

1085. Expenses Paid or Incurred for the Production of Income. An individual may deduct ordinary and necessary expenses paid or incurred for: (1) the production or collection of income; (2) the management, conservation, or maintenance of property held for the production of income: or (3) the determination, collection, or refund of any tax (¶ 1092). The expenses are deductible only if they are related to these purposes and reasonable in amount (Code Sec. 212; Reg. § 1.212-1).[152] The expenses are claimed as a miscellaneous itemized deduction on Schedule A of Form 1040, subject to the two-

References are to Standard Federal Tax Reports; Tax Research Consultant; and Practical Tax Explanations.

[145] ¶ 8634.01; INDIV: 36,300; § 7,105.10

[146] ¶ 8634.01; INDIV: 36,300; § 45,710.15

[147] ¶ 14,402; INDIV: 60,122; § 7,920.10

[148] ¶ 14,402.018; INDIV: 60,122; § 7,920.10

[149] ¶ 8524.2658; INDIV: 36,202; § 7,105.20

[150] ¶ 8524.2652, ¶ 13,601; INDIV: 36,206; § 7,105.25

[151] ¶ 6060; INDIV: 36,400; § 7,110.35

[152] ¶ 12,520, ¶ 12,521; BUSEXP: 12,050; § 7,801

percent-of-adjusted-gross-income (AGI) limitation (¶ 1079). Expenses attributable to property held for rents or royalties are deductible as an adjustment from gross income (an above the line deduction) and are not subject to the two-percent of AGI limitation (¶ 1006A). No deduction is allowed for the production of income that is allocable to interest on indebtedness incurred or continued to purchase or carry obligations earning fully tax-exempt interest or other exempt income (¶ 970).

1086. Investor's Expenses. Investment counsel fees, custodian fees, fees for clerical help, office rent, state and local transfer taxes, and similar expenses paid or incurred by an individual in connection with investments are deductible as miscellaneous itemized deductions on Schedule A of Form 1040, subject to the two-percent-of-adjusted-gross-income (AGI) limitation (¶ 1079) (Reg. § 1.212-1(g); IRS Pub. 529).[153] If an individual holds an interest in a partnership, S corporation, or nonpublicly offered mutual fund, then he or she can deduct their share of the entity's pass-through deduction of investment expenses.

Investment expenses are deductible only if they relate to investments that produce taxable income. Expenditures incurred for the acquisition or disposition of investment property generally must be capitalized (Reg. § 1.212-1(n)). A taxpayer, however, may elect a *de minimis* safe harbor not to capitalize costs to acquire investment property (¶ 903). Investment interest is deductible only to the extent of amount of net investment income (¶ 1094). A dealer or trader in securities is *not* an investor and may deduct investment expenses as business expenses, subject to the uniform capitalization (UNICAP) rules (¶ 990).[154] In addition, expenses attributable to property held for rents or royalties are deductible as an adjustment to gross income and are not subject to the two-percent of AGI floor (¶ 1006A).

1090. Expenses of Life Tenant or Income Beneficiary. In the case of business or investment property held by a life tenant, the deduction for depreciation or depletion is allowed to the life tenant and is computed as if the life tenant were the absolute owner of the property (Reg. §§ 1.167(h)-1 and 1.611-1(c)).[155] In the case of investment property held by a life tenant, the deduction is claimed as miscellaneous itemized deduction subject to the two-percent-of-adjusted-gross-income (AGI) floor (¶ 1079). After the life tenant's death, the deduction, if any, is allowed to the remainderman. For property held in trust or by an estate, the deduction is apportioned as explained at ¶ 530.

1091. Guardianship Expenses. A deduction is permitted for a reasonable amount paid or incurred for the services of a guardian or committee for a ward or minor and for other ordinary and necessary expenses incurred in connection with the production or collection of income inuring to the ward or minor, or in connection with the management, conservation, or maintenance of income-producing property belonging to the ward or minor (Reg. § 1.212-1(j)).[156] Expenses of a competency proceeding are deductible if the purpose of the proceeding is the management and conservation of income-producing property owned by the taxpayer.[157] The deduction is claimed as a miscellaneous itemized deduction on Schedule A of Form 1040, subject to the two-percent-of-adjusted-gross-income (AGI) limitation (¶ 1079).

1092. Expenses Connected with the Determination of Tax. Any ordinary and necessary expense incurred by an individual in connection with the determination, collection, or refund of any tax is deductible as a miscellaneous itemized deduction on Schedule A of Form 1040, subject to the two-percent-of-adjusted-income (AGI) limitation (¶ 1079) (Code Sec. 212(3); Reg. § 1.212-1(l)).[158] This includes tax return preparation fees allocable to an individual's Form 1040 and supporting schedules and forms. Tax preparation expenses attributable to a trade or business, rentals or royalties, or farm

References are to Standard Federal Tax Reports; Tax Research Consultant; and Practical Tax Explanations.

[153] ¶ 12,521; BUSEXP: 12,150; § 7,840.05

[154] ¶ 8521.1475, ¶ 8521.148; BUSEXP: 12,150; § 7,840.10

[155] ¶ 11,048, ¶ 23,922; DEPR: 15,258; § 5,015, § 11,015.30, § 11,605.15

[156] ¶ 12,521; BUSEXP: 12,210; § 7,801

[157] ¶ 12,523.13, ¶ 12,523.33; BUSEXP: 12,210; § 7,801

[158] ¶ 12,520, ¶ 12,521; BUSEXP: 12,064; § 7,835

income and expenses are deducted on the appropriate schedule including Schedules C, C-EZ, E, and F (Rev. Rul. 92-29, modifying Rev. Rul. 70-40).

This provision applies to income, estate, gift, property, and other taxes imposed at the federal, state, or local level. Legal expenses incurred in determining tax liability include legal fees paid for obtaining a ruling on a tax question (Rev. Rul. 89-68) and defending against a criminal indictment for tax evasion (Rev. Rul. 68-662). Expenses that pertain to both tax and nontax matters must be allocated and substantiated because only the tax element of the expense is deductible (Rev. Rul. 72-545).

Appraisal fees may be deductible as an expense paid in connection with the determination of income tax liability. Appraisal fees incurred in determining the fair market value of property donated to a charity or to establish the amount of loss are two examples of deductible expenses (Rev. Rul. 58-180; Rev. Rul. 67-461).

Credit or debit card convenience fees charged for electronic payment of federal individual income taxes, including estimated taxes, are deductible as miscellaneous itemized deductions (IRS News Release IR-2009-37).

1093. Nonbusiness Legal Expenses. Nonbusiness legal expenses of an individual are generally deductible as a miscellaneous itemized deduction on Schedule A of Form 1040, subject to the two-percent-of-adjusted-income (AGI) limitation (¶ 1079), if they are paid or incurred for the production of income or for the management, conservation, or maintenance of income-producing property (Code Sec. 212; Reg. § 1.212-1).[159] Legal expenses incurred in defending or perfecting title to property, in the acquisition or disposition of property, or in developing or improving property are *not* deductible and must be capitalized. Legal expenses paid or incurred in recovering investment property and amounts of income includible in gross income are generally deductible. The U.S. Court of Appeals for the Sixth Circuit has ruled, however, that legal expenses incurred in recovering stock are deductible only to the extent that they were allocable to the recovery of interest and dividends (*J.K. Nickell*, CA-6, 87-2 USTC ¶ 9585).

Divorce and Separation. Legal expenses paid by one spouse in resisting the other's monetary demands in connection with a divorce, separation, or support decree are generally nondeductible personal expenses (¶ 1003). Legal expenses properly attributable to producing or collecting alimony under a divorce decree, separation agreement, or support decree, however, may be deductible as a miscellaneous itemized deduction, subject to the two-percent of AGI limitation (Reg. § 1.262-1(b)(7)).[160]

Discrimination and Credit Claims. An individual can claim as an adjustment to gross income (an above-the-line deduction) in calculating adjusted gross income (AGI) (¶ 1005) for attorney's fees and court costs incurred in connection with an action involving: (1) a claim of unlawful discrimination; (2) certain claims against the federal government; or (3) a private cause of action under the Medicare Secondary Payer statute (Code Sec. 62(a)(20)).[161] The deduction is limited to the amount includible in gross income on account of a judgment or settlement, whether as a lump sum or in periodic payments. The deduction is claimed by entering the amount and "UDC" on the dotted line next to line 36 of Form 1040 and including the amount in the total for that line (Instruction to Form 1040).

Whistleblower Awards. An adjustment to gross income (an above-the-line deduction) is also allowed for court costs and attorney's fees paid by or on behalf of the taxpayer in connection with any whistleblower award under Code Sec. 7623(b) for providing information regarding tax law violations. The deduction cannot exceed the amount includible in gross income as a result of the award (Code Sec. 62(a)(21)).[162] The taxpayer claims the deduction by entering the amount and "WBF" on the dotted line next to line 36 of Form 1040 and including the amount in the total for that line (Instruction to Form 1040).

References are to Standard Federal Tax Reports; Tax Research Consultant; and Practical Tax Explanations.

[159] ¶ 12,520, ¶ 12,521; BUSEXP: 18,050; § 7,105.45, § 7,855

[160] ¶ 12,523.3273, ¶ 13,601, ¶ 13,603.223; BUSEXP: 12,302; § 7,105.45

[161] ¶ 6002; FILEIND: 9,088; § 5,805

[162] ¶ 6002; FILEIND: 9,090; § 5,001

1094. Limitation on Investment Interest Deduction. A noncorporate taxpayer may deduct on Form 4952 interest paid on investment indebtedness to the extent of the taxpayer's net investment income (Code Sec. 163(d); IRS Pub. 550; Rev. Rul. 95-16).[163] Net investment income is the excess of investment income over investment expenses. The disallowed investment interest can be carried over to a succeeding tax year.

Interest subject to the investment interest limitation is interest on debt properly allocable to property held for investment, which is generally defined as:

(1) property that produces interest, dividends, annuities, or royalties that are not derived in the ordinary course of a trade or business;

(2) property that produces gain or loss not derived in the ordinary course of a trade or business from the sale or exchange of property that either produces item (1) types of income or that is held for investment (but which is not an interest in a passive activity); and

(3) an interest in a trade or business activity that is not a passive activity and in which the taxpayer did not materially participate (¶ 1165).

Investment interest subject to the limitation also includes the taxpayer's share of investment interest from a partnership, S corporation, estate, or trust. It does not include home mortgage interest (¶ 1047), interest properly allocable to a rental real estate activity in which the taxpayer actively participates, within the meaning of the passive loss rule (¶ 1181), or interest that is taken into account in computing income or loss from a passive activity (¶ 1167).

Net capital gain from the disposition of investment property is not considered investment income. However, individuals may elect to treat all or any portion of such net capital gain as investment income by paying tax on the elected amounts at their ordinary income rates. The taxpayer may elect similar treatment for qualified dividend income (Code Sec. 163(d)(4)(B); Reg. § 1.163(d)-1).[164] Thus, the taxpayer loses the benefit of the otherwise applicable maximum capital gains tax rate with respect to the elected amount. The election must be made on Form 4952 on or before the due date of the return for the tax year in which the net capital gain or the qualified dividend income is recognized. The election is revocable with the consent of the IRS.

References are to Standard Federal Tax Reports; Tax Research Consultant; and Practical Tax Explanations.

[163] ¶ 9102, ¶ 9403.10; INDIV: 48,450; § 7,414.05

[164] ¶ 9102, ¶ 9402B; INDIV: 48,450; § 7,414.15

Chapter 11

LOSSES □ PASSIVE ACTIVITY LOSSES

	Par.
Deduction of Losses	1101
Casualty and Theft Losses	1121
Bad Debts	1135
Net Operating Losses (NOLs)	1145
At-Risk Limitations	1155
Passive Activity Limits on Losses and Credits	1165
Rental Activities Subject to Passive Activity Rules	1181
Tax-Exempt Use Property	1191
Hobby Losses	1195

Deduction of Losses

1101. Deductible Losses. A taxpayer may generally deduct losses which have not been compensated for by insurance or otherwise (Code Sec. 165(a); Reg. § 1.165-1).[1] In order to be deductible, a loss generally must be evidenced by a closed and completed transaction and fixed by identifiable events during the tax year, such as a sale, foreclosure, or condemnation. However, any loss arising from theft is treated as sustained during the tax year in which the taxpayer discovers the loss (¶ 1123). In addition, a special election exists for determining the year to deduct a loss attributable to a federally declared disaster (¶ 1133). Only a bona fide loss sustained by the taxpayer may be deducted, and the substance of a transaction, not its form, governs whether there is a deductible loss. Thus, a loss deduction may be disallowed for a transaction that lacks economic substance and is entered into solely for tax benefits.

No portion of a loss may be deducted if there is a reasonable prospect of recovery or reimbursement. Similarly, no deduction is generally allowed for a partial loss resulting from the decline in the value of property, except as reflected in inventory. An exception is provided for the deduction of an addition to a bad debt reserve and a charge-off of that part of a debt which is worthless (¶ 1137). A taxpayer may also claim a deduction for losses sustained from the abandonment of property (¶ 1109).

Losses realized by individuals may be deducted only if they are: (1) losses incurred in a trade or business; (2) losses incurred in a transaction entered into for profit; or (3) casualty and theft losses (Code Sec. 165(c); Reg. § 1.165-1(e)).[2] Individuals, as well as S corporations, partnerships, estates, and trusts, may deduct expenses attributable to activities not engaged in for profit only to the extent of the amount of gross income from the activity under the hobby loss rules (¶ 1195). Thus, an individual's personal losses that are not related to a business or profit-making activity may not be deducted unless they are the result of a casualty (¶ 1121) or theft (¶ 1123). In addition, there are a number of other special provisions that further limit an individual's ability to deduct losses, including the at-risk rules (¶ 1155), the passive activity loss rules (¶ 1165), and the related-party rules (¶ 1717). Losses from gambling or other wagering transactions are also allowed only to the extent of gains from those transactions (¶ 1113).

Amount of Loss. The amount deducted for a loss cannot exceed the taxpayer's adjusted basis in the property (Code Sec. 165(b); Reg. § 1.165-1(c)).[3] Thus, the basis of the property must be adjusted for expenses, receipts, or losses properly chargeable to capital account, and for depreciation, obsolescence, amortization, and depletion to determine the amount of loss allowable as a deduction (¶ 1604). In addition, adjustments

References are to Standard Federal Tax Reports; Tax Research Consultant; and Practical Tax Explanations.

[1] ¶ 9802, ¶ 9803; BUSEXP: 30,100; § 16,905.05

[2] ¶ 9802, ¶ 9803; BUSEXP: 30,150; § 16,901

[3] ¶ 9802, ¶ 9803; BUSEXP: 30,202; § 16,905.15

must be made for any salvage value, as well as any insurance or other compensation received by the taxpayer.

The amount or character of a loss may be limited by a number of other rules. For example, capital losses are permitted to be deducted by a taxpayer but only to the extent allowed under the capital loss limitation rules (¶ 1752) (Code Sec. 165(f); Reg. § 1.165-1(c)(3)).[4] A worthless nonbusiness bad debt is only deductible as a short-term capital loss (¶ 1143). Special rules also apply for losses on small business stock (¶ 1911), losses on worthless securities (¶ 1916), losses on wash sales of securities (¶ 1935), and losses on debt obligations required to be in registered form (¶ 1963).

1103. Loss on Sale of Residential Property. A loss realized from a sale or exchange of residential property acquired and held as a personal residence is not deductible by an individual. However, a loss on the sale or exchange of residential property realized at the time it is being rented or otherwise used for income-producing purposes is deductible (Reg. § 1.165-9).[5] If the property is used as the taxpayer's personal residence after having been acquired as income-producing property, then a loss realized on its sale or exchange at the time it is being used as a residence is not deductible. For the basis of residential or converted property, see ¶ 1626.

1105. Demolition Losses. A taxpayer may not deduct losses sustained in the demolition of buildings and their structural components, including certified historic structures. Any amount expended or loss sustained by an owner or lessee on account of the demolition of any structure must be capitalized as part of the basis of the land on which the structure was located (Code Sec. 280B).[6] The IRS has provided a safe harbor for certain structural modifications to a building that are not treated as a demolition and thus, not properly chargeable to the capital account with respect to the land on which the building is located (Rev. Proc. 95-27).[7] While demolition costs are nondeductible, a loss deduction may nonetheless be claimed by a taxpayer when depreciable business property is retired from use in a trade or business or from use in production of income (¶ 1109).

1107. Loss on Foreclosure or Tax Sale. The foreclosure of a mortgage by a judicial sale and disposition of the encumbered real estate is a sale of an asset. If the owner of an equity interest receives less than his or her basis in real estate when it is sold upon foreclosure, his or her investment may represent a deductible loss only if the property was used in a trade or business or a transaction entered into for profit.[8] The character of the loss—capital loss or ordinary loss—depends on the nature of the property foreclosed upon and whether or not it was a capital asset (¶ 1741) or section 1231 property (¶ 1747). The loss occurs when the redemption period expires or in the year the property becomes worthless. If there is no equity of redemption, however, the loss is fixed by the foreclosure sale and not by the decree of foreclosure that ordered the sale.[9] These principles also apply to a sale for delinquent taxes.[10]

If real property is disposed of by reason of foreclosure or similar proceedings, the amount of depreciation subject to recapture (¶ 1779) is determined as if the taxpayer ceased to hold the property on the date the proceedings began (Code Sec. 1250(d)(7)).[11]

1109. Abandonment and Obsolescence Losses. A taxpayer is allowed a deduction for a loss sustained in the abandonment of property used in a trade or business or a transaction entered into for profit. Depreciable property is abandoned when the taxpayer withdraws the property from use, or voluntarily and permanently gives up possession with the intention of ending ownership but without passing it on to someone else (Reg. § 1.167(a)-8(a)).[12] The abandonment loss equals the taxpayer's adjusted basis in the abandoned property, less any salvage value, insurance, or other compensation that the

References are to Standard Federal Tax Reports; Tax Research Consultant; and Practical Tax Explanations.

[4] ¶ 9802, ¶ 9803; BUSEXP: 30,102.05; § 16,901

[5] ¶ 10,102; BUSEXP: 30,158; § 16,930

[6] ¶ 14,900; BUSEXP: 39,150; § 16,915

[7] ¶ 14,901.60; BUSEXP: 39,156; § 16,915

[8] ¶ 9805.155, ¶ 10,103.54; BUSEXP: 30,268; § 18,205.20

[9] ¶ 21,817.45, ¶ 21,817.451; BUSEXP: 30,268; § 18,205.20

[10] ¶ 9808.453; BUSEXP: 30,268; § 18,205.20

[11] ¶ 31,000; DEPR: 18,260.15; § 11,710

[12] ¶ 11,020; BUSEXP: 39,104; § 16,910.05, § 16,910.10

taxpayer receives for the loss. An abandonment of property is not treated as a sale or exchange. Thus, an abandonment loss is an ordinary loss—regardless of whether or not the abandoned asset is a capital asset—and is reported on Form 4797 (IRS Pub. 544).

If nondepreciable property is abandoned following a sudden termination of its usefulness, an obsolescence loss is allowed in an amount equal to its adjusted basis. The obsolescence loss is deductible in the tax year in which it is sustained, even though the overt act of abandonment or the loss of title to the property may not occur in that year (Reg. § 1.165-2).[13]

A taxpayer cannot deduct the costs of acquiring and developing creative property (i.e., screenplays, scripts, story outlines, and similar property for film development or production) as an abandonment loss unless the taxpayer establishes either: (1) an intent to abandon the property and an affirmative act of abandonment, or (2) identifiable events which show a closed and completed transaction establishing the property's worthlessness (Rev. Rul. 2004-58).[14] Mere nonuse of an asset does not constitute abandonment, and the treatment of abandonment losses for financial reporting purposes does not control their federal tax treatment. To minimize accounting disputes, the IRS has provided a safe harbor allowing taxpayers to amortize ratably over a 15-year period any creative property costs that have been properly written off by the taxpayer under the generally accepted accounting principles (GAAP) for financial reporting purposes (¶ 1229).

1111. Interest Forfeited on Premature Withdrawals. Interest that was previously earned on a time savings account or deposit with a savings institution and that is later forfeited because of premature withdrawals is deductible by an individual in computing adjusted gross income in the year when the interest is forfeited (Code Sec. 62(a)(9)).[15]

> **Example:** Tom Smith opened a four-year time savings account in January 2015. He was credited with $400 in interest earned for 2015 and reported this income on his 2015 return. He withdrew the funds in October 2016. This premature withdrawal triggered a penalty provision so that he received only $230 of interest for 2015, plus $195 in interest earned on the account for 2016. Thus, Tom has incurred a loss of $170 that should be claimed on his 2016 return. He should also report the $195 in interest earned for 2016 on his 2016 income tax return.

The necessary information is provided on Form 1099-INT. The deduction must be claimed on Form 1040. No deduction is available on Form 1040A or Form 1040EZ.

1113. Gambling Losses. An individual can deduct gambling losses only to the extent of the amount of gambling winnings included in his or her gross income (Code Sec. 165(d); Reg. § 1.165-10).[16] For most taxpayers, deductible gambling losses are reported as miscellaneous itemized deductions not subject to the two-percent-of-adjusted-gross-income floor (¶ 1079). Professional gamblers, however, can deduct losses as an adjustment to gross income. Spouses who file a joint return can combine their gambling winnings and losses.

Casualty and Theft Losses

1121. Casualty Losses. An individual may deduct a loss from nonbusiness property only if it arises from fire, storm, shipwreck, or other casualty, or from theft (Code Sec. 165(c)(3)).[17] Each loss is subject to a $100 floor (¶ 1129), and net losses for the tax year are deductible only to the extent they exceed 10 percent of the taxpayer's adjusted gross income (AGI) (¶ 1131). However, an individual cannot claim a casualty loss deduction for damage to insured property unless a timely insurance claim is filed (Code Sec. 165(h)(4)(E)).[18] For a discussion of how to determine the amount of the deduction for a casualty loss, see ¶ 1127. Casualty and theft losses are reported on Form 4684. Theft losses are discussed at ¶ 1123.

References are to Standard Federal Tax Reports; Tax Research Consultant; and Practical Tax Explanations.

[13] ¶ 9901; BUSEXP: 39,102; § 16,910.15

[14] ¶ 9902.27; BUSEXP: 30,104.15; § 16,910.05

[15] ¶ 6002; FILEIND: 9,068; § 5,020

[16] ¶ 9802, ¶ 10,104; BUSEXP: 30,256; § 7,110.20, § 16,940.05

[17] ¶ 9802; INDIV: 54,050; § 7,701

[18] ¶ 9802; INDIV: 54,168; § 7,701

A casualty loss is generally deductible only for the tax year in which the loss is sustained (¶ 1101) (Reg. § 1.165-7(a)(1)).[19] If the extent of the damage cannot reasonably be ascertained in the year of occurrence, the deduction can be taken in a later year when the extent of the damage is known. In addition, a special election exists for determining the year to deduct a loss attributable to a federally declared disaster (¶ 1133).

Casualty Defined. A casualty is the damage, destruction, or loss of property resulting from an identifiable event due to some sudden, unexpected, or unusual cause (IRS Pub. 547).[20] Examples of casualties include earthquakes, fires (not willfully set), floods, storms, hurricanes, tornados, volcanic eruptions, government-ordered demolition or relocation, mine cave-ins, shipwrecks, sonic booms, terrorist attacks, or vandalism. A casualty also includes damage that is a result of any ordinary automobile accident whether the taxpayer, or someone else driving his or her car, is at fault in a collision, or whether the other driver is at fault (Reg. § 1.165-7(a)(3)).[21] However, if a car accident was caused by the willful act or willful negligence of the taxpayer, or his or her agent, the casualty loss deduction is not allowed.

The damage or loss of property due to progressive deterioration is not considered a casualty and is not deductible (IRS Pub. 547).[22] Examples include the weakening of property due to normal weather conditions, losses caused by drought to property not used in a trade or business or for the production of income unless the drought can be characterized as sudden or unusual, the deterioration and damage to a water heater, and damage to trees or other plants by normal infestations of fungi, disease, worms, or similar pests. The IRS takes the position that a casualty loss deduction for termite damage is not permitted because the "suddenness" test is not met, but some courts have allowed the deduction.[23]

A casualty loss is deductible only to the extent it is not compensated for by insurance or otherwise (¶ 1101). If there is no limitation on the manner in which money or property received as compensation for damaged property must be used, the amount received is a gift and does not reduce the amount of the taxpayer's casualty loss.[24] If, as the result of insurance or other reimbursement, a taxpayer realizes a gain from a casualty or theft loss, the taxpayer can defer recognition of the gain under the involuntary conversion rules by making an election and purchasing qualifying replacement property within the applicable replacement period (¶ 1715).

A casualty loss incurred with respect to either business or nonbusiness property can result in a net operating loss (NOL) (¶ 1147). The $100 floor and the 10-percent-of-AGI limitation are applied in the nonbusiness situation in determining an NOL.

1123. Theft Losses. A loss from the theft of property that is not compensated for by insurance or otherwise is generally deductible for the tax year in which the taxpayer discovers the loss (Code Sec. 165(e); Reg. § 1.165-8(a)).[25] No deduction may be claimed in the year of discovery, however, if a reimbursement claim exists with respect to which there is a reasonable prospect of recovery (Reg. § 1.165-1(d)(3)).[26] As with casualty losses (¶ 1121), an individual cannot claim a deduction for theft of insured property unless a timely insurance claim is filed (Code Sec. 165(h)(4)(E)).[27] In addition, each theft loss is subject to a $100 floor (¶ 1129), and net losses from combined personal casualty and theft losses for the tax year are deductible only to the extent they exceed 10 percent of the taxpayer's adjusted gross income (AGI) (¶ 1131).

A theft includes the taking of money or property by robbery, larceny, burglary, blackmail, embezzlement, extortion, or kidnapping for ransom. Theft does not include property that was lost or misplaced. It also does not include the decline in value of stock acquired in the open market caused by the disclosure of accounting fraud by officers or

References are to Standard Federal Tax Reports; Tax Research Consultant; and Practical Tax Explanations.

[19] ¶ 10,004; INDIV: 54,250; § 7,705.30

[20] ¶ 10,005.123—¶ 10,005.92; INDIV: 54,052, INDIV: 54,084; § 7,705.05

[21] ¶ 10,004; INDIV: 54,068; § 7,705.05

[22] ¶ 10,005.123—¶ 10,005.92; INDIV: 54,058; § 7,705.05

[23] ¶ 10,005.671; INDIV: 54,062; § 7,705.05

[24] ¶ 10,005.117; INDIV: 54,168; § 7,705.25

[25] ¶ 9802, ¶ 10,100; INDIV: 54,100; § 7,710.05, § 7,710.15

[26] ¶ 9803; BUSEXP: 30,110; § 7,710.25

[27] ¶ 9802; INDIV: 54,168; § 7,701

directors of the corporation (IRS Pub. 547).[28] The deduction for theft losses is determined in the same way as for other casualty losses (¶ 1127). Casualty and theft losses are reported on Form 4684.

Losses from Ponzi-Type Schemes. Investors who incur losses from criminally fraudulent investment arrangements such as "Ponzi" schemes are entitled to claim a theft loss, rather than a capital loss (Rev. Rul. 2009-9).[29] The loss is deductible as a loss on a transaction entered into for profit, and it is not subject to the $100 floor or the 10-percent-of-AGI limitation for personal theft losses, or the limitations on itemized deductions (¶ 1014). The theft loss is deductible in the year it is discovered, and the amount of the deduction includes the amount invested in the scheme, less any amounts withdrawn, reimbursements, and claims as to which there is a reasonable prospect of recovery. If the theft loss deduction creates or increases a net operating loss (NOL) in the year the loss is deducted, the taxpayer may carry back up to three years and forward up to 20 years the portion of the NOL attributable to the theft loss (¶ 1149).

The IRS has also provided an optional safe harbor under which a qualified investor may deduct as a theft loss up to 95 percent of a qualified investment if the investor does not pursue any potential third-party recovery, or 75 percent of a qualified investment if the investor is pursuing or intends to pursue any potential third-party recovery. The deduction is reduced by the amount of any actual recovery and any recovery from insurance or the Securities Investor Protection Corporation (Rev. Proc. 2011-58).

1125. Loss on Bank Deposits. An individual may elect to treat the loss on a nonbusiness account in an insolvent or bankrupt financial institution as a personal casualty loss in the year in which the loss can reasonably be estimated (Code Sec. 165(l)).[30] If elected, the casualty loss deduction is subject to a $100 floor (¶ 1129) and the 10-percent-of-adjusted-gross-income (AGI) limitation (¶ 1131). The election is made on Form 4684.

Alternatively, an individual can elect to treat the loss as an ordinary loss arising from a transaction entered into for profit in the year the loss can be reasonably estimated, provided that no portion of the deposit is federally insured. The maximum amount that a taxpayer may claim as ordinary loss in any tax year is limited to $20,000 ($10,000 in the case of a married individual filing separately) for each financial institution, reduced by the amount of insurance proceeds that the taxpayer can reasonably expect to receive under state law (Code Sec. 165(l)(5)). The loss is deducted on Schedule A of Form 1040 as a miscellaneous itemized deduction subject to the two-percent-of-AGI limit (¶ 1079). The name of the financial institution and "Insolvent Financial Institution" should be written on the appropriate line of Schedule A. The calculation of the deducted loss should be included with the return (IRS Pub. 529).

Once made, either election applies to all losses on deposits in the financial institution during the tax year and it is revocable only with IRS consent. A taxpayer making either election is prohibited from deducting the loss as a bad debt deduction (Code Sec. 165(l)(6) and (7)). Neither election can be made by an individual who is an owner of one percent or more of the value of the institution's stock, an officer of the institution, or a relative of an owner or officer (Code Sec. 165(l)(2)). If neither election is made, then the loss is treated as a nonbusiness bad debt in the year of final determination of the actual loss and is reported as a short-term capital loss on Form 8949 (¶ 1143 and ¶ 1752).

1127. Amount of Casualty or Theft Loss. The amount of a casualty loss (¶ 1121) which is deductible for business and income-producing property or nonbusiness property is the *lesser* of:

(1) the fair market value (FMV) of the property immediately before the casualty reduced by its FMV immediately after the casualty, or

(2) the adjusted basis of the property immediately before the casualty (Reg. § 1.165-7(b)).[31]

References are to Standard Federal Tax Reports; Tax Research Consultant; and Practical Tax Explanations.

[28] ¶ 10,101.237, ¶ 10,101.318; INDIV: 54,102; § 7,710.05, § 7,710.10

[29] ¶ 10,101.123; INDIV: 54,106.10; § 7,710.30

[30] ¶ 9802; INDIV: 54,082; § 7,105.55, § 7,705.10

[31] ¶ 10,004; BUSEXP: 30,212, INDIV: 54,152; § 7,705.10, § 7,705.15

If business or income-producing property is totally destroyed and the property's FMV immediately before the casualty is less than its adjusted basis, then the casualty loss is the adjusted basis of the property.

The amount of a theft loss (¶ 1123) which is deductible is the fair market value or the adjusted basis of the property stolen (Reg. § 1.165-8(c)).[32] When money is stolen, the theft loss is the amount stolen. The amount of a theft loss in the case of nonbusiness property other than money is the lesser of the value of the property or its adjusted basis. In the case of stolen business or income-producing property, the theft loss is the adjusted basis of the property stolen.

A personal casualty or theft loss is subject to a $100 floor (¶ 1129) and a 10-percent-of-adjusted-gross-income (AGI) limit (¶ 1131) in determining the allowable deduction. The $100 floor and AGI limit do not apply to a business or income-producing property casualty or theft loss.

A casualty or theft loss is reduced by any insurance or other compensation received by the taxpayer, and in the case of a casualty loss, it is also reduced by any salvage value (¶ 1101). An individual cannot claim a personal casualty or theft loss to the extent the loss is covered by insurance, unless a timely insurance claim is filed with respect to the loss (¶ 1121 and ¶ 1123).

When there is damage to different kinds of business property, losses must be computed separately for each single, identifiable property damaged or destroyed. This rule does not apply to nonbusiness property. For example, if a tree is blown down in the front yard of a taxpayer's residence, the loss is the difference in the FMV of the taxpayer's whole property before and after damage to the tree (Reg. § 1.165-7(b)).[33]

The taxpayer's basis for property damaged or destroyed by casualty or theft is reduced by the amount allowable as a casualty or theft loss deduction, as well as by the amount of any insurance or other recovery for the loss (Rev. Rul. 71-161).[34]

1129. $100 Floor for Personal Casualty or Theft Losses. The deduction for a personal casualty (¶ 1121) or theft loss (¶ 1123) is limited to the amount that the loss from each casualty or theft exceeds $100 (Code Sec. 165(h)(1); Reg. § 1.165-7(b)(4)).[35] The $100 floor applies separately to the loss from each single casualty or theft, regardless of how many pieces of property are involved in the event. Thus, if several items of nonbusiness property are damaged or stolen in the course of a single casualty or theft, the $100 floor is applied only once against the sum of the allowable losses. In the case of married taxpayers filing a joint return, *only one* $100 floor applies to each casualty or theft loss; it does not matter if the property is owned jointly or separately. If married taxpayers file separate returns, each spouse is subject to the $100 limitation for each casualty or theft loss. When property is used for both business and personal purposes, the $100 floor applies only to the net loss attributable to that portion of the property used for personal purposes. After the first $100 is subtracted from each personal casualty and theft loss, all personal casualty and theft losses for the tax year are netted against any personal casualty and theft gains. If personal casualty losses and theft losses exceed personal casualty and theft gains, a loss deduction is allowed to the extent that the excess is greater than 10 percent of adjusted-gross-income (AGI) (¶ 1131).

1131. 10 Percent of AGI Floor for Personal Casualty or Theft Losses. If a taxpayer's personal casualty (¶ 1121) or theft losses (¶ 1123) exceed his or her personal casualty or theft gains for the tax year, the excess generally is deductible only to the extent that it exceeds 10 percent of the taxpayer's adjusted gross income (AGI) for the year (Code Sec. 165(h)(2)).[36] For this purpose, gains and losses from personal casualties and thefts calculated on Form 4684 are netted without regard to holding periods for the initial determination of whether there was a gain or loss. The $100 floor (¶ 1129) is applied to each personal casualty or theft before this netting occurs. If the recognized

References are to Standard Federal Tax Reports; Tax Research Consultant; and Practical Tax Explanations.

[32] ¶ 10,100; BUSEXP: 30,212, INDIV: 54,152; § 7,705.10, § 7,710.20

[33] ¶ 10,004; BUSEXP: 30,212, INDIV: 54,152; § 7,705.10, § 7,705.15

[34] ¶ 10,005.16; SALES: 6,360.05; § 16,110.25

[35] ¶ 9802, ¶ 10,004; INDIV: 54,202, INDIV: 54,354; § 7,705.15

[36] ¶ 9802; INDIV: 54,204, INDIV: 54,206; § 7,705.15

gains exceed the recognized losses, the net gain is reported as a capital gain on Schedule D of Form 1040. If the recognized losses exceed the recognized gains after netting, the net loss is deductible as an itemized deduction on Schedule A of Form 1040 but only to the extent it exceeds 10 percent of the taxpayer's AGI.

Example 1: A taxpayer who has AGI of $50,000 (without regard to casualty gains or losses), a $25,000 casualty gain, and a $15,000 casualty loss (after the $100 floor) will report a $10,000 capital gain on Schedule D.

Example 2: A taxpayer who has AGI of $40,000, a $25,000 casualty loss (after the $100 floor), and a $15,000 casualty gain is allowed a $6,000 itemized deduction. The $10,000 loss resulting from netting the casualty gains against the casualty losses is deductible only to the extent that it exceeds 10 percent of AGI ($10,000 – $4,000 = $6,000).

Limitation for Estates and Trusts. The 10-percent-of-AGI limitation on personal casualty and theft losses applies to estates and trusts. AGI is computed in the same manner as it is for individuals, except that estates and trusts are allowed to deduct their administration expenses in arriving at AGI (Code Sec. 165(h)(4)(C)).[37] No deduction for a personal casualty or theft loss may be taken if, at the time of filing a decedent's return, the loss has been claimed for estate tax purposes (¶ 531).

1133. Disaster Area Loss. A taxpayer that sustains a loss occurring in a disaster area and attributable to a federally declared disaster can either (1) deduct the loss on the tax return for the year in which the loss occurred, or (2) elect to deduct the loss on the return for the preceding tax year (Code Sec. 165(i); Temporary Reg. § 1.165-11T).[38] The disaster area loss deduction is calculated using the same rules as those for any other personal casualty losses (¶ 1127). If, however, the taxpayer elects to claim a disaster area loss on the return for the year immediately preceding the loss year, the 10-percent-of-adjusted-gross-income (AGI) limit (¶ 1131) is determined with respect to the preceding year's AGI. In addition, the IRS is authorized to issue guidance allowing the use of an appraisal used to secure a federal loan or loan guarantee as a result of federally declared disaster to establish the disaster loss amount.

The election to deduct a disaster area loss in the tax year prior to the loss year is made by filing a return, an amended return, or a refund claim that clearly shows that the election is being made. The election applies to the entire loss sustained by the taxpayer in the disaster area during the disaster period. Effective for elections on or after October 13, 2016, the election generally must be made by the date that is six months after the due date of the tax return for the year of the loss without regard to extensions. For example, the election to deduct a 2016 disaster area loss in 2015 must be made on or before October 18, 2017, for a calendar-year individual. A taxpayer may revoke the election within 90 days after the required due date. Prior to October 13, 2016, the required due date was the original due date of the return, without regard to extensions. The IRS has provided procedures for taxpayers who wished to make the election pursuant to the new due date who failed to make a timely election under the old due date (Rev. Proc. 2016-53).[39]

Although a taxpayer may not deduct a loss incurred on the sale of his or her personal residence, the loss is treated as a disaster area loss if the personal residence is rendered unsafe by a disaster in an area determined by the President of the United States to warrant federal government assistance. In addition, the individual must have been ordered by the state or local government within 120 days after the area is declared a disaster area to demolish or relocate the residence (Code Sec. 165(k)).[40] The amount of the deduction is reduced by any partial payments received from the state in the form of disaster aid.

References are to Standard Federal Tax Reports; Tax Research Consultant; and Practical Tax Explanations.

[37] ¶ 9802; ESTTRST: 12,060.10; § 32,401

[38] ¶ 9802, ¶ 10,200M; INDIV: 54,302; § 7,715.10

[39] ¶ 10,201.13; INDIV: 54,304; § 7,715.10

[40] ¶ 9802, INDIV: 54,306; § 7,715.20

Bad Debts

1135. Business Bad Debts. Business bad debts can generally be deducted from gross income as an ordinary loss when and to the extent that they become totally worthless (Code Sec. 166).[41] If a business bad debt is only partially worthless and is recoverable in part, then the worthless portion is deductible to the extent it is charged off during the tax year (¶ 1137). A business debt is a debt: (1) created or acquired in connection with the trade or business of the taxpayer who is claiming the deduction, or (2) the worthlessness of which has been incurred in the taxpayer's trade or business (Reg. § 1.166-5(b)).[42] If the taxpayer's primary motive for incurring the debt is not business related, then it is a nonbusiness debt and deductible only as a short-term capital loss when the debt becomes totally worthless (¶ 1143).

Only a bona fide debt qualifies for purposes of deducting a bad debt (Reg. § 1.166-1(c)).[43] A debt is considered bona fide if it arises from a true debtor-creditor relationship based on a valid and enforceable obligation to pay a fixed or determinable amount of money. For example, a business bad debt deduction is not available to shareholders who have advanced money to a corporation as a contribution to capital.[44] In addition, the bad debt deduction rules do not apply to a debt that is evidenced by a security (Code Sec. 166(e)).[45] If a security held by a taxpayer other than a bank becomes worthless during the tax year, it is treated as sold or exchanged at a loss on the last day of the tax year (¶ 1916). A bank may treat a loss from a worthless security as a bad debt loss (¶ 2383).

Whether a debt is wholly or partially worthless is a question of fact, requiring consideration of all pertinent evidence, including the debtor's financial condition and the value of any security for the debt (Reg. § 1.166-2).[46] A debt becomes worthless when there is no longer any chance the amount owed will be paid. This can be evidenced (1) by the fact that legal action to enforce payment would result in an uncollectible judgment, or (2) upon a settlement in bankruptcy, although worthlessness may sometimes be determined after bankruptcy and before settlement. It is not necessary for the taxpayer to go to court to demonstrate worthlessness; the taxpayer only has to show that reasonable steps were taken to collect the debt, but he or she was unable to do so (IRS Pub. 535).

Guarantors. A taxpayer is eligible for a business bad debt deduction if in the course of a trade or business, the taxpayer pays an obligation as a guarantor, endorser, or indemnitor (Reg. § 1.166-9).[47] A noncorporate taxpayer is eligible for a nonbusiness bad debt deduction if the taxpayer pays an obligation as a guarantor, endorser, or indemnitor as part of a transaction entered into for profit. In the case of a business bad debt, no deduction is available if the agreement to act as guarantor, endorser, or indemnitor was not made in the course of the taxpayer's trade or business or a transaction for profit, if there is no legal obligation on the taxpayer to make the guaranty payment, or if the agreement was entered into after the debt became worthless.

Employee Loans. An employee's rendering of services for pay is a trade or business for purposes of the bad debt provisions. Therefore, a loan to an employer to protect a job can give rise to a business bad debt deduction if the employer defaults. If a loan by a shareholder-employee is intended to protect the shareholder's job rather than to protect the shareholder's investment in the company, then the failure to repay the loan results in a business bad debt deduction. The larger the shareholder's investment, the smaller his or her salary, and the larger his or her other sources of income, the more likely that a dominant nonbusiness motive exists for making the loan.[48]

References are to Standard Federal Tax Reports; Tax Research Consultant; and Practical Tax Explanations.

[41] ¶ 10,602; BUSEXP: 48,152; § 17,120.05

[42] ¶ 10,691; BUSEXP: 48,156; § 17,120.05

[43] ¶ 10,603; BUSEXP: 48,050; § 17,105

[44] ¶ 10,650.7301; BUSEXP: 48,108; § 17,120.10

[45] ¶ 10,602; BUSEXP: 48,154; § 16,555

[46] ¶ 10,604; BUSEXP: 48,250; § 17,110.05

[47] ¶ 10,753; BUSEXP: 48,400, BUSEXP: 48,402; § 17,125

[48] ¶ 10,700.241; BUSEXP: 48,160.35, BUSEXP: 48,160.40; § 17,120.10

1137. Accounting for Bad Debt Deduction. Bad debts are generally deductible in the tax year in which they become worthless (Code Sec. 166(a); Reg. § 1.166-3).[49] For a nonbusiness debt (¶ 1143), the deduction is available when the debt becomes wholly worthless. A deduction is allowed for a business debt (¶ 1135) that becomes wholly or partially worthless, but only to the extent the debt is charged off of the taxpayer's books during the tax year. The bad debt deduction is not available for nonbusiness debts that are only partially worthless. A worthless debt arising from unpaid wages, rent, interest, or a similar item is not deductible unless the income that these items represent has been reported for income tax purposes by the taxpayer (Reg. §§ 1.166-1(e) and 1.166-6(a)(2)).[50]

Generally, a taxpayer must use the specific charge-off method to claim a deduction for a business bad debt. If a business debt becomes totally worthless during the year, the taxpayer can deduct the entire amount in that year. If a business debt becomes partially worthless during the year, the taxpayer can deduct that amount of the debt charged off his or her books for the year (Reg. § 1.166-3). An exception to the charge-off rule exists for debt which has been significantly modified. Some accrual taxpayers may use the nonaccrual experience method of accounting for bad debts with respect to income to be received from the performance of services (¶ 1538). Small banks and thrift institutions can use the experience method of accounting to deduct bad debts (¶ 2383).

1139. Secured Bad Debt. When secured or mortgaged property is sold either to the secured party or to a third party for less than the amount of the debt, the creditor is entitled to a bad debt deduction (¶ 1135 and ¶ 1143) in an amount equal to the difference between the sale price and the amount of the debt, to the extent that the creditor can show that such difference is wholly or partially uncollectible (Reg. § 1.166-6).[51] No bad debt deduction is allowed if a mortgage is foreclosed and the creditor buys the mortgaged property at a price equal to the unpaid debt. However, gain or loss is realized on the transaction. It is measured by the difference between the amount of the obligations of the debtor that are applied to the purchase or bid price of the property and the fair market value of the property, to the extent that the obligations are capital or represent items the income from which has been returned by the creditor. See ¶ 1838 and ¶ 1841 for a discussion on repossession of property sold on the installment plan.

1141. Debts Owed by Political Parties. No deduction is generally allowable for a worthless debt owed by a political party. However, banks and accrual-basis taxpayers (¶ 1515) who are in the business of providing goods and services (e.g., polling, media, or organizational services) to political campaigns and candidates may deduct such bad debts (Code Sec. 271).[52]

1143. Nonbusiness Bad Debts. If a nonbusiness bad debt held by a taxpayer other than a corporation becomes *totally* worthless during the tax year, then the loss may be deducted as a short-term capital loss regardless of how long the taxpayer held the debt (Code Sec. 166(d); Reg. § 1.166-5).[53] Unlike business bad debts (¶ 1135), however, no deduction is permitted unless and until the debt becomes totally worthless. A nonbusiness bad debt is any debt *other than* one created or acquired in connection with the taxpayer's trade or business, or one that, when worthless, creates a loss that is incurred in the taxpayer's trade or business. For limitations on deduction of a capital loss, see ¶ 1752. For worthlessness of a debt evidenced by a bond or other security of a corporation or a government, see ¶ 1916.

References are to Standard Federal Tax Reports; Tax Research Consultant; and Practical Tax Explanations.

[49] ¶ 10,602, ¶ 10,605; BUSEXP: 48,250; § 17,101, § 17,112

[50] ¶ 10,603, ¶ 10,701; BUSEXP: 48,062, BUSEXP: 48,204; § 17,115

[51] ¶ 10,701; BUSEXP: 48,274, SALES: 6,064.10; § 17,110.10, § 17,115

[52] ¶ 14,306; BUSEXP: 48,068

[53] ¶ 10,602, ¶ 10,691; BUSEXP: 48,152, BUSEXP: 48,250; § 17,120.05

Net Operating Losses (NOLs)

1145. Net Operating Loss (NOL). A net operating loss (NOL) from a trade or business may be claimed as a deduction in the current tax year equal to the aggregate amount of NOLs carried back or carried forward from other tax years (¶ 1149) (Code Sec. 172(a); Reg. § 1.172-1).[54] The NOL deduction may not exceed the amount of taxable income for the year of the deduction. An NOL arises in any tax year when the taxpayer's deductible expenses for the year exceed its gross income, subject to certain adjustments (¶ 1147). The NOL deduction is available to most taxpayers, including corporations, individuals, estates and trusts, and participants in common trust funds. An NOL deduction may not be claimed by a partnership or S corporation, but partners and S corporation shareholders use their distributive shares of partnership or S corporation income to calculate their own NOLs (¶ 319 and ¶ 417). An NOL deduction also may not be claimed by regulated investment companies (¶ 2301) and life insurance companies (¶ 2370) (Code Secs. 805(b)(4) and 852(b)(2)(B)).[55]

Noncorporate Taxpayers. Individuals, estates, and trusts may use Form 1045 to claim a quick refund resulting from the *carryback* of an NOL (Code Sec. 6411; Reg. § 1.6411-1).[56] Form 1045 must be filed on or after the date for filing a tax return for the NOL year, but no later than one year after the end of the NOL year (¶ 2773). Form 1045 also contains schedules that can be used to determine the amount of NOL available for carryback or carryover, and the NOL deduction for each carryback year and the amount to be carried over.

As an alternative to Form 1045, an individual may file an amended return on Form 1040X for each carryback year to claim a refund from the *carryback* of an NOL. Form 1040X must generally be filed within three years after the due date of the return for the NOL year. Estates and trusts file an amended Form 1041 for each carryback year and check the "amended return" box. If an amended return is filed, the taxpayer must still attach the NOL computations using the Form 1045 computation schedules.

No special form is used to *carry over* an NOL deduction. If the taxpayer elects to waive the NOL deduction carryback (¶ 1149), however, a statement making the election must be attached to the return or amended return for the tax year. Individuals list an NOL carryover deduction as a negative figure on the "Other Income" line of Form 1040 or 1040NR. Estates and trusts include an NOL carryover deduction on Form 1041 with other deductions not subject to the two-percent-of-adjusted-gross-income limit.

Corporations. Corporations may file for a quick refund resulting from the *carryback* of an NOL using Form 1139. The form can be filed on or after the date on which the return for the NOL year is filed, but no later than one year after the end of the NOL year. Alternatively, a corporation may file an amended return on Form 1120X in place of Form 1139 for each carryback year. Form 1120X must be filed within three years of the due date including extensions for filing the return for the NOL year. Corporations must file Form 1120X rather than Form 1139, however, to carryback a prior year foreign tax credit, minimum tax credit, or general business credit released due to an NOL.

A corporation that expects an NOL in the current tax year may file Form 1138 to extend the time for payment of the tax for the immediately preceding tax year (Code Sec. 6164; Reg. § 1.6164-1).[57] The extension applies only to payments of tax that are required to be paid after Form 1138 is filed. The extension expires at the end of the month in which the return for the tax year of the expected NOL is required to be filed including extensions. However, if the corporation files Form 1139 before the extension period ends, the time for payments is further extended until the date that the IRS mails notice that it has allowed or disallowed the application (Reg. § 1.6164-5).[58]

References are to Standard Federal Tax Reports; Tax Research Consultant; and Practical Tax Explanations.

[54] ¶ 12,002, ¶ 12,003; BUSEXP: 45,000, BUSEXP: 45,050; § 17,001

[55] ¶ 25,770, ¶ 26,420; BUSEXP: 45,052

[56] ¶ 38,720, ¶ 38,722; BUSEXP: 45,256.05; § 17,025

[57] ¶ 37,240, ¶ 37,241; BUSEXP: 45,260; § 39,315.10

[58] ¶ 37,247; BUSEXP: 45,260.10; § 39,315.25

1147. Net Operating Loss (NOL) Defined. A net operating loss (NOL) for the tax year is the excess of allowable deductions over gross income, with certain modifications (Code Sec. 172(c); Reg. § 1.172-1).[59] For calculating the NOL, income and deductions from separate businesses are aggregated, and items that are excludable from gross income are generally excluded. The NOL for any tax year is determined under the law applicable to that tax year, without regard to the law applicable to the tax year to which the NOL is carried. A taxpayer with a short tax year cannot annualize an NOL.

Noncorporate Taxpayers. The following adjustments are made in computing the NOL of a noncorporate taxpayer (Code Sec. 172(d); Reg. § 1.172-3):[60]

(1) No deduction for NOL carryovers or carrybacks from other years is allowed.

(2) No deduction is allowed for personal or dependency exemptions.

(3) Nonbusiness capital losses are deductible only to the extent of nonbusiness capital gains determined without regard to the exclusion for gain from qualified small business stock (¶ 1905).

(4) Business capital losses are deductible only to the extent of the sum of (a) business capital gains determined without regard to the exclusion for gain from qualified small business stock, and (b) any nonbusiness capital gains that remain after deducting nonbusiness capital losses and excess nonbusiness deductions (item (5) below).

(5) Nonbusiness deductions are allowed only to the extent of nonbusiness income including net nonbusiness capital gains. Nonbusiness deductions generally include deductions not related to the taxpayer's trade or business, or employment—e.g., alimony, deductions for contributions to a retirement plan, health savings account (HSA) deductions, the standard deduction, and personal itemized deductions. Nonbusiness income generally includes income from passive investments, such as interest, dividends, annuities, as well at the taxpayer's share of nonbusiness income from a partnership or S corporation. The taxpayer's wages and salary are considered income that *is* attributable to the taxpayer's trade or business.

(6) The domestic production activities deduction (¶ 980A) is not allowed.

Corporations. The following adjustments are made in computing the NOL of a corporation (Code Sec. 172(d); Reg. § 1.172-2):[61]

(1) No deduction for NOL carryovers or carrybacks from other years is allowed.

(2) A corporation is entitled to deductions for dividends received from a domestic corporation, received on certain preferred stock of public utilities, received from certain foreign corporations, and paid on certain preferred stock of public utilities, without regard to the limitations, based on taxable income, imposed on such deductions in computing taxable income (¶ 223 and ¶ 231).

(3) The domestic production activities deduction is not allowed.

1149. Carryback and Carryforward of Net Operating Losses (NOLs). If a taxpayer has a net operating loss (NOL) for the current tax year (¶ 1147), then the loss may be carried back to prior tax years or carried forward to future years as a deduction against taxable income (¶ 1145). NOLs can generally be carried back to the two years preceding the loss year and then forward up to 20 years following the loss year (Code Sec. 172(b)(1)).[62] Special carryover periods, however, are available for NOLs attributable to casualties, disasters, farming losses, and certain other activities (¶ 1151). No deduction is allowed in the year the loss is incurred. In determining the amount of an NOL carryback or carryover, the law in effect during the year to which the NOL is carried back or carried over is applied (Code Sec. 172(e)).

References are to Standard Federal Tax Reports; Tax Research Consultant; and Practical Tax Explanations.

[59] ¶ 12,002, ¶ 12,003; BUSEXP: 45,100; § 17,005.05

[60] ¶ 12,002, ¶ 12,005; BUSEXP: 45,106; § 17,005.10

[61] ¶ 12,002, ¶ 12,004; BUSEXP: 45,104; § 17,005.15

[62] ¶ 12,002; BUSEXP: 45,150; § 17,010.05

The NOL is first carried back to the second tax year preceding the loss year, then to the next earliest carryback year, and then forward to tax years after the loss year. If an NOL carryover is not fully absorbed in a carryback or carryover year, then the following adjustments must be made to taxable income in the carryback or carryover year (but not less than zero) to determine the portion of the NOL still available to be carried to the next year in the carryback or carryover period (Code Sec. 172(b)(2); Reg. § 1.172-5).[63]

(1) The NOL deduction for the intervening year is computed by taking into account only carryback and carryovers from tax years *preceding* the loss year.

(2) For taxpayers other than corporations, capital losses are deductible only to the extent of capital gains.

(3) Personal and dependency exemptions are not allowed.

(4) The domestic production activities deduction (¶ 980A) is not allowed.

In a year in which an NOL is carried back, any income, deductions, or credits that are based on or limited to a percentage of adjusted gross income (AGI) must be recomputed based on AGI after applying the NOL deduction for the carryback year. The charitable contribution deduction, however, is *not* recomputed. Taxable income is recomputed taking into account the NOL and the preceding adjustments. Income tax, alternative minimum tax, and any credits that are based on or limited to the amount of tax are then recomputed.

Election to Forgo Carryback. A taxpayer may elect to waive the entire carryback period (Code Sec. 172(b)(3)).[64] If the election is made, the loss may be carried forward only. The election must be made by the return due date including extensions for the tax year of the NOL. The election may also be made on an amended return filed within six months of the due date of an original timely return excluding extensions. Refer to the instructions for Form 1045 or Form 1139 for specific statement requirements. Once made, the election is irrevocable.

Married Taxpayers. Married individuals who file a joint return for each year considered in figuring NOL carrybacks and carryforwrds calculate their NOL as though all the income and deductions on the return were those of one taxpayer (Reg. § 1.172-7).[65] If married individuals file separate returns for each year considered in figuring NOL carrybacks and carryovers, then each spouse is entitled to their own NOLs without regard to the income or deductions of the other spouse. Special rules apply for figuring the NOL carrybacks and carryforwards of married people whose filing status changes for any tax year considered in figuring an NOL carryback or carryforward.

1151. Special NOL Carryforward and Carryback Periods. A net operating loss (NOL) generally must be carried back to the two years preceding the loss year and then carried forward to the 20 years following the loss year (¶ 1149). Special carryover periods are available, however, for certain types of NOLs.

Casualties and Disasters. A three-year carryback period is available for: (1) an NOL of an individual arising from a fire, storm, shipwreck, other casualty, or theft, and (2) an NOL of a small business or taxpayer engaged in farming if the loss is attributable to a federally declared disaster (Code Sec. 172(b)(1)(E)).[66] A small business is one with an average annual gross receipts of $5 million or less. An eligible loss does not include a farming loss described below.

Farming Loss. A farming loss may be carried back for five years (Code Sec. 172(b)(1)(F) and (h)).[67] A farming loss is the *smaller* of (1) the amount that would be the NOL for the tax year if only income and deductions attributable to farming businesses (¶ 999) were taken into account, or (2) the NOL for the tax year. A taxpayer may

References are to Standard Federal Tax Reports; Tax Research Consultant; and Practical Tax Explanations.

[63] ¶ 12,002, ¶ 12,007; BUSEXP: 45,200; § 17,015.15

[64] ¶ 12,002; BUSEXP: 45,152; § 17,010.15

[65] ¶ 12,009; BUSEXP: 45,208.05; § 17,020

[66] ¶ 12,002; BUSEXP: 45,154.35; § 17,010.20

[67] ¶ 12,002; BUSEXP: 45,154.40; § 36,210

elect to waive the five-year carryback for a farming loss. In this case, the two-year carryback period generally applies. For ordering purposes, the farming loss is treated as a separate NOL to be taken into account *after* the remaining portion of the NOL for the tax year.

Short Tax Years. If the IRS approves a request for a change in accounting period when the short period required to effect the change is a tax year in which the taxpayer has an NOL, the taxpayer can carry back the short-period NOL only if it is either (1) $50,000 or less, or (2) less than the full 12-month period NOL beginning with the first day of the short period as determined when the 12-month period has expired.[68]

Specified Liability Losses. A 10-year carryback period applies to specified liability losses (Code Sec. 172(b)(1)(C) and (f); Notice 2005-20).[69] A specified liability loss is the portion of an NOL that (1) is attributable to product liability or (2) arises out of satisfaction of a liability under federal or state law requiring land reclamation, nuclear power plant decommissioning, drilling platform dismantling, environmental remediation, or a payment under any workers' compensation act. For ordering purposes, the specified liability loss is treated as a separate NOL to be taken into account *after* the remaining portion of the NOL for the tax year.

Real Estate Investment Trusts (REITs). An NOL from a REIT year—a tax year in which an entity operated as a REIT (¶ 2326)—cannot be carried back to any preceding tax year. An NOL from a non-REIT year cannot be carried back to a REIT year. A REIT NOL can be carried forward 20 years (Code Sec. 172(b)(1)(B); Reg. § 1.172-10).[70]

Corporate Equity Reduction Transactions (CERTs). A C corporation may not carry back a portion of its NOL if $1 million or more of interest expense is incurred in a "major stock acquisition" of another corporation or in an "excess distribution" by the corporation (Code Sec. 172(b)(1)(D) and (g)).[71] The amount subject to the limitation is the lesser of: (1) the corporation's deductible interest expense allocable to the CERT, or (2) the amount by which the corporation's interest expense for the current tax year exceeds the average interest expense for the three tax years preceding the tax year in which the CERT occurs.

1153. NOL Carryovers Between Predecessors and Successors. A net operating loss (NOL) may generally be carried back or carried forward only by the taxpayer who sustained the loss (¶ 1145). A beneficiary of an estate or trust, however, is entitled to any carryover amount remaining unused after the last tax year of the estate or trust. Similarly, a bankruptcy estate succeeds to an individual debtor's NOLs (¶ 535). A successor corporation also is allowed to carry over the NOL and certain other items of its predecessor under specified conditions (¶ 2277).

At-Risk Limitations

1155. At-Risk Limitations on Losses. A taxpayer's deductible loss with respect to an activity is generally limited to the amount that the taxpayer has at risk with respect to the activity (Code Sec. 465).[72] The at-risk rules are designed to prevent certain taxpayers (¶ 1157) from offsetting trade, business, or professional income with losses from investments in activities (¶ 1159) that are largely financed by nonrecourse loans for which they are not personally liable. Even if it has been determined that the loss is deductible under the at-risk rules, the loss may still be limited by the passive activity loss rules (¶ 1165).

Under the at-risk rules, loss deductions are limited to the amount the taxpayer has at risk in the activity. This is the money and the adjusted basis of other property the taxpayer contributes to the activity. It also includes any amounts borrowed for use in the activity if the taxpayer has personal liability for repayment of the loan (recourse) or has pledged assets not used in the activity as security for the loan (Code Sec. 465(b)).[73]

References are to Standard Federal Tax Reports; Tax Research Consultant; and Practical Tax Explanations.

[68] ¶ 12,014.30; NOL: 12,202; § 38,130.20

[69] ¶ 12,002; BUSEXP: 45,154.25; § 17,010.25

[70] ¶ 12,002, ¶ 12,012; BUSEXP: 45,154.15

[71] ¶ 12,002; NOL: 15,202

[72] ¶ 21,850; BUSEXP: 42,000; § 17,301

[73] ¶ 21,850; BUSEXP: 42,150; § 17,305.05

Amounts are not at risk if they are borrowed from (1) a person who has an interest in the activity other than as a creditor, or (2) a person related to someone other than the taxpayer who has an interest in the activity. Exceptions are available for corporations that borrow from shareholders and qualified nonrecourse financing secured by real property used in an activity. Personal liability of the taxpayer for borrowed amounts generally hinges on whether the taxpayer is the ultimate obligor of the liability with no recourse against any other party.[74] The taxpayer is not considered at risk with respect to amounts protected against loss through nonrecourse financing, guarantees, stop-loss agreements, or similar arrangements.

Any loss not allowed because of the at-risk limitation is carried over to the following tax year, to be deducted subject to the same limitation (Code Sec. 465(a)(2)). The amount allowed as a loss for any year reduces the amount at risk for later years. Conversely, if a taxpayer's amount at risk at the end of any tax year is less than zero, the loss equal to the difference is recaptured (Code Sec. 465(e)).[75] Unused amounts generally are allowed when the activity is transferred or otherwise disposed (¶ 1161).

Form 6198 is used to compute the deductible loss under the at-risk rules. An activity subject to the passive loss rules must file Form 8582. If the activity is subject to both limitations, Form 6198 is completed first, and any allowable loss must be carried over to Form 8582.

For investment tax credit at-risk rules, see ¶ 1365A.

1157. Taxpayers Affected by At-Risk Rules. The at-risk rules (¶ 1155) apply to individuals, estates, and trusts (Code Sec. 465(a)(1)).[76] They also apply to partners and S corporation shareholders at the partner or shareholder level, not at the entity level. Closely held corporations are generally subject to the at-risk rules if they meet the personal holding company stock ownership requirements (¶ 277). However, certain closely held corporations are not subject to the at-risk limits for any qualifying active business carried on; instead, each qualifying business of a corporation is treated as a separate activity (Code Sec. 465(c)(7)). In addition, if a closely held corporation is actively engaged in equipment leasing, the equipment leasing is treated as a separate activity not covered by the at-risk rules (Code Sec. 465(c)(4)).

1159. Activities Covered by At-Risk Rules. The at-risk limit on losses (¶ 1155) generally applies to all activities of a taxpayer engaged in as a trade or business or for the production of income (Code Sec. 465(c)).[77] It also specifically applies to any taxpayer engaged in: the activity of holding, producing, or distributing motion picture films or video tapes; farming; leasing of section 1245 property; or exploring for or exploiting oil and gas resources or geothermal deposits. The at-risk rules do not apply to: (1) the leasing of equipment by closely held corporations (¶ 1157); (2) a qualifying active business carried on by certain closely held corporations; or (3) the holding of real property other than mineral property acquired before 1987 as an interest in a pass-through entity engaged in holding real property placed in service before 1987.

In the case of the specifically identified activities listed previously, each film or tape, each piece of section 1245 property, each farm, and each oil, gas, or geothermal property is treated as a separate activity. However, for a partnership or an S corporation, all leased section 1245 properties that are placed in service in the same tax year are treated as a single activity (Code Sec. 465(c)(2)(B)).[78] Trade or business activities subject to the at-risk rules are aggregated and treated as a single activity if the taxpayer actively participates in the management of the trade or business or, where the trade or business is carried on by a partnership or S corporation, if 65 percent or more of the losses for the tax year are allocable to persons who actively participate in the management of the trade or business.

References are to Standard Federal Tax Reports; Tax Research Consultant; and Practical Tax Explanations.

[74] ¶ 21,893.35; BUSEXP: 42,156.05; § 17,305.05

[75] ¶ 21,850; BUSEXP: 42,206.10; § 17,315

[76] ¶ 21,850; BUSEXP: 42,050; § 17,301

[77] ¶ 21,850; BUSEXP: 42,100; § 17,310

[78] ¶ 21,850; BUSEXP: 42,106; § 17,310

1161. Application of At-Risk Rules on Disposition of Activity. Under proposed regulations, when a taxpayer transfers or otherwise disposes of an activity, any gain realized on the transfer or disposition of the activity is treated as gain from the activity, which generally permits the taxpayer to recognize any losses suspended under the at-risk rules (¶ 1155) (Prop. Reg. § 1.465-66).[79] The same rules apply if a partnership liquidates a partner's interest or an S corporation completely redeems a shareholder's interest.

Passive Activity Limits on Losses and Credits

1165. Passive Activity Defined. For purposes of the passive activity limit on losses (¶ 1169), a passive activity is one that involves the conduct of any trade or business in which the taxpayer does not materially participate (Code Sec. 469(c); Temp. Reg. § 1.469-1T(e)).[80] Any rental activity is a passive activity whether or not the taxpayer materially participates (¶ 1181). However, there are special rules for real estate rental activities (¶ 1183) and real estate professionals (¶ 1185). Trading personal property that is actively traded, such as stocks and bonds, for the account of owners of interests in the activity is not a passive activity. For example, the activity of a partnership that trades stock using money contributed by the partners is not a passive activity.

Material participation in an activity requires that a taxpayer is involved in the operations of the activity on a regular, continuous, and substantial basis (Code Sec. 469(h); Temp. Reg. § 1.469-5T).[81] Generally, an individual is considered as materially participating in an activity during a tax year if he or she satisfies one of the following tests:

(1) the individual participates more than 500 hours;

(2) the individual's participation constitutes substantially all of the participation in the activity;

(3) the individual participates for more than 100 hours and this participation is not less than the participation of any other individual;

(4) the activity is a "significant participation activity" (see following) and the individual's participation in all significant participation activities exceeds 500 hours;

(5) the individual materially participated in the activity for any five years of the 10 years that preceded the year in question;

(6) the activity is a "personal service activity" (see following) and the individual materially participated in the activity for any three years preceding the tax year in question; or

(7) the individual satisfies a facts and circumstances test that requires the individual to show participation on a regular, continuous, and substantial basis for more than 100 hours during the tax year.

With respect to test (7), an individual's participation in managing the activity does not count toward the 100-hour requirement if any other person received compensation for managing the activity or any other person spent more time managing the activity.

Special rules are provided for determining the material participation of certain retired or disabled farmers and participation in the activity of a personal service or closely held corporation (Temp. Reg. § 1.469-5T(h)).[82]

Limited Partners. A limited partner's share of income, losses, and credits from a partnership are treated as arising from a passive activity unless the limited partner participated in the activity for more than 500 hours, the limited partner materially participated in the activity five of the 10 preceding tax years, or the activity is a personal service activity in which the limited partner materially participated for any three preceding tax years. A general partner who also holds a limited partnership interest is not treated as a limited partner (Code Sec. 469(h)(2); Temp. Reg. § 1.469-5T(e)).[83]

References are to Standard Federal Tax Reports; Tax Research Consultant; and Practical Tax Explanations.

[79] ¶ 21,883; BUSEXP: 42,210; § 17,320

[80] ¶ 21,960, ¶ 21,962; BUSEXP: 33,100; § 17,420.05

[81] ¶ 21,960, ¶ 21,965; BUSEXP: 33,150; § 17,435.05

[82] ¶ 21,965; BUSEXP: 33,158, BUSEXP: 33,164; § 17,435.25, § 17,435.35

[83] ¶ 21,960, ¶ 21,965; BUSEXP: 33,160; § 17,435.20

Significant Participation Activity. A significant participation activity is one in which the taxpayer participates more than 100 hours during the tax year but does not materially participate under any of the other six tests set forth above (Temp. Reg. § 1.469-5T(c)).[84]

Personal Service Activity. A personal service activity involves the performance of personal service in the fields of health (including veterinary services), law, engineering, architecture, accounting, actuarial science, the performing arts, consulting, or any other trade or business in which capital is not a material income-producing factor (Temp. Reg. § 1.469-5T(d)).[85]

Definition of Participation. Any work done by an individual with respect to an activity in which the individual owns an interest is generally treated as participation (Reg. § 1.469-5(f)(1); Temp. Reg. § 1.469-5T(f)).[86] Participation does not include work that is not customarily done by an owner if one of the principal purposes for performing the work is to avoid the passive activity limitations. Furthermore, work done in an individual's capacity as an investor in an activity, such as studying and reviewing the activity's financial statements and operational reports, preparing summaries or analyses of the activity's finances or operations for personal use, and monitoring the finances or operations of the activity in a nonmanagerial capacity, is not counted as participation.

A married individual's participation does include the participation of his or her spouse even if the spouse does not own an interest in the activity and separate returns are filed. Participation may be established by any reasonable means. It is not necessary to maintain contemporaneous daily records of participation. An approximate number of hours of participation may be based on appointment books, calendars, or narrative summaries.

1167. Passive Activity Income and Deductions. For purposes of the passive activity limit on losses (¶ 1169), passive income or loss generally is determined by aggregating gross income and deductions from all passive activities during the year (Temp. Reg. § 1.469-2T).[87] Certain types of income and deductions from a passive activity, however, are subject to special rules and must be excluded and reported separately as nonpassive income or deductions.

Portfolio income is excluded from passive activity income and expenses directly allocable to such income are not deductible in computing passive activity losses (Code Sec. 469(e)(1)).[88] Portfolio income includes interest, dividends, annuities, royalties, and gain or loss from the disposition of investment property not derived in the ordinary course of a trade or business. No exception is provided for the treatment of portfolio income arising from working capital, i.e., amounts set aside for the reasonable needs of the business.

Passive activity income also does not include: personal service income; income or gain from investments of working capital; income from intangible property if the taxpayer's personal efforts significantly contributed to its creation; refunds of state and local taxes; reimbursements of casualty and theft losses; and cancellation of debt income. Passive activity deductions do not include: qualified home mortgage interest expense, capitalization interest expense, and most other interest expenses properly allocable to a passive activity; state and local taxes; charitable contributions; disallowed miscellaneous itemized deductions; net operating losses (NOLs); and capital loss carrybacks and carryforwards.

Certain self-charged interest income or deductions may be treated as passive activity income or deductions if the loan proceeds are used in a passive activity. Self-charged interest and expenses are items from a lending transaction between a taxpayer and a pass-through entity in which the taxpayer owns a direct or indirect interest (Reg. § 1.469-7).[89] These rules also apply to lending transactions between pass-through entities with identical ownership.

References are to Standard Federal Tax Reports; Tax Research Consultant; and Practical Tax Explanations.

[84] ¶ 21,965; BUSEXP: 33,152; § 17,435.15

[85] ¶ 21,965; BUSEXP: 33,152; § 17,435.15

[86] ¶ 21,964C, ¶ 21,965; BUSEXP: 33,154; § 17,435.10

[87] ¶ 21,963; BUSEXP: 33,350, BUSEXP: 33,400; § 17,450.05

[88] ¶ 21,960; BUSEXP: 33,354; § 17,450.10

[89] ¶ 21,965B; BUSEXP: 33,462.20; § 17,450.15

1169. Passive Activity Loss Limitations. Under the passive activity rules, losses and expenses attributable to passive activities of certain taxpayers (¶ 1173) may only be deducted from income attributable to passive activities (Code Sec. 469).[90] Similarly, tax credits attributable to passive activities may only be used to offset taxes attributable to income from passive activities. A passive activity for this purpose is any activity that involves the conduct of a trade or business in which the taxpayer does not materially participate (¶ 1165). Any rental activity is a passive activity whether or not the taxpayer materially participates (¶ 1181). However, there are special rules for real estate rental activities (¶ 1183) and real estate professionals (¶ 1185). In determining a taxpayer's allowable loss, the at-risk rules (¶ 1155) are applied before the passive activity loss rules.

To the extent that the total deductions from passive activities exceed the total income from passive activities for the tax year, the excess (the passive activity loss) is not allowed as a deduction for that year. Instead, the disallowed loss is suspended and carried forward as a deduction against income from the passive activity in the next succeeding tax year (Code Sec. 469(b)).[91] Any unused suspended losses are allowed in full when the taxpayer disposes of his or her entire interest in the activity in a fully taxable transaction (¶ 1177).

Passive Activity Credit. Tax credits arising with respect to passive activities are generally treated in the same manner as losses, except that suspended credits are not allowed on disposition of the activity (Code Sec. 469(a)(1)(B) and (d)).[92] Thus, credits may be used to offset the tax attributable to net passive income—the difference between the tax on all income, and the tax on taxable income other than net passive income. In both cases, the effect of credits is disregarded.

Unused credits can generally be carried forward indefinitely. However, the character of a credit relating to a passive activity changes, in effect, when the credit becomes allowable under the passive loss rules (either there is sufficient passive income to allow its use, or it is within the scope of the $25,000 benefit for real estate activities (¶ 1183)). At this time, the credit is aggregated with credits relating to nonpassive activities of the taxpayer to determine whether all such credits are allowable considering the other limitations that apply to the use of credits (¶ 1365).

Forms. Individuals, estates, and trusts use Form 8582 or Form 8582-CR to calculate their allowable passive losses and credits. Form 8582 generally must also be filed by a taxpayer that has an overall gain from business or rental passive activities for the year (even after including suspended passive losses from earlier tax years). However, Form 8582 does not need to be filed if the taxpayer actively participated in rental real estate activities. Form 8810 is used by personal service corporations and closely held C corporations to calculate passive activity losses and credits. Form 8825 is used by partnerships and S corporations to report income and deductible expenses from rental real estate activities.

1171. Passive Activity Losses of Publicly Traded Partnerships. Special rules apply to passive activity losses from publicly traded partnerships (PTPs) (Code Sec. 469(k)).[93] A PTP is a partnership whose interests are traded on an established securities market or are readily tradable on a secondary market or its substantial equivalent. A taxpayer's net income from a PTP may not be used to offset net losses from other PTPs or net losses from other passive activities. A disallowed loss from a PTP is carried forward and allowed as a deduction in a tax year when the PTP has net income or when the taxpayer disposes of his or her entire interest in the PTP. These rules apply to a regulated investment company or mutual fund (¶ 2301) holding an interest in a PTP, with respect to items attributable to the interest in the partnership.

References are to Standard Federal Tax Reports; Tax Research Consultant; and Practical Tax Explanations.

[90] ¶ 21,960; BUSEXP: 33,000; § 17,401

[91] ¶ 21,960; BUSEXP: 33,200; § 17,470.05

[92] ¶ 21,960; BUSEXP: 33,250; § 17,495

[93] ¶ 21,960; BUSEXP: 33,458; § 17,415.15

1173. Taxpayers Covered by Passive Activity Rules. The passive activity rules (¶ 1169) apply to individuals, estates, trusts other than grantor trusts, and personal service corporations (Code Sec. 469(a)(2)).[94] Although the passive activity rules do not apply to partnerships, S corporations, and grantor trusts directly, they are applied at the partner, shareholder, beneficiary, or grantor level. See ¶ 1171 for discussion of special rules applicable to publicly traded partnerships.

Closely Held C Corporations. C corporations are generally not subject to the passive activity rules. However, the passive activity rules do apply to a closely held C corporation (other than a personal service corporation) to the extent of its net active income. The corporation cannot use passive losses to offset portfolio income (¶ 1167). A closely held C corporation's net active income is equal to its taxable income, figured without any income or loss from a passive activity or any portfolio income or loss (Code Sec. 469(e)(2)).[95]

1175. Grouping Activities Under the Passive Activity Rules. In applying the passive activity rules (¶ 1169), one or more trade or business activities, or rental activities, may be treated as a single activity if the activities constitute an appropriate economic unit (Reg. § 1.469-4).[96] Whether activities constitute an appropriate economic unit depends upon all the relevant facts and circumstances. The following factors are given greatest weight in determining whether several activities can be combined:

- similarities or differences in types of business,
- extent of common control,
- extent of common ownership,
- geographical location, and
- business interdependencies among the activities.

Once activities are grouped together or kept separate, the taxpayer must be consistent in the treatment of these activities in subsequent tax years. A taxpayer generally may not regroup activities unless the original grouping was clearly inappropriate or became inappropriate due to a material change in facts and circumstances (Reg. § 1.469-4(e)).[97] A taxpayer is required to disclose their grouping and regrouping of activities in a written statement with the taxpayer's income tax return (Rev. Proc. 2010-13).[98] The statement must be filed for: (1) the first tax year in which two or more trade or business activities or rental activities are originally grouped as a single activity; (2) a tax year in which a taxpayer adds a new trade or business activity or a rental activity to an existing grouping; or (3) a tax year in which a taxpayer regroups activities. The IRS may disallow and regroup a taxpayer's grouping of activities if the grouping does not reflect an appropriate economic unit and has circumvention of the passive activity loss rules as a primary purpose (Reg. § 1.469-4(f)).[99]

Regrouping and Net Investment Income Tax. A one-time regrouping of activities can be made by an individual, trust, or estate in the first tax year beginning after December 31, 2013, in which it satisfies the eligibility criteria for the net investment income (NII) tax (¶ 129) (Reg. § 1.469-11(b)(3)(iv)).[100] An individual, estate, or trust was also allowed to make the regrouping for any tax year beginning in 2013 if the eligibility criteria were met for that year. The term "eligibility criteria" means that (1) an individual, estate, or trust has net investment income, and (2) the individual's modified adjusted gross income (AGI) exceeds $250,000 for joint filers and surviving spouses, $125,000 for married filing separately, and $200,000 for all other individuals, or the estate's or trust's AGI exceeds the dollar amount for which the highest income tax bracket is imposed on an estate or

References are to Standard Federal Tax Reports; Tax Research Consultant; and Practical Tax Explanations.

[94] ¶ 21,960; BUSEXP: 33,050; § 17,405.05

[95] ¶ 21,960; BUSEXP: 33,054; § 17,405.15

[96] ¶ 21,964B; BUSEXP: 33,102; § 17,415.05

[97] ¶ 21,964B; BUSEXP: 33,102; § 17,415.10

[98] ¶ 21,966.579; BUSEXP: 33,102.35; § 17,415.25

[99] ¶ 21,964B; BUSEXP: 33,102.30; § 17,415.25

[100] ¶ 21,965F; BUSEXP: 33,102.33; § 17,415.20

trust ($12,400 in 2016, $12,500 for 2017). The determination of whether a taxpayer meets the eligibility criteria for the NII tax is made without regard to the effect of the regrouping and any regrouping applies to the tax year in which the regrouping is done and all subsequent tax years. The one-time regrouping generally must be made on an original return. It may be made on an amended return only if a change reported on the amended return causes the taxpayer to meet the eligibility criteria for the first time. If it is later determined that the taxpayer did not satisfy the eligibility criteria in a tax year in which a regrouping was made, the regrouping is void for the tax year it was made and all future years, unless the taxpayer's failure to satisfy the eligibility criteria is due to the carryback of a net operating loss.

Activities Conducted Through Entities. Activities conducted through a partnership, S corporation, personal service corporation, or closely-held corporation are first grouped at the entity level (Reg. § 1.469-4(d)(5)).[101] Once the entity groups its activities, a partner or shareholder may group those activities with each other, with activities conducted directly by the partner or shareholder, and with activities conducted through other entities. However, an activity that a taxpayer conducts through a C corporation may be grouped with another activity of the taxpayer only for purposes of determining whether the taxpayer materially or significantly participates in the other activity.

Rental Activities. A taxpayer generally may not treat an activity involving the rental of real property and an activity involving the rental of personal property as a single activity (Reg. § 1.469-4(d)(2)).[102] These two activities can be treated as a single activity only if the taxpayer provides the personal property in connection with the real property or the real property in connection with the personal property.

A rental activity may not be grouped with a trade or business activity unless either: (1) the rental activity is insubstantial in relation to the trade or business activity; or (2) the trade or business activity is insubstantial in relation to the rental activity (Reg. § 1.469-4(d)(1)).[103] There is a third alternative when each owner of the trade or business has the same proportionate ownership interest in the rental activity, in which case the portion of the rental activity that involves the rental of items of property to a trade or business activity may be grouped with the trade or business activity.

> **Example:** The Getaway Partnership owns a 10-story building in which it operates a travel agency on three floors and rents seven floors to tenants. The partnership is divided into two activities: a travel agency activity and a rental real estate activity. Deductions and credits attributable to the building are allocable to the travel agency activity only to the extent that they relate to the space occupied by the travel agency during the tax year.

Partial Disposition of Activity. If the taxpayer disposes of *substantially all* of an activity, he or she may treat the interest disposed of as a separate activity, provided that the taxpayer can establish the amount of gross income, deductions and credits allocable to that part of the activity for the tax year (Reg. § 1.469-4(g)).[104] Without this rule, taxpayers generally cannot claim suspended passive losses until they have disposed of their entire interest in an activity (¶ 1177).

1177. Disposition of Interest in Passive Activity. When a taxpayer disposes of his or her entire interest in a passive activity (¶ 1165) in a taxable transaction, the taxpayer's suspended passive activity losses (¶ 1169) may be applied against his or her nonpassive income (Code Sec. 469(g)).[105] Specifically, any net passive losses must first be applied against the taxpayer's net income or gain from passive activities. Any remaining loss from the activity is then classified as nonpassive and may be used to offset income from nonpassive activities, e.g., wages. Suspended credits are not allowed on the disposition of a passive activity.

References are to Standard Federal Tax Reports; Tax Research Consultant; and Practical Tax Explanations.

[101] ¶ 21,964B; BUSEXP: 33,102.20; § 17,415.15

[102] ¶ 21,964B; BUSEXP: 33,102.25; § 17,415.15

[103] ¶ 21,964B; BUSEXP: 33,102.25; § 17,415.15

[104] ¶ 21,964B; BUSEXP: 33,652; § 17,490.10

[105] ¶ 21,960; BUSEXP: 33,652; § 17,490.05

Entire Interest. A disposition of a taxpayer's entire interest involves a disposition of the interest in all entities that are engaged in the activity. To the extent the activity is held in the form of a sole proprietorship, disposition of a taxpayer's entire interest includes disposition of all of the assets used or created in the activity. If a partnership or S corporation conducts two or more separate activities and the entity disposes of all the assets used or created in one activity, the disposition constitutes a disposition of the entire interest. The same rule applies to grantor trusts.[106] In some instances, a taxpayer may claim a deduction for suspended losses even though he or she disposes of less than his or her entire interest (¶ 1175).

Taxable Transactions. To qualify as a fully taxable disposition, the disposition generally must be a sale of the interest to a third party in an arm's-length transaction and must not be a sham, a wash sale, or a transfer of repurchase rights (Code Sec. 469(g)(1)).[107] If a taxpayer disposes of an interest in a passive activity in a taxable transaction with a related party as defined by Code Sec. 267(b) (¶ 1717) or with a controlled partnership as defined by Code Sec. 707(b)(1) (¶ 432) the suspended losses are not triggered. In these circumstances, the taxpayer is able to claim the loss only when the related person or controlled partnership disposes of the activity in a taxable transaction with an unrelated person. Abandonment is a fully taxable disposition.

Installment Sales. When a taxpayer sells his or her entire interest in a passive activity and reports the gain under the installment sale method (¶ 1801), only a portion of the suspended loss may be deducted in the year of the sale. Suspended losses are allowed in the year of sale and thereafter in the ratio that the gain recognized in a tax year bears to the total gross profit from the sale to be realized when payment is completed (Code Sec. 469(g)(3)).[108]

Death. A transfer of an individual's entire interest by reason of his or her death causes suspended losses to be allowed in the year of death to the extent that they exceed the amount by which the basis of the interest is stepped up at death (¶ 1633) (Code Sec. 469(g)(2)).[109]

Gifts. Disposition of an interest in a passive activity by gift does *not* trigger suspended losses. Instead, the basis of the transferred interest is increased by the amount of such losses (Code Sec. 469(j)(6)).[110]

Nontaxable Exchanges. An exchange of a taxpayer's interest in a passive activity in a nonrecognition transaction such as a like-kind exchange (¶ 1721) does not trigger suspended losses. However, to the extent that the taxpayer recognizes gain on the transaction (i.e., boot), the gain is treated as passive activity income against which passive losses may be deducted.[111]

Casualty or Theft. A casualty (¶ 1121) or theft (¶ 1123) loss involving property used in a passive activity does not constitute a complete disposition of the taxpayer's interest in the activity unless the casualty or theft results in a loss of all property used or created in the activity.[112]

Former Passive Activity. In the tax year that an activity ceases to be a passive activity, previously suspended losses from that activity are permitted to be claimed as deductions against the activity's net income (Code Sec. 469(f)(1)).[113] Similarly, prior year suspended passive activity credits may offset the current year's tax liability that is allocable to the current year's net income from the former passive activity. Tax liability for this purpose is figured on the net income as reduced by the prior year suspended losses.

References are to Standard Federal Tax Reports; Tax Research Consultant; and Practical Tax Explanations.

[106] ¶ 21,966.0552; BUSEXP: 33,652.10; § 17,490.10

[107] ¶ 21,960; BUSEXP: 33,652.05, BUSEXP: 33,654; § 17,490.15, § 17,490.35

[108] ¶ 21,960; BUSEXP: 33,668; § 17,490.30

[109] ¶ 21,960; BUSEXP: 33,658; § 17,490.20

[110] ¶ 21,960; BUSEXP: 33,660; § 17,490.25

[111] ¶ 21,966.0553; BUSEXP: 33,662; § 17,490.15

[112] ¶ 21,966.0553; BUSEXP: 33,652.10; § 17,490.15

[113] ¶ 21,960; BUSEXP: 33,600; § 17,440

Cessation of Closely Held C Corporation or PSC Status. If a closely held C corporation or a personal service corporation (PSC) changes its status, suspended losses from prior years continue to be subject to the limitations that were imposed before the status changed (¶ 1173). Losses arising in years after the year in which the corporation's status changes are not subject to the passive activity rules (Code Sec. 469(f)(2)).

Rental Activities Subject to Passive Activity Rules

1181. Rental Activities Subject to Passive Activity Rules. A rental activity is generally treated as a passive activity regardless of whether the taxpayer materially participates in the activity (¶ 1165) (Code Sec. 469(c)(2); Temp. Reg. § 1.469-1T(e)(3)).[114] An activity is a "rental activity" if (1) during the tax year, tangible property held in connection with the activity is used by customers or is held for use by customers, and (2) the gross income of the activity represents amounts paid mainly for the use of the tangible property. A taxpayer's rental real estate activity is not considered passive activity, however, if the taxpayer is a real estate professional (¶ 1185). In addition, if any one of the following tests is met, the activity is not considered to be a rental activity for purposes of the passive loss rules (¶ 1169):

- the average period of customer use of the property is seven days or less;
- the average period of customer use is 30 days or less and significant personal services are provided by or on behalf of the owner;
- without regard to the period of customer use, extraordinary personal services are provided by or on behalf of the owner;
- the rental of the property is incidental to a nonrental activity;
- the property is customarily made available during defined business hours for the nonexclusive use of customers; or
- the taxpayer provides property for use in an activity that is conducted by a partnership, S corporation, or joint venture in which the taxpayer owns an interest and the activity is not a rental activity.

If a taxpayer does not meet the requirements to be a real estate professional, but owns and actively participates in a rental real estate activity, then the taxpayer may deduct up to $25,000 of losses from a passive rental real estate activity from nonpassive income (¶ 1183).

1183. $25,000 Offset for Active Participation in Rental Real Estate Activity. Individuals who own and actively participate in a rental real estate activity may offset up to $25,000 of passive activity losses and credits ($12,500 for married filing separately) from the activity against nonpassive income (Code Sec. 469(i)).[115] To be eligible, the individual must own at least 10-percent by value of all interests in the activity throughout the year. The interest of an individual's spouse is taken into account in determining 10-percent ownership whether or not a joint return is filed. While the offset is available only to individual taxpayers who actively participate in rental real estate activities, a decedent's estate also qualifies for its tax years ending less than two years after the date of the decedent's death if it has an interest in a rental real estate activity in which the decedent actively participated in the year of death. A decedent's qualified revocable trust can also be treated as actively participating if both the trustee and the executor of the estate (if any) choose to treat the trust as part of the estate.

The active participation standard is less stringent than the material participation standard (¶ 1165). An individual may meet the active participation requirement if he or she participates in the making of management decisions (for example, approving new tenants, deciding on rental terms, approving expenditures) or arranges for others to provide services (for example, repairs) in a significant and bona fide sense. The requirement for active participation applies in the year in which the loss arose as well as the year in which the loss is allowed. However, real estate professionals may be able to treat rental property activities as nonpassive activities (¶ 1185).

References are to Standard Federal Tax Reports; Tax Research Consultant; and Practical Tax Explanations.

[114] ¶ 21,960, ¶ 21,962; BUSEXP: 33,106; § 17,430.05

[115] ¶ 21,960; BUSEXP: 33,700; § 17,480.05

The $25,000 maximum offset amount is reduced, but not less than zero, by 50 percent of the amount by which the taxpayer's adjusted gross income (AGI) exceeds $100,000. It is completely phased out when AGI reaches $150,000 (Code Sec. 469(i)(3)). For this purpose, AGI is computed without regard to: taxable Social Security and railroad retirement benefits (¶ 716); the exclusion for qualified U.S. savings bonds used to pay higher education expenses (¶ 863); the exclusion for employer adoption assistance payments (¶ 2063); passive activity income or loss included on Form 8582; any overall loss from a publicly traded partnership (¶ 1171); rental real estate losses allowed to real estate professionals; the domestic production activities deduction (¶ 980A); and deductions for contributions to IRAs and pension plans (¶ 2107), for one-half of self-employment tax (¶ 1027), interest on student loans (¶ 1011), and tuition and fees (¶ 1011A).

Separate Returns. For married individuals who file separate returns and live apart, up to $12,500 of passive losses may be used to offset nonpassive income. This amount is reduced by 50 percent of the amount by which the taxpayer's modified AGI exceeds $50,000. The special allowance is completely phased out when modified AGI reaches $75,000. Married individuals who file separately and live together at any time during the tax year are not eligible for the special allowance (Code Sec. 469(i)(5)).

Offset of Credits. Passive activity credits attributable to rental real estate activities in which the taxpayer actively participates may be claimed under the $25,000 offset provision, but only after all eligible losses have been used. Special rules apply for the phaseout of the rehabilitation credit (¶ 1365B), low-income housing credit (¶ 1365K), and commercial revitalization deduction (Code Sec. 1400I).

1185. Real Estate Professionals. Real estate professionals may be able to treat rental real estate activities as nonpassive and thus not subject to the passive activity rules (¶ 1165) (Code Sec. 469(c)(7); Reg. § 1.469-9(g)).[116] To qualify:

- more than one-half of the personal services performed in trades or businesses by the taxpayer during the tax year must involve real property trades or businesses in which the taxpayer or the taxpayer's spouse materially participates; and

- the taxpayer must perform more than 750 hours of service during the tax year in real property trades or businesses in which the taxpayer or the taxpayer's spouse materially participates (¶ 1165).

These two requirements must be satisfied by one spouse if married individuals file a joint return. Personal services performed as an employee are not taken into account under either requirement unless the employee owns more than a five-percent interest in the employer. A real property trade or business is a business with respect to which real property is developed or redeveloped, constructed or reconstructed, acquired, converted, rented or leased, operated or managed, or brokered.

The exception for real estate professionals is applied as if each interest of the taxpayer in rental real estate is a separate activity. However, a taxpayer may elect to treat all interests in rental real estate as a single activity for purposes of satisfying the material participation requirements. To make the election, the taxpayer must file a statement with the taxpayer's original income tax return for the tax year declaring that he or she is a qualified taxpayer for the tax year and is making the election. Certain taxpayers may be permitted to make late elections (Rev. Proc. 2011-34).[117]

A closely held corporation qualifies as a real estate professional if more than 50 percent of its annual gross receipts for the tax year are from real property trades or businesses in which it materially participates.

References are to Standard Federal Tax Reports; Tax Research Consultant; and Practical Tax Explanations.

[116] ¶ 21,960, ¶ 21,965D; BUSEXP: 33,106.40; § 17,430.15

[117] ¶ 21,966.568; BUSEXP: 33,106.40; § 17,430.15

Tax-Exempt Use Property

1191. Limits on Tax-Exempt Use Losses. A taxpayer leasing property to a government or other tax-exempt entity (i.e., sale-in, lease-out (SILO) arrangement) is not allowed to claim deductions that are related to the property (known as tax-exempt use property) to the extent that they exceed the taxpayer's income from the lease payments (a tax-exempt use loss), subject to certain exceptions (Code Sec. 470).[118] Tax-exempt use property includes property owned by a partnership or other pass-through entity that has at least one tax-exempt partner and the allocations of partnership items attempt to inappropriately transfer the deductions from the tax-exempt partner to the taxable partners (Code Sec. 168(h)).[119]

Tax-exempt losses disallowed may be carried over to the next tax year and can be deducted to the extent of the taxpayer's net income from the property for that year. If property ceases to be tax-exempt use property during the lease term, the carried-over loss cannot be used to offset income from other property. If the property is disposed of, any disallowed loss is available under rules similar to passive activity losses (¶ 1177). However, the limitation on tax-exempt use property losses is applied before the passive activity rules (¶ 1169).

Hobby Losses

1195. Hobby Expenses and Losses. Expenses incurred by individuals, S corporations, partnerships, estates, and trusts that are attributable to an activity not engaged in for profit, i.e., a hobby, are generally deductible only to the extent of income produced by the activity (Code Sec. 183; Reg. § 1.183-1).[120] Specifically, if any activity is not engaged in for profit, deductions are allowed as follows:

(1) deductions a taxpayer can claim whether or not they are incurred with a hobby, e.g., taxes, interest, and casualty losses, are allowed even if they exceed hobby income;

(2) deductions that do not result in an adjustment to the basis of property, e.g., operating expenses, supplies, are allowed, but only to the extent that gross income from the hobby exceeds the deductions under category (1); and

(3) deductions that result in an adjustment to the basis of property, e.g., depreciation, amortization, are allowed, but only to the extent that gross income from the hobby that exceeds the deductions under category (1) and (2).

Individuals must claim the deductions in categories (2) and (3) above as miscellaneous itemized deductions on Schedule A of Form 1040, subject to the two-percent-of-adjusted-gross-income limitation (¶ 1079). If a partnership or S corporation carries on a hobby, the deduction limits apply at the entity level and are reflected in the individual shareholder's or partner's distributive shares.

Whether an activity is engaged in for profit is generally determined based on the facts and circumstances. However, an activity is presumed not to be a hobby if it produced a profit (gross income exceeded deductions) in any three of five consecutive tax years ending with the tax year in question, unless the IRS proves otherwise. An activity involving the breeding, training, showing, or racing of horses is presumed not to be a hobby if it produced a profit in two out of seven consecutive tax years. A special election on Form 5213 permits suspension of the presumption until after the fourth (or sixth, for horse breeding, training, showing, or racing) tax year after which the taxpayer first engages in the activity. Filing Form 5213 automatically extends the statute of limitations for the IRS to assess a deficiency for any deductions of the activity in any year in the five-year or seven-year period to two years after the due date of the return for the last year of the period.

References are to Standard Federal Tax Reports; Tax Research Consultant; and Practical Tax Explanations.

[118] ¶ 21,970; BUSEXP: 36,000

[119] ¶ 11,250; BUSEXP: 36,050

[120] ¶ 12,170, ¶ 12,171; BUSEXP:15,000; § 17,201

Chapter 12
DEPRECIATION, AMORTIZATION AND DEPLETION

	Par.
DEPRECIATION	
Allowance for Depreciation	1201
Basis for Depreciation	1203
Section 179 Expense Election	1208
Limitations on Automobiles and Other Listed Property	1211
Depreciation Methods	1216
Leased Property	1234
Modified Accelerated Cost Recovery System (MACRS)	1236
Accelerated Cost Recovery System (ACRS)	1252
Class Life ADR System	1282
Deductions for Refiners	1285
Deduction for Energy Efficiency Improvements	1286
AMORTIZATION	
Allowance for Amortization	1287
DEPLETION	
What Is Depletion?	1289
Mineral Production Payments	1291
Percentage Depletion	1294

Allowance for Depreciation

1201. Property Subject to Depreciation. Taxpayers may deduct a reasonable allowance for the exhaustion, wear and tear of property used in a trade or business, or property held for the production of income (Reg. § 1.167(a)-1).[1] Depreciation is not allowable for property used solely for personal purposes, such as a residence.

Depreciation begins in the tax year that an asset is placed in service and ends in the tax year that it is retired from service or is fully depreciated (Reg. § 1.167(a)-10).[2] An asset is generally considered placed in service when it is in a condition or state of readiness and available for a specifically assigned function.

Methods of Depreciation. The Modified Accelerated Cost Recovery System (MACRS) (¶ 1236) applies to tangible property generally placed in service after 1986 and the Accelerated Cost Recovery System (ACRS) applies to property placed in service after 1980 and before 1987 (¶ 1252). Under MACRS and ACRS, the cost or other basis of an asset is generally recovered over a specific recovery period. Post-1980 depreciation on tangible assets first placed in service before 1981 is computed under the method elected for the years they were placed in service. For assets placed in service after 1970 and before 1981, the taxpayer had a choice of the Asset Depreciation Range (ADR) System (¶ 1282) or the general depreciation rules (¶ 1216). For tangible assets first placed in service before 1971, the taxpayer could have elected the Class Life System (CLS) for pre-1971 assets or the general depreciation rules. An asset that is not subject

References are to Standard Federal Tax Reports; Tax Research Consultant; and Practical Tax Explanations.

[1] ¶ 11,003; DEPR: 15,050; § 11,005

[2] ¶ 11,024; DEPR: 15,652, DEPR: 3,054.104; § 11,020

to MACRS or ACRS cannot be depreciated below a reasonable salvage value (Reg. § 1.167(a)-1(a)).[3]

Depreciation based on a useful life is calculated over the estimated useful life of the asset while it is actually used by the taxpayer, not over the longer period of the asset's physical life (Reg. § 1.167(a)-1(b)).[4] For rules governing the depreciation of self-constructed assets, see the uniform capitalization rules at ¶ 990–¶ 999.

Converted Residence. Depreciation may be taken on a personal residence that has been converted to an income-producing use if the taxpayer proves that (1) the house has in fact been abandoned as a personal residence, and (2) that the property is being held for the production of income.[5] For example, a vacated principle residence offered for sale may be depreciable for the period before the sale if the individual is seeking a profit based on post-conversion appreciation in value. Placing a property for sale immediately or shortly after the time of its abandonment as a residence is strong evidence that the property is not held for post-conversion appreciation in value. MACRS must be used to depreciate a residence converted to business use after 1986. For computation of depreciation when a home is used partly for business or rental purposes, see ¶ 961 and following. For depreciable basis, see ¶ 1203.

Estates and Trusts. For depreciation by an estate or trust, see ¶ 530.

Inventory. Depreciation is allowed for tangible property, but not for inventories, stock in trade, land apart from its improvements, or a depletable natural resource (Reg. § 1.167(a)-2).[6]

Farmers. Farm buildings and other physical farm property (except land) are depreciable. Livestock acquired for work, breeding, or dairy purposes may be depreciated unless included in inventory (Reg. § 1.167(a)-6(b)).[7]

Intangibles. An intangible business asset that is not amortizable over 15 years under Code Sec. 197 (¶ 1288) may be amortized under Code Sec. 167, generally using the straight-line method, provided that it has an ascertainable value and useful life that can be measured with reasonable accuracy.[8] Certain intangibles with no ascertainable useful life that are created by a taxpayer may be amortized over 15 years (Reg. § 1.167(a)-3(b)) (¶ 1288A).

Software. Computer software that is not an amortizable Code Sec. 197 intangible (¶ 1288) may be depreciated using the straight-line method over 36 months beginning on the first day of the month the software is placed in service (¶ 980) (Code Sec. 167(f)(1); Reg. § 1.167(a)-14(b)).[9] However, the cost of software developed for internal use or sale may be currently deducted as a research and development expense, amortized using the straight-line method over 60 months beginning on the date its development is complete, or amortized over 36 months from the date it is placed in service (Rev. Proc. 2000-50). Off-the-shelf computer software may be expensed under Code Sec. 179 (¶ 1208) (Code Sec. 179(d)(1), as amended by the Protecting Americans from Tax Hikes (PATH) Act of 2015 (P.L. 114-113)). Software included as part of the purchase price of a computer that has no separately stated cost is depreciated as part of the cost of the computer over a five-year recovery period (Reg. § 1.167(a)-14(b); Rev. Proc. 2000-50).

Web Site Development Costs. The IRS has not issued formal guidance on the treatment of web site development costs, but informal internal IRS guidance suggests that one appropriate approach is to treat these costs like an item of software and depreciate them over three years. It is clear, however, that taxpayers who pay large amounts to develop sophisticated sites have been allocating their costs to items such as software development (currently deductible like research and development costs under Code Sec. 174) and currently deductible advertising expense.[10]

References are to Standard Federal Tax Reports; Tax Research Consultant; and Practical Tax Explanations.

[3] ¶ 11,003; DEPR: 15,050; § 11,101

[4] ¶ 11,003; DEPR: 15,700; § 11,110

[5] ¶ 11,007.512; DEPR: 15,154; § 11,005

[6] ¶ 11,006; DEPR: 15,150; § 11,005

[7] ¶ 11,015; DEPR: 15,158, FARM: 9,078; § 36,320

[8] ¶ 11,008; DEPR: 15,162; § 11,005

[9] ¶ 11,002; DEPR: 15,162.85; § 11,535

[10] ¶ 13,720.01; BUSEXP: 18,852; § 11,005

Residential Mortgage-Servicing Rights. Depreciable residential mortgage-servicing rights that are not Code Sec. 197 intangibles may be depreciated under the straight-line method over 108 months (Code Sec. 167(f)(3)).[11]

Term Interests. The purchaser of a term interest in property held for business or investment is generally entitled to recover its cost over its expected life. However, no depreciation or amortization deduction is allowed for certain term interests in property for any period during which the remainder interest is held directly (or indirectly) by a related person (Code Sec. 167(e)).[12]

Form 4562. Form 4562 is generally used to claim the depreciation or amortization deduction and is attached to the taxpayer's tax return. Individuals and other noncorporate taxpayers (including S corporations) need not complete Form 4562 if their only depreciation or amortization deduction is for property (other than listed property (¶ 1211)) placed in service before the current tax year. Form 4562 must be filed if a section 179 deduction (including a carryover) is claimed in the current tax year.

Basis for Depreciation

1203. Cost or Other Basis Recoverable Through Depreciation Allowance. The cost of a depreciable asset, reduced by any amount claimed as an expense deduction under Code Sec. 179 (¶ 1208) or as first-year bonus depreciation (¶ 1237), may generally be recovered through depreciation. Other downward adjustments to cost may also be necessary to prevent a duplication of benefits from credits and deductions claimed with respect to the property in the tax year of purchase. See ¶ 1365A for example for the effect of the investment credit on depreciable basis. When property held for personal use, such as a residence, is converted to business or income-producing use, the basis for depreciation is the lesser of the property's fair market value or adjusted basis on the date of conversion (Reg. § 1.167(g)-1; Reg. § 1.168(i)-4(b)).[13] In the case of a residence converted to business use after 1986, the Modified Accelerated Cost Recovery System (MACRS) must be used (¶ 1236).

When a building and land are acquired for a lump sum, only the building is depreciated. The basis must be allocated between the land and the building in proportion to their relative fair market values at the time of acquisition. (Reg. § 1.167(a)-5). If property is subject to both depreciation and amortization, depreciation is allowable only for the portion that is not subject to amortization and may be taken concurrently with amortization.[14]

Section 179 Expense Election

1208. Election to Expense Certain Depreciable Business Assets. Taxpayers other than estates, trusts, and certain noncorporate lessors may elect an expense deduction for the cost of qualifying section 179 property placed in service during the tax year rather than treating the cost as a capital expenditure (Code Sec. 179).[15] The election is made on Form 4562. A taxpayer may also make, revoke, or change an election without IRS consent on an amended return filed during the period prescribed for filing an amended return (Code Sec. 179(c)(2), as amended by the Protecting Americans from Tax Hikes (PATH) Act of 2015 (P.L. 114-113); Reg. § 1.179-5).[16]

Dollar Limitation. The maximum Code Sec. 179 deduction is $500,000 for tax years beginning in 2010 through 2015 (Code Sec. 179(b)(1), as amended by P.L. 114-113). For tax years beginning in 2016 and thereafter, the $500,000 limit is adjusted for inflation (Code Sec. 179(b)(6), as added by P.L. 114-113). The inflation-adjusted dollar limitation for tax years beginning in 2016 remains $500,000 ($510,000 for tax years beginning in 2017) (Rev. Proc. 2016-14; Rev. Proc. 2016-55). Up to $250,000 of the $500,000 annual dollar limit for tax years beginning in 2010 through 2015 may be used to expense

References are to Standard Federal Tax Reports; Tax Research Consultant; and Practical Tax Explanations.

[11] ¶ 11,002; DEPR: 15,162.90; § 11,540

[12] ¶ 11,002; DEPR: 15,262; § 11,005

[13] ¶ 11,046; DEPR: 15,154; § 16,101

[14] ¶ 11,012, ¶ 11,014.021; SALES: 6,202; § 11,001

[15] ¶ 12,120, ¶ 12,126; DEPR: 12,000; § 9,801

[16] ¶ 12,120; DEPR: 12,050, DEPR: 12,150; § 9,830

qualified real property (discussed later). The $250,000 limit on qualified real property does not apply in tax years beginning after 2015. See also ¶ 1214 for a $25,000 deduction limit for any tax year on sport utility vehicles, short-bed trucks, and vans that are exempt from the luxury car depreciation caps.

De Minimis Expensing Rule. Taxpayers may claim a current deduction for amounts paid or incurred to acquire or produce relatively low-cost units of property if specific requirements are met (¶ 903).

Investment Limitation. The maximum Code Sec. 179 dollar limitation is reduced dollar for dollar by the cost of qualified property placed in service during the tax year that exceeds an investment limitation. The investment limitation is $2 million for tax years beginning in 2010 through 2015 (Code Sec. 179(b)(2), as amended by P.L. 114-113). For tax years beginning in 2016 and thereafter, the $2,000,000 investment limitation is adjusted for inflation (Code Sec. 179(b)(6), as added by P.L. 114-113). The inflation-adjusted limitation for tax years beginning in 2016 is $2,010,000 ($2,030,000 for tax years beginning in 2017) (Rev. Proc. 2016-14; Rev. Proc. 2016-55).

Taxable Income Limitation. The total cost of property that may be expensed for any tax year cannot exceed the total amount of taxable income derived from the active conduct of any trade or business during the tax year, including an employee's salary and wages (Code Sec. 179(b)(3)). An amount disallowed by the taxable income limitation is carried forward. The deduction for carryforwards and the amounts expensed for qualifying property placed in service in a carryforward year, however, may not exceed the maximum annual dollar cost ceiling, investment limitation, or taxable income limitation for that year.

Section 179 Property. To qualify as section 179 property, the property must be tangible section 1245 property (new or used), depreciable under the Modified Accelerated Cost Recovery System (MACRS), and acquired by purchase for use in the active conduct of a trade or business (Code Sec. 179(d)).[17] Property used predominantly outside of the United States, property used with respect to lodging, such as apartment buildings but not hotels and motels, and property used by tax-exempt organizations (unless the property is used predominantly in connection with an unrelated business income activity) do not qualify as section 179 property (Code Sec. 50(b)). A taxpayer may also make an election to treat qualified real property (discussed later) as section 179 property (Code Sec. 179(f)(1)).

Depreciable off-the-shelf computer software may be expensed under Code Sec. 179 (Code Sec. 179(d)(1)(A), as amended by P.L. 114-113).[18] This is software described in Code Sec. 197(e)(3)(A)(i) that is readily available for purchase by the general public, is subject to a nonexclusive license, has not been substantially modified, and is depreciable over three years under Code Sec. 167(f)(1)(A).

Qualified Real Property. A taxpayer may elect to treat the cost of qualified real property placed in service in a tax year that begins after 2009 as section 179 property (Code Sec. 179(f), as amended by P.L. 114-113; Notice 2013-59). The maximum amount of qualified real property that may be expensed in a tax year beginning in 2010 through 2015 is limited to $250,000. The expensed amount is counted toward the overall $500,000 annual expensing limit for those years, as discussed previously. The $250,000 limitation is eliminated in tax years beginning in 2016 and later (Code Sec. 179(f)(3), stricken by P.L. 114-113).

Example 1: A calendar-year taxpayer places $600,000 of qualified real property in service in 2016 and elects to treat it as section 179 property. The taxpayer also places $400,000 of other section 179 property in service in 2016. The annual dollar limit for 2016 ($500,000) is not subject to reduction under the investment limitation because the taxpayer did not place more than $2,010,000 of section 179 property in service in 2016 (only $1 million of section 179 property was placed in service). The

References are to Standard Federal Tax Reports; Tax Research Consultant; and Practical Tax Explanations.

[17] ¶ 12,120; DEPR: 12,200; § 9,810

[18] ¶ 12,120; DEPR: 12,200; § 9,810

taxpayer may elect to expense up to $500,000 of the cost of its qualified real property. If it elects to expense $500,000 of the qualified real property, then it may not elect to expense any other section 179 property in 2016 since the full $500,000 limit has been used. If the taxpayer has elected to expense only $400,000 of qualified real property, it could elect to expense up to $100,000 of its other section 179 property.

Qualified real property is defined as:

(1) qualified leasehold improvement property, described in Code Sec. 168(e)(6) (¶ 1234);

(2) qualified restaurant property (i.e., a restaurant building or improvement described in Code Sec. 168(e)(7)) (¶ 1240); and

(3) qualified retail improvement property, described in Code Sec. 168(e)(8) (¶ 1240).

The property must be depreciable and acquired by purchase for use in the active conduct of a trade or business. It does not include Code Sec. 50(b) property as discussed in *"Section 179 Property,"* previously.

No amount of a section 179 deduction attributable to qualified real property that is disallowed under the taxable income limitation may be carried over to a tax year beginning after 2015 (Code Sec. 179(f)(4), as amended by P.L. 114-113, prior to being stricken by P.L. 114-113). The taxpayer is treated as if no section 179 election had been made to the extent that any amount attributable to qualified real property is not allowed to be carried over to a tax year beginning after 2015. The amount of a disallowed carryover attributable to qualified real property placed in service in any tax year other than the taxpayer's last tax year beginning in 2015 is treated as property that was placed in service on the first day of the taxpayer's last tax year beginning in 2015. For the last tax year of the taxpayer beginning in 2015, the amount determined under the taxable business income limitation of Code Sec. 179(b)(3)(A) is determined without regard to depreciation claimed on carryforwards that are treated as placed in service in the taxpayer's last tax year beginning in 2015.

Example 2: A calendar year taxpayer pays $150,000 for qualified real property in 2014 and elects to expense the entire amount. No other amount is expensed. The taxpayer's 2014 taxable income is $50,000. The taxpayer therefore has a $100,000 carryforward attributable to qualified real property for 2015. However, the taxpayer expenses $500,000 of other property placed in service in 2015, so none of the $100,000 carryforward is deductible. The $100,000 carryforward may not be carried forward to 2016 and is treated as attributable to property placed in service on January 1, 2015, for depreciation purposes. No depreciation claimed in 2015 on the $100,000 will reduce taxable income for purposes of determining the amount of the 2015 taxable income limitation.

If a taxpayer places both qualified real property that is treated as section 179 property and other types of section 179 property in service in a tax year in which there is a carryforward due to application of the taxable income limitation, the amount of the carryforward is allocated pro rata between the qualified real property and the other types of section 179 property that the taxpayer placed in service during the tax year and elected to expense (Code Sec. 179(f)(4)(D); Notice 2013-59).

Many taxpayers filed income tax returns that treated unused section 179 carryforwards attributable to qualified real property as placed in service on the first day of the taxpayer's last tax year beginning in 2014, in accordance with the rule in effect prior to the permanent extension of the expensing election for qualified real property by P.L. 114-113. The IRS will allow such a taxpayer to either (1) continue treating the unused carryforward as property placed in service on the first day of the last tax year beginning in 2014 or (2) file an amended return for the last tax year beginning in 2014 and any subsequent affected year and treat the unused carryforward as a carryover to any tax year beginning in 2015. An amended return is allowed, however, only if the period of limitations on assessment under Code Sec. 6501(a) is still open for the last tax year beginning in 2014 as well as subsequent affected tax years for which an amended return must be filed (Rev. Proc. 2016-48, Section 3).[19]

The amount of qualified real property that is expensed under Code Sec. 179 is subject to the section 1245 ordinary income recapture rules (¶ 1785) (Code Sec. 1245(a)(3)(C)). Where only a portion of the cost of a qualified real property is expensed, a taxpayer may use any reasonable method to determine the amount of gain on the disposition of the qualified real property that is attributable to section 1245 property and section 1250 property, including the pro rata allocation methodology and gain allocation methodology described in Notice 2013-59. The section 1245 recapture amount is limited to the gain allocated to the section 1245 property.

Purchase Defined. Property is acquired by purchase unless it (1) is acquired from certain related persons, (2) is transferred between members of a controlled group, (3) has a substituted basis in whole or in part, or (4) is acquired from a decedent and has a basis determined under Code Sec. 1014(a) (generally, a fair-market value basis) (Code Sec. 179(d)(2)).

Recapture. The Code Sec. 179 expense deduction is treated as depreciation for recapture purposes (¶ 1779). Thus, gain on a disposition of section 179 property that is section 1245 property is treated as ordinary income to the extent of the Code Sec. 179 expense allowance claimed plus any depreciation claimed. Qualified real property is section 1250 property. However, as discussed previously, a section 179 expense deduction for qualified real property is subject to recapture as ordinary income under the rules that apply to section 1245 property (Code Sec. 1245(a)(3)(C)).

If business use of section 179 property does not exceed 50 percent during any year of the property's depreciation period, a portion of the amount expensed is recaptured as ordinary income (Code Sec. 179(d)(10); Reg. § 1.179-1(e)). The recapture amount is the difference between the expense claimed and the depreciation that would have been allowed on the expensed amount for prior tax years and the tax year of recapture. However, the recapture rules described at ¶ 1211 apply to listed property, such as passenger automobiles used less than 50 percent for business. Recapture is reported on Form 4797.

Empowerment Zones. The section 179 dollar limit ($500,000 for tax years beginning in 2016) is increased an additional $35,000 for section 179 property placed in service in designated empowerment zones by an enterprise zone business (Code Sec. 1397A).[20] The $35,000 increase is subject to recapture if the property is removed from the empowerment zone. In general, the qualifying property must be placed in service in the empowerment zone before January 1, 2017 (Code Sec. 1391(d)(1), as amended by P.L. 114-113; Code Sec. 1400).

Limitations on Automobiles and Other Listed Property

1211. Business Usage Requirement for Listed Property. Depreciation deductions for "listed property" are subject to special rules (Code Sec. 280F).[21] Listed property includes: passenger automobiles (¶ 1214); other forms of transportation, if the property's nature lends itself to personal use (e.g., airplanes, boats, vehicles excluded from the definition of a passenger automobile); entertainment, recreational and amusement property; computers and peripheral equipment; and any other property specified by regulation. If an item of listed property is not used more than 50 percent for business, the deductions under the Modified Accelerated Cost Recovery System (MACRS) on the property must be determined under the alternative depreciation system (ADS) (Code Sec. 280F(b)(1)) (¶ 1247).

If the listed property satisfies the more-than-50-percent business use requirement in the tax year it is placed in service but fails to meet that test in a later tax year that occurs during any year of the property's ADS recovery period, depreciation deductions (including bonus depreciation) previously taken are subject to recapture (Code Sec.

References are to Standard Federal Tax Reports; Tax Research Consultant; and Practical Tax Explanations.

[19] ¶ 12,126.65; DEPR: 12,200; § 9,825.05

[20] ¶ 32,397; DEPR: 12,116; § 9,815.05

[21] ¶ 15,100; DEPR: 3,500; § 11,301

280F(b)(2)). MACRS depreciation for years preceding the year in which the business use falls to 50 percent or less is recaptured to the extent that the MACRS depreciation (including bonus depreciation) for such years exceeds the depreciation that would have been allowed under ADS. Depreciation thereafter must be computed using ADS.

If the more-than-50-percent business use test is not satisfied in the tax year the property is placed in service, the property does not qualify for the Code Sec. 179 expensing election (¶ 1208). If the more-than-50-percent business use test is initially satisfied but is not met in a later tax year, the Code Sec. 179 expense deduction is treated as a depreciation deduction for purposes of the listed property depreciation recapture rule above. For example, if a taxpayer expenses the entire cost of a listed property, the difference between the amount expensed and the ADS deductions that would have been allowed on that amount prior to the recapture year is recaptured as ordinary income.

See ¶ 1214 for additional limits on passenger automobiles.

Reporting. Part IV of Form 4797 is used to calculate any recapture amount.

1214. Limitations on Passenger Automobiles, Including Trucks, SUVs, and Vans. The maximum depreciation deductions under the Modified Accelerated Cost Recovery System (MACRS) (including the Section 179 expensing deduction (¶ 1208) and first-year bonus depreciation allowance (¶ 1237)) that may be claimed for a passenger automobile other than a truck, including an SUV treated as a truck, or van placed in service in calendar year 2009 or later are shown in the chart below (Code Sec. 280F).[22] For earlier years, see IRS Publication 463.

For Cars Placed in Service		*Depreciation Allowable in—*				
After	*Before*	*Year 1*	*Year 2*	*Year 3*	*Year 4, etc.*	*Authority*
12/31/08	1/01/10	10,960 * 2,960	4,800	2,850	1,775	Rev. Proc. 2009-24
12/31/09	1/01/11	11,060 * 3,060	4,900	2,950	1,775	Rev. Proc. 2010-18, as modified by Rev. Proc. 2011-21
12/31/10	1/01/12	11,060 * 3,060	4,900	2,950	1,775	Rev. Proc. 2011-21
12/31/11	1/01/13	11,160 * 3,160	5,100	3,050	1,875	Rev. Proc. 2012-23
12/31/12	1/01/14	11,160 * 3,160	5,100	3,050	1,875	Rev. Proc. 2013-21
12/31/13	1/01/15	11,160 * 3,160	5,100	3,050	1,875	Rev. Proc. 2014-21, as modified by Rev. Proc. 2015-19
12/31/14	1/01/16	11,160 * 3,160	5,100	3,050	1,875	Rev. Proc. 2015-19, as modified by Rev. Proc. 2016-23
12/31/15	1/01/17	11,160 * 3,160	5,100	3,050	1,875	Rev. Proc. 2016-23

* The higher first-year limit applies if the vehicle qualifies for bonus depreciation under the general provision of Code Sec. 168(k) and no election out is made. The higher limit does not apply if bonus depreciation is claimed under the authority of any other bonus depreciation provision (¶ 1237).

Assuming that the 200-percent declining balance method and half-year convention apply, a car placed in service in 2016 on which bonus depreciation is claimed is subject to the first-year cap if the cost of the vehicle exceeds $18,600 ($9,300 bonus + (9,300 remaining basis × 20%) = $11,160).

References are to Standard Federal Tax Reports; Tax Research Consultant; and Practical Tax Explanations.

[22] ¶ 15,100; DEPR: 3,504; § 11,330.05

Trucks (including SUVs treated as trucks) and vans are subject to their own set of depreciation caps if placed in service after 2002. These caps (reproduced in the table below) reflect the higher costs associated with such vehicles. Keep in mind, however, that trucks and vans that have a loaded gross vehicle weight rating greater than 6,000 pounds are not subject to any caps (see below). *Also, certain trucks and vans placed in service after July 6, 2003, are not subject to the caps if, because of their design, they are not likely to be used for personal purposes (see below).*

For Trucks and Vans Placed in Service		*Depreciation Allowable in—*				
After	*Before*	*Year 1*	*Year 2*	*Year 3*	*Year 4, etc.*	*Authority*
12/31/08	1/01/10	11,060 * 3,060	4,900	2,950	1,775	Rev. Proc. 2009-24
12/31/09	1/01/11	11,160 * 3,160	5,100	3,050	1,875	Rev. Proc. 2010-18, as modified by Rev. Proc. 2011-21
12/31/10	1/01/12	11,260 * 3,260	5,200	3,150	1,875	Rev. Proc. 2011-21
12/31/11	1/01/13	11,360 * 3,360	5,300	3,150	1,875	Rev. Proc. 2012-23
12/31/12	1/01/14	11,360 * 3,360	5,400	3,250	1,975	Rev. Proc. 2013-21
12/31/13	1/01/15	11,460 * 3,460	5,500	3,350	1,975	Rev. Proc. 2014-21, as modified by Rev. Proc. 2015-19
12/31/14	1/01/16	11,460 * 3,460	5,600	3,350	1,975	Rev. Proc. 2015-19 as modified by Rev. Proc. 2016-23
12/31/15	1/01/17	11,560 * 3,560	5,700	3,350	2,075	Rev. Proc. 2016-23

* The higher first-year limit applies if the vehicle qualifies for bonus depreciation under the general provision of Code Sec. 168(k) and no election out is made. The higher limit does not apply if bonus depreciation is claimed under the authority of any other bonus depreciation provision (¶ 1237).

Assuming that the 200-percent declining balance method and half-year convention apply and that bonus depreciation is claimed, a truck or van placed in service in 2016 is subject to the first-year cap if the cost of the vehicle exceeds $19,266 ($9,633 bonus + ($9,633 remaining basis × 20%) = $11,560).

The above maximum annual limits (often referred to as the luxury car limits) are based on 100-percent business use. If business use is less than 100 percent, the limits must be reduced to reflect the actual business use percentage.

Passenger Automobile Defined. For purposes of the depreciation caps, a passenger automobile includes any four-wheeled vehicle manufactured primarily for use on public streets, roads, and highways that has an *unloaded* gross vehicle weight rating (GVWR) (i.e., curb weight fully equipped for service but without passengers or cargo) of 6,000 pounds or less (Code Sec. 280F(d)(5)(A)).[23] However, a truck or van is treated as a passenger automobile subject to the caps only if it has a *gross* vehicle weight rating (i.e., maximum total weight of a loaded vehicle as specified by the manufacturer) of 6,000 pounds or less (Code Sec. 280F(d)(5)(B)). A truck or van, therefore, is not subject to the depreciation caps if its GVWR exceeds 6,000 pounds. A sport utility vehicle is generally treated as a truck (even if built on a unibody (i.e., car chassis)) and, therefore, if its GVWR is in excess of 6,000 pounds it is also exempt from the caps. See footnoted material for further discussion of the definition of a "truck" as well as a list of SUVs,

References are to Standard Federal Tax Reports; Tax Research Consultant; and Practical Tax Explanations.

[23] ¶ 15,100; BUSEXP: 24,852.05, DEPR: 12,150; § 840

trucks, and vans with a GVWR in excess of 6,000 pounds.[24] Ambulances or hearses and vehicles used directly in the trade or business of transporting persons or property for hire (e.g., taxis and limousines) are not considered passenger automobiles subject to the caps regardless of their weight.

Luxury Car Depreciation Examples. The depreciation deduction that is claimed on the return for any tax year during a vehicle's recovery (depreciation) period is the lesser of the depreciation deduction for the tax year (computed as if there were no depreciation caps) or the cap that applies for the tax year.[25]

If, after the recovery period for a passenger automobile ends, the taxpayer continues to use the car in its trade or business, the unrecovered basis (referred to as "Sec. 280F unrecovered basis") may be deducted at the maximum annual rate provided in the chart above for the fourth and succeeding years. This rule permits depreciation deductions beyond the recovery period. Unrecovered basis is the difference between the cost of the vehicle and the amount of depreciation claimed on the return during the recovery period (or that would have been claimed on the return if business use had been 100 percent). The MACRS recovery period for a passenger automobile is five full years from the date the vehicle is deemed placed in service under the applicable half-year or mid-quarter convention (¶ 1245). Due to operation of the applicable convention, depreciation deductions are claimed over the six tax years that the five-year recovery period falls within.

The following example illustrates how depreciation is computed if the 50-percent bonus depreciation allowance is not claimed.

Example 1: On April 5, 2016, a calendar-year taxpayer purchased a car for $30,000. Business use of the car each year is 100 percent. Depreciation is computed under the general MACRS 200-percent declining-balance method over a five-year recovery period using a half-year convention subject to the luxury car limitations. No bonus allowance is claimed. Allowable depreciation during the regular recovery period (2016 through 2021) is computed as follows:

Year	*100% Business-Use MACRS Depreciation*	*Luxury Car Limit*	*Deduction: Lesser of Col. 2 or 3*	*Sec. 280F Unrecovered Basis*
2016	$6,000	$3,160	$3,160	$26,840
2017	9,600	5,100	5,100	21,740
2018	5,760	3,050	3,050	18,690
2019	3,456	1,875	1,875	16,815
2020	3,456	1,875	1,875	14,940
2021	1,728	1,875	1,728	13,212

Note that the unrecovered basis is computed by subtracting the depreciation that would have been allowed (taking the applicable cap into consideration) if business use was 100%, even if business use is less than 100%. Thus, for example, the unrecovered basis at the close of 2016 is $26,840 ($30,000 – $3,160). The $13,212 unrecovered basis at the close of the regular recovery period is deducted in the post recovery period years at the rate of $1,875 per year assuming 100-percent business use continues. The unrecovered basis is reduced by $1,875 each year regardless of the percentage of business use.

The following example shows how luxury car depreciation is computed if the 50-percent bonus deduction is claimed.

Example 2: On April 5, 2016, a calendar-year taxpayer purchased a new car for $30,000. Business use of the car each year is 100 percent. Depreciation is computed under the general MACRS 200-percent declining-balance method over a five-year recovery period using a half-year convention subject to the luxury car limitations. Allowable depreciation during the regular recovery period (2016 through 2021) is computed as follows:

References are to Standard Federal Tax Reports; Tax Research Consultant; and Practical Tax Explanations.

[24] ¶ 15,108.022; DEPR: 3,502.052; § 840

[25] ¶ 15,108.40; DEPR: 3,600, DEPR: 3,504.15; § 11,330.10

Year	100% Business-Use MACRS Depreciation	Luxury Car Limit	Deduction: Lesser of Col. 2 or 3	Sec. 280F Unrecovered Basis
2016	$18,000	$11,160	$11,160	$18,840
2017	4,800	5,100	4,800	14,040
2018	2,880	3,050	2,880	11,160
2019	1,728	1,875	1,728	9,432
2020	1,728	1,875	1,728	7,704
2021	864	1,875	864	6,840

Beginning in 2022, the unrecovered basis is the $6,840 difference between the $30,000 cost and the sum of the return deductions claimed in 2016 through 2021. The unrecovered basis is deducted at the rate of $1,875 per year assuming that 100-percent business use continues. However, the unrecovered basis is reduced by $1,875 each year regardless of the percentage of business use.

Special Rules for Vehicles Subject to 100-Percent Bonus Depreciation in 2010 or 2011. If the 100-percent bonus deduction was claimed in 2010 or 2011 on a new car that is subject to the caps and a safe-harbor election was not made, a taxpayer claimed the amount of the first-year cap since this was less than the bonus depreciation allowance. No depreciation may be claimed in any succeeding years of the vehicle's recovery period because the depreciation deduction for each of those years computed as if there were no depreciation caps is $0 (the full cost is deemed deducted as a bonus depreciation allowance) and $0 is less than the cap amount for each of those years. To address this anomaly, a safe harbor election allowed a taxpayer to claim a 100-percent bonus depreciation deduction in the amount of the first-year cap in the year that the vehicle was placed in service and then determine its depreciation deductions for the remaining years in the recovery period by computing those deductions as if a 50-percent bonus depreciation allowance was claimed in the year the vehicle was placed in service. A taxpayer made this election by computing its depreciation deductions in accordance with the election (Rev. Proc. 2011-26).

$25,000 Section 179 Expensing Cap on Sport Utility Vehicles, Certain Trucks, and Certain Vans That Are Exempt from Luxury Car Depreciation Caps. The maximum amount of the cost of an SUV that may be expensed under Code Sec. 179 if the SUV is exempt from the luxury car caps (e.g., has a GVWR in excess of 6,000 pounds) is limited to $25,000, effective for SUVs placed in service after October 22, 2004. The $25,000 limitation also applies to exempt trucks with an interior cargo bed length of less than six feet and exempt passenger vans that seat fewer than ten persons behind the driver's seat. Exempt cargo vans are generally not subject to the $25,000 limitation (Code Sec. 179(b)(5)).

Exclusion from Depreciation Caps for Certain Trucks and Vans Not Likely To Be Used for Personal Purposes. A truck or van that is a qualified nonpersonal use vehicle as defined in Reg. § 1.274-5(k) is excluded from the definition of a passenger automobile and is not subject to the annual depreciation limits (Reg. § 1.280F-6(c)(3)(iii)).[26] A qualified nonpersonal use vehicle generally is one that has been specially modified in such a way that it is not likely to be used more than a *de minimis* amount for personal purposes.

Reporting. The allowable depreciation deduction for any listed property, including automobiles, is reported on Form 4562 (Part V).

1215. Leased Listed Property Inclusion Amounts. The lessee of a passenger automobile (¶ 1214) used for business must include an additional amount in income to offset rental deductions for each tax year during which the vehicle is leased (Code Sec. 280F(c)(2); Reg. § 1.280F-7).[27] The inclusion amount is based on the cost of the vehicle

References are to Standard Federal Tax Reports; Tax Research Consultant; and Practical Tax Explanations.

[26] ¶ 15,107; DEPR: 3,502.05; § 11,305

[27] ¶ 15,100, ¶ 15,107; DEPR: 3,512; § 11,330.05

and generally applies to a vehicle with a fair market value exceeding an inflation-adjusted dollar amount. The inclusion amount is not required on trucks, vans, and SUVs that would be exempt from the depreciation caps if owned by the lessee (e.g., an SUV treated as a truck with a GVWR in excess of 6,000 pounds).

Lease inclusion tables are issued annually by the IRS in the same revenue procedure in which the annual depreciation caps (¶ 1214) are issued. The appropriate table is based on the calendar year that the vehicle was first leased. The same table is used for each year of the lease term.

Each revenue procedure includes a lease inclusion table for passenger automobiles and a lease inclusion table for trucks and vans (including SUVs treated as trucks). A lessee's inclusion amount for each tax year that the vehicle is leased is computed as follows: (1) use the fair market value of the vehicle on the first day of the lease term to find the appropriate dollar (inclusion) amounts on the IRS table (see following); (2) prorate the dollar amount from the table for the number of days of the lease term included in the tax year; and (3) multiply the prorated amount by the percentage of business and investment use for the tax year. For the last tax year during any lease that does not begin and end in the same tax year, the dollar amount for the preceding tax year should be used.

Example: A car costing $25,500 is leased for four years by a calendar-year taxpayer beginning on April 1, 2016, and is used 100 percent for business. The annual dollar amounts from the table for leases beginning in 2016 are: $17 for the first tax year during the lease, $38 for the second tax year, $56 for the third tax year, $67 for the fourth tax year, and $78 for the fifth and following tax years. In 2016, the inclusion amount is $12.77 (275/366 × $17). The inclusion amounts for 2017, 2018, and 2019 are $38, $56, and $67, respectively, since the vehicle is leased for the entire year during these tax years. In 2020, the inclusion amount is $16.66 (91/366 × $67 (the dollar amount for 2019, the preceding tax year, is used in the last year of the lease)).

Listed Property Other Than Passenger Automobiles. Lessees of listed property other than passenger automobiles (¶ 1211) are required to include in income a usage-based inclusion amount in the first tax year that the business use percentage of such property is 50 percent or less (Code Sec. 280F(c); Reg. § 1.280F-7(b)).[28]

Reporting. The inclusion amount is reported on Form 2106 by employees, Schedule C (Form 1040) by the self-employed, and Schedule F by farmers.

Dollar Amounts for Passenger Automobiles
(That Are Not Trucks or Vans)
With a Lease Term Beginning in Calendar Year 2016
[Rev. Proc. 2016-23, I.R.B. 2016-16

Fair Market Value of Passenger Automobile		*Tax Year During Lease*				
Over	*Not Over*	*1st*	*2nd*	*3rd*	*4th*	*5th & later*
$19,000	$19,500	6	13	20	23	27
19,500	20,000	7	15	23	27	30
20,000	20,500	8	17	26	30	35
20,500	21,000	9	19	29	33	39
21,000	21,500	10	21	31	38	42
21,500	22,000	11	23	34	41	47
22,000	23,000	12	26	39	46	53
23,000	24,000	14	30	44	54	60
24,000	25,000	16	34	50	60	69
25,000	26,000	17	38	56	67	78
26,000	27,000	19	42	62	74	85
27,000	28,000	21	46	68	81	93
28,000	29,000	23	50	73	89	101
29,000	30,000	25	53	80	95	110

References are to Standard Federal Tax Reports; Tax Research Consultant; and Practical Tax Explanations.

[28] ¶ 15,100, ¶ 15,107; DEPR: 3,512.10; § 11,330.05

Dollar Amounts for Passenger Automobiles
(That Are Not Trucks or Vans)
With a Lease Term Beginning in Calendar Year 2016
[Rev. Proc. 2016-23, I.R.B. 2016-16

Fair Market Value of Passenger Automobile		*Tax Year During Lease*				
Over	*Not Over*	*1st*	*2nd*	*3rd*	*4th*	*5th & later*
30,000	31,000	26	58	85	102	118
31,000	32,000	28	62	91	109	126
32,000	33,000	30	65	98	116	134
33,000	34,000	32	69	103	123	142
34,000	35,000	34	73	109	130	150
35,000	36,000	35	77	115	137	158
36,000	37,000	37	81	121	144	166
37,000	38,000	39	85	127	151	174
38,000	39,000	41	89	132	158	183
39,000	40,000	42	93	138	166	190
40,000	41,000	44	97	144	172	199
41,000	42,000	46	101	150	179	207
42,000	43,000	48	105	155	187	215
43,000	44,000	50	109	161	193	223
44,000	45,000	51	113	167	201	231
45,000	46,000	53	117	173	207	239
46,000	47,000	55	121	179	214	247
47,000	48,000	57	124	185	222	255
48,000	49,000	59	128	191	228	264
49,000	50,000	60	133	196	236	271
50,000	51,000	62	136	203	242	280
51,000	52,000	64	140	209	249	288
52,000	53,000	66	144	214	257	295
53,000	54,000	68	148	220	263	304
54,000	55,000	69	152	226	271	312
55,000	56,000	71	156	232	277	320
56,000	57,000	73	160	238	284	328
57,000	58,000	75	164	243	292	336
58,000	59,000	77	168	249	298	345
59,000	60,000	78	172	255	306	352
60,000	62,000	81	178	264	316	364
62,000	64,000	85	185	276	330	381
64,000	66,000	88	194	287	344	397
66,000	68,000	92	201	299	358	413
68,000	70,000	95	209	311	372	430
70,000	72,000	99	217	322	387	445
72,000	74,000	102	225	334	400	462
74,000	76,000	106	233	346	414	478
76,000	78,000	110	241	357	428	494
78,000	80,000	113	249	369	442	510
80,000	85,000	120	262	390	467	538
85,000	90,000	128	282	419	502	579
90,000	95,000	137	302	448	537	620
95,000	100,000	146	322	477	572	660
100,000	110,000	160	351	521	625	721
110,000	120,000	178	390	580	695	801
120,000	130,000	196	430	638	765	882
130,000	140,000	214	469	697	835	963
140,000	150,000	232	508	755	906	1,044
150,000	160,000	249	548	814	975	1,126
160,000	170,000	267	588	872	1,045	1,207
170,000	180,000	285	627	930	1,116	1,288
180,000	190,000	303	666	989	1,186	1,368
190,000	200,000	321	706	1,047	1,256	1,449
200,000	210,000	339	745	1,106	1,326	1,530
210,000	220,000	357	784	1,165	1,396	1,611
220,000	230,000	375	824	1,223	1,466	1,692
230,000	240,000	393	863	1,281	1,537	1,773
240,000	and over	411	902	1,340	1,607	1,854

Dollar Amounts for Trucks And Vans
With a Lease Term Beginning in Calendar Year 2016
[Rev. Proc. 2016-23]

Fair Market Value of Truck or Van		*Tax Year During Lease*				
Over	*Not Over*	*1st*	*2nd*	*3rd*	*4th*	*5th & later*
$19,500	$20,000	3	8	12	14	16
20,000	20,500	4	10	15	17	20
20,500	21,000	5	12	17	21	25
21,000	21,500	6	14	20	25	28
21,500	22,000	7	16	23	28	32
22,000	23,000	8	19	28	33	38
23,000	24,000	10	23	33	41	46
24,000	25,000	12	26	40	47	55
25,000	26,000	14	30	46	54	63
26,000	27,000	16	34	51	62	70
27,000	28,000	17	38	58	68	79
28,000	29,000	19	42	63	76	86
29,000	30,000	21	46	69	82	95
30,000	31,000	23	50	75	89	103
31,000	32,000	25	54	80	97	111
32,000	33,000	26	58	86	104	119
33,000	34,000	28	62	92	111	127
34,000	35,000	30	66	98	117	136
35,000	36,000	32	70	104	124	143
36,000	37,000	34	73	110	132	151
37,000	38,000	35	78	115	139	160
38,000	39,000	37	82	121	146	167
39,000	40,000	39	85	128	152	176
40,000	41,000	41	89	133	160	184
41,000	42,000	42	94	139	166	192
42,000	43,000	44	97	145	174	200
43,000	44,000	46	101	151	181	208
44,000	45,000	48	105	157	187	217
45,000	46,000	50	109	162	195	224
46,000	47,000	51	113	169	201	233
47,000	48,000	53	117	174	209	240
48,000	49,000	55	121	180	216	248
49,000	50,000	57	125	186	222	257
50,000	51,000	59	129	191	230	265
51,000	52,000	60	133	197	237	273
52,000	53,000	62	137	203	244	281
53,000	54,000	64	141	209	250	290
54,000	55,000	66	144	216	257	298
55,000	56,000	68	148	221	265	305
56,000	57,000	69	153	226	272	314
57,000	58,000	71	156	233	279	321
58,000	59,000	73	160	239	285	330
59,000	60,000	75	164	244	293	338
60,000	62,000	77	170	253	304	350
62,000	64,000	81	178	265	317	366
64,000	66,000	85	186	276	331	383
66,000	68,000	88	194	288	345	399
68,000	70,000	92	202	299	360	414
70,000	72,000	95	210	311	374	431
72,000	74,000	99	217	324	387	447
74,000	76,000	102	226	335	401	463
76,000	78,000	106	233	347	415	480
78,000	80,000	110	241	358	430	495
80,000	85,000	116	255	379	454	524
85,000	90,000	125	274	409	489	564
90,000	95,000	134	294	437	525	605
95,000	100,000	143	314	466	560	645
100,000	110,000	156	344	510	612	706
110,000	120,000	174	383	569	682	787
120,000	130,000	192	422	628	752	868
130,000	140,000	210	462	685	823	949
140,000	150,000	228	501	744	893	1,030
150,000	160,000	246	540	803	963	1,111

Dollar Amounts for Trucks And Vans
With a Lease Term Beginning in Calendar Year 2016
[Rev. Proc. 2016-23]

Fair Market Value of Truck or Van		*Tax Year During Lease*				
Over	*Not Over*	*1st*	*2nd*	*3rd*	*4th*	*5th & later*
160,000	170,000	264	580	861	1,033	1,192
170,000	180,000	282	619	920	1,102	1,274
180,000	190,000	300	658	979	1,172	1,354
190,000	200,000	318	698	1,036	1,243	1,435
200,000	210,000	335	738	1,095	1,313	1,516
210,000	220,000	353	777	1,154	1,383	1,597
220,000	230,000	371	816	1,212	1,454	1,678
230,000	240,000	389	856	1,270	1,524	1,759
240,000	and over	407	895	1,329	1,594	1,839

Depreciation Methods

1216. Methods of Computing Depreciation. Most tangible property placed in service after 1986 must be depreciated using the Modified Accelerated Cost Recovery System (MACRS) (¶ 1243). Depreciation for tangible property placed in service after 1980 and before 1987 is computed under ACRS (¶ 1252).

For tangible property placed in service before 1981, depreciation may be computed under the straight-line method (¶ 1224), the double declining-balance method (¶ 1226), the sum-of-the-years-digits method (¶ 1228), and other consistent methods (¶ 1231), depending on the taxpayer's election in the year the property was placed in service (Former Code Sec. 167(b)).[29] However, accelerated depreciation for pre-1981 realty is limited (Former Code Sec. 167(j)).

For an asset purchased before 1981, only a part of a full year's depreciation was allowed in the year it was placed in service. The allowable deduction was computed by multiplying the first full year's depreciation allowance by the months the property was owned and dividing by 12. The same rule applies in the year of sale.

1218. Methods for Depreciating Real Estate. Real property placed in service after 1986 is depreciated under the Modified Accelerated Cost Recovery System (MACRS) (¶ 1236). Real property placed in service after 1980 and before 1987 is depreciated under the Accelerated Cost Recovery System (ACRS) (¶ 1252). Additions and improvements to a building, including structural components of a building, placed in service after 1986 are depreciated under MACRS (¶ 1240). Post-1986 rehabilitation expenditures are also depreciated using MACRS (¶ 1236). Elements of a building that qualify as personal property may be separately depreciated under the cost segregation rules using shortened MACRS recovery periods (¶ 1240). Real property that is converted from personal use to residential rental property or nonresidential real property is depreciated as MACRS 27.5-year residential rental property or MACRS 39-year nonresidential real property even if the property was acquired for personal use prior to 1987.

1221. Change in Depreciation Method—Accounting Method Changes. A change in the method of computing depreciation is generally a change in accounting method that requires the consent of the IRS and the filing of Form 3115 (Reg. § 1.167(e)-1).[30] If the change from an impermissible accounting method to a permissible accounting method results in a negative (taxpayer favorable) Code Sec. 481(a) adjustment, the adjustment is taken into account in a single tax year. A positive adjustment is taken into account over four tax years—one-year if the positive adjustment is less than $50,000 and the taxpayer makes an election to include it in income in one year. No Code Sec. 481(a) adjustment is allowed when a taxpayer changes from one permissible method to another permissible method. These changes are applied on a "cut-off" basis.[31] Reg. § 1.446-1(e)(2)(ii)(d)(2) and (3) list changes in depreciation or amortization that are or are not considered a change in accounting method.

References are to Standard Federal Tax Reports; Tax Research Consultant; and Practical Tax Explanations.

[29] ¶ 11,037.021; DEPR: 15,306; § 10,301

[30] ¶ 11,042; DEPR: 15,304; § 11,025

[31] ¶ 11,043.021; DEPR: 15,304.15; § 11,025

Although a taxpayer has not adopted an accounting method unless two or more returns have been filed, the IRS will allow a taxpayer who has only filed one return that claimed incorrect depreciation to either file Form 3115 and claim a Code Sec. 481(a) adjustment on the current-year return, or file an amended return. The asset must have been placed in service in the tax year immediately preceding the tax year of the change (Rev. Proc. 2007-16).

For changes that are not a change in accounting method, such as mathematical or posting errors, a taxpayer may only file amended returns for open years. Changes in accounting method are generally made by filing Form 3115. Procedures for changing from an impermissible method (e.g., where incorrect or no depreciation (including bonus depreciation) was claimed) to a permissible method are generally governed by the automatic consent procedures of Rev. Proc. 2016-26 (Section 6.01), which supersedes Rev. Proc. 2015-14, effective for Forms 3115 filed on or after May 5, 2016 for a year of change ending on or after September 30, 2015. Numerous additional types of automatic accounting method changes for depreciation are provided in Section 6. For changes not listed in Section 6, the advance consent procedures of Rev. Proc. 2015-13 are followed.[32]

A taxpayer who has sold depreciable property without claiming any depreciation or all of the depreciation allowable may claim the depreciation by filing Form 3115 during the limitations period for filing an amended return for the year of the sale. The Form 3115 may be filed with the original federal tax return for the tax year in which the depreciable property is disposed (Rev. Proc. 2007-16; Rev. Proc. 2016-29, Section 6.07).[33]

For depreciable property placed in service in a tax year ending before December 30, 2003, the IRS will not assert that a change in computing depreciation is a change in accounting method (Chief Counsel Notice CC-2004-007, January 28, 2004, as clarified by Chief Counsel Notice 2004-24, July 14, 2004).[34]

1224. Straight-Line or Fixed-Percentage Method of Depreciation. The "straight-line" method of computing the depreciation deduction assumes that the depreciation sustained is uniform during the useful life of the property. The cost or other basis, less estimated salvage value, is deductible in equal annual amounts over the estimated useful life (Reg. § 1.167(b)-1).[35] An asset may not be depreciated below its salvage value. Straight-line depreciation under the Modified Accelerated Cost Recovery System (MACRS) and the Accelerated Cost Recovery System (ACRS) is generally computed in this manner, except that a recovery period is used instead of the useful life and salvage value is not considered (Code Sec. 168(b)(4))[36] (¶ 1243 and ¶ 1252).

1226. Declining-Balance Method of Depreciation. Under the declining-balance depreciation method, depreciation is greatest in the first year and smaller in each succeeding year (Reg. § 1.167(b)-2).[37] The depreciable basis (e.g., cost) is reduced each year by the amount of the depreciation deduction, and a uniform rate of 200 percent of the straight-line rate (double-declining balance or 200-percent declining balance method) or 150 percent of the straight-line rate (150-percent declining balance method) is applied to the resulting balances (Reg. § 1.167(b)-2).[38] Under the Modified Accelerated Cost Recovery System (MACRS) rules, the double-declining-balance method is used to depreciate 3-, 5-, 7-, and 10-year property and the 150-percent declining balance method is used to depreciate 15-and 20-year property (¶ 1243).

References are to Standard Federal Tax Reports; Tax Research Consultant; and Practical Tax Explanations.

[32] ¶ 11,043.021; DEPR: 15,304; § 11,025

[33] ¶ 11,043.285; DEPR: 15,304; § 11,025

[34] ¶ 11,043.015; DEPR: 15,304.22

[35] ¶ 11,033; DEPR: 15,400; § 11,130

[36] ¶ 11,250; DEPR: 3,202; § 11,130

[37] ¶ 11,034; DEPR: 15,450; § 11,130

[38] ¶ 11,034; DEPR: 15,450; § 11,130

1228. Sum-of-the-Years-Digits Method of Depreciation. Under the sum-of-the-years-digits method of depreciation, changing fractions are applied each year to the original cost or other basis, less salvage value. The numerator of the fraction each year represents the remaining useful life of the asset and the denominator, which remains constant, is the sum of the numerals representing each of the years of the estimated useful life (the sum-of-the-years digits). The taxpayer may elect this method for group, classified, or composite accounts (Reg. § 1.167(b)-3).[39]

1229. Income Forecast Method of Depreciation. The income forecast method of depreciation may be used only for film, videotape, sound recordings, copyrights, books, patents, and other property identified by IRS regulations. The income forecast method may not be used to depreciate intangible property that is amortizable under Code Sec. 197 (¶ 1288) or consumer durables subject to rent-to-own contracts (¶ 1240) (Code Sec. 167(g)(6); Rev. Rul. 60-358).[40]

Under the income forecast method, the cost of an asset (less any salvage value) is multiplied by a fraction, the numerator of which is the net income from the asset for the tax year and the denominator of which is the total net income forecast to be derived from the asset before the close of the 10th tax year following the tax year in which the asset is placed in service. The unrecovered adjusted basis of the property as of the beginning of the 10th tax year is claimed as a depreciation deduction in the 10th tax year following the tax year in which the asset was placed in service.

If the income forecast changes during the 10-year period, the formula is as follows: the unrecovered depreciable cost of the asset at the beginning of the tax year of revision is multiplied by a fraction. The numerator is the net income from the asset for the tax year of revision. The denominator is the revised forecasted total net income from the asset for the year of revision and the remaining years before the close of the 10th tax year following the tax year in which the asset was placed in service.

During the 3rd and 10th tax years after the asset is placed in service, a taxpayer is generally required to pay or may receive interest based on the recalculation of depreciation using actual income figures. This look-back rule does not apply to property that has a cost basis of $100,000 or less, or if the taxpayer's income projections were within 10 percent of the income actually earned.

Residuals and participations may be included in the adjusted basis of a property in the tax year that it is placed in service or excluded from adjusted basis and deducted in the year of payment (Notice 2006-47; Code Sec. 167(g)(7)).

Reporting. Form 8866 is used to compute the look-back interest due or owed.

Creative Property Costs of Film Makers. A taxpayer may choose to amortize creative property costs ratably over 15 years beginning on the first day of the second half of the tax year in which the cost is written off for financial accounting purposes in accordance with Statement of Position 00-2 (SOP 00-2), as issued by the American Institute of Certified Public Accountants (AICPA) on June 12, 2000 (Rev. Proc. 2004-36).[41] Creative property costs are costs to acquire and develop for purposes of potential future film development, production, and exploitation: (1) screenplays; (2) scripts; (3) story outlines; (4) motion picture production rights to books and plays; and (5) similar properties. If the election is not made, these costs are generally recovered under the income forecast method only if a film is actually produced. If a film is not made, the costs generally are not deductible as a loss (Rev. Rul. 2004-58).

Election to Expense First $15 Million of Film Costs. For qualified film and television productions commencing after December 31, 2007, and before January 1, 2017, and for live theatrical productions commencing after December 31, 2015 and before January 1, 2017, a taxpayer may elect to expense the first $15 million of production costs ($20 million for productions in low income communities or distressed areas) (Code Sec. 181, as amended by the Protecting Americans from Tax Hikes (PATH) Act of 2015 (P.L. 114-113)). Election guidance is provided in Reg. § 1.181-2.

References are to Standard Federal Tax Reports; Tax Research Consultant; and Practical Tax Explanations.

[39] ¶ 11,035; DEPR: 15,500; § 11,025

[40] ¶ 11,002; DEPR: 3,156.60, DEPR: 15,556; § 11,205

[41] ¶ 20,620.6305; DEPR: 21,500; § 11,555

1231. Other Consistent Depreciation Methods. In addition to the depreciation methods explained at ¶ 1224–¶ 1228, a taxpayer may use any other consistent method, such as the sinking fund method, if the total deductions during the first two-thirds of the useful life are not more than the total allowable under the declining-balance method (Reg. § 1.167(b)-4).[42]

Leased Property

1234. Lessee/Lessor Improvements, Lease Acquisition Costs. Unless a leasehold improvement qualifies for a 15-year recovery period by reason of being qualified leasehold improvement property (see below), qualified retail improvement property (see below), or qualified restaurant property (¶ 1240), the cost of an addition or improvement made by the lessee or lessor to real property is depreciated under the Modified Accelerated Cost Recovery System (MACRS) in the same manner as the depreciation deduction for the real property would be calculated if the real property had been placed in service at the same time as the addition or improvement (Code Sec. 168(i)(6) and (8)(A); Reg. § 1.167(a)-4).[43] For example, permanent walls installed in a commercial building (structural components) are separately depreciated as 39-year real property beginning in the month that the walls are placed in service using the mid-month convention. If, upon termination of the lease, a lessee does not retain an improvement (made by the lessee), the lessee's loss is computed by reference to the improvement's adjusted basis at the time of the lease termination. A lessor that disposes of or abandons a leasehold improvement (made by the lessor) upon termination of the lease may use the adjusted basis of the improvement at such time to determine gain or loss (Code Sec. 168(i)(8)(B); Reg. § 1.168(i)-8(c)(3)).

Leasehold additions and improvements that are section 1245 property (i.e., personal as opposed to real property) are generally depreciated over a shortened MACRS recovery period. See *Cost Segregation*, at ¶ 1240.

15-Year Qualified Leasehold Improvement Property. Qualified leasehold improvement property placed in service after October 22, 2004 is depreciated under MACRS over 15 years (39 years if the alternative depreciation system (ADS) applies) using the straight-line method and the half-year or mid-quarter convention, as applicable (Code Sec. 168(b)(3)(G) and (g)(3)(B); Code Sec. 168(e)(3)(E)(iv), as amended by the Protecting Americans from Tax Hikes (PATH) Act of 2015 (P.L. 114-113)). Qualified leasehold improvement property is defined the same way as the term is defined for bonus depreciation purposes (¶ 1237) subject to an exception that generally prohibits an individual who acquires qualified leasehold improvement property from a lessor from treating the property as 15-year qualified leasehold improvement property (Code Sec. 168(e)(6)). Thus, the improvements must be made to the interior portion of nonresidential real property that is more than three years old by the lessor or lessee under or pursuant to the terms of a lease. Elevators and escalators, internal structural framework of the building, structural components that benefit a common area, and improvements relating to the enlargement of a building do not qualify.

Lease Acquisition Costs. The cost of acquiring a lease is amortized over the lease term. A renewal period is counted as part of the lease term if less than 75 percent of the acquisition cost is attributable to the unexpired lease period (not counting the renewal period) (Code Sec. 178).[44]

Construction Allowances. A lessor must depreciate improvements made by the lessee with a qualified construction allowance as nonresidential real property (¶ 764).

1235. Sale v. Lease of Depreciable Property. Whether a transaction is treated as a lease or as a purchase is important in determining who is entitled to claim depreciation and other deductions for related business expenses.[45] In most situations, the rules for determining whether a transaction is a lease or a purchase evolved from court decisions

References are to Standard Federal Tax Reports; Tax Research Consultant; and Practical Tax Explanations.

[42] ¶ 11,036; DEPR: 15,306; § 11,025

[43] ¶ 11,250, ¶ 11,010; DEPR: 3,052; § 11,105

[44] ¶ 12,100; SALES: 42,204; § 11,515

[45] ¶ 8754.022; SALES: 42,000; § 11,015

and IRS rulings. The rules generally look to the economic substance of a transaction, not its form, to determine who owns property that the parties characterize as leased (Rev. Proc. 2001-28, Rev. Proc. 2001-29).

Motor Vehicle Leases. A qualified motor vehicle lease agreement that contains a terminal rental adjustment clause (a provision permitting or requiring the rental price to be adjusted upward or downward by reference to the amount realized by the lessor upon the sale of the vehicle) is treated as a lease if, but for the clause, it would have been treated as a lease for tax purposes (Code Sec. 7701(h)).[46] This provision applies only to qualified agreements with respect to a motor vehicle (including a trailer).

Modified Accelerated Cost Recovery System (MACRS)

1236. MACRS in General. The Modified Accelerated Cost Recovery System (MACRS) is mandatory for most tangible depreciable property placed in service after December 31, 1986, unless transitional rules apply (Code Sec. 168).[47] Under MACRS, the cost of eligible property is recovered over a 3-, 5-, 7-, 10-, 15-, 20-, 27.5-, 31.5-, or 39-year period, depending upon the type of property (¶ 1240) by using statutory recovery methods (¶ 1243) and conventions (¶ 1245). Special transferee rules apply to property received in specified nonrecognition transactions (¶ 1248).

1237. MACRS Bonus Depreciation. Under the Modified Accelerated Cost Recovery System (MACRS), a bonus depreciation deduction is allowed for qualifying MACRS property placed in service before January 1, 2020. The original use of the qualifying property must begin with the taxpayer (Code Sec. 168(k), as amended by the Protecting Americans from Tax Hikes (PATH) Act of 2015 (P.L. 114-113)).[48]

The placed-in-service-deadline is extended one year (before January 1, 2021) for long production property that is depreciable under MACRS and the original use of which begins with the taxpayer. Long production property is property that (1) is subject to the Code Sec. 263A uniform capitalization rules, (2) has a production period greater than one year and a cost exceeding $1 million, and (3) has a MACRS recovery period of at least 10 years or is "transportation property" which is defined as property used in the trade or business of transporting persons or property for hire, such as commercial aircraft. However, only pre-January 1, 2020, progress expenditures are taken into account if the extended placed-in-service deadline applies (Code Sec. 168(k)(2)(B), as amended by P.L. 114-113). The extended placed-in-service deadline also applies to certain noncommercial aircraft acquired by purchase. Unlike long production property, 2020 progress expenditures on noncommercial aircraft placed in service before January 1, 2021, are eligible for bonus depreciation (Code Sec. 168(k)(2)(C), as amended by P.L. 114-113).

The bonus depreciation rate is generally 50 percent. For property placed in service in 2018 (2019 for long production property and noncommercial aircraft) the rate is reduced to 40 percent and for property placed in service in 2019 (2020 for long production property and noncommercial aircraft) to 30 percent (Code Sec. 168(k)(6), as added by P.L. 114-113).

However, if qualifying MACRS property was acquired after September 8, 2010, and before January 1, 2012, and placed in service before January 1, 2012, the rate was increased to 100 percent.

For property placed in service before 2016, the original use of the property must begin with the taxpayer after 2007 and the property must either be acquired after 2007 (but only if no written binding contract for the acquisition was in effect before 2008) or acquired by the taxpayer pursuant to a written binding contract entered into after 2007 (Code Sec. 168(k)(2), prior to amendment by P.L. 114-113).

In the case of property placed in service after 2015, the original use of the property must begin with the taxpayer. However, the requirement that the original use cannot begin before 2008 is eliminated as unnecessary given the passage of time. The prohibitions against pre-2008 binding contracts and acquisitions of the property before 2008 are

References are to Standard Federal Tax Reports; Tax Research Consultant; and Practical Tax Explanations.

[46] ¶ 43,080; SALES: 42,104; § 11,015

[47] ¶ 11,250, ¶ 11,279; DEPR: 3,052; § 11,101

[48] ¶ 11,250; DEPR: 3,600; § 11,225

likewise eliminated. In the case of long production property eligible for an extended December 31, 2020 placed-in-service deadline, the property must be acquired by the taxpayer before 2020 or acquired pursuant to a binding contract entered into before 2020.

For purposes of the 50-percent bonus depreciation rate, property is generally deemed acquired when the taxpayer takes possession or control (i.e., taxpayer has risk of loss) (Reg. §§1.48-2(b)(6) and 1.167(c)-1(a)(2)). For purposes of the 100-percent bonus depreciation rate, property is considered acquired when its cost is paid for by a cash-basis taxpayer or incurred by an accrual-basis taxpayer (Rev. Proc. 2006-11, Section 3.02(1)(a)). Property constructed, manufactured, or produced by or for a taxpayer is deemed acquired for purposes of the 50-percent and 100-percent rates when work of a significant physical nature begins. Under an elective safe-harbor, work of a significant physical nature begins when more than 10 percent of the total cost of a project has been paid for by a cash basis taxpayer or incurred by an accrual basis taxpayer (Reg. §1.168(k)-1(b)(4)(iii); Rev. Proc. 2011-26, Section 3.02(1)(c)(2)).

If a larger self-constructed property placed in service before 2016 does not qualify for bonus depreciation because its construction began before January 1, 2008, the individual components of the larger property, whether acquired or self-constructed, also do not qualify (Reg. §1.168(k)-1(b)(4)(iii)(C)(1) and (2)). However, if a larger constructed property does not qualify for the 100-percent rate solely because its construction began after December 31, 2007, and before September 9, 2010, a taxpayer may elect to claim the 100-percent rate on individual components of the property, whether acquired or self-constructed, that separately meet the requirements for the 100-percent rate (Rev. Proc. 2011-26, Section 3.02(1)(c)(2)).

Property purchased by a taxpayer in a sale-leaseback transaction within three months after the original purchaser placed the property in service is treated as originally placed in service by the taxpayer, and, therefore the taxpayer may qualify for bonus depreciation. The last purchaser in a syndicated leasing transaction may also qualify if certain requirements are satisfied (Code Sec. 168(k)(2)(E)).

Bonus depreciation is treated as depreciation subject to recapture upon the sale of the property (Reg. §1.168(k)-1(f)(3)). Unlike the section 179 expensing allowance (¶ 1208), there is no taxable income or investment limitation on the bonus depreciation allowance. There is no limit on the overall amount of bonus depreciation that may be claimed on qualifying property. The length of the tax year or date during the tax year that the qualifying property was placed in service does not affect the amount of the bonus depreciation deduction, except that a 100-percent rate applied to property acquired after September 8, 2010, and placed in service before January 1, 2012.

2014/2015 Fiscal Year Taxpayers. Bonus depreciation was retroactively extended to apply to property placed in service in 2015 by the Protecting Americans from Tax Hikes Act of 2015 (P.L. 114-113) which was enacted on December 18, 2015. As a result some 2014/2015 fiscal year taxpayers and taxpayers with a 2015 short tax year may have failed to claim bonus depreciation on their income tax return for qualifying property placed in service in 2015. The IRS has provided guidance that applies only to these qualifying taxpayers (Rev. Proc. 2016-48).[49]

A qualifying taxpayer may claim bonus depreciation on property placed in service in 2015 by filing an amended return for the 2014/2015 fiscal tax year or 2015 short tax year if the taxpayer (1) failed to claim the bonus depreciation on its timely filed return; (2) did not elect out of bonus depreciation for the class of property in which the property placed in service in 2015 belongs; and (3) has not filed an income tax return for the first tax year following the 2014/2015 fiscal tax year or 2015 short tax year. Alternatively, the taxpayer may file an accounting method change using Form 3115 and the automatic change of accounting method procedures described in Sec. 6.01 of the applicable revenue procedure governing automatic accounting method changes (Rev. Proc. 2016-29 and Rev. Proc. 2015-14 (¶ 1221)). The Form 3115 must be filed with the taxpayer's

References are to Standard Federal Tax Reports; Tax Research Consultant; and Practical Tax Explanations.

[49] ¶ 11,279.18; DEPR: 3,600; §11,225.05

timely filed tax return for the first or second tax year succeeding the 2014/2015 fiscal year or 2015 short tax year and the taxpayer must own the property as of the first day of the year of change.

A qualifying taxpayer that fails to file an amended return or Form 3115 to claim bonus depreciation on property within a property class that was placed in service in 2015 is deemed to have elected out of bonus depreciation for all property within that class that was placed in service during the 2014/2015 fiscal tax year or 2015 short tax year provided the taxpayer claimed depreciation on the property within the class but did not claim bonus depreciation on any of the property within the class.

A qualifying taxpayer that elected out of bonus depreciation for a class of property on its timely filed 2014/2015 fiscal tax year or 2015 short tax year return may revoke that election by filing an amended return for the 2014/2015 fiscal tax year or 2015 short tax year in a manner consistent with the revocation by the later of November 11, 2016, or prior to filing the federal income tax return for the first tax year succeeding the 2014/2015 fiscal tax year or 2015 short tax year. If an election out for a property class is not revoked, it applies to property within that class that was placed in service at any time during the tax year.

Qualifying Property. The bonus depreciation allowance is available only for: (1) new property ("original use" must begin with the taxpayer) that is depreciable under MACRS and has a recovery period of 20 years or less; (2) MACRS water utility property; (3) computer software depreciable over three years under Code Sec. 167(f) (¶ 980); (4) qualified leasehold improvement property (defined below) placed in service before 2016; and (5) qualified improvement property (defined below) placed in service after 2015. Property that must be depreciated using the MACRS alternative depreciation system (ADS) (¶ 1247) does not qualify. If ADS is elected, however, the property may qualify. Listed property (¶ 1211), such as a passenger automobile (¶ 1214), that is used 50 percent or less for business, does not qualify. If business use of a listed property falls to 50 percent or less, bonus depreciation and any amount expensed under Code Sec. 179 (¶ 1208) must be recaptured. Property amortized under Code Sec. 197 (¶ 1288) also does not qualify for bonus depreciation.

Luxury Car Depreciation Caps. If the taxpayer does not elect out of bonus depreciation, the first-year Code Sec. 280F depreciation cap (¶ 1214) for a vehicle that qualifies for bonus depreciation is increased by $8,000 for vehicles acquired and placed in service after December 31, 2007, and before January 1, 2018. The increase is limited to $6,400 for a vehicle placed in service in 2018 and to $4,800 for a vehicle placed in service in 2019 (Code Sec. 168(k)(2)(F), as amended by P.L. 114-113).

AMT. Bonus depreciation is allowed in full for alternative minimum tax (AMT) purposes (¶ 1430). If bonus depreciation is claimed, no AMT adjustment is required on the regular MACRS deductions (i.e., the deductions are allowed in full for AMT purposes) (Code Sec. 168(k)(2)(G); Reg. § 1.168(k)-1(d)(iii)).

Election Out. A taxpayer may elect out of bonus depreciation with respect to any class of property (Code Sec. 168(k)(2)(D)(iii), prior to being stricken by P.L. 114-113; Code Sec. 168(k)(7), as added by P.L. 114-113).

Qualified Leasehold Improvement Property. In the case of property placed in service before January 1, 2016, bonus depreciation applies to qualified leasehold improvement property (Code Sec. 168(k)(3), prior to amendment by P.L. 114-113). Qualified leasehold improvement property, is defined as an improvement to an interior portion of nonresidential real property (whether or not depreciated under MACRS) by a lessor or lessee under or pursuant to a lease. The improvement must be placed in service more than three years after the building was first placed in service (i.e., the building must be more than three years old). The lessor and lessee may not be related persons. Expenditures for (1) the enlargement of a building, (2) any elevator or escalator, (3) any structural component that benefits a common area, or (4) the internal structural framework of the building do not qualify. Retail improvement property (¶ 1240) and restaurant improvements (¶ 1240) placed in service before January 1, 2016, that also satisfy the definitional requirements of leasehold improvement property qualify for bonus depreciation (Code Sec. 168(e)(7)(B), prior to amendment by P.L. 114-113 and (8)(D), prior to being stricken by P.L. 114-113).

Qualified Improvement Property. Effective for property placed in service after 2015, the provision which allows bonus depreciation on "qualified leasehold improvement property" is replaced with an expanded version which allows bonus depreciation on "qualified improvement property" (Code Sec. 168(k)(3), as amended by P.L. 114-113). Qualified improvement property is defined as any improvement to an interior portion of a building which is nonresidential real property (whether or not depreciated under MACRS) if the improvement is placed in service after the date the building was first placed in service by any taxpayer. Expenditures which are attributable to (1) the enlargement of a building, (2) any elevator or escalator, or (3) the internal structural framework of the building are excluded from the definition of qualified improvement property. Structural components that benefit a common area are not excluded.

Computation. The bonus depreciation deduction is claimed on the cost of the property after reduction by any Code Sec. 179 allowance (¶ 1208) claimed. Regular MACRS deductions are computed on the cost as reduced by any Code Sec. 179 allowance and bonus depreciation.

Example 1: Taxpayer purchases qualifying five-year MACRS property subject to the half-year convention for $1,500 and claims a $600 Code Sec. 179 allowance. Using the 50-percent rate, bonus depreciation is $450 (($1,500 - $600) × 50%). Regular MACRS depreciation deductions are computed on a depreciable basis of $450 ($1,500 - $600 - $450). The regular first-year MACRS allowance is $90 ($450 × 20% (first-year table percentage)).

Corporation's Election to Forgo Bonus Depreciation and Claim AMT Credit Carryforward in Tax Years Ending After 2015. A corporation may make an election on an annual basis to forgo bonus depreciation on property placed in service during its tax year and claim unused alternative minimum tax credits based on the amount of bonus depreciation that is forgone. (Code Sec. 168(k)(4), as amended by P.L. 114-113). The computation of the refundable AMT credit is made on a worksheet provided with Form 8827 (Credit for Prior Year Minimum Tax—Corporations).

For any tax year for which the election is made, bonus depreciation may not be claimed on qualified property placed in service during the tax year (i.e., property for which bonus depreciation could otherwise be claimed). The election for a tax year is revocable only with IRS consent (Code Sec. 168(k)(4)(D)(i), as amended by P.L. 114-113).

Depreciation on the qualified property is computed using the straight-line method over the regular recovery period.

The Code Sec. 53(c) limitation on the amount of unused AMT credits that may be claimed in a tax year (i.e., the limitation that allows unused AMT credits to be claimed against regular tax liability in excess of tentative minimum tax liability) is increased by the bonus depreciation amount computed for the tax year.

The bonus depreciation amount, for each asset placed in service in a tax year, is 20 percent of the difference between (1) the first year depreciation (including bonus depreciation) that could be claimed on the asset if the bonus is claimed and (2) the first-year depreciation that could be claimed on the asset if bonus depreciation is not claimed (Code Sec. 168(k)(4)(B)(i), as amended by P.L. 114-113).

The bonus depreciation amount is computed using the regular depreciation method that would otherwise apply to the property (e.g., the 200 percent declining balance method for 3-, 5-, 7-, and 10-year property and the 150 percent declining balance method for 15- and 20-year property). Elections made to use the MACRS straight-line method, 150 percent declining balance method, and alternative depreciation system are ignored.

The bonus depreciation amount computed for a tax year may not exceed the lesser of:

(1) 50 percent of the corporation's minimum tax credit under Code Sec. 53(b) for the corporation's first tax year ending after December 31, 2015, or

(2) The minimum tax credit for the tax year, determined by taking into account only the adjusted net minimum tax (as defined in Code Sec. 53(d)) for tax years ending before January 1, 2016, (determined by treating credits as allowed on a first-in, first-out basis).

The limitation above is computed in a special way by a corporation with a fiscal tax year beginning before January 1, 2016, and ending after December 31, 2015. See below.

All corporations treated as a single employer (Code Sec. 52(a)) are treated as a single taxpayer for purposes of the election. If any corporation in a group of corporations that are treated as a single employer makes the election all corporations in the group are treated as having made the election (Code Sec. 168(k)(4)(B)(iii), as amended by P.L. 114-113).

The aggregate increase in credits allowable by reason of the increased limitation resulting from the election is treated as refundable (Code Sec. 168(k)(4)(C)).

In the case of a corporation making an election which is a partner in a partnership, for purposes of determining the electing partner's distributive share of partnership items, bonus depreciation does not apply to any eligible qualified property and the straight line method is used with respect to that property (Code Sec. 168(k)(4)(D)(ii)).

In the case of a partnership having a single corporate partner owning (directly or indirectly) more than 50 percent of the capital and profits interests in the partnership, each partner takes into account its distributive share of partnership depreciation in determining its bonus depreciation amount (Code Sec. 168(k)(4)(D)(iii), as amended by P.L. 114-113).

Corporations with a fiscal tax year beginning before January 1, 2016, and ending after December 31, 2015, are subject to a transitional rule which takes into account the maximum increase amount limitation that applied in tax years ending before January 1, 2016, and the revised limitation that applies in tax years ending after December 31, 2015 (Act Sec. 143(b)(7)(B) of P.L. 114-113).

In the case of a tax year that begins before January 1, 2016, and ends after December 31, 2015, the limitation on the bonus depreciation amount is the sum of:

(1) the maximum increase amount (computed under the rules that apply to tax years ending before 2016) multiplied by a fraction, the numerator of which is the number of days in the tax year before January 1, 2016, and the denominator of which is the number of days in the tax year; and

(2) the bonus depreciation limitation (described above under the rules for tax years ending after 2015) multiplied by a fraction the numerator of which is the number of days in the tax year after December 31, 2015, and the denominator of which is the number of days in the tax year.

For tax years ending before 2016, the maximum increase amount is the lesser of $30 million or six percent of the "AMT credit increase amount" (i.e., unused AMT credits from tax years beginning before 2006) (Code Sec. 168(k)(4)(C)(ii) and (iii), prior to amendment by P.L. 113-295; Rev. Proc. 2008-65, Section 5.03).

50-Percent Bonus Depreciation Allowance for Specified Plants. Effective for specified plants that are planted or grafted after 2015 and before 2020, a taxpayer may make an annual election to claim a depreciation deduction equal to 50 percent of the adjusted basis of the specified plant in the tax year in which it is planted or grafted in the ordinary course of the taxpayer's farming business as defined in Code Sec. 263A(e)(4) (Code Sec. 168(k)(5), as added by P.L. 114-113). The deduction is reduced to 40 percent for plantings and graftings in 2018 and to 30 percent for plantings and graftings in 2019. This provision in effect accelerates the 50 percent bonus depreciation deduction that would otherwise apply in the year that the specified plant was placed in service (i.e., became productive) to the year of planting or grafting.

The deduction reduces the adjusted basis of the specified plant. If the deduction is claimed, the regular bonus depreciation deduction under Code Sec. 168(k) may not be claimed in the tax year that the specified plant is placed in service (Code Sec. 168(k)(5), as added by P.L. 114-113).

A specified plant is (1) any tree or vine which bears fruits or nuts and (2) any other plant which will have more than one yield of fruits or nuts and which generally has a pre-productive period of more than two years from the time of planting or grafting to the time at which the plant begins bearing fruits or nuts (Code Sec. 168(k)(5)(B), as added by P.L. 114-113).

If the 50 percent deduction is claimed, neither the 50 percent deduction nor any regular depreciation deductions on the specified plant are subject to AMT adjustments (i.e., the deductions are claimed in full for AMT purposes) (Code Sec. 168(k)(5)(E), as added by P.L. 114-113). The 50 percent deduction is not subject to capitalization under the uniform capitalization rules of Code Sec. 263A (Code Sec. 263A(c)(7), as added by P.L. 114-113).

50-Percent Bonus Depreciation Allowance for Mine Safety Equipment. A taxpayer may elect to deduct 50 percent of the cost of qualified advanced mine safety equipment that is placed in service before January 1, 2017 (Code Sec. 179E, as amended by P.L. 114-113).[50]

50-Percent Bonus Depreciation Allowance for Qualified Reuse and Recycling Property. A 50-percent additional depreciation allowance may be claimed on the adjusted basis of qualified reuse and recycling property acquired and placed in service during the tax year. The property must be acquired by purchase, its original use must begin with the taxpayer, it must have a useful life of a least five years, and no pre-September 1, 2008, binding acquisition contract may be in effect. Reuse and recycling property is machinery and equipment (not including buildings, real estate, rolling stock or equipment used to transport reuse and recyclable materials) that is used exclusively to collect, distribute, or recycle qualified reuse and recyclable materials. Machinery and equipment include appurtenances such as software necessary to operate the equipment. Qualified reuse and recyclable materials are scrap plastic, glass, textiles, rubber, packaging, and metal, as well as recovered fiber and electronic scrap. A taxpayer may elect out for any class of property (Code Sec. 168(m)).[51]

50-Percent Bonus Depreciation Allowance for Second Generation Biofuel Plant Property. A 50-percent additional depreciation allowance may be claimed on the adjusted basis of certain plant property acquired and placed in service after December 20, 2006, and before January 1, 2017, that is used to produce certain qualified biofuels (Code Sec. 168(l), as amended by P.L. 114-113).[52] For property placed in service after January 2, 2013, and before January 1, 2017, this bonus depreciation allowance may be claimed only on the adjusted basis of second generation biofuel plant property used to produce second generation biofuel. Second generation biofuel is defined under Code Sec. 40(b)(6)(E) and includes algae treated as qualified feedstock.

1238. Property Subject to MACRS. Most tangible depreciable property placed in service after 1986 is depreciated using the Modified Accelerated Cost Recovery System (MACRS). MACRS property is depreciable if it wears out, has a useful life that exceeds one year, and is used in a trade or business or for the production of income. MACRS property does not include: (1) property covered by the taxpayer's election to use a depreciation method not expressed in terms of years, such as the unit of production or income forecast method; (2) public utility property (unless a normalization method of accounting is used); (3) motion picture films and videotapes; (4) sound recordings; (5) intangible property; and (6) property placed in service before 1987 that is excluded from MACRS under the anti-churning rules (Code Sec. 168(f)).[53] Public utility property that does not qualify under MACRS (Code Sec. 168(f)(2))[54] is depreciated under Code Sec. 167(a)[55] using the same depreciation method and useful life as is used to compute the rate-making depreciation allowance for the property.

References are to Standard Federal Tax Reports; Tax Research Consultant; and Practical Tax Explanations.

[50] ¶ 12,139; BUSEXP: 19,000; § 10,255

[51] ¶ 11,250; DEPR: 3,800; § 11,235

[52] ¶ 11,250; DEPR: 3,850; § 11,220

[53] ¶ 11,250, ¶ 11,279.021; DEPR: 15,150; § 11,105

[54] ¶ 11,250; DEPR: 6,150; § 11,110

[55] ¶ 11,002; DEPR: 15,700; § 11,110

1239. Accounting for MACRS Property in Item, Multiple Asset, and General Asset Accounts. Under the Modified Accelerated Cost Recovery System (MACRS), property may be accounted for individually in an item account or by placing a group of identically depreciated assets (i.e., assets with the same recovery period, depreciation method, convention, and placed-in-service tax year) in a multiple asset (pool) account (Reg. § 1.168(i)-7).[56] Alternatively, a taxpayer may elect to include a single asset or a group of identically depreciated assets in a general asset account (GAA) (Reg. § 1.168(i)-1).[57]

Depreciation (including bonus depreciation) on a GAA is computed on the combined bases of the assets in the GAA (after reduction by any amounts expensed under Code Sec. 179) as if the GAA is a single asset. Depreciation allowances determined for each GAA must be recorded in a depreciation reserve account for each account (Reg. § 1.168(i)-1(d)(1)). Similar rules apply to a multiple asset account (Reg. § 1.168(i)-7).

When a taxpayer disposes of an asset in a multiple asset account, the asset is placed into a single asset account as of the first day of the tax year of disposition, and gain or loss is generally computed on the disposition. In computing the asset's adjusted depreciable basis, the depreciation allowed or allowable is computed by using the depreciation method, recovery period, and convention applicable to the multiple asset account or pool that included the asset. The unadjusted depreciable basis of the multiple asset account is reduced by the unadjusted depreciable basis of the asset as of the first day of the tax year of disposition. The depreciation reserve of the multiple asset account is reduced by the depreciation allowed or allowable for the asset in the tax years prior to the tax year of disposition (Reg. § 1.168(i)-8(h)(2)).

Generally, a disposition that is not the disposition of all of the assets or the last asset in a GAA does not reduce the unadjusted depreciable basis of the GAA. The asset is treated as having an adjusted depreciable basis of $0 immediately before the disposition and no loss is realized. The amount realized is recognized as ordinary income up to (1) the sum of the unadjusted depreciable basis of the account and the amount expensed under Code Sec. 179 for all assets in the account, and (2) reduced by amounts previously recognized as ordinary income (Reg. § 1.168(i)-1(e)(2)).

If all of the assets or the last asset in the account is disposed, a taxpayer may apply the preceding rule or elect to terminate the account and recognize gain or loss by reference to the adjusted basis of the GAA (i.e., unadjusted depreciable basis of the GAA less prior deprecation on assets in account) (Reg. § 1.168(i)-1(e)(3)(ii)).

In a "qualifying disposition" a taxpayer may also elect to recognize gain or loss by reference to the adjusted basis of the disposed asset in the GAA. However, a qualifying disposition cannot involve all of the assets or the last asset in the account, and it must be: (1) the direct result of a casualty or theft; (2) a deductible charitable contribution; (3) a direct result of a cessation, termination, or disposition of a business, manufacturing, or other income-producing process; or (4) a certain type of nonrecognition transaction (Reg. § 1.168(i)-1(e)(3)(iii)).

Partial Disposition Election. A building, including its original structural components, is treated as an asset and a taxpayer may claim a loss upon the retirement of an original structural component of a building (or an original component of any other asset, such as an original component of a machine) by making a partial disposition election (Reg. § 1.168(i)-8(d)). Without a partial disposition election, depreciation continues on the retired structural component and the basis of the building is not adjusted. The partial disposition election does not apply to assets, including buildings, that are placed in a GAA.

References are to Standard Federal Tax Reports; Tax Research Consultant; and Practical Tax Explanations.

[56] ¶ 11,276P, ¶ 11,279.0372; DEPR: 15,210; § 11,105.07

[57] ¶ 11,275B, ¶ 11,279.038; DEPR: 3,559; § 11,140

A replacement component which is separately depreciated because it is placed in service after the building is placed in service is a separate asset. If the entire component is retired then a retirement loss is claimed without regard to the partial disposition election because an entire asset has been disposed of. For example, a replacement roof is a separately depreciated asset and a retirement loss must be claimed if the entire replacement roof is again replaced. However, if the shingles on the replacement roof are replaced, a partial disposition of an asset has occurred and a loss on the remaining basis of the shingles may be claimed only if the partial disposition election is made.

The partial disposition election must be made by the due date (including extensions) of the original federal tax return for the tax year in which the portion of the asset is disposed of. No formal election statement is required. The taxpayer simply reports the loss (or gain) on the disposed asset on the appropriate form, generally Form 4797. The election may be revoked only with IRS consent (Reg. § 1.168(i)-8(d)(2)).

If a taxpayer makes a partial disposition election, the costs of related expenditures that would otherwise be deductible as repairs must be capitalized as a restoration (Reg. § 1.263(a)-3(k)(1)) (¶ 903). For example, if a taxpayer makes a partial disposition election to deduct the remaining basis of shingles on an original or replacement roof, the cost of replacing the shingles is capitalized as a restoration even though without the election the cost would be deductible as a repair. If the expenditures must be capitalized without regard to the partial disposition election (e.g., an entire original roof is replaced), the partial disposition election carries no adverse consequence.

The following transactions are treated as dispositions without making a partial disposition election (Reg. § 1.168(i)-8(d)(1)):

- a sale of a portion of an asset;
- a disposition of a portion of an asset as the result of a casualty event described in Code Sec. 165;
- a disposition of a portion of an asset for which gain (determined without regard to recapture under Code Sec. 1245 or Code Sec. 1250) is not recognized in a like kind exchange (Code Sec. 1031) or involuntary conversion (Code Sec. 1033); or
- a transfer of a portion of an asset in a step-in-the-shoes nonrecognition transaction described in Code Sec. 168(i)(7)(B) (¶ 1248).

1240. MACRS Depreciation Periods. The Modified Accelerated Cost Recovery System (MACRS) depreciation (recovery) period for an asset is based on its class life as of January 1, 1986, or is specifically prescribed by Code Sec. 168.[58] The recovery periods for MACRS assets can be found in a table that appears in IRS Pub. 946. This table is an updated version of the table that appears in Rev. Proc. 87-56. Under MACRS, an asset is classified according to its class life as follows:

Three-Year Property. Three-year property includes property with a class life of four years or less. Any race horse placed in service after December 31, 2008, and before January 1, 2017, or any other horse over 12 years old at the time it is placed in service is classified as three-year property (Code Sec. 168(e)(1) and (3), as amended by the Protecting Americans from Tax Hikes (PATH) Act of 2015 (P.L. 114-113)). A race horse that is more than two years old when it is placed in service is three-year property (seven-year property if two years old or less when placed in service) if placed in service on or before December 31, 2008, or on or after January 1, 2017.[59] Certain "rent-to-own" consumer durable property (e.g., televisions and furniture) is three-year property (Code Sec. 168(e)(3)(iii)).[60] Breeding hogs (Rev. Proc. 87-56 Asset Class 01.236) and tractor units for use over the road (Rev. Proc. 87-56 Asset Class 00.26) are three-year property. A tractor unit is a highway truck designed to tow a trailer or semitrailer and that does not carry cargo on the same chassis as the engine (Reg. § 145.4051-1(e)(1)).

References are to Standard Federal Tax Reports; Tax Research Consultant; and Practical Tax Explanations.

[58] ¶ 163.01, ¶ 11,279.021; DEPR: 15,150; § 11,110

[59] ¶ 11,250, ¶ 11,279.023; DEPR: 3,156.05; § 11,110

[60] ¶ 11,250; DEPR: 3,156.60; § 11,110

Five-Year Property. Five-year property generally includes property with a class life of more than four years and less than 10 years. This property includes: (1) cars, (2) light and heavy general-purpose trucks, (3) qualified technological equipment, (4) computer-based telephone central office switching equipment, (5) research and experimentation property that is Sec. 1245 property, (6) semi-conductor manufacturing equipment, (7) geothermal, solar and wind energy properties, (8) certain biomass properties that are small power production facilities, (9) computers and peripheral equipment, and (10) office machinery (typewriters, calculators, etc.) (Code Sec. 168(e)(1) and (3)).[61]

Furniture, appliances, window treatments, and carpeting used in residential rental property are five-year property (Announcement 99-82). Personal property used in wholesale or retail trade or in the provision of personal and professional services is five-year property if a specific recovery period is not otherwise provided (Asset Class 57.0 of Rev. Proc. 87-56). For example, a professional library used by an accountant or attorney is five-year property. Examples of *personal* service businesses include hotels and motels, laundry and dry cleaning establishments, beauty and barber shops, photographic studios and mortuaries. Examples of *professional* service businesses include services offered by doctors, dentists, lawyers, accountants, architects, engineers, and veterinarians (Rev. Proc. 77-10).

Five-year property also includes taxis (Rev. Proc. 87-56 Asset Class 00.22), buses (Rev. Proc. 87-56 Asset Class 00.23), airplanes not used in commercial or contract carrying of passengers or freight, and all helicopters (Rev. Proc. 87-56 Asset Class 00.21), trailers and trailer-mounted containers (Rev. Proc. 87-56 Asset Class 00.27), breeding cattle and dairy cattle (Rev. Proc. 87-56 Asset Class 01.21), breeding sheep and breeding goats (Rev. Proc. 87-56 Asset Class 01.21), and assets used in construction by certain contractors, builders, and real estate subdividers and developers (Rev. Proc. 87-56 Asset Class 15.0).

Seven-Year Property. Seven-year property includes property with a class life of 10 years or more but less than 16 years (Code Sec. 168(e)(1)). This property includes office furniture, equipment and fixtures that are not structural components (Rev. Proc. 87-56 Asset Class 00.11). Desks, files, safes, overhead projectors, cell phones, fax machines and other communication equipment not included in any other class fall within this category. Seven-year property also includes: assets (except helicopters) used in commercial and contract carrying of passengers and freight by air (Rev. Proc. 87-56 Asset Class 45.0); certain livestock (Rev. Proc. 87-56 Asset Class 01.1); breeding or work horses 12 years old or less when placed in service (Rev. Proc. 87-56 Asset Class 01.221); other horses that are not three-year property (Rev. Proc. 87-56 Asset Class 01.225); assets used in recreation businesses (Rev. Proc. 87-56 Asset Class 80.0); and assets used in theme and amusement parks (Rev. Proc. 87-56 Asset Class 80.0). Railroad track and property (such as a fishing vessel) that does not have a class life and is not otherwise classified is seven-year property (Code Sec. 168(e)(3)(C)).[62]

10-Year Property. Ten-year property is property with a class life of 16 years or more and less than 20 years (Code Sec. 168(e)(1)).[63] This property class includes vessels, barges, tugs, and similar means of water transportation not used in marine construction or as a fishing vessel (Rev. Proc. 87-56 Asset Class 00.28). For property placed in service after October 3, 2008, it also includes smart electric meters and qualified smart electric grid systems (Code Sec. 168(e)(3)(D)). MACRS deductions for trees or vines bearing fruit or nuts that are placed in service after 1988 are determined under the straight-line method over a 10-year recovery period (Code Sec. 168(b)(1)).[64] Single purpose agricultural or horticultural structures placed in service after 1988 are 10-year property (Code Sec. 168(e)(3)(D)(i)).

References are to Standard Federal Tax Reports; Tax Research Consultant; and Practical Tax Explanations.

[61] ¶ 11,250; DEPR: 3,156.10; § 11,110

[62] ¶ 11,250; DEPR: 3,156.15; § 11,110

[63] ¶ 11,250; DEPR: 3,156.20; § 11,110

[64] ¶ 11,250; DEPR: 3,156.20; § 11,110

15-Year Property. Property with a class life of 20 years or more but less than 25 years is generally considered 15-year property (Code Sec. 168(e)(1)). This property class includes municipal wastewater treatment plants and telephone distribution plants and other comparable equipment used for the two-way exchange of voice, data communications, and retail motor fuels outlets (Code Sec. 168(e)(3)(E)).[65] A property qualifies as a retail motor fuels outlet (as opposed, for example, to a convenience store, which is 39-year real property) if: (1) 50 percent or more of gross revenues are derived from petroleum sales; (2) 50 percent or more of the floor space is devoted to petroleum marketing sales; or (3) the property is 1,400 square feet or less (Rev. Proc. 97-10).[66]

Fifteen-year property includes car wash buildings and related land improvements, billboards, and section 1250 real property (including service station buildings) and depreciable land improvements used in marketing petroleum and petroleum products (Rev. Proc. 87-56 Asset Class 57.1). Water transportation assets (other than vessels) used in the commercial and contract carrying of freight and passengers by water are 15-year property (Rev. Proc. 87-56 Asset Class 44.0).

Otherwise depreciable land improvements that are not specifically included in any other asset class are 15-year property (Rev. Proc. 87-56 Asset Class 00.3). Examples include sidewalks, driveways, curbs, roads, parking lots, canals, waterways, drainage facilities, sewers (but not municipal sewers), wharves and docks, bridges, and nonagricultural fences. Landscaping and shrubbery is a depreciable land improvement if it is located near a building and would be destroyed if the building were replaced (Rev. Rul. 74-265; IRS Publication 946). Playground equipment attached to the ground is a land improvement (LTR 8848039).[67]

Depreciable gas utility clearing and grading costs to place pipelines into service are 15-year property (Code Sec. 168(e)(3)(E)(vi)).

15-Year Leasehold Improvement Property. See ¶ 1234.

15-Year Restaurant Improvements and Buildings. Qualified restaurant property placed in service after October 22, 2004 is 15-year MACRS property, depreciable using the straight-line method and the half-year or mid-quarter convention, as applicable (Code Sec. 168(e)(3)(E)(v), as amended by P.L. 114-113).[68] The ADS recovery period is 39 years.

Qualified restaurant property is section 1250 property that is an improvement to a building. More than 50 percent of the building's square footage must be devoted to preparation of and seating for on-premises consumption of prepared meals. For restaurant improvements placed in service before 2009, the building must also be more than three years old (Code Sec. 168(e)(3)(E)(v) and (e)(7)).

A restaurant building placed in service after December 31, 2008 is also included in the definition of qualified restaurant property and is depreciated as 15-year property using the straight-line method and half-year or mid-quarter convention if more than 50 percent of the building's square footage is devoted to preparation of and seating for the on-premises consumption of prepared meals. A 39-year ADS recovery period applies (Code Sec. 168(b)(3)(I) and (e)(7)(A)).

The Code Sec. 168(k) bonus depreciation deduction (¶ 1237) may not be claimed on qualified restaurant property placed in service after December 31, 2008 and before January 1, 2016, unless it meets the definition of qualified *leasehold* improvement property (¶ 1234) (Code Sec. 168(e)(7)(B), prior to amendment by P.L. 114-113; Rev. Proc. 2011-26). Qualified restaurant property placed in service after 2015 will qualify for bonus depreciation if it meets the definitional requirement of qualified improvement property (¶ 1237) (Code Sec. 168(e)(7)(B), as amended by P.L. 114-113).

References are to Standard Federal Tax Reports; Tax Research Consultant; and Practical Tax Explanations.

[65] ¶ 11,250; DEPR: 3,156.25; § 11,110

[66] ¶ 11,279.34; DEPR: 3,156.25; § 11,110

[67] ¶ 11,279.0518; DEPR: 6,062.10; § 11,110

[68] ¶ 11,250; DEPR: 3,156.256; § 11,215

Qualified restaurant property is a type of "qualified real property" that qualifies for expensing under Code Sec. 179. See ¶ 1208.

15-Year Qualified Retail Improvement Property. Qualified retail improvement property placed in service after December 31, 2008 is depreciated under MACRS using a 15-year recovery period, the straight-line method, and the half-year or mid-quarter convention (Code Sec. 168(e)(3)(E)(ix), as amended by P.L. 114-113).[69] The ADS recovery period is 39 years.

Qualified retail improvement property means any improvement to an interior portion of a building which is nonresidential real property if the improved portion is (1) open to the general public, (2) used in the retail trade or business of selling tangible personal property to the general public, and (3) placed in service more than three years after the date the building was first placed in service by any taxpayer. Elevators and escalators, internal structural framework of the building, structural components that benefit a common area, and improvements relating to the enlargement of a building do not qualify.

Qualified retail improvement property placed in service before 2016 is ineligible for bonus depreciation under Code Sec. 168(k) unless it also meets the definition of qualified leasehold improvement property (¶ 1234) (Code Sec. 168(e)(8); Rev. Proc. 2011-26). Qualified retail improvement property placed in service after 2015 will necessarily qualify for bonus depreciation by reason of meeting the definition of "qualified improvement" property (¶ 1237) (Code Sec. 168(k)(3), as amended by P.L. 114-113).

Qualified retail improvement property is a type of "qualified real property" that qualifies for expensing under Code Sec. 179. See ¶ 1208.

20-Year Property. Twenty-year property includes property with a class life of 25 years or more, other than Code Sec. 1250 real property with a class life of 27.5 years or more. Water utility property and municipal sewers placed in service before June 13, 1996, and farm buildings (e.g., barns and machine sheds) are included within this class (Code Sec. 168(e)(1) and (3)).[70] Depreciable electric utility clearing and grading costs incurred after October 22, 2004, to place transmission and distribution lines into service are 20-year property (Code Sec. 168(e)(3)(F)).

25-Year Property. Water utility property and municipal sewers have a 25-year recovery period (Code Sec. 168(c) and (e)(5)). The straight-line depreciation method is mandatory for 25-year property (Code Sec. 168(b)(3)(F)).

27.5-Year Residential Rental Property. Residential rental property has a recovery period of 27.5 years. Residential rental property includes buildings or structures with respect to which 80 percent or more of the gross rental income is from dwelling units (Code Sec. 168(e)(2)(A)).[71] It also includes manufactured homes that are residential rental property and elevators and escalators.

Nonresidential Real Property. Nonresidential real property is Code Sec. 1250 real property (¶ 1786) that is not residential rental property or property with a class life (as provided in Rev. Proc. 87-56) of less than 27.5 years (Code Sec. 168(e)(2)(B)).[72] The cost of nonresidential real property placed in service after May 12, 1993, is recovered over 39 years. For property placed in service after 1986 and before May 13, 1993, cost is recovered over 31.5 years.

Farm Machinery and Equipment. Machinery and equipment, grain bins, and fences (but no other land improvements) used in specified agricultural activities are MACRS 7-year property and have a 10-year ADS recovery period (Rev. Proc. 87-56 Asset Class 01.1). However, any machinery or equipment (other than any grain bin, cotton ginning asset, fence, or other land improvement) that is used in a farming business (as defined in Code Sec. 263A(e)(4)), the original use of which commences with the taxpayer after December 31, 2008, and that is placed in service before January 1, 2010, is classified as

References are to Standard Federal Tax Reports; Tax Research Consultant; and Practical Tax Explanations.

[69] ¶ 11,250; DEPR: 3,156.255; § 11,230

[70] ¶ 11,250; DEPR: 3,156.30; § 11,110

[71] ¶ 11,250; DEPR: 3,156.35; § 11,110

[72] ¶ 11,250; DEPR: 3,156.40; § 11,110

MACRS 5-year property (Code Sec. 168(e)(3)(B)(vii)) and has a 10-year ADS recovery period (Code Sec. 168(g)(3)(B)). Property used in a farming business is depreciated using the 150-percent declining balance method as explained at ¶ 1243 (Code Sec. 168(b)(2)(B)).

Indian Reservation Property. For qualified Indian reservation property that is placed in service after 1993 and before January 1, 2017, special MACRS recovery periods are provided for both regular tax and alternative minimum tax purposes that permit faster write-offs (Code Sec. 168(j), as amended by P.L. 114-113).[73]

Effective for tax years beginning after 2015, a taxpayer may make an irrevocable election to use the regular recovery periods for any class of MACRS Indian reservation property placed in service during the tax year (Code Sec. 168(j)(8), as added by P.L. 114-113).

Additions and Improvements. Additions and improvements, including the cost of capitalized structural components, are depreciated under MACRS in the same way that the improved property would be depreciated if it were placed in service at the same time as the addition or improvement (Code Sec. 168(i)(6)).[74] For example, a new floor or roof or other structural component added to a commercial building in 2015 is treated as 39-year MACRS nonresidential real property even if the building is depreciated under a pre-MACRS method. However, any elements of an addition or improvement to a building that qualify as personal property may be depreciated over a shorter recovery period as personal rather than real property under the cost segregation rule described later.

Additions or improvements, however, may qualify for a 15-year recovery period as qualified leasehold improvement property (¶ 1234, qualified retail improvement property (see previously), or qualified restaurant property (see previously).

Roofs. The replacement of an entire roof (including the sheathing and rafters) or a significant portion of a roof that has deteriorated over time is a restoration that is capitalized as an improvement (Reg. § 1.263(a)-3(k)(6)(ii)(A) and (k)(7), Example 14). The replacement of a worn and leaking waterproof membrane on a roof comprised of structural elements, insulation, and a waterproof membrane with a similar but new membrane is not required to be capitalized if the membrane was not leaking when the taxpayer placed the building in service (Reg. § 1.263(a)-3(j)(3), Example 13, and (k)(7), Example 15). Another IRS example dealing with removal costs (¶ 903) assumes that the cost of replacement shingles that are similar to shingles that became leaky while the taxpayer owned the building is not capitalized (Reg. § 1.263(a)-3(g)(2)(ii), Example 3).

Cost Segregation. The Tax Court has ruled that elements of a building that are treated as personal property under the former investment tax credit rules (Reg. § 1.48-1(c)) may be separately depreciated under MACRS and ACRS as personal property (*Hospital Corp. of America*, 109 TC 21, Dec. 52,163).[75] The IRS has acquiesced to the court's holding that the former investment tax credit rules apply in determining whether an item is a structural component (i.e., real property) or personal property (Notice of Acquiescence, 1999-35 I.R.B. 314). The separate depreciation of personal property elements of a building is referred to as "cost segregation."

The determination of whether an item is personal property or a structural component often depends on the specific facts. One important factor is whether the item is permanently attached to the building (*Whiteco Industries*, 65 TC 664, Dec. 33,596). However, items relating to the operation and maintenance of the building are structural components even if not permanently attached. The following items are examples of structural components: bathtubs, boilers, ceilings (including acoustical ceilings), central air conditioning and heating systems, chimneys, doors, electric wiring, fire escapes, floors, hot water heaters, HVAC units, lighting fixtures, paneling, partitions (if not readily removable), plumbing, roofs, sinks, sprinkler systems, stairs, tiling, walls, and windows (Reg. § 1.48-1(e)(2)).

References are to Standard Federal Tax Reports; Tax Research Consultant; and Practical Tax Explanations.

[73] ¶ 11,250; DEPR: 3,156.55; § 11,120

[74] ¶ 11,250; DEPR: 6,052; § 11,110

[75] ¶ 11,279.25; DEPR: 6,058; § 11,110

1243. MACRS Recovery Methods. Under the Modified Accelerated Cost Recovery System (MACRS), the cost of depreciable property is recovered using (1) the applicable depreciation method, (2) the applicable recovery period, and (3) the applicable convention (Code Sec. 168(a)).[76]

The cost of property in the 3-, 5-, 7-, and 10-year classes is recovered using the 200-percent declining-balance method over three, five, seven, and ten years, respectively (i.e., the applicable recovery period), and the half-year convention (unless the mid-quarter convention applies), with a switch to the straight-line method in the year when that maximizes the deduction (Code Sec. 168(b)(1)).[77] The cost of 15- and 20-year property is recovered using the 150-percent declining-balance method over 15 and 20 years, respectively, and the half-year convention (unless the mid-quarter convention applies), with a switch to the straight-line method to maximize the deduction (Code Sec. 168(b)(2)).[78] The cost of residential rental and nonresidential real property is recovered using the straight-line method and the mid-month convention over 27.5- and 39-year recovery periods, respectively (Code Sec. 168(b)(3)).[79]

Instead of the applicable depreciation method (200-percent declining balance method for 3-, 5-, 7-, and 10-year property and 150-percent declining balance method for 10- and 15-year property), taxpayers may irrevocably elect to claim straight-line MACRS deductions over the regular recovery period. The election applies to all property in the MACRS class for which the election is made that is placed in service during the tax year. A taxpayer makes the election on the return for the year the property is first placed in service (Code Sec. 168(b)(5)). For example, if the election is made for 3-year property, it applies to all 3-year property placed in service in the tax year of the election.

Taxpayers may elect to recover the cost of 3-, 5-, 7-, and 10-year property using the 150-percent declining-balance method over the regular recovery periods (the MACRS alternative depreciation system (ADS) recovery period for property placed in service before 1999) (¶ 1247) (Code Sec. 168(b)(2)(D)).[80] This election, like the straight-line election above, is made separately for each property class placed in service during the tax year of the election. A taxpayer may also elect the MACRS ADS with respect to any class of property (¶ 1247).

3-, 5-, 7-, and 10-year property used in the trade or business of farming must be depreciated under the 150-percent declining balance method unless the taxpayer elected to deduct preproductive period expenditures, in which case the ADS must be used (Code Sec. 168(b)(2)(B)). Consequently, Tables 1-8, below, may not be used for such property.

Computation of Deduction Without Tables. The MACRS deduction on personal property is computed by first determining the rate of depreciation (dividing the number one by the recovery period).[81] This basic rate is multiplied by 1.5 or 2 for the 150-percent or 200-percent declining-balance method, as applicable, to determine the declining balance rate. The adjusted basis of the property is multiplied by the declining-balance rate and the half-year or mid-quarter convention (whichever is applicable) is applied in computing depreciation for the first year. The depreciation claimed in the first year is subtracted from the adjusted basis before applying the declining-balance rate in determining the depreciation deduction for the second year.

Under the MACRS straight-line method (used, for example, on real property or if ADS applies), a new applicable depreciation rate is determined for each tax year in the applicable recovery period. For any tax year, the applicable depreciation rate (in percentage terms) is determined by dividing one by the length of the applicable recovery period remaining as of the beginning of such tax year. The rate is applied to the unrecovered basis of the property in conjunction with the appropriate convention. If as of the beginning of the tax year the remaining recovery period is less than one year, the applicable depreciation rate under the straight-line method for that year is 100 percent.

References are to Standard Federal Tax Reports; Tax Research Consultant; and Practical Tax Explanations.

[76] ¶ 11,250; DEPR: 3,200; § 11,115

[77] ¶ 11,250; DEPR: 3,202; § 11,115

[78] ¶ 11,250; DEPR: 3,202; § 11,115

[79] ¶ 11,250; DEPR: 3,202; § 11,115

[80] ¶ 11,250; DEPR: 3,202.05; § 11,115

[81] ¶ 11,279.027; DEPR: 3,204.05; § 11,130

Example 1: A calendar-year taxpayer buys an item of five-year property in January ("Year 1") for $10,000. The taxpayer does not claim any Code Sec. 179 expense allowance or bonus depreciation. The 200-percent declining-balance method and half-year convention apply. Depreciation computed without the use of the IRS tables is determined as follows: the declining-balance depreciation rate is determined and compared with the straight-line rate. A switch is made to the straight-line rate in the year depreciation equals or exceeds that determined under the declining-balance method. The applicable rate is applied to the unrecovered basis. The 200-percent declining-balance depreciation rate is 40 percent (1 divided by 5 (recovery period) times 2). The straight-line rate (which changes each year) is 1 divided by the length of the applicable recovery period remaining as of the beginning of each tax year (after considering the applicable convention in determining how much of the applicable recovery period remains as of the beginning of the year). For Year 4, the straight-line rate is .40 (1 divided by 2.5), which is the same as the declining balance rate. For Year 5, the straight-line rate is .6667 (1 divided by 1.5). For Year 6, the straight-line rate is 100 percent because the remaining recovery period is less than one year.

Year	*Method*	*Rate*		*Unrecovered Basis*				*Depreciation*
1	DB	.40	×	$ 10,000 × .5 (half-yr. conv.)			. . . .	= $ 2,000
2	DB	.40	×	(10,000 – 2,000)	=	$8,000	. .	= 3,200
3	DB	.40	×	(8,000 – 3,200)	=	4,800	. .	= 1,920
4	DB	.40	×	(4,800 – 1,920)	=	2,880	. .	= 1,152
5	SL	.6667	×	(2,880 – 1,152)	=	1,728	. .	= 1,152
6	SL	1.000	×	(1,728 – 1,152)	=	576	. .	= 576
						0		
						Total	. .	$10,000

Rev. Proc. 87-57 provides a detailed discussion of computing MACRS without tables.

Computation of Deduction Using Tables. Instead of using the rules above, taxpayers may compute depreciation using MACRS depreciation tables that contain the annual percentage depreciation rates to be applied to the unadjusted basis of property in each tax year.[82] The tables incorporate the appropriate convention and a switch from the declining-balance method to the straight-line method in the year that the latter provides a depreciation allowance equal to, or larger than, the former. The tables may be used for any item of property that qualifies for MACRS.

Selected MACRS depreciation tables are reproduced below. A complete set of tables is at ¶ 164 of the STANDARD FEDERAL TAX REPORTER and at § 820 of the Practical Tax Explanations. Tables for the TAX RESEARCH CONSULTANT are located in the "Tax Rates and Tables" publication.

The CCH "Depreciation Toolkit" located on IntelliConnect in the "Federal Tax Practice Tools" node contains an MACRS depreciation calculator which computes depreciation schedules using the MACRS depreciation tables.

An MACRS depreciation table that is used to compute the annual depreciation allowance for any item of property generally must be used throughout the entire recovery period. However, a taxpayer may not continue to use a table if there are any adjustments to the basis of the property for reasons other than (1) depreciation allowances or (2) an addition or improvement to the property that is subject to depreciation as a separate item of property. The IRS MACRS depreciation tables may not be used in situations involving short tax years (¶ 1244).

Example 2: Depreciation on five-year property purchased by a calendar-year taxpayer in January of the current tax year at a cost of $10,000 is computed under the general MACRS 200-percent declining-balance method over a five-year recovery period using the half-year convention. No amount is expensed under Code Sec. 179 or claimed as a bonus depreciation deduction.

References are to Standard Federal Tax Reports; Tax Research Consultant; and Practical Tax Explanations.

[82] ¶ 164.01; DEPR: 3,204; § 11,130

If the depreciation tables provided by the IRS are used, depreciation is computed as follows: the applicable depreciation rate in Table 1 under the column for a five-year recovery period for the applicable recovery year is applied to the cost of the property.

Year	*Rate*	*Unadj. Basis*	*Depreciation*		*Basis*		
1	.20 ×	$ 10,000 =	$ 2,000	($10,000 –	$2,000)	=	$8,000
2	.32 ×	10,000 =	3,200	(8,000 –	3,200)	=	4,800
3	.192 ×	10,000 =	1,920	(4,800 –	1,920)	=	2,880
4	.1152 ×	10,000 =	1,152	(2,880 –	1,152)	=	1,728
5	.1152 ×	10,000 =	1,152	(1,728 –	1,152)	=	576
6	.0576 ×	10,000 =	576	(576 –	576)	=	0
		Total	$10,000				

Table 1. General Depreciation System
Applicable Depreciation Method: 200 or 150 Percent
Declining Balance Switching to Straight Line
Applicable Recovery Periods: 3, 5, 7, 10, 15, 20 years
Applicable Convention: Half-year

If the Recovery Year is:	and the Recovery Period is: 3-year	5-year	7-year	10-year	15-year	20-year
	the Depreciation Rate is:					
1	33.33	20.00	14.29	10.00	5.00	3.750
2	44.45	32.00	24.49	18.00	9.50	7.219
3	14.81	19.20	17.49	14.40	8.55	6.677
4	7.41	11.52	12.49	11.52	7.70	6.177
5		11.52	8.93	9.22	6.93	5.713
6		5.76	8.92	7.37	6.23	5.285
7			8.93	6.55	5.90	4.888
8			4.46	6.55	5.90	4.522
9				6.56	5.91	4.462
10				6.55	5.90	4.461
11				3.28	5.91	4.462
12					5.90	4.461
13					5.91	4.462
14					5.90	4.461
15					5.91	4.462
16					2.95	4.461
17						4.462
18						4.461
19						4.462
20						4.461
21						2.231

Table 2. General Depreciation System
Applicable Depreciation Method: 200 or 150 Percent
Declining Balance Switching to Straight Line
Applicable Recovery Periods: 3, 5, 7, 10, 15, 20 years
Applicable Convention: Mid-quarter (property placed in service in first quarter)

If the Recovery Year is:	and the Recovery Period is: 3-year	5-year	7-year	10-year	15-year	20-year
	the Depreciation Rate is:					
1	58.33	35.00	25.00	17.50	8.75	6.563
2	27.78	26.00	21.43	16.50	9.13	7.000
3	12.35	15.60	15.31	13.20	8.21	6.482
4	1.54	11.01	10.93	10.56	7.39	5.996
5		11.01	8.75	8.45	6.65	5.546
6		1.38	8.74	6.76	5.99	5.130
7			8.75	6.55	5.90	4.746
8			1.09	6.55	5.91	4.459
9				6.56	5.90	4.459
10				6.55	5.91	4.459
11				0.82	5.90	4.459
12					5.91	4.460
13					5.90	4.459
14					5.91	4.460
15					5.90	4.459
16					0.74	4.460
17						4.459
18						4.460
19						4.459
20						4.460
21						0.565

Table 3. General Depreciation System
Applicable Depreciation Method: 200 or 150 Percent
Declining Balance Switching to Straight Line
Applicable Recovery Periods: 3, 5, 7, 10, 15, 20 years
Applicable Convention: Mid-quarter (property placed in service in second quarter)

If the Recovery Year is:	and the Recovery Period is: 3-year	5-year	7-year	10-year	15-year	20-year
	the Depreciation Rate is:					
1	41.67	25.00	17.85	12.50	6.25	4.688
2	38.89	30.00	23.47	17.50	9.38	7.148
3	14.14	18.00	16.76	14.00	8.44	6.612
4	5.30	11.37	11.97	11.20	7.59	6.116
5		11.37	8.87	8.96	6.83	5.658
6		4.26	8.87	7.17	6.15	5.233
7			8.87	6.55	5.91	4.841
8			3.33	6.55	5.90	4.478
9				6.56	5.91	4.463
10				6.55	5.90	4.463
11				2.46	5.91	4.463
12					5.90	4.463
13					5.91	4.463
14					5.90	4.463
15					5.91	4.462
16					2.21	4.463
17						4.462
18						4.463
19						4.462
20						4.463
21						1.673

Table 4. General Depreciation System
Applicable Depreciation Method: 200 or 150 Percent
Declining Balance Switching to Straight Line
Applicable Recovery Periods: 3, 5, 7, 10, 15, 20 years
Applicable Convention: Mid-quarter (property placed in service in third quarter)

If the Recovery Year is:	and the Recovery Period is: 3-year	5-year	7-year	10-year	15-year	20-year
	the Depreciation Rate is:					
1	25.00	15.00	10.71	7.50	3.75	2.813
2	50.00	34.00	25.51	18.50	9.63	7.289
3	16.67	20.40	18.22	14.80	8.66	6.742
4	8.33	12.24	13.02	11.84	7.80	6.237
5		11.30	9.30	9.47	7.02	5.769
6		7.06	8.85	7.58	6.31	5.336
7			8.86	6.55	5.90	4.936
8			5.53	6.55	5.90	4.566
9				6.56	5.91	4.460
10				6.55	5.90	4.460
11				4.10	5.91	4.460
12					5.90	4.460
13					5.91	4.461
14					5.90	4.460
15					5.91	4.461
16					3.69	4.460
17						4.461
18						4.460
19						4.461
20						4.460
21						2.788

Table 5. General Depreciation System
Applicable Depreciation Method: 200 or 150 Percent
Declining Balance Switching to Straight Line
Applicable Recovery Periods: 3, 5, 7, 10, 15, 20 years
Applicable Convention: Mid-quarter (property placed in service in fourth quarter)

If the Recovery Year is:	and the Recovery Period is: 3-year	5-year	7-year	10-year	15-year	20-year
	the Depreciation Rate is:					
1	8.33	5.00	3.57	2.50	1.25	0.938
2	61.11	38.00	27.55	19.50	9.88	7.430
3	20.37	22.80	19.68	15.60	8.89	6.872
4	10.19	13.68	14.06	12.48	8.00	6.357
5		10.94	10.04	9.98	7.20	5.880
6		9.58	8.73	7.99	6.48	5.439
7			8.73	6.55	5.90	5.031
8			7.64	6.55	5.90	4.654
9				6.56	5.90	4.458
10				6.55	5.91	4.458
11				5.74	5.90	4.458
12					5.91	4.458
13					5.90	4.458
14					5.91	4.458
15					5.90	4.458
16					5.17	4.458
17						4.458
18						4.459
19						4.458
20						4.459
21						3.901

Table 6. General Depreciation System
Applicable Depreciation Method: Straight Line
Applicable Recovery Period: 27.5 years
Applicable Convention: Mid-month

If the Recovery Year is:	And the Month in the First Recovery Year the Property is Placed in Service is: 1	2	3	4	5	6	7	8	9	10	11	12
	the Depreciation Rate is:											
1	3.485	3.182	2.879	2.576	2.273	1.970	1.667	1.364	1.061	0.758	0.455	0.152
2	3.636	3.636	3.636	3.636	3.636	3.636	3.636	3.636	3.636	3.636	3.636	3.636
3	3.636	3.636	3.636	3.636	3.636	3.636	3.636	3.636	3.636	3.636	3.636	3.636
4	3.636	3.636	3.636	3.636	3.636	3.636	3.636	3.636	3.636	3.636	3.636	3.636
5	3.636	3.636	3.636	3.636	3.636	3.636	3.636	3.636	3.636	3.636	3.636	3.636
6	3.636	3.636	3.636	3.636	3.636	3.636	3.636	3.636	3.636	3.636	3.636	3.636
7	3.636	3.636	3.636	3.636	3.636	3.636	3.636	3.636	3.636	3.636	3.636	3.636
8	3.636	3.636	3.636	3.636	3.636	3.636	3.636	3.636	3.636	3.636	3.636	3.636
9	3.636	3.636	3.636	3.636	3.636	3.636	3.636	3.636	3.636	3.636	3.636	3.636
10	3.637	3.637	3.637	3.637	3.637	3.637	3.636	3.636	3.636	3.636	3.636	3.636
11	3.636	3.636	3.636	3.636	3.636	3.636	3.637	3.637	3.637	3.637	3.637	3.637
12	3.637	3.637	3.637	3.637	3.637	3.637	3.636	3.636	3.636	3.636	3.636	3.636
13	3.636	3.636	3.636	3.636	3.636	3.636	3.637	3.637	3.637	3.637	3.637	3.637
14	3.637	3.637	3.637	3.637	3.637	3.637	3.636	3.636	3.636	3.636	3.636	3.636
15	3.636	3.636	3.636	3.636	3.636	3.636	3.637	3.637	3.637	3.637	3.637	3.637
16	3.637	3.637	3.637	3.637	3.637	3.637	3.636	3.636	3.636	3.636	3.636	3.636
17	3.636	3.636	3.636	3.636	3.636	3.636	3.637	3.637	3.637	3.637	3.637	3.637
18	3.637	3.637	3.637	3.637	3.637	3.637	3.636	3.636	3.636	3.636	3.636	3.636
19	3.636	3.636	3.636	3.636	3.636	3.636	3.637	3.637	3.637	3.637	3.637	3.637
20	3.637	3.637	3.637	3.637	3.637	3.637	3.636	3.636	3.636	3.636	3.636	3.636
21	3.636	3.636	3.636	3.636	3.636	3.636	3.637	3.637	3.637	3.637	3.637	3.637
22	3.637	3.637	3.637	3.637	3.637	3.637	3.636	3.636	3.636	3.636	3.636	3.636
23	3.636	3.636	3.636	3.636	3.636	3.636	3.637	3.637	3.637	3.637	3.637	3.637
24	3.637	3.637	3.637	3.637	3.637	3.637	3.636	3.636	3.636	3.636	3.636	3.636
25	3.636	3.636	3.636	3.636	3.636	3.636	3.637	3.637	3.637	3.637	3.637	3.637
26	3.637	3.637	3.637	3.637	3.637	3.637	3.636	3.636	3.636	3.636	3.636	3.636
27	3.636	3.636	3.636	3.636	3.636	3.636	3.637	3.637	3.637	3.637	3.637	3.637
28	1.970	2.273	2.576	2.879	3.182	3.485	3.636	3.636	3.636	3.636	3.636	3.636
29	0.000	0.000	0.000	0.000	0.000	0.000	0.152	0.455	0.758	1.061	1.364	1.667

Table 7. General Depreciation System
Applicable Depreciation Method: Straight Line
Applicable Recovery Period: 31.5 years
Applicable Convention: Mid-month

If the Recovery Year is:	And the Month in the First Recovery Year the Property is Placed in Service is:											
	1	2	3	4	5	6	7	8	9	10	11	12
	the Depreciation Rate is:											
1	3.042	2.778	2.513	2.249	1.984	1.720	1.455	1.190	0.926	0.661	0.397	0.132
2	3.175	3.175	3.175	3.175	3.175	3.175	3.175	3.175	3.175	3.175	3.175	3.175
3	3.175	3.175	3.175	3.175	3.175	3.175	3.175	3.175	3.175	3.175	3.175	3.175
4	3.175	3.175	3.175	3.175	3.175	3.175	3.175	3.175	3.175	3.175	3.175	3.175
5	3.175	3.175	3.175	3.175	3.175	3.175	3.175	3.175	3.175	3.175	3.175	3.175
6	3.175	3.175	3.175	3.175	3.175	3.175	3.175	3.175	3.175	3.175	3.175	3.175
7	3.175	3.175	3.175	3.175	3.175	3.175	3.175	3.175	3.175	3.175	3.175	3.175
8	3.175	3.174	3.175	3.174	3.175	3.174	3.175	3.175	3.175	3.175	3.175	3.175
9	3.174	3.175	3.174	3.175	3.174	3.175	3.174	3.175	3.174	3.175	3.174	3.175
10	3.175	3.174	3.175	3.174	3.175	3.174	3.175	3.174	3.175	3.174	3.175	3.174
11	3.174	3.175	3.174	3.175	3.174	3.175	3.174	3.175	3.174	3.175	3.174	3.175
12	3.175	3.174	3.175	3.174	3.175	3.174	3.175	3.174	3.175	3.174	3.175	3.174
13	3.174	3.175	3.174	3.175	3.174	3.175	3.174	3.175	3.174	3.175	3.174	3.175
14	3.175	3.174	3.175	3.174	3.175	3.174	3.175	3.174	3.175	3.174	3.175	3.174
15	3.174	3.175	3.174	3.175	3.174	3.175	3.174	3.175	3.174	3.175	3.174	3.175
16	3.175	3.174	3.175	3.174	3.175	3.174	3.175	3.174	3.175	3.174	3.175	3.174
17	3.174	3.175	3.174	3.175	3.174	3.175	3.174	3.175	3.174	3.175	3.174	3.175
18	3.175	3.174	3.175	3.174	3.175	3.174	3.175	3.174	3.175	3.174	3.175	3.174
19	3.174	3.175	3.174	3.175	3.174	3.175	3.174	3.175	3.174	3.175	3.174	3.175
20	3.175	3.174	3.175	3.174	3.175	3.174	3.175	3.174	3.175	3.174	3.175	3.174
21	3.174	3.175	3.174	3.175	3.174	3.175	3.174	3.175	3.174	3.175	3.174	3.175
22	3.175	3.174	3.175	3.174	3.175	3.174	3.175	3.174	3.175	3.174	3.175	3.174
23	3.174	3.175	3.174	3.175	3.174	3.175	3.174	3.175	3.174	3.175	3.174	3.175
24	3.175	3.174	3.175	3.174	3.175	3.174	3.175	3.174	3.175	3.174	3.175	3.174
25	3.174	3.175	3.174	3.175	3.174	3.175	3.174	3.175	3.174	3.175	3.174	3.175
26	3.175	3.174	3.175	3.174	3.175	3.174	3.175	3.174	3.175	3.174	3.175	3.174
27	3.174	3.175	3.174	3.175	3.174	3.175	3.174	3.175	3.174	3.175	3.174	3.175
28	3.175	3.174	3.175	3.174	3.175	3.174	3.175	3.174	3.175	3.174	3.175	3.174
29	3.174	3.175	3.174	3.175	3.174	3.175	3.174	3.175	3.174	3.175	3.174	3.175
30	3.175	3.174	3.175	3.174	3.175	3.174	3.175	3.174	3.175	3.174	3.175	3.174
31	3.174	3.175	3.174	3.175	3.174	3.175	3.174	3.175	3.174	3.175	3.174	3.175
32	1.720	1.984	2.249	2.513	2.778	3.042	3.175	3.174	3.175	3.174	3.175	3.174
33	0.000	0.000	0.000	0.000	0.000	0.000	0.132	0.397	0.661	0.926	1.190	1.455

Table 7A. General Depreciation System
Applicable Depreciation Method: Straight-Line
Applicable Recovery Period: 39 years
Applicable Convention: Mid-month—taken from the IRS Pub. 946

If the Recovery Year is:	And the Month in the First Recovery Year the Property is Placed in Service is:											
	1	2	3	4	5	6	7	8	9	10	11	12
	the Depreciation Rate is:											
1	2.461	2.247	2.033	1.819	1.605	1.391	1.177	0.963	0.749	0.535	0.321	0.107
2—39	2.564	2.564	2.564	2.564	2.564	2.564	2.564	2.564	2.564	2.564	2.564	2.564
40	0.107	0.321	0.535	0.749	0.963	1.177	1.391	1.605	1.819	2.033	2.247	2.461

Table 7B. Alternative Depreciation System
Applicable Depreciation Method: Straight-Line
Applicable Recovery Period: 40 years
Applicable Convention: Mid-month

If the Recovery Year is:	and the Month in the First Recovery Year the Property is Placed in Service is:											
	1	2	3	4	5	6	7	8	9	10	11	12
	the Depreciation Rate is:											
1	2.396	2.188	1.979	1.771	1.563	1.354	1.146	0.938	0.729	0.521	0.313	0.104
2—40	2.500	2.500	2.500	2.500	2.500	2.500	2.500	2.500	2.500	2.500	2.500	2.500
41	0.104	0.312	0.521	0.729	0.937	1.146	1.354	1.562	1.771	1.979	2.187	2.396

Table 8. General and Alternative Depreciation Systems
Applicable Depreciation Method: Straight Line
Applicable Recovery Periods: 2.5 — 50 years
Applicable Convention: Half-year

If the Recovery Year is:	and the Recovery Period is:														
	2.5	3.0	3.5	4.0	4.5	5.0	5.5	6.0	6.5	7.0	7.5	8.0	8.5	9.0	9.5
	the Depreciation Rate is:														
1	20.00	16.67	14.29	12.50	11.11	10.00	9.09	8.33	7.69	7.14	6.67	6.25	5.88	5.56	5.26
2	40.00	33.33	28.57	25.00	22.22	20.00	18.18	16.67	15.39	14.29	13.33	12.50	11.77	11.11	10.53
3	40.00	33.33	28.57	25.00	22.22	20.00	18.18	16.67	15.38	14.29	13.33	12.50	11.76	11.11	10.53
4		16.67	28.57	25.00	22.23	20.00	18.18	16.67	15.39	14.28	13.33	12.50	11.77	11.11	10.53
5				12.50	22.22	20.00	18.19	16.66	15.38	14.29	13.34	12.50	11.76	11.11	10.52
6						10.00	18.18	16.67	15.39	14.28	13.33	12.50	11.77	11.11	10.53
7								8.33	15.38	14.29	13.34	12.50	11.76	11.11	10.52
8										7.14	13.33	12.50	11.77	11.11	10.53
9												6.25	11.76	11.11	10.52
10														5.56	10.53

If the Recovery Year is:	and the Recovery Period is:														
	10.0	10.5	11.0	11.5	12.0	12.5	13.0	13.5	14.0	14.5	15.0	15.5	16.0	16.5	17.0
	the Depreciation Rate is:														
1	5.00	4.76	4.55	4.35	4.17	4.00	3.85	3.70	3.57	3.45	3.33	3.23	3.13	3.03	2.94
2	10.00	9.52	9.09	8.70	8.33	8.00	7.69	7.41	7.14	6.90	6.67	6.45	6.25	6.06	5.88
3	10.00	9.52	9.09	8.70	8.33	8.00	7.69	7.41	7.14	6.90	6.67	6.45	6.25	6.06	5.88
4	10.00	9.53	9.09	8.69	8.33	8.00	7.69	7.41	7.14	6.90	6.67	6.45	6.25	6.06	5.88
5	10.00	9.52	9.09	8.70	8.33	8.00	7.69	7.41	7.14	6.90	6.67	6.45	6.25	6.06	5.88
6	10.00	9.53	9.09	8.69	8.33	8.00	7.69	7.41	7.14	6.89	6.67	6.45	6.25	6.06	5.88
7	10.00	9.52	9.09	8.70	8.34	8.00	7.69	7.41	7.14	6.90	6.67	6.45	6.25	6.06	5.88
8	10.00	9.53	9.09	8.69	8.33	8.00	7.69	7.41	7.15	6.89	6.66	6.45	6.25	6.06	5.88
9	10.00	9.52	9.09	8.70	8.34	8.00	7.69	7.41	7.14	6.90	6.67	6.45	6.25	6.06	5.88
10	10.00	9.53	9.09	8.69	8.33	8.00	7.70	7.40	7.15	6.89	6.66	6.45	6.25	6.06	5.88
11	5.00	9.52	9.09	8.70	8.34	8.00	7.69	7.41	7.14	6.90	6.67	6.45	6.25	6.06	5.89
12			4.55	8.69	8.33	8.00	7.70	7.40	7.15	6.89	6.66	6.45	6.25	6.06	5.88
13					4.17	8.00	7.69	7.41	7.14	6.90	6.67	6.45	6.25	6.06	5.89
14							3.85	7.40	7.15	6.89	6.66	6.46	6.25	6.06	5.88
15									3.57	6.90	6.67	6.45	6.25	6.06	5.89
16											3.33	6.46	6.25	6.06	5.88
17													3.12	6.07	5.89
18															2.94

If the Recovery Year is:	and the Recovery Period is:														
	17.5	18.0	18.5	19.0	19.5	20.0	20.5	21.0	21.5	22.0	22.5	23.0	23.5	24.0	24.5
	the Depreciation Rate is:														
1	2.86	2.78	2.70	2.63	2.56	2.500	2.439	2.381	2.326	2.273	2.222	2.174	2.128	2.083	2.041
2	5.71	5.56	5.41	5.26	5.13	5.000	4.878	4.762	4.651	4.545	4.444	4.348	4.255	4.167	4.082
3	5.71	5.56	5.41	5.26	5.13	5.000	4.878	4.762	4.651	4.545	4.444	4.348	4.255	4.167	4.082
4	5.71	5.55	5.41	5.26	5.13	5.000	4.878	4.762	4.651	4.545	4.445	4.348	4.255	4.167	4.082
5	5.72	5.56	5.40	5.26	5.13	5.000	4.878	4.762	4.651	4.546	4.444	4.348	4.255	4.167	4.082
6	5.71	5.55	5.41	5.26	5.13	5.000	4.878	4.762	4.651	4.545	4.445	4.348	4.255	4.167	4.082
7	5.72	5.56	5.40	5.26	5.13	5.000	4.878	4.762	4.651	4.546	4.444	4.348	4.255	4.167	4.082
8	5.71	5.55	5.41	5.26	5.13	5.000	4.878	4.762	4.651	4.545	4.445	4.318	4.255	4.167	4.082
9	5.72	5.56	5.40	5.27	5.13	5.000	4.878	4.762	4.651	4.546	4.444	4.348	4.255	4.167	4.081
10	5.71	5.55	5.41	5.26	5.13	5.000	4.878	4.762	4.651	4.545	4.445	4.348	4.255	4.167	4.082
11	5.72	5.56	5.40	5.27	5.13	5.000	4.878	4.762	4.651	4.546	4.444	4.348	4.256	4.166	4.081
12	5.71	5.55	5.41	5.26	5.13	5.000	4.878	4.762	4.651	4.545	4.445	4.348	4.255	4.167	4.082
13	5.72	5.56	5.40	5.27	5.13	5.000	4.878	4.762	4.651	4.546	4.444	4.348	4.256	4.166	4.081
14	5.71	5.55	5.41	5.26	5.13	5.000	4.878	4.762	4.651	4.545	4.445	4.348	4.255	4.167	4.082
15	5.72	5.56	5.40	5.27	5.13	5.000	4.878	4.762	4.651	4.546	4.444	4.348	4.256	4.166	4.081
16	5.71	5.55	5.41	5.26	5.12	5.000	4.878	4.762	4.651	4.545	4.445	4.348	4.255	4.167	4.082
17	5.72	5.56	5.40	5.27	5.13	5.000	4.878	4.762	4.652	4.546	4.444	4.347	4.256	4.166	4.081
18	5.71	5.55	5.41	5.26	5.12	5.000	4.878	4.762	4.651	4.545	4.445	4.348	4.255	4.167	4.082
19		2.78	5.40	5.27	5.13	5.000	4.878	4.761	4.652	4.546	4.444	4.347	4.256	4.166	4.081
20				2.63	5.12	5.000	4.879	4.762	4.651	4.545	4.445	4.348	4.255	4.167	4.082
21						2.500	4.878	4.761	4.652	4.546	4.444	4.347	4.256	4.166	4.081
22								2.381	4.651	4.545	4.445	4.348	4.255	4.167	4.082
23										2.273	4.444	4.347	4.256	4.166	4.081
24												2.174	4.255	4.167	4.082
25														2.083	4.081

If the Recovery Year is:	and the Recovery Period is:														
	25.0	25.5	26.0	26.5	27.0	27.5	28.0	28.5	29.0	29.5	30.0	30.5	31.0	31.5	32.0
	the Depreciation Rate is:														
1	2.000	1.961	1.923	1.887	1.852	1.818	1.786	1.754	1.724	1.695	1.667	1.639	1.613	1.587	1.563
2	4.000	3.922	3.846	3.774	3.704	3.636	3.571	3.509	3.448	3.390	3.333	3.279	3.226	3.175	3.125
3	4.000	3.922	3.846	3.774	3.704	3.636	3.571	3.509	3.448	3.390	3.333	3.279	3.226	3.175	3.125
4	4.000	3.922	3.846	3.774	3.704	3.636	3.571	3.509	3.448	3.390	3.333	3.279	3.226	3.175	3.125
5	4.000	3.922	3.846	3.774	3.704	3.636	3.571	3.509	3.448	3.390	3.333	3.279	3.226	3.175	3.125
6	4.000	3.921	3.846	3.774	3.704	3.636	3.571	3.509	3.448	3.390	3.333	3.279	3.226	3.175	3.125
7	4.000	3.922	3.846	3.773	3.704	3.636	3.572	3.509	3.448	3.390	3.333	3.279	3.226	3.175	3.125
8	4.000	3.921	3.846	3.774	3.704	3.636	3.571	3.509	3.448	3.390	3.333	3.279	3.226	3.175	3.125
9	4.000	3.922	3.846	3.773	3.704	3.637	3.572	3.509	3.448	3.390	3.333	3.279	3.226	3.175	3.125
10	4.000	3.921	3.846	3.774	3.704	3.636	3.571	3.509	3.448	3.390	3.333	3.279	3.226	3.174	3.125
11	4.000	3.922	3.846	3.773	3.704	3.637	3.572	3.509	3.448	3.390	3.333	3.279	3.226	3.175	3.125
12	4.000	3.921	3.846	3.774	3.704	3.636	3.571	3.509	3.448	3.390	3.333	3.279	3.226	3.174	3.125
13	4.000	3.922	3.846	3.773	3.703	3.637	3.572	3.509	3.448	3.390	3.334	3.279	3.226	3.175	3.125
14	4.000	3.921	3.846	3.773	3.704	3.636	3.571	3.509	3.448	3.390	3.333	3.279	3.226	3.174	3.125
15	4.000	3.922	3.846	3.774	3.703	3.637	3.572	3.509	3.449	3.390	3.334	3.278	3.226	3.175	3.125
16	4.000	3.921	3.846	3.773	3.704	3.636	3.571	3.509	3.448	3.390	3.333	3.279	3.226	3.174	3.125
17	4.000	3.922	3.846	3.774	3.703	3.637	3.572	3.509	3.449	3.390	3.334	3.278	3.226	3.175	3.125
18	4.000	3.921	3.846	3.773	3.704	3.636	3.571	3.508	3.448	3.390	3.333	3.279	3.226	3.174	3.125
19	4.000	3.922	3.846	3.774	3.703	3.637	3.572	3.509	3.449	3.390	3.334	3.278	3.226	3.175	3.125
20	4.000	3.921	3.847	3.773	3.704	3.636	3.571	3.508	3.448	3.390	3.333	3.279	3.226	3.174	3.125
21	4.000	3.922	3.846	3.774	3.703	3.637	3.572	3.509	3.449	3.389	3.334	3.278	3.225	3.175	3.125
22	4.000	3.921	3.847	3.773	3.704	3.636	3.571	3.508	3.448	3.390	3.333	3.279	3.226	3.174	3.125
23	4.000	3.922	3.846	3.774	3.703	3.637	3.572	3.509	3.449	3.389	3.334	3.278	3.225	3.175	3.125
24	4.000	3.921	3.847	3.773	3.704	3.636	3.571	3.508	3.448	3.390	3.333	3.279	3.226	3.174	3.125
25	4.000	3.922	3.846	3.774	3.703	3.637	3.572	3.509	3.449	3.389	3.334	3.278	3.225	3.175	3.125
26	2.000	3.921	3.847	3.773	3.704	3.636	3.571	3.508	3.448	3.390	3.333	3.279	3.226	3.174	3.125
27	. . . . .	. . . . .	1.923	3.774	3.703	3.637	3.572	3.509	3.449	3.389	3.334	3.278	3.225	3.175	3.125
28	. . . . .	. . . . .	. . . . .	. . . . .	1.852	3.636	3.571	3.508	3.448	3.390	3.333	3.279	3.226	3.174	3.125
29	. . . . .	. . . . .	. . . . .	. . . . .	. . . . .	. . . . .	1.786	3.509	3.449	3.389	3.334	3.278	3.225	3.175	3.125
30	. . . . .	. . . . .	. . . . .	. . . . .	. . . . .	. . . . .	. . . . .	. . . . .	1.724	3.390	3.333	3.279	3.226	3.174	3.125
31	. . . . .	. . . . .	. . . . .	. . . . .	. . . . .	. . . . .	. . . . .	. . . . .	. . . . .	. . . . .	1.667	3.278	3.225	3.175	3.125
32	. . . . .	. . . . .	. . . . .	. . . . .	. . . . .	. . . . .	. . . . .	. . . . .	. . . . .	. . . . .	. . . . .	. . . . .	1.613	3.174	3.125
33	. . . . .	. . . . .	. . . . .	. . . . .	. . . . .	. . . . .	. . . . .	. . . . .	. . . . .	. . . . .	. . . . .	. . . . .	. . . . .	. . . . .	1.562

If the Recovery Year is:	and the Recovery Period is:														
	32.5	33.0	33.5	34.0	34.5	35.0	35.5	36.0	36.5	37.0	37.5	38.0	38.5	39.0	39.5
	the Depreciation Rate is:														
1	.	1.538	1.515	1.493	1.471	1.449	1.429	1.408	1.389	1.370	1.351	1.333	1.316	1.299	1.282	1.266
2	.	3.077	3.030	2.985	2.941	2.899	2.857	2.817	2.778	2.740	2.703	2.667	2.632	2.597	2.564	2.532
3	.	3.077	3.030	2.985	2.941	2.899	2.857	2.817	2.778	2.740	2.703	2.667	2.632	2.597	2.564	2.532
4	.	3.077	3.030	2.985	2.941	2.899	2.857	2.817	2.778	2.740	2.703	2.667	2.632	2.597	2.564	2.532
5	.	3.077	3.030	2.985	2.941	2.899	2.857	2.817	2.778	2.740	2.703	2.667	2.632	2.597	2.564	2.532
6	.	3.077	3.030	2.985	2.941	2.899	2.857	2.817	2.778	2.740	2.703	2.667	2.632	2.597	2.564	2.532
7	.	3.077	3.030	2.985	2.941	2.898	2.857	2.817	2.778	2.740	2.703	2.667	2.632	2.597	2.564	2.532
8	.	3.077	3.030	2.985	2.941	2.899	2.857	2.817	2.778	2.740	2.703	2.667	2.631	2.597	2.564	2.532
9	.	3.077	3.030	2.985	2.941	2.898	2.857	2.817	2.778	2.740	2.703	2.667	2.632	2.597	2.564	2.532
10	.	3.077	3.030	2.985	2.941	2.899	2.857	2.817	2.778	2.740	2.703	2.667	2.631	2.598	2.564	2.532
11	.	3.077	3.030	2.985	2.941	2.898	2.857	2.817	2.778	2.740	2.703	2.667	2.632	2.597	2.564	2.532
12	.	3.077	3.030	2.985	2.941	2.899	2.857	2.817	2.778	2.740	2.703	2.667	2.631	2.598	2.564	2.532
13	.	3.077	3.030	2.985	2.941	2.898	2.857	2.817	2.778	2.740	2.703	2.667	2.632	2.597	2.564	2.532
14	.	3.077	3.030	2.985	2.941	2.899	2.857	2.817	2.778	2.740	2.703	2.667	2.631	2.598	2.564	2.531
15	.	3.077	3.031	2.985	2.941	2.898	2.857	2.817	2.778	2.740	2.703	2.666	2.632	2.597	2.564	2.532
16	.	3.077	3.030	2.985	2.941	2.899	2.857	2.817	2.778	2.740	2.703	2.667	2.631	2.598	2.564	2.531
17	.	3.077	3.031	2.985	2.941	2.898	2.857	2.817	2.778	2.740	2.703	2.666	2.632	2.597	2.564	2.532
18	.	3.077	3.030	2.985	2.841	2.899	2.857	2.817	2.778	2.740	2.702	2.667	2.631	2.598	2.564	2.531
19	.	3.077	3.031	2.985	2.941	2.898	2.857	2.817	2.778	2.739	2.703	2.666	2.632	2.597	2.564	2.532
20	.	3.077	3.030	2.985	2.941	2.898	2.857	2.817	2.778	2.740	2.702	2.667	2.631	2.598	2.564	2.531
21	.	3.077	3.031	2.985	2.941	2.899	2.857	2.817	2.778	2.739	2.703	2.666	2.632	2.597	2.564	2.532
22	.	3.077	3.030	2.985	2.941	2.898	2.857	2.817	2.777	2.740	2.702	2.667	2.631	2.598	2.564	2.531
23	.	3.077	3.031	2.985	2.941	2.899	2.857	2.817	2.778	2.739	2.703	2.666	2.632	2.597	2.564	2.532
24	.	3.077	3.030	2.985	2.941	2.898	2.857	2.817	2.777	2.740	2.702	2.667	2.631	2.598	2.564	2.531
25	.	3.077	3.031	2.985	2.942	2.899	2.857	2.817	2.778	2.739	2.703	2.666	2.632	2.597	2.564	2.532
26	.	3.077	3.030	2.985	2.941	2.898	2.857	2.817	2.777	2.740	2.702	2.667	2.631	2.598	2.564	2.531
27	.	3.077	3.031	2.985	2.942	2.899	2.857	2.817	2.778	2.739	2.703	2.666	2.632	2.597	2.564	2.532
28	.	3.077	3.030	2.985	2.941	2.898	2.858	2.817	2.777	2.740	2.702	2.667	2.631	2.598	2.564	2.531
29	.	3.077	3.031	2.985	2.942	2.899	2.857	2.817	2.778	2.739	2.703	2.666	2.632	2.597	2.564	2.532
30	.	3.077	3.030	2.985	2.941	2.898	2.858	2.817	2.777	2.740	2.702	2.667	2.631	2.598	2.564	2.531
31	.	3.076	3.031	2.986	2.942	2.899	2.857	2.817	2.778	2.739	2.703	2.666	2.632	2.597	2.564	2.532
32	.	3.077	3.030	2.985	2.941	2.898	2.858	2.816	2.777	2.740	2.702	2.667	2.631	2.598	2.564	2.531
33	.	3.076	3.031	2.986	2.942	2.899	2.857	2.817	2.778	2.739	2.703	2.666	2.632	2.597	2.565	2.532
34	. . . . .		1.515	2.985	2.941	2.898	2.858	2.816	2.777	2.740	2.702	2.667	2.631	2.598	2.564	2.531
35	. . . . .				1.471	2.899	2.857	2.817	2.778	2.739	2.703	2.666	2.632	2.597	2.565	2.532
36	. . . . .						1.429	2.816	2.777	2.740	2.702	2.667	2.631	2.598	2.564	2.531
37	. . . . .								1.389	2.739	2.703	2.666	2.632	2.597	2.565	2.532
38	. . . . .										1.351	2.667	2.631	2.598	2.564	2.531
39	. . . . .												1.316	2.597	2.565	2.532
40	. . . . .														1.282	2.531

If the Recovery Year is:	and the Recovery Period is:														
	40.0	40.5	41.0	41.5	42.0	42.5	43.0	43.5	44.0	44.5	45.0	45.5	46.0	46.5	47.0
	the Depreciation Rate is:														
1	1.250	1.235	1.220	1.205	1.190	1.176	1.163	1.149	1.136	1.124	1.111	1.099	1.087	1.075	1.064
2	2.500	2.469	2.439	2.410	2.381	2.353	2.326	2.299	2.273	2.247	2.222	2.198	2.174	2.151	2.128
3	2.500	2.469	2.439	2.410	2.381	2.353	2.326	2.299	2.273	2.247	2.222	2.198	2.174	2.151	2.128
4	2.500	2.469	2.439	2.410	2.381	2.353	2.326	2.299	2.273	2.247	2.222	2.198	2.174	2.151	2.128
5	2.500	2.469	2.439	2.410	2.381	2.353	2.326	2.299	2.273	2.247	2.222	2.198	2.174	2.151	2.128
6	2.500	2.469	2.439	2.410	2.381	2.353	2.326	2.299	2.273	2.247	2.222	2.198	2.174	2.151	2.128
7	2.500	2.469	2.439	2.410	2.381	2.353	2.326	2.299	2.273	2.247	2.222	2.198	2.174	2.150	2.128
8	2.500	2.469	2.439	2.410	2.381	2.353	2.326	2.299	2.273	2.247	2.222	2.198	2.174	2.151	2.128
9	2.500	2.469	2.439	2.410	2.381	2.353	2.325	2.299	2.273	2.247	2.222	2.198	2.174	2.150	2.128
10	2.500	2.469	2.439	2.410	2.381	2.353	2.326	2.299	2.273	2.247	2.222	2.198	2.174	2.151	2.128
11	2.500	2.469	2.439	2.410	2.381	2.353	2.325	2.299	2.273	2.247	2.222	2.198	2.174	2.150	2.128
12	2.500	2.469	2.439	2.410	2.381	2.353	2.326	2.299	2.273	2.247	2.222	2.198	2.174	2.151	2.128
13	2.500	2.469	2.439	2.410	2.381	2.353	2.325	2.299	2.273	2.247	2.222	2.198	2.174	2.150	2.128
14	2.500	2.469	2.439	2.409	2.381	2.353	2.326	2.299	2.273	2.247	2.222	2.198	2.174	2.151	2.128
15	2.500	2.469	2.439	2.410	2.381	2.353	2.325	2.299	2.273	2.247	2.222	2.198	2.174	2.150	2.128
16	2.500	2.469	2.439	2.409	2.381	2.353	2.326	2.299	2.273	2.247	2.222	2.198	2.174	2.151	2.128
17	2.500	2.469	2.439	2.410	2.381	2.353	2.325	2.299	2.273	2.247	2.222	2.198	2.174	2.150	2.127
18	2.500	2.469	2.439	2.409	2.381	2.353	2.326	2.299	2.273	2.247	2.222	2.198	2.174	2.151	2.128
19	2.500	2.469	2.439	2.410	2.381	2.353	2.325	2.299	2.273	2.247	2.222	2.198	2.174	2.150	2.127
20	2.500	2.469	2.439	2.409	2.381	2.353	2.326	2.299	2.273	2.247	2.222	2.198	2.174	2.151	2.128
21	2.500	2.469	2.439	2.410	2.381	2.353	2.325	2.299	2.273	2.247	2.222	2.198	2.174	2.150	2.127
22	2.500	2.469	2.439	2.409	2.381	2.353	2.326	2.299	2.273	2.247	2.222	2.198	2.174	2.151	2.128
23	2.500	2.469	2.439	2.410	2.381	2.353	2.325	2.299	2.272	2.247	2.222	2.198	2.174	2.150	2.127
24	2.500	2.469	2.439	2.409	2.381	2.353	2.326	2.299	2.273	2.247	2.222	2.198	2.174	2.151	2.128
25	2.500	2.469	2.439	2.410	2.381	2.353	2.325	2.299	2.272	2.247	2.222	2.198	2.174	2.150	2.127
26	2.500	2.469	2.439	2.409	2.381	2.353	2.326	2.299	2.273	2.247	2.222	2.198	2.174	2.151	2.128
27	2.500	2.469	2.439	2.410	2.381	2.353	2.325	2.299	2.272	2.247	2.223	2.198	2.174	2.150	2.127
28	2.500	2.469	2.439	2.409	2.381	2.353	2.326	2.299	2.273	2.247	2.222	2.198	2.174	2.151	2.128
29	2.500	2.469	2.439	2.410	2.381	2.353	2.325	2.299	2.272	2.247	2.223	2.198	2.174	2.150	2.127
30	2.500	2.469	2.439	2.409	2.381	2.353	2.326	2.299	2.273	2.248	2.222	2.197	2.174	2.151	2.128
31	2.500	2.469	2.439	2.410	2.381	2.353	2.325	2.299	2.272	2.247	2.223	2.198	2.174	2.150	2.127
32	2.500	2.470	2.439	2.409	2.381	2.353	2.326	2.299	2.273	2.248	2.222	2.197	2.174	2.151	2.128
33	2.500	2.469	2.439	2.410	2.381	2.353	2.325	2.298	2.272	2.247	2.223	2.198	2.174	2.150	2.127
34	2.500	2.470	2.439	2.409	2.381	2.353	2.326	2.299	2.273	2.248	2.222	2.197	2.174	2.151	2.128
35	2.500	2.469	2.439	2.410	2.381	2.353	2.325	2.298	2.272	2.247	2.223	2.198	2.174	2.150	2.127
36	2.500	2.470	2.139	2.409	2.381	2.353	2.326	2.299	2.273	2.248	2.222	2.197	2.174	2.151	2.128
37	2.500	2.469	2.439	2.410	2.381	2.353	2.325	2.298	2.272	2.247	2.223	2.198	2.174	2.150	2.127
38	2.500	2.470	2.439	2.409	2.381	2.353	2.326	2.299	2.273	2.248	2.222	2.197	2.174	2.151	2.128
39	2.500	2.469	2.439	2.410	2.381	2.353	2.325	2.298	2.272	2.247	2.223	2.198	2.174	2.150	2.127
40	2.500	2.470	2.439	2.409	2.381	2.353	2.326	2.299	2.273	2.248	2.222	2.197	2.173	2.151	2.128
41	1.250	2.469	2.439	2.410	2.380	2.352	2.325	2.298	2.272	2.247	2.223	2.198	2.174	2.150	2.127
42	. . . . .	. . . . .	1.220	2.409	2.381	2.353	2.326	2.299	2.273	2.248	2.222	2.197	2.173	2.151	2.128
43	. . . . .	. . . . .	. . . . .	. . . . .	1.190	2.352	2.325	2.298	2.272	2.247	2.223	2.198	2.174	2.150	2.127
44	. . . . .	. . . . .	. . . . .	. . . . .	. . . . .	. . . . .	1.163	2.299	2.273	2.248	2.222	2.197	2.173	2.151	2.128
45	. . . . .	. . . . .	. . . . .	. . . . .	. . . . .	. . . . .	. . . . .	. . . . .	1.136	2.247	2.223	2.198	2.174	2.150	2.127
46	. . . . .	. . . . .	. . . . .	. . . . .	. . . . .	. . . . .	. . . . .	. . . . .	. . . . .	. . . . .	1.111	2.197	2.173	2.151	2.128
47	. . . . .	. . . . .	. . . . .	. . . . .	. . . . .	. . . . .	. . . . .	. . . . .	. . . . .	. . . . .	. . . . .	. . . . .	1.087	2.150	2.127
48	. . . . .	. . . . .	. . . . .	. . . . .	. . . . .	. . . . .	. . . . .	. . . . .	. . . . .	. . . . .	. . . . .	. . . . .	. . . . .	. . . . .	1.064

If the Recovery Year is:	and the Recovery Period is:					
	47.5	48.0	48.5	49.0	49.5	50.0
	the Depreciation Rate is:					
1	1.053	1.042	1.031	1.020	1.010	1.000
2	2.105	2.083	2.062	2.041	2.020	2.000
3	2.105	2.083	2.062	2.041	2.020	2.000
4	2.105	2.083	2.062	2.041	2.020	2.000
5	2.105	2.083	2.062	2.041	2.020	2.000
6	2.105	2.083	2.062	2.041	2.020	2.000
7	2.105	2.083	2.062	2.041	2.020	2.000
8	2.105	2.083	2.062	2.041	2.020	2.000
9	2.105	2.083	2.062	2.041	2.020	2.000
10	2.105	2.083	2.062	2.041	2.020	2.000
11	2.105	2.083	2.062	2.041	2.020	2.000
12	2.105	2.083	2.062	2.041	2.020	2.000
13	2.105	2.083	2.062	2.041	2.020	2.000
14	2.105	2.083	2.062	2.041	2.020	2.000
15	2.105	2.083	2.062	2.041	2.020	2.000
16	2.105	2.083	2.062	2.041	2.020	2.000
17	2.105	2.083	2.062	2.041	2.020	2.000
18	2.105	2.083	2.062	2.041	2.020	2.000
19	2.105	2.084	2.062	2.041	2.020	2.000
20	2.105	2.083	2.062	2.041	2.020	2.000
21	2.105	2.084	2.062	2.041	2.020	2.000
22	2.105	2.083	2.062	2.041	2.020	2.000
23	2.105	2.084	2.062	2.041	2.020	2.000
24	2.105	2.083	2.062	2.041	2.020	2.000
25	2.105	2.084	2.062	2.041	2.020	2.000
26	2.106	2.083	2.062	2.041	2.020	2.000
27	2.105	2.084	2.062	2.041	2.020	2.000
28	2.106	2.083	2.062	2.041	2.020	2.000
29	2.105	2.084	2.062	2.041	2.020	2.000
30	2.106	2.083	2.062	2.041	2.020	2.000
31	2.105	2.084	2.062	2.041	2.021	2.000
32	2.106	2.083	2.062	2.041	2.020	2.000
33	2.105	2.084	2.062	2.041	2.021	2.000
34	2.106	2.083	2.062	2.040	2.020	2.000
35	2.105	2.084	2.062	2.041	2.021	2.000
36	2.106	2.083	2.062	2.040	2.020	2.000
37	2.105	2.084	2.061	2.041	2.021	2.000
38	2.106	2.083	2.062	2.040	2.020	2.000
39	2.105	2.084	2.061	2.041	2.021	2.000
40	2.106	2.083	2.062	2.040	2.020	2.000
41	2.105	2.084	2.061	2.041	2.021	2.000
42	2.106	2.083	2.062	2.040	2.020	2.000
43	2.105	2.084	2.061	2.041	2.021	2.000
44	2.106	2.083	2.062	2.040	2.020	2.000
45	2.105	2.084	2.061	2.041	2.021	2.000
46	2.106	2.083	2.062	2.040	2.020	2.000
47	2.105	2.084	2.061	2.041	2.021	2.000
48	2.106	2.083	2.062	2.040	2.020	2.000
49		1.042	2.061	2.041	2.021	2.000
50				1.020	2.020	2.000
51						1.000

1244. MACRS Short Tax Years. Special rules are provided for determining deductions under the Modified Accelerated Cost Recovery System (MACRS) when: (1) property is placed in service in a short tax year (any tax year with less than 12 months); (2) a short tax year occurs during the recovery period; or (3) property is disposed of before the end of the recovery period (Rev. Proc. 89-15). In any of these situations, refinements are made to the use of the applicable conventions and the MACRS depreciation tables at ¶ 1243 may *not* be used.[83]

The mid-month convention is applied without regard to the length of the tax year. For example if residential rental property is placed in service in the first month of a six-month tax year, 5½ months depreciation is claimed.

Under the half-year convention, property placed in service or disposed of in a short tax year is deemed placed in service or disposed on the midpoint of the short tax year, which always falls on either the first day or the midpoint of the month.

Under the mid-quarter convention, property is deemed placed in service or disposed on the midpoint of the quarter, which always falls on either the first day or the midpoint of a month, in the short tax year that it is placed in service or disposed.

Depreciation for the first recovery year in the recovery period is computed by multiplying the basis in the property by the applicable depreciation rate. The depreciation allowance allocable to the first tax year that includes a portion of the first recovery year is derived by multiplying the depreciation for the first recovery year by a fraction. The numerator is the number of months (including fractions of months) the property is deemed to be in service during the tax year under the applicable convention, and the denominator is 12.

Taxpayers may use either an allocation or a simplified method to correlate a depreciation allowance between recovery years and tax years after the first tax year in the recovery period.

1245. Applicable MACRS Conventions. Specified averaging conventions apply to depreciation computations made under the Modified Accelerated Cost Recovery System (MACRS) (Code Sec. 168(d)).[84] The recovery period begins on the date the property is placed in service under the applicable convention. The depreciation table percentages take into account the applicable convention in the first and last year of the regular recovery period. However, if property is disposed of prior to the end of the regular recovery period, the result obtained by using the table percentage for the year of disposition must be adjusted to take into account the applicable convention.

No depreciation deduction is allowed if MACRS property is placed in service and disposed of in the same tax year (Reg. § 1.168(d)-1(b)(3)(ii) and (d); Reg. § 1.168(i)-4(c); IRS Pub. 946).

Half-Year Convention. Under the half-year convention, which applies to property to which the mid-quarter convention does not apply and which is not residential rental or nonresidential real property, an asset is treated as placed in service or disposed of on the midpoint of the tax year. Thus, one-half of a full year's depreciation is allowed in the tax year in which the asset is placed in service regardless of the date that the asset is placed in service.

A half-year of depreciation is allowed in the tax year in which the recovery period ends and in a tax year in which a disposition occurs, except that no depreciation may be claimed if the disposition occurs in the same tax year that the asset was placed in service.[85] The applicable table percentage for the year of disposition does not take the half-year convention into account unless the disposition falls in the tax year in which the recovery period ends; therefore, only one-half of the depreciation as computed using the applicable table percentage is allowed in a tax year other than the tax year in which the recovery period ends.

References are to Standard Federal Tax Reports; Tax Research Consultant; and Practical Tax Explanations.

[83] ¶ 11,279.053; DEPR: 3,202, DEPR: 3,350, DEPR: 3,252; § 11,130

[84] ¶ 11,250; DEPR: 3,252; § 11,125

[85] ¶ 11,279.037; DEPR: 3,252; § 11,125

Example 1: Five-year property with a depreciable basis of $1,000 and subject to the half-year convention is placed in service in 2014 by a calendar year taxpayer. Assume that the straight-line method is elected and the half-year convention applies. The recovery period begins on July 1, 2014, and ends five years later on June 30, 2019. The recovery (depreciation) period extends over 6 tax years. One-half of a full year's depreciation is allowed in 2014 and in 2019 under the half-year convention. Assume the asset is sold in 2016. Using Table 8 at ¶ 1243, 2014 depreciation is $100 ($1,000 × 10% (first-year table percentage which reflects half-year convention allowing depreciation from July 1 through December 31, 2014); 2015 depreciation is $200 ($1,000 × 20% second-year table percentage); and 2016 depreciation is $100 ($1,000 × 20% third-year table percentage × 50% to reflect half-year convention in year of disposition). If the asset was not sold in 2016, the depreciation deduction for 2019 is $100 ($1,000 × 10% sixth-year table percentage which reflects half-year convention allowing depreciation from January 1, 2019, through June 30, 2019). $100 of depreciation would also be allowed if the asset was sold in 2019 since, under the half-year convention, the asset is deemed sold on June 30, 2019, at the end of the recovery period.

Mid-Month Convention. A mid-month convention applies to residential rental property, including low-income housing, and nonresidential real property. Property is deemed placed in service or disposed of on the midpoint of the month. The deduction is based on the number of months the property was in service. Thus, one-half month's depreciation is allowed for the month the property is placed in service, as well as for the month of a disposition that occurs before the end of the recovery period. No depreciation is allowed, however, if a building is placed in service and disposed of in the same tax year.

Example 2: A commercial building costing $100,000 is purchased by a calendar-year taxpayer in February 2015 and sold in August 2016. Using Table 7A at ¶ 1243, 2015 depreciation is $2,247 ($100,000 × 2.247% (first-year percentage for property placed in service in second month of tax year)) and 2016 depreciation is $1,603 ($100,000 × 2.564% (second-year percentage for property placed in service in second month) × 7.5/12 to reflect 7.5 months in service in 2016 (January through mid-August) under the mid-month convention).

Mid-Quarter Convention. Under the mid-quarter convention, all property placed in service or disposed of during any quarter of a tax year is treated as placed in service at the midpoint of the quarter (Code Sec. 168(d)(3); Reg. § 1.168(d)-1).[86] Depreciation under the mid-quarter convention may be determined using Tables 2-5 at ¶ 1243.

The mid-quarter convention applies to all property, other than nonresidential real property and residential rental property, if more than 40 percent of the aggregate bases of the property is placed in service during the last three months of the tax year. Property placed in service and disposed of within the same tax year is disregarded for purposes of the 40-percent test since depreciation may not be claimed on such property.

The aggregate basis of property placed in service in the last three months of the tax year must be computed regardless of the length of the tax year. Thus, if a short tax year consists of three months or less, the mid-quarter convention applies regardless of when the depreciable property is placed in service during the tax year.

The bonus depreciation deduction (¶ 1237) does not reduce the aggregate basis of property taken into account for purposes of determining whether the mid-quarter convention applies. However, any amount properly expensed under Code Sec. 179 (¶ 1208) does reduce aggregate basis. Thus, a taxpayer may be able to avoid the mid-quarter convention (if desired) by allocating the Code Sec. 179 deduction to property placed in service in the last quarter. Also, the mid-quarter convention does not operate to reduce the deduction otherwise allowable under Code Sec. 179 or for bonus depreciation.

References are to Standard Federal Tax Reports; Tax Research Consultant; and Practical Tax Explanations.

[86] ¶ 11,260; DEPR: 3,252.15; § 11,125

Example 3: A calendar-year taxpayer places $100 of used five-year property in service in the first quarter of 2016 and $100 of new 10-year property in service in the fourth quarter. The taxpayer claims a 50% bonus depreciation allowance on the 10-year property. The mid-quarter convention applies to the five-year property and to the 10-year property because 50% of the aggregate adjusted basis of the property placed in service in 2016 (without regard to the bonus depreciation allowance) was placed in service in the fourth quarter. If the taxpayer did not claim bonus depreciation on the 10-year property and expensed the entire basis under section 179, the half-year convention would apply to the five-year property placed in service in the first quarter.

For purposes of the 40-percent test, depreciable basis does not include adjustments resulting from transfers of property between members of the same affiliated group filing a consolidated return.

If the MACRS deduction for property subject to the mid-quarter convention is computed without tables, depreciation for the first year is determined by computing the depreciation for the full tax year and then multiplying it by the following percentages for the quarter of the tax year the property is placed in service: first quarter, 87.5%; second quarter, 62.5%; third quarter, 37.5%; and fourth quarter, 12.5%. In the year of disposition (whether or not the table percentages are used) the deduction for a full year is multiplied by the following percentages for the quarter in which the asset is disposed of: first quarter, 12.5%; second quarter, 37.5%; third quarter, 62.5%, and fourth quarter 87.5%.

1247. MACRS Alternative Depreciation System (ADS). The Modified Accelerated Cost Recovery System (MACRS) alternative depreciation system (ADS) must be used for (1) tangible property used outside the United States, (2) tax-exempt use property, (3) tax-exempt bond-financed property, (4) property imported from a foreign country for which an Executive Order is in effect because the country maintains trade restrictions or engages in other discriminatory acts, and (5) property for which an ADS election has been made (Code Sec. 168(g)).[87] Mandatory ADS property does not qualify for bonus depreciation (¶ 1237).

Under ADS, the deduction is computed by applying the straight-line method, the applicable convention and the applicable longer recovery period (12 years for personal property with no class life, 40 years for real property, 50 years for railroad grading and tunnel bores, and the class life for all other property) for the respective class of property (Code Sec. 168(g)(2)(C)).[88] ADS is also used to compute the earnings and profits of a foreign or domestic corporation. The allowable depreciation deductions for passenger automobiles and other types of listed property used 50 percent or less in business are also determined under this method (¶ 1211 and ¶ 1214).

Electing ADS. In lieu of the regular MACRS deduction, taxpayers may irrevocably elect to apply ADS to any class of property for any tax year (Code Sec. 168(g)(7)).[89] An ADS election applies to all property in the MACRS class placed in service during the tax year. For example, an ADS election for five-year property applies to all five-year property placed in service in the tax year of the election. For residential rental property and nonresidential real property, the election is made on a property-by-property basis. Property for which ADS is elected may qualify for bonus depreciation (¶ 1237).

1248. Special Transferee Rules for Depreciation. A transferee in certain corporate and partnership transactions is treated as the transferor and must use the latter's recovery period and method in computing the deduction under the Modified Accelerated Cost Recovery System (MACRS) for the portion of the transferee's basis that does not exceed the transferor's adjusted basis in the property (Code Sec. 168(i)(7)).[90] This rule applies to nonrecognition transfers under Code Sec. 332 (subsidiary liquidations) (¶ 2261); transfers to a controlled corporation (¶ 1731); transfers related to certain reorganizations (¶ 2209); contributions to a partnership (¶ 443); certain partnership

References are to Standard Federal Tax Reports; Tax Research Consultant; and Practical Tax Explanations.

[87] ¶ 11,250; DEPR: 3,456; § 11,135

[88] ¶ 11,250; DEPR: 3,450, DEPR: 3,458; § 11,135

[89] ¶ 11,250; DEPR: 3,460; § 11,135

[90] ¶ 11,250; DEPR: 3,306.05; § 11,150

distributions (¶ 453); and transactions between members of the same affiliated group during any tax year for which the group files a consolidated return. It does not apply to transactions relating to the sale or exchange of 50 percent or more of the total interest in a partnership's capital and profits within a 12-month period (Code Sec. 708(b)(1)(B)).

1249. Recapture Upon Disposition of Depreciable Property. See ¶ 1779.

1250. Depreciable Property in Like-Kind Exchanges and Involuntary Conversions. The exchanged basis (i.e., carryover basis) of property under the Modified Accelerated Cost Recovery System (MACRS) acquired in a like-kind exchange or involuntary conversion for other MACRS property is depreciated by applying the following rules (Reg. § 1.168(i)-6).[91]

(1) If the replacement MACRS property has the same or a shorter recovery period and the same or a more accelerated depreciation method than the relinquished MACRS property, the exchanged (carryover) basis is depreciated over the remaining recovery period of, and using the depreciation method and convention of, the relinquished MACRS property.

(2) If the recovery period of the replacement MACRS property is longer than that of the relinquished MACRS property, the exchanged basis is depreciated over the remainder of the recovery period that would have applied to the replacement MACRS property if the replacement MACRS property had originally been placed in service when the relinquished MACRS property was placed in service by the acquiring taxpayer.

(3) If the depreciation method of the replacement MACRS property is less accelerated than that of the relinquished MACRS property, the exchanged basis is depreciated beginning in the year of replacement using the less accelerated depreciation method of the replacement MACRS property that would have applied to the replacement MACRS property if the replacement MACRS property had originally been placed in service when the relinquished MACRS property was placed in service by the acquiring taxpayer.

The excess basis of the replacement property (i.e., the noncarryover basis usually attributable to additional cash paid for the replacement property) is separately depreciated as if originally acquired in the year of replacement.

These rules are effective for like-kind exchanges and involuntary conversions in which the time of disposition and replacement both occur after February 27, 2004. A taxpayer, however, may apply the regulations retroactively (Reg. § 1.168(i)-6(k)). A taxpayer may also elect not to apply the regulations to a post-effective-date exchange or conversion and, instead, depreciate the entire basis of the acquired property as a single depreciable asset beginning in the tax year of replacement (Reg. § 1.168(i)-6(i) and (j)).

Bonus depreciation may be claimed on the entire basis of qualifying acquired property (¶ 1237) (Reg. § 1.168(k)-1(f)(5)). However, only the excess basis (noncarryover basis) may qualify for expensing under Code Sec. 179 even if the taxpayer elects not to apply the regulations (Reg. § 1.168(i)-6(g) and (i)).

Accelerated Cost Recovery System (ACRS)

1252. Pre-1987 ACRS in General. The Accelerated Cost Recovery System (ACRS) must be used to compute the depreciation deduction for most tangible depreciable property placed in service after 1980 and before 1987 (Code Sec. 168, prior to 1987).[92] Cost recovery methods and periods are the same for both new and used property, and salvage value is disregarded in computing ACRS allowances. Post-1980 depreciation on tangible assets first placed in service before 1981 is computed using the method elected by the taxpayer when the property was placed in service (including the Class Life ADR depreciation system (¶ 1284) and other methods of depreciation discussed at ¶ 1216).

References are to Standard Federal Tax Reports; Tax Research Consultant; and Practical Tax Explanations.

[91] ¶ 11,276K; DEPR: 3,306.30; § 18,055

[92] ¶ 11,258.01; DEPR: 3,054; § 11,001

Under ACRS, the cost of eligible property is recovered over a 3-year, 5-year, 10-year, 15-year, 18-year, or 19-year period, depending on the type of property. ACRS applies to recovery property, as defined at ¶ 1255. The deduction is determined by applying the statutory table percentage for the appropriate class of property to its unadjusted basis. The unadjusted basis of property under ACRS is the basis of the property as determined for purposes of computing gain or loss, unadjusted for depreciation, amortization or depletion. It does not include that portion of the basis that is covered by an election to amortize (¶ 1287) or to expense the cost of Code Sec. 179 property (¶ 1208) (Code Sec. 168(d)(1), prior to 1987).[93]

For personal ACRS recovery property placed in service after 1980 and before 1987, one-half year's depreciation is allowed in the year that it is placed in service, regardless of how long it is held. No deduction is allowed in the year personal recovery property is disposed of. Special prorations by month (using a mid-month convention) are provided for real recovery property (¶ 1261).

Straight-Line Election. An election to recover costs by using a straight-line method over the regular recovery period or a longer recovery period was also available under ACRS and was made on the taxpayer's return for the year in which the property was placed in service (Code Sec. 168(f)(4), prior to 1987).[94]

1255. ACRS Recovery Property. For purposes of the Accelerated Cost Recovery System (ACRS), recovery property is tangible depreciable property that is placed in service after 1980 and before 1987. It does not include property that is covered by an election to compute depreciation on a method not based on a depreciation period (unit-of-production method, income forecast method, etc.), public utility property for which the normalization method of accounting is not used, intangible assets such as patents and copyrights (¶ 1201), property covered by an election to amortize, or motion picture films and videotapes (Code Sec. 168(c) and (e), prior to 1987).[95] For purposes of determining an asset's recovery property class, recovery property is defined as either Code Sec. 1245 class property or Code Sec. 1250 class property.

Code Sec. 1245 class property includes tangible section 1245 property, as defined at ¶ 1785, other than elevators and escalators, and certain rapidly amortized realty. Code Sec. 1250 class property includes tangible section 1250 property, as defined at ¶ 1786, and elevators and escalators.

1258. ACRS Personal Property. Under the Accelerated Cost Recovery System (ACRS), the statutory percentage for personal property placed in service after 1980 and before 1987 is determined using prescribed percentage tables based on the type of property (3-year, 5-year, 10-year or 15-year). These table percentages are not reproduced because ACRS personal property should generally be fully depreciated at this time, but they appear in Prop. Reg. § 1.168-2. No recovery deduction is generally allowed in the year of disposition of ACRS personal property.

1261. ACRS Real Property. Under the Accelerated Cost Recovery System (ACRS), unadjusted basis is recovered over a period of 19 years for real property placed in service after May 8, 1985, and before 1987. For real property placed in service after March 15, 1984, and before May 9, 1985, unadjusted basis is recovered over a period of 18 years. A 15-year recovery period applies to real property placed in service after 1980 and before March 16, 1984, and to low-income housing.[96]

In computing the ACRS deduction, a full-month convention is used for real recovery property placed in service before March 16, 1984, and for low-income housing, and a mid-month convention is used for real recovery property (other than low-income housing) placed in service after March 15, 1984. Under the full-month convention, real property placed in service at any time during a particular month is treated as placed in service on the first day of such month, thereby permitting a full month's cost recovery

References are to Standard Federal Tax Reports; Tax Research Consultant; and Practical Tax Explanations.

[93] ¶ 11,258.041; DEPR: 3,104; § 11,001

[94] ¶ 11,258.031; DEPR: 3,404.15; § 11,001

[95] ¶ 11,258.01, ¶ 11,258.045; DEPR: 3,058.20; § 11,001

[96] ¶ 11,258.025; DEPR: 3,158; § 11,001

for the month the property is placed in service. No cost recovery is permitted for the month of disposition. Under the mid-month convention, real property placed in service at any time during a particular month is treated as placed in service in the middle of such month, thereby permitting one-half month's cost recovery for the month the property is placed in service. For a disposition of real property during a month before the end of a recovery period, one-half month's cost recovery is allowed for the month of disposition.

In using the following tables, there are separate rate schedules depending upon the month in the first tax year that the property is placed in service. Further, where real property is sold before the end of the recovery period, the ACRS deduction for the year of disposition should reflect only the months of the year during which the property was in service. For a short tax year, appropriate adjustments must also be made to the table amounts (¶ 1270). A complete set of ACRS depreciation tables is provided in IRS Publication 534.

Table I *18-Year Real Property (placed in service after June 22, 1984) for Which Alternate ACRS Method Over a 35-Year Period Is Elected*

	Month Placed in Service				
Year	1-2	3-6	7-10	11	12
1st	3%	2%	1%	0.4%	0.1%
2-30th	3%	3%	3%	3%	3%
31st	2%	2%	2%	2.6%	2.9%
32-35th	2%	2%	2%	2%	2%
36th		1%	2%	2%	2%

Table II *18-Year Real Property (placed in service after March 15 and before June 23, 1984) 15-Year Real Property and Low-Income Housing (placed in service before May 9, 1985) for Which Alternate ACRS Method Over a 35-Year Period Is Elected*

	Month Placed in Service		
Year	1-2	3-6	7-12
1st	3%	2%	1%
2-30th	3%	3%	3%
31-35th	2%	2%	2%
36th		1%	2%

Table III *Low-Income Housing (placed in service after May 8, 1985) for Which Alternate ACRS Method Over a 35-Year Period Is Elected*

	Month Placed in Service											
Year	1	2	3	4	5	6	7	8	9	10	11	12
1st	2.9%	2.6%	2.4%	2.1%	1.9%	1.7%	1.4%	1.2%	1.0%	0.7%	0.5%	0.2%
2-20th	2.9%	2.9%	2.9%	2.9%	2.9%	2.9%	2.9%	2.9%	2.9%	2.9%	2.9%	2.9%
21-35th	2.8%	2.8%	2.8%	2.8%	2.8%	2.8%	2.8%	2.8%	2.8%	2.8%	2.8%	2.8%
36th		0.3%	0.5%	0.8%	1.0%	1.2%	1.5%	1.7%	1.9%	2.2%	2.4%	2.7%

Table IV *19-Year Real Property for Which Alternate ACRS Method Over a 35-Year Period Is Elected*

	Month Placed in Service											
Year	1	2	3	4	5	6	7	8	9	10	11	12
1st	2.7%	2.5%	2.3%	2.0%	1.8%	1.5%	1.3%	1.1%	0.8%	0.6%	0.4%	0.1%
2-20th	2.9%	2.9%	2.9%	2.9%	2.9%	2.9%	2.9%	2.9%	2.9%	2.9%	2.9%	2.9%
21-35th	2.8%	2.8%	2.8%	2.8%	2.8%	2.8%	2.8%	2.8%	2.8%	2.8%	2.8%	2.8%
36th	0.2%	0.4%	0.6%	0.9%	1.1%	1.4%	1.6%	1.8%	2.1%	2.3%	2.5%	2.8%

Table V *18-Year Real Property (placed in service after June 22, 1984) 19-Year Real Property for Which Alternate ACRS Method Over a 45-Year Period Is Elected*

	Month Placed in Service											
Year	1	2	3	4	5	6	7	8	9	10	11	12
1st	2.1%	1.9%	1.8%	1.6%	1.4%	1.2%	1%	0.8%	0.6%	0.5%	0.3%	0.1%
2-11th	2.3%	2.3%	2.3%	2.3%	2.3%	2.3%	2.3%	2.3%	2.3%	2.3%	2.3%	2.3%
12-45th	2.2%	2.2%	2.2%	2.2%	2.2%	2.2%	2.2%	2.2%	2.2%	2.2%	2.2%	2.2%
46th	0.1%	0.3%	0.4%	0.6%	0.8%	1%	1.2%	1.4%	1.6%	1.7%	1.9%	2.1%

Table VI *18-Year Real Property (placed in service after March 15 and before June 23, 1984) 15-Year Real Property and Low-Income Housing (placed in service after December 31, 1980) for Which Alternate ACRS Method Over a 45-Year Period Is Elected*

	Month Placed in Service											
Year	1	2	3	4	5	6	7	8	9	10	11	12
1st	2.3%	2%	1.9%	1.7%	1.5%	1.3%	1.2%	0.9%	0.7%	0.6%	0.4%	0.2%
2-10th	2.3%	2.3%	2.3%	2.3%	2.3%	2.3%	2.3%	2.3%	2.3%	2.3%	2.3%	2.3%
11-45th	2.2%	2.2%	2.2%	2.2%	2.2%	2.2%	2.2%	2.2%	2.2%	2.2%	2.2%	2.2%
46th		0.3%	0.4%	0.6%	0.8%	1%	1.1%	1.4%	1.6%	1.7%	1.9%	2.1%

1264. ACRS: Predominant Use Outside the United States. Under the Accelerated Cost Recovery System (ACRS), the unadjusted basis of personal property used outside the United States is recovered over a period equal to the Asset Depreciation Range (ADR) class life for that property as of January 1, 1981 (¶ 1284).[97] No recovery deduction is generally allowed in the year of disposition of personal recovery property used predominantly outside the United States. The unadjusted basis of real property and low income housing used predominantly outside the United States is recovered over a period of 35 years. For real recovery property (other than low-income housing) placed in service after March 15, 1984, a mid-month convention is used. There are separate rate schedules depending on the month in the first tax year that the property is placed in service.

1267. ACRS: Components of Sec. 1250 Class Property. Under the Accelerated Cost Recovery System (ACRS), structural components of section 1250 class property may not be depreciated separately. Composite depreciation is required on the entire building, unless the components qualify for amortization elections (Code Sec. 168(f)(1), prior to 1987).[98] Components that are considered personal property can be separately depreciated under the cost segregation rules (¶ 1240).

Substantial Improvements. A substantial improvement to a building was treated as a separate building rather than as one or more components. The taxpayer could use the regular ACRS deduction or elect the straight-line ACRS deduction for the improvement over the regular or a longer recovery period regardless of the ACRS method that is used for the rest of the building.

Components and improvements placed in service after 1986 are depreciated using the Modified Accelerated Cost Recovery System (MACRS) even if the building is not MACRS property (¶ 1240).

1270. ACRS: Short Tax Years. For a tax year of less than 12 months, the amount of the deduction under the Accelerated Cost Recovery System (ACRS) is the amount that bears the same relationship to the amount of the deduction that would have been allowable if the recovery year were not a short tax year as the number of months and partial months in the short year bears to 12 (Code Sec. 168(f)(5), prior to 1987).[99] For real property and low-income housing placed in service or disposed of in a short tax year, this rule generally does not apply; instead, the deduction is based on the number of

References are to Standard Federal Tax Reports; Tax Research Consultant; and Practical Tax Explanations.

[97] ¶ 162.01; DEPR: 6,106; § 11,001

[98] ¶ 11,258.05; DEPR: 3,206.45; § 11,001

[99] ¶ 11,258.055; DEPR: 3,354; § 11,001

months the property is in service during the year, regardless of the length of the tax year and regardless of the recovery period and method used.

Any unrecovered allowance (the difference between the recovery allowance properly allowable for the short tax year and the recovery allowance that would have been allowable if it were not a short tax year) is claimed in the tax year following the last year in the recovery period (Prop. Reg. § 1.168-2(f)(3)).[100] However, the unrecovered allowance claimed as a recovery allowance in the tax year following the last year of the recovery period may not exceed the amount of the recovery allowance permitted for the last year of the recovery period, assuming that such year consists of 12 months. Any remainder is carried forward until exhausted.

Class Life ADR System

1282. Post-1980 Depreciation Under ADR. If the Asset Depreciation Range (ADR) System was elected for tangible assets first placed in service after 1970 and before 1981, post-1980 depreciation on such assets must be computed under the ADR System.[101]

1284. ADR in General. Under the Asset Depreciation Range (ADR) System, all tangible assets were placed in specific classes. A class life or "asset guideline period" was given for each class of assets in Reg. § 1.167(a)-11.[102] Each class of assets other than land improvements and buildings was also given a range of years or "asset depreciation range" that was about 20 percent above and below the class life. For details on the ADR system, see ¶ 11,029.01 and following of the STANDARD FEDERAL TAX REPORTER, and DEPR: 15,800 of the TAX RESEARCH CONSULTANT.

Deductions for Refiners

1285. Deduction for EPA Sulfur Regulation Compliance Costs of Small Refiners. Small business refiners may elect to immediately deduct as an expense up to 75 percent of the qualified capital costs paid or incurred during the tax year for the purpose of complying with the Highway Diesel Fuel Sulfur Control Requirements of the Environmental Protection Agency (EPA) (Code Sec. 179B).[103] Qualified costs must be paid or incurred with respect to any facility of a small business refiner during the period beginning on January 1, 2003, and ending on the earlier of the date that is one year after the date on which the taxpayer must comply with the applicable EPA regulations or December 31, 2009 (Code Sec. 45H(c)). Election guidance is provided in Temp. Reg. § 1.179B-1T(d).

1285A. Expensing Election for New or Expanded Refineries. A taxpayer may elect to expense 50 percent of the cost of qualified refinery property placed in service after August 8, 2005, and before January 1, 2014 (Code Sec. 179C; Reg. § 1.179C-1).[104] The property must be placed in service before January 1, 2010, if its construction is not subject to a written binding contract entered into after June 14, 2005, and before January 1, 2010, or, in the case of self-constructed property, construction did not begin after June 14, 2005, and before January 1, 2010. The original use of the refinery property must commence with the taxpayer. An improvement to an existing refinery can qualify if the improvement increases production capacity by specified levels. This election does not apply to property placed in service after December 31, 2013.

References are to Standard Federal Tax Reports; Tax Research Consultant; and Practical Tax Explanations.

[100] ¶ 11,252; DEPR: 3,354; § 11,001

[101] ¶ 11,029.01; DEPR: 15,800; § 11,001

[102] ¶ 11,026; DEPR: 15,812; § 11,001

[103] ¶ 12,134; BUSEXP: 18,908

[104] ¶ 12,137, ¶ 12,137A; BUSEXP: 18,900; § 10,245

Deduction for Energy Efficiency Improvements

1286. Deduction for Energy Efficiency Improvements to Depreciable Buildings. A taxpayer may deduct the cost of certain energy efficiency improvements installed on or in a depreciable building located in the United States, and placed in service after December 31, 2005, and before January 1, 2017 (Code Sec. 179D, as amended by the Protecting Americans from Tax Hikes (PATH) Act of 2015 (P.L. 114-113); Notice 2006-52, as clarified by Notice 2008-40; Notice 2012-26, modifying Notice 2008-40).[105] The deduction applies to energy efficient commercial building property, which is depreciable property installed as part of a building's (1) interior lighting systems, (2) heating, cooling, ventilation, and hot water systems, or (3) envelope as part of a certified plan to reduce the total annual energy and power costs of these systems by at least 50 percent in comparison to a reference building that meets specified minimum standards. The deduction is limited to the lesser of the cost of the qualifying property reduced by the aggregate amount deducted in any prior tax year, or the product of $1.80 and the total square footage of the building reduced by the aggregate amount deducted in any prior tax year.

A taxpayer may also claim a partial deduction for the costs of property that meets energy savings targets set by the IRS in Notice 2006-52, as modified by Notice 2012-26. The deduction is determined by substituting $.60 for $1.80.

For property placed in service on or after March 12, 2012, the taxpayer may use the following energy savings percentages to determine if a partial deduction is available: (1) building envelope—10 percent; heating, cooling, ventilation, and hot water systems—15 percent; and interior lighting systems—25 percent; or (2) building envelope—10 percent; heating, cooling, ventilation, and hot water systems—20 percent; and interior lighting systems—20 percent.

The deduction is generally claimed by the building's owner. However, the person who is primarily responsible for designing a public building may claim the deduction. The deduction reduces the depreciable basis of the building and is treated as a depreciation deduction for section 1245 recapture purposes (Code Sec. 1245(a)(3)(C)).

The Department of Energy maintains a list of the software that must be used to calculate power consumption and energy costs for purposes of certifying the required energy savings necessary to claim the deduction (Notice 2008-40). The certification is not attached to the taxpayer's return but must be retained as part of the taxpayer's books and records. The deduction is claimed on the "Other deductions" line of the taxpayer's return. There is no special form for computing the deduction.

Allowance for Amortization

1287. Property Subject to Amortization. Amortization is the recovery of certain capital expenditures, that are not ordinarily deductible, in a manner that is similar to straight-line depreciation. That portion of the basis of property that is recovered through amortization deductions may not also be depreciated.

Pollution Control Facilities. Taxpayers may elect to amortize over a 60-month period the cost of certified pollution control facilities added to or used in connection with a plant in operation before 1976. The amortization deduction is available only for the portion of the facility's basis attributable to the first 15 years of its recovery period if it has a recovery period under the Modified Accelerated Cost Recovery System (MACRS) in excess of 15 years. The remaining basis is depreciable. An air pollution control facility placed in service after April 11, 2005, in connection with a coal-fired plant placed in operation after 1975 qualifies for an 84-month amortization period (Code Sec. 169). The 60-month amortization period continues to apply to an air pollution facility placed in service after April 11, 2005, in connection with a coal-fired plant placed in operation before 1976 (Code Sec. 169).[106]

References are to Standard Federal Tax Reports; Tax Research Consultant; and Practical Tax Explanations.

[105] ¶ 12,138, ¶ 12,138D.20; BUSEXP: 18,950; § 10,250

[106] ¶ 11,502; DEPR: 21,150; § 11,501

Architectural and Transportation Barriers. Business taxpayers can elect to deduct up to $15,000 of the costs of removing certain architectural and transportation barriers for handicapped or elderly persons in the year paid or incurred instead of capitalizing and depreciating such costs (Code Sec. 190).[107]

Reforestation Expenditures. A taxpayer (other than a trust) may elect to expense up to $10,000 of qualified reforestation expenditures each tax year for each qualified timber property. Any taxpayer, including a trust or estate, may elect to amortize over 84 months amounts for which a current deduction is not elected (Code Sec. 194).[108] Election guidance is provided in Notice 2006-47.

Start-Up and Organizational Costs. See ¶ 904.

Oil and Gas Geological and Geophysical Expenditures. Geological and geophysical (G&G) expenditures paid or incurred in connection with oil and gas exploration or development in the United States must be amortized ratably over a 24-month period beginning on the mid-point of the tax year that the expenses were paid or incurred. If a property or project is abandoned or retired during the 24-month amortization period, any remaining basis must continue to be amortized (Code Sec. 167(h)).[109] Major integrated oil companies, however, must ratably amortize any G&G costs over five years (Code Sec. 167(h)(5)).

1288. Amortization of Section 197 Intangibles. The capitalized cost of goodwill and most other intangibles used in a trade or business or for the production of income are ratably amortized over a 15-year period generally beginning in the month of acquisition (Code Sec. 197).[110] Intangibles that are amortizable under this provision are referred to as "section 197 intangibles."

The following intangibles are section 197 intangibles: (1) goodwill, going concern value, and covenants not to compete entered into in connection with the acquisition of a trade or business (¶ 1743); (2) workforce in place; (3) information base; (4) a patent, copyright, formula, design, or similar item; (5) any customer-based intangible; (6) any supplier-based intangible; (7) any license, permit, or other right granted by a governmental unit or agency; and (8) any franchise, trademark, or trade name (Code Sec. 197(d)).[111]

Self-created intangibles are generally not amortized under Code Sec. 197 unless they are created in connection with the acquisition of a trade or business. Exceptions apply to government-granted licenses, permits, and rights, covenants not to compete entered into in connection with the purchase of a business, and franchises, trademarks, and trade names (Code Sec. 197(c)(2)).[112] However, certain self-created intangibles without an ascertainable useful life may be amortized over 15 years under Reg. § 1.167(a)-3(b) (¶ 1288A).

The following intangibles are specifically excluded from the definition of a section 197 intangible: (1) interests in a corporation, partnership, trust, or estate; (2) interests under certain financial contracts; (3) interests in land; (4) computer software not acquired in connection with the purchase of a business, or that is readily available for purchase by the general public, is subject to a nonexclusive license, and has not been substantially modified (¶ 980); (5) certain separately acquired rights and interests, including an interest in a patent or copyright or an interest in a film, sound recording, videotape, book, or similar property; (6) interests under existing leases of tangible property; (7) interests under existing indebtedness; (8) sports franchises acquired on or before October 22, 2004; (9) residential mortgage servicing rights not acquired in connection with the acquisition of a business; and (10) professional fees and transaction costs incurred in a corporate organization or reorganization (Code Sec. 197(e)).[113]

References are to Standard Federal Tax Reports; Tax Research Consultant; and Practical Tax Explanations.

[107] ¶ 12,260; BUSEXP: 9,102.35; § 10,220

[108] ¶ 12,330; FARM: 24,100; § 11,505

[109] ¶ 11,002; FARM: 21,176; § 11,550

[110] ¶ 12,450; DEPR: 21,050; § 11,401

[111] ¶ 12,450; DEPR: 21,052; § 11,405

[112] ¶ 12,450; DEPR: 21,052.60; § 11,415

[113] ¶ 12,450; DEPR: 21,054; § 11,410

No loss may be claimed when an amortizable section 197 intangible is disposed of if any other section 197 intangibles acquired in the same transaction are retained. The bases of the retained section 197 intangibles are increased by the amount of the unrecognized loss (Code Sec. 197(f)).[114]

1288A. 15-Year Safe-Harbor Amortization for Certain Self-Created Intangibles. A taxpayer is permitted to amortize certain self-created intangibles that do not have readily ascertainable useful lives over a 15-year period using the straight-line method and no salvage value (Reg. § 1.167(a)-3(b); Rev. Proc. 2006-12, as modified by Rev. Proc. 2006-37).[115] For example, amounts paid to acquire memberships or privileges of indefinite duration, such as a trade association membership, are covered by this safe harbor.

A taxpayer may use the 15-year amortization period on any intangible other than: (1) any intangible acquired from another person; (2) created financial interests; (3) any intangible that has a useful life that can be estimated with reasonable accuracy; or (4) an intangible asset for which an amortization period or useful life is specifically prescribed or proscribed by the Code, regulations, or published IRS guidance. In addition, amounts paid to facilitate an acquisition of a trade or business, a change in the capital structure of a business entity, and certain other similar transactions described in Reg. § 1.263(a)-5 do not qualify. The 15-year amortization period is extended to 25 years for an intangible benefit described in Reg. § 1.263(a)-4(d)(8). These are intangibles created by transferring ownership of real property to another person or by making a monetary contribution for the acquisition or improvement of real property owned by another person. However, see Rev. Rul. 2002-9, which requires developers to allocate the cost of impact fees to the basis of the buildings constructed.

What Is Depletion?

1289. Deduction for Depletion. A deduction for depletion is allowed in determining the taxable income from natural resources. The deduction is similar to depreciation in that it allows the taxpayer to recover the cost of an asset over the resource's productive life. Depletion is the exhaustion of natural resources, such as mines, wells, and timberlands, as a result of production. The right to a depletion allowance is based upon the taxpayer's economic interest in the property (Reg. § 1.611-1(b)(i)).[116] An economic interest exists if the taxpayer (1) has acquired by investment any interest in minerals in place or in standing timber, and (2) looks to the income from the extraction of the minerals or severance of the timber for a return on investment.

The basic method of computing depletion is cost depletion (Code Sec. 612).[117] The deduction is allowed on the adjusted basis of the property (Reg. § 1.612-1).[118] The part of the cost or other adjusted basis of the property that is allocable to the depletable reserves is divided by the number of units (tons, barrels, etc.) that is estimated to be in the deposit. The quotient is the cost depletion per unit. This amount, multiplied by the number of units extracted and sold during the year, determines the cost depletion deductible for the year. Each year the cost basis of the property is reduced, but not below zero, by the amount of depletion deducted for that year, whether cost or percentage depletion was used. The remaining basis is used in computing cost depletion for the next year.

An alternative method of computing depletion, known as percentage depletion, may be used for almost all depletable property other than timber (Reg. § 1.611-1(a)(1)).[119] Under this method, the depletion deduction is equal to a flat percentage of *gross income* from the property. The percentage depletion deduction may not exceed 50 percent (100 percent in the case of oil or gas properties) of the *taxable income* from the property, computed without regard to the depletion allowance or the qualified domestic production activities deduction under Code Sec. 199. See ¶ 1294 for special rules concerning

References are to Standard Federal Tax Reports; Tax Research Consultant; and Practical Tax Explanations.

[114] ¶ 12,450; DEPR: 21,056.05; § 11,425

[115] ¶ 11,008, ¶ 11,009.135; BUSEXP: 9,104.20; § 11,415

[116] ¶ 23,922; FARM: 15,052; § 11,610

[117] ¶ 23,940, ¶ 23,942; FARM: 15,100; § 11,615

[118] ¶ 23,941; FARM: 15,106; § 11,615

[119] ¶ 23,922; FARM: 24,054; § 11,620

independent producers and royalty owners. In computing taxable income, deductible mining expenses must be decreased by the amount of section 1245 gains allocable to the property (Code Sec. 613(a)).[120] The taxpayer must use cost depletion if it results in a greater deduction (Reg. § 1.613-1).[121]

Ordinarily, the lease of a mineral property requires the lessee to make an advance payment, known as a bonus or advance royalty. In such a case, the lessor's cost depletion allowance must be allocated between the advance lump-sum payment and the royalties received during the period of extraction (Reg. § 1.612-3).[122] Unlike bonuses or advance royalties, "shut-in" oil payments and delay rentals are not depletable (*F.I. Johnson*, CA-5, 61-1 USTC ¶ 9307).[123]

Coal and iron ore royalties retained upon the disposition of ore that was generally held for more than one year before mining are eligible for percentage depletion for any tax year in which the maximum rate of tax imposed on net capital gain equals or exceeds the maximum rate for ordinary income (Code Sec. 631(c)).[124]

Depletion is subject to recapture as ordinary income upon the sale or other disposition of an oil, gas, geothermal, or other mineral property at a gain (Code Sec. 1254).[125] Recapture is limited to the amount by which the depletion deduction reduced the adjusted basis of the disposed property.

Mineral Production Payments

1291. Mineral Production Payments. A mineral production payment is treated as a loan by the owner of the production payment to the owner of the mineral property (Code Sec. 636).[126] Thus, a carved-out mineral production payment—created when the owner of a mineral property sells or carves out a portion of the future production with payment secured by an interest in the minerals—is treated as a mortgage loan on the mineral property rather than as an economic interest in the property. All the income from the property is taxed to the seller (owner of the working interest) and is subject to depletion by him. The owner of the production payment does not get depletion.

When the owner of a mineral interest sells the working interest, a retained production payment is treated as a purchase money mortgage loan and not as an economic interest in the mineral property. Accordingly, all the income from the property is taxed to the purchaser and is subject to depletion by the purchaser. The seller who retains the production payment is not entitled to depletion.

Percentage Depletion

1294. Oil and Gas Production. A 22-percent depletion rate is allowed for oil and gas production in the case of regulated natural gas and natural gas sold under a fixed contract (but not certain casinghead gas contracts); a 10-percent rate applies to geopressurized methane gas wells (Code Sec. 613A(b)).[127]

For independent producers and royalty owners, a 15-percent depletion rate applies to an average daily production of 1,000 barrels of oil and six million cubic feet of gas (Code Sec. 613A(c)).[128] The percentage depletion deduction is generally limited to the lesser of 65 percent of the *taxable income* before the depletion allowance (Code Sec. 613A(d)(1))[129] or 100 percent of the *taxable income from the property* before the depletion allowance (¶ 1289). For purposes of the 65-percent limit, taxable income is computed without regard to any net operating loss carryback, capital loss carryback, or qualified domestic production activities deduction under Code Sec. 199. Any portion of a depletion

References are to Standard Federal Tax Reports; Tax Research Consultant; and Practical Tax Explanations.

[120] ¶ 23,960; FARM: 15,308; § 11,620

[121] ¶ 23,961; FARM: 15,100; § 11,620

[122] ¶ 23,946; FARM: 15,116; § 11,615

[123] ¶ 23,963.60; FARM: 15,252; § 11,615

[124] ¶ 24,150; FARM: 18,350; § 11,625

[125] ¶ 31,060; FARM: 21,200; § 16,710.05

[126] ¶ 24,170; FARM: 18,204; § 11,610

[127] ¶ 23,980; FARM: 15,202; § 11,625

[128] ¶ 23,980; FARM: 15,206; § 11,625

[129] ¶ 23,980; FARM: 15,218; § 11,625

allowance disallowed under the 65-percent limit may be carried over. Percentage depletion is also denied for lease bonuses, advance royalty payments, or other amounts payable without regard to actual production from an oil, gas or geothermal property (¶ 1296) (Code Secs. 613(e)(3) and 613A(d)(5)).[130]

The 100-percent taxable income limit on percentage depletion deductions for oil and gas properties is suspended for marginal properties for tax years (1) beginning after December 31, 1997, and before January 1, 2008, or (2) beginning after December 31, 2008, and before January 1, 2012 (Code Sec. 613A(c)(6)(H)).[131] Thus, the limitation is not suspended for tax years beginning after 2011, but is suspended for tax years beginning in 2009, 2010, and 2011.

The 15-percent depletion rate for marginal oil or gas production properties held by independent producers or royalty owners increases by one percent (up to a maximum 25-percent rate) for each whole dollar that the reference price for crude oil for the preceding calendar year is less than $20 per barrel (Code Sec. 613A(c)(6)).[132] The allowance for depletion is computed using the increased rate with respect to the portion of the taxpayer's average daily marginal production of domestic crude oil and natural gas that does not exceed the taxpayer's depletable quantities of those products. An election may be made to apply this rule to the pro rata portion of marginal production. The applicable percentage for marginal production for tax years beginning in 2001 through 2016 is 15 percent (Notice 2016-45).

1296. Geothermal Deposits. Geothermal deposits (geothermal reservoirs consisting of natural heat that is stored in rocks or in an aqueous liquid or vapor, whether or not under pressure) are eligible for a 15-percent depletion allowance (Code Sec. 613(e)).[133]

1298. Coal or Other Minerals. Percentage depletion is allowed at the following percentages of gross income from the property (Code Sec. 613(b)):[134]

(a) 22%—sulphur and uranium; and, if from deposits in the United States, anorthosite, clay, laterite, and nephelite syenite (to the extent that alumina and aluminum compounds are extracted therefrom), asbestos, bauxite, celestite, chromite, corundum, fluorspar, graphite, ilmenite, kyanite, mica, olivine, quartz crystals (radio grade), rutile, block steatite talc, and zircon, and ores of the following metals: antimony, beryllium, bismuth, cadmium, cobalt, columbium, lead lithium, manganese, mercury, molybdenum, nickel, platinum and platinum group metals, tantalum, thorium, tin, titanium, tungsten, vanadium and zinc.

(b) 15%—if from deposits in the United States, gold, silver, copper, iron ore, and oil shale (except shale described in (e) below).

(c) 14%—metal mines (other than metals from deposits in the United States to which the 22-percent rate in (a) applies), rock asphalt, and vermiculite; if (a) above and (e) and (f) below do not apply, ball clay, bentonite, china clay, sagger clay, and clay used or sold for use for purposes dependent on its refractory properties.

(d) 10%—asbestos from deposits outside the United States, brucite, coal, lignite, perlite, sodium chloride, and wollastonite.

(e) 7½%—clay and shale used or sold for use in the manufacture of sewer pipe or brick, and clay, shale, and slate used or sold for use as sintered or burned lightweight aggregates.

References are to Standard Federal Tax Reports; Tax Research Consultant; and Practical Tax Explanations.

[130] ¶ 23,960, ¶ 23,980; FARM: 15,206; § 11,625

[131] ¶ 23,980; FARM: 15,150; § 11,625

[132] ¶ 23,980; FARM: 15,216; § 11,625

[133] ¶ 23,960; FARM: 15,158; § 11,625

[134] ¶ 23,960; FARM: 15,154; § 11,625

(f) 5%—gravel, peat, pumice, sand, scoria, shale (except shale described in (b) and (e) above) and stone (except stone falling within the general 14-percent group described in (g)); clay used, or sold for use, in the manufacture of drainage and roofing tile, flower pots, and kindred products; also, if from brine wells, bromite, calcium chloride, and magnesium chloride.

(g) 14%—all other minerals not included in any of the categories listed above. For purposes of this paragraph, the term "all other minerals" does not include (A) soil, sod, dirt, turf, water, or mosses; (B) minerals from sea water, the air, or similar inexhaustible sources; or (C) oil and gas wells.

Gross income from the property is the amount of income that comes from the extraction of the ores or minerals from the ground and the application of mining processes, including mining transportation and certain specified treatment processes (Code Sec. 613(c)).[135] The percentage depletion allowance is generally based on the mined product after application of the treatment processes applied by "ordinary" miners. Hence, an integrated miner-manufacturer computes gross income from mining at the point when the nonintegrated miner disposes of the product. Gross income is computed by using the representative market or field price; or, if it is impossible to determine such a field price and where the IRS does not determine that a more appropriate method should be used, the proportionate profits method (Reg. § 1.613-4(d)).[136]

References are to Standard Federal Tax Reports; Tax Research Consultant; and Practical Tax Explanations.

[135] ¶ 23,960; FARM: 15,258; § 11,620

[136] ¶ 23,967; FARM: 15,264; § 11,620

Chapter 13
TAX CREDITS

	Par.
Nonrefundable Credits	1301
Limitation on Nonrefundable Credits	1315
Refundable Credits	1321
Health Care Credits	1331
Nonbusiness Energy Credits	1341
Alternative Motor Vehicle Credit	1345
Foreign Tax Credit	1361
General Business Credits	1365
Tax Credit Bonds	1371

Nonrefundable Credits

1301. Child and Dependent Care Credit. A nonrefundable credit is allowed for a portion of qualifying child or dependent care expenses paid for the purpose of allowing the taxpayer, and the taxpayer's spouse if filing a joint return, to be gainfully employed (Code Sec. 21).[1] The credit is computed on Form 2441 for filers of Form 1040 and 1040A. The credit cannot be claimed on Form 1040EZ. To be eligible for the credit, the taxpayer must incur employment-related expenses in providing care for one of the following qualified individuals:

- a dependent of the taxpayer who is a qualifying child of the taxpayer and has not attained the age of 13 (¶ 137A);
- a dependent of the taxpayer who is a qualifying child or qualifying relative of the taxpayer (¶ 137B) (determined without regard to whether the individual may be claimed as a dependent by another taxpayer, has income in excess of the dependency exemption amount, or files a joint return with his or her spouse), is physically or mentally incapable of caring for himself or herself, and who has the same principal place of abode as the taxpayer for more than half of the year; or
- the taxpayer's spouse, if the spouse is physically or mentally incapable of caring for himself or herself and has the same principal place of abode as the taxpayer for more than half of the year.

Amount of Credit. The maximum amount of employment-related expenses to which the credit may be applied is $3,000, if one qualifying individual is involved, or $6,000, if two or more qualifying individuals are involved, less excludable employer dependent care assistance program payments (¶ 2065) (Code Sec. 21(c)). The credit amount is equal to the amount of qualified expenses multiplied by an applicable percentage determined by the taxpayer's adjusted gross income (AGI). Taxpayers with an AGI of $15,000 or less use the highest applicable percentage of 35 percent. For taxpayers with an AGI over $15,000, the credit is reduced by one percentage point for each $2,000 of AGI, or fraction thereof, over $15,000 (Code Sec. 21(a)(2)). The minimum applicable percentage of 20 percent is used by taxpayers with an AGI greater than $43,000. Thus, the maximum dependent care credit amount is $1,050 for one qualifying dependent and $2,100 for two or more qualifying dependents.

Example: A widower paid a housekeeper $5,000 during the year to take care of his home and 10-year-old daughter while he is working. His AGI was $25,000.

References are to Standard Federal Tax Reports; Tax Research Consultant; and Practical Tax Explanations.

[1] ¶ 3502; INDIV: 57,050; § 12,201

Since there is only one qualifying child, the maximum credit he can claim is $900 (30 percent of $3,000).

Qualifying Expenses. Qualifying expenses include expenses paid for household services and for the care of a qualifying individual that allow the taxpayer, and the taxpayer's spouse if filing a joint return, to work or look for work. Services outside the home qualify if they involve the care of a qualified individual who regularly spends at least eight hours a day in the taxpayer's home. Payments to a relative may be qualifying expenses unless the taxpayer claims a dependency exemption for the relative or if the relative is the taxpayer's child and under age 19. No expenses incurred to send a child or other dependent to an overnight camp are considered qualifying expenses for credit purposes.

Qualifying employment-related expenses are considered in determining the credit only to the extent of earned income—wages, salary, remuneration for personal services, net self-employment income, etc. For married taxpayers, expenses are limited to the earned income of the lower-earning spouse. Thus, if one spouse is generally not working, no credit is allowed. However, if the nonworking spouse is physically or mentally incapable of caring for himself or herself or is a full-time student at an educational institution for at least five calendar months during the year, the earned income amount is assumed to be—for each month of disability or school attendance—$250 if there is one qualifying individual or $500 if there are two or more qualifying individuals (Code Sec. 21(d)(2)).

Claiming the Credit. A married taxpayer *must* file a joint return to claim the credit. For this purpose, a married person living apart from his or her spouse under the circumstances described at ¶ 173 is considered unmarried. Also, a divorced or legally separated taxpayer having custody of a child who is disabled or under the age 13 is entitled to the credit even though he or she has released the right to a dependency exemption for the child (¶ 139A) (Code Sec. 21(e)(5)). Taxpayers must provide each qualifying individual's taxpayer identification number in order to claim the credit (generally a Social Security number (SSN)), as well as an identifying number of the dependent care service provider (either an SSN or employer identification number (EIN)) (Code Sec. 21(e)(9) and (10)).

1302. Credit for the Elderly or Disabled. A tax credit is available to individuals who are (1) 65 years of age before the close of the tax year or (2) under age 65 but are retired and were permanently and totally disabled when they retired (Code Sec. 22).[2] Married taxpayers must file a joint return to claim the credit unless the spouses live apart throughout the tax year. The credit is computed on Schedule R of Form 1040 and 1040A.

The credit is 15 percent of an applicable initial amount based on an individual's filing status and reduced by certain income. For individuals age 65 or older, the applicable initial amount is as follows:

Single individual	$5,000
Married individuals, joint return, one spouse is a qualified individual	5,000
Married individuals, joint return, both spouses are qualified individuals	7,500
Married individual, separate return	3,750

This initial amount is then reduced by amounts received as pension, annuity, or disability benefits that are excludable from gross income and are payable under the Social Security Act (Title II), the Railroad Retirement Act of 1974, a Veterans Affairs program, or that are otherwise excludable under a non-Code provision. No reduction is made for pension, annuity or disability benefits for personal injuries or sickness payable from a Veterans Affairs program.

The maximum amount determined above is further reduced by one-half of the excess of the taxpayer's adjusted gross income (AGI) over the following levels, based on filing status (Code Sec. 22(d)):

References are to Standard Federal Tax Reports; Tax Research Consultant; and Practical Tax Explanations.

[2] ¶ 3550; INDIV: 57,100; § 12,501

Single taxpayer	$7,500
Married taxpayers, combined AGI on joint return	10,000
Married individual filing separately	5,000

For permanently and totally disabled individuals under age 65, the applicable initial amount noted may not exceed the amount of disability income for the tax year. Disability income means the total amount that is included in an individual's gross income for the tax year under Code Sec. 72 (¶ 817) or 105(a) (¶ 2015) to the extent the amount constitutes wages, or payments in lieu of wages, for periods during which the individual is absent from work due to permanent and total disability (Code Sec. 22(c)(2)(B)). Special rules apply to a married couple filing a joint return where both spouses qualify for the credit and at least one of them is under age 65.

An individual is considered permanently and totally disabled for this purpose if he or she is unable to engage in any substantial gainful activity by reason of any medically determinable physical or mental impairment that can be expected to result in death or to last for a continuous period of not less than 12 months. The impairment should be substantiated by a letter from a certified physician kept in the taxpayer's records (Code Sec. 22(e)(3)).

Example: Alex, age 66 and single, has AGI of $9,000 for the year and receives $4,000 of nontaxable Social Security benefits for the year. To determine his credit, he would make the following computation:

Initial amount	$5,000
Less: nontaxable Social Security benefits	4,000
Reduced initial amount	$1,000
Less: one-half of AGI above $7,500	750
Amount eligible for credit	$250
Credit: $250 × 15%	$38

1303. Education Credits (American Opportunity and Lifetime Learning Credits). There are two education-related tax credits: the American opportunity tax credit (AOTC) and the lifetime learning credit (LLC). The credits may be claimed on Form 8863 by individuals for qualified tuition and related expenses incurred by students pursuing college or graduate degrees, or vocational training (Code Sec. 25A, as amended by the Protecting Americans from Tax Hikes (PATH) Act of 2015 (P.L. 114-113)).[3] For tax years beginning after June 29, 2015, taxpayers must attach Copy B of Form 1098-T received from an educational institution in order to claim either credit (Code Sec. 25A(g)(3) and (8); Prop. Reg. § 1.25A-1(f)).

The credits are elective, generally nonrefundable (except for the AOTC which is 40 percent refundable), and cannot be claimed using the same expenses for which another tax benefit is also received. The credits are also not permitted to be claimed by more than one taxpayer in the same year—for example, they may be claimed either by the parents or by the dependent child, but not by both (¶ 137). Higher income parents whose adjusted gross income (AGI) would result in the phasing out of the dependency exemption may waive claiming the dependency exemption to allow their student dependent to claim an educational credit, assuming the student dependent has a sufficient tax liability to be offset by an educational credit (Reg. § 1.25A-1(f)(1)). This does not, however, entitle the student dependent to claim a personal exemption on his or her tax return (¶ 135).

American Opportunity Tax Credit (AOTC). The AOTC is an enhancement and modification of the original Hope scholarship credit (Code Sec. 25A(i), as amended by P.L. 114-113).[4] The credit amount is the sum of 100 percent of the first $2,000 of qualified tuition and related expenses, plus 25 percent of the next $2,000 of qualified tuition and related expenses for a total maximum credit of $2,500 per eligible student per year. The credit is available for the first four years of a student's post-secondary education. Up to

References are to Standard Federal Tax Reports; Tax Research Consultant; and Practical Tax Explanations.

[3] ¶ 3820; INDIV: 60,150; § 12,401

[4] ¶ 3820; INDIV: 60,152; § 12,405

40 percent of the credit amount is refundable should the taxpayer's tax liability be insufficient to offset the nonrefundable credit amount. The credit amount phases out ratably for taxpayers with modified AGI (MAGI) between $80,000 and $90,000 ($160,000 and $180,000 for joint filers). MAGI is defined as AGI determined without regard to the exclusions for foreign earned income, foreign housing expenses (¶ 2402), and U.S. possession income (¶ 2414 and ¶ 2415). The AOTC may not be taken by married taxpayers who file separate returns (Code Sec. 25A(g)).

An eligible student for the AOTC is any individual who:

- has not elected to claim the AOTC credit in any four earlier years;
- has not completed the first four years of post-secondary education before the beginning of the current tax year;
- is enrolled at least half-time in a program that leads to a degree, certificate, or other recognized educational credentials; and
- has not been convicted of any federal or state felony class drug offense for possession or distribution.

Lifetime Learning Credit (LLC). The lifetime learning credit is equal to 20 percent of the amount of qualified tuition expenses paid on the first $10,000 of tuition. In contrast to the AOTC, the maximum lifetime learning credit is calculated per taxpayer and does not vary based on the number of eligible students in the taxpayer's family. A student is eligible for the lifetime learning credit if he or she is enrolled in one or more courses at a qualified educational institution. The allowable amount of the lifetime learning credit is reduced for taxpayers who have MAGI above certain amounts. The phaseout of the credits begins for single taxpayers in 2016 when MAGI reaches $55,000 ($56,000 in 2017) and completely phases out when MAGI reaches $65,000 ($66,000 in 2017). For joint filers, the phaseout range in 2016 is $111,000 ($112,000 in 2017) to $131,000 ($132,000 in 2017) (Code Sec. 25A(d); Rev. Proc. 2015-53; Rev. Proc. 2016-55). The lifetime learning credit may not be taken by married taxpayers who file separate returns (Code Sec. 25A(g)).

Qualified Expenses. The education credits are available for qualified tuition and related expenses incurred for the taxpayer, the taxpayer's spouse, or the taxpayer's dependent who is an eligible student at a qualified educational institution (Code Sec. 25A(f) and (i)(3)). Qualified expenses generally do not include room and board, books, unless required for enrollment, as well as student health fees, or transportation. For purposes of claiming the AOTC, however, qualifying expenses include course materials. The amount of qualified tuition and related expenses paid with any tax-free funds such as scholarships or Pell grants reduces the amount available for claiming the credits. A qualified educational institution is any post-secondary educational institution eligible to participate in a student aid program administered by the Department of Education (Code Sec. 25A(f)(2)).

Coordination with Other Provisions. Educational expenses eligible for the credits must first be reduced by tax-free educational assistance such as scholarships or fellowships (¶ 865), veterans' educational assistance allowances, employer-provided educational assistance (¶ 2067), or any other educational assistance excluded from gross income, other than gifts, bequests, devises, or inheritances (Reg. § 1.25A-5(c)). Taxpayers are then permitted to elect to claim either the AOTC or the lifetime learning credit for a student in any tax year.

The expenses used to claim the education credits also reduce the amount of eligible expenses available for purposes of determining the exclusion amount of distributions from Coverdell educational savings accounts (ESAs) (¶ 867) or qualified tuition programs (QTPs) (¶ 869). Since any excess distributions from Coverdell ESAs or QTPs over the eligible educational expenses are includible in gross income and subject to a 10-percent additional tax, not claiming an educational credit may result in a lower tax liability. However, taxpayers should be aware that the 10-percent additional tax for excess distributions from Coverdell ESAs or QTPs is waived if the excess is caused by claiming an educational credit. Taxpayers who receive distributions in excess of eligible expenses from both a Coverdell ESA and a QTP in the same year must allocate the expenses between the two distributions. Finally, only after eligible expenses are reduced by an educational credit and distributions from Coverdell ESAs or QTPs, the remaining expenses may be used to determine the exclusion amount for Series EE United States Savings Bonds (¶ 730) (Code Secs. 25A(g)(2), 135(d)(2), 529(c)(3)(B), and 530(d)(2)(C)).[5]

1304. Retirement Savings Contributions Credit (Saver's Credit). Eligible low-income taxpayers may claim a nonrefundable credit for contributions to elective deferral plans or individual retirement accounts (IRAs) (Code Sec. 25B).[6] The credit is referred to as the retirement savings contributions credit or the saver's credit. The credit amount equals the eligible taxpayer's applicable percentage, determined by filing status and adjusted gross income (AGI), multiplied by the total qualified retirement savings contributions, not to exceed $2,000 for the tax year. The maximum credit amount is $1,000. The credit is in addition to the exclusion or deduction from gross income for making elective deferrals and IRA contributions that are otherwise allowed.

Eligibility. To be eligible for the credit, a taxpayer making a contribution to a qualified retirement savings plan must be at least 18 years of age at the close of the tax year, must not be claimed as a dependent by someone else (¶ 137), and must not be a full-time student (¶ 137A). A qualified retirement savings plan contribution is the sum of:

- contributions to a traditional or Roth IRA, other than rollover contributions (Code Sec. 219(e));
- any elective deferrals of compensation to a 401(k), 403(b) tax-sheltered annuity, or SIMPLE or SEP plan (Code Sec. 402(g)(3));
- any elective deferrals of compensation to a Code Sec. 457(b) plan of a state or local government or tax-exempt organization; and
- any voluntary employee contributions to any qualified retirement plan (Code Sec. 4974(c)).

The amount of contributions to be taken into account in determining the credit must be reduced by any distributions from such qualified retirement plans over a test period (Code Sec. 25B(d)(2)). The test period is the period including the current tax year, the two preceding tax years, and the following tax year up to the due date of the return including extensions. Distribution amounts that qualify as a trustee-to-trustee transfer or as a rollover distribution to another qualified retirement account are not included in the reduction calculation.

Claiming the Credit. Form 8880 is used to calculate the amount of the credit. For 2016, the credit is phased out when AGI exceeds $61,500 for joint return filers, $46,125 for heads of households, and $30,750 for single and married filing separately (Notice 2015-75). For 2017, the credit is phased out when AGI exceeds $62,000 for joint return filers, $46,500 for heads of households, and $31,000 for single and married filing separately (Notice 2016-62).

The applicable percentage is the percentage as determined by the inflation adjusted income ranges for 2016 in the following table:

Adjusted Gross Income						*Applicable percentage*
Joint return		*Head of a household*		*All other cases*		
Over	*Not over*	*Over*	*Not over*	*Over*	*Not over*	
$0	$37,000	$0	$27,750	$0	$18,500	50
37,000	40,000	27,750	30,000	18,500	20,000	20
40,000	61,500	30,000	46,125	20,000	30,750	10
61,500	—	46,125	—	30,750	—	0

References are to Standard Federal Tax Reports; Tax Research Consultant; and Practical Tax Explanations.

[5] ¶ 3820, ¶ 7550, ¶ 22,940, ¶ 22,950; INDIV: 60,150; § 1,810, § 12,420

[6] ¶ 3835; INDIV: 57,550; § 12,701

The applicable percentage is the percentage as determined by the inflation adjusted income ranges for 2017 in the following table:

Adjusted Gross Income						*Applicable percentage*
Joint return		*Head of a household*		*All other cases*		
Over	*Not over*	*Over*	*Not over*	*Over*	*Not over*	
$0	$37,000	$0	$27,750	$0	$18,500	50
37,000	40,000	27,750	30,000	18,500	20,000	20
40,000	62,000	30,000	46,500	20,000	31,000	10
62,000	—	46,500	—	31,000	—	0

1305. Child Tax Credit. Taxpayers who have one or more qualifying children that they may claim as dependents (¶ 137) may be entitled to a child tax credit of $1,000 per child (Code Sec. 24).[7] The credit is allowed only for tax years consisting of 12 months. The credit is calculated using a worksheet in the Instructions to Form 1040.

Qualifying Child. The definition of qualifying child for purposes of the child tax credit is the same as that for claiming a dependency exemption (¶ 137A) except that the child must not have attained the age of 17 by the end of the year. In addition, the qualifying child must be either a U.S. citizen, national, or resident of the United States (Code Sec. 24(c)).

Limitation on Child Tax Credit. The child tax credit begins to phase out when the taxpayer's modified adjusted gross income (MAGI) reaches $110,000 for joint filers, $55,000 for married taxpayers filing separately, and $75,000 for single taxpayers. The credit is reduced by $50 for each $1,000, or fraction thereof, of MAGI above the threshold amount (Code Sec. 24(b)). MAGI is defined as AGI determined without regard to the exclusions for foreign earned income, foreign housing expenses (¶ 2402), and U.S. possession income (¶ 2414 and ¶ 2415).

Nonrefundable Portion of Child Tax Credit. The child tax credit is generally a nonrefundable personal credit. All nonrefundable personal tax credits are allowed to the full extent of the taxpayer's regular tax liability, reduced by any allowable foreign tax credit under Code Sec. 27(a), and the alternative minimum tax (AMT) liability (Code Sec. 26(a)).[8]

Refundable Amount of Child Tax Credit. A portion of the child tax credit, referred to as the additional child tax credit (ACTC), is refundable, regardless of the amount of the taxpayer's regular tax or AMT liabilities. For claims of the refundable portion made after December 31, 2016, no refund will be issued until the 15th day of the second month, i.e., February 15th for calendar year taxpayers (Code Sec. 6402(m), as added by the Protecting Americans from Tax Hikes (PATH) Act of 2015 (P.L. 114-113)). The credit is refundable in an amount equal to the lesser of the unclaimed portion of the nonrefundable credit amount or 15 percent of the taxpayer's earned income in excess of $3,000 (Code Sec. 24(d)(4), as amended by P.L. 114-113).[9] Military families may elect to include otherwise excludable combat zone pay in their earned income when calculating the refundable portion of the credit.

Taxpayers with three or more children may use an alternative method to calculate their refundable child tax credit. Under this method, the refundable credit is the excess of the taxpayer's share of Social Security taxes, including one-half of any self-employment taxes, over his or her earned income credit for the tax year (¶ 1322). For tax years beginning after December 31, 2014, the refundable portion of the child tax credit is disallowed for any taxpayer electing to exclude any amount of foreign earned income and foreign housing expenses from gross income (Code Sec. 24(d)(5)). The additional child tax credit is claimed on Schedule 8812.

References are to Standard Federal Tax Reports; Tax Research Consultant; and Practical Tax Explanations.

[7] ¶ 3760; INDIV: 57,450; § 12,101

[8] ¶ 3850; INDIV: 57,200; § 12,005

[9] ¶ 3760; INDIV: 57,454.10; § 12,120.15

1306. Mortgage Interest Credit. Low-income homeowners who obtain qualified mortgage credit certificates (MCCs) from state or local governments may claim a tax credit on Form 8396 during any tax year for which the certificate is in effect for a portion of the interest paid or incurred (Code Sec. 25; IRS Pub. 530).[10] An MCC is in effect for interest attributable to the period beginning on the date the certificate is issued and ending when either (1) it is revoked by the issuing authority, or (2) the taxpayer sells the residence or ceases to use it as a personal residence. Any mortgage interest claimed as an itemized deduction (¶ 1047) must be reduced by any credit claimed (Code Sec. 163(g)).

Amount of Credit. The credit is equal to the product of: (1) the certificate credit rate, which may not be less than 10 percent or more than 50 percent, and (2) the interest paid or accrued by the taxpayer for the year on the remaining principal of the certified indebtedness, plus a limited carryforward, if any. If the credit rate exceeds 20 percent, the tax credit for any year may not exceed $2,000 (Code Sec. 25(a)(2)(A)).

Tax Liability Limitation. The amount of the mortgage interest credit cannot exceed the limit on nonrefundable personal credits (¶ 1315), reduced by all nonrefundable credits other than the mortgage interest credit, the adoption credit (¶ 1307), the credit for residential energy efficient property (¶ 1342), and the credit for first-time homebuyers in the District of Columbia (¶ 1308) (Code Sec. 25(e)(1)).[11] Any unclaimed credit amount may be carried over to each of three succeeding tax years. The carryover amount is added to the current year credit amount and subject to the same tax liability limitation.

Recapture of Tax Benefit. A recapture of the tax benefit received from MCCs is triggered if the home is disposed of by the taxpayer, or ceases to be the taxpayer's principal place of residence during the first nine years after the testing date (Code Secs. 25(i) and Code Sec. 143(m)). The testing date is the date the taxpayer becomes liable either in whole or in part for the federally subsidized debt on the principal residence. The recapture amount equals the product of the federally subsidized amount of indebtedness times the holding period percentage times the income percentage. This recapture amount is treated as an addition to tax for the disposition tax year and calculated using Form 8828.

1307. Adoption Credit. An individual may claim a nonrefundable credit for qualified adoption expenses for each eligible child (Code Sec. 23).[12] The maximum credit amount for the 2016 tax year is $13,460 ($13,570 for 2017). The credit is phased out ratably in 2016 for taxpayers with a modified adjusted gross income (MAGI) over $201,920 ($203,540 in 2017). No credit is allowed to taxpayers with a MAGI over $241,920 in 2016 ($243,540 in 2017) (Rev. Proc. 2015-53; Rev. Proc. 2016-55). MAGI is defined as AGI determined without regard to the exclusions for foreign earned income, foreign housing expenses (¶ 2402), and U.S. possession income (¶ 2414 and ¶ 2415).

Qualified Adoption Expenses. Qualified adoption expenses include reasonable and necessary adoption fees, court costs, attorney fees, and other expenses which are directly related to the legal adoption of an eligible child. Expenses incurred in violation of state or federal law or in connection with the adoption of a child of the taxpayer's spouse are not eligible for the credit. Costs associated with a surrogate parenting arrangement are also ineligible for use in claiming the credit (Code Sec. 23(d)(1)).

Expenses used to claim any other deduction or credit may not be used to claim the adoption credit (Code Sec. 23(b)(3)). This includes amounts excluded from gross income that are paid or incurred by an employer for the employee's qualified adoption expenses pursuant to an adoption assistance program (¶ 2063). The dollar limitation for the exclusion is identical to the dollar limitation for the credit ($13,460 for 2016; $13,570 in 2017). However, any qualified adoption expenses incurred in excess of the amount provided under an employer's adoption assistance program may be used to claim the adoption credit.

References are to Standard Federal Tax Reports; Tax Research Consultant; and Practical Tax Explanations.

[10] ¶ 3800; INDIV: 57,150; § 13,020.05

[11] ¶ 3800; INDIV: 57,158; § 13,020.10

[12] ¶ 3700; INDIV: 57,350; § 12,301

Eligible Child and Special Needs Child. For purposes of the adoption credit, an eligible child is an individual who has not attained the age of 18 as of the time of the adoption or who is physically or mentally incapable of caring for himself or herself. This definition also includes a child with special needs. A special needs child is any child who, as determined by the state, should not or cannot be returned to the home of his or her parents, is a citizen or resident of the United States, and a specific factor or condition makes it reasonable to conclude that the child cannot be placed with adoptive parents unless assistance is provided (Code Sec. 23(d)(2) and (d)(3)).

Claiming the Credit. Adoption expenses incurred or paid during a tax year prior to the year in which the adoption is finalized may be claimed as a credit in the tax year following the year the expenses were incurred. Adoption expenses incurred during the year the adoption becomes final or in the year following the finalization of the adoption are claimed in the year they were incurred (Code Sec. 23(a)(2)). Adoption expenses for any qualified child who is not a U.S. citizen or resident cannot be claimed as a credit until the adoption is finalized (Code Sec. 23(e)). Taxpayers who adopt a child with special needs are allowed to claim the full amount of the credit regardless of actual expenses paid or incurred in the year the adoption becomes final (Code Sec. 23(a)(3)). Married couples must file a joint return in order to claim the credit unless the special rules for married individuals who are separated or living apart apply (¶ 173). The credit must be claimed on Form 8839 with proper documentation attached.

Carryovers. The adoption credit may be claimed against both regular tax liability, reduced by any allowable foreign tax credit under Code Sec. 27(a), and alternative minimum tax (AMT) liability. The adoption credit can be carried forward for up to five years if the credit amount exceeds the sum of the taxpayer's regular tax liability, reduced by any allowable foreign tax credit, and the AMT liability, reduced by the sum of the other nonrefundable credits, except the adoption credit, residential energy efficient property credit, and the first-time homebuyer credit for the District of Columbia (Code Sec. 23(c)).[13]

1308. Credit for First-Time Homebuyer in the District of Columbia (Expired). First-time homebuyers who purchased a principal residence in the District of Columbia from an unrelated person before January 1, 2012, could claim a nonrefundable credit of up to $5,000 of the purchase price ($2,500 in the case of a married person filing separately) (Code Sec. 1400C).[14] Any unused credit could be carried forward to the next succeeding year (or years) (Code Sec. 1400C(d)). Form 8859 is used to claim a carryforward of any unused credit.

1309. Alternative Minimum Tax Credit. Taxpayers are permitted a tax credit against their regular income tax liability for some or all of alternative minimum tax (AMT) paid in previous years (¶ 1401). The minimum tax credit is allowed for the amount of adjusted net minimum tax for all tax years reduced by the minimum tax credit for all prior tax years (Code Sec. 53).[15] Any unused credit may be carried forward indefinitely as a credit against regular tax liability. It is limited, however, to the extent that the regular tax liability reduced by other nonrefundable credits exceeds the tentative AMT liability for the tax year. The credit may not be used to offset any future AMT liability. The credit is claimed by individuals, trusts, and estates on Form 8801 and by corporations on Form 8827.

For noncorporate taxpayers, the adjusted net minimum tax is the taxpayer's AMT liability reduced by the amount that would have been the taxpayer's AMT liability if only certain specified adjustments and preferences had been taken into account (Code Sec. 53(d)(1)).[16] The adjustments include those related to standard deduction, personal exemptions, medical and dental expenses, miscellaneous itemized deductions, taxes, and interest expenses (¶ 1435). The preference items include certain depletion deduc-

References are to Standard Federal Tax Reports; Tax Research Consultant; and Practical Tax Explanations.

[13] ¶ 3700; INDIV: 57,366; § 12,301

[14] ¶ 32,428; INDIV: 57,500; § 13,005

[15] ¶ 4870; FILEIND: 30,452; § 15,510.05

[16] ¶ 4870; FILEIND: 30,452; § 15,510.05

tions exceeding adjusted basis, tax-exempt interest on specified private activity bonds, and the exclusion of gain on the sale of qualified small business stock (¶ 1425). In determining corporate credits for prior year minimum tax liability, adjusted net minimum tax is the taxpayer's AMT for the year.

Limitation on Nonrefundable Credits

1315. Limitation on Nonrefundable Credits. Nonrefundable personal tax credits can be used against an individual's regular tax and alternative minimum tax (AMT) or minimum tax liability (Code Sec. 26(a)).[17] All nonrefundable personal tax credits are allowed to the full extent of the sum of the taxpayer's regular tax liability, reduced by any allowable foreign tax credit, and the minimum tax liability.

Refundable Credits

1321. Credit for Taxes Withheld on Wages. An individual is allowed a credit against his or her income tax liability for income taxes withheld from his or her salary or wages (Code Sec. 31).[18] A taxpayer is also allowed a special refund of any Social Security taxes which were over-withheld from his or her wages. Excess Social Security taxes may be withheld where an individual works for more than one employer during the year and earns more than the Social Security wage base in total ($118,500 in 2016; $127,200 for 2017). The maximum amount of Social Security taxes that may be withheld is 6.2 percent of the wage base (¶ 2648). The same rule applies to excess withheld railroad retirement taxes. Since there is no wage base for calculating Medicare taxes, there can be no over-withholding of such taxes. The special refund for over-withheld Social Security taxes may be claimed as a credit on Form 1040. However, if the individual is not required to file an income tax return, he or she may file a special refund claim (Reg. § 31.6413(c)-1).[19] A nonresident alien (or foreign corporation) is allowed a credit against income tax liability for taxes withheld on U.S. source income that is not effectively connected with a U.S. trade or business (Code Sec. 33).[20] For a discussion on the withholding of tax on payments other than wages to nonresident aliens, see ¶ 2455.

1322. Earned Income Credit. A refundable earned income tax credit (EIC or EITC) is available to certain low-income individuals (Code Sec. 32).[21] To be eligible to claim the credit, a taxpayer must have earned income with an adjusted gross income (AGI) below a certain level, have a valid Social Security number (SSN), use a filing status other than married filing separately, be a U.S. citizen or resident alien, have no foreign income, and not have investment income above a certain amount. The amount of credit varies depending on the number of the taxpayer's qualifying children and their AGI level.

Amount of Credit. The earned income credit is determined by multiplying an applicable credit percentage by the individual's earned income that does not exceed a maximum earned income amount. In 2016, the maximum earned income amount for taxpayers with one qualifying child is $9,920, with two or more qualifying children is $13,930, and with no qualifying children is $6,610 (Rev. Proc. 2015-53). For 2017, the amounts are $10,000, $14,040, and $6,670, respectively (Rev. Proc. 2016-55). The credit amount is then reduced by a limitation amount determined by multiplying the applicable phaseout percentage by the excess of the amount of the individual's AGI, or earned income, if greater, over a phaseout amount. The earned income amount and the phaseout amount are adjusted yearly for inflation. The amount of allowable credit is determined through the use of the tables that appear at ¶ 87.

The credit and phaseout percentages limit the maximum amount of credit that may be claimed (Code Sec. 32(b)(1)). For 2016, the maximum earned income credit for taxpayers with one qualifying child is $3,373, with two qualifying children is $5,572, with three or more qualifying children is $6,269, and with no qualifying children is $506 (Rev. Proc. 2015-53). For 2017, the amounts are $3,400, $5,616, $6,318, and $510, respectively (Rev. Proc. 2016-55).

References are to Standard Federal Tax Reports; Tax Research Consultant; and Practical Tax Explanations.

[17] ¶ 3850; INDIV: 57,200; § 12,005

[18] ¶ 4060; INDIV: 57,302, INDIV: 57,308; § 12,801, § 12,805

[19] ¶ 38,754; IRS: 33,108; § 12,801, § 12,805

[20] ¶ 4100; INTL: 3,554.05, INDIV: 57,308; § 12,801, § 12,805

[21] ¶ 4080; INDIV: 57,250; § 12,601

Credit Limitations. For 2016, the credit begins to phase out when taxpayers with a filing status of single, surviving spouse, or head of household and with one or more qualifying children have an AGI of $18,190, and with no qualifying children have an AGI of $8,270. Phaseout of the credit is complete when taxpayers with a filing status of single, surviving spouse, or head of household with one qualifying child have an AGI of $39,296; with two qualifying children have an AGI of $44,648; with three or more qualifying children have an AGI of $47,955; and with no qualifying children have an AGI of $14,880. The credit amount begins to phase out when taxpayers with a filing status of married filing jointly and with one or more qualifying children have an AGI of $23,740, and with no qualifying children have an AGI of $13,820. Phaseout of the credit is complete when taxpayers with a filing status of married filing jointly with one qualifying child have an AGI of $44,846; with two qualifying children have an AGI of $50,198; with three or more qualifying children have an AGI of $53,505; and with no qualifying children have an AGI of $20,430 (Rev. Proc. 2015-53).

For 2017, the credit begins to phase out when taxpayers with a filing status of single, surviving spouse, or head of household and with one or more qualifying children have an AGI of $18,340, and with no qualifying children have an AGI of $8,340. Phaseout of the credit is complete when taxpayers with a filing status of single, surviving spouse, or head of household with one qualifying child have an AGI of $39,617; with two qualifying children have an AGI of $45,007; with three or more qualifying children have an AGI of $48,340; and with no qualifying children have an AGI of $15,010. The credit amount begins to phase out when taxpayers with a filing status of married filing jointly and with one or more qualifying children have an AGI of $23,930, and with no qualifying children have an AGI of $13,930. Phaseout of the credit is complete when taxpayers with a filing status of married filing jointly with one qualifying child have an AGI of $45,207; with two qualifying children have an AGI of $50,597; with three or more qualifying children have an AGI of $53,930; and with no qualifying children have an AGI of $20,600 (Rev. Proc. 2016-55).

Earned Income. The credit is based on earned income, which includes all wages, salaries, tips, and other employee compensation including union strike benefits, plus the amount of the taxpayer's net earnings from self-employment determined with regard to the deduction for one-half of self-employment taxes (¶ 923). Earned income is determined without regard to community property laws (Code Sec. 32(c)(2)). It also does not include: interest and dividends; welfare benefits; veterans' benefits, including VA rehabilitation payments; pensions or annuities; alimony; Social Security and railroad retirement benefits, including disability payments; workers' compensation; unemployment compensation; taxable scholarships or fellowships that are not reported on Form W-2; nontaxable foster care payments; amounts received for services performed by prison inmates while in prison; or payments received from work activities, including work associated with the refurbishing of public housing if sufficient private sector employment is not available and from community service programs (Sections 407(d)(4) and (7) of the Social Security Act). The earned income credit calculation is based on the taxpayer's AGI (Code Sec. 2(a)(2)(B) and (c)(2)).

Members of the Armed Forces. Taxpayers who are members of the Armed Forces are allowed to elect to treat combat pay that is otherwise excludable from gross income (¶ 895) as earned income for purposes of claiming the earned income credit (Code Sec. 32(c)(2)(B)(vi)). The election applies to all excludable combat pay received by the taxpayer.

Qualifying Child. A qualifying child for purposes of claiming the earned income credit is generally the same as for claiming the dependency exemption without regard to the support test (¶ 137A) (Code Sec. 32(c)(3)). In addition, the relationship, residency, and age tests must be met with the following modifications. For the residency test, the child must have the same principal place of abode as the taxpayer for more than half of the tax year and the abode must be located within the United States. A qualifying child for the earned income credit does not include a child who is married unless the taxpayer is entitled to claim him or her as a dependent. The taxpayer claiming the qualifying child must include the name, age and taxpayer identification number (¶ 2579) of the qualifying child on his or her return. Finally, the rules for determining among several taxpayers who may claim a child as a qualifying child for purposes of the earned income credit are the same as for determining who may claim a qualifying child for the dependency exemption (¶ 139).

No Qualifying Child. An individual who does not have a qualifying child may be eligible for the credit if: (1) the principal residence of the individual is in the United States for more than half of the tax year; (2) the individual, or the spouse of the individual, is at least age 25 and under age 65 before the close of the tax year; and (3) the individual is not claimed as a dependent by another (Code Sec. 32(c)(1)(A)(ii)).

Disqualifying Income. The earned income credit may not be claimed by taxpayers whose investment income exceeds $3,400 for 2016 ($3,450 for 2017) (Code Sec. 32(i); Rev. Proc. 2015-53; Rev. Proc. 2016-55). Disqualified income includes an individual's capital gain net income and net passive income in addition to interest, dividends, tax-exempt interest, and nonbusiness rents or royalties. The credit may also not be claimed by taxpayers who are not eligible to work in the United States. For example, a nonresident alien usually cannot claim an earned income credit (Code Sec. 32(c)(1)). Also, a person who claims a foreign earned income exclusion cannot claim an earned income credit (¶ 2402).

Claiming the Credit. Taxpayers claiming the credit must provide their Social Security or taxpayer identification number, as well as the Social Security or taxpayer identification numbers of their spouse and dependents, if any. Failure to provide all required Social Security or taxpayer identification numbers is treated as a mathematical error (Code Sec. 6213(g)(2)).[22] Married persons must file a joint return in order to claim the credit. However, a married person living apart from a spouse under circumstances described at ¶ 173 need not file a joint return to claim the credit. Taxpayers with one or more qualifying children complete Schedule EIC of Form 1040 or 1040A. Taxpayers with no qualifying children may use Form 1040EZ to determine whether they are eligible to claim the earned income credit.

Credit amounts are determined by using the tables at ¶ 87. The credit may be claimed only for a full 12-month tax year, except in the case of death. Beginning with claims for refunds after December 31, 2016, no refund will be made until the 15th day of the second month following the close of the tax year (February 15 for calendar year taxpayers) if the taxpayer is allowed the earned income tax credit (Code Sec. 6402(m), as added by the Protecting Americans from Tax Hikes (PATH) Act of 2015 (P.L. 114-113)). Additionally, for tax years beginning after December 18, 2015, the Social Security or tax identification number must be issued on or before the due date of the return (Code Sec. 32(m), as amended by P.L. 114-113).

1324. First-Time Homebuyer Credit (Expired). A refundable first-time homebuyer credit was available to qualified individuals who purchased, or were under contract to purchase, a home (generally before May 1, 2010) to be used as their principal residence (Code Sec. 36).[23] Special rules were enacted for military and government personal. The credit, however, must be recaptured in years after the purchase under certain circumstances. The recapture of the credit is reported on Form 5405.

Recapture Rules. For residences purchased after April 8, 2008, and before January 1, 2009, the amount of the credit that could be claimed was equal to the lesser of 10 percent of the purchase price or $7,500 ($3,750, if married filing separately). The $7,500 credit amount must be recaptured over a 15-year period beginning in the second year after the year in which the residence is purchased, i.e., beginning with the 2010 income tax return. The recapture amount is treated as an addition to tax for each year of the recapture period and is equal to 6.67 percent of the credit amount claimed (or 1/15 of the credit amount). If the taxpayer disposes of or ceases to use the home as a principal residence within the 15-year recapture period, any remaining amount of the credit must be recaptured in the year of disposition.

References are to Standard Federal Tax Reports; Tax Research Consultant; and Practical Tax Explanations.

[22] ¶ 37,545; IRS: 27,206.50; § 39,515.10

[23] ¶ 4186; INDIV: 57,950; § 13,010

1329. Credit for Federal Tax on Gasoline, Special Fuels. A credit for federal excise taxes on gasoline and special fuels may be taken where the fuel item is used for: (1) farming purposes, (2) nonhighway purposes of a trade or business, (3) operation of intercity, local, or school buses, or (4) certain nontaxable purposes (Code Sec. 34).[24] The credit is computed on Form 4136 or the taxpayer can file a claim for refund on Form 8849 or a credit against fuel tax liability on Form 720.

1330. Credit for Capital Gain Tax. Undistributed capital gain of a regulated investment company (RIC) must be included proportionately in the gross income of its shareholders (¶ 2305). The capital gain tax that the company pays on this gain is treated as having been paid by the shareholders and is allowed as a credit against the tax (Code Sec. 852(b)(3)(D)(ii)).[25] In order to claim the credit, Copy B of Form 2439 must be attached to the taxpayer's return.

Health Care Credits

1331. Health Insurance Premium Assistance Credit. Qualified individuals who purchase health care coverage through an American Health Benefit Exchange are entitled to a refundable income tax credit equal to the premium assistance credit amount (Code Sec. 36B(a)).[26]

Eligibility for Premium Credit. A qualified individual is defined as a person who:

- is seeking to enroll in a qualified health plan in the individual market offered through an Exchange and residing in the state in which the Exchange is established,
- has a household income of at least 100 percent, but no more than 400 percent, of the federal poverty line (FPL) for the individual's family size,
- if married, must file a joint return, and
- cannot be claimed as a dependent on another taxpayer's return (¶ 137) (Code Sec. 36B(c)(1)).

A lawful resident alien who is ineligible for Medicaid and has household income below 100 percent of the FPL for the individual's family size is deemed to have a household income equal to 100 percent of the FPL and eligible for the credit (Reg. § 1.36B-2(b)(5)). An individual who is not a U.S. citizen, national, or alien lawfully present in the United States is not eligible for the credit (Code Sec. 36B(e)). In addition, qualified individuals do not include individuals who are incarcerated unless the incarceration is pending the disposition of charges (Code Sec. 5000A). The individual may, however, be allowed a tax credit if a family member is enrolled in a qualified plan (Reg. § 1.36B-2(b)(4)).

Family size is equal to the number of individuals the taxpayer is allowed as personal and dependency exemptions for the tax year. This may include individuals who are not subject to or are exempt from the penalty for failure to maintain minimum essential health care coverage (¶ 131) (Reg. § 1.36B-1(d)). Household income equals the taxpayer's modified adjusted gross income (MAGI) and includes all income of individuals who are the taxpayer's dependents if a tax return is required to be filed. Household income does not include the MAGI of a family member who files a tax return solely to report tax under a different Code section (i.e. other than the penalty for failure to maintain minimum essential health care coverage), such as a Code Sec. 72(t) early distribution penalty (Reg. § 1.36B-1(e)(1)(ii)). MAGI is AGI increased by any amount of excluded foreign income, foreign housing allowance expenses, tax-exempt interest, and Social Security and tier 1 Railroad Retirement benefits (Code Sec. 36B(d)(2)(B)).

Credit Amount. The premium assistance credit amount for any tax year is the sum of the premium assistance amounts for all of the taxpayer's coverage months during the tax year (Code Sec. 36B(b)). The premium assistance amount for any coverage month is the lesser of:

References are to Standard Federal Tax Reports; Tax Research Consultant; and Practical Tax Explanations.

[24] ¶ 4150; BUSEXP: 54,800; § 13,501

[25] ¶ 26,420; RIC: 3,260; § 19,205.05

[26] ¶ 4196; HEALTH: 3,300; § 42,015.05

- the monthly premium for one or more qualified health plans offered in the individual market Exchange within a state covering the taxpayer, the taxpayer's spouse, or any dependent of the taxpayer who is enrolled through the Exchange, or

- the excess, if any, of the adjusted monthly premium for the applicable second lowest cost silver plan with respect to the taxpayer over an amount equal to 1/12th of the product of the applicable percentage and the taxpayer's household income for the tax year.

Coverage Month. A coverage month is any month in which the taxpayer, the taxpayer's spouse, or any dependent is covered by a qualified health plan enrolled in through an Exchange and the premium is paid by the taxpayer or through advance payment of the premium assistance credit (Code Sec. 36B(c)(2)). A coverage month does *not* include any month that the individual is eligible for minimum essential coverage outside the individual market. A month also is *not* a coverage month if the taxpayer's share of premiums is not paid in full by the unextended due date for filing the taxpayer's income tax return for the tax year (Reg. § 1.36B-3(c)(1)). An employee is *not* considered to be eligible for minimum essential coverage outside of the market if the coverage is an employer-sponsored plan, including a grandfathered health plan, and either:

- the employee's required contribution is unaffordable for the employee or a related individual—it would exceed 9.66 percent of the employee's household income for 2016 (9.69 percent for 2017) (Rev. Proc. 2014-62; Rev. Proc. 2016-24); or

- the plan provides less than 60 percent coverage for total allowed costs.

An employee uses the employee's cost for self-only coverage to determine whether the coverage is affordable (Reg. § 1.36B-2(c)(3)(v)(A); Temp. Reg. § 1.36B-2T(c)(3)(v)(C)). The affordability of coverage for any related individuals of an employee is also determined by using the employee's cost of self-only coverage.

The applicable second lowest cost silver plan is the second lowest cost silver plan of the individual market Exchange in the rating area where the taxpayer resides. It must be offered through the same Exchange offering the qualified health plan and provide (1) self-only coverage for single taxpayers with no dependents or those who purchase self-only coverage, and (2) family coverage for all other taxpayers (Code Sec. 36B(b)(3)). The adjusted monthly premium for an applicable second lowest cost silver plan is the monthly premium that would be charged for the plan if each individual covered under a qualified health plan were covered by that silver plan, and the premium was adjusted only for the age of each individual. The applicable percentage is between 2.03 and 9.66 percent for 2016 (between 2.04 percent and 9.69 percent for 2017) of a taxpayer's household income for the tax year with respect to a taxpayer whose household income is between 100 and 400 percent of the FPL for that year (Rev. Proc. 2014-62; Rev. Proc. 2016-24). If there is at least one silver level plan offered on an Exchange that does not cover all members of a taxpayer's coverage family under one policy and premium, the premium for the applicable plan is the single premium or the combination of premiums that is the second lowest cost silver option for covering the entire family (Reg. § 1.36B-3(f)(3)).

The IRS has provided the following rules for determining, for purposes of the premium tax credit, whether, or when, certain individuals are eligible for minimum essential coverage (1) under the Medicaid, Medicare, Children's Health Insurance Program (CHIP), or TRICARE programs, or (2) through self-funded student health plans and state high risk pools (Notice 2013-41):

- An individual who may not re-enroll in CHIP for a period of time ("lockout period") due to a failure to pay premiums is treated as eligible for CHIP and not eligible for qualified health plan coverage subsidized by the premium tax credit during the lockout period.

- An individual who is terminated from Medicaid or CHIP for failure to pay premiums is treated as eligible for Medicaid or CHIP during any period for which the individual would be eligible for Medicaid or CHIP, but for the failure to pay premiums.
- An individual who may not enroll in CHIP during a pre-enrollment waiting period may be eligible for qualified health plan coverage subsidized by the premium tax credit during this period.
- An individual is eligible for minimum essential coverage under Medicaid or Medicare in the following circumstances only upon a favorable determination of eligibility by the responsible agency: (1) Medicaid coverage requiring a finding of disability or blindness; and (2) Medicare coverage based solely on a finding of disability or illness.
- An individual is eligible for minimum essential coverage under the following programs only if the individual is enrolled in the coverage: (1) Medicare Part A coverage requiring payment of premiums; (2) state high risk pools; (3) student health plans; and (4) TRICARE programs.

Advance Payment of Credit. The premium assistance credit must be reduced, but not below zero, by the amount of any advance payment of the credit (Code Sec. 36B(f)). If the advance payments for a tax year exceed the premium assistance credit allowed, the excess is an increase to the tax imposed for the tax year. For taxpayers with household incomes less than 400 percent of the FPL for the tax year, the increase is limited for 2016 to between $600 and $2,550 ($300 and $1,275 for unmarried taxpayers other than surviving spouses and heads of household) (Rev. Proc. 2015-53). For tax years beginning in 2017, the increase is limited to between $600 and $2,550 ($300 and $1,275 for unmarried taxpayers other than surviving spouses and heads of household) (Rev. Proc. 2016-55).

1332. Health Insurance Costs Credit. Eligible individuals may claim a refundable tax credit for the cost of qualified health insurance for themselves and qualified family members during each eligible coverage month. The credit is 72.5 percent of the costs during all coverage months beginning before January 1, 2020 (Code Sec. 35).[27] An eligible coverage month occurs when, on the first day of the month during the taxpayer's tax year, the taxpayer: (1) is an eligible individual; (2) is covered by a qualified health insurance plan on which the taxpayer paid the premiums; (3) has no other specified coverage, including under Medicare or COBRA; and (4) is not imprisoned by any federal, state, or local authority. Taxpayers determine their eligibility and claim the credit on Form 8885 and attaching it to their return along with copies of the required documentation. See IRS Pub. 502 for additional information.

Eligible Individuals. The credit is available only to individuals receiving, or who are eligible to receive, trade adjustment assistance (TAA) (or TAA-alternative payments) and retirees age 55 or older receiving benefits from the Pension Benefit Guaranty Corporation (PBGC) (Code Sec. 35(c)). A qualifying family member of an eligible individual includes the taxpayer's spouse and any dependents for whom the taxpayer is entitled to an exemption (¶ 137) (Code Sec. 35(d)). A spouse is not considered a qualifying family member if the taxpayer is married at the end of the year, both are considered eligible individuals, and each files a separate income tax return (Code Sec. 35(g)(5)). However, the rules for head of household status relating to separated parents and individuals living apart for six months apply (¶ 173). In the case of separated or divorced parents, dependents are considered qualifying family members only for the custodial parent (¶ 139A) (Code Sec. 35(d)(2)).

Qualifying Premiums. Premiums paid by taxpayers for coverage in a qualified health insurance plan (as defined in Code Sec. 35(e)(1)) are to be taken into account in determining the health insurance costs credit. Qualified health insurance does *not* include either a flexible spending or similar arrangement (¶ 2041) or any insurance whose coverage is substantially for "excepted benefits" under Code Sec. 9832(c) (Code Sec. 35(e)(3)).

References are to Standard Federal Tax Reports; Tax Research Consultant; and Practical Tax Explanations.

[27] ¶ 4170; HEALTH: 15,152; § 42,315

Insurance coverage that qualifies as other specified coverage under Code Sec. 35(f) includes: (1) any insurance which is considered to be for medical care under a health plan maintained by the employer of the taxpayer or the taxpayer's spouse where at least 50 percent of the cost is paid or incurred by the employer; (2) any insurance coverage under a cafeteria plan (¶ 2045) in which the premiums are paid or incurred by the employer in lieu of a right to receive cash benefits or other qualified benefits under a cafeteria plan; (3) participation in Medicare, Medicaid, or State Child Health Insurance Program (SCHIP); and (4) participation in a health benefits plan for federal employees and military personnel. The credit is also coordinated with the COBRA premium assistance provision (¶ 1391) to prevent double benefits.

Coordination with Other Provisions. Amounts taken into account for the determination of the health insurance costs credit may not be used in computing either the health insurance costs for the self-employed deduction (¶ 908) or the itemized deduction for medical/dental costs (¶ 1015). Amounts received from health savings account (HSAs) (¶ 2035) or Archer medical saving accounts (¶ 2037) may not be used to compute the health insurance costs credit. Payment made for the benefit of a third party who is not a qualifying family member cannot be included in the amount of premiums paid for qualified health insurance in determining the credit (Code Sec. 35(g)(1), (2) and (3)).

The premium tax credit (Code Sec. 35B) and the health insurance costs credit may not be claimed in the same month (Code Sec. 35(g)). To coordinate eligibility for the two credits, an election must be made to claim the health insurance cost credit no later than the due date, with extensions, for filing of the taxpayer's income tax return for the year (Code Sec. 35(g)(11)).

Advance Payment. The advance payment program makes monthly payments on behalf of eligible individuals directly to providers of qualified health insurance. The advance payments cannot equal more than the credit percentage (72.5 percent) of the anticipated health insurance costs of the eligible taxpayer. The aggregate amount of all advance payments during the tax year reduces the health insurance costs credit amount dollar for dollar but not below zero (Code Secs. 35(g)(8)(A) and 7527). The IRS is allowed to refund to the taxpayer amounts paid prior to the advance payment program making premiums payments.

Additional Requirements for State Plans. State health plans must make an election to be considered a qualified health insurance plan for the health insurance costs credit. In addition to the election, several additional requirements must be satisfied (Code Sec. 35(e)(2)).

1333. Small Employer Health Insurance Credit. An eligible small employer may claim a tax credit if it makes nonelective contributions that pay for at least one-half of the cost of health insurance premiums for the coverage of its participating employees (Code Sec. 45R).[28] The credit is computed on Form 8941 and is claimed as a component of the general business credit (¶ 1365).

Credit Amount. The credit amount for tax years beginning after 2013 is equal to 50 percent of the lesser of:

(1) the total amount of nonelective contributions the employer makes on behalf of its employees during the tax year under a contribution arrangement for premiums for qualified health plans offered to its employees through a state-sponsored market exchange (i.e., through a Small Business Health Options Program (SHOP)), or

(2) the total amount of nonelective contributions that would have been made during the tax year if each employee taken into account in item (1) had enrolled in a qualified health plan that had a premium equal to the average premium for the small group market in the rating area in which the employee enrolls for coverage (Code Sec. 45R(b)).

References are to Standard Federal Tax Reports; Tax Research Consultant; and Practical Tax Explanations.

[28] ¶ 4500ZN; HEALTH: 9,200; § 42,115.05

The credit amount for tax years beginning before 2014 is equal to 35 percent of the lesser of:

(1) the total amount of nonelective contributions the employer makes on behalf of its employees during the tax year under a contribution arrangement for the payment of premiums for qualified health insurance coverage (as defined in Code Sec. 9832(b)(1)) of its employees, or

(2) the total amount of nonelective contributions that would have been made during the tax year if each employee taken into account in item (1) had enrolled in a qualified health plan that had a premium equal to the average premium for the small group market in the state in which the employer is offering health insurance coverage or the area within the state specified by the Secretary of Health and Human Services (HHS) (Code Sec. 45R(a), (b) and (g)).

The contribution arrangement must require an employer to make a nonelective contribution on behalf of each employee who enrolls in a qualified health plan offered by the employer in an amount equal to a uniform percentage, but not less than 50 percent, of the premium cost of the plan (Code Sec. 45R(d)(4) and (g)(3)). An employer contribution is considered a nonelective contribution so long as it is not made through a salary reduction arrangement (Code Sec. 45R(e)(3)). For tax years beginning after 2013, the contribution arrangement must offer the insurance through an Exchange. For tax years beginning before 2014, the arrangement is not required to offer the insurance through an Exchange.

Credit Phaseout. The credit amount is reduced, but not below zero, by the sum of:

- the credit amount multiplied by the number of the employer's full-time equivalent employees for the tax year in excess of 10, divided by 15; and
- the credit amount multiplied by the employer's average annual wages in excess of the applicable dollar amount for the tax year ($25,900 in 2016; $26,200 for 2017), divided by the applicable dollar amount (Code Sec. 45R(c); Rev. Proc. 2015-53; Rev. Proc. 2016-55).

Eligible Small Employer Defined. An employer determines its status as an eligible small employer each tax year. An employer is an eligible small employer if, during the tax year:

- the employer has 25 or fewer full-time equivalent employees;
- the average annual wages of these employees is not greater than twice the applicable dollar amount for the tax year; and
- the employer has a qualified health care arrangement in effect (Code Sec. 45R(d)(1)).

Full-Time Equivalent Employee Defined. The number of full-time equivalent employees during a tax year is equal to the total number of hours for which employees were paid wages by the employer divided by 2,080. The result, if not a whole number, is rounded to the next lowest whole number. Only the first 2,080 hours of each employee's wages are taken into account. Hours in excess of this amount are not counted (Code Sec. 45R(d)(2)). For purposes of determining average annual wages and the number of full-time equivalent employees, hours of service worked by, and wages paid to, a seasonal worker are not taken into account unless the worker works for the employer on more than 120 days during the tax year (Code Sec. 45R(d)(5)(A)).

Employee Defined. For purposes of the credit, the following individuals are not considered employees (Code Sec. 45R(e)(1)):

(1) any self-employed individual (as defined in Code Sec. 401(c)(1));

(2) any two-percent shareholder (as defined in Code Sec. 1372(b)) of an eligible small business which is an S corporation;

(3) any five-percent owner (as defined in Code Sec. 416(i)(1)(B)(i)) of an eligible small business; or

(4) any individual who bears any of the familial relationships of a qualifying relative (¶ 137B) to an individual described in items (1), (2), or (3), above, or is a qualifying relative dependent with the same principal abode as the individual and is a member of the individual's household.

Leased employees as defined in Code Sec. 414(a) are considered employees (Code Sec. 45R(e)(1)).

Wages Defined. Wages for purposes of the credit are defined the same as wages for purposes of the Federal Insurance Contributions Act (FICA) but without regard to any dollar limitation (Code Sec. 45R(e)(4)) (¶ 2648).

Additional Rules. The following special rules relating to the work opportunity credit apply to the small employer health insurance credit (Code Sec. 45R(e)(5)(B)):

- an estate or trust must apportion the credit between itself and its beneficiaries based on income allocable to each (Code Sec. 52(d));
- in computing the credit, a regulated investment company (RIC), real estate investment trust (REIT), and cooperative organization (Code Sec. 1381(a)) must apply rules similar to the rules provided in Code Sec. 46(e) and (h), as in effect prior to the date of enactment of the Revenue Reconciliation Act of 1990 (P.L. 101-508) (Code Sec. 52(e)).

A third special rule seems to suggest that the small employer health insurance credit is not available to a tax-exempt organization, other than a tax-exempt cooperative described in Code Sec. 521 (Code Secs. 45R(e)(5)(B) and 52(c)). This reference appears to be erroneous. In fact, Code Sec. 45R provides special computation rules applicable to certain tax-exempt organizations. See following, under *Special Computation Rules for Tax-Exempt Eligible Small Employers.*

Certain Persons Treated as Single Employer. All controlled groups, partnerships, and affiliated service groups treated as a single employer under Code Sec. 414(b), (c), (m), or (o) are treated as one employer (Code Sec. 45R(e)(5)(A)).

General Business Credit. The small employer health insurance credit is a component of the general business credit (Code Sec. 38(b)(36)) (¶ 1365). Any portion of the credit that is not claimed by the expiration of the 20-year carryforward period may be claimed as a deduction in the first tax year after expiration of the carryforward period (Code Sec. 196(c)(14)).

Deduction for Premiums. The deduction for employer-paid premiums for qualified health plans or, in the case of tax years beginning before 2014, for health insurance coverage, is reduced by the amount of the small employer health insurance credit determined with respect to those premiums (Code Sec. 280C(h)).

Credit Period. The small employer health insurance credit may only be claimed for two consecutive tax years beginning after 2013 (Code Sec. 45R(g)). The credit period is the two-consecutive-tax-year period beginning with the first tax year in which the employer offers one or more qualified health plans to its employees through a SHOP Exchange (Code Sec. 45R(e)(2)). The credit period does not begin until the first year the employer files a return claiming the credit (Reg. § 1.45R-1(a)(3)).

No credit period is treated as beginning with a tax year beginning before 2014 (Code Sec. 45R(g)(1)). A transitional rule applies to an employer's first tax year beginning in 2014, if:

- the employer's health plan year does not begin on the first day of the tax year;
- the employer has a health plan in effect as of August 26, 2013;
- the employer offers one or more qualified health plans to its employees through a SHOP Exchange as of the first day of its 2014 plan year.

For this purpose, the employer is treated as if coverage was offered through a SHOP Exchange for the entire 2014 tax year if the health coverage that was provided from the first day of the tax year through the day prior to the first day of the 2014 plan year would have qualified for a credit under the rules applicable in the 2013 tax year discussed previously. The 2014 tax year begins the start of the two-year credit period if the employer uses this transitional rule (Reg. § 1.45R-3(i)(1)).

Special Computation Rules for Tax-Exempt Eligible Small Employers. The credit percentage for a tax-exempt eligible small employer is 35 percent for tax years beginning after 2013 (25 percent for tax years beginning before 2014) (Code Sec. 45R(b) and (g)(2)(A)). A tax-exempt eligible small employer is an eligible small employer that is a Code Sec. 501(c) organization that is exempt from tax (Code Sec. 45R(f)(2)). Other tax-exempt organizations generally are not eligible to claim the credit. However, a farmers' cooperative is eligible to claim the credit as a taxable employer if it otherwise meets the requirements (Notice 2010-82). If the credit exceeds the amount of payroll taxes of the organization during the calendar year in which the tax year begins, then the credit amount is limited to the amount of the payroll taxes (Code Sec. 45R(f)(1)).

Payroll taxes are defined as amounts required to be withheld from the tax-exempt organization's employees for Medicare and income tax withholding, and amounts of the taxes imposed on the tax-exempt organization for Medicare (Code Sec. 45R(f)(3)(A)). The special rule contained in Code Sec. 24(d)(2)(C), which treats amounts paid pursuant to an agreement entered into by American employers with respect to foreign affiliates that are the equivalent of social security taxes or railroad retirement taxes, applies (Code Sec. 45R(f)(3)(B)).

Nonbusiness Energy Credits

1341. Nonbusiness Energy Property Credit. A nonrefundable tax credit is available to individuals for the installation of nonbusiness energy property, such as residential exterior doors and windows, insulation, heat pumps, furnaces, central air conditioners, and water heaters (Code Sec. 25C, as amended by the Protecting Americans from Tax Hikes (PATH) Act of 2015 (P.L. 114-113).[29] The credit applies to qualified energy efficiency improvements and qualified energy property placed in service before January 1, 2017. The property must be installed in, or on, a dwelling unit in the United States that is owned and used by the taxpayer as the taxpayer's principal residence. Original use of the property must commence with the taxpayer.

The credit is claimed on Form 5695. It may be claimed against the sum of the regular tax and alternative minimum tax (AMT) liabilities. However, any unused credit may *not* be carried forward (Notice 2013-70). The basis of the residence is reduced by the allowed credit (Code Sec. 25C(f); Instructions to Form 5695).

Credit Amount. The credit amount is equal to 10 percent of the amount paid or incurred for qualified energy efficiency improvements during the tax year, and 100 percent of the amount paid or incurred for qualified energy property during the tax year, up to a set amount depending on the type of property (Code Sec. 25C(b)). The maximum credit amount for qualified energy property is $200 for exterior windows and skylights, reduced by the aggregate credit allowed for exterior windows and skylights in prior years; $50 for any advanced main air circulating fan; $150 for any qualified furnace or boiler; and $300 for any other item. For all nonbusiness energy property, there is a $500 maximum lifetime credit.

Qualified Energy Efficiency Improvements. Qualified energy improvements include any energy efficient building envelope component that meets certain energy conservation criteria (Code Sec. 25C(c)). A building envelope component is defined as any insulation material or system which is designed to prevent heat loss or gain, exterior windows (including skylights), exterior doors, and any metal roof with either pigmented coating or cooling granules designed to reduce heat gain.

For a building envelope components place in service after December 31, 2015, the criteria that must be satisfied to claim the nonbusiness energy property credit are; (1) in the case of roof and roof products, the applicable Energy Star program requirements, (2) in the case of exterior windows, skylights, and exterior doors, the version 6.0 Energy

References are to Standard Federal Tax Reports; Tax Research Consultant; and Practical Tax Explanations.

[29] ¶ 3839; INDIV: 57,800; § 13,201

Star program requirements, and (3) in the case of all other components, the requirements of the 2009 International Conservation Code, including supplements, in effect on February 17, 2009 (Code Sec. 25C(c)(2), as added by P.L. 114-113).

Qualified Energy Property. Qualified energy property is defined as energy-efficient building property, qualified natural gas, propane, or oil furnace or hot water boiler, or an advance main air circulating fan that meet specific performance and quality standards (Code Sec. 25C(d)). Qualified energy-efficient building property includes electric heat pump water heaters, qualified electric heat pumps, qualified central air conditioners, and qualified stoves that use biomass fuels.

1342. Residential Energy Efficient Property Credit. A nonrefundable tax credit is available to help individual taxpayers pay for residential alternative energy equipment installed on or in connection with a dwelling unit located in the United States and used as a residence by the taxpayer (Code Sec. 25D, as amended by the Protecting Americans from Tax Hikes (PATH) Act of 2015 (P.L. 114-113)).[30] The credit is available for the cost of eligible fuel cell plants, qualified small wind energy property, and qualified geothermal heat pump property placed in service before January 1, 2017, and eligible solar electric property and solar water heating property placed in service before January 1, 2022. Cooperative and condominium dwellers can claim the credit by splitting the cost of installing equipment with other unit owners. The credit is claimed on Form 5695.

Credit Amount. For property placed in service before January 1, 2017, the credit amount is equal to 30 percent of the cost of eligible property (Code Sec. 25D(a), prior to amendment by P.L. 114-113). However, the maximum amount of credit for the installation of qualified fuel cell property for any tax year is $500 per half kilowatt hour (Code Sec. 25D(b)(1)). For property placed in service after December 31, 2016 and before January 1, 2022, the credit is available only for eligible solar electric property and solar water heating property; the credit is equal to 30 percent of the cost of eligible property placed in service in 2017, 2018, or 2019; 26 percent of the cost of property placed in service in 2020; and 22 percent of the cost of property placed in service in 2021 (Code Sec. 25D(a) and (g), as amended by P.L. 114-113). The credit cannot exceed the excess of the sum of the taxpayer's regular tax, reduced by the foreign tax credit, and alternative minimum tax minus the sum of the taxpayer's other personal nonrefundable credits not including the residential energy efficient property credit. Any excess amount is carried over and added to the credit amount for the next tax year (Code Sec. 25D(c)). The credit allowed reduces the basis of the residence (Code Sec. 25D(f); Instructions to Form 5695).

Qualifying Property. Qualifying solar heating property is any property used to heat water for use in a dwelling unit that receives at least half of its energy from the sun. None of the cost allocated to heat a swimming pool or hot tub may be considered a qualified expenditure. Qualifying solar electric property is any property that generates electricity from solar energy to be used in a dwelling unit. Qualified fuel cell property is any fuel cell property with a nameplate capacity of least 0.5 kilowatt hours of electricity generated by using an electrochemical process with an electricity-generating efficiency greater than 30 percent. Qualified small wind energy property is any wind turbine that generates electricity for use in the residence of the taxpayer. It does not include any wind facility for which a credit can be claimed for electricity produced from renewable resources (¶ 1365N). Qualified geothermal heat pump property is any property that uses the ground or ground water as a thermal source to heat a dwelling unit (Code Sec. 25D(d)).

Alternative Motor Vehicle Credit

1345. Alternative Motor Vehicle Credit. Taxpayers who buy a motor vehicle may be eligible for the alternative motor vehicle credit (Code Sec. 30B).[31] The credit amount is equal to the sum of the following component credits: (1) a qualified fuel cell motor

References are to Standard Federal Tax Reports; Tax Research Consultant; and Practical Tax Explanations.

[30] ¶ 3844; INDIV: 57,850; § 13,301

[31] ¶ 4059A; INDIV: 57,702; § 12,905.05

vehicle credit (¶ 1346); (2) an advanced lean burn technology motor vehicle credit (expired); (3) a qualified hybrid motor vehicle credit (expired); (4) a qualified alternative motor vehicle credit (expired); and (5) a plug-in conversion credit (expired). Of these five component credits, only the qualified fuel cell motor vehicle credit is available. The individual components comprising the alternative motor vehicle credit are calculated based on various factors such as vehicle weight, vehicle fuel efficiency, lifetime fuel savings, etc. Each has a different phaseout or termination rule. The credit amount claimed is the sum of the components applicable to a particular vehicle, whether used for personal or business purposes. The credit is claimed on Form 8910.

Common Requirements. There are distinct requirements for each of the five components of the credit. Four requirements are, however, common to each of the components: (1) the original use of the vehicle must commence with the taxpayer; (2) the vehicle must be acquired for use or lease by the taxpayer and not for resale; (3) the vehicle must be made by a manufacturer; and (4) the vehicle must be primarily used in the United States.

Any credit amount claimed under the alternative motor vehicle credit for personal use is treated as a nonrefundable personal credit (¶ 1315). Taxpayers with qualified motor vehicles that are used in a trade or business and subject to depreciation claim the alternative motor vehicle credit as a part of, and subject to, the rules of the general business credit (¶ 1365). Thus, any unused credit in a tax year is eligible to be carried back three years and forward 20 years. A seller claiming the alternative motor vehicle credit for a vehicle sold to a tax-exempt entity can only claim the credit as a part of the general business credit.

1346. Fuel Cell Motor Vehicle Credit. One component of the alternative motor vehicle credit is a qualified fuel cell motor vehicle credit for qualifying vehicles purchased before January 1, 2017, and placed in service during the tax year (Code Sec. 30B(b), as amended by the Protecting Americans from Tax Hikes (PATH) Act of 2015 (P.L. 114-113)).[32] In addition to the common requirements for qualifying vehicles (¶ 1345), there are specific requirements for a vehicle to be classified as a qualified fuel cell motor vehicle. The vehicle must be propelled by power derived from one or more cells which convert chemical energy directly into electricity by combining oxygen with hydrogen fuel. In addition, if the vehicle is a passenger vehicle or light truck, it must be certified to meet specific environmental emission standards.

The amount of the credit is calculated based on the gross vehicle weight rating (GVWR) of the vehicle, supplemented by the fuel efficiency of the vehicle relative to the 2002 model-year city fuel economy. The credit can range from $8,000 for vehicles up to 8,500 pounds GVWR and up to $40,000 for vehicles over 26,000 pounds GVWR. Qualified fuel cell vehicles that meet the definition of either a passenger automobile or light truck and meet certain standards for increased fuel efficiency may increase their credit amount based on the increase in fuel efficiency over the 2002 city fuel economy standards. The increase in the credit amount ranges from $1,000 up to $4,000.

1351. Qualified Plug-In Electric Drive Motor Vehicle Credit. A tax credit is allowed for the purchase price of a qualified plug-in electric drive motor vehicle acquired after December 31, 2009, and placed in service during the tax year (Code Sec. 30D).[33] The credit amount is $2,500 plus $417 in the case of a vehicle which draws propulsion energy from a battery with not less than five kilowatt hours of capacity, and an additional $417 for each kilowatt hour of battery capacity in excess of five kilowatt hours. The additional amount cannot exceed $5,000. Thus, the maximum credit amount per vehicle is $7,500. For qualified vehicles used in a trade or business, the credit is claimed as a portion of the general business credit (¶ 1365). For qualified vehicles used for personal use, the credit is treated as a nonrefundable personal credit (¶ 1315). The credit is claimed using Form 8936.

References are to Standard Federal Tax Reports; Tax Research Consultant; and Practical Tax Explanations.

[32] ¶ 4059A; INDIV: 57,704; § 12,905.10

[33] ¶ 4059L; INDIV: 58,000; § 12,915.15

Qualified Vehicles. To qualify as a plug-in electric drive vehicle, the vehicle must: (1) be made by a manufacturer, (2) be acquired for use or lease but not resale, (3) have its original use commencing with the taxpayer, (4) be treated as a motor vehicle for purposes of Title II of the Clean Air Act, (5) have a gross vehicle weight rating (GVWR) of not more than 14,000 pounds, and (6) be propelled to a significant degree by an electric motor that draws electricity from a battery with a capacity of not less than four kilowatt hours and that is capable of being recharged from an external source of electricity (Code Sec. 30D(d)). The term "motor vehicle" means any vehicle that has at least four wheels and is manufactured primarily for use on public streets, roads, and highways. The plug-in electric drive motor vehicle may also be claimed for certain 2- and 3-wheeled plug-in electric vehicles (see *2- and 3-Wheeled Plug-in Electric Vehicles* discussed later).

Phaseout. The credit begins to phaseout after 200,000 vehicles have been sold for use in the United States. The phaseout period begins with the second calendar quarter following the calendar quarter in which the 200,000th unit is sold. For the first two quarters of the phaseout period, the credit is cut to 50 percent of the full credit amount. The credit is cut to 25 percent for the third and fourth quarters of the phaseout period. Thereafter, no credit is allowed (Code Sec. 30D(e)).

Special Rules. No qualified plug-in electric drive motor vehicle credit is allowed for property used predominantly outside of the United States. The amount of any other deduction or credit claimed with respect to the vehicle is reduced by the amount of the qualified plug-in electric drive vehicle credit. The individual's basis in the vehicle is reduced by the amount of credit claimed. The IRS is required to issue regulations providing for the recapture of the credit in the event the vehicle no longer qualifies for the credit. Taxpayers have the option to elect out of claiming this credit for a qualified vehicle. Finally, a vehicle is not eligible to be a qualified vehicle unless it is in compliance with the Clean Air Act for applicable makes and models of the vehicle and satisfies the motor vehicle standards under Title 49 of the United States Code (Code Sec. 30D(f)).

2- and 3-Wheeled Plug-in Electric Vehicles. A taxpayer may claim a credit for two- and three-wheeled plug-in electric vehicles (i.e., electric motorcycles) placed in service during the tax year (Code Sec. 30D(g), as amended by the Protecting Americans from Tax Hikes (PATH) Act of 2015 (P.L. 114-113)). The credit is equal to the applicable amount with respect to each new qualified 2- or 3-wheeled plug-in electric drive vehicle. The applicable amount is equal to the lesser of 10 percent of the cost of the vehicle or $2,500.

In order for a vehicle to qualify as a 2- or 3-wheeled plug-in electric drive vehicle, it must have 2 or 3 wheels, be made by a manufacturer, and be acquired for use or lease by the taxpayer and not for resale. The original use of the vehicle must begin with the taxpayer. In addition, the vehicle must:

- have a GVWR of less than 14,000 pounds;
- be primarily manufactured for use on public streets, roads, and highways;
- be able to achieve a speed of at least 45 miles an hour;
- be propelled to a significant extent by an electric motor drawing electricity from a battery having a capacity of at least 2.5 kilowatt hours that can be recharged from an external source;
- be acquired in 2012, 2013, 2015, or 2016 in the case of a 2-wheeled vehicle (no credit is available for 2-wheeled vehicle acquired in 2014); and
- be acquired in 2012 or 2013 in the case of a 3-wheeled vehicle (no credit is available for 3-wheeled vehicle acquired after 2013).

The IRS has issued guidance regarding certification of vehicles eligible for this credit (Notice 2013-67).

1355. Alternative Fuel Vehicle Refueling Property Credit. Taxpayers are permitted a credit for the installation of qualified alternative fuel refueling property, both hydrogen and non-hydrogen related, placed in service before January 1, 2017 (Code Sec.

30C, as amended by the Protecting Americans from Tax Hikes (PATH) Act of 2015 (P.L. 114-113)).[34] The credit is claimed on Form 8911 regardless of whether the property is personal or used in a trade or business. Taxpayers may elect not to have the credit apply to otherwise qualifying property.

Credit Amount. The credit amount is 30 percent of the cost of alternative fuel vehicle refueling property placed in service by the taxpayer during the tax year. There is a per-location limit of $30,000 for property subject to depreciation (a commercial or retail refueling stations). There is also a $1,000 for personal use property (residential property).

If the credit is attributable to property that is subject to depreciation, then it is considered to be part of the general business credit (¶ 1365). The amount of the credit that is not attributable to depreciable property cannot exceed the excess of the taxpayer's regular income tax liability reduced by the sum of nonrefundable personal credits and the foreign tax credit over the taxpayer's tentative minimum tax (Code Sec. 30C(d)).

Credits for property sold to a tax-exempt entity may be claimed by the seller but only if the seller discloses in a written document the amount of credit allowable. For this purpose, the property is treated as if it is depreciable property and thus is subject to the business tax credit limitation rule. Qualifying property used outside the United States cannot be used to claim the credit. The qualifying property's basis must be reduced by the amount of the credit claimed. However, should the property cease to be qualifying property, the credit may be recaptured. Taxpayers also have the option to elect not to claim this credit (Code Sec. 30(C)(e)).

Qualifying Property. Qualifying alternative fuel vehicle refueling property is property used for storing a clean-burning fuel or for dispensing clean-burning fuel into the fuel tank of a motor vehicle, but only if the property is located at the point where the fuel is delivered into the tank of the vehicle. It also includes any equipment that is used to recharge a motor vehicle that is propelled by electricity, but only if the property is located at the point where the vehicles are recharged. Only the following fuels shall be considered clean burning:

- any fuel that is at least 85 percent by volume consisting of ethanol, natural gas, compressed natural gas, liquefied natural gas, liquefied petroleum gas, or hydrogen;
- any fuel mixture that consists of a combination of at least two fuels which include biodiesel, diesel fuel, or kerosene with at least 20 percent of the volume being biodiesel without regard to any kerosene in the mixture; and
- electricity (Code Sec. 30C(c)).

Foreign Tax Credit

1361. Foreign Tax Credit. An individual taxpayer may either deduct foreign income taxes paid or accrued as an itemized deduction (¶ 1021) or claim them as a tax credit against his or her U.S. income tax liability (¶ 2475) (Code Sec. 27).[35] The credit is claimed by individuals on Form 1116 unless the total foreign taxes paid are not more than $300 for single filers ($600 for joint filers). For these taxpayers, the credit may be claimed directly on Form 1040 if all filing requirements are satisfied (¶ 2476). A corporate taxpayer may also either deduct foreign income taxes paid or accrued or elect to claim such payments as a credit against its U.S. income tax liability. Form 1118 is used by a corporation to calculate the amount of credit in a single tax year.

1362. U.S. Possessions Credit. A U.S. domestic corporation with a substantial portion of business in a U.S. possession may elect to claim a tax credit for taxes paid on business income derived from the possession and qualified investment income earned in the possession (Code Secs. 30A and 936).[36] The credit is generally unavailable to new

References are to Standard Federal Tax Reports; Tax Research Consultant; and Practical Tax Explanations.

[34] ¶ 4059F; INDIV: 57,750; § 12,910

[35] ¶ 4002; INTLOUT: 3,000; § 13,401

[36] ¶ 4058, ¶ 28,380; INTL: 27,000; § 13,435

claimants for tax years beginning after 1995 and is phased out for existing credit claimants for tax years beginning before 2006. A U.S. corporation that is an existing credit claimant with respect to American Samoa may still claim a version of the credit for tax years beginning before January 1, 2017 (Act Sec. 119(d) of the Tax Relief and Health Care Act of 2006 (P.L. 109-432), as amended by the Protecting Americans from Tax Hikes (PATH) Act of 2015 (P.L. 114-113)). In addition, other domestic corporations that have qualified production activities income (¶ 980B) from American Samoa can claim the credit for tax years beginning before January 1, 2017. Form 5735 is used to figure the credit for economic activity in American Samoa.

General Business Credits

1365. General Business Credit. The general business credit is a limited, nonrefundable credit that is claimed after all other nonrefundable credits (¶ 1315) are claimed, other than the minimum tax credit. The general business credit for a tax year is the sum of: (1) the business credit carried forward to the current year, (2) the amount of the current year business credit, and (3) the business credit carried back to that tax year (Code Sec. 38).[37]

The current year general business credit is the sum of:

- the investment credit (¶ 1365A);
- the work opportunity credit (¶ 1365G);
- the alcohol fuels credit (¶ 1365I);
- the research activities credit (¶ 1365J);
- the low-income housing credit (¶ 1365K);
- the enhanced oil recovery credit (¶ 1365L);
- the disabled access credit (¶ 1365M);
- the renewable electricity production credit (¶ 1365N);
- the empowerment zone employment credit (¶ 1365O);
- the Indian employment credit (¶ 1365Q);
- the employer Social Security credit (FICA tip credit) (¶ 1365R);
- the orphan drug credit (¶ 1365S);
- the new markets credit (¶ 1365T);
- the small employer pension plan start-up costs credit (¶ 1365U);
- the employer-provided child care facilities and services credit (¶ 1365V);
- the qualified railroad track maintenance credit (¶ 1365W);
- the biodiesel fuels credit (¶ 1365X);
- the low sulfur diesel fuel production credit (¶ 1365Y);
- the marginal oil and gas well production credit (¶ 1365KK);
- the distilled spirits credit (¶ 1365Z);
- the advanced nuclear power facility production credit (¶ 1365AA);
- the nonconventional source fuels credit (¶ 1365BB);
- the energy efficient home credit (¶ 1365CC);
- the energy efficient appliance credit (¶ 1365DD);
- the alternative motor vehicle credit (portion allocable to a trade or business) (¶ 1345);
- the alternative fuel vehicle refueling property credit (portion allocable to a trade or business) (¶ 1355);
- the mine rescue team training credit (¶ 1365GG);

References are to Standard Federal Tax Reports; Tax Research Consultant; and Practical Tax Explanations.

[37] ¶ 4250; BUSEXP: 54,000; § 13,601

- the differential wage payment credit (¶ 1365II);
- the carbon dioxide sequestration credit (¶ 1365JJ);
- the qualified plug-in electric drive motor vehicle credit (portion allocable to a trade or business) (¶ 1351);
- the small employer health insurance credit (¶ 1333);
- the credit for contributions to selected community development corporations (CDCs); and
- general credits from an electing large partnership (¶ 482–¶ 488).

Each of these credits is computed separately on its applicable IRS form. The credit computation form is attached to Form 3800, and the credit amount is reported on Form 3800. It is not necessary to attach a credit computation form if the taxpayer is not a partnership or S corporation and the taxpayer's only source for the credit is from a partnership, S corporation, estate, trust, or cooperative. However, an exception may apply if the taxpayer is claiming an investment credit (Form 3468) or a biodiesel credit (Form 8864), the taxpayer is an estate or trust and a credit is allocated to beneficiaries, or the taxpayer is a cooperative and the credit is allocated to patrons. See Form 3800 instructions for details.

Tax Liability Limitations. The general business credit may not exceed a limitation based on the amount of tax liability (Code Sec. 38(c)(1)). Specifically, the credit generally may not exceed net income tax less the greater of the taxpayer's tentative minimum tax liability or 25 percent of net regular tax liability above $25,000. The limitation, however, is determined separately for the portion of the credit attributable to the alcohol fuels credit, the low-income housing credit attributable to buildings placed in service after 2007, the renewable electricity production credit for electricity or refined coal produced at a facility placed in service after October 22, 2004, and during the 4-year period beginning on the date the facility was originally placed in service, the FICA tip credit, railroad track maintenance credit, the credit for small employer health insurance premiums, the energy credit component of the investment credit, the rehabilitation credit component of the investment credit attributable to expenditures for periods after 2007, and the work opportunity credit (Code Sec. 38(c)(4)). When calculating the limitation as it applies to these specified credits, the tentative minimum tax is to be treated as zero, which results in these credits being fully allowable against both the regular and alternative minimum tax (AMT) liabilities of the taxpayer.

For the empowerment zone employment credit (¶ 1365O), the credit amount may not exceed the excess of the net income tax over the greater of 75 percent of the taxpayer's tentative minimum tax liability or 25 percent of net regular tax liability above $25,000. This result is then reduced by the general business credit allowed for the tax year other than the empowerment zone employment credit and the specified credits listed above (Code Sec. 38(c)(2)).

For purposes of calculating these limitations, net income tax is the sum of the taxpayer's regular tax liability (¶ 1420) and AMT liability (¶ 1401), less all other nonrefundable credits (Code Secs. 21—30D). Net regular tax liability is the regular tax liability reduced by these credits (Code Sec. 38(c)(1)).

For a married couple filing separate returns, the $25,000 figure is limited to $12,500 for each spouse. If, however, one spouse has no current credit or unused credit, the spouse having current credit or unused credit may use the full $25,000 figure in determining his or her credit for the year. For a controlled group of corporations, the group may divide the $25,000 figure among its members in any way the members choose. For an estate or trust, the $25,000 figure is reduced to an amount that bears the same ratio to $25,000 as the portion of the estate's or trust's income that is not allocated to the beneficiaries bears to the total income of the estate or trust (Code Sec. 38(c)(6)).

Carrybacks and Carryforwards. If the tax liability limit is exceeded for the tax year, the components of the general business credit are generally deemed used in the order listed above (Code Sec. 38(d); Form 3800 instructions). Any excess or unused amount may be carried back one year and forward 20 years (Code Sec. 39).[38] The order in which these credits are claimed in any carryback or carryforward year is as follows: (1) carryforwards to that year on a first-in, first-out (FIFO) basis, (2) the general business credit earned in that year, and (3) the carrybacks to that year on a FIFO basis.

Eligible small business credits of an eligible small business determined for its first tax year beginning in 2010 may be carried back five years and forward 20 years (Code Sec. 39(a)(4)). Eligible small business credits are the current year business credit components of the general business credit. An eligible small business is a sole proprietorship, partnership, or non-publicly traded corporation with $50 million or less in average annual gross receipts during the three tax years preceding the first tax year beginning in 2010. The eligible small business credits determined for 2010 may be claimed against the eligible small business's regular and AMT liabilities.

Separate carryback and carryforward records must be maintained for the amount of the general business credit attributable to the empowerment zone employment credit, and to each of the other components of the general business credit. Separate recordkeeping is necessary because the empowerment zone employment credit may offset up to 25 percent of the taxpayer's AMT (Code Sec. 38(c)(2)(A)). Several of the credits that remain unused at the end of the carryforward period, or when the taxpayer ceases to exist, may be claimed as a deduction in the following year (Code Sec. 196).[39]

1365A. Investment Credit–Overview. Taxpayers may claim an investment credit which is the sum of the rehabilitation credit (¶ 1365B), the energy credit (¶ 1365C), the qualifying advanced coal project credit (¶ 1365D), the qualifying gasification project credit (¶ 1365E), and the qualifying advanced energy project credit (¶ 1365F) (Code Sec. 46).[40] The investment credit is claimed on Form 3468 and is one of the components of the general business credit, subject to the tax liability limitation and the carryover rules (¶ 1365).

The amount of investment credit allowed on investment credit property of a partnership for a tax year is generally apportioned among partners according to the ratio in which the partners divide the general profits of the partnership. The investment credit amount on an S corporation's investment credit property for a tax year is apportioned among the shareholders on a daily basis according to each shareholder's proportion of ownership. The investment credit amount allowed on investment credit property of an estate or trust is apportioned between the estate or trust and the beneficiaries on the basis of the income allocable to each.

At-Risk Limitation. No investment credit is allowed for investment credit property to the extent that the property is financed with nonqualified nonrecourse borrowing (Code Sec. 49).[41] Thus, the credit base of investment credit property is reduced by the amount of nonqualified nonrecourse financing regarding the property, as determined at the close of the tax year in which the property is placed in service.

Nonqualified nonrecourse financing is any nonrecourse financing which is not qualified commercial financing. Qualified commercial financing is any financing of property if: (1) the property is acquired from an unrelated person; (2) the amount of the nonrecourse financing does not exceed 80 percent of the property's credit base; and (3) the financing is borrowed from a qualified person, or represents a loan from any Federal, state or local government or instrumentality, or which is guaranteed by any Federal, state or local government or instrumentality. The credit base is equal to the sum of the portion of the basis of a qualified rehabilitation building attributable to qualified rehabilitation expenditures, the basis of energy property, and the basis of any property that is part of a qualifying advanced coal project, a qualifying gasification project, or a qualified advanced energy project. A qualified person is any person who actively and regularly engages in the business of lending money and is not the person from whom the property

References are to Standard Federal Tax Reports; Tax Research Consultant; and Practical Tax Explanations.

[38] ¶ 4300; BUSEXP: 54,058; § 13,605.15

[39] ¶ 12,400; BUSEXP: 54,058.10; § 13,605.20

[40] ¶ 4502; BUSEXP: 51,050; § 13,701

[41] ¶ 4750; BUSEXP: 51,400; § 13,730.05

was acquired, a person who receives a fee with respect to the taxpayer's investment in the property, or a person who is related to the taxpayer (Code Sec. 49(a)(1)(D)).

Decreases in nonqualified recourse financing on the property in tax years following the year in which the property was placed in service increase the credit base of the property. This rule does not apply if the decrease occurs through the surrender or other use of property financed by nonqualified nonrecourse financing. Similarly, increases in nonqualified nonrecourse financing on the property in tax years following the year in which the property was placed in service decrease the credit base of the property and trigger recapture (Code Sec. 49(a)(2) and (b)).

The limitation applies to investment credit property placed in service by individuals and by certain closely held corporations engaged in business activities that are subject to the loss limitation rules of the at-risk rules (¶ 1155). For a partnership or S corporation, the investment credit at-risk limitation applies at the partner or shareholder level (Code Sec. 49(a)(1)(E)).

The investment credit at-risk limitation does not apply to certain energy property. To come within this exception, nonqualified nonrecourse financing may not exceed 75 percent of the basis of energy property at the close of the tax year in which the property is placed in service. In addition, any nonqualified nonrecourse financing for such property must be a level payment loan (a loan repaid in substantially equal installments, including both principal and interest).

An increase in the amount at risk is treated as if it occurred in the year that the property was first placed in service for purposes of computing the investment credit and for computing any recapture of the credit. However, the investment credit attributable to the increase in the amount at risk is claimed by the taxpayer during the tax year in which the decrease in the amount of nonqualified nonrecourse financing occurs.

If at the close of a tax year there is a net increase in the amount of nonqualified nonrecourse financing regarding such property, thereby causing a decrease in the taxpayer's amount at risk, the investment credit must be recomputed and the decrease in investment credits for previous tax years is recaptured as additional tax in the year that the net increase in nonqualified nonrecourse financing occurs.

Ineligible Property. No investment credit is allowed for: (1) property used predominantly outside the United States except in limited circumstances; (2) property used predominantly to furnish lodging (or in connection with the furnishing of lodging), except in the case of non-lodging commercial facilities, a hotel or motel furnishing accommodations predominantly to transients, certified historic structures to the extent of that portion of the basis attributable to qualified rehabilitation expenditures, and energy property; and (3) property used by a tax-exempt organization (other than a farmers' cooperative) unless it is used predominantly in an unrelated trade or business (Code Sec. 50(b)).[42] Property used by, or leased to, a governmental unit, foreign person, or foreign entity is generally not eligible for the investment credit. The portion of the property attributable to qualified rehabilitation expenditures or held under a short-term lease (generally under six months) does, however, qualify for the investment credit.

Basis Reduction. The basis of property for which an investment credit is claimed is reduced by the full amount of the credit, except for the energy credit property whose basis is reduced by 50 percent of the credit amount (¶ 1365B) (Code Sec. 50(c)).[43] The reduced basis is used to compute depreciation and any gain or loss on the disposition of property.

If the investment credit is recaptured on property for which an investment credit downward basis adjustment was made, the basis of the property immediately before the event resulting in recapture must be increased by the recapture amount and by 50 percent of the recapture amount for an energy credit. In determining the amount of gain that is recaptured as ordinary income on a sale or disposition of depreciable personal property (Code Sec. 1245) or depreciable real property (Code Sec. 1250), the amount of

References are to Standard Federal Tax Reports; Tax Research Consultant; and Practical Tax Explanations.

[42] ¶ 4752; BUSEXP: 51,250; § 13,701

[43] ¶ 4752; BUSEXP: 51,056; § 13,740

the investment credit downward basis adjustment is treated as a deduction allowed for depreciation. Thus, the basis adjustment is treated as depreciation subject to ordinary income recapture. For section 1250 property, the recapture applies only to the excess of depreciation claimed over depreciation computed under the straight-line method, with the latter computed on the basis without reduction for the applicable investment credit downward basis adjustment.

If an investment credit for which a downward basis adjustment was made does not result in a tax benefit because it remains unused at the end of the 20-year credit carryover period for tax years after December 31, 1997, a deduction is allowed under Code Sec. 196 to the taxpayer for 50 percent of the unused energy and 100 percent of any other unused investment credit attributable to the basis reduction.

Special Investment Credit Rules. Special limitations apply to the amount of investment credit that may be claimed by regulated investment companies (RICs or mutual funds), real estate investment trusts (REITs), noncorporate lessors, and certain other regulated companies (Code Sec. 50(d)).[44]

Early Disposition. When investment credit property is disposed of by the taxpayer (including dispositions due to casualties or thefts), or ceases to be investment credit property before the end of its recapture period, the tax for the year of disposal or cessation is increased by the amount of the credit that is recaptured (Code Sec. 50(a)).[45] A taxpayer subject to recapture must file Form 4255.

The amount of the recapture is a percentage of the original credit claimed, depending on how long the property is held before recapture is required. The recapture percentages are 100 percent within the first full year after placement in service, 80 percent within the second full year, 60 percent within the third full year, 40 percent within the fourth full year, 20 percent within the fifth full year, and zero thereafter. Advance rehabilitation or energy credits on progress expenditures are also subject to recapture. Special recapture rules apply to certain energy property.

The recapture rules do not apply: (1) a transfer between spouses or incident to divorce (¶ 778) (but a later disposition by the transferee will result in recapture to the same extent as if the disposition had been made by the transferor at that later date), (2) a transfer because of death, and (3) a transfer to which Code Sec. 381(a) (concerning carryovers after corporate acquisitions) applies. Similarly, the recapture rules do not apply where there is a mere change in the form of operating a business, provided that the property is retained in the business and the taxpayer retains a substantial interest in the business.

1365B. Rehabilitation Credit. A part of the investment credit (¶ 1365A), the rehabilitation investment credit is 20 percent of qualified rehabilitation expenses (QREs) for certified historic structures and 10 percent of QREs for qualified rehabilitated buildings (QRBs) first placed in service before 1936 (other than certified historic structures) (Code Sec. 47).[46] An election may also be made to claim an advance rehabilitation investment credit. No energy credit (¶ 1365C) is allowed on that portion of the basis of property that is attributable to QREs (Code Sec. 48(a)(2)(B)). Certain restrictions also apply to property which is used as lodging (Code Sec. 50(b)).

Eligibility. A building and its structural components constitute a QRB if they are substantially rehabilitated for the tax year and placed in service by any person before the beginning of the rehabilitation. Property other than a certified historic structure must also satisfy: (1) the applicable wall retention test, (2) an age requirement, and (3) a location-of-rehabilitation requirement (Code Sec. 47(c)(1); Reg. § 1.48-12(b)).[47] Property is considered substantially rehabilitated only if the expenditures during an elected 24-month measurement period (60-month period for phased rehabilitations) ending with or within the tax year are greater then the adjusted basis of the property or $5,000.

References are to Standard Federal Tax Reports; Tax Research Consultant; and Practical Tax Explanations.

[44] ¶ 4752; BUSEXP: 51,650, BUSEXP: 51,606; § 13,701

[45] ¶ 4752; BUSEXP: 51,450, BUSEXP: 51,500; § 13,735

[46] ¶ 4600; BUSEXP: 51,152; § 13,705

[47] ¶ 4600, ¶ 4609; BUSEXP: 51,154; § 13,705

QREs do not include: (1) an enlargement or new construction; (2) the cost of acquisition; (3) non-certified rehabilitation of a certified historic structure; (4) rehabilitation of tax-exempt use property; (5) expenditures, generally, that are not depreciated under the MACRS straight-line method over specified recovery periods; or (6) a lessee-incurred expenditure if, on the date the rehabilitation of the building is completed, the remaining term of the lease (determined without regard to renewal periods) is less than the applicable recovery period (Reg. § 1.48-12(c)).

The rehabilitation investment credit for QREs generally must be claimed in the tax year in which the property attributable to the expenditures is placed in service, provided that the building is a QRB for such tax year (Code Sec. 47(b)). The credit may be claimed before the date the property is placed in service under the rules for qualified progress expenditures (Code Sec. 47(d)).

Advance Credits for Progress Expenditures. An election may be made to claim an advance rehabilitation investment credit for progress expenditures on certain rehabilitated buildings before such property is placed in service (Code Sec. 47(d)).[48] Property qualifying for an advance rehabilitation investment credit on progress expenditures includes a building that is being rehabilitated by, or for, the taxpayer, if the normal rehabilitation period for the building is two or more years and it is reasonable to expect that the building will be a QRB when it is placed in service.

The amount of QREs that are considered progress expenditures for which an advance rehabilitation investment credit may be claimed is the amount of QREs properly chargeable to the capital account for self-rehabilitated buildings. For non-self-rehabilitated buildings, the amount is the lesser of: (a) the QRE paid to another person for the rehabilitation of the building during the tax year, or (b) the portion of the overall cost of the rehabilitation completed during the tax year.

1365C. Energy Credit. A part of the investment credit (¶ 1365A), the business energy investment credit is generally equal to a percentage of the taxpayer's basis in qualified energy property placed in service during the tax year (Code Sec. 48, as amended by the Protecting Americans from Tax Hikes (PATH) Act of 2015 (P.L. 114-113)).[49] The credit percentage before January 1, 2017, is: (1) 10 percent for combined heat and power system property, as well microturbine property—property that uses the ground or ground water as a thermal energy source or sink; (2) 30 percent for qualified fuel cell property, equipment that uses solar energy to illuminate the inside of a structure using fiber-optic distributed sunlight, and qualified small wind energy property. For equipment that uses solar energy to generate electricity, heat or cool a structure, or provide solar process heat (but not to heat a swimming pool), the credit percentage is 30 percent if construction of the property begins before 2020; 26 percent if construction begins during 2020; 22 percent if construction begins during 2021; and 10 percent if construction begins before 2022 but the property is not placed in service before 2024. The credit for qualified fuel cell property may not exceed $1,500 for each 0.5 kilowatt of capacity.

To qualify for the credit, the energy property must be depreciable or amortizable, and must meet performance and quality standards prescribed by IRS regulations. The taxpayer must complete the construction, reconstruction, or erection of the property, or be the first person to use acquired property. The basis of all energy property prior to the credit determination is reduced by any tax-exempt or subsidized financing. No energy credit is allowed for that portion of the basis of property for which a rehabilitation investment credit (¶ 1365B) is claimed. An advance energy investment credit may be claimed under special rules for progress expenditures. The energy credit may be claimed against the alternative minimum tax.

Investment Credit Election. A taxpayer may make an irrevocable election to treat certain qualified property that is part of a qualified investment credit facility as energy property eligible for a 30-percent investment credit (Code Sec. 48(a)(5), as amended by P.L. 114-113). If the election is made, no renewable electricity production credit is

References are to Standard Federal Tax Reports; Tax Research Consultant; and Practical Tax Explanations.

[48] ¶ 4600; BUSEXP: 51,160; § 13,705

[49] ¶ 4651; BUSEXP: 51,102; § 13,710

allowed (¶ 1365N) for any tax year with respect to the facility. Qualified investment credit facilities are facilities that are placed in service after 2008, otherwise eligible for the renewable electricity production credit, and produce electricity using wind or solar power, closed-loop biomass, open-loop biomass, geothermal energy, landfill gas, municipal solid waste (trash), hydropower, or marine and hydrokinetic renewable energy. Construction of the facility generally must begin before 2017. For a wind facility, construction must begin before 2020, but the credit is reduced by 20 percent if construction begins in 2017, by 40 percent if construction begins in 2018, and by 60 percent if construction begins in 2019. Qualified investment credit property must also be depreciable or amortizable tangible personal property or other tangible property (not including a building or its structural components) that is used as an integral part of the qualified investment credit facility. In addition, it must be constructed, reconstructed, erected, or acquired by the taxpayer, with the original use of the property commencing with the taxpayer.

Coordination With Section 1603 Grants. The Secretary of Treasury is authorized to provide a grant to each person who places into service specified energy property that is either: (1) an electricity production facility otherwise eligible for the renewable electricity production credit, or (2) qualifying property otherwise eligible for the energy investment credit (Act Sec. 1603(a) of the American Recovery and Reinvestment Act of 2009 (P.L. 111-5), as amended by the Tax Relief, Unemployment Insurance Reauthorization, and Job Creation Act of 2010 (P.L. 111-312)). In order to be eligible for the grant, the specified energy property must be:

- placed in service during 2009, 2010, or 2011, or
- placed in service after 2011 and before the credit termination date for such property, if construction of the property began during 2009, 2010, or 2011.

No energy credit or electricity production credit is allowed for the year of the grant or any subsequent year (Code Sec. 48(d)). In the event that a credit amount was claimed for the facility prior to the grant being made, the credit amount is recaptured by adding the prior claimed credit amounts to the tax liability of the grant year. The taxpayer must adjust any carryovers of general business credits to reflect the amount of the recaptured credit. The energy credit and electricity production credit may not be claimed on account of the reduction of a section 1603 grant by reason of the sequestration rules (Notice 2014-39).

1365D. Qualified Advanced Coal Project Credit. A qualifying advanced coal project credit may be claimed as a component of the investment credit (¶ 1365A) (Code Sec. 48A).[50] The credit is available only to taxpayers who have applied for and received certification that their project satisfies the relevant requirements outlined by the IRS, in consultation with the Secretary of Energy. The credit is equal to 20 percent of qualified investments in integrated combined cycle projects, 15 percent of qualified investments in other advanced coal-based projects, and 30 percent of qualified investments in advanced coal-based generation technology projects. The IRS is required to recapture any tax benefits should the project fail to maintain carbon dioxide separation and sequestration.

1365E. Qualified Gasification Project Credit. A qualifying gasification project credit may be claimed as a component of the investment credit (¶ 1365A) (Code Sec. 48B).[51] The credit is available only to taxpayers who have applied for and received certification that their project satisfies the relevant requirements outlined by the IRS, in consultation with the Secretary of Energy. The credit is equal to 20 percent of qualified investments in qualifying gasification projects, increased to 30 percent for qualifying gasification projects that include equipment that separates and sequesters at least 75 percent of the project's total carbon dioxide emissions. A qualifying gasification facility is one that combines coal, petroleum residue, biomass, or other materials with steam under high pressure to create a synthetic gas, or "syngas." The IRS is authorized to recapture any tax benefits if the project fails to attain or maintain the 75-percent separation and sequestration requirement.

References are to Standard Federal Tax Reports; Tax Research Consultant; and Practical Tax Explanations.

[50] ¶ 4672; BUSEXP: 51,700; § 13,715

[51] ¶ 4676; BUSEXP: 51,750; § 13,720

1365F. Advanced Energy Project Credit. A tax credit is allowed equal to 30 percent of a taxpayer's qualified investment for the tax year with respect to any qualifying advanced energy project (Code Sec. 48C).[52] The credit is part of the investment credit (¶ 1365A) and the basis of any property that is part of a qualifying advanced energy project is included in the credit base for purposes of applying the investment credit at-risk limitation rules. The credit is not allowed for any qualified investment for which a credit is also allowed for the energy credit (¶ 1365C), the qualifying advanced coal project credit (¶ 1365D), or the qualifying gasification project credit (¶ 1365E).

A qualifying advanced energy project is a project that re-equips, expands, or establishes a manufacturing facility for the production of: (1) property designed to be used to produce energy from the sun, wind, or geothermal deposits or other renewable resources; (2) fuel cells, microturbines, or an energy storage system for use with electric or hybrid-electric motor vehicles; (3) electric grids to support the transmission of intermittent sources of renewable energy, including storage of such energy; (4) property designed to capture and sequester carbon dioxide emissions; (5) property designed to refine or blend renewable fuels or to produce energy conservation technologies (including energy-conserving lighting technologies and smart grid technologies); (6) new qualified plug-in electric drive motor vehicles or components which are designed specifically for use with such vehicles, including electric motors, generators, and power control units; or (7) other advanced energy property designed to reduce greenhouse gas emissions as may be determined by the Secretary of Treasury (Code Sec. 48C(c)(1)). Any portion of the qualified investment in the qualifying project must be certified by the Secretary of Treasury as eligible for the credit. A qualifying project does not include any portion of a project for the production of any property used in the refining or blending of any transportation fuel, other than renewable fuels.

1365G. Work Opportunity Tax Credit. The work opportunity credit is available for wages paid by employers who hire individuals from certain targeted groups of hard-to-employ individuals (Code Sec. 51, as amended by the Protecting Americans from Tax Hikes (PATH) Act of 2015 (P.L. 114-113)).[53] The credit is generally 40 percent of the first $6,000 of qualified wages ($3,000 for qualified summer youth employees) paid to each member of a targeted group during the first year of employment and 25 percent in the case of wages attributable to individuals meeting only minimum employment levels. Any business deduction for such wages must be reduced by the amount of the credit, as computed on Form 5884.

Tax Liability Limitations. Although the work opportunity credit is a component of the general business credit (¶ 1365), credit amounts are not subject to the general business credit tax liability limitation rule but are to be calculated separately. The credit limitation formula is changed to treat the tentative minimum tax as zero, allowing taxpayers to fully utilize the credit against both the regular tax and the minimum tax liabilities (Code Sec. 38(c)(4)). The credit limitation calculation applies to any carrybacks of such credit amounts to any previous year. No credit is allowed for wages paid to an individual for services rendered at the employer's plant or facility that are substantially similar to services performed by employees who are participants in a strike or who are affected by a lockout.

Minimum Employment Period. An employee must have completed a minimum of 120 hours of service for the wages to be taken into account for calculation of the work opportunity credit. The hours-of-service test is the only way the minimum employment period is measured for purposes of the credit. If the 120-hour test is met but the employee fails to perform at least 400 hours of service, the employer is entitled to a credit of 25 percent. For 400 or more hours of service, the percentage is 40 percent of the employee's wages (Code Sec. 51(i)(3)).

References are to Standard Federal Tax Reports; Tax Research Consultant; and Practical Tax Explanations.

[52] ¶ 4685; BUSEXP: 51,800; § 13,725

[53] ¶ 4800; BUSEXP: 54,250; § 13,805.05

Target Groups. Wages paid to individuals who are certified members of one of the following groups qualify for the work opportunity credit (Code Sec. 51(d)):

- a qualified IV-A recipient (the individual must be a member of a family that received Temporary Assistance for Needy Families (TANF) assistance for any 9 of the 18 months before the hire date);
- a qualified veteran;
- a qualified ex-felon (the individual must have a hire date within one year of being released from prison);
- a designated community resident (the individual must be at least 18 years of age but less than 40 years of age on the hiring date and live in an empowerment zone or rural renewal county while such designation is in effect);
- a vocational rehabilitation referral (the individual must have a physical or mental handicap resulting in a substantial handicap to employment and be referred to the employer upon completion of rehabilitative services);
- a qualified summer youth employee (the individual must be a new hire who performs services between May 1 and September 15, be 16 or 17 years of age on the later of the hire date or May 1, and must live in an empowerment zone while such designation is in effect) (the maximum qualified wages is $3,000 with the maximum credit amount being $1,200);
- a qualified food stamps recipient (the individual must be at least 18 of age but younger than 40 years of age and be a member of a family that either received food stamp benefits for the six months before the hire date or received food stamp benefits for three of the five months before the hire date but lost the benefits for failure to comply with the program's work requirements);
- a qualified supplemental security income (SSI) recipient (the individual must have received SSI within 60 days before the hire date);
- a long-term family assistance recipient (the individual must be a member of a family that received the maximum amount of IV-A (TANF) assistance over an 18-month period ending within two years of the hire date) (up to $10,000 are considered qualified first year wages, up to $10,000 are considered qualified second year wages, and the credit percentage equals 50 percent for the second year (maximum credit amount of $5,000)); or
- a long-term unemployment recipient who begins work for the employer after December 31, 2015 (an individual unemployed for at least 27 weeks, including periods in which he or she was receiving unemployment compensation under State or Federal law (Code Sec. 51(d)(1)(J) and (d)(15), as added by P.L. 114-113)).

Certifications. An employer of an individual who is a member of a targeted group must either have the individual certified by an authorized local agency prior to the individual's first day of work or file an application for certification of the individual within 28 days of the first day of work (Code Sec. 51(d)(12)). Employers use Form 8850 to prescreen employees and to make a written request that the local agency certify an employee as being a member of a targeted group. Employers are permitted to submit Form 8850 electronically. Two alternative methods of certification using electronic signatures are also permitted (Notice 2012-13). Employers claiming the work opportunity credit for certain targeted group members hired from January 1, 2015, through May 31, 2016, were granted an extension of time to comply with certification requirements (Notice 2016-22, modified by Notice 2016-40).

Special Rules for Qualified Veterans. A veteran is a qualified veteran if the veteran is certified as falling within one of the following categories (Code Sec. 51(d)(3) and (d)(13)(D)):

- a member of a family receiving assistance under a supplemental nutrition assistance program under the Food and Nutrition Act of 2008 for at least a three-month period ending during the 12-month period ending on the hiring date;
- a veteran entitled to compensation for a service-connected disability and either has a hiring date which is not more than one year after discharge or release

from active duty or has aggregate periods of unemployment during the one-year period ending on the hiring date which equal or exceed six months;

- a veteran with aggregate periods of unemployment during the one-year period ending on the hiring date which equal or exceed four weeks (but less than six months); or

- a veteran with aggregate periods of unemployment during the one-year period ending on the hiring date which equal or exceed six months.

Although the qualified wage limit is generally $6,000 for a targeted group member, the limit is increased to: (a) $12,000 for an individual who is a qualified veteran by reason of being entitled to compensation for a service-connected disability and having a hiring date which is not more than one year after discharge; (b) $24,000 for an individual who is a qualified veteran by reason of being entitled to compensation for a service-connected disability and having aggregate periods of unemployment during the one-year period ending on the hiring date which equal or exceed six months; and (c) $14,000 for an individual who is a qualified veteran by reason of having aggregate periods of unemployment during the one-year period ending on the hiring date which equal or exceed six months (Code Sec. 51(b)(3)).

Tax-Exempt Organizations and Qualified Veterans. Tax-exempt organizations, other than exempt farmers' cooperatives (¶ 698) generally cannot claim the work opportunity credit (Code Sec. 52(c)). However, Code Sec. 501(c) exempt organizations (¶ 602 and ¶ 692) that employ qualified veterans may take advantage of the credit. The credit rate in such circumstances is reduced from 40 percent to 26 percent of qualified wages. These exempt organizations must use Form 5884-C to claim the credit. The form is filed separately and is not attached to any other return filed by the exempt organization. The credit is allowed against the tax-exempt employer's FICA tax obligation on wages paid to the veteran within one year of hiring (Code Sec. 3111(e)). The liability on the organization's employment tax return is not reduced by the credit; rather, the credit is processed separately and the amount properly claimed is refunded to the exempt organization. This is likely to occur after the filing of the return, so organizations are cautioned not to reduce their FICA obligation on their returns in anticipation of the refund (Notice 2012-13).

1365I. Alcohol Fuels Credit. Producers of alcohol fuels or alcohol fuel mixtures are entitled to a tax credit for any sale or use unless the alcohol fuels was produced outside the United State for use as a fuel outside the United States (Code Sec. 40).[54] The credit is the sum of the second generation biofuel producer credit (formerly, the cellulosic biofuel producer credit), alcohol mixture credit (expired), the alcohol credit (expired), and the small ethanol producer credit (expired). With the exception of the second generation biofuel producer credit, the alcohol fuels credit may not be claimed with respect to sales or uses after December 31, 2011. The credit is computed on Form 6478 and is a component of the general business credit (¶ 1365), but the credit limitation is calculated separately from the general business credit limitation. The credit amount may be claimed against both the regular and the alternative minimum tax liabilities.

Second Generation Biofuel Producer Credit (formerly, Cellulosic Biofuel Production Credit). The second generation biofuel producer credit is equal to $1.01 per gallon of qualified second generation biofuel produced by a qualified second generation biofuel producer before January 1, 2017 (Code Sec. 40(b)(6), as amended by the Protecting Americans from Tax Hikes (PATH) Act of 2015 (P.L. 114-113)). Second generation biofuel is defined as any liquid fuel produced from lignocellulosic or hemicellulosic matter or, with respect to fuels sold or used after January 2, 2013, from any cultivated algae, cyanobacteria, or lemna, that is available on a renewable or recurring basis and that meets the Environmental Protection Agency registration requirements for fuel and fuel additives established under section 211 of the Clear Air Act. The fuel called "black liquor," as well as crude tall oil (made by reacting acid with black liquor soap), does not

References are to Standard Federal Tax Reports; Tax Research Consultant; and Practical Tax Explanations.

[54] ¶ 4302; BUSEXP: 54,100; § 14,205

qualify for the credit. Renewable sources of lignocellulosic and hemicellulosic matter include energy crops and trees, wood and wood residues, plants, grasses, agricultural residues, fibers, animal wastes, and other waste material, including municipal solid waste.

The second generation biofuel must be used by the producer for specific purposes or sold to another person who will use the second generation biofuel for those purposes. The specified purposes are: (1) to use in a trade or business to produce an alcohol mixture (other than casual off-farm production), (2) to use as a fuel in a trade or business, or (3) to sell to another person at retail and putting the ethanol in the buyer's fuel tank. A qualified second generation biofuel producer is one that is registered with the IRS as a second generation biofuel producer whose production is produced and used in its entirety within the United States. The second generation biofuel claimed under Code Sec. 40 cannot also be claimed under Code Sec. 40A as renewable diesel or biodiesel (¶ 1365X).

Special Rules. Special rules apply for partnerships, S corporations, and other pass-through entities which include allocation to patrons of farm cooperatives. All taxpayers have the option of electing to not claim the alcohol fuels credit. Any excise tax exemption claimed with respect to alcohol produced for alcohol fuels reduces the amount of the income tax credit. The carryforward period for the alcohol fuels credit is limited to three tax years after the relevant fuel's termination year. An alcohol fuels credit carryforward that is unused at the end of the carryforward period is deductible in the following tax year (Code Sec. 196).

Recapture of Credit. If the alcohol fuels credit is claimed, the producer must pay a tax on each gallon at the original credit rate if the producer separates alcohol from the mixture, uses the alcohol mixture other than as fuel, mixes alcohol on which the credit was allowed for retail sale, uses the alcohol other than as fuel, or for ethanol fuel or second generation biofuel, does not use the fuel for the required purpose (Code Sec. 40(d)(3)). The tax must be reported on Form 720.

1365J. Credit for Increased Research Expenditures. A credit for incremental research expenses (computed on Form 6765) is claimed as one of the components of the general business credit (¶ 1365) (Code Sec. 41).[55] The credit has been made permanent by the Protecting Americans from Tax Hikes Act of 2015 (P.L. 114-113).

The credit is subject to the general business credit's tax liability limitation and carryover rules (¶ 1365). The research credit that remains unused at the end of the carryforward period is allowed as a deduction in the year following the expiration of such period (Code Sec. 196). The credit does not apply to unused amounts claimed under the reduced research credit election.

In the case of an eligible small business, the research credit is treated as a "specified credit" that may offset alternative minimum tax as well as regular tax, effective for credits determined for tax years beginning after December 31, 2015 (Code Sec. 38(c)(4), as amended by P.L. 114-113). An eligible small business is a partnership, sole proprietorship, or corporation without publicly traded stock that has average annual gross receipts of less than $50 million in the three preceding tax years (Code Sec. 38(c)(5)(C)(i)).

Amount of Credit. Unless an election is made to use the alternative simplified credit computation (discussed later), the research credit is the sum of: (1) 20 percent of the excess of qualified research expenses for the current tax year over a base period amount; (2) 20 percent of the basic research payments made to a qualified organization; and (3) 20 percent of the amounts paid or incurred by a taxpayer in carrying on any trade or business to an energy research consortium for qualified energy research (Code Sec. 41(a)). Special base period adjustments are required where there is an acquisition or disposition of the major portion of a business that paid or incurred research expenses.

References are to Standard Federal Tax Reports; Tax Research Consultant; and Practical Tax Explanations.

[55] ¶ 4350; BUSEXP: 54,150; § 13,901

Base Amount. The base period amount is the product of the taxpayer's fixed-base percentage and average annual gross receipts for the four tax years preceding the credit period (Code Sec. 41(c)). The base amount may not be less than 50 percent of the qualified research expenses for the credit year. The fixed-base percentage (aggregate qualified research expenses compared to aggregate gross receipts for 1984 through 1988 tax years) may not exceed 16 percent.

Start-Up Company. A start-up company's fixed-base percentage is three percent for each of the first five tax years for which it has qualified research expenses. The fixed-base percentage for the sixth through tenth tax years in which qualified research expenses were incurred is a portion of the percentage which qualified research expenses bear to gross receipts for specified preceding years. For subsequent tax years, the fixed-base percentage is the whole percentage that qualified research expenses bear to gross receipts for any five years selected by the taxpayer from the fifth through tenth tax years. The definition of a start-up company includes a taxpayer who has both gross receipts and qualified research expenses for the first time in a tax year that begins after 1983 (Code Sec. 41(c)(3)(B)).

Alternative Simplified Credit. Taxpayers may elect an alternative method to calculate the research credit amount using an alternative simplified credit (Code Sec. 41(c)(5)). Under the alternative simplified credit method, a taxpayer can claim an amount equal to 14 percent of the amount by which the qualified research expenses exceed 50 percent of the average qualified research expenses for the three preceding tax years (Code Sec. 41(c)(5)). If the taxpayer has no qualified research expenses for any of the preceding three years, then the credit is equal to six percent of the qualified research expenses for the current tax year. If the taxpayer makes the election to use the alternative simplified credit method, the election is effective for succeeding tax years unless revoked with the consent of the IRS.

Deduction for Research and Experimental Expenditures. A taxpayer claiming the credit must reduce the business deduction for research and experimental expenditures (¶ 979) by the amount of the research credit (Code Sec. 280C(c)). Capitalized expenses must also be reduced by the amount of the research credit that exceeds the amount otherwise allowable as a deduction for such expenses. An annual irrevocable election is available to claim a reduced research credit and thereby avoid reducing the research expense deduction or capital expenditures. Under the election, the research credit must be reduced by the product of the research credit computed in the regular manner and the maximum corporate tax rate.

Qualified Research Expenses. Qualified research expenses for purposes of calculating the credit are the same as those for the business deduction (¶ 979) other than expenses for foreign research, research in the social sciences, arts or humanities, or subsidized research. However, research eligible for the credit is limited to research undertaken to discover information that is technological in nature and intended to be useful in the development of a new or improved business component. Further, the research must relate to elements of a process of experimentation for a functional purpose, i.e., it must relate to a new or improved function, performance, reliability, or quality.

Qualified research expenses cover in-house expenses for the taxpayer's own research (i.e., wages, including income from employees' exercise of stock options, for substantially engaging in or directly supervising or supporting research activities, supplies, and computer use charges) and 65 percent of amounts paid or incurred for qualified research done by a person other than an employee of the taxpayer. The percentage is increased to 75 percent of amounts paid or incurred for qualified research performed by a qualified research consortium. This is a tax-exempt organization under either Code Sec. 501(c)(3) or (c)(6) that must be operating primarily to conduct energy research. In addition, the consortium must have at least five unrelated customers, with no single person accounting for more than 50 percent of the revenues of the organization.

Qualified Energy Research Expenditures. The 20-percent credit amount applies to expenditures to an energy research consortium for qualified energy research only. The percent limitation placed on outside research does not apply to energy research. Amounts paid or incurred for any energy research conducted outside of the United States, Puerto Rico, or U.S. possession cannot be taken into account in determining the 20 percent of amounts paid or incurred by a taxpayer in carrying on any trade or business during the tax year to an energy research consortium (Code Sec. 41(f)(6)(C)).

Special Rule for Pass-Through Entities. For individuals with interests in unincorporated businesses, partners, trust or estate beneficiaries, or S corporation shareholders, any allowable pass-through of the credit cannot exceed the amount of tax attributable to the individual's taxable income allocable to that individual's interest in the entity (Code Sec. 41(g)).

Payroll Tax Credit in Lieu of Research Credit. In tax years beginning after December 31, 2015, a qualified small business may elect to apply a portion of its research credit against the 6.2 percent payroll tax imposed on the employer's wage payments to employees (Code Sec. 41(h), as added by P.L. 114-113). A partnership or corporation (including an S corporation) is a qualified small business during a tax year if its gross receipts are less than $5 million and the entity did not have gross receipts in any tax year preceding the five-tax-year period that ends with the tax year of the election. A taxpayer other than a partnership or a corporation, e.g., an individual, is also a qualified small business during a tax year if the taxpayer's gross receipts for the election year are less than $5 million and it had no gross receipts in any tax year preceding the five-tax-year period that ends with the tax year of the election. Gross receipts for this purpose are determined by taking into account gross receipts received by the taxpayer in carrying on all of its trades or businesses.

1365K. Low-Income Housing Credit. A nonrefundable income tax credit is available on a per-unit basis for low-income units in qualified low-income buildings in qualified low-income housing projects (Code Sec. 42).[56] The owner of a qualified low-income housing project that is constructed, rehabilitated, or acquired may claim the credit over a 10-year period in an amount equal to the applicable credit percentage appropriate to the type of project, multiplied by the qualified basis allocable to the low-income units in each qualified low-income building.

The taxpayer begins to claim the credit with the tax year in which the project is placed in service or, at the taxpayer's election, the next tax year (but only if the building is a qualified low-income building as of the close of the first year of such period). The first-year credit is reduced to reflect the time during the year that any low-income units are unoccupied. If the reduction is made, a credit is allowed in the eleventh year in an amount equal to the reduction. The credit is calculated on Form 8586 and is a component of the general business credit. Thus, it is subject to the general business credit's tax liability limitation and carryover rules (¶ 1365).[57] The credit cannot be claimed for otherwise qualified buildings unless the owner of the building is subject to an enforceable 30-year low-income use agreement with the housing agency (Code Sec. 42(h)(6)). However, the credit is not limited or disallowed by the rules applicable to activities not entered into for profit (¶ 1195) (Reg. § 1.42-4).[58]

The applicable credit rates are the appropriate percentages issued by the IRS for the month in which the building is placed in service (¶ 86). Different percentages are provided for new construction or rehabilitation, subsidized construction or rehabilitation, and the acquisition of existing housing. An irrevocable election is available to determine the credit percentage applicable to a building in advance of the date that it is placed in service.

Rehabilitation expenditures are generally treated as expenditures for a separate new building provided that the expenditures are allocable to, or substantially benefit, low-income units and that they are incurred during any 24-month period and are at least equal to the greater of 20 percent of the adjusted basis of the building or $6,000 per low-

References are to Standard Federal Tax Reports; Tax Research Consultant; and Practical Tax Explanations.

[56] ¶ 4380; BUSEXP: 54,200; § 14,420

[57] ¶ 4380; BUSEXP: 54,224; § 14,420

[58] ¶ 4384A; BUSEXP: 54,218; § 14,420

income unit, adjusted annually for inflation ($6,700 in 2016; $6,700 in 2017) (Code Sec. 42(e); Rev. Proc. 2015-53; Rev. Proc. 2016-55). The limits are 10 percent of adjusted basis and $3,000 for buildings that are allocated a credit dollar amount on or before July 30, 2008. A qualified low-income housing project is any project for residential rental property that meets requirements for low-income tenant occupancy, gross rent restrictions, state credit authority, and IRS certification. The project must continue to meet these requirements for 15 years or recapture of a portion of the credit may be required using Form 8611. A qualified low-income building must be subject to MACRS depreciation.

State Allocations. The low-income housing credit can be claimed for any tax year, but generally only to the extent that the owner of a qualified low-income building receives a housing credit allocation from a state or local housing credit agency (Code Sec. 42(h)).

1365L. Enhanced Oil Recovery Credit. An enhanced oil recovery (EOR) credit is available in an amount up to 15 percent of the eligible costs attributable to a qualified domestic EOR project for increasing the production of crude oil or for production of Alaskan natural gas (Code Sec. 43(a) and (e)).[59] The amount of the credit allowable is phased out as the average wellhead price of uncontrolled domestic oil rises from $28 to $34 per barrel in the preceding calendar year. The reference price for 2015 calendar year is $44.39 which does not exceed $28 times the inflation adjustment factor for 2015 of 1.6464. Thus, any EOR credit for qualified costs paid or incurred in 2016 is determined without regard for the phaseout for crude oil increases (Notice 2016-44). This credit is claimed as one of the components of the general business credit. Thus, it is subject to the tax liability limitation and the carryover rules (¶ 1365). Any unused credit remaining after the expiration of the carry forward period is deductible (Code Sec. 196).

1365M. Disabled Access Credit. An eligible small business is entitled to a nonrefundable tax credit for expenditures incurred to make a business accessible to disabled individuals (Code Sec. 44).[60] The credit is 50 percent of the amount of eligible access expenditures for a year that exceed $250 but that do not exceed $10,250. The credit is computed on Form 8826 and is a component of the general business credit. Thus, it is subject to the tax liability limitation and the carryover rules of the general business credit (¶ 1365). Any unused credit remaining at the end of the carryforward period is lost. No other deduction or credit is permitted for any amount for which a disabled access credit is allowed.

Eligibility. An eligible small business is any person that had gross receipts (less returns and allowances) for the preceding tax year that did not exceed $1 million or that employed no more than 30 full-time employees during the preceding tax year. Eligible access expenditures include reasonable and necessary amounts paid or incurred by an eligible small business for the purpose of enabling the business to comply with the requirements of the Americans with Disabilities Act of 1990.

Eligible expenditures also include expenditures: (1) for the purpose of removing architectural, communication, physical, or transportation barriers that prevent a business from being accessible to, or usable by, disabled individuals (other than amounts for new construction); (2) to provide qualified interpreters or other effective methods of making aurally delivered materials available to hearing-impaired individuals; (3) to provide qualified readers, taped texts, and other effective methods of making visually delivered materials available to visually impaired individuals; (4) to acquire or modify equipment or devices for disabled individuals; or (5) to provide other similar services, modifications, materials, or equipment.

1365N. Credit for Electricity Produced from Renewable Sources. A credit is available for electricity produced from qualified energy resources at a qualified facility in the United States and sold to an unrelated third party (Code Sec. 45, as amended by the Protecting Americans from Tax Hikes (PATH) Act of 2015 (P.L. 114-113)).[61] The credit is also allowed with respect to Indian coal and certain types of refined coal produced at a

References are to Standard Federal Tax Reports; Tax Research Consultant; and Practical Tax Explanations.

[59] ¶ 4386; BUSEXP: 54,302; § 14,210.

[60] ¶ 4400; BUSEXP: 54,350; § 14,101

[61] ¶ 4410; BUSEXP: 54,550; § 14,215

domestic qualified facility and sold to an unrelated person. The credit for refined coal production may not be claimed, however, if production from the facility was eligible for the nonconventional fuel source credit for any tax year (¶ 1365BB).

Credit Amounts and Limitations. The credit amount for electricity produced in a qualified wind, closed-loop biomass, geothermal energy, or solar facility is 2.3 cents per kilowatt hour in 2016. Electricity produced in qualified open-loop biomass, small irrigation power, landfill gas, trash combustion, qualified hydroelectric, and marine and hydrokinetic energy facilities generate a credit amount of 1.2 cents in 2016. The credit amount for production of refined coal in 2016 is $6.810. The credit for Indian coal has been extended through 2016. The credit amount for calendar year 2016 is $2.387 (Notice 2016-34).

The credit is reduced in the same ratio as the excess of the reference price for the calendar year in which the sale occurs over eight cents bears to three cents. The reference price and the eight-cent threshold amount are each adjusted annually by multiplying them by an inflation adjustment factor for the calendar year in which the sale occurs.

For 2016, the inflation adjustment factor for qualified energy resources and refined coal is 1.5556. The reference price for electricity produced from wind is 4.50 cents per kilowatt-hour; for refined coal production the reference price for 2002 is $31.90 and for 2016 is $53.74 per ton; the reference prices for electricity produced from closed-loop biomass, open-looped biomass, geothermal energy, solar energy, small irrigation power, municipal solid waste, and qualified hydropower production facilities has not been determined for calendar year 2016. The phaseout of the credit for electricity produced by wind does not apply for calendar year 2016, nor does it apply to refined coal sold in calendar year 2016. The phaseout of the credit for production of electricity from closed-loop biomass, open-looped biomass, geothermal energy, solar energy, small irrigation power, municipal solid waste, qualified hydroelectric production, and marine and hydrokinetic energy does not apply during calendar year 2016 (Notice 2016-34).

The credit is claimed on Form 8835 and is one of the components of the general business credit (¶ 1365). The credit limitation for the renewable energy source credit is determined separately from the other general business credits. In the calculation of the tax liability limitation, the tentative minimum tax is to be treated as zero. The result is that the renewable energy source credit amounts are available to be used against both the regular and the alternative minimum tax liabilities for the current year (Code Sec. 38(c)(4)).

Qualified Energy Facilities. The credit for electricity from renewable energy sources can be claimed over a 5-or 10-year period depending on the facility. The following facilities qualify for the 5-year period: (1) open-loop biomass facilities that use agricultural livestock waste nutrients originally placed in service after October 22, 2004, and on or before August 8, 2005; (2) open-loop biomass facilities that do not use agricultural livestock waste nutrients originally placed in service before January 1, 2005; (3) geothermal facilities originally placed in service after October 22, 2004, and on or before August 8, 2005; (4) solar facilities originally placed in service after October 22, 2004, and on or before August 8, 2005; (5) small irrigation power facilities originally placed in service after October 22, 2004, and on or before August 8, 2005; (6) landfill gas facilities originally placed in service after October 22, 2004, and on or before August 8, 2005; and (7) trash combustion facilities (or certain new units placed in service in connection with an existing trash combustion facility) originally placed in service after October 22, 2004, and on or before August 8, 2005.

The following facilities qualify to claim the credit for the 10-year period for electricity from a renewable energy source: (1) wind facilities originally placed in service after December 31, 1993, and the construction of which begins before January 1, 2020 (the credit is reduced by 20 percent if construction begins in 2017, by 40 percent if construction begins during 2018, and by 60 percent if construction begins in 2019); (2) open-loop biomass facilities originally placed in service after August 8, 2005, and the construction of which begins before January 1, 2017; (3) closed-loop biomass facilities modified to use closed-loop biomass to co-fire with coal, other biomass, or both originally placed in service after December 31, 1992, and the construction of which begins before January 1, 2017; (4) any other closed-loop biomass facilities originally placed in service after December 31, 1992, and the construction of which begins before January 1, 2017; (5) geothermal facilities originally placed in service after August 8, 2005, and the construction of which begins before January 1, 2017; (6) solar facilities originally placed in service after August 8, 2005, and before January 1, 2006; (7) small irrigation power facilities originally placed in service after August 8, 2005, and before October 3, 2008; (8) landfill gas facilities originally placed in service after August 8, 2005, and the construction of which begins before January 1, 2017; (9) trash facilities (or new units placed in service in connection with an existing trash facility) originally placed in service after August 8, 2005, and the construction of which begins before January 1, 2017; (10) refined coal production facilities placed in service after October 22, 2004, and before January 1, 2012; (11) qualified hydropower facilities placed in service after August 8, 2005, and the construction of which begins before January 1, 2017 (and 10-year period begins on date such improvements are placed in service); and (12) marine and hydrokinetic renewable energy facility, originally placed in service on or after October 3, 2008, and the construction of which begins before January 1, 2017 (Code Sec. 45(d), as amended by P.L. 114-113). The Indian coal credit applies to coal produced and sold during the eleven-year period beginning on January 1, 2006 (through 2016) (Code Sec. 45(e)(10), as amended by P.L. 114-113).

Construction Starting Date. Construction on a facility is deemed to begin before the deadline if a taxpayer either begins physical work of a significant nature or pays or incurs at least five percent of the total cost of the facility prior to the deadline. If a single project consists of multiple facilities, a taxpayer that pays or incurs at least three percent but less than five percent of the total cost of the project before the deadline may treat the number of individuals facilities with a total aggregate cost not greater than twenty times the amount paid or incurred before the deadline as eligible for the credit (Notice 2013-29, Notice 2013-60, Notice 2014-46, and Notice 2015-25, as clarified and modified by Notice 2016-31).

1365O. Empowerment Zone Credit. Employers located in empowerment zones are entitled to a 20-percent wage credit on the first $15,000 of annual wages paid or incurred for services performed within an empowerment zone by residents of the empowerment zone (Code Sec. 1396).[62] The empowerment zone designation has been extended through December 31, 2016 (¶ 999B). The empowerment zone employment credit is computed on wages paid during the calendar year that ends within the employer's tax year. The credit is claimed on Form 8844 and, although part of the general business credit, is not a part of the general business credit tax liability limitation computation (¶ 1365).

1365Q. Indian Employment Credit. A nonrefundable credit is available to employers for certain wages and health insurance costs paid or incurred in a tax year beginning before January 1, 2017, for qualified full- or part-time employees, or their spouses, who are enrolled members of an Indian tribe (Code Sec. 45A, as amended by the Protecting Americans from Tax Hikes (PATH) Act of 2015 (P.L. 114-113)).[63] The credit is equal to 20 percent of the excess of eligible employee qualified wages and health insurance costs paid or incurred during a tax year over the amount of the costs paid or incurred during 1993. However, the credit is available only for the first $20,000 of qualified wages and health insurance costs paid for each qualified employee. Also, no deduction is allowed for the portion of wages equal to the amount of the credit. Qualified wages are wages paid or incurred by an employer for services performed by a qualified employee, excluding wages for which a work opportunity credit (¶ 1365G) is allowed. Qualified health insurance costs are costs paid or incurred by an employer for a qualified employee, except for costs paid under a salary reduction agreement.

Eligibility. An individual who receives more than 50 percent of wages from services performed in the trade or business of the employer is a qualified employee for any period *only* if: (1) the individual was an enrolled member of an Indian tribe or the spouse thereof; (2) substantially all of the services performed during the period by the em-

References are to Standard Federal Tax Reports; Tax Research Consultant; and Practical Tax Explanations.

[62] ¶ 32,393; BUSEXP: 54,650; § 13,810

[63] ¶ 4430; BUSEXP: 54,700; § 13,815

ployee for the employer were performed within an Indian reservation; and (3) the principal place of abode of the employee while performing the services was on or near the reservation on which the services are performed. Ineligible employees include employees who receive wages exceeding an dollar amount, adjusted for inflation ($45,000 for 2015 and 2016 (Code Sec. 45A(c)(3); Instructions Form 8845)).

The credit is calculated on Form 8845 and is claimed as one of the components of the general business credit (¶ 1365). Thus, it is subject to the tax liability limitation and carryover rules. Any unused credit at the end of the carryforward period is allowed as a deduction in the year following the expiration of the period (Code Sec. 196).

1365R. Credit for Employer-Paid Social Security Taxes on Employee Cash Tips (FICA Tip Credit). An employer in the food and beverage industry may claim a nonrefundable income tax credit for a portion of the employer's Social Security and Medicare taxes (FICA taxes) paid or incurred on employee tips (Code Sec. 45B).[64] Employee tip income is treated as employer-provided wages for purposes of FICA taxes (Code Sec. 3121(q)). The credit is equal to the employer's FICA obligation to an employee attributable to excess tips treated as wages for purposes of satisfying the minimum wage provisions of the Fair Labor Standards Act. No credit may be claimed for the employer's portion of FICA taxes on the tips used to meet the Federal minimum wage rate. For purposes of calculating the credit only, the minimum wage rate has been permanently established at the amount in effect on January 1, 2007, or $5.15 per hour.

The credit is allowed for tips received from customers in connection with the providing, delivering, or serving of food or beverages for consumption if the tipping of employees delivering or serving food or beverages by customers is customary. The credit is available whether or not the employee reported the tips and regardless of where the services were performed. The employer may not deduct any amount considered in determining this credit to claim any other tax benefit. An election may be made to have this credit not apply.

The FICA tip credit is claimed on Form 8846 and is a component of the general business credit (¶ 1365). For purposes of determining the amount of the FICA tip credit that may be claimed in the current tax year and any credit carrybacks from the current tax year, the tentative minimum tax is considered zero and the credit amount is not subject to the general business credit tax liability limitation rule but is calculated separately (Code Sec. 38(c)(4)(A)). The result of setting the minimum tax at zero and reducing the net tax liability allows taxpayers to claim the maximum amount of the FICA tip credit against both their regular and the alternative minimum tax liabilities. Any credit that remains unused at the end of the carryover period is lost.

1365S. Orphan Drug Credit. A credit, commonly known as the orphan drug credit, is allowed for an amount equal to 50 percent, subject to limitations, of the clinical testing expenses to develop drugs to treat rare diseases and conditions (Code Sec. 45C).[65] The credit is claimed on Form 8820 and is a component of the general business credit. Thus, it is subject to the general business credit's tax liability limitation and carryover rules (¶ 1365).

1365T. New Markets Tax Credit. The new markets tax credit is available for equity investments made in low-income communities through a qualified community development entity (CDE) (Code Sec. 45D, as amended the Protecting Americans from Tax Hikes (PATH) Act of 2015 (P.L. 114-113)).[66] The equity investment must be made within five years after the CDE receives an allocation of the national credit limitation amount for the calendar year ($3.5 billion for each of the calendar years through 2019). The credit is equal to five percent of the equity investment for the first three allowance dates and six percent of the equity investment for the next four allowance dates. The total credit available is equal to 39 percent of the investment over seven years. Active involvement of the low-income communities is required with strict penalties if the investment is terminated before seven years.

References are to Standard Federal Tax Reports; Tax Research Consultant; and Practical Tax Explanations.

[64] ¶ 4450; BUSEXP: 54,400; § 14,005

[65] ¶ 4470; BUSEXP: 54,450; § 14,405

[66] ¶ 4480; BUSEXP: 54,900; § 14,430

The new markets tax credit is a component of the general business credit, subject to its tax liability limitation and carryover rules (¶ 1365). The credit is calculated on Form 8874. Any unused credit at the end of the carryforward period is allowed as a deduction in the following tax year under Code Sec. 196. Any termination event requires recapture of the credit amount claimed, treated as an addition to tax in the termination year. Any amount carried forward or carried back will need to be adjusted accordingly. Finally, claiming the new markets tax credit necessitates an adjustment in the basis of the investment in the CDE.

1365U. Small Employer Pension Plan Startup Costs Credit. Eligible small businesses may claim a credit for qualified startup costs incurred in establishing and administering an eligible employer benefit plan for their employees (Code Sec. 45E).[67] The credit equals 50 percent of the qualified startup costs incurred to create or maintain a new employee retirement plan. The credit is limited to $500 in any tax year and it may be claimed for qualified costs incurred in each of the three years beginning with the tax year in which the plan becomes effective. The credit is part of the general business credit and subject to the tax liability limitation and carryover rules of the general business credit (¶ 1365). Form 8881 is used to calculate and claim the credit.

Eligibility. An eligible small business is one that has not employed more than 100 employees who received at least $5,000 of compensation from that employer in the preceding year. A business is not eligible if during the preceding three tax years it established or maintained a qualified employer plan with respect to which contributions were made, or benefits were accrued, for substantially the same employees as are in the new qualified employer plan. An eligible plan includes a new qualified defined contribution or defined benefit plan (¶ 2101), savings incentive match plans for employees (SIMPLEs) (¶ 2187), or simplified employee pension plans (SEP) (¶ 2189).

Qualified startup costs are any ordinary and necessary expenses incurred to establish or administer an eligible plan or to educate employees about retirement planning. Qualified costs are not deductible to the extent that they are effectively offset by the tax credit. The credit is applied to the first $1,000 of qualified costs incurred in the first year the new plan is effective and in each of the following two years. The employer may elect to take the credit in the year immediately preceding the first year the new plan is effective or elect not to claim the credit for a tax year.

1365V. Employer-Provided Child Care Credit. Businesses may claim a tax credit for qualified expenses related to either an employer-provided child care center or a service related to locating qualified child care (Code Sec. 45F).[68] The credit for a given tax year is the sum of 25 percent of the qualified child care expenditures and 10 percent of the qualified resource and referral expenditures. The maximum amount of credit allowed in any given year is $150,000. Form 8882 is used to calculate and claim the credit. The credit is part of the general business credit and is subject to its tax liability limitation and carryover rules (¶ 1365).

No double benefit is allowed for expenditures used to claim the employer-provided child care credit and the basis of the qualified child care facility must be reduced by the amount of the credit taken. In addition, there is no deduction allowed in the year following the final year of any carryforward of unused employer-provided child care credit. If a qualified child care facility ceases to operate as a qualified child care facility (or there is a change in ownership), the business may have to recapture part or all of the credit claimed. In the event of recapture, the tax liability of that tax year must be increased by an amount equal to the applicable percentage times the aggregate decrease in the general business credit as if all previously allowed employer-provided child care credits with respect to the employer's child care facility had been zero. Any carryforward or carryback amounts of the employer-provided child care credit must also be adjusted.

References are to Standard Federal Tax Reports; Tax Research Consultant; and Practical Tax Explanations.

[67] ¶ 4491; BUSEXP: 54,950; § 14,010

[68] ¶ 4493; BUSEXP: 55,000; § 14,015

Qualifying Facility. A qualified child care facility is a facility whose principal use is to provide child care assistance and that meets the requirements of all applicable laws and regulations of the state and local government in which it is located, including the licensing requirements applicable to a child care facility. The principal use requirement is waived for facilities located in the principal residence of the operator of the facility. Additional requirements include that: (1) enrollment must be open to the employees of the taxpayer during the tax year; (2) at least 30 percent of the enrollees at the facility are the dependents of the taxpayer's employees (¶ 133) in the event the facility is the principal trade or business of the taxpayer; and (3) the use of the child care facility cannot discriminate in favor of highly compensated employees (¶ 2017).

Qualifying Expenditures. Qualified child care expenditures are amounts paid or incurred: (1) to acquire, construct, rehabilitate, or expand property which is to used as a qualified child care facility of the taxpayer; (2) for the operating costs of a qualified child care facility, including the costs related to the training of employees, scholarship programs, and providing increased compensation for employees with high levels of child care training; or (3) under a contract with a qualified child care facility to provide child care services to the taxpayer's employees. Costs associated with item (1) must qualify for depreciation or amortization and must not be the principal residence of the taxpayer. Expenses for items (2) and (3) cannot exceed the fair market value of such care. Further, qualified child care resources and referral expenditures are expenses paid or incurred by the taxpayer under a contract to provide child care services to the taxpayer's employees. These expenditures cannot discriminate in favor of highly compensated employees.

1365W. Railroad Track Maintenance Credit. An income tax credit is available to small-and mid-sized railroad companies for qualified railroad track maintenance expenses (Code Sec. 45G, as amended by the Protecting Americans from Tax Hikes (PATH) Act of 2015 (P.L. 114-113)).[69] The credit is equal to 50 percent of the qualified expenses paid or incurred by an eligible taxpayer in tax years beginning before January 1, 2017. The credit cannot exceed $3,500 multiplied by the number of miles of railroad track owned or leased by the eligible taxpayer as of the close of the tax year. Eligible taxpayers are Class II and Class III railroad companies and persons who operate over their rail lines or provide related rail services. The credit is a part of the general business credit but is not subject to the tax liability limitation rule. Instead, the credit is allowed against the sum of the regular income tax and alternative minimum tax liabilities (Code Sec. 38(c)). The credit is subject to the general business credit's carryover rules (¶ 1365). No provision is made for deduction of unused credits at the end of the carryforward period or if the taxpayer ceases to exist. The credit is claimed on Form 8900.

1365X. Biodiesel Fuels Credit. A producer of biodiesel fuels may claim a credit equal to the sum of the biodiesel mixture credit, the biodiesel credit, and the small agri-biodiesel producer credit (Code Sec. 40A, as amended by the Protecting Americans from Tax Hikes (PATH) Act of 2015 (P.L. 114-113)).[70] The credit is computed on Form 8864 and may be claimed for fuels sold or used before January 1, 2017. The credit is part of the general business credit and is subject to its tax liability limitation and carryover rules (¶ 1365). Any unused credit at the end of the carryforward period, or if the taxpayer ceases to exist, may be claimed as a deduction (Code Sec. 196). No credit is allowed for any biodiesel which is produced outside the United States for use as a fuel outside the United States.

The biodiesel mixture credit is $1.00 for each gallon of biodiesel used by the taxpayer in the production of a qualified biodiesel mixture. A qualified biodiesel mixture is a mixture of biodiesel and diesel fuel, determined without regard to any use of kerosene, which is sold by the taxpayer producing the mixture to any person for use as a fuel or is used as a fuel by the taxpayer producing the mixture. The sale or use by the taxpayer must be in the taxpayer's trade or business. Casual off-farm production is not eligible for the credit (Code Sec. 40A(b)(1)).

References are to Standard Federal Tax Reports; Tax Research Consultant; and Practical Tax Explanations.

[69] ¶ 4495; BUSEXP: 55,050; § 14,415

[70] ¶ 4310; BUSEXP: 55,100; § 14,220

The biodiesel credit is $1.00 for each gallon of biodiesel which is not in a mixture with diesel fuel and which is used by the taxpayer as a fuel in a trade or business or is sold by the taxpayer at retail to a person and placed in the fuel tank of the person's vehicle (Code Sec. 40A(b)(2)). Biodiesel fuels are defined as monoalkyl esters of long chain fatty acids derived from plant or animal matter that meet the requirements for fuels or fuel additives imposed by the Environmental Protection Agency and which meet the requirements of the American Society of Testing and Materials D6751 (Code Sec. 40A(d)(1)).

The small agri-biodiesel producer credit of any eligible small agri-biodiesel producer is 10 cents for each gallon of qualified agri-biodiesel production. Qualified agri-biodiesel production means any agri-biodiesel which is produced by an eligible small agri-biodiesel producer and: (1) is sold by the producer to another person (a) for use by the other person in the production of a qualified biodiesel mixture in the other person's trade or business (other than casual off-farm production), (b) for use by the other person as a fuel in a trade or business, or (c) who sells the agri-biodiesel at retail to another person and places the agri-biodiesel in the fuel tank of such other person; or (2) is used or sold by the producer for any of these purposes.

An eligible agri-biodiesel fuel producer's production of qualified agri-biodiesel cannot exceed 15 million gallons per tax year (Code Sec. 40A(b)(4)). An eligible small agri-biodiesel producer is a person with a productive capacity for agri-biodiesel not in excess of 60 million gallons per tax year (Code Sec. 40A(e)(1)). Agri-biodiesel is biodiesel derived solely from virgin oils, including esters derived from virgin vegetable oils from corn, soybeans, sunflower seeds, cottonseeds, canola, crambe, rapeseeds, safflowers, flaxseeds, rice bran, and mustard seeds, camelina, and animal fats (Code Sec. 40A(d)(2)).

If a credit was claimed on biodiesel used in the production of a qualified biodiesel fuel mixture, a tax equal to the $1 per gallon credit rate is imposed on any person who separates the biodiesel from the mixture or does not use the mixture as a fuel. A $1 per gallon tax is imposed on any person who mixes biodiesel or uses it other than as a fuel if the biodiesel credit was claimed with respect to the retail sale of the biodiesel. A 10 cent per gallon tax is imposed on a person who does not use agri-biodiesel production for which a credit was claimed for one of the qualifying purposes described previously (Code Sec. 40A(d)(3)).

1365Y. Low Sulfur Diesel Fuel Production Credit (Expired). A credit of five cents per gallon was available to small business refiners for the production of low sulfur diesel fuel unless an election out from claiming the credit was made (Code Sec. 45H).[71] The credit was intended to subsidize the costs incurred by small refiners to comply with Environmental Protection Agency (EPA) regulations requiring refiners to produce diesel fuel with a low sulfur content (15 parts per million or less). The maximum credit available was 25 percent of the qualified costs incurred by the refiner in bringing the refining facility into compliance with the EPA's Highway Diesel Fuel Sulfur Control Requirements. The credit applied only to costs incurred between January 1, 2003, and December 31, 2009, or if earlier, one year after the date on which the taxpayer had to comply with the EPA requirements. The credit was claimed on Form 8896.

1365Z. Distilled Spirits Excise Tax Carrying Credit. An income tax credit is available for wholesalers, qualified distillers, and importers that carry distilled spirits subject to excise taxes in inventory (Code Sec. 5011).[72] The credit is generally calculated to equal the approximate interest charges that the eligible taxpayer would incur while holding the distilled spirits in inventory. The credit is a component of the general business credit and is subject to its tax liability limitation and carryover rules (¶ 1365). The credit is claimed on Form 8906.

References are to Standard Federal Tax Reports; Tax Research Consultant; and Practical Tax Explanations.

[71] ¶ 4497; BUSEXP: 55,150; § 14,225

[72] ¶ 34,965; BUSEXP: 55,250

1365AA. Advanced Nuclear Power Facilities Production Credit. A tax credit is available to taxpayers that produce electricity from an advanced nuclear power facility (Code Sec. 45J).[73] The credit is equal to 1.8 cents times the number of kilowatt hours of electricity produced at a qualifying advanced nuclear power facility and sold to an unrelated person during the tax year. It may only be claimed during the eight-year period beginning on the date the facility was originally placed in service. A qualifying advanced nuclear power facility is any advanced nuclear facility owned by the taxpayer that uses nuclear energy to produce electricity and was placed in service after August 8, 2005, and before January 1, 2021. Any nuclear facility with a reactor design (or a substantially similar design of comparable capacity) approved before 1994 by the Nuclear Regulatory Commission is not a qualifying advanced nuclear power facility. Certain limitations restrict the amount of credit that may be claimed in any tax year, including that the credit is part of the general business credit and as such is subject to the tax liability limitation and carryover rules (¶ 1365).

1365BB. Nonconventional Source Fuel Production Credit (Expired). A tax credit is allowed for the domestic production of qualified fuels derived from nonconventional sources produced by the taxpayer within the United States or U.S. possession and sold to unrelated persons (Code Sec. 45K).[74] The credit was available for coke or coke gas produced in facilities placed in service before January 1, 1993, or after June 30, 1998, and before January 1, 2010, that was sold during the period beginning after the later of January 1, 2006, or the year the facility is placed in service but no later than four years after the start of such period. The credit has expired for fuel produced from biomass and liquid, gaseous, or solid synthetic fuels.

The credit is a component of the general business credit and is subject to the tax liability limitation and carryover rules of the general business credit (¶ 1365). The credit amount is reduced pro rata by any grants, tax-exempt bonds, and subsidized energy financing the project receives. No double benefits are allowed as the credit amount is reduced by any credit amount claimed as an energy credit (¶ 1365C) and/or enhanced oil recovery credit (¶ 1365L). The credit is claimed on Form 8907.

Credit Amount. The credit for coke or coke gas was equal to $3 multiplied by the barrel-of-oil equivalent of qualified fuels produced and sold by the taxpayer to an unrelated third party. The $3 amount is annually adjusted for inflation (Code Sec. 45K(a) and (b)(2)). The inflation factor is determined and published no later than April 1st for the preceding calendar year. The credit for coke or coke gas expired in calendar year 2013.

1365CC. Energy Efficient Home Credit. Eligible contractors who build an energy-efficient home acquired by a person for use as a residence before January 1, 2017, can claim an income tax credit of up to $2,000 (Code Sec. 45L, as amended by the Protecting Americans from Tax Hikes (PATH) Act of 2015 (P.L. 114-113)).[75] Eligible contractors also include manufacturers of energy-efficient manufactured homes. A residence qualifies as an energy-efficient home if it is located in the United States and is certified to have an annual heating and/or cooling consumption at least 50 percent less than a comparable house with at least 10 percent of the 50 percent saving coming from the building envelope. A reduced credit of $1,000 is available for homes with a heating or cooling consumption at least 30 percent less than a comparable house and for homes with the Energy Star label. The credit is a component of the general business credit and is subject to the tax liability limitation and carryover rules (¶ 1365). The credit is claimed on Form 8908.

1365DD. Energy Efficient Appliance Credit (Expired). An income tax credit is available to taxpayers that manufacture energy-efficient home appliances in calendar years before 2014 (Code Sec. 45M).[76] The total credit available for a tax year is equal to

References are to Standard Federal Tax Reports; Tax Research Consultant; and Practical Tax Explanations.

[73] ¶ 4500A; BUSEXP: 55,300; § 14,235

[74] ¶ 4050; BUSEXP: 54,500; § 14,240

[75] ¶ 4500I; BUSEXP: 55,350; § 14,315

[76] ¶ 4500N; BUSEXP: 55,400; § 14,320

the sum of the credit separately calculated for each type of qualified energy-efficient appliance (dishwashers, clothes washers, and refrigerators) produced by the taxpayer during the calendar year ending with or within that tax year. The credit for each type of qualified appliance is determined by multiplying the eligible production for that type of appliance by the type's applicable amount. The maximum credit is reduced each subsequent year by the amount of credit, if any, claimed in the prior year. In addition, there are sub-limits for each type of home appliance. This credit is a component of the general business credit and is subject to its tax liability limitations and carryover rules (¶ 1365). The credit is claimed on Form 8909.

1365GG. Mine Rescue Team Training Credit. Eligible employers are entitled to a tax credit for mine rescue team training expenses paid or incurred in tax years beginning before January 1, 2017 (Code Sec. 45N, as amended by the Protecting Americans from Tax Hikes (PATH) Act of 2015 (P.L. 114-113)).[77] The credit is equal to the lesser of: (1) 20 percent of the training program costs paid or incurred during the tax year for each qualified mine rescue team employee, including wages paid while attending the training program, or (2) $10,000. An eligible employer is any taxpayer that employs individuals as miners in underground mines located in the United States. A qualified mine rescue team employee is a full-time miner employee who is eligible for more than six months of the tax year to serve as a mine rescue team member because he or she has met certain training requirements. To prevent any double benefits that may arise from the claiming of this credit, eligible mine employers cannot claim as a wage the amount of any mine rescue team training credit determined for the tax year (Code Sec. 280C). The mine rescue team training credit is claimed on Form 8923 and is a component of the general business credit subject to its tax liability limitation and carryover rules (¶ 1365).

1365II. Employer Credit for Differential Wage Payments to Military Personnel. A qualified employer that makes a differential wage payment to a qualified employee may claim a tax credit equal to 20 percent of the payment made to the employee (Code Sec. 45P, as amended by the Protecting Americans from Tax Hikes (PATH) Act of 2015 (P.L. 114-113)).[78] An eligible differential wage payment is a payment that: (1) is made by an employer to an individual with respect to any period during which the individual is performing services in the uniformed armed forces on active duty for a period of more than 30 days, and (2) represents all or a portion of the wages that the individual would have received from the employer if the individual were performing services for the employer (Code Sec. 3401) (¶ 895 and ¶ 2609). The differential wage payment is limited to $20,000 per employee paid during the tax year.

A qualified employee is an individual who has been employed by the employer for a period of 91 days immediately preceding the period for which any differential wage payments were made. Effective for tax years beginning before January 1, 2016, a qualified employer is a small business employer that: (1) employs an average of fewer than 50 individuals on any day during the tax year, and (2) provides differential wage payments to every qualified employee under a written plan (Code Sec. 45P(a) and (b)(3), prior to being amended by P.L. 114-113). For tax years beginning after December 31, 2015, however, a qualified employer is an employer of any size, rather than only eligible small businesses.

The differential wage payment credit is claimed on Form 8932 and is a component of the general business credit subject to the tax liability and carryover rules (¶ 1365). The amount of the credit claimed reduces the employer's deduction of wages paid to an employee as a business expense, as well as any other credit related to compensation paid to the employee.

1365JJ. Carbon Dioxide Capture Credit. Taxpayers may claim a tax credit for the capture and transport of carbon dioxide from an industrial source for use in enhanced oil recovery or for permanent storage in a geologic formation (Code Sec. 45Q).[79] The credit

References are to Standard Federal Tax Reports; Tax Research Consultant; and Practical Tax Explanations.

[77] ¶ 4500S; BUSEXP: 55,450; § 14,435

[78] ¶ 4500Z; BUSEXP: 55,500; § 14,020

[79] ¶ 4500ZH; BUSEXP: 55,600; § 14,450

is $20 per metric ton of qualified carbon dioxide that is captured by the taxpayer at a qualified facility and disposed of in secure geological storage. The credit is $10 per metric ton of qualified carbon dioxide that is captured by the taxpayer at a qualified facility, used as a tertiary injectant in a qualified enhanced oil or natural gas recovery project, and disposed of in secure geologic storage. The credit amounts are adjusted annually for inflation, and are $22.14 and $11.07 per metric ton, respectively, for calendar year 2016 (Notice 2016-53).

The credit is recaptured with respect to any qualified carbon dioxide that ceases to be captured, disposed of, or used as a tertiary injectant in accordance with the credit requirements. It is attributable to the person that captures and physically or contractually ensures the disposal, or the use as a tertiary injectant, of the qualified carbon dioxide, except to the extent provided by regulations. The credit applies with respect to qualified carbon dioxide before the end of the calendar year in which the IRS, in consultation with the Environmental Protection Agency, certifies that 75-million metric tons of qualified carbon dioxide have been captured or disposed of or used as a tertiary injectant. The credit is a component of the general business credit subject to its tax liability limitation and carryover rules (¶ 1365). The credit is claimed on Form 8933.

Eligibility. Qualified carbon dioxide is carbon dioxide captured from an industrial source that would otherwise be released into the atmosphere as an industrial emission of greenhouse gas and that is measured at the source of capture and verified at the point of disposal or injection. Qualified carbon dioxide includes the initial deposit of captured carbon dioxide used as a tertiary injectant, but does not include carbon dioxide that is recaptured, recycled, and reinjected as part of the enhanced oil and natural gas recovery process. Only carbon dioxide captured and disposed of or used within the United States or its possessions (including the continental shelf areas as defined in Code Sec. 638) is taken into account in computing the credit.

1365KK. Credit for Producing Oil and Gas from Marginal Wells (Phased Out). Taxpayers owning interest in qualified marginal wells producing crude oil or natural gas could have claimed a credit for the amount of oil and gas produced (Code Sec. 45I).[80] The credit was equal to $3 per barrel of qualified crude oil or 50 cents per 1000 cubic feet of qualified natural gas production. The credit began to phase out when the reference price of crude oil exceeded $15 per barrel and $1.67 per metric cubic foot (mcf). The credit is completely phased out if the reference price exceeds $18 per barrel or $2.00 per mcf, respectively (both adjusted for inflation after 2005). The credit for producing oil and gas from marginal wells is completely phased out due to continued high oil and gas wellhead prices and, therefore, unavailable to taxpayers.

Tax Credit Bonds

1371. Tax Credit Bonds. As an alternative to traditional tax-exempt bonds, state and local governments may issue tax credit bonds for certain purposes. Unlike tax-exempt bonds, tax credit bonds are not interest-bearing obligations. Rather, the taxpayer holding a tax credit bond on a credit-allowance date is entitled to a tax credit. The credit can be claimed against both the regular income tax and alternative minimum tax liabilities. To standardize the tax treatment of these bonds, they must meet certain requirements regarding the determination of the amount of the credit bond holders are entitled to receive. In addition, in order for a bondholder to qualify for the tax credit, the bond must meet certain requirements with respect to proceeds, expenditures, arbitrage, maturity limitations, and conflicts of interest (Code Sec. 54A)).[81]

Credit Amount. A taxpayer holding a tax credit bond on a credit-allowance date is entitled to a tax credit calculated on Form 8912. If the bond is held by a partnership or S corporation, the allocation of the credit to the partners or shareholders is treated as a distribution (Code Sec. 54A(g)). If the bond is held by a regulated investment company (RIC) or real estate investment trust (REIT), the credit is allocated and any interest

References are to Standard Federal Tax Reports; Tax Research Consultant; and Practical Tax Explanations.

[80] ¶ 4500.01 BUSEXP: 55,200 § 14,230

[81] ¶ 4882; BUSEXP: 55,800; § 14,501

treated as gross income is distributed to the shareholders or beneficiaries under procedures to be prescribed by the Secretary of the Treasury (Code Sec. 54A(h)).

The amount of the credit with respect to any allowance date is 25 percent of the annual credit amount determined on that allowance date (Code Sec. 54A(b)). The allowance dates are: March 15, June 15, September 15, and December 15. The annual credit amount is determined by multiplying the bond's applicable credit rate by the face amount on the holder's bond. The applicable credit rate is set by the Secretary of the Treasury at a rate that would permit issuance of a tax credit bond without discount and interest cost to the issuer. The taxpayer holding a tax credit bond on a quarterly credit-allowance date is entitled to a tax credit (Code Sec. 54A(a) and (e)(1)). The credit accrues quarterly and is includible in gross income as if it were an interest payment on the bond (Code Sec. 54A(f)).

The credit in a tax year cannot be larger than the sum of the taxpayer's regular tax liability plus minimum tax liability, minus the total of the taxpayer's credits against tax. The subtracted credits do not include refundable credits or the qualified tax bond credit itself (Code Sec. 54A(c)). Unused qualified tax credit bond amounts may be carried over to succeeding tax years. Special rules apply to S corporation, partnership, regulated investment companies, and real estate investment trust bond holders.

Reporting Requirements. The qualified issuer must submit reports similar to reports required under Code Sec. 149(e) for tax-exempt bonds (Code Sec. 54A(d)(3)). For other return purposes, the credit is reported as an interest payment (Code Sec. 6049(d)(9)). Holders of tax credit bonds receiving a credit amount of $10 or more are issued a Form 1099-INT.

Refundable Credit Election. To stimulate the rebuilding and improvement of local and state infrastructure, issuers of certain tax credit bonds may elect to claim a refundable credit generally equal to the amount of interest that would be payable to the holders of the bonds (Code Sec. 6431(f)). The election may be made only for bonds issued after March 18, 2010. The election can be made by issuers of new clean renewable energy bonds (¶ 1374), qualified energy conservation bonds (¶ 1375), qualified zone academy bonds other than those issued under the 2011 bond limitation or any carryforward of such allocation (¶ 1376), and qualified school construction bonds (¶ 1377). The election is similar to the alternative election available to issuers of Build America bonds (¶ 1378).

1373. Qualified Forestry Conservation Bonds. State and local governments, or qualified nonprofit organizations, may generally issue up to $500 million in qualified forestry conservation credit bonds (QFCB) after May 22, 2008, for the acquisition of forest and forest lands that are subject to conservation restrictions (Code Sec. 54B).[82] The purpose of the bonds is the acquisition of forest and forest lands from an unrelated third person that meets the following requirements: (1) some portion of the land acquired must be adjacent to United States Forest Service Land; (2) at least half of the land acquired must be transferred to the United States Forest Service at no net cost, and not more than half of the land acquired may either remain with or be donated to a state; (3) all of the land must be subject to a habitat conservation plan for native fish approved by the United States Fish and Wildlife Service; and (4) the amount of acreage acquired must be at least 40,000 acres. QFCB are tax credit bonds subject to rules similar to those that apply to qualified tax credit bonds (¶ 1371).

1374. New Clean Renewable Energy Bonds (NCREBs). New clean renewable energy bonds (NCREBs) provide a federal subsidy to allow nonprofit electricity producers, including cooperatives and government-owned utilities, to compete more evenly with for-profit companies that can take advantage of the credit for electricity produced from renewable sources (Code Sec. 54C).[83] NCREBs are tax credit bonds subject to rules similar to those that apply to qualified tax credit bonds (¶ 1371).

References are to Standard Federal Tax Reports; Tax Research Consultant; and Practical Tax Explanations.

[82] ¶ 4890; BUSEXP: 55,804; § 14,510.10

[83] ¶ 4897; BUSEXP: 55,806; § 14,510.15

An NCREB is a bond issued as part of an issue if: (1) 100 percent of the available project proceeds of the issue are to be used for capital expenditures incurred by governmental bodies, public power providers, or cooperative electric companies for one or more qualified renewable energy facilities; (2) the bond is issued by a qualified issuer; and (3) the issuer designates the bond as an NCREB (Code Sec. 54C(a)). Qualified renewable energy facilities are facilities that produce electrical power and are owned by a public power provider, a governmental body or a cooperative electric company and that qualify under the renewable electricity production credit (Code Sec. 45). Qualified facilities include wind facilities, closed-loop biomass facilities, open-loop biomass facilities, geothermal or solar energy facilities, small irrigation power facilities, landfill gas facilities, trash combustion facilities, and qualified hydropower facilities (Code Sec. 54C(d)(1)).

1375. Qualified Energy Conservation Bonds. State and local governments, or qualified nonprofit organizations, are authorized to issue qualified energy conservation bonds (QECBs) to finance energy conservation projects, including capital expenditures, research expenditures, expenses for mass commuting facilities, demonstration projects, and public education campaigns (Code Sec. 54D).[84] The bonds are subject to the requirements for tax credit bonds (¶ 1371) with the annual tax credit limited to 70 percent of the face amount times the applicable credit rate.

1376. Qualified Zone Academy Bond Credit. State and local governments are authorized to issue qualified zone academy bonds (QZAB) through 2016 to be used to improve certain eligible public schools (Code Secs. 54E, as amended by the Protecting Americans from Tax Hikes (PATH) Act of 2015 (P.L. 114-113) and 1397E).[85] QZABs issued after October 3, 2008, are subject to the requirements for qualified tax credit bonds (¶ 1371). QZABs issued prior to October 3, 2008, are subject to the provisions under Code Sec. 1397E.

1377. Qualified School Construction Tax Credit Bonds. Tax credit bonds known as qualified school construction bonds could be issued through December 31, 2010 (Code Sec. 54F).[86] The bonds must satisfy the requirements for qualified tax credit bonds (¶ 1371) (Code Sec. 54A(d)(1)(E)). A bond is a qualified school construction bond if: (1) 100 percent of the available project proceeds of the issue of which it is a part are to be used for the construction, rehabilitation, or repair of a public school facility or to acquire land on which a facility funded by the same issue is to be built; (2) the bond is issued by a state or local government within the jurisdiction of which the school is located; and (3) the issuer designates the bond as a qualified school construction bond (Code Sec. 54F(a)).

1378. Build America Bonds. State and local governments could issue taxable build America bonds through January 1, 2011, which provide the bondholder with both taxable interest and a tax credit (Code Sec. 54AA).[87] A build America bond is any obligation, other than a private activity bond, that meets these three requirements: (1) the bond must be issued before January 1, 2011; (2) the issuer must make an irrevocable election to have Code Sec. 54AA apply to the bond; and (3) but for that election, the interest on the bond would have been excludable under Code Sec. 103 (Code Sec. 54AA(d)(1)).

For purposes of the rules under Code Sec. 149(b) that exclude federally guaranteed bonds from the category of tax-exempt bonds, build America bonds are not treated as federally guaranteed by virtue of their cash payment or credit features. Also, for purposes of the rules under Code Sec. 148 that exclude arbitrage bonds from the category of tax-exempt bonds, the yield on build America bonds must be determined without regard to the credit. Finally, build America bonds cannot have an issue price that has more than a *de minimis* amount of premium over the stated principal amount of

References are to Standard Federal Tax Reports; Tax Research Consultant; and Practical Tax Explanations.

[84] ¶ 4902; BUSEXP: 55,808; § 14,510.20

[85] ¶ 4910, ¶ 32,405; BUSEXP: 57,150; § 14,510.25

[86] ¶ 4918; BUSEXP: 55,812; § 14,510.30

[87] ¶ 4932; BUSEXP: 55,814; § 14,515

the bond (a *de minimis* amount is generally ¼ of one percent of the stated redemption price at maturity, multiplied by the number of years to maturity) (Code Sec. 54AA(d)(2)).

Unlike tax credit bonds, which provide a tax credit in lieu of interest payments, build America bonds pay interest to the bondholders and also provide a tax credit. The bondholder must include the interest in gross income but is allowed a credit against federal income tax liability for a portion of the interest payments received (Code Sec. 54AA(a) and (f)(1)). The credit is itself treated as interest that is includible in gross income (Code Sec. 54AA(f)(2)). The tax credit is equal to 35 percent of the interest payable on the interest payment date of the bond (Code Sec. 54AA(b)). The interest payment date is any date on which the bondholder of record is entitled to a payment of interest under the bond (Code Sec. 54AA(e)).

Tax Liability Limitations. The credit cannot exceed the excess of the sum of the bondholder's regular tax liability and alternative minimum tax liability over the sum of the credits allowed under Code Secs. 21 through 54E, not including Code Secs. 31 through 37 and the build America bond credit itself. Any unused credit may be carried forward to succeeding tax years (Code Sec. 54AA(c)).

Rules similar to Code Sec. 54(g), (h) and (i) apply for purposes of the credit (Code Sec. 54AA(f)(2)). Thus, in the case of a build America bond held by a partnership or S corporation, the allocation of the credit to the partners or shareholders is treated as a distribution. For build America bonds held by a real estate investment trust (REIT), the credit is allowed to the respective beneficiaries (and any gross income included in income with respect to the credit is treated as distributed to them) under procedures to be prescribed by the Treasury Secretary.

Qualified Bonds Issued Before 2011. State and local governments were allowed to elect to issue certain build America bonds as qualified bonds before January 1, 2011. Qualified bonds are issued in exchange for a payment credit, determined in accordance with Code Sec. 6431. The payment credit to the issuer is in lieu of the credit that would otherwise be allowed to the bondholder and is generally equal to 35 percent of the interest paid on the bond (Code Sec. 54AA(g)(1)).

1385. Mutual Fund Election to Pass-Through Tax Credit Bond Credits. Regulated investment companies (RICs or mutual funds) may elect to pass through to their shareholders credits attributable to tax credit bonds held by the entity, replacing the required pass through of the credits (Code Sec. 853A).[88] If the election is made, the RIC is not allowed any credits attributable to the tax credit bonds and includes in gross income, as interest, the amount of income that the entity would have included if the election did not apply, increasing the amount of the dividends paid by the same amount.

In order to qualify for the election, a RIC must hold directly or indirectly, one or more tax credit bonds on one or more applicable dates during the tax year and must also meet the 90 percent distribution requirements of a RIC (¶ 2301). The RIC must also have been taxed as a RIC for all tax years ending on or after November 8, 1983, or have no accumulated earnings and profits from a tax year to which the RIC provisions did not apply.

Where the election is made, shareholders of the RIC are to include in income the shareholder's proportionate share of the interest income attributable to the credits and are simultaneously allowed the proportionate share of credits. A RIC must report to shareholders in a written notice the shareholder's proportionate share of credits and gross income in respect of the credits. The shareholder's proportionate share of credits and gross income in respect of the credits cannot exceed the amounts so designated by the RIC in the notice.

References are to Standard Federal Tax Reports; Tax Research Consultant; and Practical Tax Explanations.

[88] ¶ 26,448; RIC: 3,366; § 14,505

Chapter 14

ALTERNATIVE MINIMUM TAX

	Par.
AMT Liability	1401
AMT Preferences and Adjustments	1425
Credits Against Minimum Tax	1470

AMT Liability

1401. Alternative Minimum Tax (AMT) Liability. The alternative minimum tax (AMT) is a separate method of determining tax liability designed to ensure that taxpayers do not completely avoid income tax through the use of deductions, exemptions, losses, and credits. All taxpayers subject to regular income tax are generally subject to the AMT, including individuals, estates, trusts, and corporations (Code Secs. 55(a) and 59(c)).[1] Partnerships and S corporations are not subject to the AMT. Instead, partners and shareholders compute their AMT liability separately by taking into account their share of partnership or S corporation items. Special rules apply, however, to partners of an electing large partnership using a simplified pass-through system (¶ 1455).

A taxpayer's AMT for a tax year is the excess of the taxpayer's tentative minimum tax over regular tax liability. AMT must be paid in addition to the regular tax liability and other federal taxes owed (¶ 1420). For example, if a taxpayer's tentative minimum tax for a tax year is $75,000 while regular tax liability is $50,000, the taxpayer must pay an AMT liability of $25,000 in addition to the $50,000 regular tax liability for a total tax liability of $75,000.

Tentative Minimum Tax. For an individual, estate, or trust, tentative minimum tax is equal to 26 percent of the taxpayer's alternative minimum taxable income (AMTI) up to a certain threshold amount, plus 28 percent of any AMTI in excess of the threshold amount (Code Sec. 55(b) and (d)(4); Rev. Proc. 2015-53; Rev. Proc. 2016-55).[2] For tax years beginning in 2016, the threshold amount is $186,300 ($93,150 for married filing separately). For tax years beginning in 2017, the threshold amount is $187,800 ($93,900 for married filing separately). For corporations, tentative minimum tax is 20 percent of AMTI, but certain small corporations and corporations in their first year of existence are exempt from the AMT (¶ 1415). AMTI is the taxpayer's regular taxable income increased by AMT tax preference items and modified by AMT adjustments (¶ 1405). A certain amount of AMTI is exempt from tax (¶ 1410).

Both corporate and noncorporate taxpayers may claim the AMT foreign tax credit in computing their tentative minimum tax (¶ 1470). Subject to limits, AMT liability may also be reduced by nonrefundable personal credits and general business credits (¶ 1475). Individuals use Form 6251 to compute AMT. Estates and trusts use Schedule I of Form 1041. Corporations use Form 4626.

Net Capital Gain and Qualified Dividends. The taxation of net capital gains and qualified dividends for AMT purposes is the same as for regular income tax purposes (¶ 1736 and ¶ 1738), including the netting of capital gains and losses by noncorporate taxpayers into separate tax-rate groups (¶ 1739) (Code Sec. 55(b)(3)). The capital gain or loss amounts, however, may differ from the regular tax amounts because of AMT tax preferences and adjustments affecting the basis of capital assets in computing AMTI.

References are to Standard Federal Tax Reports; Tax Research Consultant; and Practical Tax Explanations.

[1] ¶ 5100, ¶ 5400; FILEIND: 30,000; § 15,005

[2] ¶ 5100; FILEIND: 30,400; § 15,005, § 15,110.05

Minimum Tax on a Minor Child. A child who is subject to the kiddie tax (¶ 103) is subject to the AMT. The child computes tentative minimum tax in the same manner as any individual taxpayer. Thus, all adjustments and preferences apply, and AMT liability on the child's net unearned income is computed under the rules that apply to other taxpayers except that the child's exemption amount is limited (¶ 1410). The child's exemption amount and ultimate AMT liability are not dependent on the parent's AMTI or AMT exemption amount.

1405. Alternative Minimum Taxable Income (AMTI). Alternative minimum taxable income (AMTI) for purposes of determining alternative minimum tax (AMT) liability (¶ 1401) is the taxpayer's regular taxable income modified by AMT tax preference items and various AMT adjustments (Code Sec. 55(b)(2); Reg. § 1.55-1).[3] All provisions of the Code and regulations that apply in determining regular taxable income also generally apply in determining AMTI. If, however, the taxpayer's regular income tax is determined by reference to an amount other than regular taxable income, then that amount is treated as taxable income for AMT purposes (e.g., unrelated business taxable income (¶ 655), real estate investment trust (REIT) taxable income (¶ 2329), and life insurance company taxable income (¶ 2370)). Nonresident aliens and foreign corporations only include income effectively connected with a U.S. trade or business in their AMTI (¶ 2429). AMTI does not include fixed or determinable annual or periodic (FDAP) income (¶ 2431).

Tax preference items are deductions or exclusions that are allowed in computing regular taxable income but are not allowed in computing AMTI. This includes the exclusion of gain from qualified small business stock, depletion deductions for natural resources, and interest earned on tax-exempt private activity bonds (¶ 1425). Thus, tax preferences items can only increase a taxpayer's AMTI. Taxpayers may avoid having some of these deductions classified as tax preference items if they elect to capitalize the expenses and deduct them ratably over specified periods for regular tax purposes (¶ 1450).

AMT adjustments are items of income or deductions that are computed differently in determining AMTI than they are for regular taxable income. This means that adjustments may increase or decrease AMTI. For example, taxpayers must recompute depreciation, the expensing of mining exploration and development costs, income from long-term contracts, and net operating losses (NOLs) in computing AMTI (¶ 1430).

Individuals, estates, and trusts must also make adjustments for itemized deductions, personal exemptions, the standard deduction, and incentive stock options (¶ 1435). In determining the AMTI of an individual, estate, or trust, however, any reference to the taxpayer's adjusted gross income (AGI) or modified AGI is treated as a reference to AGI or modified AGI as determined for regular tax purposes (Reg. § 1.55-1(b)). Corporations must make adjustments to various items that only pertain to them, including adjusted current earnings (¶ 1440). In addition, the reduction or cutback of certain corporate preference items for regular tax purposes must generally be applied before a corporation applies the AMT rules (¶ 1445).

In computing the AMTI of a noncorporate taxpayer, the passive activity loss limitations generally apply with certain modifications (¶ 1460). However, a taxpayer cannot deduct any losses from tax-shelter farming activities. The limitations on the deductibility of other losses, including losses subject to the at-risk rules (¶ 1155), partnership losses claimed by partners (¶ 425), and S corporation losses claimed by shareholders (¶ 321), do apply in determining a taxpayer's AMTI (Code Sec. 59(h)).[4] These limitations are applied separately, taking into account all AMT tax preferences and adjustments. Thus, the amount of losses suspended and carried over may differ for AMT and regular tax purposes.

1410. AMT Exemption Amounts. A certain amount of a taxpayer's alternative minimum taxable income (AMTI) (¶ 1405) is exempt from the alternative minimum tax

References are to Standard Federal Tax Reports; Tax Research Consultant; and Practical Tax Explanations.

[3] ¶ 5100; ¶ 5100B; FILEIND: 30,050; § 15,005, § 15,110.05

[4] ¶ 5400; FILEIND: 30,150; § 15,401

(AMT) (Code Sec. 55(d); Rev. Proc. 2015-53; Rev. Proc. 2016-55).[5] The exemption amounts for individuals, estates, and trusts are adjusted annually for inflation for tax years beginning after 2012.

For individuals, the AMT exemption amount for tax years beginning in 2016 is $83,800 for married filing jointly or surviving spouse, $53,900 for single or head of household, and $41,900 for married filing separately. The AMT exemption amount for 2017 is $84,500 for married filing jointly or surviving spouse, $54,300 for single or head of household, and $42,250 for married filing separately.

For estates and trusts (other than electing small business trusts (¶ 304)), the AMT exemption amount is $23,900 for tax years beginning in 2016. For 2017 the exemption amount is $24,100. The AMT exemption is zero for the portion of an electing small business trust that is treated as a separate trust (Code Sec. 641(c)(2)(B)).[6]

For corporations, the AMT exemption amount is $40,000 for any tax year; it is *not* adjusted annually for inflation. All members of a controlled group of corporations (¶ 291) share a single $40,000 exemption (Code Sec. 1561(a)(3)).[7]

Phaseout of AMT Exemption Amount. For all taxpayers (individuals, estates, trusts, and corporations), the AMT exemption amount is phased out or reduced 25 percent for each $1 of the excess of the taxpayer's AMTI over certain threshold amounts (Code Sec. 55(d)(3) and (d)(4); Rev. Proc. 2015-53; Rev. Proc. 2016-55).[8] The thresholds for individuals, estates, and trusts are adjusted annually for tax years beginning after 2012.

For individuals, the threshold amount for tax years beginning in 2016 is $159,700 for married filing jointly or surviving spouse, $119,700 for single or head of household, and $79,850 for married filing separately. The AMT exemption amount is completely phased out in 2016 when AMTI reaches $494,900 for married filing jointly or surviving spouse, $335,300 for single or head of household, and $247,450 for married filing separately.

For 2017, the threshold amount is $160,900 for married filing jointly, $120,700 for single or head of household, and $80,450 for married filing separately. The AMT exemption amount is completely phased out for 2017 when AMTI reaches $498,900 for married filing jointly or surviving spouse, $337,900 for single or head of household, and $249,450 for married filing separately.

For estates or trusts, the threshold amount for tax years beginning in 2016 is $79,850, and the AMT exemption amount is completely phased out when AMTI reaches $175,450. For 2017, the threshold amount is $80,450, and the AMT exemption amount is completely phased out when AMTI reaches $176,850.

For corporations, the threshold amount is $150,000 for any tax year and is not adjusted annually for inflation. Thus, the $40,000 AMT exemption amount of a corporation is completely phased out when its AMTI reaches $310,000 for any tax year.

AMT Exemption Amount for a Child. A child who is subject to the kiddie tax (¶ 103) is subject to the AMT and computes tentative minimum tax in the same manner as any other individual taxpayer. The AMTI exemption amount of a child subject to the kiddie tax, however, is limited to the sum of the child's earned income for the year, plus $7,400 for 2016 ($7,500 for 2017) (Code Sec. 59(j); Rev. Proc. 2015-53; Rev. Proc. 2016-55).[9]

1415. AMT Exemption for Small Corporations. A corporation is generally subject to the alternative minimum tax (AMT) at a flat rate of 20 percent (¶ 1401) on alternative minimum taxable income (AMTI) (¶ 1405). However, a small corporation that meets a gross receipts test is not liable for the AMT so long as it remains a small corporation—its tentative minimum tax is treated as zero (Code Sec. 55(e)).[10]

For a corporation to qualify as an exempt small corporation, its average gross receipts must not exceed $7.5 million for all three-tax-year periods prior to the year for

References are to Standard Federal Tax Reports; Tax Research Consultant; and Practical Tax Explanations.

[5] ¶ 5100; FILEIND: 30,402; § 15,015, § 15,115

[6] ¶ 24,260; SCORP: 166.35; § 32,605.25

[7] ¶ 33,340; CCORP: 42,058

[8] ¶ 5100; FILEIND: 30,402; § 15,015, § 15,115

[9] ¶ 5400; FILEIND: 30,404.15; § 1,515

[10] ¶ 5100; STAGES: 9,120.15; § 15,105.15

which qualification is sought. The threshold is reduced to $5 million for the corporation's first three-year-period (or portion thereof). A corporation is generally treated as an exempt small corporation in its first year of existence regardless of its gross receipts. In applying the small corporation exemption, any reference to the corporation includes its predecessor and any related corporation. An exempt small corporation may also be exempt from using the accrual method of accounting (¶ 1515).

Once a corporation qualifies as a small corporation, it is exempt from AMT for so long as its average annual gross receipts for all three prior tax-year periods does not exceed $7.5 million. If a corporation ceases to be a small corporation, it cannot qualify as such for any subsequent tax year. The AMT in such circumstances will only apply prospectively.

Example: XYZ is a calendar-year corporation that is incorporated in 2015. It is neither aggregated with an existing related corporation, nor treated as having a predecessor. It will qualify as a small corporation for 2015, regardless of its gross receipts for the year. In order to qualify as a small corporation for 2016, XYZ's gross receipts for 2015 must be $5 million or less. If XYZ qualifies for 2016, it will also qualify for 2017 if its average gross receipts for the two-tax-year period including 2015 and 2016 is $5 million or less. If XYZ does not qualify for 2016, it cannot qualify for 2017 or any subsequent year. If XYZ qualifies for 2017, it will qualify for 2018 if its average gross receipts for the three-tax-year period including 2015, 2016, and 2017 is $7.5 million or less.

AMT Credit for Small Corporations. Taxpayers may be eligible to claim a tax credit based upon their AMT liability for the prior tax year (¶ 1309). However, the credit allowed against the regular tax of an exempt small corporation is limited to the amount by which the corporation's regular tax liability (reduced by other credits) exceeds 25 percent of the excess (if any) of the corporation's regular tax (reduced by other credits) over $25,000 (Code Sec. 55(e)(5)).[11]

1420. Regular Tax Compared with Tentative Minimum Tax. A taxpayer is subject to the alternative minimum tax (AMT) to the extent that tentative minimum tax exceeds regular tax liability (¶ 1401). A taxpayer's regular tax liability is regular income tax liability reduced by the foreign tax credit used for regular income tax purposes (¶ 1361), and by the U.S. possession or Puerto Rico economic activity credit (¶ 1362) (Code Sec. 55(c)).[12] It does not include any increase in tax due to the recapture of the investment tax credit (¶ 1365A) or the low-income housing credit (¶ 1365K). The income averaging rules for farmers and fishermen also do not apply when determining regular tax liability (¶ 767). Taxes excluded from regular tax liability are (Code Sec. 26(b)):

- alternative minimum tax (AMT);
- additional tax on early distributions from retirement plans (Code Sec. 72(m)(5)(B), (q), (t), and (v));
- tax on recaptured federal subsidies for mortgage bonds (Code Sec. 143(m));
- the additional tax on certain distributions from Coverdell education savings accounts (Code Sec. 530(d)(4));
- accumulated earnings tax (Code Sec. 531);
- tax on personal holding companies (Code Sec. 541);
- tax on foreign expropriation loss recoveries (Code Sec. 1351(d));
- tax on an S corporation's built-in gains (Code Sec. 1374);
- tax on an S corporation's passive investment income (Code Sec. 1375);
- tax on nonqualified withdrawals from certain Merchant Marine capital construction funds (Code Sec. 7518(g)(6));

References are to Standard Federal Tax Reports; Tax Research Consultant; and Practical Tax Explanations.

[11] ¶ 5100; FILEIND: 30,404.30; § 15,105.25

[12] ¶ 5100; FILEIND: 30,400, INDIV: 57,200; § 15,005, § 15,110.05

- 30-percent withholding tax on the fixed or determinable annual or periodical (FDAP) income of nonresident aliens and foreign corporations (Code Secs. 871(a) and 881);
- excise tax on the transfer of a residual interest in a real estate mortgage investment company (REMIC) to a "disqualified organization" (Code Sec. 860E(e));
- foreign corporations' branch profits taxes (Code Sec. 884);
- interest on tax liabilities deferred under the installment method (Code Secs. 453(l)(3) and 453A(c));
- the "tax" on certain transfers of high-yield interests to disqualified holders (Code Sec. 860K);
- the additional tax on Archer medical savings account (MSA) distributions not used for qualified medical expenses (Code Sec. 220(f)(4));
- the penalty imposed for distributions from Medicare Advantage medical savings accounts that were not used for qualified medical expenses (Code Sec. 138(c)(2));
- taxes relating to certain failures to maintain high deductible health plan coverage (Code Secs. 106(e)(3)(A)(ii), 223(b)(8)(B)(i)(II), and 408(d)(9)(D)(i)(II));
- tax relating to recapture of certain deductions for fractional gifts (Code Sec. 170(o)(3)(B));
- the additional tax on health savings account (HSA) distributions not used for qualified medical expenses (Code Sec. 223(f)(4));
- the additional tax under Code Sec. 409A(a)(1)(B) and (b)(5)(A) on income from nonqualified deferred compensation plans;
- the recapture of the first-time homebuyer credit under Code Sec. 36(f);
- the tax (including interest and an additional tax) on certain compensation that is deferred under a nonqualified deferred compensation plan (Code Sec. 457A(c)(1)(B)); and
- the additional tax on nonqualified distributions from ABLE accounts under Code Sec. 529A(c)(3)(A).

AMT Preferences and Adjustments

1425. AMT Tax Preference Items. In determining alternative minimum taxable income (AMTI) (¶ 1405), a taxpayer's regular taxable income for the tax year is increased by certain tax preference items (Code Sec. 57).[13] A corporation generally must also reduce or cut back certain tax preference items before calculation of its AMTI (¶ 1445). Tax preference items include the following:

- Seven percent of any gain realized on the sale of qualified small business stock and excluded from gross income under Code Sec. 1202 is treated as a tax preference item (¶ 1905) if the taxpayer acquired the stock before September 28, 2010. For qualified stock acquired after February 17, 2009, and before September 28, 2010, 75 percent of the gain is excluded, so 5.25 percent of the realized gain is treated as a tax preference item. For qualified stock acquired before February 17, 2009, 50 percent of the gain is excluded, so 3.5 percent of the gain is treated as a tax preference item. For qualified stock acquired after September 27, 2010, the excluded gain is not a tax preference item.[14]
- Tax-exempt interest (less any related expenses) on certain tax-exempt private activity bonds issued after August 7, 1986, is a tax preference item (except for bonds issued in 2009 and 2010).

References are to Standard Federal Tax Reports; Tax Research Consultant; and Practical Tax Explanations.

[13] ¶ 5300; FILEIND: 30,100, FILEIND: 30,250; § 15,301

[14] ¶ 30,372; FILEIND: 30,256; § 15,305

• The amount by which the depletion deduction (¶ 1289) claimed by a taxpayer (other than an independent oil and gas producer) for an interest in a property exceeds the adjusted basis of the interest at the end of a tax year is a tax preference item.

• If a taxpayer deducts intangible drilling costs (IDCs) (¶ 989), the difference between the amount allowed as a deduction and the amount that would have been deductible if the costs had been capitalized and ratably amortized over a 120-month period is a tax preference item to the extent it exceeds 65 percent of the taxpayer's net income from oil, gas, and geothermal properties. An independent producer is not subject to this rule, but its AMTI may not be reduced by more than 40 percent of the AMTI that would otherwise be determined if the taxpayer took the IDC tax preference into account and did not compute an alternative tax net operating loss deduction (¶ 1430). A taxpayer may avoid having deductions for IDCs classified as a tax preference item by electing to capitalize the expenses and deduct them over a 60-month period for regular income tax purposes (¶ 1450).

• The accelerated depreciation of real property, leased personal property, leased recovery property, and pollution control facilities placed in service before 1987 is treated as a tax preference item to the extent that it was a preference item under prior law, unless the taxpayer elected to apply MACRS to the property for regular tax purposes.

1430. AMT Adjustments for All Taxpayers. In determining alternative minimum taxable income (AMTI) (¶ 1405), certain deductions must be recomputed in a less favorable manner than is allowed when determining regular taxable income. The adjustments are usually intended to eliminate time value tax savings that result from the acceleration of deductions or the deferral of income. Some adjustments are made solely by noncorporate taxpayers (¶ 1435), while others are made solely by corporate taxpayers (¶ 1440). Both noncorporate and corporate taxpayers must make the following adjustments when determining AMTI.

Depreciation. For MACRS property placed in service after 1998, if the 200-percent declining balance method is used for regular tax purposes for 3-, 5-, 7-, or 10-year property, then the 150-percent declining balance method and regular tax depreciation period must be used in calculating AMTI (Code Sec. 56(a)(1)).[15] For all other MACRS property placed in service after 1998, no AMT adjustment is required as AMT and regular tax depreciation are computed in the same way.

For MACRS property placed in service after 1986 and before 1999, if the 200-percent declining balance method is used for regular income tax purposes for 3-, 5-, 7-, or 10-year property, then the 150-percent declining balance method and the alternative depreciation system (ADS) recovery period must be used in calculating AMTI. If the 150-percent declining balance method is used for 15-or 20-year property, then the 150-percent declining balance method and the ADS recovery period are used in calculating AMTI. If the 150-percent declining balance method election is in effect for regular tax purposes for 3-, 5-, 7-, 10-, 15-, or 20-year property, then no adjustment is required for AMT purposes as the AMT and regular tax depreciation are computed the same way.

For 27.5-year residential real property and 31.5- or 39-year real property placed in service after 1986 and before 1999, AMT depreciation is computed using the straight-line method and ADS recovery period (40 years). If the straight-line election is in effect for regular tax purposes for 3-, 5-, 7-, 10-, 15-, or 20-year property, then for AMT purposes the straight-line method and ADS recovery period must be used. If the ADS method (elective or nonelective) is used for regular tax purposes, then no adjustment is required in calculating AMTI, as AMT and regular tax depreciation are computed the same way on real and personal property subject to the ADS method.

It should be noted that a benefit of the AMT depreciation adjustment is that depreciation for all property is combined in calculating AMTI. This allows the netting of

References are to Standard Federal Tax Reports; Tax Research Consultant; and Practical Tax Explanations.

[15] ¶ 5200; FILEIND: 30,102; § 15,230

excess MACRS deductions with excess AMT deductions. A taxpayer with excess MACRS deductions on new property may offset them against AMT deductions on old property and, thus, may be able to avoid paying AMT on these deductions.

No AMT adjustment of depreciation is required for the following property:

- any qualified property for which bonus depreciation or special depreciation allowance was claimed (¶ 1237) if the basis for AMT purposes is the same as for regular income tax purposes (Code Sec. 168(k)(2)(G)), including qualified disaster assistance property (Code Sec. 168(n)(2)(D)), qualified reuse and recycling property (Code Sec. 168(m)(2)(D)), cellulosic biofuel plant property (Code Sec. 168(l)(5)), qualified New York Liberty Zone property (Code Sec. 1400L(b)(2)(E)), qualified Gulf Opportunity Zone property (Code Sec. 1400N(d)(4)), and Kansas disaster area qualified recovery assistance property (Act Sec. 15345(a)(1) and (d)(1) of P.L. 110-246);
- any portion of property the taxpayer elected to expense under Code Sec. 179 (¶ 1208), as well as any other property depreciated under a method not expressed in a term of years such as the unit-of-production method (but not the retirement-replacement-betterment or similar method) (Code Sec. 56(a)(1)(B));
- motion picture films, videotapes, or sound recordings;
- public utility property if a normalization method of accounting is not used;
- certain natural gas gathering lines placed in service after April 11, 2005, which are treated as MACRS 7-year property regardless of whether owned by a producer or a nonproducer; and
- any qualified Indian reservation property (Code Sec. 168(j)(3)).

Disposition of Property. The AMT adjustments for depreciation, pollution control facilities, incentive stock options, and circulation, research, and experimental expenses (¶ 1435) are taken into account in determining the related property's basis for AMT purposes. Thus, the AMT gain or loss from the disposition of the property may be different from the gain or loss for regular tax liability. The difference between regular tax gain or loss and AMT gain or loss is an adjustment in computing the taxpayer's AMTI (Code Sec. 56(a)(6) and (b)(3)).[16] The difference is taken into account as a negative adjustment in calculating AMTI if the AMT gain is less than the regular tax gain, the AMT loss is more than the regular tax loss, or there is an AMT loss and a regular tax gain.

Example: A taxpayer purchased a piece of property for $100,000 and claimed a total of $25,000 of depreciation deductions resulting in an adjusted basis of $75,000 for regular tax purposes. In AMTI calculations made during the same tax years, the taxpayer claimed adjusted depreciation deductions totaling $10,000 resulting in an adjusted basis of $90,000 for AMT purposes. If the taxpayer sells the property in the current tax year for $150,000, his regular tax gain is $75,000 ($150,000 – $75,000) and his AMT gain is $60,000 ($150,000 – $90,000). The $15,000 difference is a negative adjustment in calculating the taxpayer's AMTI.

Mining Exploration and Development Costs. A taxpayer who has expensed mining exploration and development expenses (or amortized the costs in computing regular tax liability (¶ 987 and ¶ 988)) must capitalize and amortize the expenses over a 10-year period in calculating AMTI, beginning with the tax year the expenses were incurred (Code Sec. 56(a)(2)).[17] If a tax loss is incurred from a mine, the deduction from AMTI is the lesser of the loss allowed for the costs had they remained capitalized or all expenses that have been capitalized but not yet amortized. When property that generated mining exploration and development deductions is sold, its adjusted basis must be computed under the AMT rules in order to determine the gain or loss from the sale for AMT purposes. The AMT adjustment for mining exploration and development costs does not have to be made if the taxpayer elects an optional 10-year amortization period for regular tax purposes (¶ 1450).

References are to Standard Federal Tax Reports; Tax Research Consultant; and Practical Tax Explanations.

[16] ¶ 5200; FILEIND: 30,054; § 15,245, § 15,425

[17] ¶ 5200; FILEIND: 30,106; § 15,255

Long-Term Contracts. A taxpayer must use the percentage-of-completion method of accounting (¶ 1551) to determine AMTI from long-term contracts (other than home construction contracts) (Code Sec. 56(a)(3)).[18] A long-term contract is a building, installation, construction, or manufacturing contract that is not completed during the tax year it is entered into. This method replaces all other accounting methods, such as the completed contract or cash basis method. The percentage-of-completion is determined using simplified cost allocation procedures for construction contracts of certain small contractors if the contract has an estimated duration of less than two years.

Alternative Tax Net Operating Losses. Net operating loss (NOL) deductions must be recomputed in calculating AMTI (Code Sec. 56(a)(4) and (d)).[19] The alternative tax NOL (ATNOL) is generally computed in the same manner as an ordinary NOL (¶ 1145) except that all AMT adjustments are taken into account first, and tax preference items reduce ATNOL (¶ 1425) to the extent they increased the amount of the NOL for the tax year. The ATNOL may not offset more than 90 percent of AMTI, determined without regard to the ATNOL deduction and the domestic production activities deduction. Unused ATNOLs are carried forward or back to the earliest year in which they can be used, according to the rules for NOLs including the election to forgo the carryback period (¶ 1149). The amount of ATNOLs carried forward or back is reduced by 90 percent of the AMTI for any year to which they are carried, whether or not the taxpayer is liable for the AMT in that year.

Example: A taxpayer's income for a tax year is $75,000, while her losses total $100,000, of which $20,000 is from tax preference items. Her NOL for regular taxation is $25,000. In computing AMTI, tax preference items cannot be used. Consequently, only $80,000 of the losses may offset income, leaving the taxpayer with an ATNOL of $5,000.

Pollution Control Facilities. For property placed in service after 1986 and before 1999, the five-year amortization method for depreciating pollution control facilities (¶ 1287) must be replaced by the alternative depreciation system (ADS) (¶ 1247) (Code Sec. 56(a)(5)).[20] The pollution control facility adjustment is computed under MACRS using the straight-line method for property placed in service after 1998. When the pollution control facility is sold, its adjusted basis must be computed under the AMT rules in order to determine the gain or loss from the sale for AMT purposes.

Domestic Production Activities Deduction. The domestic production activities deduction is allowed for both individuals and corporations against the AMT (¶ 980A). The deduction is equal to nine percent of the lesser of (1) the taxpayer's qualified production activities income determined without regard to available AMT adjustments, or (2) the taxpayer's taxable income (or a corporation's AMTI), determined without regard to the deduction (Code Sec. 199(a) and (d)(6)).

1435. AMT Adjustments for Noncorporate Taxpayers. In addition to alternative minimum tax (AMT) adjustments that affect all taxpayers (¶ 1430), individuals and other noncorporate taxpayers must make a number of adjustments to various tax items that pertain only to them in calculating alternative minimum taxable income (AMTI) (¶ 1405).

Itemized Deductions. Individuals may claim itemized deductions in calculating AMTI with certain adjustments (Code Sec. 56(b)).[21] The limit on itemized deductions that applies for regular tax purposes does not apply for AMT purposes (¶ 1014).

An individual may not deduct state, local, or foreign income or property taxes paid during the tax year (including state and local sales taxes paid in lieu of income taxes) (¶ 1021) in calculating AMTI. Tax refunds are not included in AMTI even though the recovered taxes are included in gross income for regular tax purposes. The only taxes that reduce a noncorporate taxpayer's AMTI are business taxes that reduce adjusted gross income (AGI) and generation-skipping transfer taxes paid on income distributions.

References are to Standard Federal Tax Reports; Tax Research Consultant; and Practical Tax Explanations.

[18] ¶ 5200; FILEIND: 30,202; § 15,240

[19] ¶ 5200; FILEIND: 30,156; § 15,415

[20] ¶ 5200; FILEIND: 30,110

[21] ¶ 5200; FILEIND: 30,300; § 15,205

Itemized deductions for medical expenses may be claimed in computing AMTI to the extent they exceed 10 percent of the taxpayer's AGI (¶ 1015). The adjustment is applicable to all individuals, including taxpayers who otherwise may claim medical expenses to the extent they exceed 7.5 percent of AGI for regular tax purposes. This includes (i) individuals who have attained age 65 in any tax year after December 31, 2012, and before January 1, 2017, and (ii) all individuals for tax years beginning before January 1, 2013.

An itemized deduction may also be claimed in computing AMTI for qualified housing interest, which is similar to the qualified residence interest deduction that may be claimed for regular tax purposes (¶ 1047) (Code Sec. 56(e)).[22] However, qualified housing interest is limited to interest paid on acquisition debt for a house, apartment, condominium, or mobile home; it does not include interest paid on home equity debt.

Investment interest expenses are generally deductible in computing AMTI to the same extent as regular tax liability—thus, the deduction is limited to the taxpayer's net investment income (¶ 1094) (Code Sec. 56(b)(1)(C)). However, investment interest does not include qualified housing interest for AMT purposes even if it is otherwise allocable to property held for investment. In addition, tax-exempt interest on private activity bonds is included in investment income for AMT purposes, and interest expended to carry the bonds is included in investment interest expenses.

A noncorporate taxpayer cannot claim any miscellaneous itemized deductions subject to the two-percent of AGI floor in calculating AMTI (¶ 1079). For example, legal expenses are generally deductible as a miscellaneous itemized deduction and therefore cannot be deducted for AMTI. Attorney fees and court costs paid in connection with an unlawful federal discrimination claim or whistleblower award for providing information on tax law violations, however, are deductions taken into account as an above-the-line deduction in computing the individual's AGI and can therefore be claimed as a deduction for AMTI (¶ 1093).

Personal Exemptions and the Standard Deduction. Personal exemption deductions may not be claimed against AMTI, including the personal exemption deduction allowed to a decedent's estate or a trust (¶ 133 and ¶ 534). In addition, the standard deduction is not allowed in computing AMTI, including the additional standard deduction for elderly and blind taxpayers (¶ 126) (Code Sec. 56(b)(1)(E)).[23]

Incentive Stock Options. An individual does not recognize gain or loss for regular tax purposes when an incentive stock option (ISO) is granted or exercised (¶ 1925). Instead, gain or loss is recognized when the stock is sold. The individual, however, must make an adjustment for AMT purposes by increasing AMTI by the amount the stock's fair market value exceeds the option price at the time the individual's rights to the stock are freely transferable or not subject to a substantial risk of forfeiture (Code Sec. 56(b)(3)).[24] This generally occurs when the option is exercised. The basis of stock acquired through the exercise of the ISO is increased for AMT purposes by the amount of the AMT adjustment. There is no AMT adjustment of basis if the stock is nontransferable and subject to a substantial risk of forfeiture. The individual in such circumstances may make a Code Sec. 83(b) election to take the AMT adjustment into account in the tax year (¶ 713). There is no AMT adjustment if the option is exercised and the stock is disposed of in the same tax year. Although the exercise of an ISO can trigger an AMT liability, a taxpayer may be able to recover the liability through the AMT credit in future years (¶ 1309).

It should be noted that the price of stock acquired through an ISO may substantially decrease in value after the option is exercised. As a result, the taxpayer may not realize any actual income or a loss when the stock is sold. If the stock is sold at a loss, the taxpayer would be subject to $3,000 limit on deducting capital losses for regular tax purposes. Thus, even though the individual could have a significant AMT liability from exercising the ISO, he or she could have a loss for regular tax purposes from selling the stock which cannot be used against the AMT liability. Before 2013, a taxpayer could use

References are to Standard Federal Tax Reports; Tax Research Consultant; and Practical Tax Explanations.

[22] ¶ 5200; FILEIND: 30,310.05; § 15,220.05

[23] ¶ 5200; FILEIND: 30,302; § 15,205

[24] ¶ 5200; FILEIND: 30,204; § 15,245

any long-term unused AMT credit to offset regular tax liability arising from excess losses. However, this offset is no longer available. (¶ 1327).

Circulation, Research, and Experimental Expenses. Circulation expenses that are expensed for regular tax purposes (¶ 971) must be capitalized for AMTI calculations and ratably amortized over a three-year period starting with the tax year they are incurred. Similarly, research and experimental expenses which are expensed for regular tax purposes (¶ 979) must be capitalized for AMT purposes and ratably amortized over a 10-year period (Code Sec. 56(b)(2)).[25] The adjustment for circulation expenses applies to any individual or personal holding company (¶ 277). The adjustment for research and experimental expenses applies only to an individual, unless the individual has materially participated (¶ 1165) in the activity that generated the expenses. Neither adjustment has to be made if the taxpayer elects to amortize the circulation, research, or experimental expenses for regular income tax purposes (¶ 1450).

If a loss is sustained on property that generated the circulation, research, or experimental expenses, a deduction is allowed equal to the lesser of the unamortized expenses or the amount that would be allowed as a loss had the expenses remained capitalized. The adjusted basis of such property must be computed under the AMT rules in order to determine the gain or loss from the sale for AMT purposes (¶ 1430). The difference between the regular tax gain or loss and the recomputed AMT gain or loss is a tax preference adjustment in the year of sale.

1440. AMT Adjustments for Corporate Taxpayers. In addition to alternative minimum tax (AMT) adjustments that affect all taxpayers (¶ 1430), corporations must make a number of adjustments to various tax items that pertain only to them in calculating alternative minimum taxable income (AMTI) (¶ 1405).

Adjusted Current Earnings. A portion of the difference between the AMTI and the adjusted current earnings (ACE) of a corporation—other than an S corporation, regulated investment company (RIC) (¶ 2301), real estate investment trust (REIT) (¶ 2326), or real estate mortgage investment conduit (REMIC) (¶ 2343)—is treated as an adjustment to AMTI (Code Secs. 56(c)(1) and (g)).[26] This adjustment does not attempt to recapture the tax benefit a corporation derives from the use of a particular tax deduction or exclusion. Instead, it is aimed at recapturing some of the overall tax savings enjoyed by a corporation that reports large earnings to its shareholders and creditors, but pays little or no tax. To achieve recapture, a corporation's AMTI must be increased by 75 percent of the amount by which its ACE exceeds its AMTI, computed without the adjustments for ACE or alternative tax net operating losses (ATNOLs) (¶ 1430).

Example: A corporation has AMTI of $100,000 before it makes adjustments for ACE or ATNOLs. The current tax year's ACE amounts to $200,000, leaving the corporation with an ACE adjustment of $75,000 (.75 × ($200,000 – $100,000)), which increases AMTI to $175,000 ($100,000 + $75,000).

Similarly, a corporation's AMTI is reduced by 75 percent of the excess of the corporation's pre-adjustment AMTI over its ACE. The reduction cannot exceed the excess of the total positive adjustments for all prior years over the total negative adjustments for all prior years. In a given tax year, this ceiling is determined by limiting the amount of AMTI available for reduction to the excess of prior year increases in AMTI caused by the ACE adjustment over prior year reductions caused by an ACE shortfall.

Example: In a corporation's current tax year it calculates ACE of $50,000 and AMTI of $70,000. Multiplying the difference between AMTI and ACE by 0.75 leaves the corporation with $15,000 that may possibly be used to reduce AMTI. In its prior tax years, the corporation calculated an overall positive ACE adjustment of $10,000. This amount serves as a limit on the amount by which AMTI may be reduced in the current year, leaving the corporation with only a $10,000 reduction of AMTI rather than a $15,000 reduction. The possible reduction of $5,000 that remains may not be carried over to later tax years.

References are to Standard Federal Tax Reports; Tax Research Consultant; and Practical Tax Explanations.

[25] ¶ 5200; FILEIND: 30,112; § 15,250, § 15,252

[26] ¶ 5200; STAGES: 9,120.05; § 15,125.05

The computation of a corporation's ACE begins with its AMTI as a base, but determined without regard to the ACE adjustment and the ATNOL deduction. This AMTI is then adjusted to determine ACE. Many of the adjustments are similar to the adjustments made in determining the corporation's earnings and profits for purposes of taxing its dividend distributions to shareholders (¶ 748). The adjustments include, but are not limited to, the following:

- A corporation that has pre-1994 depreciable assets remaining in service must adjust the depreciation in calculating ACE. For most depreciable property placed in service before 1994, ACE depreciation is computed using the alternative depreciation system (ADS) (straight-line method) (¶ 1247).

- Income that is exempt from regular tax and AMT liability but that is included in the computation of earnings and profits must be included in the computation of ACE. For example, ACE includes tax-exempt interest from investments in state or local bonds (except bonds issued in 2009 and 2010 and certain housing bonds). Income from the discharge of indebtedness, however, does not have to be included in this adjustment. Expenses incurred in earning tax-exempt income, while not deductible in determining regular tax or AMT, are deductible in determining ACE.

- A deduction that is not claimed against earnings and profits generally may not be claimed in the computation of ACE (except for certain 100-percent dividends and dividends from 20-percent-owned corporations).

- Intangible drilling costs (IDC) (¶ 989), the costs of organizing a corporation (¶ 237), and the costs of circulating periodicals (¶ 971) that may be expensed or amortized for regular tax purposes must be capitalized in computing ACE.

- ACE must be increased or decreased by an increase or decrease in a corporation's LIFO recapture amount, which is the amount by which the value of the corporation's inventory under the first in, first out (FIFO) method of inventory valuation exceeds the value under the last in, first out (LIFO) method.

- The installment method of accounting (¶ 1801) may not be used in the computation of ACE except to the extent that it is used to calculate preadjustment AMTI. Rather, income from installment sales must be included in ACE in the year in which property is sold.

- Income that has built up on a life insurance contract must be included in a corporation's ACE.

- Corporations other than independent oil and gas producers and royalty owners must use the cost depletion method (¶ 1289) to determine depletion deductions.

- A corporation that has undergone an ownership change in which new shareholders have acquired more than half of the value of the corporation's stock must undertake a wholesale recomputation of the basis of its assets so that the adjusted basis of each asset immediately after an ownership change becomes its proportionate share of the fair market value of the assets immediately before the change.

- ACE may not include a loss from the exchange of one pool of debt obligations for another pool that consists of obligations with the same effective interest rates and maturities as obligations in the first pool.

- The adjusted basis of assets for purposes of making ACE adjustments is determined under these ACE adjustment rules.

- No adjustment related to the earnings and profits effect of charitable contributions is made to ACE.

- A property and casualty insurance company that elects to be taxed only on taxable investment income for regular tax purposes determines its ACE without regard to underwriting income and expense.

Merchant Marine Capital Construction Funds. Contributions made by shipping companies to capital construction funds (established under § 607 of the Merchant Marine Act of 1936, 46 U.S.C. 1177) may not be deducted and a fund's earnings (including gains or losses) may not be excluded from AMTI (Code Sec. 56(c)(2)).[27] Amounts withdrawn from a fund that have been included in AMTI do not reduce the basis of a vessels, barges, and containers.

Blue Cross and Blue Shield Organizations. The special deduction from regular tax allowed to Blue Cross and Blue Shield organizations under Code Sec. 833 for 25 percent of their annual claims and administrative expenses (less the prior tax year's adjusted surplus) may not be claimed against AMTI (Code Sec. 56(c)(3)).[28]

1445. AMT Interaction with Corporate Preference Cutbacks. The tax benefit a corporation derives from certain tax preferences generally must be reduced or cut back 20 or 30 percent (Code Secs. 59(f) and 291).[29] The cutback rules of Code Sec. 291 are applied before the calculation of a corporation's alternative minimum taxable income (AMTI) (¶ 1405). The cutbacks are made to the following tax preferences:

- If a corporation sells or otherwise disposes of section 1250 property (¶ 1786), the 20 percent of any excess of the amount that would have been treated as recapture income had the property been section 1245 property (¶ 1785), over the amount recaptured as ordinary income under Code Sec. 1250, must be recaptured as ordinary income. The cutback does not apply to the extent Code Sec. 1250 does not apply, or to property that was part of a certified pollution control facility that elected to amortize expenses (¶ 1287). Also, if a real estate investment trust (REIT) (¶ 2326) disposes of section 1250 property, gain that is treated as not coming from ordinary income and is distributed to shareholders as a capital gain dividend is excluded from ordinary income treatment. Corporate shareholders of a REIT must treat capital gain dividends as subject to the 20-percent ordinary income treatment.

- A corporation's percentage depletion deduction (¶ 1298) for iron ore and coal (including lignite) must be reduced by 20 percent of the excess of the percentage depletion deduction (determined before the 20-percent reduction is made), over the adjusted basis (determined without including the depletion deduction) of the minerals at the close of the tax year.

- There must be a 20-percent reduction in the amount of deductions claimed by a financial institution (defined under Code Sec. 585) for certain interest expenses on debts incurred to purchase tax-exempt obligations acquired after December 31, 1982, and before August 8, 1986.

- The basis of certified pollution control facilities that are used for computing rapid amortization deductions must be reduced by 20 percent. ACRS depreciation must be used to depreciate the reduced basis.

- A corporation's (including an integrated oil company's) deductions for intangible drilling costs and mineral exploration and development costs (¶ 987, ¶ 988, and ¶ 989) must be reduced by 30 percent. Reduced deductions may be deducted ratably over a 60-month period that starts with the month the costs are paid or incurred. If the related property is disposed, the deductions may be recaptured.

1450. Election to Avoid Tax Preference Status. A taxpayer can avoid having an alternative minimum tax (AMT) preference or adjustment for certain expenses by electing to capitalize the expenses and deduct them ratably over specified periods for regular tax purposes beginning with the tax year (or month) in which the expenses were made (Code Sec. 59(e)).[30] Taxpayers may limit their elections to only a portion of their deductions, leaving the remaining deductions subject to AMT. A three-year period may be claimed for circulation expenses (¶ 971), a 60-month period may be claimed for

References are to Standard Federal Tax Reports; Tax Research Consultant; and Practical Tax Explanations.

[27] ¶ 5200; INDIV: 33,558

[28] ¶ 5200; EXEMPT: 15,160.10

[29] ¶ 5,400, ¶ 15,190; DEPR: 18,266, FARM: 15,154.35, FARM: 21,154.10; § 26,020.05

[30] ¶ 5400; FILEIND: 30,114; § 15,250, § 15,252, § 15,255, § 15,320

intangible drilling costs (IDC) that begins with the month in which they are paid or incurred (¶ 989), and a 10-year period may be claimed for research and experimental expenses (¶ 979) and mineral exploration and development expenses (¶ 987 and ¶ 988). The election for deductions allowed to partnerships and S corporations is made by the partners or shareholders, rather than by the partnership or the corporation.

1455. Net AMT Adjustment of Electing Large Partnerships. A partnership is not subject to the alternative minimum tax (AMT) and its partners generally compute their AMT liability separately by taking into account their shares of partnership items (¶ 1401). However, an electing large partnership using a simplified reporting system for partnership items (¶ 482), computes AMT tax preference items and adjustments at the partnership level with the partnership reporting to its partners a net AMT adjustment for passive loss limitation activities and other activities (Code Sec. 772).[31] The net AMT adjustment is determined by using the adjustments applicable to individuals in the case of noncorporate partners (¶ 1435) and the adjustments applicable to corporations in the case of corporate partners (¶ 1440). Except as provided in regulations, the applicable net AMT adjustment is treated as a deferral tax preference for purposes of computing the minimum tax credit (¶ 1309).

1460. Losses Not Allowed for AMT. In computing alternative minimum taxable income (AMTI) (¶ 1405), most taxpayers subject to the passive activity loss rules (¶ 1169) may claim passive activity losses only to the extent they exceed income from passive activities. However, an insolvent taxpayer may claim the otherwise disallowed losses. Losses from a tax shelter farm activity are also not allowed in computing AMTI unless the taxpayer is insolvent.

Passive Activity Losses. The passive activity rules of Code Sec. 469 apply in computing the AMTI of an individual, estate, trust, closely-held C corporation, or personal service corporation (Code Sec. 58(b)).[32] Thus, deductions for passive losses may be claimed only against passive income. The taxpayer must take into account AMT adjustments and tax preference items before computing income, deductions, and credits from a passive activity for AMT purposes. AMT passive activity gain or loss is computed without regard to qualified housing interest, as opposed to qualified residence interest for regular tax purposes (¶ 1435). The amount of a disallowed AMT passive activity loss is reduced by the amount of a taxpayer's insolvency at the close of the tax year (Code Sec. 58(c)).

> **Example:** In calculating his regular tax, a taxpayer has a passive loss deduction of $15,000 for net losses from real estate rentals. The losses are partially based on MACRS deductions. His AMT liability must be determined by computing depreciation deductions under the alternative depreciation system (ADS). This leaves him with a passive loss deduction of only $5,000 against AMTI. Since he already has adjusted his depreciation deductions in determining whether there is a passive loss, he does not have to include them as part of any adjustment for depreciation in calculating AMTI.

Passive Farm Tax Shelter Losses. Noncorporate taxpayers, as well as personal service corporations, may not deduct losses from a tax shelter farm activity in computing AMTI (Code Sec. 58(a)).[33] A tax shelter farm activity is a farm syndicate (¶ 1521) or passive farm activity in which the taxpayer (or the taxpayer's spouse) is not a material participant (¶ 1165). The taxpayer must take into account AMT adjustments and tax preference items in determining the amount of gain or loss from a tax shelter farm activity. The amount of a disallowed loss is reduced by the amount of a taxpayer's insolvency at the close of the tax year (Code Sec. 58(c)). Taxpayers may not net income and losses from various farming tax shelters to determine an overall loss or gain. Each tax shelter must be regarded separately. Farm losses that have been disallowed as deductions from AMTI in one tax year may be claimed as deductions from farm income from the same farm activity in the succeeding tax year. Taxpayers who dispose of their interest in a tax shelter farm activity may claim their losses against AMTI.

References are to Standard Federal Tax Reports; Tax Research Consultant; and Practical Tax Explanations.

[31] ¶ 25,608; PART: 18,452.25; § 15,025

[32] ¶ 5350; FILEIND: 30,152; § 15,405

[33] ¶ 5350; FILEIND: 30,154; § 15,410

1465. AMT Liability of REITs, RICs, and Common Trust Funds. Tax preference items and adjustments that are treated differently for alternative minimum tax (AMT) purposes (¶ 1405) and regular tax purposes must be apportioned between regulated investment companies (RICs) (¶ 2301) or real estate investment trusts (REITs) (¶ 2326), and their shareholders and holders of beneficial interests. Participants in common trust funds must apportion these items among themselves on a pro rata basis (Code Sec. 59(d)).[34]

Credits Against Minimum Tax

1470. Alternative Minimum Tax Foreign Tax Credit. The alternative minimum tax (AMT) foreign tax credit may be claimed by taxpayers in computing their tentative minimum tax (¶ 1401). The AMT foreign tax credit is similar to the foreign tax credit for regular income tax purposes (¶ 2475), except that it is limited to the foreign tax on foreign source alternative minimum taxable income (AMTI) instead of foreign tax on regular taxable income (Code Sec. 59(a)).[35] Thus, the AMT foreign tax credit cannot exceed the taxpayer's tentative minimum tax multiplied by the ratio of the taxpayer's foreign source AMTI to worldwide AMTI. Alternatively, the taxpayer may elect to compute the AMT foreign tax credit limit by multiplying the tentative minimum tax by the ratio of the taxpayer's foreign source regular taxable income to worldwide AMTI. Amounts disallowed by the foreign tax credit limitation may be carried back one year and forward 10 years, subject to the same limitation in those years for both regular tax and AMT purposes.

1475. Other Tax Credits Under AMT. An individual's nonrefundable personal credits are allowed in full against the taxpayer's combined regular tax liability and alternative minimum tax (AMT) liability (Code Sec. 26(a)).[36] A taxpayer's regular tax liability for this purpose is reduced by the foreign tax credit used for regular income tax purposes and the U.S. possession credit (¶ 1420).

A taxpayer's general business credit (¶ 1365) may not exceed the excess of net income tax over the greater of (1) the taxpayer's tentative minimum tax or (2) 25 percent of the taxpayer's net regular tax liability that exceeds $25,000 (Code Sec. 38(c)).[37] For this purpose, net income tax is the sum of the taxpayer's regular tax liability and AMT liability, reduced by all other nonrefundable and other credits. The tax liability limitation is determined separately for the general business credit attributable to the alcohol fuels credit (¶ 1365I), the low-income housing credit (¶ 1365K), the renewable electricity production credit (¶ 1365N), the FICA employer tip credit (¶ 1365R), the railroad track maintenance credit (¶ 1365W), the small employer health insurance credit (¶ 1333), the rehabilitation credit (¶ 1365B), the business energy credit (¶ 1365C), and the work opportunity credit (¶ 1365G). The limitation is also made separately for the empowerment zone employment credit (¶ 1365O), substituting 75 percent of tentative AMT for 100 percent of AMT.

1480. AMT and Possessions Tax Credit. Corporate income for which the Puerto Rico economic activity credit or the possessions tax credit may be claimed (¶ 1362) is not includible in alternative minimum taxable income (AMTI) (¶ 1405) and therefore is not subject to the minimum tax (Code Sec. 59(b)).[38]

References are to Standard Federal Tax Reports; Tax Research Consultant; and Practical Tax Explanations.

[34] ¶ 5400; FILEIND: 30,404.25; § 15,025

[35] ¶ 5400; FILEIND: 30,352; § 15,505

[36] ¶ 3850; INDIV: 57,200; § 12,005

[37] ¶ 4250; BUSEXP: 54,056; § 15,515.15

[38] ¶ 5400; INTL: 27,066

Chapter 15

TAX ACCOUNTING

	Par.
Accounting Period	1501
Accounting Method	1515
Timing of Income and Expenses	1533
Long-Term Contracts	1551
Inventories	1553
Allocation and Reconstruction of Income	1573

Accounting Period

1501. Tax Year. Taxable income is computed on the basis of a taxpayer's tax year (Code Sec. 441).[1] A tax year is the annual accounting period regularly used by a taxpayer in keeping books and records to compute income. This period is usually a calendar year of 12 months ending on December 31 or a fiscal year of 12 months ending on the last day of any month other than December. A taxpayer may elect to use a 52-53 week fiscal year that always ends on the same day of the week, rather than the last day of the month (¶ 1503). A taxpayer with a short tax year must file a return for a period that is less than 12 months (short-period return) under special rules (¶ 1505).

> **Example 1:** A corporation began doing business on August 15, 2016. The end of its first tax year cannot be later than July 31, 2017, because a tax year may not cover more than a 12-month period and must end on the last day of a month, unless it is a 52-53 week tax year.

A new taxpayer may adopt either a calendar or a fiscal year on their first tax return, but certain taxpayers must adopt a specific tax year (Reg. § 1.441-1).[2] An existing taxpayer must follow IRS procedures to change a tax year (¶ 1513). If a taxpayer adopts an improper tax year, such as a fiscal year (other than a 52-53 week tax year) that does not end on the last day of a calendar month, the IRS may require the taxpayer to adopt a proper tax year or to request IRS approval to change tax years (Rev. Rul. 85-22).[3]

> **Example 2:** Assume that the new corporation in Example 1 determines there is no advantage in keeping its books on the basis of any year other than the calendar year. Therefore, it adopts the calendar year as its tax year. It should close its books as of December 31, 2016, and file its first return for the short period from August 15, 2016, through December 31, 2016. This short period is its first tax year. All its later tax years will be full calendar years until its dissolution or until it changes to a fiscal year.

A fiscal year will be recognized only if it is established as the taxpayer's annual accounting period and only if the taxpayer keeps books and records on the same basis. A taxpayer who has no annual accounting period, does not keep adequate records, or whose present tax year does not qualify as a fiscal year must compute taxable income on a calendar-year basis (Reg. § 1.441-1).[4]

Partnerships. A partnership generally must use the same tax year as that of its owners, unless the partnership can establish a business purpose for having a different tax year (Code Sec. 706(b); Reg. § 1.706-1).[5] The tax year of the owners is the tax year of the partner(s) owning the majority interest in the partnership—that is, the tax year of

References are to Standard Federal Tax Reports; Tax Research Consultant; and Practical Tax Explanations.

[1] ¶ 20,302; ACCTNG: 24,050; § 38,101

[2] ¶ 20,303; ACCTNG: 24,052; § 38,105

[3] ¶ 20,307.70; ACCTNG: 24,058; § 38,135.20

[4] ¶ 20,303; ACCTNG: 24,052; § 38,110

[5] ¶ 25,160, ¶ 25,161; ACCTNG: 24,352; § 30,120.05

the partner(s) owning in total more than a 50-percent interest in partnership profits and capital (¶ 416). If there is no majority interest tax year, the partnership must adopt the same tax year as that of its principal partners, each of whom must have at least a five-percent interest in partnership profits or capital. When neither condition is met, the partnership must use the tax year that produces the least aggregate deferral of income to the partners.

Corporations. An S corporation or a personal service corporation (PSC) (¶ 273) must use the calendar year unless the entity can establish a business purpose for having a different tax year (Code Secs. 441(i) and 1378(b)).[6] The ownership tax year of an S corporation generally satisfies the business purpose requirement. A corporation is not considered a PSC unless more than 10 percent of its stock, by value, is held by employee-owners. If a corporation is a member of an affiliated group filing a consolidated return, all members of that group must be considered in determining whether the corporation is a PSC.

Section 444 Election of Nonrequired Year. A partnership, S corporation, or PSC may make a section 444 election on Form 8716 to use a tax year other than a required tax year if the deferral period of the elected year is not longer than three months (Code Sec. 444).[7] To neutralize the tax benefits resulting from using a tax year other than a required tax year, an electing partnership or S corporation must compute and make any required payments exceeding $500. Required payments are the amount of tax that would otherwise be due from partners and stockholders had the entity used the required tax year (Code Sec. 7519; Temp. Reg. § 1.7519-2T).[8] The required payment is due on or before May 15 of the calendar year following the calendar year in which the section 444 election year begins. An electing PSC must make minimum distributions to its employee-owners by the end of a calendar year falling within a tax year to avoid certain deduction deferrals for amounts paid to employee-owners (Code Sec. 280H).[9]

The section 444 election must be made by the earlier of: (1) the 15th day of the fifth month following the month that includes the first day of the tax year for which the election is first effective, or (2) the due date, without extensions, of the return that results from the election (Code Sec. 444(d); Temp. Reg. § 1.444-3T).[10] The election will remain in effect until the entity changes its tax year or otherwise terminates the election. The election may not be made by an entity that is a member of a tiered structure unless the tiered structure consists only of partnerships or S corporations or both, all of which have the same tax year.

Common Trust Funds. Common trust funds maintained by a bank (¶ 2389) are required to adopt the calendar year as their tax year (Code Sec. 584(i)).[11]

DISCs. The tax year of a domestic international sales corporation (DISC) (¶ 2498) must be the same as that of the shareholder or group of shareholders with the same tax year who have the highest percentage of voting power (Code Sec. 441(h)).[12]

1503. 52- or 53-Week Accounting Period. A taxpayer may elect to use a fiscal tax year (¶ 1501) that varies from 52 to 53 weeks if that period always ends on the same day of the week (Monday, Tuesday, etc.) and that day is either the last such day in a calendar month or the closest such day to the last day of a calendar month (Code Sec. 441(f); Reg. § 1.441-2).[13]

References are to Standard Federal Tax Reports; Tax Research Consultant; and Practical Tax Explanations.

[6] ¶ 20,302, ¶ 32,260; ACCTNG: 24,354, ACCTNG: 24,356; § 27,120, § 28,410.15

[7] ¶ 20,600; ACCTNG: 24,450; § 38,115.05

[8] ¶ 42,770, ¶ 42,773; ACCTNG: 24,500; § 38,115.10

[9] ¶ 15,160; ACCTNG: 24,550; § 38,115.15

[10] ¶ 20,600, ¶ 20,604; ACCTNG: 24,450; § 38,115.05

[11] ¶ 23,630; RIC: 12,304.15

[12] ¶ 20,302; ACCTNG: 24,110.10

[13] ¶ 20,302, ¶ 20,304; ACCTNG: 24,302; § 38,105

Example: A new taxpayer wishes to have its accounting period end on the last Thursday in August. In 2016, its tax year ends on August 25, completing a 52-week year (August 28, 2015, through August 25, 2016). In 2017, its tax year ends on August 31, completing a 53-week year (August 26, 2016, through August 31, 2017). With this type of tax year, most of the taxpayer's tax years are 52 weeks long. As an alternative, the taxpayer could select a tax year that ends on the Thursday that is nearest to the end of August. In 2016, therefore, the tax year ends on September 1 (the Thursday nearest the end of August). In 2017, the tax year ends on August 31.

If a pass-through entity, owner of a pass-through entity, or both, use a 52-53-week tax year and the tax year of the entity and owner end with reference to the same calendar month, then for purposes of determining the tax year in which items of income, gain, loss, deductions, or credits from the entity are taken into account by the owner, the owner's tax year is deemed to end on the last day of the entity's tax year. Under this rule, a pass-through entity is a partnership, S corporation, trust, estate, closely held real estate investment trust (REIT) (¶ 2326), common trust fund (¶ 2389), controlled foreign corporation (CFC) (¶ 2487), or passive foreign investment company (PFIC) (¶ 2490) (Reg. § 1.441-2(e)).[14]

1505. Short-Period Return. A short-period return is a tax return for a period of less than 12 months. A taxpayer may need to file a short-period return if the taxpayer changes its annual accounting period (¶ 1513) or is in existence during only part of what would otherwise be the tax year (Code Sec. 443; Reg. § 1.443-1).[15]

Taxpayers who are not in existence for a full 12-month period include:

- a corporation that begins business or goes out of business at any time other than the beginning or end of its accounting period,
- an individual who dies prior to the end of the accounting period, and
- a decedent's estate that comes into existence on the date of the decedent's death and adopts an accounting period ending less than 12 months from that date.

If the taxpayer is not in existence for a full tax year, the tax is computed as if the return had actually covered a full tax year. When a short period occurs as a result of a change in accounting period, the tax is computed on an annualized basis (¶ 1507). An alternative relief method is also available for taxpayers that change their accounting period (¶ 1509). However, short-period returns of decedents and dissolving corporations, and the first return of a new corporation are not required to be annualized.

If a change to or from a 52-53 week tax year results in a short period of 359 days or more, the tax is computed as if the return had actually covered a full tax year. If the short period is less than seven days, the short period becomes part of the following tax year. If the short period is more than six days but less than 359 days, the tax is computed under the annualized method (Code Sec. 441(f)(2)).[16] Special annualization rules apply to taxpayers that make such a change (¶ 1507).

1507. General Method for Annualizing Income for Short Periods. When there has been a change in an accounting period that requires filing a short-period return (¶ 1505), income for the short period must be converted to an annual basis. This conversion is generally accomplished by: (1) multiplying the taxpayer's modified taxable income for the short period by 12, and (2) dividing the result by the number of months in the short period. The tax is computed on the resulting taxable income except that individuals must use the tax rate schedules to compute the tax and not the tax tables. The tax computed is divided by 12 and multiplied by the number of months in the short period (Code Sec. 443).[17] See ¶ 1509 for an alternative method for annualizing income for short periods.

References are to Standard Federal Tax Reports; Tax Research Consultant; and Practical Tax Explanations.

[14] ¶ 20,304; ACCTNG: 24,308; § 38,105

[15] ¶ 20,500, ¶ 20,501; ACCTNG: 24,250; § 38,140.05

[16] ¶ 20,302; ACCTNG: 24,306; § 38,140.15

[17] ¶ 20,500; ACCTNG: 24,260; § 38,140.10, § 38,140.15

The modified taxable income for the short period is the gross income for the period less any allowable deductions. However, in the case of an individual, no standard deduction is allowed (¶ 126), only itemized deductions (¶ 1014) (Code Sec. 63(c)(6)(C)). In addition, the deduction for personal exemptions (¶ 133) is only allowed in proportion to the ratio that the number of months in the short period bears to 12.

Example: Tom has been making his returns on the basis of a fiscal year ending April 30. He changes to a year ending June 30 in 2016. He must file his return for the year ending April 30, 2016, on or before August 15, 2016. On or before October 15, 2016, he must file his return for the short period of two months beginning May 1, 2016, and ending June 30, 2016. His gross income for the short period is $9,600, and his itemized deductions total $600. He is married, age 60, and has no dependents. His wife has no income or deductions. Tom's income tax liability on before credits on their joint return for the short period is computed as follows:

Gross income	$9,600
Itemized deductions*	600
Net income	9,000
Less 2/12 of $8,100 (2 × $4,050) exemptions	1,350
Modified taxable income for short period	7,650
Annualized taxable income—$7,650 × 12/2	45,900
Tax on $45,900	5,958
Tax for short period, 2/12 of $5,958	993

* Assume that the itemized deductions are not miscellaneous itemized deductions and that amounts are rounded to the nearest dollar.

When a short-period return is filed, the taxpayer's self-employment tax (¶ 2664) is computed on the actual amount of self-employment income earned for the short period and not prorated for a portion of a 12-month period.[18] A net operating loss deduction (¶ 1145) is applied against actual income for the short period before annualizing (Reg. § 1.443-1(b); Rev. Proc. 2002-39, modified by Rev. Proc. 2003-34 and Rev. Proc. 2003-79).[19]

A taxpayer that is changing to or from a 52-53-week fiscal tax year and that must annualize income will apply the same rules as other taxpayers in determining the income of the short period. However, the taxpayer will calculate income on an annual basis by multiplying the income of the short period by 365 and dividing the result by the number of days in the short period (Code Sec. 441(f)(2)(B)(iii)). Tax is computed on that annualized income and then is multiplied by the ratio of the number of days in the short period to 365; the resulting figure is the tax for the short year.

1509. Alternative Method for Annualizing Income for Short Periods. An alternative method is provided for annualizing income when computing tax for a short-period return (¶ 1505) (Code Sec. 443(b)(2); Reg. § 1.443-1(b)(2)).[20] Under this method, the tax for the short period is the greater of:

(1) a tax on the actual taxable income for the 12-month period beginning with the start of the short period (using the law in effect for that 12-month period), multiplied by the modified taxable income (¶ 1507) for the short period and divided by the modified taxable income for the 12-month period, or

(2) a tax on the modified taxable income for the short period.

If a taxpayer does not exist at the end of the 12-month period described in (1) above, or if a corporate taxpayer has distributed substantially all its assets before the end

References are to Standard Federal Tax Reports; Tax Research Consultant; and Practical Tax Explanations.

[18] ¶ 35,203.30; INDIV: 63,058; § 38,140.15

[19] ¶ 20,501, ¶ 20,406.27; ACCTNG: 24,260.10; § 38,140.15

[20] ¶ 20,500, ¶ 20,501; ACCTNG: 24,260.15; § 38,140.25

of that period, the tax is computed by using a 12-month period ending with the last day of the short period. In such cases, in order to claim the benefits of the alternative method, the taxpayer must attach a return covering the 12-month period ending on the last day of the short year to the return initially filed with tax computed for the short period.

If there was a change in accounting period resulting in a short period (¶ 1513), the taxpayer must first compute the tax using the general annualization method and file the return. If the alternate method would result in lower taxes, a claim for credit or refund must be filed no later than the due date by which a return would have been required to be filed if the 12-month period beginning with the short period were considered a tax year. The application for use of the alternate method is considered as a claim for credit or refund.

1513. Change of Accounting Period. A change from one accounting period (¶ 1501) to another generally requires prior permission of the IRS and requires filing a return for the short period (¶ 1505). To request IRS approval to change, Form 1128 must be filed by the due date of the taxpayer's return, not including extensions, for the first effective year. A change in the accounting period will be approved where it is established that a substantial business purpose exists for making the change. It will generally not be approved where the sole purpose of the change is to maintain or obtain a preferential tax status (Reg. § 1.442-1(b)).[21]

The IRS will consider all the facts and circumstances relating to the change, including the tax consequences. Among the non-tax factors is the effect of the change on the taxpayer's annual cycle of business activity. The agreement between the taxpayer and the IRS under which the change is carried out will, in appropriate cases, provide terms, conditions, and adjustments necessary to prevent a substantial distortion of income that would otherwise result from the change. For example, effects that would constitute substantial distortions of income include:

- deferring a substantial portion of the taxpayer's income or shifting a substantial portion of deductions from one year to another so as to reduce substantially the taxpayer's tax liability;
- causing a similar deferral or shift in the case of any other person, such as a partner, a beneficiary, or an S corporation shareholder; or
- creating a short period in which there is either: (i) a substantial net operating loss, capital loss or credit, including a general business credit; or (ii) a substantial amount of income to offset an expiring net operating loss, capital loss, or credit (Reg. § 1.442-1(b)(3)).[22]

Non-Individual Taxpayers. Automatic approval procedures are provided for certain corporations that have not requested a tax year change within the most recent 48-month period ending with the last month of the requested tax year (Rev. Proc. 2006-45, modified by Rev. Proc. 2007-64).[23] Automatic approval procedures are also provided for trusts and certain partnerships, S corporations, electing S corporations, and personal service corporations that have not requested a tax year change within the most recent 48-month period ending with the last month of the requested tax year and that meet certain conditions (Rev. Proc. 2006-46).[24] If the automatic approval procedures do not apply, the IRS has provided other procedures for taxpayers to follow in order to obtain the IRS's approval of an adoption, change, or retention of an annual accounting period through application to the IRS national office with payment of a user fee (Reg. § 1.442-1(b)(3); Rev. Proc. 2002-39, modified by Rev. Proc. 2003-34 and Rev. Proc. 2003-79).[25]

References are to Standard Federal Tax Reports; Tax Research Consultant; and Practical Tax Explanations.

[21] ¶ 20,401, ¶ 20,406.41; ACCTNG: 24,200; § 38,130.05

[22] ¶ 20,401; ACCTNG: 24,200; § 38,120.20, § 38,125.10, § 38,130.25

[23] ¶ 20,406.17; CCORP: 45,202; § 38,125.05

[24] ¶ 20,406.123; ACCTNG: 24,168; § 38,120.05

[25] ¶ 20,401, ¶ 20,406.123; ACCTNG: 24,200; § 38,120.05, § 38,125.05, § 38,130.05

Individuals. A newly married individual who is adopting the annual accounting period of his or her spouse in order to file a joint return can make the change in tax year without IRS consent (Reg. § 1.442-1(d); Rev. Proc. 2003-62).[26] In addition, the IRS has provided procedures for individuals filing federal income tax returns on a fiscal year to obtain automatic approval to change their annual accounting method to a calendar year.

Improper Tax Year. As an alternative to the above procedures, any taxpayer may correct a prior adoption of an improper tax year by filing Form 1128 with an amended return on a calendar year basis (Rev. Proc. 85-15).[27]

Accounting Method

1515. Cash v. Accrual Basis. Taxable income must be computed not only on the basis of a fixed accounting period (¶ 1501) but also according to the method of accounting regularly employed in keeping the taxpayer's books (Code Sec. 446; Reg. § 1.446-1(a)).[28] A method of accounting includes the overall method of accounting for income and expenses, as well as the method of accounting for special items such as depreciation. There are two common overall methods of accounting for income: the cash basis and the accrual basis.

The cash basis (cash receipts and disbursements) is the accounting method used by most individuals. Income is generally reported in the year that it is actually or constructively received in the form of cash, or its equivalent, or other property. Income is constructively received when it is within the taxpayer's control, but has not been actually received (¶ 1533). There is no constructive receipt, however, if there are substantial limits or restrictions on the right to receive the income. Deductions or credits are generally taken for the year in which the related expenditures were actually paid, unless they should be taken in a different period to more clearly reflect income, such as depreciation allowances and prepaid expenses (¶ 1539) (Reg. § 1.446-1(c)(1)(i)).[29]

Under the accrual method, income is accounted for when the taxpayer has the right to receive it—when all events that determine that right have occurred. It is not the actual receipt but the *right to receive* that governs. Expenses are deductible on the accrual basis in the year incurred—when all the events have occurred that fix the amount of the item and determine the liability of the taxpayer to pay it (Reg. § 1.446-1(c)(1)(ii)).[30] See ¶ 1540 for a discussion of the all-events test as it relates to economic performance.

The accounting method used by a taxpayer must clearly reflect income (¶ 1525). An approved standard method of accounting (i.e., the cash basis or the accrual basis) ordinarily is regarded as clearly reflecting income. An individual may use one accounting method to keep his or her personal books and another for the books of his or her trade or business. A taxpayer may use different accounting methods if the taxpayer has two or more separate businesses as long as separate and distinct sets of records are maintained. However, the use of multiple accounting methods is not permitted if there is a creation or shifting of profits or losses between the taxpayer's various trades or businesses (Reg. § 1.446-1).[31] Generally, and except as otherwise required, a hybrid method combining two or more methods of accounting—such as a combination of the cash method as the taxpayer's overall method of accounting and the accrual method for inventories—may be used so long as the combination clearly reflects income and is consistently used (Reg. § 1.446-1(c)(1)(iv)).[32]

Taxpayers that are required to use inventories (¶ 1553) must use the accrual method to account for purchases and sales (Reg. § 1.446-1(c)(2)).[33] Furthermore, the

References are to Standard Federal Tax Reports; Tax Research Consultant; and Practical Tax Explanations.

[26] ¶ 20,401, ¶ 20,406.21; ACCTNG: 24,152; § 38,110

[27] ¶ 20,406.15; ACCTNG: 24,166; § 38,110

[28] ¶ 20,606, ¶ 20,607; ACCTNG: 200; § 38,201

[29] ¶ 20,607; ACCTNG: 208; § 38,210, § 38,215.05

[30] ¶ 20,607; ACCTNG: 210; § 38,220.05

[31] ¶ 20,607; ACCTNG: 208.05; § 38,205.05

[32] ¶ 20,607; ACCTNG: 6,400; § 38,225

[33] ¶ 20,607; ACCTNG: 15,060; § 38,215.05

following taxpayers must generally use the accrual method of accounting as their overall method of accounting for tax purposes:

(1) C corporations,

(2) partnerships that have a C corporation as a partner,

(3) charitable trusts that are subject to the tax on unrelated trade or business income (¶ 655), but only for that income, and

(4) tax shelters (Code Sec. 448(a) and (d)(6)).[34]

Qualified personal service corporations (¶ 273) are treated as individuals rather than as corporations for purposes of category (2), above.

Notwithstanding the general requirement that these taxpayers use the accrual method, the cash method of accounting may be used instead if the entity is not a tax shelter and:

(1) is engaged in a farming or tree-raising business, unless the taxpayer is a corporation or has a corporation as a partner (¶ 1519),

(2) is a qualified personal service corporation, or

(3) is an eligible small business (Code Sec. 448(b)).

A small business is exempt from using the accrual method if it has met a $5-million-or-less gross receipts test for all prior tax years beginning after 1985. An entity meets the $5 million gross receipts test if its average annual gross receipts for the three tax years ending with the prior tax year do not exceed $5 million (Temp. Reg. § 1.448-1T(f)).[35] Furthermore, most businesses that are required to account for inventories may use the cash method if average annual gross receipts do not exceed $1 million (Rev. Proc. 2001-10). Certain other small businesses required to account for inventories may also use the cash method if average annual gross receipts do not exceed $10 million (Rev. Proc. 2002-28).[36]

1516. Prorating Income of Accrual-Method Taxpayers. When the effective date of a tax rate change occurs within a tax year, an accrual-method taxpayer (¶ 1515) must compute the tax for the entire tax year by using both the old and the new rates (Code Sec. 15).[37] The final tax is the sum of: (1) the tax calculated at the old rates that is proportionate to the portion of the tax year before the effective date of the new tax, and (2) the tax calculated at the new rates that is proportionate to the portion of the tax year beginning with the effective date. When the tax rate change involves the highest rate of income tax, the taxpayer must compute the tax for the year by using a weighted average of the highest rates before and after the change determined on the basis of the respective portions of the tax year before the date of change and on or after the date of change.

1519. Accrual Accounting for Farm Corporations. Corporations and partnerships having a corporation as a partner that are engaged in the business of farming are required to use the accrual method of accounting (¶ 1515) (Code Sec. 447).[38] In addition, these taxpayers are required to capitalize their preproductive period expenses (¶ 999). All farming corporations are subject to the accrual accounting rule except:

- S corporations,
- corporations or partnerships engaged in the trade or business of operating a nursery or sod farm, or raising or harvesting trees, other than fruit and nut trees, and
- corporations having annual gross receipts of $1 million or less for each prior tax year beginning after 1975, including the receipts of predecessor corporations and members of a controlled group.

References are to Standard Federal Tax Reports; Tax Research Consultant; and Practical Tax Explanations.

[34] ¶ 20,800; ACCTNG: 6,050; § 38,215.05

[35] ¶ 20,801B; ACCTNG: 208.15; § 38,215.10

[36] ¶ 20,803.75; ACCTNG: 6,050, ACCTNG: 15,058; § 38,215.10

[37] ¶ 3385; ACCTNG: 24,310.10, FILEIND: 15,054.25; § 38,140.10

[38] ¶ 20,700; FARM: 3,060; § 36,315.10

A family corporation is not required to use the accrual method if its gross receipts do not exceed $25 million for each prior tax year beginning after 1985. A family corporation is defined as:

- any corporation in which at least 50 percent of the total combined voting power of all classes of voting stock and at least 50 percent of all other classes of the corporation's stock are owned by members of the same family, or
- any of the closely held corporations described in Code Sec. 447(h).

If a corporation or qualified partnership (each of the partners of which is a corporation) has for a 10-year period ending with its first tax year after 1975, and for all subsequent years, used an annual accrual method of accounting with respect to its trade or business of farming, and the entity raises crops that are harvested a year or more after planting, it may continue to use this method.

1521. Expenses of Farming Syndicates. A farming syndicate is a tax shelter and must use the accrual method of accounting (¶ 1515) (Code Secs. 448(d) and 461(i)(4)).[39] A farming syndicate is any farming partnership or enterprise, other than a corporation that is not an S corporation, if at any time: (1) interests in the enterprise or partnership have been offered for sale in an offering required to be registered with any federal or state agency having authority to regulate such offering, or (2) more than 35 percent of the losses during any period are allocable to limited partners or limited entrepreneurs (Code Sec. 461(j)[k]). An individual is not treated as a limited partner or limited entrepreneur if the individual:

(1) has his or her principal residence on the farm on which the farming enterprise is being carried on;

(2) has an interest attributable to active participation in management of the farming enterprise for a period of not less than five years;

(3) actively participates in the management of a farming enterprise as his or her principal business activity, regardless of whether he or she actively participates in the management of the enterprise in question; or

(4) actively participates in the management of another farming enterprise involving the raising of livestock (or is so treated under either (1) or (2)) and owns an interest in an enterprise involving the further processing of the livestock raised in the enterprise.

If an individual meets any of these conditions, any member of his or her family who owns an interest in a farming enterprise that is attributable to the individual's active participation is not treated as a limited partner or limited entrepreneur.

1525. Accounting Method Prescribed by IRS. The IRS can prescribe a method of accounting (¶ 1515) that will clearly reflect income if, in its opinion, the method used by the taxpayer fails to do so (Code Sec. 446(b)).[40] If the IRS requires a change in accounting methods, the taxpayer must compute an income adjustment due to the change, referred to as a section 481(a) adjustment (¶ 1531).

1529. Change of Accounting Method. A taxpayer generally may not change his or her method of accounting (¶ 1515) without obtaining advance permission from the IRS (Code Sec. 446(e); Reg. § 1.446-1(e)).[41] A change of accounting method includes a change in the overall plan of accounting as well as a change in the treatment of any material item. In most cases, a method of accounting is not established for an item unless there is a pattern of consistent treatment. A change in the treatment of a material item is one involving the timing of its inclusion in income or deduction; not the traditional accounting meaning dealing with the relationship of amounts.

IRS consent is required whether the change is made from an acceptable or an unacceptable method. If the taxpayer fails to file a request to change his or her method

References are to Standard Federal Tax Reports; Tax Research Consultant; and Practical Tax Explanations.

[39] ¶ 20,800, ¶ 21,802; ACCTNG: 12,352

[40] ¶ 20,606; ACCTNG: 21,110; § 38,620

[41] ¶ 20,606, ¶ 20,607; ACCTNG: 21,102; § 38,610.05

of accounting, the absence of IRS consent to the change will not prevent the imposition of or diminish any resulting penalties (i.e., additions to tax) (Code Sec. 446(f)).[42] A taxpayer that changes its method of accounting for a tax year generally must make certain adjustments to its income, referred to as section 481(a) adjustments (¶ 1531).

Changes in accounting method include, but are not limited to:

- a change from the cash to the accrual basis;
- any change in the method of valuing inventories (¶ 1571);
- a change in depreciation or amortization method (¶ 1221);
- a change from the cash or accrual basis to one of the long-term contract methods (¶ 1551), from one of the long-term contract methods to the cash or accrual basis, or from one long-term contract method to another;
- a change involving the adoption, use, or discontinuance of any other specialized method (i.e., the crop method) (¶ 1569); and
- a change where the Code and regulations specifically require that IRS consent be obtained.

The IRS will automatically approve certain changes of accounting method. This approval is granted for the tax year for which the taxpayer requests the change if the taxpayer complies with the automatic change procedures included in Rev. Proc. 2015-13.[43] Rev. Proc. 2016-29 contains the list of accounting method changes to which the automatic change procedures apply. Rev. Proc. 2016-29 also includes specific procedures for each of the listed changes. The list is updated to add or remove changes as needed (Rev. Proc. 2016-29).[44] For changes of accounting method which are not granted automatic approval by the IRS, taxpayers must comply with the advance consent procedures in Rev. Proc. 2015-13.[45]

Application for permission to change the taxpayer's method of accounting must generally be filed on Form 3115 during the tax year in which the taxpayer desires to make the proposed change (Reg. § 1.446-1(e)(3)(i)).[46]

1531. Adjustments Required by Changes in Method of Accounting. Taxpayers who voluntarily change their method of accounting with the IRS's permission (¶ 1529), or who are compelled by the IRS to make a change because the method used does not clearly reflect income (¶ 1525), must make certain adjustments to income in the year of the change (Code Sec. 481(a); Reg. § 1.481-1).[47] The adjustments are those determined to be necessary to prevent duplication or omission of items.

The adjustment period for most voluntary accounting method changes is one tax year (the year of change) for a net negative section 481(a) adjustment and four tax years (the year of change and next three tax years) for a net positive section 481(a) adjustment. A net positive section 481(a) adjustment is taken into account ratably over the adjustment period for taxpayers that agree to the IRS conditions. A taxpayer may elect to use a one-year adjustment period (the year of change) in lieu of the four-year adjustment period otherwise provided for a positive adjustment if the net adjustment is less than $50,000 (Rev. Proc. 2015-13).[48] Moreover, a taxpayer may request approval of an alternative method of allocating the amount of the adjustments (Reg. § 1.481-4; Rev. Proc. 2015-13).[49] A change in accounting method resulting from limitations placed on the use of the cash method of accounting (¶ 1515) is treated as a change initiated by the taxpayer with the consent of the IRS. The related section 481(a) adjustment is includible in income over a period generally not exceeding four years (Code Sec. 448(d)(7)).[50]

References are to Standard Federal Tax Reports; Tax Research Consultant; and Practical Tax Explanations.

[42] ¶ 20,606; ACCTNG: 21,050; § 38,610.05

[43] ¶ 20,620.284; ACCTNG: 21,300; § 38,610.10

[44] ¶ 20,620.285; ACCTNG: 21,300; § 38,610.10

[45] ¶ 20,620.284; ACCTNG: 21,200; § 38,610.20

[46] ¶ 20,607; ACCTNG: 21,104; § 38,615

[47] ¶ 22,270, ¶ 22,271; ACCTNG: 21,150; § 38,625.05

[48] ¶ 22,277.70; ACCTNG: 21,204; § 38,625.05

[49] ¶ 22,275; ACCTNG: 21,104.15; § 38,625.05

[50] ¶ 20,800; ACCTNG: 21,164.15; § 38,625.05

Since the adjustments for the year of change might result in the bunching of income, two statutory methods of limiting the tax in the changeover year may be applied if the adjustments for the changeover year increase taxable income by more than $3,000 (Code Sec. 481(b); Reg. § 1.481-2).[51] If both limitations apply, the one resulting in the lower tax should be used.

Under the first method, the old method of accounting must have been used in the two preceding years; if so, the tax increase in the changeover year is limited to the tax increases that would result if the adjustments were spread ratably over that year and the two preceding years. Under the second method, the taxpayer must be able to reconstruct his or her income under the new method of accounting for one or more consecutive years immediately preceding the changeover year. The increase in the changeover year's tax because of the adjustments may not be more than the net tax increases that would result if the adjustments were allocated back to those preceding years under the new method. Any amounts that cannot be allocated back must be included in the changeover year's income for purposes of computing the limitation.

Timing of Income and Expenses

1533. Constructive Receipt of Income for Cash-Basis Taxpayers. It is not always necessary that a taxpayer take possession of money or property representing income before it is considered received. Income that is constructively received is taxed to a cash-basis taxpayer (¶ 1515) as though it had been actually received (Reg. § 1.451-2(a)).[52] There is constructive receipt when income is credited without restriction and made available to the taxpayer. There must be no substantial limitation or condition on the taxpayer's right to bring the funds within his or her control. An insubstantial forfeiture provision, a notice requirement, or the loss of bonus interest for deposits or accounts in certain financial institutions is not a substantial limitation.

Common examples of constructive receipt include matured and payable interest coupons, interest credited on savings bank deposits, and dividends unqualifiedly made subject to a stockholder's demand. However, if a dividend is declared payable on December 31 and the corporation follows a practice of paying the dividend by checks mailed so that the shareholders will not receive them until January of the following year, the dividend is not considered to be constructively received by the stockholders in December (Reg. § 1.451-2(b)).[53] For the time of receipt by shareholders of certain mutual fund dividends, see ¶ 2309. Accrued interest on an unwithdrawn insurance policy dividend is gross income to the taxpayer for the first tax year during which the interest may be withdrawn.

Salaries credited on corporate books are taxable to an officer in the year when the officer may withdraw the compensation at will if the corporation has funds available to pay the salaries without causing financial difficulties. Bonuses that are based on yearly sales and that are otherwise not available to an officer are taxable in the year of receipt.[54]

Accrued interest on a deposit that may not be withdrawn at the close of an individual's tax year because of an institution's actual or threatened bankruptcy or insolvency is not includible in the depositor's income until the year in which that interest is withdrawable (Code Sec. 451(g)).[55]

Constructive receipt does not give rise to constructive payment. For example, a negotiable note of a responsible and solvent maker received in payment of salary, interest, rent, etc., must be reported as income by a cash-basis recipient to the extent of its fair market value when received. IT does not mean that the cash-basis maker may also deduct the same amount at that time. Delivery of a note is not a payment on the cash basis, and the deduction may be taken only in the year when the note is paid.

References are to Standard Federal Tax Reports; Tax Research Consultant; and Practical Tax Explanations.

[51] ¶ 22,270, ¶ 22,272; ACCTNG: 21,152; § 38,625.10

[52] ¶ 21,007; ACCTNG: 6,150; § 38,315.05

[53] ¶ 21,007, ¶ 21,009.1235; ACCTNG: 6,210, ACCTNG: 6,218; § 3,101, § 38,315.15

[54] ¶ 21,009.17; ACCTNG: 6,152.10; § 38,315.05

[55] ¶ 21,002; ACCTNG: 6,218; § 38,315.15

Giving collateral to secure the note does not change the promise to pay into an actual payment.[56]

1537. Prepaid Income. Payments received by a taxpayer in advance of future services or property are usually income to an accrual-basis or cash-basis taxpayer (¶ 1515) in the year of receipt, provided that there is no restriction on the use of the payments. This is true even though the prepayments are returnable on the happening of some specified event. A distinction must be made, however, between prepayments that may be refunded for services or goods, and deposits over which the taxpayer does not have complete dominion and control on receipt.[57] For example, a utility company was not required to include deposits from uncreditworthy customers in income on receipt because it was required to return the deposit on request by a customer who established creditworthiness.

Prepaid Merchandise. Inclusion in the year of receipt is required for advance payments received on the sale of merchandise. However, under certain circumstances the IRS permits accrual-basis sellers to include certain advance payments in income in the tax year in which those payments are properly accruable under the method of accounting used for tax purposes if they are reported at that time or later for financial reporting purposes (Reg. § 1.451-5).[58] If the method used for financial reporting results in an earlier accrual, then the advance payments are taxed according to the financial reporting method. When a long-term contract method of accounting (¶ 1551) is used, advances are included in income under that method without regard to how the income from these payments is accounted for in the seller's financial reports.

An advance payment for this purpose is any amount received by an accrual-basis taxpayer under an agreement: (1) for the sale or other disposition in a future tax year of goods held by the taxpayer primarily for sale to customers in the ordinary course of its trade or business, or (2) for the building, installation, construction, or manufacture of items by the taxpayer where the agreement is not completed within that tax year. An exception exists where substantial advance payments for inventoriable goods have been received and goods are on hand or available to satisfy the agreement in the year of receipt. Payments for gift certificates are substantial when received, but in other cases, advance payments are not substantial until they exceed the cost of goods to be sold. In such cases, all advance payments received by the last day of the second tax year following the year in which the substantial advance payments are received and not previously included in income under the taxpayer's method of accounting must be included in income in the second tax year (Reg. § 1.451-5(c)).[59]

Certain manufacturers, wholesalers, and retailers that receive advance payments for multi-year service warranty contracts may elect to recognize income from the payments as a series of equal payments over the life of the contracts. The election is permitted only if an eligible taxpayer purchases insurance to cover its obligations under a service warranty contract within 60 days after the sale of the contract (Rev. Proc. 97-38).[60]

Prepaid Services and Mixed Prepayments. Taxpayers who receive advance payments for services and advance payments for the transfer of both goods and services are allowed a limited deferral beyond the tax year of receipt for certain advance payments (Rev. Proc. 2004-34, modified by Rev. Proc. 2011-18, modified by Rev. Proc. 2013-29).[61] Excludable payments generally include: the payment for services; the sale of goods other than those for which the taxpayer uses a method of deferral allowed for advance payments of goods discussed previously; the use of intellectual property, including license or lease; the use of property ancillary to the provision of services (e.g., hotel rooms, booths at trade shows, campsites, and banquet facilities); the sale, lease, or license of computer software; guaranty or warranty contracts ancillary to any of the

References are to Standard Federal Tax Reports; Tax Research Consultant; and Practical Tax Explanations.

[56] ¶ 21,817.185; ACCTNG: 6,262; § 38,315.05

[57] ¶ 21,005.7039; ACCTNG: 6,152, ACCTNG: 9,104; § 38,310.05

[58] ¶ 21,016; ACCTNG: 9,200; § 38,310.10

[59] ¶ 21,016; ACCTNG: 9,206; § 38,310.10

[60] ¶ 20,620.20; ACCTNG: 9,484.25

[61] ¶ 21,005.7043; ACCTNG: 27,154; § 38,310.10

above; subscriptions; memberships in an organization; an eligible gift card sale; or any combination of the above. An eligible gift card sale is a sale in which the taxpayer is primarily liable to the customer and the gift card is redeemable by the taxpayer or an entity legally obligated to the taxpayer.

The term "advance payment" does not include: rent, other than that paid for the use of intellectual property, computer software, and property ancillary to the provision of services; insurance premiums to the extent governed by the taxation of insurance companies; payments with respect to financial instruments, such as debt instruments, deposits, letters of credit, notional principal contracts, options, forward contracts, futures contracts, foreign currency contracts, credit card agreements, and financial derivatives; payments with respect to service warranty contracts; payments with respect to warranty and guaranty contracts under which a third party is the primary obligor; certain payments with respect to nonresident aliens and foreign corporations; and payments in property transferred in connection with the performance of services to which the restricted property rules of Code Sec. 83 apply (¶ 713).

Qualifying taxpayers generally may defer including advance payments in gross income to the next succeeding tax year for federal income tax purposes to the extent the advance payments are not recognized in revenues for financial statement purposes or, in certain cases, are not earned in the tax year of receipt. Except in the case of certain short tax years, the IRS does not permit deferral to a tax year later than the next succeeding tax year. These rules neither restrict a taxpayer's ability to use the methods of deferral for the advance payment of merchandise (see "*Prepaid Merchandise,*" previously), nor limit the period of deferral available.

Example 1: Advance payment for 48 dancing lessons under a one-year contract is received on November 1, 2016, by a calendar-year dance studio. Eight lessons are given in 2016. The remaining lessons are provided in 2017. In its applicable financial statement, the dance studio recognizes 1/6 of the payment in revenues for 2016 and 5/6 of the payment in revenues for 2017. If the dance studio is an accrual-basis taxpayer and elects the deferral method, 1/6 of the payment is includible in 2016 income and 5/6 of it is taxable as 2017 income, even if not all of the remaining 40 lessons are given in 2017.

Example 2: Assume the same facts as in Example 1, except that the advance payment is received for a 2-year contract under which up to 96 lessons are provided. The dance studio provides eight lessons in 2016, 48 lessons in 2017, and 40 lessons in 2018. In its applicable financial statement, the studio recognizes 1/12 of the payment in revenues for 2016, 6/12 of the payment in revenues for 2017, and 5/12 of the payment in gross revenues for 2018. For federal income tax purposes, the studio must include 1/12 of the payment in gross income for 2016 and the remaining 11/12 of the payment in gross income for 2017.

Certain accrual-basis membership organizations and publishers can defer prepaid dues and subscription income (Code Secs. 455 and 456).[62]

Accrued Income. In certain situations, cash-basis taxpayers may be required to report income that has not yet been received, and accrual-basis taxpayers may compute income in a manner that differs from general accrual principles. For example, both accrual-basis and cash-basis taxpayers may be required to use present value concepts to compute and report income arising out of a section 467 rental agreement (¶ 1541), original issue discount (OID) from any debt obligation held by the taxpayer (¶ 1952), and amounts arising from debt instruments issued for property (¶ 1868 and ¶ 1954). In addition, an accrual-method publisher of magazines, paperbacks, or records may elect to exclude from gross income the income attributable to the qualified sale of magazines, paperbacks, or records that are returned before the close of the merchandise return period (Code Sec. 458).[63]

References are to Standard Federal Tax Reports; Tax Research Consultant; and Practical Tax Explanations.

[62] ¶ 21,510, ¶ 21,520; ACCTNG: 9,250, ACCTNG: 9,300; § 38,320.45

[63] ¶ 21,540; ACCTNG: 12,206; § 38,320.20

1538. Accruing Income Doubtful of Collection. If a taxpayer is on the accrual basis of accounting (¶ 1515), income such as interest is taxable as it accrues even though it is received at a later date. However, if there is a real doubt that the interest is collectible when it becomes due, it need not be accrued.[64] On the other hand, where the uncollectible item arises from a sale of property, the proper procedure is to report the sale and then take a bad debt deduction as appropriate (¶ 1135 and ¶ 1143).

An accrual-basis taxpayer that elects to use the nonaccrual-experience (NAE) accounting method is generally not required to accrue as income any amount to be received for the performance of services that, based on experience, will not be collected (Code Sec. 448(d)(5); Reg. § 1.448-2(a)).[65] The NAE method is limited to amounts to be received for the performance of qualified services (health, law, engineering, architecture, accounting, actuarial science, performing arts, or consulting) and for services provided by certain small businesses.

1539. Prepaid Expenses of Cash-Basis Taxpayers. Cash-basis taxpayers (¶ 1515) may deduct certain prepaid *expenses* in the year paid under certain conditions (Code Sec. 461; Reg. § 1.461-1).[66] A distinction is made between expenditures that are more in the nature of expenses and those that are capital in nature. If the payment creates an asset having a useful life extending substantially beyond the end of the tax year in which the payment is made, the expenditure may not be deductible, or may be deductible only in part, in that year. If payment is made for a capital asset or is capital in nature, a deferment and charge-off for depreciation, amortization, or other comparable allowance is proper (¶ 1201). Taxpayers are generally not required to capitalize amounts paid for a right or benefit such as rent or insurance that does not extend beyond the earlier of: (1) 12 months after the first date on which the taxpayer realizes the right or benefit, or (2) the end of the tax year following the tax year in which the payment is made (Reg. § 1.263(a)-4(f)(1)).[67] Special rules apply to certain rental agreements (¶ 1541).

> **Example:** Mathis is a calendar-year taxpayer who uses the cash basis of accounting. He signs a three-year business property lease on December 1 of the tax year and agrees to pay $18,000 up front, plus a monthly rental of $1,000 for 36 months. He can deduct only $1,500 for the tax year ($1,000 rent plus 1/36 of $18,000). The $18,000 is an amount paid for securing the lease and must be amortized over the lease term.

Cash-basis farmers and ranchers can deduct prepaid feed costs in the year of payment if:

- the advance feed expenditure is a payment and not a deposit;
- the payment is for a business purpose; and
- the deduction does not cause a material distortion of income.[68]

No deduction is generally allowed, however, to a cash-basis farmer in the year of prepayment for advance payments for feed, seed, fertilizer, or other supplies to the extent those prepayments exceed 50 percent of total deductible farming expenses, excluding prepaid supplies (Code Sec. 464(d)).[69] For rules applicable to farming syndicates, see ¶ 1521. The limitation does not apply to a farm-related taxpayer if:

- the aggregate prepaid farm supplies for the preceding three tax years are less than 50 percent of the aggregate deductible farming expenses, other than prepaid farm supplies, for that period, or
- the taxpayer has excess prepaid farm supplies for the tax year by reason of any change in business operation directly attributable to extraordinary circumstances.

References are to Standard Federal Tax Reports; Tax Research Consultant; and Practical Tax Explanations.

[64] ¶ 5704.32; ACCTNG: 9,058; § 38,220.10

[65] ¶ 20,800, ¶ 20,802; ACCTNG: 9,058.10; § 38,320.25

[66] ¶ 21,802, ¶ 21,805; ACCTNG: 6,266; § 38,410.05

[67] ¶ 13,704C; BUSEXP: 9,104.20; § 10,210.40

[68] ¶ 21,817.205; FARM: 9,054; § 38,410.20

[69] ¶ 21,840; FARM: 9,054; § 38,410.20

A farm-related taxpayer is one whose principal residence is on a farm, who has a principal occupation of farming, or who is a family member of such a taxpayer. The family of an individual includes brothers and sisters, whether by whole or half blood, spouse, ancestors, and lineal descendants (Code Sec. 461(j)[k](2)(E)). It may also include a corporation that is engaged full-time in farming activities.

Estimated state income taxes paid in advance are deductible by a cash-basis taxpayer in the year paid (Rev. Rul. 56-124).[70]

See ¶ 1055 for a discussion of the allowance of deductions for prepaid interest payments.

1540. Expenses of Accrual-Basis Taxpayers. Under the all-events test, an accrual-basis taxpayer (¶ 1515) generally deducts the face amount of an accrued expense in the tax year in which: (1) all of the events have occurred that determine the fact of liability, and (2) the amount of the liability can be determined with reasonable accuracy (Code Sec. 461(h)).[71] The all-events test is not treated as met before economic performance occurs with respect to the particular item of expense or obligation that underlies the taxpayer's liability. For a liability of a taxpayer that requires a payment for property or services, economic performance is deemed to occur as the property or services are provided to the taxpayer. If the liability arises out of the taxpayer's use of property, economic performance occurs as the taxpayer uses the property (Reg. § 1.461-4(d)).[72]

> **Example 1:** A taxpayer on the accrual basis contractually obligates itself in October 2016 to pay a corporation $10,000 for research and development to be performed in 2017. No amount is deductible before performance is rendered in 2017.

Taxpayers are permitted to accrue payments before services are rendered or property is received if the taxpayer can reasonably expect the services or property to be provided within 3½ months after payment.

> **Example 2:** An accrual-method, calendar-year taxpayer makes payment on December 1, 2016, for goods it expects to receive by March 12, 2017. It may deduct the payment or otherwise take it into account for its 2016 tax year.

If the taxpayer's liability requires the taxpayer to provide services or property, then economic performance occurs as the taxpayer incurs costs. However, economic performance with respect to the drilling of an oil or gas well is considered to have occurred within a tax year if drilling commences within 90 days after the close of the tax year.

> **Example 3:** Zop Corp., a calendar-year, accrual-method taxpayer, sells lawn mowers under a three-year warranty that obligates it to make reasonable repairs to each mower it sells. In 2016, Zop repairs 12 mowers sold in 2015 at a cost of $2,500. Economic performance with respect to Zop's liability to perform services under the warranty occurs as Zop incurs costs in connection with the liability. Consequently, the $2,500 expense incurred by Zop is a deduction for the 2016 tax year.

Certain manufacturers, wholesalers, and retailers that make advance payments to purchase insurance policies that cover their obligations under multi-year service warranty contracts must capitalize the cost of the policies and deduct that cost ratably over the life of the policies. This rule applies regardless of whether the taxpayer uses the cash or accrual method of accounting (Rev. Proc. 97-38).[73]

Economic performance generally occurs only when payment is made to the person to whom the liability is owed. Payment is considered to be economic performance for the following:

References are to Standard Federal Tax Reports; Tax Research Consultant; and Practical Tax Explanations.

[70] ¶ 21,817.1875; ACCTNG: 6,318; § 38,410.25

[71] ¶ 21,802; ACCTNG: 12,050, ACCTNG: 12,100; § 38,430.05

[72] ¶ 21,810; ACCTNG: 12,102; § 38,435.05

[73] ¶ 20,620.20; ACCTNG: 9,484.25

- liabilities to another person arising out of any workers' compensation, tort, or breach of contract claims against the taxpayer or any violation of law by the taxpayer;
- rebates and refunds;
- awards, prizes, and jackpots;
- insurance, warranty, and service contracts; and
- taxes other than creditable foreign taxes (Reg. § 1.461-4(g)).[74]

Under certain limited circumstances, an irrevocable payment to a court-ordered settlement fund that completely extinguishes specified tort liabilities will also constitute economic performance (Code Sec. 468B).[75]

Recurring Items. Certain recurring items are treated as incurred in advance of economic performance by taxpayers other than tax shelters. Under this exception, an item is treated as incurred during a tax year if:

- the all-events test, without regard to economic performance, is satisfied during that year;
- the economic performance test is met within the shorter of 8½ months or a reasonable time after the close of the year;
- the item is recurring in nature and the taxpayer consistently treats similar items as incurred in the tax year in which the all-events test is met; and
- either the item is not material or accrual of the item in the year that the all-events test is met results in a better matching against the income to which it relates than accrual of the item in the tax year of economic performance (Code Sec. 461(h)(3); Reg. § 1.461-5).[76]

In determining whether an item is material or whether a more proper matching against income results from deduction of an expense prior to economic performance, the treatment of the expense on financial statements is to be taken into account but will not necessarily govern the tax treatment of the expense.

An item is recurring if it can generally be expected to be incurred from one tax year to the next (Reg. § 1.461-5(b)(3)). However, a taxpayer may treat a liability as recurring even if it is not actually incurred in each tax year. Also, a liability that has never previously been incurred may be treated as recurring if it is reasonable to expect that it will be incurred on a recurring basis in the future.

A taxpayer may adopt the recurring item exception as part of its method of accounting for any type of expense for the first tax year in which that type of expense is incurred. Any change to or from the recurring item exception is generally treated as a change in the taxpayer's method of accounting (¶ 1529) (Reg. § 1.461-5(d)). Tax shelters are generally prohibited from using the recurring item exception (Code Sec. 461(i)).[77]

Ratable Service Contract Safe Harbor. A taxpayer can use a safe harbor accounting method for a ratable service contract, such as a janitorial service contract, with a term of 12 months or less. Under this method, the taxpayer treats economic performance as occurring on a ratable basis over the term of the service contract (Rev. Proc. 2015-39).[78]

1540A. Accruing Uncertain and Contingent Liabilities. On the accrual-basis of accounting (¶ 1515), expenses are deductible in the tax year when all events have occurred that fix the amount of the item and determine the liability of the taxpayer to pay it (¶ 1540). Thus, there can be no accrual of an expense until any contingency is resolved and the liability becomes fixed and certain (Reg. § 1.461-1).[79] Similarly, an accrual-method taxpayer generally cannot accrue a liability that the taxpayer is con-

References are to Standard Federal Tax Reports; Tax Research Consultant; and Practical Tax Explanations.

[74] ¶ 21,810; ACCTNG: 12,102.20; § 38,435.05

[75] ¶ 21,950; ACCTNG: 12,214; § 38,435.20

[76] ¶ 21,802, ¶ 21,811; ACCTNG: 12,104.10; § 38,435.10

[77] ¶ 21,802; ACCTNG: 12,354; § 38,435.10

[78] ¶ 21,817.2377; ACCTNG: 12,102.05; § 38,435.05.

[79] ¶ 21,805; ACCTNG: 12,056; § 38,430.10

testing, as the liability is not fixed and certain. However, if the taxpayer is contesting an asserted liability and transfers money or property to provide for the satisfaction of the liability, the taxpayer can take a deduction in the year of the transfer if the contest continues to exist after the transfer and the liability would otherwise be allowed as a deduction in the year of transfer or an earlier tax year (Code Sec. 461(f)).[80]

See ¶ 1547 for a discussion of reserves for contingent or estimated expenses.

1540B. Accruing Interest and Expenses Owed to Related Taxpayers. When different methods of accounting (¶ 1515) are used by related taxpayers, accrued interest and expenses owed to a related taxpayer may not be deducted until the interest or expense payment is includible in the gross income of the cash-basis payee (Code Sec. 267(a)(2)).[81] Thus, an accrual-basis payor is placed on the cash basis for the purpose of deducting business expenses and interest owed to a related cash-basis taxpayer. The deduction is deferred until the cash-basis payee takes the item into income.

A related person for this purpose includes persons described in Code Sec. 267(b) (¶ 1717), as well as a personal service corporation (PSC) and any of its employee-owners (¶ 273). Thus, a PSC may not deduct payments made to owner-employees before the tax year in which such persons must include the payment in gross income. A special pass-through entity rule treats a partnership or S corporation as related to a taxpayer who owns any capital or profits interest in the partnership or stock of the S corporation and persons related to that taxpayer (Code Sec. 267(e)).

1541. Deferred Payments Under Certain Rental Agreements. Lessors and lessees of certain leaseback and long-term rental agreements that involve the use of property must report income and expenses arising out of those agreements by applying statutory accrual-basis and present-value principles (Code Sec. 467; Reg. § 1.467-1).[82] This treatment, in effect, is an extension of the principles governing the taxation of original issue discount (OID) (¶ 1952). Although the Code Sec. 467 rules apply to the use of property, the IRS is authorized to extend similar rules to agreements for services.

Section 467 rental agreements cover tangible property with respect to which either: (1) at least one payment allocable to the use of property in the calendar year is to be paid after the close of the following calendar year (deferred payments); or (2) there are increases in the amount to be paid as rent under the agreement (stepped rents). A section 467 rental agreement does not encompass a rental agreement in which the sum of the amounts to be paid is $250,000 or less.

Regardless of the accounting method used (¶ 1515), the lessor or lessee of any section 467 rental agreement must report for any tax year the sum of the accrued rental payments, and any interest for the year (calculated at the rate of 110 percent of the applicable federal rate compounded semiannually (¶ 83)) on unpaid rents (i.e., amounts that were attributed to a prior tax year but are still unpaid as of the current tax year).

The accrued rental payments—except in tax-avoidance transactions and agreements that do not allocate rents—are calculated by allocating rents in accordance with the agreement, and including the present value of rents allocable to the period but paid after the close of the period. In tax-avoidance transactions and agreements that do not allocate rents, the rent that accrues during the tax year is equal to the allocable portion of the constant rental amount. This is the amount which, if paid as of the close of each lease period, would result in an aggregate present value equal to the present value of the aggregate payments required under the lease.

1543. Claim-of-Right Doctrine. Under the claim-of-right doctrine, payments must be included in gross income if the taxpayer receives them without restriction under a claim of right.[83] This is true even though the taxpayer may discover in a later year that

References are to Standard Federal Tax Reports; Tax Research Consultant; and Practical Tax Explanations.

[80] ¶ 21,802; ACCTNG: 12,058; § 38,430.15

[81] ¶ 14,150; ACCTNG: 12,150, ACCTNG: 12,152.10; § 9,140, § 27,125.25

[82] ¶ 21,910, ¶ 21,910D; REAL: 12,356; § 38,410.35

[83] ¶ 21,005.1251; ACCTNG: 27,000; § 38,310.05

he or she had no right to the payments in the earlier year and is required to repay the same amount. The taxpayer may deduct the repayments in the year in which they are made.

When the repayments exceed income for the year of repayment, or when the income (after subtraction of those repayments) is taxed at a rate lower than that at which the income in the year of inclusion was taxed, the deduction does not compensate the taxpayer adequately for the tax paid in the earlier year. The law eliminates this inequity if the amount repaid exceeds $3,000. In that case, the taxpayer is required to reduce his or her tax for the year of repayment by the amount of tax for the previous year which was attributable to inclusion of this amount; any excess is to be claimed as a refund. If a smaller tax liability results from simply deducting the repaid amount in the year of repayment, the taxpayer should claim the deduction instead (Code Sec. 1341; Reg. § 1.1341-1).[84]

In either case, the adjustment is made for the year of repayment. The return for the prior year—the year in which the item was received—is not reopened; in no case will there be an allowance for interest on the tax paid for the earlier year.

Example: In 2015, a single taxpayer reported taxable income of $55,000 (adjusted gross income of $65,300 minus $4,000 personal exemption, minus $6,300 standard deduction), consisting entirely of sales commissions, on which he paid a tax of $9,544. In 2016, it is determined that the commissions were erroneously computed for 2015. Accordingly, the taxpayer pays back $6,000 of the commissions. His taxable income for 2016, without regard to the $6,000 repayment, is $13,200.

The tax for 2016 will be computed as follows:

(1) Tax on $7,200 ($13,200 less $6,000)		$720
(2) Tax on $13,200		1,516
Less: Difference between—		
Tax paid for 2015 on $55,000	9,544	
Tax payable in 2015 on $49,000 ($55,000 – $6,000)	8,044	1,500
		16

The tax for 2016 is the lesser of the amount computed under (1) or (2). In this case, the amount computed under (2) is less than the amount computed under (1). Thus, the tax for 2016 is $16, the amount computed under (2).

When the tax for the year of restoration under a claim of right is reduced by the amount of the tax already paid on the item in a previous year, the amount restored is not considered for any purpose. For example, taxpayers cannot use that amount in computing a net operating loss for the year of restoration (Reg. § 1.1341-1(b)(2)).[85] The reduction of tax in the year of repayment does not apply where the taxpayer did, in fact, have an unrestricted right to receive the amount in the prior year and the obligation to repay arose as the result of subsequent events.

1545. Dealer's Reserve for Income. Dealers who discount customers' installment paper with financial institutions that withhold a small percentage of the price and credit it to a reserve account as security for the dealer's guaranty of payment of the installment paper must accrue those credits as income in the year when the installment paper is transferred to the financial institution.[86] This rule has been applied to an accrual-basis home seller who guaranteed a buyer's loan by requiring the home seller to accrue as income in the year of sale the proceeds pledged as loan security to the lender. As to a cash-basis dealer, however, the pledged amounts are taxable to the dealer only as they become available for withdrawal (i.e., where the pledged amount was in a restricted savings account and could be withdrawn in specified amounts only as the buyer reduced the loan principal by certain amounts).

References are to Standard Federal Tax Reports; Tax Research Consultant; and Practical Tax Explanations.

[84] ¶ 31,880, ¶ 31,881; ACCTNG: 27,500; § 4,230.05

[85] ¶ 31,881; ACCTNG: 27,558; § 38,310.05

[86] ¶ 31,882.25; ACCTNG: 9,406; § 38,320.05

1547. Reserve for Estimated Expense. Although reserves for contingent liabilities are often set up in business practice, amounts credited to them are generally not deductible for income tax purposes because the fact of liability is not fixed.[87] For example, advance deductions have been denied for additions to a reserve for expected cash discounts on outstanding receivables, amounts credited by a manufacturer to a reserve for possible future warranty service, and additions to a reserve covering estimated liability of a carrier for tort claims. However, to the extent that the Code specifically provides for a deduction for a reserve for estimated expenses, the economic performance rules (¶ 1540) do not apply (Code Sec. 461(h)(5)).[88]

1549. Accrual of Vacation and Sick Leave Pay. The deduction by an employer for vacation and sick leave pay is generally limited to the amount of pay earned during the year to the extent: (1) the amount is paid to employees during the year, or (2) the amount is vested as of the last day of the tax year and is paid to employees within 2.5 months after the end of the year. If the vacation or sick leave pay is not paid until after the expiration of that period, the employer may deduct vacation pay when paid and sick leave pay in its tax year that includes the last day of the employee's tax year for which the payment is reported as income by the employee (Code Sec. 404(a)(5); Temp. Reg. § 1.404(b)-1T).[89] However, vacation and sick leave pay incurred with respect to the production of real and tangible personal property, or with respect to property acquired for resale, is considered a direct labor cost that must be capitalized by taxpayers subject to the uniform capitalization rules (¶ 991) (Reg. § 1.263A-1(e)(2)(i)(B)).[90]

Regardless of whether or not vested vacation pay is considered deferred compensation, FICA and FUTA taxes may be deducted by an accrual-basis taxpayer prior to the tax year that the FICA and FUTA taxes are actually paid if: (1) all events have occurred to establish the fact of the taxpayer's liability for the FICA and FUTA taxes, (2) the amount of the payroll tax liability can be determined with reasonable accuracy, and (3) the taxpayer properly adopts the recurring item exception (¶ 1540) as a method of accounting with respect to the payroll taxes (Rev. Rul. 2007-12).[91]

Long-Term Contracts

1551. Long-Term Contract Method of Accounting. Taxable income from a long-term contract generally must be accounted for under the percentage-of-completion method of accounting (Code Sec. 460).[92] However, a taxpayer who has entered into a small construction contract or home construction contract may use an exempt contract method of accounting (¶ 1552).

A long-term contract is a building, installation, construction, or manufacturing contract that is not completed within the tax year in which it is entered into. A manufacturing contract is not considered long term unless the contract involves the manufacture of: (1) unique items not normally carried in the finished goods inventory, or (2) items normally requiring more than 12 calendar months to complete, regardless of the duration of the actual contract.

Percentage-of-Completion Method. Under the percentage-of-completion method, gross income is reported annually according to the percentage of the contract completed in that year. The completion percentage is determined by comparing costs allocated and incurred before the end of the tax year to the estimated total contract costs (cost-to-cost method or simplified cost-to-cost method). Thus, for a particular tax year, the business includes a portion of the total contract price in gross income as it incurs allocable contract costs for the year. Any contract income that has not been included in the taxpayer's gross income by the end of the tax year in which the contract is completed is

References are to Standard Federal Tax Reports; Tax Research Consultant; and Practical Tax Explanations.

[87] ¶ 21,817.688; ACCTNG: 12,200; § 38,430.10

[88] ¶ 21,802; ACCTNG: 12,104; § 38,430.10

[89] ¶ 18,330, ¶ 18,354; ACCTNG: 12,300; § 38,435.15

[90] ¶ 13,811; ACCTNG: 15,208.10; § 10,310.10

[91] ¶ 21,817.128; ACCTNG: 12,052.15; § 9,365

[92] ¶ 21,550; ACCTNG: 33,000; § 38,230.05

included in gross income for the following tax year (Code Sec. 460(b); Reg. § 1.460-4(b)).[93]

Modified Percentage-of-Completion Method (10-Percent Method). A taxpayer may elect to defer the recognition of income and accounting for costs until the first tax year in which at least 10 percent of the estimated total costs of the contract have been incurred (Code Sec. 460(b)(5)).

Look-Back Rule. To the extent that the percentage-of-completion method applies to a long-term contract, a business that errors in its estimate of the contract price or costs must look back and recompute its tax liability on the basis of the actual contract price and costs for the years for which that method was used. The business will either pay or receive interest at the rate for overpayment of tax (¶ 2765), compounded daily and figured on Form 8697, on the amount by which the recomputed tax liability for a year exceeds or is less than the previously reported tax liability (Code Sec. 460(b); Reg. § 1.460-6).[94] Only one rate of interest will apply for each accrual period—the period which begins on the date after the original return due date for the tax year and which ends on the original return due date for the following tax year. The applicable overpayment rate of interest is the overpayment rate in effect for the calendar quarter in which the accrual period begins. The look-back method does not have to be applied in computing taxable income with respect to home construction contracts and long-term construction contracts of small businesses and small long-term contracts. Taxpayers can also elect not to apply the look-back method when the differences between estimated and actual amounts are *de minimis.*

Pass-through entities such as partnerships, S corporations, and trusts that are not closely held must use a simplified look-back method if substantially all of the income under a long-term contract is from sources in the United States (Code Sec. 460(b)(4)). A closely held entity is an entity where 50 percent or more of the value of the beneficial interests are owned by five or fewer persons. The amount of taxes deemed overpaid or underpaid under a contract in any year is determined at the entity level and is the product of the amount of contract income overreported or underreported for the year times the top marginal tax rate applicable for the year (i.e., the top corporate tax rate, or the top individual tax rate if more than 50 percent of the beneficial interests in the entity are held by individuals).

Allocation and Capitalization of Costs. A taxpayer generally must allocate costs to long-term contracts accounted for under the percentage-of-completion method in the same manner as direct and indirect costs are capitalized to property produced by a taxpayer under the uniform capitalization rules (Code Sec. 460(c); Reg. § 1.460-5).[95] Thus, the taxpayer must allocate to each long-term contract all direct costs and certain indirect costs properly allocable to the long-term contract. While bonus depreciation (¶ 1237) is generally taken into account when allocating contract costs, solely for purposes of determining the percentage of completion, the cost of qualified property is taken into account as if the bonus depreciation rules had not been enacted. In general, this provision applies to property with a recovery period of seven years or less that is placed in service in 2010, or after December 31, 2012, and before January 1, 2020 (Code Sec. 460(c)(6)(B)).

Under the general cost allocation method, research and experimental expenses, other than independent research and development expenses, must be allocated to the contract. However, independent research and development expenses, expenses incurred in making unsuccessful bids and proposals, and marketing, selling, and advertising costs may be expensed. Production period interest generally must be allocated to the contract (¶ 1561). Contributions to a pension or annuity plan, whether related to current or past services, are subject to the long-term contract rules and are treated as costs allocable to a long-term contract.

References are to Standard Federal Tax Reports; Tax Research Consultant; and Practical Tax Explanations.

[93] ¶ 21,550, ¶ 21,555; ACCTNG: 33,100; § 38,230.20

[94] ¶ 21,550, ¶ 21,557; ACCTNG: 33,200; § 38,230.55

[95] ¶ 21,550, ¶ 21,556; ACCTNG: 33,300; § 38,230.55

A taxpayer can elect to use a simplified cost-to-cost method of allocation if all the taxpayer's contracts are accounted for under the percentage-of-completion method and the 10-percent method is not used (Reg. § 1.460-5(c)). Small construction and home construction contracts accounted for under an exempt contract method are not subject to the general cost allocation rules (¶ 1552). Special rules are also provided for allocating costs to cost-plus long-term contracts and to federal long-term contracts.

1552. Exempt Contract Methods of Accounting. Although taxable income from a long-term contract generally must be accounted for under the percentage-of-completion method of accounting (¶ 1551), income from a small construction contract or a home construction contract may be taken into account using the exempt-contract-percentage-of-completion method or the completed contract method. The look-back rule and the cost allocation rules, except for the allocation of production period interest, are also not required for these contracts (Code Sec. 460(e); Reg. § 1.460-4).[96] The contractor may change its method of accounting to conform with either of these special methods only after securing permission from the IRS (¶ 1529). Eligible taxpayers are not required to use these methods of accounting and may instead elect any other permissible method, such as a cash, accrual, or hybrid method (¶ 1515).

Small Construction Contracts. A small construction contract is a construction contract expected to be completed within two years that is performed by a taxpayer whose average annual gross receipts for the three prior tax years does not exceed $10 million.

Home and Residential Construction Contracts. A home construction contract is any construction contract where 80 percent or more of the estimated total contract costs are reasonably expected to be attributable to dwelling units contained in buildings with four or fewer dwelling units, and to improvements to real property related to such dwelling units. A home construction contract related to buildings with more than four dwelling units is a residential construction contract, for which the availability of the exempt contract methods is limited (see below).

Exempt-Contract-Percentage-of-Completion Method. Under the exempt-contract-percentage-of-completion method, the taxpayer includes in income the portion of the total contract price that corresponds to the percentage of the entire contract that the taxpayer has completed during the tax year. The percentage is determined by using any method of cost comparison that clearly reflects income and is used consistently (Reg. § 1.460-4(c)).

Completed Contract Method. Under the completed contract method, the taxpayer does not report income until the tax year in which the contract is completed and accepted (Reg. § 1.460-4(d)). Expenses allocable to the contract are deductible in the year in which the contract is completed. Expenses not allocated to the contract (i.e., period costs) are deductible in the year in which they are paid or incurred, depending on the method of accounting used.

Percentage-of-Completion/Capitalized-Cost Method. For residential construction contracts, the taxpayer may report 70 percent of the income using the percentage-of-completion method and the remaining 30 percent using an exempt contract method (Reg. § 1.460-4(e)).

Inventories

1553. Requirement to Use Inventories. A taxpayer generally must use inventories to clearly reflect income where the production, purchase, or sale of merchandise is an income-producing factor (Code Sec. 471(a); Reg. § 1.471-1).[97] To figure taxable income, a taxpayer must value inventory at the beginning and end of each tax year. This valuation depends on the items included in inventory (¶ 1557) and the method of valuation (¶ 1559). Inventory practices must be consistent from year to year. A taxpayer whose

References are to Standard Federal Tax Reports; Tax Research Consultant; and Practical Tax Explanations.

[96] ¶ 21,550, ¶ 21,555; ACCTNG: 33,066, ACCTNG: 33,152; § 38,230.15, § 38,230.30

[97] ¶ 22,202, ¶ 22,203; ACCTNG: 15,052; § 38,501

average annual gross receipts do not exceed $1 million or a taxpayer engaged in an eligible trade or business whose average annual gross receipts do not exceed $10 million is generally not required to use inventories or the accrual method of accounting (Rev. Procs. 2002-28 and 2001-10). However, a taxpayer who does not otherwise use inventories must treat merchandise inventory in the same manner as a material or supply that is not incidental (¶ 903). A farmer may also use the cash method of accounting for purchases and sales. However, see the accrual method requirement for certain farming corporations at ¶ 1519. Any taxpayer, including a farmer, who uses inventories must use the accrual method of accounting for purchases and sales.

1557. Items Included in Inventory. An inventory is an itemized list, with valuations, of goods held for sale or consumption in a manufacturing or merchandising business. Taxpayers must usually verify the amount of items in inventory by a physical count of the items as of the last day of the tax year. Taxpayers may use estimates of inventory shrinkage that are confirmed by a physical count after year-end if the taxpayer normally does a physical inventory count at each location on a regular and consistent basis and makes proper adjustments to those inventories and to its estimating methods to the extent the estimates are greater than or less than the actual shrinkage (Code Sec. 471(b)).[98]

Inventory should include all finished or partly finished goods and only those raw materials and supplies that have been acquired for sale or will physically become a part of merchandise intended for sale (Reg. § 1.471-1).[99] Merchandise should be included in inventory only if title to it is vested in the taxpayer. A seller should include in inventory goods under contract for sale but not yet segregated and applied to the contract, and goods out on consignment. The seller should not include goods sold, including containers, in inventory where title has passed to the buyer. A buyer should include goods purchased, including containers, in inventory where title has passed to the buyer, even where the goods are in transit or have not been physically received.

It is necessary to identify the particular goods in inventory so that proper costs can be applied to items. Identification of inventories is ordinarily accomplished by the first-in, first-out (FIFO) rule (¶ 1564), unless the items are specifically identified. A taxpayer can also elect to identify inventory items by use of the last-in, first-out (LIFO) rule (¶ 1565).

Real property held for sale by a dealer may not be inventoried because each parcel of real estate is unique.[100] Likewise, capital assets, equipment, accounts, notes, investments, cash, or similar assets may not be included in inventories. For inventories of farmers and dealers in securities, see ¶ 1569 and ¶ 1903, respectively.

1559. Valuation of Inventory. An inventory must conform to the best accounting practice in the particular trade or business and must clearly reflect income (Reg. § 1.471-2(a) and (b)).[101] An inventory that, under the best accounting practice, can be used in a balance sheet showing the financial position of the taxpayer will generally be regarded as clearly reflecting income. In determining whether income is clearly reflected, great weight is given to consistency in inventory practice, but a legitimate accounting system will be disallowed where it distorts income.

Two methods commonly used to value inventories are the cost method (¶ 1561) and the lower of cost or market method (¶ 1563) (Reg. § 1.471-2(c) and (d)).[102] Opening and closing inventories must be valued by the same method. If the lower of cost or market method is used, it must be consistently applied to each item in the inventory. Cost and market value are determined as to each item, and the lower amount is included in the inventory valuation. A taxpayer is not permitted to inventory the entire stock at cost and also at market and use the lower of the two results (Reg. § 1.471-4).[103]

References are to Standard Federal Tax Reports; Tax Research Consultant; and Practical Tax Explanations.

[98] ¶ 22,202; ACCTNG: 15,252.20; § 38,515.10

[99] ¶ 22,203; ACCTNG: 15,056; § 38,505.05

[100] ¶ 22,204.36; ACCTNG: 15,058.15; § 38,505.05

[101] ¶ 22,205; ACCTNG: 15,152; § 38,501

[102] ¶ 22,205; ACCTNG: 15,250; § 38,535.05

[103] ¶ 22,209; ACCTNG: 15,254.05; § 38,535.15

Deviations are permitted, however, for goods inventoried under the last-in, first-out (LIFO) identification method (¶ 1565) and animals inventoried under the unit-livestock-price method (¶ 1569).

The IRS will also generally accept the rolling-average inventory valuation method used to value inventories for financial accounting purposes as clearly reflecting income for federal income tax purposes (Rev. Proc. 2008-43, modified by Rev. Proc. 2008-52). However, if inventory is held for several years or costs fluctuate substantially, the rolling-average cost method may not clearly reflect income, depending on the particular facts and circumstances. Moreover, if the taxpayer does not use the rolling-average method for financial accounting purposes, then that method may not accurately determine costs or clearly reflect income for tax purposes. Special rules apply to dealers in securities (¶ 1903).

Whether the cost or the lower of cost or market method is used, inventoried goods that are unsalable, or unusable in normal transactions because of wear and tear, obsolescence, or broken lots, should be valued at bona fide selling price, less cost of selling (Reg. § 1.471-2(c)).[104] A bona fide selling price is the actual offering of goods during a period ending not later than 30 days after inventory date. Adjustment of the valuation on a reasonable basis, not less than scrap value, is permitted in the case of unsalable or unusable raw material or partly finished goods.

1561. Inventory at Cost: Uniform Capitalization Rules. Uniform capitalization rules govern the inclusion in inventory or capital accounts of all allocable costs that are incurred with respect to real and tangible personal property that is produced by the taxpayer or acquired for resale and would otherwise be considered in computing taxable income (Code Sec. 263A(a) and (b); Reg. § 1.263A-2).[105] For this purpose, tangible personal property includes a film, sound recording, videotape, book, or similar property. Except for the interest capitalization rules, the uniform capitalization rules also apply to costs incurred with respect to real or personal property, whether tangible or intangible, that is acquired for resale. Certain small businesses with average annual gross receipts of $10 million or less for the three previous years that acquire personal property for resale are exempt from these rules.

Costs attributable to inventory must be added to costs of producing or acquiring the inventory, and costs attributable to producing other property must be capitalized. Direct material and labor costs, as well as the portion of indirect costs allocable to that property, are subject to these rules (Reg. § 1.263A-1(a)(3)).

The uniform capitalization rules replace the inventory cost rules of Code Sec. 471 (see below) in the case of property to which they apply. The uniform capitalization rules do not apply to inventories valued at market under either the market method or the lower of cost or market method (¶ 1563) if the market valuation used by the taxpayer generally equals the property's fair market value (i.e., price of sale to customers less direct disposition costs). However, the uniform capitalization rules do apply in determining the market value of any inventory for which market is determined with reference to replacement cost or reproduction cost.

The uniform capitalization rules do not apply to property produced for personal use or pursuant to a long-term contract (¶ 1551); timber, including certain ornamental trees; costs deductible as Code Sec. 174 research and experimental expenditures (¶ 979); costs associated with certain oil, gas, and other mineral property, foreign drilling, and amortizable or developmental expenditures; and costs, other than circulation expenditures, subject to the 10-year amortization rule for certain alternative minimum tax preference items (¶ 1450). Certain costs incurred by an individual or personal service corporation (¶ 273) engaged in the business of being a writer, photographer, or artist (¶ 990A) that are otherwise deductible are also exempt from those rules. In addition, the following costs may be currently deducted: marketing and selling expenses and general

References are to Standard Federal Tax Reports; Tax Research Consultant; and Practical Tax Explanations.

[104] ¶ 22,205; ACCTNG: 15,256.05; § 38,515.20

[105] ¶ 13,800, ¶ 13,817; ACCTNG: 15,200; § 38,535.10

and administration expenses that do not directly benefit production or the acquisition of inventory (¶ 992) (Code Sec. 263A(c) and (h)); Reg. § 1.263A-1(e)(4)).[106]

Interest Capitalization Rules. Interest costs paid or incurred during the production period and allocable to real property or tangible personal property produced by the taxpayer must be capitalized if the property has: (1) a long useful life (real property or any other property that has a class life of 20 years or more), (2) an estimated production period exceeding two years, or (3) an estimated production period exceeding one year and a cost exceeding $1 million (Code Sec. 263A(f)).[107] See ¶ 993.

Farming Businesses. For the uniform capitalization rules pertaining to farm businesses, see ¶ 999.

Inventory at Cost: Code Sec. 471 Rules. The following rules are to be used to value inventory at cost where the uniform capitalization rules do not apply. For merchandise on hand at the beginning of the year, cost is the amount at which it was included in the closing inventory of the preceding period. For merchandise *bought* after the beginning of the year, cost means the invoice price less trade or other discounts, except cash discounts approximating a fair interest rate, which may be deducted from cost, or reported as income, at the option of the taxpayer. Cost also includes transportation or other acquisition charges. For merchandise *produced* by the taxpayer, the costs attributed to inventoried goods must be determined under the uniform capitalization rules (see above).

1563. Inventory at "Cost or Market". If the lower of cost or market inventory method is used, the market value of each item is compared with the cost of the item (¶ 1561), and the lower of the two values is used for that item (Reg. § 1.471-4).[108]

Example: A lumber dealer has three grades of lumber at the end of his tax year. They are valued as follows:

Grade	*Cost*	*Market*	*Lower of Two*
A	$45,000	$60,000	$45,000
B	20,000	15,000	15,000
C	5,000	5,000	5,000
	$70,000	$80,000	$65,000

If the lumber dealer is using the cost method, his ending inventory is valued at $70,000. If the dealer is using the lower of cost or market method, the ending inventory is valued at $65,000.

Under normal conditions, market value is the prevailing current bid price at the inventory date in the volume in which the items are usually purchased by the taxpayer. If a current bid price is unobtainable, the best available evidence of fair market value must be used. Specific purchases or sales by the taxpayer or others, or compensation paid for cancellation of contracts for purchase commitments, may be used.

The market value of goods in process and finished goods, for a manufacturer or processor, is reproduction cost. This is the total that materials, labor, and factory burden or overhead would cost at current prices to bring the article to a comparable state of completion. The market price basis does not apply to goods on hand or in the process of manufacture for delivery under firm sale contracts at fixed prices entered into before the inventory date where the taxpayer is protected against actual loss. Such goods must be inventoried at cost.

A merchant may also use the retail method to approximate the lower of cost or market of goods in inventory (Reg. § 1.471-8).[109] The retail selling prices of goods on hand at the end of the year are multiplied by a ratio or cost complement to arrive the value of ending inventory.

References are to Standard Federal Tax Reports; Tax Research Consultant; and Practical Tax Explanations.

[106] ¶ 13,800, ¶ 13,811; BUSEXP: 9,050; § 10,305.05

[107] ¶ 13,800; BUSEXP: 9,060; § 10,330.05

[108] ¶ 22,209; ACCTNG: 15,254; § 38,535.15

[109] ¶ 22,217B; ACCTNG: 15,256.35; § 38,535.20

If inventories are valued at cost under the lower of cost or market method, that valuation is subject to the uniform capitalization rules at ¶ 1561.

1564. "First-In, First-Out" (FIFO) Rule. The "first-in, first-out" (FIFO) method of identifying inventory assumes that items purchased or produced first are the first items sold, consumed, or otherwise disposed (Code Sec. 471; Reg. § 1.471-2).[110] Accordingly, items in inventory at the end of the year are matched with the costs of similar items that were most recently purchased or produced. The FIFO method is used for items in inventory that have been so commingled that they cannot be identified with specific invoices; thus, they are considered to be the items most recently purchased or produced. The cost is the actual cost of the items purchased and produced during the period in which the quantity of items in inventory was acquired. In the absence of an election to use the last-in, first-out (LIFO) method (¶ 1565), inventory is identified under the FIFO method.

1565. "Last-In, First-Out" (LIFO) Rule. The "last-in, first-out" (LIFO) method of identifying inventory is based on cost values (Code Sec. 472).[111] Under the LIFO method, inventory is taken at cost, but the items contained in the inventory are treated as being those contained in opening inventory to the extent of the opening inventory (whether or not they are physically on hand), and then those acquired during the tax year. The items treated as still in the opening inventory are taken in order of acquisition, except for the first year in which the method is used. For that year, the items in the opening inventory are taken at the average cost of those items. The closing inventory of the preceding year must also be adjusted and an amended return filed to reflect the changes. In the case of a retailer or certain manufacturers, items deemed to have been purchased during the year (i.e., inventory increases) may be taken at the taxpayer's election on the basis of the most recent purchases, at average cost for the year, or in order of acquisition.

A taxpayer need not obtain advance permission from the IRS to elect to use the LIFO method but must adopt it on the return for the year in which the method is first used. In addition, the taxpayer must file a Form 970 with the return and accept any modifications or adjustments required by the IRS. The election applies only to the class or classes of goods specified in the application. Although the election to adopt LIFO must generally cover the entire inventory of a business, manufacturers or processors may elect to have the method apply to raw materials only, including those in finished goods and work-in-process (Reg. § 1.472-1(h)).[112] Furthermore, if LIFO is used for tax purposes, it generally must also be used in preparing annual financial statements for credit purposes or for the purpose of reports to stockholders, partners, or proprietors. For purposes of this reporting rule, all members of the same group of financially related corporations are treated as one taxpayer.

As an alternative to the regular LIFO method, a taxpayer with numerous items in an inventory may use the dollar-value LIFO method (¶ 1567).

1567. Dollar-Value LIFO Method. Instead of determining quantity increases of each item in the inventory and then pricing them, as is required under the regular last-in, last (LIFO) method (¶ 1565), the dollar-value LIFO method may be used (Reg. § 1.472-8).[113] The increase in LIFO value is determined by comparing the total dollar value of the beginning and ending inventories at base year prices (the first LIFO year) and then converting any dollar-value increase to current prices by means of an index. Under the dollar-value LIFO method, taxpayers are allowed to determine base year dollars through the use of government indexes (Code Sec. 472(f)).[114]

References are to Standard Federal Tax Reports; Tax Research Consultant; and Practical Tax Explanations.

[110] ¶ 22,202, ¶ 22,205; ACCTNG: 15,154.05; § 38,520

[111] ¶ 22,230; ACCTNG: 18,050; § 38,525.05

[112] ¶ 22,231; ACCTNG: 18,100; § 38,525.07

[113] ¶ 22,239; ACCTNG: 18,200; § 38,525.10

[114] ¶ 22,230; ACCTNG: 18,204; § 38,525.10

Simplified Dollar-Value LIFO Method. Small businesses, those with average gross receipts for the three preceding years of $5 million or less, may elect to use a simplified dollar-value LIFO method to account for inventories (Code Sec. 474).[115] The method requires separate inventory pools for each major category in the applicable government price index. The election applies to all succeeding years unless the taxpayer obtains IRS permission to change to another method or becomes ineligible to use that method. If elected, it must be used to value all LIFO inventories.

1569. Special Inventory Valuation Methods for Farmers. In addition to the standard cost (¶ 1561) and the lower of cost or market (¶ 1563) methods for valuing inventory, a farmer on the accrual basis of accounting has a choice of two other systems. The farm-price method provides for the valuation of inventories at market price less the direct cost of disposition. If this method is used, it must be applied to the entire inventory except livestock which the taxpayer has elected to inventory under the unit-livestock-price method (Reg. § 1.471-6(d)).[116]

The unit-livestock-price method—adoptable when the farmer raises his or her own livestock or purchases young animals and raises them to maturity—provides for the valuation *of different classes* of animals at a standard unit price for each animal within a class. This method, once elected, must be applied to all livestock raised to maturity or purchased before maturity and raised to maturity, whether held for sale or for breeding, draft, or dairy purposes. This includes unweaned calves. Unit prices assigned to classes must account for normal cost of production. For purchased livestock, the cost should be increased in accordance with unit prices only for animals acquired in the first six months of the tax year (Reg. § 1.471-6(g)).[117]

The crop basis of accounting may be used with IRS consent for crops which have not been gathered and disposed of during the tax year in which they are planted (Reg. § 1.61-4(c)).[118] The entire cost of producing the crop must be deducted no earlier than in the year in which the crop income is realized.

1571. Change in Inventory Accounting. A change in the method used to account for an inventory can be made only when authorized by the IRS. A change from a cash method to an inventory method is, in effect, a change to the accrual method of accounting for purchases and sales (Reg. § 1.446-1(c)(2)).[119] Permission to make such a change must generally be requested within the tax year that the change is to be effective (¶ 1529), with the exception of an election to change to the last-in, first-out (LIFO method) (¶ 1565). An election to use this method may be made by a statement on Form 970 attached to the first tax return in which it is used; however, adjustments will be required to prevent duplications and omissions of income and expenses (Reg. §§ 1.472-3 and 1.472-4).[120]

Allocation and Reconstruction of Income

1573. Allocation of Income and Deductions by IRS. When two or more organizations, trades, or businesses are owned or controlled by the same interests, the IRS may allocate gross income, deductions, or credits between them if it determines that this action is necessary to prevent evasion of taxes or to clearly reflect income (Code Sec. 482).[121] Moreover, the IRS is specifically authorized by statute to allocate any income, deduction, credit, exclusion, or other allowance between certain personal service corporations (¶ 273) and their employee-owners when the principal purpose of forming or using such a corporation is to avoid or evade income tax (¶ 1575).

References are to Standard Federal Tax Reports; Tax Research Consultant; and Practical Tax Explanations.

[115] ¶ 22,260; ACCTNG: 18,250; § 38,525.15

[116] ¶ 22,213; FARM: 3,110; § 36,325

[117] ¶ 22,213; FARM: 3,112; § 36,325

[118] ¶ 5601; FARM: 3,064; § 36,315.15

[119] ¶ 20,607, ¶ 20,620.243; ACCTNG: 15,300; § 38,601

[120] ¶ 22,234, ¶ 22,235; ACCTNG: 18,102; § 38,601

[121] ¶ 22,280; ACCTNG: 30,050; § 38,010.10

1575. Acquisitions to Avoid Tax. If a taxpayer acquires control of a corporation, directly or indirectly, to evade or avoid income tax by securing the benefit of a deduction, credit, or other allowance that would not otherwise be enjoyed, then that deduction, credit or other allowance will not be permitted. The same rules of disallowance apply to a corporation that acquires property of another corporation that was not controlled by the acquiring corporation or its stockholders and that acquires a basis determined by reference to the basis in the hands of the transferor corporation (Code Sec. 269).[122] The IRS is authorized to deny an acquiring corporation the carryover and other tax benefits of a subsidiary corporation, acquired in a qualified stock purchase for which an election of asset acquisition treatment is not made, if the subsidiary corporation is liquidated under a plan adopted within two years of the acquisition date and the principal purpose of the liquidation is tax avoidance or evasion. For a discussion of the use or formation of a personal service corporation (PSC) by another entity to avoid or evade income tax and the IRS's authority to allocate amounts between the PSC and its employee-owners in order to clearly reflect income, see ¶ 273.

1577. Income Reconstruction. When a taxpayer has kept either inadequate or no books or records, the IRS has authority to compute income in order to clearly reflect the taxpayer's income (Code Sec. 446(b)).[123] The methods for reconstructing income vary depending on the facts and circumstances, and the records that are available. The IRS has developed several methods for reconstructing a taxpayer's income.

Bank Deposits and Expenditures Method. All bank deposits are assumed to represent income unless the taxpayer can establish otherwise. Although the taxpayer is given an opportunity to show that the deposits do not represent income, the IRS is not required to link the bank deposits with an identified income-producing activity.[124]

Net Worth Method. An opening net worth or total value of assets at the beginning of a given year is established. The IRS then shows increases in the taxpayer's net worth for each subsequent year and calculates the difference between the adjusted net values of the assets at the beginning and end of each year under examination. Nondeductible expenses are added to the increases. If the resulting amount is greater than reported taxable income for that year, then the excess is treated as unreported taxable income.[125]

Percentage or Unit Mark-Up Method. This method is used where inventories are a necessary income-producing factor but have not been kept or were incorrectly taken. Net income is determined by applying certain percentages, such as gross profits to sales, net income to gross income, or net income to sales, derived from other taxpayers in similar types of businesses.[126]

References are to Standard Federal Tax Reports; Tax Research Consultant; and Practical Tax Explanations.

[122] ¶ 14,250; CONSOL: 71,050; § 9,135

[123] ¶ 20,606; ACCTNG: 3,152; § 39,730.05

[124] ¶ 20,620.416; ACCTNG: 3,156; § 39,730.15

[125] ¶ 20,620.52; ACCTNG: 3,154; § 39,730.15

[126] ¶ 20,620.548; ACCTNG: 3,162; § 39,730.15

Chapter 16

BASIS FOR GAIN OR LOSS

	Par.
Computing Gain or Loss	1601
Property Acquired by Purchase	1611
Property Acquired by Gift or Bequest	1630
Property Acquired by Exchange	1648
Other Acquired Property	1678
Valuation Rules	1695

Computing Gain or Loss

1601. Basis. The rules on determining the basis for computing gain or loss or depreciation on property acquired in most common transactions are outlined below, with references to the paragraphs where additional details appear. This basis, after adjustments described at ¶ 1611—¶ 1617, is subtracted from the amount realized to determine the amount of gain or loss from a sale or other disposition (Code Sec. 1001).[1] Except where other rules are prescribed, the basis for gain or loss is determined under the law in effect when the property is sold or disposed.

Type of acquisition	Basis for gain or loss
Bargain purchases	
arm's-length	Cost (¶ 789)
corporation's, from nonstockholder	Cost (¶ 1660)
corporation's, from stockholder	Cost, unless saving is paid-in surplus (¶ 1660)
employee's	Cost plus amount taxable as compensation for services (¶ 789)
relative or friend	Cost, unless saving is a gift (¶ 1630)
stockholder's	Cost plus amount taxable as a dividend (¶ 789)
Bequests	Generally, fair market value at the date of the decedent's death, but no more than the estate tax value or value reported to IRS (¶ 1633)
Cash purchases	Cost (¶ 1604)
mortgage also assumed, or property taken subject to the mortgage	Full price, including mortgage amount (¶ 1611)
purchase money mortgage also given	Full purchase price (¶ 1611)
purchase notes also given	Full purchase price (¶ 1611)
redeemable ground rent assumed, or property taken subject to ground rent	Full purchase price (¶ 1611)
Community property	
survivor (death of spouse)	See "Bequests," above
Corporate property	
acquired for stock by controlled corporation	Transferor's basis (¶ 1660)
acquired for stock in taxable exchange	Fair market value of stock at time of exchange (¶ 1648)
contributions by nonstockholders	Zero (¶ 1660)
paid-in surplus	Transferor's basis (¶ 1660)
Dividend property	
corporate, stockholder of domestic corporation	Fair market value (¶ 735)
corporate, stockholder of foreign corporation	Fair market value (¶ 735)
noncorporate, stockholder	Fair market value (¶ 735)

References are to Standard Federal Tax Reports; Tax Research Consultant; and Practical Tax Explanations.

[1] ¶ 29,220; SALES: 9,050; § 16,015

Type of acquisition	Basis for gain or loss
Divorce or separation agreement	Transferors' basis (¶ 1734)
Gift property	Donor's basis, increased by gift tax in some cases; basis for loss *limited* to lesser of donor's basis or fair market value at time of gift (¶ 1630)
Inventory	Last inventory value (¶ 1559)
Joint tenancy	
after death of one tenant	Basis depends on amount contributed by each joint tenant toward the original purchase price (¶ 1634, ¶ 1636)
Lessor's acquisitions of lessee's improvements	Zero, if excluded from income (¶ 764)
Life estate	Zero, if disposed of after October 9, 1969 (¶ 1633)
Livestock	
inventory	Last inventory value (¶ 767)
purchased	Cost (¶ 767)
raised by accrual-basis farmer	Cost of raising (¶ 767)
raised by cash-basis farmer	Zero, if costs were charged to expense (¶ 767)
Mortgaged property (or property subject to redeemable ground rent)	Basis includes mortgage (or ground rent) (¶ 1611)
Partners' property	
partnership interest in exchange for contribution	Partners' adjusted basis of property contributed (¶ 443)
partnership interest purchased	Cost (¶ 434)
received in distribution other than liquidation	Partnership's adjusted basis at time of distribution (limited to partner's basis of his interest) (¶ 456)
received in partnership liquidation	Adjusted basis of partnership interest less cash received (¶ 456)
Partnership property	
after transfer of partnership interest or distributions to partners	Unaffected, unless election is made to adjust values (¶ 459, ¶ 467)
capital contribution	Partner's adjusted basis (¶ 443)
Purchase for more than value	Cost (¶ 1604), but excess may be a gift
Rehabilitated buildings, other than certified historic structures	Basis is reduced by allowable investment credit and the recaptured credit is added to basis (¶ 1365A)
Repossessed property after installment sale	
personal property	Fair market value (¶ 1838)
real property reacquired in satisfaction of purchaser's indebtedness secured by property	Adjusted basis of indebtedness plus gain resulting from reacquisition and reacquisition costs (¶ 1843)
Spousal transfers	Transferor's basis (¶ 1734)
Stock	
acquired in wash sale	Basis of stock sold, adjusted for difference between selling price of sold stock and purchase price of acquired stock (¶ 1935)
bonus stock	Allocable portion of basis of old stock (¶ 1620, ¶ 1682)
nontaxable stock dividend	Allocable share of basis of stock on which declared (¶ 1620, ¶ 1682)
qualified small business stock rollover	Cost, reduced by gain rolled over (¶ 1907)
purchased	Cost, if adequately identified (¶ 1975)
received for services	Amount reported as income, plus cash paid (¶ 1681)
S corporation	See ¶ 315, ¶ 317
specialized small business investment company stock rollover	Cost, reduced by gain rolled over (¶ 1907)
taxable stock dividend	Fair market value when issued (¶ 733A)
Stock rights	
nontaxable	Allocable share of basis of stock unless rights value is less than 15% of stock value (¶ 733A, ¶ 1682)
taxable	Fair market value when issued (¶ 733A)
Transfer in trust	Grantor's basis, plus gain or minus loss, upon transfer (¶ 1678)

1604. Adjusted Basis of Property. To determine the gain or loss from a sale or other disposition of property, the amount realized must be compared with the basis of the property to the taxpayer—generally measured by the original capital investment, adjusted to the date of sale (¶ 1611—¶ 1617) (Code Sec. 1011; Reg. § 1.1011-1).[2] In most situations, the basis of property is its cost to the taxpayer (Code Sec. 1012).[3] When property is acquired in a fully taxable exchange, the cost of the property acquired is the fair market value of the property given up.[4] Since, in an arm's-length transaction, both are presumed to be equal in value, the basis of the acquired property can be expressed as its fair market value.

1607. "Substituted" or Carryover Basis. A "substituted" basis is one that is continued or carried over from one taxpayer to another, or from one piece of property to another. The taxpayer has a substituted or carryover basis in property received as a gift (¶ 1630), in a transfer in trust (¶ 1678), in a tax-free exchange (¶ 1651), or acquired from a decedent dying in 2010 whose estate elects not to have federal estate tax apply (¶ 1636). The taxpayer also has a substituted basis in a personal residence purchased before May 7, 1997, if the recognition of gain realized on the sale of a prior residence was deferred under former Code Sec. 1034.[5]

Property Acquired by Purchase

1611. Additions to Basis of Property. In computing gain or loss on the sale of business or investment property, or gain on the sale of personal property, the cost or other basis must be *adjusted* for any expenditure, receipt, loss, or other item that is a capital expenditure (Code Sec. 1016(a)(1); Reg. § 1.1016-2).[6] This necessitates an addition for improvements made to the property since its acquisition.[7] For example, the cost of capital improvements such as an addition, new roof, newly installed central air conditioning, or electrical rewiring is added to the owner's basis. Other components that add to the cost basis of property include: brokers' commissions and lawyers' fees incurred in buying real estate; expenditures incurred in defending or perfecting the title to property;[8] zoning costs;[9] the capitalized value of a redeemable ground rent (Code Sec. 1055);[10] and sales tax, freight, installation and testing costs, excise taxes, and revenue stamps.[11]

Settlement Fees and Other Costs. The basis of real property includes settlement fees and closing costs such as abstract fees, charges for installing utility services, legal fees (including title search and preparation of the sales contract and deed), recording fees, surveys, transfer taxes, and owner's title insurance. Also included in basis are amounts owed by the seller but paid by the buyer, such as back taxes or interest, recording or mortgage fees, charges for improvements or repairs, and sales commissions (Code Sec. 1012; Reg. § 1.1012-1(b); Rev. Rul. 68-528).[12] However, amounts placed in escrow for future payments of items such as insurance and taxes do not increase basis. The creation of a mortgage does not diminish the owner's basis in a property. When a buyer assumes an existing mortgage and pays cash or other consideration, the buyer's basis in the property includes the outstanding portion of the mortgage and the value of the other consideration, and the seller realizes a benefit in the amount of the assumed mortgage and the additional consideration (*B.B. Crane*, SCt, 47-1 USTC ¶ 9217).[13] Fees and costs related to getting a loan to purchase the property are not included in the basis of the property.

References are to Standard Federal Tax Reports; Tax Research Consultant; and Practical Tax Explanations.

[2] ¶ 29,310, ¶ 29,311; SALES: 6,350, SALES: 9,050; § 16,005

[3] ¶ 29,330; SALES: 6,050; § 16,105.05

[4] ¶ 29,335.33; SALES: 6,060; § 16,105.15

[5] ¶ 29,426.01; SALES: 6,250; § 16,101

[6] ¶ 29,410, ¶ 29,413; SALES: 6,352; § 16,110.10

[7] ¶ 29,412.84; SALES: 6,352.05; § 16,110.10

[8] ¶ 29,412.844, ¶ 29,412.9901; SALES: 6,352.20; § 16,105.30

[9] ¶ 13,709.659; SALES: 6,352.05; § 16,110.10

[10] ¶ 29,940; SALES: 6,054.10; § 16,105.05

[11] ¶ 29,335.967, ¶ 29,335.577; SALES: 6,056.05; § 16,110.10

[12] ¶ 29,330, ¶ 29,331, ¶ 29,313.40; BUSEXP: 9,402.05; § 16,110.10

[13] ¶ 29,313.60; SALES: 6,054; § 18,505.05

Assessments. Assessments for improvements or other items that increase the value of property are added to the basis of the property and not deducted as a tax. Such improvements may include streets, sidewalks, water mains, sewers, and public parking facilities. The amount of an assessment may be a depreciable asset. For example, the cost of a mall enclosure paid for by a business through an assessment is depreciable. Assessments for maintenance or repairs, or for meeting interest charges on the improvements, are currently deductible as a real property tax, although the burden is on the taxpayer to show the allocation of the amounts assessed to the different purposes (Code Sec. 164(c)(1); Reg. § 1.164-4; Rev. Rul. 70-62).[14] Legal fees for obtaining a decrease in an assessment levied against property to pay for local improvements are added to the basis of the property and are not a deductible business expense.

Taxes. Any tax paid in connection with the acquisition of a property is treated as part of the cost of the property. A tax paid in connection with the disposition of a property reduces the amount realized on the disposition (Code Sec. 164(a)).[15]

In computing the cost of real property, the buyer cannot take into account any amount paid to the seller as reimbursement for real property taxes which are treated as imposed upon the purchaser (¶ 1032). This rule applies whether or not the sales contract calls for the buyer to reimburse the seller for real estate taxes paid or to be paid by the seller. However, where the buyer pays or assumes liability for real estate taxes imposed upon the seller, the taxes are considered part of the cost of the property. It is immaterial whether or not the sales contract specifies that the sale price has been reduced by, or is in any way intended to reflect, real estate taxes allocable to the seller (Reg. § 1.1012-1(b)).[16]

Checklist. Common expenses and the corresponding deduction rules may be found at ¶ 57.

1614. Additions to Basis for Carrying Charges. A taxpayer may elect to treat taxes or other carrying charges (such as interest) on some property as capital charges rather than as an expense of the tax year (Code Sec. 266; Reg. § 1.266-1).[17] The items chargeable to the capital account are:

(1) in the case of unimproved and unproductive real property: annual taxes, interest on a mortgage, and other carrying charges;

(2) in the case of real property, whether improved or unimproved and whether productive or unproductive: interest on a loan, taxes of the owner of such property measured by compensation paid to the owner's employees, taxes of the owner on the purchase of materials or on the storage, use or other consumption of materials, and other necessary expenditures, paid or incurred for the development or improvement of the property up to the time the development or construction work has been completed;

(3) in the case of personal property, taxes of an employer measured by compensation for services rendered in transporting machinery or other fixed assets to the plant or installing them, interest on a loan to buy such property or to pay for transporting or installing it, and taxes of the owner imposed on the purchase of such property or on the storage, use or other consumption, paid or incurred up to the date of installation or the date when the property is first put to use by the taxpayer, whichever is later; and

(4) any other taxes and carrying charges, otherwise deductible, which are chargeable to the capital account under sound accounting principles.

The election must be made by filing a statement with the taxpayer's original return indicating which items the taxpayer elects to treat as chargeable to the capital account (Reg. § 1.266-1(c)).[18] The election in (1) above is effective only for the year in which it is

References are to Standard Federal Tax Reports; Tax Research Consultant; and Practical Tax Explanations.

[14] ¶ 8526.453, ¶ 9500, ¶ 9508; REAL: 3,104; § 7,315.05

[15] ¶ 9500; SALES: 6,354; § 16,110.25, § 16,430

[16] ¶ 29,331; REAL: 15,302; § 16,105.25

[17] ¶ 14,100, ¶ 14,101; SALES: 6,354, BUSEXP: 9,304; § 10,220

[18] ¶ 14,101; SALES: 6,354.05; § 10,220

made. The election in (2) is effective until the development or construction work has been completed. The election in (3) is effective until the property is installed or first put to use, whichever date is later. The IRS determines whether the election in (4) is effective.

1617. Reductions in Basis. In order to determine the amount of gain or loss realized on the sale, exchange, or other disposition of property (or for figuring allowable depreciation, depletion, or amortization), the unadjusted basis of property (¶ 1601) must be decreased by any items that represent a return of capital for the period during which the property has been held by the taxpayer (Code Sec. 1016(a)).[19] These include:

- deductions previously allowed or allowable for depreciation, depletion, or amortization (¶ 1201 and following);
- the Code Sec. 179 expense deduction for certain depreciable business assets (¶ 1208), as well as the expense deduction for energy efficient commercial business property (¶ 1286) and small business refiner capital costs incurred to comply with Environmental Protection Agency sulfur regulations (¶ 1285);
- any loss recognized from an involuntary conversion, as well as any money received that was not invested in replacement property (¶ 1687);
- gain from the sale of qualified small business stock or publicly traded securities excluded from gross income and rolled over to the basis of qualified replacement stock (¶ 1907 and ¶ 1909);
- casualty or theft loss deductions, as well as the amount of any insurance or other recovery for the loss (¶ 1127);
- tax-free dividends by corporations (¶ 733A) and nonliquidating distributions by a partnership to a partner (¶ 447); and
- the investment credit (except for 50 percent of the energy credits) (¶ 1365A).

Depreciation. The basis of property is reduced by the amount of depreciation claimed, or if greater, the depreciation which should have been claimed under the method chosen (Code Sec. 1016(a)(2); Reg. § 1.1016-3).[20] If no depreciation or insufficient depreciation was claimed, the basis is nonetheless reduced by the full amount of depreciation that should have been claimed. In order to mitigate the effect of this rule, the IRS has issued procedures that allow the taxpayer to change to a proper method of accounting for depreciation and claim a downward adjustment to income that reflects the additional amount of depreciation that should have been claimed (¶ 1221). If excess depreciation was claimed on an asset, the basis of the asset is reduced by the amount of depreciation that should have been claimed plus the part of the excess depreciation deducted that actually reduced the taxpayer's tax liability.

Percentage Depletion. Even though a percentage depletion allowance is in excess of cost or other basis, it is not necessary to use a negative basis (less than zero) in computing gain on the sale of mineral property (¶ 1294–¶ 1298).[21]

Motor Vehicles. The basis of a motor vehicle is reduced by any deduction or tax credit the taxpayer claimed with respect to the purchase, including the credit for qualified fuel cell motor vehicles (¶ 1346), the credit for new qualified plug-in electric drive motor vehicles purchased after 2009 (¶ 1351), and the credit for alternative fuel vehicle refueling property, whether commercial or residential (¶ 1355). The basis of an automobile must also be reduced by the amount of any gas guzzler tax imposed by Code Sec. 4064 when use of the vehicle begins not more than one year after the first retail sale (Code Sec. 1016(d)).[22]

References are to Standard Federal Tax Reports; Tax Research Consultant; and Practical Tax Explanations.

[19] ¶ 29,410; SALES: 6,350; § 16,110.25

[20] ¶ 29,410, ¶ 29,414; SALES: 6,364; § 16,110.20

[21] ¶ 29,412.675; FARM: 18,068; § 11,610

[22] ¶ 29,410; SALES: 6,372.50

Easements. Generally, the amount received for granting an easement for a limited use or for a limited period reduces the basis of the affected part of the property (Rev. Rul. 68-291).[23] Gain is recognized to the extent that the amount received exceeds the basis of the affected part. The granting of a perpetual easement that denies the grantor any beneficial use of the property may be considered a sale of property even though the grantor retains legal title.

Residential Property. The basis of a personal residence or dwelling unit is reduced by certain tax credits the taxpayer claimed with respect to the property. This includes the nonbusiness energy credit allowed for qualified energy efficiency improvements and residential energy property (¶ 1341), and the residential energy efficient property credit allowed for amounts spent on alternative energy equipment such as solar or fuel cell equipment (¶ 1342). An eligible contractor who has constructed and claimed a credit a for qualified new energy-efficient home must also reduce his or her basis in the property to the extent that the credit is claimed (¶ 1365CC). In addition, the basis of a dwelling unit for which an excludable energy conservation subsidy was provided by a public utility must be reduced by the amount of the subsidy (¶ 889).

Homes Purchased Before May 7, 1997. The basis of a home purchased before May 7, 1997, must be reduced to reflect any gain realized on the sale of the prior home but deferred under former Code Sec. 1034.

Adoption Credit. The basis of a residence must be reduced by the amount of the adoption tax credit that was claimed with respect to improvements that increased that basis of the home (¶ 1307).

Child Care Credit. The basis of facilities acquired, constructed, rehabilitated, or expanded, and with respect to which an employer-provided child care credit (¶ 1365V) is allowed, must be reduced by the amount of the credit. If there is a recapture of the credit on the disposition of such property, the basis of the property is increased by the amount recaptured (Code Sec. 1016(a)(28)).

Canceled Debt. A taxpayer must reduce certain tax attributes by an amount excluded from gross income as the result of a discharge of indebtedness in a Title 11 bankruptcy case, a discharge of indebtedness during insolvency, or a discharge of qualified farm indebtedness (¶ 855).

Railroad Track. For tax years before January 1, 2017, eligible small and mid-sized railroad companies must reduce the basis of track on which they have been allowed a railroad track maintenance credit (¶ 1365W).

Substituted Basis. Where the basis of the property is a substituted basis (¶ 1607), the same adjustments must be made for the period the property was held by the transferor, donor, or grantor, or during the period the property was held by the person for whom the basis is to be determined (Code Sec. 1016(b)).[24]

1620. Apportionment of Cost or Other Basis. When a sale is made of parts of property purchased as a unit, as in a subdivision of real estate, allocation of the total basis is required (Reg. § 1.61-6).[25] Other instances where allocation of the cost or other basis is necessary include stock of different classes received as a dividend or pursuant to a reorganization, a split-up, split-off, or spin-off (¶ 2205); stock received as a bonus with the purchase of stock of a different character; stock purchase warrants attached to debenture bonds; and depreciable and nondepreciable property purchased for a lump sum.

Trade or Business Purchased. Applicable asset acquisition rules require the allocation of the purchase price of a trade or business among the assets in proportion to their fair market values in the following classes and in the following order (Code Sec. 1060; Reg. § § 1.338-6 and 1.1060-1):[26]

References are to Standard Federal Tax Reports; Tax Research Consultant; and Practical Tax Explanations.

[23] ¶ 29,412.813; SALES: 6,356.05; § 16,110.25

[24] ¶ 29,410; SALES: 6,374; § 16,101

[25] ¶ 5605; SALES: 6,200, SALES: 6,216; § 16,115

[26] ¶ 16,281, ¶ 30,060, ¶ 30,061; SALES: 33,052; § 18,401

- Class I asset: Cash and general deposit accounts (including savings and checking accounts), other than certificates of deposits held in banks, savings and loan associations, and other depository institutions.
- Class II asset: Actively traded personal property, as well as certificates of deposit and foreign currency, even if they are not actively traded personal property.
- Class III asset: Assets that the taxpayer marks to market at least annually for federal income tax purposes.
- Class IV asset: Stock in trade of the taxpayer or other property of a kind that would properly be included in the inventory of the taxpayer if on hand at the close of the tax year, or property held by the taxpayer primarily for sale to customers in the ordinary course of its trade or business.
- Class V asset: All assets other than Class I, II, III, IV, VI, and VII assets.
- Class VI asset: Code Sec. 197 intangibles, except goodwill and going concern value.
- Class VII asset: Goodwill and going concern value whether or not they qualify as section 197 intangibles.

Before making the allocation, the purchase price is first reduced by any cash and general deposit accounts (savings and checking) which the acquired business holds as assets. The buyer and seller of the assets of a trade or business are bound by any written agreements allocating consideration to the transferred assets. However, any allocation that is not found to be fair market value will be disregarded. The buyer and seller must attach Form 8594 to their income tax returns for the year of sale to report the allocation.

Land and Buildings. When a building and land are purchased for a lump sum, the purchase price must be allocated between the land and building on the basis of their fair market values. If the fair market values are uncertain, the allocation may be based on their assessed values for real estate tax purposes (Reg. § § 1.61-6(a) and 1.167(a)-5).[27]

Subdivided Lots. The basis of each lot of a subdivided property is equal to the purchase price of the entire property multiplied by a fraction, the numerator of which is the fair market value of the lot and the denominator of which is the fair market value of the entire property. The cost of common improvements is also allocated among the individual lots. A developer who sells subdivided lots before development work is completed may include, with IRS consent, an allocation of the estimated future cost for common improvements in the basis of the lots sold (Rev. Proc. 92-29).[28] There is a special rule relating to the recognition of capital gain on the sale of subdivided lots (¶ 1762).

1623. Allocation of Basis—Bargain Sale to Charity. If a charitable deduction is available (¶ 1062), the basis of property sold to charity for less than its fair market must be allocated between the portion of the property "sold" and the portion "given" to charity, based on the fair market value of each portion. Thus, the seller-donor realizes some taxable gain even if the selling price did not exceed the seller-donor's cost or other basis for the entire property (Code Sec. 1011(b); Reg. § 1.1011-2).[29] The adjusted basis of the portion of property sold to a charity is computed as:

$$\frac{\text{Amount realized (fair market value of part sold)}}{\text{Fair market value of entire property}} \times \text{Adjusted basis of entire property}$$

1626. Basis of Residential or Converted Property. Where property has been continually occupied by the taxpayer as a residence since its acquisition, no adjustment of the basis is made for depreciation because none is allowable. The cost of permanent improvements to the property is added to the basis, as are special assessments paid for

References are to Standard Federal Tax Reports; Tax Research Consultant; and Practical Tax Explanations.

[27] ¶ 5605, ¶ 11,012; SALES: 6,202.05; § 16,115

[28] ¶ 29,313.576; SALES: 6,216; § 16,560.20

[29] ¶ 29,310, ¶ 29,312; INDIV: 51,302; § 7,530

local benefits that improve the property (¶ 1611). Recoveries against a builder for defective construction reduce the basis.[30]

If residential property is converted to rental property, an adjustment should be made for depreciation from the date of the conversion. Thus, the basis for gain in the case of rented residential property is the taxpayer's cost or other statutory basis, less depreciation allowable while the property was rented or held for rental.

The basis for loss may not exceed the value at the time the residence was converted to rental use, taking into account subsequent basis adjustments, including reduction for allowable depreciation. This is only a limitation; if a smaller loss results from the use of the adjusted cost basis, it must be used (Reg. § 1.165-9(b)).[31] The value of the property upon conversion to rental use has no effect on the basis for gain. If converted property is sold for a price that is greater than the basis for loss but less than the basis for gain, there is no gain or loss.

If rental property is converted to a personal residence, adjustments to basis for depreciation end on the date of the conversion. Any gain on the sale of the property will be recognized (subject to the exclusion rules at ¶ 1705) and may be subject to depreciation recapture (¶ 1779). Loss will not be recognized.

Property Acquired by Gift or Bequest

1630. Basis of Property Acquired by Gift. For property acquired by gift, the basis to the donee is generally the same as it would be in the hands of the donor or the last preceding owner by whom it was not acquired by gift (Code Sec. 1015(a); Reg. § 1.1015-1).[32] However, the basis for loss is the adjusted basis of the property prior to the date of the gift (¶ 1611—¶ 1617) or the fair market value of the property at the time of the gift, whichever is lower. In some cases, there is neither gain nor loss on the sale of property received by gift because the selling price is less than the basis for gain and more than the basis for loss.

If a gift was made on or after September 1, 1958, and before 1977, the basis of the property is increased by the amount of the gift tax paid (¶ 2903), but not above the fair market value of the property at the time of the gift. As to gifts made before September 2, 1958, and held by the donee on that date, the basis is also increased by the amount of the gift tax, but not by more than any excess of the fair market value of the property at the time of the gift over the basis of the property in the hands of the donor at the time of the gift (Code Sec. 1015(d); Reg. § 1.1015-1).[33]

In the case of a gift made after 1976 on which the gift tax is paid, the basis of the property is increased by the amount of gift tax attributable to the net appreciation in value of the gift. The net appreciation for this purpose is the amount by which the fair market value of the gift exceeds the donor's adjusted basis immediately before the gift (Code Sec. 1015(d)(6)).[34]

Zero basis generally applies to a life estate acquired by gift (¶ 1633).

1633. Basis of Property Acquired from a Decedent. The basis of any real or personal property acquired from a decedent is generally its fair market value on the date of the decedent's death or on the alternate valuation or special use valuation date (¶ 2922) (Code Sec. 1014).[35] If there is no federal estate tax liability, the basis of the property is its fair market value as of the date of the decedent's death for the purpose of state inheritance or transmission taxes (Reg. § 1.1014-3(a); Rev. Rul. 54-97).[36] Fair market value is presumptive, and may be rebutted by clear and convincing evidence. There are certain exceptions to the basis of property acquired from a decedent equaling fair market value (¶ 1636 and ¶ 1639), including property subject to a qualified conservation easement and income in respect of the decedent (¶ 182) (Code Sec. 1014(a)(4) and (c)).[37]

References are to Standard Federal Tax Reports; Tax Research Consultant; and Practical Tax Explanations.

[30] ¶ 29,412.9968; SALES: 6,356.10; § 16,110.10

[31] ¶ 10,102; REAL: 15,054; § 16,930

[32] ¶ 29,390, ¶ 29,391; SALES: 6,102; § 16,205

[33] ¶ 29,390, ¶ 29,391; SALES: 6,104.10; § 16,210.05, § 28,605.25

[34] ¶ 29,390; SALES: 6,104.05; § 16,210.15

[35] ¶ 29,370; ESTGIFT: 54,000; § 16,305.05

[36] ¶ 29,373, ¶ 29,380.38; ESTGIFT: 54,058.05; § 16,305.15

[37] ¶ 29,370; ESTGIFT: 54,102, ESTGIFT: 15,758; § 16,305.40, § 32,930

Consistency of Basis. Effective for property with respect to which an estate tax return is filed after July 31, 2015, the basis of property received by reason of a decedent's death must be consistent with the value for estate tax purposes (Code Sec. 1014(f).[38] Thus, the basis of any property to which the stepped-up basis rules apply may not exceed the value of the property determined on the decedent's federal estate tax return or the value reported to the IRS and the taxpayer on a separate information return, Form 8971 (¶ 2938). The consistency in reporting is only applicable to property that was includible in the decedent's gross estate and resulted in increased estate tax liability (reduced by applicable credits) on the estate. The accuracy-related penalty will be imposed for inconsistent estate basis reporting (Code Sec. 6662(b)(8) and (k)).[39]

The IRS has released proposed regulations addressing consistency of basis requirements. These regulations may not be relied upon by taxpayers, but comprise the only guidance that has been released by the IRS regarding the requirements (Prop. Reg. §§1.1014-10 and 1.6035-1; NPRM REG-127923-15).[40]

Decedents Dying in 2010. Effective for decedents dying in 2010, the executor of the decedent's estate had the option to elect out of the federal estate tax. If the election was made, a modified carryover basis rule applied to property acquired from the decedent. For a complete discussion of the modified carryover basis rule as it applies to property acquired from a decedent who died in 2010, see ¶ 1636.

Term Interests. In most instances, a zero basis is assigned to a life estate that was acquired by gift or bequest and sold or disposed of after October 9, 1969. Interests covered by this exception to the usual rules are: (1) life interests in property; (2) interests for a term of years in property; and (3) income interests in trusts. The zero basis requirement does not apply where the life tenant and remainderman sell their interests simultaneously so that the entire ownership of the property is transferred to another person or group of persons (Code Sec. 1001(e); Reg. §§1.1001-1 and 1.1014-5(b)).[41] Special rules also are provided in determining a beneficiary's basis in a term interest in a charitable remainder trust (CRT) upon a sale or other disposition of all interests in the trust to the extent that the basis consists of a share of adjusted uniform basis (Reg. §1.1014-5(c)).[42]

1634. Basis in Property Held in Joint Tenancy. A decedent's interest in property held in a joint tenancy (with a right of survivorship) or as tenants by the entirety that passes to the other owner by operation of law is considered property acquired from a decedent (Code Sec. 1014(b)(9); Reg. §§1.1014-2(b) and 1.1014-6(a)(1)).[43] Thus, the basis of the property in the hands of the survivor will generally depend upon the amount contributed by each joint tenant toward the original purchase price and, in the case of depreciable property, the manner in which income is divided under local (state) law.

Example 1: Tom Smith and Susan Jones (unmarried) purchased a townhouse for $100,000, which they held as joint tenants with right of survivorship. Tom contributed $30,000 and Susan $70,000. Susan died when the property was worth $200,000; 70 percent of the fair market value ($140,000) is included in her estate. Tom's basis in the property is $170,000 ($30,000 + $140,000).

Example 2: Assume the same facts as in Example 1, except that Tom and Susan held the townhouse as a rental property and that $25,000 of depreciation was allowed prior to Susan's death. If Tom and Susan are entitled to one-half of the income from the property under local law, Tom's basis would be reduced by $12,500 to $157,500 ($170,000 – $12,500).

References are to Standard Federal Tax Reports; Tax Research Consultant; and Practical Tax Explanations.

[38] ¶ 29,370; ESTGIFT: 54,050, SALES: 6,156; § 16,305.45

[39] ¶ 39,651; SALES: 6,156, PENALTY: 3,102; § 16,305.45

[40] ¶ 29,379D, ¶ 35,472B; SALES: 6,156, PENALTY: 3,102; § 16,305.45

[41] ¶ 29,220, ¶ 29,221, ¶ 29,375; ESTGIFT: 54,056; § 2,115.30

[42] ¶ 29,375; ESTGIFT: 45,206; § 2,115.30

[43] ¶ 29,370, ¶ 29,372, ¶ 29,376; ESTGIFT: 54,206; § 16,305.20

For purposes of the federal estate tax, the entire value of jointly held property with the right of survivorship is included in a decedent's gross estate except for the portion of the property for which the surviving joint tenant furnished consideration (¶ 2919). If the joint tenants are spouses, then the property is a qualified joint interest and it does not matter who furnished the consideration for it—one-half of the value is included in the gross estate of the first spouse to die. The surviving spouse's basis in the remaining portion of the qualified joint interest is one-half of the original cost (regardless of the amount that the survivor actually contributed) reduced by any depreciation deductions allocable to the surviving spouse (IRS Pub. 559).

Example 3: Assume the same facts as in Example 1, except that Tom and Susan are married. Tom's basis in the property is $150,000 ($50,000 (one-half of original cost) + $100,000 (one-half of fair market value included in Susan's estate).

1636. Carryover Basis Elections. Effective for decedents dying in 2010, the executor of the decedent's estate had the option to elect out of the federal estate tax. If the election was made, a modified carryover basis rule applied to property acquired from the decedent (former Code Sec. 1022).[44] Specifically, the property recipient received a basis equal to the lesser of the property's adjusted basis in the hands of the decedent or its fair market value on the date of the decedent's death. Executors had the option to elect to increase the basis of estate property by up to $1.3 million (plus an increase for certain carryovers and unrealized losses of the decedent), with an additional basis increase of up to $3 million in the case of property passing to a surviving spouse. However, the basis of any property could not be increased above its fair market value in the decedent's hands on the date of the decedent's death. The IRS provided optional safe harbor procedures for determining modified carryover basis (Rev. Proc. 2011-41).[45]

Executors and administrators of estates of decedents dying after 1976 and before November 7, 1978, could elect to determine the basis under the otherwise repealed carryover basis rules.[46] The time for elections expired July 31, 1980, but valid elections will continue to affect computation of gain on dispositions of property to which such elections apply.

1639. Appreciated Property Reacquired by Donor from Decedent. For property acquired from a decedent who dies after December 31, 1981, the basis of the property when reacquired by the donor following the decedent's death is equal to the decedent's adjusted basis in the property immediately before the decedent's death if: (1) appreciated property was acquired by the decedent after August 13, 1981, as a gift; (2) the decedent received the gift within one year before his death; and (3) following the decedent's death, the donor of the gift, or the donor's spouse, reacquires the property (Code Sec. 1014(e)).[47]

Property Acquired by Exchange

1648. Basis of Property Transferred to Corporation in a Taxable Exchange. When a corporation acquires property for its stock in an exchange taxable to the transferor, its basis for the property is the fair market value of the stock on the date of the exchange. If the stock has no established market value at that time, it may be considered to be the equivalent of the fair market value of the property received.[48]

1651. Basis of Property Acquired in a Tax-Free Exchange. If property is acquired in an exchange on which no gain or loss is recognized, the basis of the property is the same as that for the property exchanged (Code Sec. 1031(d); Reg. § 1.1031(d)-1).[49] Substitute basis (¶ 1607) applies to:

- like-kind exchange of property held for productive use or investment (¶ 1721), as well as the exchange of government obligations for similar obligations (¶ 1726);

References are to Standard Federal Tax Reports; Tax Research Consultant; and Practical Tax Explanations.

[44] ¶ 29,496; ESTGIFT: 51,060.10; § 16,310

[45] ¶ 29,498.10; ESTGIFT: 51,060.10; § 16,310

[46] ¶ 44,438.70; ESTGIFT: 54,060

[47] ¶ 29,370; ESTGIFT: 54,104; § 16,305.35

[48] ¶ 29,225.272; SALES: 6,060, SALES: 6,068; § 16,105.15

[49] ¶ 29,602, ¶ 29,612; SALES: 6,250; § 18,040

- exchange of stock for stock of the same corporation (¶ 1728);
- exchange of property solely for stock or securities of a "controlled" corporation (¶ 1731); and
- exchange of stock or securities solely for stock or securities in a reorganization (¶ 2229).

Trade-in arrangements under which a taxpayer sells old equipment used in a trade or business to a dealer and purchases new equipment of like kind from the dealer are like-kind exchanges qualifying for nonrecognition treatment if the sale of the old equipment and the purchase of the new equipment are mutually dependent transactions, even if they are not simultaneous. The basis of the new equipment, for gain or loss or depreciation, is ordinarily the total of the adjusted basis of the trade-in plus whatever additional cash is needed. In effect, the basis of the new property is its purchase price, increased or decreased according to whether the trade-in value of the old equipment is greater or less than its depreciated cost. Special depreciation rules may apply to like-kind exchanges (¶ 1250).

1657. Basis of Boot Acquired in an Otherwise Tax-Free Exchange. In a like-kind exchange, a taxpayer may receive money or other property (commonly referred to as boot) that is not of a like-kind (¶ 1723). The taxpayer recognizes gain from the transaction to the extent of the boot's fair market value. In such exchanges, the cost or other applicable basis of the property acquired is the same as that of the property exchanged, decreased by the amount of any money received by the taxpayer in the transaction and increased by the amount of gain or decreased by the amount of loss recognized in the exchange. If boot is received in an exchange that is tax free in part, the cost or other basis of the property disposed of must be allocated between the property received tax free and such "other property," assigning to the "other property" an amount equivalent to its fair market value (Code Sec. 1031(d)).[50]

1660. Basis of Property Transferred to a Corporation. The basis of property acquired by a corporation from a shareholder in exchange for stock in a Code Sec. 351 transaction in which the shareholder controls the corporation immediately after the exchange (¶ 203), as well as the basis of property from a shareholder as paid-in surplus or as a contribution to capital, is the same to the corporation as it was in the hands of the shareholder, increased by the amount of gain recognized by the shareholder on the transfer (Code Sec. 362(a); Reg. § 1.362-1).[51] If property is acquired by a corporation in a reorganization, the basis of the transferor (increased by any recognized gain) generally also follows through to the transferee corporation. However, carryover basis will not apply if the property acquired by the corporation consists of stock or securities in another corporation that is a party to the reorganization unless the stock or securities were acquired as consideration for the transfer (Code Sec. 362(b)). Rules for property acquired subject to a built-in loss (¶ 1667) and for property acquired upon liquidation of a subsidiary may apply (¶ 2261).

Property contributed to a corporation by nonstockholders on or after June 22, 1954, has a zero basis. Money contributed by an outsider on or after that date reduces the basis of corporate property acquired with it within 12 months after the contribution is received. To the extent that the contribution is not used to acquire property within this 12-month period, it reduces, as of the last day of the period, the basis of any other property held by the company (Code Sec. 362(c)).

1667. Limitations on Built-In Losses. If a corporation receives property in an exchange with an owner who is *not* subject to U.S. tax, and the property's fair market value is less than the transferee's adjusted basis of all property received in the exchange (i.e., there is a built-in loss), the corporate transferee's basis in the property received is its fair market value immediately after the transfer (Code Sec. 362(e)).[52] Thus, the foreign loss is not recognized for U.S. tax purposes. This treatment applies to property

References are to Standard Federal Tax Reports; Tax Research Consultant; and Practical Tax Explanations.

[50] ¶ 29,602; SALES: 6,252; § 18,040

[51] ¶ 16,610, ¶ 16,611; CCORP: 3,204, CCORP: 39,302; § 26,135

[52] ¶ 16,610; CCORP: 39,304.10; § 26,135

acquired by the corporation from a shareholder in exchange for stock in a Code Sec. 351 transaction in which the shareholder controls the corporation immediately after the exchange (¶ 203), as well as the basis of property from a shareholder as paid-in surplus or as a contribution to capital (¶ 1660).

If a corporation acquires property in a section 351 exchange with an owner who *is* subject to U.S. tax, and the transferred property's adjusted basis exceeds its fair market value, the corporate transferee's basis in the property is also generally limited to its fair market value immediately after the transaction. Any required basis reduction is allocated among the transferred properties in proportion to their built-in losses immediately before the transaction. The transferor owner and transferee controlled corporation can make an irrevocable election to limit the owner's basis in the stock received—rather than the corporation's basis in the property—to the aggregate fair market value of the transferred property (Reg. § 1.362-4(d)).[53] If a transaction involves multiple transferors, the limitation on the transfer of built-in losses is determined separately for each transferor (Reg. § 1.362-4(b)).

1669. Assumption of Liabilities. The assumption of liabilities by a shareholder in a Code Sec. 351 exchange with a controlled corporation (¶ 203) or in a reorganization (¶ 2229) is generally not treated as the equivalent of cash or boot (¶ 2233). However, the assumption of a liability is treated as money received for the purpose of determining the basis of the property or stock received in such transfers (Code Secs. 358(d) and 1031(d)).[54] Thus, the corporation's assumption of a liability generally results in a reduction of the basis of the property the shareholder receives in the exchange. An exception applies to an assumption of a liability that would give rise to a deduction, provided the incurrence of such liabilities did not result in the creation or increase of basis of any property.

1672. Discharge of Debt. Under some conditions, a taxpayer realizes no income from a discharge of debt (¶ 855). Any amount of debt discharged and excluded from gross income reduces the basis of the property securing the debt (Code Sec. 1017).[55] Regulations prescribe the sequence of allocation where the debt is, or must be treated as, a general liability (Reg. § § 1.108-4 and 1.1017-1).[56]

Other Acquired Property

1678. Basis of Property Transferred in Trust. If property is acquired by a transfer in trust, other than by a transfer in trust by gift, bequest, or devise, its basis is the same as it would be in the hands of the trust's grantor, increased by the gain or decreased by the loss recognized to the grantor under the law in effect as of the date of such transfer (Code Sec. 1015(b)).[57] When an existing charitable remainder trust is split pro rata into separate trusts, one for each beneficiary, the original trust's basis in the assets is split pro rata among the new trusts (Rev. Rul. 2008-41).

1681. Basis of Stock or Other Property Received for Services. If stock or other property is given to an employee as compensation for personal services instead of cash, the fair market value of the property is income to the employee unless the property is subject to a substantial risk of forfeiture (¶ 713). The fair market value of the property included in income becomes its basis to the employee (Code Sec. 83; Reg. § 1.83-4(b)).[58] If the property is sold to the employee for less than its market value, the difference between the amount paid and the value of the property is also income. In this case, the employee's basis for the property is the cash cost, plus the amount reported as income.

A taxpayer who receives property subject to a substantial risk of forfeiture may make a Code Sec. 83(b) election to include the fair market value of the property (less any amount paid for the property) in income in the year that the property is received (¶ 713). For property transfers made on or after January 1, 2016, a taxpayer is no longer required to file a copy of the election with is or her income tax return (Reg. § 1.83-2(c)).

References are to Standard Federal Tax Reports; Tax Research Consultant; and Practical Tax Explanations.

[53] ¶ 16,611CE; CCORP: 39,304.10; § 26,135

[54] ¶ 16,550, ¶ 29,602; SALES: 27,300, CCORP: 39,256.05; § 26,130

[55] ¶ 29,430; SALES: 6,368; § 3,420.15

[56] ¶ 7003E, ¶ 29,431; SALES: 6,368.10; § 3,420.10

[57] ¶ 29,390; SALES: 6,110; § 16,205

[58] ¶ 6380, ¶ 6384; SALES: 6,062; § 21,430.05

The basis for determining gain or loss when the property is sold is the amount included in income in the election year, plus the amount paid for the property (Reg. § 1.83-2(a)).[59]

Corporations may grant their employees the option to purchase stock in the corporation (¶ 1923—¶ 1931). For purposes of determining an individual's basis in property transferred in connection with the performance of services, rules similar to the annuity basis rules for nonresident aliens apply (Code Sec. 83(c)(4)) (¶ 821).

1682. Basis of Stock Received in Nontaxable Distributions. If a shareholder in a corporation receives stock or stock rights in a nontaxable distribution (¶ 733A), the basis of the old stock is allocated between the old stock and new stock in proportion to the fair market value of each on the date of the distribution (not the record date) (Code Sec. 307; Reg. § 1.307-1).[60] If only part of the stock dividend is nontaxable, the basis of the old stock is allocated between the old stock and the part of the new stock that is not taxable.

This rule applies with respect to stock rights only if such rights are exercised or sold. If exercised, the basis of the stock rights is added to the cost of the stock acquired. If sold, the basis allocable to the stock rights is used to determine the taxpayer's gain or loss. If the stock rights are allowed to expire, the basis of the shares with respect to which the rights were distributed remains intact.

If the fair market value of the stock rights on the date of distribution is less than 15 percent of the fair market value of the stock with respect to which the distribution is made, the basis of the stock rights is deemed to be zero unless the taxpayer elects to make a basis allocation (Code Sec. 307(b); Reg. § 1.307-2).[61] The election must be made in a statement attached to the shareholder's return for the year in which the rights are received. It is irrevocable with respect to the rights for which it is made. The election must be made for all the rights received in a particular distribution by the shareholder on stock of the same class received by the shareholder at the time of the distribution.

Example: Bob bought 100 shares of Yeta Company common stock at $125 per share and later received 100 rights entitling him to purchase 20 shares of new common stock in Yeta Company at $100 per share. When the rights were distributed, the old shares had a fair market value of $120 per share, and the rights had a fair market value of $3 each. Three weeks later, Bob sold his rights for $4 each. He elects to apportion basis.

Cost of old stock on which rights were distributed	$12,500.00
Market value of old stock at date of distribution of rights	12,000.00
Market value of rights at date of distribution	300.00
Cost apportioned to old stock after distribution of rights (12,000/12,300 of $12,500)	12,195.12
Cost apportioned to rights (300/12,300 of $12,500)	304.88
Selling price of rights	400.00
Gain ($400 – $304.88)	$95.12

In determining gain or loss from any later sale of the stock on which the rights were distributed, the adjusted cost of the old stock is $12,195.12, or $121.95 a share.

The holding period of nontaxable stock rights includes the holding period of the stock on which the rights are distributed. The holding period of the stock acquired by the exercise of the rights begins on the date that the rights are exercised (Code Sec. 1223(4) and (5); Reg. § 1.1223-1(e) and (f)).[62]

1684. Basis of Equipment for Which Medical Deduction Claimed. The basis of equipment whose cost qualifies as a medical expense (¶ 1016) does not include that portion of its cost that has been claimed as an itemized deduction because such amounts are not properly capitalized. However, the equipment's basis includes that portion of the

References are to Standard Federal Tax Reports; Tax Research Consultant; and Practical Tax Explanations.

[59] ¶ 6382; COMPEN: 18,302; § 21,475.05

[60] ¶ 15,500, ¶ 15,501; SALES: 6,302.10; § 26,235.10

[61] ¶ 15,500, ¶ 15,501B; SALES: 6,302.15; § 26,235.10

[62] ¶ 30,460, ¶ 30,461; SALES: 15,162.30; § 16,540.05

cost that is nondeductible because of the 10-percent of adjusted gross income (AGI) floor (7.5-percent of AGI floor if the taxpayer or his or her spouse has attained age 65 before 2017) (¶ 1015).

To determine this portion, the total amount of the AGI limitation is multiplied by a fraction whose numerator is the cost of the equipment and whose denominator is the total amount of the taxpayer's medical expenses. Similarly, if a taxpayer's total allowable itemized deductions exceed the taxpayer's AGI, or are limited by the overall limitation on itemized deductions of high-income taxpayers (¶ 1014), that portion of the equipment's cost attributable to the nondeductible expenses may also be included in the equipment's basis (Reg. § 1.1016-2).[63]

1687. Basis of Property Acquired Through Involuntary Conversion. The basis of property purchased as the result of an involuntary conversion (¶ 1713) on which gain is not recognized is the cost of the replacement property less the amount of gain not recognized on the conversion (Code Sec. 1033(b); Reg. § 1.1033(b)-1).[64] If qualifying replacement property is received as the result of an involuntary conversion, the replacement property's basis is the same as the basis of the involuntarily converted property decreased by any loss recognized on the conversion and any money received and not spent on qualifying replacement property. The basis is increased by any gain recognized on the conversion and any cost of acquiring the replacement property. Special depreciation rules may apply (¶ 1250).

1693. Basis of Property Transferred Between Spouses. No gain or loss is recognized on a transfer of property from an individual to, or in trust for the benefit of, a spouse or a former spouse if the transfer to the former spouse is incident to the divorce of the parties (¶ 1734). In such case, the basis of the transferred property in the hands of the transferee is the transferor's adjusted basis in the property. The carryover basis rule does not apply to a spouse (or former spouse) who is a nonresident alien (Code Sec. 1041(d)). Nonrecognition of gain is not permitted with respect to the transfer of property in trust to the extent that the sum of the amount of any liabilities assumed, plus the amount of any liabilities to which the property is subject, exceeds the total of the adjusted basis of the property transferred (Code Sec. 1041(e)).[65] The transferee's basis is adjusted to take into account any gain recognized.

Valuation Rules

1695. Indeterminate Fair Market Value. Only in rare and extraordinary cases does property have no determinable fair market value (Reg. § 1.1001-1).[66] If the fair market value of an asset received in an exchange (such as a contract to receive royalties) cannot be determined with fair certainty, gain is not realized on the exchange until after the total payments received under the contract exceed the cost (or other basis) of the property surrendered in exchange.[67] The Tax Court has applied the *Cohan* rule (estimated or approximate value) to estimate the value of patents, patent applications, and stock rights, where the taxpayer could not prove their exact value.[68]

1697. Valuation of Securities and Real Estate. The fair market value of securities traded on the open market, or on a recognized exchange, is ordinarily the average of the high and low quoted prices on the valuation date. If only a minimal number of shares are traded on the valuation date, or if other abnormal market conditions exist, an alternative valuation method may be necessary.[69]

References are to Standard Federal Tax Reports; Tax Research Consultant; and Practical Tax Explanations.

[63] ¶ 29,413; SALES: 6,360.10; § 7,285.10

[64] ¶ 29,640, ¶ 29,644; SALES: 6,254; § 18,145.05

[65] ¶ 29,800; SALES: 6,262; § 18,230

[66] ¶ 29,221; VALUE: 1,000; § 16,405

[67] ¶ 29,225.153; ACCTNG: 6,114; § 16,405

[68] ¶ 8520.586, ¶ 16,612.175; SALES: 6052; § 26,410.15

[69] ¶ 29,225.187, ¶ 29,225.242; VALUE: 3,100; § 34,110.20

When corporate stock is not sold on the open market, its fair market value depends upon many factors, including the nature and history of the business, economic outlook and condition of the industry, book value of stock and financial condition of the business, earning capacity of the company, dividend-paying capacity, goodwill, prior sales, size of the block to be valued, and market price of similar but listed stock.[70] Isolated sales of small portions of the stock or forced sales are not considered evidence of fair market value.[71]

Restrictive sales agreements must be considered in the valuation of stock. If the stock is subject to a repurchase option, its value may not exceed the amount for which it may be repurchased. If there are restrictions making sale of stock impossible, and its value is highly speculative, it does not have a fair market value.[72]

There are three principal methods used in determining the fair market value of real property:[73]

(1) the comparable sales method, which involves gathering information on sales of property similar to the subject property and then making adjustments (both positive and negative) for various differences between the *comparables* and the property being appraised;

(2) the capitalization of income method, which estimates a property's fair market value based upon future benefits (cash-flow) to be derived from the ownership of the property; and

(3) the replacement cost method, which is based on the principle of substitution and estimates the fair market value of real property based on the assumption that a prudent person (in other words, a willing buyer) would not pay more for a property than it would cost to acquire a similar site and erect a comparable structure (less accrued depreciation).

Other factors that may be appropriate to consider with regard to a fair market value determination of real property include:

(1) the development potential of the property with regard to its highest and best potential and realistic use;

(2) the possibility of zoning changes that may either enhance or diminish the marketability of the property;

(3) the taxpayer's ability to acquire adjacent parcels of property allowing for expanded and, in many cases, enhanced uses;

(4) leases, debt, and other encumbrances on the property; and

(5) environmental concerns, restrictions, and hazards.

Appraisal affidavits of a retrospective nature, standing alone, are generally not accorded great weight.[74]

References are to Standard Federal Tax Reports; Tax Research Consultant; and Practical Tax Explanations.

[70] ¶ 29,225.228; VALUE: 9,050; § 34,110.20

[71] ¶ 29,225.234; VALUE: 9,062.05; § 34,110.20

[72] ¶ 29,225.2563; VALUE: 9,200; § 34,110.20

[73] ¶ 11,660.555; VALUE: 15,100

[74] ¶ 29,225.1055; VALUE: 1,104; § 7,600.25

Chapter 17
SALES AND EXCHANGES
CAPITAL GAINS

	Par.
SALES AND EXCHANGES	
Sales and Exchanges of Property	1701
Gain or Loss from Sale of Residence	1705
Involuntary Conversion	1713
Transactions Between Related Persons	1717
Tax-Free Exchanges	1719
CAPITAL GAINS	
Treatment of Capital Gain or Loss	1735
Section 1231	1747
Capital Loss Limitation, Carryover, Carryback	1752
Subdivision of Real Estate	1762
Patents, Royalties, and Franchises	1767
Disposition of Depreciable Property	1779
Farmers' Recapture	1797

Sales and Exchanges of Property

1701. Gain or Loss from Sale or Exchange of Property. Gain or loss from the sale or exchange of property generally must be recognized (Code Sec. 1001(c)).[1] The seller has gain if the amount realized is more than the seller's adjusted basis in the property. The seller has a loss when the adjusted basis of the property is more than the amount realized (Code Sec. 1001(a)).[2] Part of the basis in a larger property generally must be allocated to any portion of that property that is disposed of. However, if basis or fair market value cannot be ascertained or apportioned, the open-transaction doctrine may defer recognition of any gain until the taxpayer's basis in the larger property has been recovered (*E.A. Fisher*, FedCl, 2008-2 USTC ¶ 50,481, aff'd, per curiam, CA-FC, 2010-1 USTC ¶ 50,289).[3]

To determine the tax consequences of a sale or exchange, the following questions must be answered:

(1) What is the amount realized in the transaction (¶ 1703)?

(2) What is the taxpayer's adjusted basis in the property (¶ 1601—¶ 1697)?

(3) Is the gain or loss on the transaction recognized (¶ 1719—¶ 1734)?

(4) Do the capital gain and loss provisions apply (¶ 1735—¶ 1744)?

(5) Is any part of the gain attributable to depreciation recapture (¶ 1779)?

Installment Payments. When a nondealer sells real or personal property and part or all of the selling price is to be paid after the year of sale, the recognized gain must be reported on the installment method, unless the taxpayer elects otherwise (¶ 1801).

Rollover into SSBICs. Individuals and C corporations may elect to defer the recognition of capital gain from the sale of publicly traded securities that is invested in the stock of, or a partnership interest in, a specialized small business investment company (SSBIC). These rollovers are subject to cumulative limits (¶ 1909).

References are to Standard Federal Tax Reports; Tax Research Consultant; and Practical Tax Explanations.

[1] ¶ 29,220; SALES: 9,050; § 16,005, § 16,010

[2] ¶ 29,220; SALES: 9,052; § 16,015

[3] ¶ 5700.225; SALES: 36,404; § 16,105.15

Gain from Small Business Stock. A noncorporate seller's gain on the sale or exchange of qualified small business stock may qualify for two tax benefits. First, if the stock was issued after August 10, 1993 and the seller held it for more than five years, a percentage of the gain is generally excludable from gross income (¶ 1905). Second, a seller that held the stock for more than six months may elect to roll over the realized gain into other small business stock that is purchased during the 60-day period beginning on the date of sale (¶ 1907).

Virtual Currency. Convertible virtual currency, such as Bitcoin, that has an equivalent value in or acts as a substitute for real currency is property for federal tax purposes (¶ 785) (Notice 2014-21).[4] Thus, the sale or exchange of virtual currency results in gain or loss, which is capital in nature if the virtual currency was a capital asset in the hands of the seller. The basis of virtual currency that a taxpayer "mines" or receives as payment for goods or services is the fair market value of the virtual currency in U.S. dollars on the date of receipt.

Gift Taxes. A taxpayer who makes a gift of property on condition that the donee pay the resulting gift taxes realizes gain to the extent that the gift taxes paid by the donee exceed the donor's basis in the property (*V.P. Diedrich*, SCt, 82-1 USTC ¶ 9419).[5]

Insurance Company Demutualization. A mutual insurance company is demutualized when it converts into a stock company and issues cash and/or shares to its policyholders in exchange for their equity interests. The IRS has held that a policyholder has zero basis in the surrendered equity interest (Rev. Rul. 71-233), but some courts disagree, and instead treat demutualization proceeds as a return of capital.[6]

1703. Amount Realized. The amount realized on a sale or exchange of property is the total of monies received plus the fair market value of all other property or services received (Code Sec. 1001(b); *International Freighting Corp., Inc.*, CA-2, 43-1 USTC ¶ 9334).[7] Property with no readily determinable fair market value is generally equal in value to the property for which it was exchanged (*Philadelphia Park Amusement Co.*, CtCls, 54-2 USTC ¶ 9697).[8] The amount realized normally includes any liabilities from which the seller is relieved as a result of the sale or exchange (Reg. § 1.1001-2).[9]

The amount realized on the receipt of an annuity in exchange for property is the fair market value of the annuity contract at the time of the exchange. The entire gain or loss is recognized at the time of the exchange, regardless of the taxpayer's method of accounting (Prop. Reg. § 1.1001-1(j)).[10]

Gain or Loss from Sale of Residence

1705. Exclusion of Gain from Sale of Principal Residence. An individual may exclude from gross income up to $250,000 of gain ($500,000 for joint return filers and surviving spouses) realized on the sale or exchange of a principal residence (Code Sec. 121).[11] The individual (1) must meet ownership and use tests for at least two years during the five years preceding the sale or exchange (¶ 1707), and (2) must not have used the exclusion for a disposition during the two years preceding the sale or exchange. A partial or reduced exclusion may be available for taxpayers who do not meet these tests (¶ 1709).

Married Individuals. The maximum exclusion is $500,000 for married individuals filing jointly for the tax year of the sale or exchange if:

(1) either spouse meets the ownership test,

(2) both spouses meet the use test, and

(3) neither spouse excluded gain on a sale or exchange of a residence within the prior two years (Code Sec. 121(b)(2); Reg. § 1.121-2).[12]

References are to Standard Federal Tax Reports; Tax Research Consultant; and Practical Tax Explanations.

[4] ¶ 29,225.1038; SALES: 45,600; § 19,601

[5] ¶ 29,226.3062; SALES: 3,056.10; § 32,830.30

[6] ¶ 29,225.1726, ¶ 31,829.13; INDIV: 30,100

[7] ¶ 29,220, ¶ 29,225.1013; SALES: 9,100; § 16,401

[8] ¶ 29,225.1523; SALES: 9,104.10; § 16,405

[9] ¶ 29,223; SALES: 9,108; § 16,410

[10] ¶ 29,221D; SALES: 9,106; § 3,245.10

[11] ¶ 7260; REAL: 15,152; § 1,601

[12] ¶ 7260, ¶ 7262; REAL: 15,152.10; § 1,615.10

A married couple's exclusion is determined on an individual basis. For instance, if Spouse A is eligible for the exclusion, but Spouse B used the exclusion within the previous two years, Spouse A is entitled to a maximum exclusion of $250,000.

Surviving Spouse. A surviving spouse may use the full $500,000 exclusion if the sale occurs within two years after the other spouse's death and the spouses satisfied the three requirements listed above immediately before the death (Code Sec. 121(b)(4); Reg. § 1.121-4(a)).[13] A surviving spouse who does not remarry before the sale is treated as having owned and lived in the home for the same period as the deceased spouse (Code Sec. 121(d)(2)).

Example 1: Erik purchases and begins living in his home in 2005. On July 10, 2015, he marries Helen and she moves into his home. Erik dies on March 3, 2016, and Helen inherits the home. On June 1, 2016, Helen, who has not remarried, sells the home. Helen satisfies the ownership and use tests because she can include the time that Erik owned and used the home.

Gain Allocable to Nonqualified Use. Gain that is allocable to periods of nonqualified use may not be excluded from gross income (Code Sec. 121(b)(5)).[14] Nonqualified use is generally any use other than as a principal residence; thus, this rule significantly limits the exclusion for second homes and vacation homes. However, a period of nonqualified use does not include: (1) any portion of the five-year period ending on the date of the sale that is after the last date the home was used as the taxpayer's principal residence; (2) any period of 10 years or less when the taxpayer or the taxpayer's spouse is serving on qualified official extended duty as a member of the U.S. uniformed services or U.S. Foreign Service, or an employee of the intelligence community; or (3) any period of two years or less for temporary absence due to a change of employment, health conditions, or other unforeseen circumstances.

Example 2: On January 1, 2016, Eleanor buys a residence for $400,000 and uses it as rental property for two years, claiming $20,000 of depreciation deductions. On January 1, 2018, she converts the property to her principal residence. She moves out on January 13, 2020, and sells the property for $700,000 on January 1, 2021. The portion of the gain attributable to the depreciation deductions ($20,000) is included in income (see "*Gain Recognized to Extent of Depreciation*," later). Of the remaining $300,000 gain, 40 percent (two years divided by five years), or $120,000, is allocated to nonqualified use and is not eligible for the exclusion. The period from January 14, 2020, to January 1, 2021, is after she last used the home as her primary residence, so it is not a period of nonqualified use. Thus, the remaining gain of $180,000 is excluded from Eleanor's gross income.

Like-Kind Exchanges. The exclusion does not apply to a home that was acquired in a like-kind exchange (¶ 1721) if the taxpayer (or any person whose basis in the property is derived from the taxpayer's basis) sells or exchanges the residence within five years after the acquisition (Code Sec. 121(d)(10)).[15]

Example 3: Wallace obtains a single family home in a like-kind exchange on September 1, 2011. After renting it out for 18 months, he begins using it as his principal residence on March 1, 2013. If Wallace sells the home before September 1, 2016, he cannot exclude any gain on the sale.

Gain Recognized to Extent of Depreciation. The exclusion of gain on the sale or exchange of a principal residence does not apply to the extent of any depreciation allowable with respect to the rental or business use of the residence after May 6, 1997 (Code Sec. 121(d)(6); Reg. § 1.121-1(d)(1)).[16] This rule applies to the amount of depreciation allowed if the taxpayer can establish that it was less than the amount allowable (Code Sec. 1250(b)(3)).[17]

Remainder Interests. The exclusion applies to gain on the sale or exchange of a remainder interest in a principal residence, provided the buyer is not a member of the

References are to Standard Federal Tax Reports; Tax Research Consultant; and Practical Tax Explanations.

[13] ¶ 7260, ¶ 7264; REAL: 15,152.10; § 1,615.15

[14] ¶ 7260; REAL: 15,152.05; § 1,615.20

[15] ¶ 7260; REAL: 15,160; § 1,640

[16] ¶ 7260, ¶ 7261; DEPR: 18,112; § 1,615.25

[17] ¶ 31,000; DEPR: 18,262.10; § 11,710

taxpayer's family or other related entity as defined by Code Secs. 267(b) or 707(b) (Code Sec. 121(d)(8)).[18] See ¶ 432 and ¶ 1717 for discussion of related persons.

Expatriates. The exclusion is not available to nonresident aliens who relinquish U.S. citizenship or long-term resident status and are subject to the mark-to-market rules for higher-income expatriates (¶ 2412) (Code Sec. 121(e)).[19]

Involuntary Conversions. For purposes of the exclusion, the destruction, theft, seizure, requisition, or condemnation of the property is a sale or exchange (Code Sec. 121(d)(5); Reg. § 1.121-4(d)).[20] In addition, the ownership and use of the replacement property generally includes the ownership and use of the converted property. For purposes of the involuntary conversions rules (¶ 1713), the amount realized on the conversion is reduced by the excluded gain.

Inherited Property. Estates, heirs and revocable trusts established by a decedent generally cannot exclude any gain on the sale of the decedent's principal residence. However, the exclusion can be used if the decedent died in 2010 and the estate elects to have the modified carryover basis rules apply (¶ 1633) (Code Sec. 121(d)(11), prior to repeal by the Tax Relief, Unemployment Insurance Reauthorization, and Job Creation Act of 2010 (P.L. 111-312); Act Sec. 301 of P.L. 111-312).[21]

Reporting Requirements. If all of the gain from the sale of a home is excludable, the sale does not have to be reported on the seller's tax return. If, however, the individual can exclude only some of the gain or receives a Form 1099-S, the sale or exchange is reported on Form 8949. If the home is sold under the installment method and gain is recognized (¶ 1801), the sale is reported on Form 6252. Sale of the business or rental portion of the property (¶ 1707) may have to be reported on Form 4797.

1707. Ownership and Use Requirements. An individual may exclude gain on the sale or exchange of a principal residence (¶ 1705) if, during the five-year period that ends on the date of the sale or exchange, the individual owned and used the property as a principal residence for periods aggregating two years or more (at least 730 days (365 × 2)) (Code Sec. 121(a); Reg. § 1.121-1(c)).[22] The seller may meet the ownership and use tests during nonconcurrent periods, as long as both tests are satisfied during the five years preceding the sale. A reduced exclusion may be available for owners who do not meet the ownership and use requirements, or who used the exclusion for a disposition that occurred within two years before the sale or exchange (¶ 1709).

The home or dwelling unit does not have to be the taxpayer's principal residence at the time it was purchased or sold. Although a principal residence may include the surrounding land, the exclusion applies only if the home itself satisfies the ownership and use tests (*D.A Gates*, 135 TC 1, Dec. 58,259).[23] Short temporary absences for vacations or seasonal absences are counted as periods of use, even if the taxpayer rents out the property during these periods. However, absence for an entire year is not considered a short temporary absence.

Divorce. If the residence is transferred to the transferor's spouse (or former spouse incident to divorce), the period the transferor owned the property is added to the period the transferee owns the property (Code Sec. 121(d)(3); Reg. § 1.121-4(b)).[24] Similarly, a homeowner is deemed to use the home as a principal residence during the time his or her spouse or former spouse has use of the home under a divorce or separation agreement.

Incapacity. A homeowner who becomes physically or mentally incapable of self-care is deemed to use the home as a principal residence while residing in a licensed care facility, such as a nursing home, as long as he or she owned and used the home as a principal residence for periods totalling at least one year during the five years preceding the sale or exchange (Code Sec. 121(d)(7)).[25]

References are to Standard Federal Tax Reports; Tax Research Consultant; and Practical Tax Explanations.

[18] ¶ 7260; REAL: 15,152.05; § 1,625.10

[19] ¶ 7260; REAL: 15,152.05; § 1,610.25

[20] ¶ 7260, ¶ 7264; REAL: 15,158; § 1,625.15

[21] ¶ 7260; REAL: 15,150; § 1,610.30

[22] ¶ 7260, ¶ 7261; REAL: 15,156; § 1,610.05

[23] ¶ 7266.72; REAL: 15,156.10; § 1,610.05

[24] ¶ 7260, ¶ 7264; REAL: 15,152.10; § 1,610.10

[25] ¶ 7260; REAL: 15,156.10; § 1,610.15

Military, Foreign Service, Peace Corps, and Intelligence Personnel. A homeowner may elect to suspend the running of the five-year ownership and use period for up to 10 years while the homeowner (or spouse) serves on qualified official extended duty as a member of the U.S. uniformed services or U.S. Foreign Service, or an employee of the intelligence community; or serves outside the United States as a Peace Corps employee on qualified official extended duty or as a Peace Corps enrolled volunteer or volunteer leader (Code Sec. 121(d)(9) and (12); Reg. § 1.121-5).[26] The taxpayer makes the election by not including the gain in gross income on the tax return filed for the year of the sale. The election may be made for only one property, but it may be revoked at any time.

Qualified official extended duty is any extended duty while serving at a duty station that is at least 50 miles from the principal residence or while residing in government quarters under government orders (Code Sec. 121(d)(9)(C)). Extended duty is any period of active duty due to a call or order for more than 90 days or for an indefinite time.

Allocation for Partial Use. The exclusion does not apply to any gain that is allocable to any portion of the property that is separate from the actual residence (the dwelling unit) and not used as a residence (Reg. § 1.121-1(e)).[27] The sale is treated as a sale of two properties: the dwelling unit and the nonresidential property. Basis and the amount realized must be allocated under the same method used to determine depreciation adjustments. The IRS has provided a number of examples to illustrate the allocation rules in various situations.

However, if part of the dwelling unit itself was used for a business, such as a home office, or to produce rental income, these rules do not apply. Instead, the seller must recognize gain to recapture depreciation (¶ 1705).

> **Example:** Bob meets the ownership and use tests to exclude the $30,000 in gain that he realizes on the sale of his home. However, he had previously claimed $500 in depreciation on his home office. Because the business office was part of his home (not separate from it), he does not have to allocate the basis and amount realized between the business and residential portions of the property. In addition, he does not have to report any part of the gain on Form 4797. Bob reports his gain, exclusion, and taxable gain of $500 on Form 8949.

Trusts and Single-Owner Entities. An individual is treated as owning a residence while (1) it is owned by a grantor trust (¶ 571) and the individual is treated as the owner of the trust or the portion of the trust that includes the residence, or (2) it is owned by the individual's single-member disregarded entity (¶ 402A) (Reg. § 1.121-1(c)(3)).[28]

Co-ops. A taxpayer who owns stock in a cooperative housing corporation as a tenant-stockholder (¶ 1040) may be able to exclude gain on the sale or exchange of the stock if, during the five-year period ending on the date of sale or exchange, the taxpayer owned the stock for at least two years and lived in the house or apartment as a principal residence for at least two years (Code Sec. 121(d)(4); Reg. § 1.121-4(c)).[29]

1709. Reduced Exclusion of Gain from Sale of Principal Residence. The maximum exclusion of gain on the sale of a principal residence (¶ 1705) is available only if the homeowner satisfies ownership and use requirements (¶ 1707) and has not used the exclusion for a sale within the previous two years. However, a reduced exclusion is available when a seller does not meet these tests if, based on the facts and circumstances, the primary reason for the sale is a qualified individual's change in place of employment, health reasons, or unforeseen circumstances (Code Sec. 121(c); Reg. § 1.121-3).[30] A qualified individual is the taxpayer, the taxpayer's spouse, a co-owner of the residence, or a person whose principal place of abode is in the same household as the taxpayer.

References are to Standard Federal Tax Reports; Tax Research Consultant; and Practical Tax Explanations.

[26] ¶ 7260, ¶ 7265; REAL: 15,156.15; § 1,610.20

[27] ¶ 7261; REAL: 15,156.20; § 1,610.35

[28] ¶ 7261; REAL: 15,156.05; § 1,610.25

[29] ¶ 7260, ¶ 7264; REAL: 9,304, REAL: 15,156.05; § 1,610.25

[30] ¶ 7260, ¶ 7263; REAL: 15,166; § 1,620.05

The IRS considers all the facts and circumstances when determining whether the primary-reason test is satisfied, including: (1) the circumstances giving rise to the sale; (2) the taxpayer's financial ability to maintain the property; (3) material changes that impact the suitability of the property as the taxpayer's residence; and (4) the taxpayer's use of the property as a residence during the ownership period (Reg. § 1.121-3(b)). Safe harbors are also available.

Change in Place of Employment. The primary reason test is satisfied if the sale or exchange is due to a change in the location of a qualified individual's employment (Reg. § 1.121-3(c)). The safe harbor applies if the new place of employment is at least 50 miles farther from the residence sold or exchanged than was the former place of employment; or, if there was no former place of employment, the new place of employment is at least 50 miles away from the residence sold or exchanged. Employment includes beginning a job with a new employer, continuing a job with an existing employer, or beginning or continuing self-employment.

Health. The primary reason test is satisfied if the reason for the sale or exchange is to obtain, provide, or facilitate the diagnosis, cure, mitigation, or treatment of a qualified individual's disease, illness, or injury; or to obtain or provide medical or personal care for a qualified individual suffering from a disease, illness, or injury (Reg. § 1.121-3(d)). For this purpose, a qualified individual includes a qualified individual's child, sibling, parent, niece, nephew, or in-law, and a descendant of the taxpayer's grandparent. A sale or exchange that is merely beneficial to the individual's general health does not qualify. The safe harbor applies if a physician recommends a change of homes for health reasons (Reg. § 1.121-3(f)).

Unforeseen Circumstances. The primary reason test is satisfied if the sale or exchange is due to an event that the taxpayer could not reasonably have anticipated before buying and occupying the residence (Reg. § 1.121-3(e)). A sale or exchange to move to a preferred home or to improve financial position does not qualify. The safe harbor applies in the following situations:

- involuntary conversion of the home (¶ 1713);
- damage to the home from natural or man-made disasters or acts of war or terrorism;
- a qualified individual's:
  - — death,
  - — loss of employment that qualifies for unemployment compensation,
  - — change in employment status resulting in the taxpayer's inability to pay housing costs and reasonable basic living expenses,
  - — divorce or legal separation, or
  - — multiple births resulting from a single pregnancy; and
- other events that the IRS designates as safe harbors.

Computing the Reduced Exclusion. The reduced exclusion is computed by multiplying the maximum allowable exclusion ($250,000 or $500,000) by a fraction (Reg. § 1.121-3(g)). The numerator is the shortest of (a) the period that the taxpayer owned the property during the five-year period ending on the sale or exchange date; (b) the period that the taxpayer used the property as a principal residence during the five-year period ending on the sale or exchange date; or (c) the period between the current sale and the sale for which the taxpayer last used the exclusion. The denominator of the fraction is either 730 days or 24 months, depending on the whether the numerator is expressed in days or months.

Example 1: Al is an unmarried taxpayer who owns and occupies his principal residence for 12 months. He sells the home after an accident leaves him unable to care for himself. He did not exclude gain from the sale of a residence within the prior two years. He may exclude up to $125,000 of any gain that he realizes from the sale ($250,000 maximum exclusion × 12/24 = $125,000).

Example 2: On September 1, 2015, Bill and Ruth Green purchase a townhouse in Boston for $450,000. Ten months later, Ruth accepts a job in Atlanta, and on July 1, 2016, the Greens sell the townhouse and move to Atlanta. They did not exclude gain from the sale of a residence within the prior two years. Because they owned and resided in the townhouse for 10 months, they may exclude up to $208,333 of their realized gain ($500,000 maximum exclusion × 10/24 = $208,333).

Involuntary Conversion

1713. Gain or Loss from Involuntary Conversion. An involuntary conversion occurs when (1) property is destroyed, stolen, seized, condemned, or disposed of under threatened or imminent condemnation; and (2) the taxpayer receives other property or money (usually insurance proceeds or a condemnation award) as compensation. To the extent the compensation exceeds the basis of the converted property, the taxpayer realizes gain (¶ 1701).

In two circumstances, however, the taxpayer does not have to recognize gain on a conversion (Code Sec. 1033; Reg. § § 1.1033(a)-1, 1.1033(a)-2):[31]

- When property is converted involuntarily or by compulsion into other property that is similar or related in service or use, no gain is currently recognized. The basis of the old property is transferred to the new property (¶ 1687). This nonrecognition rule is mandatory.

- When property is involuntarily converted into money or property that is not similar or related to the converted property in service or use, the owner may elect to postpone recognizing gain that is invested in replacement property within the replacement period (¶ 1715). Thus, an electing taxpayer recognizes gain on the conversion only to the extent that the amount realized exceeds the cost of the replacement property. A taxpayer elects to defer the reinvested gain by simply excluding it from gross income on the tax return for the tax year in which it is realized, and providing details of the involuntary conversion in a statement attached to the return (see "*Reporting Requirements,*" later).

Loss. Loss from an involuntary conversion is deductible if the converted property was used in a business or for the production of income (¶ 1101). Some casualty or theft losses on personal property may also be deductible (¶ 1121 and ¶ 1123). Some gains and losses from involuntary conversions may be treated as capital gains and losses (¶ 1748).

Residence. An individual whose principal residence is involuntarily converted may be able to exclude up to $250,000 of the realized gain ($500,000 for joint return filers and surviving spouses) as if the home had been sold (¶ 1705) (Code Sec. 121(d)(5)).[32] Nonexcludable gain may be deferred if it is used to purchase replacement property. The sale of the underlying land within a reasonable period of time following the destruction of a principal residence can qualify as part of the involuntary conversion of the residence (Rev. Rul. 96-32).[33]

Livestock. Livestock is involuntarily converted if it is destroyed, sold or exchanged because of disease (Code Sec. 1033(d); Reg. § 1.1033(d)-1).[34] A sale or exchange of livestock (except poultry) that is made solely on account of drought, flood, or other weather-related conditions may also qualify as an involuntary conversion to the extent it exceeds the number that would normally be sold (Code Sec. 1033(e); Reg. § 1.1033(e)-1).[35] The generally applicable two-year period for purchasing replacement property is extended to four years when the weather-related condition makes the area eligible for assistance from the federal government. The IRS can further extend the replacement period if the weather-related condition continues for more than three years. For instance, the replacement period for livestock that is involuntarily converted due to persistent drought in the taxpayer's region is extended until the end of the taxpayer's first tax year ending after the region's first drought-free year (Notice 2006-82). Each

References are to Standard Federal Tax Reports; Tax Research Consultant; and Practical Tax Explanations.

[31] ¶ 29,640, ¶ 29,641, ¶ 29,642; SALES: 27,050; § 18,101

[32] ¶ 7260; REAL: 15,158, SALES: 27,104; § 1,625.15

[33] ¶ 29,650.508; SALES: 27,104; § 18,140.10

[34] ¶ 29,640, ¶ 29,646; FARM: 3,206; § 18,115

[35] ¶ 29,640, ¶ 29,647; FARM: 3,206; § 36,015.10

year, the IRS publishes a list of the counties that suffered droughts sufficient to extend the replacement period (Notice 2016-60).[36]

If, due to drought, flood, other weather-related conditions, or soil or other environmental contamination, it is not feasible for a farmer to reinvest the proceeds from involuntarily converted livestock in property that is similar or related in service or use, the proceeds may be invested in other property used for farming (Code Sec. 1033(f)).[37] If the conversion was due to soil or other environmental contamination, even real property can qualify as replacement property.

Reporting Requirements. Form 4797 is used to report the gain or loss from an involuntary conversion (other than casualty or theft) of business property, as well as capital assets used in a business or in connection with a transaction entered into for profit. Form 4684 is used to report involuntary conversions from casualties and thefts. Gains from involuntary conversions (other than casualty or theft) of capital assets not held for business or profit are reported by individuals, estates, and trusts on Form 8949.

A separate statement that reports all details connected to the involuntary conversion must be attached to the tax return for the year in which gain is realized (Reg. § 1.1033(a)-2(c)(2)).[38] These details include a description of the property, the date and type of conversion, computation of the gain, the decision to replace the converted property, and expiration of the replacement period. If the taxpayer elects to defer gain, but then decides not to replace the converted property, or fails to invest all of the deferred gain in replacement property during the replacement period, the taxpayer must recompute the tax liability in an amended return for the year(s) for which the election was made. If the taxpayer elects nonrecognition after filing the return and paying tax for the tax year(s) in which gain is realized but before the replacement period expires, the taxpayer should file a credit or refund claim for each year that gain was reported. The taxpayer must report all of the details of the replacement of converted property in the return for the year of replacement, even if no gain is realized in that year.

The IRS may assess a deficiency attributable to realized gain on an involuntary conversion within three years from the date the taxpayer notifies the IRS of the replacement of the converted property, an intention not to replace, or a failure to replace within the required period (Code Sec. 1033(a)(2)(C); Reg. § 1.1033(a)-2(c)(5)).

1715. Replacement Property. A taxpayer does not recognize gain on an involuntary conversion (¶ 1713) to the extent that the converted property is replaced with property that is similar or related in service or use (Code Sec. 1033(a)).[39] Thus, money or dissimilar property that is received for the converted property must be invested in qualifying replacement property within the replacement period. Gain that is not invested in replacement property must be recognized.

Replacement Property. Replacement property can be (1) other property similar or related in service or use to the property converted, or (2) stock with a controlling interest (at least 80-percent control) in a corporation owning such property. The taxpayer must actually purchase the property or stock; an enforceable contract to purchase is not sufficient.[40] If real property used in the taxpayer's trade or business (other than inventory or property held primarily for sale) or held for investment is condemned or disposed of under threat of condemnation, replacement property includes "like-kind" (¶ 1721) property that the taxpayer holds for productive use in trade or business or for investment (Code Sec. 1033(g); Reg. § 1.1033(g)-1).[41] The like-kind test does not apply to acquisitions of 80-percent control of a corporation owning such property or to involuntary conversions by fire, storm, or other casualty. A taxpayer may elect to treat an outdoor advertising display (billboard) as real property as long as the display was not subject to a Code Sec. 179 expense election (¶ 1208).

References are to Standard Federal Tax Reports; Tax Research Consultant; and Practical Tax Explanations.

[36] ¶ 29,650.127; FARM: 3,206; § 36,015.10

[37] ¶ 29,640; SALES: 27,160; § 18,130

[38] ¶ 29,642; SALES: 27,200; § 18,160

[39] ¶ 29,640; SALES: 27,150; § 18,125, § 18,135.05

[40] ¶ 29,650.204; SALES: 27,152; § 18,125

[41] ¶ 29,640, ¶ 29,648; SALES: 27,158; § 18,135.20

Basis of Replacement Property. If property is compulsorily or involuntarily converted directly into property that is similar or related in service or use, the basis of the acquired property is the same as the basis of the converted property (¶ 1687). If the taxpayer uses conversion proceeds to acquire the replacement property, the basis of the replacement property is its cost, decreased by any unrecognized gain. If the taxpayer purchases more than one piece of replacement property, the basis is allocated to the properties in proportion to their respective costs.

Property Acquired from Related Persons. Certain taxpayers cannot defer the recognition of gain on an involuntary conversion if the replacement property is acquired from a related person, unless the related person obtained the property from an unrelated person during the replacement period (Code Sec. 1033(i)).[42] See ¶ 432 and ¶ 1717 for discussion of related persons. The prohibition applies to a C corporation, a partnership if more than a 50 percent of its interest is owned by C corporations, and any other taxpayer who realizes gain of more than $100,000 during the year from involuntary conversions. If the property is owned by a partnership or S corporation, the $100,000 limitation applies to both the entity and each partner or shareholder.

Replacement Period. Purchase of the replacement property, or of 80-percent control of a corporation that owns such property, must be completed within a period that begins on the actual date of the destruction, condemnation, etc., or the date on which the threat or imminence of condemnation or requisition begins, whichever is earlier (Code Sec. 1033(a)(2)(B)).[43] The replacement period generally ends two years after the close of the first tax year in which any gain on the conversion is realized. The replacement period is three years for certain real property used in a trade or business or held for investment. The replacement period is four years for a principal residence (¶ 1705) in a federally declared disaster area, and for certain involuntarily converted livestock (¶ 1713). Taxpayers may also apply for an extension of the applicable time period (see "*Application for Extension,*" later).

Example: Laura has a $100,000 basis in a commercial building when it is destroyed by fire. She receives a $120,000 settlement from her insurance company, thus realizing a gain of $20,000. If she acquires a new building for the same use for $120,000 (or more) within the prescribed replacement period, she may elect not to recognize any gain on the involuntary conversion. If she elects nonrecognition and the replacement building costs only $110,000, she must recognize $10,000 of gain. Without her election, she must recognize the entire $20,000 gain.

Real Property. If business or investment real property (other than inventory) is condemned or disposed of under the threat of condemnation, the replacement period ends three years, rather than two years, after the close of the first tax year in which any of the gain is realized (Code Sec. 1033(g)(4)).[44]

Principal Residence in Federal Disaster Area. Special rules apply to a principal residence, including its contents, that is located in a disaster area and is involuntarily converted as the result of a federally declared disaster (Code Sec. 1033(h)(1)).[45] Generally, insurance proceeds for the residence and its scheduled contents are treated as a common pool of funds received for the conversion of a single item of property. The taxpayer recognizes gain only to the extent that this pool of funds exceeds the cost of replacement property that is similar or related in service or use to the converted residence or its contents. No gain is recognized on insurance proceeds for unscheduled contents, regardless of how those funds are used (Rev. Rul. 95-22).[46]

The replacement period for a principal residence involuntarily converted as the result of a federally declared disaster is four years after the close of the first tax year in which any gain upon the conversion is realized (Code Sec. 1033(h)(1)(B)). For this purpose, a principal residence can include a home that the taxpayer does not own (Code Sec. 1033(h)(4)).

References are to Standard Federal Tax Reports; Tax Research Consultant; and Practical Tax Explanations.

[42] ¶ 29,640; SALES: 27,152.05; § 18,135.15

[43] ¶ 29,640; SALES: 27,164; § 18,135.05

[44] ¶ 29,640; SALES: 27,164; § 18,135.20

[45] ¶ 29,640; SALES: 27,066; § 18,140.10

[46] ¶ 29,650.317; SALES: 27,066; § 18,140.10

Business or Investment Property in Federal Disaster Area. Business or investment property that is located in a disaster area and is compulsorily or involuntarily converted as a result of a federally declared disaster may be replaced by tangible property held for productive use in a trade or business, even if it is not similar or related in service or use (Code Sec. 1033(h)(2)).[47] The replacement period is generally two years.

Application for Extension. The IRS may extend the replacement period upon a written application submitted to the Internal Revenue Center where the taxpayer's return is filed (Code Sec. 1033(a)(2)(B); Reg. § 1.1033(a)-2(c)(3)).[48] The IRS does *not* provide a form for extension requests. The application should explain in detail why the taxpayer is unable to replace the converted property within the replacement period. It should be filed before the statutory replacement period expires, but the IRS may accept a late request if it is made within a reasonable period of time after the replacement period expires and there is reasonable cause for the untimely filing. The IRS may grant an extension if the replacement property is being built during the replacement period, but it will not grant an extension based on the scarcity or high price of replacement property (Rev. Rul. 60-69).[49]

1716. Condemnation Award. If only a portion of a tract of land is appropriated by a government authority, the condemnation award may have two components: (1) compensation for the converted portion; and (2) severance damages for the retained portion. Severance damages may be paid, for example, when access to the owner's land is impaired, or because the owner must replace fences and plant trees to restore the retained property to its former use. The entire award is considered compensation for the condemned property unless both parties stipulate that a specific amount was paid for severance damages (Rev. Rul. 59-173).[50] The owner's net severance damages (gross severance damages minus legal expenses and other costs) reduce the basis of the retained property. Any excess of the severance damages over the owner's basis is gain (Rev. Rul. 68-37). However, the owner may elect not to recognize gain that is reinvested in replacement property (¶ 1715) (Rev. Rul. 83-49).

Transactions Between Related Persons

1717. Losses Not Allowed in Transactions Between Related Persons. A loss from a sale or exchange is generally not recognized when the parties to the transaction are related persons (Code Sec. 267(a); Reg. § 1.267(a)-1).[51] However, a loss might be recognized when the buyer subsequently sells or exchanges the property at a gain.

Related Persons. Related persons include:

(1) An individual and members of his or her family (spouse, plus brothers, sisters, ancestors, and lineal descendants);

(2) An individual and a corporation if the individual owns (directly or indirectly) more than 50 percent in value of the outstanding stock;

(3) Corporations that are members of the same controlled group;

(4) A grantor and a fiduciary of the same trust;

(5) Fiduciaries of different trusts with the same grantor;

(6) A fiduciary and a beneficiary of the same trust;

(7) A fiduciary and a beneficiary of different trusts with the same grantor;

(8) A trust fiduciary and a corporation, if more than 50 percent in value of the outstanding stock is directly or indirectly owned by or for the trust or its grantor;

(9) An exempt charitable or educational organization and a person who controls it (including an individual's family members);

References are to Standard Federal Tax Reports; Tax Research Consultant; and Practical Tax Explanations.

[47] ¶ 29,640; SALES: 27,066; § 18,140.15

[48] ¶ 29,640, ¶ 29,642; SALES: 27,164; § 18,135.05

[49] ¶ 29,650.202; SALES: 27,164; § 18,135.05

[50] ¶ 29,650.504; SALES: 27,106, § 18,105

[51] ¶ 14,150, ¶ 14,151; SALES: 39,100; § 17,601

(10) A corporation and a partnership if the same persons own more than 50 percent in value of the outstanding stock of the corporation, and more than 50 percent of the capital interest or profits interest in the partnership;

(11) S corporations if the same persons own more than 50 percent in value of the outstanding stock of each corporation;

(12) An S corporation and a C corporation if the same persons own more than 50 percent in value of the outstanding stock of each corporation; and

(13) An executor and a beneficiary of the same estate, unless the sale or exchange satisfies a pecuniary bequest (Code Sec. 267(b); Reg. § 1.267(b)-1).[52]

Stock Ownership. In determining stock ownership: (1) stock held by a corporation, partnership, estate, or trust is considered owned proportionately by its shareholders, partners, or beneficiaries; and (2) an individual is considered to own stock owned by his or her family members (as defined previously) and partners (Code Sec. 267(c)).[53]

Previously Disallowed Loss. The related transferee's gain on a subsequent disposal of the property is generally reduced (but not below zero) by the amount of any loss that was denied to the original transferor because of the related-person rules. However, a transferor's unrecognized loss on a sale or exchange with a related person after December 31, 2015, does not reduce the transferee's gain on a subsequent disposition if the loss (if allowed) would not have been considered in calculating the transferor's income tax, or any tax computed like an income tax (Code Sec. 267(d), as amended by the Protecting Americans from Tax Hikes (PATH) Act of 2015 (P.L. 114-113)).[54]

Example : Asa sells business property with a $15,000 basis to his son, Ben, for $5,000. Asa's $10,000 realized loss is not deductible because he sold the property to a related person. Later, Ben sells the property for $18,000 to an unrelated person. Ben's realized gain is $13,000 ($18,000 minus $5,000). However, he recognizes only $3,000 ($13,000 realized gain minus Asa's $10,000 unrecognized loss).

Tax-Free Exchanges

1719. Gain or Loss from Exchange of Property. Gain from an exchange of property generally must be recognized (Code Sec. 1001(c)).[55] Some types of exchanges, however, do not result in recognized gain or deductible loss. These include like-kind exchanges (¶ 1721—¶ 1723); exchanges of insurance or annuity contracts (¶ 1724), mortgaged real estate (¶ 1725), or government obligations (¶ 1726); stock exchanged for stock in the same corporation (¶ 1728) or for property (¶ 1729); transfers of property to the transferor's controlled corporation (¶ 1731); exchanges by certain government employees to avoid conflicts of interest (¶ 1732); sales of stock to an employee stock ownership plan (¶ 1733); and transfers between spouses or former spouses (¶ 1734).

1721. Like-Kind Exchanges. No gain or loss is recognized on the exchange of property held for productive use in a trade or business or for investment if the property received is of a like kind and is held either for productive use in a business or for investment (Code Sec. 1031(a)(1); Reg. § 1.1031(a)-1).[56] This nonrecognition rule generally does not apply to stock in trade or other property held primarily for sale, stocks, bonds, notes, certificates of trust, beneficial interests, partnership interests, securities, evidences of indebtedness or interest, and choses in action (Code Sec. 1031(a)(2)).[57] However, stock in certain mutual ditch, reservoir, or irrigation companies can qualify as like-kind property if it is treated as real property or an interest in real property under applicable state law (Code Sec. 1031(i)).

The like-kind exchange rules also do not apply to exchanges of property the taxpayer uses for personal purposes, such as homes and family cars (IRS Pub. 544). However, a vacation home or other dwelling unit is generally treated as held for business purposes if (1) the taxpayer rented out the unit for at least two weeks in each of

References are to Standard Federal Tax Reports; Tax Research Consultant; and Practical Tax Explanations.

[52] ¶ 14,150, ¶ 14,153; SALES: 39,150; § 17,605.10

[53] ¶ 14,150; SALES: 39,154.25; § 17,605.15

[54] ¶ 14,150; ¶ 14,155; SALES: 39,110; § 17,605.20

[55] ¶ 29,220; SALES: 3,050; § 16,010

[56] ¶ 29,602, ¶ 29,603; SALES: 30,000; § 18,001, § 18,005.05

[57] ¶ 29,602; SALES: 30,120; § 18,010.05

the two years before the exchange, and rents out the property received for at least two weeks in each of the first two years after the exchange, and (2) the taxpayer's personal use of the units in those years is minimal (Rev. Proc. 2008-16).[58] The disposition of a home that was converted to business use may be both a like-kind exchange and a sale of a principal residence qualifying for an exclusion of gain (¶ 1705) (Rev. Proc. 2005-14).

Trade-in Arrangements. A like-kind exchange occurs when a taxpayer sells old trade or business equipment to a dealer and purchases new equipment of like kind from the same dealer in reciprocal and mutually dependent transactions, even though the parties execute separate contracts and treat the sale and purchase as unrelated transactions for recordkeeping purposes (Rev. Rul. 61-119).[59]

Related Persons. If property received in a like-kind exchange between certain controlled partnerships (¶ 432) or related persons (¶ 1717) is disposed of within two years after the last transfer involved in the exchange, the original exchange does not qualify for nonrecognition treatment (Code Sec. 1031(f)). The taxpayer takes the previously unrecognized gain or loss into account on the date of the subsequent disposition of the exchanged property by the taxpayer or the related party. The parties cannot circumvent this rule by using a qualified intermediary. The running of the two-year period may be suspended when the holder of the exchanged property has substantially diminished the risk of loss by the use of a put option (¶ 1921), short sale (¶ 1944), another person's right to acquire the property, or any other transaction (Code Sec. 1031(g)).[60] These related-person rules do not apply if the avoidance of federal income tax was not a principal purpose of the original exchange or the subsequent disposition, or if the disposition was due to the death of either related party or the compulsory or involuntary conversion of the property (¶ 1713) (Code Sec. 1031(f)(2)).

Like-Kind Property Defined. Properties are of like kind if they are of the same nature or character (Reg. § 1.1031(a)-1(b) and (c)).[61] All facts and circumstances are considered in determining whether properties are of like kind, including state law and federal tax law classifications. Federal income tax law determines whether the properties are of the same nature or character (CCA 201238027).[62]

Most exchanges of real property qualify as like-kind exchanges. However, real property located in the United States and real property located outside the United States are not like-kind (Code Sec. 1031(h)(1)).[63] Leaseholds with at least 30 years to run are generally like-kind to fee simple interests (Reg. § 1.1031(a)-1(c)).[64]

Personal properties are of like kind if they are of a like kind or class. Depreciable tangible personal properties are of a like class if they fall within the same general asset class or the same product class (Reg. § 1.1031(a)-2(b)).[65] Asset classes are those used for depreciation purposes, as set forth in Rev. Proc. 87-56 (¶ 1240). Product classes are established by the six-digit product codes of the North American Industrial Classification System (NAICS). Personal property that is predominantly used in the United States is not like-kind to personal property that is predominantly used outside of the United States (Code Sec. 1031(h)(2)).[66]

Intangible personal property and nondepreciable tangible personal property in a like kind exchange must be of like kind, because like classes are not provided for such properties (Reg. § 1.1031(a)-2(c)).[67] For example, a copyright on a novel is generally like-kind to a copyright on another novel, but not to a copyright on a song. The goodwill or going concern value of different businesses are not like-kind. Intangibles such as trademarks, trade names, mastheads and other customer-based intangibles that can be separately described and valued apart from goodwill can qualify as like-kind property.[68]

References are to Standard Federal Tax Reports; Tax Research Consultant; and Practical Tax Explanations.

[58] ¶ 29,608.2495; SALES: 30,200, § 18,005.10, § 18,060

[59] ¶ 29,608.1178; SALES: 30,312; § 18,015.20

[60] ¶ 29,602, ¶ 29,608.2493; SALES: 30,206; § 18,020

[61] ¶ 29,603; SALES: 30,100; § 18,005.15

[62] ¶ 29,608.1103; SALES: 30,100; § 18,005.15

[63] ¶ 29,602; SALES: 30,100; § 18,010.20

[64] ¶ 29,603; SALES: 30,110, § 18,005.15

[65] ¶ 29,606; SALES: 30,102; § 18,005.15

[66] ¶ 29,602; SALES: 30,102; § 18,010.20

[67] ¶ 29,606; SALES: 30,118; § 18,010.05

[68] ¶ 29,608.2654; SALES: 30,104; § 18,010.05

Substituted Basis. For the basis of property received in a like-kind exchange, see ¶ 1651.

Reporting. Like-kind exchanges are reported on Form 8824. If any gain is recognized because the taxpayer transferred and received more than one group of like-properties or boot (¶ 1723), then Schedule D (Form 1040) is used to report gains on capital assets not held for business or profit, Form 4797 is used to report gains on assets held for business or profit, or Form 6252 is used to report gain from an installment sale.

1722. Deferred Like-Kind Exchanges. A like-kind exchange (¶ 1721) may occur even if the replacement property is received after the relinquished property has been transferred, provided that identification and receipt requirements are satisfied (Code Sec. 1031(a)(3); Reg. § 1.1031(k)-1).[69] This type of transaction is known as a "Starker exchange." The replacement property must be (1) identified within 45 days after the relinquished property is transferred, and (2) received within 180 days of the transfer or, if earlier, by the due date (including extensions) of the income tax return for the tax year in which the relinquished property was transferred. The deadlines may be extended if the parties are affected by a federally declared disaster (Rev. Proc. 2007-56).[70] Property not in existence or still under construction may qualify as replacement property in a deferred exchange (Reg. § 1.1031(k)-1(e)).[71]

Identifying Replacement Property. The period for identifying replacement property begins on the date that the relinquished property is transferred and ends at midnight on the 45th day thereafter (Code Sec. 1031(a)(3)(A); Reg. § 1.1031(k)-1(b)(2)).[72] The replacement property must be unambiguously described and designated as replacement property in: (1) a written agreement covering the exchange that is signed by all parties before the end of the identification period; or (2) a written document signed by the taxpayer and hand delivered, mailed, telecopied, or otherwise sent before the end of the identification period to a person involved in the exchange (such as an intermediary, escrow agent, or title company) other than the taxpayer, the taxpayer's agent, or a related party (Reg. § 1.1031(k)-1(c)).[73] A street address or legal description adequately identifies most real property. A taxpayer may identify up to three replacement properties regardless of their fair market values, or any number of replacement properties whose aggregate value does not exceed 200 percent of the aggregate value of all relinquished properties.

Safe Harbors. The taxpayer may not actually or constructively receive cash or other property and then use the proceeds to buy the replacement property (Reg. § 1.1031(k)-1(f)). However, a party to a deferred like-kind exchange is not considered to be in actual or constructive receipt of money or other property if the transaction involves: (1) qualifying security or guarantee arrangements; (2) qualified escrow accounts or trusts; (3) a qualified intermediary; or (4) the transferor's entitlement to receive interest or a growth factor (Reg. § 1.1031(k)-1(g)).[74]

Parking Transactions. An additional safe harbor may apply to a "reverse-Starker exchange" or "parking transaction"—an exchange in which replacement property is acquired before the relinquished property is transferred (Rev. Proc. 2000-37, modified by Rev. Proc. 2004-51).[75] The replacement property is "parked" with a third party (the accommodation party) until it is transferred to the ultimate transferee in a simultaneous or deferred exchange. The parties use a qualified exchange accommodation arrangement (QEAA) in which a person other than the taxpayer or a disqualified person (persons related to or acting as agents for the taxpayer) holds title to the property. The combined time period that the relinquished and replacement properties are held in the QEAA cannot exceed 180 days. The IRS will not challenge the qualification of the replacement property or the relinquished property or the treatment of the exchange accommodation titleholder (EAT) as the beneficial owner of the property. The safe

References are to Standard Federal Tax Reports; Tax Research Consultant; and Practical Tax Explanations.

[69] ¶ 29,602, ¶ 29,619; SALES: 30,600; § 18,015.05

[70] ¶ 29,620.80; SALES: 36,102.30; § 18,015.30

[71] ¶ 29,619; SALES: 30,606; § 18,015.15

[72] ¶ 29,602, ¶ 29,619; SALES: 30,602; § 18,015.10

[73] ¶ 29,619; SALES: 30,602.10; § 18,015.10

[74] ¶ 29,619; SALES: 30,608, SALES: 30,610; § 18,035.05

[75] ¶ 29,620.10; SALES: 30,614; § 18,015.25

harbor is not available if the taxpayer owned the replacement property during the 180-day period ending on the date that title or other qualified indicia of ownership is transferred to the EAT.

Interest on Funds Held by Intermediaries. Escrow accounts, trusts, and funds used to facilitate deferred exchanges (exchange funds) are generally treated as loaned by the taxpayer to an exchange facilitator (Reg. § 1.468B-6).[76] An exchange facilitator is a qualified intermediary (QI), transferee, escrow holder, trustee or other party that holds exchange funds for a taxpayer in a deferred exchange under an escrow, trust or exchange agreement. Interest is imputed to the taxpayer under Code Sec. 7872 (¶ 795), unless the exchange facilitator pays sufficient interest. The exchange facilitator is deemed to receive the same amount as compensation for its services, and has an offsetting deduction for its interest "payment" to the taxpayer. The exchange facilitator must take into account all items of income, deduction, and credit attributable to the exchange fund. Exchange funds include relinquished property, cash, or cash equivalents held in an escrow account, trust, or fund to secure the transferee's obligation to transfer replacement property or the proceeds from a transfer of the relinquished property. Exchange funds are not treated as loans if the escrow agreement, trust agreement, or exchange agreement specifies that the earnings attributable to the exchange funds are payable to the taxpayer; however, the taxpayer must take into account all items of income, deduction, and credit attributable to the exchange funds.

Safe Harbor for Bankrupt Qualified Intermediaries. The IRS has provided a safe harbor method for reporting gain or loss for a taxpayer undertaking a deferred like-kind exchange if the qualified intermediary defaults on its obligations (Rev. Proc. 2010-14).[77] Taxpayers are generally allowed to avoid recognition of gain until payment is received.

Direct Deeding of Property. An exchange of real property involving three parties—the taxpayer, a qualified intermediary, and a third party that supplies the replacement property—may qualify as like kind even if the third party deeds the replacement property directly to the taxpayer (Rev. Rul. 90-34).[78] Therefore, it is not necessary for the transferee to take title to the replacement property and then transfer title to the taxpayer.

1723. Cash or Other Property Received in a Like-Kind Exchange. If money or property not of a like kind (commonly referred as to "boot") is received by a taxpayer as part of a like-kind exchange (¶ 1721), the taxpayer recognizes gain from the transaction to the extent of the boot's fair market value (Code Sec. 1031(b); Reg. § 1.1031(b)-1).[79] A taxpayer who receives boot cannot deduct any loss on the exchange (Code Sec. 1031(c); Reg. § 1.1031(c)-1).[80] Boot may consist of cash, relief from indebtedness (¶ 1725), property that is not like kind to the property being exchanged, or property excluded from like-kind treatment. Boot is often given to equalize the value of the like-kind properties being exchanged.

> **Example:** Bill exchanges real estate, with a basis of $10,000, for real estate with a fair market value of $12,000 and $4,000 in cash. His *realized* gain of $6,000 ($16,000 received minus $10,000 basis) is *recognized* only to the extent of the $4,000 cash he receives. His basis for the replacement property is $10,000 ($10,000 basis in old property, minus $4,000 cash received, plus $4,000 recognized gain).

See ¶ 1728 for situations involving stock exchanged for stock in the same corporation, and ¶ 1731 for discussion of the tax-free transfer of property to a controlled corporation.

1724. Exchange of Insurance or Annuity Contracts. A life insurance, endowment, annuity, or qualified long-term care insurance policy is considered property for federal tax purposes, so any gain or loss realized on a sale or exchange of the policy is ordinarily taxable. However, no gain or loss results from an exchange of:

References are to Standard Federal Tax Reports; Tax Research Consultant; and Practical Tax Explanations.

[76] ¶ 21,950H; ACCTNG: 12,222; § 18,035.15

[77] ¶ 29,621.75; SALES: 30,610.15; § 18,035.20

[78] ¶ 29,621.30; SALES: 30,510

[79] ¶ 29,602, ¶ 29,609; SALES: 30,250; § 18,030

[80] ¶ 29,602, ¶ 29,611; SALES: 30,250; § 18,030

- a life insurance contract for another life insurance contract or an endowment, annuity, or qualified long-term care insurance contract;

- an endowment contract for another endowment contract that provides for regular payment beginning at a date no later than the date payments would have begun under the contract exchanged, or for an annuity or long-term care insurance contract;

- an annuity contract for another annuity contract that is payable over the life of the same annuitant, or for a qualified long-term care insurance contract; or

- a qualified long-term care insurance contract for another qualified long-term care insurance contract (Code Sec. 1035; Reg. § 1.1035-1).[81]

Gain or loss may be recognized if the exchange has the effect of transferring property to any person other than a United States person. Policyholders who surrender life insurance or annuity contracts of a financially troubled insurance company may qualify for nonrecognition treatment if, within 60 days, all cash received is reinvested in another policy or contract issued by another insurance company or in a single custodial account (Rev. Proc. 92-44; Rev. Proc. 92-44A).[82]

A partial exchange of the cash surrender value of an existing annuity contract for a second annuity contract is a tax-free exchange only if no amount, other than an amount received as an annuity for a period of 10 years or more or during one or more lives, is received during the 180 days beginning on the date of the transfer (Rev. Proc. 2011-38).[83] A subsequent direct transfer is not taken into account. These rules do not apply to partial annuitizations (¶ 817).

1725. Like-Kind Exchange of Mortgaged Real Estate. A taxpayer who relinquishes mortgaged real estate in a like-kind exchange (¶ 1721) receives boot (¶ 1723) equal to the amount of the mortgage from which the taxpayer is relieved (Code Sec. 1031(d); Reg. § § 1.1031(b)-1(c), 1.1031(d)-2).[84] If mortgaged property is exchanged for mortgaged property, the net reduction of the mortgage indebtedness is treated as boot. It is immaterial whether a mortgage is assumed by the purchaser or whether the property is acquired subject to a mortgage.

Example: Kathy's relinquished property has a fair market value of $100,000 and an adjusted basis of $75,000, and is subject to a $70,000 mortgage. Her replacement property has a fair market value of $60,000 and is subject to a $30,000 mortgage. Her entire realized gain must be recognized because it is less than the $40,000 net mortgage reduction:

Fair market value of property received	$60,000
Less mortgage on that property	30,000
	$30,000
Mortgage on property transferred by Kathy	70,000
Total consideration received	$100,000
Less basis of property transferred	75,000
Gain realized	$25,000

1726. Exchange of Government Obligations. Obligations issued by the United States may be exchanged tax-free for other such obligations, except to the extent that money is received in the exchange (Code Sec. 1037; Reg. § 1.1037-1).[85] Municipal or state bonds may be exchanged under a refunding agreement with no recognized gain or loss, provided that there are no material differences in the terms of the exchanged bonds (Rev. Rul. 81-169).[86]

References are to Standard Federal Tax Reports; Tax Research Consultant; and Practical Tax Explanations.

[81] ¶ 29,680, ¶ 29,681; INDIV: 30,502; § 3,250.10

[82] ¶ 29,682.30; INDIV: 30,502; § 3,250.10

[83] ¶ 29,682.108; INDIV: 30,502.10; § 3,250.10

[84] ¶ 29,602, ¶ 29,609, ¶ 29,614; SALES: 30,258; § 18,030

[85] ¶ 29,720, ¶ 29,721; SALES: 27,252; § 18,220

[86] ¶ 29,226.1117; SALES: 24,510

1728. Stock Exchanged for Stock of the Same Corporation. An exchange of common stock for common stock of the same corporation, or preferred stock for preferred stock of the same corporation, does not result in recognized gain or deductible loss (Code Sec. 1036; Reg. § 1.1036-1).[87] However, gain (but not loss) may be recognized if cash or other property (boot) is received (¶ 1723). Nonqualified preferred stock is not treated as stock for these purposes.

1729. Stock Exchanged for Property. A corporation does not recognize gain or loss upon the receipt of money or other property in exchange for its own stock, including treasury stock, regardless of the nature of the transaction or the facts and circumstances involved (Code Sec. 1032; Reg. § 1.1032-1).[88] The corporation may receive its own stock, as long as it is received in exchange for its own stock. A corporation also does not recognize gain or loss on the lapse or acquisition of an option, or with respect to a securities futures contract, to buy or sell its own stock, including treasury stock. See ¶ 736 for discussion of the nonrecognition of gain or loss when a corporation distributes its stock to shareholders.

1731. Tax-Free Transfer of Property to Controlled Corporation. No gain or loss is recognized if one or more persons (individuals, trusts or estates, partnerships, or corporations) transfer property to a corporation solely in exchange for its stock if, immediately after the transfer, the transferors are in control of the transferee corporation (Code Sec. 351; Reg. § 1.351-1).[89] See ¶ 203 for further discussion of tax-free contributions of property to a corporation in exchange for stock. See ¶ 1660 for discussion of the basis of the property transferred to the controlled corporation.

1732. Dispositions of Property to Avoid Conflicts of Interest. An officer or employee of the executive branch or a judicial officer of the federal government who sells property in order to comply with conflict-of-interest requirements may elect to recognize gain only to the extent that the amount realized is more than the adjusted basis of any permitted property that the taxpayer purchases during the 60-day period beginning on the sale date (Code Sec. 1043).[90] Permitted property includes any U.S. obligation or diversified investment fund approved by the Office of Government Ethics. The nonrecognized gain reduces basis in the permitted property. This option is also available to any spouse, minor, or dependent child whose ownership of property is attributable to the federal officer or employee under applicable conflict-of-interest laws. These deferral rules also apply to sales by a trustee if any person subject to the rules has a beneficial interest in the principal or income of the trust. Form 8824 is used to report conflict-of-interest sales.

1733. Tax-Free Sale of Stock to ESOP. Taxpayers (other than C corporations) may elect to sell qualified securities to an employee stock ownership plan (ESOP) (¶ 2103) or worker-owned cooperative and replace the securities with other securities without recognizing gain (Code Sec. 1042; Temp. Reg. § 1.1042-1T).[91] The taxpayer makes the election by attaching a statement to its original or amended return for the tax year of the sale.

1734. Transfers of Property Between Spouses or Former Spouses. No gain or loss is recognized on transfers of property from an individual to a spouse or to a former spouse incident to a divorce (Code Sec. 1041; Temp. Reg. § 1.1041-1T).[92] The transferor's basis in the transferred property carries over to the transferee. A transfer to a former spouse must occur within one year after the date on which the marriage ceased, or must be related to the cessation of the marriage. The nonrecognition rule does not apply if the transferee is a nonresident alien.

References are to Standard Federal Tax Reports; Tax Research Consultant; and Practical Tax Explanations.

[87] ¶ 29,700, ¶ 29,701; SALES: 27,300; § 18,215

[88] ¶ 29,622, ¶ 29,623; CCORP: 3,152; § 26,801

[89] ¶ 16,402, ¶ 16,403; CCORP: 3,050; § 26,110.05

[90] ¶ 29,840; SALES: 27,350; § 18,240

[91] ¶ 29,820, ¶ 29,821; RETIRE: 75,354.05; § 24,825.15

[92] ¶ 29,800, ¶ 29,801; INDIV: 21,050; § 18,230

Treatment of Capital Gain or Loss

1735. Characterization of Gain or Loss. Gain or loss on the disposition of property generally is recognized for federal income tax purposes (¶ 1701). The character of the gain or loss determines its tax treatment. Gain or loss on the sale or exchange of property that is not a capital asset is ordinary income or ordinary loss, respectively (Code Secs. 64 and 65).[93] Individuals, estates, and trusts may be eligible for lower tax rates on their net long-term gain from the sale of capital assets (¶ 1736). Whether a capital gain or loss is long-term or short-term depends on whether the taxpayer held the capital asset for at least one year (¶ 1737). Corporate taxpayers must include both net long-term and short-term capital gains in gross income (¶ 1738). Deductions for capital losses that exceed capital gains may be limited for all taxpayers (¶ 1752).

Capital gain or loss can arise only from a sale or exchange of a capital asset (¶ 1741 and ¶ 1742). Taxpayers must follow specific procedures in calculating their recognized capital gain or loss (¶ 1739). Special rules prevent taxpayers from converting all or a part of what would otherwise be capital gain into ordinary income (¶ 1740).

Reporting Requirements. Taxpayers report the details of their sales and other dispositions of capital assets on Form 8949, and then carry the relevant dollar amount totals to Schedule D of their tax returns.

1736. Tax on Capital Gains—Individual, Estate, Trust. For individuals, estates, and trusts, a number of different tax rates can apply to net capital gains for regular income tax and alternative minimum tax (AMT) purposes. The capital gains rate on net capital gains and qualified dividend income (¶ 733) for individuals is 20 percent for taxpayers in the 39.6-percent income tax bracket, 15 percent for the 25-, 28-, 33-, or 35-percent income tax brackets, and 0 percent for the 10- or 15-percent income tax brackets. For estates and trusts, the rate is 20 percent for the 39.6-percent income tax bracket, 15 percent for the 25-, 28-, or 33-percent income tax brackets, and 0 percent for the 15-percent income tax bracket (Code Sec. 1(h)(1)).[94] The capital gains tax rate is 25 percent for unrecaptured Code Sec. 1250 gain (¶ 1779), and 28 percent for gain on collectibles and qualified small business stock (¶ 1905).

To calculate net capital gain (or loss) for the tax year, a noncorporate taxpayer must first net short-term and long-term capital gains and losses for each of the rate groups separately (¶ 1739). Capital gain or loss is short- or long-term depending on how long the taxpayer held the property prior to its sale or other disposition (¶ 1737). Net capital gain that the taxpayer elects to treat as investment interest (¶ 1094) is subtracted from the total net capital gain that is subject to the maximum capital gains rate (Code Sec. 1(h)(2)).

Depreciable Real Estate. A 25-percent tax rate applies to long-term capital gain attributable to certain prior depreciation that was claimed on real property (Code Sec. 1(h)(1)(E) and (6)(A)).[95] This depreciation, known as "unrecaptured Section 1250 gain," is the excess of:

(1) long-term capital gain (not otherwise treated as ordinary income) that would be treated as ordinary income if Code Sec. 1250(b)(1) included all depreciation and the applicable percentage under Code Sec. 1250(a) were 100 percent, over

(2) the excess of 28-percent rate loss over 28-percent rate gain.

Even under these capital gains rules, Code Sec. 1250 still treats some prior claimed depreciation as ordinary income (¶ 1779) (usually the amount claimed in excess of the amount allowable under the straight-line method).

Example: William sells a building for $1 million, realizing a $600,000 gain. He bought the building for $700,000, and had claimed $300,000 in depreciation, including $100,000 that was in excess of that allowed under the straight-line method. Thus, $200,000 of the total claimed depreciation is unrecaptured Section 1250 gain, because if Code Sec. 1250 had applied to all depreciation rather than just

References are to Standard Federal Tax Reports; Tax Research Consultant; and Practical Tax Explanations.

[93] ¶ 6030, ¶ 6040; SALES: 15,050; § 16,020

[94] ¶ 3260; SALES: 15,200; § 16,525.10

[95] ¶ 3260; SALES: 15,202.70; § 16,525.10

additional depreciation, $300,000 of William's long-term capital gain would have been treated as ordinary income. The $100,000 in excess depreciation is taxed as ordinary income, the $200,000 in unrecaptured Section 1250 gain is subject to a capital gains rate of 25 percent, and the remaining $300,000 of gain is subject to regular capital gains rates.

Under MACRS, all depreciation on real property must be computed under the straight-line method (¶ 1780). As a result, any gain on the sale of MACRS real property that was held more than 12 months and that is due to claimed depreciation is unrecaptured Section 1250 gain and subject to a maximum capital gains rate of 25 percent.

Collectibles. Generally, gain on collectibles, such as stamps, antiques, gems, and most coins, is taxed at a 28-percent rate even if the seller held the collectible for more than 12 months (Code Sec. 1(h)(4)(A)(i) and (5)).[96]

Small Business Stock. Noncorporate taxpayers may exclude from gross income a certain percentage of capital gain from the sale or exchange of qualified small business stock issued after August 10, 1993 and held for more than five years (¶ 1905). This excluded capital gain is not used in computing the taxpayer's long-term capital gain or loss, and it is not investment income subject to the investment interest limitation. However, the capital gain that is not excluded (section 1202 gain) is taxed at the maximum 28-percent capital gains rate (Code Sec. 1(h)(4)(A)(ii) and (7)).[97]

Pass-Through Entities. A pass-through entity—including an S corporation, partnership, estate, trust, regulated investment company (mutual fund), and real estate investment trust (REIT)—allocates capital gains to its shareholders or beneficiaries (Code Sec. 1(h)(10)).[98] Capital gain distributions from a mutual fund are taxed as long-term capital gains regardless of how long the shareholder owned the fund shares (¶ 2311). If capital gain distributions are automatically reinvested in the fund, the reinvested amount is the basis of the additional shares (IRS Pub. 550).

1737. Holding Period for Capital Assets. The holding period for a capital asset (¶ 1741) is the length of time that the taxpayer owns the property before disposing of it. The tax treatment of recognized gain or loss (¶ 1736 and ¶ 1739, respectively) depends, in part, on whether the taxpayer's holding period is short-term or long-term. Long-term gain or loss arises from assets held for more than one year, while short-term gain or loss arises from assets held for one year or less (Code Secs. 1222 and 1223; Reg. § 1.1223-1).[99]

Calculating the Holding Period. When determining how long an asset was held, the taxpayer generally begins counting on the date after the day the property was acquired. The same date of each following month is the beginning of a new month regardless of the number of days in the preceding month (Rev. Rul. 66-7).[100] The date the asset is disposed of is part of the holding period. If an asset is acquired on the last day of a month, the first day on which it may be considered to have been held for more than one year is the first day of the *13th* calendar month following the calendar month of acquisition. However, there are special rules for assets acquired in a tax-free exchange, by gift or inheritance, or in an involuntary conversion.

Example: An asset acquired on March 31, 2015, must be held until April 1, 2016, to be held for more than one year.

Tax-Free Exchange. When property is received in a tax-free exchange (¶ 1719), the holding period of the property given up by the taxpayer is added ("tacked on") to the holding period of the property that the taxpayer receives (Code Sec. 1223).[101]

Gift. The holding period of property acquired by gift or transfer in trust includes the time the property was held by both the donor and the donee if, as is usually the case, the

References are to Standard Federal Tax Reports; Tax Research Consultant; and Practical Tax Explanations.

[96] ¶ 3260; SALES: 15,202.65; § 16,525.10

[97] ¶ 3260; SALES: 15,300; § 16,525.10

[98] ¶ 3260; SALES: 15,202.90; § 16,525.10

[99] ¶ 30,440, ¶ 30,460, ¶ 30,461; SALES: 15,150; § 16,540.05

[100] ¶ 30,463.3997, ¶ 30,463.4099; SALES: 15,152; § 16,540.05

[101] ¶ 30,460; SALES: 15,178; § 16,540.15

donee takes the donor's basis (Code Sec. 1223(2)).[102] However, when the fair market value at the time of the gift is used as the donee's basis (¶ 1630), the holding period starts the day after the gift was made (IRS Pub. 544).

Inherited. When property is acquired from a decedent, its basis in the hands of the heir or beneficiary is stepped up to its fair market value, and it is automatically deemed to have been held for more than one year (Code Sec. 1223(9)).[103] However, if the decedent died in 2010 and the executor elected to have the carryover basis rule (¶ 1633) rather than the estate tax apply, the taxpayer's holding period of the property is the same as the decedent's, whether or not the executor allocates any basis increase to the property (Rev. Proc. 2011-41).[104]

Involuntary Conversion. The holding period of involuntarily converted property (¶ 1713) is added to the holding period of qualified replacement property if the basis of the replacement property is determined by reference to the basis of the converted property (Code Sec. 1223(1)(A)).[105]

Stock. The holding period for stock and securities purchased on an exchange begins on the day following the purchase (the trade date), and ends on, and includes, the date of sale, rather than the day when payment is received and delivery is made (the settlement date) (Rev. Rul. 66-97; Rev. Rul. 93-84).[106] The holding period for stock received in a nontaxable stock distribution or in a "spin-off" includes the holding period of the related stock on which the distribution is made (Code Sec. 1223(1) and (4)).[107]

Options. When assets are acquired by the exercise of a purchase option, the holding period starts the day after the option is exercised.[108]

Partnership Property. A partner's holding period for property received in a partnership distribution includes the period the partnership held the property (Code Sec. 735(b)).[109]

Treasury Obligations. In determining the holding period of U.S. Treasury notes and bonds sold at auction on the basis of yield, the acquisition date is the date the Secretary of Treasury identifies the successful bidder in a news release (Rev. Rul. 78-5).[110] The acquisition date of U.S. Treasury notes sold through an offering on a subscription basis at a specified yield is the date the subscription is submitted.

1738. Corporate Capital Gains. A corporation must include both long-term and short-term capital gains in gross income to the extent they exceed capital losses for the year. Thus, a corporation's capital gains are generally taxed at ordinary corporate income tax rates (¶ 219). However, the maximum tax rate on corporate capital gains is effectively capped at 35 percent (Code Secs. 1201(a) and 1222(11)).[111]

See ¶ 1752 and ¶ 1756 for treatment of corporate capital losses.

1739. Netting of Gains and Losses. Noncorporate taxpayers must use netting procedures to calculate their recognized capital gain or loss for the tax year (Code Sec. 1(h)(1); Notice 97-59).[112] The gains and losses within each tax rate group are netted in order to arrive at a net gain or loss for the group. Generally, there are three tax rate groups—15 percent (20 percent for individuals, estates, and trusts in the 39.6-percent income tax bracket), 25 percent, and 28-percent (¶ 1736). After each group has been netted, the following ordering rules are applied:

References are to Standard Federal Tax Reports; Tax Research Consultant; and Practical Tax Explanations.

[102] ¶ 30,460; SALES: 15,178.05; § 16,540.25

[103] ¶ 30,460; SALES: 15,164; § 16,540.30

[104] ¶ 29,380.762; ESTGIFT: 51,060.10; § 16,310

[105] ¶ 30,460; SALES: 15,178.30; § 18,145.05

[106] ¶ 30,463.3746, ¶ 30,463.4383; SALES: 15,162; § 16,540.10

[107] ¶ 30,460; SALES: 15,178.25; § 16,540.10

[108] ¶ 30,463.4013; SALES: 15,154.05; § 16,540.10

[109] ¶ 25,400; SALES: 15,178.15; § 30,535.10

[110] ¶ 30,463.67; SALES: 15,162.45

[111] ¶ 30,352, ¶ 30,440; SALES: 15,210; § 16,527.10

[112] ¶ 3260, ¶ 3285.55; SALES: 15,206.15; § 16,525.05

• *Short-term capital gains and losses.* Short-term capital losses (including short-term capital loss carryovers (¶ 1754)) are applied first to reduce short-term capital gains, if any, that would otherwise be taxable at ordinary income tax rates. A net short-term loss is then used to reduce any net long-term capital gain from the 28-percent group. Any remaining short-term loss is then used to reduce gain from the 25-percent group, and then to reduce net gain from the 15-percent group (20-percent group for taxpayers in the 39.6-percent income tax bracket).

• *Long-term capital gains and losses.* A net loss from the 28-percent group (including long-term capital loss carryovers) is used first to reduce gain from the 25-percent group, then to reduce net gain from the 15-percent group (20-percent group for taxpayers in the 39.6-percent income tax bracket). A net loss from the 15-percent group (20-percent group) is used first to reduce net gain from the 28-percent group, and then to reduce gain from the 25-percent group.

1740. Gain from Conversion Transactions. Capital gain from the disposition or termination of a position that is part of a financial "conversion transaction" may be recharacterized as ordinary income (Code Sec. 1258).[113] A conversion transaction is generally a transaction in which a taxpayer's return on an investment is attributable to the time value of money, but appears to be attributable to market risk so that it seems to be capital gain rather than ordinary income, if (1) the taxpayer acquires property and on a substantially contemporaneous basis enters into a contract to sell it or substantially identical property at a predetermined price; (2) the transaction qualifies as a tax straddle (¶ 1948); (3) the transaction is marketed or sold as producing capital gains from a transaction in which the taxpayer's expected return is substantially from the time value of the net investment; or (4) the transaction is specified by the IRS in regulations.

The capital gain treated as ordinary income is generally equal to the interest that would have accrued on the taxpayer's net investment at a yield equal to 120 percent of the applicable federal rate (AFR) compounded semiannually (¶ 83), or 120 percent of the federal short-term rates compounded daily if the term of the conversion transaction is indefinite.

Example: Sam purchases stock on January 2, 2014, for $100 and agrees on the same day to sell it to Wendell on January 2, 2016, for $115. A portion of Sam's $15 gain from the sale of the stock equal to 120 percent of the AFR compounded semiannually for two years and applied to the $100 investment is recharacterized as ordinary income.

Transactions of options dealers and commodities traders in the normal course of their trade or business of dealing in options or trading section 1256 contracts (¶ 1947) are *not* conversion transactions (Code Sec. 1258(d)(5)).[114] This exception does not apply to certain gains allocated to limited partners and limited entrepreneurs as defined in Code Sec. 461(j)[k](4).

Constructive Ownership Transactions. The amount of long-term capital gains that a taxpayer may recognize from certain constructive ownership transactions that arise from specified financial assets may be limited (Code Sec. 1260).[115] These financial assets include any equity interest in a pass-through entity (a partnership, S corporation, regulated investment company (mutual fund), or real estate investment trust). The long-term gain is limited to the amount of gain that the taxpayer would have recognized if the taxpayer had directly held the financial asset during the term of the derivative contract. Any additional gain is recognized as ordinary income. Tax liability is increased by the amount of interest that would have accrued on the underpayment that would have arisen if the recharacterized ordinary income had been included in gross income.

1741. Capital Asset. A capital gain or loss arises from the sale or exchange of a capital asset. A capital asset is any property held by a taxpayer, whether or not connected with a trade or business (Code Sec. 1221; Reg. § 1.1221-1).[116] The following items, however, are *not* capital assets:

References are to Standard Federal Tax Reports; Tax Research Consultant; and Practical Tax Explanations.

[113] ¶ 31,125; SALES: 15,250

[114] ¶ 31,125; SALES: 15,252.25

[115] ¶ 31,140; SALES: 45,500

[116] ¶ 30,420, ¶ 30,421; SALES: 15,100; § 16,505.05

- stock in trade, inventory, and property held primarily for sale to customers in the ordinary course of the taxpayer's trade or business;
- a note or account receivable acquired in the ordinary course of trade or business for services rendered or from the sale of stock in trade or property held primarily for sale in the ordinary course of business;
- depreciable business property;
- real property used in the taxpayer's trade or business;
- a copyright, a literary, musical or artistic composition, a letter or memorandum, or similar property (but not a patent or invention) held by the taxpayer who created it, or by a taxpayer whose basis in the property is determined by reference to the basis of the person who created it, or in the case of a letter, memorandum or similar property, a taxpayer for whom such property was prepared or produced;
- a U.S. government publication (including the *Congressional Record*) held by a taxpayer who received it (or by another taxpayer whose basis in the publication is determined in whole or in part by reference to the original recipient's basis) other than by purchase at the price at which the publication is offered to the public;
- commodities derivative financial instruments held by commodities derivatives dealers;
- hedging transactions (¶ 1949) entered into in the normal course of the taxpayer's business; and
- supplies of a type regularly used or consumed by the taxpayer in the ordinary course of business.

Although creative works are generally not capital assets in the hands of their creators, a musical composition or a copyright in a musical work may be treated as a capital asset by a taxpayer whose personal efforts created it, or whose basis is determined by the reference to the creator's basis (Code Sec. 1221(b)(3); Reg. § 1.1221-3).[117] The taxpayer may elect capital gains treatment separately for each composition or copyright sold by reporting the transaction as a sale of a capital asset on Form 8949.

Personal Property. Gain from the sale of an individual's household furnishings, personal residence, or automobile is generally taxed under the capital gains rates. However, loss from the sale is not recognized unless the property was held for the production of income (¶ 1003 and ¶ 1101) (Reg. § 1.262-1(b)(4)).[118] For example, an individual who sells a residence that was partially used as rental property must allocate the original cost of the building, the selling price, depreciation (applicable to the rental portion only), and selling expenses between the personal and rental portions of the building as if there were two separate transactions (¶ 1707). Only the loss allocable to the rental portion of the home may be a capital loss. The gain or loss associated with the sale of a personal residence is discussed at ¶ 1103, ¶ 1626, and ¶ 1705.

Securities. Stock and securities generally are held for production of income so that a loss on their sale is a capital loss, except for a dealer who holds them for sale to customers (¶ 1903).[119] Gain or loss from the sale, exchange or termination of a securities futures contract may be eligible for capital gain treatment (Code Sec. 1234B).[120]

Noncapital Assets. The sale or exchange of noncapital assets results in ordinary income or loss. The definition of "capital asset" must be broadly interpreted, so a noncapital asset must come within one of the statutory categories of noncapital assets listed previously (*Arkansas Best Corp.*, SCt, 88-1 USTC ¶ 9210).[121] Ordinary income and loss treatment does not apply to an asset that is otherwise capital simply because it is acquired for business purposes. Therefore, bank stock that a holding company acquired to prevent damage to its own business reputation was a capital asset even though it was acquired for a business purpose, because the stock did not fall within any of the exclusion categories. In an earlier decision, the Supreme Court ruled that assets held as part of hedging transactions that were an integral part of a business's inventory-purchase system were noncapital assets because they were inventory (*Corn Products Refining*, SCt, 55-2 USTC ¶ 9746).[122]

References are to Standard Federal Tax Reports; Tax Research Consultant; and Practical Tax Explanations.

[117] ¶ 30,420, ¶ 30,425; SALES: 15,108.15; § 16,505.20

[118] ¶ 13,601; SALES: 15,206.05; § 8,201

[119] ¶ 30,422.684; SALES: 15,104.30; § 16,505.05

[120] ¶ 30,640; SALES: 45,550; § 18,845.10

[121] ¶ 30,422.6865; SALES: 15,118.05

[122] ¶ 30,426.15; SALES: 15,118.10

Special Rules. Special rules apply when the sale involves section 1231 property (¶ 1747), patents (¶ 1767), depreciable property (¶ 1779), farm property (¶ 1797), and partnership interests (¶ 434).

1742. Sale or Exchange Requirement. The capital gain and loss provisions (¶ 1735) apply to the sale or exchange of a capital asset (¶ 1741) (Code Sec. 1222; Reg. § 1.1222-1).[123] A sale or exchange of real estate occurs on the conveyance date or, if earlier, the date when the burden and benefits of ownership pass to the purchaser.[124] A sale or exchange occurs when there is a corporate liquidation (¶ 2253), when securities become worthless (¶ 1916), and upon any failure to exercise a privilege or option on property that would have been a capital asset if acquired (¶ 1919).

When bonds with past-due interest are purchased "flat" (that is, with none of the price allocated to the past-due interest), aggregate interest payments that are for the prepurchase period and are more than the purchase price but less than the face value of the bonds are capital gains, because they are considered to be amounts received on retirement of the bonds (Rev. Rul. 60-284).[125] The sale of an endowment insurance policy before its maturity or of a paid-up annuity contract before the annuity starting date results in ordinary income (*E.J. Arnfeld*, CtCls, 58-2 USTC ¶ 9692).[126]

1743. Sale of a Trade or Business. The sale of a trade or business is generally treated as if each asset of the business was sold separately (Rev. Rul. 55-79).[127] The purchase price must be allocated among the assets by the seller to determine the amount and character of any recognized gain or loss; and by the buyer to determine basis and allowable depreciation or amortization (Code Sec. 1060(a); Reg. § 1.1060-1(a)).[128] The buyer and seller may agree in writing to allocations of part or all of the consideration involved in the transaction and the fair market value of any assets transferred. The allocation is binding on both parties, unless the IRS determines that it is inappropriate (¶ 1620).

Reporting. The purchaser and the seller each must file Form 8594 to report the sale of assets used in a trade or business when the purchaser's basis in the assets is determined wholly by the amount paid. The form is attached to the tax return for the year in which the sale took place.

1744. Sale of Depreciable Assets Between Related Taxpayers. Capital gain treatment (¶ 1735) is denied when depreciable property (including patent applications) is sold or exchanged between related taxpayers (Code Sec. 1239; Reg. § 1.1239-1).[129] This rule applies to sales or exchanges between (a) a person and all entities that the person controls; (b) a taxpayer and any trust in which the taxpayer or the taxpayer's spouse has a beneficiary interest that is not a remote contingent interest; or (c) an executor and a beneficiary of the same estate, unless the sale or exchange is in satisfaction of a pecuniary bequest.

Entities that are controlled by a taxpayer include:

- a corporation if the taxpayer owns (directly or indirectly) more than 50 percent of the value of its stock;
- a partnership if the taxpayer owns (directly or indirectly) more than 50 percent of the capital or profits interest; and
- certain entities that are related persons with respect to the taxpayer, including two corporations that are members of the same controlled group, a corporation and a partnership if the same persons own more than 50 percent of each, and two S corporations, or an S corporation and a C corporation, if the same persons own more than 50 percent of the stock of each.

References are to Standard Federal Tax Reports; Tax Research Consultant; and Practical Tax Explanations.

[123] ¶ 30,440, ¶ 30,441; SALES: 15,050; § 16,520.05

[124] ¶ 21,005.8838; SALES: 3,110; § 16,540.10

[125] ¶ 5704.3075; SALES: 24,508; § 45,415.15

[126] ¶ 30,422.58; INDIV: 30,212, INDIV: 30,356; § 45,450.10

[127] ¶ 30,422.125; SALES: 33,050; § 18,401

[128] ¶ 30,060, ¶ 30,061; SALES: 33,052; § 18,401

[129] ¶ 30,730, ¶ 30,731; SALES: 39,200; § 17,615

Section 1231

1747. Section 1231 Property Used in Trade or Business. Business real estate and depreciable business property generally is not a capital asset (¶ 1741). However, if the business property is "section 1231 property," gain or loss realized from its sale, exchange, or involuntary conversion may qualify as capital gain or loss. Specifically, when section 1231 gains exceed section 1231 losses, all of the section 1231 gains and losses are generally treated as long-term capital gains and losses (¶ 1736) (Code Sec. 1231(a)).[130] On the other hand, if section 1231 losses exceed section 1231 gains, all of the section 1231 gains and losses are treated as ordinary income and losses. Taxpayers use Form 4797 to report the sale or exchange of section 1231 property.

Section 1231 Property. Section 1231 property includes:

- depreciable property used in the taxpayer's trade or business and held more than one year, other than property includible in inventory; property held primarily for sale to customers; a copyright, a literary, musical or artistic composition, or a letter, memorandum, or similar property; and certain federal government publications;
- real property used in the trade or business and held for more than one year, other than property that is includible in inventory or held primarily for sale to customers;
- trade or business property held for more than one year and compulsorily or involuntarily converted (¶ 1748);
- capital assets held for more than one year in connection with a trade or business or a transaction entered into for profit, and compulsorily or involuntarily converted;
- an unharvested crop on land used in the trade or business and held for more than one year, if the crop and land are sold, exchanged, or involuntarily converted at the same time to the same person;
- certain livestock, but not poultry (¶ 1750); and
- timber, domestic iron ore, and coal (¶ 1772) (Code Sec. 1231(b); Reg. §§ 1.1231-1 and 1.1231-2).[131]

When section 1231 property is subject to depreciation recapture, the section 1231 gain is the amount by which the total gain exceeds the amounts recaptured and taxed at ordinary income rates (¶ 1779). The recapture of certain farmland expenses may also reduce section 1231 gain (¶ 1797). A gain or loss that is disallowed by other rules, such as a loss on a sale between family members, is not taken into account in determining section 1231 gains and losses (Code Sec. 1231(a)(4); Reg. § 1.1231-1(d)).

Recapture of Net Section 1231 Losses. A taxpayer with a net section 1231 gain for the tax year (section 1231 gains that exceed section 1231 losses) must recapture past net section 1231 losses by treating the current year's net section 1231 gain as ordinary income to the extent of the unrecaptured net section 1231 losses for the five previous tax years (Code Sec. 1231(c)).[132] The losses are recaptured on a first-in, first-out (FIFO) basis (IRS Pub. 544).

Example: Mary has a net section 1231 gain of $23,000 for 2016. She had a net section 1231 loss of $12,000 in 2014 and a net section 1231 loss of $15,000 in 2015. For 2016, Mary must include her $23,000 net section 1231 gain as ordinary income in order to recapture her $12,000 loss from 2014 and $11,000 of her $15,000 loss from 2015. The $4,000 balance of her 2015 loss remains outstanding, and available for recapture if Mary realizes any net section 1231 gain during 2017-2020.

References are to Standard Federal Tax Reports; Tax Research Consultant; and Practical Tax Explanations.

[130] ¶ 30,572; SALES: 21,100; § 16,805

[131] ¶ 30,572, ¶ 30,573, ¶ 30,574; SALES: 21,100; § 16,805

[132] ¶ 30,572; SALES: 21,250; § 16,830

1748. Compulsory or Involuntary Conversion of Section 1231 Property. The capital gain and ordinary loss rules of Code Sec. 1231 (¶ 1747) can apply to gains and losses from the compulsory or involuntary conversion of section 1231 property unless the nonrecognition rules for involuntary conversions (¶ 1713) apply (Code Sec. 1231(a)(3)(A)(ii); Reg. § 1.1231-1(d)(4) and (e)).[133] Recognized gains and losses resulting from a theft, seizure, requisition, or condemnation are section 1231 gains or losses. When casualty or theft gains and losses result in a net loss, the transactions are not grouped with other section 1231 transactions. Instead, the net loss is an ordinary loss. Since personal assets (those not used in a trade or business or for investment) are not Section 1231 property, casualty and theft losses on personal assets are excluded from Code Sec. 1231. For taxation of personal casualty gains and losses, see ¶ 1129 and ¶ 1131.

1750. Livestock as Section 1231 Property. Capital gain and ordinary loss treatment under Code Sec. 1231 applies to the sale, exchange, or involuntary conversion of livestock (not including poultry) held for draft, breeding, dairy or sporting purposes (¶ 1747) (Code Sec. 1231(b)(3); Reg. § 1.1231-2).[134] Horses and cattle must be held for at least 24 months and all other livestock must be held for at least 12 months. The holding period begins on the date the animal is acquired rather than the date it is put to one of the prior uses. Livestock includes fur-bearing animals such as chinchillas, mink, and foxes.[135] For involuntary conversions of livestock due to disease or weather conditions, see ¶ 1713. For forced sales due to weather conditions, such as flood or drought, see ¶ 767.

1751. Canceled Leases and Distributor's Agreements. An amount received by a lessee for cancellation of a lease is treated as received in exchange for the lease. This rule also applies also to amounts that a distributor of goods receives for the cancellation of a distributor's agreement if the taxpayer has a substantial capital investment in the distributorship (Code Sec. 1241; Reg. § 1.1241-1).[136] If the lease or agreement is section 1231 property (¶ 1747), the taxpayer has a section 1231 gain or loss (Rev. Rul. 2007-37).[137]

Capital Loss Limitation, Carryover, Carryback

1752. Limitation on Capital Losses. To determine the deductibility of capital losses (¶ 1735), the taxpayer totals all capital gains and losses, both long term and short term, incurred during the year. Capital losses are deductible only to the extent of the capital gains plus, in the case of noncorporate taxpayers, up to $3,000 in ordinary income (Code Sec. 1211(b); Reg. § 1.1211-1(b)).[138] Thus, both net long-term capital losses and net short-term capital losses may be used to offset up to $3,000 of an individual's ordinary income ($1,500 for married individuals filing separate returns). There are special rules for married persons, whether filing joint or separate returns (¶ 1757). Unused losses are carried forward (¶ 1754).

> **Example:** Pat is a single individual with $30,000 of ordinary income, a net short-term capital loss of $3,500 a net long-term capital loss of $300, and no capital gain. Pat's capital loss deduction is limited to $3,000 for the current tax year. The remaining $800 is carried forward.

Corporations. A corporation may use capital losses to offset only capital gains and not ordinary income (Code Sec. 1211(a); Reg. § 1.1211-1(a)).[139] However, its capital losses may be carried back or carried forward (¶ 1756).

1754. Capital Loss Carryover of Noncorporate Taxpayers. Individuals and other noncorporate taxpayers may carry over a net capital loss (¶ 1739) to future tax years until the loss is used (Code Sec. 1212(b)).[140] The carried-over loss retains its long-term

References are to Standard Federal Tax Reports; Tax Research Consultant; and Practical Tax Explanations.

[133] ¶ 30,572, ¶ 30,573; SALES: 21,052; § 16,820

[134] ¶ 30,572, ¶ 30,574; FARM: 3,252; § 16,805

[135] ¶ 30,575.154; FARM: 3,252; § 16,805

[136] ¶ 30,750, ¶ 30,751; SALES: 24,354.05; § 16,520.30

[137] ¶ 30,752.24; SALES: 24,354.05; § 16,520.30

[138] ¶ 30,390, ¶ 30,391; SALES: 15,206.05; § 16,530

[139] ¶ 30,390, ¶ 30,391; SALES: 15,210, SALES: 15,212; § 16,535

[140] ¶ 30,400; SALES: 15,208; § 16,530

or short-term character. In determining the amount of the carryover, short-term capital gain is increased by the lesser of:

- the ordinary income offset (whether $3,000 or the amount of the overall net loss), or
- taxable income increased by the sum of that offset and the deduction for personal exemptions (¶ 133), with any excess of allowable deductions over gross income for the loss year treated as negative taxable income.

A short-term capital loss carryover first offsets short-term gain in the carryover year. Any remaining net short-term capital loss first offsets net long-term capital gain, and then up to $3,000 of ordinary income ($1,500 for married individuals filing separate returns) (¶ 1752). A long-term capital loss carryover first reduces long-term capital gain in the carryover year, then net short-term capital gain, and finally up to $3,000 of ordinary income.

Example: Jack has taxable income of $30,000 and files a joint return. In computing taxable income, he reports a net short-term capital loss of $1,000 and a net long-term capital loss of $6,000. He uses his $1,000 net short-term loss to offset $1,000 of ordinary income; he then uses $2,000 of his net long-term capital loss to offset $2,000 of ordinary income. The remaining $4,000 of his net long-term capital loss is carried over to the following tax year because it is less than his taxable income of $30,000 increased by the ordinary income offset of $3,000 and the deduction for personal exemptions.

Code Sec. 1256 Contract Loss. An individual (but not an estate, trust, or corporation) may elect to carry back a net section 1256 contract loss (¶ 1947) to the three prior tax years (Code Sec. 1212(c)).[141]

1756. Corporate Capital Loss Carryover and Carryback. A corporation may carry back a net capital loss (¶ 1738) to the three tax years preceding the loss year (Code Sec. 1212(a); Reg. § 1.1212-1(a)).[142] Any excess may be carried forward for five years following the loss year. However, the carryback cannot cause or increase a net operating loss (¶ 1145) in the carryback year. Any carryback or carryover is a short-term capital loss for the carryover year that is grouped with other capital losses for that year and used to offset any capital gains. Any undeducted loss remaining after the three-year carryback and the five-year carryover is not deductible.

Foreign expropriation losses can be carried forward for 10 years but are ineligible for the three-year carryback. A foreign expropriation capital loss is the sum of the capital losses sustained (either directly or on securities that become worthless) because of the expropriation, intervention, seizure, or similar taking of property by a foreign country's government or its political subdivision, agency, or instrumentality.

A regulated investment company or mutual fund (¶ 2301) can carry forward net capital losses indefinitely, with the carried over losses maintaining their long-term or short-term character (Code Sec. 1212(a)(3)).

A quick refund procedure is available for corporate net operating loss carrybacks or capital loss carrybacks (¶ 2773).

1757. Capital Gain or Loss of Spouses. Spouses who file a joint return compute their aggregate capital gains and losses (¶ 1735) as if they were the gains and losses of one person (Reg. § 1.1201-1(d)).[143] If the spouses file separate returns, the capital loss deduction (¶ 1752) for each is limited to $1,500 (one-half of the limit for a joint return) (Code Sec. 1211(b)(1)).[144] If they file separate returns for a year after a net capital loss was reported on a joint return, any carryover is allocated on the basis of the individual net capital loss of the spouses for the prior year (Reg. § 1.1212-1(c)).[145]

References are to Standard Federal Tax Reports; Tax Research Consultant; and Practical Tax Explanations.

[141] ¶ 30,400; SALES: 48,108; § 45,420.10

[142] ¶ 30,400, ¶ 30,401; SALES: 15,214; § 16,535

[143] ¶ 30,353; SALES: 15,206.10; § 16,530

[144] ¶ 30,390; SALES: 15,206.10; § 16,530

[145] ¶ 30,401; SALES: 15,208; § 16,530

1758. Capital Gain or Loss of Partnerships and S Corporations. The capital gains and losses of a partnership or S corporation are generally segregated from its ordinary net income and carried separately into the income of the partners or shareholders. The distributive shares of the capital gain or loss are treated as if they were the partners' (¶ 431) or shareholders' (¶ 309) own capital gain or loss. The same rule applies for Code Sec. 1231 transactions (¶ 1747) (Code Secs. 702(a) and 1366(a)).[146] S corporations may be taxed on capital gains in very limited situations (¶ 337).

Reporting. Generally, partnerships and S corporations use Form 8949 to report capital gains and losses that are not required to be reported on any other form. Partnerships then use Schedule D of Form 1065 to determine the overall gain or loss from the transactions reported on Form 8949. The net gains and losses from Schedule D are entered on Schedule K, and each partner's share is entered on Schedule K-1 of Form 1065. S corporations similarly use Schedule D of Form 1120S to determine the overall gain or loss from the transactions reported on Form 8949. The net gains and losses from Schedule D are entered on Schedule K, and each shareholder's share is entered on Schedule K-1 of Form 1120S.

1760. Gains or Losses of Investors, Dealers, and Traders. Whether a taxpayer's gains or losses on securities are ordinary or capital in nature (¶ 1735) depends on whether the taxpayer entered into the transaction as an investor, dealer, or trader.

Investors. Investors' activities are limited to occasional transactions for their own accounts. The level of activity is less than that associated with a trade or business.[147] An investor's gains and losses are capital in nature (¶ 1736).

Dealers. A dealer regularly purchases securities from, and sells securities to, customers in the ordinary course of a trade or business. Because dealers are in the business of buying and selling, their gains and losses are ordinary unless the securities are held primarily for personal investment (Code Sec. 1236).[148] Securities that a dealer holds for personal investment must be clearly identified in the dealer's records before the close of the day on which they were acquired and must never be held primarily for sale to the dealer's customers. Similarly, capital gain and loss treatment does not apply to real estate sales by a dealer in realty unless the property was held as an investment (¶ 1762). See ¶ 1903 for discussion of the mark-to-market requirement for dealers in securities.

Traders. Securities traders, including "day traders," buy and sell securities for their own accounts. A trader seeks to profit from short-term changes in value rather than long-term investments. A trader's trading activity must be substantial, frequent, regular, and continuous.[149] Because a trader's securities are not held primarily for sale to customers (¶ 1741), the gains and losses are generally capital in nature, and are reported on Form 8949. However, traders that make a mark-to-market election report their gains and losses on Form 4797. Traders claim their business expenses on Schedule C of Form 1040 because they are in the business of trading. For the rules concerning the commissions paid by traders when buying and selling securities, see ¶ 1983.

Subdivision of Real Estate

1762. Subdivision and Sale of Real Estate. Noncorporate taxpayers and S corporations are not treated as real estate dealers solely because they subdivide a tract of land for sale (Code Sec. 1237(a)).[150] At least part of the gain on the sale of a lot or parcel is capital gain when:

(1) the taxpayer has not previously held the tract, or any lot or parcel of it, for sale in the ordinary course of business and, in the same tax year as the sale occurs, does not hold any other real estate for sale in the ordinary course of business (this rule automatically disqualifies a real estate dealer);

References are to Standard Federal Tax Reports; Tax Research Consultant; and Practical Tax Explanations.

[146] ¶ 25,080, ¶ 32,080; PART: 18,104, SCORP: 402; § 28,405, § 30,410

[147] ¶ 8521.1475; SALES: 45,052; § 7,840.10

[148] ¶ 30,670; SALES: 45,054; § 18,805.05

[149] ¶ 30,422.6811; SALES: 45,058; § 18,805.15

[150] ¶ 30,690; REAL: 15,500; § 16,560.05

(2) no substantial improvements are made while the tract is held by the taxpayer or under a sale contract between the taxpayer and the buyer; and

(3) the taxpayer either held the lot for at least five years, or acquired it by inheritance or devise.

Certain improvements, such as water, sewage, drainage, or road installations, are not considered substantial improvements if: (1) the property (including inherited property) is held for at least 10 years; (2) the property would not have been marketable at the prevailing local price for similar building sites without such improvements; and (3) the taxpayer elects not to adjust the basis of the property (or other property) for the improvement costs or deduct them as expenses (Code Sec. 1237(b)(3); Reg. § 1.1237-1(c)).[151] The election is reported with the tax return for the year in which the lots covered by the election are sold. The election must include additional information, including a plat of the subdivision and a list of all the improvements.

The profits realized on the sales of the first five lots or parcels from the same tract are capital gains (Code Sec. 1237(b)(1); Reg. § 1.1237-1(e)(2)).[152] However, beginning in the year in which the sixth sale or exchange is made, gain on each sale is ordinary income to the extent of five percent of the selling price. Selling expenses are deducted first from this ordinary income, and then are used to reduce the capital gain on the sale or exchange (Code Sec. 1237(b)(2)). The selling expenses cannot be deducted from other income as ordinary business expenses.

Example 1: Mark subdivides a tract of land that he bought approximately 10 years ago and sells three lots for $50,000 each. The adjusted basis for each lot is $30,000. Selling expenses for each lot total $600. Mark has a long-term capital gain of $19,400 from the sale of each lot ($50,000 - $30,000 - $600).

Example 2: Same facts as in Example 1, except that Mark sells three additional lots under the same terms. Because he sold more than five lots, five percent of the selling price, or $2,500, could be characterized as ordinary income. However, this amount is reduced by his $600 in selling expenses. Thus, the sale of each lot produces $1,900 in ordinary income ($2,500 - $600), and $17,500 in long-term capital gain ($50,000 - $30,000 - $2,500).

If five years pass without the taxpayer selling or exchanging any other lots from the parcel, the taxpayer can sell another five lots without any of the gain taxed as ordinary income (Reg. § 1.1237-1(g)(2)).[153]

A taxpayer that buys a tract of land with the intent to subdivide and sell it as separate lots or parcels must measure gain or loss on every lot or parcel sold on the basis of an equitable (not ratable) apportionment (such as their relative assessed valuations for real estate tax purposes) of the cost of the subdivision (Reg. § 1.61-6(a)).[154]

Patents, Royalties, and Franchises

1767. Sale or Exchange of Patents. The transfer of all substantial rights to a patent, or an undivided interest in such rights, is treated as the sale of a capital asset (¶ 1741) held for more than 12 months (Code Sec. 1235(a); Reg. §§ 1.1235-1 and 1.1235-2).[155] The payment for the patent may be a lump-sum, a periodic payment, or contingent upon the productivity or use of the property transferred. These rules do not apply to transfers by gift or inheritance. The rules do apply to a transfer by the original inventor or another individual who acquired the patent from the original inventor before the invention was tested successfully under operating conditions. The inventor's employer and certain related persons are not eligible for long-term capital gain treatment if they acquire the patent from the inventor.

References are to Standard Federal Tax Reports; Tax Research Consultant; and Practical Tax Explanations.

[151] ¶ 30,690, ¶ 30,691; REAL: 15,510; § 16,560.20

[152] ¶ 30,690, ¶ 30,691; REAL: 15,504; § 16,560.10

[153] ¶ 30,691; REAL: 15,506; § 16,560.10

[154] ¶ 5605; REAL: 15,504; § 3,015, § 16,560.10

[155] ¶ 30,650, ¶ 30,651, ¶ 30,652; SALES: 24,050; § 18,705.05

1772. Timber, Coal or Iron Ore. A taxpayer may elect to treat the cutting of timber for sale or for use in a trade or business as a sale or exchange of the timber. The taxpayer must have owned the timber or held the contract right to cut it for more than one year (Code Sec. 631; Reg. § 1.631-1).[156] Under Code Sec. 1231, this timber is property used in the trade or business, so the gain may be treated as long-term capital gain under certain conditions (¶ 1747). An electing taxpayer must generally file Form T with the tax return for the year in which the election is effective.

Timber, coal, or domestic iron ore royalties are generally subject to Code Sec. 1231 treatment when the owner or a holder (including a lessee) disposes of the timber, coal or ore while retaining an economic interest in it (Code Sec. 631(b) and (c); Reg. § § 1.631-2 and 1.631-3).[157] An outright sale of timber also qualifies. This treatment is not available for iron ore mined outside the United States, or for coal or iron ore dispositions between related parties or persons owned and controlled by the same interests.

1774. Transfers of Franchises, Trademarks, or Trade Names. Amounts received from the transfer of a franchise, trademark, or trade name are generally ordinary income if the transferor retains any significant power, right, or continuing interest over the transferred asset (Code Sec. 1253).[158] Ordinary income treatment also applies to amounts received from the transfer, sale, or other disposition of a franchise, trademark, or trade name that are contingent on the transferred asset's productivity, use, or disposition. Amounts paid or incurred on account of the transfer of a franchise, trademark, or trade name are amortized over 15 years under Code Sec. 197 (¶ 1288). Amortization is claimed on Form 4562.

Contingent serial payments paid or incurred on account of a transfer, sale, or other disposition of a trademark, trade name, or franchise may be a deductible business expense (¶ 901) if: (1) the payments are contingent on the asset's productivity, use, or disposition; and (2) the contingent amounts are paid as part of a series of payments that are payable at least annually throughout the term of the transfer agreement, and are substantially equal in amount or payable under a fixed formula (Code Sec. 1253(d)(1)).

Disposition of Depreciable Property

1779. Depreciation Recapture Rules. A taxpayer that sells or disposes of certain depreciable or amortizable property must treat realized gain as ordinary income (rather than capital gain) to the extent of depreciation or amortization deductions previously allowed or allowable for the property. The recapture of depreciation or amortization applies to section 1245 property (¶ 1785) and section 1250 property (¶ 1786). The recapture rules apply notwithstanding any other Code provision (Reg. § § 1.1245-6 and 1.1250-1(c)).[159]

Section 1245 Property. Gain realized from the disposition of section 1245 property is ordinary income to the extent the adjusted basis of the property is exceeded by the lower of: (1) the recomputed basis of the property; (2) the amount realized upon a sale, exchange, or involuntary conversion of the property; or (3) the fair market value of the property in any other disposition (Code Sec. 1245(a)).[160] Recomputed basis is the property's adjusted basis plus previously allowed or allowable depreciation or amortization. Amortization deductions include amounts expensed for the following: Code Sec. 179 property (¶ 1208); capital costs of compliance with EPA sulfur regulations (¶ 1285); refinery property (¶ 1285A); energy efficient commercial buildings (¶ 1286); mine safety equipment (¶ 989A); film, television production, and live theatrical production costs (¶ 977B); and expenditures for removal of architectural and transportation barriers to the handicapped and elderly, reforestation (¶ 1287), and tertiary injectants.

References are to Standard Federal Tax Reports; Tax Research Consultant; and Practical Tax Explanations.

[156] ¶ 24,150, ¶ 24,151; FARM: 24,150; § 11,615.20, § 16,805

[157] ¶ 24,150, ¶ 24,153, ¶ 24,155; FARM: 18,360, FARM: 24,200; § 11,615.20, § 11,625.25, § 16,805

[158] ¶ 31,040; SALES: 24,300; § 18,745

[159] ¶ 30,908, ¶ 31,001; DEPR: 18,054; § 16,815

[160] ¶ 30,902; DEPR: 18,200; § 11,705.05

Section 1250 Property. Gain on the sale or other disposition of section 1250 property is treated as ordinary income to the extent of the excess of post-1969 depreciation allowances over the depreciation that would have been available under the straight-line method (¶ 1780) (Code Sec. 1250).[161] However, if section 1250 property is held for one year or less, all depreciation (and not just the excess over straight-line depreciation) is recaptured (Code Sec. 1250(b)(1)). See ¶ 1736 for capital gains treatment of unrecaptured Section 1250 gain. In a sale to a related party (¶ 1717), gain that is not recaptured may still be treated as ordinary income (¶ 1744). Different holding periods and recapture percentages may apply to substantial improvements made to section 1250 property that are considered separate property for recapture purposes, and also to property that consists of more than one element (Code Sec. 1250(f)).[162]

For residential rental property, certain types of government assisted housing, subsidized housing, section 1250 property for which rapid depreciation of rehabilitation expenditures was claimed, and property mortgaged under the Housing Act of 1949, depreciation recapture is reduced by one percent for each full month the property is held over a specified period (Code Sec. 1250(a)(1)(B) and (2)(B)).

Dispositions. Depreciation recapture is triggered by the disposition of depreciable property, including sales, exchanges, and involuntary conversions. Special rules apply for transfers by gift or at death (¶ 1788), certain tax-free corporate or partnership transactions (¶ 1789), disposal in a like-kind exchange or involuntary conversion where gain is not recognized (¶ 1790), and property distributed by a partnership (¶ 1792). A disposition of section 1245 property includes a sale in a sale-and-leaseback transaction and a transfer upon the foreclosure of a security interest, but it does not include a mere transfer of title between a debtor and a creditor upon the creation or termination of a security interest (Reg. § 1.1245-1).[163]

Installment Sale. In an installment sale of section 1245 or section 1250 property, gain recaptured as ordinary income is recognized in the year of the disposition, and gain in excess of the recapture income is reported under the installment method (¶ 1823).

Investment Credit Basis Reductions. For recapture purposes, the amount of an investment credit downward basis adjustment is treated as a deduction allowed for depreciation (¶ 1365A).

Additional Recapture for Corporations. For C corporations, the amount treated as ordinary income on the sale or other disposition of section 1250 property is increased by 20 percent of the additional amount that would be treated as ordinary income if the property were subject to recapture under the rules for section 1245 property (Code Sec. 291(a)(1)).[164]

Reporting Recapture. Form 4797 is used to calculate and report the amount of recaptured depreciation. A taxpayer subject to recapture of an investment credit downward basis adjustment must file Form 4255.

1780. Depreciation Subject to Recapture. In general, depreciation on tangible property placed in service after 1986 is determined under the Modified Accelerated Cost Recovery System (MACRS). Property placed in service after 1980 and before 1987 is subject to the Accelerated Cost Recovery System (ACRS). See ¶ 1216 and following for the methods of computing allowable depreciation deductions.

MACRS. Gain on the disposition of tangible personal property is ordinary income to the extent of previously-allowed MACRS deductions (¶ 1779). If property from a general asset account is disposed of, the full amount of proceeds realized on the disposition is ordinary income to the extent the unadjusted depreciable basis of the account (increased by amounts allowed as deductions under Code Secs. 179 and 190 for assets in

References are to Standard Federal Tax Reports; Tax Research Consultant; and Practical Tax Explanations.

[161] ¶ 31,000; DEPR: 18,250; § 11,710

[162] ¶ 31,000; DEPR: 18,264

[163] ¶ 30,903; DEPR: 18,052; § 11,705.05

[164] ¶ 15,190; DEPR: 18,266; § 26,020.10

the account) exceeds previously recognized ordinary income from prior dispositions (Code Sec. 168(i)(4); Reg. § 1.168(i)-1(e)).[165]

Residential rental property and nonresidential real property that is placed in service after 1986 and is subject to MACRS must be depreciated under the straight-line MACRS method (¶ 1243). Thus, there is no recapture of depreciation upon disposition of such property because no depreciation in excess of straight-line depreciation could have been taken.

ACRS. Gain on the disposition of personal recovery property and nonresidential real recovery property is treated as ordinary income to the extent of previously-allowed ACRS deductions (¶ 1779).[166] Gain on the disposition of residential rental real recovery property is treated as ordinary income to the extent that ACRS deductions exceed straight-line ACRS depreciation over the recovery period applicable to the property. Consequently, there is no recapture if the straight-line ACRS method was elected for real property.

On the disposition of assets from mass asset accounts, taxpayers recognize the amount of the proceeds realized as ordinary income to the extent of the unadjusted basis in the account less any amounts previously included in income. Any excess proceeds realized are capital gain, unless a nonrecognition provision applies. Regarding the recovery of depreciation, the mass asset account is treated as though there was no disposition of the asset, and the unadjusted basis of the property is left in the capital account until fully recovered in future years (Prop. Reg. § 1.168-2(h)).[167]

Amounts Excluded from Depreciation Adjustments. In determining the amount of additional depreciation taken before the disposition of section 1250 property, depreciation adjustments do not include amortization of emergency facilities, pollution control facilities, railroad grading and tunnel bores, and child care facilities; expenditures to remove architectural and transportation barriers to the handicapped and elderly; or tertiary injectant expenses (Code Sec. 1250(b)(3)).[168]

1785. Code Sec. 1245 Property. Code Sec. 1245 property is property that is or has been depreciable (or subject to amortization under Code Sec. 197) and is either:

- personal property (tangible and intangible); or
- other tangible property (not including a building or its structural components) used as an integral part of (1) manufacturing, production, or extraction; or (2) the furnishing of transportation, communications, electrical energy, gas, water, or sewage disposal services (Code Sec. 1245(a)(3); Reg. § 1.1245-3).[169]

The term "other tangible property" includes research facilities or facilities for the bulk storage of fungible commodities used in connection with the activities listed above. A leasehold of section 1245 property is also treated as section 1245 property. Livestock is considered section 1245 property, and depreciation on purchased draft, breeding, dairy and sporting livestock is recaptured as ordinary income when sold. Raised livestock generally has no basis for depreciation, but to the extent that it does have a basis and is depreciated, it is subject to recapture (IRS Pub. 225).

Section 1245 property also includes any real property that has an adjusted basis reflecting adjustments for special amortization for the following: Code Sec. 179 property (¶ 1208); capital costs of compliance with EPA sulfur regulations (¶ 1285); refinery property (¶ 1285A); energy efficient commercial buildings (¶ 1286); mine safety equipment (¶ 989A); railroad grading and tunnel bores; child care facilities; and expenditures for removal of architectural and transportation barriers to the handicapped and elderly, reforestation (¶ 1287), or tertiary injectants. Section 1245 property also includes single purpose agricultural and horticultural structures, and storage facilities used in connection with the distribution of petroleum products.

References are to Standard Federal Tax Reports; Tax Research Consultant; and Practical Tax Explanations.

[165] ¶ 11,250, ¶ 11,275B; DEPR: 3,554; § 11,145

[166] ¶ 30,909.023; DEPR: 18,166; § 11,001

[167] ¶ 11,252; DEPR: 3,560

[168] ¶ 31,000; DEPR: 18,262; § 11,710

[169] ¶ 30,902, ¶ 30,905; DEPR: 18,150; § 11,705.10

1786. Code Sec. 1250 Property. Code Sec. 1250 property is any real property that is or has been depreciable under Code Sec. 167 but is not subject to recapture under Code Sec. 1245. This includes all intangible real property (such as leases of land or section 1250 property), buildings and their structural components, and all other tangible real property except section 1245 property (Code Sec. 1250(c); Reg. § 1.1250-1(e)).[170] For real property that is section 1245 property rather than section 1250 property, see ¶ 1785.

1788. Disposition of Depreciable Property by Gift or Death. The recapture of depreciation as ordinary income upon the sale or disposition of section 1245 or section 1250 property (¶ 1779) does not apply to dispositions by gift or transfers at death, other than taxable transfers of section 1245 or section 1250 property in satisfaction of a specific bequest of money (Code Secs. 1245(b) and 1250(d); Reg. § § 1.1245-4 and 1.1250-3).[171] Upon a later sale, however, the donee realizes the same amount of ordinary income that the donor would have realized had the donor retained the property and sold it (unless the donee is tax-exempt). Also, if a taxpayer contributes section 1245 or section 1250 property to a charitable organization, the allowable charitable contribution deduction is reduced by the amount that would have been treated as ordinary income had the taxpayer sold the asset at its fair market value (¶ 1062).

1789. Disposition of Depreciable Property in Tax-Free Corporate or Partnership Transaction. When section 1245 or section 1250 property is disposed of in certain tax-free transactions (i.e., Code Secs. 332, 351, 361, 721, or 731), the transferor takes into account the depreciation recapture treated as ordinary income (¶ 1779) only to the extent that gain is recognized under those sections (Code Secs. 1245(b)(3) and 1250(d)(3); Reg. § § 1.1245-4(c) and 1.1250-3(c)).[172] However, when there is an otherwise tax-free transfer to a tax-exempt organization (other than a cooperative described in Code Sec. 521), the gain is recognized in full to the transferor. On a later sale of section 1245 or section 1250 property received in one of these tax-free transactions, the transferee realizes depreciation recapture to the extent of the transferor's unrecognized unrecaptured section 1245 or section 1250 gain plus depreciation deducted by the transferee (not to exceed the actual gain).

1790. Disposition of Depreciable Property in Like-Kind Exchange or Involuntary Conversion. If section 1245 or section 1250 property is exchanged for like-kind property (¶ 1721) or is involuntarily converted (¶ 1713), depreciation recapture (¶ 1779) is recognized to the extent of any gain recognized on the exchange (if money or other property is received) or on the conversion (when the conversion proceeds are not all spent on replacement property), plus the fair market value of any property received in the exchange or acquired as replacement property that is not section 1245 or section 1250 property (Code Secs. 1245(b)(4) and 1250(d)(4); Reg. § § 1.1245-4(d) and 1.1250-3(d)).[173] The basis of the acquired property is determined under the like-kind exchange or involuntary conversion rules (Reg. § § 1.1245-5 and 1.1250-3(d)).[174]

> **Example:** Greg exchanges section 1245 property with an adjusted basis of $10,000 for like-kind property with a fair market value of $9,000 and unlike property with a fair market value of $3,500. He must recognize gain of $2,500 because he received unlike property. His basis in the acquired property is $12,500 ($10,000 adjusted basis of the transferred property plus $2,500 recognized gain), of which $3,500 (fair market value) is allocated to the unlike property and the remaining $9,000 is allocated to the like-kind property.

References are to Standard Federal Tax Reports; Tax Research Consultant; and Practical Tax Explanations.

[170] ¶ 31,000, ¶ 31,001; DEPR: 18,252; § 11,710

[171] ¶ 30,902, ¶ 30,906, ¶ 31,000, ¶ 31,003; DEPR: 18,102, DEPR: 18,104; § 11,705.15, § 11,710

[172] ¶ 30,902, ¶ 30,906, ¶ 31,000, ¶ 31,003; DEPR: 18,106; § 11,705.15, § 11,710

[173] ¶ 30,902, ¶ 30,906, ¶ 31,000, ¶ 31,003; DEPR: 18,108; § 18,145.05

[174] ¶ 30,907, ¶ 31,003; SALES: 30,452; § 11,705.20, § 11,710

1792. Partnership Distribution of Depreciable Property. For purposes of the depreciation recapture rules (¶ 1779), the basis of section 1245 or section 1250 property distributed by a partnership to a partner is determined by reference to the partnership's adjusted basis in the property (Code Secs. 1245(b)(5) and 1250(d)(5); Reg. §§ 1.1245-4(f) and 1.1250-3(f)).[175]

For recomputing the basis of the property in the hands of the partner, the amount of the depreciation or amortization adjustments for section 1245 property, or the additional depreciation for distributed section 1250 property, attributable to pre-distribution periods is equal to: (1) the amount of gain that would have been treated as ordinary income under the recapture rules had the partnership sold the property at fair market value immediately before the distribution; minus (2) any gain treated as ordinary income under the partnership rules for distributions of receivables or inventory items (¶ 436).

1793. Corporate Distribution of Depreciable Property. A corporation that distributes a dividend consisting of section 1245 or section 1250 property might be required to recognize ordinary income under the depreciation recapture rules (¶ 1779), even though it would not normally recognize gain under the corporate distribution rules (¶ 736) (Reg. §§ 1.1245-1(a), 1.1245-6(b), and 1.1250-1(c)).[176]

A corporation's transfer of section 1245 property or section 1250 property to a shareholder for less than fair market value is not treated as a sale, exchange, or involuntary conversion for depreciation recapture purposes (Reg. §§ 1.1245-1(c) and 1.1250-1(a)). Accordingly, the corporation's gain for recapture purposes is the amount by which the property's adjusted basis is exceeded by the lower of the property's fair market value on the disposition date or the property's recomputed basis.

If a corporation transfers section 1245 property or section 1250 property to a shareholder in a sale or exchange for less than fair market value, the disposition is not treated as a sale, exchange, or involuntary conversion for depreciation recapture purposes (Reg. §§ 1.1245-1(c) and 1.1250-1(a)). Accordingly, the corporation's gain for recapture purposes is the amount by which the property's adjusted basis is exceeded by the lower of the property's fair market value on the disposition date or the property's recomputed basis.

If the transferee's basis in the property is determined solely by the corporate distribution rules (¶ 735), no depreciation adjustments are reflected in the adjusted basis of section 1245 property, and no additional depreciation is reflected in the adjusted basis of section 1250 property, on the date that the transferee acquires the property (Reg. §§ 1.1245-2(c) and 1.1250-2(e)).[177]

Farmers' Recapture

1797. Recapture on Land Sale. If farm land held for less than 10 years is disposed of, the lesser of the gain realized or a percentage of the total deductions for soil and water conservation (¶ 982) and land clearing expenses must be recaptured as ordinary income on Form 4797 (Code Sec. 1252).[178] The recapture percentage is 100 percent if the land is held for five years or less, and declines 20 percent for each additional year (to 80 percent in the sixth year, 60 percent in the seventh year, 40 percent in the eighth year, and 20 percent in the ninth year). There is no recapture after the ninth year. This recapture rule does not apply to transfers by gift, transfers at death, and transfers in certain tax-free transactions (Reg. § 1.1252-2).[179]

References are to Standard Federal Tax Reports; Tax Research Consultant; and Practical Tax Explanations.

[175] ¶ 30,902, ¶ 30,906, ¶ 31,000, ¶ 31,003; DEPR: 18,106.05; § 30,535.20, § 30,555

[176] ¶ 30,903, ¶ 30,908, ¶ 31,001; DEPR: 18,054

[177] ¶ 30,904, ¶ 31,002; DEPR: 18,204.05, DEPR: 18,262

[178] ¶ 31,020; FARM: 9,168; § 36,030.10

[179] ¶ 31,022; FARM: 9,168.20; § 36,030.10

Chapter 18
INSTALLMENT SALES
DEFERRED PAYMENTS

	Par.
INSTALLMENT SALES	
Installment Method	1801
Computation of Income	1813
Related-Party Sales	1833
Repossessions of Property	1838
Dispositions of Installment Obligations	1846
Corporate Liquidations	1856
DEFERRED PAYMENTS	
Imputed Interest	1859
Treatment of Interest	1883

Installment Method

1801. Use of Installment Method. The installment method is a special way of reporting gains (not losses) from sales of property when at least one payment is received in a tax year after the year of sale (deferred payments). Under the installment method, gain from the sale is prorated and recognized over the years in which payments are received (Code Sec. 453).[1] As a result, each payment received usually consists of interest, return of basis, and gain on the sale.

The installment method must be used for installment sales unless the taxpayer elects not to use the installment method (¶ 1803) or it is otherwise prohibited. This rule applies to both cash and accrual basis taxpayers (¶ 1515). The installment method generally is not available for most sales by dealers (¶ 1808), sales of property of a type that would be included in inventory (¶ 1553), sales of personal property under a revolving credit plan (¶ 1805), sales of publicly traded property (¶ 1805), or sales of depreciable property between related taxpayers (¶ 1835). Thus, payments for such sales are treated as if they are received in the year of disposition, even if the taxpayer expects to receive some payments in future years.

Gain Calculation. The amount of gain from an installment sale that is taxable in a given year is calculated by multiplying the payments received in that year by the gross profit ratio for the sale (Code Sec. 453(c)).[2] The gross profit ratio is equal to the anticipated gross profit divided by the total contract price (¶ 1813). However, gain from installment sales of depreciable property subject to recapture under Code Sec. 1245 or Code Sec. 1250 is determined under a special rule (¶ 1823).

Example: On December 1, 2016, Bob Smith sells vacant land that he has held for investment purposes for a number of years. His basis in the land is $12,000. The total contract price is $15,000. Bob receives a $5,000 down payment, with the $10,000 balance due in monthly installments of $500 each, plus interest at the applicable federal rate, beginning on January 1, 2017. His anticipated gross profit from the sale is $3,000. His gross profit percentage is 20% ($3,000 gross profit ÷ $15,000 contract price). Under the installment method, Bob must report $1,000 ($5,000 × 20%) as long-term capital gain in 2016, $1,200 ($6,000 × 20%) in 2017, and $800 ($4,000 × 20%) in 2018. The interest is reported as ordinary income.

References are to Standard Federal Tax Reports; Tax Research Consultant; and Practical Tax Explanations.

[1] ¶ 21,402; SALES: 36,050; § 18,301

[2] ¶ 21,402; SALES: 36,100; § 18,320

Although use of the installment method determines when gain from an installment sale is reported, it does not affect the characterization of the gain as capital gain or ordinary income. The proper characterization depends on the nature of the asset sold (¶ 1735 and ¶ 1741).

Reporting Requirements for Gain. Gain from an installment sale is reported on Form 6252, which must be filed with the tax return in the year of sale and in each year payments are received. The gain calculated on Form 6252 is carried over and entered on Schedule D of the taxpayer's return or Form 4797, or both, as appropriate.

1803. Election Not to Use Installment Method. If a taxpayer elects not to use the installment method (¶ 1801), the entire gain is reported in the year of the sale, even though not all of the sale proceeds are received in that year (Code Sec. 453(d); Temp. Reg. § 15A.453-1(d)).[3] The election is made by individuals, corporations, partnerships, estates, and trusts by simply reporting the gain on Form 8949 or Form 4797, whichever applies. The election must be made by the due date, including extensions, of the tax return for the year in which the installment sale occurs. If a taxpayer files a timely return without an election out, the taxpayer can elect out by filing an amended return within six months of the due date, excluding extensions (Reg. § 301.9100-2). The IRS will otherwise permit late elections only in rare circumstances where the taxpayer can show good cause for not making the election by the due date. An election out can be revoked only with IRS approval, but revocation is not allowed if one of its purposes is to avoid federal income tax, or if the tax year in which any payment was received has closed.

1805. Publicly Traded Property and Revolving Credit Plans. The installment method (¶ 1801) may *not* be used for: (1) sales of personal property under a revolving credit plan; (2) sales of stock or securities that are traded on an established securities market; or (3) to the extent provided by regulations, sales of other kinds of property that are regularly traded on an established market. All payments to be received from such sales are treated as received in the year of disposition (Code Sec. 453(k)).[4]

1808. Dealer Dispositions by Installment Sale. Dealers in real or personal property may not use the installment method to report the gain from dealer dispositions (Code Sec. 453(b)(2)(A) and (l)(1)).[5] A dealer disposition includes:

- any disposition of personal property by a person who regularly sells or otherwise disposes of such property on an installment plan; and
- any disposition of real property that is held by the taxpayer for sale to customers in the ordinary course of the taxpayer's trade or business.

Certain types of installment transactions by a dealer, however, are not considered dealer dispositions and the installment method of reporting may be used (Code Sec. 453(l)(2)).[6] These include:

- the disposition of any property used or produced in the trade or business of farming;
- the disposition in the ordinary course of the taxpayer's trade or business of:
  - — any residential lot, provided that the dealer or any related person is not obligated to make any improvements to the lot; or
  - — a timeshare right to use or own residential real property for not more than six weeks per year, or a right to use specified campgrounds for recreational purposes.

A timeshare right to use or own property held by an individual's spouse, children, grandchildren, or parents is treated as held by the individual.

Payment of Interest. To use the installment method for the sale of residential lots and timeshares, the taxpayer must pay interest on the amount of tax attributable to the

References are to Standard Federal Tax Reports; Tax Research Consultant; and Practical Tax Explanations.

[3] ¶ 21,402, ¶ 21,404; SALES: 36,056; § 18,315

[4] ¶ 21,402; SALES: 36,052.05; § 18,310.20, § 18,310.25

[5] ¶ 21,402; SALES: 36,250; § 18,310.10

[6] ¶ 21,402; SALES: 36,054; § 18,310.10

installment payments received during the year. The interest is calculated for the period beginning on the date of sale and ending on the date the payment is received (Code Sec. 453(l)(3)).[7] The amount of interest is based upon the applicable federal rate in effect at the time of sale, compounded semiannually (¶ 1875).

Computation of Income

1813. Amount of Income for Installment Sales. For most nondealer dispositions of property (¶ 1808), the amount of income reported from an installment sale in any tax year (including the year of sale) is equal to the payments received during the year multiplied by the gross profit ratio for the sale (Code Sec. 453(c); Temp. Reg. § 15A.453-1(b)(2)).[8] Payments include all amounts actually or constructively received in the tax year under the installment obligation (¶ 1819). Different computations are required for installment sales of property that are not subject to the depreciation recapture provisions of Code Sec. 1245 or Code Sec. 1250 (¶ 1823)

The gross profit ratio is the gross profit on the installment sale divided by the total contract price. The gross profit is the selling price of the property minus its adjusted basis. The selling price of the property is not reduced by any existing mortgage or encumbrance, or by any selling expenses, but is reduced by any imputed interest (¶ 1859).

The total contract price (denominator of gross profit ratio) is the selling price minus that portion of qualifying indebtedness (¶ 1815) which the buyer assumes or takes the property subject to that does not exceed the seller's basis in the property (adjusted to reflect commissions and other selling expenses). In the case of an installment sale that is a partially nontaxable like-kind exchange (¶ 1723), the gross profit is reduced by that portion of the gain that is not recognized, and the total contract price is reduced by the value of the like-kind property received (Code Sec. 453(f)(6)).[9]

For certain nondealer sales of property over $150,000, a special interest charge may apply (¶ 1825).

1815. Qualifying Indebtedness for Installment Sales. For the purpose of determining the total contract price of an installment sale of property (¶ 1813), qualifying indebtedness includes:

(1) any mortgage or other indebtedness encumbering the property; and

(2) any indebtedness not secured by the property but incurred or assumed by the purchaser incident to the acquisition, holding or operation of the property in the ordinary course of business or investment (Temp. Reg. § 15A.453-1(b)(2)(iv)).[10]

Qualifying indebtedness does not include an obligation of the seller incurred incident to the *disposition* of the property, or an obligation functionally unrelated to the acquisition, holding or operation of the property. Any obligation incurred or assumed in contemplation of disposition of the property is not qualifying indebtedness if recovery of the seller's basis is accelerated.

Wrap-Around Mortgage. When property encumbered by an outstanding mortgage is sold in exchange for an installment obligation equal to the mortgage, the installment obligation is said to "wrap around" the mortgage. The seller generally uses the payments received from the installment obligation to pay the "wrapped" mortgage. In this situation, the IRS will follow the Tax Court's position and will not treat the buyer as having taken the property subject to, or as having assumed, the seller's mortgage (*Professional Equities, Inc.*, 89 TC 165, Dec. 44,064 (1987) (Acq.)).[11] As a result, the seller does not have to reduce the total contract price by the amount of the wrapped mortgage.

References are to Standard Federal Tax Reports; Tax Research Consultant; and Practical Tax Explanations.

[7] ¶ 21,402; SALES: 36,054.10; § 18,310.10

[8] ¶ 21,402, ¶ 21,404; SALES: 36,100; § 18,320.05

[9] ¶ 21,402; SALES: 36,114.05; § 18,350

[10] ¶ 21,404; SALES: 36,106; § 18,320.05

[11] ¶ 21,412.80; SALES: 36,106; § 18,325

1819. Installment Payments. When determining the amount of reportable income under the installment method (¶ 1813), a payment includes all amounts actually or constructively received in the tax year under an installment obligation, as well as:

(1) evidence of indebtedness of a person other than the buyer;

(2) evidence of indebtedness of the buyer that is payable on demand or readily tradable, including a bond issued with coupons or in registered form;

(3) a bank certificate or treasury note;

(4) qualifying indebtedness (¶ 1815) assumed or taken subject to by the buyer, to the extent it exceeds the seller's basis for the sold property as adjusted for selling expenses;

(5) seller's indebtedness to the buyer that is canceled; and

(6) indebtedness on the sold property (for which the seller is not personally liable) when the buyer is the obligee of the indebtedness (Code Sec. 453(f)(3), (f)(4), and (f)(5); Temp. Reg. § 15A.453-1(b)(3)).[12]

Debt instruments in registered form that the seller can establish are not readily tradable are not considered payments. In addition, like-kind property received in a partially tax-free exchange (¶ 1723) that is part of an installment sale transaction is not treated as a payment for purposes of determining the amount of income to be reported under the installment method (Code Sec. 453(f)(6)).[13]

1821. Contingent Payment Sales. A contingent payment sale must be reported on the installment method (¶ 1801) unless the seller elects not to use the installment method (Temp. Reg. § 15A.453-1(c)).[14] A contingent payment sale is a sale or other disposition of property in which the total selling price is not determinable by the close of the tax year in which the sale or disposition occurs. It does not include transactions with respect to which the installment obligation represents, under applicable principles of tax law: (1) a retained interest in the property which is the subject of the transaction; (2) an interest in a joint venture or partnership; (3) an equity interest in a corporation; or (4) similar transactions, regardless of the existence of a stated maximum selling price or a fixed payment term.

In a contingent payment sale, the basis of the property sold (including selling expenses, but not those of real estate dealers) is allocated to payments received in each tax year and recovered as follows:

- for sales with a stated maximum selling price, basis is recovered according to a profit ratio based on the stated maximum selling price;
- for sales with a fixed payment period, basis is recovered ratably over the fixed period; and
- for sales with neither a maximum selling price nor a fixed payment period, basis is recovered ratably over a 15-year period.

Alternate methods of basis recovery may be required when the normal method would substantially and inappropriately accelerate or defer the recovery of basis.

1823. Installment Sale of Property Subject to Depreciation Recapture. For installment sales of real or personal property to which the depreciation recapture provisions of Code Sec. 1245 or Code Sec. 1250 apply (¶ 1779), any recapture income must be reported in the year of disposition, whether or not an installment payment is received in that year (Code Sec. 453(i)).[15] The amount of ordinary income reported in the year of sale is added to the property's basis, and this adjusted basis is used in determining the remaining profit on the disposition. The remaining profit amount is used to compute the gross profit percentage to be applied to each installment payment.

References are to Standard Federal Tax Reports; Tax Research Consultant; and Practical Tax Explanations.

[12] ¶ 21,402, ¶ 21,404; SALES: 36,102; § 18,325

[13] ¶ 21,402; SALES: 36,114.05; § 18,350

[14] ¶ 21,404; SALES: 36,112; § 18,330.05

[15] ¶ 21,402; SALES: 36,108; § 18,355.05

Example: On December 1, 2016, Bob sells a rental building for a total contract price of $100,000, plus interest at the applicable federal rate. He receives a note due in yearly installments of $20,000, plus interest, beginning January 1, 2017. Bob's adjusted basis in the building is $20,000. Assume that $10,000 of the total $80,000 gain is attributable to depreciation that must be recaptured as ordinary income under Code Sec. 1250 (¶ 1779). The $10,000 must be included in Bob's ordinary income for 2016 (the year of sale). The $10,000 is added to his $20,000 adjusted basis for purposes of determining the gross profit on the remaining gain. Therefore, gross profit is, $70,000 ($100,000 – $30,000). Of each $20,000 payment received in the following years, $14,000 is includible in income ($20,000 × ($70,000 ÷ $100,000)).

If a portion of the capital gain from an installment sale of depreciable real property consists of unrecaptured section 1250 gain, and another portion consists of other capital gains (¶ 1736), the taxpayer is required to take the unrecaptured section 1250 gain into account before the other capital gains are received (Reg. § 1.453-12).[16]

1825. Special Interest Rule for Nondealers of Property. A special interest charge may apply to an installment obligation that arises from a nondealer disposition of real or personal property (¶ 1813) under the installment method if the sales price is over $150,000 (Code Sec. 453A).[17] The interest charge does not apply to nondealer dispositions of property used in the business of farming or personal use property. For this purpose, personal use property is property that is not substantially used in connection with the taxpayer's trade or business or in an investment activity. The interest charge also does not apply to dispositions of timeshares and residential lots (but the interest payment rule described in ¶ 1808 does apply).

Generally, the interest charge is imposed on the tax deferred under the installment method with respect to outstanding installment obligations. However, the interest charge will not apply unless the face amount of all obligations held by the taxpayer that arose during and remain outstanding at the close of the tax year exceeds $5 million.

If any indebtedness is secured by a nondealer installment obligation that arises from the disposition of any real or personal property having a sales price over $150,000, the net proceeds of the secured indebtedness will be treated as a payment received on the installment obligation on the later of the date that the indebtedness is secured or the date that the net proceeds are received.

The interest is not reported on Form 6252, but rather is entered as an additional tax on the taxpayer's return. For individuals, it is included on the line for "Other taxes" on Form 1040. For estates and trusts, it is included on the line for "Total tax" on Schedule G of Form 1041. For corporations, it is entered on Schedule J of Form 1120.

Related-Party Sales

1833. Installment Sale to Related Persons. When a person makes an installment sale of property (¶ 1801) to a related person who sells the property before the installment payments are made in full, the amount realized by the related person from the second sale is treated as being received by the initial seller at the time of the second sale (Code Sec. 453(e)).[18] However, the resale rule does not generally apply if the second sale takes place more than two years after the first sale. A related person for this purpose includes the seller's spouse, child, grandchild and other lineal descendants, parent, grandparent and other ancestors, brother, sister, controlled corporation, partnership, certain trusts, estate, or executor (Code Sec. 453(f)(1)).

In applying the resale rule, the amount treated as received by the initial seller is limited to:

(1) the *lesser* of—

(a) the total amount realized from the second disposition before the close of the tax year of disposition; or

(b) the total contract price for the first disposition;

References are to Standard Federal Tax Reports; Tax Research Consultant; and Practical Tax Explanations.

[16] ¶ 21,425; SALES: 36,100; § 18,355.05

[17] ¶ 21,450; SALES: 36,150

[18] ¶ 21,402; SALES: 36,200; § 18,360

(2) *minus* the sum of—

(a) the total amount received from the first disposition before the close of the year of the second disposition; and

(b) the total amount treated as received for prior years under the resale rule.

There are a number of exceptions to the resale rule. Any sale or exchange of stock to the issuing corporation is not treated as a first disposition. An involuntary conversion (¶ 1713), and any transfer thereafter, is not treated as a second disposition if the first disposition occurred before the threat or imminence of the conversion. Any transfer after the earlier of the death of the person making the first disposition or the death of the person acquiring the property in the first disposition, and any transfer thereafter, is not treated as a second disposition. Further, the resale rule does not apply if it is established to the IRS's satisfaction that neither disposition had federal income tax avoidance as one of its principal purposes.

1835. Installment Sale of Depreciable Property Between Related Persons. The installment method (¶ 1801) generally cannot be used for installment sales of depreciable property between related persons. As a result, all payments are deemed received in the year of sale. However, the installment method may be used if the IRS is satisfied that tax avoidance was not one of the principal purposes of the sale (Code Sec. 453(g)).[19] For this purpose, the term "related person" is defined in Code Sec. 1239(b) (¶ 1744) and includes corporations and partnerships that are more than 50-percent owned, either directly or indirectly, by the same person.

Repossessions of Property

1838. Repossession of Personal Property. When personal property that was sold in an installment sale (¶ 1801) is repossessed, the repossession is treated as a disposition of the installment obligation (¶ 1846) (IRS Pub. 537).[20] Gain or loss is measured by subtracting the seller's basis in the obligation from the fair market value of the property on the date of repossession (and the value of any other property received from the buyer). If the seller did not use the installment method to report the gain on the original sale, the seller's basis in the obligation is equal to the face value of the obligation minus all principal payments that the seller received on the obligation. If the seller used the installment method to report the gain on the original sale, the seller's basis in the obligation is determined by multiplying the unpaid balance of the obligation by the seller's gross profit percentage, and then subtracting that amount from the unpaid balance. The character of the gain or loss, if any, on the repossession is the same as on the original sale.

If the installment obligation is not completely satisfied by repossession of the property, and the seller is unable to collect the balance of the debt, the seller may be able to claim a bad debt deduction for the portion of the obligation that is not satisfied through repossession (¶ 1135 and ¶ 1143).

1841. Repossession of Real Property. When real property is sold on the installment method (¶ 1801) and the seller accepts an installment debt secured by the property, the seller will recognize only a limited amount of gain and no loss upon repossession of the property (Code Sec. 1038; Reg. § 1.1038-1).[21] Gain on the repossession is limited to the lesser of:

(1) the amount by which the amount of money and the fair market value of other property (other than obligations of the purchaser) received, prior to the reacquisition, with respect to the sale of such property, exceeds the amount of the gain on the sale of such property returned as income for periods prior to the reacquisition; or

References are to Standard Federal Tax Reports; Tax Research Consultant; and Practical Tax Explanations.

[19] ¶ 21,402; SALES: 36,204; § 18,310.30

[20] ¶ 21,406.048; SALES: 36,452; § 18,365.10

[21] ¶ 29,740, ¶ 29,741; SALES: 36,454; § 18,365.15

(2) the amount by which the price at which the real property was sold exceeded its adjusted basis, reduced by the sum of (a) the amount of the gain on the sale of such property returned as income for periods prior to the reacquisition of such property, and (b) the amount of money and the fair market value of other property (other than obligations of the purchaser received with respect to the sale of such property) paid or transferred by the seller in connection with the reacquisition of such property.

The same rules apply when an estate or beneficiary repossesses real property that had been sold by a decedent on the installment method (Code Sec. 1038(g)).[22]

Repossession of Principal Residence. Special rules apply if a seller repossesses a principal residence that was sold under the installment method and gain realized from the sale was excluded from gross income (¶ 1705). If the seller resells the residence within one year of repossession, the original sale and the resale are treated as one transaction and realized gain is determined on the combined sale and resale (Code Sec. 1038(e); Reg. § 1.1038-2).[23] If the resale does not take place within one year, the general rules for repossessions of real property apply.

1843. Basis After Repossession of Real Property. The seller's basis in repossessed real property (¶ 1841) is generally the adjusted basis of the debt secured by the property (determined at the time of the repossession), increased by any gain recognized at the time of the repossession and by the seller's repossession costs (Code Sec. 1038(c)).[24] If the debt to the seller is not discharged as a result of the repossession, the basis of the debt is zero. If, before repossession, the seller has treated the secured debt as having become worthless or partially worthless, then, upon repossession, the seller is considered to have received an amount equal to the amount that was treated as worthless. However, the seller's adjusted basis in the debt is increased by the same amount (Code Sec. 1038(d)).

Dispositions of Installment Obligations

1846. Dispositions or Transfers of Installment Obligations. Gain or loss is generally recognized when an installment obligation is sold, disposed of, or satisfied other than at face value (Code Sec. 453B).[25] The character of any resulting gain or loss on the disposition of an installment obligation is determined by the character of the original asset that was sold (¶ 1741). The amount of gain or loss is the difference between the basis of the obligation and either:

(1) the amount realized, if the obligation is satisfied other than at face value or is sold or exchanged; or

(2) the fair market value of the obligation, if the obligation is distributed or disposed of other than by sale or exchange.

For this purpose, the basis of the obligation to the transferor is the excess of the face value of the obligation over the income that would have been returnable had the obligation been satisfied in full. To determine the basis, the unpaid balance of the installment obligation is multiplied by the gross profit percentage, and the result is subtracted from the unpaid balance. The result is the basis in the installment obligation (IRS Pub. 537).

The cancellation or lapse of an installment obligation is treated as a disposition other than a sale or exchange. This includes a self-canceling installment note that is extinguished at the death of the holder (*R.E. Frane Est.*, CA-8, 93-2 USTC ¶ 50,386).[26] Therefore, gain or loss is computed based on the fair market value of the obligation.

Transfers Between Spouses. The transfer of an installment obligation between spouses or incident to divorce (other than a transfer in trust) will not trigger recognition

References are to Standard Federal Tax Reports; Tax Research Consultant; and Practical Tax Explanations.

[22] ¶ 29,740; ESTTRST: 9,166; § 18,365.15

[23] ¶ 29,740, ¶ 29,742; REAL: 6,156.35; § 18,365.20

[24] ¶ 29,740; REAL: 6,156.25; § 18,365.15

[25] ¶ 21,470; SALES: 36,350; § 18,370

[26] ¶ 21,471.15; SALES: 36,352.15

of gain (Code Sec. 453B(g)).[27] Thus, the same tax treatment applies to the transferee spouse that would have applied to the transferor spouse.

Transfers at Death. The transfer of an installment obligation at the death of the obligee (other than to the buyer) is not a taxable disposition requiring the recognition of any gain or loss (Code Sec. 453B(c)).[28] Instead, the gain portion of any installment obligation acquired from a decedent is considered income in respect of a decedent (¶ 182). The taxpayer who receives such installment payments (estate, beneficiary, etc.) must report as income the same portion of the payments that would have been taxable income to the decedent. The amount considered to be an item of gross income in respect of the decedent is the excess of the face value of the obligation over its basis in the hands of the decedent.

While the transfer of an installment obligation upon a seller's death is generally not a taxable disposition, the seller's estate is deemed to have made a taxable disposition if the obligation is transferred by bequest, devise, or inheritance to the obligor or if the estate allows the obligation to become unenforceable. If the decedent and obligor-recipient of the obligation were related persons (¶ 1833), the fair market value of the obligation may not be determined at less than its face amount (Code Sec. 691(a)(5)).[29]

Corporate Liquidations

1856. Installment Obligations Received from Liquidating Corporations. Liquidating corporations, other than certain liquidating S corporations (¶ 1858), that distribute installment obligations to shareholders in exchange for their stock must currently recognize gain or loss from the distribution (¶ 1846). However, a shareholder that receives a qualifying installment obligation may treat the exchange as though it were an ordinary sale of stock for an installment obligation. Thus, the shareholder may be able to use the installment method to report the gain from the exchange (Code Sec. 453(h)(1)(A); Reg. § 1.453-11(a)(1)).[30]

If the liquidating corporation is traded on an established securities market, installment sale treatment is generally not available (¶ 1805). However, a shareholder *may* use the installment method if the stock of the liquidating corporation is not traded on an established market, even if the obligation arose from the sale by the liquidating corporation of securities that are traded on an established market (so that the liquidating corporation could not have used the installment method). For this rule to apply, the liquidating corporation must not have been formed or used to avoid the prohibition against using the installment method for publicly traded stock (Reg. § 1.453-11(c)(5)).

Gain on the transfer of a qualifying installment obligation to a shareholder during a liquidation is not immediately taxed to the shareholder. Instead, the payments received under the installment obligation are treated as payments for the stock, and any gain is included in the shareholder's income as payments are received. This rule applies when:

(1) stockholders exchange their stock in the corporation in a Code Sec. 331 liquidation (¶ 2253);

(2) the corporation, during the 12-month period beginning with the adoption of the plan of liquidation, had sold some or all of its assets in exchange for an installment note;

(3) the corporation, within that 12-month period, distributes the installment notes acquired in connection with those sales to the shareholders in exchange for their stock; and

(4) the liquidation is completed within that 12-month period.

This rule does not apply to obligations arising from a sale of inventory, stock in trade, or assets held for sale to customers in the ordinary course of business, unless those assets are sold in a bulk sale (Code Sec. 453(h)(1)(B)).

References are to Standard Federal Tax Reports; Tax Research Consultant; and Practical Tax Explanations.

[27] ¶ 21,470; SALES: 36,354.40; § 18,230

[28] ¶ 21,470; SALES: 36,354.35; § 18,370

[29] ¶ 24,900; SALES: 36,352.15; § 18,370

[30] ¶ 21,402, ¶ 21,419; SALES: 36,354.20; § 26,710

Subsidiary Liquidations. In a complete liquidation of a subsidiary, in which gain or loss on distributions of property is generally not recognized by the parent or the subsidiary (¶ 2261), the distribution of installment obligations will not cause recognition of gain or loss (Code Sec. 453B(d)).[31]

1858. Installment Obligation Received in S Corporation Liquidations. If an installment obligation is distributed by an S corporation in a complete liquidation (¶ 2253), and the receipt of the obligation is not treated as payment for stock in a complete 12-month liquidation (¶ 1856), then the corporation generally does not recognize gain or loss on the distribution. This is true even for accrual-basis S corporations (Code Sec. 453B(h)).[32]

Imputed Interest

1859. Inadequate or Unpaid Interest on Deferred Payments. When a sale or exchange of property involves the issuance of a debt instrument with deferred payments, such as with an installment sale (¶ 1801), the instrument generally should provide for the payment of adequate interest. If the instrument does not provide for the payment of adequate stated interest, interest income must be imputed to the seller or holder of the debt under the original issue discount (OID) rules of Code Sec. 1274 (¶ 1954) or the unstated interest rules of Code Sec. 483 (¶ 1868). The unstated interest rules will apply only if the transaction does not come within the scope of the OID rules (Code Sec. 483(d)(1)).[33]

If neither the unstated interest rules nor OID rules apply, interest may be imputed under other Code sections (Reg. § 1.483-1(a) and (c)(3); Reg. § 1.1274-1(b)).[34] For example, interest is imputed to certain obligations given in exchange for services or for the use of property under Code Secs. 404 and 467 (¶ 906 and ¶ 1541). Further, the interest imputation rules of Code Sec. 7872 apply to certain below-market demand loans (¶ 795).

In addition, the unstated interest rules and OID rules do not apply to transfers of property between spouses or incident to divorce (¶ 778), to cash method debt instruments (¶ 1954), or to a purchaser who gives debt when buying personal use property.

The following steps should be taken with respect to deferred contracts:

(1) determine whether the transaction is covered by either the unstated interest rules or the OID rules (¶ 1868 and ¶ 1954);

(2) test for unstated interest or OID;

(3) compute the total unstated interest or OID under the contract; and

(4) apportion the unstated interest or OID over the payments.

1868. Scope of Code Sec. 483. The unstated interest rules of Code Sec. 483 impute interest income (¶ 1872) on any payments on the sale or exchange of property that are due more than six months after the sale or exchange if any payments are due more than one year after the sale or exchange (Code Sec. 483).[35] The rules under Code Sec. 483 do not apply in the following situations:

(1) debt instruments for which an issue price is determined under Code Sec. 1273(b)(1), (2) or (3), or Code Sec. 1274;

(2) sales for $3,000 or less;

(3) with respect to the buyer, any purchase of personal property or educational services (under Code Sec. 163(b)) on an installment basis if the interest charge cannot be ascertained and is treated as six percent; and

(4) sales or exchanges of patents (¶ 1767) to the extent of any payments that are contingent on the productivity, use or disposition of the property transferred.

References are to Standard Federal Tax Reports; Tax Research Consultant; and Practical Tax Explanations.

[31] ¶ 21,470; SALES: 36,354.20; § 18,370

[32] ¶ 21,470; SCORP: 352.45; § 28,905.10

[33] ¶ 22,290; ACCTNG: 36,304.05; § 18,355.10

[34] ¶ 22,291, ¶ 31,301; ACCTNG: 36,154.05

[35] ¶ 22,290; ACCTNG: 36,300; § 19,505.05

1872. Testing for and Imputing Unstated Interest. The imputed interest rules of Code Sec. 483 apply (¶ 1868) when there is "unstated interest," which is the excess of the total payments (excluding any interest payments) due more than six months after the date of sale over the total of their present values (including the present values of any interest payments). Generally, present value is determined by using a discount rate equal to the applicable federal rate (AFR) determined under Code Sec. 1274(d) (¶ 1875) (Code Sec. 483(b); Reg. § § 1.483-2 and 1.483-3).[36] However, the discount rate will not exceed six percent, compounded semiannually, in the case of transfers of land between family members. This rule only applies if the aggregate sales price of all land sales between the family members does not exceed $500,000, and if no party to the sale is a nonresident alien (Code Sec. 483(e); Reg. § 1.483-3(b)).[37] In addition, a discount rate not in excess of nine percent (if less than the AFR), compounded semiannually, applies to most debt instruments given in consideration for the sale or exchange of property if the stated principal amount does not exceed a certain amount adjusted for inflation (¶ 1954).

1875. Adequate Stated Interest. A debt instrument with deferred payments is considered to have adequate stated interest for purposes of the unstated interest rules of Code Sec. 483 (¶ 1868) if the stated principal amount is less than or equal to its imputed principal amount (Code Secs. 483(b) and 1274(b) and (c); Reg. § § 1.483-2(b) and 1.1274-2(c)).[38] The imputed principal amount is determined by totaling the present values of all principal and interest payments due on the instrument discounted at the applicable federal rate (AFR) (¶ 83). Payments within six months after the sale are taken into account.

The AFR is the lowest rate in effect for any month in the three-calendar-month period ending with the first calendar month in which there is a binding written contract. It is determined by reference to the term of the debt instrument, including renewal and extension options, as shown in the following table (Code Sec. 1274(d); Reg. § § 1.483-3(a) and 1.1274-4(a)).[39]

Term of Debt Instrument:	*Applicable Federal Rate:*
Not over 3 years	Federal short-term rate
Over 3 years but not over 9 years	Federal mid-term rate
Over 9 years	Federal long-term rate

For sale and leaseback transactions, the discount rate is 110 percent of the AFR, compounded semiannually (Code Sec. 1274(e); Reg. § 1.1274-4(a)(2)).[40] For transactions in which a debt instrument is given in consideration for the sale or exchange of property (other than new Code Sec. 38 property) and the stated principal amount of the instrument does not exceed an inflation-adjusted amount ($5,664,800 for 2016), a nine-percent rate may be substituted for the AFR (Code Sec. 1274A; Rev. Rul. 2015-24).[41] The discount rate will not exceed six percent, compounded semiannually, in the case of certain transfers of land between family members (¶ 1872).

1881. Assumptions of Debt. If any person in connection with the sale or exchange of property assumes any debt instrument or acquires any property subject to any debt instrument, the assumption or acquisition is not generally taken into account in determining whether the unstated interest rules apply. However, when the instrument's terms and conditions are modified in a manner that would constitute an exchange, the unstated interest rules may be applied (Reg. § 1.483-1(d)).[42]

References are to Standard Federal Tax Reports; Tax Research Consultant; and Practical Tax Explanations.

[36] ¶ 22,290, ¶ 22,292, ¶ 22,294; ACCTNG: 36,310; § 19,510.10

[37] ¶ 22,290, ¶ 22,294; ACCTNG: 36,308.25; § 19,510.15

[38] ¶ 22,290, ¶ 22,292, ¶ 31,300, ¶ 31,302; ACCTNG: 36,310; § 19,510.05

[39] ¶ 22,294, ¶ 31,300, ¶ 31,304; ACCTNG: 36,162; § 19,410.10

[40] ¶ 31,300, ¶ 31,304; ACCTNG: 36,308.20

[41] ¶ 31,320, ¶ 31,322.30; ACCTNG: 36,308; § 19,315.10

[42] ¶ 22,291; ACCTNG: 36,264; § 19,505.10

Treatment of Interest

1883. Treatment of Imputed Interest. The amount of unstated interest determined under Code Sec. 483 is classified as interest for tax purposes (Reg. § 1.483-1(a)(2)).[43] As a result, it may be deductible by the buyer. Unstated interest is not deductible, however, by the issuer of a debt instrument given in consideration for the sale or exchange of personal use property (Reg. § 1.483-1(c)(3)).[44] Instead, the unstated interest must be accrued by the holder. Personal use property means any property substantially all the use of which by the taxpayer is not in connection with the taxpayer's trade or business or activities engaged in for profit (Code Sec. 1275(b)(3)).[45]

Reporting Requirements. The reporting of unstated interest depends upon whether the seller is on the cash or accrual basis. Cash basis sellers include unstated interest as interest income in the year payments are received. Sellers on the accrual basis include unstated interest in income in the year payments are due (Reg. § 1.446-2(a)).[46]

References are to Standard Federal Tax Reports; Tax Research Consultant; and Practical Tax Explanations.

[43] ¶ 22,291; ACCTNG: 36,302; § 19,515

[44] ¶ 22,291; ACCTNG: 36,306.30; § 19,505.10

[45] ¶ 31,340; ACCTNG: 36,224.10; § 19,315.10

[46] ¶ 20,610; ACCTNG: 36,200; § 19,310.05

Chapter 19

SECURITIES TRANSACTIONS

	Par.
Taxation of Securities Transactions	1901
Gains and Losses on Small Business Stock	1905
Worthless Securities	1916
Options	1919
Wash Sales	1935
Short Sales	1944
Commodities and Related Instruments	1947
Corporate Bonds and Other Debt Instruments	1950
Accounting Issues	1973

Taxation of Securities Transactions

1901. Securities Transactions. Securities such as stocks and bonds held for investment are generally capital assets. Gain or loss from the sale of securities is calculated as it is for other capital assets (¶ 1701). There are, however, a number of special rules that apply to the sale or exchange of certain securities, including securities held by dealers (¶ 1903), worthless securities (¶ 1916), options to buy securities (¶ 1919), wash sales (¶ 1935), short sales (¶ 1944), tax straddles (¶ 1948), and a corporation dealing in its own stocks or bonds (¶ 1729). In addition, gain on the sale of qualified small business stock may be excluded from gross income (¶ 1905) or rolled over to other small business stock (¶ 1907). A taxpayer may also roll over gain from the sale of publicly traded securities to an interest in a specialized small business investment company (¶ 1909). Losses from the sale of stock in certain small businesses may be treated as ordinary losses (¶ 1911 and ¶ 1913).

1903. Dealer in Securities. Securities held by dealers for sale to their customers in the ordinary course of a trade or business are not capital assets (¶ 1741). Thus, gain or loss realized from the sale or disposition is treated as ordinary gain or loss unless the securities are held primarily for personal investment (Code Sec. 1236; Reg. § 1.1236-1).[1] Securities that are held by a dealer for personal investment must be clearly identified in the dealer's records before the close of the day on which they are acquired and must never be held primarily for sale to the dealer's customers. See ¶ 1760 for a discussion of the distinction between a dealer, trader, and investor.

Mark-to-Market Requirements. Dealers in securities must use the mark-to-market method of accounting to report gains and losses from the disposition of securities (Code Sec. 475(a)).[2] Under the mark-to-market rules, any security that is inventory in the hands of a dealer must be included in inventory at its fair market value. The dealer may use the fair market value reported on its financial statements (Reg. § 1.475(a)-4).[3]

Any security that is not classified as inventory in the dealer's hands and that is held at the close of the tax year is treated as if it were sold at its fair market value on the last business day of the year. The dealer must recognize any gain or loss that would result from the deemed sale and take it into account when calculating gain or loss on the actual sale or exchange of the security.

The mark-to-market rules generally apply to all securities held by a dealer, other than those held as investments or not for sale to customers in the ordinary course of the

References are to Standard Federal Tax Reports; Tax Research Consultant; and Practical Tax Explanations.

[1] ¶ 30,670, ¶ 30,671; SALES: 45,054; § 18,805.05

[2] ¶ 22,265; SALES: 45,350; § 38,235.05

[3] ¶ 22,265E; SALES: 45,362; § 38,235.05

dealer's trade or business (Code Sec. 475(b)).[4] The rules also do not apply to debt instruments acquired in the ordinary course of a trade or business or securities that are hedges of certain positions (¶ 1949). In order for a security to be exempt from the mark-to-market requirements, it must be clearly identified in the dealer's records before the close of the day on which it is acquired, originated, or entered into.

Commodity dealers and traders in securities or commodities may elect to apply the mark-to-market rules to their noninvestment positions (Code Sec. 475(e) and (f)).[5] The election applies to commodities held by a commodities dealer in the same manner as securities held by a dealer. A trader in securities or commodities that elects mark-to-market treatment must recognize gain or loss on any security or commodity held in connection with the trading business as if the security or commodity were sold at fair market value on the last business day of the tax year.

The mark-to-market election must be made by the due date (not including extensions) of the tax return for the year prior to the year for which the election becomes effective. For example, the election must have been made by April 15, 2016, to be effective for 2016. The election is made by attaching a statement to the taxpayer's timely filed return or request for a filing extension (Rev. Proc. 99-17; Rev. Proc. 2015-13; Rev. Proc. 2016-29).[6] A taxpayer that is not required to file a tax return makes the election by placing a statement in its books and records no later than March 15 of the election year. The election may be made without the consent of the IRS, and in the case of trader of securities or commodities, may be made separately for each trade or business of the taxpayer. Once made, the election continues to apply to every tax year of the taxpayer until it is revoked with the IRS's consent.

Gains and Losses on Small Business Stock

1905. Exclusion of Gain from Small Business Stock. A noncorporate taxpayer can exclude from gross income 100 percent of gain from the sale or exchange of most qualified small business stock acquired after September 27, 2010, and held for more than five years (Code Sec. 1202, amended by the Protecting Americans from Tax Hikes (PATH) Act of 2015 (P.L. 114-113)).[7] The exclusion is 75 percent for qualified small business stock acquired after February 17, 2009, and before September 28, 2010, and 50 percent for qualified stock acquired before February 18, 2009. The exclusion is 60 percent for gain attributable to periods before 2019 if the stock is issued by a corporation in an empowerment zone (¶ 999B) and the taxpayer acquires the stock after December 21, 2000. For stock acquired before September 28, 2010, seven percent of the excluded gain is a tax preference item for alternative minimum tax (AMT) purposes (¶ 1425). The sale or exchange of qualified small business stock is reported on Form 8949.

Excludable gain on dispositions of stock from any single issuer for any given tax year is limited to the greater of: (1) $10 million reduced by the aggregate amount of eligible gain on the issuer's stock that the taxpayer excluded in prior years ($5 million for married individuals filing separately); or (2) 10 times the taxpayer's adjusted basis in all of the issuer's qualified stock disposed of during the tax year.

Qualified Small Business Stock. Qualified small business stock is stock issued after August 10, 1993, and acquired by the taxpayer at its original issue (directly or through an underwriter) in exchange for money or property, or as compensation for services provided to the corporation (Code Sec. 1202(c) and (d); Reg. § 1.1202-2).[8] Qualified stock acquired by exercising options or warrants or by converting debt is deemed acquired at original issue. The issuing corporation must be a domestic C corporation (other than a regulated investment company (RIC) (¶ 2301), cooperative, or other similar pass-through corporation).

References are to Standard Federal Tax Reports; Tax Research Consultant; and Practical Tax Explanations.

[4] ¶ 22,265; SALES: 45,354; § 38,235.15

[5] ¶ 22,265; SALES: 45,360; § 38,235.20

[6] ¶ 22,268.20; SALES: 45,360.15; § 38,235.20

[7] ¶ 30,372; SALES: 15,300; § 16,605.05

[8] ¶ 30,372, ¶ 30,374; SALES: 15,304.05; § 16,605.10

Both before and immediately after the qualified stock's issuance, the corporation's aggregate gross assets must not exceed $50 million. All corporations that are members of the same parent-subsidiary controlled group are treated as one corporation in applying this test. In addition, during substantially all of the taxpayer's holding period, at least 80 percent of the value of the corporation's assets must be used in the active conduct of one or more qualified trades or businesses (Code Sec. 1202(e)). The performance of services in the fields of health, law, engineering, architecture, etc., are not qualified trade or business, nor are the hospitality, farming, insurance, finance or mineral extraction industries. However, a specialized small business investment company (SSBIC), licensed under section 301(d) of the Small Business Investment Act of 1958, meets the active business test (¶ 1909). Small business stock is not qualified if it has been the subject of certain redemptions that are more than *de minimis*.

Qualified stock that is converted to other stock of the corporation (such as preferred stock) remains qualified stock (Code Sec. 1202(f)). A taxpayer who acquires qualified stock by gift or inheritance is treated as having acquired it in the same manner as the transferor and adds the transferor's holding period to his or her own (Code Sec. 1202(h)). Gain on dispositions of qualified stock held by a pass-through entity (partnership, S corporation, RIC, or common trust fund) for more than five years is excludable when it is passed through to partners, shareholders, and participants who held interests in the entity when it acquired the stock and at all times thereafter. However, the exclusion cannot reflect any increase in that person's share of the entity after the entity acquired the stock (Code Sec. 1202(g)).

1907. Rollover of Gain from Small Business Stock. A noncorporate taxpayer may elect to roll over capital gain from the sale of qualified small business stock (¶ 1905) held for more than six months if other qualified small business stock is purchased during the 60-day period beginning on the date of sale (Code Sec. 1045; Reg. § 1.1045-1).[9] The replacement stock must meet the active business requirement for the six-month period following its purchase. Except for purposes of applying the six-month active business test, the holding period of the stock purchased includes the holding period of the stock sold. Gain is recognized only to the extent that the amount realized on the sale exceeds the cost of the replacement stock. The basis of the newly purchased stock is reduced by the amount of gain rolled over. Special rules apply for partnerships that want to roll over gain from a business that is held in the form of qualified small business stock. The sale of the stock is reported on Form 8949.

1909. Rollover of Gain from Publicly Traded Securities. Individuals and C corporations may elect to defer recognition of capital gain realized on the sale of publicly traded securities if the sale proceeds are used within 60 days to purchase common stock or a partnership interest in a specialized small business investment company (SSBIC) (Code Sec. 1044; Reg. § 1.1044(a)-1).[10] Gain must be recognized to the extent that the sale proceeds exceed the cost of the SSBIC common stock or partnership interest. An SSBIC is a corporation or partnership licensed under section 301(d) of the Small Business Investment Act of 1958 to finance small business concerns owned by disadvantaged persons.

The exclusion for an individual (including spouses who file a joint return) is limited to $50,000 in any single tax year and $500,000 over the taxpayer's lifetime ($25,000 and $250,000, respectively, for a married individual filing separately). Gain excluded on a joint return is allocated equally between the spouses in applying the $500,000 lifetime limit. For a C corporation, the annual and cumulative limits are $250,000 and $1 million, respectively. All corporations that are members of the same controlled group are treated as one taxpayer, and any gain excluded by the predecessor of a C corporation is treated as gain excluded by the successor corporation. The deferred gain generally reduces the taxpayer's basis in the acquired stock or partnership interest. However, if the stock is

References are to Standard Federal Tax Reports; Tax Research Consultant; and Practical Tax Explanations.

[9] ¶ 29,850, ¶ 29,852; SALES: 15,308; § 16,610.05

[10] ¶ 29,845, ¶ 29,845B; SALES: 27,400; § 16,615, § 18,245

qualified small business stock, basis is not reduced when calculating gain eligible for the exclusion for qualified small business stock (¶ 1905).

The election to roll over gain into an SSBIC must be made by the due date (including extensions) for the taxpayer's return for the year in which the publicly traded securities are sold. The election is made by reporting the entire gain from the sale on Form 8949. The taxpayer must also attach a statement showing how the nonrecognized gain was calculated, the SSBIC in which the sale proceeds were invested, the date the SSBIC stock or partnership interest was purchased, and the basis of the SSBIC interest. Once made, the election is revocable only with the IRS's consent.

1911. Losses on Small Business Stock (Section 1244 Stock). An individual's loss on the sale, exchange, or worthlessness of small business stock (section 1244 stock) may be treated as an ordinary loss, even if the stock is a capital asset (Code Sec. 1244).[11] The maximum amount deductible as an ordinary loss in any tax year is $50,000 ($100,000 for married individuals filing a joint return).

The ordinary loss is treated as a loss from the taxpayer's trade or business in computing a net operating loss (NOL) for the tax year (¶ 1145) and is reported on Form 4797. Any loss that exceeds the annual limit is treated as a capital loss and reported on Form 8949. Any gain on the disposition of section 1244 stock is capital gain if the stock was a capital asset in the taxpayer's hands (¶ 1741).

Section 1244 stock is stock of a domestic corporation (including preferred stock) issued after November 6, 1978, that meets the following requirements (additional requirements apply to stock issued after June 30, 1958, and before November 7, 1978):

- the stock must have been issued to the taxpayer, or a partnership in which the taxpayer was a partner, in exchange for money or property other than stock or securities;

- the issuing corporation must be a small business corporation, meaning that at the time the stock was issued the aggregate amount of money and other property (taken into account at its adjusted basis) received by the corporation as contributions to capital and as paid-in surplus (not only for the stock in question but any previously issued stock) did not exceed $1 million (so S corporation stock does not automatically qualify as section 1244 stock); and

- during the corporation's five most recent tax years ending before the date the stock is sold by the taxpayer, more than 50 percent of its gross receipts must have been derived from sources other than royalties, rents, dividends, interest, annuities, and gains from the sales of securities (since the corporation must be largely an operating company, stock in corporations with little or no gross receipts is not eligible for ordinary loss treatment) (Reg. § § 1.1244(c)-1 and 1.1244(c)-2).[12]

1913. Losses on Small Business Investment Company Stock (SBIC). A loss on the sale, exchange, or worthlessness of stock in a small business investment company (SBIC) (¶ 2392) may be treated as an ordinary loss on Form 4797, even if the stock is a capital asset in the taxpayer's hands (Code Sec. 1242; Reg. § 1.1242-1(b)).[13] The SBIC must be licensed to operate as an SBIC when the loss is sustained. The loss is not subject to the limitations on the allowance of nonbusiness deductions in computing net operating losses (NOLs) (¶ 1145). When a taxpayer has several transactions involving SBIC stock, each transaction is considered separately; they are not netted to determine if the taxpayer has an overall gain or loss. A loss on a short sale of SBIC stock (¶ 1944) with other SBIC stock acquired only for the purpose of closing the short sale is a capital loss under the short sale rules, rather than an ordinary loss (Rev. Rul. 63-65).

References are to Standard Federal Tax Reports; Tax Research Consultant; and Practical Tax Explanations.

[11] ¶ 30,790; SALES: 18,200; § 16,620.05

[12] ¶ 30,793, ¶ 30,794; SALES: 18,100; § 16,620.15

[13] ¶ 30,753, ¶ 30,754; SALES: 18,304; § 45,410.15

Worthless Securities

1916. Worthless Securities. A security that becomes completely worthless during the tax year is treated as sold or exchanged on the last day of the tax year (Code Sec. 165(g); Reg. § 1.165-5).[14] If the security is a capital asset (¶ 1741), the loss is generally a capital loss subject to the limits on capital losses (¶ 1752). If the security is not a capital asset, the loss is an ordinary loss subject to the limits on ordinary losses (¶ 1101). The amount of the loss is the taxpayer's adjusted basis in the security, less any amount compensated for by insurance.

> **Example:** On December 10, 2015, Judy Green purchased shares of Xetco Corporation for $5,000. On May 1, 2016, she received formal notification that the shares of Xetco were worthless. In claiming a capital loss for the worthless shares on her 2016 tax return, Judy must treat the shares as becoming worthless on December 31, 2016. As a result, her $5,000 capital loss is a long term loss even though she did not own the shares for more than 12 months before they became worthless.

A security becomes totally worthless when it has no value or potential value as the result of an identifiable event. The abandonment of a security establishes its worthlessness to the taxpayer. To abandon a security, the taxpayer must permanently surrender and relinquish all rights in it and receive no consideration for the exchange. Deductions for partial worthlessness are generally not allowed.

A security includes stock, the right to subscribe for or receive stock, and bonds, debentures, notes, certificates, or other evidence of indebtedness issued with interest coupons or in registered form by a corporation or government to pay a fixed or determinable sum of money. A worthless debt that does not meet the definition of a security (e.g., because it was not issued by a corporation or government) is treated as a bad debt (¶ 1135 and ¶ 1143).

Securities held by a securities dealer as inventory are not capital assets, so a dealer's loss from worthlessness is an ordinary loss (¶ 1903). An ordinary loss may also be claimed for losses from worthless securities that are section 1244 stock (¶ 1911), issued by a small business investment company (SBIC) (¶ 1913), held by a small business investment company (¶ 2392), securities in an affiliated corporation, or securities held by a bank or other financial institution (¶ 2383).

Options

1919. Options to Buy or Sell Property. Gain or loss from the sale or exchange of an option to buy or sell property, including a cash settlement option and an option on a section 1256 contract (¶ 1947), is considered gain or loss from the sale or exchange of the underlying property (Code Sec. 1234; Reg. § 1.1234-1).[15] Thus, the gain or loss is capital only if the option covers property that would be a capital asset in the taxpayer's hands (¶ 1741). The length of time the taxpayer held the option determines whether a capital gain or loss is short term or long term unless the sale or exchange is part of a hedging transaction (¶ 1949). If the underlying property is section 1231 property, gain or loss on the sale or exchange of the option may be section 1231 gain or loss (¶ 1747).

If a loss arises from an option holder's failure to exercise an option, the option is deemed to have been sold or exchanged on the date it expired. For the grantor of an option for stock, securities, commodities, or commodity futures (including an option granted as part of a straddle (¶ 1948)), gain or loss from any closing transaction and gain on the lapse of the option is a short-term capital gain or loss. See ¶ 1921 for a discussion of holders and writers of options on securities (i.e., puts and calls).

These characterization rules do not apply to gain or loss realized on the sale or exchange of an option by a dealer who holds options primarily for sale to customers (¶ 1903). They also do not apply to gain realized from the sale or exchange of an

References are to Standard Federal Tax Reports; Tax Research Consultant; and Practical Tax Explanations.

[14] ¶ 9802, ¶ 10,000; BUSEXP: 30,262; § 16,935

[15] ¶ 30,610, ¶ 30,611; SALES: 45,202; § 19,110, § 19,115

employee stock option (¶ 1925 and ¶ 1927), an option to lease property, an option to buy or sell inventory, an option equivalent to a dividend, an option involving section 306 stock (¶ 739), and an option included as part of a short sale (¶ 1944).

1921. Puts and Calls. Puts are options to sell, and calls are options to buy, stock, securities, or commodities at a set price on or before a specified date. Puts and calls are issued by writers (grantors) to holders for premiums. They end when the holder exercises the option, the option lapses, or the option is effectively terminated at its current fair market value in a closing transaction (Rev. Rul. 78-182; IRS Pub. 550).[16]

Holders of Puts and Calls. The purchase of a put option or call option is not a taxable event. The cost of purchasing the put or call is a nondeductible capital expenditure (Rev. Rul. 71-521).[17] If the holder sells a put or call without exercising it, the difference between its cost and the amount received is either a long-term or short-term capital gain or loss, depending on how long it was held (¶ 1919). If the option expires, its cost is either a long-term or short-term capital loss, depending on the taxpayer's holding period, which ends on the expiration date. If the holder exercises a call, its cost is added to the basis of the security purchased. If the holder exercises a put, the amount realized on the sale of the underlying security is reduced by the cost of the put when computing gain or loss on the sale of the security. That gain or loss is long term or short term depending on the taxpayer's holding period for the underlying security (Rev. Rul. 78-182; IRS Pub. 550).[18] The acquisition of a put is considered a short sale, and the exercise, sale, or lapse of the put is a closing of the short sale (¶ 1944).

Writers of Puts and Calls. If a taxpayer writes or grants a call or put option, the premium received is not included in income at the time of receipt. Instead it is deferred until the option expires, the taxpayer buys or sells the underlying security when the option is exercised, or the taxpayer engages in a closing transaction.

When the option expires, the premium can then be treated as a short-term capital gain. If a call is exercised and the taxpayer sells the underlying security, the premium is added to the amount realized on the sale and any gain or loss is long-term or short-term depending on how long the taxpayer held the security. If a put is exercised and the taxpayer buys the underlying security, then the premium reduces its basis in the security. The taxpayer's holding period on the security begins on the date of the purchase, not on the date the put was written.

The taxpayer can also terminate a put or call through a closing transaction—such as repurchasing the option or substituting the original option by purchasing another option with identical terms. The difference between the premium originally received and the amount paid in the closing transaction is short-term capital gain or loss.

Example 1: Ten call options were issued on April 8 for $4,000. The options expired in December without being exercised. The holder (buyer) of the options recognizes a short-term capital loss of $4,000. The writer of the options recognizes a short-term capital gain of $4,000.

Example 2: Assume the same facts as in Example 1, except that on May 10, the options were sold for $6,000. The holder (buyer) of the options who sold them recognizes a short-term capital gain of $2,000. If the writer of the options bought them back, he or she would recognize a short-term capital loss of $2,000.

Example 3: Assume the facts as in Example 1, except that the options were exercised on May 27. The holder (buyer) adds the $4,000 cost of the options to the basis of the stock bought through the exercise of the options. The writer adds the $4,000 received from writing the options to the amount realized from selling the stock. The gain or loss is short term or long term, depending on the holding period of the stock.

References are to Standard Federal Tax Reports; Tax Research Consultant; and Practical Tax Explanations.

[16] ¶ 30,614.14; SALES: 45,200; § 19,105

[17] ¶ 30,592.70; SALES: 45,202; § 19,120

[18] ¶ 30,614.14; SALES: 45,200; § 19,105

1923. Nonstatutory Stock Options. An employee or independent contractor granted a stock option as compensation for services rendered is generally subject to the rules regarding restricted property transfers (¶ 713) when the option is granted or exercised, unless it is an incentive stock option (ISO) (¶ 1925) or an option granted under an employee stock purchase plan (ESPP) (¶ 1929) (Code Sec. 83(e)(1); Reg. § 1.83-7).[19]

If a nonstatutory stock option has a readily ascertainable fair market value (FMV) when it is granted, the restricted property rules apply on the grant date. The taxpayer has ordinary income equal to the stock's fair market value on the grant date, less any amount paid. If a nonstatutory stock option does not have a readily ascertainable FMV when it is granted, the restricted property rules apply when the option is exercised or disposed of by the taxpayer, even if the FMV becomes ascertainable before exercise or disposition. If the option is exercised, the taxpayer has ordinary income equal to the stock's FMV at the exercise date or when substantially vested, less the exercise price.

If a nonstatutory stock option is sold or disposed of in an arm's-length transaction, the taxpayer is considered to have exercised the option and has income equal to the money or property received, less the exercise price. If the sale or disposition is not an arm's-length transaction, the taxpayer is not considered to have exercised the option. The taxpayer must, nonetheless, include in income as compensation the amount of money or property received. In addition, when the transferee exercises the option, the taxpayer (transferor) has additional income equal to the FMV of stock acquired by the transferee, less the exercise price and any amount the taxpayer received from the sale of the option. A sale or disposition to a related person is not an arm's-length transaction. If the holder of an option incurs a loss on failure to exercise the option, then it is deemed to have been sold or exchanged on the date it expired (¶ 1919).

Readily Ascertainable Market Value. A stock option generally has a readily ascertainable FMV if it is actively traded on an established securities market (Reg. § 1.83-7(b)).[20] An option that is not actively traded on an established securities market has a readily ascertainable value if the taxpayer can demonstrate that the option is transferable and immediately exercisable, there is no condition or restriction on the underlying property that would have a significant effect on its FMV, and the FMV of the option privilege is readily ascertainable.

Sale of Stock. Stock acquired through the exercise of a nonstatutory stock option is treated as any other investment property when sold or exchanged (IRS Pub. 525). The taxpayer's basis is the amount paid for the stock, plus any amount included in income upon grant or exercise of the option. The taxpayer's holding period begins when the option was acquired if it had a readily ascertainable value, or the date the option was exercised if it did not.

Employer's Deduction. An employer may deduct the value of a nonqualified stock option as a business expense for the tax year in which the option is included in the employee's gross income (Code Sec. 83(h); Reg. § 1.83-6(a)).[21] When the employer and the employee have different tax years, the employer generally claims the deduction in the tax year in which, or with which, the employee's tax year ends. If the option's market value, however, is not readily ascertainable at the time of grant, and the employee's rights in the stock are substantially vested upon exercise, the employer may take the deduction in accordance with its usual method of accounting.

Reporting Requirements. In most situations, when an employee exercises a nonqualified stock option, the employer must report the excess of the fair market value of the stock received over the amount that the employee paid for that stock (i.e., "the spread") on the employee's Form W-2.

1925. Incentive Stock Options. An incentive stock option (ISO) is an option granted by an employer corporation (or related corporation) that gives an employee the

References are to Standard Federal Tax Reports; Tax Research Consultant; and Practical Tax Explanations.

[19] ¶ 6380, ¶ 6388; COMPEN: 18,500; § 21,701

[20] ¶ 6388; COMPEN: 18,502, COMPEN: 18,504; § 21,710.05

[21] ¶ 6380, ¶ 6386; COMPEN: 18,508; § 21,720

right to purchase stock of the employer, often at a discount. Unlike with a nonstatutory stock option (¶ 1923), the employee generally does not realize gain or loss when an ISO is granted or exercised if certain requirements are met (Code Sec. 421(a)).[22] Instead, the employee is not subject to income tax until the shares acquired by the exercise of the option are sold. See ¶ 1927 for a discussion of ISO plan requirements.

Gain or loss from the sale of the stock received in an ISO is a capital gain or loss if the taxpayer holds the stock for at least two years after the option is granted and for at least one year after the option is exercised (Code Sec. 422(a); Reg. § 1.422-1(a)).[23] The amount of gain or loss is the difference between the amount the taxpayer paid for the stock (the option price) and the amount received when the taxpayer sold the stock. The taxpayer must remain an employee of the corporation from the time the option is granted until three months before the option is exercised (one year if employment ends because of the taxpayer's permanent and total disability). If the holder of an ISO dies, the deceased's executor, administrator, or representative may exercise the option and receive the same treatment but does not have to do so within three months after the death of the employee (Reg. § 1.421-2(c)).[24]

If the employee sells the stock before the required holding period ends (a disqualifying disposition), gain on the sale is ordinary income to the extent that the fair market value of the stock when the option was exercised exceeds the exercise price (Code Sec. 421(b); Reg. § 1.421-2(b)).[25] Any additional gain is capital gain, and any loss is a capital loss. The gain is recognized for the tax year in which the sale occurs. Gain from a disqualifying disposition is excluded from wages for FICA and FUTA tax purposes and is not subject to income tax withholding (Code Secs. 3121(a)(22) and 3306(b)(19)).

Basis of ISO. An employee's basis in an ISO is the amount that the employee paid for the option. If the employee did not pay for the option and the option lapses, the employee does not have a deductible loss because there is no basis. An employee's basis in stock purchased through an ISO is the amount paid for the stock when the option was exercised, plus any amount paid for the option.

Annual Dollar Limit. The maximum value of stock with respect to which ISOs may first become exercisable in any one year is $100,000. Stock is valued when the option is granted. Options are taken into account in the order in which they are granted, and options issued under ISO plans of any parent, subsidiary, or predecessor corporation are taken into account (Code Sec. 422(d)).[26]

Minimum Tax. The favorable tax treatment of ISOs does not apply for purposes of the alternative minimum tax (AMT). Instead, the *excess* of the (1) fair market value of the stock received upon the exercise of the option, over (2) the amount paid for the stock, plus any amount paid for the ISO, must generally be recognized as an AMT adjustment (¶ 1435). As a result, individuals who have exercised ISOs to purchase stock with a high fair market value that declined before they were able to sell it could be left with large AMT liabilities and no cash to pay them.

1927. Incentive Stock Options Plan Requirements. A stock option granted by an employer to an employee must satisfy several requirements to qualify for favorable tax treatment as an incentive stock option (ISO) (¶ 1925) (Code Sec. 422(b); Reg. § 1.422-2).[27] ISOs must be granted under a plan adopted by the granting corporation that sets out the total number of shares that may be issued under options and the employees who may receive the options. The plan must be approved by the stockholders within 12 months before or after the corporation adopts it.

The options must be granted within 10 years from the date the plan is adopted or approved, whichever is earlier, and the options must be exercisable within 10 years from

References are to Standard Federal Tax Reports; Tax Research Consultant; and Practical Tax Explanations.

[22] ¶ 19,602; COMPEN: 24,050; § 21,510

[23] ¶ 19,800, ¶ 19,801A; COMPEN: 24,150; § 21,525.05

[24] ¶ 19,609; COMPEN: 24,152; § 21,520.15

[25] ¶ 19,602, ¶ 19,609; COMPEN: 24,056, COMPEN: 24,154; § 21,530.10

[26] ¶ 19,800; COMPEN: 24,116; § 21,515.40

[27] ¶ 19,800, ¶ 19,801C; COMPEN: 24,100; § 21,515.05

the date of the grant. The option price may not be less than the fair market value of the stock at the time the option is granted, and the option may not be transferable other than at the grantee's death. The option may be exercised only by the employee. In addition, the employee, *at the time the option is granted,* may not own stock with more than 10 percent of the total combined voting power of all classes of stock of the employer corporation or its parent or any subsidiary.

1929. Employee Stock Purchase Plans. An employee stock purchase plan (ESPP) may grant employees the option to purchase stock in their employer or the employer's parent or subsidiary. Unlike with a nonstatutory stock option (¶ 1923), the employee generally does not realize gain or loss when an option is granted or exercised under an ESPP, if certain requirements are met (Code Sec. 421(a)).[28] Instead, the employee is not subject to income tax until the shares acquired by the exercise of the option are sold. See ¶ 1931 for a discussion of ESPP plan requirements.

Gain or loss from the sale of the stock received in an ESPP is a capital gain or loss if the taxpayer holds the stock for at a least two years after the option is granted and for at least one year after the option is exercised (Code Sec. 423(a)).[29] The amount of gain or loss is the difference between the amount the taxpayer paid for the stock (the option price) and the amount the taxpayer received when he or she sold the stock. The taxpayer must remain an employee of the corporation from the time the option is granted until three months before the option is exercised (one year if employment ends because of the taxpayer's permanent and total disability). If the employee dies, his or her executor, administrator, or representative may exercise the option and receive the same treatment but does not have to do so within three months after the employee's death (Reg. § 1.421-2(c)).[30]

If the option price is less than 100 percent (but not less than 85 percent) of the fair market value of the stock, then the favorable tax treatment does not apply when the taxpayer disposes of the stock (Code Sec. 423(c)).[31] Instead, the employee recognizes ordinary income equal to the *lesser* of:

- the excess of the fair market value of the shares when sold or on the employee' death, over the option price, or
- the excess of the fair market value of the shares when the option was granted, over the option price.

The balance of any gain is capital gain. Any loss from the sale is a capital loss.

If the employee sells the stock before the required holding period ends (a disqualifying disposition), gain on the sale is ordinary income equal to the fair market value of the stock when the option was exercised, less the exercise price (Code Sec. 421(b); Reg. § 1.421-2(b)).[32] Any additional gain is capital gain, and any loss is a capital loss. The gain is recognized for the tax year in which the sale occurs. Gain from a disqualifying disposition is excluded from wages for FICA and FUTA tax purposes and is not subject to income tax withholding (Code Secs. 3121(a)(22) and 3306(b)(19)).

An ESPP is different from an employee stock ownership plan (ESOP) (¶ 2103). While both plans involve employee ownership of company stock, an ESOP is a retirement plan that holds employer stock for the benefit of participating employees.

1931. Employee Stock Purchase Plan Requirements. An employee stock purchase plan (ESPP) must satisfy several requirements in order for options acquired under the plan to qualify for favorable tax treatment (¶ 1929) (Code Sec. 423(b)).[33] ESPPs are written, shareholder-approved plans under which employees are granted options to purchase shares of their employer's stock or the stock of a parent or subsidiary corporation.

References are to Standard Federal Tax Reports; Tax Research Consultant; and Practical Tax Explanations.

[28] ¶ 19,602; COMPEN: 21,050; § 21,601

[29] ¶ 19,900; COMPEN: 21,054; § 21,625.10

[30] ¶ 19,609; COMPEN: 21,054.15; § 21,625.10

[31] ¶ 19,900; COMPEN: 21,054.10; § 21,625.10

[32] ¶ 19,602, ¶ 19,609; COMPEN: 21,054; § 21,625.10

[33] ¶ 19,900; COMPEN: 21,052; § 21,610.05

An ESPP cannot grant options to any employee who has more than five percent of the voting power or value of the employer's stock, or that of any parent or subsidiary of the employer. The plan must include all full-time employees except those with less than two years of employment, highly compensated employees (¶ 2114), part-time employees, and seasonal workers. The plan must be nondiscriminatory, though it may limit the amount of stock any employee can buy, and the amount of stock that each employee may become entitled to buy may be tied to compensation.

The option price must be at least equal to the *lesser* of: (1) 85 percent of the fair market value of the stock at the time the option is granted, or (2) 85 percent of the fair market value of the stock at the time the option is exercised. The option must be exercised within 27 months after it is granted (or within five years if the option price test considers the fair market value of the stock at the time the option is exercised). No employee can acquire the right to buy more than $25,000 of stock per year (valued at the time the option is granted).

Wash Sales

1935. Wash Sales of Stock or Securities. Under the wash sale rule, a loss on a sale or other disposition of stock or securities is not deductible unless it is incurred in the ordinary course of a securities dealer's trade or business (¶ 1903) (Code Sec. 1091; Reg. § 1.1091-1).[34] A wash sale occurs if the taxpayer sells or disposes of stock or securities, and within 30 days before or after the disposition date (the 61-day period), the taxpayer acquires substantially identical stock or securities (¶ 1937). Stock and securities acquisitions include contacts and options to acquire them, and acquisition by the taxpayer's traditional IRA or Roth IRA (Rev. Rul. 2008-5).

Only a portion of the total loss is disallowed if a taxpayer acquires less stock or securities during the 61-day period than the taxpayer sold. The nondeductible loss is allocated to the stock or securities disposed of in the order of their time of acquisition. When the amount of stock and securities acquired during the 61-day period is more than the amount sold, the shares acquired that resulted in the nondeductibility of the loss are determined by the order of their acquisition.

A loss realized on the closing of a short sale of stock or securities (¶ 1944) is disallowed under the wash sale rule if within 30 days before or after the closing, the taxpayer sells substantially identical stock or securities or enters into another short sale of substantially identical stock or securities. The wash sale rule also applies to a loss realized on the sale, exchange, or termination of a securities futures contract to sell stock or securities. However, it does not apply to losses from sales or trades of commodity futures contracts and foreign currencies.

The disallowance of a loss under the wash sale rule does not apply to stock or securities acquired in a nontaxable exchange (¶ 1719). This includes stock or securities acquired by gift, bequest, or devise, or through a nonrecognition transaction such as a like-kind exchange, exchange of property for stock, exchange of stock for stock, and spousal transfer incident to divorce. The wash sale rule also does not apply to any loss attributable to a section 1256 contract (¶ 1947) (Code Sec. 1256(f)(5)).[35]

A loss that is disallowed because of the wash sale rule is added to the cost basis of the new stock or securities unless they are acquired through an IRA. The adjustment postpones the loss deduction until the disposition of the new stock or securities (Code Sec. 1091(d); Reg. § 1.1091-2).[36] The taxpayer's holding period of the new stock or securities includes the holding period of the stock or securities sold (Code Sec. 1223(3)).[37]

References are to Standard Federal Tax Reports; Tax Research Consultant; and Practical Tax Explanations.

[34] ¶ 30,180, ¶ 30,181; SALES: 45,150; § 18,905

[35] ¶ 31,100; SALES: 45,150; § 18,910

[36] ¶ 30,180, ¶ 30,182; SALES: 45,164; § 18,920

[37] ¶ 30,460; SALES: 45,164; § 18,925

Example: Betty buys 100 shares of Rapid Corporation stock for $1,000 on January 1, 2016. She sells these shares on January 2, 2017, for $750. Within 30 days from the sale, she buys another 100 shares of Rapid Corporation for $800. Because Betty purchased substantially identical stock, she cannot deduct the $250 loss that she realized on the sale. However, she adds the disallowed loss of $250 to the cost of her new shares. As a result, her basis in the new shares is $1,050 ($800 cost, plus the $250 loss she could not claim under the wash sale rule). If she sells the new shares on March 31, 2017, any gain is long-term capital gain.

The wash sale rule applies without regard to gain or loss realized on the sale of separate lots of the same stock or security. Thus, a disallowed loss on one lot does not reduce gain realized on a separate lot (Rev. Rul. 70-231).[38] The wash sale rule also does not specifically apply when stock is sold at a loss and a related party, such as the seller's spouse, reacquires the stock within the prohibited 61-day period; however, the loss may be disallowed under the related party rules of Code Sec. 267 (¶ 1717) on the ground that there is an indirect sale to the spouse (*J. P. McWilliams*, SCt, 47-1 USTC ¶ 9289).[39]

1937. Substantially Identical Stock or Securities. In determining whether stock or securities are substantially identical under the wash sale rule (¶ 1935), all facts and circumstances must be considered. Ordinarily, stocks or securities of one corporation are not considered substantially identical to stocks or securities of another corporation. They may, however, be substantially identical in some cases such as in a reorganization—the stocks and securities of the predecessor and successor corporations may be substantially identical (IRS Pub. 550).

A corporation's bonds or preferred stock are not ordinarily substantially identical to its common stock. When the bonds or preferred stock are convertible into common stock, however, the relative values, price changes, and other circumstances may make them substantially identical to common stock (Rev. Rul. 77-201).[40]

1942. Share Lending Agreements. No gain or loss is recognized on an exchange of securities that is part of a qualifying securities lending arrangement in which the taxpayer transfers the securities and later receives identical securities in return (Code Sec. 1058).[41] In effect, the taxpayer is merely lending securities to the other party to the transaction. This provision is intended to mitigate delays that a broker may face in obtaining securities by allowing the broker to borrow securities without creating tax consequences for the lender. However, the provision applies to any taxpayer that lends securities, not just those that lend to brokers. The securities lending agreement must require the borrower to return securities to the taxpayer that are identical to those that were lent. The taxpayer's basis in the securities received is the same as the taxpayer's basis in the securities that were loaned to the borrower.

Short Sales

1944. Short Sales. A short sale is a transaction in which a taxpayer sells shares of stock or property that he or she does not own or wish to transfer at the time of the sale. The taxpayer sells short by: (1) borrowing property (usually from a broker) and delivering it to the buyer; and (2) closing or covering the transaction at a later date by purchasing substantially identical property and delivering it to the lender, or making delivery out of property the taxpayer held at the time of the sale (Code Sec. 1233(a); Reg. § 1.1233-1(a)).[42]

The seller generally does not recognize gain or loss on a short sale transaction until the property is delivered to the lender and the short sale is closed. However, if the property that has been sold short becomes substantially worthless, the seller must recognize gain as if the short sale were closed when the property became substantially

References are to Standard Federal Tax Reports; Tax Research Consultant; and Practical Tax Explanations.

[38] ¶ 30,183.11; SALES: 45,160; § 18,930

[39] ¶ 30,183.109; SALES: 45,166.10

[40] ¶ 30,183.14; SALES: 45,154; § 18,915

[41] ¶ 30,000; SALES: 3,302.35; § 18,855

[42] ¶ 30,590, ¶ 30,591; SALES: 45,100; § 19,001

worthless (Code Sec. 1233(h)).[43] In addition, a short sale of an appreciated financial position may cause the taxpayer to be treated as making a constructive sale at the time that the taxpayer entered into the transaction (¶ 1945). A taxpayer can avoid the prohibition on recognizing losses from a short sale if the position is part of a mixed straddle (¶ 1948).

Gain or loss on a closed short sale is the difference between the amount realized on the sale of the borrowed property and the taxpayer's adjusted basis in the property used to close the transaction. The character of that gain or loss generally depends on the character of the property used to close the sale in the hands of the taxpayer. Thus, a taxpayer has capital gain or loss if the property used to close the short sale is a capital asset (¶ 1741). Hedging transactions, however, generally result in ordinary income or loss (¶ 1949). If a short seller has a gain on the transaction when the replacement property is purchased, the gain is recognized at that time. A loss is not recognized until the replacement property is delivered to the lender (Rev. Rul. 2002-44).[44]

Holding Period. The short-term or long-term nature of a short seller's capital gain or loss generally depends on how long the seller held the property that is delivered to the lender to close out the sale.

> **Example:** On January 2, Mary Edwards agrees to sell 100 shares of Niftexo Corp. for $10 a share to Susan Croft. Mary does not own any Niftexo shares, so she borrows the 100 shares from her broker and delivers them to Susan. On May 1, Mary buys 100 shares of Niftexo at a price of $15 a share, and immediately delivers them to her broker to replace the shares she had borrowed. Her recognized loss of $500 is short term because her holding period of the Niftexo shares she delivered to her lender (the broker) is determined by the amount of time she held the shares (i.e., less than one day).

Gain from the short sale of a capital asset is short-term capital gain if the taxpayer owned substantially identical property for one year or less on the date of the short sale, or if the taxpayer acquired substantially identical property after the short sale and by the date the sale is closed (Code Sec. 1233(b); Reg. § 1.1233-1(c)).[45] The holding period of the substantially identical property begins on the closing of the short sale or on the date the property is sold, whichever happens first. Any loss realized on the short sale of a capital asset is a long-term capital loss if the taxpayer owned substantially identical property for more than one year even when the property used to close the short sale is held by the seller for one year or less (Code Sec. 1233(d)).

Special holding period rules apply to brokers' arbitrage transactions (Code Sec. 1233(f); Reg. § 1.1233-1(f)).[46] Losses on short sales of stock or securities are also subject to the wash sales rule (¶ 1935).

1945. Constructive Sale of Appreciated Positions. Appreciated financial positions are treated as constructively sold when the taxpayer enters into certain transactions (Code Sec. 1259(a)).[47] The taxpayer must recognize gain as if the position were sold, assigned, or otherwise terminated at its fair market value *as of the date of the constructive sale* and immediately repurchased. Any gain or loss subsequently realized on the position is adjusted to reflect the gain recognized. A new holding period begins on the date of the constructive sale.

An appreciated financial position is generally any position with respect to any stock, debt instrument, or partnership interest if gain would arise if the position were sold, assigned, or otherwise terminated at its fair market value (Code Sec. 1259(b)). It does not include any position that is subject to mark-to-market requirements (¶ 1903), including section 1256 contracts (¶ 1947). It also does not include any position or hedge of a position with regard to straight debt if:

References are to Standard Federal Tax Reports; Tax Research Consultant; and Practical Tax Explanations.

[43] ¶ 30,590; SALES: 45,120; § 19,005

[44] ¶ 30,463.4383; SALES: 45,102

[45] ¶ 30,590, ¶ 30,591; SALES: 45,104; § 19,010.10

[46] ¶ 30,590, ¶ 30,591; SALES: 45,112

[47] ¶ 31,130; SALES: 45,450

- the debt unconditionally entitles the holder to receive a specified principal amount;
- interest payments are payable based on a fixed rate or, to the extent provided in regulations, at a variable rate; and
- the debt is not convertible into stock of the issuer or any related person as defined by Code Secs. 267(b) or 707(b) (¶ 432 and ¶ 1717).

A constructive sale generally is one of four specified types of transactions offsetting an appreciated financial position that have the effect of substantially eliminating both the taxpayer's risk of loss and chance for further gain on the position. They include: short sales (¶ 1944); notional principal contracts; forward or futures contracts; and the purchase of property to cover the position if the appreciated position is itself a short position (Code Sec. 1259(c)). A contract for the sale of appreciated financial assets that are not publicly traded is not a constructive sale if the contract settles within one year after the date it was entered. A safe harbor may apply to certain short-term hedges that would otherwise be treated as constructive sales if:

- the transaction is closed on or before the end of the 30th day after the end of the tax year in which the transaction was entered;
- the taxpayer holds the appreciated financial position throughout the 60-day period beginning on the date the transaction is closed; and
- at no time during that 60-day period is the taxpayer's risk of loss with respect to the position reduced by a circumstance that would be described in Code Sec. 246(c)(4) if the position was treated as stock.

The closed transaction exception also applies to certain reestablished positions.

1946. Payments in Lieu of Dividends on Short Sales. A taxpayer who borrows stock to make a short sale (¶ 1944) may have to make payments to the lender in lieu of dividends distributed during the short position. The payments may be treated by an individual as an itemized deduction for investment interest expense (¶ 1094) if the short sale is held open for at least 46 days (more than one year if extraordinary dividends are involved). If the short sale is closed by the 45th day after the date of the short sale (one year or less if extraordinary dividends are involved), the short seller cannot claim the deduction and must instead increase the basis of the stock used to close the short sale by the amount of the payment (Code Sec. 263(h)).[48] The 45-day and one-year periods are suspended for any period in which the borrower holds options to buy substantially identical property or holds one or more positions in such property.

Commodities and Related Instruments

1947. Section 1256 Contracts. Each section 1256 contract held by a taxpayer at the end of the tax year is generally subject to mark-to-market requirements that treat the contract as sold at its fair market value on the last business day of the year (Code Sec. 1256).[49] The mark-to-market rule also applies if the taxpayer's obligations (or rights) under a section 1256 contract are terminated or transferred during the tax year.

Capital gains or losses resulting from the mark-to-market requirement for section 1256 contracts are 60 percent long-term and 40 percent short-term without regard to the taxpayer's actual holding period. Taxpayers use Form 6781 to report gains and losses from all section 1256 contracts that are open at the end of the year or that were closed during the year. An individual may elect to carry back a net section 1256 contract loss for three years instead of carrying it over to the next year (¶ 1754).

A section 1256 contract includes regulated futures contracts, foreign currency contracts, nonequity options, dealer equity options, and dealer securities futures contracts. The mark-to-market rules do not apply to hedging transactions (¶ 1949), equity options, and section 1256 contracts that are part of a mixed straddle if the taxpayer elects to exclude them from mark-to-market treatment (¶ 1948).

References are to Standard Federal Tax Reports; Tax Research Consultant; and Practical Tax Explanations.

[48] ¶ 13,700; SALES: 45,118.05; § 19,015

[49] ¶ 31,100; SALES: 48,100; § 18,830.05

1948. Tax Straddles. A tax straddle is any set of offsetting positions such as a futures contract, a forward contract, or an option on actively traded personal property (including stock) that seeks to diminish an investor's risk of loss (Code Sec. 1092).[50] Loss realized with respect to a straddle position is deductible only to the extent that the loss exceeds the taxpayer's unrealized gain in the offsetting position. Unused losses are carried forward to the taxpayer's next tax year. A taxpayer uses Form 6781 to report each position in actively traded personal property (whether or not it is part of a straddle) on which the taxpayer has unrecognized gain at the end of the tax year.

The loss deferral rule does not apply if a straddle is identified on the taxpayer's books before the close of the day on which it is acquired. If there is a loss from any position in an identified straddle, the taxpayer must increase the basis of each of the positions that offset the loss position by the same ratio to the loss as the unrecognized gain for the offsetting position bears to the total unrecognized gain for all the offsetting positions. The loss deferral rule also does not apply to hedging transactions (¶ 1949), straddles consisting entirely of qualified covered call options, and straddles consisting entirely of section 1256 contracts (¶ 1947).

Wash Sale and Short Sales. A modified wash sale rule (¶ 1935) applies to any disposition of a position in a straddle and denies a deduction of a loss if there is unrecognized gain in a successor position (Temp. Reg. § 1.1092(b)-1T).[51] In addition, a modified short sale rule (¶ 1944) applies to a straddle suspending the taxpayer's holding period during the time the taxpayer holds offsetting and successor positions (Temp. Reg. § 1.1092(b)-2T).[52]

Mixed Straddles. A mixed straddle is a straddle in which at least one, but not all, of the positions is a section 1256 contract (¶ 1947), with each position being properly identified as part of the straddle. A taxpayer may elect not to have the mark-to-market rules apply to the section 1256 contracts that are a part of the mixed straddle (Code Sec. 1256(d)).[53] If the taxpayer elects out of the mark-to-market rules, the straddle is subject to the loss deferral rule, the modified wash sale rule, and the modified short sale rule. Alternatively, a taxpayer may elect to offset gains and losses from positions that are part of a mixed straddle by (1) separately identifying each mixed straddle to which such treatment applies, or (2) establishing a mixed straddle account with respect to a class of activities for which gains and losses will be recognized and offset on a periodic basis (Code Sec. 1092(b); Temp. Reg. § § 1.1092(b)-3T and 1.1092(b)-4T).[54]

Interest and Carrying Charges. Interest and carrying charges incurred with respect to a straddle position can only be offset by current income generated by the position. Any excess must be capitalized (Code Sec. 263(g)).[55]

1949. Hedging Transactions. A hedging transaction is a transaction in the normal course of business that is primarily intended to reduce the risk of changes in interest rates, price changes, or currency fluctuations (Code Sec. 1221(a)(7); Reg. § 1.1221-2).[56] The property involved in a hedging transaction is generally not classified as a capital asset (¶ 1741). As a result, gain or loss on most hedging transactions is ordinary income or loss. This rule also applies when a short sale or option is part of a hedging transaction (¶ 1944). The determination of whether a transaction was intended to manage the taxpayer's business risk is based upon all the facts and circumstances. A transaction that is not a hedging transaction may be a straddle (¶ 1948).

Identification. The hedging transaction must be identified before the close of the day on which the taxpayer entered into the transaction (Reg. § 1.1221-2(f)). The taxpayer must identify the property that is being hedged within 35 days after the transaction is entered into. The taxpayer's identification of the hedged property must be unambiguous and become part of the taxpayer's books and records.

References are to Standard Federal Tax Reports; Tax Research Consultant; and Practical Tax Explanations.

[50] ¶ 30,200; SALES: 48,150; § 45,425.30

[51] ¶ 30,201; SALES: 48,156; § 45,425.30

[52] ¶ 30,202; SALES: 48,158; § 45,425.30

[53] ¶ 31,100; SALES: 48,200; § 45,425.30

[54] ¶ 30,200, ¶ 30,203, ¶ 30,204; SALES: 48,200; § 45,425.30

[55] ¶ 13,700; SALES: 48,160, BUSEXP: 9,502.05; § 45,425.30

[56] ¶ 30,420, ¶ 30,424; SALES: 15,114, SALES: 48,250; § 16,505.40

Corporate Bonds and Other Debt Instruments

1950. Corporate Bond Discounts, Premiums, and Issue Expenses. The tax effects of a corporation's issuance or reacquisition of bonds depends on whether the bonds are issued at face value, at a discount, or at a premium. A corporation generally does not realize gain or loss upon the issuance of a bond or other debt instrument (Reg. § 1.61-12(c)).[57] However, a corporation that repurchases a bond for less than its adjusted issue price realizes income from the discharge of indebtedness (¶ 855). For bonds repurchased at a discount during 2009 or 2010, the corporation can elect to defer the discharge of indebtedness income and recognize it ratably over a five-year period beginning in 2014 and through 2018 (Code Sec. 108(i)).[58]

For bonds issued at a discount, the discount is amortized and deductible by the corporation over the life of the bond. If bonds are issued at a premium on or after March 2, 1998, the premium is amortized as an offset to the corporation's otherwise allowable interest deduction with the portion of bond premium allocable to the accrual period based on constant yield (Reg. § 1.163-13(a)).[59] Any amount allocable to a bond's conversion feature is not part of the bond premium (Code Sec. 171(b)(1)).[60] See ¶ 1967 for the tax treatment of a premium paid by the buyer of a bond. Any expenses related to issuing the bond (i.e., printing, advertising, legal fees) are amortized over the life of the bond and deducted as business expenses.[61]

1952. Original Issue Discount. If a debt instrument has original issue discount (OID), the holder's gross income must include an amount equal to the sum of the daily portions of the OID for each day during the tax year that the holder held the instrument (Code Sec. 1272).[62] The holder's basis in the instrument is increased by the OID that must be included in gross income. The OID requirement does not apply to short-term obligations with a fixed maturity of less than one year, tax-exempt obligations, U.S. savings bonds, and certain loans between natural persons. It also does not apply if the holder purchased the debt instrument at a premium or if the holder is a life insurance company.

OID on a debt instrument is the excess of the stated redemption price at maturity over the issue price (Code Sec. 1273).[63] Under a special *de minimis* rule, if the difference is less than 0.25 percent of the redemption price multiplied by the number of full years from the date of issue to the date of maturity, then the OID is zero.

The stated redemption price at maturity includes all payments provided by the obligation other than qualified interest payments. Qualified interest is stated interest that is actually and unconditionally payable at fixed, periodic intervals of one year or less, based on a fixed interest rate and outstanding principal amount. Debt instruments that are publicly offered or that are issued for money or publicly traded property have their issue price determined based on those objective features. Special rules determine issue price when publicly offered debt instruments are part of investment units. For debt instruments that are issued for property, services, or the right to use property, but are not publicly traded, the issue price may be the stated principal amount, or the imputed principal amount (¶ 1954).

Interest Deduction. For a debt instrument issued after July 1, 1982, the portion of OID that the issuer may deduct for any tax year is equal to the aggregate daily portions of the OID for days during that tax year (Code Sec. 163(e)).[64] The daily portion of OID for any day is determined by allocating to each day in any accrual period a ratable portion of the increase during the accrual period in the adjusted issue price of the debt instrument (Code Sec. 1272(a)(3)).[65]

References are to Standard Federal Tax Reports; Tax Research Consultant; and Practical Tax Explanations.

[57] ¶ 5,801; CCORP: 3,158; § 3,401

[58] ¶ 7002; SALES: 12,252; § 3,420.40

[59] ¶ 9,302D; BUSEXP: 21,214

[60] ¶ 11,850; CCORP: 3,154; § 11,530

[61] ¶ 5804.22; CCORP: 3,156; § 19,350

[62] ¶ 31,260; ACCTNG: 36,200; § 19,310.05

[63] ¶ 31,280; ACCTNG: 36,100; § 19,315.05

[64] ¶ 9102; BUSEXP: 21,102; § 7,405.20

[65] ¶ 31,260; ACCTNG: 36,214; § 19,310.10

Information Statements. An issuer with any outstanding bond or any other evidence of indebtedness in registered form issued at a discount must generally furnish the holder and the IRS with an information statement (Form 1099-OID) for the calendar year if there is OID of at least $10 (Code Sec. 6049).[66]

Stripped Bonds and Stripped Coupons. Special OID rules govern stripped bonds and stripped coupons purchased or sold after July 1, 1982 (Code Sec. 1286(a)).[67] Under this type of arrangement, one taxpayer strips an interest coupon from a bond and sells either the bond or the coupon. The bond and the coupon are treated as separate debt instruments issued with OID. For the buyer of a stripped bond, OID is the bond's value at maturity minus the price paid. For the buyer of a stripped coupon, OID is the interest to be paid on the due date of the coupon minus the price paid.

The seller of stripped bonds or stripped coupons must include in income the interest that accrued before the date of sale that was not previously included in income. Market discount must also be included in the seller's income. Both of these included items increase the seller's basis in the bonds and coupons. The seller then allocates the adjusted basis between the item kept (e.g., the bond) and the item sold (e.g., the coupon) based on their fair market values. The difference between the sales price of the item and its adjusted basis is the seller's gain or loss.

Stripped Stock. Preferred stock purchased after April 30, 1993, that has been stripped of some or all of its dividend rights is treated like stripped bonds. OID is equal to the stated redemption price minus the amount paid for the stock (Code Sec. 305(e)).[68]

Tax-Exempt and Stripped Tax-Exempt Bonds. OID on a tax-exempt bond is generally treated as tax-exempt interest (¶ 1956). However, when a tax-exempt bond is stripped, only a portion of the OID is treated as coming from a tax-exempt obligation (Code Sec. 1286(d)).[69] The balance is treated as OID on a taxable obligation. The Code contains the rules for determining the tax-exempt portion of the OID.

1954. Original Issue Discount for Debt Instruments Issued for Property. In determining the original issue discount (OID) of certain debt instruments issued for property (¶ 1952), the issue price is the stated principal amount of the instrument when there is adequate stated interest, or the imputed principal amount if there is not adequately stated interest (Code Sec. 1274).[70] This rule applies to debt instruments given in consideration for the sale or exchange of property if: (1) the stated redemption price at maturity exceeds either the stated principal amount (when there is adequate stated interest) or the imputed principal amount; and (2) some or all of the payments due under the instrument are due more than six months after the date of the sale or exchange. The rule does not apply to:

- sales for $250,000 or less;
- sales of principal residences by individuals (¶ 1707);
- sales of farms by individuals, estates, testamentary trusts, or small business corporations or partnerships for $1 million or less;
- certain land transfers between related parties covered by the imputed interest rules of Code Sec. 483(e) (¶ 1872);
- sales of patents for amounts that are contingent on the productivity, use, or disposition of the property transferred (¶ 1767); or
- in the case of the borrower, sales or exchanges of personal use property (Code Sec. 1275(b)).[71]

References are to Standard Federal Tax Reports; Tax Research Consultant; and Practical Tax Explanations.

[66] ¶ 36,020; ACCTNG: 36,550; § 19,320.10

[67] ¶ 31,480; ACCTNG: 36,350; § 19,335

[68] ¶ 15,400; ACCTNG: 36,356

[69] ¶ 31,480; ACCTNG: 36,500; § 19,335

[70] ¶ 31,300; ACCTNG: 36,150; § 19,315.10

[71] ¶ 31,340; ACCTNG: 36,154.45; § 19,315.10

Certain annuity contracts are also excluded from the definition of debt instrument (Code Sec. 1275(a)(1)(B)).[72] A debt-for-property transaction that is not covered by these rules may be subject to the imputed interest rules of Code Sec. 483 (¶ 1868).

Adequate Stated Interest. A debt instrument generally provides for adequate stated interest if its stated principal amount is less than or equal to the imputed principal amount—the sum of the present value of all principal and interest payments due on the instrument (Code Sec. 1274(c)(2)).[73] Except for potentially abusive situations, the present value of all payments due on the instrument is generally determined based on the lowest applicable federal rate (AFR) in effect (¶ 83) in the three-month period ending with (1) the first month in which there is a binding written contract, or (2) the month in which the sale or exchange occurred (Code Sec. 1274(b)). The AFR is determined by reference to the term of the debt instrument, including renewal and extension options. If the imputed interest rules of Code Sec. 483 apply to a debt instrument (¶ 1868), payments due within six months after the sale are taken into account at face value. For a sale-leaseback transaction, a rate equal to 110 percent of the AFR applies in determining the present value of payments (Code Sec. 1274(e)).

The discount rate may not exceed nine percent, compounded semiannually, if a debt instrument is given in consideration for the sale or exchange of property (other than new Code Sec. 38 property) and the stated principal amount of the instrument does not exceed an inflation-adjusted amount ($5,664,800 for 2016) (Code Sec. 1274A; Rev. Rul. 2015-24).[74] The discount rate may not exceed six percent, compounded semiannually, when determining unstated interest on deferred payments in a transfer of land between family members if the aggregate sales price of all prior land sales between the family members during the calendar year is $500,000 or less. However, this limit does not apply if any party to the sale is a nonresident alien (Code Sec. 483(e); Reg. § 1.483-3(b)).[75]

Joint Election. For sales or exchanges of property (other than new Code Sec. 38 property), the lender and borrower may jointly elect out of the rules for OID on debt issued for property, and take the interest on the debt instrument into account under the cash method of accounting (Code Sec. 1274A(c); Rev. Rul. 2015-24).[76] The election can be made only if:

- the stated principal amount of the instrument does not exceed an inflation-adjusted amount ($4,046,300 for 2016);
- the lender is on the cash-basis method of accounting and is not a dealer with respect to the property sold or exchanged; and
- these rules would otherwise have applied to the transaction.

1956. Original Issue Discount on Tax-Exempt Bonds. For tax-exempt obligations issued after September 3, 1982, and acquired after March 1, 1984, original issue discount (OID) is accrued like OID on obligations issued by corporations and others under the constant yield method (¶ 1952) when determining the interest expense deduction and the holder's adjusted basis (Code Sec. 1288).[77] For purposes of determining the interest expense deduction, the reduction normally required where a subsequent holder pays an acquisition premium is disregarded. For tax-exempt obligations with a maturity of less than one year, interest is computed as it is for short-term taxable obligations. The tables at ¶ 84 show applicable federal interest rates that are adjusted to account for tax-exempt interest.

References are to Standard Federal Tax Reports; Tax Research Consultant; and Practical Tax Explanations.

[72] ¶ 31,340; ACCTNG: 36,054.05

[73] ¶ 31,300; ACCTNG: 36,158, ACCTNG: 36,160; § 19,315.10

[74] ¶ 31,320, ¶ 31,322.30; ACCTNG: 36,162.20; § 19,315.10

[75] ¶ 22,290, ¶ 22,294; ACCTNG: 36,308.25; § 19,510.15

[76] ¶ 31,320, ¶ 31,322.30; ACCTNG: 36,154.65; § 19,315.10

[77] ¶ 31,520; ACCTNG: 36,502.10, ACCTNG: 36,502.15; § 3,105.05

1958. Market Discount Bonds. Gain from the sale of a market discount bond is treated as ordinary interest income to the extent of accrued market discount (Code Sec. 1276(a)).[78] A market discount bond is a bond that was purchased at a discount, other than obligations that mature within one year of issuance, U.S. savings bonds, certain installment obligations, and tax-exempt bonds purchased before May 1, 1993.

The accrued market discount on a bond is generally determined under a ratable accrual method where the accrued market discount equals the amount bearing the same ratio to the market discount on the bond as the number of days that the taxpayer held the bond bears to the number of days after the date of acquisition to the maturity date (Code Sec. 1276(b)(1)). Alternatively, the taxpayer can make an irrevocable election to determine the accrued market discount for a bond under a constant interest method where the accrued market discount is equal to the total amount that would have been includible in gross income using the constant yield method for debt instruments with original issue discount (OID) for all periods the taxpayer held the bond (Code Sec. 1276(b)(2)). The election is made by filing a statement with the taxpayer's timely filed tax return that states that the market discount has been included in income, and indicates how the included amount was calculated (Code Sec. 1276(b)(2)(C); Rev. Proc. 92-67; Rev. Proc. 2011-14; Rev. Proc. 2015-13; Rev. Proc. 2015-14).[79]

Any partial payment of principal on a market discount bond is ordinary income to the extent of accrued market discount on the bond for obligations acquired after October 22, 1986 (Code Sec. 1276(a)(3)).[80] The payment that is included in gross income reduces the amount of accrued market discount.

Net direct interest expenses on debt incurred to purchase or continue a market discount bond acquired after July 18, 1984, may be deducted only to the extent that the expenses exceed the market discount allocable to the number of days the bond is held by the taxpayer (Code Sec. 1277).[81] The taxpayer may elect to take any deferred interest deduction in a subsequent year to the extent of net interest income from the market discount bond. Any deferred interest expense that remains (whether or not the election is made) is deducted in the year of disposition.

1961. Discount on Short-Term Obligations. Certain holders of short-term obligations must include in gross income: (1) an amount equal to the sum of the daily portions of the acquisition discount for each day during the tax year that the holder held the bond; and (2) any other interest payable on the obligation (Code Sec. 1281).[82] The amounts included in gross income increase the holder's basis in the obligation. Obligations include a bond, debenture, note, certificate, or other evidence of debt (but not a tax-exempt obligation) with a fixed maturity date not more than one year from the date of issue (Code Sec. 1283(a)(1)).[83] For short-term, nongovernmental obligations, the accrual requirement applies to original issue discount (OID), as opposed to acquisition discount.

Acquisition discount on short-term obligations must be accrued by: accrual method taxpayers; banks; brokers and dealers who hold short-term obligations for sale to customers in the ordinary course of trade or business; regulated investment companies (RICs) (¶ 2301) and common trust funds (¶ 2389); persons who identify short-term obligations as part of a hedging transaction (¶ 1949); persons who strip a short-term bond of its interest coupons (¶ 1952); and any person whose basis in the instrument is determined by reference to the basis in the hands of any other listed person. Accrual of acquisition discount and interest is also mandatory for obligations held by a pass-through entity (i.e., partnership, S corporation, or trust) that acquires the obligation during the required accrual period or acquires the obligation to avoid mandatory accrual.

References are to Standard Federal Tax Reports; Tax Research Consultant; and Practical Tax Explanations.

[78] ¶ 31,360; ACCTNG: 36,400; § 19,325.05

[79] ¶ 31,361.40; ACCTNG: 36,404; § 19,325.05

[80] ¶ 31,360; ACCTNG: 36,408.15; § 19,325.05

[81] ¶ 31,380; ACCTNG: 36,410; § 19,325.10

[82] ¶ 31,420; ACCTNG: 36,452; § 19,330.05

[83] ¶ 31,460; ACCTNG: 36,452; § 19,330.05

Net direct interest expense incurred with respect to a short-term obligation is deductible only to the extent that it exceeds the sum of: (1) acquisition discount (excess of stated redemption price over basis) for each day during the year that the taxpayer holds the bond, and (2) any interest payable on the obligation that accrues during the year but is not included in gross income because of the taxpayer's accounting method. The daily portion of the acquisition discount is equal to the total discount divided by the number of days from the acquisition date to the maturity date (Code Secs. 1282(a) and 1283(b)(1)).[84] The interest deduction is deferred in a manner similar to that applicable to market discount bonds (¶ 1958).

1963. Unregistered Obligations. Most corporate and government debt obligations must be in registered form for the payor to deduct interest (Code Sec. 163(f)(1)).[85] An excise tax applies to issues of registration-required obligations (other than tax-exempt bonds) that are not in registered form (Code Sec. 4701).[86] The excise tax is equal to one percent of the principal amount of the obligation multiplied by the number of calendar years (or portions thereof) during the period beginning on the issue date of the obligation and ending on the date of maturity.

If a registration-required obligation is not in registered form, any gain realized on its sale or other disposition is ordinary income (Code Sec. 1287)[87] and any loss is not deductible (Code Sec. 165(j))[88] unless the issuance of the obligation was subject to the excise tax or certain other specified exceptions apply. The issuer cannot reduce earnings and profits by the amount of any interest on the obligation (Code Sec. 312(m)).[89]

1965. Exchanges of U.S. Obligations. Some types of U.S. savings bonds may be exchanged tax free for other types of U.S. savings bonds (¶ 730) (Code Sec. 1037).[90] If the original bond was issued at a discount, an amount equal to what would have been ordinary income from original issue discount (OID) (¶ 1952) if the exchange had been taxable is treated as ordinary income when the bond received in exchange is disposed of or redeemed at a gain.

1967. Amortized Bond Premium. A bond owner who pays a premium over the face amount of a taxable bond has the option of (1) amortizing the premium by deducting it over the life of the bond, or (2) not amortizing and adding the premium to the basis of the bond (Code Sec. 171(a); Reg. § 1.171-4).[91] A holder elects to amortize the premium by reporting the amortization on the tax return for the first year the election is to apply and attaching a statement to the tax return that the amortization election is being made. Any premium paid for tax-exempt bonds cannot be amortized; instead, the premium reduces the basis of the bond (Code Sec. 1016(a)(5)).[92] For a dealer in municipal bonds, see ¶ 1970.

The amount of bond premium that can be amortized for the tax year (and deducted currently) is calculated under a constant yield method (Code Sec. 171(b); Reg. § 1.171-2).[93] Under this method, the amount of the amortizable bond premium and the amount attributable to a particular tax year must be determined on the basis of the taxpayer's yield to maturity, using the taxpayer's basis in the obligation and compounding at the close of each accrual period. If a bond is received in an exchange and the basis of the bond is determined at least in part from the basis of the property given up in the exchange, the basis of the bond cannot exceed its fair market value immediately after the exchange for purposes of determining bond premium. This rule generally does not apply to an exchange of securities in a reorganization.

Premium on Convertible Bond. Amortization is not allowed for any part of a premium that is paid for the conversion feature in a convertible bond. A corporation's deduction

References are to Standard Federal Tax Reports; Tax Research Consultant; and Practical Tax Explanations.

[84] ¶ 31,440, ¶ 31,460; ACCTNG: 36,458; § 19,330.10

[85] ¶ 9102; BUSEXP: 30,252; § 19,340

[86] ¶ 33,941; BUSEXP: 30,252; § 19,340

[87] ¶ 31,500; SALES: 24,404; § 19,340

[88] ¶ 9802; SALES: 24,404

[89] ¶ 15,600; CCORP: 12,104.30

[90] ¶ 29,720; SALES: 27,250; § 18,220

[91] ¶ 11,850, ¶ 11,854; DEPR: 21,200; § 45,415.20

[92] ¶ 29,410; DEPR: 21,210; § 45,415.20

[93] ¶ 11,850, ¶ 11,852; DEPR: 21,200; § 45,415.20

for the premium it is called upon to pay to repurchase its own convertible indebtedness is generally limited to the amount of the normal call premium (Code Sec. 249(a)).[94]

1970. Dealer in Tax-Exempt Bonds. A dealer in tax-exempt obligations must amortize any premiums just as if the interest on the bonds had been taxable. A dealer who does not inventory securities or who inventories them at cost must reduce the adjusted basis of any municipal bonds sold during the year by the total amortization for the period they were held. A dealer who values inventories other than at cost (for example, market value) must annually reduce the cost of securities sold by the amortization on municipal bonds held during the year (Code Sec. 75; Reg. § 1.75-1).[95]

When a purchased tax-exempt obligation is sold or otherwise disposed of within 30 days after acquisition, matures, or is callable more than five years after it is acquired, an amortization adjustment must be made unless the bond is sold or disposed of at a gain. Thus, a dealer who inventories securities other than cost and holds at the end of the year a tax-exempt bond maturing or callable more than five years after acquisition, does not have to reflect amortization in the bond in the cost of securities sold. If the bond is sold at a gain, no amortization adjustment is made. If it is not sold at a gain, the cost of securities sold is reduced by the amortization for the entire period it was held.

Accounting Issues

1973. Time of Sale for Publicly Traded Securities. A cash or accrual method taxpayer other than a dealer (¶ 1903) who sells stock or securities traded on an established securities market generally must recognize gains and losses on the trade date, rather than the settlement date (Rev. Rul. 93-84).[96] The holding period for the stock or securities is also measured by using the trade date as the date sold (¶ 1737). Gain or loss on a short sale of securities, however, is recognized on the settlement date as set by exchange rules (¶ 1944). The installment method of reporting is not available for sales of stock or securities traded on an established securities market (¶ 1805).

1975. Identification of Securities Sold. If a taxpayer can adequately identify the shares of securities sold or exchanged, the seller's basis is the cost or other basis of the particular shares of stock or bond. Shares are adequately identified if the taxpayer can show the certificates representing shares of stock from a lot that the taxpayer acquired on a certain date or for a certain price, and that were delivered to the taxpayer's broker or other transferee. If a taxpayer buys and sells securities at various times in varying quantities and cannot adequately identify the shares that are sold, then the basis and holding period of the shares sold are generally determined on a first-in, first-out (FIFO) basis (Reg. § 1.1012-1(c)).[97] Most courts hold, however, that after a nontaxable reorganization in which the taxpayer receives shares of stock in another corporation in exchange for the original shares, the FIFO rule is not applicable.[98] In the case of the sale, exchange, or other disposition of a specified security on or after an applicable date (¶ 1980), the basis reported by the broker on Form 1099-B must be calculated on an account by account basis (Code Sec. 1012(c)).[99] Thus, the broker may be required to use different basis computation methods for different accounts.

A shareholder in a regulated investment company (RIC) or mutual fund (¶ 2301) may elect to figure gain or loss on identical shares using an average basis if the shareholder: (1) acquired the shares at various times and prices, and (2) left the shares on deposit in an account handled by a custodian or agent who acquires or redeems shares of the RIC or mutual fund (Code Sec. 1012(d); Reg. § 1.1012-1(e)).[100] Shares are identical if they have the same Committee on Uniform Security Identification Procedure (CUSIP) number or other security identifier number permitted by the IRS. The option to use average basis is available only with respect to mutual fund shares and dividend

References are to Standard Federal Tax Reports; Tax Research Consultant; and Practical Tax Explanations.

[94] ¶ 13,400; BUSEXP: 9,454.05

[95] ¶ 6250, ¶ 6251; ACCTNG: 15,256.15

[96] ¶ 21,005.892; SALES: 45,300; § 18,310.25

[97] ¶ 29,331; SALES: 6,212; § 16,115

[98] ¶ 29,336.451; SALES: 6,212.25; § 16,115

[99] ¶ 29,330; SALES: 6,068; § 39,120.12

[100] ¶ 29,330, ¶ 29,331; SALES: 6,212.35, SALES: 6,212.45; § 19,220.05, § 19,220.20

reinvestment plans. Average basis is determined by averaging the basis of all shares of identical stock in an account regardless of the taxpayer's holding period.

1980. Basis and Holding Period Reporting for Securities. If a broker is required to file a return on Form 1099-B to report the gross proceeds from the sale of a covered security (¶ 2565), the broker must also report the customer's adjusted basis in the security and whether any gain or loss with respect to the security is long-term or short-term (Code Sec. 6045(g); Reg. § 1.6045-1; Temp. Reg. § 1.6045-1T).[101] A "covered security" is any specified security that was acquired through a transaction in the account in which the security was held, or was transferred to that account from an account in which the security was a covered security if the broker receiving custody of the security receives a statutory statement with respect to the transfer.

A "specified security" includes: (1) a share of stock in a corporation; (2) a note, bond, debenture or other evidence of indebtedness, other than certain interests in a real estate mortgage investment conduit (REMIC) (¶ 2343), a debt instrument where payments may be accelerated, and pools of debt instruments affected by prepayments; (3) a commodity, or a contract or a derivative with respect to a commodity; (4) a securities futures contract; (5) an option on one or more specified securities, or a warrant or stock right; and (6) other financial instruments as determined by the IRS. Special rules apply to broker reporting on sales by S corporations, short sales (¶ 1944), certain stock held in connection with dividend reinvestment plan, and options transactions.

The applicable date for the basis reporting requirements depends on the type of specified security that is sold. The applicable date is:

- January 1, 2011, for corporate stock, generally;
- January 1, 2012, for stock in a regulated investment company (RIC) or mutual fund (¶ 2301) and stock acquired in connection with a dividend reinvestment plan (DRP);
- January 1, 2014, for an option granted or acquired on or after that date (but see below);
- January 1, 2014, for a debt instrument for which a yield and maturity can be determined (e.g., a debt instrument that provides a single fixed payment schedule or alternative payment schedule); however, short-term debt instruments with a fixed maturity of less than one year are exempted from basis reporting;
- January 1, 2016, for a debt instrument with more complex features (e.g., variable rate, inflation-indexed, or contingent payment), convertible debt, stripped bond or coupon, tax credit bond, and a debt instrument issued by a non-U.S. issuer or that requires payment in a foreign currency;
- January 1, 2016, for an option, stock right, or warrant acquired on or after that date if it is issued as part of an investment unit; and
- January 1, 2016, for an option granted or acquired on or after that date, if the property underlying the option is a debt instrument that is issued by a non-U.S. person or that provides for payments in a foreign currency.

The broker must generally determine adjusted basis of a covered security under the first-in, first-out (FIFO) method (¶ 1975) unless the taxpayer adequately identifies the stock sold. For any stock for which an average basis method is allowed, such as stock in a mutual fund acquired in connection with a dividend reinvestment plan, the customer's adjusted basis is determined according to the broker's default method, unless the customer notifies the broker that he or she elects another acceptable method regarding the account in which the stock is held. Basis is determined without regard to the wash sale rule (¶ 1935) unless the acquisition and sale transactions resulting in a wash sale occur in the same account and are in identical securities.

References are to Standard Federal Tax Reports; Tax Research Consultant; and Practical Tax Explanations.

[101] ¶ 35,920, ¶ 35,923, ¶ 35,924; FILEBUS: 9,252, FILEBUS: 9,256; § 39,120.12

Securities Transfers Between Accounts. Every broker (and any other person specified in regulations) that transfers a covered security to another broker must furnish to the transferee broker a written statement that permits the transferee broker to satisfy the basis and holding-period reporting requirements (Code Sec. 6045A; Reg. § 1.6045A-1).[102] The written statement must be furnished no later than 15 days after the date of the transfer, except as provided otherwise by the IRS, or the transferor could be subject to a penalty (¶ 2823).

Organizational Actions Affecting Basis. Issuers of specified securities must file Form 8937 describing any organizational action (e.g., stock split, merger, acquisition) that affects the basis of the security, the quantitative effect on basis from the action, and any other information required by the IRS (Code Sec. 6045B; Reg. § 1.6045B-1).[103] A copy of Form 8937 must also be given to each security holder of record or the holder's nominee as of the date of the organizational action. Form 8937 must be filed by the earlier of 45 days after the organizational action or January 15 of the year following the calendar year during which the organizational action took place. However, no return is required for organizational actions that occur before the applicable date for that security.

An issuer does not have to file Form 8937 if, by the filing due date, the issuer posts a completed and signed Form 8937 in a readily accessible format in a dedicated area of its primary public website and keeps that form accessible on its website (or its successor's primary public website) for 10 years. An issuer that satisfies these public reporting requirements is treated as having furnished a copy of Form 8937 to all holders and nominees. Form 8937 also does not have to be filed if: (1) the issuer reasonably determines that all recipients of the securities are exempt recipients; or (2) the issuer is an S corporation that reports the information on a timely filed Schedule K-1 of Form 1120S. Penalties may be imposed for failure to file correct information returns in connection with organizational actions, failure to furnish correct statements to holders or nominees, or failure to provide required publicly available information (¶ 2823).

1983. Commissions Paid on Securities. Commissions and other transaction costs paid to facilitate the sale of securities generally must be capitalized (Reg. § 1.263(a)-1(e)).[104] For securities dealers, however, commissions and other amounts paid to facilitate the sale of a security are ordinary and necessary business expenses. For traders and investors, the amounts capitalized reduce the amount realized from the sale and are taken into account in either the tax year in which the sale occurs or the tax year in which the sale is abandoned if a loss deduction is permitted. The capitalized amount is not added to the basis of the property. See ¶ 1760 for information concerning the proper classification of a taxpayer as a trader, dealer, or investor. Ordinary and necessary expenses for investment advice, including a "wrap fee" on a brokerage account paid by an investor in lieu of commissions on individual trades, are deductible investment expenses and are claimed as miscellaneous itemized deductions in the year paid (¶ 1086) (Reg. § 1.212-1(g)).[105]

References are to Standard Federal Tax Reports; Tax Research Consultant; and Practical Tax Explanations.

[102] ¶ 35,931, ¶ 35,932; FILEBUS: 9,252, FILEBUS: 9,256; § 39,120.12

[103] ¶ 35,934, ¶ 35,935; FILEBUS: 9,380; § 39,120.12

[104] ¶ 13,701; SALES: 9,152; § 7,105.40

[105] ¶ 12,521; BUSEXP: 12,154.05; § 7,840.05

Chapter 20
HEALTH AND EMPLOYEE BENEFITS

	Par.
Employer Health Insurance Mandate	2001
Health and Welfare Benefits	2011
HSAs, HRAs, and FSAs	2035
Cafeteria Plans	2045
Other Employee Benefits	2055
Fringe Benefits Under Code Sec. 132	2085

Employer Health Insurance Mandate

2001. Employer Health Insurance Mandate. For any month beginning on or after January 1, 2015 (for employers with 100 or more full-time employees), and January 1, 2016 (for employers with 50 or more full-time employees), an applicable large employer may be assessed a nondeductible penalty known as a shared responsibility payment if either:

- the employer fails to offer at least 95 percent of its full-time employees and their dependents the opportunity to enroll in minimum essential coverage under an eligible employer-sponsored plan (¶ 2003), or
- the employer offers its full-time employees and their dependents the opportunity to enroll in minimum essential coverage under an eligible employer-sponsored plan but the coverage is unaffordable to the employee or does not provide minimum value (¶ 2005) (Code Sec. 4980H; Notice 2013-45; T.D. 9655).[1]

An applicable large employer may be liable for either type of assessable payment in any calendar month, but not both. Minimum essential coverage for this purpose means coverage under an employer-sponsored plan offered in the small or large group market within a state and which meets the requirements for group health plans or group health insurance coverage under section 2791 of the Public Health Service Act (Code Sec. 5000A(f); Reg. § 54.4980H-1(a)(27)).[2]

Applicable Large Employer. An applicable large employer is any employer that employed on average at least 50 full-time employees, full-time equivalents (FTEs), or some combination on business days during the preceding calendar year (Code Sec. 4980H(c)(2); Reg. § § 54.4980H-1(a)(4) and 54.4980H-2).[3] An individual who has medical coverage under the TRICARE program or the Veterans' Administration is not considered an employee in determining whether an employer meets the 50-employee threshold.

FTEs are determined by adding all hours of service for the month for employees who were not full-time employees (but no more than 120 hours per employee), and dividing by 120. An employer not in existence during an entire preceding calendar year is an applicable large employer for the current year if it is reasonably expected to employ an average of 50 or more full-time employees (including FTEs) on business days during the current calendar year.

An exemption to the 50-employee threshold applies if the employer has more than 50 employees for 120 days or less during the preceding calendar year, but the employees in excess of 50 are seasonal workers. A seasonal worker is an employee who performs labor or services on a seasonal basis including, but not limited to, certain agricultural workers and retail workers employed during holiday season.

References are to Standard Federal Tax Reports; Tax Research Consultant; and Practical Tax Explanations.

[1] ¶ 34,619ZA, ¶ 34,619ZD.35; HEALTH: 6,050; § 42,101

[2] ¶ 34,619ZBF, ¶ 34,962; HEALTH: 6,050; § 42,101

[3] ¶ 34,619ZA, ¶ 34,619ZBF, ¶ 34,619ZBI; HEALTH: 6,052; § 42,105

In applying the 50-employee threshold, an employer means all common law employers, including for-profit businesses, tax-exempt organizations, and government entities (federal, state, local, and Indian tribes). Employers with common ownership such as controlled groups under Code Sec. 414(b) or (c), or related employers such as an affiliated service group under Code Sec. 414(m), are combined for the 50-employee threshold. Moreover, any references to an employer include references to the employer's predecessors and successors.

Full-Time Employee. A full-time employee for purposes of determining applicable large employer status is an employee who was employed on average at least 30 hours of service per week or 130 hours of service in a calendar month (Code Sec. 4980H(c)(4); Reg. §§54.4980H-1(a)(21) and 54.4980H-3).[4] Employee is defined under the common law standard, i.e., right to control, direct, etc. It does not include a leased employee, sole proprietor, partner in partnership, or two-percent or more S corporation shareholder, unless services are provided as both an employee and nonemployee.

An hour of service includes each hour for which the employee is paid or entitled to be paid for services performed in the United States for the employer, including periods of paid leave. For hourly employees, the employer calculates hours of service using records of hours worked and for which payment is made or due. For non-hourly employees, an employer can count actual hours worked and for which payment is due, or apply a days-worked equivalency (8 hours of service) or weeks-worked equivalency (40 hours of service). An employer may use different methods for different classifications of non-hourly employees as long as the categories are reasonable and consistently applied.

Safe harbors are provided allowing an employer the option of using either a look-back method or monthly measurement method to determine full-time employee status (Reg. §54.4980H-3).[5] Look-back measurements are provided for ongoing employees, new employees, and employees with a change in employment status.

Offer of Coverage. An employer is treated as offering coverage for a calendar month if it offers the coverage for that month to at least 95 percent of its full-time employees and their dependents (Reg. §§54.4980H-4(b) and 54.4980H-5(b)).[6] An offer occurs if the employee has the opportunity to elect to enroll in or decline coverage at least once during the plan year. Failure to offer coverage for any day of a calendar month is treated as failure to offer coverage for the entire month.

A full-time employee is treated as having been offered coverage only if the employer also offers coverage to the employee's dependents. A dependent is the employee's child who is under the age of 26. It does not include anyone other than children, such as the employee's spouse. If an employee or dependent enrolls in coverage but fails to pay his or her share of premiums on a timely basis, the employer is nonetheless treated as offering coverage for that coverage period.

Reporting Requirements. Employers and insurers are required to file an annual information return with the IRS reporting health care coverage provided to employees and other individuals (¶ 2567) (Code Secs. 6055 and 6056; Notice 2013-45).

2003. Penalty for Employers Not Offering Health Care Coverage. Applicable large employers (¶ 2001) are liable for a shared responsibility payment (assessable payment) if:

- the employer fails to offer to its full-time employees and their dependents the opportunity to enroll in minimum essential coverage under an eligible employer-sponsored group health plan for any month, and
- at least one full-time employee is certified as having enrolled in a qualified health plan through a Health Insurance Exchange and eligible to receive a premium tax credit (¶ 1331) or cost-sharing reduction payment (Code Sec. 4980H(a); Reg. §54.4980H-4; Notice 2013-45).[7]

References are to Standard Federal Tax Reports; Tax Research Consultant; and Practical Tax Explanations.

[4] ¶ 34,619ZA, ¶ 34,619ZBF, ¶ 34,619ZBL; HEALTH: 6,052; § 42,110

[5] ¶ 34,619ZBL; HEALTH: 6,056; § 42,110

[6] ¶ 34,619ZBO, ¶ 34,619ZBR; HEALTH: 6,054; § 42,125

[7] ¶ 34,619ZA, ¶ 34,619ZBO, ¶ 34,619ZD.35; HEALTH: 6,054; § 42,130.10

The assessable payment for an employer not offering coverage with respect to any calendar month equals the number of the employer's full-time employees reduced by 30, multiplied by 1/12 of $2,160 for 2016 (Code Sec. 4980H(a), (c)(1) and (c)(5); T.D. 9655; Notice 2015-87).

The 30-employee reduction applies only for purposes of calculating the assessable payment (Code Sec. 4980H(c)(2)(D)). It does not apply for determining if the employer is an applicable large employer (i.e., 50-employee threshold). Also, a full-time employee does not include a full-time equivalent (FTE) employee for purposes of the payment calculation (Code Sec. 4980H(c)(2)(E)). Employers with common ownership or otherwise related are allowed only one 30-employee reduction which is allocated ratably among all the related employers.

An employer must pay the assessable payment upon notice and demand by IRS; it is not required to be included with the employer's tax return (Code Sec. 4980H(d)). The payment is assessed and collected in the same manner as an assessable penalty. However, it is not deductible as a business expense (Code Sec. 4980H(c)(7)).

2005. Penalty for Employers Offering Health Care Coverage. Applicable large employers (¶ 2001) are liable for a shared responsibility payment (assessable payment) if:

- the employer offers minimum essential coverage under an eligible employer-sponsored group health plan to its full-time employees and their dependents for any month, but
- at least one full-time employee is certified as having enrolled in a qualified health plan through a Health Insurance Exchange and eligible to receive an applicable premium tax credit (¶ 1331) or cost-sharing reduction payment because the coverage is not affordable to the employee or does not provide minimum value (Code Sec. 4980H(b); Reg. § 54.4980H-5; Notice 2013-45).[8]

Affordability. Coverage for an employee is affordable if the employee's share of the premium for self-only coverage, not family coverage, does not exceed 9.66 percent of the employee's annual household income for 2016 (9.69 percent for 2017) (Rev. Proc. 2014-62, Rev. Proc. 2016-24). The affordability test applies to the lowest-cost option available to the employee that also meets the minimum value requirement.

Safe harbors are provided for an employer to determine if coverage is affordable to an employee based on the employee's Form W-2 wages, the employee's rate of pay, or the federal poverty line. An employer may choose one or more safe harbors for all of its employees or any reasonable category of employees, so long as it is done on a uniform and consistent basis. The safe harbors only apply for purposes of the assessable payment; they do not affect an employee's eligibility for a premium tax credit.

Minimum Value. An employer-sponsored group health plan fails to provide minimum value if the plan's share of the total allowed costs of benefits provided under the plan is less than 60 percent of the costs, and generally fails to offer substantial coverage for in-patient hospitalization services and physician services (Prop. Reg. § 1.36B-6).[9] An eligible employer-sponsored plan may determine whether it provides minimum value by: (1) a minimum value calculator provided by the IRS and the Department of Health and Human Services (HHS); (2) actuarial certification; (3) certain safe harbor plan designs that will be specified in future guidance; or (4) for plans in the small group market, meeting the requirements for bronze, silver, gold, or platinum level coverage.

Calculation of Assessable Payment. The assessable payment for an employer offering health care coverage with respect to any calendar month equals the number of the employer's full-time employees who receive a premium tax credit or cost-sharing reduction, multiplied by 1/12 of $3,240 in 2016 (Code Sec. 4980H(b) and (c)(5); Reg. § 54.4980H-5; Notice 2015-87).[10]

References are to Standard Federal Tax Reports; Tax Research Consultant; and Practical Tax Explanations.

[8] ¶ 34,619ZA, ¶ 34,619ZBR, ¶ 34,619ZD.35; HEALTH: 6,054; § 42,130.15

[9] ¶ 4196U; HEALTH: 3,310; § 42,120

[10] ¶ 34,619ZA, ¶ 34,619ZBR; HEALTH: 6,054; § 42,130.15

The assessable payment for any calendar month is capped at the number of the employer's full-time employees for the month reduced by 30, multiplied by 1/12 of $2,160 for 2016 (Notice 2015-87). The cap ensures that the payment for an employer that offers coverage can never exceed the assessable payment the employer would owe if it did not offer coverage (¶ 2003).

An employer must pay the assessable payment upon notice and demand by the IRS; it is not required to be included with the employer's tax return (Code Sec. 4980H(d)). The payment is assessed and collected in the same manner as an assessable penalty. However, it is not deductible as a business expense (Code Sec. 4980H(c)(7)).

Health and Welfare Benefits

2011. Welfare Benefit Plans. A welfare benefit plan or welfare benefit fund is any fund through which an employer provides welfare benefits to employees, independent contractors, or their beneficiaries (Code Sec. 419).[11] Welfare benefits are benefits other than deferred compensation or transfers of restricted property, such as accident or health benefits, disability or death benefits, unemployment benefits, severance benefits, vacation, or similar benefits.

An employer may deduct contributions paid or accrued to a welfare benefit fund to the extent that the contributions do not exceed the qualified cost of the fund for the tax year, reduced by the after-tax income of the fund. If the employer's contributions to the fund are more than its qualified cost, the excess is carried over to the next tax year. Welfare benefits provided directly by an employer are deductible only in the tax year the employee includes the benefits in gross income or would include such benefits in gross income if they were taxable to the employee (¶ 906) (Code Sec. 404(b)(2)(A)).[12] An employer may not accrue and deduct unpaid welfare benefits.

A welfare benefit fund's qualified cost is the direct cost the employer would have been able to deduct using the cash method of accounting if it paid for the benefits directly (Code Sec. 419(c)). It also includes any addition to a qualified asset account—a reserve set aside for the payment of disability benefits, medical benefits, supplemental unemployment benefits (SUB) or severance pay benefits, and life insurance or death benefits (Code Sec. 419A).[13]

The allowable addition to a qualified asset account for a tax year is the amount that will bring the account to a level (the "account limit") that is reasonably and actuarially necessary to fund the payment of incurred but unpaid benefits. In the case of post-retirement medical and life insurance benefits, the allowable addition is the amount required to fund the payment of such benefits on a level basis over the working lives of the covered employees based on current medical costs. For employers who do not support higher additions to a qualified asset account by actuarial certifications, there are safe harbor additions for the various benefits. Limits are placed on the level of disability and SUB or severance pay benefits that may be considered in establishing the account limit for such benefits.

VEBAs. Collectively bargained voluntary employees' beneficiary associations (VEBAs) are exempt from the account limits applicable to welfare benefit funds (Code Sec. 419A(f)(5)). Thus, employer contributions to VEBAs are deductible and earnings on assets of such VEBAs are tax exempt. In addition, VEBAs that are funded solely with employee contributions are also exempt from the account limits if: (1) the VEBA covers at least 50 employees; and (2) no employee is entitled to a refund with respect to amounts in the fund, other than a refund based on the experience of the entire fund. VEBAs are tax-exempt trusts that provide life, sickness, accident and other benefits to members, or their dependents or beneficiaries, and meet certain nondiscrimination requirements (Code Secs. 501(c)(9) and 505).[14]

References are to Standard Federal Tax Reports; Tax Research Consultant; and Practical Tax Explanations.

[11] ¶ 19,295; COMPEN: 42,100; § 9,345

[12] ¶ 18,330; COMPEN: 42,050; § 9,345

[13] ¶ 19,298; COMPEN: 42,150; § 9,345

[14] ¶ 22,602, ¶ 22,711; COMPEN: 54,100; § 33,005

2013. Employer Contributions to Accident and Health Plans. Contributions by an employer to an accident or health plan that provides coverage for personal injuries or sickness incurred by the employee and his or her spouse, dependent, or child under the age of 27, are excluded from the employee's gross income (Code Sec. 106; Reg. § 1.106-1).[15] If a plan provides other benefits in addition to accident and health benefits, the exclusion applies only to the part of the employer's contributions that is allocable to accident and health benefits. See ¶ 2015 for a further discussion of accident and health plans. See ¶ 322 and ¶ 421 for a discussion of accident and health insurance premiums paid by a partnership or S corporation.

An employer generally contributes to an accident or health plan by paying a portion of the premium for accident and health insurance, or by contributing to a separate trust or fund that provides benefits directly or through insurance. A qualified long-term care insurance contract is generally treated as an accident and health insurance contract for this purpose (¶ 2019). Employer contributions for the cost of long-term care insurance provided through a flexible spending account or similar arrangement (¶ 2041) are included in the employee's wages for income tax purposes, but they are excluded from wages for FICA and FUTA purposes (Code Sec. 106(c)).

Employer contributions to an employee's health savings account (HSA) (¶ 2035) or Archer medical savings account (MSA) (¶ 2037) may be excluded from an employee's gross income as employer-provided coverage for medical expenses under an accident or health plan to the extent they do not exceed the HSA or MSA limits (Code Sec. 106(b) and (d)). If an employer makes such contributions, it must make comparable contributions on behalf of all employees with comparable coverage during the same period (Code Secs. 4980E and 4980G).[16] Employer contributions paid for COBRA continuation coverage of a former employee (¶ 2021) may also be excluded as coverage under an accident or health plan (IRS Pub. 15-B).

2015. Accident and Health Benefits. Amounts received by an employee under an employer-financed accident and health plan are generally excluded from gross income if received as:

- reimbursements for medical care of the employee, his or her spouse, dependent, or child under the age of 27 to the extent the medical expenses were not deducted by the employee in a prior tax year (Code Sec. 105(b); Reg. § 1.105-2);[17] or
- payments for permanent injury or loss of bodily function (i.e., disability) of the employee, spouse, or dependent, so long as the payments are based on the nature of the injury rather than length of time the employee is absent from work (Code Sec. 105(c); Reg. § 1.105-3).[18]

Amounts received by an employee through an accident and health insurance that are not reimbursements of medical expenses, but are instead payments for personal injuries or sickness, generally are included in gross income if they are attributable to contributions by the employer that were not included in the employee's gross income or paid directly by the employer (¶ 2014) (Code Sec. 105(a); Reg. § 1.105-1).[19] Amounts the employee receives that are not attributable to employer contributions, such as benefits attributable to the employee's own contributions, are not included in gross income.

Employee. An employee for this purpose includes any current, retired, and former employee, as well as a widow or widower of a retired employee and any individual who dies while an employee. It also includes a leased employee who provides services on substantially full-time basis (IRS Pub. 15-B). Self-employed individuals are not considered employees and the cost of their employer-provided accident and health insurance is included in their gross income (Code Sec. 105(g); Reg. § 1.105-5(b)).[20] However, a self-

References are to Standard Federal Tax Reports; Tax Research Consultant; and Practical Tax Explanations.

[15] ¶ 6800, ¶ 6801; HEALTH: 12,102; § 42,220

[16] ¶ 34,615, ¶ 34,619B; HEALTH: 9,306; § 42,515.35, § 42,615.10

[17] ¶ 6700, ¶ 6703; HEALTH: 12,104; § 42,215

[18] ¶ 6700, ¶ 6705; HEALTH: 12,200; § 42,215

[19] ¶ 6700, ¶ 6701; HEALTH: 12,104; § 42,215

[20] ¶ 6700, ¶ 6708; HEALTH: 12,100; § 42,215

employed individuals may deduct from gross income 100 percent of amounts paid for health insurance coverage (¶ 908). Partners in a partnership and two-percent or greater shareholders of an S corporation who are employees are considered to be self-employed.

Dependents. The definition of a dependent for this purpose is the same as for claiming the dependency exemption, but without regard to whether the dependent claims dependency exemptions (¶ 137), files a joint return (¶ 138), or has gross income in excess of the exemption amount for the year (¶ 137A). If certain conditions are met, the IRS will treat the child of divorced or separated parents as a dependent of both parents under an employer accident and health plan (Code Sec. 105(b)).

Same-Sex Spouses. A marriage of two individuals is recognized for federal tax purposes if the marriage would be recognized by the state, possession, or territory of the United States in which the marriage was entered into, regardless of where the individuals are domiciled (¶ 152) (Reg. § 301.7701-18).[21]

Accident and Health Plan. An accident and health plan is any arrangement of an employer that provides benefits to employees and their spouses, dependents, and children under age 27 in the event of personal injury or sickness (Code Sec. 105(e); Reg. § 1.105-5(a)).[22] The plan may be insured or not insured, and does not need to be in writing. A qualified long-term care insurance contract is generally treated as an accident and health insurance contract for this purpose (¶ 2019). A sickness and disability fund for employees maintained by a state, the District of Columbia, or Indian tribal government are also treated the same as an employer accident and health plan (Code Sec. 7871(a)(6)(A)). Qualified health care benefits provided by an Indian tribal government may also be excluded from gross income (¶ 2027). An employer's accident and health plan must not discriminate in favor of highly compensated individuals (¶ 2017).

COBRA Coverage. A group health plan provided by an employer must offer each qualified beneficiary who would otherwise lose coverage as a result of a qualifying event, an opportunity to elect continuation coverage referred to as COBRA continuation coverage (¶ 2021).

Railroad Unemployment Insurance. Benefits paid to an employee under the Railroad Unemployment Insurance Act for sick days are included in the employee's gross income unless an illness is due to an on-the-job injury (Code Sec. 105(i)).[23]

Annuity Rules. Amounts received as accident or health benefits are generally not taxable under the annuity rules of Code Sec. 72 (Reg. § 1.72-15).[24] However, some employer-established plans pay participants both amounts taxable under the annuity rules (¶ 817) and amounts excludable from gross income as payments under an accident or health plan. Specific rules are provided for determining which amounts are excludable in these cases. Benefits attributable to the employee's contributions are excludable from gross income under the rules at ¶ 851.

2017. Nondiscrimination Requirements for Employer Health Plans. An employer's self-insured medical reimbursement plan must not discriminate in favor of highly compensated individuals in terms of eligibility for coverage or benefits offered under the plan (Code Sec. 105(h); Reg. § 1.105-11).[25] For plan years beginning on or after September 23, 2010, similar nondiscrimination requirements apply to group health plans other than self-insured plans. However, compliance for group health plans will not be required until additional guidance is issued (Code Sec. 9815; Notice 2011-1). For a discussion of employer health reimbursement arrangements (HRAs), see ¶ 2039.

Excess reimbursements paid to a highly compensated individual under a plan that fails to meet the nondiscrimination requirements are includible in the individual's gross income. A highly compensated employee for this purpose is an employee who is one of

References are to Standard Federal Tax Reports; Tax Research Consultant; and Practical Tax Explanations.

[21] ¶ 3320.15; FILEIND: 3,200; § 1,210.10

[22] ¶ 6700, ¶ 6708; HEALTH: 12,104; § 42,225

[23] ¶ 6700; HEALTH: 12,104

[24] ¶ 6124; INDIV: 30,152.05; § 42,225

[25] ¶ 6700, ¶ 6711; HEALTH: 9,050; § 42,155.10

the five highest paid officers, among the highest paid 25 percent of all employees, or a shareholder owning more than 10 percent in value of the company's stock.

The entire amount of a reimbursement with respect to a benefit that is available only to highly compensated individuals is treated as an excess reimbursement includible in income. In the case of a plan that discriminates in terms of eligibility, the includible excess reimbursement is equal to all the medical expenses for which the highly compensated individual was reimbursed times a fraction—the numerator of which is the total amount reimbursed to all participants who are highly compensated individuals and the denominator is the total amount reimbursed to all employees under the plan for such plan year. If the plan discriminates in terms of eligibility *and* benefits, any amount which is included in income by reason of the benefits not being available to all other participants is not to be taken into account in determining the excess reimbursements that result from the plan being discriminatory in terms of eligibility.

There is no eligibility discrimination if the plan benefits (1) at least 70 percent of all employees or 80 percent of all eligible employees if at least 70 percent of all employees are eligible, or (2) a class of employees found by the IRS not to be discriminatory in favor of highly compensated individuals. Certain employees, such as part-time workers, employees with less than three years of service, employees under age 25, and employees excluded as a result of a collective bargaining agreement, may be excluded from coverage. There is no benefits discrimination if the self-insured medical expense plan provides the same benefits for non-highly compensated employees as it does for highly compensated employees.

2019. Long-Term Care Insurance. A qualified long-term care insurance contract is treated as an accident and health insurance contract, and any employer plan providing coverage under a qualified long-term care insurance contract is treated as an accident and health plan (Code Sec. 7702B).[26] Amounts received under the contract other than dividends and refunds are excluded from the recipient's gross income as amounts received for personal injuries and sickness (¶ 2015). The exclusion does not apply to long-term care insurance coverage provided under a cafeteria plan (¶ 2045) or flexible spending arrangement (¶ 2041) (Code Secs. 106(c) and 125(f)).[27] Premiums paid by an individual for a qualified long-term care insurance contract may be deducted as a medical expense (¶ 1019).

A qualified long-term care insurance contract is an insurance contract that only provides coverage of qualified long-term care services, including necessary diagnostic, preventive, and treatment services, or personal care services required by a chronically ill individual and prescribed by a licensed health care practitioner (Code Sec. 7702B(b) and (c)).[28] In addition, the contract must be guaranteed renewable, must not provide a cash surrender value, and must meet certain consumer protection provisions.

2021. COBRA Continuation Coverage. A group health plan provided by an employer with 20 or more employees must offer each covered employee, as well as his or her spouse and dependent, who would lose coverage as a result of a qualifying event, an opportunity to elect to continue coverage referred to as COBRA coverage (Code Sec. 4980B).[29] A qualifying event with respect to a covered employee includes death, termination of employment or reduction of hours, divorce or legal separation, eligibility for Medicare, a dependent child ceasing to be a dependent, or bankruptcy of the employer. Group health plans that fail to provide COBRA coverage to qualified beneficiaries are subject to an excise tax.

The option to elect COBRA coverage must allow the qualified beneficiary to purchase medical coverage under the company plan at group, rather than individual, rates for at least 18 months for most qualified beneficiaries (36 months in limited circumstances). The plan may require the beneficiary to pay premiums for the continua-

References are to Standard Federal Tax Reports; Tax Research Consultant; and Practical Tax Explanations.

[26] ¶ 43,166; HEALTH: 12,150; § 7,240.15

[27] ¶ 6800, ¶ 7320; HEALTH: 12,150

[28] ¶ 43,166; HEALTH: 12,150; § 7,240.15

[29] ¶ 34,600; HEALTH: 24,100; § 42,801

tion coverage not to exceed 102 percent of the applicable premium for the coverage period. The continuation coverage must be identical to the coverage provided to similarly situated beneficiaries under the plan for whom no qualifying event has occurred.

2023. Wellness Programs; Employee Assistance Programs. Wellness programs or employee assistance programs (EAPs) are generally part of an employer's overall health promotion for employees and may be one of several methods used to reduce health care costs. Although many EAPs are initiated to deal with drug and alcohol abuse, EAPs may also address family problems, stress, job termination, finances, and retirement. Because EAPs commonly provide treatment for drug and alcohol abuse and other similar health and medical problems, they often qualify as employee welfare benefit plans (¶ 2011). However, if an EAP merely provides referrals and does not pay for any services or benefits, the EAP will not be deemed to be an employee welfare benefit plan (Pension Welfare Benefits Administration (PWBA) Opinion Letter 91-26A).

2025. Disability Benefits. Disability income plans are employer plans, some mandated by state law, that provide full or partial income replacement for employees who become disabled. To the extent an employer offers such coverage under an accident and health plan, whether benefits received by employees are taxable depends on who pays for the premiums and whether they are paid on an after-tax basis (¶ 2015) (Code Sec. 105(a)).

2027. Indian Health Care Benefits. Qualified health care benefits provided by Indian tribal governments to a member of an Indian tribe, or to a member's spouse or dependent, are excluded from the beneficiary's gross income (Code Sec. 139D).[30] A qualified health care benefit includes:

- any health service provided or purchased by the Indian Health Service through a grant, contract or compact with an Indian tribe or tribal organization, or through a program funded by the Indian Health Service;
- medical care provided or purchased, or reimbursements for such medical care, by an Indian tribe or tribal organization for a member of an Indian tribe, the member's spouse or dependent;
- coverage under an accident or health insurance plan provided by an Indian tribe or tribal organization for medical care to a member of an Indian tribe, the member's spouse or dependent; and
- any other medical care provided by an Indian tribe or tribal organization that supplements, replaces or substitutes for medical care programs and services provided by the federal government to Indian tribes or their members.

The exclusion does not apply to Indian health care benefits that are not includible in the beneficiary's gross income under another provision in the Code or to any benefit for which the beneficiary may claim a deduction.

2028. Indian General Welfare Benefits. Indian general welfare benefits provided to, or on behalf of, a member of an Indian tribe, the member's spouse, or dependents are excluded from the recipient's gross income (Code Sec. 139E).[31] An Indian general welfare benefit is any payment made, or services provided, under an Indian tribal government program administered under specific guidelines and which does not discriminate in favor of members of the governing body of the Indian tribe. A program will not fail to be treated as an Indian tribal government program solely by reason of it being established by tribal custom or government practice. Benefits under the program must be available to any tribal member and must be for the promotion of general welfare. In addition, benefits must not be lavish or extravagant, and not provided as compensation for services. Any items of cultural significance, reimbursement of costs, or cash honorarium for participation in cultural or ceremonial activities for the transmission of tribal culture will not be treated as compensation.

References are to Standard Federal Tax Reports; Tax Research Consultant; and Practical Tax Explanations.

[30] ¶ 7649N; INDIV: 33,512; § 3,715

[31] ¶ 7649V; INDIV: 33,364; § 4,050

2029. Subsidies for Retiree Prescription Drug Plans. An employer that provides a qualified retiree prescription drug plan to its retired employees is eligible for a special subsidy payment each year from the federal government based on the cost of providing the coverage to qualified retirees (Social Security Act, § 1860D-22). The subsidy payment is excludable from the employer's gross income for both regular income tax and alternative minimum tax (AMT) purposes (Code Sec. 139A).[32] The amount otherwise allowable as a deduction to the employer for retiree prescription drug costs is reduced by the amount of the excludable subsidy received by the employer.

2031. Medical Loss Ratio Rebates. Health insurance issuers may be required to pay medical loss ratio (MLR) rebates to policyholders in the form of either cash payments or premium reductions. For policies purchased on the individual insurance market, MLR rebates are taxable or nontaxable depending on whether the individual deducted the premium payments (www.irs.gov, IRS FAQs, Medical Loss Ratio (MLR)). If the individual did not deduct the premiums for the year, an MLR rebate received in the following year is excluded from income whether received as cash or premium reduction. If the individual deducted the premiums, then an MLR rebate received in the following year is treated as the recovery of an itemized deduction under the tax benefit rule (¶ 799).

For policies purchased by an employee through an employer-sponsored group health plan, MLR rebates are taxable or nontaxable depending on whether the employee used pre-tax or after-tax dollars to pay the health insurance premiums. If the employee used pre-tax dollars, then any MLR rebate received is subject to income and employment taxes. If the employee used after-tax dollars and MLR rebates are paid only to employees who participated in the plan both in the year the premiums were paid and in the year the rebates are received, then a rebate is not included in income if the employee did not deduct the premiums. If, however, MLR rebates are provided to all employees participating in the group health plan in the year the rebates are paid, regardless of whether the employee participated in the plan in the year the premiums were paid, then the rebates are not included in income if the employee used after-tax dollars.

HSAs, HRAs, and FSAs

2035. Health Savings Accounts (HSAs). A health savings account (HSA) is a trust or custodial account established for the exclusive purpose of paying for qualified medical expenses of the account beneficiary (Code Sec. 223).[33] HSAs can be established by an employee through an employer's cafeteria plan (¶ 2045) or by individual outside the employment context.

Eligibility. To be eligible to establish an HSA in any month, an individual:

- must be covered by a high-deductible health plan (HDHP) on the first day of the month,
- must not be covered by any other plan that is not a HDHP,
- must not be enrolled in Medicare, and
- cannot be claimed as a dependent on another person's tax return (Code Sec. 223(c)(1)).[34]

Exceptions exist for permitted coverage under certain non-HDHPs. Permitted coverage includes coverage for accidents, disability, dental care, vision care, long term care or prescription drugs. Also allowed is permitted insurance for a specified disease or illness, insurance paying a fixed amount per day (or other period) for hospitalization, and insurance if substantially all the coverage relates to liabilities for workers' compensation, ownership or use of property (for example, auto insurance), or torts. Effective for months beginning after December 31, 2015, an individual will not fail to be treated as an eligible individual solely because he or she receives hospital care or medical services under any law administered by the Department of Veterans Affairs for a service-connected disability (Code Sec. 223(c)(1)).

References are to Standard Federal Tax Reports; Tax Research Consultant; and Practical Tax Explanations.

[32] ¶ 7649; HEALTH: 9,250

[33] ¶ 12,776; INDIV: 42,450; § 42,501

[34] ¶ 12,776; INDIV: 42,460.05; § 42,510.05

While covered by an HSA, an individual generally may not be covered by a health flexible spending arrangement (FSA) (¶ 2041) or health reimbursement account (HRA) (¶ 2039) sponsored by the individual's employer or spouse's employer unless it is a limited purpose FSA or HRA, a suspended HRA, a post-deductible health FSA or HRA, or a retirement HRA. Coverage under a general purpose health FSA during a grace period is disregarded in determining if tax deductible contributions can be made to an HSA for that period if the balance in the health FSA at the end of the plan year is zero or the entire remaining balance in the health FSA at the end of the plan year is contributed to an HSA in a qualified HSA distribution.

A taxpayer who is an eligible individual for an HSA on the first day of the last month of a tax year is treated as eligible during every month of that tax year. If the taxpayer ceases to be eligible during the period beginning with the last month of the tax year and ending on the last day of the 12th month following that month, he or she must include in gross income an amount equal to the amount actually contributed minus the sum of the monthly contribution limits to which the individual would otherwise have been entitled. An additional 10-percent tax is imposed on this amount. Recapture does not apply if the taxpayer is ineligible due to death or disability (Code Sec. 223(b)(8); Notice 2008-52).[35]

Dependent. The definition of a dependent for purposes of an HSA is the same as for claiming a dependency exemption, but determined without regard to whether the dependent claims dependency exemptions (¶ 137), files a joint return (¶ 138), or has gross income in excess of the exemption amount for the year (¶ 137A) (Code Sec. 223(d)(2)(A)). If certain conditions are met, the IRS will treat the child of divorced or separated parents as a dependent of both parents, without a declaration by the custodial parent releasing the claim to the dependency exemption (¶ 139A) (Rev. Proc. 2008-48).[36]

Contributions. Cash contributions may be made to an HSA by the eligible individual, the individual's employer, or any other person on behalf of the eligible individual. Contributions made by an individual outside the employment context are deductible as an above-the-line deduction in calculating adjusted gross income (AGI) (Code Secs. 62(a)(19) and 223(a)). Employer contributions to an employee's HSA may be excluded from the employee's gross income (¶ 2013). An individual must report all contributions to his or her HSA on Form 8889.

The maximum amount that can be contributed for 2016 is $3,350 for self-only coverage or $6,750 for family coverage (Rev. Proc. 2015-30). The maximum amount that can be contributed for 2017 is $3,400 for self-only coverage or $6,750 for family coverage (Rev. Proc. 2016-28). The contribution limit is increased $1,000 if the individual reaches age 55 by the end of the tax year. The annual limit applies to all HSAs of the eligible individual combined, and all contributions made by anyone to the accounts. The limit is decreased for any month the participant is not an eligible individual. Excess contributions are subject to a six-percent excise tax. Contributions cannot be made after the participant attains age 65 or is enrolled in Medicare (Notice 2008-59, amplifying Notice 2004-2; Notice 2004-50).[37]

Married Taxpayers. For married taxpayers, if either spouse has family coverage under any health plan, then both will be treated as having only family coverage under the plan. If each spouse has family coverage under different plans, then both spouses are treated as having coverage under the plan with the lowest deductible (Code Sec. 223(b)(5)). If only one spouse is an eligible individual, only that spouse may contribute to an HSA (Notice 2004-50). If one or both spouses have family coverage, the contribution limit is the lowest deductible amount, divided equally between the spouses unless they agree on a different division, and further reduced by any contribution to an Archer MSA. Both spouses may make the catch-up contributions for individuals age 55 or over without exceeding the family coverage limit (Notice 2008-59, amplifying Notice 2004-2).

References are to Standard Federal Tax Reports; Tax Research Consultant; and Practical Tax Explanations.

[35] ¶ 12,776, ¶ 12,785.25; HEALTH: 18,050; § 42,515.10

[36] ¶ 6702.27; PLANIND: 3,254.05, INDIV: 42,460.05; § 1,215.40

[37] ¶ 12,785.25, ¶ 12,785.50; INDIV: 42,454.05; § 42,540

If a husband and wife are each eligible to make catch-up contributions, each spouse can make such contributions only to his or her own HSA. The maximum annual contribution limit for a married couple is the statutory maximum for family coverage where: (1) one spouse has family coverage and the other spouse has self-only coverage, regardless of whether the family coverage includes the spouse with self-only coverage; or (2) both spouses have family coverage, regardless of whether each spouse's family coverage covers the other spouse. A married taxpayer covered under an HDHP can contribute to an HSA for use with qualifying out-of-pocket medical expenses even if his or her spouse's coverage is nonqualifying family coverage, as long as the taxpayer is not covered by the spouse's policy (Rev. Rul. 2005-25).

HDHP Defined. An HDHP is a plan with (1) an annual deductible of at least $1,300 for 2016 ($1,300 for 2017) for self-only coverage, or $2,600 for 2016 ($2,600 for 2017) for family coverage; and (2) an annual out-of-pocket expenses limit of $6,550 for 2016 ($6,550 for 2017) for self-only coverage or $13,100 for 2016 ($13,100 for 2017) for family coverage (Rev. Proc. 2015-30; Rev. Proc. 2016-28). Out-of-pocket expenses include deductibles, co-payments and other amounts (other than premiums) that must be paid for plan benefits (Code Sec. 223(c)(2); Notice 2008-59, amplifying Notice 2004-2).[38]

Distributions. Distributions from an HSA are excluded from the account beneficiary's gross income only if used to pay or be reimbursed for qualified medical expenses incurred during the coverage period (Code Sec. 223(f)).[39] Qualified medical expenses are those specified in the plan that would generally qualify as an itemized deduction and incurred by the account beneficiary, his or her spouse, or dependents (¶ 1016). Nonprescription medicines (other than insulin) are not considered qualified medical expenses under an HSA (Code Sec. 223(d)(2)). In addition, health insurance premiums are not qualified medical expenses under an HSA unless for long-term care insurance, COBRA continuation coverage, health care coverage while receiving unemployment compensation, or Medicare. Distributions from an HSA not used for qualified medical expenses are included in the account beneficiary's gross income and subject to a 20 percent additional tax, unless made after the beneficiary reaches age 65, dies, or becomes disabled. The additional tax is not treated as a tax liability for purposes of the alternative minimum tax (¶ 1420).

Contributions by Partnership or S Corporation. Contributions made by a partnership or S corporation to a partner's or shareholder's HSA are generally treated as payments to the partner or shareholder and includible in gross income. The individual partner or shareholder may treat the contribution as an above-the-line deduction (an adjustment to gross income). However, a contribution to the partner's HSA by the partnership for services rendered is treated as a guaranteed payment, and the partnership may deduct the contribution as a business expense. Similarly, a contribution by a S corporation to a two-percent shareholder's HSA for services rendered is deductible by the S corporation and included in the shareholders income (Notice 2005-8).[40]

Distributions to Fund HSAs. An eligible individual can make a one-time qualified HSA distribution directly from his or her IRA to his or her HSA (¶ 2165). The amount that can otherwise be contributed to the HSA for the tax year of the distribution is reduced by the amount contributed from the IRA, and the individual cannot deduct the distribution amount as an HSA contribution (Code Sec. 223(b)(4)(C); Notice 2008-51).[41] An eligible individual can also roll over distributions from another HSA or Archer MSA into an HSA. The taxpayer does not have to be an eligible individual to make a rollover contribution from an existing HSA to a new HSA (Code Sec. 106(e)).

2037. Archer Medical Savings Accounts (MSAs). An Archer medical savings account (MSA) is a trust or custodial account established for the exclusive purpose of paying for qualified medical expenses of the account beneficiary, his or her spouse, or dependents (Code Sec. 220).[42] Archer MSAs operate almost exactly the same as health

References are to Standard Federal Tax Reports; Tax Research Consultant; and Practical Tax Explanations.

[38] ¶ 12,776, ¶ 12,785.25, ¶ 12,785.50; INDIV: 42,450; § 42,510.10

[39] ¶ 12,776; INDIV: 42,460; § 42,520.10, § 42,525

[40] ¶ 12,785.25; INDIV: 42,454.10; § 42,515.05

[41] ¶ 12,776; HEALTH: 9,306; § 42,515.40

[42] ¶ 12,670; INDIV: 42,500, INDIV: 42,510; § 42,601

savings accounts (HSAs) (¶ 2035). New Archer MSAs may *not* be established after 2007. However, an individual can still utilize an Archer MSA if he or she was an active participant in the MSA before January 1, 2008, or he or she became an active participant for a tax year ending after December 31, 2007, by reason of coverage under a high deductible health plan (HDHP) of an Archer MSA participating employer.

To qualify for an Archer MSA, an individual or spouse must be either an employee of a small employer or self-employed person that maintains high-deductible health plan (HDHP). A small employer for this purpose is generally an employer who had an average of 50 or fewer employees during either of the last two calendar years. Like HSAs, the individual can have no other health care coverage, including under Medicare. An HDHP under an Archer MSA has higher annual deductibles and lower out-of-pocket limits than under an HSA: (1) for individual coverage, the minimum deductible is $2,250 for 2016 ($2,250 for 2017), the maximum deductible is $3,350 for 2016 ($3,350 for 2017), and the maximum out-of-pocket limitation is $4,450 for 2016 ($4,500 for 2017); and (2) for family coverage, the minimum deductible is $4,450 for 2016 ($4,500 for 2017), the maximum deductible is $6,700 for 2016 ($6,750 for 2017), and the maximum out-of-pocket limitation is $8,150 for 2016 ($8,250 for 2017) (Rev. Proc. 2015-53; Rev. Proc. 2016-55).

Contributions. Cash contributions may be made to an Archer MSA by the eligible individual or the individual's employer. Contributions made by the individual outside of the employment contact are deductible as an above-the-line deduction in calculating adjusted gross income (AGI) (Code Secs. 62(a)(16) and 220(a)). Employer contributions to an employee's MSA may be excluded from the employee's gross income (¶ 2013). An individual must report all contributions to an MSA on Form 8853. Annual contributions to an Archer MSA are limited to 75 percent of the deductible of the required health insurance plan (65 percent if a self-only plan). Contributions are also limited by an employee's compensation or the income earned from a self-employed individual's business (Code Sec. 220(b)). Excess contributions are subject to an excise tax.

Distributions. Distributions from an Archer MSA are excluded from the account beneficiary's gross income only if used to pay or be reimbursed for qualified medical expenses incurred during the coverage period (Code Sec. 220(f)). Qualified medical expenses are those specified in the plan that would generally qualify as an itemized deduction and incurred by the account beneficiary, his or her spouse, or dependents (¶ 1016). Nonprescription medicines (other than insulin) are not considered qualified medical expenses under an MSA. In addition, health insurance premiums are not qualified medical expenses under an MSA unless for long-term care insurance, COBRA continuation coverage, and health care coverage while receiving unemployment compensation. Distributions from an MSA not used for qualified medical expenses are included in the account beneficiary's gross income and subject to a 20 percent additional tax, unless made after the beneficiary reaches age 65, dies, or becomes disabled. The additional tax is not treated as a tax liability for purposes of the alternative minimum tax (¶ 1420).

Medicare Advantage MSAs. Medicare Advantage MSAs are medical savings accounts that must be used in conjunction with a high deductible Medicare Advantage MSA health plan (Code Sec. 138).[43] Individuals eligible for Medicare are permitted to have their Medicare benefits deposited directly into a Medicare Advantage MSA and can make trustee-to-trustee transfers from Archer MSAs to these MSAs. Income earned on the account and withdrawals used to pay health care expenses are not included in the individual's income.

2039. Health Reimbursement Arrangements (HRAs). A health reimbursement arrangement (HRA) is an employer-funded plan that reimburses employees for qualified medical care expenses (Notice 2002-45, amplified by Rev. Rul. 2006-36).[44] An HRA is funded solely by employer contributions and may not be funded through employee salary deferrals under a cafeteria plan (¶ 2045). The plan must provide reimbursements

References are to Standard Federal Tax Reports; Tax Research Consultant; and Practical Tax Explanations.

[43] ¶ 7630; INDIV: 42,466; § 42,615

[44] ¶ 6702.73; HEALTH: 18,100; § 42,401

up a maximum dollar amount for a coverage period. Any unused amounts in the HRA can be carried forward for reimbursements in later years.

To the extent an HRA constitutes an employer-provided accident or health plan (¶ 2015), coverage and reimbursements of qualified medical care expenses are generally excludable from the employee's gross income. An HRA may be offered in conjunction with other provided health benefits, such as a group health plan or health FSA (¶ 2041). HRAs must be integrated with an employer's minimum essential coverage, and reimbursements cannot be used to obtain individual coverage on a health exchange (except for stand-alone retiree plans and plans with fewer than two participants).[45]

Distributions from an HRA can only be used to reimburse the employee for his or her qualified medical expenses incurred during the coverage period. Qualified medical expenses are those specified in the plan that would generally qualify as an itemized deduction and incurred for the employee, spouse, dependent, or child under the age of 27 (¶ 1016). Nonprescription medicines (other than insulin) are not considered qualified medical expenses under an HRA (Code Sec. 106(f)).[46]

2041. Flexible Spending Arrangements (FSAs). A flexible spending arrangement (FSA) is an employer-established benefit program under which amounts credited to an employee's account may be used to reimburse the employee for health care, dependent care, or adoption expenses that would otherwise be excludable from the employee's gross income if paid by the employer (Prop. Reg. § 1.125-5).[47] An FSA may be funded by employer contributions or by a salary reduction agreement with pre-tax dollars as part of a cafeteria plan (¶ 2045).

The plan must provide either a maximum dollar limit or maximum percentage of compensation that can be contributed through a cafeteria plan. In the case of a health FSA, the maximum contribution is limited to $2,550 for 2016 ($2,600 for 2017) (Code Sec. 125(i); Rev. Proc. 2015-53; Rev. Proc. 2016-55).[48] If the plan allows salary reduction contributions to a health FSA in excess of the annual dollar amount, then the employee will be subject to tax on distributions from the health FSA. In the case of a dependent or adoption FSAs, the maximum contribution is limited to the amount the employee could exclude under a adoption assistance program (¶ 2063) or dependent care assistance program (¶ 2065).

An FSA may not be used to defer compensation; any balance remaining in the account at the end of the plan year is generally forfeited (use-it-or-lose-it rule) (Prop. Reg. § 1.125-5(c); Notice 2005-42).[49] However, a plan may permit a grace period of up to 2½ months after the end of the plan year (March 15 for calendar year plans) during which qualified expenses incurred during the period can be paid from any amounts left in the account at the end of the previous year. The employer is not permitted to refund any balance in an FSA account to an employee.

A cafeteria plan may allow also up to $500 of any balance remaining in a health FSA at the end of the year to be carried over to pay or reimburse qualified medical expenses incurred in the next year (Notice 2013-71). The carried over amount does not count against the maximum contribution an employee can make to the health FSA ($2,550 for 2016; $2,600 for 2017) (Rev. Proc. 2015-53; Rev. Proc. 2016-55). Any unused amount in a health FSA at the end of the year in excess of $500 (or lower amount specified in the plan) is forfeited. A plan that adopts the carryover option may not also provide the 2½ month grace period.

Special Rules for Health FSAs. Health FSA plans must comply with the rules applicable to other accident and health plans, including the nondiscrimination requirements for highly compensated employees (¶ 2017). Distributions from a health FSA can only be used to reimburse the employee for qualified medical expenses incurred during the coverage period. Qualified medical expenses are those specified in the plan that would generally qualify as an itemized deduction and incurred for the employee, spouse,

References are to Standard Federal Tax Reports; Tax Research Consultant; and Practical Tax Explanations.

[45] ¶ 34,963.054; HEALTH: 18,108; § 42,405

[46] ¶ 6800; HEALTH: 18,100; § 42,401

[47] ¶ 7323F; COMPEN: 51,200; § 42,701

[48] ¶ 7320, ¶ 7324.45; COMPEN: 51,200; § 42,701

[49] ¶ 7323F; COMPEN: 51,212; § 42,710

dependent, or child under the age of 27 (¶ 1016). Nonprescription medicines (other than insulin) are not considered qualified medical expenses under an FSA (Code Sec. 106(f)).[50]

Qualified Reservist Distribution. A cafeteria plan may allow for distribution of any remaining balance of a health FSA for any reason to a participant who is called to active duty for a period of at least 180 days due to his or her membership in a reserve unit of the military (Code Sec. 125(h)). The distribution must be made between the date of the order and the last day for which reimbursements can be made during the plan year.

Family and Medical Leave Act. The Family and Medical Leave Act (P.L. 103-3) (FMLA) imposes certain requirements on employers regarding coverage, including family coverage, under group health plans for employees taking FMLA leave and regarding the restoration of benefits to employees who return from FMLA leave. Reg. § 1.125-3 provides guidance on the effect of the FMLA on the operation of cafeteria plans.

Cafeteria Plans

2045. Cafeteria Plans. Cafeteria plans are employer-sponsored benefit packages that offer employees a choice between taking cash and receiving qualified benefits which may be excluded from gross income (Code Sec. 125; Prop. Reg. § 1.125-1).[51] If a participant chooses cash, it is includible in gross income as compensation. If qualified benefits are chosen, they are excludable to the extent allowed under the Code. A cafeteria plan cannot offer anything other than cash or qualified benefits. An employer who maintains a cafeteria plan is required to file an information return, but the reporting requirement has been suspended indefinitely (Code Sec. 6039D; Notice 2002-24).[52]

Cafeteria plan elections must be made before the start of the plan year and are generally irrevocable unless the employee experiences a change in status (i.e., marital status, number of dependents, etc.). An employer may permit elections to be revoked for employees expected to average less than 30 hours of service per week who nevertheless are still eligible for coverage under the employer plan, and employees who would like to cease employer coverage and buy coverage through an American Health Benefit Exchange (see later) without a period of duplicate or no coverage (Notice 2014-55).

A cafeteria plan may include any of the following qualified benefits: accident and health benefits (¶ 2015) including benefits under a flexible spending arrangement (¶ 2041), adoption assistance benefits (¶ 2063), dependent care assistance benefits (¶ 2065), disability coverage (¶ 2025), group-term life insurance (¶ 2055), health savings accounts (HSAs) (¶ 2035), and 401(k) plans (¶ 2104). A qualified benefit does *not* include benefits under an Archer MSA (¶ 2037), scholarships and fellowship grants (¶ 865), educational assistance benefits (¶ 2067), long-term care insurance (¶ 2019), or statutory fringe benefits under Code Sec. 132 (¶ 2085). A plan that provides deferred compensation is generally *not* included in the definition of a cafeteria plan. However, elective contributions under a qualified cash or deferred arrangement, profit-sharing plan, stock bonus plan, such as a 401(k) plan (¶ 2121), or contributions by an educational institution for post-retirement group life insurance are permitted.

Highly compensated employees (¶ 2114) are not entitled to exclude any benefit under a cafeteria plan attributable to a plan year in which the plan discriminates in favor of the highly compensated employees with respect to participation, contributions, and benefits. Key employees (¶ 2132) are not entitled to exclude any benefit attributable to a plan year in which the statutory qualified benefits provided to all key employees exceed 25 percent of the total of such benefits provided to all employees under the plan. In such cases, the benefits must be included in the gross income of the highly compensated employee or key employee for the tax year in which the plan year ends (Code Sec. 125(b)).

American Health Benefit Exchange Plans. An American Health Benefit Exchange (otherwise known as a Marketplace Exchange) and Small Business Health Options

References are to Standard Federal Tax Reports; Tax Research Consultant; and Practical Tax Explanations.

[50] ¶ 6800; HEALTH: 18,150; § 42,710

[51] ¶ 7320, ¶ 7321; COMPEN: 51,000; § 20,801

[52] ¶ 35,660, ¶ 35,661.50; COMPEN: 51,058; § 39,155.25

Program (SHOP) Exchange, run either by a state or the federal government, are generally available in every state and provide qualified individuals and small businesses with access to health plans, possibly at subsidized prices. Qualified health plans offered through such an exchange cannot be provided by employers through a cafeteria plan unless the employer is exchange-eligible (Code Sec. 125(f)(3)). An exchange-eligible employer is a small employer electing to make all of its full-time employees eligible for one or more qualified health plans offered in the small group market through an exchange (Act Sec. 1312(f)(2)(A) of the Patient Protection and Affordable Care Act (P.L. 111-148)).

A small employer is an employer who employed an average of at least one, but not more than 50, employees on business days during the preceding plan year and employs at least one employee on the first day of the current plan year. States have the option to treat employers with 51 to 100 employees as small employers (Act Sec. 1304(b)(2) of P.L. 111-148, as amended by Act Sec. 2(a) of the Protecting Affordable Coverage for Employees (PACE) Act (P.L. 114-60)). The small group market is the health insurance market under which employees obtain health insurance coverage through a group health plan maintained by a small employer (Act Sec. 1304(a)(3) of P.L. 111-148). Beginning in 2017, states may expand the definition of an exchange-eligible employer to include large employers in addition to small employers (Act Sec. 1312(f)(2)(B) of P.L. 111-148).

2047. Simple Cafeteria Plans. Certain small employers can establish simple cafeteria plans under which the nondiscrimination requirements applicable to regular cafeteria plans (¶ 2045), as well as the nondiscrimination rules applicable to group-term life insurance (¶ 2055), accident and health plans (¶ 2015), and dependent care assistance programs (¶ 2065), are considered satisfied (Code Sec. 125(j)).[53] A simple cafeteria plan is a cafeteria plan established and maintained by an eligible employer that meets certain contribution, eligibility, and participation requirements.

Eligible Employers. To be eligible to establish a simple cafeteria plan, an employer must have employed an average of 100 or fewer employees on business days during either of the two preceding years. An employer that was not in existence throughout the preceding year may be considered as an eligible employer if it reasonably expects to average 100 or fewer employees on business days during the current year. If an employer has 100 or fewer employees for the year and establishes a simple cafeteria plan, then it is treated as an eligible employer for any subsequent year even if the employer employs more than 100 employees in the subsequent year, unless the employer employs an average of 200 or more employees during the subsequent year.

For purposes of determining the qualification of a business that has changed ownership, the fact that the previous owner had 100 or fewer employees in a preceding year is used to determine eligibility of the current ownership to establish a simple cafeteria plan. Also, all persons treated as a single employer for purposes of the work opportunity credit (¶ 1365G) or the deferred compensation rules for leased employees under Code Sec. 414(n) or Code Sec. 414(o) are treated as one person for purposes of simple cafeteria plans.

Contribution Requirements. The contribution requirements of a simple cafeteria plan are met if the employer is required by the plan to make a contribution to provide qualified benefits on behalf of each qualified employee in an amount equal to: (1) a uniform percentage of at least two percent of the employee's compensation for the year; or (2) at least six percent of the employee's compensation for the plan year or twice the amount of the salary reduction contributions of each qualified employee, whichever is less (Code Sec. 125(j)(3)). If the employer bases the satisfaction of the contribution requirements on the second option, it will not be treated as met if the rate of contributions with respect to any salary reduction contribution of a highly compensated (¶ 2114) or key employee (¶ 2132) is greater than that with respect to any other employee.

References are to Standard Federal Tax Reports; Tax Research Consultant; and Practical Tax Explanations.

[53] ¶ 7320; COMPEN: 51,250; § 20,840.05

Employee Eligibility and Participation Requirements. The minimum eligibility and participation requirements of a simple cafeteria plan are met if all employees who had at least 1,000 hours of service for the preceding plan year are eligible to participate. In addition, each employee eligible to participate may elect any benefit under the plan, subject to terms and conditions applicable to all participants (Code Sec. 125(j)(4)). An employer may elect to exclude from the plan, regardless of the satisfaction of the 1,000 hour requirement, employees: (1) who have not attained the age of 21 before the close of the plan year; (2) who have less than one year of service with the employer; (3) who are covered under a collective bargaining agreement; or (4) who are nonresident aliens working outside the United States whose income did not come from a U.S. source.

Other Employee Benefits

2055. Group-Term Life Insurance. An employee may exclude from gross income the cost of the first $50,000 of group-term life insurance on the employee's life provided under a policy carried directly or indirectly by the employer (Code Sec. 79(a) and (c); Reg. §§ 1.79-1 and 1.79-3).[54] The cost of coverage in excess of $50,000 is included in the employee's gross income and subject to employment taxes, reduced by any amount the employee paid toward the insurance. The cost in excess of $50,000 is not the employer's actual cost in providing coverage. Instead, the cost is determined under a Uniform Premium Table (see below) which provides a per-month premium cost for $1,000 of insurance based on the employee's age as of the end of the employee's tax year. The $50,000 limit relates to the group-term life insurance coverage which the employee receives during any part of the tax year.

In the case of certain disabled or retired employees, the full cost of employer-provided group-term life insurance coverage is excluded from the employee's income (Code Sec. 79(b) and (d); Reg. § 1.79-2; Temp. Reg. § 1.79-4T).[55] A full exclusion is also available if the employer or a charity is the beneficiary of the insurance benefits. On the other hand, key employees (¶ 2132) must include the cost of all benefits they receive under plans that do not satisfy nondiscrimination requirements. In addition, coverage on the life of the employee's spouse or dependents is not excluded unless it qualifies as a *de minimis* fringe benefit (¶ 2089).

Group-term life insurance is insurance that provides for a general death benefit that is excluded from gross income (¶ 803) and provided to a group of at least 10 full-time employees at some time during the year (Reg. § 1.79-1; IRS Pub. 15-B). An employee includes any current common-law employee, former employee, or leased employee, as well as a statutory employee who is a full-time salesperson. An employee does not include a self-employed person, partner, or two-percent or more S corporation shareholder. The amount of insurance provided to each employee must be computed under a formula that precludes individual selection. In addition, the policy must not provide any permanent benefits.

Table 1

Cost Per $1,000 of Protection for One-Month Period

Age	*Cost*
Under 25	5 cents
25 through 29	6 cents
30 through 34	8 cents
35 through 39	9 cents
40 through 44	10 cents
45 through 49	15 cents
50 through 54	23 cents
55 through 59	43 cents
60 through 64	66 cents
65 through 69	$1.27
70 and above	$2.06

References are to Standard Federal Tax Reports; Tax Research Consultant; and Practical Tax Explanations.

[54] ¶ 6360, ¶ 6362, ¶ 6364; COMPEN: 48,100; § 21,005.05

[55] ¶ 6360, ¶ 6363, ¶ 6366; COMPEN: 48,100; § 21,005.05

Example: X Corp. pays the premiums on a $70,000 group-term insurance policy on the life of its president, Fox, who is 51 years old at the end of 2016. The IRS-established uniform cost for $1,000 of group-term coverage for twelve months is $2.76 ($0.23 × 12) (Reg. § 1.79-3(d)(2)). The cost of the policy includible in Fox's gross income is computed as follows:

Total insurance coverage	$70,000.00
Tax-free insurance	50,000.00
Insurance coverage subject to tax	$20,000.00
Taxable cost of policy includible in Fox's gross income ($2.76 × 20)	$55.20

2057. Split-Dollar Life Insurance. A split-dollar life insurance arrangement is an arrangement where the premiums, cash-surrender value, or death benefits are split between an owner and non-owner of a life insurance policy (Reg. § 1.61-22).[56] Ownership and benefits are most often split between an employer and an employee, but they may also be split between a corporation and shareholder, or between family members. A split-dollar arrangement entered into, or materially modified after September 17, 2003, is taxed under either the economic benefit rule or the loan rule depending upon which party owns the contract, and the relationship of the owner to the non-owner.

Owner of the Contract. The owner of a contract is generally the person named as the policy owner (Reg. § 1.61-22(c)). If two or more persons are named as policy owners and each has an undivided interest in every right and benefit, those persons are treated as owners of separate contracts. However, an employer is treated as the owner of the policy if the only benefit available under the arrangement is the value of the current life insurance protection (i.e., in a non-equity arrangement).

Economic Benefit Rule. Under the economic benefit rule, the owner of the life insurance contract is treated as transferring economic benefits to the non-owner (Reg. § 1.61-22(d)). Depending on the relationship between the parties, the economic benefits may constitute compensation, a distribution under Code Sec. 301, a gift, or another type of income. Both the owner and non-owner must account for the economic benefits fully and consistently, reduced by any consideration paid by the non-owner for the economic benefits. The economic benefit rule generally applies to compensatory arrangements in which the employer is the owner of the contract—for example, endorsement split-dollar arrangements, in which the employer is formally designated as the owner of the insurance contract and endorses the contract to specify the portion of the insurance proceeds payable to the employee's beneficiary (Reg. § 1.61-22(b)(3)(ii)). The value of the benefit provided under such an arrangement is the cost of any current life insurance protection provided to the employee (Reg. § 1.61-22(d)).

Loan Rule. Under the loan rule, the non-owner is treated as lending premium payments to the owner (Reg. § 1.7872-15). The rule generally applies to collateral assignments in which the employee is designated as the owner of the contract and the employer pays all or a portion of the premiums, the payment is a loan under general principals of federal tax law, and repayment is secured by the insurance policy's death benefits or cash surrender value. If a split-dollar loan does not provide for sufficient interest, the loan is a below-market split-dollar loan and is subject to the below market interest rules (¶ 795).

Deferred Compensation. Because certain types of split-dollar life insurance arrangements provide for deferred compensation, the requirements of Code Sec. 409A may apply (¶ 2197).

Pre-September 18, 2003, Arrangements. For a split-dollar arrangement entered into on or before September 17, 2003, or not materially modified thereafter, an employee is taxed on the value of economic benefits received. The economic benefit primarily consists of the value of the protection the employee receives over the premiums the employee pays. Certain other benefits might also be taxed, such as policy dividends received by the employee. The value of the economic benefit is determined using the

References are to Standard Federal Tax Reports; Tax Research Consultant; and Practical Tax Explanations.

[56] ¶ 5906E; COMPEN: 48,150; § 21,010.05

P.S. 58 rate table contained in Rev. Rul. 55-747,[57] the insurance company's lower published term rates, or the Table 2001 group-term rates (¶ 2055) (Notice 2002-8).

2059. Employer-Provided Vehicle. An employee who uses an employer-provided vehicle for more than *de minimis* personal use receives a taxable fringe benefit from his or her employer (Reg. § 1.61-21(a)).[58] The fair market value (FMV) of the fringe benefit is included in the employee's wages for income and employment tax purposes, and may be deducted by the employer as compensation. The FMV is generally the cost to the employee of leasing a comparable car at a comparable price for a similar period in an arms-length transaction (Reg. § 1.61-21(b)(4)). Under certain conditions, however, the employer may elect to use one of the following special valuation rules: automobile lease valuation, cents-per-mile valuation, or commuting valuation (Reg. § 1.61-21(c)). Separate rules are used for valuing flights by an employee on employer-provided noncommercial aircraft.

Automobile Lease Valuation. The value of the personal use of an employer-provided car may be computed under annual lease value tables (Reg. § 1.61-21(d)).[59] The annual lease value of an automobile is computed by first determining the FMV of the automobile on the first date it was made available to any employee for personal use. Under a safe-harbor, the employer's cost can be substituted for FMV, provided certain conditions are met. FMV is reduced when an employee contributes an amount toward the purchase or lease of the automobile. In addition, if the automobile is part of a fleet of at least 20, then the FMV of each automobile can be treated as equal to the fleet-average value. The maximum fleet-average value for employer-provided vehicles first made available for personal use by employees in calendar year 2016 is $21,200 for passenger automobiles and $23,100 for a truck or van (Notice 2016-12).

Once the FMV is established, the annual lease value table prepared by the IRS and reproduced below, is used to determine the annual lease value that corresponds to the FMV. The annual lease values include the FMV of maintenance and insurance for the automobile but do not include the cost of gasoline provided by the employer. The fuel provided can be valued either at its FMV or at 5.5 cents per mile for all miles driven within the United States, Canada, or Mexico by the employee. If continuous personal use of a company car is for less than a year, but at least 30 days, the employee may prorate the car's annual lease value. The values in the table are based on an assumed four-year lease term.

Automobile fair market value (1)	*Annual Lease Value (2)*
$ 0 to 999	$600
1,000 to 1,999	850
2,000 to 2,999	1,100
3,000 to 3,999	1,350
4,000 to 4,999	1,600
5,000 to 5,999	1,850
6,000 to 6,999	2,100
7,000 to 7,999	2,350
8,000 to 8,999	2,600
9,000 to 9,999	2,850
10,000 to 10,999	3,100
11,000 to 11,999	3,350
12,000 to 12,999	3,600
13,000 to 13,999	3,850
14,000 to 14,999	4,100
15,000 to 15,999	4,350
16,000 to 16,999	4,600
17,000 to 17,999	4,850
18,000 to 18,999	5,100
19,000 to 19,999	5,350
20,000 to 20,999	5,600
21,000 to 21,999	5,850

References are to Standard Federal Tax Reports; Tax Research Consultant; and Practical Tax Explanations.

[57] ¶ 5508.24; COMPEN: 48,150; § 21,005.20

[58] ¶ 5906; COMPEN: 33,150; § 8,035

[59] ¶ 5906; COMPEN: 33,152; § 8,055.10

Automobile fair market value (1)	*Annual Lease Value* (2)
22,000 to 22,999	6,100
23,000 to 23,999	6,350
24,000 to 24,999	6,600
25,000 to 25,999	6,850
26,000 to 27,999	7,250
28,000 to 29,999	7,750
30,000 to 31,999	8,250
32,000 to 33,999	8,750
34,000 to 35,999	9,250
36,000 to 37,999	9,750
38,000 to 39,999	10,250
40,000 to 41,999	10,750
42,000 to 43,999	11,250
44,000 to 45,999	11,750
48,000 to 49,999	12,750
50,000 to 51,999	13,250
52,000 to 53,999	13,750
54,000 to 55,999	14,250
56,000 to 57,999	14,750
58,000 to 59,999	15,250

For vehicles having a fair market value in excess of $59,999, the Annual Lease Value is equal to: (0.25 × the fair market value of the automobile) + $500.

Cents-Per-Mile Valuation. The value of the personal use of an employer-provided vehicle may be determined by multiplying personal use mileage, provided it is at least 10,000 miles, by the standard mileage rate (54 cents per mile in 2016) if certain requirements are satisfied (Reg. § 1.61-21(e); Rev. Proc. 2010-51; Notice 2016-1).[60] For a passenger automobile first made available to an employee in calendar year 2016, the FMV of the vehicle cannot exceed $15,900, and for a truck or van, the FMV cannot exceed $17,700 (Notice 2016-12). Fuel provided by the employer must be valued separately, at either its FMV or at 5.5 cents per mile for miles driven in North America (Reg. § 1.61-21(d)(3)(ii)(B)).

Commuting Valuation. If certain requirements are met, the use of an employer-provided commuting vehicle is valued at $1.50 each way (i.e., to and from work), per employee (Reg. § 1.61-21(f)).[61] Even if two or more employees commute in the vehicle such as a car pool, each employee includes $1.50 each way in income. To qualify, personal use of the vehicle must be *de minimis* and the employer must require the employee or employees to commute to and/or from work in the vehicle for bona fide noncompensatory business reasons.

Employer-Provided Transportation Due to Unsafe Conditions. If it is unsafe for an employee, who would normally do so, to walk or use public transportation to get to work and certain other requirements are met, the employee includes only $1.50 per one-way commute ($3.00 per round trip commute) in income with respect to cab fare or an employer-provided vehicle (Reg. § 1.61-21(k)).[62]

Chauffeur Services. The FMV of chauffeur services is determined separately from the value of the availability of an employer-provided automobile (Reg. § 1.61-21(b)(5)). The services of a chauffeur may generally be valued by reference to either (1) the FMV of these services as determined in an arm's-length transaction, or (2) the compensation of the chauffeur.

Noncommercial Aircraft Flights. The value of personal flights, domestic or international, on employer-provided noncommercial aircraft is determined under an IRS formula that is based on Standard Industry Fare Level (SIFL) flight mileage rates, a terminal charge and the weight of the aircraft (Reg. § 1.61-21(g)).[63] If a trip made

References are to Standard Federal Tax Reports; Tax Research Consultant; and Practical Tax Explanations.

[60] ¶ 5906; COMPEN: 33,154; § 8,055.15

[61] ¶ 5906; COMPEN: 33,156; § 8,055.20

[62] ¶ 5906; COMPEN: 33,152.20, COMPEN: 33,156, COMPEN: 33,160; § 21,130.10, § 21,130.15

[63] ¶ 5906; COMPEN: 33,202; § 21,105.10

primarily for business purposes includes business and personal flights, the excess of the value of all the actual flights over the value of the flights that would have been taken if there had been no personal flights is includible in gross income. If the trip is primarily personal, the value of the personal flights that would have been taken if there had been no business flights is includible in gross income. No amount is included in income if the employee takes a personal trip on a noncommercial aircraft and at least one-half of the aircraft's seating capacity is occupied by employees whose flights are primarily business related and excludable from income.

Frequent Flyer Miles. The IRS will not tax the personal use of airline frequent flyer miles or other in-kind promotional benefits attributable to the taxpayer's business or official travel. Any future guidance on the taxability of these benefits will be applied prospectively. This relief does not apply to travel or other promotional benefits that are converted to cash, to compensation that is paid in the form of travel or other promotional benefits, or to other circumstances where these benefits are used for tax-avoidance purposes (Announcement 2002-18).[64]

2063. Adoption Assistance Programs. Qualified adoption expenses incurred by a taxpayer for the adoption of an eligible child and paid to a third party or reimbursed to an employee by an employer under a written adoption assistance program are excludable from the employee's gross income (Code Sec. 137).[65] An adoption assistance program is a written plan that (1) benefits employees who qualify under rules set up by the employer which do not favor highly compensated employees (¶ 2114) or their dependents (¶ 152); (2) does not pay more than five percent of its payments each year to shareholders or owners of more than five percent of the stock; (3) provides for adequate notice to employees of their eligibility; and (4) requires employees to provide reasonable substantiation of qualified expenses that are to be paid or reimbursed.

The rules for the exclusion generally parallel the rules for the adoption expense credit. Thus, an eligible child and qualified adoption expenses are defined as they are for purposes of the credit (¶ 1307). The aggregate amount of payments that may be excluded from income (for both special needs adoptions and other adoptions) is $13,460 for 2016 ($13,570 for 2017) (Rev. Proc. 2015-53; Rev. Proc. 2016-55). The exclusion is phased out for higher income taxpayers the same as for the adoption credit when modified adjusted gross income is between $201,920 and $241,920 for 2016 (between $203,540 and $243,540 for 2017).

2065. Dependent Care Assistance Benefits. An employee may exclude from gross income amounts paid or incurred by an employer for dependent care assistance services provided to the employee under a written plan (Code Sec. 129).[66] The maximum amount excluded cannot exceed $5,000 for the tax year ($2,500 if married filing separately). Any amount exceeding the limit is includible in the employee's gross income for the year in which the services are provided, even if the payment for the services is received in a subsequent year. The exclusion also cannot exceed the employee's earned income if unmarried, or earned income of the lower-earning spouse if married.

Dependent care assistance means the payment for services (or providing services) which if paid by the employee would entitle him or her to claim the child and dependent care credit (¶ 1301). In other words the expenses must be incurred for household services for care of a child or other dependent to enable the employee to work. A dependent care assistance plan generally must not discriminate in favor of employees who are highly compensated (¶ 2114). If a plan would qualify as a dependent care assistance program except for the fact that it fails to meet discrimination, eligibility, or other requirements, then despite the failure the plan may still be treated as a dependent care assistance program in the case of employees who are not highly compensated.

The exclusion of dependent care assistance benefits does not apply unless the name, address, and taxpayer identification number of the person performing the child or dependent care services are included on the return of the employee benefiting from the exclusion. The exclusion may be claimed even though the information is not provided if

References are to Standard Federal Tax Reports; Tax Research Consultant; and Practical Tax Explanations.

[64] ¶ 5907.35; BUSEXP: 24,906.15; § 3,085

[65] ¶ 7600; COMPEN: 36,650; § 4,025

[66] ¶ 7380; COMPEN: 36,600; § 20,001

it can be shown that the taxpayer exercised due diligence in attempting to provide this information.

2067. Educational Assistance Programs. Up to $5,250 of payments received by an employee for tuition, fees, books, supplies, etc., under an employer's educational assistance program may be excluded from gross income (Code Sec. 127; Reg. §§ 1.127-1 and 1.127-2).[67] This benefit is available for both undergraduate and graduate-level courses. Excludable assistance payments may not cover tools or supplies that the employee retains after completion of the course or the cost of meals, lodging, or transportation. Although the courses covered by the plan need not be job related, an exception applies to courses involving sports, games, or hobbies. These courses may only be covered if they involve the employer's business or are required as part of a degree program.

An educational assistance program is a separate written plan that provides educational assistance only to employees, subject to various limitations. An employee for this purpose includes a current employee, as well as a former employee who retired, left on disability, or was laid off. It also includes a partner who performs services for a partnership and a leased employee who has provided services on a substantially full-time basis for at least a year (Rev. Rul. 96-41). A program that provides benefits to spouses or dependents of employees is not a qualified program.

Reports and Records. An employer who maintains an educational assistance plan must maintain records and file an information return for the plan, but the reporting requirement has been suspended indefinitely (Code Sec. 6039D; Notice 2002-24).[68]

2069. Employee Achievement Award. An employee achievement award is excludable from an employee's gross income to the extent the cost of the award is deductible by the employer ($400 for nonqualified awards or $1,600 for qualified awards) (Code Sec. 74(c); Prop. Reg. § 1.74-2).[69] See ¶ 919 for a discussion of the employer's deduction and the definition of an employee achievement award. If the cost of an award exceeds the dollar limitations, then the employee must include in gross income the greater of excess of the fair market value or the cost to the employer of the award over the dollar limitation, but not in excess of the fair market value of the award. The exclusion is not available for any award made by a sole proprietorship to the sole proprietor.

2071. Vacation Pay. A vacation pay plan is an employer plan that provides compensation to employees for specified periods of vacation, including vacation time that has been earned but not actually taken. Such a plan also generally includes compensation for specified holidays, whether or not those days are actually taken.[70]

Vacation pay plans, like other employee benefit plans, can take a wide variety of forms: the benefits may be vested or unvested; the plan may be funded or unfunded; and the plan may be a single-employer plan or a multiemployer plan. Vacation pay is taxable and is subject to income tax withholding (Code Sec. 61; Reg. § 31.3401(a)-1(b)(3)). Vacation pay is also subject to FICA and FUTA taxes (Code Secs. 3121(a) and 3306(b)).

Vacation pay is generally deductible by an employer as reasonable compensation for prior services rendered (Code Sec. 162; SeeReg. § 1.162-7). See ¶ 1549 for a discussion of the accrual of vacation and sick leave pay. See ¶ 2073 for a discussion of employer-sponsored leaving programs.

2073. Leave Sharing Programs. An employee who deposits accrued leave in an employer-sponsored leave-sharing program for use by other employees adversely affected by a major disaster does not realize income or wages with respect to the deposited leave, provided the plan treats the amounts paid to the leave recipient as wages subject to income tax withholding and payroll taxes (Notice 2006-59).[71] The employee may not claim a charitable contribution, business expense, or loss deduction on account of the deposit of the leave or its use by a leave recipient.

References are to Standard Federal Tax Reports; Tax Research Consultant; and Practical Tax Explanations.

[67] ¶ 7350, ¶ 7351, ¶ 7352; COMPEN: 36,554; § 20,101

[68] ¶ 35,660, ¶ 35,661.50; PENALTY: 3,208.20; § 39,155.25

[69] ¶ 6200, ¶ 6203; INDIV: 33,154; § 3,060.15

[70] ¶ 5507.47; COMPEN: 12,212; § 22,110.10

[71] ¶ 11,620.522; COMPEN: 6054; § 3,005.25, § 22,110.10

Similarly, if an employee participates in a leave donation program under which employees may elect to forgo vacation, sick, or personal leave in exchange for employer making cash contributions to charitable organizations, the contributing employee may not claim charitable contribution, business expense, or loss deduction for the contributed leave. However, the IRS will not assert that such cash payments constitute gross income or wages of the employee with respect to donations made to a charitable organization: (1) before January 1, 2018, for relief of victims of severe storms and flooding in Louisiana that began on August 11, 2016; (2) before January 1, 2016, for the relief of victims of the Ebola virus disease outbreak in Guinea, Liberia, and Sierra Leone; and (3) before January 1, 2014, for the relief of victims of Hurricane Sandy (Notice 2016-55; Notice 2014-68; Notice 2012-69).[72]

Amounts deposited in a leave bank to be used by employees experiencing medical emergencies are not taxable to contributing employees but they are included in the gross income of the recipients subject to income tax withholding and payroll taxes (Rev. Rul. 90-29). The IRS has not granted favorable tax treatment to other leave-sharing plans.

2075. Severance Pay. A severance pay plan is a plan that provides payments to employees upon termination of employment. Depending upon the facts and circumstances, severance pay arrangements can qualify as a welfare benefit plan (¶ 2011) or retirement plan (¶ 2111), or may be exempt from certain federal requirements. Generally, the payments are proportionate to length of employment.[73] The plan may be a permanent program or a limited program—e.g., an "open-window" program that offers a group of employees cash payments, increased pension benefits, or both as inducements to voluntarily retire or to separate from employment within a certain time period. The plan may cover voluntary separations, involuntary separations, or both, and may place conditions on payment of benefits—e.g., no benefits are provided if the employee goes to work for a competitor or for a successor employer. In addition, the plan may deny benefits if the employee is terminated for cause.

Golden Parachutes. In a golden parachute agreement, a corporate employer states that it will pay a key employee (¶ 2132) or a number of key employees an amount over and above other compensation in the event of a change in ownership or control of the corporation or a substantial portion of the corporation's assets (¶ 907). The tax consequences applicable to golden parachute payments are triggered merely by the payment of the requisite amount of compensation, and a termination of employment is not literally required. As a practical matter, however, golden parachute payment provisions in an employment agreement or employer's benefits plan usually are designed to be triggered upon loss of employment within a designated period of time following the acquisition of the employer.

2077. Domestic Partner Benefits. Employers may offer benefits to an employee's domestic partner, including health care insurance (medical, dental, vision), access to an employee assistance plan, and dependent life insurance. Employers often require a written affidavit affirming the relationship and may require various documentation, such as joint mortgage or lease, proof of registration under a local ordinance, drivers' license, tax returns, bank statements, or joint credit statements.

A marriage of two individuals is recognized for federal tax purposes if the marriage would be recognized by the state, possession, or territory of the United States in which the marriage was entered into, regardless of where the individuals are domiciled (¶ 152). However, a marriage for federal tax purposes does not include registered domestic partnerships, civil unions, or other similar relationships recognized under state law that are not denominated as a marriage under that state's law (Reg. § 301.7701-18).[74] Thus, while employer-provided health benefits are tax free for spouses (including same-sex spouses) and dependents of an employee (¶ 2015), the cost of providing the benefit to a domestic partner who is not legally married to the employee or cannot be claimed as the employee's dependent (¶ 137) is included in the employee's gross income. Additionally, if a domestic partner is not the employee's spouse or dependent, contributions for a

References are to Standard Federal Tax Reports; Tax Research Consultant; and Practical Tax Explanations.

[72] ¶ 11,620.1005; INDIV: 27,208; § 22,110.10

[73] ¶ 5507.297; COMPEN: 27,202; § 9,345

[74] ¶ 43,166; FILEIND: 3,202; § 45,901

partner's coverage must be on an after-tax basis, and the domestic partner is not eligible for reimbursement from health care FSAs.

Specific guidance has been provided for employers and employees to make claims for refunds or adjustments of overpayments of employment taxes and income tax withholding for benefits provided to same-sex spouses (Notice 2013-61).[75]

Fringe Benefits Under Code Sec. 132

2085. Fringe Benefits Under Code Sec. 132. Certain fringe benefits provided by an employer to an employee are excluded from an employee's gross income for income tax purposes, and from wages for purposes of income tax withholding and FICA and FUTA taxes (Code Sec. 132).[76] These include: no-additional-cost services (¶ 2087), qualified employee discounts (¶ 2088), *de minimis* fringe benefits (¶ 2089), working condition fringe benefits (¶ 2090), qualified transportation fringe benefits (¶ 2091), qualified moving expense reimbursements (¶ 2092), qualified retirement planning services (¶ 2093), on-premises athletic facilities (¶ 2094), and qualified military base realignment and closure fringe benefits (¶ 2095). Employers providing fringe benefits must meet certain nondiscrimination requirements in order for such benefits to apply to favored groups.

Any fringe benefit that does not qualify for exclusion under Code Sec. 132, or any other Code provision, is includible in the recipient's gross income and wages at the excess of its fair market value over any amount paid by the employee for the benefit (unless excluded under another specific statutory provision) (¶ 713). Employers are generally allowed a trade or business expense deduction for the value or a portion of the value of the fringe benefit provided to employees (¶ 906).

For purposes of no-additional-cost services, qualified employee discounts, and on-premise athletic facilities, the exclusion under Code Sec. 132 applies to benefits provided to: (1) employees, their spouses, and dependent children; (2) former employees who separated from service because of retirement or disability, as well as their spouses and dependent children; (3) the widow or widower of a deceased employee; and (4) the dependent children of deceased employees (Code Sec. 132(h); Reg. § 1.132-1(b)).[77] For purposes of working condition fringes, the exclusion applies to benefits provided to employees, independent contractors, directors, and partners who perform services for a partnership.

2087. No-Additional-Cost Services. No-additional-cost services provided by an employer to employees are excluded from gross income and wages as a fringe benefit (¶ 2085) (Code Sec. 132(b); Reg. § 1.132-2).[78] No-additional-cost services are free services provided to all employees by an employer where the employer incurs no substantial additional cost in providing the service, and the service is normally offered to the employer's customers in the line of business, such as free travel on a standby basis for airline employees. The exclusion is available only if the service is available to employees on a nondiscriminatory basis.

2088. Qualified Employee Discounts. Discounts provided to employees on their purchase of qualified property or services of their employer are excluded from gross income and wages as a fringe benefit (¶ 2085) (Code Sec. 132(c); Reg. § 1.132-3).[79] Qualified employee discounts are discounts provided to all employees on the selling price of certain property or services in the ordinary line of business. In the case of merchandise, the discount cannot exceed the gross profit percentage of the price at which the property is offered to customers. For services, the discount cannot exceed 20 percent of the price at which the service is offered to customers. In order to be excluded, the discounts must be available to employees on a nondiscriminatory basis. Moreover, employees do not receive income if they pay at least fair market value for damaged, distressed, or returned property.

References are to Standard Federal Tax Reports; Tax Research Consultant; and Practical Tax Explanations.

[75] ¶ 38,519.395, ¶ 38,770.13; PAYROLL: 9,352; § 22,235.25

[76] ¶ 7420; COMPEN: 36,000; § 21,101

[77] ¶ 7420, ¶ 7422; COMPEN: 33,050; § 21,101

[78] ¶ 7420, ¶ 7423; COMPEN: 36,050; § 21,105.05

[79] ¶ 7420, ¶ 7424; COMPEN: 36,100; § 21,110.05

2089. *De Minimis* Fringe Benefits. If the value of any property or service provided to an employee is so minimal that accounting for the property or service would be unreasonable or administratively impracticable for an employer, it is a *de minimis* fringe benefit that is excluded from the employee's gross income and wages (¶ 2085) (Code Sec. 132(e); Reg. § 1.132-6).[80] Examples include limited use of copy machines, occasional parties or picnics, meal money or transit fare due to overtime work, holiday gifts with a small market value, tickets occasionally provided for entertainment events, and employer-furnished coffee and doughnuts. In determining whether the *de minimis* exclusion applies, the frequency with which similar fringe benefits are provided by an employer to its employees is taken into account. A subsidized eating facility operated by an employer for the benefit of employees is treated as a *de minimis* fringe benefit if the eating facility is located on or near the employer's business premises, and the revenue derived from such facility normally equals or exceeds the direct operating costs of such facility (Reg. § 1.132-7).

Meals and Lodging. Meals are excluded from an employee's gross income and wages as a *de minimis* fringe benefit if furnished on the business premises of the employer for the convenience of the employer (Code Sec. 119; Reg. § 1.119-1).[81] Lodging is also excluded from an employee's gross income and wages if furnished for the convenience of the employer on the business premises of the employer, and as a condition of employment.

Meals are regarded as furnished for the convenience of the employer if they are furnished for a substantial noncompensatory business reason of the employer (even if the meals also serve a compensatory purpose). If more than one-half of the employees who are furnished meals by the employer are furnished meals for the convenience of the employer, then all meals furnished on the premises of the employer are considered to be for the convenience of the employer. Therefore, the meals are fully deductible by the employer, instead of possibly being subject to the 50-percent limit on business meal deductions, and excludable by the employees (¶ 916). The business premises of the employer for this purpose generally means the place of employment of the employee. It can include a camp located in a foreign country if an employee is furnished lodging (¶ 2406).

Faculty Housing. The value of campus lodging furnished to employees by educational or medical research institutions is excludable from the employee's gross income and wages if an adequate rental is charged. A rental is considered *inadequate* and thus the exclusion will not apply to the extent of the excess of: (1) the lesser of (a) five percent of the appraised value of the lodging or (b) an amount equal to the average of the rentals paid by nonemployees or nonstudents during the year for comparable lodging provided by the institution; over (2) the rent paid by the employee for the calendar year (Code Sec. 119(d)).[82] The appraised value of lodging will be determined as of the close of the calendar year in which the tax year begins or, in the case of a rental period not greater than one year, at any time during the calendar year in which such period begins.

2090. Working Condition Fringe Benefits. Working condition fringe benefits provided to an employee may be excluded from gross income and wages as a fringe benefit (¶ 2085) provided the cost of the property or service would have been deductible by the employee as a business expense or depreciation had the employee paid for it on his or her own (Code Sec. 132(d); Reg. § 1.132-5).[83] The general nondiscrimination rules applicable to fringe benefits do not apply to working condition fringes; therefore, they can be provided exclusively, or on more favorable terms, to executives. Examples of working condition fringes include use of a company vehicle, airplane transportation, travel expenses including meals and lodging, allowances for business use of cell phones, computers, internet service, entertainment, and club dues. Denial of a deduction to an

References are to Standard Federal Tax Reports; Tax Research Consultant; and Practical Tax Explanations.

[80] ¶ 7420, ¶ 7427; COMPEN: 36,300; § 21,120.05

[81] ¶ 7220, ¶ 7221; COMPEN: 36,500; § 21,205, § 21,210

[82] ¶ 7220; COMPEN: 36,508; § 21,230

[83] ¶ 7420, ¶ 7426; COMPEN: 36,250; § 21,115.05

employer for its payment of travel expenses of a spouse, dependent, or other individual accompanying an employee on business travel does not preclude those items from qualifying as working condition fringe benefits.

Employer-Provided Cell Phones. An employer-provided cell phone and similar equipment provided to an employee for noncompensatory business purposes is excluded from an employee's gross income and wages as a working condition fringe benefit (Notice 2011-72).[84] In addition, the business substantiation requirements for the working condition fringe exclusion are automatically satisfied for a employer-provided cell-phone. A noncompensatory business purpose is any substantial reason relating to the employer's business, other than providing compensation, such as the employer's need to contact employees during work-related emergencies, or the employer's requirement that the employee be available to speak with clients away from the office or outside normal workday hours. Personal use of an employer-provided cell-phone, provided primarily for noncompensatory business purposes, is excluded from an employee's gross income and wages as a *de minimis* fringe benefit (¶ 2089). Employers that require employees to use their personal cell phones primarily for noncompensatory business reasons may treat reimbursements of the employees' reasonable expenses as nontaxable. This does not mean, however, that cell phones used for primarily personal reasons are exempt from tax or from the substantiation requirements.

Employer-Provided Vehicles. The value of an employee's *business use* of an employer-provided automobile is excludable from the employee's gross income and wages as a working condition fringe benefit. The value of employee's *personal use* of an employer-provided automobile is generally included in the employee's income and wages (¶ 2059). The employer, however, may elect not to withhold income tax on the value of the employee's personal use (Code Sec. 3402(s)).[85] The employer must notify the employee of the election, and must include the value of the benefit on a timely filed Form W-2. An employer who elects not to withhold income tax for an employer-provided automobile is still required to withhold FICA taxes.

2091. Qualified Transportation Fringe Benefits. Commuting expenses to and from a place of business and home are generally not deductible. However, qualified transportation fringe benefits provided by an employer to an employee may be excluded from the employee's gross income and wages as a fringe benefit (¶ 2085) (Code Sec. 132(f), as amended by the Protecting Americans from Tax Hikes (PATH) Act of 2015 (P.L. 114-113); Reg. § 1.132-9).[86] A qualified transportation fringe benefit includes employer-provided transit passes, qualified parking, van pooling, and qualified bicycle commuting reimbursement.

For 2016, the maximum that may be excluded for qualified parking, transit passes, and van pooling is $255 per month (Rev. Proc. 2015-53, as modified by Rev. Proc. 2016-14). For 2017, the maximum that may be excluded for qualified parking, transit passes, and van pooling is $255 per month (Rev. Proc. 2016-55). The exclusion for qualified bicycle commuting reimbursement is limited to a per employee limitation of $20 per month, multiplied by the number of qualified bicycle commuting months during the calendar year.

An employer may simultaneously provide an employee with a transit pass, qualified parking, and van pooling. However, an employee may not receive a bicycle commuting expense reimbursement for any month in which the employee receives any other qualified transportation fringe benefit. Employers who provide any qualified transportation fringe benefits for their employees may offer employees a choice between cash and one or more qualified transportation benefits without causing the employees to lose the exclusion from income for noncash transportation fringe benefits. The amount of cash offered is includible in the employee's income only to the extent that the employee chooses the cash option.

Qualified parking for this purpose is parking provided on or near the business premises of the employer, or on or near a location from which the employee commutes

References are to Standard Federal Tax Reports; Tax Research Consultant; and Practical Tax Explanations.

[84] ¶ 7438.80; COMPEN: 36,258; § 21,115.22

[85] ¶ 33,542; COMPEN: 33,350; § 22,110.10

[86] ¶ 7420, ¶ 7429B; COMPEN: 36,350; § 21,125.05

to work by mass transit, in a commuter highway vehicle, or by car pool. It does not include parking on or near property used by the employee for residential purposes. Van pooling is transportation in a qualifying commuter highway vehicle if that transportation is in connection with travel between the employee's residence and the place of employment. A qualifying commuter vehicle must seat at least six adults (excluding the driver) and at least 80 percent of its mileage use must be reasonably expected to be for employees' commuting purposes and for trips when the vehicle is at least one-half full (excluding the driver).

2092. Qualified Moving Expenses Reimbursements. An employee may exclude any qualified moving expenses reimbursement from gross income and wages as a fringe benefit (¶ 2085) (Code Sec. 132(g)).[87] A qualified moving expenses reimbursement includes any amount received, directly or indirectly, by the employee from the employer as payment or reimbursement of expenses that would be deductible as moving expenses if directly paid or incurred by the employee (¶ 1073). It does not include a payment for, or a reimbursement of, an expense actually deducted by the employee in a prior tax year. Expenses that would be deductible if paid directly or incurred by the employee include the reasonable expenses of moving household goods and personal effects from a former residence to a new residence, as well as the expense of traveling to the new residence, including lodging during the period of travel.

2093. Qualified Retirement Planning Services. Qualified retirement planning services provided to an employee and his or her spouse by an employer that maintains a qualified plan are excludable from the employee's gross income and wages as fringe benefits (¶ 2085) (Code Sec. 132(m)).[88] Qualified retirement planning services consist of retirement planning advice and information. The exclusion applies to a highly compensated employee (¶ 2114) only if retirement planning services are available on substantially the same terms to each member of the group of employees that is normally provided with education and information about the employer's qualified plan. In determining the exclusion's application to highly compensated employees, the IRS may allow employers to take into account employee circumstances other than compensation and position in providing advice to classifications of employees.

2094. Athletic Facilities. The value of an on-premises athletic facility provided by an employer is a fringe benefit (¶ 2085) that is excluded from an employee's gross income (Code Sec. 132(j)(4); Reg. § 1.132-1(e)(3)).[89] The athletic facility must be located on the employer's premises, operated by the employer, and be used on a substantially exclusive basis by employees, their spouses, and dependent children. The athletic facility need not be located on the employer's business premises, only on premises owned or leased by the employer. However, the exclusion does not apply to any athletic facility that is a facility for residential use. In addition, employer-paid country club or health club memberships are not qualifying athletic facilities unless owned (or leased) and operated by the employer and substantially all the use of the facility is by employees, their spouses, and dependent children.

2095. Military Base Realignment and Closure Benefits. Qualified military base realignment and closure payments are excluded from an individual's gross income and wages as a fringe benefit (¶ 2085) (Code Sec. 132(n)).[90] The exclusion applies to payments made under the Department of Defense Homeowners Assistance Program (HAP) as in effect February 17, 2009, where: (1) there was a base closure or realignment; (2) the property was purchased before July 1, 2006, and sold between July 1, 2006, and September 30, 2012; (3) the property is the owner's primary residence; and (4) the owner has not previously received benefits under HAP. The payments are intended to compensate military personnel and certain civilian employees for a reduction in the fair market value (FMV) of their homes resulting from military or Coast Guard base closure or realignment.

References are to Standard Federal Tax Reports; Tax Research Consultant; and Practical Tax Explanations.

[87] ¶ 7420; COMPEN: 33,116; § 21,135

[88] ¶ 7420; COMPEN: 36,700; § 21,145

[89] ¶ 7420, ¶ 7422; COMPEN: 36,450; § 21,140

[90] ¶ 7420; COMPEN: 6,610; § 4,065.25

Chapter 21
RETIREMENT PLANS

	Par.
Types of Retirement Plans	2101
Qualified Plan Requirements	2111
Taxation of Distributions and Rollovers	2141
Traditional IRAs	2155
Roth IRAs	2171
SIMPLE Plans and SEPs	2181
Sec. 403(b), Sec. 457, and Nonqualified Plans	2191

Types of Retirement Plans

2101. Retirement Plans—Introduction. An employer may establish a pension, profit-sharing, or stock bonus plan that qualifies for certain tax benefits (Code Sec. 401).[1] These are called "qualified plans" and they are entitled to certain tax benefits, including: (1) a tax exemption for the trust established to provide benefits (Code Sec. 501(a); Reg. § 1.401(f)-1(c)(1));[2] (2) a current deduction by the employer for contributions made to the trust (Code Sec. 404);[3] and (3) tax deferral for the employee on the employer's contributions and earnings (Code Secs. 402(a) and 403(a)(1)).[4] To receive these benefits, an employer-provided retirement plan must meet the qualification requirements of Code Sec. 401 (¶ 2111).

There are two broad categories of qualified retirement plans: defined contribution plans and defined benefit plans. Defined contribution plans include profit-sharing, stock bonus, and money purchase plans in which a separate account is provided for each employee covered by the plan and the employee's retirement benefit is based on the contributions to the account, as well as any income, expenses, gains, losses, and any forfeitures of other accounts that may be allocated to the account (Code Sec. 414(i)).[5] Defined benefit plans include pension and annuity plans that offer a specific retirement benefit to employees, usually in the form of a monthly retirement pension based on a formula that takes the employee's wages and years of service into account (Code Sec. 414(j)).[6] An employer's annual contributions to the plan are based on actuarial assumptions and are not allocated to individual accounts maintained for the employees (Reg. § 1.401-1(b)(1)(i)).[7]

As an alternative to a qualified plan, an employer may establish and contribute to an individual retirement account (IRA) based plan such as a savings incentive match plan for employees (SIMPLE IRA) (¶ 2181) or simplified employee pension (SEP) (¶ 2189), or an employer may merely enable employees to choose to make direct contributions via payroll deductions to an IRA they have established. An eligible small business with 100 or fewer employees may claim a credit for the start-up costs incurred in establishing certain benefit plans (¶ 1365U). Outside the employment relationship, individuals who have compensation during a year may establish and make contributions to a traditional IRA (¶ 2155) or Roth IRA (¶ 2171) to save for their retirement. Educational employers (¶ 2191) and tax exempt and government employers (¶ 2193) may establish specialized plans. All of these plans and accounts mirror the tax treatment accorded to qualified plans: current deduction for the employers, tax-free accumulation of earnings, and

References are to Standard Federal Tax Reports; Tax Research Consultant; and Practical Tax Explanations.

[1] ¶ 17,502; RETIRE: 100; § 24,101

[2] ¶ 18,100, ¶ 22,602; RETIRE: 100; § 24,101

[3] ¶ 18,330; RETIRE: 100; § 24,101

[4] ¶ 18,202, ¶ 18,270; RETIRE: 100; § 24,101

[5] ¶ 19,150; RETIRE: 3,000; § 24,115

[6] ¶ 19,150; RETIRE: 6,000; § 24,120.05

[7] ¶ 17,504; RETIRE: 100; § 24,120.10

deferral of tax for the participant until the benefits are received. Rules vary, but they tend to favor nondiscriminatory benefits that reach rank and file employees.

Nonqualified deferred compensation plans are different. In general, the employer's deduction is matched to the tax year of the service provider's inclusion in income. These plans are typically aimed narrowly at executives or directors rather than rank and file employees, and may be conditioned on performance (¶ 2197).

2102. Profit-Sharing and Money Purchase Plans. A profit-sharing retirement plan is a type of defined contribution plan (¶ 2101) to which the employer makes discretionary contributions, so long as the plan provides a definite formula for allocating the contributions among participants and distributing accumulated funds (Code Sec. 401(a)(27); Reg. § 1.401-1(b)(1)(ii)).[8] The term "profit-sharing plan" is a misnomer because the employer does not have to make a profit for the year in order to make a contribution (unless the individual is self-employed), and the plan may be maintained by a tax-exempt organization. In fact, the employer is not required to contribute every year or any particular percentage of profits or other particular amount, but contributions must be substantial and recurring. A profit-sharing plan can also be coordinated with the employer's paid time off plan so that the cash value of each employee's unused time off, either at the end of each year or at the termination of the employee's employment, is contributed to the employee's account under the plan as an employer contribution or as an elective deferral by the employee (¶ 2104). In either case, the contributions are subject to the generally applicable nondiscrimination rules (¶ 2114) and limits on contributions (¶ 2115). A money purchase plan is a type of defined contribution plan that operates like a profit-sharing plan except that the employer's annual contributions are fixed under the terms of the plan (Reg. § 1.401-1(b)(1)(i)).[9] For example, under a money purchase plan, the employer may be required to contribute five percent of each participating employee's wages, regardless of whether the employer shows a profit for the year.

2103. Stock Bonus Plans and ESOPs. A stock bonus plan is a defined contribution plan (¶ 2101) that must generally follow the same rules as a profit-sharing plan (¶ 2102) except that distributed benefits usually are in the form of employer stock (Reg. § 1.401-1(b)(1)(iii)).[10] An employee stock ownership plan (ESOP) is a special type of stock bonus plan that, if certain requirements are met, provides special tax advantages including the following (Code Secs. 409 and 4975(e)(7)):[11]

- An ESOP will qualify for an exemption from certain prohibited transaction rules that apply in the case of loans made by disqualified persons to qualified plans (¶ 2136) (Code Sec. 4975(d)(3)).[12]
- Under some circumstances, a shareholder, other than a C corporation, may elect not to recognize gain on the sale of qualified securities to an ESOP (Code Sec. 1042).[13] Nonrecognition depends upon the shareholder purchasing qualified replacement property within a specific period of time.
- A C corporation is entitled to a deduction for dividends on its stock held by an ESOP that are: (1) paid in cash directly to participants in the ESOP, (2) paid to the ESOP and subsequently distributed to the participants in cash no later than 90 days after the end of the plan year in which the dividends are paid to the ESOP, or (3) used to repay an ESOP loan (Code Sec. 404(k)).[14] In addition, C corporations may deduct dividends that are, at the election of plan participants or their beneficiaries, paid to an ESOP and reinvested in qualified employer securities.
- Contributions to an ESOP that are used to pay the principal on loans that were incurred to purchase employer securities may be deducted to the extent that they do not exceed 25 percent of the compensation paid to participants (Code Sec. 404(a)(9)).[15] This contribution rule does not apply to S corporations.

References are to Standard Federal Tax Reports; Tax Research Consultant; and Practical Tax Explanations.

[8] ¶ 17,502, ¶ 17,504; RETIRE: 3,100; § 24,115.10

[9] ¶ 17,504; RETIRE: 33,206; § 24,115.20

[10] ¶ 17,504; RETIRE: 3,450; § 24,115.15

[11] ¶ 18,950, ¶ 34,400; RETIRE: 75,000; § 24,801

[12] ¶ 34,400; RETIRE: 75,302; § 24,825.10

[13] ¶ 29,820; RETIRE: 75,350; § 24,825.15

[14] ¶ 18,330; RETIRE: 75,204; § 24,815.15

[15] ¶ 18,330; RETIRE: 75,202.15; § 24,815.10

2104. 401(k) Plans (Cash or Deferred Arrangements). A profit-sharing (¶ 2102) or stock-bonus (¶ 2103) retirement plan can include a cash or deferred arrangement (CODA) under which each participating employee has the option of receiving an amount of their compensation in cash or having it contributed pre-tax to the plan (Code Secs. 401(k) and 402(e)(3); Reg. §§ 1.401(k)-1 and 1.402(a)-1(d)).[16] The contribution is referred to as an elective contribution or elective deferral. A profit-sharing or stock-bonus plan with this type of arrangement is known as a 401(k) plan. If the plan meets certain requirements, the normal constructive receipt rules are preempted and the employees do not have to recognize the deferred amounts immediately in gross income. Certain eligible employers (¶ 2187) may also adopt a savings incentive match plan for employees (SIMPLE) option as part of a 401(k) plan. Generally, a SIMPLE 401(k) must meet the same requirements that apply to other 401(k) plans except for the nondiscrimination and top-heavy rules. It is also subject to special rules on contributions, deductions, and vesting (¶ 2185).

A partnership may maintain a 401(k) plan and individual partners may make elective deferrals to the plan based on their compensation for the services they provide to the partnership (Reg. § 1.401(k)-1(a)(6)(i)).[17] A sole proprietor is also permitted to maintain a 401(k) plan with elective deferrals based on net earnings from the business. In fact, many self-employed individuals will find that their tax deductible contributions to a 401(k) plan will be greater than those allowed to other types of self-employed retirement plans (¶ 2107). The Federal Thrift Savings Plan provides federal employees with the same savings and tax benefits that private employers offer their employees with 401(k) plans (¶ 2110).

A 401(k) plan must meet the following specific requirements, in addition to the general requirements for all qualified plans (¶ 2111):

- the plan must not require as a condition of participation that an employee complete more than one year of service with the employer;
- the plan must not condition any other employee benefit (apart from matching contributions) upon an employee's election to make contributions to the 401(k) plan;
- the plan must provide that the participant's right to the value of his or her account that is attributable to elective contributions be fully vested at all times;
- the plan must not provide for distributions merely by reason of a stated period of participation or the lapse of a fixed number of years; and
- the plan must be prohibited from distributing amounts attributable to elective contributions of a plan participant *earlier* than:
  - — the participant' severance from employment, death, or disability;
  - — termination of the plan without establishment or maintenance of another defined contribution plan (¶ 2101) (Code Sec. 401(k)(10));
  - — attainment of age 59½ by the plan participant; or
  - — hardship of the participant (¶ 2129), except that distributions after age 59½ or for hardship are not permitted in the case of a money purchase pension plan.

A 401(k) plan that includes a qualified Roth contribution program (¶ 2121) may permit a qualified rollover contribution from a participant's non-Roth account to the participant's designated Roth account within the same plan (¶ 2147) (Code Sec. 402A(c)(4)(B)).

References are to Standard Federal Tax Reports; Tax Research Consultant; and Practical Tax Explanations.

[16] ¶ 17,502, ¶ 18,202, ¶ 18,110B, ¶ 18,203; RETIRE: 3,200; § 24,701

[17] ¶ 18,110B; RETIRE: 3,206; § 24,705.10

2105. Pension and Annuity Plans. A pension or annuity plan is a employer-provided defined benefit plan (¶ 2101) providing specific benefits to an employee or beneficiaries generally in the form of an annuity based on a formula reflecting the compensation and years of service of the employee. For example, under a flat benefit plan, the benefit for each participant is a fixed dollar amount, as long as a minimum number of years of service is reached. A formula for this type of plan could base a monthly retirement benefit upon a flat percentage of monthly compensation. On the other hand, under a unit benefit plan, greater benefits are generally provided for a long-service employee than for a short-term employee with the same average compensation. A formula for this type of plan could be a monthly retirement benefit based on a percentage of monthly compensation multiplied by years of service.

In either case, the employer (or other sponsor) must make required minimum contributions to the plan based on actuarial assumptions and calculations of the amount necessary to fund the promised benefits (¶ 2133). Employee contributions are sometimes required or voluntary. Instead of funding the plan directly, an employer may buy an insurance policy or annuity contract to fund the plan (Code Secs. 403(a)(1) and 404(a)(2)).[18] Employers with 500 or fewer employees may establish a plan that combines a defined benefit plan with a 401(k) plan (¶ 2109).

2106. IRA-Based Retirement Plans. In addition to individuals being able to set up a individual retirement account (IRA) (¶ 2155 and ¶ 2171), an employer may also establish and contribute to an IRA-based plan for providing retirement benefits to employees. In these arrangements, a separate IRA account is established and maintained on behalf of each participating employee. The employer's contributions to the accounts are deductible as compensation, but generally are not recognized as income by the employee until distributed. There are three types of IRA-based plans. Under a simplified employee pension (SEP) plan, the employer makes contributions directly to a traditional IRA (called a SEP-IRA) set up by or for each eligible employee (¶ 2189). Certain eligible employers may also establish a savings incentive match plan for employees (SIMPLE) in which employees are allowed salary reduction contributions to an IRA and the employer makes matching or nonelective contributions to the account (¶ 2181). Under a payroll deduction IRA, an employer may establish a traditional or Roth IRA to which an employee authorizes a payroll deduction to be contributed to the account.

2107. Retirement Plans Covering Self-Employed Participants. No distinction is generally made between pension, profit-sharing, and other retirement plans (¶ 2101) established by corporations and those established by partnerships and sole proprietors. Retirement plans maintained by self-employed individuals are generally referred to by the name used for that particular plan type—SEP-IRA (¶ 2189), self-employed 401(k) plan (¶ 2104), or SIMPLE IRA (¶ 2181).

Even though there is general parity between retirement plans established by a self-employed individual and plans established by other business entities, special rules have to be considered. For example, the term "employee" generally includes a participant in a plan of an unincorporated enterprise who is a partner or a sole proprietor (Code Sec. 401(c)).[19] When references are made to the employer, a sole proprietor is treated as his or her own employer. However, a partnership is considered to be the employer of each partner. As a result, sole proprietors may establish their own retirement plans. Only a partnership may establish a retirement plan for its partners.

Contributions and deductions for a self-employed participant covered by a qualified plan are subject to the same basic rules that apply to participants who are common law employees. However, a special computation must be made to figure the maximum deduction for contributions made by a self-employed taxpayer as an employer for himself or herself. Generally, the deduction limits are based, in part, on the compensation paid to eligible employees participating in the plan. For this purpose, a self-employed individual's compensation is his or her earned income, defined as the net

References are to Standard Federal Tax Reports; Tax Research Consultant; and Practical Tax Explanations.

[18] ¶ 18,270, ¶ 18,330; RETIRE: 6,150, RETIRE: 33,254; § 24,120.15

[19] ¶ 17,502; RETIRE: 60,052; § 24,135.10

earnings from self-employment (¶ 2670) reduced by: (1) the deduction allowed for contributions made on behalf of the self-employed participant, and (2) the deduction from gross income that is allowed for 50 percent of the self-employment tax paid by the self-employed participant (¶ 923) (Code Sec. 401(c)(2)(A)).[20]

Since a self-employed individual's deductions for contributions on his or her own behalf and his or her net earnings are dependent on each other, the deduction for the taxpayer's own contributions must be determined indirectly by reducing the contribution rate provided in the plan (referred to as the percentage equivalent adjustment). IRS Pub. 560 provides a rate table or rate worksheet to determine the reduced contribution rate for this purpose, depending on whether the plan's contribution rate is a whole percentage or not. For example, under the rate table, if the maximum plan contribution rate is 15 percent, the maximum deduction percentage for contributions to the self-employed individual's own plan is 13.0435 percent, while the 15 percent rate applies to other employees. Similarly, if the plan's maximum contribution rate is 25 percent, a 20 percent rate applies to the self-employed individual, and the 25 percent rate applies to other employees.[21]

401(k) Plan for the Self Employed. In general, the same rules that apply to 401(k) plans established by other types of entities apply to the 401(k) plans of self-employed individuals (¶ 2104) (Reg. § 1.401(k)-1(a)(6)(i)). This makes a 401(k) plan more advantageous than other types of self-employment plans because the taxpayer may make both employer contributions and elective employee contributions subject to the general limit for additions to defined contributions plans (¶ 2115). Self-employed 401(k) plans may also offer the possibility of being able to make loans to participating employees (¶ 2152).

Retirement Contribution for Partner. A partnership's deduction for retirement contributions on behalf of a partner must be allocated solely to that partner (Reg. § 1.404(e)-1A(f)).[22] It cannot be allocated among all of the partners pursuant to the partnership agreement (¶ 428).

Deduction of Contributions. Contributions to a qualified plan on behalf of a self-employed individual who is treated as an employee are considered to be ordinary and necessary expenses. They are deductible to the extent of the individual's earned income from the trade or business and not allocated to the purchase of life, accident, health, or other insurance (Code Sec. 404(a)(8)(C)).[23] However, the contributions not deductible on Schedule C of Form 1040 or on Form 1065 are also not deductible in calculating self-employment tax (¶ 2670). For a sole proprietorship, the contribution is claimed as an adjustment to gross income on Form 1040 (¶ 1027). For a partnership, the contribution is shown on Schedule K-1 of Form 1065 and deducted from gross income on the partner's Form 1040 (¶ 431).

2108. Hybrid Benefit Plans. There are several types of hybrid plans that combine elements of defined contribution plans and defined benefit plans (¶ 2101).

Cash Balance Plans. Cash balance plans are hybrid defined benefit plans that provide guaranteed benefits for employees that are insured by the Pension Benefit Guaranty Corporation (PBGC). These plans establish a separate hypothetical account for each employee. The employer credits a specified percentage of compensation to each account and credits each account with interest earned to mimic the allocations of actual contributions under a defined contribution plan such as a money purchase plan. The amounts to be contributed are actuarially determined to ensure sufficient funds to provide the promised benefit. If at retirement the balance in a participant's individual account is less than the amount promised by the employer, the participant will receive the promised amount. Participants may elect to receive their benefit in a lump-sum or as an annuity. Since benefits are not based solely on actual contributions and forfeitures allocated to an employee's account and the actual investment experience and expenses of the plan allocated to the account, the arrangement is treated as a defined benefit plan

References are to Standard Federal Tax Reports; Tax Research Consultant; and Practical Tax Explanations.

[20] ¶ 17,502; RETIRE: 60,100; § 24,330.05

[21] ¶ 17,933.036; RETIRE: 60,202; § 24,330.05

[22] ¶ 18,359; PART: 21,260; § 24,305.30

[23] ¶ 18,330; RETIRE: 60,214; § 24,330.05

rather than as a defined contribution plan. Accordingly, the plan is required to provide definitely determinable benefits, use a fixed interest rate, and adhere to the minimum funding standards.[24]

Floor Offset Plans. A floor offset plan is a defined contribution plan with a defined benefit floor. Under such a plan, an employee who leaves employment before retirement age receives the amount in his or her individual account. However, an employee who continues to work until retirement receives the greater of the defined contribution accumulation or the promised defined benefit pension. The defined contribution and defined benefit portions of the combined floor-offset plan must comply with statutory requirements applicable to both plans (i.e., the actuarial equivalence rule governing lump-sum distributions of accrued benefits).[25]

Pension Equity Plans. Under a pension equity plan (PEP plan), benefits accrue on a level basis. Employee earn credits for each year they have worked. Upon termination, employees receive a lump-sum payment or an annuity that is based on accumulated credits and final average pay.[26]

Target Benefit Plan. A target benefit plan is a plan under which an employer establishes a target benefit for its employees but where each employee's actual benefit is based on the amount in his or her individual account. The IRS defines a target benefit plan as a money purchase pension plan (¶ 2102) in which:

(1) the plan indicates a stated benefit commencing at the plan's normal retirement date;

(2) contributions necessary to fund the stated benefit with respect to a participant are determined under the individual level premium funding method using actuarial assumptions or factors stated in the plan;

(3) the contributions, and any forfeitures reducing those contributions, are allocated and separately accounted for with respect to each such participant; and

(4) the benefits provided under the plan are provided solely from the contribution amounts allocated in paragraph (3), employee contributions and any income, expenses and gains, reduced by any losses.

Because it is a money purchase pension plan, it is considered a defined contribution plan. However, the employer contributions are determined actuarially, as though the plan were a defined benefit plan. The employer does not guarantee the targeted amount; its only obligation is to pay whatever benefit can be provided by the amount in the participant's account.[27]

Small Employer Combined Plans. Small employers may establish a combined qualified retirement plan that consists of a defined benefit plan and a defined contribution plan incorporating a cash or deferred arrangement (401(k) plan) (¶ 2109).

2109. Defined Benefit and 401(k) Plans (DB/K Plans). Small employers may establish a combined defined benefit/401(k) plan (a "DB/K" plan) under which the relevant Code provisions are applied separately to the defined benefit (¶ 2101) portion of the plan and the 401(k) portion (¶ 2104) (Code Sec. 414(x)).[28] A small employer for this purpose is an employer who employed an average of at least two but not more than 500 employees on business days during the preceding calendar year and who employs at least two employees on the first day of the plan year.

The assets of the DB/K plan must be held in a single trust and must be clearly identified and allocated to the defined benefit plan and the applicable defined contribution plan to the extent necessary for the separate application of the Code and ERISA. Thus, for example, the Code Sec. 415 limitations apply separately to contributions under the 401(k) plan and to benefits under the defined benefit plan, both of which are part of the DB/K plan (¶ 2115). Similarly, the spousal protection rules apply to the defined

References are to Standard Federal Tax Reports; Tax Research Consultant; and Practical Tax Explanations.

[24] ¶ 19,076.0345; RETIRE: 39,058; § 24,270.05

[25] ¶ 17,710; RETIRE: 39,206; § 24,120.17

[26] ¶ 19,050; RETIRE: 39,058; § 24,001

[27] ¶ 19,200; RETIRE: 36,304; § 24,115.20

[28] ¶ 19,150; RETIRE: 3,500; § 24,901

benefit plan but not to the 401(k) plan. In addition, the DB/K plan must also meet certain benefit, contribution, vesting, and nondiscrimination requirements.

Defined Benefit Plan Requirements. A defined benefit plan that is part of a DB/K plan must provide each participant with a benefit of not less than the applicable percentage of the participant's final average pay. For this purpose, final average pay is determined using the consecutive-year period (not exceeding five years) during which the participant has the greatest aggregate compensation. The applicable percentage is the lesser of one percent multiplied by the participant's years of service or 20 percent (Code Sec. 414(x)(2)(B)(i) and (ii)). Any benefits provided under a defined benefit plan that is part of a DB/K plan (including any benefits provided in addition to required benefits) must be fully vested after three years of service (Code Sec. 414(x)(2)(D)(i)).[29]

Cash Balance Plans. A special rule applies to an applicable defined benefit plan, under which the accrued benefit is calculated as the balance of a hypothetical account or as an accumulated percentage of the participant's final average compensation, and which meets certain interest credit requirements (Code Sec. 414(x)(2)(B)(iii) and (iv)). The plan is treated as meeting the benefit requirement if each participant receives a pay credit for each plan year of not less than a certain percentage of compensation that is determined based on the participant's age. If the participant is age 30 or less, then the percentage is two percent; if the participant is over age 30 but less than age 40, then the percentage is four percent; if the participant is age 40 or over but less than age 50, then the percentage is six percent; and if the participant is age 50 or over, the percentage is eight percent. A defined benefit plan that is part of a DB/K plan must provide the required benefit to each participant, regardless of whether the participant makes elective deferrals to the applicable defined contribution plan that is part of the DB/K plan.

Defined Contribution Plan Requirements. Certain automatic enrollment and matching contribution requirements must be met with respect to a 401(k) plan that is part of a DB/K plan. First, the qualified cash or deferred arrangement under the plan must constitute an automatic contribution arrangement (Code Sec. 414(x)(2)(C)(i)(I)). It generally must provide that each employee eligible to participate in the arrangement is treated as having elected to make elective contributions in an amount of four percent of the employee's compensation. The employee, however, may elect not to make the contributions or to make contributions at a different rate. The automatic contribution arrangement must also meet certain notice requirements (Code Sec. 414(x)(5)(B)).[30]

Second, the employer must make matching contributions on behalf of each employee eligible to participate in the arrangement in an amount equal to 50 percent of the employee's elective deferrals, but no more than four percent of the compensation. The rate of matching contributions with respect to any elective deferrals for highly compensated employees (¶ 2114) must not be greater than the matching contribution rate for non-highly compensated employees. Matching contributions in addition to the required matching contributions can also be made (Code Sec. 414(x)(2)(C)(i)(II)).

The employer can also make nonelective contributions under the 401(k) plan. These contributions, however, are not taken into account in determining whether the matching contribution requirement is met (Code Sec. 414(x)(2)(C)(ii)). Matching contributions under the 401(k) plan (including contributions in excess of the required matching contributions) are fully vested when made, while nonelective contributions are fully vested after three years of service.

2110. Federal Thrift Savings Plan. The Federal Thrift Savings Plan (TSP) provides employees of the federal government with the same savings and tax benefits that private employers offer their employees with 401(k) plans (¶ 2104) (Code Sec. 7701(j)).[31] However, nondiscrimination rules that apply to cash or deferred arrangements do not apply to the TSP.

References are to Standard Federal Tax Reports; Tax Research Consultant; and Practical Tax Explanations.

[29] ¶ 19,150; RETIRE: 3,502; § 24,910

[30] ¶ 19,150; RETIRE: 3,504; § 24,915

[31] ¶ 43,080; RETIRE: 3,400; § 24,701

Qualified Plan Requirements

2111. Qualified Retirement Plan Requirements—Introduction. A qualified retirement plan is a pension plan that features a tax-exempt trust to which employers contribute. These contributions are currently deductible, earnings accumulate tax-free, and participants are taxed on the payment of benefits. To be a qualified plan, the plan must satisfy the requirements of Code Sec. 401. A plan that is out of compliance risks losing its qualified status causing, among other things, participants to be taxed immediately for current and past employer contributions, the trust income becoming taxable, and rollovers being prohibited (¶ 2101).[32]

A qualified plan must be written, permanent, and for the exclusive benefit of employees or their beneficiaries. In addition, the plan must meet requirements regarding:

- participation and coverage (¶ 2112);
- minimum vesting standards (¶ 2113);
- nondiscrimination requirements for contributions and benefits (¶ 2114);
- limitations on contributions and benefits (¶ 2115);
- deduction of employer contributions (¶ 2117);
- elective deferrals to 401(k) and other plans (¶ 2121);
- distributions of benefits (¶ 2125);
- minimum distributions requirements (¶ 2127);
- payment of joint and survivor annuities (¶ 2130);
- anti-assignment of benefits (¶ 2131);
- top-heavy plans (¶ 2132);
- minimum funding standards (¶ 2133); and
- prohibited transactions of retirement plans (¶ 2136).

The annual accounting period adopted by the plan is called the plan year and it may or may not coincide with the employer's tax year. If there is a trust associated with plan, then it must be a valid written domestic trust established by the employer.

Not all employer-sponsored pension plans are Code Sec. 401 qualified plans. Such plans include Code Sec. 403(b) plans for educational employers (¶ 2191), Code Sec. 457 plans for government and tax-exempt employers (¶ 2193), and IRA-based plans for small employers (¶ 2181 and ¶ 2189). These plans are taxed similarly to qualified plans, and they are subject to similar though simplified participation, coverage and nondiscrimination requirements.

2112. Participation and Coverage Requirements for Retirement Plans. A qualified retirement plan (¶ 2111) must satisfy minimum participation and coverage requirements (Code Sec. 410).[33]

Participation. The minimum participation requirement provides that a qualified plan may generally not condition an employee's participation in the plan on the completion of more than one year of service or the attainment of more than 21 years of age, whichever occurs later (Code Sec. 410(a)).[34] Once these conditions are met, an employee must be eligible to participate within six months or, if earlier, by the first day of the plan's next accounting year. However, participation may be conditioned on completion of two years of service if, after no more than two years of service, each participant has a vested right to their entire accrued benefit under the plan

Coverage. The minimum coverage requirement limits the ability of a plan to adopt employee classification standards that disproportionately favor highly compensated employees (¶ 2114) in comparison to non-highly compensated employees. The requirement may be met in one of two ways:

References are to Standard Federal Tax Reports; Tax Research Consultant; and Practical Tax Explanations.

[32] ¶ 17,507; RETIRE: 100; § 24,201

[33] ¶ 18,970; RETIRE: 12,000; § 24,250.05, § 24,255.05

[34] ¶ 18,970; RETIRE: 12,150, RETIRE: 12,200; § 24,250.05

- *Ratio percentage test*—The percentage of rank-and-file employees who benefit from the plan divided by the percentage of highly compensated employees who benefit must equal at least 70 percent (Code Sec. 410(b)(1); Reg. § 1.410(b)-2(b)(2)).[35]

- *Average benefit test*—The plan must benefit employees under a classification set up by the employer and found by the IRS not to discriminate in favor of highly compensated employees. In addition, the average benefit percentage for non-highly compensated employees must be at least 70 percent of the average benefit percentage for highly compensated employees. An employee's benefit percentage comprises the employer-provided contributions (including forfeitures) or benefits under all qualified plans of the employer, expressed as a percentage of the employee's compensation (Code Sec. 410(b)(2); Reg. § § 1.410(b)-2, 1.410(b)-4, and 1.410(b)-5).[36]

A defined benefit plan (¶ 2101) must also benefit at least the lesser of: 50 employees, or the greater of 40 percent of all employees or two employees (one employee if there is only one employee) (Code Sec. 401(a)(26)).[37]

2113. Vesting Requirements for Retirement Plans. A qualified retirement plan (¶ 2111) must satisfy minimum vesting requirements (Code Sec. 411(a)).[38] Employee contributions must be vested (i.e., nonforfeitable) at all times, including those made through elective deferral of compensation (¶ 2121).

For defined contribution plans (¶ 2101), employer contributions (including matching contributions) must be vested at least as quickly as they would be under one of the following methods (Code Sec. 411(a)(2)(B)):[39]

- *Graded Vesting*—20 percent of an employee's accrued benefit derived from employer contributions must vest after two years of service and an additional 20 percent must vest after each additional year of service; after six years of service, the employee must be 100 percent vested;

- *Cliff Vesting*—an employee has no vested interest in the accrued benefit derived from employer contributions until the employee has completed three years of service, but then must be 100 percent vested.

For defined benefit plans (¶ 2101), all employees' interests in their accrued benefits derived from employer contributions must vest at least as quickly as they would under either a three-to-seven-years graded vesting schedule or a five-year cliff vesting schedule (Code Sec. 411(a)(2)(A)).[40]

2114. Nondiscrimination Requirements for Retirement Plans. A qualified retirement plan (¶ 2111) must provide either contributions or benefits that do not discriminate in favor of highly compensated employees (Code Sec. 401(a)(4)).[41] This is satisfied if: (1) either the contributions or benefits provided are nondiscriminatory in amount; (2) the benefits, rights, and features under the plan are available in a nondiscriminatory manner; and (3) the plan is nondiscriminatory in effect, including plan amendments, terminations, and grants of past service credit.

Highly Compensated Employees. An employee is generally considered highly compensated for this purpose if he or she: (1) was a five-percent owner at any time during the current or preceding year, or (2) had compensation from the employer for the preceding year in excess of $120,000 for 2016 ($120,000 for 2017) (Code Sec. 414(q)(1); Notice 2015-75; Notice 2016-62).[42] The employer may elect to limit employees treated as highly compensated employees under item (2) above to those who are in the top 20 percent of employees when ranked on the basis of compensation paid during the year.

References are to Standard Federal Tax Reports; Tax Research Consultant; and Practical Tax Explanations.

[35] ¶ 18,970, ¶ 18,988; RETIRE: 12,056; § 24,255.10

[36] ¶ 18,970, ¶ 18,988, ¶ 18,990, ¶ 18,991; RETIRE: 12,058; § 24,255.15

[37] ¶ 17,502; RETIRE: 12,100; § 24,120.25

[38] ¶ 19,050; RETIRE: 18,050; § 24,260

[39] ¶ 19,050; RETIRE: 18,102; § 24,260

[40] ¶ 19,050; RETIRE: 18,102; § 24,260

[41] ¶ 17,502; RETIRE: 39,000; § 24,245.05

[42] ¶ 19,150; RETIRE: 3,210.30; § 24,140

Part-time employees, minors, union members, and any employee who works less than six months during the year may be excluded from the top-paid group.

Actual Contribution Percentage (ACP) Test. A special nondiscrimination test applies to employee contributions and matching contributions by employers to a qualified plan (Code Sec. 401(m); Reg. § 1.401(m)-1).[43] Matching contributions are those made by the employer on account of a contribution by a participant or because of an elective contribution by a participant under a 401(k) plan. The test is satisfied if the actual contribution percentage (ACP) for the group of eligible highly compensated employees for the plan year does not exceed the greater of: (1) 125 percent of ACP for all other eligible employees for the preceding plan year, or (2) the lesser of 200 percent of ACP for all other eligible employees for the preceding plan year or ACP for all other eligible employees for the preceding plan year, plus two percentage points. The ACP test can be satisfied by the plan adopting one of the alternative safe harbors for meeting the actual deferral percentage (ADP) test for 401(k) plans (¶ 2123).

Failure to satisfy the ACP test will not result in disqualification of the plan if the excess contributions (and the income allocable to them) are distributed within 12 months following the plan year in which they arose (Code Sec. 401(m)(6)).[44] However, the employer is subject to a 10-percent tax based on the amount of the excess contributions unless the contributions (and the income allocable to them) are distributed to the highly compensated employees within 2½ months after the plan year in which they arose (Code Sec. 4979(f)).[45] The amount of a corrective distribution (other than the portion representing the employee's contributions) is included in the employee's gross income. The 10-percent additional tax on early distributions (¶ 2151) does not apply (Code Sec. 401(m)(7)).[46]

2115. Contribution and Benefit Limits for Retirement Plans. A qualified retirement plan (¶ 2111) must limit the contributions and benefits that may be provided to each individual plan participant (Code Sec. 415).[47] See ¶ 2117 and ¶ 2119 for the limits imposed on the deduction of employer contributions.

Defined Contribution Plan. The maximum annual addition that may be made to a participant's account in a defined contribution plan (¶ 2101) may not exceed the *lesser* of 100 percent of the participant's compensation or $53,000 for 2016 ($54,000 for 2017) (Code Sec. 415(c); Notice 2015-75; Notice 2016-62).[48] The term "annual addition" includes employer and employee contributions, as well as forfeitures allocated to the account under the plan.

Defined Benefit Plan. The maximum annual retirement benefit for any participant of a defined benefit plan (¶ 2101) may not exceed the *lesser* of 100 percent of the participant's average compensation for the participant's three consecutive calendar years of highest compensation or $210,000 for 2016 ($215,000 for 2017) (Code Sec. 415(b); Notice 2015-75; Notice 2016-62).[49] The maximum annual benefit is actuarially reduced when retirement benefits are paid before age 62 and increased when benefits are not paid until after age 65. If certain requirements are met, an annual benefit of up to $10,000 may be provided by the plan even if that exceeds the 100 percent of compensation limit. The benefit limit and the compensation limit are reduced in the case of individuals with less than 10 years of service with the employer.

Compensation Limit. The maximum compensation that may be taken into account when determining the limit on contributions and benefits of an employee, and when applying the nondiscrimination rules (¶ 2114), is $265,000 for 2016 ($270,000 for 2017) (Code Sec. 401(a)(17); Reg. § 1.401(a)(17)-1(a); Notice 2015-75; Notice 2016-62).[50] For purposes of the limitation on contributions to a defined contribution plan, an employee's

References are to Standard Federal Tax Reports; Tax Research Consultant; and Practical Tax Explanations.

[43] ¶ 17,502, ¶ 18,121; RETIRE: 27,150; § 24,705.35

[44] ¶ 17,502; RETIRE: 27,154; § 24,705.35

[45] ¶ 34,520; RETIRE: 27,154; § 24,705.35

[46] ¶ 17,502; RETIRE: 27,154; § 24,705.35

[47] ¶ 19,200; RETIRE: 36,050; § 24,275.05

[48] ¶ 19,200, ¶ 19,218.27; RETIRE: 36,200; § 24,275.15

[49] ¶ 19,200, ¶ 19,218.27; RETIRE: 36,150; § 24,275.10

[50] ¶ 17,502, ¶ 17,902; RETIRE: 36,350; § 24,145

compensation includes any compensation received from the employer maintaining the plan included in gross income or net earnings from self-employment, as well as any elective deferrals (¶ 2121) or other amounts contributed by the employer at the employee's election that may be excluded from an employee's gross income (e.g., cafeteria plan benefits (¶ 2045)) (Code Sec. 415(c)(3)).[51]

2117. Deduction of Employer Contributions to Retirement Plans. Subject to annual limits (¶ 2119), employers are allowed to deduct their contributions to a qualified retirement plan (¶ 2111) to the extent they are otherwise deductible under the Code as an ordinary and necessary expense or paid for the production of income (Code Sec. 404(a)).[52] The deductions are allowed whether or not the rights of the employees to the contributions are forfeitable. However, contributions are generally deductible only for the tax year when paid regardless of whether the employer uses the cash or accrual method of accounting, unless contributions in excess of the annual limits must be carried over to later years.

A deductible contribution is generally deemed made on the last day of the tax year if it is paid no later than the due date, including extensions, of the employer's income tax return. In the case of most defined benefit plans, however, the minimum required contribution for a plan year must be paid (¶ 2133) within 8½ months after the close of the plan year (Code Sec. 430(j)). As a result, the required funding date may actually come before the last day for making deductible contributions. Payments made on a date other than the valuation date for the plan year of a defined benefit plan must be adjusted for interest accruing for the period from the valuation date to the payment date. Elective and matching contributions under a 401(k) plan (¶ 2121) and other types of defined contribution plans are not deductible by the employer for a tax year if they are attributable to compensation earned by participants after the end of that tax year (Rev. Rul. 90-105; Rev. Rul. 2002-46).[53]

S Corporations. A retirement plan established by an S corporation is generally governed by the same rules that apply to plans established by other corporations. As a result, S corporation shareholders are not entitled to claim retirement plan deductions based on their pro rata share of pass-through income from the S corporation. A court has ruled that this income could not be treated as earnings from self-employment for retirement plan purposes (*A.R. Durando*, CA-9, 95-2 USTC ¶ 50,615).[54]

2119. Limits on Deduction of Employer Contributions to Retirement Plans. There are limits on the annual deductions that may be claimed for an employer's contributions to a qualified retirement plan (¶ 2117).

Defined Contribution Plans. The maximum deduction allowed for contributions to a defined contribution plan (¶ 2101), including profit-sharing, stock-bonus, and money purchase plans (except as provided otherwise in regulations), is 25 percent of the compensation of all the participants in the plan (Code Sec. 404(a)(3)).[55] However, contributions that are in excess of the maximum amount allowed to be made to the plan (¶ 2115) may not be deducted (Code Sec. 404(j)).[56] See ¶ 2181 and ¶ 2185 for the deduction limits that apply to SIMPLE IRAs and SIMPLE 401(k) plans, respectively.

Defined Benefit Plans. The maximum deduction allowed for contributions to a defined benefit plan (¶ 2101) generally is determined actuarially based on the expected costs of the plan (Code Sec. 404(a)(1)).[57] The deduction is subject to both a floor of the annual contributions necessary to satisfy the minimum funding standard (¶ 2133) and a ceiling of the full funding limitation for the plan. The amount that can be deducted for any year cannot exceed the greater of the following:

References are to Standard Federal Tax Reports; Tax Research Consultant; and Practical Tax Explanations.

[51] ¶ 19,200; RETIRE: 36,100; § 24,145

[52] ¶ 18,330; RETIRE: 33,354; § 24,305.05

[53] ¶ 18,347.27; RETIRE: 33,356; § 24,305.30

[54] ¶ 17,933.656; RETIRE: 60,102.05; § 28,820.30

[55] ¶ 18,330; RETIRE: 33,202, RETIRE: 60,202; § 24,305.15

[56] ¶ 18,330; RETIRE: 33,200; § 24,310

[57] ¶ 18,330; RETIRE: 33,252; § 24,305.10

• *Level Funding Method*—The limit is an amount necessary to provide, for all participants under the plan, the remaining unfunded cost of their past and current service credits distributed as a level amount or level percentage of compensation over the remaining service of each participant. Under this method, the past service liability for each participant is deducted ratably over the employee's projected years of service until retirement.

• *Normal Cost Method*—The limit is an amount equal to the normal ("current") cost of the plan plus, if past service or other supplementary credits are provided, an amount not in excess of that necessary to amortize the credits in equal payments over 10 years. However, all defined benefit plans may deduct 100 percent of their unfunded current liability.

Employer Maintaining More Than One Type of Plan. If an employer makes contributions to a defined contribution plan and also to a defined benefit plan, there is an overall limit on the deduction of these contributions. The deduction is limited to the *greater* of: (1) 25 percent of the compensation paid or accrued for that year to the participants in all such plans, or (2) the amount necessary to satisfy the minimum funding standards. The overall limitation does not apply when no individual is a participant in more than one plan maintained by the employer (Code Sec. 404(a)(7)).[58] Also, the overall deduction limit does not apply when only elective deferrals are made to any of the employer's defined contribution plans during the tax year.

Elective Deferrals. Elective deferrals (¶ 2121) made by employees are not taken into account when determining deduction limits for stock bonus and profit-sharing plans, combination defined benefit and defined contribution plans, and ESOPs (Code Sec. 404(n)).

Compensation. In applying the annual deduction limits, the amount of an employee's compensation that may be taken into account is limited in the same manner as for determining contributions and benefits (¶ 2115) (Code Sec. 404(l)).[59] However, compensation for purposes of the deduction limits includes certain amounts that are generally excluded from gross income (e.g., elective deferrals and certain disability benefits and elective deferrals) (Code Sec. 404(a)(12)).

Carryovers. When an employer's contribution exceeds the maximum deductible amount for the year, the excess amount may be carried over and deducted in later tax years. However, the total of the carryovers and the regular contributions in the carryover year may not exceed the deductible limit for that year (Code Sec. 404(a)(1)(E) and (3)(A)(ii)).[60] Similarly, if the 25 percent overall limit for contributions to different types of plans is exceeded, the excess may be carried over. The combination of carryovers and regular deductions for any succeeding year may not exceed 25 percent of the compensation paid to participants in that year (Code Sec. 404(a)(7)(B)).[61]

2121. Elective Deferrals to 401(k) Plans. A qualified retirement plan (¶ 2111) may include a cash or deferred arrangement, i.e., 401(k) plan, under which a participating employee has the option of receiving compensation in cash or having it contributed on a pre-tax basis to the plan (¶ 2104). The contribution is referred to as an elective contribution or elective deferral and is subject to an annual limit ($18,000 for 2016; $18,000 for 2017) (Code Sec. 402(g); Notice 2015-75; Notice 2016-62).[62] The limit does not just apply to each 401(k) plan to which the employee makes elective deferrals, but instead applies to the aggregate amount of all the elective deferrals made by the employee for the year to all plans which permit such contributions, including other 401(k) plans, SEP-IRAs (¶ 2181), and 403(b) annuity plans (¶ 2191) (but not 457 plans (¶ 2193)). Special nondiscrimination rules for 401(k) plans may further limit the amount of elective deferrals (but not catch-up contributions) that can be made by highly compensated employees (¶ 2123).

References are to Standard Federal Tax Reports; Tax Research Consultant; and Practical Tax Explanations.

[58] ¶ 18,330; RETIRE: 33,306; § 24,305.20

[59] ¶ 18,330; RETIRE: 36,350; § 24,305.10, § 24,305.15

[60] ¶ 18,330; RETIRE: 33,300; § 24,305.10, § 24,305.15

[61] ¶ 18,330; RETIRE: 33,306; § 24,305.20

[62] ¶ 18,202, ¶ 18,221.10; RETIRE: 3,254; § 24,710.10

Example: Tony, age 45, works for two employers. Each of the employers offers a 401(k) plan and Tony participates in both plans. During 2016, Tony deferred $12,000 of his wages into the 401(k) plan of Employer A and $6,500 of his wages into the 401(k) plan of Employer B. For 2016, Tony has made an excess deferral of $500 ($18,500 in aggregate deferrals – $18,000 maximum deferral allowable).

Catch-Up Contributions. An individual who will be at least 50 years of age by the end of the tax year may make additional "catch-up" contributions to a qualified plan allowing elective deferrals including 401(k) plan, 403(b) annuity plan, 457 plan, SIMPLE 401(k), SIMPLE IRA, and certain SEPs. The maximum amount of the catch-up contribution depends upon the type of plan involved. The maximum catch-up contribution to a 401(k), 403(b) annuity plan, 457 plan, and certain SEPs is $6,000 for 2016 ($6,000 for 2017). The maximum catch-up contribution to a SIMPLE 401(k) or SIMPLE IRA is $3,000 for 2016 ($3,000 for 2017) (Code Sec. 414(v); Notice 2015-75; Notice 2016-62).[63] Catch-up contributions may only be made if the plan permits this type of contribution.

Excess Deferrals. Elective deferrals that exceed the annual limit are included in the employee's income and subject to a 10-percent penalty (Code Secs. 402(g) and 4979).[64] The employee may generally withdraw the excess contribution from the plan before April 15 of the following tax year along with any attributable income. If the employee has made elective deferrals to more than one plan, then the employee can designate the amount of the excess that is to be withdrawn from each plan. If the excess contribution remains in the plan past the April 15 distribution date, it will be taxed a second time when distributed (Reg. § 1.402(g)-1(e)(8)(iii)).[65] The 10-percent penalty will not apply if the excess is distributed within 2½ months following the plan year in which the excess contribution was made.

Matching Contributions. Matching contributions made to a 401(k) plan by the employer are not treated as an employee's elective contributions and therefore, not subject to the annual limit on deferrals. In addition, matching contributions made by a self-employed person to a 401(k) plan are not treated as part of the individual's elective contributions (Code Sec. 402(g)(8)).[66]

After-Tax Roth Contributions. Plans that allow employees to make pre-tax elective deferrals may also allow participating employees to designate all or part of their elective deferrals to the plan to be treated as after-tax Roth contributions (Code Sec. 402A).[67] The designated Roth contributions are generally treated the same as pre-tax elective deferrals under the plan for purposes of limits on deferrals and nondiscrimination requirements, except that the plan must account for them separately. While the employee must include the Roth contributions in gross income, distributions are subject to rules similar to the rules applicable to distributions from a Roth IRA (¶ 2173). However, unlike a Roth IRA, amounts held in a Roth 401(k) account are subject to the required minimum distribution (RMD) rules (¶ 2127).

2123. Nondiscrimination Requirements for 401(k) Plans. A special nondiscrimination requirement applies to elective deferrals made to a 401(k) plan (but not catch-up contributions) (¶ 2121) (Code Sec. 401(k)(3); Reg. § 1.401(k)-2).[68] The plan will not be treated as qualified unless the actual deferral percentage (ADP) for eligible highly compensated employees (¶ 2114) for the plan year bears a relationship to the ADP for all other eligible employees for the preceding plan year that meets either of the following tests:

- the ADP for the group of eligible highly compensated employees is not more than the actual ADP of all other eligible employees multiplied by 1.25, or
- the excess of the ADP for the group of eligible highly compensated employees over that of all other eligible employees is not more than 2 percentage points, and the ADP for the group of eligible highly compensated employees is not more than the ADP of all other eligible employees multiplied by 2.

References are to Standard Federal Tax Reports; Tax Research Consultant; and Practical Tax Explanations.

[63] ¶ 19,150, ¶ 19,198.25; RETIRE: 27,102.35; § 24,710.15

[64] ¶ 18,202, ¶ 34,520; RETIRE: 3,254.05; § 24,710.10

[65] ¶ 18,220, ¶ 34,520; RETIRE: 3,254; § 24,710.10

[66] ¶ 18,202; RETIRE: 3,210.20, RETIRE: 3,254.05; § 24,710.25

[67] 18,230; RETIRE: 3,258; § 24,725.05

[68] ¶ 17,502, ¶ 18,111; RETIRE: 3,210; § 24,705.35

The employer may elect to calculate the ADP test for rank-and-file employees with reference to the current year rather than the preceding year. However, the election once made may not be revoked without IRS consent. In the case of a test year which is the first year of the plan (other than a successor plan), the ADP of rank-and-file employees for the preceding plan year will be deemed to be three percent or, if the employer elects, the ADP calculated on the basis of rank-and-file employees for the first plan year. If the 401(k) plan provides for matching employer contributions or allows employees contributions to be made on an after-tax basis, then a separate nondiscrimination test generally applies to those contributions.

A plan can avoid failing to satisfy the ADP test by having the employer make qualified nonelective contributions or qualified matching contributions that are treated as elective contributions under the plan and that, in combination with the elective deferrals, satisfy the nondiscrimination requirements. The plan can also limit the elective deferrals by highly compensated employees to prevent any excess contributions or allow the highly compensated employees the option to have any excess contributions distributed back to them or recharacterized (Code Sec. 401(k)(8); Reg. § 1.401(k)-2(b)(1)). An employer may also adopt one of three designed-based safe harbors to satisfy the ADP test for its 401(k) plan. The ADP test will be deemed satisfied if:

- a prescribed level of matching or nonelective contributions are made under the plan on behalf of all eligible non-highly compensated employees and if employees are provided a timely notice describing their rights and obligations under the plan (Code Sec. 401(k)(12) and (m)(11); Reg. § 1.401(k)-3);[69]
- the plan meets the requirements for a qualified automatic contribution arrangement where eligible employees are uniformly treated as having elected to have the employer make elective contributions equal to a qualified percentage of compensation (no more than 10 percent, but at least three percent in the first year, four percent for the second year, five percent for the third year, and six percent for the fourth year) (Code Sec. 401(k)(13) and (m)(12)); or
- the plans meets the contribution and vesting requirements applicable to SIMPLE 401(k) plans (¶ 2185).

2125. Distribution Requirements for Retirement Plans. An qualified retirement plan (¶ 2111) must provide that the payment of benefits under the plan will begin, unless the participant elects otherwise, no later than the 60th day after the *latest* of the close of the plan year in which:

- the participant attains the earlier of age 65 or the normal retirement age specified in the plan;
- the participant marks the 10th anniversary of enrollment in the plan; or
- the participant terminates service with the employer (Code Sec. 401(a)(14)).[70]

See ¶ 2141 for a discussion of the taxation of distributions from retirements plans.

Mandatory Cash-Outs. Generally, a qualified plan is restricted from distributing any portion of a participant's accrued benefits in any form without the participant's (or surviving spouse's) consent. However, the plan may pay out the balance of a participant's account without the participant's consent if the present value of the benefit does not exceed $5,000 (Code Sec. 411(a)(11)(A)).[71] If the present value of the benefit exceeds $1,000, and the participant does not elect otherwise, a mandatory distribution must be transferred directly to a traditional IRA (¶ 2155) established by the plan for the benefit of the participant (Code Sec. 401(a)(31)(B); Notice 2005-5).

Phased Retirement Arrangements. A qualified plan is allowed to provide that a distribution may be made to an employee who has attained age 62 and who is not

References are to Standard Federal Tax Reports; Tax Research Consultant; and Practical Tax Explanations.

[69] ¶ 17,502, ¶ 18,111C; RETIRE: 3,210.60; § 24,705.35

[70] ¶ 17,502; RETIRE: 42,106; § 24,425

[71] ¶ 19,050; RETIRE: 42,104; § 24,430

separated from employment at the time of the distribution but instead is in a phased retirement program (i.e., working retirement) (Code Sec. 401(a)(36)).

Death Benefits for Participants Serving in the Military. Survivors of a participant who has died while performing qualified military service are entitled to any benefits that would have been provided under the plan (other than benefit accruals relating to the period of military service) had the participant returned from service and then terminated employment on account of death (Code Sec. 401(a)(37)). Thus, survivor benefits such as accelerated vesting or ancillary life insurance benefits that are contingent upon a participant's termination of employment on account of death must be provided to the beneficiaries of a participant who has died during qualified military service. This requirement applies to qualified plans, 403(b) annuity plans (¶ 2191), and 457 plans (¶ 2193).

2127. Required Minimum Distributions (RMDs). All types of qualified retirement plans (¶ 2101), as well as traditional IRAs (¶ 2155), 403(b) annuity plans (¶ 2191), and 457 plans (¶ 2193) must satisfy a minimum distribution requirement in which distribution of an employee's or IRA owner's interest must begin by the required beginning date (Code Sec. 401(a)(9); Reg. § 1.401(a)(9)-1).[72] For most individuals, this is April 1 of the calendar year following *the later of*: (1) the calendar year in which the participant attains age 70½, or (2) the calendar year in which the employee retires. In the case of a five-percent owner (¶ 2132) or IRA owner, the required beginning date is April 1 of the year following the year in which the individual reaches age 70½.

If the employee's entire interest is not distributed by the required beginning date, then the employee's interest must generally be paid out over a period that does not exceed the life or life expectancy of the participant, or the combined lives or life expectancies of the participant and his or her designated beneficiary (Code Sec. 401(a)(9)(A)).[73] The required minimum distribution (RMD) rules vary depending upon whether distributions begin before or after the employee's death. However, distributions made to a participant or the beneficiary of a participant must satisfy the RMD rules in each calendar year.

The RMD for a particular year is generally equal to the participant's accrued benefit or account balance as of the end of the prior year, divided by the appropriate distribution period (Reg. §§ 1.401(a)(9)-5 and 1.401(a)(9)-6).[74] A plan participant may exclude the value of a Qualifying Longevity Annuity Contract (QLAC) purchased on or after July 2, 2014, from the account balance used to determine RMDs prior to annuitization. QLACs are permissible for qualified plans, as well as for Code Sec. 403(b) plans and IRAs (Reg. §§ 1.403(b)-6(e)(9) and 1.408-8, Q&A 12).[75]

Required Distributions Before Participant's Death. If RMDs begin while the participant is alive, the distribution period is derived from one of two tables (Reg. § 1.401(a)(9)-9). The *Uniform Lifetime Table* (reproduced later) is used to determine the distribution period for lifetime distributions to an unmarried individual or to a married individual if the individual's spouse is either: (1) not the sole designated beneficiary or (2) the sole designated beneficiary and not more than 10 years younger than the individual. The *Joint and Last Survivor Table* is used to determine the distribution period for lifetime distributions to a married individual whose spouse is the sole beneficiary and is more than 10 years younger than the individual.

Required Distributions After Participant's Death. If required distributions have been made to the participant before his or her death, then any remaining benefit payable to a beneficiary may be payable over the longer of the life expectancy of the beneficiary or of the participant (Code Sec. 401(a)(9)(B)(i); Reg. § 1.401(a)(9)-5, Q&A-5(a)).[76]

References are to Standard Federal Tax Reports; Tax Research Consultant; and Practical Tax Explanations.

[72] ¶ 17,502, ¶ 17,723C; RETIRE: 42,150; § 24,440.10

[73] ¶ 17,502; RETIRE: 42,158.10; § 24,440.15

[74] ¶ 17,725G, ¶ 17,725I; RETIRE: 42,158.10; § 24,440.15

[75] ¶ 18,278H, ¶ 18,917A; RETIRE: 42,174.45; § 24,440.15

[76] ¶ 17,502, ¶ 17,725G; RETIRE: 42,160; § 24,440.20

If required distributions have not been made to the participant before his or her death, then the participant's entire interest is to be distributed to the beneficiary within five years after the death (Code Sec. 401(a)(9)(B)(ii); Reg. § 1.401(a)(9)-5, Q&A-5(b)).[77] However, most beneficiaries will be able to take advantage of one of two exceptions to the five-year distribution rule. First, the five-year rule does not apply when:

- any portion of the participant's interest is payable to, or for the benefit of, a designated beneficiary;
- the portion of the participant's interest to which the beneficiary is entitled will be distributed over the life of the beneficiary or over a period not extending beyond the life expectancy of the beneficiary (for this purpose, the *Single Life Table* provided in the regulations and reproduced following is used to determine an individual beneficiary's life expectancy) (Reg. § 1.401(a)(9)-9); and
- the distributions commence no later than one year after the date of the participant's death (Code Sec. 401(a)(9)(B)(iii)).[78]

Second, the five-year rule does not apply if:

- the designated beneficiary is the participant's surviving spouse;
- the portion of the participant's interest to which the surviving spouse is entitled will be distributed over the life of that spouse (or over a period not exceeding his or her life expectancy); and
- the distributions commence no later than the date on which the participant would have attained age 70½ (Code Sec. 401(a)(9)(B)(iv)).[79]

If the surviving spouse dies before payments are required to begin, the five-year rule is to be applied as if the surviving spouse were the participant. Payments to a surviving spouse under a qualified joint and survivor annuity (¶ 2130) will satisfy this second exception.

Estate planners use these rules strategically to maximize the distribution period for an inherited IRA by pegging the distribution period to an individual's (preferably, a young individual's) life expectancy to preserve IRA assets as long as possible (Reg. § 1.401(a)(9)-5, Q&A-5(b), (c)).[80]

Final Determination of Beneficiary. A beneficiary must be designated as of the date of the employee's death. However, the final determination of who is a beneficiary is not made until September 30 of the year following the calendar year of death (Reg. § 1.401(a)(9)-4, Q&A-4(a)). As a result, if an individual does not remain a beneficiary on the September 30 deadline, the individual is not taken into consideration when determining the RMDs that must be made from the retirement account. For example, individuals who are named beneficiaries as of the time of the participant's death may not be beneficiaries by the September 30 deadline because they have disclaimed their right to any portion of the retirement account.

Penalty for Failure to Receive RMDs. An excise tax is imposed on an employee or beneficiary who does not take an RMD. The tax is 50 percent of the amount by which the RMD exceeds the distribution actually made (Code Sec. 4974).[81] Part or all of the tax may be waived if any of the RMD shortfall is due to reasonable error and if steps are taken to correct it. The penalty is reported on Form 5329. If the individual believes that part or all of the tax should be waived due to reasonable error, a statement of explanation should be attached along with Form 5329. Any tax due must be paid at the time Form 5329, along with the statement of explanation, is filed.

References are to Standard Federal Tax Reports; Tax Research Consultant; and Practical Tax Explanations.

[77] ¶ 17,502, ¶ 17,725G; RETIRE: 42,162; § 24,440.20

[78] ¶ 17,502; RETIRE: 42,162.10; § 24,440.20

[79] ¶ 17,502; RETIRE: 42,162.15; § 24,440.20

[80] ¶ 17,725G; RETIRE: 66,456.20

[81] ¶ 34,380; RETIRE: 42,652; § 24,450.15

Uniform Lifetime Table

Age of employee	*Distribution period*	*Age of employee*	*Distribution period*
70	27.4	92	10.2
71	26.5	93	9.6
72	25.6	94	9.1
73	24.7	95	8.6
74	23.8	96	8.1
75	22.9	97	7.6
76	22.0	98	7.1
77	21.2	99	6.7
78	20.3	100	6.3
79	19.5	101	5.9
80	18.7	102	5.5
81	17.9	103	5.2
82	17.1	104	4.9
83	16.3	105	4.5
84	15.5	106	4.2
85	14.8	107	3.9
86	14.1	108	3.7
87	13.4	109	3.4
88	12.7	110	3.1
89	12.0	111	2.9
90	11.4	112	2.6
91	10.8	113	2.4
		114	2.1
		115+	1.9

Single Life Table (for use by beneficiaries)

Age	*Life Expectancy*	*Age*	*Life Expectancy*	*Age*	*Life Expectancy*	*Age*	*Life Expectancy*
0	82.4	27	56.2	55	29.6	83	8.6
1	81.6	28	55.3	56	28.7	84	8.1
2	80.6	29	54.3	57	27.9	85	7.6
3	79.7	30	53.3	58	27.0	86	7.1
4	78.7	31	52.4	59	26.1	87	6.7
5	77.7	32	51.4	60	25.2	88	6.3
6	76.7	33	50.4	61	24.4	89	5.9
7	75.8	34	49.4	62	23.5	90	5.5
8	74.8	35	48.5	63	22.7	91	5.2
9	73.8	36	47.5	64	21.8	92	4.9
10	72.8	37	46.5	65	21.0	93	4.6
11	71.8	38	45.6	66	20.2	94	4.3
12	70.8	39	44.6	67	19.4	95	4.1
13	69.9	40	43.6	68	18.6	96	3.8
14	68.9	41	42.7	69	17.8	97	3.6
15	67.9	42	41.7	70	17.0	98	3.4
16	66.9	43	40.7	71	16.3	99	3.1
17	66.0	44	39.8	72	15.5	100	2.9
18	65.0	45	38.8	73	14.8	101	2.7
19	64.0	46	37.9	74	14.1	102	2.5
20	63.0	47	37.0	75	13.4	103	2.3
21	62.1	48	36.0	76	12.7	104	2.1
22	61.1	49	35.1	77	12.1	105	1.9
23	60.1	50	34.2	78	11.4	106	1.7
24	59.1	51	33.3	79	10.8	107	1.5
25	58.2	52	32.3	80	10.2	108	1.4
26	57.2	53	31.4	81	9.7	109	1.2
		54	30.5	82	9.1	110	1.1
						111+	1.0

2129. Hardship Distributions from 401(k) Plans. A 401(k) plan may allow hardship distributions up to the amount of the participant's elective deferrals (¶ 2121). A hardship distribution is one that (1) is made because of the employee's immediate and heavy financial need, and (2) does not exceed the amount necessary to satisfy that need (Reg. § 1.401(k)-1(d)(3)).[82] Types of expenses that satisfy the requirement of immediate and heavy financial need include:

- medical expenses of the employee, spouse, and dependents;
- expenditures (excluding mortgage payments) to purchase a principal residence for the employee;
- post-secondary tuition for the employee, spouse, or dependents;
- expenditures to stave off eviction or foreclosure with respect to the employee's principal residence;
- burial or funeral expenses for the employee's deceased parent, spouse, or dependents; and
- expenses for the repair of casualty damage to the employee's principal residence.

An immediate and heavy financial need also includes any amounts necessary to pay any income taxes or penalties reasonably anticipated to result from the distribution. To the extent allowed under the plan, if medical, tuition, or funeral expenses incurred on behalf of the employee's spouse or dependent are deemed to be an immediate and heavy financial need, the same expenses with regard to the employee's beneficiary under the plan can also be considered an immediate and heavy financial need (Notice 2007-7).

A distribution will be treated as necessary to satisfy the employee's immediate and heavy financial need if the following requirements are met:

- the distribution is not in excess of the amount needed to satisfy the financial need;
- the employee has obtained all distributions and nontaxable loans available under all plans of the employer; and
- the distribution triggers the suspension of elective contributions on behalf of the employee and other employee contributions to any deferred compensation plan of the employer for at least six months.

Example: Bill takes a hardship distribution from his 401(k) plan on April 1, 2016. In order to satisfy one of the safe harbor requirements, Bill will not be able to make any elective deferrals or after-tax contributions to the plan until October 1, 2016.

A hardship distribution is included in the employee's income and subject to the 10-percent additional tax on early distributions unless an exception applies (¶ 2151). A hardship distribution generally may *not* be rolled over into an IRA or other type of retirement plan (Code Sec. 402(c)(4)(C)).[83]

2130. Joint and Survivor and Pre-Retirement Annuities. A qualified retirement plan (¶ 2111) that pays benefits in the form of an annuity generally must provide for the payment in the form of a joint and survivor annuity for the participant and his or her surviving spouse (Code Secs. 401(a)(11)(A)(i) and 417).[84] The annuity must be the actuarial equivalent of an annuity for the single life of the employee, and the survivor portion may not be less than 50 percent of the annuity paid during the joint lives of the employee and spouse. A pre-retirement survivor annuity must be provided for the surviving spouse of a vested participant who dies prior to the earliest retirement age. An employee may elect out of either the joint and survivor or pre-retirement survivor annuity. However, the election may only be made with the written consent of the spouse and the consent must be witnessed by a notary public or plan representative. The spouse's consent cannot be given in a prenuptial agreement (Reg. § 1.401(a)-20).[85]

References are to Standard Federal Tax Reports; Tax Research Consultant; and Practical Tax Explanations.

[82] ¶ 18,110; RETIRE: 3,302; § 24,715.15

[83] ¶ 18,202; RETIRE: 3,302; § 24,455.10

[84] ¶ 17,502, ¶ 19,260; RETIRE: 42,200; § 24,435.05

[85] ¶ 17,729; RETIRE: 42,212; § 24,435.25

2131. Anti-Assignment of Retirement Plan Benefits. A qualified retirement plan (¶ 2111) must provide that benefits under the plan may not be assigned or otherwise transferred (Code Secs. 401(a)(13) and 414(p)).[86] An exception is made for assignments ordered by a qualified domestic relations order (QDRO) issued under a state's domestic relations law (¶ 2144). In addition, a participant's benefits may be reduced when the individual has committed a breach of fiduciary duty or committed a criminal act against the plan.

2132. Top-Heavy Retirement Plans. More stringent qualification requirements must be met by qualified retirement plans (¶ 2111) and 403(b) annuity plans (¶ 2191) that primarily benefit an employer's key employees. These plans are referred to as "top-heavy plans" (Code Sec. 416(a)).[87] Most qualified plans must include language stating that they will comply with the top-heavy rules if they become top heavy. However, the top-heavy requirements do not apply to SIMPLE IRAs (¶ 2181) or SIMPLE 401(k) (¶ 2185). A plan is top heavy if the accrued benefits or account balances of key employees are more than 60 percent of the total benefits or balances under the plan.

Accelerated Vesting. For any plan year in which a plan is top heavy, the benefits of each employee for that year must *either* be: (1) 100 percent vested if the employee has at least three years of service, or (2) 20 percent vested after two years of service with a 20 percent increase for each later year of service (Code Sec. 416(b)).[88] See ¶ 2113 for the general vesting requirements.

Minimum Benefits and Contributions. In any plan year in which a defined benefit plan is top heavy, each participating non-key employee must be provided with a retirement benefit that is not less than two percent of average annual compensation (¶ 2115) for the employee's five consecutive years of highest compensation, multiplied by years of service (up to a maximum of ten years of service) (Code Sec. 416(c)(1)).[89] In any plan year in which a defined contribution plan is top heavy, each participating non-key employee must be provided with a contribution that is not less than three percent of such employee's compensation for that year. Employer matching contributions are taken into account when determining if this contribution requirement has been met. If the contribution rate for the key employee receiving the largest contribution is less than three percent, then the contribution rate for such key employee is used to determine the minimum contribution for non-key employees (Code Sec. 416(c)(2)).[90]

Key Employee Defined. A key employee is defined as an employee who, at any time during the plan year, is:

- an officer with compensation in excess of $170,000 for 2016 ($175,000 for 2017) (Code Sec. 416(i)(1); Notice 2015-75; Notice 2016-62);[91]
- a more-than-five-percent owner, or
- a more-than-one-percent owner who received more than $150,000 (not subject to inflation adjustment) in compensation.

In the case of a corporate employer, an employee is a five-percent owner when the employee owns more than five percent of the employer's outstanding stock or stock possessing more than five percent of the total combined voting power of all of the employer's stock. When the employer is not a corporation, a five-percent owner is any employee who owns more than five percent of the capital or profits interest in the employer. An employee is also treated as owning stock owned by certain members of the employee's family or, in the case of any employer that is not a corporation, by partnerships, estates, trusts, or corporations in which the employee has an interest (Code Sec. 416(i)(1)(B)). The same rules apply to determine whether an individual owner is a one-percent owner.

2133. Minimum Funding Standards of Defined Benefits Plans. Employers maintaining single-employer defined benefit plans (¶ 2101) are required to make minimum contributions to the plan each year based on the plan's assets (reduced by credit

References are to Standard Federal Tax Reports; Tax Research Consultant; and Practical Tax Explanations.

[86] ¶ 17,502, ¶ 19,150; RETIRE: 9,300; § 24,230.20

[87] ¶ 19,250; RETIRE: 21,050; § 24,280.05

[88] ¶ 19,250; RETIRE: 21,302; § 24,280.10

[89] ¶ 19,250; RETIRE: 21,354.05; § 24,280.15

[90] ¶ 19,250; RETIRE: 21,356; § 24,280.15

[91] ¶ 19,250; RETIRE: 21,102; § 24,280.20

balances), funding target, and target normal cost (Code Secs. 412, 430, and 436).[92] Full funding of plans is required, with existing shortfalls generally required to be eliminated over seven years, unless a special funding schedule has been elected. Multiemployer collectively bargained plans and Cooperative and Small Employer Charity (CSEC) plans operate under different sets of rules (substantially the same rules under which all plans operated prior to 2008) that require a funding standard account (Code Secs. 431 and 433).[93] Failure to meet minimum funding requirements or correct shortfalls will generally subject the employer to an excise tax (Code Sec. 4971).[94] However, a temporary waiver of the minimum funding requirements may be provided to an employer that is unable to satisfy the minimum funding standard for a plan year without "substantial business hardship." The employer may be required to provide security to the plan as a condition for the waiver. In addition, no plan amendment that has the effect of increasing plan liabilities may generally be adopted during the waiver period.

2136. Prohibited Transactions of Retirement Plans. Certain transactions between a qualified employees' trust (¶ 2101) and a plan fiduciary or other "disqualified person" are prohibited (Code Sec. 4975(c)).[95] The disqualified person who engages in the prohibited transaction is liable for excise taxes based upon the amount of the prohibited transaction. The basic excise tax rate is 15 percent. If the prohibited transaction is not corrected before the IRS assesses the tax or mails a notice of deficiency regarding it, the excise tax rate increases to 100 percent (Code Sec. 4975(b)).[96]

Plan Loans. Loans of plan assets to owners of the employer, including owner-employees, are generally prohibited transactions. Loans of IRA assets to the account owner are always prohibited, but a loan from an employer plan may qualify for an exception to the rule (Code Sec. 4975(f)(6)(B)(iii)). Loans from employer plans to disqualified persons are not prohibited if (Code Sec. 4975(d)(1)):

- loans are available to all participants on a reasonably equivalent basis;
- the plan must explicitly provide for such loans;
- the loan must have a reasonable rate of interest; and
- the loan must be adequately secured.

For this purpose, the term "owner-employee" is defined as: (1) a self-employed person who owns the entire interest in an unincorporated trade or business (i.e., a sole proprietor), or (2) an individual who owns more than a 10-percent capital or profits interest in a partnership (Code Sec. 401(c)(3)).[97]

2137. Retirement Plan Returns (Form 5500). An employer or plan administrator of a qualified retirement plan (¶ 2111) generally must file Form 5500 (and accompanying schedules) each tax year to report detailed information with respect to qualification, financial condition, and operations of the plan (Code Sec. 6058).[98] Small plans meeting certain eligibility requirements (generally plans with less than 100 participants) must file Form 5500-SF. One-participant plans may file a simpler Form 5500-EZ if a plan's only participants are an individual and spouse who together own the business (whether or not incorporated) for which the plan is established. Form 5500-EZ may also be used by the plan of a partnership if the only participants are partners and their spouses. Form 5500-SF or 5500-EZ need not be filed if certain conditions are met, e.g., the plan, and any other plan of the employer, had total assets of $250,000 or less at the end of the plan year, unless it is the plan's final year.

If a Form 5500 series return has to be filed, the form and its required schedules generally have to be filed no later than the last day of the seventh month after the plan year ends (July 31 for calendar year plans). A one-time extension of up to 3½ months (November 15 for calendar year plans) may be obtained by filing Form 5558 (¶ 1.6081-11). An automatic extension for filing will be granted if certain conditions are

References are to Standard Federal Tax Reports; Tax Research Consultant; and Practical Tax Explanations.

[92] ¶ 19,100, ¶ 20,151, ¶ 20,211; RETIRE: 30,000; RETIRE: 57,200; § 24,120.30

[93] ¶ 20,171, ¶ 20,202; RETIRE: 30,500; RETIRE: 30,650; RETIRE: 57,200; § 24,120.30

[94] ¶ 34,320; RETIRE: 30,502; § 24,120.30

[95] ¶ 34,400; RETIRE: 48,250; § 24,020.20

[96] ¶ 34,400; RETIRE: 48,250; § 24,020.05

[97] ¶ 17,502; RETIRE: 48,322; § 24,020.25

[98] ¶ 36,500; RETIRE: 78,052; § 24,530.05

met, e.g., the plan year and the employer's tax year are the same and the employer has been granted an extension to file its tax return. Form 5500 and Form 5500-SF are filed with the Department of Labor and must be filed electronically if the plan administrator and employer are required in the aggregate to file at least 250 returns during the calendar year that includes the first day of the plan year (Reg. § 301.6058-2). The electronic filing requirement applies to returns required to be filed for plan years that begin on or after January 1, 2015, but only for filings with a filing deadline (without regard to extensions) after December 31, 2015. Form 5500-EZ can only be filed on paper with the IRS. A one-participant plan that is eligible to file may elect to file Form 5500-SF electronically through the Department of Labor's system rather than filing a Form 5500-EZ on paper with the IRS.

A plan may also be required to file the stand-alone Form 8955-SSA to report certain information regarding separated participants with deferred vested benefits under the plan. Form 8955-SSA must be filed with the IRS by the last day of the seventh month following the last day of that plan year plus extensions. It should not be filed with Form 5500 or Form 5500-SF. A one-time extension to file Form 8955-SSA (up to 3½ months) may be obtained by filing Form 5558 on or before the normal due date not including any extensions. Form 8955-SSA must be filed electronically if the plan administrator is required to file at least 250 returns during the calendar year that includes the first day of the plan year (Reg. § 301.6057-3). This electronic filing requirements applies to Form 8955-SSAs filed for plan years that begin on or after January 1, 2014, but only for filings with a filing deadline, without regard to extensions, on or after July 31, 2015. The IRS will provide hardship waiver of the electronic filing requirements for Form 8955-SSA only in limited circumstances (Rev. Proc. 2015-47).

Various penalties may be imposed for the failure to timely file the required Form 5500 series form, schedules, reports, or Form 8955-SSA (Code Secs. 6652 and 6692).[99]

The IRS has implemented a permanent program to grant administrative and certain penalty relief to plan sponsors of one-participant and certain foreign plans for failure to timely file their annual reports on Form 5500-EZ (Rev. Proc. 2015-32; Rev. Proc. 2014-32).[100]

2138. Retirement Plans Terminations. An employer that establishes a qualified retirement plan (¶ 2111) can terminate the plan when it has sufficient assets to satisfy benefit liabilities or in a distress situation. On termination, partial termination, or complete discontinuance of contributions to plan, all affected employees have certain nonforfeitable rights. Depending on type of plan being terminated and whether termination is standard termination or distress termination, the plan administrator must comply with specific requirements. For this purpose, whether a partial termination has occurred is determined on a case-by-case basis (Reg. § 1.411(d)-2(b)).[101] A special rule applies where a defined benefit plan ceases or reduces future benefit accruals. In this case, a partial termination occurs if a potential reversion to the employer or employees who maintain the plan is created or increased. Multiemployer plans are subject to the vesting, participation, and benefit accrual rules that generally apply to all qualified plans. However, there are special funding and termination rules for multiemployer plans regarding special amortization periods (Code Sec. 412(b)(2)).

A defined contribution plan (¶ 2101) is considered terminated on the date when it is voluntarily terminated by the employer or employers who maintain it. A defined benefit plan is terminated when it is voluntarily terminated by the plan administrator or when it is terminated by the Pension Benefit Guaranty Corporation (PBGC) (Reg. § 1.411(d)-2(c)). The PBGC is a corporation operated under the Department of Labor whose primary purpose is to administer a pension plan termination insurance program for beneficiaries provided in ERISA.

Voluntary Termination. A qualified defined benefit plan may be voluntarily terminated through either a standard termination or a distress termination. The type of termination that the plan administrator uses depends on whether there are, or appear to

References are to Standard Federal Tax Reports; Tax Research Consultant; and Practical Tax Explanations.

[99] ¶ 39,480, ¶ 39,935; RETIRE: 78,052.10; § 24,530.05

[100] ¶ 39,490.1295; RETIRE: 78,052.10; § 24,530.05

[101] ¶ 19,070; RETIRE: 45,100

be, assets sufficient to satisfy PBGC guaranteed benefits. In determining if there are sufficient plan assets to pay benefits in a standard termination, claims are divided into six categories: (1) voluntary employee contributions that are nonforfeitable; (2) mandatory employee contributions, plus interest; (3) annuities provided with employer contributions that have been, or could have been, in pay status at least three years prior to plan termination; (4) the participant's basic-type benefits that do not exceed the guarantee limits; (5) all other nonforfeitable benefits; and (6) all plan benefits not allocated to the other categories (29 CFR § 4044, Secs. 11-16).

On the other hand, a distress termination of a defined benefit plan may be initiated by the plan administrator or the PBGC. Initiating a distress termination requires several steps: (1) notice of intent to terminate given to participants, (2) filing forms with PBGC, (3) PBGC review, (4) determination of whether requirements are met, (5) notice of benefit distribution, (6) issuances of notices, (7) distribution of benefits, and (8) filing of post-distribution certificate (ERISA § 4041).

Involuntary Terminations. A defined benefit may be involuntarily terminated by the PBGC if it makes a determination that: (1) the plan has not met the minimum funding standard; (2) the plan will be unable to pay benefits when due; (3) there has been a distribution under the plan to a participant who is a substantial owner, the distribution has a value of $10,000 or more, the distribution is not made by reason of the death of the participant, and, immediately after the distribution, the plan has nonforfeitable benefits that are not funded; or (4) the possible long-run loss to the PBGC may be expected to increase unreasonably if the plan is not terminated (ERISA § 4042(a)). When a termination occurs, (1) the termination must not have the effect of discriminating in favor of highly compensated employees (¶ 2114), (2) the plan administrator must notify the IRS, (3) all benefits or contributions that are not allocated to employees must be so allocated, (4) benefits must become nonforfeitable, and (5) the plan's assets must be distributed as soon as administratively feasible.

2139. Employee Plan Compliance Resolution System (EPCRS). The Employee Plan Compliance Resolution System (EPCRS) is a comprehensive system of correction programs for sponsors of plans intended to be qualified retirement plans (¶ 2111), 403(b) annuity plans (¶ 2191), SIMPLE IRAs (¶ 2181), and SEPs (¶ 2189) that have not met the qualification requirements for a period of time. Plan sponsors should generally follow the correction procedures found in Rev. Proc. 2016-51, modifying and superseding Rev. Proc. 2013-12.[102] EPCRS includes the following correction programs.

Self-Correction Program (SCP). The SCP is available to correct operational failures for qualified plans and 403(b) annuity plans, as well as SEPs and SIMPLE IRAs provided the SEP or SIMPLE IRA is established and maintained on a document approved by the IRS. In addition, in the case of a qualified plan that is the subject of a favorable determination letter or in the case of a 403(b) annuity plan, the plan sponsor generally may correct significant and insignificant operational failures without payment of any fee or sanction. SEPs and SIMPLE IRAs are eligible for SCP only to correct insignificant operational failures. SCP may also be used to correct significant operational failures for qualified plans or 403(b) plans. A plan can self correct an operational failure if the failure is insignificant. Self correction is available even if the plan or sponsor is under examination and even if the operational failure is discovered on examination.

Voluntary Correction Program (VCP). The VCP provides general procedures for correction of operational, plan document, demographic, and employer eligibility qualification failures for qualified plans, 403(b) annuity plans, SEPs, and SIMPLE IRAs. A plan sponsor may, at any time prior to audit, pay a limited fee and receive the IRS's approval for a correction. Under VCP, there are special procedures for anonymous submissions and group submissions. If the plan or plan sponsor is under examination, VCP is not available. However, while the plan or plan sponsor is under examination, insignificant operational failures can be corrected under the SCP and, if correction has been substantially completed before the plan or plan sponsor is under examination, significant operational failures can be corrected under SCP. VCP is for correction of failures raised

References are to Standard Federal Tax Reports; Tax Research Consultant; and Practical Tax Explanations.

[102] ¶ 17,507.331; RETIRE: 51,452; § 24,515

by the plan sponsor or failures identified by the IRS in processing the application. Consideration under VCP does not preclude a subsequent examination of the plan or plan sponsor by the IRS with respect to the tax year(s) involved with respect to matters outside the compliance statement. Absent unusual circumstances, a plan that has been properly submitted under VCP will not be examined while the submission is pending. This does not, however, preclude concurrent examination of the plan sponsor's other plan.

Closing Agreements Programs (Audit CAP). If a failure is identified on audit and has not been corrected through the SCP or the VCP, the plan sponsor may correct the failure and pay a sanction. The sanction imposed will take into account the nature, extent and severity of the failure as well as the extent to which correction occurred before audit. The Audit Closing Agreement Program (Audit CAP) is available for qualified plans for correction of all failures found on examination that have not been corrected in accordance with SCP or VCP. If the IRS and the plan sponsor cannot reach an agreement regarding the correction or the failure(s) or the amount of the sanction, the plan will be disqualified or, in the case of a 403(b) annuity plan, SEP, or SIMPLE IRA, the plan cannot rely on the effect of EPCRS. The sanction under Audit CAP is a negotiated percentage of the maximum payment amount. For 403(b) annuity plans, SEPs and SIMPLE IRAs, the sanction is a negotiated percentage of the total sanction amount.

Taxation of Distributions and Rollovers

2141. Taxation of Distributions from Retirement Plans. Generally, distributions from a qualified retirement plan (¶ 2111) are taxed to the recipient unless the distribution is an eligible rollover distribution (¶ 2145) or attributable to designated Roth contributions (¶ 2121). The tax treatment of a distribution depends on the form of the distribution. If the plan distribution takes the form of an annuity, it is taxable under the annuity rules (¶ 817 and ¶ 839) (Code Secs. 402(a) and 403(a)(1)).[103] For this purpose, the benefits derived from the employee's contributions to a defined contribution plan and the earnings on them may be treated as a separate contract from benefits derived from the employer's contributions (Code Sec. 72(d)(2)).[104] A participant's separate account in a defined benefit plan is treated as a defined contribution plan if the plan provides a benefit derived from employer contributions that is based partly on the balance of the separate account (Code Sec. 414(k)(2)).[105]

If a plan distribution is not in the form of an annuity, the following rules apply (Code Sec. 72(e); Reg. § 1.72-11):[106]

- If a distribution is made *before* the annuity starting date, it is treated in much the same way as an annuity distribution; that is, there is excluded from gross income that portion of the distribution that bears the same ratio to the distribution as the investment in the contract bears to the value of the contract. The total amount excluded cannot exceed the employee's investment in the contract.

- A non-annuity distribution made *on or after* the annuity starting date is generally included in full in gross income unless it reduces the dollar amount of subsequent annuity payments.

U.S. Civil Service Retirement Benefits. Retired federal employees generally receive annuity payments under the Civil Service Retirement System (CSRS) or the Federal Employee Retirement System (FERS). The portion of the payment that represents the employee's after-tax contributions to the retirement plan is not taxed. Form 1099-R will generally show the nontaxable portion of the CSRS or FERS payment as calculated under the simplified method (¶ 839) (IRS Pub. 721).

References are to Standard Federal Tax Reports; Tax Research Consultant; and Practical Tax Explanations.

[103] ¶ 18,202, ¶ 18,270; RETIRE: 42,300; § 24,405.10

[104] ¶ 6102; RETIRE: 42,302; § 24,405.10

[105] ¶ 19,150; RETIRE: 42,302; § 24,405.10

[106] ¶ 6102, ¶ 6113; RETIRE: 42,550, INDIV: 30,100; § 24,405.15

Death In Line of Duty. The amount paid as a survivor annuity to the spouse, former spouse, or child of a public safety officer killed in the line of duty is generally excludable from the recipient's gross income when the annuity is provided under a governmental retirement plan (Code Sec. 101(h)). A public safety officer includes law enforcement officers, firefighters, and members of an ambulance crew, or public rescue squad (Act Sec. 1204 of the Omnibus Crime Control and Safe Streets Act of 1968 (P.L. 90-351)). A chaplain killed in the line of duty may also be classified as a public safety officer for purposes of this exclusion.

Victims of Terrorism. If certain requirements are met, death benefits paid by an employer due to the death of an employee who was a victim of a terrorist act may be excluded from income (Code Sec. 101(i)). For this purpose, a self-employed individual may be considered an employee.

Employer Securities. Distributions of an employer's securities under circumstances not involving a lump-sum distribution (¶ 2143) are subject to the above rules except for unrealized appreciation attributable to shares that were purchased with the employee's own contributions (Code Sec. 402(e)(4)(A)).[107] That appreciation is not taxed until the securities are sold.

Loss. An employee may claim a loss on his or her return if the employee receives, entirely in cash or worthless securities, a distribution of his or her entire benefit from a qualified plan and the distribution is less than the employee's remaining basis in the plan (Rev. Rul. 72-305). The deductible loss is claimed on as a miscellaneous itemized deduction subject to the two-percent of adjusted gross income (AGI) limitation (¶ 1079).

2143. Lump-Sum Distributions from Retirement Plans. Special rules apply in determining the taxable portion of a lump-sum distribution from a qualified retirement plan (¶ 2111). A lump-sum distribution is a distribution of a participant's entire interest in a qualified plan within a single tax year of the recipient due to one of the following circumstances:

- the death of the employee,
- the employee has attained age 59½,
- on account of the employee's separation from service from the employer (as common-law employee), or
- after a participant who is a self-employed individual becomes totally and permanently disabled (Code Sec. 402(e)(4)(D)).[108]

The rules applicable to lump-sum distributions are applied without regard to community property laws. As a result, a lump-sum distribution is considered to belong entirely to the participant, rather than half to the participant and half to his or her spouse (*R.L. Karem*, 100 TC 521, Dec. 49,091).[109] However, a spouse may acquire an interest in retirement plan assets by means of a qualified domestic relations order (QDRO) (¶ 2144).

Determining Taxable Amount. The entire amount of the lump-sum distribution is not always subject to taxation. To determine the taxable portion of the lump-sum distribution, the following items must be subtracted from the total amount of the distribution:

- nondeductible amounts contributed to the plan by the participant (less any previous distributions the participant received that were not includible in gross income),
- any premiums paid by the plan to furnish a participant with life insurance protection that were included in gross income,
- any repayments of loans from the plan that were included in gross income (¶ 2152),
- the current actuarial value of any annuity contract that was included in the lump-sum distribution, and
- net unrealized appreciation in any employer securities that were distributed as part of the lump-sum distribution (unless the taxpayer elects to be taxed on this appreciation).

References are to Standard Federal Tax Reports; Tax Research Consultant; and Practical Tax Explanations.

[107] ¶ 18,202; RETIRE: 42,402; § 24,301

[108] ¶ 18,202; RETIRE: 42,360.05; § 24,405.20

[109] ¶ 18,207.11; RETIRE: 42,058.10; § 24,405.20

If the net unrealized appreciation is excluded from gross income upon distribution of the securities, tax is deferred until the securities are sold or exchanged. The cost or other basis of the employer securities is included in the taxable portion of the distribution (Code Sec. 402(e)(4)(B)).[110]

Born Before January 2, 1936. Employees born before January 2, 1936, may elect to have their lump-sum distributions from a qualified plan taxed under favorable rates. The election is also available to the employee's beneficiaries, including a spouse or former spouse who was named as an alternate payee under a QDRO. The recipient (employee, beneficiary, or alternate payee) must elect to use this special tax treatment for all such amounts received during the tax year (Code Sec. 402(d)(4)(B), prior to amendment by the Small Business Job Protection Act of 1996 (P.L. 104-188)). Also, this special treatment is *not* available if any portion of the lump-sum distribution is rolled over into another plan (Code Sec. 402(d)(4)(K), prior to amendment by P.L. 104-188).[111]

2144. Retirement Plans Distributions Incident to Divorce or Separation. A distribution made by a qualified retirement plan (¶ 2111) to an alternate payee (e.g., spouse, ex-spouse, child or other dependent of the participant) under the terms of a qualified domestic relations order (QDRO) is taxable to the alternate payee and not to the participant (Code Secs. 402(e)(1)(A) and 414(p)).[112] A QDRO is a judgment, decree, or order (including approval of a property settlement agreement) made under a state's domestic relations or community property law. The QDRO must relate to the provision of child support, alimony, or marital property rights to a spouse, former spouse, child, or other dependent of a plan participant. In order to be qualified, the order must meet specified requirements as to content and generally may not require the plan to pay benefits that are not otherwise payable under the terms of the plan.

Payment of the entire amount due the spouse or ex-spouse under a QDRO is eligible for special tax averaging treatment for lump-sum distributions if it would be eligible had it been paid to the participant (¶ 2143). All qualified plans must permit a participant, or spouse or ex-spouse of a participant who is an alternate payee under a QDRO, to elect to have any distribution that is eligible for rollover treatment transferred directly to an eligible transferee plan specified by the participant (¶ 2145). The participant's investment in the contract is allocated between the participant, spouse, or ex-spouse, pro rata on the basis of the present value of all benefits awarded to the spouse or ex-spouse, and the present value of all benefits reserved to the participant (Code Sec. 72(m)(10)).[113]

Rollover Distributions. When a participant's spouse or former spouse is awarded all or part of the participant's interest in a qualified retirement plan by a QDRO, the distribution of any part of that interest to the spouse or former spouse may be rolled over on the same terms that would apply if the distribution were made to the participant (¶ 2145) (Code Sec. 414(p)(10)).[114]

Transfers of IRAs. The transfer of all or a portion of an IRA to a spouse or former spouse under a divorce or separation instrument (¶ 772) is a nontaxable transaction as to both parties, and the IRA is thereafter treated as that of the spouse or former spouse (Code Sec. 408(d)(6)).[115] Accordingly, the spouse or former spouse may roll over to another IRA all or any part of the interest transferred to him or her (¶ 2167).

2145. Rollovers Distributions from Retirement Plans. A distribution from an qualified retirement plan (¶ 2111) may be excluded from gross income if the recipient rolls over the distribution to another qualified plan or IRA (Code Sec. 402(c)).[116] All distributions from a qualified plan are eligible for rollover treatment except:

References are to Standard Federal Tax Reports; Tax Research Consultant; and Practical Tax Explanations.

[110] ¶ 18,202; RETIRE: 42,356; § 24,410

[111] ¶ 18,202; RETIRE: 42,360.15; § 24,405.20; § 46,640.15

[112] ¶ 18,202, ¶ 19,150; RETIRE: 42,250; § 24,460.05

[113] ¶ 6102; RETIRE: 42,304; § 24,460.15

[114] ¶ 19,150; RETIRE: 9,308.05; § 24,460.15

[115] ¶ 18,902; RETIRE: 66,462; § 25,460

[116] ¶ 18,202; RETIRE: 42,450; § 25,445.05

- a distribution that is one of a series of substantially equal periodic payments, made over the life (or life expectancy) of the participant or the joint lives (or joint life expectancies) of the participant and his or her beneficiary;
- a distribution that is one of a series of substantially equal periodic payments made over a specified period of 10 years or more;
- distributions required under the minimum distribution rules (¶ 2127); and
- hardship distributions from 401(k) plans (¶ 2129) (Code Sec. 402(c)(4)).[117]

Eligible rollover distributions from qualified plans, 403(b) annuity plans, and 457 plans may be rolled over to any type of plan. Similarly, distributions from a traditional IRA generally are permitted to be rolled over into any type plan (¶ 2167). A distribution from a designated Roth account in a qualified plan may be rolled over only to another designated Roth account or to a Roth IRA (¶ 2175). Special rules apply for rollover distributions by successor after death of participant (¶ 2148) and incident to divorce or separation (¶ 2144). SIMPLE IRA plans can receive rollover distributions after December 18, 2015, from a qualified plan, 403(b) annuity plan, 457 plan, or traditional IRA after an initial period of two years (¶ 2183).

A rollover generally must be made within 60 days of receipt of the distribution. The IRS has the authority to grant a waiver of the 60-day rule in situations involving equity, good conscience, or situations beyond the control of the individual. Acceptable excuses might include: (1) military service in a combat zone or during a Presidentially declared disaster; (2) errors committed by a financial institution; or (3) inability to complete a rollover due to death, disability, hospitalization, incarceration, restrictions imposed by a foreign country, or postal error (Code Sec. 402(c)(3)).

The IRS has provided procedures to obtain a waiver of the 60-day requirement, including an automatic waiver in the event of an error by a financial institution (Rev. Proc. 2003-16, modified by Rev. Proc. 2016-47).[118] In addition, effective August 24, 2016, taxpayers may qualify for an automatic waiver and a self-certification procedure in the following circumstances: a misplaced distribution check was never cashed; a distribution was deposited into and remained in an account the taxpayer mistakenly thought was an eligible retirement plan; the taxpayer's home was severely damaged; a family member died; the taxpayer or a family member was seriously ill; the taxpayer was incarcerated; restrictions were imposed by a foreign country; the party making the distribution to which the rollover relates delayed providing information that the receiving plan or IRA required to complete the rollover despite the taxpayer's reasonable efforts to obtain the information; the post office made an error; or the distribution was made on account of an IRS levy and the proceeds of the levy have been returned to the taxpayer.

Direct Transfers. A qualified plan must allow an employee to elect to have any distribution that is eligible to be rolled over transferred directly to another qualified plan or traditional IRA unless it reasonably believes that the employee will receive distributions eligible to be rolled over of less than $200 (Code Secs. 401(a)(31)(C) and 402(c)(2), Reg. § 1.401(a)(31)-1).[119] Plans that are eligible to receive direct rollovers generally are the same plans that can receive rollovers, except qualified plans are required to allow direct transfers to qualified plans only if they are defined contribution plans (Code Sec. 401(a)(31)(E)). The defined contribution plan that accepts the transfer must agree to separately account for the pre-tax and after-tax portions of the amount that is transferred. After-tax contributions from qualified retirement plans can also be rolled over in a direct trustee-to-trustee transfer to a defined benefit plan or a 403(b) annuity plan. The transferee plan must separately account for after-tax contributions and earnings. A traditional IRA to which the pre-tax and post-tax amounts are rolled over does not have to separately account for these amounts. A rollover that includes both pre-tax and post-tax amounts is considered as coming first from pre-tax amounts.

References are to Standard Federal Tax Reports; Tax Research Consultant; and Practical Tax Explanations.

[117] ¶ 18,202; RETIRE: 42,450; § 24,455.10

[118] ¶ 18,922.0335; RETIRE: 42,454; § 25,445.35

[119] ¶ 17,502, ¶ 18,202, ¶ 17,925A; RETIRE: 42,500; § 24,455.40

Mandatory Rollovers. A qualified plan must provide for a direct rollover, i.e., a trustee to trustee transfer, from the plan into an IRA when the plan makes a mandatory distribution of the participant's benefit (an involuntary cash-out) (Code Sec. 401(a)(31)). The rule applies when a mandatory distribution from a qualified plan exceeds $1,000 and the plan specifies that nonforfeitable benefits that do not exceed $5,000 must be distributed immediately. However, the employee must have the right to elect to receive the distribution or have it rolled over into another IRA or qualified plan (Notice 2005-5).

Withholding. If a distributee does not elect a direct transfer, and receives the distribution and then transfers the funds to an eligible plan within 60 days, the payor of the distribution must withhold 20 percent of the distribution (Code Sec. 3405(c)).[120] If the distributee does elect a direct transfer, there is no withholding.

Written Explanation. The plan administrator must provide a written explanation to a recipient of the distribution options, including the direct trustee-to-trustee transfer option, within a reasonable period of time before making an eligible rollover distribution (Code Sec. 402(f); Notice 2009-68, modified by Notice 2014-74).[121] The IRS has provided two safe harbor explanations that may be provided to recipients of eligible rollover distributions from an employer plan.

2147. Rollover Distributions of After-Tax Roth Contributions. A qualified retirement plan (¶ 2111) that allows participating employees to designate part of their elective deferrals as after-tax Roth contributions (¶ 2121) may permit a rollover of a distribution from a participant's non-Roth account to the participant's designated Roth account within the same plan (Code Sec. 402A(c)(4)).[122] The intra-plan non-Roth to Roth rollover rules mirror the eligible retirement plan to Roth IRA rollover rules (¶ 2175). Both kinds of rollovers adopt the traditional IRA to Roth IRA conversion rules. The distribution to be rolled over must be otherwise allowed under the plan; thus, an employer may have to amend its non-Roth plan to allow in-service distributions or distributions prior to normal retirement age. The converted amount is includible in gross income as a distribution for the tax year in which the amount is distributed or transferred. This amount is reduced by any after-tax contributions included in the amount rolled over. Any election for any distribution during a tax year may not be changed after the due date for such tax year.

2148. Rollover Distributions After Death of Participant. When a distribution from a qualified retirement plan (¶ 2111) that would be eligible for rollover treatment if made to the employee is received by the participant's surviving spouse, the spouse may roll that distribution into an account maintained in the survivor's name under the same terms and conditions that would have applied to the employee (¶ 2145) (Code Sec. 402(c)(9)).[123] A successor other than a surviving spouse who receives a distribution from a qualified plan is not entitled to roll over the distribution to an IRA or to another qualified plan account in his or her own name. Instead, a nonspouse beneficiary can roll a qualified plan distribution into an IRA established in the name of the decedent. The IRA is treated as an inherited IRA. This allows the beneficiary to take distributions from the IRA in accordance with the required minimum distribution rules (¶ 2127) instead of including the entire distribution into gross income in the year of the plan distribution (Code Sec. 402(c)(11)). The surviving spouse of the owner of an IRA is also eligible to roll over any amount received from that IRA to another IRA or qualified plan (¶ 2167). However, this cannot be done by any other successor to the IRA.

2151. Penalty for Early Distribution from Retirement Plans. Taxable distributions from a qualified retirement plan (¶ 2141) or traditional IRA (¶ 2165) are generally subject to an 10-percent additional tax if they are made before the participant reaches age 59½ (Code Sec. 72(t)).[124] However, the 10-percent additional tax will *not* apply to:

References are to Standard Federal Tax Reports; Tax Research Consultant; and Practical Tax Explanations.

[120] ¶ 33,620; RETIRE: 42,700; § 24,445.20

[121] ¶ 18,202, ¶ 18,218A.23; RETIRE: 42,466; § 24,455.40

[122] ¶ 18,230; RETIRE: 3,260; § 24,725.27, § 25,235.30

[123] ¶ 18,202; RETIRE: 42,460.05; § 24,455.30

[124] ¶ 6102; RETIRE: 66,454; § 25,450.25

- eligible distributions that are timely and properly rolled over into an IRA or other qualified plan (¶ 2145);
- distributions upon death or disability of the participant;
- distributions after separation from service that are part of a series of substantially equal periodic payments (not less frequently than annually) over the life (or life expectancy) of the participant or the joint lives (or life expectancies) of the participant and the beneficiary;
- distributions other than from a SEP (¶ 2189) or traditional IRA (¶ 2163) after the participant's separation from service, provided the separation from service occurred during or after the calendar year in which the participant reached age 55; the age for separation of service is only 50 in the case of distributions from a government plan that is a defined benefit plan (and defined contribution plans beginning after 2015) to a retired police officer, firefighter, emergency medical services provider (and beginning after 2015, specified federal law enforcement officers, customs and border protection officers, federal firefighters, air traffic controllers, nuclear materials couriers, United States Capitol Police, Supreme Court Police, and diplomatic security special agents) (Code Sec. 72(t)(10)(B), as amended by the Defending Public Safety Employees' Retirement Act (P.L. 114-26) and the Protecting Americans from Tax Hikes Act of 2015 (P.L. 114-113));
- distributions to a nonparticipant under a qualified domestic relations order (QDRO) (¶ 2144);
- distributions not exceeding deductible medical expenses, determined without regard to whether deductions are itemized (¶ 1015);
- certain distributions by employee stock ownership plans (ESOPs) of dividends on employer securities;
- distributions made on account of the IRS's levy against the participant's account;
- qualified reservist distributions (¶ 2160); and
- distributions from federal retirement plans that are made under a phased retirement program.

Additional Tax on IRA Distributions. The exceptions to the 10-percent additional tax generally apply to IRA distributions except for distributions to a participant who has reached age 55 and has separated from service. Also, though the transfer of an IRA interest under a divorce or separation agreement is not a taxable event, subsequent distributions from a transferred IRA are not excluded from the additional tax. Some additional exceptions to the tax apply for IRA distributions only (¶ 2169).

SIMPLE Plan Penalty. For employees who withdraw any amount from a SIMPLE IRA (¶ 2181) during the first two years of participation, the 10-percent additional tax is increased to 25 percent (Code Sec. 72(t)(6)).

Reporting Requirements. The 10-percent additional tax on early distributions is generally reported on Form 5329. If an exception to the tax exists, the individual should provide this information on Form 5329. However, if no exception exists and distribution "Code 1" (i.e., early distribution) is correctly shown in the Form 1099-R received by the individual, then Form 5329 does not need to be filed. Instead, the amount of the additional tax should be reported directly on the individual's Form 1040.

2152. Retirement Plan Loans. Unless certain requirements are met, a loan to a participant from a qualified retirement plan is treated as a distribution and included in the participant's gross income. A pledge or assignment of any part of a participant's interest in a plan is treated as a loan for this purpose (Code Sec. 72(p); Reg. § 1.72(p)-1).[125] The exceptions do not apply unless loan limitations and level amortization of the loan is required, with payments that occur not less frequently than quarterly. The loan must also be subject to an enforceable agreement.

References are to Standard Federal Tax Reports; Tax Research Consultant; and Practical Tax Explanations.

[125] ¶ 6102, ¶ 6133; RETIRE: 42,802.05; § 24,465.15

Allowable Loans. Subject to specific dollar limits, a loan will not be treated as a distribution if the loan must be repaid within five years or the loan proceeds must be used (within a reasonable time after the date of the loan) to acquire a dwelling unit that is to be used as the principal residence of the participant. When determining if a plan loan is allowable, all plans of the employer are treated as a single plan. As a general rule, the *refinancing* of a home loan does not qualify under this exception. However, the repayment of a loan from a third party that was used to acquire the principal residence may qualify under the exception.

> **Example 1:** On July 1, 2016, Betty purchased a home that she used as a principal residence. She paid a portion of the purchase price with a $50,000 loan from Global Bank. On August 1, 2016, Betty borrowed $50,000 from her 401(k) plan. A few days later, Betty used the money from the plan loan to pay the $50,000 she owed Global Bank. Based on these facts, the plan loan would be treated as having been used to acquire Betty's principal residence. As a result, Betty's plan loan would *not* be treated as a taxable distribution.

Loan Limits. A loan from a qualified plan will be treated as a distribution only to the extent that, when added to the balances of all other loans to the participant (whenever made), the proceeds exceed the *lesser* of $50,000 or half the present value (but not less than $10,000) of the plan participant's vested benefits under the plan. The $50,000 amount must be reduced by the excess (if any) of: (1) the highest outstanding balance of loans from the plan during the one-year period ending on the day preceding the date of the loan over (2) the outstanding balance of those loans on the date of the loan (Code Sec. 72(p)(2)).[126]

> **Example 2:** Jane Smith is a participant in her employer's qualified profit-sharing plan. She wishes to borrow the maximum amount subject to the five-year repayment rule on July 1, 2016. On that date, the value of her vested interest in the plan is $120,000. Her highest loan balance during the period July 1, 2015, through June 30, 2016, was $40,000, and her balance on July 1, 2016, is $35,000. The maximum amount that Jane may borrow on July 1, 2016, is $10,000. This is the amount that, when added to her $35,000 loan balance, does not exceed $45,000. The $45,000 amount is determined by reducing the $50,000 loan limit by the excess of her highest loan balance for the past year ($40,000) over the loan balance at the time of the new loan ($35,000).

Traditional IRAs

2155. Traditional Individual Retirement Accounts (IRAs). An individual who receives compensation, including alimony, that is includible in gross income and who is under age 70½ throughout the tax year is entitled to make contributions to traditional individual retirement accounts (IRAs) (Code Sec. 219).[127] Amounts earned in a traditional IRA are not taxed until distributions are made (Code Sec. 408(e)(1)).[128] Contributions to a traditional IRA generally may be deducted. However, when the individual, or the individual's spouse, is an active participant in an employer-maintained retirement plan, the deduction may be reduced or eliminated based on the individual's modified adjusted gross income (¶ 2157). Nondeductible contributions may be made to a traditional IRA (¶ 2160). Roth IRAs are discussed at ¶ 2171.

IRA Contributions. The maximum combined contribution that can be made to all of an individual's traditional and Roth IRAs is $5,500 for 2016 ($5,500 for 2017) (Code Sec. 219(b); Notice 2015-75; Notice 2016-62).[129] An individual who will be at least 50 years of age by the end of the tax year may generally make additional "catch-up" contributions to a traditional or Roth IRA of $1,000.

Individuals have until the due date of their tax returns to make contributions to their IRAs for the return year (generally April 15). Filing extensions are *not* taken into account. If the contribution is made by the due date, it will be treated as having been

References are to Standard Federal Tax Reports; Tax Research Consultant; and Practical Tax Explanations.

[126] ¶ 6102; RETIRE: 42,804.05; § 24,465.15

[127] ¶ 12,650; RETIRE: 66,000; § 25,401

[128] ¶ 18,902; RETIRE: 66,500; § 25,401

[129] ¶ 12,650; RETIRE: 66,202; § 25,410

made on the last day of the tax year for which the return is filed (Code Sec. 219(f)(3)).[130] A deduction may be claimed for a contribution even though the contribution had not yet been made when the return is filed. However, the contribution must be made by the due date of the tax return (Rev. Rul. 84-18).[131]

If a contribution to a traditional IRA is *less* than the allowable maximum for that year, the individual cannot contribute more in a later year to make up the difference. If a contribution is *more* than the allowable maximum, the excess contribution may be withdrawn on or before April 15 or carried over and deducted in later years to the extent that the actual contributions in those later years are less than the allowable maximum (Code Sec. 219(f)(6)).[132] However, the excess contribution is subject to a six percent excise tax each year until it is corrected (Code Sec. 4973(a)).[133] The individual reports the six percent excise tax on Form 5329. Individuals with low to moderate incomes may be able to claim a nonrefundable credit based upon their contributions to IRAs (traditional and/or Roth), as well as other types of qualified retirement plans (¶ 1304).

Compensation. For purposes of determining an individual's eligibility to make contributions to an IRA, the term "compensation" includes earned income and alimony. It also includes differential wage payments received by a reservist from his or her civilian employer (Code Sec. 219(f)(1)). Compensation does *not* include pensions, annuities, or other forms of deferred compensation. However, under a safe-harbor rule, the IRS will accept as compensation the amount properly shown on the individual's Form W-2 as wages, tips, and other compensation, less any amount properly shown for nonqualified plans (Rev. Proc. 91-18).[134] The compensation of a self-employed person is the individual's earned income (¶ 2107). Combat pay earned by a member of the Armed Forces excluded from gross income (¶ 895) may be treated as compensation for purposes of the limit on IRA contributions.

Tax Refunds. A taxpayer may choose to have a refund of federal income taxes directly deposited into up to three separate accounts, including an IRA. The IRA must be established before the request for the direct deposit is made. The deposit counts against the taxpayer's annual contribution limit. Thus, the taxpayer should inform the IRA trustee which year the direct deposit contribution is made. The taxpayer must also verify that the direct deposit is made to the IRA by the due date of his or her return for that year without regard to extensions. A direct deposit request of an entire refund into an IRA should be made on a taxpayer's Form 1040. If a taxpayer chooses to have a refund split and deposited in up to three different accounts, then Form 8888 is used.

Allowable Investments. Although IRAs may hold almost any investment, they are generally prohibited from investing in "collectibles", e.g., antiques and stamps. However, certain U.S. gold and silver bullion coins minted since October 1986 may be held by an IRA. An IRA may also hold certain platinum and state-issued coins, as well as gold, silver, platinum, and palladium bullion (Code Sec. 408(m)(3)).[135]

Deemed IRAs. Qualified retirement plans (¶ 2111) may allow employees to make voluntary contributions to a separate account that will be deemed to be a traditional IRA or Roth IRA if the account meets all the requirements of the particular type of IRA (Code Sec. 408(q); Reg. § 1.408(q)-1(a)). The employee must designate the contribution as a deemed IRA contribution. An employee's contributions to the account count against the annual limit on IRA contributions.

Modified Adjusted Gross Income. When determining the taxpayer's AGI for deduction limitation rules, the taxpayer's AGI is modified by taking into account the inclusion in income of Social Security and Railroad Retirement benefits (¶ 716) and the disallowance of passive activity losses (¶ 1169), but not the exclusion of interest on educational U.S. savings bonds (¶ 863), the exclusion of employer-paid adoption assistance (¶ 2063), the deduction for student loan interest (¶ 1011), the deduction for tuition and related expenses (¶ 1011A), the deduction for domestic production activities (¶ 980A), the

References are to Standard Federal Tax Reports; Tax Research Consultant; and Practical Tax Explanations.

[130] ¶ 12,650; RETIRE: 66,208; § 25,425.05

[131] ¶ 18,922.87; RETIRE: 66,208; § 25,425.05

[132] ¶ 12,650; RETIRE: 66,356.15; § 25,430.05

[133] ¶ 34,360; RETIRE: 66,354; § 25,430.05

[134] ¶ 18,922.1063; RETIRE: 66,206; § 25,415.10

[135] ¶ 18,902; RETIRE: 66,458.10; § 25,470

foreign earned income and housing exclusion (¶ 2402), and the deduction for contributions to IRAs (¶ 2157) (Code Sec. 219(g)(3)(A)).[136]

2157. Deductible Contributions to IRAs—In General. Contributions to a traditional IRA generally may be deducted subject to the contribution limits (¶ 2155). The maximum deduction may be reduced when the individual or spouse is an active participant in a qualified retirement plan (¶ 2111), SIMPLE IRA (¶ 2181), SEP (¶ 2189), or a Code Sec. 501(c)(18) trust created before June 25, 1959 (Code Sec. 219(g); Reg. § 1.219-2).[137] An eligible 457 deferred compensation plan (¶ 2193) is not treated as a plan for this purpose. When an individual is an active participant in an employer's plan, the amount of the deductible IRA contribution depends upon the individual's modified adjusted gross income (AGI) and filing status. See ¶ 2158 for phaseout for married individuals filing jointly. See ¶ 2159 for phaseout for married individuals filing separately and single filers. See ¶ 2160 for discussion of nondeductible contributions.

Active Participant Defined. The determination on active participant status is made without regard to whether an individual's rights under an employer-sponsored plan are nonforfeitable (Code Sec. 219(g)). In the case of a defined benefit plan, an individual who is not excluded under the eligibility provisions of the plan is considered to be an active participant if he or she is eligible to participate for any part of the plan year ending with or within the tax year, even though the individual has elected not to do so, has failed to make a mandatory contribution, or has failed to meet the minimum service requirements (Reg. § 1.219-2). In the case of a defined contribution plan, an individual is considered an active participant if contributions or forfeitures are allocated to the individual's account for the plan year that ends with or within that tax year. Finally, an individual is an active participant for any tax year in which the individual makes a voluntary or mandatory employee contribution (Notice 87-16).[138]

Social Security and Railroad Retirement (Tier I or Tier II) are not retirement arrangements for purposes of determining active participation. If an individual receives benefits from a previous employer's plan, the individual is not covered by the plan. An individual is also *not* considered an active participant in an employer-sponsored plan merely because the individual's spouse is an active participant (Code Sec. 219(g)(7)).[139] An employer should have marked the box labeled "Retirement Plan" on the employee's Form W-2 if the employee participated in an employer plan for the year.

Social Security Recipients. An employed individual, either the taxpayer or the spouse, who is covered by a retirement plan, currently receiving Social Security benefits, and wants to determine the allowable deduction for contributions to a traditional IRA must compute taxable Social Security benefits twice. The first computation is for the purpose of determining the tentative amount of Social Security benefits that must be included in gross income if the individual did not make any IRA contribution. This computation determines the amount of hypothetical AGI for purposes of the IRA phaseout provision. The second computation determines the actual amount of taxable Social Security benefits by taking into account the deductible IRA contribution that was determined under the first computation. The worksheets necessary for these computations are found in IRS Pub. 590-A (¶ 716).

2158. Deductible IRA Contribution Limits—Married Filing Jointly. When a married couple files a joint return, each spouse may make deductible contributions to his or her IRA. For 2016, the IRAs of the spouse with the greater amount of compensation ("higher-paid spouse") may claim deductible contributions of up to the *lesser* of: (1) $5,500, or $6,500 if catch-up contributions are allowable ($5,500 and $6,500, respectively, for 2017), as reduced for active participation, or (2) his or her compensation (Code Sec. 219(c); Notice 2015-75; Notice 2016-62).[140] The IRAs of the spouse with the lesser amount of compensation ("lower-paid spouse") may claim deductible contributions for 2016 equal to the *lesser* of:

References are to Standard Federal Tax Reports; Tax Research Consultant; and Practical Tax Explanations.

[136] ¶ 12,650; RETIRE: 66,202; § 25,415.15

[137] ¶ 12,650, ¶ 12,653; RETIRE: 66,202; § 25,415.15

[138] ¶ 18,922.865; RETIRE: 66,202; § 25,415.15

[139] ¶ 12,650; RETIRE: 66,202; § 25,415.15

[140] ¶ 12,650; RETIRE: 66,302; § 25,415.15

- $5,500, or $6,500 if catch-up contributions are allowable ($5,500 and $6,500, respectively, for 2017), as reduced for active participation, or
- the sum of:
  - — the compensation of the lower-paid spouse, and
  - — the compensation of the higher-paid spouse, reduced by: (i) the deduction allowed to the higher-paid spouse for IRA contributions, (ii) the amount of any designated nondeductible IRA contribution on behalf of the higher-paid spouse, and (iii) the amount of any contribution on behalf of the higher-paid spouse to a Roth IRA (¶ 2171).

AGI Limits for Joint Filers. If both individuals on a joint return are active participants in an employer's qualified retirement plan, their ability to claim a deduction for contributions made to traditional IRAs depends upon the amount of their modified adjusted gross income (AGI) (¶ 2155). The allowable IRA deduction for joint filers will be reduced when modified AGI is between $98,000 and $118,000 for 2016 (between $99,000 and $119,000 for 2017) (Notice 2015-75; Notice 2016-62). For information regarding the IRA deduction limits for married persons filing separately and single filers, see ¶ 2159. See ¶ 2160 for discussion of nondeductible contributions.

Example 1: Ralph and Alice file a joint return for 2016. They are both employed and both are covered by their employers' qualified plans. Their modified AGI for 2016 is $120,000. Since they are both active participants in qualified plans sponsored by their employers and their modified AGI exceeds the phaseout range for 2016 ($98,000 to $118,000), they are not allowed to make deductible IRA contributions for 2016. They may make nondeductible contributions to traditional IRAs. As an alternative, they should consider the tax advantages of making their contributions to Roth IRAs.

An individual will *not* be considered an active participant in an employer-sponsored plan merely because the individual's spouse is treated as an active participant (Code Sec. 219(g)(7)).[141] However, if an individual is not an active participant and is married to someone who is covered, the deductible contribution is phased out if the couple's modified AGI (jointly computed) is between $184,000 and $194,000 for 2016 (between $186,000 and $196,000 for 2017).

Example 2: Bob is covered by a 401(k) plan sponsored by his employer. His wife, Betty, is not employed. The couple files a joint income tax return for 2016, with a modified AGI of $120,000. Betty may make a deductible contribution to a traditional IRA for the year because she is not an active participant in an employer-sponsored retirement plan and their combined modified AGI is below the phaseout range for a married couple where only one spouse is an active participant ($184,000 to $194,000 for 2016). Bob may not make a deductible IRA contribution because their combined modified AGI is above the phaseout range for active participants who are married and filing jointly ($98,000 to $118,000 for 2016).

Example 3: Assume the same facts as in Example 2 above, except that the couple's modified AGI was $200,000 for 2016. Neither Bob nor Betty would be able to make a deductible contribution to a traditional IRA.

2159. Deductible IRA Contribution Limits—Single or Married Filing Separately. For a single individual, head of household, or a married individual who files separately, contributions to traditional IRAs are generally deductible to the extent that they do not exceed the *lesser* of: (1) the individual's compensation for that year that is includible in gross income; or (2) for 2016, $5,500, or $6,500 if catch-up contributions are allowable ($5,500 and $6,500, respectively, for 2017) (Code Sec. 219(b)(1); Notice 2015-75; Notice 2016-62).[142] The maximum allowable deduction may be reduced when the individual is an active participant in an employer-maintained retirement plan (¶ 2157). For information regarding the IRA deduction limits for married individuals filing jointly, see ¶ 2158. See ¶ 2160 for discussion of nondeductible contributions.

References are to Standard Federal Tax Reports; Tax Research Consultant; and Practical Tax Explanations.

[141] ¶ 12,650; RETIRE: 66,202; § 25,415.15

[142] ¶ 12,650; RETIRE: 66,200, RETIRE: 66,202; § 25,415.15

Single or Head of Household. When a single individual or head of household is an active participant in an employer's retirement plan, the IRA deduction begins to phase out when modified adjusted gross income (AGI) (¶ 2155) is between $61,000 and $71,000 for 2016 ($62,000 and $72,000 for 2017) (Code Sec. 219(g); Notice 2015-75; Notice 2016-62).

Married Filing Separately. When an individual files as married filing separately and the individual, or the spouse, is an active participant in an employer's retirement plan, the IRA deduction begins to phase out when the individual's modified AGI exceeds $0. The deduction is completely phased out when modified AGI is $10,000 or more. This phaseout range is not adjusted for inflation. When determining if an individual is married or single for the purpose of determining which IRA deduction limit applies, spouses who file separate returns and live apart at all times during a tax year are *not* considered to be married during that tax year (Code Sec. 219(g)(4)).

2160. Nondeductible Contributions to Traditional IRAs. An individual may make nondeductible contributions to a traditional IRA (¶ 2155). These contributions may not exceed the *excess* of: (1) the maximum allowable contribution for the year over (2) the amount actually allowed as a deduction for the year (¶ 2157) (Code Sec. 408(o)).[143] In applying this rule, an individual may elect to treat otherwise deductible contributions as nondeductible contributions. However, the tax advantages of funding a Roth IRA should be considered before making nondeductible contributions to a traditional IRA (¶ 2171).

> **Example:** In 2016, Bill Webb, age 48 and single, had earned income of $53,000 and a modified adjusted gross income (AGI) of $62,000. He is an active participant in his employer's 401(k) plan. Since his modified AGI exceeds $61,000, a maximum contribution to a traditional IRA would not be fully deductible. Bill determines that his maximum deductible contribution would be $4,950. As a result, he could make an additional $550 nondeductible IRA contribution.

Nondeductible contributions may be made up to and including the due date of the return for the tax year. A filing extension does *not* extend the due date for making the contribution (Code Sec. 219(f)(3)). The same deadline applies to deductible IRA contributions and Roth IRA contributions. Nondeductible contributions to a traditional IRA must be reported on Form 8606, which is attached to the individual's return.

Reservist Contributions. Certain qualified reservist distributions are not subject to the tax on early distributions and may be recontributed to an IRA as a nondeductible contribution without counting against the dollar limits applicable to IRA contributions (Code Sec. 72(t)(2)(G)).[144] A qualified reservist distribution is a distribution that is made:

- from an IRA or from an individual's elective deferrals under an employer plan such as a 401(k) plan or 403(b) annuity plan (¶ 2121);
- to an individual who is a reservist who was called to active duty for a period of more than 179 days or for an indefinite period; and
- during the period beginning on the date the reservist was called to active duty and ending on the date the active duty ended.

The distribution may be recontributed at any time within the two years after the end of the active duty period. A reservist who took a distribution after being called up and paid the early distribution penalty may file a claim for refund of the penalty.

2161. Excess Contributions to IRAs. Annual contributions to a traditional IRA (¶ 2155) and/or Roth IRA (¶ 2171) in excess of the allowable amount are subject to a cumulative six percent excise tax, which is reported on Form 5329 (Code Sec. 4973).[145] See ¶ 2165 for a discussion on the taxation of distributions from a traditional IRA.

References are to Standard Federal Tax Reports; Tax Research Consultant; and Practical Tax Explanations.

[143] ¶ 18,902; RETIRE: 66,250; § 25,420

[144] ¶ 6102; RETIRE: 66,454.25; § 24,480

[145] ¶ 34,360; RETIRE: 66,350; § 25,430.05

2163. Distribution Requirements of Traditional IRAs. Traditional IRAs (¶ 2155) are subject to the same required minimum distribution (RMD) rules that apply to qualified employer-provided retirement plans (¶ 2127) (Code Sec. 408(a)(6) and (b)(3); Reg. § 1.408-8).[146] This means that distributions to the owner or beneficiary of a traditional IRA must begin no later than April 1 following the calendar year in which the owner reaches age 70½. A few special rules, however, apply to RMDs from IRAs.

Inherited Traditional IRA: Spouse. A surviving spouse may elect to treat an inherited traditional IRA as his or her own by having the account redesignated as an account belonging to the surviving spouse as owner rather than beneficiary. Alternatively, the surviving spouse will be treated as having made this election if: (1) any amounts in the IRA are not distributed within the time period that applied to the decedent, or (2) the surviving spouse makes contributions (including rollover contributions) to the inherited IRA that are subject, or are deemed subject, to the lifetime distribution requirements. In order to make the election, the surviving spouse must be the sole beneficiary of the IRA and have an unlimited right to withdraw amounts from it (Reg. § 1.408-8, Q&A-5).[147] When a trust is named as the beneficiary of the IRA, this requirement has not been satisfied even if the spouse is the sole beneficiary of the trust. When the surviving spouse makes the election, he or she is treated as the owner of the IRA for all purposes. If the election is not made, then the RMDs are determined as though the spouse was the beneficiary of the IRA.

Inherited Traditional IRA: Nonspouse. A nonspouse beneficiary who inherits an IRA cannot treat it as his or her own account but must take RMDs determined under the rules applicable to beneficiaries receiving distributions from a qualified plan. When an individual other than the decedent's spouse receives a lump sum distribution from an IRA, then the individual may generally not roll over that distribution into another IRA; it must be distributed within a certain period (Code Sec. 408(d)(3)(C); Rev. Rul. 92-47).[148] The distribution, minus the aggregate amount of the owner's nondeductible IRA contributions, is taxed as ordinary income in the year the distribution is received.

Trust Named as Beneficiary. When a trust is named as the beneficiary of the IRA, the beneficiaries of the trust will be treated as the deceased individual's beneficiaries if certain requirements are met (Reg. § 1.401(a)(9)-4, Q&A-5).[149] The requirements include: (1) validity of the trust, (2) identification of the trust's beneficiaries, and (3) the delivery of proper documentation to the plan administrator (Reg. § 1.401(a)(9)-4, Q&A-6).

More Than One IRA. If an individual is required to receive an RMD from more than one traditional IRA in a calendar year, the amount of the minimum distribution from each IRA must be calculated separately and the separate amounts totalled. However, the total may be withdrawn from one or more of the IRAs in whatever amounts the individual chooses (Reg. § 1.408-8, Q&A-9).[150]

Planning and Due Diligence Considerations. For families that are not in immediate need of inherited IRA funds, it can make sense to stretch out the RMD period as long as possible in order to protect the IRA assets from tax. Careful designation of beneficiaries can help to peg the RMD period to the life expectancy of an individual beneficiary. Inherited IRAs are subject to a number of special rules and deadlines in the year following the owner's death, including rules for identifying designated beneficiaries, disclaiming interests, providing the IRS with trust information, and slicing an inherited IRA into multiple IRAs.[151]

2165. Taxation of Distributions from Traditional IRAs. If an individual only made deductible contributions to a traditional IRA (¶ 2160), then any distributions from the IRA are fully taxable to the owner or beneficiary as ordinary income unless it is rolled over to another IRA or qualified retirement plan (¶ 2167) (Code Sec. 408(d)(1) and (2);

References are to Standard Federal Tax Reports; Tax Research Consultant; and Practical Tax Explanations.

[146] ¶ 18,902, ¶ 18,917A; RETIRE: 66,400, RETIRE: 66,450; § 25,475.05

[147] ¶ 18,917A; RETIRE: 42,160.20; § 25,445.30

[148] ¶ 18,902, ¶ 18,922.26; RETIRE: 66,702.10; § 25,445.30

[149] ¶ 17,725E; RETIRE: 42,164.20; § 24,440.30, § 24,440.35

[150] ¶ 18,917A; RETIRE: 66,456; § 25,475.05

[151] ¶ 18,917A; RETIRE: 66,456.20; RETIRE: 66,812; RETIRE: 66,814; § 25,475.10

Reg. § 1.408-4(a)).[152] If nondeductible contributions were made, the owner has a *cost basis* in the IRA equal to the sum of the nondeductible contributions made to the IRA minus any prior withdrawals or distributions of nondeductible contributions (Notice 87-16). The recovery of this basis is not recognized as taxable income. As a result, the individual must determine how much of the IRA distribution is nontaxable. The nontaxable portion of the distribution is generally determined under the same rules that apply to annuity payments (¶ 817). When applying these rules:

- all traditional IRAs of an individual, including SIMPLE IRAs (¶ 2181) and SEPs (¶ 2189), are treated as a single contract;
- all distributions during the individual's tax year are treated as one distribution;
- the value of the contract, the income on the contract, and the investment in the contract are calculated (after adding back distributions made during the year) as of the close of the calendar year in which the tax year of the distribution begins; and
- total withdrawals excludable from income in all tax years cannot exceed the taxpayer's investment in the contract in all tax years.

Pro Rata Rule. The amount representing a nontaxable return of basis for any traditional IRA distribution is a pro rata amount based on the ratio between the owner's total basis in all of the owner's IRAs to the total value of all of the owner's IRAs.[153]

Example: Walt Long has two IRAs—IRA-1 is worth $50,000 with $10,000 in nondeductible contributions, and IRA-2 is worth $50,000 with no nondeductible contributions. Collectively, Walt's IRAs are worth $100,000 with $10,000 in basis. If he withdraws $10,000 from IRA-1, either to use or to roll over, $1,000 is treated as a nontaxable return of basis. The same would hold true for a $10,000 distribution from IRA-2.

The pro rata rule does not apply to distributions from an employer plan that includes both taxable and nontaxable amounts: these amounts can be separately allocated to different destinations (for example, a nontaxable basis amounts can go to a Roth IRA while taxable amounts to a traditional IRA) (¶ 2175). In addition, in a rollover from an IRA with basis to a qualified employer plan (such as a 401(k) plan) the basis remains in the IRA and only taxable amounts are rolled over (Reg. § 1.402(c)-2, Q&A 3(b)(3)).[154] The basis in an inherited IRA is also not aggregated either with the basis in the IRAs the beneficiary holds as an owner, or with the basis of any other inherited IRA from a different decedent (though if the beneficiary is a spouse who treats the IRA as his or her own, then basis is aggregated) (IRS Pub. 590-B).[155]

Charitable Distributions. Individuals age 70 ½ or older may distribute up to $100,000 tax-free from their IRAs to certain charitable organizations without including the distribution in gross income (Code Sec. 408(d)(8)).[156] The entire distribution must otherwise be deductible as a charitable contribution, disregarding the percentage limitations, even though the individual cannot claim a charitable deduction for the donation (¶ 1058).

HSA Funding Distributions. An individual may make a one-time transfer of funds from his or her IRA distribution directly to his or her health savings account (HSA) without recognizing income on the distribution (Code Sec. 408(d)(9); Notice 2008-51).[157] The transfer can only be made, however, if it would otherwise be a taxable distribution. The dollar amount excluded cannot exceed the annual limitation on the individual's HSA contribution for the year (¶ 2035). The exclusion is lost if the individual ceases to be eligible to contribute to an HSA during the twelve months after the contribution. In such a case, the distribution is subject to tax and a 10-percent penalty is imposed.

Reporting Requirements. Form 8606 is used to report the taxable portion of an IRA distribution if the individual ever made nondeductible contributions to an IRA. Income tax withholding is optional.

References are to Standard Federal Tax Reports; Tax Research Consultant; and Practical Tax Explanations.

[152] ¶ 18,902, ¶ 18,910; RETIRE: 66,500; § 25,450.10, § 25,450.15

[153] ¶ 18,922.0326; RETIRE: 66,502; § 25,450.15

[154] ¶ 18,922.041; RETIRE: 42,458; § 25,445.15

[155] ¶ 18,922.041; RETIRE: 66,808; § 25,445.15

[156] ¶ 18,902; RETIRE: 66,514; § 25,450.35

[157] ¶ 18,902; RETIRE: 66,454.30; § 25,450.45

Estate Tax. If the distributee of an IRA distribution is the beneficiary of the IRA owner and the value of the IRA is included in the owner's estate for federal estate tax purposes, the distributee is entitled to deduct the estate tax allocable to the IRA (¶ 191) (Rev. Rul. 92-47).[158]

Return of Contributions. A distribution from a traditional IRA that represents the return of a contribution made for a particular tax year will not be included in the individual's income if (Code Sec. 408(d)(4)):[159]

- the distribution is made before the due date, including extensions, of the individual's tax return for that year;
- no deduction is allowed with respect to the contribution; and
- the distribution includes any net income earned by the contribution.

The net income earned by the contribution is included in income for the tax year in which the contribution was made even if the distribution is received in the following year.

Recognizing Loss on an IRA. An IRA owner can recognize a loss on traditional IRA investments, but only when all amounts from all of the owner's traditional IRA accounts have been distributed and the total distributions are less than any unrecovered basis in the accounts. The recognized loss is claimed as a miscellaneous itemized deduction subject to the two-percent-of-adjusted-gross-income (AGI) limitation (¶ 1079) (IRS Pub. 590-B). If the individual never made nondeductible contributions to any of the traditional IRAs, the realized loss cannot be deducted because the individual has no tax basis in the IRAs.

2167. Rollover Distributions from IRAs. A distribution from a traditional IRA (¶ 2163) may be excluded from gross income if the recipient rolls over the distribution to another traditional IRA or returns it to the same IRA (Code Sec. 408(d)(3); Rev. Proc. 2003-16).[160] A distribution from a traditional IRA may also be rolled over into a qualified plan (¶ 2111), 403(b) annuity plan (¶ 2191), or 457 plan (¶ 2193) provided that the plan accepts rollover contributions. All distributions from a qualified plan are eligible for rollover treatment except for required minimum distributions (RMDs) (¶ 2127). A rollover of after-tax Roth contributions can be made from one IRA to another IRA. However, after-tax Roth contributions in an IRA cannot be rolled over into an employer's qualified plan. See ¶ 2175 regarding a rollover from a traditional IRA into a Roth IRA. See ¶ 2181 regarding rollovers from a SIMPLE IRA.

The rollover or return of an IRA distribution must generally be accomplished within 60 days after the withdrawal. It is not necessary that the entire amount withdrawn be transferred, but only the amount that is transferred during the 60-day period will be excluded from gross income. Any portion of the withdrawal that is not rolled over within the 60-day period will be taxed as ordinary income and may be subject to the 10-percent additional tax for early distributions (¶ 2169). The IRS has the authority to grant a waiver of the 60-day rule in situations involving equity, good conscience, or situations beyond the control of the individual.

Once-Per-12-Month Rule. Once an individual has made a tax-free rollover, he or she must wait at least one year from the date of receipt of the amount withdrawn before becoming eligible to engage in another rollover (Code Sec. 408(d)(3)(B)). Historically, the IRS applied this rule generously for taxpayers by applying it on an IRA-by-IRA basis, rather than on a taxpayer-by-taxpayer basis. For example, a taxpayer with multiple IRAs could roll over amounts from each IRA during the course of a 12-month period, as long as the taxpayer only did it once per IRA. Starting in 2015, however, the once-per-12-month rule applies on a taxpayer-by-taxpayer basis. Accordingly, if a taxpayer has multiple IRAs, a rollover from one prevents the taxpayer from rolling over again within 12-months from any of the taxpayer's IRAs. Under transition relief, rollover distributions

References are to Standard Federal Tax Reports; Tax Research Consultant; and Practical Tax Explanations.

[158] ¶ 18,922.26; RETIRE: 66,502.05

[159] ¶ 18,902; RETIRE: 66,356.05; § 25,430.10

[160] ¶ 18,902; RETIRE: 42,450, RETIRE: 66,700; § 25,445.05

in 2014 do not count against rollovers in 2015 (Announcement 2014-32).[161] Note that the once-per-12-month rule does not apply to trustee-to-trustee direct transfers.

2169. Penalty for Early Distributions from IRAs. Generally, if an individual is under age 59½, a distribution from a traditional IRA (¶ 2165) or nonqualified distribution from a Roth IRA (¶ 2173) is subject to the 10-percent additional tax on early distributions. Many of the exceptions to the tax on early distributions that apply to distributions from qualified employer-provided retirement plans (¶ 2151) also apply to early distributions from an IRA with the exception for early retirements (Code Sec. 72(t)(3)(A)).[162] In addition, the following exceptions apply to early distributions from an IRA but not to distributions from a qualified retirement plan. If an exception applies, it may be necessary to file Form 5329.

Medical Insurance Premiums of Unemployed Individuals. Distributions from an IRA, SIMPLE IRA (¶ 2181), or SEP (¶ 2189) to certain unemployed individuals for use in paying qualified medical insurance premiums are *not* subject to the 10-percent additional tax (Code Sec. 72(t)(2)(D)).[163] Eligible unemployed individuals are those who have received federal or state unemployment compensation for 12 consecutive weeks. A self-employed individual will be treated as having received unemployment compensation if, under federal or state law, the individual would have received unemployment compensation but for being self-employed.

Qualifying premiums are deductible premiums for the medical care of the unemployed individual, spouse, and dependents. The distributions must be received in the tax year during which unemployment compensation is received or in the following year. In determining whether the premiums are deductible, the adjusted gross income (AGI) floor for claiming medical expenses as an itemized is ignored (¶ 1015). This exception to the 10-percent additional tax ceases to apply after the individual has been reemployed for 60 days (not necessarily consecutive) after initial unemployment.

Education Expenses. The 10-percent additional tax does not apply if the individual uses the IRA distribution to pay for qualified higher education expenses for the individual, the individual's spouse or child, or a grandchild of the individual or the individual's spouse. Qualified expenses include tuition at a post-secondary educational institution, books, fees, supplies and equipment (Code Sec. 72(t)(2)(E)).[164]

First-Time Homebuyer Expenses. The 10-percent additional tax does not apply if the individual uses the IRA distribution for certain expenses of a first-time homebuyer. Only $10,000 during the individual's lifetime may be withdrawn without a penalty for this purpose. Qualified expenses include acquisition costs, settlement charges, and closing costs. The principal residence may be for the individual or the individual's spouse, child or grandchild, or an ancestor of the individual or the individual's spouse. In order to be considered a first-time homebuyer, the person buying the residence (and spouse, if married) must not have had an ownership interest in a principal residence during the two-year period ending on the date that the new home is acquired (Code Sec. 72(t)(2)(F)).[165]

Return of Nondeductible Contributions. The 10-percent additional tax does not apply to the portion of the distribution that represents a return of nondeductible IRA contributions (¶ 2165).

Roth IRAs

2171. Roth IRAs. A Roth IRA is a type of IRA consisting of after-tax contributions (Code Sec. 408A).[166] A Roth IRA generally is treated like a traditional IRA (¶ 2155) except that contributions to a Roth IRA cannot be deducted from income and qualified distributions from the Roth IRA are excludable from gross income (¶ 2173).

References are to Standard Federal Tax Reports; Tax Research Consultant; and Practical Tax Explanations.

[161] ¶ 18,922.75; RETIRE: 66,704; § 25,445.10

[162] ¶ 6102; RETIRE: 66,506; 25,450.25

[163] ¶ 6102; RETIRE: 42,554.216; 25,450.25

[164] ¶ 6102; INDIV: 60,056; 25,450.25

[165] ¶ 6102; RETIRE: 42,554.224; § 25,450.25

[166] ¶ 18,925; RETIRE: 66,750; § 25,501

Roth IRA Contributions. The maximum contribution that can be made to individual's Roth and traditional IRAs is $5,500 for 2016 ($5,500 for 2017) (Code Sec. 408A(c); Reg. § 1.408A-3; Notice 2015-75; Notice 2016-62).[167] The limit is the amount that may be contributed to *both* types of IRAs combined, not the amount that may be contributed to each type. An individual who will be at least 50 years of age by the end of the tax year may generally make additional catch-up contributions to a traditional or Roth IRA of $1,000 (Code Sec. 219(b)(5)). Rollover contributions into a Roth IRA are not counted against the annual contribution limit. In addition, unlike traditional IRAs, individuals may make contributions to a Roth IRA after reaching age 70½.

Income Limits. The ability of an individual to make a contribution to a Roth IRA depends upon the amount of the individual's modified adjusted gross income (MAGI) (Notice 2015-75; Notice 2016-62). For 2016, the MAGI phaseout range is between $117,000 and $132,000 for single filers, and between $184,000 and $194,000 for joint filers. For 2017, the allowable Roth IRA contribution is phased out when MAGI is between $118,000 and $133,000 for single filers, and between $186,000 and $196,000 for joint filers. The phaseout range is between $0 and $10,000 for individuals who are married filing separately. MAGI is generally calculated as it is for traditional IRAs. However, for Roth IRA purposes, MAGI does not include the income reported from the conversion of a traditional IRA into a Roth IRA (¶ 2175).

Deemed Roth IRAs. Qualified employer-provided retirement plans may allow employees to make voluntary contributions to an account that will be deemed to be a Roth IRA if the account meets all the requirements of a Roth IRA (Code Sec. 408(q)).[168] An employee's contribution to this account counts towards the maximum annual contribution that may be made to a Roth IRA.

Losses in Roth IRA. Like a traditional IRA, the owner of a Roth IRA can recognize a loss on investments in the account only when all the amounts in all the owner's Roth IRA accounts have been distributed and the total distributions are less than the individual's unrecovered basis in the accounts. The basis is the total amount of the nondeductible contributions in the Roth IRAs. The recognized loss is claimed as a miscellaneous itemized deduction subject to the two-percent-of-adjusted-gross-income (AGI) limitation (¶ 1079) (IRS Pub. 590-B). The loss rule applies separately to each kind of IRA. Thus, to report a loss on a Roth IRA, all the Roth IRAs owned by the individual have to be liquidated, and to report a loss on a traditional IRA, all the traditional IRAs owned by the individual have to be liquidated.

Military Death Gratuity. An individual who receives a military death gratuity or payment under the Servicemembers' Group Life Insurance (SGLI) program may contribute an amount up to the sum of the gratuity and SGLI payments received to a Roth IRA, notwithstanding the annual contribution limit and the income phaseout of the contribution limit that otherwise apply. The contribution must be made within one year of the receipt of the payment (Code Sec. 408A(e)). These contributions are generally treated as though they were a rollover from another Roth IRA. This option is available for amounts paid in connection with deaths from injuries occurring on or after June 17, 2008.

myRA. Entry level retirement accounts called "myRAs" are available through the Treasury Department to individuals and for use by employers. These accounts are cost-free, guaranteed by the government, flexible, and structured similar to and follow the rules for Roth IRAs. The IRS has also added myRAs to Form 8888 to allow part or all of an income tax refund to be deposited into this type of retirement account. For more information on myRAs, go to https://myra.gov.

2173. Taxation of Distributions from Roth IRAs. Qualified distributions from a Roth IRA (¶ 2171) are not included in the recipient's gross income nor are they subject to the 10-percent additional tax for early withdrawals (¶ 2169) (Code Sec. 408A(d); Reg. § 1.408A-6).[169] To be treated as a qualified distribution, the Roth IRA distribution, including distributions allocable to rollover contributions, may not be made before the end of the five-year period beginning with the first tax year for which the individual

References are to Standard Federal Tax Reports; Tax Research Consultant; and Practical Tax Explanations.

[167] ¶ 18,925, ¶ 18,927; RETIRE: 66,752; § 25,510

[168] ¶ 18,902; RETIRE: 66,058.10; § 25,405.25

[169] ¶ 18,925, ¶ 18,928; RETIRE: 66,758; § 25,525.10

made a contribution to the Roth IRA. The five-year holding period ends on the last day of the individual's fifth consecutive tax year after the holding period started. Generally, each Roth IRA owner has only one five-year period for all of the Roth IRAs that the individual owns.

Example: Jack Martin made his first contribution to a Roth IRA on September 15, 2012, for the 2012 tax year. On December 27, 2013, Jack made another contribution to a Roth IRA for the 2013 tax year. On December 30, 2014, he made another contribution to a Roth IRA for the 2014 tax year. The five-year holding period for all of Jack's Roth IRAs is considered to have started on January 1, 2012. Distributions made after December 31, 2016, will have satisfied the five-year holding period.

In addition to satisfying the five-year holding period, a distribution will constitute a qualified distribution only if it is (Code Sec. 408A(d)(2)):[170]

- made on or after the date on which the individual attains age 59½,
- made to a beneficiary (or the individual's estate) on or after the individual's death,
- attributable to the individual being disabled, or
- a distribution to pay for qualified first-time homebuyer expenses (¶ 2169).

Pre-Death Requirements. The *pre-death* required minimum distribution (RMD) requirements (¶ 2127) that apply to qualified retirement plans and traditional IRAs do *not* apply to Roth IRAs (Code Sec. 408A(c)(5)).[171] Thus, owners of Roth IRAs are not required to take distributions by April 1 of the year following the calendar year in which they attain age 70½. As a general rule, the *post-death* RMD rules do apply to Roth IRAs (Reg. § 1.408A-6, Q&A-14). If the sole beneficiary is the decedent's spouse, the spouse may delay distributions until the decedent would have attained age 70½ or may treat the Roth IRA as his or her own.

Nonqualified Distributions. When an individual receives a nonqualified distribution from a Roth IRA, a portion of the distribution may be includible in gross income. In order to determine the amount that is includible in gross income, specific ordering rules are applied under which regular Roth contributions are deemed to be withdrawn first, then amounts transferred from traditional IRAs starting with amounts first transferred (Code Sec. 408A(d)(4)). Withdrawals of transferred amounts are then treated as coming first from amounts that were included in income. Earnings are treated as withdrawn after contributions (Reg. § 1.408A-6, Q&A-8). Thus, no amount is includible in gross income until all the after-tax contributions have been distributed. If an individual receives a nonqualified distribution from a Roth IRA that is includible in gross income, then the 10-percent additional tax for early distributions will generally apply. However, the same exceptions that apply to early distributions from traditional IRAs (¶ 2169) will also apply to the nonqualified Roth IRA distributions.

Reporting Roth IRA Distributions. Distributions from Roth IRAs are reported on Form 8606. If the 10-percent additional tax on early distributions applies, it is reported on Form 5329.

2175. Rollovers and Conversions of Roth IRAs. Taxpayers can make qualified rollover contributions to a Roth IRA (¶ 2171) from another Roth IRA, a traditional IRA (¶ 2155), and from certain qualified retirement plans (Code Sec. 408A(c)(6) and (e)).[172] However, unlike rollovers to traditional IRAs (¶ 2145), qualified rollovers to Roth IRAs may result in the inclusion in income of an amount equal to the amount that would be includible if it were not part of a qualified rollover distribution.

Rollovers from Roth IRAs. In the case of a qualified rollover from another Roth IRA, amounts distributed from the Roth IRA must be contributed either to the same or to another Roth IRA within 60 days of receiving the distribution. Once a qualified rollover has been made, any other distributions received within the twelve months after the distribution rolled over is received cannot also be rolled over.

References are to Standard Federal Tax Reports; Tax Research Consultant; and Practical Tax Explanations.

[170] ¶ 18,925; RETIRE: 66,758; § 25,525.10

[171] ¶ 18,925; RETIRE: 66,758; § 25,525.10

[172] ¶ 18,925; RETIRE: 66,760; § 25,530

Conversions of Traditional IRAs. A taxpayer can convert a traditional IRA to a Roth IRA as long as the amount contributed to the Roth IRA satisfies the definition of a qualified rollover contribution for a traditional IRA (¶ 2167) (Code Sec. 408A(e); § 1.408A-4).[173] Generally, amounts transferred or converted from a traditional IRA into a Roth IRA must be included in gross income for the tax year in which the amount is distributed or transferred to the extent it does not represent a return of basis.

The 10-percent additional tax on early distributions does not apply to the taxable conversion amount. However, if within the five-year period starting with the year in which an individual made a conversion contribution of an amount from a traditional IRA to a Roth IRA, the individual takes a distribution from a Roth IRA of an amount that is attributable to the portion of the conversion contribution that was included in income, then the individual will be liable for the 10-percent additional tax unless one of the exceptions to the tax applies (¶ 2169) (Reg. § 1.408A-6, Q&A-5).[174] The five-year period is separately determined for each conversion contribution made to a Roth IRA. Individuals can correct a failed Roth conversion by making a proper recharacterization election (¶ 2177).

Rollovers from Qualified Plans. Distributions from qualified retirement plans (¶ 2145), 403(b) annuity plans (¶ 2191), or 457 plans (¶ 2193) can be rolled over directly into a Roth IRA. Such rollovers are treated the same as under the conversion rules for traditional IRAs, though rollovers from designated Roth accounts are treated as rollovers from another Roth IRA (Notice 2009-75). In addition, the rollover contribution must meet the rollover requirements applicable to the specific type of retirement plan.

A plan participant who rolls over a distribution that includes both pre-tax and after-tax contributions may allocate the pre-tax amounts to a different destination than the post-tax amounts. For example, a plan participant may allocate pre-tax amounts to a traditional IRA and post-tax amounts to a Roth IRA as long as the participant re-contributes the amounts within 60-days of distributions. For distributions on or after September 18, 2014, this rule applies to direct trustee-to-trustee transfers as well, so plan participants can take advantage of it without having to pay withholding (Notice 2014-54).[175]

2177. Recharacterization of IRA Contributions. An individual who has made contributions to a traditional IRA (¶ 2155) or Roth IRA (¶ 2171) may later decide that a contribution to an IRA of the other type is more advantageous. If certain requirements are met, the contribution can be recharacterized and treated as having been originally made to the desired type of IRA (Code Sec. 408A(d)(6); (Reg. § 1.408A-5).[176] Recharacterizing an IRA contribution requires transferring amounts previously contributed to a traditional or Roth IRA (plus any resulting net income or minus any resulting net loss) to a new IRA of the opposite type and electing to have the amounts treated as having been transferred to the second IRA at the time they actually were contributed to the first IRA. The transfer must be from trustee to trustee. Generally, taxpayers have until the due date, including extensions, of the tax return for the year in which the contribution was made to make the recharacterization. A recharacterization must be reported on the taxpayer's tax return as directed by Form 8606, along with a statement explaining the nature of the recharacterization (IRS Pub. 590-A). Once a Roth IRA has been recharacterized back to a (new) traditional IRA, the (new) traditional IRA can be (re)converted back to a Roth IRA, provided the taxpayer meets the eligibility requirements in the reconversion year (¶ 2179).

2179. Roth IRA Reconversions. A reconversion is a conversion from a traditional IRA (¶ 2155) to a Roth IRA (¶ 2171) of an amount that had previously been recharacterized as a contribution to the traditional IRA after having been earlier converted to a Roth IRA (¶ 2177). An IRA owner who converts an amount from a traditional IRA to a Roth IRA during any tax year and then transfers that amount back to a traditional IRA by

References are to Standard Federal Tax Reports; Tax Research Consultant; and Practical Tax Explanations.

[173] ¶ 18,925, ¶ 18,927B; RETIRE: 66,760; § 25,515.05

[174] ¶ 18,925, ¶ 18,928; RETIRE: 66,760; § 25,515.15

[175] ¶ 18,922.0343; RETIRE: 3,314; § 24,455.20

[176] ¶ 18,925, ¶ 18,927D; RETIRE: 66,762; § 25,520.05

means of a recharacterization may not reconvert that amount from the traditional IRA to a Roth IRA before the *later* of:

- the beginning of the tax year following the tax year in which the amount was converted to a Roth IRA; or
- the end of the 30-day period beginning on the day on which the IRA owner transfers the amount from the Roth IRA back to a traditional IRA by means of a recharacterization (regardless of whether the recharacterization occurs during the tax year in which the amount was converted to a Roth IRA or the following tax year) (Reg. § 1.408A-5, Q&A-9(a)(1)).[177]

SIMPLE Plans and SEPs

2181. SIMPLE IRA Plans. An eligible small employer (¶ 2187) may adopt a Savings Incentive Match Plan for Employees (SIMPLE) IRA retirement plan for its employees (Code Sec. 408(p)).[178] A SIMPLE IRA plan is a written salary reduction agreement that lets eligible employees elect to have the employer make payments as elective contributions to a SIMPLE IRA of the employee or to the employee directly in cash. The plan may be designed so that elective contributions are made only if the employee affirmatively elects to have them made or as an automatic contribution unless the employee affirmatively opts out (Notice 2009-66). The employer is required to make contributions to its employees' SIMPLE IRAs as either matching contributions of up to three percent of compensation or as nonelective contributions. No contributions other than the employee's salary reduction contributions and employer contributions may be made to a SIMPLE IRA. However, a rollover from another SIMPLE IRA may be received (Code Sec. 408(d)(3)(G)).[179] See ¶ 2183 for a discussion of employee and employer contributions to a SIMPLE IRA.

All contributions under a SIMPLE IRA plan must be made to SIMPLE IRA set up by the employer for each eligible employee. A SIMPLE IRA must meet the same requirements that apply to traditional IRAs (¶ 2155). It may not be designated as a Roth IRA (¶ 2171), but contributions to a SIMPLE IRA are not taken into account in determining the Roth IRA contribution limit (Code Sec. 408A(f)). Each eligible employee must have the right to elect during the 60-day period preceding the beginning of any calendar year (and the 60-day period preceding the employee's first day of eligibility) to participate in the plan for that calendar year or to modify the amount of his or her elective contributions for that calendar year (Code Sec. 408(p)(5)).[180] In addition, an employee may terminate participation in the SIMPLE plan at any time during a calendar year. However, the plan may prohibit reentry until the beginning of the following calendar year.

Distributions from a SIMPLE IRA are taxable to the employee (or the beneficiary or estate of the employee) under the same rules that govern distributions from traditional IRAs (¶ 2163) (Code Sec. 402(h)(3) and (k)).[181] This includes the 10-percent additional tax that applies to early distributions from an IRA (¶ 2169) except that the tax is increased to 25 percent when the employee takes an early distribution within two years after the employee's first participation in a SIMPLE IRA plan (Code Sec. 72(t)(6); Notice 98-4).[182] The two-year period begins on the first day on which contributions made by the individual's employer are deposited in the individual's SIMPLE IRA. If the employee has participated in the SIMPLE IRA for at least two years, a distribution may be rolled over (¶ 2167) into other types of retirement plans including qualified employer-provided retirement plans (¶ 2111), 403(b) annuity plans (¶ 2191), and 457 plans (¶ 2193). If the employee has not participated in the SIMPLE plan for two years, the distribution may only be rolled over into another SIMPLE plan (Code Sec. 408(d)(3)(G)).[183]

References are to Standard Federal Tax Reports; Tax Research Consultant; and Practical Tax Explanations.

[177] ¶ 18,927D; RETIRE: 66,764; § 25,520.15

[178] ¶ 18,902; RETIRE: 63,550; § 25,101

[179] ¶ 18,902; RETIRE: 63,756; § 25,145.10

[180] ¶ 18,902; RETIRE: 63,606; § 25,125.05

[181] ¶ 18,202; RETIRE: 63,756; § 25,145.10

[182] ¶ 6102, ¶ 18,922.40; RETIRE: 63,756; § 25,145.10

[183] ¶ 18,902; RETIRE: 63,756; § 25,145.10

Establishing SIMPLE IRAs. The IRS has issued two model forms that may be used by employers that want to establish a SIMPLE IRA for their employees. Form 5304-SIMPLE is used when the employer permits each employee to choose the financial institution that will receive the SIMPLE IRA contributions. Form 5305-SIMPLE is used when the employer designates the financial institution that will receive the contributions. In that case, an employee must be given a reasonable period of time each year in which to transfer his or her SIMPLE IRA balance without cost or penalty from the designated financial institution to a SIMPLE IRA at another financial institution. Both forms also contain information that can be used to notify employees of the existence of the plan. Although the completed forms do not have to be filed with the IRS, they must be kept in order to show that the plan was adopted by the employer.

2183. SIMPLE IRAs—Employee and Employer Contributions. Contributions to an employee's SIMPLE IRA (¶ 2181) are limited to: (1) employee contributions made under a salary reduction agreement, and (2) employer contributions that are made as either matching contributions or nonelective contributions (Code Sec. 408(p)(2)).[184] However, a rollover from another SIMPLE IRA may be received (Code Sec. 408(d)(3)(G)).[185] A rollover may also be received from another plan (including traditional IRAs, SEP plans, qualified plans, tax-favored annuity plans, and nonqualified deferred compensation plans for state and local government employees) after an initial period of two years for contributions made after December 18, 2015 (Code Sec. 408(p)(1))).

Employee Contributions. An employee's elective contributions to a SIMPLE IRA under a salary reduction agreement are limited to $12,500 for 2016 ($12,500 for 2017) (Code Sec. 408(p)(2); Notice 2015-75; Notice 2016-62).[186] In addition, employees who will be at least age 50 by the end of the year are allowed to make additional catch-up contributions of $3,000 for 2016 ($3,000 for 2017) (Code Sec. 414(v)). The maximum dollar limit is the only limit on employee contributions. An employer may not place a limit on the percentage of salary an employee may elect to defer in the plan (except in order to comply with the annual dollar limit). The employer must deposit the employee's elective contributions into the SIMPLE IRA within 30 days after the end of the month in which the amounts would have been paid to the employee. Elective contributions by an employee are fully vested when made (Code Sec. 408(p)(3)).[187]

Matching Contributions. If an employee makes an elective contribution to a SIMPLE IRA, then the employer generally must make a matching contribution in an amount not exceeding three percent of the employee's compensation for the calendar year (¶ 2185). An employer may elect to limit its matching contribution to a smaller percentage of compensation but not less than one percent. The election may *not* be made by an employer in more than two out of every five years. If the SIMPLE account did not exist during the full five-year period, the election may still be made in up to two of the years in which it did exist. Employees must be notified of the employer's election to contribute less than three percent a reasonable time before the beginning of the 60-day period at the end of each calendar year during which employees designate the amount of their election contributions for the following calendar year. Matching contributions to SIMPLE IRAs that are made on behalf of self-employed individuals are not treated as elective contributions made by the individuals (Code Sec. 408(p)(9)).

> **Example 1:** Ralph, age 52, participates in his employer's SIMPLE IRA plan and for 2016 his salary will be $50,000. He elects to defer the maximum amount into the plan ($15,500). Under the plan, the employer makes a maximum matching contribution for each participating employee, up to the three percent limit. Therefore, the employer will make a $1,500 ($50,000 × three percent) matching contribution to Ralph's SIMPLE IRA.

References are to Standard Federal Tax Reports; Tax Research Consultant; and Practical Tax Explanations.

[184] ¶ 18,902; RETIRE: 63,652, RETIRE: 63,654.05; § 25,145.10

[185] ¶ 18,902; RETIRE: 63,756; § 25,145.10

[186] ¶ 18,902; RETIRE: 63,650; § 25,120.10

[187] ¶ 18,902; RETIRE: 63,612, RETIRE: 63,614; § 25,130.05

Nonelective Contributions. Instead of making matching contributions, an employer may elect to make nonelective contributions of two percent of the compensation for each employee who is eligible to participate in the plan and who has at least $5,000 of compensation from the employer for the calendar year (Code Sec. 408(p)(2)(B)).[188]

> **Example 2:** Assume the same facts as in Example 1 above, except that Ralph's employer decided to base its contributions on the nonelective contributions option. In this situation, Ralph would still be allowed to contribute $15,500 to his SIMPLE IRA. However, the employer's contribution would be $1,000 ($50,000 × two percent).

Vesting. The employee's right to both matching contributions and nonelective contributions of the employer (and the earnings on these contributions) in a SIMPLE IRA must be fully vested at all times (Code Sec. 408(p)(3)).[189]

Employer's Deduction. An employer can deduct SIMPLE IRA contributions in the tax year with or within which the calendar year for which the contributions were made ends. Contributions for a particular tax year may be deducted if they are made for that tax year and are made by the due date, including extensions, of the employer's tax return for that year (Code Sec. 404(m)).[190]

2185. SIMPLE 401(k) Plans. An eligible small employer (¶ 2187) may adopt a Savings Incentive Match Plan for Employees (SIMPLE) retirement plan as part of a 401(k) plan (¶ 2104). A SIMPLE 401(k) is a simplified plan which generally must meet the same requirements that apply to other 401(k) plans except that in lieu of satisfying the nondiscrimination test for elective deferrals and matching contributions (¶ 2123), a SIMPLE 401(k) plan must satisfy the following requirements and also will not be subject to the rules for top-heavy plans (¶ 2132).

Employee Contributions. Each employee eligible to participate in the SIMPLE 401(k) plan must have the right to make annual elective contributions, expressed as a percentage of compensation but not exceeding $12,500 for 2016 ($12,500 for 2017) (Code Sec. 401(k)(11)(B); Notice 2015-75; Notice 2016-62).[191] An employee age 50 or over may make an additional catch-up contribution of $3,000 for 2016 ($3,000 for 2017) (Code Sec. 414(v)). Nondeductible employee contributions and rollover contributions may not be made to a SIMPLE 401(k).

Employer Contributions. The employer generally must make matching contributions for each participant in a SIMPLE 401(k) in an amount not exceeding three percent of the employee's compensation (Code Sec. 401(k)(11)(B)).[192] Instead of making matching contributions, an employer may elect to make nonelective contributions of two percent of compensation for each employee who is eligible to participate in the arrangement and who has at least $5,000 of compensation. Employees must be notified that the employer has chosen to make the two-percent contribution within a reasonable period of time before the 60th day before the beginning of the calendar year.

Compensation. SIMPLE compensation means the sum of wages, tips, and other compensation from the eligible employer subject to federal income tax withholding. It also includes the employee's elective contributions made under any other qualified plan, including a SIMPLE IRA plan, a salary reduction simplified employee pension (SARSEP), a 403(b) annuity plan, and compensation deferred under a section 457 plan required to be reported by the employer on Form W-2. For self-employed individuals, SIMPLE compensation means net earnings from self-employment determined prior to subtracting any contributions made under the SIMPLE 401(k) plan on behalf of the individual (Reg. § 1.401(k)-4(e)(5)).[193]

References are to Standard Federal Tax Reports; Tax Research Consultant; and Practical Tax Explanations.

[188] ¶ 18,902; RETIRE: 63,654.10; § 25,120.20

[189] ¶ 18,902; RETIRE: 63,612, RETIRE: 63,614; § 25,130.05

[190] ¶ 18,330; RETIRE: 63,700; § 25,145.15

[191] ¶ 17,502; RETIRE: 27,102.20; § 24,720.15

[192] ¶ 17,502; RETIRE: 3,350; § 24,720.15

[193] ¶ 18,111F; RETIRE: 3,350; § 24,720.15

Employer's Deduction. An employer's deduction for contributions to a defined contribution plan is generally limited to the *greater* of: (1) 25 percent of the compensation paid or accrued during the tax year to beneficiaries under a stock bonus or profit-sharing plan, or (2) the amount that the employer is required to contribute to a SIMPLE 401(k) plan for the year (Code Sec. 404(a)(3)(A)(i)).[194] Thus, an employer's deduction for its contributions to a SIMPLE 401(k) may be greater than the general limit of 25 percent of compensation paid (¶ 2119).

Vesting. All contributions to a SIMPLE 401(k) must be fully vested when made, and the plan cannot impose any restrictions on withdrawals (Code Sec. 401(k)(11)(A)).[195]

Establishing a SIMPLE 401(k). The IRS has issued a model amendment that may be used by employers that want to adopt a plan that contains a SIMPLE 401(k) plan (Rev. Proc. 97-9).[196] The model amendment includes provisions for employee contributions, employer options concerning its contributions, and notification to employees.

2187. SIMPLE Plans—Eligible Employers and Employees. A SIMPLE IRA plan (¶ 2181) or SIMPLE 401(k) (¶ 2185) may only be established by an employer that has 100 or fewer eligible employees who received at least $5,000 in compensation during the preceding tax year (Code Secs. 401(k)(11)(D) and 408(p)(2)(C)(i)).[197] Any type of employer can establish a SIMPLE plan, including tax-exempt entities, governmental entities, and employers of domestic workers even though the compensation of domestic workers may not be subject to income tax withholding. The employer may generally not make contributions to any other qualified plan starting with the year the SIMPLE plan goes into effect. However, employers may adopt a SIMPLE plan for noncollectively bargained employees and at the same time maintain a qualified plan for collectively bargained employees (Code Sec. 408(p)(2)(D)).[198]

If the employer has established a SIMPLE plan, an employee must be eligible to participate in any calendar year if he or she received at least $5,000 of compensation from the employer during *any* of the *two* preceding calendar years and is reasonably expected to receive at least $5,000 in compensation during the current calendar year (Code Sec. 408(p)(4)).[199] Nonresident alien employees and employees covered by a collective bargaining agreement may be excluded from participation.

If an individual is not self-employed, compensation means the amount wages, tips, and other compensation from the employer subject to income tax withholding (¶ 2604), and the total amount of elective deferrals to qualified retirement plans (¶ 2121) including deferrals to 401(k) plans, 403(b) annuity contract, and salary reduction SEP (SARSEP), as well as elective contributions made under a SIMPLE IRA plan and section 457 plan (Code Sec. 408(p)(6); Notice 98-4).[200] Compensation does not include amounts deferred under a cafeteria plan (¶ 2045).

A self-employed individual is treated as an employee and may participate in a SIMPLE plan if the minimum compensation requirement is met (Code Sec. 408(p)(6)).[201] For this purpose, compensation means net earnings from self-employment from Schedule SE of Form 1040 before subtracting any contributions made to a SIMPLE IRA. A self-employed individual who has elected out of the self-employment tax on religious grounds (¶ 2667) may base his or her retirement plan contributions, including contributions to SIMPLE IRAs, on his or her self-employment income that is exempt from self-employment tax.

2189. Simplified Employee Pensions (SEPs). A simplified employee pension (SEP) is an arrangement under which an employer makes contributions to the IRAs of each of its employees (Code Sec. 408(k)).[202] Annual contributions by an employer to a

References are to Standard Federal Tax Reports; Tax Research Consultant; and Practical Tax Explanations.

[194] ¶ 18,330; RETIRE: 63,700; § 24,305.15

[195] ¶ 17,502; RETIRE: 3,350; § 24,720.25

[196] ¶ 18,112.80; RETIRE: 3,352; § 24,720.35

[197] ¶ 17,502, ¶ 18,902; RETIRE: 3,350, RETIRE: 63,552; § 24,720.10 § 25,110.05

[198] ¶ 18,902; RETIRE: 63,552; § 25,110.15

[199] ¶ 18,902; RETIRE: 63,602; § 25,115.05

[200] ¶ 18,902, ¶ 18,922.40; RETIRE: 63,602; § 25,115.05

[201] ¶ 18,902; RETIRE: 63,602; § 25,115.05

[202] ¶ 18,902; RETIRE: 63,050; § 25,005

SEP are excluded from the employee's gross income to the extent that the contributions do not exceed the *lesser* of 25 percent of the participant's compensation or $53,000 for 2016 ($54,000 for 2017) (Code Sec. 402(h); Notice 2015-75; Notice 2016-62).[203] The maximum amount of compensation that may be considered is $265,000 for 2016 ($270,000 for 2017). If the employer exceeds the annual limit on contributions, the employee is generally taxed on the amount of the excess contribution and subject to a six-percent excise tax if not withdrawn (¶ 2161). In the case of a SEP established by an unincorporated employer, the compensation of a self-employed participant (partner or proprietor) is earned income.

The employer must decide each year whether and how much to contribute to a SEP plan. If any contribution is made to a plan, nondiscriminatory employer contributions must be made for each employee who has reached age 21, performed services for the employer during at least three of the immediately preceding five years, and received at least $600 for 2016 ($600 for 2017) (Code Sec. 408(k)(2); Notice 2015-75; Notice 2016-62).[204] Unlike traditional IRAs, the account owner of a SEP-IRA can make contributions after reaching age 70½ (Code Sec. 219(b)(2)).

In order to deduct its SEP contributions for a particular year, the employer must make the contributions by the due date, including extensions, of its tax return for that tax year (Code Sec. 404(h)).[205] The contributions are made to the SEP-IRAs that have been established by, or for, each eligible employee. Although the employer's deduction cannot exceed 25 percent of the employee's compensation (¶ 2119), any excess can be carried over and deducted in later years subject to the percentage limitation. In addition, when an employer maintains another type of defined contribution plan, the contributions to a SEP must be taken into account when determining compliance with the annual limit imposed on deductible contributions to the plans.

Employee Contributions. In plan years beginning before 1997, an employer could include a salary reduction agreement (cash or deferred arrangement) as part of its SEP—commonly know as SARSEP. New SARSEPs cannot be established after 1996 (Sec. 1421(c) of Small Business Job Protection Act of 1996 (P.L. 104-188)).[206] However, SARSEPs established before 1997 are allowed to continue and take on new participants. SARSEPs are generally subject to the same elective contribution rules as 401(k) plans (¶ 2121) after an initial period of two years for contributions made after December 18, 2015.

Establishing a SEP-IRA. Most employers are able to establish a SEP plan by completing a Form 5305-SEP. The form is *not* filed with the IRS, but it is retained by the employer as evidence that a SEP plan has been established. All eligible employees must be given a copy of the Form 5305-SEP. Certain employers should not use Form 5305-SEP, e.g., employers that are currently maintaining another qualified plan or use the services of leased employees. An employer may establish a SEP-IRA for a particular year as late as the due date, including extensions, for its income tax return for that year.

Distributions. Distributions from a SEP are taxed under the rules that apply to distributions from a traditional IRA (¶ 2163) (Code Secs. 402(h)(3) and 408(d)).[207]

Top-Heavy SEP. If a SEP is top heavy (¶ 2132), each participant who is not a key employee must be provided with a contribution that is not less than three percent of his or her compensation. If the rate for the key employee receiving the largest contribution is less than three percent, the contribution rate for that employee is used to determine the minimum contribution for non-key employees (Code Sec. 408(k)(1)(B)).[208]

Sec. 403(b), Sec. 457, and Nonqualified Plans

2191. Sec. 403(b) Plans (Tax Sheltered Annuities). A public school system or tax-exempt educational, charitable, or religious organization may provide retirement benefits for its employees through the purchase of annuities or by contributing to a custodial

References are to Standard Federal Tax Reports; Tax Research Consultant; and Practical Tax Explanations.

[203] ¶ 18,202; RETIRE: 63,050; § 25,015

[204] ¶ 18,902; RETIRE: 63,102; § 25,010.10

[205] ¶ 18,330; RETIRE: 63,202, RETIRE: 63,204; § 25,015

[206] ¶ 18,902; RETIRE: 63,150; § 25,020

[207] ¶ 18,202, ¶ 18,902; RETIRE: 63,256; § 25,010.20

[208] ¶ 18,902; RETIRE: 63,114; § 25,010.30

account invested in mutual funds (Code Sec. 403(b)).[209] This type of retirement plan is commonly referred to as a 403(b) annuity plan or tax-sheltered annuity (TSA). Generally, the employee's rights in the annuity or account must be nonforfeitable.

Limit on Annual Addition. There is a limit imposed on the total amount of the annual addition that may be made to an employee's 403(b) account. This annual limit is sometimes called the maximum amount contributable (MAC). The annual addition or MAC is made up of the following three types of contributions:

- elective contributions made by the employee,
- nonelective contributions made by the employer, and
- after-tax contributions made by the employee (Code Sec. 403(b)(1)).[210]

Generally, the annual addition cannot be more than the *lesser* of 100 percent of the employee's compensation or $53,000 for 2016 ($54,000 for 2017) (¶ 2115). There are also limits on the amount of elective deferrals that generally apply to all of an employee's deferrals (¶ 2121) under any 403(b) annuity plan, 401(k) plan, SIMPLE 401(k) (¶ 2185), and SEP (¶ 2189). Employees are not required to coordinate their maximum deferral under a 457 plan (¶ 2193) with their contributions made to 403(b) plans. Employees who will be at least age 50 by the end of the year may make catch-up contributions to a 403(b) plan. The maximum catch-up contribution to a 403(b) plan is $6,000 for 2016 ($6,000 for 2017) (Code Sec. 414(v); Notice 2015-75; Notice 2016-62). Qualified employees of certain organizations, e.g., schools, hospitals, churches, and home health service organizations, who are covered by an annuity contract under a 403(b) plan may defer additional amounts of their compensation (Code Sec. 402(g)(7)).[211] For this purpose, a qualified employee is one who has completed 15 years of service with the organization.

Distributions. Payments to an employee from a 403(b) plan are taxed under the annuity rules (¶ 817). However, any employee contributions that were excluded from wages are not treated as part of the employee's investment in the contract. Distributions may generally be made because of the employee's death, disability, severance from employment, attainment of age 59½, or financial hardship (Code Sec. 403(b)(7)(A) and (b)(11)).[212] Distributions that do not meet these requirements are subject to the 10-percent additional tax on early distributions (¶ 2151). The required minimum distribution (RMD) rules also apply (¶ 2127) (Code Sec. 403(b)(10); § 1.403(b)-6(e)).[213]

Rollovers. Distributions from a 403(b) annuity plan may be rolled over into an IRA or another 403(b) plan, as well as to other types of qualified employer-provided retirement plans to the extent they accept rollover contributions (Code Sec. 403(b)(8)).[214] The spousal rollover rules that apply to other types of employer sponsored plans and the written explanation requirements also apply to a beneficiary under a qualified annuity plan (Code Sec. 403(a)(4)(B)). A 403(b) plan that includes a qualified Roth contribution program may permit a qualified rollover contribution from a participant's non-Roth account to the participant's designated Roth account within the same plan (Code Sec. 402A(c)(4)(B)).

2193. Sec. 457 Plans (Deferred Compensation Plans of Exempt Employers). Special rules apply to certain deferred compensation plans sponsored by state and local governments and private tax-exempt organizations, commonly referred to as 457 plans (Code Sec. 457(a)).[215] Under a state or local government plan, compensation deferred under the plan is only included in income when it is paid to the employee. However, for plans of tax-exempt organizations, deferred compensation is includible when paid or made available. As with other types of qualified retirement plans, special requirements have to be met by 457 plans.

References are to Standard Federal Tax Reports; Tax Research Consultant; and Practical Tax Explanations.

[209] ¶ 18,270; RETIRE: 69,050; § 25,201

[210] ¶ 18,270; RETIRE: 69,200; § 25,215.05

[211] ¶ 18,202; RETIRE: 69,204; § 25,215.15

[212] ¶ 18,270; RETIRE: 69,250; § 25,230.10

[213] ¶ 18,270, ¶ 18,278H; RETIRE: 69,254; § 25,230.05

[214] ¶ 18,270; RETIRE: 69,260; § 25,230.20

[215] ¶ 21,531; COMPEN: 15,150; § 25,301

Availability of Benefits. Compensation is deferred for any calendar month under a 457 plan only if an agreement providing for deferral is entered into before the beginning of that month (Code Sec. 457(b)(4); Reg. § 1.457-7(c)).[216] Benefits are not considered to be made available under the plan if the participant or beneficiary may elect, before any benefits become payable, to defer payment of some or all of them to a fixed or determinable future time. In addition, amounts deferred under an eligible plan are not considered to be made available to the participant solely because the individual may choose among various investment options under the plan, whether before or after benefit payments have commenced. After benefits have become payable but before payments have commenced, the participant or beneficiary may elect to defer them to a date later than that originally elected. Only one such election may be made (Code Sec. 457(e)(9)(B)).[217]

Limitation on Deferral. The maximum amount that can be deferred under a 457 plan is the *lesser* of 100 percent of the participant's includible compensation or $18,000 for 2016 ($18,000 for 2017) (Code Sec. 457(e)(15); Notice 2015-75; Notice 2016-62).[218] Participants in a 457 plan are permitted to make additional deferrals of income for one or more of the last three tax years that end before normal retirement age (Code Sec. 457(b)(3)). The allowable deferral for such participants is increased, up to a limit of twice the standard dollar amount for the year, by the amount of allowable deferrals not made in previous plan years. Alternatively, employees covered by a 457 plan who will be at least 50 years of age by the end of the year are able to make special catch-up contributions to the plan (Code Sec. 414(v); Notice 2015-75). The maximum catch-up contribution is $6,000 for 2016 ($6,000 for 2017). However, during the last three years of employment that end before attaining normal retirement age, a special formula is used to determine the maximum contribution (Code Sec. 457(e)(18)).

Other Requirements. A 457 plan must satisfy the required minimum distribution (RMD) rules that are generally imposed on qualified plans (¶ 2127) (Code Sec. 457(d)).[219] Distributions of deferred amounts must not be made available before the calendar year in which the participant attains age 70½, is severed from employment, or is faced with an unforeseen emergency. An unforeseeable emergency must be defined in the plan as: (1) a severe financial hardship to the participant that results from a sudden unexpected illness or accident of the participant, or his or her spouse or dependent, or (2) a loss of the participant's property due to casualty or other similar extraordinary and unforeseeable circumstances beyond the control of the participant.

Hardship withdrawals may not be made to the extent that the financial hardship can be relieved by insurance, liquidation of the participant's assets (if liquidation would not cause financial hardship), or by stopping deferrals under the plan. In addition, withdrawal of amounts for unforeseeable emergencies is permitted only to the extent reasonably needed to satisfy the emergency (Reg. § 1.457-6(c)).[220] The need for funds to purchase a new home or to meet the college expenses of the participant's children is *not* an unforeseeable emergency. To the extent allowed under the plan, if the occurrence of an event with regard to the employee's spouse or dependent would be a hardship, the occurrence of the same event with regard to the employee's beneficiary under the plan would also be a hardship (Notice 2007-7, Q&A-5).

Rollovers. An employee participating in a 457 plan may roll over distributions into an IRA, 401(k) plan, and 403(b) annuity plan (Code Sec. 457(e)(16)). Similarly, in some circumstances, assets from these plans may be rolled over into another 457 plan. A 457 plan that includes a qualified Roth contribution program may permit a qualified rollover contribution from a participant's non-Roth account to the participant's designated Roth account within the same plan (Code Sec. 402A(c)(4)(B)).

Roth 401(k) Plans. A 457 plan may allow participants to designate elective deferrals as Roth contributions. An applicable retirement plan for purposes of offering a qualified

References are to Standard Federal Tax Reports; Tax Research Consultant; and Practical Tax Explanations.

[216] ¶ 21,531, ¶ 21,535M; COMPEN: 15,156; § 25,310.10

[217] ¶ 21,531; COMPEN: 15,156; § 25,310.10

[218] ¶ 21,531; COMPEN: 15,152.25; § 25,305.20

[219] ¶ 21,531; COMPEN: 15,152.40; § 25,305.30

[220] ¶ 21,535J; COMPEN: 15,152.40; § 25,305.05

Roth contribution program includes eligible deferred compensation plans offered by state and local governments (Code Sec. 402A(e)(1)(C)). Elective deferrals for these purposes include any elective deferral of compensation by an individual under an eligible deferred compensation plan of an eligible employer that is a state or local government (Code Sec. 402A(e)(2)(B)).

Ineligible Plans. Compensation deferred under a nonqualified deferred compensation plan (¶ 2197) of a state or local government or other tax-exempt organization that is not an eligible 457 plan is includible in the income of a participant or beneficiary for the first tax year in which there is no substantial risk of forfeiture (Code Sec. 457(f)(1)(A) and (2)(E)).[221]

2195. Sec. 457A Plans (Tax-Indifferent Parties). Compensation which is deferred under a nonqualified deferred compensation plan (¶ 2197) of a nonqualified entity is includible in the service provider's gross income when there is no substantial risk of forfeiture of the rights to the compensation (Code Sec. 457A).[222] If the amount of any compensation is not determinable at the time that it is otherwise includible in gross income, then additional taxes apply to such compensation when the amount is determinable and includible in gross income. The increase is 20 percent of the amount of the compensation, plus an interest charge.

A nonqualified entity for this purpose includes a foreign corporation unless substantially all its income is effectively connected with the conduct of a U.S. trade or business (¶ 2429) or is subject to a comprehensive foreign income tax (Code Sec. 457A(b)). It also includes a partnership (domestic or foreign) unless substantially all its income is allocated to persons other than: (1) foreign persons with respect to whom such income is not subject to a comprehensive foreign income tax; and (2) organizations that are exempt from U.S. income tax.

A nonqualified deferred compensation plan of a nonqualified entity is defined in the same manner as for purposes of Code Sec. 409A (¶ 2193), except that it also includes any arrangement under which compensation is based on the increase in value of a specified number of equity units of the service recipient (Code Sec. 457A(d)(3)). Thus, a nonstatutory stock option to purchase service recipient stock is not included, as well as a stock appreciation right that at all times by its terms is settled in service recipient stock (Rev. Rul. 2014-18). Nonqualified deferred compensation includes earnings with respect to previously deferred amounts (Code Sec. 457A(d)(5)). Compensation is not treated as deferred if the service provider receives payment of the compensation not later than 12 months after the end of the first tax year of the service recipient during which the right to the payment of such compensation is no longer subject to a substantial risk of forfeiture.

2197. Nonqualified Deferred Compensation Plans. An employer may maintain a retirement or other deferred compensation plan for a group of selected employees that is not a qualified retirement plan (¶ 2111). Unless certain plan design and funding requirements are met, all compensation deferred under a nonqualified plan for the current year and all preceding tax years is includible in income of plan participants to the extent they are not subject to a substantial risk of forfeiture (¶ 713) and not previously included in gross income (Code Sec. 409A(a)(1)).[223] Any amount included in gross income will also be subject to a penalty of 20 percent of the deferred compensation, plus interest. See ¶ 2199 for a discussion of funding rules for nonqualified plans.

Distributions. To avoid immediate inclusion of deferrals and the penalty, a nonqualified plan must allow distributions only if they are permissible payments triggered by the employee's separation from service from the employer, the employee's death or disability, a time specified under the plan, upon a change in the effective ownership or control of the employer, or in the event of an unforeseeable emergency (Code Sec.

References are to Standard Federal Tax Reports; Tax Research Consultant; and Practical Tax Explanations.

[221] ¶ 21,531; COMPEN: 15,158; § 22,110.20

[222] ¶ 21,537; COMPEN: 15,350, COMPEN: 15,352; § 25,620

[223] ¶ 18,952; COMPEN: 15,050; § 25,601

409A(a)(2)).[224] Distributions to key employees (¶ 2132) resulting from a separation from service must also not be allowed until six months after the separation, unless the former employee dies in the interim.

Actual distributions from a nonqualified plan are included in the income of the employee in the year in which the distributions are made in accordance with the rules applicable to annuities (¶ 817) (Code Secs. 402(b) and 403(c)).[225] If the distributions do not take the form of an annuity, they are considered to be derived first from plan earnings and asset appreciation (taxable gain), rather than from the employee's investment (basis) in the plan. The participant's basis in a nonqualified plan is increased by any amounts included in his or her income for contributions, if any, made by the plan sponsor.

Acceleration of Benefits. A nonqualified plan generally cannot permit the acceleration of the time or schedule of any payment under the plan (Code Sec. 409A(a)(3)).[226] Exceptions are permitted for: domestic relations orders; *de minimis* cash-out provisions; payment of employment taxes; cancellations of deferrals due to disability, hardships, or unforeseen circumstances; and as an offset of debts.

Election Rules. A nonqualified plan must meet certain requirements regarding the participants' elections to defer compensation and to receive distributions (Code Sec. 409A(a)(4)).[227] Compensation for services performed during a tax year generally can be deferred only if the participant's election to defer is made before the close of the preceding tax year. In the case of any performance-based compensation that is based on services performed over a period of at least 12 months, the election may be made no later than six months before the end of the period. For new employees, a deferral election may be made within 30 days after the date the participant becomes eligible to participate. A participant is "new" for this purpose if at least 24 months have passed since the employee was an active participant in the plan or the plan aggregated with the plan.

Reporting. The total amount of deferrals under a nonqualified deferred compensation plan are required to be shown on an individual's Form W-2 or Form 1099-MISC even if the amount of deferred compensation is not currently taxable (Code Secs. 6041(g) and 6051(a)(13)).

2199. Nonqualified Deferred Compensation Plans—Funding Rules. The income tax treatment of contributions to a nonqualified deferred compensation plan (¶ 2197) depends on whether the plan is funded or unfunded. If an employer funds a nonqualified plan with contributions or the payment of premiums for an annuity, it is transferring restricted property to the plan participant under Code Sec. 83 in connection with the performance of services (¶ 713). The plan participant generally must include the contributions or amount of the premiums in gross income in the first year that the rights to the contributions or premium amounts are transferable or are not subject to a substantial risk of forfeiture (Code Secs. 402(b)(1) and 403(c)). If, however, one of the reasons the deferred compensation plan fails to be a qualified deferred compensation plan is the failure to satisfy the minimum participation or coverage requirements (¶ 2112), then highly compensated employees (¶ 2114) must include their vested accrued benefits, reduced by their own investment, in gross income for the tax year with or within which the tax year of the trust ends (Code Sec. 402(b)(4)).[228] Contributions to unfunded deferred compensation plans are discussed at ¶ 723 and ¶ 906.

Employer's Deduction. The employer is entitled to a deduction for contributions to, or premiums paid under, a nonqualified deferred compensation plan on behalf of an employee in the tax year of the employer in which an amount attributable to the contribution is includible in the gross income of the employee (Code Sec. 404(a)(5)).[229] If more than one employee participates, this rule applies only if separate accounts are maintained for each employee.

References are to Standard Federal Tax Reports; Tax Research Consultant; and Practical Tax Explanations.

[224] ¶ 18,952; COMPEN: 15,056; § 25,601

[225] ¶ 18,202, ¶ 18,270; COMPEN: 15,200; § 25,610.10

[226] ¶ 18,952; COMPEN: 15,056.30; § 25,601

[227] ¶ 18,952; COMPEN: 15,060; § 25,601

[228] ¶ 18,202; RETIRE: 39,700; § 24,105.10

[229] ¶ 18,330; COMPEN: 15,250; § 25,605

Plan Income. In the case of a nonqualified plan funded through a trust, the trust is not tax-exempt and the plan's earnings are generally taxable to the trust (Code Sec. 641).[230] The grantor trust rules (¶ 571) ordinarily do not apply to a nonqualified plan. Therefore, the participant is not usually treated as the owner of his or her share of the trust's assets and is not subject to tax on the trust's income. However, if a participant's contributions as of any date exceed the employer's contributions on behalf of the participant, the participant is treated as the owner of the portion of the trust attributable to his or her contributions and is subject to tax on the income from that portion (Reg. § 1.402(b)-1(b)(6)).[231]

Other Funding Rules. If a nonqualified deferred compensation plan uses an offshore trust, or places assets outside the United States, the plan will generally *not* defer the compensation (Code Sec. 409A(b)).[232] Also, if the plan provides that its assets will become restricted to the payment of benefits under the plan if there is a change in the employer's financial health, or if the assets actually become so restricted, the plan will not defer compensation. These rules apply to all deferred compensation, regardless of when it was deferred.

A nonqualified plan will also not defer compensation to the extent of contributions made on behalf of or restricted to benefits for certain employees at a time when the employer or its defined benefit plan are experiencing financial difficulties. This provision applies if the plan is in at-risk status under Code Sec. 430(i), if the plan sponsor is in bankruptcy, and if, during the 12-month period beginning six months before the plan terminates, the plan is underfunded.

References are to Standard Federal Tax Reports; Tax Research Consultant; and Practical Tax Explanations.

[230] ¶ 24,260; PLANIND: 15,064; § 25,610.10

[231] ¶ 18,208; COMPEN: 15,106; § 25,610.10

[232] ¶ 18,952; PLANRET: 3,206.40; § 25,610.20, § 45,040.10

Chapter 22
CORPORATE ACQUISITIONS REORGANIZATIONS LIQUIDATIONS

	Par.
Corporate Division	2201
Corporate Reorganization	2205
Corporate Liquidation	2253
Carryforwards	2277

Corporate Division

2201. Spin-Off, Split-Off, Split-Up, and Splint-Off Exchanges. No gain or loss is recognized by shareholders or security holders upon the receipt of stock or securities of a corporation controlled by the distributing corporation (at least 80-percent stock ownership) in certain distributions known as "spin-offs," "split-offs," "split-ups," or "splint-offs" (Code Sec. 355; Reg. § 1.355-1).[1]

Spin-Off. A spin-off occurs when a corporation distributes pro rata stock or securities in a controlled corporation. Shareholders do not typically surrender any of their stock in the controlling corporation. A new or existing corporation may be used for the spin-off.

Split-Off. In a split-off, a parent corporation distributes to some or all of its shareholders stock in a newly formed or pre-existing controlled corporation, under the same conditions as in a "spin-off," except that the shareholders surrender a part of their stock in the parent corporation for the stock in the controlled corporation. The distribution may be pro rata but usually is not.

Split-Up. In a split-up, the distributing corporation's shareholders surrender all shares held in the distributing corporation and in return receive new shares in two or more subsidiaries the distributing corporation controlled immediately before the distribution. The subsidiaries may be pre-existing or newly formed.

Splint-Off. In a splint-off, some of the distributing corporation's shareholders surrender their shares of the corporation in exchange for stock of a controlled corporation (as in a split-off). Other shareholders receive stock of the controlled corporation pro rata without surrendering any of their stock of the distributing corporation (as in a spin-off).

To attain nonrecognition treatment in a spin-off, split-off, split-up, or splint-off, the distributing and controlled corporations must immediately after the transaction be engaged in the active conduct of a trade or business (Code Sec. 355(b); Reg. § 1.355-3).[2] This requirement does not apply to the distributing corporation if immediately before the distribution, it had no assets other than stock in the controlled corporation. The trade or business must have been actively conducted throughout the five-year period immediately preceding the date of the distribution.

In addition to the active business requirement, the transaction must have a valid corporate business purpose, and it cannot be primarily a tax-avoidance device (Reg. § 1.355-2(b)).[3] If, however, a corporate business purpose can be achieved through a nontaxable transaction that does not involve the distribution of stock of a controlled corporation and which is neither impractical nor unduly expensive, then the separation

References are to Standard Federal Tax Reports; Tax Research Consultant; and Practical Tax Explanations.

[1] ¶ 16,460, ¶ 16,462; REORG: 30,050, REORG: 30,052

[2] ¶ 16,460, ¶ 16,464; REORG: 30,106

[3] ¶ 16,463; REORG: 30,114

is not carried out for that corporate business purpose. Other limitations relate to continuity of interest on the part of the owners (Reg. § 1.355-2(c)),[4] the amount of securities distributed, taxable acquisitions within five years, and receipt of other property or "boot" (Code Sec. 355(a)(3)).[5]

Basis Rules. With an exchange of stock or securities, the basis of the old stock or securities becomes the basis of the new stock or securities ("substituted basis") (Code Sec. 358).[6] If the exchange is partially taxable, the basis of the old stock or securities is decreased by the sum of the money and fair market value of other property or boot received and increased by the amount of gain recognized and the amount treated as a dividend. If any loss is recognized, the basis of the property received is decreased by that amount. If some old stock is retained, the basis is allocated as though the stock were first surrendered and then received in the exchange.

Morris Trust Rules. Restrictions have been imposed on certain spin-offs that follow the fact pattern of *Morris Trust*, SCt, 66-2 USTC ¶ 9718 (Code Sec. 355(e)).[7] If either the controlled or distributing corporation is acquired pursuant to a plan or arrangement in existence on the date of the distribution, gain is generally recognized by the distributing corporation as of the date of the distribution. Recognition can be avoided if more than 50 percent of the historical shareholders retain ownership in the distributing and acquiring corporations. Acquisitions occurring within the four-year period beginning two years before the date of distribution are presumed to have occurred pursuant to a plan or arrangement.

Real Estate Investment Trusts. Nonrecognition treatment generally does not apply to distributions on or after December 7, 2015, if either the distributing corporation or controlled corporation is a real estate investment trust (REIT) (¶ 2326), except where both corporations are REITs or where, at all times during a three-year period ending on the date of distribution, the distributing corporation was a REIT, the controlled corporation is a taxable REIT subsidiary (¶ 2340), and the distributing corporation had control of the controlled corporation (Code Sec. 355(h), as added by the Protecting Americans from Tax Hikes (PATH) Act of 2015 (P.L. 114-113)).

Reporting Requirements. The distributing corporation in a divisive Code Sec. 355 transaction is required to file a statement with its tax return for the year of the distribution (Reg. § 1.355-5).[8] A shareholder or security holder of the distributing corporation that is a significant distributee must also file an information statement with its return for the tax year in which the distribution is received. A significant distributee is any shareholder of the distributing corporation who received stock in the distribution and owned, immediately before the distribution, at least five percent (by vote or value) of the stock of the distributing corporation if the stock owned by the shareholder is publicly traded, or at least one percent (by vote or value) of the distributing corporation's stock if the stock owned by the shareholder is not publicly traded.

The distributing corporation and its shareholders and security holders who are required to file information statements in connection with the Code Sec. 355 transaction must keep records that contain information regarding the amount, basis and fair market value of all property distributed or exchanged in the transaction, and any liabilities assumed or extinguished as part of the transaction.

Corporate Reorganization

2205. Tax-Free Exchange in Reorganization. A corporation that is a party to a reorganization (¶ 2221), as well at its shareholders and security holders, are eligible for nonrecognition of gain or loss on the reorganization exchange. To achieve the favorable tax treatment, reorganization transactions must satisfy strict statutory and nonstatutory requirements (¶ 2209).

A corporation generally recognizes no gain or loss on the exchange of property solely for stock or securities of another corporation if the corporation is a party to the reorganization and the exchange is made pursuant to a plan of reorganization (Code Sec. 361).[9] If the corporation receives other property or money ("boot") in addition to the

References are to Standard Federal Tax Reports; Tax Research Consultant; and Practical Tax Explanations.

[4] ¶ 16,463; REORG: 30,116
[5] ¶ 16,460; REORG: 30,104.05
[6] ¶ 16,550; REORG: 30,152.15
[7] ¶ 16,460, ¶ 16,466.10; REORG: 30,112
[8] ¶ 16,465C; REORG: 30,158
[9] ¶ 16,580; CCORP: 39,302

stock or securities, it does not recognize gain on the exchange if the boot is distributed pursuant to the plan of reorganization. The transferee corporation does not recognize gain or loss on the receipt of property in exchange for its own stock (Code Sec. 1032).[10]

No gain or loss is generally recognized by shareholders or security holders who exchange, pursuant to a plan of reorganization, stock or securities of a corporation that is a party to the reorganization solely for stock or securities of that corporation or another corporation that is a party to the reorganization (Code Sec. 354).[11] However, gain (but not loss) may be recognized on the receipt of boot (Code Sec. 356).[12] The recognized gain equals the lesser of the amount of gain realized on the exchange or the amount of boot received. Gain on the boot is typically capital gain, unless the exchange has the effect of the distribution of a dividend, in which case the boot is taxed as ordinary income (¶ 2237).

Basis Rules. The basis of stock and securities received by a corporate transferor in a reorganization is generally the same as the basis of the property transferred to the acquiring corporation, adjusted for any gain or loss recognized on the exchange and the value of any boot received (Code Sec. 358(a)).[13] The basis of boot received by the transferor corporation from the acquiring corporation is its fair market value at the time of the exchange. Property received by the transferee corporation has the same basis in the hands of the transferee as it had in the hands of the transferor ("carryover basis"), increased by the amount of gain recognized by the transferor on the transfer (Code Sec. 362(b)).[14] The property acquired by the transferee corporation does not take a carryover basis, however, if it consists of stock or securities in a corporation that is a party to the reorganization.

The basis of stock or securities received by shareholders in the reorganization exchange is the same as the basis of stock or securities they surrendered in the exchange (Code Sec. 358(a)).[15] If boot is received, the basis of the nonrecognition property received by a shareholder is equal to the basis of the stock or securities exchanged in the reorganization, increased by the amount of gain recognized and any amount treated as a dividend (¶ 2237), and decreased by the amount of boot received and the amount of any loss recognized on the exchange. The basis determined for nonrecognition stock and securities must be allocated among all classes of stock or securities involved in the transaction. The shareholder's basis in any boot received is its fair market value.

2209. "Reorganization" Defined. A qualified reorganization must fall within one of seven categories—each referred to by a letter corresponding to the statutory provisions of Code Sec. 368 (Code Sec. 368; Reg. § 1.368-2).[16] In each category, there cannot be a tax-free reorganization unless there is an exchange of properties as distinguished from a sale.

Type A reorganization: a statutory merger or consolidation (that is, a merger or consolidation accomplished pursuant to state law or the laws of a foreign jurisdiction, including certain mergers involving disregarded entities) (Reg. § 1.368-2(b));[17]

Type B reorganization: the acquisition by one corporation of the stock of another corporation, in exchange solely for all or a part of its own or its parent's voting stock (¶ 2211), if the acquiring corporation has control of the other corporation immediately after the acquisition, whether or not it had control before the acquisition;

Type C reorganization: the acquisition by one corporation of substantially all of the properties of another corporation (¶ 2217) in exchange solely for all or a part of its own voting stock or its controlling parent's voting stock (¶ 2211), followed by the acquired corporation's distribution of all its property pursuant to the plan of reorganization (unless this requirement is waived by the IRS);

References are to Standard Federal Tax Reports; Tax Research Consultant; and Practical Tax Explanations.

[10] ¶ 29,622; CCORP: 39,304.05
[11] ¶ 16,431; CCORP: 39,252
[12] ¶ 16,490; CCORP: 39,254
[13] ¶ 16,550; CCORP: 39,302.15
[14] ¶ 16,610; CCORP: 39,304.10
[15] ¶ 16,550; CCORP: 39,256
[16] ¶ 16,750, ¶ 16,752; CCORP: 39,052
[17] ¶ 16,752; REORG: 6,050

Type D reorganization: a transfer by a corporation of all or a part of its assets to another corporation if, immediately after the transfer, the transferor and/or one or more of its shareholders (who were shareholders immediately before the transfer) are in control of the corporation to which the assets are transferred, but only if the stock or securities of the corporation to which the assets are transferred are distributed under the plan of reorganization in a transaction described at ¶ 2201 or ¶ 2205;

Type E reorganization: a recapitalization (¶ 2225);

Type F reorganization: a mere change in the identity, form, or place of organization of one corporation; or

Type G reorganization: a transfer by a corporation in bankruptcy of all or part of its assets to another corporation, but only if stock or securities of the transferee corporation are distributed to the shareholders tax free or partially tax free (¶ 2247).

80-Percent Control Test. For purposes of the corporate reorganization rules, the term "control" means the ownership of stock possessing at least 80 percent of the combined voting power of all classes of stock entitled to vote and at least 80 percent of the total number of shares of all other classes of stock of the corporation (Code Sec. 368(c)).[18] The 80-percent control requirement is changed to 50 percent in the case of nondivisive D reorganizations (Code Secs. 304(c) and 368(a)(2)(H)(i)).[19]

In order for the control requirement to be satisfied, it is not necessary that the acquiring corporation acquire 80 percent (or 50 percent) of the target's stock in the reorganization, nor that control be attained in the transactions that constitute the reorganization. Rather, it is sufficient that the acquiring corporation is in control of the target corporation immediately after the transaction (Code Sec. 368(a)(1)(B)).[20] Thus, a corporation can acquire stock in one of its subsidiaries in a tax-free reorganization.

S Corporation Reorganization Using QSubs. When an S corporation merges into a newly formed corporation in a transaction qualifying as a Type F reorganization, the newly formed surviving corporation meets the requirements of an S corporation, and the acquiring corporation elects to treat the transferor S corporation as a qualified subchapter S subsidiary (QSub), the reorganization does not terminate the S election (Rev. Ruls. 64-250 and 2008-18).[21] The QSub must retain and use its employer identification number (EIN) when it is treated as a separate corporation for federal tax purposes.

Triangular Reorganizations. Tax-free reorganizations are often structured as triangular reorganizations, which involve use of a subsidiary to acquire the target corporation. There are five types of triangular reorganizations (Reg. § 1.358-6(b)(2)):[22]

(1) triangular B reorganizations;

(2) triangular C reorganizations;

(3) triangular G reorganizations;

(4) forward triangular mergers (the acquiring corporation uses the stock of its parent to acquire substantially all the properties of the target corporation); and

(5) reverse triangular mergers (parent stock is used to acquire the target corporation, but an acquisition subsidiary of the parent merges into the target, and the target becomes an 80-percent-owned subsidiary of the parent).

2211. Exchange of Stock or Property Solely for Voting Stock. In a B reorganization (¶ 2209), the exchange of stock "solely for voting stock" means that the acquiring corporation cannot use cash or nonvoting stock in the exchange, or the reorganization becomes taxable (Reg. § 1.368-2(c)).[23]

The "solely" requirement is relaxed for a C reorganization (¶ 2209) in that "substantially all the assets" (¶ 2217) must be acquired solely for voting stock. If at least 80 percent of the value of all the property of the transferor corporation is acquired solely for voting stock, the remaining properties may be acquired for money or other property (Code Sec. 368(a)(2)(B)).[24] If the acquiring corporation does transfer money or property

References are to Standard Federal Tax Reports; Tax Research Consultant; and Practical Tax Explanations.

[18] ¶ 16,750; CCORP: 39,052, REORG: 12,054, REORG: 15,058

[19] ¶ 15,375, ¶ 16,750; REORG: 18,052.10

[20] ¶ 16,750; CCORP: 39,052, REORG: 12,054

[21] ¶ 32,053.69; SCORP: 304.10; § 28,920

[22] ¶ 16,552F; REORG: 9,050, REORG: 9,100, REORG: 27,400

[23] ¶ 16,752; REORG: 12,052

[24] ¶ 16,750; REORG: 15,100

in addition to voting stock, then for the purpose of determining whether at least 80 percent of the assets are acquired for voting stock, the amount of any liability assumed by the acquiring corporation or the amount of any liability to which the property acquired is subject is also treated as money paid for the property.

2217. "Substantially All" Requirement in C Reorganizations. What constitutes "substantially all" of the properties of a corporation for purposes of a C reorganization (¶ 2209) is not precisely defined in the Code or regulations. A special rule provides that a reorganization may still qualify as a C reorganization if the acquiring corporation acquires at least 80 percent of all of the target corporation's property solely for voting stock of the acquiring corporation or its parent (Code Sec. 368(a)(1)(C) and (a)(2)(B)).[25] Some courts have held that a transfer of approximately two-thirds in value of the assets, or 68 percent or even 75 percent of all the corporate property, is not "substantially all." Other courts have held that 85.2 percent or even 90 percent, which included all property except cash, is substantially all. The IRS interprets the substantially all requirement, for the purpose of issuing ruling letters, as requiring a transfer of assets representing at least 90 percent of the fair market value of the net assets and at least 70 percent of the fair market value of the corporation's gross assets held immediately before the transfer (Rev. Proc. 77-37).[26]

2221. Party to a Reorganization—Plan of Reorganization. The reorganization provisions provide for the nonrecognition solely of the gains and losses of the parties to reorganization, and their shareholders and security holders (¶ 2205 and ¶ 2229). A party to a reorganization includes a corporation resulting from a reorganization and both corporations in a reorganization resulting from the acquisition by one corporation of stock or properties of another (Code Sec. 368(b); Reg. § 1.368-2(f)).[27] In an A, B, C, or G reorganization (¶ 2209), a party to a reorganization includes a controlling corporation if its stock is exchanged and likewise includes a controlled subsidiary that receives any of the assets or stock exchanged.

A plan of reorganization is required in connection with a tax-free exchange (Reg. § 1.368-2(g)).[28] The plan does not need to be a formal written document. However, the safest practice is to incorporate the plan into the corporate records. The plan may be amended as circumstances change so long as the reorganization remains in compliance with the reorganization requirements (¶ 2209).

2225. Recapitalization. For a transaction to qualify as a recapitalization or E reorganization (¶ 2209), there must be a reshuffling of the capital structure of a corporation (*Southwest Consolidated Corp.*, SCt, 42-1 USTC ¶ 9248).[29] For example, an E reorganization occurs when a corporation discharges outstanding bond indebtedness by issuing preferred stock to the shareholders in exchange for the bonds instead of paying them off in cash, when 25 percent of a corporation's preferred stock is surrendered for cancellation and no-par-value common stock is issued, or when previously authorized but unissued preferred stock is issued in exchange for outstanding common stock (Reg. § 1.368-2(e)).[30]

2229. Receipt of Stock, Securities or Other Property. No gain or loss is generally recognized by a shareholder or security holder if stock or securities in a corporation that is party to a reorganization (¶ 2221) are exchanged solely for stock or securities of another corporation that is also a party to the reorganization, and the exchange is made pursuant to a plan of reorganization (¶ 2209) (Code Sec. 354).[31] This nonrecognition treatment also applies to shareholders or security holders who receive stock or securities of a controlled corporation in a corporate division (¶ 2201) (Code Sec. 355; Reg. § 1.355-1).[32] An exchange of securities in a reorganization or corporate division is tax free only to the extent that the principal amount received does not exceed the principal amount surrendered. Nonrecognition treatment also does not apply if securities are received and no securities are surrendered. The term "securities" is not defined by the

References are to Standard Federal Tax Reports; Tax Research Consultant; and Practical Tax Explanations.

[25] ¶ 16,750; REORG: 15,056

[26] ¶ 16,753.53; REORG: 15,056

[27] ¶ 16,750, ¶ 16,752; CCORP: 39,054

[28] ¶ 16,752; CCORP: 39,056, REORG: 3,200

[29] ¶ 16,753.476; REORG: 24,050

[30] ¶ 16,752; REORG: 24,052

[31] ¶ 16,431; CCORP: 39,250

[32] ¶ 16,460, ¶ 16,462; REORG: 30,152

Code or regulations for this purpose. Under case law, however, an instrument with a term of less than five years generally is not a security.[33]

If a shareholder or security holder receives money or other property ("boot") in the exchange, it can result in gain recognition, dividend treatment (¶ 2237), or in the case of a corporate division, treatment as a corporate distribution (Code Sec. 356).[34] Securities received in a Code Sec. 351 exchange are treated as boot for this purpose (¶ 1731). In addition, nonqualified preferred stock is treated as boot (Code Sec. 351(g)).[35] However, any liabilities of the shareholder or security holder assumed by a party to the organization are not considered boot (¶ 2233).

If no boot is received in a corporate reorganization or division, the shareholders or security holders retain the same basis in the stock or securities they receive that they had in the stock or securities they surrendered in the exchange (Code Sec. 358).[36] If boot is received, the basis of the nonrecognition property received by a shareholder or security holder is equal to the basis of the stock or securities exchanged in the reorganization, increased by the amount of gain recognized and any amount treated as a dividend (¶ 2237), and decreased by the amount of boot received and the amount of any loss recognized on the exchange. The basis determined for nonrecognition stock and securities must be allocated among all classes of stock or securities involved in the transaction. The basis of any boot is its fair market value.

2233. Assumption of Liabilities in Reorganizations. A release from liabilities assumed by a transferee or a disposition of property subject to liabilities in a reorganization (¶ 2209), a transfer of property to a controlled corporation (¶ 1731), or certain bankruptcy reorganizations or foreclosures (¶ 2247) is not money or other property ("boot") received by the taxpayer and does not prevent the transaction from being tax free (Code Sec. 357).[37] However, if the principal purpose of the assumption of liabilities is to avoid income tax, or the purpose is not a bona fide business purpose, the liability assumed is treated as boot (unless the taxpayer can prove to the contrary).

If the liabilities assumed, or to which the property is subject, exceed the total basis of all the properties transferred in a Code Sec. 351 exchange or divisive D reorganization involving a corporate division, the excess is treated as gain from a sale or exchange of a capital asset or a noncapital asset, depending on the nature of the encumbered asset transferred (Code Sec. 357(c)). See ¶ 1669 for a discussion of the basis of property after an assumption of liabilities. A liability is excluded from this exception if the payment of the liability by the transferor would give rise to a deduction or would be basically the equivalent of a payment made in liquidation of the interest of a retiring or deceased partner, unless such liability resulted in the creation of, or the increase in, the basis of any property.

2237. Dividend Distribution in Reorganization. A distribution of money or other property ("boot") to a shareholder as part of a plan of reorganization or in a corporate division (¶ 2229) may be taxed as a dividend if it has the effect of a taxable dividend, even if the money or other property is received in an exchange which is, in part, tax free (Code Sec. 356; Reg. § 1.356-1).[38] The constructive ownership rules discussed at ¶ 743 are applied in determining dividend equivalency. For this purpose, a distribution is taxable as a dividend, not to exceed the recognized gain, to the extent the distributing corporation has earnings and profits sufficient to cover the distribution.

2241. Liquidation as Part of Reorganization. Under a plan of reorganization (¶ 2209), a corporation often acquires for all or part of its stock, all of the stock in another corporation from the shareholders of the latter. As a final step in the reorganization, the acquiring corporation may liquidate the latter corporation, acquiring those assets by surrendering its own stock. This last step in the reorganization may be accomplished tax free under Code Sec. 332 (¶ 2261).

References are to Standard Federal Tax Reports; Tax Research Consultant; and Practical Tax Explanations.

[33] ¶ 16,433.61; CCORP: 39,252.05

[34] ¶ 16,490; CCORP: 39,254

[35] ¶ 16,402; CCORP: 3,102.05

[36] ¶ 16,550; CCORP: 39,256

[37] ¶ 16,520; CCORP: 39,252.15, CCORP: 39,302.20; § 26,125.05

[38] ¶ 16,490, ¶ 16,491; CCORP: 39,254.15

2247. Reorganizations of Bankrupt or Insolvent Corporations. Corporate restructurings ordered pursuant to certain bankruptcy, foreclosure, or similar proceedings may qualify as G reorganizations (¶ 2209) (Code Sec. 368(a)(1)(G)).[39] To qualify for nonrecognition treatment, a G reorganization must meet six requirements:

- the debtor/target corporation must transfer all or part of its assets to an acquiring corporation;
- the transfer must take place in a Title 11 or similar case;
- the stock or securities of the acquiring corporation must be distributed as part of a plan of reorganization;
- there must be continuity of interest;
- there must be continuity of business enterprise; and
- there must be a business purpose for the transaction.

2249. Reporting Requirements. Each corporation that is a party to a reorganization (¶ 2221) must file a statement with its tax return for the tax year of the reorganization exchange (Reg. § 1.368-3(a)).[40]

Certain shareholders and security holders of the target corporation ("significant holders") must also file an information statement with their return for the tax year of the reorganization exchange (Reg. § 1.368-3(b) and (c)).[41] A target shareholder is a significant holder if the shareholder receives stock in the reorganization exchange and owns, before the exchange, at least five percent (by vote or value) of the target's total outstanding stock if the stock owned by the shareholder is publicly traded or at least one percent (by vote or value) of the target's total outstanding stock if the stock owned by the shareholder is not publicly traded. A security holder in the target corporation who receives stock or securities in the exchange is a significant holder and is required to file a statement if, immediately before the exchange, the security holder owned securities in the target with a basis of $1 million or more.

Corporate parties and shareholders and security holders who are required to file information statements in connection with a reorganization must keep records that contain information regarding the amount, basis, and fair market value of all property transferred or exchanged in the transaction, and any liabilities assumed or extinguished as part of the transaction (Reg. § 1.368-3(d)).[42]

Corporate Liquidation

2253. Gain or Loss to Shareholders in Corporate Liquidations. Amounts distributed in a complete liquidation of a corporation are usually treated as full payment in exchange for the stock (Code Sec. 331; Reg. § 1.331-1).[43] The shareholder's gain or loss from a liquidating distribution is determined by comparing the amount distributed to the cost or other basis of the stock. Assuming that the stock is a capital asset, the gain or loss to the shareholder is capital.

If property is received in a distribution in a complete liquidation and gain or loss is recognized on receipt of the property, the basis of the property in the hands of the person receiving it is the fair market value of the property at the time of the distribution (Code Sec. 334(a)).[44] When a parent corporation liquidates an 80-percent controlled subsidiary, the parent corporation's basis in the property received is generally the same as the liquidating subsidiary's basis in the property unless the subsidiary recognizes gain from the transfer (¶ 2261). If property received in a complete liquidation is subject to a liability, the recipient's recognition of gain or loss is adjusted accordingly (¶ 1672).

A distribution that is one of a series of distributions in redemption of all of a corporation's stock pursuant to a plan is treated as a complete liquidation (Code Sec. 346(a)).[45] If a distribution is made as one of a series of distributions intended eventually to result in a complete liquidation of the corporation, no gain is realized by the shareholder until the entire cost of the stock is recovered. If a complete liquidation

References are to Standard Federal Tax Reports; Tax Research Consultant; and Practical Tax Explanations.

[39] ¶ 16,750; REORG: 27,050
[40] ¶ 16,754; REORG: 3,252
[41] ¶ 16,754; REORG: 3,254
[42] ¶ 16,754; REORG: 3,252, REORG: 3,254
[43] ¶ 16,002, ¶ 16,003; CCORP: 27,100; § 26,710
[44] ¶ 16,150; CCORP: 27,122; § 26,710
[45] ¶ 16,351; CCORP: 27,050

covers two or more consecutive tax years, the distribution first offsets the shareholder's basis for the stock and the excess is gain in the year received. The gain is not allocable to all of the years in which distributions were received (Rev. Rul. 85-48).[46]

Partial Liquidation. A distribution of corporate assets to a *noncorporate* shareholder is treated as made in exchange for stock (whether or not stock is actually surrendered) if the distribution is in a partial liquidation of the corporation. The distribution must not be essentially equivalent to a dividend (determined by reference to the effect on the corporation rather than the effect on the shareholders), but rather must be made pursuant to a plan and must occur within the tax year in which the plan is adopted or within the succeeding tax year. A distribution qualifies as a partial liquidation if it is attributable to the corporation ceasing to conduct a trade or business that it actively conducted for at least five years ending with the date of the distribution and if the corporation continues to conduct at least one other trade or business immediately after the distribution (Code Sec. 302(b)(4) and (e)).[47] A corporation may also rely on the common law doctrine of "corporate contraction"—contraction of the business of the corporation—to establish a partial liquidation.

2257. Recognition of Gain or Loss by Corporation in Complete Liquidation. Property distributed in a complete liquidation of a corporation is generally deemed to have been sold by the corporation at its fair market value and any gain or loss is recognized by the liquidating corporation (Code Sec. 336).[48] If the distributed property is subject to a liability or if the distributee assumes a liability upon the distribution, the fair market value of the property is deemed to be no less than the amount of the liability. The following exceptions to this general recognition rule apply:

(1) No gain or loss is recognized upon any distribution of property to shareholders in a tax-free reorganization (¶ 2205 and ¶ 2209), except that gain may be recognized on the distribution of appreciated property that is not a qualified property (Code Secs. 336(c) and 361(c)(4)).[49]

(2) No gain or loss is generally recognized in connection with the complete liquidation of a controlled subsidiary into its parent corporation, except that gain (but not loss) is recognized with respect to any property distributed to minority shareholders (¶ 2261).

(3) No loss is recognized with respect to a distribution of property to a related person within the meaning of Code Sec. 267 (¶ 1717), unless the property (a) is distributed to all shareholders on a pro rata basis, and (b) was not acquired by the liquidating corporation in a Code Sec. 351 transaction or as a contribution to capital during the five years preceding the distribution (Code Sec. 336(d)(1)).[50]

(4) Recognition of loss may be limited if the distributed property was initially acquired by the liquidating corporation, either by tax-free transfer to a controlled corporation or as a contribution to capital, as part of a plan a principal purpose of which was the recognition of loss on the property in connection with the liquidation. In these circumstances, the basis of the property for purposes of determining loss is reduced, but not below zero, by the excess of the adjusted basis of the property on the date of contribution over its fair market value. There is a presumption of a tax-avoidance purpose with respect to any such transfer within the two-year period prior to the adoption of the plan of liquidation (Code Sec. 336(d)(2)).[51]

(5) No gain or loss is recognized if a corporation owning 80 percent or more of the voting power and value of another corporation elects to treat any disposition (sale, exchange, or distribution) of the subsidiary's stock as a disposition of all of the subsidiary's assets (¶ 2263) (Code Sec. 336(e); Reg. §§ 1.336-0—1.336-5).[52]

References are to Standard Federal Tax Reports; Tax Research Consultant; and Practical Tax Explanations.

[46] ¶ 16,004.163; CCORP: 27,108

[47] ¶ 15,325; CCORP: 21,700; § 26,330.05

[48] ¶ 16,200; CCORP: 27,150; § 26,715

[49] ¶ 16,200, ¶ 16,580; CCORP: 27,156

[50] ¶ 16,200; CCORP: 27,160.05; § 26,720.10

[51] ¶ 16,200; CCORP: 27,160.15; § 26,720.15

[52] ¶ 16,200, ¶ 16,201—¶ 16,211; CCORP: 27,250

2259. Reporting Requirements for Complete Liquidations. Certain shareholders of a liquidating corporation who transfer stock to the liquidating corporation in exchange for property must file a statement with their return for the tax year of the liquidating exchange (Reg. § 1.331-1(d)).[53] The statement must include the fair market value and basis of the transferred stock and a description of the property received in the exchange.

The reporting requirement applies to a "significant shareholder"—a shareholder who owns at least five percent (by vote or value) of the liquidating corporation's total outstanding stock if the stock owned by the shareholder is publicly traded or at least one percent (by vote or value) of the liquidating corporation's total outstanding stock if the stock owned by the shareholder is not publicly traded. A shareholder need not file a statement if the property is part of a distribution made pursuant to a resolution providing that the distribution is made in a complete liquidation, and the liquidating corporation is completely liquidated and dissolved within one year after the distribution.

The liquidating corporation must file Form 966 within 30 days after it adopts a plan of liquidation (Code Sec. 6043(a); Reg. §§ 1.6043-1 and 1.6043-2).[54] The liquidating corporation must also file a separate Form 1099-DIV for each shareholder to whom a liquidating distribution of $600 or more is made and furnish a copy to the shareholder.

2261. Liquidation of Subsidiary. If distributions in a complete liquidation are made by a subsidiary to a parent corporation (owning at least 80 percent by value and voting power of the subsidiary), then no gain or loss on the distributions is recognized by either the parent corporation or the liquidating subsidiary (Code Secs. 332 and 337).[55] For this purpose, the 80-percent control requirement must be met by direct ownership and not by reason of the aggregation rules. In addition, property distributed to a controlling domestic corporation in satisfaction of a debt owed by the liquidating subsidiary is treated as a distribution in a complete liquidation for these purposes (Code Sec. 337(b)(1)). However, the distribution of earnings by a U.S. holding company to a foreign corporation in a complete liquidation is treated as a taxable dividend if the U.S. holding company was in existence for less than five years (Code Sec. 332(d)).

If a minority shareholder receives property in such a liquidation, the minority shareholder may recognize gain or loss on the distribution (¶ 2253), while the liquidating corporation may recognize gain, but not loss (¶ 2257). Gain or loss also is recognized on distributions to 80-percent distributees that are foreign corporations (¶ 2492), as well as tax-exempt organizations unless the property is used by that tax-exempt organization in a trade or business unrelated to its exempt purpose (Code Sec. 337(b)(2)).

Basis. After a complete liquidation of a subsidiary, the parent corporation usually holds the distributed assets with the same basis that the assets formerly had in the hands of the subsidiary. However, the basis of the property in the hands of the parent corporation is the fair market value at the time of the distribution if: (1) the subsidiary recognizes gain or loss with respect to the property; or (2) the parent's aggregate adjusted basis in the property exceeds its fair market value immediately after the liquidation in the case of a loss importation transaction where the built-in loss property was not subject to tax in the hands of the subsidiary but is subject to tax in the hands of the parent (Code Sec. 334(b); Reg. § 1.334-1(b)).[56]

Reporting Requirements. The parent corporation must include a statement with its tax return for the year in which it receives a distribution from the liquidating subsidiary (Reg. § 1.332-6(a)).[57] The liquidating subsidiary must timely file Form 966 and its final income tax return (Code Sec. 6043(a); Reg. §§ 1.332-6(b) and 1.6043-1).[58] Both the liquidating subsidiary and the parent corporation must also retain permanent records

References are to Standard Federal Tax Reports; Tax Research Consultant; and Practical Tax Explanations.

[53] ¶ 16,003; CCORP: 27,054

[54] ¶ 35,880, ¶ 35,881, ¶ 35,883; FILEBUS: 9,352, CCORP: 27,054; § 26,740

[55] ¶ 16,050, ¶ 16,225; CCORP: 27,202, CCORP: 27,210; § 26,730.10, § 26,730.20

[56] ¶ 16,150, ¶ 16,151; CCORP: 27,214.05; § 26,730.10

[57] ¶ 16,051E; CCORP: 27,202.30

[58] ¶ 35,880, ¶ 16,051E, ¶ 35,881; FILEBUS: 9,352, CCORP: 27,202.30; § 26,740

regarding the liquidation (Reg. § 1.332-6(d)).[59] These records must specifically include information regarding the amount, basis, and fair market value of the distributed property, and any liability assumed or extinguished as part of the liquidation.

2263. Code Sec. 336(e) Election. A corporation that owns at least 80 percent of the total voting power and 80 percent of the total value of the stock of another corporation (a target corporation) and sells, exchanges, or distributes 80 percent or more of the total voting power and 80 percent or more of the total value of the stock in a qualified stock disposition may make an election to treat the sale, exchange, or distribution as a disposition of all the assets of the target corporation (a Code Sec. 336(e) election). In such circumstance, no gain or loss is recognized on the sale, exchange, or distribution of the stock (Code Sec. 336(e); Reg. § 1.336-2).[60] The Code Sec. 336(e) election is available for qualified stock dispositions occurring on or after May 15, 2013.

A qualified stock disposition is any disposition or series of dispositions in which the seller sells, exchanges, or distributes—or any combination thereof—stock equal to 80 percent or more of the voting power and 80 percent or more of the total value of a domestic target corporation during the 12-month disposition period. Thus, the seller may retain a portion of the target stock. The 12-month disposition period is the 12-month period beginning with the date of the first sale, exchange, or distribution of stock included in a qualified stock disposition (Reg. § 1.336-1(b)).[61]

A disposition is any sale, exchange, or distribution of stock, but only if: (1) the basis of the stock in the hands of the purchaser is not determined by reference to the adjusted basis of the stock in the hands of the person from whom the stock is acquired or from a decedent; (2) the stock is not sold, exchanged, or distributed in a transaction to which Code Sec. 351, 354, 355, or 356 applies and is not sold, exchanged, or distributed in any transaction described in regulations in which the transferor does not recognize the entire amount of the gain or loss realized in the transaction (an exception applies to a distribution of stock to an unrelated person in which the full amount of stock gain would be recognized in certain Code Sec. 355 transactions); and (3) the stock is not sold, exchanged, or distributed to a related person.

Stock disposed of by the seller to another person that is reacquired by the seller during the 12-month disposition period is not considered as disposed of by the seller. If a seller retains any target stock after the 12-month disposition period, the seller is treated as purchasing the retained stock from an unrelated person on the day after the disposition date for its fair market value. The holding period for the retained stock starts on the day after the disposition date. For this purpose, the fair market value of all the target stock equals the grossed-up amount realized on the sale, exchange, or distribution of recently disposed stock of the target corporation.

A seller for this purpose is any domestic corporation that makes a qualified stock disposition of stock of another corporation. A seller includes both a transferor and a distributor of target stock. A purchaser is one or more persons that receive the stock of another corporation in a qualified stock disposition. A target corporation is any domestic corporation the stock of which is sold, exchanged, or distributed by another domestic corporation in a qualified stock disposition.

2265. Acquisition of Stock Treated as Acquisition of Assets. If a corporation (the acquiring corporation) purchases 80-percent control of a second corporation (the target) within a 12-month period, the acquiring corporation may irrevocably elect to have the target treated as if it had sold and purchased its own assets (a Code Sec. 338 election) (Code Sec. 338; Reg. § 1.338-3).[62] If the election is made, the target is treated as a new corporation after the date of acquisition of 80-percent control, holding its assets with a stepped-up basis. The hypothetical sale is deemed to have occurred on the date of acquisition of control.

The target's tax year as the "selling corporation" ends on that date, and its carryovers and other tax attributes disappear. As the "purchasing corporation," the

References are to Standard Federal Tax Reports; Tax Research Consultant; and Practical Tax Explanations.

[59] ¶ 16,051E; CCORP: 27,202.30

[60] ¶ 16,200, ¶ 16,205; CCORP: 27,250

[61] ¶ 16,203; CCORP: 27,250.

[62] ¶ 16,275, ¶ 16,278; CCORP: 30,000

target is treated as if it had purchased the assets on the day following the acquisition date. The target becomes a member of the affiliated group including the acquiring corporation on the day following the acquisition date. Gain or loss is recognized by the target as though it had sold all of its assets at fair market value in a single transaction on the acquisition date. Gain or loss from the deemed asset sale is reported, and recapture items are typically taken into account, on the final return of the "selling corporation." The election is to be made no later than the 15th day of the ninth month beginning after the month in which 80-percent control is acquired. The acquiring corporation is not required to liquidate the target, but if it does, it succeeds to the basis of the target's assets, as increased by the hypothetical purchase.

There are detailed rules to ensure consistency of treatment for acquisitions of stock or assets by and from members of an affiliated group of corporations (Reg. § § 1.338-4(h) and 1.338-8).[63] A consolidated group may treat a sale of its 80-percent-controlled target as a sale of the target's underlying assets. The assets receive a stepped-up basis to fair market value, and the selling consolidated group recognizes gain or loss attributable to the assets, but there is no separate tax on the seller's gain attributable to the stock. This treatment also applies in situations where the selling affiliated group owns 80 percent of the target's stock by value and voting power but does not file a consolidated return (Code Sec. 338(h)(10)).[64]

Carryforwards

2277. Carryovers in Certain Corporate Acquisitions. In a tax-free asset acquisition, certain tax attributes may be transferred or are carried over to the acquiring corporation (Code Sec. 381; Reg. § 1.381(a)-1).[65] This applies to a parent after a complete liquidation of a subsidiary (¶ 2261), as well as to an acquiring corporation after a tax-free A, C, D, F, or G reorganization (¶ 2209). In the case of D and G reorganizations, however, the carryover of certain tax attributes only applies to acquisitive reorganizations, where substantially all of the assets are acquired and distributed, not to divisive reorganizations.

The carryover provisions are mandatory, even though in some cases they work to the disadvantage of the successor. They do not apply after a split-up, split-off, spin-off, or splint-off type of divisive reorganization (¶ 2201) or a partial liquidation. The tax-attribute items covered are listed in Code Sec. 381(c) and include, but are not limited to, net operating losses (NOLs), unused general business credits, capital loss carryovers, method of computing depreciation, and method of accounting. Even if a tax attribute properly carries over to an acquiring corporation, the acquiring corporation's ability to use the attribute may be limited (¶ 2281). If an acquiring corporation makes an election to treat the target corporation as having purchased its own assets (¶ 2265), there is no carryforward of attributes of the subsidiary for the periods prior to the parent's acquisition.

Carrybacks. Carrybacks of net operating losses (¶ 1149) and net capital losses (¶ 1756) are permitted from one corporate entity to another only in the case of an F reorganization—a mere change in identity, form, or place of organization (¶ 2209).

2281. Limitations on Use of Carryforwards in Corporate Acquisitions. After a reorganization or other change in corporate ownership, the use of certain carryforwards may be limited or prohibited (¶ 2277). The carryforwards involved concern:

(1) net operating losses (NOLs);
(2) unused general business credit;
(3) corporate minimum tax credit;
(4) foreign tax credit; and
(5) capital loss carryovers (Code Secs. 382 and 383).[66]

After an ownership change, the amount of *income* that a corporation may offset each year by preacquisition NOL carryforwards (¶ 2285) is generally limited to an amount

References are to Standard Federal Tax Reports; Tax Research Consultant; and Practical Tax Explanations.

[63] ¶ 16,279, ¶ 16,282B; CCORP: 30,300

[64] ¶ 16,275; CCORP: 30,250

[65] ¶ 17,002, ¶ 17,003; REORG: 33,150

[66] ¶ 17,101, ¶ 17,200; REORG: 33,200, REORG: 33,250

determined by multiplying the value of the equity of the corporation just prior to the ownership change by the federal long-term tax-exempt rate (¶ 85) in effect on the date of the change (Code Sec. 382).[67] Any unused limitation may be carried forward and added to the next year's limitation. In addition, NOL carryforwards are eliminated completely unless the business continuity requirements for reorganizations are satisfied for the two-year period following the ownership change. The annual income limitation is reduced by the recognition of any built-in losses and increased by the recognition of built-in gains. An exception to the limitations on NOL carryforwards is provided in bankruptcy situations, with certain restrictions.

Two kinds of ownership changes can trigger the income limitation: a change involving a five-percent shareholder, and any tax-free reorganization other than divisive and F reorganizations (¶ 2209). In either case, one or more of the five-percent shareholders must have increased their percentage of ownership in the corporation by more than 50 percent over their lowest pre-change ownership percentage (generally within three years of the ownership change). Similar rules apply to the other carryforwards, including those for net capital losses, unused general business credit, and foreign taxes (Code Sec. 383; Reg. § 1.383-1).[68]

Pre- and Post-change Allocation. A loss corporation must allocate NOLs or taxable income and net capital loss or gain for the change year between the pre-change period and the post-change period either by: (1) ratably allocating an equal portion to each day in the change year; or (2) electing to treat its books as closed on the date of the change (Reg. § 1.382-6).[69] If a "closing of the books" election is made, the amounts allocated to either period may not exceed the NOL or taxable income and net capital loss or gain for the change year.

Worthless Stock. In order to prevent a double tax benefit, the NOLs of a corporation may not be carried forward after an ownership change if a shareholder with 50-percent-or-more control (prior to the ownership change) claims, within three years, a worthless stock deduction with respect to the stock (Code Sec. 382(g)(4)(D)).[70]

Tax Avoidance Purpose. NOLs and other carryforwards may be disallowed if an acquisition is made with a tax avoidance purpose (¶ 1575).

2285. Limitation on Preacquisition Losses. A corporation (or any member of its affiliated group) may not use its preacquisition losses (net operating losses (NOLs), net built-in losses, net capital losses, and credit carryforwards, ¶ 2281) against the built-in gains of a corporation:

(1) whose assets are acquired in an A, C, or D reorganization (¶ 2209); or

(2) that becomes directly or indirectly controlled (80-percent ownership of its stock by vote and value) by the acquiring corporation.

The restriction generally applies to built-in gains recognized within five years of the acquisition date, unless 50 percent or more of the gain corporation has been owned by the loss corporation (or a member of its group) for five years prior to the acquisition (Code Sec. 384).[71]

The unrealized built-in gains of either the acquired or acquiring corporation are subject to the restriction. It applies to any successor corporation to the same extent as to its predecessor, and all members of the same affiliated group before the acquisition are treated as one corporation.

References are to Standard Federal Tax Reports; Tax Research Consultant; and Practical Tax Explanations.

[67] ¶ 17,101; REORG: 33,200

[68] ¶ 17,200, ¶ 17,204; REORG: 33,250

[69] ¶ 17,111; REORG: 33,208

[70] ¶ 17,101; REORG: 33,200

[71] ¶ 17,300; REORG: 33,300

Chapter 23

SPECIAL CORPORATE STATUS

	Par.
Mutual Funds	2301
Real Estate Investment Trusts	2326
Real Estate Mortgage Investment Conduits	2343
Insurance Companies	2370
Other Special Entities	2383

Mutual Funds

2301. Qualification as a Mutual Fund. Mutual funds (regulated investment companies or RICs) are domestic corporations that act as investment agents for their shareholders, typically investing in corporate and government securities and distributing income earned from the investments as dividends. Mutual funds may escape corporate taxation because, unlike ordinary corporations, they are entitled to claim a deduction for dividends paid (¶ 259) to shareholders against their ordinary income and net capital gain. A corporation qualifies as a mutual fund if it makes an irrevocable election to be treated as such by filing Form 1120-RIC, and it meets all of the following requirements (Code Sec. 851; Reg. § § 1.851-1—1.851-7).[1]

- The corporation must be registered under the Investment Company Act of 1940 as a management company, unit investment trust, business development company, or as a type of common trust fund.
- At least 90 percent of its gross income must be derived from dividends, interest, payments with respect to certain securities loans, gains from the sale or disposition of stock, securities, or foreign currencies, or other income derived from the business of investing, including the net investment income of qualified publicly traded partnerships.
- At the close of each quarter of the tax year, at least 50 percent of its total assets must be invested in cash, government securities, securities of other mutual funds, or the securities of other issuers (so long as the securities of any given issuer do not exceed five percent of the value of the mutual fund's assets or 10 percent of the issuer's outstanding voting securities).
- At the close of each quarter of the tax year, no more than 25 percent of the total value of its assets may be invested in the securities of any one issuer (other than government securities or securities of other mutual funds), the securities of two or more issuers controlled by the mutual fund and engaged in a related trade or business, or the securities of one or more qualified publicly traded partnerships.
- The corporation must distribute at least 90 percent of its annual investment company taxable income (¶ 2303) and its net tax-exempt interest income (¶ 2307) to its shareholders (there is no threshold for net capital gains) (Code Sec. 852(a)).[2]

2303. Taxation of Mutual Funds. A mutual fund (regulated investment company) (¶ 2301) is subject to taxation at regular corporate income tax rates on its investment company taxable income (Code Sec. 852(b); Reg. § 1.852-3).[3] Investment company taxable income is computed on Form 1120-RIC in the same manner as the taxable income of an ordinary corporation (¶ 221) with the following adjustments:

References are to Standard Federal Tax Reports; Tax Research Consultant; and Practical Tax Explanations.

[1] ¶ 26,400, ¶ 26,401—¶ 26,407; RIC: 3,000, RIC: 3,050; § 19,201, § 45,430.05

[2] ¶ 26,420; RIC: 3,060; § 19,201, § 45,430.05

[3] ¶ 26,420, ¶ 26,424; RIC: 3,200; § 19,201, § 45,430.05

- gross income is the fund's ordinary income (net capital gains are not included);
- a deduction is allowed for any ordinary dividends paid (¶ 259), but no deduction is allowed for dividends of capital gains or tax-exempt interest;
- no deduction is allowed for dividends received;
- no deduction is allowed for net operating losses (NOLs);
- taxable income of a short tax year is not annualized;
- if the fund so elects, taxable income is computed by disregarding the short-term discount obligation rules of Code Sec. 454(b); and
- a deduction is allowed for the tax imposed on the fund if it fails to meet the asset test or gross income test (¶ 2301).

For purposes of the dividends-paid deduction, dividends declared and payable by a mutual fund in October, November, or December of a calendar year are treated as paid on December 31 of that year if they are actually paid in January of the following calendar year (Code Sec. 852(b)(7)).[4] See ¶ 2323 for discussion of the treatment of certain dividends declared after the close of the mutual fund's tax year.

A mutual fund, other than a publicly traded mutual fund, generally may not claim a deduction for dividend distributions if it singles out one class of shareholders or one or more members of a class of shareholders for special dividend treatment, unless such treatment was originally intended when the dividend rights were created (Code Sec. 562(c); Rev. Rul. 89-81).[5] However, the IRS has issued guidance describing the conditions under which distributions to mutual fund shareholders may vary and nevertheless be deductible, including the treatment of distributions to shareholders that differ as a result of the allocation and payment of fees and expenses (Rev. Proc. 99-40).[6]

Excise Taxes. A nondeductible excise tax is generally imposed on a mutual fund that does not satisfy minimum distribution requirements (Code Sec. 4982).[7] The tax is four percent of the excess of any required distribution for the calendar year over the amount actually distributed for the calendar year. For this purpose, the required distribution is the sum of 98 percent of the fund's ordinary income for the year, plus 98.2 percent of its net capital gain income for the one-year period ending October 31 of the calendar year. Special rules apply to how a mutual fund treats post-October 31 capital gains and foreign currency losses. For excise tax purposes, amendments made in 2010 to the capital loss carryover rules (¶ 2305) apply beginning with any net capital loss recognized in the period that determines a mutual fund's required distribution for calendar year 2011 (Rev. Rul. 2012-29).[8]

Built-in Gains Tax. A mutual fund may be subject to a modified version of the built-in gains tax imposed on S corporations (¶ 337) if property owned by a C corporation becomes property of the mutual fund when the corporation qualifies as a mutual fund, or if property of a C corporation is transferred to the mutual fund (Reg. § 1.337(d)-7).[9] The tax does not apply, however, if the corporation makes a deemed sale election to recognize gain and loss as if it sold the converted property to an unrelated person at fair market value. The tax also does not apply if the corporation otherwise recognizes gain or loss on the conversion transaction, or if the corporation's gain is not recognized in a like-kind exchange or an involuntary conversion.

2305. Capital Gains and Losses of Mutual Funds. A mutual fund (regulated investment company) (¶ 2301) may avoid corporate level tax on its net capital gains by distributing such gains to shareholders. If the mutual fund elects to retain some of its net capital gains, then it is subject to tax at regular capital gains rates (¶ 1738) on the excess of its net capital gains for the tax year over the amount of any capital gains

References are to Standard Federal Tax Reports; Tax Research Consultant; and Practical Tax Explanations.

[4] ¶ 26,420; RIC: 3,460; § 19,205.50

[5] ¶ 23,470, ¶ 26,433.50; RIC: 3,204.10

[6] ¶ 26,433.28; RIC: 3,204.10

[7] ¶ 34,640; RIC: 3,212; § 19,201, § 45,430.05

[8] ¶ 34,642.10; RIC: 3,212; § 19,201, § 45,430.05

[9] ¶ 16,241H; RIC: 3,550

dividends paid during the year (Code Sec. 852(b)(3)).[10] Form 2438 is used to figure and report the fund's capital gains. Although the fund is taxed on its undistributed net capital gains, it may elect to designate to its shareholders some or all of its undistributed gains and the tax paid on those gains. Form 2439 is used to notify each shareholder of his or her portion of the undistributed capital gains and tax paid for the year (¶ 2309 and ¶ 2311). The mutual fund must also report any undistributed long-term capital gains not designated to shareholders and any net short-term capital gain on Form 8949 and Schedule D (Form 1120).

Capital Loss Carryovers. If a mutual fund has a net capital loss for a tax year, any excess of the net short-term capital loss over the net long-term capital gain is treated as a short-term capital loss arising on the first day of the next tax year, and any excess of the net long-term capital loss over the net short-term capital gain is treated as a long-term capital loss arising on the first day of the next tax year (Code Sec. 1212(a)(3)(A)).[11] There is no limit to the number of tax years that a net capital loss of a mutual fund may be carried over.

If a net capital loss under the general corporate capital loss carryback and carryover rules (¶ 1756) is carried over to a tax year of a mutual fund, amounts treated as a long-term or short-term capital loss arising on the first day of the next tax year under the capital loss carryover rules for mutual funds (discussed above) are determined without regard to amounts treated as a short-term capital loss under the general corporate capital loss carryover rule. Further, in determining the reduction of a carryover by capital gain net income for a prior tax year under the general corporate capital loss carryover rule, any capital loss treated as arising on the first day of the prior tax year under the capital loss carryover rules for mutual funds is taken into account in determining capital gain net income for the prior year (Code Sec. 1212(a)(3)(B)). Capital gain net income is the excess of gains from the sale or exchange of capital assets over losses from such sales or exchanges (Code Sec. 1222(9)).[12]

2307. Tax-Exempt Interest of Mutual Funds. A mutual fund (regulated investment company) (¶ 2301) may pay tax-exempt interest earned on state or local bonds to its shareholders in the form of exempt-interest dividends, but only if the bonds represent at least 50 percent of the value of the fund's assets at the close of each quarter of its tax year (Code Sec. 852(b)(5)).[13] Form 1099-INT is used to inform shareholders of dividends identified as tax-exempt interest dividends (¶ 2309 and ¶ 2311).

An upper-tier mutual fund that is a qualified fund of funds may pass through exempt-interest dividends to its shareholders without having to meet the 50-percent asset requirement (Code Sec. 852(g)).[14] A qualified fund of funds is a mutual fund if, at the close of each quarter of the tax year, at least 50 percent of the value of its total assets is represented by interests in other mutual funds.

If a mutual fund shareholder receives an exempt-interest dividend with respect to any share held for six months or less, then any loss on the sale or exchange of such share is generally disallowed to the extent of the exempt-interest dividend (Code Sec. 852(b)(4)).[15] However, the disallowance of a loss on the sale or exchange of mutual fund shares on which exempt-interest dividends have been paid does not apply, except as otherwise provided by regulations, to a regular dividend paid by a mutual fund that declares exempt-interest dividends on a daily basis in an amount not less than 90 percent of its net tax-exempt interest and distributes such dividends on a monthly or more frequent basis.

2309. Designation of Mutual Fund Distributions. A mutual fund (regulated investment company) (¶ 2301) must report in written statements furnished to its shareholders the portions of distributions made during the tax year that are capital gains dividends (¶ 2305) and exempt-interest dividends (¶ 2307), as well as any foreign tax credits

References are to Standard Federal Tax Reports; Tax Research Consultant; and Practical Tax Explanations.

[10] ¶ 26,420; RIC: 3,250; § 19,205.05, § 45,430.10

[11] ¶ 30,400; RIC: 3,252; § 16,535

[12] ¶ 30,440; SALES: 15,202.45; § 16,535

[13] ¶ 26,420; RIC: 3,300; § 19,205.05, § 45,430.10

[14] ¶ 26,420; RIC: 3,302; § 19,205.35

[15] ¶ 26,420; RIC: 3,304, SALES: 45,406.20; § 19,230.10

(¶ 2320), tax credit bond credits (¶ 2320), dividends that qualify for the dividends-received deduction (¶ 223), and passed-through ordinary dividends eligible for the reduced tax rate for qualified dividends (¶ 2311) (Code Secs. 852(b)(3)(C) and (5), 853(c), 853A(c), and 854(b)).[16] Capital gain dividends, dividends received from a tax-exempt corporation, and dividends received from a qualified real estate investment trust (REIT) (¶ 2326) are not eligible for the dividends-received deduction (Code Sec. 854(a) and (b)(2)). The aggregate amount that the mutual fund can report as dividends eligible for the dividends-received deduction is limited to its aggregate dividends received from domestic corporations for the tax year. The aggregate amount that the mutual fund can report as qualified dividend income is limited to its qualified dividend income for the tax year (Code Sec. 854(b)(1)(C)).

Additionally, within 60 days after the close of its tax year, a mutual fund must report and notify its shareholders of the portion of distributions made during the tax year that is designated as undistributed capital gain (Code Sec. 852(b)(3)(D)).

2311. Taxation of Mutual Fund Distributions. The tax treatment of a distribution received from a mutual fund (regulated investment company) (¶ 2301) depends on how the distribution is designated (¶ 2309). Distributions not designated as capital gain dividends are generally treated by shareholders as ordinary income to the extent of the fund's earnings and profits. However, all or a portion of the distribution of an ordinary dividend may be a qualified dividend eligible to be taxed at capital gains rates (¶ 733) if the aggregate amount of qualified dividends received by the fund during the year is less than 95 percent of its gross income (Code Sec. 854(b)(1)(B)).[17] Distributions reported as tax-exempt interest dividends may generally be excluded from the shareholder's gross income (Code Sec. 852(b)(5)(B)).[18] However, exempt-interest dividends derived from private activity bonds constitute tax preference items for alternative minimum tax (AMT) purposes (¶ 1425).

Distributions received from a mutual fund reported as capital gain dividends may be treated as long-term capital gains by the shareholder for income and AMT purposes, regardless of how long the shareholder held the shares (Code Sec. 852(b)(3)(B)).[19] Similarly, capital gains that the fund elects to pass through to the shareholder are treated as long-term capital gains (¶ 2305). The shareholder is entitled to a credit or refund for its portion of any capital gain taxes paid by the mutual fund on the undistributed capital gains (Code Sec. 852(b)(3)(D)). In addition, the shareholder may increase the basis of its mutual fund shares by the difference between the undistributed capital gains and its deemed portion of taxes paid. The mutual fund must designate distributions as undistributed capital gain dividends, reporting the designation and providing shareholders a written notice within 60 days of the end of its tax year (¶ 2309).

If a shareholder receives a capital gain dividend or has capital gain passed through by the fund with respect to any share or beneficial interest, and holds the share for six months or less, then any loss on the sale of that share is treated as a long-term capital loss to the extent of any long-term capital gain (Code Sec. 852(b)(4)).[20] In addition, the amount of loss that may be claimed must also be reduced by the amount of any exempt-interest dividend received on the shares. These rules do not apply to losses incurred on the disposition of mutual fund shares or beneficial interests pursuant to a plan that provides for the periodic liquidation of such shares or interests. For purposes of determining whether a taxpayer has held mutual fund shares for six months or less, rules similar to those for the dividends-received deduction are applied (¶ 223). A mutual fund shareholder may also not claim a loss from the sale or exchange of mutual fund shares if the wash sale rules apply (¶ 1935).

A distribution that is not out of a mutual fund's earnings and profits is a return of the shareholder's investment. Return-of-capital distributions are generally not subject to tax,

References are to Standard Federal Tax Reports; Tax Research Consultant; and Practical Tax Explanations.

[16] ¶ 26,420, ¶ 26,440, ¶ 26,448, ¶ 26,460; RIC: 3,400; § 19,205.05

[17] ¶ 26,460; RIC: 3,400; § 19,205.10, § 19,205.15

[18] ¶ 26,420; RIC: 3,304; § 19,205.35

[19] ¶ 26,420; RIC: 3,250; § 19,205.20, § 19,205.25

[20] ¶ 26,420; RIC: 3,258; § 19,230.15

and they reduce the shareholder's basis in the mutual fund shares. On the other hand, mutual fund distributions that are automatically reinvested by the shareholder into more shares of the fund are taxed as if they had actually been received by shareholder in cash. Thus, reinvested ordinary dividends and reinvested capital gain distributions are generally taxed as income, reinvested exempt-interest dividends are not reported as income, and reinvested return-of-capital distributions are reported as a return of capital (IRS Pub. 550).

Deferral of Late-Year Losses. A mutual fund can elect to defer certain post-October capital losses for a tax year, as well as certain late-year ordinary losses for that year, to the first day of the following tax year (Code Sec. 852(b)(8); Notice 2015-41).[21] The mutual fund makes the election by giving effect to the deferral in computing its capital gains and losses for the tax year in question, and completing its income tax return (including any necessary schedules) for that year according to the instructions for those items that apply to the election.

Capital Gains Tax Rates. The IRS has provided guidance that mutual funds and their shareholders must use in applying the net capital gain tax rates (¶ 1736) to capital gain dividends (Notices 97-64, 2004-39, and 2015-41).[22]

2313. Earnings and Profits of Mutual Funds. Dividends from a mutual fund (regulated investment company), just like dividends from most other corporations, must be paid out of earnings and profits (¶ 747—¶ 757) (Code Secs. 301, 312, 316, 561, 562(a), and 852(a)(1)).[23] Thus, a mutual fund must maintain sufficient current or accumulated earnings and profits to satisfy annual dividend distribution requirements. There should also be enough earnings and profits to avoid the excise tax on the undistributed income (¶ 2303).

A mutual fund's earnings and profits are generally computed under the rules that apply to ordinary corporations. However, mutual funds do not reduce their current earnings and profits by any amount they are unable to claim as a deduction from taxable income in that year (Code Sec. 852(c)(1)).[24] Net capital loss for a tax year is not taken into account in determining earnings and profits. Also, deductions disallowed in computing mutual fund taxable income with respect to tax-exempt interest are allowed in calculating a mutual fund's current earnings and profits (but not accumulated earnings and profits).

If a mutual fund that is not a calendar-year taxpayer makes distributions to its shareholders with respect to any class of stock of the company in excess of the sum of its current and accumulated earnings and profits (i.e., a portion of the distribution constitutes return of capital or capital gain), its current earnings and profits must be allocated first to distributions during the mutual fund's tax year that are made before January 1 (Code Sec. 316(b)(4)).[25] If a mutual fund has more than one class of stock, this rule applies separately to each class of stock, so that distributions made during the corporation's tax year are considered to be made to the shares with higher priority before they are made to shares with lower priority (Rev. Rul. 69-440).[26]

A company that has failed to qualify as a mutual fund because it has not purged itself of non-mutual fund earnings and profits may still qualify if it distributes those earnings and profits with interest to its shareholders (Code Sec. 852(e)).[27] In order to qualify, distributions must be specifically designated as non-mutual fund distributions and take place within the 90-day period that begins on the date the corporation is determined not to be a mutual fund (¶ 2317). This option is not available if the corporation was determined not to be a mutual fund because it engaged in fraudulent tax evasion.

References are to Standard Federal Tax Reports; Tax Research Consultant; and Practical Tax Explanations.

[21] ¶ 26,420, ¶ 26,433.16; RIC: 3,254

[22] ¶ 26,433.16; RIC: 3,254; § 19,205.20

[23] ¶ 15,302, ¶ 15,600, ¶ 15,702, ¶ 23,450, ¶ 23,470, ¶ 26,420; RIC: 3,204.15; § 26,601

[24] ¶ 26,420; RIC: 3,204.15; § 19,201

[25] ¶ 15,702; RIC: 3,204.15

[26] ¶ 15,704.755; CCORP: 12,166, RIC: 3,204.15

[27] ¶ 26,420; RIC: 3,202

2315. Redemption of Mutual Fund Shares. A redemption of stock by a corporation, including a mutual fund (regulated investment company) (¶ 2301), is generally treated as an exchange of stock if the redemption falls within one of four categories of transactions (Code Sec. 302):[28] (1) a redemption that is not essentially equivalent to a dividend; (2) a substantially disproportionate redemption; (3) a redemption that terminates the shareholder's interest in the corporation; or (4) a partial liquidation, in the case of a noncorporate shareholder. Redemptions of corporate stock are discussed in ¶ 742—¶ 745. Because transactions that fall within one of these four categories are treated as exchanges of stock, they normally result in capital gain treatment to the shareholder. If the redemption does not fall within any of these categories, it is treated as a Code Sec. 301 distribution of property that generally results in dividend treatment.

Special rules apply to redemptions of mutual fund shares. A distribution in redemption of stock of a publicly offered mutual fund is treated as an exchange for stock if the redemption is upon the demand by the stockholder and the mutual fund issues only stock that is redeemable upon the demand of the stockholder. A publicly offered mutual fund is a fund whose shares are: (1) continuously offered pursuant to a public offering; (2) regularly traded on an established securities market; or (3) held by or for no fewer than 500 persons at all times during the tax year (Code Sec. 67(c)(2)(B)).[29] Additionally, the loss disallowance and deferral rules for transactions between related persons (¶ 1717) do not apply to any redemption of stock of a fund-of-funds mutual fund if the mutual fund issues only stock that is redeemable upon the demand of the stockholder and the redemption is upon the demand of another mutual fund (Code Sec. 267(f)(3)(D)).[30]

2317. Deficiency Dividends of Mutual Funds. If there is a determination that adjustments are needed to certain amounts that a mutual fund (regulated investment company) (¶ 2301) reports for a tax year, and if the adjustments could cause the entity to lose its mutual fund status, the mutual fund may avoid disqualification by making deficiency dividend distributions, and may claim a deduction for such dividends paid (Code Sec. 860; Reg. §§ 1.860-1—1.860-5).[31] A deficiency dividend is a distribution of property (including money) that would have been includible in calculating the entity's dividends-paid deduction had the property been distributed during the tax year. The distribution must be made within 90 days after the determination date, and before the entity files a deficiency dividend deduction claim, which must be filed on Form 976 within 120 days after the determination date.

For a mutual fund, an adjustment can be: (1) an increase in its investment company taxable income, determined without regard to the dividends-paid deduction; (2) an increase in the amount of the excess of its net capital gain over its deduction for capital gain dividends paid; or (3) a decrease in its dividends-paid deduction (determined without regard to capital gains dividends). A determination is a final decision by a court, a closing agreement, an agreement between the IRS and the entity relating to its tax liability, or a statement by the entity attached to its amendment or supplement to a tax return for the relevant tax year. Filing Form 8927 is treated as a "self-determination" by the entity for these purposes (Rev. Proc. 2009-28).[32]

The deficiency dividend deduction is not available if part of the adjustment is due to fraud with intent to evade tax or willful failure to file a timely income tax return.

2318. Basis in Mutual Fund Shares. A shareholder's basis in the shares of a mutual fund (regulated investment company) (¶ 2301) is usually the cost to purchase the shares, including any fees or load charges incurred to acquire or redeem them (¶ 1975). Fees or load charges are not added to the shareholder's original basis if the shareholder acquires a reinvestment right, disposes of the shares within 90 days of being purchased, and acquires new shares in the same (or another) mutual fund for

References are to Standard Federal Tax Reports; Tax Research Consultant; and Practical Tax Explanations.

[28] ¶ 15,325; CCORP: 21,104; § 26,301

[29] ¶ 6060; RIC: 3,204.10; § 19,210.07

[30] ¶ 14,150; SALES: 39,100; § 19,210.07

[31] ¶ 26,580, ¶ 26,581—¶ 26,585; RIC: 3,500

[32] ¶ 42,625.435; RIC: 3,500

which the fee or load charge is reduced or waived because of the reinvestment right (Code Sec. 852(f)).[33] In such cases, the omission of the load charge from basis applies to the extent the charge does not exceed the reduction in the load charge for the new investment. To the extent that a load charge is not taken into account in determining the purchaser's gain or loss, it is treated as incurred in connection with the acquisition of the second-acquired shares.

The treatment of load charges applies only if the original mutual fund stock is disposed of within 90 days after the date it was originally acquired and the taxpayer acquires stock in the same or another mutual fund during the period beginning on the date of the disposition of the original stock, and ending on January 31 of the calendar year following the calendar year that includes the date of such disposition for this rule to apply.

The original basis of mutual fund shares acquired by reinvesting distributions (even exempt-interest dividends) is the amount of the distributions used to buy each full or fractional share (¶ 1975). A shareholder's original basis in shares acquired by gift is generally the donor's adjusted basis (¶ 1630). However, if the fair market value of the shares was more than the donor's adjusted basis, then the shareholder's basis is the donor's adjusted basis at the time of the gift, plus all or part of any gift tax paid. A shareholder's basis in mutual fund shares that are inherited is generally the fair market value of the shares at the decedent's death (or the alternate valuation date if the estate chooses) (¶ 1633). No matter how a shareholder's original basis is determined, it must be adjusted for post-acquisition occurrences such as reinvestment of distributions and return of capital distributions (¶ 2311).

2320. Tax Credit Elections. A mutual fund (regulated investment company) (¶ 2301) may elect to have its foreign tax credit (¶ 2475) claimed by its shareholders on their tax returns instead of its own. The election can only be made if more than 50 percent of the value of the fund's total assets at the close of the tax year consists of stock or securities in foreign corporations and it has distributed at least 90 percent of its investment company taxable income (¶ 2303) and net tax-exempt interest (¶ 2307) for the year (Code Sec. 853).[34]

An upper-tier mutual fund that is a qualified fund of funds may pass through foreign tax credits to its shareholders without having to meet the 50-percent asset requirement (Code Sec. 852(g)).[35] A qualified fund of funds is a mutual fund at least 50 percent of the total value of whose assets (as measured at the close of each quarter of its tax year) is represented by interests in other mutual funds.

A mutual fund may also elect to pass through to its shareholders credits attributable to tax credit bonds (¶ 1371) held by the mutual fund (Code Sec. 853A).[36]

2323. Mutual Fund Distributions After Tax Year Ends. A mutual fund (regulated investment company) may declare and pay spillover dividends after the close of a tax year that are considered made out of the mutual fund's earnings and profits for that year (Code Sec. 855(a); Reg. § 1.855-1).[37] Spillover dividends are included in the calculation of mutual fund taxable income for that year and are considered in determining whether the mutual fund met its distribution requirements for the year. Spillover dividends must be declared no later than the fifteenth day of the ninth month following the close of the tax year to which the dividend relates, or the extended due date for the mutual fund's return for the tax year, whichever comes later. The dividend must be paid to shareholders in the 12-month period after the close of the tax year to which the dividend relates, but no later than the date of the first dividend payment *of the same type of dividend* (e.g., capital gains or ordinary) after the declaration.

References are to Standard Federal Tax Reports; Tax Research Consultant; and Practical Tax Explanations.

[33] ¶ 26,420; SALES: 6,068, SALES: 45,404.05; § 19,215.05

[34] ¶ 26,440; RIC: 3,350; § 19,240.10

[35] ¶ 26,420; RIC: 3,352; § 19,240.10

[36] ¶ 26,448; RIC: 3,364; § 14,505

[37] ¶ 26,480, ¶ 26,481; RIC: 3,450

The shareholder generally must treat such a dividend as received in the tax year in which the distribution is made. This does not apply, however, to dividends declared in October, November, or December that are treated as paid on December 31 of a calendar year even though they are actually paid in January of the following calendar year (¶ 2303) (Code Sec. 855(b)).

Real Estate Investment Trusts

2326. Qualification as a REIT. A corporation, trust, or association that acts as an investment agent specializing in real estate and real estate mortgages may elect to be a real estate investment trust (REIT) (Code Sec. 856).[38] REITs may escape corporate taxation because, unlike ordinary corporations, they are entitled to claim a deduction for dividends paid to shareholders against their ordinary income and net capital gains (¶ 259). An entity qualifies as a REIT if it makes an election to be treated as such by filing Form 1120-REIT, and it meets certain requirements as to ownership and organization, source of income, investment of assets, and distribution of income to shareholders. The REIT election may be revoked voluntarily, but the organization will be prohibited from making a new REIT election for the four tax years after revocation. An organization may elect REIT status even if it fails the ownership test in the first year.

Ownership and Organization Requirements. To be eligible for REIT status, an entity must be taxable as a domestic corporation (Code Sec. 856(a)). Foreign corporations, trusts, and associations, as well as financial institutions such as banks and insurance companies, are not eligible. An eligible entity must be managed by one or more trustees or directors during the entire tax year. It must also adopt a calendar-year accounting period (Code Sec. 859).[39] An entity making a REIT election may change its accounting period to a calendar year without seeking IRS approval.

Beneficial ownership in a REIT must be evidenced by transferable shares or certificates of interest. The REIT must have at least 100 beneficial owners for at least 335 days of a 12-month tax year (Code Sec. 856(a) and (b)). Ownership cannot be closely held as determined under the personal holding company rules (¶ 285) (Code Sec. 856(h)).[40] However, attribution to another partner in a partnership is ignored. In addition, a pension trust generally is not treated as a single owner, but any REIT shares or certificates of interest held by the trust are treated as directly held by its beneficiaries. The look-through rule does not apply if persons disqualified from dealings with the pension trust own five percent or more of the value of the REIT and the REIT has accumulated earnings and profits attributable to a year it did not qualify as a REIT.

Generally, a corporation that was either a distributing or controlled corporation in a distribution on or after December 7, 2015, which qualified for nonrecognition treatment under Code Sec. 355 (¶ 2201) will not be eligible to make a REIT election during the ten-year period after the date of distribution (Code Sec. 856(c)(8), as added by the Protecting Americans from Tax Hikes (PATH) Act of 2015 (P.L. 114-113)).

Income Requirements. An entity must satisfy the following income tests each tax year in order to qualify as a REIT (Code Sec. 856(c)(2) and (3)):[41]

- at least 95 percent of the entity's gross income must be from rents from real property, gain from the disposition of real property, dividends, interest, gains from dispositions of stock and securities, abatements and refunds of real property taxes, income and gain from foreclosure property, consideration received or accrued for agreeing to make loans secured by real property mortgages or interests or to purchase or lease real property, and certain mineral royalty income earned from real property owned by a timber REIT; and
- at least 75 percent of the entity's gross income, excluding income from prohibited transactions (¶ 2329), must be from real property sources, which include rents from real property, interest on real property mortgages, gain from

References are to Standard Federal Tax Reports; Tax Research Consultant; and Practical Tax Explanations.

[38] ¶ 26,500; RIC: 6,050; § 19,201, § 45,440.05

[39] ¶ 26,560; RIC: 6,050, RIC: 6,052; § 38,135.10

[40] ¶ 26,500; RIC: 6,052.30

[41] ¶ 26,500; RIC: 6,054; § 45,440.05

the disposition of a real estate asset (other than a nonqualified publicly offered REIT debt instrument), dividends and gain from the disposition of shares in other qualifying REITs, abatements and refunds of real property taxes, income and gain from foreclosure property, consideration received or accrued for agreeing to make loans secured by real property mortgages or interests or to purchase or lease real property, and qualified temporary investment income.

For both tests, an entity's gross income does not include the gross income from prohibited transactions, foreign currency gains in the form of passive foreign exchange gains, or real estate foreign exchange gains (Code Sec. 856(n)),[42] as well as gains from hedging transactions (including counteracting hedges in tax years after December 31, 2015) entered into by the entity to reduce the risk of debt incurred to acquire or hold real estate or to manage the risk of currency fluctuations (Code Sec. 856(c)(5)(G), as amended by P.L. 114-113)).[43] The IRS has the authority to designate income as not constituting gross income for purposes of the REIT income tests. Alternatively, the IRS may designate nonqualified income as qualified income (Code Sec. 856(c)(5)(J)).[44]

Real property is defined for these purposes as land and improvements to land. For tax years beginning after August 31, 2016, the definition of real property includes land, inherently permanent structures and structural components of inherently permanent structures (Reg. § 1.856-10).[45] Rents from real property generally include: rents from interests in real property; amounts received for customary services (utilities, maintenance), even if separate charges are made for such services; and rent attributable to personal property incidental to rental of real property if the amount allocable to personal property is 15 percent or less of the total rent (Code Sec. 856(d)).[46] Rents from real property do *not* include amounts received from: (1) any noncorporate person in which the REIT owns 10 percent or more in that person's assets or profits; (2) a corporation, if the REIT owns 10 percent or more of either the voting stock or the value of all shares issued by the corporation; or (3) amounts received based on income or profits of a tenant or debtor (unless certain conditions are met). Rents from real property also do not include rents that depend on income or profits derived by any person from the property; exceptions exist to this general prohibition.

Amounts paid to a REIT by a taxable REIT subsidiary (¶ 2340) are not excluded from the definition of rents from real property if at least 90 percent of the property at issue is rented to unrelated parties at rents comparable to those paid by other tenants for comparable space (Code Sec. 856(d)(8)). In addition, a taxable REIT subsidiary may lease a qualified lodging facility or a qualified health care property, and the rents paid are treated as rents from real property so long as the facility is operated by an eligible independent contractor for a fee.

An entity that fails to meet either of the income tests for any tax year may still qualify as a REIT if it identifies the failure on a separate schedule prescribed by the IRS and the failure is due to reasonable cause and not willful neglect (Code Sec. 856(c)(6)).[47] The REIT also must pay a tax equal to the greater of the amount by which the entity fails to meet either the 95-percent or 75-percent income test, multiplied by the fraction of the REIT's taxable income over its gross income for the tax year (Code Sec. 857(b)(5)).[48]

Asset Requirements. A REIT must meet the following requirements regarding its assets at the close of each quarter of the tax year:

- at least 75 percent of the value of its total assets must consist of real estate assets (including interests in a REMIC (¶ 2343)), cash items (including receivables), and government securities;
- no more than 25 percent of the value of its total assets can be invested in securities other than those representing real estate assets or government securities;

References are to Standard Federal Tax Reports; Tax Research Consultant; and Practical Tax Explanations.

[42] ¶ 26,500; RIC: 6,054.05

[43] ¶ 26,500; RIC: 6,054.05, RIC: 6,054.15

[44] ¶ 26,500; RIC: 6,054

[45] ¶ 26,512; RIC: 6,072

[46] ¶ 26,500; RIC: 6,056

[47] ¶ 26,500; RIC: 6,054.20

[48] ¶ 26,520; RIC: 6,054.20

- no more than 25 percent of the value of its total assets can be invested in securities of taxable REIT subsidiaries (20 percent for tax years beginning after December 31, 2017) (¶ 2340);
- no more than 25 percent of the value of its total assets can be invested in nonqualified publicly offered REIT debt instruments, as defined under Code Sec. 856(c)(5)(L)(ii); and
- except for government securities and securities of taxable REIT subsidiaries, no more than five percent of the value of its total assets can be invested in the securities of any one issuer, and investment in the securities of any one issuer cannot exceed 10 percent of the total value or voting power of that issuer's outstanding securities (Code Sec. 856(c)(4), as amended by P.L. 114-113).[49]

For purposes of the limitation that a REIT may not hold more than 10 percent of the value of the outstanding securities of a single issuer, certain obligations are not treated as securities of an issuer, including straight debt securities, loans to an individual or estate, section 467 rental agreements (¶ 1541), or any obligation to pay rents from real property (Code Sec. 856(m)).[50] A straight debt security is debt payable on demand or on a specified date where the interest rate and interest payments are not contingent on profits, the borrower's discretion, or similar factors, and there is no convertibility (directly or indirectly) into stock (Code Sec. 1361(c)(5)(B)).[51] However, special rules permit certain contingencies of straight debt.

Ancillary Personal Property. In tax years beginning after December 31, 2015, both the 75-percent asset test and the 75-percent income test can include rents from personal property that is ancillary to real property as well as obligations secured by mortgages where no more than 15 percent of the total FMV of all secured property is represented by personal property (Code Sec. 856(c)(9), as added by P.L. 114-113).

An entity that fails to meet any of the asset requirements for a particular tax quarter (other than the 5-percent and 10-percent asset tests) may still qualify as a REIT if:

(1) it identifies the failure on a separate schedule prescribed by the IRS;

(2) failure is due to reasonable cause and not willful neglect;

(3) the assets causing the failure are disposed of within six months of the last day of the quarter in which the failure occurred; and

(4) the REIT pays an excise tax (Code Sec. 856(c)(7)).[52]

The tax is the greater of $50,000 or the tax on the net income generated by the assets during the period of failure at the highest corporate rate (¶ 219). A REIT will not lose its exempt status for a *de minimis* failure to meet the 5- or 10-percent asset requirements if the failure is due to ownership of assets the total value of which does not exceed the lesser of one percent of the total value of the REIT's assets at the end of a tax quarter or $10 million. The REIT must dispose of the assets causing the failure within six months of the last day of the quarter in which the failure occurred.

Distribution of Income. To qualify as a REIT, an entity generally must distribute to its shareholders during the tax year the sum of 90 percent of its ordinary taxable income (determined without the deduction for dividends paid and excluding net capital gain) (¶ 2329) and 90 percent of its net income from foreclosure property (less the tax imposed on that income), minus its excess noncash income (Code Sec. 857(a)).[53] The IRS has the authority to waive this requirement if the REIT's failure to meet it is due to distributions necessary to avoid imposition of the excise tax on undistributed REIT income.

Other Failures. If an entity fails to satisfy one or more requirements of REIT qualification other than the income tests or asset requirements, then the entity may still retain REIT qualification if the failure is due to reasonable cause and not willful neglect. However, the REIT must pay a penalty of $50,000 for each failure (Code Sec. 856(g)(5)).[54]

References are to Standard Federal Tax Reports; Tax Research Consultant; and Practical Tax Explanations.

[49] ¶ 26,500; RIC: 6,072
[50] ¶ 26,500; RIC: 6,072.10
[51] ¶ 32,021; RIC: 6,072.10
[52] ¶ 26,500; RIC: 6,072.25
[53] ¶ 26,520; RIC: 6,074
[54] ¶ 26,500; RIC: 6,078.05

2329. Taxation of REITs. An entity that qualifies as a real estate investment trust (REIT) (¶ 2326) is subject to regular corporate income tax rates on its taxable income (Code Sec. 857(b)).[55] A REIT's taxable income is computed on Form 1120-REIT in the same manner as an ordinary corporation with the following adjustments:

- A deduction is allowed for dividends paid (¶ 259), but without regard to dividends attributable to the net income from foreclosure property.
- Net income from foreclosure property or a prohibited transaction is disregarded.
- The special deductions available to corporations (¶ 223—¶ 231), including the dividends-received deduction, are not allowed, but the deduction for organizational expenditures (¶ 237) is allowed.
- Any tax imposed on redetermined rents, redetermined deductions, and excess interest under Code Sec. 857(b)(7), and any tax imposed for failures to meet the income, asset, or other REIT qualification requirements (¶ 2326), are deducted.
- Taxable income is not annualized in the case of a change in accounting periods.

For purposes of the dividends-paid deduction, dividends declared and payable in October, November, or December of a calendar year are treated as paid on December 31 of that year if they are actually paid in January of the following calendar year (Code Sec. 857(b)(9)).[56] See ¶ 2339 for discussion of the treatment of dividends declared after the close of the REIT's tax year.

Capital Gains. If a REIT has any net capital gains in the tax year, the tax imposed on REIT taxable income is the lesser of: (1) the regular corporate tax on REIT taxable income; or (2) the regular corporate tax on REIT taxable income, determined by excluding net capital gains and by computing the deduction for dividends paid without capital gain dividends, plus 35 percent on the excess of the net capital gain minus any capital gain dividends paid (Code Sec. 857(b)(3)).[57]

A REIT may avoid the tax on its net capital gains by distributing the gains to its shareholders (¶ 2331). The REIT must designate any distributions as capital gain dividends in a written notice to the shareholders or beneficiaries with its annual report or within 30 days of the end of the tax year. For purposes of determining the maximum amount of capital gain dividends that a REIT may pay for a tax year, the REIT may not offset its net capital gains with the amount of any net operating losses (NOLs) (¶ 1145). In addition, the REIT must increase the amount of any NOL carryover to the extent it pays capital gains dividends in excess of its net income.

If the REIT does retain any net capital gains, it may elect to designate to its shareholders some or all of those undistributed amounts and the tax it paid on those gains. The REIT must make the designation in a written notice to its shareholders at any time before the end of the 60-day period after the close of its tax year, or that is mailed with its annual report for the tax year. The REIT uses Form 2438 to report and determine its tax on undistributed capital gains, and Form 2439 to inform each shareholder of his or her portion of the undistributed gains and any tax paid. Form 2439 must be provided within 60 days of the close of the REIT's tax year. The REIT must also report any undistributed long-term capital gains not designated to shareholders and any net short-term capital gain on Form 8949 and Schedule D (Form 1120).

Net Operating Losses. NOLs in a tax year that an entity is a REIT may only be carried forward, while NOLs in a tax year an entity is not a REIT may not be carried back to any year the entity was a REIT (¶ 1151) (Code Sec. 172(b)(1)(B)).[58]

References are to Standard Federal Tax Reports; Tax Research Consultant; and Practical Tax Explanations.

[55] ¶ 26,520; RIC: 6,100

[56] ¶ 26,520; RIC: 6,104; § 19,205.50

[57] ¶ 26,520; RIC: 6,108

[58] ¶ 12,002; RIC: 6,110

Built-in Gains Tax. A REIT may be subject to a modified version of the built-in gains tax imposed on S corporations (¶ 337) if property owned by a C corporation becomes property of the REIT when the corporation qualifies as a REIT (¶ 2326) or is transferred to the REIT (Reg. § 1.337(d)-7), or if a C corporation engages in a conversion transaction involving a REIT (Temp. Reg. § 1.337(d)-7T).[59] The tax does not apply, however, if the corporation makes a deemed sale election to recognize gain and loss as if it sold the converted property to an unrelated person at fair market value. The tax also does not apply if the corporation otherwise recognizes gain or loss on the conversion transaction, or if the corporation's gain is not recognized in a like-kind exchange or an involuntary conversion.

Other Taxes. In addition to the tax on its taxable income, a REIT may be subject to the following additional taxes:

- a tax for failure to meet the REIT asset or income requirements for the tax year (¶ 2326);
- a tax at the highest corporate rate on net income from foreclosure property (Code Sec. 857(b)(4));[60]
- a 100-percent tax on the net income derived from a prohibited transaction (e.g., disposition of property, other than foreclosure property, that is held for sale to customers in the ordinary course of business) (Code Sec. 857(b)(6));[61]
- a four-percent excise tax on the amount of any taxable income that is undistributed at the end of the tax year, and calculated and paid on Form 8612 (Code Sec. 4981);[62] and
- a 100-percent tax on the excess portion of rents, deductions, and interest that must be reduced to clearly reflect income when a REIT and taxable REIT subsidiary (¶ 2340) engage in transactions other than those at arm's length (Code Sec. 857(b)(7)).[63]

2331. Taxation of REIT Distributions. Distributions received from a real estate investment trust (REIT) (¶ 2326) not designated as capital gain dividends are generally treated by shareholders as ordinary income to the extent of the REIT's earnings and profits. However, all or a portion of the distribution of an ordinary dividend may be a qualified dividend eligible to be taxed at capital gains rates (¶ 733). The amount a REIT can designate as qualified dividend income is limited to the sum of: (1) the REIT's qualified dividend income for the tax year; (2) the excess of the sum of REIT taxable income for the preceding tax year and the income subject to tax under the Code Sec. 337(d) regulations for that preceding tax year, over the taxes payable by the REIT under the REIT rules (¶ 2329) and the Code Sec. 337(d) regulations for that preceding tax year; and (3) the amount of earnings and profits that were distributed by the REIT for the tax year and accumulated in tax years in which the entity was not a REIT. The amount of qualified dividends must be specified by the REIT in a written notice to shareholders no later than 60 days after the close of the tax year (Code Sec. 857(c)(2)).[64]

Distributions in excess of the REIT's earnings and profits (other than deficiency dividends (¶ 2337)) constitute a return of the shareholder's basis (¶ 754). Dividends received from a REIT do not qualify for the dividends-received deduction for corporations (¶ 223).

Distributions designated as capital gain dividends are treated as long-term capital gains by the shareholders, regardless of how long they held their interests in the REIT (Code Sec. 857(b)(3)).[65] This includes any undistributed capital gains designated by the REIT (¶ 2329). Shareholders are entitled to a credit or refund for their portion of any capital gain taxes paid by the REIT on the undistributed capital gains. In addition, a shareholder must increase the basis of his or her REIT shares by the difference between

References are to Standard Federal Tax Reports; Tax Research Consultant; and Practical Tax Explanations.

[59] ¶ 16,241H; RIC: 6,124
[60] ¶ 26,520; RIC: 6,114
[61] ¶ 26,520; RIC: 6,116
[62] ¶ 34,620; RIC: 6,120
[63] ¶ 26,520; RIC: 6,122
[64] ¶ 26,520; RIC: 6,150, RIC: 6,200; § 19,205.05, § 45,440.10
[65] ¶ 26,520; RIC: 6,108, RIC: 6,200; § 19,205.20, § 45,440.10

his or her portions of the undistributed capital gains and the deemed taxes paid. Certain capital gain distributions from REITs to foreign investors are treated as REIT dividends that are not capital gains (Code Sec. 857(b)(3)(F)).

If a shareholder receives a capital gain dividend or the REIT has designated undistributed capital gains with respect to any share or beneficial interest, and the shareholder holds the share for six months or less, then any loss on the sale of that share is treated as a long-term capital loss to the extent of the long-term capital gain dividend (Code Sec. 857(b)(8)).[66] This rule does not apply to losses incurred on the disposition of REIT stock or a beneficial interest under a plan that provides for the periodic liquidation of such shares or interests. For purposes of determining whether a taxpayer has held REIT stock or a beneficial interest for six months or less, rules similar to those for the dividends-received deduction are applied (¶ 223).

Capital Gains Tax Rates. The IRS has provided guidance that REITs and their shareholders must use in applying the net capital gain tax rates (¶ 1736) to capital gain dividends (Notices 97-64 and 2004-39).[67]

2337. Deficiency Dividends of REITs. If there is a determination that adjustments are needed to certain amounts that a real estate investment trust (REIT) (¶ 2326) reports for a tax year, and if the adjustments could cause the entity to lose its REIT status, the REIT may avoid disqualification by making deficiency dividend distributions, and may claim a deduction for the dividends paid (Code Sec. 860; Reg. §§ 1.860-1—1.860-5).[68] For a REIT, an adjustment can be: (1) an increase in the sum of its taxable income (determined without regard to its dividends-paid deduction and excluding any net capital gain), plus the excess of its net income from foreclosure property minus the tax on the foreclosure property net income; (2) an increase in the amount of the excess of its net capital gain over its deduction for capital gain dividends paid; or (3) a decrease in its dividends-paid deduction (determined without regard to capital gains dividends). See ¶ 2317 for further discussion of the deficiency dividend procedure, which is the same as that for mutual funds (regulated investment companies).

2339. REIT Distributions After Tax Year Ends. A real estate investment trust (REIT) (¶ 2326) that declares a dividend (including a capital gain dividend) before the due date for filing its return for a tax year (including extensions), but distributes the dividend after the close of the tax year, can treat the dividend as having been paid during the tax year if the entire declared dividend is paid within the 12-month period following the close of the tax year and no later than the date of the first regular dividend payment after the declaration (Code Sec. 858; Reg. § 1.858-1).[69] The shareholder must generally treat the dividend as received in the tax year in which the distribution is made. This rule does not apply, however, to dividends declared in October, November, or December that are treated as paid on December 31 of a calendar year even though they are actually paid in January of the following calendar year (¶ 2329).

2340. REIT Subsidiaries. A real estate investment trust (REIT) (¶ 2326) may own a qualified REIT subsidiary and treat all of the subsidiary's assets, liabilities, and items of income, deduction, and credit as its own (Code Sec. 856(i)).[70] A qualified subsidiary is any corporation other than a taxable REIT subsidiary, all of the stock of which is held by the REIT. A taxable REIT subsidiary is any corporation that is owned, in whole or in part, by the REIT and that both entities jointly elect (using Form 8875) to treat as a taxable REIT subsidiary (Code Sec. 856(l)). A taxable REIT subsidiary can be used by the REIT to provide noncustomary services to its tenants or to manage and operate properties without causing the amounts received or accrued to be disqualified as rents from real property. The election to be treated as a taxable REIT subsidiary can only be revoked with the consent of both the REIT and the subsidiary.

References are to Standard Federal Tax Reports; Tax Research Consultant; and Practical Tax Explanations.

[66] ¶ 26,520; RIC: 6,150; § 19,230.15, § 45,440.10

[67] ¶ 26,433.16; RIC: 6,104.15; § 19,205.20

[68] ¶ 26,580, ¶ 26,581—¶ 26,585; RIC: 6,106

[69] ¶ 26,540, ¶ 26,541; RIC: 6,104.05

[70] ¶ 26,500; RIC: 6,072.20, RIC: 6,072.30

Real Estate Mortgage Investment Conduits

2343. Qualification as a REMIC. A real estate mortgage investment conduit (REMIC) is an entity that holds a fixed pool of mortgages and issues multiple classes of interests to investors (Code Sec. 860D; Reg. § 1.860D-1).[71] A REMIC is treated like a partnership for federal tax purposes with its income passed through to its interest holders (¶ 2344). Thus, a REMIC is not subject to taxation on its income, although it is subject to taxes on prohibited transactions (¶ 2355), income from foreclosure property (¶ 2356), and on certain contributions received after its start-up day (¶ 2357). It also may be required to withhold taxes on amounts paid to foreign holders of regular or residual interests (¶ 2367).

An entity qualifies as REMIC if it makes an irrevocable election to be treated as such by filing Form 1066 during its first tax year of existence, and if it meets certain requirements as to its investors (¶ 2344) and assets (¶ 2345). If an entity ceases to qualify as a REMIC at any time during the tax year, it will not be treated as a REMIC for that or any later tax year. A REMIC is required to file an information return with the IRS on Form 8811 within 30 days of its start-up day (and 30 days from any change of information provided in a previously-filed Form 8811) identifying its representative for reporting tax information (Reg. § 1.6049-7).[72]

2344. Investors' Interests. In order to qualify as a real estate mortgage investment conduit (REMIC) (¶ 2343), all of the interests in the entity must be either regular interests or residual interests, and there must be only one class of residual interests (Code Sec. 860D; Reg. § 1.860D-1).[73] However, a *de minimis* interest that is neither a regular nor a residual interest can be created to facilitate the REMIC creation.

A regular interest is any interest that is issued on the start-up day of the REMIC with fixed terms and that is designated as a regular interest (Code Sec. 860G(a)(1); Reg. § 1.860G-1).[74] A regular interest may be issued in the form of debt, stock, interest in a partnership or trust, or any other form permitted by state law, as long as it unconditionally entitles the holder to receive a specific principal amount and interest based on a fixed rate (or permitted variable rate). An interest-only regular interest may also be issued that entitles the holder to receive interest payments determined by reference to the interest payable on qualified mortgages, rather than a specified principal amount.

An interest does not fail to qualify as a regular interest merely because the timing of principal payments may be contingent on the prepayments on qualified mortgages or the amount of income from permitted investments (¶ 2345). In addition, an interest does not fail to be a regular interest solely because the specified principal amount may be reduced as a result of a nonoccurrence of a contingent payment with respect to a reverse mortgage loan held by the REMIC if the REMIC's sponsor reasonably believes on the start-up day that all principal and interest due under the regular interest will be paid at or prior to the REMIC's liquidation. The REMIC must file Form 1099-INT for each regular interest holder (and provide a copy to the interest holder) that has been paid or to which has accrued $10 or more of interest during the calendar year (Reg. § 1.6049-7).[75] If the REMIC is also reporting original issue discount (OID) (¶ 1952), it can report both the interest and OID on Form 1099-OID.

A residual interest is an interest issued on the REMIC's start-up day that is not a regular interest and that is designated as a residual interest (Code Sec. 860G(a)(2)).[76] There may be only one class of residual interests, and any distribution with respect to such interests must be pro rata. Furthermore, a REMIC must have reasonable arrangements to ensure that residual interests are not held by certain disqualified organizations (governments, exempt organizations, cooperatives) (Code Sec. 860D(a)(3) and (6)).[77] For each quarter of its tax year, a REMIC must send a Schedule Q of Form 1066 to

References are to Standard Federal Tax Reports; Tax Research Consultant; and Practical Tax Explanations.

[71] ¶ 26,660, ¶ 26,661; RIC: 9,050; § 45,445.05

[72] ¶ 36,036; RIC: 9,052

[73] ¶ 26,660, ¶ 26,661; RIC: 9,050; § 45,445.05

[74] ¶ 26,720, ¶ 26,720A; RIC: 9,056; § 45,445.10

[75] ¶ 36,036; RIC: 9,052, RIC: 9,204, RIC: 9,206; § 39,110.10

[76] ¶ 26,720; RIC: 9,058

[77] ¶ 26,660; RIC: 9,062

residual interest holders reporting their share of the REMIC's income or loss (Reg. § 1.860F-4(e)).[78]

REMIC Interests as Assets in Other Contexts. Regular and residual interests in a REMIC are treated as real estate assets for purposes of determining whether an organization qualifies as a real estate investment trust (REIT) (¶ 2326). However, if for any calendar quarter less than 95 percent of the REMIC's assets are real estate assets, the REIT is treated as holding directly its proportionate share of the assets and income of the REMIC (Code Sec. 856(c)(5)(E); Reg. § 1.856-3(b)).[79] If one REMIC owns interests in another REMIC, then the character of the second REMIC's assets flow through for purposes of making this determination. Any regular or residual interest in a REMIC can also qualify as an asset for purposes of determining whether an organization is a domestic building and loan association (Code Sec. 7701(a)(19); Reg. § 301.7701-13A).[80] If 95 percent or more of REMIC assets qualify as an asset for this purpose, then the entire interest in the REMIC can qualify as an asset.

2345. Qualified Mortgages and Permitted Investments of REMICs. In order to qualify as a real estate mortgage investment conduit (REMIC) (¶ 2343), substantially all of an entity's assets must consist of qualified mortgages and permitted investments at the close of the third month beginning after the start-up day and all times thereafter (Code Sec. 860D(a)(4)).[81] A qualified mortgage is any obligation that is principally secured by an interest in real property and that:

(1) is transferred to the REMIC on the start-up day in exchange for a regular or residual interest;

(2) is purchased by the REMIC within three months after the start-up day pursuant to a fixed price contract in effect on the start-up day; or

(3) represents an increase in the principal under the original terms of the obligation, if the increase (i) is attributable to an advance made to the obligor under the terms of a reverse mortgage or other obligation, (ii) occurs after the start-up day, and (iii) is purchased by the REMIC pursuant to a fixed price contract in effect on the start-up day (Code Sec. 860G(a)(3)).[82]

A qualified mortgage may also include any qualified replacement mortgage, or a regular interest in another REMIC transferred on the start-up day in exchange for a regular or residual interest.

Permitted investments include "cash flow" investments of amounts received under qualified mortgages for a temporary period, intangible property held for payment of expenses as part of a qualified reserve fund, and foreclosure property acquired in connection with the default of a qualified mortgage (Code Sec. 860G(a)(5)).[83]

2349. Transfer of Property to REMICs. No gain or loss is recognized when property is transferred to a real estate mortgage investment conduit (REMIC) in exchange for a regular or residual interest (¶ 2344) (Code Sec. 860F(b); Reg. § 1.860F-2(b)).[84] The basis of a regular or residual interest received in the exchange is equal to the total adjusted basis of the property transferred, plus any organizational expenses. If the transferor receives more than one interest in the REMIC (both a regular and residual interest), then the basis must be allocated among the interests in accordance with their respective fair market values. The basis of the property received by the REMIC in exchange for a regular or residual interest is its fair market value immediately after the transfer.

The issue price of a regular or residual interest is generally determined under the same rules as for determining the issue price for the original issue discount (OID) of debt instruments (¶ 1952) (Code Sec. 860G(a)(10)).[85] If the issue price of a regular

References are to Standard Federal Tax Reports; Tax Research Consultant; and Practical Tax Explanations.

[78] ¶ 26,701; RIC: 9,052, RIC: 9,252.30

[79] ¶ 26,500, ¶ 26,504; RIC: 6,072.05

[80] ¶ 43,080, ¶ 43,109; RIC: 12,056

[81] ¶ 26,660; RIC: 9,060; § 45,445.05

[82] ¶ 26,720; RIC: 9,060.05; § 45,445.05

[83] ¶ 26,720; RIC: 9,060.10; § 45,445.05

[84] ¶ 26,700, ¶ 26,700B; RIC: 9,100

[85] ¶ 26,720; RIC: 9,106

interest in a REMIC exceeds its adjusted basis, then the excess is included in the transferor's gross income as if it were a market discount bond (¶ 1958) (Code Sec. 860F(b)(1)(C); Reg. § 1.860F-2(b)(4)). If the issue price of a residual interest exceeds its adjusted basis, then the excess is included in the transferor's gross income ratably over the anticipated weighted average life of the REMIC. If the adjusted basis of a regular interest exceeds the issue price, then the excess is allowable as a deduction to the transferor under the rules similar to those governing amortizable bond premiums (¶ 1967) (Code Sec. 860F(b)(1)(D); Reg. § 1.860F-2(b)(4)). If the adjusted basis of a residual interest exceeds the issue price, then the excess is allowed as a deduction to the transferor over the anticipated weighted average life of the REMIC.

2352. Taxable Income or Loss of REMICs. A real estate mortgage investment conduit (REMIC) (¶ 2343) is not generally taxed on its income (Code Sec. 860A).[86] However, its taxable income must still be determined for purposes of the taxation of residual interest holders (¶ 2361). REMIC taxable income is determined in the same manner as that of an individual, except that it must use the accrual method of accounting and make the following adjustments:

- Regular interests in the REMIC are treated as debt.
- Market discount on any bond is included in gross income as the discount accrues.
- No item of income, gain, loss, or deduction from a prohibited transaction is taken into account (¶ 2355).
- The deductions for personal exemptions, foreign taxes, charitable contributions, net operating losses (NOLs), itemized deductions for individuals (except ordinary and necessary expenses paid or incurred for the production of income), and depletion are not allowed.
- The amount of any net income from foreclosure property is reduced by the amount of tax imposed on that income.
- Gain or loss from the disposition of assets, including qualified mortgages and permitted investments, is treated as ordinary gain or loss rather than gain or loss from a capital asset.
- Interest expenses (other than the portion allocable to tax-exempt interest) may be deducted without regard to the investment interest limitation.
- Debts owed to the REMIC are not treated as nonbusiness debts for purposes of the bad debt deduction.
- The REMIC is not treated as carrying on a trade or business, and ordinary and necessary operating expenses may only be deducted as expenses incurred for the production of income (without regard to the two-percent floor on itemized deductions (¶ 1079)) (Code Sec. 860C(b); Reg. § 1.860C-2).[87]

A REMIC's net loss is determined by subtracting its gross income from allowable deductions, taking into account the same modifications listed above.

2355. Prohibited Transactions of REMICs. A real estate mortgage investment conduit (REMIC) (¶ 2343) is required to pay a 100-percent tax on its *net income* from a prohibited transaction; losses are not taken into account for this purpose (Code Sec. 860F(a)).[88] The disposition of any qualified mortgage is considered a prohibited transaction, but not if the disposition is due to:

- the substitution of a qualified replacement mortgage for a qualified mortgage (or the repurchase in lieu of substitution of a defective obligation);
- the bankruptcy or insolvency of the REMIC;
- a disposition incident to foreclosure or default of a mortgage; or
- a qualified liquidation.

References are to Standard Federal Tax Reports; Tax Research Consultant; and Practical Tax Explanations.

[86] ¶ 26,600; RIC: 9,150; § 45,445.10

[87] ¶ 26,640, ¶ 26,640B; RIC: 9,254

[88] ¶ 26,700; RIC: 9,152

A significant modification of a mortgage is considered a disposition (Reg. § 1.860G-2(b)).[89] The IRS has issued procedures that set forth conditions under which modifications of certain mortgage loans, as well as subprime mortgage loans, will not be considered a disposition of a qualified mortgage and a prohibited transaction of a REMIC or investment trust that holds the loans (Rev. Proc. 2010-30; Rev. Proc. 2009-45; Rev. Proc. 2009-23).[90]

Prohibited transactions of a REMIC also include: the receipt of any income from an asset that is neither a qualified mortgage nor a permitted investment (¶ 2345); the receipt of any amount that represents a fee or compensation for services; and the receipt of gain from the disposition of any cash flow investment, unless the disposition is made pursuant to a qualified liquidation. A disposition is not treated as a prohibited transaction if it is required to prevent default on a regular interest where the threatened default results from a default on one or more qualified mortgages, or is undertaken to facilitate a cleanup call.

2356. Net Income from Foreclosure Property. A real estate mortgage investment conduit (REMIC) is subject to tax at the highest corporate income tax rate (¶ 219) on its *net income* from foreclosure property for the tax year (Code Sec. 860G(c)).[91] For this purpose, net income from foreclosure property is the excess of gain from the sale or other disposition of foreclosure property as described in Code Sec. 1221(a)(1) (i.e., stock in trade or property held by the REMIC for sale to customers in the ordinary course of trade or business), plus the gross income derived from foreclosure property during the tax year, over deductions derived from the production of such income (Code Sec. 857(b)(4)(B)).[92] Foreclosure property is any interest in real property, and personal property incident to the real property, acquired by a REMIC as a result of a default of a lease on the property or a debt securing the property. A REMIC must elect to treat property as foreclosure property by the due date (including extensions) of its annual return for the year in which it acquires the property. Property ceases to be foreclosure property: (1) as of the close of the third tax year after the tax year in which it is acquired, unless an extension is granted, or (2) if the property's foreclosure property status terminates prior to that date (Code Sec. 856(e)).[93]

2357. Post-Startup Contributions to REMICs. A real estate mortgage investment conduit (REMIC) (¶ 2343) that receives contributions of property after its start-up day is subject to a tax equal to the full value of the contribution (Code Sec. 860G(d)).[94] Exceptions to the tax are provided for cash contributions that are: made to facilitate a cleanup call or a qualified liquidation; in the nature of a guarantee; made during the three-month period that begins on the start-up day; made by a holder of a residual interest in the REMIC to a qualified reserve fund; or permitted under regulations.

2358. Taxation of Regular Interests. Holders of regular interests in a real estate mortgage investment conduit (REMIC) (¶ 2344) are taxed as if their interests were debt instruments, except that income derived from their interests must be computed under the accrual method of accounting (Code Sec. 860B).[95] Gain on the disposition of a regular interest is treated as ordinary income to the extent of unaccrued original issue discount (OID) (¶ 1952), computed at 110 percent of the applicable federal rate (AFR) effective at the time the interest was acquired. The REMIC must report interest payments of $10 or more to regular interest holders and the IRS on Form 1099-INT.

2361. Taxation of Residual Interests. Holders of residual interests in a real estate mortgage investment conduit (REMIC) (¶ 2344) must take into account their daily portions of the taxable income or net loss of the REMIC (¶ 2352) for each day during the tax year on which they hold their interests (Code Sec. 860C; Reg. § 1.860C-1).[96] The daily portion is determined on the basis of quarterly computations of the REMIC's taxable income or net loss with such amounts being allocated among all residual

References are to Standard Federal Tax Reports; Tax Research Consultant; and Practical Tax Explanations.

[89] ¶ 26,720B; RIC: 9,152.10

[90] ¶ 26,721.70; RIC: 9,152.10

[91] ¶ 26,720; RIC: 9,154

[92] ¶ 26,520; RIC: 6,114

[93] ¶ 26,500; RIC: 6,068.10, RIC: 6,068.15; RIC: 9,060.10

[94] ¶ 26,720; RIC: 9,156

[95] ¶ 26,620; RIC: 9,202; § 45,445.10

[96] ¶ 26,640, ¶ 26,640A; RIC: 9,250, RIC: 9,252; § 45,445.10

interests in proportion to their respective holdings on each day during the quarter (reported on Schedule Q of Form 1066). The holder treats his or her portion of taxable income and net loss as ordinary income or loss. However, the amount of loss that the holder may take into account in any calendar quarter cannot exceed his or her adjusted basis in the residual interest (as determined without regard to any required basis decreases for the daily portions of the REMIC's net loss). Any allocated loss that is disallowed may be carried forward to succeeding calendar quarters indefinitely, but it may only be used to offset income from the same REMIC.

Distributions made by the REMIC to a holder of a residual interest are received tax free to the extent that they do not exceed that holder's adjusted basis in his or her interest. Any excess is treated as gain from the sale or exchange of the interest. The basis of a holder's residual interest is increased by the daily portion of REMIC taxable income allocated to the interest. The holder's basis is decreased, but not below zero, by the amount of any distribution received and the daily portion of the REMIC net loss allocated to the interest holder. When a residual interest in a REMIC is disposed of by the holder, these adjustments are treated as occurring immediately before the disposition.

Income in Excess of Daily Accruals. A holder of a residual interest may not reduce his or her taxable income (or alternative minimum taxable income) for the tax year below his or her excess inclusion for the year (Code Sec. 860E; Reg. § 1.860E-1).[97] A holder's excess inclusion is equal to the excess of the net income passed through to the holder each calendar quarter over a deemed interest component referred to as the "daily accrual." The effect is to prevent a holder from offsetting his or her excess inclusion by any net operating losses (NOLs) (¶ 1145) or in calculating alternative minimum tax (AMT) (¶ 1401). Excess inclusions are also treated as unrelated business taxable income for tax-exempt holders (¶ 655). Where a residual interest is held by a mutual fund (regulated investment company or RIC), real estate investment trust (REIT), common trust fund, or cooperative, a portion of the dividends paid by such organizations to their shareholders are treated as excess inclusions.

Application of Wash Sale Rules. Except as provided in the regulations, the wash sale rules (¶ 1935) apply to dispositions of residual interests where a seller of the interest acquires any residual interest in any REMIC (or any interest in a taxable mortgage pool (¶ 2368) that is comparable to a residual interest) within a period beginning six months before the date of sale or disposition and ending six months after that date (Code Sec. 860F(d)).[98]

Residual Interests Held by Disqualified Organizations. If a disqualified organization (government, exempt organization, cooperative) holds a residual interest in a REMIC at any time during the tax year, then an excise tax is imposed against the person or entity that has transferred the interest to the organization (Code Sec. 860E(e); Reg. § 1.860E-2).[99] The tax is the highest corporate income tax rate (¶ 219) imposed on the present value of the total excess inclusion that is anticipated for the interest after the transfer takes place. If the transfer is through an agent of the disqualified organization, the agent must pay the tax.

Noneconomic Interests. The transfer of a noneconomic residual interest is disregarded for federal tax purposes if a significant purpose of the transfer was to impede the assessment or collection of tax (Reg. § 1.860E-1(c)).[100] A noneconomic residual interest is one for which anticipated distributions are insufficient to meet anticipated tax liabilities.

References are to Standard Federal Tax Reports; Tax Research Consultant; and Practical Tax Explanations.

[97] ¶ 26,680, ¶ 26,680A; RIC: 9,256

[98] ¶ 26,700; RIC: 9,262

[99] ¶ 26,680, ¶ 26,680B; RIC: 9,062, RIC: 9,258.05

[100] ¶ 26,680A; RIC: 9,258.10

2367. Foreign Holders of REMIC Interests. If the holder of a residual interest in a real estate mortgage investment conduit (REMIC) (¶ 2361) is a nonresident alien or foreign corporation, then for withholding and income tax purposes (¶ 2425): (1) amounts includible in the holder's gross income are taken into account when paid or distributed, or when the interest is disposed of; and (2) no exemption from the 30-percent tax imposed on U.S.-source income not effectively connected with a U.S. business applies to any excess inclusion (¶ 2431) (Code Sec. 860G(b)).[101]

2368. Taxable Mortgage Pools. If a mortgage pool does not elect to be or qualify as a real estate mortgage investment conduit (REMIC) (¶ 2343) or as a financial asset securitization investment trust (FASIT) formed prior to January 1, 2005 (¶ 2394), it may qualify as a taxable mortgage pool. An entity is a taxable mortgage pool if:

(1) substantially all the assets of which consist of debt obligations (or interests therein) and more than 50 percent of the obligations (or interests) consist of real estate mortgages;

(2) the entity is the obligor under debt obligations with two or more maturities; and

(3) under the terms of the entity's debt obligations, payments on the obligations referred to in (2) are related to payments on the obligations or interests referred to in (1) (Code Sec. 7701(i)).[102]

A taxable mortgage pool is taxed as a separate corporation and may not join with any other corporation in filing a consolidated return. Any portion of an entity that meets the requirements above is treated as a taxable mortgage pool. However, no domestic savings and loan association can qualify to be a taxable mortgage pool.

Insurance Companies

2370. Taxation of Life Insurance Companies. A life insurance company is generally taxed on its life insurance company taxable income at regular corporate income tax rates (¶ 219) (Code Sec. 801).[103] If it has net capital gains, however, the company is taxed at the 35-percent corporate capital gain rate (¶ 1738) on its net capital gain, and at regular corporate tax rates on the excess of its life insurance company taxable income minus the net capital gain, if this results in a lower tax amount.

Life insurance company taxable income for this purpose is the sum of the life insurance company's net premiums, net decreases in reserves, and other items of income, minus deductions for the following: claims, benefits, and losses accrued; net increases in various reserves (¶ 2372); policyholder dividends (¶ 2373); dividends received (subject to limitations); operational losses (¶ 2377); consideration paid for another person's assumption of the company's insurance and annuity liabilities; and dividend reimbursements paid to another insurance company (Code Secs. 803, 804, and 805).[104]

All other deductions allowed to a corporation are also permitted, subject to some modifications (for example, no deduction for net operating losses (NOLs) is allowed). Small life insurance companies (gross assets of less than $500 million at the close of a tax year) may claim an additional deduction based on their tentative taxable income (Code Sec. 806).[105] A life insurance company uses Form 1120-L to figure and report its taxable income.

A business entity qualifies as a life insurance company if: (1) more than half of its business activities consist of issuing life insurance or annuity contracts, or reinsuring risks underwritten by other insurance companies; and (2) more than half of its total reserves for paying off insurance obligations consist of life insurance reserves, plus unearned premiums, and unpaid losses on noncancellable life, accident, or health policies that are not included in life insurance reserves (Code Sec. 816).[106]

References are to Standard Federal Tax Reports; Tax Research Consultant; and Practical Tax Explanations.

[101] ¶ 26,720; RIC: 9,252.20, INTL: 33,110.30

[102] ¶ 43,080; RIC: 9,300

[103] ¶ 25,710

[104] ¶ 25,730, ¶ 25,750, ¶ 25,770

[105] ¶ 25,790; FILEBUS: 3,056

[106] ¶ 25,990

2372. Net Change in Reserves. Life insurance companies (¶ 2370) may deduct the net increase in certain reserves and must include in income the net decrease in such reserves that have occurred during the tax year (Code Sec. 807).[107] The net increase or decrease is generally computed by comparing the closing balance for reserves to the opening balance of the reserves. The closing balance is reduced by the policyholders' shares of tax-exempt interest and shares of the increase in cash values of insurance and annuity contracts for the year.

Items that must be taken into account in determining whether reserves have had a net increase or decrease include:

- life insurance reserves;
- unearned premiums and unpaid losses (Code Sec. 846);[108]
- discounted amounts necessary to satisfy obligations arising under contracts that did not involve life, accident, or health contingencies;
- dividend accumulations and other amounts held in connection with insurance and annuity contracts;
- advanced premiums and liabilities for premium deposit funds; and
- reasonable special contingency reserves for group term life insurance or group accident and health contracts.

Insurance companies that are required to discount unpaid losses may claim an additional deduction up to the excess of undiscounted unpaid losses over related discounted unpaid losses (Code Sec. 847).[109]

2373. Policyholder Dividends. Life insurance companies (¶ 2370) may claim a deduction for dividends or similar distributions paid or accrued to policyholders during the tax year (Code Sec. 808).[110] A policyholder dividend includes excess interest, premium adjustments, experience-rated refunds, and any amount paid or credited to policyholders not based on a fixed amount in the contract but dependent on the experience rate of the company or the discretion of management. The policyholder dividends deduction must be reduced by the amount by which the deduction was accelerated due to a change in the life insurance company's business practice.

2377. Operations Loss Deduction. A life insurance company (¶ 2370) may claim an operations loss deduction, which equals the sum of operations loss carryovers and carrybacks to the tax year. The company's loss from operations for a tax year is the excess of its life insurance deductions over its life insurance gross income (subject to limitations). An operations loss may be carried back three years and carried forward 15 years (Code Sec. 810).[111] The company may elect to forgo the entire carryback period for an operations loss for any tax year. In addition, if the company qualifies as a new life insurance company, the operations loss for any tax year may be carried forward 18 years.

2378. Taxation of Other Insurance Companies. Insurance companies that do not meet the definition of a life insurance company (¶ 2370) (property and casualty companies) are subject to taxation at regular corporate income tax rates (¶ 219) on their taxable income (Code Secs. 831(a) and 832).[112] However, such companies are exempt from tax if gross receipts for the tax year do not exceed $600,000 and more than 50 percent of such receipts consist of premiums ($150,000 and 35 percent, respectively, for mutual insurance companies) (Code Sec. 501(c)(15)).[113] A property and casualty insurance company with net written premiums of no more than $1.2 million for the tax year may elect to be taxed only on its taxable investment income. This is the company's gross investment income less deductions for tax-free interest, investment expenses, real estate expenses, depreciation, paid or accrued interest, capital losses, trade or business deductions, and certain corporate deductions (Code Secs. 831(b) and 834).[114]

References are to Standard Federal Tax Reports; Tax Research Consultant; and Practical Tax Explanations.

[107] ¶ 25,810
[108] ¶ 26,330
[109] ¶ 26,350
[110] ¶ 25,830
[111] ¶ 25,870; NOL: 9,250
[112] ¶ 26,130, ¶ 26,150; CCORP: 100
[113] ¶ 22,602; EXEMPT: 9,650; § 33,005.05
[114] ¶ 26,130, ¶ 26,190; EXEMPT: 9,650

Effective for tax years beginning after December 31, 2016, eligibility rules for small property and casualty insurance companies to elect Code Sec. 831(b) status have been modified to increase the premium limit and index it to inflation, and to add certain diversification requirements (Code Sec. 831, as amended by the Protecting Americans from Tax Hikes (PATH) Act of 2015 (P.L. 114-113)). The existing $1.2 million limit on net written premiums or direct written premiums (whichever is greater) is increased and adjusted for inflation, and is $2,250,000 for tax years beginning in 2017 (Code Sec. 831(b)(2)(A)(i), as amended by P.L. 114-113; Rev. Proc. 2016-55).

A diversification requirement has also been added to the Code Sec. 831(b) eligibility requirements. There are two methods of meeting this requirement. The primary method—the "risk diversification test"—is to have no more that 20 percent of the company's net written premiums (or, if greater, direct written premiums) attributable to one policyholder in a tax year (Code Sec. 831(b)(2)(B)(i)(I), as added by P.L. 114-113). Small insurance companies that fail to meet this test may be able to meet the alternative "relatedness test" requirements. This second chance requires that no person who holds (directly or indirectly) an interest in the company be a "specified holder" with aggregate interests in the company (held directly or indirectly) that are a higher percentage of the entire interests in that insurance company than a *de minimis* percentage of interests in the specified assets with respect to the company held (directly or indirectly) by the specified holder (Code Sec. 831(b)(2)(B)(i)(II), as added by P.L. 114-113).

2380. Foreign Insurance Companies. A foreign company carrying on an insurance business within the United States that would otherwise qualify as an insurance company if it were a domestic company is taxable as an insurance company on its income effectively connected with the conduct of any U.S. trade or business (¶ 2429) and is taxable on its remaining income from U.S. sources (¶ 2431) (Code Sec. 842).[115]

Other Special Entities

2383. Banks and Other Financial Institutions. Banks and other financial institutions are generally subject to the same tax rules as corporations. However, unlike other taxpayers, banks are not subject to capital loss limitations with respect to the worthlessness of debt securities (¶ 1916). Instead, banks may treat these losses as bad debt losses. In addition, if one bank directly owns at least 80 percent of each class of stock of another bank, the first bank's losses on worthless stock and stock rights in the second bank are not treated as losses from the sale or exchange of capital assets (Code Sec. 582).[116]

The method that is used to deduct bad debts of a bank depends on the type and size of the institution in question (Code Sec. 585; Reg. §§1.585-1—1.585-8).[117] A small bank (average adjusted basis of all assets of $500 million or less) may add to its bad debt reserves an amount based on its actual experience as shown by losses for the current and preceding five tax years. A thrift institution that would be treated as a small bank may utilize this method as well. Large banks are generally required to use either a specific charge-off method in which the bank's debt reserves are recaptured over a four-year period, or the cutoff method in which recoveries and losses are reflected as adjustments to the bank's reserve account.

Definition of a Bank. For this purpose, a bank is defined as a corporation with a substantial part of its business consisting of either receiving deposits and making loans or exercising fiduciary powers similar to those permitted to national banks. This includes commercial banks and trust companies, mutual savings banks, building and loan associations, cooperative banks, and federal savings and loan associations (Code Sec. 581; Reg. §1.581-2).[118] These latter "banks," however, are allowed a deduction for dividends paid or credited to depositors (Code Sec. 591).[119]

References are to Standard Federal Tax Reports; Tax Research Consultant; and Practical Tax Explanations.

[115] ¶ 26,250; INTLIN: 3,108

[116] ¶ 23,608; BUSEXP: 30,102.15, BUSEXP: 48,154, RIC: 12,114.15

[117] ¶ 23,650, ¶ 23,651—¶ 23,661; RIC: 12,202

[118] ¶ 23,602, ¶ 23,604; RIC: 12,050

[119] ¶ 23,690; CCORP: 9,062

Sale or Exchange of Securities. In the case of certain financial institutions, the sale or exchange of a bond, debenture, note, certificate, or other evidence of indebtedness is not considered a sale or exchange of a capital asset (Code Sec. 582(c)).[120] Instead, net gains and losses from such transactions are treated as ordinary income and losses. A financial institution includes commercial banks, mutual savings banks, domestic building and loan associations, cooperative banks, business development corporations, and small business investment companies (¶ 2392).

2389. Common Trust Funds. A common trust fund is an investment vehicle established by a bank in the form of a state-law trust to handle the investment and reinvestment of money contributed to it in its capacity as a trustee, executor, administrator, guardian, or as a custodian of a Uniform Gifts to Minors account (Code Sec. 584).[121] For tax purposes, a common trust fund is treated in a manner similar to that of a partnership. Instead of the trust being subject to tax, each participant that invests in the trust fund must include his or her proportionate share of the trust fund's income or loss on his or her own return. This includes a participant's share of dividends received by the fund that are eligible for the reduced tax rate on qualified dividends (¶ 733). The admission and withdrawal of a participant, however, does not result in a gain or loss to the common trust fund.

2392. Small Business Investment Companies. A small business investment company (SBIC) is a private corporation that operates under the Small Business Investment Act of 1958 to provide capital to small business concerns through the purchase of convertible debentures. An SBIC is generally treated as a corporation for federal tax purposes with a few exceptions. First, an SBIC may claim an ordinary loss deduction for any loss on the sale or exchange of stock of a small business concern if the stock was received under the conversion privilege of a debenture acquired on the providing of equity capital to small business concerns (Code Sec. 1243).[122] Second, an SBIC may deduct 100 percent (rather than 70 percent) of the dividends it receives from taxable domestic corporations (Code Sec. 243(a)(2)).[123] See ¶ 1913 for discussion of the treatment of losses on SBIC stock and ¶ 1909 for discussion of the rollover of gain from the sale of publicly traded securities into stock or a partnership interest in a specialized SBIC.

2394. Financial Asset Securitization Investment Trusts (Repealed). Prior to January 1, 2005, a qualified entity could elect to be treated as a financial asset securitization investment trust (FASIT) (Code Secs. 860H—860L, prior to repeal by the American Jobs Creation Act of 2004 (P.L. 108-357)).[124] A FASIT is a passthrough entity used to securitize debt obligations such as credit card receivables, home equity loans, and auto loans. A FASIT must be entirely owned by a taxable C corporation. Any residual income of the FASIT is passed through and taxed to the owner. The advantage offered by a FASIT is that asset-backed securities issued by a FASIT are treated as debt for federal tax purposes. Thus, interest paid to investors is deductible.

The rules regarding FASITs are repealed as of January 1, 2005, but the repeal does not apply to any FASIT in existence on October 22, 2004, to the extent that regular interests already issued by the FASIT remain outstanding in accordance with their original terms.

References are to Standard Federal Tax Reports; Tax Research Consultant; and Practical Tax Explanations.

[120] ¶ 23,608; RIC: 12,214

[121] ¶ 23,630; RIC: 12,300

[122] ¶ 30,770; SALES: 18,304; § 18,245

[123] ¶ 13,051; CCORP: 9,056; § 26,505

[124] ¶ 26,730—¶ 26,738; RIC: 18,000

Chapter 24
FOREIGN INCOME AND TRANSACTIONS

	Par.
Overview	2401
U.S. Citizens and Residents Living Abroad	2402
Nonresident Aliens and Foreign Corporations	2425
Reporting Foreign Assets of U.S. Taxpayers	2465
Foreign Tax Credit or Deduction	2475
U.S. Shareholders of Foreign Corporations	2487
Other Foreign Tax Rules	2495

Overview

2401. Taxation of Worldwide Income. The United States taxes the worldwide income of U.S. citizens, resident aliens, and domestic corporations without regard to whether the income arose from a transaction or activity originating outside its geographic borders (¶ 2402). Nonresident aliens and foreign corporations are generally taxed in the same manner as U.S. citizens and domestic corporations on income that is effectively connected with a U.S. trade or business (¶ 2425). Income not effectively connected with a U.S. trade or business, such as fixed, determinable, annual, or periodical (FDAP) income, is generally taxed at a 30-percent rate, absent a lower treaty rate (¶ 2431). To prevent income from being subject to double taxation—once in the United States and once in a foreign country—U.S. taxpayers may be entitled to a credit or deduction for foreign income taxes paid or accrued during the tax year (¶ 2475). Special rules apply with regard to the taxation of U.S. shareholders of controlled foreign corporations (CFCs) (¶ 2487). U.S. persons are also subject to a number of foreign asset reporting requirements (¶ 2570 and ¶ 2572).

U.S. Citizens and Residents Living Abroad

2402. Foreign Earned Income Exclusion. A qualifying individual (¶ 2404) who lives and works abroad may elect (¶ 2408) to exclude from gross income a certain amount of foreign earned income attributable to his or her residence in a foreign country during the tax year (Code Sec. 911(a)(1) and (b)(2)).[1] The maximum amount of foreign earned income that may be excluded is $101,300 for 2016 ($102,100 for 2017) (Rev. Proc. 2015-53; Rev. Proc. 2016-55). The exclusion is computed on a daily basis. Therefore, the maximum limit must be reduced ratably for each day during the calendar year that the taxpayer does not qualify for the exclusion. The exclusion is also limited to the excess of the individual's foreign earned income for the year over his or her foreign housing exclusion (¶ 2403). In the case of married taxpayers, each spouse may compute the limitation separately and without regard to community property laws (if otherwise applicable). Thus, it is possible for a married couple to exclude up to $202,600 for 2016 ($204,200 for 2017) if each spouse is qualified to claim the exclusion (Reg. § 1.911-5).[2]

> **Example 1:** Andy is a U.S. citizen who qualified as a bona fide resident of Costa Rica for all of 2015 and who received $78,000 in salary for work he did in Costa Rica. Assuming he claimed no foreign housing exclusion, Andy was able to exclude all of the salary from his gross income for 2015. Andy continues to work in Costa Rica until October 31, 2016, when his employer permanently reassigns him to the United States. During this time, Andy received a salary of $90,000 for his work in Costa Rica in 2016. Assuming he claimed no foreign housing exclusion, the maximum amount of foreign earned income he can exclude from his gross income

References are to Standard Federal Tax Reports; Tax Research Consultant; and Practical Tax Explanations.

[1] ¶ 28,040; EXPAT: 12,100; § 37,510.05

[2] ¶ 28,045; EXPAT: 12,400; § 37,510.25

in 2016 is $84,417 ($101,300 multiplied by ratio of the number of days he was a bona fide resident of Costa Rica (305/366).

Foreign Earned Income. Foreign earned income includes wages, salaries, professional fees, and other amounts received as compensation for personal services actually rendered when the taxpayer's tax home is located in a foreign country and the taxpayer meets either the bona fide residence or physical presence test (Code Sec. 911(b)(1) and (d)(2); Reg. § 1.911-3).[3] If the taxpayer engages in a sole proprietorship or partnership where both personal services and capital are material income-producing factors, no more than 30 percent of the taxpayer's share of the net profits can be treated as earned income (30 percent of gross profits if no net profits). Any salary received from a corporation is earned income to the extent it represents reasonable compensation for personal services performed.

Foreign earned income does not include any compensation received after the close of the tax year following the year in which the personal services were performed. It also does not include any reimbursements received under an accountable plan for expenses incurred on an employer's behalf (¶ 952A), the value of meals and lodging that are furnished for the convenience of an employer and excluded from gross income (¶ 2089 and ¶ 2406), employer contributions to a nonqualified retirement plan, or any recaptured moving expenses. Foreign earned income also does not include amounts received as a pension, annuity, or social security payments, amounts paid by the United States or its agencies to its employees, or income earned in a country in which the United States imposes travel restrictions.

A taxpayer who elects to claim the foreign earned income exclusion (or foreign housing exclusion) is prohibited from claiming any deduction, exclusion, or tax credit (including the foreign tax credit) that is properly allocable to the excluded amounts (Code Sec. 911(d)(6); Reg. § 1.911-6(a)).[4] For example, a taxpayer may not deduct unreimbursed employee business expenses against wages that are excluded as foreign earned income.

Determination of Tax Liability. If an individual elects to exclude foreign earned income or foreign housing expenses (or both), then his or her income tax liability and alternative minimum tax liability on the nonexcluded amount is determined using the tax rates that would have applied had the exclusion(s) not been claimed (Code Sec. 911(f)).[5] If the taxpayer's net capital gains exceed his or her taxable income or alternative minimum taxable income, then the excess reduces the taxpayer's net capital gains without regard to qualified dividend income, and then qualified dividend income. The excess is also treated as a long-term capital loss in computing the taxpayer's adjusted net capital gain, unrecaptured section 1250 gain, and 28-percent rate gain. The Foreign Earned Income Worksheet in the Form 1040 Instructions or Form 6251 Instructions is used to calculate tax liability for this purpose.

2403. Foreign Housing Exclusion or Deduction. In addition to the election to exclude foreign earned income (¶ 2402), a qualified individual (¶ 2404) may elect (¶ 2408) to exclude from gross income a certain amount of foreign housing expenses paid for with employer-provided amounts included in the taxpayer's foreign earned income (for example, housing allowance or reimbursement) (Code Sec. 911(a)(2)).[6] The amount of foreign housing expenses or foreign earned income excluded from an individual's gross income is used to determine the taxpayer's regular income tax and alternative minimum tax liability on his or her nonexcluded income (¶ 2402).

The maximum housing amount that may be excluded is limited to 14 percent of the maximum foreign earned income exclusion for the year (Code Sec. 911(c)). This is the excess of: (1) the taxpayer's reasonable "foreign housing expenses" for the tax year (generally limited to 30 percent of the maximum foreign earned income exclusion for the year), over (2) a "base housing amount" equal to 16 percent of the maximum foreign

References are to Standard Federal Tax Reports; Tax Research Consultant; and Practical Tax Explanations.

[3] ¶ 28,040, ¶ 28,043; EXPAT: 12,200; § 37,510.10

[4] ¶ 28,040, ¶ 28,046; EXPAT: 12,250; § 37,525.05

[5] ¶ 28,040; EXPAT: 12,100; § 37,520

[6] ¶ 28,040; EXPAT: 12,150; § 37,515.05

earned income exclusion amount for the year. The exclusion is computed on a daily basis and multiplied by the number of days of foreign residence or presence by the taxpayer for the year.

For 2016, the maximum amount of foreign housing expenses that generally may be excluded is $14,182 or $38.75 per day. This is 14 percent of the maximum foreign exclusion amount for 2016 ($101,300), and is the difference between 30 percent of the exclusion amount ($30,390 or $83.03 per day), and 16 percent of the exclusion amount ($16,208, or $44.28 per day) (Rev. Proc. 2015-53). For 2017, the maximum amount of foreign housing expenses that generally may be excluded is $14,294 or $39.16 per day. This is 14 percent of the maximum foreign exclusion amount for 2017 ($102,100), and is the difference between 30 percent of the exclusion amount ($30,630 or $83.92 per day), and 16 percent of the exclusion amount ($16,336, or $44.76 per day) (Rev. Proc. 2016-55). Foreign housing expenses may be excluded only to the extent of the lesser of the expenses attributable to employer-provided amounts or the individual's foreign earned income for the tax year.

The reasonable amount of expenses that may be used in calculating the maximum exclusion limit, i.e., the 30 percent of the maximum foreign earned income exclusion, may be adjusted annually by the IRS for specific geographic locations that have higher housing costs relative to the United States (Notice 2016-21).[7] For this purpose, the taxpayer must actually reside within the geographic limits of the high-cost location identified by the IRS to claim the adjusted limit; the taxpayer cannot reside in a suburb of the location. The limits for high-cost localities are listed in the Instructions for Form 2555.

Housing Expenses. A individual's foreign housing expenses are the reasonable costs paid or incurred during the tax year to provide housing in a foreign country for the taxpayer and for his or her spouse and dependents if they reside with the taxpayer (Reg. § 1.911-4).[8] This may include reasonable expenses related to a second foreign household for the taxpayer's spouse and dependents if they do not reside with the taxpayer due to adverse conditions near the taxpayer's tax home. Eligible expenses include rent or the fair rental value of housing provided in kind by an employer, utilities (other than telephone charges), real or personal property insurance, household repairs, rental of furniture and accessories, and residential parking. Excluded are expenses that are otherwise deductible (depreciation, interest, taxes) or that are extravagant. Also excluded is the cost of buying property (including mortgage payments), capital improvements to property, purchased furniture or accessories, or the cost of domestic labor. If a husband and wife are both qualified individuals with foreign earned income, special rules apply which may allow them both to claim the foreign housing exclusion or deduction, depending on whether separate households are maintained (Reg. § 1.911-5).[9]

Self-Employment. A self-employed individual is entitled to deduct from gross income a certain amount of foreign housing expenses in lieu of the exclusion for employer-provided amounts (Code Sec. 911(c)(4); Reg. § 1.911-4(e)).[10] The deduction is limited to the amount by which the taxpayer's foreign earned income for the tax year exceeds his or her foreign earned income and housing exclusion. Any amount that exceeds the deduction limit can be carried forward one tax year. If the taxpayer has foreign earned income that consists of both employer-provided amounts and self-employment amounts, then the taxpayer may elect to exclude the part of the housing expenses that are paid for with employer-provided amounts and may claim a deduction for any remaining housing expenses attributed to self-employment income.

2404. Eligibility for Foreign Earned Income and Housing Exclusions. In order to qualify for the foreign earned income exclusion (¶ 2402) or foreign housing exclusion (¶ 2403), an individual's tax home must be in a foreign country and he or she must satisfy either the bona fide residence test or the physical presence test (Code Sec. 911(d)(1); Reg. § 1.911-2).[11] A foreign country is any territory, including airspace and

References are to Standard Federal Tax Reports; Tax Research Consultant; and Practical Tax Explanations.

[7] ¶ 28,049.225; EXPAT: 12,152; § 37,515.05

[8] ¶ 28,044; EXPAT: 12,154; § 37,515.10

[9] ¶ 28,045; EXPAT: 12,400; § 37,515.25

[10] ¶ 28,040, ¶ 28,044; EXPAT: 12,162; § 37,515.20

[11] ¶ 28,040, ¶ 28,042; EXPAT: 12,050; § 37,505.05

territorial waters, under the sovereignty of a government other than the United States. A foreign country does not include Antarctica or U.S. possessions such as Puerto Rico, Guam, the Commonwealth of the Northern Mariana Islands, the U.S. Virgin Islands, and Johnston Island. A bona fide resident of American Samoa (¶ 2414) or Puerto Rico (¶ 2415) may be eligible to exclude income from the possession for U.S. tax purposes. The foreign earned income and housing exclusions are denied if the taxpayer is present in a foreign country in which travel is generally restricted (Code Sec. 911(d)(8)).

Tax Home. "Tax home" for this purpose has the same meaning as it does for determining the deductibility of travel expenses away from home (¶ 950). An individual's tax home is where his or her principal place of business is located, regardless of where he or she maintains a family home (Code Sec. 911(d)(3)). The location of a taxpayer's tax home often depends on whether a work assignment is temporary or indefinite. An individual is not considered to have a tax home in a foreign country for any period during which his or her abode is in the United States. Temporary presence or maintenance of a dwelling in the United States does not necessarily mean that an abode is in the United States during that time, even if the taxpayer's spouse or dependents use the dwelling.

Bona Fide Residence. A U.S. citizen (or resident alien subject to a U.S. income tax treaty) may qualify for the foreign earned income or housing exclusions if he or she is a bona fide resident of a foreign country for an uninterrupted period that includes a full tax year (Code Sec. 911(d)(1)(A) and (d)(5)). This determination is based on all of the facts and circumstances, including the taxpayer's intentions regarding the length and nature of the stay. It is not determined by the taxpayer's status under the laws of the foreign country, nor by merely living in a foreign country for a year. The taxpayer does not have to be a bona fide resident of the same foreign country for the entire period and the foreign country in which the taxpayer is a bona fide resident does not have to be the primary place of employment. Once the bona fide residence requirement is met, the taxpayer is permitted the exclusions for any tax year in which the period of residence began or ended.

Example 1: Barney is a calendar-year taxpayer whose salary is $120,000 per year. On January 1, 2015, he establishes bona fide residence in Canada. His residence lasts until March 31, 2016. Assuming he claims no foreign housing exclusion, he qualifies in 2015 for the maximum exclusion of $100,800 for his foreign earned income because he established residence for the full year in a foreign country. He also qualifies for the exclusion of $25,187 of his foreign earned income ($101,300 × 91/366) for the portion of the 2016 tax year he was a resident in Canada.

Physical Presence. A U.S. citizen or resident alien may qualify for the foreign income or housing exclusions if he or she is present in a foreign country (or countries) for 330 full days out of any consecutive 12-month period (Code Sec. 911(d)(1)(B)). The taxpayer does not have to be present in the foreign country solely for business purposes and the 330 days do not have to be consecutive. In addition, the taxpayer can select any 12-month period in which he or she meets the physical presence test.

Example 2: Betty is a U.S. citizen who leaves New York on February 3, 2016, and arrives in Spain on that same day. During December 2016, Betty vacations in France for 10 days. She leaves Spain to move back to the United States on January 10, 2017. Betty will meet the 330-day test during either the 12-month period beginning February 4, 2016, or the 12-month period ending January 10, 2017.

Waiver of Time Requirements. Relief from either the bona fide residence or the physical presence test is provided to an individual if he or she was forced to flee a foreign country because of civil unrest, war, or other adverse conditions (Code Sec. 911(d)(4)). To qualify for the relief, the individual must have been a bona fide resident of, or present in, the foreign country on or prior to the date the IRS determines that adverse conditions exist in the foreign country and individuals are required to leave. In addition, the taxpayer must establish that he or she could reasonably be expected to have satisfied the residency requirement had the adverse conditions not arisen. The IRS publishes annually the names of countries for which the waiver is available.[12]

2406. Camps Located in a Foreign Country. In addition to the exclusion of foreign earned income (¶ 2402) and foreign housing expenses (¶ 2403), an individual may be able to exclude from gross income and wages as a *de minimis* fringe benefit (¶ 2089) the value of meals and lodging provided by his or her employer in a camp located in a foreign country if three requirements are met (Code Sec. 119(c)).[13] First, the lodging must be provided for the convenience of the employer because the place where the employee's services are performed is in a remote area where satisfactory housing is unavailable. Second, the location of the camp must be as near as practicable to the place where the employee's services are performed. Third, the lodging must be provided in a common area, not open to the public, that normally accommodates 10 or more employees. An employee who works for a U.S. military contractor on a foreign military base cannot exclude from income the value of lodging provided by his or her employer, as the lodging is not considered to be on the employer's business premises (*P.M. Middleton*, Dec. 57,464(M), TC Memo. 2008-150).[14]

2408. Electing the Foreign Earned Income and Housing Exclusions. A qualified individual (¶ 2404) must make a separate election with respect to the foreign earned income exclusion (¶ 2402) and the foreign housing exclusion (¶ 2403). The elections are made by filing Form 2555 or Form 2555-EZ with the taxpayer's timely-filed income tax return (including extensions), amended return, or a late-filed return if filed within one year after the due date of the return (not including extensions) (Code Sec. 911(e); Reg. § 1.911-7).[15] Once made, the election will remain in effect for the current tax year and all subsequent years unless revoked. A taxpayer who revokes the election will be prohibited from making a new election for at least five tax years without IRS approval. If both a taxpayer and his or her spouse qualify for the exclusions, each must file a separate Form 2555 regardless of whether they file a joint return or separate returns. A self-employed taxpayer does not have to make an election in order to claim the foreign housing deduction.

An individual that claims either the foreign earned income or foreign housing exclusion may not claim the foreign tax credit or deduction (¶ 2475) for any income excluded. If a taxpayer attempts to claim the foreign tax credit or deduction, then the election for the foreign earned income and foreign housing exclusions will be considered revoked (IRS Pub. 54). In addition, a taxpayer cannot claim either of the exclusions and also the earned income tax credit (¶ 1322) or the additional child tax credit (¶ 1305).

2409. Resident Aliens. A resident alien is generally taxed in the same manner as a U.S. citizen. For this purpose, residency is determined under the lawful permanent residence test ("green card") or the substantial presence test (Code Sec. 7701(b)(1)).[16] An alien who does not qualify under either test is generally treated as a nonresident alien for federal income, employment, and excise tax purposes (but not estate and gift tax purposes). Some individuals may be eligible to elect resident status (¶ 2410). In addition, an individual can have a dual-status tax year and be both a resident and nonresident alien during the year (¶ 2411). In the case of an individual who is considered both a U.S. resident and a resident of a foreign country during the year (dual resident taxpayer), a tax treaty may override the normal treatment of the individual as a resident alien for all purposes under the treaty. The green card test and substantial presence test determine whether an alien is a resident of a U.S. possession or territory whose income tax laws mirror those of the United States. They do not determine whether an individual is a bona fide resident of other U.S. possessions or territories (¶ 2414) (Reg. § 301.7701(b)-1(d)).[17]

References are to Standard Federal Tax Reports; Tax Research Consultant; and Practical Tax Explanations.

[12] ¶ 28,049.5775; EXPAT: 12,058; § 37,505.15, § 37,505.20

[13] ¶ 7220; EXPAT: 12,302; § 21,235

[14] ¶ 7222.63; EXPAT: 12,302; § 21,235

[15] ¶ 28,040, ¶ 28,047; EXPAT: 12,108, EXPAT: 12,166; § 37,530.05

[16] ¶ 43,080; EXPAT: 3,000; § 37,101

[17] ¶ 43,117; EXPAT: 3,100; § 37,145

Green Card Test. An alien who is a lawful permanent resident of the United States under U.S. immigration laws (i.e., receives a "green card") is considered a resident alien for federal tax purposes (Reg. § 301.7701(b)-1(b)).[18] Resident status begins in the first calendar year in which the alien is a lawful resident and is physically present in the United States for at least one day (¶ 2411). Resident status continues until permanent resident status is terminated or abandoned (¶ 2412).

Substantial Presence Test. An alien is considered a U.S. resident if the individual is physically present in the United States for at least 31 days during the calendar year and 183 days for the current and two preceding calendar years (¶ 2411). For purposes of the 183-day requirement, each day present in the United States during the current calendar year counts as a full day, each day in the first preceding year as ⅓ of a day, and each day in the second preceding year as ⅙ of a day (Code Sec. 7701(b)(3); Reg. § 301.7701(b)-1(c)).[19] There are exceptions as to what days an alien is considered to be physically present in the United States, including days for: (1) regular commuters from Canada or Mexico; (2) days in transit between two places outside the United States; (3) medical conditions preventing departure; (4) exempt individuals including teachers, trainees, and students on temporary visas, as well as professional athletes competing in a charitable event; (5) crew members of foreign vessels; and (6) foreign government workers. Form 8843 must be completed to exclude days of physical presence in the United States due to a medical condition or as an exempt individual. Presence in U.S. territories or possessions does not count as presence in the United States.

An individual who otherwise meets the substantial presence test may still be treated as a nonresident alien if the individual has a tax home in a foreign country during the tax year, has a closer connection to the foreign country, and was physically present in the United States for less than 183 days during the year. An alien must fully complete Form 8840 and attach it to his or her return for the relevant tax year to prove that he or she satisfies the closer connection exception.

2410. Elective Resident Status. There are two ways alien individuals are permitted to elect resident status if they do not otherwise qualify as a resident alien (¶ 2409). First, an individual who otherwise fails to meet the green card or substantial presence test may elect to be a resident alien for part of the current year (Code Sec. 7701(b)(4); Reg. § 301.7701(b)-4(c)(3)).[20] To qualify for the election, the individual:

- must not be a resident alien in the prior calendar year;
- must meet the substantial presence test in the calendar year following the election year;
- must be present in the United States for at least 31 consecutive days in the election year; and
- must be present in the United States for at least 75 percent of the days during the period from the first day of the 31-day presence period through the end of the election year.

If these requirements are met, the individual's election to be treated as a U.S. resident alien is effective for that portion of the year that begins on the first day of the earliest testing period that the 31-day and 75 percent requirements are met. The election is made by attaching a signed statement to the individual's tax return for the election year indicating that the individual meets the election requirements. The election cannot be made before the individual has met the substantial presence test for the calendar year following the election year. Once made, the election can be revoked only with the IRS's consent.

References are to Standard Federal Tax Reports; Tax Research Consultant; and Practical Tax Explanations.

[18] ¶ 43,117; EXPAT: 3,050; § 37,105

[19] ¶ 43,080, ¶ 43,117; EXPAT: 3,100; § 37,110.05

[20] ¶ 43,080, ¶ 43,120; EXPAT: 3,200; § 37,130

The second way an alien may elect resident status is if the individual is married to a U.S. citizen or resident alien at the end of the tax year—then the election may be made in order to file a joint return (Code Sec. 6013(g) and (h)).[21] The taxpayer may be either a nonresident or resident alien at the end of the tax year for the election to be made. Both spouses must join in the election by attaching a statement to a joint return for the first tax year for which the election applies. It is effective for the entire tax year and all subsequent tax years for federal income tax and withholding purposes unless neither spouse is a U.S. citizen or resident alien at any time during the year. The election may also be jointly revoked by the couple or terminated by reason of death, separation, divorce, or by the IRS for failure of the couple to keep adequate records. Once terminated, the election may not be made again by the couple.

2411. Dual-Status Tax Years. An individual can be both a resident and nonresident alien during the same tax year (¶ 2409). This usually occurs the year of arrival in, or departure from, the United States. An individual who is a dual-status alien has a dual-status tax year. Thus, the individual's income tax liability is computed as a resident alien for the period of residence and as a nonresident alien for the period of nonresidence (¶ 2425) (Reg. § 1.871-13).[22]

If an alien individual is filing a tax return for a dual-status year, then the standard deduction cannot be claimed, the deduction for personal and dependency exemptions cannot exceed taxable income for the period the individual is a resident alien, and head of household filing status may not be used. A married individual may also not use joint filing status and tax rates for joint filers for the period of residency unless he or she is married to a U.S. citizen or resident alien and the election to be treated as a resident alien for the year is made (¶ 2410) (IRS Pub. 519). The education credits, earned income credit, and the elderly or disabled credit may also not be claimed unless the individual is married and elects to be treated as a resident alien by filing a joint return.

Residency Starting Date and Termination Date. If an alien meets the green card test, residency starts the first day the individual is physically present in the United States while a lawfully admitted resident. If an alien meets the substantial presence test, residency starts the first day the individual is physically present in the United States during the calendar year. A *de minimis* exception allows up to 10 days to be disregarded in determining the residency starting date under the substantial presence test if the individual has a closer connection to a foreign country. For an alien that satisfies both tests, residency starts on the earlier date when either test is satisfied (Reg. § 301.7701(b)-4).[23] If the individual was a resident alien in the previous tax year, then residency begins on the first day of the current tax year regardless of whether residency status is determined under the green card test or substantial presence test. Residency status may terminate before the end of the tax year under either test, but only if the individual is not a U.S. resident alien at any time during the following tax year.

Departure Requirements. Generally, no alien (whether resident or nonresident) is permitted to depart the United States or a U.S. possession without first obtaining a certificate of compliance from the IRS (i.e., sailing or departure permit). The certificate is proof that the individual has discharged all of his or her U.S. income tax liability (Code Sec. 6851(d); Reg. § 1.6851-2).[24] The certificate must be obtained at least two weeks before the individual leaves the United States. Resident aliens (whether they have taxable income or not) and nonresident aliens having no taxable income for the tax year must file Form 2063 to obtain the certificate. Nonresident aliens with taxable income for the tax year must file Form 1040-C to obtain the certificate. The forms do not constitute an individual's final tax return and Form 1040 or Form 1040NR must still be filed after the individual's tax year ends. Payment of any tax is not required prior to departure if it is determined that tax collection will not be jeopardized by the alien's departure. Individuals who abandon U.S. citizenship or long-term residency for tax avoidance purposes are subject to special rules (¶ 2412).

References are to Standard Federal Tax Reports; Tax Research Consultant; and Practical Tax Explanations.

[21] ¶ 35,160; EXPAT: 3,200; § 37,125.05

[22] ¶ 27,341; EXPAT: 3,150; § 37,120.05

[23] ¶ 43,120; EXPAT: 3,150; § 37,120.05

[24] ¶ 40,402, ¶ 40,405; FILEIND: 18,062.10; § 37,010.35

2412. Expatriation to Avoid Tax. Individuals who are covered expatriates are subject to a mark-to-market tax regime under which they are taxed on the unrealized gain in their property to the extent it exceeds $693,000 for 2016 ($699,000 for 2017) (Code Sec. 877A; Notice 2009-85; Rev. Proc. 2015-53; Rev. Proc. 2016-55).[25] For this purpose, a covered expatriate is considered to own any interest in property that would generally be taxable as part of his or her gross estate for federal estate tax purposes (¶ 2912) if the individual died on the day before the expatriation date. For example, an installment obligation held by a covered expatriate was property subject to tax because it would be included in the expatriate's estate (*G. Topsnik*, Dec. 60,501, 146 TC No. 1 (2016)). Special rules apply for deferred compensation items, specified tax deferred accounts, and interests in nongrantor trusts (¶ 566). A U.S. citizen or resident alien is also subject to a special transfer tax upon receipt of property by gift, devise, bequest, or inheritance from a covered expatriate (¶ 2948).

The exclusion amount must be allocated among all built-in gain property that is subject to the mark-to-market regime and is owned by the covered expatriate on the day before the expatriation date. Gain is determined as if a sale of the property for fair market value had taken place on the day before the expatriation date without regard to other Code provisions. Losses from the deemed sale, however, are generally taken into account as otherwise provided in the Code, except that the wash sale rules do not apply (¶ 1935). The taxpayer must make adjustments to the basis of any property by the amount of gain or loss taken into account.

Covered Expatriate. A covered expatriate is any U.S. citizen who relinquishes citizenship or any long-term U.S. resident who ceases to be a lawful permanent resident of the United States (¶ 2409), if the individual: (1) has an average annual net income tax liability for the five preceding years ending before expatriation that exceeds $161,000 for 2016 ($162,000 for 2017); (2) has a net worth of $2 million or more on the expatriation date; or (3) fails to certify under penalties of perjury that he or she has complied with all U.S. tax obligations for the preceding five years or fails to submit evidence of compliance required by the IRS on Form 8854 (Code Sec. 877A(g); Notice 2009-85; Rev. Proc. 2015-53; Rev. Proc. 2016-55). Dual citizens and minors may be excepted from the tax liability and net worth requirements.

Election to Defer Tax. A covered expatriate may make an irrevocable election to defer payment of the mark-to-market tax that would otherwise be imposed on the deemed sale of property (Code Sec. 877A(b); Notice 2009-85).[26] The election cannot be made without providing adequate security such as a bond or letter of credit to ensure payment of the tax. In addition, no election can be made unless the individual makes an irrevocable waiver of any rights under an income tax treaty that would preclude assessment or collection of the tax.

The election is made on an asset-by-asset basis. The tax for each piece of property is determined by multiplying the total mark-to-market tax by the ratio of the gain on the deemed sale of the property over the total gain taken into account with respect to all property deemed sold. The election defers payment of the tax until the due date for the return for the tax year in which the property is disposed of or the taxpayer's death. Payment may not be extended beyond the due date for the return for the tax year in which the covered expatriate dies.

Reporting Requirements. In addition to any other requirements for filing a return, a covered expatriate must also file an information return on Form 8854 in each tax year he or she is subject to the mark-to-market tax (Code Sec. 6039G; Notice 2009-85).[27] The return is also to be used to provide notice that the individual has relinquished his or her U.S. citizenship or long-term residency status.

References are to Standard Federal Tax Reports; Tax Research Consultant; and Practical Tax Explanations.

[25] ¶ 27,430, ¶ 27,438.10, ¶ 27,438.15; EXPAT: 3,314; § 37,025.05

[26] ¶ 27,430, ¶ 27,438.15; EXPAT: 3,322; § 37,025.10

[27] ¶ 27,438.15, ¶ 35,692; EXPAT: 3,324; § 39,135.25

2414. Resident of U.S. Possessions. Generally, an individual who is a bona fide resident of a U.S. possession during the tax year is subject to U.S. taxation as a U.S. citizen or resident alien (¶ 2409), rather than as a nonresident alien (Code Sec. 876).[28] A U.S. possession for this purpose includes American Samoa, Guam, the Northern Mariana Islands, and Puerto Rico. Separate rules apply to a bona fide resident of the U.S. Virgin Islands (¶ 2416).

An individual is a bona fide resident of a U.S. possession if the person is physically present in the possession for a certain number of days during the tax year, does not have a tax home outside the possession, and does not have a closer connection to the United States or a foreign country than to the possession during the tax year (Code Sec. 937; Reg. § 1.937-1).[29] An individual with worldwide gross income of more than $75,000 must file Form 8898 for the tax year in which the individual becomes or ceases to be a bona fide resident of a U.S. possession. A spouse's income is not included when calculating an individual's worldwide gross income for this purpose. Thus, if married individuals are each required to file Form 8898, then a separate Form 8898 must be filed for each spouse regardless of whether a joint return is filed.

A U.S. citizen or resident alien who is a bona fide resident of American Samoa for the entire tax year may exclude from gross income for U.S. tax purposes any income derived from sources within the possession or that is effectively connected with a trade or business by the individual in the possession (Code Sec. 931).[30] The exclusion does not apply to income that is received for services performed as an employee of the United States. The individual may also not claim a tax credit or deduction that is attributable to the amount of excluded income. Form 4563 is used to claim the exclusion and must be attached to a Form 1040 filed with the IRS. A similar rule applies to a bona fide resident of Puerto Rico (¶ 2415).

2415. Resident of Puerto Rico. A U.S. citizen or resident alien (¶ 2409) who is also a bona fide resident of Puerto Rico (¶ 2414) during the entire tax year may exclude from gross income for U.S. tax purposes any income derived from sources within Puerto Rico (Code Sec. 933).[31] If the taxpayer gives up Puerto Rican residence after having been a bona fide resident for at least two years, then the taxpayer may claim a partial exclusion for the tax year of the residence change. In either case, the exclusion does not apply to income received for services performed as an employee of the United States. The taxpayer may also not claim any tax credit or deduction (except a personal exemption) which is attributable to the amount of excluded income.

A U.S. citizen or resident alien who has income from Puerto Rican sources is liable for the payment of taxes to Puerto Rico and may have to file a tax return with the United States as well. Generally, a U.S. citizen or resident alien who is a bona fide resident of Puerto Rico for the entire tax year must pay taxes to Puerto Rico on income from worldwide sources. If U.S. source income is also reported on an individual's Puerto Rican tax return, a credit may be claimed up to the amount allowable for income taxes paid to the United States.

2416. Resident of U.S. Virgin Islands. A U.S. citizen or resident alien (other than a bona fide resident of the U.S. Virgin Islands (¶ 2414)) who has income from sources within the U.S. Virgin Islands or effectively connected with a trade or business in the U.S. Virgin Islands is required to file an income tax return with both the United States and the U.S. Virgin Islands (Code Sec. 932).[32] The tax owed to the U.S. Virgin Islands is determined on Form 8689 by multiplying the total tax owed on the United States return (after certain adjustments) by the ratio of adjusted gross income (AGI) from the U.S. Virgin Islands to worldwide AGI. The U.S. Virgin Islands' tax liability (if paid) is credited against the individual's total U.S. tax liability. An individual who qualifies as a bona fide resident of the U.S. Virgin Islands (or who files a joint U.S. return with a U.S. citizen or resident with U.S. Virgin Islands income) will generally have no U.S. tax liability so long as the taxpayer reports all income from all sources on the return filed with the U.S. Virgin Islands.

References are to Standard Federal Tax Reports; Tax Research Consultant; and Practical Tax Explanations.

[28] ¶ 27,400; INTL: 24,300; § 37,145

[29] ¶ 28,395, ¶ 28,396; INTL: 24,300; § 37,145

[30] ¶ 28,240; INTL: 24,300; § 46,005.35

[31] ¶ 28,300; INTL: 24,050

[32] ¶ 28,280; INTL: 24,100; § 37,145

Nonresident Aliens and Foreign Corporations

2425. Taxation of Nonresident Aliens and Foreign Corporations. A nonresident alien (¶ 2409) and foreign corporation are generally taxed in the same manner as a U.S. citizen or domestic corporation on all income that is effectively connected with the conduct of a trade or business in the United States (¶ 2429). For this purpose, gain or loss from the disposition of a U.S. real property interest is treated as effectively connected income (¶ 2442). If any U.S. source income (¶ 2427) received by a nonresident alien or foreign corporation is not effectively connected with a U.S. trade or business, such as fixed, determinable, annual, or periodical (FDAP) income (¶ 2431), then it will generally be taxed at a flat 30-percent rate, absent a lower treaty rate. A nonresident alien and foreign corporation may generally only claim deductions and credits related to effectively connected income (¶ 2446). A flat 30-percent tax rate also applies to the profits (and certain interest amounts) of a U.S. branch of a foreign corporation that are remitted to the foreign corporation during the tax year (¶ 2433).

A nonresident alien or foreign corporation who engages in trade or business in the United States at any time during the tax year or who has taxable income must generally file an income tax return (Code Secs. 6012 and 6072(c)).[33] Form 1040NR or Form 1040NR-EZ is used by a nonresident alien, and Form 1120-F is used by a foreign corporation. The returns are generally due on or before the 15th day of the 6th month following the close of the tax year (June 15 for calendar year taxpayers). However, the due date is 15th day of the 4th month following the close of the tax year (April 15 for calendar year taxpayers) if the nonresident alien has wages subject to income tax withholding or the foreign corporation has an office or place of business in the United States. Filing extensions can be obtained under the same rules applicable to other taxpayers (¶ 2509). Nonresident aliens and foreign corporations do not need to file a return in certain circumstances, including if the taxpayer's full U.S. tax liability was withheld at the source.

2427. Source of Income Rules. The U.S. taxation of nonresident aliens and foreign corporations (¶ 2425), as well as the application of the foreign tax credit limitations (¶ 2479), is dependent on the determination of the source of a taxpayer's income. Income is generally derived from U.S. sources or foreign sources in the following manner (Code Secs. 861, 862, and 865).[34]

- Interest income is generally sourced to the residence or country of incorporation of the obligor. The method and place of payment are irrelevant (see exceptions following). Interest for the guarantee of a debt is analogous to interest paid on a loan and is U.S. source income if paid by a noncorporate U.S. resident, domestic corporation, or any foreign person if effectively connected with a U.S. trade or business (¶ 2429).

- Dividend income, scholarships, grants, prizes, and awards are sourced to the residence of the payor (see exceptions following).

- Compensation for personal services is sourced to the place where the services are rendered. The location of the payor's residence, where the services are contracted for, and place of payment are irrelevant. If services are performed only partly within the United States, compensation is generally sourced on the basis of time spent working in each location.

- Rents and royalties are sourced to the location of the property.

- Gain on the sale of real property is sourced to the location of the property (¶ 2442).

- Gain on the sale of inventory is sourced to where the sale occurs (where title to the inventory passes).

- Gain on the sale of personal property that is not inventory is sourced to the residence of the seller (except for depreciable personal property, intangible property, or stock of an affiliate).

References are to Standard Federal Tax Reports; Tax Research Consultant; and Practical Tax Explanations.

[33] ¶ 35,142, ¶ 36,720; INTL: 3,750; § 37,010.10, § 37,015.10

[34] ¶ 27,120, ¶ 27,151, ¶ 27,200; INTL: 3,000; § 37,205.05

Special source rules apply to income that is derived from transportation, space, ocean, and communications activities. Other items of income are allocated or apportioned to sources within or without the United States as provided in regulations or other IRS rulings (for example, mixed-source income) (Code Sec. 863).[35] Where allocation of an item of income is not provided, then it must be construed.

Interest Income Exceptions. Interest paid by a foreign corporation or foreign partnership engaged in a U.S. trade or business is treated as U.S. source income rather than foreign source income if paid by the U.S. trade or business (Code Secs. 861(a)(1) and 884(f)).[36] However, interest on deposits in foreign branches of U.S. commercial banks is treated as foreign source income. A qualified fails charge is also treated similar to interest but is sourced to the residence of the recipient or the taxpayer's qualified business unit (QBU), unless the income is effectively connected with a U.S. trade or business. Qualified fails charges are amounts paid for the failure to deliver designated securities on the settlement date in a delivery-versus-payment transaction (Reg. § 1.863-10).[37]

Dividend Exceptions. A portion of the dividends paid by a foreign corporation are U.S. source income rather than foreign sourced if: (1) 25 percent or more of the corporation's gross income for a three-year period is effectively connected with a U.S. trade or business, or (2) it is required to figure the dividends received deduction by a U.S. corporation (¶ 223) (Code Sec. 861(a)(2)).[38] Dividends paid by a U.S. corporation electing to be treated as a possession corporation (¶ 1362) are treated as foreign source income.

Allocation of Expenses. U.S. taxpayers are allowed deductions directly related to U.S. source or foreign source income to determine taxable income. Deductions are generally first allocated to the activity or property from which the class of income is derived. If any expense or loss is not directly related to any specific item of income, then it must be apportioned ratably between certain statutory and residual groupings (Code Secs. 861(b) and 862(b); Reg. § 1.861-8; Temp. Reg. § 1.861-8T).[39] Special apportionment rules are provided for interest expenses, research and development expenses, losses from the disposition of property, net operating losses, income taxes, and legal, accounting, and stewardship fees.

Interest expenses are considered related to all income-producing activities and assets of a taxpayer. They are generally allocated to all gross income that the assets of the taxpayer generate (Code Sec. 864(e); Reg. § 1.861-9; Temp. Reg. § 1.861-9T).[40] As a result, allocation and apportionment of interest expenses must be made on the basis of the taxpayer's assets, and the various statutory groupings or classes. Taxpayers may choose to value their assets on the basis of fair market value, tax book value, or an alternative tax book value method. Exceptions exist for qualified nonrecourse debt, assets acquired in integrated financial transactions, and certain related controlled foreign corporation (CFC) debt.

In the case of an affiliated group of corporations, interest expenses must be allocated and apportioned to members based on asset values as if all members were a single taxpayer (the one-taxpayer rule) (Code Sec. 864(e) and (f); Reg. § 1.861-11; Temp. Reg. § 1.861-11T).[41] For tax years beginning after 2020, a one-time election may be made to determine foreign source taxable income of an affiliated group, by allocating and apportioning interest expense of the domestic members of the affiliated group on a worldwide basis, as if all members of the group were a single corporation.

References are to Standard Federal Tax Reports; Tax Research Consultant; and Practical Tax Explanations.

[35] ¶ 27,160; INTL: 3,000

[36] ¶ 27,120, ¶ 27,540; INTL: 3,100

[37] ¶ 27,173; INTL: 3,325

[38] ¶ 27,120; INTL: 3,150; § 37,205.15

[39] ¶ 27,120, ¶ 27,138, ¶ 27,139, ¶ 27,151; INTL: 6,000; § 37,210.05

[40] ¶ 27,139C, ¶ 27,140, ¶ 27,180; INTL: 6,100; § 37,210.10

[41] ¶ 27,140, ¶ 27,141E, ¶ 27,142; INTL: 6,108

2429. Income Effectively Connected With U.S. Trade or Business. A nonresident alien (¶ 2409) and foreign corporation are taxed in the same manner as a U.S. citizen or domestic corporation on income that is effectively connected with the conduct of a trade or business in the United States (Code Secs. 871(b) and 882(a)).[42] Generally, all income, gain, or loss from sources within the United States is treated as effectively connected with the conduct of a U.S. trade or business for this purpose, including gain from the disposition of U.S. real property interests (¶ 2442) and any scholarship or fellowship grant of a visiting student, teacher, or trainer (¶ 2448) (Code Sec. 864(c)(3)).[43] There are two exceptions.

First, fixed, determinable, annual, or periodical (FDAP) income (¶ 2431) from *U.S. sources*, as well as capital gains from U.S. sources (¶ 2435) are treated as income effectively connected with a U.S. trade or business only if: (1) the income, gain, or loss is derived from assets used or held for use in the conduct of a U.S. trade or business, or (2) the activities of a U.S. trade or business are a material factor in the realization of the income, gain, or loss. In applying these factors, consideration is given to whether or not the asset or income involved was separately accounted for by the trade or business. In addition, a nonresident alien or foreign corporation who is a member of a partnership or the beneficiary of an estate or trust, which at any time within the tax year is engaged in a trade or business within the United States, is considered to be engaged in a U.S. trade or business (Code Sec. 875).[44] A nonresident alien and foreign corporation may elect to treat investment income from U.S. real property interests as effectively connected income (¶ 2432).

Second, income, gain, or loss from *foreign sources* is treated as effectively connected with the conduct of a U.S. trade or business if the nonresident alien or foreign corporation maintains an office or other fixed place of business in the United States at any time during the tax year to which the income, gain, or loss is attributable (Code Sec. 864(c)(4)).[45] Under these circumstances, the following foreign source income (or the economic equivalent of such income) is treated as effectively connected with a U.S. trade or business:

- rents and royalties derived from the use of intangible property;
- dividends, interest, or amounts received for the guarantees of debt that is either (1) derived from the active conduct of a banking, financial, or similar business through securities or debt obligations, or (2) received by a corporation the principal business of which is trading in stocks or securities for its own account; or
- income from the disposition of inventory or personal property held for sale in the normal course of business through a U.S. office.

Trade or Business. Whether a nonresident alien or foreign corporation is conducting a trade or business within the United States is a facts and circumstances test determined on a yearly basis (Reg. § 1.864-2(e)).[46] The conduct of a U.S. trade or business denotes a considerable, continuous, and regular course of activity by the taxpayer or through an agent, partnership, estate, or trust. Thus, the taxpayer need not be present in the United States to be engaged in a U.S. trade or business.

For this purpose, a trade or business includes the performance of personal services within the United States at any time during the tax year unless the services are performed by a nonresident alien who is temporarily present in the United States for a period of 90 days or less, compensation received for the services does not exceed $3,000, and the services are performed for another nonresident alien, foreign corporation, or foreign partnership (Code Sec. 864(b)).[47] A trade or business also does not generally include the trading of stocks, securities, or commodities through a resident broker, commission agent, custodian, or other independent agent unless the individual or foreign corporation is a dealer.

References are to Standard Federal Tax Reports; Tax Research Consultant; and Practical Tax Explanations.

[42] ¶ 27,320, ¶ 27,500; INTLIN: 3,100; § 37,010.20, § 37,015.20

[43] ¶ 27,180; INTLIN: 3,104; § 37,010.20, § 37,015.20

[44] ¶ 27,380; INTLIN: 3,052.10; § 37,010.20, § 37,015.20

[45] ¶ 27,180; INTLIN: 3,106; § 37,010.20, § 37,015.20

[46] ¶ 27,182; INTLIN: 3,052; § 37,010.20, § 37,015.20

[47] ¶ 27,180; INTLIN: 3,050; § 37,010.20, § 37,015.20

2431. Fixed, Determinable, Annual, or Periodical (FDAP) Income. Fixed, determinable, annual, or periodical (FDAP) income of a nonresident alien or foreign corporation received from U.S. sources is generally taxed at a flat 30-percent rate (or lower rate permitted under a tax treaty) if the income is not effectively connected with the conduct of a U.S. trade or business (¶ 2429). To ensure collection and payment, the tax must be withheld from the payment of FDAP income by a withholding agent (¶ 2455).

FDAP income includes interest, dividends, rents, salaries, wages, premiums, annuities, compensation, remunerations, emoluments, and any other item of annual or periodical gain, profit, or income (Code Secs. 871(a) and 881(a)).[48] It also includes royalties for timber, coal, and iron ore, as well as payments contingent on the productivity, use, or disposition of patents, copyrights, secret processes and formulas, and other like property. A nonresident alien and foreign corporation, however, may elect to treat income from U.S. real property interests as effectively connected income (¶ 2432).

A dividend equivalent payment is treated as a dividend from U.S. sources in determining FDAP income (Code Sec. 871(m); Reg. § 1.871-15; Temp. Reg. § 1.871-15T).[49] A dividend equivalent payment is any payment (or substantially similar payment) made pursuant to a securities lending or sale-repurchase transaction, or a specified notional principal contract (NPC) determined by, or contingent upon, payment of U.S. source dividends. For payments made on or after January 1, 2017, a dividend equivalent payment includes payments pursuant to a specified equity-linked instrument (ELI) and both specified NPCs and ELIs are described based on the delta of the contract.

Social Security Benefits. For purposes of computing a nonresident alien's taxable income (as well as for withholding purposes), 85 percent of any Social Security benefits received is considered FDAP income (Code Sec. 871(a)(3)).[50]

Original Issue Discount. For a sale or exchange of an original issue discount (OID) obligation (¶ 1952), the amount of OID accruing while the obligation is held by a nonresident alien or foreign corporation is considered FDAP income. A payment on an OID obligation is also subject to tax to the extent that the payment reflects OID accruing while the obligation is held by the nonresident alien or foreign corporation (Code Secs. 871(a)(1)(C) and 881(a)(3)).[51] For this purpose, an OID obligation includes any bond or other evidence of indebtedness having OID (Code Sec. 871(g)). It does not include any obligation payable 183 days or less from its date of original issue or any tax-exempt obligation.

Portfolio Interest. U.S. source portfolio interest is generally not considered FDAP income. Exempt portfolio interest includes any interest (including OID) accrued on an obligation issued after March 18, 2012, that is in registered form and held by the nonresident alien or foreign corporation (Code Secs. 871(h) and 881(c); Reg. § 1.871-14(a); Temp. Reg. § 1.871-14T).[52] For registered obligations, the exception is generally available only if the beneficial owner has provided the withholding agent with Form W-8BEN or other statement certifying that the beneficial owner is not a U.S. person (with exceptions for certain foreign-targeted obligations issued before January 1, 2016) (Notice 2012-20; Temp. Reg. § 1.871-14T(e)). For obligations issued on or before March 18, 2012, the portfolio interest exemption applies if the obligation is in bearer or registered form (Temp. Reg. § 1.871-14T(b)).

Exempt portfolio interest does not include contingent interest or interest received by a nonresident alien or foreign corporation that is a 10-percent shareholder. Interest is generally contingent if it is determined by reference to any receipts, income, or change in value of property of the debtor or a related person (¶ 432 and ¶ 1717). Other types of contingent interest may be identified by the IRS to prevent tax avoidance. A 10-percent shareholder is any person who owns 10 percent or more of the total combined voting power of all classes of stock in a corporation or 10 percent or more of a capital or profits interest in a partnership.

References are to Standard Federal Tax Reports; Tax Research Consultant; and Practical Tax Explanations.

[48] ¶ 27,320, ¶ 27,480; INTLIN: 3,102, INTL: 3,558; § 37,010.15, § 37,015.15

[49] ¶ 27,320, ¶ 27,341D, ¶ 27,341E; INTL: 3,558.25; § 37,010.15, § 37,015.15

[50] ¶ 27,320; INTL: 3,556; § 37,010.15

[51] ¶ 27,320, ¶ 27,480; INTL: 3,558.10; § 37,010.15, § 37,015.15

[52] ¶ 27,320, ¶ 27,341B; ¶ 27,341C, ¶ 27,480; INTL: 3,558.20; § 37,010.15, § 37,015.15

Other Interest and Dividend Income. FDAP does not include a portion of any dividend received by a nonresident alien or foreign corporation paid by a U.S. corporation primarily engaged in an active trade or business in a foreign country (80/20 company), but only if the corporation was an 80/20 company before 2011 (Code Secs. 871(i) and (l), and 881(d)).[53] Payments made by a corporation not in existence as of January 1, 2011, are not eligible for the exemption. A grandfathered corporation must meet a modified 80-percent foreign business requirement for each subsequent tax year (rather than over a three year period). The grandfathered corporation must also not have a substantial new line of business after August 10, 2010.

FDAP income of a nonresident alien and foreign corporation does not include other types of interest and dividends, including: (1) interest paid on bank deposits not effectively connected with a U.S. trade or business; (2) income derived by a foreign bank of central issue from bankers' acceptances; and (3) the portion of a dividend that is paid by a foreign corporation and treated as U.S. source income (¶ 231) (Code Secs. 871(i)(2) and 881(d)). It also does not include certain interest-related dividends and short-term capital gain dividends received from a regulated investment company or mutual fund (¶ 2301) (Code Sec. 871(k), as amended by the Protecting Americans from Tax Hikes (PATH) Act of 2015 (P.L. 114-113)).

U.S. Possession Corporations. A corporation created or organized in, or under the laws of, Guam, American Samoa, the Northern Mariana Islands, or the U.S. Virgin Islands is not considered a foreign corporation and thus is not subject to the tax on FDAP income if certain requirements are met. However, U.S. source dividends paid to a Puerto Rico corporation is considered FDAP income and subject to U.S. taxation and withholding at a 10-percent rate (Code Sec. 881(b)).[54]

2432. Election to Treat Real Property Income as Effectively Connected Income. A nonresident alien (¶ 2409) and foreign corporation may elect to treat income from U.S. real property interests (¶ 2442) held for investment purposes as effectively connected with the conduct of a U.S. trade or business (Code Secs. 871(d) and 882(d)).[55] The election is available where the income would not otherwise qualify as effectively connected income (¶ 2429), thus allowing the taxpayer to claim deductions associated with the property (¶ 2446). The election applies to all income of the taxpayer from all U.S. real property interests, including rents or royalties from mines, wells, or other natural deposits, as well as certain timber, iron ore, and coal royalties. It does not include mortgage interest, dividends from a real estate investment trust (¶ 2331), income from personal property, and income of a nonresident alien from real property which is not held for the production of income, such as a personal residence (Reg. §§ 1.871-10 and 1.882-2).[56] The election is made by attaching a statement to the taxpayer's timely filed return or amended return. Once made, the election applies to the current tax year and all subsequent tax years until revoked by filing a timely amended return for all affected years. If the election is revoked, the taxpayer may not make a new election for five years without the IRS's consent.

2433. Branch Profits Tax. A foreign corporation that operates a trade or business in the United States may be required to pay a branch profits tax and a branch-level interest tax in addition to the tax on income effectively connected with the conduct of a U.S. trade or business (¶ 2429). The branch profits tax is 30 percent (or lower if permitted by a tax treaty) of the foreign corporation's dividend equivalent amount (Code Sec. 884).[57] This is the amount of the foreign corporation's effectively connected after-tax earnings that are not reinvested in a U.S. trade or business by the close of the tax year or disinvested in a later tax year. The branch interest tax is 30 percent (or lower if permitted by a tax treaty) of the amount of interest paid by a U.S. branch of a foreign corporation with respect to a liability and notional excess interest amounts. If there is a conflict between the branch profits tax or branch-level interest tax with any U.S. income tax treaty, special rules are provided to determine the extent to which the treaty takes priority.

References are to Standard Federal Tax Reports; Tax Research Consultant; and Practical Tax Explanations.

[53] ¶ 27,320, ¶ 27,480; INTL: 3,558.25; § 37,010.15, § 37,015.15

[54] ¶ 27,480; INTL: 33,158; § 37,015.15

[55] ¶ 27,320, ¶ 27,500; INTLIN: 3,114.05; § 37,020

[56] ¶ 27,338, ¶ 27,502; INTLIN: 3,114.05; § 37,020

[57] ¶ 27,540; INTLIN: 3,150

2435. Capital Gains of Nonresident Aliens and Foreign Corporations. U.S. sourced capital gains of a nonresident alien (¶ 2409) or foreign corporation may be completely exempt from U.S. taxation if they are not: (1) effectively connected with the conduct of a U.S. trade or business (¶ 2429); (2) gains from the sale of U.S. real property interests (¶ 2442); or (3) fixed, determinable, annual, or periodical (FDAP) income (¶ 2431) (Code Secs. 871(a)(2) and 881(a)).[58] In the case of a nonresident alien, net capital gains that do not fall into one of these three categories are exempt from U.S. tax if the individual is not present in the United States for at least 183 days (whether or not consecutive) during the tax year. If the 183-day limitation is exceeded, the individual's net capital gains not effectively connected to conduct of a U.S. trade or business are subject to a flat 30-percent tax rate. For purposes of this rule, gains and losses are determined without regard to the exclusion of gain from the sale of qualified small business stock (¶ 1905) or the carryover of capital losses (¶ 1754).

2438. Community Income of Nonresident Aliens. If a nonresident alien (¶ 2409) is married to a U.S. citizen or resident and does not elect to be treated as a resident (¶ 2410), then any community income is to be treated as follows:

- earned income (other than from a trade or business or the distributive share of partnership income) is treated as income of the spouse who earned it;
- trade or business income (other than from a partnership) is treated as the separate income of the spouse carrying on the trade or business (unless carried on jointly);
- a distributive share of partnership income is treated as the income of the spouse who is the partner with no portion attributed to the other spouse; and
- all other community income from separate property of one spouse is treated as the income of that spouse (Code Sec. 879).[59]

2442. Sale or Disposition of U.S. Real Property Interest. The gain or loss derived by a nonresident alien (¶ 2409) or foreign corporation from the sale, exchange, or other disposition of a U.S. real property interest is treated as gain or loss effectively connected with the conduct of a U.S. trade or business (¶ 2429) (Code Sec. 897).[60] Income from a U.S. real property interest held for investment purposes is not considered income effectively connected with a U.S. trade or business. However, a nonresident alien and foreign corporation may elect to treat income from U.S. real property interests held for investment purposes as effectively connected income in order to claim deductions associated with the property (¶ 2446). A foreign corporation that holds a U.S. real property interest may also elect to be treated as a domestic corporation for this purpose if, under any treaty obligation of the United States, it is entitled to nondiscriminatory treatment of its U.S. real property interests (Code Sec. 897(i)).

Cash or property received by a nonresident alien or foreign corporation in exchange for an interest in a partnership, trust, or estate is considered received from the sale or disposition of U.S. real property interest to the extent attributable to the sale or disposition of a U.S. real property interest (Code Sec. 897(g)). Similarly, special look-through rules apply for distributions by qualified investment entities attributable to dispositions of U.S. real property interests (¶ 2444).

U.S. real property interests held by qualified foreign pension funds (or any entity that has all of its interests held by a qualified pension fund) are not subject to these rules, for dispositions and distributions after December 18, 2015 (Code Secs. 897(l), as added by the Protecting Americans from Tax Hikes Act of 2015 (P.L. 114-113) and 1445(f), as amended by P.L. 114-113; Reg. § 1.1445-2(b)(2)).[61]

Real Property Interests. A U.S. real property interest is any interest in real property (including a mine, well, or other natural deposit) located in the United States or the U.S.

References are to Standard Federal Tax Reports; Tax Research Consultant; and Practical Tax Explanations.

[58] ¶ 27,320, ¶ 27,480; INTL: 3,560; § 37,010.15, § 37,015.15

[59] ¶ 27,460; INDIV: 24,156; § 23,210.35, § 45,920.10

[60] ¶ 27,700; INTLIN: 6,050; § 37,410.05, § 37,425

[61] ¶ 27,700, ¶ 32,780, ¶ 32,782; INTLIN: 6,052.05; § 37,410.05, § 37,415.10

Virgin Islands (Code Sec. 897(c); Reg. § 1.897-1).[62] Real property includes land and improvements, personal property associated with the use of the real property, and unsevered timber, crops, and minerals. The nonresident alien's or foreign corporation's interest can be any interest (other than solely as a creditor), such as a direct ownership, fee-ownership, co-ownership, as well as any leasehold or option to acquire the property.

An interest in U.S. real property also includes any interest (other than solely as a creditor) in a U.S. real property holding corporation (USRPHC), unless the corporation was not a USRPHC during the shorter of the five-year period ending on the date of disposition, or the period the taxpayer held the interest in the corporation. A corporation is a USRPHC if the fair market value of its U.S. real property interests is at least 50 percent of the fair market value of all of its real property interests and any other property used in its business (Reg. § 1.897-2).[63] For this purpose, a corporation is considered to own a proportionate share of the assets held through a partnership, trust, or estate, as well as a domestic or foreign corporation in which it holds a controlling interest.

Whether a corporation is a USRPHC is generally determined as of the last day of the corporation's tax year, the date on which the corporation acquires a U.S. real property interest, *and* the date on which the corporation disposes of a real property interest located outside the United States or disposes of other assets used in a trade or business during the calendar year. The IRS has issued simplified procedures for a taxpayer to request relief for late filings establishing that a domestic corporation is not a USRPHC or that nonrecognition of gain or treaty provisions apply (Rev. Proc. 2008-27).[64]

A U.S. real property interest does not include any interest in a USRPHC if, as of the date of disposition, the corporation has already disposed of all of its U.S. real property interests in a transaction in which it recognized gain (the cleansing rule) (Code Sec. 897(c)(1)(B); Reg. § 1.897-2(f)(2)).[65] For dispositions on or after December 18, 2015, the cleansing rule will not apply if the corporation or its predecessor was a regulated investment company (RIC) or real estate investment trust (REIT) during the testing period (Code Sec. 897(c)(1)(B)(iii), as added by P.L. 114-113; Reg. § 1.897-2(f)(2)(iii)). In addition, if a corporation has a class of stock that is regularly traded on an established securities market, then such stock will be treated as a U.S. real property interest only in the hands of a taxpayer who owns more than five percent of the total fair market value of that class of stock.

A U.S. real property interest generally does not include the stock of a REIT held directly, or indirectly through partnerships, by a qualified shareholder with respect to distributions and dispositions on or after December 18, 2015. A qualified shareholder is: (1) a foreign person eligible for treaty benefits under a U.S. income tax treaty with an exchange of information agreement and with the principal class of its interests listed and regularly traded on a recognized stock exchange, or (2) certain foreign limited partnerships organized in a jurisdiction with an exchange of information agreement with the United States and a class of limited partnership units traded on the New York Stock Exchange or Nasdaq, the value of which is greater than 50 percent of the value of all partnership units. The qualified shareholder must also be a qualified collective investment vehicle and maintain records on persons who own directly five percent or more of a class of interest in the foreign person. A collective investment vehicle is a foreign person: (1) allowed reduced rates of withholding on dividends paid by a REIT under a U.S. income tax treaty, (2) which is a publicly traded foreign withholding partnership that would, if it were a U.S. corporation, be a USRPHC during the 5-year period ending on the date of disposition of, or distribution with respect to, the partnership's interest in the REIT, or (3) designated as a qualified collective investment vehicle by the IRS. The exception is limited in the case of applicable investors of the qualified shareholder (i.e., the investor holds more than 10 percent of the REIT stock) (Code Sec. 897(k)(2), as added by P.L. 114-113).[66]

References are to Standard Federal Tax Reports; Tax Research Consultant; and Practical Tax Explanations.

[62] ¶ 27,700, ¶ 27,701; INTLIN: 6,056; § 37,405

[63] ¶ 27,702; INTLIN: 6,058; § 37,405

[64] ¶ 27,711.60; INTLIN: 6,058.35; § 37,405

[65] ¶ 27,700, ¶ 27,702; INTLIN: 6,058.40.

[66] ¶ 27,700, INTLIN: 6,056.20; § 37,405.

Distributions of U.S. Real Property Interests. If a foreign corporation distributes a U.S. real property interest with respect to its stock, then the corporation recognizes gain (but not loss) to the extent the fair market value of the property at the time of distribution exceeds its adjusted basis (Code Sec. 897(d); Temp. Reg. § 1.897-5T(c)).[67] A foreign corporation may avoid recognizing gain if at the time of the distribution, the distributee would be subject to U.S. taxation on a subsequent disposition of the property and if the fair market value of the distributed property in the hands of the distributee is no greater than its basis increased by any amount of gain recognized by the distributing corporation. The foreign corporation is required to file a U.S. income tax return to report the distribution, even if it has no tax liability.

Nonrecognition Exchanges. Nonrecognition provisions of the Code apply to the exchange of a U.S. real property interest by a nonresident alien or foreign corporation if the property is exchanged for another U.S. real property interest that would be subject to U.S. tax upon its subsequent disposition and the transferor meets certain filing requirements (Code Sec. 897(e); Temp. Reg. § 1.897-6T).[68] Nonrecognition provisions for this purpose include like-kind exchanges (¶ 1721), involuntary conversions (¶ 1713), contributions and distributions related to partnerships (¶ 443 and ¶ 453), and corporate liquidations and reorganizations (¶ 2205 and ¶ 2253). The transfer of a U.S. real property interest in exchange for stock in a foreign corporation may also qualify for nonrecognition treatment. This includes contributions to capital or as paid in surplus (Code Sec. 897(j)).

Withholding. In order to ensure that a foreign investor will pay taxes on gain realized on the sale or disposition of a U.S. real property interest, the transferee is generally required to withhold and deduct a tax equal to 10 percent of the amount realized on the disposition, for dispositions on or before February 16, 2016, and a tax equal to 15 percent of the amount realized on the disposition, for dispositions after February 16, 2016 (Code Sec. 1445, as amended by P.L. 114-113; Reg. § 1.1445-1; Reg. § 1.1445-2).[69] Special rules and withholding rates apply for distributions and other transactions by corporations, partnerships, estates, trusts, and qualified investment entities.

There are certain exemptions and exceptions from withholding. For example, an exemption from withholding applies if the amount realized on the disposition of a residence does not exceed $300,000. The withholding rate is lowered from 15 percent to 10 percent for amounts realized in excess of $300,000, but not in excess of $1 million, for dispositions after February 16, 2016.

If the transferee fails to withhold the required tax, then it may be held liable for the tax, as well as any applicable penalties or interest. The transferee must file Form 8288 and Form 8288-A to report and transmit the amount withheld to the IRS within 20 days of the transfer of the property.

2444. Look-Through Rules for Disposition of U.S. Real Property Interests. Any distribution by a qualified investment entity to a nonresident alien (¶ 2409), foreign corporation, or other qualified investment entity to the extent attributable to gain from the sale or exchange of a U.S. real property interest, must be treated by the recipient as gain from the sale or exchange of a U.S. real property interest (¶ 2442) A qualified investment entity includes any real estate investment trust (REIT) (¶ 2326) and any regulated investment company (RIC) or mutual fund (¶ 2301) that is a U.S. real property holding company (USRPHC). However, in determining whether a RIC is a USRPHC, the regularly traded stock exception in defining a USRPHC does not apply. In addition, the

References are to Standard Federal Tax Reports; Tax Research Consultant; and Practical Tax Explanations.

[67] ¶ 27,700, ¶ 27,706; INTLIN: 6,060

[68] ¶ 27,700, ¶ 27,707; INTLIN: 6,062

[69] ¶ 32,780, ¶ 32,781, ¶ 32,782; INTLIN: 6,100; § 37,415.05

RIC must include its interest in any other domestically controlled REIT or RIC that is a USRPHC (Code Sec. 897(h), as amended by the Protecting Americans from Tax Hikes Act of 2015 (P.L. 114-113)).[70]

The look-through rule does not apply to any distribution from a qualified investment entity with respect to a class of stock that is regularly traded on an established securities market in the United States if the foreign distributee did not own more than five percent of the class of stock at any time within one year of the distribution. The ownership threshold is increased to 10 percent for distributions and dispositions on or after December 18, 2015 (Code Sec. 897(k)(1), as added by P.L. 114-113). To the extent this exception applies, the distribution from the qualified investment entity is treated as a dividend, and not as income effectively connected with a U.S. trade or business.

An interest in a domestically controlled qualified investment entity (less than 50 percent of the stock's value is held by foreign persons) is not treated as a U.S. real property interest and any gain from the sale of the interest does not pass through to a nonresident alien or foreign corporation. However, the gain is passed through if a wash sale transaction is involved. For this purpose, a wash sale transaction is one in which: (1) the interest in a domestically controlled qualified investment entity is disposed of within 30 days prior to a distribution by the qualified entity that would be treated as gain from the sale or exchange of a U.S. real property interest; and (2) a substantially identical interest is reacquired within 61 days of the distribution. For purposes of the exception for domestically controlled qualified investment entities, a number of rules and presumptions are applied to determine if the stock owner is a U.S. or foreign person, effective December 18, 2015 (Code Sec. 897(h)(4)(E), as added by P.L. 114-113).

2446. Taxable Income of Nonresident Aliens and Foreign Corporations. A nonresident alien (¶ 2409) and foreign corporation are subject to U.S. income tax on income effectively connected with a U.S. trade or business (¶ 2429) and fixed, determinable, annual, periodical (FDAP) income from U.S. sources (¶ 2431). Generally, all exclusions from gross income permitted to U.S. citizens and domestic corporations may also be excluded by nonresident aliens and foreign corporations (Code Secs. 872 and 883).[71] In addition, earnings on certain categories of cross-border transactions may also be excluded, such as compensation paid by a foreign employer to an exchange student, teacher, trainee, or specialist (¶ 2448), gambling winnings derived from a legal wager initiated outside the United States, and earnings from the international operation of a ship or aircraft.

A nonresident alien or foreign corporation may only claim deductions and tax credits related to effectively connected income in determining taxable income (Code Secs. 873, 874 and 882(c)).[72] This includes the foreign tax credit subject to the same limitations that apply to U.S. citizens and domestic corporations (¶ 2479) (Code Sec. 906).[73] Deductions and credits are generally not allowed in determining the tax on U.S. sourced FDAP income. However, a charitable contribution deduction can be claimed whether or not related to effectively connected income. Similarly, a nonresident alien may deduct one personal exemption (with certain exceptions) and casualty or theft losses (so long as the property is located in the United States). A nonresident alien and foreign corporation may elect to treat income from U.S. real property interests as effectively connected income in order to claim the deductions associated with the property (¶ 2432).

A nonresident alien or foreign corporation must file an accurate and timely return to claim any allowable deduction or credit. If a return is not filed, then the IRS may prepare one for the taxpayer but no deductions and credits will be allowed other than the credits for withheld taxes, gasoline and special fuels, and for nonresident aliens for taxes paid by a regulated investment company on undistributed capital gains (¶ 2305).

References are to Standard Federal Tax Reports; Tax Research Consultant; and Practical Tax Explanations.

[70] ¶ 27,700; INTLIN: 6,068; § 19,205.30

[71] ¶ 27,344, ¶ 27,520; INTL: 3,558.35, INTL: 3,604; § 37,010.25

[72] ¶ 27,360, ¶ 27,363, ¶ 27,500; INTL: 3,554.05; § 37,010.20, § 37,015.20

[73] ¶ 27,920; INTLOUT: 3,152.10; § 13,405.15

2448. Foreign Students, Teachers, or Trainees. A nonresident alien (¶ 2409) who is not otherwise engaged in a U.S. trade or business but who is temporarily present in the United States under immigration laws on a F, J, M, or Q visa as a visiting student, teacher, trainee, or specialist is considered to be engaged in a U.S. trade or business (Code Sec. 871(c)).[74] This means that any portion of a scholarship or fellowship grant from U.S. sources (including incidental expenses) that is not excludable from gross income (¶ 865) is income effectively connected with the conduct of a U.S. trade or business (¶ 2429). The income is subject to a special withholding rate of 14 percent (¶ 2455) (Code Sec. 1441(b); Reg. § 1.1441-4(c)).[75] Compensation paid by a foreign employer to a person in the United States as a visiting student, teacher, trainee, or specialist is exempt from tax (Code Sec. 872(b)(3)).[76]

2450. Tax Treaties. The United States has negotiated a network of tax treaties with other countries to avoid the double taxation of taxpayers on the same income and to prevent taxpayers from evading taxation. In addition, the United States has enacted strict anti-abuse rules to prevent individuals from treaty shopping, and has incorporated exchange of information clauses in many tax treaties to facilitate the enforcement of these rules. These anti-abuse rules deny treaty benefits to nonresidents of either the United States or its treaty partner that funnel income through the treaty country only to take advantage of reduced tax rates.

Generally, the Code is to be applied to a taxpayer with "due regard" to treaty obligations of the United States (Code Sec. 894).[77] In instances where a U.S. taxpayer takes the position that a treaty overrules or modifies the Code or regulations, disclosure of the position must generally be made with the taxpayer's tax return on Form 8833 (Code Sec. 6114; Reg. § 301.6114-1).[78] If a return is not otherwise required to be filed, a return must nevertheless be filed for purposes of making the required disclosure. The determination of whether a treaty-based return position is required to be reported is made by comparing the taxpayer's tax liability under current law to that same tax liability as it would exist if the relevant treaty positions did not exist. Any difference must be reported. Failure to disclose the difference may result in a penalty (Code Sec. 6712).[79]

Tax treaties between the United States and foreign countries generally reduce the tax rate for income paid. Some countries allow the withholding of tax at the treaty-reduced rate. Other countries, however, withhold tax at their statutory tax rate and refund any difference upon receiving proof of residency. To apply for certification of U.S. residency to receive the benefits under a tax treaty, a taxpayer must file Form 8802 at least 45 days before the certificate is needed. If the application is approved, the IRS will provide the residency certification to the taxpayer on Form 6166. A nonresident alien or foreign corporation is not entitled under any U.S. income tax treaty to any reduced rate of withholding on an item of income derived through an entity treated as a partnership (or other fiscally transparent entity) if: (1) the income is not treated by the treaty partner as an item of income of such foreign person; (2) the foreign country does not impose tax on a distribution of the item by the U.S. entity to the foreign person; and (3) the treaty does not contain a provision addressing its applicability in the case of an item of income derived through a partnership (Code Sec. 894(c)).[80]

2452. Corporate Inversions. Special rules apply for the tax treatment of corporate inversion transactions where a U.S. corporation reincorporates in a foreign jurisdiction and thereby replaces the U.S. parent corporation of a multinational corporate group with a foreign parent corporation. Inversion transactions may take many different forms, including stock inversions, asset inversions, and various combinations. In any case, if former shareholders of a U.S. corporation hold 80 percent or more (by vote or value) of the stock of a foreign corporation after the transaction, the foreign corporation will be

References are to Standard Federal Tax Reports; Tax Research Consultant; and Practical Tax Explanations.

[74] ¶ 27,320; EXPAT: 3,108.25, EXPAT: 3,108.30; § 37,320.20

[75] ¶ 32,702, ¶ 32,708; INTL: 33,110.35; § 37,320.20

[76] ¶ 27,344; INTL: 3,558.35; § 37,010.25

[77] ¶ 27,640; INTL: 18,060; § 37,605

[78] ¶ 37,060, ¶ 37,061; FILEBUS: 12,056; § 37,605

[79] ¶ 40,135; FILEBUS: 12,056; § 37,605

[80] ¶ 27,640; INTL: 18,060; § 37,605

treated as a domestic corporation for U.S. tax purposes (Code Sec. 7874).[81] If the former shareholders hold at least 60 percent but less than 80 percent of the stock of the foreign corporation after the transaction, then the inversion transaction is respected but any applicable corporate-level tax imposed as a result of the transaction cannot be offset by tax attributes such as a net operating loss (NOL) or foreign tax credit.

An inversion transaction for this purpose is a transaction in which, pursuant to a plan or a series of related transactions, the following three requirements are met:

(1) the foreign corporation must acquire substantially all of the properties of the domestic corporation or that constitute the trade or business of a domestic partnership;

(2) the former U.S. shareholders must hold 60 percent or more (by vote or value) of the stock of the foreign corporation after the transaction (ownership fraction); and

(3) the expanded affiliated group (EAG) must not conduct substantial business activities in the foreign country in which the foreign acquiring entity is created or organized, compared to the total business activities of the expanded affiliated group (Code Sec. 7874(a)(2); Temporary Reg. § 1.7874-12T).[82]

A number of rules apply to disregard certain stock of the foreign acquiring corporation in determining the ownership fraction. For example, the stock may be disregarded under a modified statutory public offering rule or if it is attributable to passive assets (Code Sec. 7874(c)(2)(B); Temporary Reg. §§ 1.7874-4T and 1.7874-7T).[83] An EAG has substantial business activities in the relevant foreign country only if at least 25 percent of the group employees, group assets, and group income are located or derived in the relevant country, and the foreign acquiring country corporation is subject to tax as a resident of the relevant foreign country (Reg. § 1.7874-3; Temporary Reg. § 1.7874-3T).[84]

2455. Withholding of Tax on Nonresident Aliens and Foreign Corporations. A foreign person is generally subject to U.S. tax on U.S. source income received during the tax year (¶ 2425). To ensure collection and payment, the tax must be withheld from the payment of the U.S. source income to the foreign person by a withholding agent (Code Secs. 1441 and 1442).[85] Most types of U.S. source income received by a foreign person are subject to a 30-percent withholding rate. Different rates may apply, however, to wages paid to a nonresident alien employee (including pensions paid for personal services), scholarship or fellowship grants of a foreign exchange student (¶ 2448), dispositions of U.S. real property interests (¶ 2442), a foreign partner's distributive share of effectively connected income of a partnership, gross investment income paid to foreign private foundations (¶ 631), and dividends paid to a Puerto Rican corporation. Reduced rates of withholding may also apply, including an exemption, under a tax treaty or convention with the foreign person's country of residence (¶ 2450).

Persons Subject to Withholding. All nonresident aliens and foreign corporations, foreign partnerships, foreign trusts, and foreign estates are subject to withholding on U.S. source income. Withholding also applies to the foreign branch of a U.S. financial institution that furnishes an intermediary withholding certificate on Form W-8IMY to the withholding agent (Temp. Reg. § 1.1441-1T(b)(1) and (c)(2)).[86] A nonresident alien is any individual who is not a U.S. citizen or resident alien and includes any bona fide resident of Puerto Rico, Guam, the Northern Mariana Islands, the U.S. Virgin Islands, or American Samoa (Reg. § 1.1441-1(c)(3)).[87] A nonresident alien who elects resident status for income tax purposes (¶ 2410) is still considered a foreign person for nonresident alien withholding purposes on all income except wages. Withholding may also be required for payments made to certain foreign financial institutions (FFIs) (¶ 2469) and

References are to Standard Federal Tax Reports; Tax Research Consultant; and Practical Tax Explanations.

[81] ¶ 43,969; INTL: 30,082.05

[82] ¶ 43,969, ¶ 43,970Q; INTL: 30,082.05

[83] ¶ 43,969, ¶ 43,970H, ¶ 43,970L; INTL: 30,082.10, INTL: 30,082.30

[84] ¶ 43,970F, ¶ 43,970G; INTL: 30,082.25

[85] ¶ 32,702, ¶ 32,720; INTL: 33,000; § 37,301

[86] ¶ 32,703E; INTL: 33,050; § 37,305

[87] ¶ 32,703; INTL: 33,050; § 37,305

nonfinancial foreign entities (NFFEs) (¶ 2473) if certain requirements are not met. Under coordination rules, withholding does not apply if there is withholding under these provisions (Temp. Reg. § 1.1441-1T(b)(1)).

Income Subject to Withholding. U.S. source income subject to the withholding requirements includes: (1) fixed, determinable, annual, or periodical (FDAP) income (¶ 2431); (2) certain gains on the disposal of timber, coal, or domestic iron ore; and (3) gains relating to contingent payments received from the sale or exchange of patents, copyrights, and similar intangible property. If the source of the income cannot be determined at the time of payment (¶ 2427), it is treated as U.S. source income (Code Sec. 1441(b); Reg. § 1.1441-2(a)).[88] In addition, income payable for personal services performed in the United States is treated as from sources within the United States, regardless of where the location of the contract for the services was entered, the place of payment, or residence of payer. Income effectively connected with the conduct of a U.S. trade or business is not subject to the withholding requirements for foreign persons, including income received as wages (¶ 2429). Instead, such income is generally subject to the tax and withholding rules as if the foreign person were a U.S. citizen, resident, or domestic entity. However, special rules apply to the effectively connected income of a partnership (foreign or domestic) that is allocable to its foreign partners (Code Sec. 1446).[89]

Withholding Agent. The withholding agent is the person or entity required to deduct, withhold, and pay any tax on income paid to a foreign person (Reg. § 1.1441-7; Temp. Reg. § 1.1441-7T).[90] The duty is imposed on all persons (acting in whatever capacity) that have control, receipt, custody, disposal, or payment of any items of income which are subject to withholding. Thus, the withholding agent may be any individual, corporation, partnership, trust, or other entity (including a foreign intermediary or partnership). A withholding agent may designate an authorized agent on its behalf.

The withholding agent is personally liable for any tax required to be withheld except in the case of certain conduit financing arrangements (Code Sec. 1461).[91] This liability is independent of the tax liability of the foreign person for whom the tax was withheld from a payment of income. Even if the foreign person pays the tax, the withholding agent may still be liable for any interest, penalty, or addition to tax for failure to withhold (Code Sec. 1463).[92] A refund or credit of any overpayment is made to the withholding agent unless the tax was actually withheld (Code Sec. 1464).[93] The withholding agent is indemnified against any person claiming any tax properly withheld.

A withholding agent is not required to withhold any amount if the payee is a U.S. person or a foreign person that is the beneficial owner of the income and is entitled to a reduced rate of withholding. Absent actual knowledge or reason to know, the withholding agent must obtain valid documentation from the payee that it is either a U.S. payee or beneficial owner. Generally, a U.S. payee is any person required to furnish Form W-9. While such persons are not subject to withholding as a foreign person, they may be subject to Form 1099 reporting and withholding requirements. A beneficial owner is any foreign person or entity that is required to furnish Form W-8BEN, Form W-8BEN-E, Form W-8ECI or Form W-8EXP. Payment to an intermediary (whether qualified or not), flow-through entity, or U.S. branch of a foreign entity may be treated as a payee for these purposes so long as valid documentation is provided on Form W-8IMY. In all cases in which valid documentation cannot be provided, the withholding agent may presume a person to be a U.S. payee or beneficial owner under specified rules.

The IRS has announced that it intends to issue regulations regarding the claiming of refunds or credits for withheld amounts due to concerns with non-compliant foreign withholding agents (Notice 2015-10). The regulations will provide that otherwise allowable claims for refund or credit by the beneficial owner of the withheld payment will be

References are to Standard Federal Tax Reports; Tax Research Consultant; and Practical Tax Explanations.

[88] ¶ 32,702, ¶ 32,704; INTL: 33,100, INTL: 33,150, INTL: 33,200; § 37,320.05

[89] ¶ 32,800; INTL: 33,106; § 37,350.05

[90] ¶ 32,714, ¶ 32,714G; INTL: 33,054; § 37,315.05

[91] ¶ 32,820; INTL: 33,056; § 37,315.05

[92] ¶ 32,860; INTL: 33,056; § 37,315.05

[93] ¶ 32,880; INTL: 33,056; § 37,315.05

limited to the amount actually deposited by the withholding agent. The regulations will also provide an allocation method for the amounts available when the withholding agent has only partially satisfied the deposit requirements. The regulations will apply to claims for refunds or credits for amounts withheld in the 2015 calendar year and thereafter.

Returns. A withholding agent must file an annual information return on Form 1042-S to report income paid to a foreign person during the tax year that is subject to withholding unless an exception applies (Reg. §§1.1461-1 and 1.6302-2).[94] A separate Form 1042-S must be filed for each recipient, as well as for each type of income that is paid to the same recipient. A copy of Form 1042-S must also be provided to the recipient. Form 1042 is used by the withholding agent to report and pay the taxes withheld from the payments of income. The forms are also used by withholding agents making payments to foreign financial institutions (FFIs) (¶ 2469) and non-financial foreign institutions (NFFEs) (¶ 2473).

Both forms must be filed by March 15 of the year following the calendar year the income was paid. An automatic six-month extension for filing Form 1042 can be obtained by filing Form 7004. The extension of time to file does not extend the time to pay the withheld tax. An automatic 30-day extension for filing Form 1042-S can be obtained by filing Form 8809. A second extension request may be submitted by filing a second Form 8809 before the end of the initial extended due date. Form 1042-S *must* be filed electronically if 250 or more returns are filed or if returns are filed by a financial institution (¶ 2503) (Reg. §301.1474-1(a); Temp. Reg. §1.1461-1T(c)(5)).[95] Paper Forms 1042-S must be accompanied by Form 1042-T.

The amount of tax required to be withheld will determine whether the withholding agent must deposit the taxes prior to the due date for filing the returns and how frequently such amounts must be deposited. Penalties may be imposed for failure to file, failure to provide complete and correct information, as well as failure to pay any taxes.

Reporting Foreign Assets of U.S. Taxpayers

2465. FBAR Reporting (Foreign Financial Assets). A United States person is required to disclose any interest in or signature over any financial account outside the United States if the aggregate value of the account exceeds $10,000 at any time during the calendar year (FBAR) (31 CFR Reg. §1010.350). The disclosure is required to be made electronically on the Treasury Department Financial Crimes Enforcement Network (FinCEN) Form 114 through FinCEN's BSA E-Filing System.[96] See ¶ 2570 for a further discussion of FBAR reporting.

2467. FATCA Reporting of Specified Foreign Financial Assets (Form 8938). Under the Foreign Account Tax Compliance Act (FATCA), an individual is required to disclose his or her interest in a specified foreign financial asset during the tax year if the aggregate value of all the assets exceeds an applicable threshold amount. The reporting requirement also applies to any domestic entity that is "formed or availed of" for purposes of holding, directly or indirectly, specified foreign financial assets (¶ 2572) (Code Sec. 6038D; Reg. §§1.6038D-2 and 1.6038D-6).[97] The information is reported on Form 8938.

2469. FATCA Reporting and Withholding Obligations for Foreign Financial Institutions (FFIs). Under the Foreign Account Tax Compliance Act (FATCA), a foreign financial institution (FFI) is required to report to the IRS certain information about financial accounts held by U.S. taxpayers or by foreign entities in which U.S. taxpayers hold substantial ownership interests (Code Sec. 1471).[98] If an FFI fails to meet the FATCA requirements, a U.S. withholding agent must deduct and withhold a tax equal to 30 percent on any "withholdable payment" made to the FFI after June 30, 2014, unless the withholding agent can reasonably rely on documentation that the payment is exempt

References are to Standard Federal Tax Reports; Tax Research Consultant; and Practical Tax Explanations.

[94] ¶ 32,821, ¶ 38,062; INTL: 33,056; §37,330

[95] ¶ 32,821E, ¶ 32,899H; INTL: 33,056; §37,330

[96] ¶ 36,551D; FILEBUS: 9,104; §37,705

[97] ¶ 35,593, ¶ 35,594AH, ¶ 35,594AS; FILEBUS: 9,108; §37,710

[98] ¶ 32,883; INTL: 36,000; §37,725.05

from withholding (Code Sec. 1471(a); Temp. Reg. § 1.1471-2T(a)(1)).[99] The withholding requirement applies without regard to whether the FFI receives a withholdable payment as a beneficial owner or as a qualified intermediary (QI). No withholding is required, however, if an FFI enters into an agreement with the IRS to provide the required information (participating FFI). An FFI may also be deemed to meet the requirements of the agreement (deemed-compliant FFI). For a discussion of the requirements for FFI agreements, see ¶ 2471.

Foreign Financial Institutions. An FFI is a foreign entity that accepts deposits in the ordinary course of a banking business, holds financial assets for the account of others as a substantial part of its business (i.e., mutual fund), or is an investment entity whose gross income is primarily attributable to investing, reinvesting, or trading in financial assets (i.e., hedge fund, private equity fund) (Code Sec. 1471(d)(4); Reg. § 1.1471-5(d) and (e)).[100] In the case of an entity that is resident in a country that has in effect a Model 1 or Model 2 Intergovernmental Agreement with the United States (Model 1 IGA or Model 2 IGA), an FFI is any entity that is treated as an FFI pursuant to the Model 1 or Model 2 IGA.

Withholdable Payment. A withholdable payment includes any payment of U.S. source fixed or determinable, annual or periodical (FDAP) income (¶ 2431), and, for any sales or other dispositions occurring after December 31, 2018, any gross proceeds that can produce interest or dividends that are U.S. source FDAP income (Code Sec. 1473(1); Reg. § 1.1473-1(a); Notice 2015-66).[101] Withholdable payments do not include items of income effectively connected with a U.S. trade or business (¶ 2429), payments of interest or original issue discount (OID) on short-term obligations, and other specified nonfinancial payments, such as payments for services, leases of property, and interest payable from the acquisition of goods and services.

Withholding is not required with respect to any payment under a grandfathered obligation or from any gross proceeds from the disposition of a grandfathered obligation (Reg. § 1.1471-2(b); Temp. Reg. § 1.1471-2T(b)).[102] A grandfathered obligation is generally any legally binding agreement or instrument outstanding on July 1, 2014, such as a debt instrument, line of credit, derivatives transaction, life insurance contract, and immediate annuity contract. It also includes collateral associated with the obligation. It does not include any legal agreement or instrument treated as equity for U.S. tax purposes or that lacks a stated expiration or term (for example, savings deposits, demand deposits, or deferred annuity contract). Similarly, it does not include a brokerage agreement, custodial agreement, investment insurance or annuity contract, or similar agreement to hold financial assets in an account for another person. A material modification of a grandfathered obligation will result in the obligation being treated as newly issued and subject to withholding. A payment made under a grandfathered obligation does include a payment made to a flow-through entity such as a partnership or trust. This includes a payment made with respect to the entity's disposition of the obligation. A foreign passthru payment does not include any payment made under a grandfathered obligation, or any gross proceeds from the disposition of such an obligation. Withholding is also not required with respect to any payment to an exempt beneficial owner including most governmental entities, nonprofit organizations, certain small, local financial institutions, and certain retirement entities (Code Sec. 1471(f); Reg. § 1.1471-6; Temp. Reg. § 1.1471-6T).[103]

Withholding Agent. A withholding agent for FATCA reporting purposes includes any U.S. or foreign person, in whatever capacity having the control, receipt, custody, disposal, or payment of any withholdable payment or foreign pass-through payment (Code Sec. 1473(4); Reg. § 1.1473-1(d)).[104] A U.S. withholding agent, participating FFI, qualified intermediary, or any other person that fails to withhold and deposit tax as

References are to Standard Federal Tax Reports; Tax Research Consultant; and Practical Tax Explanations.

[99] ¶ 32,883, ¶ 32,884J; INTL: 36,050; § 37,725.05

[100] ¶ 32,883, ¶ 32,884T; INTL: 36,056; § 37,725.05

[101] ¶ 32,893, ¶ 32,895, ¶ 32,887.35; INTL: 36,054; § 37,725.05

[102] ¶ 32,884H, ¶ 32,884J; INTL: 36,054; § 37,725.05

[103] ¶ 32,883, ¶ 32,884X; ¶ 32,884Z; INTL: 36,054; § 37,725.05

[104] ¶ 32,893, ¶ 32,895; INTL: 36,054; § 37,725.05

required is liable for the tax and penalties, but is indemnified against claims and demands of anyone for the amount of the payments (Code Sec. 1474; Reg. §§1.1474-1 and 301.1474-1; Temp. Reg. §1.1474-1T).[105] Form 1042 is used to report and pay taxes withheld during the tax year. In addition, an annual information return must be filed on Form 1042-S and a copy furnished to the recipient of the withholdable payment, including any qualified intermediaries, withholding foreign partnerships, and withholding foreign trusts. Both forms are due by March 15 of the calendar year following the year the withholdable payment was made to the recipient.

The IRS publishes a list of registered and approved FFIs and their Global Intermediary Identification Numbers (GIINs) every month. Withholding agents may rely on the IRS published list to verify an FFI's GIIN and not withhold on payments made to the FFI.

2471. Foreign Financial Institution (FFI) Agreements. A foreign financial institution (FFI) meets its reporting requirements under the Foreign Account Tax Compliance Act (FATCA) (¶ 2469) by: (1) entering into an FFI agreement with the IRS (participating FFI); (2) being deemed to comply with the FATCA requirements without the need to enter into an FFI agreement (deemed-compliant FFI); or (3) being a resident in a country that has in effect a Model 1 or Model 2 Intergovernmental Agreement with the United States (Model 1 IGA or Model 2 IGA). The reporting requirements the FFI must meet include:

- identifying U.S. accounts it maintains in accordance with certain verification and due diligence procedures;
- reporting certain information to the IRS regarding the U.S. accounts and accounts held by a U.S. person who is unwilling to provide the required information (recalcitrant account holder); and
- deducting and withholding tax on any payment of U.S. source income by the FFI to a recalcitrant account holder or nonparticipating FFI (Code Sec. 1471(b); Reg. §1.1471-4(a); Temp. Reg. §1.1471-4T(a)).[106]

An FFI (including a reporting Model 2 FFI) may register itself and its branches on the IRS's FATCA registration website (or on a paper copy of Form 8957) to enter into an FFI agreement as a participating FFI, a registered-deemed compliant FFI, a limited FFI or branch unable under foreign law to perform reporting and other acts with respect to U.S. accounts, or a sponsoring entity that agrees to perform the reporting obligations for one or more FFIs. The availability of a limited FFI or branch will terminate on January 1, 2017 (Notice 2015-66). Upon approval, a registered FFI or sponsoring entity will receive a Global Intermediary Identification Number (GIIN) from the IRS, unless the FFI is treated as a limited FFI. An FFI or sponsoring entity uses its GIIN to identify that it is registered and approved to withholding agents and the IRS. The IRS publishes a list of registered and approved FFIs and their GIINs monthly. Withholding agents may rely on the IRS published list to verify an FFI's GIIN and not withhold on payments made to the FFI.

Identification Requirement. A participating FFI is required to identify and document the status of each holder of an account maintained by the FFI to determine if the account is a U.S. account, non-U.S. account, or an account held by a recalcitrant account holder or nonparticipating FFI (Reg. §1.1471-4(c)(1)). A U.S. account is a financial account held by one or more specified U.S. persons or U.S.-owned foreign entities, including any depository or custodial account maintained by the FFI, and any equity or debt interest in the FFI other than an interest regularly traded on an established securities market (Code Sec. 1471(d); Reg. §§1.1471-5(a) and 1.1473-1(c)).[107] A specified U.S. person is any U.S. person *other than* a: dealer in securities, commodities, or derivative financial instruments; broker; publicly traded corporation; tax exempt organization, trust, or individual retirement plan; bank, real estate investment trust (REIT), regulated investment company (RIC or mutual fund), common trust fund or charitable remainder trust; or government entity.

References are to Standard Federal Tax Reports; Tax Research Consultant; and Practical Tax Explanations.

[105] ¶ 32,898, ¶ 32,899D, ¶ 32,899F; ¶ 32,899H; INTL: 36,150; §37,725.05, §37,730

[106] ¶ 32,883, ¶ 32,884P; ¶ 32,884R; INTL: 36,060; §37,725.10

[107] ¶ 32,883, ¶ 32,884T, ¶ 32,895; INTL: 36,060; §37,725.10

An FFI must follow due diligence procedures for identifying and documenting account holders based on the value and risk profile of the account. FFIs in many cases are permitted to rely on information they already collect (Reg. § 1.1471-4(c)). Generally, accounts with a balance or value of more than $50,000 ($250,000 for a cash value insurance or annuity contract) but less than $1 million are only subject to electronic review of searchable data for indicia of U.S. status. Accounts with a balance that exceeds $1 million are subject to review of electronic and non-electronic files for U.S. indicia, including an inquiry of the actual knowledge of any relationship manager associated with the account. A preexisting account of an individual with a balance or value of $50,000 or less, as well as certain cash value insurance contracts with a value of $250,000 or less, are excluded from the due diligence review unless the FFI elects otherwise. Preexisting accounts of an entity with account balances of $250,000 or less are also exempt from review until the account balance exceeds $1 million.

Reporting Requirement. A participating FFI is required to report annually to the IRS the name, address, and taxpayer identification number (TIN) of each holder of a U.S. account which is a specified U.S. person. In the case of any account holder which is a U.S.-owned foreign entity, the participating FFI must report the name, address, and TIN of each substantial U.S. owner of the entity (Code Sec. 1471(c); Reg. § 1.1471-4(d) and (i)). The FFI must also report the account number, the year-end account balance or value in U.S. dollars, and the gross amount and character of dividends, interest, or other income paid or credited to the account. This includes the gross proceeds from the sale or redemption of property paid or credited to the account. Special rules are provided for a participating FFI to report information regarding its recalcitrant account holders. If an FFI is prohibited by foreign law from reporting the required information with respect to an account, then it must close the account within a reasonable period of time or must otherwise block or transfer the account.

A participating FFI reports the required information on Form 8966 with respect to each account maintained at any time during the calendar year. The form must be filed electronically with the IRS by March 31 of the year following the end of the calendar year to which it relates. Form 8809-I is used to request an automatic 90-day extension. For calendar years 2015 and 2016, a separate Form 8966 must be filed for each account maintained for a nonparticipating FFI to report aggregate foreign source payments (Temporary Reg. § 1.1471-4T(d)(2)(ii)(F)). As an alternative to filing Form 8966, the FFI may elect to be subject to the same reporting requirements of U.S. institutions. Thus, the institution must provide a full Form 1099 reporting for every account with a U.S. person or U.S. foreign entity as an account holder. As a result, both U.S. and foreign source amounts (including gross proceeds) are subject to reporting under this election regardless of whether the amounts are paid inside or outside the United States.

Withholding Requirement. A participating FFI is required to deduct and withhold 30 percent from any withholdable payment (¶ 2469) made by the FFI to an account held by a recalcitrant account holder or to a nonparticipating FFI after June 30, 2014 (Temp. Reg. § 1.1471-4T(b)(1)). If an FFI is prohibited by foreign law from withholding as required with respect to an account, then it must close the account within a reasonable period of time or must otherwise block or transfer the account (Reg. § 1.1471-4(a)(1)). A participating FFI is not required to deduct and withhold tax on a foreign passthru payment made by the FFI to an account held by a recalcitrant account holder or to a nonparticipating FFI before the later of January 1, 2019, or the date final regulations are issued defining foreign passthru payments. A participating FFI may elect not to withhold on any withholdable payments, but instead have a U.S. withholding agent withhold tax on payments the electing FFI receives which are allocable to a recalcitrant account holder or a nonparticipating FFI (Code Sec. 1471(b)(3); Notice 2015-66).[108]

2473. FATCA Reporting and Withholding Obligations for Non-Financial Foreign Entities (NFFEs). Under the Foreign Account Tax Compliance Act (FATCA), if a non-financial foreign entity (NFFE) is the beneficial owner of a withholdable payment

References are to Standard Federal Tax Reports; Tax Research Consultant; and Practical Tax Explanations.

[108] ¶ 32,883, ¶ 32,887.35;
INTL: 36,054; § 37,725.05

(¶ 2469) made to the NFFE after June 30, 2014, then the NFFE is required to report certain information to the withholding agent (Code Sec. 1472(b); Reg. § 1.1472-1; Temp. Reg. § 1.1472-1T).[109] The reporting requirement is satisfied if the NFFE reports the name, address, and taxpayer identification number (TIN) of each substantial U.S. owner or if it certifies that it does not have any substantial U.S. owners. If the NFFE or other payee fails to meet the reporting requirement, then the withholding agent must deduct and withhold a tax of 30 percent from the withholdable payment.

An NFFE for this purpose is any foreign entity that is not a financial institution, meaning the entity does not accept deposits in the ordinary course of a banking business, does not hold financial assets for the account of others as a substantial part of its business, and is not engaged primarily in investing. A substantial U.S. owner is:

- in the case of a corporation, a U.S. person that owns, directly or indirectly, more than 10 percent of the corporate stock by vote or value;
- in the case of a partnership, a U.S. person that owns directly or indirectly, more than 10 percent of the capital or profits interests of the partnership; and
- in the case of a trust, a U.S. person treated as an owner of any portion of the trust under the grantor trust rules and any U.S. person holding more than 10 percent of the beneficial interests (Code Sec. 1473(2); Reg. § 1.1473-1(b)).[110]

A withholding agent that receives information about substantial U.S. owners of an NFFE must report the information to the IRS on or before March 15 of the calendar year following the year in which the withholdable payment is made. This includes the name of the NFFE and the name, TIN, and address of each U.S. substantial owner. If withholding is required, Form 1042 is used to report and pay taxes withheld during the tax year. In addition, an annual information return must be filed on Form 1042-S and a copy furnished to the recipient of the withholdable payment (Code Sec. 1472(b); Reg. § 1.1472-1(e)).[111]

So long as the NFFE and the withholding agent satisfy their reporting requirements, withholding is not required unless the withholding agent knows or has reason to know that any information provided about substantial U.S. owners is incorrect. A withholding agent is also not required to withhold taxes if the withholding agent may treat the payment as beneficially owned by an excepted NFFE. An excepted NFFE includes a publicly traded corporation and its related entities, territory entities, the government of a foreign country or U.S. possession, an international organization, or any foreign central bank of issue. Additionally, active NFFEs, direct reporting NFFEs and sponsored direct NFFEs are excepted NFFEs (Code Sec. 1472(c); Reg. § 1.1472-1(c); Temp. Reg. § 1.1472-1T(c)). An active NFFE is any NFFE if less than 50 percent of its gross income for the preceding tax year is passive income, and less than 50 percent of its assets produce or are held for the production of dividends, interest, rents and royalties (other than those derived in the active conduct of a trade or business), annuities, or other passive income. A direct reporting NFFE elects to report directly to the IRS. A sponsored direct reporting NFFE is a direct reporting NFFE with a sponsoring entity that acts on its behalf. In addition, entities which are by definition not financial institutions are considered excepted NFFEs, including certain holding companies, start-up companies, NFFEs that are liquidating or emerging from reorganization or bankruptcy, and certain hedging entities.

Withholding is not required with respect to any payment under a grandfathered obligation or from any gross proceeds from the disposition of such an obligation. A grandfathered obligation is any legal obligation outstanding on July 1, 2014, that produces or could produce a withholdable payment or pass-through payment. It does not include any instrument treated as equity for U.S. tax purposes or any legal agreement that lacks a definitive expiration or term (Reg. § 1.1471-2(b); Temp. Reg. § 1.1471-2T(b)).[112]

References are to Standard Federal Tax Reports; Tax Research Consultant; and Practical Tax Explanations.

[109] ¶ 32,888, ¶ 32,890, ¶ 32,890B; INTL: 36,100; § 37,730

[110] ¶ 32,893, ¶ 32,895; INTL: 36,060; § 37,730

[111] ¶ 32,888, ¶ 32,890; INTL: 36,100; § 37,730

[112] ¶ 32,884H, ¶ 32,884J; INTL: 36,100; § 37,730

Foreign Tax Credit or Deduction

2475. Foreign Tax Credit or Deduction. Subject to certain limitations (¶ 2479), a U.S. taxpayer may elect a credit or deduction against U.S. income liability for foreign taxes paid or accrued to a foreign country or U.S. possession during the tax year (Code Sec. 901; Reg. § 1.901-1).[113] The credit and deduction are intended to relieve U.S. taxpayers of double taxation on foreign source income. The election is made on an annual basis (¶ 2476) and is applicable to all creditable foreign taxes paid or incurred during the tax year (¶ 2477). A separate foreign tax credit can be claimed by individuals and corporations against alternative minimum tax liability (AMT) (¶ 1470).

Taxpayers entitled to claim the foreign tax credit or deduction against income liability include U.S. citizens, resident aliens (¶ 2409), bona fide residents of Puerto Rico for the entire tax year (¶ 2415), domestic corporations, and nonresident aliens and foreign corporations with respect to foreign taxes paid or accrued on foreign source income effectively connected with the conduct of a U.S. trade or business (¶ 2429). A taxpayer who is a partner in a partnership, shareholder in an S corporation, or beneficiary of an estate or trust may claim the credit or deduction with respect to the taxpayer's proportionate share of creditable foreign taxes paid or accrued by the entity (Code Secs. 901(b) and 1373(a)).[114] Similarly, a shareholder of a regulated investment company or mutual fund may be able to claim the credit or deduction based on the shareholder's share of creditable foreign taxes paid by the entity (¶ 2320).

Income Matching. If there is a foreign tax credit splitting event, the foreign tax credit or deduction may not be claimed by a taxpayer until the related income is taken into account for U.S. income tax purposes (Code Sec. 909; Reg. § 1.909-2).[115] A foreign tax credit splitting event occurs with respect to a foreign income tax if in connection with a splitter arrangement the related income is (or will be) taken into account by a covered person. A covered person is a person or entity that has a specified relationship with the taxpayer—at least 10 percent ownership interest, related party, or otherwise specified by the IRS. In the case of a partnership, S corporation, or trust, the matching requirement is applied at the partner, shareholder, or beneficiary level. Special rules apply to a foreign tax credit splitting event involving a Code Sec. 902 corporation, including the application of the matching rule to foreign income taxes paid or accrued in pre-2011 tax years for purposes of applying the deemed paid foreign tax credit (¶ 2485) for periods after 2010 (Reg. §§ 1.909-5 and 1.909-6).[116] The IRS intends to issue regulations addressing the separation of related income from foreign taxes paid by a Code Sec. 902 corporation pursuant to a foreign-initiated adjustment. The regulations will apply to foreign income taxes paid on or after September 15, 2016 (Notice 2016-52).

2476. Election of Foreign Tax Credit or Deduction. The election to claim the foreign tax credit or deduction (¶ 2475) is made on an annual basis. It may be made or changed anytime within 10 years from the due date for filing a return for the year in which the taxes were actually paid or accrued, unless the period is extended by agreement with the IRS (Code Sec. 6511(d)(3); Reg. § 1.901-1(d) and (e)).[117] For partnerships and S corporations, the election is made by the individual partners and shareholders, respectively (Code Secs. 702(a)(6), 703(b)(3), and 1366(a)(1)).[118] Corporations in an affiliated group make the election and compute the credit on a consolidated basis for a consolidated return year (Reg. § 1.1502-4).[119]

A taxpayer claims the foreign tax credit by filing Form 1116 (for individuals, estates, and trusts) or Form 1118 (for corporations) with the taxpayer's income tax return. An individual may elect to claim the foreign tax credit without filing Form 1116 by entering the credit directly on his or her tax return if: (1) all of the individual's foreign source income is passive income; (2) all of the income and any foreign taxes paid on the income

References are to Standard Federal Tax Reports; Tax Research Consultant; and Practical Tax Explanations.

[113] ¶ 27,820, ¶ 27,821; INTLOUT: 3,050; § 13,401

[114] ¶ 27,820, ¶ 32,180; INTLOUT: 3,152; § 13,405.05

[115] ¶ 27,971, ¶ 27,973D; INTLOUT: 3,300; § 13,432

[116] ¶ 27,974I, ¶ 27,974N; INTLOUT: 3,304; § 13,432

[117] ¶ 39,060, ¶ 27,821; INTLOUT: 3,054; § 13,413

[118] ¶ 25,080, ¶ 25,100, ¶ 32,080; INTLOUT: 3,054; § 13,405.20

[119] ¶ 33,148; INTLOUT: 3,054

is reported on a qualified payee statement (i.e., Form 1099); and (3) the total creditable foreign taxes is less than $300 ($600 for joint filers) (Code Sec. 904(j)).[120] If an individual makes the election, then the foreign tax credit limitations will not apply (¶ 2479). However, the individual cannot carry over any excess credit to another tax year. The election is not available to estates, trusts, or corporations. An election to take the credit or deduction on a joint return applies to the qualifying foreign taxes paid or accrued by both spouses. If married taxpayers file separate returns, either may take the credit or deduction without regard to the other.

Credit vs. Deduction. Generally, it is more advantageous for a U.S. taxpayer to elect the foreign tax credit rather than the deduction because the credit is taken against the taxpayer's U.S. liability on a dollar-for-dollar basis. In contrast, a deduction for foreign taxes merely reduces a taxpayer's income subject to tax. In addition, an individual who deducts foreign taxes must claim the taxes as an itemized deduction.

The election to claim the credit or deduction applies to all creditable foreign taxes paid or incurred by the taxpayer during the tax year for which a U.S. return is required (¶ 2477). A taxpayer cannot claim a credit for some creditable foreign taxes and a deduction for other creditable foreign taxes in the same tax year. Partial credits and partial deductions are not permitted except in limited circumstances (Code Sec. 275(a)(4)).[121]

2477. Creditable Foreign Taxes. A U.S. taxpayer is allowed a foreign tax credit or deduction (¶ 2475) against U.S. income tax liability for any income tax, including war profits, and excess profits taxes, paid or accrued to a foreign country or U.S. possession during the tax year on foreign source income. This includes taxes paid or accrued in lieu of income taxes imposed by the foreign country or U.S. possession (Code Secs. 901 and 903; Reg. § 1.901-2).[122] A U.S. corporation is also allowed a foreign tax credit for creditable foreign taxes paid by a foreign subsidiary in which it owns at least 10 percent of the voting stock and from which it receives a dividend (¶ 2485).

A creditable foreign tax is a levy the predominant character of which is that of a compulsory income tax according to U.S. tax principles (Reg. § 1.901-2).[123] A penalty, fine, interest payment, customs duty, or similar obligation is not a tax; nor is any payment to a foreign government in exchange for a specific economic benefit that is not available on substantially the same terms to all persons. A foreign tax paid for retirement, unemployment, or disability benefits is generally not a payment for a specific economic benefit. However, no credit or deduction is allowed for social security taxes paid or accrued to a foreign country with which the United States has a social security agreement. The IRS may disallow foreign tax credits generated in transactions it views as abusive such as structured passive investment arrangements. The foreign tax credit or deduction is also not available for the withholding of otherwise creditable foreign taxes on dividends and other items of gain or income from property unless certain holding period requirements are met (Code Sec. 901(k) and (l)).

The foreign tax credit or deduction can only be claimed by the taxpayer upon whom the foreign law imposes legal liability, and who actually pays or accrues the tax. In the case of combined income of two or more persons, foreign law is considered to impose legal liability on each person on a pro rata basis (Reg. § 1.901-2(f)).[124] This includes the combined income of a husband and wife, or a corporation and one or more of its subsidiaries. However, income which is subject to a special tax rate, is exempt from tax, or for which certain deductions or credits are allowed under the foreign law must be allocated only to the person(s) with that type of income. The income subject to preferential treatment must be computed separately and the tax on that income allocated separately.

A U.S. taxpayer may not claim the foreign tax credit or deduction for any foreign taxes paid or accrued on income excluded from U.S. gross income. This includes

References are to Standard Federal Tax Reports; Tax Research Consultant; and Practical Tax Explanations.

[120] ¶ 27,880; INTLOUT: 6,102.05; § 13,425.20

[121] ¶ 14,500; INTLOUT: 3,050; § 13,413

[122] ¶ 27,820, ¶ 27,822, ¶ 27,860; INTLOUT: 3,100; § 13,410.05

[123] ¶ 27,822; INTLOUT: 3,100; § 13,410.10

[124] ¶ 27,822; INTLOUT: 3,113; § 13,410.25

income excluded under the foreign earned income or foreign housing exclusions (¶ 2402 and ¶ 2403), or income from a U.S. possession (¶ 2414). The taxpayer may also not claim a credit or deduction for foreign taxes paid or accrued to the extent that: (1) the taxpayer is certain to receive a refund or credit, or the tax is used as a subsidy; (2) the liability is dependent on the availability of a foreign tax credit in another jurisdiction; (3) the taxes are paid or accrued to a country with which the United States does not conduct diplomatic relations or which is designated as supporting acts of international terrorism; or (4) the taxes are attributable to boycott income (¶ 2496). The amount of foreign taxes a taxpayer may claim will be reduced if the taxpayer controls a foreign corporation (CFC) or partnership that fails to file Form 5471 or Form 8865, respectively (¶ 2487 and ¶ 2494).

Covered Asset Acquisitions. In the case of a covered asset acquisition, a taxpayer may not take into account in determining the foreign tax credit the disqualified portion of any foreign income tax determined with respect to income or gain attributable to the relevant foreign assets (Code Sec. 901(m)).[125] A covered asset acquisition includes: (1) a qualified stock purchase under Code Sec. 338 (¶ 2265); (2) any transaction that is treated as the acquisition of assets for U.S. tax purposes and as the acquisition of stock (or is disregarded) for purposes of the foreign income taxes; (3) any acquisition of an interest in a partnership that has an election in effect under Code Sec. 754 (¶ 459); and (4) any other transaction as determined by the IRS.

The disqualified portion of any covered asset acquisition for any tax year is generally the aggregate basis difference allocable to the tax year with respect to all relevant foreign assets, divided by the income on which the foreign income tax is determined (Code Sec. 901(m)(3)(B); Notice 2014-44; Notice 2014-45).[126] However, the basis difference allocated to the tax year of disposition of any relevant foreign asset is the basis difference of the asset over the aggregate basis differences from prior years (the "unallocated basis difference"). No basis difference with respect to the asset will be allocated to any subsequent tax year. The IRS intends to issue regulations that will provide that a disposition for this purpose means an event that results in gain or loss being recognized for U.S. income tax or foreign income tax purposes with respect to the relevant foreign asset. The portion of the basis difference that will be taken into account for a tax year will depend on whether the disposition is fully taxable or not. The regulations will generally apply to dispositions occurring on or after July 21, 2014. They will also apply to determine the tax consequences of an entity classification election and whether a disposition results from the election and the treatment of any unallocated basis difference, for an election filed on or after July 29, 2014, that is effective on or before July 21, 2014.

2479. Foreign Tax Credit Limitations. The foreign tax credit or deduction (¶ 2475) is subject to a two-part limitation calculated on Form 1116 or Form 1118 that prevents the use of foreign taxes to reduce U.S. income tax liability on U.S. source income. First, an overall limitation provides that the total amount of a taxpayer's foreign tax credit may not exceed the taxpayer's entire U.S. income tax liability (determined without regard to the credit), multiplied by a fraction equal to the taxpayer's foreign source taxable income over worldwide taxable income from all sources (Code Sec. 904(a)).[127] Second, the limitation must be calculated separately for certain categories or baskets of foreign source income (¶ 2481). Special rules also apply if the taxpayer has an overall foreign loss (¶ 2483). The IRS may recharacterize the income of an affiliated group of corporations or modify the consolidated return regulations to the extent necessary to prevent avoidance of the foreign tax credit limitation rules (Code Sec. 904(i); Reg. § 1.904(i)-1).[128]

Foreign source taxable income is the taxpayer's gross income from all geographic sources outside the United States (regardless of the country), less any applicable

References are to Standard Federal Tax Reports; Tax Research Consultant; and Practical Tax Explanations.

[125] ¶ 27,820; INTLOUT: 3,110.30

[126] ¶ 27,820, ¶ 27,826.2204; INTLOUT: 3,110.30

[127] ¶ 27,880; INTLOUT: 6,050; § 13,425.05

[128] ¶ 27,880, ¶ 27,900C; INTLOUT: 6,404

deductions that properly relate to the income and an allocation of deductions unrelated to any specific item of income (Code Sec. 904(b)).[129] An individual, estate, or trust may not claim deductions for personal and dependency exemptions in calculating taxable income. In the case of a corporation, taxable income does not include any portion of income taken into account for purposes of the possession tax credit (¶ 1362). For all taxpayers, foreign source capital gains and losses are subject to (1) a capital gain net income limitation adjustment (i.e., U.S. capital loss adjustment), and (2) a capital gain rate differential adjustment (Reg. § § 1.904(b)-1 and 1.904(b)-2).[130]

De Minimis Exemption. An individual with $300 or less of creditable foreign taxes ($600 if married filing jointly) is exempt from the overall foreign tax credit limitation provided he or she has no foreign source income other than qualified passive income (¶ 2476). The exemption is not automatic and an individual must elect to take the exemption for the tax year directly on Form 1040.

U.S.-Owned Foreign Corporations. Certain amounts derived from U.S.-owned foreign corporations that would otherwise be treated as foreign source income are treated as U.S. source income for purposes of the foreign tax credit limitations (Code Sec. 904(h); Reg. § 1.904-5(m)).[131] The sourcing rule applies to subpart F income inclusions from a controlled foreign corporation (CFC) (¶ 2488), income from a qualified electing fund (¶ 2490), and interest and dividends paid by a foreign corporation where not less than 10 percent of the corporation's earnings and profits for the tax year are attributable to U.S. sources. A U.S.-owned foreign corporation is generally any foreign corporation (including a Code Sec. 902 corporation (¶ 2485)) if 50 percent or more of the total combined voting power of all classes of stock in the corporation entitled to vote, or of the total value of the stock of the corporation, is held by U.S. persons.

Carryover of Unused Foreign Taxes. When the amount of creditable foreign taxes paid or accrued by a taxpayer during the tax year exceeds the overall limitation for that year (as well as the separate limitation for each separate basket of foreign source income), the unused portion may be carried back one year and then forward ten years (Code Sec. 904(c); Reg. § 1.904-2).[132] The amount that may be carried back and forward is limited to the amount by which the credit limitation in the carryback or forward year exceeds the amount of foreign taxes paid or accrued in that year. In addition, any unused foreign tax must be carried back and forward to its own separate basket of income. It cannot offset other taxes imposed on income in another basket.

If any unused foreign tax credit is carried back or forward to a tax year in which a foreign tax deduction is claimed (¶ 2476), the taxpayer must compute a foreign tax credit limit as if the credit was elected for that year. Any excess generated in the deduction year cannot be deducted or claimed as a credit for any year, but reduces the amount of unused foreign taxes that can be carried over to another tax year. Alternatively, an amended return may be filed within 10 years from the due date of the return of the deduction year to claim the foreign tax credit rather than the deduction (¶ 2475). For any portion of a foreign tax credit carryback from a tax year attributable to the carryback of a net operating loss or capital loss from a later tax year, the carryback stops the running of interest until the filing date for the later tax year (Code Sec. 6601(d)).[133] An individual electing the *de minimis* exemption may not carryback or carryforward any excess foreign taxes to an election year.

2481. Separate Foreign Tax Limitation Categories. A taxpayer is generally required to compute the foreign tax credit limitation (¶ 2479) separately for two main categories or baskets of foreign source income: passive category income and general category income (Code Sec. 904(d); Reg. § 1.904-4).[134] Passive category income includes investment income such as dividends, interest, rents, royalties, annuities, net gain from the sale of non-income-producing investment property or property that generates passive income, and income from a qualified electing fund (¶ 2490). It does not include

References are to Standard Federal Tax Reports; Tax Research Consultant; and Practical Tax Explanations.

[129] ¶ 27,880; INTLOUT: 6,050; § 13,425.10

[130] ¶ 27,889, ¶ 27,890; INTLOUT: 6,060; § 13,425.10

[131] ¶ 27,880, ¶ 27,886; INTLOUT: 6,054.15

[132] ¶ 27,880, ¶ 27,883; INTLOUT: 6,300; § 13,425.25

[133] ¶ 39,410; INTLOUT: 6,304; § 13,425.25

[134] ¶ 27,880, ¶ 27,885; INTLOUT: 6,100; § 13,425.15

gains or losses from the sale of inventory or property held mainly for sale to customers in the ordinary course of a trade or business, any rents or royalties that are derived in the active conduct of a trade or business, certain export financing interest, and highly taxed income. Any foreign source income that is not included in the passive income basket is considered part of the general income basket.

To determine taxable income in each category, a taxpayer must allocate expenses, losses, and other deductions directly related to the foreign source income allocated to each basket. Similarly, foreign taxes paid or accrued may only include those taxes that are related to income in that basket. If a tax is related to more than one basket, the taxpayer must apportion the tax. However, if creditable foreign taxes were imposed on amounts that do not constitute income under U.S. tax law ("base difference items"), then they will be treated as imposed on general category income.

Look-Through Rules. Foreign source income received by a U.S. shareholder from a controlled foreign corporation (CFC) (¶ 2487) is categorized by applying look-through rules that require identification of underlying income to specific foreign tax credit limitation categories (Code Sec. 904(d)(3) and (4); Reg. § 1.904-5).[135] Tracing rules prescribe classification of subpart F income (¶ 2488), interest, rents, royalties, and dividends to various limitation categories. The look-through rules also apply in the case of payments made by Code Sec. 902 corporations (¶ 2485), certain domestic corporations, partnerships, and related look-through entities. In the case of a partner in a partnership, the look-through rule will apply with respect to the partner's distributive share of partnership income unless the partner owns less than 10 percent of the partnership, in which case the income is treated as passive income.

Other Limitations. In addition to the separate foreign tax credit limitations for passive category income and general category income, separate foreign tax credit limitations must be determined for certain special categories of income (Reg. § 1.904-4(m)).[136] This includes: (1) any income sourced under a tax treaty as foreign source income including any income derived from foreign sources; (2) income from sanctioned countries; (3) for purposes of the alternative minimum tax (AMT), dividends received from a corporation that qualifies for the possession tax credit if the dividends-received deduction is disallowed under the alternative current earnings (ACE) rules; (4) dividends received from 10-percent owned foreign corporations (¶ 231); (5) gain from the sale of stock in a foreign corporation or intangible property that is treated as foreign source under a tax treaty; (6) lump-sum distributions from retirement plans for which the special averaging treatment is used to figure tax; and (7) combined foreign oil and gas income including foreign oil and gas extraction income (FOGEI) and foreign oil-related income (FORI) (Code Sec. 907).[137]

2483. Recapture of Foreign and U.S. Losses. An overall foreign loss (OFL) is subject to recapture to prevent a double tax benefit from using the OFL to reduce U.S. tax liability on U.S. source income and claiming the foreign tax credit (¶ 2475) on the same income. If a taxpayer has an OFL in any tax year, then a portion of the taxpayer's foreign source income earned in a subsequent year is recharacterized as U.S. source income (Code Sec. 904(f)).[138] For this purpose, an OFL is the amount by which gross income from foreign sources is exceeded by the sum of expenses, losses, and other deductions properly allocable to such income, but without taking into account any net operating losses (NOL), foreign expropriation losses, and uncompensated casualty or theft losses. A foreign loss must be determined for each separate foreign tax credit category or basket (¶ 2481), referred to as a separate limitation loss (SLL). Thus, a taxpayer can have an OFL, an SLL for passive income, and a SLL for general income in any given tax year. Foreign losses in one separate foreign tax credit category or basket must be offset against income in other foreign categories before offsetting U.S. income.

The amount of foreign source income that must be recaptured and recharacterized as U.S. source income is generally limited to the lesser of the taxpayer's OFL (to the

References are to Standard Federal Tax Reports; Tax Research Consultant; and Practical Tax Explanations.

[135] ¶ 27,880, ¶ 27,886; INTLOUT: 6,200

[136] ¶ 27,885; INTLOUT: 6,114; § 13,425.15

[137] ¶ 27,940; INTLOUT: 6,350

[138] ¶ 27,880; INTLOUT: 6,250; § 13,425.30

extent not used in prior tax years) or 50 percent of the taxpayer's foreign source taxable income for the tax year. If a taxpayer disposes of assets used in its trade or business predominantly outside the United States in a taxable disposition, or disposes of stock in a controlled foreign corporation (CFC) (¶ 2487) in which it owns more than 50 percent, then 100 percent of the gain must be recaptured. Fifty percent of the recognized gain is recaptured under the general rule above and the remainder recaptured to the extent of the taxpayer's OFL balance. Special recapture rules also apply if the disposition is nontaxable. For these purposes, property is considered used predominantly outside the United States if, during a three-year period ending on the date of disposition, the property was located outside the United States more than 50 percent of the time. Similar recapture rules apply to an overall domestic loss (ODL) requiring U.S. source income earned in a subsequent year to be recharacterized as foreign source income. Special ordering rules are used to allocate NOLs, net capital losses, U.S. source losses and SLLs, and for the recapture of SLLs, OFLs, and ODLs (Reg. § 1.904(g)-3).[139]

2485. Deemed Paid or Indirect Foreign Tax Credit. The foreign tax credit (¶ 2475) is available to a U.S. corporate shareholder that owns 10 percent or more of the voting stock in a foreign corporation from which it receives a dividend (or deemed to receive a dividend through an affiliated group or a partnership) (Code Sec. 902).[140] The amount of the "deemed paid" or "indirect" credit is determined by reference to the portion of the foreign corporation's foreign income taxes that the dividend received by the domestic corporation bears to the foreign corporation's undistributed earnings. However, the deemed paid credit does not include the disqualified portion of any foreign income tax paid by a Code Sec. 902 corporation in a covered asset acquisition and determined with respect to income or gain attributable to the relevant foreign assets (¶ 2477). A corporation electing to take the deemed paid credit must increase ("gross up") its tax base by including not only the dividend but the tax deemed paid by the foreign corporation (Code Sec. 78).[141] Additionally, the deemed paid credit is subject to the foreign tax credit limitation (¶ 2479).

The deemed paid credit is allowed to a domestic shareholder for foreign taxes paid by a lower-tier foreign corporation if the foreign corporation is a member of a qualified group and the foreign corporation owns 10 percent or more of the voting stock of the member of the qualified group from which it receives a dividend (Code Sec. 902(b)). A qualified group includes any foreign corporation in a chain that includes the first-tier corporation and foreign corporations through the sixth-tier. A corporation below the third-tier will not be included in the qualified group unless it is a controlled foreign corporation (CFC) (¶ 2487) and the domestic corporation is a U.S. shareholder. Whether the ownership requirements are met is determined at the time dividends are received. A qualified group cannot aggregate their shares in a foreign corporation to meet the ownership requirements.

U.S. Shareholders of Foreign Corporations

2487. Controlled Foreign Corporations (CFCs). A U.S. shareholder of a foreign corporation that is a controlled foreign corporation (CFC) for an uninterrupted period of 30 days or more during the tax year must include in gross income its pro rata share of the CFC's subpart F income (¶ 2488) (whether distributed or not) and earnings invested in U.S. property during the year (Code Sec. 951).[142] A foreign corporation is a CFC if more than 50 percent of its total voting power or value is owned by U.S. shareholders (Code Sec. 957).[143] A U.S. shareholder is any U.S. person (U.S. citizen, resident alien, domestic corporation, partnership, estate, or trust) that owns directly, indirectly, or constructively 10 percent or more of the total combined voting power of the foreign corporation (Code Sec. 958).[144]

The U.S. shareholder includes subpart F income and earnings in gross income in its tax year in which the CFC's tax year ends but only if it is a shareholder on the last day of

References are to Standard Federal Tax Reports; Tax Research Consultant; and Practical Tax Explanations.

[139] ¶ 27,900AM; INTLOUT: 6,260; § 13,425.30

[140] ¶ 27,840; INTLOUT: 3,200; § 13,420

[141] ¶ 6350; INTLOUT: 3,200; § 13,420

[142] ¶ 28,470; INTLOUT: 9,000

[143] ¶ 28,590; INTLOUT: 9,050

[144] ¶ 28,610; INTLOUT: 9,056

the CFC's tax year. In addition, the shareholder only includes income from that portion of the year that the corporation qualifies as a CFC. The income is treated as a deemed dividend (¶ 733). Actual distributions are excluded from gross income to the extent they have already been accounted for by the shareholder (Code Sec. 959).[145] To prevent double taxation, the basis of the U.S. shareholder's CFC stock and basis in property the shareholder is considered owning through the CFC is increased by the amount of subpart F income required to be included in income and decreased by any distribution that is excluded from income (Code Sec. 961).[146]

A U.S. shareholder of CFC that is a domestic corporation is allowed a foreign tax credit (¶ 2475) for any foreign taxes paid (or deemed paid) by the CFC for income that is attributed or distributed to it as a U.S. shareholder (Code Sec. 960).[147] The credit is limited to the taxes that would have been deemed paid if the foreign corporation had made an actual distribution to the domestic corporation. A deemed-paid credit is also available to any individual U.S. shareholder who elects to be taxed at domestic corporate income tax rates on amounts included in gross income (Code Sec. 962).[148]

Investment of Earnings. U.S. shareholders of a CFC are taxed on their pro rata share of the CFC's earnings that are invested in U.S. property during the tax year and not distributed or otherwise taxed (Code Sec. 956).[149] The amount of earnings invested in U.S. property is the economic equivalent of a dividend deemed to have been paid, but it is not a qualified dividend eligible to be taxed at capital gains rates because it is not actually distributed (*O. Rodriguez*, CA-5, 2013-2 USTC ¶ 50,420). A CFC acquires a direct interest in U.S. property when it acquires an adjusted basis in the property. U.S. property includes tangible real or personal property located in the United States, stock of domestic corporations, obligations of U.S. persons, and the right to use a patent, copyright, invention, etc., in the United States. Certain properties acquired in normal commercial transactions without the intention that they remain in the United States indefinitely are not to be treated as U.S. property.

Sale or Exchange of CFC Stock. Any gain recognized by a U.S. shareholder from the sale, exchange, or redemption of stock in a CFC is included in gross income as an ordinary dividend to the extent of the corporation's earnings and profits allocable to the stock (Code Sec. 1248).[150] Any gain exceeding the CFC's earnings and profits is treated as capital gain. The shareholder may claim a foreign tax credit for the taxes paid by the CFC on the income. However, the credit may be less than the indirect credit (¶ 2485) because it will not apply to as many tiers of foreign corporations.

Returns. Every U.S. person (U.S. citizen, resident alien, domestic corporation, domestic partnership, or domestic estate or trust) who is a U.S. shareholder of a CFC must file an information return on Form 5471 with their income tax return (Code Sec. 6038).[151] Failure to timely file the form may result in penalties and a reduced foreign tax credit. The taxpayer must include information on acquisitions, reorganizations, and dispositions of ownership interests in a CFC during the tax year (Code Sec. 6046).[152] U.S. shareholders of controlled foreign partnerships are subject to similar reporting requirements using Form 8865.

2488. Subpart F Income. Subpart F income of a controlled foreign corporation (CFC) (¶ 2487) is the sum of the corporation's insurance income, foreign base company income, boycott income (¶ 2496), illegal payments (¶ 2497), and income from countries not diplomatically recognized by the U.S. government (Code Sec. 952).[153] It does not include income from sources within the United States that is effectively connected with the conduct of a trade or business by the corporation (¶ 2429) unless that income is exempt from tax or taxed at a reduced rate pursuant to a tax treaty. Subpart F income for the tax year is also limited to the CFC's total earnings and profits for that year, and may be reduced in certain circumstances to accumulated deficits of earnings and profits.

References are to Standard Federal Tax Reports; Tax Research Consultant; and Practical Tax Explanations.

[145] ¶ 28,630; INTLOUT: 9,350
[146] ¶ 28,670; INTLOUT: 9,360
[147] ¶ 28,650; INTLOUT: 9,358
[148] ¶ 28,690; INTLOUT: 9,362
[149] ¶ 28,570; INTLOUT: 9,250
[150] ¶ 30,960; INTLOUT: 9,400
[151] ¶ 35,540; INTLOUT: 9,450; § 39,135.05
[152] ¶ 35,940; INTLOUT: 9,456; § 39,135.05
[153] ¶ 28,490; INTLOUT: 9,100

Subpart F insurance income is any income that is attributable to the issuance or reissuance of any insurance or annuity contract (Code Sec. 953, as amended by the Protecting Americans from Tax Hikes (PATH) Act of 2015 (P.L. 114-113)).[154] The income must be of a type that would be taxed (with some modifications) under the rules that apply to domestic insurance companies. It does not include insurance income in connection with risks located outside of the United States.

Foreign base company income of a CFC is made up of income from a foreign personal holding company (FPHC) and foreign base company sales, services, and oil-related income (Code Sec. 954, as amended by P.L. 114-113).[155] FPHC income is generally the major component of foreign base company income and includes dividends, interest (including otherwise tax-exempt interest), rents, royalties, and annuities. It also includes: amounts received under a contract to furnish personal services; any item of income, gain, deduction, or loss from a notional principal contract; and the excess of gains over losses from the sale or exchange of property (including foreign currency and commodities) unless the CFC is a regular dealer. FPHC income does not include rents and royalties from an active trade or business, certain income from related persons, and export financing interest. It also does not include income derived in the active conduct of a banking, financing or similar business (active financing income), income derived in the active conduct of an insurance business (active insurance income), or qualified insurance investment income.

For purposes of determining FPHC income, the sale of a partnership interest by a CFC is treated as a sale of the proportionate share of partnership assets attributable to that interest, including subpart F income. On the other hand, for tax years beginning before January 1, 2020, a no look-through rule applies to dividends, interest, rents and royalties received by a CFC from a related CFC to the extent that it creates or increases a deficit that reduces subpart F income of either the payor or another CFC (Code Sec. 954(c)(6), as amended by P.L. 114-113).

2490. Passive Foreign Investment Company. A U.S. shareholder of a passive foreign investment company (PFIC) who receives an excess distribution with respect to its stock or disposes of its PFIC stock must allocate the income or gain pro rata over the shareholder's holding period for the stock unless the shareholder elects to treat the PFIC as a qualifying electing fund (QEF) or makes a mark-to-market election (Code Sec. 1291).[156] The amount allocated to the shareholder's current tax year, and to the tax years in its holding period before the foreign corporation qualified as a PFIC (pre-PFIC years), are taxed as ordinary income. The amount allocated to any other tax year in the shareholder's holding period is taxed at the highest income tax rate applicable for that year, plus interest from the due date for the taxpayer's return for that year. For this purpose, an excess distribution is any part of a distribution received from the PFIC which is greater than 125 percent of the average distribution received by the shareholder during the three preceding tax years or, if shorter, during the period the shareholder held the stock.

A PFIC is any foreign corporation that derives 75 percent or more of its gross income for the tax year from passive investments or at least 50 percent of its average total assets held for the year produce passive income or are held for the production of passive income (Code Sec. 1297).[157] Passive income generally is the type of income that would be foreign personal holding company income (¶ 2488). Miscellaneous rules apply regarding stock attribution, start-up companies and business changes, the leasing of tangible personal property, intangible assets, and the interaction of the PFIC rules with the taxation of accumulated earnings and subpart F income (Code Sec. 1298).[158] Even if a foreign corporation ceases to qualify as a PFIC, a U.S. shareholder is subject to the PFIC rules for any period stock is held that the corporation was a PFIC. To avoid the PFIC rules, the shareholder can purge PFIC stock by making a deemed sale or deemed dividend election.

References are to Standard Federal Tax Reports; Tax Research Consultant; and Practical Tax Explanations.

[154] ¶ 28,510; INTLOUT: 9,102

[155] ¶ 28,530; INTLOUT: 9,104

[156] ¶ 31,540; INTLOUT: 18,200

[157] ¶ 31,620; INTLOUT: 18,202

[158] ¶ 31,640; INTLOUT: 18,200

A U.S. person that is a direct or indirect shareholder of a PFIC generally must file Form 8621 with its tax return for each tax year in which the person receives an excess distribution, disposes of its PFIC stock, or makes an election to purge its PFIC stock, including a QEF or mark-to-market election. The reporting requirement may also meet the FATCA requirements for disclosing information with respect to specified foreign financial assets on Form 8938 (¶ 2570). A separate Form 8621 must be filed for each PFIC in which stock is held.

Qualified Electing Fund. Instead of paying the additional tax on deferrals (or deemed sale or deemed dividend elections), a U.S. shareholder of a PFIC may elect to treat the corporation as a QEF. If the election is made, the shareholder must include in gross income each year as ordinary income its pro rata share of earnings of the corporation, and as long-term capital gain, its pro rata share of the net capital gain of the corporation (Code Secs. 1293 and 1295).[159] The inclusions are made for the shareholder's tax year in which, or with which, the QEF's tax year ends. Once made, the QEF election is revocable only with the IRS's consent and is effective for the current tax year and all subsequent tax years. Under certain circumstances, the U.S. shareholder can elect to defer payment of the tax on any undistributed earnings of the QEF (Code Sec. 1294).[160]

Mark-to-Market Election. A U.S. shareholder of a PFIC may also avoid the additional tax on the deferral of income by making a mark-to-market election with respect to its PFIC stock that is marketable (Code Sec. 1296).[161] If the election is made, the shareholder annually includes in gross income as ordinary income an amount equal to the excess of the fair market value of the PFIC stock as of the close of the tax year over its adjusted basis. If the stock has declined in value, an ordinary loss deduction is allowed limited to the net amount of gain previously included in income.

2491. Sale or Exchange of Patent, Etc. to Foreign Corporations. A U.S. person who controls a foreign corporation (at least 50 percent of voting power of all stock) directly or indirectly must recognize gain from the sale or exchange of a patent, invention, model, design, copyright, secret formula or process, or any other similar property right to the foreign corporation as ordinary income rather than capital gain (Code Sec. 1249).[162]

2492. Reorganization Involving Foreign Corporations. A U.S. person is generally required to recognize gains (but not losses) on the transfer of appreciated property to a foreign corporation (outbound transfers) that would otherwise be tax-free under the corporate organization (¶ 203), reorganization (¶ 2205), and liquidation rules (¶ 2253) (Code Sec. 367(a); Temp. Reg. § 1.367(a)-1T).[163] Similarly, transfers by a foreign corporation to a U.S. corporation (inbound transfers) or transfers by a foreign corporation to another foreign corporation (foreign-to-foreign transfers) may require U.S. shareholders to recognize income currently, or defer recognition of gain by making basis, and earnings and profits adjustments (Code Sec. 367(b); Reg. § 1.367(b)-3; Reg. § 1.367(b)-4).[164]

Active Trade or Business. Recognition of gain on outbound transfers does not apply to any property transferred for use by the foreign corporation in the active conduct of a trade or business outside the United States, provided the U.S. person transferring the property complies with the reporting requirements of Code Sec. 6038B by filing Form 926 (Code Sec. 367(a)(3); Temp. Reg. § 1.367(a)-2T(a)).[165] The exception does not apply to outbound transfers of certain tainted assets such as inventory, accounts receivable, intangible property, and certain leased property (Temp. Reg. § 1.367(a)-5T).[166] The exception also does not apply in the case where a U.S. person transfers assets of a foreign branch with previously deducted losses to a foreign corporation (Temp. Reg. § 1.367(a)-6T).[167]

References are to Standard Federal Tax Reports; Tax Research Consultant; and Practical Tax Explanations.

[159] ¶ 31,560, ¶ 31,600; INTLOUT: 18,206

[160] ¶ 31,580; INTLOUT: 18,206.15

[161] ¶ 31,610; INTLOUT: 18,202.30

[162] ¶ 30,980; § 18,705.05

[163] ¶ 16,640, ¶ 16,641; INTL: 30,050

[164] ¶ 16,640, ¶ 16,647E, ¶ 16,647F; INTL: 30,050

[165] ¶ 16,640, ¶ 16,642AC; INTL: 30,068

[166] ¶ 16,645C; INTL: 30,072

[167] ¶ 16,646; INTL: 30,080

Transfers of Stock or Securities. Recognition of gain on outbound transfers does not apply to any transfer of stock or securities of a party to the exchange (Code Sec. 367(a)(2); Reg. § 1.367(a)-3; Temp. Reg. § 1.367(a)-3T).[168] An outbound transfer of foreign stock or securities is not subject to tax if the U.S. person owns less than five percent of the transferee foreign corporation or enters into a five-year gain recognition agreement (GRA) with the IRS (Reg. § 1.367(a)-8).[169] An outbound transfer of domestic stock or securities is not subject to tax if: (1) the U.S. person receives 50 percent or less of the voting power and stock value of the transferee; (2) U.S. officers, directors, five percent or more shareholders of U.S. corporation do not own more than 50 percent of voting power and stock value of the transferee; (3) the U.S. person is not a five-percent or more shareholder of the transferee or must enter into a GRA with the IRS; and (4) the transferee has been actively engaged in business for at least three years.

Code Sec. 361 Exchanges. If a U.S. person transfers property to a foreign corporation in a Code Sec. 361 exchange (¶ 2205), the exceptions above will generally not apply and the transferor will recognize gain under the outbound transfer rules (Code Sec. 367(a)(5); Temp. Reg. § 1.367(a)-3T(e)).[170] However, recognition of gain only applies if the transferring corporation is controlled by five or fewer domestic corporations, and basis adjustment and other conditions provided in the regulations are met.

2493. Transfers of Property to Foreign Trusts. Any U.S. person that transfers property to a foreign trust (other than the trust of an employee benefits plan or tax-exempt organization) with a U.S. beneficiary is treated as the owner of the portion of the trust attributable to the property (Code Sec. 679; Reg. § 1.679-1).[171] If the transferor and another person would be treated as owner of the same portion of the trust, then the U.S. transferor will be treated as the owner. Thus, any income received by the trust with respect to the property is taxable to the transferor under the grantor trust rules (¶ 571).

This rule applies without regard to whether the transferor retains any power or interest in the property. It also applies regardless of whether the transfer is direct or indirect. Exceptions exist for foreign trusts established by a will, transfers made by reason of death of the U.S. person (transferor), or transfers of property to the foreign trust in exchange for consideration equal to its fair market value. A U.S. person who is treated as the owner of any portion of a foreign trust under the grantor trust rules is required to ensure that the trust files an annual information return on Form 3520-A and furnishes the required annual statements to its U.S. owners and beneficiaries, or be subject to a penalty (Code Secs. 6048(b) and 6677(a)).[172]

The IRS may presume that when a U.S. person transfers property to a foreign trust the trust has a U.S. beneficiary unless the U.S. person demonstrates otherwise (Code Sec. 679(d)). Thus, an amount will be treated as either paid or accumulated for the benefit of a U.S. person if: (1) the U.S. person's interest in the trust is contingent on a future event; (2) a loan of cash or marketable securities, or the use of any other trust property, is made to any U.S. person; (3) any person has the discretion of making a distribution from the trust to any class of persons that may include a U.S. person; or (4) the U.S. person who transferred property to the trust is involved in any agreement or understanding that may result in trust income or corpus being paid to or accumulated for the benefit of a U.S. person.

2494. Information Reporting on Foreign Partnerships. A number of reporting requirements apply with respect to foreign partnerships. First, a foreign partnership must file a U.S. partnership return (Form 1065) if it has gross income that is either U.S. source income (¶ 2427) or income effectively connected with a U.S. trade or business (¶ 2429) (Code Sec. 6031(e)).[173] A U.S. partner cannot claim distributive shares of any partnership deduction, loss, or credit if a partnership return is not filed (Code Sec. 6231(f)).[174] Second, every U.S. person that controls a foreign partnership (more than 50

References are to Standard Federal Tax Reports; Tax Research Consultant; and Practical Tax Explanations.

[168] ¶ 16,640, ¶ 16,642B, ¶ 16,643; INTL: 30,074, INTL: 30,075

[169] ¶ 16,647A; INTL: 30,074

[170] ¶ 16,640, ¶ 16,643; INTL: 30,072

[171] ¶ 24,820, ¶ 24,820B; INTL: 30,252; § 32,805.10

[172] ¶ 36,000, ¶ 39,815; EST-TRST: 36,258.10; § 39,135.15

[173] ¶ 35,381; PART: 18,410.05; § 39,155.10

[174] ¶ 37,770; PART: 18,410.05; § 39,155.10

percent interest) is required to file an annual information return on Form 8865 with their income tax return (¶ 2487). Additionally, any U.S. person that owns at least a 10-percent interest in a foreign partnership must report on Form 8865 any changes to his or her ownership in the partnership during the tax year (Code Sec. 6046A).[175] Failure to file Form 8865 will result in a $10,000 penalty per occurrence (Code Sec. 6679).[176] A U.S. person who transfers property to a foreign partnership in a nontaxable transfer must report the transfer on Form 926 if the U.S. person has at least a 10-percent interest in the partnership or if the value of the property transferred exceeds $100,000 (Code Sec. 6038B).[177]

Other Foreign Tax Rules

2495. Foreign Currency Transactions. All federal income tax determinations must be made in the taxpayer's functional currency (Code Sec. 985).[178] Generally, the functional currency of a U.S. taxpayer will be the U.S. dollar. However, in the case of a qualified business unit (QBU), the functional currency is the currency in which the taxpayer conducts a significant part of its activities and which is used in keeping books and records. For this purpose, a QBU is any separate and clearly identified unit of a trade or business of the taxpayer which maintains its own books and records (for example, a foreign subsidiary of a U.S. corporation or a foreign corporation) (Code Sec. 989).[179] Special rules apply in determining when foreign earnings and profits and foreign income taxes must be translated into U.S. dollars, as well as the use of a foreign branch of a U.S. taxpayer (Code Secs. 986 and 987).[180]

Foreign currency gain or loss attributable to a nonfunctional currency transaction is treated separately from the underlying transaction. Generally, it is treated as ordinary gain or loss but is not treated as interest income or expenses (Code Sec. 988).[181] However, gain of an individual from the disposition of foreign currency in a personal transaction is not taxable, provided that the gain realized does not exceed $200. A personal transaction is any transaction other than one with respect to which properly allocable expenses are deductible as trade or business expenses or expenses incurred in the production of income. It also refers to an individual's currency exchange transactions that are entered into in connection with business travel but do not affect tax treatment of capital losses (¶ 1754).

2496. International Boycotts. Participation by a taxpayer in, or cooperation with, an international boycott will result in the reduction or denial of the foreign tax credit (¶ 2475), the deferral of tax allowed to foreign subsidiaries (¶ 2485), and the deferral of tax allowed to domestic international sales corporation (DISC) shareholders (¶ 2498) (Code Sec. 999; Temp. Reg. § 7.999-1).[182] The amount of the benefits to be denied is determined from the ratio of the value of the sales or purchases of goods and services (or other transactions) arising from the boycott activity to the total value of the foreign sales or purchases of goods and services (or other transactions).

Participation in or cooperation with an international boycott occurs when a person, in order to do business in a certain country, agrees not to do business with a specified second country or with other countries doing business in specified countries. An agreement not to hire employees of, or to do business with, other companies whose employees are of a specified nationality, race or religion is also boycott activity. The following countries may require participation in, or cooperation with, an international boycott: Iraq, Kuwait, Lebanon, Libya, Qatar, Saudi Arabia, Syria, United Arab Emirates, and the Republic of Yemen.[183] The reduction of foreign tax credit extends to the credit that the taxpayer is entitled to as a shareholder as well as to the credit for foreign taxes

References are to Standard Federal Tax Reports; Tax Research Consultant; and Practical Tax Explanations.

[175] ¶ 35,960; PART: 18,410.15; § 39,135.05

[176] ¶ 39,835; PART: 18,410.15; § 39,135.05

[177] ¶ 35,580; INTL: 30,352.10; § 39,135.10

[178] ¶ 28,840; INTLOUT: 21,050; § 46,020.10

[179] ¶ 28,920; INTLOUT: 21,052; § 46,020.10

[180] ¶ 28,860, ¶ 28,880; INTLOUT: 21,200, INTLOUT: 21,250; § 46,020.10

[181] ¶ 28,900; INTLOUT: 21,100

[182] ¶ 29,080, ¶ 29,081; INTL: 21,000

[183] ¶ 29,083.15; INTL: 21,050

the taxpayer paid himself or herself (Code Sec. 908).[184] Taxpayers who participate in or cooperate with a boycott and derive income from such activities must report such information to the IRS by filing Form 5713 when their income tax return is due, including extensions.

2497. Illegal Payments. If an illegal bribe, kickback, or other payment is made by, or on behalf of, a controlled foreign corporation (CFC) (¶ 2487) or a domestic international sales corporation (DISC) (¶ 2498), either directly or indirectly, to an official, employee, or agent-in-fact of a foreign government, the amount of the bribe, kickback or other payment will affect shareholders. In the case of a CFC, the amount is included as subpart F income for the year (¶ 2488) and thus is included in the shareholder's income (Code Sec. 952(a)(4)).[185] In the case of a DISC, the amount is considered a constructive dividend and must be included in the shareholder's income (Code Sec. 995(b)(1)(F)(iii)).[186] However, such payments may be deductible in certain circumstances, despite their possible illegality (¶ 972).

2498. Foreign Trade Income. Prior to 2005, the Code contained a number of rules designed to promote the export of U.S. manufactured products. For example, a percentage of income generated through a domestic international sales corporation (DISC) could be deferred for U.S. tax purposes, while a certain percentage of income from the sale of qualified export property by a foreign sales corporation (FSC) could be completely exempt from U.S. tax. Similarly, any U.S. taxpayer was entitled to exclude from gross income extraterritorial income (ETI) to the extent it was qualifying foreign trade income. These rules have been effectively repealed. However, a DISC geared toward small businesses may still exist if the income deferred by shareholders is limited and an interest charge is paid on such deferred amounts (Code Sec. 995).[187] The election to be treated as an interest-charge DISC is made on Form 4876-A.

2499. Information from Foreign Sources. The IRS may make a formal document request for foreign records if the normal summons procedure fails to produce the requested documentation (Code Sec. 982).[188] The request for formal documentation supplements the administrative summons procedure and does not prevent the use of any other Code provisions to obtain documents.

References are to Standard Federal Tax Reports; Tax Research Consultant; and Practical Tax Explanations.

[184] ¶ 27,964; INTL: 21,306; § 13,410.05

[185] ¶ 28,490; INTLOUT: 9,154

[186] ¶ 29,020; INTL: 21,312

[187] ¶ 29,020; INTLOUT: 11,000

[188] ¶ 28,820; IRS: 21,260

Chapter 25

RETURNS □ PAYMENT OF TAX

	Par.
Filing Returns	2501
Payment of Tax	2525
Deadlines	2549
Information Returns and Payment at Source	2565
Reportable Transactions and Tax Shelters	2591

Filing Returns

2501. Income Tax Returns—Types of Returns. Individuals who must file income tax returns use Form 1040, 1040A, or 1040EZ, along with any appropriate schedules; fiduciaries of estates and trusts who must file income tax returns use Form 1041; corporations must file income tax returns on Form 1120; and partnerships must file information returns on Form 1065.

The following specialized income tax return forms for individuals also exist: Form 1040-C for a departing alien; Form 1040NR or Form 1040NR-EZ for a nonresident alien; Form 1040-SS (self-employment) for a resident of the Virgin Islands, Guam, American Samoa or the Northern Mariana Islands; and Form 1040-PR or 1040-SS (self-employment) for a resident of Puerto Rico.

Specialized forms for certain types of corporations also exist:

(1) Schedule PH, attached to Form 1120 for a U.S. personal holding company;

(2) Schedule UTP, attached to the Form 1120 series return for a corporation with at least $10 million in assets (was $50 million for 2013 tax year) that has taken an uncertain tax position;

(3) Form 1120-C for a cooperative association;

(4) Form 1120-F for a foreign corporation;

(5) Form 1120-FSC for a foreign sales corporation;

(6) Form 1120-H for a homeowners association;

(7) Form 1120-IC-DISC for an interest charge domestic international sales corporation;

(8) Form 1120-L for a life insurance company;

(9) Form 1120-ND for a nuclear decommissioning fund;

(10) Form 1120-PC for a property and casualty insurance company;

(11) Form 1120-POL for a political organization;

(12) Form 1120-REIT for a real estate investment trust;

(13) Form 1120-RIC for a regulated investment company;

(14) Form 1120S for an S corporation; and

(15) Form 1120-SF for a settlement fund.

Rules for determining which individuals must file an income tax return are at ¶ 101; rules for determining who must pay estimated tax are at ¶ 2682; rules for corporation returns are at ¶ 211; rules for S corporations are at ¶ 351; rules applicable to partners and partnerships are at ¶ 406; and rules for estates and trusts are at ¶ 510.

Employers must file quarterly returns on Form 941 to report wages paid to employees and income tax withheld on the wages, tips employees have received, both the employer's and the employee's share of Social Security and Medicare taxes, and additional Medicare taxes withheld from employees (¶ 2650). Employers with an estimated employment tax liability of $1,000 or less ("small employers") may instead file an annual return on Form 944. Employers who pay wages for agricultural labor must file Form 943. In addition, employers must file Form 940 annually to report and pay federal unemployment taxes.

Individuals who pay annual cash wages of $2,000 or more in 2016 ($2,000 or more in 2017) for domestic services in their private homes must file Schedule H of Form 1040 to report and pay both the employer and employee share of Social Security and Medicare taxes, and any income tax withheld at the employee's request. Individuals also use Schedule H to pay and report federal unemployment taxes if they paid total cash wages of $1,000 or more to household employees in any calendar quarter (¶ 2652) (IRS Pub. 926).

2503. Electronic Filing. Electronic filing allows qualified filers to transmit tax return information directly to the IRS over the internet. Taxpayers may e-file their tax returns through a paid preparer (or an electronic return originator (ERO)), by using a personal computer and commercial tax preparation software, or by qualifying for and enrolling in the Free File program. Individual taxpayers who e-file their returns can authorize direct debit payment from their checking or savings account on a specified date. Taxpayers may also charge their taxes by credit card or pay their taxes electronically through the Electronic Federal Tax Payment System (EFTPS) (IRS Fact Sheet FS-2011-7).

Free File is a public-private sector initiative with commercial software providers to provide free tax return preparation and electronic filing service for middle- and low-income taxpayers who meet certain adjusted gross income requirements. A Free File Fillable Tax Forms option is also available which allows all taxpayers, regardless of income level, to fill out and file their tax forms electronically (IRS News Release IR-2011-5). Free File is available at the IRS website at https://www.irs.gov/uac/free-file-do-your-federal-taxes-for-free.

Taxpayers who file their tax returns electronically must use electronic signatures (IRS Fact Sheet FS-2011-7). Electronic filers use a Self-Select Personal Identification Number (PIN), or if using a paid preparer, that preparer's Practitioner PIN (IRS Pub. 1345).

Form 8453 is used to transmit certain forms and supporting paper documents that are specifically listed on Form 8453 and are required to be submitted to the IRS with e-filed returns. If paper documentation must be submitted that is not listed on Form 8453, the return cannot be e-filed (Instructions to Form 8453).

Corporations, S corporations, partnerships, and exempt organizations may also elect to electronically file, respectively, Forms 1120, 1120S, 1065, and 990. However, certain organizations are required to submit those returns electronically. Corporations and S corporations with assets of $10 million or more, and that file 250 or more returns during the year, must file Forms 1120 and 1120S electronically (Reg. § 301.6011-5; Reg. § 301.6037-2).[1] A partnership with more than 100 partners must file Form 1065 (and Schedules K-1 and related forms) electronically (Reg. § 301.6011-3).[2] Exempt organizations with assets of $10 million or more, and that file 250 or more returns annually, must file Form 990 electronically. If a private foundation or a Code Sec. 4947(a)(1) trust files 250 or more returns annually, regardless of asset size, it must file Form 990-PF electronically (Reg. § 301.6033-4).[3] Exempt organizations with gross receipts of $50,000 or less generally must file Form 990-N electronically (¶ 625). Although electronic filing is not required for organizations not described above, the IRS encourages such organizations to do so, e.g., an S corporation or an exempt organization filing less than 250 returns during the calendar year. The IRS has updated the procedures that corporations,

References are to Standard Federal Tax Reports; Tax Research Consultant; and Practical Tax Explanations.

[1] ¶ 35,129J, ¶ 35,522C; FILEBUS: 3,052.05, FILEBUS: 12,300; § 26,030.10, § 29,010.15, § 39,225.10b

[2] ¶ 35,126F; FILEBUS: 12,300, FILEBUS: 12,302.35; § 30,435

[3] ¶ 35,424C; EXEMPT: 12,252.15, EXEMPT: 12,252.20, FILEBUS: 12,300; § 33,245, § 33,605.05

S corporations, and tax-exempt organizations must use to request a waiver of the electronic filing requirement (Notice 2010-13).

For income tax returns of individuals, estates, or trusts (i.e., individual income tax returns) electronic filing is required if the return is prepared and filed by a specified tax return preparer for the calendar year during which the return is filed. With respect to any calendar year, a "specified tax return preparer" means any tax return preparer (¶ 2517), unless the preparer reasonably expects to file 10 or fewer individual income tax returns during the calendar year (Code Sec. 6011(e)(3)).[4]

An individual income tax return is considered "filed" by a specified return preparer if the preparer submits the return to the IRS on the taxpayer's behalf. A return is not considered filed by a specified return preparer if the preparer obtains a hand-signed and dated statement from the taxpayer that the taxpayer chooses to file the return in paper format and that the taxpayer, and not the preparer, will submit the paper return to the IRS (Reg. § 301.6011-7(a)(4)).[5]

The IRS may grant waivers of the electronic filing requirement for specified return preparers in cases of undue hardship (Reg. § 301.6011-7(c)(1)).[6] Such waivers generally are intended to be granted for undue hardships that can be identified in advance before the preparers would otherwise be required to file individual income tax returns electronically for a particular calendar year and will ordinarily be granted only in rare cases. Requests for a hardship waiver are made by filing Form 8944 (Rev. Proc. 2011-25).

The IRS has provided further administrative exemptions to the electronic filing requirement for certain classes of specified tax return preparers (Notice 2011-26). They include: exempt preparers (preparer members of certain religious groups; foreign preparers without Social Security numbers; and certain preparers ineligible for IRS e-file); exempt individual income tax returns due to preparer's technological difficulties (rejected returns; forms or schedules not supported by the preparer's software package; and other technological difficulties); and exempt individual income tax returns due to IRS e-file limitations (returns currently not accepted and required documentation not accepted electronically). Exemptions are automatic and do not have to be requested, but preparers will be required to show entitlement to exemption upon request by the IRS. Form 8948 is used to explain why an individual tax return that was able to be filed electronically was filed in a paper format.

Foreign Accounts. The IRS is authorized to require a financial institution to electronically file returns with respect to withheld taxes for which the institution is liable as a withholding agent under the nonresident alien and foreign corporation withholding rules (¶ 2455), or under the foreign account withholding rules (¶ 2469), even though the financial institution files less than 250 returns during the tax year (Code Sec. 6011(e)(4)).

2504. Signatures on Returns. Forms 1040, 1040A, and 1040EZ must be signed by the individual taxpayer (Code Sec. 6061; Reg. § 1.6061-1).[7] In the case of married individuals filing a joint return, both spouses must sign. If the taxpayer did not prepare the return, the return must be signed by the taxpayer and the tax return preparer (¶ 2517 and ¶ 2518). If a decedent's return is filed by a representative, the representative should sign the return on the line indicated for the taxpayer and attach a written power of attorney. Taxpayers who file their tax returns electronically must use electronic signatures (¶ 2503). All returns filed with the IRS must contain a declaration that they are made under the penalties of perjury (Code Sec. 6065).[8]

2505. Income Tax Returns—When to File. Subject to an exception for deadlines falling on a Saturday, Sunday, or a legal holiday (¶ 2549), the due dates for income tax returns are as follows.

References are to Standard Federal Tax Reports; Tax Research Consultant; and Practical Tax Explanations.

[4] ¶ 35,120; FILEBUS: 12,302; § 41,803

[5] ¶ 35,129OC; FILEBUS: 12,302; § 41,803

[6] ¶ 35,129OC; FILEBUS: 12,302; § 41,803

[7] ¶ 36,602, ¶ 36,603; FILEBUS: 12,100, FILEIND: 15,250; § 1,330.05, § 39,010.25, § 41,810.15

[8] ¶ 36,680; FILEBUS: 12,100; § 39,010.25

Individual, trust, and estate income tax returns are due on or before the 15th day of the fourth month following the close of the tax year, typically April 15 in the case of a calendar-year taxpayer (Code Sec. 6072(a); Reg. § 1.6072-1(a)).[9] The final income tax return of a decedent for a fractional part of a year is due on the same date as would apply had the taxpayer lived the entire year (i.e., the 15th day of the fourth month following the close of the 12-month period that began on the first day of the fractional year) (Reg. § 1.6072-1(b)).[10]

For tax years beginning before January 1, 2016, a partnership's income tax return (¶ 406) is due on or before the 15th day of the *fourth* month following the close of the tax year (April 15 for a calendar-year partnership) (Code Sec. 6072(b); Reg. § 1.6031(a)-1).[11] For tax years beginning after December 31, 2015, a partnership's return is due on or before the 15th day of the *third* month following the close of the tax year (March 15 for a calendar-year partnership).

For tax years beginning before January 1, 2016, a domestic or foreign C corporation having a U.S. office must file its U.S. corporate income tax return (¶ 211) on or before the 15th day of the *third* month following the close of the its tax year (March 15 for a calendar year corporation) (Code Sec. 6072; Reg. § 1.6072-2).[12] For tax years beginning after December 31, 2015, a C corporation's return generally must be filed on or before the 15th day of the *fourth* month following the close of the corporation's tax year (April 15 for a calendar year corporation). However, in the case of a C corporation with a fiscal tax year ending on June 30, its return must still be filed on or before 15th day of the *third* month following the close of the its tax year for tax years beginning before December 31, 2025. A corporation whose foreign sales corporation election is still in effect must file its U.S. income tax return by the 15th day of the third month after the end of its tax year (Instructions for Form 1120-FSC). The return of an interest charge domestic international sales corporation (IC-DISC), an exempt farmers' cooperative, or other cooperative organization is due on or before the 15th day of the ninth month following the close of the tax year (September 15 for a calendar-year taxpayer) (Reg. § 1.6072-2).[13]

An S corporation's income tax return is due on or before the 15th day of the third month following the close of the tax year (March 15 for a calendar-year S corporation) (Code Sec. 6072(b); Reg. § 1.6037-1(b)).[14]

The due date for income tax returns of tax-exempt organizations, other than employees' trusts under Code Sec. 401(a), subject to the unrelated business income tax (¶ 655 and ¶ 658) is the 15th day of the fifth month following the close of the tax year (May 15 for calendar-year organizations) (Reg. § 1.6072-2(c)).[15]

The due date for an income tax return of nonresident alien who is not subject to income tax withholding on wages (¶ 2601) and a foreign corporation not having an office or place of business in the United States is the 15th day of the sixth month after the close of the tax year (June 15 for calendar-year taxpayers) (Code Sec. 6072(c); Reg. §§ 1.6072-1(c) and 1.6072-2(b)).[16] A nonresident alien who has wages subject to income tax withholding, however, is required to file a return on or before the 15th day of the fourth month following the close of the tax year.

Amended Returns. A taxpayer may correct an error in a return, without incurring interest or penalties, by filing an amended return (for individuals, Form 1040X) and paying any additional tax due on or before the last day prescribed for filing the original return. An amended return filed after the due date may be accepted, rejected, or ignored by the IRS in its sole discretion, and in the absence of an abuse of discretion the courts will not grant relief to the taxpayer. Ordinarily, the amended return will be accepted by

References are to Standard Federal Tax Reports; Tax Research Consultant; and Practical Tax Explanations.

[9] ¶ 36,720, ¶ 36,721; FILEIND: 18,052.20; § 39,205.10

[10] ¶ 36,721; FILEIND: 18,052.20; § 38,145.05

[11] ¶ 36,720, ¶ 35,383; PART: 18,160.05; § 39,205.15

[12] ¶ 36,720, ¶ 36,724; FILEBUS: 3,052.05; § 26,030.05

[13] ¶ 36,724; FILEBUS: 3,052.05, INTLOUT: 15,058.20; § 39,205.05

[14] ¶ 35,521, ¶ 36,720; SCORP: 500; § 29,010.10

[15] ¶ 36,724; EXEMPT: 12,252; § 39,205.20

[16] ¶ 36,720, ¶ 36,721, ¶ 36,724; FILEIND: 100, FILEIND: 15,200, CCORP: 36,060; § 37,010.10,

the IRS if it is filed within the statutory period of limitations, generally within three years from the due date of the original return (¶ 2726).[17]

2509. Extension of Time to File Returns. An individual is granted an automatic extension of six months for filing a return, but *not* for payment of tax, by properly filing Form 4868 on or before the normal due date of the return (¶ 2505) (Reg. § 1.6081-4).[18] Form 4868 may be filed electronically or by mail. A filing extension can be obtained without making tax payments, so long as the taxpayer properly estimates his or her tax liability on the form. If the taxpayer does not properly estimate his or her tax liability, the extension request will be denied and the IRS will charge interest and a penalty for late payment. If the amount of tax included with the extension request is less than sufficient to cover the taxpayer's liability, the taxpayer will be charged interest on the overdue amount. However, no late-payment penalty will be imposed if the income tax paid through withholding, estimated tax payments, or any payment accompanying Form 4868 is at least 90 percent of the total tax due with Form 1040 and if the remaining unpaid balance is paid with the return within the extension period (¶ 2809) (Reg. § 1.6081-4; Reg. § 301.6651-1).[19] An automatic extension should not be requested if the taxpayer has asked the IRS to compute the tax or if the taxpayer is under a court order to file the return by the original due date.

Individuals Residing Outside the United States. U.S. citizens or residents living outside the United States and Puerto Rico, including military personnel, are granted an automatic extension up to June 15 (the 15th day of the sixth month following the close of their tax year) for filing an income tax return and paying the tax if they attach a statement to their return showing that they are entitled to such an extension (Reg. § 1.6081-5).[20] However, interest will be assessed on any unpaid tax from the original due date of the return (April 15 for calendar-year individuals), without regard to the automatic extension, until the tax is paid (IRS Pub. 54). The automatic filing extension runs concurrently with the automatic six-month extension allowed to all individuals. Thus, the maximum automatic extension is only six months from the regular due date. The application for the automatic six-month extension is timely if it is filed by the due date established by the automatic two-month extension. If an individual outside the United States needs more than the automatic extension in order to meet either the bona fide residence or the physical presence test for the foreign earned income or housing exclusion, Form 2350 should be filed by the due date for filing the return (June 15 for calendar-year citizens or residents living outside the United States and Puerto Rico). Such filing will entitle the individual to additional time for filing the return but not for paying the tax.

Corporations. A C corporation or an S corporation is generally entitled to an automatic extension of six months for filing its return, provided that it timely and properly files Form 7004 and deposits the full amount of the tax due (Code Sec. 6081(b); Reg. § 1.6081-3).[21] The IRS may terminate the extension at any time by mailing a notice to the corporation (or the parent corporation for an affiliated group filing a consolidated return) at least 10 days prior to the termination date. In the case of a C corporation return for a tax year ending on December 31, the maximum extension allowed is five months for filing its return in tax years beginning before January 1, 2026. In the case of a C corporation return for a tax year ending on June 30, the maximum extension allowed is seven months for filing its return for tax years beginning before January 1, 2026.

Other Entities. An automatic five-month extension of time (through the 15th day of the sixth month following the close of the tax year) for filing a return and paying the tax is granted to a partnership that keeps its books and records outside the United States and Puerto Rico, a domestic corporation that transacts its business and keeps its books and records outside the United States and Puerto Rico, a foreign corporation that maintains an office or place of business within the United States, and a domestic

References are to Standard Federal Tax Reports; Tax Research Consultant; and Practical Tax Explanations.

[17] ¶ 35,141.40; FILEBUS: 3,150, FILEIND: 18,150; § 1,315

[18] ¶ 36,793; FILEBUS: 15,100; § 39,215.10

[19] ¶ 36,793, ¶ 39,472; FILEBUS: 15,100; § 39,215.10

[20] ¶ 36,795; FILEBUS: 15,100; § 1,325.10

[21] ¶ 36,780, ¶ 36,790; FILEBUS: 15,100; § 39,215.15

corporation whose principal income is from sources within U.S. possessions (Reg. § 1.6081-5(a)).[22] The automatic filing extension runs concurrently with the automatic six-month filing extension allowed for most businesses.

Partnerships filing Form 1065 or Form 8804, and estates and trusts filing Form 1041, should use Form 7004 to apply for an automatic filing extension (Reg. § § 1.6081-2 and 1.6081-6).[23]

For a partnership filing Form 1065 for tax years beginning before January 1, 2016, an automatic *five-month* extension is available. An automatic *six*-month extension is available for calendar-year partnerships filing Form 1065 for tax years beginning after December 31, 2015 (Act Sec 2006(b) of Surface Transportation and Veterans Health Care Choice Improvement Act of 2015 (P.L. 114-41)).

For an estate filing Form 1041, and for a trust filing Form 1041 for tax years beginning before January 1, 2016, an automatic *five*-month extension is available. An automatic *five-and-a-half-month* extension is available for calendar-year trusts filing Form 1041 for tax years beginning after December 31, 2015 (Act Sec 2006(b) of P.L. 114-41).

The following entities must use Form 8868 to apply for extensions of time for filing returns: various trusts filing Forms1041-A, 5227, and 6069; certain exempt organizations filing Forms 990, 990-PF, 990-EZ, or 990-BL, certain exempt organizations or corporations filing Form 990-T, and Form 4720; and certain charitable organizations filing Form 8870 (Reg. § 1.6081-9).[24] Real estate mortgage investment conduits filing Form 1066 or Form 8831 should use Form 7004 to apply for an automatic six-month filing extension (Reg. § 1.6081-7).[25]

2513. Place for Filing Paper Returns. An individual, estate, or trust must file paper returns with the IRS Service Center indicated in the instructions to the taxpayer's return, except for certain charitable and split-interest trusts and pooled-income funds (Instructions for Form 1040; Instructions for Form 1041).

A corporation, S corporation, or partnership must file its return with the Service Center indicated in the instructions to the entity's return (Instructions for Form 1120; Instructions for Form 1120S; Instructions for Form 1065).

The place to file certain elections, statements, returns and other documents can be found at the IRS website, at www.irs.gov/uac/Where-to-File-Certain-Elections-Statements-Returns-and-Other-Documents (Notice 2010-53).

2517. Tax Return Preparers. A person who prepares for compensation, or who employs persons to prepare for compensation, all or a substantial portion of *any* tax return or refund claim is a "tax return preparer" (Code Sec. 7701(a)(36); Reg. § 301.7701-15).[26] Preparers are divided into two categories for purposes of the return preparer penalties (¶ 2518): signing tax return preparers and nonsigning tax return preparers. A signing tax return preparer is the individual preparer with primary responsibility for the overall substantive accuracy of the preparation of tax returns or refund claims. A nonsigning tax return preparer is any preparer who is not a signing tax return preparer but who prepares a substantial portion of a return or refund claim regarding events that have occurred at the time advice is rendered.

In addition to the prohibition against disclosure of return information (¶ 2894), a tax return preparer is subject to the following rules:

(1) The signing tax return preparer must sign a tax return electronically using a Self-Select Personal Identification Number (PIN) or a Practitioner PIN (IRS Pub. 1345). The preparer need not sign an electronic return before presenting a completed copy to the taxpayer, but must furnish all information that will be transmitted as the electronically signed return to the taxpayer at the same time that the preparer furnishes Form 8879 or a similar IRS e-file signature form. The

References are to Standard Federal Tax Reports; Tax Research Consultant; and Practical Tax Explanations.

[22] ¶ 36,795; FILEBUS: 15,100

[23] ¶ 36,788, ¶ 36,797; FILEBUS: 15,104.20; § 30,435, § 32,610.15, § 39,215.20

[24] ¶ 36,798K; FILEBUS: 15,104.35; § 33,245, § 33,605.05, § 33,945

[25] ¶ 36,798; FILEBUS: 15,104.20; § 39,215.05

[26] ¶ 43,080, ¶ 43,113; IRS: 6,050; § 41,410.05

signing tax return preparer must actually sign a paper return after its completion but before its presentation to the taxpayer for signature (Code Sec. 6695(b); Reg. § 1.6695-1(b)).[27] Paper returns require the preparer to manually sign the return or use any of three alternative methods that include either a facsimile of the preparer's signature or the individual preparer's printed name: (1) rubber stamp, (2) mechanical device, or (3) computer software program (Notice 2004-54).

(2) The signing tax return preparer must include his or her identifying number on the taxpayer's return after its completion but before its presentation to the taxpayer. The identifying number is the individual's preparer tax identification number (PTIN) or other number prescribed by the IRS. If the preparer is employed by another person, the employer must furnish the identifying numbers of both the employer and the employee-preparer (Code Sec. 6109(a)(4); Reg. § 1.6109-2; Notice 2011-6).[28]

(3) The signing tax return preparer must provide the taxpayer with a completed copy of the prepared return, in either paper or electronic form, no later than the time the original return is presented for signing. The copy must be in any media acceptable to both the taxpayer and the preparer, and must include all information submitted to the IRS to enable the taxpayer to determine what schedules, forms, electronic files, and other supporting materials have been filed. The copy need not contain the identification number of the paid tax return preparer. The signing tax return preparer must also keep, for three years following the close of the return period, a copy of the return (in either paper or electronic form) or a list of the names, identification numbers, and tax years of taxpayers for whom returns were prepared, and the name of the individual tax return preparer required to sign the return (Code Sec. 6107; Reg. § 1.6107-1).[29] The preparer need not sign the taxpayer's copy of the return.

(4) If a tax return preparer, or any person, employs any signing tax return preparers to prepare returns for other persons (i.e., not the employer's return), the preparer must keep a record, for three years following the close of the return period to which the record relates, of the name, taxpayer identification number (TIN), and principal place of work of each tax return preparer employed by the preparer at any time during the return period (Code Sec. 6060; Reg. § 1.6060-1).[30] Any individual signing tax return preparer who is not employed by another preparer is treated as his or her own employer. The "return period" is defined as the 12-month period beginning on July 1 of each year.

PTIN Requirement. All tax return preparers must have a PTIN or other prescribed identifying number that was applied for and received at the time and in the manner prescribed by the IRS, including the payment of a user fee. To obtain a PTIN, a tax return preparer must be an attorney, certified public accountant (CPA), enrolled agent, or registered tax return preparer authorized to practice before the IRS (Reg. § 1.6109-2(d); Notice 2011-6).[31] The IRS will also allow individuals who are 18 years old or older, but are not one of these specific types of professionals, to pay the applicable user fee and obtain a PTIN if: (1) the individual is supervised by an attorney, CPA, enrolled agent, enrolled retirement plan agent, or enrolled actuary authorized to practice before the IRS under Circular 230 § 10.3(a)-(e); (2) the supervising attorney, CPA, enrolled agent, enrolled retirement plan agent, or enrolled actuary signs the tax returns or refund claims prepared by the individual; (3) the individual is employed at the law firm, CPA firm, or other recognized firm of the tax return preparer who signs the tax return or refund claim; or (4) the individual passes the requisite tax compliance check and suitability check when available.

References are to Standard Federal Tax Reports; Tax Research Consultant; and Practical Tax Explanations.

[27] ¶ 39,965, ¶ 39,966; IRS: 6,104; § 41,510

[28] ¶ 36,960, ¶ 36,961C; IRS: 6,106; § 41,515

[29] ¶ 36,920, ¶ 36,921; IRS: 6,108, IRS: 6,110.05; § 41,520.05, § 41,520.10

[30] ¶ 36,560, ¶ 36,561; IRS: 6,110.10; § 41,520.20

[31] ¶ 36,961C; IRS: 6,106.05; § 41,515.05

The PTIN can generally be obtained or renewed online at http://www.irs.gov/Tax-Professionals/PTIN-Requirements-for-Tax-Return-Preparers. Alternatively, a paper application may be submitted on Form W-12. A U.S. citizen or foreign person without a Social Security number must also submit with their application Form 8945 or Form 8946. All PTINs must be renewed on a calendar year basis, and the required user fee paid. The renewal period begins after October 15 and runs through December 31 of the calendar year. PTINs obtained or renewed during the calendar year will expire on December 31 of the calendar year.

Voluntary Certification Program. The IRS has established a voluntary certification program, the Annual Filing Season Program (AFSP), designed to encourage unenrolled tax preparers to complete continuing education courses for the purpose of increasing his or her knowledge of relevant federal tax law necessary for preparation of tax returns (Rev. Proc. 2014-42, modifying and superseding Rev. Proc. 81-38).[32] The voluntary program neither restricts any individual from preparing and signing tax returns or claims for refund, nor changes the requirement that paid tax return preparers must obtain a PTIN. Upon successful completion each year of certain requirements, the IRS will issue a Record of Completion. The Record of Completion is only valid for tax returns or claims for refund prepared and signed during the calendar year for which it has been issued. Thus, a Record of Completion is valid from the later of January 1 of the year covered by the Record of Completion or the date the Record of Completion is issued until December 31st of that year. The application for a Record of Completion is made on Form W-12 and all applications must be received no later than April 15th of the year for which the Record of Completion is sought.

Unenrolled tax return preparers who obtain an AFSP Record of Completion are permitted to represent taxpayers before the IRS during examination of tax returns and claim for refund that he or she prepared and signed, or prepared if there is no signature space on the form, provided the individual had a valid Record of Completion for the year the return or claim of refund was prepared and a valid Record of Completion for the year or years in which the representation occurs. The representation is limited to exam, and the individual may not appear before an appeals officer, a revenue officer, Counsel, or similar IRS officer or employee.

2518. Tax Return Preparer Penalties. Several penalties may be assessed against tax return preparers.

Failure to Follow Procedures. A tax return preparer who fails to meet the requirements described in ¶ 2517 may be assessed the following penalties, unless the failure is due to reasonable cause and not to willful neglect:

(1) $50 (for 2016 and 2017) for each failure to sign a return, to furnish an identifying number, or to furnish the taxpayer with a copy of the prepared return (up to a maximum penalty per calendar year of $25,500 for 2016 and 2017);

(2) $50 (for 2016 and 2017) for each failure to retain and make available a copy of prepared returns or a list of taxpayers for whom returns were prepared, and the name of the individual preparer required to sign the return (up to a maximum penalty per return period of $25,500 for 2016 and 2017); and

(3) $50 (for 2016 and 2017) for each failure to retain and make available a record of preparers employed, or each failure to include an item required in such record (up to a maximum penalty per return period of $25,500 for 2016 and 2017)).

A preparer who endorses or negotiates a taxpayer's refund check is also subject to a penalty ($510 in 2016 and 2017). The penalty will not apply to a bank preparer who negotiates customers' refund checks for bank account deposits (Code Sec. 6695; Reg. § 1.6695-1; Rev. Proc. 2015-53; Rev. Proc. 2016-55).[33]

Understatement of Taxpayer's Liability. A penalty may be imposed against a return preparer for each tax return or claim for refund that understates the taxpayer's liability

References are to Standard Federal Tax Reports; Tax Research Consultant; and Practical Tax Explanations.

[32] ¶ 43,808.43; IRS: 6,252.30; § 41,025

[33] ¶ 39,965, ¶ 39,966; IRS: 6,112; § 41,535.05

due to an unreasonable position that the preparer knew, or reasonably should have known. The penalty is the greater of $1,000 or 50 percent of the income derived, or to be derived, by the preparer with respect to the return or refund claim (Code Sec. 6694(a); Reg. § § 1.6694-1 and 1.6694-2; Rev. Proc. 2016-13).[34] The penalty will not be imposed if the preparer shows that there was reasonable cause for the understatement and the preparer acted in good faith. Modified rules apply to nonsigning preparers.

A position is treated as unreasonable unless: (1) there is or was substantial authority for the position; (2) the position is adequately disclosed and has a reasonable basis; or (3) if the position pertains to a tax shelter (¶ 2870) or a reportable transaction (¶ 2591), it is reasonable to believe that the position would more likely than not be sustained on its merits. Under interim guidance, the term "substantial authority" has the same meaning as it does for the 20-percent accuracy-related penalty for a substantial understatement of income tax (¶ 2858). The guidance also contains penalty compliance rules for tax shelter transactions (Notice 2009-5).[35]

The understatement penalty increases to the greater of $5,000 or 50 percent of the income derived, or to be derived, by the preparer with respect to the return or refund claim if the understatement is willful or reckless (Code Sec. 6694(b), as amended by Protecting Americans from Tax Hikes (PATH) Act of 2015 (P.L. 114-113); Reg. § 1.6694-3).[36] For tax returns prepared for tax years ending after December 18, 2015, preparers are subject to a penalty of the greater of $5,000 or 75 percent of the income derived from the preparation of the return if the preparer willfully understates a client's tax liability or takes a position in reckless disregard for the rules or regulations. The IRS has concluded that this penalty can be assessed (1) if the preparer made an amended return that was never filed, so long as the preparer signed the return, and (2) if an amended return was filed, but the IRS disallowed the refund. Conversely, the IRS ruled that both this penalty and the penalty for understatement of a taxpayer's liability due to an unreasonable position (see above), as well as the penalty for aiding or abetting in an understatements of tax liability (see below) may not be assessed if the preparer made and filed a claim for refund after the period of limitations for refund claims has expired (CCA 201519029).

Lack of Diligence in Claiming Earned Income Credit. Tax return preparers must comply with due diligence requirements for returns or refund claims asserting eligibility for the earned income credit (Code Sec. 6695(g); Reg. § 1.6695-2; Rev. Proc. 2015-53; Rev. Proc. 2016-55).[37] Among the requirements, tax return preparers are required to file (or submit to the taxpayer for filing) Form 8867 (or a self-created alternate computation record) with any federal return claiming the earned income credit. Each failure to meet the requirements regarding the amount of, or eligibility for, the credit will result in a penalty of $510 in 2016 ($510 in 2017). The penalty is in addition to any other penalty imposed.

Aiding or Abetting in Tax Liability Understatement. A penalty of $1,000 may also be imposed on persons for aiding or abetting in an understatement of tax liability on a return, claim, or other document. The penalty increases to $10,000 for aiding or abetting an understatement of liability on a corporate return (Code Sec. 6701).[38] Only one penalty may be imposed per taxpayer per period; however, the tax period may not necessarily be a tax year. For instance, understatements on quarterly employment tax returns may give rise to four separate penalties for a calendar year. According to the Sixth and Eighth Circuit Court of Appeals, no statute of limitations applies to bar the penalty.[39] Generally, this penalty may be imposed in addition to other penalties. However, it will not be imposed if either the tax return preparer penalty for understatements due to unreasonable positions or the penalty for promoting abusive tax shelters has been applied with respect to the same tax return or refund claim.

References are to Standard Federal Tax Reports; Tax Research Consultant; and Practical Tax Explanations.

[34] ¶ 39,955, ¶ 39,956, ¶ 39,957, ¶ 39,960.20; IRS: 6,150; § 41,610

[35] ¶ 39,960.70; IRS: 6,156; § 41,610.10

[36] ¶ 39,955, ¶ 39,957E; IRS: 6,158; § 41,615

[37] ¶ 39,965, ¶ 39,968; IRS: 6,116; § 12,640

[38] ¶ 40,033; PENALTY: 3,258; § 41,620

[39] ¶ 40,035.10; PENALTY: 3,258; § 41,620

2521. Penalty for Frivolous Tax Return. A civil penalty of $5,000 is imposed upon any person (including an individual, trust, estate, partnership, association, company, or corporation) who files a purported tax return (income or otherwise) if: (1) the purported return fails to contain sufficient information from which the substantial correctness of the amount of tax liability can be judged, or contains information that on its face indicates that the amount of tax shown is substantially incorrect; and (2) such conduct arises from a frivolous position or from a desire to delay or impede administration of the tax laws. The penalty is imposed in addition to any other penalties imposed on the taxpayer (Code Sec. 6702).[40]

A $5,000 civil penalty may also be imposed on any person who files a "specified frivolous submission." This is a specified submission that either is based on a position that has been identified as frivolous in a prescribed frivolous positions list by the IRS, or reflects a desire to delay or impede the administration of federal tax laws. A "specified submission" is a request for a collection due process hearing or an application for an installment agreement, offer in compromise, or taxpayer assistance order. If a person withdraws a submission within 30 days after receiving notice that the return is a specified frivolous submission, the penalty will not be imposed.

The penalty may be reduced to $500 at the discretion of the Secretary of the Treasury in order to promote compliance with, and administration of, the federal tax laws (Rev. Proc. 2012-43). If a person satisfies all eligibility criteria under the procedure, including filing all tax returns and paying all outstanding taxes, penalties (other than the frivolous return penalty), and related interest, then the IRS will usually reduce all unpaid frivolous return penalties assessed against that person to $500, regardless of the number of penalties assessed. Any employer applying for relief must have deposited all employment taxes for the current quarter and the prior two quarters.

A prescribed list of frivolous positions may be found in Notice 2010-33. The list is not conclusive, and will be periodically revised. Returns or submissions that contain positions not prescribed in the Notice, but which on their face have no basis for validity in existing law, or which have been deemed frivolous in a published opinion by the U.S. Tax Court or other court of competent jurisdiction may also be subject to the $5,000 penalty.

Up to $25,000 may be assessed by the Tax Court against a taxpayer who institutes or maintains proceedings primarily for delay or on frivolous grounds or who unreasonably fails to pursue available administrative remedies. Other courts may require a taxpayer to pay a penalty of up to $10,000 if the taxpayer's action against the IRS for unauthorized collection activities appears to be a frivolous or groundless proceeding (Code Sec. 6673).[41] The Tax Court has held that a penalty for instituting proceedings primarily for delay is properly assessed against the tax matters person of an S corporation, rather than against the entity or its other shareholders.[42]

2523. Requirement to Keep Books and Records. Taxpayers are required to keep accurate, permanent books and records so as to be able to determine the various types of income, gains, losses, costs, expenses, and other amounts that affect their income tax liability for the year (Reg. § 1.6001-1(a)).[43] The records must be retained for as long as they may be, or may become, "material" for any federal tax purpose. Generally, records that support an item of income or a deduction on a tax return should be kept at least for the period of limitation for that return. See ¶ 2726, ¶ 2732, ¶ 2734, ¶ 2738, and ¶ 2517 (for tax return preparers) regarding applicable limitation periods.

References are to Standard Federal Tax Reports; Tax Research Consultant; and Practical Tax Explanations.

[40] ¶ 40,040; PENALTY: 3,260; § 40,220

[41] ¶ 39,785; LITIG: 6,816; § 40,220.05

[42] ¶ 39,790.47; LITIG: 6,816; § 40,220.05

[43] ¶ 35,102; ACCTNG: 3,052.05; § 39,055

Payment of Tax

2525. Place for Paying Tax. The amount of tax shown on a return of individuals, estates, and trusts must be paid to the internal revenue officer with whom the return is filed. In the case of corporations, the tax must be deposited with an authorized depository (Code Sec. 6151(a); Reg. § 1.6302-1).[44] See ¶ 2513.

The IRS requests that individuals use a payment voucher, Form 1040-V, for any balance due on any Forms 1040. See ¶ 2545 regarding electronic funds withdrawal.

2529. Time of Payment. The tax shown on an income tax return is generally to be paid, without assessment or notice and demand, at the time fixed for filing the return, determined without regard to any extension of time for filing the return (¶ 2505). Exceptions apply when:

(1) a taxpayer shows that payment on the return due date will result in undue hardship (¶ 2537);

(2) a taxpayer is residing outside the United States on the return due date (¶ 2509); or

(3) a taxpayer elects to have the IRS compute the tax (¶ 105), in which case payment is due within 30 days after the IRS mails a notice and demand (Code Sec. 6151(b)(1)).[45]

The IRS also has the authority to enter into a written agreement with the taxpayer, allowing for the full or partial payment of any tax in installments, if such an agreement will facilitate the collection of a tax liability (Code Sec. 6159).[46] There are four types of installment agreements.

First, referred to as guaranteed installment agreements, must be accepted by the IRS if an individual taxpayer's tax liabilities, without regard to interest, penalties, additions to tax, and any other additional amounts, total $10,000 or less and certain other conditions are met (Code Sec. 6159(c)). Second, referred to as streamlined installment agreements, are for individuals who do not qualify for the guaranteed agreement and businesses. if the taxpayer owes no more than $50,000, without regard to interest, penalties, additions to tax, or any other additions, and the taxpayer agrees to pay the amount due in full within six years (IRM 5.14.5.2). Small business taxpayers are allowed to enter into streamlined agreements if they agree to pay the amount due in full within two years and a direct debit installment agreement is entered into (IRS News Release IR-2011-20). Streamlined agreements do not require a financial analysis and do not involve filing liens.

The third type of installment agreement is the in-business trust fund express agreement available to businesses with trust fund liabilities, such as employment taxes. The total balance may not exceed $25,000 and generally must be paid within 24 months. No financial statement is required, and the IRS does not determine any trust fund recovery penalty. The fourth type of installment agreement is for taxpayers owing more than $50,000 of income taxes. These agreements are accepted on a case-by-case basis if the IRS determines the taxpayer can eventually pay off the debt, and the agreement will facilitate the collection of the debt.

For taxpayers with $50,000 or less in combined tax liability, interest and penalties, an interactive Online Payment Agreement (OPA) application is available at the IRS website for requesting an installment agreement. Otherwise, a taxpayer can request an installment agreement by filing Form 9465. The user fee for entering into an installment agreement is $120. The fee is $52 if the taxpayer pays by a direct debit from their bank account, and $43 for certain low-income taxpayers, regardless of the method of payment. The fee for reinstating a defaulted agreement, or restructuring an existing agreement, is $50, regardless of income level. For installment agreements entered into on or after January 1, 2017, the IRS has proposed a general user fee of $225 and a fee of $107 for taxpayers who pay by direct debit. Alternatively, the IRS has proposed a user fee of $149

References are to Standard Federal Tax Reports; Tax Research Consultant; and Practical Tax Explanations.

[44] ¶ 37,080, ¶ 38,061; FILEBUS: 6,106.10, FILEIND: 21,152; § 39,305, § 39,320

[45] ¶ 37,080; FILEBUS: 6,100; § 39,305

[46] ¶ 37,180; FILEBUS: 6,104.40, FILEIND: 21,154.40; § 39,325.05

for taxpayers who apply for an installment agreement through the OPA process, and $31 for taxpayers who apply through the OPA process and pay by direct debit. The user fee for low-income taxpayers is proposed to remain at $43, but is $31 if the taxpayer applies through the OPA process and pays by direct debit. The proposed user fee for restructuring and reinstating an installment agreement is $89, and $43 for low-income taxpayers (Reg. § § 300.1 and 300.2; Prop. Reg. § § 300.1(b) and 300.2(b)).[47]

2533. Taxes of Member of Armed Forces upon Death. The tax liability of a member of the U.S. Armed Forces is forgiven in the tax year the individual dies (1) while in active service in a combat zone (¶ 895), (2) from wounds, disease, or injury incurred while serving in a combat zone, or (3) from wounds or injury incurred in a terrorist or military action (IRS Pub. 3). Any unpaid taxes of such individual that relate to tax years prior to service in a combat zone may also be abated. In the case of a joint return, only the decedent's portion of joint tax liability is forgiven. A similar tax forgiveness rule applies to U.S. military and civilian employees who die as the result of wounds or injury occurring outside the United States in a terroristic or military action against the United States or any of its allies (Code Sec. 692).[48]

2537. Extension of Time for Payment of Tax. An extension of time for filing a tax return ordinarily does not postpone the time for payment (¶ 2509). The IRS, however, may extend the time for payment of the tax shown on the return for up to six months, or longer if the taxpayer is abroad, upon a showing of undue hardship. A taxpayer applying for an extension of the time to pay tax must file Form 1127 on or before the original due date for payment of the tax. The application must be accompanied by evidence showing the undue hardship that would result if the extension were refused, a statement of the assets and liabilities of the taxpayer, and a statement of the receipts and disbursements of the taxpayer for the three months preceding the original due date for payment of tax (Code Sec. 6161(a); Reg. § 1.6161-1).[49] If an extension of time for payment of tax is granted, interest on the tax liability will accrue (¶ 2838) from the original due date until the date on which the balance is fully paid. As a condition to the granting of an extension, the taxpayer may be required to furnish a bond (Code Sec. 6165; Reg. § 1.6165-1).[50]

Military and Government Personnel. Armed Forces members and civilians serving in support of the Armed Forces who serve in a designated combat zone (¶ 895) or in a contingency operation, or are hospitalized outside the United States as a result of an injury received while serving in a combat zone/contingency operation, qualify for an extension for filing returns and paying tax for the period of combat/contingency operation service or hospitalization plus 180 days (Code Sec. 7508).[51] This extension is also available to such a taxpayer's spouse who wishes to file a joint return.

Disaster Areas. The IRS is authorized to postpone deadlines for filing returns and paying taxes for up to one year for taxpayers affected by a federally declared disaster (Code Sec. 7508A).[52] This includes taxpayers affected by terroristic or military actions. A list of recent federally declared disaster areas may be found on the IRS website at https://www.irs.gov/uac/tax-relief-in-disaster-situations.

2541. Extension of Time for Payment of Deficiency in Tax. An extension of time for payment of a deficiency of tax may be granted for a period of not more than 18 months where timely payment of the deficiency would result in undue hardship. The extension may be applied for according to the procedure for an extension of time for payment of tax outlined in ¶ 2537. An additional period of not more than 12 months may be granted in an exceptional case. A request for an extension will be refused if the deficiency was due to negligence, intentional disregard of income tax rules and regulations, or fraud (Code Sec. 6161(b); Reg. § 1.6161-1(a)(2) and (c)).[53]

References are to Standard Federal Tax Reports; Tax Research Consultant; and Practical Tax Explanations.

[47] ¶ 37,180C, ¶ 37,180CD, ¶ 37,180D, ¶ 37,180DB; FILEBUS: 6,104.40, FILEIND: 21,154.40; § 39,325.05

[48] ¶ 24,920; COMPEN: 6,604, ESTTRST: 6,300; § 1,005.15

[49] ¶ 37,200, ¶ 37,201; FILEBUS: 6,104, FILEIND: 15,302, FILEIND: 21,154; § 39,310.05

[50] ¶ 37,260, ¶ 37,261; FILEBUS: 6,104; § 39,310.10

[51] ¶ 42,686; FILEIND: 21,154.30; § 39,215.30

[52] ¶ 42,687A; FILEBUS: 6,104, FILEBUS: 15,100; § 39,215.35

[53] ¶ 37,200, ¶ 37,201; FILEBUS: 6,104.15, FILEIND: 21,154.15; § 39,310.05

2545. Forms of Payment. Payment of taxes must be made by a commercially acceptable means deemed appropriate by the IRS. Such means of payment include personal or cashier's check, money order, credit, debit or charge cards, or electronic funds withdrawal (Code Sec. 6311; Reg. § 301.6311-2).[54] Payments can be made online, by phone, or by mail whether the taxpayer files electronically or on paper. Credit card payments may be charged to VISA, MasterCard, American Express, and Discover cards, although the private companies that process such payments may charge a convenience fee (IRS Fact Sheet FS-2008-6; IRS Pub. 17). The convenience fee may be deductible (¶ 1092).

Electronic funds withdrawal is free and allows taxpayers to schedule payments to be withdrawn directly from their bank accounts. Additionally, taxpayers may use the Electronic Federal Tax Payment System (EFTPS), a free tax payment system that allows taxpayers to pay online or via telephone (IRS Pub. 966). The EFTPS must be used for all federal tax deposits, including deposits of employment taxes, corporate income and corporate estimated taxes, unrelated business income taxes paid by tax-exempt organizations, private foundation excise taxes, taxes withheld on nonresident aliens and foreign corporations, estimated taxes on certain trusts, railroad retirement taxes, nonpayroll taxes, FUTA taxes, and excise taxes reported on Form 720 (Reg. § § 1.6302-1, 1.6302-2, 1.6302-3, and 1.6302-4).[55]

Individual taxpayers may use the IRS web-based Direct Pay system, which allows individuals with Social Security numbers or "eligible" IRS-issued individual taxpayer identification numbers (ITINs) (¶ 2579) to pay tax bills or make estimated tax payments directly from their checking or savings accounts without fees or, unlike EFTPS, preregistration (IRS News Release IR-2014-67; IRM 21.2.1.48.1). An eligible ITIN has a fourth and fifth digit that falls in the 70-88 range (the IRS expects to eventually correct this technical limitation).

Deadlines

2549. Deadlines Falling on a Weekend or Holiday. If the last day for performing any act such as filing a return, paying tax, or filing a claim for credit or refund, falls on Saturday, Sunday, or a legal holiday, the act is timely if it is performed on the next day that is not a Saturday, Sunday, or a legal holiday (Code Sec. 7503; Reg. § 301.7503-1).[56] A legal holiday includes a legal holiday in the District of Columbia, including Emancipation Day. When a legal holiday in the District of Columbia falls on a Sunday, the next Monday is treated as a legal holiday. When a legal holiday in the District of Columbia, other than Inauguration Day, falls on a Saturday, the preceding Friday is treated as a legal holiday (DC Code Annotated § 28-2701 (2010); Notice 2011-17, amplified by Rev. Rul. 2015-13). For the 2017 calendar year, Emancipation Day in the District of Columbia falls on Sunday, April 16, 2017, and is officially observed on Monday, April 17, 2017. Thus, the filing deadline for all tax forms and payments required to be filed or completed by April 15 is Tuesday, April 18, 2017.

In the case of a return, statement, or other document required to be filed with an IRS office, a legal holiday also includes a statewide legal holiday in the state in which the office is located, such as Patriots' Day in Massachusetts and Maine. This extension for filing a return, statement, or other document required to be filed with an IRS office for statewide legal holidays does not, however, include the payment of estimated taxes if the designated depository is located in another non-celebrating state. Thus, if the first payment of estimated taxes for a resident of Massachusetts falls on the statewide holiday of Patriots' Day, the first payment must still be made on that day since the designated depository for estimated payments for residents of Massachusetts is in Connecticut, which does not celebrate Patriots' Day.

References are to Standard Federal Tax Reports; Tax Research Consultant; and Practical Tax Explanations.

[54] ¶ 38,085, ¶ 38,088; FILEIND: 21,156; § 39,320.10

[55] ¶ 38,061, ¶ 38,062, ¶ 38,063, ¶ 38,063C; FILEBUS: 6,106.10; § 22,240.05, § 22,345.05, § 37,355, § 39,320.20

[56] ¶ 42,630, ¶ 42,631; FILEBUS: 15,056; § 39,210.10

2553. Timely Mailing as Timely Filing and Paying (Mailbox Rule). Any return, claim, statement, or document that must be filed with the IRS or the Tax Court, or any payment required to be made on or before a particular date is regarded as having been timely filed or paid if, on or before the due date, including extensions granted, it is deposited in the mail in the United States in an envelope or other appropriate wrapper, postage prepaid and properly addressed, and the date of the U.S. postmark falls on or before the due date (Code Sec. 7502(a); Reg. § 301.7502-1).[57] The postmark date is deemed the date of delivery or payment. Federal tax returns, including claims, statements, or other documents, mailed from outside the United States are timely if they bear the official timely dated postmark of the foreign country (Rev. Rul. 2002-23). The timely-mailed-is-timely-filed rule applies to designated private delivery services. See ¶ 5 for a listing of the available delivery services.

Documents or payments properly sent by registered mail are considered to have been filed on time if the registration date falls on or before the due date of the document. Such documents or payments properly sent by certified mail are timely filed if the certified mail sender's receipt is postmarked on or before the due date of the document. Delivery by properly registered or certified mail is presumed to have occurred if the envelope or package was properly addressed to the appropriate agency, officer, or office for filing or payment. Proof of use of a designated private delivery service under criteria established by the IRS is entitled to a similar presumption of delivery (Code Sec. 7502(c); Reg. § 301.7502-1(c)(2) and (e)).[58]

The timely-mailed-is-timely-filed rule also covers documents filed electronically (Reg. § 301.7502-1(d)). The date of an electronic postmark that is given by an authorized electronic return transmitter and is on or before the filing due date will be deemed to be the filing date.

A tax deposit received by an authorized depository after the due date for the deposit is timely if it has been properly mailed at least two days before the prescribed due date. However, if any person is required to deposit tax more than once a month and the deposit amounts to $20,000 or more, the deposit must be received on or before the prescribed due date to be timely (Code Sec. 7502(e); Reg. § 301.7502-2).[59]

Information Returns and Payment at Source

2565. Payments Made in Course of Trade or Business. Every person engaged in a trade or business, including a partnership and a nonprofit organization, must file information returns for each calendar year for certain payments made during the year in the course of the payor's trade or business (Code Secs. 6041—6050W).[60] In many cases the information contained on such returns must be reported to the IRS by means of electronic filing through the IRS FIRE (Filing Information Returns Electronically) System (IRS Pub. 1220). Recipients must be furnished a copy of the information return or a comparable statement. While payee statements are generally required to be in written form, persons required to furnish recipients with copies of forms in the Form 1099 series and any other information return may furnish electronic payee statements (Sec. 401 of the Job Creation and Worker Assistance Act of 2002 (P.L. 107-147)). Payee statements for Form W-2 may also be filed electronically (Reg. § 31.6051-1).[61]

The following information returns are among those currently being filed:

Form 1098. Persons file this form if they receive $600 or more in mortgage interest from an individual in the course of a trade or business. Points paid directly by a borrower, including seller-paid points, for the purchase of a principal residence must be reported on Form 1098. Refunds and reimbursements of overpaid mortgage interest, and mortgage insurance premiums of $600 or more must also be reported on Form 1098. Applicable to returns and statements required to be furnished after December 31, 2016, the following information must also be reported on Form 1098: (1) the amount of

References are to Standard Federal Tax Reports; Tax Research Consultant; and Practical Tax Explanations.

[57] ¶ 42,620, ¶ 42,621; FILEIND: 15,206, FILEBUS: 15,052; § 39,210.05

[58] ¶ 42,620, ¶ 42,621; FILEIND: 15,206, FILEBUS: 15,052; § 39,210.05

[59] ¶ 42,620, ¶ 42,623; PAYROLL: 9,202; § 39,210.05

[60] ¶ 35,820 et seq.; FILEBUS: 9,200; § 39,105

[61] ¶ 36,421; PAYROLL: 3,356.50; § 39,140.10

outstanding principal of the mortgage as of the beginning of the calendar year, (2) the address of the property securing the mortgage, and (3) the loan origination date (Code Sec. 6050H); Reg. § 1.6050H-2).[62]

Form 1098-E. Financial institutions, governmental units, and educational institutions must file this form when, in the course of a trade or business, they receive interest of $600 or more in a calendar year on a student loan that is used solely to pay for qualified higher education expenses (Code Sec. 6050S, as amended by the Protecting Americans from Tax Hikes (PATH) Act of 2015 (P.L. 114-113); Reg. § 1.6050S-3).[63]

Form 1098-T. An educational institution must file this form with respect to each individual enrolled for an academic period to report payments received (or amounts billed if paid before 2016) for qualified tuition and related expenses. Also, any person engaged in a trade or business of making payments to any individual under an insurance arrangement as reimbursements or refunds, or similar arrangements, of qualified tuition and related expenses must file this form for each individual for whom reimbursements or refunds are made during the calendar year (Code Sec. 6050S, as amended by the Protecting Americans from Tax Hikes (PATH) Act of 2015 (P.L. 114-113)); Reg. § § 1.6050S-1 and 1.6050S-2).[64]

Form 1099-A. Persons who lend money in connection with their trade or business and, in full or partial satisfaction of the debt, acquire an interest in property that is security for the debt, must file this form. The form must also be filed if the person has reason to know that the property securing the debt has been abandoned (Code Sec. 6050J).[65]

Form 1099-B. Brokers are to use this form to report sales, including short sales, of stock, bonds, commodities, regulated futures contracts, foreign currency contracts, forward contracts, and debt instruments. In this case of a "covered security", a brokers must also report the customer's adjusted basis in the security (¶ 1980). Brokers that holds shares for a customer in a corporation that a broker knows or has reason to know has engaged in a transaction of acquisition of control or substantial change in capital structure must also file this form. Barter exchanges are to use the form to report exchanges of property or services through the exchange. For 2016 transactions, brokers must furnish Form 1099-B to customers by February 15, 2017 (Code Sec. 6045).[66] Trustees and middlemen of widely held fixed investment trusts (WHFITs) must use Form 1099-B to report the *non-pro rata* partial principal payments, trust sales proceeds, redemption asset proceeds, redemption proceeds, sales asset proceeds and the sales proceeds that are attributable to a trust interest holder (TIH) for the calendar year. Trustees and middlemen of WHFITs must furnish the required statement by March 15, 2017.

Form 1099-C. Financial institutions, credit unions, federal agencies and any organization that lends money on a regular and continuing basis must file this form for each debtor for whom a debt of $600 or more was cancelled. Multiple discharges of debt of less than $600 during a year need not be aggregated unless the separate discharges occurred with the purpose of evading the reporting requirements. The returns must be filed regardless of whether the debtor is subject to tax on the discharged debt. For example, debts discharged in bankruptcy must be reported (Code Sec. 6050P; Reg. § 1.6050P-1).[67]

Form 1099-DIV. Corporate payors file this form for each person:

(1) to whom payments of $10 or more in distributions, such as dividends, capital gains, or nontaxable distributions, were made on stock;

(2) for whom any foreign tax was withheld and paid on dividends and on other distributions on stock if the recipient can claim a credit for the tax;

References are to Standard Federal Tax Reports; Tax Research Consultant; and Practical Tax Explanations.

[62] ¶ 36,180, ¶ 36,184; REAL: 6,106; § 18,501, § 39,105.05

[63] ¶ 36,319A, ¶ 36,319AJ; FILEBUS: 9,374; § 5910

[64] ¶ 36,319A, ¶ 36,319AD, ¶ 36,319AG; FILEBUS: 9,370; § 12,405

[65] ¶ 36,220; FILEBUS: 9,354; § 18,525.10

[66] ¶ 35,920; FILEBUS: 9,250; § 39,120.20

[67] ¶ 36,310, ¶ 36,311B; SALES: 12,450; § 3,401

(3) for whom any federal income tax was withheld under the backup withholding rules; or

(4) to whom payments of $600 or more were made as part of a liquidation (Code Sec. 6042).[68]

S corporations use this form only to report distributions made during the calendar year out of accumulated earnings and profits.

Form 1099-G. Government units use this form to report payments of $10 or more for unemployment benefits and state and local tax refunds, credits, or offsets, payments of $600 or more in taxable grants or alternative trade adjustment assistance payments, and agricultural subsidy payments made during the year (Code Secs. 6050B and 6050E).[69]

Form 1099-H. Health insurance providers are required to file this return to report any advance payments of the credit for health insurance costs they are entitled to receive on behalf of individuals under Code Sec. 7527 (¶ 1332) (Code Sec. 6050T).[70]

Form 1099-INT. Payors file this form for each person to whom payments of $10 or more in interest were paid, including interest on bearer certificates of deposit and interest on U.S. Savings Bonds, Treasury bills, Treasury notes, and Treasury bonds (Code Sec. 6049).[71] Interest of $600 or more is also reportable if paid for a person in the course of a trade or business, such as interest on delayed death benefits paid by a life insurance company, interest received with damages, or interest on a state or federal income tax refund. Form 1099-INT must also be filed to report interest of $10 or more (other than original issue discount) accrued to a real estate mortgage investment conduit (REMIC), a financial asset securitization investment trust (FASIT) regular interest holder, or a holder of a collateralized debt obligation (CDO). Additionally, trustees and middlemen of WHFITs must report the gross amount of interest exceeding $10 that is attributable to a trust interest holder (TIH) for the calendar year on this form.

Form 1099-K. Banks and other processors of merchant payment card transactions (e.g., credit and debit cards and internet payment systems) must use this form to report a merchant's annual gross payment card receipts to the IRS and to the merchant (Code Sec. 6050W; Reg. §§ 1.6050W-1 and 1.6050W-2).[72] A third-party settlement organization must report information concerning a merchant's third-party network transactions only if, for the calendar year, the aggregate value of reportable payment transactions for the merchant exceeds $20,000 and the aggregate number of transactions exceeds 200.

Form 1099-MISC. This form is filed by payors for each person to whom at least $10 in gross royalty payments or broker payments in lieu of dividends or tax-exempt interest, or $600 for rents or services in the course of a trade or business, was paid. Some of the items reported on this form are:

(1) payments for real estate, machine and pasture rentals;

(2) royalties paid to authors;

(3) prizes and awards that were not paid for services rendered;

(4) amounts withheld as backup withholding;

(5) payments by medical and health care insurers to each physician or health care provider under health, accident and sickness insurance programs;

(6) compensation such as fees, commissions and awards, and golden parachute payments paid to a nonemployee for services, including payments to attorneys for legal services (Code Sec. 6045(f));

(7) notification of the occurrence of sales of $5,000 or more of consumer products to a person on a buy-sell or commission basis for resale anywhere other than in a permanent retail establishment;

References are to Standard Federal Tax Reports; Tax Research Consultant; and Practical Tax Explanations.

[68] ¶ 35,860; FILEBUS: 9,154; § 26,240

[69] ¶ 36,060, ¶ 36,120; FILEBUS: 9,308; § 3080

[70] ¶ 36,320; HEALTH: 15,158; § 42,315.15

[71] ¶ 36,020; FILEBUS: 9,158; § 39,110

[72] ¶ 36,376, ¶ 36,378C, ¶ 36,378G; FILEBUS: 9,320; § 39,130

(8) fishing boat proceeds;

(9) fish purchases of $600 or more paid in cash for resale (Code Sec. 6050R);

(10) crop insurance proceeds of $600 or more; and

(11) any deferrals for the year under a nonqualified deferred compensation plan (Code Sec. 6041(g)).

For 2016 payments, this form must be furnished to recipients by February 15, 2017, if substitute payments in lieu of dividends or tax-exempt interest are being reported in box 8 or gross proceeds paid to an attorney are being reported in box 14. Effective for payments made after the 2015 tax year, the form must be provided to recipients by January 31 if nonemployee compensation is reported in box 7.

Form 1099-OID. Issuers of bonds or certificates of deposit, and trustees and middlemen of WHFITs use this form to report original issue discount of $10 or more (Code Sec. 6049(d); Reg. § 1.6049-4; Temp. Reg. § 1.6049-4T).[73]

Form 1099-PATR. Cooperatives use this form to report patronage dividends and other distributions of $10 or more to patrons (Code Sec. 6044).[74]

Form 1099-R. Payors file this form to report any distributions of $10 or more from retirement or profit-sharing plans, individual retirement arrangements (IRAs), simplified employee pensions (SEPs), annuities, or insurance contracts. Reports must be furnished to the participants by January 31 following the year of distribution.

Form 1099-S. This form is used to report the sale or exchange of real estate, as well as the real property taxes imposed on the purchaser of a residence. Included are sales or exchanges of residences, land (including air space), commercial buildings, condominium units, stock in cooperative housing corporations, and noncontingent interests in standing timber (Reg. § 1.6045-4).[75] The form must be filed by the person responsible for closing the real estate transaction or, if no such person exists, by the mortgage lender, the transferor's broker, the transferee's broker or the transferee, in that order. Payments of timber royalties under a "pay-as-cut" contract are also reported on the form. For 2016 transactions, this form must be furnished to recipients by February 15, 2017.

Forms 3921 and *3922.* These forms must be filed by a corporation to report certain stock transfers to an employee. Form 3921 is used to report a transfer of stock pursuant to an employee's exercise of an incentive stock option. Form 3922 is used to report a transfer of stock pursuant to an employee's exercise of an option granted under an employee stock purchase plan where the exercise price is less than 100 percent of the value of the stock, or is not fixed or determinable, on the date of grant (Code Sec. 6039).[76]

Form 5498. This form is filed by the account trustee for each person for whom an IRA, a deemed IRA, or a simplified employee pension (SEP) was maintained. Contributions made during the year to the IRA, including rollover contributions and contributions under a SEP plan, and the fair market value of the IRA or SEP account on December 31 must be reported here. The form must be furnished to a plan participant by January 31 following the plan year for the value of the account and the required minimum distribution (RMD) (if applicable) or May 31 following the plan year for contribution information (Code Secs. 408(i) and 408A(d)(3)(D); Reg. § 1.408-5).[77]

Form 8027. Each employer that runs a large food or beverage establishment (¶ 2605) must file an annual return of the receipts from food or beverage operations and tips reported by employees (Code Sec. 6053).[78] In addition, in certain circumstances, the employer is required to allocate amounts as tips to employees. Establishments filing 250 or more Forms 8027 must file electronically (Rev. Proc. 2012-37).

References are to Standard Federal Tax Reports; Tax Research Consultant; and Practical Tax Explanations.

[73] ¶ 36,020, ¶ 36,025, ¶ 36,027; FILEBUS: 9,158; § 19,320

[74] ¶ 35,900; FARM: 12,118.20; § 36,040

[75] ¶ 35,929; REAL: 15,458; § 39,115

[76] ¶ 35,600; COMPEN: 24,404, COMPEN: 21,352; § 21,545, § 21,635

[77] ¶ 18,902, ¶ 18,912, ¶ 18,925; RETIRE: 66,604.05, COMPEN: 21,352; § 21,545, § 21,635

[78] ¶ 36,460; FILEBUS: 12,302; § 21,305.20

Form 8300. Each person engaged in a trade or business who, in the course of such trade or business, receives more than $10,000 in cash in one transaction (or two or more related transactions) must file this form. The form is to be filed with the IRS by the 15th day after the transaction, and a similar statement is to be provided to the payor on or before January 31 of the calendar year following the year of receipt (Code Sec. 6050I).[79]

Form W-2. Employers use this form to report wages, tips, other compensation, and withheld income and FICA taxes to both the recipient and the Social Security Administration (SSA) (Code Sec. 6051).[80] Bonuses, vacation allowances, severance pay, moving expense payments, some kinds of travel allowances and third-party payments of sick pay are included. Employers are required to use the form to report the aggregate cost of certain employer-sponsored health coverage provided to employees if the employer was required to file at least 250 Forms W-2 for 2015 (¶ 2567). Form W-3 must be filed along with Form W-2 if submitting a paper copy of the form to the SSA.

Due Dates. Unless otherwise specified, the above information returns for 2016 are to be provided to the IRS by February 28, 2017, if filed on paper and March 31, 2017, if filed electronically. The due date for sending payee statements to recipients is January 31, 2017. The due date for filing 2016 Forms W-2 and W-3 with the SSA is January 31, 2017, whether being filed on paper or electronically (Code Sec. 6071, as amended by P.L. 114-113)).[81] Form 8809 is used to request an automatic 30-day extension of time to file Forms 1098, 1099, W-2G, 1042-S, 5498 and 8027 with the IRS. One additional 30-day extension may also be obtained by filing Form 8809 before the expiration of the first 30-day extension, but the requester must explain in detail why additional time is needed. For filings on or after January 1, 2017, Form 8809 is also used to request one 30-day extension of time to file Form W-2 with the SSA (other than Form W-2G), but the extension is not automatic and the IRS will grant the request only in extraordinary circumstances. Form 8809 *cannot* be used to request an extension of time to furnish required statements to recipients (Reg. § 1.6081-8; Temporary Reg. § 1.6081-8T).[82]

Other Information Returns. Other information returns are required with respect to the following:

(1) a U.S. person that owns at least a 10-percent interest in a foreign partnership must report on Form 8865 any changes in his or her ownership during the tax year (¶ 2494) (Code Sec. 6046A);

(2) in cases of liquidation or dissolution of a corporation, including an exempt organization, Form 966 must be filed (¶ 2259) (Code Sec. 6043(a) and (b));

(3) corporate recapitalizations are reported on Form 8806 and Form 1099-CAP (Code Sec. 6043(c));

(4) corporate mergers and acquisitions are reported on Form 8806 and Form 1099-CAP (Code Sec. 6043A);

(5) formations or reorganizations of foreign corporations are reported on Form 5471 (¶ 2487) (Code Sec. 6046);

(6) foreign trusts with a U.S. grantor report ownership and certain transactions on Form 3520 and Form 3520-A is the annual information return of the trust (¶ 588 and ¶ 2493) (Code Sec. 6048);

(7) U.S. persons who own interests in foreign partnerships or corporations must file Form 5471 (¶ 2487) (Code Sec. 6038);

(8) U.S. persons who transfer property to foreign partnerships or corporations report the transaction on Form 8865 or Form 966, respectively (Code Sec. 6038B);

(9) payors of long-term care benefits must file Form 1099-LTC (Code Sec. 6050Q);

References are to Standard Federal Tax Reports; Tax Research Consultant; and Practical Tax Explanations.

[79] ¶ 36,200; FILEBUS: 9,322; § 39,125

[80] ¶ 36,420; PAYROLL: 3,356; § 22,401

[81] ¶ 36,700; FILEBUS: 15,050; § 39,205

[82] ¶ 36,798F; FILEBUS: 15,106.25; § 39,145.05

(10) U.S. persons, other than tax-exempt organizations, that receive foreign gifts during the tax year totaling more than $15,671 in 2016 ($15,797 in 2017) report the gifts on Form 3520 (Code Sec. 6039F; Rev. Proc. 2015-53; Rev. Proc. 2016-55);

(11) individuals who lose citizenship, and long-term residents who terminate residency in the United States, are required to file Form 8854 annually (¶ 2412) (Code Sec. 6039G);

(12) Alaska Native Settlement Trusts may elect to have special rules apply to the trust and its beneficiaries using Form 1041-N (Code Sec. 6039H);

(13) dispositions by charitable donees within three years of donated property with a value in excess of $5,000 are reported on Form 8282 by the donee and Form 8283 by the donor (¶ 627) (Code Sec. 6050L(a));

(14) charitable organizations that receive or accrue net income from a qualified intellectual property contribution must file Form 8899 and provide a copy to the donor (¶ 1062A) (Code Sec. 6050L(b));

(15) employer-owned life insurance contracts (also known as company-owned life insurance (COLI) contracts) must be reported by the policyholder on Form 8925 (¶ 804) (Code Sec. 6039I);

(16) charges or payments made for qualified long-term insurance contracts under combined arrangements are reported on Form 1099-R (Code Sec. 6050U); and

(17) federal executive agencies must report information about persons with whom they have entered contracts with for product or service on Form 8596 and Form 8596-A, as well file Form 1099-MISC if in the course of a trade or business it pays remuneration of $600 or more in a calendar year to any person for services provided by that person (Code Secs. 6041A and 6050M).

2567. Health Care Coverage Reporting. Employers are required to disclose the aggregate cost of employer-sponsored health insurance coverage provided to their employees on the employee's Form W-2 (Code Sec. 6051(a)(14); Notice 2012-9).[83] The aggregate cost of the coverage reported includes both the portion of coverage paid by the employer and the employee, as well as any portion of the cost of coverage that is includible in the employee's gross income for the employee's spouse, dependent, or child under the age of 27. It does not include salary reduction contributions to a health savings account (HSA) (¶ 2035) or Archer medical savings account (MSA) (¶ 2037) of the employee or the employee's spouse, or salary reduction contributions to a flexible spending arrangement under a cafeteria plan (¶ 2041). Reporting the cost of health care coverage on the Form W-2 does not mean that the coverage is taxable—it is for informational purposes only. Form W-2 is not required to be issued by an employer solely to report the value of the coverage for retirees or former employees.

The reporting requirement was generally required beginning with the 2012 calendar year. Pending further guidance from the IRS and under transitional relief, the reporting requirement is optional for employers who are required to file fewer than 250 Forms W-2 for the preceding year. For example, if an employer files fewer than 250 Forms W-2 for 2015 calendar year, the employer is not subject to the reporting requirements for Forms W-2 for the 2016 calendar year (the Forms W-2 that are generally furnished to employees in January 2017). Transitional relief is also available for certain other types of coverage and situations (Notice 2012-9).

Offers of Coverage. An applicable large employer (¶ 2001) must report whether full-time employees and their dependents are offered the opportunity to enroll in minimum essential coverage under an eligible employer-sponsored plan, along with other related

References are to Standard Federal Tax Reports; Tax Research Consultant; and Practical Tax Explanations.

[83] ¶ 36,420; HEALTH: 6,102; § 42,180.05

information (Code Sec. 6056; Reg. §§301.6056-1 and 301.6056-2; Notice 2013-45)).[84] For this purpose, a return must be filed with the IRS on or before February 28 (March 31 if filed electronically) of the year succeeding the calendar year to which it relates. A statement must be furnished to each full-time employee on or before January 31 of the following calendar year. The employer's return to the IRS may be made on Forms 1094-C (transmittal) and 1095-C (employee statement) or on a substitute form. An applicable large employer that is self-insured (see below) may combine Code Sec. 6055 reporting on Form 1095-C. A separate return is required for each full-time employee, accompanied by a single transmittal form for all of the returns filed for a given calendar year. Electronic filing is required for employers filing 250 of more applicable large employer information returns during the calendar year. The employee statement may be made by furnishing to the full-time employee a copy of Form 1095-C or a substitute statement. An electronic statement may instead be furnished with the employee's consent. Failure to follow these rules may subject the employer to a penalty (¶ 2816 and ¶ 2823).

Insurer Reporting. Every insurer who provides minimum essential health care coverage to an individual during a calendar year, including an employer who self-insures, is also required to file an information return reporting such coverage (Code Sec. 6055; Reg. §1.6055-1; Prop. Reg. §1.6055-1; Notice 2013-45).[85] The reporting entity must file the information on Form 1095-B with the IRS on or before February 28 (or March 31 if filed electronically) of the year following the calendar year. The return must be submitted to the IRS with transmittal Form 1094-B. Self-insured employers that are also applicable large employers subject to shared responsibility reporting (see above) can instead combine insurance provider reporting on Forms 1095-C and 1094-C. A statement must also be furnished to each full-time employee on or before January 31 of the following calendar year. The statement may be furnished electronically if affirmative consent is given (Reg. §1.6055-2). Failure to follow these rules may subject the employer to a penalty (¶ 2816 and ¶ 2823).

2570. Reporting Foreign Financial Accounts (FBAR). A U.S. person is required to disclose any financial interests in, signature authority over, or other authority over foreign financial accounts if the aggregate value of the accounts exceeds $10,000 at any time during the calendar year (31 CFR §1010.350).[86] The information is reported electronically on FINCen Report 114 (commonly referred to as FBAR) through the Treasury's Financial Crimes Enforcement Network (FinCEN) BSA E-Filing System. The filing of the FBAR does not relieve a taxpayer of the requirement to file Form 8938 to report specified foreign financial assets (¶ 2572).

For tax years beginning after December 31, 2015, the FBAR is to be filed by April 15 of the succeeding year, with a maximum extension of six months ending on October 15. In addition, any penalty for failure to timely file a request for an extension to file the FBAR may be waived by the IRS for first-time filers (Act Sec. 2006(b)(11) of the Surface Transportation and Veterans Health Care Choice Improvement Act of 2015 (P.L. 114-41)). For tax years beginning before January 1, 2016, the FBAR must be *received*, not just filed, with the Department of Treasury for each calendar year, on or before June 30, of the succeeding year. The June 30 deadline may generally not be extended. However, relief from FBAR reporting is provided for certain individuals who have signature authority over one or more foreign financial accounts, but no financial interest in the accounts. Under this relief, the deadline for filing FBAR for signature authority held during the 2015 calendar year (as well as the reporting deadlines previously extended for 2011, 2012, 2013, and 2014) is extended until April 15, 2017 (FinCEN Notice 2015-1).

U.S. persons subject to FBAR reporting are U.S. citizens, resident aliens, and entities created, organized, or formed under U.S. laws, including but not limited to domestic corporations, partnerships, limited liability companies (LLCs), trusts, and

References are to Standard Federal Tax Reports; Tax Research Consultant; and Practical Tax Explanations.

[84] ¶ 36,467, ¶ 36,470, ¶ 36,470C; HEALTH: 6,106; §42,135.10

[85] ¶ 36,465E, ¶ 36,466A, ¶ 36,466AB; HEALTH: 6,104; §42,135.15

[86] ¶ 36,555.33; FILEBUS: 9,104; §37,705

estates. The federal tax treatment of a person or entity does not determine whether an FBAR filing is required. For example, an entity disregarded for federal tax purposes must still file an FBAR if otherwise required. Participants and beneficiaries in qualified retirement plans, including individual retirement accounts (IRAs) are not required to file FBARs with respect to a foreign financial account held by or on behalf of the plan. A beneficiary of a trust in which a U.S. person has 50 percent or more interest is also not required to file FBAR if the trust, trustee, or agent of the trust is a U.S. person that files an FBAR for the trust's foreign financial assets.

FinCen Form 114a, Record of Authorization to Electronically File FBARs, is used by a U.S. person to authorize a third party preparer (i.e., CPA, enrolled agent, or attorney) to file the FBAR on his or her behalf, or to jointly file the FBAR with his or her spouse. Form 114a is not filed with Treasury, but must be maintained by the foreign account holder and the filer and made available upon request by Treasury or the IRS.

2572. Reporting Specified Foreign Financial Assets (Form 8938). Under the Foreign Account Tax Compliance Act (FATCA), any individual who holds an interest in a specified foreign financial asset during the tax year must attach Form 8938 to his or her tax return to report certain information for each asset if the total value of all such assets exceeds an applicable threshold amount (Code Sec. 6038D).[87] The requirement applies to any U.S. citizen and individual who is a resident alien for any part of the tax year. A nonresident alien who makes the election to be treated as a resident alien for purposes of filing a joint return for the tax year must also file Form 8938, as well as a nonresident alien who is a bona fide resident of American Samoa or Puerto Rico. Form 8938 is also required to be filed by any domestic entity which is formed or availed of for purposes of holding, directly or indirectly, specified foreign financial assets, in the same manner as if the entity were an individual. Applicable to tax years beginning after December 31, 2015, specified domestic entities subject to the reporting requirement include certain closely-held domestic corporations or partnerships, as well as certain domestic trusts (Reg. § 1.6038D-6).

A "specified foreign financial asset" includes (1) a depository, custodial, or other financial account maintained by a foreign financial institution, (2) a stock or security issued by a person other than a U.S. person, (3) a financial instrument or contract held for investment that has an issuer or counterparty other than a U.S. person, and (4) an interest in an entity that is not a U.S. person. The filing of Form 8938 does not relieve an individual of the requirement to file the FBAR (¶ 2570) for disclosing foreign financial accounts. Similarly, the filing of the FBAR does not relieve an individual of the requirement to file Form 8938. An individual may be required to file both Form 8938 and FBAR to report the same information on certain foreign accounts. The FBAR, however, is not filed with the individual's federal income tax return.

The applicable threshold amount that determines whether a taxpayer must file Form 8938 depends on the taxpayer's filing status and whether the individual lives in the United States or abroad. The total value of specified foreign financial assets for this purpose is the asset's fair market value as determined in U.S. dollars using the Treasury's currency exchange rate on the last day of the tax year (Reg. § 1.6038D-2; Instructions for Form 8938).[88] The applicable threshold amounts are as follows:

- Unmarried taxpayers living in the United States must file Form 8938 if the total value of specified foreign financial assets is more than $50,000 on the last day of the tax year or more than $75,000 at any time during the tax year.

References are to Standard Federal Tax Reports; Tax Research Consultant; and Practical Tax Explanations.

[87] ¶ 35,593; FILEBUS: 9,108; § 37,710

[88] ¶ 35,594AH; FILEBUS: 9,108; § 37,710

• Married taxpayers living in the United States and filing a joint income tax return must file Form 8938 if the value of specified foreign financial assets is more than $100,000 on the last day of the tax year or more than $150,000 at any time during the tax year.

• Married taxpayers living in the United States and filing separate income tax returns must file Form 8938 if the value of specified foreign financial assets is more than $50,000 on the last day of the tax year or more than $75,000 at any time during the tax year.

• Married taxpayers living abroad and filing a joint return must file Form 8938 if the value of specified foreign assets is more than $400,000 on the last day of the tax year or more than $600,000 at any time during the year.

• Other taxpayers living abroad must file Form 8938 if the total value of specified foreign assets is more than $200,000 on the last day of the tax year or more than $300,000 at any time during the year.

The individual must disclose the asset's maximum value during the tax year and provide specific information based on the asset type. For a financial account, the individual must provide the name and address of the financial institution in which the account is maintained, and the account number. For stock or security, the individual must provide the issuer's name and address, and any other information needed to identify the asset's class or issue. For any other instrument, contract, or interest, the individual must provide any information needed to identify the asset, and the names and addresses of all issuers and counterparties. An individual who fails to furnish the required information in timely manner will subject the individual to a penalty. Additionally, a 40-percent accuracy-related penalty (¶ 2864) may be imposed for any underpayment of tax attributable to an undisclosed foreign financial asset and an extended statute of limitations may be extended or suspended depending on the circumstances.

2579. Taxpayer Identification Number. Persons filing returns and other documents must record on such items a taxpayer identification number (TIN) (Code Sec. 6109(a); Reg. § 301.6109-1).[89] A person may also be required to furnish a TIN to another person or request an identifying number from another person using Form W-9 for filing information returns (¶ 2565). The TIN used on an information return or payee statement, however, may be a truncated taxpayer identification number (TTIN) (Reg. § 301.6109-4).[90]

Individuals generally use their Social Security number as their TIN. Executors of individuals' estates who must file Form 706 are to use both their Social Security number and the decedent's Social Security number. An individual who needs a Social Security number must file an application on Form SS-5 with the Social Security Administration (Reg. § 301.6109-1(d)(1)). A prospective adoptive parent can apply for an adoption taxpayer identification number (ATIN) for a child who is in the process of being adopted (Reg. § 301.6109-3).[91] Application for an ATIN must be made on Form W-7A.

Individual taxpayer identification numbers. Foreign persons and other individuals who do not have, and are unable to obtain, a Social Security number may use an IRS-issued individual taxpayer identification number (ITIN) (Code Sec. 6109(i), as added by the Protecting Americans from Tax Hikes Act of 2015 (P.L. 114-113); (Reg. § 301.6109-1(d)(1)).[92] Form W-7 is used to apply for an ITIN and generally must be filed with the individual's original tax return for which the ITIN is needed. The individual must include with the application original or certified copy of documents proving his or her identity, foreign status, and U.S. residency. Form W-7 packets may be submitted by mail or in person to an employee of the IRS. Effective for applications made after December 18, 2015, individuals residing in the United States may also submit the Form W-7 packets to a community-based certified acceptance agent. Until further guidance is

References are to Standard Federal Tax Reports; Tax Research Consultant; and Practical Tax Explanations.

[89] ¶ 36,960, ¶ 36,961; FILEBUS: 12,106; § 39,010.20

[90] ¶ 36,964I; FILEBUS: 12,106.15; § 39,142

[91] ¶ 36,964D; FILEBUS: 12,106; § 39,010.20

[92] ¶ 36,960, ¶ 36,961; FILEBUS: 12,106; § 39,010.20

issued, applicants residing in the United States may continue to submit their Form W-7 packets to certified acceptance agents (CAAs) under existing procedures (Notice 2016-48; Rev. Proc. 2006-10).[93]

ITINs issued after December 31, 2012, will remain in effect unless the individual does not file a return, or is not included as a dependent on a return, for three consecutive tax years. If an ITIN is not used during the three-year period, then it expires on the last day of the third year. ITINs issued before January 1, 2013, will remain in effect until the earlier of the end of the three-year period of nonuse or (i) January 1, 2017, in the case of an ITIN issued before January 1, 2008; (ii) January 1, 2018, in the case of an ITIN issued in 2008; (iii) January 1, 2019, in the case of an ITIN issued in 2009 or 2010; and (iv) January 1, 2020, in the case of an ITIN issued in 2011 or 2012 (Code Sec. 6109(i)(3), as added by P.L. 114-113). However, because ITIN holders may not know when their ITIN was issued, the IRS will administer the expiration and renewal process for ITINs issued before 2013 based upon the fourth and fifth digits (middle digits) in the ITIN. Individuals that have an expired ITIN may renew it by a new submitting Form W-7 packet (Notice 2016-48).

Employer identification number (EIN). For corporations, partnerships, nonprofit associations, estates and trusts, and other business entities their TIN is the employer identification number (EIN). An individual who is engaged in a trade or business as a sole proprietor uses both his Social Security number and EIN of his or her business when supplying a TIN on returns, statements or other documents, depending on which number is required by the IRS. Any person needing an EIN is required to file an application on Form SS-4 (Reg. § 301.6109-1(d)(2)).[94]

Penalties. A penalty of $50 per failure applies to a taxpayer who omits his or her own TIN from a required return, statement, or document. Failure to furnish one's TIN to another person when so required or to include another person's TIN in any document for information reporting purposes will also give rise to a $50 penalty. The maximum penalty per calendar year for failure to include TINs is $100,000 (Code Secs. 6723 and 6724(d)(3)).[95]

Reportable Transactions and Tax Shelters

2591. Reportable Transactions. Reporting and disclosure requirements apply to taxpayers (¶ 2592) and material advisors (¶ 2593) with respect to reportable transactions. A reportable transaction is any transaction with respect to which information is required to be included with a return or statement because the transaction is of a type that the IRS has determined under regulations as having a potential for tax avoidance or evasion (Code Sec. 6707A(c)(1)).[96]

There are five categories of reportable transactions: listed transactions, confidential transactions, transactions with contractual protection, loss transactions, and transactions of interest (Reg. § 1.6011-4(b)).[97] A transaction is not considered a reportable transaction, or it is excluded from any individual category of reportable transaction, if the IRS makes a determination by published guidance that the transaction is not subject to the reporting requirements. The IRS may make a determination by individual letter.

2592. Disclosure of Reportable Transactions by Taxpayers. Every taxpayer that is required to file a tax return and has participated directly or indirectly in a reportable transaction (¶ 2591) must disclose its participation in the transaction (Reg. § 1.6011-4(a)).[98] The fact that a transaction is a reportable transaction does not affect the legal determination of whether the taxpayer's treatment of the transaction is proper.

Form 8886 is used to disclose information for each reportable transaction in which the taxpayer participated. A separate Form 8886 must be filed for each reportable transaction. The form must be attached to the taxpayer's tax return for each tax year for

References are to Standard Federal Tax Reports; Tax Research Consultant; and Practical Tax Explanations.

[93] ¶ 36,965.10, ¶ 36,965.1702; FILEBUS: 12,106; § 39,010.20

[94] ¶ 36,961; FILEBUS: 12,106; § 39,010.20

[95] ¶ 40,250, ¶ 40,275; PENALTY: 3,200; § 40,230

[96] ¶ 40,091; FILEBUS: 9,450; § 39,015.05

[97] ¶ 35,127; FILEBUS: 9,458; § 39,015.05

[98] ¶ 35,127; FILEBUS: 9,456; § 39,015.05

which the taxpayer participates in a reportable transaction. A copy of the disclosure statement must be sent to the Office of Tax Shelter Analysis (OTSA) at the same time that any disclosure statement is first filed with the taxpayer's tax return (Reg. § 1.6011-4(d) and (e)). If a reportable transaction results in a loss that is carried back to a prior year, Form 8886 is attached to the taxpayer's application for tentative refund or amended tax return for the prior year.

In the case of a taxpayer that is a partnership, an S corporation, or a trust, Form 8886 must be attached to the partnership's, S corporation's, or trust's tax return for each tax year in which the partnership, S corporation, or trust participates in the transaction. A taxpayer who is a partner, S corporation shareholder, or a beneficiary of a trust who receives a Schedule K-1 less than 10 calendar days before the due date of its return, including extensions, has a 60-day extension to file Form 8886 with the OTSA if the taxpayer determines from the Schedule K-1 that it participated in a reportable transaction.

Failure to file Form 8886 regarding a reportable transaction is subject to a penalty (¶ 2594). Special reporting rules apply to listed transactions and transactions of interest. Also, in some cases, taxpayers must make multiple disclosures of a reportable transaction (Reg. § 1.6011-4(e)).

A taxpayer may submit a request to the IRS for a ruling as to whether a transaction is subject to the disclosure requirements (Reg. § 1.6011-4(f)). If a taxpayer requests a ruling on the merits of a specific transaction on or before the date that disclosure would otherwise be required and receives a favorable ruling, the disclosure rules are satisfied. The ruling request must fully disclose all relevant facts relating to the transaction. If a taxpayer is uncertain whether a transaction must be disclosed, the taxpayer may make a protective disclosure. The taxpayer must disclose the transaction and indicate on the disclosure statement that the taxpayer is uncertain whether the transaction is required to be disclosed and that the disclosure statement is being filed on a protective basis. The taxpayer must retain a copy of all documents and other records related to a transaction subject to disclosure (Reg. § 1.6011-4(g)). The retained documents and records are those that are material to an understanding of the tax treatment or tax structure of the transaction.

2593. Disclosure of Reportable Transactions by Material Advisors. Each material advisor is required to timely file an information return with the IRS for any reportable transaction (¶ 2591) (Code Sec. 6111; Reg. § 301.6111-3).[99] The disclosure is made on Form 8918 and generally must be filed with the Office of Tax Shelter Analysis (OTSA) by the last day of the month that follows the calendar quarter in which the advisor became a material advisor with respect to the reportable transaction or in which circumstances occur to require an amended disclosure statement.

The material advisor's disclosure on Form 8918 must include: (1) information identifying and describing the transaction; (2) information describing any potential tax benefits expected to result from the transaction; and (3) whatever other information the IRS may require. This includes enough information about the transaction to identify if any other person that the material advisor knows or has reason to know acted as a material advisor with respect to the transaction. A single Form 8918 may be filed for substantially similar transactions. An amended form must be filed if information previously provided is no longer accurate, if additional information becomes available, or if there are material changes to the transaction. If a potential material advisor is uncertain whether a transaction must be disclosed, a protective disclosure may be made. Any material advisor who fails to file Form 8918 when required or files a false or incomplete form is subject to a penalty (¶ 2595).

A material advisor is any person: (1) who provides material aid, assistance, or advice with respect to organizing, promoting, selling, implementing, or carrying out any

References are to Standard Federal Tax Reports; Tax Research Consultant; and Practical Tax Explanations.

[99] ¶ 37,000, ¶ 37,001D; FILEBUS: 9,452, PENALTY: 3,254

reportable transaction; and (2) who directly or indirectly derives gross income in excess of $250,000 ($50,000 in the case of a reportable transaction substantially all of the tax benefits from which are provided to natural persons) for that aid, assistance, or advice. If more than one material advisor is required to disclose a reportable transaction, the material advisors may designate by written agreement a single material advisor to disclose the transaction.

2594. Penalty for Failure to Disclose Reportable Transaction. A penalty is imposed on any taxpayer who fails to disclose its participation in a reportable transaction that is required to be included on the taxpayer's return (¶ 2592) (Code Sec. 6707A; Reg. § 301.6707A-1).[100] The penalty is equal to 75 percent of the decrease in tax shown on the return as a result of the transaction, or that would have resulted from the transaction if the transaction had been respected for federal tax purposes. The *minimum* penalty, however, is $10,000 ($5,000 in the case of a natural person). The maximum penalty is $50,000 ($10,000 in the case of a natural person), but in circumstances involving listed transactions, the maximum penalty is $200,000 ($100,000 in the case of a natural person). The penalty for failure to disclose is imposed in addition to any other penalty, including a special accuracy-related penalty for an understatement of tax resulting from a reportable transaction (¶ 2870).

For reportable transactions other than listed transactions, the penalty can be rescinded or abated only in exceptional circumstances, and abatement of the penalty must promote compliance with the tax laws and effective tax administration. Factors that are taken into account in deciding whether to grant rescission include: (1) the taxpayer, on becoming aware of the failure to properly disclose a reportable transaction, filed a complete and proper, although untimely, Form 8886; (2) the failure to properly disclose was due to an unintentional mistake of fact that existed despite the taxpayer's reasonable attempts to determine the correct facts; (3) the taxpayer has an established history of properly disclosing reportable transactions and complying with tax laws generally; (4) the failure to file was beyond the taxpayer's control; (5) the taxpayer cooperates with the IRS; and (6) assessment of the penalty weighs against good conscience, and the taxpayer demonstrates it acted in good faith with respect to the failure.

Any person seeking rescission of a penalty must make a written request within 30 days after the date that the IRS sends notice and demand for payment of the penalty. If the penalty is paid (not including interest) prior to the date that notice and demand is sent, the written request must be made within 30 days from the date of payment. In order to request rescission, the person must have either exhausted the administrative remedies available within the IRS Office of Appeals or agreed in writing to the assessment of the penalty and not to file or prosecute a claim for refund or credit of the penalty. The IRS has provided guidance on the information required to be included with any rescission request, as well as factors considered in granting or denying the request (Rev. Proc. 2007-21; Announcement 2016-1).[101] The IRS's collection efforts are not suspended because a rescission request has been made.

2595. Material Advisor Penalty for Reportable Transactions. A penalty is imposed on any material advisor who fails to file an information return or who files a false or incomplete information return regarding a reportable transaction (¶ 2593) (Code Sec. 6707; Reg. § 301.6707-1).[102] Generally, a $50,000 penalty is assessed for failure to furnish required information with respect to a reportable transaction. In the case of the failure to file an information return with respect to a listed transaction, the penalty assessed is the greater of $200,000 or 50 percent of the gross income derived by the person required to file the return with respect to aid, assistance, or advice that is provided. The 50-percent limit is raised to 75 percent in cases involving an intentional failure to act. Only one penalty applies in the case of a transaction that is both a listed transaction and a reportable transaction. The penalty that applies in these cases is the higher penalty for listed transactions. If there is a failure with respect to more than one reportable or listed

References are to Standard Federal Tax Reports; Tax Research Consultant; and Practical Tax Explanations.

[100] ¶ 40,091, ¶ 40,092; PENALTY: 3,252.10; § 39,015.05

[101] ¶ 40,093.70; PENALTY: 3,252.10; § 39,015.05

[102] ¶ 40,085, ¶ 40,088; PENALTY: 3,254

transaction, a material advisor will be subject to a separate penalty for each transaction. The penalty with respect to reportable transactions other than listed transactions may be rescinded only in exceptional circumstances similar to those for rescission of the penalty for failure to disclose reportable transactions by taxpayers (¶ 2594). The penalty with respect to a listed transaction cannot be waived.

Each material advisor with respect to any reportable transaction is required to maintain a list identifying each person with respect to whom that advisor acted as a material advisor with respect to the transaction and containing any other information required by the IRS (Code Sec. 6112; Reg. § 301.6112-1).[103] Regulations set forth the requirements for the preparation and maintenance of advisee lists, including persons required to be included on lists, contents of the list, definitions, and requirements for retention and furnishing of the lists. All information that is required to be included in the advisee lists must be retained for seven years. Any person required to maintain advisee lists with respect to reportable transactions who receives a written request from the IRS, but who fails to make the lists available within 20 business days, may be assessed a $10,000 penalty for each day of failure after the 20th business day (Code Sec. 6708; Reg. § 301.6708-1).[104]

2597. Abusive Tax Shelters Penalty. A penalty is imposed against any person who organizes, assists in organizing, or participates in the sale of any interest in a tax shelter if he or she makes or furnishes or causes another person to make or furnish: (1) a statement concerning the allowability of any tax benefit obtained through participation in the tax shelter that the person knows or has reason to know is false or fraudulent; or (2) a gross valuation overstatement concerning any matter that is material to the tax shelter (Code Sec. 6700).[105] The penalty is 50 percent of the gross income derived, or to be derived, from the abusive plan or arrangement activities engaged in, other than promotion activities involving gross valuation overstatements. The penalty for promotion of activities involving gross valuation overstatements is an amount equal to the lesser of $1,000 or 100 percent of the gross income derived, or to be derived, by the promoter from the activity.

In applying the penalty, promotion of each entity or activity is a separate activity and each sale of an interest in the shelter is a separate activity. The penalty is imposed in addition to all other penalties that may be imposed, except with respect to any documents if an aiding and abetting penalty is imposed on that person with respect to the same document (¶ 2518).

2598. Injunctions Related to Tax Shelters. An injunction may be obtained with respect to the following acts: (1) promoting an abusive tax shelter (¶ 2597); (2) aiding someone in understating a tax liability in a return or other document (¶ 2518); (3) failing to furnish information about a reportable transaction (¶ 2593); or (4) failing to maintain a list of advisees (¶ 2595) (Code Sec. 7408).[106] Once a court has enjoined a person from engaging in one or more of the above activities, the court may expand the injunction to include any other activity that is subject to a penalty under tax law.

References are to Standard Federal Tax Reports; Tax Research Consultant; and Practical Tax Explanations.

[103] ¶ 37,020, ¶ 37,021; PENALTY: 3,254.10

[104] ¶ 40,095, ¶ 40,095B; PENALTY: 3,254.10

[105] ¶ 40,025; PENALTY: 3,256

[106] ¶ 41,670; PENALTY: 3,256.20

Chapter 26

WITHHOLDING ☐ ESTIMATED TAX

	Par.
WITHHOLDING	
Withholding on Wages	2601
Computation of Withholding on Wages	2612
Withholding on Non-Wage Payments	2642
FICA and FUTA Taxes	2648
Return and Payment by Employer	2650
Self-Employment Tax	2664
ESTIMATED TAX	
Payment of Estimated Taxes	2682

Withholding on Wages

2601. Withholding of Income Tax on Wages. An employer is generally required to deduct and withhold income taxes from wages actually or constructively paid to each employee (Code Sec. 3402(a); Reg. § 31.3402(a)-1).[1] Wages include all remuneration (other than fees paid to a public official) for services performed by an employee for an employer, including the cash value of all remuneration (including benefits) paid in any medium other than cash (¶ 2604). Thus, salaries, fees, bonuses, commissions on sales or insurance premiums, taxable fringe benefits, pensions, and retirement pay (unless taxed as an annuity) are subject to income tax withholding if paid as compensation for services.

The term "employer" generally means any person for whom an individual has performed any service as an employee, regardless of the nature of the service. However, if the person for whom services are performed does not have legal control over the payment of wages, then the employer is the person actually controlling the payment of the wages (Code Sec. 3401(d); Reg. § 31.3401(d)-1).[2] The services do not need to be continuing at the time the wages are paid in order for employer status to exist. An employer includes not only individuals and organizations engaged in trade or business, but also tax-exempt organizations and federal, state, and local government units, including the District of Columbia and Puerto Rico. An employer also includes any person paying wages on behalf of a nonresident alien individual, foreign partnership, or foreign corporation not engaged in trade or business within the United States or Puerto Rico.

An individual is an employee if the employer for whom the services are performed has the right to control and direct the individual not only as to the result to be accomplished by the work, but also as to the details and the means by which that result is accomplished (Code Sec. 3401(c); Reg. § 31.3401(c)-1).[3] An employee also includes any officer, employee, or elected official of a federal, state, or local government unit, as well as an officer of a corporation, but not a director. Professionals such as physicians, lawyers, contractors, and others who follow an independent trade, business, or profession in which they offer their services to the public generally are not employees. If an employer-employee relationship exists, it does not matter what the parties call it (independent contractor, agent, etc.); it also does not matter how wages are measured, or whether the employee works full or part time (¶ 2602).

An employer that is required to deduct and withhold income taxes from an employee's wages is generally liable for paying the taxes, even if the taxes are not

References are to Standard Federal Tax Reports; Tax Research Consultant; and Practical Tax Explanations.

[1] ¶ 33,542, ¶ 33,543; PAYROLL: 3,000; § 22,105.05

[2] ¶ 33,502, ¶ 33,537; PAYROLL: 3,052; § 22,105.15

[3] ¶ 33,502, ¶ 33,536; COMPEN: 3,000; § 22,005.15

withheld (Code Sec. 3403).[4] If an employer's agent pays or controls the payment of wages, both the agent and the employer are liable (Code Sec. 3504).[5] Any third party who pays wages directly to employees of an employer or to the employee's agent is liable for any required withholding on those wages (Code Sec. 3505).[6] However, effective for wages for services performed on or after January 1, 2016, a certified professional employer organization (CPEO) is treated as the sole employer of an employee performing services for a customer of the CPEO (¶ 2660).

2602. Employee v. Independent Contractor. Employees must be distinguished from independent contractors because an employer does not generally have employment tax obligations with respect to independent contractors. The IRS for many years relied on a 20-factor test to determine whether individuals are employees or independent contractors (Rev. Rul. 87-41).[7] However, it has shifted its analysis to focus on a three-part behavioral analysis—behavioral control, financial control, and relationship of the parties (IRS Pub. 15-A). A worker that may be an independent contractor under this analysis may nevertheless be treated as an employee for FICA and FUTA tax purposes if the worker is classified as a statutory employee (¶ 941B). Either an employer or employee, with or without the other's knowledge or assent, may file Form SS-8 to request that the IRS determine whether or not a particular worker is an employee.

If an employer erroneously classifies an employee as an independent contractor and has no reasonable basis for doing so, the employer is liable for taxes under the income tax withholding (¶ 2601) and FICA and FUTA tax provisions (¶ 2648 and ¶ 2649). An employer may be eligible for reduced rates with respect to income tax withholding (1.5 percent of employee's wages) and the employer's share of FICA tax (20 percent of the amount otherwise due) (Code Sec. 3509).[8] These rates are doubled if the employer failed to file forms consistent with the employer's treatment of the worker as an independent contractor. The reduced rate for FICA taxes is not available for statutory employees. If the employer had a reasonable basis for not treating an individual as an employee, the employer may be relieved of liability for employment taxes with respect to that individual if the employer has consistently treated the worker as a nonemployee (Section 530 of the Revenue Act of 1978).[9]

The IRS has established the Voluntary Classification Settlement Program to allow an eligible business to voluntarily reclassify some or all of its workers as employees for future tax periods while limiting employment tax liability for past nonemployee treatment (Announcement 2012-45, modifying Announcement 2011-64).[10] Form 8952 is used to apply for the program.

An employee who has been misclassified as an independent contractor uses Form 8919 to figure and report the employee's share of uncollected Social Security and Medicare taxes due on his or her compensation.

2604. Wages Subject to Income Tax Withholding. Wages subject to income tax withholding (¶ 2601) generally include all remuneration (other than fees paid to a public official) for services performed by an employee for an employer (Code Sec. 3401(a); Reg. § 31.3401(a)-1(a)).[11] It includes salaries, fees, bonuses, and commissions. Withholding is based on *gross* wage payments before deductions such as those for federal or state unemployment insurance, pensions (except deductible contributions to IRAs), insurance, etc., or liabilities of the employee paid by the employer. An employer is required to withhold income tax from wages paid for employment regardless of the circumstances

References are to Standard Federal Tax Reports; Tax Research Consultant; and Practical Tax Explanations.

[4] ¶ 33,591; PAYROLL: 6,252; § 22,105.15

[5] ¶ 33,720; PAYROLL: 6,254.05; § 22,105.15

[6] ¶ 33,740; PAYROLL: 6,254.10; § 22,205.25

[7] ¶ 33,538.66; COMPEN: 3,102; § 22,015.05

[8] ¶ 33,820; PAYROLL: 9,306; § 22,020.10

[9] ¶ 33,538.5056; COMPEN: 3,110; § 22,020.15

[10] ¶ 33,538.5057; COMPEN: 3,350; § 22,020.22

[11] ¶ 33,502, ¶ 33,503; PAYROLL: 3,150; § 22,110.05

under which the employee is employed or the frequency or size of the individual wage payments.[12] Tax must be withheld from wages paid for *each* payroll period.[13]

If an employee works on two jobs for the same employer, and only a part of the remuneration is wages—for example, a construction worker who also works on his employer's farm (exempt employment)—all of the remuneration is treated alike. Thus, either: (1) all of the wages are subject to withholding if more than one-half of the time is spent performing services for which wages are received; or (2) all the remuneration is excluded from wages if more than one-half of the time spent is in exempt services, provided the payroll period is no longer than 31 consecutive days (Code Sec. 3402(e); Reg. § 31.3402(e)-1).[14]

Compensation. Other forms of compensation besides salaries, fees, bonuses, and commissions are subject to withholding, including tips and other gratuities (¶ 2605), reimbursed employee expenses paid through a nonaccountable plan (¶ 2607), other supplemental wages such as fringe benefits (¶ 2606), employee expenses in excess of per diem rates (¶ 2608), and payments for the stoppage of work such as severance payments and strike benefits (Reg. § 31.3401(a)-1).[15] Some types of compensation are specifically excluded from the definition of wages for income tax withholding purposes (¶ 2609).

Supplemental unemployment compensation benefit (SUB) payments are treated as wages for income tax withholding purposes, but withholding applies only to the extent that such benefits are includible in the employee's gross income (Code Sec. 3402(o)).[16] SUB payments are also wages for FICA purposes, but may be excluded from wages for FICA (¶ 2648) and FUTA (¶ 2649) tax purposes if payable based upon state unemployment benefits (*In re Quality Stores, Inc.*, SCt, 2014-1 USTC ¶ 50,228; Rev. Rul. 90-72).[17] Guaranteed annual wage payments made during periods of unemployment under a collective bargaining agreement are wages subject to withholding.[18] However, strike benefits (other than hourly wages received for strike-related duties) paid by a union to its members are not subject to withholding.[19]

Although the value of noncash compensation generally must be included in wages, when a retail commission salesperson is occasionally paid other than in cash, the employer is not required to withhold income tax for the noncash payments (Code Sec. 3402(j); Reg. § 31.3402(j)-1).[20] However, the fair market value of the noncash payments (such as prizes) must be included on the Form W-2 furnished to the employee as part of the total pay earned during the calendar year.

Withholding is available if the payee so requests for wage continuation payments (i.e., sick pay) received from a third party under a health or accident plan in which the employer participates (Code Sec. 3402(o); Reg. § 31.3402(o)-3).[21] Payments of sick pay made directly by employers to their employees are automatically subject to withholding. Employers who are third-party payors of sick pay are not required to withhold income taxes from payments unless the employee has requested withholding on Form W-4S. Sick pay is exempt for FICA and FUTA purposes after six calendar months following the month the employee last worked for the employer (Code Secs. 3121(a)(4) and 3306(b)(4)).

Wages subject to withholding include amounts received under a nonqualified deferred compensation plan that are includible in an employee's gross income under Code Sec. 409A for the year of inclusion (¶ 2197) (Code Sec. 3401(a)).

References are to Standard Federal Tax Reports; Tax Research Consultant; and Practical Tax Explanations.

[12] ¶ 33,593.165; PAYROLL: 6,058; § 22,110.05

[13] ¶ 33,544.20; PAYROLL: 6,056; § 22,110.05

[14] ¶ 33,542, ¶ 33,551; PAYROLL: 6,058; § 22,105.10

[15] ¶ 33,503; PAYROLL: 3,150; § 22,110.05

[16] ¶ 33,542; PAYROLL: 3,178; § 22,110.40

[17] ¶ 33,506.3683; PAYROLL: 3,178; § 22,210.40, § 22,310.40

[18] ¶ 33,506.3683; PAYROLL: 3,150; § 22,110.40

[19] ¶ 33,506.3678; PAYROLL: 3,178; § 22,110.40

[20] ¶ 33,542, ¶ 33,574; PAYROLL: 6,208; § 22,105.10

[21] ¶ 33,542, ¶ 33,584; PAYROLL: 3,206; § 22,125.10

Differential Wage Payments. Differential wage payments are treated as wages for federal income tax withholding purposes (Code Sec. 3401(h)).[22] A differential wage payment is any payment that: (1) is made by an employer to an individual with respect to any period during which the individual is performing service in the uniformed services while on active duty for a period of more than 30 days, and (2) represents all or a portion of the wages the individual would have received from the employer if the individual were performing services for the employer. Differential wage payments are considered supplemental wages and subject to the special rules that apply to such payments (¶ 2606). They are not treated as wages for FICA and FUTA purposes (Rev. Rul. 2009-11).

2605. Tips and Gratuities Subject to Withholding. An employee must account for cash tips paid directly to him or her by a customer and charged tips paid over to the employee (¶ 717) in a written statement furnished to the employer on or before the 10th day of the month following the month when they are received (Code Sec. 6053(a)).[23] The employee reports the tips on Form 4070 or similar statement. If tips received in the course of his or her employment for a single employer are less than $20 in a calendar month, then the employee is not required to report the tips. The employer uses the employee's report to figure the amount of income tax to withhold for the pay period on both wages and reported tips (Code Sec. 3401(a)(16)).[24] It is also used to figure the amount of FICA and FUTA taxes to withhold for the pay period (Code Secs. 3121(a)(12) and 3306(s)). A service charge added to a bill or fixed by the employer that the customer must pay is not a tip. A payment is a tip rather than wages only if it is made free from compulsion, the amount is freely determined by the customer, the payment is not negotiated or dictated by the employer, and the customer decides who receives the payment (Rev. Rul. 2012-18).

A large food and beverage establishment (one normally with more than 10 employees on a typical business day and in which tipping is customary) must file annual information returns using Form 8027 (¶ 2565). These returns must report gross food and beverage sales receipts, employee-reported tip income, total charge receipts, and total charge tips (Code Sec. 6053(c); Reg. § 31.6053-3).[25] The employer must allocate during the payroll period among its employees who customarily receive tip income an amount equal to the excess of eight percent of gross receipts over reported tips. The allocation is not required if the employees voluntarily report total tips equal to at least eight percent of gross sales. If it can be shown that average tips are less than eight percent of gross sales, the employer or a majority of its employees may apply to the IRS to have the allocation reduced from eight percent, but not to below two percent.

2606. Supplemental Wages Subject to Withholding. Special withholding rules apply when an employee is paid supplemental wages (e.g., bonus, overtime pay, back pay, commissions, vacation allowance, taxable fringe benefits, etc.). If supplemental wages are paid at the same time as regular wages, the two are added together and income tax withholding is computed on the total as a single wage payment. If the supplemental wages are not paid at the same time as the regular wages, the supplemental wages may be added either to the regular wages for the preceding payroll period or for the current payroll period within the same calendar year (Reg. § 31.3402(g)-1).[26]

Under an alternative method, the employer may treat supplemental wages as wholly separate from regular wages, and withhold at a flat rate equal to the third lowest income tax rate (25 percent) without any allowance for exemptions or reference to any regular payment of wages. Once the total of supplemental wage payments made to an employee within a calendar year exceeds $1 million, the excess is subject to withholding at the highest income tax rate (39.6 percent). This rule applies regardless of the method otherwise used to withhold supplemental wages paid to the employee (Reg. § 31.3402(g)-1; IRS Pubs. 15 and 505).

References are to Standard Federal Tax Reports; Tax Research Consultant; and Practical Tax Explanations.

[22] ¶ 33,502; PAYROLL: 6,058; § 22,110.45

[23] ¶ 36,460; PAYROLL: 3,154; § 21,310

[24] ¶ 33,502; PAYROLL: 3,154; § 21,310, § 21,315.05, § 21,320

[25] ¶ 36,460, ¶ 36,463; PAYROLL: 3,406.05; § 21,305.20

[26] ¶ 33,561; PAYROLL: 6,066; § 22,120.50

An employer must collect both income tax and an employee's share of Social Security or railroad retirement tax on tips reported by the employee from wages due the employee or other funds that the employee makes available. Tips may be treated as if they were supplemental wages subject to the flat withholding rate (25 percent) without allowance for exemptions, provided that income tax has been withheld on the employee's regular wages. Otherwise, the tips must be treated as part of the current or preceding wage payment of the same calendar year and are subject to the regular graduated withholding rates (Rev. Rul. 66-190).[27]

2607. Employee Expense Reimbursements Subject to Withholding. An employer's withholding obligations with respect to amounts paid to employees under an expense allowance or reimbursement arrangement depend upon whether the amounts are paid under an accountable or a nonaccountable plan (¶ 943 and ¶ 952A). Amounts paid under an accountable plan may be excluded from an employee's gross income to the extent of the employee's substantiated expenses, and are not required to be reported on the employee's Form W-2. Thus, the payments are exempt from employment tax obligations (income tax withholding, FICA, FUTA, railroad retirement, and railroad unemployment taxes) (Reg. § § 1.62-2 and 31.3401(a)-4).[28] Amounts paid under a nonaccountable plan are included in the employee's gross income, reported on Form W-2, and are subject to withholding as supplemental wages (¶ 2606). If expenses are reimbursed under an accountable plan, but either the expenses are not substantiated within a reasonable time period or amounts in excess of substantiated expenses are not returned within a reasonable time period, the unsubstantiated or excess amounts are treated as paid under a nonaccountable plan and are subject to withholding no later than the first payroll period following the end of the reasonable time period.

Expense reimbursements that are subject to withholding may be added to the employee's regular wages for the appropriate payroll period, and withheld taxes may be computed on the total. Alternatively, the employer may withhold at the flat rate that applies to supplemental wages (¶ 2606) if the expense reimbursement or allowance is paid separately or is separately identified (Reg. § 31.3401(a)-4(c)).

2608. Per Diem Allowances Subject to Withholding. If the amount of an employee's business expenses are substantiated through the use of an IRS-approved per diem allowance, any amounts paid by the employer to the employee exceeding the amounts deemed substantiated are treated as paid under a nonaccountable plan (¶ 2607) and subject to income tax withholding and other employment taxes (Reg. § § 1.62-2(h)(2)(i)(B) and 31.3401(a)-4(b)(1)(ii)).[29] See ¶ 947 for standard mileage rate and FAVR allowances for automobile expenses, and see ¶ 954 for per diem methods relating to meal and lodging expenses.

For per diem or mileage allowances paid in advance, withholding on any excess must occur no later than the first payroll period following the payroll period in which the expenses paid (i.e., the days or miles of travel) are substantiated by the employee. For a per diem or mileage allowance paid as a reimbursement, the excess amounts reimbursed are subject to withholding when paid.

2609. Compensation Not Subject to Withholding. Some types of compensation are excluded from the definition of wages for income tax withholding purposes (¶ 2601). This includes amounts paid for or for the services of:

- newspaper carriers under age 18 delivering to customers;
- newspaper and magazine vendors who buy at fixed prices and retain the excess from sales to customers;
- agricultural workers who are not subject to FICA withholding;
- household employees;
- cash or noncash tips of less than $20 per month;

References are to Standard Federal Tax Reports; Tax Research Consultant; and Practical Tax Explanations.

[27] ¶ 33,506.3687; PAYROLL: 6,066, PAYROLL: 6,068; § 22,120.50

[28] ¶ 6004, ¶ 33,508A; PAYROLL: 3,168; § 22,110.45, § 22,210.45, § 22,310.45

[29] ¶ 6004, ¶ 33,508A; PAYROLL: 3,168; § 10,120.10

- certain employer contributions to IRAs and deferred compensation plans,
- individuals not working in the course of the employer's business (less than $50 paid and less than 24 days worked during the current or preceding quarter);
- employees of foreign governments and international organizations;
- armed forces personnel serving in a combat zone;
- foreign earned income if excludable from gross income; and
- members of a religious order performing services for the order or associated institution (Code Sec. 3401(a)).[30]

Fringe benefits are generally included in supplemental wages. However, certain qualified employee fringe benefits—such as no-additional-cost services, qualified employee discounts, working condition fringe benefits, *de minimis* fringe benefits, qualified transportation fringe benefits, qualified moving expense reimbursements, qualified retirement planning services, qualified military base realignment and closure fringe benefits, and certain employer-provided cell phones—are not subject to income tax withholding if it is reasonable to believe the recipient will be able to exclude them from gross income (¶ 2085) (Code Sec. 3401(a)(19); IRS Pub. 15-B).[31] Accident and health insurance premiums paid by a partnership on behalf of a partner, and premiums paid by an S corporation on behalf of a two-percent shareholder-employee, are not excludable from gross income (Rev. Rul. 91-26). Thus, they are wages subject to income tax withholding, but not for FICA and FUTA purposes (Code Secs. 3121(a)(2)(B) and 3306(b)(2)(B)).

An employer's cost of group-term life insurance, including any amount in excess of $50,000 coverage that is taxable to the employee as compensation (¶ 2055), is exempt from income tax withholding (Code Sec. 3401(a)(14); Reg. § 31.3401(a)(14)-1).[32] However, the employer must report the cost of the insurance coverage includible in the employee's gross income on Form W-2 (Reg. § 1.6052-1).[33] An employer's reimbursement of an employee's moving expenses is also exempt if it is reasonable to believe a moving expense deduction will be allowable to the employee (¶ 1073) (Code Sec. 3401(a)(15)).[34] In addition, the value of any meals or lodging excludable by the employee from gross income (¶ 2089) is exempt from income tax withholding (Reg. § 31.3401(a)-1(b)(9)).[35] See ¶ 2607 and ¶ 2608 for information concerning amounts paid to employees as advances or reimbursements for traveling, meals, etc.

Benefits provided by an employer to an employee in the form of certain educational assistance (¶ 2067), dependent care assistance (¶ 2065), fellowship or scholarship grants (¶ 865), National Health Service Corps loan repayments, employee achievement awards (¶ 2069), or qualified military benefits for dependent care assistance and for certain travel (¶ 896) are not subject to income tax withholding if it is reasonable to believe that the employee is entitled to exclude the payment from income (Code Sec. 3401(a)(18) and (19)).[36] Benefits provided by the employer in the form of medical care reimbursement made to, or for the benefit of, an employee under a self-insured medical reimbursement plan are excluded from wages for withholding purposes (¶ 2015) (Code Sec. 3401(a)(20)).[37] Benefits paid under workers' compensation laws (other than nonoccupational disability benefits) are not taxable compensation for services performed and are not subject to withholding for income, FICA, and FUTA tax purposes (Code Secs. 104, 3121(a)(2)(A), and 3306(b)(2)(A)).[38]

An employee's elective contributions to a traditional Code Sec. 401(k) retirement plan, simplified employee pension (SEP), Code Sec. 403(b) annuity plan, or SIMPLE retirement account are not included in wages for income tax withholding purposes, but

References are to Standard Federal Tax Reports; Tax Research Consultant; and Practical Tax Explanations.

[30] ¶ 33,502; PAYROLL: 3,000; § 22,110.05

[31] ¶ 33,502; PAYROLL: 3,200; § 22,110.10

[32] ¶ 33,502, ¶ 33,527; PAYROLL: 3,202; § 22,110.10

[33] ¶ 36,441; PAYROLL: 3,356.15; § 21,005.45

[34] ¶ 33,502; PAYROLL: 3,170; § 22,110.10

[35] ¶ 33,503; PAYROLL: 3,208; § 22,110.10

[36] ¶ 33,502; COMPEN: 33,350; § 22,110.10

[37] ¶ 33,502; PAYROLL: 3,206; § 22,110.10

[38] ¶ 6660; PAYROLL: 3,206; § 3,705.05

they are wages for FICA and FUTA purposes (Code Secs. 3401(a)(12), 3121(a)(5), and 3306(b)(5)).[39]

Death benefit payments to beneficiaries or to the estates of deceased employees, and payments to such persons of compensation due but unpaid at the time of the decedent's death, are not subject to withholding.[40]

Effective for stock acquired under an option exercised after October 22, 2004, withholding is not required on a disqualifying disposition of stock acquired through exercise of either an incentive stock option (¶ 1925) or through an employee stock purchase plan (ESPP) (¶ 1929) (Code Sec. 421(b)).[41] Further, no withholding is required when compensation is recognized in connection with an ESPP discount (Code Sec. 423(c)).[42]

Voluntary Withholding. If remuneration is taxable to the employee but is exempt from withholding, the employee may voluntarily request that the employer increase the amount withheld from the employee's other compensation. In many cases, the employee and employer may enter into a mutual agreement for the employer to withhold from the remuneration that would be otherwise exempt from withholding (¶ 2629).

Computation of Withholding on Wages

2612. Calculation of Income Tax Withholding. To calculate an employee's income tax withholding (¶ 2601), an employer should follow a few basic steps:

- determine the payroll period, such as weekly, biweekly, or monthly (¶ 2621);
- calculate the employee's wages for the applicable payroll period (¶ 2604);
- determine the number of the employee's allowances from his or her filled-out Form W-4 (¶ 2634); and
- choose the withholding method (¶ 2614).

Other factors to consider in the calculation include whether the employee is a recent hire or only works part-time, whether the employee has more than one employer, and whether the employee receives any supplemental wage payments (¶ 2606).

2614. Methods of Income Tax Withholding. An employer will generally elect to use one of the two major methods of computing the income tax to be withheld from wages: the percentage method (¶ 2616) or the wage bracket method (¶ 2619) (Code Sec. 3402; Reg. § 31.3402(a)-1).[43] For other permissible withholding methods, see ¶ 2627. Regardless of which method is used, the amount of withholding depends upon the amount of wages paid (¶ 2604), the number of exemptions claimed by the employee on the withholding allowance certificate (Form W-4) (¶ 2632 and ¶ 2634), the employee's marital status, and the employee's payroll period (¶ 2621) (IRS Pub. 15).

2616. Percentage Method of Income Tax Withholding. If the employer selects the percentage method of withholding (¶ 2614), the employer must:

(1) multiply the amount of one withholding exemption for the payroll period by the number of allowances claimed on the employee's Form W-4 (¶ 2634);

(2) subtract the amount determined in (1) from the employee's wages; and

(3) apply the appropriate percentage rate table to the resulting figure to determine the amount of withholding (Code Sec. 3402(b)).[44]

Each withholding exemption is equal to one personal exemption for the year (¶ 133) prorated to the payroll period (¶ 2621). Thus, for 2016, if the payroll period is monthly and the personal exemption is $4,050 (Rev. Proc. 2015-53), the amount of one withholding exemption is $4,050 divided by 12, or $337.50. In 2017, the amount of one

References are to Standard Federal Tax Reports; Tax Research Consultant; and Practical Tax Explanations.

[39] ¶ 33,502; PAYROLL: 3,300; § 22,110.20

[40] ¶ 33,506.1856; PAYROLL: 3,150; § 22,110.45

[41] ¶ 19,602; COMPEN: 21,058; § 22,110.15

[42] ¶ 19,900; COMPEN: 21,058; § 22,110.15

[43] ¶ 33,542, ¶ 33,543; PAYROLL: 6,050; § 22,120.05

[44] ¶ 33,542; PAYROLL: 6,054.05; § 22,120.10

withholding exemption is $337.50, based on a monthly payroll period and a personal exemption amount of $4,050 (Rev. Proc. 2016-55).

Percentage method withholding tables are provided for determining the amount of tax to be withheld, and each payroll period has a separate table for single individuals (including heads of household) and married individuals. The IRS has also provided alternative formula tables for percentage method withholding that are devised for computing withheld tax under different payroll systems. See IRS Pub. 15.

2619. Wage Bracket Method of Income Tax Withholding. The wage bracket method of withholding (¶ 2614) is based on the employee's marital status, pay period, and claimed exemptions. Unlike the percentage method (¶ 2616), the wage bracket method generally does not require the employer to make separate computations. Instead, the actual withholding amounts are pre-calculated in wage bracket tables covering weekly, biweekly, semimonthly, and monthly payroll periods (Code Sec. 3402(c)).[45] Separate tables for each period are provided for single individuals (including heads of household) and married individuals. The proper columns for the employer to use are determined by the total number of allowances claimed on the employee's withholding allowance certificate (¶ 2634). The wage bracket method tables produce results similar to those of the percentage method tables, and are designed to accommodate different payroll systems. If the wage bracket tables cannot be used because wages are more than the amount shown in the last bracket of the table, the employer should use the percentage method tables. See IRS Pub. 15.

2621. Payroll Period. For purposes of calculating income tax withholding (¶ 2612), the employee's payroll period, or the period of service for which a payment of wages is ordinarily made to an employee, determines the exemption amount to be used if the employer uses the percentage method (¶ 2616) or the correct table to be used if the employer uses the wage bracket method (¶ 2619). Daily, weekly, biweekly, semimonthly, monthly, quarterly, semiannual, and annual payroll periods have separate tables for the percentage computation. Any other payroll period is a miscellaneous payroll period. Wages may also be paid for periods that are not payroll periods (¶ 2624).

2624. Calculation of Income Tax Withholding Allowance. If an employee has an established payroll period (¶ 2621), the amount of the withholding allowance for the percentage method (¶ 2616) is determined by the payroll period, without regard to the time the employee is actually engaged in performing services during such period. If the payment is for a period that is not a payroll period, such as when wages are paid upon completion of a particular project, the withholding allowance under the percentage method or the amount withheld under the wage bracket method (¶ 2619) is computed based on a miscellaneous payroll period containing a number of days (including Sundays and holidays) equal to those in the period covered by the payment (Code Sec. 3402(b); Reg. § 31.3402(c)-1(c)).[46]

If the wages are paid without regard to any period, the tax to be withheld is the same as for a miscellaneous payroll period containing the number of days equal to the days (including Sundays and holidays) which have elapsed since the later of: (1) the date of the last payment of wages by the employer during the calendar year, (2) the date employment began with the employer during such year, or (3) January 1 of such year.

2627. Alternative Methods of Income Tax Withholding. An employer may withhold income taxes based on average wages (using estimated quarterly wages paid to an employee), annualized wages, cumulative wages, or any method which produces substantially the same withholding amount as the percentage method or the wage bracket method (¶ 2614) (Code Sec. 3402(h)).[47] See IRS Pub. 15-A.

2629. Voluntary Income Tax Withholding. An employee may request on Form W-4 that the employer withhold additional amounts of income from the employee's wages. An employer must comply with such a request, but only to the extent the

References are to Standard Federal Tax Reports; Tax Research Consultant; and Practical Tax Explanations.

[45] ¶ 33,542; PAYROLL: 6,054.10; § 22,120.15

[46] ¶ 33,542, ¶ 33,547; PAYROLL: 6,056; § 22,115.05

[47] ¶ 33,542; PAYROLL: 6,054; § 22,120.45

additional withholding amount does not reduce the employee's net pay (after other deductions required by law) below zero (Code Sec. 3402(i); Reg. §§31.3402(i)-1 and 31.3402(i)-2).[48]

An employee and employer may also enter into an agreement for the employer to withhold from certain types of income that are not subject to mandatory withholding (¶ 2609). For example, magazine vendors, domestic workers, etc., may enter into an agreement with their employer to have income tax withheld. To effectuate this agreement, the employee must submit Form W-4 to the employer, and the employer must begin withholding (Code Sec. 3402(p); Reg. §31.3402(p)-1).[49] Taxpayers may use Form W-4V to request voluntary withholding from certain federal payments, including Social Security benefits, crop disaster payments, Commodity Credit Corporation loans, and unemployment compensation.

2632. Claiming Withholding Exemptions and Allowances. An employee must file Form W-4 (¶ 2634) with his or her employer showing the number of exemptions from income tax withholding to which he or she is entitled (Code Sec. 3402(f); Reg. §31.3402(f)(1)-1).[50] Every employee is entitled to his or her own withholding exemption and one for each dependent (¶ 137). A married employee may claim a withholding exemption for his or her spouse if the latter does not claim one. An employee who can be claimed as a dependent on another individual's tax return, such as a parent's return, may not claim a withholding exemption for himself or herself. No withholding exemption is allowed for unborn children, even if the birth is expected to occur within the same tax year. Employees with more than one job may not claim an exemption that is currently in effect with another employer.

In order to avoid excess withholding, a standard deduction allowance equal to one withholding exemption may be claimed by an employee provided that the employee: (1) does not have a spouse who is receiving wages subject to withholding; and (2) does not have withholding certificates in effect with more than one employer. However, these restrictions do not apply if the wages earned by the spouse or by the employee from another employer are $1,500 or less, combined (Instructions to Form W-4).

Additional withholding allowances are available to an employee who can show that he or she will have large itemized deductions, deductible alimony payments, moving expenses, employee business expenses, retirement contributions, net losses from Schedules C, D, E, and F of Form 1040, or tax credits (Code Sec. 3402(m); Reg. §31.3402(m)-1).[51]

2634. Employee's Withholding Allowance Certificate (Form W-4). Before an employee is allowed any withholding exemptions (¶ 2632), he or she must file a withholding allowance certificate on Form W-4 with the employer, showing the number of exemptions to which the employee is entitled (Code Sec. 3402(f)(2); Reg. §31.3402(f)(2)-1).[52] Otherwise, withholding must be computed as if the employee were single and claiming no other exemptions. A widow or widower may claim married status for withholding purposes if he or she qualifies as a surviving spouse (¶ 175) (Code Sec. 3402(l)(3)).

An employee who certifies to the employer that he or she had no income tax liability for the preceding tax year and anticipates none for the current tax year may be exempt from the withholding rules (Code Sec. 3402(n); Reg. §31.3402(n)-1).[53] Form W-4 should be used and renewed annually by any employee claiming the exemption.

A $500 civil penalty may be assessed against any individual who decreases his or her withholding rate by claiming withholding allowances on Form W-4 without a reasonable basis (Code Sec. 6682).[54] In addition, a criminal penalty may be imposed

References are to Standard Federal Tax Reports; Tax Research Consultant; and Practical Tax Explanations.

[48] ¶ 33,542, ¶ 33,571, ¶ 33,572; PAYROLL: 6,104; §22,125.05

[49] ¶ 33,542, ¶ 33,586; PAYROLL: 6,104; §22,125.25

[50] ¶ 33,542, ¶ 33,553; PAYROLL: 6,060; §22,115.10, §22,115.15

[51] ¶ 33,542, ¶ 33,579; PAYROLL: 6,064; §22,115.15

[52] ¶ 33,542, ¶ 33,554; PAYROLL: 6,062; §22,115.25

[53] ¶ 33,542, ¶ 33,580; PAYROLL: 6,062; §22,115.20

[54] ¶ 39,845; PAYROLL: 6,062.15; §22,115.25

against any individual who willfully supplies false or fraudulent withholding information, or willfully fails to supply information that would increase the amount withheld (Code Sec. 7205).[55]

Most Forms W-4 are retained by the employer and only need to be submitted to the IRS if directed to do so. The IRS may issue a notice to the employer that specifies the maximum number of withholding exemptions a particular employee may claim. Generally, the employer is bound by this determination until otherwise advised by the IRS (Reg. § 31.3402(f)(2)-1(g)).[56]

2637. Changes to Withholding Exemptions and Allowances. An employee may file an amended withholding exemption certificate (¶ 2634) to increase the number of exemptions at any time that he or she becomes eligible for an additional dependency exemption or an extra allowance based on certain deduction and credits (¶ 2632). An employee must file a new certificate within 10 days if the number of exemptions decreases after the occurrence of any of the following events (Code Sec. 3402(f)(2)(B); Reg. § 31.3402(f)(2)-1(b)):[57]

- the employee divorces or legally separates from his or her spouse for whom the employee has been claiming an exemption, or the employee's spouse claims his or her own exemption on a separate Form W-4;
- the support of a claimed dependent is taken over by someone else, and the employee no longer expects to claim that individual as a dependent;
- the employee discovers that a dependent (other than a qualifying child) for whom an exemption was claimed will receive sufficient income of his or her own for the calendar year to disqualify that individual as a dependent (¶ 137); or
- circumstances have changed so that the employee is no longer entitled to claim an exemption based on one of the deduction or credit items.

An employee who claimed "no liability" must file a new Form W-4 within 10 days from the time the employee anticipates that he or she will incur liability for the year, or before December 1 if the employee anticipates liability for the next year (Reg. § 31.3402(f)(2)-1(c)).

The death of a spouse or dependent does not affect the withholding exemption for that year unless the employee's tax year is not a calendar year and the death occurs in that part of the calendar year preceding the employee's tax year (Reg. § 31.3402(f)(2)-1(b)(1)(ii)).[58]

A Form W-4 furnished to the employer that replaces an existing certificate can be effective for the first payment after the form is received if so elected by the employer. However, the replacement certificate must be effective for the first payroll period that ends on or after the 30th day after the day on which the new Form W-4 is furnished (Code Sec. 3402(f)(3)(B)).[59]

Withholding on Non-Wage Payments

2642. Withholding on Certain Gambling Winnings. Income tax withholding is required at a flat rate of 25 percent for winnings of more than $5,000 from sweepstakes, wagering pools, and lotteries, and other types of gambling (including pari-mutual pools with respect to horse races, dog races, and jai alai) if the winnings are at least 300 times the wager. No withholding is required on winnings from bingo, keno, or slot machines (Code Sec. 3402(q)).[60]

The payor must report gambling winnings to the taxpayer and the IRS on Form W-2G if the winnings are subject to withholding or if the winner receives: $1,200 or more from a bingo game or slot machine; $1,500 or more from keno; more than $5,000 from a poker tournament; or for other gambling winnings, $600 or more and at least 300 times

References are to Standard Federal Tax Reports; Tax Research Consultant; and Practical Tax Explanations.

[55] ¶ 41,325; PAYROLL: 6,358; § 22,115.25

[56] ¶ 33,554; PAYROLL: 6,062.10; § 22,115.25

[57] ¶ 33,542, ¶ 33,554; PAYROLL: 6,062; § 22,115.25

[58] ¶ 33,554; PAYROLL: 6,062; § 22,115.10

[59] ¶ 33,542; PAYROLL: 6,062; § 22,115.25

[60] ¶ 33,542; PAYROLL: 3,404.10; § 39,435

the amount of the wager (Temp. Reg. § 7.6041-1).[61] If reporting is required, backup withholding must occur if the winner of the reportable amount does not furnish his or her taxpayer identification number (TIN) to the payor (¶ 2645). All withheld income reported on Form W-2G must also be reported on Form 945.

2643. Withholding on Pensions, Annuities, and Certain Deferred Income. For taxable payments from an employer-sponsored pension, annuity, profit-sharing, stock bonus, or other deferred compensation plan, income tax withholding is required unless the recipient elects not to have tax withheld (Code Sec. 3405).[62] The same rule applies to an IRA or an annuity, endowment, or life insurance contract issued by a life insurance company. The recipient's election not to have withholding apply remains in effect until revoked. The payor must notify the recipient of his or her right to make or revoke such election. The election is generally not available for payments delivered outside the United States or a U.S. possession, unless the recipient certifies to the payor that he or she is not a U.S. citizen, a U.S. resident alien, or a tax-avoidance expatriate.

The amount withheld depends on whether the distributions are periodic payments or nonperiodic payments. For periodic payments (annuity and similar periodic payments), withholding is made as though the payment was a payment of wages for the appropriate payroll period. If the recipient does not have a withholding exemption certificate (Form W-4P) in effect, he or she is treated as a married individual claiming three exemptions. The exemptions are not available to a payee failing to file a certificate if the payee fails to furnish a taxpayer identification number (TIN) to a payor or if the IRS notifies the payor that the payee's TIN is incorrect.

The withholding rate on nonperiodic distributions is 10 percent. The withholding rate on distributions that were eligible for rollover but not directly transferred from the distributing plan to an eligible transferee plan is 20 percent. Withholding is mandatory, and distributees cannot elect to forego withholding on rollover eligible distributions.

2645. Backup Withholding. The backup withholding system requires a payor to deduct and withhold income tax at a flat rate of 28 percent from reportable payments, such as interest or dividends, if:

- the payee fails to furnish a correct taxpayer identification number (TIN) to the payor in the manner required;
- the IRS notifies the payor that the TIN furnished by the payee is incorrect;
- the IRS notifies the payor that the payee has underreported reportable payments; or
- the payee is required, but fails, to certify that he or she is not subject to withholding (Code Sec. 3406).[63]

Backup withholding is reported on Form 945.

FICA and FUTA Taxes

2648. FICA Tax. Under the Federal Insurance Contributions Act (FICA), an employer is required to withhold an employee's share of Social Security and Medicare taxes from FICA wages paid to the employee during the year, and to pay a matching amount as the employer's share of these taxes (Code Secs. 3101, 3111, and 3121(a)).[64] Even if an employee claims exemption from income tax withholding, the employer must withhold FICA taxes. The employer is required to report FICA taxes withheld (¶ 2650) and to deposit the amounts paid and withheld (¶ 2651).

FICA Tax Rate and Base. The employee and employer are each subject to a tax rate of 7.65 percent of wages paid for FICA purposes, consisting of a 6.2-percent rate for old-age, survivors, and disability insurance (OASDI) (i.e., Social Security) and a 1.45-percent rate for hospital insurance (HI) (i.e., Medicare). The Social Security tax rate applies only

References are to Standard Federal Tax Reports; Tax Research Consultant; and Practical Tax Explanations.

[61] ¶ 35,835; PAYROLL: 3,404.10; § 39,435

[62] ¶ 33,620; RETIRE: 42,700; § 22,140

[63] ¶ 33,640; FILEBUS: 18,150; § 39,401

[64] ¶ 114; PAYROLL: 9,050; § 22,201

to wages paid up to the Social Security wage base limit for the year ($118,500 in 2016; $127,200 in 2017). The wage base applies separately to each common-law employer, with exceptions for successor employers and common paymasters, as well as certain motion picture project employers (Code Sec. 3512, as added by the Protecting Americans from Tax Hikes (PATH) Act of 2015 (P.L. 114-113)). There is no limit on wages subject to the Medicare tax.

Additional 0.9% Medicare Tax. The employee's portion of the Medicare component of FICA taxes is increased by an additional 0.9 percent (to 2.35 percent) for wages in excess of $200,000 ($250,000 in the case of a joint return, $125,000 in the case of a married taxpayer filing separately). For a joint return, the additional tax is imposed on the couple's combined wages (Code Sec. 3101(b)(2); Reg. § 31.3102-4).

Although the employer is generally required to withhold the employee's portion from the employee's wages, the employer is not obligated to withhold the additional Medicare tax unless (and until) the employee receives wages from the employer in excess of $200,000. For this purpose, the employer is permitted to disregard the amount of wages received by the employee's spouse. Thus, because an employee may receive wages from more than one employer, or because the employee's spouse may receive wages, an employee may be subject to the additional Medicare tax without the tax being withheld from the employee's wages. The employee is responsible for any portion of the additional 0.9-percent tax that is not withheld.

If an employer fails to withhold the additional Medicare tax and the employee pays it, the employer is not obligated to pay the tax but may be subject to penalties and additions to tax for failing to withhold (Code Sec. 3102(f)). If the tax is overwithheld, the employee may claim a credit against income tax. The employee takes any underwithheld or overwithheld amount into account in calculating the tax on Form 8959, which must be attached to his or her tax return for the year.

Multiple Employers. If an individual works for more than one employer, each employer must withhold and pay FICA taxes on the wages paid. In such instances, the employee's FICA tax withheld for the year might exceed the maximum employee portion of the tax for the year. If this happens, the employee must take the excess as a credit against income tax liability. If the employee is not required to file an income tax return, then he or she may file a special refund claim (¶ 1321) (Reg. §§ 1.31-2 and 31.6413(c)-1). The same rule applies to taxes withheld under the Railroad Retirement Tax Act.

If an individual is concurrently employed by two or more related corporations and all remuneration is disbursed to the individual through a common paymaster for the group, the common paymaster is responsible for the reporting and payment of FICA and FUTA taxes. However, the other related corporations remain jointly and severally liable for their appropriate share of the taxes (Reg. § 31.3121(s)-1).

FICA Wages. Wages for FICA tax purposes generally has the same meaning as for income tax withholding, and includes all remuneration for services performed by an employee for the employer with certain exceptions (¶ 2604). In the case of employees performing domestic services in a private home of the employer or performing agricultural labor, if the employer pays the employee's liability for FICA taxes or state unemployment taxes without deduction from the employee's wages, those payments are not wages for FICA purposes (Code Sec. 3121(a)(6)). Other special rules apply to domestic workers (¶ 2652).

2649. FUTA Tax. The Federal Unemployment Tax Act (FUTA) imposes a tax on employers: (1) who employed one or more individuals in covered employment (10 or more individuals for agricultural labor) for at least part of one day in any 20 or more different weeks during the current or preceding calendar year; or (2) who paid wages (in covered employment) of at least $1,500 ($20,000 for agricultural labor, $1,000 for household employees) in any calendar quarter in the current or preceding calendar year. The tax rate is 6 percent, but the employer is allowed a partial credit against the tax based on its state unemployment insurance tax liability (Code Secs. 3301 and 3302).[65] The tax rate applies only to first $7,000 of wages paid to each employee in the calendar year. The wage base applies separately to each common-law employer, with exceptions for successor employers and common paymasters, as well as certain motion picture project employers (Code Sec. 3512, as added by the Protecting Americans from Tax Hikes (PATH) Act of 2015 (P.L. 114-113)).

FUTA Wages. Wages for FUTA tax purposes generally has the same meaning as for income tax withholding, and includes all remuneration for services performed by an employee for the employer with certain exceptions (¶ 2604). In the case of employees performing domestic services in a private home of the employer or performing agricultural labor, if the employer pays the employee's liability for FICA taxes or state unemployment taxes without deducting those taxes from the employee's wages, the amounts paid by the employer are not wages for FUTA purposes (Code Sec. 3306(b)(6)). Other special rules apply to domestic workers (¶ 2652).

Return and Payment by Employer

2650. Employer Returns for Employment Taxes. An employer who is required to withhold federal income tax on wages (¶ 2601) or pays wages subject to FICA taxes (¶ 2648) generally must file a quarterly return on Form 941 (Reg. § 31.6011(a)-1; Reg. § 31.6011(a)-4).[66] The employer uses the form to report wages paid, tips employees have received, federal income tax withheld, both the employer's and the employee's share of FICA taxes, the additional Medicare tax withheld, and any adjustments to FICA taxes for sick pay, tips, and group-term life insurance. Small employers with an estimated annual employment tax liability of $1,000 or less may report employment taxes annually using Form 944 (discussed later). Taxes on wages for agricultural employees, including domestic services on a farm operated for profit, are reported annually on Form 943. Nonpayroll items, such as pension and annuity payments (¶ 2643), are reported annually on Form 945. Employers who must pay FUTA tax (¶ 2649) generally must file an annual return using Form 940.

Form 941 is due on or before the last day of the month following the quarter involved. Forms 940, 943, 944, and 945 are all due January 31 of the year following the calendar year for which the return is made. For all of these forms, including Form 941, an extension of time for filing is automatically granted to the 10th day of the second month following the close of the calendar quarter if the return is accompanied by receipts showing timely deposits in full payment of taxes due for the period (Reg. § 31.6071(a)-1).[67]

Forms W-2 and W-3 must be filed with the Social Security Administration (SSA) by January 31 of the year following the year included in the return, whether filed electronically or on paper (Code Sec. 6071(c), as added by the Protecting Americans from Tax Hikes Act of 2015 (P.L. 114-113)).[68] The SSA transmits the income tax information on the return to the IRS. Forms W-2 and W-3 related to calendar years before 2016 were required to be filed with the SSA by the last day of February of the year following the year included in the return (March 31 if filed electronically) (Reg. § 31.6071(a)-1).[69]

Form 944 Program. The Form 944 Program allows certain small employers to file an annual Form 944 rather than quarterly on Form 941. Form 944 is generally due January 31 of the year following the year for which the return is filed (Reg. § § 31.6011(a)-1(a)(5) and 31.6011(a)-4(a)(4)).[70]

Eligibility for the Form 944 Program is limited to employers with an annual estimated employment tax liability of $1,000 or less, who are notified in writing by the IRS that they must file Form 944. An employer that believes it is qualified for the program can contact the IRS to express its desire to file Form 944 instead of Form 941,

References are to Standard Federal Tax Reports; Tax Research Consultant; and Practical Tax Explanations.

[65] ¶ 114; PAYROLL: 9,100; § 22,301

[66] ¶ 35,131; PAYROLL: 3,352; § 22,130.05, § 22,235.05

[67] ¶ 36,702; PAYROLL: 6,202; § 22,130.05, § 22,235.05, § 22,340.05

[68] ¶ 36,700; PAYROLL: 3,354.05; § 22,405.10

[69] ¶ 36,702; PAYROLL: 3,354.05; § 22,405.10

[70] ¶ 35,131; PAYROLL: 3,352.15; § 22,130.15, § 22,235.15

but cannot file Form 944 unless it receives written notice from the IRS that it is eligible to do so (Rev. Proc. 2009-51). Employers may opt out of filing Form 944 for any reason by calling or writing the IRS before the applicable due date.

Most participating employers can pay their employment taxes annually with their Form 944, rather than making monthly or semiweekly deposits (¶ 2651). A participating employer, however, may not discover that its actual annual employment tax liability exceeded the $1,000 threshold until it files its Form 944 on the following January 31. These employers can avoid the penalty for failing to make a timely monthly deposit of their January taxes, so long as they fully pay their January employment taxes by March 15 (Reg. § 31.6302-1).[71]

A modified lookback period applies for determining whether a participating employer that eventually discovers that it is not eligible for the Form 944 Program is a monthly or semiweekly depositor. For those employers, the lookback period is the second calendar year preceding the current calendar year. For instance, the lookback period for 2017 is calendar year 2015 (Reg. § 31.6302-1(b)(4)).

An employer in the Form 944 Program whose actual total employment tax liability exceeds the $1,000 threshold but whose employment tax liability for a quarter is less than $2,500 is eligible for the *de minimis* deposit rules that apply to quarterly Form 941 filers (¶ 2651). The employer is allowed to apply the *de minimis* rules if it deposits the employment taxes that accumulated during a quarter by the last day of the month following the close of the quarter. If an employer's tax liability for a quarter does not qualify for *de minimis* treatment, the employer must make deposits either monthly or semiweekly, whichever is appropriate, in order to avoid the failure-to-deposit penalty (¶ 2658).

2651. Employer Deposit of Withheld Taxes. An employer generally must deposit withheld income taxes (¶ 2601) and FICA taxes (¶ 2648) on either a monthly or semiweekly basis. An employer's status as a monthly or semiweekly depositor for a given calendar year is determined based on the employer's employment tax reporting history during a lookback period. An employer must also deposit FUTA taxes quarterly (¶ 2649). All employers are required to make deposits by electronic funds transfer (EFT) using the Electronic Federal Tax Payment System (EFTPS) unless the IRS authorizes an exemption, such as for a small business that would suffer a hardship if required to make EFT deposits (Reg. § 31.6302-1).[72] A deposit of taxes by EFT is deemed made when the amount is withdrawn from the employer's account. Employers that fail to deposit the full amount of taxes in a timely manner or fail to use EFT will be subject to penalties (¶ 2658).

Depositing Income Taxes and FICA Taxes. For calendar year 2017, an employer generally must deposit withheld income and FICA taxes on a monthly basis during the 12-month lookback period from July 1, 2015, through June 30, 2016, if the amount of the aggregate employment taxes reported was $50,000 or less. For new employers, during the first calendar year of business, the tax liability for each quarter of the lookback period is considered to be zero. Therefore, the employer is a monthly depositor for the first calendar year of business. Monthly depositors are required to deposit each month's taxes on or before the 15th day of the following month. If the 15th day is a Saturday, Sunday, or legal holiday in the District of Columbia (¶ 2549), the employer has until the next succeeding business day to make the deposit.

An employer that reported more than $50,000 in aggregate employment taxes during the lookback period from July 1, 2015, through June 30, 2016, will be a semiweekly depositor for calendar year 2017. Semiweekly depositors generally are required to deposit their taxes by the Wednesday after payday, if the payday falls on a Wednesday, Thursday, or Friday. For all other paydays, the deposit is due by the Friday following payday. Semiweekly depositors always have at least three business days after the payday to make the deposit.

References are to Standard Federal Tax Reports; Tax Research Consultant; and Practical Tax Explanations.

[71] ¶ 38,055B; PAYROLL: 3,352.15; § 22,130.15, § 22,235.15

[72] ¶ 38,055B; PAYROLL: 6,106; § 22,135.05, § 22,240.05, § 22,345.05

For agricultural employers filing Form 943, the lookback period used to determine monthly or semiweekly depositing status is the second calendar year preceding the current calendar year. For example, the lookback period for calendar year 2017 is calendar year 2015.

Notwithstanding these general requirements, under the one-day rule, employers with $100,000 or more of accumulated liability during a monthly or semiweekly period are required to deposit the funds by the next day that is not a Saturday, Sunday, or legal holiday in the District of Columbia. Monthly depositors subject to the one-day rule must switch to making deposits semiweekly.

As a safe harbor, employers that fail to deposit the full amount of employment taxes will not be penalized (¶ 2658) if the shortfall does not exceed the greater of $100 or two percent of the amount of taxes required to be deposited, provided that the shortfall is deposited on or before a prescribed makeup date. For a monthly depositor, the makeup date is the due date of the return for the period in which the shortfall occurred. For a semiweekly depositor, the makeup date is the earlier of the due date of the return for the period of the shortfall, or the first Wednesday or Friday (whichever comes first) that falls on or after the 15th of the month following the month in which the shortfall occurred. Penalties may also be abated if an employer shows that a failure to deposit the full amount of taxes was due to reasonable cause.

Amounts withheld under the backup withholding requirements (¶ 2645) are treated as employment taxes subject to the deposit rules. Employers are permitted to treat the backup withholding amounts separately from other employment taxes for purposes of the deposit rules (Reg. § 31.6302-3).[73] Different monthly and semimonthly deposit requirements apply to taxes withheld from nonresident aliens and foreign corporations (Reg. § 1.6302-2).[74]

Depositing FUTA Taxes. Although Form 940 is an annual return, an employer generally must deposit FUTA taxes quarterly. For deposit purposes, the employer determines the FUTA tax for each of the first three calendar quarters by multiplying the amount of wages paid during the quarter by 0.006. If at the end of the quarter the employer owes, but has not yet deposited, more than $500 in FUTA tax for the year, the employer must make a deposit by the last day of the month following the end of the quarter (Reg. § 31.6302(c)-3(a)(1)). For example, for the quarter ending March 31, deposits of FUTA are due by April 30. If the last day of the month is a Saturday, Sunday, or legal holiday in the District of Columbia, the employer has until the next succeeding business day which is not a Saturday, Sunday, or legal holiday to make the deposit.

De Minimis Exceptions. Two *de minimis* rules allow small employers to make payments with Form 941 or Form 943 rather than make deposits (Reg. § 31.6302-1(f)(4)).[75] First, deposits are not required if the employer's accumulated employment taxes for the current quarter are less than $2,500. Secondly, deposits are not required if the total accumulated employment taxes for the preceding quarter were less than $2,500 and the one-day rule does not require a deposit at the close of the next business day. An additional exception to the deposit requirement exists for employers in the Form 944 Program (¶ 2650).

2652. Household Employees (Nanny Tax). An employer generally must withhold and pay FICA taxes (¶ 2648) for a household employee only if the employer has paid the employee cash wages during the calendar year at least equal to the threshold amount for that year ($2,000 in 2016; $2,000 in 2017) (Code Sec. 3121(a)(7)(B) and (x)).[76] An employer must pay FUTA taxes for a household employee if the employer has paid aggregate cash wages of $1,000 or more to the employee in a calendar quarter (Code Sec. 3306(c)(2)).[77]

An employer must report and pay required employment taxes for household employees on Schedule H of the employer's Form 1040 or Form 1040A. While withheld

References are to Standard Federal Tax Reports; Tax Research Consultant; and Practical Tax Explanations.

[73] ¶ 38,055D; PAYROLL: 6,106; § 39,405.15

[74] ¶ 38,062; PAYROLL: 6,106, PAYROLL: 9,200; § 37,335

[75] ¶ 38,055B; PAYROLL: 6,106.05; § 22,240.05

[76] ¶ 114; PAYROLL: 3,358; § 22,235.30

[77] ¶ 114; PAYROLL: 3,106; § 22,340.20

amounts do not have to be deposited on a monthly basis, the employer does need an employer identification number (EIN) to include on the employee's Form W-2 (¶ 2655) and the employer's Schedule H. To obtain an EIN, an employer should complete Form SS-4.

An employer must increase either his or her quarterly estimated tax payments or the income tax withholding on his or her own wages in order to satisfy employment tax obligations with respect to household employees. Failure to withhold results in liability for the penalty for underpayment of estimated tax (¶ 2682).

2654. Withholding for Disregarded Entities. A disregarded entity (¶ 402A) is treated as a separate entity responsible for employment tax liabilities (Reg. § 301.7701-2(c)(2)(iv)).[78] Thus, a an otherwise disregarded entity is liable for employment taxes on wages paid to its employees and responsible for other employment tax obligations, such as making timely tax deposits, filing returns, and providing Forms W-2 to employees. This rule applies to disregarded entities such as a qualified subchapter S subsidiary (QSub) and a single-member limited liability company (LLC). The entity continues to be disregarded for other federal tax purposes, including self-employment taxes (¶ 2667) for which the owner of the entity is personally liable.

2655. Employee Wage Statements (Form W-2). On or before January 31, an employer is required to furnish an employee with copies of Form W-2 for income taxes and FICA taxes withheld from the employee's wages during the preceding calendar year. With the employee's consent, the employer may elect to furnish an electronic payee statement of Form W-2, rather than a paper statement (Code Sec. 6051(a); Reg. § 31.6051-1).[79] When employment terminates before the end of the calendar year, there is no reasonable expectation of reemployment, and the employee submits a written request for the information, Form W-2 must be furnished within 30 days of the written request if the 30-day period ends before January 31.

Form W-2 is a multiple-part wage statement with several copies: Copy A is sent to the Social Security Administration (SSA), Copy 1 is sent to the state where the employee resides, Copy B is kept by the employee and attached to his or her federal tax return, Copy C is retained for the employee's records, Copy 2 is attached to the employee's state, city, or local tax return, and Copy D is kept in the employer's records. Employers must file electronically with the SSA if 250 or more Forms W-2 are to be filed. Hardship waivers may be requested (Reg. § 301.6011-2(c)).[80]

If FICA taxes imposed on tips reported by the employee exceeds the tax that has been collected by the employer, the employer is required to furnish the employee with a statement showing the amount of the excess (Code Sec. 6053(b)).[81]

Effective December 18, 2015, the use of a truncated Social Security number (or truncated tax identification number) is permitted on Form W-2 (Code Sec. 6051(a)(2), as amended by the Protecting Americans from Tax Hikes Act of 2015 (P.L. 114-113)).[82]

2658. Employment Tax Penalty for Employers. An employer is primarily liable for deducting and paying employment taxes whether or not the taxes are actually collected from the employee (¶ 2601). The employer may be subject to civil and criminal penalties for failing to deduct and withhold employment taxes. For example, any responsible person—typically a corporate officer or employee—who willfully fails to withhold, account for, or pay over any tax to the government is subject to a penalty equal to 100 percent of such tax, a $10,000 criminal fine, and up to five years imprisonment (Code Secs. 6672 and 7202).[83] The civil penalty is a collection device, usually assessed only when the tax cannot be collected from the employer, and results in a personal liability not dischargeable by bankruptcy. Civil and criminal penalties can also be imposed if an

References are to Standard Federal Tax Reports; Tax Research Consultant; and Practical Tax Explanations.

[78] ¶ 43,082; PAYROLL: 9,162; § 31,405.10

[79] ¶ 36,420, ¶ 36,421; PAYROLL: 6,204; § 22,415.05

[80] ¶ 35,125; FILEBUS: 12,302; § 22,405.05

[81] ¶ 36,460; PAYROLL: 3,406.30; § 21,305.15

[82] ¶ 36,425.01; PAYROLL: 3,356.05; § 22,401.

[83] ¶ 39,775, ¶ 41,310; PAYROLL: 6,300; § 40,315.05

employer willfully fails to furnish, or furnishes a false or fraudulent, Form W-2 statement (¶ 2655) to an employee (Code Secs. 6674 and 7204).[84]

Failure to Make Timely Deposits. A graduated penalty applies to failures to make timely deposits of tax (¶ 2651), unless the failure is due to reasonable cause and not willful neglect (Code Sec. 6656).[85] The penalty amount varies with the length of time within which the taxpayer corrects the failure to make the required deposit. The penalty is assessed as follows:

- two percent of the underpayment amount if the failure is for not more than five days;
- five percent of the underpayment amount if the failure is for more than five days but not more than 15 days; and
- 10 percent of the underpayment amount if the failure is for more than 15 days.

The penalty imposed is 15 percent of the underpayment amount if a required tax deposit is not made on or before the earlier of (1) the day that is 10 days after the date of the first delinquency notice to the taxpayer, or (2) the day on which notice and demand for immediate payment of tax is given in cases of jeopardy. A failure to deposit includes a failure to make deposits electronically when required to do so (¶ 2651).

Deposits generally are applied to the most recent tax liability within the quarter. Any depositor to whom the IRS mails a penalty notice may, within 90 days of the date of the notice, designate how the payment is to be applied in order to minimize the amount of the penalty.

2660. Certified Professional Employer Organizations. Employers sometimes contract with professional employer organizations (PEOs), also called employee-leasing organizations, to help the employer lower health and worker's compensation insurance costs or to provide other employee benefits. They also complete and file returns, and pay and withhold employment taxes with respect to wages paid to employees. Under an employee-leasing arrangement, a PEO provides payroll, worker's compensation, human resources, and employee benefits administration to customer-employers. The PEO essentially becomes the workers' employer for tax and insurance purposes, while the lessee-employer retains control of the workers' day-to-day activities.

Effective for wages for services performed on or after January 1, 2016, a *certified* professional employer organization (CPEO) is treated as the sole employer of a work-site employee performing services for a customer of the CPEO with respect to remuneration paid to the employee. A CPEO is a legal entity that is certified by the IRS as meeting certain requirements (Code Secs. 3511 and 7705).[86] For the CPEO to qualify as the sole employer of a particular individual, at least 85 percent of the individuals performing services for the CPEO's customer at the work site at which the individual works must be employed under contract with the CPEO (Code Sec. 7705(e)(3)).

A CPEO is considered the employer with respect to remuneration remitted to an individual (other than a work-site employee or individual with net earnings from self-employment derived from the trade or business of the CPEO's customer) who is performing services covered by a contract meeting the service contract requirements for purposes of liability for the CPEO's employment tax and other obligations under Subtitle C (Employment Taxes) of the Code. The exceptions, exclusions, definitions, and other rules that are based on type of employer and that would otherwise apply to the taxes imposed on the individual's remuneration still apply to the remuneration (Code Sec. 3511(c)).

User fee. A annual fee of no more than $1,000 per year may be imposed on a CPEO in connection with the certification program (Code Sec. 7528(b)(4)).[87]

References are to Standard Federal Tax Reports; Tax Research Consultant; and Practical Tax Explanations.

[84] ¶ 39,795, ¶ 41,320; PAYROLL: 6,350; § 40,325.25

[85] ¶ 39,580; PAYROLL: 6,106; § 40,315.15

[86] ¶ 33,860, ¶ 43,200; PAYROLL: 3,058; § 22,501

[87] ¶ 42,816U; PAYROLL: 3,058

Voluntary Certification Program. The IRS is required to establish a voluntary certification program for CPEOs (Code Sec. 7705(h); Act Sec. 206(h) of the Stephen Beck, Jr., Achieving a Better Life Experience Act of 2014 (P.L. 113-295)). As part of the certification process, the IRS will (1) complete background, credit, and tax compliance checks; (2) verify that the CPEO has an active and approved surety bond; (3) verify that the CPEO satisfies the service agreement and financial review requirements; (4) collect a user fee; and (5) provide public disclosure of CPEOs and of any person whose certification has been suspended or revoked. To qualify for and maintain IRS certification, CPEOs will need to adhere to bonding and independent financial review requirements, and observe ongoing reporting and recordkeeping responsibilities. Certification is not intended to create any inference in determining who is an employee or employer for federal tax purposes (Code Sec. 7705(g)).

The Treasury and IRS have issued proposed regulations that taxpayers can rely on for guidance on a CPEO's federal employment tax liabilities and other obligations under Code Sec. 3511, as well as temporary regulations that contain the requirements a person must satisfy in order to become and remain a CPEO (Prop. Reg. §§31.3511-1 and 301.7705-1; Temp. Reg. §§301.7705-1T and 301.7705-2T).[88] The IRS also has provided detailed procedures for applying to become a CPEO, and interim guidance that modifies and clarifies certain application requirements (Rev. Proc. 2016-33; Notice 2016-49). The IRS began accepting online CPEO applications in July 2016.

Self-Employment Tax

2664. Self-Employment Tax Rate. Every taxpayer who has self-employment income (¶ 2667 and ¶ 2670) for a tax year must pay a self-employment tax in addition to any other applicable taxes. The combined rate of tax on self-employment income generally is 15.3 percent, consisting of a 12.4-percent component for Social Security (old-age, survivors, and disability insurance (OASDI)) and a 2.9-percent component for Medicare (hospital insurance (HI)) (Code Sec. 1401).[89]

If net earnings from self-employment are less than $400, no self-employment tax is payable. The amount of self-employment income subject to the Social Security tax rate in a tax year is limited to the amount of the Social Security wage base for the year ($118,500 for 2016; $127,200 for 2017). If the taxpayer receives wages subject to FICA or railroad retirement tax during the year, the Social Security wage base is reduced by the amount of wages on which these taxes were paid (Code Sec. 1402(b)).[90] There is no cap on self-employment income subject to the Medicare tax.

Additional 0.9% Medicare Tax. The Medicare portion of the self-employment tax rate is increased by an additional 0.9 percent (to 3.8 percent) for self-employment income in excess of $200,000 ($250,000 in the case of a joint return, $125,000 in the case of a married taxpayer filing separately). In the case of a joint return, the additional tax is imposed on the combined self-employment income of the taxpayer and his or her spouse. If a taxpayer, or a taxpayer and his or her spouse, receives both self-employment income and wages which may be subject to the additional Medicare tax that applies for FICA purposes (¶ 2648), then the threshold amount for determining the additional Medicare tax for self-employment purposes is reduced by the taxpayer's wages, but not below zero (Code Sec. 1401(b)(2); Reg. §1.1401-1(d)).[91]

Under these rules, a taxpayer's self-employment tax rate is 15.3 percent (12.4 percent + 2.9 percent) of the taxpayer's self-employment income up to the Social Security wage base in effect for the year, 2.9 percent of self-employment income above the Social Security wage base not in excess of the threshold amount for the additional 0.9-percent tax, and 3.8 percent (2.9 percent + 0.9 percent) of any self-employment income above that threshold amount.

References are to Standard Federal Tax Reports; Tax Research Consultant; and Practical Tax Explanations.

[88] ¶ 33,862, ¶ 43,201B, ¶ 43,202, ¶ 43,204; PAYROLL: 3,058; § 22,501

[89] ¶ 32,541; INDIV: 63,060; § 23,105

[90] ¶ 32,560; INDIV: 63,050; § 23,110.10

[91] ¶ 32,541, ¶ 32,542; INDIV: 69,100; § 23,105

Example: Carl, a single filer, has $130,000 in wages and $145,000 in self-employment income. Carl's wages are not in excess of the $200,000 threshold for single filers, so he is not liable for the additional Medicare tax on these wages for FICA purposes. Before calculating the additional Medicare tax on self-employment income, the $200,000 threshold for single filers is reduced by Carl's $130,000 in wages, resulting in a reduced self-employment income threshold of $70,000. Carl is liable to pay the additional Medicare tax on $75,000 of self-employment income ($145,000 minus $70,000).

Reporting Requirements. The self-employment tax is computed on Schedule SE of Form 1040, is treated as part of the taxpayer's income tax liability, and must be taken into account for purposes of the estimated tax (¶ 2682). A married couple filing a joint return must file separate Schedules SE if each spouse is self-employed. Taxpayers subject to the additional Medicare tax must complete Form 8959 and attach it to their return.

2667. Persons Subject to Self-Employment Tax. An individual who is self-employed is subject to a self-employment tax (¶ 2664) if he or she earns $433.13 or more of self-employment income in a year (¶ 2670). An individual is generally self-employed if he or she carries on a trade or business as a sole proprietor or independent contractor (¶ 2602), or is a member of a partnership that carries on a trade or business (Code Sec. 1402(c)).[92] A trade or business does not include the performance of services by an individual as an employee, but certain employee services are treated as a trade or business and are therefore subject to self-employment tax.

Members of religious orders who have taken vows of poverty are not subject to self-employment tax when they perform duties connected with their religious order (Code Sec. 1402(c)(4) and (5)).[93] Also, a duly ordained, commissioned, or licensed minister of a church, a member of a religious order (who has not taken a vow of poverty), or a Christian Science practitioner may elect not to be covered by Social Security by filing an exemption certificate on Form 4361 indicating that he or she is opposed by conscience or religious principle to the acceptance of any public insurance. The statement must include a declaration that the individual has informed the ordaining, commissioning, or licensing body of the church of the individual's opposition to such insurance. A qualified individual must apply for the exemption on or before the due date of the income tax return for the second tax year for which the individual had net earnings from self-employment of $400 or more from religious activities (Code Sec. 1402(e)). An individual who has conscientious objections to accepting private or public insurance by reason of an adherence to established tenets or teachings of a religious sect of which he or she is a member may also be exempt from the self-employment tax (Code Sec. 1402(g)).

Services performed by employees for a church or church-controlled organization may be excluded from Social Security coverage if the church or organization makes a valid election under Code Sec. 3121(w) to be exempt from the employer portion of FICA taxes. However, the employees remain liable for FICA or self-employment tax on remuneration paid for such services unless the remuneration is less than $100 per year (Code Sec. 1402(a)(14) and (j)).[94]

A U.S. citizen who works for an employer that is exempt from the Social Security tax because it is either a foreign government or instrumentality, or an international organization, is treated as self-employed (Code Sec. 1402(c)(2)).[95] Nonresident aliens are not subject to self-employment tax, but the tax may apply to a resident of Puerto Rico, the Virgin Islands, Guam, the Commonwealth of the Northern Mariana Islands, or American Samoa who is not a citizen of the United States (Code Sec. 1402(b); IRS Pub. 334).[96]

References are to Standard Federal Tax Reports; Tax Research Consultant; and Practical Tax Explanations.

[92] ¶ 32,560; INDIV: 63,300; § 23,001

[93] ¶ 32,560; INDIV: 63,400; § 23,501

[94] ¶ 32,560; INDIV: 63,308; § 23,045.10

[95] ¶ 32,560; INDIV: 63,154; § 23,045.10

[96] ¶ 32,560; INDIV: 63,302; § 23,110.20

2670. Self-Employment Income. The self-employment tax (¶ 2664) is imposed on self-employment income derived by an individual during the tax year. Self-employment income is generally defined as net earnings from self-employment which consists of: (1) the gross income derived from any trade or business, less allowable deductions attributable to the trade or business, and (2) the taxpayer's distributive share of the ordinary income or loss of a partnership engaged in a trade or business (Code Sec. 1402(b); Reg. § 1.1402(a)-1).[97] A trade or business does not include services performed as an employee other than services relating to certain newspaper and magazine sales, sharing of crops, foreign organizations, and sharing of fishing catches (Code Sec. 1402(c)(2)).[98]

There are special rules for computing net earnings from self-employment, including a special optional method for nonfarm self-employment (¶ 2673) (Code Sec. 1402(a)).[99] Rents from real estate and from personal property leased with the real estate, and the attributable deductions, are also excluded from net earnings from self-employment unless received by the individual in the course of his or her business as a real estate dealer. Rental real estate income that is otherwise excludable does not become self-employment income merely because it is held in a qualified joint venture (¶ 402) (CCA 200816030). Authorities are split, however, on whether Conservation Reserve Program (CRP) payments from the federal government to a nonfarmer are excludible from net earnings from self-employment as rental income from real estate (¶ 2676).[100]

Dividends and interest from any bond, debenture, note, certificate or other evidence of indebtedness issued with interest coupons or in registered form by any corporation are excluded from net earnings from self-employment income unless received by a dealer in stocks and securities in the course of his or her business (Code Sec. 1402(a)(2)). Other interest received in the course of any trade or business is not excluded. Gain or loss from the sale or exchange of property that is not stock in trade or held primarily for sale is excluded, as is gain or loss from the sale or exchange of a capital asset (Code Sec. 1402(a)(3)).

Termination payments received by former insurance salespersons are excludable from net earnings from self-employment if the amount is received after the termination of the individual's agreement to perform services for the company and the individual performs no services for the company after the termination and before the close of the tax year. In addition, the payment must be conditioned upon the salesperson agreeing not to compete with the company for at least one year following termination. The payment also must depend primarily on policies sold by or credited to the individual during the last year of the agreement and/or the extent to which the policies remain in force for some period after the termination, and must not depend on the length of service or overall earnings from services performed for the company (Code Sec. 1402(k)).[101]

Even though the rental value of a parsonage (¶ 875) and the value of meals and lodging furnished for the convenience of the employer (¶ 2089) are not included in a minister's gross income for income tax purposes, they are taken into account in calculating net earnings from self-employment (Code Sec. 1402(a)(8)).[102] The same is true of amounts excluded from gross income as foreign earned income (¶ 2402). However, self-employment income does not include a minister's retirement benefits received from a church plan or the rental value of a parsonage allowance, as long as each was furnished after the date of retirement.

One business deduction that cannot be taken in calculating net earnings from self-employment for the tax year is the deduction allowed for self-employment tax paid during the year (¶ 923). However, the law provides a substitute for that deduction. This is an amount determined by multiplying net earnings from self-employment (calculated without regard to the substitute deduction) by one-half of the self-employment tax rate

References are to Standard Federal Tax Reports; Tax Research Consultant; and Practical Tax Explanations.

[97] ¶ 32,560, ¶ 32,561; INDIV: 63,100; § 23,205

[98] ¶ 32,560; INDIV: 63,154; § 23,045.10

[99] ¶ 32,560; INDIV: 63,050; § 23,210.05

[100] ¶ 32,578.280; INDIV: 63,102.30; § 23,405.10

[101] ¶ 32,560; INDIV: 63,100; § 23,210.25

[102] ¶ 32,560; INDIV: 63,402; § 23,505.05

(¶ 2664) (Code Sec. 1402(a)(12)).[103] Thus, the deduction equals 7.65 percent of the net earnings from self-employment. Taxpayers who reduce self-employment income by an amount equal to one-half of the combined self-employment tax rate do not include the additional 0.9-percent Medicare tax in the rate used to make such computation.

Example: Aileen, a self-employed individual, has $40,000 of net earnings from self-employment during the year (determined without regard to the substitute deduction). Her self-employment tax is computed as follows:

Self-employment net earnings	$40,000
Less: $40,000 × 7.65%	3,060
Reduced self-employment net earnings	$36,940
Tax rate on self-employment income	× 15.3%
Self-employment tax	$5,652

2673. Optional Method for Nonfarm Self-Employment. A taxpayer may be able to use an optional method to compute net earnings from self-employment if the net earnings from nonfarm self-employment for 2016 are less than $5,457 and less than 72.189 percent of gross nonfarm income. In addition, the optional method may only be used if the taxpayer had net earnings from self-employment of $400 or more in at least two of the three years immediately preceding the year in which the nonfarm optional method is elected (Code Sec. 1402(a) and (l)).[104]

If the taxpayer is eligible to use the optional method, he or she may report two-thirds of the gross income from the nonfarm business as net earnings from self-employment, provided the gross income from all nonfarm trades or businesses is less than 72.189 percent of gross nonfarm income. If, however, the gross income from all nonfarm trades or businesses is more than $5,040, the individual may report $5,040 as net earnings from nonfarm self-employment. The optional nonfarm method may not be used to report an amount less than actual net earnings from self-employment. The purpose of this optional method is to permit taxpayers to pay into the Social Security system and obtain or increase their benefits, even though they are not otherwise eligible because their net earnings from self-employment is under $400. This optional method may not be used more than five times by any individual. Note that the $5,040 amount refers to net earnings after reduction by the 7.65-percent deduction amount (¶ 2670).

2676. Farmer's Self-Employment Income. A special method for determining self-employment net earnings is provided for farm operators whether they own the land they farm, rent on a fixed rental basis, or rent under a share-farming arrangement. Rentals received by the owner or tenant of the land under a share-farming arrangement—where the farm is operated by a third party such as a share-farmer who may be a subtenant—are treated as self-employment income (¶ 2670) if the owner or tenant materially participates with the share-farmer working the land in the production, or management of the production, of an agricultural or horticultural commodity. There is no material participation if the owner or tenant does not participate in operations and has turned over management of the land to an agent, such as a professional farm management company. The share-farmer is also considered a self-employed farmer (Code Sec. 1402(a)(1); Reg. §§ 1.1402(a)-4, 1.1402(a)-13; IRS Pub. 225).[105]

Payments made by the U.S. Department of Agriculture under its Conservation Reserve Program (CRP) are considered earnings from a trade or business and are includible in the self-employment income of farmers, regardless of whether the farmer actively engages in farming or ceases all farming activities (Notice 2006-108). Authorities are split, however, on whether CRP payments to a nonfarmer are included in net earnings from self-employment as rental income from real estate.[106] Regardless of the

References are to Standard Federal Tax Reports; Tax Research Consultant; and Practical Tax Explanations.

[103] ¶ 32,560; INDIV: 63,060; § 23,210.30

[104] ¶ 32,560; INDIV: 63,056; § 23,215.10

[105] ¶ 32,560, ¶ 32,564, ¶ 32,573; INDIV: 63,450, INDIV: 63,254; § 23,215.15

[106] ¶ 32,578.280; INDIV: 63,102.30; § 23,405.10

recipient's farming activities, CRP payments are excluded from an individual's net earnings from self-employment, provided the individual is receiving retirement or disability benefits from Social Security.

A self-employed farmer has to pay the self-employment tax if his or her net earnings from self-employment are $400 or more (Code Sec. 1402(b)). However, an optional method for reporting income from farming, providing for greater credit toward benefits under Social Security old-age and survivors insurance, is available to a farmer. If the farmer's gross income for 2016 is not more than $7,560 ("upper limit"), he or she can report two-thirds of gross income as net earnings from self-employment (Code Sec. 1402(a)). If the farmer has more than $7,560 of gross income from farm operations in 2016, he or she may report either actual net earnings or, if net earnings are less than $5,040 ("lower limit"), $5,040 as net earnings. As in the case of the nonfarm optional method (¶ 2673), the $5,040 amount refers to net earnings after reduction by the 7.65-percent deduction (¶ 2670). There is no limit on the number of times a taxpayer may use this optional method.

> **Example:** Breanna Jones owns and operates her own farm. She receives all her income from the operation of the farm. Her gross income (receipts minus cost of goods sold) for 2016 is $7,800, but her net earnings for that year are only $4,000. She cannot simply report $5,200 (⅔ of $7,800) because her gross income is over $7,560, but she can report $5,040 as her net earnings from self-employment even though her actual net earnings are only $4,000. In electing to pay the self-employment tax on $5,040 rather than on $4,000, she will pay a greater tax. The positive effect, however, is that she will theoretically receive a greater credit toward Social Security benefits.

Payment of Estimated Taxes

2682. Estimated Taxes for Individuals. Individuals may need to pay a portion of their tax liability through estimated tax payments over the course of the tax year rather than when they file their return. Estimated taxes are generally used to pay tax on income that is not subject to withholding, such as interest, dividends, and gains from the sale of assets. An individual may also have to pay estimated tax if the amount of tax being withheld from wages or other income is not enough. Thus, estimated taxes are used to pay income and self-employment tax for the tax year, as well as other taxes reported on the taxpayer's return, including the 3.8-percent tax on net investment income (¶ 129) and the 0.9-percent additional Medicare tax (¶ 2648 and ¶ 2664), less any estimated credits against tax.

While the law does not directly impose an obligation to pay estimated taxes, it does impose a penalty (or addition to tax) on individuals for failure to pay enough tax either through withholding or estimated taxes (¶ 2875) (Code Sec. 6654).[107] To avoid the penalty, an individual must generally make four required installment payments of estimated taxes based on his or her required annual payment. In general, each installment is 25 percent of the lesser of:

- 90 percent of the tax shown on the individual's tax return for the current year; or
- 100 percent of the tax shown on the prior year's return (110 percent in the case of an individual with adjusted gross income in excess of $150,000; $75,000 for a married individual filing separately), unless the prior year was not a 12-month period (Code Sec. 6654(d)).[108]

A lower required installment payment may be made if the individual annualizes his or her tax at the end of each payment period based on a reasonable estimate of income,

References are to Standard Federal Tax Reports; Tax Research Consultant; and Practical Tax Explanations.

[107] ¶ 39,550; FILEIND: 15,350; § 1,401

[108] ¶ 39,550; FILEIND: 15,352; § 1,405.05

deductions, and credits. The annualized installment method may be used if the taxpayer does not receive income evenly throughout the year. Special rules also apply for farmers and fishermen (¶ 2691). Regardless of whether an individual uses the regular or annualized installment method, each required installment must be paid by its due date (¶ 2685), with an exception for the fourth (last) installment if the taxpayer pays the required amount and files his or her tax return by January 31 of the following year (¶ 2688).

An individual uses Form 1040-ES to figure his or her required installment of estimated taxes. In calculating estimated tax payments, taxes withheld from an individual's wages or other income are treated as payments of estimated tax (Code Sec. 6654(g)). Thus, an equal part of withheld taxes is deemed paid on each due date for the tax year, unless the taxpayer establishes the dates when all taxes were actually withheld. See ¶ 241 and ¶ 511, respectively, for rules on payment of estimated tax by a corporation or trusts and estates.

Exceptions to Penalty. The penalty for failure to pay estimated tax will not apply to an individual whose tax liability for the year is less than $1,000 after credits for withheld taxes and refundable personal credits. Also, a U.S. citizen or resident alien will not be subject to the penalty if he or she had no tax liability for the preceding tax year, provided such year was a 12-month period. The penalty may also be waived under certain other circumstances or hardship, or following an individual's retirement or disability (Code Sec. 6654(e)).[109]

Married Taxpayers. Individuals who are married may make a joint estimated tax payment, even if they are living separate and apart (Reg. § 1.6654-2(e)(5)).[110] Joint estimated payments are not allowed if:

- there is a decree of divorce or separate maintenance;
- the married taxpayers have different tax years; or
- the taxpayer's spouse is a nonresident alien (including a bona fide resident of Puerto Rico or U.S. possession for the entire tax year (¶ 2414)), unless an election has been made to treat the spouse as a resident alien (¶ 2410), or the spouse becomes a resident alien during the tax year.

Joint estimated payments are based on the spouses' estimated aggregate taxable income. In the event of married taxpayers filing separately, however, the amount of estimated self-employment tax is based on the separate estimated income of each individual.

Household Employees. Employers of domestic workers who fail to satisfy their obligations for FICA and FUTA withholding (¶ 2652) through regular estimated tax payments or increased tax withholding from their own wages, may be liable for estimated tax penalties (IRS Pub. 926).

2685. Estimated Tax Payment Due Dates for Individuals. For estimated tax purposes of individuals (¶ 2682), the year is broken down into four payment periods (Code Sec. 6654(c)(2)).[111] When the due date falls on a Saturday, Sunday, or legal holiday in the District of Columbia (¶ 2549), the individual has until the next succeeding business day to make the payment. For the 2017 tax year, a calendar-year individual is required to pay estimated tax in four installments as follows:

Installment	*Due date*
First	April 18, 2017
Second	June 15, 2017
Third	September 15, 2017
Fourth	January 16, 2018

If a taxpayer files his or her tax return for the current year and pays the full tax due by January 31 of the following year, then the taxpayer does not have to make the fourth estimated tax installment that would otherwise have been due on January 15 (¶ 2688).

References are to Standard Federal Tax Reports; Tax Research Consultant; and Practical Tax Explanations.

[109] ¶ 39,550; FILEIND: 15,354; § 1,435.05

[110] ¶ 39,553; FILEIND: 15,352; § 1,415

[111] ¶ 39,550; FILEIND: 15,352; § 1,410

For fiscal-year individuals, the due dates for the four estimated tax payments are:

- the 15th day of the fourth month of the fiscal year;
- the 15th day of the sixth month of the fiscal year;
- the 15th day of the ninth month of the fiscal year; and
- the 15th day of the first month after the end of the fiscal year.

If an individual is not liable for estimated tax on March 31, 2017, but his or her tax situation changes so that he or she becomes liable for estimated tax at some point after March 31, then the individual must make estimated tax payments as follows:

- If the individual becomes required to pay estimated tax after March 31 and before June 1, then he or she should pay 50 percent of estimated tax on or before June 15, 2017, 25 percent on September 15, 2017, and 25 percent on January 16, 2018.

- If the individual becomes required to pay estimated tax after May 31 and before September 1, then he or she should pay 75 percent of estimated tax on or before September 15, 2017, and 25 percent on January 16, 2018.

- If the individual becomes required to pay estimated tax after August 31, then he or she should pay 100 percent of estimated tax by January 16, 2018 (Form 1040-ES; IRS Pub. 505).

Nonresident Alien Individuals. Nonresident aliens who do *not* have wages subject to federal income tax withholding must pay estimated taxes for 2017 in three installments (June 15, 2017, September 15, 2017, and January 16, 2018). Fifty percent of the annual payment must be made on the first installment due date and 25 percent on each of the remaining two installment due dates (Code Sec. 6654(j)).[112]

2688. Return as Substitute for Last Installment of 2016 Estimated Tax. The fourth (last) tax installment of an individual (¶ 2685) for the 2016 tax year need not be made if the taxpayer files Form 1040 or Form 1040A and pays the balance of the tax on or before January 31, 2017, or for a fiscal year on or before the last day of the month following the close of the fiscal year. Filing a final 2016 return by January 31, 2017, with payment of any tax due will not avoid an addition to tax for underpayment of any of the first three installments that were due for the year, but it will terminate the period of underpayment (and, therefore, the accrual of further additions) as of the normal due date for the last installment (Code Sec. 6654(h); IRS Pub. 505).[113]

2691. Estimated Taxes of Farmer or Fisherman. A farmer or fisherman who expects to receive at least two-thirds of his or her gross income for the tax year from farming or fishing, or who received at least two-thirds of gross income for the previous tax year from farming or fishing, may pay estimated tax for the year in one installment. Thus, a qualifying farmer or fisherman may make the 2016 estimated tax payment on January 17, 2017. The entire amount of the 2016 estimated tax generally must be paid at that time. The January 17 payment date may be ignored if the farmer or fisherman files his or her income tax return for 2016 and pays the entire tax due by March 1, 2017. The penalty for underpayment of estimated tax (¶ 2875) does not apply unless a farmer or fisherman underpays the tax by more than one-third (Code Sec. 6654(i); IRS Pub. 505).[114] If a joint return is filed, a farmer or fisherman must consider his or her spouse's gross income in determining whether at least two-thirds of gross income is from farming or fishing.

References are to Standard Federal Tax Reports; Tax Research Consultant; and Practical Tax Explanations.

[112] ¶ 39,550; FILEIND: 21,052.25; § 1,420

[113] ¶ 39,550; FILEIND: 15,352; § 1,410

[114] ¶ 39,550; FILEIND: 21,052.20; § 36,510.05

Chapter 27
EXAMINATION OF RETURNS COLLECTION OF TAX

	Par.
Organization of IRS	2701
Examination	2708
Assessment and Collection of Tax	2711
Liens and Levies	2751
Mitigation of Effect of Statute of Limitations	2756
Refunds and Credits	2759
The Courts	2776

Organization of IRS

2701. IRS Organization and Functions. The Internal Revenue Service (IRS) is the bureau of the Treasury Department responsible for determining, assessing, and collecting federal taxes and enforcing the Internal Revenue Code.

The IRS is organized into four operating divisions serving groups of taxpayers with similar needs. These operating divisions are:

(1) Wage and Investment, serving individual taxpayers with wage and investment income,

(2) Small Business/Self-Employed, serving self-employed individuals and small businesses with assets of $10 million or less,

(3) Large Business and International, serving C corporations, S corporations and partnerships with assets of greater than $10 million, and

(4) Tax-Exempt and Government Entities, serving employee plans, exempt organizations, and government entities.

IRS field offices also include a number of IRS service centers. These service centers currently receive and process tax and information returns, manage accounts, and conduct simple audits. The IRS also maintains a national computer center located near Martinsburg, West Virginia.

In addition, a nine-member IRS Oversight Board has been created to ensure that the IRS is organized and operated to carry out its mission to place a greater emphasis on serving the public and meeting taxpayers' needs (Code Sec. 7802).[1]

2702 Office of the Commissioner. Federal tax laws are administered and enforced under the supervision of the Secretary of the Treasury. The Treasury Secretary delegates the responsibility for administering the tax laws to the IRS Commissioner. The IRS Commissioner is the official immediately in charge of the IRS. The duties of the IRS Commissioner are specifically listed, rather than left to the complete discretion of the Treasury Secretary. The listed duties, all of which are subject to delegation by the Treasury Secretary, are: (1) to administer, manage, direct and supervise the execution and application of the tax laws and tax treaty provisions; and (2) to recommend candidates for Chief Counsel to the President when a vacancy occurs or recommend the removal of Chief Counsel (Code Sec. 7803(a)(2)).[2].

References are to Standard Federal Tax Reports; Tax Research Consultant; and Practical Tax Explanations.

[1] ¶ 43,254; IRS: 3,060

[2] ¶ 43,258; IRS: 3,052

The Commissioner must ensure that IRS employees are familiar with, and act in accordance with, certain taxpayer rights. Included in this list of rights are the right to: (1) be informed, (2) quality service, (3) pay no more than the correct amount of tax, (4) challenge the position of the IRS and be heard, (5) appeal a decision of the IRS in an independent forum, (6) finality, (7) privacy, (8) confidentiality, (9) retain representation, and (10) a fair and just tax system (Code Sec. 7803(a)(3), as added by the Protecting Americans from Tax Hikes Act of 2015 (P.L. 114-113)).[3]

2703. Office of Chief Counsel. The legal work of the IRS is performed by the Office of the Chief Counsel (Code Sec. 7803(b)).[4] The Chief Counsel is a member of the Commissioner's executive staff and acts as counsel and legal adviser to the Commissioner in all matters pertaining to the administration and enforcement of the Internal Revenue Code. There are also Division Counsels, subject to the general supervision of the Chief Counsel, in each of the IRS operating divisions (¶ 2701).

2705. Appeals Procedure. If a tax return is examined by the IRS and the taxpayer does not agree with the results of the examination, further appeal within the IRS is permitted (Reg. § 601.106).[5] Once the IRS has issued a preliminary 30-day letter, the taxpayer has the right to appeal to a local Appeals Office by filing a written request for appellate consideration. This is the only level of appeal within the IRS, disregarding the functions of the National Taxpayer Advocate (¶ 2707). Appeals conferences are conducted in an informal manner. A taxpayer who requests a conference may also need to file a formal written protest. If the protested amount is not more than $25,000 for any tax period, however, a taxpayer may make a small case request instead of a formal written protest (IRS Pub. 556). Taxpayers who wish to forego the right to submit a protest to the Appeals Office after receiving a 30-day letter can file a petition in the Tax Court within 90 days after the receipt of a statutory notice of deficiency.

The IRS is required to develop certain appeals dispute resolution procedures (Code Sec. 7123).[6] Accordingly, the IRS has established procedures under which any taxpayer may request early referral of issues from the examination or collection division to the Office of Appeals (Rev. Proc. 99-28). Additionally, procedures have been developed under which either a taxpayer or the Office of Appeals may request nonbinding mediation of any unresolved issue at the conclusion of the appeals procedure or an unsuccessful attempt to enter into a closing agreement or an offer in compromise (Rev. Proc. 2014-63). An appeals arbitration process under which the Office of Appeals and the taxpayer may jointly request binding arbitration has been eliminated due to lack of use (Rev. Proc. 2015-44).

In addition, the Secretary of the Treasury is required to establish procedures under which an organization that is either exempt from tax under Code Sec. 501(a) because of its status as a Code Sec. 501(c) organization (or belief that it qualifies for status as a 501(c) organization) can request an administrative appeal—together with a conference related to that appeal, if so desired—in response to receiving an adverse determination (Code Sec. 7123(c), as added by the Protecting Americans from Tax Hikes (PATH) Act of 2015 (P.L. 114-113)). For this purpose, an adverse determination is one that is adverse to the organization's exempt status, regardless of whether that involves the organization's initial qualification or the continuing classification of the organization, concerning whether the organization is: (1) an organization described in Code Sec. 170(c)(2), (2) exempt from tax under Code Sec. 501(a), (3) a private foundation under Code Sec. 509(a), or (4) a private operating foundation under Code Sec. 4942(j)(3).

Small business and self-employed taxpayers can resolve their tax disputes through fast-track mediation (Rev. Proc. 2003-41). Disputes will be resolved through this expedited process within 40 days, compared to several months using the regular appeals process.

References are to Standard Federal Tax Reports; Tax Research Consultant; and Practical Tax Explanations.

[3] ¶ 43,258; IRS: 3,052

[4] ¶ 43,258; IRS: 3,056

[5] ¶ 43,336; IRS: 24,050; § 39,605, § 39,615

[6] ¶ 41,132, ¶ 41,135.10, ¶ 41,135.40; IRS: 24,106; § 39,740.05

Large- and mid-size businesses can resolve their tax disputes through a fast-track settlement program (Rev. Proc. 2003-40). The goal for this program is to reach settlement within 120 days. A similar fast-track settlement program exists for small businesses and self-employed taxpayers as well (Announcement 2011-5). A fast-track settlement program for tax-exempt and government entities has also been established (Announcement 2012-34). The goal for both this program and the small business and self-employed taxpayer program is to reach settlement within 60 days. Additional criteria may be found on the Appeals Mediation Programs webpage on the IRS website.

2707. Taxpayer Assistance Orders. The National Taxpayer Advocate assists taxpayers in resolving problems with the IRS and has the authority to issue a taxpayer assistance order if a taxpayer is suffering, or is about to suffer, significant hardship as a result of the IRS's actions (Code Secs. 7803(c) and 7811; Reg. § 301.7811-1).[7] "Significant hardship" means any serious privation caused to the taxpayer as the result of the IRS's administration of revenue laws. Mere economic or personal inconvenience to the taxpayer does not constitute significant hardship. The following four specific factors, among other things, must be considered by the Advocate when determining whether there is a significant hardship:

(1) whether there is an immediate threat of adverse action,

(2) whether there has been a delay of more than 30 days in resolving the taxpayer's account problems,

(3) whether the taxpayer will incur significant costs, including fees for professional representation, if relief is not granted, and

(4) whether the taxpayer will suffer irreparable injury, or a long-term adverse impact, if relief is not granted.

An application for a taxpayer assistance order may be filed by the taxpayer or a duly authorized representative, who may request remedial action, such as the release of the taxpayer's property from IRS levy or the immediate reissuance of a lost refund check. Form 911 is to be used for this purpose. Any relevant limitations period is suspended from the date on which the application is filed until the Advocate makes a decision on the application, unless the order provides for the continuation of the suspension beyond the date of the order. These orders are binding on the IRS unless modified or rescinded by the Advocate, IRS Commissioner or Deputy Commissioner. The Advocate can take independent action and issue an assistance order without an application by the taxpayer. The statute of limitations, however, is not suspended when the Advocate issues an order independently.

Examination

2708. Examination of Return. The IRS examines a taxpayer's books and records either at the place of business where the books and records are maintained (i.e., a field examination) or at an IRS office (Reg. § 601.105).[8]

The Taxpayer Bill of Rights requires the IRS to provide a written statement detailing the taxpayer's rights and the IRS's obligations during the audit, appeals, refund, and collection process. Additionally, at or before the first in-person interview with a taxpayer relating to the determination of any tax, the IRS must provide the taxpayer with an explanation of the audit process and the taxpayer's rights under the process (Code Sec. 7521(b)).[9]

The taxpayer has the right to make an audio recording of any in-person interview conducted by the IRS upon 10 days' advance notice (Code Sec. 7521(a); Notice 89-51).[10] Moreover, a taxpayer is guaranteed the right to be represented by any individual currently permitted to practice before the IRS, unless the IRS notifies the taxpayer that

References are to Standard Federal Tax Reports; Tax Research Consultant; and Practical Tax Explanations.

[7] ¶ 43,258, ¶ 43,304, ¶ 43,308; IRS: 3,058, IRS: 45,112; § 41,315

[8] ¶ 43,332; IRS: 15,100; § 39,715

[9] ¶ 42,790; IRS: 45,112; § 39,705

[10] ¶ 42,790, ¶ 42,791.30; IRS: 15,110; § 39,715.15

the representative is responsible for unreasonable delay or hindrance (Code Sec. 7521(c)).[11] Any interview must be suspended when the taxpayer clearly requests the right to consult with a representative. Further, unless it issues an administrative summons, the IRS cannot require the taxpayer to accompany the representative to the interview.

The IRS may provide administrative relief to taxpayers in hostage situations or in a combat zone, who are continuously hospitalized as a result of injuries received in a combat zone, or who are affected by a federally declared disaster area, by suspending tax examination and collection actions during this time (Code Secs. 7508 and 7508A).[12] Examination and collection actions that can be precluded or suspended include tax return audits, mailings of notices, and other actions involving the collection of overdue taxes. The collection period for taxpayers hospitalized for combat zone injuries may not be suspended by reason of any period of continuous hospitalization or the 180 days thereafter (Code Sec. 7508(e)(3), as added by the Protecting Americans from Tax Hikes Act of 2015 (P.L. 114-113)).[13] As a result, the collection period expires 10 years after assessment, plus the actual time spent in a combat zone, regardless of the length of the postponement period available for hospitalized individuals to comply with their tax obligations.

2708A. Power of Attorney. A taxpayer generally may choose a person to represent him or her before the IRS by filing a power of attorney (Reg. § 601.501(a)).[14] A power of attorney is a written authorization for an individual to act on behalf of another individual or an entity in tax matters. Form 2848 can be used to grant a power of attorney, or another equivalent document can be used. If the authorization is not limited, the individual can generally perform all acts that the taxpayer granting the power can perform. The holder of a power of attorney cannot, however, represent the taxpayer before the IRS unless the holder is one of the persons authorized to practice before the IRS (CCA 200321017).

A taxpayer may change his or her representative by filing a new power of attorney (Reg. § 601.505(a)).[15] The new power revokes any prior power that the taxpayer granted to someone else concerning the same matter unless the new power contains a clause stating that it does not revoke the prior power. A taxpayer may also revoke a power of attorney without authorizing a new representative.

A taxpayer who only wants to have someone answer any questions that may arise regarding his or her income tax return does not have to file a power of attorney. Instead, the taxpayer can designate anyone to do this, not just a person qualified to practice before the IRS, by checking the appropriate box on his or her tax return (Instruction to Form 1040).

2709. Third-Party Summonses. The IRS may issue summonses to third-party recordkeepers (attorneys, enrolled agents, banks, brokers, accountants, etc.) and other third parties for the production of records concerning the business transactions or affairs of a taxpayer (Code Sec. 7609).[16] The taxpayer is to be notified of the summons within three days of service of the summons, but no later than 23 days before the examination of the summoned person or records is scheduled to take place. However, notice is not required with respect to any summons:

(1) served on the person with respect to whose liability the summons is issued, or any officer or employee of the person,

(2) issued to determine whether or not records of the business transactions or affairs of an identified person have been made or kept,

References are to Standard Federal Tax Reports; Tax Research Consultant; and Practical Tax Explanations.

[11] ¶ 42,790; IRS: 18,202; § 39,715.10

[12] ¶ 42,686, ¶ 42,687A; FILEBUS: 15,100; § 39,215.30, § 39,215.35

[13] ¶ 42,686; FILEIND: 15,204.20; § 39,215.30

[14] ¶ 43,408; IRS: 3,208.05; § 41,205.05

[15] ¶ 43,424; IRS: 3,208.15; § 41,210

[16] ¶ 42,890; IRS: 21,100, IRS: 21,150; § 39,810

(3) issued solely to determine the identity of any person having a numbered account or similar arrangement with a bank or similar institution,

(4) issued to aid the collection of (a) an assessment or judgment against the person with respect to whose liability the summons is issued, or (b) the liability of that person's transferee or fiduciary, or

(5) issued in certain criminal investigations.

Any taxpayer who is entitled to notice may intervene in any proceeding for the enforcement of the summons in question. The taxpayer also has the right to begin a proceeding to quash the summons if, within 20 days after the day the notice of summons was served on or mailed to him or her, the taxpayer files a petition to quash the summons in a district court having jurisdiction and notifies the IRS and the third party by mailing a copy of the petition by certified or registered mail to each one. Although notice is not required for a "John Doe" summons (i.e., a summons that does not identify the person whose liability is at issue), these summonses may be issued only after the IRS has shown adequate grounds for serving the summons, and an ex parte court proceeding is held to determine its validity.

If a taxpayer intervenes in a dispute between the IRS and a third party and the dispute is not resolved within six months, the statute-of-limitations period will be suspended beginning on the date that is six months after the summons is served and continuing until the dispute is resolved. This provision also applies with respect to "John Doe" summonses (Code Sec. 7609(e)).[17]

The IRS is required to provide reasonable notice in advance to a taxpayer before contacting third parties with respect to examination or collection activities regarding the taxpayer (Code Sec. 7602(c); Reg. § 301.7602-2).[18] However, notice is *not* required: (1) with respect to any contact authorized by the taxpayer, (2) if the IRS determines that the notice would jeopardize collection of any tax, or (3) with respect to any pending criminal investigation. IRS contractors may participate in summons interviews with certain limitations (Reg. § 301.7602-1).[19]

Assessment and Collection of Tax

2711. Assessment of Deficiency. The IRS is authorized to assess taxes (Code Sec. 6201; Reg. § 301.6201-1).[20] There are, however, certain procedures that must be followed before assessing a deficiency. A deficiency is the excess of (1) the correct tax liability, over (2) the tax shown on the return, if any, plus amounts previously assessed or collected without assessment as a deficiency, and minus any rebates made to the taxpayer (Code Sec. 6211).[21] For this purpose, the tax shown on the return is the amount of tax before credits for estimated tax paid, withheld tax, or amounts collected under a termination assessment.

The deficiency process begins when a notice of deficiency is sent to the taxpayer's last known address by registered or certified mail (Code Sec. 6212).[22] In each deficiency notice, the IRS must provide a description of the basis for the assessment, an identification of the amount of tax, interest, and penalties assessed (Code Sec. 7522),[23] and the date determined to be the last day on which the taxpayer may file a petition with the Tax Court (Code Sec. 6213(a)).[24] However, the failure by the IRS to specify the last day on which to file a petition will not invalidate an otherwise valid deficiency notice if the taxpayer was not prejudiced by the omission.[25]

Within 90 days after notice of the deficiency is mailed (or within 150 days if the notice is mailed to an address outside the United States), the taxpayer may file a petition

References are to Standard Federal Tax Reports; Tax Research Consultant; and Practical Tax Explanations.

[17] ¶ 42,890; IRS: 21,114; § 39,810

[18] ¶ 42,820, ¶ 42,824; IRS: 21,106; § 39,810

[19] ¶ 42,824; IRS:21,050; § 39,805.

[20] ¶ 37,502, ¶ 37,503; IRS: 27,200; § 39,501

[21] ¶ 37,535; IRS: 27,052; § 39,510.10

[22] ¶ 37,540; IRS: 27,150; § 39,510.15

[23] ¶ 42,800; IRS: 27,154; § 39,510.05

[24] ¶ 37,545; IRS: 27,154; § 39,510.05

[25] ¶ 37,544.25; IRS: 27,154.05; § 39,510.05

with the Tax Court for a redetermination of the deficiency (Code Sec. 6213).[26] Payment of the assessed amount after the deficiency notice is mailed does not deprive the Tax Court of jurisdiction over the deficiency (Reg. § 301.6213-1(b)(3)).[27]

If the taxpayer does not file a Tax Court petition within the required time period, the tax may be assessed. After giving notice and demand for payment of the tax, the IRS may take action to collect (¶ 2735). A taxpayer's property may be seized to enforce collection if there is a failure to pay an assessed tax within 30 days after notice of intent to levy (Code Sec. 6331).[28] However, the notice and waiting period does not apply if the IRS finds that the collection of tax is in jeopardy (¶ 2713). Notices of levy must provide a description of the levy process in simple and nontechnical terms.

Last Known Address. As noted previously, the collection process begins when a notice of deficiency is sent to the taxpayer's last known address by registered or certified mail. A taxpayer's last known address is the address that appears on the taxpayer's most recently filed federal tax return. However, if the taxpayer gives the IRS clear and concise notification of a different address, that address is the taxpayer's last known address (Reg. § 301.6212-2).[29] The IRS uses the National Change of Address database maintained by the U.S. Postal Service to update a taxpayer's last known address. A taxpayer can change his or her last known address with the IRS through any of several means (Rev. Proc. 2010-16).[30] First, the taxpayer can file a return with new address information. Second, the taxpayer can provide clear and concise written notification to an appropriate IRS address using Form 8822, Form 8822-B for employers, or other written notice satisfying the requirements including returning IRS correspondence with corrections marked (IRS Pub. 15). Next, the taxpayer can provide clear and concise written or oral notification of a change of address to an IRS employee who contacts the client regarding the filing of a return or an adjustment in his or her account. Finally, the taxpayer can provide the IRS with clear and concise electronic notification through one of the secure applications found on the IRS website.

Mathematical or Clerical Errors. A notice of tax due because of mathematical or clerical errors is not a deficiency notice, and the taxpayer has no right to file a petition with the Tax Court for redetermining the deficiency. A taxpayer who receives notice of additional tax due to mathematical or clerical error has 60 days after the notice is sent in which to file a request for abatement of any part of the assessment. Any reassessment must be made under the regular notice-of-deficiency procedures. During the 60-day period, the IRS cannot proceed to collect upon the summary assessment (Code Sec. 6213(b)(1) and (f)).[31]

Criminal Restitution. Criminal restitution for a failure to pay tax, ordered by a court pursuant to 18 USC § 3556, is assessed and collected as if it were such a tax (Code Sec. 6201(a)(4)(A)).[32] The restitution assessment is excepted from the general restrictions on assessments and filing of Tax Court petitions for deficiency redetermination. The restitution amount may be assessed, or a court proceeding for its collection may begin without assessment, at any time.

2712. Waiver of Deficiency Restrictions. The taxpayer has the right to waive the restrictions on assessment and collection of all or part of a deficiency at any time, whether or not a notice of deficiency has been issued (Code Sec. 6213(d)).[33] This is done by executing Form 870. Execution of a waiver of the restrictions on assessment and collection of the entire deficiency in advance of the statutory ("90-day") notice relieves the IRS of sending such a notice and precludes appeal to the Tax Court. However, an appeal to the Tax Court is not precluded if the waiver covers only part of the deficiency or is executed after receipt of the 90-day deficiency notice. Payment of an

References are to Standard Federal Tax Reports; Tax Research Consultant; and Practical Tax Explanations.

[26] ¶ 37,545; IRS: 27,158; § 39,510.05

[27] ¶ 37,546; LITIG: 6,100; § 39,510.05

[28] ¶ 38,185; IRS: 51,054; § 39,945.15

[29] ¶ 37,542; IRS: 27,160; § 39,510.15

[30] ¶ 37,544.28, ¶ 37,549.5023; IRS: 27,160.05; § 39,510.15

[31] ¶ 37,545; IRS: 27,206.15; § 39,515.10

[32] ¶ 37,502; IRS: 27,206.70; § 39,515.10

[33] ¶ 37,545, ¶ 37,549.9612; IRS: 27,208; § 39,540.15

amount of tax before issuance of the statutory notice has the effect of a waiver, and, if the amount paid equals or exceeds the amount of a subsequently determined deficiency, it deprives the Tax Court of jurisdiction (Reg. § 301.6213-1(b)(3)).[34]

2713. Jeopardy and Termination Assessments. The IRS can immediately determine and assess income tax in a termination assessment if it finds that tax collection is in jeopardy because a taxpayer is leaving the country, or seeking to hide assets, or doing any other act that tends to render collection ineffective (Code Sec. 6851).[35] Similarly, the IRS can immediately assess a deficiency if tax assessment or collection would be jeopardized by delay (Code Sec. 6861).[36] If a jeopardy assessment is made prior to the mailing of the notice of deficiency, the notice must be mailed to the taxpayer within 60 days after the assessment (Code Sec. 6861(b)).[37] If a termination assessment is made, the assessment ends the taxpayer's tax year only for purposes of computing the amount of tax that becomes immediately due and payable. It does not end the tax year for any other purpose. In the case of a termination assessment, the IRS must issue the taxpayer a notice of deficiency within 60 days of the later of (1) the due date, including extensions, of the taxpayer's return for the full tax year or (2) the day on which the taxpayer files the return (Code Sec. 6851(b)).[38]

The IRS may presume that the collection of tax is in jeopardy if an individual in physical possession of more than $10,000 in cash or its equivalent does not claim either ownership of the cash or that it belongs to another person whose identity the IRS can readily ascertain and who acknowledges ownership of the cash. In this case, the IRS may treat the entire amount as gross income taxable at the highest rate specified in Code Sec. 1. The possessor of the cash is entitled to notice of, and the right to challenge, the assessment. However, should the true owner appear, he or she will be substituted for the possessor and all rights will vest in the true owner (Code Sec. 6867).[39]

2719. Injunction to Restrain Collection. The Code prohibits a suit to restrain the assessment or collection of any tax or to restrain the enforcement of liability against a transferee or fiduciary (Code Sec. 7421).[40] Nevertheless, injunctive relief may be available in rare cases if irreparable harm will be done to the taxpayer and the taxpayer shows, at the outset of the suit, that the government could not collect the tax under any circumstances.[41] However, injunctive relief may be obtained for assessment or collection actions (other than jeopardy or termination assessments) if a notice of deficiency has not been mailed to the taxpayer, the period for filing a Tax Court petition has not expired, or a Tax Court proceeding with respect to the tax is pending (Code Sec. 6213(a)).[42]

2721. Closing Agreement. The IRS is authorized to enter into a written agreement with a taxpayer in order to determine conclusively the tax liability for a tax period that ended prior to the date of the agreement (Form 866) or to determine one or more separate items affecting the tax liability for any tax period (Form 906). A closing agreement may also be entered for tax periods that end subsequent to the date of the agreement. Closing agreements may be entered into in order to finally resolve questions of tax liability (Code Sec. 7121; Reg. §§ 301.7121-1 and 601.202).[43] For example, a fiduciary may desire a final determination before an estate is closed or trust assets distributed. Closing agreements are final, conclusive, and binding upon both parties. They cannot be reopened or modified except upon a showing of fraud or malfeasance or the misrepresentation of a material fact.[44] Generally, the IRS is not precluded from later determining additions to tax absent terms in the agreement that specifically address the issue of additions to tax.

References are to Standard Federal Tax Reports; Tax Research Consultant; and Practical Tax Explanations.

[34] ¶ 37,546; LITIG: 6,110; § 39,540.15

[35] ¶ 40,402; IRS: 54,100; § 39,520, § 39,530.10

[36] ¶ 40,460; IRS: 54,050; § 39,520, § 39,525.05

[37] ¶ 40,460; IRS: 54,050; § 39,525.15

[38] ¶ 40,402; IRS: 54,102; § 39,530.20

[39] ¶ 40,580; IRS: 54,152; § 39,525.10

[40] ¶ 41,680; IRS: 45,152; § 39,940

[41] ¶ 41,683.69, ¶ 41,683.70; IRS: 45,152; § 39,940

[42] ¶ 37,545; IRS: 45,152; § 39,940

[43] ¶ 41,080, ¶ 41,081, ¶ 43,364; IRS: 39,050; § 40,405.15

[44] ¶ 41,090.279; IRS: 39,150; § 40,405.15

2723. Compromise of Tax and Penalty. The IRS may generally compromise a tax liability before it has been referred to the Department of Justice for prosecution or defense. The Attorney General or a delegate may compromise any case after the referral. Interest and penalties, as well as tax, may be compromised (Code Sec. 7122; Reg. § 301.7122-1).[45] Offers-in-compromise based on doubt as to collectibility or effective tax administration are submitted on Form 656, and must be accompanied by a financial statement on Form 433-A (OIC) for an individual or Form 433-B (OIC) for a business. Offers-in-compromise based on doubt as to liability are submitted on Form 656-L (Reg. § 601.203(b)).[46] If the IRS accepts an offer-in-compromise, and the terms of the offer (and collateral agreement, if any) provide for the allocation of payments, the payments will be allocated under the terms of the agreement. If the offer or agreement do not provide for the allocation of payments, the IRS will apply payments, whether paid in installments or in a lump sum, to the periods in the order of priority that the IRS determines will best serve the government's interest (Rev. Proc. 2002-26).[47]

A $186 user fee is generally required when an offer-in-compromise is submitted (Reg. § 300.3).[48] However, no user fee is imposed with respect to offers:

(1) that are based solely on doubt as to liability, or

(2) that are made by low-income taxpayers (i.e., taxpayers whose total monthly income falls at or below income levels based on the U.S. Department of Health and Human Services poverty guidelines).

The IRS has issued a proposed amendment to Reg. § 300.3 that increases the user fee for an offer in compromise. The increase will become final upon the proposed amendment being adopted and published in the Federal Register. The processing fee for offers submitted on or after February 27, 2017, will be $300 (Notice of Proposed Rulemaking (NPRM) REG-108934-16).

If an offer is accepted to promote effective tax administration or is accepted based on doubt as to collectibility and a determination that collecting more than the amount offered would create economic hardship, the fee will be applied to the amount of the offer or, upon the taxpayer's request, refunded to the taxpayer. The fee will not be refunded if an offer is withdrawn, rejected, or returned as nonprocessible. The IRS treats offers received by taxpayers in bankruptcy as nonprocessible; however, some courts have held that the IRS must consider such offers.[49] The IRS has issued detailed procedures for the submission and processing of offers-in-compromise (Rev. Proc. 2003-71).

Partial Payment Requirement. Taxpayers are required to make nonrefundable partial payments with the submission of any offer-in-compromise based on doubt as to collectibility or effective tax administration (Code Sec. 7122(c)). Taxpayers who submit a lump-sum offer (any offer that will be paid in five or fewer installments) must include a payment of 20 percent of the amount offered. Taxpayers who submit a periodic payment offer must include payment of the first proposed installment with the offer and continue making payments under the terms proposed while the offer is being evaluated. Offers that are submitted to the IRS without the required partial payments will be returned to the taxpayer as nonprocessable. Partial payments are not required for offers based solely on doubt as to liability or filed by low-income taxpayers (Notice 2006-68).

The required partial payments are applied to the taxpayer's unpaid liability and are not refundable. Taxpayers may specify the liability to which they want their payments applied. Additionally, the user fee (see previously) is applied to the taxpayer's outstanding tax liability. Any offer that is not rejected within 24 months of the date it is submitted is deemed to be accepted. However, any period during which the tax liability to be compromised is in dispute in any judicial proceeding is not taken into account in determining the expiration of the 24-month period (Code Sec. 7122(f)).

References are to Standard Federal Tax Reports; Tax Research Consultant; and Practical Tax Explanations.

[45] ¶ 41,110, ¶ 41,111; IRS: 42,050; § 39,920.05

[46] ¶ 43,372; IRS: 42,100; § 39,920.25

[47] ¶ 9104.63; IRS: 42,150; § 39,920.25

[48] ¶ 41,120; IRS: 42,106; § 39,920.25

[49] ¶ 41,130.18; IRS: 42,106

The IRS will return any filed offers in compromise application where the taxpayer has not filed all required tax returns.

2724. Partial Payments. Specific written directions from a taxpayer regarding the application of partial payments of assessed federal income taxes, penalties, and interest made by the taxpayer will be respected (Rev. Proc. 2002-26).[50] A partial payment on deficiencies received without instructions for its application will be applied to tax, penalties, and interest, in the order of priority that best serves the government's interest.

2726. Statute of Limitations for Assessment and Collection. Generally, all income taxes must be assessed within three years after the original return is filed (the last day prescribed by law for filing if the return was filed before the last day) (Code Sec. 6501; Reg. § 301.6501(a)-1).[51] In the case of pass-through entities, the three-year rule begins to run at the time the pass-through entity's shareholder or other beneficial owner files an individual income tax return. A return filed prior to its due date is deemed to have been filed on the due date. A return executed by an IRS official or employee in which the taxpayer has not filed a return will not start the running of the statute of limitations. A proceeding in court without assessment for collection of the tax must commence within the same period. The period can be extended by a written agreement between the taxpayer and the IRS (Code Sec. 6501(c)(4); Reg. § 301.6501(c)-1(d)).[52] Interest on any tax may be assessed and collected at any time during the period within which the tax itself may be collected (Code Sec. 6601(g); Reg. § 301.6601-1(f)).[53]

If, within the 60-day period ending on the last day of the assessment period, the IRS receives an amended return or written document from the taxpayer showing that additional tax is due for the year in question, the period in which to assess such additional tax is extended for 60 days after the day on which the IRS receives the amended return or written document (Code Sec. 6501(c)(7)).[54]

If unused foreign tax credits have been carried back, the statute of limitations on assessment and collection for the year to which the carryback is made will not close until one year after the expiration of the period within which a deficiency may be assessed for the year from which the carryback was made (Code Sec. 6501(i); Reg. § 301.6501(i)-1).[55] Deficiencies attributable to carryback of a net operating loss, a capital loss, or the general business and research credit, may be assessed within the period that applies to the loss or credit year. Deficiencies attributable to the carrying back of one of those credits as a result of the carryback of another credit, a net operating loss or a capital loss, may be assessed within the period that applies to the loss or other credit year (Code Sec. 6501(h) and (j)).

2728. Request for Prompt Assessment. A corporation that is contemplating dissolution, is in the process of dissolving, or has actually dissolved, or a decedent or an estate of a decedent (for taxes other than the estate tax imposed by chapter 11), may request a prompt assessment (Code Sec. 6501(d); Reg. § 301.6501(d)-1).[56] If such a request is made, an assessment or a proceeding in court without assessment for the collection of any tax must begin within 18 months after the receipt of a written request for a prompt assessment. In the case of a corporation, however, the 18-month period will not apply unless the corporation has completed or will eventually complete its dissolution at or before the end of the 18-month period. This provision does not apply in the cases described at ¶ 2732 and ¶ 2734. It also does not apply for personal holding company taxes in certain instances or where a waiver filed by the taxpayer extends the assessment period beyond the 18-month period.

References are to Standard Federal Tax Reports; Tax Research Consultant; and Practical Tax Explanations.

[50] ¶ 39,415.329, ¶ 39,780.14; PENALTY: 9,058.10; § 39,320.35

[51] ¶ 38,960, ¶ 38,961; IRS: 30,050; § 39,505.05

[52] ¶ 38,960, ¶ 38,966; IRS: 30,250; § 39,905

[53] ¶ 39,410, ¶ 39,412; PENALTY: 9,052; § 40,105

[54] ¶ 38,960; IRS: 30,056; § 39,505.05

[55] ¶ 38,960, ¶ 38,977; IRS: 30,122; § 39,505.30

[56] ¶ 38,960, ¶ 38,968; IRS: 30,118; § 26,740

2732. Assessment Period for False Returns or No Return. There is no limitation period on an assessment or a court proceeding to collect tax if:

(1) the return is false or fraudulent,

(2) there is a willful attempt to evade tax, or

(3) no return is filed (Code Sec. 6501(c); Reg. § 301.6501(c)-1).[57]

In addition, in the case of a fraudulent return, the government may impose additional taxes at any time, without regard to statutes of limitations, although the burden of proof falls on the government to prove fraud by the taxpayer (Code Sec. 7454(a)).[58]

2733. Assessment Period for Listed Transactions. If a taxpayer fails to include with a return any information required relating to a listed transaction (¶ 2591), the statute of limitations with respect to that transaction will not expire before one year after the earlier of: (1) the date on which the information is furnished to the IRS or (2) the date that a material advisor to the listed transaction satisfies certain list maintenance requirements (¶ 2595) with respect to the transaction (Code Sec. 6501(c)(10)).[59]

2734. Assessment Period for Omission of Over 25 Percent of Income. If the taxpayer omits from gross income (total receipts, without reduction for cost) an amount in excess of 25 percent of the amount of gross income stated in the return, a six-year limitations period on assessment and collection of tax applies. An item will not be considered as omitted from gross income if information sufficient to apprise the IRS of the nature and amount of such item is disclosed in the return or in any schedule or statement attached to the return (Code Sec. 6501(e); Reg. § 301.6501(e)-1(a)).[60] A taxpayer's overstatement of its basis in an asset that resulted in an understatement of gross income from the asset's sale will trigger the six-year limitations period as an omission from gross income (Code Sec. 6501(e)(1)(B)). This is a legislative repeal of the U.S. Supreme Court's invalidation of Reg. § 301.6501(e)-1(a)(1)(iii) (*Home Concrete &Supply, LLC*, SCt, 2012-1 USTC ¶ 50,315).

2735. Collection After Assessment. After assessment of tax made within the statutory period of limitations (¶ 2726), the tax may be collected by levy or a proceeding in court commenced within 10 years after the assessment or within any period for collection agreed upon in writing between the IRS and the taxpayer before the expiration of the 10-year period (Code Sec. 6502(a); Reg. § 301.6502-1).[61] The period agreed upon by the parties may be extended by later written agreements, so long as they are made prior to the expiration of the period previously agreed upon. The IRS has to notify taxpayers of their right to refuse an extension each time one is requested (Code Sec. 6501(c)(4)).[62] If a timely court proceeding has commenced for the collection of the tax, then the period during which the tax may be collected is extended until the liability for tax, or a judgment against the taxpayer, is satisfied or becomes unenforceable.

The 10-year limitations period on collections is generally suspended for any period during which the IRS is prohibited from levying on the taxpayer's property. The collection period may also be extended by agreement between a taxpayer and the IRS. If the taxpayer entered into an installment agreement with the IRS, however, the 10-year limitations period may be extended for the period that the limitations period was extended under the original terms of the installment agreement plus 90 days.

Interest accrues on a deficiency from the date the tax was due (determined without regard to extensions) until the date payment is received at the rate specified at ¶ 2838

References are to Standard Federal Tax Reports; Tax Research Consultant; and Practical Tax Explanations.

[57] ¶ 38,960, ¶ 38,966; IRS: 30,102, IRS: 30,104, IRS: 30,106; § 39,505

[58] ¶ 42,081; IRS: 30,104; § 39,505.15

[59] ¶ 38,960; IRS: 30,052, PENALTY: 3,252.10; § 39,015.05

[60] ¶ 38,960, ¶ 38,970; IRS: 30,152; § 39,505.10

[61] ¶ 39,010, ¶ 39,011; IRS: 45,200; § 39,910

[62] ¶ 38,960; IRS: 30,254; § 39,905

(Code Sec. 6601(g); Reg. § 301.6601-1(a)(1)).[63] Interest may be assessed and collected during the period in which the related tax may be collected.

2736. Suspension of Assessment Period. When an income, estate, or gift tax deficiency notice is mailed, the running of the period of limitations on assessment and collection of any deficiency is suspended for 90 days (150 days for a deficiency notice mailed to persons outside the United States) not counting Saturday, Sunday, or a legal holiday in the District of Columbia, plus an additional 60 days thereafter (Code Sec. 6503(a)(1); Reg. § 301.6503(a)-1).[64] If a petition is filed with the Tax Court, the running of the period of limitations is suspended until the Tax Court's decision becomes final and for an additional 60 days thereafter.

The 10-year statute of limitations for collection after assessment is also suspended from the date the IRS wrongfully seizes or receives a third party's property to 30 days after the date the IRS returns the property or the date on which a judgment secured in a wrongful levy action becomes final. Similarly, with respect to wrongful liens, the 10-year limitations period is suspended from the time the third-party owner is entitled to a certificate of discharge of lien until 30 days after the earlier of (1) the date that the IRS no longer holds any amount as a deposit or bond that was used to satisfy the unpaid liability or that was refunded or released, or (2) the date that the judgment in a civil action becomes final (¶ 2755) (Code Sec. 6503(f)).[65]

For federal bankruptcy cases, the running of the period of limitations is suspended during the period of the automatic stay on collection of taxes and for an additional period ending 60 days after the day the stay is lifted for assessments and for six months thereafter for collection (Code Sec. 6503(h)).[66] Additionally, in receivership and bankruptcy cases where a fiduciary is required to give written notice to the IRS of an appointment or authorization to act, the assessment period is suspended from the date the proceedings are instituted and ending 30 days after the day of notice to the IRS of such appointment. The extension period cannot exceed two years (Code Sec. 6872).[67]

If the taxpayer and the IRS agree to the rescission of a deficiency notice, the statute of limitations again begins to run as of the date of the rescission and continues to run for the period of time that remains on the date the notice was issued (Code Sec. 6212(d)).[68]

2738. Suit for Recovery of Erroneous Refund. The government may sue to recover an erroneous refund (including, but not limited to, one made after the applicable refund period described in ¶ 2763) within two years after such refund was paid. However, a suit may be commenced within five years if any part of the refund was induced by fraud or misrepresentation of a material fact (Code Sec. 6532(b); Reg. § 301.6532-2).[69]

2740. Criminal Prosecution. A criminal prosecution must generally be started within three years after the offense is committed (Code Sec. 6531).[70] However, a six-year period applies in a case where there is:

(1) fraud or an attempt to defraud the United States or an agency thereof, by conspiracy or otherwise,

(2) a willful attempt to evade or defeat any tax or payment,

(3) willful aiding or assisting in the preparation of a false return or other document,

(4) willful failure to pay any tax or make any return (except certain information returns) at the time required by law,

References are to Standard Federal Tax Reports; Tax Research Consultant; and Practical Tax Explanations.

[63] ¶ 39,410, ¶ 39,412; IRS: 30,114, PENALTY: 9,050; § 40,105

[64] ¶ 39,030, ¶ 39,031; IRS: 30,202; § 39,910

[65] ¶ 39,030; IRS: 45,204; § 39,910

[66] ¶ 39,030; IRS: 30,208; § 39,550.15

[67] ¶ 40,640; IRS: 30,208; § 39,550.15

[68] ¶ 37,540; IRS: 30,202; § 39,510.20

[69] ¶ 39,270, ¶ 39,272; IRS: 45,162; § 40,060.05

[70] ¶ 39,240; IRS: 66,454; § 40,245.05

(5) a false statement verified under penalties of perjury or a false or fraudulent return, statement or other document,

(6) intimidation of a U.S. officer or employee,

(7) an offense committed by a U.S. officer or employee in connection with a revenue law, or

(8) a conspiracy to defeat tax or payment.

2743. Collection from Transferee of Property. The liability of a transferee of property is generally assessed and collected in the same manner as is any other deficiency imposed by the IRS (Code Sec. 6901; Reg. § 301.6901-1(a)).[71] The term "transferee" includes an heir, legatee, devisee, distributee of an estate of a deceased person, the shareholder of a dissolved corporation, the assignee or donee of an insolvent person, the successor of a corporation, a party to a Code Sec. 368(a) reorganization, and a member of any other class of distributees. Such term also includes, with respect to the gift tax, a donee (without regard to the solvency of the donor) and, with respect to the estate tax, any person who, under Code Sec. 6324(a)(2), is personally liable for any part of such tax.

2745. Transferee Assessment and Collection Period. Unless a taxpayer has filed a false return with intent to evade tax (¶ 2732), an assessment against a transferee or fiduciary must be made within the following periods:

(1) in the case of an initial transferee, within one year after the expiration of the period of limitations for assessment against the taxpayer,

(2) in the case of a transferee of a transferee, within one year after the expiration of the period of limitations for assessment against the preceding transferee or three years after the expiration of the period of limitations for assessment against the taxpayer, whichever of these two periods expires first,

(3) if a timely court proceeding has been brought against the taxpayer or last preceding transferee, within one year after the return of execution in such proceeding, or

(4) in the case of a fiduciary, within one year after the liability arises or within the limitations period for collection of the tax (¶ 2726), whichever is the later (Code Sec. 6901; Reg. § 301.6901-1(c)).[72]

2747. Collection from Fiduciary. In order to receive advance notice from the IRS with respect to assessments, every fiduciary must give written notice to the IRS of his or her fiduciary capacity. If this notice (Form 56) is not filed, the IRS may proceed against the property in the hands of the fiduciary after mailing notice of the deficiency or other liability to the taxpayer's last known address, even if the taxpayer is then deceased or is under legal disability. The fiduciary may be relieved of any further liability by filing with the IRS written notice and evidence of the termination (Reg. § 301.6903-1).[73]

2750. Assessment in Bankruptcy or Receiverships. When a taxpayer's assets are taken over by a receiver appointed by the court, the IRS may immediately assess the tax if it has not already been lawfully assessed. The IRS may also assess the tax on (1) the debtor's estate under U.S. Code Title 11 bankruptcy proceedings or (2) the debtor if the tax liability has become *res judicata* pursuant to a Title 11 bankruptcy determination (Code Sec. 6871).[74] Tax claims may be presented to the court before which the receivership or a Title 11 bankruptcy is pending, despite the pendency of proceedings in the Tax Court. However, in the case of a receivership proceeding, no petition may be filed with the Tax Court after the appointment of the receiver. The trustee of the debtor's estate in a Title 11 bankruptcy proceeding may intervene on behalf of the debtor's estate in any Tax Court proceeding to which the debtor is a party (Code Sec. 7464).[75]

References are to Standard Federal Tax Reports; Tax Research Consultant; and Practical Tax Explanations.

[71] ¶ 40,700, ¶ 40,701; IRS: 60,250; § 39,545.05

[72] ¶ 40,700; IRS: 60,256; § 39,545.05

[73] ¶ 40,730, ¶ 40,811; IRS: 60,200; § 39,545.05

[74] ¶ 40,610; IRS: 57,056; § 39,550.05

[75] ¶ 42,120; IRS: 57,056; § 39,550.10

Liens and Levies

2751. Property Subject to Liens. If a taxpayer fails to pay an assessed tax after notice and demand for payment, the United States acquires a lien for the amount due, including interest and penalties, against all the taxpayer's property (real, personal, tangible, and intangible), including after-acquired property and rights to property (Code Sec. 6321; Reg. § 301.6321-1).[76] Whether the taxpayer owns or has an interest in property is determined under the appropriate state law. Once the taxpayer's rights in the property are established, federal law determines priorities among competing creditors (Code Sec. 6323).[77] Federal law also controls whether specific property is exempt from levy (¶ 2753). Once a tax lien arises, it continues until the tax liability is paid or the lien becomes unenforceable due to a lapse of time (Code Sec. 6322).[78] Therefore, the lien period generally coincides with the statutory period for collection, which is 10 years from the date of assessment (Code Sec. 6502(a)).[79] However, the collection period may be suspended or extended.

2753. Property Subject to Levy. Although a tax lien attaches to all of the debtor's property, some property is exempt from levy. The following are among the items that are exempt from levy to some extent:

(1) wearing apparel and school books;

(2) fuel, provisions, furniture, and personal effects: up to $9,120 for 2016 ($9,200 for 2017);

(3) unemployment benefits;

(4) books and tools of a trade, business, or profession: up to $4,560 for 2016 ($4,600 for 2017);

(5) undelivered mail;

(6) certain annuity and pension payments;

(7) workers' compensation;

(8) judgments for support of minor children;

(9) certain public assistance payments, supplemental security income for the aged, blind, and disabled, state and local welfare payments, and Job Training Partnership Act payments;

(10) certain amounts of wages, salary, and other income; and

(11) certain service-connected disability payments (Code Sec. 6334; Rev. Proc. 2015-53; Rev. Proc. 2016-55).[80]

Certain specified payments are not exempt from levy if the Secretary of the Treasury approves a continuous levy (Code Sec. 6334(f)).[81] The IRS, under the Federal Payment Levy Program (FPLP), can approve a continuous levy on up to 15 percent (100 percent for payments due to a vendor of goods and services and sales or leases of real property; 30 percent for payments owed to a Medicare provider; and 100 percent for payments owed a Medicare provider) of any federal payment other than: a payment for which eligibility is not based on the income or assets or both of the payee; unemployment benefits, worker's compensation payments, wages, or salary; Social Security disability payments; welfare and public assistance payments; and annuity or pension payments or benefits under the Railroad Retirement Act or Railroad Unemployment Insurance Act (Code Sec. 6331(h), as amended by the Medicare Access and CHIP Reauthorization Act of 2015 (P.L. 114-10)).

The IRS may not seize any real property used as a residence by the taxpayer or any real property of the taxpayer (other than rental property) that is used as a residence by another person in order to satisfy a liability of $5,000 or less (including tax, penalties,

References are to Standard Federal Tax Reports; Tax Research Consultant; and Practical Tax Explanations.

[76] ¶ 38,135, ¶ 38,135A; IRS: 48,050, IRS: 48,100; § 39,925.05

[77] ¶ 38,145; IRS: 48,150; § 39,925.20

[78] ¶ 38,140; IRS: 48,050; § 39,925.10

[79] ¶ 39,010; IRS: 45,202; § 39,925.10

[80] ¶ 38,210; IRS: 51,062; § 39,930.15

[81] ¶ 38,210; IRS: 51,060.35; § 39,930.20

and interest). In the case of the taxpayer's principal residence, the IRS may not seize the residence without written approval of a federal district court judge or magistrate (Code Sec. 6334(a)(13) and (e)).[82] Unless collection of tax is in jeopardy, tangible personal property or real property (other than rented real property) used in the taxpayer's trade or business may not be seized without written approval of an IRS district or assistant director. Such approval may not be given unless it is determined that the taxpayer's other assets subject to collection are not sufficient to pay the amount due and the expenses of the proceedings. Where a levy is made on tangible personal property essential to the taxpayer's trade or business, the IRS must provide an accelerated appeals process to determine whether the property should be released from levy (Code Sec. 6343(a)(2)).[83] See ¶ 2755.

Levies are prohibited if the estimated expenses of the levy and sale exceed the fair market value of the property (Code Sec. 6331(f)).[84] Also, unless the collection of tax is in jeopardy, a levy cannot be made on any day on which the taxpayer is required to respond to an IRS summons (Code Sec. 6331(g)).[85] Further, financial institutions are required to hold amounts garnished by the IRS for 21 days after receiving notice of the levy to provide the taxpayer time to notify the IRS of any errors (Code Sec. 6332(c)).[86]

2754. Recording and Priority of Tax Liens. Until notice of a tax lien has been properly recorded, it is not valid against any bona fide purchaser for value, mechanic's lienor, judgment lien creditor, or holder of a security interest (e.g., a mortgagee or pledgee) (Code Sec. 6323(a)).[87] Also, even a properly recorded tax lien may not be valid against so-called superpriorities, which include purchases of securities and automobiles, retail purchases, casual sales of less than $1,530 for 2016 ($1,540 for 2017), certain possessory liens securing payment for repairs to personal property, real property taxes and special assessment liens, mechanic's liens for repairs and improvements of not more than $7,630 for 2016 ($7,690 for 2017) to certain residential property, attorneys' liens, certain insurance contracts and deposit secured loans (previously referred to as passbook loans) (Code Sec. 6323(b); Rev. Proc. 2015-53; Rev. Proc. 2016-55).[88] In addition, security interests arising from commercial financing agreements may be accorded superpriority status (Code Sec. 6323(c)).[89]

Notice of a federal tax lien must be filed in one office designated by the state in which the property is situated (Code Sec. 6323(f); Reg. § 301.6323(f)-1).[90] Generally, personal property is considered situated in the state where the taxpayer resides, rather than where domiciled; for real property, the situs is its physical location. If, in the case of either real or personal property, the state designates more than one office or does not designate an office where notice must be filed, notice of the lien must be filed with the Clerk of the U.S. District Court for the district in which the property is situated. If state law provides that a notice of lien affecting personal property must be filed in the county clerk's office located in the taxpayer's county of residence and also adopts a federal law that requires a notice of lien to be filed in another location in order to attach to a specific type of property, the state is deemed to have designated only one office for the filing of the notice. Thus, to protect its lien, the IRS need only file its notice in the county clerk's office located in the taxpayer's home county (Reg. § 301.6323(f)-1(a)(2)). Notice regarding property located in the District of Columbia is filed with the Recorder of Deeds of the District of Columbia. Special rules apply in a state that requires public indexing for priority liens against realty.

A forfeiture under local law of property seized by any law enforcement agency or other local governmental branch relates back to the time the property was first seized,

References are to Standard Federal Tax Reports; Tax Research Consultant; and Practical Tax Explanations.

[82] ¶ 38,210; IRS: 51,062.05; § 39,930.15

[83] ¶ 38,270; IRS: 51,154; § 39,930.15

[84] ¶ 38,185; IRS: 51,054; § 39,930.05

[85] ¶ 38,185; IRS: 51,054; § 39,930.05

[86] ¶ 38,185; IRS: 51,064.35; § 39,930.25

[87] ¶ 38,145; IRS: 48,150; § 39,925.20

[88] ¶ 38,145; IRS: 48,160; § 39,925.20

[89] ¶ 38,145; IRS: 48,160; § 39,925.20

[90] ¶ 38,145, ¶ 38,153; IRS: 48,056; § 39,925.20

unless, under local law, a claim holder would have priority over the interest of the government in the property (Code Sec. 6323(i)(3)).[91]

The IRS may not levy against property while a taxpayer has a pending offer in compromise or installment agreement (Code Sec. 6331(k)).[92] If the offer in compromise or installment agreement is ultimately rejected, the levy prohibition remains in effect for 30 days after the rejection and during the pendency of any appeal of the rejection, providing the appeal is filed within 30 days of the rejection. No levy may be made while the installment agreement is in effect. If the installment agreement is terminated by the IRS, no levy may be made for 30 days after the termination and during the pendency of any appeal.

2754A. Notice and Opportunity for Hearing. The IRS must notify any person subject to a lien of the existence of the lien within five days of the lien being filed (Code Sec. 6320; Reg. § 301.6320-1).[93] Among other requirements, the notice must address the person's right to request a hearing during the 30-day period beginning on the sixth day after the lien is filed. Similarly, at least 30 days prior to levying on any person's property or right to property, the IRS must provide the taxpayer with notice of its intent to levy and of the taxpayer's the right to a hearing, commonly referred to as a Collection Due Process (CDP) hearing (Code Sec. 6330; Reg. § 301.6330-1).[94] Whether in connection with the notice of lien or notice of intent to levy, the hearing is to be held by the IRS Office of Appeals. At the hearing, the taxpayer may raise any issue relevant to the appropriateness of the proposed collection activity if such issue was not raised at a previous hearing. The taxpayer has 30 days after the hearing determination to appeal the determination to the Tax Court, which has exclusive jurisdiction over appeals of hearing determinations. A taxpayer subject to a levy for the collection of employment taxes cannot request a hearing if the taxpayer already requested a hearing regarding unpaid employment taxes arising in the two-year period before the beginning of the tax period at issue.

2755. Release of Tax Liens and Levies. Taxpayers may appeal the filing of a notice of lien in the public record and petition for release (Code Sec. 6326; Reg. § 301.6326-1).[95] If filed in error, the IRS must release the lien and state that the lien was erroneous. The request for relief must be based on one of the following grounds:

(1) the tax liability had been satisfied before the lien was filed;

(2) the assessing of the tax liability violated either the notice of deficiency procedures or the Bankruptcy Code; or

(3) the limitations period for collecting the liability had expired prior to the filing of the lien.

Further, the IRS may withdraw a public notice of tax lien before payment in full if:

(1) the filing of the notice was premature or not in accord with administrative procedures;

(2) the taxpayer has entered into an installment agreement to satisfy the tax liability;

(3) withdrawal of the notice would facilitate the collection of the tax liability; or

(4) withdrawal of the notice would be in the best interest of the taxpayer and the government, as determined by the National Taxpayer Advocate (Code Sec. 6323(j)).[96]

The withdrawal of a notice of tax lien does not affect the underlying tax lien; rather, the withdrawal simply relinquishes any lien priority the IRS had obtained when the notice was filed.

References are to Standard Federal Tax Reports; Tax Research Consultant; and Practical Tax Explanations.

[91] ¶ 38,145; IRS: 48,154; § 39,925.20

[92] ¶ 38,185; IRS: 51,054; § 39,930.05

[93] ¶ 38,132, ¶ 38,133; IRS: 48,058.05; § 39,945.10

[94] ¶ 38,182, ¶ 38,183; IRS: 51,056.05; § 39,945.15

[95] ¶ 38,175, ¶ 38,176; IRS: 48,200; § 39,925.25, § 39,930.30

[96] ¶ 38,145; IRS: 48,052.10; § 39,925.25

The IRS is required to release a levy if:

(1) the underlying liability is satisfied or becomes unenforceable due to lapse of time;

(2) the IRS determines that the release of the levy will facilitate the collection of tax;

(3) an installment payment agreement has been executed by the taxpayer with respect to the liability;

(4) the IRS determines that the levy is creating a financial hardship; or

(5) the fair market value of the property exceeds the liability, and the partial release of the levy would not hinder the collection of tax (Code Sec. 6343(a)).[97]

In addition, a taxpayer may request that the IRS sell the levied property (Code Sec. 6335(f); Reg. § 301.6335-1(d)).[98]

The IRS has been given authority to return property that has been levied upon if:

(1) the levy was premature or not in accordance with administrative procedure;

(2) the taxpayer has entered into an installment agreement to satisfy the tax liability, unless the agreement provides otherwise;

(3) the return of the property will facilitate collection of the tax liability; or

(4) with the consent of the taxpayer or the Taxpayer Advocate, the return of the property would be in the best interests of the taxpayer and the government (Code Sec. 6343(d)).[99]

Property is returned in the same manner as if the property had been wrongfully levied upon, except that the taxpayer is not entitled to interest.

A taxpayer may bring a suit in federal district court if an IRS employee knowingly or negligently fails to release a tax lien on the taxpayer's property after receiving written notice from the taxpayer of the IRS's failure to release the lien (Code Sec. 7432; Reg. § 301.7432-1).[100] The taxpayer may recover actual economic damages plus the costs of the action. Injuries such as inconvenience, emotional distress, and loss of reputation are not compensable damages unless they result in actual economic harm. Costs of the action that may be recovered are limited generally to certain court costs and do not include administrative costs or attorney's fees, although attorney's fees may be recoverable (¶ 2796). A two-year statute of limitations, measured from the date on which the cause of action accrued, applies.

Third-Party Owners. A third-party owner of property against which a federal tax lien has been filed may obtain a certificate of discharge with respect to the lien on such property (Code Sec. 6325(b)(4); Reg. § 301.6325-1(b)(4)).[101] The certificate is issued if (1) the third-party owner deposits with the IRS an amount of money equal to the value of the government's interest in the property as determined by the IRS or (2) the third-party owner posts a bond covering the government's interest in the property in a form acceptable to the IRS. A third-party owner who is a co-owner of property with the taxpayer against whom the underlying tax was assessed may no longer be automatically barred from obtaining a certificate of discharge with respect to a lien on the property. Third-party owners may request the discharge of a tax lien on property that they own with the person whose tax liability gave rise to the lien.

If the IRS determines that (1) the liability to which the lien relates can be satisfied from other sources or (2) the value of the government's interest in the property is less than the IRS's prior determination of the government's interest in the property, then the

References are to Standard Federal Tax Reports; Tax Research Consultant; and Practical Tax Explanations.

[97] ¶ 38,270; IRS: 51,154; § 39,930.30

[98] ¶ 38,230, ¶ 38,231; IRS: 51,202; § 39,930.30

[99] ¶ 38,270; IRS: 51,154.05; § 39,930.30

[100] ¶ 41,760, ¶ 41,761; IRS: 48,210; § 39,925.25

[101] ¶ 38,165, ¶ 38,166; IRS: 48,204.15; § 39,925.25

IRS will refund, with interest, the amount deposited and release the bond applicable to such property. Within 120 days after a certificate of discharge is issued, the third-party owner may file a civil action against the United States in a federal district court for a determination of whether the government's interest in the property, if any, has less value than that determined by the IRS (Code Sec. 7426(a)(4) and (b)(5)).[102]

Mitigation of Effect of Statute of Limitations

2756. Correction of Errors in Certain Cases. The Code provides relief from some of the inequities caused by the statute of limitations and other provisions that would otherwise prevent equitable adjustment of various income tax hardships (Code Secs. 1311–1314; Reg. §§ 1.1311(a)-1–1.1314(c)-1).[103] Adjustments are permitted, even though the limitations period for assessment or refund for the year at issue may have otherwise expired, when a determination under the income tax laws:

(1) requires the inclusion in gross income of an item that was erroneously included in the income of the taxpayer for another tax year or in the gross income of a "related taxpayer," e.g., spouse, beneficiary, partner, member of affiliated group of corporations, etc.;

(2) allows a deduction or credit that was erroneously allowed to the taxpayer for another tax year or to a related taxpayer;

(3) requires the exclusion from gross income of an item included in a return filed by the taxpayer or with respect to which tax was paid and which was erroneously excluded or omitted from the gross income of the taxpayer for another tax year or from the gross income of a related taxpayer for the same or another tax year;

(4) allows or disallows, in certain situations, deductions or inclusions for a trust or an estate, and there has been no appropriate corresponding change in the income of beneficiaries, heirs, or legatees;

(5) establishes the basis of property by making adjustments to such basis for items that should have been added to, or deducted from, income of preceding years;

(6) requires the allowance or disallowance of a deduction or credit to a corporation where a correlative deduction or credit was erroneously allowed, or disallowed, to a related taxpayer that is a member of an affiliated group of corporations where there is an 80% common ownership;

(7) requires the exclusion from gross income of an item not included in a return filed by the taxpayer and with respect to which the tax was not paid but which is includible in the gross income of the taxpayer for another tax year or in the gross income of a related taxpayer; or

(8) disallows a deduction or credit that should have been allowed, but was not allowed, to the taxpayer for another tax year or to a related taxpayer for the same or another tax year (Code Sec. 1312).[104]

Refunds and Credits

2759. Claim for Refund or Credit. A claim for refund for an overpayment of income taxes is generally made on the appropriate income tax return. However, once the return has been filed and the taxpayer believes the tax is incorrect, the claim for refund by an individual who filed Form 1040, 1040A, or 1040EZ is made on Form 1040X. The refund claim is made on Form 1120X by a corporation that filed Form 1120. A claim for refund or credit for an overpayment of income taxes for which a form other than Form 1040, 1040A, 1040EZ, 1120, or 990T was filed is made on the appropriate amended

References are to Standard Federal Tax Reports; Tax Research Consultant; and Practical Tax Explanations.

[102] ¶ 41,710; IRS: 48,204.15; § 39,925.25

[103] ¶ 31,800–¶ 31,865; IRS: 30,300; § 40,401

[104] ¶ 31,820; IRS: 30,300; § 40,405, § 40,410.05

tax return (Reg. § 301.6402-3).[105] Form 843 should be filed for any claim for refund or credit if no other form is prescribed (Reg. § 301.6402-2(c)).[106]

2760. Amendment of Refund Claim. A timely claim for refund based upon one or more specific grounds may not be amended to include other and different grounds after the statute of limitations has expired (Reg. § 301.6402-2(b)).[107]

2761. Refund or Credit After Appeal to Tax Court. Where the taxpayer has been mailed a notice of deficiency and has filed a petition with the Tax Court (¶ 2778), the taxpayer may not bring a separate refund suit in any other court for recovery of any part of the tax at issue in the Tax Court (Code Sec. 6512).[108] The taxpayer is permitted, however, to institute a claim for credit or refund in another court for the same tax year to recover:

(1) an overpayment determined by a decision of the Tax Court that has become final,

(2) any amount collected in excess of an amount computed in accordance with a final decision of the Tax Court,

(3) any amount collected after the expiration of the period of limitations upon the beginning of levy or a proceeding in court for collection,

(4) overpayments attributable to partnership items,

(5) any amount that was collected within the period following the mailing of a notice of deficiency during which the IRS is prohibited from collecting by levy or through a court proceeding, and

(6) any amount that is not contested on an appeal from a Tax Court decision.

The Tax Court can order the refund of a tax overpayment plus interest if the IRS has not made a refund to the taxpayer within 120 days after the decision fixing the amount of the refund has become final (Code Sec. 6512(b)).[109]

The Tax Court is empowered to resolve disputes regarding the amount of interest to be charged on a tax deficiency redetermined pursuant to a Tax Court order. The action must be brought within one year from the date on which the decision ordering the redetermination of taxes became final. Further, the taxpayer must pay the entire redetermined deficiency, plus the entire amount of interest, before the Tax Court can hear the case (Code Sec. 7481(c)).[110]

2763. Limitations on Credit or Refund. A taxpayer may generally file a claim for refund within three years from the time the return was filed or within two years from the time the tax was paid, whichever is later. If no return was filed by the taxpayer, the claim must be filed within two years from the time the tax was paid (Code Sec. 6511(a)).[111] For this purpose, a return filed before the due date is treated as filed on the due date (Code Sec. 6513(a)).[112] Taxpayers who fail to file a return as of the date the IRS mails a deficiency notice may recover in the Tax Court taxes paid during the three years preceding the IRS mailing date (Code Sec. 6512(b)(3)).[113]

If the claim relates to the deductibility of bad debts or worthless securities, the period is seven years; if it relates to the credit for foreign taxes, the period is 10 years. If the refund claim relates to a net operating loss (NOL) or a capital loss carryback, the period is that period which ends three years after the time prescribed by law for filing the return, including extensions, for the tax year of the NOL or capital loss carryback. To the extent that an overpayment is due to unused credit carrybacks that arise as the

References are to Standard Federal Tax Reports; Tax Research Consultant; and Practical Tax Explanations.

[105] ¶ 38,517; IRS: 33,150; § 40,010.10

[106] ¶ 38,516; IRS:33,154.10; § 40,010.10.

[107] ¶ 38,516; IRS: 33,200; § 40,010.25

[108] ¶ 39,090; LITIG: 3,102; § 40,001

[109] ¶ 39,090; LITIG: 6,100; § 40,001

[110] ¶ 42,420; LITIG: 6,114; § 40,001

[111] ¶ 39,060; IRS: 36,050; § 40,040.05

[112] ¶ 39,120; IRS: 36,050; § 40,040.05

[113] ¶ 39,090; IRS: 36,116; § 40,040.05

result of the carryback of an NOL or capital loss, the claim may be filed during the period that ends three years after the time prescribed by law for filing the return, including extensions, for the tax year of the unused credit that results in the carryback (Code Sec. 6511(d); Reg. § 301.6511(d)-2).[114]

The statute of limitations on refund claims is suspended during any period that an individual is financially disabled, i.e., under a medically determinable mental or physical impairment that: (1) can be expected to result in death or that has lasted or can be expected to last for a continuous period of not less than one year, and (2) renders the person unable to manage his or her financial affairs (Code Sec. 6511(h)).[115] The suspension of the limitations period does not apply for any period during which the taxpayer's spouse or another person is authorized to act on behalf of the individual in financial matters.

Retired Military Personnel. The time period for retired military personnel to file claims for credits or refunds related to disability determinations by the Department of Veterans Affairs, e.g., determinations after the tax return is filed, is extended until one year after the date of the disability determination if that period is later than the normal three-year period of limitations (Code Sec. 6511(d)(8)).[116] This provision does not apply to any tax year that began more than five years before the date of the disability determination.

2764. Refund Reduction for Past-Due, Legally Enforceable Debts. The Treasury Department's Financial Management Service (FMS) will reduce the amount of any tax refund payable to a taxpayer by the amount of any past-due, legally enforceable nontax debt that is owed to any federal agency. Debts that are less than $25 are exempt. In most cases, the creditor federal agencies must have first attempted to collect the debt by using salary offset and administrative procedures. The federal agency is also required to notify the taxpayer that a debt will be referred to the FMS for refund offset if the debt remains unpaid after 60 days or if there is insufficient evidence that the debt is either not past due or not legally enforceable (31 CFR § 285.2).

The FMS has also promulgated rules governing the offset of tax refunds against past-due child and spousal support (31 CFR § 285.3) and against state income tax debts reduced to judgment (31 CFR § 285.8). Tax refunds may also be offset against past-due debts owed to a state for (1) erroneous payment of unemployment compensation due to fraud or failure to report earnings, or (2) failure to make contributions to a state's unemployment fund for which the state has determined the person to be liable (Code Sec. 6402(f)).[117]

2765. Interest on Refund. When a return has been properly filed in processable form, interest is allowed on a refund from the date of overpayment to a date preceding the date of the refund check by not more than 30 days (Code Sec. 6611(b)(2) and (3)).[118] If a return is filed late, no interest is allowed for any day before the date on which it is filed. No interest is payable on a refund arising from an original tax return if the refund is issued by the 45th day after the later of the due date for the return, determined without regard to any extensions, or the date the return is filed (Code Sec. 6611(e)). Similarly, if a refund claimed on an amended return or claim for refund is issued within 45 days after the date the amended document was filed, interest is not payable for that period, although interest is payable from the due date of the original return to the date the amended document was filed. If a refund is not issued within the 45-day grace period, interest is payable for the period from the due date of the original return to the date the refund is paid.

References are to Standard Federal Tax Reports; Tax Research Consultant; and Practical Tax Explanations.

[114] ¶ 39,060, ¶ 39,067; IRS: 36,100; § 40,045.05

[115] ¶ 39,060; IRS: 36,052; § 40,040.05

[116] ¶ 39,060; IRS: 36,052; § 40,045.05

[117] ¶ 38,510; IRS: 33,304.20; § 40,015.05

[118] ¶ 39,430; PENALTY: 9,100; § 40,115.05

The interest rate the IRS must pay for overpayment of taxes by noncorporate taxpayers is equal to the federal short-term rate (¶ 83) plus three percentage points (which is equal to the interest rate on underpayments of tax). The interest rate on overpayments by corporate taxpayers is the short-term federal rate plus two percentage points (Code Sec. 6621).[119] For large corporate overpayments, i.e., any portion that exceeds $10,000, the rate is reduced to the sum of the short-term federal rate plus one-half of one percentage point. These rates are adjusted quarterly, with each successive rate becoming effective two months after the date of each quarterly adjustment. The rates for the first quarter of 2016 were 3 percent for noncorporate taxpayers and 2 percent for corporate taxpayers (0.5 percent for large corporate overpayments); for the second, third, and fourth quarters of 2016 were 4 percent for noncorporate taxpayers and 3 percent for corporate taxpayers (1.5 percent for large corporate overpayments).[120]

Overlapping Overpayments and Underpayments. The interest rates for overpayments and underpayments have been equalized (also referred to as "global interest netting") for any period of mutual indebtedness between taxpayers and the IRS (Code Sec. 6621(d)).[121] No interest is imposed to the extent that underpayment and overpayment interest run simultaneously on equal amounts. The net zero interest rate applies regardless of whether an underpayment otherwise would be subject to the increased interest rate imposed on large corporate underpayments or an overpayment otherwise would be subject to a reduced interest rate because it was a corporate overpayment in excess of $10,000. Although global interest netting is available to both corporate and noncorporate taxpayers, its effect on noncorporate taxpayers is mitigated due to the equalization of the underpayment and overpayment interest rates for such taxpayers.

2768. Refunds Disregarded for Means-Tested Assistance Programs. Any federal tax refund, or advance payment with respect to a refundable federal tax credit made to any individual cannot be taken into account as income or as resources for a period of 12 months from receipt, for purposes of determining the individual's eligibility (or that of any other individual) for benefits or assistance, or for the amount or extent of benefits or assistance, under (1) any federal program, or (2) any state or local program financed in whole or in part with federal funds (Code Sec. 6409).[122]

2773. Quick Carryback Refund and Postponement of Tax Payment. A corporation other than an S corporation that has an overpayment of tax as a result of a net operating loss (NOL), capital loss, business and research credits, or a claim-of-right adjustment can file an application on Form 1139 for a tentative adjustment or refund of taxes for a year affected by the carryback of such loss or credits or by such adjustment. A noncorporate taxpayer can apply for similar adjustments on Form 1045 (Code Sec. 6411; Temp. Reg. § 5.6411-1).[123] For provisions on the quick refund of a capital loss carryback, see ¶ 1145.

The application itself is not a formal refund claim and its rejection in whole or in part cannot be made the basis of a refund suit. However, the taxpayer can file a regular claim for refund within the limitations period (¶ 2763), and this claim can be made the basis for a suit. For losses and credits, the IRS must allow or disallow the refund or credit within 90 days from the later of (1) the date the application is filed or (2) the last day of the month in which the return for the loss or unused credit year is due (giving effect to extensions of time). For claim-of-right adjustments, the IRS must allow or disallow the refund or credit within 90 days from the later of (1) the date the application is filed or (2) the date of the overpayment.

References are to Standard Federal Tax Reports; Tax Research Consultant; and Practical Tax Explanations.

[119] ¶ 39,450; PENALTY: 9,152; § 40,115.05

[120] ¶ 39,455.51; PENALTY: 9,152

[121] ¶ 39,450; PENALTY: 9,056.05; § 40,120.15

[122] ¶ 38,702; IRS: 33,300; § 40,001

[123] ¶ 38,720, ¶ 38,726; IRS: 33,352; § 40,025

If a corporation expects a NOL carryback from the current (unfinished) tax year, it can, subject to certain limitations, extend the time for payment of all or a part of the tax still payable for the immediately preceding year by filing a statement on Form 1138 (Reg. § 1.6164-1).[124]

The Courts

2776. Organization of Tax Court. The primary function of the U.S. Tax Court is to review deficiencies asserted by the IRS for additional income, estate, gift, or self-employment taxes or special excise taxes (Code Secs. 6512 and 7442).[125] The Tax Court is not an agency of, and is independent of, the Executive Branch of the Government (Code Sec. 7441, as amended by the Protecting Americans from Tax Hikes (PATH) Act of 2015 (P.L. 114-113). The Tax Court is the only judicial body from which relief may be obtained without the payment of tax. The Tax Court also may issue declaratory judgments on the initial or continuing qualification of a retirement plan under Code Sec. 401, a tax-exempt organization under Code Sec. 501(c), Code Sec. 501(d) or Code Sec. 170(c)(2), a private foundation under Code Sec. 509(a), a private operating foundation under Code Sec. 4942(j)(3), or a tax-exempt farmers' cooperative under Code Sec. 521. However, a revocation of tax-exempt status for failure to file an annual information return or notice is not subject to an action for declaratory judgment relief. The Tax Court also may rule on the tax-exempt interest status of a government bond issue (Code Secs. 7428, 7476, and 7478; Tax Court Rule 210).[126] Declaratory judgment powers are also provided for (1) estate tax installments, (2) gift tax revaluations, and (3) employment status determinations.

The Tax Court may establish procedures for filing complaints with respect to the conduct of any judge or special trial judge (Code Sec. 7466, as added by P.L. 114-113). The Tax Court has the same general management, administrative and expenditure authorities that are available to other courts and may conduct annual judicial conferences and charge reasonable registration fees (Code Sec. 7470 and Code Sec. 7470A, as added by P.L. 114-113). All fees received by the Tax Court, except for annual conference registration fees and periodic practice fees, must be deposited into a Treasury special fund (Code Sec. 7473, as amended by P.L. 114-113).

The Tax Court's offices and trial rooms are located in Washington, D.C., but trials are also conducted in principal cities throughout the country. At the time of filing a petition, the taxpayer should file a request indicating where he or she prefers the trial to be held. The court imposes a filing fee of $60 (Code Sec. 7451).[127]

In any Tax Court case, other than small tax cases (¶ 2784), the findings of fact and opinion must generally be reported in writing. In appropriate cases, a Tax Court judge may state orally, and record in the transcript of the proceedings, the findings of fact or opinion in the case (Code Sec. 7459).[128] In these cases, the court must provide to all parties in the case either a copy of the transcript pages, which record the findings or opinion, or a written summary of such findings or opinion (Tax Court Rule 152).[129]

2778. Appeal to the Tax Court. Before the IRS can assess a deficiency, it generally must mail a deficiency notice to the taxpayer. The taxpayer then has an opportunity to appeal, within 90 days after the notice is mailed, to the Tax Court (¶ 2711). A notice based solely upon a mathematical or clerical error is not considered a notice of deficiency (Code Sec. 6213; Reg. § 301.6213-1).[130] If the notice is mailed to a person outside the United States, the period is 150 days instead of 90 days. The period is counted from midnight of the day on which the notice is mailed. Saturday, Sunday, or a legal holiday in the District of Columbia is not counted as the 90th or 150th day.

References are to Standard Federal Tax Reports; Tax Research Consultant; and Practical Tax Explanations.

[124] ¶ 37,241; FILEBUS: 6,104.20; § 40,025

[125] ¶ 39,090, ¶ 42,057; LITIG: 6,100

[126] ¶ 41,720, ¶ 42,134, ¶ 42,154, ¶ 42,370; LITIG: 6,100

[127] ¶ 42,072; LITIG: 6,050

[128] ¶ 42,110; IRS: 27,206

[129] ¶ 42,312; LITIG: 6,802

[130] ¶ 37,545, ¶ 37,546, ¶ 37,549.34; LITIG: 6,202, LITIG: 6,204

When a petition to the Tax Court is properly addressed and mailed within the prescribed time for filing, with the postage prepaid, the date of the U.S. postmark stamped on the cover in which the petition is mailed is the date of filing. For a petition that is mailed from a foreign country, this rule applies only if the petition is given to a designated international delivery service (Rev. Rul. 2002-23). If a petition is sent by registered or certified mail, the date of registration or certification is the date of mailing and is prima facie evidence that the petition was delivered to the Tax Court. Similarly, the proper use of a private delivery service, under criteria established by the IRS, also constitutes prima facie evidence that the petition was delivered to the Tax Court (Reg. § 301.7502-1).[131]

If a taxpayer has filed a Tax Court petition before a jeopardy assessment or levy is made, the Tax Court is given concurrent jurisdiction with the federal district courts with respect to the taxpayer's challenge of the jeopardy assessment or levy (Code Sec. 7429(b)(2)).[132] Similarly, if there is a premature assessment of tax made while a proceeding with respect to that tax is pending in the Tax Court, the Tax Court has concurrent jurisdiction with the federal district court to restrain the assessment and collection of tax (Code Sec. 6213).[133]

2782. Burden of Proof. The IRS has the burden of proof in the Tax Court with respect to a factual issue that is relevant to determining a taxpayer's tax liability if the taxpayer presents credible evidence with respect to that issue *and* satisfies three applicable conditions (Code Sec. 7491):[134]

(1) The taxpayer must comply with the substantiation and recordkeeping requirements of the Code and regulations.

(2) The taxpayer must cooperate with reasonable requests by the IRS for witnesses, information, documents, meetings and interviews.

(3) Taxpayers *other than individuals* must meet the net worth limitations that apply for awarding attorneys' fees under Code Sec. 7430. Thus, corporations, trusts, and partnerships whose tax worth exceeds $7 million cannot benefit from this provision.

Further, in any court proceeding where the IRS solely uses statistical information from unrelated taxpayers to reconstruct an item of an *individual* taxpayer's income, such as the average income for taxpayers in the area in which the taxpayer lives, the burden of proof is on the IRS with respect to that item of income. Also with respect to individuals, the IRS must initially come forward with evidence that it is appropriate to apply a penalty, addition to tax, or additional amount before the court can impose the penalty.

In cases in which the burden of proof does not shift to the IRS, the taxpayer generally has the burden of proof in the Tax Court. However, a taxpayer must only establish that the IRS is in error and not whether any tax is owed (Tax Court Rule 142).[135] The IRS bears the burden of proof with respect to any new matter, increase in deficiency, or affirmative defenses raised in its answer. Further, the burden of proving fraud and liability as a transferee is upon the IRS (Code Secs. 6902 and 7454).[136] The IRS also has the burden of proof in proceedings involving a manager of a private foundation where the manager knowingly participated in an act of self-dealing, participated in an investment which jeopardizes the carrying out of an exempt purpose, or agreed to the making of a taxable expenditure.

2784. Small Tax Cases. The Tax Court maintains relatively informal procedures for the filing and handling of cases where neither the tax deficiency in dispute (including additions to tax and penalties) nor the amount of claimed overpayment exceeds $50,000. Usually taxpayers represent themselves, although they may be represented by anyone

References are to Standard Federal Tax Reports; Tax Research Consultant; and Practical Tax Explanations.

[131] ¶ 42,621; LITIG: 6,214

[132] ¶ 41,725; IRS: 54,204

[133] ¶ 37,545; LITIG: 6,136

[134] ¶ 42,515; LITIG: 3,200

[135] ¶ 42,302, ¶ 42,302.615; LITIG: 6,704

[136] ¶ 40,780, ¶ 42,081; LITIG: 6,708

admitted to practice before the Tax Court. Each decision is final and cannot be appealed by either the taxpayer or the government (Code Sec. 7463).[137] The filing fee is $60 (¶ 2776).

2786. Appeal from Tax Court Decision. A taxpayer who loses in the Tax Court may appeal the case (unless the case was tried as a small tax case (¶ 2784)) to the proper U.S. Court of Appeals by filing a notice of appeal with the clerk of the Tax Court. The notice must be filed within 90 days after the Tax Court decision is entered. However, if one party to the proceeding files a timely notice of appeal, any other party to the proceeding may take an appeal by filing a notice of appeal within 120 days after the decision of the Tax Court is entered (Code Sec. 7483).[138] A taxpayer who wants the assessment postponed pending the outcome of the appeal must file an appeal bond with the Tax Court guaranteeing payment of the deficiency as finally determined (Code Sec. 7485).[139]

2788. Acquiescence and Nonacquiescence by Commissioner. The IRS may announce in the Internal Revenue Bulletin if it has decided to acquiesce or not acquiesce in a regular decision of the Tax Court. Any acquiescence or nonacquiescence may be withdrawn, modified, or reversed at any time and any such action may be given retrospective, as well as prospective, effect.[140]

An acquiescence or nonacquiescence relates only to the issue or issues decided adversely to the government. Acquiescence means the IRS accepts the conclusion reached and does not necessarily mean acceptance and approval of any or all of the reasons assigned by the court for its conclusions. Acquiescences are to be relied on by IRS officers and others concerned as conclusions of the IRS only with respect to the application of the law to the facts in the particular case.

2790. Suits for Refund of Tax Overpayments. After the IRS rejects a refund claim for an alleged tax overpayment, suit can be maintained in the U.S. Court of Federal Claims or a U.S. District Court. A suit may be brought in the Court of Federal Claims against the United States to recover any overpayment of tax, regardless of amount (Judicial Code Sec. 1491).[141] Final decisions of the U.S. Court of Federal Claims are appealable to the U.S. Court of Appeals for the Federal Circuit (Judicial Code Sec. 1295).[142] All civil actions against the United States for the recovery of any internal revenue tax alleged to have been erroneously or illegally assessed or collected may be brought against the United States as defendant in a U.S. District Court with right of trial by jury in any action if either party makes a specific request for a jury trial (Judicial Code Secs. 1346 and 2402).[143] Filing a proper claim for refund or credit (¶ 2759) is a condition precedent to a suit for recovery of overpaid taxes (Code Sec. 7422(a)).[144]

If, prior to the hearing on a taxpayer's refund suit in a District Court or the Court of Federal Claims, a notice of deficiency is issued on the subject matter of the taxpayer's suit, then the District Court or Court of Federal Claims proceedings are stayed during the period of time in which the taxpayer can file a petition with the Tax Court (¶ 2778) and for 60 days thereafter. If the taxpayer files a petition with the Tax Court, then the District Court or the Court of Federal Claims loses jurisdiction as to any issues over which the Tax Court acquires jurisdiction. If the taxpayer does not appeal to the Tax Court, the United States may then counterclaim in the taxpayer's suit within the period of the stay of proceedings even though the time for such pleading may otherwise have expired (Code Sec. 7422(e)).[145]

2792. Time to Bring Suit. A suit or proceeding based upon a refund claim must be brought within two years from the date the IRS mails, by registered or certified mail, notice of disallowance of the part of the claim to which such suit or proceeding relates or

References are to Standard Federal Tax Reports; Tax Research Consultant; and Practical Tax Explanations.

[137] ¶ 42,118; LITIG: 7,000
[138] ¶ 42,477; LITIG: 6,960
[139] ¶ 42,500; LITIG: 6,966
[140] ¶ 43,282.20; IRS: 12,354
[141] ¶ 41,571; LITIG: 9,050
[142] ¶ 41,555; LITIG: 9,210
[143] ¶ 41,560, ¶ 41,589; LITIG: 9,052
[144] ¶ 41,685; LITIG: 9,056
[145] ¶ 41,685; LITIG: 3,102, LITIG: 9,106

within two years from the date the taxpayer waives notification of disallowance of his or her claim (Code Sec. 6532(a)).[146] The two-year period of limitations for filing suit may be extended by written agreement between the taxpayer and the IRS. Unless a bankruptcy proceeding has begun, no action can be brought before the expiration of six months from the date of filing the refund claim unless the IRS renders a decision on the claim before the six months are up. In bankruptcy proceedings, the six-month period is reduced to 120 days.

2794. Supreme Court. Either party may seek a review of a U.S. Court of Appeals decision by the U.S. Supreme Court through a petition for a writ of certiorari (Code Sec. 7482(a); Judicial Code Sec. 2101).[147]

2796. Attorneys' Fees and Court Costs. A "prevailing party"—any party, other than the United States or a creditor of the taxpayer, who has substantially prevailed with respect to the amount in controversy or the most significant issue or issues—may be awarded reasonable litigation costs in most civil tax litigation, including declaratory judgment proceedings (Code Sec. 7430).[148] In addition, a prevailing party can recover reasonable administrative costs incurred in connection with such administrative proceeding with the IRS.

These awards may be made if the taxpayer meets certain net worth limitations and the IRS fails to prove that its position was substantially justified. When litigation costs are involved, the IRS's position is the government's position taken in the litigation proceeding or administratively by the IRS District Counsel. In the case of administrative costs, the IRS's position is the position taken as of the earlier of (1) the date the taxpayer received a decision notice from the IRS Office of Appeals or (2) the date of the deficiency notice.

Reasonable administrative costs include (1) administrative fees or similar charges imposed by the IRS, and (2) the reasonable expenses incurred with respect to compensating expert witnesses, financing necessary studies and reports, and paying attorneys' fees. The costs can only be awarded if incurred after the earlier of:

(1) the date the taxpayer received the decision notice from the IRS Office of Appeals,

(2) the date of the deficiency notice, or

(3) the date on which the first letter of proposed deficiency is sent that allows the taxpayer an opportunity for administrative review in the IRS Office of Appeals.

Reasonable litigation costs include:

(1) expenses of expert witnesses;

(2) costs of any study, analysis, engineering report, test, or project, which was found by the court to be necessary for the preparation of its case;

(3) fees of an individual authorized to practice before the court or the IRS, whether or not an attorney (generally not in excess of $200 per hour for 2016; $200 per hour for 2017), unless an affidavit is presented that establishes a special factor for a higher rate, such as the unavailability of qualified representatives at the customary rate; and

(4) court costs.

To be recoverable, litigation costs must generally be paid or incurred by the taxpayer. However, a taxpayer may recover costs paid by a third party if the taxpayer assumes either a noncontingent obligation to repay the advanced fees or a contingent obligation to repay the fees in the event of their eventual recovery *(B.F. Morrison*, CA-9, 2009-1 USTC ¶ 50,387).

References are to Standard Federal Tax Reports; Tax Research Consultant; and Practical Tax Explanations.

[146] ¶ 39,270; LITIG: 9,058; § 40,010.25

[147] ¶ 41,583, ¶ 42,440; LITIG: 6,954

[148] ¶ 41,740; LITIG: 3,150; § 41,230.05

For purposes of both reasonable administrative costs and reasonable litigation costs, reasonable attorneys' fees may be awarded to attorneys and specified persons who represent prevailing parties on a pro bono basis or for a nominal fee. Thus, the amount awarded may be more than the amount of fees actually paid or incurred. The award must be paid to the attorney or the attorney's employer.

In order to establish that the taxpayer was a prevailing party, the taxpayer needs to establish that he has substantially prevailed with respect to the amount in controversy or with respect to the most significant issue or set of issues presented (Code Sec. 7430(c)(4); Reg. § 301.7430-5).[149] A taxpayer who meets the timely filing and net worth requirements may be treated as a prevailing party if the taxpayer's liability is determined to be equal to or less than it would have been had the government accepted the taxpayer's last qualified offer to settle the case (including interest). A qualified offer is a written offer made at any time during the time from the issuance of the 30-day letter to a date 30 days before the date the case is first set for trial (Code Sec. 7430(g); Reg. § 301.7430-7).[150]

No costs will be awarded where the prevailing party failed to exhaust all of the administrative remedies within the IRS (Code Sec. 7430(b); Reg. § 301.7430-1).[151] The tender of a qualified settlement offer does not satisfy the requirement to exhaust all administrative remedies (*Haas & Associates Accounting Corporation*, 117 TC 48, Dec. 54,447, aff'd CA-9, 2003-1 USTC ¶ 50,253). Further, costs will be denied for any portion of the proceeding where the prevailing party caused unreasonable delay (Code Sec. 7430(b)(4)).[152] A taxpayer who prevails in an IRS proceeding must apply to the IRS for administrative costs before the 91st day after the date the final IRS determination of tax, interest or penalty was mailed to the taxpayer. If the IRS denies the application for costs, the taxpayer must petition the Tax Court within 90 days of the IRS mailing of the denial.

An order granting or denying an award for litigation costs becomes part of the decision or judgment in the case and is subject to appeal in the same manner as the decision or judgment (Code Sec. 7430(f)).[153]

2798. Suit for Damages in Connection with Collection of Tax. A taxpayer may bring a suit in federal district court for damages sustained in connection with the collection of any federal tax because an IRS employee recklessly or intentionally disregarded any provision of the Internal Revenue Code, any IRS regulations or certain provisions of the Bankruptcy Code (Code Sec. 7433; Reg. § 301.7433-1).[154] A suit may also be brought for negligent disregard of the Internal Revenue Code or any IRS regulations. Except as provided in Code Sec. 7432 relating to damage awards for failure to release liens (¶ 2755), this action is the taxpayer's exclusive remedy for recovering damages caused by reckless, intentional or negligent disregard of such provisions and regulations by IRS employees. The suit must be brought within two years after the right of action accrues.

The award is limited to the costs of the action plus any actual direct economic damages sustained by the taxpayer, up to a maximum award of $1 million for reckless or intentional actions and $100,000 for acts of negligence. The IRS must comply with certain provisions of the Fair Debt Collection Practices Act so that the treatment of tax debtors by the IRS is at least equal to that required of private sector debt collectors (Code Sec. 6304). Taxpayers may bring a damages action under Code Sec. 7433 against the IRS for violations of these provisions.

References are to Standard Federal Tax Reports; Tax Research Consultant; and Practical Tax Explanations.

[149] ¶ 41,740, ¶ 41,742E, ¶ 41,742H; LITIG: 3,154; § 41,230.15

[150] ¶ 41,740, ¶ 41,742H; LITIG: 3,154; § 41,230.15

[151] ¶ 41,740, ¶ 41,742; LITIG: 3,150; § 41,230.20

[152] ¶ 41,740; LITIG: 3,154; § 41,230.30

[153] ¶ 41,740; LITIG: 3,158; § 41,230.40

[154] ¶ 41,770, ¶ 41,771; IRS: 45,114; § 39,950.05

Chapter 28

PENALTIES □ INTEREST

	Par.
Failure to File Returns or Pay Tax	2801
Document and Information Return Penalties	2814
Underpayments of Tax—Interest	2838
Underpayments of Tax—Penalties	2854
Underpayments of Estimated Tax	2875
Erroneous Tax Refund Claims	2891
Unauthorized Return Disclosures or Inspections	2892
Criminal Penalties	2898

Failure to File Returns or Pay Tax

2801. Failure to File Returns. A failure to file any tax return within the time prescribed by the Code may result in an addition to tax, i.e., a penalty. The penalty is five percent of the unpaid tax shown on the return for one month, with an additional five percent for each month or part of a month that the failure continues, up to 25 percent. If the tax return is not filed within 60 days of the prescribed due date, including extensions, the penalty will *not* be less than the lesser of $205 for 2016 ($210 for 2017) or 100 percent of the tax due on the return (Code Sec. 6651(a) and (i), as amended by the Trade Facilitation and Trade Enforcement Act of 2015 (P.L. 114-125); Rev. Proc. 2016-55).[1] The late-filing addition runs for the period up to the date the IRS actually receives the late return (Rev. Rul. 73-133).[2] The penalty is computed only on the net amount of tax due, if any, on the return after application of credits for payments of tax through withholding and estimated tax, as well as any other tax credits claimed on the return (Code Sec. 6651(b); Reg. § 301.6651-1(a), (b) and (d)).[3]

The fraud and accuracy-related penalties (¶ 2854) do not apply in the case of a fraudulent failure to file a return. Instead, the failure-to-file penalty ranges from 15 percent to 75 percent of the unpaid tax shown on the return (Code Sec. 6651(f)).[4]

The failure-to-file penalty is not imposed when the taxpayer can show that the failure to file was due to reasonable cause and not to willful neglect. Mere absence of willful neglect is not reasonable cause.[5] For example, reasonable cause did *not* exist when: (1) the taxpayer relied upon the advice of an agent; (2) the taxpayer relied on the accountant to perform the purely ministerial function of filing;[6] or (3) an officer of the corporate taxpayer misjudged the extension date.[7] However, failure to file a return upon a lawyer's or certified public accountant's advice that there was no income to report, or that the taxpayer was not liable for tax, has been held to be reasonable cause when the taxpayer supplied complete information to the tax professional.[8]

2805. Failure to Pay Tax. A penalty is imposed for failure to pay, when due, those taxes (other than estimated taxes) shown by a taxpayer on a return, unless the failure is due to reasonable cause (Code Sec. 6651(a)(2)).[9] A penalty is also imposed on additional taxes determined to be due on audit for which the IRS has made a demand for payment,

References are to Standard Federal Tax Reports; Tax Research Consultant; and Practical Tax Explanations.

[1] ¶ 39,470; PENALTY: 3,050; § 40,205.15

[2] ¶ 39,475.33; PENALTY: 3,056; § 40,205.15

[3] ¶ 39,470, ¶ 39,472; PENALTY: 3,054; § 40,205.15

[4] ¶ 39,470; PENALTY: 3,052; § 40,205.15

[5] ¶ 39,475.34; PENALTY: 3,060; § 40,205.15

[6] ¶ 39,475.42, ¶ 39,475.72; PENALTY: 3,060; § 40,205.15

[7] ¶ 39,475.705; PENALTY: 3,060; § 40,205.15

[8] ¶ 39,475.41; PENALTY: 3,060; § 40,205.15

[9] ¶ 39,470; PENALTY: 3,062; § 40,205.20

but this penalty runs only for the period of nonpayment beginning after the 21st *calendar* day (10th *business* day if the amount demanded is at least $100,000) following the demand (Code Sec. 6651(a)(3)).

In both cases, the addition to tax is one-half of one percent of the tax not paid, for each month or part of a month the tax remains unpaid, up to a maximum of 25 percent. The penalty increases to one percent per month beginning with either the 10th day after notice of levy is given or the day on which notice and demand is made in the case of a jeopardy assessment (¶ 2713). For taxpayers who enter into installment agreements (¶ 2529) with the IRS, the penalty for failure to timely pay taxes is reduced to one-quarter of one percent of the tax not paid (Code Sec. 6651(h); Reg. § 301.6651-1(a)(4)).[10]

If a taxpayer files a late return that is subject to both the failure-to-file penalty (¶ 2801) and the failure-to-pay penalty, the former may be reduced by the latter. However, if no return is filed or if a late-filed return understates the amount required to be shown on the return, the failure-to-pay penalty attributable to additional tax demanded by the IRS may not be used to offset any portion of the failure-to-file penalty. If the penalty for failure to file beyond 60 days applies, the penalty may not be reduced by a failure-to-pay penalty that is also imposed below the lesser of $205 for 2016 ($210 in 2017) or 100 percent of the tax due (Code Sec. 6651(a), (c), (d), and (i), as amended by the Trade Facilitation and Trade Enforcement Act of 2015 (P.L. 114-125); Rev. Proc. 2016-55).[11]

2809. Automatic Extension of Time for Filing. An automatic extension of time to file a tax return (¶ 2509) is not an extension of time to pay the tax due under the return (Reg. §§ 1.6081-3(b) and 1.6081-4(c)).[12] However, an individual taxpayer can avoid a failure-to-pay penalty (¶ 2805) by making an estimate of the tax due and paying that estimate with the request for extension of time to file. The estimate may be reduced by any amounts already paid through withholding or estimated tax payments over the course of the tax year. If the balance of tax due is remitted when the income tax return is filed by an individual or corporation, no penalty for failure to pay will apply unless the unpaid amount is more than 10 percent of the total tax liability (Reg. § 301.6651-1(c)(3) and (4)).[13]

2811. Frivolous Return Penalty. In addition to other penalties that may be imposed, there is a $5,000 penalty for filing a frivolous return (Code Sec. 6702).[14] A frivolous return is one that omits information necessary to determine the taxpayer's tax liability, shows a substantially incorrect tax, is based upon a frivolous position (e.g., that wages are not income), or is based upon the taxpayer's desire to impede the collection of tax. The IRS periodically updates a list of frivolous positions (Notice 2010-33). For example, a return based on the taxpayer's altering or striking out the "penalty of perjury" language above the signature line constitutes a frivolous return.

In certain limited circumstances, the IRS will reduce the $5,000 frivolous return penalty to $500 (Rev. Proc. 2012-43). If a person satisfies all eligibility criteria under the procedures, including filing all tax returns and paying all outstanding taxes, penalties (other than the frivolous return penalty), and related interest, the IRS will generally reduce all unpaid frivolous return penalties assessed against that person to $500, regardless of the number of penalties assessed. Any employer applying for relief must have deposited all employment taxes for the current quarter and the prior two quarters.

2813. Abatement of Penalties and/or Interest. The IRS must abate certain penalties that result from reliance on incorrect IRS advice if (1) the advice was furnished in writing in response to a specific written request from the taxpayer, and (2) the taxpayer reasonably relied upon the advice (Code Sec. 6404(f); Reg. § 301.6404-3).[15] However,

References are to Standard Federal Tax Reports; Tax Research Consultant; and Practical Tax Explanations.

[10] ¶ 39,470, ¶ 39,472; PENALTY: 3,062; § 40,205.20

[11] ¶ 39,470; PENALTY: 3,064; § 40,205.20

[12] ¶ 36,790, ¶ 36,793; FILEBUS: 15,102; § 39,215.05

[13] ¶ 39,472; PENALTY: 3,062.20; § 39,215.10

[14] ¶ 40,040, ¶ 40,043.50; PENALTY: 3,250; § 40,220.10

[15] ¶ 38,570, ¶ 38,576; IRS: 33,400; § 40,250.15

penalties will be abated only if the taxpayer furnished adequate and accurate information in making the request. Taxpayers entitled to abatement should file Form 843 with copies of the relevant written documents attached.

If the IRS extends the due date for filing income tax returns and for paying any tax due for taxpayers located in a federally declared disaster area, the IRS will abate the interest that would otherwise accrue for the extension period (Code Secs. 6404(i) and 7508A).[16]

The accrual of interest and penalties will be suspended after 36 months unless the IRS sends the taxpayer a notice following the later of: (1) the original due date of the return (without regard to extensions); or (2) the date on which a timely return is filed (Code Sec. 6404(g)).[17] The suspension of interest and penalties is available only for individuals and only for income taxes. Although the suspension pertains only to tax that is related to timely filed returns, the IRS has expanded this rule to cover additional tax voluntarily reported by a taxpayer, after a timely original return has been filed, on an amended return, or in correspondence with the IRS (Rev. Rul. 2005-4). The suspension begins on the day after the end of the 36-month period and ends on the day that is 21 days after the date on which the notice is made. The suspension does not stop the accrual of:

(1) the failure-to-file (¶ 2801) and failure-to-pay (¶ 2805) penalties;

(2) any interest, penalty, or other addition to tax in a case involving fraud;

(3) any interest, penalty, addition to tax, or additional amount with respect to any tax liability shown on the return;

(4) any interest, penalty, or other addition to tax with respect to any gross misstatement;

(5) any interest, penalty, or other addition to tax with respect to any reportable avoidance transaction or listed transaction (¶ 2591); or

(6) any criminal penalty (¶ 2898).

Document and Information Return Penalties

2814. Information Reporting Penalties. Three categories of penalties apply to failures to file required information returns and payee statements:

(1) failure to file an information return or to include correct information on an information return (¶ 2816) (Code Sec. 6721);

(2) failure to file a payee statement or to include correct information on a payee statement (¶ 2823) (Code Sec. 6722); and

(3) failure to comply with other information reporting requirements, which includes all reporting failures not covered by the other two categories (¶ 2833) (Code Sec. 6723).

2816. Failure to File Correct Information Returns. A time-sensitive three-tier penalty structure is imposed for: (1) any failure to file correct information returns (¶ 2565) with the IRS on or before the required filing date (other than a failure due to reasonable cause and not to willful neglect); (2) any failure to include all the information required to be shown on a return; or (3) the inclusion of incorrect information (Code Sec. 6721).[18] The penalty applies also to any failure to file electronically when required, but is imposed only if the taxpayer is filing 250 or more information returns (100 information returns in the case of a partnership having more than 100 partners) (Code Sec. 6724(c)).[19]

References are to Standard Federal Tax Reports; Tax Research Consultant; and Practical Tax Explanations.

[16] ¶ 38,570, ¶ 42,687A; FILEBUS: 15,110; § 39,215.35

[17] ¶ 38,570; PENALTY: 3,350, PENALTY: 9,056; § 40,030.30, § 40,250.10

[18] ¶ 40,210; PENALTY: 3,202; § 40,305.10

[19] ¶ 40,275; PENALTY: 3,202; § 40,305.10

The total amount of each penalty that may be imposed during a calendar year is subject to a maximum limit. The annual maximum penalty is reduced for small businesses whose average annual gross receipts for the three most recent tax years before the calendar year are $5 million or less. The penalty amounts and maximum limits are adjusted annually for inflation and are as follows:

(1) If a person files a correct information return after the required filing date but on or before the date that is 30 days after the required filing date, the amount of the penalty is (first-tier penalty):

(a) for tax years beginning in 2016, $50 per return, with a maximum penalty of $532,000 (for small businesses the maximum penalty is $186,000) (Code Sec. 6721(b)(1) and (d)(1)(B); Rev. Proc. 2015-53), and

(b) for tax years beginning in 2017, $50 per return, with a maximum penalty of $536,000 (for small businesses the maximum penalty is $187,500) (Code Sec. 6721(b)(1) and (d)(1)(B); Rev. Proc. 2016-55);

(2) If a person files a correct information return after the date that is 30 days after the prescribed filing date but on or before August 1 of the calendar year in which the required filing date occurs, the amount of the penalty is (second-tier penalty):

(a) for tax years beginning in 2016, $100 per return, with a maximum penalty of $1,596,500 (for small businesses the maximum penalty is $532,000 (Code Sec. 6721(b)(2) and (d)(1)(C); Rev. Proc. 2015-53),

(b) for tax years beginning in 2017, $100 per return, with a maximum penalty of $1,609,000 and (for small businesses the maximum penalty is $536,000) (Code Sec. 6721(b)(2) and (d)(1)(C); Rev. Proc. 2016-55);

(3) If a correct information return is not filed on or before August 1 of the calendar year in which the required filing date occurs, the amount of the penalty is (third-tier penalty):

(a) for returns required to be filed in 2016, $260 per return, with a maximum penalty of $3,193,000 (for small businesses the maximum penalty is $1,064,000 Code Sec. 6721(a)(1) and (d)(1)(A); Rev. Proc. 2015-53, and

(b) for returns required to be filed in 2017, $260 per return, with a maximum penalty of $3,218,500 (for small businesses the maximum penalty is $1,072,500) (Code Sec. 6721(a)(1) and (d)(1)(A), as amended by P.L. 114-27); Rev. Proc. 2016-55).

A certain *de minimis* number of returns timely filed with incorrect or omitted information that are corrected on or before August 1 of the calendar year in which the returns are due will be treated as having been filed correctly, and no penalty will be imposed on them. This exception is limited to the greater of 10 returns or one-half of one percent of the total number of information returns required to be filed during the calendar year. The *de minimis* exception does not apply to a failure to file an information return (Code Sec. 6721(c)).

A safe harbor is provided for *de minimis* dollar amount errors on information returns and payee statements required to be filed or provided after December 31, 2016 (Code Secs. 6721(c)(3) and 6722(c)(3), as added by the Protecting Americans from Tax Hikes (PATH) Act of 2015 (P.L. 114-113). A return or payee statement that is otherwise correct will be treated as filed or provided with all correct required information if no single erroneous dollar amount differs from the correct amount by more than $100, and no single amount reported for tax withheld differs from the correct amount by more than $25. The person to whom a payee statement must be provided may elect that the safe harbor does not apply to a payee statement. (Code Sec. 6722(c)(3)(B), as added by P.L. 114-113)). A broker must determine the adjusted basis in a covered security by treating as correct any incorrect dollar amount that does not need to be corrected due to the *de minimis* safe harbor (Code Sec. 6045(g)(2)(B)(iii), as added by P.L. 114-113).

Intentional Disregard. If the failure to file an information return or to include all the required correct information is due to intentional disregard of the filing requirements, neither the three-tier penalty nor the *de minimis* exception will apply (Code Sec. 6721(e)). Instead, the penalty for each failure, for tax years beginning in 2016 is:

(1) $530 per return, or

(2) if greater,

(a) 10 percent of the aggregate amount of the items required to be reported correctly in the case of a return other than a return required under Code Sec. 6045(a) (brokers' transactions with customers), Code Sec. 6041A(b) (payments of remuneration for direct sales), Code Sec. 6050H (information on mortgage interest received in a trade or business from individuals), Code Sec. 6050I (information on cash receipts from a trade or business), Code Sec. 6050J (information on foreclosures and abandonments of security), Code Sec. 6050K (information on exchanges of certain partnership interests), or Code Sec. 6050L (information on certain dispositions of donated property);

(b) five percent of the aggregate amount of the items required to be properly reported under Code Secs. 6045(a), 6050K, or 6050L;

(c) for informational returns required under Code Sec. 6050I(a) (cash receipts of more than $10,000 in a trade or business), the greater of $26,600 or the amount of cash received in the transaction or related transactions, up to a maximum of $106,000; or

(d) in the case of a return filed under Code Sec. 6050V, 10 percent of the value of the benefit of any contract with respect to which information is required to be include on the return (Rev. Proc. 2015-53).

The penalty for each failure, for tax years beginning in 2017, is:

(1) $530 per return, or

(2) if greater,

(a) 10 percent of the aggregate amount of the items required to be reported correctly in the case of a return other than a return required under Code Sec. 6045(a) (brokers' transactions with customers), Code Sec. 6041A(b) (payments of remuneration for direct sales), Code Sec. 6050H (information on mortgage interest received in a trade or business from individuals), Code Sec. 6050I (information on cash receipts from a trade or business), Code Sec. 6050J (information on foreclosures and abandonments of security), Code Sec. 6050K (information on exchanges of certain partnership interests), or Code Sec. 6050L (information on certain dispositions of donated property);

(b) five percent of the aggregate amount of the items required to be properly reported under Code Secs. 6045(a), 6050K, or 6050L;

(c) for informational returns required under Code Sec. 6050I(a) (cash receipts of more than $10,000 in a trade or business), the greater of $26,820 for the amount of cash received in the transaction or related transactions, up to a maximum of $107,000; or

(d) in the case of a return filed under Code Sec. 6050V, 10 percent of the value of the benefit of any contract with respect to which information is required to be include on the return (Rev. Proc. 2016-55).

In addition, the intentional disregard penalties are not considered in figuring the yearly maximum penalty for the third-tier penalty for failures not attributable to intentional disregard (generally, $3,193,000 for 2016 and $3,218,500 for 2017; but $1,064,000 for 2016 and $1,072,500 for 2017 for small businesses).

No penalty is imposed for inconsequential omissions and inaccuracies that do not prevent or hinder the IRS from adequately processing the return. Errors and omissions that relate to a taxpayer identification number (TIN), to the surname of a person required to receive a copy of the information provided, or to any monetary amounts are never considered inconsequential (Code Sec. 6721(c); Reg. § 301.6721-1(c)). Beginning after December 31, 2015, however, educational institutions will not be subject to the failure to provide a correct information return provided they certify they requested and were unable to obtain the required information (Code Sec. 6724(f)).[20] In addition, the penalties were waived for Forms 1098-T filed for the 2015 calendar year, solely because they fail to include a student's correct TIN (Announcement 2016-3).

2823. Failure to Furnish Correct Payee Statement. The statutory structure of the penalties for failure to timely furnish a correct payee statement resembles the three-tier Code Sec. 6721 penalties for failure to timely file a correct information return, including reduced maximum penalties for small businesses whose average annual gross receipts for the three most recent tax years before the calendar year are $5 million or less (¶ 2816) (Code Sec. 6722).[21] The penalty amounts and maximum limits are adjusted annually for inflation and are as follows:

(1) If a person furnishes a correct payee statement up to 30 days after the date prescribed for furnishing such statement, the amount of the penalty is (first-tier penalty):

(a) for tax years beginning in 2016, $50 per statement, with a maximum penalty of $532,000 per calendar year ($186,000 for small businesses), and

(b) for tax years beginning in 2017, $50 per statement, with a maximum penalty of $536,000 (for small businesses the maximum penalty is $187,500) (Code Sec. 6722(b)(1) and (d)(1)(B); Rev. Proc. 2015-53; Rev. Proc. 2016-55;

(2) If a person furnishes a correct payee statement more than 30 days after the prescribed filing date but on or before August 1 of the calendar year in which the date prescribed for furnishing such statement occurs, the amount of the penalty is (second-tier penalty):

(a) for tax years beginning in 2016, $100 per statement, with a maximum penalty of $1,596,500 per calendar year ($532,000 for small businesses), and

(b) for tax years beginning in 2017, $100 per statement, with a maximum penalty of $1,609,000 (for small businesses, the maximum penalty is $536,000) (Code Sec. 6722(b)(2) and (d)(1)(C); Rev. Proc. 2015-53; Rev. Proc. 2016-55);

(3) If a correct payee statement is not furnished on or before August 1 of the calendar year in which the date prescribed for furnishing such statement occurs, the amount of the penalty is (third-tier penalty):

(a) for tax years beginning in 2016, $260 per statement, with a maximum penalty of $3,193,000 per calendar year ($1,064,000 for small businesses), and

(b) for tax years beginning in 2017, $260 per statement, with a maximum penalty of $3,218,500 (for small businesses the maximum penalty is $1,072,500) (Code Sec. 6722(a)(1) and (d)(1)(A), as amended by P.L. 114-27); Rev. Proc. 2015-53; Rev. Proc. 2016-55).

Payee statements include the following (Code Sec. 6724(d):[22]

(1) pass-through income, deductions, etc., to partners in a partnership under Code Sec. 6031(b) or (c), to beneficiaries of estates and trusts under Code Sec. 6034A, and to S corporation shareholders under Code Sec. 6037(b);

(2) certain stock options under Code Sec. 6039(b);

(3) information-at-source payments under Code Sec. 6041(d);

(4) payments in connection with services and direct sales under Code Sec. 6041A(e);

References are to Standard Federal Tax Reports; Tax Research Consultant; and Practical Tax Explanations.

[20] ¶ 40,275; PENALTY: 3,206.10; § 40,305.20

[21] ¶ 40,230; PENALTY: 3,204; § 40,305.15

[22] ¶ 40,275; PENALTY: 3,204; § 40,305.05

(5) statements relating to returns regarding payments of dividends and corporate earnings and profits under Code Sec. 6042(c);

(6) taxable mergers and acquisitions under Code Sec. 6043A;

(7) statements regarding payments of patronage dividends under Code Sec. 6044(e);

(8) brokers under Code Sec. 6045(b) or (d);

(9) statements to brokers relating to the transfer of covered securities under Code Sec. 6045A (however, transitional relief from the penalty was provided for certain 2011 transfers (Notice 2010-67));

(10) statements relating to organizational actions affecting basis of specified securities under Code Sec. 6045B (however, transitional relief from the penalty was provided for any organization action in 2011 (Notice 2011-18));

(11) statements regarding interest payments under Code Sec. 6049(c);

(12) catch shares of certain fishing boat crews under Code Sec. 6050A(b);

(13) mortgage interest payments under Code Sec. 6050H(d) and (h)(2);

(14) cash payments in excess of $10,000 under Code Sec. 6050I(e), (g)(4), or (g)(5);

(15) foreclosures and abandonments of security under Code Sec. 6050J(e);

(16) exchanges of certain partnership interests under Code Sec. 6050K(b);

(17) certain dispositions of donated property under Code Sec. 6050L(c);

(18) payments of royalties under Code Sec. 6050N(b);

(19) statements relating to the cancellation of indebtedness by certain financial entities under Code Sec. 6050P(d);

(20) long-term care benefits under Code Sec. 6050Q(b);

(21) payments for certain purchases of fish for resale under Code Sec. 6050R;

(22) income tax withheld from employees' wages under Code Sec. 6051;

(23) group-term life insurance under Code Sec. 6052(b);

(24) tip income reportable by employers under Code Sec. 6053(b) or (c);

(25) foreign trust reporting requirements under Code Sec. 6048(b)(1)(B);

(26) distributions from individual retirement accounts under Code Sec. 408(i) and from employee benefit plans under Code Sec. 6047(d);

(27) payments relating to qualified tuition and related expenses under Code Sec. 6050S;

(28) returns relating to certain company-owned life insurance held by a natural person where a trade or business is directly or indirectly the beneficiary under the policy under Code Sec. 264(f)(5)(A)(iv);

(29) returns filed with respect to the credit for health insurance costs of eligible individuals under Code Sec. 6050T;

(30) charges or payments for qualified long-term insurance contracts under combined arrangements of Code Sec. 6050U;

(31) payments made in settlement of payment card transactions under Code Sec. 6050W;

(32) statements relating to information regarding health insurance coverage under Code Sec. 6055(c);

(33) statements relating to certain employers required to report on health insurance coverage under Code Sec. 6056(c); and

(34) statements to be provided by an executor of an estate to all parties receiving property from a decedent relating to the value of those interests under Code Sec. 6035.

In the case of intentional disregard of the requirements with respect to payee statements, the penalty imposed is identical to that for failures to file an information return or to include correct information (¶ 2816). Similarly, the intentional disregard penalty is not considered in applying the yearly maximum penalty for the third-tier penalty for failures not attributable to intentional disregard. In addition, the exception from the imposition of the penalty in the case of inconsequential omissions and inaccuracies on a payee statement applies. Beginning after December 31, 2015, however, educational institutions will not be subject to the failure to provide a correct payee statement provided they certify they requested and were unable to obtain the required information (Code Sec. 6724(f), as added by P.L. 114-27).[23]

2833. Failure to Comply with Other Information Reporting Requirements. A penalty of $50 is imposed for each failure to comply with any specified information reporting requirement on or before the prescribed time, up to a maximum of $100,000 for a calendar year (Code Sec. 6723).[24] The penalty will *not* be imposed if it can be shown that the failure was due to reasonable cause and not to willful neglect.

The specified information reporting requirements that are subject to the penalty include:

(1) the requirement that a transferor of an interest in a partnership promptly give notice to the partnership concerning the transfer;

(2) the requirement that a person include his or her taxpayer identification number (TIN) on any return, statement, or other document (other than an information return or payee statement), furnish his or her TIN to another person, or include the TIN of another person on any return, statement, or other document made with respect to that person;

(3) the requirement on returns reporting alimony payments that the TIN of the payee be furnished to the payor or that the payee's TIN be included on the payor's return;

(4) the requirement that a person include the TIN of any dependent on his or her return; and

(5) the requirement that a person who deducts qualified residence interest (¶ 1047) on any seller-provided financing include the name, address, and TIN of the person to whom such interest is paid or accrued (Code Sec. 6724(d)(3)).[25]

Underpayments of Tax—Interest

2838. Interest on Underpayment of Tax. Interest on underpayments of tax is imposed at the federal short-term rate plus three percentage points (Code Sec. 6621(a)(2)).[26] The interest rates, which are adjusted quarterly, are determined during the first month of a calendar quarter and become effective for the following quarter.

Interest accrues from the date the payment was due, determined without regard to any extensions of time, until it is received by the IRS, although no underpayment interest accrues for failure to timely pay individual or corporate estimated tax. Interest is compounded daily (Code Secs. 6601 and 6622).[27] For the first quarter in 2016, the interest rate on underpayments is three percent. For the second, third and fourth quarters, the interest rate is four percent.[28]

References are to Standard Federal Tax Reports; Tax Research Consultant; and Practical Tax Explanations.

[23] ¶ 40,275; PENALTY: 206.10; § 40,305.20

[25] ¶ 40,275; PENALTY: 3,204; § 40,305.20

[27] ¶ 39,410, ¶ 39,460; PENALTY: 9,050; § 40,105.05

[26] ¶ 39,450; PENALTY: 9,152; § 40,105.05

[28] ¶ 175.01; PENALTY: 9,152

If a carryback of a net operating loss, net capital loss, or other credit carryback eliminates or reduces a deficiency otherwise due for such earlier year, the taxpayer remains liable for interest on unpaid income taxes, including deficiencies later assessed by the IRS, for the carryback year. The entire amount of the deficiency will be subject to interest from the last date prescribed for payment of the income tax of the carryback year up to the due date, excluding extensions, for filing the return for the tax year in which the loss or credit occurred (Code Sec. 6601(d); Reg. § 301.6601-1(e)).[29]

Large Corporate Tax Underpayments. Interest on large underpayments of tax by corporations is imposed at the federal short-term rate plus five percentage points (Code Sec. 6621(c); Reg. § 301.6621-3).[30] A large corporate underpayment is any tax underpayment by a C corporation that exceeds $100,000 for any tax period. For purposes of determining the $100,000 threshold, underpayments of different types of taxes (e.g., income and employment taxes) as well as underpayments relating to different tax periods are not added together. The tax period is the tax year in the case of income tax or, in the case of any other tax, the period to which the underpayment relates.

The interest rate for large underpayment by corporations applies to time periods after the 30th day after the earlier of: (1) the date the IRS sends the first letter of proposed deficiency that allows the taxpayer an opportunity for administrative review in the IRS Office of Appeals (a 30-day letter); or (2) the date the IRS sends a deficiency notice (a 90-day letter) (¶ 2711). The 30-day period does not begin unless the underpayment shown in the letter or notice exceeds $100,000. An IRS notice that is later withdrawn because it was issued in error will not trigger the higher rate of interest on large corporate underpayments. If the underpayment is not subject to deficiency payments, the 30-day period begins to run following the sending of any letter or notice by the IRS that notifies the taxpayer of the assessment or proposed assessment of the tax. A letter or notice is disregarded if the full amount shown as due is paid during the 30-day period. For the first quarter of 2016, the interest rate on large corporate underpayments is five percent. For the second, third, and fourth quarters, the interest rate is six percent.[31]

Overlapping Overpayments and Underpayments. The interest rates for overpayments and underpayments have been equalized (also referred to as "global interest netting") for any period of mutual indebtedness between taxpayers and the IRS (¶ 2765).

Abatement of Interest. The IRS has the authority to abate interest in cases where the additional interest was caused by IRS errors or delays (Code Sec. 6404(e)).[32] However, the IRS may act only if there was an error or delay in performing either a ministerial act or a managerial act, including loss of records by the IRS, transfers of IRS personnel, extended illness, extended personnel training, or extended leave, and only if the abatement relates to a tax of the type for which a notice of deficiency is required. These taxes would be those relating to income, generation-skipping transfers, estate, gift, and certain excise taxes, but not employment taxes or other excise taxes. Taxpayers requesting an abatement of interest generally must file a separate Form 843 for each tax period for each type of tax with the IRS Service Center where their tax return was filed or, if unknown, with the Service Center where their most recent tax return was filed. Taxpayers may file a petition to review a claim for interest abatement with the Tax Court in cases in which the IRS has failed to issue a final determination within the 180-day period following the filing of claim (Code Sec. 6404(h), as amended by the Protecting Americans from the Tax Hikes (PATH) Act of 2015 (P.L. 114-113). The Tax Court also has jurisdiction over interest abatement actions in cases to be conducted using small tax case procedures where the total amount of interest abatement sought does not exceed $50,000 (Code Sec. 7463(f), as amended by P.L. 114-113).

References are to Standard Federal Tax Reports; Tax Research Consultant; and Practical Tax Explanations.

[29] ¶ 39,410, ¶ 39,412; PENALTY: 9,056.10; § 40,105.15

[30] ¶ 39,450, ¶ 39,453; PENALTY: 9,152.05; § 40,120.15

[31] ¶ 175.01; PENALTY: 9,152.05; § 40,105.05

[32] ¶ 38,570; PENALTY: 9,056.20; § 40,030.15

Suspension of Interest. In order to avoid the accrual of underpayment interest, a taxpayer may make a cash deposit with the IRS for future application against an underpayment of income, gift, estate, generation-skipping, or certain excise taxes that have not been assessed at the time of the deposit (Code Sec. 6603; Rev. Proc. 2005-18).[33] To the extent that a deposit is used by the IRS to pay a tax liability, the tax is treated as paid when the deposit is made, and no underpayment interest is imposed. Furthermore, if the dispute is resolved in favor of the taxpayer or the taxpayer withdraws the deposited money before resolution of the dispute, interest is payable on the deposit at the federal short-term rate.

2845. Interest on Additions and Penalties. Interest on additions to tax, i.e., penalties, for failure to file a return (¶ 2801), for failure to pay the stamp tax, and for accuracy-related (¶ 2854) and fraud penalties (¶ 2866) will be imposed for the period beginning on the due date of the return, including extensions, and ending on the date of payment. If payment is made within 21 *calendar* days after notice and demand is made (10 *business* days if the amount demanded is at least $100,000), then interest will stop running after the date of notice and demand. For all other penalties, interest will be imposed only if the addition to tax or penalty is not paid within the 21-or 10-day period after notice and demand is made and then only for the period from the date of notice and demand to the date of payment (Code Sec. 6601(e)).[34] For rules governing the allocation of interest on tax liabilities paid pursuant to a compromise or partial payment, see ¶ 2723 and ¶ 2724, respectively.

Underpayments of Tax—Penalties

2854. Accuracy-Related Penalty. An accuracy-related penalty of 20 percent is imposed on the portion of any underpayment of tax that is due to negligence or disregard of rules or regulations (¶ 2856), substantial understatement of income tax (¶ 2858), substantial valuation misstatement (¶ 2860), substantial overstatements of pension liabilities (¶ 2862), substantial estate or gift tax valuation understatement (¶ 2862A), transactions lacking economic substance (¶ 2863), and inconsistent estate basis reporting, and (¶ 2863A) (Code Sec. 6662)[35] In addition, a 40-percent accuracy-related penalty is imposed for an underpayment of tax due to an undisclosed foreign financial asset understatement (¶ 2864). If any part of an underpayment of tax required to be shown on a return is due to fraud, a separate penalty equal to 75 percent of the portion of the underpayment is imposed (¶ 2866).

The accuracy-related penalty is entirely separate from the failure-to-file penalty (¶ 2801) and will not be imposed if no return is filed, other than a return prepared by the IRS when a person fails to make a required return (Code Sec. 6664(b)).[36] In addition, the accuracy-related penalty will not apply to any portion of a tax underpayment on which the fraud penalty is imposed. Also, with the exception of the penalty for underpayments attributable to transactions lacking economic substance, no penalty is imposed with respect to any portion of any underpayment if the taxpayer shows that there was reasonable cause for the underpayment and that the taxpayer acted in good faith (Code Sec. 6664(c)).[37]

2856. Penalty for Negligence or Disregard of Rules and Regulations. If any part of an underpayment of tax is due to negligence or careless, reckless, or intentional disregard of rules and regulations, a 20-percent accuracy-related penalty (¶ 2854) will be imposed on that portion of the underpayment attributable to the negligence or intentional disregard of rules and regulations (Code Sec. 6662(a) and (c); Reg. § 1.6662-3).[38] Negligence includes the failure to reasonably comply with tax laws, to exercise reasonable care in preparing a tax return, to keep adequate books and records, or to substantiate items properly. Taxpayers may not avoid the negligence penalty merely by adequately disclosing a return position which is "not frivolous" on Form 8275 or Form 8275-R

References are to Standard Federal Tax Reports; Tax Research Consultant; and Practical Tax Explanations.

[33] ¶ 39,426, ¶ 39,428.20; IRS: 36,056.25; § 40,110.15

[34] ¶ 39,410; PENALTY: 9,060; § 40,105.05

[35] ¶ 39,651; PENALTY: 3,100; § 40,210.05

[36] ¶ 39,660; PENALTY: 3,102; § 40,210.05

[37] ¶ 39,660; PENALTY: 3,102; § 40,210.40

[38] ¶ 39,651, ¶ 39,651E; PENALTY: 3,106; § 40,210.15

2858. Penalty for Substantial Understatement of Income Tax. A 20-percent accuracy-related penalty (¶ 2854) may be imposed on a taxpayer when there is a substantial understatement of income tax for the tax year (Code Sec. 6662(d); Reg. § 1.6662-4).[39] A substantial understatement exists when the understatement for the year exceeds the greater of 10 percent of the tax required to be shown on the return, including self-employment tax, or $5,000. In the case of corporations (other than S corporations or personal holding companies), a substantial understatement exists when the understatement exceeds the lesser of 10 percent of the tax required to be shown on the return (or, if greater, $10,000) or $10 million.

Taxpayers generally may avoid all or part of the penalty by showing:

(1) that they acted in good faith and there was reasonable cause for the understatement;

(2) that the understatement was based on substantial authority; or

(3) if there was a reasonable basis for the tax treatment of an item, the relevant facts affecting the item's tax treatment were adequately disclosed on Form 8275 or Form 8275-R.

Substantial authority generally means that the likelihood that a taxpayer's position is correct is somewhere between 50 percent and the more lenient reasonable basis standard used in applying the negligence penalty. The disclosure exception does not apply to tax shelter items. Further, a corporation does not have a reasonable basis for its tax treatment of an item attributable to a multi-party financing transaction if the treatment does not clearly reflect the income of the corporation. Some items may be disclosed on the taxpayer's return, instead of on Form 8275 or Form 8275-R (Rev. Proc. 2016-13, updating, Rev. Proc. 2015-16, updating Rev. Proc. 2014-15).[40]

Only the following are authority for purposes of determining whether a position is supported by substantial authority:

(1) the Internal Revenue Code and other statutory provisions;

(2) proposed, temporary, and final regulations construing the statutes;

(3) revenue rulings and procedures;

(4) tax treaties and the regulations thereunder, and Treasury Department and other official explanations of such treaties;

(5) court cases;

(6) Congressional intent as reflected in committee reports, joint explanatory statements of managers included in conference committee reports, and floor statements made prior to enactment by one of a bill's managers;

(7) General Explanations of tax legislation prepared by the Joint Committee on Taxation (the Blue Book);

(8) private letter rulings and technical advice memoranda issued after October 31, 1976;

(9) actions on decisions and general counsel memoranda issued after March 12, 1981, as well as general counsel memoranda published in pre-1955 volumes of the Cumulative Bulletin;

(10) IRS information and press releases; and

(11) notices, announcements, and other administrative pronouncements published by the IRS in the Internal Revenue Bulletin (Reg. § 1.6662-4).[41]

References are to Standard Federal Tax Reports; Tax Research Consultant; and Practical Tax Explanations.

[39] ¶ 39,651, ¶ 39,651H; PENALTY: 3,108; § 40,210.20

[40] ¶ 39,652.102; PENALTY: 3,108.15; § 40,210.20

[41] ¶ 39,651H; PENALTY: 3,108; § 40,210.20

2860. Penalty for Substantial Valuation Misstatement. A 20-percent accuracy-related penalty (¶ 2854) is imposed on any portion of an underpayment of tax resulting from any substantial income tax valuation misstatement (Code Sec. 6662(e)).[42] There is a substantial valuation misstatement if:

(1) the value of any property, or adjusted basis of any property, claimed on a tax return is 150 percent or more of the amount determined to be the correct amount of the valuation or the adjusted basis;

(2) the price for any property, or use of property, or services in connection with any transaction between persons described in Code Sec. 482 is 200 percent or more, or 50 percent or less, of the correct Code Sec. 482 valuation; or

(3) the net Code Sec. 482 transfer price adjustment exceeds the lesser of $5 million or 10 percent of the taxpayer's gross receipts.

The penalty is doubled to 40 percent in cases of gross valuation misstatements where claimed value or adjusted basis exceeds the correct value or adjusted basis by 200 percent or more (Code Sec. 6662(h)). A gross valuation misstatement with respect to a controlled taxpayer transaction (Code Sec. 482) occurs if the price claimed exceeds 400 percent or more, or 25 percent or less, of the amount determined to be the correct price, or the net Code Sec. 482 transfer price adjustment for the year exceeds the lesser of $20 million or 20 percent of the taxpayer's gross receipts.

No penalty is imposed unless the portion of the underpayment attributable to the substantial valuation misstatement exceeds $5,000, or $10,000 in the case of corporations other than S corporations or personal holding companies. The penalty will not be imposed if it is shown that there was reasonable cause for an underpayment and the taxpayer acted in good faith. However, there is no reasonable cause exception for underpayments due to gross valuation misstatements on charitable deduction property, although the exception still exists for substantial valuation misstatements on charitable deduction property and for gross valuation misstatements on property for which a charitable deduction is not being claimed (Code Sec. 6664(c)).[43]

2862. Penalty for Substantial Overstatement of Pension Liabilities. A 20-percent accuracy-related penalty (¶ 2854) is imposed on any portion of any underpayment of tax resulting from a substantial overstatement of pension liabilities (Code Sec. 6662(b)(4), (f), and (h)).[44] A substantial overstatement occurs if the actuarial determination of pension liabilities is 200 percent or more of the amount determined to be correct. The penalty is doubled to 40 percent of the underpayment if a portion of the substantial overstatement to which the penalty applies is attributable to a gross valuation misstatement of 400 percent or more. The penalty applies only if the portion of the underpayment attributable to the overstatement exceeds $1,000. The penalty will not be imposed if it is shown that there was a reasonable cause for an underpayment and the taxpayer acted in good faith (Code Sec. 6664(c)).[45]

2862A. Penalty for Substantial Estate or Gift Tax Valuation Understatements. A 20-percent accuracy-related penalty (¶ 2854) is imposed on the portion of an underpayment of tax that is due to a substantial estate or gift tax valuation understatement (Code Sec. 6662(b)(5), (g), and (h)).[46] There is a substantial estate or gift tax valuation understatement if the value of any property claimed on any estate or gift tax return is 65 percent or less of the amount determined to be the correct amount of the valuation. The penalty will not be imposed unless the portion of the underpayment attributable to the valuation understatements for the taxable period or for the estate of the decedent exceeds $5,000. The penalty is increased to 40 percent if the valuation understatement is

References are to Standard Federal Tax Reports; Tax Research Consultant; and Practical Tax Explanations.

[42] ¶ 39,651; PENALTY: 3,110; § 40,210.25

[43] ¶ 39,660; PENALTY: 3,110; § 40,210.25

[44] ¶ 39,651; PENALTY: 3,112; § 40,210.30

[45] ¶ 39,660; PENALTY: 3,116; § 40,210.40

[46] ¶ 39,651; PENALTY: 3,114; § 40,210.35

a gross valuation misstatement. A valuation understatement is a gross valuation understatement if the value of any property claimed on any estate or gift tax return is 40 percent or less of the amount determined to be the correct amount of the valuation. The penalty will not be imposed if it is shown that there was a reasonable cause for an underpayment and the taxpayer acted in good faith (Code Sec. 6664(c)).[47]

2863. Penalty for Underpayment Attributable to Transactions Lacking Economic Substance. A 20-percent accuracy-related penalty (¶ 2854) is imposed for an underpayment of tax attributable to any disallowance of claimed tax benefits by reason of a transaction lacking economic substance, or failing to meet the requirements of any similar rule of law (Code Sec. 6662(b)(6)).[48] A transaction is treated as having economic substance if: (1) apart from the federal income tax effects, it changes in a meaningful way the taxpayer's economic position; and (2) the taxpayer has a substantial purpose for entering into the transaction (Code Sec. 7701(o); Notice 2010-62).[49] The term transaction, including related transactions, generally includes all the factual elements relevant to the expected tax treatment of any investment, entity, plan, or arrangement, and any and all steps that are carried out as part of the plan. Whether a plan's steps should be aggregated or disaggregated is a facts and circumstances analysis. The phase "similar rule of law" means a rule or doctrine that disallows the tax benefits in the Code related to a transaction because the taxpayer's economic position does not change in a meaningful way apart from the Federal income tax effects, or the taxpayer does not have a substantial purpose, apart from the Federal income tax effects, for entering into the transaction (Notice 2014-58, amplifying Notice 2010-62).

Although the IRS will continue to rely on relevant case law handed down prior to the codification of the economic substance doctrine for transactions entered into after March 30, 2010, when applying the two-prong test, taxpayers may not rely on case law that treats a transaction as having economic substance unless the transaction satisfies *both* prongs of the test.

The penalty is increased to 40 percent for an underpayment attributable to a nondisclosed noneconomic substance transaction (Code Sec. 6662(i)).[50] A nondisclosed noneconomic substance transaction is any portion of a transaction lacking economic substance with respect to which the relevant facts affecting the tax treatment are not adequately disclosed in the return or in a statement attached to the return. The determination of whether a position is a nondisclosed noneconomic substance transaction will generally be based on the return as originally filed or as amended by the taxpayer prior to being contacted by the IRS.

To satisfy the adequate disclosure requirements, the taxpayer must: (1) disclose the relevant facts on a timely filed original return or a qualified amended return; (2) file Form 8275 or Form 8275-R; and (3) if the transaction is a reportable transaction (¶ 2591), satisfy all disclosure requirements for such transactions (¶ 2592).

No exceptions, including the reasonable cause exception, are available to the imposition of a penalty for any underpayment or reportable transaction understatement attributable to a transaction lacking economic substance (Code Sec. 6664(c)(2) and (d)(2)).[51]

2863A Inconsistent Estate Basis Reporting. A 20-percent accuracy-related penalty (¶ 2854) is imposed for inconsistent estate basis reporting, applicable to property with respect to which an estate tax return is filed after July 31, 2015 (Code Sec. 6662(b)(8)).[52] Inconsistent estate basis reporting is defined as basis on a return that exceeds the basis of property as determined under Code Sec. 1014(f) (¶ 1633).

References are to Standard Federal Tax Reports; Tax Research Consultant; and Practical Tax Explanations.

[47] ¶ 39,660; PENALTY: 3,116; § 40,210.40

[48] ¶ 39,651; PENALTY: 3,122; § 40,210.36

[49] ¶ 39,654AF.40, ¶ 43,080; PENALTY: 3,122; § 40,210.36

[50] ¶ 39,651; PENALTY: 3,122; § 40,210.36

[51] ¶ 39,660; PENALTY: 3,122; § 40,210.36

[52] ¶ 39,651; PENALTY:3,100; § 40,210.05

2864. Penalty for Underpayment Attributable to Undisclosed Foreign Financial Assets. A 40-percent accuracy-related penalty (¶ 2854) is imposed for underpayment of tax that is attributable to an undisclosed foreign financial asset understatement (Code Sec. 6662(b)(7) and (j)).[53] An undisclosed foreign financial asset understatement for any tax year is the portion of the understatement for the year that is attributable to any transaction involving undisclosed foreign financial assets. An undisclosed foreign financial asset includes any asset that is subject to the information reporting requirements of Code Sec. 6038 (information reporting with respect to certain foreign corporations and partnerships (¶ 2487)), Code Sec. 6038B (notice of certain transfers to foreign persons (¶ 2492)), Code Sec. 6046A (returns as to interests in foreign partnerships (¶ 2494)), Code Sec. 6048 (information with respect to certain foreign trusts (¶ 588)), and Code Sec. 6038D (information with respect to foreign financial assets (¶ 2572)), but for which the required information was not provided by the taxpayer as required under the applicable reporting provisions.

2866. Penalty for Fraud. A penalty is imposed at the rate of 75 percent on the portion of any underpayment of tax that is attributable to fraud (Code Sec. 6663).[54] The fraud penalty will not apply, however, if no return is filed other than a return prepared by the IRS when a person fails to make a required return (Code Sec. 6664(b)).[55] Although the failure-to-file penalty is entirely separate from the fraud penalty, in cases of a fraudulent failure to file, the failure-to-file penalty will be imposed at a higher rate (¶ 2801). If any portion is attributable to fraud, it is presumed that the entire underpayment is attributable to fraud, unless the taxpayer establishes otherwise by a preponderance of the evidence with respect to any item. The accuracy-related penalty will not apply to any portion of an underpayment on which the fraud penalty is imposed (¶ 2854). The IRS must meet its burden of proof in establishing fraud by clear and convincing evidence (Code Sec. 6663(b)).[56]

2870. Penalty for Tax Shelters. An accuracy-related penalty is imposed for understatement of tax attributable to any listed transaction and any reportable transaction with a significant tax avoidance purpose (¶ 2591) (Code Sec. 6662A).[57] The 20-percent accuracy-related penalty on understatements attributable to reportable transactions will not be imposed if the 40-percent penalty is imposed on an underpayment attributable to one or more undisclosed noneconomic substance transactions (¶ 2863).

Underpayments of Estimated Tax

2875. Underpayment of Estimated Tax by Individuals. An underpayment of estimated tax by an individual and most trusts and estates will result in imposition of an addition to tax equal to the applicable underpayment rate of interest (¶ 2838) that accrues on the underpayment for the period of the underpayment (Code Sec. 6654(a)).[58] In determining the addition to tax for an underpayment of individual estimated tax, the federal short-term rate that applies during the third month following the tax year of the underpayment will also apply during the first 15 days of the fourth month following such tax year (Code Sec. 6621(b)(2)(B); Reg. § 301.6621-1).[59] Changes in the interest rate apply to amounts of underpayments outstanding on the date of change or arising thereafter. An individual can avoid any penalty for underpayment of estimated tax by making payments as set forth in ¶ 2682. See ¶ 511 for the rules regarding trusts and estates.

References are to Standard Federal Tax Reports; Tax Research Consultant; and Practical Tax Explanations.

[53] ¶ 39,651; PENALTY: 3,120; § 40,210.37

[54] ¶ 39,656; PENALTY: 6,100; § 40,215

[55] ¶ 39,660; PENALTY: 6,112; § 40,215

[56] ¶ 39,656; PENALTY: 6,106, PENALTY: 6,158; § 40,215

[57] ¶ 39,655; PENALTY: 3,252.05

[58] ¶ 39,550; FILEIND: 21,050; § 1,430.05

[59] ¶ 39,450, ¶ 39,451; FILEIND: 21,056; § 1,430.05

Under certain circumstances, a taxpayer is not subject to the penalty for underpaying estimated taxes (¶ 2682). The IRS is also authorized to waive the penalty for underpayment of estimated tax of an individual if the underpayment is due to casualty, disaster, or other unusual circumstances, and the imposition of the penalty would be against equity and good conscience (Code Sec. 6654(e)(3)).[60] The penalty may also be waived for an individual who retired after having attained age 62, or who became disabled, in the tax year for which the estimated payment was due or in the preceding tax year and the underpayment was due to reasonable cause and not to willful neglect.

The amount of an underpayment of estimated tax and the amount of the resulting penalty is computed on Form 2210 and attached to the individual's income tax return; farmers and fishermen use Form 2210-F. If Form 2210 is not completed and attached to the individual's return, the IRS will compute the penalty for the taxpayer. When the IRS computes the penalty, however, it will investigate any reason why the penalty should be waived.

2890. Underpayment of Estimated Tax by Corporations. An underpayment of estimated tax by a corporation, including an S corporation, will result in the imposition of an addition to tax equal to the applicable underpayment rate or interest (¶ 2838) that accrues on the underpayment for the period of the underpayment (Code Sec. 6655).[61] See ¶ 241 for more information on the penalty for underpayment of corporate estimated taxes.

Erroneous Tax Refund Claims

2891. Erroneous Refund or Credit Claims. Erroneous income tax refund or credit claims made for an excessive amount are subject to a penalty equal to 20 percent of the excessive amount (Code Sec. 6676).[62] The penalty does not apply to claims for refunds or credits relating to the earned income credit (¶ 1322), which has a separate set of rules.

An excessive amount is the amount by which the refund or credit claim exceeds the amount allowable under the Code for the tax year. However, if it can be shown that the claim for the excessive amount has a reasonable basis, the penalty will not apply. In addition, the penalty does not apply to any portion of the excessive amount of a refund claim or credit that is subject to an accuracy-related penalty (¶ 2854 and ¶ 2870), or the fraud penalty (¶ 2866).

Unauthorized Return Disclosures or Inspections

2892. Disclosure of Return Information by Government Employees. Returns and tax return information are confidential and may not be disclosed to federal or state agencies or employees except as provided in Code Sec. 6103.[63] A return is defined as any tax return, information return, declaration of estimated tax, or claim for refund filed under the Internal Revenue Code. Return information includes the taxpayer's identity, the nature, source or amount of income, payments, receipts, deductions, net worth, tax liability, deficiencies, closing (and similar) agreements, and information regarding the actual or possible investigation of a return. All officers and employees of the United States, of any state, and of any local child support enforcement agency are prohibited from disclosing tax returns and return information. The prohibition also applies to most other persons who have had access to returns or return information by virtue of permitted disclosures of such returns or information under Code Sec. 6103. A taxpayer may bring a damage action against a person who knowingly or negligently makes an unauthorized disclosure or inspection of any return or return information of the taxpayer (¶ 2893).

References are to Standard Federal Tax Reports; Tax Research Consultant; and Practical Tax Explanations.

[60] ¶ 39,550; FILEIND: 21,056.10; § 1,435.10

[61] ¶ 39,565; FILEBUS: 6,050; § 26,015.15

[62] ¶ 39,801; PENALTY: 3,332; § 40,240

[63] ¶ 36,880; IRS: 9,050; § 41,215.15

Agreements and information received under a tax convention with a foreign government, including a U.S. possession, are also confidential and generally cannot be disclosed (Code Sec. 6105).[64]

2893. Remedies for Unauthorized Disclosures or Inspections of Return Information. A taxpayer may bring a civil action against the United States if a government employee knowingly or negligently discloses or inspects any return or return information with respect to the taxpayer under Code Sec. 6103 (¶ 2892) without authorization. A taxpayer may also bring a civil action against any person who is *not* a United States employee who knowingly or negligently discloses or inspects any return or return information with respect to the taxpayer under Code Sec. 6103 or a tax-exempt organization under Code Sec. 6104 (¶ 625) (Code Sec. 7431).[65] Upon a finding of liability, the taxpayer may recover the greater of $1,000 for each unauthorized disclosure or the amount of the actual damages sustained as a result of the disclosure. Punitive damages, as well as litigation costs, may be recovered if the disclosure was willful or grossly negligent. Criminal penalties can also be brought against individuals who have made unauthorized and willful disclosures of any return or return information including present and former federal employees, and any other person who obtains returns and return information in the course of processing, storing and reproducing returns and return information (Code Sec. 7213).[66]

In addition, criminal penalties for unauthorized inspections may be imposed against any federal employee, as well as any state employee or other person who acquires the return or return information under Code Sec. 6103 or Code Sec. 6104, which permits the use of federal return information for other government purposes, such as state tax and child support collection, law enforcement, social welfare program administration, and statistical use (Code Sec. 7213A).[67]

It is permissible for the IRS to release information regarding investigations of unauthorized disclosure or inspection of return information, to the person making the allegation of a violation of privacy, or that person's designee (Code Sec. 6103(e)(11), as added by the Protecting Americans from Tax Hikes (PATH) Act of 2015 (P.L. 114-113)).

2894. Disclosure of Return Information by Return Preparers. A return preparer who uses return information for any purpose other than to prepare a return, or who makes an unauthorized disclosure of return information, is subject to a $250 penalty for each disclosure, up to a maximum of $10,000. If the action is undertaken knowingly or recklessly, the preparer may be subject to criminal penalties or a fine of up to $1,000, or up to a year in jail, or both, together with the cost of prosecution (Code Secs. 6713 and 7216).[68] A taxpayer may bring a civil action for damages against the U.S. government if an IRS employee offers the taxpayer's representative favorable tax treatment in exchange for information about the taxpayer (Code Sec. 7435).[69]

Criminal Penalties

2898. Criminal Penalties. Criminal penalties may be incurred when the taxpayer: (1) willfully fails to make a return, keep records, supply required information, or pay any tax or estimated tax; (2) willfully attempts in any manner to evade or defeat the tax; or (3) willfully fails to collect and pay over the tax. In addition to the felony charges listed in the preceding sentence, misdemeanor charges can be brought for making fraudulent statements to employees, filing a fraudulent withholding certificate, or failing to obey a summons. The criminal penalties are in addition to the civil penalties (Code Secs. 7201—7212). A good faith misunderstanding of the law or a good faith belief that one is not violating the law negates the willfulness element of a tax evasion charge.[70]

References are to Standard Federal Tax Reports; Tax Research Consultant; and Practical Tax Explanations.

[64] ¶ 36,912; IRS: 9,550

[65] ¶ 41,750; IRS: 9,350; § 41,625.05

[66] ¶ 41,350; IRS: 66,360

[67] ¶ 41,354; IRS: 66,360

[68] ¶ 40,155, ¶ 41,365; IRS: 6,114; § 41,625.05

[69] ¶ 41,785; IRS: 45,116

[70] ¶ 41,318.136; IRS: 66,050; § 40,245.10

Chapter 29

ESTATE, GIFT AND GENERATION-SKIPPING TRANSFER TAX

	Par.
Transfer Tax System	2901
Gift Tax	2903
Estate Tax	2912
Generation-Skipping Transfer Tax	2942
Transfer Tax on Gifts and Bequests from Expatriates	2948

Transfer Tax System

2901. Estate, Gift, and Generation-Skipping Transfer Tax System. The estate, gift, and generation-skipping transfer (GST) taxes are designed to form a unified transfer tax system on the transfer of property at death (estate tax), during life (gift tax), and on transfers that skip a generation (GST tax). The maximum marginal tax rate is 40 percent for the estates of decedents dying and gifts and GSTs made after December 31, 2012 (¶ 40). The estate and gift tax exclusion amount and the GST exemption amount is $5 million, which is indexed annually for inflation; the exclusion and exemption amounts are $5.45 million for 2016 ($5.49 million for 2017) (¶ 41). A decedent's estate may elect to allow the unused portion of the decedent's applicable exclusion amount to be available to his or her surviving spouse or the spouse's estate (referred to as "portability"). As a result, the applicable exclusion amount of a surviving spouse may include the predeceased spouse's unused exclusion amount, potentially allowing the spouse to transfer up to $10.9 million in 2016 ($10.98 million in 2017) (¶ 2934 and ¶ 2938).

Same-Sex Couples. For federal tax purposes, same-sex couples are treated as married if they are legally married in a jurisdiction that recognizes same-sex marriages, even if they live in or move to a jurisdiction that does not (Reg. § § 20.7701-2, 25.7701-2, 26.7701-2, 301.7701-18). Thus, same-sex married couples may take advantage of the same benefits previously enjoyed only by opposite-sex married couples, such as split gifts (¶ 2905), the estate and gift tax marital deductions (¶ 2908 and ¶ 2926), and portability (¶ 2934). Same-sex couples in a civil union, registered domestic partnership, or similar formal relationship under state or foreign law are not afforded the same treatment, however, if the jurisdiction does *not* denominate such a relationship as a marriage.

Gift Tax

2903. Transfers Subject to Gift Tax. A gift tax applies to the transfer of property by gift, whether the gift is direct or indirect, and whether the transfer is in trust or otherwise. The property transferred may be real, personal, tangible, or intangible (Code Sec. 2511; Reg. § 25.2511-1(a)).[1] The donor makes a gift to the extent that the value of the property transferred exceeds the consideration, i.e., any property or services received in return for the transfer (Code Sec. 2512(b)). The transferred property or evidence of it must be delivered to the donee and the donor must relinquish all control over the property for the gift to be completed (Reg. § 25.2511-2).[2] Transfers to qualifying

References are to Federal Estate & Gift Tax Reports; Tax Research Consultant; Practical Tax Explanations.

[1] ¶ 10,514, ¶ 10,528, ¶ 10,555.06; ESTGIFT: 3,050; § 34,805

[2] ¶ 10,568; ESTGIFT: 3,056, ESTGIFT: 3,060; § 34,805.05

political organizations are not considered gifts (Code Sec. 2501(a)(4)).[3] Transfers to organizations that are described in Code Sec. 501(c)(4), (5) or (6) (¶ 692) and are exempt from tax under Code Sec. 501(a) are not subject to federal gift tax (Code Sec. 2501(a)(6)).[4]

Indirect gifts, such as transfers in trust and the cancellation of indebtedness, are subject to the gift tax (Code Sec. 2511). Other examples of indirect gifts include certain assignments of benefits, permission to withdraw funds deposited by a donor from a joint account, and below-market interest rate loans (Reg. § 25.2511-1(c) and (h)). However, a waiver of the right to a joint and survivor annuity in a qualified plan is not a gift (Code Sec. 2503(f)).[5]

A gratuitous transfer of property by a corporation is considered to be a gift by the shareholders to the donee, while a gift to a corporation is considered to be a gift to its shareholders (Reg. § 25.2511-1(h)). In addition, a gift may occur at the creation of a family limited partnership or when transferring control of a closely held company.[6] Transfers of stock or securities are gifts even if the securities are exempt from tax. The transfer of an option is a gift. Also, gratuitous transfers made by guardians or conservators under court orders are gifts. Conversely, a transfer pursuant to a will contest settlement entered into at arm's length is generally not a gift. The treatment of income earned by domestic partners as community property by operation of state law is also not considered a gift.[7]

Valuation. Generally, the value of property for gift tax purposes is its fair market value on the date of the gift. That is, the price at which the property would change hands between a willing buyer and a willing seller, both having reasonable knowledge of relevant facts (Code Sec. 2512; Reg. § 25.2512-1).[8] Special valuation rules apply for determining the amount of a gift if the transferor retains (1) an equity interest in a corporation or partnership transferred to a family member, or (2) an interest in a trust to or for the benefit of a family member (Code Secs. 2701, 2702 and 2704).[9] Regulations under Code Secs. 2701 and 2704 were proposed that would restrict the ability to achieve minority and lack-of-control valuation discounts with respect to the transfer of interests in many family-owned entities. The regulations do not take effect until published as final in the *Federal Register*.[10]

Qualified Disclaimers. The donee of a gift may make a qualified disclaimer of the entire interest or a portion of it without making a taxable gift. To be a qualified disclaimer: (1) the disclaimer must be in writing; (2) the disclaimer must be received by the transferor or the transferor's representative within nine months of the date of the transfer; (3) the beneficiary may not accept any of the benefits from the transferred property; and (4) the property being disclaimed must pass to someone other than, and without direction from, the disclaiming beneficiary (Code Sec. 2518).[11]

Nonresident Alien Donors. A donor who is a nonresident alien is subject to gift tax on transfers of real and tangible property situated in the United States (Code Sec. 2501(a); Reg. § 25.2501-1).[12] Transfers of intangible property by a nonresident alien generally are not subject to gift tax (Code Sec. 2501(a)(2)). A donor who relinquishes his or her U.S. citizenship or terminates his or her long-term residency is subject to special expatriation rules (Code Sec. 2501(a)(3)).[13] For the transfer tax imposed on

References are to Federal Estate & Gift Tax Reports; Tax Research Consultant; Practical Tax Explanations.

[3] ¶ 9245, ¶ 9340.05; ESTGIFT: 3,150; § 34,805

[4] ¶ 9340.052; ESTGIFT: 3,172; § 34,801

[5] ¶ 9649, ¶ 10,181.05; ESTGIFT: 3,100; § 34,805

[6] ¶ 10,514, ¶ 10,555.07; ESTGIFT: 3,154; § 34,801

[7] ¶ 9340.05, ¶ 9340.80; ESTGIFT: 33,000; § 34,601

[8] ¶ 10,622, ¶ 10,649; ESTGIFT: 100; § 34,810.05

[9] ¶ 13,551, ¶ 14,001, ¶ 14,651; ESTGIFT: 18,600; § 34,810

[10] ¶ 13,690.10, ¶ 14,720.05, ¶ 14,790.01, ¶ 14,790.10, ¶ 14,790.20; ESTGIFT: 18,608; § 34,810.20.

[11] ¶ 11,339, ¶ 11,419.03; ESTGIFT: 100; § 34,805.20

[12] ¶ 9245, ¶ 9290; ESTGIFT: 60,050; § 35,010

[13] ¶ 9245; ESTGIFT: 60,250; § 35,015.05

recipients of gifts from "covered expatriates," see ¶ 2948. Taxable gifts are taxed at the same rates that apply to U.S. citizens (Code Sec. 2501(a)(1)).[14]

2905. Gift Tax Annual Exclusion. The first $14,000 of gifts of a present interest made by a donor during calendar year 2016 ($14,000 in 2017) to each donee is not included in the total amount of the donor's taxable gifts during that year (Code Sec. 2503(b); Rev. Proc. 2015-53; Rev. Proc. 2016-55).[15] Therefore, these amounts are not taxed and do not use up any of the donor's lifetime gift tax applicable credit amount. Also, spouses who consent to split their gifts may transfer a total of $28,000 per donee in 2016 ($28,000 in 2017), free of gift and generation-skipping transfer (GST) tax (Code Sec. 2513(a)).[16]

If the donor's spouse is not a U.S. citizen, an annual exclusion of $148,000 in 2016 ($149,000 in 2017) is allowed for present interest gifts to the spouse that would qualify for the marital deduction if the spouse were a U.S. citizen (Code Sec. 2523(i)(2); Rev. Proc. 2015-53; Rev. Proc. 2016-55).[17] The annual exclusion is available to all donors, including nonresident citizens.

The annual exclusion is allowed for gifts of present interests, but not for gifts of future interests in property. Present interests include any interests, whether vested or contingent, that are available for the donee's immediate use, possession, or enjoyment (Reg. § 25.2503-3(b)). A transfer of property for the benefit of a minor pursuant to the Uniform Transfers to Minors Act (UTMA), the Uniform Gifts to Minors Act (UGMA), or the Gifts of Securities to Minors Act (GSMA) is considered to be a completed gift of the full fair market value of the property.[18]

Transfers in Trust. The number of annual exclusions available for a gift in trust is determined by the number of trust beneficiaries who have a present interest in the gifted property. A transfer to a trust that allows a beneficiary the unrestricted right to the immediate use, possession, or enjoyment of the transferred property or the income from the property, such as a life estate or term certain, is a present interest gift that qualifies for the annual exclusion (Reg. § 25.2503-3(b)). However, such unrestricted gifts through a trust are rarely made. Normally, limits are placed on the beneficiary's right to use, possess, or enjoy the trust property. A gift of the right to demand a portion of a trust corpus is a gift of a present interest, so long as the donee-beneficiary is aware of his or her right to make the demand. Typically, the beneficiary of such a trust (known as a *Crummey* trust) is given the right to demand an amount of corpus equal to the annual gift tax exclusion for a limited period of time, such as 60 days. If the persons who have a right of withdrawal do not have a present income interest in the trust or a vested remainder interest, however, the IRS may question the claimed annual exclusion.[19]

Gifts to Minors. Gifts to minors may qualify for the annual exclusion if they meet the requirements of Code Sec. 2503(c).[20] The property and income from it must be expended by or for the benefit of the minor, and any income and principal not expended must be paid to the minor at age 21, or to his or her estate if the minor dies before age 21 (Code Sec. 2503(c); Reg. § 25.2503-4(a)).[21] However, if a transfer of property is made under a parent's legal obligation to support a minor, the transfer is not a gift, as is the case with child support.[22]

2907. Exclusion for Educational or Medical Payment. In addition to the annual exclusion (¶ 2905), an unlimited gift tax exclusion is allowed for amounts paid on behalf of a donee *directly* to an educational organization, provided such amounts constitute

References are to Federal Estate & Gift Tax Reports; Tax Research Consultant; Practical Tax Explanations.

[14] ¶ 7575.09, ¶ 9245; ESTGIFT: 60,100; § 35,010

[15] ¶ 9,649; ESTGIFT: 6,050; § 34,820.10

[16] ¶ 10,960, ¶ 10,987.06; ESTGIFT: 6,054; § 34,820.10

[17] ¶ 11,662, ¶ 11,850, ¶ 11,884.05; ESTGIFT: 6,050; § 35,010.15

[18] ¶ 9649, ¶ 9950.335, ¶ 10,041.05; ESTGIFT: 6,058, ESTGIFT: 6,060; § 34,820.10

[19] ¶ 9649, ¶ 9842.055, ¶ 9891, ¶ 9950.07; ESTGIFT: 6,060; § 34,820.10

[20] ¶ 9649, ¶ 9842.05, ¶ 9996; ESTGIFT: 6,060.10; § 34,820.10

[21] ¶ 9649, ¶ 9996, ¶ 10,041.05; ESTGIFT: 12,056; § 34,820.10

[22] ¶ 11,311, ¶ 11,324.05; ESTGIFT: 12,100; § 34,820.10

tuition payments. Amounts paid for books, dormitory fees, or board on behalf of the donee are not eligible for the exclusion. Likewise, amounts paid *directly* to health care providers for medical services on behalf of a donee also qualify for the unlimited gift tax exclusion. Medical expense payments are excludable without regard to the percentage limitations imposed for income tax purposes. Both the medical and tuition exclusions are available without regard to the relationship between the donor and donee (Code Sec. 2503(e)).[23]

2908. Gifts to Spouse. In computing the taxable gifts of a married donor, a marital deduction is allowed for property that passes to the donor's spouse. As a result, an unlimited amount of property, other than certain terminable interests, can be transferred between spouses. The gift tax marital deduction is not available, however, if the donor's spouse is not a U.S. citizen at the time of the gift. Instead, gifts to a noncitizen spouse are eligible for a gift tax annual exclusion of up to $148,000 in 2016 ($149,000 in 2017) (Code Sec. 2523; Rev. Proc. 2015-53; Rev. Proc. 2016-55).[24]

In addition, a gift tax marital deduction is not allowed for transfers of terminable interests in property. A terminable interest in property is an interest that will terminate or fail on the lapse of time or on the occurrence or failure to occur of some contingency. For example, terminable interests include life estates, terms for years, and annuities. However, a gift tax marital deduction will be allowed if the donee spouse is given a life estate with a general power of appointment or a qualified terminable interest property (QTIP), or if the donor and spouse are named as the only non-charitable beneficiaries of a qualified charitable remainder trust (¶ 2926).[25]

2909. Gifts to Charity. In determining a donor's taxable gifts, a gift tax charitable deduction is available for transfers to charitable organizations (federal, state, and local governmental entities, fraternal societies (if the property is used for charitable purposes), or veterans' organizations). The charitable deduction is not limited to gifts for use within the United States, unless the donor is a nonresident alien at the time of the gift (Code Sec. 2522).[26] A deduction may also be allowed for the value of the charitable interest in a split-interest transfer (a transfer in which there are both charitable and noncharitable beneficiaries) provided the charitable interest is in a qualified form (i.e., charitable remainder annuity trust, charitable remainder unitrust, charitable lead annuity trust, charitable lead unitrust, or a pooled income fund) (¶ 2932).

2910. Computing the Gift Tax Liability. The gift tax is calculated by first determining the total value of the donor's gifts for the current calendar year. The value of a gift is its fair market value on the date of the gift (¶ 2903). This amount is reduced by any exclusions—annual (¶ 2905), and educational and medical (¶ 2907)—and deductions—marital (¶ 2908) and charitable (¶ 2909). The sum of all taxable gifts made by the donor in all prior years is then added to the current year's taxable gifts to arrive at the total taxable gifts. The donor's tentative gift tax liability is then determined by (1) calculating a tentative tax on the sum of all taxable gifts made in the calendar year and in preceding calendar periods, (2) calculating a tentative tax on only the taxable gifts in preceding calendar periods, and (3) then subtracting the tentative tax determined in step (2) from the tentative tax determined in step (1) (Code Sec. 2502).[27]

The donor is allowed a unified credit (or applicable credit) against gift tax, equal to (1) the estate tax applicable credit amount in effect for the calendar year of the gift (¶ 2934), minus (2) the sum of all applicable credits allowable to the donor for gifts made in all prior calendar periods. For 2016, the basic exclusion amount is $5.45 million, and the gift tax credit amount is $2,125,800 (Code Secs. 2010(c) and 2505(a); Rev. Proc.

References are to Federal Estate & Gift Tax Reports; Tax Research Consultant; Practical Tax Explanations.

[23] ¶ 9649, ¶ 10,095, ¶ 10,139.05; ESTGIFT: 6,100; § 34,820.15

[24] ¶ 11,662, ¶ 11,689.01, ¶ 11,884.05; ESTGIFT: 42,050; § 34,815.10

[25] ¶ 11,709.05; ESTGIFT: 42,058, ESTGIFT: 42,060, ESTGIFT: 42,062; § 34,815.10

[26] ¶ 11,486, ¶ 11,513.01; ESTGIFT: 45,050, ESTGIFT: 45,100, ESTGIFT: 45,350; § 34,815.15

[27] ¶ 9385, ¶ 9494.07; ESTGIFT: 100; § 34,830

2015-53).[28] For 2017, the basic exclusion amount is $5.49 million, and the gift tax credit amount is $2,141,800 (Rev. Proc. 2016-55). The applicable credit amount might be higher for any year if the donor is a surviving spouse and the estate of his or her predeceased spouse has elected portability of the deceased spouse's unused exclusion (DSUE) amount (¶ 2934 and ¶ 2938). For gifts made after 2009, any unified credit allocated to prior periods must be redetermined using current gift tax rates, rather than the rates that were in effect when the prior gifts were made (Code Sec. 2505(a)).

Thus, it should be noted that the $5.45 million and first dollar (that is, the first dollar that becomes taxable) is taxed at the rate that would apply to gifts in the amount of $5,450,001 (40 percent in 2016) rather than the rate that would apply to a gift of $1 (18 percent).

If a gift is adequately disclosed on the gift tax return and the gift tax statute of limitations has expired, the IRS may not revalue the donor's lifetime gifts when computing the estate tax liability upon the donor's death (Code Sec. 2001(f)). There is a three-year statute of limitations for gift tax returns (Code Sec. 2504(c)).[29]

Filing Requirements. Form 709 must be filed, and any gift tax must be paid, on an annual basis. Generally, the due date for filing the annual gift tax return will be the same as the due date for the income tax return. However, for the calendar year in which the donor dies, the gift tax return is due on the earlier of the due date, with extensions, for filing the donor's estate tax return, or the "normal" due date with respect to the gifts (Code Sec. 6075(b)).[30] Taxpayers filing gift tax returns for gifts made in 2016 must file by April 18, 2017.

2911. Donor Is Primarily Liable to File Return and Pay Gift Tax. Gift tax returns must be filed by individual donors for gifts of more than $14,000 in 2016 ($14,000 in 2017) that do not qualify for an exclusion. Gift tax returns must be filed on Form 709. The donor is primarily liable for the payment of the gift tax (Code Sec. 6019).[31]

Estate Tax

2912. Gross Estate. The federal estate tax is imposed on the transfer of a person's property at the time of that person's death. The amount of the tax is determined by applying the relevant tax rates to the taxable estate—the gross estate reduced by any deductions. The gross estate of a U.S. citizen or resident decedent includes the value of all property described in Code Sec. 2033 through Code Sec. 2044, whether real or personal, tangible or intangible, wherever situated. Effectively executed disclaimers prevent the property subject to the disclaimer from being included in the disclaimant's gross estate (Code Secs. 2046 and 2518).[32]

Qualified terminable interest property (QTIP) for which an election was made to qualify it for the marital deduction in the estate of the first spouse to die (¶ 2926), or on the gift tax return of the donor spouse, is included in the gross estate of the surviving or donee spouse (Code Sec. 2044(a)).[33]

Form 706 includes specific schedules on which the estate must provide details for specific types of property included in the decedent's gross estate. Real estate that the decedent owned or had contracted to purchase is reported on Schedule A. Stocks and bonds included in the gross estate are reported on Schedule B. Mortgages and notes payable to the decedent at the time of death, as well as cash that the decedent possessed on the date of death, are reported on Schedule C. Other Form 706 schedules are specifically designated for other types of property. If an asset in the gross estate is not required to be reported on any other schedule, it must be reported on Schedule F.

References are to Federal Estate & Gift Tax Reports; Tax Research Consultant; Practical Tax Explanations.

[28] ¶ 10,403, ¶ 10,448.03; ESTGIFT: 100; § 34,820.20

[29] ¶ 10,235, ¶ 10,368.05; ESTGIFT: 3,300; § 34,835

[30] ¶ 20,301, ¶ 20,330.05; ESTGIFT: 3,300; § 34,830

[31] ¶ 9245, ¶ 20,125, ¶ 20,135.05, ¶ 20,301; ESTGIFT: 3,300; § 34,830

[32] ¶ 5980, ¶ 5990.05, ¶ 11,339, ¶ 11,419.03; ESTGIFT: 15,050; § 34,170

[33] ¶ 5901, ¶ 5940.05; ESTGIFT: 15,500; § 34,160

2913. Transferred Property in Which Decedent Retained an Interest. When a decedent retains some control over gifts of property made during life, the property may be added back to the decedent's gross estate. The transfers subject to this rule include:

(1) gifts in which the decedent retains a life estate or the right to the income, possession, or enjoyment of the property, or the right to designate who will enjoy the property, including gifts of stock in which voting rights are retained (Code Sec. 2036);[34]

(2) gifts in which the decedent retains a right to a reversionary interest that exceeds five percent of the value of the transferred property and possession or enjoyment of the property can be obtained only by surviving the decedent (Code Sec. 2037(a));[35] and

(3) gifts in which the decedent holds a power to alter, amend, revoke, or terminate the gift (Code Sec. 2038(a)(1); Reg. § 20.2038-1(a)).[36]

If income from transferred property is used to discharge a legal obligation of the decedent, such as the decedent's obligation to support his or her dependents, the decedent is considered to have a right to income from the property and the property is includible in his or her gross estate (Reg. § 20.2036-1(b)(2)).[37] Such transfers are generally reported on Schedule G of Form 706.

An estate valuation freeze is a technique used to limit the value of closely held business interests owned by an individual by transferring the future appreciation in value of the business to the next generation of the owner's family while retaining certain interests in the business. This technique has been severely limited by the special valuation rules (Code Secs. 2701—2704), which treat transfers of family business interests unfavorably for gift tax purposes by assigning a value of zero to certain types of interests retained by the donor in such exchanges.[38]

If a lifetime transfer with a retained interest is a sale for adequate and full consideration, the property that is transferred is not included in the transferor's gross estate (Code Sec. 2036(a); Reg. § 20.2036-1(c)).[39] However, if the transfer is not for adequate and full consideration, the amount included in the decedent's estate is the full value of the property subject to the decedent's retained interest. If the interest or right is reserved over only part of the property transferred, only the reserved portion is included in the gross estate.

2914. Gifts Made Within Three Years of Death. Gifts made within three years of the donor's death ordinarily are not includible in the donor's gross estate. However, gifts made within three years of death are included in the donor's gross estate if the gift consists of interests in property that would otherwise be included in the gross estate because of the donor's retained powers, such as the power to alter, amend, revoke, or terminate the gift (¶ 2913) (Code Sec. 2035(a)).[40] Similarly, a gift of life insurance that would have been includible in the decedent's gross estate because of his or her retention of incidents of ownership in the policy is includible if the policy was transferred within three years of the decedent's date of death (¶ 2915). Gifts made from a decedent's revocable trust within three years of death are not included in the decedent's gross estate, but instead are treated as if made directly by the decedent (Code Secs. 2035(e) and 2038). Gift tax paid on all transfers made within three years of death is included in the gross estate (Code Sec. 2035(b)).

Such transfers are generally reported on Schedule G of Form 706.

References are to Federal Estate & Gift Tax Reports; Tax Research Consultant; Practical Tax Explanations.

[34] ¶ 4901, ¶ 4955.06, ¶ 4980.05; ESTGIFT: 18,400, ESTGIFT: 18,450, ESTGIFT: 18,600; § 34,135.10

[35] ¶ 5001, ¶ 5075.01; ESTGIFT: 18,500; § 34,135.15

[36] ¶ 5101, ¶ 5135, ¶ 5170.05; ESTGIFT: 18,550; § 34,135.20

[37] ¶ 4925; ESTGIFT: 18,304; § 34,135.10

[38] ¶ 13,551, ¶ 13,670, ¶ 13,690.05, ¶ 14,001, ¶ 14,501, ¶ 14,651; ESTGIFT: 18,600; § 34,810

[39] ¶ 4901, ¶ 4925, ¶ 4955.05; ESTGIFT: 18,100; § 34,135.05

[40] ¶ 4801, ¶ 4845.01, ¶ 4845.091; ESTGIFT: 18,200; § 34,150

2915. Life Insurance. Proceeds of insurance on a decedent's life payable to or for the benefit of his or her estate, and insurance payable to other beneficiaries in which the decedent retained incidents of ownership, are included in the decedent's gross estate (Code Sec. 2042(1) and (2); Reg. § 20.2042-1(b)(1)).[41] Insurance that is paid to a named beneficiary, but that must be used to satisfy a legal obligation to meet expenses of the decedent's estate, such as debts and taxes, is also included in the decedent's gross estate (Reg. § 20.2042-1(c)(1)).

Incidents of Ownership. If proceeds of insurance on the life of a decedent are payable to a beneficiary other than the decedent's estate, they are included in the decedent's gross estate if the decedent has retained an incident of ownership in the life insurance policy on the date of death (Code Sec. 2042(2); Reg. § 20.2042-1(c)). The term "incidents of ownership" is not limited in its meaning to ownership of the policy. The term refers to the right of the insured or the insured's estate to the economic benefits of the policy. Some incidents of ownership include the power to change the beneficiary, the ability to pledge the policy as security for a loan, the ability to borrow against the policy, or a reversionary interest by which the insured or the insured's estate may regain one of the previously stated rights under certain circumstances. If the decedent transfers a life insurance policy or an incident of ownership in the policy within three years of his or her death, the proceeds are included in the decedent's gross estate (Code Sec. 2035(a)).[42] However, generally only one-half of the proceeds of life insurance purchased with community property is included in the estate of the insured spouse, even if the decedent possessed an incident of ownership (Reg. § 20.2042-1(b)(2)).[43]

A person insured under a key-employee insurance arrangement usually has no interest in the insurance. None of its proceeds will be included in the insured's gross estate. However, the arrangement will be taken into account in determining a value for any stock that the insured may have owned in the company.[44]

In the case of split-dollar life insurance, death proceeds from the employee's portion of the policy are included in the employee's estate if:

(1) the proceeds are payable to, or for the benefit of, the employee's estate; or

(2) the employee holds an incident of ownership in the policy at death or transfers an incident of ownership to a third party within three years before death.

Gift tax liability for employer-paid premiums may arise if a co-owner of the policy is neither the employer nor the employee.[45]

Life insurance that is included in a decedent's gross estate is generally reported on Schedule D of Form 706. For each policy listed, a separate Form 712, Life Insurance Statement, must be completed and attached to Schedule D.

2917. Annuities and Retirement Benefits. The value of an annuity or other payment received by any beneficiary by reason of surviving the decedent is generally included in the decedent's gross estate. The annuity or other payment is not taxable under the rules unless it is payable under a contract by agreement and the following factors exist:

(1) the contract or agreement was entered into after March 31, 1931;

(2) the contract or agreement is not a policy of insurance on the decedent's life;

(3) the decedent possessed the right to receive the payments during his or her lifetime; and

(4) payments under the contract are determined by reference to the decedent's life or life expectancy (Code Sec. 2039(a)).[46]

References are to Federal Estate & Gift Tax Reports; Tax Research Consultant; Practical Tax Explanations.

[41] ¶ 5651, ¶ 5715, ¶ 5740.05; ESTGIFT: 21,050; § 34,120

[42] ¶ 4801, ¶ 4845.09, ¶ 5651; ESTGIFT: 21,100; § 34,120

[43] ¶ 5670, ¶ 5715, ¶ 5740.05; ESTGIFT: 21,200; § 34,120

[44] ¶ 5760, ¶ 5780.03; ESTGIFT: 21,150; § 34,105

[45] ¶ 5780.045, ¶ 5780.183; COMPEN: 48,150; § 34,105

[46] ¶ 5201, ¶ 5245.05; ESTGIFT: 24,050; § 34,145

The value of an annuity or other payment included in a decedent's gross estate is the portion of its value attributable to the portion of the purchase price contributed by the decedent. Any contribution made by a decedent's employer or former employer by reason of his or her employment is considered to be made by the decedent (Code Sec. 2039(b)).[47]

Annuities that are included in a decedent's gross estate are generally reported on Schedule I of Form 706.

With respect to the estate tax valuation of a qualified account, i.e., an IRA, the value of the account is the fair market value of the assets in the account without any discount for the income tax liability that would be triggered if the estate or beneficiary was to take a distribution of the assets in order to sell them.[48]

2918. Powers of Appointment. Property subject to a general power of appointment is included in the gross estate of the holder of the power if the power exists at the holder's death (Code Sec. 2041(a)(2)). The exercise or release of a general power during the life of the holder is a transfer subject to gift tax (Code Sec. 2514(b)).[49] A power of appointment is a right to dispose of the property given to someone other than the donor of the property. The holder of the power of appointment has a general power if the holder may exercise it in favor of himself or herself, the holder's creditors, the holder's estate, or the creditors of the holder's estate (Code Secs. 2041(b) and 2514(c)). Powers that expressly cannot be exercised in favor of any of these are special or limited powers (Reg. § 20.2041-1(c)(1)). A power is not general if its exercise is limited by an ascertainable standard (Code Secs. 2041(b)(1)(A) and 2514(c)(1)). A power is not general if the creator of the power must join in its exercise or if a co-holder of the power has a substantial adverse interest (Code Secs. 2041(b)(1)(C) and 2514(c)(3)(A)). The power holder's incompetence or lack of capacity to exercise the power does not affect whether the power is taxable to the power holder.[50]

Property subject to a power of appointment that is included in a decedent's gross estate is generally reported on Schedule H of Form 706.

2919. Jointly Held Property. The entire value of jointly held property with the right of survivorship, including joint bank accounts and U.S. savings bonds registered in two names, is included in a decedent's gross estate except for the portion of the property for which the surviving joint tenant furnished consideration. If the joint property was received by the decedent and the other joint tenants as a gift or bequest, the decedent's fractional share of the property is included in the decedent's gross estate (Code Sec. 2040(a)).[51] If the joint tenants are spouses, it generally does not matter who furnished the consideration for the property; one-half of the value of a qualified joint interest is included in the gross estate of the first spouse to die (Code Sec. 2040(b)).[52]

Jointly held property that is included in a decedent's gross estate is generally reported on Schedule E of Form 706.

The creation of a joint interest in property results in a taxable gift by the person supplying the consideration to the noncontributing joint tenant. Creation of a joint bank account or joint brokerage account is not a taxable gift until a joint owner withdraws funds (Reg. § 25.2511-1(h)). If a donor purchased property and conveyed title to himself or herself and another as joint tenants with rights of survivorship, and those rights may be defeated by either owner severing his or her interest, the donor made a gift to the other joint owner in the amount of one-half of the property's value. A transfer of joint property to a third party is a gift of the value of each joint owner's share.[53]

2921. Community Property. Community property is all property acquired by means other than gift, devise, bequest, and inheritance by spouses domiciled in commu-

References are to Federal Estate & Gift Tax Reports; Tax Research Consultant; Practical Tax Explanations.

[47] ¶ 5201, ¶ 5245.07; ESTGIFT: 24,100; § 34,145

[48] ¶ 3100, ¶ 3220.41; ESTGIFT: 15,202.15; § 34,145

[49] ¶ 5501, ¶ 11,054; ESTGIFT: 27,100; § 34,140, § 34,805.10

[50] ¶ 5630.231; ESTGIFT: 27,050; § 34,805

[51] ¶ 5401, ¶ 5475.05; ESTGIFT: 30,050; § 34,125

[52] ¶ 5401, ¶ 5475.07; ESTGIFT: 30,060; § 34,125

[53] ¶ 10,528, ¶ 10,555.24; ESTGIFT: 30,100; § 34,805.15

nity property jurisdictions. Separate property is property other than community property.[54] One-half of the value of all community property owned by a married couple is includible in the gross estate of the first of the spouses to die (Code Sec. 2033). This rule of inclusion applies even though the surviving spouse elects to allow his or her share of the community property to pass according to the will of the decedent spouse.[55]

2922. Valuation of Gross Estate. The value of property that is included in the gross estate is its fair market value on decedent's date of death (Code Sec. 2031; Reg. § 20.2031-1(b)).[56] The fair market value of property includible in the gross estate is the price at which it would change hands between a willing buyer and a willing seller, both having reasonable knowledge of relevant facts.

Alternate Valuation. Instead of valuing property includible in the gross estate as of the date of death, the executor may elect to value the gross estate at the fair market value of the property on the alternate valuation date, which is the date six months after the date of the decedent's death (Code Sec. 2032; Reg. § 20.2032-1).[57] To use the alternate valuation election, the value of the gross estate must have decreased and the amount of estate and GST taxes imposed on the property included in the gross estate must also decrease. The alternate valuation election is irrevocable. The election is made on Form 706. The amount of any marital or charitable deduction is adjusted based on the alternate value of assets passing to charity or a surviving spouse (Code Sec. 2032(b); Reg. § 20.2032-1(g)). When the alternate valuation election is made, all property included in the gross estate is valued as of the alternate valuation date (Reg. § 20.2032-1(d)).[58] However, if property is sold, exchanged, distributed, or otherwise disposed of during the six-month period, it is valued on the date of disposition rather than the alternate valuation date (Code Sec. 2032(a)(1)).[59]

Special Use Valuation. If a farm or real property used in a closely held business is included in the gross estate, the executor may elect to value the property at its "current use" rather than at its "highest and best use." Special use valuation is obtained pursuant to an irrevocable election by an executor to value real property used in a farm, trade, or business (Code Sec. 2032A).[60] The limitation on the reduction in value resulting from special use valuation is $1,110,000 in 2016 ($1,120,000 in 2017) (Rev. Proc. 2015-53; Rev. Proc. 2016-55).

Special use valuation is elected on the estate tax return (Part 3, line 2 of Form 706) by, among other things, completing the notice of election (Schedule A-1) and submitting a recapture agreement.[61] If the qualified heir ceases to use the farm property for farming or sells the property to a non-family member within 10 years of the decedent's date of death, an additional estate tax, the recapture tax, is due and Form 706-A must be filed (Code Sec. 2032A(c)).[62]

2925. Deductions from Gross Estate—Expenses. A deduction from the gross estate is allowed for funeral expenses, administration expenses, claims against the estate, certain taxes, and unpaid mortgages or other indebtedness allowable under the local law governing the administration of the decedent's estate (Code Sec. 2053; Reg. § 20.2053-1).[63] For expenses that are not paid before filing the estate tax return, an estimated amount may be deducted if the amount is ascertainable and there is reasonable certainty that the amount will be paid. Contested and contingent claims and expenses cannot be ascertained with reasonable certainty. Estate administration expenses may generally be deducted on either the decedent's estate tax return or the estate's income tax return, but not on both (Code Sec. 642(g); Reg. § 1.642(g)-1).[64]

References are to Federal Estate & Gift Tax Reports; Tax Research Consultant; Practical Tax Explanations.

[54] ¶ 4620, ¶ 4675.04; ESTGIFT: 33,050; § 34,601

[55] ¶ 4675.11; ESTGIFT: 33,100; § 34,125

[56] ¶ 3011, ¶ 3100, ¶ 3125.01; ESTGIFT: 100; § 34,101

[57] ¶ 3801, ¶ 3830, ¶ 3870.05; ESTGIFT: 36,050, ESTGIFT: 36,100; § 34,205

[58] ¶ 3830; ESTGIFT: 36,102; § 34,205

[59] ¶ 3801; ESTGIFT: 36,150; § 34,205

[60] ¶ 4001, ¶ 4240.05; ESTGIFT: 36,200; § 34,210

[61] ¶ 4001; ESTGIFT: 36,300; § 34,210

[62] ¶ 4001, ¶ 4240.35; ESTGIFT: 36,350; § 34,210

[63] ¶ 6040, ¶ 6050, ¶ 6060.025, ¶ 6060.055; ESTGIFT: 39,050, ESTGIFT: 39,100, ESTGIFT: 39,150; § 34,305

[64] ¶ 16,675, ¶ 16,825, ¶ 16,875.05, ¶ 16,875.07; ESTGIFT: 39,050, ESTGIFT:

Expenses incurred in connection with the decedent's funeral, including reasonable expenses for a tombstone, mausoleum, or burial lot, are deductible (Code Sec. 2053(a)(1)).[65] Administration expenses are deductible if actually and necessarily incurred in the administration of the estate. Administration expenses include fees paid to surrogates, appraisers, and accountants. Reasonable attorney's fees that meet the requirements of Reg. § 20.2053-1 are deductible (Code Sec. 2053(a)(2); Reg. § 20.2053-3(c)).[66] Fees incurred by beneficiaries incident to litigation with regard to their interests are not deductible, unless the litigation is essential to the proper settlement of the estate. An executor or administrator may deduct the amount of his or her commissions from the decedent's gross estate in an amount actually paid or an amount that is reasonably ascertainable and will be paid (Reg. § 20.2053-3(b)).[67] Miscellaneous expenses necessarily incurred in preserving and distributing estate assets are also deductible as administration expenses (Reg. § 20.2053-3(d)).[68]

Funeral and administrative expenses are generally reported on Schedule J of Form 706.

Claims that are a personal obligation of the decedent are deductible, provided that they are existing and enforceable against the decedent at the time of his or her death, are allowable under local law, and have actually been paid or meet the requirements of Reg. § 20.2053-1(d)(4). Liabilities imposed by law or arising out of torts committed by the decedent are also deductible. In certain circumstances, an executor may deduct the current value of a claim or claims that concern the same or similar issue or asset, even if the claim has not yet been paid (Reg. § 20.2053-4).[69] The full value of any unpaid mortgage or other indebtedness charged against property for which the decedent is personally liable, plus interest accrued on the debt to the date of death, is deductible if the property's entire value undiminished by the mortgage or indebtedness is included in the gross estate (Code Sec. 2053(a)(4); Reg. § 20.2053-7).[70]

Debts, mortgages, and liabilities of the decedent are generally reported on Schedule K of Form 706.

Federal estate taxes are not deductible. State estate, succession, legacy, or inheritance taxes actually paid to any state or the District of Columbia from the value of the gross estate are deductible (¶ 2933), as are unpaid gift taxes on gifts made before death. Unpaid income taxes are deductible if they are on income properly includible in an income tax return of a decedent for a period before his or her death (Reg. § 20.2053-6).[71] A deduction is also allowed for losses arising from fires, storms, shipwrecks, or other casualties or thefts that are incurred during estate administration and not compensated for by insurance (Code Sec. 2054).[72]

Such losses and taxes, except for the state death tax deduction (¶ 2933), are generally reported on Schedule L of Form 706.

2926. Estate Tax Marital Deduction. In determining a married decedent's taxable estate, an unlimited deduction is allowable for property that passes to the decedent's surviving spouse (Code Sec. 2056).[73] In order to qualify for the deduction, the decedent must be married and survived by his or her spouse, the spouse must be a U.S. citizen, the property must be included in the decedent's gross estate and pass to the surviving spouse, and the property must not be a nondeductible terminable interest. The estate tax marital deduction is not available if the decedent's surviving spouse is not a U.S. citizen unless the spouse becomes a citizen before the estate tax return is filed or the property passes to a qualified domestic trust (QDOT) (Code Secs. 2056(d) and 2056A).[74]

(Footnote Continued)

39,100, ESTGIFT: 39,150; § 34,305

[65] ¶ 6040, ¶ 6070, ¶ 6080.03; ESTGIFT: 39,100; § 34,305.10

[66] ¶ 6040, ¶ 6090, ¶ 6100.03, ¶ 6130, ¶ 6140.05; ESTGIFT: 39,150, ESTGIFT: 39,158; § 34,305.15

[67] ¶ 6110, ¶ 6120; ESTGIFT: 39,154; § 34,305.15

[68] ¶ 6150, ¶ 6160.05; ESTGIFT: 39,160; § 34,305.15

[69] ¶ 6170, ¶ 6180.01; ESTGIFT: 39,200; § 34,305.20

[70] ¶ 6040, ¶ 6230, ¶ 6240.05; ESTGIFT: 39,250; § 34,305.25

[71] ¶ 6210, ¶ 6220.05; ESTGIFT: 39,300; § 34,305.20

[72] ¶ 6320, ¶ 6340.03; ESTGIFT: 39,350; § 34,310

[73] ¶ 6501; ESTGIFT: 42,100; § 34,320

[74] ¶ 6501, ¶ 7001, ¶ 7045.05, ¶ 7045.10; ESTGIFT: 42,100, ESTGIFT: 42,150; § 34,320

Estates of decedents who are in a same-sex marriage may claim the estate tax marital deduction (*E. Windsor*, SCt, 2013-2 USTC ¶ 60,667).[75]

Passing Requirement. Property must pass from the decedent to a surviving spouse for a transfer to be deductible (Code Sec. 2056(a)). Bequests and inheritances, dower and curtesy interests, joint property, property received under antenuptial agreements, annuities, and life insurance may pass from the decedent to the surviving spouse. Property received by a spouse under a state law right of election against the will satisfies the passing requirement (Code Sec. 2056(c); Reg. § 20.2056(c)-2(c)). Property passing to the spouse as a result of another person's qualified disclaimer (¶ 2905) is considered to pass from the decedent (Reg. § 20.2056(d)-2(b)).[76]

Terminable Interest Rule. The terminable interest rule bars a deduction for any nondeductible terminable interest. A terminable interest in property is an interest that terminates or fails because of the lapse of time or the occurrence of an event (Code Sec. 2056(b)(1) and (3); Reg. § 20.2056(b)-3).[77] A nondeductible terminable interest is an interest in which a person, other than the surviving spouse, receives an interest in property from the decedent and, upon the termination of the spouse's interest in the same property, the other person may possess or enjoy the property. Property interests passing to a spouse that are conditioned on the spouse's survival of a period of six months or less, or on the spouse's survival in a common disaster, are not subject to the terminable interest rule.

Qualified Terminable Interest Property. Qualified terminable interest property (QTIP) is excluded from the terminable interest rule. To qualify as QTIP, the surviving spouse must have the right to all the income from the property for life, payable no less frequently than annually (Code Sec. 2056(b)(7); Reg. § 20.2056(b)-7(a)).[78] A surviving spouse's income interest may be contingent upon the executor's QTIP election and still be considered a "qualifying income interest for life." In addition, no person may have a power to appoint any of the property to any person other than the surviving spouse during the surviving spouse's life. An election on Schedule M of Form 706 is necessary to designate property as QTIP. Once the QTIP election is made, the surviving spouse must include the property remaining at death in his or her gross estate even though the surviving spouse has no control over its disposition (Code Sec. 2044). However, the estate tax that is attributable to the QTIP included in the spouse's estate may be recovered from the QTIP (Code Sec. 2207A).[79]

Life Estate with Power of Appointment. A life estate with a power of appointment qualifies for the marital deduction if:

(1) the surviving spouse is entitled to all the income from the entire interest or a specific portion of the interest for life;

(2) the income is payable at least annually;

(3) the spouse has the power to appoint the property, or the specific portion, to himself or herself or to his or her estate;

(4) the power is exercisable by the spouse alone and in all events; and

(5) no other person has the power to appoint property to anyone but the surviving spouse (Code Sec. 2056(b)(5)).

There is a similar exception to the terminable interest rule for life insurance proceeds held by an insurer in which the spouse has a right to all payments and a power of appointment (Code Sec. 2056(b)(6); Reg. § 20.2056(b)-6(c)).[80]

References are to Federal Estate & Gift Tax Reports; Tax Research Consultant; Practical Tax Explanations.

[75] ¶ 6580.035; ESTGIFT: 42,102; § 34,320.10

[76] ¶ 6501, ¶ 6920.03, ¶ 6935, ¶ 6975; ESTGIFT: 42,150; § 34,320

[77] ¶ 6501, ¶ 6701, ¶ 6725.03; ESTGIFT: 42,200; § 34,320.15

[78] ¶ 6501, ¶ 6825; ESTGIFT: 42,250; § 34,320.20

[79] ¶ 5901, ¶ 6501, ¶ 8800; ESTGIFT: 42,260, ESTGIFT: 42,262; § 34,320.20

[80] ¶ 6501, ¶ 6801, ¶ 6815.05; ESTGIFT: 42,300; § 34,320.20

Amount of the Marital Deduction. The marital deduction is limited to the net value of property passing to the spouse. Death taxes, debts, and administration expenses payable from the marital bequest, mortgages on property passing to the spouse, and insufficient estate assets to fund the marital bequest all reduce the amount of the deduction (Code Sec. 2056(b)(4); Reg. § 20.2056(b)-4).[81] However, administration expenses allocable to an estate's income do not necessarily reduce the amount of the marital deduction (*O. Hubert Est.*, SCt, 97-1 USTC ¶ 60,261).[82]

Transfers for which an estate is taking the estate tax marital deduction are generally reported on Schedule M of Form 706.

2932. Estate Tax Charitable Deduction. An unlimited estate tax charitable deduction is available for transfers to: federal, state, and local governmental entities; charitable organizations; fraternal societies (if the property is used for charitable purposes); veterans' organizations; or an employee stock ownership plan if the transfer qualifies as a qualified gratuitous transfer. The bequest must have a public rather than a private purpose (Code Secs. 2055(a)).[83]

Transfers of Partial Interests. If an interest in property passes from a transferor to a charity and an interest in the same property passes to a noncharitable recipient, the transfer must take one of the following forms:

(1) charitable remainder annuity trust, which provides for a fixed-dollar amount to be paid to the noncharitable income beneficiary annually, or charitable remainder unitrust, which provides for a fixed percentage of trust assets, valued annually, to be paid to the noncharitable income beneficiary annually (Code Secs. 2055(e)(2)(A) and 2522(c)(2)(A); Reg. § 20.2055-2(e)(2));[84]

(2) charitable lead trust with guaranteed annuity or unitrust amount paid to charity (Code Secs. 170(f)(2), 2055(e)(2)(B), and 2522(c)(2)(B); Reg. § 20.2055-2(e)(2));[85]

(3) remainder interest in a farm or personal residence (Code Sec. 2055(e)(3)(I); Reg. § 20.2055-2(e)(2));[86]

(4) copyrighted work of art separate from its copyright (Code Secs. 2055(e)(4) and 2522(c)(3); Reg. § 20.2055-2(e)(1));[87] or

(5) qualified conservation contribution (Code Sec. 170(f)(3); Reg. § 20.2055-2(e)(2)).[88]

The amount of the estate tax charitable deduction must be reduced by the administration expenses and death taxes paid from the property transferred to charity (Code Sec. 2055(c); Reg. § 20.2055-3(a)).[89] However, administration expenses allocable to an estate's income do not necessarily reduce the amount of the charitable deduction (*O. Hubert Est.*, SCt, 97-1 USTC ¶ 60,261).[90]

Transfers for which an estate is taking the estate tax charitable deduction are generally reported on Schedule O of Form 706.

2933. State Death Tax Deduction. A deduction from the gross estate is allowed for estate, inheritance, legacy, or succession taxes actually paid to any state or the District of Columbia as a result of the decedent's death (Code Sec. 2058).[91] A limitations period

References are to Federal Estate & Gift Tax Reports; Tax Research Consultant; Practical Tax Explanations.

[81] ¶ 6501, ¶ 6745; ESTGIFT: 42,350; § 34,320.10

[82] ¶ 6755.674; ESTGIFT: 42,356; § 34,320.10

[83] ¶ 6360, ¶ 6370; ESTGIFT: 45,050, ESTGIFT: 45,100, ESTGIFT: 45,350; § 34,315

[84] ¶ 6360, ¶ 6390, ¶ 11,486, ¶ 16,901; ESTGIFT: 45,150, ESTGIFT: 45,200; § 34,315.20

[85] ¶ 6360, ¶ 6390, ¶ 11,486, ¶ 16,901; ESTGIFT: 45,250, ESTGIFT: 45,300; § 34,315.15

[86] ¶ 6360, ¶ 6390; ESTGIFT: 45,158; § 34,315.15

[87] ¶ 6360, ¶ 6390; ESTGIFT: 45,154; § 34,315.30

[88] ¶ 6390; ESTGIFT: 45,160; § 34,315.15

[89] ¶ 6360, ¶ 6430; ESTGIFT: 45,352, ESTGIFT: 45,354; § 34,315.05

[90] ¶ 6380.18; ESTGIFT: 45,352; § 34,315.05

[91] ¶ 7450, ¶ 7460.05; ESTGIFT: 39,304; § 34,330

is imposed that allows a deduction only for those state death taxes paid and a deduction claimed before the later of:

(1) four years after filing the estate tax return;

(2) if a timely petition for redetermination has been filed with the Tax Court, 60 days after the Tax Court decision becomes final;

(3) if an extension of time has been granted for payment of estate tax or of a deficiency, the date the extension expires; or

(4) if a timely refund claim has been filed, then the latest of the expiration of (a) 60 days from the mailing of a notice to the taxpayer of a disallowance of the refund claim, (b) 60 days after a court decision on the merits of the claim becomes final, or (c) two years after a notice of waiver of disallowance is filed under Code Sec. 6532(a)(3).

A refund based on the deduction may be made if the refund claim is filed within the above-defined period. Any refunds made will be without interest.

The state death tax deduction is taken on Part 2, line 3b of Form 706.

2934. Credits Against the Estate Tax. A number of credits are available to offset a decedent's federal estate tax liability. The most important credit is the applicable credit amount (formerly, the unified credit), which is determined by calculating a tentative estate tax on the basic exclusion amount (adjusted annually for inflation) (Code Sec. 2010(c); Reg. § 20.2010-1).[92] The basic exclusion amount can be used to offset an estate tax liability on a taxable estate of $5.45 million in 2016 ($5.49 million in 2017) resulting in an applicable credit amount of $2,125,800 for 2016 ($2,141,800 for 2017) (Rev. Proc. 2015-53; Rev. Proc. 2016-55).

Portability of Unused Applicable Exclusion Amount. The applicable exclusion amount for a surviving spouse whose predeceased spouse's estate elected portability is the sum of (1) the basic exclusion amount ($5.45 million in 2016; $5.49 million in 2017), plus (2) the aggregate deceased spousal unused exclusion (DSUE) amount (Code Sec. 2010(c)(2) and (4); Reg. § § 20.2010-2 and 20.2010-3).[93] The DSUE amount is the lesser of (1) the basic exclusion amount in effect in the year of the deceased spouse's death or (2) the last deceased spouse's applicable exclusion amount minus the amount with respect to which the tentative tax is determined on the last deceased spouse's estate. To take advantage of this special provision, the predeceased spouse must have died after December 31, 2010, and the predeceased spouse's estate must have made an election on Form 706 (¶ 2938). If portability is elected, the surviving spouse can apply the predeceased spouse's unused exclusion amount toward lifetime gifts, and any remaining unused exclusion amount can generally be applied by the surviving spouse's estate upon his or her death. Special rules limit the use of unused exclusion amounts by a surviving spouse with multiple predeceased spouses.

An executor electing portability must make the election on a timely-filed Form 706, including extensions actually granted, even if there is no estate tax liability. If the executor must otherwise file an estate tax return, but does not wish to make the portability election, the executor should make an affirmative statement to that effect on the return (Reg. § 20.2010-2(a)(3)). Not timely filing Form 706 will also effectively prevent the election (Notice 2011-82). Guidance on the interplay between the portability election and the qualified terminable interest property (QTIP) election, where the QTIP election was unnecessary to reduce the estate tax to zero but was done to maximize the DSUE amount portable to the surviving spouse, is provided in Rev. Proc. 2016-49.

References are to Federal Estate & Gift Tax Reports; Tax Research Consultant; Practical Tax Explanations.

[92] ¶ 1401, ¶ 1410, ¶ 1450.01; ESTGIFT: 51,052.05; § 34,010.40

[93] ¶ 1401, ¶ 1415, ¶ 1420, ¶ 1450.08; ESTGIFT: 51,060; § 34,010.45

State Death Tax Credit (Repealed). The state death tax credit, which had been repealed for estates of decedents dying after December 31, 2004, and before January 1, 2013, was permanently repealed for the estates of decedents dying after December 31, 2012. Instead, such estates may claim a state death tax *deduction* (¶ 2933) for estate, inheritance, legacy, or succession taxes actually paid to any state or the District of Columbia (Code Sec. 2058).[94]

Federal Estate Tax Paid on Prior Transfers. A credit is available for federal estate tax paid on prior transfers to the decedent from a person who died within 10 years before or two years after the decedent (Code Sec. 2013).[95] The credit is limited to the lesser of the estate tax attributable to the transferred property in the transferor's estate or the estate tax attributable to the transferred property in the decedent's estate. If the transferor predeceased the decedent by more than two years, the allowable credit is reduced by 20 percent for each full two-year period by which the death of the transferor preceded the transferor's death. The credit is claimed on Schedule Q of Form 706.

Foreign Death Taxes. A credit against estate tax is available for foreign death taxes paid on property located in a foreign country, but included in the gross estate of a U.S. citizen or resident (Code Sec. 2014).[96] The credit is limited to the lesser of the foreign or the U.S. tax attributable to the property. If a treaty exists with the foreign country, the credit provided for under the treaty or Code Sec. 2014 may be used, whichever results in the lower amount of estate tax. The credit cannot be allowed until the foreign tax has been paid. The credit is claimed on Schedule P of Form 706 and Form 706-CE must be attached to support any credit claimed.

Credit for Gift Taxes on Pre-1977 Gifts. For gifts made before 1977, the gift tax paid on gifts included in the gross estate is a credit against the estate tax (Code Sec. 2012).[97] The credit is limited to the lesser of the gift tax paid or the estate tax attributable to inclusion of the gift in the gross estate.

2937. Computing the Estate Tax Liability. The estate tax computation begins with a calculation of the gross estate (¶ 2912—¶ 2921). The gross estate is valued at the fair market value on the decedent's date of death or, if elected, on the alternate valuation date, which is six months after the date of death (¶ 2922). Deductions for charitable (¶ 2932) and marital bequests (¶ 2926), state death taxes (¶ 2933), and estate administration expenses (¶ 2925), as well as other allowable deductions are subtracted from the gross estate to determine the taxable estate (Code Sec. 2051). The amount of adjusted taxable gifts made after 1976 is added to the taxable estate. A tentative tax is computed by applying the applicable tax rates from the unified rate schedule (¶ 40) to the sum of the amount of the taxable estate and the adjusted taxable gifts. The tentative tax is then reduced by the amount of gift tax payable on the post-1976 gifts. The resulting amount is the gross estate tax, which is reduced by any allowable credits (¶ 2934), including the applicable credit amount, credits for foreign death taxes paid, the credit for tax on prior transfers, and the credit for gift tax paid on pre-1977 gifts included in the gross estate. For estates of decedents dying after 2009, the estate tax rates in effect at the time of the decedent's death are used to recompute (1) the gift tax imposed on post-1976 gifts made in prior years and (2) the unified credit allowed against such gift taxes (Code Sec. 2001(g)).[98]

An estate tax reduction is available for the estates of U.S. citizens or residents who are active members of the Armed Forces and who are killed in action while serving in a combat zone (Code Sec. 2201).[99] This special treatment has been extended to include a "specified terrorist victim," as defined by Code Sec. 692(d)(4) (¶ 2533) and any astronaut whose death occurs in the line of duty.

References are to Federal Estate & Gift Tax Reports; Tax Research Consultant; Practical Tax Explanations.

[94] ¶ 1551, ¶ 7450; ESTGIFT: 39,304, ESTGIFT: 48,050; § 34,330, § 34,501

[95] ¶ 2001, ¶ 2045; ESTGIFT: 48,100; § 34,515

[96] ¶ 2301; ESTGIFT: 48,150; § 34,520

[97] ¶ 1901; ESTGIFT: 48,200; § 34,510

[98] ¶ 1201, ¶ 1250.02, ¶ 6010, ¶ 6030.01; ESTGIFT: 100; § 34,010

[99] ¶ 8325, ¶ 8375.05, ¶ 8375.10; ESTGIFT: 100; § 34,010.60

Qualified Family-Owned Business Interest (Repealed). The qualified family-owned business interest (QFOBI) deduction, which had been repealed for estates of decedents dying after December 31, 2003, and before January 1, 2013, is permanently repealed for estates of decedents dying after December 31, 2012 (Code Sec. 2057).[100] For estates that had been allowed to elect QFOBI treatment, a recapture tax applied if a specified recapture event occurred within the 10-year period following the decedent's death and before the death of the qualified heir. To report a taxable event for recapture tax purposes, the heir was required to file Form 706-D.

2938. Filing Estate Tax Return and Liability for Payment. Form 706 must be filed for every U.S. citizen or resident decedent whose gross estate exceeds the basic exclusion amount (¶ 2934) for the year of the decedent's death ($5.45 million in 2016, $5.49 million in 2017), or whose executor makes the portability election (discussed following) regardless of the size of the gross estate.

Filing the Return. The estate tax return must be filed by the executor, administrator, or person in possession of the estate's assets (Code Secs. 2203 and 6018(a)).[101] The return is due within nine months of the decedent's date of death, but a six-month extension of time to file is available (Code Sec. 6075(a); Reg. § 20.6075-1).[102] The six-month extension is automatically available if: (1) Form 4768 is filed on or before the due date for the estate tax return; (2) the application is filed with the IRS office designated in the application's instructions; and (3) an estimate of the amount of estate and generation-skipping transfer (GST) tax liability is included.

Basis Reporting Requirement. Executors and beneficiaries who are required to file an estate tax return under Code Sec. 6018 after July 31, 2015, must also furnish an information statement to the IRS and to each person acquiring an interest in property included in the decedent's gross estate. The statement must identify the value of each property interest as reported on the estate tax return and provide any other information required by the IRS. The statement generally must be furnished no later than the *earlier* of (1) 30 days after the due date for filing the estate tax return (including extensions) or (2) 30 days after the estate tax return has been filed. However, the due date is June 30, 2016, for statements required to be furnished before or after July 31, 2015 (Code Sec. 6035); Notice 2016-27, Notice 2016-19 and Notice 2015-57).[103] For discussion of rules requiring consistent basis reporting between a decedent's estate and a person who acquires property from the decedent, see ¶ 1633.

The information is reported on Form 8971. Each beneficiary receiving property from an estate should be given Schedule A of Form 8971, describing the property received. The executor or beneficiary must also provide any other information as directed by the IRS.[104]

Paying the Tax. The estate tax must be paid within nine months after the decedent's date of death (Code Secs. 6075(a) and 6151(a)) by the executor or person in possession of the estate's property (Code Sec. 2002; Reg. § 20.2002-1).[105] The tax may be paid by check, money order, draft, credit card, or debit card (Code Sec. 6311(a)). The time for payment of the estate tax may be extended, upon reasonable cause, for a period of one year past the due date (Code Sec. 6161(a)(1)).[106] If reasonable cause exists, the time for payment may be extended for up to 10 years (Code Sec. 6161(a)(2)).[107]

References are to Federal Estate & Gift Tax Reports; Tax Research Consultant; Practical Tax Explanations.

[100] ¶ 7391, ¶ 7398.01, ¶ 7398.05; ESTGIFT: 15,700; § 34,325.05

[101] ¶ 8425, ¶ 20,075; ESTGIFT: 51,050; § 34,405.05

[102] ¶ 20,301, ¶ 20,310, ¶ 20,315.05; ESTGIFT: 51,050; § 34,405.10

[103] ¶ 20,184, ¶ 20,188.05; SALES: 6,156; § 16,305.45

[104] ¶ 17,675.024, ¶ 20,188.05; SALES: 6,156; § 39,137.

[105] ¶ 1301, ¶ 1340, ¶ 20,301, ¶ 20,501; ESTGIFT: 51,000; § 34,410.05

[106] ¶ 20,575, ¶ 20,845; ESTGIFT: 51,108; § 34,410.10

[107] ¶ 20,575; ESTGIFT: 51,110, ESTGIFT: 51,112; § 34,410.10

Portability Election for Unused Applicable Exclusion Amount. Executors of the estates of decedents dying after 2010 can make an election allowing the decedent's surviving spouse to use the unused portion of the decedent spouse's applicable exclusion amount (¶ 2934) (Code Sec. 2010(c)(4) and (5)).[108] The executor of the predeceased spouse's estate must file Form 706 within the required filing period, including extensions actually granted, to make the election, even if Form 706 is not otherwise required to be filed (Reg. § 20.2010-2(a)).

2939. Election to Pay Estate Tax in Installments. If an estate includes a farm or closely held business whose value exceeds 35 percent of the adjusted gross estate, the executor may elect to pay the estate and generation-skipping transfer (GST) taxes in 10 annual installments following a deferral period of five years (Code Sec. 6166).[109] The amount of tax that may be deferred is limited to the tax attributable to the business interest. A *two-percent* interest rate applies to that portion of the estate tax deferred on the first $1 million in *taxable* value of the closely held business (Code Sec. 6601(j)). The $1 million amount is indexed annually for inflation: $1,480,000 for estates of decedents dying in 2016 ($1,490,000 for decedents dying in 2017) (Rev. Proc. 2015-53; Rev. Proc. 2016-55). A closely held corporation may redeem stock from the estate of a decedent or from the beneficiaries of the estate to pay estate taxes and administrative expenses if the stock comprises 35 percent of the gross estate. This redemption of stock is generally not treated as a disqualifying disposition for purposes of the installment payment of the estate tax (Code Sec. 6166(g)(1)(B)).

The election to pay the estate and GST taxes in installments is made by checking "Yes" on Part 3, line 3 of Form 706 and attaching a statement as described in the instructions to Form 706.

2940. Estate Taxation of Nonresident Aliens. A decedent who is a nonresident alien is subject to estate tax on real, tangible, and intangible property situated in the United States (Code Secs. 2101 and 2103).[110] Intangible property situated in the United States includes stock in domestic corporations, bonds, and debt obligations of U.S. obligors, U.S. partnership assets, and U.S. property owned by a trust in which the nonresident alien has an interest. The value of such property in a nonresident alien's gross estate is not reduced by indebtedness secured by the property if the decedent was personally liable for the debt, even though the personal debt deduction allowed a nonresident alien may fall short of the amount actually owed (*H.H. Fung Est.,* CA-9 (unpub. op.), 2003-1 USTC ¶ 60,460, aff'g, 117 TC 247, Dec. 54,560 (2001)).[111]

The estate of a nonresident alien is taxed at the same estate tax rates that apply to U.S. citizens' estates (Code Sec. 2101(b); Reg. § 20.2101-1).[112] Except where provided by treaty, the unified credit is $13,000 (Code Sec. 2102). The estate may claim deductions for a pro rata share of expenses, debts, and losses, a marital deduction if the surviving spouse is a U.S. citizen, and a charitable deduction (Code Sec. 2106(a)(1); Reg. § 20.2106-2(a)(2)).[113] An estate tax return must be filed if a nonresident alien's gross estate situated in the United States exceeds $60,000 (Code Sec. 6018(a)(2)).[114] The estate must file Form 706-NA.

If a former citizen or long-term resident who is subject to the alternative tax regime of Code Sec. 877(b) dies within 10 years of relinquishment of citizenship or residency, an estate tax is imposed on the transfer of U.S.-situs property, including the decedent's pro rata share of the U.S. property held by a foreign corporation. The estate tax is computed on the taxable estate using the same estate tax rate schedule used for the estate of a U.S. citizen or resident (Code Secs. 2107(a) and 2501(a)(3)(B); Reg. §§ 20.2107-1(a) and 25.2511-1(b)).[115]

References are to Federal Estate & Gift Tax Reports; Tax Research Consultant; Practical Tax Explanations.

[108] ¶ 1401, ¶ 1415, ¶ 1420, ¶ 1450.08, ¶ 10,415, ¶ 10,448.03; ESTGIFT: 51,060; § 34,010.45

[109] ¶ 20,650, ¶ 21,620; ESTGIFT: 51,150; § 34,410.20

[110] ¶ 7525, ¶ 7725; ESTGIFT: 60,050; § 35,005

[111] ¶ 8075.55; ESTGIFT: 60,150; § 35,005.15

[112] ¶ 7525, ¶ 7550; ESTGIFT: 60,200; § 35,005.05

[113] ¶ 8025, ¶ 8055, ESTGIFT: 60,200; § 35,005.15

[114] ¶ 20,075; ESTGIFT: 60,200; § 35,005.30

[115] ¶ 8125, ¶ 8150, ¶ 9245, ¶ 10,528; ESTGIFT: 60,250; § 35,015.05

The estate and gift tax Code provisions may be affected by provisions contained in foreign tax treaties (Code Sec. 7852(d)).[116]

Generation-Skipping Transfer Tax

2942. Transfers Subject to Tax. To ensure that property transfers are subject to transfer tax at least once at each generation, a generation-skipping transfer (GST) tax is imposed on certain transfers (Code Sec. 2601). The GST tax rate is 40 percent for 2013 and thereafter (¶ 2901).

A GST may take one of three forms: a direct skip, a taxable termination, or a taxable distribution to a skip person. A direct skip is a transfer to a skip person that is also subject to estate or gift tax (Code Sec. 2612(c)). A skip person is defined as (1) a person two generations or more younger than the transferor, or (2) a trust for the benefit of one or more skip persons (Code Sec. 2613(a); Reg. § 26.2612-1). However, if the parent of the skip person predeceases the transferor, a gift to the skip person is not a GST (Code Sec. 2651(e)(1)). A taxable termination occurs when an interest in property held in trust terminates and trust property is held for or distributed to a skip person (Code Sec. 2612(a)). A taxable distribution is any distribution from a trust to a skip person that is not a taxable termination or a direct skip (Code Sec. 2612(b)). Transfers that are not subject to gift tax because of the unlimited exclusion for direct payment of medical and tuition expenses (¶ 2907), certain transfers to the extent that the property transferred was previously subject to the GST tax, as well as direct skips and certain transfers to trusts that qualify for the annual gift tax exclusion (¶ 2905) or the medical and tuition expense payment exclusion, are not subject to GST tax (Code Secs. 2611(b) and 2642(c)(1)).[117]

2943. Allocation of Lifetime Exemption and Computation of Tax Rate. Individuals are entitled to a lifetime exemption from generation-skipping transfer (GST) tax (Code Sec. 2631). The GST exemption is $5.45 million for GSTs occurring in 2016 ($5.49 million in 2017) (Code Sec. 2631(c); Rev. Proc. 2015-53; Rev. Proc. 2016-55). The exemption amount is not transferable between spouses, but married couples may elect to "split" a transfer and treat it as being made one-half by each spouse, pursuant to the rules applicable to split gifts (¶ 2905) (Code Sec. 2652(a)(2); Reg. § 26.2652-1(a)(4)).

The GST tax is computed by multiplying the taxable amount of the transfer by the applicable rate (Code Sec. 2602). The applicable rate is a flat rate equal to the product of the maximum estate tax rate—40 percent for 2013 and thereafter (¶ 40)—and the "inclusion ratio" with respect to the transfer (Code Sec. 2641(a); Reg. § 26.2641-1).

The inclusion ratio represents the portion of the transfer that is *not* exempted from the GST tax by the transferor's exemption amount. The inclusion ratio for any property transferred in a GST is the excess, if any, of 1 over the "applicable fraction" determined for the trust from which a GST is made or, in the case of a direct skip, the applicable fraction determined for such a skip.

Conversely, the applicable fraction represents the proportion of the transfer, whether in trust or as a direct skip, that is free of tax due to an allocation of the transferor's exemption amount. The numerator of the applicable fraction is the amount of the GST exemption allocated to the trust, or to the property transferred in a direct skip. The denominator is the value of the property transferred to the trust or involved in the direct skip, reduced by the sum of any federal estate or state death tax attributable to the property that was recovered from the trust and any estate or gift tax charitable deductions allowed with respect to the property (Code Sec. 2642; Reg. § 26.2642-1).[118]

The GST tax exemption may be allocated by an individual, or the individual's executor, to any property with respect to which the individual was the transferor (Code Sec. 2632(a)). In the case of property held in trust, the GST tax exemption is allocated to

References are to Federal Estate & Gift Tax Reports; Tax Research Consultant; Practical Tax Explanations.

[116] ¶ 22,870; ESTGIFT: 63,050, ESTGIFT: 63,100; § 35,001

[117] ¶ 12,025, ¶ 12,225, ¶ 12,295, ¶ 12,315, ¶ 12,750, ¶ 12,940; ESTGIFT: 57,050; § 34,710

[118] ¶ 12,585, ¶ 12,625, ¶ 12,690, ¶ 12,710, ¶ 12,750, ¶ 12,770, ¶ 12,790, ¶ 12,940, ¶ 12,960; ESTGIFT: 57,100; § 34,725

the entire trust rather than to specific assets (Reg. § 26.2632-1). In the case of a lifetime direct skip, any unused GST tax exemption is automatically deemed allocated to the property transferred in an amount necessary to make such property's inclusion ratio equal to zero (Code Sec. 2632(b)(1)). An individual may elect out of this automatic allocation for lifetime direct skips (Code Sec. 2632(b)(3)).

2944. Filing the Return and Paying the GST Tax. For direct skips occurring at death, the executor must file the return (Form 706, Schedules R and R-1) and pay the tax. The transferor is responsible for filing the return (Form 709) and paying the tax on lifetime direct skips. The trustee is responsible for filing the return (Form 706-GS(T)) and paying the tax on taxable terminations. The transferee is responsible for filing the return (Form 706-GS(D)) and paying the tax on taxable distributions (Code Sec. 2603(a); Reg. § 26.2662-1(c)(1)).[119]

Transfer Tax on Gifts and Bequests from Expatriates

2948. Gifts and Bequests from Expatriates. A U.S. citizen or resident who directly or indirectly receives a "covered gift or bequest"—a gift, devise, bequest, or inheritance from a covered expatriate (¶ 2412)—after the date of expatriation must pay a tax equal to the value of the covered gift or bequest multiplied by the highest rate in effect under Code Sec. 2001(c) (Code Sec. 2801(a) and (b)). The maximum tax rate under Code Sec. 2001(c) is 40 percent for 2013 and thereafter (¶ 40). This special transfer tax applies only to the extent that the value of the covered gifts and bequests received by any person during the calendar year exceeds the annual gift tax exclusion amount in effect under Code Sec. 2503(b) ($14,000 for 2016; $14,000 for 2017) (Code Sec. 2801(c); Rev. Proc. 2015-53; Rev. Proc. 2016-55).[120] The tax is reduced by the amount of any gift or estate tax paid to a foreign country with respect to such covered gift or bequest (Code Sec. 2801(d)). The IRS has issued proposed regulations on the tax treatment of covered gifts and bequests, which will be effective when published as final regulations in the *Federal Register*. The IRS intends to issue Form 708 for reporting the tax once the regulations are finalized (Prop. Reg. § § 28.2801-0—28.2801-7; NPRM REG-112997-10).[121]

A covered gift or bequest made to a domestic trust is subject to tax in the same manner as for a U.S. citizen or resident, and as the recipient, the trust is required to pay the tax imposed (Code Sec. 2801(e)(4)(A)). A covered gift or bequest made to a foreign trust is also subject to tax, but only at the time a distribution, whether from income or principal, is made to a U.S. citizen or resident from the trust that is attributable to the covered gift or bequest (Code Sec. 2801(e)(4)(B)(i)).[122] The recipient is allowed an income tax deduction under Code Sec. 164 for the amount of tax paid or accrued under Code Sec. 2801 by reason of a distribution from a foreign trust, but only to the extent the tax is imposed on the portion of the distribution included in the recipient's gross income (Code Sec. 2801(e)(4)(B)(ii)). For purposes of Code Sec. 2801 only, a foreign trust may elect to be treated as a domestic trust (Code Sec. 2801(e)(4)(B)(iii)).[123]

References are to Federal Estate & Gift Tax Reports; Tax Research Consultant; Practical Tax Explanations.

[119] ¶ 12,150, ¶ 13,160, ¶ 13,200, ¶ 13,225; ESTGIFT: 57,150; § 34,715.25, § 34,740.05

[120] ¶ 15,501, ¶ 15,575.01, ¶ 15,575.05; ESTGIFT: 60,256; § 35,020

[121] ¶ 15,510—¶ 15,545; ESTGIFT: 60,256; § 35,020

[122] ¶ 15,501, ¶ 15,575.07; ESTGIFT: 60,256; § 35,020

[123] ¶ 15,501, ¶ 15,575.07; ESTGIFT: 60,256; § 35,020

Topical Index

References are to paragraph (¶) numbers

A

Abandonment loss
. deductibility 1109

Abatement of taxes
. private foundations 647

ABLE accounts
. qualifications 131
. requirements 870

Accelerated Cost Recovery System (ACRS), pre-1987 rules—see also Modified Accelerated Cost Recovery System (MACRS)
. automobiles 1211
. conventions 1252
. election to use modified ACRS 1252
. expensing election 1208
. . recapture 1780
. mass asset election 1249
. personal property 1258
. placed in service 1252
. property used outside U.S. 1264
. recapture 1780
. recovery property
. . dispositions . . . . . 1249; 1779—1793
. . excludable property 1255
. . general 1261
. . public utility property 1255
. . Sec. 1245 class property 1255
. . Sec. 1250 class property 1255; 1261
. . transfers 1248
. sale or exchange during tax year 1252
. Sec. 1250 property 1267
. short tax years 1270
. straight-line election 1252
. transferee rules 1248
. transitional rules 1261

Accelerated depreciation . . . . . 1216—1270

Accident and health plans—see Health and accident plans

Accident insurance benefits
. taxability . . . . . 851—852; 2015

Accident insurance premiums 908
. medical expense deductibility 1019

Accountable v. nonaccountable plans
. automobile expenses substantiation 947
. employee business expenses 952A
. . withholding of tax 2607
. meals and lodging expenses
. . substantiation . . . . . 952A—954B
. uniforms and work clothes reimbursements . 1083

Accountant's expenses
. deductibility 981

Accounting methods and periods
. accrual method
. . defined 1515
. . farming corporations 221
. . income collection doubtful 1538
. . liability contested 1540A
. . liability uncertain 1540A
. . personal service corporations 221
. accrued expenses 1540
. accrued income 1537
. application for change of method 1529
. application for change of period 1513
. calendar year v. fiscal year 1501
. cash method
. . defined 1515

Accounting methods and periods—continued
. change of method 1529
. . adjustments required by 1531
. . advance consent procedures 1529
. . automatic change procedures 1529
. . inventories 1571
. . long-term contracts 1552
. . material item 1529
. . permission to change 1529
. . section 481(a) adjustment 1531
. change of period 1513
. . partners and partnerships 416
. . permission to change 1513
. change of tax year
. . annualization 1507; 1509
. . short-period return 1505
. contested liabilities 1540A
. decedent's income 182
. deferred income 1537
. estate, first return 510
. examination of returns 2708
. farmers' inventories 1569
. 52-53 week year 1503
. home construction contracts 1552
. hybrid method 1515
. installment method—see also Installment sales 1801
. inventories 1553
. . FIFO rule 1564
. . LIFO rule 1565
. IRS, method prescribed by 1525
. long-term contracts 1551
. mark-to-market method
. . securities dealers 221
. married persons 152
. nonaccrual experience method 1538
. partnerships 419
. prepaid expenses 1539
. prepaid income 1537
. real estate investment trust 2326
. related taxpayers, amounts owed 1540B
. reserves for estimated expenses 1547
. residential construction contracts 1552
. S corporations 355
. securities transactions . . . . . 1973—1983
. small construction contracts 1552
. tax shelters 1515
. tax year 1501
. . change of 1513
. . improper 1513
. trust, first return 510
. uncertain liabilities 1540A
. uniform capitalization rules . . . . . 995—999

Accrual basis of accounting
. all-events test 1540
. bad debts 1137
. cash basis v. 1515
. change from 1529
. compensation 906
. contested liabilities 1540A
. corporations 1515
. . charitable contributions 927
. economic performance rule 1540
. farms 767; 1519
. income collection doubtful 1538
. interest paid 1043
. interest received 793
. inventories 1553
. mortgage discounts, commissions on loans . . 793
. prepaid income 1537
. . gift cards, sales of 1537

Accrual basis of accounting—continued
. proration of tax 1516
. publishers 1537
. real property tax
. . deduction timing 1031
. required use of 1515
. . inventories 1515
. . small business exception 1515
. sick leave 1549
. taxes accrued
. . year deductible 1034
. uncertain liabilities 1540A
. U.S. savings bond interest 730
. vacation pay 1549

Accumulated earnings tax . . . . . 251—269
. accumulated earnings credit 261
. . minimum amount 261
. accumulated taxable income 253
. . adjustments to taxable income 253
. . holding or investment company 253
. closely held corporations 251
. controlled foreign corporation
. . subpart F income 253
. divedends-paid deduction
. . consent dividends 259
. dividends-paid deduction 259
. effectively connected income 253
. liability for 263
. . liquidity 263
. personal service corporations
. . credit 261
. publicly held corporations 251
. rates of tax 37; 251
. reasonable business needs 265
. . acceptable grounds for income accumulation 265
. . burden of proof 267
. . operating-cycle approach 265
. . stock redemptions 265
. . unacceptable grounds for income accumulation 265
. source of income 253
. tax avoidance intent 269
. . mere holding or investment company 269
. U.S.-owned foreign corporations 253

Accumulation distributions, throwback rules 567

Accuracy-related penalty 2854

Acquiescence in Tax Court case by Commissioner 2788

Acquired intangibles, amortization 1288

Acquisition indebtedness
. corporations 937
. exempt organizations 689
. indebtedness on or before October 13, 1987
. . dollar limitation 1048
. interest paid or accrued
. . dollar limitation 1048
. residence 1047; 1048A
. . defined 1048
. . mortgage insurance premiums 1048A

Acquisitions, corporate
. carryovers and carrybacks 2277; 2281
. . tax avoidance purpose 2281
. loss corporations 2285
. net operating losses (NOLs)
. . tax avoidance purpose 2281
. preacquisition losses, limitation 2285
. stock acquisitions
. . Code Sec. 338 elections 2265
. . treated as asset acquisitions 2265

Acquisitions, corporate—continued
. stock as assets 2265
. successor corporations 2285
. tax avoidance 1575

Acquisitions to avoid tax 1575

Active participation rules, IRAs 2157
. married persons 2158

Addiction treatment
. medical expense 1016

Additions to tax, interest on—see also Penalties 2845

Addresses for filing returns 5

Adequate interest
. debt interests issued for property 1954

Adjusted current earnings (ACE)
. alternative minimum tax (AMT) 1440

Adjusted gross income (AGI)
. above-the-line-deductions 1005
. alimony or separate maintenance paid . . . 1008
. charitable contributions base 1058
. deductions allowed 1005
. definition of 1005
. itemized deductions
. . estates and trusts 528
. . two-percent-of-adjusted-gross-income floor 1079
. jury pay 1010
. legal fees
. . deductibility 1093
. loss from sale or exchange of property . . . 1007
. phaseout thresholds 4
. rents and royalty expenses 1006A
. supplemental unemployment benefits repaid 1009
. trade or business expenses 1006

Administration of estate or trust
. expenses, deductibility
. . estate tax 2925
. . income tax 528; 529
. taxable period 507

Administrative fees, award of 2796

Adoption 1307; 2063
. adoption tax identifying number (ATIN) 116
. assistance programs 2063
. dependency exemption 137A

Adoption credit 1307
. credits against tax 1307

Advance payments
. income deferral 1537
. interest deduction
. . cash-basis taxpayer 1055
. royalties 1289

Advanced clean coal projects
. credits against tax 1365D

Advanced energy project credit
. credits against tax 1365F

Advanced nuclear power facilities production credit
. credits against tax 1365AA

Advertising expenses
. deductibility 969

Advertising profits
. exempt organization UBTI 685

Affiliated corporations—see also Controlled corporate groups
. consolidated returns 295; 297
. dividends received deduction 223; 229
. . life insurance companies 229

Affiliated corporations—see also Controlled corporate groups—continued
. foreign tax credit 229

Affiliated groups—see also Controlled corporate groups
. consolidated returns 295; 297

Agents—see also Fiduciaries
. information returns 2565
. minor, incompetent, or disabled taxpayers, returns filed by agents 504

Agri-biodiesel fuels
. credits against tax 1365X

Agricultural organizations
. exempt organizations 692

Alaskan whale hunting activities
. charitable contributions 1058

Alcohol fuels credit
. credits against tax 1365I

Alimony or separate maintenance payments
. child support 776
. deductibility 1008
. deduction from gross income 771
. divorce or separation instruments 772
. estates, payment by 529
. failure to provide TIN 2833
. in general 771
. inclusion in gross income 771
. indirect payments 775
. property transfers 778
. recapture of excess 774
. three-year recapture of excess payments . . . 774
. year deductible or taxable 773

All-events test
. accrual method of accounting 1515; 1540

Allocation of income
. community property income 711
. family partnerships 474
. joint return 156

Alternate valuation
. in general 2922

Alternative depreciation system
. averaging conventions
. . half-year 1245
. . mid-month 1245
. . mid-quarter 1245
. elections
. . alternative depreciation system 1243
. . straight-line 1243

Alternative fuel vehicle refueling property credit
. credits against tax 1355

Alternative fuels credit
. credit against tax 1365BB

Alternative minimum tax (AMT)
. adjusted current earnings (ACE) 1440
. adjustments required
. . all taxpayers 1430
. . corporate taxpayers 1440
. . noncorporate taxpayers 1435
. alternative minimum taxable income (AMTI) 1405
. . at-risk rules 1405
. . partnership losses 1405
. . passive activity losses 1405
. . S corporation losses 1405
. Blue Cross/Blue Shield organizations 1440
. calculation of 1401
. capital gains 1401
. children 1401
. circulation expenditures 1435
. common trust funds 1465

Alternative minimum tax (AMT)—continued
. corporations 219
. . adjustments 1430; 1440
. . preference cutbacks 1445
. . preference items 1425
. . small corporations 1415
. . tax rate 1401
. credits against later years regular tax 1309
. credits against minimum tax
. . foreign tax credit 1470
. . general business credits 1475
. . nonrefundable personal tax credits 1475
. . other tax credits 1475
. depletion 1425
. depreciation 1425; 1430
. dividends 1401
. domestic production activities 1430
. estates 516; 1401
. exemption amount 1410
. foreign tax credit 1470
. incentive stock options 1435; 1925
. intangible drilling and development costs . . 1425
. itemized deductions 1435
. long-term contracts 1430
. loss limitations 1460
. Merchant Marine capital construction funds . 1440
. minimum tax credit 1309
. mining exploration and development costs . 1430
. net operating loss deduction 1430
. partners and partnerships 1401
. partnerships 1455
. passive business activity losses 1460
. passive farm tax shelter losses 1460
. personal exemptions 1435
. pollution control facilities 1430
. possessions tax credit 1480
. private activity bonds 1425
. property and casualty insurance companies 1440
. real estate investment trusts 1465
. regular tax compared 1420
. regulated investment companies 1465
. research and experimental expenditures . . 1435
. S corporations 1401
. small business stock 1425
. small corporations 219; 1415
. standard deduction 1435
. state and local taxes paid 1435
. tax preference items 1425
. . election to avoid 1450
. tax rate 1401
. tentative minimum tax 1401; 1420
. trusts 516; 1401

Alternative motor vehicle credit
. credits against tax 1345
. fuel cell motor vehicle credit 1346

Amended returns 107
. refunds or credits 2759; 2760

American Opportunity tax credit (AOTC)
. credits against tax 1303

American Samoa
. corporations, withholding 2431
. income earned in 2414
. self-employment tax 2667

American Samoa possessions credit
. credits against tax 1362

Amortization 1287
. acquired intangibles 1288
. barrier removal costs 1287
. bond premium 1967
. . dealer in municipal bonds 1970
. computer software costs 980
. covenants not to compete 1288

Amortization—continued
. geological and geophysical expenditures . . 1287
. lease acquisition costs 1234
. licenses 1288
. 15-year safe harbor
. . self-created intangibles 1288A
. organizational expenditures 237
. pollution control facilities 1287
. reforestation expenses 1287
. Sec. 197 intangibles 1288
. self-created intangibles 1288
. start-up expenditures 904
. supplier-based intangibles 1288
. trademarks and trade names 1288
. workforce in place 1288

Annuities and annuity contracts
. annual exclusion computation 825
. annuity starting date 823
. borrowed funds used to purchase
. . interest deduction 909
. charitable annuity trusts 590
. discharge of annuity obligation 841
. dividends received 809
. employees' annuities
. . distributions 839
. estate distributions 548
. exchanged for property
. . amount realized 1703
. exchanges of contracts 1724
. exclusion for first year 835
. exclusion ratio 817
. exempt organization unrelated business
income 673
. expected return computation 825
. foreign sourced contributions 821
. fractional part of year 835
. gross estate 2917
. health and accident plans 2015
. installment options 843
. investment in the contract 821
. . June 30, 1986, before and after 825
. life expectancy 817
. loans to purchase 909
. military personnel 891
. partial annuitization 817
. preretirement survivor 2130
. refund annuity contract 837
. retirement plans
. . distributions 839
. safe-harbor roles
. . pre-November 19, 1996 839
. sale prior to maturity 1742
. simplified method
. . post-November 18, 1996 839
. tables, use of 825
. taxability
. . discharge of annuities 841
. temporary life annuities 829
. transfer for value
. . exceptions 845
. trust distributions 548
. types of annuities 829
. variable annuities 829
. withholding of tax at source 2643

Annuity trusts 590
. beneficiaries, tax treatment of 590B
. charitable contributions
. . deductibility 1061
. taxation of 590A

Antiques
. capital gains rate 1736

Apostolic associations
. exempt status 604

Appeals
. Claims Court decisions 2790
. Court of Appeals decisions 2794
. IRS determinations 2705
. Tax Court decisions 2778; 2786

Applicable federal rates (AFRs) 83
. imputed interest 1875
. long-term tax-exempt rates 85
. low-income housing 86
. original issue discount 84

Application for exempt status
. determination letter 623

Appraisals
. charitable contributions 1071
. deductibility of fees 1071; 1092

Appreciated financial position
. constructive sale 1945

Appreciated inventory
. sale of partnership interest 436

Appreciated property
. charitable contributions
. . deductibility 1062
. corporate distributions 1729
. unrealized appreciation 702

Arbitrage bonds 724

Archer medical savings accounts (MSAs) . . 2035; 2037
. deductibility 2037
. health and accident plans 2037

Armed forces
. allowances 893
. combat zone
. . examination and collection relief 2708
. Health Professions Scholarship and
Financial Assistance Program 829
. refund claims
. . retired military personnel 2763
. withholding of tax
. . differential wage payments 2604

Articles of incorporation
. exempt organizations 602

Artists
. expenses exempt from uniform
capitalization rules 990A; 1561
. expenses of performing artists 941A
. uniform capitalization rules 1561

Artworks, gain from sale 1741

Assessment of tax . . . . . 2711—2740
. collection after assessment 2735
. criminal restitution 2711
. failure to file return 2732
. gross error on return 2734
. injunction to restrain 2719
. interest on deficiencies 2735
. jeopardy assessment 2713
. limitations period 2726
. . fraudulent return 2732
. mathematical and clerical errors 2711
. partial payments 2724
. partnerships 415
. prompt assessment, request 2728
. six-year limitations period 2734
. suspension of assessment period 2736
. termination assessments 2713
. three-year limitations period 2726
. transferee liability 2745
. waiver of restrictions 2712

Assessments for local benefits
. deductibility 1026

Asset acquisitions
. foreign tax credit 2477
. stock acquisitions treated as 2265

Asset depreciation range (ADR) 1282; 1284

Asset sales
. losses 1007

Assignment of benefits, qualified plans . . . 2131

Assignment of income 705

Associations
. partnership v. 401
. trusts v. 502

Assumption of liabilities
. gain or loss basis 1669
. tax-free exchanges 2233

At-risk rules
. activity defined 1159
. alternative minimum tax (AMT) 1405
. carry over of losses 1155
. disposition of activity 1161
. investment tax credit
. . limitations 1365A
. limitation on loss deduction 1155
. nonrecourse financing
. . real estate 426
. partners 426
. partnerships
. . real estate special rules 426
. S corporations 309
. taxpayers subject to 1157

Athletic scholarships
. exempt income 865

Attorneys' fees—see also Legal expenses
. awarded prevailing party in court
proceedings 2796
. deductibility 981; 1093
. from unlawful discrimination suits
. . deductibility 1093
. from whistle blower suits
. . deductibility 1093
. personal injury awards
. . taxability 852
. unlawful discrimination awards
. . taxability 852
. whistle blower suits
. . taxability 852

Attribution, stock ownership 743
. losses
. . sale or exchange 1717
. personal holding company 285

Audits 2708
. partnerships 415

Automatic extension of time for filing returns 2509

Automobiles
. charitable donation 627
. . substantiation 1070A
. charitable use 1061
. depreciation 1211; 1214
. . leases of motor vehicles 1235
. expenses . . . . . 945—948
. . fixed and variable rate (FAVR) method . . . 947
. . interest on automobile loans 948
. fixed and variable rate (FAVR) method 947
. inclusion amount 1215
. rural mail carriers' expenses for 947
. standard mileage rate
. . business 947
. . charitable activities 1061
. . medical expenses 1016
. . moving expenses 1073

Automobiles—continued
. standard mileage rate—continued
. . rural mail carriers' deduction 947
. . substantiation 947
. . withholding on reimbursed expenses . . . 2608

Awards and prizes
. employee achievement awards 919; 2069

Away-from-home expenses . . . . . 949—960

B

Back pay
. damage awards 852
. withholding of tax 2606

Backup withholding 2645
. certification failure 2645
. estates 540
. gambling winnings 2642
. trusts 540

Bad debts
. political parties 1141

Bad debts, deductibility . . . . . 1135—1143
. accrual basis 1137
. banks
. . reserves 2383
. . worthless securities 1916
. bonds 1916
. business bad debts 1135
. cash basis 1137
. estates and trusts 531
. installment sales 1838
. loan guaranty 1135
. mortgage foreclosure 1139
. nonbusiness bad debts 1143
. political parties 1141
. reserves
. . banks 2383
. secured bad debts 1139
. shareholders paying corporate debts 1135
. treatment of deduction 1135
. year deductible 1137

Bank deposit method
. reconstruction of income 1577

Bank deposits
. losses, deductibility 1125
. premature withdrawals, interest forfeited
. . deductibility 1111

Bankruptcy
. corporations 203

Bankruptcy Act, transfer ordered under . . . 2247

Bankruptcy and receivership
. bankruptcy estate 505; 506
. . carrybacks 535
. . tax attributes, succession to and from 535
. cancellation of indebtedness income 855
. collection of tax 2750
. fiduciaries v. receivers 506
. penalties for nonpayment of tax 2750
. reorganizations 2247
. returns filed for corporations or
partnerships 506
. statute of limitations 2736
. suits for refunds 2792
. trustees for individual debtors 505

Banks—see also Financial institutions
. bad debt reserves 2383
. bad debts
. . worthless securities as 1916
. cancellation of debt, information returns . . . 2565
. cooperative 2383

Banks—see also Financial institutions—continued
. foreign bank interests, information returns . 2570; 2572
. insolvent or bankrupt, depositors' losses . . 1125
. institutions treated as 2383
. interest paid 970
. liability for tax 2383
. mutual savings banks, taxability 2383
. personal holding company income 281
. personal holding status 277
. securities sold or exchanged 2383
. worthless securities, deduction for 1916

Bargain purchases of corporate property
. taxability 789

Bargain sales to charity, allocation of basis 1623

Barrier removal costs, current deduction . . 1287

Bartered services
. inclusion in gross income 785

Bartering
. income from 785

Basis adjustments 1604
. cancellation of indebtedness
. . stock, S corporation 317
. charitable deductions
. . stock, S corporation 317
. damaged property
. . casualty loss 1127
. depreciation 1617
. easements 1617
. energy efficiency and conservation
. . business 1617
. . residential 1617
. investment tax credit 1365A
. motor vehicles 1617
. partner's interest, increase or decrease 445
. partnership assets 443; 459; 467; 470
. partnership interest
. . built-in loss 467
. recapture 1779
. reorganization 2205
. return of capital 1617
. Sec. 1245 property 1790
. Sec. 1250 property 1790
. stock, S corporation 317
. stock, surrender of 1916
. subdivided lots 1620

Basis of property received
. consistency
. . estate tax value 1633; 2938

Basis—see also Gain or loss—see also Basis adjustments
. adjusted basis 1604
. allocation 1620
. . purchase of trade or business 1620
. assumption of liabilities 1669
. built-in losses 1667
. carryover basis, property valued under . . . 1636
. charitable bargain sale 1623
. chart, basis for gain or loss 1601
. condemnation awards 1716
. cost depletion 1289
. covered securities, information reporting . . 1980
. depreciation and cost recovery 1203
. discharge of indebtedness 1672
. divorce 1693
. gifts 1630
. gifts reacquired, decedent-donee 1639
. incentive stock options 1925
. involuntary conversion 1687
. joint tenancy 1634

Basis—see also Gain or loss—see also Basis adjustments—continued
. medical equipment 1684
. organizational actions affecting stock basis, information reporting 1980
. partnership distributions 456
. partnership interests or assets . . . . . 443—470
. . increase or decrease in basis of partner's interest 445
. regulated investment companies (RIC)
. . shares 2318
. reorganization 2205
. repossessed real estate 1843
. residence 1626
. securities
. . wash sales 1935
. specified securities, information reporting . . 1980
. spousal transfer 1693
. stepped-up basis 1633
. . decedent, property acquired from 1633
. stock
. . information reporting 1980
. . nontaxable distribution 1682
. . received for services 1681
. stock and stock rights, nontaxable 1682
. stock, S corporation 317
. substituted basis 1607
. . spin-offs, split-offs, split-ups and splint-offs 2201
. tax-free exchange 1648
. transfer to corporation 1660
. trust transfer 1678
. valuation of property 1695

Below-market loans
. imputed interest 795

Beneficiaries
. annuities and annuity contracts . . . . . 817—845
. basis of property acquired from decedent . 1633—1639
. capital gain or loss 562
. complex trusts
. . distributions deduction 545
. . income 556; 559
. depletion deduction 530
. depreciation deduction 530
. distributable net income 543
. distributions deduction, estates or complex trusts 545
. . 65-day election 546
. distributions deduction, simple trusts 544
. estate or complex trust, taxation 556; 559
. estate or trust having different tax year 565
. estate tax deduction 191
. excludable death benefit 813
. foreign tax credit 540
. gifts and bequests 564
. income . . . . . 554—565
. . from charitable remainder trusts 590
. income in respect of decedent 182; 189
. joint and survivor annuity 827
. life insurance 803
. life insurance proceeds 805
. loss carryovers 535
. multiple beneficiaries, separate shares 557
. net operating losses 535; 1153
. nonresident alien, fiduciary return 510
. qualified disclaimers 2903
. real estate investment trusts 2331
. simple trusts 554
. 65-day election, distributions 546
. termination of estate or trust 535
. transfer to, taxability of gain 526
. trusts defined 501

Benefits
. accident and health benefits 851; 2015
. beneficiaries of public safety officers 851
. military personnel
. . disability payments 851
. no-fault insurance
. . sickness or injury payments 851
. retirement plans
. . mandatory cash-outs 2125
. . military participants, death benefits 2125
. . phased-retirement arrangements 2125
. social security
. . taxability 716
. strike 849
. unemployment compensation
. . taxability 722
. workers' compensation
. . taxability 851; 2015

Bequests—see also Gifts
. basis of property acquired 1633
. exclusion from income 564; 847
. income from property 847

Bicycle commuting
. fringe benefits 2091

Biodiesel fuels credit
. credit against tax 1365X

Black lung benefit trusts
. exempt status 692
. information returns 625

Blindness
. additional standard deduction 126

Body scan
. medical expense 1016

Bonds
. amortization of premium 1967
. . dealers in municipal bonds 1970
. arbitrage bonds 724
. bad debts 1916
. convertible bonds, amortization of premium . 1967
. corporation's own bonds 1950
. discount, issued at
. . deductible amounts 1950
. . original issue discount . . . . . 1952—1956
. . reporting requirements 1952
. . tax-free exchange 1965
. discount, market; gain on sale 1958
. education
. . savings bond income 863
. enterprise zone private activity bonds 729
. government
. . exchange 1726
. interest expense deduction, OID 1952
. interest income 724
. . imputed interest 727
. . private activity bonds 729
. . transaction between interest dates 728
. interest past-due, purchased with; capital gains 1742
. issued at discount 1950
. issued at premium 1950
. municipal and state bonds
. . dealer in municipal bonds, amortization of bond premium 1970
. . exchange 1726
. . interest 729
. . interest income 724; 1970
. . original issue discount 1956
. . private activity bonds 729
. . unregistered 1963
. nonrecognition of gain or loss, corporation's own bonds 1950
. original issue discount . . . . . 1952—1956

Bonds—continued
. premium
. . amortization by bondholder 1967
. . amortization by dealer in municipal bonds 1970
. . issued at 1950
. private activity bonds 729
. registration 1963
. stripped bonds 1952
. U.S. savings bonds 730
. . exclusion for education 863
. unregistered 1963

Bonus depreciation 1237
. accelerated AMT credit election 1237
. alternative minimum tax 1237
. computation 1237
. election out 1237
. election to claim accelerated amt credit . . . 1237
. in general 1237
. long production period property 1237
. qualifying property 1237
. self-constructed property 1237

Bonuses
. deductibility as compensation 906
. gross income 713
. $1-million compensation limitation 906
. repayment 1543
. withholding of tax 2604
. year income taxable 1533

Books and records
. examination by IRS 2708
. inadequate or none kept 1577
. reconstruction of income by IRS 1577
. recordkeeping requirements 2523
. retention requirements 2523
. substantiation of business expenses 953
. tax year 1501
. third-party summons 2709
. travel expense substantiation 953

Boot
. corporate reorganizations 2205
. excess principal amount of securities 2229
. gain recognized on exchange 2229
. nonqualified preferred stock in exchange transaction 2229
. spin-offs, split-offs, split-ups and splint-offs . 2201

Bootstrap sales to exempt organizations . . . 687

Boycott income, foreign source 2496

Branch profits tax, foreign corporations . . . 2433

Bribe payments 972; 2497

Brokers
. covered securities, information reporting . . 1980
. foreign corporations, business for 2429
. information returns by 1980; 2565
. personal holding company income
. . dividend and interest exclusions 281
. specified securities, information reporting . . 1980
. stock and securities, information reporting . 1980
. transfers between accounts, information reporting 1980

Brother-sister controlled corporate group . . 291

Build America bonds
. credits against tax 1378

Building and loan associations
. REMIC interests as assets of 2344
. securities sold or exchanged 2383
. taxability 2383

Built-in gains
. preacquisition losses 2285
. real estate investment trusts (REIT) 2329

Built-in gains—continued
. regulated investment companies (RIC) . . . 2303
. S corporations 337

Burden of proof
. accumulated earnings tax liability
. . reasonable business needs 267
. fraud 2866
. Tax Court, credible evidence 2782

Business assets, sale of
. capital gains and losses on 1747
. loss from sale 1007
. reporting 1747

Business expenses . . . . . 901—999
. accident and health plan contributions 2013
. advertising 969
. automobiles 946
. bad debts 1135
. bribe payments 972
. capital expenditures v. 903
. charitable contributions . . . . . 927—931
. circulation costs 971
. club dues 913A
. compensation paid 906
. . employee benefits 908
. . golden parachute contracts 907
. . life insurance premiums paid 909
. corporations
. . stock redemption costs 742
. deductibility
. . generally 901; 941
. deductions
. . from adjusted gross income 1006
. disability payments 908A
. . includible as gross income 908A
. economically distressed communities . . . 999A—999D
. . District of Columbia 999D
. . empowerment zones 999B
. . generally 999A
. . renewal communities 999C
. education 1082
. employees
. . substantiation 943
. employment agency fees 1081
. entertainment
. . exceptions 915
. . meal and gift expenses . . . . . 910—919
. entertainment deduction
. . associated entertainment 912
. . directly related 911
. farmers . . . . . 982—985
. federal government employees, substantiation 953
. Federal National Mortgage Association stock purchase 975
. fines paid 972
. gifts 918
. home office
. . limitations 963
. . requirements 961
. impairment-related work expenses 941
. insurance premiums
. . fire and casualty 968
. . future remediation costs, reimbursement . . 968
. . life insurance premiums paid 909
. interest expense 937
. job-hunting expenses 1081
. kickbacks 972
. legal expenses 973
. lobbying expenses 974
. lodging, employee
. . local 949
. materials and supplies 903

Business expenses—continued
. meal and entertainment expenses . 910; 914; 916
. . exceptions 917
. . percentage limit 916
. meals and lodging
. . per diem allowances . . . . . 954—954B
. . travel away from home 949; 960
. merchants and manufacturers . . . . . 978—980
. mileage rate, standard 947
. military reserve members
. . per diem, limitations 941E
. . travel expenses 941E
. National Guard members 941E
. ordinary and necessary
. . defined 901
. other business expenses 901
. penalties paid 972
. performing artists 941A
. political contributions 976
. professional expenses 981
. professional organization dues 913A
. public service organization dues 913A
. related taxpayers 905
. rents 986
. retirement plan contributions, self-employed 2107
. school teachers 941C
. securities traders, commissions 1983
. short sales, expenses of 1946
. social club dues 913A
. start-up expenses 904
. state and local government officials 941D
. statutory employees 941B
. substantiation 953
. taxes paid . . . . . 920—924
. teachers 941C
. telephone, residential 961
. travel expenses . . . . . 945—960
. uniforms and special clothing 1083
. union dues 1080

Business income
. credits against tax 760
. gross income 759
. tax-exempt organizations . . . . . 655—685

Business leagues
. exempt status 692

Business property
. capital gains and losses 1741; 1747
. cost recovery, ACRS 1252
. personal use 961

Business, sale of
. residual method
. . reporting 1743

Business trusts 502

Business use of residence . . . . . 961—967

C

C Corporations—see also Corporations 201

Cafeteria plans 2045
. accident insurance benefits 2045
. cash alternative 2045
. dependent care assistance programs 2045
. family medical leave act 2045
. flexible spending arrangements 2041
. . use it or lose it rule 2045
. group legal services plans 2045
. group-term life insurance 2045
. health and accident plans 2045
. permissible benefits 2045
. simple cafeteria plans 2047

Calendar of due dates 6

Calendar-year taxpayers
. accounting periods 1501

Campaign contributions
. deductibility 976

Cancellation of debt income
. gross income, inclusion in 785

Cancellation of indebtedness income
. bankruptcy or insolvency exception 855
. estates and trusts, beneficiary's obligation . . 556
. information returns 2565
. nonrecourse debt 855
. qualified farm indebtedness exception 855
. qualified principal residence indebtedness exception 855
. qualified real property business indebtedness exception 855
. student loan forgiveness exception 855

Cancellation of lease or distributor's agreement
. gain or loss 1751

Capital assets
. defined 1741
. exceptions 1741

Capital contributions
. corporation 1660
. . basis, built-in loss limitation 1667
. nonstockholders 1660
. partnership 428; 443

Capital expenditures
. business expenses v. 903
. carrying charges 1614
. circulation expenses 971
. expensing election 1208
. . recapture 1780
. home improvements
. . medical expenses 1016
. mines 987; 988
. oil wells 989
. uniform capitalization rules . . . . 990—997; 1561

Capital gain tax credit
. credits against tax 1330
. regulated investment companies (RICs)
. . credits against tax 1330

Capital gains and losses
. alternative tax, corporations 1738
. appreciated financial position 1945
. artistic works 1741
. business property sold 1747
. business purposes, asset held for 1741
. business, sale of
. . reporting 1743
. cancellation of lease or distributor's agreement 1751
. capital assets 1741
. capital loss carrybacks
. . corporate 1756
. capital loss carryovers
. . corporate 1756
. . noncorporate taxpayers 1754
. coal royalties 1772
. commodity futures transactions 1944
. constructive ownership transactions 1740
. constructive sale 1945
. conversion transactions 1740
. copyright 1741
. corporations 1738
. . carrybacks and carryovers 1756
. . loss limitations 1752
. dealers 1760
. depreciable real estate 1736
. estates and trusts 562; 1736
. . carryover deduction 535

Capital gains and losses—continued
. exclusion of gain
. . District of Columbia Enterprise Zone 999D
. . renewal community 999C
. foreign corporations 2435
. foreign expropriations
. . carryovers 1756
. franchise grants and sales 1774
. futures transactions 1945
. holding period 1737
. in general 1735
. individuals 1736
. . limitation on deduction 1752
. investment interest 1736
. investors 1760
. involuntary conversions 1748
. iron ore royalties 1772
. joint returns 1757
. liquidation distributions 2253
. livestock 1750
. long-term 1735; 1737
. married persons 1757
. maximum rates for noncorporate taxpayers . 1736
. mortgage foreclosure 1107
. musical compositions and copyrights 1741
. netting procedures 1739
. nonrecognition of gain
. . empowerment zone investment 999B
. nonresident aliens 2435
. options, failure to exercise 1742; 1919
. options, sale or exchange 1919
. ordinary loss rule, Sec. 1231 assets 1751
. partnership 1758
. partnership interest 1741
. . sale or exchange of 434
. patents 1767
. property used in trade or business 1747
. rate of tax 1736
. . corporations 1738
. real estate dealers 1760
. real estate investment trusts 2329; 2331
. real estate, subdivision and sale 1762
. regulated investment company (RICs) 2305
. . capital gain dividends 2311
. . capital gain tax credit 1330
. reorganizations 2253
. reporting 1735
. residence 1741
. returns 128
. S corporations 341; 1758
. sale of trade or business 1743
. sale or exchange, requirement of 1742
. sales between related taxpayers 1744
. sales to controlled corporations 1744
. Sec. 1231 assets . . . . . 1747—1751
. securities dealers 1760
. short sales 1944
. short-term 1735; 1737
. small business stock 1736
. . empowerment zone investment 999B
. stock option holding periods 1923
. tax on capital gains
. . corporations 1738
. tax rates 1736
. timber 1772
. traders in securities 1760
. transactions treated as sales or exchanges . 1742
. unrecaptured Sec. 1250 gain 1736
. wash sales 1935
. worthless securities 1742

Car expenses
. business deductions . . . . . 946—948

Carbon dioxide capture credit
. credits against tax 1365JJ

Carpooling
. transportation fringe benefits 2091

Carrybacks
. acquiring corporations 2277
. anticipated, quick refunds 2773
. corporate capital loss 1756
. foreign tax credit 2479
. . statute of limitations 2726
. liquidations 2277
. net operating loss deduction . . . . . 1145—1153
. refund claims, limitation period 2763
. specified liability losses 1151

Carryforwards
. nonbusiness bad debts 1145

Carrying charges
. additions to basis 1614
. real property
. . deductibility 1028

Carryover basis election
. decedents dying in 2010 1636

Carryovers
. acquiring corporation 2277; 2281
. capital loss, corporations 1756
. charitable contributions
. . corporations 927
. . individuals 1060
. foreign tax credit 2479
. general business credit 1365
. investment interest 1094
. liquidations 2277
. losses suspended under at-risk rules 1161
. net capital loss 1754
. . noncorporate taxpayers 1754
. net operating loss deduction . . . . . 1145—1153
. qualified conservation contributions 1060
. retirement plan contributions 2119
. successor corporations 2277; 2281
. suspended passive activity losses and credits 1177

Carved-out mineral production payments . . 1291

Cash balance plans 2108

Cash basis of accounting
. accrual basis v. 1515
. bad debts 1137
. change from 1529
. constructive receipt 1533
. farming income 767
. gross receipts test 1515
. interest paid 1043
. . deductibility 1055
. interest received 724; 793
. mortgage discounts or commissions on loans 793
. prepaid expenses 1539
. qualified personal service corporation 1515
. real property taxes
. . buyers deductibility 1034
. . sellers deductibility 1034
. U.S. savings bond interest 730
. year income taxable
. . income not yet received 1537

Casualty insurance premiums paid
. deductibility 968

Casualty losses . . . . . 1121—1133
. $100 floor 1129
. adjusted gross income (AGI) limitation 1131
. amount of 1127
. bank deposits 1125
. basis of damaged property 1127
. causes, generally 1121
. corrosive drywall 1121

Casualty losses—continued
. disaster loss
. . federally declared 1133
. drought 1121
. federally declared disaster 1133
. netting requirement 1131
. netting requirement, gains and losses 1748
. passive activity losses 1177
. personal assets 1748
. personal casualties 1129; 1131
. reimbursement for living expenses
. . exclusion from income 877
. trusts and estates 531

Catch-up contributions
. 401(k) plans 2121

Cellular telephones, listed property 1211

Certificates of deposit
. interest income 724

Certified mail 2553

Certified professional employer organiations (CPEOs)
. employment taxes 2660

Charitable bequests 2932

Charitable contributions, deductibility
. Alaskan whale hunting activities 1058
. annuity trust donee 1061
. appraisal
. . valuation 1071
. appraisals
. . fees 1071
. appreciated property 1062
. automobile expenses 1061
. automobiles 627
. . substantiation 1070A
. bargain sale 1623
. capital gain property 1062
. cash donation substantiation 1070A
. charitable remainder trusts 590
. charitable trusts, gifts to 538
. charity workers out-of-pocket expenses . . . 1061
. clothing 1061
. Combined Federal Campaign payment . . . 1070A
. contributions charged to credit card 1058
. corporations
. . accrual basis 927
. . carryover 927
. . computer equipment 930
. . inventory contributed 930
. . limits 927
. . scientific property contributed 930
. . special rules 931
. declaratory judgments on qualified donees . . 623
. defined 1061
. disclosure
. . nondeductibility 627
. . *quid pro quo* contributions 627
. disposal of donated property
. . recapture of tax benefits 1062
. distributions from IRAs 1058
. donee eligibility 1061
. donor advised funds
. . contributions 1061
. estate and gift taxes 2909; 2932
. estates 537; 538
. facade easement restrictions 1063
. food inventories 930A; 1062
. foreign corporations 2446
. fractional interests, additional contributions of 1063
. fundraising events 1061
. future interests 1069
. household items 1061

Charitable contributions, deductibility—continued
. individual retirement account (IRA) distributions . . . 1058
. individuals . . . 1058—1071
. . five-year carryover . . . 1060
. . limitations . . . 1059
. . noncash . . . 1061
. intellectual property, donee income . . 627; 1062A
. interest reduction . . . 1065
. leave-based donation programs . . . 1061
. lobbying activities . . . 1061
. noncash donations
. . appraisals . . . 1071
. . substantiation . . . 1070A
. nondeductible donations . . . 1061
. nonresident aliens . . . 2446
. ordinary income property . . . 1062
. partial interests . . . 1063
. partnerships . . . 417; 1058
. payroll deductions . . . 1070A
. private foundation donee . . . 1061
. prohibited transaction . . . 538
. Puerto Rico residents . . . 1059
. qualified conservation contributions . . 1059; 1063
. . carryover . . . 1060
. . corporations . . . 927
. qualified organizations . . . 1061
. recapture of tax benefits . . . 1062; 1063
. recordkeeping requirements . . . 1070A
. reduction for liability assumed . . . 1065
. reporting donations . . . 1070A
. services . . . 1061
. special rules . . . 931
. student maintained in the home . . . 1064
. substantiation requirements . . . 1070A
. ticket purchases . . . 1061
. token benefits . . . 1061
. transfer in trust . . . 1070
. travel expenses . . . 1061
. trusts . . . 537; 538
. $250 or more, substantiation . . . 1070A
. unitrust donee contributions . . . 1061
. use of property . . . 1063
. vehicle substantiation . . . 627; 1070A
. year deductible . . . 1058; 1061

Charitable organizations
. application for exempt status . . . 623
. churches and religious organizations . . . 604
. disclosure requirements . . . 627
. donor advised funds . . . 610
. exempt purposes . . . 602
. hospitals . . . 602
. lobbying activities . . . 613
. operational test . . . 602
. organizational test . . . 602
. political activities . . . 613
. political expenditures . . . 614
. private benefits . . . 602; 617
. private foundation status . . . 631
. supporting organizations . . . 607

Charitable purpose
. exempt organizations . . . 602

Charitable remainder trusts
. beneficiaries, tax treatment of . . . 590B
. charitable contribution deduction limits . . . 538
. division . . . 590
. estate tax . . . 2932
. private foundations . . . 591
. qualifying as . . . 590
. reporting . . . 590
. taxation of . . . 590A

Check-the-box regulations
. choosing partnership status . . . 402A

Check-the-box regulations—continued
. corporation classification . . . 201
. default classifications . . . 402A
. disregarded entities . . . 402A
. foreign entities . . . 402A
. S corporations . . . 306

Checklist
. deductions—see also specific headings . . . 57
. gross income items—see also specific headings . . . 55
. medical expenses deductions . . . 59
. tax credits . . . 61

Checks, payment of tax . . . 2545

Chief Counsel, Office of . . . 2703

Child and dependent care credit
. credit against tax . . . 1301

Child care, employer-provided . . . 2065
. cafeteria plans . . . 2045
. credit for employer . . . 1365V
. in general . . . 2065

Child support
. alimony or separate maintenance payments . . . 776

Child tax credit
. credit against tax . . . 1305
. qualifying child . . . 1305
. refundable portion . . . 1305

Children—see also Minors . . . 137
. adoption of
. . adoption credit . . . 1307
. alternative minimum tax . . . 1401
. alternative minimum tax exemption amount . 1410
. kidnapped or missing
. . dependency exemption . . . 150
. special needs
. . adoption credit . . . 1307
. under age 18
. . unearned income of . . . 571

Christian Science practitioners
. self-employment tax . . . 2667

Chronically ill individuals
. accelerated death benefits . . . 803
. long-term care expenses . . . 1016

Churches
. convention or association of churches . . . 604
. exempt status . . . 604
. information returns . . . 625
. lobbying expenses . . . 613
. notification requirements . . . 623

Circulation expenditures
. alternative minimum tax . . . 1435
. magazine circulation expenses . . . 971
. newspaper circulation expenses . . . 971

Civic leagues
. exempt status . . . 692

Civil unions
. joint returns . . . 152

Claim of right doctrine . . . 1543

Claims Court . . . 2790
. attorney fee awards . . . 2796

Class life asset depreciation range system . 1282; 1284

Clergy
. housing or rental allowance . . . 875
. mortgage interest . . . 1050
. real estate taxes
. . deductibility . . . 1028
. self-employment tax . . . 2667
. withholding of tax on wages . . . 2609

Clinical testing expenses
. credit against tax 1365S
Closely held business
. installment payment of estate tax 2939
Closely held corporations
. compensation repayment agreements 906
Closing agreements 2721
Clothing
. charitable contributions 1061
. cleaning costs
. . travel 952
. uniforms and special work clothes 1083
Club dues
. business expenses 913A
Coal
. percentage depletion 1289; 1298
. royalties, capital gain treatment 1772
COBRA continuation coverage 2015; 2021
COBRA continuation coverage rules
. accident and health plans 2021
. health and accident plans 2015
***Cohan* rule**
. business expenses substantiation 953
Coins
. capital gains rate 1736
Collectibles
. capital gains rate 1736
Collection of tax
. bankruptcy 2750
. check for payment 2545
. closing agreements 2721
. damages, suits by taxpayers 2798
. deficiencies, waiver of restrictions 2712
. Direct Pay system 2545
. distraint 2735
. expenses of
. . deductibility 1092
. fiduciaries, from 2747
. injunction to restrain collection 2719
. interest on deficiencies 2735
. levy 2735
. limitations period 2726; 2735
. notice and demand for tax 2845
. partial payments 2724
. private debt collection agencies 2735
. receivership 2750
. statute of limitations 2726
. suit for collection without assessment 2726
. transferees 2743; 2745
College
. Coverdell education savings accounts 867
. credits for higher education tuition 1303
. qualified tuition programs 869
. scholarship or fellowship grant 865
Combat zone
. designated areas 895
. examination and collection relief 2708
. military personnel in
. . filing of joint return 152
. pay for military personnel
. . exclusion from gross income 895
Combined group controlled corporate group 291
Commercial property
. energy-efficient buildings
. . deductibility 977D
Commissioner of IRS
. acquiescence by 2788
Commissions
. securities transactions 1983
. taxability 713
. withholding of tax 2604
Commodities
. traders
. . mark-to-market election 1903
Commodity Credit Corporation loans
. gross income 769
Commodity futures transactions
. short sales 1944
. wash sales 1935
Common trust funds 595; 2389
. alternative minimum tax 1465
. tax year 1501
Community Living Assistance Services and Supports (CLASS) program
. deductibility 1019
Community property
. allocation of income 711
. domestic partners
. . gift tax 2903
. gross estate 2921
. income 710
. . estate v. surviving spouse 520
. . foreign spouse 2438
. joint v. separate return 711
. registered domestic partners (RDPs) 710
. same-sex married couples (SSMCs) 710
. separate return
. . dependency exemption 141
. separated spouses 711
Commuter vehicle
. employer-provided 2091
Commuting expenses
. exclusion 2091
. nondeductibility of 945
Company-owned life insurance policies (COLIs)
. limited exclusion of proceeds 804
Compensation
. gross income 713
. retirement plan contributions 2115
. withholding of tax 2604
Compensation limitation
. executives, TARP 907
. $1-million limitation
. . covered employee 906
Compensation paid, deductibility 906
. deferred compensation 906
. deferred compensation plans 906
. employee achievement awards 919
. golden parachute payments
. . defined 907
. . excise tax 907
. health insurance providers 906
. life insurance premium paid 907
. officer-shareholder
. . repayment agreements 906
. $1-million compensation limitation
. . covered employee 906
. partners 421
. self-insurance 908
. TARP limitations 906
Compensation received, taxability 713
. accrued but unpaid 1533
. damages for lost wages 852
. deferred compensation 723
. employee benefits 713
. excessive salaries 715
. government employees 714

Compensation received, taxability—continued
. injury or sickness 2015
. meals and lodging 2089
. partners 421
. property, gain or loss basis 1681
. property transferred as payment 720
. reasonableness 715
. stock, gain or loss basis 1681
. surviving spouse, salary continuation 719
. use of property, personal holding company income 281

Completed contract method
. long-term contracts 1552

Complex trusts 542
. beneficiary, taxation of 556
. computation of income 559
. deduction for distributions 545
. . 65-day election 546
. exemption 534
. rules, operation of 559
. taxation 556

Compromise agreements 2723

Computation
. table percentages
. . with tables 1243
. . without tables 1243

Computation of tax
. annual basis, short tax year 1507
. . alternative method 1509
. by IRS 105
. consolidated returns 295
. individuals . . . . . 123—131
. joint return 156
. personal holding company 275
. tax rate schedules . . . . . 11—19; 128
. tax tables . . . . . 25—33; 128

Computer equipment donation
. charitable deduction, corporations 930

Computer software
. costs
. . amortization, deduction, depreciation 980
. royalties
. . personal holding company income 281

Condemnation awards 1716
. federal disaster area
. . involuntary conversions 1716
. involuntary conversions
. . federal disaster area 1716

Condominium associations
. exempt status 699

Confidentiality of returns 2892

Conflicts of interest, property exchanged to avoid 1732

Congress members
. tax home 950

Conservation expenses
. cost-sharing payments
. . exclusion from gross income 881
. energy conservation subsidies 889
. soil and water conservation 982

Consolidated returns 295
. advantages and disadvantages 297
. includible corporations 295

Construction allowance 1234
. exclusion from gross income 764

Constructive receipt 1533
. cash basis 1533
. interest 724

Constructive sale
. appreciated financial position 1945

Consumer debt
. deductibility of interest 1043

Consumer durable property
. depreciation, income forecast method 1240

Contested liabilities, accrual-basis taxpayer 1540A

Contested taxes
. deductible expenses 1092

Contingent payment sales 1821

Contraceptives
. medical expense 1016

Contracts
. annuities 817
. depreciation 1201
. exchange of 1724
. long-term, accounting for 1551

Contributions
. ABLE accounts 131
. defined contribution plans 2115
. . catch-up 2121
. 401(k) plans
. . catch-up 2121
. . elective deferrals 2121; 2123
. . matching 2121
. . Roth contributions 2121
. . SIMPLE 401(k) plans 2185
. 403(b) plans 2191
. 457A plans 2195
. partnership 443
. qualified plans
. . deduction limits 2119
. . deductions 2117
. Roth IRAs 2171
. SIMPLE IRAs
. . matching 2183
. . nonelective 2183
. . salary reduction 2181
. traditional IRAs
. . contributions, excess 2161
. . contributions, limits 2157
. . contributions, married filing separately . . . 2159
. . contributions, single persons 2159

Controlled corporate groups
. accumulated earnings credit 289
. accumulated earnings tax
. . credit 261
. allocation of tax benefits 289
. alternative minimum tax 289
. brother-sister controlled corporate group . . . 291
. combined group 291
. defined 291
. dividends-received deduction 289
. expenses, losses, interest 293
. loss defferal 293
. matching rule 293
. parent-subsidiary controlled corporate group 291
. rates of tax 34
. related-party transaction rules 293
. types of 291

Controlled corporations
. defined 203
. estimated tax 243
. exempt organizations 673
. property transferred to 1660; 1731
. . basis, built-in loss limitation 1667
. . liabilities assumed 1669
. rates of tax 34
. redemption of related corporation's stock . . . 744

Controlled corporations—continued
. sales to 1744
. stock as assets 2265
. stock exchanged for property 1731

Controlled foreign corporations (CFC) 2487
. accumulated earnings tax 253
. defined 2487
. passive foreign investment companies . . . 2490
. returns 2487
. stock sold, exchanged, or redeemed 2487
. subpart F income
. . accumulated earnings tax 253; 2488
. tiered corporations 2485
. undistributed earnings 2487
. U.S. shareholder defined 2487

CONUS travel
. per diem rates 954A; 954B

Convention expenses 959
. foreign conventions 960
. professional persons 981

Conventions and tradeshows
. exempt organizations 685

Conversion transactions
. capital gains and losses 1740
. straddles 1948

Convertible bond premium amortization . . 1967

Cooperative housing
. condominium associations
. . exempt status 699
. interest and taxes paid 1040
. sale 1707
. taxes deductible by owners 1028
. tenant-stockholders
. . deductions 1040

Cooperative service organizations
. cooperative educational organizations 699
. hospitals 699

Cooperative banks 2383

Copyright
. capital asset 1741
. controlled foreign corporation
. . sale or exchange with 2491
. depreciation 1201

Corporate Equity Reduction Transactions (CERTs)
. net operating loss carryback 1151

Corporate-owned life insurance
. S corporations
. . accumulated adjustments account 325

Corporations 201
. accounting period, change of 1513
. accrual-method of accounting
. . farming operations 221
. . required use of 221; 1515
. accumulated earnings tax . . . . . 251—269
. acquisition indebtedness
. . interest on 937
. active foreign business 2427
. affiliated corporations
. . consolidated returns . . . . . 295—297
. alternative minimum tax—see Alternative minimum tax (AMT)
. . adjustments 1430; 1440
. . reductions in tax benefits 1445
. . small corporations 219
. alternative tax on capital gains 1738
. bankruptcy, transfer of assets 203
. business and investment trusts 502
. capital gains 1738
. . timber gains 1738
. capital loss limitation 1752

Corporations—continued
. carryback expected, extension of time for tax payment 2773
. carryover from predecessor 2277
. carryover/carryforward from predecessor
. . net operating losses 1153
. charitable contributions . . . . . 927—931; 1062
. check-the-box regulations 201; 402A
. classification as 201
. closely held
. . compensation repayment agreements 906
. consolidated returns . . . . . 295—297
. constructive ownership of stock 743
. contributions of property 203
. contributions to capital 1660
. . basis, built-in loss limitation 1667
. control, defined 203
. controlled groups . . . . . 289—293
. debt
. . bona fide debt 227
. debt-equity guidelines 227
. debt instruments . . . . . 1950—1970
. . issuer's characterization 733B
. defined 201
. deposits of estimated tax 243
. dissolution 211
. distributions—see also Distributions by corporations 733A
. dividends paid . . . . . 733—754
. . stock redemptions as 742
. dividends received deduction 223; 229
. earnings and profits . . . . . 747—757
. . LIFO reserves 757
. elections
. . Code Sec. 336(e) election 2263
. . electing "association" status under check-the-box rules 402A
. . liquidations 2263
. estimated tax
. . annualization method 245
. . due dates 215; 243
. . electronic deposits 243
. . installment payments 243
. . large corporations 243
. . seasonal income method 245
. . underpayment 241
. exempt status 692
. farming operations
. . accrual method of accounting 221
. farming, taxability 767
. formation 203
. information returns 2565
. inversion transactions 2452
. investment companies
. . transfers to 203
. large corporations
. . estimated tax 243
. liabilities, assumption of 203
. life insurance
. . transfer for value 807
. limited liability companies 402B
. limited liability companies v. 201
. liquidations
. . elections 2263
. . reporting requirements 2259
. . subsidiaries 2263
. minority shareholders 2261
. net operating losses (NOL) 1147
. nonstockholders, transfers by 1660
. operating deficits 749
. organizational expenditures 237
. . syndication expenses contrasted 237
. partnerships v. 201; 401
. payments to, information returns 2565

Corporations—continued
. personal service corporations 273
. . accrual method of accounting 221
. publicly held
. . $1-million dollar compensation limitation . . 906
. . accumulated earnings tax 251
. purchase and sale of own stock 1729
. qualified conservation contributions . . 1059; 1063
. . carryover 1060
. rates of tax . . . . . 33—39; 219
. receivers filing returns for 506
. refunds of tax
. . quick refunds 247
. related-party debt 227
. . debt treated as stock 227
. . documentation requirements 227
. . expanded group 227
. . modified expanded group 227
. . part debt-part stock treatment 227
. . regulations 227
. reorganization expenditures 237
. returns 203
. . due date 211
. . extensions of time for filing 2509
. . fiscal year 211
. . forms 211
. . short period 211; 1505
. . time for filing 2505
. S corporations . . . . . 301—355
. S corporations v. 201
. Sec. 1250 property, additional recapture . . 1779
. sole proprietorships v. 201
. special deductions 221
. stock distributions
. . spin-offs, split-offs, split-ups and splint-offs 2201
. stock exchanged for property
. . bankruptcy 203
. . boot received 203
. . gain recognized 203
. . liabilities assumed 203
. . reporting requirements 203
. stock redemption costs 742
. stock surrendered 1916
. stock v. corporate debt, issuer's characterization 733B
. subdisiaries
. . liquidations 2263
. tax rates
. . qualified timber gains 219
. tax year 211
. taxable income 221
. taxable mortgage pool (TMP) 2368
. taxation
. . double taxation 201
. transfers to controlled corporations 203
. . reporting requirements 203
. treasury stock
. . property exchanged for 1729
. underpayments of tax, large 2838
. worthless stock 1916

Cosmetic surgery
. medical expenses 1016

Cost depletion 1289

Cost segregation 1240

Cost-sharing payments
. conservation expenses
. . exclusion from gross income 881

Coupons stripped from bonds 1952

Court costs, award of 2796

Courts of Appeals, U.S.
. appeals from decisions of 2794

Courts of Appeals, U.S.—continued
. jurisdiction 2786

Covenant not to compete
. amortization 1288
. sale of business 1743

Coverdell education savings accounts
. educational expenses
. . exclusion from gross income 867

Credit cards, payment of tax 2545

Credit counseling organizations
. exempt status 699

Creditors
. discounted loans 793

Credits against tax
. adoption credit 1307
. advanced clean coal project credit 1365D
. advanced energy project credit 1365F
. advanced nuclear power facilities credit . . 1365AA
. agri-biodiesel fuels credit 1365X
. alcohol fuels credit 1365I
. alternative fuel vehicle refueling property credit 1355
. alternative fuels credit 1365BB
. alternative minimum tax 1470; 1475; 1480
. . credit against regular tax for prior year liability 1309
. alternative motor vehicle credit 1345
. . fuel cell motor vehicle credit 1346
. American Opportunity tax credit (AOTC) . . 1303
. American Samoa possessions credit 1362
. biodiesel fuels credit 1365X
. build America bonds 1378
. carbon dioxide capture credit 1365JJ
. checklist 61
. child and dependent care 1301
. child tax credit 1305
. clinical testing expenses 1365S
. corporations
. . gross income 760
. differential wage payment credit 1365II
. disabled access credit 1365M
. distilled spirits excise tax carrying credit . . . 1365Z
. dividends by foreign subsidiaries 2485
. earned income credit (EIC) 1322
. elderly and permanently disabled tax credit . 1302
. elective deferrals and IRA contribution credit 1304
. electricity production from renewable resources 1365N
. employer-provided child care credit 1365V
. empowerment zone employment credit . . 1365O
. energy credit 1365C
. energy efficient appliances 1365DD
. energy efficient home credit 1365CC
. enhanced oil recovery credit 1365L
. estates 540
. excess Social Security taxes withheld 1321
. excessive employment tax withheld 2648
. FICA obligations of employers
. . tip income 1365R
. first-time homebuyer credit
. . recapture 1324
. first-time homebuyer in D.C. 1308
. foreign corporations 2446
. foreign taxes 1361; 2475
. gasification project credit 1365E
. gasoline and special fuels credit 1329
. general business credit 1365
. health insurance costs 1332
. health insurance premium assistance credit 1331
. home mortgage credit—see also Mortgage credit certificates 1306

Credits against tax—continued
. Hope scholarship credit 1303
. Indian employment credit 1365Q
. investment tax credit 1365A
. . advanced clean coal project credit 1365D
. . advanced energy project credit 1365F
. . energy credit 1365C
. . gasification project credit 1365E
. . rehabilitation credit 1365B
. lifetime learning credit 1303
. low-income housing 1365K
. low sulfur diesel fuel production credit 1365Y
. mine rescue team training credit 1365GG
. mortgage credit certificates 1306
. new clean renewable energy bonds (NCREBs) 1374
. new market credit 1365T
. nonbusiness energy property credit 1341
. nonconventional sources fuel production . 1365BB
. nonrefundable credits
. . limitations 1315
. nonresident aliens 2446
. oil and gas from marginal wells producer credit 1365KK
. order taken 105
. orphan drugs credit 1365S
. partnerships 431
. plug-in electric drive motor vehicles 1351
. prior-year minimum tax liability 1309
. qualified energy conservation bonds (QECDs) 1375
. qualified energy research expenditures . . . 1365J
. qualified forestry conservation bonds 1373
. qualified school construction bonds 1377
. qualified small agri-biodiesel producers credit 1365X
. qualified tax credit bonds 1371
. railroad track maintenance credit 1365W
. recoveries 799
. regulated investment company (RICs)
. . capital gain tax credit 1330
. rehabilitation credit 1365B
. research expenditures credit 1365J
. residential energy efficiency property credit . 1342
. retirement savings contribution credit 1304
. savers credit 1304
. small employer health insurance credit . . . 1333
. small employer pension plan startup costs credit 1365U
. tax-credit bond credits
. . mutual fund election to pass through tax-credit bond credits 1385
. tax credit bonds
. . build America bonds 1378
. . mutual fund election to pass-through bond credits 1385
. . new clean renewable energy bonds (NCREBs) 1374
. . qualified energy conservation bonds 1375
. . qualified forestry conservation bonds . . . 1373
. . qualified school construction bonds 1377
. . qualified zone academy bonds 1376
. trusts 540
. U.S. possessions tax credit 1362
. withheld taxes 1321
. work opportunity credit 1365G
. zone academy bonds 1376

Criminal penalties
. deficiency in tax 2898

Criminal prosecutions, statute of limitations 2740

Criminal restitution
. assessment of tax 2711

Crop basis of accounting 1569

Crop disaster payments 767

Crop sold with land 1747

Customer-based intangibles
. amortization 1288

D

Damages 972
. collection of tax, suits by taxpayers 2798
. corporations
. . lost profit or capital 759
. deductibility of attorney fees and court costs 852; 1093
. personal injuries 702; 852

Day care operators
. home use
. . business deduction 961; 964

Day traders
. gains and losses 1760

DB/K plans 2109

De minimis expensing safe harbor 903

Dealers
. installment sales 1808
. reserves
. . security for payment 1545

Dealers in securities
. capital gains and losses 1760
. defined 1760; 1903
. municipal bonds 1970
. ordinary gains and losses 1760
. personal holding company income
. . adjusted ordinary gross income 283
. . dividend and interest exclusions 281

Dealer's reserves 1545

Death benefit payments
. astronauts 813
. lump-sum distributions 2143
. public safety officer 813
. rollovers 2148
. terrorist actions 813
. withholding of tax 2609

Death gratuity payments
. exclusion from gross income 896

Death or retirement of partner 410
. income in respect of decedent 440
. liquidation distributions 438; 456

Death—see also Decedents
. dependency exemption 149
. joint returns . . . . . 164—168; 175
. property transmitted at, basis 1633

Death taxes
. deduction 191
. estate tax credit for foreign death taxes . . . 2934
. estate tax credit for state death taxes . . 43; 2934
. estate tax deduction for state death taxes . . 2933
. redemption of stock to pay 745

Debt
. basis
. . S corporations 318
. corporations
. . bona fide debt 227
. interest paid . . . . . 1043—1056
. refund offset for past-due debts owed to federal agencies 2764
. S corporations
. . basis 318

Debt-financed portfolio stock
. dividends received deduction 223

Debt-financed property
. exempt organizations
. . acquisition indebtedness 689
. . exceptions 691

Debt-financed property, unrelated business income . . . . . 687—691

Debt instruments—see also Bonds and also see Notes
. adequate interest 1954
. issued for property 1954
. . exemptions 1954
. . joint election 1954
. issuer's characterization 733B

Decedents
. short tax year 178

Decedent's final return
. accounting methods 182
. annualization exception 1505
. death taxes 191
. deductions 187
. due date 180; 2505
. expenses 187
. gain from sale of depreciable property 182
. income, how treated 182
. installment obligations 184
. interest paid by 187
. losses 531
. recipient, treatment 189
. taxes paid by 187
. who must file 178

Decedents—see also Death
. basis of property acquired from . . . . 1633—1639
. deductions 187; 191
. joint returns 164; 175
. medical expenses 1018
. new refinery construction costs 977C
. personal exemption 149
. property acquired from
. . basis . . . . . 1633—1639
. . Sec. 1245 or 1250 property 1788

Declaratory judgments
. court costs, award of 2796
. exempt organization status 623
. Tax Court jurisdiction 2776

Declining-balance method of depreciation . 1226

Deductions—see also specific headings
. above-the-line deductions 1005
. adjusted gross income 1005
. alimony and separate maintenance payment 771; 1008
. allocation by IRS 1573
. appreciated property
. . charitable contributions 1061
. Archer medical savings accounts (Archer MSAs) 2037
. bad debts 1135
. banks 2383
. bribe payments 972
. business expenses
. . employment agency fees 1081
. . generally 901
. . job hunting expenses 1081
. . uniforms and special clothing 1083
. business or profession 901; 981
. capital expenditures 903
. capital loss
. . annual limit 1752
. charitable contributions by corporations . 927—931
. charitable contributions by individuals . . . . . 1058—1071
. . limitations 1059
. checklist 57

Deductions—see also specific headings—continued
. compensation paid 906
. consumer debt interest 1043
. cooperative housing payments 1040
. decedents 187
. deductions
. . net operating losses (NOL) 1145
. defined benefit plan contributions 2119
. depletion 1289
. depreciation 1201
. domestic production activities 980A
. . allocation of costs and deductions 980G
. . construction, engineering, architectural . . 980F
. . corporations 239
. . domestic production gross receipts 980D
. . manufacturer's deduction 980A
. . partnerships 431A; 980H
. . qualified production activities income . . . 980B
. . qualified production property 980E
. . S corporations 312
. . W-2 wage limitation 980C
. educational expenses
. . business expenses 1082
. . interest on student loans 1011
. . teachers 1011B
. . tuition and fees 1011A
. employer contributions to employee welfare benefit plans 908
. energy-efficient buildings 977D
. energy-efficient commercial building property 1286
. entertainment expenses 910
. estate life tenant or income beneficiary . . . 1090
. estate tax
. . estate v. beneficiary 191
. estates . . . . . 528—537
. exempt organizations 682
. fee-based government officials 941D
. film and television production cost 977B
. fines paid 972
. foreign corporations 2446
. foreign housing expenses 2403
. guardianship expenses 1091
. handicapped individuals
. . employment-related expenses 1084
. health savings accounts (HSAs) 2035
. home office expenses . . . . . 961—966
. . safe harbor 963
. individuals 1001
. insurance premiums 1019
. insurance premiums paid 968
. interest on education loans 1011
. interest on tax deficiencies 1043
. interest paid or accrued—see also Interest paid or accrued . . . . . 1043—1056
. interest paid or accrued
. . exceptions and limitations 1043
. investment expenses 1085
. investors' expenses 1086
. itemized deductions 1079
. jury pay remitted to employer 1010
. long term care insurance premiums 1019
. losses . . . . . 1101—1195
. manufacturing 239; 312; 431A
. manufacturing corporations 239
. medical expenses . . . . . 1015—1019
. miscellaneous itemized deductions 1079
. mortgage insurance premiums 1048A
. mortgage interest . . . . . 1047—1048A
. moving expenses . . . . . 1073—1078
. net operating loss . . . . . 1145—1153
. nonbusiness expenses . . . . . 1001—1094
. nonresident aliens 2446

Deductions—see also specific headings—
continued
. partnerships 417
. penalties paid 972
. performing artist's expenses 941A
. personal expenses 1003
. prepaid interest 1055
. real estate taxes . . . . . 1028—1040
. recoveries 799
. . real estate taxes 1034
. redeemable ground rents 1049
. renewal community 999C
. rental or royalty property expenses 1006A
. repatriated earnings 2487
. repayment of items previously included in income 1543
. research or experimental expenditures 979
. retirement plan contributions 2117; 2119
. school teachers 941C
. self-employed health insurance premiums . 1019
. small refiners
. . low sulfur production 977A
. state and local government officials . . 105; 941D
. statutory employee's expenses 941B
. sulfur compliance costs 1285
. supplemental unemployment benefits repaid 1009
. taxes paid 920; 1021
. teacher's classroom expenses 1011B
. trade or business expenses . . . . . 901—905
. transportation costs . . . . . 945—948
. travel expenses . . . . . 949—960
. trusts 528; 535
. uniforms and special clothing 1083
. union dues 1080

Deferral of prepaid income 1537

Deferred compensation 906
. paid, deductibility 906
. received, taxability 723

Deferred compensation plans
. exempt employers 2193
. exempt employers, foreign 2195

Deferred like-kind exchanges 1722

Deferred payments
. applicable federal rate 1875
. rental agreements 1541
. sales . . . . . 1801; 1859—1883

Deficiency dividends
. personal holding companies 287
. real estate investment trusts 2337
. regulated investment companies 2317

Deficiency in tax
. accuracy-related penalty 2854
. assessment 2711
. criminal penalties 2898
. definition 2711
. disregard of rules and regulations, penalty . 2856
. extension of time for payment 2541
. interest
. . deductibility 1043
. judicial review 2786; 2790; 2792
. negligence penalty 2856
. notice 2778
. . joint liability 162
. . partnerships 415
. notice of deficiency
. . last known address 2711
. partial payments 2724
. penalties . . . . . 2854—2890
. waiver of restriction on collection 2712

Defined benefit and 401(k) plans (DB/K plans)
. combined qualified plans 2109

Defined benefit plans 2105
. benefit limits 2115
. contribution limits 2119
. flat benefit plan 2105
. minimum funding standards 2133
. plan termination insurance 2138
. requirements 2105
. unit benefit plan 2105
. vesting 2113

Defined contribution plans 2101
. compensation limits 2115
. contributions 2115
. contributions, catch-up 2121
. coverage 2112
. ESOPs 2103
. 401(k) plans 2104
. money purchase plans 2102
. nondiscrimination 2114
. participation 2112
. plan loans 2152
. profit-sharing plans 2102
. requirements 2111
. returns 2137
. rollovers 2145
. rollovers, from IRAs 2167
. Roth contributions 2121
. SEP plans 2189
. SIMPLE 401(k) plans 2185
. SIMPLE plans 2185
. stock bonus plans 2103
. thrift and savings plans 2110
. top-heavy plans 2132
. vesting 2113

Delinquent returns, penalties 2801

Delivery services
. filing returns 5

Demolition costs
. deductibility 1105

Demutualization
. insurance companies 1701

Dental expenses
. deductibility . . . . . 1015—1019

Department of Transportation
. hours of service rules
. . meal expenses 916

Dependency exemption
. adopted children 137A
. amount 133
. children of divorced parents 139A
. claiming the same child
. . tie-breaking rules 139
. divorced and/or separated parents
. . tie-breaking rules 139A
. effect of death 149
. foster children 137A
. income of qualifying relative 143
. kidnapped or missing children 150
. married dependents 138
. Midwestern disaster area 137
. qualifying child 137A
. qualifying relative 137B
. . adopted child 137B
. . foster children 137B
. . support test 147
. requirements 137
. separate returns filed 141
. students 137A

Dependent care assistance
. qualified military benefit
. . combat zone compensation 896

Dependent care assistance programs 2065

Dependent care assistance programs—continued
. cafeteria plans 2045
. exclusion from gross income
. . limitations 2065

Dependents
. blind exemption 126
. child and dependent care credit 1301
. children under the age of 27 908
. estate deduction for dependent allowance . . 549
. exemption
. . dependent's return 103
. head of household defined 173
. medical expenses 1015
. qualifying relative
. . earnings limitation 143
. returns 101
. standard deduction 126
. taxability of income 103
. travel expense deduction 952

Depletion—see also Percentage depletion
. alternative minimum tax
. . tax preference item 1425
. basis for allowance 1289
. beneficiary of estate or trust, deduction by . . 530
. coal 1298
. cost depletion 1289
. deduction 1289
. estates and trusts
. . apportionment of deduction 530
. gain or loss basis 1617
. life tenant's allowance 1090
. mineral production payments 1291
. mineral property 1289
. oil and gas wells 1289
. percentage depletion . . . . . 1289; 1294—1298
. timber 1289

Deposits of tax payments
. corporations, estimated tax 243
. employment taxes 2651
. . returns 2651
. failure to make timely deposits
. . penalties 2651; 2658

Depreciable property, disposition of
. adjustments to basis 1790
. corporate distributions 1793
. gifts 1788
. installment sales 1779
. investment credit recapture 1779
. involuntary conversions 1790
. like-kind exchanges 1790
. ordinary income treatment 1779
. partnership distributions 1792
. property acquired from decedent 1788
. related party 1835
. Sec. 1245 property 1779; 1785
. Sec. 1250 property 1786
. . additional recapture 1779
. tax-free transactions 1789

Depreciation . . . . . 1201—1284
. accelerated 1216
. Accelerated Cost Recovery System
(ACRS) . . . . . 1252—1270
. adjusted basis 1203
. alternative minimum tax
. . adjustment required 1430
. . tax preference item 1425
. automobiles 1211; 1214; 1215
. barrier removal costs for benefit of
handicapped and elderly 1287
. basis 1203
. beneficiary of estate or trust, deduction by . . 530
. bonus depreciation 1237
. change in method of computing 1221

Depreciation—continued
. computation of . . . . . 1216—1270
. computer software 980
. consumer durable property 1240
. converted residence 1201; 1203
. copyrights 1201
. cost segregation 1240
. depreciable property
. . what is depreciable 1201
. dispositions of depreciable property 1779
. double declining-balance method 1226
. earnings and profits, effect on 755
. election to expense 1208
. . recapture 1780
. energy efficiency improvements to
buildings 1286
. estates and trusts
. . apportionment of deduction 530
. exhaustion of property 1201
. expensing election 1208
. . recapture 1780
. films and theatrical productions
. . expensing election 1229
. films
. . income forecast method 1229
. fixed-percentage method 1224
. Form 4562 1201
. gain or loss basis 1617
. income beneficiary 1090
. income forecast method
. . consumer durable property 1240
. inventory 1201
. involuntary conversions 1250
. leased property 1234
. life tenant 1090
. like-kind exchanges 1250
. listed property 1211
. methods of 1216
. . change in 1221
. . miscellaneous methods 1231
. . real estate 1218
. Modified Accelerated Cost Recovery
System (MACRS) . . . . . 1236—1250
. property subject to 1201
. real estate 1218
. recapture 1779; 1780
. . installment sales 1823
. refineries 1285A; 1285
. related taxpayer sales 1744
. residential mortgage servicing rights 1201
. section 179 1208
. sinking fund method 1231
. straight-line method 1224
. structural components 1240
. sum of the years-digits method 1228
. term interests 1201
. transfer of property 1744
. web site development costs 1201

Design costs
. advertising
. . deductibility v. amortization 969

Development expenditures—see also Research and experimental expenditures
. farmers 984

Diagnostic testing
. medical expenses 1016

Diesel fuel credit
. credits against taxes 1329

Differential wage payment credit
. credits against tax 1365II

Disability benefits 2025
. health and accident plans 2015

Disability benefits—continued
. occupational
. . taxability 851
. terrorist attack 851

Disability insurance
. deductibility 968

Disability payments
. deductibility 908A

Disabled access credit
. credit against tax 1365M

Disabled individuals
. elderly and permanently disabled tax credit . 1302
. returns of
. . agent filing return 504

Disaster areas
. extensions for filing and paying 2537

Disaster losses 1133
. federally declared disaster
. . adjusted gross income (AGI) limitation . . 1133
. involuntary conversion of property 1715

Disaster relief payments
. exclusion from gross income 887

Disclosure
. charitable contributions
. . nondeductibility 627
. . *quid pro quo* contributions 627
. exempt organizations
. . public inspection 625
. listed transactions 2592
. reportable transactions 2592; 2593
. return information
. . penalties 2894
. . remedies 2893

Discounts
. short-term obligations 1961
. tax-exempt obligations 1952

Discrimination suits
. attorney fees and court costs
. . deductibility 852; 1093

Dispositions
. charitable contributions
. . donated property 627

Disqualified persons
. excess benefit transactions 617

Disregard of rules and regulations, penalty . 2856

Disregarded entities
. withholding 2654

Dissolution of corporations
. distributions
. . information returns 211
. short tax years 1505

Distilled spirits
. excise tax
. . credits against tax 1365Z

Distributable net income (DNI)
. estates and trusts 543; 559; 564

Distributions
. ABLE accounts 131
. annuities and annuity contracts
. . employees' annuities 839
. real estate investment trusts (REIT) 2331
. . after end of tax year 2339
. regulated investment companies (RIC) 2309; 2311
. . after end of tax year 2303; 2323

Distributions by corporations—see also Dividends paid; Dividends received
. appreciated property 1729

Distributions by corporations—see also Dividends paid; Dividends received—continued
. common and preferred stock 733A
. compensation paid v. 715
. computation of earnings and profits 748
. convertible preferred stock 733A
. depreciable property 1793
. disproportionate 733A; 742
. earnings or profits, effect on 747
. fractional shares 733A
. gain or loss 736
. information returns 2565
. liquidations . . . . . 2253—2265
. loss, earnings and profits affected 750
. noncash 733A
. nontaxable distributions
. . effect on earnings 753
. other than dividends 754
. partial liquidation 2253
. personal holding company 281
. preferred stock, dividend 733A
. property distributed 748
. proportionate interest increased 733A
. redemption of stock
. . death taxes paid 745
. . earnings and profits 751
. . related corporations 744
. reorganization 2237
. . earnings and profits 752
. sources of 747
. stock dividends 733A
. stock rights 733A

Distributions by estates and trusts
. annuities 548
. beneficiaries' tax . . . . . 554—565
. . 65-day election 546
. deduction for
. . complex trusts 545
. . estates 545
. . simple trusts 544
. distributable net income 543
. property or corpus transfer 526
. surviving spouse or dependent allowance . . . 549

Distributions by partnerships
. basis of property 456
. disposition of distributed property 462
. encumbered property 453
. gain or loss 453
. . distribution within five years of contribution 454
. liabilities, decrease 447
. liquidation of interest of retiring or deceased partner 438; 456
. marketable securities 453
. partners . . . . . 428—432
. partnership assets . . . . . 453—470
. property, basis of 436; 456
. property, precontribution gain 453; 454

Distributions by retirement plans
. divorce or separation 2144
. early distribution 2151
. 403(b) plans 2191
. 457A plans 2195
. IRAs
. . charitable contributions 1058
. penalty, early distribution 2151
. required minimum distributions (RMDs) . . . 2127

Distributor's agreement, cancellation
. gain or loss 1751

District Court
. attorney fee awards 2796
. jurisdiction 2790

District of Columbia
. enterprise zone
. . exclusion of gain 999D
. homebuyers credit 999D

Dividends paid
. backup withholding 2645
. deduction
. . accumulated earnings tax 259; 2303
. . real estate investment trusts (REIT) 2329
. earnings and profits, effect on 747
. information returns 2565
. preferred dividends
. . consolidated returns 297
. stock sold short 1946
. withholding of tax at source 2645

Dividends received
. affiliated groups
. . life insurance companies 229
. amount of dividend 733
. declaration v. receipt 734
. deductions by corporations 223
. . affiliated corporations 223; 229
. . debt-financed portfolio stock 223
. . extraordinary dividends 223
. . foreign corporation dividends 231
. . holding period 223
. . repatriated earnings 2487
. definition of dividend 733
. distribution in reorganization 2237
. distributions not dividends 754
. dividends received by corporations
. . qualifying dividends 229
. exchange of stock v. 742
. exempt organizations 673
. extraordinary dividends
. . deductions by corporations 223
. gross income 733
. holding period 733
. life insurance 809
. paid in property 735
. personal holding company income 281
. qualified dividends 733; 1736
. redemption of stock as dividend 742
. regulated investment company
shareholders 2309; 2311
. Sec. 306 stock 739
. stock dividends 733A
. stock redemption, death taxes paid 745

Divorce
. alimony or separate maintenance 1008
. child's medical expenses
. . deductibility 1015
. deductibility of legal expenses 1093
. dependency exemptions 139A
. interlocutory decree
. . effect on joint return 152
. retirement plans
. . rollovers 2144
. transfers incident to
. . basis of property transferred 1693
. . property transfers and settlements . . . 778; 1734
. . sale of residence, gain exclusion 1707

Divorce or separation instruments
. alimony or separate maintenance 772

Dollar amounts
. rounding off 105

Domestic international sales corporation (DISC) 2498
. returns 2505
. tax year 1501

Domestic partner benefits 2077

Domestic partnerships, registered
. joint returns 152

Domestic production activities 980A
. allocation of costs and deductions 980G
. alternative minimum tax 1430
. calculation
. . QPAI 980H
. . W-2 wages 980H
. construction, engineering, architectural . . . 980F
. deduction 980A
. domestic production gross receipts 980D
. eligible entity
. . definition 980H
. estates 536
. film or television production
. . S corporations 312
. partnerships 431A
. qualified production activities income 980B
. qualified production property 980E
. S corporations 312
. trusts 536
. W-2 wage limitation 431A; 980C
. . partnerships 431A
. . S corporations 312

Domestic production activities deduction
. corporations 239

Donations
. dispositions of 627
. intellectual property 627
. vehicles 627

Donor advised funds
. charitable contribution
. . deductibility 1061
. defined 610
. excess benefit transactions 617
. excess business holdings 640
. excise tax 610
. information returns 625
. prohibited benefits 610
. taxable distributions 610

Donor lists
. exempt organizations
. . unrelated business income 667

Double declining-balance method of depreciation 1226

Drawing accounts of partners 453

Drilling expenses
. oil or gas 989

Drought
. casualty losses 1121

Drug dealers' deductions 972

Drugs
. deductibility 1017

Dual resident companies
. consolidated returns 297

Due dates
. calendar 6
. corporation taxes 215; 2505
. decedent's return 180
. estate returns 510
. estimated tax 243; 2685
. . corporations 215
. fiduciary returns 510
. foreign corporations 2425
. individual returns 107; 2505
. nonresident aliens 2425
. partnership returns 406
. payment of tax 2529
. . installment agreements 2529
. trust returns 510

Due dates—continued
. weekends and holidays 2549
Dues paid
. deductibility 981

E

Earned income
. child and dependent care credit
. . defined 1301
. foreign earned income 2402
. self-employed persons, retirement plans . . 2107
Earned income credit (EIC)
. credits against tax 1322
. due diligence requirements 1322
. tables 87
Earnings and profits
. regulated investment companies (RIC) . . . 2313
Earnings and profits of corporation
. computation 748
. depreciation effect on 755
. dividends paid, effect of 747
. installment sales effect on 756
. LIFO reserves 757
. S corporations . . . . . 323—333
Earnings stripping
. interest payments nondeductible 937
Easements
. basis 1617
. facade easements
. . charitable contributions 1063
. gain or loss 1617
Economic interests
. oil and gas properties 1289
Economic performance rule 1540
. recurring item exception 1540
. tax shelters 1540
Economic substance
. transactions lacking
. . penalty 2863
Education expenses
. business expenses 1082
. credits against tax
. . American Opportunity tax credit (AOTC) . 1303
. . Hope scholarship credit 1303
. . lifetime learning credit 1303
. employees 1082
. employer-provided assistance programs . . 2067
. forgiveness of debt for qualified student loans 855
. gift tax exclusion 2907
. handicapped student
. . medical expenses 1016
. interest on education loans 1011
. IRAs
. . education IRAs/Coverdell education savings accounts 867
. . eligible educational institutions 867
. . qualified higher education expenses 867
. qualified tuition programs 869
. travel as education 1082
. . business expense deduction 958
. tuition and fees 1011A
. tuition reduction
. . exclusion from income 865
. U.S. savings bond income 863
Education IRAs
. Coverdell accounts 867
Education tax credits
. credits against tax 1303
Educational assistance programs 2067
. employer-provided 2067
. grants 865
Educational organizations, exempt status . . 602; 699
Effectively connected U.S. source income . 2429
Elderly and permanently disabled tax credit
. credit against tax 1302
Elections
. alternative minimum tax
. . tax preference status, avoidance 1450
. bonus depreciation 1237
. carryover basis, prior law 1636
. complex trusts, 65-day election 546
. depreciation
. . alternative MACRS method 1247
. . class life asset depreciation range system 1282
. . expensing election 1208
. . mass asset election 1249
. disaster losses 1133
. expatriation
. . deferral of tax 2412
. foreign earned income exclusion 2408
. foreign housing expense exclusion 2408
. foreign tax credit or deduction 2476
. installment method
. . election out of 1803
. joint v. separate returns 154
. mark-to-market
. . dealers 1903
. . expatriation 2412
. . traders 1903
. . U.S. shareholders of PFICs 2490
. nonresident aliens 2410
. partners and partnerships
. . qualified joint ventures 402
. partnership provision exclusion 402
. partnerships 419
. . tax year 1501
. passive activity losses
. . separate activity 1175
. personal service corporations
. . tax year 1501
. real estate
. . subdivision 1762
. . U.S. real property interests 2432
. regulated investment companies 2320
. . tax credit bonds 2320
. resident aliens 2410
. S corporations 303; 304; 305; 306; 333
. . domestic eligible entities 306
. . late elections 306
. . limited liability companies 306
. . tax year 1501
. Sec. 179 expense 1208
. specialized small business investment companies 1909
. tax year
. . partnerships, personal service corporations, and S corporations 1501
Elective deferrals
. 401(k) plans 2123
Electricity production from renewable resources
. credit against tax 1365N
Electronic Federal Tax Payment System (EFTPS) 2503
Electronic filing of returns
. Electronic Federal Tax Payment System (EFTPS) 2503
. Filing Information Returns Electronically (FIRE) system 2565

Electronic filing of returns—continued
. income tax returns 2503
Electronic funds transfers of tax payments . 2545
. employer deposits 2651
Embezzlement
. losses, deductibility 1123
Employee achievement awards
. deductibility 919
. exclusion 2069
Employee assistance programs (EAPs) . . . 2023
Employee benefits
. employer contributions
. . Archer medical savings account (MSA) . . 2037
. . flexible spending arrangement (FSA) . . . 2041
. . health reimbursement arrangement (HRA) 2039
. . health savings account (HSA) 2035
. exclusion from gross income
. . employer-financed 873
Employee discounts 2088
Employee parking
. transportation fringe benefit 2091
Employee Plan Compliance Resolution System (EPCRS) 2139
. Audit Closing Agreements Program (AuditCAP) 2139
. Self-Correction Plans (SCP) 2139
. Voluntary Correction with Service Approval (VCP) 2139
Employee stock ownership plans (ESOP)
. exchange of stock to 1733
. stock bonus plan, requirements 2103
. S corporations 323
. tax advantages 2103
Employee stock purchase plans (ESPP) . . . 1929; 1931
Employees
. automobile expenses . . . . . 945—948
. . fixed and variable rate (FAVR) method . . . 947
. . standard mileage rate 947
. . withholding 2608
. bargain purchases from employer 789
. business expenses . . . . . 941—943
. . accountable v. nonaccountable plans 943; 952A; 2607
. . automobile expenses . . . . . 945—948
. . employment agency fees 1081
. . job-hunting expenses 1081
. . performing artist's expenses 941A
. . reimbursed expenses 941; 942
. . school teachers 941C
. . statutory employees 941B
. . substantiation 942; 943
. . union dues 1080
. . unreimbursed 941
. cafeteria plans 2045
. . taxability 713
. conventions 959
. credit for withheld taxes 1321
. deductions for expenses 941; 942
. educational assistance plans 2067
. educational expenses 1082
. employment agency fees 1081
. entertainment 910
. flexible spending arrangements 2041
. fringe benefits 2085
. group-term life insurance 2055
. health and accident plans 2015
. home office deduction 965
. impairment-related work expenses
. . deductibility 1084
Employees—continued
. incentive stock options . . . . . 1925—1927
. independent contractors distinguished 2602
. job-hunting expenses 1081
. jury pay remitted to employer 1010
. meals and lodging
. . fringe benefits 2089
. . travel expenses . . . . . 949—960
. misclassification 2602
. moving expenses
. . deductibility . . . . . 1073—1077
. . exclusion from gross income 2085
. . reimbursement, withholding on 2609
. nonqualified stock options 1923
. performing artist's expenses 941A
. prizes and awards 919
. qualified stock options 1929
. reimbursement of expenses
. . business 942
. . medical 2609
. . moving 2609
. . withholding 2607
. simple cafeteria plans 2047
. state and local government officials 941
. statutory employees 941B
. . business expenses 941B
. stock options
. . employer's deduction 1923
. . fair market value, readily ascertainable . . 1923
. . holding period, determination of 1923
. . in general 1919
. . incentive stock options . . . . . 1925—1927
. . lapse of options 1923
. . nonqualified stock options 1923
. . qualified stock options 1929
. . stock purchase plans . . . . . 1929—1931
. stock purchase plans 1929; 1931
. tax home 950
. transportation expenses . . . . . 945—948
. transportation fringe benefits 2091
. travel expenses
. . Federal employees 951
. . per diem . . . . . 954—954B
. . substantiation 943
. . withholding 2608
. uniforms and special clothing 1083
. union dues deduction 1080
. unreimbursed expenses 942
. welfare benefits 2011
Employees' annuities
. annuities and annuity contracts
. . distributions 839
Employer-provided child care credit
. credit against tax 1365V
Employer-provided daycare
. business expense 908B
. S-Corporation, sole shareholder 908B
Employer-provided vehicles
. compensation 713; 2059
Employers
. adoption assistance programs 2063
. awards to employees
. . deductibility 919
. cafeteria plans 2045
. . simple cafeteria plans 2047
. child and dependent care services 2065
. commuter vehicles 2091
. contributions to employees' welfare benefit plans
. . deductibility 908
. domestic partner benefits 2077
. educational assistance plans 2067
. educational assistance programs 2067

Employers—continued
. employee assistance programs (EAPs) . . . 2023
. FICA obligations of employers
. . certified professional employer organizations (CPEOs) 2660
. . tip income 1365R
. flexible spending arrangements (FSAs) . . . 2041
. health and accident plans
. . contributions 2013
. health care coverage, information returns . . 2567
. health insurance coverage cost, information returns 2567
. health insurance mandate 2001
. . applicable large employer 2001
. . full-time employees 2001
. . minimum essential coverage 131; 2001
. . offer of coverage 2001
. . penalty for not offering coverage 2003
. . penalty when offering coverage 2005
. . reporting requirements 2567
. health reimbursement arrangements (HRAs) 2039
. large employers, health care coverage reporting 2567
. penalties, failure to withhold 2658
. simple cafeteria plans 2047
. stock option plans, taxation 1923
. transportation-related fringe benefits 2091
. withholding, liability
. . certified professional employer organizations (CPEOs) 2660
. withholding, liability for 2601; 2648

Employment agency fees
. deductibility 1081

Employment taxes . . . . . 49; 921—923
. certified professional employer organizations (CPEOs) 2660
. deductibility 921
. deposits 6; 2651
. FICA 2648
. FUTA 2649
. household employees 2652
. nanny tax 2652
. per diem and mileage allowances 2608
. rates
. . FICA 2648
. . FUTA 2649
. returns 2650
. social security taxes (FICA) 923
. state income 924
. unemployment taxes 922

Empowerment zone
. employer credit 1365O
. employment credit 999B
. section 179 allowance 1208

Endowment insurance proceeds
. discharge of annuity obligations 841
. exclusion ratio 817

Endowment policies
. exchanges 1724
. loans to purchase
. . interest deduction 909
. transfer for value 845

Energy conservation bonds 1375

Energy conservation subsidies
. exclusion from gross income 889

Energy-efficient appliances
. credits against tax 1365DD

Energy-efficient homes
. credits against tax 1365CC

Energy investment credit
. credit against tax 1365C

Energy research
. credits against tax 1365J

Enhanced oil recovery credit
. credits against tax 1365L

Enterprise zone—see also Empowerment zone
. exempt facility bonds 729

Entertainment expenses . . . . . 910—919
. business deduction
. . associated entertainment 912
. . directly related 911
. entertainment facility 913
. exceptions 915
. . business meetings 915
. . employee reimbursements 915
. . expenses for goods and services 915
. . expenses of stockholders 915
. hunting lodge 913
. meals and entertainment expenses
. . exceptions to 50% limitation 917
. recreational facility 913
. yacht 913

Estate basis
. inconsistency
. . accuracy penalty 1633

Estate taxes—see also Generation-skipping transfer (GST) tax; Gift taxes . . 2901
. adequate consideration for transfer 2913
. administration expenses 2925
. charitable deduction 2932
. computation of tax 2937
. credit, applicable 2901
. credit, unified 41
. credits against estate taxes 2934
. . prior transfers 2934
. . state death taxes 43
. decedent's medical expenses 1018
. deductible expenses 2925
. deduction by estate or beneficiary 191
. estate tax valuation freeze 2913
. excluded amount under applicable credit . . 2901
. excluded amount under unified credit 41
. family-owned business deduction 2937
. funeral expenses 2925
. income from transferred property 2913
. interest 1043
. marital deduction 2926
. . life estate 2926
. . qualified terminable interest property (QTIP) 2926
. nonresident aliens 40; 41; 2940
. payment of tax 2938
. . installment payments 2939
. portability of spouse's unused applicable exclusion amount 2934; 2938
. qualified disclaimers 2912
. qualified terminable interest property 2912
. returns 2938
. state death tax credit 43; 2934
. state death tax deduction 2933
. unified transfer tax system 2901
. . rate schedule 40
. . unified credit 41

Estates and trusts—see also Trusts
. accounting period, first return 510
. accumulated income of 520
. administration period 507
. alimony payments 529
. alternative minimum tax 516; 1401
. annuities distributable from income or corpus 548

Estates and trusts—see also Trusts—continued
. backup withholding, credit for 540
. bad debts, deductibility 531
. beneficiaries
. . depletion deduction 530; 1090
. . depreciation deduction 530; 1090
. . different tax year 565
. . gain on transfer to 526
. . separate shares as separate trusts or estates 557
. . taxation 556
. capital gains and losses 562; 1736
. capital loss carryover 535
. charitable deduction 537; 538
. charitable trusts . . . . . 590—593
. common trust fund 595
. computation of tax 516
. corporation v. trust 502
. credits 540
. deductions allowable . . . . . 528—538
. . two-percent floor on miscellaneous itemized deductions 528
. defined 501
. dependent allowance 549
. depletion deduction 530
. depreciation deduction 530
. distributable net income 543; 559
. distributions by
. . deductibility 544; 545
. . income taxed to beneficiary 554; 556
. domestic production activities 536; 980H
. double deductions 529
. estate tax deduction 191
. estimated tax 511
. excess deductions on termination 535
. exclusion of gain from small business stocks 538; 543
. exemptions 534
. expenses incurred 529
. fiduciary returns 510; 512
. foreign estates 501; 527
. foreign tax credit 540
. foreign trusts 501
. Form 1041 510
. Form 1041, Schedule J 567
. Form 4970 567
. fuels, credit against tax 540
. general business credit 1365
. gifts and bequests 564
. gross income . . . . . 520—527
. . community property states 520
. hobby expenses and losses 1195
. income, defined 514
. information returns 510
. interest paid or accrued, deductibility 533
. loss of estate, carryover to beneficiary 535
. losses 531
. manufacturer's deduction 536; 980H
. net investment income tax 517
. net operating loss, beneficiary's refund claim 556
. passive activity losses 531
. payment of tax, time for 510
. personal exemption 534
. personal holding company income 281
. personal property, income from 523
. pooled income funds 593
. private foundation taxes on trusts 591
. prohibited transactions, charitable deduction effect 538
. rates of tax 19
. . capital gains tax 1736
. real property, income from 522
. regulated investment company credit 540
. returns 510

Estates and trusts—see also Trusts—continued
. sale of property by 524
. separate entity, status of estate as 514
. 65-day election, distributions 546
. surviving spouse, widow's allowance 549
. tax year 510
. taxation of, generally 514
. taxes—see also Estate taxes 514; 2901
. . deductibility 532
. . tax preference items 516
. termination, deductions 507
. . excess deductions 535
. unused loss carryovers 535
. widow's allowance 549
. withholding of tax on wages, credit for 540

Estimated expenses
. reserves for 1547

Estimated tax
. corporations 241
. . adjusted seasonal installments 245
. . annualization method 245
. . controlled group 243
. . due dates 215; 243
. . electronic deposits 243
. . installment payments 243
. . large corporations 243
. . payments, time, and amount 243
. . seasonal income method 245
. . underpayment 241; 2890
. estates 511
. exempt organizations
. . investment income 633
. . unrelated business taxable income 658
. farmer or fisherman 2691
. individuals 117
. . due dates 2685
. . final installment 117; 2688
. . installment amount 2682
. . liability for 2682
. . overpayment 117
. . underpayment 117; 2875
. quick refunds for corporations 247
. trusts 511

Examination of books and records 2708

Examination of returns 2708
. foreign-source documents 2499
. unauthorized inspection, penalties 2893

Excess benefit transactions
. disqualified persons 617
. donor advised funds 617
. exempt organizations 617
. supporting organizations 617

Excess business holdings
. exempt organizations 640
. supporting organizations 617

Excess parachute payments—see also Golden parachute contracts 907

Exchange visitors 2448

Exchanges of property—see also Sales or exchanges of property
. gain or loss 1719
. government obligations 1726
. losses
. . related persons 1717
. Sec. 1245 or 1250 property 1790
. tax-free . . . . . 1719—1734

Excise tax table 53

Excise taxes
. donor advised funds 610
. exempt organizations
. . excess benefits transactions 617

Excise taxes—continued
. exempt organizations—continued
. . excess lobbying expenditures 613
. . political expenditures 614
. . tax shelters 619
. private foundations
. . abatement of taxes 647
. . accumulation of income 637
. . excess business holdings 640
. . investment income 633
. . investments jeopardizing exempt purpose 642
. . self-dealing 635
. . taxable expenditures 644
. real estate investment trusts
. . undistributed income 2329
. regulated investment companies 2303
. retirement plans
. . minimum funding standards, defined benefit plans 2133
. . prohibited transactions 2136
. . required minimum distributions 2127
. supporting organizations
. . excess benefits transactions 617
. . excess business holdings 640
. unregistered obligations 1963

Excludable death benefits
. payment to beneficiaries
. . incidental death benefits 813
. . public safety officer 813

Excluded income . . . . . 801—896

Exclusion from gross income
. ABLE accounts 131
. annuities and annuity contracts
. . first year exclusion 835
. . part year exclusion 835
. benefits
. . Indian health care 2027
. casualties
. . reimbursed living expenses 877
. disaster relief payments 887
. energy conservation subsidies 889
. foreign earned income 2402
. . election 2408
. . eligibility 2404
. foreign housing expenses 2403
. . election 2408
. . eligibility 2404
. foster care payments 883
. fringe benefits 2085
. health and accident benefits 2015
. health savings accounts 2013
. Holocaust payment or restitution 889
. human trafficking victims 889
. Indian health care benefits 2027
. IRA distributions to charity 1058
. meals and lodging
. . foreign camp, employer-provided 2406
. medical loss ratio rebates 889; 2031
. Native American health care benefits 889
. Native American litigation settlement 889
. other income 889
. residence, sale 1705; 1709
. retiree prescription drug plans 2029
. U.S. possessions 2414
. veteran's benefits
. . U.S. Public Health Services 891
. wrongfully incarcerated individuals 889

Exclusion ratio
. annuities and annuity contracts 817
. formula 819

Executors
. decedent's return filed by 178

Exempt-contract-percentage-of-completion method
. long-term contracts 1552

Exempt income—see also specific headings 801
. accident and health plans 2015
. agricultural cost-sharing payments 881
. American Samoa, income earned by bona fide residents 2414
. annuities and annuity contracts . . . . . 817—845
. . annuity starting date 823
. . exclusion ratio 819
. . investment in the contract 821
. bequests 847
. cancellation of indebtedness 855
. casualties
. . reimbursement for living expenses 877
. child or dependent care services 2065
. . employer-provided 2065
. combat zone compensation 895
. damages for personal injuries 702; 852
. disability benefits 851
. educational savings bonds 863
. employee's death benefits 813
. endowment insurance proceeds 817
. energy conservation subsidies 889
. expenses 970
. fellowships 865
. foster care payments 883
. fringe benefits, employees 2085
. gifts 849
. interest 729
. . dividends, regulated investment companies 2307
. involuntary conversion, gain from 1713
. life insurance policy, transfer for value 807
. life insurance proceeds 803
. . installment options 805
. loans to purchase exempt obligations 970
. meals and lodging 2089
. minister's rental allowance 875
. moving expenses 2092
. scholarships 865
. sickness and disability benefits . . . . . 851—852
. small business stock
. . gain on sale of 871
. transportation fringe benefits 2091
. treaty-exempt income 2450
. U.S. possessions, income from 2414
. working conditions fringe benefits 2090

Exempt obligations—see also Bonds
. expenses to carry 970
. original issue discount 1952; 1956

Exempt organizations . . . . . 601—699
. accumulated earnings tax 251
. acquisition indebtedness 689
. advertising income 685
. agricultural organizations 692
. application and modification of exempt status 623
. appreciated property contributions 1062
. black lung benefit trusts 692
. bootstrap sales 687
. business leagues 692
. charitable contributions 1061
. charitable organizations 602
. . hospitals 602
. . operational test 602
. . organizational test 602
. . private benefits 602
. charitable purpose 602
. civic leagues 692
. consolidated returns 295
. conventions 685

Exempt organizations—continued
. cooperative hospital service organization . . . 699
. cooperative service organizations of educational organizations 699
. cooperatives 698
. corporations 692
. credit card programs, royalties from 673
. credit counseling organizations 699
. debt-financed acquisitions 687
. declaratory judgments, status determinations in court 623
. disclosure
. . information returns 625
. . nondeductibility 627
. . *quid pro quo* contributions 627
. . UBTI returns 625
. . vehicle donations 627
. disqualified person 617; 637
. dissolution 625
. donations
. . intellectual property 627
. . property, disposed of 627
. . vehicles 627
. donor advised funds 610
. estimated tax
. . investment income 633
. . unrelated business taxable income 658
. excess benefits transactions 617
. feeder organizations 694
. 403(b) plans 2191
. fraternal beneficiary societies 692
. homeowners' associations 699
. horticultural organizations 692
. information returns 625
. investment income 673
. investment tax credit 1365A
. labor organizations 692
. lease-back income 687
. lobbying expenditures
. . public charities 613
. . reporting of 625
. loss of exempt status 623
. low-cost articles 667
. membership organizations 673
. notification requirements 623
. notional principal contracts, income from . . . 673
. political expenditures 614
. political organizations 696
. prohibited transactions 538
. proof of exemption 625
. qualifying organizations 601
. reinstatement of exempt status 623
. religious or apostolic 604
. rents 676
. residual interests in REMICs held by 2361
. return requirement 2505
. revocation of exempt status 623
. S corporation shareholders 304
. sales or exchanges of property 679
. scientific organizations 692
. self-dealing 635
. social clubs 692
. social welfare organizations 692
. sponsorship income 685
. supplemental unemployment benefits (SUB) trust 692
. supporting organizations 607
. . excess benefit transactions 617
. . excess business holdings 640
. tax shelters 619
. title holding corporations 692
. trade shows 685
. types 601
. unrelated business income . . . . . 655—685

Exempt organizations—continued
. unrelated business taxable income
. . look-through rules 673
. VEBAs 692
. veterans' organizations 692

Exemptions
. alternative minimum tax
. . income exemption amount 1410
. . personal exemptions 1435
. dependents 133
. . requirements 137
. personal 135
. personal exemptions . . . . . 133—150
. phaseout repeal 133
. withholding exemptions . . . . . 2632—2637

Expatriates
. distributions from trust, withholding 566
. estates of 2940
. gift or bequest to trust 516
. . deduction of tax 1021
. gifts and bequests from 2948
. mark-to-market tax 2412
. reporting requirements 2412
. residence, sale 1705

Expenses
. decedent's final return 187
. exempt income, nonbusiness expenses—;see Nonbusiness expenses
. . costs of acquiring 970

Expensing election, depreciation 1208
. recapture 1780

Exploration expense
. mines 987
. . foreign 988A

Extensions of time
. carrybacks anticipated 2773
. filing returns 109; 2509
. . corporations 2509
. . estates 510
. . individuals 2509
. . penalties 2809
. . trusts 510
. form of request for 2509
. payment of deficiency 2541
. . interest on tax 2537
. returns 2509

Extraterritorial income exclusion 2498

F

Failure to distribute income
. private foundations 637

Fair market value
. determination of gain or loss 1695
. nonrecourse indebtedness 1695
. stock options
. . readily ascertainable 1923

Family estate trusts 571

Family medical leave act
. cafeteria plans 2045
. flexible spending arrangements 2045

Family-owned business
. estate tax deduction 2937

Family partnerships 474

Family transactions
. losses not recognized 1717
. partnerships 474
. trusts 571

Farm cooperatives
. dividends received from 223

Farm cooperatives—continued
. information returns 625; 2565
. patronage dividends
. . taxability 768

Farm-price method of inventory 1569

Farmers and farming
. accrual basis 767
. cancellation of debt 855
. cash basis 767
. corporate farmers, accrual method 1519
. cost-sharing payments
. . conservation expenses 881
. crop basis of accounting 1569
. crop disaster payments 767
. depreciation 1201; 1240; 1243
. development expenses 984
. disaster-forced sales of livestock 767
. endangered species recovery 982
. estimated tax 2691
. expenses
. . deductibility . . . . . 982—985
. farm-price method of accounting 1569
. fertilizer costs 985
. foreclosure 855
. gasoline and special fuels credit 1329
. hobby expenses and losses 1195
. income averaging election 767
. income from, taxability 767
. insolvency 855
. installment payment of estate tax 2939
. inventories 767; 1569
. involuntary conversions
. . livestock 1713
. land-clearing expenses 983
. land sold with growing crop 1747
. livestock sales 1747; 1750
. losses 767
. . loss limitation, Schedule F 982
. machinery 1240
. net operating loss carryback 1151
. prepaid feed costs, deferral
. . year deductible 1539
. qualified conservation contributions . . 1059; 1063
. . carryover 1060
. recapture on land sale 1797
. returns 767
. self-employment tax 2676
. soil and water conservation expense 982
. syndicates, expenses 1521
. uniform capitalization rules 999
. unit-livestock-price method of accounting . . 1569
. well-drilling costs 982

Farmers' cooperatives
. exempt status 698
. patronage dividends, taxability 698
. per-unit retain certificates 698
. return 698

FATCA reporting requirements
. foreign financial institutions (FFIs) 2469
. . participating FFI agreements 2471
. individuals 2467; 2572
. non-financial foreign entities (NFFEs) 2473
. specified foreign financial assets 2467; 2572

FBAR reporting requirements 2465; 2570

Federal government agencies
. refund offset for past-due debts owed to . . . 2764

Federal government employees
. taxability of compensation 714

Federal National Mortgage Association
. stockholders 975

Federally declared disasters
. casualty losses
. . adjusted gross income (AGI) limitation . . 1133
. disaster losses 1133
. involuntary conversions 1715

Feed costs, deferral 1539

Feeder organizations 694

Fees
. taxability 713

Fertility enhancement
. medical expenses 1016

Fertilizer expenses 985

FICA benefits
. nonresident aliens 2431

FICA taxes 2648
. certified professional employer
organizations (CPEOs) 2660
. deposits 2651
. domestic workers 2652
. due dates for deposits 6
. employer deductions 923
. excess withholding 2648
. household employees 2652
. Medicare 2648
. . additional tax 2648
. penalties 2658
. rate 49; 2648
. returns 2650
. Social security 2648
. tip income
. . credit against tax for FICA obligation 1365R
. vacation and sick pay 1549

Fiduciaries
. amounts paid to 529
. collection of tax from 2747
. defined 501
. liability of 512
. receiver distinguished 506
. returns of estates and trusts 510
. . charitable remainder trusts 590
. . fiduciary as agent 504
. . nonresident alien beneficiary 510
. time for filing returns 2505
. trustee distinguished 506

FIFO inventories 1564

Fifteen-year property 1240

Filing of returns 101; 111
. bankrupt estate 505
. charitable trusts 537
. children 103
. corporations 211
. dependents 103
. due dates 107
. . calendar of due dates 6
. . weekends and holidays 2549
. estate tax return 2938
. estates, income tax 510
. extensions for filing 109
. fiduciary returns 504
. gift tax return 2910
. identifying numbers 116
. individuals
. . requirements 101
. nonresident aliens 101
. partnerships 406
. resident aliens 101
. trusts, income tax 510
. types of returns 2501
. U.S. citizens 101
. where to file 111
. who must file returns 101

Filing status
. head of household 173
. marital status 152
. single 176
. surviving spouse 175

Film and television productions
. production cost
. . deductibility 977B

Financial asset securitization investment trusts (FASIT) 2394

Financial institutions—see also Banks
. bad debt reserves 2383
. cancellation of debt, information returns . . . 2565
. foreign
. . withholding 2469
. interest paid 970
. mutual nonprofit corporations 692
. securities, sale or exchange 2383

Fines paid
. deductibility 972

Fire insurance premiums
. deductibility 968

First-in, first-out rule 1564
. identification of stock 1975

First-time homebuyer credit
. credits against tax
. . recapture 1324

First-time homebuyer in D.C.
. credit against tax 1308

Fiscal tax year
. 52-53 week year 1503
. . short tax year 1505

Fiscal-year taxpayers
. accounting periods 1501
. election under Code Sec. 444 1501

Five-year property 1240

Fixed and variable rate (FAVR) method
. automobile expenses of employees 947

Fixed-percentage method of depreciation . . 1224

Flat benefit plans 2105

Flexible spending arrangements (FSA) . . . 2041
. cafeteria plans 2045
. domestic partners 2077
. use it or lose it rule 2045

Floor offset plans 2108

Food inventories
. charitable contributions 1062

Foreclosure losses, deductibility 1107

Foreign bank, interest in
. information returns 2570

Foreign convention expenses 960

Foreign corporations
. American Samoa, Guam, Northern Mariana Islands and Virgin Islands corporations 2431
. branch profits tax 2433
. capital gains 2435
. consolidated returns 295
. deductions 2446
. dividends from 231
. . debt-financed portfolio stock 231
. effectively connected U.S. source income . . 2429
. . foreign insurance companies 2380
. fixed or determinable income 2431
. foreign tax credit 2446
. functional currency transactions 2495
. interest income 2429; 2431
. investments in U.S. 2431

Foreign corporations—continued
. life insurance companies 2380
. nonfunctional currency transactions 2495
. original issue discount 2431
. qualified business unit (QBU) 2495
. rates of tax 38; 219
. real property in U.S. owned by
. . effectively connected income 2432
. . qualified investment entities 2444
. . sale or exchange 2442
. REMIC ownership 2367
. reorganizations 2492
. returns 2425; 2501
. . controlled corporation 2487
. subsidiary of domestic corporation 2485
. taxable income 2446
. taxation 2425
. trade or business 2429
. trading in securities 2429
. U.S. sources, income from 2427
. withholding of tax 2455

Foreign countries
. moving expenses 1073

Foreign earned income
. defined 2402
. exclusion 2402
. . bona fide residence test 2404
. . effect on tax rates 2402
. . election 2408
. . eligibility 2404
. . physical presence test 2404
. . waiver of time requirements 2404

Foreign entities, transfers involving
. foreign trusts 2493
. intangibles 2492
. patent, copyright, etc. 2491

Foreign estates 501
. income of 527
. returns 510

Foreign expropriation losses, capital loss carryover 1756

Foreign financial assets
. interests in 2572
. undisclosed
. . penalty 2864

Foreign financial institutions (FFIs)
. FATCA reporting requirements 2469
. . participating FFI agreements 2471

Foreign government officials and employees
. bribes to 972
. self-employment tax 2667
. withholding of tax 2609

Foreign governments, expropriation of property by 1756

Foreign housing expenses
. deduction for self-employed individuals . . . 2403
. exclusion 2403
. . bona fide residence test 2404
. . effect on tax rates 2403
. . election 2408
. . eligibility 2404
. . physical presence test 2404
. . waiver of time requirements 2404

Foreign losses, recapture 2483

Foreign moves
. deductible moving expenses 1073
. retirees 1075
. return to U.S. 1075

Foreign partnerships
. information returns 2494

Foreign Sales Corporations (FSC)
. defined 2498
. returns, due date 2505

Foreign ships and aircraft 2446

Foreign students and exchange visitors . . . 2448

Foreign tax
. credit against tax 2475
. deductibility . . . . . 1023; 2475—2485
. refunds of 2475

Foreign tax credit . . . . . 1361; 2475—2485
. alternative minimum tax 1470
. beneficiaries 540
. carryback and carryover 2479
. claiming the credit 2475
. corporations 2475
. covered asset acquisitions 2477
. creditable foreign taxes 2477
. credits against tax 1361
. credits or deductions 2476
. deemed paid credit 2485
. election 2476
. estates 540
. foreign corporations 2446
. foreign subsidiary, taxes of 2485
. . S corporation 349
. holding period 2477
. income matching 2475
. limitations on 2479
. . separate limitation baskets 2481
. look-through rules 2481
. nonresident aliens 2446
. partnerships 2475
. Puerto Rican residents 2475
. regulated investment company shareholders 2320
. S corporation 349
. special computation for certain income categories 2481
. trusts 540

Foreign travel
. business expenses
. . deductibility 955

Foreign trust with U.S. beneficiary 588
. expatriate, gift or bequest from 516
. . tax deduction 1021
. loan by 542

Foreign trusts—see also Trusts 501
. grantor trust rules 588
. returns 510

Foreign wells
. drilling expenses 989

Forestry conservation bonds
. credits against tax 1373

Forms 63

Foster care payments
. exclusion from gross income 883

Foster children
. dependency exemption 137A
. qualifying relative 137B

401(k) plans
. catch-up contributions 2121
. contributions
. . catch-up 2121
. . elective deferrals 2123
. . excess 2121
. . matching 2121
. distributions
. . hardship 2129
. hardship distributions 2129
. requirements 2104

403(b) plans
. requirements 2191

457 plans 2193

457A plans 2195

Franchises
. amortization 1288; 1774
. contingent payments 1774
. grant, income from 1774

Fraternal beneficiary societies
. exempt status 692

Fraud penalties 2866
. burden of proof 2782

Fraudulent returns 2732

Fringe benefits 2085
. accident and health insurance
. . taxability 2015
. bicycle commuting 2091
. de minimis 2089
. . cell phones 2089
. . meals 2089
. educational assistance programs 2067
. exclusions from income 2085
. flight mileage rates 2059
. gross income 713
. military base realignment and closure 2095
. moving expense reimbursement 2092
. moving expenses, employer provided 2092
. no-additional cost services 2085; 2087
. on-premise athletic facilities 2094
. partners 421
. qualified employee discounts 2085; 2088
. retirement planning services 2093
. S corporations 322
. transportation, employer-provided 2091
. transportation fringe benefits 2091
. . vanpooling 2091
. withholding tax 2606
. working condition fringe benefits 2090

Fringe benefits. working condition fringe benefits 2095

Frivolous return, additional penalty 2811

Fruit growers' associations, exempt status . . 698

Fuel cell motor vehicle credit
. credits against tax 1346

Fuels
. credits against tax
. . alternative fuels 1365BB
. . biodiesel fuels 1365X
. . estates and trusts claims for 540
. . nonconventional source fuels 1365BB
. . second generation biofuel producers credit 1365I

Functional currency transactions 2495

Funding target
. defined benefit plans 2133

Funeral expenses
. estate tax deduction 2925
. funeral trusts 575
. medical expenses 1016

FUTA benefits
. repayment 1009

FUTA taxes 2649
. certified professional employer organizations (CPEOs) 2660
. deductibility 921
. deposits 2651
. due dates for deposits 6
. penalties 2658
. rates 49; 2649

FUTA taxes—continued
. returns 2650
. vacation and sick pay 1549

Future interests
. charitable contributions
. . deductibility 1069

Futures transactions
. gain or loss 1948
. hedging transactions 1949
. short sales 1944
. wash sales 1935

G

Gain or loss
. amount realized 1703
. basis
. . additions to basis 1611
. . adjusted basis 1604
. . apportionment 1620
. . assumption of liability 1669
. . bargain sale to charity 1623
. . built-in loss, limitation 1667
. . carrying charges 1614
. . chart 1601
. . controlled corporations, transfer to 1660
. . converted property 1626
. . corporations, transfers to 1660
. . cost 1604
. . damaged property, casualty loss 1127
. . discharge of indebtedness 1672
. . divorce transfers 1693
. . gift 1630
. . improvements 1611
. . involuntary conversions 1687
. . joint tenancy 1634
. . lessee improving property 764
. . liquidation of subsidiary 2261
. . medical equipment 1684
. . partner's interest 434; 443; 445
. . partnership property distributed . . . . . 453—462
. . property acquired by gift 1630
. . property acquired by purchase . . . 1611—1626
. . property acquired in exchange . . . 1648—1693
. . property, compensation received 1681
. . property transferred for stock 1648
. . rental property 1626
. . reorganization 1660
. . repossession of real estate 1843
. . residential property 1626; 1705
. . spouses, transfers between 1693
. . stock, compensation received 1681
. . substituted basis of property 1607
. . subtractions from 1617
. . tax-free exchange 1607; 1651; 1657
. . trade-in of equipment 1651
. . transfers in trust 1678
. . wash sale 1935
. bonds as bad debts 1916
. built-in loss limitations
. . transfers to corporations by foreign taxpayers 1667
. commodity transactions 1948
. constructive sale 1945
. corporate distributions 1793
. corporations, stock and stock rights 736
. dealers in securities 1903
. depreciable property sold 1249
. . computation of amount 1779
. dividends paid by corporation 733A
. divorce transfers
. . residence ownership 1707
. employee stock purchase plan 1929

Gain or loss—continued
. exchange of property 1719
. fair market valuation of property 1695
. futures transactions 1944
. gifts
. . taxes paid by donee 1701
. hedging transactions 1949
. identification of stock 1975
. incentive stock option 1925
. installment obligations, disposition 1846
. installment sales 1801
. involuntary conversions 1713
. liabilities, effect of 1703
. like-kind exchanges 1721
. liquidation distributions
. . corporation 2257
. . installment obligations 1856
. . shareholders 2253
. nonstautory stock options 1923
. options 1919
. property exchanged for annuity 1703
. publicly traded securities
. . rollover 1909
. puts and calls 1921
. real estate
. . fair market value 1697
. . sold in parcels 1762
. realized
. . sale of property 1703
. recapture of Sec. 1231 losses 1747
. recognition
. . controlled corporations, transfers to 1731
. . divorce property settlements 778
. . exchange of property 1719
. . residential property 1705
. . sale or exchange of property 1701
. recovery property 1779
. residence, sale
. . exclusion of gain 1705
. sale or exchange 1701
. section 1256 contracts 1947
. securities transactions 1901
. . fair market value 1697
. share lending agreements 1942
. short sales 1944
. small business stock
. . exclusion of gain 1905
. . losses 1911
. . rollover of gain 1907
. . Sec. 1244 stock 1911
. small business stock, exclusion of gain from 1701
. stock
. . nontaxable distribution 1682
. surrender of stock 1916
. tax straddles 1948
. wash sales 1935
. worthless stock 1916

Gains and losses
. exempt organizations
. . unrelated business income 679

Gambling
. income from 785
. losses, deductibility 1113
. withholding of tax on winnings 2642

Gasification projects
. credit against tax 1365E

Gasoline and special fuels credit
. credits against tax 1329

Gems, capital gains 1736

General asset accounts
. in general 1239

General business credit—see also names of component credits
. credits against tax 1365
. estates and trusts 540
. limitations
. . carry over of unused credit 1365

Generation-skipping transfer (GST) tax
. computation 2943
. deductibility 1021
. exemption 41; 2943
. payment of tax 2944
. returns 2944
. tax rate 40
. transfers subject to tax 2942

Geothermal deposits
. percentage depletion 1296

Geothermal wells
. drilling expenses 989

Gift taxes—see also Estate taxes
. annual gift tax exclusion 41; 2905
. . transfers in trust 2905
. charitable deduction 2909
. community property
. . domestic partners 2903
. computation 2910
. credit against estate taxes 2934
. educational expenses 2907
. excluded amount under unified credit 41
. gift defined 2903
. gift splitting 2905
. gifts made within three years of death 2914
. jointly held property 2919
. liability to file return; pay tax 2911
. lifetime use of spouse's unused applicable exclusion amount (portability) 2910
. marital deduction 2908
. . life estate 2908
. . qualified terminable interest property (QTIP) 2908
. medical expenses 2907
. nonresident aliens 40; 41; 2903
. returns 2910
. state death tax credit table 43
. transfers in trust annual exclusion 2905
. transfers subject to tax 2903
. unified transfer tax system 2901
. . applicable credit 2901
. . unified credit 41
. . unified transfer rate schedule 40

Gifts
. business expenses 918
. employees 713
. estate or trust beneficiary 564
. future interests
. . charitable contribution 1069
. gain or loss basis 1630
. gross income v. 702
. holding period 1737
. husband and wife, transfers between 1734
. income from gift 849
. made within three years of death 2914
. passive activity losses 1177
. reacquired from decedent-donee
. . basis 1639
. Sec. 1245 property 1788
. Sec. 1250 property 1788
. substantiation 953
. substituted basis 1630
. surviving spouse, salary continuation 719
. taxes—see also Gift taxes . . . . 849; 2901—2911
. . paid by donee, recognition of gain 1701
. tips 849

Going-concern value
. amortization 1288

Golden parachute contracts 907
. base amount 907
. consolidated returns 297
. exceptions 907
. payment, excess 907
. payment, limitation 907

Goodwill
. amortization 1288
. entertainment expenses to promote 912
. sale of business 1743

Government assistance payments
. gross income 702

Government bonds
. exchanges 1726

Government obligations
. exchange of 1726
. interest on 730
. unregistered 1963

Government publications as capital asset . 1741

Grandfathered debt
. acquisition indebtedness 1048

Grantor trusts
. foreign trust, U.S. beneficiary 588
. in general 571
. income for benefit of grantor 584
. income taxable to person other than grantor 585
. power to control beneficial enjoyment 579
. power to revoke trust 582
. powers held by grantor's spouse 578
. retention of administrative powers 581
. return requirement 586
. reversionary interest 576
. S corporation shareholder 304

Gross estate 2912
. alternate valuation date 2922
. annuities 2917
. community property 2921
. gifts made within three years of death 2914
. incidents of ownership in life insurance policy 2915
. jointly held property 2919
. life insurance 2915
. powers of appointment 2918
. property in which decedent held interest . . . 2912
. retirement benefits 2917
. special use valuation 2922
. transferred property in which decedent held interest 2913
. valuation 2922

Gross income 701
. accident and health plans 2015
. alimony and separate maintenance payments 771
. annuities
. . distributions 841
. assignments of income 705
. bargain purchases from employer 789
. bartered services 785
. business income 759
. capital or labor 702
. checklist of includible items 55
. child's income—see also Kiddie tax 103
. child's unearned income—see also Kiddie tax 706
. Commodity Credit Corporation loans 769
. community property income 710; 711
. corporations
. . dealing in own stock 1729

Gross income—continued
. corporations—continued
. . dividends received 733
. credits against tax 760
. damages 702
. damages for lost profit or capital 759
. debt canceled 855
. debt cancelled 785
. deferred compensation 723
. definition 701
. dividends received 733
. . declaration v. receipt 734
. estates . . . . . 520—527
. exclusions from . . . . . 801—896
. farming income 767
. frequent flyer miles 2059
. fringe benefits 713
. . partners 421
. . S corporation shareholders 322
. gifts v. 702
. government assistance payments 702
. housing assistance payments 702
. illegal transactions 785
. includible
. . checklist 55
. inclusions in 701
. interest received 724
. joint tenancy 709
. lessors
. . improvements by lessee 764
. . obligations paid by lessee 765
. life insurance, group-term 2055
. life insurance, split-term 2055
. nonresident alien 2429
. omission, more than 25% 2734
. options 1919
. pensions 718
. railroad retirement benefits 716
. rental income 762
. rewards 713
. royalties 763
. salaries 713
. salary continuation payments 719
. social security benefits 716
. stock options . . . . . 1919—1931
. strike and lockout benefits 702
. tenancy in common 709
. tips 717
. trusts 520
. unemployment compensation 722
. wages 713
. who must report 704

Ground rents
. redeemable
. . deductibility 1049

Group health plans
. coverage
. . requirements 2015

Group legal services plans
. cafeteria plans 2045

Group-term life insurance 2055
. cafeteria plans 2045
. withholding of tax 2609

Guam
. corporations
. . foreign corporation status 2431
. income earned in 2414
. self-employment tax 2667

Guaranteed payments to partners 421

Guarantors
. bad debt 1135

Guardians—see also Fiduciaries
. minor, incompetent, or disabled taxpayers, returns filed by guardians 504

Guardianship expenses
. deductibility 1091

Gulf Opportunity Zone
. section 179 expense allowance 1208

H

Handicapped individuals
. barrier removal costs 1287
. disabled access credit 1365M
. medical expenses 1016
. state payments for children 147

Handicapped person's employment-related expenses
. miscellaneous itemized deductions 1084

Hardship
. sale of residence 1709

Hardship distributions, 401(k) plans 2129

Head of household
. qualifications 173
. standard deduction 126
. status 173
. tax rate schedules 17

Health and accident plans
. Archer medical savings accounts (Archer MSAs) 2037
. benefits
. . application of annuity rules 2015
. . taxability 851; 2015
. cafeteria plans 2045
. COBRA continuation coverage 2021
. disability benefits 2015
. domestic partners 2077
. employer contributions 2013
. employer health insurance mandate 2001
. . applicable large employer 2001
. . full-time employees 2001
. . minimum essential coverage 2001
. . offer of coverage 2001
. . penalty for not offering coverage 2003
. . penalty when offering coverage 2005
. . reporting requirements 2567
. employer-provided coverage 2015
. flexible spending arrangements (FSAs) . . . 2041
. health reimbursement arrangements (HRAs) 2039
. health savings accounts (HSAs) 2035; 2037
. Indian health care benefits 2027
. Indian tribe members 2027
. long-term care insurance 2019
. medical loss ratio rebates 2031
. medical savings accounts (MSAs) 2037
. nondiscrimination requirements 2017
. partners 421
. payments, information returns 2565
. premiums
. . deductibility 1019
. premiums paid
. . S corporations 322
. retiree prescription drug plans 2029
. S corporations 322

Health insurance benefits
. exclusion from gross income . . . 851; 2015; 2045
. taxability 851; 2015

Health insurance costs credit
. advance payments
. . information returns 2565
. credits against tax 1332

Health insurance penalty
. individuals without insurance 131

Health insurance premium assistance credit
. advance payment 1331
. credits against taxes 1331

Health insurance premiums 908
. medical expense deductibility 1019
. S corporations 322
. self-employed persons 908

Health reimbursement arrangements (HRAs) 2039

Health savings accounts (HSAs) 2035; 2037
. deductibility 2035
. exclusion from gross income 2035

Hedging transactions
. capital assets 1741
. constructive sale 1945
. defined 1949
. short sales 1945
. tax treatment 1949

High-income taxpayers
. exemption phaseout repeal 133
. itemized deductions
. . phaseout 1014
. personal exemption reduction 133

Hobbies
. income from 785

Hobby losses
. deductibility 1195

Holding period
. capital assets 1735
. . determination 1737
. corporations
. . dividends received 733
. covered securities, information reporting . . 1980
. gift property 1737
. incentive stock options 1925
. inherited property 1737
. livestock 1750
. nontaxable stock distributions 1682
. partner, distributions to 1737
. partnership property distributions 456
. property acquired from decedent 1737
. property received in tax-free exchange . . . 1737
. Sec. 1250 property 1779
. specified securities, information reporting . . 1980
. stock
. . acquired as stock dividend 1737
. . dividends received deduction 223
. . information reporting 1980
. . settlement date 1737
. . trade date 1737
. Treasury notes or bonds 1737
. wash sales 1935

Holiday, deadline falling on 2549

Holocaust payment or restitution
. exclusion from gross income 889

Home construction contracts
. long-term contract method 1552

Home equity indebtedness
. defined 1048
. interest paid or accrued
. . dollar limitation 1048

Home improvements
. medical expenses 1016
. nonbusiness energy property credit 1341
. residential energy efficient property credit . . 1342
. sale of residence
. . basis 1626

Home mortgage interest—see also Qualified residence interest
. mortgage insurance premiums 1048A
. points paid to obtain 1055

Home mortgage interest credit
. credit against tax 1306

Home office expenses
. auction sellers 961
. business use of home 961
. consignment sellers 961
. day care services 964
. employees 965
. limitation on deduction 963
. optional safe harbor for deductibility 963
. principal place of business 961
. transportation expenses
. . deductibility 945

Home—see also Personal residence; Principal residence
. tax home defined
. . travel expenses 950

Home workers
. business expenses of 941B

Homebuyer credits
. first-time
. . recapture 1324

Homeowner credits
. mortgage interest certificates 1306
. nonbusiness energy property 1341
. residential energy efficient property 1342

Homeowners associations
. exempt status 699

Hope scholarship tax credit
. credit against tax 1303

Horticultural organizations
. exempt organizations 692

Hospitalization premiums and benefits
. deductibility 1019

Hospitals
. charitable hospitals 602

Hospitals, exempt status
. service organizations 699
. unrelated business income 667

Hostages in combat zone, administrative relief 2708

Household employment
. FUTA taxes 2649
. nanny tax 2652
. withholding of tax 2609

Household items
. charitable contributions 1061

Housing allowance
. minister of the gospel 875

Housing assistance payments
. gross income 702

Housing expenses, working abroad 2403

Hunting lodge expenses
. deductible entertainment expense 913

Hybrid accounting methods 1515

Hybrid retirement plans 2108
. cash balance plans 2108
. floor offset plans 2108
. pension equity plans 2108
. target benefit plans 2108

I

Illegal payments
. controlled foreign corporation (CFC) 2497
. domestic international sales corporation (DISC) 2497
. foreign government officials 972
. illegal transactions, income from 785

Improvements to property
. ACRS, use of 1267
. additions to basis 1611
. capital expenditures 903
. cost recovery on 1234
. lessee improvements 764
. materials and supplies 903
. repair regulations 903
. repairs 903

Imputed interest
. applicable federal rates (AFRs) 1875
. application of Code Sec. 483 1868
. assumptions of debt 1881
. below-market loans 795
. bond interest 727
. deferred payment sales . . . . . 1859—1881
. reporting 1883
. testing for inadequate interest 1872

Incentive stock options (ISOs)
. alternative minimum tax 1435; 1925
. basis 1925
. plan requirements 1927
. tax treatment 1925

Incidental expenses
. deduction only
. . optional method 954B

Inclusion amount
. automobiles 1215

Income
. defined
. . trusts and estates 514

Income averaging
. farmers 767

Income distributable to grantor 584

Income forecast method 1229

Income in respect of decedent 182; 189
. beneficiaries 189
. deduction for estate tax 191
. installment obligations 184
. partner 440

Income items, checklist 55

Income—see also Gross income
. allocation by IRS 1573
. checklist of includible items 55
. claim of right 713
. collection doubtful 1538
. conversion transaction, capital gains 1740
. damages for personal injuries 852
. defined . . . . . 701—702
. frequent flyer miles 2059
. gift property 1788
. ownership of . . . . . 704—711
. reconstruction by IRS 1577
. recoveries 799
. repayment of items previously included . . . 1543
. U.S. possession 2414
. U.S.-source, effectively connected 2429
. vacation pay 713
. worldwide, taxation of 2401

Income tax
. federal 924
. state 924

Indefinite v. temporary travel
. test 951

Independent contractors
. employees distinguished 2602
. misclassification 2602
. self-employment tax . . . . . 2664—2670

Independent producers of oil and gas 1294

Indian employment credit
. credit against tax 1365Q

Indians
. health care benefits 2027
. reservation property, depreciation of 1240

Individual health insurance mandate
. minimum essential coverage 131
. shared responsibility payment 131

Individual retirement accounts (IRAs)
. contributions
. . credit against tax 1304
. . deductibility 2157
. . married filing jointly 2158
. . maximum allowable deduction 2159
. . nondeductible 2160
. . return of, inclusion in income 2165
. deductions 2155
. distributions
. . charitable 2165
. . charitable contributions 1058
. . early 2169; 2169
. . requirements, minimum 2163
. . taxation 2165
. early distributions
. . penalty 2169
. . permissible 2169
. eligibility 2155
. excess contributions
. . penalty 2161
. generally 2106
. HSA funding
. . limitations 2165
. investments, allowable 2155
. Roth IRAs 2171
. . conversions 2175
. . deemed 2171
. . distributions, nonqualified 2173
. . distributions, qualified 2173
. . income limits 2171
. . losses 2171
. . recharacterizations 2177
. . reconversions 2179
. . rollovers 2175
. SARSEPs 2189
. SEPs 2189
. SIMPLE IRAs 2181
. . contributions, salary reduction 2181
. . eligible employees 2187
. . eligible employers 2187
. withholding of tax on wages to be contributed 2609

Individuals
. accounting period, change of 1513
. bankrupt 505
. capital loss carryover 1754
. capital loss limitation 1752
. carryback, refunds 2773
. computation of tax . . . . . 105; 123—128
. health insurance penalty
. . individuals without insurance 131
. itemized deductions 126; 1014
. loss from sale or exchange of property . . . 1007
. net investment income tax 129
. net operating losses (NOL) 1147
. protest returns 2521

Individuals—continued
. rate schedules, computation . . . . . 11—17
. tax rate schedules . . . . . 11—17; 128
. tax rate tables 128
. tax tables 25
. trade and business expenses 1006

Information bases, amortization 1288

Information from foreign sources 2499

Information returns 1980; 2565
. basis, stock and securities 1980
. brokers 1980; 2565
. corporations, payments to 2565
. covered securities 1980
. dissolution of corporation 211
. estates 510
. exempt organizations
. . acquisition of life insurance contracts . . . 2565
. . dispositions of donated property 2565
. . failure to file 625
. . lobbying expenditures 625
. . qualified intellectual property 2565
. failure to file correct 2816
. Filing Information Returns Electronically (FIRE) system 2565
. foreign bank account interest 2570
. foreign partnerships 2494
. grantor trusts, foreign 588
. guide to 64
. health care coverage, minimal essential . . . 2567
. health insurance coverage, employer-sponsored 2567
. holding period, stock and securities 1980
. interest payments 2565
. . foreign bank accounts 2570
. life insurance contracts
. . combined arrangements 2565
. . employer-owned 2565
. . exempt organizations 2565
. liquidating corporation 211
. magnetic tape 2565
. mortgage interest 2833
. nonemployee payments 2565
. partnership 406
. patronage dividends 2565
. payment card transactions 2565
. penalties relating to . . . . . 2814—2833
. . amounts 2816
. . de minimis exception 2816
. . intentional disregard 2816
. . payee statements, failure to furnish correct 2823
. private foundations 625
. rental real estate 2565
. specified securities 1980
. stock and securities, basis and holding period 1980
. third-party network transactions 2565
. tips 2605
. trusts 510
. trusts, charitable contributions 537
. who must file 2565

Inherited IRAs
. traditional 2163

Injunctions
. tax shelter promoters 2598
. to restrain collection 2719

Injured spouse claims
. requirements 163

Injury, damages
. personal injury damages 702; 852
. taxability 851
. withholding of tax 2609

Innocent spouse relief 711
. community property states 711
. election 162
. partnership administrative proceedings 415

Inspection of returns, unauthorized
. penalties 2893

Installment agreements 2529

Installment obligations
. decedent, acquired from 184
. liquidations 1856
. S corporation liquidations 1858

Installment option
. annuities and annuity contracts 843

Installment payment of estate tax
. farm or closely held business 2939

Installment sales
. bad debt 1838
. computation of income . . . . . 1813—1825
. contingent payment sales 1821
. contingent payments 1774
. contract price
. . indebtedness, qualifying 1815; 1813
. dealers 1808
. depreciable property
. . recapture 1779
. depreciation
. . recapture 1779; 1823
. disposition of installment obligations 1846
. earnings and profits, effect on 756
. election out of installment method 1803
. gain or loss 1701
. gains, reporting of 1801
. gross profit ratio 1813
. interest charge rule 1825
. liquidations 1856
. mortgages 1815
. passive activity losses 1177
. payments received 1819
. personal property
. . dealer dispositions 1808
. publicly traded property 1805
. recapture
. . depreciation 1779; 1823
. related party, sales to 1833; 1835
. repossession 1838
. . principal residence 1841
. . real estate 1841; 1843
. revolving credit plans 1805
. S corporations
. . built-in gains 337
. Sec. 1245 property 1823
. Sec. 1250 property 1823
. self-cancelling installment note 1846
. selling price 1813
. use of installment method 1801
. wrap-around mortgage 1815

Insurance
. casualty insurance
. . living expenses reimbursed 877
. casualty insurance premiums
. . deductibility 968
. deductibility of premiums 909; 968; 1019
. fire insurance premiums
. . deductibility 968
. future remediation costs, reimbursement . . . 968
. long-term care insurance
. . accident and health plan 2019
. long-term care insurance premiums
. . deductibility 1016
. long-term care premium
. . deductibility 1019
. mortgage insurance premiums 1048A

Insurance—continued
. payment of premiums
. . partnership 421
. . S corporation 322

Insurance companies
. demutualization 1701

Insurance companies—see also Life insurance companies . . . . . 2370—2380
. consolidated returns 295
. demutualization 1701
. exempt status 692
. foreign insurance companies 2380
. net operating losses 1145
. rates of tax 36
. taxation of 2378

Intangible assets (Sec. 197 intangibles), amortization of 1288

Intangible drilling and development costs (IDCs)
. alternative minimum tax
. . tax preference item 1425
. deductibility 989

Intellectual property
. charitable contribution
. . deductibility 1062A
. charitable contributions 627

Interest capitalization rules 993

Interest on deficiencies . . . . . 2838—2845
. abatement of interest 2838
. assessment and collection 2735
. compromise agreements 2723
. deductibility 937A; 1043
. estimated tax 241
. . avoidance of penalty 2875
. . corporations 2890
. . individuals 2875
. interest rate 2838
. large corporate underpayments 2838
. penalties, interest on 2845
. suspension of interest 2838
. Tax Court jurisdiction 2761

Interest on overpayments of tax
. refunds 2765

Interest paid or accrued
. accrual basis of accounting 1043
. acquisition indebtedness 1048
. annuity contract 909
. automobile loans 948
. backup withholding 2645
. business or investment expense 937
. capitalization rules
. . inventories 1561
. cash basis of accounting 1043
. construction period interest and taxes
. . deductibility 1028
. consumer debt 1043
. cooperative housing 1040
. corporate acquisition indebtedness 937
. decedents 187
. deductibility 1043
. . exceptions and limitations 1043
. . qualified residence interest 1047; 1048
. earnings stripping 937
. education loans
. . deductibility 1011
. estates, deductibility by 533
. exempt obligations 970
. home equity indebtedness 1048
. information returns 2565
. installment sales 1825
. insurance contract purchased 909
. investment expense
. . trade or business 937

Interest paid or accrued—continued
. investment interest expense 1094
. liability for charitable contribution 1065
. loans on life insurance policies 909
. mortgage credit certificates 1306
. mortgage insurance premiums 1048A
. mortgage interest 1047; 1048
. . clergy 1050
. . military personnel 1050
. penalties 2845
. personal interest 1043
. points 1055
. prepaid interest
. . cash-basis taxpayers 1055
. redeemable ground rents 1049
. related taxpayers 905; 1043; 1540B
. stripped bonds 1952
. taxes
. . interest on 937A
. trusts, deductibility by 533
. uniform capitalization rules 993
. unwithdrawn deposit
. . bankruptcy or insolvency of institution . . . 1533
. unwithdrawn insurance dividend 1533
. VA/FHA loan origination fees 1055
. withholding of tax at source 2645

Interest rates
. deficiency in tax 2838
. large corporate underpayments 2838
. overpayments 2765
. refunds 2765

Interest received
. creditors 793
. deferred payment, unstated interest . 1859—1881
. exempt 724
. exempt organization 673
. foreign bank accounts, information returns . 2570
. foreign tax credit 2481
. imputed interest 727
. investment interest 1736
. life insurance premiums prepaid 724
. limitation 1094
. mortgage interest 726
. nonresident aliens 2431
. original issue discount—see Original issue discount 2431
. personal holding company income 281
. . adjusted ordinary gross income 283
. premature withdrawals, interest forfeited
. . deductibility 1111
. seller-provided financing 726
. six-month certificates 724
. source of income 2427
. state or municipal bonds 724
. "thank you" points, redemption of 724
. U.S. obligations 731
. U.S. savings bonds 730
. unpaid bequests
. . taxability 847

Internal Revenue Service
. accounting methods prescribed 1525
. acquiescences and nonacquiescences . . . 2788
. allocation of income and deductions 1573
. appeals procedure 2705
. change of accounting method, approval . . . 1529
. Chief Counsel 2703
. compromise of tax or penalty 2723
. damage suits by taxpayers 2798
. examination of returns 2708
. incorrect advice, abatement of penalties . . 2813
. interviews with taxpayers 2708
. organization and functions 2701
. tax liability
. . computation 105

Internal Revenue Service—continued
. written statement of taxpayer rights 2708

International boycott
. participation 2496

International organization employees, withholding of tax 2609

Interns
. stipends
. . exempt income 865

Inventories
. accrual basis of accounting 1553
. change in basis of 1571
. charitable contributions
. . corporations 930
. cost
. . uniform capitalization rules 1561
. cost method 1559; 1561
. dealers in securities 1903
. farmers 767; 1569
. first-in, first-out rule 1564
. gross receipts test 1553
. identification of goods 1557
. interest capitalization rules 1561
. items included in 1557
. last-in, first-out rule 1565
. . dollar-value method 1567
. lower of cost or market method 1559; 1563
. need for 1553
. noncapital assets 1741
. partnership, appreciated 436
. retail method 1563
. rolling-average method 1559
. uniform capitalization rules 995; 1561
. unit-livestock-price method 1569
. valuation of 1559

Inventors, long-term capital gains 1767

Inversion transactions 2452

Investment companies
. regulated investment companies . . . 2301—2323

Investment expenses
. deductibility 1085; 1086
. interest paid
. . deductibility 1094

Investment in the contract
. annuities and annuity contracts 821
. foreign sourced contributions 821

Investment income
. child's 128
. exempt organizations 673
. private foundations 633
. net investment income tax 129

Investment tax credit
. components
. . advanced energy project credit 1365F
. . energy investment credit 1365C
. . qualified advanced coal project 1365D
. . qualified gasification project 1365E
. . rehabilitation investment credit 1365B
. credit against tax 1365A

Investment trusts 502

Investors
. capital gains and losses 1760
. dealers v. 1903
. expenses 1086
. investment interest
. . limitation 1094
. transactions by . . . . . 1901—1983

Involuntary conversions of property
. basis 1687
. capital gain or loss 1748

Involuntary conversions of property—continued
. casualty losses 1748
. condemnation awards 1715; 1716
. depreciation 1250
. disaster losses 1715
. federally declared disasters 1715
. gain or loss 1713; 1715
. . holding period 1737
. . netting requirement 1748
. livestock 1713; 1750
. nonrecognition of gain 1713
. outdoor advertising display 1715
. replacement of converted property 1715
. . replacement property acquired from related party 1715
. replacement period 1715
. replacement property 1687
. reporting requirements 1713
. residential property 1713; 1715
. . treatment as sale or exchange 1705
. Sec. 1231 property 1748
. Sec. 1245 property 1790
. Sec. 1250 property 1790
. severance damages 1716
. theft losses 1748

Iron ore royalties 1289; 1772

Itemized deductions 126
. alternative minimum tax 1435
. average amount claimed, table 88
. casualty and theft losses 1121
. charitable contributions . . . . . 1058—1071
. . limitations 1059
. education and related expenses 1082
. guardianship expenses 1091
. handicapped person's employment-related expenses 1084
. interest . . . . . 1043—1056
. investor's expenses 1086
. job hunting expenses 1081
. legal expenses 1093
. medical expenses . . . . . 1015—1019
. miscellaneous itemized deductions 1079
. mortgage insurance premiums 1048A
. mortgage interest 1047; 1048
. phaseout threshold 1014
. production or collection of income expenses 1085
. qualified residence interest 1047; 1048
. recoveries 799
. rent or royalty property 1006A
. taxes . . . . . 1021—1040
. . convenience fee for electronic payment . . 1092
. . expenses for determination 1092
. two-percent floor
. . estates and trusts 528
. two-percent-of-adjusted-gross-income floor 1079
. . not subject to limitation 1079
. uniforms and special clothing 1083
. union dues 1080

J

Jeopardizing investments
. exempt organizations 642

Jeopardy and termination assessments . . . 2713
. Tax Court jurisdiction over jeopardy assessments 2778

Jeopardy levies, Tax Court jurisdiction . . . 2778

Job-hunting expenses
. deductibility 1081

Joint and survivor annuities
. qualified plans 2130

Joint and survivor annuities—continued
. surviving spouse 827
. table, use of 827

Joint returns
. accounting periods and methods 152
. advantages of filing 156
. capital gains and losses 1757
. charitable contributions 1058
. citizen with nonresident alien spouse . . 711; 2410
. civil unions 152
. community property income 711
. death of one spouse 164
. . surviving spouse remarried 166
. decedent's return 168; 178
. dependency exemptions 141
. disadvantages of filing 156
. election to file 154
. exemption amount 133
. injured spouse claims 163
. innocent spouse relief 162
. itemized deductions
. . phaseout threshold 1014
. liability for tax 162
. . injured spouse claims 163
. . innocent spouse relief 162
. marriage penalty relief 156
. medical expenses 1015
. nonresident aliens 152; 2410
. personal exemptions 141
. qualifying widow(er) 175
. registered domestic partners 152
. rental real estate, passive activity losses . . 1185
. resident aliens 2410
. resident with nonresident alien spouse . . . 2410
. same-sex married couples (SSMCs) 152
. separate returns after filing joint return 154
. separate v. 156
. separated spouses 152
. signatures 2504
. splitting of income 156
. spouses of military personnel
. . missing in action 152
. standard deduction 126
. surviving spouse . . . . . 164—168; 175
. tax rate schedules 13
. who may file 152

Joint tenancy
. basis 1634
. gross estate 2919
. income 709
. qualified joint interests 1634

Joint ventures, partnerships 401

Jurisdiction
. Claims Court 2790
. Courts of Appeals, U.S. 2786
. District Court 2790
. Supreme Court 2794
. Tax Court 2778

Jury duty pay 941
. adjustment to gross income 1010
. income from 785

K

Key employees, retirement plans
. defined contribution plans 2132

Kickbacks 972; 2497

Kiddie tax 103; 706
. alternative minimum tax 1401
. alternative minimum tax exemption amount . 1410
. election to pay on parent's return 103
. family trusts 571

Kiddie tax—continued
. Form 8615 128
. standard deduction 126

Kidnapped or missing children
. dependency exception 150

Know-how, amortization 1288

L

Labor organizations
. exempt organizations 692

Land-clearing expenses
. farmers 983
. recapture 1797

Land improvements 1240

Land sold with growing crop 1747

Last-in, first-out rule 1565

Leasehold improvement property 1234

Leases—see also Lessors and lessees
. acquisition costs 1234
. cancellation 1751
. depreciation and cost recovery 1234
. disposition of 1779
. motor vehicle leases, depreciation 1235
. . luxury automobile leases 1215
. sale and leaseback
. . exempt organization 687
. sale v. 1235
. tax-exempt use property 1191

Leave-based donation programs
. employee's tax consequences 1061
. employer's deduction 1061

Leave sharing 2073

Legal expenses 973
. deductibility 1093

Legislators, travel expenses
. Congress members
. . tax home 950
. state legislators 956

Lessors and lessees
. capital expenses 1234
. conditional sales contracts 986
. depletion 1289
. depreciation and cost recovery 1234
. lessee paying expenses 762; 765; 986
. lessee's improvements
. . depreciation 1234
. . taxability 764
. lessor's obligations paid by lessee 765
. listed property 1215
. luxury automobiles 1215

Levy for taxes
. notice and opportunity for hearing 2754A
. property exempt from 2753
. property subject to 2753
. release of 2755

Liability for tax
. banks 2383
. beneficiary of estate or trust 554; 556
. child or dependent 103
. fiduciaries 512
. joint returns 162
. ownership of income 704
. transferees 2743

Licenses, amortization 1288

Lien for taxes
. notice and opportunity for hearing 2754A
. notice of 2754
. property subject to 2751

Lien for taxes—continued
. recording and priority of 2754
. release of 2755
. third-party owners 2755

Life estates
. power of appointment 2908; 2926

Life insurance
. accelerated death benefits 803
. company-owned life insurance policies (COLIs) 804
. contract defined 803
. deposit for future premiums 909
. disability benefits 851
. dividends on unmatured policies 809
. dividends paid to military personnel taxability 891
. exchange of contract 1724
. gross estate 2915
. group-term 2055
. indebtedness to purchase 909
. interest
. . prepaid premium 724
. interest on policy loans 909
. key employee
. . excluded from gross estate 2915
. policy transferred as gift 807
. policy transferred in tax-free transaction 807
. premiums paid
. . deductibility 909
. salesperson, full-time
. . expenses of 941B
. split-dollar
. . employee's gross estate 2915
. . premiums paid by employer 2055
. transfer for value 807; 845
. welfare benefits 2011

Life insurance companies
. affiliated groups
. . dividends received 229
. foreign companies 2380
. . effectively connected income 2380
. increase in reserves 2372
. operations loss deduction 2377
. policyholder dividends 2373
. qualifying as 2370
. small life insurance companies 2370
. taxation of 2370

Life insurance proceeds
. discharge of annuity obligations 841
. exclusion from gross income 803
. installment options 805
. interest paid on 805

Life insurance trusts
. grantor as beneficiary, taxability 584

Life tenant and remainderman deductions . 1090

Lifetime learning tax credit
. credit against tax 1303

LIFO inventories 1565
. dollar-value
. . simplified method 1567
. reserve changes
. . effect on earnings and profits 757
. S corporations 339

Like-kind exchanges . . . . . 1721—1725
. cash and other property (boot) 1723
. contracts, exchange of 1724
. deferred
. . identification 1722
. . safe harbors 1722
. depreciation 1250
. direct deeding of property 1722

Like-kind exchanges—continued
. installment sales 1819
. like-kind property 1721
. mortgaged real estate 1725
. parking transactions 1722
. qualified intermediary, use of 1722
. residential property
. . treatment of gain on sale 1705
. reverse-Starker exchange 1722
. Sec. 1245 property 1790
. Sec. 1250 property 1790
. Starker exchange 1722

Limited liability companies (LLC)
. check-the-box regulations 402A
. conversions from corporation to LLC 402B
. conversions from partnership to limited liability company 402B
. conversions from S corporation to LLC . . . 402B
. corporations v. 201
. S corporation stock ownership 304
. series LLCs 402B

Limited partnership
. definition 401A

Liquidating distributions, partnerships
. retiring or deceased partner 438; 456

Liquidating trusts 503

Liquidations of corporations
. asset acquisitions 2265
. basis of property received
. . subsidiary liquidated 2261
. complete liquidations 2253
. distributions . . . . . 2253—2265
. . capital gain or loss 1742
. . information returns 211; 2565
. dividend equivalence 2253
. elections
. . Code Sec. 336(e) election 2263
. . subsidiaries 2263
. foreign corporation 2492
. gain or loss 2253
. . recognition of 2257
. liquidating corporation
. . reporting requirements 2259
. loss limitation rules 2257
. partial liquidation, distributions 2253
. reorganization, part of 2241
. reporting requirements 2259
. . significant shareholder 2259
. shareholders
. . corporate 2253
. . installment method 1856
. . minority shareholders 2261
. . noncorporate 2253
. . reporting requirements 2259
. subsidiaries
. . elections 2263
. . reporting requirements 2261
. subsidiary 2261
. . gain or loss 2261
. . installment obligations, distribution 1856
. tax-avoidance purpose 2257

Listed property
. automobiles 1211; 1214
. business use test 1211
. depreciation 1211
. leased property restrictions 1215
. substantiation
. . employees 943

Literary organizations
. exempt status 602

Litigation
. costs, award of 2796

Livestock
. depreciation recapture 1785
. involuntary conversion 1713; 1750
. sales 767; 1750

Livestock sales
. Form 4797 767

Loans
. automobile loan interest
. . deductibility 948
. below-market interest loans 795
. commissions on 793
. guaranty of, bad debt deduction 1135
. home equity indebtedness 1048
. interest-free 795

Lobbying expenses
. deductibility 974; 1061
. private foundations 644
. public charities 613
. reporting requirements for exempt organizations 625

Long-term capital gain or loss . . 1735; 1736; 1737

Long-term care
. insurance premiums
. . deductibility 1016; 1019

Long-term contracts
. accounting methods 1551
. . exempt methods 1552
. alternative minimum tax 1430
. cost allocation and capitalization 1551
. look back rule 1551
. pass-through entities 1551

Look-through rules
. exempt organizations
. . unrelated business income 673

Losses
. distributions by corporation
. . earnings and profits affected 750

Losses, deductibility . . . . . 1101—1195; 1155
. abandonment loss 1109
. alternative minimum tax 1460
. amount of loss 1101
. at-risk limitation 1155
. . partners 426
. bank deposits 1125
. bonds, worthlessness 1916
. casualty loss 1127
. character of loss 1101
. contested liability 1540A
. creative property 1109
. demolition losses 1105
. disaster 1133
. embezzlement 1123
. estates and trusts 531
. farmers 767
. foreclosure losses 1107
. foreign losses 2483
. gambling 1113
. hobby 1195
. limitation
. . alternative minimum tax 1460
. . farming 982
. obsolescence loss 1109
. partial losses 1101
. partner's loss, limited to basis 425
. partnership losses, limitations . . . . . 425—427A
. partnerships, allocation 410; 428
. personal loss limitation 1101
. personal residence 1741
. Ponzi schemes 1123
. premature withdrawals, interest forfeited . . 1111
. principal residence, sale of 1103
. related taxpayers 905; 1717

Losses, deductibility—continued
. Roth IRAs 2171
. sales or exchanges 1007
. Sec. 1231 losses, recapture 1747
. Sec. 1244 stock 1911
. small business investment company shareholders 1913
. specified liability losses 1151
. stock, surrender of 1916
. stock, worthlessness 1916
. tax-exempt use property 1191
. tax sales 1107
. theft 1123
. theft loss 1127
. trade or business 1101
. traditional IRAs 2165
. voluntary removal of buildings 1105
. wash sales 1935
. year deductible 1101

Lottery
. income from 785

Low-cost articles
. exempt organizations
. . unrelated business income 667

Low-income housing
. ACRS 1261
. applicable credit percentages, table 86
. credit against tax 1365K
. depreciation 1261

Low sulfur diesel fuel production credit
. credit against tax 1365Y

Lump-sum distributions
. taxable portion 2143

Luxury automobiles
. depreciation 1211; 1214
. . leased property restrictions 1215

Luxury water travel
. business expenses
. . deductibility 957

M

MACRS bonus depreciation
. alternative minimum tax 1237
. computation 1237
. election out 1237
. qualifying property 1237

Magazines
. circulation expenditures 971
. vendors
. . self-employment tax 2670
. . withholding 2609

Mailbox rule 2553

Mailing addresses for returns 5

Manufacturer's deduction
. computer software costs 980
. domestic production activities 980A
. . partnerships 431A
. . s corporations 312
. ordinary and necessary 978
. research costs 979

Margin trading accounts
. interest paid 937

Marginal properties
. percentage depletion 1294

Marital status
. determination 152

Mark-to-market rules
. expatriation 2412
. section 1256 contracts 1947

Mark-to-market rules—continued
. securities dealers 221; 1903
. securities traders 1903
. U.S. shareholders of CFCs 2490

Market discount bonds 1958

Market research costs
. deductibility 979

Marriage counseling fees
. medical expenses 1016

Marriage penalty relief
. joint returns 156

Married dependents
. dependency exemption 138

Married individuals
. capital gains and losses 1757
. different accounting method and periods . . . 152
. estate and gift taxes
. . jointly held property 2919
. . marital deduction 2926
. filing status 152
. foreign spouse, community income 2438
. general business credit
. . joint v. filing separately 1365
. injured spouse claim 163
. IRAs
. . AGI limits 2158
. . spouse with no compensation 2158
. jointly held property 2919
. net operating losses 1149
. S corporation shareholders 303
. sale of residence 1705
. standard deduction 126
. tax rate schedules
. . filing jointly 13
. . filing separately 15
. transfers of property between 1693; 1734
. travel expenses 952

Matching contributions, retirement plans
. 401(k) plans 2121

Material advisors
. disclosure 2593
. list maintenance requirement 2595
. penalties 2595

Material participation
. passive activities 1165
. rental real estate, passive activity losses . . 1185

Materials and supplies 903

Meals and incidental expenses (M&IE)
. leased employees 916
. per diem allowances . . . . . 954—954B

Meals and lodging
. business meals
. . entertainment 914
. . entertainment and gift expenses 910; 916
. . percentage limit on deduction 916
. employer-provided 2089
. . camps in foreign country 2406
. foreign camp, employer-provided 2406
. foreign travel expenses 955
. medical expenses 1016
. per diem allowances . . . . . 954—954B
. substantiation requirements . . . . . 953—954B
. support of dependent 147
. transportation industry employees 916
. travel expenses . . . . . 949—960
. . charitable services 1061
. . substantiation . . . . . 953—954B

Medical expenses
. Archer medical savings accounts (Archer MSAs) 2037

Medical expenses—continued
. decedents 1018
. deductibility 1015
. deductible expenditures 1016
. deduction
. . checklist 59
. gift tax exclusion 2907
. health savings accounts (HSAs) 2035
. insurance premiums 1019
. Medicare Advantage medical savings accounts 2037
. medicine and drugs 1017
. withholding of tax 2609

Medical loss ratio rebates 889; 2031

Medical savings accounts (MSAs) 2035
. Archer MSAs 2037
. health and accident plans 2037

Medicare Advantage MSAs
. deductibility 2037

Medicare hospital insurance
. FICA taxes 2648
. self-employment tax 2664

Medicare premiums paid 49
. deductibility 1019

Medicine
. deductibility 1017

Membership organizations
. exempt organizations 673

Merchant Marine capital construction funds
. alternative minimum tax 1440

Merchants' expenses . . . . . 978—980
. computer software costs 980
. research costs 979

Mergers
. carryovers/carryforwards and carrybacks, net operating losses 1153
. reorganizations 2209

Midwestern disaster area
. charitable contributions
. . travel expenses 1061

Military personnel
. allowances, housing and cost-of-living 893
. annuities 891
. base realignment and closure fringe benefits 2095
. benefits 891
. . qualified plans 2125
. combat zone
. . compensation 895
. . examination and collection relief 2708
. . withholding of tax 2609
. death benefit, Roth IRAs 2171
. death in combat zone 2533
. disability benefit payments 851
. dividends paid on insurance contracts 891
. employer credit 1365II
. extension of time for payment of tax 2537
. missing in action
. . filing of joint returns 152; 175
. mortgage interest 1050
. moving expenses 1073; 1075
. pensions 891
. real property taxes
. . deductibility 1028
. reservist distributions
. . IRA contributions, nondeductible 2160
. retirement pay 891
. serving in a combat zone
. . filing of joint return 152
. subsistence allowances 893
. veterans' organizations, exempt status 692

Military personnel—continued
. withholding of tax 2609
Mine rescue team training credit
. credit against tax 1365GG
Mineral property—see also Mines and mining
. depletion 1289; 1298
. percentage depletion 1298
. personal holding company income 281
. . adjusted ordinary gross income 283
. royalty income 763
. sale, production payment retained 1291
Mines and mining—see also Mineral property
. exploration and development expenditures . . 987; 988
. . alternative minimum tax 1430
. . foreign 988A
. mine safety equipment expense 989A
. operating expenditures 988
. production payments 1291
Minimum distributions
. IRAs 2163
. qualified plans 2127
Minimum essential coverage
. individuals without insurance
. . penalty 131
Minors—see also Children
. gift tax annual exclusion 2905
. returns of 101
. . agent filing return 504
Miscellaneous and other income
. gross income 785
Miscellaneous income
. types 785
Miscellaneous itemized deductions
. employment agency fees 1081
. handicapped person's employment-related expenses 1084
. investor's expenses 1086
. job-hunting expenses 1081
. legal expenses 1093
. production or collection of income expenses 1085
. taxes
. . convenience fee for electronic payment . . 1092
. . expenses for determination 1092
. two-percent floor
. . entertainment expenses, employees 910
. . estates and trusts 528
. two-percent-of-adjusted-gross-income floor 1079
. . not subject to limitation 1079
. uniforms and work clothes 1083
. union dues 1080
Missing in action
. military personnel
. . filing of joint returns 152; 175
Mitigation of effect of statute of limitations . 2756
Modified Accelerated Cost Recovery System—see also Depreciation and Accelerated Cost Recovery System (ACRS), pre-1987 rules 1236
. additions and improvements 1240
. alternative depreciation system (ADS) 1247
. alternative MACRS method 1247
. automobiles 1211
. averaging conventions 1245
. . half-year 1245
. . mid-month 1245
. . mid-quarter 1245
. . short tax years 1244
Modified Accelerated Cost Recovery System—see also Depreciation and Accelerated Cost Recovery System (ACRS), pre-1987 rules—continued
. biofuel plant property 1237
. bonus depreciation 1237
. computation
. . table percentages 1243
. . with tables 1243
. . without tables 1243
. cost segregation 1240
. depreciable property
. . classes of 1240
. . improvements by lessee 1234
. . recapture 1779; 1780
. . sale of purchase during taxable year 1252
. depreciation periods 1240
. depreciation tables 1243
. disaster assistance property 1237
. disposition of property 1249
. elections
. . alternative depreciation system (ADS) . . . 1243; 1247
. . straight-line 1243
. expensing election 1208
. farm machinery 1240
. farm property 1243
. fifteen-year property 1240
. five-year property 1240
. general asset accounts 1239
. horses 1240
. improvements by lessor 1234
. income forecast method 1229
. Indian reservation property 1240
. involuntary conversions 1250
. item accounts 1239
. land improvements 1240
. leasehold improvement property 1234
. like-kind exchanges 1250
. mine safety equipment 1237
. multiple asset accounts 1239
. nonresidential real property 1240
. 150 percent declining balance 1243
. partial disposition election 1239
. property subject to 1238
. public utility property 1238
. recovery methods 1243
. residential rental property 1240
. restaurant improvements 1240
. retail improvement property 1240
. reuse and recycling property 1237
. roof 903; 1239; 1240
. seven-year property 1240
. short tax years 1244
. specific recovery periods for various types of property 1240
. sport utility vehicles 1214
. structural components 1239
. tables of depreciation percentages 1243
. tax-free transfers 1248
. ten-year property 1240
. three-year property 1240
Money purchase plans 2102
Mortgage credit certificates
. credit against tax 1306
Mortgages
. exchange of mortgaged real estate 1725
. foreclosure
. . bad debt deduction 1139
. interest paid—see also Qualified residence interest 1047; 1048; 1306
. . clergy 1050
. . military personnel 1050

Mortgages—continued
. mortgage insurance premiums 1048A
. penalty for prepayment 1055
. points paid to obtain
. . deductibility 1055
. redeemable ground rents 1049
. taxable mortgage pool (TMP) 2368
. wrap-around
. . installment sale 1815

Motion pictures
. at-risk loss limitations 1159
. creative property costs 1229
. expensing film costs 1229
. income forecast method 1229

Motor vehicle leases, depreciation 1235
. luxury automobile leases 1215

Moving expenses
. commencement of work test 1075
. deduction from gross income . . . . . 1073—1078
. distance test 1075
. exclusion from gross income 2092
. foreign moves 1073
. length of employment test 1075
. military personnel 1073; 1075
. reimbursements 1073; 2092
. . withholding on 2609
. self-employed individuals
. . deductibility 1073

Multiple support agreement
. dependent 147

Municipal and state bonds
. private activity bonds 729

Musical compositions and copyrights
. capital asset treatment, election 1741
. UNICAP rules 990A

Mutual insurance companies
. consolidated returns 295
. taxation of 2378

Mutual savings banks 2383
. exempt status 692

N

Nanny tax 2652

Native Americans
. employment credit 1365Q
. health care benefits
. . exclusion from gross income 889; 2015
. litigation settlement
. . exclusion from gross income 889

Negligence penalty 2856

Negligent inspection of returns, penalties . . 2893

Net earnings from self-employment 2670

Net investment income
. exempt organizations 633

Net investment income tax
. distributable net income, beneficiary's share of 554; 556
. estates 517
. individuals 129
. passive activities 1175
. S corporation shareholders 314
. trusts 517
. . grantor trusts 571

Net operating losses (NOL) . . . . . 1145—1153
. alternative minimum tax 1430
. beneficiaries 1153
. carryback . . . . . 1145—1153
. carryforwards 1145

Net operating losses (NOL)—continued
. carryover . . . . . 1145—1153
. . allocation 2281
. . closing-of-the-books election 2281
. . estates and trusts 531
. . federal long-term tax-exempt rates, table . . . 85
. . successor corporation 2277; 2281
. . tax avoidance purpose 2281
. carryover and carryback 1149
. carryover/carryforward 1151
. corporations 1147
. deduction 1145
. definition 1147
. election to forego carryback 1149
. estates and trusts, beneficiary's refund claim 556
. farmers 1151
. individuals 1147
. insurance companies 1145
. married individuals 1149
. noncorporate taxpayers 1147
. partners 427A
. predecessor corporation 1153
. real estate investment trusts 2329
. refund claims 1145
. regulated investment company 1145
. short tax years 1151
. specified liability losses, carrybacks 1151
. successor corporation 1153

Net worth method
. reconstruction of income 1577

Netting procedures
. capital gains and losses 1739

New clean renewable energy bonds
. credit against tax (NCREBs) 1374

New market credit
. credit against tax 1365T

Newspapers
. circulation expenditures 971
. prepaid subscriptions 1537
. vendors
. . self-employment tax 2670
. withholding of tax 2609

No-additional cost services 2087

No-fault insurance
. disability benefits 851

Non-Financial Foreign Entities (NFFEs)
. FATCA reporting requirements 2473

Nonaccrual experience method of accounting 1538

Nonbusiness bad debts 1135; 1143
. bank deposits 1125

Nonbusiness expenses
. guardianship expenses 1091
. income beneficiaries 1090
. investment interest limitation 1094
. investors 1086
. legal expenses 1093
. life tenants 1090
. penalty mortgage prepayment 1055
. production or collection of income 1085
. rental or royalty property 1006A
. short sales, expenses of 1946
. taxes
. . expenses of contesting 1092

Noncapital assets 1741

Nonconventional source fuels credit
. credits against tax 1365BB

Noncorporate taxpayers
. net operating losses (NOL) 1147

Nondeductible taxes
. defined 1025
Nondeductibles
. commuting costs 945
. contributions to exempt organizations 627
. personal expenses 1003
. personal interest expense 1043
Nonfunctional currency transactions 2495
Nonqualified retirement plans
. deduction, employer 2199
. election rules 2039
. funding 2199
. in general 2039
. income
. . participant 2199
. . plan 2199
. payments, permissible 2039
. reporting, W-2s 2039
. requirements 2039
Nonqualified stock options 1923
Nonrecognition of gain or loss—see also Gain or loss: recognition
. involuntary conversions of property 1713
. sale of principal residence 1705
Nonrecourse indebtedness
. cancellation of debt 855
. partnerships 448
Nonrefundable credits
. limitations 1315
Nonresident aliens
. capital gains 2435
. certain interest and dividend income 2431
. change of residence 2411
. community property 2438
. credits against tax 2446
. deductions 2446
. defined 2409
. departure from U.S. 2411
. dual status 2411
. effectively connected U.S. source income . . 2429
. estates of 40; 41; 2940
. estimated taxes 2685
. exemptions 2446
. expatriation to avoid tax 2412
. fixed or determinable income 2431
. foreign tax credit 2446
. gift tax 2903
. interest income 2429; 2431
. joint returns 152; 2410
. . community property 711
. net investment income tax 129
. original issue discount 2431
. portfolio investment interest 2431
. rates of tax
. . estate and gift tax 40
. real property in U.S. owned by
. . effectively connected income 2432
. . qualified investment entities 2444
. . sale or exchange 2442
. REMIC ownership 2367
. resident spouse
. . community income 711
. . joint return 152; 2410
. . net investment income tax 129
. returns 2425; 2501
. scholarships and fellowships 2448
. sources of income 2427
. taxable income 2446
. taxation of 2425
. temporary employee in U.S. 2429
. trade or business 2429
. trading in securities 2429
Nonresident aliens—continued
. transfers between spouses or incident to divorce 778
. trust, beneficiary of 588
. U.S. sources, income from 2427
. withholding of tax 2455
Nonresident citizens
. foreign government employees
. . self-employment tax 2667
Nonstatutory stock options 1923
Nontaxable distributions
. distribution by corporation
. . effect on earnings 753
Nontaxable stock distributions
. basis 1682
. holding period 1682
Northern Mariana Islands
. foreign corporation status 2431
. income earned in 2414
. self-employment tax 2667
Notes
. exclusion from capital assets 1741
. installment sales 1819
. . installment obligations, disposition 1846
Notice and demand for tax 2845
Notice of lien for taxes 2754
Nursing home care
. medical expenses 1016

O

OCONUS travel
. per diem rates 954A; 954B
. self-employed persons 954B
Offer-in-compromise 2723
Oil and gas from marginal wells producer credit
. credits against tax 1365KK
Oil and gas property
. at-risk loss limitations 1159
. carved-out mineral production payments . . 1291
. depletion 1289; 1294
. drilling and development expenses 989
. geological and geophysical expenditures . . . 987; 1287
. mineral interests 1289
. percentage depletion 1294
. royalties
. . personal holding companies, adjusted ordinary gross income 281
. . personal holding company income, adjusted ordinary gross income 283
. royalty income 763
Old age, survivors and disability insurance (OASDI)
. FICA tax rate 49; 2648
. self-employment tax rate 47; 2664; 2670
. . deductible 923
150 percent declining balance 1250
Operating deficits
. corporations 749
Operational test
. exempt organizations 602
Options—see also Stock options . . . 1919—1931
. commodity transactions 1944
. failure to exercise 1742; 1919
. futures transactions 1944
. puts and calls 1921
. sale or exchange 1919

Ordinary and necessary
. business expenses
. . defined 901

Organizational expenses
. corporations 237
. partnerships 477
. start-up expenses vs. 904

Organizational test
. exempt organizations 602

Original issue discount 1952
. applicable federal rates (AFRs)
. . tables 84
. discounted U.S. bonds, tax-free exchange . 1965
. election out of rules 1954
. foreign corporations 2431
. nonresident aliens 2431
. short-term obligations 1961
. stripped preferred stock 1952
. tax-exempt bonds 1956

Orphan drug credit
. credit against tax 1365S

Overpayment of tax
. estimated tax 117
. interest on overpayment 2765
. offset for past-due debts owed to federal agencies 2764
. suit for recovery 2790

Overtime pay
. withholding of tax 2606

Owner-employee
. retirement plan contributions 2107

P

Package design costs
. capitalization of 992
. deductible as advertising expense 969

Paid-in surplus, basis of property 1660

Parent-subsidiary controlled corporate groups 291

Parking transaction
. like-kind exchanges 1722

Parsonage allowance
. exclusion from gross income 875
. self-employment income 2670

Partial disposition election 1239

Partial liquidation distributions 2253

Partial losses
. deductibility 1101

Partners and partnerships . . . . . 401—488
. abandonment of partnership interest 453
. accounting period, change of 1513
. accounting periods and methods 416; 419
. accrual method of accounting 1515
. adjustments to partner's basis 445
. administrative proceedings 415
. . innocent spouse relief 415
. . small partnership exception 415
. allocation of basis in liquidation 456
. allocation of income or loss 410; 428
. allocation of liabilities among partners 448
. alternative minimum tax (AMT) 1401; 1405
. anti-abuse regulations 418
. association v. 401
. at-risk limitation of losses 426
. at-risk limitations 1157; 1159
. audits 415
. audits and adjustments
. . early election of post-2017 rules 413
. . post-2017 rules 413

Partners and partnerships—continued
. bankrupt partnership 506
. basis
. . adjustment by partnership 467
. . contributions 443
. . interests and assets . . . . . 443—470
. . membership, change in 467
. . optional adjustments 459
. . partnership assets, optional adjustment . . . 459
. . property, transferee partner 456
. capital gains and losses 1758
. . holding period 1737
. change in membership 410
. charitable contributions 417; 1061
. . deductibility 1058
. check-the-box regulations 402A
. classification as 401
. consistency requirements 415
. contributed property 428
. contributions to
. . gain or loss 443
. . inventory items 443
. . property 428
. . unrealized receivables 443
. controlled partnerships, transactions between 432
. conversion to S corporation 303
. conversions from partnership to limited liability company 402B
. cost or basis of interests or assets . . . . 443—470
. . increase or decrease in basis of partner's interest 445
. credits, partners 431
. deductions not allowed 417
. deemed distribution, relief from liabilities as . . 448
. disguised sales 432
. disproportionate distributions 430
. dissolution 410
. distribution of property
. . partner's optional adjustment of basis 456
. distributive share . . . . . 404; 428—432
. domestic production activities 431A; 980H
. . QPAI and W-2 wages, calculation 980H
. drawing accounts 453
. electing 1987 partnerships 403
. electing large partnerships 482
. . alternative minimum tax (AMT) 1455
. . audit procedures 482
. . capital gains and losses 482
. . Code Sec. 1231 gains and losses 482
. . deductions and credits 482
. . gains and losses 482
. . reporting 482
. . TEFRA 482
. elections 419
. . basis adjustment 470
. elective adjustment of basis by partnership . . 467; 470
. estate as partner 440
. exclusion from partnership provisions, election 402
. family partnerships 474
. farm partnerships 767
. final partnership administrative adjustment (FPAA) 415
. foreign partners
. . built-in gains 428
. . withholding of tax at source 2455
. fringe benefits 421
. gain or loss
. . contributions of property 428
. . distributed property, disposition . . . . . 453—462
. gift of interest 410
. goodwill 438

Partners and partnerships—continued
. guaranteed payments 421
. health and accident insurance premiums paid 421
. hobby losses, deductibility 1195
. income
. . computation 417
. . decedent, in respect of 440
. . partnership . . . . . 410; 417—427
. interests
. . abandonment 434
. . adjusted basis 443; 445
. . capital asset 1741
. . sale or exchange 410; 434; 436
. . transferor, information at source 2833
. inventories 434
. . appreciated 436
. . inventory basis allocation 456
. . inventory contributions 443
. . substantially appreciated 430
. . substantially appreciated inventories 436
. investment interest limitation 1094
. liabilities 426
. . allocation among partners 448
. . treated as distributions or contributions . . . 447
. life insurance
. . transfer for value 807
. limited liability companies 402B
. limited liability limited partnerships 401B
. limited liability partnerships 401B
. limited partnerships 401A
. liquidating distribution 435
. liquidation of partnership
. . basis of property distributed 456
. loss denial rule 432
. loss limitations . . . . . 425—427A
. . at-risk rules 426
. majority-interest taxable year 416
. manufacturer's deduction 431A; 980H
. master limited partnerships 403
. net operating losses 427A
. nonrecognition transactions 462
. nonrecourse liabilities
. . allocation among partners 448
. organization fees 477
. partner nonrecourse loans and guarantees . . 448
. partner's interest redeemed by partnership . . 436
. partnership liabilities
. . adjusted basis 447
. pass-through entity, partnership as 417
. passive activity loss rules . 427; 1171; 1173; 1175
. passive loss rules
. . publicly traded partnerships 403
. publicly traded partnerships 403
. . passive loss rules 403; 1171
. purchase or sale of interest 434
. real estate rules for nonrecourse financing . . 426
. reallocation of income 418
. receipt of interest for services 443
. recourse liabilities
. . allocation among partners 448
. redemption of partner's interest 435
. reorganization 410
. required tax year 416
. . Code Sec. 444 election 416
. retired partner, interest 410; 438
. retirement plan contributions 2107
. returns 406; 2505
. . failure to file 406
. . incomplete, penalties 406
. salaries and interest paid to partners 421
. sale of partnership interest
. . adjustment of basis 467
. sale or purchase of interest 434; 436
. Sec. 751 assets defined 436

Partners and partnerships—continued
. Sec. 1245 property
. . basis 436
. . distribution of 1792
. Sec. 1250 property
. . distribution of 1792
. separate reporting of partnership items 431
. start-up expenditures 481
. substantial economic effect 428
. substantially appreciated inventory 430
. syndication fees 477
. tax credits 431
. tax year 416; 1501
. taxation of partners 404
. TEFRA audit rules 415
. . small partnership exception 402B; 415
. termination of partnership 410
. tiered partnerships 410; 434
. transactions between partner and partnership 432
. unrealized receivables . . 434; 436—438; 443; 456
. withdrawing partners 410

Partnerships
. corporations v 201

Pass-through entities
. capital gains pass-through 1736
. partnership as 417

Passive activity losses . . . . . 427; 1165—1177
. alternative minimum tax (AMT) 1405; 1460
. current credits 1169
. current losses 1169
. definition of passive activity 1165
. disposition of activity 1175; 1177
. general rules 1169
. limited partners 1165
. material participation 1165
. net investment income tax 1175
. partners and partnerships 427; 1171; 1173
. passive income
. . portfolio income 1167
. . self-charged interest 1167
. personal service activity 1165
. publicly traded partnerships 1171
. rental activities
. . active participation exception 1183
. . general rules 1181
. . grouping of activities 1175
. . real estate professionals 1185
. S corporations 309; 1173; 1175
. significant participation activity 1165
. suspended losses and credits 1169; 1177
. tax-exempt use property 1191
. taxpayers covered 1173
. trusts and estates 531

Passive farm tax shelter losses
. alternative minimum tax 1460

Passive foreign investment companies (PFIC)
. accumulated earnings tax 251
. definition 2490
. mark-to-market election 2490

Passive investment income
. S corporation 341

Patents
. capital gains 1767
. controlled foreign corporations 2491
. deductibility
. . research expenditure 979
. transfer by gift or inheritance 1767

Patronage dividends 698
. information returns 2565
. taxability 768
. withholding of tax 2645

Payee statements, penalties for failure to furnish correct 2823

Payment of tax—see also Withholding of tax on wages
. checks 2545
. credit cards 2545
. due dates 6; 2529
. estates and trusts 510
. extension of time for 2537
. . deficiency in tax 2541
. . disaster areas, presidentially declared . . . 2537
. forms of payment 2545
. military personnel, death 2533
. nonresident aliens 2455
. notice and demand 2845
. partners, distributive share . . . . . 428—432
. partnerships 404
. penalties for failure to make 2854
. . criminal penalties 2898
. place for 2525
. self-employment tax 2664
. timely mailing 2553
. withholding taxes
. . deposits 2651

Payments
. type of
. . checklist 65

Payroll period
. withholding of tax 2621

Penalties
. abatement, declared disaster area 2813
. abatement, incorrect advice by IRS 2813
. accuracy-related penalty 2854
. bankrupt taxpayer 2750
. civil . . . . . 2801—2894
. compromise by IRS 2723
. criminal 2898
. deductibility of 972
. deficiency in tax . . . . . 2854—2890; 2898
. delinquent returns 2801
. early distributions
. . exceptions 2151
. . IRAs 2169
. . retirement plans 2151
. economic substance
. . transactions lacking 2863
. employer health insurance mandate 2001
. . penalty for not offering coverage 2003
. . penalty when offering coverage 2005
. erroneous refund claims 2891
. estate or gift tax valuation, understatement . 2862A
. estimated tax of corporations 241; 2890
. estimated tax of individuals
. . avoidance of penalty 2875
. . failure to pay 117
. . underestimation 117; 2682; 2875
. . waiver of penalty 2875
. evasion of tax 2898
. excess contributions
. . 401(k) plans 2121
. exempt organizations
. . disclosure of nondeductibility 627
. . disclosure of *quid pro quo* contributions . . . 627
. . donated intellectual property 627
. . donated property 627
. . donated vehicles 627
. . failure to disclose information returns 625
. . failure to file information returns 625
. . information on dissolution 625
. failure to file return 2732; 2801; 2898
. failure to furnish withholding statement . . . 2658
. failure to pay tax . . . . . 2805; 2854—2890; 2898
. . extended filing period 2809

Penalties—continued
. failure to provide TIN 2579
. Form 5500 2137
. fraud 2866
. frivolous return, additional penalty 2811
. health insurance coverage
. . individuals without insurance 131
. information returns . . . . . 2814—2833
. . amounts 2816
. . de minimis exception 2816
. . failure to file correct 2816
. . failure to provide TIN 2833
. . inconsequential omission and inaccuracies 2816
. . intentional disregard 2816
. . payee statements, failure to furnish correct 2823
. interest on 2845
. misdemeanors 2898
. negligence 2856
. nonpayment of tax . . . . 2805; 2854—2890; 2898
. . avoidance of penalty 2875
. . Form 2210 2875
. partnership, failure to file return 406
. pension liabilities, substantial overstatement of 2862
. protest returns 2521
. reportable transactions 2592
. shared responsibility payment
. . computation 131
. tax return preparers 2518; 2521; 2894
. tax shelter promoters 2597
. tax shelters
. . accuracy-related penalty 2870
. . penalties for failure to disclose 2594
. unauthorized return inspection 2893
. underpayment of estimated tax
. . corporations 241; 2890
. . individuals 117; 2682; 2875
. . waiver 2875
. understatement of income tax, substantial . 2858
. undisclosed foreign financial assets 2864
. valuation misstatement 1071
. valuation misstatement, substantial 2860
. withholding exemptions, excessive 2634
. withholding taxes 2651; 2658

Pension Benefit Guaranty Corporation (PBGC) 2138

Pension equity plans 2108

Pensions—see also Retirement plans; Self-employed individuals: retirement plans
. disability retirement 851
. government deferred compensation plans . . 723
. gross income 718
. liabilities, substantial overstatement of 2862
. military personnel 891
. withholding of tax at source 2643

Per diem allowances . . . . . 954—954B
. federal rates, allowances exceeding 954
. high-low method 954A
. lodging plus M&IE allowance 954A
. M&IE-only allowances 954B
. types of 954
. withholding and employment taxes 2608

Per-unit retain certificates 698

Percentage depletion 1289
. coal and other minerals 1298
. geothermal deposits 1296
. oil and gas property 1294
. rates 1298

Percentage method of withholding 2616

Percentage-of-completion/capitalized-cost method
. long-term contracts 1552

Percentage-of-completion method
. long-term contracts 1551

Percentage or unit mark-up method
. reconstruction of income 1577

Performing artist's expenses
. deductibility 941A

Personal exemptions
. amount 133
. dependent's return 103
. effect of death 149
. estate 534
. head of household 173
. joint returns 141
. married individuals 135
. nonresident aliens 2446
. resident aliens 135
. spouse 135
. taxpayer 135
. trust 534

Personal expenses
. deductibility 1003

Personal expenses, deductibility
. commuting costs 945
. personal interest expense 1043

Personal holding companies . . . . . 275—287
. accumulated earnings tax 251
. adjusted ordinary gross income 283
. deficiency dividend deduction 287
. definition of 277
. dividends-paid deduction
. . accumulated earnings tax 259
. exceptions 277
. income of 281
. rates of tax 35; 275
. royalties 281
. . adjusted ordinary gross income 283
. stock ownership 285
. . constructive ownership 285
. stock ownership requirement 277
. undistributed personal holding company income 275

Personal injury, damages 702; 852

Personal property—see also Depreciable property, disposition of
. ACRS 1249; 1258
. . use outside U.S. 1264
. estate's income from 523
. installment sales
. . dealer dispositions 1808
. uniform capitalization rules 990
. . reasonable position rule 990
. use outside U.S.
. . ACRS 1264

Personal property taxes
. deductibility 1021

Personal residence—see also Residential property
. business use of residence . . . . . 961—967
. capital asset 1741
. home improvements
. . medical expenses 1016
. involuntary conversions 1713; 1715
. loss on sale
. . deductibility 1103
. minister's home or rental allowance exclusion 875
. rental, information returns 2565
. sale of residence 1705
. . basis 1626
. . exclusion 1705

Personal service contract payments v. personal holding company income 281

Personal service corporations
. accounting 221
. accounting period, change of 1513
. accrual method of accounting 221
. definition 273
. employee-owners 273
. rates of tax 219
. related taxpayers, interest and expenses owed 1540B
. tax year 1501
. uniform capitalization rules for writers, photographers, and artists 1561

Phased-retirement arrangements, payment of benefits 2125

Phaseout threshold - itemized deductions . 1014

Phaseout thresholds
. adjusted gross income (AGI) 4

Photographers
. uniform capitalization rules 990A; 1561

Physical examination
. medical expenses 1016

Physicians expenses
. deductibility 981

Place for filing returns 2513

Place for paying tax 2525

Plan loans
. allowable loans 2152
. limits 2152

Plug-in electric drive motor vehicle credits
. vehicle credit 1351

Points paid
. amortization 1055
. deductibility 1055
. principal residence
. . purchase or improvement 1055
. refinancing 1055
. seller-paid points
. . deductibility 1055

Political activities
. charitable organizations 613

Political campaign contributions
. advertising 969
. deductibility 976

Political expenditures
. exempt organizations 614

Political organizations
. excise taxes 614
. exempt functions 696
. exempt status 696
. return 696

Political parties
. bad debts, deductibility 1141

Pollution control facilities
. alternative minimum tax 1430
. amortization 1287

Ponzi schemes
. losses, deductibility 1123

Pooled income funds 593
. set-aside deduction, charitable contributions 537

Possessions of U.S., income from
. bona fide resident 2414
. . Puerto Rico 2415
. . Virgin Islands 2416
. foreign tax credit 2475
. individuals 2414

Possessions of U.S., income from—continued
. residents, returns required 2501
. U.S. possessions tax credit 1362

Possessions tax credit
. distributions
. . dividends received deduction 223

Power of attorney 2708A

Powers of appointment 2918

Powers, trusts
. administrative powers, retention by grantor . . 581
. control of beneficial enjoyment 579
. powers held by grantor's spouse 578
. reversionary 576
. revocation of trust 582

Pregnancy test kit
. medical expenses 1016

Premature withdrawals, interest forfeited
. deductibility 1111

Prepaid expenses
. accounting for 1539
. tax shelters 1540
. year deductible 1539

Prepaid interest deduction
. cash-method taxpayers 1055

Prepaid mortgage interest
. deductibility 1055

Preparers of tax returns—see Tax return preparers 2517

Preretirement survivor annuity 2130

Prescription drugs
. deductibility 1017

Principal place of business
. home office deduction 961

Principal residence
. conversion to rental use 967
. deemed sale 1705
. divorce transfers
. . period of ownership 1707
. exchange
. . exclusion of gain 1705
. exclusion of gain
. . married individuals 1705
. . ownership and use 1707
. . surviving spouse 1705
. gain or loss
. . home office 1707
. incapacity
. . period of ownership 1707
. involuntary conversions 1713; 1715
. levy, exemption from 2753
. like-kind exchange 1705
. military personnel
. . suspension period 1707
. nonqualified use
. . exclusion of gain 1705
. ownership and use
. . exclusion of gain 1707
. partial exclusion 1707; 1709
. reporting requirements 1705
. repossession by seller 1841
. sale
. . business purpose 1705
. . business use 1707
. . exclusion of gain 1705
. . remainder interest 1705
. . rental use 1707
. trust or single-owner entity 1707

Priority of liens 2754

Private activity bonds—see also Bonds 729

Private activity bonds—see also Bonds—continued
. alternative minimum tax
. . tax preference item 1425
. municipal and state bonds 729

Private benefits
. exempt organizations 602

Private debt collection agencies
. collection of tax 2735

Private delivery services
. filing returns 5

Private foundations
. abatement of taxes 647
. accumulation of income 637
. charitable contributions
. . deductibility 1061
. charitable contributions deduction
. . qualified appreciated stock 1062
. declaratory judgments 623
. definition 631
. information returns 625
. investment income, tax on 633
. . estimated tax 633
. investments jeopardizing exempt purpose . . 642
. lobbying and other prohibited expenditures . . 644
. notification requirements 623
. operating foundation 633
. self-dealing, prohibitions against 635
. taxable expenditures 644
. termination of status 649
. trusts, applicability of rules to 591
. unrelated business, excess holdings 640
. unrelated business income 655

Prizes
. employee achievement awards 919; 2069

Prizes and awards
. income from 785

Production or collection of income expenses
. deductibility 1085
. investor expenses 1086

Professional expenses
. deductibility 981
. dues 981
. subscription costs 981

Professional organizations
. business expenses
. . dues 913A

Profit-sharing plans 2102

Prohibited expenditures
. private foundations 644

Prohibited transactions
. plan loans 2136
. retirement plans 2136

Property
. acquisition expenses 903
. assignment of 705
. charitable contributions 1062
. . fractional interests 1063
. . partial interests 1063
. depreciation and cost recovery 1203
. distribution by corporations 733A; 735
. improvements 903
. intangible property 903
. Sec. 179, expense deduction 1208
. . recapture 1780
. transfer as payment
. . taxability 720

Property and casualty insurance companies
. alternative minimum tax 1440
. taxation of 2378

Proration of tax, accrual-method taxpayers . 1516

Protest returns 2521
Psychiatric treatment
. medical expenses 1016
Public charities, lobbying 613
Public safety officers
. death benefit payments 813
Public service organizations
. dues
. . business expenses 913A
Public utilities
. preferred stock
. . dividends received deductions 223
Public utility property, depreciation . . 1238; 1255
Publicly traded partnerships
. special rules 403
Publicly traded property
. installment method of accounting 1805
Publishers
. circulation expenditures 971
. merchandise returns 1537
. prepaid subscriptions 1537
Puerto Rico
. charitable contributions by residents 1059
. foreign tax credit 2475
. resident, taxability 2415
. self-employment tax 2667
Punitive damages
. gross income 702
. taxability 852
Puts and calls
. defined 1921

Q

Qualified ABLE programs—see ABLE accounts
Qualified appraisal
. charitable contributions 1071
. . clothing 1061
. . household items 1061
Qualified appraiser
. charitable contributions 1071
Qualified business unit (QBU) 2495
Qualified conservation contributions
. charitable deduction
. . carryover 1060
. charitable deductions 1063
. deductibility 1059
. defined 1063
. facade easement restrictions 1063
Qualified dividend
. corporations
. . dividends received 733
Qualified domestic relations order (QDRO)
. anti-assignment provision 2131
. distributions
. . divorce or separation 2144
. . lump-sum 2143
. rollovers
. . divorce or separation 2144
Qualified domestic trusts (QDOT) 501; 2926
Qualified electing fund
. foreign tax credit 2490
. personal foreign investment company 2490
Qualified energy conservation bonds (QECDs)
. credits against tax 1375
Qualified joint venture 402
Qualified military benefits
. exclusion from gross income
. . military personnel 896
Qualified nonprofit health insurance
. excess benefit transactions 617
Qualified plans
. defined 2111
. requirements 2111
Qualified production activities 312; 431A
Qualified residence interest
. acquisition indebtedness 1048
. defined 1047
. failure to provide TIN 2833
. home equity indebtedness 1048
. indebtedness on or before October 13, 1987
. . dollar limitation 1048
. mortgage insurance premiums 1048A
Qualified revocable trust 516
Qualified school construction bonds
. credits against tax 1377
Qualified subchapter S trust 304
Qualified terminable interest property (QTIP) 2908; 2926
Qualified tuition programs
. educational expenses
. . exclusion from gross income 869
Qualified Zone Academy Bonds (QZABs) . . 1376
Qualifying child
. child and dependent care credit 1301
. child tax credit 1305
. earned income credit (EIC) 1322
. requirements 137A
Qualifying relative
. adoption of children
. . dependency exemption 137B
. dependency exemption 137B
. . income limitation 143
. . support test 147
. foster children
. . dependency exemption 137B
Qualifying widow(er)
. filing status 175
***Quid pro quo* contributions**
. charitable organizations, disclosure requirement 627

R

Raffle tickets
. deductibility of purchase price 1061
Railroad Retirement Act pensions
. taxability 716; 839
Railroad track maintenance credit
. credit against tax 1365W
Real estate
. basis
. . additions 1611
. . assessments 1611
. . settlement fees 1611
. . taxes 1611
. . zoning costs 1611
. components 1218; 1267
. dealer
. . defined 1762
. deferred payment sales, repossession 1841; 1843
. depreciation and cost recovery
. . methods of 1218

Real estate—continued
. depreciation and cost recovery—continued
. . recapture 1779
. . unrecaptured gain 1736
. discharge of indebtedness income exclusion 855
. estate's income from 522
. foreign corporation owning U.S.
. . sale or exchange 2442
. installment sales
. . mortgages 1815
. . repossession 1841; 1843
. involuntary conversion 1715
. . disaster losses 1715
. like-kind exchanges . . . . . 1721—1725
. located outside U.S.
. . like-kind exchanges 1721
. management associations 699
. mortgaged, tax-free exchanges 1725
. nonresident alien owning U.S.
. . sale or exchange 2442
. 15-year property, ACRS 1261
. parcels, sale in 1762
. passive activity losses, real estate professionals 1181
. qualified conservation contributions . . 1059; 1063
. . carryover 1060
. rehabilitation expenditures
. . low-income housing credit 1365K
. rental real estate
. . information returns 2565
. . passive activity losses 1175; 1181
. subdivision and sale 1762
. uniform capitalization rules 990
. U.S. real property interests
. . effectively connected income 2432
. . qualified investment entities 2444
. . sale or exchange 2442
. use outside U.S., ACRS 1264
. valuation 1697

Real estate dealers
. capital gains and losses 1760; 1762
. installment method 1808
. passive activity losses 1181

Real estate investment trusts (REIT) . 2326—2340
. accounting period 2326
. alternative minimum tax 1465
. asset tests 2326
. beneficiaries 2331
. built-in gains 2329
. capital gains and losses 2331
. consolidated returns 295
. definition of 2326
. distributions 2326
. distributions from 2331
. . after end of tax year 2339
. . deficiency dividends 2337
. dividends
. . capital gains 2329
. dividends-paid deduction
. . accumulated earnings tax 259
. dividends received deduction 223
. election 2326
. . failure to qualify 2326
. . revocation 2326
. excise taxes
. . undistributed income 2329
. income tests 2326
. investment tax credit 1365A
. net operating loss 2329
. . carryback, carryforward 1151
. organization test 2326
. ownership test 2326

Real estate investment trusts (REIT)—continued
. penalties 2326; 2329
. pension fund investment in REITs 2326
. qualification as 2326
. qualified dividends 2331
. qualified subsidiaries 2340
. rates of tax 39
. real property 2326
. REMIC interests as real estate assets 2344
. rents from real property 2326
. taxable subsidiaries 2340
. taxation of 2329

Real estate mortgage investment conduits (REMIC) . . . . . 2343—2367
. accrual method of accounting requirement . 2352
. adjustments to income 2352
. clean-up calls 2357
. contributions made after startup day 2357
. excess inclusion 2361
. expense deductions 2352
. fees for services 2355
. foreclosure property 2356
. foreign taxpayers 2367
. forms 2343
. information returns 2343
. interest
. . contingent payments 2344
. interests as real estate assets 2344
. investors' interests 2344
. . gain on disposition 2358
. . issue price 2349
. . regular, taxation of 2358
. . residual, taxation of 2361
. . treatment as real estate assets for REIT purposes 2344
. losses of 2352
. mortgages
. . significant modifications 2355
. permitted investments 2345
. prohibited transactions 2355
. property transferred to 2349
. qualification as 2343
. qualified dispositions 2355
. qualified liquidations 2357
. qualified mortgages 2345
. qualified replacement mortgages 2345; 2355
. regular interests 2344
. . taxation of 2358
. residual interests 2344
. . basis 2361
. . distributions on 2361
. . taxation of 2361
. taxable income 2352
. transfer of interests
. . transfers of residual interests 2361

Real estate taxes
. deductibility 1021
. . accrual-basis buyers and sellers 1034
. . accrual method taxpayers 1031
. . apportionment upon sale 1032
. . carrying charges 1028; 1614
. . cash-basis buyers 1034
. . cash-basis sellers 1034
. . construction period interest and taxes . . . 1028
. . cooperative housing 1040
. . excess deduction 1028; 1034
. . property sold before or after real property tax year 1034
. . tax year defined 1032
. recurring item 1031

Real property holding corporation (RPHC)
. status 2442

Reasonable compensation 715

Reasonable position
. uniform capitalization rules 990

Recapitalization 2225

Recapture
. additional recapture for corporations 1779
. agricultural cost-sharing payments 881
. alimony or separate maintenance, excess payments 774
. basis adjustment, investment tax credit . . . 1779
. charitable contributions 1062; 1063
. depreciation and cost recovery 1779; 1780
. . installment sales 1823
. farm land, soil and water conservation expenditures 1797
. farm losses 1797
. foreign losses 2483
. investment tax credit 1365A
. land conservation expenditures
. . recapture 1797
. LIFO
. . S corporation 339
. mine exploration payments 987
. reporting requirements 1779
. safe-harbor lease 1779
. Sec. 1231 losses 1747
. Sec. 1245 and 1250 property . . . . . 1779—1793
. soil and water conservation expenses
. . exempt transfers 1797
. soil conservation expenditures
. . recapture 1797
. U.S. losses 2483

Recharacterization, Roth IRAs 2179

Reconstruction of income 1577
. bank deposits method 1577
. net worth method 1577
. percentage or unit mark-up method 1577

Reconversion, Roth IRAs 2171

Recordkeeping
. books and records 2523
. . retention requirements 2523

Records
. Form 4070A 717

Recourse indebtedness
. partnerships 448

Recoveries
. claim of right 1543
. erroneous refund, suit for 2738
. income from 785
. tax benefit rule 799
. taxes paid 2790
. . real property taxes 1034

Recovery property
. dispositions . . . . . 1249; 1779—1793
. MACRS 1236
. transfers 1248

Redeemable ground rent
. mortgage treatment 1049

Redemption of stock
. appreciated property used 1729
. death taxes and expenses 745
. dividend status 742
. earnings and profits 751
. foreign corporation 2487; 2492
. related corporations 744
. S corporation 325

Redemptions
. regulated investment companies (RIC) . . . 2315

Reductions in basis
. return of capital 1617

Refineries
. deduction for low sulfur fuel 977A
. expensing election 1285A
. new construction cost
. . deductibility 977C
. sulfur compliance costs 1285

Reforestation expenditures
. amortization 1287
. estates and trusts 530

Refund annuities 837

Refund claims 2759
. amendment of 2760
. carrybacks, limitations period 2763
. excessive employment tax withheld 2648
. interest allowable 2765
. limitations period 2763
. . retired military personnel 2763
. net operating loss deduction 1145
. past-due debts owed to federal agencies, offset procedures 2764
. return form as 2759
. Tax Court determination 2761
. Tax Court jurisdiction 2761

Refunds of tax
. deductible expenses 1092
. foreign taxes 2475
. government assistance eligibility
. . disregard of tax refunds in determining . . 2768
. interest on 2765
. limitation on amount of 2763
. means-tested assistance programs
. . disregard of tax refunds in determining . . 2768
. offset by past-due debts owed to federal agencies 2764
. quick refund procedure 2773
. quick refunds for corporations 247
. recovery of erroneous refund 2738
. suits for refund 2790; 2792
. Tax Court appeal filed 2761
. Tax Court jurisdiction 2761

Regional offices of Internal Revenue Service 2701

Registered domestic partners (RDPs)
. community property 710
. joint returns 152

Registered mail 2553

Regulated investment companies (RIC)
. alternative minimum tax 1465
. basis in shares 2318
. . mutual fund load charges 2318
. built-in gains 2303
. capital gain dividends 2309; 2311
. capital gain tax credit 1330
. capital gains 2305
. . undistributed net capital gains 2305
. capital loss carryover 1756
. capital losses 2305
. . carryovers 2305
. consolidated returns 295
. credit bond pass-through election 1385
. definition of 2301
. distributions from 2309
. . after the tax year ends 2303; 2323
. . deficiency dividend procedures 2317
. dividend requirements 2309; 2431
. dividends
. . designation of 2309
. . exempt-interest 2311
. . reporting requirements 2309
. dividends received
. . reinvested dividends 2311

Regulated investment companies (RIC)—continued
. dividends-paid deduction 2303
. . accumulated earnings tax 259
. dividends-received deduction 223
. earnings and profits 2313
. elections 2301
. . foreign tax credits 2320
. . tax credit bonds 2320
. estates 540
. exempt-interest dividends 2307
. failure to qualify
. . deficiency dividends 2317
. foreign tax credit 2320
. forms 2301; 2305
. investment company taxable income 2303
. investment tax credit 1365A
. net operating losses 1145
. rates of tax 36
. redemptions 2315
. return of capital distributions 2311
. sale
. . basis 1975
. shares
. . basis 2318
. tax-exempt interest 2305; 2307
. taxation of 2303
. taxation of shareholders 2311
. trusts 540

Rehabilitation expenditures
. depreciation 1218
. low-income housing credit 1365K

Rehabilitation investment credit
. credit against tax 1365B

Reimbursements
. automobile expenses 946
. casualty losses
. . living expenses 877
. educational expenses 1082
. employee business expenses 942
. . accountable v. nonaccountable plans 943; 952A; 2607
. medical expenses 1015
. . withholding 2609
. moving expenses 1073
. per diem and mileage allowances . . . 954—954B
. . withholding and employment taxes 2608
. travel expenses . . . . . 953—954B

Related interests
. losses 905; 1717
. sales between 1744
. unstated interest . . . . . 1859—1883

Related-party debt
. debt treated as stock 227
. documentation requirements 227
. expanded group 227
. modified expanded group 227

Related-party transaction rule
. controlled corporate group 293

Related taxpayers
. expenses and interest 1540B
. expenses, losses, interest 905
. installment sales between 1833
. installment sales of depreciable property . . 1835
. like-kind exchanges 1721
. losses
. . previously disallowed losses 1717
. matching of income and deduction 1540B
. personal service corporations 1540B
. sale of depreciable property 1744

Relationship test
. exempt organizations
. . supporting organizations 607

Religious organizations
. exempt status 602; 604

Remainder interests, gifts of 590

Removal costs 903

Renewal community
. capital gain exclusion 999C
. employment credit 999C

Rent-to-own contracts and property
. depreciation 1240

Rental property
. income from 762; 785
. real estate
. . information returns 2565
. residential
. . recapture 1780

Rents
. advance payment 986
. conditional sales contracts 986
. deductible expenses 1006A
. deferred payments 1541
. exempt organizations 676
. gross income 762
. information returns by payors 2565
. passive activity losses 1181
. . active participation exception 1183
. . deductibility by real estate professionals . 1181
. personal holding company income 281
. . adjusted ordinary gross income 283
. production or collection of income expenses 1085

Reorganizations
. assumption of liabilities 2233
. bankruptcy 2247
. basis rules 2205
. boot received in addition to stock 2229
. boot relaxation rule 2211
. C reorganizations 2211; 2217
. . substantially all requirement 2217
. capital loss carryovers 2281
. carryovers to successor corporation . . 2277; 2281
. control, defined 2209
. corporate minimum tax credit 2281
. corporate parties
. . reporting requirements 2249
. defined 2209
. dividend distribution in 2237
. divisive 2209
. documentation 2221
. E reorganization 2225
. earnings and profits 752
. foreign corporation 2492
. foreign tax credit 2281
. G reorganizations 2247
. general business credit 2281
. information statements 2249
. liquidation of subsidiary 2261
. liquidations of corporations 2241
. mergers 2209
. net operating losses (NOLs) 2281
. nondivisive 2209
. partnerships 410
. party to reorganization 2221
. plan of reorganization 2221
. property or securities for securities 2229
. . nonqualified preferred stock 2229
. recapitalization 2225
. reporting requirements 2249
. . significant holder 2249
. S corporations 307
. . qualified subchapter S subsidiary 2209
. securities
. . promissory notes v. 2209

Reorganizations—continued
. solely for voting stock 2211
. spin-offs, split-offs, split-ups and splint-offs
. . Real Estate Investment Trusts 2201
. . reporting requirements 2201
. stock for assets 2217
. substantially all property acquired . . . 2209; 2217
. substantially all requirement 2217
. target shareholders
. . reporting requirements 2249
. transfers, gain or loss basis 1660
. triangular 2209
. triangular c reorganizations 2217
. voting stock acquired 2209

Repair regulations 903
. accounting method changes 903
. acquired or produced tangible property 903
. adaptations 903
. betterments 903
. building improvements safe harbor 903
. de minimis expensing safe harbor 903
. election to capitalize per books 903
. materials and supplies 903
. removal costs 903
. restorations 903
. rotable, temporary, ... 903
. routine maintenace safe harbor 903
. unit of property 903

Repairs
. deductibility of expense 903

Repayment of items previously included in income 1543

Reportable transactions
. advisee lists 2595
. definition 2591
. disclosure 2592; 2593
. material advisor 2593; 2595
. partnerships 2592
. penalties
. . accuracy-related panelty 2870
. . failure to disclose 2594
. . material advisors 2595
. S corporations 2592
. trusts 2592

Repossession of property . . . . . 1838—1843
. basis 1841
. residence 1841

Required minimum distributions (RMDs) . . 2127

Research and experimental expenditures
. alternative minimum tax 1435
. credit against tax 1365J
. deductibility 979
. qualified energy research 1365J

Reserves
. bad debts
. . banks 2383
. bad debts, deductibility 1137
. dealers
. . security for payment
. . year income taxable 1545
. estimated expenses 1547
. life insurance companies 2372
. warranties 1547

Reservist distributions
. IRA contributions, nondeductible 2160

Resident aliens
. active foreign business 2427
. change of residence 2411
. defined 2409
. departure from U.S. 2411
. dual status 2411

Resident aliens—continued
. elective status 2410
. exemptions 135
. expatriation to avoid tax 2412
. green card test 2409
. substantial presence test 2409
. taxation of 2409

Residential construction contracts
. long-term contract method 1552

Residential energy efficiency property
. credits against tax 1342

Residential energy improvements
. credits against tax 1341

Residential property
. bed and breakfast inns 966
. business use . . . . . 961—967
. casualty loss
. . reimbursed living expenses 877
. conversion to rental use 967
. . basis for gain or loss 1626
. day care services 964
. energy conservation subsidies 889
. . exclusion from gross income 889
. home construction contracts 1552
. installment sale
. . repossession 1841
. involuntary conversion 1713
. long-term contracts 1552
. loss on sale
. . deductibility 1103
. rental-residential property
. . deductibility of expenses 966
. . limitations on expense deduction 966
. sale
. . change in place of employment 1709
. . death of spouse 1705
. . gain or loss basis 1626
. . gain or loss recognition 1705
. . health reasons 1709
. . reporting requirements 1705
. . unforeseen circumstances 1709

Residual method
. business, sale of 1743

Restricted property transfers
. gross income 713

Retail method
. inventories
. . lower of cost or market 1563

Retired partner
. payments in liquidation 438

Retirement planning services 2093

Retirement plans
. ADP test 2114
. anti-assignment 2131
. Audit Closing Agreement Programs (AuditCAP) 2139
. benefit limit 2115
. checklists
. . tax planning 2111
. contribution limit 2115
. coverage 2112
. deduction 2117
. deduction limit 2119
. defined contribution plans 2101; 2111
. distributions 2125
. . annuity payment safe-harbor rule 839
. . annuity payment simplified method calculation 839
. . federal employees 2141
. . lump-sum 2143
. . minimum required 2127

Retirement plans—continued
. distributions—continued
. . penalty 2151
. . public safety officers 2141
. . special circumstances 2141
. . taxation 2141
. . withholding of tax at source 2643
. . rollovers 2145
. early distribution penalty 2151
. EPCRS 2139
. exempt trusts 692
. Form 5500 2137
. 401(k) plans 2104
. gross estate 2917
. hardship distributions 2129
. highly compensated employees (HCEs) . . . 2114
. hybrid plans 2108
. information returns 2565
. involuntary termination 2138
. loans 2152
. minimum funding standards 2133
. nondiscrimination 2114
. nonqualified plans 2197
. participation 2112
. prohibited transactions 2136
. qualifying longevity annuity contracts (QLACs) 2127
. real estate investment trusts, investments in 2326
. required minimum distributions (RMD) 2127
. rollover of distributions
. . withholding of tax at source 2643
. rollovers . . . . . 2145—2148
. . after participant's death 2148
. . non-Roth to Roth 2147
. rollovers, between qualified plans 2145
. rollovers, to traditional IRAs 2145
. Self-Correction Plans (SCP) 2139
. self-employed individuals 2107
. termination 2138
. top-heavy 2132
. types of plans 2138
. uniform lifetime table 2127
. unrelated business income, property received from troubled financial institutions 679
. vesting 2113
. Voluntary Correction with Service Approval (VCP) 2139
. voluntary termination 2138
. required minimum distributions (RMD)

Retirement savings contributions credit
. credit against tax 1304

Return of capital
. gross income 702

Returns
. amended 2505
. child's return 101; 103
. claim for refund 101
. confidentiality 2892
. consolidated . . . . . 295—297
. corporate returns
. . due date 211
. corporations 203; 211
. . foreign 2425; 2487; 2505
. . Form 1120 211
. . short-period returns 211
. cost of preparing 1092
. decedents . . . . . 178—191; 2505
. . joint return 168
. . partner 410
. delinquency penalty 2801
. dependents 103

Returns—continued
. disregard of rules and regulations 2856
. dollar amounts
. . rounding 105
. electronic filing 2503
. . Filing Information Returns Electronically (FIRE) system 2565
. . free online filing 2503
. estate tax 2938
. estates and trusts
. . Form 1041 510
. estimated tax
. . final installment 2688
. . individuals 117
. examination by IRS 2708
. executed by IRS 2726
. exempt organizations 625
. extensions of time for filing 109; 2509
. . armed forces personnel 109
. . U.S. citizens living abroad 109
. failure to file
. . assessment of tax 2732
. . penalties 406; 2898
. fiduciary 504; 510
. filing requirements . . . . . 101—116
. foreign corporations 2425; 2505
. . controlled 2487
. foreign earned income 2408
. foreign estates and trusts 510
. foreign housing expenses 2408
. fraudulent 2732
. frivolous, additional penalty 2811
. generation-skipping transfer (gst) tax 2944
. gift taxes 2911
. gross error 2734
. head of household 173
. individuals . . . . . 5; 101—191
. . Form 1040 105
. . Form 1040A 105
. . Form 1040EZ 105
. . Form 1040X 2759
. . place for filing 5
. . time for filing 2505
. joint v. separate 156
. late, penalties 2801
. married persons living apart 173
. minimum gross income amounts 101
. nonresident aliens 101; 2425; 2501
. partnerships 406
. private delivery services 5
. protest 2521
. qualifying widow(er) 175
. resident aliens 101
. retirement plans 2137
. S corporations 351
. . due date 351
. . lack of income, requirement to file 351
. self-employment tax . . . . . 2664—2676
. signatures 2504
. 65 or over 101
. substantiation of employee's expenses on . . 943
. surviving spouse 164; 175
. time for filing 2505
. . timely mailing as timely filing 2553
. . weekend and holiday deadlines 2549
. trusts, Form 1041 510
. when to file 107; 2505
. where filed 5; 111; 2513
. who must file 101; 2501
. withheld taxes 2442; 2455; 2650

Revocable trusts
. power to revoke 582
. treat as part of estate, election to 516

Revolving credit plans
. installment method of accounting 1805
Rights of taxpayers 2708
. interviews with IRS 2708
. levies 2755
. lien for taxes 2755
. ombudsman 2707
. suit for damages, collection of tax 2798
. taxpayer assistance orders 2707
. written statement of, provided by IRS 2708
Rollovers
. divorce or separation 2144
. general rules 2145
. IRAs
. . IRA to IRA 2167
. . IRA to qualified plan 2167
. non-Roth account to Roth account 2147
. qualified plans
. . direct rollovers 2145
. . to IRAs 2145
. . withholding of tax 2145
. small business investment company publicly traded securities 1909
. small business stock 1907
. successor, after participant's death 2148
. withholding of tax at source 2643
Roth 401(k) contributions 2104
Roth IRAs
. conversions 2175
. deemed Roth IRAs 2171
. distributions
. . nonqualified 2173
. . qualified 2173
. . required minimum distributions 2173
. in general 2171
. income limits 2171
. losses 2171
. military personnel, death benefit 2171
. recharacterizations 2177
. reconversions 2179
Rounding
. dollar amounts 105
Routine maintenance safe harbor 903
Royalties
. coal, capital gains treatment 1772
. computer software
. . personal holding company income 281
. . personal holding company income, adjusted ordinary gross income 283
. deductible expenses 1006A
. exempt organization 673
. gross income 763
. iron ore 1772
. oil and gas 1294
. patents 1767
. personal holding company income 281
. . adjusted ordinary gross income 283
. production or collection of income expenses 1085
. timber 1772
Rule of 78's 793
Rulings by the Internal Revenue Service
. incorrect advice, abatement of penalties . . 2813

S

S corporations
. accident and health insurance premiums . . . 322
. accounting period 355
. accounting period, change of 1513
. accumulated adjustments account 325
. . corporate-owned life insurance 325
S corporations—continued
. accumulated adjustments account—continued
. . distributions, effect of 323
. . post-termination distributions 329
. accumulated earnings and profits . . . . 307—333
. adjustment to basis of shareholders' stock . . 317
. alternative minimum tax (AMT) 1401
. annual return
. . extension of time to file 351
. at-risk limitations 309; 1157; 1159
. banks 304
. basis
. . shareholder basis in debt 318
. basis of shareholder debt
. . adjustments 317
. basis of shareholder stock 315
. . adjustments 317
. . decedent, shares acquired from 315
. . gift, shares acquired by 315
. built-in gains 335
. . installment sales 337
. . recognition period 337
. . tax on 337
. business tax credit carryovers 337
. C corporation rules, subject to 301
. cancellation of indebtedness 317
. capital gains 335; 341
. capital gains and losses 320; 1758
. charitable contributions 319; 320; 321; 1061
. . basis, effect on 317
. check-the-box elections 306
. class of stock 305
. Code Sec. 179 expensing 320
. Code Sec. 1231 gains and losses 320
. contributed property 309
. contributions to capital 301
. conversion from partnership 303
. corporations v 201
. debt
. . corporate debt 318
. . shareholder guarantees 318
. deductions
. . suspended deductions 321
. disposition of stock 312; 314
. distributions 301; 323
. . accumulated adjustments account 325
. . distribution of earnings, election 333
. . earnings and profits, effect on 323
. . election to distribute earnings first 333
. . post-termination 329
. domestic eligible entities 303
. . check-the-box elections 303
. domestic production activities 312; 980H
. . QPAI and W-2 wages, calculation 980H
. earnings and profits . . . . . 323—333
. electing small business trusts 304; 501; 516
. election of S status 306
. . community property states 306
. . domestic eligibility entities 306
. . eligibility 303; 304
. . late elections 306
. . revocation 307
. . termination 307
. elections
. . due date 306
. . to distribute earnings first 333
. . to end tax year 307
. eligible corporations 303
. . domestic international sales corporations . . 303
. . financial institutions 303
. . insurance companies 303
. . Puerto Rico and possessions tax credit . . . 303
. . reserve method of accounting 303
. eligible shareholders 304

S corporations—continued
. employee stock ownership plans (ESOP) 322; 323
. excess net passive income 341
. family ownership 303
. final tax year 329
. foreign income 349
. foreign loss recapture 349
. foreign taxes 320
. former C corporations 337
. fringe benefits 322
. gambling 320
. health insurance premiums 322
. hobby losses, deductibility 1195
. income
. . nonseparately stated items 320
. . separately stated items 320
. income, credit, deduction, and loss 301; 309
. indebtedness
. . adjustments to basis 317
. ineligible shareholders 304
. installment sales
. . built-in gains 337
. interest
. . investment interest 320
. investment credit, recapture of 335
. itemized deductions 320
. LIFO recapture 335; 339
. liquidations 301
. . distribution of installment obligation 1858
. losses
. . suspended losses 321
. low-income housing credit 320
. manufacturer's deduction 312; 980H
. medical and dental expenses 320
. net investment income tax 314
. net operating losses 319
. net passive income 341
. nonbusiness bad debts 320
. number of shareholders 303
. organizational expenditures 319
. passive activities 320
. passive activity loss rules 309; 1175
. passive income 335
. passive investment income 307; 341
. passthrough entity status 301
. penalties 353
. . failure to file 353
. . jurisdiction of court 353
. portfolio income or loss 320
. post-termination distributions 329
. post-termination tax consequences 329
. post-termination transition period 329
. qualified small business stock 309
. qualified subchapter S subsidiaries 304
. qualified subchapter S trusts
. . at-risk rules 309
. . income beneficiaries 304
. . passive activity loss rules 309
. real estate activities 320
. redemption of stock 301; 314; 325
. rental activities 320
. reorganization using QSUB 2209
. reorganizations 301; 307
. . ineligible shareholder 307
. returns
. . extension of time to file 351
. . penalties 353
. revocation of election 307
. shareholder taxation
. . domestic production activities 312; 980H
. . net investment income tax 314
. . stock, adjustments to basis 317

S corporations—continued
. shareholder taxation—continued
. . taxable income 319
. shareholders
. . alternative minimum tax 320
. . basis in debt 318; 321
. . basis in stock 321
. . bona fide debt 321
. . charitable contributions 321
. . charitable remainder trusts 304
. . disallowed losses 321
. . duty of consistency 309
. . electing small business trusts 304
. . estates 304
. . exempt organizations 304
. . family members 303
. . grantor trusts 304
. . husband and wife 303
. . individual retirement accounts (IRAs) 304
. . individuals 304
. . limitations on deductions 321
. . limited liability companies 304
. . qualified subchapter S trusts 304
. . spouses 321
. . trusts 304
. shareholders, taxation of
. . in general 309
. . separately stated items 309
. short tax years 307
. single class of stock
. . options 305
. . redemption agreements 305
. . restricted stock 305
. . voting rights 305
. small business corporation, definition 303
. stock for services
. . basis 315
. stock options 305
. subdivided real estate 1762
. subsidiaries 304
. . dividends, as passive investment income . . 307
. tax-exempt income 320
. tax matters person 2521
. tax years 355; 1501
. taxable income 309; 319
. taxation of corporation 335
. termination of election 307
. . consent 307
. . effective date 307
. . inadvertent termination 307
. two-percent shareholders
. . fringe benefits 322
. wagering 320

Safe harbor de minimis expensing election . . 903

Safe harbor plans
. defined contributions plans 2114

Safe-harbor rules for reporting annuity distributions
. pre-November 19, 1996 839

Salaries
. excessive 715
. partners 421
. taxability 713
. withholding of tax 2604

Salary continuation payments
. surviving spouse 719

Salary reduction SEP (SARSEP) 2189

Sale-leasebacks
. exempt organization 687

Sale v. lease 1235

Sales or exchanges of property—see also Exchanges of property; Involuntary conversions
. losses from
. . at-risk rules 1161
. . deductibility 1007

Sales or exchanges of property—see also Exchanges of property; Like-kind exchanges
. amount realized 1703
. business property sold 1747
. business sold 1741
. capital gain or loss
. . requirement of 1742
. conflicts of interest, property exchanged to avoid 1732
. crops and land 1747
. depreciation deduction, mid year 1252
. estates and trusts 523; 524
. exempt organization 679
. franchise grant v. 1774
. government obligations 1726
. installment sales 1801
. leases v. 1235
. lots sold 1762
. patents 1767
. principal residence 1705
. property acquired from decedent 1705
. real estate
. . apportionment of taxes 1032
. recovery property, ACRS 1255
. related interests 1717; 1744
. trade or business
. . basis of assets 1620
. . gain or loss 1743
. U.S. real property interest, foreign taxpayer . 2442

Salesperson
. business expenses of 941B

Salvage value 1201

Same-sex married couples (SSMCs)
. community property 710
. joint returns 152

Saturday and Sunday deadlines 2549

Savers credit
. credits against tax 1304

Savings deposits
. premature withdrawals, interest forfeited
. . deductibility 1111

Savings incentive match plan for employees (SIMPLEs) 2181; 2185
. SIMPLE 401(k) plans 2185
. SIMPLE IRA 2181
. . contributions, matching 2183
. . contributions, nonelective 2183
. . distributions 2181
. . employees 2187
. . employers 2181

Scholarships and fellowships
. athletic 865
. dependent student 147
. employer-related 865
. exempt income 865
. nonresident aliens 2448
. teaching or research, payments for 865

School teachers
. business expenses
. . deductibility 941C

Scientific organizations
. exempt status 602

Scientific property
. charitable contribution by corporation 930

Sec. 179 property 1208
. disposition 1249
. empowerment zone 999B
. expense deduction 1208
. . recapture 1780
. qualified real property 1208
. sport utility vehicles 1214

Sec. 197 intangible assets, amortization of . 1288

Sec. 306 stock 739
. special rules and exception 740

Sec. 444 election 1501

Sec. 529 plans
. educational expenses
. . exclusion from gross income 869

Sec. 751 assets defined 436

Sec. 1231 assets . . . . . 1747—1751; 1758; 1772

Sec. 1244 stock
. losses on 1911

Sec. 1245 property—see also Depreciable property, disposition of 1785
. ACRS 1255
. defined 1785
. disposition 182; 1779
. installment sales 1823
. partnerships 1792
. recapture of depreciation . . . . . 1779—1793

Sec. 1250 property
. ACRS 1255; 1267
. components, ACRS 1267
. defined 1786
. depreciation adjustments 1780
. disposition 182; 1779
. installment sales 1823
. partnerships 1792
. recapture of depreciation . . . . . 1779—1793
. unrecaptured gain
. . capital gains rate 1736

Sec. 1256 contract loss
. carryback 1754

Sec. 1256 contracts
. mark-to-market rules 1947
. mixed straddles 1948

Second generation biofuel producers credit
. credits against tax 1365I

Secure bad debts
. deductibility 1139

Securities—see also Securities transactions; Stock
. basis, information reporting 1980
. bonds 2383
. capital asset 1741
. covered securities, information reporting . . 1980
. definition of, reorganizations 2229
. exchanges of, in reorganization 2229
. financial institution, sale or exchange 2383
. holding period, information reporting 1980
. organizational actions affecting basis, information reporting 1980
. other property v. 2229
. transfers between accounts, information reporting 1980
. valuation 1697
. worthless, capital gain or loss 1742; 1916

Securities transactions . . . . . 1901—1983
. bonds as bad debts 1916
. bonds issued at discount 1950
. commissions paid, deductibility 1983
. commodities 1944
. controlled foreign corporation stock 2487

Securities transactions—continued
. dealers
. . mark-to-mark accounting method 221
. dealers and nondealers 1903
. deductible items 1950
. first-in, first-out rule
. . identification 1975
. futures 1944
. gain or loss 1901
. holding period, wash sales 1935
. identification of stock 1975
. income from 1903
. market discount bonds 1958
. nontaxable stock distributions 1682
. original issue discount 1952
. . short-term obligations 1961
. reorganization stock 1975
. share lending agreements 1942
. short sales 1944
. . dividends and payments in lieu of dividends 1946
. straddles 1948
. substantially identical securities
. . wash sales 1937
. surrender of stock 1916
. time of sale 1973
. unregistered obligations 1963
. wash sales 1935
. worthless securities 1916
. wrap fees paid, deductibility 1983
. year-end sales 1973

Security deposits
. year income taxable 1537

Self-cancelling installment note 1846

Self-created intangibles
. amortization 1288

Self-dealing
. private foundations 635

Self-employed individuals
. automobile loans 948
. foreign housing expenses 2403
. health insurance 322; 908
. health insurance premiums
. . deductibility 1019
. moving expenses
. . deductibility 1073
. retirement plans 2107
. travel
. . per diem rates 954B

Self-employment tax
. additional Medicare tax 2664
. American Samoan residents 2667
. citizens in U.S. possessions 2667
. clergy 2667
. computation 2670
. . farmers 2670; 2676
. . optional method 2670; 2673
. decedent's return 178
. deductibility 1027
. farmers and farming 2676
. Guam residents 2667
. income included and excluded 2670
. . farm income 2676
. . nonfarm income 2673
. Northern Mariana Islands residents 2667
. payment of tax 2664
. persons subject to tax 2667
. Puerto Rico residents 2667
. rate 47; 2664
. reporting 2664
. self-employment income, computation 2670
. Virgin Islands residents 2667

Self-employed
. accident and health plans 2015

Seller-paid points
. deductibility 1055

Separate returns
. community property income 711
. dependency exemption 141
. exemption amount 133
. itemized deductions
. . phaseout threshold 1014
. joint returns after filing separate returns 154
. joint v. 156
. marriage penalty relief 156
. personal exemptions 141
. standard deduction 126
. tax rate schedules 15

Separate shares as separate trusts or estates 557

Separated parents
. dependency exemption
. . tie-breaking rules 139

Series LLCs
. definition 402B

Settlement date
. stock 1737; 1973

Seven-year property 1240

Severance damages
. basis adjustments to retained property . . . 1716

Severance pay 2075
. key employees
. . golden parachutes 2075
. taxability 713

Share lending agreements
. securities transactions 1942
. wash sales 1942

Shared responsibility payments
. employers health insurance mandate 2001
. individual health insurance mandate 131
. penalties
. . computation 131

Sharing economy
. income from 785

Short sales
. appreciated financial positions 1945
. capital gains and losses 1944
. constructive sales 1945
. payments in lieu of dividends 1946

Short tax years . . . . . 1505—1509
. ACRS deduction 1270
. annualization 1507
. . alternative method 1509
. computation of tax 1507
. . self-employment tax 1507
. corporations
. . dissolution 211
. . dissolving 1505
. . liquidation 211
. . new 1505
. decedents 178; 1505; 2505
. dissolving corporations 211
. MACRS deduction 1244
. net operating losses 1151

Short-term capital gain or loss 1735; 1737

Short-term obligations
. discount 1961

Sick leave
. accrual, employer deduction 1549

Sickness or injury benefit payments
. exclusion from gross income 851

Sickness or injury benefit payments—continued
. taxability 851
Signatures on returns 2504
Simple cafeteria plans 2047
SIMPLE IRAs 2181
. distributions
. . taxation 2181
Simple trusts 542
. beneficiary, taxation of 554
. deduction for distributions 544
. exemption 534
Simplified employee pension (SEP) plans . . 2189
. salary reduction SEPs (SARSEPs) 2189
Simplified method for reporting annuity distributions
. post-November 18, 1996 839
Single
. filing status 176
Single individuals
. exemption amount 133
. rates of tax 11
. standard deduction 126
65 or over
. additional standard deduction 126
. dependent
. . medical expenses 1015
. elderly and permanently disabled tax credit . 1302
. returns 101
Skyboxes
. business expenses 917
Small business corporations 1911
. definition 1911
. losses on stock 1911
. net operating losses (NOL) 1911
. S corporations 303
Small business investment companies (SBIC)
. dividends received 223
. investors' losses 1913
. personal holding company status 277
. taxation of, generally 2392
Small business losses 1151
Small business stock 1905
. alternative minimum tax
. . tax preference item 1425
. capital gains 1736
. definition 1905
. exclusion of gain 871; 1736; 1905
. issuing corporation 1905
. losses 1911
. rollover of gain 1907
. S corporations 309
. Sec. 1244 stock 1911
Small business trusts
. alternative minimum tax
. . exemption amount 1410
. tax rate 516
Small employer health insurance credit
. credits against tax 1333
Small employer pension plan startup costs credit
. credit against tax 1365U
Small tax cases, Tax Court procedure 2784
Smoking cessation program
. medical expenses 1016
Social clubs
. business expenses
. . dues 913A
. exempt status 692
. homeowner's association 699
Social clubs—continued
. unrelated business income 664; 673
Social security benefits, taxation of 716
. IRA deduction 2157
. nonresident aliens 2431
Social security number
. adoption 116
Social security tax 2648
. credits against tax
. . excess withholding 1321
. employer deductions 923
. excess withholding 2648
. . credits against tax 1321
. FICA 2648
. rate 49
. self-employment 2664
. tip income
. . credit against tax for FICA obligation 1365R
. withholding 2648
Social welfare organizations
. excess benefit transactions 617
. exempt status 692
Soil and water conservation expense 982
. recapture 1797
Sole proprietorships
. corporations v 201
Source of income 2427
Specific recovery periods for various types of property 1240
Specified liability losses
. net operating losses 1151
Spin-offs, split-offs, split-ups and splint-offs
. limitations
. . Real Estate Investment Trusts 2201
. Morris Trust rules 2201
. reporting requirements
. . significant distributee 2201
Split-interest trusts . . . . . 590—595
. charitable deduction limits 537
. excise taxes 591
Sponsorship income, exempt organizations 685
Sport utility vehicles
. expensing limits 1214
. luxury car caps 1214
Stamp taxes
. interest on penalties 2845
Stamps, collectible
. capital gains 1736
Standard deduction 126
. additional amounts
. . automobile sales and excise tax 126
. alternative minimum tax 1435
. blind individuals 126
. dependents 126
. itemized deductions versus 126
. marriage penalty relief 126
. over-65 years old 126
Standard mileage rate
. charitable services 1061
. moving expense rate 1073
Standard mileage rate, automobiles
. business 947
. medical care 1016
. rural mail carriers' deduction 947
Starker exchanges
. like-kind exchanges 1722
. reverse exchange 1722

Start-up expenditures 481
. amortization of 904
. deduction of 904
. organizational expenses vs 904

Start-up expenses
. corporations 237
. . organizational expenses contrasted 237

State and local government employees
. state legislators
. . travel expenses 956
. taxability of compensation 714

State and local taxes
. alternative minimum tax 1435
. deductibility 1021
. deduction for
. . advance payment of tax 1022
. . employer deduction for unemployment insurance and disability fund contributions 922
. . estate and trust deduction 532
. estate tax credit for state death taxes . . 43; 2934
. estate tax deduction for state death taxes . . 2933
. refunds, information returns 2565

State and municipal bonds
. dealer in municipal bonds 1970
. exchange 1726

State death taxes
. estate tax credit 43; 2934
. estate tax deduction 2933; 2934

State legislators
. travel expenses 956

Statute of limitations
. assessment of tax 2726
. assessment period, suspension 2736
. bankruptcy 2736
. carrybacks 2773
. collection of tax 2735
. criminal prosecutions 2740
. erroneous refund, recovery of 2738
. false return or no return filed 2732
. gross error on return 2734
. joint return after separate return 154
. mitigation of effect of 2756
. refunds and credits 2763
. return executed by IRS 2726
. suits for refunds 2792
. transferee liability 2745

Statutory employee
. deductible expenses 1079

Stock bonus plans 2103

Stock dividends
. taxability 733A

Stock options . . . . . 1919—1931
. employee purchase plans . . . . . 1929—1931
. fair market value
. . readily ascertainable 1923
. holders 1921
. holding period, determination of 1923
. incentive stock options . . . . . 1925—1931
. lapse of options 1923
. nonqualified stock options 1923
. puts and calls 1921
. qualified stock options 1925; 1929
. S corporation stock, treatment as 305
. wash sales 1935
. writers 1921

Stock rights
. nontaxable distributions 1682
. nontaxable rights
. . basis after exercise 1682
. taxability 733A

Stock—see also Securities and Securities transactions
. attribution rules 743
. basis, information reporting 1980
. capital asset 1741
. charitable contributions
. . appreciated stock 1062
. compensation received 1681
. constructive ownership
. . corporate distributions 743
. . personal holding companies 285
. . related party losses 1717
. controlled corporation
. . transferred for property 1731
. corporate debt v. 733B
. corporation purchasing own 1729
. debt-financed portfolio stock 231
. exchange v. dividend 742
. exchanged for property 1729
. exchanged for stock of same corporation . . 1728
. first-in, first-out rule 1975
. fractional shares 733A
. holding period
. . dividends received deduction 223
. holding period, information reporting 1980
. issued at discount 1729
. issued at premium 1729
. nontaxable distributions 1682
. organizational actions affecting basis, information reporting 1980
. personal holding companies 285
. . constructive ownership 285
. preferred
. . interest deduction 937
. redemptions 742; 745
. reorganization 1975
. Sec. 306 stock 739
. . special rules and exceptions 740
. Sec. 1244 stock 1911
. short sales 1944
. . payments in lieu of dividends 1946
. stripped preferred 1952
. surrendered, loss 1916
. time of sale
. . trade date 1973
. transfers between accounts, information reporting 1980
. treasury 1729
. worthless 1916

Stockholders
. bargain purchases of corporate property . . . 789
. capital contributions 1660
. controlled foreign corporations 2487
. corporate debt paid 1135
. liquidations, gain or loss 2253

Straddles 1948
. conversion transaction, capital gains . . 1740; 1948

Straight-line method of depreciation 1224

Strike benefits
. gift 849
. gross income 702

Stripped bonds 1952

Stripped coupons 1952

Stripped preferred stock 1952

Structural components
. partial disposition election 1239

Students
. deductible education expenses 1082
. foreign students and exchange visitors . . . 2448
. loans
. . forgiveness of debt 855
. . interest on education loans 1011

Students—continued
. unrelated student in home
. . charitable deduction 1064
Subdivided real estate
. basis 1620
. taxation of 1762
Subpart F income
. defined 2488
Subscription income, prepaid 1537
Subsidiaries
. acquired corporations
. . stock as assets 2265
. foreign, dividends of 2485
. liquidation of 2261
. . installment obligations, gain or loss on distribution of 1856
. liquidations
. . elections 2263
. . reporting requirements 2261
. Real estate investment trusts (REIT) 2340
. redemption of parent's stock 744
Subsistence allowances to military personnel
. taxability 893
Substantial authority for return position . . . 2858
Substantial risk of forfeiture
. compensation 713
Substantial understatement of tax 2858
Substantially appreciated inventory
. sale of partnership interest 436
Substantially identical securities
. wash sale 1935
Substantiation of charitable contributions . 1070A
Substantiation of expenses
. accountable plan 952A
. automobile expenses 947
. employees 943
. meals and incidental expenses 943
. per diem methods, travel away from home . 954—954B
. travel away from home . . . . . 953—954B
Substituted basis
. spin-offs, split-offs, split-ups and splint-offs . 2201
Suits by taxpayers 2790; 2792
. attorneys' fees 2796
. damages, collection of tax 2798
. unauthorized disclosures 2893
. unauthorized inspection of returns 2893
Suits by United States
. attorneys' fees 2796
. erroneous refund recovery 2738
Sulfur compliance costs
. deduction 1285
Sum of the years-digits depreciation method 1228
Summons, third-party 2709
Sunday due date 2549
Supplemental unemployment benefits
. repayment 1009
. withholding of tax 2604
Supplemental wages
. withholding of tax 2606
Supplier-based intangibles
. amortization 1288
Supporting organizations 607
. excess benefit transactions 617
. excess business holdings 640
. private foundation distributions 637
Supporting organizations—continued
. private foundations 631
. . accumulation of income 637
. public charity status 607; 631
. reporting requirements 625
Supreme Court, review 2794
Surrender of stock 1916
Surviving spouse
. annuities
. . joint and survivor 2130
. . preretirement survivor 2130
. community property
. . income from 520
. election against estate
. . effect on charitable remainder trusts 590
. estate deduction for widow allowance 549
. filing status 175
. joint returns 164; 175
. . remarriage 166
. returns 175
. rollovers
. . distributions, retirement plan 2148
. salary payment continuation 719
. standard deduction 126
. tax rate schedules 13
Syndicates, expenses 477; 1521
Syndication fees, partnerships 477

T

Tables
. depreciation tables 1243
. federal long-term tax-exempt rates 85
. life insurance costs 2055
. tax tables 25
. ten-year averaging, lump-sum distributions . 2143
Target benefit plans 2108
Tax avoidance
. accumulated earnings 269
. acquisitions 1575
Tax benefit rule
. real property taxes, excess deduction 1034
. recoveries 799
Tax calendar 6
Tax computation worksheet 20
Tax Court
. appeals from 2786
. appeals to 2778
. . refunds after 2761
. attorney fee awards 2796
. bankruptcy cases, intervention 2750
. burden of proof 2782
. final partnership administrative adjustments 415
. jurisdiction
. . declaratory judgments 2776
. . deficiency in tax 2761; 2776
. . jeopardy assessments and levies 2778
. . overpayment of tax 2761
. organization of 2776
. overpayments, suit for 2790
. penalty for delay or frivolous position 2521
. petitions 2778
. small tax case procedure 2784
Tax-credit bond credits
. mutual fund election to pass through tax-credit bond credits 1385
Tax credit bonds
. build America bonds 1378
. credits against tax 1371

Tax credit bonds—continued
. new clean renewable energy bonds (NCREBs) 1374
. qualified energy conservation bonds 1375
. qualified forestry conservation bonds 1373
. qualified school construction bonds 1377
. qualified zone academy bonds 1376

Tax-exempt use property
. depreciation 1247
. limits on losses 1191
. rehabilitation credit 1365B

Tax-favored savings accounts
. ABLE accounts 870

Tax-free exchanges 1719
. assumption of liabilities 2233
. bankruptcy 2247
. depreciable property, disposal of 1789
. discounted U.S. bonds received in 730; 1965
. divorce transfers 1734
. exchange of stock to ESOP 1733
. gain or loss basis
. . substituted basis 1651
. government obligations 1726
. holding period of property received 1737
. like-kind exchanges
. . receipt of cash or other property (boot) . . 1723
. passive activity losses 1177
. reorganizations 2205
. securities 1728
. spin-offs, split-offs, split-ups and splint-offs . 2201
. stock for property 1729
. stock for stock of same corporation 1728
. tax-free in part
. . allocation of basis 1657
. . gain or loss basis 1657
. transfer to controlled corporation 1731
. transfers between spouses or former spouses 1734
. triangular reorganizations 2209

Tax home
. defined 950; 2404

Tax legislation 2

Tax preference items
. depletion 1425
. depreciation 1425
. intangible drilling and development costs . . 1425
. private activity bonds 1425
. small business stock 1425

Tax rates and tables
. accumulated earnings tax 37; 251
. alternative tax, corporations 1738
. applicable federal rates 83
. capital gains
. . corporations 1738
. . individuals, trusts, and estates 1736
. controlled corporate groups 34
. controlled corporations 34
. corporations . . . . . 33—39; 219
. . large corporate underpayments 2838
. deficiencies
. . interest rate . . . . . 2838—2845
. . large corporate underpayments 2838
. depreciation tables 1243
. earned income credit 87
. estate and gift taxes
. . unified transfer tax rate schedule 40
. estates and trusts 19
. federal long-term tax-exempt rates 85
. FICA taxes 49; 2648
. foreign corporations 38; 219; 2425
. foreign earned income exclusion
. . effect on 2402

Tax rates and tables—continued
. foreign housing exclusion
. . effect on 2403
. FUTA taxes 49; 2649
. head of household 17; 173
. individuals
. . tax rate schedules . . . . . 11—17; 128
. . tax tables 25; 128
. insurance companies 36
. itemized deductions, average 88
. life insurance companies 2370
. low-income housing, applicable credit percentage for 86
. nonresident aliens 2425
. personal holding companies 35
. personal holding company 275
. personal service corporations 219
. qualified personal service corporations 219
. real estate investment trusts (REITs) 39
. regulated holding companies 36
. regulated investment companies 2303
. self-employment tax 47; 2664
. small business trusts 516
. social security taxes 49; 2648
. surviving spouse 13
. tax computation worksheet 128
. tax rate schedules, estate and gift tax 40
. tax rate schedules, estates 19
. tax rate schedules, individuals . . . . . 11—17
. . computation of tax 128
. . head of household 17
. . husband and wife 13; 15
. . surviving spouse 13
. . unmarried individuals 11
. tax rate schedules, trusts 19
. tax tables 25
. ten-year averaging, lump-sum distributions . 2143
. unemployment taxes 49; 2649
. unrelated business taxable income 658

Tax return preparers
. deductible fees 1092
. disclosures, prohibition against 2894
. penalties 2518; 2894
. special rules 2517
. Voluntary Certification Program 2517

Tax sale losses
. deductibility 1107

Tax shelters
. accounting method 1515
. accuracy-related penalty 2870
. exempt organizations 619
. injunctions 2598
. material advisors 2595
. penalties for failure to disclose 2594
. penalty for abusive shelters 2597

Tax straddles 1948

Tax tables—see also Tax rates and tables 25

Tax treaties 2450

Tax years—see also Accounting methods and periods 416; 1501
. corporations 211
. estates and trusts 510
. partners and partnerships 416
. real estate sales 1034
. real estate taxes 1032
. S corporations 355

Taxable distributions
. donor advised funds 610

Taxable income
. computation 105; 123
. corporations 221
. estates 516

Taxable income—continued
. S corporations 319
. trusts 516
. worldwide income 2401

Taxable mortgage pool (TMP) 2368

Taxes
. capital charges
. . election 1614
. expenses of contesting 1092

Taxes paid
. deductibility
. . foreign income and profits taxes 1023

Taxes paid, deductibility 920
. automobile registration and license fees . . . 1021
. business expenses 920
. corporate income taxes 924
. decedent 187
. estates 532
. expatriates, gift or bequest from 1021
. expense of determining 1092
. federal corporate income taxes 924
. foreign income taxes . . . . . 2475—2485
. improvement taxes 1026
. interest on tax 937A; 1043
. lessee paying 765
. nondeductible taxes 1025
. personal property taxes 920; 1021
. real property assessments 1026
. real property taxes—see Real estate taxes 1028—1040
. . accrual-basis taxpayers 1034
. . apportionment upon sale 1032
. . cash-basis buyers 1034
. . cash-basis sellers 1034
. . election to ratably accrue 1031
. self-employment tax 1027
. social security 923
. state and local taxes 1021
. state income taxes 924
. state income taxes, advance payment of . . 1022
. state unemployment and disability fund contributions 922
. tenant-stockholders
. . cooperative housing 1040
. trusts 532
. unemployment insurance taxes 921
. year deductible 1022

Taxidermy property
. charitable contributions
. . capital gain property 1062

Taxpayer advocate 2707

Taxpayer assistance orders (TAO) 2707

Taxpayer identification number (TIN) 2579
. adoption 116
. failure to supply 2579
. . penalty 2833
. nonresident aliens
. . IRS-issued identification number (ITIN) . . 2579

Teachers
. deductible classroom expenses 1011B
. education expenses
. . business expense deduction 1011B
. retirement fund association, exempt status . . 692

Teaching or research assistants
. tuition reduction 865

Telephone
. business expenses 961
. cellular phones, listed property 1211

Temporary v. indefinite test
. travel expenses deductibility 951

Ten-year averaging, lump-sum distributions 2143

Ten-year property 1240

Tenancy in common
. gross income 709

Tentative carryback adjustment 2773

Term interests
. basis 1633

Terminable interest rule 2908; 2926

Terminally ill individuals
. accelerated death benefits 803

Termination assessments 2713

Termination of status
. private foundations 649

"Thank you" points
. redemption of
. . interest received 724

Theft loss, deductibility 1123
. $100 floor 1129
. adjusted gross income (AGI) limitation 1131
. amount of 1127
. netting requirement 1131; 1748
. passive activity losses 1177

Third-party summons, books and records . 2709

Three-year property 1240

Thrift and savings plans 2110

Throwback rule, trusts 567

Tickets
. collegiate sporting events 917
. entertainment expenses 917

Tie-breaking rules
. dependency exemption
. . claiming the same child 139
. . divorced and/or separated parents 139A

Tiered corporations
. controlled foreign corporations (CFC) 2485

Tiered partnerships 410; 434

Timber
. cutting
. . Election to treat as sale or exchange 1772
. cutting, capital gains and losses 1772
. depletion 1289

Time deposits
. interest income 724
. premature withdrawals, interest forfeited
. . deductibility 1111

Timely mailing as timely filing 2553

Timeshare associations, income 699

Tips
. credit against tax for FICA obligation on tip income 1365R
. gifts 849
. gross income 717
. withholding of tax 2605

Tools
. transportation of 945

Top-heavy retirement plans 2132

Trade date
. stock 1973

Trade-ins
. like-kind exchanges 1651

Trade or business
. bad debts, deductibility 1135
. basis, allocation among assets 1620
. losses, deductibility 1101

Trade or business—continued
. nonresident aliens 2429
. sale or exchange
. . allocation of purchase price 1743
. . reporting 1743

Trade show income, unrelated business income 685

Trademarks and trade names
. amortizations 1288; 1774
. contingent payments 1774
. transfers of 1774

Traders in securities
. capital gains and losses 1760
. defined 1760
. expenses 1760
. mark-to-market 1903
. nonresident aliens 2429

Transactions between interest dates
. bonds 728

Transferee liability 2743
. assessment period 2745
. burden of proof 2782
. collection from transferees 2743
. collection period 2745

Transferees
. recovery property, ACRS rules 1248; 1255

Transfers in trust
. charitable contributions
. . deductibility 1070
. gain or loss basis 1678

Transportation
. automobiles—see Automobiles
. . commuting expenses 945
. . employee expenses . . . . . 945—948
. . home office expenses 945
. expenses—see also Travel expenses . . 945—948
. fringe benefits 2085
. mileage rate 947

Transportation fringe 2091

Transportation industry employees
. deduction for meal expenses 916

Travel expenses—see also Transportation . . 949
. charitable contribution
. . services to charity 1061
. convention attendance 959
. cruise ships 959
. deductible expenses 952
. education, travel as 958
. employee's deduction 949
. foreign conventions 960
. foreign travel 955
. home for tax purposes 950
. local lodging 949
. luxury water travel
. . deductibility 957
. medical treatment 1016
. mileage rate, standard 947
. outside the U.S. 955
. production of income expenses 959
. spouse and dependents
. . elimination of deduction 952
. substantiation . . . . . 943; 953—954B; 2608
. . employees 943
. . employers 953
. . per diem methods . . . . . 954—954B
. temporary v. indefinite test 951
. . federal employees 951
. travel as education 1082
. withholding of tax 2608

Treasure trove
. inclusion in gross income 785

Treasury stock, exchange by corporation . . 1729

Troubled Asset Relief Program (TARP)
. executive compensation, limitation 907

Trustees
. bankruptcy of individual debtor 505; 2750
. fiduciaries v. 506

Trusts—see also Estates and trusts
. accumulation distributions 567
. administration period 507
. administrative control 581
. alternative minimum tax 516; 1401
. annuities distributable from income or corpus 548
. associations v. 502
. backup withholding, credit for 540
. bad debts, deductibility 531
. beneficiaries . . . . . 554—556
. . different tax year 565
. . gain on transfer to 526
. . separate shares as separate trusts 557
. business and investment trusts 502
. capital gains and losses 562
. . loss carryover 535
. casualty losses 531
. charitable . . . . . 590—593
. charitable contributions 537; 538; 1070
. common trust fund 595
. complex 545; 559
. complex trusts 542; 546; 556
. computation of tax 516
. corporations v. 502
. credits 540
. deductions 528
. . distributions to beneficiaries 544; 545
. . excess deductions on termination 535
. defined 501
. depletion deduction 530
. depreciation deduction 530
. disability trusts 534
. distributable net income 543
. domestic production activities 536
. electing small business trusts 304; 501; 516
. estimated tax 511
. exclusion of gain from small business stocks 538; 543
. exempt status 692
. exemptions 534
. expatriates
. . gift or bequest from 516
. . withholding on distributions 566
. expenses incurred 529
. family estate trusts 571
. family trusts 571
. fiduciary returns . . . . . 510—512
. financial asset securitization investment trusts (FASIT) 2394
. foreign tax credit 540
. foreign trusts 501
. . grantor trust rules 588
. . income of 527
. . loan by 542
. fuels, credit against tax 540
. funeral trusts 575
. gifts and bequests 564
. grantor trusts
. . defined 571
. . return for 586
. gross income . . . . . 520—527
. income
. . defined 514
. . for grantor's benefit 584
. . required to be distributed . . . . . 554—565
. . taxable to person other than grantor 585
. information returns 510

Trusts—see also Estates and trusts—continued
. interest paid or accrued, deductibility 533
. investment trusts 502
. liquidating trusts 503
. losses 531
. . carryover to beneficiary 535
. manufacturer's deduction 536
. multiple trusts 515
. net investment income tax 517
. ordinary trust rules . . . . . 501—567
. passive activity losses 531
. pooled income funds 593
. powers . . . . . 578—582
. private foundation rules, application of 591
. prohibited transactions, charitable deduction 538
. qualified domestic trusts 501; 2926
. qualified revocable trusts 516
. qualified subchapter S trusts 304
. rates of tax 19
. regulated investment company credit 540
. related parties, transactions between
. . losses 1717
. reversionary interest 576
. revocable trust
. . treat as part of estate, election to 516
. revocable trust taxable to grantor 582
. S corporation shareholders 304
. sales of property by 524
. separate entities, status as 514
. simple trusts 542; 544; 554
. 65-day election, distributions 546
. tax year 516
. taxation of, generally 514
. taxes paid by 532
. termination, deduction and loss carryovers . . 535
. termination, deductions 507
. throwback rule 567
. transfers in
. . gain or loss basis 1678
. . gift tax exclusion 2905
. withholding of tax on wages, credit for 540

Tuition
. Coverdell education savings accounts 867
. deductibility 1011A
. educational assistance programs 2067
. paid by employer 2067
. reduction for employees 865
. scholarships and fellowships 865
. Sec. 529 plans 869
. tax credits 1303
. teaching or research assistants 865
. U.S. savings bonds 863

U

Underpayment of tax, penalties—see also Penalties . . . . . 2838—2890

Understatement of tax, substantial 2858

Undistributed income
. private foundations 637

Unearned income
. net investment income tax 129

Unearned income of certain child—see also Kiddie tax 128

Unemployment benefits
. repayment 1009
. supplemental benefits (SUB) trust 692
. . unrelated business income 664; 673
. taxability 722

Unemployment insurance taxes
. federal
. . employer deduction 921
. state
. . employer deduction 922

Unified transfer tax 2901
. applicable credit 2901
. credit 41
. rate schedule 40

Uniform capitalization rules . . . . 990—999; 1561
. costs not required to be capitalized 992
. costs required to be capitalized 991
. creative costs of writers, photographers, or artists 990A
. farming and ranching 999
. interest capitalization rules 993
. inventories
. . adjustments 1561
. . costs 1561
. inventory adjustments 995
. production costs, simplified accounting method 996
. reasonable position rule 990
. resale costs
. . simplified accounting methods 995
. resale, property acquired for 994
. simplified service cost method 997
. writers, photographers, or artists 990A

Uniform expenses
. deductibility 1083

Union benefits received
. gross income 702
. strike benefits
. . gifts 849

Union dues
. deductibility 1080

Unit benefit plan 2105

Unit-livestock-price method of inventory . . 1569

U.S. obligations
. interest received 731

U.S. possessions tax credit
. alternative minimum tax 1480
. credits against tax 1362

U.S. Postal Service employees
. mileage deduction 947

U.S. Public Health Service benefits
. exclusion from gross income 891

U.S. real property interests
. effectively connected income 2432
. qualified investment entities 2444
. sale or exchange 2442
. withholding 2442

U.S. savings bonds
. exchange, discounted bonds 730; 1965
. higher education, income used for 863
. interest income 730; 1965

Unitrusts 590
. beneficiaries, tax treatment of 590B
. charitable contributions deductibility 1061
. taxation of 590A

Unlimited estate and gift tax marital deduction 2908; 2926

Unrealized appreciation
. gross income 702

Unrealized receivables of partnership . . 436; 443
. defined 436
. distributions 456
. retiring parties 438
. sale of partnership interest 434

Unrelated business income, exempt organizations . . . 655—685
. advertising activities . . . 685
. credit card programs, royalties from . . . 673
. deductions . . . 682
. donor lists, exchange or sale . . . 667
. exempt types of . . . 670
. feeder organizations . . . 694
. investment income . . . 673
. organizations subject to tax on . . . 655
. rates and payment . . . 658
. regular carrying on . . . 664
. relatedness to other functions . . . 667
. rents . . . 676
. sales or exchanges . . . 679
. social clubs . . . 664; 673
. supplemental unemployment benefit (SUB) trusts . . . 664; 673
. unrelated business taxable income defined . . 670
. VEBAs . . . 664; 673

Unrelated debt-financed income, exempt organizations
. acquisition indebtedness . . . 689
. computing the tax . . . 687
. exempt properties . . . 691

Useful life . . . 1201

V

VA/FHA loan origination fees
. deductibility . . . 1055

Vacation home rental expenses
. deductibility rules . . . 966

Vacation pay . . . 2071
. accrual, employer deduction . . . 1549
. capitalization . . . 1549
. taxability . . . 713
. withholding of tax . . . 2606

Valuation
. basis of property . . . 1695
. . indeterminate value . . . 1695
. . real estate . . . 1697
. . securities . . . 1697
. . substantial misstatement, penalty . . . 2860
. charitable contributions
. . appraisals . . . 1071
. gift tax . . . 2903
. gross estate . . . 2922
. securities
. . restrictive sales agreements . . . 1697
. substantial misstatement penalty . . . 1071

Vanpooling
. transportation fringe benefit . . . 2091

Variable annuities
. annuities and annuity contracts . . . 829

Vesting, retirement plans
. defined benefit plans . . . 2113
. defined contribution plans . . . 2113

Veteran benefits
. exclusion from gross income . . . 891

Veteran's bonuses and payments
. qualified military benefit
. . combat zone compensation . . . 896

Viatical settlements
. accelerated death benefits
. . terminally or chronically ill individuals . . . 803

Virgin Islands
. foreign corporation status . . . 2431
. resident, taxation . . . 2416
. self-employment tax . . . 2667

Virtual currency
. sales and exchanges . . . 1701

Virtual currency transactions
. inclusion in gross income . . . 785

Voluntary Classification Settlement Program . . . 2602

Voluntary employees' beneficiary associations . . . 664; 673
. exempt status . . . 692
. unrelated business income . . . 664; 673
. welfare benefits . . . 2011

W

Wage bracket method of withholding . . . 2619

Waivers
. assessment and collection of tax deficiency . . . 2712
. estimated tax of individuals, penalty for underpayment . . . 2875

Warranties
. reserve for
. . year-deductible . . . 1547

Wash sales . . . 1935
. basis of stock or security . . . 1935
. holding period . . . 1935
. REMIC transactions . . . 2361
. share lending agreements . . . 1942
. substantially identical securities . . . 1935; 1937

Water conservation expenses
. deductibility . . . 982
. recapture . . . 1797

Water travel
. expenses, luxury water travel . . . 957

Website development
. costs . . . 980; 1201

Weight-reduction program
. medical expenses . . . 1016

Welfare benefits, employer-provided
. disability benefits . . . 2025
. employer contributions
. . deductibility . . . 908
. funded welfare benefit plans
. . employer deductions . . . 2011
. health insurance . . . 2015
. in general . . . 2011
. leave sharing . . . 2073
. life insurance benefits . . . 2011
. severance pay . . . 2075
. unfunded welfare benefit plans
. . employer deductions . . . 2011
. vacation pay . . . 2071
. voluntary employees' beneficiary associations . . . 2011

Whistleblower suits
. attorney fees and court costs
. . deductibility . . . 1093

Who must file returns . . . 2501

Withholding exemptions . . . 2632—2637

Withholding of tax at source
. agents . . . 2455
. annuities . . . 2643
. backup withholding . . . 2565; 2645
. dividends . . . 2645
. expatriates, trust distribution to . . . 566
. foreign corporations . . . 2455
. foreign financial institutions . . . 2469
. foreign partners . . . 2455
. gambling winnings . . . 2642
. interest . . . 2645

Withholding of tax at source—continued
. non-financial foreign entities 2473
. nonresident aliens 2455
. patronage dividends 2645
. pensions 2643
. per diem and mileage allowances 2608
. rates 2455
. returns 2455
. rollover distributions 2145; 2643
. U.S. real property interest, foreign taxpayer . 2442
. voluntary withholding 2609

Withholding of tax on wages
. advance payment of earned income credit . 2565
. allowances 2624; 2632
. annual returns of employers
. . Form 944 program 2650
. annuities 2643
. back pay 2606
. bonuses 2604; 2606
. certified professional employer
organizations (CPEOs) 2660
. clergy 2609
. commissions 2604; 2606
. compensation 2604
. computation of
. . allowances 2624
. . withholding 2612
. credit for withheld taxes 1321
. death benefits to beneficiaries 2609
. deferred compensation 2604
. deposits of tax payments
. . monthly/semi-weekly deposit system . . . 2651
. differential wage payments 2604
. disregarded entities 2654
. domestic workers 2609
. employee business expenses 2607
. employees 2601
. employer defined 2601
. estates 540
. exempt remuneration 2609
. exemptions . . . . . 2632—2637
. . amended exemption certificate 2637
. . certificate 2634
. . changing number allowed 2637
. . claiming exemptions 2632
. expense account or reimbursement
arrangement 2607
. FICA taxes 2648
. foreign earned income 2609
. foreign government employees 2609
. foreign students 2455
. Form W-2 2655
. fringe benefits 2604; 2606; 2609
. FUTA taxes 2649
. group-term life insurance premiums 2609
. household employees 2652
. household employment 2609
. in general 2601
. international organization employees 2609
. magazine vendors 2609
. medical expenses 2609
. methods of withholding 2614
. . alternative methods 2627
. . percentage method 2616
. . wage bracket method 2619
. military personnel 2609
. moving expenses 2609
. nanny tax 2652
. newspaper carriers and vendors 2609
. noncash payment of wages 2604
. overtime pay 2606
. payroll period 2621
. penalties against employers 2651; 2658
. pensions 2643

Withholding of tax on wages—continued
. per diem and mileage allowances 2608
. percentage method 2616
. quarterly returns of employers 2650
. reimbursements 2609
. retirement plans 2609
. returns by employer 2650
. sick pay 2604
. statement to employees 2655
. stock options 2609
. supplemental unemployment
compensation 2604
. supplemental wages 2606
. tips 2605
. trusts 540
. vacation pay 2606
. voluntary withholding 2609; 2629
. wage bracket method 2619
. wages subject to withholding
. . excluded wages 2609
. . included wages 2604

Withholding statements 2655

Work opportunity credit
. credit against tax 1365G

Worker-owned cooperatives
. tax-free exchange of stock to 1733

Workers' compensation awards
. taxability 851

Workforce in place
. amortization 1288

Working condition fringe benefits
. employer-provided cell phones 2090
. exempt income 2085

Worldwide income, taxation of 2401

Worthless stock or securities
. deductibility of loss 1916

Wrap-around mortgages
. installment sales 1815

Wrap fees paid, deductibility 1983

Writers
. uniform capitalization rules 990A; 1561

Wrongfully incarcerated individuals
. restitution awards
. . exclusion from gross income 889

Y

Yacht
. business use 913

Year deductible
. accrual basis 1515
. . accrued expenses 1540
. . contested liability 1540A
. . liability to related parties 1540B
. accrual method taxpayers
. . real property taxes 1031
. accrued income 1537
. alimony or separate maintenance 773
. bad debts 1137
. cash basis 1515
. . prepaid expenses 1539
. charitable contributions 1058
. deferred income 1537
. estimated expenses
. . reserves for 1547
. long-term contract method 1551
. losses 1101
. medical and dental expenses 1015
. prepaid interest
. . cash basis 1055

Year deductible—continued
. real property taxes
. . tax year defined 1032
. rental agreements
. . deferred payments 1541
. sick leave 1549
. tax shelters, cash-basis 1540
. taxes paid 1022
. vacation pay
. . accrual of 1549

Year income taxable 1515
. accrual basis 1515
. alimony or separate maintenance 773
. cash basis 1515
. compensation accrued 1533
. dealers' reserves 1545
. loan commissions 793

Year income taxable—continued
. long-term contract method 1551
. rental agreements
. . deferred payments under 1541
. securities, sale 1973

Z

Zero-coupon bonds 1952

Zip code
. filing returns 5

Zone
. combat 2533; 2537; 2708
. empowerment 999B

Zone academy bond
. credit against tax 1376